KU-792-244

Britain

THE ROUGH GUIDE

There are more than one hundred and fifty Rough Guide titles
covering destinations from Amsterdam to Zimbabwe

Forthcoming titles include
Beijing • Cape Town • Croatia • Ecuador • Switzerland

Rough Guide Reference Series
Classical Music • Drum 'n' Bass • English Football • European Football
House • The Internet • Jazz • Music USA • Opera • Reggae
Rock Music • Techno • World Music

Rough Guide Phrasebooks
Czech • Dutch • Egyptian Arabic • European Languages • French • German
Greek • Hindi & Urdu • Hungarian • Indonesian • Italian • Japanese
Mandarin Chinese • Mexican Spanish • Polish • Portuguese • Russian
Spanish • Swahili • Thai • Turkish • Vietnamese

Rough Guides on the Internet
www.roughguides.com

ROUGH GUIDE CREDITS

Text editors: Judith Bamber and James McConnachie
Series editor: Mark Ellingham
Editorial: Martin Dunford, Jonathan Buckley, Jo Mead, Kate Berens, Amanda Tomlin, Ann-Marie Shaw, Paul Gray, Helena Smith, Orla Duane, Olivia Eccleshall, Ruth Blackmore, Sophie Martin, Geoff Howard, Claire Saunders, Gavin Thomas, Alexander Mark Rogers, Polly Thomas, Joe Staines, Lisa Nellis, Andrew Tomičić, Claire Fogg, Richard Lim, Duncan Clark, Peter Buckley (UK); Andrew Rosenberg, Mary Beth Maioli (US)
Production: Susanne Hillen, Andy Hilliard, Link Hall, Helen Ostick, Julia Bovis, Michelle Draycott, Katie Pringle, Robert Evers, Neil Cooper, Niamh Hatton

Cartography: Melissa Baker, Maxine Repath, Nichola Goodliffe, Ed Wright
Picture research: Louise Boulton, Sharon Martins
Online editors: Kelly Cross, Loretta Chilcoat (US)
Finance: John Fisher, Gary Singh, Edward Downey, Mark Hall, Tim Bill
Marketing & Publicity: Richard Trillo, Niki Smith, David Wearn, Jemima Broadbridge (UK); Jean-Marie Kelly, Myra Campolo, Simon Carloss (US)
Administration: Tania Hummel, Charlotte Marriott, Demelza Dallow

ACKNOWLEDGEMENTS

The editors would like to thank: Justin Bell, Kate Hughes and Silke Kerwick for updates to basics; Helena Smith and Dan Smith for additional material in and updates to contexts; Robert Evers for typesetting, Maxine Repath for cartography, Anne Hegerty for proofreading and Tania Hummel for the index.

PUBLISHING INFORMATION

This third edition published March 2000 by
Rough Guides Ltd, 62–70 Shorts Gardens,
London, WC2H 9AB.
Distributed by the Penguin Group:
Penguin Books Ltd, 27 Wrights Lane, London W8 5TZ
Penguin Books USA Inc., 375 Hudson Street, New York 10014, USA
Penguin Books Australia Ltd, 487 Maroondah Highway, PO Box 257, Ringwood, Victoria 3134, Australia
Penguin Books Canada Ltd, 10 Alcorn Avenue, Toronto, Ontario, Canada M4V 1E4
Penguin Books (NZ) Ltd, 182–190 Wairau Road, Auckland 10, New Zealand
Typeset in Linotron Univers and Century Old Style to an original design by Andrew Oliver.
Printed in England by Clays Ltd, St Ives Plc.
Illustrations in Part One and Part Three by Edward Briant.

Britain

THE ROUGH GUIDE

written and researched by

Rob Andrews, Jules Brown, Rob Humphreys, Phil Lee, Mike Parker, Donald Reid, Paul Tarrant and Paul Whitfield

THE ROUGH GUIDES

THE ROUGH GUIDES

 We set out to do something different when the first Rough Guide was published in 1982. Mark Ellingham, just out of university, was travelling in Greece. He brought along the popular guides of the day, but found they were all lacking in some way. They were either strong on ruins and museums but went on for pages without mentioning a beach or taverna. Or they were so conscious of the need to save money that they lost sight of Greece's cultural and historical significance. Also, none of the books told him anything about Greece's contemporary life – its politics, its culture, its people, and how they lived.

So with no job in prospect, Mark decided to write his own guidebook, one which aimed to provide practical information that was second to none, detailing the best beaches and the hottest clubs and restaurants, while also giving hard-hitting accounts of every sight, both famous and obscure, and providing up-to-the-minute information on contemporary culture. It was a guide that encouraged independent travellers to find the best of Greece, and was a great success, getting shortlisted for the Thomas Cook travel guide award, and encouraging Mark, along with three friends, to expand the series.

The Rough Guide list grew rapidly and the letters flooded in, indicating a much broader readership than had been anticipated, but one which uniformly appreciated the Rough Guide mix of practical detail and humour, irreverence and enthusiasm. Things haven't changed. The same four friends who began the series are still the caretakers of the Rough Guide mission today: to provide the most reliable, up-to-date and entertaining information to independent-minded travellers of all ages, on all budgets.

We now publish more than 150 titles and have offices in London and New York. The travel guides are written and researched by a dedicated team of more than 100 authors, based in Britain, Europe, the USA and Australia. We have also created a unique series of phrasebooks to accompany the travel series, along with an acclaimed series of music guides, and a best-selling pocket guide to the Internet and World Wide Web. We also publish comprehensive travel information on our web site:

www.roughguides.com

READERS' LETTERS

We would like to thank all the readers who have taken the time and trouble to write in with comments, suggestions and helpful advice. Thanks, especially to:

S.E. Anderton, Chloë Anderton-Brown, Leanne Armstrong, Peter Atkinson, A.J. Barclay, Dorothy Baxter, L. Bramley, Perry Bramlett, Michael Briggs, Graham Bryant, James and Catherine Cape, Nicola Cheyne, Kim Church, Lisette Cohen, Celia Couslon, Sue and Dick Courchée, David A. Crerar and Julia E. Lawn, Karen Cunningham, April Darsch, Sandra Day, Jane and Mark Eaton, Tamara Edwards-Playne, Carolyn Ellenberger, Louise Fournier and Roger Simard, Diane Frazer, Anita Garside, Carole Gray and Jane Thompson, John Guest, Colin and Jennifer Hawskworth, Linda Dalrymple Henderson, Sarah Holtom, W.G. Hopkin, Professor Richard and Gaynor Hudson, Mrs A. Hughson, John and Rachel Hyde, Richard Ingamells, Helen Jones, A. Johnston, Helen Kara, Karine (from Oslo), A. Kemph, Lynn Kopac, B. Kowalski, Julia E. Lawn, Mark Leach, Alice Lear, Suzanne Lenton, Richard D. Lysons, Josephine Maltby, Doreen McCarthy, Scott McMenomey, Julie McMillan, P.S. Metcalfe, Dr Shayne Mitchell, Lily Neal, Ann Ohlenschlager, Catriona Picken, Max Rathmell, Diana Rawnsley, Elizabeth Raymont, Liz Raynort, Kevin Reagan, Stephen Ainsleigh Rice and Jennifer Halliday, Peter Richards, A.D. Ridgewell, Dr Francis M. Russell, Mrs S.M. Salter, Ingrid van Sambeek and Marian Huisenan, Kay Sayer, Monica S. Staaf, Iain Stewart, Margaret Steyer, Paulette Staats, Claire Stolkm, Maxy Stone, Robert Sulley, Alan Thwaite, Marco Varenkamp, Caroline Ward, Dr R.J. Washington, Susan Bartlett Weber, Philippa Whittaker, M. Williams, Nathan Williams, Elizabeth Wilson, Amanda Wood, David Wood, Gavin Yamey.

CONTENTS

Introduction xiii

• CHAPTER 8: THE NORTHWEST 499–536

• CHAPTER 9: CUMBRIA AND THE LAKES 537–562

• CHAPTER 10: YORKSHIRE 563–619

• CHAPTER 11: THE NORTHEAST 620–656

PART THREE   WALES   657

• CHAPTER 12: SOUTHEAST WALES 659–685

● CHAPTER 13: SOUTHWEST WALES 686–704

● CHAPTER 14: POWYS AND THE DEE VALLEY 705–726

● CHAPTER 15: THE CAMBRIAN COAST 727–742

●CHAPTER 16: SNOWDONIA AND THE LLŶN 743–763

● CHAPTER 17: THE NORTH COAST AND ANGLESEY 764–779

PART FOUR   SCOTLAND   781

● CHAPTER 18: EDINBURGH AND AROUND 783–831

● CHAPTER 25: THE HIGHLAND REGION 1010–1062

● CHAPTER 26: ORKNEY AND SHETLAND 1063–1097

PART FIVE CONTEXTS 1099

LIST OF MAPS

MAP SYMBOLS

M4 Motorway	Ⓜ Metro station	♦ Museum
Main road	🅿 Parking	△ Youth hostel (Wales maps)
Minor road	★ Bus stop	Ⓐ Campsite
Pedestrianized street	🏛 Stately home	◉ Accommodation
Path	♖ Castle	ⓘ Tourist office
Railway	🏠⚓ Abbey	⊠ Post office
Ferry route	∴ Ruins	▬▪ Gate
Waterway	⬤ Cave	Building
National border	♈ Public gardens	Church
County border	▲ Mountain peak	⁺₊⁺ Cemetery
Chapter division boundary	Hill	Park
Wall	⬭ Waterfall	National Park
♦ General point of interest	Marshland	Forest
✗ Airport	⚓ Lighthouse	Beach
⊖ London Underground station	Ⓗ Hospital	

INTRODUCTION

There's a decidedly upbeat air about Britain today. In the vibrant music scene, in its fashionable new restaurants, bars and clubs, and in a burgeoning film industry, there's a buzz, a "feel-good" factor, heralded by the press as "Cool Britannia". And yet in many respects, this cool new world isn't so new: Britain has maintained its creative momentum consistently from the "Swinging Sixties" to the present day. From The Beatles to Oasis, from Hockney to Hirst, there's always been an innovative flair to British popular culture, which contrasts sharply with the bucolic view of Britain that many of us favour. The countryside may yield all manner of delights, from walkers' trails around the hills and lakes, through prehistoric stone circles, to traditional villages and their pubs; but Britain's urban culture – amongst the most characterful and multi-ethnic in Europe – is fast becoming as popular a draw as its countryside and its history have ever been.

Yet the monuments to the past are still a major part of Britain's attraction – in the cities and in its many ancient towns, especially in **England**, the dominant and most urbanized member of the British partnership. Virtually every town bears a mark of former wealth and power, whether it be a Gothic cathedral financed from a monarch's treasury, a parish church funded by the tycoons of medieval trade, or a triumphalist Victorian civic building, raised on the income of the British Empire. In the south of England you'll find old dockyards from which the navy patrolled the oceans, while in the north there are mills that employed whole town populations. Britain's museums and galleries – several of them ranking among the world's finest – are full of treasures trawled from Europe and farther afield. And in their grandiose stuccoed terraces and wide esplanades the old resorts bear testimony to the heyday of the British holiday towns, when Brighton, Bath and diverse other towns were as fashionable and elegant as any European spa.

In Wales and in Scotland – the two other countries which, along with Northern Ireland, constitute Great Britain* – there is a marked contrast with their English neighbour. As soon as you cross the border into predominantly rural **Wales**, you are aware that you have entered a Celtic land; and in **Scotland** – a land whose absorption into Britain was a rather more recent event – the presence of a profoundly non-English worldview is just as striking. In both countries there are areas in which the ancient language predominates, and in both there's an active nationalist movement striving to convert a cultural identity into political terms. In 1997, nationalist feeling finally held sway when both the Scots and the Welsh voted for a devolution of power from the London-based British government. As yet it is unclear exactly how much power will move to the two new legislative bodies: although the Scots have always retained a separate legal and educational system, and will now have the power to levy Scottish taxes independently of London, little seems likely to change for the Welsh, who will remain – despite devolution – more securely subservient to a country that's been in control for some seven hundred years.

---

*Northern Ireland, constitutionally part of the United Kingdom, is a region to explore in conjunction with the rest of the island of Ireland. If that's your destination, you'll want a copy of *The Rough Guide to Ireland*, the most comprehensive guidebook to the Republic and the North.

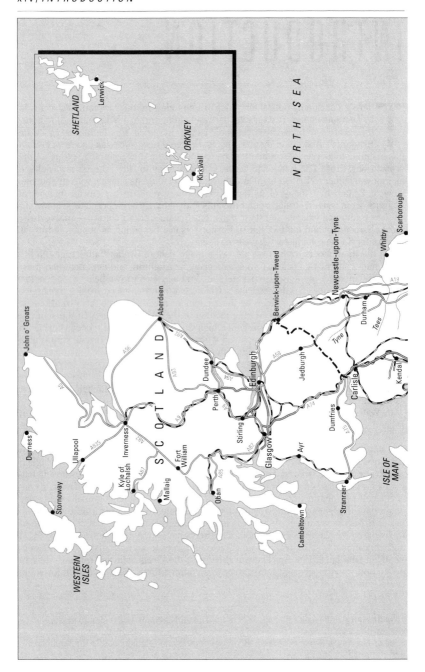

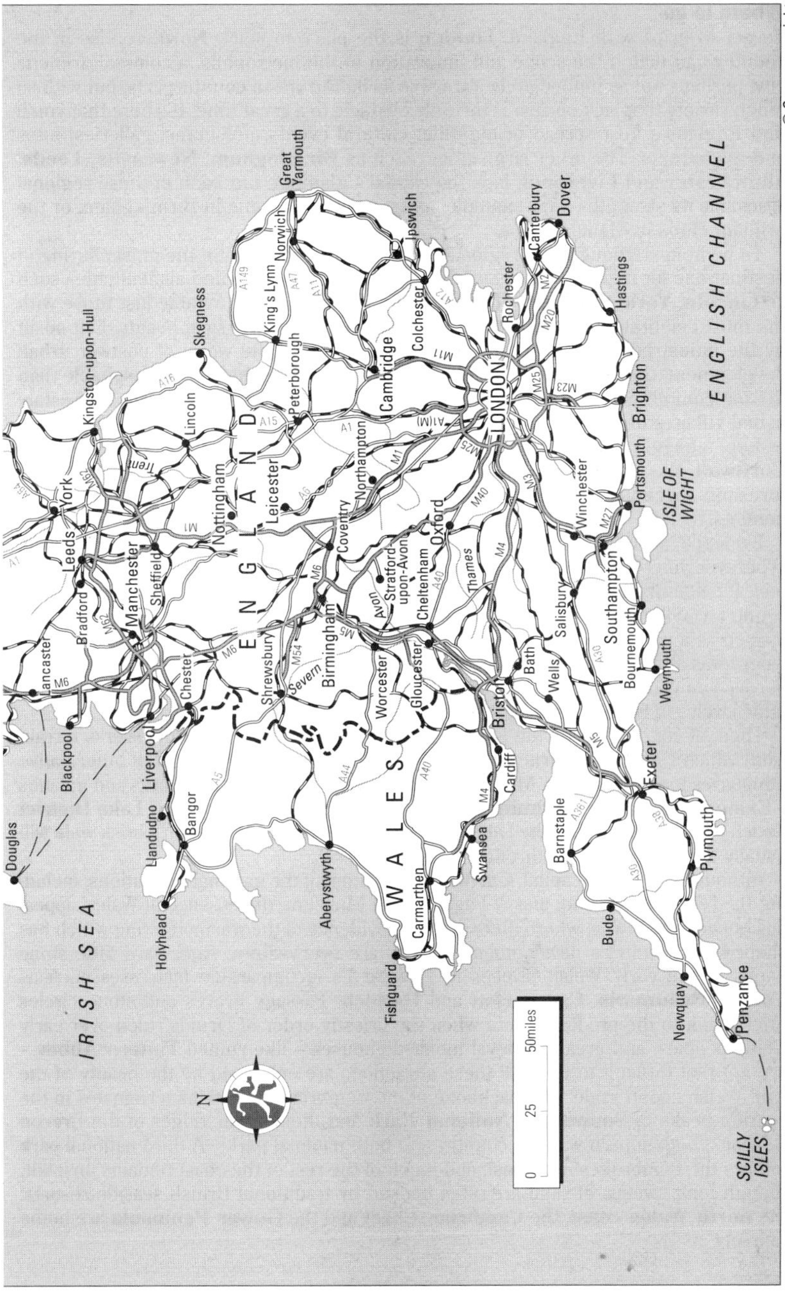
ENGLAND
WALES
IRISH SEA
ENGLISH CHANNEL
ISLE OF WIGHT
SCILLY ISLES
LONDON
Douglas
Blackpool
Lancaster
Liverpool
Llandudno
Holyhead
Bangor
Chester
Manchester
Bradford
Leeds
York
Sheffield
Kingston-upon-Hull
Lincoln
Skegness
Nottingham
Leicester
Peterborough
King's Lynn
Norwich
Great Yarmouth
Ipswich
Colchester
Cambridge
Northampton
Coventry
Birmingham
Shrewsbury
Aberystwyth
Fishguard
Carmarthen
Swansea
Cardiff
Bristol
Bath
Wells
Gloucester
Cheltenham
Worcester
Stratford-upon-Avon
Oxford
Salisbury
Winchester
Southampton
Portsmouth
Bournemouth
Weymouth
Brighton
Hastings
Rochester
Canterbury
Dover
Exeter
Barnstaple
Plymouth
Bude
Newquay
Penzance
Severn
Avon
Thames
Trent
M1
M4
M5
M6
M11
M20
M23
M25
0
25
50miles
N

Where to go

To get to grips with England, **London** is the place to start. Nowhere else in the country can match the scope and innovation of the metropolis, a colossal, frenetic city, perhaps not as immediately attractive as its European counterparts, but with so much variety that lack of cash is the only obstacle to a great time. It's here that you'll find England's best spread of nightlife, cultural events, museums, galleries, pubs and restaurants. The other large cities, such as **Birmingham**, **Newcastle**, **Leeds**, **Manchester** and **Liverpool**, lack the capital's glamour, but each of these regional cities has its strengths – for example, a resurgent arts scene in Birmingham, or the brilliant clubs in Manchester.

To be honest, though, the regional centres don't rank among the most alluring of destinations for many tourists, and they come a long way behind ancient cities such as **Lincoln**, **York**, **Salisbury**, **Durham** and **Winchester** – to name just those with the most celebrated of England's cathedrals – for sheer physical beauty. Left adrift by the industrialization of the last century and spared the worst of postwar urban development, these cities remain small-scale and manageable, more hospitable than the big commercial and industrial centres. Most beguiling of all are the long-established villages of England, hundreds of which amount to nothing more than a pub, a shop, a gaggle of cottages and a farmhouse offering bed and breakfast – **Devon**, **Cornwall**, the **Cotswolds** and the **Yorkshire Dales** harbour some especially picturesque specimens, but every county can boast a decent showing of photogenic hamlets.

Evidence of England's pedigree is scattered between its settlements as well. Wherever you're based, you're never more than a few miles from a ruined castle, a majestic country house, a secluded chapel or a monastery, and in some parts of the country you'll come across the sites of civilizations that thrived here before England existed as a nation. In the southwest there are remnants of a Celtic culture that elsewhere was all but eradicated by the Romans, and from the south coast to the northern border you can find traces of prehistoric settlers – the most famous being the megalithic circles of **Stonehenge** and **Avebury**.

Then, of course, there's the English countryside, an extraordinarily diverse terrain from which Constable, Turner, Wordsworth, Emily Brontë and a host of other native luminaries took inspiration. Most dramatic and best known are the moors and uplands – **Exmoor**, **Dartmoor**, **Bodmin Moor**, the **North York Moors** and the **Lake District** – each of which, especially the Lakes, has its over-visited spots, though a brisk walk will usually take you out of the throng.

Although the Welsh capital, **Cardiff**, boasts most of the national institutions, including the National Museum and St Fagan's Folk Museum, the essence of Wales' appeal lies outside the towns, where there is ample evidence of the warmongering which has shaped the country's development. Castles are everywhere, from hard little stone keeps of the early Welsh princes to Edward I's incomparable fortresses such as **Conwy**, **Beaumaris**, **Caernarfon** and **Harlech**. Passage graves and stone circles offer a link to the pre-Roman era when the priestly order of Druids ruled over early Celtic peoples, and great medieval monastic houses – like ruined **Tintern Abbey** – are not that difficult to find. All these attractions are enhanced by the beauty of the wild Welsh countryside. The backbone of the Cambrian Mountains terminates in the soaring peaks of **Snowdonia National Park** and the angular ridges of the Brecon Beacons, both superb walking country and both national parks. A third national park follows the Pembrokeshire Coast, and much of the rest of the coast remains unspoilt, though long sweeps of sand are often backed by traditional British seaside resorts: the **north Wales coast**, the **Cambrian Coast** and the **Gower Peninsula** are home to many.

The majority of visitors begin their tour of Scotland in the capital, **Edinburgh**, a handsome and ancient city famous for its magnificent castle and the Palace of Holyroodhouse, as well as for the excellence of its museums – not to mention the **Edinburgh International Festival**, a world-acclaimed arts shindig held for three weeks in August and early September. From here it's just a short journey west to the capital's rival, **Glasgow**, a sprawling industrial metropolis that was once the second city of the British Empire. Though its industrial base remains in decline, Glasgow has done much to improve its image in recent years, making the most of the impressive architectural legacy of its late eighteenth- and nineteenth-century heyday – a rejuvenation that has generated a brisk tourist trade.

Southern Scotland, often underrated, features some gorgeous scenery, but nothing quite to compare to the shadowy glens and well-walked hills of the **Trossachs**, nor to the **Highlands**, whose multitude of mountains, sea cliffs, glens and lochs cover the northern two-thirds of the country. **Inverness** is an obvious base for exploring the region, although Fort William, at the opposite end of the Great Glen close by **Ben Nevis**, Scotland's highest peak, is a possible alternative. Britain's most thrilling wilderness experiences are to be had here and on the Scottish islands, the most accessible of which extend in a long rocky chain off Scotland's Atlantic coast, from **Arran**, through **Skye** (the most visited of the Hebrides) to the Western Isles, where the remarkably hostile terrain harbours some of the last bastions of the Gaelic language. At Britain's northern extreme lie the sea- and wind-buffeted **Orkney** and **Shetland** islands, whose rich Norse heritage makes them distinct in dialect and culture from mainland Scotland, while their wild scenery offers some of Britain's finest bird watching and some stunning archeological remains.

When to go

Considering the temperateness of the British climate, it's amazing how much mileage the locals get out of the subject – a two-day cold snap is discussed as if it were the onset of a new Ice Age, and a week in the upper 70s starts rumours of a heatwave. The fact is that summers rarely get hot and the winters don't get very cold, except in the north of Scotland and on the highest points of the Welsh and Scottish uplands. Rainfall is fairly even, though again the mountainous areas of Wales and Scotland get higher rainfall throughout the year (the west coast of Scotland is especially damp, and Llanberis, at the foot of Snowdon, gets more than twice as much rainfall as Caernarfon, seven miles away), and in general the south of the country gets more hours of sunshine than the north.

The bottom line is that it's impossible to say with any degree of certainty what the weather will be like. May might be wet and grey one year and gloriously sunny the next, and the same goes for the autumnal months – November stands an equal chance of being crisp and clear or foggy and grim. Obviously, if you're planning to lie on a beach, or camp in the dry, you'll want to go between June and September – a period when you shouldn't go anywhere without booking your accommodation in advance. Elsewhere, if you're balancing the likely fairness of the weather against the density of the crowds, the best months to explore Britain are April, May, September and October.

AVERAGE TEMPERATURES

	Jan	Feb	March	April	May	June	July	Aug	Sept	Oct	Nov	Dec
Birmingham	42	43	48	54	60	66	68	68	63	55	48	44
	5	6	9	12	16	19	20	20	17	13	9	7
Cardiff	45	45	50	56	60	68	69	69	64	58	51	46
	7	7	10	13	16	20	21	21	18	14	11	8
Edinburgh	42	43	46	51	56	64	65	64	60	54	48	44
	5	6	8	11	13	17	18	18	16	12	9	7
Fort William	43	44	48	52	58	60	62	63	60	54	49	45
	6	7	9	11	14	16	17	17	16	12	9	7
London	43	44	50	56	62	69	71	71	65	58	50	45
	6	7	10	13	17	21	22	22	19	14	10	7
Plymouth	47	47	50	54	59	64	66	67	64	58	52	49
	8	8	10	12	15	18	19	19	18	14	11	9
York	43	44	49	55	60	67	70	69	64	57	49	45
	6	7	10	13	16	19	21	21	18	14	9	7

The figures above represent average daily maximum temperatures in°F/°C

AVERAGE RAINFALL

	Jan	Feb	March	April	May	June	July	Aug	Sept	Oct	Nov	Dec
Birmingham	3	2.1	2	2.1	2.5	2	2.7	2.7	2.4	2.7	3.3	2.6
	75	54	50	54	64	50	69	69	61	69	84	67
Cardiff	4.3	2.8	2.5	2.6	3	2.5	3.5	3.8	3.9	4.3	4.7	4.3
	108	72	63	65	76	63	89	97	99	109	116	108
Edinburgh	2.2	1.5	1.5	1.5	2.1	1.9	3.3	3	2.2	2.6	2.4	2.2
	57	39	39	39	54	47	84	78	57	65	62	57
Fort William	5.8	4.3	3.3	3.5	2.8	3.4	4.7	4.6	5.6	6.7	5.8	6.8
	146	109	84	90	72	87	120	116	141	169	146	172
London	2.1	1.6	1.5	1.5	1.8	1.8	2.2	2.3	1.9	2.2	2.5	1.9
	54	40	37	37	45	45	57	59	49	57	64	48
Plymouth	3.9	2.9	2.7	2.1	2.5	2.1	2.8	3	3.1	3.6	4.5	4.3
	99	74	69	54	63	54	70	77	79	91	113	110
York	2.3	1.8	1.5	1.6	2	2	2.4	2.7	2.2	2.2	2.6	2
	59	46	37	41	50	50	62	68	55	56	65	50

The figures above represent average monthly rainfall in inches/millimetres

GETTING THERE FROM NORTH AMERICA

For visitors from the US and Canada, the range of options will always be greatest – and the fares will usually be lowest – flying into London, Britain's busiest gateway city. Two of London's airports – Heathrow and Gatwick – handle transatlantic flights, and in terms of convenience they are about equal. If you're planning to tour the north of England, Scotland or Wales, you might consider one of the growing number of direct flights into Manchester, Birmingham or Glasgow (there are no transatlantic flights into Wales). Birmingham airport is the one best equipped to get you on your way around England or Wales quickly, since it's directly linked to the rail network. It's also possible to connect in London to several other regional airports, such as Newcastle or Aberdeen, on one of Britain's domestic carriers. Domestic services to Cardiff are minimal and you are better off reaching Wales overland. See p.23 for full details on domestic flights.

SHOPPING FOR TICKETS

Given the enormous volume of air traffic crossing the Atlantic, you should have no problem finding a seat – the problem will be sifting through all the possibilities. Basic fares, especially to London, are kept very reasonable by intense competition, and discounts by bulk agents and periodic special offers from the airlines themselves can drive prices still lower. Any local **travel agent** should be able to access airlines' up-to-the-minute fares, although in practice they may not have time to research all the possibilities – you might want to call a few airlines direct (see box on p.5).

The cheapest tickets widely available from the airlines are **Apex** tickets, which carry certain restrictions: you have to book – and pay – at least 21 days before departure, spend at least seven days abroad (maximum stay one month), and you tend to get penalized if you change your schedule. There are also winter **Super Apex** tickets, sometimes known as "Eurosavers" – slightly less expensive than an ordinary Apex, but limiting your stay to between 7 and 21 days. Some airlines also issue Special Apex tickets to those under 24, often extending the maximum stay to a year.

Whatever the airlines are offering, however, any number of specialist travel companies should be able to beat it. These are the outfits you'll see advertising in the Sunday newspaper travel sections, and they come in several forms. **Consolidators** buy up large blocks of tickets which airlines don't think they'll be able to sell at their published fares, and sell them at a discount. Many advertise fares on a one-way basis, enabling you to fly into one city and out from another without penalty. Besides being cheap, consolidators normally don't impose advance purchase requirements (although in busy times you'll want to book ahead just to be sure of getting a ticket), but they often charge very stiff fees for date changes; note also that airlines generally won't alter tickets after they've gone to a consolidator, forcing you to make changes only through the consolidator. Also, these companies' margins are pretty tiny, so they make their money by dealing in volume – don't expect them to entertain lots of questions.

Discount agents also wheel and deal in blocks of tickets off-loaded by the airlines, but they tend to be most worthwhile to students and under-26s, who can often benefit from their special fares and deals. Agents can also offer a range of other travel-related services such as travel insurance, rail passes, youth and student ID cards, car rentals, tours and the like. Some agencies specialize in **charter flights**, which may be even cheaper than any available scheduled flight, but again there's a trade-off: departure dates are fixed and cancellation penalties are high.

Discount travel clubs are another option for those who travel a lot – most charge an annual membership fee, which may be worth it for discounts on air tickets, car rental and the like.

Incidentally, don't automatically assume that tickets purchased through a travel specialist will be the least expensive on offer – once you get a quote, check with the airlines and you may turn up an even cheaper promotional fare. Be advised also that the pool of travel companies is swimming with sharks – exercise caution with any outfit that sounds shifty or impermanent, and never deal with a company that demands cash up front or refuses to accept payment by credit card.

Regardless of where you buy your ticket, the fare will depend on **when you travel**. Fares to Britain are highest from around early June to mid-September; they drop during the shoulder seasons, mid-September to early November and mid-April to early June, and you'll get the best deals during the low season, November through to April (excluding Christmas). The Christmas–New Year holiday period is a thing unto itself – if you want to travel at this time, book at least two or three months ahead, and be prepared for fares even higher than those in summer.

A further possibility is to see if you can arrange a **courier flight**, although the hit-or-miss nature of these makes them most suitable for the single traveller who travels light and has a very flexible schedule. In return for shepherding a parcel through customs and possibly giving up your baggage allowance, you can expect to get a highly discounted ticket. A couple of courier brokers are listed in the box opposite; for more options, consult *A Simple Guide to Courier Travel* (Pacific Data Sales Publishing).

Prices quoted in the sections below are based on the lowest typical Apex fares, exclusive of tax (which is around $50–100). Youth/student and consolidator tickets will usually be cheaper on high-volume routes, but not necessarily on the more obscure ones. Flying at weekends ordinarily adds $20–60.

FLIGHTS FROM THE US

Dozens of airlines fly from New York to London, and a few fly direct from other **East Coast** and Midwestern cities. The best low-season fares from New York to London hover around $500 round-trip. Low-season fares to London can also start as low as $470 from Boston, $380 from Washington DC and $410 from Chicago; Delta flies from Atlanta starting from around $420; Virgin and British Airways from Miami or Orlando for $660; and Continental from Houston for about $430. For high-season fares, add $150–340.

Don't assume you'll have to change planes when flying from the **West Coast** – American, British Airways, United and Virgin all fly non-stop from LA. Several carriers connect with flights to London from Los Angeles or San Francisco, with low-season midweek fares from both cities starting at around $460. Northwest offers direct service from Seattle to London for as low as $468. High-season fares will be at least $200 higher.

MAJOR NORTH AMERICAN AIRLINES AND ROUTES

Only direct routes are listed below; many other routings are possible through these "gateway" cities.

Aer Lingus US ☎1-800/223-6537; *www.aerlingus.ie*. New York, Newark, Los Angeles, Chicago and Boston via Dublin or Shannon to London and Manchester.
Air Canada Canada ☎1-800/555-1212 for local toll-free number; US ☎1-800/776-3000; *www.aircanada.ca*. Calgary, Edmonton, Halifax, Montreal, Ottawa, Toronto and Vancouver to London; Toronto to Manchester and Glasgow.
American Airlines US ☎1-800/433-7300; *www.aa.com*. Boston, Chicago, Dallas-Fort Worth, Los Angeles, Miami, Newark, New York and Raleigh-Durham to London; Chicago to Manchester and Birmingham, plus Glasgow in summer.
British Airways US ☎1-800/247-9297; *www.british-airways.com*. Atlanta, Baltimore, Boston, Charlotte, Chicago, Denver, Dallas-Fort Worth, Detroit, Houston, Los Angeles, Miami, Montreal, New York, Orlando, Philadelphia, Phoenix, San Diego, San Francisco, Seattle, Tampa, Toronto, Vancouver and Washington DC to London (with extensive connections on to other UK destinations); also New York to Manchester.
Canadian Airlines Canada ☎1-800/665-1177; US ☎1-800/426-7000; *www.cdnair.ca*. Calgary, Ottawa, Toronto, Vancouver and London.

Continental Airlines ☎1-800/231-0856; *www.flycontinental.com*. Houston, Newark, and Cleveland to London; Newark to Manchester and Birmingham.
Delta Airlines ☎1-800/221-1212; *www.delta-air.com*. Atlanta to London and Manchester; Cincinnati to London.
Kuwait Airways ☎1-800/458-9248. New York to London.
Northwest Airlines ☎1-800/447-4747; *www.nwa.com*. Detroit, Minneapolis, Los Angeles and Seattle to London.
TWA ☎1-800/221-2000; *www.twa.com*. St Louis to London.
United Airlines ☎1-800/538-2929; *www.ual.com*. Chicago, Denver, Los Angeles, Newark, New York, Seattle, San Diego, San Francisco and Washington DC to London (with many other onward connections possible through a co-operative agreement with British Midland).
Virgin Atlantic Airways ☎1-800/862-8621; *www.fly.virgin.com*. Boston, Chicago, Los Angeles, Miami, Newark, New York, Orlando, San Francisco and Washington DC to London (with many onward connections possible through a co-operative agreement with British Midland).

Several airlines fly direct to a few of Britain's **regional airports**, notably **Manchester** (from New York with British Airways, from Chicago with American Airlines, from Newark with Continental, and from Atlanta with Delta), **Birmingham** (British Airways from New York and American from Chicago) and **Glasgow** (American Airlines from Chicago through the summer); for onward connections, British Airways has the greatest selection of destinations. These airports are "common rated" with London, which means that the Apex fare should be the same. However, it's much harder to find discounted fares (consolidators and discount agents tend to deal only in high-volume destinations), and there are far fewer direct flights to these destinations than there are to London. If you fly to London on a discounted ticket, expect to pay $100–150 each way for an onward connection within Britain.

FLIGHTS FROM CANADA

In Canada, you'll get the best deal flying to London from the big gateway cities of **Toronto** and **Montreal**, where low-season midweek fares start at around $600 round-trip; direct flights from Ottawa and Halifax will probably cost only slightly more. From **Edmonton** and **Calgary**, London flights start at $1020, from Vancouver around the same. High-season travel can add a premium of $300–400 to all these fares.

Only Air Canada flies nonstop to **Manchester** and **Glasgow** (both from Toronto), but you can pick up direct or connecting flights from many Canadian cities to Birmingham, Manchester and Newcastle (usually via London), and to Glasgow from Vancouver, often at no extra cost over the fare to London. Again, British Airways is the best source for onward connections.

ROUND-THE-WORLD TICKETS

If Britain is only part of a longer journey, you might want to consider buying a **round-the-world (RTW) ticket**. Some travel agents can sell you an "off-the-shelf" RTW ticket that will stop in about half a dozen cities, in which London is very easily included; connections to other parts

---

NORTH AMERICAN ROUTES TO BRITAIN

Bargain Boating ☎1-800/637-0782. Self-crewed boat rentals for canal trips.
BCT Scenic Walking ☎1-800/473-1210; www.bctwalk.com. Extensive line-up of walking trips (7–16 days) in regions including the Cotswolds; Cornwall; the Lake District; the Pembrokeshire Coast; and the Scottish Borders, Highlands, and Isles.
British Travel International ☎1-800/327-6097; www.britishtravel.com. Agent for independent arrangements: rail, bus passes, and hotels, with a comprehensive cottage rental and B&B reservation service; also apartment rentals in London.
CIE Tours International ☎1-800/243-8687; www.cietours.com. All-inclusive coach tours, independent travel arrangements, accommodation and car rental deals.
Contiki Tours ☎1-800/CONTIKI; www.contiki.com. Organized tours with a party-like atmosphere geared toward 18–35-year-olds.
English Lakeland Ramblers ☎1-800/724-8801; www.ramblers.com. Walking tours in the Lake District, the Cotswolds and the Scottish Highlands.
English Experience Travels Limited ☎1-800/892-9317; www.english-experience.com. Small-group tours focusing on British life; some homestay options.

Especially Britain ☎1-800/869-0538; www.expresspages.com/e/especiallybritain. Fly-drives and independent rail tours built around accommodation in B&Bs, country houses and castles.
Home at First ☎1-800/5CELTIC; www.homeatfirst.com. Independent travel packages including airfare, ground transportation, and cottage, house, or apartment rental.
Insight International Tours ☎1-800/582-8380; www.insightvacations.com. Fully escorted coach tours.
Le Boat ☎1-800/922-0291; www.leboat.com. Inland waterway travel on hotel boats, self-crewed boats and yacht charters; also golf cruises.
Sterling Tours ☎1-800/727-4359; www.sterlingtours.com. Offers a variety of independent itineraries and some packages.
Select Travel Service ☎1-800/752-6787; www.selecttravel.com. Customized history, literature, theatre, horticulture, and other specialized tours.
Value Golf Vacations ☎1-800/786-7634. Golf tours through England and Scotland.
All these tours can be booked through a travel agent at no extra cost.

of Britain will probably have to be added on separately. Others will assemble a route for you, which can be tailored to your needs but is apt to be more expensive. Prices start at around $2000 for a simple RTW ticket stopping in London.

PACKAGES AND ORGANIZED TOURS

Although you'll want to see Britain at your own speed, you shouldn't dismiss out of hand the idea of a **package deal**. Many agents and airlines put together very flexible deals, sometimes amounting to nothing more restrictive than a flight plus accommodation and car or rail pass, and these can actually work out cheaper than the same arrangements made on arrival – especially car rental, which is expensive in Britain. A package can also be great for your peace of mind, if only to ensure a worry-free first week while you're finding your feet for a longer tour.

There are hundreds of tour operators specializing in travel to the British Isles. Most can do packages of the standard highlights, but of greater interest are the outfits that help you explore Britain's unique points: many organize walking or cycling trips through the countryside, boat trips along canals, and any number of theme tours based around Britain's literary heritage, history, pubs, gardens, theatre, golf – you name it. A few of the possibilities are listed in the box opposite, and a travel agent will be able to point out others. For a full listing, contact the British Tourist Authority (see p.20).

Be sure to examine the fine print of any deal, and bear in mind that everything in brochures always sounds great. Choose only an operator that is a member of the United States Tour Operator Association (USTOA) or has been approved by the American Society of Travel Agents (ASTA).

GETTING THERE FROM AUSTRALIA AND NEW ZEALAND

The route from Australia and New Zealand to Britain's main entry point, London, is a highly competitive one, with flights via Southeast Asia generally being the cheapest option. There are a few direct flights to Manchester, in northern England, but none to Scotland or Wales, so you will generally have to route through London.

Fares are **seasonally adjusted** – low season is October to mid-November and mid-January to

February; high season is May to August and December to mid-January; the rest of the year is classed as shoulder season. Tickets purchased direct from the airlines tend to be expensive, travel agents offer much better deals on fares and have the latest information on limited special deals and stopovers with some of the best discounts through Flight Centres and STA, who can also advise on visa regulations.

FLIGHTS FROM AUSTRALIA

Fares from Australia's **eastern cities** are common rated while flights from Perth via Asia and Africa are around $200 less, and via the Americas about $400 more. The cheapest **scheduled flights are** via Asia with Garuda, Gulf Air, Korean Air, Japan Airlines (JAL) and Royal Brunei from around $1350; these usually involve a transfer in the carrier's hub city. For a little more Virgin Atlantic/Malaysian Airlines can get you to London via Kuala Lumpur from around $1600. In the mid range are Cathay Pacific, Malaysian Airlines, Thai Airways and Singapore Airlines, all at around $1650–1850. British Airways and Qantas both quote direct-flight fares from $1700

AIRLINES IN AUSTRALIA AND NEW ZEALAND

Air New Zealand New Zealand ☎09/357 3000 or 0-800 737000; *www.airnz.co.nz*; Australia ☎13/2476; *www.airnz.com.au*. Daily flights to London from Brisbane, Melbourne and Sydney (code share with Ansett from other major cities in Australia) via Asia and from New Zealand via Los Angeles.

Airtours & Britannia Airways Australia ☎02/9247 4833; New Zealand ☎09/308 3360. Several flights a month (Nov–March only) from Adelaide, Auckland, Brisbane, Perth and Sydney to London and once a week to Manchester via Singapore and Bahrain.

British Airways Australia ☎02/8904 8800; *www.britishairways.com/regional/australia*; New Zealand ☎09/356 8690. Daily direct flights from Brisbane, Melbourne, Perth and Sydney. Code share with Qantas (part owners of the company) from other major cities to London via Los Angeles and Singapore and twice weekly via Harare or Johannesburg from Sydney; daily from Auckland via Los Angeles. Onward connections to other destinations in Britain.

Canadian Airlines Australia ☎1-300/655767; New Zealand ☎09/309 0735; *www.cdnair.ca*. Several flights a week from Auckland, Melbourne and Sydney to London via Toronto or Vancouver.

Cathay Pacific Australia ☎13/1747; New Zealand ☎09/379 0861; *www.cathaypacific.com/australia*. Several flights a week from Auckland, Brisbane, Cairns, Melbourne, Perth and Sydney to London and Manchester via Hong Kong.

Garuda Australia ☎1-300/365330; New Zealand ☎09/366 1855 or 0-800/128510; *http://151.196.75.122/garuda*. Several flights weekly from Australia and New Zealand to London via Denpasar or Jakarta.

Gulf Air Australia ☎02/9244 2199; New Zealand ☎09/308 3366; *www.gulfairco.com*. Several flights weekly from Sydney to London via Singapore and Bahrain or Abu Dhabi.

Japanese Airlines (JAL) Australia ☎02/9272 1111; New Zealand ☎09/379 3202; *www.jal.co.jp*. Daily flights from Brisbane and Sydney to London via Osaka or Tokyo and several weekly from Auckland and Cairns, also via Osaka and Tokyo. Code share with Air New Zealand. Onward connections to Edinburgh.

KLM Australia ☎02/9231 6333 or 1-800/505747; *www.klm.com.au*. Twice weekly flights from Sydney to London via Singapore and Amsterdam.

Korean Air Australia ☎02/9262 6000; New Zealand ☎09/303 0166; *www.koreanair.com*. Several flights a week via Seoul from Auckland, Brisbane and Sydney to London and once a week from Christchurch.

Malaysia Airlines (MAS) Australia ☎13/2627; New Zealand ☎09/373 2741 or ☎0-08/657472; *www.malaysiaairlines.com.my*. Several flights a week from Auckland, Melbourne, Perth and Sydney to London via Kuala Lumpur. With onward connections to the northwest of England.

Qantas Australia ☎13/1313; New Zealand ☎09/357 8900 or 0-800/808 767; *www.qantas.com.au*. Daily flights from major Australasian cities to London via Bangkok or Singapore. Onward connections with British Airways to regional UK airports.

Royal Bruei Airlines Australia ☎02/3221 7757; *www.bruneiair.com*. Several flights weekly from Brisbane, Darwin and Perth to London via Singapore or Abu Dhabi.

South African Airways (SAA) Australia ☎02/9223 4402; *www.sairways.com.au*; New Zealand ☎09/379 3708. Four flights a week to London from Sydney and Perth via Johannesburg.

Singapore Airlines Australia ☎13/1011; *www.singaporeair.com.au*; New Zealand ☎09/303 2129 or 0-800/808 909; *www.singaporeair.co.nz*. Daily flights from Auckland, Brisbane, Christchurch, Melbourne, Perth and Sydney and several weekly from Adelaide and Cairns to London and Manchester via Singapore.

Thai Airways Australia ☎1-300/651960; New Zealand ☎09/377 3886; *www.thaiair.com*. Several flights a week from Auckland, Brisbane, Melbourne, Perth and Sydney to London Heathrow via Bangkok.

United Airlines Australia ☎13/1777; New Zealand ☎09/379 3800; *www.ual.com*. Daily flights from Auckland, Melbourne and Sydney to London and Manchester via Los Angeles and Chicago, New York or Washington.

Virgin Atlantic Australia ☎02/9244 2747 or 1-800/646747; *www.fly.virgin.com.au*; New Zealand ☎09/308 3377. Daily flights from Sydney and several weekly from Melbourne to London via Kuala Lumpur. Code share with Malaysia Airlines for the first leg.

DISCOUNT TRAVEL AGENTS

Anywhere Travel, 345 Anzac Parade, Kingsford, Sydney, NSW 2032 (☎02/9663 0411, *anywhere@ozemail.com.au*).

Budget Travel, 16 Fort St, Auckland; plus branches around the city (☎09/366 0061 or 0800/808 040).

Destinations Unlimited, 87 Albert St, Auckland (☎09/373 4033).

Flight Centres Australia: 82 Elizabeth St, Sydney, NSW 2000 (☎13/1600; *www.flightcentre.com.au*), plus branches nationwide. New Zealand: 350 Queen St, Auckland (☎09/358 4310), plus branches nationwide.

Northern Gateway, 22 Cavenagh St, Darwin, NT 0800 (☎08/8941 1394, *oztravel@norgate.com.au*).

STA Travel Australia: 855 George St, Ultimo, Sydney, NSW 2007; 256 Flinders St, Melbourne, VIC 3000; plus branches nationwide (nearest branch ☎13/1776; telesales ☎1300/360 960). New Zealand: 10 High St, Auckland (☎09/309 0458; telesales ☎09/366 6673, *traveller@statravelaus.com.au* or *www.statravel.com.au*), plus branches nationwide.

Student Uni Travel, 92 Pitt St, Sydney, NSW 2000 (☎02/9232 8444); plus branches in Brisbane, Cairns, Darwin, Melbourne and Perth.

Thomas Cook Australia: 175 Pitt St, Sydney, NSW 2000; 257 Collins St, Melbourne, VIC 3000; plus branches nationwide (local branch ☎13/1771, telesales ☎1800/801 002). New Zealand: 191 Queen St, Auckland (☎09/379 3920; *www.thomascook.com.au*).

Trailfinders, 8 Spring St, Sydney, NSW 2000 (☎02/9247 7666; *www.trailfinders.com.au/australia*) plus branches in Brisbane and Cairns.

Travel.com, 76–80 Clarence St, Sydney, NSW 2000 (☎02/9262 3555, *consultant@travel.com.au* or *www.travel.com.au*).

UK Flight Shop, 7 Macquarie Place, Sydney, NSW 2000 (☎02/9247 7833; *www.ukflightshop.com.au*); plus branches in Melbourne and Perth.

Usit Beyond, corner of Shortland St and Jean Batten Place, Auckland (☎09/379 4224 or 0800/788336; *www.usitbeyond.co.nz*); plus branches in Christchurch, Hamilton, Palmerston North and Wellington.

SPECIALIST AGENTS

Adventure Specialists, 1st Floor, 69 Liverpool St, Sydney, NSW 2000 (☎02/9261 2927; *www.adventurespec.citysearch.com.au*). A selection of walking and cycling holidays throughout Britain.

Adventure Travel Company, 164 Parnell Rd, Parnell, East Auckland (☎09/379 9755). New Zealand agents for Peregrine Adventures.

Adventure World Australia: 73 Walker St, North Sydney, NSW 2060 (☎02/9956 7766 or 1-800/221 931; *www.adventureworld.com.au*). New Zealand: 101 Great South Rd, Remuera, Auckland (☎09/524 5118). A wide variety of tours around England and based in London.

Best of Britain, 352a Military Rd, Cremorne, Sydney, NSW 2090 (☎02/9909 1055). Can arrange flights, accommodation, car rental, tours, canal boats and B&Bs.

Explore Holidays, 55 Blaxland Rd, Ryde, NSW 2112 (☎02/9857 6200). Organizes accommodation throughout Britain, as well as special interest and rambling trips.

Peregrine Adventures, 258 Lonsdale St, Melbourne, VIC 3000 (☎03/9663 8611;

www.peregrine.net.au), plus branches in Adelaide, Brisbane, Perth and Sydney. Specializes in small-group walking, cycling and canoeing trips, with travel between main points by minibus.

Sundowners, Suite 15, 600 Lonsdale St, Melbourne, VIC 3000 (☎03/9600 1934 or 1800/337089; *www.sundowners.com.au*). Russian and Trans-Siberian Railway specialists; escorted group tours and independent travel by train to London via Moscow.

Wiltrans/Maupintour, Level 10, 189 Kent St, Sydney, NSW 2000 (☎02/9225 0899). Fully escorted tours around Britain's historic homes and gardens, staying in upmarket accommodation.

YHA Travel Centre Australia: 422 Kent St, Sydney, NSW 2000 (☎02/9261 1111); 205 King St, Melbourne, VIC 3000 (☎03/9670 9611; *www.yha.com.au*). New Zealand: corner of Shortland St and Jean Batten Place, Auckland (☎09/379 4224; *www.yha.co.nz*). Organizes budget accommodation throughout Britain for Hostelling International members.

in low season up to $2500 in high season. Many of the airlines also offer **free stopovers** in their hub cities; JAL flies from Brisbane, Cairns and Sydney several times a week including an overnight hotel stopover in Osaka or Tokyo. British Airways and Qantas offer fares through to **Edinburgh** for $1750. Otherwise, the cost of an add-on flight from London to Glasgow or Edinburgh will be anything from A$150 to A$300, depending on the season.

Currently, the best fares on offer are the Airtours/Britannia Airways **charter flights** to London and Manchester via Singapore and Bahrain which run several times a month between November and March. Fares start at $1100 in low season and range up to $1800 in high season.

The lowest fares for routes **via Africa** are with Qantas/British Airways via Johannesburg via Harare, returning via Southeast Asia from around A$2000. South African Airways has a route via Johannesburg starting at $2230 from Sydney and $2200 from Perth.

Flights are generally pricier **via North America**, with United Airlines offering the cheapest deal via Los Angeles and either Chicago, New York or Washington for $1950–2430 while Air New Zealand flies via Auckland and Los Angeles – and Canadian Airlines via Toronto or Vancouver – for around $1975–2450.

FLIGHTS FROM NEW ZEALAND

The most direct route from **New Zealand** is **via North America**, with Air New Zealand offering the best value, stopping in Los Angeles for $2200 low season and $2900 in high season, while United Airlines has a similar deal for around $2275–2975. Canadian Airlines flies via Vancouver or Toronto, starting at $2095.

Garuda, JAL, Korean Air and Thai Airways fly to London **via Asia** with either a transfer or stopover in their home city for around $1900–2300; for a little more money and comfort Qantas/British Airways fly via Sydney and Bangkok to London from $2175 or $2475, including onward connections to other destinations in Britain.

As with Australia, the cheapest fare is Airtours or Britannia Airways' **charter flights** from Auckland to London and Manchester, running several times a month from November to March; fares are from $1620 low season, $1850 shoulder season and $2110 high season.

ROUND-THE-WORLD FARES

If you're planning a long trip, a **round-the-world ticket (RTW)** that includes London can be very good value. Currently the best deals on offer are the "Global Explorer" and "One World" tickets (Qantas/British Airways), and the "Star Alliance" deal (United/Air New Zealand/Thai/Lufthansa/Air Canada/SAS/ANA/Ansett and Varig) – all of which allow a minimum of four stopovers on several continents on a mileage basis, from A$2400/NZ$3000 to A$2700/NZ$3400. Note that while it's easy enough to include London on your itinerary, a stop in Scotland may involve backtracking and can be harder to arrange.

GETTING THERE FROM IRELAND AND THE CONTINENT

Stiff competition on routes between **Ireland** and Britain has kept the cost of **flights** relatively low, with several airlines offering return tickets from Dublin at off-peak periods for as little as IR£44. Ryanair (☎01/609 7800; *www.ryanair.ie*) flies to eleven destinations in Britain from Cork, Kerry and Knock, and is generally the cheapest, with its best deals being to Stansted; booking a week ahead brings the price of a return ticket to IR£70. Aer Lingus (☎01/705 3333) offers a greater choice of departure points, with fares from IR£87 if your journey includes a Saturday night, and British Airways (☎1800/626747) often gives good discounts on its published fares from Dublin. Flying from Belfast, however, your best bet is Easyjet (☎0870/600 0000; *www.easyjet.com*) whose cheapest return flight to Luton Airport costs £48. British Midland (☎0870/607 0555; *www.britishmidland.com*) flies to Heathrow from £67 and BA (☎08457/222111; *www.british-airways.com*) also covers this route, with open returns at a published fare of £283 – though booking through a travel agent will undercut this – and special off-peak deals from £89 if you travel mid-week and your journey includes a Saturday.

Flying cuts out a long overland and ferry journey, but if you're keeping costs to a minimum, then take the **coach**. Eurolines (☎01232/333000, 01/836 6111 or 0990/143219; *www.eurolines.com*) runs a service from Belfast (from £49 return) and Dublin (from IR£34) via Birmingham to London, with connections throughout Ireland. Considering the distances involved, this is great value; the downside is that the

trip to London, with an overnight ferry crossing to Holyhead, takes around ten hours from Belfast, twelve hours from Dublin and up to fourteen hours from elsewhere. Travelling from the Republic by train is marginally less uncomfortable, but if you're starting from the south or west the best ferry crossings are the more expensive Cork to Swansea, or Rosslare to Fishguard or Pembroke routes, which can bring the train fare to around the same as a flight. For more information, contact British and European Rail (☎01/703 4095).

Driving is the other option, although the cost of taking your car on the ferry can make this an expensive alternative if you're travelling alone and can't split the fare. A full rundown of the ferry routes between Ireland and England appears overleaf; fares fluctuate wildly depending on the time of year and the day of the week you travel, and also the length of your car, but expect to pay IR£120–280 for a small vehicle and up to five adults between Dublin and Holyhead, or IR£90–185 on the Cork–Swansea route.

Drivers **from Europe** also have the option of using **Eurotunnel** (☎0990/353535; *www.eurotunnel.com*), crossing underneath the Channel on freight trains which carry coaches, cars and motorbikes. You can just turn up, but booking is advised, especially at weekends; tickets are fully flexible. A five-day return for a car and passengers travelling off-peak costs from £169, £215 in peak season. Travelling between 10pm and 6am brings the price down to £139.

For foot passengers there are frequent through trains between Paris, Brussels, Lille and London run by **Eurostar** (☎0990/186186; *www.eurostar.co.uk*). The least expensive return fare (which must be booked three days in advance and include a Saturday night) is £89 from Paris, £79 from Brussels and £69 from Lille. Full fares with no restrictions are £249 from Paris and Brussels and £210 from Lille. Youth tickets (for under-26s) have no restrictions attached and cost £79 from Paris, £69 from Brussels and £65 from Lille. Eurostar also offers frequent promotional fares.

Tariffs on the **ferries** are bewilderingly complex: prices vary with the month, day or even hour at certain times of the year, not to mention how long you're staying and the size of your car.

FERRY CONNECTIONS

	Company	Frequency	Duration
From Belgium			
Ostend–Dover	Hoverspeed (SeaCat)	4–7 daily	2hr
Zeebrugge–Hull	P&O North Sea Ferries	1 daily	14hr
From Denmark			
Esbjerg–Harwich	Scandinavian/Stena	3–4 weekly	18hr
From France			
Boulogne–Folkestone	Hoverspeed SeaCat	April–Sept 4 daily	55min
Caen–Portsmouth	Brittany	Jan–mid-Nov 2–3 daily	6hr
Calais–Dover	P&O Stena	30–35 daily	75 min
Calais–Dover	Hoverspeed (hovercraft/SeaCat)	6–20 daily	35min/50 min
Cherbourg–Poole	Brittany	Jan–mid-Nov 1–2 daily	4hr 15min
Cherbourg–Portsmouth	P&O Portsmouth	1–5 daily	3hr–5hr
Dieppe–Newhaven	P&O Stena	2 daily	4hr
Dieppe–Newhaven	Hoverspeed (Super SeaCat)	April–Sept 3 daily	2 hr
St Malo–Poole (via Jersey)	Condor	May–Oct 1 daily	5hr40min
St Malo–Weymouth (via Jersey)	Condor	May–Oct I daily	5hr
St Malo–Portsmouth	Brittany	Jan–mid-Nov 1–7 weekly	8hr 45min
Le Havre–Portsmouth	P&O Portsmouth	2–3 daily	5hr–8hr
Roscoff–Plymouth	Brittany	Jan–mid-Nov 1–3 daily	6hr
From Germany			
Hamburg–Harwich	Scandinavian	3–4 weekly	19hr
Hamburg–Newcastle	Scandinavian	May–Sept 2weekly	22hr
From Holland			
Amsterdam–Newcastle	Scandinavian	2–7 weekly	14hr
Hook of Holland–Harwich	Stena (catamaran)	2 daily	3hr 40min
Rotterdam–Hull	North Sea	1 daily	14hr
From Ireland			
Cork–Swansea	Swansea–Cork Ferries	mid-March–Nov 4–6 weekly	10hr
Dun Laoghaire–Holyhead	Stena (catamaran)	4–5 daily	99min
Dublin–Holyhead	Stena/Irish Ferries	2–6 daily	1hr 50min/3hr 15min
Dublin–Liverpool	Isle of Man Steam Packet (SuperSeaCat)	March–Sept 1–2 daily	3hr 45min

FERRY CONNECTIONS

	Company	Frequency	Duration
Rosslare–Fishguard	Stena/Stena Sea Lynx	2–6 daily	1hr 35min–3hr 30min
Rosslare–Pembroke	Irish Ferries	2 daily	4hr
From Norway			
Stavanger/ Bergen–Newcastle	Fjord Line	4–6 weekly	20–27hr
Kristiansand–Newcastle	DFDS Scandinavian	2 weekly	18hr
Bergen–Lerwick	Smyril	mid-May–mid-Sept 1 weekly	12 hr
From Spain			
Bilbao–Portsmouth	P&O	2 weekly	29hr–40hr
Santander–Plymouth	Brittany	March–mid-Nov 1–2 weekly	24hr
From Sweden			
Gothenburg–Newcastle	Scandanavian	Feb–Dec 2 weekly	26hr

FERRY COMPANIES IN BRITAIN, IRELAND AND EUROPE

Brittany Ferries UK ☎0990/360360; France ☎02.31.36.36.36; Spain ☎42 22 00 00; *www.brittany-ferries.com*

Condor UK ☎01305/761551; France ☎02.99.20.03.00; *www.condorferries.co.uk*

DFDS Scandinavian Seaways UK ☎0990/333000; Denmark ☎79.17.79.17; Germany ☎040/389 0371; Holland ☎0255/03456; Sweden ☎031/650650; *www.scansea.com*

Fjord Line UK 0191/296 1313; Norway ☎55/548600; *www.fjordline.com*

Hoverspeed/SeaCat UK ☎08705/240241; France ☎3.21.46.14.14; *www.hoverspeed.co.uk*

Irish Ferries UK ☎08705/171717; Ireland ☎01/638 3333; *www.irishferries.ie*

Isle of Man Steam Packet UK ☎08705/523523; *www.steam-packet.com*

P&O ☎0870/600600; France ☎08.02.01.00.20; *www.posl.com*

P&O European Ferries UK ☎0870/242 4666; France ☎08.03.01.30.13; *www.poef.com*

P&O North Sea Ferries UK ☎01482/980980; Belgium ☎050.54.34.30; Holland ☎0181/255555; *www.ponsf.com*

P&O Portsmouth UK ☎0870/242 4999; *www.poportsmouth.com*

P&O Scottish Ferries UK ☎01224/572615; *www.poscottishferries.co.uk*

Sea France ☎0990/711711; *www.seafrance.com*

Smyril Line UK ☎01224/572615; Norway ☎55/320970

Stena Line UK & Ireland ☎0990/707070; Holland ☎017/438 9333; *www.posl.com*

Swansea–Cork Ferries UK ☎01792/456116; Ireland ☎021/271166.; *www.swansea-cork.ie*

Another thing to bear in mind is that some kind of sleeping accommodation is often obligatory on the longer crossings if made at night, pushing the price way above the basic rate. As an indication of cost, two people driving in a small car from Calais, Boulogne, Dieppe, Zeebrugge or Ostend to one of the English Channel ports could expect to pay £80–95 (the return fares are usually just twice the price); for a foot passenger the single fare is £24. The Gothenburg–Newcastle route, one of the longest crossings, costs over £175 at the least expensive time of the year, and £400 in high season for a car and up to five passengers, with prices from £54 for a foot passenger. All current crossings, including foot-passenger, hovercraft and catamaran services, are listed in the box on p.13.

You can, of course, also catch **buses** from a long list of European countries to Britain. Given the low cost of air fares from many cities, however, you'd have to be a masochist to want to travel by bus from, say, Athens – a journey of two nights and three days that actually costs more than the price of a three-and-a-half-hour flight to London. Eurolines is Britain's largest international coach company, with departures to London from 48 European cities, including Amsterdam, Brussels, Frankfurt, Hamburg, Madrid, Paris and Rome.

VISAS, CUSTOMS, REGULATIONS AND TAX

Citizens of all the countries of Europe – other than Albania, Romania, Bulgaria and the republics of the former Soviet Union (with the exception of the Baltic states) – can enter Britain with just a passport, generally for up to three months. US, Canadian, Australian and New Zealand citizens can enter the country for up to six months with just a passport. All other nationalities require a visa, obtainable from the British Consular office in the country of application.

For stays of longer than six months, **US**, **Canadian**, **Australian** and **New Zealand** citizens should apply to the British Embassy or High Commission (see box opposite). If you want to extend your visa, you should write, before the expiry date given on the endorsement in your passport, to: The Under Secretary of State, Home Office, Immigration and Nationality Dept, Lunar House, Wellesley Rd, Croydon CR9 2BY (☎0181/686 0688), enclosing your passport or National Identity Card and form IS120 (if these were your entry documents).

WORKING IN BRITAIN

Unless you're a **resident of an EU country**, you need a permit to work legally in the UK, although without the backing of an established employer or company this can be very difficult to obtain. Persons aged between 17 and 27 may, however, apply for a Working Holiday-Maker Entry Certificate, which entitles you to a two-year stay in the UK during which it is permitted to undertake work of a casual nature (ie, not in a profession, or as a sportsperson or entertainer). The certificates are only available abroad, from British embassies and consulates, and when you apply you must be able to convince the officer you have a valid return or onward ticket, and the means to support yourself while you're in Britain without having to claim state benefits of any kind. Note, too, that the certificates are valid from the date of entry into Britain – you won't be able to recoup time spent elsewhere in the two-year period of validity.

In **North America**, full-time college students can get temporary work permits through BUNAC, 30 Southbury, CT 06488 (☎1/800-GO-BUNAC; *www.bunac.org*). Permits are valid for up to six months and cost $225; send an application form, college verification form and two passport photos to the above address; allow two to three weeks to process the application.

Other visitors entitled to work in Britain are **Commonwealth citizens** with a parent or grandparent who was born in the UK. If you fall into this category, you can apply for a Certificate of Entitlement to the Right of Abode. If you're unsure about whether or not you may be eligible for one of these, contact your nearest British Mission (embassy or consulate), or the Foreign and Commonwealth Office in London (☎0171/270 1500 or 238 4633).

The kind of work you can expect to find in England as a visitor is generally unskilled **employment** in hotels, restaurants, cleaning companies and on farms. Working conditions may not be up to much, and as a casual employee you can be fired at short notice. Pay is poor, too (£3–4 per hour), and will bring in barely enough to survive. So unless you're desperate, try to save at home before travelling. With **voluntary work**, the choice of jobs improves considerably, ranging from farm camps to placements with service organizations. Scores of useful addresses are featured in a guide called *Working Holidays*, published by the Central Bureau for Educational Visits and Exchanges (CBEVE), available from 10 Spring Gardens, London SW1A 2BN (£9.99). *Summer Jobs in Britain* by David Woodworth (£8.99) gives comprehensive information on paid seasonal work in the UK.

If you're between 17 and 27, and don't have kids, you might also consider **working as an au pair**. This enables you to live for a maximum of two years with an English-speaking family. In return for your accommodation, food and a small amount of pocket money (say £40 per week), you'll be expected to help around the house and to look after the children for a maximum of five hours each day. The easiest way to find au pair work is through a licensed agency. The Federation of Recruitment and Employment Services (FRES), 36–38 Mortimer St, London W1N 7RB (☎0800/320558; *www.fres.co.uk*), will send you a list of reputable agents (ie, those that are vetted annually by the government) for £3.75.

CUSTOMS

Since the inauguration of the EU Single Market, travellers coming into Britain directly from another EU country do not have to make a declaration to Customs at their place of entry. In other words, you can bring almost as much French wine or German beer across the Channel as you like – the guidance levels are 90 litres of wine and 110 of beer, which should suffice for anyone's requirements – any more than this, and you'll have to provide proof that it's for personal use only. If you're travelling to or from a non-EU country, you can still buy duty-free goods, but within the EU, this perk no longer exists. The duty-free allowances are as follows:

BRITISH EMBASSIES AND HIGH COMMISSIONS ABROAD

Australia British High Commission, Commonwealth Ave, Yarralumla, Canberra, ACT 2600 (☎1902/941555; *www.uk.emb.gov.au*).

Canada British High Commission, 80 Elgin St, Ottawa, ON K1P 5K7 (☎613/237-1530).

Ireland 29 Merrion Rd, Dublin 4 (☎01/205 3700).

New Zealand British High Commission, 44 Hill St, Wellington (☎04/495 0889; *www.brithighcomm.org.nz*).

USA 3100 Massachusetts Ave, NW, Washington DC 20008 (☎202/462-1340).

OVERSEAS REPRESENTATION IN BRITAIN

American Embassy, 24 Grosvenor Square, London W1A 1AE (☎0171/499 9000).

Australian High Commission, Australia House, The Strand, London WC2B 4LA (☎0171/379 4334; *www.australia.org.uk*).

Canadian High Commission, 1 Grosvenor Square, London W1X 0AB

(☎0171/258 6600; *www.canada.org.uk*).

Irish Embassy, 17 Grosvenor Place, London SW1 (☎0171/235 2171; *www.irlgov.ie*).

New Zealand High Commission, New Zealand House, 80 Haymarket, London SW1Y 4TQ (☎0171/930 8422; *www.newzealandhc.org*).

• **Tobacco**: 200 cigarettes; or 100 cigarillos; or 50 cigars; or 250 grammes of loose tobacco.

• **Alcohol**: 2 litres of still wine plus 1 litre of drink over 22 percent alcohol; or 2 litres of alcoholic drinks not over 22 percent.

• **Perfumes**: 60ml of perfume plus 250ml of toilet water.

• Plus **other goods** to the value of £145.

There are **import restrictions** on a variety of articles and substances, from firearms to furs derived from endangered species, none of which should bother the normal tourist. However, if you need any clarification on British import regulations, contact HM Customs and Excise, Dorset House, Stamford St, London SE1 9PY (☎0171/202 4227). You are not allowed to bring **pets** into Britain.

Most goods in Britain, with the chief exceptions of books and food, are subject to **Value Added Tax (VAT)**, which increases the cost of an item by 17.5 percent. Visitors from non-EU countries can save a lot of money through the **Retail Export Scheme**, which allows a refund of VAT on goods to be taken out of the country. (Savings will usually be minimal for EU nationals, because of the rates at which the goods will be taxed upon import to the home country.) Note that not all shops participate in this scheme (those doing so will display a sign to this effect) and that you cannot reclaim VAT charged on hotel bills or other services.

MONEY, BANKS AND COSTS

The easiest and safest way to carry your money is in travellers' cheques, available for a small commission (normally one percent) from any major bank. The most commonly accepted travellers' cheques are American Express, followed by Visa and Thomas Cook – most cheques issued by banks will be one of these three brands. You'll usually pay commission again when you cash each cheque, normally another one percent or so, or a flat rate – though no commission is payable on Amex cheques exchanged at Amex branches. Keep a record of the cheques as you cash them, and you can get the value of all uncashed cheques refunded immediately if you lose them.

You'll find that most hotels, shops and restaurants in Britain accept the major **credit cards** – MasterCard, Visa, American Express and Diners Club – although they're less useful in the most rural areas, and smaller establishments all over the country, such as B&B accommodation, will often accept cash only. Your card will also enable you to get cash advances from certain **ATMs** (known as cashpoints in Britain) – call the issuing bank or credit company to get a list of British locations. In addition, you may be able to make withdrawals using your ATM cash card – your bank's international banking department should be able to advise on this. Make sure you have a personal identification number (PIN) that's designed to work overseas.

BANKS AND BUREAUX DE CHANGE

Every sizeable town in **England and Wales** has a branch of at least one of the big four **high-street banks**: National Westminster, Barclays, Lloyds TSB and HSBC. Basic **opening hours** are Monday to Friday 9.30am to 4.30pm, though many branches in larger towns open at 9am, close at 5.30pm and also remain open until 3pm or 4pm on Saturdays.

In Scotland the big high-street names are Bank of Scotland, Royal Bank of Scotland, Clydesdale and Lloyds TSB, all open Monday to Friday 9.15am to 4.45pm, and in larger towns on Saturday mornings. In remoter parts of Scotland, however, there may be only a mobile bank that runs to a timetable, usually available from the local post office.

Almost everywhere banks are the best places to change money and cheques. Outside banking hours you're best advised to go to a **bureau de change**; these can be found in most city centres, often at train stations or airports. Try to avoid changing money or cheques in hotels, where the rates are normally the poorest on offer.

If, as a foreign visitor, you run out of money or there is some kind of emergency, the quickest way to get **money sent out** is to contact your bank at home and have them wire the cash to the nearest bank. You can do the same thing through Thomas Cook or American Express if there is a branch nearby. Americans, Canadians and Australians can have cash sent out through Western Union (☎1-800/325-6000) or American Express MoneyGram (☎1-800/543-4080). Fees depend on the destination and the amount being transferred, but as an example, wiring $1000 to England will cost around $75. The funds should be available for collection at Western Union's or Amex's local office within minutes of being sent.

There are **no exchange controls** in Britain, so you can bring in as much cash as you like and change travellers' cheques up to any amount.

CURRENCY

The British **pound sterling** (£; *punt* in Welsh) is a decimal currency, divided into 100 pence (p; c in Wales for *ceiniogau*). Coins come in denominations of 1p, 2p, 5p, 10p, 20p, 50p and £1 and £2. Notes come in denominations of £5, £10, £20 and £50; shopkeepers will carefully scrutinize any £20 or £50 notes, as forgeries are widespread, and you'd be well advised to do the same. The quickest test is to hold the note up to the light to make sure there's a thin wire filament running through the note from top to bottom; this is by no means foolproof, but it will catch most fakes.

Bank of England and Northern Ireland banknotes are accepted **in Scotland**, where the Bank of Scotland, the Royal Bank of Scotland and the Clydesdale Bank also issue their own banknotes in denominations of £1, £5, £10, £20, £50 and £100. Although these Scottish banknotes are legal tender in the rest of Britain, some traders south of the border may be unwilling to accept them.

Britain remains sceptical about the euro, and despite moves in other EU countries, it's unlikely to become currency in this country until well after the next election, if then.

COSTS

Britain has become an expensive place to visit. The **minimum expenditure**, if you're camping, or hostelling, using public transport, buying picnic food and eating in pubs and cafés, would be in the region of £25–35 a day. Couples staying at budget B&Bs, eating at unpretentious restaurants and visiting a fair number of tourist attractions are looking at around £40–50 each per day, and if you're renting a car, staying in comfortable B&Bs or hotels and eating well, budget on at least £80 each per day. Single travellers should count on spending around 60 percent of what a couple would spend (single rooms cost more than half a double), and on any visit to London, work on the basis that you'll need at least an extra £15 per day to get any pleasure out of the place. On the other hand, costs are often lower in rural areas, and average costs in Scotland and Wales can be marginally lower than in England. For more detail on the cost of accommodation, transport and eating, see the relevant sections below.

YOUTH AND STUDENT DISCOUNTS

Various official and quasi-official youth/student ID cards are widely available and most will pay for themselves in savings pretty soon. Full-time students are eligible for the **International Student ID Card (ISIC)**, which entitles the bearer to special fares on local transport, and discounts at museums, theatres and other attractions; for Americans and Canadians there's also a health benefit (see overleaf). The card costs $20 for Americans, CDN$16 for Canadians, A$15 for Australians, NZ$17 for New Zealanders and £5 in the UK, and is available from branches of Council Travel, STA and Travel CUTS around the world (see pp.4 & 9).

You only have to be 25 or younger to qualify for the **Travel Cuts Go-25 Card**, which costs the same as the ISIC and carries the same benefits. It can be purchased through Council Travel in the US, Travel Cuts in Canada and STA in Australia (see boxes on pp.4 & 9).

STA also sells its own ID card that's good for some discounts, as do various other travel organizations. A university photo ID might open some doors, too.

INSURANCE, HEALTH AND EMERGENCIES

Wherever you're travelling from, it's a very good idea to have some kind of **travel insurance**. The amount of cover you get varies according to the premium you pay, but a standard policy should always cover the cost of cancellation and curtailment of flights, medical expenses, travel delay, accident, missed departures, lost baggage, lost passport, personal liability and legal expenses. **In the UK**, low-cost policies start at around £13 per month, and it is usually worth shopping around. Good companies to phone for quotes include Columbus Travel Insurance (☎0171/375 0011), Worldwide (☎01892/833338), Endsleigh Insurance (☎0171/436 4451) and Marcus Hearne & Co Ltd (☎0171/739 3444). Note that some insurance companies refuse to cover travellers over 65, or have upper limits of 69 or 74 years of age, and most that do accept them charge hefty premiums; the best policies with no upper age limit are offered by Age Concern (☎01883/346964).

Whatever your policy, and regardless of who you buy it from, if you have anything stolen, get a copy of the police report of the incident, as this is essential to substantiate your claim.

In the **US and Canada** you should carefully check the insurance policies you already have before taking out a new one. You may discover that you're covered already for medical and other losses while abroad. Canadians especially are usually covered by their provincial health plans. Holders of an official student/teacher/youth card, such as ISIC (see p.17), are entitled (outside the USA) to be reimbursed for accident coverage and hospital in-patient benefits, with up to $3000 in emergency

medical coverage and $100 a day for up to sixty days in hospital, plus a 24-hour hotline to call in the event of a medical, legal or financial emergency. Students may also find their health coverage extends during vacations, and many bank and charge accounts include some form of travel cover; insurance is also sometimes included if you pay for your trip with a credit card. Premiums vary, so shop around. The best deals are usually to be had through student/youth travel agencies – ISIS now offers STA Travel Insurance for travellers under the age of 60. Coverage is worldwide and is structured to offer you either a comprehensive package or the option of excluding medical protection if your private health insurance covers you away from home. STA policies come in packages covering seven days ($35), fifteen days ($55), one month ($115) and two months ($180) – add an extra $55 for each additional month on longer stays. If you're planning to do any **dangerous sports**, be sure to ask whether these activities are covered: some policies add a hefty surcharge.

Note that most North American travel policies apply only to items lost, stolen or damaged while in the custody of an identifiable, responsible third party – hotel porter, airline, luggage consignment, etc – and very few insurers will arrange on-the-spot payments in the event of a major expense or loss; you will usually be reimbursed only after going home.

Travel insurance policies in **Australia and New Zealand** tend to be put together by the airlines and travel agent groups, which are all fairly similar in terms of coverage and price – but if you plan to indulge in **high-risk activities** such as mountaineering, bungee jumping or scuba diving, check the policy carefully to make sure you'll be covered. A typical policy for the UK covering medical bills, lost baggage and personal liability will cost around A\$110/NZ\$140 for two weeks, A\$160/NZ\$200 for one month, A\$265/NZ\$330 for two months. The companies listed in the box opposite offer some of the widest cover available which can be arranged through most travel agents.

MEDICAL MATTERS

No vaccinations are required for entry into Britain. Citizens of all EU countries and those with a reciprocal health care agreement with this country are entitled to free medical treatment at National Health Service hospitals. If you don't fall into either of these categories, you will be charged for all medical services, in which case **health insurance** is strongly advised.

There are no particular health risks in Britain, though if you're visiting Scotland you should be prepared to encounter the **midge** (*culicoides*) – a tiny biting fly prevalent in the Highlands and islands. To most people these insects are merely a nuisance; others have a violent allergic reaction when bitten. Unless you visit in the winter, midges are hard to avoid: they love still, damp, shady conditions and are at their most vicious around sunrise and sunset. You'll soon notice if they're near; cover up arms and legs and try to avoid wearing dark colours, which attract them. Various repellents, widely available from pharmacists, are worth a try.

Pharmacists (known as chemists in Britain) can dispense only a limited range of drugs without a doctor's prescription. Most pharmacies are **open** **standard shop hours**, though in large towns some may stay open as late as 10pm – local newspapers carry lists of late-opening pharmacies. **Doctor's surgeries** tend to be open from about 9am to noon and then for a couple of hours in the evenings; outside **surgery hours**, you can turn up at the casualty department of the local hospital for complaints that require immediate attention – unless it's an **emergency**, in which case ring for an ambulance, ☎999.

POLICE

Although the traditional image of the friendly British "bobby" has become increasingly tarnished by stories of corruption, racism and crooked dealings, the **police** continue to be approachable and helpful. If you're lost in a major town, asking a police officer is generally the quickest way to pinpoint your destination – alternatively, you could ask a **traffic warden**, a species of law-enforcer much maligned in car-loving Britain. Most traffic wardens are distinguishable by their security guardish uniforms and by the fact that they are generally armed with a hand-set for dispensing parking-fine tickets; police officers on street duty generally wear a distinctive domed hat with a silver tip, and are armed with just a truncheon.

As with any country, the major towns of England have their dangerous spots, but these tend to be inner-city housing estates where no tourist has any reason to be. The chief risk on England's streets is pickpocketing, and there are some virtuoso villains at work in London, especially on the big shopping streets and the Underground. Carry only as much money as you need, and keep all bags and pockets fastened. Should you have anything stolen or be involved in some incident that requires reporting, go to the local police station; the ☎999 number should only be used **in emergencies**.

EMERGENCIES

For Police, Fire Brigade, Ambulance and, in certain areas, Mountain Rescue or Coastguard, dial ☎999.

INFORMATION AND MAPS

If you want to do a bit of research before arriving in Britain, you could contact the **British Tourist Authority (BTA)** in your country – the addresses are given in the box below. The BTA will send you a wealth of free literature, some of it just rose-tinted advertising copy, but much of it extremely useful – especially the maps, city guides and event calendars. If you want more hard facts on a particular area, you should approach the **regional tourist offices** in Britain, which are listed opposite. Some are extremely helpful, others give the impression of being harassed to breaking point by years of understaffing, but all of them will have a few leaflets worth scanning before you set out.

Tourist offices (usually called Tourist Information Centres, or TICs for short) exist in virtually every British town – you'll find their phone numbers and opening hours in the relevant sections of the guide. The average opening hours are much the same as standard shop hours, with the difference that in summer they'll often be open on a Sunday and for a couple of hours after the shops have closed on weekdays; opening hours are generally shorter in winter, and in more remote areas the office may even be closed. All centres offer information on accommodation (which they can often book – see p.32), local public transport, attractions and restaurants, as well as town and regional maps. In many cases this is free, but a growing number of offices make a small charge for an accommodation list or a town guide with an accompanying street plan. Areas designated as **National Parks** (such as the Lake District, Dartmoor or Snowdonia) also have a fair sprinkling of National Park Information Centres, which are generally more expert in giving guidance on local walks and outdoor pursuits.

MAPS

The most comprehensive series of maps, renowned for their accuracy and clarity, are produced by the **Ordnance Survey**. The 204 maps in its 1:50,000 (a little over one-inch-to-one-mile) Landranger Series cover the whole of Britain and show enough detail to be useful for most walkers. More detailed, and invaluable for serious hiking, are the 1:25,000 Outdoor Leisure maps, which deal with National Parks and areas of outstanding beauty, and the Explorer set of maps which is gradually replacing the Pathfinder series; between them they cover the entire country. Less well known is the Goldeneye series, a range of fairly ordinary road touring maps for various English counties, but made interesting with the addition of historical and recreational details on the back. The full range of Ordnance Survey maps is only available at a few big-city stores (see box

REGIONAL TOURIST OFFICES IN ENGLAND

Britain Visitor Centre, 1 Regent St, London SW1Y 4NS (no telephone enquiries; *www.visitbritain.com*).

Cumbria Tourist Board, Ashleigh, Holly Rd, Windermere, Cumbria LA23 2AQ (☎01539/444444; *www.cumbria-the-lake-district.co.uk*).

East of England Tourist Board, Toppesfield Hall, Hadleigh, Suffolk IP7 5DN (☎01473/822922; *www.visitbritain.com*).

Heart of England Tourist Board, Woodside, Larkhill Rd, Worcester WR5 2EZ (☎01905/763436; *www.visitbritain.com*); Premier House, 15 Wheeler Gate, Nottingham NG1 2NA (☎0115/959 8383; *www.visitbritain.com*).

London Tourist Board, Glen House, Stag Place, London SW1E 5LT (no telephone enquiries; *www.LondonTown.com*).

North West England Tourist Board, Swan House, Swan Meadow Road, Wigan Pier, Wigan WN3 5BB (☎01942/821222; *www.visitbritain.com*).

Northumbria Tourist Board, Aykley Heads, Durham DH1 5UX (☎0191/375 3000; *www.ntb.org.uk*).

South East England Tourist Board, The Old Brew House, Warwick Park, Tunbridge Wells, Kent TN2 5TU (☎01892/540766; *www.seetb.org.uk*).

Southern Tourist Board, 40 Chamberlayne Rd, Eastleigh, Hampshire SO50 5JH (☎01703/620006; *www.visitbritain.com*).

West Country Tourist Board, 60 St David's Hill, Exeter, Devon EX4 4SY (☎01392/425426; *www.wctb.co.uk*).

Yorkshire Tourist Board, 312 Tadcaster Rd, York YO24 1GS (☎01904/707961; *www.ytb.org.uk*).

REGIONAL TOURIST OFFICES IN SCOTLAND

Aberdeen and Grampian Tourist Board, 27 Albyn Place, Aberdeen AB10 1YL (☎01224/632727; *www.agtb.org*).

Angus and City of Dundee Tourist Board, 7–21 Castle Street, Dundee DD1 3AA (☎01382/434664; *www.angusanddundee.co.uk*).

Argyll, the Isles, Loch Lomond, Stirling & Trossachs Tourist Board, Old Town Jail, St John St, Stirling FK8 1EA (☎01786/475019; *www.scottish.heartlands.org*).

Ayrshire and Arran Tourist Board, Burns House, Burns Statue Square, Ayr KA7 1UT (☎01292/288688; *www.ayrshire-marran.com*).

Dumfries and Galloway Tourist Board, 64 Whitesands, Dumfries DG1 2RS (☎01387/253862; *www.galloway.co.uk*).

Edinburgh and Lothians Tourist Board, 4 Rothesay Terrace, Edinburgh EH3 7RY (☎0131/473 3800; *www.edinburgh.org*).

Greater Glasgow & Clyde Valley Tourist Board, 11 George Square, Glasgow G2 1DY (☎0141/204 4400; *www.glasgowtourist.co.uk*).

Highlands of Scotland Tourist Board, Peffery House, Strathpeffer, IV14 9HA (☎01997/421160 or 0870/5143070; *www.host.co.uk*).

Kingdom of Fife Tourist Board, 7 Hanover Court, North St, Glenrothes KY7 5SB (☎01334/472021; *www.sta.co.uk*).

Orkney Tourist Board, 6 Broad St, Kirkwall, Orkney KW15 1NX (☎01856/872856; *www.orkneyislands.com*).

Perthshire Tourist Board, Lower City Mills, West Mill Street, Perth PH1 5QP (☎01738/627958; *www.perthshire.co.uk*).

Scottish Tourist Board, 19 Cockspur St, London SW1 5BL (☎0171/930 8661; *www.holiday.scotland.net*).

Scottish Borders Tourist Board, Shepherds Mills, Whinfield Rd, Selkirk TD7 5DT (☎01750/20555; *www.scotborders.co.uk*).

Shetland Island Tourism, Market Cross, Lerwick, Shetland ZE1 0LU (☎01595/693434; *www.shetland-tourism.co.uk*).

Western Isles Tourist Board, 26 Cromwell St, Stornoway, Isle of Lewis HS1 2DD (☎01851/703088; *www.witb.co.uk*).

WELSH TOURIST BOARD OFFICES

Wales Tourist Board, Head Office: Brunel House, 2 Fitzalan Rd, Cardiff CF24 0UY (☎01222/499909; *www.tourism.wales.gov.uk*). Written requests for information should be sent to: WTB, Dept RJ3, PO Box 1, Cardiff CF1 2XN.

Wales Information Bureau, Britain Visitor Centre, 1 Regent St, London SW1Y 4NS (☎0171/808 3838; *www.visitwales.com*).

North Wales Tourism, 77 Conway Rd, Colwyn Bay, LL29 7LN (☎01492/531731 or 0800/834820; *www.nwt.co.uk*).

Mid Wales Tourism, The Station, Machynlleth, SY20 8TG (☎01654/702653 or 0800/273747; *www.mid-wales-tourism.org.uk*).

Tourism South and West Wales, Charter Court, Phoenix Way, Enterprise Park, Swansea SA7 9DB (☎01792/781212 or 0800/243731).

MAP OUTLETS

UNITED KINGDOM

London: Daunt Books, 83 Marylebone High St, W1M 3DE (☎0171/224 2295) and 193 Haverstock Hill, NW3 4QL (☎0171/794 4006); National Map Centre, 22–24 Caxton St, SW1H 0QU (☎0171/222 2466); Stanfords, 12–14 Long Acre, WC2E 9LP (☎0171/836 1321); 52 Grosvenor Gardens, SW1W 0AG (☎0171/730 1314) and within the British Airways offices at 156 Regent St, W1R 5TA (☎0171/434 4744); The Travel Bookshop,

13–15 Blenheim Crescent, W11 2EE (☎0171/229 5260).

Cardiff: Blackwell's, 13–17 Royal Arcade, CF1 2PR (☎01222/395036).

Glasgow: John Smith and Sons, 57–61 St Vincent St, G2 5TB (☎0141/221 7472).

Maps are also available by **mail order** from Stanfords (☎0171/836 1321).

NORTH AMERICA

Chicago: Rand McNally, 444 North Michigan Ave, IL 60611 (☎312/321-1751).

Los Angeles: Map Link Inc, 30 S LaPatera Lane, Suite 5, Santa Barbara, CA 93117 (☎805/692-6777).

Montreal: Ulysses Travel Bookshop, 4176 St-Denis (☎514/843-9447).

New York: BritRail's British Travel Shop, 551 5th Ave (☎212/490-6688); The Complete Traveler Bookstore, 199 Madison Ave, NY 10016 (☎212/685-9007); Rand McNally, 150 East 52nd St, NY 10022 (☎212/758-7488); Traveler's Choice Bookstore, 2 Wooster St, NY 10013 (☎212/941-1535).

San Francisco: The Complete Traveler Bookstore, 3207 Fillmore St, CA 94123

(☎415/923-1511); Rand McNally, 595 Market St, CA 94105 (☎415/777-3131); Phileas Fogg's Books & Maps, Stanford Shopping Center, Suite 87, Palo Alto, CA 94304 (☎1-800/233-FOGG in California; ☎1-800/533-FOGG elsewhere in US).

Seattle: Elliot Bay Book Company, 101 South Main St, WA 98104 (☎206/624-6600).

Toronto: Open Air Books and Maps, 25 Toronto St, M5C 2R1 (☎416/363-0719).

Vancouver: International Travel Maps and Books, 552 Seymour, BC V6B 3J5 (☎604/687-3320).

Washington DC: Rand McNally, 7101 Democracy Blvd, Bethesda, MD 20817 (☎301/365-6277).

AUSTRALIA

Adelaide: The Map Shop, 16a Peel St, SA 5000 (☎08/8231 2033).

Auckland: Specialty Maps, 58 Albert St (☎09/307 2217).

Brisbane: Worldwide Maps and Guides 187 George St, Brisbane QLD 4000 (☎07/3221 4330).

Melbourne: Mapland, 372 Little Bourke St, VIC 3000 (☎03/9670 4383).

Sydney: Travel Bookshop, Shop 3, 175 Liverpool St, NSW 2000 (☎02/9261 8200).

Perth: Perth Map Centre, 1/884 Hay St, WA 6000 (☎08/9322 5733).

above), but in any walking district of Britain you'll find the relevant maps in local shops or information offices. Virtually every service station stocks one or more of the big road atlases.

Scotland's official tourist map series, published by **Estate Publications**, is perfect if you're driving or cycling round one particular region since it marks all the major tourist sights as well as youth hostels and campsites. The best **road atlases** are the large-format items produced by the AA, RAC, Collins and Ordnance Survey, which cover all of Britain at around three miles to one inch and include larger-scale plans of major towns.

USEFUL WEB SITES

Weaving your way in and out of the numerous websites before leaving for Britain is a good way to familiarize yourself with the place, book up accommodation and arm yourself with tips and information. We've indicated relevant Web sites throughout this chapter, but listed here are some useful general sites.

www.backpackers.co.uk Gives information on travel, jobs and independent hostels.
www.britishtravel.com Details hotel accommodation, cottage rental, bus and rail information.
www.city-net/countries/ united-kingdom/england A county by county guide, listing top attractions, accommodation, and some all-important tips on etiquette.
www.dedicate.co.uk Gives a useful list of links of sites.
www.knowhere.co.uk A self-styled user's guide to Britain. Up-to-date info, with readers' comments, including best-of and worst-of sections.

www.mtn.co.uk Information on mountaineering courses, holidays, gear and books.
www.ordsvy.gov.uk Details the full range of Ordnance Survey maps, including digital maps.
www.rcahms.gov.uk Information on Scotland's historic buildings and ancient monuments.
www.seaview.co.uk/ferries/ferlinks.html For comprehensive information on all ferries.
www.tiac.net/users/namarie/ The site is named Anglophilia and provides a host of links to other sites from shops to bands.
www.ukonline.co.uk Gives a guide to events in the regions, sport, up-to-the-minute news and access to telephone books.

GETTING AROUND

As you'd expect of such a small and densely populated island, just about every place in Britain is accessible by train or bus. However, the costs of Britain's public transport are among the highest in Europe – London's commuters spend more on getting to work than any of their European counterparts, while cross-country travel can eat up a large part of your budget. It pays to plan ahead and make sure you're aware of all the passes and special deals on offer – note that some are only available outside England, and must be purchased before you arrive. It's often cheaper to drive yourself around the country though fuel and car rental costs again are among the highest in Europe and will seem prohibitive to North Americans. Congestion around the main cities can be bad, and even the motorways (notoriously the M25, London's orbital road) are liable to sporadic gridlocks, especially on public holidays when what seems like half the population takes to the roads.

INTERNAL FLIGHTS

Since the distances involved are so small, **internal flights** are not the most obvious choice for getting around Britain. The domestic traffic handled by the main regional airports of Birmingham, Bristol, Manchester, Glasgow and Edinburgh is generally aimed at commuters and saves little time over the equivalent train journey. The only flight you might seriously consider taking is one from England to Scotland.

You can fly to Scotland's main airports – Edinburgh, Glasgow and Aberdeen – in an hour or so from all three London airports (Heathrow, Gatwick and Stansted), as well as from various provincial

AIRLINES

KLM UK ☎08705/074074; *www.klmuk.com.*
London to Edinburgh and Glasgow.

British Airways ☎08457/222111; *www. british-airways.com.* London, Birmingham, Manchester, Bristol and Plymouth to Edinburgh, Glasgow and Aberdeen; London and Birmingham to Inverness.

British Airways/Loganair ☎08457/222111. Flights within Scotland only.

British Midland ☎0870/607 0555; *www. britishmidland.com.* London, Manchester and East Midlands to Edinburgh and Glasgow.

Easyjet ☎0870/600 0000; *www.easyjet.com.* London to Aberdeen, Edinburgh, Glasgow and Inverness.

Go ☎08456/054 321; *www.go-fly.com.* London to Edinburgh, Glasgow and Aberdeen.

Manx Airlines ☎08457/256256; *www. manx-airlines.com.* Isle of Man to Glasgow.

Ryanair ☎08701/569569; *www.ryanair.com.* Stansted to Prestwick.

FLIGHT AGENTS IN BRITAIN

Campus Travel, 52 Grosvenor Gardens, London SW1 0AG (☎0171/730 3402; *www.usitcampus.co.uk*). Also many branches around the country.

Council Travel, 28A Poland St, London W1V 3DB (☎0171/437 7767). Flights and student discounts.

Destination Group, 14 Greville St, London EC1N 8SB (☎0171/400 7077; *www.destination-group.com*). Good discount fares.

STA Travel, 86 Old Brompton Rd, London SW7

3LQ (☎0171/361 6161; *www.statravel.co.uk*). Offices nationwide.

Trailfinders, 215 Kensington High St, London W8 7RG (☎0171/937 5400; *www.trailfinders.com*). Branches nationwide.

Travel Bug, 597 Cheetham Hill Rd, Manchester M8 5EJ (☎0161/721 4000; *www.travel-bug.co.uk*). Large range of discounted tickets.

Travel CUTS 295A Regent St, London W1R 7YA (☎0171/255 1944; *www.travelcuts.co.uk*). Discounted and student fares.

airports. There's usually a confusingly wide range of fares. The best deals are **special-offer tickets**, sold at least three days in advance on specific flights; these tend to fly at less social hours and are subject to availability and certain restrictions, but the savings can make the extra effort well worthwhile. The next cheapest seats are **Apex** tickets, available on all flights, at about half the price of a full-price economy-class ticket. The full amount for Apex must be paid at least two weeks before departure, and only fifty percent of the price will be returned if the booking is cancelled. Anyone under 26 should also check out a specialist agency such as Campus Travel or STA Travel, as they offer special youth deals, including Domestic Air Passes (aka "Skytrekker Passes") on British Airways flights, which can get you to Inverness and the Hebrides for a fraction of the published fare. Addresses for discount agents are listed in the box above.

There are flights almost hourly to Edinburgh and Glasgow from London, and nearly as many to

Aberdeen. As a broad guide to what you're likely to pay, reckon on £30 for a rock-bottom one-way ticket from Luton or Stansted to Edinburgh or Glasgow with Easyjet or Go. Full return fares for British Airways, British Midland or KLM UK, the three main carriers, start at around £100, rising to more than double that for the most flexible tickets; Apex rates and reductions for young persons and students apply in most cases. Note, too, that airport tax, currently around £21, is levied on all domestic flights to Scotland.

If you're short of time, Scotland's 22 internal airports, many of them on the islands, can be useful. Inter-island flights are mainly operated by British Airways flying between Edinburgh, Glasgow, Aberdeen and Inverness and the main islands. For £169 you can get a Highland Rover pass which gives you five internal flights (excluding local flights within Orkney and Shetland); you must stay for a minimum of seven days and book seven days before your first flight. Call BA (☎08457/222111) for information.

RAIL TRAVEL

A chronic lack of investment and a foolhardy privatization process has caused a severe decline in **rail travel** over the last decade. With the track and stations now being owned by Railtrack, and the trains and services being run by a tangle of private companies, there's also no little confusion when it comes to trying to figure out routes and prices. Still, despite the fears of many, few lines and services have been axed so far and there aren't many major towns that cannot be reached by rail, although travelling across the country – rather than out from London – can involve making connections with several different services.

You can buy **tickets** at the train station on the day of travel, but it should hardly come as a surprise to find that booking as far ahead as possible (at least two weeks) ensures the cheapest fares – or that travelling most places on a Friday is the most expensive way to go.

At the time of going to press, there were five types of **reduced-fare ticket** – Saver, SuperSaver, SuperAdvanced, Apex and SuperApex – all with byzantine restrictions which are often different from route to route and company to company (for instance, it's often cheaper to travel return from the north to London, rather than from London to the north). **Apex** tickets are issued in limited numbers on certain InterCity journeys of 150 miles or more, and have to be booked at least seven days before travelling; a seat reservation is included with the ticket. The rock-bottom **SuperApex** tickets have to be booked fourteen days in advance, and are available in limited numbers on InterCity services between London and selected towns and cities. To take the London–Newcastle service as an example, an ordinary return fare costs £144; a Saver is £77.40; a SuperSaver £66; a SuperAdvanced is £54; an Apex is £43; and a SuperApex £31. For all special-offer tickets you should book as far in advance as you possibly can – many Apex and SuperApex tickets are sold out weeks before the travel date.

Children aged between 5 and 15 pay half the adult fare on most journeys – but there are no discounts on Apex and SuperApex tickets. Under-5s travel free, although they are not entitled to a seat on crowded trains.

At weekends and on public holidays, many long-distance services have a special deal whereby you can convert your second-class ticket to a first-class one by buying a first-class supplement, which costs between £3 and £10 and is well worth paying if you're facing a five-hour journey

---

RAIL OFFICES AND AGENCIES

NORTH AMERICA AND AUSTRALIA

BritRail's British Travel Shop, 551 5th Ave, NY (☎212/490-6688) All British rail passes, rail-drive and multi-country passes and Channel Tunnel tickets.

CIT Rail, 9501 W Devon Ave, Suite 502, Rosemont IL 60018 (☎1-800/248-7245). Eurail passes, and BritRail passes.

Rail Europe US: 500 Mamaroneck Ave, Suite 314 Harrison, NY 10528 (Rail Europe ☎1-800/438-7245; BritRail ☎1-800/677-8585). Canada: 2087 Dundas East, Suite 105,

Mississauga, L4X 1M2 (Rail Europe ☎1-800/361-7245; BritRail ☎1-800/555-2748). Eurail, BritRail passes, ferry passes between UK and Ireland, Netherlands, Channel Tunnel passes.

Student Flights, 5010 E Shea Blvd, Suite 104A, Scottsdale, AZ 85254 (☎1-800/255-8000; *www.isecard.com*). Free shipping and $20 discount for BritRail and Eurail passes for everyone.

Rail Plus, Level 8, 114 William St, Melbourne, VIC 3000 (☎03/9642 8644 or 1300/555003); Level 6, 76 Symonds St, Auckland (☎09/303 2484).

RAIL INFORMATION AND BOOKING IN BRITAIN

For all timetable and fare information, **call National Rail Enquiries** (☎08457/484950; *www.rail.co.uk* or *www.scotrail.co.uk*). Calls are charged at local rates – at peak times you may have to wait ten minutes or more for a reply. Credit card bookings can only be made directly with the privatized rail companies – National Rail Enquiries will tell you which company you need (and their credit card booking number).

on a popular route – every Brit has a horror story about having to stand all the way from London to Newcastle in a smelly second-class carriage.

The ticket offices at many rural and commuter stations are closed at weekends; in these instances there's often a vending machine on the platform. If there isn't a functioning machine, you can buy your ticket on board – but if you've embarked at a station that does have a machine and you've got on the train without buying a ticket, the inspector is entitled to charge you the full fare to your destination and issue you with an on-the-spot fine of £10 or twice the standard single fare.

RAIL PASSES

For foreign visitors who anticipate covering a lot of ground around Britain, a **rail pass** is a wise investment. The standard **BritRail Pass**, which must be bought before you enter the country, is available from BritRail Travel International (see box on p.25) and many specialist tour operators outside Britain (see pp.4 & 9). It gives unlimited travel in England, Scotland and Wales for eight days ($265), fifteen days ($400), 22 days ($505) or one month ($600). The **BritRail Flexipass** is good for standard-class travel on four days out of two months ($235), eight days out of one month ($340), or fifteen days out of two months ($515). Note that with both these passes there are discounts for those under 26 (**BritRail Youth Pass**) or over 60 (**BritRail Senior Pass**). Families should consider the **BritRail Family Pass** – buy one of the special passes listed above (such as the Flexipass) and one accompanying child gets a pass of the same type free, other children getting the appropriate pass at half price.

There are several passes which give discounts on all regular train journeys throughout Britain. The **Young Person's Railcard** costs £18 and gives a reduction of one-third on all standard, Saver and SuperSaver fares to full-time students and those aged between 16 and 25; while the over-60s can get the same reductions with the **Senior Citizens' Railcard**, which also costs £18. The **Family Railcard** costs £20 and gives a variety of discounts for up to four adults travelling with children; even more enticingly, it allows up to four children aged 5 to 15 to travel anywhere in the country for a flat fare of £2 each (which includes a seat reservation).

There are also a number of regional passes available, such as the **Network Card**, which costs £20 and gives a discount of one-third off off-

peak services throughout London and the south (including Oxford, Cambridge, Salisbury, Exeter and all the Home Counties). Up to four adults can travel on one card, along with up to four children (who will be charged a flat fare of £1 for each journey). In Scotland there are two regional passes: the **Highland Rover**, which costs £39 for four out of eight days and allows unlimited travel in the Glasgow to Mallaig area and from Thurso to Aberdeen; and the **Festival Cities Rover**, which costs £29 for three out of seven days and includes routes from Glasgow to Edinburgh and Stirling. For more comprehensive coverage of Scotland try the **Freedom of Scotland Travelpass**, which allows unlimited travel on the whole ScotRail system for varying periods – prices range from £69 for four days' travel out of eight consecutive days, to £119 for twelve out of fifteen days. The pass is also valid on all CalMac west coast ferry links (for ferry information see p.31), and provides a one-third reduction on many buses and on some P&O Orkney and Shetland ferries. Three passes cover the Welsh lines specifically, the most comprehensive being the **Freedom of Wales Flexipass**, which allows travel throughout the Welsh rail network and costs £75 for eight out of fifteen days and £39 for four out of eight days. The **North and Mid-Wales Rail Rover**, available for seven days for £40.90 or three days out of seven for £26.30, covers the Welsh and connecting English lines north of Aberystwyth. Most regions other than South Wales also have their own local **Day Ranger tickets** (£16.90), valid after 9.30am on weekdays and at any time on weekends, which may be worthwhile if you're not straying far.

BUSES AND COACHES

Inter-town **bus services** (known as **coaches** in Britain) duplicate many rail routes, very often for half the price of the train fare or less. The frequency of services is often comparable to rail, and in some instances the difference in journey time isn't great enough to be a deciding factor; coaches are comfortable, and the ones on longer routes often have drinks and sandwiches available on board. There's a plethora of regional companies operating buses and coaches, but by far the biggest national operator is National Express (☎0990/808080; *www.nationalexpress.co.uk*) and its subsidiary Scottish Citylink Coaches (☎0990/505050; *www.citylink.co.uk*), whose network extends to every corner of England and Scotland and the main centres in Wales. With rail prices becoming exorbitant, these coach services are so popular that for busy routes and on any route at weekends and during holidays it's advisable to book ahead.

One of the longest journeys you may wish to make, the twelve-hour trip from London to Inverness, costs £44 return, £36 if you book a week in advance. However, UK residents under 25, in full-time education or over 50 can buy a **National Express Discount Coach Card**, which costs £8, is valid for one year and entitles the holder to a thirty percent discount on all journeys. A Citylink Explorer Pass would cost you £30 for three days unlimited travel, £60 for five out of ten days and £90 for eight out of sixteen days, as well as fifty percent off CalMac passenger fares. Foreign travellers of any age can purchase a **Tourist Trail Pass**, which offers unlimited travel on the National Express and Citylink network: unlimited travel for two consecutive days (£39 for students and under-23s, £49 for others), five days out of ten (£69/£85), seven days out of 21 (£94/£120) or fourteen days out of thirty (£143/£187). In Britain you can obtain both passes from major travel agents, at Gatwick and Heathrow airports, at the Britain Visitor Centre in London (see p.21), or at the main National Express office in Victoria Coach Station, Buckingham Palace Rd, London SW1 (☎0990/808080). Scottish outlets include the main bus stations in Glasgow and Edinburgh. In North America these passes are available for the dollar equivalent through specialist tour operators (see box on p.6) or direct from British Travel International, PO Box 299, Elkton, VA 22827 (☎540/298-1395).

Local bus services are run by a bewildering array of companies, most private, a few not. In many cases, timetables and routes are well integrated, but it's increasingly the case that private companies duplicate the busiest routes in an attempt to undercut the commercial opposition, leaving the remoter spots neglected. Thus if you want to get from one end of a big city to another, you'll probably have a choice of buses all offering cut-price fares and cheap day passes, but to get out into the suburbs or to a satellite village, you may have to wait several hours; services are even less frequent in the evenings and at weekends. As a rule, the further away from urban areas you get, the less frequent and more expensive bus services become; however, there are very few rural areas that aren't connected by at least the occasional privately owned minibus. For all local

bus details, call the information and hotline numbers listed in the guide where appropriate.

Many rural areas not covered by other forms of public transport are served by the **Post Bus Network**, which operates minibuses carrying mail and about eight fare-paying passengers. They set off in the morning – usually around 8am – from the main post office and collect mail (or deliver it) from/to the outlying regions. It's a cheap way to travel, and can be a convenient way of getting to hidden-away B&Bs, although it is often excruciatingly slow. You can get a booklet of routes and timetables for England and Wales from the Royal Mail, Road Transport Consultancy, Room BT 20/3rd Floor, Rowland Hill House, Boythorpe Rd, Chesterfield S49 1HQ (☎01246/546329) and for Scotland from the Royal Mail Communications Centre, 102 West Port, Edinburgh EH3 9HS (☎0131/228 7407). The network is especially useful in Scotland, where it's often the only way to reach many far-flung spots.

DRIVING

In order to drive in Britain you need **a current full driving licence**. If you're bringing your own vehicle you should also carry your **vehicle registration or ownership document** at all times. Furthermore, you must be adequately insured, so be sure to check your existing policy.

In Britain you **drive on the left**, a situation which can lead to a few tense days of acclimatization for overseas drivers. Speed limits are 30–40mph (50–65kph) in built-up areas, 70mph (110kph) on motorways (freeways) and dual carriageways and 60mph (100kph) on most other roads. As a rule, assume that in any area with street lighting the speed limit is 30mph (50kph) unless otherwise stated.

Out in the remoter regions, particularly in Wales and Scotland, many roads are steep, single-track lanes, with passing places – try to remember the last one you passed and be prepared to reverse into it if you meet a vehicle coming the other way. In the **Highlands of Scotland**, the roads are littered with sheep which are entirely oblivious to cars, so slow down and edge your way past – should you kill one, it is your duty to inform the local farmer; **in Wales** you may have to stop to open gates designed to keep sheep from straying.

Fuel is expensive compared to North American prices – unleaded petrol (gasoline) costs in the

MOTORING ORGANIZATIONS

American Automobile Association (AAA), 1000 AAA Dr, Heathrow, FL 32746 (☎407/444-7000).

Australian Automobile Association, 212 Northbourne Ave, Canberra, ACT 2601 (☎02/6247 7311).

Automobile Association, Fanum House, Basingstoke, Hants RG21 4EA (☎0990/500600).

Canadian Automobile Association, 1145 Hunt Club Rd, Suite 200, Ottawa, K1V 0Y3 (☎613/247-0117).

Green Flag National Breakdown, Green Flag House, Cote Lane, Leeds LS28 5GF (☎0800/000111).

New Zealand Automobile Association, 17/99 Albert St, Auckland (☎09/377 4660).

Royal Automobile Club, RAC House, 1 Forest Rd, Feltham, Middlesex TW13 7RR (☎0181/917 2500 or 0800/550055).

CAR RENTAL FIRMS

UK

Avis ☎0990/900500; *www.avis.com*

Budget ☎0800/181181; *www.budget.com*

Europcar BCR ☎08457/222525; *www.europcar.com*

National Car Rental ☎01895/233300; *www.nationalcar.com*

Hertz ☎0870/844 8844; *www.hertz.com*

Holiday Autos ☎0990/300400; *www.holidayautos.co.uk*

Thrifty ☎0990/168238, *www.thrifty.co.uk*

NORTH AMERICA

Alamo US ☎1-800/522-9696; Canada ☎1-800/GO-ALAMO.

Avis US ☎1-800/331-1084; Canada ☎1-800/331-1084.

Budget US ☎1-800/472-3325; Canada ☎1-800/472-3325.

Europe By Car US ☎1-800/223-1516; Canada ☎1-800/223-1516 or 212/581-3040.

Hertz US ☎1-800/654-3001; Canada ☎1-800/654-3001.

Kenwel Holiday Autos US ☎1-800/678-0678; Canada ☎1-800/678-0678.

National Car Rental US & Canada ☎1-800/CAR-EURO.

AUSTRALIA

Avis ☎1800/225533.

Budget ☎1300/362848.

Hertz ☎1800/550067.

NEW ZEALAND

Avis ☎09/579 5231 or 0-800/655111.

Budget ☎0-800/652227.

Hertz ☎09/309 0989 or 0-800/655955.

region of 72p per litre, leaded 4-star 80p, and diesel 75p. The lowest prices of all are charged at out-of-town supermarkets; suburban service stations are usually fairly reasonable; and the highest prices are charged by motorway stations.

The Automobile Association (AA), the Royal Automobile Club (RAC) and Green Flag National Breakdown all operate 24-hour emergency **breakdown services** with the first two also providing many other motoring services including a reciprocal arrangement for free assistance with many overseas motoring organizations – check the situation with your association before setting out. On motorways the AA and RAC can be called

from roadside booths; elsewhere ring ☎0800/887766 for the AA; ☎0800/828282 for the RAC; and ☎0800/400600 for Green Flag. You can use these emergency numbers even if you are not a member of the respective organization, although a substantial fee will be charged.

Car parking in cities and in popular tourist spots can be a nightmare and will also cost you a small fortune. If you're in a tourist city for a day, look out for the **Park-and-Ride** schemes where you can park your car and take a cheap or free bus to the centre. Parking in the long or short stay car parks will be cheaper than using meters which restrict parking time to two hours at the most. As a rule, the smaller the town, the cheaper the parking. A yellow line along the edge of the road indicates **parking restrictions**; check the nearest sign to see exactly what they are. A double-yellow line means no parking at any time, though you can stop briefly to unload or pick up people or goods (maximum stop two minutes), but if the lines are red, that means absolutely no stopping at all.

CAR AND MOTORBIKE RENTAL

Compared to rates in North America, car rental in Britain is expensive, and you'll probably find it cheaper to arrange things in advance through one of the multinational chains, or by opting for a fly-drive deal. If you do **rent a car** from a company in Britain, the least you can expect to pay is around £135 a week, which is the rate for a small hatchback from Holiday Autos, the most competitive company; reckon on paying £40 a day for something direct from one of the multinationals, £10 or so less with a local firm. Rental agencies prefer you to pay by credit card, otherwise you may have to leave a deposit of at least £100 on top of the rental charge. There are very few automatics at the lower end of the price scale – if you want one, you should book well ahead. To rent a car you need to show your driving licence; few companies will rent to drivers with less than one year's experience and most will only rent to people between 21 and 70 years of age.

Motorbike rental is ludicrously expensive if you go to a specialized agent such as Scootabout Ltd, 1 Leeke St, London WC1X 9HZ (☎0171/833 4607), which charges around £300 per week for a Deauville, or £365 for a Pan-European ST1100. These prices include insurance cover, 250 miles free (after which it's 10p per mile), and the bikes are kept in top condition. However, you'll save a fortune by taking a chance on an ex-dispatch machine, which can be rented from as little as £50 per week from London-based courier companies such as World's End (☎0181/746 3595), Banjax (☎0171/729 5228) and Mike's Bikes (☎0181/983 4896). The last currently offers the best deals, with a Honda CB350 going for £55 per week (plus a £55 deposit), and NTV650s for £85 per week (£200 deposit). They also have CG125s for pottering around the city at £50 per week, and do very competitive insurance deals, including short-term third-party policies from around £50 per month. You don't have to be a dispatch rider to rent from these companies, although you'll need a full bike licence, and some places only take clients aged 23 or over.

If you're touring Scotland by motorbike, bear in mind, too, that some regions of the country, particularly the far north, have comparatively few garages and fuel stops. Breakdowns are frequent because of the demanding terrain, so invest in comprehensive recovery insurance with the AA or RAC, preferably a policy with home relay – spare parts can be hard to get hold of in the Highlands, and most standard policies will only get you to the nearest garage, where you can find yourself stranded for days until the part you need is sent from Inverness or Glasgow.

CAR AND CAMPER VAN PURCHASE

If you're with a group and visiting for months, rather than weeks, you might consider it worthwhile **buying a car or camper van**. Both types of vehicle will give you greater independence and flexibility of travel, and the camper van has the added benefit of providing your sleeping needs, too. The best way to get a decent vehicle – a car for under £1000 and a van for £2000 or under – is to scour the pages of either the weekly *Autotrader* or the local ads papers such as *Loot*. If you can find a professional car mechanic to look your bargain over for you, so much the better – a few pounds spent this way could save you a lot in the long run. If the car is more than three years old, make sure it has a Ministry of Transport (MOT) certificate and, if possible, tax, as these are transferred to the new owner. Otherwise you'll end up paying for a minimum six months tax at £85.50, an MOT test and any subsequent repairs necessary for the certificate. Shop around for the compulsory insurance which is probably going to be at least £200. You'll find all information you need about licensing and registering procedures in the form V100, available from any post office.

HITCHING AND LIFT SHARING

It's inadvisable for anyone, alone or not, to **hitch** in Britain. Only in exceptionally remote areas, such as parts of the Scottish Highlands, is there a tradition of giving lifts, but even there locals clearly have priority and you may have to wait a long time before you're picked up. Due to the decrease in popularity of hitching in the UK, **lift-sharing deals** have started to appear as a cheap and safer way of getting around the country. There is currently no organized lift-share agency in the UK, so the best option is to consult the noticeboards of specialist travellers' bookshops and hostels or put up your own notice; Nomad Books at 781 Fulham

Rd, London SW6 5HA (☎0171/736 4000), has a particularly good noticeboard downstairs. The travel magazine *Wanderlust* has a useful "Connections" page worth consulting for possible lift shares/travel companions; you can **place an advertisement** on this page (£5 for up to 50 words), though you should plan well ahead as the magazine is only published once every two months. Address mail to: Connections, Wanderlust, PO Box 1832, Windsor SL4 6YP (☎01753/620426). Another option is to look in the small ads sections of local papers.

TAXIS

Taxis are useful option for finding that hostel or sight that's off the beaten track or when time is limited. Also, if you're with a group, hiring a taxi can work out as cheap as taking a bus. Reckon on paying around £3 for the first mile and £1 for subsequent miles in cities, and £1.40 a mile in country districts. **Black cabs** are generally a little more expensive than **minicabs**, but are usually more reliable. You can hail a black cab on the street, but you must book minicabs by phone – we have given numbers for reliable minicab services throughout the book.

ORGANIZED TOURS

A popular service pitched at budget travellers and backpackers is the **minibus trips** run by Stray and Outback UK. The Stray tour starts in London and travels three days each week (April–Oct) in a clockwise direction via Windsor, Bath, Snowdonia, Liverpool, the Lakes, Edinburgh, York, Stratford, and Oxford, before heading back to the capital. Tickets cost £129, and are valid for up to four months. There is also a shorter trip from London to Liverpool. You can use this bus as a "Jump-On-Jump-Off" option or as a six-day guided tour, either arranging accommodation (average price £10 per night) along the way yourself or letting the company do the hard work for you. Contact Stray, 171 Earls Court Rd, Earls Court, London SW5 9RF (☎0171/373 7737, *www.straytravel.com*). Outback UK's guided tours of Britain set off from the Earls Court Youth Hostel in London on Saturdays. Their fourteen-day tour takes in Windsor, Devon, Dorset, Cornwall, Bath, Stratford, the Brecon Beacons, Snowdonia, Liverpool, the Peak District, York, the Lake District, the Scottish Lowlands and Edinburgh before returning to London. The complete package costs £490 and includes accommodation, two

meals a day, activities – including riding in the Brecon Beacons and ghost walks in York – and all entrance fees as well as the cost of travel. Passengers have the option of joining just part of this tour, paying a daily rate of about £35 for the part they join. For further information, contact Outback UK at The Cottage, Church Green, Badby, Northants NN11 3AS (☎01327/704115; *www.outbackuk.clara.net*) or call in at any Campus Travel Agency.

Trafalgar, 15 Grosvenor Place, London SW1X 7HH (☎0171/574 7444), offer round **coach trips from London**, taking in either Devon and Cornwall in five days, England and Scotland in four or six days, and Scotland only in five days. Sights include Stratford-upon-Avon, Hadrian's Wall, Edinburgh, and York. The England with Scotland trips run all year, the others between April and October and include all meals and hotel accommodation; four-day trips cost from £245, five days from £280 and six days from £295. Similar escorted tours from London are organized by two other companies. Insight, Gareloch House, 6 Gareloch Rd, Port Glasgow PA14 5XH (☎0870/514 3433), offer four-, seven- and twelve-day tours of Britain, running from March to November and costing from £255 for four days, £435 for seven days and £725 for twelve days. Contiki, Wells House, 15 Elmfield Rd, Bromley, Kent BR1 1LS (☎0181/290 6422; *www.contiki.com*), have a ten-day tour of Great Britain travelling as far as Inverness in the north and Stonehenge in the south, which runs all year and costs from £515. The five-day tour of Scotland, costing from £349, includes Edinburgh, Inverness, the Isle of Skye and Glasgow, and runs from June to September.

In Scotland, MacBackpackers operates a "Jump-On-Jump-Off" service out of Edinburgh, stopping at Dunkeld, Inverness, Kyle of Lochalsh, Fort William, Oban, and Glasgow in the summer, before returning to Edinburgh. The service runs daily in summer and five days a week in winter, and gives you the freedom to stay as long as you like in each place, and a ticket for one circuit costs £55, excluding accommodation. The company also offers a week's car rental and accommodation from £115 per person. For further details contact MacBackpackers, 105 High St, Edinburgh EH1 1SG (☎0131/558 9900; *www.macbackpackers.com*). Haggis Backpackers, at 11 Blackfriars St, Edinburgh EH1 1TB (☎0131/557 9393; *www.haggis-backpackers.com*), offer a similar service in large Mercedes buses complete with punchy sound systems for £95, which takes you as far as Ullapool and the Isle of Skye. Both of these companies also run backpacker-oriented minibus tours of Scotland. Prices start at £65 for a three-day round trip from Edinburgh, taking in Loch Ness, Skye, Glen Coe and other Highland highlights, while a six-day guided tour, combining most of Scotland's main tourist destinations, costs £139; these fares do not include food and accommodation, but the tour companies can help with hostel booking. The same applies to the popular Rabbie's Trail Burners tours, which also start in Edinburgh (207 High St, Edinburgh EH1 1PE; ☎0131/226 3133), offering a range of one-, two-, three- or five-day tours in sixteen-seater Mercedes minicoaches, with knowledgeable driver-guides. A three-day tour would cost around £80.

SCOTLAND'S FERRIES

Scotland has 130 inhabited islands, and **ferries** play an important part in travelling around the country. Most ferries carry cars and vans, for which advance reservations can be made – highly advisable, particularly during the busy summer season (April–Oct). Of the major operators, Caledonian MacBrayne (abbreviated by most people and throughout this book to CalMac) covers the majority of routes.

CalMac has a virtual monopoly on services on the River Clyde and those to the Inner and Outer Hebrides, sailing to 23 islands altogether. They aren't cheap, but they do have two types of reduced fare options, Island Hopscotch and Island Rover tickets. The Hopscotch offers a range of special economy fares for cars and passengers on seventeen pre-planned routes; valid for one month from the date of the first journey, it's the best option for anyone planning to make several ferry trips between islands. The Island Rover tickets are valid for unlimited travel on either eight or fifteen consecutive days; the eight-day pass costs £41 for passengers and £199 for cars, the fifteen-day option £59/£299. Schedules vary and are highly complicated, but you can get details from the address in the box, and it's advisable to book ahead, especially at peak times.

P&O Scottish Ferries sail to Orkney and Shetland in high season from Aberdeen and Scrabster (Thurso). Shetland to Aberdeen (13hr)

standard single fare is £56 for a foot passenger (reclining seat), plus £80 or so for a small car; to Orkney (8hr) it costs £41, plus £63 for a car; and Scrabster to Orkney (1hr 45min) £15.50, plus a further £30 for a car. For both routes you should book if you are taking a vehicle. There is a ten percent reduction for students and senior citizens.

In addition, **Western Ferries** operate between Gourock and Dunoon across the Clyde. The various Orkney islands are linked by the services run by the Orkney Ferries Ltd and the Shetlands by a service run by the Shetland Islands Council. Numerous small operators round the Scottish coast run day-excursion trips; their phone numbers are listed in the relevant chapters in the Guide.

It is possible to **book ferry tickets in advance** in North America, if you're organized enough to know exactly when you'll be making the crossing. For sailings to or from France, Belgium or the Netherlands, contact BritRail Travel International (☎1-800/677-8585) or Scots American (☎1-201/768-1187); to or from Scandinavia, contact Bergen Line (☎1-800/323-7436) or Scandinavian Seaways (☎1-800/533-3755); and to or from Ireland, try Lynott Tours (☎1-800/221-2474). In Australia and New Zealand, you can book ferry tickets in advance at branches of Thomas Cook.

FERRY OFFICES AND INFORMATION IN SCOTLAND

Caledonian MacBrayne Ltd, The Ferry Terminal, Gourock, Renfrewshire PA19 1QP (☎01475/650100; *www.calmac.co.uk*).

Orkney Ferries, Shore St, Kirkwall KW15 1LG (☎01856/872044; *www.orkneyislands. com/travel/orkfer*).

P&O Scottish Ferries, PO Box 5, Jamieson's Quay, Aberdeen AB11 5NP (☎01224/572615; *www.poscottishferries.co.uk*).

Shetland Islands Council, Environment and Transportation Dept, Grantfield, Lerwick ZE1 0NT (☎01595/744800).

Western Ferries Ltd, Hunter's Quay, Dunoon, Argyll PA23 8HJ (☎01369/704452).

ACCOMMODATION

Britain has scores of upmarket hotels, ranging from bland business-oriented places to plush country mansions and ancient castles, as well as budget accommodation in the form of hundreds of bed and breakfast places (B&Bs) and youth hostels. Nearly all tourist offices will book rooms for you, although the fee for this service varies considerably. In some areas you will pay a deposit that's deducted from your first night's bill (usually ten percent), in others the office will take a percentage or flat-rate commission – on average around £3. Another useful service operated by the majority of tourist offices is the *Book-a-bed-ahead* service, which locates accommodation in your next port of call for a charge of about £3. For a full explanation of the price-coding system used in this book see the box below.

HOTELS AND B&BS

There is no formalized system for grading hotel accommodation in Britain as a whole, but the tourist authorities and various private organizations classify **hotels**, **B&Bs** and **guest houses** on a system of stars, crowns, rosettes or similar badges, with five stars typically the top rank. The grades used by the **AA** and **RAC** are the most reliable, as they combine evaluation of facilities with a degree of subjective judgement – thus a hotel offering a whirlpool in each room will not earn its five stars if the management is unhelpful or the hotel food atrocious.

Though there's no hard-and-fast correlation between standards and **price**, you'll probably be paying in the region of £50–60 per night for a double room at a one-star hotel (breakfast included), rising to around £100 in a three-star and from around £200 for a five-star – in Scotland and Wales you might pay around twenty percent less, in London the price doubles. In some towns and cities you'll find that the larger hotels often offer cut-price deals on Saturdays and Sundays to fill the rooms vacated by the week's business trade, but these places tend to be soulless multinational chain operations. If you have money to throw around, stay in a nicely refurbished old building – the historic towns of Britain are chock-full of top-quality old coaching inns and similar ancient hostelries, while out in the countryside there are numerous converted mansions, manor houses and castles, often with brilliant restaurants attached.

At the lower end of the scale, it's sometimes difficult to differentiate between a hotel and a bed-and-breakfast (B&B) establishment. At their most basic, these typically British places – often known as guest houses in resorts and other tourist towns – are ordinary private houses with a couple of bedrooms set aside for paying guests and a dining room for the consumption of a rudimentary breakfast. At their best, however, B&Bs offer rooms as well furnished as those in hotels, but for half the price, with delicious home-prepared

ACCOMMODATION PRICE CODES

Throughout this guide, hotel and B&B accommodation is priced on a scale of ① to ⑨, the number indicating the lowest price you could expect to pay per night in that establishment for a double room in high season. The prices indicated by the codes are as follows:

① under £40	④ £60–70	⑦ £110–150
② £40–50	⑤ £70–90	⑧ £150–200
③ £50–60	⑥ £90–110	⑨ over £200

breakfasts, and an informal hospitality that a larger place can't match. B&Bs are graded by the same organizations mentioned above, but using diamonds instead of stars. As a guideline on costs, it's easy to find a one-diamond place for under £40 per night. Since many B&Bs, even the pricier ones, have a very small number of rooms, you should book as far in advance as possible. An important point to remember is that some hotels and B&Bs in rural areas, particularly in Scotland, are only open between Easter and October; where this is the case, we've said so in the guide.

Finally, don't assume that a B&B is no good if it's ungraded. There are so many B&Bs in Britain that the grading inspectors can't possibly keep track of them all, and in the rural backwaters some of the most enjoyable accommodation is to be found in welcoming and beautifully set houses whose facilities may technically fall short of official standards.

HOSTELS

The **Youth Hostels Association** network consists of over 230 properties in England and Wales, with the **Scottish Youth Hostels Association** responsible for around eighty properties in Scotland, all offering bunk-bed accommodation in single-sex dormitories or smaller rooms of four to six beds. A few new hostels and many refurbished older ones also now have double and family rooms available, and in cities the facilities are often every bit as good as some hotels. Indeed, although a few places are spartan establishments of the sort traditionally associated with the wholesome, fresh-air ethic of the first hostels, most have moved well away from the old-fashioned, institutional ambience.

Membership of the YHA is open only to residents of England and Wales and costs £5.50 per year for under-18s, £11 for others; Scottish nationals can join the SYHA for £6 a year, £2.50 for under-18s. You can join by either writing to the associations (see box below for addresses) or in person at any YHA and most SYHA hostels. The membership fee also gives you membership of the hostelling associations of the sixty countries affiliated to Hostelling International (HI); visitors who belong to any HI association have automatic membership of the YHA and SYHA; if you aren't a member of such an organization, you can join the HI at any English or Welsh and most Scottish hostels for a £11 fee or alternatively by collecting six Welcome stamps at £1.80 each from hostels as you go along.

Throughout most of Britain, **accommodation prices** for under-18s range from £4.10 per night, and from £6.10 for the over-18s. Students aged 18–25 can get a £1 reduction on production of a valid student card. Length of stay is normally unlimited, and the hostel warden will provide a linen sleeping bag for a small charge. The cost of hostel meals is similarly low: breakfast is around £3.20, a packed lunch is about £3.50 and evening meals start at just £4.60. Nearly all hostels have kitchen facilities for those who prefer self-catering.

At any time of year it's best to **reserve your place** well in advance, and it's essential at Easter and Christmas, and from May to August. Most hostels accept payment by Mastercard or Visa; with those that don't, you should confirm your reservation in writing, with payment, at least

---

YOUTH HOSTEL ASSOCIATIONS

Australia: Australian Youth Hostels Association, 422 Kent St, Sydney, NSW 2000 (☎02/9261 1111; *www.yha.com.au*).

Canada: Hostelling International–Canada (HI), 205 Catherine St, Suite 400, Ottawa, K2P 1C3 (☎613/237-7884 or 1-800/663-5777).

England: Youth Hostels Association (YHA), Trevelyan House, 8 St Stephen's Hill, St Albans, Herts AL1 2DY (☎01727/845047; *www.yha.org.uk*).

Ireland: An Oige, 61 Mountjoy St, Dublin 7 (☎01/830 4555; *www.irelandyha.org*).

New Zealand: Youth Hostels Association of New Zealand, PO Box 436, Christchurch 1 (☎03/379 9970; *www.yha.co.nz*).

Northern Ireland: Youth Hostel Association of Northern Ireland, 22 Donegal Rd, Belfast BT12 5JN (☎01232/324 733; *www.hini.org.uk*).

Scotland: Scottish Youth Hostels Association, 7 Glebe Crescent, Stirling FK8 2JA (☎01786/451181; *www.syha.org.uk*).

USA: Hostelling International–American Youth Hostels (HI-AYH), 733 15th St NW, Suite 840, Washington, DC 20005 (☎202/783-6161).

seven days before arrival. Reservations made less than seven days in advance will be held only until 6pm on the day of arrival. If you're tempted to turn up on the spur of the moment, bear in mind that very few hostels are open year-round, many are closed at least one day a week even in high season, and several have periods during which they accept reservations from groups only. To give the full details of **opening times** within this guide would be impossibly unwieldy, so always phone – we've given the number for every hostel mentioned. Most hostels are closed from 10am to 5pm, with an 11.30pm curfew, although all seven of the London hostels offer 24-hour access. If you're planning to make full use of the system, it's worth getting hold of the annual Hostelling International handbook for Europe and the Mediterranean (free to members), which includes a listing for every property with copious details of opening hours and facilities.

At best, **independent hostels**, which are more likely to be found in town centres than in the backwoods, offer facilities commensurate with those of YHA/SYHA places and at a lower price. However, many of these hostels make their money by over-cramming their rooms with beds; kitchens are often inadequate or non-existent and washing facilities can be similarly poor. That said, a lot of people find the lack of curfews and lock-outs ample compensation. A useful publication to have is *The Independent Hostel Guide* (£3.95) published by The Backpackers Press, 2 Rockview Cottages, Matlock Bath, Derbyshire, DE4 3PG, which fills you in on hostels in the UK and Ireland.

In Scotland, ninety hostels, mainly situated in the Highlands and islands, have banded together to form the **Independent Backpackers Hostels Association**. Most are family-run places, with no membership or curfew, and open all year, charging from £6.50–£9 per person per night. Housed in buildings ranging from croft-houses to converted churches, they all have decent facilities and kitchens, while several organize outdoor activities. A brochure listing all the properties is available if you send a stamped addressed envelope to Peter Thomas, Croft Bunkhouse, 7 Portnalong, Isle of Skye IV47 8SL (☎01478/640254; *wwwhostel-scotland.co.uk*). Detailed reviews of most independent hostels in Scotland are also featured in the Guide section of this book, and in more detail in the excellent *Accommodation For Groups* by Sam Dalley (£2.95, Backpacker Press), distributed by Cordee Books

and Maps, 3a De Montfort St, Leicester LE1 7HD (☎0116/254 3579).

In addition, some cities throughout Britain have **YMCA** and **YWCA** hostels, though these are only attractive if you're staying for at least a week, in which case you can get discounts on rates that are otherwise no better than budget B&Bs.

In British university towns you can usually find out-of-term accommodation in **student halls**, generally one-bedded rooms either with their own or shared bathrooms. In some instances, this may be the only budget accommodation on offer in the centre of town – for example, if you were to arrive in Durham in high summer with nothing booked in advance. All the useful university addresses are given in the guide, but if you want a list of everything that's on offer, write to the British Universities Accommodation Consortium, Box 1781, University Park, Nottingham NG7 2RD (☎0115/950 4571; *www.buac.co.uk*).

In the wilder parts of England and Wales, such as the north Pennines, North Yorkshire, Dartmoor, Exmoor and Snowdonia, the YHA administers basic accommodation for walkers in **camping barns**. Holding up to twenty people, these agricultural outbuildings are often unheated and are very sparsely furnished, with wooden sleeping-platforms, or bunks if you're lucky, a couple of tables, a toilet and a cold-water supply; but they are weatherproof, extremely good value (from £3.35 a night) and perfectly situated for walking tours. You do not have to be a YHA member to stay in any of these. Similar barns, often called bunkhouses, are run by private individuals in these areas – the useful ones are mentioned in the guide. Primitive croft accommodation in the Hebridean Islands is provided by the charitable Gatliff Hebridean Hostels Trust, which is allied to the SYHA.

CAMPING AND CARAVANNING

There are hundreds of **campsites** in Britain, charging from £5 per tent per night to around £12 for the plushest sites, with amenities such as laundries, shops and sports facilities. Some YHA hostels have small campsites on their property, charging half the indoor overnight fee. In addition to these official sites, farmers may offer pitches for as little as £2 per night, but don't expect tiled bathrooms and hair dryers for that kind of money. Even farmers without a reserved camping area may let you pitch in a field if you ask first, and may even charge you nothing for the privilege; setting up a tent without asking is an act of trespass,

SELF-CATERING ACCOMMODATION FIRMS

Brecon Beacons Holiday Cottages, Brynoyre, Talybont-on-Usk, Brecon, Powys LD3 7YS (☎01874/676446; *www.wiz.to/beacons*). Around 200 cottages in the Brecon Beacons National Park, Black Mountains and Wye Valley.

CKD Finlayson Hughes, 45 Church St, Inverness IV1 1DR (☎01463/224707; *www.finlaysonhughes. uk.com*). Just under 200 properties across Scotland from castles to bothies.

Coastal Cottages of Pembrokeshire, 2 Riverside Quay, Haverford West, Pembrokeshire SA6 12LJ (☎01437/767600; *www.coastalcottages.co.uk*). Around 500 cottages, chalets, flats and houses in the Welsh Pembrokeshire coast area.

Country Holidays, Spring Mill, Earby, Lancs BB94 60AA (☎01282/445400; *www.country -holidays.co.uk*). More than 5000 properties all over England.

English Country Cottages, Stoney Bank, Earby, Barnoldswick, Lancs BB9 40EF (☎0870/585 1100 or ☎01328/864041). Around 2000 cottages in various parts of rural England.

Forest Holidays, Forestry Commission, 231 Corstorphine Rd, Edinburgh EH12 7AT (☎0131/334 0303; *www.forestry.gov.uk*). Mostly purpose-built cabins in beautiful woodland areas, often with pony trekking and similar outdoor activities available at or near the site.

Gwyliau Cymreig (Welsh Holidays), Snowdonia Tourist Services, High St, Porthmadog, Gwynedd LL49 9PG (☎01766/513829; *www.snowdoniatourist.com*). Best and cheapest of the many companies offering self-catering accommodation in Snowdonia and North Wales.

Landmark Trust, Shottesbrooke, Maidenhead, Berks SL6 3SW (☎01628/825925; *www. landmarktrust.uk*). The firm's £9.50 brochure lists some 150 converted historic properties, ranging from restored forts and Martello towers to a tiny radio shack used in the last war.

National Trust (Enterprises) Ltd, PO Box 536, Melksham, Wilts SN2 8SX (☎01225/791199). About 250 NT-owned cottages and farmhouses, most set in their own gardens or grounds.

National Trust for Scotland, 5 Charlotte Square, Edinburgh EH2 4DU (☎0131/226 5922). There are 37 NTS-owned converted historic cottages and houses around Scotland.

Powell's Cottage Holidays, Dolphin House, High St, Saundersfoot, Dyfed SA69 9EJ (☎01834/812791; *www.powells.co.uk*). Some 300 properties in South Wales and the Gower, and in the southwest of England.

Quality Cottages, Cerbid, Solva, Haverfordwest, Dyfed SA62 6YE (☎01348/837871; *www.qualitycottages.co.uk*). Coastal cottages throughout Wales.

Rural Retreats, Station Rd, Blockley, Moreton-in-Marsh, Gloucestershire GL56 9DZ (☎01386/701177; *www.ruralretreats.co.uk*). Upmarket apartments in restored old buildings, many of them listed buildings.

Wales Holidays, Bear Lanes, Newton, Powys SY16 2QZ (☎01686/628200l; *www.wales-holidays.co.uk*). A varied selection of over 500 properties all over Wales.

Vivat Trust, 61 Pall Mall, London, SW1Y 5HZ (☎0171/930 8030; *www.vivat.org.uk*). Small, select range of historic properties in Shropshire, Dorset, Cumbria and Derbyshire – including North Lees Hall, Charlotte Brontë's inspiration for Thornfield Hall in *Jane Eyre*.

which will not be well received. Free camping is illegal in national parks and nature reserves.

For **North Americans** planning to do a lot of camping, an **international camping carnet** is a sound investment, available from home-motoring organizations, or from Family Campers and RVers (FCRV), 4804 Transit Rd, Building 2, Depew NY 14043 (☎1-800/245-9755) in the US; and 181 Melrose Ave, Halifax, Nova Scotia B3N 2E8 (☎1-800/245-9755) in Canada. The carnet is good for discounts at member sites and serves as useful

identification; otherwise you will usually have to deposit your passport overnight. FCRV annual membership costs $25, and the carnet an additional $10.

The problem with many campsites in the most popular parts of Britain – especially England's West Country coast, the Welsh coastline and national parks and the Scottish Highlands and islands – is that tents have to share the space with **caravans**. Every summer the country's byways are clogged by migrations of these cumbersome trailers. The great majority of caravans, however, are permanently moored at their sites, where they are rented out to families for self-catering holidays, and the ranks of nose-to-tail trailers in the vicinity of most of the UK's best beaches might make you think that half the population of Britain shacks up in a caravan for the midsummer break. Visitors from outside Britain tend to prefer more robust self-catering accommodation, and there are thousands of tourist-board-approved properties for rent by the week, ranging from city penthouses to secluded cottages. The least you can expect to pay for four-berth self-catering accommodation in summer would be around £200 per week, but for something more attractive – such as a small house near the West Country moors – you should budget for twice that amount. The BTA list *Britain: Self-*

Catering Holiday Homes includes a good range of accommodation.

Detailed annually revised **guidebooks** to Britain's camping and caravan sites include the AA's *Caravan and Camping in Britain and Ireland* (£8.99), which lists their inspected and graded sites, and Cade's *Camping, Touring and Motor Caravan Site Guide* (£4.75), published by Marwain. Alternative sources of information on all types of self-catering accommodation, from canal boats to ex-lighthouses, are *Dalton's Weekly* (available from most newsagents) and the Sunday newspapers, and of course most British travel agents can offer a range of self-catering holiday packages. Some of the more interesting firms offering accommodation only are listed in the box on p.35.

FOOD AND DRINK

Though the British still tend to regard eating as a functional necessity rather than a focal point of the day, great advances towards a more sophisticated appreciation of the culinary arts have been made in recent years. Every major town has its top-range restaurants, many of them boasting awards for excellence, while it's nearly always possible to eat well and inexpensively, thanks chiefly to the influence of Britain's various immigrant communities. However, the pub will long remain the centre of social life in Britain, a drink in a traditional "local" often making the best introduction to the life of a town.

EATING

In many hotels and B&Bs you'll be offered what's termed an **"English breakfast"**, which is basically sausage, bacon and eggs plus tea and toast. This used to be the typical working-class start to the day, but these days the British have adopted the healthier cereal alternative, and most places will give you this option as well. A **"Scottish breakfast"** is likely to include porridge – properly made with genuine oatmeal and traditionally eaten with salt rather than sugar, though the latter is always on offer. You may also be served kippers or Arbroath smokies (delicately smoked haddock with butter), or a large piece of haddock with a poached egg on top. Oatcakes (plain savoury biscuits) and a "buttery" – not unlike a French croissant – will often feature.

For most overseas visitors the quintessential British meal is **fish and chips** (known in Scotland as a "fish supper", even at lunchtime), a dish that can vary from the succulently fresh to the indigestibly oily – it's little wonder that lashings of salt, vinegar and tomato ketchup or the fruitier brown sauce are common additions. The classier places have tables, but more often they serve **takeaway** (takeout) food only, sometimes supplying a disposable fork so that you can guzzle your roadside meal with a modicum of decorum. Fish-and-chip shops ("**chippies**") can be found on most high streets and main suburban thoroughfares throughout Britain, although in larger towns they're beginning to be outnumbered by **pizza**, **kebab** and **burger** outlets.

Other sources of straightforward food throughout the day are "**greasy spoons**" (which tend to close at around 6–7pm), and **pubs** (which usually stop serving food by 9pm), where you'll often find plain "meat-and-two-veg" dishes: steak-and-kidney pie, shepherd's pie (minced lamb or beef covered in mashed potato, and baked), chops and steaks, accompanied by boiled potatoes, carrots or some such vegetable. However, a lot of British pubs now take their food very seriously indeed, having separate dining areas and menus that can compete with some of the better mid-range restaurants. In the smallest villages the pub may be the only place you can eat. Another recent development is the growing number of specialist **vegetarian restaurants**, especially in the larger towns, and the increasing awareness of vegetarian preferences in other eating places. In Wales especially you'll come across dozens of small,

---

RESTAURANT PRICES

Our restaurant listings include a mix of high-quality and good-value establishments, but if you're intent on a culinary pilgrimage, you would do well to arm yourself with a copy of the *Good Food Guide* (£14.99), which is updated annually and includes nearly 1300 detailed recommendations.

Throughout this book, we've supplied the phone number for all restaurants where you may need to book a table. At places categorized as "inexpensive", you can expect to pay under £10 per head, without drinks; "moderate" means £10–20, "expensive" £20–30, and "very expensive" over £30.

inexpensive wholefood cafés, often doubling up as alternative resource centres. Also on the rise in the major towns are vaguely French **brasseries**, informal **bar/restaurants** offering simple meals from around £10–12 per head and often with a set lunchtime menu for around half that.

Britain has its diverse immigrant communities to thank for the range of foods in the mid-range category. Of the innumerable types of **ethnic restaurants** offering good-value high-quality meals you'll find Chinese, Indian and Bangladeshi specialities in every town of any size, with the widest choice in London and the industrial cities of the Midlands and the north. Other Asian restaurants, particularly Thai and Indonesian, are now becoming more widespread in England, but are generally a shade more expensive, while further up the economic scale there's no shortage of French and Italian places – by far the most popular European cuisines, though most cities also have their share of Spanish tapas bars. Japanese food has been one of the success stories of recent years, with sushi bars joining the expense-account restaurants that have been established for some time in the business centres of England.

The ranks of Britain's **gastronomic restaurants** grow with each passing year, with cordon-bleu chefs producing high-class French-style dishes, California-influenced menus, internationalist hybrid creations, and traditional British meat and fish dishes that are as delicious as the more arty creations of their cross-Channel counterparts. London of course has the highest concentration of top-flight places, but wherever you are in Britain you're never more than half an hour's drive from a really good meal – some of the very best dining rooms are to be found in the countryside hotels. The problem is that fine food costs more in Britain than it does anywhere else in Europe. If a place has any sort of reputation in foodie circles you're unlikely to be spending less than £30 per head, and for the services of the country's glamour chefs you could be paying up to a preposterous £120.

REGIONAL CUISINE

England is not particularly celebrated for its variety of regional cuisines, though most areas have a speciality or two, generally rather robust in character. Lincolnshire, for example, is known for its **sausages**, Lancashire and Yorkshire for their **black puddings** (a type of sausage), Cornwall for its **pasty** (a stodgy envelope of pastry filled with meat, potatoes and other root vegetables), and

Melton Mowbray for its leaden **pork pies**. England's traditional **cakes** – among them, Bath buns, Bakewell puddings or tarts and Eccles cakes – can be found in bakeries on any high street, though they're at their most authentic in their place of origin. A few delicacies are seasonal, such as hot cross buns, available in the few weeks leading up to Easter. More refined dishes are to be had along the coasts – the best **seafood** is found in Cornwall, while oysters are a speciality in Whitstable – and a few English **cheeses**, notably Stilton, enjoy world recognition. England's regional beers are perhaps more distinctive than its food, however, and you'll find a much stronger emphasis on traditional cooking in Scotland and Wales.

The quality of **Scottish food** has improved by leaps and bounds in recent years. Scottish produce – superb meat, fish and game, a wide range of dairy products and a bewildering variety of traditional baked goodies – is of outstanding quality and has to some extent been rediscovered of late. The quintessential Scottish dish is **haggis**, a sheep's stomach stuffed with spiced liver, offal, oatmeal and onion and traditionally eaten with bashed neeps (mashed turnips) and chappit tatties (mashed potatoes). Among other native staples is **stovies**, a tasty mash of onion and fried potato heated up with minced beef. Home-made soup is generally welcome in what can be a cold climate: try **Scots broth**, made with various combinations of lentil, split pea, mutton stock or vegetables and barley.

Welsh cooking is similarly in resurgence, as attested to by the many restaurants, hotels and pubs displaying the "Taste of Wales" (*Blas ar Cymru*) badge. Traditional dishes, such as the delicious native **lamb**, fresh **salmon** and **trout**, can be found on an increasing number of menus, frequently combined with the national vegetable, the **leek**. Particularly Welsh specialities include **laver bread** (*bara lawr*), a thoroughly tasty seaweed and oatmeal cake often included in a traditional fried breakfast; **bara brith**, a fruit bread found in all teashops, **Glamorgan sausages**, a vegetarian combination of local cheese and spices; **cawl**, a chunky mutton broth; and **cockles**, trawled from the estuary north of the Gower. Dairy products feature highly in such a predominantly rural country, and there's a superb range of Welsh **cheeses**. The best known is Caerphilly, a soft crumbly white cheese that is mixed with beer and toasted on bread to form an authentic **Welsh Rarebit**.

DRINKING

The combination of an inclement climate and an English temperamental aversion to casual chat makes the simple **café** a rare phenomenon outside the biggest cities – there are probably more in London's Soho and the surrounding area than in the rest of the country combined. A growing number of pubs now serve **tea and coffee** during the day, but in most places you'll attract consternation by asking for a cup; in the more genteel tourist towns (eg Stratford, Harrogate and York), you'll find plenty of **teashops**, unlicensed establishments where the normal procedure is to order a slice of cake or some other pastry with your tea or coffee – the former is far more popular. Increasingly common in the big cities are **brasseries** or equivalent establishments, where the majority of customers are there for a bite to eat, but where you're generally welcome to spend half an hour nursing a cappuccino or glass of wine.

Nothing is likely to dislodge the **pub** from its status as the great British social institution. Originating as wayfarers' hostelries and coaching inns, pubs have outlived the church and marketplace as the focal points of communities, and at their best they can be as welcoming as the full name – "public house" – suggests. Pubs are as varied as the country's townscapes: in larger market towns you'll find huge oak-beamed inns with open fires and polished brass fittings; in the remoter upland villages there are stone-built pubs no larger than a two-bedroomed cottage; and in the more inward-looking parts of industrial Britain you'll come across no-nonsense pubs where something of the old division of the sexes and classes still holds sway – the "spit and sawdust" public bar is where working men can bond over a pint or two, the plusher saloon bar, with a separate entrance, is the preferred haunt of mutually preoccupied couples, the middle classes and unaccompanied women. Whatever the species of pub, its **opening hours** are daily 11am–11pm (in quieter spots, closed between about 3pm and 5.30pm), with "last orders" called by the bar staff about twenty minutes before closing time. The legal drinking age is eighteen and unless there's a special family room or a beer garden, children are not usually welcome.

Most pubs are owned by large breweries who favour their own **beers** and **lagers**, as well as some "guest beers", all dispensed by the pint or

half-pint (a pint costs anything from £1.20 to £2.70, depending on the brew and the locale of the pub; see below for more on types of beer). **Cider**, the fermented produce of apples, is a sweet, alcoholic beverage produced in the West Country, where it's often preferred to beer; the far more potent and less refined **scrumpy** is the type consumed by aficionados of the apple. The cider sold in pubs all over Britain is a fizzy drink that only approximates the real thing. As with beer, the best scrumpy is available within a short radius of the factory, but the drink has nothing like the variety of beer. **Wines** sold in pubs are generally appalling, a strange situation in view of the excellent range of wine available in off-licences and supermarkets. The wine lists in brasseries and **wine bars** are nearly always better, but the mark-ups are often outrageous, and any members of the party who prefer beer will have to be content with bottled drinks. Nonetheless, many people are prepared to pay the extra in return for a less boozy and less male-dominated atmosphere.

BEER

The most widespread type of English beer is **bitter**, an uncarbonated and dark beverage that should be pumped by hand from the cellar and served at room temperature. Though virtually extinct in England, the sweeter, darker "**mild**" beer and the even stronger porter are quite common in Welsh pubs. The indigenous Scottish beer is ale, much like the English **bitter** (in Scotland known as "**heavy**"). In recent years, boosted by aggressive advertising, **lager** has overtaken beer in popularity, and every pub will have at least two brands on offer, but the major breweries are now capitalizing on a backlash against foreign-sounding, pale, chilly and often tasteless drinks, a reaction in large part due to the work of **CAMRA** (Campaign for Real Ale). Some of the beer touted as good traditional ale is nothing of the sort (if the stuff comes out of an electric pump, it probably isn't the real thing), and some of the genuine beers have been adulterated since being taken over by the big companies, but the big breweries do widely distribute some very good beers – for example, Directors, produced by the giant Courage group, is a very classy strong bitter. Guinness, a very dark, creamy Irish stout, is also on sale virtually everywhere, and is an exception to the high-minded objection to electrically pumped beers (though purists will tell you that the stuff the English drink does not compare with the stuff sold in Ireland). Smaller operations whose fine ales are available over a wide area include Young's, Fuller's, Wadworth's, Adnams, Greene King, Flowers and Tetley's.

Scottish beers are graded by the shilling: a system used since the 1870s and indicating the level of potency – the higher the shilling mark, the stronger or "heavier" the beer. Scotland's biggest-name breweries are McEwan's and Younger's, part of the mighty Scottish and Newcastle group, and Tennents, owned by the English firm Bass. The beers produced by these companies tend to be heavier, smoother and stronger than their English equivalents, especially McEwan's Export, a mass-produced, highly potent brew, and Tennents' Velvet, a famously smooth ale. Younger's Tartan, though less flavoursome, is Scotland's biggest seller.

However, if you really want to discover how good British beer can be, you should sample the products of the innumerable small local breweries producing **real ales** to traditional recipes. Every region has its distinctive brew, frequently available at free houses – independently run establishments that sell what they please and are generally more characterful than so-called "tied pubs". In **Scotland**, Edinburgh's Caledonian Brewery makes nine good cask beers, operating from Victorian premises that preserve much of their original equipment. Others to look out for are Belhaven, a brewery near Edinburgh whose 80-shilling Export is a typical Scottish ale; Maclays, a hoppy, lightish ale brewed in Alloa; and in the Borders, Traquair Brewery, the only British brewery still to ferment its ale in oak, does a wonderfully smooth House Ale. The Orkney Brewery's Raven Ale could be a life-saver in the north, where good beer is hard to come by. Among beers worth sampling in **Wales** are the brews produced by the Cardiff-based Brains, whose Dark, Bitter and SA Best Bitter are among the finest pints in the UK. Llanelli-based Felinfoel and Crown Buckley also produce a number of excellent bitters.

For some serious research, CAMRA's annual *Good Beer Guide* (£10.99) is essential; if you see a recent CAMRA sticker on the window of a pub, the beer inside is certainly worth a try. Also useful is the *Good Pub Guide* (£14.99, Ebury Press), a thousand-page yearly handbook that rates each pub's ambience and food as well as its beer.

WHISKY

Scotland's national drink is **whisky** – *uisge beatha*, the "water of life" in Gaelic – traditionally drunk in pubs with a half-pint of beer on the side, a combination known as a "nip and a hauf". Whisky has been produced in Scotland since the fifteenth century, and really took off in popularity after the 1780 tax on claret made wine too expensive for most people. The taxman soon caught up with illicit whisky distilling and drove the stills underground, and today many malt distilleries operate on the site of simple cottages that once distilled the stuff illegally. In 1823 Parliament revised its Excise Laws, in the process legalizing whisky production, and today the drink is Scotland's chief export. There are two types of whisky: **single malt**, made from malted barley, and grain, which, relatively cheap to produce, is made from maize and a small amount of malted barley in a continuous still. **Blended whisky**, which accounts for more than 90 percent of all sales, is, as the name suggests, a blend of the two types.

Grain whisky forms about 70 percent of the average bottle of blended whisky, but the distinctive flavour of the different blends comes from the malt whisky which is added to the grain in different quantities. The more expensive the blend, the higher the proportion of skilfully chosen and aged malts that has gone into it. Among many brand names, Johnnie Walker, Bell's, Teacher's and Famous Grouse are some of the most widely available. All have a similar flavour, and are often drunk with mixers such as lemonade or mineral water.

Despite the dominance of the blended whiskies, single malt whiskies are infinitely superior, and best drunk neat to appreciate their distinctive flavours. They vary enormously depending on the peat used for drying, the water used, and the type of oak cask in which they are matured, but they fall into four distinct groups – Highland, Lowland, Campbeltown and Islay, with the majority falling into the Highland category and produced largely on Speyside. You can get the best-known makes – among them Glenlivet, Glenmorangie, MacAllan, Talisker, Laphroaig, Highland Park and Glenfiddich, the top seller – in most of the pubs.

POST AND PHONES

Virtually all **post offices** (*swyddfa'r post* in Wales) are open Monday to Friday from 9am to 5.30pm and Saturday from 9am to 12.30 or 1pm; in small communities you'll find sub-post offices operating out of a shop, but these are open the same hours, even if the shop itself is open for longer. **Stamps** can be bought at post office counters, from vending machines outside, or from an increasing number of newsagents, although in the last case usually only in books of four or ten stamps. A first-class letter to anywhere in the British Isles currently costs 26p and should – in theory – arrive the next day; second-class letters cost 19p, and take two to four days. **Airmail** letters of less than 20g (0.7oz) to EU countries cost 30p and elsewhere overseas from 44p for 10g, and 64p for 20g. Pre-stamped aerogrammes conforming to overseas airmail weight limits of under 10g can be bought for 37p from post offices only. For more information about Royal Mail postal ser-

vices, contact ☎08457/740740.

Most, although no longer all, **public payphones** in England are operated by British Telecom (BT) and, in towns, at least, are widespread. Many BT payphones take all coins from 10p upwards, although an increasing proportion only accept phonecards, available from post offices and newsagents which display BT's green logo. These cards come in denominations of £3, £5 and £10; an increasing number of phones accept credit cards too.

Inland calls are cheapest at weekends and between 6pm and 8am on weekdays. **Reduced rate periods** for most international calls are 6pm to 8am from Monday to Friday and all day on Saturday and Sunday. A cheaper way to call is from one of the number of independent telecom centres, though you're likely to find these only in the major cities.

Throughout this guide, every telephone number is prefixed by the area code and separated from the subscriber number by an oblique slash; the latter is omitted if dialling from within the area covered by that prefix. However, some prefixes relate to the cost of calls rather than the location of the subscriber, and should never be omitted: numbers with an ☎0800 and 0808 prefix are free of charge to the caller; ☎0345 and 08457 numbers are charged at local rates, ☎0870 up to the national rate, irrespective of where in the country you are calling from.

A **reconfiguration of telephone numbers** is currently taking place in the UK – a process that began in the summer of 1999, but that is not due to be completed until some time in autumn 2000. Throughout the book we have

---

OPERATOR SERVICES

Domestic operator ☎100   Domestic directory assistance ☎192 (free from payphones, otherwise 35p)
International operator ☎155   International directory assistance ☎153 (free from payphones, otherwise 80p)

INTERNATIONAL CALLS

To call Britain from overseas, dial the international access code (☎011 from the US and Canada; ☎0011 from Australia; and ☎00 from New Zealand) followed by 44, the area code minus its initial zero, and then the number. To dial overseas

from Britain it's ☎00 followed by the country code, area code (with the exception of Italy and Czech Republic, without the zero if there is one) and subscriber number. Country codes are as follows:

US and Canada ☎1   Ireland ☎353   Australia ☎61   New Zealand ☎64

TELEPHONE NUMBERS IN THE UK

On April 22, 2000, the UK's telephone-numbering system will change. Six regions will be given **new area codes** – Cardiff, Coventry, London, Northern Ireland, Portsmouth and Southampton – and special-rate numbers will be reconfigured.
Until September 16, 2000, if phoning **from outside an affected area**, you can use either the old number or the new one. However, there is no change-over period for **locally dialled numbers**: the new local numbers won't work until April 22, 2000, and only those numbers will work after that.
The numbers for the affected areas will be reconfigured as follows:

CARDIFF:

(01222) xxx xxx becomes **(029) 20**xx xxxx

PORTSMOUTH:

(01705) xxx xxx becomes **(023) 92**xx xxxx

COVENTRY:

(01203) xxx xxx becomes **(024) 76**xx xxxx

SOUTHAMPTON:

(01703) xxx xxx becomes **(023) 80**xx xxxx

LONDON:

(0171) xxx xxxx becomes **(020) 7**xxx xxxx
(0181) xxx xxxx becomes **(020) 8**xxx xxxx

*BELFAST:

(01232) xx xxxx becomes **(028) 90**xx xxxx

The process of reconfiguring **special-rate numbers** (numbers with four-digit prefixes starting 08 or 09) started in autumn 1999, but the latest information is that old and new numbers should work side by side until at least autumn 2000.

*Belfast is used purely as an example. The Northern Ireland code will change to 028, with local 5- and 6-digit numbers all becoming 8 digits long. For changes to other Northern Ireland numbers or queries about special-rate numbers, **call directory enquiries** on ☎192.

used the old telephone-numbering system, which will – in most cases – work in tandem with the new numbers throughout the change-over period. Throughout the text, in accounts of areas where numbers will be reconfigured, the relevant changes are outlined in a small box. For full details of the changes, see the box above.

OPENING HOURS AND HOLIDAYS

General **shop hours** are Monday to Saturday from 9am to 5.30 or 6pm, although there's an increasing amount of Sunday and late-night shopping in the larger towns, with Thursday or Friday being the favoured evenings for late opening. The big supermarkets also tend to stay open until 8pm or 9pm from Monday to Saturday and between 10am and 4pm on Sundays in England and Wales, as do many of the stores in the shopping complexes that are springing up on the outskirts of many major towns. It's also not unusual to find some of the supermarkets in cities and large towns open 24 hours. In Scotland you can't buy alcohol in shops on Sundays. Many provincial towns still retain an "**early closing day**" when shops close at 1pm – Wednesday is the favourite. It's worth noting that not all service stations on motorways are open for 24 hours although you can usually get fuel around the clock in the larger towns and cities.

In England and Wales most fee-charging sites are open on **Bank Holidays (public holidays)**, when Sunday hours usually apply. In Scotland, "bank holidays" mean just that – they are literally days when the banks are closed rather than general public holidays, and they vary from year to year; January 1 is the only fixed public holiday in Scotland, but all Scottish towns and cities have a one-day holiday in both spring and autumn – dates vary from place to place but normally fall on a Monday. If you want to know the exact dates, you can get a booklet detailing them from Glasgow Chamber of Commerce, 30 George Square, Glasgow G2 1EQ (☎0141/204 2121).

PUBLIC HOLIDAYS IN ENGLAND AND WALES

January 1

Good Friday – late March to early April

Easter Monday – as above

First Monday in May

Last Monday in May

Last Monday in August

December 25

December 26

Note that if January 1, December 25 or December 26 falls on a Saturday or Sunday, the next weekday becomes a public holiday.

SIGHTS, MUSEUMS AND MONUMENTS

Most attractions in England and Wales are open daily in summer and closed one or two days a week in winter, though the major state museums are open daily all year. In Scotland the tourist season runs from Easter to October and only the biggest museums and most popular indoor attractions are open outside this period, although ruins and gardens are normally accessible year-round. We've given full details of opening hours throughout the guide.

Many of Britain's most treasured sites – from castles, abbeys and great houses to tracts of protected landscape – come under the control of the private **National Trust**, 36 Queen Anne's Gate, London SW1H 9AS (☎0171/222 9251; *www. nationaltrust.org.uk*), and **National Trust for Scotland**, 5 Charlotte Square, Edinburgh EH2 4DU (☎0131/226 5922). Both organizations charge an entry fee for the majority of their sites, and these can be quite high, especially for the more grandiose estates. If you think you'll be visiting more than half a dozen of their properties, denoted "**NT**" or "**NTS**" in the guide, it's worth taking out **annual membership** (NT £29, £14.50 for under-25s; NTS £26, £10 for under-25s), which allows free entry to both sets of properties, although you'll only receive mailings from the one that you join.

A great many of Britain's other sites are controlled by the state-run **English Heritage**, 23 Savile Row, London W1X 1AB (☎0171/973 3000; *www.english-heritage.org.uk*); **Historic Scotland**, Longmore House, Salisbury Place, Edinburgh EH9 1SH (☎0131/668 8600; *www. historic-scotland.gov.uk*); and **CADW Welsh**

Historic Monuments, Cathays Park, Cardiff CF10 3NQ (☎01222/500200), which we've denoted as "**EH**", "**HS**" and "**CADW**" respectively. Annual membership of any one of the three (EH £26, £16 for under-20s; HS £24, £17 for students; CADW £22, £15 for under-20s) entitles you to half-price entry to properties run by the other two.

A lot of **stately homes** remain in the hands of the landed gentry, who tend to charge in the region of £5 for admission to edited highlights of their domain – even more if, as at Longleat, they've added some theme-park attractions to the historic pile. Many other old buildings, albeit rarely the most momentous structures, are owned by the local authorities, which are generally more lenient with their admission charges, sometimes allowing free access. You may find that a history museum or a similar collection has been installed in the local castle or half-rebuilt ruin, and in these cases there's usually a modest entry charge. However, **municipal art galleries and museums** are often free, as are many of the great **state museums** – both the British Museum and the National Gallery are free, for example, though Cardiff's National Museum of Wales is not. On the other hand, these cash-starved institutions are nowadays obliged to request voluntary donations, as are several **cathedrals**. Most cathedrals charge a pound or two for admission to the most beautiful parts of the structure – usually the chapter house or cloister. **Churches**, increasingly, are kept locked except for services, but when they are open entry is free.

You will certainly have to pay to visit any of Britain's burgeoning **heritage museums**, which in some instances are large multi-building sites staffed by people in period costume, but more often consist of interactive displays – some of which take the form of hi-tech animatronic tableaux, while others amount to little more than a few mannequins with video monitors for heads. Tickets for these can cost anywhere between £5 and £10, and expense is not necessarily an indication of quality. However, the most expensive attractions in Britain are those aimed squarely at tourists with cash to spend – Madame Tussaud's, the country's number one earner of foreign cash, now charges £12 for admission.

The majority of fee-charging attractions in England have **reductions** for senior citizens, the unemployed, full-time students and children under 16, with under-5s being admitted free almost everywhere. Proof of eligibility will be required in most cases, though even the flintiest desk clerk will probably take on trust the age of a babe-in-arms. The entry charges given in the guide are the full adult charges; as a rule, adult reductions are in the range of 25–35 percent, while reductions for children are around 50 percent.

Finally, foreign visitors planning on seeing more than a dozen stately homes, monuments or gardens might find it worthwhile to buy a **Great British Heritage Pass**, which gives free admission to some six hundred sites, many of which are not run by the National Trust or English Heritage. Costing under £30/US$42 for seven days, £42/US$64 for fifteen days and £56/US$90 for a month the pass can be purchased through most travel agents at home, on arrival at any large UK airport, from most major tourist offices and the Britain Visitor Centre, 1 Regent St, London W1 (walk-in service only).

THE MEDIA

NEWSPAPERS AND MAGAZINES

English daily newspapers are predominantly right wing, with the Murdoch-owned *Times* and the staunchly Conservative *Daily Telegraph* occupying the "quality" end of the market, trailed by the *Independent*, which strives worthily to live up to its self-righteous name, and the *Guardian*, which inhabits a niche marginally to the left of centre. At the opposite end of the scale in terms of intellectual weight and volume of sales is the pernicious *Sun*, the sleaziest occupant of the Murdoch stable; its chief rivals in the sex and scandal stakes are the *Daily Star* and self-consciously ridiculous *Daily Sport* but the only tabloid that manages anything approximating to a thought-out response to the *Sun's* reactionary politics is the *Daily Mirror*. The middle-brow daily tabloids – the *Daily Mail* and the *Daily Express* – show a depressing preoccupation with the royal family and TV celebrities. The scene is a little more varied on a Sunday, when the *Guardian*-owned *Observer*, England's oldest **Sunday newspaper**, supplements the Sunday editions of the dailies, whose ranks are also swelled by the amazingly popular *News of the World*, a smutty rag commonly known as "The News of the Screws".

All the above publications are available in **Wales**, though they don't cover Welsh news in much depth. The only quality Welsh daily is the *Western Mail*, an uneasy mix of local, Welsh, British and token international news, though its attempts to give a Welsh slant to British stories can sometimes be ludicrous. The national Sunday paper, *Wales on Sunday*, is far superior.

In **Scotland**, the principal English papers are widely available, often as specific Scottish editions. The Scottish press produces two major daily papers, the liberal-left *Scotsman* and the slightly less-so *Herald*, published in Edinburgh and Glasgow respectively. Scotland's best selling daily paper, though, is the downmarket *Daily Record*, from the same group as the *Daily Mirror*. Many national Sunday newspapers have a Scottish section north of the border, but Scotland's own Sunday "heavy" is the wholly serious and somewhat dull *Scotland on Sunday*. Far more fun is the anachronistic *Sunday Post*, read by over half of the population.

Every town in Britain seems to publish one or more **local papers**, ranging from quality regional news sheets to little more than a collection of adverts. Even these can, however, be a useful source for local events information; we've given details of specific listings magazines in the relevant parts of the Guide.

When it comes to **specialist periodicals**, British newsagents can offer a range covering just about every subject, with motoring, music, sport, computers, gardening and home improvements all well served. One noticeably poor area is current events – the only high-selling weekly commentary magazine is the *Economist*, which is essential reading in the boardrooms of England. The socialist alternative, the *New Statesman*, is subsidized by a few socialist millionaires and is complemented by the glossy monthly *Red Pepper*. The satirical bi-weekly *Private Eye* is a much-loved institution that prides itself on printing the stories the rest of the press won't touch, and on surviving the consequent stream of libel suits. If you feel you can stomach a descent into the scatological pit of the English male psyche, take a look at *Viz*, a fortnightly comic which has managed to lodge its grotesque caricatures in the collective consciousness. Scottish monthly magazines include the widely read *Scots Magazine*, an old-fashioned middle-of-the-road publication that promotes family values. There's a profusion of Welsh monthlies – *Planet*, an English-language overview of the arts, history and politics, is the best of the bunch.

Australians and New Zealanders in London will be gratified to find the weekly free magazine *TNT*, which provides news from the home countries as well as adverts for jobs, accommodation and events in the capital. For **North Americans**, *USA Today* and the *International Herald Tribune* are widely distributed as are the magazines *Time* and *Newsweek*.

TELEVISION AND RADIO

In Britain **terrestrial television** stations are divided between the state-owned BBC, with two public service channels, and three independent commercial channels, ITV, Channel 4 and Channel 5. Though assailed by critics in the Conservative Party, who think that a nationalized TV station – indeed the very notion of a nationalized anything – is a Leninist throwback, the BBC is just about maintaining its worldwide reputation for in-house quality productions, ranging from expensive costume dramas to intelligent documentaries. BBC2 is the more offbeat and heavyweight BBC channel; BBC1 is avowedly mainstream. Various regional companies together form the ITV network, but they are united by a more tabloid approach to programme-making – necessarily so, because if they don't get the advertising they don't survive. Channel 4, a partly subsidized institution, is the most progressive of the bunch, with a reputation for broadcasting an eclectic spread of "arty" and minority-pleasing programmes, and for supporting small-budget motion pictures. The most recent newcomer is Channel 5, a self-consciously "young 'n' fun" alternative distinguished by its lurid colour schemes and breathless presenters. The principal Welsh channel is S4C (*Sianel Pedwar Cymru*), which, like Channel 4, sponsors diverse animation and feature-film projects. Welsh-language programmes are broadcast at lunchtime and for most of the evening, with the rest of the schedule reverting to Channel 4's UK-wide output. Rupert Murdoch's multi-channel Sky network has a monopoly on the **satellite** business, presenting a blend of movies, news, sport, reruns and overseas soaps. It has an increasing number of rivals in the form of cable TV companies, which are making big inroads in London especially. Within a few years these commercial stations will probably be making life uncomfortable for the BBC and ITV networks, but for the time being the old terrestrial stations still attract the majority of viewers. All these services can be accessed by means of the latest technological development, the **digital** system, through which the BBC presents its News 24, Knowledge, Parliament and Choice channels.

Market forces are eating away rather more quickly at the BBC's **radio network**, which has five stations: Radio 1 plays almost exclusively pop music, with a chart-biased view of the rock world; Radio 2 is bland music and chat; Radio 3 is predominantly classical music; Radio 4 a blend of current affairs, arts and drama; and Radio 5, a sports and news channel. Radio 1 has rivals on all fronts, with Virgin running a youth-oriented nationwide commercial network, and a plethora of local commercial stations – like London's Capital Radio and the Kiss FM soul station – attracting large sections of Radio 1's target audience. Melody Radio has whittled away at the Radio 2 easy-listening market, as has Jazz FM, while Classic FM has lured listeners away from Radio 3 by offering a less earnest approach to its subject, though it frequently degenerates into a "Greatest Hits" view of the most renowned composers. The BBC also operates a number of regional stations, but they are usually rather like listening to a broadcast of the local newspapers interspersed with the Top Twenty; the commercial stations, some of them real "fly-by-night" operations, tend to be far livelier.

One BBC institution that has stayed in front despite the arrival of downmarket pretenders is the **Radio Times**, a weekly publication that gives full details on national TV and radio programmes, not just the ones broadcast by the BBC.

ANNUAL EVENTS

In terms of the number of tourists they attract, the biggest occasions in the **English calendar** are the rituals that have associations with the ruling classes – from the courtly pageant of the Trooping of the Colour to the annual rowing race between Oxford and Cambridge universities. **In Scotland** many visitors home straight in on bagpipes, ceilidhs and Highland Games; such anachronisms certainly reflect the endemic British taste for nostalgia, but to gauge the spirit of the nation you should sample a wider range of events. London's large-scale festivals range from the riotous street party of the Notting Hill Carnival to the Promenade concerts, Europe's most egalitarian high-class music season, while the Edinburgh Festival and Welsh National Eisteddfod are vast cultural jamborees that have attained international status. Every major town in Britain has its own local arts festival, the best of which, along with various other local fairs and commemorative shows, are mentioned in the main part of the Guide; the very biggest ones are also listed in the box overleaf – and for the complete low-down on festivals throughout the country, get a copy of *The Great British Festival Guide* (Summersdale Press; £9.99).

To see Britain at its most idiosyncratic, take a look at one of the numerous regional celebrations that perpetuate **ancient customs**, the origins and meanings of which have often been lost or conveniently forgotten. The sight of the entire population of a village scrambling around a field after a barrel (that they call a bottle), or chasing a cheese downhill is not easily forgotten. Some of these strange rituals are mentioned in the Guide and included in the list below. Bear in mind that at a few of the smaller, more obscure events casual visitors are not always welcome. If in doubt, check with the local tourist office.

Also included in the list are the main **sports events**, which may often be difficult to get tickets for, but are invariably televised. In addition to these, there are of course football matches every Saturday (and some Sundays) from late August till early May, and cricket matches every day throughout the summer – both interesting social phenomena even for those unenthralled by team sports.

SCOTTISH HIGHLAND GAMES

Despite their name, **Highland Games** are held all over Scotland from May until mid-September: they vary in size and differ in the range of events they offer, and although the most famous are at Braemar, Oban and Cowal, the smaller ones are often more fun. They probably originated in the fourteenth century as a means of recruiting the best fighting men for the clan chiefs, and were popularized by Queen Victoria to encourage the traditional dress, music, games and dance of the Highlands; various royals still attend the Games at Braemar. The most distinctive events are known as the "**heavies**" – tossing the caber, putting the stone, and tossing the weight over the bar – all of which require prodigious strength and skill. Tossing the caber is the most spectacular, when the athlete must run carrying an entire tree trunk and attempt to heave it end over end in a perfect, elegant throw. Just as important as the sporting events are the **piping competitions** – for individuals and bands – and **dancing competitions**, where you'll see girls as young as three years old tripping the quick, intricate steps of such traditional dances as the Highland Fling.

The list includes some of the better-known Games; for the smaller, local games, check at individual tourist offices.

EVENTS CALENDAR

January 1: Kirkwall Boy's and Men's Ba' Games, Orkney. Mass, drunken football game through the streets of the town, with the castle and the harbour the respective goals. As a grand finale the players jump into the harbour.

January: Celtic Connections. International folk festival at Glasgow.

Last Tuesday in January: Up-Helly-Aa, Lerwick, Shetland. Norse fire festival culminating in the burning of a specially built Viking longship. Visitors can attend celebrations in the town hall.

End of January: Burns Night. Burns suppers. Held all over Scotland to commemorate Scotland's greatest poet; haggis, whisky and lots of poetry recital.

February: Scottish Curling Championship held in a different (indoor) venue each year.

Mid-February: Chinese New Year. Festivities in London's and Manchester's Chinatowns.

Shrove Tuesday: Purbeck Marblers and Stonecutters Day, Corfe Castle, Dorset. Ritual football game through the streets of the village.

February to March: Five Nations rugby championship.

March 1: St David's Day. Hwyrnos and celebrations all over Wales.

Mid-March: Cheltenham Gold Cup meeting. The country's premier national hunt horseracing event.

End of March or early April: University Boat Race. Hugely popular rowing contest on the Thames, between the teams of Oxford and Cambridge.

Maundy Thursday: The Queen dispenses the Royal Maundy Money, at a different cathedral every year.

Easter Monday: Hare Pie Scramble and Bottle-Kicking, Hallaton, Leicestershire.

Early April: Edinburgh Folk Festival.

April: Scottish Grand National at Ayr. Not quite as testing as the English equivalent steeplechase but an important event on the Scottish racing calendar.

April: Shetland Folk Festival.

Saturday in late March or early April: Grand National meeting, Aintree, Liverpool. Cruelly testing steeplechase that entices most of Britain's population into the betting shops.

April 30 to May 3: Minehead Hobby Horse, Minehead, Somerset.

May: Scottish FA Cup Final in Glasgow.

May: Mayfest. Glasgow's recent and very successful answer to the Edinburgh Festival.

May to July: Glyndebourne Opera Festival, East Sussex. The classiest and most snobbish arts festival in the country.

May 1: Padstow Hobby Horse, Padstow, Cornwall.

May 1: Beltane Fire festival on Calton Hill in Edinburgh.

May 8: Helston Furry Dance, Helston, Cornwall.

Early May: FA Cup Final, Wembley, London. The deciding contest in the premier football tournament.

Late May: Atholl Highlanders Parade at Blair Castle, Perthshire. The annual parade and inspection of Britain's last private army by their colonel-in-chief, the Duke of Atholl.

Late May: Hay-on-Wye Festival of Literature. London's literati flock to the Welsh borders for a week.

Last week in May: Chelsea Flower Show, Royal Hospital, Chelsea, London. Essential event for England's green-fingered legions.

Last week in May: St David's Cathedral Festival. Superb setting for classical concerts and recitals.

Spring Bank Holiday Monday: Cheese Rolling, Brockworth, Gloucestershire. Pursuit of a cheese wheel down a murderous incline – one of the weirdest customs in England.

Late May and early June: Bath International Festival. International arts jamboree.

June: Shinty Camanachd Cup Final, usually in Inverness. Finals of the intensely competitive games between the northern towns who play Scotland's own stick-and-ball game.

June: Royal Highland Agricultural Show, Ingliston, near Edinburgh. Scotland's biggest and best.

June: Highland Games at Campbeltown, Aberdeen and Grantown-on-Spey.

June: Aldeburgh Festival. Jamboree of classical music held on the Suffolk coast; established by Benjamin Britten.

First week in June: Derby week, Epsom racecourse, Surrey. The world's most expensive horse flesh competing in the Derby, the Coronation Cup and the Oaks.

First week in June: Eisteddfod Genedlaethol Urdd. The largest youth festival in Europe, alternating between North and South Wales.

Early June: Cotswold Olimpicks, Chipping Campden, Gloucestershire. Rustic sports festival and torchlight procession.

First or second Saturday in June: Trooping the Colour, Horse Guards Parade, London. Equestrian pageantry for the Queen's Official Birthday.

Mid-June: Royal Ascot, Berkshire. High-class horseracing attended by high-class people; the best seats go to royalty and their satellites, while the proles mill around in the outfield.

Mid-June: Cardiff Singer of the World competition. Huge, televised week-long music festival, with a star-studded list of international competitors.

Late June: Glastonbury Festival, Somerset. Hugely popular festival, with international bands and loads of hippies.

Last week of June and first week of July: Lawn Tennis Championships, Wimbledon, London. Queues are phenomenal even for the early rounds, and you need to know a freemason or ex-champion to get into the big games.

June to August: Riding of the Marches in the border towns of Hawick, Selkirk, Annan, Dumfries, Duns, Peebles, Jedburgh, Langholm and Lauder. The Rides originated to check the boundaries of common land owned by the town and also to remember the bloody warfare between the Scots and the English. Nowadays individual Ridings have their own special ceremonies, though they all start with a parade of pipes and brass bands.

July: Scottish Open Golf Championship held at a different venue annually.

July: Highland Games at Caithness, Elgin, Glengarry, North Uist, Inverness, Inveraray, Mull, Lewis, Durness, Lochaber, Dufftown, Halkirk.

First week in July: Henley Royal Regatta, Oxfordshire. Rowing event attended by much the same crew as that which populates the grandstands at Ascot.

First week in July: Tynwald Ceremony, St Johns, Isle of Man.

Second weekend in July: Gûyl Werin y Cnapan, Ffostrasol, near Lampeter, Ceredigion. The best folk and Celtic music festival in the world.

Early July: Llangollen International Music Eisteddfod. Over 12,000 participants from all over the world, including choirs, dancers, folk singers, groups and instrumentalists.

Mid-July: British Open Golf Championship, at a different venue annually. The season's last Grand Slam golf tournament.

Late July: Cambridge Folk Festival. Biggest event of its kind in England.

Late July: Womad, Reading. Three-day world music festival.

Third week in July: Swan Upping, River Thames from Sunbury to Pangbourne. Ceremonial registering of the Thames cygnets.

Last week in July: Royal Tournament, Earls Court Exhibition Centre, London. Precision military displays.

Last week in July to first week in August: Cardiff Festival. Incorporates music, art, drama, opera, literature and street entertainment.

July to early September: The Promenade Concerts, Royal Albert Hall, London. Classical music concerts ending in the fervently patriotic Last Night of the Proms.

August: Edinburgh International Festival and Fringe. One of the world's great arts jamborees.

August: Edinburgh Military Tattoo held on the Castle esplanade. Massed pipe bands and drums by floodlight.

August: World Pipe Band Championship at Glasgow.

August: Highland Games at Dunoon (Cowal), Mallaig, Skye, Dornoch, Aboyne, Strathpeffer, Assynt, Bute, Glenfinnan, Argyllshire, Glenurquhart and Invergordon.

First week in August: Royal National Eisteddfod. Wales' biggest single annual event: fun, very impressive and worth seeing if only for the overblown pageantry. Bardic competitions, readings, theatre, TV, debates and copious help for the Welsh language learner.

August Bank Holiday: Notting Hill Carnival, West London. Vivacious celebration by London's Caribbean community – plenty of music, food and floats.

Continues over

EVENTS CALENDAR (CONT.)

August Bank Holiday: Reading Festival, Berkshire. Three-day indie-rock jamboree.

Last Sunday in August: Plague Memorial, Eyam, Derbyshire.

September: Highland Games at Braemar.

September: Ben Nevis Race for amateurs to the top of the highest mountain in Scotland and back down again.

Early September to early November: Blackpool Illuminations, Lancashire. Five miles of exotic light displays.

First Monday after September 4: Abbots Bromley Horn Dance, Abbots Bromley, Staffordshire; vaguely pagan mass dance in mock-medieval costume – one of the most famous ancient customs.

October: The National Mod. Competitive festival of all aspects of Gaelic performing arts, held in varying Scottish venues.

October: Glenfiddich Piping Championships at Blair Atholl for the world's top ten solo pipers.

October: Swansea Festival of Music and the Arts. Concerts, jazz, drama, opera, ballet and art events throughout the city.

Late October to early November: Huddersfield Contemporary Music Festival. One of Europe's premier showcases for up-to-the-minute highbrow music.

First Sunday in November: London to Brighton Veteran Car Rally. Ancient machines lumber the 57 miles down the A23 to the seafront.

November 5: Guy Fawkes Night. Nationwide fireworks and bonfires commemorating the foiling of the Gunpowder Plot in 1605. Especially raucous celebrations at Ottery St Mary, Devon and Lewes, East Sussex.

Mid-November: Lord Mayor's Procession and Show, the City of London. Cavalcade to mark the inauguration of the new mayor.

November 30: St Andrew's Day celebrations at St Andrews.

December 31: Tar Barrels Parade, Allendale Town, Northumberland.

December 31: New Year Walk-In, Llanwrtyd Wells, Powys. A boozy stagger around the town.

December 31 and January 1: Hogmanay and Ne'er Day. More important to the Scots than Christmas. Festivities revolve around the "first-footing", when at midnight crowds of revellers troop into neighbours' houses bearing gifts.

OUTDOOR PURSUITS

No matter where you are in Britain, you're never far from a stretch of countryside where you can lose the crowds on a brief walk or cycle ride. For tougher specimens, there are numerous long-distance footpaths, as well as opportunities for the more extreme disciplines of rock climbing and potholing (caving). On the coast and many of the inland lakes you can follow the more urbane pursuits of sailing and windsurfing, and there are plenty of fine beaches for less structured fresh-air activities or just slobbing around.

WALKING AND CLIMBING

Walking routes trace many of Britain's wilder areas, amid landscapes varied enough to suit anyone. More sedate walkers will be happy enough in England, where many of the footpaths traverse moorlands, but if you're after more demanding exercise, or a feeling of isolation, head for Wales or Scotland. Welsh Snowdonia and the Scottish highlands offer Britain's best **climbing** and have acted as training grounds for some of the world's greatest mountaineers.

Numerous short walks and several major walks are covered in the Guide – however, you should use these notes only as general outlines and always in conjunction with a good **map**. Where possible we have given details of the best maps to use – in most cases one of the Ordnance Survey (OS) series (see p.20) – along with advice, leaflets and specialist guidebooks from tourist offices and shops in walking areas. In England

SAFETY IN THE BRITISH HILLS

British mountains are not high by European standards, but, due to rapid weather changes, they are potentially extremely dangerous and should be treated with respect. Every year, in every season, climbers and hill walkers die on mountains in Scotland, Wales and the English Lake District. If the weather looks as if it's closing in, get down fast. It is essential that you are properly equipped – even for what appears to be an easy expedition in apparently settled weather – with proper warm and waterproof layered clothing, supportive footwear and adequate maps, a compass (which you should know how to use) and food. Always leave word of your route and what time you expect to return; and remember to contact the person again to let them know that you are back.

and Wales you need to keep to established routes as you'll often be crossing private land, even within the National Parks: all OS maps mark public rights of way. Scotland, in contrast, has a tradition of **free public access** to most of the countryside, restricted only at certain times of the year.

IN ENGLAND

England's finest **walking areas** are the granite moorlands and spectacular coastlines **of Devon and Cornwall** in the southwest, and the highlands of the north – the low limestone and millstone crags of the **Peak District**, between Sheffield and Manchester; the **Yorkshire Dales**, the stretch of the Pennines to the north of the **Peak District**; the **North York Moors**, a bleak, treeless upland to the east of the Pennines; and the glaciated Cumbrian Mountains, better known as the **Lake District**. On summer weekends the more accessible reaches of these regions can get very crowded with day-trippers, but at any time of the year you'll find yourself in relative isolation if you undertake one of the **Long Distance Footpaths (LDPs)**. Defined as any route over twenty miles long, LDPs exist all over the country and are marked at frequent intervals with an acorn waymarker. **Youth hostels** are littered along most routes, though you may need a tent for some of the more heroic hikes.

WALKING HOLIDAY SPECIALISTS

Adventureline, North Trefula Farm, Redruth, Cornwall TR16 5ET (☎01209/820847; *www.chyycor.co.uk/adventureline*). Small group tours with local guides around the Celtic landscapes of Cornwall.

Assynt Guided Holidays, Birchbank, Knockan Elphin, Sutherland (☎01854/666215). Mountain walks, or glen and loch-side ambles, and fishing trips, with one of Scotland's most knowledgeable guides.

C-N-Do Scotland, 32 STEP, Stirling FK7 7RP (☎01786/445703; *www.cndoscotland.com*). Complete range of mountain activities including Munro bagging for novices and experts, in small groups and with qualified leaders.

English Wanderer, 6 George St, Ferryhill, County Durham DL17 0DT (☎01740/653169). Guided or independent walking holidays along the coastal paths of northeast England.

Footpath Holidays, 16 Norton Bavant, nr Warminster, Wiltshire BA12 7BB (☎01985/840049; *www.dmac.co.uk/footpath.html*). Packages to various hill and mountain districts in England, with experienced group leaders.

Glencoe Mountain Sport, 37 Park Rd, Ballachulish, Argyll PA39 4JS (☎01855/811472; *www.glencoe-mountain-sport.co.uk*). Year-round programmes of climbs, walks and scrambles on Skye, and around Glen Coe/Ben Nevis.

HF Walking Holidays, Imperial House, Edgware Road, London NW9 5AL (☎0181/905 9388). A wide choice of locations, and lodging in comfortable country houses.

Instep Walking Holidays, 35 Cokeham Rd, Lancing, West Sussex BN15 0AE (☎01903/766475; *www.instep.demon.co.uk*). Self-guided holidays with accommodation in small country hotels and guest houses, mainly in the south of England.

North-West Frontiers, 18A Braes, Ullapool IV26 2BZ (☎01854/612628; *www.nwfrontiers.com*). Graded walking tours all year round in the Scottish Highlands and islands.

Rua Reidh Lighthouse, Melvaig, Gairloch, Wester Ross (☎01445/771263; *www.scotlandinfo.co.uk/ruareidh.htm*). Accompanied and self-guided wilderness walks on the west coast; from three-nights to one-week itineraries. Family multi-activity holidays also available.

Walker's Britain, 131A Heston Rd, Hounslow, Middlesex TW5 0RD (☎0181/577 2717). At-your-own-pace, self-guided walks between country pubs all over England. and West Wales.

IN SCOTLAND

The whole of **Scotland** offers good opportunities for gentle hill walking, from the smooth, grassy hills and moors of the **Southern Uplands** to the wild and rugged country of the northwest. Scotland has three **Long Distance Footpaths (LDPs)**, each of which takes days to walk, though you can of course just cover sections of them. The **Southern Upland Way** crosses Scotland from coast to coast in the south, and is the country's longest at 212 miles; the best known is the **West Highland Way**, a 95-mile hike from Glasgow to Fort William via Loch Lomond and Glen Coe; and the gentler **Speyside Way**, in Aberdeenshire, is a mere thirty miles. The green signposts of the Scottish Rights of Way Society point to these and many other cross-country routes; while in the wilder parts the accepted freedom to roam allows extensive mountain walking, rock climbing, orienteering and allied activities.

Scotland's main **climbing areas** are in the Highlands, which boast many challenging peaks as well as great hill walks. There are 279 mountains over 3000ft (914m) in Scotland, known as **Munros** after the man who first classified them: many walkers "collect" them, and it's possible to chalk up several in a day. Serious climbers will probably head for **Glen Coe** or **Torridon** which offer difficult routes in spectacular surroundings. These and some of the other finest Highland areas (Lawers, Kintail, West Affric) are in the ownership of the National Trust for Scotland, while Blaven and Ladhar Bheinn (Knoydart) are John Muir Trust properties; both allow year-round access. Elsewhere there may be restricted access during lambing (dogs are particularly unwelcome during April and May) and deer-stalking seasons (mid-August to the third week in October). The **booklet** *Heading for the Scottish Hills* (published by the Scottish Mountaineering Club or "SMC"; £6.95) provides such information on all areas.

Beginners should contact the Mountaineering Council of Scotland, 4A St Catherine's Rd, Perth, Perthshire PH1 5SE (☎01738/ 638227) for information on courses.

Among the many **guidebooks** available for serious walking and climbing, the SMC's series of District Guides offer blow-by-blow accounts of climbs written by professional mountaineers. For other good walking guides see the "Books" section of Contexts.

IN WALES

Wales's best **walking country** is to be found within its three national parks. Almost the whole of the northwestern corner of Wales is taken up with the **Snowdonia National Park**, a dozen of the country's highest peaks separated by dramatic glaciated valleys and laced with hundreds of miles of ridge and moorland paths. From Snowdonia, the Cambrian Mountains stretch south to the **Brecon Beacons National Park**, with its striking sandstone scarp at the head of the South Wales coalfield, and lush, cave-riddled limestone valleys to the south. One hundred and seventy miles of Wales's southwestern peninsula make up the third park – the **Pembrokeshire Coast National Park**, best explored by the **Pembrokeshire Coast Path** that traverses the cliff-tops, frequently dipping down into secluded coves. This is only one of Wales' four frequently walked **Long Distance Paths** – the other three LDPs are the 168-mile-long **Offa's Dyke Path** that traces the England–Wales border; the 274-mile **Cambrian Way**, cutting north–south over the Cambrian Mountains, and **Glyndŵyr's Way**, which weaves through mid-Wales for 120 miles. For details on specialist walking guides, see Contexts, or contact the Long Distance Walkers' Association (Bank House, High St, Wrotham, Kent TN15 7AE).

As well as being superb walking country, Wales offers some of Britain's best **rock climbing** and some challenging scrambles – ascents that fall somewhere between walks and climbs, requiring some use of your hands. There are a couple of noted climbing spots around the Pembrokeshire coast and in the Brecon Beacons but the vast majority are in Snowdonia, with its predominance of low-lying crags and easy access. The best general **guide** for experienced climbers is *Rock Climbing in Snowdonia* by Paul Williams (£12.95, Constable). Beginners should contact the

British Mountaineering Council, 177–179 Burton Rd, Manchester M20 2BB (☎0161/445 4747).

CYCLING

Despite the recent boom in the sale of mountain bikes, **cyclists** are treated with notorious disrespect by many motorists and by the people who plan the country's traffic systems. In spite of the efforts of organizations such as SUSTRANS (see overleaf), few of England's towns as yet have proper cycle routes and British cyclists are estimated to be twelve times more likely to be killed or injured (per miles cycled) than their counterparts in Denmark, where a network of safe cycle paths and traffic-calming schemes has been created. Surprisingly, **cycle helmets** are not compulsory in Britain – but if you're hellbent on tackling the congestion, pollution and aggression of city traffic, you're well advised to get one. You do have to have a **rear reflector** and front and back lights when riding at night, and are not allowed to carry children without a special child seat. It is also illegal to cycle on pavements (sidewalks) and in most public parks. A secure **lock** (preferably some kind of "D" lock) is also indispensable – cycle theft in Britain has become an organized racket in recent years, and it's always a good idea to make a note of your frame number in case you have to report a loss to the police.

The backroads of rural England (those labelled with the prefix "B") are infinitely more enjoyable than trunk routes (or "A" roads), with a sufficient density of pubs and B&Bs to keep the days manageable. Your main problem out in the countryside will be getting hold of any spare parts – only inner tubes and tyres are easy to find.

Off-road riding is popular in the highland walking areas, but cyclists should remember to keep to rights of way designated on maps as Bridleways, BOATs ("Byways Open To All Traffic") or RUPPs ("Roads Used As Public Footpaths") and to pass walkers at considerate speeds. Footpaths, unless otherwise marked, are for pedestrian use only. Other rules of the road to bear in mind are that cycles are not permitted on motorways (labelled with the prefix "M").

Every region of England offers rich potential for cyclists, with varied scenery and miles of sleepy country lanes to explore. Armed with a detailed **OS map** of any area, you can improvise scenic routes of your own that avoid the main roads. For the less map literate, most good bookshops also

CARRYING YOUR BIKE ON PUBLIC TRANSPORT

The majority of **airlines** will carry bicycles as part of your luggage allowance on plane journeys, although protruding parts, such as pedals and handlebars, have to be removed, and the tyres deflated; some carriers also require you to stash the machine in a bike bag or cardboard cover. Check with your airline well in advance to find out exactly what their terms and conditions are, and bear in mind that you may have to pay excess baggage. Transporting cycles by **ferry** is also free, but a lot more straightforward; you just wheel them on and off, and reservation is not normally required. **Coach** companies, on the other hand, rarely accept cycles unless they're of the special stowaway variety. One exception is European Bike Express, 31 Baker St, Middllesborough, Cleveland TS1 2LF (☎01642/251440), which tacks trailers on the back of their luxury coaches for journeys to and from a range of destinations on the continent.

Carrying your bike by **train** is a good way of getting to the interesting parts of England without a lot of stressful or boring pedalling. For some reason, however, the newly privatized rail companies seem hellbent on making life difficult for cyclists by slapping on hefty surcharges. Most suburban trains will carry cycles outside the rush hours of 7.30am to 9.30am and 4pm to 6pm, but they are not allowed at all on some InterCity express trains (or Eurostar), while those that do accept cycles charge between £1 and £3; this usually has to be paid at least 24 hours in advance, and for each separate leg of the trip, which can work out to be ridiculously expensive if your journey involves a couple of changes. If you book 48 hours in advance, Eurotunnel will carry you and your bike for £15 on the 11am or 6pm train from Calais and the 8am or 3.30pm train from Folkestone. Call ☎01303/288933.

CYCLING HOLIDAY SPECIALISTS

For those who want a guaranteed hassle-free **cycling holiday**, there are various companies offering easy-going packages. These can take all sorts of forms, but generally include transport of your gear to each night halt, pre-booked accommodation, detailed route instructions, a packed lunch and back-up support. Nor need they necessarily cost a fortune. Most companies offer some budget cycling holidays, with hostels or B&Bs instead of hotels. Below is a list of reliable and established operators worth phoning for quotes and brochures:

Acorn Activities, PO Box 120, Hereford HR4 8YB (☎01432/830083; *www.acornactivities.co.uk*). Weekend, one-week and fourteen-day tours, with bikes, accommodation, luggage transportation and maps provided.

Bespoke Highland Tours, The Bothy, Camusdarach, Arisaig, Inverness-shire PH39 4NT (☎01687/450272; *www.scotland-info.co.uk/ tours*). Cycling holidays in the Scottish Highlands.

Byways Bike Breaks, 25 Mayville Rd, Liverpool L18 0HG (☎0151/722 8050; *www.byways-breaks.com*). Tours of the gentle Cheshire countryside.

Compass Holidays, 48 Shurdington Rd, Cheltenham Spa GL53 0JE (☎01242/250642). Guided or independent tours in the Cotswolds and Warwickshire.

Country Lanes, 9 Shaftesbury St, Fordingbridge,

Hampshire SP6 1JF (☎01425/655022; *www.countrylanes.co.uk*). Countrywide trips. Also rents out bikes at train stations.

Orchard Cycle Tours, 1 The Orchard, Appleton, Oxfordshire OX13 5LF (☎01865/863773). Tours through the quintessentially English villages of Oxfordshire and the Thames Valley.

Rough Tracks, 6 Castle St, Calne SN11 0DU (☎0700/560749). Mountain bike tours across the country.

Scottish Border Trails, Venlaw High Rd, Peebles EH45 8RL (☎01721/722934). Trips in border country.

Scottish Cycling Holidays, 87 Perth St, Blairgowrie, Perthshire PH10 6DT (☎01250/876100; *www.sol.co.uk/s/scotcycl/*). Trips throughout Scotland, from Glasgow northwards.

stock a range of **cycling guides**, featuring suggestions for rides of varying length, with coloured maps and detailed route descriptions. Currently the best series in this line is Ordnance Survey's

One-Day Routes by Nick Cotton, which covers the country's most inspiring cycling areas, including the major national parks and coastal regions, in user-friendly ring-binder books, with sections of

OS Landranger Maps, details of mileage, terrain, gradients, refreshments and places of interest along the way. Other recommended maps for popular cycling regions such as the Lake District and Cotswolds are those published by Goldeneye; these come in a handy showerproof format, feature height shading, campsites, hostels and many off-road itineraries, and are available direct from Goldeneye, PO Box 5, Cheltenham, Glos GL52 6XQ (☎01242/575943).

Many of the routes featured in these guides include stretches of traffic-free cycle tracks, of which there are currently 3000 miles in England. Funded by a £42-million grant by the Millennium Commission, in partnership with local authorities and organizations like the National Trust and Countryside Commission, the charity **SUSTRANS** (which stands for Sustainable Transport) hopes by 2005 to expand this to a 8,500-mile National Cycle Network, passing within two miles of some twenty million people. A large proportion of the network is made up of quiet backroads, dubbed "Cycleways", but more than half runs along disused railways and canal towpaths, including the showpiece section connecting the cities of Bath and Bristol. Maps of the network are available from SUSTRANS, 37–41 Prince St, Bristol BS1 4PS (☎0117/929 0888; *www.sustrans.org.uk*).

With more time, you may want to take on one of England's challenging **long-distance routes**. The Cycle Touring Club or CTC (Cotterell House, 69 Meadrow, Godalming, Surrey GU7 3HS; ☎01483/417217; *www.CTC.org.uk*) publishes special maps for some of these, and supplies members with touring and technical advice as well as insurance. The classic cross-Britain route is Land's End, in the far southwest of England, to John O'Groats, on the northeast tip of Scotland – roughly one thousand miles that you can cover in two to three weeks, depending on which of the three CTC-recommended routes you choose. Another favourite coast-to-coast option is the journey from Lowestoft Ness, in the southeast home county of Suffolk, to the Ardnamurchan peninsula in northwest Scotland. The CTC suggests a ten-day itinerary, but you could easily spend twice that long scaling the English watershed. The same applies to the wonderful 130-mile Wye Valley route, which winds from the Severn Estuary through the forests and moorlands of the Welsh borders to the rough mountains of mid-Wales. Other tempting long-distance tours could take you around the

Yorkshire Dales, Pennines, and Peak District, around Dartmoor and the Cornish coast, or across the austere North Yorkshire Moors. For a full rundown of tour routes in these and other regions, ask for copies of their leaflets costing £2–4, or *Cycling Great Britain* by Tim Hughes and Joanna Cleary (£8.95, Bicycle Books Inc).

Bike rental is available at cycle shops in most large towns, and at villages within National Parks and other scenic areas; the addresses and telephone numbers of these appear in the relevant sections of the Guide. Although increasing numbers of rental outfits have quality multi-geared mountain bikes, many of the machines on offer are often old and unwieldy – all right for a brief spin, but not for any serious touring. Expect to pay in the region of £10–15 per day, with discounts for longer periods.

BEACHES

Britain is ringed by fine beaches and bays, the best of which are readily accessible by public transport – though of course that means they tend to get very busy in high summer. For a combination of decent climate and good sand, southwest **England** is the best area, especially the coast of north Cornwall and Devon. The beaches of England's southern coast become more pebbly as you approach the southeastern corner of the country – resorts round here are more garish than their southwestern counterparts. Moving up the east coast, the East Anglian shore is predominantly pebbly and very exposed, making it ideal for those who want to escape the crowds rather than bask in the sun, while right up in the northeast there are some wonderful sandy strands and old-fashioned seaside resorts, though the North Sea breezes often require a degree of stoicism. Over in the northwest, the inland hills of Cumbria are a greater attraction than anything on the coast, though Blackpool has a certain appeal as the apotheosis of the "kiss-me-quick" holiday town.

Many of **Scotland's** beaches and bays are deserted even in high summer – perhaps hardly surprising given the bracing winds and icy water. Though you're unlikely to come here for a beach holiday, it's worth sampling one or two beaches, even if you never shed as much as a sweater. A rash of slightly melancholy seaside towns lies within easy reach of Glasgow, while on the east coast, the relatively low cliffs and miles of sandy beaches are ideal for walking. Despite the low

BRITAIN'S DIRTIEST BEACHES

This is a list of British beaches where the shore and bathing waters failed to meet EU standards in 1999 (the latest available figures). An asterisk (*) denotes places that failed for the previous two years as well.

ENGLAND

Aldingham* (Cumbria)
Alnmouth (Northumberland)
Askham-in-Furness* (Cumbria)
Bardsea* (Cumbria)
Bantham (Devon)
Beadnell (Northumberland)
Blackpool – North, Central and South* (Lancashire)
Blue Anchor (Somerset)
Blyth – South Beach (Northumberland)
Broadstairs
Burnham-on-Sea (Somerset)
Cawsand Bay (Cornwall)
Crimdon Park (Durham)
Doniford (Somerset)
Douglas – Palace (Isle of Man)
Felpham (West Sussex)
Folkestone* (Kent)
Gansey Bay (Isle of Man)
Harlyn Bay (Cornwall)
Hartland Quay (Devon)
Haverigg* (Cumbria)
Hope Cove (Devon)
Instow (Devon)
Jurby (Isle of Man)
Kingsand Bay (Cornwall)
Kirk Michael (Isle of Man)
Looe – East* (Cornwall)
Minehead – Terminus (Somerset)
Morecambe – South* (Lancashire)
Mother Ivey's Bay (Cornwall)
Newbiggin (Cumbria)
Peel (Isle of Man)
Plymouth Hoe West* (Devon)
Port St Mary (Isle of Man)
Port Soderick (Isle of Man)
Porthluney Cove (Cornwall)
Roan Head (Cumbria)

Saltburn (North Yorkshire)
Sandsend (North Yorkshire)
Saunton Sands (Devon)
Seaham – Beach*, Remand Home (Durham)
Seaton Sluice (North Tyneside)
South Shields (North Tyneside)
Spittal (Northumberland)
St Anne's – North* (Lancashire)
Staithes* (North Yorkshire)
Walney West Shore* (Cumbria)
The Warren, Folkestone
White Strand (Isle of Man)

SCOTLAND

Anstruther (Fife)
Ayr (South Ayrshire)
Barassie (South Ayrshire)
Broughty Ferry (Angus)
Burntisland (Fife)
Croy (South Ayrshire)
Cruden Bay (Aberdeenshire)
Dunnet Bay/Murkle Bay (Highland)
East Largo (Fife)
Eyemouth (The Borders)
Fraserburgh (Aberdeenshire)
Girvan* (South Ayrshire)
Greenan (South Ayrshire)
Irvine – Beach Park (North Ayrshire)
Kinghorn (Fife)
Kirkcaldy Linktown (Fife)
Largs (North Ayrshire)
Leven – East (Fife)
Longniddry (East Lothian)
Lossiemouth – East (Moray)
Lower Largo (Fife)
Maidens – Turnberry (South Ayrshire)
Millport – Cumbrae (North Ayrshire)

Monifieth (Angus)
Montrose (Angus)
Nairn – East (Moray)
Newburgh (Aberdeenshire)
Prestwick (South Ayrshire)
Rockcliffe (Dumfries & Galloway)
Saltcoats (North Ayrshire)
Sandend Bay (Aberdeenshire)
Sandyhills (Dumfries & Galloway)
St Cyrus (Aberdeenshire)
Seamill (North Ayrshire)
Stevenston (North Ayrshire)
Stonehaven – Carron (Aberdeenshire)
Turnberry* (South Ayrshire)
Wonderwest World (South Ayrshire)

WALES

Aberfan – East (Neath & Port Talbot)
Abersoch (Gwynedd)
Broughton Bay (Swansea)
Criccieth (Gwynedd)
East Tywyni – Ynyslas Estuary (Ceredigion)
Ferryside (Carmarthenshire)
Garreg Wen (Gwynedd)
Llandulas (Conwy)
Llanfairfechn (Conwy)
Llanina (Ceredigion)
Llanstephan & Tywi Estuary (Carmarthenshire)
Morfa Aberech (Gwynedd)
Patch (Ceredigion)
Penrhyn Bay (Conwy)
Poppit Sands (Pembrokeshire)
Saundersfoot – Wiseman's Bridge (Pembrokeshire)
Swansea Bay*
Three Cliffs Bay (Swansea)

temperature of the water, the beaches in the northeast are beginning to figure on surfers' itineraries, attracting enthusiasts from all over Europe. Perhaps the most beautiful beaches of all are to be found on Scotland's islands: endless, isolated stretches that on a sunny day can seem the epitome of the Scottish Hebridean dream.

In **Wales** the best areas to head for for sunbathing and swimming are the Gower peninsula, the Pembrokeshire coast, the Llŷn and the southwest coast of Anglesey. The southwest-facing beaches of Wales offer the best conditions for surfing, key spots being Rhossili, at the western tip of the Gower, and Whitesands Bay near St David's. Windsurfers tend to congregate at Barmouth, Borth, around the Pembrokeshire coast and at The Mumbles. Though the north coast has more resorts than any other section of the Welsh coastline, its beaches are certainly not the most attractive and nor is it a good place to swim.

It has to be said that Britain's beaches are not the cleanest in Europe, and many of those that the British authorities declare to be acceptable actually fall below **EU standards**. Although steps are being taken to improve the situation, far too many stretches of the coastline are contaminated by seaborne effluent or other rubbish. The box opposite gives the latest state of play. For annually updated, detailed information on the condition of Britain's beaches, the *Good Beach Guide*, compiled by the Marine Conservation Society (9 Gloucester Rd, Ross-on-Wye, Herefordshire HR9 5BU, ☎01989/566017; *www.goodbeachguide.co.uk*), is the definitive source.

SURFING

For most people, surfing in Britain means surfing in Newquay, and while it's true that the southwest of England is the heartland of the British **surf scene**, it would be a mistake to think that there aren't decent waves elsewhere. You don't get the sunshine of Hawaii, and the waves are steely-grey rather than turquoise-blue, but there are world-class waves to be found if you know where to go. The major difference between Britain and the States or Australasia, of course, is the water temperature, which even in mid-summer rarely exceeds 15°C, and in winter can drop to as low as 7°C or colder (on the north coast of Scotland you're surfing at the same latitude as Alaska and Iceland). For this reason, if you're planning to surf in the UK – particularly in winter – make sure you have a good wetsuit, and ideally a 5/3mm "steamer", wetsuit boots and, outside summer, gloves and a hood. You'll also need a shedload of enthusiasm to get out into the waves, although when you do eventually paddle out, you may be pleasantly surprised.

In **England**, the northeast coast, from Yorkshire to Northumberland, has a growing population of hardy surfers willing to endure low temperatures to surf clean northerly groundswells. The coastline here is often spectacular, and although the more popular breaks such as Cayton Bay and Saltburn are now crowded, you can find relative isolation off the beaten track. Nevertheless, the southwest, or more specifically Newquay, Cornwall, remains the country's undisputed surf Mecca. Visitors are often amazed to see the hype surrounding this self-styled "surf city". In summer, every other male seems to be a "surfie", sporting regulation bleached hair and designer gear, but the majority only turn up to cruise surf babes. It can still be hectic out in the water though, especially at the main break, Fistral, which regularly hosts international contests. Head out of town, however, and things quieten down noticeably. Try spots such as Perranporth or Polzeath, or travel up to Devon, which also gets decent waves, despite the overcrowding of its main break, Croyde.

Surfing in **Wales** tends to be concentrated on the south coast, around the Gower peninsula, which boasts a good variety of beach and reef breaks, and a lively social scene. One thing to bear in mind if you surf here, though, is the enormous tidal range of the Bristol Channel – it can be up to thirteen metres, and this can have a major effect on the surf. The tidal range drops as you head west towards Pembrokeshire, where the coastline becomes more scenic, and numbers in the water diminish considerably. This area, comprising Britain's only coastal national park, is where you'll find the most consistent surf beach in Wales, Freshwater West, as well as seals, porpoise, dolphins, basking sharks and sunfish in the water. Washed by the Irish Sea, the west coast gets much less surf than the south, with the waves breaking mostly in winter. Aberystwyth is the main centre hereabouts, and its local breaks tend to be pretty busy. Heading further north, you come to the Llŷn peninsula, in the shadow of Snowdonia, where Hell's Mouth has the best and most consistent waves in North Wales, drawing lots of weekend surfers from northern England throughout the year.

BRITAINS TOP TWENTY BREAKS

Listed below, in alphabetical order, is a selection of top British breaks. All of them are well known, and can thus get crowded, but you'll find plenty of less frequented alternatives in the same regions. For a fuller rundown of these, and dozens more hot surfing spots in Britain, check out *Surf UK* by Wayne "Alf" Alderson (£13.95, Fernhurst Books) which covers 400 breaks, or the less detailed *Stormrider Guide* by Tim Rainger and Oliver Fitzjones (£24.95, Low Pressure Publications); both should be available from any well-stocked bookstore. Any large newsagent will also offer a selection of surfing magazines, including *Surf* (£3.00, bi-monthly), the most "grass roots" on the market, along with *Wavelength* (£2.99, bi-monthly) and *Carve* (£2.95, bi-monthly).

An asterisk (*) denotes beaches suitable for experienced surfers only.

1. **Bamburgh**, Northumberland, northeast England. A wonderfully scenic quiet beach, with seals in the water and a spectacular castle as a backdrop.

2. **Constantine**, Cornwall, southwest England. Picks up a lot of swell.

3. **Croyde Bay**, Devon, southwest England. Good beach breaks, but crowds can be a problem.

4. **Fistral**, Newquay, Cornwall, southwest England. Hype, crowds, but still a good wave if you can get one to yourself.

5. **Freshwater West**, Pembrokeshire, South Wales. Quality beach and reef breaks. Beware of currents.

6. **Hell's Mouth**, Llŷn Peninsula, North Wales. Popular, quality break.

7. **Llangennith**, Gower, South Wales. Long beach with peaks along its length. Busy.

8. **Newgale**, Pembrokeshire. South Wales. Two-mile-long beach with peaks along its length.

9. **Pease Bay**, near Dunbar, 26 miles east of Edinburgh, Scotland. A popular break suited to all abilities.

*10. **Pete's Reef**, Gower, South Wales. Picks up most swells. Popular.

*11 **Porthleven**, Cornwall, southwest England. Heavy reef break, heavy locals.

12. **Machrihanish Bay**, Mull of Kintyre. Four miles of beach breaks on one of Scotland's loneliest peninsulas.

13. **Sandwood Bay**, a day's hike south of Cape Wrath in Sutherland. Beach breaks on one of the most scenic and remote shorelines in Britain, only accessible on foot.

14. **Sennen Cove**, Cornwall, southwest England. Picks up any swell going.

15. **Saltburn**, Cleveland, northeast England. Another good beach break, with atmosphere to match.

*16 **Skirza Harbour**, three miles south of John O'Groats, northeast Scotland. An excellent left-hand reef break on the far northeast tip of Scotland.

*17 **Staithes**, Yorkshire, northeast England. Excellent reef breaks, crowded and jealously guarded by locals.

*18. **Thurso East**, just below the castle, Thurso, northern Scotland. One of the best right-hand reef breaks in Europe.

*19. **Torrisdale Bay**, Bettyhill, on the north coast of the Scottish Highlands. An excellent right-hand rivermouth break.

*20. **Valtos**, on the Uig peninsula, Lewis, Outer Hebrides, Scotland. A break on one of the Outer Hebrides' most exquisite shell-sand beaches.

Scotland may not seem the most promising destination for surfers, but is fast gaining a reputation for the high quality of its breaks. The number one spot is Thurso on the north coast, which has hosted the European Surfing Championships, and has what is widely acknowledged to be one of the finest reef breaks in Europe. Elsewhere along this coastline are waves which compare to those of Hawaii, Australia and Indonesia. Nor do you have to go all the way to Thurso to get tubed. Many of the best breaks lie within easy reach of

large cities (eg Pease Bay, near Edinburgh, and Fraserburgh near Aberdeen), while the spectacular west coast has numerous possibilities: try Sandwood Bay, the most isolated beach in Britain, or the waves of the Outer Hebrides. All are surrounded by stunning scenery, and you'd be unlucky to encounter another surfer for miles, which is an important consideration in itself. The fact that many of the breaks are quite isolated, the water is cold, and the surf often big and powerful means that, in general, Scottish surf is best left to experienced surfers. If you're a beginner, get local advice before you go in and be aware of your limitations; remember, if you get caught in a current off the west coast the next stop might be Iceland.

GOLF

There are over 400 **golf courses** in **Scotland**, where the game is less elitist, cheaper and more accessible than anywhere else in the world. The game as it's known today took shape in the sixteenth century on the dunes of Scotland's east coast, and today you'll find some of the oldest courses in the world on these early coastal sites, known as "links". If you want a round of golf, it's often possible just to turn up and play, though it's sensible to phone ahead and book, and essential for the championship courses (see below). It's worth asking at the tourist office for the Golf Pass Scotland which will give you a discount on courses for either three or five days. Prices vary according to area.

Public courses are owned by the local council, while **private courses** belong to a club. You can play on both – occasionally the private courses require that you be a member of another club, and the odd one asks for introductions from a member, but these rules are often waived for overseas visitors and all you need to do is pay a one-off fee. The cost of one round will set you back between around £5 for small, nine-hole courses, up to more than £20 for eighteen holes. Simply pay as you enter and play. In remote areas the courses are sometimes unmanned – just put the admission fee into the honour box. Most courses have **resident professionals** who give lessons, and some rent equipment at reasonable rates. Renting a caddy car will add an extra few pounds depending on the swankiness of the course you are playing.

Scotland's **championship courses**, which often host the British Open tournament, are renowned for their immaculately kept greens and challenging holes, and though they're favoured by serious players, anybody with a valid handicap certificate can enjoy them. **St Andrews** (☎01334/475757; *www.standrews.org.uk*) is the top destination for golfers: it's the home of the Royal and Ancient Golf Club, the international controlling body that regulates the rules of the game. Of its six courses, the best known is the Old Course, a particularly intriguing ground with eleven enormous greens and the world-famous "Road Hole". If you want to play, there's no introduction needed, but you'll need to book months in advance and for the Old and the New Courses have a handicap certificate – handicap limits are 24 for men and 36 for women. You could also enter your name for the daily lottery – call before 2pm on the day you'd like to play. One of the easier championship courses to get into is Carnoustie, in Angus (☎01241/853249), though you should still try and book as far ahead as possible; a handicap certificate is required – 28 for men and 36 for women. Other championship courses include **Gleneagles** in Perthshire (☎01764/694469), **Royal Dornoch** in Sutherland (☎01862/810219) and **Turnberry** in Ayrshire (☎01655/331000). A round of golf at any of these will set you back at least £45, with an extra £25–30 if you hire a caddy – and you'll be expected to tip over and above that. Near Edinburgh, Muirfield, considered by professional players to be one of the most testing grounds in the world, is also one of the most reactionary – women can only play on Tuesdays and Thursdays and then only if accompanied by a man, and they aren't allowed into the clubhouse at any time.

SPECTATOR SPORTS

As a quick glance at the national press will tell you, sport in Britain is a serious matter, with each defeat of the national side being taken as an index of the country's slide down the scale of world powers. Football, rugby and cricket are the major spectator sports, and horseracing also has a big following, though a fair proportion of its public has little interest beyond the Grand National, the country's most popular opportunity for a gamble until the National Lottery came along. The calendar is chock-full of one-off quality sports events, ranging from the massed masochism of the London Marathon to the Wimbledon championship, one of the world's greatest tennis tournaments.

For the top international events it can be almost impossible to track down a ticket without resorting to the services of a grossly overcharging ticket agency, but for many fixtures you can make credit card bookings. Should you be thwarted in your attempts to gain admission, you can often fall back on TV or radio coverage. BBC Radio 5 has live commentaries on major sporting events, while TV carries live transmission of the big international rugby and cricket matches; you'll find that Rupert Murdoch's Sky satellite station makes greater inroads into the terrestrial channels with each passing year. As it is, to watch live Premier League (and some international) football, you'll need to find a set that has Sky TV – many pubs offer Sky games (sometimes on big screens) to draw in custom.

FOOTBALL

English football teams may have lost ground to the more cultured continentals in recent years, but it is still the most passionately supported sport in the land, and if you have the slightest interest in the game, then catching a league or FA Cup fixture is a must. The season runs from mid-August to early May, when the **FA Cup Final** at Wembley (for which tickets are almost impossible to obtain) rounds things off. There are four league divisons for England and Wales: three, two, one and, at the top of the pyramid, the twenty-club **Premier League**. Currently, this is dominated by Manchester United who are challenged most regularly by other northern clubs – Liverpool, who signed the phenomenal star Michael Owen, and

Leeds and Newcastle. In the Midlands, Coventry and Birmingham's Aston Villa are the strongest clubs, while in London the contest is between Arsenal, Chelsea and Tottenham. **Wales's** big three teams are Cardiff City and Wrexham, which play in the second division, and Swansea City, which plays in the third; the rest of the Welsh clubs play in the feeble Konica League of Wales. **Scotland** has three divisions, each with fewer teams than the equivalent south of the border, and of considerably lower standard. Glasgow Rangers has dominated the top flight in recent years, and together with Glasgow Celtic are the only Scottish clubs to currently have the clout or the cash to make big-name signings. Top British clubs also take part in European matches played midweek, particularly early in the season.

The team with the biggest following is Manchester United, whose matches are almost always a sell-out, regardless of how the team is playing. Of the other glamorous English clubs, Liverpool and Newcastle United also command so ardent a following that tickets for their matches are often like gold dust. It's easy enough to get tickets, if booked in advance, for most other Premier League games, unless two local sides are playing each other. In Scotland, only the "Old Firm" clash between Rangers and Celtic (representing the Protestant and Irish Catholic communities of Glasgow respectively) is a certain full house.

Most **fixtures** kick off at 3pm on Saturday (highlights of the day's best games are shown on BBC1's *Match of the Day* on Saturday night), though there are generally a few midweek games (usually 7.30pm on Wednesday), and one each on Sunday (kick-off between 2pm and 4pm) and Monday (kick-off at 8pm), both broadcast live on Sky TV. **Tickets** cost from about £20 for Premier games, falling to less than £15 in the lower divisions.

Since the introduction of all-seater Premiership stadiums in 1994, top-flight games have lost their reputation for tribal violence, and there's been a striking increase in the numbers of women and children attending. Nonetheless, it's an intense business, with a lot of foul language, and being stuck in the middle of a few thousand West Ham supporters as their team goes 3–0 down is not one of life's more uplifting experiences.

CRICKET

In the glory days of the Empire the **English** took cricket to the colonies as a means of instilling the gentlemanly values of fair play while administering a sound thrashing to the natives. These days the former colonies, such as Australia, the West Indies and India, all beat England on a regular basis, so to see the game at its best you should try to get into one of the series of three, five or six **Test matches** played between England and the summer's touring team. These international matches are played in the middle of the cricket season, which runs from April to September. Two of these matches are played in London – the second is always played at Lord's, the home of English cricket, and the last is held at The Oval in Kennington, London; the other Test grounds are Trent Bridge (Nottingham), Old Trafford (Manchester), Headingley (Leeds) and Edgbaston (Birmingham). In tandem with the full-blown five-day Tests, there's also a series of **one-day internationals**, two of which are again usually held in London.

Getting to see England play one of the big teams may be difficult unless you book months in advance. If you can't wangle your way into a Test, you could watch it live on TV (the Test series is always televised), listen to ball-by-ball commentary on BBC radio, or settle down to an inter-county match, either in the **county championship** (these are four-day games) or in one of the three fast and furious one-day competitions: the Benson and Hedges Cup and the Nat West Trophy (both knockout competitions), or the CGU National league. Of the eighteen county teams (divided into two divisions) in the championship, two are based in London – Middlesex, who play at Lord's, and Surrey, who play at The Oval.

THE RULES OF CRICKET

The laws of cricket are so complex that the official rule book runs to some twenty pages. The basics, however, are by no means as byzantine as the game's detractors make out.

There are two teams of eleven players. A team wins by scoring more runs than the other team and dismissing all the opposition – in other words, a team could score many runs more than the opposition, but still not win if the last enemy batsman doggedly stays in (hence ensuring a draw). The match is divided into innings, when one team bats and the other fields. The number of innings varies depending on the type of competition; one-day matches have one per team, Test matches and county championship matches have two.

The aim of the fielding side is to limit the runs scored and get the batsmen "out". Two players from the batting side are on the pitch at any one time. The bowling side has a bowler, a wicket keeper and nine fielders. Two umpires, one standing behind the stumps at the bowler's end and one square on to the play, are responsible for adjudicating if a batsman is out. Each innings is divided into overs, consisting of six deliveries, after which the wicket keeper changes ends, the bowler is changed and the fielders move positions.

The batsmen score runs either by running up and down from wicket to wicket (one length is one "run"), or by hitting the ball over the boundary rope, scoring four runs if it crosses the boundary having touched the ground, and six runs if it flies over. The main ways a batsman can be dismissed are: by being "clean bowled", where the bowler dislodges the bails of the wicket (the horizontal pieces of wood resting on top of the stumps); by being "run out", which is when one of the fielding side dislodges the bails with the ball while the batsman is running between the wickets; by being caught, which is when any of the fielding side catches the ball after the batsman has hit it and before it touches the ground; or "LBW" (leg before wicket), where the batsman blocks with his leg a delivery that would otherwise have hit his stumps.

These are the rudimentaries of a game whose beauty lies in the subtlety of its skills and tactics. The captain, for example, chooses which bowler to play and where to position his fielders to counter the strengths of the batsman, the condition of the pitch, and a dozen other variables. Cricket also has a beauty in its esoteric language, used to describe such things as fielding positions ("silly mid-off", "cover point", etc) and the various types of bowling delivery ("googly", "yorker", etc). For beginners, some enlightenment may be gained by watching the TV coverage, or befriending a spectator – cricket fans tend to be congenial types, eager to introduce newcomers to the mysteries of the true faith.

Prices for Test matches cost £15–40 per day; for one-day internationals you can expect to pay £20–50, but tickets for the sparsely attended county games start at as little as £7.

RUGBY

Rugby gets its name from Rugby public school, where the game mutated from football (soccer) in the nineteenth century. A rugby match may at times look like a bunch of weightlifters grappling each other in the mud – as the old joke goes, rugby is a hooligan's game played by gentleman, while football is a gentleman's game played by hooligans – but it is in reality a highly tactical and athletic game. What's more, England's rugby teams have represented the country with rather more success in the last few years than the cricket and football squads, even if they can't quite match the power and attacking panache of the southern hemisphere sides – Australia, New Zealand and South Africa.

There are two types of rugby played in Britain, both professional. Fifteen-a-side **Rugby Union** is very strong in working-class Wales, especially in the valleys of the former South Wales coal fields, but has upper-class associations in England, where it is the preferred character-building sport of the great fee-paying schools. The maintenance of the amateur status of Rugby Union in England contributed to its officer-class image until 1995, when the sport finally went professional. The thirteen-a-side **Rugby League** is played almost exclusively in the north of England (though the final of its knockout trophy is played at Wembley). Union's move towards professionalism was in part brought about by the tendency of League clubs to poach the top Union players – such as Welsh golden boy Jonathan Davies, who defected to Widnes (half the Welsh national side is these days made up of former League players). Currently Bristol is the contender for the Union championship vying with Leicester, which is never far away from the top, and among top players Martin Johnson (Leicester) and Lawrence Dallaglio (Wasps), who both also play for England, lead the way. As for the League, it's not too much of an exaggeration to say that the real competition in recent years has been for second place – Wigan win whenever they feel like it.

The Union season runs from September until the end of April, finishing off with the **Pilkington Cup**, Union's equivalent of the FA Cup; the League finishes in May, with the **Challenge Cup** final at

Wembley. The Pilkington Cup Final, international Rugby Union Test matches and some games in the Five Nations Cup (a round-robin tournament between England, Scotland, Wales, Ireland and France) are played at Twickenham stadium in west London. The other international Union grounds are Murrayfield in Edinburgh and Cardiff Arms Park in Cardiff. Unless you are affiliated to one of the 2000 clubs of the Rugby Union, or willing to pay well over the odds at a ticket agency, it is tough to get a ticket for one of these big games – as it is for League internationals, which are played at Wembley or at one of the larger club grounds. For Union and League club games, however, there should be no problem getting tickets at the gate; expect to pay from £5.

TENNIS

Tennis in England is synonymous with **Wimbledon**, the only Grand Slam tournament to be played on grass, and for many players the ultimate goal of their careers. The Wimbledon championship lasts a fortnight, in the last week of June and the first week of July. Most of the tickets, especially those with seats for the main show courts (Centre and No. 1), are allocated in advance to Wimbledon's members, other tennis clubs and corporate "sponsors" – as well as by public ballot – and by the time these have taken their slice there's not a lot left for the general public.

It is possible, however, to turn up on the day and buy tickets, and if you're rich enough you could buy through ticket agencies (although these sales are technically illegal). On tournament days, queues start to form around dawn and if you arrive by around 7am you have a reasonable chance of securing the limited number of Centre and No. 1 court tickets held back for sale on the day. If you're there by around 9am, you should get admission to the outside courts (where you'll catch some top players in the first week of the tournament). Either way, you then have a long wait until play commences at noon.

If you want to see big-name players in Britain, an easier opportunity is the **Stella Artois Championship** at Queen's Club in Hammersmith, London, which finishes a week before Wimbledon. Many of the stars use this tournament to acclimatize themselves to British grass-court conditions. As with Wimbledon, you have to apply for tickets in advance, although there is a limited number of returns on sale at 10am each day.

For the unlucky, there's the consolation of **TV coverage**, which is pretty well all-consuming for the two weeks that the Wimbledon tournament lasts.

HORSE RACING

For most of the British population there is just one important day in the horseracing calendar – the last Saturday in March or the first in April, when the **Grand National**, the "World's Greatest Steeplechase", is run at Liverpool's Aintree course. Millions of people risk a quid or two on the race, and watch the proceedings anxiously on TV, where it's broadcast live and then repeated at least twice before the end of the day. The National is by far the most arduous (some would say cruel) race of the steeplechasing and hurdling season, which runs from August to April, with races taking place on Saturdays and midweek at a vast array of courses, ranging from ovals of grass in the depths of the countryside to prestigious venues like Windsor. Ticket prices range from £5 to £35.

The horses and the clientele are often more upmarket when it comes to racing on the flat, which is a summer sport, observing an April to October season. Whereas the big events in the steeplechasing season draw a broad-based crowd, the showcase races on the flat are largely about upper-crust networking. That said, thousands of Londoners treat themselves to a day out at **Epsom** on Derby Day, the first Saturday in June. The Derby, a mile-and-a-half race for three-year-old thoroughbreds, is the most prestigious of the five classics of the flat season, and is preceded in the three-day Derby meeting by another classic, the **Oaks**, which is for fillies only – the other Classics are the **1000 Guineas**, **2000 Guineas** (both run at Newmarket) and the **St Leger** (run at Doncaster).

BETTING

Most of the money spent by Britain's gamblers is blown on the horses, though only a small minority of punters actually goes to the races. At the course itself you can place a bet with one of the independent trackside book-makers (or "tic-tac men" as they are known, from the bizarre sign language with which they signal the odds), or with the state-run Tote, a system by which the total money placed on a race is divided among the winners.

Competing with Tote and the small bookies are the representatives of the big nationwide betting organizations, such as Ladbrokes, Coral and William Hill, who make their money by taking bets on anything from the result of the 4.15 at Epsom to the name of the rider who will finish fourth in the Tour de France or the likelihood of snow at Christmas.

Anyone aged eighteen or over can place a bet, on which a nine percent tax is levied – you can have it deducted either from the stake or from your hypothetical winnings.

For sheer snobbery nothing can match the **Royal Ascot** week in mid-June, when the Queen and selected members of the royal family are in attendance, along with half the nation's blue bloods. As with the Derby, the best seats are the preserve of the gentry, but the rabble are allowed into the public enclosure for a mere £8–10, and can get considerably closer to the action for from £37–45, providing they dress smartly. Prices are slightly lower at the country's other flat-racing meetings, where the class divisions of British society are generally less glaring. Many of these meetings take place on courses used for steeplechasing in the winter, though some of the better courses – such as Goodwood – are reserved for the flat.

GAY AND LESBIAN BRITAIN

Homosexual acts between consenting males were legalized in Britain in 1967, but it wasn't until as recently as 1994 that the age of consent was finally reduced from 21 to 18 (still two years older than that for heterosexuals). Lesbianism has never specifically been outlawed, apocryphally owing to the fact that Queen Victoria refused to believe that such a thing existed.

As with so many other aspects of British life, attitudes on homosexuality are riven with contradictions. Despite its draconian laws and the sensationalist trash in the tabloid press, England, at least, offers one of the most diverse and accessible lesbian and gay scenes to be found anywhere in Europe. Nearly every town of any size has some kind of organized gay life – pubs, clubs, community groups, campaigning organizations, shops and phone lines – with the **major scenes** being found in London, Manchester and Brighton. The Scottish scene is lively in Edinburgh and in Glasgow, but pretty much non-existent in the more rural areas. In Wales things are a lot more muted, with few venues outside the main centres of Cardiff, Newport and Swansea. We've listed many venues throughout this book, and you'll be able to pick up a free gay listings sheet in almost any one of them.

Of the **nationwide publications**, the weekly *Pink Paper* is informative and contains limited listings; also worth checking are the frothy weekly *Boyz*, and its monthly women's sibling, *Diva*. The best bet for a comprehensive national directory of pubs, clubs, groups, gay accommodation and local lesbian and gay switchboards is the glossy monthly *Gay Times*, available from many newsagents and alternative bookshops. Gay Men's Press produce guidebooks aimed primarily at gay men, although with some lesbian information included too; there's currently *London Scene*, which includes Brighton. Much of the information in such publications applies both to men and women, as the British scene is far more mixed than in most other European nations.

DISABLED TRAVELLERS

Britain has numerous specialist **tour operators** catering for physically disabled travellers, and the number of non-specialist operators who welcome clients with disabilities is increasing. For more **information** on these operators and on facilities for the disabled traveller, you should get in touch with the Royal Association for Disability and Rehabilitation (RADAR), 250 City Rd, London EC1V 8AF (☎0171/250 3222, Minicom ☎0171/250 4119; *www.radar.org.uk*), which publishes its own guide to holidays and travel abroad (see opposite), as well as being a good source of all kinds of information and advice. If you're planning a trip to Scotland, contact Disability Scotland, Princes House, 5 Shandwick Place, Edinburgh EH2 4RG (☎0131/229 8632), which publishes its own directory and is happy to deal with queries. The Wales Council for the Disabled, Llys Ifor, Crescent Rd, Caerphilly, Mid-Glamorgan CF83 1XL (☎01222/887325), distributes the *Discovering Accessible Wales* booklet (£3). There's also the Holiday Care Service, 2nd Floor, Imperial Buildings, Victoria Rd, Horley, Surrey RH6 7PZ (☎01293/774535; Minicom ☎01293/776943), which publishes numerous fact sheets on disabled travel abroad and deals with all sorts of queries. You might also want to contact the charity Tripscope, at the Courtyard, Evelyn Road, London W4 5JL (☎0181/994 9294), who provide a national telephone information service offering free advice on transport, travel and access in England for those with a mobility problem.

In **North American** contact Mobility International, PO Box 10767, Eugene, OR 97440 (☎541/343-1284; *www.miusa.org*). Other useful organizations for North Americans are the Society for the Advancement of Travel for the Handicapped, 347 5th Ave, Suite 610, New York, NY 10016 (☎212/447-7284; *www.sath.org*), a non-profit-making travel-industry referral service that passes queries on to its members, and the Travel Information Service, Moss Rehabilitation Hospital, 1200 West Tabor Rd, Philadelphia, PA 19141 (☎215/456-9600; *www.mossresourcenet.org*), a telephone information and referral service. Undiscovered Britain, 11978 Audubon Pl,

Philadelphia, PA 19116 (☎215/969-0542; *www.undiscoveredbritain.com*), can organize comprehensive group or independent tours in the UK and Ireland, as well as provide useful information to those traveling independently.

Disabled travellers in **Australia** and **New Zealand** can get information and advice from ACROD, PO Box 60, Curtin, ACT 2605 (☎02/6282 4333), which has compiled lists of organizations, accommodation, travel agencies and tour operators, Barrier Free Travel, 36 Wheatley St, North Bellingen, NSW 2454 (☎02/6655 1733), a fee-based travel access information service, or the Disabled Persons Assembly, PO Box 10, 138 The Terrace, Wellington (☎04/472 2626).

Should you go it alone, you'll find that British **attitudes towards travellers** with disabilities are often begrudging and guilt-ridden, and are years behind advances towards independence made in North America and Australia. Access to theatres, cinemas and other public places has improved recently, but public transport companies rarely make any effort to help disabled people, though some rail services now accommodate wheelchair users in comfort. Wheelchair users and blind or partially sighted people are automatically given 30–50 percent reductions on train fares, and people with other disabilities are eligible for the **Disabled Persons Railcard** (£14 per year), which gives a third off most tickets but can take up to two weeks to process. There are no bus discounts for the disabled, while of the major **car-rental** firms only Hertz offers models with hand controls at the same rate as conventional vehicles, and even these are in the more expensive categories. **Accommodation** is the same story, with modified suites for people with disabilities available only at higher-priced establishments and perhaps at the odd B&B.

Useful **publications** include RADAR's annually updated *Holidays in the British Isles: A Guide For Disabled People* (£7.50), *Getting There: a Guide to Long Distance Travel* (£5) and *Access to the Skies* (£5). The AA publishes the *Disabled Travellers' Guide* (£4.99), free to members. RADAR also produces an *Access Guide to London* (£7.50). Two helpful **Web sites** are *www.disabilitynet.co.uk* and *access-able.com*.

DIRECTORY

Cigarettes The last decade has seen a dramatic change in attitudes towards smoking and a significant reduction in the consumption of cigarettes. Smoking is now outlawed from just about all public buildings and on public transport, and many restaurants and hotels have become non-smoking establishments. Smokers are advised, when booking a restaurant table or a room, to check that their vice is tolerated there.

Drugs Likely-looking visitors coming to Britain from Holland or Spain can expect scrutiny from customs officers on the lookout for hashish (marijuana resin). Being caught in possession of a small amount of hashish or grass will lead to a fine, but possession of larger quantities or of "harder" narcotics could lead to imprisonment or deportation.

Electricity In Britain the current is 240V AC. North American applicances will need a transformer and adaptor; Australasian appliances will only need an adaptor.

Laundry Coin-operated laundries (launderettes) are to be found in most British towns and are

open about twelve hours a day from Monday to Friday, with shorter hours at weekends. A wash followed by a spin or tumble dry costs about £3, with "service washes" (your laundry done for you in a few hours) about £1 more.

Public toilets These are found at all train and bus stations and are signposted on town high streets. In urban locations a fee of 10p or 20p is usually charged.

Time Greenwich Mean Time (GMT) is used from late October to late March, when the clocks go forward an hour for British Summer Time (BST). GMT is five hours ahead of the US Eastern Standard Time and ten hours behind Australian Eastern Standard Time.

Tipping and service charges In restaurants a service charge is usually included in the bill; if it isn't, leave a tip of 10–15 percent. Some restaurants are in the habit of leaving the total box blank on credit card counterfoils, to encourage customers to add another few percent on top of the service charge – if you're paying by credit card, check that the total box is filled in before you sign. Taxi drivers expect a tip in the region of 10 percent. You do not generally tip bar staff – if you want to show your appreciation, offer to buy them a drink.

Videos Visitors from North America should note that there is a different format for videotapes in Britain than there is in the US and Canada – so even though they look the same, VHS tapes recorded in Britain (in what's called the PAL format) will not work when you get them home and try to play them back on your VCR (which is NTSC format). If you are shooting with your own camera, however, you can use a blank tape purchased in Britain to record your trip's highlights, since your camera will format the tape while it records.

PART TWO

ENGLAND

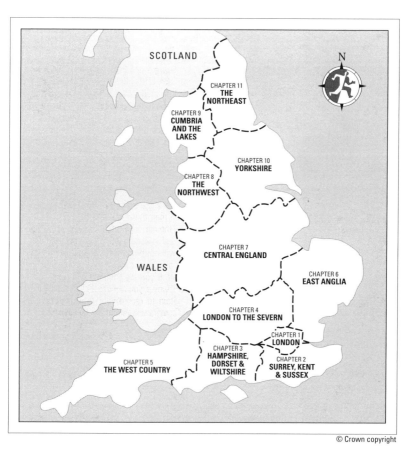

SCOTLAND

N

CHAPTER 11
THE NORTHEAST

CHAPTER 9
CUMBRIA AND THE LAKES

CHAPTER 10
YORKSHIRE

CHAPTER 8
THE NORTHWEST

CHAPTER 7
CENTRAL ENGLAND

WALES

CHAPTER 6
EAST ANGLIA

CHAPTER 4
LONDON TO THE SEVERN

CHAPTER 1
LONDON

CHAPTER 3
HAMPSHIRE, DORSET & WILTSHIRE

CHAPTER 2
SURREY, KENT & SUSSEX

CHAPTER 5
THE WEST COUNTRY

CHAPTER ONE

LONDON

hat strikes visitors more than anything about **London** is the sheer size of the place. With a population of around seven million, it is still by far Europe's largest city, spreading across an area of more than 620 square miles from its core on the River Thames. London is also pre-eminent in England: it's where the country's news and money are made and, as far as its inhabitants are concerned, provincial life begins beyond the circuit of the orbital motorway. Londoners' sense of superiority causes enormous resentment in the regions, yet it's undeniable that the capital has an unmatched charisma, a unique aura of excitement and success. In many walks of life, it's still the case that if you want to get on, you've got to get on in London.

Despite its dominant role, London remains the only capital city to have entered the new millennium without its own governing body, a symptom of more than a decade and a half's political indifference from previous Conservative governments. This neglect, compounded by a political culture that penalizes the unfortunate, has resulted in a city of spiralling extremes – ostentatious private affluence and increasing public squalor. At night, the West End is packed with theatregoers, while the doorways and shopfronts continue to serve as dormitories for London's dispossessed. London's problems are perfectly illustrated by the city's chaotic transport system, which is one of the most expensive in the world. Despite the huge expense, the tube network remains at breaking point, and the buses are notoriously unreliable and overcrowded.

London should undoubtedly be better than it is, but it is still a thrilling place. Its museums and galleries are among the finest in the world, while monuments from the capital's more glorious past are everywhere to be seen, from Roman ruins through great Baroque churches to the eclectic Victorian architecture of the triumphalist British Empire. The major sights – from Big Ben to the Tower of London – draw in millions of tourists, but there is enjoyment to be had from the quiet squares, narrow alleyways and surprisingly large expanses of greenery: Hyde Park, Green Park and St James's Park are all within a few minutes' walk of the West End shops.

You could also spend days just shopping in London, hobnobbing with the ruling classes in Harrods, or sampling the offbeat weekend markets, the seedbed of London's famously innovative street fashions, which provide fertile ground for the capital's own home-grown talent. The music, clubbing and gay/lesbian scene is second to none, and mainstream arts are no less exciting, with regular opportunities to catch brilliant theatre companies, dance troupes, exhibitions and opera. Restaurants, these days, are an attraction, too. London has caught up with its European rivals and offers something to suit every taste and budget, from three-star Michelin establishments to low-cost high-quality Indian cafés. Meanwhile, the city's pubs have heaps of atmosphere, especially away from the centre – and an exploration of the farther-flung communities is essential to get the feel of this dynamic metropolis.

A brief history of London

The Romans founded Londinium in 43 AD as a stores depot on the marshy banks of the Thames. Despite frequent attacks – not least by Queen Boudicca, who razed it in 61 AD – the port became secure in its position as capital of Roman Britain by the end of the century. London's expansion really began, however, in the eleventh century, when it

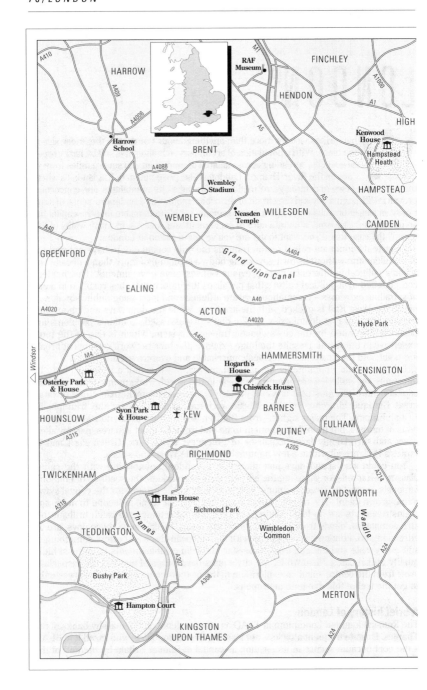

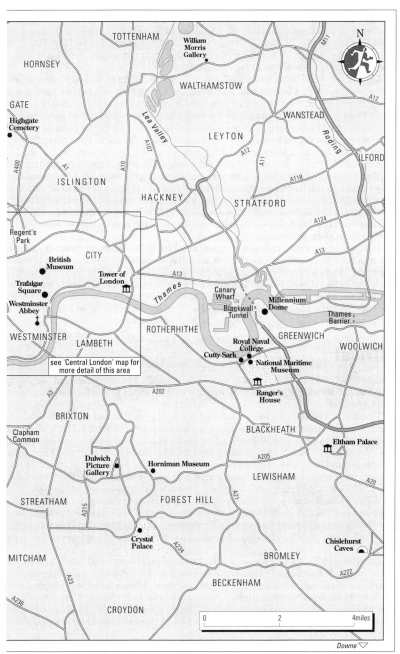

N

TOTTENHAM

William
Morris
Gallery

HORNSEY

WALTHAMSTOW

GATE

WANSTEAD

Highgate
Cemetery

A12

Lea Valley

LEYTON

ILFORD

Roding

A400

A1

A10

A107

A12

A11

A118

ISLINGTON

HACKNEY

STRATFORD

A124

Regent's
Park

CITY

A13

British
Museum

A13

Tower of
London

Trafalgar
Square

Thames

Canary
Wharf

Millennium
Dome

Westminster
Abbey

Blackwall
Tunnel

Thames
Barrier

WESTMINSTER

ROTHERHITHE

Royal Naval
College

GREENWICH

WOOLWICH

LAMBETH

Cutty Sark

National Maritime
Museum

see 'Central London' map for
more detail of this area

A202

Ranger's
House

A3

BRIXTON

BLACKHEATH

Clapham
Common

Eltham Palace

Dulwich
Picture
Gallery

Horniman Museum

A205

LEWISHAM

A20

STREATHAM

A215

FOREST HILL

A21

Crystal
Palace

A234

Chislehurst
Caves

MITCHAM

BROMLEY

A23

A222

BECKENHAM

A236

CROYDON

0   2   4miles

Downe ▽

became the seat of the last successful invader of Britain, the Norman duke who became **William I of England** (aka "the Conqueror"). Crowned king of England in Westminster Abbey, William built the White Tower – centrepiece of the Tower of London – to establish his dominance over the merchant population, the class that was soon to make London one of Europe's mightiest cities.

Little is left of medieval or Tudor London. Many of the finest buildings were wiped out in the course of a few days in 1666 when the **Great Fire of London** annihilated more than thirteen thousand houses and nearly ninety churches, completing a cycle of destruction begun the year before by the Great Plague, which killed as many as a hundred thousand people. Chief beneficiary of the blaze was Sir Christopher Wren, who was commissioned to redesign the city and rose to the challenge with such masterpieces as St Paul's Cathedral and the Royal Naval Hospital in Greenwich.

Much of the public architecture of London was built in the eighteenth century and during the reign of Queen Victoria, when grand structures were raised to reflect the city's status as the financial and administrative hub of the invincible **British Empire**. However, in comparison to many other European capitals much of London looks bland, due partly to the German bombing raids in World War II, and partly to some postwar development that has lumbered London with the sort of concrete-and-glass mediocrity that gives modern architecture a bad name.

Yet London's special atmosphere comes not from its buildings, but from the life on its streets. A cosmopolitan city since at least the seventeenth century, when it was a haven for Huguenot immigrants escaping persecution in Louis XIV's France, today it is truly multicultural, with over a third of its permanent population originating from overseas. This century has seen the arrival of thousands from the Caribbean, the Indian subcontinent, the Mediterranean and the Far East, all of whom play an integral part in defining a metropolis that is unmatched in its sheer diversity.

Arrival

Flying into London, you'll arrive at one of the capital's four **international airports**: Heathrow, Gatwick, Stansted or City Airport, each of which is less than an hour from the city centre.

Heathrow, twelve miles west of the city, has four terminals, and two train/tube stations: one for terminals 1, 2 and 3, and a separate one for Terminal 4. The high-speed **Heathrow Express** trains travel nonstop to Paddington Station (every 15min; 15–20min) for £10 each way. A much cheaper alternative is to take the **Piccadilly Underground line** into central London (every 2–5min; 40–50min) for £3.40. If you plan to make several journeys on your arrival day, buy a multi-zone One-Day Travelcard for £4.50 (see "City Transport", opposite). There are also **Airbuses**, which run from outside all four Heathrow terminals to several destinations in the city (every 20–30min; 1hr) and cost £6 single, £10 return. After midnight, you'll have to take the **night bus** #N97 to Trafalgar Square (hourly; 1hr 15min) for a bargain £1.50. **Taxis** are plentiful, but cost at least £35 to central London and take around an hour (longer in the rush hour).

Gatwick, thirty miles to the south, has two terminals, North and South, connected by a monorail. The nonstop **Gatwick-Express** train runs day and night between the South Terminal and Victoria Station (every 15–30min; 30min) for £9.50. Other options include the **Connex South Central** service to Victoria (every 30min; 40min) for £8.20, and **Thameslink** to King's Cross (every 15–30min; 50min) for £9.50. **Flightline coaches** run from both terminals to Victoria Coach Station (hourly; 1hr 15min) and cost £7.50 single, £11 return.

Stansted, London's swankiest international airport, lies 34 miles northeast of the capital and is served by the **Stansted Skytrain** to Liverpool Street (every 30min; 45min), which costs £10.40. **Flightline coaches** also run to Victoria Coach Station (hourly; 1hr 15min) and cost £9 single, £13 return.

London's smallest airport, **City Airport**, is situated in Docklands, nine miles east of central London. It handles European flights only, and is connected by shuttle bus with Canary Wharf (every 10min; 10min; £2), and Liverpool Street (every 10min; 25–35min; £4). Another option is to take the North London Line to Silvertown, which is ten minutes' walk from the airport.

Arriving by **train** from elsewhere in Britain, you'll come into one of London's numerous mainline stations, all of which have adjacent Underground stations linking into the city centre's tube network. **Eurostar** trains arrive at **Waterloo International**, south of the river. Trains from the Channel ports arrive at Liverpool Street, Charing Cross and Victoria train stations; **coaches** terminate at **Victoria Coach Station**, a couple of hundred yards south of the train station, down Buckingham Palace Road.

Information

The **London Tourist Board** (LTB) has a desk in arrivals at Heathrow Terminal 3 (daily 6am–11pm), and another in the Underground station concourse for Heathrow terminals 1, 2 and 3 (daily 8am–6pm), but the **main central office** is in the forecourt of Victoria Station (Easter–Oct daily 8am–7pm; Nov–Easter Mon–Sat 8am–6pm, Sun 8.30am–4pm). Other centrally located offices can be found near Piccadilly Circus in the British Visitor Centre, 1 Regent St (June–Aug Mon–Fri 9am–6.30pm, Sat 9am–5pm, Sun 10am–4pm; rest of year Mon–Fri 9am–6.30pm, Sat & Sun 10am–5pm), in the arrivals hall of Waterloo International (daily 8.30am–10.30pm) and in Liverpool Street Underground station (Mon–Fri 8am–6pm, Sat & Sun 8.45am–5.30pm).

Individual boroughs also run tourist offices at various prime locations. The two most useful are to the south of St Paul's Cathedral (April–Sept daily 9.30am–5pm; Oct–March Mon–Fri 9.30am–5pm, Sat 9.30am–12.30pm; ☎0171/332 1456) and at 46 Greenwich Church St, SE10 (daily: April–Oct 10am–5pm; Oct–March 11am–4pm; ☎0181/858 6376). Both these offices will answer enquiries by phone; the LTB offices can only offer a spread of pre-recorded phone announcements – these are a very poor service indeed, and the calls are charged at an exorbitant rate.

City transport

London's transport network is among the most complex and expensive in the world. The **London Transport information office**, at Piccadilly Circus tube station (daily 9am–6pm), will provide free transport maps; there are other desks at Euston, King's Cross, Liverpool Street, Oxford Circus, Piccadilly Circus, St James's Park and Victoria

---

TELEPHONE NUMBERS

On April 22, 2000, all **telephone numbers** in London will change. There will be a **new area code, 020**, and all local numbers will become eight digits long: old 0171 numbers being prefixed with a 7, old 0181 numbers with an 8. For further information on the changes to the telephone numbering system in the UK, see the box on p.42.

LONDON WHITE CARD

Serious museum addicts should consider buying the **London White Card**, which gives you free entry into over fifteen of the big arts and cultural museums, including the V&A, MOMI and the Courtauld Institute. The three-day card costs £16, while the seven-day card costs £26. Even better value is the Family Card, which covers two adults and up to four children and costs £32 for three days or £50 for seven. The cards are available from participating museums and galleries; for more information call ☎0171/923 0807.

---

stations. There's also a 24-hour phone line for transport information (☎0171/222 1234). If you can, avoid travelling during the **rush hour** (Mon–Fri 8–9.30am & 5–6.30pm) when tubes become unbearably crowded and some buses get so full that you literally won't be allowed on.

The fastest way of moving around the city is by Underground or **tube**, as it's known to all Londoners. The eleven different tube lines cross much of the metropolis, although London south of the river is not very well covered. Each line has its own colour and name – all you need to know is which direction you're travelling in: northbound, eastbound, southbound or westbound. Services operate from around 5.30am until shortly after midnight and you rarely have to wait more than five minutes for a train from central stations. **Tickets** must be bought in advance from the machines or booths in the station entrance hall; if you cannot produce a valid ticket, you will be charged an on-the-spot Penalty Fare of £10. A single journey in the central zone costs an unbelievable £1.40; a **carnet** of ten tickets costs £10. If you're intending to travel about a lot, a Travelcard is by far your best bet (see box opposite).

The network of **buses** is very dense, but much slower going than the tube. Bus tickets cost a minimum of 70p, rising to a maximum of £1.20. Normally you pay the driver on entering, but some routes are covered by older Routemaster buses, staffed by a conductor and with an open rear platform. Note that at request stops, you must stick your arm out to hail the bus you want. In addition to the Travelcards mentioned in the box opposite, a **One-Day Bus Pass** is also available and can be used before 9.30am, and costs £2 (Zones 2, 3 & 4) or £2.70 (All Zones). Regular buses run between about 6am and midnight; **Night Buses** (prefixed with the letter "N") operate outside this period. Night bus routes radiate out from Trafalgar Square at hourly intervals, more frequently on some routes and on Friday and Saturday nights. Fares are a flat £1.50 from central London; One-Day and Weekend Travelcards are not valid.

Large areas of London's suburbs are best reached by the **suburban train** network (Travelcards valid). Wherever a sight can only be reached by overground train, we've indicated the nearest train station and the central terminus from which you must depart. If you're planning to use the railway network a lot, you might want to purchase a **Network Card**, which is valid for a year, costs £20, and gives you up to a third off fares to destinations in and around the southeast. To find out about a particular service, phone **National Rail Enquiries** on ☎0345/484950.

If you're in a group of three or more, London's metered **black cabs** can be an economical way of getting around the centre – a ride from Euston to Victoria, for example, should cost around £10. A yellow light over the windscreen tells you if the cab is available – just stick your arm out to hail it. (If you want to book one in advance, call ☎0171/272 0272.)

Minicabs are less reliable than black cabs, but considerably cheaper, so you might want to take one back from a late-night club. Most minicabs are not metered, so always establish the fare beforehand. If you want to be certain of a woman driver, call Ladycabs (☎0171/254 3501), or a gay/lesbian driver, call Freedom Cars (☎0171/734 1313).

TRAVELCARDS

To get the best value out of the public transport system, buy a **Travelcard**. Available from machines and booths at all tube and train stations and at some newsagents as well (look for the sticker), they are valid for the bus, tube, Docklands Light Railway and suburban rail networks. **One-Day Travelcards**, valid on weekdays from 9.30am and all day at weekends, cost £3.80 (central Zones 1 & 2), rising to £4.50 for All Zones (1–6, including Heathrow); the respective **Weekend Travelcards**, for unlimited travel on Saturdays and Sundays, cost £5.70 and £6.70. If you need to travel before 9.30am on a weekday, but don't need to use suburban trains, you can buy a **One-Day LT Card**, which costs from £4.50 (Zones 1 & 2) to £7.30 (All Zones). **Weekly Travelcards** are even more economical, beginning at £14.30 for Zone 1; for these cards you need a **Photocard**, available free of charge from tube and train stations on presentation of a passport photo.

Accommodation

There's no getting away from the fact that **accommodation** in London is expensive. Compared with most European cities, you pay over the odds in every category. The city's hostels are among the most expensive in the world, while venerable institutions such as *Claridge's*, *The Dorchester* and *The Connaught* charge the very top international prices – up to £300 or more per luxurious night. All of the **hotels** listed here, however, cost significantly less than that and have been grouped by location rather than in price brackets, with the emphasis on value for money. The capital has plenty of **hostel** space, both in YHA properties and student halls, though these can be booked up weeks in advance over the summer.

If you want to avoid the hassle of contacting individual hotels and B&Bs, you could turn to one of the various **accommodation agencies**. All the LTB offices listed on p.73 operate a room-booking service, which costs £5 plus fifteen percent of the room fee in advance; credit card holders can also book through the LTB by phone (☎0171/824 8844). In addition, **Thomas Cook** has accommodation desks at Gatwick airport (☎01293/529372), Victoria (☎0171/828 4646), King's Cross (☎0171/837 5681) and Paddington (☎0171/723 0184) train stations. Most of these are open daily from around 7am till 11pm, and will book anything from youth hostels through to four-star hotels for around £5.

Try also the **British Hotel Reservation Centre** (BHRC) at 13 Grosvenor Gardens (☎0171/828 2425), at either Heathrow Underground station (☎0181/564 8808 or 564 8211), Gatwick airport (☎01293/502433), Victoria train station (☎0171/828 1027) or Victoria Coach Station (☎0171/824 8232). The Victoria train station office, open daily from 6am to midnight, has the longest opening hours; all offer their services free of charge.

A brief word on **London addresses**: the name of each street is followed by a letter giving the geographical location (E for "east", WC for "west central" and so on) and a number that specifies the postal area. However, this is not a reliable indication of the remoteness of the locale – W5, for example, lies beyond the more remote sounding NW10 – so it's always best to check a map before taking a room at what may sound like a fairly central area.

Hotels and B&Bs

With **hotels** you get less for your money in London than elsewhere in the country – generally breakfasts are more meagre and rooms more spartan than in similarly priced places in the provinces. In high season you should phone as far in advance as you can if

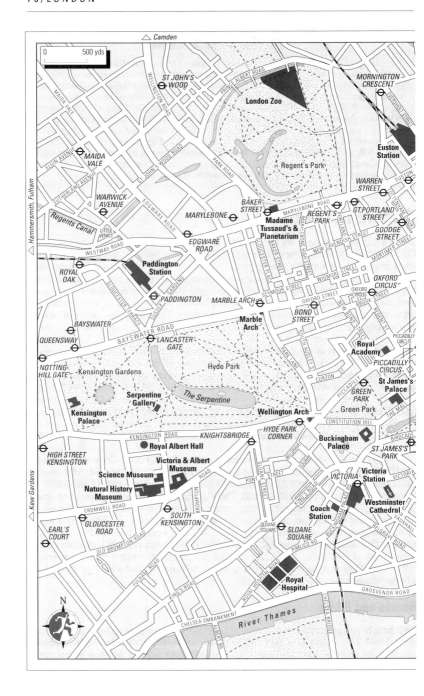

0   500 yds

△ Camden

MORNINGTON
CRESCENT

St JOHN'S
WOOD

London Zoo

Euston
Station

MAIDA
VALE

Regent's Park

WARREN
STREET

WARWICK
AVENUE

Regents Canal

LITTLE
VENICE

BAKER
STREET

REGENT'S
PARK

GT. PORTLAND
STREET

MARYLEBONE

Madame
Tussaud's &
Planetarium

GOODGE
STREET

ROYAL
OAK

EDGWARE
ROAD

WESTWAY ROAD

Paddington
Station

OXFORD
CIRCUS

PADDINGTON

MARBLE ARCH

OXFORD STREET

BOND
STREET

BAYSWATER

Marble
Arch

QUEENSWAY

BAYSWATER ROAD

LANCASTER
GATE

Hyde Park

Royal
Academy

PICCADILLY
CIRCUS

NOTTING
HILL GATE

Kensington Gardens

The Serpentine

PICCADILLY
CIRCUS

St James's
Palace

Serpentine
Gallery

GREEN
PARK

Kensington
Palace

Wellington Arch

Green Park

HYDE PARK
CORNER

Buckingham
Palace

ST JAMES'S
PARK

HIGH STREET
KENSINGTON

KENSINGTON ROAD — KNIGHTSBRIDGE

Royal Albert Hall

Victoria & Albert
Museum

Victoria
Station

Science Museum

Natural History
Museum

CROMWELL ROAD

SOUTH
KENSINGTON

Coach
Station

Westminster
Cathedral

EARL'S
COURT

GLOUCESTER
ROAD

SLOANE
SQUARE

OLD BROMPTON ROAD

Royal
Hospital

GROSVENOR ROAD

N

CHELSEA EMBANKMENT

River Thames

CHELSEA BRIDGE

△ Hammersmith, Fulham

△ Kew Gardens

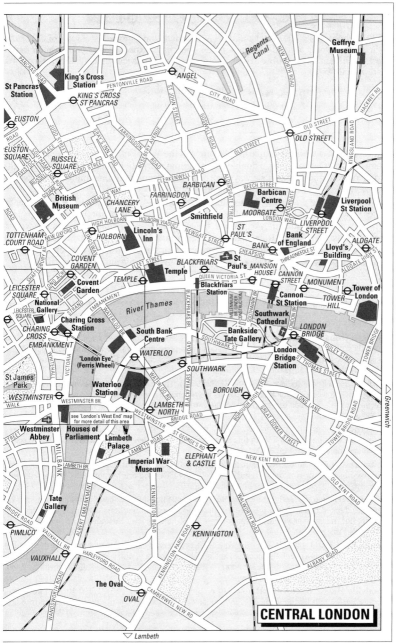

CENTRAL LONDON

ACCOMMODATION PRICE CODES

Throughout this guide, hotel and B&B accommodation is priced on a scale of ① to ⑨, the number indicating the **lowest price** you could expect to pay per night in that establishment for a **double room** in high season. The prices indicated by the codes are as follows:

① under £40	④ £60–70	⑦ £110–150
② £40–50	⑤ £70–90	⑧ £150–200
③ £50–60	⑥ £90–110	⑨ over £200

---

you want to stay within a couple of tube stops of the West End, and expect to pay no less than £40 for an unexceptional double room without a private bathroom. If travelling with two or more companions, it's always worth asking the price of the family rooms, which generally sleep four and can save you a few pounds.

When choosing your **area**, bear in mind that the West End – Soho, Covent Garden, St James's, Mayfair and Marylebone – and the western districts of Knightsbridge and Kensington, are dominated by expensive, upmarket hotels. For cheaper rooms, the widest choice is close to the main train stations of Victoria and Paddington, and the budget B&Bs of Earl's Court. Those close to King's Cross cater for people on welfare, or charge by the hour, although neighbouring Bloomsbury is both inexpensive and very central.

Victoria

Dover Hotel, 42–44 Belgrave Rd, SW1 (☎0171/821 9085, *dover@rooms.demon.co.uk*). One of the best B&Bs in this area. All rooms are tastefully decorated, and have a shower, toilet, telephone and TV. Victoria tube. ③.

Elizabeth Hotel, 37 Eccleston Square, SW1 (☎0171/828 6812). Comfortable and elegantly furnished hotel, very close to the coach and train stations and providing en-suite and more basic rooms at decent prices. Large TV lounge, and the gardens and tennis courts of Eccleston Square can be used by hotel residents. Victoria tube. ④.

The Goring, 15 Beeston Place, SW1 (☎0171/396 9000). This Edwardian hotel, owned and run by the Goring family for three generations, succeeds in creating an atmosphere of elegance and tranquillity. Afternoon tea is served on the delightful private garden-terrace in fine weather; breakfast is not included. Victoria tube. ③.

Limegrove Hotel, 101 Warwick Way, SW1 (☎0171/828 0458). Just about the cheapest decent rooms with washbasins and TVs in this area. Showers and toilets are shared; English breakfast is served in rooms. Victoria tube. ①.

Melbourne House Hotel, 79 Belgrave Rd, SW1 (☎0171/828 3516). One of the best B&Bs along Belgrave Road: family-run, totally refurbished, offering clean and bright rooms, excellent communal areas and friendly service. Victoria or Pimlico tube. ⑤.

Sanctuary House, 33 Tothill St, SW1 (☎0171/799 4044). Situated above a Fuller's pub, run by them and decked out like one, too – smart, pseudo-Victoriana. Breakfast is extra, and is served in the pub, but this is a very central location, right by St James's Park. Ask about the weekend deals. St James's Park tube. ⑥.

Windermere Hotel, 142–144 Warwick Way, SW1 (☎0171/834 5163). Situated at the western end of Warwick Way, this is a tastefully decorated and quietly stylish place, with a few good-value doubles with shared facilities and en-suite doubles for considerably more. There's a good restaurant downstairs, too. Sloane Square, Pimlico or Victoria tube. ④.

Woodville House & Morgan House, 107 & 120 Ebury St, SW1 (☎0171/730 1048). Two above-average B&Bs, run by the same friendly couple. Great breakfasts, patio garden, with an iron and fridge for guests to use. All rooms at *Woodville* are with shared facilities; some at *Morgan* are en suite. Victoria tube. ③.

Knightsbridge, Kensington and Chelsea

Abbey House Hotel, 11 Vicarage Gate, W8 (☎0171/727 2594). Inexpensive B&B in a quiet street just north of Kensington High Street, maintained to a high standard by its attentive owners. Rooms are large and bright – prices are kept down by sharing facilities. Full English breakfast, with free tea and coffee available all day. High Street Kensington tube. ④.

Blakes, 33 Roland Gardens, SW7 (☎0171/370 6701, *blakes@easynet.co.uk*). Blakes's dramatically designed interior and glamorous suites have long attracted visiting celebs. A faintly *Raffles*esque flavour pervades, with bamboo furniture and old travelling trunks mixing with unusual *objets d'art*, tapestries and prints. Doubles are smart but small; fully equipped suites are spectacular, as they should be for over £300. Gloucester Road tube. ⑧.

The Gore, 189 Queen's Gate, SW7 (☎0171/584 6601, *reservations@gorehotel.co.uk*). Popular, privately owned century-old hotel, awash with oriental rugs, rich mahogany, walnut panelling and other Victoriana. An award-winning restaurant adds to the allure, and it's only a step away from Hyde Park. South Kensington, Gloucester Road or High Street Kensington tube. ⑧.

The Hempel, 31–35 Craven Hill Gardens, W2 (☎0171/298 9000, *the-hempel@easynet.co.uk*). Deeply fashionable minimalist hotel, designed by the actress Anouska Hempel, with a huge and very empty atrium entrance. White-on-white rooms start at around £260 a double, and there's an excellent postmodern Italian/Thai restaurant called *I-Thai*. Lancaster Gate or Queensway tube. ⑨.

Hotel 167, 167 Old Brompton Rd, SW5 (☎0171/373 0672). Nicely furnished Victorian B&B with en-suite facilities, double-glazing and a fridge in all rooms. Breakfast is a continental-style buffet. Gloucester Road tube. ⑤.

Number Five, 5 Sumner Place, SW7 (☎0171/584 7586, *no.5@dial.pipex.com*). Discreetly luxurious B&B in one of South Ken's prettiest terraces. Breakfast is served in the house's lovely conservatory. South Kensington tube. ⑦.

Vicarage Hotel, 10 Vicarage Gate, W8 (☎0171/229 4030, *jim@vichotel.demon.co.uk*). Ideally located B&B. Clean rooms with shared facilities and a full English breakfast. High Street Kensington tube. ④.

Wilbraham, 1 Wilbraham Place, SW1 (☎0171/730 8296). Superb location, just off Sloane Street, with lots of original Victorian fittings in the rooms. A pleasant, old-fashioned place to stay. Sloane Square tube. ⑥.

Earl's Court

Philbeach Hotel, 30–31 Philbeach Gardens, SW5 (☎0171/373 1244). Friendly gay hotel, with basic and en-suite rooms, a pleasant TV lounge area and popular *Wilde About Oscar* restaurant. Earl's Court tube. ③.

Rushmore Hotel, 11 Trebovir Rd, SW5 (☎0171/370 3839). A cut above the average, with its colourful murals and imaginative room decor in this often dreary area. The attic rooms are especially spacious and comfortable. Full continental breakfast. Earl's Court tube. ⑤.

York House Hotel, 28 Philbeach Gardens, SW5 (☎0171/373 7519). B&B in a quiet crescent right next to the Exhibition Centre; some en-suite rooms and more basic alternatives, all including English breakfast. Friendly service and a lovely garden. Earl's Court tube. ②.

Paddington, Bayswater and Notting Hill

The Columbia, 95–99 Lancaster Gate, W2 (☎0171/402 0021). The spacious public lounge, wellworn decor and useful 24-hour bar make this a rock-band favourite. All rooms are en suite. Lancaster Gate tube. ⑤.

Garden Court Hotel, 30–31 Kensington Garden Square, W2 (☎0171/229 2553). Presentable, familyrun B&B close to Portobello market; less expensive rooms with shared facilities also available. English breakfast included. Queensway or Bayswater tube. ②.

The Gresham Hotel, 116 Sussex Gardens, W2 (☎0171/402 2920, *sales@the-gresham-hotel.co.uk*). B&B with a touch more class than many in the area. Rooms are small but tastefully kitted out, and all have TV. Continental breakfast included. Paddington tube. ⑤.

Inverness Court Hotel, 1 Inverness Terrace, W2 (☎0171/229 1444). Late-Victorian facade, reception area, bar and lounges lend a charming ambience, even if most of the bedrooms are in an undistinguished modern style. Bayswater or Queensway tube. ⑥.

Pavilion Hotel, 34–36 Sussex Gardens, W2 (☎0171/262 0905). The successful rock star's home-from-home, with outrageously over-the-top decor and every room individually themed. Paddington tube. ⑥.

Pembridge Court Hotel, 34 Pembridge Gardens, W11 (☎0171/229 9977). Attractively converted town house close to Portobello market, with spacious, fully equipped rooms. Two cats add to the homely feel, as does the lively *Caps Restaurant and Bar*. Notting Hill Gate or Holland Park tube. ④.

St James's, Mayfair and Marylebone

Edward Lear Hotel, 28–30 Seymour St, W1 (☎0171/402 5401, *edwardlear@aol.com*). A great location close to Oxford Street and Hyde Park, lovely flower boxes and a plush foyer. The rooms themselves need a bit of a makeover, but the low prices reflect this and the fact that most only have shared facilities. Kids free at the weekend. Marble Arch tube. ④.

Hotel La Place, 17 Nottingham Place, W1 (☎0171/486 2323). Just off the busy Marylebone Road, this is a small, good-value place; rooms are all en suite, equipped with all the gadgets usually found in grander establishments, and comfortably furnished. Baker Street tube. ⑥.

The Metropolitan, Old Park Lane, W1 (☎0171/447 1000, *sales@metropolitan.co.uk*). Very trendy new hotel run by Christina Ong, the *Met* adheres to the current fad for minimalism. The staff are kitted out in DKNY clothes, and the hotel bar was the place to be seen when it opened a few years ago. Green Park or Hyde Park Corner tube. ⑨.

Wigmore Court Hotel, 23 Gloucester Place, W1 (☎0171/935 0928). Better than average B&B, boasting a high tally of returning clients. Comfortable rooms with en-suite facilities, plus two doubles with shared facilities for just £45. Unusually, there's also a laundry and basic kitchen for guests' use. Marble Arch or Baker Street tube. ⑤.

Soho, Covent Garden and The Strand

Covent Garden Hotel, 10 Monmouth St, WC2 (☎0171/806 1000, *covent@firmdale.co.uk*). Stylish new conversion from a French Hospital just off Shaftesbury Avenue, with rooms decorated in a fairly traditional English style. All mod cons, including stereo, video, fax and voicemail. Bar and brasserie on the ground floor. Covent Garden or Leicester Square tube. ④.

The Fielding Hotel, 4 Broad Court, Bow St, WC2 (☎0171/836 8305). Quietly situated on a traffic-free and gas-lit court, this excellent hotel is one of Covent Garden's hidden gems. A firm favourite with visiting performers, since it's just a few yards from the Royal Opera House. Breakfast is extra. Covent Garden tube. ⑤.

Hazlitt's, 6 Frith St, W1 (☎0171/434 1771). This early eighteenth-century building is a Soho hotel of real character and charm, offering en-suite rooms decorated and furnished in a style as close to that period as convenience and comfort allow. Continental breakfast is served in the rooms. Tottenham Court Road tube. ⑧.

Manzi's, 1–2 Leicester St, W1 (☎0171/734 0224). Set over the Italian and seafood restaurant of the same name, *Manzi's* is one of very few West End hotels in this price range. Noise might prove to be a nuisance. Continental breakfast is included in the price. Leicester Square tube. ⑤.

One Aldwych, 1 Aldwych, WC2 (☎0171/300 1000, *sales@onealdwych.co.uk*). Following the minimalist trend, this fashionable new luxury hotel is a conversion of one of London's few vaguely Art Nouveau buildings, built in 1907 for the *Morning Post*. Little survives from those days – the draws now are the underwater music in the hotel's vast pool and the TVs in the bathrooms. Covent Garden or Temple tube. ⑨.

Strand Continental Hotel, 143 Strand, WC2 (☎0171/836 4880). This tiny Indian-run hotel near Aldwych offers very basic rooms with shared facilities; plus continental breakfast. Rooms have recently had a lick of paint, but nothing too drastic, making this an unbeatable central London bargain. Covent Garden or Temple tube. ②.

Bloomsbury

Avalon Hotel, 46–47 Cartwright Gardens, WC1 (☎0171/387 2366). Friendly, old-fashioned B&B. All rooms have washbasin and TV, a few are en suite, and English breakfast is included. Euston or Russell Square tube. ③.

Hotel Cavendish, 75 Gower St, WC1 (☎0171/636 9079). A real bargain, with lovely owners, two beautiful overrun gardens and some quite well-preserved original features. All rooms have shared facilities, and there are some good-value family rooms, too. Goodge Street tube. ②.

Crescent Hotel, 49–50 Cartwright Gardens, WC1 (☎0171/387 1515). Very comfortable and taste-fully decorated B&B – definitely a cut above the rest. Lovely blacked-up range in the breakfast room. All doubles are en suite, but there are a few bargain singles with shared facilities. Euston or Russell Square tube. ⑤.

Harlingford Hotel, 61–63 Cartwright Gardens, WC1 (☎0171/387 1551). Another good option in this fine Georgian crescent. All rooms are en suite with TV, the lounge has a real fire, and the break-fast room is bright and cheery. Euston or Russell Square tube. ⑤.

Jenkins Hotel, 45 Cartwright Gardens, WC1 (☎0171/387 4654). Smartly kept family-run place with just fourteen fairly small but well-equipped rooms. The lovely in-house black labrador is a big hit with visitors. Euston or Russell Square tube. ④.

Ridgemount Hotel, 65–67 Gower St, WC1 (☎0171/636 1141). Old-fashioned, family-run place, with small rooms, mostly with shared facilities, a garden, free hot-drinks machine and a laundry. Goodge Street tube. ②.

Hotel Russell, Russell Square, WC1 (☎0171/837 6470, *anon@forte.com*). From its grand 1898 exterior to its opulent interiors of marble, wood and crystal, this late-Victorian landmark fully retains its period atmosphere. No two rooms are identical in size or facilities but all are well appointed and decorated in a homely manner. Half-price weekend deals are available. Russell Square tube. ⑧.

Hampstead

Dillons Hotel, 21 Belsize Park, NW3 (☎0171/794 3360). Bargain B&B in a lovely big Victorian house on a leafy residential street, close to Belsize Park "village". Rooms are very plain, shared facil-ities only, but quite spacious. TV lounge. Belsize Park tube. ①.

La Gaffe, 107–111 Heath St, NW3 (☎0171/435 4941). Small, warren-like hotel situated over an Italian restaurant and bar in the heart of Hampstead, two minutes' walk from the Heath. All rooms are en suite, and there's a communal roof garden. Hampstead tube. ⑤.

Hampstead Village Guest House, 2 Kemplay Rd, NW3 (☎0171/435 8679, *hvguesthouse@dial.pipex.com*). Lovely non-smoking B&B in an old house set in a quiet backstreet between Hampstead Village and the Heath. Rooms have "lived-in" clutter which makes a change from anodyne hotels and spartan B&Bs. Hampstead tube. ⑤.

Sandringham Hotel, 3 Holford Rd, NW3 (☎0171/435 1569). Utterly charming small hotel on a quiet, leafy street right by the Heath. The decor has bags of character, service is relaxed, and there's a beautiful garden. Hampstead tube. ⑧.

Hostels, student halls and camping

London's seven **YHA hostels** are generally the cleanest, most efficiently run and most expensive hostels in the capital. They are always busy, so you'll have to arrive as early as possible or book in advance to stand a chance of getting a room. Members of any association affiliated to Hostelling International have automatic membership of the YHA; non-members can join at any of the hostels. In addition to the official hostels, there's a wide range of **private hostels** which charge less and tend to be more laid-back; unlike YHA hostels, however, there's no quality control, so standards can vary wildly. Some accommodation in **student halls of residence** is available outside term time, but the prices aren't all that attractive and the rooms get booked up quickly. London's **campsites** are all out on the perimeters of the city, offering pitches for around £2–4, plus a fee of around £3–4 per person per night (reductions for children and out of season).

YHA hostels

City of London, 36 Carter Lane, EC4 (☎0171/236 4965). Opposite St Paul's Cathedral; two hundred beds, mostly in four and five-bed dorms, with triple bunks in larger dorms. St Paul's tube.

Earl's Court, 38 Bolton Gardens, SW5 (☎0171/373 7083). Better than a lot of accommodation in Earl's Court, but only offering dorms of four to sixteen beds, and the triple-bunks take some getting used to. Kitchen, restaurant and large garden. No school groups. Earl's Court tube.

Hampstead Heath, 4 Wellgarth Rd, NW11 (☎0181/458 9054). One of the biggest and best-appointed hostels, set in its own grounds near Hampstead Heath. Golders Green tube.

Holland House, Holland Walk, W8 (☎0171/937 0748). Idyllically situated in a converted Jacobean house, and fairly convenient for the centre, this extensive hostel offers a decent kitchen, inexpensive restaurant and Internet access, and tends to be popular with school groups. Holland Park or High Street Kensington tube.

Oxford Street, 14 Noel St, W1 (☎0171/734 1618). Its unbeatable West End location and modest size (ninety beds in rooms of two, three and four beds) mean that this hostel tends to be full even out of high season. No children. Oxford Circus or Tottenham Court Road tube.

Rotherhithe, Island Yard, Salter Rd, SE16 (☎0171/232 2114). Purpose-built for the YHA, this large hostel is located in a redeveloped area that has little going for it compared to other hostels, but it's only twenty minutes by tube from the West End, and very convenient for the Dome. Rooms have two, four, five or ten beds. Rotherhithe tube.

St Pancras, 79–81 Euston Road, NW1 (☎0171/388 9998). London's newest YHA hostel is housed in six floors of a converted police station, directly opposite the new British Library, on the busy Euston Road. Rooms are very clean, bright, triple-glazed and air-conditioned – some even have en-suite facilities. Family rooms available with TVs. King's Cross or Euston tube.

Private hostels

Albert Hotel, 191 Queen's Gate, SW7 (☎0171/584 3019). Battered budget accommodation in a plush area. It's a long walk to the nearest tube, but only a minute or two to Hyde Park and the South Ken museums. No kitchen, but breakfast is included and there's a laundry. South Kensington, Gloucester Road or High Street Kensington tube.

Chelsea Hotel, 33–41 Earl's Court Square, SW5 (☎0171/244 6892). A 260-bed ramshackle hostel offering cheap dorm beds and en-suite twins. Facilities include a TV lounge, restaurant, bar with pool table and a laundry. Breakfast included. Earl's Court tube.

Generator, Compton Place, off Tavistock Place, WC1 (☎0171/388 7666). The neon- and UV-lighting and post-industrial decor may not be to everyone's tastes, but the youthful clientele certainly enjoy the cheap bar that's open daily until 2am. You don't share with strangers, so prices get progressively cheaper the more there are in your posse. Russell Square or Euston tube.

Leinster Hotel, 7–12 Leinster Square, W2 (☎0171/229 9641, *astorhostels@msn.com*). The biggest and liveliest of the Astor Hostels, with a party atmosphere, and two bars open until the wee small hours. Under-30s only. Queensway or Notting Hill Gate tube.

Museum Hostel, 27 Montague St, WC1 (☎0171/580 5360, *astorhostels@msn.com*). In a lovely Georgian house in Bloomsbury, this is the quietest of the Astor hostels. There's no bar, though it's still a sociable, laid-back place, and well situated. Small kitchen, TV lounge and baths as well as showers. Under-30s only. Russell Square tube.

Tonbridge Club, 120 Cromer St, WC1 (☎0171/837 4406). This is a real last resort, but if you're desperate (and a non-British passport holder), you can sleep on a mattress on the floor for £5 per person. Hot showers, TV room. Check-in 9pm–midnight. King's Cross tube.

Student halls

Carr Saunders Hall, 18–24 Fitzroy St, W1 (☎0171/323 9712). Student accommodation belonging to the London School of Economics; prices include breakfast. Open July–Sept. Warren Street tube.

International Student House, 229 Great Portland St, NW1 (☎0171/631 8300, *accom@ish.org.uk*). Hundreds of beds in a vast complex at the southern end of Regent's Park. Open year-round. Great Portland Street or Regent's Park tube.

King's Campus Vacation Bureau, 552 King's Rd, SW10 (☎0171/928 3777). King's College has a range of accommodation mostly in the Kensington, Chelsea and Westminster areas, with some less expensive alternatives in Hampstead, Wandsworth and Denmark Hill. Open July–Sept.

Ramsay Hall, 20 Maple St, W1 (☎0171/387 4537). Fairly central and comfortable, with over 400 beds, mostly singles. Open Easter & June–Sept. Warren Street or King's Cross tube.

Campsites

Abbey Wood, Federation Rd, Abbey Wood, SE2 (☎0181/311 7708). Enormous site east of Greenwich, ten miles from central London. Train from Charing Cross to Abbey Wood.

Crystal Palace, Crystal Palace Parade, SE19 (☎0181/778 7155). Maximum stay of two weeks in summer, three weeks in winter. Train from London Bridge or Victoria to Crystal Palace.

Tent City Acton, Old Oak Common Lane, W3 (☎0181/743 5708). The cheapest beds in London either in your own tent or in dorm accommodation in fourteen large tents. Closed mid-Sept to July. East Acton tube.

Tent City Hackney Camping, Millfields Rd, Hackney Marshes, E5 (☎0181/985 7656). Dorm tents for £5 a night, plus tent pitches. Big, but very inconvenient, way over in the east of the city with poor transport connections. Closed Sept–May. Bus #38 from Victoria or Angel tube, then #236 or #276.

THE CITY

The majority of London's sights are situated to the north of the **River Thames**, which loops through the city from west to east, but there is no single predominant focus of interest, for London has grown not through centralized planning but by a process of agglomeration – villages and urban developments that once surrounded the core are now lost within the amorphous mass of Greater London.

One of the few areas which is manageable on foot is **Westminster** and **Whitehall**, the city's royal, political and ecclesiastical power base, where you'll find the **National Gallery** and a host of other London landmarks from **Buckingham Palace** to **Westminster Abbey**. The grand streets and squares of **St James's**, **Mayfair** and **Marylebone**, to the north of Westminster, have been the playground of the rich since the Restoration, and now contain the city's busiest shopping zones.

East of Piccadilly Circus, **Soho** and **Covent Garden** form the heart of the **West End** entertainment district, containing the largest concentration of theatres, cinemas, clubs, flashy shops, cafés and restaurants. To the north lies the university quarter of **Bloomsbury**, home to the ever-popular **British Museum**, and the secluded quadrangles of **Holborn**'s Inns of Court, London's legal heartland.

The area known specifically as **the City** – or the City of London, to give it its full title – is at one and the same time the most ancient and the most modern part of London. Settled since Roman times, it is now one of the world's great financial centres, yet retains its share of historic sights, notably the **Tower of London** and a fine cache of Wren churches that includes **St Paul's Cathedral**. Impoverished and working class, the **East End**, to the east of the City, is not conventional tourist territory, but to ignore it entirely is to miss out a crucial element of contemporary London. **Docklands** is the converse of the down-at-heel East End, with the Canary Wharf tower, the country's tallest building, epitomizing the pretensions of the Thatcherite dream.

Lambeth and **Southwark** comprise the small slice of central London that lies south of the Thames. The **South Bank Centre**, London's little-loved concrete culture bunker, is set to be one of the focal points of the millennial celebrations. Neighbouring Southwark is also due to rise into prominence, with a new pedestrian bridge linking the City with **Bankside**, whose former power station is set to become the new **Tate Gallery of Modern Art**.

The largest park in central London is **Hyde Park**, a segment of greenery which separates wealthy **Kensington** and **Chelsea** from the city centre. The museums of South Kensington – the Victoria and Albert Museum, the Science Museum and the Natural History Museum – are a must; and if you have shopping on your agenda, you'll want to check out the hive of plush stores in the vicinity of Harrods.

The capital's trendiest weekend market takes place around **Camden Lock** in North London. Further out, in the literary suburbs of Hampstead and Highgate, there are unbeatable views across the city from half-wild **Hampstead Heath**, the favourite parkland of thousands of Londoners. The glory of s**outheast London** is **Greenwich**, with its nautical associations, royal park and observatory. Finally, there are plenty of rewarding day trips along the Thames from **Chiswick** to **Windsor**, most notably to Hampton Court Palace and Windsor Castle.

Westminster and Whitehall

Political, religious and regal power has emanated from **Westminster** and **Whitehall** for almost a millennium. It was Edward the Confessor who first established Westminster as London's royal and ecclesiastical power base, some three miles west of the City of London. The embryonic English parliament met in the abbey in the fourteenth century and eventually took over the old royal palace of Westminster. In the nineteenth century, Whitehall became the "heart of the Empire", its ministries ruling over a quarter of the world's population. Even now, though the UK's world status has diminished, the institutions that run the country inhabit roughly the same geographical area: Westminster for the politicians, Whitehall for the civil servants.

The monuments and buildings in and around Whitehall and Westminster also span the millennium, and include some of London's most famous landmarks – **Nelson's Column**, **Big Ben** and the **Houses of Parliament**, **Westminster** Abbey and **Buckingham Palace**, plus two of the city's finest permanent art collections, the **National Gallery** and the **Tate Gallery**. This is a well-trodden tourist circuit since it's also one of the easiest parts of London to walk round, with all the major sights within a mere half-mile of each other, linked by two of London's most triumphant avenues, **Whitehall** and **The Mall**.

Trafalgar Square

Despite being little more than a glorified, sunken traffic island, infested with scruffy urban pigeons, **Trafalgar Square** is still one of London's grandest architectural setpieces. John Nash designed the basic layout in the 1820s, but died long before the square took its present form. The Neoclassical National Gallery (see below) filled up the northern side of the square in 1838, followed five years later by the square's central focal point, **Nelson's Column**; the famous bronze lions didn't arrive until 1868, and the fountains – a rarity in a London square – didn't take their present shape until the eve of World War II.

As one of the few large public squares in London, Trafalgar Square has been both a tourist attraction and a focus for **political demonstrations** since the Chartists assembled here in 1848 before marching to Kennington Common. On a more festive note, the square is graced each December with a giant Christmas tree, donated by Norway in thanks for liberation from the Nazis, and on **New Year's Eve**, thousands of inebriates sing in the New Year here.

Stranded on a traffic island to the south of the column, and predating the entire square, is the **equestrian statue of Charles I**, erected shortly after the Restoration on the very spot where eight of those who had signed the king's death warrant were disembowelled. Charles's statue also marks the original site of the thirteenth-century **Charing Cross**, from where all distances from the capital are measured – a Victorian imitation now stands outside Charing Cross train station.

The northeastern corner of the square is occupied by James Gibbs's church of **St Martin-in-the-Fields**, fronted by a magnificent Corinthian portico and topped by an elaborate and distinctly unclassical tower and steeple. Completed in 1726, the interior is purposefully simple, though the Italian plasterwork on the barrel vaulting is exceptionally rich; it's best appreciated while listening to one of the church's free lunchtime concerts. There's a licensed café in the roomy **crypt**, not to mention a shop, gallery and brass-rubbing centre (Mon–Sat 10am–6pm, Sun noon–6pm).

The National Gallery

Unlike the Louvre or the Hermitage, the **National Gallery**, on the north side of Trafalgar Square (Mon–Sat 10am–6pm, Wed until 8pm, Sun noon–6pm; free; Leicester

Square or Charing Cross tube), is not based on a royal collection, but was begun as late as 1824 when the government bought 38 paintings belonging to a Russian emigré banker, John Julius Angerstein. The gallery's canny acquisition policy has resulted in a collection of more than 2200 paintings, but the collection's virtue is not so much its size as the range, depth and sheer quality of its contents.

However, with over a thousand paintings on permanent display in the main galleries, you'll need visual endurance to see everything in one day. To view the collection chronologically, begin with the Sainsbury Wing, the softly-softly, postmodern adjunct which playfully imitates elements of the gallery's original Neoclassicism. One welcome innovation is the **Gallery Guide Soundtrack**, a brief audio commentary on each of the more than 1000 paintings on display. The Soundtrack is available free of charge, though you'll be pressured into paying a "voluntary contribution" of £3. Another possibility is to join up with one of the free **guided tours** (Mon–Fri 11.30am & 2.30pm, Wed also 6.30pm, Sat 2 & 3.30pm), which set off from the Sainsbury Wing foyer.

THE SAINSBURY WING
Prince Charles was outraged upon seeing the original winning design for the **Sainsbury Wing**, blustering that it would be a "monstrous carbuncle on the face of a much-loved and elegant friend." As a result the structure that was eventually built is only timidly postmodern, blending well with the older building. The first room you enter (room 51) contains the earliest works in the collection, but also boasts the **Leonardo Cartoon**, enshrined behind bullet-proof glass in its own dimly lit side-chapel. The drawing, *The Virgin and Child with St Anne and St John the Baptist*, is a study for a painting commissioned by the king of France; like so many of Leonardo's projects it was never completed. Outside the cartoon's room hangs one he did finish, *The Virgin of the Rocks*, a melancholy scene in a brooding landscape.

Room 53 features the extraordinarily vivid **Wilton Diptych**, a portable altarpiece painted by an unknown fourteenth-century artist for the young King Richard II, who is depicted being presented by saints to Mary, Jesus and assorted angels. During recent restoration, a minuscule map was discovered in the orb atop the banner, showing a green island, a white castle and a boat in full sail, symbolizing Richard's island kingdom.

Paolo Uccello's *Battle of San Romano*, which dominates room 55, is a transitional work, mixing elements of medieval decoration and early Renaissance experiments with linear perspective – note the foreshortened body in the foreground and the broken lances ranged on the ground. Painted for the Medici family, the panel shows a minor skirmish between the Florentines and the Sienese, and is centred on the mercenary captain Niccolò da Tolentino, who races into battle on a delightful white horse.

Room 56 introduces the Dutch contingent, notably **Jan van Eyck's** *Arnolfini Marriage*, one of the few surviving full-length double portraits from the fifteenth century; signed "Van Eyck Was Here" in Latin above the mirror, the painting is thought by some to have served as both a commemorative portrait and a marriage contract in which the painter is witness.

Botticelli's elongated *Venus and Mars* dominates room 58, with a naked Mars in a deep post-coital sleep, watched over by a beautifully calm Venus, fully clothed and less overcome. Inspired by a Dante sonnet, the painting was a wedding present – some think it was intended as a headboard for the marital bed, others say it was to decorate the lid of a casket. Either way, it is generally agreed to have been painted for the Vespucci family – *vespa* is the Italian for wasp, a swarm of which buzz around Mars's head.

Room 61 holds some fine examples of **Mantegna's** "cameo" paintings, which imitate the effect of classical stone reliefs, reflecting the craze among fashionable Venetian society for collecting antique engraved marbles and gems. The largest of them, *The Introduction of the Cult of Cybele*, the artist's last work, was commissioned by Francesco

Cornaro, a Venetian nobleman who claimed descent from one of the greatest Roman families. The Venetian theme is continued with **Bellini**'s *Doge Leonardo Loredan*, one of the artist's greatest portraits.

Piero della Francesca's monumental religious paintings are at the opposite end of the wing in room 66. *The Baptism of Christ*, dating from the 1450s, is one of his earliest surviving pictures and displays his immaculate compositional technique, derived from Piero's innovative work as a mathematician.

THE WEST WING

Displayed in the **West Wing** are the National's High Renaissance works. Room 9, linked to the Sainsbury Wing, has a fine array of large-scale Venetian works, including **Titian**'s colourful early masterpiece *Bacchus and Ariadne* and his much later, much gloomier *Death of Acteon*, and **Veronese**'s lustrous *The Family of Darius Before Alexander*, a remarkable demonstration of his eye for colour.

Next door, in room 8, **Bronzino**'s disturbing and erotic *Venus, Cupid, Folly and Time* and **Raphael**'s trenchant *Pope Julius II* keep company with the gallery's works by **Michelangelo**, the most startlingly innovative of which is his unfinished *Entombment*. In place of earlier, static lamentations, this painting shows Christ's body being hauled into the tomb, and has no fixed iconography by which to identify the figures – either of the women could be Mary Magdalene, for example, and it is arguable whether the man in red is John the Evangelist or Nicodemus. Michelangelo also provided drawings for the *Raising of Lazarus* by **Sebastiano del Piombo**, the largest painting in the room, which was planned as the altarpiece for Narbonne Cathedral.

Among the north Europeans in room 4, **Holbein** stands out, with his masterfully detailed double portrait, *The Ambassadors*, and his intriguing portrait *A Lady with a Squirrel and a Starling*, painted in 1527 during the artist's first visit to England. The blue background and half-length format are familiar Holbein traits, but the presence of the two animals is more mysterious – they may be oblique references to the name of the unidentified sitter, who was probably a regular at the court of Henry VIII.

THE NORTH WING

The North Wing is particularly strong in seventeenth- and eighteenth-century Dutch painting. The Dutch works in room 16 include **Vermeer**'s serene *A Young Woman Standing at a Virginal*, whose subject is now thought to be Vermeer's eldest daughter Maria, though nobody is quite sure of the relevance of the picture of Cupid above her.

Claude Lorrain's *Enchanted Castle* in room 19 caught the imagination of the Romantics, supposedly inspiring Keats's *Ode to a Nightingale*, while **Turner** left specific instructions in his will for two of his Claude-influenced paintings to be hung alongside a couple of the French painter's landscapes in room 15. Claude's dreamy classical landscapes and seascapes and the mythological scenes of **Poussin** were favourites of aristocrats on the Grand Tour, and made both artists very famous in their time. Nowadays, though Poussin has a strong academic following, his works strike many people as empty and dull. Hardly surprising then that rooms 19 and 20, which are given over entirely to these two, are among the quietest in the gallery.

Room 27 is completely given over to **Rembrandt**'s works. Two of his self-portraits, painted thirty years apart, regard each other across the room: the melancholic *Self-Portrait Aged 63*, from the last year of his life, making a strong contrast with the sprightly early work. Three adjoining rooms, known collectively as room 28, are dominated by the fleshy expansive canvases of **Rubens**, including his lurid *Samson and Delilah* (which many believe was actually executed by one of his pupils) and the famous portrait of his sister-in-law, known strangely as *Le chapeau de paille* (The Straw Hat) – the hat is actually black felt, decorated with white feathers.

Velázquez dominates the Spanish paintings in room 29, with his astounding portraits and the remarkable *Rokeby Venus*, an ambiguously narcissistic image that was slashed in 1914 by suffragette Mary Richardson, who loved the painting but was revolted by the way it was leered at. Next door, in room 30, **Van Dyck**'s *Portrait of Charles I* is a fine example of the work that made the painter the favourite of the Stuart court, romanticizing the monarch as a dashing horseman. The inscription on the tree declares in Latin that this is Charles, King of England, in case anyone should be confused. Close by in room 32, **Caravaggio**'s melodramatic art is represented by *Christ at Emmaus* and the erotic *Boy Bitten by Lizard*.

THE EAST WING
The East Wing, housing paintings from 1700 to 1900, begins in room 33 with some wistful gallantries from **Watteau** and **Fragonard** and a splendid assembly of portraits, including the dapper self-portrait by **Louise Vigée le Brun**, one of only three women artists in the whole collection.

Next door, room 34 contains a roll-call of the best of English art: **Turner**'s *Fighting Téméraire*, showing the veteran of Trafalgar being towed to the shipyard at sunset; **Gainsborough**'s feathery and translucent *Morning Walk*; and **Constable**'s *Hay Wain*, a painting so familiar that it's difficult to appreciate it properly any more. In room 35 hangs **Hogarth**'s lively satire on loveless marriage, *Marriage à la Mode*. Room 38 contains **Canaletto**'s glittery vistas of Venice and in room 40 there's the airy draughtsmanship of **Tiepolo**, father and son.

Delacroix, who was profoundly impressed by Constable's dappled application of paint, is shown in room 41 alongside **Ingres**' elegant portrait of the banker's wife *Madame Moitessier*, completed when the artist was 76, having taken twelve years to finish. This room also features the only two paintings in the country by **Jacques-Louis David**, as well as the perennially popular, but phoney, *Execution of Lady Jane Grey* by **Paul Delaroche**.

Five magnificent rooms (42–46) of Impressionist and early twentieth-century paintings close the proceedings, starring, in room 43, **Manet**'s unfinished *Execution of Maximilian*. This was one of three versions, and was cut into pieces during the artist's lifetime, then bought and reassembled by Degas after Manet's death. Other major Impressionist pieces here include seminal works such as **Renoir**'s *Umbrellas* and **Monet**'s *Thames below Westminster* – with, of course, *Waterlilies* close at hand. Also here are **Van Gogh**'s dazzling *Sunflowers*, **Seurat**'s *Bathers at Asnières*, one of Europe's most comprehensive showings of **Cézanne** and a few choice works by **Picasso**, dovetailing the National's collection into that of the Tate (see p.92).

The National Portrait Gallery
Around the back of the National Gallery lurks the **National Portrait Gallery** (Mon–Sat 10am–6pm, Sun noon–6pm; free; Leicester Square or Charing Cross tube), which was founded in 1856 to house uplifting depictions of the good and the great. Though it has some fine works in its collection, many of the studies are of less interest than their subjects and the overall impression is of an overstuffed shrine to famous Brits rather than a museum offering any insight into the history of portraiture. However, it is fascinating to trace who has been deemed worthy of admiration at any moment: aristocrats and artists in previous centuries, warmongers and imperialists in the early decades of this century, writers and poets in the 1930s and 40s and, latterly, footballers and film- and pop-stars.

The NPG's **new extension** opened in the spring of 2000, with new Tudor and contemporary galleries to expand the section that's by far the most popular. To view the gallery chronologically, you need to head for the Tudor gallery, which has the NPG's earliest works. The **Sound Guide**, which gives useful biographical background information to some of the pictures, is provided free of charge, though you're strongly invited to give a "voluntary contribution" of £3.

The Mall and St James's Park

The southwestern exit of Trafalgar Square is marked by the bombastic **Admiralty Arch**, from where you get a fantastic view down the tree-lined sweep of **The Mall**. This dead-straight avenue was laid out early this century as a memorial to Queen Victoria, along with the triumphal arch itself and, half a mile away, the Victoria Memorial in front of Buckingham Palace. There had, however, been a thoroughfare here since 1660, and Regency architect John Nash was responsible for many of its finest buildings. **Carlton House Terrace**, for example, a graceful stretch of town houses just beyond Admiralty Arch, is typical of his best work, and houses the trendy **Institute of Contemporary Arts**, or ICA (Mon–Sat noon–1am, Sun noon–10.30pm; day pass £1.50, £2.50 Sat & Sun), the city's main forum for avant-garde exhibitions, films and performances. Many people pay the day membership for access to the bar alone, one of London's hippest bouncer-free meeting places.

Flanking nearly the whole length of The Mall, **St James's Park** was originally created for Henry VIII as recreational land between his palaces at Whitehall and St James's. Developed as a public park by Charles II, it was landscaped by Nash into its present elegant appearance for George IV in 1828, in a style that established the trend for Victorian city parks. Today the pretty tree-lined lake is an inner-city reserve for wildfowl, in particular pelicans (descendants of the pair presented to Charles II by the Russian ambassador), and a favourite picnic spot for the civil servants of Whitehall. The view to Westminster and Whitehall from the bridge is one of the best – and even the ineffably dull facade of Buckingham Palace looks good from here.

Buckingham Palace

The graceless colossus of **Buckingham Palace** (Aug & Sept daily 9.30am–4.15pm; £9.50; Green Park tube) has served as the monarch's permanent London residence since the accession of Victoria. It began its days in 1702 as the Duke of Buckingham's city residence, built on the site of a notorious brothel, and was sold by the duke's son to George III in 1762. The building was overhauled in the late 1820s by Nash and again in 1913, producing a palace that's as bland as it's possible to be. For ten months of the year there's little to do here save watch the Changing of the Guard, a thirty-minute ceremony in which a detachment of the Queen's Foot Guards marches to appropriate martial music from St James's Palace (May–Aug daily 11.30am; Sept–April alternate days; no ceremony if it rains).

Since 1993, the hallowed portals have been grudgingly nudged open for two months of the year. Tickets are sold from the tent-like box office in Green Park, at the western end of The Mall; queues vary enormously, but can be long, after which there's a further long wait until your allocated visiting time. Once inside, despite the voyeuristic pleasure of a glimpse behind those forbidding walls, it's a bit of an anticlimax: of the palace's 660 rooms you're permitted to see just eighteen, and there's little sign of life, as the Queen decamps to Scotland every summer (see p.998).

Beyond the enormous courtyard, from where you can see the Nash portico that looked over St James's Park until it was closed off by Queen Victoria, you hit the **Grand Hall**, the Duke of Buckingham's original hall. Now a frenzy of red and gold decorated to the taste of Edward VII, it's dominated by Nash's winding, curlicued **Grand Staircase**. Past a range of dull royal portraits, all beautifully lit by Nash's glass dome, the Guard Room is decorated with Gobelin tapestries and nineteenth-century sculpture, leading into the Green Drawing Room, a blaze of unusually bright green walls, red carpet and enormous chandeliers. Disappointingly, there's no regal throne in the **Throne Room**, just two pink his'n'hers chairs initialled ER and P.

Nash's vaulted **Picture Gallery**, however, stretching right down the centre of the palace, is breathtaking. On show here is a selection of the Queen's art collection (over three times larger than the National Gallery's) – among them several Van Dycks, two Rembrandts and an excellent Vermeer. Of the remaining rooms a few stand out: the stultifyingly scarlet and gilt **State Dining Room**, for example, and Nash's **Blue Drawing Room**, with thirty fake onyx columns, flock wallpaper and an extraordinary Sèvres porcelain table made for Napoleon. The frothy **White Drawing Room**, full of priceless French antiques, is the incongruous setting of an annual royal prank – when hosting the reception for the diplomatic corps, for some mystifying reason the Queen and family emerge from a secret door behind the fireplace to greet the ambassadors.

You can see a further selection of the monarch's art collection at the **Queen's Picture Gallery** (daily 9.30am–4.30pm; £4; Victoria tube), round the side of the palace on Buckingham Palace Road. The exhibitions usually include some works by Reynolds, Gainsborough, Vermeer, Rubens, Rembrandt and Canaletto, which make up the bulk of the collection.

There's more pageantry on show at the Nash-built **Royal Mews** (April–Sept Tues–Thurs noon–4pm; Oct–Dec Wed only; £3.50; Victoria tube), further along Buckingham Palace Road. The royal carriages, lined up under a glass canopy in the courtyard, are the main attraction, in particular the Gold Carriage, made for George III in 1762, smothered in 22-carat gilding and weighing four tons, its axles supporting four life-size figures.

Whitehall

Whitehall, the broad avenue connecting Trafalgar Square to Parliament Square, is synonymous with the faceless, pin-striped bureaucracy charged with the day-to-day running of the country. Since the sixteenth century, nearly all the key governmental ministries and offices have migrated here, rehousing themselves on an ever-increasing scale. The statues dotted about Whitehall recall the days when this street stood at the centre of an empire on which the sun never set. Nowadays, with the Scots, Welsh and Northern Irish all with their own assemblies, Whitehall's remit is greatly reduced.

During the sixteenth and seventeenth centuries Whitehall was also synonymous with royalty, since it was the permanent residence of the kings and queens of England. The original **Whitehall Palace** was the London seat of the Archbishop of York, confiscated and greatly extended by Henry VIII after a fire at Westminster forced him to find alternative accommodation; it was here that Henry celebrated his marriage to Anne Boleyn in 1533, and here that he died fourteen years later.

In 1698, a fire destroyed much of the palace and the royal residence shifted to St James's. The chief section to survive the fire was the **Banqueting House** (Mon–Sat 10am–5pm; £3.50), the first Palladian building to be built in England, begun by Inigo Jones in 1619. The one room now open to the public has no original furnishings, but is well worth seeing for the superlative **Rubens** ceiling paintings glorifying the Stuart dynasty and commissioned by Charles I in the 1630s. Charles himself walked through the room for the last time in 1649 when he stepped onto the executioner's scaffold from one of its windows.

Across the road, two mounted sentries of the Queen's Household Cavalry and two horseless colleagues, all in ceremonial uniform, are posted daily from 10am to 4pm. Ostensibly they are protecting the **Horse Guards** building, originally built as the old palace guard house, but now guarding nothing in particular. The mounted guards are changed hourly and those standing, every two hours. Try to coincide your visit with the Changing of the Guard (Mon–Sat 11am, Sun 10am), when a squad of twelve mounted troops in full livery arrive from Hyde Park Barracks via Hyde Park Corner, Constitution Hill and the Parade Ground to the rear.

Further down this west side of Whitehall is London's most famous road, **Downing Street**. Number 10 has been the residence of the prime minister since the house was presented to Sir Robert Walpole by George II in 1732; along with no. 11 – home of the chancellor of the exchequer – and no. 12, it's the only bit remaining of the original seventeenth-century terrace, the rest of the street dating from 1868. The public have been kept at bay since 1990 when Margaret Thatcher ordered a pair of iron gates to be installed at the junction with Whitehall, a highly symbolic act, and less than effective – a year later the IRA lobbed a mortar into Downing Street, coming within a whisker of killing the Cabinet. Just beyond the Downing Street gates, in the middle of the road, stands Edwin Lutyens' **Cenotaph**, eschewing any kind of Christian imagery, and inscribed simply with the words "The Glorious Dead". The memorial remains the focus of the Remembrance Sunday ceremony in November.

In 1938, in anticipation of Nazi air raids, the basement of the civil service buildings on the south side of King Charles Street were converted into the **Cabinet War Rooms**, now open to the public (daily 10am–6pm; £4.40). It was here that Winston Churchill directed operations and held cabinet meetings for the duration of World War II. The rooms have been left pretty much as they were when they were finally abandoned on VJ Day 1945, and make for an atmospheric underground trot through wartime London. The museum's free acoustophone commentary helps bring the place to life and includes various eye-witness accounts by folk who worked there.

The Houses of Parliament

Clearly visible at the south end of Whitehall is one of London's best-known monuments, the Palace of Westminster, better known as the **Houses of Parliament**. The city's finest Victorian Gothic Revival building and symbol of a nation once confident of its place at the centre of the world, it is distinguished above all by the ornate, gilded clock tower popularly known as **Big Ben**, after the thirteen-ton main bell that strikes the hour (and is broadcast across the world by the BBC).

The original Westminster Palace was built by **Edward the Confessor** in the first half of the eleventh century, so that he could watch over the building of his abbey. It then served as the seat of all the English monarchs until a fire forced Henry VIII to decamp to Whitehall. The Lords have always convened at the palace, but it was only following Henry's death that the House of Commons moved from the abbey's chapter house into the palace's St Stephen's Chapel, thus beginning the building's associations with parliament.

In 1834 the old palace burned down. Virtually the only relic of the medieval building is the bare expanse of **Westminster Hall** (guided tours only, see below), on the north side of the complex. Built by William Rufus in 1099, it's one of the most magnificent secular medieval halls in Europe. The **Jewel Tower** (April–Oct daily 10am–6pm; Nov–March Wed–Sun 10am–4pm; £1.50; EH), across the road from parliament, is another remnant of the medieval palace, now housing an excellent exhibition on the history of parliament.

To watch the proceedings in either the House of Commons or the Lords, simply join the queue for the **public galleries** (known as Strangers' Galleries) outside St Stephen's Gate. The public are let in slowly from about 4.30pm onwards from Monday to Thursday and from 10am on Fridays; the security checks are very tight, and the whole procedure can take an hour or more. If you want to avoid the queues, turn up an hour or more later, when the crowds have usually thinned. Recesses (holiday closures) of both Houses occur at Christmas, Easter, and from August to the middle of October; phone ☎0171/219 4272 for more information.

To see Question Time (Mon–Thurs 2.30–3.30pm) you need to book a **ticket** several weeks in advance from your local MP (if you're a UK citizen) or your embassy in

London (if you're not). To contact your MP, simply phone ☎0171/219 3000 and ask to be put through. MPs and embassies can also arrange **guided tours**, which take place in the morning on Mondays, Tuesdays and Thursdays and on Friday afternoons. The full price of a guided tour is around £25, but individuals can usually ask to join up with a pre-booked group, thus cutting the cost to around £2.50 per person. If you want to climb **Big Ben** before or after your tour, say so, as it may be possible to arrange.

Westminster Abbey

The Houses of Parliament dwarf their much older neighbour, **Westminster Abbey** (Mon–Fri 9am–4pm, Sat 9am–2pm & 4–5pm, also Wed 6–7.45pm; £4; Westminster or St James's Park tube), yet this single building embodies much of the history of England. Founded in the eighth century, rebuilt in the eleventh by Edward the Confessor, then again – in honour of Edward – by Henry III in the mid-thirteenth century, it has been the venue for all but two coronations from the time of William the Conqueror onwards and the site of more or less every royal burial during the half-millennium between the reigns of Henry III and George II. Scores of the nation's most famous citizens are honoured here, too – though many of the stones commemorate people buried elsewhere.

Entry is currently via the north transept, cluttered with monuments to politicians and traditionally known as Statesmen's Aisle, shortly after which you come to the abbey's most dazzling architectural set-piece, the **Lady Chapel**, added by Henry VII in 1503 as his future resting place. With its intricately carved vaulting and fan-shaped gilded pendants, the chapel represents the final spectacular gasp of the English Perpendicular style. At the very east end of the chapel, under the Battle of Britain stained glass window, a plaque marks the spot where Oliver Cromwell rested until the Restoration, whereupon his body was disinterred, hanged at Tyburn and beheaded. The aisle north of this chapel is the resting place of Henry VII's granddaughters, Queen Elizabeth I and Queen Mary; in the south aisle you'll find the exquisite tomb of Henry's mother, Margaret Beaufort.

Unfortunately, the public are no longer admitted to the **Shrine of Edward the Confessor**, the sacred heart of the building, though you do get to inspect Edward I's **Coronation Chair**, a decrepit oak throne dating from around 1300, which used to squat above the great slab of the Stone of Scone – the Scottish coronation stone pilfered in 1297 by Edward – until it was given back to the Scots in 1996 as a sop to their nationalism.

Nowadays, the abbey's royal tombs are upstaged by **Poets' Corner**, in the south transept, though the first occupant, **Geoffrey Chaucer**, was in fact buried here not because he was a poet, but because he lived nearby. By the eighteenth century this zone had become an artistic Pantheon, since when the transept has been filled with tributes to all shades of talent. On the south wall stands the memorial to William Shakespeare – who, like T. S. Eliot, Byron, Tennyson and various other luminaries, is not actually buried here.

Doors in the south choir aisle lead to the **Great Cloisters** (daily 8am–6pm), rebuilt after a fire in 1298 and now home to a shop and brass-rubbing centre. At the eastern end of the cloisters lies the octagonal **Chapter House** (daily: April–Oct 10am–5.30pm; Nov–March 10am–4pm; £2.50; EH), where the House of Commons met from 1257 until Henry VIII's reign. The thirteenth-century decorative paving stones and wall-paintings have survived intact. Chapter House tickets include entry to the nearby **Pyx Chamber** (daily 10.30am–4pm), which displays the abbey's plate, and to one of the few surviving Norman sections of the abbey, now the **Undercroft Museum** (daily 10.30am–4pm), filled with generations of royal death masks, including those of Edward III and Henry VII. Wax funeral effigies include representations of Charles II, William III and Mary (the king on a stool to make him as tall as his wife) and Lady Frances Stuart, complete with stuffed parrot.

It's only after exploring the cloisters that you get to see the **nave** itself: narrow, light and, at over a hundred feet in height, by far the tallest in the country. Close by the west door is a doleful fourteenth-century portrait of Richard II, the oldest-known image of an English monarch painted from life. The most famous monument is the **Tomb of the Unknown Soldier**; it stands right in front of the west door, which now serves as the main exit.

Westminster Cathedral

Halfway down Victoria Street, which runs east from Westminster Abbey, you'll find one of London's most surprising churches, the stripey neo-Byzantine concoction of the Roman Catholic **Westminster Cathedral**. Begun in 1895, it is one of the last and wildest monuments to the Victorian era: constructed from more than twelve million terracotta-coloured bricks, decorated with hoops of Portland stone, it culminates in a magnificent tapered campanile which rises to 274 feet, served by a lift (April–Oct daily 9am–5pm; Nov–March Thurs–Sun only; £2). The **interior** is only half finished, so to get an idea of what the place will look like when it's finally completed, explore the series of **side chapels** whose rich, multi-coloured decor makes use of over one hundred different marbles from around the world.

The Tate Gallery

From Parliament Square the unprepossessing Millbank runs south along the river to the **Tate Gallery** (daily 10am–5.50pm; free; Pimlico tube). Founded in 1897 with money from Sir Henry Tate, inventor of the sugar cube, the Tate is currently undergoing the biggest period of change in its hundred-year history. Having struggled to perform a difficult dual function as both the nation's chief collection of British art and its primary gallery for international modern art, the Tate is finally going to have two separate buildings to reflect its split personality. The new Tate Gallery of Modern Art opens in spring 2000 in the disused Bankside Power Station (see p.120). The following year, the newly expanded premises on Millbank will officially re-open as the Tate Gallery of British Art.

Until then, the Millbank gallery will continue to house a sampling of modern international art, with first-rate pieces from most of the century's Western art movements. It's a pretty safe bet that there'll be works by **Surrealists**, Dalí, Magritte and Miró, plus works from the key periods of Picasso's life, one or two by Matisse, and the odd sculpture by Rodin. In addition, the Tate owns works by **Expressionists** such as Munch, Grosz and Kirchner, leading **Abstract** artists Mondrian, Malevich and Kandinsky, and later Abstract Expressionists Pollock and Rothko. **Pop Art** is represented by Warhol and Lichtenstein, and the **Minimalist** collection includes Carl André's infamous pile of bricks, less well known as *Equivalent VIII*.

The permanent collection of **British art** from Tudor times to the twentieth century includes a fine array of works by Hogarth, Constable, Gainsborough and Reynolds, plus twelve large colour prints of the Creation by Blake, and a range of works by the ever-popular Pre-Raphaelite Brotherhood. From established greats such as Stanley Spencer and Francis Bacon to living artists like David Hockney, R.B. Kitaj and Damien Hirst, twentieth-century British art is currently scattered throughout the modern section described above. It is work by these British artists that will eventually expand to fill the space left by the departure of the international twentieth-century pieces to Bankside.

Lastly, don't miss the Tate's outstanding **Turner collection**, displayed in the Clore Gallery extension. The gallery also offers audioguides, called **TateInform** – one for the British collection 1500–1925 and one for the Turner collection – for £2 each or £3 for both. In its new reincarnation, the Millbank Tate will showcase contemporary British artists and continue to sponsor the **Turner Prize**, the country's most prestigious modern art prize.

St James's, Mayfair and Marylebone

St James's, **Mayfair** and **Marylebone** emerged in the late seventeenth century as London's first real suburbs, characterized by grid-plan streets feeding into grand, formal squares. This expansion set the westward trend for middle-class migration, and as London's wealthier consumers moved west, so too did the city's more upmarket shops and luxury hotels, which are still a feature of the area.

Aristocratic **St James's**, the rectangle of land to the north of St James's Park, was one of the first areas to be developed and remains the preserve of the seriously rich. **Piccadilly**, which forms the border between St James's and Mayfair, is no longer the fashionable promenade it once was, but a whiff of exclusivity still pervades **Bond Street** and its tributaries. **Regent Street** was created as a new "Royal Mile", a tangible borderline to shore up these new fashionable suburbs against the chaotic maze of Soho and the City, where the working population still lived. Now, along with **Oxford Street**, it has become London's busiest shopping district – it's here that Londoners mean when they talk of "going shopping up the West End".

Marylebone, which lies to the north of Oxford Street, is another grid-plan Georgian development, a couple of social and real-estate leagues below Mayfair, but a wealthy area nevertheless. It boasts a very fine art gallery, the **Wallace Collection**, and, in its northern fringes, one of London's biggest tourist attractions, **Madame Tussaud's**, the oldest and largest wax museum in the world.

St James's

St James's, the exclusive little enclave sandwiched between The Mall and Piccadilly, was laid out in the 1670s close to St James's Palace. Royal and aristocratic residences predominate along its southern border, gentlemen's clubs cluster along Pall Mall and St James's Street, while jacket-and-tie restaurants and expense-account gentlemen's outfitters line Jermyn Street. Hardly surprising, then, that most Londoners rarely stray into this area.

St James's does, however, contain some interesting architectural set-pieces, such as **Lower Regent Street**, which was the first stage in John Nash's ambitious plan to link George IV's magnificent Carlton House with Regent's Park. Like so many of Nash's grandiose schemes, it never quite came to fruition, as George IV, soon after ascending the throne, decided that Carlton House – the most expensive palace ever to have been built in London – wasn't quite luxurious enough, and had it pulled down. Instead, Lower Regent Street now opens up into **Waterloo Place**, at the centre of which stands the Guards' Crimean Memorial, fashioned from captured Russian cannon and featuring a statue of Florence Nightingale. Clearly visible, beyond, is the "Grand Old" **Duke of York's Column**, erected in 1833, ten years before Nelson's more famous one in Trafalgar Square.

Cutting across Waterloo Place, **Pall Mall** – named after the croquet-like game of *paglio e maglio* (literally "ball and mallet") that was popular at the time – leads west to **St James's Palace**, whose main red-brick gate-tower is pretty much all that remains of the Tudor palace erected here by Henry VIII. When Whitehall Palace burned down in 1698, St James's became the principal royal residence and, in keeping with tradition, an ambassador to the UK is still known as "Ambassador to the Court of St James", even though the court moved down the road to Buckingham Palace when Queen Victoria ascended the throne. The rambling, crenellated complex now provides a bachelor pad for Prince Charles and is off limits to the public, with the exception of the **Chapel Royal** (Oct–Easter Sun 8.30am & 11.15am), situated within the palace, and the **Queen's Chapel** (Easter–July Sun 8.30am & 11.15am), on the other side of Marlborough Road – both are open for services only.

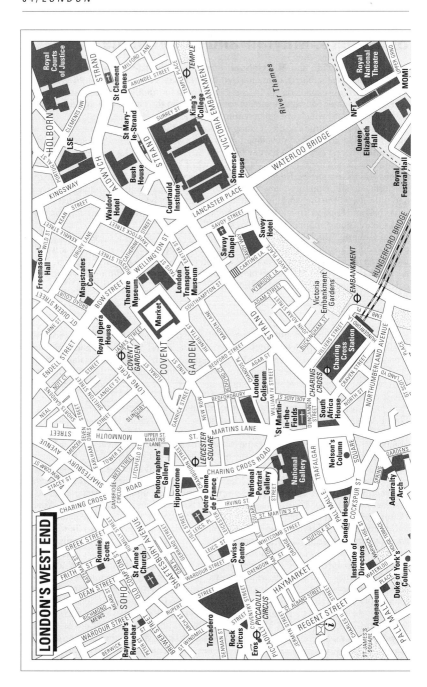

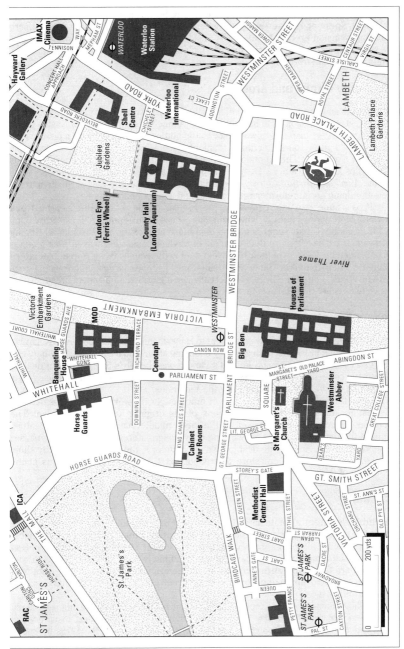

© Crown copyright

One palatial St James's residence you can visit, however, is Princess Diana's ancestral home, **Spencer House** (Feb–July & Sept–Dec Sun 11.30am–4.45pm; £6), a superb Palladian mansion erected in the 1750s. Inside, tour guides take you through nine of the state rooms, the most outrageous of which is Lord Spencer's Room, with its astonishing gilded palm-tree columns.

Piccadilly Circus and around

Anonymous and congested it may be, but **Piccadilly Circus**, is, for many Londoners, the nearest their city comes to having a centre. A much-altered product of Nash's grand 1812 Regent Street plan and now a major traffic bottleneck, it may not be a picturesque place, but it's prime tourist territory, thanks to its celebrated aluminium statue, popularly known as **Eros**. The fountain's archer is one of the city's top attractions, a status that baffles all who live here. Despite the bow and arrow, it's not the god of love at all but the *Angel of Christian Charity*, erected to commemorate the Earl of Shaftesbury, a bible-thumping social reformer who campaigned against child labour.

If Eros's fame remains a mystery, the regular queue outside the nearby **Rock Circus** (Mon, Wed, Thurs & Sun 10am–8pm, Tues 11am–8pm, Fri & Sat 9am–8pm; £8.25; Piccadilly Circus tube) is a good deal more perplexing. Billed as an all-singing extravaganza, it's little more than an array of Madame Tussaud's waxen rock legends accompanied by snippets of their hits. Next door is the equally tacky **Pepsi Trocadero** (Mon–Fri 11am–midnight, Sat & Sun 10am–1am), Europe's largest indoor virtual-reality theme park. For all the hype, this is really just a glorified amusement arcade with a few virtual-reality rides thrown in.

Regent Street

Regent Street is London's only equivalent to Haussmann's Parisian boulevards. Drawn up by John Nash in 1812 as both a luxury shopping street and a triumphal way between George IV's Carlton House and Regent's Park, it was the city's first attempt at dealing with traffic congestion, and its first stab at slum clearance and planned social segregation, which would later be perfected by the Victorians.

Despite the subsequent destruction of much of Nash's work in the 1920s, it's still possible to admire the stately intentions of his original Regent Street plan. The increase in the purchasing power of the city's middle classes in the last century brought the tone of the street "down" and heavyweight stores catering for the masses now predominate. Among the best known are Hamley's, the world's largest toy shop, and Liberty, the department store that popularized Arts and Crafts designs at the beginning of this century.

Piccadilly

Piccadilly apparently got its name from the ruffs or "pickadills" worn by the dandies who used to promenade here in the late seventeenth century. Despite its fashionable pedigree, it's no place for promenading in its current state, with traffic careering down it nose to tail most of the day and night. Infinitely more pleasant places to window-shop are the **nineteenth-century arcades**, originally built to protect shoppers from the mud and horse-dung on the streets, but now equally useful for escaping exhaust fumes.

Piccadilly may not be the shopping heaven it once was, but there are still several old firms here that proudly display their royal warrants. One of the oldest institutions is **Fortnum & Mason**, the food emporium at no. 181, established in the 1770s by one of George III's footmen, Charles Fortnum and his partner, Hugh Mason. In a kitsch addition dating from 1964, the figures of Fortnum and Mason bow to each other on the hour every day as the clock over the main entrance clanks out the Eton school anthem.

Further along Piccadilly, with its best rooms overlooking Green Park, stands the **Ritz Hotel**, a byword for decadence since it first wowed Edwardian society in 1906; the hotel's design, with its two-storey French-style mansard roof and long arcade, was based on the buildings of Paris's Rue de Rivoli. For a prolonged look inside, you'll need to be in good appetite (and book in advance) for the famous afternoon tea in the hotel's Palm Court.

Across the road from Fortnum & Mason, the **Royal Academy of Arts** (Mon–Thurs, Sat & Sun 10am–6pm, Fri 10am–8.30pm; £3–6; Green Park or Piccadilly Circus tube) occupies the enormous Burlington House, one of the few survivors from the ranks of aristocratic mansions that once lined the north side of Piccadilly. The Academy itself was the country's first-ever formal art school, founded in 1768 by a group of English painters including Thomas Gainsborough and Joshua Reynolds. Reynolds went on to become the Academy's first president, and his statue now stands in the courtyard, palette in hand ready to paint the cars.

The Academy has always had a conservative reputation for its teaching and, until recently, most of its shows. The **Summer Exhibition**, which opens in June each year, remains a stop on the social calendar of upper middle-class England. Anyone can enter paintings in any style, and the lucky winners get hung, in rather close proximity, and sold. Supposed gravitas is added by the RA "Academicians", who are allowed to display six of their own works – no matter how awful. The result is a bewildering display, which gets panned annually by the critics.

Along the west side of the Royal Academy runs the **Burlington Arcade**, built in 1819 for Lord Cavendish, then owner of Burlington House, to prevent commoners throwing rubbish into his garden. It's Piccadilly's longest and most expensive nineteenth-century arcade, lined with mahogany-fronted jewellers, gentlemen's outfitters and the like. Upholding Regency decorum, it is still illegal to whistle, sing, hum, hurry or carry large packages or open umbrellas on this small stretch, and the arcade's beadles (known as Burlington Berties), in their Edwardian frock-coats and gold-braided top hats, take the prevention of such criminality very seriously.

Bond Street

While Oxford Street, Regent Street and Piccadilly have all gone downmarket, **Bond Street**, which runs parallel with Regent Street, has carefully maintained its exclusivity. It is, in fact, two streets rolled into one: the southern half, laid out in the 1680s, is known as Old Bond Street; its northern extension, which followed less than fifty years later, is known as New Bond Street. In contrast to their international rivals, Rue de Rivoli or Fifth Avenue, they are both pretty unassuming streets architecturally: a mixture of modest Victorian and Georgian town houses. The shops that line them, however, are among the flashiest in London, dominated by perfumeries, **jewellers** and designer clothing stores like Prada, Versace, Donna Karan, Gucci, Nicole Farhi, YSL and so on.

In addition to fashion, Bond Street is also renowned for its **auction houses** and for its **fine art galleries**. Sotheby's, 34–35 New Bond St, is the oldest of the auction houses, and its viewing galleries are open free of charge. Bond Street's art galleries – exclusive mainstays of the street – are actually outnumbered by those on neighbouring **Cork Street**. The main difference between the two locations is that the Bond Street dealers are basically heirloom offloaders, whereas Cork Street galleries sell largely contemporary art. Both have impeccably presented and somewhat intimidating staff, but if you're interested, walk in and look around. They're only shops, after all.

Oxford Street

As wealthy Londoners began to move out of the City in the eighteenth century in favour of the newly developed West End, so **Oxford Street** – the old Roman road to Oxford – gradually became London's main shopping street. Today, despite successive recessions and sky-high rents, this scruffy, two-mile hotchpotch of shops is still one of the world's busiest streets.

East of Oxford Circus, the street forms the border between Soho and Fitzrovia, and features the city's two main record stores, HMV and Virgin Megastore. West of Oxford Circus, the street is dominated by more upmarket stores, including one great landmark, **Selfridge's**, a huge Edwardian pile fronted by giant Ionic columns, with the Queen of Time, riding the ship of commerce and supporting an Art Deco clock, above the main entrance. The store was opened in 1909 by Chicago millionaire Gordon Selfridge, who flaunted its 130 departments under the slogan, "Why not spend a day at Selfridge's?", but was later pensioned off after running into trouble with the Inland Revenue.

Broadcasting House: the BBC Experience

Just north of Oxford Circus, beyond **All Souls**, Nash's simple and ingenious little Bath stone church, lies the totalitarian-looking **Broadcasting House**, BBC radio headquarters since 1931 and now home to the new interactive **BBC Experience** (Mon 1–4.30pm, Tues–Fri 9.30am–4.30pm, Sat & Sun 9.30am–5.30pm; £6.50; Oxford Circus tube). A word of warning is necessary to TV addicts, however, as the museum is almost exclusively concerned with radio (Broadcasting House is the home of BBC radio, but not television). The museum is part guided tour, part hands-on experience, so visits are carefully orchestrated, with tours setting off every thirty minutes (every fifteen at peak times). As well as the usual static displays and audio-visuals extolling the virtues of the "Beeb", you get to record a short radio play with your fellow visitors, and play around in the museum's interactive section, mixing records, fine-tuning your sports commentary and presenting the weather.

The Wallace Collection

One block north of Wigmore Street and just a couple of minutes from Oxford Street, but eons away from its frenetic pace, Hertford House on Manchester Square holds one of London's most important art galleries, the **Wallace Collection** (Mon–Sat 10am–5pm, Sun 2–5pm; free; Bond Street tube). This wonderful array, best known for its eighteenth-century French paintings and decorative art, was bequeathed to the nation by the widow of Sir Richard Wallace, an art collector and, as the illegitimate son of the fourth Marquess of Hertford, inheritor of the elegant mansion and its treasures. If you visit the collection before the summer of 2000, you'll probably be aware of the museum's new-building works, which are due to be completed around that time.

The ground floor rooms, set around an open-air courtyard, have some interesting medieval and Renaissance pieces, an extensive armoury, and a group of fine nineteenth-century pictures, including **Richard Parkes Bonington**'s translucent watercolours and paintings by his close friend Delacroix. However, the most famous works are on the first floor, the tone of which is set by **Boucher**'s sumptuous mythological scenes over the staircase. Here you'll find furniture from the courts of Louis XV and XVI, decorative gold snuff boxes and fine Sèvres porcelain. Of the paintings, portraits include Sir Joshua Reynolds's doe-eyed moppets and Greuze's winsome adolescents, and two by Louise Vigée le Brun, one of the most successful portraitists of pre-revolutionary France. Among the Rococo delights are **Fragonard**'s coquettes, the most famous of whom flaunts herself to a smitten beau in *The Swing,* some elegiac scenes by **Watteau** and

Boucher's gloriously florid portrait of Madame de Pompadour, Louis XV's mistress and patron of many of the great French artists of the period.

In addition to all this French finery there's a good collection from the Dutch and Venetian schools: **de Hooch**'s *Woman Peeling Apples*, the contrasting vistas by **Canaletto** and **Guardi**, **Titian**'s *Perseus and Andromeda*, **Rembrandt**'s affectionate portrait of his teenage son, Titus, who was helping administer his father's estate after bankruptcy charges, and **Hals**'s arrogant *Laughing Cavalier*, the subject of which remains unknown. In the same vast hall as the Hals you'll find **Velázquez**'s typically searching *Lady with a Fan*, and **Gainsborough**'s deceptively innocent portrait of the actress Mary Robinson, in which she insouciantly holds a miniature of the Prince of Wales, her lover (later George IV).

Baker Street, Madame Tussaud's and the Planetarium

A small percentage of tourists emerging from **Baker Street** tube station are on the trail of English literature's languid super-sleuth, Sherlock Holmes, who's celebrated in the **Sherlock Holmes Museum** at no. 239 (the sign on the door actually says 221B). It's a competent exercise in period reconstruction, but the building has no proven connection with Holmes or his creator, Sir Arthur Conan Doyle. Nor is there any attempt to impart any insights, or even basic facts about Holmes or Doyle, yet the narrow staircases are crowded every day with fans from all over the world.

Just round the corner on Marylebone Road, **Madame Tussaud's** (June to mid-Sept daily 9am–5.30pm; mid-Sept to May Mon–Fri 10am–5.30pm, Sat & Sun 9.30am–5.30pm; £9.25; combined ticket with Planetarium £11.50) has been pulling in the crowds ever since the good lady arrived in London from Paris in 1802 bearing the sculpted heads of guillotined aristocrats (she herself only just managed to escape the same fate – her uncle, who started the family business, was less fortunate). The entrance fee might be extortionate, the likenesses occasionally dubious and the automated dummies inept by *Jurassic Park* standards, but you can still rely on finding London's biggest queues here – an hour's wait is the summertime norm.

The best photo opportunities come in the first section, an all-star garden party peppered with contemporary politicians, TV and sports personalities. The next section, called **200 Years**, is more offbeat, with dismembered heads and limbs of outdated personalities – Rudolf Nureyev, Sophia Loren, Nikita Khrushchev – ranged on a shelf as in a butcher's shop, along with a fire-damaged model of George IV with a melted eye. Close by, the very first Tussaud figure, Madame du Barry gently respires (thanks to a motorized heart).

The **Grand Hall**, a po-faced gathering of statesmen, clerics, royalty and generals, is lined with oil paintings to add a dash of respectability, but the veracity is a bit suspect – Margaret Thatcher looks like a kindly aunt. The **Chamber of Horrors**, the most popular section of all, is irredeemably tasteless and includes a reconstruction of a foggy East End street, strewn with one of Jack the Ripper's mutilated victims.

The tour of Tussaud's ends with the **Spirit of London**, a manic five-minute romp through the history of London in a miniaturized black taxi. It begins well, dropping witty visual jokes as it careers from Elizabethan times through to Swinging London, ending in a postmodern heritage nightmare, with a cacophony of punks and Beefeaters, before shuddering to a halt by a slobbering Benny Hill.

The adjoining and equally crowded **London Planetarium** (same hours; shows every 40min; £5.65) has a permanent exhibition featuring a giant revolving Earth circled by satellites, live weather satellite transmissions, images from a space telescope and touchscreen computers. All this is just a taster, however, for the thirty-minute virtual-reality presentation, "Planetary Quest", a standard romp through the history of astronomy accompanied by cosmic astro-babble commentary.

Soho

Soho gives you the best and worst of London. It's here you'll find the city's street fashion on display, its theatres, mega-cinemas and the widest variety of restaurants and cafés – where, whatever hour you wander through, there's always something going on. Uniquely, though, Soho retains an unorthodox and slightly raffish air born of an immigrant history as rich as that of the East End. The porn joints that made the district notorious in the 1970s are still in evidence, especially to the west of Wardour Street, as are the yuppies who pushed up the rents in the 1980s.

In the 1990s, Soho transformed itself again, this time into one of Europe's leading gay centres, with bars and cafés bursting out from the Old Compton Street area. Nevertheless, the area continues to boast a lively fruit and vegetable market on **Berwick Street** and a nightlife that has attracted writers and ravers to the place since the eighteenth century. The big movie houses on **Leicester Square** always attract crowds of punters and the tiny enclave of **Chinatown** continues to double as a focus for the Chinese community and a popular place for inexpensive Chinese restaurants.

Leicester Square and Chinatown

By night, when the big cinemas and discos are doing good business, and the buskers are entertaining the crowds, **Leicester Square** is one of the most crowded places in London, particularly on a Friday or Saturday when huge numbers of tourists and half the youth of the suburbs seem to congregate here. By day, queues form for half-price deals at the Society of West End Theatres booth at the south end of the square, while touts haggle with tourists over the price of dodgy tickets for the top shows and clubbers hand out flyers to likely looking punters.

It wasn't until the mid-nineteenth century that the square actually began to emerge as an entertainment zone, with accommodation houses (for prostitutes and their clients) and music halls such as the grandiose Empire and the Hippodrome (just off the square), edifices which survive today as cinemas and discos. Cinema moved in during the 1930s, a golden age evoked by the sleek black lines of the Odeon on the east side, and maintains its grip on the area. The Empire, at the top end of the square, is the favourite for the big royal premieres and, in a rather half-hearted imitation of the Hollywood (and Cannes) tradition, there are hand prints visible in the pavement by the southwestern corner of the square.

Chinatown, hemmed in between Leicester Square and Shaftesbury Avenue, is a self-contained jumble of shops, cafés and restaurants that makes up one of London's most distinct and popular ethnic enclaves. **Gerrard Street**, Chinatown's main drag, has been endowed with ersatz touches – telephone kiosks rigged out as pagodas and fake oriental gates – and few of London's 60,000 Chinese actually live in the three small blocks of Chinatown. Nonetheless, it remains a focus for the community, a place to do business or the weekly shopping, celebrate a wedding, or just meet up for meals, particularly on Sundays, when the restaurants overflow with Chinese families tucking into *dim sum*.

Old Compton Street and around

If Soho has a main drag, it has to be **Old Compton Street**, which runs parallel with Shaftesbury Avenue. The corner shops, peep shows, boutiques and trendy cafés here are typical of the area and a good barometer of the latest Soho fads. Soho has been a permanent fixture on the **gay scene** for much of this century, but the approach is much more upfront nowadays, with gay bars, clubs and cafés jostling for position on Old

Compton Street and round the corner in Wardour Street. And it doesn't stop there: there's now a gay travel agency, a gay financial adviser and, even more convenient, a gay taxi service.

The streets off Old Compton Street are lined with Soho institutions past and present. One of the best known is London's longest-running jazz club, *Ronnie Scott's*, on Frith Street, founded in 1958 and still capable of pulling in the big names. Opposite is the *Bar Italia*, an Italian café with a big screen for satellite TV transmissions of Italian football games, and late-night hours popular with Soho's clubbers. It was in this building, appropriately enough for such a media-saturated area, that John Logie Baird made the world's first public television transmission in 1926.

At the western end of Old Compton Street is **Wardour Street**, a kind of dividing line between the trendier, eastern half of Soho and the seedier western zone. Immediately west of Wardour Street, the **vice and prostitution** rackets still have the area well staked out. However, straight prostitution makes up a small proportion of what gets sold here, and has been since Paul Raymond – now Britain's richest man – set up his Folies-Bergère style *Revue Bar* in the late 1950s, now complemented by the transvestite floor show next door at *Madame Jo-Jo's*. These last two are paragons of virtue compared with the dodgy videos, short con outfits and rip-off joints that operate in the neighbouring streets.

Until the 1950s, **Carnaby Street** was a backstreet on Soho's western fringe, occupied, for the most part, by sweatshop tailors who used to make up the suits for Savile Row. Then, sometime in the mid-1950s, several trendy boutiques opened catering for the new market in flamboyant men's clothing. In 1964 – the year of the official birth of the Carnaby Street myth – Mods, West Indian Rude Boys and other "switched-on people", as the *Daily Telegraph* noted, began to hang out here. The area quickly became the epicentre of Swinging Sixties' London, and its street sign the image on London's most popular postcard. A victim of its own hype, Carnaby Street equally quickly declined into an avenue of overpriced tack, and so it has remained, despite a fairly recent facelift.

Covent Garden

A little more sanitized and unashamedly commercial than Soho, **Covent Garden** today is a far cry from its heyday when the piazza was the great playground (and red-light district) of eighteenth-century London. The buskers in front of St Paul's Church, the theatres round about and the Royal Opera House on Bow Street are survivors in this tradition, and on a balmy summer evening, Covent Garden Piazza is still an undeniably lively place to be. Another positive side-effect of the market development has been the renovation of the run-down warehouses to the north of the piazza, especially around the Neal Street area, which now boast some of the trendiest shops in the West End, selling everything from shoes to skateboards.

Covent Garden Piazza

London's oldest planned square, laid out in the 1630s by Inigo Jones, **Covent Garden Piazza** was initially a great success, its novelty value alone attracting a rich and aristocratic clientele, but over the next century the tone of the place fell as the fruit and vegetable market expanded, and theatres and coffee houses began to take over the peripheral buildings. When the market closed in 1974, the piazza narrowly survived being turned into an office development. Instead, the elegant Victorian market hall and its environs were restored to house shops, restaurants and arts-and-crafts stalls. Boosted by buskers and street entertainers, the piazza has now become one of London's major tourist attractions, its success prompting a wholesale gentrification of the streets to the north of the market.

Of Jones's original piazza, the only remaining parts are the two rebuilt sections of north-side arcading, and **St Paul's Church**, facing the west side of the market building. The church's proximity to so many theatres has made it known as the "Actors' Church" and it's filled with memorials to international thespians from Boris Karloff to Gracie Fields. The space in front of the Tuscan portico – where Eliza Doolittle was discovered selling violets by Henry Higgins in George Bernhard Shaw's *Pygmalion* – is now a legalized venue for buskers and street performers, who must audition for a slot months in advance.

The piazza's history of entertainment goes back to May 1662, when the first recorded performance of Punch and Judy in England was staged by Italian puppeteer Pietro Gimonde, and witnessed by Samuel Pepys. This historic event is commemorated every second Sunday in May by a **Punch and Judy Festival**, held in the gardens behind the church; for the rest of the year the churchyard provides a tranquil respite from the activity outside (access is from King Street, Henrietta Street or Bedford Street).

The Piazza's museums

An original flower-market shed on the piazza's east side is occupied by the **London Transport Museum** (daily 10am–6pm, Fri from 11am; £4.95; Covent Garden tube). A herd of old buses, trains and trams make up the bulk of the exhibits, though there's enough interactive fun – touch-screen computers and the odd costumed conductor and vehicles to climb on – to keep most children amused. London Transport's stylish maps and posters are also displayed here in their very own gallery, and you can buy reproductions, plus countless other LT paraphernalia, at the shop on the way out.

The rest of the old flower market now houses the **Theatre Museum** (Tues–Sun 11am–7pm; £3.50), displaying three centuries of memorabilia from every conceivable area of the performing arts in the West (the entrance is on Russell Street). The corridors of glass cases cluttered with props, programmes and costumes are not especially exciting. The long-term temporary shows such as "Slap", a history of stage make-up, tend to be a lot more fun, with a make-up artist on hand to give you a hideous scar or bullet wound. The museum also runs a **booking service** for West End shows and has an unusually good selection of cards and posters.

Not strictly a museum, but more than just a shop, the **Cabaret Mechanical Theatre** (Mon–Sat 10am–6.30pm, Sun 11am–6.30pm; £1.95), on the lower floor of the market building, contains a quirky permanent collection of fifty or so eccentric inventions, handmade gadgets and witty automata, many of which are for sale. Jokes, from the slapstick to the erudite, are plentiful and the devices within the museum function at the touch of a button.

Bloomsbury

Bloomsbury gets its name from its medieval landowners, the Blemunds, though nothing was built here until the 1660s. Through marriage, the Russell family, the earls and later dukes of Bedford, acquired much of the area and established the many formal, bourgeois squares which are the main distinguishing feature of the area. The Russells named the grid-plan streets after their various titles and estates, and kept the pubs and shops to a minimum to maintain the tone of the neighbourhood.

This century, Bloomsbury acquired a reputation as the city's most learned quarter, dominated by the dual institutions of the **British Museum** and **London University** and home to many of London's chief book publishers, but perhaps best known for its literary inhabitants. Today, the British Museum is clearly the star attraction, but there are other sights, such as the **Dickens House Museum**, that are high on many people's itineraries. In its northern fringes, the character of the area changes dramatically, becoming steadily more seedy as you near the two big mainline train stations of **Euston** and **King's Cross**, where cheap B&Bs and run-down council estates provide fertile territory for prostitutes and drug dealers, and an unlikely location for the new **British Library**.

The British Museum

The **British Museum** (Mon–Sat 10am–5pm, Sun noon–6pm; free; Russell Square, Tottenham Court Road or Holborn tube) is one of the great museums of the world and, after Blackpool, is England's most popular tourist attraction, with in excess of six million visitors a year. With over four million exhibits ranged over two and a half miles of galleries, the BM contains one of the most comprehensive collections of antiquities, prints, drawings and books to be housed under one roof. Its collection of Roman and Greek art is unparalleled, its Egyptian collection is the most significant outside Egypt and, in addition, there are fabulous treasures from Anglo-Saxon and Roman Britain, from China, Japan, India and Mesopotamia – not to mention an enormous collection of prints and drawings, only a fraction of which can be displayed at any one time.

The building itself, begun in 1823, is the grandest of London's Greek Revival buildings, dominated by the giant Ionic colonnade and portico that forms the main entrance. With the British Library now settled into its new premises at St Pancras (see p.106), the museum is currently undergoing a £100 million redevelopment plan, which will allow for the return of its ethnographical department, the opening-up of the British Library's former Round Reading Room – due to re-open at the end of 2000 – where Karl Marx wrote *Das Kapital*, and the surrounding Great Court, which will feature a glass roof designed by Norman Foster. The final completion date for the whole project is 2003.

Greek and Roman antiquities

Greek and Roman antiquities make up the largest section in the museum, spread over three floors. Treasures from Ancient Greece and Rome are ranged to the side of the Assyrian collection on the ground floor, beginning with Cycladic figures, Minoan artefacts, Archaic black-figured vases and later red-figured vases from Greece's Classical age. Beyond here is a glut of wonders: the marble frieze including the **Temple of Apollo at Bassae** (mezzanine room 6) and the reconstructed **Nereid monument**, mighty tomb of a ruler of Xanthos, fronted with Ionic columns and finely carved sea-nymphs.

A huge purpose-built room (no. 8) is devoted to the museum's most famous relics, the **Elgin Marbles**, a series of exquisite friezes, metopes and pedimental sculptures, carved between 447 and 432 BC under the supervision of the great sculptor Pheidias for the **Parthenon**, the sanctuary of the goddess Athena. Removed from Athens in 1801 by Lord Elgin, British ambassador to Constantinople, ostensibly in order to protect them from damage, the sculptures were bought by the British government in 1816 for £35,000 and have caused more controversy than any other of the museum's trophies, with the Greek government repeatedly requesting that they be returned. A CD audioguide (£3) is available to rent, but it's by no means essential as the explanatory panels and video are good enough.

Past the Nereid monument in room 9, you come to two more of Lord Elgin's appropriations: a single column and one of the six caryatids from the **Erechtheum** on the Acropolis. Room 12 contains fragments from one of the Seven Wonders of the Ancient World: two huge figures, an Amazonian frieze and a marble horse the size of an elephant from the tomb of **King Mausolos at Halicarnassus** (source of the word "mausoleum"). A fragment from another Wonder lies in room 14: a giant sculpted marble column drum from the colossal **Temple of Artemis at Ephesus**.

Upstairs, rooms 69 to 73 are dedicated to less spectacular classical artefacts, grouped under specific themes, such as gladiators, music, women and so on. The highlight of these first-floor rooms, though, is the **Portland Vase** (room 70); made from cobalt-blue blown glass and decorated with opaque white cameos, it dates from around the beginning of the first millennium.

The bulk of the British Museum's **Roman statuary** is in the basement, best approached by the west stairs, which are lined with mosaic pavements. The best stuff forms part of the Townley Collection (room 84) and includes two curiously gentle marble greyhounds, a claw-footed sphinx, a chariot-shaped latrine and a Roman copy of the Greek bronze Discobolus (the discus thrower).

The western Asiatic antiquities

Just before reaching the Egyptian sculpture on the ground floor, the attendant gods, their robes smothered in inscriptions, fix their gazes on you and serve as a prelude to the **Assyrian sculptures and reliefs** ranged in a corridor (rooms 19–21) parallel to the Egyptian hall. Guarded by two colossal five-legged, human-headed winged bulls, the collection sets off with a full-scale reconstruction of the **Balawat Gates** from Shalmaneser III's palace, leading into room 19 lined with reliefs from the **palace at Nimrud** (883–859 BC); also on display here is a black obelisk carved with hieroglyphs and images of foreign rulers paying tribute to Shalmaneser III.

Another room (no. 17) is lined with splendidly legible friezes, showing **royal lion hunts** of Ashurbanipal, which involved rounding up the beasts before letting them loose in an enclosed arena so the king could kill them, a practice which effectively eradicated the species in Assyria; the succession of graphic death scenes features one in which the king slaughters the cats with his bare hands. From here it's a convenient trot down into the basement (room 89), where smaller **Mesopotamian friezes** and domestic objects include an iron bathtub-cum-coffin from Ur, thought to be the first great city on earth, dating from 2500 BC.

Up the west stairs, in room 56, are some of the BM's oldest artefacts, dating from Mesopotamia in the third millennium BC. The most extraordinary treasures hail from Ur: the enigmatic **Ram in the Thicket**, a midnight blue and white shell statuette of a goat on its hind legs, peering through golden branches; and the equally mysterious **Standard of Ur**, a small hollow box showing scenes of battle on one side, with peace and banqueting on the other, all fashioned in shell, red limestone and lapis lazuli, set in bitumen. A selection of Mesopotamian cuneiform tablets scratched with infinitesimal script includes the **Flood Tablet**, a fragment of the Epic of Gilgamesh, perhaps the world's oldest story.

The Egyptian collection

The BM's collection of Egyptian antiquities is one of the finest in the world. On the ground floor, just past the entrance to the Assyrian section (see above), two seated black statues of **Amenophis III** guard the entrance to the main Egyptian Hall (room 25), where the cream of the British Museum's Egyptian antiquities are on display. The name "Belzoni", scratched under the left heel of the larger statue, was carved by the Italian circus strong man responsible for dragging some of the heftiest Egyptian treasures to the banks of the Nile, prior to their export to England.

Beyond, a crowd usually hovers around the **Rosetta Stone**, a black slab found in the Nile delta in 1799, whose trilingual inscription enabled scholars to decode Egyptian hieroglyphs for the first time. Beyond the stone, a sombre trio of life-sized granite statues of **Sesotris III** makes a doleful counterpart to the colossal pink-speckled granite head of **Amenophis III**, whose enormous arm lies on the floor next to him. Glass cases in the central atrium display a fascinating array of smaller objects, from signet rings to eye-paint containers in the shape of hedgehogs, as well as a bronze of the cat goddess Bastet, with gold nose and earrings. Further on still, another giant head and shoulders, made of two pieces of different-coloured stone, still bears the hole drilled by French soldiers in an unsuccessful attempt to remove it from the mortuary temple of **Rameses II**.

Climbing the west stairs brings you to the **upper floor** and the huge **Egyptian mummy** collection (rooms 60 & 61). The sheer number of exhibits here is overwhelming – one display cabinet to make for is that containing mummies of various animals, including cats, apes, crocodiles and falcons, along with their highly ornate coffins – there's even an eel, whose bronze coffin depicts the deceased as a cobra with a human head.

The Oriental collections

The BM's **Oriental collection** (rooms 33–34 & 91–94) – best approached from the back entrance on Montague Place – is unrivalled in the West, covering Buddhism, Taoism and Confucianism. The Chinese collection is particularly good and the collection of Indian sculpture is easily as good as anything at the V&A (where you now have to pay to get in).

The Chinese collection occupies the eastern half of the Hotung Gallery (room 33), with garish "three-colour" statuary occupying the centre and far end of the room. There's a great cabinet of miniature landscapes popular among bored bureaucrats during the Manchu Empire, and an incredible array of **snuff boxes** in lapis lazuli, jade, crystal, tortoiseshell and quartz. Beyond the superlative collection of **Chinese porcelain**, you enter the Southeast Asian half of the room, which kicks off with a beautiful gilt-bronze statue of the Bodhisattva Tara, who, it said, was born from one of the tears wept by Avalokitesvara, a companion of Buddha. At the far end of the room, past the **Tibetan musical instruments** and larger-scale Indian sculptures, is the showpiece of the collection: a dazzling cluster of limestone reliefs, dome sculptures and drum slabs purloined from the **Buddhist stupa of Amaravati**.

The museum's **Islamic antiquities** (room 34), from as far apart as Spain and southern Asia, are in the gallery below, adjacent to the north entrance. The bulk of the collection is made up of thirteenth- to fifteenth-century **Syrian brass** objects, and blue, green and tomato-red **Iznik** ceramics. The best stuff is at the far end of the room, where Moorish lustre pottery resides alongside thirteenth-century astrolabes, scimitars and sabres, and a couple of Mughal hookahs encrusted with lapis lazuli and rubies set in gold. Most unusual, however, is the naturalistic green Kashgar jade terrapin, discovered in Allahabad in 1600.

The other collections

One of the most famous exhibits of the (rather loosely defined) Prehistoric and Romano-British collections, on the first floor, is the **Mildenhall Treasure** (room 49), 28 pieces of silver tableware from the fourth century AD. Further on, in room 50 a glass case holds the remains of the two-thousand-year-old **Lindow Man**, preserved in a Cheshire bog after his sacrificial death at the hands of druids. It's an unsettling introduction to the brilliant displays of **Celtic craftwork**, where two of the most distinctive objects are bronze wine flasks from France, inlaid with coral. Showing Persian and Etruscan influences, they are supreme examples of Celtic art, with happy little ducks on the lip and rangy dogs for handles.

The medieval, Renaissance and modern collections cover more than a millennium, from the Dark Ages to the interwar period. Most visitors, though, come here to see the Saxon **Sutton Hoo** ship burial in room 41. Discovered in Suffolk in 1939, this enormous haul includes silver bowls, gold jewellery decorated with cloisonné enamel and an iron helmet bejewelled with gilded bronze and garnets. Further on, in room 42, among the splendid Viking brooches and coins, are the thickset **Lewis chessmen**, wild-eyed Scandinavian figures carved from walrus ivory and originally painted dark red, which were discovered in the Western Isles (see p.963).

The BM's ethnography department is gradually returning to Bloomsbury, and will be clustered around the current **Mexican Gallery** (room 33c), a dramatically lit display, covering a huge period of Mexican art from the second millennium BC to the sixteenth century AD. A new gallery for the North American collection has also just opened, and there are further galleries devoted to the Oceanic and Asian collections, due to open over the course of the next few years. In the meantime, an ethnography showcase, in room 35, at the top of the main stairs, will continue to display a few tempting hors d'oeuvres.

The BM also has a new **Money Gallery** (room 68) – sharp right at the top of the main stairs – which traces the history of money from the use of grain in Mesopotamia around 2000 BC to the advent of coins in around 625 BC in Greek cities in Asia Minor, to printed money in China in the tenth century AD. It's an attractive and informative gallery, and the modern section has coins from all over the world from Siberia to Papua New Guinea.

Minor Bloomsbury museums

A couple of Bloomsbury's lesser museums, although dwarfed by the British Museum, are worth dipping into. **Dickens's House**, 48 Doughty St (Mon–Sat 10am–5pm; £3.50; Russell Square tube), is the area's only house museum – surprisingly, given the plethora of blue plaques marking the residences of local luminaries. Dickens moved here in 1837 shortly before his marriage to Catherine Hogarth, and they lived here for two years, during which time he wrote *Nicholas Nickleby* and *Oliver Twist*. This is the only one of Dickens's fifteen London addresses to survive intact, but only the drawing room has been restored to its original Regency style. Letters, manuscripts, the earliest-known portrait and the annotated books he used during extensive lecture tours in Britain and the States, are the rewards for those with more than a passing interest in the novelist.

Of the various collections linked to university departments, the **Petrie Museum of Egyptian Archeology** (Mon–Fri 10am–noon & 1.15–5pm; free; Goodge Street tube), on the first floor of the Watson building down Malet Place, has a haphazard display of prehistoric to Coptic pottery and jewellery, while tucked away in the southeast corner of Gordon Square at no. 53, the **Percival David Foundation of Chinese Art** (Mon–Fri 10.30am–5pm; free; Russell Square tube) is a fine collection of ceramics ranging from fragile tea cups to opulent bowls glazed with extraordinarily rich colour. The most famous pieces are on the second floor – the vivid blue-and-white "David" vases, made in the fourteenth century that so influenced Western tastes in crockery.

Gordon Square itself, once the centre of the Bloomsbury Group, is less landscaped and quieter than Russell Square and used mainly by swotting students from the various university departments in the surrounding buildings. Plaques mark the residences of Lytton Strachey (no. 51) and Keynes (no. 46), while another (no. 50) commemorates the **Bloomsbury Group** as a whole (see p.193).

The British Library

After fifteen years of hassle and £500 million of public money, the new **British Library** (Mon & Wed–Fri 9.30am–6pm, Tues 9.30am–8pm, Sat 9.30am–5pm, Sun 11am–5pm; free; King's Cross or Euston tube), located on the busy Euston Road on the northern fringes of Bloomsbury, finally opened to the public in 1998. As the country's most expensive public building, it's hardly surprising that the place has come under fierce criticism from all sides. Architecturally the charge has been led, predictably enough, by Prince Charles, who compared it to an academy for secret policemen. Yet while it's true that the architect, Colin St John Wilson, has a penchant for red-brick brutalism that's horribly out of fashion, and compares unfavourably with its cathedralesque Victorian neighbour, the former *Midland Grand Hotel*, the interior of the library has met with general approval and the new high-tech exhibition galleries are superb.

With the exception of the reading rooms, the library is open to the general public. The three exhibition galleries are to the left as you enter; straight ahead, is the spiritual heart of the BL, a multi-storey glass-walled tower housing the vast **King's Library**, collected by George III and donated to the museum by George IV in 1823; to the side of the King's Library is the philatelic collection. If you want to explore the parts of the building not normally open to the public, you must sign up for a **guided tour** (Mon, Wed, Fri & Sun 3pm, Sat 10.30am & 3pm; £3).

The first of the three exhibition galleries to head for is the dimly lit **John Ritblat Gallery**, where a superlative selection of the BL's ancient manuscripts, maps, documents and precious books, including the richly illustrated Lindisfarne Gospels, are displayed. One of the most appealing innovations is "**Turning the Pages**", a small room off the main gallery, where you can turn the pages of four selected texts "virtually" on a computer terminal. The **Pearson Gallery of Living Words** houses a more educative exhibition and includes a reading area, where you can peruse a selection of books – for adults and children – on sale in the library's bookshop. The **Workshop of Words, Sounds and Images** is a hands-on exhibition of more universal appeal, where you can design your own literary publication.

Holborn and the Inns of Court

Bounded by Kingsway to the west, the City to the east, the Strand to the south and Theobald's Road to the north, **Holborn** (pronounced "Ho-bun") is a fascinating area to explore. Strategically placed between the royal and political centre of Westminster and the mercantile and financial might of the City, this wedge of land became the hub of the English legal system in the early thirteenth century. Hostels, known as **Inns of Court**, were established where lawyers could eat, sleep and study English Common Law (which was not taught in the universities at the time). Nowadays, the Inns of Court make for an interesting stroll, their archaic, cobbled precincts exuding the rarefied atmosphere of an Oxbridge college, and sheltering one of the city's oldest churches, the twelfth-century **Temple Church**. Close by the Inns, in Lincoln's Inn Fields, is **Sir John Soane's Museum**, one of the most memorable and enjoyable of London's small museums, packed with architectural illusions and an eclectic array of curios.

Aldwych

The wide crescent of **Aldwych**, forming a neat "D" with the eastern part of the Strand, was driven through the slums of this zone in the last throes of the Victorian era. A confident ensemble occupies the centre, with the enormous **Australia House** and **India House** sandwiching **Bush House**, home of the BBC's World Service since 1940. Despite its thoroughly British associations, Bush House was actually built by the American speculator Irving T. Bush, whose planned trade centre flopped in the 1930s. The giant figures on the north facade and the inscription, "To the Eternal Friendship of English-speaking Nations", thus refer to the friendship between the US and Britain, and are not, as many people assume, the declaratory manifesto of the current occupants.

Somerset House: Courtauld Institute

South of Aldwych and the Strand stands **Somerset House**, sole survivor of the grandiose edifices which once lined this stretch of the riverfront, its four wings enclosing a large courtyard rather like a Parisian *hôtel*. The present building was begun in 1776 by William Chambers as a purpose-built governmental office development. From 2000, the south wing will be open to the public in order to display the **Gilbert Collection** of European silver and gold.

Part of the north wing has, for some time now, been home to the galleries of the **Courtauld Institute** (Mon–Sat 10am–6pm, Sun 2–6pm; £4, free after 5pm; Temple or Covent Garden tube), chiefly known for its dazzling collection of Impressionist and Post-Impressionist paintings, whose virtue is quality rather than quantity. Among works by Gauguin, Toulouse-Lautrec, Seurat, Van Gogh and Modigliani are one or two highly prized paintings: a small-scale version of Manet's *Déjeuner sur l'herbe*, Renoir's *La Loge* and Degas' *Two Dancers*, plus a whole heap of Cézanne's canvases, including one of his series of *Card Players*. The Courtauld also boasts earlier works by the likes of Rubens, van Dyck, Tiepolo and Cranach the Elder.

Temple and the Royal Courts of Justice

Temple is the largest and most complex of the Inns of Court, where every barrister in England must study before being called to the Bar. Temple itself is an amalgamation of two Inns – **Middle Temple** and **Inner Temple** – both of which lie to the south of the Strand and, strictly speaking, just within the boundaries of the City of London. A few very old buildings survive here, but the overall scene is dominated by the soulless neo-Georgian reconstructions that followed the devastation of the Blitz. Still, the maze of courtyards and passageways is fun to explore – especially after dark, when Temple is gas-lit.

There are several points of access, simplest of which is Devereux Court. Medieval students ate, attended lectures and slept in the **Middle Temple Hall** (Mon–Fri 10–11.30am & 3–4pm), across the courtyard, still the Inn's main dining room. The present building was constructed in the 1560s and provided the setting for many great Elizabethan masques and plays – probably including Shakespeare's *Twelfth Night*, which is believed to have been premiered here in 1602. The hall is worth a visit for its fine hammer-beam roof, wooden panelling and decorative Elizabethan screen.

The two Temple Inns share use of the complex's oldest building, **Temple Church** (Wed–Sun 10am–4pm), built in 1185 by the Knights Templar. An oblong chancel was added in the thirteenth century, and the whole building was damaged in the Blitz, but the original round church – modelled on the Church of the Holy Sepulchre in Jerusalem – still stands, with its striking Purbeck marble piers, recumbent marble effigies and tortured grotesques grimacing in the spandrels of the blind arcading.

Across the Strand from Temple, the **Royal Courts of Justice** (Mon–Fri 8.30am–4.30pm), a daunting nineteenth-century Gothic Revival complex, is home to the Court of Appeal and the High Court, where the most important civil cases are tried. Appeals and libel suits are heard here – it was from here that the Guildford Four and Birmingham Six walked to freedom, and it is where countless pop and soap stars have battled it out with the tabloids. The fifty-odd courtrooms are open to the public, though you have to go through stringent security checks first.

Lincoln's Inn Fields

North of the Law Courts lies **Lincoln's Inn Fields**, London's largest square, laid out in the early 1640s, with **Lincoln's Inn** (Mon–Fri 9am–6pm), the first and in many ways the prettiest of the Inns of Court, on its east side. The Inn's fifteenth-century **Old Hall** is open by appointment only (☎0171/405 1393), but you can view the early seventeenth-century **chapel** (Mon–Fri noon–2.30pm), with its unusual fan-vaulted open undercroft and, on the first floor, its late Gothic nave, hit by a Zeppelin in World War I and much restored since.

The south side of Lincoln's Inn Fields is occupied by the gigantic **Royal College of Surgeons**, home to the **Hunterian Museum** (Mon–Fri 9am–5pm; free; Holborn tube), a fascinating collection of pickled bits and bobs. Also on view are the skeletons of the Irish giant, O'Brien (1761–83), who was seven feet ten inches tall and the Sicilian midget Caroline Crachami (1815–24), who was just one foot ten and a half inches when she died.

A group of buildings on the north side of Lincoln's Inn Fields house **Sir John Soane's Museum** (Tues–Sat 10am–5pm; first Tues of the month also 6–9pm; free; Holborn tube), one of London's best-kept secrets. Soane (1753–1837), architect of the Bank of England, was an avid collector who designed this house not only as a home and office, but also as a place to stash his large collection of art and antiquities – everything from an Egyptian sarcophagus to paintings by the likes of Hogarth and Reynolds. Arranged much as it was in his lifetime, the ingeniously planned house has an informal, treasure-hunt atmosphere, with surprises in every alcove. At 2.30pm every Saturday, a fascinating, hour-long **free guided tour** takes you round the museum and the enormous research library, next door, containing architectural drawings, books and cork and wood models.

Gray's Inn and Staple Inn

North of Lincoln's Inn, **Gray's Inn** (Mon–Fri 10am–4pm), entered from High Holborn, is named for the de Grey family, who owned the original mansion. The entrance is through an anonymous cream-coloured building next door to the venerable *Cittie of Yorke* pub. Established in the fourteenth century, most of what you see today was rebuilt after the Blitz, with the exception of the **Hall** (by appointment only; ☎0171/405 8164), with its fabulous Tudor screen and stained glass, where the premiere of Shakespeare's *Comedy of Errors* is thought to have taken place in 1594.

Heading east along Holborn, it's worth pausing to admire **Staple Inn**, on the right, not one of the Inns of Court, but one of the now defunct Inns of Chancery, which used to provide a sort of foundation course for those aspiring to the Bar. Its overhanging half-timbered facade and gables date from the sixteenth century and are the most extensive in the whole of London; they survived the Great Fire, which stopped just short of Holborn Circus, but had to be extensively rebuilt after the Blitz.

The City

The City is where London began. Long established as the financial district, it stretches from Temple Bar in the west to the Tower of London in the east – administrative boundaries that are only slightly larger than those marked by the Roman walls and their medieval successors. However, in this Square Mile (as the City is sometimes referred to), you'll find few leftovers of London's early days, since four-fifths of the area burnt down in the Great Fire of 1666. Rebuilt in brick and stone, the City gradually lost its centrality as London swelled westwards, though it has maintained its position as Britain's financial heartland. What you see on the ground is mostly the product of three fairly recent building phases: the Victorian construction boom of the late nineteenth century; the postwar reconstruction following the Blitz; and the money-grabbing frenzy of the Thatcherite 1980s, in which nearly fifty percent of the City's office space was rebuilt.

When you consider what has happened here, it's amazing that so much has survived to pay witness to the City's two-thousand-year history. Wren's spires still punctuate the skyline here and there and his masterpiece, **St Paul's Cathedral**, remains one of London's geographical pivots. At the eastern edge of the City, the **Tower of London** still stands protected by some of the best-preserved medieval fortifications in Europe. Other relics, such as the City's few surviving medieval alleyways, Wren's **Monument** to the Great Fire and London's oldest synagogue and church, are less conspicuous, and even locals have problems finding the more modern attractions of the **Museum of London** and the **Barbican** arts complex.

Perhaps the biggest change of all, though, has been in the City's population. Up until the eighteenth century the majority of Londoners lived and worked in or around the City; nowadays 300,000 commuters spend the best part of Monday to Friday here, but only 5000 people remain at night and at weekends. The result of this demographic shift is that the City is fully alive only during office hours. This means that by far the best time to visit is during the week, since many pubs, restaurants and even some tube stations and tourist sights close down at the weekend.

Fleet Street

In 1500 a certain Wynkyn de Worde, a pupil of William Caxton, moved the Caxton presses from Westminster to **Fleet Street**, to be close to the lawyers of the Inns of Court and to the clergy of St Paul's. However, the street really boomed two hundred years later when, in 1702, the now defunct *Daily Courant*, Britain's first daily newspaper, was published here. By the nineteenth century all the major national and provincial dailies had their offices and printing presses in the Fleet Street district, a situation that prevailed until the 1980s, when the press barons relocated their operations elsewhere.

The best source of information about the old-style Fleet Street is the so-called "journalists' and printers' cathedral", the church of **St Bride's** (Mon–Sat 8am–5pm; Blackfriars tube), which boasts Wren's tallest and most exquisite spire (said to be the inspiration for the tiered wedding cake). The crypt contains a little **museum of Fleet Street history**, with information on the *Daily Courant* and the *Universal Daily Register*, which later became *The Times*, claiming to be "the faithful recorder of every species of intelligence...circulated for a particular set of readers only".

Numerous narrow alleyways lead off the north side of Fleet Street, two of which – Bolt Court and Hind Court – eventually open out into Gough Square, on which stands **Dr Johnson's House** (May–Sept Mon–Sat 11am–5.30pm; Oct–April Mon–Sat 11am–5pm; £3; Blackfriars tube). Here, the great savant, writer and lexicographer lived from 1747 to 1759, whilst compiling the 41,000 entries for the first dictionary of the English language, two first editions of which can be seen in the grey-panelled rooms of the house. You can also view the open-plan attic, in which Johnson and his six helpers put together the dictionary.

St Paul's Cathedral

St Paul's Cathedral (Mon–Sat 8.30am–4pm; £4; combined ticket with galleries £7.50; St Paul's tube), the City's finest old building, is the fifth church on this site. Its immediate predecessor, a huge Gothic cathedral, was irreparably damaged in the Great Fire and Wren was given the task of building a replacement – just one of over fifty church commissions he received in the wake of the blaze. Topped by an enormous lead-covered dome that's second in size only to St Peter's in Rome, St Paul's remains a dominating presence in the City, despite the encroaching tower blocks – its showpiece west facade is particularly magnificent and is at its most impressive at night when bathed in sea-green arc lights. Westminster Abbey has the edge when it comes to celebrity corpses, pre-Reformation sculpture, royal connections and sheer atmosphere. St Paul's, by contrast, is a soulless but perfectly calculated architectural set-piece, a burial place for captains rather than kings, though it does contain more artists than Westminster Abbey.

The best place from which to appreciate the glory of St Paul's is beneath the **dome**, decorated (against Wren's wishes) by Thornhill's trompe l'oeil frescoes. By far the most richly decorated section of the cathedral, however, is the **chancel**, in particular the spectacular, swirling, gilded mosaics of birds, fish, animals and greenery, dating from the 1890s. The intricately carved oak and limewood **choir stalls**, and the imposing organ case, are the work of Wren's master carver, Grinling Gibbons. Meanwhile, in the south-choir aisle is the only complete effigy to have survived from Old St Paul's, the upstanding shroud of **John Donne**, poet, preacher and one-time Dean of St Paul's.

A series of stairs, beginning in the south aisle, lead to the dome's three **galleries**, the first of which is the internal **Whispering Gallery**, so called because of its acoustic properties – words whispered to the wall on one side are distinctly audible over one hundred feet away on the other, though the place is usually so busy you can't hear very much above the hubbub. The other two galleries are exterior: the **Stone Gallery**, around the balustrade at the base of the dome, and ultimately the **Golden Gallery**, below the golden ball and cross which top the cathedral.

Although the nave is crammed full of overblown monuments to military types, burials in St Paul's are confined to the **crypt**, reputedly the largest in Europe. The whitewashed walls and bright lighting, however, make this one of the least atmospheric mausoleums you could imagine. Immediately to your right you'll find **Artists' Corner**, which boasts as many painters and architects as Westminster Abbey has poets, including Christopher Wren himself. The crypt's two other star tombs are those of **Nelson** and **Wellington**, both occupying centre stage and both with more fanciful monuments upstairs.

Paternoster Square to Newgate

The Blitz destroyed the area immediately to the north of St Paul's. In its place the City authorities built the brazenly modernist **Paternoster Square**, a grim pedestrianized piazza whose buildings are currently due for demolition. They will be replaced with Sir William Whitfield's restrained masterplan, seen as a compromise choice in the modernism versus classicism debate.

To the north of Paternoster Square, next to the hollowed-out shell of Wren's **Christ Church** is the **National Postal Museum** (Mon–Fri 9.30am–4.30pm; free), housed in the city's former General Post Office building. The ornate ground floor, where the service counters once were, is now given over to a general history of the postal service, while the museum's world-class collection of stamps is displayed in pull-out drawers on the second floor of the building, along with a short video on the history of post office sorting techniques.

A short distance along Newgate Street, you'll find the Central Criminal Court, more popularly known as the **Old Bailey**. Built on the site of the notoriously harsh Newgate Prison, where folk used to come to watch public hangings, the Old Bailey is now the venue for all the country's most serious criminal court cases; you can watch the proceedings from the visitors' gallery (Mon–Fri 10.30am–1pm & 2–4pm), but note that bags and cameras are not allowed in, and there is no cloakroom.

The Museum of London and the Barbican

Despite London's long pedigree, very few of its ancient structures are now standing. However, numerous Roman, Saxon and Elizabethan remains have been discovered during the City's various rebuildings and many of these finds are now displayed at the **Museum of London** (Tues–Sat 10am–5.50pm, Sun noon–5.50pm; £5, free after 4.30pm; St Paul's or Barbican tube), hidden above the western end of London Wall, in the southwestern corner of the Barbican complex. The museum's permanent exhibition is basically an educational trot through London's history from prehistory to the present day. This is interesting enough (and attracts a lot of school groups), but the real strength of the museum lies in the excellent temporary exhibitions, lectures, walks and videos it organizes throughout the year.

The City's only large residential complex is the **Barbican**, a phenomenally ugly and expensive concrete ghetto built on the heavily bombed Cripplegate area. The zone's solitary prewar building is the heavily restored sixteenth-century church of **St Giles Cripplegate** (Mon–Fri 9.30am–5.15pm, Sat 9am–noon), situated across from the famously user-repellent **Barbican Arts Centre**, the "City's gift to the nation", which was formally opened in 1982. The complex does, however, serve as home to the London Symphony Orchestra and the London chapter of the Royal Shakespeare Company, and holds various free gigs in the foyer.

The financial centre

Bank is the finest architectural arena in the City. Heart of the finance sector and the busy meeting point of eight streets, it's overlooked by a handsome collection of Neoclassical buildings – among them, the Bank of England, the Royal Exchange and Mansion House (the Lord Mayor's official residence) – each one faced in Portland stone.

Sadly, only the **Bank of England**, which stores the nation's vast gold reserves in its vaults, actually encourages visitors. Established in 1694 by William III to raise funds for the war against France, the so-called "Grand Old Lady of Threadneedle Street" wasn't erected on its present site until 1734. All that remains of the building on which Sir John Soane spent the best part of his career from 1788 onwards, is the windowless, outer curtain wall, which wraps itself round the 3.5-acre island site. However, you can view a reconstruction of Soane's Bank Stock Office, with its characteristic domed skylight, in the **museum** (Mon–Fri 10am–5pm; free), which has its entrance on Bartholomew Lane.

East of Bank, beyond Bishopsgate, stands Richard Rogers' glitzy **Lloyd's Building**, completed in 1984. A startling array of glass and blue steel pipes – a vertical version of Rogers' own Pompidou Centre – this is easily the most popular of the new City buildings, at least with the general public. Its claims of ergonomic and environmental efficiency have, however, proved to be false, its open-plan trading floor remains extremely unpopular with the workers themselves and the exterior piping is already in need of extensive repairs.

Just south of the Lloyd's building you'll find the picturesque **Leadenhall Market**, whose richly painted, graceful Victorian cast-ironwork dates from 1881. Inside, the traders cater mostly for the lunchtime City crowd, their barrows laden with exotic seafood and game, fine wines, champagne and caviar.

If you walk down Gracechurch Street from Leadenhall Market, you should be able to make out Wren's **Monument** (April–Sept Mon–Fri 10am–5.40pm, Sat & Sun 2–5.40pm; Oct–March Mon–Sat 10am–5.40pm; £1; Monument tube), which was designed by Wren to commemorate the Great Fire of 1666. Crowned with spiky gilded flames, this plain Doric column stands 202 feet high, making it the tallest isolated stone column in the world; if it were laid out flat it would touch the bakery where the Fire started, east of Monument. The bas-relief on the base, now in very bad shape, depicts Charles II and the Duke of York in Roman garb conducting the emergency relief operation. The 311 steps to the viewing gallery once guaranteed an incredible view; nowadays it is dwarfed by the buildings around it.

The Tower of London and around

The **Tower of London** (March–Oct Mon–Sat 9am–6pm, Sun 10am–6pm; Nov–Feb Mon–Sat 9am–5pm, Sun 10am–5pm; £9.50; Tower Hill tube), one of London's main tourist attractions, overlooks the river at the eastern boundary of the old city walls.

Despite all the hype and heritage claptrap, it remains one of London's most remarkable buildings, site of some of the goriest events in the nation's history and somewhere all visitors and Londoners should explore at least once. Chiefly famous as a place of imprisonment and death, it has variously been used as a royal residence, armoury, mint, menagerie, observatory and – a function it still serves – a safe-deposit box for the Crown Jewels. It was also the home of the royal menagerie: the keeper of the king's leopard during the reign of Edward II was paid sixpence a day for the sustenance of the beast, one penny for himself.

Amidst the crush of tourists and the weight of history surrounding the place, it's easy to forget that the Tower is, above all, the most perfectly preserved (albeit heavily restored) medieval fortress in the country. Begun by William the Conqueror as a simple watchtower, much of what's visible today was already in place by the end of the thirteenth century. Before you set off to explore the Tower complex, it's a good idea to get your bearings by taking one of the free **guided tours**, given every thirty minutes by one of the forty-odd **Beefeaters** (officially known as Yeoman Warders), ex-servicemen in Tudor costume, who can get you into areas otherwise inaccessible.

Visitors today enter the Tower along Water Lane, but in times gone by most prisoners were delivered through **Traitors' Gate**, on the waterfront. The nearby **Bloody Tower**, which forms the main entrance to the Inner Ward, is where the twelve-year-old Edward V and his ten-year-old brother were accommodated "for their own safety" in 1483 by their uncle, the future Richard III, and later murdered. It's also where **Sir Walter Raleigh** was imprisoned on three separate occasions, including a thirteen-year stretch.

William's **White Tower**, adorned with corner cupolas in Henry VIII's reign, houses a small sample of the **Royal Armouries** collection, the majority of which now reside in Leeds (see p.569). On the second floor, however, you can visit the **Chapel of St John**, London's oldest church, which is said to have been where Henry VI was buried after his murder in 1471. Today the once highly decorated blocks of pale Norman limestone are starkly unadorned, the chapel's beauty coming from its smooth curves and perfect rounded apse.

Surrounding the White Tower, **Tower Green** was where the executions took place of those traitors lucky enough to be spared being put to death in front of jeering crowds on Tower Hill. A brass plate marks the spot where Lady Jane Grey, Anne Boleyn, Catherine Howard and four other privileged individuals met their end (less fortunate folk were hung, drawn and quartered in front of the mob on nearby Tower Hill). They and other noble Tower prisoners, including Thomas More, are buried in the **Chapel of St Peter-ad-Vincula**, a Tudor church close by the scaffold site, only accessible on guided tours. Prisoners at the **Queen's House**, on the far side of Tower Green, included Lady Jane Grey and Rudolf Hess, after his unexplained parachute jump into Scotland in 1941.

The green is also home to two of the Tower's eight famous **ravens**, their wings clipped so they can't fly away – legend says that the Tower and the kingdom will fall if they do. The birds are descendants of early scavengers attracted by the waste from palace kitchens, and are the latest in a long line protected by royal decree since the reign of Charles II. They even have their own graveyard, in the moat near the ticket barrier.

The castellated Waterloo Barracks, just north of the White Tower, holds the **Crown Jewels**, the majority of which postdate the Commonwealth (1649–60), when many of the royal riches were melted down. These days, the displays are efficient and disappointingly swift – visitors are sped along on moving walkways which allow just 28 seconds' viewing. Look out for the **Imperial State Crown**, sparkling with a 317-carat diamond, a sapphire from a ring said to have been buried with Edward the Confessor, and assorted emeralds, rubies and pearls. This mind-blowing display of wealth includes the three largest cut diamonds in the world, the most famous of which, the **Koh-i-Noor**, is set into a crown made for the Queen Mother in 1937 and is displayed separately near the exit. The crowds here are usually phenomenal, so get here as early as possible.

The Lanthorn and Wakefield towers, on the wall of the inmost ward, have been reconstructed to represent Edward I's medieval palace, although the king only lived here intermittently. A few panels in the **Lanthorn Tower** describe the king's domestic and public life, while the **Wakefield Tower**, the second largest in the complex, re-creates two of the king's private chambers, with period-clad actors on hand to answer questions. A tablet on the floor in the state reception room marks the spot where, it is believed, Henry VI was murdered at prayer by Edward IV during the Wars of the Roses. Candlelight and heavy incense enhance the aura of authenticity.

You can also walk along the eastern section of the walls, beginning at the **Salt Tower**, which features prisoners' graffiti. The **Broad Arrow Tower** is decked out as it would have been when Sir Simon de Burley – tutor to Richard II and later to be beheaded on Tower Hill – took refuge here during the 1381 Peasants' Revolt. The **Martin Tower**, at the far end, now houses an exhibition featuring lots of discarded royal crowns, without their precious stones, or with replicas fitted.

Tower Bridge

Tower Bridge (daily: April–Oct 10am–6.30pm; Nov–March 10am–5.15pm; £5.95; Tower Hill tube) is just over one hundred years old, yet it ranks with Big Ben as the most famous of all London landmarks. Completed in 1894, its neo-Gothic towers are clad in Cornish granite and Portland stone, but conceal a steel frame, which, at the time, represented a considerable engineering achievement, allowing a road crossing that could be raised to give tall ships access to the upper reaches of the Thames. The raising of the bascules (from the French for "see-saw") remains an impressive sight (ring ahead to find out when the next opening is). The elevated walkways linking the summits of the towers (intended for public use) were closed from 1909 to 1982 due to their popularity with prostitutes and the suicidal. You can only visit them now on an overpriced **guided tour**, dubbed the "Tower Bridge Experience", that employs videos and an animatronic chirpy Cockney to describe the history of the bridge.

The East End and Docklands

Few places in London have engendered so many myths as the **East End** (a catch-all title which covers just about everywhere east of the City, but has its heart closest to the latter). Its name is synonymous with slums, sweatshops and crime, as epitomized by antiheroes such as Jack the Ripper and the Kray Twins, but also with the rags-to-riches careers of the likes of Harold Pinter and Vidal Sassoon, and whole generations of Jews who were born in the most notorious of London's cholera-ridden quarters and have now moved to wealthier pastures. Old East Enders will tell you that the area's not what it was – and it's true, as it always has been. The East End is constantly changing as newly arrived immigrants assimilate and move out.

The East End's first immigrants were French Protestant Huguenots, fleeing religious persecution in the late seventeenth century. Within three generations the Huguenots were entirely assimilated, and the Irish became the new immigrant population, but it was the influx of Jews escaping pogroms in eastern Europe and Russia that defined the character of the East End in the second half of the nineteenth century. The area's Jewish population has now dispersed throughout London, though the East End remains at the bottom of the pile; even the millions poured into the **Docklands** development have failed to make much impression on local unemployment and housing problems. Unfortunately, racism is still rife, and is directed, for the most part, against the extensive Bengali community, who came here from the poor rural area of Sylhet in Bangladesh in the 1960s and 1970s.

Most visitors to the East End come for its famous Sunday **markets** since the area is not an obvious place for sightseeing, and certainly no beauty spot – Victorian slum clearances, Hitler's bombs and postwar tower blocks have all left their mark. However, there's plenty more to get out of a visit, including several **Hawksmoor churches**, and the vast **Docklands** redevelopment, which has to be seen to be believed.

Whitechapel and Spitalfields

The districts of **Whitechapel** and, in particular, **Spitalfields**, within sight of the sleek tower blocks of the financial sector, represent the old heart of the East End, where the French Huguenots settled in the seventeenth century, where the Jewish community was at its strongest in the late nineteenth century, and where today's Bengali community eats, sleeps, works and prays. If you visit just one area in the East End, it should be this zone, which preserves mementoes from each wave of immigration.

The easiest approach is from Liverpool Street Station, a short stroll west of **Spitalfields Market**, the strange-looking red-brick and green-gabled market hall, built in 1893 and extended in the 1920s, which forms the centrepiece of the area. The dominant architectural presence in Spitalfields, however, is **Christ Church** (Mon–Fri noon–2.30pm), built between 1714 and 1729 to a characteristically bold design by Nicholas Hawksmoor and now facing the market hall. Best viewed from Brushfield Street, the church's main features are its huge 225-foot-high broach spire and a giant Tuscan portico, raised on steps and shaped like a Venetian window (a central arched opening flanked by two smaller rectangles), a motif repeated in the tower and doors.

Whitechapel Road – as Whitechapel High Street and the Mile End Road are collectively known – is still the East End's main street, shared by all the many races who live in the borough of Tower Hamlets. The East End institution that draws in more outsiders than any other is the **Whitechapel Art Gallery** (Tues & Thurs–Sun 11am–5pm, Wed 11am–8pm; free), a little further up the High Street in a beautiful crenellated 1899 Arts and Crafts building by Charles Harrison Townsend, architect of the similarly audacious Horniman Museum (see p.134). The gallery puts on some of London's most innovative exhibitions of contemporary art, as well as hosting the biennial Whitechapel Open, a chance for local artists to get their work shown to a wider audience.

Just before the point where Whitechapel Road turns into Mile End Road stands the gabled entrance to the former Albion Brewery, where the first bottled brown ale was produced in 1899. Next door lies the **Blind Beggar**, the East End's most famous pub since March 8, 1966, when Ronnie Kray walked into the crowded pub and shot gangland rival George Cornell for calling him a "fat poof". This murder spelled the

---

EAST END SUNDAY MARKETS

Most visitors to the East End come here for the **Sunday markets**. Approaching from Liverpool Street, the first one you come to is **Petticoat Lane**, not one of London's prettiest streets, but one of its longest-running Sunday markets, specializing in cheap (and often pretty tacky) clothing. The authorities renamed the street Middlesex Street in 1830 to avoid the mention of ladies' underwear, though the original name has stuck.

To the north lies **Spitalfields Market**, once the capital's premier wholesale fruit and vegetable market, now specializing in organic food, plus clothes and jewellery. Further east lies **Brick Lane**, heart of the Bengali community, famous for its bric-a-brac Sunday market, wonderful curry houses and non-stop bagel bakery. From Brick Lane's northernmost end, it's a short walk to **Columbia Road**, the city's best market for flowers and plants.

end of the infamous Kray Twins, Ronnie and Reggie, both of whom were sentenced to life imprisonment, though their well-publicized gifts to local charities created a Robin Hood image that still persists in these parts of town.

East End museums

The East End boasts two fascinating museums, both of them open to the public free of charge. The easiest one to get to is the Bethnal Green **Museum of Childhood** (Mon–Thurs & Sat 10am–5.50pm, Sun 2.30–5.50pm; free), situated opposite Bethnal Green tube station. The open-plan wrought-iron hall, originally part of the V&A (see p.124), was transported here in the 1860s to bring art to the East End. The variety of exhibits means that there's something here for everyone from three to ninety-three, but the museum's most frequent visitors are children. The ground floor is best known for its unique collection of antique dolls' houses dating back to 1673. It's a good idea to take a pile of 20p pieces with you to work the automata – Wallace the Lion gobbling up Albert is always a firm favourite. Elsewhere, there are puppets, a jumble of toys, a vast doll collection and excellent temporary exhibitions.

The **Geffrye Museum** (Tues–Sat 10am–5pm, Sun 2–5pm; free; bus #67, #149 or #242 from Liverpool Street tube), housed in a peaceful little enclave of eighteenth-century iron-mongers' almshouses, set back from Kingsland Road, is essentially a furniture museum. A series of period living rooms, ranging from the oak-panelled seventeenth century through refined Georgian and cluttered Victorian, leads to the state-of-the-art New Gallery Extension, housing the new café and the excellent twentieth-century section, with a room devoted to virtually every decade, and temporary exhibitions in the basement.

Docklands

The architectural embodiment of Thatcherism, a symbol of 1980s smash-and-grab culture according to its critics; a blueprint for inner-city regeneration to its free-market supporters – the **Docklands** redevelopment provokes extreme reactions. Despite its catch-all name, however, Docklands is far from homogeneous. Canary Wharf, with its Manhattan-style skyscraper, is only its most visible landmark; industrial-estate sheds and huge swathes of dereliction are more indicative. Wapping, the westernmost district, has retained much of its old Victorian warehouse architecture, while the Royal Docks, further east, remain a relatively undisturbed industrial wasteland.

The docks were originally built from 1802 onwards to relieve congestion on the Thames quays, eventually becoming the largest enclosed cargo dock system in the world. However, competition from the railways and, later, the development of container ships signalled the closure of the docks in the 1960s. In 1981, at the height of the recession, the **London Docklands Development Corporation** (LDDC) was set up and regeneration began in earnest. No one thought the old docks could ever be rejuvenated; the LDDC, on the other hand, predicted a resident population of over 100,000 and a working population twice that. Seventeen years later, the LDDC was wound up having achieved more than many thought possible, and less than some had hoped.

Travelling through on the overhead railway, Docklands comes over as an intriguing open-air design museum, not a place one would choose to live or work – most people stationed here see it as a bleak business-oriented outpost – but a spectacular sight nevertheless. The best way to view Docklands is from one of the pleasure boats that course up and down the Thames, or from the driverless, overhead **Docklands Light Railway** (DLR), which sets off from Bank, or from Tower Gateway, close to Tower Hill tube. Travelcards are valid on the DLR, or you can get a Docklander ticket for £2.50, giving you unlimited travel on the network after 9.30am. If you're heading for Greenwich, and fancy taking a boat back into town, it might be worth considering a Sail & Rail ticket (£7.20), which allows unlimited travel on the DLR, plus the boat trip between Greenwich and Westminster piers.

From St Katharine's Dock to the Isle of Dogs

An alternative to taking the DLR is to walk from Wapping to Limehouse, along the Riverside Walk, which sticks to, or close to, the riverbank. You begin at **St Katharine's Dock**, immediately east of the Tower of London, and the first of the old docks to be renovated way back in the 1970s. The dock's redeeming qualities are the old swing bridges and the boats themselves, many of them beautiful old sailing ships. Continue along desolate **Wapping High Street**, lined with tall brick-built warehouses, most now tastefully converted into yuppie flats, and you will eventually find yourself in **Limehouse**, beyond which lies the Isle of Dogs. The walk is about two miles in length, and will bring you eventually to Westferry DLR station – for details of riverside pubs along the way, see p.153.

The Thames begins a dramatic horseshoe bend at Limehouse, thus creating the **Isle of Dogs**, currently the geographical and ideological heart of the new Docklands, which reaches its apotheosis in **Canary Wharf**, the strip of land in the middle of the former West India Docks, previously a destination for rum and mahogany, later tomatoes and bananas (from the Canary Islands – hence the name). This is the only really busy bit of the new Docklands, best known as home to Britain's tallest building, Cesar Pelli's landmark tower, officially known as **One Canada Square**, which at 800ft is the highest building in Europe after Frankfurt's Messerturm. The world's first skyscraper to be clad in stainless steel, it's an undeniably impressive sight, both from a distance (its flashing pinnacle is a feature of the horizon at numerous points in London) and close up. Unless you work here, however, there is no public access, except to the marble atrium.

The warehouses to the north of Canary Wharf are to be converted into flats, bars, restaurants and a **Docklands Museum** (scheduled to open sometime in 2000), and will be incorporated into a new complex including a thirty-storey tower block and a multiplex cinema. Until this opens, there's little point in getting off the DLR, which cuts right through the middle of the Canary Wharf office buildings under a parabolic steel and glass canopy.

The rest of the Isle of Dogs remains surreally lifeless, an uneasy mix of drab highrises, council estates, warehouses converted into expensive apartments and a lot of new architecture – some of it startling, some of it crass, much of it empty. Stay on the DLR and you will eventually come to the southernmost terminus at **Island Gardens**, starting point for the 1902 foot-tunnel to Greenwich (see p.135) and Christopher Wren's favourite spot from which to contemplate his own masterpieces across the river, the Royal Naval College and Old Royal Observatory.

Lambeth and Southwark

Until well into the seventeenth century, the only reason for north-bank residents to cross the Thames, to what is now **Lambeth** and **Southwark**, was to visit the disreputable Bankside entertainment district around the south end of London Bridge, which lay outside the jurisdiction of the City. South London (a catch-all term for everything south of the river) still has a reputation, among north Londoners at least, as a boring, sprawling, residential district devoid of any local culture or life.

As it turns out, this is not too far from the truth: **Lambeth**, for one, is mostly residential, but along its riverbank lie several important cultural institutions, collectively known as the **South Bank Centre**. Although a mess architecturally, these galleries, theatres and concert halls, plus the Museum of the Moving Image, draw large numbers across the river for night-time entertainment.

There are more sights further east in **Bankside**, home to a reconstruction of Shakespeare's Globe Theatre and the new **Tate Gallery of Modern Art** (due to open in the summer of 2000). Neighbouring **Southwark** also has a range of popular museums around Tooley Street. Further east still, **Butler's Wharf** is a thriving little warehouse development, centred on the excellent **Design Museum**.

The South Bank

In 1951, the South Bank Exhibition, held on derelict land south of the Thames, formed the centrepiece of the **Festival of Britain**, an attempt to revive postwar morale by celebrating the centenary of the Great Exhibition (when Britain really did rule over half the world). The most striking features of the site were the Royal Festival Hall (which still stands), the Ferris wheel (which returned to the South Bank for the millennium), the saucer-shaped Dome of Discovery (inspiration for the current Millennium Dome), and the cigar-shaped Skylon tower.

The festival's success provided the impetus for the eventual creation of the **South Bank Centre**, home to institutions such as the National Theatre and National Film Theatre. Sadly, the South Bank has become London's much unloved culture bunker, a mess of "weatherstained concrete, rain-swept walkways, urine-soaked stairs", as one critic aptly put it. On the plus side, the South Bank is currently under inspired artistic direction and stands at the heart of the capital's arts scene. Its unprepossessing appearance is softened, too, by its riverside location, its avenue of trees, and its occasional buskers and skateboarders.

The South Bank also hosts one of London's highest-profile millennium projects, the **BA London Eye** (formerly known as the Millennium Wheel), set to revolve over the River Thames from the Jubilee Gardens from 2000 onwards. Standing 495 feet high, the Millennium Wheel is the largest Ferris wheel ever built, and a ride in one of its sixty capsules, symbolizing seconds and minutes, will cost £7.45 for a twenty-minute, one-rotation ride (0870 5000 600).

The Museum of the Moving Image

Slotted adroitly under Waterloo Bridge, the **Museum of the Moving Image (MOMI)** (daily 10am–6pm; £6.25; Waterloo tube) covers an impressive amount in its somewhat cramped space, reeling through a spirited history of film and cinema, with actors on hand to enliven the proceedings. It begins with a vast array of optical toys, but the real fun starts in the following rooms, where, among the memorabilia, you can audition for a screen test in a 1920s-style casting session, make your own cartoons in an animation room and watch a shoot on a Hollywood film set, complete with egotistical director.

There's also plenty of opportunity to watch films, often in witty settings: to see the newsreels, for example (including footage of the Hindenburg disaster, Mussolini's pompous posturing and V-Day celebrations), you climb onto the roof of a news van, thus mimicking the logo of the Pathé newsreels. The television section, pandering shamelessly to twenty- and thirty-something Anglo-nostalgia, leads to the bit that's most popular with children, where you get to read the television news and be interviewed by a televisual Barry Norman.

County Hall to the Imperial War Museum

South of the South Bank Centre proper, beyond Jubilee Gardens, stands the colonnaded crescent of **County Hall**, the only truly monumental building in this part of town. Designed to house the London County Council, it was completed in 1933 and enjoyed its greatest moment of fame as the headquarters of the GLC (Greater London Council), abolished by Mrs Thatcher in 1986, leaving London as the only European city without an elected authority. London is due, once more, to get an elected body, and its own mayor, but neither will reside at County Hall, which is now in the hands of a Japanese property company.

Its vast floor space is now home to, among other things, a glorified amusement arcade called Namco Station, a two-hundred-bed Marriott Hotel and, as of 1999, a Football Museum, run by the Premier League. By far the most popular attraction so far, though, is the **London Aquarium** (daily 10am–6pm; £7; Waterloo or Westminster tube), laid out across three floors of the basement. With some super-large tanks, and everything from dog-face puffers to piranhas, this is somewhere that's pretty much guaranteed to please younger kids. The Beach where children can actually stroke the (non-sting) rays is particularly popular. Impressive in scale, the aquarium is fairly conservative in design, however, with no walk-through tanks and only the very briefest of information on any of the fish.

On the south side of Westminster Bridge, in the midst of **St Thomas's Hospital**, on Lambeth Palace Road, is the **Florence Nightingale Museum** (Tues–Sun 10am–5pm; £3.50; Waterloo or Westminster tube), celebrating the woman who revolutionized the nursing profession by establishing the first school of nursing at St Thomas's in 1859. The exhibition hits just the right note, putting the two years she spent in the Crimea in the context of a lifetime of tireless social campaigning.

A short walk south of St Thomas's is the Kentish ragstone church of St Mary-at-Lambeth, which now contains a café and an unpretentious little **Museum of Garden History** (March–Dec Mon–Fri 10.30am–4pm, Sun 10.30am–5pm; free; Lambeth North tube). The graveyard has been transformed into a small **seventeenth-century garden**, where two interesting sarcophagi lurk among the foliage: one belongs to **Captain Bligh**, the commander of the *Bounty* in 1787; the other is a memorial to **John Tradescant**, gardener to James I and Charles I.

Vauxhall, half a mile south of St Mary-at-Lambeth and once famous for its pleasure gardens, is now a bleak traffic-plagued spot, but it harbours the largest tethered helium balloon in the world, behind the tube station in Spring Gardens. The **London Balloon**, or **Big Bob** as it's affectionately known, rises slowly to a height of 400 feet, to provide the capital's only high viewpoint (until the Ferris wheel gets going in 2000). A fifteen-minute ride costs a hefty £12 (Sun–Thurs 10am–dusk, Fri & Sat until midnight; Vauxhall tube).

The domed building at the east end of Lambeth Road, formerly the infamous lunatic asylum of Bethlehem Royal Hospital (better known as Bedlam), is now the **Imperial War Museum** (daily 10am–6pm; £5, free after 4.30pm; Lambeth North, Waterloo or Elephant & Castle tube), by far the best military museum in the capital. The treatment of the subject is impressively wide-ranging and fairly sober, with the main hall's militaristic display of guns, tanks and planes offset by the lower-ground-floor array of documents and images attesting to the human damage of war, including a harrowing section on the liberation of Belsen in 1945. In addition to the static displays, you can walk through re-creations of a World War I trench and a bomb-ravaged street in the Blitz.

Southwark

Southwark, the district ranged around the southern end of London Bridge, was a lively Roman red-light district whose brothels continued to do a thriving illegal trade until 1161 when they were licensed by royal decree. This measure imposed various restrictions on the prostitutes, who could now be fined three shillings for "grimacing to passers-by", and brought in a lot of revenue for the bishops of Winchester, who owned the area for the four centuries after the Norman Conquest. Under the bishops' rule, bull- and bear-baiting, drinking, cockfighting and gambling were also rife, especially on Bankside and although, after 1556, Southwark came under the jurisdiction of the City, it was not subject to its regulations on entertainment. So Southwark remained the pleasure quarter of Tudor and Stuart London, where brothels and other disreputable institutions banned in the City – notably theatres – continued to flourish until the Puritan purges of the 1640s.

Bankside

Bankside, east of Blackfriars Bridge, was the most nefarious street in London in Elizabethan times, thanks to its brothels, bearpits and theatres. Nowadays, the biggest crowds currently to be found along Bankside are milling around a spectacular recon-struction of **Shakespeare's Globe Theatre,** the polygonal playhouse where most of the Bard's later works were first performed. The thatched theatre uses only natural light and the minimum of scenery, and currently puts on shows from mid-May to mid-September. Every half an hour, informative **guided tours** (daily: mid-May to mid-Sept 9am–12.15pm & 2–4pm; rest of year 10am–5pm; £5; London Bridge, Southwark or Blackfriars tube) take you round the theatre itself.

Architecturally, Bankside is now dominated by the austere **Bankside Power Station**. Closed down in 1908, the power station has been redesigned by the Swiss duo Herzog & de Meuron, to become the **Tate Gallery of Modern Art**. The gallery should be open from the summer of 2000 and will house the modern collection from the Tate Gallery at Millbank (see p.92). At the same time, a new pedestrian bridge, designed by Norman Foster, will link the new Tate with the steps of Peter's Hill, below St Paul's Cathedral.

East of Bankside, beyond Southwark Bridge, in the suitably dismal confines of dark and narrow Clink Street, is the **Clink Prison Museum** (daily 10am–4pm; £4; London Bridge tube), built on the site of the former Clink Prison, origin of the expression "in the clink". The prison began as a dungeon for disobedient clerics under the Bishop of Winchester's Palace – the rose window of the palace's Great Hall survives just east of the museum – and later became a dumping ground for heretics, prostitutes and a mot-ley assortment of Bankside lowlife. The exhibition features a handful of prison life tableaux and dwells on the torture and grim conditions within, but, given the rich his-tory of the place, this is a disappointingly lacklustre museum.

In St Mary Overie Dock, round the corner from the Clink, you'll find another timber reconstruction, this time the **Golden Hinde** (daily 10am–7pm; £2.30; London Bridge tube), the galleon in which Sir Francis Drake sailed round the world in 1577–80. The ship is surprisingly small and, with a crew of eighty-plus, conditions must have been cramped to say the least. There's a refreshing lack of interpretive panels, so it's worth paying the little bit extra and getting a guided tour from one of the folk in period garb, who will show you the ropes, so to speak, and demonstrate how to fire a cannon, use the ship's toilet and so forth.

Southwark Cathedral

Close by the Golden Hinde, bang next door to London Bridge, is **Southwark Cathedral**, originally built in the thirteenth and fourteenth centuries as the Augustinian priory church of St Mary Overie. It miraculously survived the nineteenth century, which saw its East End chapel demolished to make way for London Bridge, railways built within a few feet of its tower and some very heavy-handed Victorian restoration. As if in compensation, the church was granted cathedral status in 1905 and has since had a lot of money spent on it. Of the cathedral's original features, the splendid choir is the most striking. Built in 1207, and thus probably the oldest Gothic structure in London, it has a beautiful sixteenth-century stone altar screen. The build-ing houses hundreds of monuments, including one, in the southwest corner of the nave, to the 47 people who died when the *Marchioness* pleasure boat collided with a barge on the Thames in 1989. Others include a thirteenth-century oak effigy of a knight, the brightly painted tomb of poet John Gower, Chaucer's contemporary, and an early twentieth-century memorial to Shakespeare – for whom a birthday service is held here annually. His younger brother Edmund, an actor at the Globe, was buried here in 1607.

Old Operating Theatre Museum and Herb Garret

The most educative and strangest of Southwark's museums is the **Old Operating Theatre Museum and Herb Garret** on St Thomas Street (daily 10am–4pm; £2.50), built in 1821 at the top of a church tower, where the hospital apothecary's herbs were stored. Despite being entirely gore-free, the museum is as stomach-churning as the London Dungeon (see below), for this theatre dates from the pre-anaesthetics era. The surgeons who used this room concentrated on speed and accuracy (most amputations took less than a minute), but there was still a thirty percent mortality rate, many patients simply dying of shock, many more from bacterial infection, about which very little was known. This is clear from the design of the theatre itself, which has no sink and is made almost entirely of mahogany and pine, which would have harboured bacteria even after vigorous cleaning. Sawdust was sprinkled on the floor to soak up the blood and prevent it dripping onto the heads of the worshippers in the church below.

The London Dungeon, Britain at War and HMS Belfast

A walk past the railway bridges and warehouses of Tooley Street brings you round the back of London Bridge train station to the cold dark vault of the **London Dungeon** (daily: April–Sept 10am–6.30pm; Oct–March closes 5.30pm; £8.95; London Bridge tube), a crowd-pleasing show playing on the foreigners' fascination with English Gothic horror. Among the life-size waxwork tableaux include a hanging at Tyburn gallows, a man being hung, drawn and quartered and one being boiled alive, the general hysteria being boosted by actors dressed as top-hatted Victorian vampires pouncing out of the darkness. Queues form for the "River of Death" boat ride, an historical journey to your execution (not for the faint-hearted); this is immediately followed up by the "Jack the Ripper Experience", an exploitative and voyeuristic trawl through post-mortem photos and wax mock-ups of the victims; lastly you pass through the rather limp "Theatre of the Guillotine".

A little further east on Tooley Street is **Winston Churchill's Britain at War** (daily: April–Sept 10am–5.30pm; Oct–March closes 4.30pm; £5.95; London Bridge tube), which, despite its jingoistic name, is an illuminating exhibition of every aspect of London life during the Blitz. It begins with a rickety elevator ride down to a mock-up of a tube air-raid shelter, a prelude to hundreds of sometimes bizarre wartime artefacts. You can sit in an Anderson shelter beneath the chilling whistle of the doodlebugs, tune in to contemporary radio broadcasts, and as a grand finale walk through the chaos of a just-bombed street – pitch dark, noisy, smoky and hot.

There's more World War II history, from a more aggressive angle, at **HMS Belfast** (daily: March–Oct 10am–6pm; Nov–Feb closes 5pm; £4.70; London Bridge tube), a huge cruiser permanently moored between London Bridge and Tower Bridge. Armed with six torpedoes and six-inch guns with a range of over fourteen miles, the *Belfast* spent over two years of the war in the Royal Naval shipyards, after being hit by a mine in the Firth of Forth at the beginning of hostilities. Decommissioned after the Korean War, the ship contains tired-looking historical exhibitions, but the maze of cabins, spread across seven decks, is fun to explore.

Butler's Wharf

In contrast to the brash offices on Tooley Street, **Butler's Wharf**, east of Tower Bridge, has retained its historical character. **Shad Thames**, the narrow street at the back of Butler's Wharf, has kept the wrought-iron overhead gangways by which the porters used to transport goods from the wharves to the warehouses further back from the river, and is one of the most atmospheric alleyways in the whole of Bermondsey. The eight-storey **Butler's Wharf Warehouse** itself, with its shops and restaurants, forms part of Terence Conran's commercial empire and caters for a monied clientele, but the wide promenade on the riverfront is open to the public.

The big attraction of Butler's Wharf is Conran's superb riverside **Design Museum** (daily 10am–6pm; £3.50; Tower Hill or Bermondsey tube), at the eastern end of Shad Thames. The stylish white edifice, a Bauhaus-like conversion of an old 1950s warehouse, is the perfect showcase for an unpretentious display of mass-produced industrial design from classic cars to Tupperware. The constantly evolving Collections Gallery is on the top floor; the first-floor Review Gallery acts as a showcase for new ideas, including prototypes and failures, as well as hosting temporary exhibitions on important designers, movements or single products. The small coffee-bar in the foyer is a great place to relax and there's a pricey Conran restaurant on the top floor.

The **Bramah Tea and Coffee Museum** (daily 10am–6pm; £3.50), housed in an old tea warehouse, Tamarind House, behind the Design Museum on Maguire Street, is not quite in the same league as its neighbour. Still, it's a fun museum and well worth a visit. Founded in 1992 by Edward Bramah, who began his career on an African tea garden in 1950, the museum's emphasis is firmly on tea. There's an impressive array of teapots, from Wedgwood to novelty, and coffee machines, from huge percolator siphons to espresso machines spanning the twentieth century.

Hyde Park, Kensington and Chelsea

Hyde Park, together with its westerly extension, Kensington Gardens, covers a distance of two miles from Speakers' Corner in the northeast to **Kensington Palace** in the southwest. At the end of your journey, you've made it to one of London's most exclusive districts, the Royal Borough of Kensington and Chelsea. Other districts go in and out of fashion, but this area has been in vogue ever since royalty moved into Kensington Palace in the late seventeenth century.

Aside from the shops around Harrods in Knightsbridge, however, the popular tourist attractions lie in **South Kensington**, where three of London's top museums – the **Victoria and Albert**, **Natural History** and **Science museums** – stand on land bought with the proceeds of the Great Exhibition of 1851. **Chelsea**'s character is slightly more bohemian; in the 1960s, the **King's Road**, the district's main thoroughfare, carved out its reputation as London's catwalk, while in the late 1970s it was the epicentre of the punk explosion. Nothing so risqué goes on in Chelsea now, though its residents like to think of themselves as rather more artistic and intellectual than the purely monied types of Kensington.

Hyde Park

Seized from the Church by Henry VIII to satisfy his desire for yet more hunting grounds, **Hyde Park** was first opened to the public by James I and soon became a fashionable gathering place for the beau monde, who rode round the circular drive known as the Ring, pausing to gossip and admire each other's equipage. Hangings, muggings and duels, the Great Exhibition of 1851 and numerous public events have all taken place in Hyde Park – and it is still a popular gathering point or destination for political demonstrations. For most of the time, however, the park is simply a leisure ground – a wonderful open space which allows you to lose all sight of the city beyond a few persistent tower blocks.

Located at the treeless northeastern corner of the park, **Marble Arch** was originally erected in 1828 as a triumphal entry to Buckingham Palace, but now lies stranded on a ferociously busy traffic island at the west end of Oxford Street. This is the most historically charged spot in Hyde Park, as it marks the site of **Tyburn gallows**, the city's main public execution spot until 1783. It's also the location of **Speakers' Corner**, once an entertaining and peculiarly English Sunday tradition, featuring an assembly of characterful speakers and hecklers – now, sadly, a forum for soap-box religious extremists.

A better place to enter the park is at **Hyde Park Corner**, the southeast corner, where **Constitution Arch** stands in the midst of another of London's busiest traffic interchanges. Erected in 1828 to commemorate Wellington's victories in the Napoleonic Wars, the arch originally served as the northern gate into Buckingham Palace grounds. Close by stands **Apsley House** (Tues–Sun 11am–5pm; £3; Hyde Park Corner tube), Wellington's London residence, now a museum to the the "Iron Duke". Unless you're a keen fan of the Duke, the highlight of the museum is the art collection; much of it used to belong to the King of Spain. Among the best pieces are works by de Hooch, van Dyck, Velázquez, Goya, Rubens and Murillo, displayed in the Waterloo Gallery on the first floor. The famous, more than twice life-size, nude statue of Napoleon by Antonio Canova stands at the foot of the main staircase.

The park is divided in two by the **Serpentine Lake**, which has a popular **Lido** (May–Sept daily 10am–6pm; £2.50) on its south bank. By far the prettiest section of the lake, though, is the upper section known as the **Long Water**, which narrows until it reaches a group of four fountains, laid out symmetrically in front of an Italianate summerhouse designed by Wren.

The western half of the park is officially known as **Kensington Gardens** and is, strictly speaking, a separate entity, though you hardly notice the change. Its two most popular attractions are the **Serpentine Gallery** (daily 10am–6pm; free), which has a reputation for lively, and often controversial, contemporary art exhibitions, and the richly decorated Gothic **Albert Memorial**, clearly visible to the west. Erected in 1876, the memorial is as much a hymn to the glorious achievements of Britain as to its subject, Queen Victoria's husband (who died of typhoid in 1861). Recently restored to his former gilded glory, Albert occupies the central canopy, clutching a catalogue for the 1851 Great Exhibition that he helped organize.

The Exhibition's most famous feature, the gargantuan glasshouse of the Crystal Palace, no longer exists, but the profits were used to buy a large tract of land south of the park, now home to South Kensington's remarkable cluster of **museums and colleges**, plus the vast **Royal Albert Hall**, a splendid iron-and-glass-domed concert hall, with an exterior of red brick, terracotta and marble that became the hallmark of South Ken architecture. The hall is venue for Europe's most democratic music festival, the Henry Wood Promenade Concerts, better known as the **Proms**, which take place from July to September, with standing-room tickets for as little as £3.

Kensington Palace

On the western edge of Kensington Gardens stands **Kensington Palace** (May–Sept daily 9.45am–5pm; £6; High Street Kensington tube), a modestly proportioned Jacobean brick mansion bought by William and Mary in 1689, and the chief royal residence for the next fifty years. KP, as it's fondly known in royal circles, is, of course, best known today as the place where Princess Diana lived up until her death in 1997. It was, in fact, the official London residence of both Charles and Di until the couple formally separated. In the weeks following Diana's death, literally millions of flowers, mementoes, poems and gifts were deposited at the gates to the south of the palace.

Visitors don't get to see Diana's apartments, which were on the west side of the palace, where various minor royals still live. Instead, they get to view some of the Queen's frocks in the **Royal Ceremonial Dress Collection** and are then given an audioguide which takes them round the sparsely furnished state apartments. The highlights are the trompe l'oeil ceiling paintings by William Kent, in particular the Cupola Room, and the oil paintings in the King's Gallery. En route, you also get to see the tastelessly decorated rooms in which the future Queen Victoria spent her unhappy childhood. To recover from the above, take tea in the exquisite **Orangery** (daily: Easter–Sept 10am–6pm; Oct–Easter 10am–4pm), to the north of the palace.

The Victoria and Albert Museum

The **Victoria and Albert Museum** (daily 10am–5.45pm; £5, free after 4.30pm; South Kensington tube) began its days as the Museum of Manufactures, a gathering of objects from the Great Exhibition and a motley collection of plastercasts – it being Albert's intention to rekindle Britain's industrial dominance by inspiring factory workers, students and craftspeople with examples of excellence in applied art and design. This notion disappeared swiftly as exotica poured in from around the world, and today, in addition to being the world's finest collection of decorative arts, the museum encompasses sculpture, musical instruments, paintings and photography, all beautifully, if rather haphazardly, displayed across a seven-mile, four-storey maze of halls and corridors. As if all this were not enough, the V&A's temporary shows are among the best in Britain, ranging from surveys of specialized areas of craft and technology to overviews of entire cultures.

Floor plans from the information desks at the **main entrance** on Cromwell Road and the **side entrance** on Exhibition Road can help you decide on which areas to concentrate. There are also free guided orientation tours every day; enquire at the main information desk. Like all London's major museums, the V&A also has big plans for the millennium, with a £75 million multi-faceted extension, known as the "**Spiral**" and designed by the controversial Polish-born architect Daniel Libeskind, in the pipeline.

The ground floor

The ground floor holds the best of the V&A. The **Raphael cartoons** (room 48a), seven full-colour designs for tapestries intended for the Sistine Chapel, are to the left of the main entrance and beyond the museum shop. These drawings, reproduced in countless tapestries and engravings in the seventeenth and eighteenth centuries, were probably more familiar and influential than any of the artist's paintings. Across the hall, the excellent **dress collection** (room 40) starts at 1540 and comes right up-to-date with clothes by contemporary British designers such as Paul Smith, Helen Storey and Vivienne Westwood.

There follows a string of superb eastern galleries. The Nehru Gallery (room 41), for example – which shows only a fraction of the biggest assembly of **Indian art** outside the subcontinent – features an exquisitely carved white jade wine cup belonging to the Emperor Shah Jahan, a golden chair that belonged to Ranjit Singh, all manner of jewels, sandstone screens and delicate watercolours, not to mention Tippoo's Tiger, a life-size wooden automaton devouring an officer of the East India Company. Next comes the **Islamic gallery** (room 42), a dramatic gathering of vivid blue tiles and carved wooden pulpits, dominated by the stupendous sixteenth-century Ardabil carpet and the exquisite "Chelsea" carpet, bought in Chelsea but of unknown origin.

The **Medieval Treasury** (room 43), full of reliquaries, religious sculpture and other devotional items, including the Norman masterpiece called the Gloucester candlestick, is adjacent to the **Chinese Art** collection (room 44), which ranges from green-tinged Shang bronzes and Tang horses to ceramics produced in the Cultural Revolution. Next door, the most intriguing objects in the understated **Japanese room** (room 45), among all the silk, lacquer and samurai armour, are the tiny carved jade and marble *netsuke* (belt toggles), portraying such quirky subjects as "spider on aubergine" and "starving dog on a bed of leaves".

Turn right at the main information desk and you'll arrive at the **sculpture and architecture** gallery (rooms 50a & 50b), with its array of funerary monuments and portrait busts. The statue of Handel, created in 1738, was highly radical in its day, showing the composer slouching in inspired disarray, one shoe hanging from his foot. Also here is the original plaster model for the tomb of Victoria and Albert, on which they both appear to be 42 years old (the age Albert died) – Albert is raised slightly higher than the Queen, in accordance with her wishes.

Passing from here through the minimalist gallery of **Korean art**, where you are encouraged to touch one of the huge ceramic bowls, you come to the two enormous **Cast Courts** (rooms 46a & 46b), which were created so that ordinary Londoners, who couldn't afford to travel, would be able to experience the glories of classical and ancient art. Even today, the rooms, still painted in heavy Victorian red and green, are an astonishing sight – a life-size replica of Michelangelo's *David* towers opposite Donatello's smaller bronze of the same subject; the cast of the colossal Trajan's Column, from the forum in Rome, is sliced in half to fit in the room; while the rest of the space is crammed with full-scale replicas of the doors of Hildesheim cathedral, Spanish altars, the pulpit of Pisa's cathedral and scores of other sculptural masterpieces. An interesting little gallery (room 46) between the two cast rooms is lined with **fakes and forgeries**, among them a "fourteenth-century" wooden oratory which the museum bought in good faith in 1912, only to be informed it was a fake by the carpenter's son.

Most of the remainder of the ground floor is given over to the **Italian Renaissance** (rooms 12–20), including a room of Donatello and his followers. Whatever you do, however, don't miss the museum's new **Canon Photography Gallery** (room 38), nor the original refreshment rooms at the back of the main galleries. The eastern **Poynter Room**, a wash of decorative blue tiling, is where the hoi polloi ate; the dark green **Morris Room**, with its Pre-Raphaelite panels, accommodated a better class of diner – in between is the largest and grandest of the rooms, the **Gamble Room**, richly decorated with Minton tiles and now, once more, a cake and coffee halt.

The upper floors

If you go up to the **first floor** you come to a series of rooms covering **Britain 1500 to 1750** (rooms 52–58) and featuring a restored music room, Spitalfields silks and Huguenot silver, an early seventeenth-century oak-panelled interior thought to have been James I's hunting lodge, and the legendary Great Bed of Ware, a king-sized oak monstrosity mentioned by Shakespeare and Ben Jonson and thought to have belonged to Edward IV. Beyond here, the **Twentieth-century Galleries** (rooms 70–74) make a diffident attempt to address contemporary questions of design, ranging from Constructivist fabrics to Olivetti typewriters and Swatch watches.

Beyond the refurbished **Silver Galleries**, which house a dazzling display of silverwork from the medieval to modern, you come to a dimly lit room, hung with medieval tapestries, and the exemplary **Textile Study Rooms** (nos 95–100), displaying all manner of lace, Danish cottons, Chinese damask and robes from Palestine and Afghanistan. The heavily-guarded **jewellery** collection (rooms 91–93) is equally splendid, sparkling with Egyptian amulets, Celtic chokers, Roman snake bracelets, precious gems and 1960s perspex bangles.

There are more works from **Britain 1750–1900** on the **second floor** (rooms 118–126), with a Chippendale bed, a plaster model of the Albert Memorial and furniture shown at the Great Exhibition. A room devoted to William Morris is adorned with his wallpaper, carpets and tiles, as well as furniture designed by his followers, and the collection comes up-to-date with a small selection of Henry Moore sculptures. Lastly, also on the second floor, there's the high-tech **glass gallery** (room 131), with touch-screen computers and a spectacular, modern glass staircase and balustrade.

The **top floor** is given almost exclusively to pottery and earthenware, with Far Eastern ceramics, European porcelain and Islamic tiles, but is often closed in the summer.

The Henry Cole Wing

The **Henry Cole Wing**, named after the museum's first director, can easily be overlooked, as its main entrance is on Exhibition Road and it's only linked to the rest of the building on the ground floor. Highlights here include the **Frank Lloyd Wright** gallery on level 2, centred on an office created by the architect for a Pittsburgh department store owner – a typically organic design in luxuriant wood. Also on this floor is the **European ornament** gallery, demonstrating the influences and fashions in decoration of all kinds: antiquities, Rococo figurines and architectural plans share space with 1920s cotton hangings, inspired by Howard Carter's discovery of Tutankhamen's tomb, and kitsch 1950s china.

Portrait miniatures by Holbein, Hilliard and others feature on level 4, the rest of which is, mostly, taken up with nineteenth-century oil paintings, densely hung in the manner of their period. The largest collection of Swiss landscape paintings outside Switzerland and sentimental Victorian genre works are unlikely to pull in the crowds, but persevere and you'll discover Carracciolo's *Panorama of Rome*, paintings by the Barbizon School, an Arts and Crafts piano, a Burne-Jones sideboard and several Pre-Raphaelite works. Level 6 is largely devoted to the paintings of **John Constable**, four hundred of whose works were left to the museum by his daughter. The finished works include *Salisbury Cathedral* and *Dedham Mill*, and there are studies for the *Hay Wain* and *Leaping Horse* plus a whole host of his alfresco cloud studies and sketches. In addition, there's an impressive collection of statues by **Rodin**, most of them donated by the sculptor himself in 1914.

The Science Museum

Established as a technological counterpart to the V&A, the **Science Museum**, on Exhibition Road (daily 10am–6pm; £6.50, free after 4.30pm; South Kensington tube), is undeniably impressive, filling seven floors with items drawn from every conceivable area of science, including space travel, telecommunications, time measurement, chemistry, computing, photography and medicine. Keen to dispel the enduring image of museums devoted to its subject as boring and full of dusty glass cabinets, the Science Museum is gradually updating its galleries with more interactive displays and puts on daily demonstrations to show that not all science teaching has to be deathly dry.

The real problem, though, is that, for a science museum, the whole place remains a long way from the cutting edge of technology. All this is set to change in the summer of 2000, with the opening of the new **Wellcome Wing**, which aims to keep its displays up-to-date with the latest in computer technology. In the meantime, there's considerable disruption on the ground floor, where the **Power, Space and Transport** exhibition, charting British innovation during the Industrial Revolution, resides.

The **Launch Pad** on the first floor makes a good attempt to present lively, hands-on demonstrations of basic scientific principles and is usually mobbed by kids. Its success has spawned further hands-on galleries in the basement: the "Garden", aimed at 3- to 6-year-olds, and the "Things", for 7- to 11-year-olds. More educative by half, however, is the **Food for Thought** exhibition: interactive displays on nutrition, an exercise bicycle for kids who need to pedal off excess energy and possibly the healthiest branch of *McDonald's* in the world (it doesn't serve food). There's another spectacular new permanent gallery on the first floor, called the **Challenge of Materials**, with some wacky exhibits, including a pair of chocolate shoes, a steel wedding dress and a Bakelite coffin.

One of the most educative and fascinating sections of the whole museum is the **Science and Art of Medicine** gallery, tucked away right on the top floor. Using an anthropological approach, this is a visual and cerebral feast, galloping through ancient medicine, medieval and Renaissance pharmacy, alchemy, quack doctors, royal healers, astrology and military surgery. Offbeat artefacts include African fetishes, an Egyptian mummified head, an eighteenth-century Florentine model of a female torso giving birth, and George Washington's dentures.

The Natural History Museum

Alfred Waterhouse's purpose-built mock-Romanesque colossus ensures the **Natural History Museum** (Mon–Sat 10am–5.50pm, Sun 11am–5.50pm; £6, free after 4.30pm; South Kensington tube) its status as London's most handsome museum. Caught up, without huge public funds, in the current enthusiasm for museum redesign and accessibility, the contents are a mishmash of truly imaginative exhibits slotted in among others little changed since the museum's opening in 1881.

The main entrance brings you straight into the Central Hall of the **Life Galleries**, dominated by a plaster cast skeleton of a Diplodocus. The "side chapels" are filled with wonders of the natural world – the largest egg, a sabre-tooth tiger – but it's the **dinosaur gallery** that pulls in the crowds, a show of massive-jawed skeletons and models much enlivened by a stimulating exhibition on Tyrannosaurus Rex and his pea-brained cronies. Best of all is the grisly life-size animatronic tableau of two reptiles tearing apart a Tenontosaurus, with much roaring, slurping and oozing blood.

The other firm favourite with kids is the insect room, known as **Creepy-crawlies**, with its giant models of bugs, arachnids and crustaceans, plus real-life displays on the life-cycle of the house fly and other unlovely creatures. Opposite the creepy-crawlies is the entrance to the high-tech **ecology gallery**, a child-friendly exhibition with a serious message, only slightly marred by the fact it's sponsored by British Petroleum. The rest of the museum, on the upper floors, is more old-fashioned, and you're best off heading across to the former Geological Museum, now known as the **Earth galleries**, whose main entrance is on Exhibition Road.

From the central hall, an escalator takes you through a revolving, partially formed globe to "**The Power Within**", a big exhibition on volcanoes and other acts of God. The most popular section is the slightly tasteless Kobe earthquake simulator, where you enter a Japanese supermarket and see the soy sauce bottles wobble while watching an in-store video of the real event. On the other side of the same floor is **Restless Surface**, an interactive display on the earth's elements, soil and rock erosion and, of course, global warming. Other new galleries worth exploring include **Earth's Treasury**, a dimly lit high-tech display of lustrous minerals and crystals, gemstones and jewels.

Kensington

Shopper-thronged **Kensington High Street** is dominated architecturally by the twin presences of Sir George Gilbert Scott's neo-Gothic church of **St Mary Abbots**, whose 250-foot spire makes it London's tallest parish church, and the Art Deco colossus of Barkers department store.

Kensington's sights are mostly hidden away in the backstreets, the one exception being the **Commonwealth Institute** (☎0171/603 4535), housed in a bold 1960s building set back from the High Street. The whole place is currently undergoing a massive restoration and refurbishment programme, aiming to re-open fully in 2000 as a rather more up-to-date, interactive museum.

Two paths along the side of the Commonwealth Institute lead to densely wooded **Holland Park**, the former grounds of a Jacobean mansion, whose east wing alone still stands. Theatrical and musical performances are staged here throughout the summer, and several formal gardens surround the house, most notably the Japanese-style Kyoto Gardens.

A number of wealthy Victorian artists rather self-consciously founded an artists' colony in the streets that lie between the High Street and Holland Park. The most remarkable is **Leighton House** at 12 Holland Park Rd (Mon–Sat 11am–5.30pm; free; Kensington High Street tube). "It will be opulence, it will be sincerity", Lord

Leighton opined before starting work on the house in the 1860s – he later became President of the Royal Academy and was ennobled on his deathbed. The big attraction is the domed Arab Hall, decorated with Saracen tiles, gilded mosaics and woodwork drawn from all over the Islamic world. The other rooms are less spectacular but, in compensation, are hung with paintings by Lord Leighton and his Pre-Raphaelite friends.

East of the Commonwealth Institute, two blocks north of the High Street, is **Linley Sambourne House**, 18 Stafford Terrace (March–Oct Wed 10am–4pm, Sun 2–5pm; £3), where the highly successful *Punch* cartoonist lived until his death in 1910. A grand, though fairly ordinary, stuccoed terrace house by Kensington standards, it's less a tribute to the artist and more a showpiece for the Victorian Society, which maintains the house in all its cluttered, late Victorian excess.

Knightsbridge and Harrods

Knightsbridge is irredeemably snobbish, revelling in its reputation as the swankiest shopping area in London, largely through **Harrods** on Brompton Road (Mon, Tues & Sat 10am–6pm, Wed–Fri 10am–7pm; Knightsbridge tube). London's most famous department store started out as a family-run grocery store in 1849, with a staff of two. The current 1905 terracotta building is now owned by the Egyptian Mohammed Al Fayed and employs in excess of 3000 staff. Tourists flock to Harrods – it's thought to be the city's third top tourist attraction – though much of what the shop stocks you can buy more cheaply if you can do without the Harrods carrier bag.

The store does, however, have a few sections that are architectural sights in their own right, in particular the Food Hall, with its exquisite Arts and Crafts tiling, and the Egyptian Hall, with its pseudo-hieroglyphs and sphinxes. The Egyptian escalators are an added attraction, now that the Di and Dodi fountain is in place, but don't bother taking them to the first-floor "washrooms", unless you want to pay £1 for the privilege of relieving yourself. Note, too, that the store has a draconian dress code: no shorts, no ripped jeans, no vest T-shirts and no backpacks.

Chelsea

It wasn't until the latter part of the nineteenth century that **Chelsea** began to earn its reputation as London's very own Left Bank. Its household fame, however, came through the role of the King's Road as the unofficial catwalk of the "Swinging Sixties". The road remained a fashion parade for hippies, too, and in the Jubilee Year of 1977 it witnessed the birth of punk, masterminded from a shop called Sex, run by Vivienne Westwood and Malcolm McLaren. The posey cafés and boutiques still persist, but these days the area has a more subdued feel, with high rents and house prices keeping things staid, and interior design shops rather than avant-garde fashion the order of the day.

The area's other aspect, oddly enough considering its boho reputation, is a military one. For among the most nattily attired of all those parading down the King's Road are the scarlet- or navy-blue-clad Chelsea Pensioners, army veterans from the nearby **Royal Hospital** (Mon–Sat 10am–noon & 2–4pm, Sun 2–4pm; free; Sloane Square tube), founded by Charles II in 1681. The hospital's plain, red-brick wings and grassy courtyards became a blueprint for institutional and collegiate architecture all over the English-speaking world.

The concrete bunker next door to the Royal Hospital, on Royal Hospital Road, houses the **National Army Museum** (daily 10am–5.30pm; free; Sloane Square tube). The militarily obsessed are unlikely to be disappointed by the succession of uniforms and medals, but there is very little here for non-enthusiasts. The temporary exhibitions staged on the ground floor are the museum's strong point, but overall it's a disappointing museum – you're better off visiting the infinitely superior Imperial War Museum (see p.119).

Cheyne Walk

The quiet riverside locale of **Cheyne Walk** (pronounced "chainy") drew artists and writers here in great numbers during the nineteenth century. Since the building of the Embankment and the increase in the volume of traffic, however, the character of this peaceful haven has been lost. Novelist Henry James, who lived at no. 21, used to take "beguiling drives" in his wheelchair along the Embankment; today, he'd be hospitalized in the process.

The chief reason to come here nowadays is to visit the **Chelsea Physic Garden** (April–Oct Wed 2–5pm & Sun 2–6pm; £3.50; Sloane Square tube), which marks the beginning of Cheyne Walk. Founded in 1673, this small walled garden is the oldest botanical garden in the country after Oxford's. At the entrance (on Swan Walk) you can pick up a map of the garden with a list of the month's most interesting flowers and shrubs, whose labels are slightly more forthcoming than the usual terse Latinate tags. The garden also has an excellent tea house, serving tea and delicious home-made cakes.

It's also worth popping into the nearby **Chelsea Old Church** (daily 9.30am–1pm & 2–4.30pm), halfway down Cheyne Walk, where Thomas More built his own private chapel in the south aisle. The church was badly bombed in the last war, but an impressive number of monuments were retrieved from the rubble and continue to adorn the church's interior.

A short distance inland from Cheyne Walk, at 24 Cheyne Row, is **Carlyle's House** (April–Oct Wed–Sun 11am–5pm; £3.20; NT; Sloane Square tube), where the historian Thomas Carlyle set up home, having moved down from his native Scotland in 1834. The house became a museum just fifteen years after Carlyle's death and is a typically dour Victorian abode, kept much as the Carlyles would have had it: the historian's hat still hanging in the hall, his socks in the chest of drawers. The top floor contains the garret study where Carlyle tried in vain to escape the din of the neighbours' noisy roosters in order to complete his final magnum opus on Frederick the Great.

Notting Hill

In the 1950s **Notting Hill** was described as "a massive slum, full of multi-occupied houses, crawling with rats and rubbish", and was populated by offshoots of the Soho vice and crime rackets. These insalubrious dwellings became home to a large contingent of Afro-Caribbean immigrants, who had to compete for jobs and living space with the area's similarly downtrodden white residents. Now, the region has been gentrified, with richer folk having taken over large houses in the leafy crescents and trendy bars and restaurants springing up all over.

Nowadays, Notting Hill is best known for two things – the **Carnival** (see below) and **Portobello Road Market**, a mish-mash of stalls selling anything from valuable antiques to junky bric-a-brac and West Indian vegetables. The initial stretch of London's most popular market contains a mixture of overpriced, touristy stalls and some genuine shops selling classy antiques. In its lower stretches the market gets a lot more funky and the emphasis switches to street clothes and jewellery, odd trinkets, records and books.

Within easy walking distance of Portobello Road, on the other side of the railway tracks, gasworks and canal, is **Kensal Green Cemetery** (daily: April–Sept

Notting Hill Carnival began unofficially in 1959 as a response to the the previous year's race riots. In 1965, Carnival took to the streets and has grown into the world's biggest street festival outside Rio, with an estimated one million revellers turning up each August bank holiday. During the 1960s, it was little more than a few church hall events and a carnival parade, inspired by that of Trinidad – home of many of the area's immigrants. Today the carnival still belongs to West Indians (from all parts of the city), but there are participants, too, from London's Latin American and Asian communities, and, of course, everyone turns out to watch the bands and parades, and hang out.

The main sights of Carnival are the costume parades, known as the *mas* (masquerades), which take place on the Sunday (for kids' groups) and Monday (adults) from around 10am until late afternoon. The processions consist of floats, drawn by trucks, with costume themes and steel bands – the "pans" which are one of the chief sounds of the carnival (and have their own contest on the Saturday). The parade makes its way around a three-mile route, starting at the top end of Ladbroke Grove, heading south under the Westway, then turning into Westbourne Grove, before looping north again via Chepstow Road, Great Western Road and Kensal Road. In addition to the parades, there are three or four stages for live music – Portobello Green and Powis Square are regular venues – where you can catch reggae, ragga, jungle, a bit of hip-hop and maybe Caribbean soca. And everywhere you go, between Westbourne Grove and the Westway, there are sound systems on the street, blasting out reggae and black dance sounds.

Over the last few years, Carnival has been fairly relaxed, considering the huge numbers of people it attracts. However, this is not an event for you if you are at all bothered by crowds – you can be wedged stationary during the parades – and very loud music. It is worth taking more than usual care about crime, too: leave your camera and jewellery at home, and just bring enough money for the day, as pickpockets turn up from all over. As far as safety goes, don't worry unduly about the media's horror stories; if there's going to be any trouble, it tends to come after 7pm each day, when the carnival proper winds down and the police look to disperse the sound systems. If you feel at all uneasy, head home early.

Getting to and from Carnival is an event in itself. Ladbroke Grove tube station is closed for the duration, while Notting Hill Gate and Westbourne Park are open only for incoming visitors. The nearest fully operative tube stations are Latimer Road and Royal Oak. Alternatively, there's a whole network of buses running between most points of London and Notting Hill Gate.

8am–6pm; Oct–March 9am–5pm; free), opened in 1833 and still a functioning cemetery. Graves of the more famous incumbents – Thackeray, Trollope and the Brunels – are less interesting architecturally than those arranged on either side of the Centre Avenue, which leads from the easternmost entrance on Harrow Road (Kensal Rise tube).

Regent's Park and Camden

Regent's Park, framed by Nash-designed architecture and home of London Zoo, is one of London's finest parks. Within easy walking distance, to the northeast is **Camden Town**, whose vast weekend market has now become one of the city's biggest tourist attractions – a warren of stalls selling street fashion, books, records and ethnic goods.

REGENT'S CANAL BY BOAT

Three companies run boat services on the Regent's Canal between Camden (Camden Town tube) and Little Venice (Warwick Avenue tube), stopping off at London Zoo on the way and passing through the Maida Hill tunnel en route. The Jenny Wren (Easter–Oct; ☎0171/485 4433) starts off at Camden, while Jason's (Easter–Oct; ☎0171/286 3428) starts off at Little Venice, and the London Waterbus Company (year round; ☎0171/482 2660) sets off from both places. Whichever you choose, you can board at either end; tickets cost around £5–6 return and journey time is 35–45 minutes one-way.

Those interested in the history of the canal should head off to the **London Canal Museum** (Tues–Sun 10am–4.30pm; £2.50), on the other side of York Way, down New Wharf Road, ten minutes' walk from King's Cross Station.

Regent's Park

As with almost all of London's royal parks, we have Henry VIII to thank for **Regent's Park**, which he confiscated from the Church for yet more hunting grounds. However, it wasn't until the reign of the Prince Regent (later George IV) that the park began to take its current form. According to the masterplan, devised by John Nash in 1811, the park was to be girded by a continuous belt of terraces, and sprinkled with a total of 56 villas, including a magnificent pleasure palace for the Prince himself, which would be linked by Regent Street to Carlton House in St James's. The plan was never fully realized, due to lack of funds, but enough was built to create something of the idealized garden city that Nash and the Prince Regent envisaged.

To appreciate the special quality of Regent's Park, take a closer look at the architecture, starting with the Nash terraces, which form a near-unbroken horseshoe of cream-coloured stucco around the Outer Circle. Within the Inner Circle is the Open Air Theatre, which puts on summer performances of Shakespeare, opera and ballet, and **Queen Mary's Gardens**, by far the prettiest section of the park. A large slice of the gardens is taken up with a glorious rose garden, featuring some 400 varieties, surrounded by a ring of ramblers.

Clearly visible on the western edge of the park is the shiny copper dome and minaret of the **London Central Mosque**, an entirely appropriate addition given the Prince Regent's taste for the Orient. Non-Muslim visitors are welcome to look in at the information centre and glimpse inside the hall of worship, which is packed out with a diversity of communities for the lunchtime Friday prayers.

The northeastern corner of the park is occupied by **London Zoo** (daily: March–Oct 10am–5.30pm; Nov–Feb 10am–4pm; £8.50; Camden Town, Regent's Park or Great Portland Street tube), founded in 1826. It may not be the most uplifting place for animal lovers, but kids will love the place, especially the children's enclosure, where they can actually handle the animals, and the regular "Animals in Action" displays in the Lifewatch House. The zoo boasts some striking architectural features, too, most notably the 1930s modernist, spiral-ramped, concrete penguin pool (where Penguin Books' original colophon was sketched), designed by the Tecton partnership, led by Russian emigré Berthold Lubetkin.

Camden Town

For all the gentrification of the last twenty years, **Camden Town** retains a seedy air, compounded by the various railway lines that plough through the area, the canal, and the market, now the district's best-known attribute.

Having started out as a tiny crafts market in the cobbled courtyard by the lock, **Camden Market** has since mushroomed out of all proportion. More than 100,000 shoppers turn up here each weekend and parts of the market now stay open week-long, alongside a similarly oriented crop of shops, cafés and bistros. The market's overabundance of cheap leather, DM boots and naff jewellery is compensated for by the sheer variety of what's on offer: from bootleg tapes to furniture, along with a mass of street fashion that may or may not make the transition to mainstream stores. To avoid the crowds, which can be overpowering on a summer Sunday afternoon, you'll need to come either early – before 10am – or late – say, after 4pm, when many of the stalls will be packing up to go.

Despite having no significant Jewish associations, Camden is now home to London's **Jewish Museum** at 129–131 Albert St, just off Parkway (Mon–Thurs & Sun 10am–4pm; £3; Camden Town tube). The purpose-built premises are smartly designed, but the conventional style and contents of the museum are disappointing. Apart from the usual displays of Judaica there's a video and exhibition explaining Jewish religious practices and the history of the Jewish community in Britain. More challenging temporary exhibitions are held in the museum's Finchley branch on East End Road.

Hampstead

Beyond Camden, up Haverstock Hill, the suburb of **Hampstead** developed as a spa resort in the eighteenth century and retains an upper-crust small-town atmosphere. It's long been a bolt-hole of the high-profile intelligentsia, and you can get some idea of its tone from the fact that its MP is the actress Glenda Jackson.

Whichever route you take north of Hampstead tube, you will probably end up at the small triangular green on **Holly Bush Hill**, on the north side of which stands the late seventeenth-century **Fenton House** (April–Oct Wed–Fri 2–5pm, Sat & Sun 11am–5pm; £4; NT; Hampstead tube). As well as housing a collection of European and Oriental ceramics, the house contains the superb Benton-Fletcher collection of early musical instruments, chiefly displayed on the top floor. Among the many spinets, virginals and clavichords are the earliest extant English grand piano and an Unverdorben lute dating from 1580 (one of only three in the world).

One of the most poignant of London's house museums is the **Freud Museum**, hidden away in the leafy streets of south Hampstead at 20 Maresfield Gardens (Wed–Sun noon–5pm; £3; Finchley Road tube). Having lived in Vienna for his entire adult life, Freud, by now a semi-invalid with only a year to live, was forced to flee the Nazis, arriving in London in the summer of 1938. The ground-floor study and library look exactly as they did when Freud lived here; the collection of erotic antiquities and the famous couch, sumptuously draped in Persian carpets, were all brought here from Vienna. Upstairs, home movies of family life in Vienna are shown continually and a small room is dedicated to his daughter, Anna, herself an influential child analyst, who lived in the house until her death in 1982.

Hampstead's newest attraction is **2 Willow Road** (guided tours April–Oct Thurs–Sat noon–5pm every 45min; £4; NT; Hampstead tube), a modernist red-brick terraced house, built in the 1930s by the Hungarian-born architect Ernö Goldfinger. When Goldfinger moved in, this was a state-of-the-art house, but Goldfinger changed little of it in the following sixty years, so what you see is a 1930s avant-garde dwelling preserved in aspic, a house at once both modern and old-fashioned. An added bonus is that the rooms are packed with works of art by the likes of Max Ernst, Duchamp, Henry Moore and Man Ray. There are a limited number of tickets for the **guided tours**, so it's worth booking ahead. Incidentally, James Bond's adversary is indeed named after Ernö, as Ian Fleming lived close by and had a deep personal dislike of both Goldfinger and his modernist abode.

Hampstead's most lustrous figure is celebrated at **Keats' House** (April–Oct Mon–Fri 10am–1pm & 2–6pm, Sat 10am–1pm & 2–5pm, Sun 2–5pm; Nov–March Mon–Fri 1–5pm, Sat 10am–1pm & 2–5pm, Sun 2–5pm; free; Hampstead tube), an elegant, whitewashed Regency double villa on Keats Grove, a short walk south of Willow Road. Inspired by the peacefulness of Hampstead and by his passion for girl-next-door Fanny Brawne (whose house is also part of the museum), Keats wrote some of his most famous works here, before leaving for Rome, where he died in 1821. The neat, rather staid interior contains books and letters, Fanny's engagement ring and the four-poster bed in which the poet first coughed up blood, confiding to his companion, Charles Brown, "that drop of blood is my death warrant".

Hampstead Heath and Kenwood

Hampstead Heath, north London's "green lung", is the city's most enjoyable public park. It may not have much of its original heathland left, but it packs in a wonderful variety of bucolic scenery in its 800 acres. At its southern end are the rolling green pastures of **Parliament Hill**, north London's premier spot for kite-flying. On either side are numerous ponds, three of which – one for men, one for women and one mixed – you can swim in. The thickest woodland is to be found in the West Heath, beyond Whitestone Pond, as is the most formal section, **Hill Garden**, a secretive and romantic little gem with eccentric balustraded terraces and a ruined pergola. Beyond, lies **Golders Hill Park**, where you can gaze on pygmy goats and fallow deer and inspect the impeccably maintained aviaries, home to flamingos, cranes and other exotic birds.

Finally, don't miss the landscaped grounds of Kenwood, in the north of the Heath, which are focused on the whitewashed, Neoclassical mansion of **Kenwood House** (daily: April–Sept 10am–6pm; Oct 10am–5pm; Nov–March 10am–4pm; free; EH). The house is now home to the **Iveagh Bequest**, a collection of seventeenth- and eighteenth-century art, including a handful of real masterpieces by the likes of Vermeer, Rembrandt, Boucher, Gainsborough and Reynolds. Of the house's period interiors, the most spectacular is Robert Adam's sky-blue and gold **Library**, its book-filled apses separated from the central entertaining area by paired columns. To the south of the house a grassy amphitheatre slopes down to a lake where outdoor **classical concerts** are held on summer evenings.

Highgate

Northeast of Hampstead Heath, and fractionally lower than Hampstead (appearances notwithstanding), **Highgate** lacks the literary cachet of Hampstead, but makes up for it with London's most famous cemetery, resting place of Karl Marx. It also retains more of its village origins, especially around **The Grove**, Highgate's finest row of houses, the oldest dating back as far as 1685.

To get to the cemetery, head south down Highgate High Street and **Highgate Hill**, with its amazing views towards the City. When you get to the copper dome of "Holy Joe", the Roman Catholic Church which stands on Highgate Hill, pop into the pleasantly landscaped **Waterlow Park**, next door, with its fine café and restaurant.

The park provides a through route to **Highgate Cemetery**, which is ranged on both sides of Swain's Lane. Highgate's most famous corpse, that of **Karl Marx**, lies in the **East Cemetery** (daily: April–Sept 10am–5pm; Oct–March 10am–4pm; £1; Archway or Highgate tube). Marx himself asked for a simple grave topped by a headstone, but by 1954 the Communist movement decided to move his grave to a more prominent position and erect the vulgar bronze bust that now surmounts a granite plinth. Close by lies the grave of the author George Eliot.

What the **East Cemetery** lacks in atmosphere is in part compensated for by the fact that you can wander at will through its maze of circuitous paths, whereas to visit the more atmospheric and overgrown **West Cemetery**, with its spooky Egyptian Avenue and terraced catacombs, you must go round with a guided tour (Mon–Fri noon, 2pm & 4pm, Sat & Sun hourly 11am–4pm; £3). Among the prominent graves usually visited are those of artist Dante Gabriel Rossetti and lesbian novelist Radclyffe Hall.

Southeast London: Dulwich to Greenwich

Now largely built up into a patchwork of Victorian terraces, one area of **southeast London** stands head and shoulders above all the others in terms of sightseeing, and that is **Greenwich**. At its heart is the outstanding architectural set-piece of the **Royal Naval College** and the **Queen's House**, courtesy of Christopher Wren and Inigo Jones respectively. Most visitors, however, come to see the **Cutty Sark**, the **National Maritime Museum** and the **Old Royal Observatory** in Greenwich Park, though Greenwich also pulls in an ever-increasing volume of Londoners in search of bargains at its Sunday market.

Greenwich is, of course, also famous as the "home of time", thanks to its status as the **Prime Meridian of the World** from where time all over the globe is measured. It's partly for this reason that Greenwich was chosen as the centrepiece of the country's millennium celebrations, though the **Millennium Dome** is, in fact, situated in the reclaimed industrial wasteland of North Greenwich, a mile or so northeast of Greenwich town centre.

The only other suburban sights that stand out are the **Dulwich Picture Gallery**, a public art gallery even older than the National Gallery, and the eclectic **Horniman Museum**, in neighbouring Forest Hill.

Dulwich and Forest Hill

Dulwich Village, one of southeast London's prettier patches, is built on land owned in the seventeenth century by the actor Edward Alleyn, who founded **Dulwich College** in 1619 as almshouses and a school for poor boys on the profits of his whorehouses and bear-baiting pits on Bankside (see p.120). Alleyn is buried in the chapel of the new Dulwich College, a grand Italianate structure with an impressive roll-call of old boys, including Raymond Chandler, P.G. Wodehouse and World War II traitor Lord Haw-Haw, though they tend to keep quiet about the last of the trio.

The original college is a short walk away down College Road, right next to the **Dulwich Picture Gallery** (Tues–Fri 10am–5pm, Sat 11am–5pm, Sun 2–5pm; £3, free on Fri; West Dulwich train station, from Victoria), the nation's oldest public art gallery, designed by Sir John Soane and opened in 1817. Soane created a beautifully spacious building, awash in natural light. Crammed with superb paintings from the collection assembled in the 1790s by the French dealer Noel Desenfans, then bequeathed to Francis Bourgeois, who in turn passed it on to the college, highlights include elegiac landscapes by Cuyp; a fine array of Gainsborough portraits (including his famous *Linley Sisters* and a likeness of Samuel Linley, said to have been painted in less than an hour); Rembrandt's *Portrait of a Young Man*; one of the world's finest Poussin series; and splendid works by Tiepolo, Hogarth, Van Dyck, Canaletto and Rubens.

If you walk for a mile or so across Dulwich Park and south down Lordship Lane, you'll reach the wacky **Horniman Museum** (Mon–Sat 10.30am–5.30pm, Sun 2–5.30pm; free; Forest Hill train station, from Victoria or London Bridge), which occupies a striking building designed by Harrison Townsend, architect of the Whitechapel

Gallery (see p.115). Horniman, a tea trader with a passion for collecting, financed construction of the purpose-built gallery in 1901, and today the museum revels in its Victorian eclecticism. Ascending the staircase, which is lined with a freshwater aquarium, you reach the old museum with its cases of stuffed birds and skeletons sharing space with half a fruit bat and an orang-utang's foot. The museum has a wide-ranging anthropology section, a musical department, with over 1500 instruments from Chinese gongs to electric guitars, and puts on excellent temporary exhibitions. The newest gallery is its "centre for understanding the environment", known as **"cue"**, a timber-clad extension with hands-on displays concerned with green issues and aimed primarily at youngsters. In the lovely gardens round the back of the museum there's a graceful Victorian conservatory and a small collection of live animals.

Greenwich

Greenwich is one of London's most beguiling spots and the one place in southeast London that draws large numbers of visitors. It boasts one of the capital's finest architectural set-pieces in the former Royal Naval College overlooking the Thames. To the west lies Greenwich town centre, while to the south lies the National Maritime Museum and the Old Royal Observatory, Greenwich's two prime tourist sights. If you're heading straight for either the Maritime Museum or the Observatory, the quickest way to get there is to take the train from Charing Cross (every 30min) to Maze Hill, on the eastern edge of Greenwich Park. Those wanting to start with the town or the *Cutty Sark* should alight at Greenwich station.

A more scenic way of getting to Greenwich is to take a **boat** (every 30–45min) from Charing Cross, Tower Bridge or Westminster piers. At the moment, it's also considerably more expensive, though it is hoped that a new, cheaper "hopper" service from central London will be in place by the millennium. A third possible option is to take the **Docklands Light Railway** (DLR) to Island Gardens, where the Greenwich Foot Tunnel leads under the Thames emerging beside the *Cutty Sark* – the advantage of this approach being the fabulous view of the Wren buildings from across the river.

THE MILLENNIUM DOME

The **Millennium Dome**, clearly visible from the riverside at Greenwich, is located over a mile downstream at North Greenwich, and open to the public from January 1, 2000. As most grand projects do, it's had a rough ride in the press. Public opinion and the Labour Party – then in opposition – were vehemently against the project, though, of course, once in power, Labour did an abrupt U-turn, and even gave the Dome its own minister. The Church of England, in particular, criticized the project for being "too secular", arguing, with some justification, that, without Jesus, there would be no millennium.

Nevertheless, the Dome, completed at a total cost of something approaching £800 million, is estimated to pull in around 12 million punters in 2000 alone. Designed by Richard Rogers (of Lloyd's Building and Pompidou Centre fame), the Dome's geodesic dome is by far the world's largest – 1km in circumference and 50m in height – held up by a dozen 90-metre-tall yellow steel masts. The interior is divided into twelve themed zones, each of which is replete with interactive and virtual-reality gadgetry. At the centre a high-tech, live, multimedia extravaganza is performed at regular intervals.

Getting to the Dome is an experience in itself. The site has its very own Jubilee line tube station designed by Norman Foster, and part of a tube extension that has cost more to build per mile than the Channel Tunnel. There are also several options of arriving by boat and an aerial cable car link with East India DLR station on the north bank of the Thames.

The town centre

Greenwich town centre, laid out in the 1820s with the Nash-style terraces, is currently plagued with heavy traffic. To escape the busy streets, filled with nautical nick-nack shops and bookshops, head for the old covered market, now at the centre of the weekend **Greenwich Market** (Sat & Sun 9am–5pm), a lively antique, crafts and clothes market which has spread far beyond the perimeters of its predecessor, spilling out up the High Road, Stockwell Road and Royal Hill. The best sections are the indoor secondhand book markets, flanking the Central Market on Stockwell Road; the antiques hall, further down on Greenwich High Road; and the flea market on Thames Street.

A short distance in from the old covered market, on the opposite side of Greenwich Church Street, rises the Doric portico and broken pediment of Nicholas Hawksmoor's **St Alfege's Church** (daily: April–Oct noon–3pm; Nov–March noon–2pm). Built in 1712–18, the church was flattened in the Blitz, but it has been magnificently repaired.

Wedged in a dry dock by the Greenwich Foot Tunnel is the majestic **Cutty Sark** (May–Sept Mon–Sat 10am–6pm, Sun noon–6pm; Oct–March closes 5pm; £3.50), the world's last surviving tea clipper, built in 1869. The *Cutty Sark* lasted just eight years in the China tea trade, and it was as a wool clipper that it actually made its name, making a return journey to Australia in just 72 days. Inside, there's little to see beyond the exhibition in the main hold which tells the ship's story from its inception to its arrival in Greenwich in 1954.

It's entirely appropriate that the one London building that makes the most of its river-bank location should be the former **Royal Naval College** (daily 2.30–4.45pm; free), Wren's beautifully symmetrical Baroque ensemble, initially built as a royal palace, but eventually converted into a hospital for disabled seamen. From 1873 until quite recently, it was home to the Royal Naval College, but is now set to house the University of Greenwich and the Trinity College of Music.

The two grandest rooms, situated underneath Wren's twin domes, are open to the public and well worth visiting; they must be approached from the King William Walk entrance. The magnificent **Painted Hall**, in the west wing, is dominated by James Thornhill's gargantuan allegorical ceiling painting and his trompe l'oeil fluted pilasters. The **RNC Chapel**, in the east wing, is an altogether colder and more formal affair. The current chapel was designed by James "Athenian" Stuart and features exquisite pastel-shaded plasterwork and spectacular, decorative detailing.

The National Maritime Museum

The west wing of the former Naval Asylum, to the south of the Royal Naval College, now houses the **National Maritime Museum** (daily: 10am–5pm; £7.50), which has undergone a spectacular redevelopment programme for the new millennium. The **Neptune Court** has re-opened, so you can now see the museum's four late seventeenth-century river barges, including the magnificent 63-foot Royal Barge, a gilded Rococo confection designed by William Kent for Prince Frederick, the much-unloved eldest son of George II.

The **Nelson Gallery**, meanwhile, contains the museum's vast collection of Nelson-related memorabilia, including Turner's *Battle of Trafalgar, 21st October, 1805*, his largest work and only royal commission. There's a new hands-on gallery, called **All Hands**, where children can have a go at radio transmission, loading miniature cargo, firing a cannon and so forth. In fact, only a couple of old-fashioned galleries remain now: **Ship of War**, the museum's collection of model sailing ships dating from 1650 to 1815, and **Twentieth-century Seapower**, which employs a tad more theatre to explain modern naval conflicts.

Inigo Jones's **Queen's House**, originally built amidst a rambling Tudor royal palace, is now the focal point of the Greenwich ensemble and an integral part of the Maritime

Museum. As royal residences go, it's an unassuming country house, but as the first Neoclassical building in the country, it has enormous architectural significance. An audio commentary on the house is available from the desk in the **Great Hall**, off which is the beautiful **Tulip Staircase**, Britain's earliest cantilevered spiral staircase – its name derives from the floral patterning in the wrought-iron balustrade. The ground floor is given over to temporary exhibitions from the Maritime Museum, while the **Royal Apartments** on the first floor have been decked out with skilful repro furniture, rush matting and damask silk wall hangings.

The Old Royal Observatory

Crowning the hill in Greenwich Park, behind the National Maritime Museum, the **Old Royal Observatory** (daily 10am–5pm; £5; combined ticket with the National Maritime Museum £9.50) was established by Charles II in 1675 to house the first Astronomer Royal, John Flamsteed. Flamsteed's chief task was to study the night sky in order to discover an astronomical method of finding the longitude of a ship at sea, the lack of which was causing enormous problems for the emerging British Empire. Astronomers continued to work here at Greenwich until the postwar smog forced them to decamp to Herstmonceux Castle and the clearer skies of Sussex (they've since moved to the Pacific); the old observatory, meanwhile, is now a very popular museum.

Greenwich's greatest claim to fame is, of course, as the home of Greenwich Mean Time (GMT) and the Prime Meridian – a meridian being any north–south line used as a basis for astronomical observations, and therefore also for the calculation of longitude and time. Since 1884, Greenwich has occupied zero longitude, which means the entire world sets its clocks by GMT. What the Old Royal Observatory don't tell you is that the meridian has, in fact, moved. Nowadays, longitude is calculated by a differential Global Positioning Receiver, served by several US military satellites, which places the meridian 336ft to the east of the brass strip.

The oldest part of the observatory is the Wren-built **Flamsteed House**, whose northeastern turret sports a bright red Time-Ball that climbs the mast at 12.58pm and drops at 1pm GMT precisely; it was added in 1833 to allow ships on the Thames to set their clocks. Passing quickly through Flamsteed's restored apartments and the **Octagon Room**, where the king used to show off to his guests, you reach the **Chronometer Gallery** which focuses on the search for longitude, and displays four different precision clocks designed by **John Harrison**, who eventually won the Longitude Prize in 1763.

Flamsteed's own meridian line is a brass strip in the floor of the Meridian Building. Edmund Halley, Flamsteed's successor, who charted the comings and goings of the famous comet, worked out his own version of the meridian, and the Bradley Meridian Room reveals yet another meridian, standard from 1750 to 1850 and still used for Ordnance Survey maps. Finally, you reach a room that's split in two by the present-day Greenwich Meridian, fixed by the cross-hairs in Airy's "Transit Circle", the astronomical instrument that dominates the room.

The exhibition ends on a soothing note in the **Telescope Dome** of the octagonal Great Equatorial Building, home to Britain's largest telescope. In addition, there are half-hourly presentations in the **Planetarium** (Mon–Fri 2.30pm; £2), housed in the adjoining South Building.

The Ranger's House and the Fan Museum

Southwest of the observatory and backing onto Greenwich park's rose garden, is the **Ranger's House** (April–Oct daily 10am–6pm; Oct–March Wed–Sun 10am–4pm; £2.50; EH), a red-brick Georgian villa on the southwestern edge of Greenwich Park, that houses a collection of paintings donated by the nineteenth Countess of Suffolk, whose portrait by John Singer Sargent hangs in the foyer. Built in the early eighteenth century, it was lived in after 1749 by the Earl of Chesterfield, who extended the bow window of the large gallery to just within the boundaries of the Royal Park, pushing the rent on the window up to £10 a year, compared to a total rent of six shillings and eight pence on the rest of the house. The high points of the art collection are William Larkin's full-length portraits of a Jacobean wedding party, particularly the twin bridesmaids in slashed silver brocade dresses, and the arrogant Richard Sackville, a dissolute aristocrat resplendent in pompom shoes. The Architectural Study Centre, in the courtyard, is a collection of plaques, mantels, fireplaces and chimneys saved from London's historic buildings – the spiral staircase snaking through the centre of the room was retrieved from the old Covent Garden market hall.

A steepish walk back towards Greenwich proper down Croom's Hill, which runs along the western edge of the park, brings you to the **Fan Museum** at no. 12 (Tues–Sat 11am–4.30pm, Sun noon–4.30pm; £2.50). It's a fascinating little place (and an extremely beautiful house), revealing the importance of the fan as a social and political document. The permanent exhibition on the ground floor traces the history of the materials employed, from peacock feathers to straw. Temporary exhibitions on the first floor explore conditions of production, the fan's link with the Empire and changing fashion.

Out west: Chiswick to Windsor

Most people experience west London en route to or from Heathrow airport, from either the confines of the train or tube, which runs overground at this point, or the motorway. The city and its satellites seem to continue unabated, with only fleeting glimpses of the countryside. However, in the five-mile stretch from Chiswick to Osterley there are several former country retreats, now surrounded by suburbia, which are definitely worth checking out.

The Palladian villa of **Chiswick House** is perhaps the best known of these attractions. However, it draws nothing like as many visitors as **Syon House**, most of whom come for the gardening centre rather than for the house itself, a showcase for the talents of Robert Adam, who also worked at **Osterley House**, another Elizabethan conversion, now owned by the National Trust.

Running through much of the area is the **River Thames**, once known as the "Great Highway of London" and still the most pleasant way to travel in these parts during the summer. Boats plough up the Thames all the way from central London via the **botanical gardens of Kew** and the picturesque riverside at **Richmond**, as far as **Hampton Court**, home of the country's largest royal residence and the famous maze. To reach the heavily touristed royal outpost of **Windsor Castle**, however, you really need to take the train.

Chiswick

Chiswick House (April–Sept daily 10am–6pm; first three weeks of Oct daily 10am–5pm; late Oct to March Wed–Sun 10am–4pm; £3; EH; Chiswick train station, from Waterloo) is a perfect little Neoclassical villa, designed in the 1720s by Richard Boyle, Earl of Burlington, and set in one of the most beautifully landscaped gardens in London. Like its prototype, Palladio's Villa Rotonda near Vicenza, the house was purpose-built as a "temple to the arts" – here, amid his fine art collection, Burlington could entertain artistic friends such as Swift, Handel and Pope. Visitors enter via the **lower floor**, where you can pick up an audioguide, before heading up to the **upper floor**, a series of cleverly interconnecting rooms, each enjoying a wonderful view out onto the gardens – all, that is, except the Tribunal, the central octagonal hall, where the earl's finest paintings and sculptures would have been displayed.

To do a quick circuit of the **gardens**, head across the smooth carpet of grass, punctuated by urns and sphinxes that sit under the shadow of two giant cedars of Lebanon. A great place from which to admire the northwest side of the house is from the stone benches of the exedra, the set of yew-hedge niches harbouring lions and copies of Roman statuary, situated beyond the cedars. Elsewhere, there's an Italian garden, a maze of high-hedge alleyways, a lake and a grassy amphitheatre, centred on an obelisk in a pond and overlooked by an Ionic temple.

If you leave Chiswick House gardens by the northernmost exit, beyond the conservatory, it's just a short walk (to the east) along the thunderous A4 road, to **Hogarth's House** (April–Sept Tues–Fri 1–5pm, Sat & Sun 1–6pm; Oct–March closes an hour earlier; closed Jan; free), where the artist spent each summer with his wife, sister and mother-in-law from 1749 until his death in 1764. Nowadays, it's hard to believe that Hogarth came here for peace and quiet, but in the eighteenth century the house was almost entirely surrounded by countryside. In addition to scores of Hogarth's engravings, you can see copies of his satirical series *An Election*, *Marriage à la Mode* and *A Harlot's Progress*, and compare the modern view from the parlour with the more idyllic scene in *Mr Ranby's House*.

Syon House

Across the water from Kew stands **Syon** (April–Sept Wed–Sun 11am–5pm; Oct Sun only; £5.50, including entry to the gardens; bus #237 or #267, from Gunnersbury tube or Kew Bridge train station); seat of the Duke of Northumberland since Elizabethan times, it is now more of a working commercial concern than a family home, embracing a garden centre, a wholefood shop, a trout fishery, an aquatic centre stocked with tropical fish, a mini-zoo and a butterfly house, as well as the old aristocratic mansion and its gardens.

From its rather plain castellated exterior, you'd never guess that **Syon House** contains the most opulent eighteenth-century interiors in the whole of London. The splendour of Robert Adam's refurbishment is immediately revealed, however, in the pristine **Great Hall**, an apsed double cube with a screen of Doric columns at one end and classical statuary dotted around the edges. There are several more Adam-designed rooms to admire in the house, plus a smattering of works by Van Dyck, Lely, Gainsborough and Reynolds.

While Adam beautified Syon House, Capability Brown laid out its **gardens** (daily 10am–6pm or dusk; £2.50) around an artificial lake, surrounding it with oaks, beeches, limes and cedars. The gardens' chief focus now, however, is the crescent-shaped **Great Conservatory**, an early nineteenth-century addition which is said to have inspired Joseph Paxton, architect of the Crystal Palace. Those with young children will be compelled to make use of the **miniature steam train** which runs through the park at weekends from April to October, and on Wednesdays during the school holidays.

Another plus point for kids is Syon's **Butterfly House** (daily: May–Sept 10am–5pm; Oct–April 10am–3.30pm; £2.90), a small, mesh-covered hothouse, where you can walk amid hundreds of exotic butterflies from all over the world, as they flit about the foliage. However, if your kids show more enthusiasm for life-threatening reptiles than delicate insects, then you could skip the butterflies and go instead for the adjacent **London Aquatic Experience** (daily: April–Sept 10am–6pm; Oct–March 10am–5pm; £3), a purpose-built centre with a mixed range of aquatic creatures from the mysterious basilisk, which can walk on water, to the perennially popular piranhas.

Osterley Park and House

Robert Adam redesigned another colossal Elizabethan mansion three miles northwest of Syon at **Osterley Park** (daily 9am–7.30pm or dusk; free), which maintains the impression of being in the middle of the countryside, despite the presence of the M4 to the north of the house. The park itself is well worth exploring, and there's a great café in the Tudor stables, but anyone with a passing interest in Adam's work should pay a visit to **Osterley House** (April–Oct Wed–Sat 2–5pm, Sun 1–5pm; £4; NT; Osterley tube). If you arrive by public transport, you get a £1 reduction off the price of your ticket.

From the outside, Osterley bears some similarity to Syon, the big difference being Adam's grand entrance portico, with its tall, Ionic colonnade. From here, you enter a characteristically cool **Entrance Hall**, followed by the so-called State Rooms of the south wing. Highlights include the **Drawing Room**, with Reynolds portraits on the damask walls and a coffered ceiling centred on a giant marigold, and the **Etruscan Dressing Room**, in which every surface is covered in delicate painted trelliswork, sphinxes and urns, a style that Adam (and Wedgwood) dubbed "Etruscan", though it is in fact derived from Greek vases found at Pompeii.

Kew and Richmond

Established in 1759, the **Royal Botanical Gardens** (daily 9.30am to 7.30pm or dusk; £5; Kew Gardens tube) have grown from their original eight acres into a 300-acre site in which more than 33,000 species are grown in plantations and glasshouses, a display that attracts over a million visitors every year, most of them with no specialist interest at all. The only drawbacks with Kew are the prohibitive entry fee, and the fact that it lies on the main flight path to Heathrow. There's always something to see whatever the season, but to get the most out of the place, come some time between spring and autumn, bring a picnic and come for the day.

There are four entry points to the gardens, but the majority of people arrive at Kew Gardens tube and train station, a few minutes' walk east of the **Victoria Gate**. Of all the glasshouses, by far the most celebrated is the **Palm House**, a curvaceous mound of glass and wrought iron, designed by Decimus Burton in the 1840s. Its drippingly humid atmosphere nurtures most of the known palm species, while in the basement there's a small but excellent tropical aquarium. The largest of the glasshouses, however, is the **Temperate House**, to the south, which contains plants from every continent, including one of the largest indoor palms in the world, the sixty-foot Chilean Wine Palm.

Kew's origins as an eighteenth-century royal pleasure garden are evident in the numerous follies dotted about Kew, the most conspicuous of which is the ten-storey 163-foot-high **Pagoda**. Unfortunately, **Kew Palace**, the three-storey red-brick mansion bought by George II as a nursery for his many children, will be closed for renovation until at least 2000. As a consolation, you could explore **Queen Charlotte's Cottage** (April–Sept Sat & Sun 10.30am–4pm; free), a tiny thatched summerhouse built in the 1770s as a royal picnic spot for George III's wife in the thickly wooded, southwestern section of the park – a sure way to lose the crowds.

On emerging from the station at **Richmond**, you'd be forgiven for wondering why you're here, but the procession of chain stores spread out along the one-way system is only half the story. To see Richmond's more interesting side, take one of the narrow pedestrianized alleyways off busy George Street, which bring you to the wide open space of **Richmond Green**, one of the finest village greens in London, and no doubt one of the most peaceful before it found itself on the main flight path into Heathrow. Handsome seventeenth- and eighteenth-century houses line the south side of the green, where the medieval royal palace of **Richmond** once stood, though only its unspectacular **Tudor Gateway** survives.

The other place to head for in Richmond is the **Riverside**, pedestrianized, terraced and redeveloped by Quinlan Terry, Prince Charles's favourite purveyor of ersatz classicism, in the late 1980s. The real joy of the waterfront, however, is **Richmond Bridge**,

London's oldest extant bridge, an elegant span of five arches made from Purbeck stone in 1777. The old town hall, set back from the new development, houses the **tourist office** (April–Oct Mon–Fri 10am–6pm, Sat 10am–5pm, Sun 10.15am–4.15pm; rest of year closed Sun) and, on the second floor, the **Richmond Museum** (April–Oct Tues–Sat 11am–5pm, Sun 2–5pm; Nov–March Tues–Sat 11am–5pm; £2), but most folk prefer to ensconce themselves in the riverside pubs, or head for the numerous boat and bike rental outlets.

Richmond's greatest attraction, though, is the enormous **Richmond Park** (daily: March–Sept 7am–dusk; Oct–Feb 7.30am–dusk; free), at the top of Richmond Hill – 2500 acres of undulating grassland and bracken, dotted with coppiced woodland and as wild as anything in London. Eight miles across at its widest point, this is Europe's largest city park, famed for its red and fallow deer, which roam freely, and for its ancient oaks. For the most part untamed, the park does have a couple of deliberately land-scaped plantations which feature splendid springtime azaleas and rhododendrons, in particular the Isabella Plantation.

If you continue along the towpath beyond Richmond Bridge, after a mile or so, you will eventually leave the rest of London far behind and arrive at **Ham House** (April–Oct Mon–Wed, Sat & Sun 1–5pm; £5), home to the Earls of Dysart for nearly three hundred years. Expensively furnished in the seventeenth century, but little altered since then, the house boasts one of the finest Stuart interiors in the country, from the stupendously ornate Great Staircase to the Long Gallery, featuring six "Court Beauties" by Peter Lely. Elsewhere, there are several fine Verrio ceiling paintings, some exquisite parquet flooring and works by Van Dyck and Reynolds. Another bonus is the formal seventeenth-century **gardens** (all year Mon–Wed, Sat & Sun 10.30am–6pm; £1.50), especially the Cherry Garden, laid out with a pungent lavender parterre, surrounded by yew hedges and pleached hornbeam arbours. The Orangery, overlooking the original kitchen garden, currently serves as a tearoom.

Hampton Court

Thirteen miles southwest of London you'll find the finest of Tudor palaces, **Hampton Court Palace** (mid-March to mid-Oct Mon 10.15am–6pm, Tues–Sun 9.30am–6pm; rest of year closes 4.30pm; £9.25; Hampton Court train station, from Waterloo); a sprawling red-brick ensemble on the banks of the Thames, thirteen miles southwest of London, it is the finest of England's royal abodes. Built in 1516 by the upwardly mobile **Cardinal Wolsey**, Henry VIII's Lord Chancellor, it was purloined by Henry himself after Wolsey fell from favour. Charles II laid out the gardens, inspired by what he had seen at Versailles, while William and Mary had large sections of the palace remodelled by Wren. Finally abandoned as a royal residence by George III, Hampton Court was opened to the public by Queen Victoria in 1838.

The royal apartments are divided into six thematic walking tours, for which guided tours and audio tours are available at no extra cost. The highlight of **Henry VIII's State Apartments** is the Great Hall, with its astonishing double hammer-beam roof. Further on is the Haunted Gallery, home to the ghost of Henry's fifth wife, nineteen-year-old Catherine Howard. Another high point is the Chapel Royal, which boasts false-timber vaulting wrought in plaster and decorated with gilded, music-making cherubs. The **Queen's Apartments**, approached by the grandiose trompe l'oeil Queen's Staircase, feature several marvellous marble fireplaces, fiery frescoes, Gobelin tapestries and *chinoiserie*. The tour of the so-called **Georgian Rooms** takes you through the brightly decorated **Wolsey Closet**, one of the few rooms remaining from Wolsey's apartments, and the Cartoon Gallery, hung with Brussels tapestries, some of which are copies of Raphael's cartoons (now in the V&A) for which the room was originally intended.

The **King's Apartments**, approached via the magnificent King's Staircase and the armoury of the King's Guard Chamber, are furnished in the same period as the Queen's, with only the throne-like velvet toilet for light relief. The **Renaissance Picture Gallery** is chock-full of treasures, among them paintings by Tintoretto, Lotto, Titian, Cranach, Breugel and Holbein. After the opulence of the rest of the palace, the workaday **Tudor Kitchens** come as something of a relief. To make the most of this route, you really do need the audio tour, which sets the vast complex of reconstructed kitchens alight.

Tickets to the Royal Apartments cover entry to the rest of the sites in the grounds. Those who don't wish to visit the apartments are free to wander around the gardens, but will have to pay extra to visit the curious **Royal Tennis Courts** (50p), the palace's famously tricky hedge **Maze** (£2.10), laid out in 1714 north of the palace, and the **South Gardens** (£2.10), where you can view Andrea Mantegna's colourful, heroic canvases, *The Triumphs of Caesar*, housed in the Lower Orangery, and the celebrated **Great Vine**, grown from a cutting in 1768 and now averaging about seven hundred pounds of black grapes per year and sold at the palace each September. Further afield, across Hampton Court Road, Wren's royal road, Chestnut Avenue, cuts through the semi-wild **Bushy Park**, which sustains a few fallow deer.

Windsor and Eton

Every weekend trains from Waterloo and Paddington are packed with people heading for **Windsor**, the royal enclave 21 miles west of London, where they join the human conveyor belt round **Windsor Castle** (daily: March–Oct 10am–5pm; Nov–Feb 10am–4pm; £9.50, £7.50 on Sun). Towering above the town on a steep chalk bluff, the castle is an undeniably awesome sight, its chilly grey walls, punctuated by mighty medieval bastions, continuing as far as the eye can see. Once there, the small selection of state rooms open to the public are unexciting, though the magnificent St George's Chapel and the chance to see another small selection of the Queen's private art collection make the trip worthwhile. On a fine day, it pays to put aside some time for exploring Windsor Great Park, which stretches for several miles to the south of the castle.

The castle began its days as a wooden fortress built by William the Conqueror, and numerous later monarchs had a hand in its evolution: Henry II rebuilt it in stone, Henry III and Edward III improved it, and George IV restored it. Some of their work was undone by a huge fire in November 1992, which gutted a number of rooms, including St George's Hall. Most have been rebuilt exactly as they were before the fire, but one or two have been redesigned in a safe neo-Gothic style.

Once inside the castle, it's best to head straight for the **St George's Chapel** (Mon–Sat 10am–4pm), a glorious Perpendicular structure ranking with Henry VII's Chapel in Westminster Abbey, and the second most important resting place for royal corpses after the Abbey. Entry is via the south door and a one-way system operates, which brings you out by the **Albert Memorial Chapel**, built by Henry VII as a burial place for Henry VI, completed by Cardinal Wolsey for his own burial, but eventually converted for Queen Victoria into a High Victorian memorial to her husband, Prince Albert.

Before entering the State Apartments, pay a quick visit to **Queen Mary's Dolls' House**, a palatial micro-residence designed for the wife of George V, and the **Gallery,** where special exhibitions culled from the Royal Art Collection are staged. Most visitors just gape in awe at the monotonous, gilded grandeur of the **State Apartments**, while the real highlights – the paintings from the Royal Collection that line the walls – are rarely given a second glance. The **King's Dressing Room**, for example, despite its small size, contains a feast of art treasures, including a dapper Rubens self-portrait, Van Dyck's famous triple portrait of Charles I, and *The Artist's Mother*, a perfectly observed portrait of old age by Rembrandt.

You'd hardly know that Windsor suffered the most devastating fire in its history in 1992, so thorough (and uninspired) has the restoration been in rooms such as the **St George's Hall**. By contrast, the octagonal **Lantern Lobby**, beyond, is clearly an entirely new room, a safe neo-Gothic design replacing the old chapel. At this point, those visiting during the winter season are given the privilege of seeing four **Semi-State Rooms**, created in the 1820s by George IV, and still used in the summer months by the royal family.

Over the footbridge, at the end of Thames Avenue in Windsor village, is **Eton**, a one-street village lined with bookshops and antique dealers, but famous all over the world for **Eton College** (Easter, July & Aug daily 10.30am–4.30pm; mid-April to June, Sept & Nov daily 2–4.30pm; £2.50; guided tours daily 2.15 & 3.30pm; £3.50), the ultra-exclusive and inexcusably powerful school founded by Henry VI in 1440 and now charged with educating the heirs to the throne, princes William and Henry. Within the rarefied complex you can visit the Gothic chapel, with its medieval wall paintings and a small self-congratulatory museum telling the history of the school – Percy Bysshe Shelley is a rare rebellious figure in the roll-call of Establishment greats.

EATING, DRINKING AND NIGHTLIFE

No matter what your taste in food, drink or entertainment, you'll find what you're looking for in London, a city that in many ways becomes a more appealing place after dark. The capital's rich ethnic mix and concentration of creative talent give it a diversity and energy that no other town in England comes close to matching – Birmingham might have a better concert hall, Manchester might have a couple of hot clubs, but nowhere can match the capital's consistent quality and choice. The weekly calendar of gigs, movies, plays and other events is charted most completely in *Time Out*, the main listings magazine, and there are any number of specialist publications for those who want to make sure they are not missing a thing – from solemn books on the foodie shrines of London to esoteric little mags for the rave cognoscenti. However, the listings that follow should be more than enough for any visitor who's planning on spending less than a couple of months in the city.

Eating

London is a great place to eat. You can sample more or less any kind of cuisine here, and – wherever you come from – you should find something new and possibly unique. London is home to some of the best **Cantonese** restaurants in Europe, is a noted centre for **Indian and Bangladeshi** food, and has numerous French, Greek, Italian, Japanese, Spanish and Thai restaurants. And within all these cuisines you can choose anything from simple meals to gourmet spreads. Traditional and **Modern-British** food is available all over town, and some of the best venues are reviewed below. Another bonus is that there are plenty of places to eat around the main tourist drags of the West End – **Soho** has long been renowned for its eclectic and fashionable restaurants and new eateries appear every month, while **Chinatown**, on the other side of Shaftesbury Avenue, offers value-for-money eating right in the centre of town.

There are also plenty of spots to pick up a street **snack** or cheap **lunch** – and some of these quick-stop places are good standbys for an evening filler. The inexpensive places that rely on a rapid turnover are listed under "Snacks, sandwiches, cakes and coffee", and "breakfasts, lunches and quick meals", but there are plenty of more relaxed eateries suitable for a quick bite, such as the pizza and pasta joints, Chinese restaurants, many of which do excellent *dim sum*, and the ever-expanding ranks of London's French-style bistros.

Snacks, sandwiches, cakes and coffee

As well as the places we've listed below, there are several London-wide chains that are well worth checking out. Try **Aroma**, with its bright Aztec colours, designer sandwiches, Portuguese pastries and good coffee in varying strengths; **Caffè Nero**, which serves terrific coffee, a range of Italian cakes, and pasta, calzone and pizza; **Häagen-Dazs**, offering a huge range of interesting ice-cream flavours, plus cakes, sundaes, shakes and coffee; **Pret à Manger**, with its excellent ready-made sandwiches, imaginative salads, hot stuffed croissants and sushi selections; or **Starbucks**, the clean-cut American operation serving some of the best coffee in town.

Mayfair and Marylebone

La Madeleine, 5 Vigo St, W1. This is an authentic French patisserie and café with mountains of tempting patisserie from which to indulge yourself while seated at the tables towards the front of the café; those at the back are for punters who want more substantial bistro fare. Green Park or Piccadilly Circus tube. Closed Sun.

Patisserie Valerie at Sagne, 105 Marylebone High St, W1. Founded as *Maison Sagne* in the 1920s, and preserving its wonderful decor from those days, the café is now run by Soho's fab patisserie makers, and is without doubt Marylebone's finest. Bond Street tube.

Soho

Bar Italia, 22 Frith St, W1. A tiny café that's a Soho institution, serving coffee, croissants and sandwiches more or less around the clock – as it has been since 1949. Popular with late-night clubbers and those here to watch the Italian-league soccer on the giant screen. Leicester Square tube.

Java Java, 26 Rupert St, W1. Wide range of coffee, a staggering array of teas, and free papers and magazines are all on offer in this cross between a French and an American café. Leicester Square or Piccadilly Circus tube.

The Living Room, 3 Bateman St, W1. Hidden away in a Soho backstreet, this is a welcoming, laidback café with groovy music, sandwiches and cakes, and great armchairs and tatty sofas to chill out in. Tottenham Court Road tube.

Maison Bertaux, 28 Greek St, W1. Long-standing, old-fashioned, downbeat Soho patisserie, with tables on two floors (and one or two outside) and a loyal clientele that keeps them busy. You'll be tempted in by the window full of elaborate cakes, but be warned, when it comes to coffee, they only do café au lait. Leicester Square tube.

Patisserie Valerie, 44 Old Compton St, W1. Popular coffee, croissant and cake emporium dating from the 1920s and attracting a loud-talking, arty, people-watching Soho crowd. The same outfit now run *Maison Sagne* in Marylebone (see above). Leicester Square or Piccadilly Circus tube.

INTERNET CAFES

Internet cafés are useful if you need to send a quick email to someone and, occasionally, to visit in their own right. Below are a couple worth trying:

Cyberia, 39 Whitfield St, W1 (☎0171/209 0983, *cyberia@easynet.co.uk*). The city's first Internet café, with trip-hop in the background, chilled beers, coffee and cakes for refuelling, and eleven computers lined up for their netizens. Internet access, £3 per half-hour. Goodge Street tube. Daily 9.30am–10pm.

Global Café, 15 Golden Square, W1 (☎0171/287 2242, *webmasters@globalcafe.co.uk*). A pleasant, roomy Soho café, with helpful staff, and a choice of bagels, double-decker sandwiches, coffee, tea and beer. Access to one of the seven terminals costs £2.50 per half-hour; Saturday nights are women-only. Piccadilly Circus tube. Mon–Sat 10am–11pm.

Covent Garden and Bloomsbury

Coffee Gallery, 23 Museum St, WC1. An excellent, if a little small, café close by the British Museum, serving mouth-watering Italian sandwiches and more substantial dishes at lunchtime. Get there early to grab a seat. Closed Sun. Tottenham Court Road tube.

Coffee Matters, 4 Southampton Row, WC1. Campaigning organic café on the edge of Holborn, serving fairly traded espresso, cappuccino or latte to accompany your organic brownies and biscotti. Freshly squeezed organic juices also available. Closed Sat & Sun. Holborn tube.

Mode, 57 Endell St, WC2. The best things about this stylish Covent Garden café are the Italian sandwiches, the cheeses from nearby Neal's Yard Dairy and the laid-back, groovy atmosphere. Closed Sun. Covent Garden tube.

Monmouth Coffee Company, 27 Monmouth St, WC2. The marvellous aroma's the first thing you notice, while the cramped wooden booths and daily newspapers on hand evoke an eighteenth-century coffee-house atmosphere – pick and mix your coffee from a fine selection (or buy the beans to take home). No smoking. Covent Garden or Leicester Square tube.

Notting Hill

Lisboa Patisserie, 57 Golborne Rd, W10. Authentic Portuguese *pastelaria*, with the best custard tarts this side of Lisbon – also coffee, cakes and a friendly atmosphere. The *Oporto* at no. 62a (closed Mon) is a good fallback if this place is full. Ladbroke Grove tube.

Maison Blanc, 102 Holland Park Ave, W11. French patisserie (with other branches in St John's Wood, Hampstead, Chelsea and Richmond) where you can guarantee you'll get the real thing when it comes to croissants and the like. Holland Park tube.

Kensington and Chelsea

Raison d'Etre, 18 Bute St, SW7. Smack in the middle of South Kensington's French quarter, this is a top-notch patisserie/boulangerie, serving excellent coffee. Closed Sun. South Kensington tube.

Camden

Marine Ices, 8 Haverstock Hill, NW3. Splendid old-fashioned Italian ice-cream parlour with a reputation for ices that spreads far and wide; pizza and pasta served in the adjacent restaurant. Chalk Farm tube.

Greenwich

Pistachio's Café, 15 Nelson Rd, SE10. Very good sandwich café in the centre of Greenwich, serving excellent coffee, and with a small garden out back. Greenwich train station.

Breakfasts, lunches and quick meals

There are cafés and small, basic restaurants all over London that can rustle up an **inexpensive meal**. You should be able to fill up at all of the places listed in this section for under £10, including tea or coffee.

Most of these cafés also feature big **English breakfasts**, served most often till 11am, then move over to pies, fish and chips, and the like – a few offer breakfast all day. Some cafés, and many of the Italian places listed, are also open in the evening, but the turnover is fast, so don't expect to linger. They are best seen as fuel stops before – or in a few cases, after – a night out elsewhere.

London-wide chains worth checking out are **Cranks**, the veggie (and vegan) eating house that spawned a thousand imitators with its wholemeal decor, keen staff, lentil bakes, exotic fruit juices and no-smoking policy; **Ed's Easy Diner**, 1950s-theme diners dishing up some of the city's best burgers and fries for middling prices; and **Stockpot**, which serve big portions at rock-bottom prices.

Piccadilly and Soho

Bar du Marché, 19 Berwick St, W1. A weird find in the middle of raucous Berwick Street market: a French café serving quick snacks, meals and fried breakfasts. Licensed bar. Closed Sun. Tottenham Court Road tube.

Bonbonnière, 36 Great Marlborough St, W1. A good find in the Oxford Circus neighbourhood – cheap, plain fry-ups and Italian dishes, served in a no-nonsense dining room. Wine served by the carafe. Closed Sun. Oxford Circus tube.

Centrale, 16 Moor St, W1. Tiny Italian café that serves up huge plates of steaming, garlicky pasta, as well as omelettes, chicken and chops. You'll almost certainly have to wait for – or share – a table. Bring your own booze; there's a 50p corkage charge. Leicester Square tube.

Hotei, 39 Great Windmill St, W1 (plus other branches at 4 Glasshouse St, W1 and 1 Addle St, EC1). Tiny Japanese-run sushi and noodle bar with a simple, inexpensive menu of rah-men (noodle soup) or yaki-soba (fried noodles). Piccadilly Circus tube.

Indian YMCA, 41 Fitzroy Square, W1. Don't take any notice of the signs saying the canteen is only for students – this place is open to the public, just press the bell and pile in. The entire menu is portioned up into pretty little bowls; go and collect what you want and pay at the till. The food is great and the prices unbelievably low. Goodge Street tube.

Pollo, 20 Old Compton St, W1. This place has a reputation – some say unjustified – for the best-value Italian food in town, which means that even though there are two floors, you'll either have to wait in line or share a table. Alcohol is served. Leicester Square tube.

Wren at St James's, 35 Jermyn St, SW1 (right by the church). Useful vegetarian café to know about, as the area is short on cheap options. There's outdoor courtyard seating in summer. Piccadilly Circus tube.

Covent Garden and the Strand

Café in the Crypt, St Martin-in-the-Fields, Duncannon St, WC2. Below the church, in the crypt, the good-quality buffet food – including veggie dishes – makes this an ideal spot to fill up before hitting the West End. Charing Cross tube.

Diana's Diner, 39 Endell St, WC2. Cramped wooden benches, a friendly welcome for regulars and improbably large plates of home-made pies, omelettes, grills and chips. A favourite with local office workers. Covent Garden tube.

Food for Thought, 31 Neal St, WC2. A sympatico veggie restaurant and takeaway counter – the food is good, with daily changing specials, and vegan and wheat-free options. Expect to queue and don't expect to linger at peak times. Closed Sun eve. Covent Garden tube.

Frank's Cafe, 52 Neal St, WC2. Italian café/sandwich bar with easy-going service. All-day breakfasts, plates of pasta and omelettes on offer; come either side of lunch to make sure of a table. Closed Sun. Covent Garden tube.

Gaby's, 30 Charing Cross Rd, WC2. Jewish café and takeaway joint serving a wide range of home-cooked veggie and Middle Eastern specialities. Hard to beat for value, choice or long hours. It's licensed, too. Leicester Square tube.

India Club, 143 Strand, WC2. There's a faded period charm to this long-established first-floor Anglo-Indian eatery, whose chilli bhajis are to be taken very seriously. Lunchtime only; closed Sun. Covent Garden or Temple tube.

Juice, 7 Earlham St, WC2. Spartan, antiseptic café serving a wde range of wild juices, quiche, salad and sandwiches that appeals to Covent Garden's clubby crowd, who feel the need to cleanse their bodies. Covent Garden or Leicester Square tube.

Neal's Yard Tearoom, 6 Neal's Yard, WC2. Ramshackle first-floor room above superb organic co-operative bakery. Order your food downstairs before heading for the rickety seats upstairs. Closed Sun. Covent Garden tube.

Clerkenwell

Al's Café Bar, 11–13 Exmouth Market, EC1. This is a trendy little spot – a designer greasy spoon with a media-luvvie clientele, who are served up Italian breads, Mediterranean dishes, nachos, decent coffee and good soups alongside the chips and grills. Angel or Farringdon tube.

Clark & Sons, 46 Exmouth Market, EC1. Exmouth Market is currently undergoing something of a transformation, so it's all the more surprising to find this genuine eel and pie shop still going strong. Angel or Farringdon tube. Closed Sun.

Restaurants

Many of the restaurants we've listed will be busy on most nights of the week, particularly on Thursday, Friday and Saturday, and you're best advised to **reserve a table** wherever you're headed. As for **prices**, you can pay an awful lot for a meal in London, and if you're used to North American portions, you're not going to be particularly impressed by the volume in most places.

St James's, Mayfair and Marylebone

Abu Ali, 136–138 George St, W1 (☎0171/724 6338). Honest Lebanese fare that's terrific value for money from the *tabbouleh* to the kebabs – wash it all down with fresh mint tea. Closed Sun. Marble Arch tube. Moderate.

Browns, 47 Maddox St, W1 (☎0171/495 4565). Bustling, popular chain, whose reputation is founded on its steak, mushroom and Guinness pie, but which also offers pastas, hot sandwiches and salads. Closed Sun. Oxford Circus or Bond Street tube. Moderate.

The Criterion, 224 Piccadilly, W1 (☎0171/930 0488). One of the city's most beautiful restaurants, right by Piccadilly Circus. Refurbishment has made the huge dining room sparkle, and the menu has been devised by that scourge of the faint-hearted, Marco Pierre White. Closed Sun lunch. Piccadilly Circus tube. Expensive.

Mandalay, 444 Edgware Rd, W2 (☎0171/258 3696). Pure and unexpurgated Burmese cuisine – a melange of Thai, Malaysian and Indian. The portions are huge, the service friendly and the prices low. Closed Sun. Edgware Road tube. Inexpensive.

Quaglino's, 16 Bury St, SW1 (☎0171/930 6767). Huge 1930s ballroom revived by Terence Conran as one of the capital's busiest and most fashionable eating spots, so you'll need to book well in advance. Dishes don't always work but the splendid surroundings and an unmistakable buzz are the reward. Green Park tube. Expensive.

Sea-Shell, 49–51 Lisson Grove, NW1 (☎0171/723 8703). Top-quality, no-nonsense fish and chips in the heart of Marylebone. Closed Sun eve. Marylebone tube. Moderate.

La Spighetta, 43 Blandford St, W1 (☎0171/486 7340). Not a spaghetti house, in fact, but a pizza and pasta joint – spighetta means wheat – and a very good one at that. Bond Street tube. Moderate.

Soho

China City, White Bear Yard, 25 Lisle St, WC2 (☎0171/734 3388). Large restaurant tucked into a little courtyard off Lisle Street; fresh and bright, with *dim sum* that's up there with the best, service that is "Chinatown brusque", and a menu with eminently reasonable prices. Leicester Square tube. Moderate.

Chuen Cheng Ku, 17 Wardour St, W1 (☎0171/437 1398). Big Cantonese restaurant that's one of the closest in spirit to Hong Kong's cavernous diners. There's a massive range of dishes – the best are on the Chinese-only menu (ask for the day's special). Authentic *dim sum*, too, served from circulating trolleys until 6pm. Leicester Square tube. Moderate.

Kettner's, 29 Romilly St, W1 (☎0171/734 6112). Despite the expensive-looking Baroque decor and the pianist, this place serves cheap pizzas and the like. You can't book and might be forced to hang out a while in the noisy Champagne Bar – no great hardship. Closed Sun. Leicester Square tube. Moderate to Expensive.

Kulu Kulu, 76 Brewer St, W1 (☎0171/734 7316). Small, friendly, *kaiten* (or conveyor-belt) sushi restaurant, which pulls off the unlikely trick of serving really good sushi without being intimidating. Closed Sun. Piccadilly Circus tube. Moderate.

Mezzo, 100 Wardour St, W1 (☎0171/314 4000). *Mezzo* is big, busy and very noisy. Considering the numbers served here, the French/Med food is pretty good. The extraction system is so good you can't even smell the Havanas (served by the "cigarette girl") smoked on your own table. Watch out for the £5 "music-cover charge" after 10.30pm. Piccadilly Circus or Tottenham Court Road tube. Moderate to Very Expensive.

Mr Kong, 21 Lisle St, WC2 (☎0171/437 7341). One of Chinatown's finest, with a chef-owner who pioneered many of the modern Cantonese dishes now on menus all over town. You may have to be firm with staff if you want the more unusual dishes – order from the "Today's" and "Chef's Specials" menu and don't miss the mussels in black-bean sauce. Leicester Square tube. Inexpensive to Moderate.

Randall & Aubin, 16 Brewer St, W1 (☎0171/287 4447). Converted butcher's, now a champagne-oyster bar, rotisserie, sandwich shop and charcuterie, to boot – in the summer, this is a wonderfully airy place to eat. Closed Sun. Piccadilly Circus tube. Moderate to Very Expensive.

Zilli Fish, 36–40 Brewer St, W1 (☎0171/734 8649). Bright, brittle and brash, *Zilli Fish* is a hectic place that appeals to Soho's media luvvies. Serves consistently good fish dishes. Closed Sat & Sun. Oxford Circus or Piccadilly Circus tube. Expensive.

Covent Garden

Livebait, 21 Wellington St, WC2 (☎0171/836 7161). Innovative, irrepressible restaurant, with a large, bustling, black-and-white-tiled dining room, and fish so fresh you expect to see it flapping on the slab. Closed Sun. Covent Garden tube. Expensive.

Mon Plaisir, 21 Monmouth St, WC2 (☎0171/836 7243). One of London's best imitations of a Parisian bistro. The set lunch is a bargain at around £15; otherwise pay up for some of the most pleasing French food in town. Closed Sat lunch & Sun. Covent Garden or Leicester Square tube. Moderate to Expensive.

Stephen Bull, 12 Upper St Martin's Lane, WC2 (☎0171/379 7811). The Bauhaus decor and Modern-British food are a bold statement and this restaurant has plenty of admirers – the fish dishes and desserts are particularly recommended. Reasonably priced set lunches are a bonus. Closed Sun. Leicester Square tube. Moderate to Expensive.

Fitzrovia and Bloomsbury

Chutney's, 124 Drummond St, NW1 (☎0171/388 0604). Tasty, varied veggie Indian food is guaranteed. The buffet lunch for £5 is a bargain as is the deluxe thali for just £7. Euston Square tube. Inexpensive.

Efes, 80 Great Titchfield St, W1 (☎0171/636 1953). Vast Turkish kebab restaurant with 1970s decor – a reliable and friendly place, with doner and shish kebabs big enough to sink a battleship, and some great starters. There's a takeaway counter at the front. Closed Sun. Oxford Circus or Great Portland Street tube. Moderate.

Great Nepalese, 48 Eversholt St, NW1 (☎0171/388 6737). One of very few places in London serving genuine spicy Nepalese dishes. Euston tube. Inexpensive to Moderate.

Ikkyu, 67a Tottenham Court Rd, W1 (☎0171/636 9280). Busy, basement Japanese restaurant, good enough for a quick lunch or a more elaborate dinner. Either way, prices are infinitely more reasonable than elsewhere in the capital, and the food is tasty and authentic. Closed Sat & Sun lunch. Goodge Street tube. Moderate to Expensive.

Malabar Junction, 107a Great Russell St, WC1 (☎0171/580 5230). Inexpensive Keralan restaurant with two separate kitchens, one serving mouth-watering veggie dishes, the other dishing out meat and fish fare. Tottenham Court Road tube. Inexpensive to Moderate.

Mash London, 19–21 Great Portland St, W1 (☎0171/637 5555). Buzzy modern bar/café/restaurant, with its own micro-brewery, that offers an eclectic roster of dishes from its wood-fired oven and grill. Oxford Circus tube. Moderate to Expensive.

R.K. Stanley, 6 Little Portland St, W1 (☎0171/462 0099). Sausages from all over the globe, served in modern surroundings, and washed down with ale, lager, stout or porter. Closed Sun. Oxford Circus tube. Moderate.

Wagamama, 4 Streatham St, WC1 (☎0171/323 9223). Austere, minimalist place where the waiters take your orders on hand-held computers. Diners share long benches and slurp huge bowls of noodle soup or stir-fried plates. You may have to queue, however, and the rapid turnover means it's not a place to consider for a long, romantic dinner. Closed Sun. Tottenham Court Road tube. Inexpensive to Moderate.

Clerkenwell and the City

Cicada, 132 St John St, EC1 (☎0171/720 5433). Part bar, part restaurant, *Cicada* offers an unusual Thai-based menu that allows you to mix and match from small, large and side dishes ranging from fishy *tom yum* to ginger noodles or sushi. Closed Sat lunch & Sun. Farringdon tube. Moderate.

St John, 26 St John St, EC1 (☎0171/251 0848). Decidedly English restaurant, only a stone's throw from Smithfield meat market and specializing in offal. All those strange and unfashionable cuts of meat that were once commonplace in rural England – brains, bone marrow, meat from a cow's sternum – are on offer at this white-painted former smokehouse. Closed Sat & Sun. Farringdon tube. Expensive.

Singapura, 1–2 Limeburner Lane, EC4 (☎0171/329 1133). Beautiful, large, modern restaurant off Ludgate Hill specializing in Nonya cuisine – a sort of fusion of Malayan and Chinese traditions – from Singapore. The food is spicy, garlicky and delicious. Closed Sat & Sun. Blackfriars or St Paul's tube. Expensive.

East End

Arkansas Café, 12 Old Spitalfields Market, E1 (☎0171/377 6999). American-barbie fuel stop, using only the very best ingredients. Try Bubb's own smoked beef brisket and ribs, and be sure to taste his home-made barbie sauce (made to a secret formula). Closed Mon–Sat eve. Liverpool Street tube. Inexpensive to Moderate.

Café Spice Namaste, 16 Prescott St, E1 (☎0171/488 9242). Very popular East End Indian, where the menu is a touch more varied than in many of its rivals – Goan and Kashmiri dishes are often included, and you're as likely to find squid or potato cakes as your usual favourites. Closed Sun. Tower Hill tube. Moderate.

Lahore Kebab House, 3 Umberstone St, E1 (☎0171/481 9737). Despite refurbishment, the food is still good and spicy, the prices low, and the service brusque. In addition, the *Lahore* serves long-stewed sheep's feet – *paya* (Fridays only) – the hallmark of any genuine Pakistani restaurant. Whitechapel tube. Inexpensive.

Viet Hoa Café, 72 Kingsland Rd, E2 (☎0171/729 8293). Large, light and airy Vietnamese café in the wasteland of Shoreditch; serving splendid "meals in a bowl", soups and noodle dishes with everything from spring rolls to tofu. Be sure to try the *pho* soup, a Vietnamese staple that's eaten at any and every meal. Closed Mon. Bus #67, #149 or #242 from Liverpool Street Station. Inexpensive to Moderate.

Lambeth and Southwark

Blue Print Café, Design Museum, Butler's Wharf, SE1 (☎0171/378 7031). The oldest of Terence Conran's gastrodomes – expect to pay higher than average prices for a higher than average meal, and a fabulous view from the terrace windows (for which you must book ahead). Closed Sat lunch. Tower Hill tube. Very Expensive.

Butler's Wharf Chop House, 36e Shad Thames, SE1 (☎0171/403 3403). Conran-owned restaurant showcasing British meat, fish and cheeses. Prices are high, but the *Chop House* tries to cater for all: you could enjoy a simple dish at the bar, a well-priced set lunch, or an extravagant dinner. You can't reserve the terrace tables but try and book ahead for a window seat. Closed Sat lunch. Tower Hill tube. Moderate to Expensive.

Cantina del Ponte, Butler's Wharf, Shad Thames, SE1 (☎0171/403 5403). Another, cheaper Conran place, offering earthy Italian fare in designer surroundings. Again, to enjoy the window tables, or the alfresco terrace, you should book ahead. Tower Hill tube. Moderate to Expensive.

County Hall Restaurant, Queens Walk, SE1 (☎0171/902 8000). Located within the *Marriot Hotel* that now occupies much of County Hall, this restaurant serves ambitious Med-influenced food in sumptuous surroundings, and offers superb views across the Thames to the Houses of Parliament. Westminster tube. Expensive.

Fina Estampa, 150 Tooley St, SE1 (☎0171/403 1342). This may be London's only Peruvian restaurant, but it also happens to be the very best, bringing a little of downtown Lima to London Bridge. The menu is traditional Peruvian, with a big emphasis on seafood. Closed Sun. London Bridge tube. Moderate to Expensive.

Little Saigon, 139 Westminster Bridge Rd, SE1 (☎0171/207 9747). Great Vietnamese spring rolls, grilled squid-cake and crystal pancakes, all served with a wonderful array of sauces, plus great crispy fried noodles. Closed Sat & Sun lunch. Waterloo tube. Moderate to Expensive.

RSJ, 13a Coin St, SE1 (☎0171/928 4554). Regularly high standards of Anglo-French cooking make this a good spot for a meal after or before an evening at a South Bank theatre or concert hall. The set meals for around £15 are particularly popular. Closed Sat lunch & Sun. Waterloo tube. Moderate to Very Expensive.

Kensington and Chelsea

Hunan, 51 Pimlico Rd, SW1 (☎0171/730 5712). Probably England's only restaurant serving Hunan food, a relative of Szechuan food with the same spicy kick to most dishes, and a fair wallop of pepper in those that aren't actively riddled with chillis. Most people opt for the £21 "leave-it-to-us feast" which lets the chef, Mr Peng, show what he can do. Closed Sun lunch. Sloane Square tube. Expensive.

Jenny Lo's Teahouse, 14 Ecclestone St, SW1 (☎0171/259 0399). Bright, bare, utilitarian Chinese restaurant, whose prices make you think you're in the politest cafeteria in the world. Be sure to check out the therapeutic teas. Closed Sun. Victoria tube. Inexpensive.

New Culture Revolution, 305 King's Rd, SW3 (☎0171/352 9281). Great name, great concept – big bowls of freshly cooked noodles in sauce or soup, dumplings and rice dishes, all offering a one-stop meal at bargain prices in simple, minimalist surroundings. Not a place to linger. Sloane Square tube. Inexpensive.

O Fado, 49–50 Beauchamp Place, SW3 (☎0171/589 3002). Probably the oldest Portuguese restaurant in London, which speaks volumes for its authenticity. It can get rowdy what with the live *fado* ballads, and the family parties, but that's half the enjoyment. You'll need to reserve a table. Closed Sun eve. Knightsbridge tube. Expensive.

Wódka, 12 St Alban's Grove, W8 (☎0171/937 6513). The food is cooked with a little imagination, which makes the smart *Wódka* the place to go if you want to experience the best that Polish cuisine has to offer. It's not an expensive place to eat until you start ladling out the ice-cold, flavoured vodkas. Closed Sat & Sun lunch. High Street Kensington or Gloucester Road tube. Moderate to Expensive.

Bayswater and Notting Hill

Alounak, 44 Westbourne Grove, W2 (☎0171/229 0416). Don't be put off by the dated sign outside – this place turns out really good, really cheap Iranian food. Bayswater tube. Inexpensive.

Hung Toa, 51 Queensway, W2 (☎0171/727 5753). Cantonese and Szechuan barbecued meats, noodle dishes and noodle soups at keen prices on this busy street. Queensway or Bayswater tube. Inexpensive.

The Mandola, 139 Westbourne Grove, W11 (☎0171/229 4734). Strikingly delicious "urban Sudanese" food at sensible prices, served by extremely laid-back staff. Check out the Sudanese spiced coffee at the end. Notting Hill Gate tube. Inexpensive to Moderate.

Rodrizio Rico, 111 Westbourne Grove, W11 (☎0171/792 4035). No menu, no prices, but no problem either as this Brazilian eatery specializes in smoky, grilled meat. Carvers come round and lop off chunks of freshly grilled meats, while you help yourself from the salad bar and hot buffet to prime your plate. Closed Sun. Notting Hill Gate or Queensway tube. Moderate.

Rotisserie Jules, 133a Notting Hill Gate, W11 (☎0171/221 3331). One of three restaurants – the other two being at 6 Bute St, SW7 and 338 King's Rd, SW3 – that excels in freshly roasted chicken at sound prices. Notting Hill Gate tube. Inexpensive to Moderate.

Camden and Hampstead

Cheng Du, 9 Parkway, NW1 (☎0171/485 8058). Probably London's best Szechuan restaurant, full of Camden trendies soaking up the spices in a most un-Chinese-restaurant-like environment, with prices more West End than rustic. Camden Town tube. Moderate to Expensive.

El Parador, 245 Eversholt St, NW1 (☎0171/387 2789). Small, no-frills Spanish restaurant a stone's throw from Camden High Street, serving up tasty *tapas*. Service is friendly and laid-back and there's a lovely garden, with tables for alfresco eating. Closed Sat & Sun lunch. Mornington Crescent tube. Moderate.

Lemonia, 89 Regent's Park Rd, NW1 (☎0171/586 7454). Spirited Greek taverna, doing all the basics well, especially the charcoal-grilled meats and fish – the fish meze is splendid. It's extremely popular, so book ahead. If you can't get in, try the associated *Limani* at no. 154 opposite (☎0171/483 4492), with similarly fine food at roughly the same prices. Closed Sat lunch & Sun eve. Chalk Farm tube. Moderate.

Solly's, 146–150 Golders Green Rd, NW11 (☎0171/455 2121). *Solly's*, downstairs, is a small kosher restaurant and deli specializing in epic felafel; *Solly's Exclusive*, upstairs, is a huge, bustling kosher restaurant. Closed Fri eve & Sat lunch. Golders Green tube. Moderate.

Trojka, 101 Regent's Park Rd, NW1 (☎0171/483 3765). Unpretentious restaurant in the heart of Primrose Hill, offering hearty portions of Russian, Ukrainian and Polish food, to the accompaniment of East European music. Chalk Farm tube. Moderate.

Greenwich

The North Pole, 131 Greenwich High Rd, SE10 (☎0181/853 3020). Pub-like from the outside, bright and bar-like on the ground floor, the *North Pole* offers "East meets West" cuisine upstairs, combining Pacific Rim style cooking with European ingredients. Be sure to check out the goldfish-bowl lamps. Closed Mon. Greenwich train station. Moderate to Expensive.

Tai Won Mein, 49 Greenwich Church St, SE10 (☎0181/858 1668). Good quality fast-food noodle bar that gets very busy at the weekend. Decor is functional and minimalist; choose between rice, fried or soup noodles and *ho fun* (a flatter, softer, ribbon-like noodle). Greenwich train station. Inexpensive.

Chiswick to Richmond

Chez Lindsay, 11 Hill Rise, Richmond, Surrey (☎0181/948 7473). Small, bright authentic Breton crepe and galetterie, which also serves more formal French main courses, including lots of fresh fish and shellfish, all washed down with Breton cider in earthenware bolées. Richmond tube. Inexpensive to Moderate.

The Gate, 51 Queen Caroline St, W6 (☎0181/748 6932). Gourmet vegetarian dining that's rich, calorific and naughty in a striking little restaurant tucked behind the Hammersmith Apollo. Closed Sat & Sun. Hammersmith tube. Expensive.

Springbok Café, 42 Devonshire Rd, W4 (☎0181/742 3149). Small, informal, authentic South African restaurant, with an open-plan barbie-oriented kitchen. Many of the ingredients are imported, so there's plenty of biltong, smoked ostrich and the like to please ex-pats. Closed Mon–Sat lunch & Sun. Turnham Green tube. Expensive.

Drinking

Virtually every street in central London has its **pub** and, although generally you'll find the best places away from the centre, there are one or two watering holes in the West End that have kept their character. The greatest concentrations of unspoilt pubs within a tube-hop of the centre are to be found on the east side of town, between Aldwych and the City – some can be uncomfortably packed on weekdays before 8pm, but after that, when the City types have gone home, they are far more appealing. The traditional image of London pub food is dire – a pseudo "ploughman's lunch" of bread and cheese, or a murky-looking pie and chips – but the last couple of decades has seen a lot of change for the better. At many of the pubs listed below you can get a palatable lunchtime meal, and at a few of them you're looking at cooking worthy of high restaurant praise.

According to English **licensing laws**, pubs are allowed to open Monday to Saturday from 11am to 11pm and Sundays from noon to 10.30pm. Most London pubs stick to these hours, but you may find that some of the less busy establishments still follow the old Sunday hours of noon to 3pm and 7 to 10.30pm. It's also worth noting that many pubs in the City are open from Monday to Friday only, and some close earlier than 11pm. For drinking beyond the standard 11pm last orders at a pub, you're probably best off heading for one of the city's **bars**, whose numbers have increased enormously over the past few years. These are very different places from your average pub, catering to a somewhat cliquey, often youngish crowd, with designer interiors and drinks; they're also expensive, often levying an entry charge after 11pm. We've listed a fair few – while covering those tied to, or more like, clubs and dance venues on p.157.

Whitehall and Westminster

Albert, 52 Victoria St, SW1. Roomy High Victorian pub, with big bay windows and glass partitions. Good food, with an excellent upstairs carvery. St James's Park tube.

ICA Bar, 94 The Mall, SW1. You have to be a member to drink at the *ICA Bar* – but anyone can join on the door (Mon–Fri £1.50, Sat & Sun £2.50). It's a cool drinking venue, with a *noir* dress code observed by the arty crowd and staff. Piccadilly Circus or Charing Cross tube.

Paviour's Arms, Page St, SW1. Original, stylish 1930s Art Deco pub, close to the Tate Gallery and offering Thai food along with the beer. Closed Sat & Sun. Pimlico tube.

St James's, Mayfair and Marylebone

Devonshire Arms, 21a Devonshire St, W1. Beautiful interior with lots of brass, frosted mirrors and original tiling, plus newspapers to read. Closed Sun. Baker's Street or Regent's Park tube.

Mulligans, 13–14 Cork St, W1. A fine Irish pub with an odd mix of clientele – Cork Street gallery staff and Irish lads – and the best Guinness in London. Also has a high-class restaurant downstairs, with fine Modern-British cooking. Closed Sun. Green Park or Piccadilly tube.

O'Conor Don, 88 Marylebone Lane, W1. Stripped bare anti-theme Irish pub with table service, excellent Guinness and a pleasantly measured pace. Closed Sun. Bond Street tube.

Red Lion, 2 Duke of York St, SW1. Popular little gin palace, which has preserved its classic Victorian decor. Closed Sun. Green Park or Piccadilly Circus tube.

Soho and Fitzrovia

Coach & Horses, 29 Greek St, W1. Long-standing – and, for once, little-changed – haunt of the ghosts of old Soho, *Private Eye*, nightclubbers, and art students from nearby St Martin's College. Fifties red plastic stools and black formica tables guaranteed. Leicester Square tube.

Dog & Duck, 18 Bateman St, W1. Tiny Soho pub that retains much of its old character, beautiful Victorian tiling and mosaics, and a loyal clientele that often includes jazz musicians from nearby *Ronnie Scott's* club. Closed Sat & Sun lunch. Leicester Square or Tottenham Court Road tube.

French House, 49 Dean St, W1. The tiny French pub has been a Soho institution since before World War I. Free French and literary associations galore, half pints only at the bar (no real ale) and a fine little restaurant upstairs. Leicester Square tube.

The Hope, 15 Tottenham St, W1. Chiefly remarkable for its sausage (veggie ones included), beans and mash lunches, and its real ales. Goodge Street tube.

Newman Arms, 23 Rathbone St, W1. What the *Hope* is to sausages, the *Newman Arms* is to pies, with every sort from gammon to steak-and-kidney. Closed Sat lunch & Sun. Tottenham Court Road tube.

Covent Garden

The Chandos, 29 St Martin's Lane, WC2. If you can get one of the booths downstairs or the leather sofas upstairs in the Opera Room, then you'll find it difficult to leave. Leicester Square tube.

Lamb & Flag, 33 Rose St, WC2. Busy, tiny and highly atmospheric pub, tucked away down an alley between Garrick Street and Floral Street, where John Dryden was attacked in 1679 for writing scurrilous verses about one of Charles II's mistresses. Leicester Square tube.

Punch & Judy, 40 The Market, WC2. Horribly mobbed and expensive, but unbeatable location with a balcony overlooking the Piazza – and a stone-flagged cellar. Covent Garden tube.

Salisbury, 90 St Martin's Lane, WC2. One of the most beautifully preserved Victorian pubs in the capital, with cut, etched and engraved windows, bronze figures and lincrusta ceiling. Leicester Square tube.

Soho Brewing Company, 41 Earlham St, WC2. Busy, brick-vaulted basement brewery with wrought-iron pillars, lots of brushed steel and pricey, strong brews, in particular a very fine wheat beer. Covent Garden tube.

Bloomsbury

Lamb, 94 Lamb's Conduit St, WC1. Pleasant pub with a marvellously well-preserved Victorian interior of mirrors, old wood and "snob" screens. Russell Square tube.

Museum Tavern, 49 Great Russell St, WC1. Large and characterful old pub, right opposite the main entrance to the British Museum, erstwhile drinking hole of Karl Marx. Tottenham Court Road or Russell Square tube.

The Strand, Holborn and Clerkenwell

Café Kick, 43 Exmouth Market, EC1. Stylish take on a local French-style café-bar in the heart of newly fashionable Exmouth Market, with table football to complete the retro theme. Closed Sun. Farringdon or Angel tube.

Eagle, 159 Farringdon Rd, EC1. The first of London's pubs to go foodie, this place is heaving at lunch and dinnertimes, as *Guardian* workers tuck into Med dishes, but you should be able to find a seat at other times. Closed Sun. Farringdon tube.

Fox & Anchor, 115 Charterhouse St, EC1. Handsome Smithfield market pub famous for its early opening hours and huge breakfasts (served 7–10am). Closed Sat & Sun. Farringdon or Barbican tube.

Gordon's, 47 Villiers St, WC2. A real, claustrophobic, cave-like wine bar specializing in ports, right next door to Charing Cross station. The excellent and varied wine list, decent buffet food and genial atmosphere make this a favourite with local office workers. Closed Sat lunch & Sun. Charing Cross or Embankment tube.

Jerusalem Tavern, 55 Britton St, EC1. Cosy little converted Georgian parlour, stripped bare and slightly "distressed", serving tasty food along with the beer. Closed Sat & Sun. Farringdon tube.

O'Hanlon, 8 Tysoe St, EC1. Small Irish pub serving its own brews, including the best stout in London, plus great Irish food. Closed Sun. Angel tube.

Princess Louise, 208 High Holborn, WC1. Old-fashioned place, with highly decorated ceilings, lots of glass, brass and mahogany, and a good range of real ales. Closed Sun. Holborn tube.

The City: Fleet Street to St Paul's

Blackfriar, 174 Queen Victoria St, EC4. A gorgeous, utterly original pub, with Art Nouveau marble friezes of boozy monks and a wonderful highly decorated alcove – all original, dating from 1905. Closed Sat eve & Sun. Blackfriars tube.

Old Bank of England, 194 Fleet St, EC4. Not the actual Bank of England, but the former Law Courts' branch, this imposing High Victorian banking hall is now a magnificently opulent ale and pie pub. Closed Sat & Sun. Temple or Chancery Lane tube.

Old Cheshire Cheese, Wine Office Court, 145 Fleet St, EC4. A famous seventeenth-century watering hole, with several snug, dark panelled bars and real fires. Popular with tourists, but by no means exclusively so. Closed Sun eve. Temple or Blackfriars tube.

The City: Bank to Bishopsgate

The Counting House, 50 Cornhill, EC2. Another City bank conversion, with fantastic high ceilings, a glass dome, chandeliers and a central oval bar. Naturally enough, given the location, it's wall-to-wall suits. Closed Sat & Sun. Bank tube.

Hamilton Hall, Liverpool Street Station, EC2. Cavernous, gilded, former ballroom of the *Great Eastern* hotel, adorned with nudes and chandeliers. Packed out with City commuters tanking up before the train home, but a great place nonetheless. Liverpool Street tube.

Jamaica Wine House, St Michael's Alley, EC3 (☎0171/626 9496). An old City institution tucked away down a narrow alleyway. Despite the name, this is really just a pub, divided into four large "snugs" by high wooden-panelled partitions. Closed Sat & Sun. Bank tube.

East End and Docklands

Dickens Inn, St Katharine's Way, E1. Eighteenth-century timber-framed warehouse transported on wheels from its original site, and then much altered. Still, it's a remarkable building, with a great view, but very firmly on the tourist trail. Tower Hill tube.

Ferry House, 26 Ferry St, E14. Nice, laid-back, old pub, with no pretensions. Conveniently located near the Greenwich foot tunnel. Island Gardens DLR.

Grapes, 76 Narrow St, E14. The *Grapes'* fame is assured thanks to a mention in Dickens' *Our Mutual Friend*; it has a riverside balcony out back, great bar meals and an expensive fish restaurant upstairs. Closed Sat lunch. Westferry DLR.

The Gun, 27 Cold Harbour, E14. An old dockers' pub with lots of maritime memorabilia, and – the main attraction – an unrivalled view of the Millennium Dome. South Quay or Blackwall DLR.

Prospect of Whitby, 57 Wapping Wall, E1. London's most famous riverside pub with a flagstone floor, a cobbled courtyard and great views. Wapping tube.

Town of Ramsgate, 62 Wapping High St, E1. Dark, narrow medieval pub located by Wapping Old Stairs, which once led down to Execution Dock. Captain Blood was discovered here with the crown jewels under his cloak, and Admiral Bligh and Fletcher Christian were regular drinking partners in pre-mutiny days. Wapping tube.

Lambeth and Southwark

Anchor Bankside, 34 Park St, SE1. While the rest of Bankside has changed almost beyond all recognition, this pub still looks much as it did when first built in 1770 (on the inside, at least). Good for alfresco drinking by the river. London Bridge tube.

George Inn, 77 Borough High St, SE1. London's only surviving coaching inn, dating from the seventeenth century and now owned by the National Trust; it also serves a good range of real ales. Borough or London Bridge tube.

NFT Bar, South Bank, SE1. The National Film Theatre's newly refurbished bar is the only river-front bar on the South Bank between Westminster and Blackfriars bridges – worth checking out not only for the views, but also for the food and the congenial crowd. Waterloo tube.

Knightsbridge, Kensington and Chelsea

Bunch of Grapes, 207 Brompton Rd, SW3. This popular High Victorian pub, complete with "snob" screens, is the perfect place for a post-V&A pint. South Kensington tube.

Front Page, 35 Old Church St, SW3. Centre of boho Chelsea and infinitely preferable to anything on offer on the King's Road. Sloane Square tube.

Orange Brewery, 37 Pimlico Rd, SW1. The area may be posh, but this is a fairly down-to-earth, gas-lit boozer with its very own micro-brewery. Sloane Square tube.

Paxton's Head, 153 Knightsbridge, SW1. Wonderful Edwardian pub, with lincrusta ceiling tiles, mahogany bar and etched mirrors, and very unpretentious given the locale. Avoid the bar food. Knightsbridge tube.

Notting Hill

The Cow, 89 Westbourne Park Rd, W2. Pub owned by Tom Conran, son of gastro-magnate Terence, which pulls in the beautiful W11 types, thanks to its spectacular food, including a daily supply of fresh oysters. Westbourne Park tube.

Pharmacy, 150 Notting Hill Gate, W11. Don't come here if you despise the work of artist Damien Hirst, as this bar/restaurant is his little conceit. Still, the medicinal joke is worth at least one laugh: stools that look like giant pills, staff in surgical boots. Closed Sun lunch. Notting Hill Gate tube.

Prince Bonaparte, 80 Chepstow Rd, W2. Pared-down, minimalist pub, with acres of space for sitting and supping or enjoying the excellent Mediterranean food. Closed Tues lunch. Westbourne Park tube.

Retro, 183 Portobello Rd, W11. Another trendy Notting Hill bar – lined with old sofas, and serving sushi and cocktails. Closed Sun & Mon. Ladbroke Grove tube.

St John's Wood and Maida Vale

Prince Alfred, 9 Formosa St, W9. A fantastic period-piece Victorian pub with all its original 1862 fittings intact, right down to the glazed "snob" screens. The beer and Thai food are good, too. Warwick Avenue tube.

Warrington, 93 Warrington Crescent, W9. Yet another architectural gem – this time flamboyant Art Nouveau – in an area replete with them. Thai restaurant upstairs. Warwick Avenue or Maida Vale tube.

Camden Town

Crown & Goose, 100 Arlington St, NW1. Cross between a pub, bar and restaurant, situated a block away from the High Street and not too badly mobbed, even during the market. Food's a bit special, too. Camden Town tube.

The Engineer, 65 Gloucester Ave, NW1. Smart, grandiose pub for the smart, grandiose types in Primrose Hill – the food is exceptional though pricey, and it's advisable to book if you're intending to nosh. Chalk Farm tube.

Lansdowne, 90 Gloucester Ave, NW1. Big, bare-boards minimalist pub with comfy sofas, in elegant Primrose Hill. Pricey, tasty food. Chalk Farm tube. Closed Mon lunch.

Hampstead and Highgate

Flask, 14 Flask Walk, NW3. Convivial Hampstead local, which retains its original Victorian "snob" screen. Serves good food and fine ale. Hampstead tube.

Flask, 77 Highgate West Hill, N6. Ideally situated at the heart of Highgate village green, with a rambling low-ceilinged interior and a summer terrace. Highgate tube.

Freemason's Arms, 32 Downshire Hill, NW3. Big, smart pub close to the Heath, of interest primarily for its large beer garden and its basement skittle alley. Hampstead tube.

Holly Bush, 22 Holly Mount, NW3. A lovely old gas-lit pub, tucked away in the steep backstreets of Hampstead village. Mobbed on the weekend. Hampstead tube.

Dulwich and Greenwich

Crown & Greyhound, 73 Dulwich Village, SE21. Grandiose Victorian pub with ornate plaster-work ceiling and a nice summer beer garden. Convenient for the Picture Gallery. North Dulwich train station.

Cutty Sark, Ballast Quay, off Lassell St, SE10. The nicest riverside pub in Greenwich, yet much less touristy than the *Trafalgar Tavern* (it's a couple of minutes walk further east, following the river). Maze Hill train station.

Trafalgar Tavern, 5 Park Row, SE10. Great riverside position and a mention in Dickens' *Our Mutual Friend* have made this Regency-style inn a firm tourist favourite. Good whitebait and other snacks. Maze Hill train station.

Chiswick to Richmond

Dove, 19 Upper Mall, W6. Old, old riverside pub with literary associations, the smallest back bar in the UK (4ft by 7ft), and Thai food in the evening. Ravenscourt Park tube.

White Cross Hotel, Water Lane, Richmond. With a longer pedigree and more character than its rivals, the *White Cross* is also closer to the river, has a garden out back and serves filling pub food. Richmond tube.

White Swan, Riverside, Twickenham. Decent food and beer and a quiet riverside location – with a beer pontoon overlooking Eel Pie Island if you want to get even closer to the water. Twickenham train station.

Nightlife

On any night of the week London offers a vast range of things to do after dark, rang-ing from top-flight opera and theatre to clubs with a life span of a couple of nights. The **listings magazine** *Time Out*, which comes out every Wednesday, is essential if you want to get the most out of this city, giving full details of prices and access, plus previews and reviews.

Don't believe the hype over the last couple of years about the new, Cool Britannia: as far as London is concerned, there's been a bewildering range of places to go after dark for at least the last couple of decades. The live music scene remains amazingly diverse, encompassing all variations of **rock, blues, roots and world music**. And although London's **jazz clubs** aren't on a par with those in the big American cities there's a highly individual scene of home-based artists, supplemented by top-name visiting players.

London is seriously into **dance music** – from hardcore to house, from techno to trance. Venues once used exclusively by performing bands now pepper the week with club nights, and you often find dance sessions starting as soon as the band's stopped playing. Bear in mind, then, that there's an overlap between "live music venues" and "clubs" in the listings below; we've indicated which places serve a double function.

London has enjoyed a reputation for quality **theatre** since the time of Shakespeare, and despite the increasing prevalence of fail-safe blockbuster musicals and revenue-spinning star vehicles, the city still provides a platform for innovation. **Cinema** is rather less healthy, for London's repertory film theatres are a dying breed, edged out by the multiscreen complexes, which show mainstream Hollywood fare some months behind America. There are a few excellent independent cinemas, though, including the National Film Theatre, which is the focus of the richly varied **London International Film Festival**, in November.

Live music venues

London is hard to beat for its musical mix: whether you're into **jazz**, **indie rock**, **R&B**, **blues** or **world music** you'll find something worth hearing on almost any night of the week. Entry prices for gigs run from a couple of pounds for an unknown band thrashing it out in a pub to around £30 for the likes of U2, but £10–15 is the average price for a good night out – not counting expenses at the bar.

Rock and blues clubs and pubs

12 Bar Club, 22–23 Denmark Place, WC2. Seven nights a week this club plays a combination of live blues and contemporary country. Tottenham Court Road tube.

Astoria, 157 Charing Cross Rd, WC2. One of London's best and most central venues. A large, balconied one-time theatre that goes for slightly alternative bands, with club nights on Friday and Saturday. LA2, next door, is primarily a club, but also attracts less well-known bands. Tottenham Court Road tube.

Borderline, Orange Yard, off Manette St, W1. Intimate basement joint with diverse musical policy. Good place to catch new bands, although big ones sometimes turn up under a pseudonym. Also has club nights. Tottenham Court Road tube.

Brixton Academy, 211 Stockwell Rd, SW9. This refurbished Victorian hall, complete with Roman decorations, can hold 4000, and usually does, but manages to seem small and friendly, probably because no one is forced to sit down. Hosts mainly mid-league bands, and has renowned club all-nighters too. Brixton tube.

Forum, 9–17 Highgate Rd, NW5. The Forum is perhaps the capital's best medium-sized venue – large enough to attract established bands, and with great views and good bars. Kentish Town tube.

The Mean Fiddler, 24–28a Harlesden High St, NW10. An excellent, if unfortunately located, small venue with a main hall and smaller acoustic room. The music veers from rock to world to folk to soul (and even, occasionally, gospel). Willesden Junction tube.

The Orange, 3 North End Crescent, W14. Pub-like venue for serious-minded jazz-funkers. There are also club nights (nights vary). West Kensington tube.

Rock Garden, 35 The Piazza, WC2. Central, loud-music joint where you can get in free if you dine at the attached burger place first. Covent Garden tube.

Roadhouse, 35 The Piazza, WC2. American food, 1950s American decor and a line-up of mainly blues and rock'n'roll bands performing to an older, nostalgic crowd. Covent Garden tube.

Station Tavern, 41 Bramley Rd, W10. Arguably London's best blues venue, with free and occasionally great blues six nights a week. Latimer Road tube.

Subterania, 12 Acklam Rd, W10. One of the original live music/club crossover venues in an arch under a bridge. The crowd is as trendy as the music. Ladbroke Grove tube.

Underworld, 174 Camden High St, NW1. This labyrinthine venue is good for new bands and has sporadic club nights. Camden Town tube.

Jazz, world music and roots

100 Club, 100 Oxford St, W1. After a brief spell as a stage for punk bands, the *100 Club* is once again an unpretentious and inexpensive trad jazz venue. Tottenham Court Road tube.

606 Club, 90 Lots Rd, SW10. A rare for London all-jazz venue, located off the untrendy end of the King's Road. You can book a table, and the licensing laws dictate that you must eat if you want to drink, but there's no cover charge. Fulham Broadway tube.

Africa Centre, 38 King St, WC2. African bands perform here in a packed old hall. The atmosphere is usually great, as most of the audience are London-based Africans. It also has a market. Covent Garden tube.

Jazz Café, 5 Parkway, NW1. Slick modern venue with an adventurous booking policy exploring Latin, rap, funk, hip-hop and other unlikely avenues. Die-hard trad-jazz fans won't be happy. Camden Town tube.

Ronnie Scott's, 47 Frith St, W1. The most famous jazz club in London: small and smoky and still going strong, even though the great man himself has passed away. The place for top-line names, who play two sets – one at around 10pm, the other after midnight. Book a table, or you'll have to stand. Leicester Square tube.

Clubs and discos

More than ten years after the explosion of acid-house, London is still up for it. The sheer diversity of dance music has enabled London to maintain its status as Europe's **dance capital** – and is still a port of call for DJs from around the world. Recent relaxations in late-night licensing have allowed many venues to keep serving alcohol until 6am or even later. This resurgence in alcohol in clubland (much to the relief of the breweries) has been echoed by the meteoric rise of the club-bar (see box below).

Nearly all **dance clubs** open their doors between 10pm and midnight. Some are open six or seven nights a week, some keep irregular days, others just open at the weekend – and very often a venue will host a different club on each night of the week. Admission **charges** vary enormously, with small midweek nights starting at around £3 and large weekend events charging as much as £25; around £10 is the average for a Friday and Saturday night, but bear in mind that profit margins at the bar are even more outrageous than at live music venues.

Club venues

333, 333 Old St, EC1. Three floors of drum'n'bass, twisted disco and breakbeat madness. Old Street tube.

Aquarium, 256 Old St, EC1. The place with the pool – when all the beautiful young things get hot and sweaty they can dive in and cool off. Popular for speed garage nights. Old Street tube.

The Arches, 53 Southwark St, SE1. A good place to head if you like your music retro. Soul, funk and disco from the Seventies and Eighties. London Bridge tube.

CLUB-BARS

The most notable event in the clubbing world of late has been the arrival of the **club-bar**: essentially a bar with modern decor, dance music and a club clientele. Some of the places listed below are more like bars and not all of them have DJs, but all are more about socializing rather than dancing. However, there's no denying it gets tedious when you have to yell.

A.K.A., West Central St, WC1. Minimalist bar, next door to *The End*. Chrome balcony overlooks the main floor, which includes a well-stocked bar where you can eat such delights as butternut squash and chive soup. Tottenham Court Road tube.

Alphabet, 61–63 Beak St, W1. Upstairs is light and spacious with decadent leather sofas and mouth-watering food; downstairs, the dimmed coloured lights and car seats make for an altogether seedier atmosphere. Oxford Circus tube.

Atlantic, 20 Glasshouse St, W1. Still a popular choice for the glitzy crowd. Three bars designed in the Art Deco style attract a mixed clientele. Oxford Circus tube.

Bar Vinyl, 6 Inverness St, NW1. Funky glass-bricked place complete with record shop downstairs. Has a breakbeat and trip-hop vibe. Camden Town tube.

Detroit, 35 Earlham St, WC2. Cavernous underground venue mixing open-plan bar area and secluded Gaudiesque booths. Stocks a huge range of spirits. DJs take over at the weekends, with underground house popular on Saturdays. Covent Garden tube.

Dog House, 187 Wardour St, W1. Dark, smoky basement bar popular for hip-hop, funk and acid-jazz. Leicester Square tube.

Jerusalem, 33–34 Rathbone Place, W1. At the time of writing, this is the place to be seen. Decor is all chandeliers and velvet drapes; astonishing diversity of music. Tottenham Court Road tube.

The Notting Hill Arts Club, 21 Notting Hill Gate, W11. Basement bar, popular for everything from Latin-inspired funk, jazz and disco through to soul, house and garage. Notting Hill Gate tube.

Astoria, 157 Charing Cross Rd, W1. Massive dancefloor packed with up-for-it clubbers on Friday and Saturday nights. Loads of room for everyone and a nice bar area upstairs for those with no energy left. Tottenham Court Road tube.

Bagley's, King's Cross Goods Yard, off York Way, N1. Vast warehouse-style venue. The perfect place for enormous raves, with a different DJ in each of the three rooms, and a chill-out bar complete with sofas. King's Cross tube.

Bar Rumba, 36 Shaftesbury Ave, W1. Small West End venue with a programme of Latin, jazz-based and funk dance. Many of the punters are regulars. An unpretentious place frequented by happy people and well noted in clubbing circles for its amazing diversity. Piccadilly Circus tube.

Blue Note, 1–5 Parkfield St, N1. Everything from Indian music on Mondays to a live acoustic set on Saturdays. Other floors play a funky mix of house, garage, hip-hop and swing, with a great sound system and a lively crowd. The massive Sunday night drum'n'bass session (*Metalheadz*) is always rammed. Angel tube.

Café de Paris, 3 Coventry St, W1. Elegantly restored ballroom that plays house, garage and disco to a smartly dressed, trendy crowd – no jeans or trainers. Leicester Square tube.

Camden Palace, 1 Camden High St, NW1. Most often home to Balearic beats; great lights, great sound, heaving crowds. Camden Town tube.

Chunnel Club, 101 Timworth St, SE1. Chiefly a house venue and justly famous for *Sunny Side Up* which runs all day on Sundays. Dress code is a smile. Vauxhall tube.

Cloud 9, 67–68 Albert Embankment, SE1. Friendly venue, under the arches. One arch for full-on house and techno and the other for the chill-out. Vauxhall tube.

The Cross, Goods Way Depot, off York Way, N1. Hidden underneath the arches the favourite flavours of this renowned club are hard-house, house and garage. It's bigger than you imagine, but always rammed with chic clubby types, and there's a fabulous garden – perfect for those chill-out moments. King's Cross tube.

Electric Ballroom, 184 Camden High St, NW1. Attracts a mixed crowd with a wide range of sounds: from rock to hip-hop, jazz to house. Camden Town tube.

The End, 18 West Central St, WC1. A club designed for clubbers, by clubbers – large and spacious with chrome minimalist decor. Well known for all music styles, and especially noted for monthly nights hosted by other clubs or record labels. Holborn tube.

Fridge, Town Hall Parade, Brixton Hill, SW2. South London's big night out, with a musical policy running from funk to garage. Great psyche nights and top techno tunes. Occasional home to *Escape from Samsara*, the night with the psychedelic, trancy vibe and hippie market. Brixton tube.

Gardening Club, 4 The Piazza, WC2. Unusually for a central London club, the *Gardening Club* is surprisingly good. A popular choice for house and garage, but be warned, early on you'll be sharing the dance floor with beer-boys and bemused tourists. Covent Garden tube.

Gossips, 69 Dean St, W1. Cave-like basement club that seems to have been around forever. Located deep in the heart of Soho, it's a popular stop for reggae and hip-hop fans. Tottenham Court Road tube.

Hanover Grand, 6 Hanover St, W1. A former Masonic hall, that's now a cool and extravagant club, with a great lights and sound system, a fine dancefloor, lots of alcoves – and air conditioning. Popular with the glammed-up, glittery and beautiful crew. Oxford Circus tube.

HQs, West Yard, Camden Lock, NW1. Smallish venue by the canal with a range of nights, although the emphasis is on uplifting house through to salsa. Friendly vibe. Camden Town tube.

Iceni, 11 White Horse St, W1. Three-floor club patronized by a slightly older, self-consciously stylish, well-off crowd. Music ranges from funk and rap to house, but is always the last word in drop-dead cool. Green Park tube.

LA2, 157 Charing Cross Rd. Fantastic Nineties-house-meets-disco place with gay and straight nights. The legendary *Carwash* (on Saturdays) is the epitome of all things Seventies – you'll have to dress up to get in. Tottenham Court Road tube.

The Leisure Lounge, 121 Holborn, EC1. This place has had its share of the big name nights, and is always a good place to check out the latest grooves. Two dancefloors – one a full-on dance zone, the other a more relaxed bar area. Chancery Lane or Farringdon tube.

Ministry of Sound, 103 Gaunt St, SE1. A vast, state of the art club based on New York's legendary *Paradise Garage*, with an exceptional sound system. Corporate clubbing and full of tourists, but it still draws the top talent. Elephant & Castle tube.

Office, 3–5 Rathbone Place W1. Various music styles but noted as home to the original mid-week session where you can play silly board games like Ker-Plunk. Booking a table in advance is advised. Tottenham Court Road tube.

Plastic People, 37–39 Oxford St, W1. Surprisingly undiscovered for such a central location. Small, but perfectly formed; funky deep-house, cheerful punters and reasonable prices. Tottenham Court Road tube.

Salsa! 96 Charing Cross Rd, WC2. Funky salsa-based club where you can book a table to eat as you jive. Leicester Square tube.

Subterania, 12 Acklam Rd, W10. In the heart of trendy Notting Hill, worth a visit for its diverse (but dressy) club nights on Fridays and Saturdays. Ladbroke Grove tube.

SW1, 191 Victoria St, SW1. Serious clubbers congregate at this Edwardian oak-panelled dance hall for some hard-house and speed garage. Sunday afternoons attract a less sweaty crowd. Victoria tube.

Turnmills, 63 Clerkenwell Rd, EC1. Swanky coffee bar upstairs, fantastic alien-invasion style bar and funky split-level dancefloor in the main room. *Heavenly Jukebox* on Saturdays is followed at 4am by the awesomely glorious gay extravaganza, *Trade*. Farringdon tube.

The Velvet Room, 143 Charing Cross Rd, WC2. Very cool velvet-dripping interior, with house, techno and drum'n'bass nights. Tottenham Court Road tube.

The Wag Club, 35 Wardour St, W1. In need of an overhaul, but still going strong, with two floors of sounds. The dance music and Eighties-revival nights are popular. Wild, psychedelic interior with funky music to match. Leicester Square or Piccadilly Circus tube.

Gay and lesbian bars and clubs

Lesbian and gay Londoners have a lot to be cheerful about, with a scene that is the envy of most other world capitals and a political climate that seems increasingly to embrace the sexual diversity of its population. **Soho** remains the country's most vibrant "gay village", though it's less male-dominated than it was. Details of most events appear in *Time Out* and the many free gay **listings guides** distributed in bars, clubs and bookshops, or you can tune in to the Thursday night *Lavender Lounge* radio programme on GLR (94.5FM). Another excellent source of information is the London **Lesbian and Gay Switchboard** (☎0171/837 7324), which operates around the clock.

Bars and cafés

There are loads of lesbian and gay watering holes in London, many of them operating as **cafés** by day and transforming into **drinking dens** at night. Lots have **disco nights** and are open until the early hours, making them a fine alternative to the more expensive clubs. This selection will give you a good idea of the range on offer, but almost every corner of London has its own gay local.

79CXR, 79 Charing Cross Rd, WC2. Busy, cruisey men's den on two floors, with industrial decor, late licence and a no-messing atmosphere. Leicester Square tube.

Angel, 65 Graham St, N1. Relaxed, Mediterranean-style lesbian and gay café-bar, attracting a mixed but generally upmarket crowd, and especially popular with women. The food is good, the exhibitions eye-catching, and the sofas comfy. Angel tube.

Balans, 60 Old Compton St, W1. This relaxed (but not especially cheap) café-bar is open all night at weekends, late during the week, and always packed, with a singer or cabaret after 11pm. Be warned though – you may have to promise to eat to get in at busy times, even if you just want a coffee. Leicester Square tube.

Bar Code, 3–4 Archer St, W1. Stylish, busy men's cruise- and dance-bar on two floors in the middle of Soho. Piccadilly tube.

The Black Cap, 171 Camden High St, NW1. North London cabaret institution – a big venue on the drag scene, with live acts almost every night. A friendly mixed (mainly male) crowd joins in the fun. *Mrs Shufflewick's Bar* upstairs is quieter, and opens onto a lush and lovely roof garden. Camden Town tube.

The Box, 32–34 Monmouth St, WC2. Bright, gay-owned café-bar serving good food for a mixed gay/straight crowd during the day, and becoming queerer as the night draws in. *Box Babes* on Sunday nights sees girlpower take it over. Covent Garden or Leicester Square tube.

Brief Encounter, 41–43 St Martin's Lane, WC2. One of the longest-running gay bars in London. One bar is bright and busy, the other dim and busy. A popular pre-*Heaven* or post-opera hang-out (it's next door to the Coliseum). Leicester Square tube.

Candy Bar, 4 Carlisle St, W1. Britain's first seven-day all-girl bar is right in the heart of gay-boys' land and offers three floors of varied lesbo action: a retro-style cocktail bar upstairs, beer and elbows-in-yer-face on ground level, and a range of club nights in the packed basement. Gay men welcome as guests. Be warned, some nights you can queue and queue and queue. Tottenham Court Road tube.

Compton's, 53 Old Compton St, W1. Large, traditional-style pub in the centre of Soho, always busy and with a youngish crowd, but still a relaxed place to cruise or just hang out. Lesbians are a rare, but not unwelcome, sight. Leicester Square or Piccadilly tube.

First Out, 52 St Giles High St, WC2. The first gay café-bar in the West End and still packed, serving good veggie food at reasonable prices. Upstairs is airy and non-smoking, downstairs dark and smoky. *Girl Friday* is a women-only pre-club Friday night session; gay men welcome as guests. Tottenham Court Road tube.

Freedom, 60–66 Wardour St, W1. Hip, busy café/bar, popular and occasionally just a little posey. Fashionably health-conscious beverages complement the more decadent liquids on offer. The theatre space downstairs occasionally transforms itself into a seriously funky basement club. Leicester Square or Piccadilly tube.

The Glass Bar, West Lodge, Euston Square Gardens, 190 Euston Rd, NW1. Difficult to find, but never forgotten, this friendly and intimate women-only bar is housed in a listed building with a wrought-iron spiral staircase. Open to members (you become one once you've found it) Tuesday to Saturday till late, with a mellow soundtrack and live jazz monthly. Euston tube.

Her/She Bar at *Jacomo's*, 88–89 Cowcross St, EC1. This new women's bar boasts stylish but strangely soulless decor, although it does have a good selection of board games. Weekly indie DJs and live music on Sundays jazz it up a bit. Gay men welcome as guests during the week, women-only at weekends. Farringdon tube.

Old Compton Café, 34 Old Compton St, W1. Open all day, every day, this gay coffee-bar is the obvious answer to pre- or post-party peckishness. Tottenham Court Road tube.

Village Soho, 81 Wardour St, W1. Elegant bi-level café-bar attracting more pretty boys than women, but striving to redress the balance. Leicester Square tube.

The Yard, 57 Rupert St, W1. Attractive café-bar, making full use of its courtyard and loft areas. Good food, weekly cabaret – including *Screamers*, the queer comedy club – and fortune tellers. Piccadilly Circus tube.

Clubs

The majority of lesbian and gay **clubs** are still one-nighters at established venues (listed in the mainstream "clubs and discos" above), such as DTPM at The End, G.A.Y. at the Astoria, and Popstartz at the Leisure Lounge. Those listed below are the city's permanent gay and lesbian clubs.

Ace of Clubs, 52 Piccadilly, W1. It calls itself legendary, and it's certainly an institution. This weekly Saturday night women-only club for all ages and styles has been packing them in for years and shows no sign of losing its appeal. Piccadilly Circus tube.

Heaven under The Arches, Villiers St, WC2. This legendary, 2000-capacity club has had major cosmetic surgery of late and emerged with its reputation as the UK's most popular gay club unscathed. Big nights are Mondays (Popcorn), Wednesdays (Fruit Machine) and Saturdays (Just Heaven). More boys than girls. Charing Cross or Embankment tube.

The Hoist, Railway Arch 47c South Lambeth Rd, SW8. Weekend men's cruise-bar with leather/rubber/industrial/uniform dress code. Also hosts SM Gays every third Thursday. Vauxhall tube.

Underground at Central Station, 37 Wharfdale Rd, N1. The basement of this friendly, three-tiered pub yields sleazy late-night cruising seven nights a week and is also host to Gummi, Europe's only rubber-only club, every second Sunday of the month. Equally picturesque theme nights include Blacksmiths, Meatpackers, Locker Room and Glory Hole. King's Cross tube.

Theatre and cinema

London's two big government-subsidized theatre companies are the National Theatre, performing in three theatres on the South Bank (☎0171/452 3000), and the Royal Shakespeare Company, whose productions transfer to the two houses in the Barbican (☎0171/638 8891) after their run in Stratford. For a show that's had good reviews, tickets under £10 are difficult to come by at either, but it's always worth ringing their box offices for details of standby deals, which can get you the best seat in the house for as little as £5 if you're a student, otherwise £10. Similar deals are offered by many of London's scores of theatres. Venues with a reputation for challenging productions include the Almeida, Bush, Donmar Warehouse, Royal Court, Young Vic, Tricycle and the ICA.

The Society of London Theatres ticket booth (Mon–Sat 2.30–6.30pm; matinees only noon–2.30pm) in Leicester Square sells half-price tickets for that day's performances at all the West End theatres, but they specialize in the top end of the price range. The Charing Cross Road and Leicester Square areas also have offices that can get tickets for virtually all shows, but the mark-up can be outrageous. Beware that if you buy from touts, there's no guarantee that the tickets aren't fakes.

There are an awful lot of cinemas in the West End, but only a very few places committed to non-mainstream movies, and even fewer repertory cinemas programming serious films from the back catalogue. London's main repertory cinemas in the centre are the National Film Theatre (☎0171/928 3232) on the South Bank and the ICA (☎0171/930 3647), both of which charge for day membership on top of the ticket price. It's always worth checking what's on at the Renoir (Brunswick Square; Russell Square tube), the Gate (Notting Hill Gate), the Metro (Rupert Street, near Leicester Square), and the cut-price Prince Charles (Leicester Square). November's London Film Festival, which occupies half a dozen West End cinemas, is so popular that most of the films sell out within a couple of days of the publication of the festival's programme.

Classical music, opera and dance

For classical concerts the principal venue is the South Bank Centre, where the biggest names appear at the Royal Festival Hall, with more specialized programmes staged in the Queen Elizabeth Hall and Purcell Room (all three halls ☎0171/960 4242). Programmes in the massive concert hall of the Barbican Centre, Silk Street, EC2 (☎0171/638 8891), are too often pitched at the corporate audience, though it has the occasional classy recital. For chamber music, the intimate and elegant Wigmore Hall, 36 Wigmore St, W1 (☎0171/935 2141), is many a Londoner's favourite. Tickets for all these venues begin at about £7, with cheap standbys sometimes available to students on the evening of the performance.

From July to September each year, the Proms at the Royal Albert Hall (☎0171/589 8212) feature at least one concert daily, with hundreds of standing seats sold for just £3 on the night. The acoustics aren't the world's best, but the calibre of the performers is unbeatable and the programme is a fascinating mix of standards and new or obscure works. The hall is so vast that only megastars like Jessye Norman can pack it out, so if you turn up half an hour before the show starts there should be little risk of being turned away. All year round, from Monday to Friday, there are **free lunchtime concerts** in many of London's churches, with performances of chamber music or solo works by students or professionals.

Covent Garden's **Royal Opera House**, expensively refurbished for the new millennium, is hoping to dispel its elitist, but not its classy, reputation. The **English National Opera** at the Coliseum, St Martin's Lane (☎0171/632 8300), has more radical producers and is a more democratic institution – tickets begin at £8 and any unsold seats are released on the day of the performance at greatly reduced prices; all works are sung in English. In addition to the big two opera houses, smaller halls often stage more innovative productions by touring companies such as Opera North – the Queen Elizabeth Hall is a regular venue. Nowadays the Royal Opera House has a better reputation for **ballet** than for singing, as its resident **Royal Ballet Company** can call on the talents of Darcy Bussell and Sylvie Guillem, to name just two of its most glamorous stars. Visiting classical companies also appear regularly at the Coliseum, and less frequently at the Royal Albert Hall. London's **contemporary dance** scene is no less exciting – adventurous programmes are staged at the South Bank, the ICA, Sadler's Wells, The Place, as well as at numerous more ad hoc venues.

Listings

Airlines American Airlines (☎0345/789789); British Airways (☎0345/222111); Lufthansa (☎0345/737747); Virgin Atlantic (☎01293/747747).

Airport enquiries Gatwick (☎01293/535353); Heathrow (☎0181/759 4321); London City (☎0171/646 0000); Stansted (☎01279/680500).

American Express 6 Haymarket, SW1 (Mon–Fri 9am–5.30pm, Sat 9am–6pm, Sun 10am–1pm & 2–5pm; ☎0171/930 4411).

Bike rental Bikepark, 14 Stukeley St, WC1 (☎0171/430 0083).

Books Foyles, 119 Charing Cross Rd, WC2, is London's most famous bookshop but is chaotically organized. Neighbouring Waterstones is preferable, as is Books Etc and Blackwells across the road, and the university bookshop Dillons, 82 Gower St, WC1. For more radical publications, call in at Compendium, 234 Camden High St, NW1, a London institution for everything from anarchy to Zen Buddhism. For maps and travel books, go to Stanford's, 12 Long Acre, WC2 or The Travel Bookshop, 13 Blenheim Crescent, W11.

Bus information Long-distance coach services depart from Victoria Coach Station, Buckingham Palace Rd (Victoria tube). National Express have ticket offices here (☎0990/808080) and can tell you about European services operated by Eurolines.

Car rental You'll find cheapish rates at Holiday Autos (☎0990/300400). The multinational firms also have outlets all over London; ring their central switchboards to find the nearest one: Avis (☎990/900500), Budget (☎0800/181181), Hertz (☎0990/996699).

Dentist Emergency treatment: Guy's Hospital, St Thomas's St, SE1 (Mon–Fri 9am–3pm; ☎0171/955 4317).

Embassies Australia, Australia House, The Strand, WC2 (☎0171/379 4334); Canada, 1 Grosvenor Square, W1 (☎0171/258 6600); Ireland, 17 Grosvenor Place, SW1 (☎0171/235 2171); New Zealand, New Zealand House, 80 Haymarket, SW1 (☎0171/930 8422); South Africa, South Africa House, Trafalgar Square, WC2 (☎0171/930 4488); USA, 24 Grosvenor Square, W1 (☎0171/499 9000).

Exchange Shopping areas such as Oxford Street and Covent Garden are littered with private exchange offices, and there are 24-hour booths at the biggest central tube stations, but their rates are always worse than the banks. Oxford Street, Regent Street and Piccadilly are where you'll find the major branches of all the main banks.

Hospitals The most central hospitals with 24-hour emergency units are: Chelsea & Westminster, 369 Fulham Rd, SW10 (☎0181/746 8000); Royal London Hospital, Whitechapel Rd, E1 (☎0171/377 7000); St Mary's Hospital, Praed St, W2 (☎0171/886 6666); University College Hospital, Grafton Way, WC1 (☎0171/387 9300).

Left luggage AIRPORTS Gatwick: North Terminal (daily 6am–10pm; ☎01293/502013); South Terminal (24hr; ☎01293/502014). Heathrow: Terminal 1 (daily 6am–11pm; ☎0181/745 5301); Terminal 2 (daily 6am–10.30pm; ☎0181/745 4599); Terminal 3 (daily 5.30am–10.30pm; ☎0181/759 3344); Terminal 4 (daily 5.30am–11pm; ☎0181/745 7460). London City Airport (Mon–Fri 6am–9.30pm, Sat 6am–1pm, Sun 10.30am–9.30pm; ☎0171/646 0000). Stansted Airport (24hr; ☎01279/662082). TRAIN STATIONS Charing Cross (daily 7.15am–11pm; ☎0171/839 4282); Euston (daily 6.45am–11.15pm; ☎0171/320 0528); Paddington (Mon–Sat 7am–10pm, Sun 8am–10pm; ☎0171/313 1514); Victoria (daily 7am–10.15pm, plus lockers; ☎0171/928 5151 ext 29887); Waterloo (daily 7am–11pm; ☎0171/928 2424).

London Transport enquiries 24-hour information on ☎0171/222 1234.

Lost property AIRPORTS Gatwick (daily 7.30am–5.30pm; ☎01293/50316); Heathrow (Mon–Fri 8am–5pm, Sat & Sun 8am–4pm; ☎0181/745 7727); London City (Mon–Fri 6am–9.30pm, Sat

6am–1pm, Sun 10.30am–9.30pm; ☎0171/646 0000); Stansted (daily 5.30am–11pm; ☎01279/680500). TRAIN STATIONS Euston (Mon–Sat 9am–5pm, Sun 11am–7pm; ☎0171/922 6477); King's Cross (daily 8am–7.45pm; ☎0171/922 9081); Liverpool Street (Mon–Fri 7am–7pm, Sat & Sun 7am–2pm; ☎0171/928 9158); Paddington (Mon–Sat 7am–10pm, Sun 8am–10pm; ☎0171/313 1514); Victoria (daily 7am–10.15pm, ☎0171/922 9887); Waterloo (Mon–Fri 7.30am–8pm; ☎0171/401 7861). TUBE TRAINS London Regional Transport (☎0171/486 2496).

Markets Camden, Camden High Street to Chalk Farm Road – mainly clothes and cheap jewellery (Wed–Sun 9am–5pm; Camden Town tube); Brick Lane – everything from sofas to antique cameo brooches (Sunday from dawn to around midday; Aldgate East tube); Greenwich, Market Square – small arty-crafty market (Sat & Sun 9am–5pm; Greenwich train station); Petticoat Lane, Middlesex Street and Goulston Street – cheap and cheerful clothes (Sun 9am–4pm; Aldgate East or Liverpool Street tube); Portobello, Portobello Rd – mostly boho-chic clothes and portable antiques (Sat 9am–5pm; Notting Hill or Ladbroke Grove tube); Spitalfields, Commercial Street – arty-crafty during the week plus organic fruit and veg on Fridays and Sundays (Mon–Fri 11am–3pm, Sun 9am–3pm).

Pharmacies Every police station keeps a list of emergency pharmacies in its area.

Police The most central police station is at 10 Vine St, W1 (☎0171/437 1212), just off Regent Street. In emergencies dial ☎999.

Post offices The Trafalgar Square post office (24–28 William IV St, WC2 4DL) has the longest opening hours (Mon–Fri 8am–8pm, Sat 9am–8pm). It's to this post office that Poste Restante mail should be sent.

Train stations and information As a broad guide, Euston handles services to northwest England and Glasgow; King's Cross northeast England and Edinburgh; Liverpool Street eastern England; Paddington western England; Victoria and Waterloo southeast England. For information, call national rail enquiries on ☎0345/484950.

Travel agents Campus Travel, 52 Grosvenor Gardens, SW1 (☎0171/730 3402); Council Travel, 28a Poland St, W1 (☎0171/437 7767); STA Travel, 86 Old Brompton Rd, SW7 (☎0171/361 6161); Trailfinders, 42–50 Earl's Court Rd, SW5 (☎0171/938 3366).

travel details

Trains from:

London Charing Cross to: Dover Priory (2 hourly; 1hr 45min–2hr).

London Euston to: Birmingham New St (2 hourly; 1hr 40min); Carlisle (every 1–2hr; 3hr 50min); Chester (3 daily; 2hr 40min); Crewe (hourly; 2hr); Lancaster (8 daily; 3hr); Liverpool Lime St (hourly; 2hr 45min); Manchester Piccadilly (hourly; 2hr 30min).

London King's Cross to: Brighton (every 10–40min; 1hr 15min); Cambridge (2 hourly; 50min); Durham (every 1–2hr; 2hr 50min); Leeds (hourly; 2hr 20min); Newcastle (2 hourly; 2hr 40min–3hr); York (2 hourly; 1hr 40min–2hr).

London Liverpool Street to: Cambridge (hourly; 1hr 20min); Harwich (every 2hr; 1hr 10min); Norwich (hourly; 2hr); Stansted (every 30min; 45min).

London Paddington to: Bath (1–2 hourly; 1hr 25min); Bristol Parkway (1–2 hourly; 1hr 20min); Exeter St Davids (hourly; 2hr 10min); Oxford (1–2 hourly; 50min–1hr); Penzance (7 daily; 5hr); Plymouth (every 1–2hr; 3hr–3hr 40min); Worcester (11 daily; 2hr–2hr 15min).

London St Pancras to: Leicester (every 30min; 1hr 15min); Nottingham (hourly; 1hr 50min); Sheffield (hourly; 2hr 20min).

London Victoria to: Brighton (2 hourly; 1hr–1hr 20min); Canterbury East (2 hourly; 1hr 30min); Canterbury West (hourly; 1hr 50min); Dover Priory (hourly; 1hr 50min); Gatwick (frequently; 30min) ; Ramsgate (hourly; 1hr 50min).

London Waterloo to: Portsmouth Harbour (2 hourly; 1hr 35min); Southampton Central (3 hourly; 1hr 15min); Winchester (3 hourly; 1hr–1hr 5min).

Buses from Victoria Coach Station to:

Bath (11 daily; 3hr 15min); **Birmingham** (hourly; 2hr); **Brighton** (hourly; 1hr 45min); **Bristol** (hourly; 2hr 20min); **Cambridge** (hourly; 2hr); **Canterbury** (hourly; 1hr 50min); **Carlisle** (3–4 daily; 6hr); **Chester** (5–6 daily; 5hr 30min); **Dover** (hourly; 2hr 45min); **Exeter** (8 daily; 4hr); **Gloucester** (10 daily; 3hr); **Liverpool** (5–6 daily; 4hr 30min); **Manchester** (9 daily; 4hr 15min); **Oxford** (frequently; 1hr 30min); **Plymouth** (7 daily; 4hr 40min); **York** (3 daily; 4hr 20min).

KENT, SUSSEX & SURREY

T he southeast corner of England was traditionally where London went on holiday. In the past, trainloads of East Enders were shuttled to the hop fields and orchards of Kent for a working break from the city; boats ferried people down the Thames to the beach at Margate; and everyone from royalty to cuckolding couples enjoyed the seaside at Brighton, a blot of decadence in the otherwise sedate county of Sussex. Of the three, Surrey is the least pastoral and historically significant – the home of wealthy metropolitan professionals prepared to commute from what has become known as the "stockbroker belt".

The late twentieth century has brought big changes to the southeast region. In purely administrative terms the three counties have become four, since local government reorganization split Sussex into East and West. More significantly, many of the coastal towns have faced an uphill struggle to keep their tourist custom in the face of ever more accessible foreign destinations. To make matters worse, Brighton, long known as "London beside the sea", now matches the capital with one of the highest proportions of homeless people in the country.

The proximity of Kent and Sussex to the continent has dictated the history of this region, which has served as a gateway for an array of invaders, both rapacious and benign. **Roman** remains dot the landscape – the most spectacular are at **Bignor**, near Arundel – and many roads, including the London-to-Dover A2 and Watling Street, follow the straight lines laid by the legionaries. When post-Roman **Christianity** spread through Europe, it arrived in Britain on the **Isle of Thanet** – the northeast tip of Kent, although older orders already existed among the Celts in the north and west of the country. In 597 AD Augustine moved inland and established a monastery at **Canterbury**, still the home of the Church of England and the county's prime historic attraction. (Surprisingly, Sussex was among the last counties to accept the Cross – due more to the region's then impenetrable forest than to its innate ungodliness.)

The last successful invasion of England took place in 1066, when the **Normans** overran King Harold's army near **Hastings**, on a site now marked by **Battle Abbey**. The Normans left their mark all over this corner of England and Kent remains unmatched in its profusion of medieval castles, among them **Dover**'s sprawling cliff-top fortress guarding against continental invasion and **Rochester**'s huge, box-like citadel, close to the old dockyards of **Chatham**, power base of the formerly invincible British Navy.

ACCOMMODATION PRICE CODES

Throughout this guide, hotel and B&B accommodation is priced on a scale of ① to ⑨, the number indicating the **lowest price** you could expect to pay per night in that establishment for a **double room** in high season. The prices indicated by the codes are as follows:

① under £40	④ £60–70	⑦ £110–150
② £40–50	⑤ £70–90	⑧ £150–200
③ £50–60	⑥ £90–110	⑨ over £200

Away from the great historic sites, you can spend unhurried days in elegant old towns such as **Rye**, **Royal Tunbridge Wells** and **Lewes**, or enjoy the less elevated charms of the traditional resorts, of which **Brighton** is far and away the best, combining the buzz of a university town with a good-time atmosphere and an excellent range of eating options. Dramatic scenery may be in short supply, but in places the **South Downs Way** offers an expanse of rolling chalk uplands that, as much as anywhere in the crowded southeast, gets you away from it all. And of course Surrey, Kent and Sussex harbour some of the country's finest **gardens**, ranging from the lush flowerbeds of **Sissinghurst** to the great landscaped estates of **Petworth** and **Sheffield Park**.

The North Kent coast

It's a commonly held view that the northern part of Kent is a scenic and cultural wasteland, a prejudice that stems partly from the fact that most visitors only glimpse the area as they race to or from the Channel ports. However, the region has its fair share of attractions, all of which are easily accessible from London. The knot of historic sites at **Chatham** and **Rochester** are followed by the seaside towns of **Whitstable**, **Margate**, **Broadstairs** and **Ramsgate**, once-popular resorts that now make an interesting mix of the stuffy and the purely frivolous.

Rochester and around

ROCHESTER was first settled by the Romans, who built a fortress on the site of the present **Castle** (daily: April–Sept 10am–6pm; Oct 10am–5pm; Nov–March 10am–4pm; £3.50; EH) at the northwest end of the High Street; some kind of fortification has remained here ever since. In 1077, William I gave Gundulf, architect of the White Tower at the Tower of London, the see of Rochester and the job of improving the defences on the Medway's northernmost bridge on Watling Street. The castle remains one of the best-preserved examples of a Norman fortress in England. The stark 100-foot-high keep glowers over the town, while its interior is all the better for having lost its floors, allowing clear views up and down the dank interior. It has three square towers and one cylindrical (the southwest), which was rebuilt following its collapse during the siege of 1215, when the bankrupt King John eventually wrested the castle from its archbishop. The outer walls and two of the towers retain their corridors and spiral stairwells, allowing access to the uppermost battlements.

The foundations of the adjacent **Cathedral** (daily 8.30am–5.30pm; free) were also Gundulf's work, but the building has been much modified over the past nine hundred years. Plenty of Norman touches have endured, particularly in the west front, with its pencil-shaped towers, blind arcading and richly carved portal and tympanum above the doorway. Norman round arches, decorated with zigzags and made from lovely honey-coloured Caen stone, also line the nave. The cathedral once enshrined the remains of one St William of Perth, a pious baker from Scotland, who in 1201 embarked on a pilgrimage to the Holy Land, but got only as far as Rochester, where he was murdered and robbed. The monks of Rochester, envying the popular appeal of St Thomas à Becket's shrine at nearby Canterbury, used William's demise as an opportunity to establish a rival shrine – indeed, substantial additions to the cathedral were financed by donations from pilgrims paying their respects to the canonized baker's tomb, which has long since disappeared. Some fine paintings which survived the Dissolution of the Monasteries decorate the interior, most notably on the walls of the choir where the thirteenth-century depiction of the Wheel of Fortune (only half of which survives) is shown as a treadmill, a trenchant image of medieval life's relentless slog.

Rochester's most famous son is **Charles Dickens**, who spent his youth around here but would seem to have been less than impressed by the place – it appears in two of his novels as "Mudfog" and "Dullborough". Many town buildings, such as the *Royal Victoria & Bull Hotel* at the top of the High Street, also feature in his novels, while most of his last book, the unfinished *Mystery of Edwin Drood*, was set here. A gritty picture of Victorian life is conjured up by the tableaux at the **Charles Dickens Centre** in

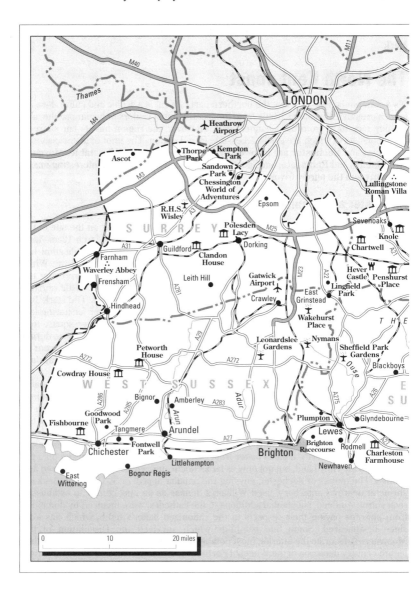

Eastgate House at the east end of the High Street (daily 10am–5.30pm; £3.50). Key scenes from his well-known books are enacted at the push of a button and the whole place is entertaining and informative whether you're a Dickens enthusiast or not. Further down the High Street stands **Watts' Charity** (March–Oct Tues–Sat 2pm–5pm; free), a sixteenth-century almshouse featuring galleried Elizabethan bedrooms and immortalized in Dickens' short story *The Seven Poor Travellers*.

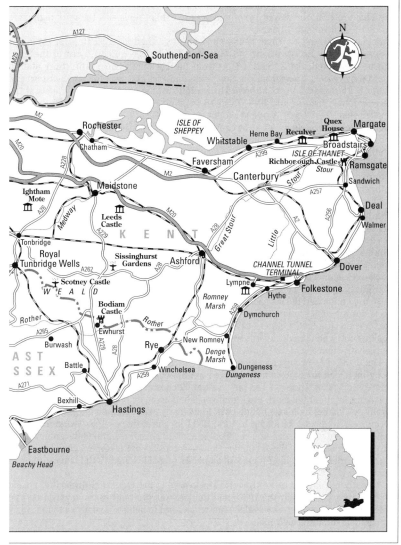

Not all town museums are worth close scrutiny but Rochester's excellent **Guildhall Museum**, at the castle end of the High Street (daily 10am–5.30pm; free), is an exception. Inside, you'll find a vivid model of King John's siege of the castle and a chilling exhibition on the prison ships or **hulks** once moored near the Medway towns. Following American independence from Britain in 1776, England was stuck for a place to transport her growing numbers of convicts – an increase caused as much by desperate poverty and draconian sentencing as any wave of criminality. Until the new penal colony of Botany Bay was established a decade or so later, criminals were housed in appalling and overcrowded conditions inside decommissioned naval vessels moored in the Thames. With the clever use of mirrors the exhibit replicates the grim nightmare inside these floating prisons.

Rochester's **tourist office** stands opposite the cathedral at 95 High St (Mon–Sat 10am–5pm, Sun 10.30am–5pm; ☎01634/843666); its free guided tours of the town (Easter–Sept Wed, Sat & Sun) set off from the Dickens Centre. The **train station** (served by regular trains from Charing Cross and Victoria) is at the southeastern end of the High Street. You could **spend the night** with some Dickensian ghosts at the ancient *Royal Victoria and Bull Hotel*, 16–18 High St (☎01634/846266; ⑤) or at the smaller *Blue Boar Guest House* at no. 99 (☎01634/827373; ②). Other options include B&Bs, such as *Grayling House*, 54 St Margaret's St (☎01634/826593; ①), west of the cathedral. The nearest youth hostel (☎01722/400788) is at Capstone Farm, two miles southeast of Chatham (bus #114). The best **places to eat** are all Italian – choose from *Giannino's* in the *Victoria and Bull* or the modest, family-run *Casa Lina,* at 145 High St. Alternatively, try *Coopers Arms* on St Margaret's Street, just west of the castle and cathedral, which serves good lunches in its small beer garden.

Chatham

CHATHAM, less than a mile or so east of Rochester and one stop further on by train, has none of the charms of its neighbour. Its chief attraction is its **Historic Dockyard** (April–Oct daily 10am–5pm; Feb, March & Nov Wed, Sat & Sun 10am–4pm; £8.50), originally founded by Henry VIII, and once the major base of the Royal Navy – many of whose vessels were built, stationed and victualled here – it commanded worldwide supremacy from the Tudor era until the end of the Victorian age. Well sheltered, yet close to London and the sea, and lined with tidal mud flats which helped support ships' keels during construction, the port expanded quickly and by the time of Charles II it had become England's largest naval base. This era of shipbuilding came to an ignominious end when the dockyards were closed in 1984, re-opening soon afterwards as a tourist attraction.

The dockyards occupy a vast eighty-acre site about a mile north of the town centre along the Dock Road; it's a not very pleasant fifteen-minute walk from Chatham town centre, or a short ride on the bus (ask at Rochester's tourist office for the latest timetable). Behind the stern brick wall you'll find an array of historically and architecturally fascinating buildings dating back to the early eighteenth century. In addition to an impressive display of fifteen historic RNLI lifeboats, there's the **"Wooden Walls" gallery**, where you can experience life as an apprentice in the eighteenth-century dockyards. The main part of the exhibition, however, consists of the Ropery complex including the former rope-making room – at a quarter of a mile long, it's the longest room in the country.

Recently introduced to the Historic Dockyards is the **Ocelot Submarine**, a Cold War warrior dating from the 1960s and the last warship built in the dockyards. The cramped conditions the crew had to endure are hard to believe, and a visit to the sub is a definite no-no for claustrophobes.

Whitstable

Peculiarities of silt and salinity have made **WHITSTABLE** an oyster-friendly environment since classical times, when the Romans feasted on the region's marine delicacies. Before the modern era, oysters were thought of as poor people's food and during the 1950s the town prospered, with offshore **oyster** beds covering five thousand acres and fishing and seaside tourism bringing additional revenue – but then sea pollution, as well as the changing patterns in holidaymaking, brought about Whitstable's reversion to humbler status. These days, small-scale boatbuilding and a mildly Bohemian ambience make Whitstable one of the few pleasant spots along the north Kent coast and it's a popular day-trip destination for Londoners.

Back in 1830, Whitstable became the northern terminus for one of Britain's first steam-powered passenger railway services – the so-called "Crab & Winkle Line" which linked the town via a half-mile tunnel (the world's longest at that time) with Canterbury, ten miles to the south. Relics of this line survive at the **Chuffa Trains Railmania Museum**, 82 High St (Mon–Sat 10am–3pm, open till 5pm in school holidays; £1.50). If you're not satisfied simply eating the local oysters, you can learn more about them at the **Whitstable Oyster and Fishery Exhibition** (April–Oct Mon, Tues & Thurs–Sun 10am–4pm; £1), on the East Quay; kids get to touch some marine life, while the adults can take part in oyster tastings for a further £2.50. If your fascination with Whitstable's maritime history is still not sated, head for the more staid **Whitstable Museum and Gallery** in Oxford Street (Mon, Tues & Thurs–Sat 10.30am–1pm & 2–4pm; free), the southern continuation of High Street, with displays on diving and some good photographs of the town's heyday.

Whitstable's **train station** is a five-minute walk east of the High Street, while the **tourist office** is at 7 Oxford St (Mon–Sat 10am–4pm; ☎01227/275482), the southern continutation of the High Street. For **accommodation** along the seafront, try *Copeland House*, 4 Island Wall (☎01227/266207; ②), west of the High Street, with a garden which backs on to the beach; the *Hotel Continental*, 29 Beach Walk (☎01227/280280; ③); or the simply converted self-contained units, the *Fisherman's Huts*, at Sea Wall (☎01227/280280; ⑤). For **campsites**, you're best off heading to *Seaview Caravan Park* (☎01227/792246; closed Nov–March), which backs onto the beach towards Herne Bay.

Whitstable's fishing background is reflected in its **eating** places, from any number of fish-and-chip outlets along the High Street to the very popular *Royal Native Oyster Stores* by the seafront (☎01227/276856; closed Sun eve & Mon), the town's best restaurant, with its own art-house cinema above. If it's full, *Pearsons Crab & Oyster House* right opposite (☎01227/272005) is a good second choice. *Tea & Times*, 36 High St, caters for the town's arty fringe and serves a decent English breakfast with real coffee and newspapers. For a **drink** and excellent atmosphere check out the *Old Neptune*, standing alone in its white weatherboards on the shore.

The Thanet resorts

The **Isle of Thanet**, a featureless plain fringed by low chalk cliffs and the odd sandy bay, became part of the mainland when the navigable Wantsum Channel began silting up, around the time of the first Roman invasion. This northeastern corner of Kent has witnessed successive waves of incursions. In 43 AD, nearly a century after Julius Caesar's exploratory visit, the Romans got into their stride when they landed near Pegwell Bay and established the port of Richborough in preparation for the march inland. The Saxons followed them four hundred years later (the island is named after the "tenets", which were fire beacons used to warn local residents of the Saxons' raids) and Augustine arrived here in 597 on a divine mission to end English paganism. The evangelist is supposed to have met King Ethelbert of Kent and preached his first sermon at a spot three miles west of Ramsgate – a cross marks the location at Ebbsfleet, next to St Augustine's Golf Club.

Over the next thousand years or so, civilization advanced to the point at which, in 1751, a resident of Margate, one Mr Benjamin Beale, invented the bathing machine, a wheeled cubicle that enabled people to slip into the sea without undue exhibitionism. It heralded the birth of sea bathing as a recreational and recuperative activity, and led to the growth of **seaside resorts**. By the mid-twentieth century the Isle's intermittent expanses of sand had become fully colonized as the "bucket and spade" resorts of the capital's leisure-seeking proletariat. That heyday has passed, but these earliest of resorts still cling to their traditional attractions to varying degrees.

Margate

MARGATE – memorably summarized by Oscar Wilde as "the nom-de-plume of Ramsgate" – is a ragged assortment of cafés, shops and amusement arcades wrapped around a broad bay, a rather less elegant place than the one with which it's been twinned, the Black Sea resort of Yalta. Yet two centuries of tourism are embodied by Margate: at its peak thousands of Londoners were ferried down the Thames every summer's day, to be disgorged at the pier – precursor of all such seaside structures.

Other than the agreeable, if small, beach, Margate's main attraction along its unashamedly tacky seafront is **Dreamland** on Marine Terrace (Easter–June & Sept daily 11am–6pm; July & Aug 10am–10pm), an amusement park, with a rollercoaster dating back to 1863. If this doesn't appeal you could always visit the **Shell Grotto** (Easter to mid-Oct Mon–Fri 10am–5pm, Sat & Sun 10am–4pm; £1.50), Grotto Hill, off Northdown Road, which claims to be the world's only underground shell temple and has been open to the public since it was discovered by some children in 1835. Its passages are intricately decorated with shell mosaics and its caverns were once linked to the less interesting **Margate Caves** down Northdown Road (April–June & Oct daily 10am–4pm; July–Sept Mon–Sat 10am–5pm; £1.50) – if nothing else, a good place to cool off on a hot day.

Margate's **train station** is on All Saint's Avenue, just a couple of minutes' walk from Dreamland, while the **tourist office** is at 22 High St (Easter–Sept Mon–Fri 9am–5pm, Sat 9am–4pm, Sun 10am–4pm; Oct–Easter Mon–Sat 9am–4pm; ☎01843/220241). There are plenty of **B&Bs** lining the Regency crescents of the Cliftonville suburb to the east – try the family-run *Ocean View Hotel*, 8–10 Ethelbert Terrace (☎01843/220641; ①), or *Crescent House*, 24 Fort Crescent (☎01843/223092; ①), which also overlooks the sea. Prosaic **seaside food** is on offer at any of the seafront greasy spoons and fish-and-chip shops, but if you're staying in the Cliftonville area, you can get very fine **pastries** and snacks from *Batchelor's Patisserie*, at 246 Northdown Rd. For **pubs**, try the tiny *Rose & June*, on Trinity Square, or for real ales (and pizzas), try the *Spread Eagle*, 20 Victoria Rd.

Broadstairs

Said to have been established on the profits of smuggling, **BROADSTAIRS** is the smallest, quietest and most pleasant of Thanet's three resort towns, overlooking the pretty Viking Bay from its cliff-top setting. The town's main claim to fame, though, is as Dickens' holiday retreat: throughout his most productive years he stayed in various hostelries here, and eventually rented an austere dwelling overlooking the bay from Fort Road, since renamed **Bleak House** (daily: March–June & Sept to mid-Dec 10am–6pm; July & Aug 10am–9pm; £3). It was here that he planned the novel of that name as well as finishing *David Copperfield*, and three rooms in the house have been preserved as the author would have known them. There's more of the same at the **Dickens House Museum** in Victoria Parade on the main cliff-top seafront (April to mid-Oct daily 2–5pm; £1.20).

Broadstairs' **train station** is a ten-minute walk from the seafront up the High Street; its **tourist office** is at 6B High St (April–Sept daily 9am–5pm; Oct–March Mon–Sat 9am–4pm; ☎01843/862242). The comfortable but pricey **hotel**, the *Royal Albion* on Albion Street (☎01843/868071; ⑤), cashes in on its association with Dickens – he wrote part of *Nicholas Nickleby* here. There are several ivy-covered establishments in Belvedere Road, behind the High Street: the *Admiral Dundonald Hotel* at no. 43 (☎01843/862236; ②) and the *Hanson Hotel* next door (☎01843/868936; ②) are both good value. There is also a **youth hostel** (☎01843/604121; closed mid-Oct to mid-March; £9.15), a Victorian villa just two minutes' walk from the train station, at 3 Osborne Rd with a family atmosphere. For **food** there are plenty of fish-and-chip shops at the bottom of Harbour Street and elsewhere in Broadstairs; *Peter's Fish Factory* run chippies throughout the area and claim to be the cheapest and the best, while the cheapest pub, the *Tartar Frigate*, has a seafood restaurant upstairs For a popular and friendly **pub**, serving the tasty Faversham Shepherd Neame beers, check out the *Neptune's Hall*, further along at 1–3 Harbour St.

Ramsgate

If Thanet had a capital, it would be **RAMSGATE**, a handsome resort and a working port, with daily catamarans crossing the Channel to Dunkerque and Ostend. Rich in robust Victorian red brick, the town is set high on a cliff linked to the seafront and harbour by broad, sweeping ramps, with the villas on the seaward side displaying wrought iron verandas and bricked-in windows – a legacy of the tax on glazed windows. Overall the port has avoided Margate's vulgarity while retaining some of Broadstairs' class.

The most entertaining sight in Ramsgate is the subterranean **Motor Museum** at West Cliff Hall, just by the ferry terminal (Easter–Oct daily 10.30am–5.30pm; Nov–Easter Sun only 10am–5pm; £2.50), which spices up its eclectic collection of cars and motorbikes by placing each vehicle in its historical context. A 1905 Rex pushbike is on show alongside a newspaper proclaiming the increase of third-class steamer fares to the USA to £6 and a 1904 De Dion Bouton is displayed along with details of events from the same year – the founding of Rolls Royce and the arrest of a New York woman for a shocking crime, smoking in public. Ramsgate's other sight, the Clock House Maritime Museum, in the middle of the harbour (April–Sept daily 10am–5pm; Oct–March Mon–Fri 9.30am–4.30pm; £1), is brightened only by an illuminating section on the Goodwin Sands sandbanks – six miles southeast of Ramsgate – the occasional playing field of the eccentric Goodwin Sands Cricket Club. Opened in 1999 in a converted church near the top of the High Street, the **Thanet Movie Centre** on Meeting St (daily 10am–5pm; £3.50) is a film and TV museum covering the early history of the media. You can get hands-on experience of a TV newsroom and editing equipment, and a close-up of all the paraphernalia involved in making a movie.

Ramsgate's **train station** is about a mile northwest of the centre, at the end of Wilfred Road, off the High Street, and the **tourist office** is at 19–21 Harbour St (Mon–Sat 9.30am–5pm, Sun 10am–4pm; ☎01843/591086). For an overnight stay the York House, 7 Augusta Rd (☎01843/596775; ①), in Eastcliff, offers all the modern comforts in an 1830s building; the Victorian *Eastwood Guest House*, 28 Augusta Rd (☎01843/591505; ③), has some rooms with balconies, while *Goodwin View*, 19 Wellington Crescent (☎01843/591419; ①), is an attractive seafront option. The nearest **campsite** to Ramsgate is *Nethercourt*, just two miles southwest of the town centre (☎01843/595485; closed Nov–March).

The *Falstaff* **pub**, on Addington Street by the seafront, does a decent ploughman's lunch, or there's the *Camden Arms*, in nearby La Belle Alliance Square, for good-value fish and chips – for cliff-top views, real ales and occasional live music, head for the *Churchill Tavern* on the Paragon.

Canterbury

One of England's most venerable cities, **CANTERBURY** offers a rich slice through two thousand years of history, with Roman and early Christian ruins, a Norman castle, and a famous cathedral that dominates a medieval warren of time-skewed Tudor dwellings. The city began as a Belgic settlement that was overrun by the Romans and renamed **Durovernum**, from where they proceeded to establish a garrison, supply base and system of roads that was to reach as far as the Scottish borders. With the Roman Empire's collapse came the Saxons, who renamed the town **Cantwarabyrig**; it was a Saxon king, Ethelbert, who in 597 welcomed Augustine, dispatched by the pope to convert the British Isles to Christianity. By the time of his death, Augustine had founded two Benedictine monasteries, one of which – Christ Church, raised on the site of the Roman basilica – was to become the first cathedral in England.

At the turn of the millennium Canterbury suffered repeated sackings by the Danes until Canute, a recent Christian convert, restored the ruined Christ Church, only for it to be destroyed by fire a year before the Norman invasion. As the new religion became a tool of control, a struggle for power developed between the archbishops, the abbots from the nearby Benedictine abbey and King Henry II, culminating in the assassination of Archbishop Thomas à Becket in 1170, a martyrdom that effectively established the autonomy of the archbishops and made this one of Christendom's greatest shrines. Geoffrey Chaucer's *Canterbury Tales*, written towards the end of the fourteenth century, portrays the unexpectedly festive nature of pilgrimages to Becket's tomb, which was plundered and destroyed at the orders of Henry VIII.

In 1830 a pioneering passenger railway service linked Canterbury to the sea and prosperity grew until the city suffered extensive German bombing in the notorious **Baedeker Raids**, when Hitler ordered the destruction of the most treasured historic sites described in the Baedeker travel guide series. The cathedral and compact town centre, however, survived, enclosed on three sides by medieval walls, and today remain the focus for leisure-motivated pilgrims from across the globe.

Arrival, information and accommodation

Canterbury has two **train stations**, Canterbury East for services from London Victoria and Dover Priory, and Canterbury West for slower services from London Charing Cross and Folkestone – the stations are northwest and south of the centre respectively, each a ten-minute walk from the cathedral. National Express coaches and local **buses** use the bus station just inside the city walls on St George's Lane. The busy **tourist office** is at 34 St Margaret's St (May–Sept Mon–Sat 9.30am–6pm, Sun 9.30am–5pm; rest of year closed Sun; ☎01227/766567), right in the middle of the city centre, south of the High Street.

Hotels and B&Bs

Ann's House, 63 London Rd (☎01227/768767). Restored Victorian villa, with some comfortable rooms. ①.

Cathedral Gate Hotel, 36 Burgate (☎01227/464381). Built in 1438 and set in the city's medieval heart, this venerable pilgrims' hostelry combines crooked floors and exposed timber beams with modern amenities. ②.

The Chaucer, Ivy Lane (☎01227/464427). Big hotel just beyond the city walls, fully refurbished with modern comforts but retaining some of its early Georgian charm. ⑥.

Ebury Hotel, 65–67 New Dover Rd (☎01227/768433). Very comfortable and spacious Victorian hotel, fifteen minutes' walk from the centre; indoor pool and well-appointed rooms. ④.

St John's Court Guest House, St John's Lane (☎01227/456425). Good-value guest house, offering B&B accommodation in a quiet but central location, south of the old town. ①.

Slatters Hotel, St Margaret's St (☎01227/463271). Refreshingly unstuffy luxury hotel with an excellent designer bar and restaurant and great central location. ⑤.

Thanington Hotel, 140 Wincheap (☎01227/453227). Comfortably converted Georgian building, ten minutes' walk from the city centre with an indoor pool, games room and friendly, attentive service. ④.

The White House, 6 St Peter's Lane (☎01227/761836). Small and friendly guest house in a fine Regency building, midway between the cathedral and Canterbury West station. ②.

Wincheap Guest House, 94 Wincheap (☎01227/762309). Good-value Victorian B&B, with shared facilities, close to Canterbury East station. ①.

Hostels and campsites

KiPPS, 40 Nunnery Fields, (☎01227/786121). Self-catering hostel-type accommodation in dormitories a few minutes' walk from Canterbury East station.

St Martin's Caravan & Camping Site, Bekesbourne Lane (☎01227/463216). Large caravan park, one and a half miles east of the city off the A257 Sandwich road.

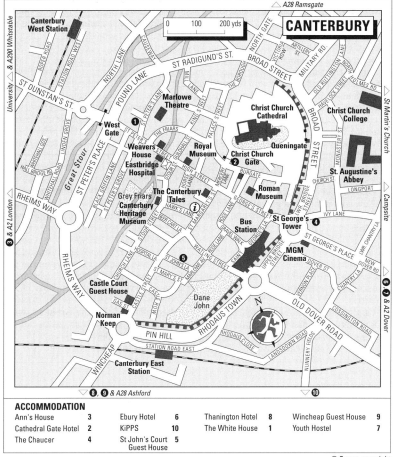

ACCOMMODATION

Ann's House	3	Ebury Hotel	6	Thanington Hotel	8	Wincheap Guest House	9
Cathedral Gate Hotel	2	KiPPS	10	The White House	1	Youth Hostel	7
The Chaucer	4	St John's Court Guest House	5				

Youth Hostel, 54 New Dover Rd (☎01227/462911, *canterbury@yha.org.uk*). Half a mile out of town, and a fifteen-minute walk from Canterbury East station, this friendly hostel is set in a Victorian villa. Closed Jan.

The City

Despite the presence of a university and art college, England's second most visited city is a surprisingly small place with a population of just 35,000. The town centre, ringed by ancient walls, is virtually car-free, but this doesn't stop the High Street seizing up all too frequently with tourists, two million of whom arrive each year. Having said that, the very reason for the city's popularity is its rich tapestry of historical sites, combined with a good selection of places to stay, eat and drink, and no visit to southeast England would be complete without, at the very least, a quick stop here.

The Cathedral

Mother Church of the Church of England, seat of the Primate of All England, **Canterbury Cathedral** (Mon–Fri 9am–5.30pm, Sat 9am–2.30pm, Sun 12.30–2.30pm & 4.30–5.30pm; closes earlier in winter; £3, free on Sun) is ecclesiastically supreme and fills the northeast quadrant of the city with a befitting sense of authority, even if architecturally it's perhaps not among the country's most impressive. A cathedral has stood here since 602, but in 1070 the first Norman archbishop, Lanfranc, levelled that Saxon structure and work began on a replacement. Over successive centuries the masterpiece was heavily modified, and with the puritanical lines of the Perpendicular style gaining ascendancy in late medieval times, the cathedral now derives its distinctiveness from the thrust of the 235-foot-high Bell Harry Tower, completed in 1505. The precincts (daily 7am–9pm) are entered through the superbly ornate early sixteenth-century **Christ Church Gate**, where Burgate and St Margaret's Street meet. This junction, the city's medieval core, is known as the Buttermarket, where religious relics were once sold to pilgrims hoping to prevent an eternity in damnation. Having paid your entrance fee, you pass through the gatehouse and get one of the finest views of the cathedral, foreshortened and crowned with soaring towers and pinnacles.

Once in the magnificent **interior**, look for the tomb of Henry IV and his wife, Joan of Navarre, and for the gilded effigy of Edward III's son, the Black Prince, all of them to be found in the Trinity Chapel, behind the main altar. The **shrine of Thomas à Becket**, in the northwest transept, is marked by the Altar of Sword's Point, where a crude sculpture of the assassins' weapons is suspended above the spot where Becket died and was later enshrined – until Henry VIII's act of ecclesiastical vandalism in 1538. Steps from here descend to the low, Romanesque arches of the **crypt**, one of the few remaining relics of the Norman cathedral and considered the finest such structure in the country, with some amazingly well-preserved carvings on the capitals of the columns.

On the cathedral's north flank are the fan-vaulted colonnades of the **Great Cloister**, from where you enter the **Chapter House**, with its intricate web of fourteenth-century tracery supporting the roof and a wall of stained glass, which illustrates scenes from St Thomas's life and death. In 1935 it was a fitting venue for the inaugural performance of T.S. Eliot's *Murder in the Cathedral*.

The rest of the city

Passing through the cathedral grounds and out through the city walls at the Queningate exit, you come to the vestigial remains of **St Augustine's Abbey** (daily: April–Sept 10am–6pm; Oct–March 10am–4pm; £2.50; EH), occupying the site of the church founded by Augustine in 598. It was built outside the city because of a Christian tradition which forbade burials within the walls, and became the final resting place of

Augustine, Ethelbert and successive archbishops and kings of Kent, although no trace remains either of them or of the original Saxon church. Shortly after the Normans arrived, the church was demolished in the same construction frenzy which saw the rebuilding of the cathedral. It was replaced by a much larger abbey, most of which was destroyed in the Dissolution so that today only the ruins and foundations remain. To help bring the site to life, pick up an audio tour (free) from the abbey's excellent new interpretive centre.

Nearby, on the corner of North Holmes Road and Pretoria Road is **St Martin's Church**, one of England's oldest churches, built on the site of a Roman villa or temple and used by the earliest Christians. Although medieval additions obscure the original Saxon structure, it was here that King Ethelbert was himself baptized, making this perhaps the earliest Christian site in Canterbury.

Back in the city centre, redevelopment of the Longmarket area in the early 1990s exposed Roman foundations and mosaics that are now part of the **Roman Museum** (June–Oct Mon–Sat 10am–5pm, Sun 1.30–5pm; rest of year closed Sun; £2.30). The extant remnants of the larger building are pretty dull and better mosaics can be seen at Lullingstone (see p.188), but the display of recovered artefacts and general design of the museum are tasteful, with re-created Roman domestic scenes as well as a computer-generated view of Durovernum two thousand years ago.

From here a walk down the **High Street** to Mercery Lane and a glance up towards Christ Church Gate presents you with one of the most photographed views in the city: a narrow, medieval street of crooked, overhanging houses behind which loom the turreted gatehouse and the cathedral's towers. Turning in the other direction down St Margaret's Street leads to the former church that's now **The Canterbury Tales** (March–June, Sept & Oct daily 9.30am–5.30pm; July & Aug daily 9am–5.30pm; Nov & Dec Mon–Fri & Sun 10am–4.30pm; £5.25), a quasi-educational show based on Geoffrey Chaucer's book, which was the first ever to be printed in English. Genuinely educational and better value is **Canterbury Heritage Museum**, round the corner in Stour Street (June–Oct Mon–Sat 10.30am–5pm, Sun 1.30–5pm; rest of year closed Sun; £2.30), an interactive exhibition spanning local history from the splendour of Durovernum through to the contemporary literary figures of Joseph Conrad (buried in the cemetery in London Road) and local-born Mary Tourtel, creator of the check-trousered philanthropist Rupert Bear. Back on St Margaret's Street, continue to the end to see the simple (but inaccessible) shell of the Norman castle's **keep**.

Where the High Street passes over a branch of the River Stour and turns into St Peter's Street stands **Eastbridge Hospital** (Mon–Sat 10am–5pm; £1), founded in the twelfth century to provide poor pilgrims with shelter. Downstairs is an exhibition on Chaucer's life, where storytellers in feudal garb recite parts of his book. Over the road is the wonky, half-timbered **Weavers' House**, built around 1500 and once inhabited by Huguenot textile workers who had been offered religious asylum in post-Reformation England. St Peter's Street terminates at the two massive crenellated towers of the **West Gate**, between which local buses just manage to squeeze. The only one of the town's seven city gates to have survived intact, the West Gate's towers house a small **museum** (Mon–Sat 11am–12.30pm & 1.30–3.30pm; £1), which displays contemporary armaments and weaponry used by the medieval city guard, as well as giving access to the battlements.

Eating, drinking and nightlife

The combination of a large student population and the tourist trade means Canterbury has a good selection of places to **eat and drink**, with many establishments in genuinely old settings. Head for *Tapas en las Trece*, 13 Palace St, for tasty Spanish snacks (and occasional live music), or the popular and moderately priced *Café des Amis*, 95 St

Dunstans St, for authentic Mexican food. The refined delights of Thai cuisine are available at a reasonable price at *Chaopraya River*, 2 Dover St, while *Kudos*, 52 Dover St, is an inexpensive Chinese restaurant, serving excellent food. For classy Italian dishes at moderate prices, try the *Tuo e Mio*, a long-established restaurant at 16 The Borough.

Nightlife in Canterbury keeps a low profile – check what's happening in the free *What, Where, When* listings sheet available at the tourist office. **Pubs** to go for include the *Bell & Crown*, a cramped medieval hostelry on Palace Street; the *City Arms*, 7 Butchery Lane, the art students' pub; or the *Miller's Arms*, good for a riverside pint in summer. At *Alberry's* wine bar, opposite the tourist office, and *Simple Simon's*, Radigund's Hall, 3 Church Lane, you can catch the occasional live music act. Also in Northgate, the recently revived Penny Theatre presents local and global live music. The University puts on a good range of arty **films**, and also houses the Gulbenkian Theatre, a venue which shares the city's more edifying cultural events with the Marlowe Theatre in The Friars.

The Dover area

Dover, just 21 miles from the Continent (Calais' low cliffs are visible on a clear day), is the southeast's principal cross-Channel port, but as a town it is not immensely appealing, even though its key position has left it with a clutch of historic attractions. To its north lie **Sandwich**, once the most important of the Cinque Ports (see box opposite) but now no longer even on the coast, and the pleasant resort towns of **Deal** and **Walmer**, each with its own set of distinctive fortifications as well as a smattering of traditional seaside B&Bs.

Sandwich and around

SANDWICH, situated on the River Stour four miles north of Deal, is best known nowadays for giving rise to England's favourite culinary contribution when, in 1762, the fourth Earl of Sandwich, passionately absorbed in a game of cards, demanded some meat between two bits of bread for a quick snack. Aside from this incident, the town's main interest lies in its maritime connections – it was chief among the Cinque Ports (see box opposite) until the Stour silted up. Unlike other former harbour inlets, however, the Stour hasn't silted up completely here and still flows through town, its grassy willow-lined banks adding to the once great medieval port's present charm.

By the bridge over the Stour stands the sixteenth-century **Barbican**, a stone gateway where tolls were once collected. Running parallel to the river is **Strand Street**, whose crooked half-timbered facades front antique shops and private homes. The genteel town is separated from the sandy beaches of Sandwich Bay by the **Royal St George** golf course – frequent venue of the British Open tournament – and a mile of nature reserves. The reserve that most ornithologists make for is the **Gazen Salts Nature Reserve**, three miles north of town, across the Stour.

Overlooking the doleful expanse of Pegwell Bay, two miles northwest of Sandwich, is **Richborough Castle** (April–Sept daily 10am–6pm; Oct daily 10am–5pm; £2.50; EH), one of the earliest coastal strongholds built by the Romans along what later became known as the Saxon Shore on account of the frequent raids by the Germanic tribe. Like Reculver, ten miles northwest, it guarded the southern entrance to the Wantsum Channel, which then isolated the Isle of Thanet from the mainland. Rumour has it that Emperor Claudius once rode through a triumphal arch erected inside the castle on an elephant on his way to London, but all that remains now within the well-preserved Roman walls are the relics of an early Saxon church. Richborough's historical significance far outshines its present appearance, especially as Pegwell Bay is now blighted by an ugly chemical works.

THE CINQUE PORTS

In 1278, Dover, Hythe, Sandwich, New Romney and Hastings – already part of a long-established but unofficial confederation of defensive coastal settlements – were formalized under Edward I's charter as the five **Cinque Ports** (pronounced "sink", despite its French origin). In return for providing England with maritime support when necessary – chiefly in the transportation of troops and supplies to the Continent during times of war – the five ports were given trading privileges and other liberties, which enabled them to prosper while neighbouring ports struggled to survive. Some took advantage of this during peacetime, boosting their wealth by various nefarious activities such as piracy and smuggling of tax-free contraband.

Later, Rye and Winchelsea were added to the confederation along with several other "limb" ports on the southeast coast which joined up at various times. The confederation continued until 1685, when the ports' privileges were revoked. Their maritime services were no longer necessary as Henry VIII had founded a professional navy and, due to a shifting coastline, several of the ports' harbours had silted up anyway. Nowadays, only Dover is still a major working port, though the post of Lord Warden of the Cinque Ports still exists. This honorary title, appointed by the presiding monarch, is currently held by the Queen Mother.

Finding **accommodation** in Sandwich shouldn't be much of a problem – the local **tourist office**, housed in the lovely sixteenth-century Guildhall (April–Oct daily 10am–4pm; ☎01304/613565), will provide you with a list of local hotels and guesthouses. The golfers' choice, the *Bell Hotel* by the Barbican (☎01304/613388; ⑥), is out of most people's range; better value are the en-suite rooms at the old coaching inn, the *Fleur de Lis*, near the Guildhall at 6–8 Delf St (☎01304/614944; ③), or the modest *Le Trayas* bungalow at 57 St George's St (☎01304/611056; ①). Alternatively, there's the Crispin, an attractive fifteenth-century pub in the village of Worth, a mile or so south of Sandwich (☎01304/612081; ③). Your best choice for top-class food is the pricey Fisherman's Wharf on the quayside (☎01304/613636; closed Sun), which serves excellent seafood; for something less expensive try one of the pubs by the Barbican or the *Haven*, 20A King St, for good coffee, light lunches and evening meals. For the definitive Sandwich sandwich, head for the twee *Little Cottage Tearooms*, on the quay.

Deal and Walmer

One of the most unusual of Henry VIII's forts is the diminutive castle at **DEAL**, six miles southeast of Sandwich and site of Julius Caesar's first successful landfall in Britain in 55 BC. The **castle** (April–Sept daily 10am–6pm; Oct daily 10am–5pm; Nov–March Wed–Sun 10am–4pm; £3; EH) is situated off the Strand at the south end of town. Its unusual shape – viewed from the air it looks like a Tudor rose – is as much an affectation as a defensive design, based on the premise that rounded walls would be better at deflecting missiles. Inside, the comprehensive display on the other similar forts built during Henry VIII's reign is well worth a visit. Much more recently, the town was the focal point of Kent's small-scale coal industry, until the pits were shut down during the bitterly fought retrenchments of the 1980s.

Walmer Castle (times as above; £4.50; EH), a mile south of Deal, is another rotund Tudor-rose-shaped affair, albeit with a more conventional interior, commissioned when the castle became the official residence of the Lord Warden of the Cinque Ports in 1730. Now it resembles a heavily fortified stately home more than a military stronghold. The best-known Lord Warden was the Duke of Wellington, who died here in 1842 – the house is devoted primarily to his life and times; busts and portraits of the Iron

Duke crowd the rooms and corridors, where you'll also find the armchair in which he expired and the original Wellington boots in which he triumphed at Waterloo.

Deal's **tourist office** (Mon–Fri 9am–12.30pm & 1.30–5pm; mid-May to mid-Sept also Sat 9am–2pm; ☎01304/369576) is situated on the High Street near the sea, about a ten-minute walk from the **train station**. In Deal there's a whole host of places offering **accommodation** on Beach Street: try the winsome *King's Head* pub (☎01304/368194; ③), or the nearby town house of *Channel View*, at no. 17, run by the same proprietor (same phone number and prices). Another option is *Dunkerley's*, next door at no. 19 (☎01304/375016; ⑤), whose **restaurant** is Deal's finest (and priciest). For more reasonably priced seafood try the *Lobster Pot* on Beach Road (☎01304/374713), opposite the concrete pier.

Dover

Badly bombed during the war **DOVER**'s town centre and seafront just don't have what it takes to induce many travellers to linger before speeding onwards to Europe, or inland to London or Canterbury. That said, the town authorities have put a lot of effort and money into sprucing the place up, particularly the early Victorian New Bridge development along the Esplanade. Despite such valiant attempts, Dover Castle is still by far the most interesting of the numerous attractions which plug the port's defensive history. Entertainment of a saltier nature is offered by Dover's legendary **White Cliffs**, which dominate the town and have long been a source of inspiration for lovers, travellers and soldiers sailing off to war.

Dover Castle

The town's chief attraction is **Dover Castle** (daily: April–Sept 10am–6pm; Oct 10am–5pm; Nov–March 10am–4pm; £6; EH), a superbly positioned defensive complex, begun in 1168 and in continuous military use until the 1980s. The **Romans** put Dover on the map when they chose its harbour as the base for their northern fleet, and erected a lighthouse here to guide the ships into the river mouth. Beside the lighthouse stands a Saxon-built church, **St Mary in Castro**, dating from the seventh century, with motifs graffitied by irreverent Crusaders still visible near the pulpit. Further up the hill is the impressive, well-preserved **Norman keep**, built by Henry II as a palace. Inside, there's an interactive exhibition on spying; you can also climb its spiral stairs to the lofty battlements for views over the sea to France. The castle's other main attraction is its network of **secret wartime tunnels** dug during the Napoleonic war. Extended during World War II and used as a headquarters to plan the Dunkirk evacuation, "**Hellfire Corner**" – the tunnels' wartime nickname – can be seen on a fifty-minute guided tour (every 20min). The tour is spiced up with a little gore, and reveals the quaintly low-tech communications systems and war rooms of the Navy's command post.

CROSS-CHANNEL TRANSPORT SERVICES FROM DOVER AND FOLKESTONE

Dover Eastern Docks to Calais: P&O Stena Line (30 daily; journey time 1hr 15min); Seafrance (15 daily, journey time 1hr 30min).

Dover Western Docks to Calais: Hoverspeed (10 daily; journey time 35min by Hovercraft, 50min by SeaCat).

Folkestone to Boulogne: Hoverspeed SeaCat (4 daily; journey time 55min).

Folkestone to Calais: Eurotunnel (up to 4 hourly; journey time 35min).

Reservations: Eurotunnel (☎0990/353535); Hoverspeed (☎08705/240241 or 01304/865000); P&O Stena Line (☎08706/000600); SeaFrance (☎0990/711711).

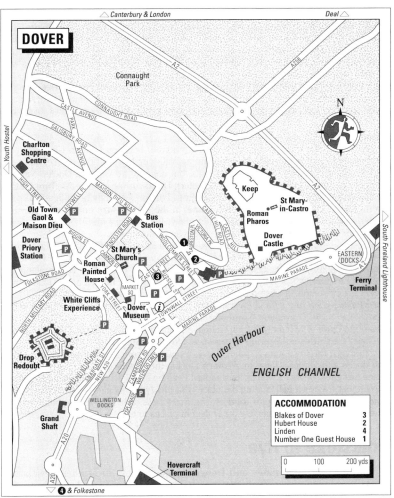

© Crown copyright

The town centre

Postwar rebuilding has made Dover **town centre** a grim place, but in 1970 the construction of a car park on New Street did at least lead to the discovery of an ancient guest house. The **Roman Painted House** (April–Sept Tues–Sun 10am–5pm; £2) possesses some reasonable Roman wall paintings, the remains of an underground Roman heating system and some mosaics – it's worth a look if you've some time to kill.

Views of Dover's famous cliffs are best enjoyed from a boat several miles out to sea, but the **White Cliffs Experience** on Market Square (April–Oct daily 10am–6pm; Nov–March 10am–4pm; last admission 1hr before closing; £5.75) – an indoor theme museum with animated mannequins – offers an alternative historical view of the port.

Less expensive and less frivolous is the new **museum** below the White Cliffs gift shop (daily: summer 10am–6pm; winter 10am–5.30pm; £1.70, free with ticket for White Cliffs Experience), which has three floors packed with informative displays on Dover's past. At the **Old Town Gaol** (May–Sept Tues–Sat 10am–4.30pm, Sun 2–4.30pm; Oct–April Wed–Sat 10am–4.30pm; £3.50), beneath the Town Hall on Biggin Street, dummies with TVs for heads describe the misery of penal incarceration during Victorian times. The high ground to the west of town, originally the site of a Napoleonic-era fortress, retains one interesting oddity, the **Grand Shaft** (July & Aug Tues–Sun 2–5pm; £1.25), a triple staircase by which troops could descend at speed to defend the port in case of attack.

Practicalities

There are regular services (every 30min; 1hr 30min) between London Charing Cross and Dover Priory **train station**, a ten-minute walk northwest of the centre; there are regular shuttle buses to the Eastern Docks, but none to the Western Docks. National Express **buses** from London run to the Eastern Docks, or the town-centre **bus station** on Pencester Road. If you miss the last train to London, you may be obliged to spend the night in Dover. If so, the **tourist office**, in the town centre underneath the ugly high-rise *County Hotel* on Townwall Street (daily: July & Aug 8am–7.30pm; rest of year 9am–6pm; ☎01304/205108), can advise about accommodation.

    Rooms are plentiful: Hubert House, 9 Castle Hill Rd (☎01304/202253; ②), is a friendly B&B, convenient for the Eastern Dock, as is the *Number One Guesthouse*, 1 Castle Hill Rd (☎01304/202007; ②). *Linden*, at no. 231, is one of the better B&Bs along the Folkestone Road (☎01304/205449; ①). There's a busy **youth hostel**, a mile inland from Dover Priory station, in a listed Georgian town house at 306 London Rd (☎01304/201314, *dover@yha.org.uk*), but with an overspill building in Godwyne Road, half a mile north of town. The most convenient **campsite** is *Hawthorn Farm* (☎01304/852658; closed Dec–Feb) close to Martin Mill train station, one stop up the line towards Ramsgate.

    Given the town's uninspiring appearance, Dover's **pubs** are surprisingly characterful, although the town gets a rather rough reputation from its shift workers servicing the docks and ferries. Close to Western Docks, the *Cinque Ports Arms* on Clarence Place has guest beers as well as its standard Fremlin's ales, while the *Park Inn* on Park Street near the town hall is a big old place with plenty of real ales to choose from. You could do worse than eat pub **food** at *The Eight Bells*, a big Weatherspoon's pub on Cannon Street, as Dover has few other decent places to eat.

Folkestone to Rye

In Roman times, the **Romney and Denge marshes** – now the southernmost part of Kent – were submerged beneath the English Channel. Then the lowering of the sea levels in the Middle Ages and later reclamation created a forty-square-mile area of marshland which, until the last century, was afflicted by malaria and various other malaises. Contrasting strongly with the wooded pastures of Kent's interior, the sheep-speckled marshes have an eerie, forlorn appearance, as if still unassimilated with the mainland and haunted by their maritime origins. The ancient town of **Hythe** is on the eastern edge of the reclaimed marshes and is linked with Rye in East Sussex on the marshes' western edge, by the arc of the 23-mile Royal Military Canal. **Folkestone**, Kent's other major port, five miles east of Hythe, and site of the British entrance to the **Channel Tunnel**, is a drab and utterly missable introduction to this swathe of coast.

Folkestone

In theory, **FOLKESTONE**, with its narrow cobbled streets and cliff-top promenade, should be a more appealing place than, say, Dover, but the truth is that, rather like the Channel Tunnel itself, the good times seem to have passed Folkestone by. The only passenger vessels that arrive in Folkestone these days are the Hoverspeed SeaCats from Boulogne, which dock adjacent to **Folkestone Harbour train station** and connect with trains to London Charing Cross (these also call in at **Folkestone Central**, a twenty-minute walk from the harbour). Eurostar passengers for Paris and Brussels can climb aboard at the new pompously named Ashford International train station, just up the line from Folkestone. National Express **coaches** to London leave from the **bus station** on Bouverie Square, between the Central and Harbour stations. The **tourist office** is in Harbour Street, near the quayside (daily: July & Aug 9am–7pm; Sept–June Mon–Sat 9am–5.30pm, Sun 9am–1pm & 2–4pm; ☎01303/258594).

If you need **to stay** overnight, the nicest part of Folkestone to try is west along the Leas: the red-brick and terracotta *Burlington* in Earls Avenue (☎01303/255301; ⑤), the *Chilton House Hotel*, 14 Marine Parade (☎01303/249786; ①) and*Westward Ho!*, at no. 13 on the lovely Clifton Crescent (☎01303/221515; ②) are the best options among the scores of hotels and B&Bs.

Hythe to Dungeness

Separated from Folkestone by the massive earthworks of the Channel Tunnel, **HYTHE** is a sedate seaside resort bisected by the disused waterway of the Royal Military Canal, built as a defensive obstacle during the perceived threat of Napoleonic invasion. Hythe's receding shoreline reduced its usefulness as a port and the nearby coast is now just a sweep of beach punctuated by **Martello towers**, part of the chain of 74 citadels built along the southeast coastline for the same reasons as the canal.

There's little to do in Hythe other than enjoy its tranquil antiquity, although a ride on the world's largest toy train – or smallest public railway – the **Romney, Hythe & Dymchurch Railway** (R, H & DR), a fifteen-inch-gauge line which runs the fourteen miles from Hythe to Dungeness, makes a fun day out. Built in the 1920s as a tourist attraction linking the resorts along the shore, its fleet of steam locomotives is now maintained by volunteers (Easter–Sept daily; March & Oct Sat & Sun only;

THE CHANNEL TUNNEL

In the autumn of 1994 passenger services through the Channel Tunnel finally began, 160 years after the idea was first suggested by French engineer Aimé Thome de Gamond, whose geological survey of the seabed concluded that such a link was feasible. As a result of his work, a tunnel over a mile long was driven out from the English coast in 1882, while French engineers began to dig from Sangatte – the present location of the French terminal. All was going remarkably well until Queen Victoria became paranoid about the possibility of invasion, and work was halted.

In 1973 a pang of Euro-optimism led to another attempt, until cash problems forced the British to pull out of the "Chunnel", as it was dubbed, and things didn't go any smoother when the French and British finally agreed on proposals at the end of the Eighties for a pair of rail tunnels and a third service tunnel. Britain's biggest-ever civil engineering project was dogged by delays, overspending and disagreements between Trans Manche Link (the tunnellers) and Eurotunnel (who put up the money), while the British government dithered over the routing of a new high-speed rail link to London, which is not expected to be completed until well into the next century. In the meantime the Eurostar travels at close to 200mph from Paris or Brussels to the tunnel, zips through at 100mph to surface at Folkestone and then crawls with the commuter traffic to its terminal at Waterloo.

☎01797/362353). At New Romney station, three stops southwest of Hythe, the R, H & DR has a permanent **model train** exhibition (same days as the railway 10am–5pm; £1).

DUNGENESS, six miles south of New Romney, is the southern terminus for the R, H & DR, set in the sort of wasteland normally used as an army firing-range, but in this case the site of a nuclear power station. The barren environment of the Denge Marsh supports a unique floral ecology and all around you'll see tiny communities of wild-flowers struggling against the unrelenting breeze. On the road to the power station, the flotsam sculptures in the late film director **Derek Jarman's garden** (not open to the public) make an eye-catching sight, though the non-indigenous flora he planted around them has attracted the wrath of the local conservation authorities.

Hythe's **tourist office** is, bizarrely, situated in the old toilets in Red Lion Square (April–June & Sept daily 9am–5.30pm; July & Aug daily 9am–7pm; Oct–March Mon–Sat 9am–5.30pm, Sun 10am–4pm; ☎01303/267799). For **accommodation** check out the *White House*, 27 Napier Gardens (☎01303/266252; ②), just a couple of minutes from the sea, or *Fern Lodge*, a mile east of the town centre at 87 Seabrook Rd (☎01303/267315; ②). The *Capri*, 32–34 High St (☎01303/269898) serves good Italian **food**.

Rye and around

Perched on a hill overlooking the Romney Marshes, the town of **RYE** lies over the county border in East Sussex. Added as a "limb" to the original Cinque Ports, the town then became marooned two miles inland with the retreat of the sea and the silting up of the River Rother. It is now one of the most popular places along the Sussex coast – half-timbered, skew-roofed and quintessentially English, but also very commercialized.

From Strand Quay, head up The Deals to Rye's most picturesque street, the sloping cobbled lane of **Mermaid Street**, which will bring you eventually to the peaceful oasis of Church Square. Henry James, who strangely suggested that "Rye would . . . remind you of Granada", spent the last years of his life at **Lamb House** (April–Oct Wed & Sat 2pm–6pm; £2.50; NT) at the east end of Mermaid Street. The house's three rooms and garden are of interest chiefly to fans of James's novels, or to admirers of the novelist E.F. Benson, who lived here after James. A blue plaque in the High Street also testifies that Radclyffe Hall, author of the seminal lesbian novel *The Well of Loneliness*, was also once a resident of the town. At the centre of Church Square stands **St Mary's Church**, boasting the oldest functioning pendulum clock in the country; the ascent of the church tower – whose bells were looted by French raiders in 1377 and then retrieved with similar audacity – offers fine views over the clay-tiled roofs and grid of narrow lanes. In the far corner of the square stands the modest **Rye Castle** (daily: April–Oct 10.30am–5.30pm; Nov–March Sat & Sun 10.30am–4pm; £3), whose Ypres Tower was formerly used to keep an eye out for cross-Channel invaders and now functions as a museum housing relics from those days.

Practicalities

Rye **train station** lies on the Eastbourne–Ashford International rail line and is a short walk north of the town; local **buses** use the station forecourt. The town's **tourist office** is on Strand Quay (April–Oct daily 9am–5.30pm; Nov–March daily 10am–4pm; ☎01797/226696). Rye's popularity with weekending Londoners gives it an excellent choice of **accommodation**: try the luxurious fifteenth-century *Mermaid Inn* on Mermaid Street itself (☎01797/223065; ⑦), or the deservedly popular *Jeake's House*, also on Mermaid Street (☎01797/222828; ②). Alternatively, there's the *Old Vicarage Guest House* at 66 Church Square (☎01797/222119; ②), a lovely pink Georgian house next to the church, not to be confused with Rye's hotel of the same name; and *Owlet* B&B, 37 New Rd, east of the centre on the A259, one of Rye's least expensive options

(☎01797/222544; ①). The *Mermaid* is by far the best **pub** in town; the pricey *Landgate Bistro* at 5 Landgate (☎01797/222829; closed Mon & Sun) is also recommended; alternatively, you can sample reasonably priced local seafood at the *Old Forge* on Wish Street (☎01797/223227; closed Mon & Sun, also Tues & Wed lunch), or the intimate *Gatehouse Restaurant*, 1 Tower St (☎01797/222327; closed Mon lunch).

Winchelsea

WINCHELSEA, two miles southwest of Rye and easily reached by train, bus, foot or bike, shares Rye's indignity of having become detached from the sea, but has a very different character. Rye gets all the visitors, whereas Winchelsea feels positively deserted, an impression augmented as you pass through the Strand Gate and see the ghostly ruined **Church of St Thomas à Becket**. The original settlement was washed away in the great storm in 1287, after which Edward I planned a new port with a chequerboard pattern of streets. Even at the height of Winchelsea's economic activity, however, not all the plots on the grid were used. The town also suffered from incursions by the French in the fourteenth and fifteenth centuries, at which time the church was pillaged; its remains constitute Sussex's finest example of the Decorated style. Head south for a mile and a half and you get to **Winchelsea beach**, a long expanse of pebbly sand.

The fourteenth-century *Strand House* (☎01797/226276; ②), at the foot of the cliff below Strand gate, is the best **accommodation** option.

Hastings and Battle

During the twelfth and thirteenth centuries, **HASTINGS** flourished as an influential Cinque Port. In 1287 its harbour creek was silted up by the same storm which washed away nearby Winchelsea, forcing the settlement to be temporarily abandoned. These days, Hastings is a curious mixture of traditional seaside resort, arty retreat popular with painters (there's even a street and quarter named Bohemia) and unpretentious fishing port. William, Duke of Normandy, landed at Pevensey Bay a few miles west of town and made Hastings his base, but his forces met Harold's army – exhausted after quelling a Nordic invasion near York – at **Battle**, six miles northwest of Hastings. Battle today boasts a magnificent abbey built by William in thanks for his victory, which makes for a good afternoon's excursion from Hastings.

Hastings

Hastings' **Old Town**, east of the pier, holds most of the appeal of this fading seaside resort. With the exception of the oddly neglected Regency architecture of **Pelham Crescent**, directly beneath the castle ruins, **All Saints Street** is the most evocative thoroughfare, punctuated with the odd rickety, timber-framed dwelling from the fifteenth century. The thirteenth-century **St Clements** church stands in the High Street, on the other side of The Bourne. By a louvred window at the top of the church's tower rests a cannonball that was lodged there by a Dutch galleon in the 1600s – its poignancy rather lost by a companion fitted in the eighteenth century for the sake of symmetry.

Down by the seafront, the area known as The Stade is characterized by its tall, black weatherboard **net shops**, dating from the mid-nineteenth century. To raise Hastings' tone, the town council attempted to shift the fishermen and their malodorously drying nets from the beach by increasing rents per square foot and these sinister-looking towers were their response. There's a trio of nautical attractions on the adjacent Rock-a-Nore Road: the **Fisherman's Museum** (daily: April–Oct

11am–5pm; Nov–March 11am–4pm; free), a converted seaman's chapel, offers an account of the port's commercial activities; the neighbouring **Shipwreck Heritage Centre** (daily 10.30am–5pm; £2.20), details the dramas of unfortunate mariners; while the **Sea-Life Centre**, opposite (daily 10am–5pm; £5.25), features walk-through tunnels and magnified tanks housing marine creatures.

Castle Hill, separating the Old Town from the visually less interesting modern quarter, can be ascended by the **West Hill Cliff Railway**, one of two Victorian funicular railways in Hastings (daily: April–Sept 10.30am–5.30pm; Oct–March 11am–4pm; 80p). On top of the hill is where William the Conqueror erected his first **castle** in 1066, one of several wooden prefabricated structures brought over from Normandy in sections. In the thirteenth century storms caused the cliffs to subside, tipping most of the castle into the sea; the surviving ruins, however, offer an excellent prospect of the town. The castle is home to **The 1066 Story** (daily: April–Sept 10am–5pm; Oct–March 11am–3.30pm; £3), in which the events of the last successful invasion of the British mainland are described inside a mock-up of a siege tent. More fun is the **Smugglers' Adventure** (daily: Easter–July & Sept 10am–5pm; Aug 10am–5.30pm; Oct–Easter 11.30am–3.30pm; £4.50; combined ticket with 1066 Story £6.45), over the hill. Here the labyrinthine St Clement's caves have been converted to house a number of amusing and educational dioramas depicting the town's long history of duty-dodging.

Practicalities

The **train station** is a ten-minute walk from the seafront along Havelock Road; National Express services operate from the **bus station** at the junction of Havelock and Queen's roads. The **tourist office** is located within the Town Hall on Queen's Road (daily: June–Aug 9.30am–6pm; rest of year Mon–Sat 10am–5pm; ☎01424/718888); there's also a smaller seafront office (April–Sept daily 9.30am–6pm; Oct–March Sat & Sun 11am–4pm; ☎01424/781120) near the Boating Lake on East Parade by the old town.

Accommodation available in town includes the *Argyle Guest House*, 32 Cambridge Gardens (☎01424/421294; ①), with sea views; timber-framed *Lavender & Lace*, right in the Old Town at 106 All Saints St (☎01424/716290; ①); and the *Jenny Lind Hotel*, 69 High St (☎01424/421392; ②), above a moderately priced fish restaurant in the Old Town. The nearest youth hostel and campsite (☎01424/812373) are in a large manor house at Guestling, three miles along the road to Rye (bus #711).

By far the best prospects for **eating and drinking** are on the High Street and its pedestrianized offshoot, George Street. The *Jenny Lind*, on the High St, offers imaginative, moderately priced fish and seafood dishes, while the smell of garlic from *Bella Napoli* is positively enticing. The best fish and chips in town are at the eat-in *Mermaid*, 2 Rock-a-Nore, right by the beach. There are more than thirty **pubs** to choose from in Hastings: the local fishermen's favourite is the *Lord Nelson* right by the front on the Bourne; others to check out are the ever-popular *First In Last Out,* 15 High St in the Old Town, or the trendy clubby bar, *The Street*, accessible via a tiny entrance on Cambridge Road in the new town centre.

Battle

The town of **BATTLE** – a ten-minute train ride from Hastings – occupies the site of the most famous land battle in British history. Here, on October 14, 1066, the invading Normans overcame the Anglo-Saxon army of King Harold, who was killed not by an arrow through the eye – a myth resulting from the misinterpretation of the Bayeux Tapestry – but from a workaday clubbing about the head. Before the battle took place, William vowed that, should he win the engagement, he would build a religious foundation on the very spot of Harold's slaying to atone for the bloodshed and, true to his word, **Battle Abbey** (daily: April–Sept 10am–6pm; Oct 10am–5pm; Nov–March

10am–4pm; £4; EH) was built four years later and subsequently occupied by a fraternity of Benedictines. The magnificent structure, though partially destroyed in the Dissolution and much rebuilt and revised over the centuries, still dominates the town with the huge gatehouse, added in 1338, now containing a good audio-visual exhibition on the battle. You can wander through the ruins of the abbey to the spot where Harold was clubbed – the site of the high altar of William's abbey, now marked by a memorial stone.

Though nothing can match the resonance of the abbey, the rest of the town is worth a stroll. At the far end of the High Street, packed with antique shops and other tourist outlets, is the fourteenth-century **Almonry** (Mon–Sat 10am–4.30pm; £1) – the present town hall – which contains a miniature model of Battle and the oldest Guy Fawkes in the country. Every year, on the Saturday nearest to November 5, this three-hundred-year-old effigy is paraded along the High Street at the head of a torch-lit procession culminating in a huge bonfire in front of the abbey gates; similar celebrations occur in Lewes (see p.190).

The **tourist office** is at 88 High St (April to mid-Oct daily 10am–6pm; mid-Oct to March Mon–Sat 10am–4pm, Sun 10am–2pm; ☎01424/773721). Battle's **accommodation** tends to be agreeable but expensive – a couple of less pricey **B&Bs** are *Abbey View*, Caldbec Hill (☎01424/775513; ③), only two minutes' walk from town, and the 270-year-old Georgian *Kitchenham Farm* at Ashburnham (☎01424/892 221; ②), a working farm near the village of Ninfield, about seven miles southwest of Battle. Town-centre **pubs** serving decent food include the *Old Kings Head* on Mount Street, the *1066* at 12 High St – both of which serve real ales – and the *Chequers Inn* at Lower Lake, on the High Street.

The Weald

The Weald is usually taken to refer to the region around the spa town of **Royal Tunbridge Wells**, but in fact it stretches across a much larger area between the North and South Downs and includes parts of both Kent and Sussex, though the majority of its attractions are in Kent. During Saxon times, much of The Weald was covered in thick forest – the word itself derives from the Germanic word *wald*, meaning forest, and the suffixes -hurst (meaning wood) and -den (meaning clearing) are commonly found in Wealden village names. Now, however, the region is epitomized by gentle hills, sunken country lanes and somnolent villages as well as some of England's most beautiful gardens – **Sissinghurst** being the best known.

Burwash, Batemans and Bodiam Castle

Thirteen miles northwest of Hastings on the A265, halfway to Tunbridge Wells, **BURWASH**, with its red-brick and weatherboard cottages and Norman church tower, exemplifies the pastoral idyll of inland Sussex. Half a mile south of the village lies the main attraction, **Batemans** (April–Oct Mon–Wed, Sat & Sun 11am–5.30pm; £5; NT), home of the Nobel Prize-winning writer and journalist Rudyard Kipling from 1902 until his death in 1936. Built by a local ironmaster in the seventeenth century and set amid attractive gardens, the house features a working watermill converted by Kipling to generate electricity. Inside, the house is laid out as he left it, with letters, early editions of his work and mementoes from his travels on display. Next to the house, a garage houses the last of Kipling's Rolls Royces, one of the many that he owned during his lifetime, although he never actually drove them, preferring the services of a chauffeur.

Bodiam Castle (Feb–Oct daily 10am–6pm or dusk; Nov–Dec Tues–Sun 10am–4pm or dusk; £3; NT), eleven miles north of Hastings, is a classic, stout, square castle with rounded corner turrets, battlements and a moat. When it was built in 1385 to guard what were the lower reaches of the River Rother, Bodiam was state-of-the-art military architecture, but during the Civil War a company of Roundheads breached the fortress and removed its roof to reduce its effectiveness as a possible stronghold for the King. Over the next 250 years Bodiam fell into neglect until restoration earlier this century by the philanthropic Lord Curzon. Nowadays, the castle particularly appeals to children who enjoy clambering up the narrow spiral staircases which lead to crenellated battlements, and watching the absorbing fifteen-minute video portraying medieval life in a castle.

For **accommodation** and **food**, head for the lovely village of **Ewhurst**, two miles southeast of Bodiam, which houses an idyllic country pub, *The White Dog Inn* (☎01580/830264; ②).

Royal Tunbridge Wells and around

ROYAL TUNBRIDGE WELLS – not to be confused with the more mundane Tonbridge, a few miles to the north – is the home of the mythical whingeing right-wing letter-writer known as "Disgusted of Tunbridge Wells". Most British people, therefore, view it with derision, but don't be misled – this prosperous spa town, surrounded by gorgeous countryside, is an elegant and diverting place. It was founded in 1606, when Lord North discovered a bubbling spring, and reached its height of popularity during the Regency period, when such restorative cures were in vogue. The well-mannered architecture of that period, surrounded by parklands in which the rejuvenated gentry exercised, gives the southern and western part of town its special character.

The icon of those genteel times, and the best place to start your wanderings, is the **Pantiles**, an elegant colonnaded parade of shops, ten minutes' walk south of the train station, where the fashionable once gathered to promenade and take the waters. The name stems from the chunky Kent tiles made of baked clay, which were put down as paving during Queen Anne's reign. Hub of the Pantiles is the original **chalybeate spring** (March–Sept daily 10am–5pm) in the Bath House, where a "Dipper" has been employed since the late eighteenth century to serve the ferrous waters. A period-dressed incumbent will fetch you a glass from the cool spring for 25p – or, if you bring your own cup, you can help yourself for free from the adjacent source. The Bath House itself was built in 1804 but failed as an enterprise as the water turns a nasty colour when heated; it closed in 1847 and now houses a chemist's shop.

You can view one of the original "pantiles" in the exhibition, **A Day at the Wells** (daily: April–Oct 10am–5pm; Nov–March 10am–4pm; £4.95), situated in the basement of the nearby Corn Exchange. An audio tour, narrated as if by Richard "Beau" Nash – self-appointed arbiter of good taste – attempts to re-create, with the help of various historical tableaux, eighteenth-century spa life.

Apart from tiles, Tunbridge also produced domestic ceramics, on view with other local relics and historical artefacts in the **Museum and Art Gallery** built in the 1950s at the top of Mount Pleasant Road (Mon–Sat 9.30am–5pm; free), a fifteen-minute walk up the old-fashioned High Street from the Pantiles.

Tunbridge Wells' **train station**, on the line between London Charing Cross and Hastings, is in the centre of town, where the High Street becomes Mount Pleasant Road. The **tourist office** is in the Old Fish Market, The Pantiles (Oct–April Mon–Sat 9am–5pm, Sun 10am–4pm; May & Sept Mon–Sat 9am–5pm, Sun 10am–5pm; June–Aug Mon–Sat 9am–6pm, Sun 10am–5pm; ☎01892/515675). For **B&B**, *Ephraim Lodge* (☎01892/523053; ③), on The Common, and the nearby *Clarken Guest House*, a large Victorian house with gardens at 61 Frant Rd (☎01892/533397; ②), are good value. The *Swan Hotel* in the Pantiles (☎01892/541450; ⑤) is pricey but worth a splurge.

For a small town, Tunbridge Wells has a fair selection of **restaurants** – one of the best (and most expensive) being *Thackeray's House*, one-time home of the writer at 85

London Rd (☎01892/511921; closed Sun eve & Mon). The cheaper end of the market is dominated by the chains: the reliable *Pizza Express* have a branch at 81 High St; *Pierre Victoire* on Mount Pleasant Road offers a bargain three-course lunch. *Flippers*, 9 High St (closed Sun), fry superior fish and chips, while veggies can have lunch or pre-theatre grub at the *Trinity Arts Centre Café* in a converted church on Church Road (closed Sun).

Sissinghurst and Leeds Castle

Sissinghurst, twelve miles east of Tunbridge Wells (April to mid-Oct Tues–Fri 1–6.30pm, Sat & Sun 10am–5.30pm; £6; NT), was described by Vita Sackville-West as "a garden crying out for rescue" when she and her husband took it over in the 1920s. Gradually, they transformed the five-acre plot into one of England's greatest and most popular modern gardens. Spread over the site of an Elizabethan mansion (of which only one wing remains today), the gardens were designed around the linear pattern of the former building's walls. Sissinghurst's appeal derives from the way that the flowers are allowed to spill over onto the narrow walkways, defying the classical formality of the great gardens that preceded it. The brick tower Vita restored and used as her study acts as a focal point and offers the best views of the walled gardens. Most impressive are the **White Garden**, composed solely of white flowers and silvery-grey foliage, and the **Cottage Garden**, featuring flora in shades of orange, yellow and red. Sissinghurst gets so busy in summer that timed tickets for half-hourly visits are issued. Food options in the gardens are limited and overpriced – your best bet is to bring a picnic.

    Leeds Castle, fifteen miles north of Sissinghurst, on the edge of the North Downs (daily: March–Oct 10am–5pm; Nov–Feb 10am–3pm; £9.30), is more like a fairytale palace than a defensively efficient fortress. The present stone castle dates from Norman times and is set half on an island in the middle of a lake and half on the mainland surrounded by landscaped parkland. Following centuries of regal and noble ownership (and service as a prison) the castle is now run as a commercial concern, hosting conferences as well as sporting and cultural events. Its interior fails to match the castle's stunning external appearance and, in places, twentieth-century renovations have quashed any of its historical charm; possibly the most unusual feature inside is the dog-collar museum. In the grounds, there's a fine aviary with some colourful exotic specimens, as well as manicured gardens and a mildly challenging maze.

Penshurst and Hever Castle

Tudor timber-framed houses and shops line the high street of the attractive village of **PENSHURST**, five miles northwest of Tunbridge Wells. Its village church, St John the Baptist, is capped by an unusual four-spired tower and is entered under a beamed archway which conceals a rustic post office. However, the main reason for coming here is to visit **Penshurst Place** (house: March Sat & Sun noon–5.30pm; April–Sept daily noon–5.30pm; grounds same days 11am–6pm; house & grounds £5.70; grounds only £4.20), home to the Sidney family since 1552 and birthplace of the Elizabethan soldier and poet, Sir Philip Sidney. The fourteenth-century Barons Hall, built for Sir John de Pulteney, four times Mayor of London, is the chief glory of the interior, with its sixty-foot-high chestnut roof still in place. The ten acres of grounds include a formal Italian garden with clipped box hedges, and double herbaceous borders mixed with an abundance of yew hedges.

    The moated and much-altered **Hever Castle** (daily: April–Oct noon–5pm; March & Nov noon–4pm; £7.30), three miles further west, is where Anne Boleyn, second wife of Henry VIII, grew up, and where Anne of Cleves, Henry's fourth wife, lived after their divorce. In 1903, having fallen into disrepair, the castle was bought by William

Waldorf-Astor, American millionaire owner of *The Times*, who assiduously restored the house, panelling the rooms with reproductions of Tudor woodcarvings. In the Inner Hall hang two fine portraits of Henry VIII and Elizabeth I by Holbein. Upstairs, in Anne of Cleves' room, there's a well-preserved tapestry, depicting the marriage of Henry's sister to King Louis XII, with Anne Boleyn as one of the ladies-in-waiting. Outside in the grounds, next to the gift shop, is the absorbing **Guthrie Miniature Model Houses Collection**, showing the development of aristocratic seats from feudal times onwards. The best feature of the grounds, though, is the beautiful **Italian Garden**, built on reclaimed marshland and decorated with Roman statuary.

Sevenoaks and around

Set among the Greensand ridges of west Kent, 25 miles from London, **SEVENOAKS** lost all but one of the ageing oaks from which it derives its name in the storm that struck southern England in October 1987. With mere saplings having taken their place, the only real reason to come to the town is to visit the immense baronial estate of **Knole** (April–Oct Wed–Sat noon–4pm, Sun 11am–5pm; £5; NT), accessible from the south end of Sevenoaks High Street. Knole House was transformed into a palace in 1456 by Archbishop Thomas Bourchier, for himself and succeeding archbishops of Canterbury. Designed to numerically match the calendar with 7 courtyards, 52 staircases and 365 rooms, it was appropriated by Henry VIII, who lavished further expense on it and hunted in the thousand acres of parkland, still home to several hundred deer. Elizabeth I passed the estate on to her cousin, Thomas Sackville, and it has remained in the family's hands ever since. Vita Sackville-West was born here, and her one-time lover Virginia Woolf derived inspiration for her novel *Orlando* from her frequent visits to the house. Only thirteen rooms are open to the public, featuring an array of fine, if well-worn, furnishings and tapestries. Paintings by Gainsborough and Van Dyck are on display, as are Reynolds' depictions of George III and of Queen Charlotte – between them hangs a painting of their strutting, dandified progeny, George IV, one of the fifteen children she bore the king.

Sevenoaks' **train station** is fifteen minutes' walk north of the town centre on the London Road. The **bus station** is in Buckhurst Lane, off the High Street. The **tourist office** is in the library building, just opposite the bus station (April–Sept Mon–Sat 9.30am–5pm; Oct–March Mon–Fri 9.30am–5pm, Sat 9.30am–4.30pm; ☎01732/450305). Reasonable **accommodation** options include the self-catering "family room" at the elegant *Red House* (☎01732/460506; ②), ten minutes northeast of the High Street at 23 Bayham Rd, or the spacious room at *Burley Lodge* (☎01732/455761; ①), close to the entrance to Knole. The nearest **youth hostel** is in Kemsing, four miles northeast of Sevenoaks, and a two-mile hike from Kemsing station (☎01732/761341; closed Jan). Alternatively, take bus #425/6 or #433 from Sevenoaks to Kemsing post office, which is close by – note that no public transport runs to Kemsing on Sundays.

For truly delicious **food**, you need to go to the *Sycamore* restaurant at the *Royal Oak Hotel* on Upper High Street just beyond the entrance to Knole Park, which offers a two-course lunch for over £10, though in the evening one main dish will cost you more than that. At this point, you might prefer to head for the bistro (in other words the bar) which is also good – and half the price.

Lullingstone, Chartwell and Ightham Mote

Lullingstone Roman Villa (daily: April–Sept 10am–6pm; Oct 10am–5pm; Nov–March 10am–4pm; £2.50; EH), seven miles north of Sevenoaks and half a mile south of Eynsford train station, has some of the best-preserved Roman mosaics in southeast England on show, in a pleasant location alongside the trickle of the River Darent. Believed to have been the first-century residence of a farmer, the site has yielded some fine marble busts (now in the British Museum) and a superb floor depicting the despatching of the chimera, a mythical fire-breathing beast with a lion's head, goat's body and a serpent's tail. Excavation in a nearby chamber has revealed early Christian iconography, suggesting that the villa may have become a Romano-Christian chapel in the third century, pre-empting the official arrival of Christianity by three hundred years and making Lullingstone one of the earliest sites of clandestine Christian worship in England.

The residence of Winston Churchill from 1924 until his death in 1965, **Chartwell**, six miles west of Sevenoaks (April–June, Sept & Oct Wed–Sun 11am–5pm; July & Aug Tues–Sun 11am–5pm; £5.50; NT), is one of the most visited National Trust properties. It's an unremarkable, heavily restored Tudor building whose main appeal is the wartime premier's memorabilia, including his paintings, which show an unexpectedly contemplative side to the famously gruff statesman. At peak times entry to the house is by timed ticket – expect long queues.

The secluded, moated manor house of **Ightham Mote**, six miles southeast of Sevenoaks just off the A227 (April–Oct Mon, Wed–Fri & Sun 11am–5.30pm; £5; NT), originates from the fourteenth century and is one of the southeast's most picturesque National Trust properties, though the original defensive appearance of this half-timbered ragstone building has been muted by Tudor alterations. A tour of the interior reveals a mixture of architectural styles ranging from the fourteenth-century Old Chapel and crypt, through a barrel-vaulted Tudor chapel with a painted ceiling to an eighteenth-century Palladian window. This idyllically situated medieval dwelling is being restored by the National Trust, whose efforts are described in a small exhibition on the ground floor.

Eastbourne and around

Like so many of the southeast's seaside resorts, **EASTBOURNE** was kick-started into life in the 1840s, when the Brighton, Lewes & Hastings railway company built a branch line from Lewes to the sea. Past holidaymakers include George Orwell, the composer Claude Debussy – who finished writing *La Mer* here – as well as Marx and Engels. Nowadays Eastbourne has a solid reputation as a retirement town – albeit one that's a touch livelier than the nearby custom-built Peacehaven. Eastbourne's elegant three-mile seafront consists of houses and hotels and is tainted by barely a shop, but the greatest draw around is the South Downs, which the sea has ground into a series of dramatic chalk cliffs around **Beachy Head**, just west of town.

Eastbourne

Conforming to traditions, Eastbourne's **pier** is the focal point of its seafront: opened in 1872 and among the finest on the south coast. The promenade is framed by two prominent red-brick Martello forts: the northeastern one, the **Redoubt Fortress**, now houses a military museum (Easter–Nov daily 10am–5.30pm; £1.85) and the other, the **Wish Tower** – the name is an old Sussex word meaning "marsh" – has been transformed into a **puppet museum** (Easter–Nov daily 10am–5pm; £1.80). One bright spark in sedate Eastbourne is the **Towne Gallery and Museum** on the corner of High Street and the Borough in the Old Town (Tues–Sat noon–5pm, Sun 2–5pm; free), a ten-minute walk west of the train station – it shows a refreshingly contemporary and ever-changing range of work.

Eastbourne **train station** is a splendid Italianate terminus ten minutes' walk from the seafront; the **bus station** is on Cavendish Place right by the pier; and the **tourist office** is at 3 Cornfield Rd, on the corner of Hyde Gardens (Mon–Sat 9.30am–5.30pm, Sun

---

THE SOUTH DOWNS WAY

Following the undulating crest of the South Downs, from the village of Buriton on the Sussex/Hampshire border, two miles southwest of Petersfield train station, to their spectacular end at Beachy Head, the **South Downs Way** rises and dips over eighty miles along the chalk uplands, offering the southeast's finest walks. If undertaken in its entirety, the bridleway is best traversed from west to east, taking advantage of the prevailing wind, Eastbourne's better transport services and accommodation, and the psychological appeal of ending at the sea. **Steyning**, the halfway point, marks a transition between predominantly wooded sections and more exposed chalk uplands – to the east of here you'll pass the modern **youth hostel** at Truleigh Hill (☎01903/813419; closed Oct–March). Other hostels are at Telscombe (see p.194) and Alfriston (☎01323/870423, *alfriston@yha.org.uk*; closed mid-Dec to Jan), a traditional Sussex flint building in the Cuckmere Valley, where a southern loop can be taken which brings you to Eastbourne along the cliffs of the Seven Sisters.

10am–1pm; ☎01323/411400). Eastbourne has hundreds of places to **stay**: try *Seabreeze Guest House*, 6 Marine Rd (☎01323/725440; ①), a hundred yards from the sea, or *Sea Beach House Hotel*, 39–40 Marine Parade (☎01323/410458; ③). The **youth hostel** is on East Dean Road (☎01323/721081; closed Oct–March), a mile and a half west of town, with spectacular views across Eastbourne; take bus #712. Terminus Road, between the train station and the sea, boasts an excellent Thai **restaurant**, *Seeracha*, at no. 94 (☎01323/642867), plus the town's best Italian, *Luigi's*, at 72 Seaside Rd (☎01323/736994; closed Sun), off Terminus Road; both are moderately priced. The best **pubs** are some distance from the seafront: the *Hurst Arms* at 76 Willingdon Rd, a ten-minute walk inland from the station up Upperton Road, has Harvey's locally brewed beers on tap.

Beachy Head and the Seven Sisters

A short walk west from Eastbourne takes you out along the most dramatic stretch of Sussex coastline, where the chalk uplands of the Sussex Downs are cut by the sea into a sequence of splendid cliffs. The most spectacular, **Beachy Head**, is 575ft high, with a diminutive-looking lighthouse below, but no beach – the headland's name derives from the French *beau chef* meaning "beautiful head". The beauty certainly went to Friedrich Engels' head – he insisted his ashes be scattered here and depressed individuals regularly try to join him by leaping to their doom from this well-known suicide spot. West of the headland the scenery softens into a diminishing series of cliffs, a landmark known as the **Seven Sisters**. The country park after which they are named provides some of the most impressive walks in the county, taking in the cliff-top walk and the lower valley of the meandering River Cuckmere, into which the Seven Sisters subside.

Lewes and around

East Sussex's county town, **LEWES** straddles the River Ouse as it carves a gap through the South Downs on its final stretch to the sea. The town's core is remarkably good-looking: Georgian and crooked older dwellings still line the High Street and the narrow lanes – or "Twittens" – lead off this main street and its continuations, with views onto the downs. Following the Norman Conquest, William's son-in-law, William de Warenne, built a priory and castle here, the latter still dominating the High Street. In 1264 Henry III's incompetence caused a baronial revolt led by Simon de Montfort which culminated in the king's surrender at the Battle of Lewes, although de Montfort and his reduced force were annihilated within a year at the Battle of Evesham. De

THE BONFIRE SOCIETIES

Each November 5, while the rest of Britain lights small domestic bonfires or attends municipal firework displays to commemorate the foiling of a Catholic plot to blow up the Houses of Parliament, Lewes puts on a more dramatic show, whose origins lie in the deaths of the town's Protestant martyrs. By the end of the eighteenth century, Lewes' **Bonfire Boys** had become notorious for the boisterousness of their anti-Catholic demonstrations, in which they set off fireworks indiscriminately and dragged rolling tar barrels through the streets – a tradition still practised today, although with a little more caution. In 1845 events came to a head when the incorrigible pyromaniacs of Lewes had to be read the Riot Act, instigating a night of violence between the police and Bonfire Boys. Lewes' first **bonfire societies** were established soon afterwards, to try to get a bit more discipline into the proceedings, and earlier this century they were persuaded to move their street fires to the town's perimeters.

Today's tightly knit bonfire societies, each with its quasi-militaristic motto ("Death or Glory", "True to Each Other", etc), spend much of the year preparing the Bonfire Night shenanigans, when their members dress up in traditional costumes and parade through the town carrying flaming torches, before marching off onto the Downs for their society's big fire. At each of the fires effigies of Guy Fawkes and the Pope are burned alongside contemporary, but equally reviled, figures – Chancellors of the Exchequer and Prime Ministers are popular choices.

Montfort's name crops up all over the town, as do references to the Lewes Martyrs, the seventeen Protestants burned here in 1556, at the height of Mary Tudor's militant revival of Catholicism – an event commemorated in spectacular fashion every November 5. Intellectual nonconformity is something of a Lewes trademark, its roll call of free-thinkers featuring pioneer paleontologist Gideon Mantell, and the radical humanist Tom Paine, whose works inspired or supported the revolutions in France and America. The conservative spirit triumphed in 1914, however, after a pair of local enthusiasts commissioned a version of Rodin's majestic sculpture *The Kiss*, depicting Paolo and Francesca – lovers from Dante's *Inferno* – clinched in a full-on embrace. Local sentiment was outraged when the piece was unveiled in Lewes Town Hall, leading to its rapid removal amid a flurry of controversy (the sculpture was re-exhibited in the town hall in June 1999, 85 years after the scandal).

The Town

The best way to begin a tour of Lewes from the train station, is to walk up Station Road, then left down the High Street. The town's **Castle** (Mon–Sat 10am–5.30pm, Sun 11am–5.30pm; £3.50) is hidden from view behind the houses on your right. Inside the castle complex – unusual for being built on two mottes, or mounds – the shell of the eleventh-century keep remains, and both the towers can be climbed for excellent views over the town's roofs to the surrounding Downs. Tickets for the castle include admission to the **museum** (same opening hours as castle), by the castle entrance, which is much better than the usual stuffy town museum. The highlight is a half-hourly audiovisual history of Lewes, aided by the vast Lewes Living History Model on which places of interest within the town are spotlit as the tale unfolds.

A few minutes' walk further west along the High Street past St Michael's Church, with its unusual twin towers – one arcaded and wooden and the other round flint – you come to the steep cobbled and much photographed **Keere Street**, down which the reckless Prince Regent is alleged to have driven his carriage. Keere Street leads eventually to **Southover Grange** (Mon–Sat 8am–dusk, Sun 9am–dusk; free), with its lovely gardens. Built in 1572 from the priory's remains, the Grange was also the childhood home of the diarist John Evelyn. Past the gardens, a right turn down Southover High Street leads to the Tudor-built **Anne of Cleves House** (mid-Feb to Nov Mon–Sat 10am–5.30pm, Sun noon–5.30pm; Dec to mid-Feb Tues, Thurs & Sat only; £2.30; combined ticket with castle £4.80), given to her in settlement after her divorce from Henry VIII (although she never actually lived here), now an absorbing museum. The magnificent oak-beamed Tudor bedroom is impressive, with its cumbersome "bed wagon", a bed-warming brazier which would fail the slackest of fire regulations and which the four-hundred-year-old Flemish four-poster has managed to survive. The house's decor dates from the sixteenth century when the Wealden iron industry was flourishing and Sussex produced most of England's iron, with Lewes being a centre of cannon manufacture.

On the opposite side of the road and closer to the train station, is the church of **St John the Baptist**, with its squat, brick tower capped by a six-foot shark for a weather vane; inside there's some superb stained glass and a tiny chapel with the lead coffins of William de Warenne and his wife Gundrada, William I's daughter. De Warenne was one of the six barons presiding over the new administrative provinces – known as the **Rapes of Sussex** – created by the Normans soon after the Conquest. Behind the church are the ruins of de Warenne's **St Pancras Priory**, once one of Europe's principal Cluniac institutions, with a church the size of Westminster Abbey. Sadly it was dismantled to build town houses following the Dissolution and is now an evocative ruin surrounded by playing fields.

Returning to the town centre, the **Star Brewery Studio** off Fisher Street, north of the High Street, displays the creative talents of a collective of artists, bookbinders, carpenters and other artisans; the attached **Star Gallery** (Mon–Sat 10.30am–5.30pm; free) presents a changing series of exhibitions. At the east end of the High Street, School Hill descends towards Cliffe Bridge, built in 1727 and entrance to the commercial centre of the medieval settlement, although Cliffe High Street's appearance is now predominantly nineteenth century. For the energetic, a path leads up onto the Downs from the end of Cliffe High Street – site of England's worst avalanche disaster in 1836, when a bank of snow slid onto Cliffe village, killing eight people. The path passes close to an obelisk, commemorating the town's seventeen Protestant martyrs.

Practicalities

The **train station**, south of the High Street on Station Road, has regular services from London Victoria and along the coast to Brighton, Eastbourne, Hastings and the ferry port at Newhaven, from where Hoverspeed run ferries and catamarans to Dieppe (☎08705/240241). **Buses** to the rest of East Sussex leave from the **bus station** on Eastgate Street, by the river. The **tourist office** (Easter–Sept Mon–Fri 9am–5pm, Sat 10am–5pm, Sun 10am–2pm; Oct–Easter Mon–Fri 9am–5pm; ☎01273/483448) is at the junction of the High Street and Station Road. For **accommodation** try *Millers*, a timber-framed house at 134 High St (☎01273/475631; ②) or *Castle Bank Cottages*, a beamed period house with great views at no. 4 Castle Banks (☎01273/476291; ③); the *Crown Hotel* on the High Street, close to the tourist office (☎01273/480670; ③), is a reasonable fallback. The nearest **youth hostel** is in the village of Telscombe, six miles south of Lewes (see below); there's another – a rustic wooden cabin with basic facilities – eleven miles northeast of Lewes at Blackboys (☎01825/890607; closed mid-Sept to March; £7.50). Lewes is home to the excellent Harvey's brewery and most of the **pubs** serve its products. The *Brewers' Arms* is central and pleasant enough, as is the *Lewes Arms* tucked behind the *Star Brewery Studios*. **Food** options include the inexpensive Indian *Dilraj*, at 12 Fisher St, a moderately priced Italian joint *La Cucina*, at 13 Station St, or the inexpensive *Pailin* Thai restaurant, opposite at no. 20 (☎01273/473906).

Around Lewes: Glyndebourne, Rodmell and Charleston

Glyndebourne, Britain's only unsubsidized opera house, is situated near the village of Glynde, three miles east of Lewes. Founded in 1934, the Glyndebourne Festival season, which runs from May to August, is an indispensable part of the high-society calendar, with ticket prices and distribution excluding all but the most devoted opera lovers. On one level, Glyndebourne is a repellent spectacle, its lawns thronged with gentry and corporate bigwigs ingesting champagne and smoked salmon – productions have one massive interval to allow for an unhurried repast. On the other hand, the musical values are of the highest standard, mixing young talent with starrier names, and taking the sort of risks Covent Garden wouldn't dream of. The acoustically outstanding new theatre (seating 1200) has broadened the appeal of this exclusive venue to a wider audience. Some tickets are available at reduced prices for dress rehearsals or if you are prepared to stand (☎01273/813813). Tickets for Glyndebourne Touring Opera, which uses the same productions but with up-and-coming singers, are both cheaper and easier to obtain.

Three miles south of Lewes lies the village of **Rodmell**, whose main source of interest is the **Monk's House** (April–Oct Wed & Sat 2–5.30pm; £2.50; NT), former home of Virginia Woolf, a leading figure of the Bloomsbury Group (see box below). She and her husband Leonard moved to the weatherboard cottage in 1919 and Leonard stayed there until his death in 1969; both Virginia's and Leonard's remains are interred in the gardens. Nearby lies the River Ouse where Virginia killed herself in 1941 by walking into the water with her pockets full of stones. The house's interior is nothing special and will only really be of interest to Bloomsbury fans, who can look round the study where

---

THE BLOOMSBURY GROUP

The **Bloomsbury Group** were essentially a bevy of upper middle-class friends, who took their name from the Bloomsbury area of London, where most of them lived before acquiring houses in the Sussex countryside. The Group revolved around Virginia, Vanessa, Thoby and Adrian Stephen, who lived at 46 Gordon Square, the London base of the Bloomsbury Group. Thoby's Thursday evening gatherings and Vanessa's Friday Club for painters attracted a whole host of Cambridge-educated snobs who subscribed to Oscar Wilde's theory that "aesthetics are higher than ethics". Their diet of "human intercourse and the enjoyment of beautiful things" was hardly revolutionary, but their behaviour, particularly that of the two sisters (unmarried, unchaperoned, intellectual and artistic), succeeded in shocking London society, especially through their louche sexual practices (most of the group swung both ways).

All this, though interesting, would be forgotten were it not for their individual work. In 1922 Virginia declared, without too much exaggeration, "Everyone in Gordon Square has become famous": Lytton Strachey had been the first to make his name with *Eminent Victorians*, a series of unprecedently frank biographies; Vanessa, now married to the art critic Clive Bell, had become involved in Roger Fry's prolific design firm, Omega Workshop; and the economist John Maynard Keynes had become an adviser to the Treasury (he later went on to become the leading economic theorist of his day). The Group's most celebrated figure, Virginia, married Leonard Woolf and became an established novelist; she and Leonard also founded the Hogarth Press, which published T.S. Eliot's *Waste Land* in 1922.

Eliot was just one of a number of writers, such as Aldous Huxley, Bertrand Russell and E.M. Forster, who were drawn to the interwar Bloomsbury set, but others, notably D.H. Lawrence, were repelled by the clan's narcissism and snobbish narrow-mindedness. Whatever their limitations, the Bloomsbury Group were Britain's most influential intellectual coterie of the interwar years, and their appeal shows little sign of waning – even now scarcely a year goes by without the publication of the biography and or memoirs of some Bloomsbury peripheral.

Virginia wrote several of her novels, and her bedroom, laid out with period editions of her work. Three miles south of Rodmell, in the village of **Telscombe**, is a quiet **youth hostel** (☎01273/301357; closed mid-Sept to March; £7.50), whose simple accommodation is in two-hundred-year-old cottages.

Six miles east of Lewes, off the A27, is another Bloomsbury Group shrine, **Charleston Farmhouse** (April–Oct Wed–Sun 2–5pm; July & Aug Wed–Sat 11.30am–5pm, Sun 2–5pm; £5.50), home to Virginia Woolf's sister Vanessa Bell, Vanessa's husband Clive Bell and her lover Duncan Grant. As conscientious objectors, the trio moved here during World War I so that the men could work on local farms (farm labourers were exempted from military service). The farmhouse became a gathering point for other members of the Bloomsbury Group, including the biographer Lytton Strachey, the economist Maynard Keynes and the novelist E.M. Forster. Duncan Grant continued to live in the house until his death in 1978. Unless it's a Sunday, you have to join a fifty-minute guided tour in order to view the interior of the farmhouse, where almost every surface is painted and the walls are hung with paintings by Picasso, Renoir and Augustus John, alongside the work of the markedly less talented residents. Many of the fabrics, lampshades and other artefacts bear the unmistakable mark of the Omega Workshop, the Bloomsbury equivalent of William Morris's Arts and Crafts Movement.

Brighton

Recorded as the tiny fishing village of Brithelmeston in the Domesday Book, **BRIGHTON** seems to have slipped unnoticed through history until the mid-eighteenth-century sea-bathing trend established a resort that has never looked back. The fad received royal approval in the 1770s when the decadent Prince Regent, later George IV, began patronizing the town in the company of his mistress, thus setting a precedent for the "dirty weekend", Brighton's major contribution to the English collective consciousness. Trying to shake off this blowsy reputation, Brighton now highlights its Georgian charm, its upmarket shops and classy restaurants and its thriving conference industry. Yet, however much Brighton tries to present itself as a comfortable middle-class town, the essence of its appeal is its faintly bohemian vitality, a buzz that comes from a mix of English holidaymakers, thousands of young foreign students from the town's innumerable language schools, a thriving gay community and an energetic local student population from the art college and two universities.

Arrival, information and accommodation

Brighton **train station** is at the head of Queen's Road, which descends to the Clock Tower and then becomes West Street which eventually collides with the seafront – a distance of about half a mile. **Buses** arrive at Pool Valley bus station, tucked just in from the seafront on the south side of the Old Steine. The **tourist office** is at 10 Bartholomew Square, behind the town hall on the southern side of the Lanes (June–Sept Mon–Fri 9am–6pm, Sat 10am–5pm, Sun 10am–4pm; Oct–May Mon–Sat 9am–5pm, Sun 10am–4pm; ☎01273/292599), a maze of narrow alleyways marking Brighton's Old Town. You'll find most budget **accommodation** clustered around the Kemp Town district, to the east of the Palace Pier, with the more elegant and expensive hotels west of the town centre around Regency Square, opposite the West Pier. Brighton's official **campsite** is the year-round *Sheepcote Valley* site (☎01273/626546), just north of Brighton Marina; take bus #1 or #1A to Wilson Avenue, or take the Volks railway and walk up Arundel Road to Wilson Avenue.

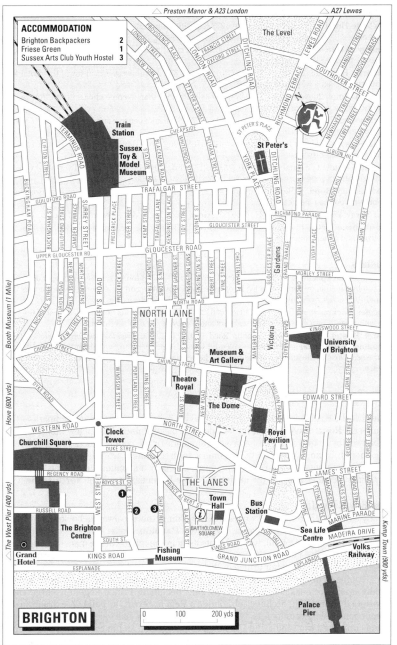

© Crown copyright

Hotels, B&Bs and guest houses

Adelaide Hotel, 51 Regency Square (☎01273/205286). Topnotch guest house in the fancier part of town. ④.

Ainsley House, 28 New Steine (☎01273/605310). Friendly, upmarket guest house in an attractive Regency terrace. ②.

Andorra Hotel, 15–16 Oriental Place (☎01273/321787). At the west end of town, this hotel has comfortable rooms with good facilities. ②.

Arlanda Hotel, 20 New Steine (☎01273/699300). Plusher than average choice in the New Steine square, with a wide price range. ③.

Cornerways Hotel, 18–20 Caburn Rd (☎01273/731882). Inexpensive and friendly B&B, a couple of minutes west of the train station. ①.

Four Seasons, 3 Upper Rock Gardens (☎01273/681496). Cosy B&B in the Kemp Town area, with good vegetarian breakfast options. ①.

Oriental Hotel, 9 Oriental Place (☎01273/205050). Friendly, laid-back staff and very funky decor throughout; full veggie breakfasts are served in the hotel's mellow café. ③.

Queensbury Hotel, 58 Regency Square (☎01273/325558). Comfortable guest house in Brighton's definitive Georgian district. ③.

Sea Spray, 25 New Steine (☎01273/680332). Good value B&B with showers in all rooms. ②.

Westbourne Hotel, 46 Upper Rock Gardens (☎01273/686920). Well appointed B&B close to the seafront and all amenities. ②.

Hostels

Brighton Backpackers, 75 Middle St (☎01273/777717). Brighton's established independent hostel run by tuned-in owners with a lively, easy-going atmosphere and vivid murals. A new annex just round the corner overlooks the seafront and offers a quieter alternative.

Baggies Backpackers, 33 Oriental Place (☎01273/733740). Spacious house a little west of the centre with large bright dorms, decent showers and plenty of room to spread out.

Youth Hostel, Patcham Place, London Road (☎01273/556196, *brighton@yha.org.uk*; closed Jan). Brighton's YHA hostel is housed in a splendid Queen Anne mansion, in parkland four miles north of the sea, close to the junction of the roads to Lewes and London. Take bus #5 or 5a from the town centre.

The Town

Any visit to Brighton inevitably begins with a visit to its two most famous landmarks – the exuberant **Royal Pavilion** and the wonderfully tacky **Palace Pier**, a few minutes away – followed by a stroll along the seafront promenade or the pebbly beach. Just as interesting, though, is an exploration of Brighton's car-free **Lanes**, where some of the town's diverse restaurants, bars and tiny bric-a-brac, jewellery and antique shops can be found; or an idle meander through the quaint, but more bohemian streets of **North Laine**.

The Royal Pavilion

In any survey to find England's most loved building, there's always a bucketful of votes for Brighton's exotic extravaganza, the **Royal Pavilion** (daily: June–Sept 10am–6pm; Oct–May 10am–5pm; £4.50), which flaunts itself in the middle of the main thoroughfare of Old Steine. The building that originally stood here was a conventional farmhouse. Then in 1787, the fun-loving Prince of Wales commissioned something more regal, and for a couple of decades the prince's south-coast pied-à-terre was a Palladian villa, with mildly oriental embellishments. Shortly after becoming Prince Regent, George commissioned John Nash, architect of London's Regent Street, to build an extraordinary confection of slender minarets, twirling domes, pagodas, balconies and miscellaneous motifs imported from India and China and supported on an innovative cast-iron frame, creating an exterior profile that defines a genre of its own – Oriental-Gothic. Queen

Victoria was not amused by George's taste in architecture, and shifted the royal seaside residence to the Isle of Wight, taking the pavilion's valuable fittings back to Buckingham and Kensington palaces and selling the building to the town. The pavilion was then pressed into a series of humdrum roles – tearoom, hospital, concert hall, radar station, ration office – but has now been brilliantly restored.

Inside the pavilion the exuberant compendium of Regency exotica has been enhanced by the return of many of the objects which Victoria had taken away. One of the highlights – approached via the restrained Long Gallery – is the **Banqueting Room**, which erupts with ornate splendour and is dominated by a one-tonne chandelier hung from the jaws of a massive dragon cowering in a plantain tree. Next door, the huge, high-ceilinged kitchen, fitted with the most modern appliances of its time, has iron columns disguised as palm trees. Nearby, the stunning **Music Room**, the first sight of which reduced George to tears of joy, has a huge dome lined with more than 26,000 individually gilded scales and hung with exquisite umbrella-like glass lamps. After climbing the famous cast-iron staircase with its bamboo-look bannisters, you can go into Victoria's sober and seldom-used bedroom and the North Gallery where the King's portrait hangs, along with a selection of satirical cartoons. More notable, though, is the **South Gallery**, decorated in sky blue with trompe l'oeil bamboo trellises and a carpet which appears to be strewn with flowers.

The rest of the town

Tucked between the pavilion and the seafront is a warren of narrow, pedestrianized thoroughfares known as **the Lanes** – the core of the old fishing village from which Brighton evolved. Long-established antiques shops, designer outlets and a concentration of bars, pubs and restaurants generate a lively and intimate atmosphere in this part of town. **North Laine**, which spreads north of North Street along Kensington, Sydney, Gardner and Bond streets, is more bohemian with its hub along pedestrianized Kensington Gardens. Here the shops are more eclectic, selling secondhand records, clothes, bric-a-brac and New Age objects, and mingle with earthy coffee shops and downbeat cafés.

Most of the seafront is an ugly mix of shops, entertainment complexes and hotels, ranging from the impressively pompous plasterwork of the *Grand* – scene of the IRA's attempted assassination of the Conservative cabinet in October 1984 – to the green-glass monstrosity on the seaward side of the Lanes. To appreciate fully the tackier side of Brighton, you must take a stroll along the **Palace Pier**. The pier has yet to gain a replacement for the splendid theatre that once occupied its seaward end, but every inch of the structure is devoted to fun and money-making, from the cacophonous Palace of Fun to the Pleasure Dome, and from the state-of-the-art video games to the fairground rides and karaoke sessions at the end of the pier. Brighton's architecturally superior West Pier, built in 1866 half a mile west along the seafront, was damaged in World War II and then fell into disrepair, but looks set to be restored to its former glory in time for the year 2002.

Across the road from the Palace Pier, on Marine Parade, is the **Sea Life Centre** (daily 10am–5pm; £5.50), one of the best marine life displays of its kind, with a transparent tunnel passing through a huge aquarium – a walk along the bottom of the sea with sharks and rays gliding overhead. Nearby, the antiquated locomotives of **Volk's Electric Railway** (April to mid-Sept; £1) – the first electric train in the country – run eastward towards the Marina and the nudist beach, usually the preserve of just a few thick-skinned souls.

Brighton's museums

Across the gardens from the pavilion stands the **Brighton Museum and Art Gallery** (Mon, Tues & Thurs–Sat 10am–5pm, Sun 2–5pm; free), which is entered just around the corner on Church Street. The paintings here are generally nondescript, but there's an interesting collection of classic Art Deco and Art Nouveau furniture as well as Dali's famous sofa, based on Mae West's lips. There's also a large selection of pottery, from basic Neolithic earthenware to delicate porcelain figurines popular in the eighteenth century.

Brighton's other big municipal museum is the **Booth Museum of Natural History** (Mon–Wed, Fri & Sat 10am–5pm, Sun 2–5pm; free), a mile up Dukes Road from the centre of town. Purpose-built to house Mr E.T. Booth's prodigious collection of stuffed birds, this is a wonderfully fusty old Victorian museum with beetles, butterflies and animal skeletons galore, but which also puts on very imaginative temporary shows.

Perhaps more immediately gratifying for younger children is the **Sussex Toy and Model Museum** (Mon–Fri 10am–1pm & 2–5pm, Sat 11am–1pm & 2–5pm; £3), housed in an old stables underneath the train station. The collection is impressive, ranging from an entire cabinet full of Smurfs to a set of Pelham puppets, but it's the working model railways that are likely to be the focus of most children's attention.

Eating, drinking and nightlife

Brighton has the greatest concentration of **restaurants** in the southeast, second only to London. Around North Laine are some great, inexpensive **cafés**, but for classier establishments head to the Lanes and out towards Hove. Many of the cheaper places fight hard to attract the large student market with discounted deals of around ten percent, so if you have a student ID, use it. **Nightlife** is hectic and compulsively pursued throughout the year, making Brighton unique in the sedate southeast. There are a couple of outstanding clubs, lots of live music and more cinema screens per head than anywhere else in Britain. Midweek entry into the clubs can cost just a couple of pounds and cinema seats are similarly priced before 6pm. For up-to-date details of what's on, pick up a copy of the monthly *Impact* (50p) from the tourist office, or the trendy listings magazines *The Latest* (30p) or *New Insight* (45p). Every May the three-week-long **Brighton Festival** (☎01273/706771; *www.brighton-festival.org.uk*) takes place in various venues around town. This arty celebration includes fun fairs, exhibitions, street theatre and concerts from classical to jazz. Brighton is hoping to emulate Berlin by staging its very own version of the latter's Love Parade, a day-and-night-long **Dance Parade**, held in mid-July.

Cafés and bars

Bar Centro, Ships St. Brighton's biggest, most spacious pre-club bar with occasional in-house DJs spinning tunes.

Disco Biscuit Café, 14 Queen's Rd. Clubbers' choice with big bright sofas, furry dalmatian chairs and all-day breakfasts.

Grinder, 10 Kensington Gardens. Upstairs trip-hoppy café serving tasty cheap snacks, with a great balcony for watching life in North Laine go by.

Mock Turtle, 4 Pool Valley. Old-fashioned teashop crammed with bric-a-brac and cheap homemade cakes. Closed Mon.

The Sanctuary, 51 Brunswick St East, Hove. Cool and arty vegetarian café with soft furnishings and a cosy, relaxed ambience. Deservedly popular, despite its not-very-central location.

Zanzibar, 129 St James's St. Premier pre-club gay bar, situated up towards Kemp Town.

Restaurants

Al Duomo, 7 Pavilion Buildings (☎01273/326741). Brilliant pizzeria with a genuine wood-burning oven. Has a more intimate sister restaurant *Al Forno*, at 36 East St. Inexpensive.

Black Chapati, 12 Circus Parade (☎01273/699011). Innovative Asian cooking with Japanese and Thai influences as well as more conventional Indian dishes, which are brilliantly executed. Something of a Brighton landmark despite its out-of-the-way location, more than a mile inland, at the point where the London road enters town. Moderate.

Browns, 3–4 Duke St (☎01273/323501). A mixture of steak, seafood and pasta dishes as well as traditional favourites like Guinness-marinated steak-and-mushroom pie, served in a sophisticated continental setting with wooden floors, palms and background jazz. Moderate.

Casa Don Carlos, 5 Union St (☎01273/327177). Small, long-established tapas bar in the Lanes with outdoor seating and daily specials. Also serves more substantial Spanish dishes and drinks. Inexpensive.

English's Oyster Bar, 29–31 East St (☎01273/327980). Three fishermen's cottages knocked together to house a marble and brass oyster bar and a red velvet dining room. Seafood's the speciality with a mouthwatering menu and better value than you might expect, especially the set menus. A Brighton institution famed for its atmosphere as much as its food. Closed Sun evening. Expensive.

Food for Friends, 17 Prince Albert St (☎01273/202310). Brighton's ever-popular wholefood veggie eatery is imaginative enough to please die-hard meat-eaters. It's frequently busy but well worth the squeeze and offers discounts for students. Inexpensive.

Le Gastronome, 3 Hampton Place (☎01273/777399). Well known for its good-value classic French cuisine, friendly service and outstanding selection of wines. Closed Sun & Mon. Moderate.

Havana, 33 Duke St (☎01273/773388). Very stylish continental brasserie with just a hint of colonial ambience to evoke tropical luxury and a feeling of being pampered. The menu is eclectic ranging from Med to Thai – the lunchtime menu is particularly good value. Moderate.

Melrose Restaurant, 132 Kings Rd (☎01273/326 520). Traditional and decent seafront establishment which has been serving seafood, roasts and custard-covered puddings for over forty years. The *Regency Restaurant* next door is a similar and smaller option. Inexpensive.

Piccolo, 58 Ship St (☎01273/380380). Informal Italian restaurant with pizza and pasta dishes from around £4 and special deals for students. Inexpensive.

Tamarind Tree, 48 Queen's Rd (☎01273/298816). Mellow Caribbean café decked in turquoise and wickerwork, with a surprisingly large range of veggie dishes. Moderate.

Terre-à-Terre, 7 Pool Valley (☎01273/729051). Imaginative, global, veggie cuisine in a small, modern arty setting, just off Old Steine. Closed Mon lunch. Inexpensive.

Thai Spice Market, 13 Boyces St (☎01273/325195). Classical Thai interior and cuisine, serving meat, seafood and vegetarian varieties. Inexpensive to Moderate.

Yum Yum Noodle Bar, 22–23 Sydney St (☎01273/606777). Serves anything Southeast Asian – Chinese, Thai, Indonesian and Malaysian noodle dishes at good-value prices – situated above a Chinese supermarket. Lunchtimes only. Inexpensive.

Pubs

The Albert, 48 Trafalgar St. A listed building, right by the train station, popular with students, live rock upstairs, real ale downstairs; free pool in the afternoon.

Cricketers, 15 Black Lion St. Just west of the Lanes, this is Brighton's oldest pub and it looks it too; very popular with good pub grub.

Dr Brighton's, 16 King's Rd. Popular gay venue near the Queens Hotel.

Druids Head, 9 Brighton Place. Great, old pub in the heart of the Lanes with a flagstone floor and a raucous juke box.

Font & Firkin, Union St. Spacious and imaginatively converted chapel with a bar in place of the altar.

Hand in Hand, 33 Upper St James's St. An agreeable pub with its own brewery out the back.

Queens Head, 10 Steine St. Popular, gay pub in the heart of the town centre.

Smugglers, 10 Ship St. A young crowd packs out this place, with a good jazz club upstairs, dance club downstairs, and free pool during the day.

Nightlife

Casablanca, *Churchill Palace Hotel*, 2–5 Middle St (☎01273/321817). Mostly Brazilian funky jazz and reggae.

Escape, 10 Marine Parade (☎01273/606906). Brighton's trendiest nightclub packs them in night after night, specializing in funk and rave music.

The Jazz Place, *Smugglers Inn*, 10 Ship St (☎01273/328439). Popular jazz venue in the basement with the livelier *Reforming Club* upstairs catering for active ravers and fronting the occasional abstract dance troupe.

Lift, above the *Pig in Paradise*, 11–12 Queens Rd (☎01273/779411). Regular and varied jazz, jungle and funk events.

Paradox, 78 West St (☎01273/321628). The best option after the *Zap Club*. Its *Wild Fruits* gay nights on first Mondays of the month are particularly popular.

Revenge, 32 Old Steine (☎01273/606064). The south's largest gay club with Monday night cabarets plus upfront dance and retro boogie on two floors.

Swifts Club, West St (☎01273/327701). Popular venue for retro sounds from the Sixties onwards with the *Cavern* below playing hip-hop, ragga jungle and some truly wicked street soul.

Zap Club, Kings Rd Arches (☎01273/821588). Brighton's most durable club, right on the seafront. A popular venue even for Londoners.

Mid-Sussex

The principal attraction of **mid-Sussex** is its wealth of fine gardens, ranging from the majestic **Sheffield Park** to the luscious flowerbeds of **Nymans** and the landscaped lakes of **Leonardslee**. Exploring this region by public transport isn't really feasible unless you take your bike on the train; tourist information is thin on the ground too, so get clued up at Brighton's tourist office before you go.

Sheffield Park and the Bluebell Railway

Around twenty miles northeast of Brighton lies the country estate of **Sheffield Park**, its centrepiece a Gothic mansion built for Lord Sheffield by James Wyatt. The house is closed to the public, but you can roam around the hundred-acre **gardens** (Jan & Feb Sat & Sun 10.30am–4pm or dusk; March, Nov & Dec Tues–Sun 10.30am–4pm; April–Oct Tues–Sun 10.30am–6pm or dusk; £4.20; NT), which were laid out by Capability Brown, the Christopher Wren of the grassy knoll. A mile south of the gardens lies the southern terminus of the **Bluebell Railway** (May–Sept daily; Oct–April Sat, Sun & school holidays; day ticket £7.20; information ☎01825/723777), whose vintage steam locomotives chuff nine miles north via Horsted Keynes to Kingscote. Although the service gets extremely crowded on weekends – especially in May, when the bluebells blossom in the woods through which the line passes – it's an entertaining and nostalgic way of travelling through the Sussex countryside and your day ticket lets you go to and fro as often as you like.

Nymans and Leonardslee

Nymans (March–Oct Wed–Sun 11am–6pm or dusk; £5; NT), fifteen miles north of Brighton near the village of Handcross (bus #773 from Brighton to Crawley can drop you off on the A23 beside the village), was created by Ludwig Messel, an inspired gardener and plant collector. The **gardens** contain a valuable collection of exotic trees and shrubs as well as more everyday plants, of which the colourful rhododendrons are particularly prolific. Nymans consists of a series of different enclosures and gardens, the highlight of which is the large, romantic walled garden, almost hidden from sight by an abundance of climbing plants and housing a collection of rare Himalayan magnolia trees. The gardens are centred around the picturesque ruins of a mock-Tudor manor house, now covered in wisteria, roses and honeysuckle, and are laced with gently sloping paths linking the huge beds of rhododendrons, azaleas and roses.

The most picturesque of all the mid-Sussex gardens are those at **Leonardslee** (daily: April–Oct 9.30am–6pm; £4, £5 during May), four miles southwest of Nymans, near the village of Crabtree; bus #107 from Brighton to Horsham passes by the garden gates. Set in a wooded valley, the seventy-acre gardens are crisscrossed by steep paths, which link six lakes created – like those at Sheffield Park – in the sixteenth century to power waterwheels for iron foundries. The range of flora is especially impressive here, featuring many hybrid species of rhododendron that were created specifically for this garden and are at their best in May when opening hours are specially extended (and admission charges raised). Wallabies, sika and fallow deer roam freely, adding to the edenic atmosphere.

Arundel and around

The hilltop town of **ARUNDEL**, eighteen miles west of Brighton, has for seven centuries been the seat of the Dukes of Norfolk, whose fine castle looks over the valley of the River Arun. The medieval town's well-preserved appearance and picturesque setting draws in the crowds on summer weekends, but at any other time a visit reveals one of West Sussex's least spoilt old towns. Arundel also has a unique place in English cricket: traditionally, the first match of every touring side is played against the Duke of Norfolk's XI on the ground beneath the castle.

Arundel Castle (April–Oct Mon–Fri & Sun noon–5pm; £6.70 castle, grounds & chapel; grounds & chapel £2), towering over the High Street, is what first catches the eye and, despite its medieval appearance, most of what you see is only a century old. The structure dated from Norman times, but was ruined during the Civil War, then lavishly reconstructed during the nineteenth century by the eighth, eleventh and fifteenth dukes. From the top of the keep, you can see the current duke's spacious residence and the pristine castle grounds. Inside the castle, the renovated quarters include the impressive Barons Hall and the library, which boasts paintings by Gainsborough, Holbein and Van Dyck. On the edge of the castle grounds, the fourteenth-century **Fitzalan Chapel** houses tombs of past dukes of Norfolk including twin effigies of the seventh duke – one as he looked when he died and, underneath, one of his emaciated corpse. The Catholic chapel belongs to the Norfolk estate, but is actually physically joined to the parish church of St Nicholas, whose entrance is in London Road. It is separated from the altar of the main Anglican church by an iron grille and a glass screen. Although traditionally Catholics, the dukes of Norfolk have shrewdly played down their papal allegiance in sensitive times – such as during the Tudor era when two of the third duke's nieces, Anne Boleyn and Catherine Howard, became Henry VIII's wives.

West of the parish church, further along London Road is Arundel's other major landmark, the towering Gothic bulk of **Arundel Cathedral**. Constructed in the 1870s by the fifteenth Duke of Norfolk over the town's former Catholic church, the cathedral's spire was designed by John Hansom, inventor of the hansom cab, the earliest taxi. Inside are the enshrined remains of St Philip Howard, the fourth duke's son, exhumed from the Fitzalan Chapel after his canonization in 1970. Following a wayward youth, Howard returned to the Catholic fold at a time when the Armada's defeat saw anti-Catholic feelings soar. Caught fleeing overseas and sentenced to death for praying for Spanish victory, he spent the next decade in the Tower of London, where he died. The cathedral's impressive outline is more appealing than the interior, but it fits in well with the townscape of the medieval seaport. The rest of Arundel is pleasant to wander round, with the antique-shop-lined Maltravers and Arun streets the most attractive thoroughfares.

Practicalities

The **train station** is half a mile south of the town centre over the river on the A27, with **buses** arriving either on the High Street or River Road. The **tourist office** is at 61 High St (June–Aug Mon–Fri 9am–5pm, Sat & Sun 10am–5pm; Sept–May Mon–Fri 9am–5pm, Sat & Sun 10am–3pm; ☎01903/882268). For **accommodation**, try *Bridge*

House, just south of the Queen Street bridge (☎01903/882142; ②), a friendly place offering good-value en-suite rooms, or the venerable *Swan Hotel* at the bottom of High Street (☎01903/882314; ④), a fine old house with a cosy adjoining restaurant. *Castle View* (☎01903/883029; ②), next door to the tourist office, above the tearooms of the same name is reasonable, and neighbouring *Dukes Restaurant*, with its spectacular gilded ceiling, also has a few reasonable rooms (☎01903/883847; ④). Arundel's **youth hostel** (☎01903/882204; closed Nov to mid-Feb) is in a large Georgian house by the river at Warningcamp, a mile and a half northeast of town. You can **camp** at the hostel, or try the *Maynards* site (☎01903/882075) at the top of the hill on the A27 two miles southeast of town.

Bignor and Petworth

Six miles north of Arundel, the excavated second-century ruins of the **Bignor Roman Villa** (March–May & Oct Tues–Sun 10am–5pm; June–Sept daily 10am–6pm; £3.35) include some well-preserved mosaics, of which the Ganymede is the most outstanding. The site, first excavated between 1811 and 1819, is superbly situated at the base of the South Downs and features the longest extant section of mosaic in England, as well as the remains of a hypocaust, the underfloor heating system developed by the Romans.

In the pretty little village of **PETWORTH**, eleven miles north of Arundel, is **Petworth House** (April–Oct Mon–Wed, Sat & Sun 1–5.30pm; park daily 8am–dusk, house £5.50; park free; NT), one of the southeast's most impressive stately homes. Built in the late seventeenth century, the house contains an outstanding art collection, including paintings by Van Dyck, Titian, Gainsborough, Bosch, Reynolds, Blake and Turner – the last a frequent guest here. Highlights of the interior decor are Louis Laguerre's murals around the Grand Staircase and the Carved Room, where carvings by Grinling Gibbons and Holbein's full-length portrait of Henry VIII can be seen. The seven-hundred-acre grounds were landscaped by Capability Brown and are considered one of his finest achievements.

Chichester

The county town of West Sussex and its only city, **CHICHESTER** is an attractive, if stuffy, market town, which began life as a Roman settlement – the Roman cruciform street plan is still evident in the four-quadrant symmetry of the town centre, spread around the Market Cross. The city has built itself up as one of southern England's cultural centres, hosting the **Chichester Festival** in early July, its focus a fairly safe programme of middle-brow plays, though the studio theatre is a bit more adventurous. The racecourse at **Goodwood Park**, north of the city, hosts one of England's most fashionable racing events at the same time. The Gothic cathedral is the chief permanent attraction in the city, but two miles west of the town are the restored Roman ruins of **Fishbourne**, one of the most visited ancient sites in the county.

The City

The main streets lead off to the compass's cardinal points from the Gothic **Market Cross**, a bulky octagonal rotunda topped by ornate finials and a large crown, and built in 1501 to provide shelter for the market traders, although it appears far too small for its function.

A short stroll down West Street brings you to the neat form of the **Cathedral** (daily: Easter to mid-Sept 7.30am–7pm; mid-Sept to Easter 7.30am–5pm), whose slender spire – a nineteenth-century addition – is visible from out at sea. Building began in the

1070s, but the church was extensively rebuilt following a fire a century later and has been only minimally modified since about 1300, except for the spire and the unique, free-standing fifteenth-century bell tower, which now houses the cathedral shop. The **interior** is renowned for its contemporary devotional art, which includes a stained-glass window by Marc Chagall and an enormous altar-screen tapestry by John Piper. Other points of interest are the sixteenth-century painting in the north transept of the past bishops of Chichester, and the fourteenth-century Fitzalan tomb which inspired a poem by Philip Larkin. However, the highlight is a pair of **reliefs** in the south aisle, close to the tapestry – created around 1140, they show the raising of Lazarus and Christ at the gate of Bethany. Originally highly coloured, the reliefs once featured semi-precious stones set in the figures' eyes and are among the finest Romanesque stone carvings in England.

Across South Street in the well-preserved Georgian quadrant of the city known as the Pallants, you'll find **Pallant House**, 9 North Pallant (Tues–Sat 10am–5.15pm; £2.50). Stone dodos stand guard over the gates of this fine mansion, which houses artefacts and furniture from the early eighteenth century. Modern works of art are also included, among them pieces by Henry Moore and Barbara Hepworth and George Sutherland's portrait of Walter Hussey, the former Dean of Chichester, who commissioned much of the cathedral's contemporary art.

Continuing in an anticlockwise direction around the town and crossing East Street to head north up Little London brings you to the **Chichester District Museum** (Tues–Sat 10am–5.30pm; free), housed in an old white weatherboarded corn store. Inside, the modest but entertaining display on local life includes a portable oven carried by Joe Faro, the city pieman, as well as the portable stocks used for the ritual humiliation of petty criminals. The **Guildhall** (June–Aug Sat noon–4pm; free), a branch museum within a thirteenth-century Franciscan church in the middle of Priory Park, at the north end of Little London, has some well-preserved medieval frescoes. It was formerly a town hall and court of law; the poet, painter and visionary William Blake was tried here for sedition.

Practicalities

A regular rail service runs from London Victoria to Chichester's **train station** at the foot of South Street, with the **bus station** next door. From either station it's a ten-minute walk north to the Market Cross, passing the **tourist office** at 29a South St (April–Sept Mon–Sat 9.15am–5.15pm, Sun 10am–4pm; Oct–March Mon–Sat only; ☎01243/775888).

There should be no problem finding **accommodation**, except during the festival when it's advisable to book ahead. If you want to splash out, the *Ship* on North Street (☎01243/778000; ⑥) is a comfortable and characterful inn in the centre of town. Less expensive central B&B options include *Riverside Lodge*, 7 Market Ave, in the Pallants quarter (☎01243/783164; ②) and *Friary Close*, on Friary Lane (☎01243/527294; ③), east of the town centre. You can **camp** at the *Red House Farm*, Brookers Lane, Earnley (☎01243/512959; closed Nov–Easter), six miles southwest of town, a mile or so from the beach.

The *Ship* is a good place for a **drink**, or you could try *Rainbow*, 56 St Paul's Rd, northwest of the town centre, which also has an excellent range of Sussex beers. For something to **eat**, the *Medieval Crypt Brasserie* at 12 South St (☎01243/537033) has wonderful stone vaulting and main courses for around £8; further down the street there's a branch of *Pizza Express*. For authentic French/Med food, go for the stylish *Little London* restaurant in Little London, which offers set-price two- and three-course dinners at moderate prices.

Fishbourne Roman Palace

Fishbourne, two miles west of Chichester (March–July, Sept & Oct daily 10am–5pm; Aug daily 10am–6pm; Nov to mid-Dec daily 10am–4pm; mid-Dec to Feb Sat & Sun 10am–4pm; £4.20), is the largest and best-preserved Roman palace in the country. Roman relics have long been turning up here and in 1960 a workman unearthed their source – the site of a depot used by the invading Romans in 43 AD which, it is thought, later became the vast, hundred-room palace of the Romanized Celtic aristocrat Cogidubnus. A pavilion has been built over the north wing of the excavated remains, where floor mosaics depict Fishbourne's famous dolphin-riding cupid as well as the more usual geometric patterns. Like the remains at Bignor (see p.202), only the residential wing of the former quadrangle has been excavated – other parts of the dwelling fulfilled mundane service roles and probably lacked the mosaics which give both sites their singular appeal. The underfloor heating system has also been well restored and an audio-visual programme gives a fuller picture of the palace as it was in Roman times. The extensive gardens attempt to re-create the appearance of the palace grounds as they would have been then.

To get to Fishbourne take the **train** to Fishbourne station, turn right as you leave the station and the palace is a few minutes' walk away. Buses #700 or #56 from Chichester also run to Fishbourne; both services drop you to the bottom of Salt Hill Road, from where it's a clearly signposted five-minute walk to Fishbourne.

Surrey

Effectively a rural suburb of southern London, for those who can afford it, **SURREY** is bisected laterally by the chalk escarpment of the **North Downs** which rise west of Guildford, peak around Box Hill near Dorking and continue east into Kent. The portion of Surrey within the M25 orbital motorway has little natural and virtually no historical appeal, being a collection of satellite towns and light industrial installations serving the capital, although an enjoyable day can be spent at **Sandown Park** or **Epsom** racecourses, or trying the rides at one of Surrey's theme parks, **Thorpe Park** or **Chessington World of Adventures**. Outside the M25's ring Surrey takes on a more pastoral demeanour, with the county town of **Guildford**, the open heathland of Surrey's western borders and **Farnham**, which houses the county's only intact castle.

Guildford

Thirty-five miles southwest of London, **GUILDFORD**, the county capital, is a moderately interesting town, whose cobbled **High Street** retains a great deal of architectural interest. Several picturesque narrow lanes and courts lead off to the adjoining North Street. As you look up the High Street, you can't fail to notice the wonderful gilded **clock** projecting over the street that has marked the town's time for more than three hundred years. The clock belongs to the **Guildhall** (guided tours Tue & Thurs 2pm, 3pm & 4pm; free) with its elaborate Restoration facade disguising Tudor foundations. A little further up the High Street is the **Archbishop Abbot's Hospital**, a hospice built for the elderly in 1619 fronted by a palatial red-brick Tudor gateway. You can take a peek at the pretty courtyard, but if you want to inspect the Flemish stained glass and oak beams that characterize the interior you must sign up for a guided tour (by appointment; contact the tourist office for details). Back down towards the river on the right, at no. 72, is the **Undercroft** (Easter–Sept Tues & Thurs 2–4pm, Sat noon–4pm; free), a well-preserved thirteenth-century basement of vaulted arches.

Guildford's ruined Norman **Castle** keep (April–Sept daily 10am–6pm; 85p) sits on its motte behind the High Street, surrounded by flower-filled gardens. Beneath the castle,

NORTH SURREY THEME PARKS

Less than an hour's drive southwest of central London lie two popular **theme parks**, both owned by the Tussauds Group and both ranked in the top twenty most visited attractions in the UK – **Chessington** comes in at number five with over one and a half million visitors annually and **Thorpe Park** at number twenty with just under a million visitors. Both parks primarily appeal to the 8–14 age group, and can get extremely crowded during school holidays; an early arrival on summer weekends will avoid long queues for the more popular rides. If it's action you're after, Chessington has the edge, but both easily return their seemingly pricey entrance fees with activities that fill the best part of a day.

Thorpe Park
The purpose-built and water-oriented **Thorpe Park** (times vary, call to check on ☎01932/562633; £17.50) is well signposted off the A320 south of Staines and easily reached by train from London's Waterloo to Staines or Chertsey station, with buses taking you on to the park itself. Set in an old gravel pit next to a concrete works whose machinery is easily mistaken for the latest ride, the park continues to develop new attractions, but is still fairly low-key. Swimwear is a good idea for younger children as the better rides can include a soaking, and it allows them to romp around in the play pool. The watery rides provide grins of amusement rather than screams of delight with the *Loggers Leap* involving an exhilarating fifty-foot drop-off and *Thunder River* being an enjoyable whitish water descent in a huge tyre-like raft. Small children are excluded from these sorts of rides for safety reasons, but are well catered for in the *Octopus's Garden* and the train or boat ride to the small animal farm.

Chessington World of Adventures
Smaller and more animated, but marginally tackier, than Thorpe Park is **Chessington World of Adventures** (April to mid-July, Sept & Oct daily 10am–5pm; mid-July & Aug daily 10am–9pm; last admission 2hr before closing; £19). Located in a former zoo, the park is signposted off the A243, twelve miles southwest of London, and reached from London's Waterloo train station (to Chessington South) or bus #777 from Victoria. The best way to get the measure of the place is to take the yellow *Safari Skyway* monorail, which introduces you to the few remaining animals, then hop on the *Chessington Railroad* which does a round tour of the rest of the park. Of the better rides the *Dragon River*, *Runaway Minetrain* and *Terrortomb* are all fun rather than frightening, *Seastorm* is a watery favourite, as is *Rameses' Revenge*, though it's slightly scarier.

the town **museum** (Mon–Sat 11am–5pm; free) houses mementoes of writer Lewis Carroll (aka Rev Charles Dodgson), author of the children's classic *Alice's Adventures in Wonderland*. An imaginative sculpture of Alice passing through the looking glass is a recent addition to the Castle Gardens and Dodgson's grave can be visited in the cemetery off The Mount, on the other side of the river. At the bottom of the High Street runs the **River Wey**, a rather neglected feature of the town, although the once crucial River Wey and Godalming Navigation Canal has been restored into a picturesque waterway. From Easter to October, you can **hire boats** and take pleasure cruises up the river from the town quay, at the bottom of the High Street (July & Aug Mon–Sat 2pm & 3.30pm; £4.25), and from the Boat House, off Millbrook, a couple of hundred yards upstream (Sun 2.15 & 3.15pm; £2.75; ☎01483/504494).

Finally, it's difficult to miss Guildford's monumentally unremarkable modern Gothic **Cathedral** (daily 8.30am–5.30pm), ostentatiously perched on Stag Hill, a mile northwest of the centre. Resembling an outsized crematorium and consecrated in 1961, the cathedral's plain, bright interior has all the spirituality of a concert hall, but without the acoustics. Its most notable claim to fame is having been a location in the film *The Omen*.

Practicalities

Guildford's main **train station** lies just over the river west of the town centre; the **bus station** is between the town centre and the train station, at the foot of North Street. The county's main **tourist office** is at 14 Tunsgate opposite the Guildhall (May–Sept Mon–Sat 9am–6pm, Sun 10am–5pm; Oct–April Mon–Sat 9.30am–5.30pm; ☎01483/444333). Inexpensive **accommodation** options in town include *Hillcote*, 11 Castle Hill (☎01483/563324; ①), or the similar *Greyfriars* next door (☎01483/561795; ①).

The High Street area offers a fairly routine range of **eating options** – *Café de Paris* at no. 35 (☎01483/564555; closed Sun), a busy French-style brasserie in a listed building, offers three-course meals from around £14 – while *Olivo*, at 53 Quarry St (☎01483/564555; closed Sun), is an innovative *focacceria* serving delicious regional Italian dishes, housed in the town's sixteenth-century dispensary. Guildford's better **pubs** include the *King's Head* in Quarry Street, with a courtyard and inexpensive meals, and *Ye Olde Ship Inn*, the town's oldest hostelry, on Portsmouth Road.

Farnham and around

Tucked into Surrey's southwestern corner, ten miles west of Guildford along the exposed ridgetop of the Hog's Back, lies **FARNHAM**. Smaller and, in parts, more charming than Guildford, Farnham moves at a slower pace. Despite its thousand-year history, the majority of Farnham's architecture dates from the eighteenth century, when the town enjoyed a boom period based on hop farming.

Farnham is home to Surrey's only intact **castle**, built around 1160 by Henry de Blois, Bishop of Winchester, as a convenient residence halfway between his diocese and London. The castle was continuously occupied until 1927, but now houses a conference venue. Its **keep** (April–Sept daily 10am–6pm; Oct 10am–5pm or dusk; £2; EH), from where there are good views over Farnham's red-tile roofs to the Downs beyond, is the only part open to the public and holds a well shaft excavated from an earlier Saxon structure. Farnham's refined Georgian dwellings are at their best along the broad **Castle Street**, which links the town centre with the castle.

The **train station**, with frequent trains to London Waterloo, is over the river on the south edge of town, along South Street and over the bypass. The **tourist office** is in the council offices on South St (Mon–Fri 9.30am–5.15pm, Sat 9am–12.30pm; ☎01252/715109) and has a list of **accommodation** in and around Farnham – though most are hard to find without a car. A good central option is the *Stafford House Hotel*, 22 Firgrove Hill (☎01252/724336; ②), close to the station south of town. About a mile south of Farnham Station off the Tilford Road, *High Wray*, 73 Lodge Hill Rd (☎01252/715589; ②), is located in a peaceful, semi-rural setting, conveniently close to the start of the North Downs Way – it's a little off the beaten track, so be sure to ask for clear directions. Back in town, the French-style brasserie *Café Rouge* on the Borough (☎01252/733688; closed Sun) does decent **food**, while the *Jolly Sailor* **pub** offers reasonable bar meals; there's also a *Pizza Express* on Castle Street.

t r a v e l   d e t a i l s

Trains

Battle to: Hastings (hourly; 15min); London Charing Cross (2 hourly; 1hr 15min); Sevenoaks (hourly; 45min); Tunbridge Wells (hourly; 30min).
Brighton to: Chichester (2 hourly; 1hr); Gatwick Airport (every 10–20min; 30–40min); Hastings (2

hourly; 1hr 10min); Lewes (Mon–Sat 3 hourly, Sun hourly; 15min); London King's Cross (2–4 hourly; 1hr 15min); London Victoria (2 hourly; 1hr–1hr 20min).
Broadstairs to: London Victoria (hourly; 2hr 45min); Ramsgate (2–3 hourly; 5min).
Canterbury East to: Dover Priory (hourly; 30min); London Victoria (hourly; 1hr 30min).

Canterbury West to: London Charing Cross (hourly; 1hr 40min); London Victoria (hourly; 1hr 40min); Ramsgate (hourly; 20min).

Chatham to: Dover Priory (hourly; 50min); London Charing Cross (2 hourly; 1hr 10min); London Victoria (every 10–30min; 40min–1hr).

Chichester to: London Victoria (2 hourly; 1hr 45min).

Dorking to: Farnham (hourly; 1hr); London Waterloo (2 hourly; 40min).

Dover Priory to: Canterbury (2 hourly; 15–30min); Folkestone Central (2 hourly; 15min); London Charing Cross (hourly; 1hr 40min); London Victoria (2 hourly; 1hr 50min).

Eastbourne to: Gatwick Airport (2 hourly; 1hr); Hastings (1–3 hourly; 30min); Lewes (1–3 hourly; 20–30min); London Victoria (hourly; 1hr 30min).

Folkestone Central to: London Charing Cross (2 hourly; 1hr 30min).

Folkestone West to: London Charing Cross (2 hourly; 1hr 30min).

Gatwick Airport to: Brighton (3–4 hourly; 40min); London Victoria (every 10min; 30min).

Hastings to: Battle (2 hourly; 15min); Brighton (hourly; 1hr); Eastbourne; Gatwick Airport (hourly; 1hr 30min); London Charing Cross (hourly; 1hr 40min); London Victoria (hourly; 2hr); Rye (railbus every 20min); Tunbridge Wells (2 hourly; 35–45min).

Lewes to: Brighton (4 hourly; 15min); London Victoria (hourly; 1hr 15min).

Maidstone East to: London Charing Cross (hourly; 1 hr); London Victoria (hourly; 1hr).

Margate to: Canterbury West (hourly; 35–45min); London Victoria (hourly; 1hr 10min).

Ramsgate to: Broadstairs (2 hourly; 5min); Canterbury (hourly; 20min); London Charing Cross (2 hourly; 2hr–2hr 20min); London Victoria (hourly; 2hr 30min).

Rochester to: Dover Priory (hourly; 1hr–1hr 10min); Herne Bay (hourly; 1hr); London Charing Cross (hourly; 1hr–1hr 15min); London Victoria (hourly; 40min).

Rye to: Hastings (railbus every 20min).

Sandwich to: Dover Priory (hourly; 30min); Ramsgate (hourly; 15min).

Sevenoaks to: London Blackfriars (Mon–Sat 2–4 hourly; 1hr); London Charing Cross (2–4 hourly; 30min).

Tunbridge Wells to: Battle (2 hourly; 30min); London Victoria (Mon–Fri 2 hourly; 50min).

Whitstable to: London Victoria (hourly; 1hr 20min); Ramsgate (every 30min; 40min).

Buses

All buses go to London's Victoria Coach Station

Brighton to: London (hourly; 2hr).

Canterbury to: London (hourly; 1hr 50min).

Chichester to London (2 daily; 3hr)

Dover Eastern Docks to: London (hourly; 2hr 45min).

Eastbourne to: London (3 daily; 2hr 40min).

Folkestone to: London (4 daily; 2hr 30min).

Hastings to: London (2 daily; 2hr 40min).

Ramsgate to: London (4 daily; 2hr 50min).

Rochester to: London (hourly; 1hr 30min).

Tunbridge Wells to: London (1 daily; 1hr 40min).

CHAPTER THREE

HAMPSHIRE, DORSET AND WILTSHIRE

The distant past is perhaps more tangible in **Hampshire**, **Dorset** and **Wiltshire** than in any other part of England. Predominantly rural, these three counties overlap substantially with the ancient kingdom of **Wessex**, whose most famous ruler, Alfred, repulsed the Danes in the ninth century and came close to establishing the first unified state in England. Before Wessex came into being, however, many earlier civilizations had left their stamp on the region. The chalky uplands of Wiltshire boast several of Europe's greatest Neolithic sites, including **Stonehenge** and **Avebury**, while in Dorset you'll find **Maiden Castle**, the most striking Iron Age hill fort in the country, and the **Cerne Abbas Giant**, source of many a legend. The Romans tramped all over these southern counties, leaving the most conspicuous signs of their occupation at the amphitheatre of **Dorchester** – though that town is more closely associated with the novels of Thomas Hardy and his distinctively gloomy vision of Wessex.

None of the landscapes of this region could be described as grand or wild, but the countryside is consistently seductive, its appeal exemplified by the crumbling fossil-bearing cliffs around **Lyme Regis**, the managed woodlands of the **New Forest**, or the gentle, open curves of **Salisbury Plain**. Its towns are also generally modest and slow-paced, with the notable exceptions of the two great maritime bases of **Portsmouth** and, to a lesser extent, **Southampton**, a fair proportion of whose visitors are simply passing through on their way to the more genteel pleasures of the **Isle of Wight**. This is something of an injustice, though neither place can compete with the two most interesting cities in this part of England – **Salisbury** and **Winchester**, each of which possesses a stupendous cathedral amid an array of other historic sights. Of these counties' great houses, **Wilton**, **Stourhead**, **Longleat** and **Kingston Lacy** are the ones that attract the crowds, but every cranny has its medieval church, manor house or unspoilt country inn – there are few parts of the

---

ACCOMMODATION PRICE CODES

Throughout this guide, hotel and B&B accommodation is priced on a scale of ① to ⑨, the number indicating the **lowest price** you could expect to pay per night in that establishment for a **double room** in high season. The prices indicated by the codes are as follows:

① under £40	④ £60–70	⑦ £110–150
② £40–50	⑤ £70–90	⑧ £150–200
③ £50–60	⑥ £90–110	⑨ over £200

country in which an aimless meander can be so rewarding. If it's straightforward seaside fun you're after, **Bournemouth** leads the way, with Weymouth and Lyme Regis heading the ranks of the minor resorts, along with the yachties' havens over on the Isle of Wight.

Portsmouth

Britain's foremost naval station, **PORTSMOUTH** occupies the bulbous peninsula of Portsea Island, on the eastern flank of a huge, easily defended harbour. The ancient Romans raised a fortress on the northernmost edge of this inlet, and a small port developed during the Norman era, but this strategic location wasn't fully exploited until Tudor times, when Henry VII established the world's first dry dock here and made Portsmouth a royal dockyard. It has flourished ever since and nowadays Portsmouth is a large industrialized city, its harbour clogged with naval frigates, ferries bound for the continent or the Isle of Wight, and swarms of dredgers and tugs. Portsmouth was heavily bombed during the last war due to its military importance and tower blocks from the nadir of British architecture now give the city an ugly profile. Only **Old Portsmouth**, based around the original harbour, preserves some Georgian and a little Tudor character. East of here is **Southsea**, a residential suburb of terraces with a half-hearted resort strewn along its shingle beach, where a mass of B&Bs face stoic naval monuments and tawdry seaside amusements.

The Royal Naval Base

For most visitors, a trip to Portsmouth begins and ends at the Historic Ships, in the **Royal Naval Base** (daily: March–Oct 10am–5.30pm; Nov–Feb 10am–5pm; last entry 1hr before closing) at the end of Queen Street. The complex comprises three ships and as many museums, with each ship visitable separately (£5.95 each), though most people do the lot on an all-ships ticket (£11.90), which also includes entry to the Royal Naval Museum. There's also an all-inclusive ticket, taking in all the ships, various exhibitions and a harbour tour (£14.90) – to cover all this would easily take half a day. Note that visits to the *Victory* are guided, with limited numbers at set times, and you may have to wait up to a couple of hours to take your turn.

Nearest the entrance to the complex is the youngest ship, **HMS Warrior**, dating from 1860. It was Britain's first armoured, or "iron-clad" battleship, complete with sails and steam engines, and was the pride of the fleet in its day. Longer and faster than any previous naval vessel, and the first to be fitted with washing machines, the *Warrior* was described by Napoleon III as a "black snake amongst the rabbits". Despite being amply prepared – with weaponry, including rifles, pistols and sabres _ the *Warrior* was never challenged and she did not even fire a cannon in her 22 years at sea. **HMS Victory** was already forty years old when she set sail from Portsmouth for Trafalgar on September 14, 1805, returning victorious three months later, but bearing the corpse of Admiral Nelson. Shot by a sniper from a French ship at the height of the battle, Nelson expired below decks three hours later, having been assured that victory was in sight. The usual fate of casualties at sea was to be sewn into their hammocks with a cannon ball and thrown overboard, but Nelson didn't wish to be buried at sea, so his body was preserved in a huge vat of brandy pending his eventual burial in St Paul's Cathedral. In a shed behind the *Victory* are the remains of the **Mary Rose**, Henry VIII's flagship, which capsized before his eyes off Spithead in 1545 while engaging French intruders, sinking swiftly with almost all her seven-hundred-strong crew. In 1982 a massive conservation project raised the remains of the hull, which silt had preserved beneath the seabed. The ship itself is a bit disappointing; the exhibition close to the *Warrior*, displaying thousands of objects which were found near the wreck, is rather more absorbing.

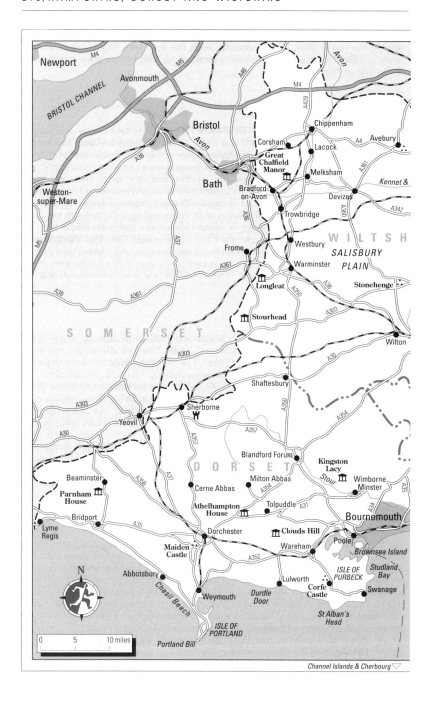

Channel Islands & Cherbourg ▽

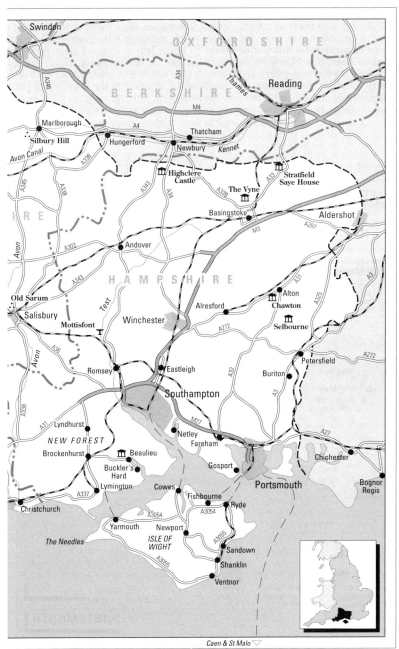

Caen & St Malo ▽

© Crown copyright

Opposite the *Victory*, various buildings house the exhaustive **Royal Naval Museum** (£3.50; free with ticket with *HMS Victory*). Tracing the story from Alfred the Great's fleet to the present day, this is the most resistible attraction in the complex. The naval theme is continued at **Submarine World** on Haslar Jetty in Gosport (daily: April–Oct 10am–5.30pm; Nov–March 10am–4.30pm; last tour 1hr before closing; £3.75), reached by taking the passenger ferry from Harbour train station jetty (daily 5.30am–midnight; every 10–15min; £1.50 return), just south of the entrance to the Royal Naval Base. Alternatively, take the water-bus from the same jetty, which gives you a thirty-minute tour of the harbour before dropping you in Gosport (Easter–Oct 10.30am–5pm; £3). Allow yourself a couple of hours to explore these slightly creepy vessels – a guided tour inside *HMS Alliance* gives you an insight into life on board and the museum elaborates evocatively on the long history of submersible craft.

From the pontoon beside *HMS Warrior*, regular ferries depart (Wed & Sat 1.30pm, Sun 2pm) for the mile-long ride to **Spitbank Fort** (£6.50, including boat trip), an off-shore bastion of granite, iron and brick little altered since its construction in the 1860s. With over fifty rooms linked by passages and steps on two floors, the complex includes a 430-foot deep well which still draws fresh water from below the seafloor, and an inner

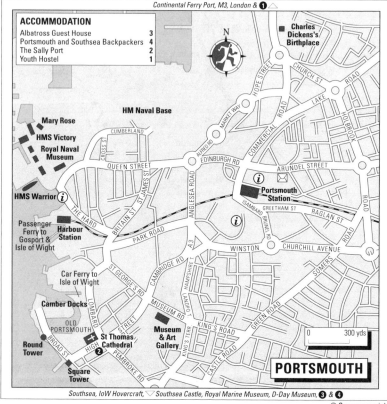

courtyard holds a café and sheltered terrace. The artificial island hosts theme nights, for which there are special evening boat excursions; ask at the tourist office for details, or call ☎01329/664286. You can also stay here (see p.214).

Old Portsmouth, Southsea and Portchester Castle

Back at the Harbour train station in Portsmouth, it's a well-signposted twenty-minute walk south to what remains of **Old Portsmouth**. Along the way in the High Street, you pass the simple **Cathedral of St Thomas**, whose twelfth-century features have been obscured by post-Civil War and post-World War II rebuilding. The High Street ends at a maze of cobbled Georgian streets huddling behind a fifteenth-century wall protecting the **Camber**, or old port, where Walter Raleigh landed the first potatoes and tobacco from the New World. Nearby, the Round and Square Towers, which punctuate the Tudor fortifications, are popular vantage points for observing nautical activities. The remainder of Portsmouth has little else of interest apart from **Dickens's Birthplace** at 393 Commercial Rd (April–Oct daily 10.30am–5.30pm; Dec 1–20 10am–4.30pm; £2), half a mile north of the town centre, where Dickens was born in 1812.

    Southsea's main attraction is the **D-Day Museum** on Clarence Esplanade (April–Oct daily 10am–5.30pm; Nov–March Mon 1–5pm, Tues–Sun 10am–5pm; £4.75), relating how Portsmouth had a chance to avenge its wartime bombing by being the main assembly point for the D-Day invasion, code-named "Operation Overlord". Next door to the museum the squat profile of **Southsea Castle** (April–Oct daily 10am–5.30pm; Nov–March Sat & Sun 10am–4.30pm; £2), built from the remains of Beaulieu Abbey (see p.225), may have been the spot where Henry VIII watched the *Mary Rose* sink in 1545. A mile further along the shore, just past South Parade pier, the **Royal Marines Museum** (daily 10am–4.30pm; £3.75) describes the origins and greatest campaigns of the Navy's elite fighting force. Outside, a junior assault course gives aspirant young commandos a chance to get in shape.

    The city's outstanding monument is six miles away – just past the burgeoning marina development at Port Solent – where, in the third century, the Romans founded **Portchester Castle** (daily: April–Sept 10am–6pm; Oct 10am–5pm; Nov–March 10am–4pm; £2.70; EH). Over twenty feet high and incorporating some twenty bastions, this Roman fort is the finest surviving example in northern Europe and is so robust that the Normans felt no need to alter it when they moved in. In later years a castle was built within its precincts by Henry II, which Richard II extended and Henry V used as his garrison when assembling the army that was to fight the Battle of Agincourt. Today its grassy enclosure makes a sheltered spot for a congenial game of cricket.

Practicalities

Portsmouth's main **train station** is in the city centre, but the line continues to **Harbour Station**, the most convenient stop for the main sights and old town. Passenger **ferries** leave from the jetty at the Harbour station for Ryde on the Isle of Wight (see p.216), and Gosport, on the other side of Portsmouth Harbour; car ferries depart from the ferry port off Gunwharf Road for Fishbourne (see p.216). There are three **tourist offices** in Portsmouth: one on The Hard, by the entrance to the dockyards (daily: Easter–Sept 9.30am–5.45pm; Oct–Easter 9.30am–5.15pm; ☎023/9282 6722); another opposite the main train station, at 103 Commercial Rd (Mon–Sat 10am–5pm; ☎023/9283 8382); and a third on Southsea's seafront, next to the Sea Life Centre (Easter–Sept daily 9.30am–1.30pm & 2.30–5.45pm; ☎023/9283 2464).

    One of the nicest **places to stay** is *The Sally Port*, 57–58 High St (☎02392/821860; ③), an old pub opposite the cathedral, which serves good bar food. *Albatross Guest*

House, 51 Waverley Rd (☎023/9282 8325; ①), is one of many good-value Southsea B&Bs. The official **youth hostel** (☎023/9237 5661; closed Jan) is housed in an attractive Tudor manor on Old Wymering Lane, in Cosham, ten minutes walk west of Cosham train station and a couple of miles north of the centre; take bus #5, #5a or #12 from city centre. There's also an independent hostel, *Portsmouth & Southsea Backpackers* at 4 Florence Rd in Southsea (☎023/9283 2495; bus #4). In summer, a four-bed apartment in **Spitbank Fort** (☎01329/664286) is available for nightly or weekly rent for around £120 per night: book early.

Places to eat are surprisingly scarce in the old town: the best **restaurants** are all in Southsea. Among these, *Bistro Montparnasse*, 103 Palmerston Rd (☎02392/816754), stands out for its good-quality French and seafood dishes; a cheaper alternative is the wholefood *Country Kitchen*, 59a Marmion Rd, Southsea. In Old Portsmouth, try the **Quayhaven**, Broad St (☎023/9282 0607), for its traditional English and seafood dishes, or either of the two **pubs** on Bath Square, *Spice Island* and the *Still & West*, where you'll find good food, beer and views over the harbour.

Southampton

A glance at the map gives some idea of the strategic maritime importance of **SOUTHAMPTON**, which stands on a triangular peninsula formed at the place where the rivers Itchen and Test flow into Southampton Water, an eight-mile inlet from the Solent. Sure enough, Southampton has figured in numerous stirring events: it witnessed the exodus of Henry V's Agincourt-bound army, the Pilgrim Fathers' departure in the *Mayflower* in 1620, and the maiden voyages of such ships as the *Queen Mary* and the *Titanic*. Unfortunately, since its pummelling by the Luftwaffe and some disastrous postwar planning, the thousand-year-old city is now a sprawling conurbation low on most tourists' list of priorities.

King Canute is alleged to have commanded the waves to retreat at Southampton – not, as legend has it, from a misguided sense of his kingly powers, but to rebuke his fawning courtiers. Whatever his motive, the task would have been especially difficult here, for Southampton, like other Solent ports, enjoys the phenomenon of "double tides" – a prolonged period of high water as the Channel swirls first up the westerly side of the Solent, then, two hours later, backs up round Spithead. This means that exceptionally large vessels can berth here and, even though ocean-going liners are rare nowadays, there'll certainly be some large-scale vessels either in the Eastern Docks, or in the **Western Docks**, home to England's largest commercial dry dock.

The core of the modern town is the **Civic Centre**, a short walk east of the train station. Its clock tower is the most distinctive feature of the skyline, and it houses an excellent **art gallery** (Tues–Sat 10am–5pm, Sun 1–4pm; free) that's particularly strong on twentieth-century British artists such as Sutherland, Piper and Spencer. The **Western Esplanade**, curving southward from the station, runs alongside the best remaining bits of the old city **walls**. Rebuilt after a French attack in 1338, they feature towers with evocatively chilly names like Windwhistle, Catchcold and God's House Tower – the last of these, at the southern end of the old town in Winkle Street, houses a good **museum of archeology** (Tues–Fri 10am–noon & 1–5pm, Sat 10am–noon & 1–4pm, Sun 2–5pm; free). Best preserved of the city's seven gates is **Bargate**, at the opposite end of the old town at the head of the High Street; an elaborate structure, cluttered with lions, classical figures and machicolations (defensive apertures used to drop missiles), it was formerly the guildhall and courthouse.

Other ancient buildings survive amid the piecemeal redevelopment of the High Street area. The oldest church is **St Michael's**, to the west of the High Street, with a twelfth-century font of black Tournai marble. The nearby **Tudor House museum** in Bugle

Street (same times as the archeology museum; free) is an impressive fifteenth-century timber-framed building, outshining its exhibits of Victorian and early twentieth-century social history, a banqueting hall and a reconstructed Tudor garden. On the opposite side of the High Street, the ruined **Holy Rood** church stands as a monument to the merchant navy men killed in World War II, and also has a memorial fountain to the crew of the *Titanic*, many of whom came from Southampton. Down at the southwest corner of the old town, by the seafront, the **Wool House** is a fine fourteenth-century stone warehouse; formerly used as a jail for Napoleonic prisoners, it now houses a **maritime museum** (Tues–Fri 10am–1pm & 2–5pm, Sat 10am–1pm & 2–4pm, Sun 2–5pm; free). The museum also offers the opportunity to listen to the recorded voices of various survivors of the *Titanic* tragedy relating their experiences, while *Titanic* obsessives can follow a "*Titanic* Trail" walking tour around Southampton – ask for the free pamphlet at the tourist office.

If you're an aviation enthusiast you should visit the **Hall of Aviation** (June–Sept Mon–Sat 10am–5pm, Sun noon–5pm; Oct–May closed Mon; £3) in Albert Road South, by the car ferry terminal. Dedicated to local aviation designer R.J. Mitchell, it has sixteen of his aircraft on display, including the Spitfire, the Sandringham Flying Boat and the Supermarine seaplane, which in 1931 won the Schneider Trophy by whizzing round the Isle of White at an average speed of 340mph.

Practicalities

The **train station** is centrally located in Blechynden Terrace, west of the civic centre; the **bus** and **coach stations** are immediately south and north of the civic centre. The **tourist office** is at 9 Civic Centre Rd (Mon–Wed, Fri & Sat 9am–5pm, Thurs 10am–5pm; ☎023/8022 1106). Southampton isn't a wildly attractive **place to stay**, but there are plenty of possibilities in the centre, including *Elizabeth House* at 43–44 The Avenue (☎023/8022 4327; ⑤), or *Linden*, just north of the train station on The Polygon (☎023/8022 5653; no credit cards; ①). For grander lodging, try the *Star* (☎023/8033 9939; ④) or the *Dolphin* (☎023/8033 9995; ⑧) hotels, both at the bottom of the High Street and both providing comfortable accommodation. There's not a great choice of original **eating** places in town either: try *Buon Gusto,* at 1 Commercial Rd (☎023/8033 1543; closed Sun), an inexpensive Italian restaurant; *The Town House,* 59 Oxford St, for vegetarian specialities; *Kuti's Brasserie,* 39 Oxford St (☎023/8022 1585), a top-class, moderately priced Bengali restaurant; or *La Brasserie,* a busy French restaurant with good lunchtime deals, at 33 Oxford St (☎023/8063 5043; closed Sun). As for pubs, the tiny old *Platform Tavern* in Winkle Street at the south end of the High Street is your best bet.

The Isle of Wight

Having achieved county status after years of being lumped in with Hampshire, the **ISLE OF WIGHT** still has difficulty in shaking off its image as a mere adjunct of rural southern England – comfortably off, scrupulously tidy and desperately unadventurous. Yet the Isle of Wight – less than 23 miles at its widest point – packs a surprising variety of landscapes and coastal scenery within its bounds. The island is divided fairly neatly by a chalk spine that runs east to west across its centre: north of the ridge is a terrain of low-lying woodland and pasture, deeply cut by meandering rivers; to the south is open chalky downland fringed by high cliffs. Two **Heritage Coast** paths follow the best of the shoreline and, what's more, the island harbours several historic buildings and a splendid array of well-preserved Victoriana clad in fretted bargeboards and pseudo-Gothic gables. All of which is scarcely surprising, since the founding Victorian herself felt most at home here – **Osborne House**, originally designed as a summer retreat for the royal family, became Victoria's permanent home after Albert died.

SEA ROUTES TO THE ISLE OF WIGHT

Wightlink Ferries, PO Box 59, Portsmouth PO1 2XB (☎0990/827744) has three year-round ferry routes to the Isle of Wight, including a faster but more expensive catamaran service to Ryde.

Portsmouth–Ryde: 4.30am–12.20am every 30–60min; 15min; £10.50 for foot passengers only.

Portsmouth–Fishbourne: 3am–1.30am every 30–60min; 35min; £8.20 for foot passengers; £58.10–£72.30 for car and driver plus £8.20 per passenger.

Lymington–Yarmouth: every 30–60min 6.15am–9.30pm; 30min; £8.20 for foot passengers; £58.10–£72.30 for car and driver plus £8.20 per passenger.

Hovertravel, Quay Road, Ryde, Isle of Wight PO33 2HB (☎023/9281 1000 or 01983/811000) runs a year-round hovercraft service from Southsea to Ryde.

Southsea–Ryde: Mon–Fri 7.10am–8.10pm, Sat & Sun 8.15am–8.10pm every 15–30min; 9min; £10.20 for foot passengers only.

Red Funnel, 12 Bugle Street, Southampton, SO14 2JY (☎023/8033 4010) operates year-round ferries on two routes, one of them a high-speed service.

Southampton–East Cowes: daily 4am–1am every 1–2hr; 55min; £7.80 for foot passengers; £60 for car and driver plus £7.80 per passenger.

Southampton–West Cowes: daily 5.55am–10.30pm every 30min–1hr; 22min; £11.80 for foot passengers only.

All the prices quoted are for a 90-day (Red Funnel and Hovertravel) or 1-year (Wightlink) return ticket. Wightlink and Red Funnel both offer overnight or 5-day deals for cars, with discounts of around 35 percent.

If you're dependent upon **public transport**, pick up the Southern Vectis bus route map and timetable from the tourist office or bus station at your point of arrival. The company's hourly Island Explorer buses (routes #7 and #7A) circle the island in about four hours. A Rover Ticket allows you unlimited travel on the bus network, costing £6.25 for a summer Day Rover and £25.50 for a Weekly Rover, with discounts of about thirty percent in winter (information ☎01983/827005). The **rail line** is a short east-coast stretch linking Ryde, Sandown and Shanklin (☎08457/484950). **Bikes** are carried free on all ferry services, but beware that in summer the island's narrow lanes can get very busy.

Ryde and around

As a major ferry terminal, **RYDE** is the first landfall many visitors make on the island, but one where few choose to linger despite some grand nineteenth-century architecture and decent beach amusements. Ferries dock at the functional half-mile-long pier reaching out over the shallows of Ryde Sands, from which former London Underground rolling stock carries the seasonal throngs inland. Union Street rises steeply from the pier's base to the town centre and at its crest sits All Saints church, whose spire can be seen from vantage points all across the east of the island and even from parts of the mainland.

The **tourist office** (Aug Mon–Thurs & Sun 9am–7pm; Fri & Sat 9am–9pm; rest of year daily 9am–5pm; ☎01983/562905), **bus station, Hovercraft terminal** and Esplanade **train station** are all located near the base of the pier. **Boat trips** to the Solent ports leave from Ryde jetty; for details contact *Solent Cruises* (☎01983/564602). **Accommodation** and fine Italian cooking are available just over the road from the jetty in the *Biskra House Hotel and Restaurant*, 17 St Thomas St (☎01983/567913; ④). Other

B&Bs to try include *Trentham Guest House*, 38 The Strand (☎01983/563418; no credit cards; ③), and *Vine Guest House*, 16 Castle St (☎01983/566633; ③) – both are south of the Esplanade. **Eating** options include *Joe Daflo's Café Bar* at 24 Union St, which has an appealing continental menu, while the *Redan* at no. 70 is an unusual and inexpensive pub and café.

As elsewhere on the island, just a couple of miles can remove you from an undistinguished urban setting into one of idyllic rusticity. Just ouside the village of **BINSTEAD**, two miles west of Ryde's centre, lies **Quarr Abbey**, founded in 1132, but now little more than an ivy-clad archway, hanging picturesquely over a farm track. In 1907 a new abbey was founded just west of the ruins, a striking rose-brick building with Byzantine overtones (daily 9am–9pm). At Wootton Bridge, three miles west of Binstead, the **Isle of Wight Steam Railway** (late March to Oct 10.30am–4.15pm; £6.50) starts its delightful ten-mile round trip to Smallbrook on the main Ryde–Shanklin line to the east. Though it doesn't stop anywhere of interest along the way, the impeccably restored carriages in traditional green livery pass through lovely unspoilt countryside.

The village of **BRADING**, four miles south of Ryde on the busy A3055, boasts a surprisingly disparate collection of ancient and modern sites. Just south of the village are the remains of **Brading Roman Villa** (April–Oct daily 9.30am–5pm; £2.50), one of two Roman "villas" on the island (the other is in Newport; see p.220) which were probably sites of bacchanalian worship. The Brading site is renowned for its superbly preserved mosaics, including intact images of Medusa and depictions of Orpheus, the latter associated with the cult of Bacchus.

Nunwell House (July to mid-Sept Mon–Wed 1–5pm; £4), signposted off the A3055 less than a mile northwest of Brading, was where, in 1647, Charles I spent his last night of freedom before being taken to Carisbrooke Castle and eventual execution in Whitehall. The house has been in the Oglander family for nearly nine hundred years, with the present building being a mix of Jacobean and Georgian styles with Victorian additions. Nunwell sits in five acres of lovely gardens and remains very much the family home of the present owners, whose military legacy is reflected inside in a small exhibition commemorating the Home Guard, the defence force of volunteers recruited during the early years of World War II when the island prepared to resist Nazi occupation.

Sandown and Shanklin

SANDOWN is the island's holidaymaking epicentre and possesses its only surviving pleasure **pier**, bedecked with amusement arcades, cafeterias, dodgems and a large theatre with nightly entertainment in season. Those with children might consider a visit to the **Tiger Sanctuary and Isle of Wight Zoological Gardens** (daily: Easter–Nov 10am–5pm; call for winter opening times; ☎01983/403883; £4.95) at Yaverland, just east of town, which houses an exhaustive selection of spiders and snakes, including huge pythons, as well as some frisky lemurs and monkeys, tigers, panthers and other big cats.

Being separated from the shore by hundred-foot cliffs has helped preserve **SHANKLIN** from the tawdry excesses of its northern neighbour, although it hasn't stopped the zealous promotion of the Old Village's rose-clad, thatched charm. Nevertheless, with the adjacent **Shanklin Chine** (daily: Easter–May & Oct 10am–5pm; June–Sept 10am–10pm; £2), a twisting pathway descending a mossy ravine and decorated at night with fairy lights, it all adds up to a picturesque spot, popular since early Victorian times when local resident John Keats drew his Romantic imagery from the environs.

Sandown's **tourist office** is at 8 High St (Easter to late July, Sept & Oct daily 9am–6pm; late July & Aug 9am–8.45pm; Nov–Easter Mon–Sat 10am–4pm; ☎01983/403886). The Shanklin equivalent is at 67 High St (same times; ☎01983/862942). Both towns have Island

Line train stations about half a mile inland from their beachfront centres. For **accommodation**, try *St Catherine's Hotel*, 1 Winchester Park Rd (☎01983/402392; ③), a comfortable B&B five minutes from Sandown beach, or the attractive Victorian *Osborne House Hotel*, 20 Esplanade (☎01983/862501; ③), near Shanklin beach. More secluded is **Luccombe Hall**, Luccombe Rd, Shanklin (☎01983/862719; *reservations@luccombehall.co.uk*; ⑤), a finely situated country house hotel, a mile from the Old Village in Shanklin. *Sandown Youth Hostel* (☎01983/402651; closed Nov–March; £9.15) is in a converted house in the town centre on Fitzroy Street. **Eating** options in Sandown include the *Kings Bar Café*, a continental-style licensed café on the High Street with great views over the sea. In Shanklin, head for the *Fisherman's Cottage Free House*, an atmospheric seafaring pub at the southern end of the Esplanade on Appley Beach, serving wholesome food. Alternatively, try the excellent **Francine's Restaurant**, 16 High St, Sandown (☎01983/403289; closed Dec–Easter), which offers a good variety of English and seafood dishes.

Ventnor and around

The attractive seaside resort of **VENTNOR** sits at the foot of St Boniface Down (787ft), the island's highest point. The Down periodically disintegrates into landslides creating the jumbled terraces known locally as the **Undercliff**, whose sheltered, south-facing aspect and mild winter temperatures have turned Ventnor into a fashionable health spa. Thanks to these unique factors, the town possesses rather more character than the island's other resorts, its Gothic Revival buildings clinging dizzily to zigzagging bends. The floral terraces of the **Cascade** curve down to the slender Esplanade and narrow beach, where former boatbuilders' cottages now provide more recreational services. From the Esplanade, it's a pleasant mile-long stroll to Ventnor's famous **Botanical Gardens**, where 22 landscaped acres of subtropical vegetation flourish.

Ventnor's **tourist office** is at 34 High St (Easter–Oct daily 9.30am–5.30pm; ☎01983/853625). For **accommodation**, try the *Spyglass Inn* (☎01983/855338; ②) on Ventnor's Esplanade, which boasts a great location, or the *Bonchurch Inn* (☎01983/852611; ②), off the Shute in the suburb of Bonchurch. Also in Bonchurch is the *Under Rock Hotel* (☎01983/855274; no credit cards; ②), a small Georgian country house in a sub-tropical rock garden. The best of the many **restaurants** in Ventnor town centre is the *Thistle Café*, 30 Pier St, offering inexpensive seafood and vegetarian meals as well as a decent all-day breakfast.

Appuldurcombe House and St Catherine's Point

Follow the B3327 for a couple of miles inland, over St Boniface Down to Wroxall, where a track leads left for half a mile to the ruins of **Appuldurcombe House** (April–Oct daily 10am–6pm or dusk; Nov to mid-Dec & March Sat & Sun 10am–4pm; £2; EH), built in the late eighteenth century in the Palladian style, its gardens landscaped by Capability Brown. The house was the home of Lord Yarborough before impecunity and neglect led to its semi-abandonment earlier this century. What makes Appuldurcombe unusual is that it has been preserved in this state of decay, a partially roofed but intact shell where the evidence of a former owner's extravagant raising of all floor levels and doorways is clear.

A footpath runs southwestwards along the coast to the most southerly tip of the island, **St Catherine's Point**, with St Catherine's Oratory, a prominent landmark known locally as the "Pepper Pot", on the downs behind. In fact it's a medieval lighthouse, reputedly built in 1325 as an act of expiation by Walter de Goditon who attempted to pilfer a cargo of wine owned by a monastic community whose ship was wrecked off Atherfield Point in 1313. A short distance west lies **Blackgang Chine** (daily: late March to late May & mid-Sept to late Oct 10am–5.30pm; late May to mid-Sept 10am–10pm; £5.50), which opened as a landscaped garden in 1843 and gradually evolved into a theme park, possibly the world's first. It now offers a half-dozen exhibits from Smugglerland to Dinosaurland, a giant maze and a rendition of a Victorian quay.

Yarmouth and around

Situated, as its name suggests, at the mouth of the River Yar, the pleasant town of **YARMOUTH** was the island's first purpose-built port. Although razed by the French in 1377, the port began to prosper again after **Yarmouth Castle** (daily: April–Sept 10am–6pm; Oct 10am–5pm; £2; EH), tucked between the quay and the pier, was built by Henry VIII. Although there is little more to see in town, Yarmouth, linked to Lymington in the New Forest by car ferry, makes an appealing arrival or departure point. The **tourist office** is on Yarmouth Quay (Easter–Oct daily 9.30am–5.45pm; Nov–Easter Mon & Fri–Sun 10am–4pm; ☎01983/760015). There's a good range of **accommodation** in town – *Jireh House* in St James's Square (☎01983/760513; ②) is a seventeenth-century guest house with tearooms that also serves evening meals in summer; or try the cosy *Bugle Hotel* opposite (☎01983/760272; ⑤), also one of the town's many good **pubs**. There's good **food** too at the Bugle's *Poacher's Restaurant, Barnacles* on Bridge Street or *Gossips* at the base of the pier.

Yarmouth is also a good base for exploring the isle's western tip, whose focal point is **Alum Bay**'s multichrome cliffs, best viewed from the chair lift (£2.50 return), and the chalk stacks of **The Needles**, best seen from a boat trip leaving from Alum Bay (Needles Pleasure Cruises; 25min; £2.60; ☎01983/754477), or from the tunnel by the Old Battery, a fort dating from 1862. Taking the southern road from Freshwater Bay you'll pass the *Farringford Hotel*, on Bedbury Lane (☎01983/752500, *farringford@netgates.co.uk*; ⑥), Tennyson's former home. There's also a **youth hostel** between the Needles and Yarmouth, at Totland Bay (☎01983/752165).

Cowes and around

COWES, at the island's northern tip, is inextricably associated with sailing craft and boatbuilding: Henry VIII built a castle here to defend the Solent's expanding naval dockyards and in the 1950s the world's first hovercraft made its test runs here. In 1820 the Prince Regent's patronage of the yacht club gave the port its cachet with the *Royal Yacht Squadron*, now one of the world's most exclusive sailing clubs and permitted to fly the St George's Ensign, guaranteeing free entry to all foreign ports. Only its three hundred members and their guests are permitted within the hallowed precincts of the club house in the remains of Henry VIII's castle, and the club's landing stage is sacrosanct. The first week of August sees the international yachting festival known as **Cowes Week**, which visiting royalty turns into a high-society gala, although most summer weekends see some form of yachting or powerboat racing off Cowes.

The town is bisected by the River Medina with West Cowes being the older and more interesting half, its High Street meandering up from the waterfront Parade. Along the High Street you'll find shops reflecting the town's gentrified heritage, with boatyards, chandlers and *Bekens'* famous yachting gallery – a photo by Bekens of your yacht is considered as prestigious as a family portrait by Snowdon. Cowes **tourist office** is at the Arcade, Fountain Quay (April–Oct Mon–Sat 9am–5pm, Sun 10am–4pm, with extended hours during Cowes Week; Nov–March Mon–Sat 10am–4pm; ☎01983/291914). **Boat trips** upriver and around the harbour leave from The Parade; for details contact *Solent Cruises* (☎01983/564602).

Central **accommodation** options include the *Union Inn* (☎01983/293163; ①) in Watch House Lane; the *Wishing Well Guest House*, 10b High St (☎01983/297322; ②); or the *Doghouse* on Crossways Road, East Cowes (☎01983/293677; ②). The town boasts a decent selection of places to **eat**: *Baan Thai,* 10 Bath Rd, and the *Ocean Tandoori,* 38

Birmingham Rd (the east end of the High Street) both offer good-quality oriental food at moderate prices. There are numerous wholesome snack and sandwich shops along the High Street as well as the traditional pub meals served at the *Fountain*, *Anchor* and *Harbour Lights*, all on the High Street.

Osborne House and Whippingham

A floating bridge (pedestrians free, cars £1.30) connects West Cowes to the more industrial East Cowes, where the only place of interest is Queen Victoria's family home, **Osborne House** (daily: April–Sept daily 10am–6pm; Oct 10am–5pm; £6.90; EH), signposted one mile southeast of town. The house was built between 1845 and 1851 by Prince Albert and Thomas Cubitt, as an Italianate villa with balconies and large terraces overlooking the landscaped gardens towards the Solent. The state rooms, used to entertain visiting dignitaries, possess an expected formality while the private apartments feel more homely like an affluent family's holiday residence, which is what Osborne was – far removed from the pomp and ceremony of state affairs in London.

Following Albert's death, the desolate Victoria spent much of her time at Osborne where she eventually died in 1901. Since that time and according to her wishes the house has remained virtually unaltered, allowing an unexpectedly intimate glimpse into Victoria's family life. A mile to the south is another of Albert's architectural extravaganzas, the Gothic Revival **Royal Church of St Mildred** (April & Oct daily 10am–4pm; May–Sept Mon–Fri 10am–5pm). The German Battenberg family, who later adopted the anglicized name Mountbatten, have a chapel here and the parents of the present Queen's late uncle, Earl Mountbatten, the island's last governor, are buried in the churchyard.

Newport and Carisbrooke Castle

NEWPORT, the capital of the Isle of Wight, sits at the centre of the island at a point where the Medina's commercial navigability ends. Apart from a few pleasant old quays dating from its days as an inland port, the town serves as the island's municipal and commercial centre, where familiar chain stores draw in the shoppers. The town's main attraction is the hilltop fortress of **Carisbrooke Castle** (daily: April–Sept 10am–6pm; Oct 10am–5pm; Nov–March 10am–4pm; £4.50; EH), on the southwest outskirts. The austere Norman keep's most famous visitor was Charles I, detained here (and caught one night ignominiously jammed between his room's bars while attempting escape) prior to his execution in London. The **museum** in the centre of the castle features many relics from his incarceration as well as those of the last royal resident, Princess Beatrice, Queen Victoria's youngest daughter. The castle's other notable curiosity is the sixteenth-century well house where donkeys still trudge inside a huge, hamster-like treadmill to raise a barrel 160ft up the well shaft.

Winchester

Nowadays a tranquil, handsome market town, set amid docile hay meadows and watercress beds, **WINCHESTER** was once the fifth largest town in Roman Britain. It was **Alfred the Great**, however, who really put Winchester on the map, when he made it the capital of his Wessex kingdom in the ninth century. For the next couple of centuries it ranked alongside London, its status affirmed by William the Conqueror's coronation in both cities, and his commissioning of the local monks to prepare the **Domesday Book**. It wasn't until after the Battle of Naseby in 1645, when Cromwell took the city, that Winchester began its decline into provinciality. Hampshire's county town now has a scholarly and slightly anachronistic air, embodied by the ancient almshouses that still provide shelter for senior citizens of "noble poverty" – the pensioners can be seen wandering the town in medieval black or mulberry-coloured gowns with silver badges. A trip to this secluded old city is a must – not only for the magnificent **cathedral**, chief relic of Winchester's medieval glory, but for the all-round well-preserved ambience of England's medieval capital.

The City

The first minster to be built in Winchester was raised by Cenwalh, the Saxon king of Wessex in the mid-seventh century, and traces of this building have been unearthed adjacent to the present **cathedral**, which was begun in 1079. Its construction lasted for three hundred years, producing a church whose elements range from early Norman to Perpendicular styles. The exterior is not its best feature – squat and massive, the cathedral crouches stumpily over the tidy lawns of the Cathedral Close. The interior is rich

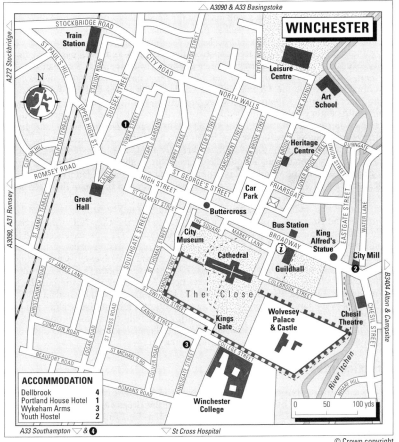

© Crown copyright

and complex, however, and its 556-foot nave makes this Europe's longest medieval church. Outstanding features include its carved Norman font of black Tournai marble, the fourteenth-century misericords (the choir stalls are the oldest complete set in the country) and some amazing monuments – Bishop **William of Wykeham's Chantry**, halfway down the nave on the right, is one of the best. Jane Austen, who died in Winchester, is commemorated by a stone close to the font, though she's recorded simply as the daughter of a local clergyman. Above the high altar lie the mortuary chests of pre-Conquest kings, including Canute, while William Rufus – killed hunting in the New Forest in 1100 (see p.224) – lies in the presbytery. The Norman crypt contains the tomb of St Swithun, originally buried outside in the churchyard. When his remains were interred inside the cathedral where the "rain of heaven" could no longer fall on him, he took revenge and the heavens opened for forty days, hence the legend that if it rains on St Swithun's Day (July 15) it will continue for another forty.

The Norman **crypt** is open only in the summer, since it's flooded for much of the winter – the cathedral's original foundations were dug in marshy ground, and at the beginning of this century a steadfast diver, William Walker, spent five years replacing the rotten timber foundations with concrete. A small statue stands at the eastern end of the nave, although it erroneously portrays an assistant diver rather than Walker himself. If the crypt is open, have a look inside at the fourteenth-century statues of William of Wykeham and St Swithun as well as Anthony Gormley's standing figure, one of the country's most adventurous recent ecclesiastical commissions.

Walk west along the High Street, north of the cathedral, and you'll pass close to the **City Museum** on The Square (April–Sept Mon–Fri 10am–5pm, Sat 10am–1pm & 2–5pm, Sun 2–5pm; rest of year closed Mon; free), a basic local history display, and eventually arrive at the **Great Hall** in Castle Street (April–Oct daily 10am–5pm; Nov–March Mon–Fri 10am–5pm, Sat & Sun 10am–4pm), the vestigial remains of a thirteenth-century castle destroyed by Cromwell. Sir Walter Raleigh heard his death sentence here in 1603, though he wasn't finally dispatched until 1618, and Judge Jeffreys held one of his Bloody Assizes in the castle after Monmouth's rebellion in 1685. The main interest now, however, is a brightly painted eighteen-foot disc slung on one wall like some curious antique dartboard. This is alleged to be **King Arthur's Round Table**, but the woodwork is probably fourteenth-century, later repainted as a PR exercise for the Tudor dynasty – the portrait of Arthur at the top of the table bears an uncanny resemblance to Henry VII.

If instead you walk east, past the Guildhall and the august bronze statue of King Alfred on the Broadway, you reach the River Itchen and the **City Mill** (March Sat & Sun 11am–4.45pm; April–Oct Wed–Sun 11am–4.45pm; £1; NT), now part-occupied by a youth hostel. Turning right before the bridge you pass what remains of the Saxon walls, which bracket the ruins of the twelfth-century **Wolvesey Castle** (daily: April–Sept 10am–6pm, Oct 10am–dusk; £1.80) and the Bishop's Palace, built by Christopher Wren. Immediately to the west up College Street stand the buildings of **Winchester College**, the oldest public school in England – established in 1382 by William of Wykeham for "poor scholars", it now educates few but the wealthy and privileged. The cloisters and chantry are open during term time, the chapel is open all year. The thirteenth-century **Kings Gate**, at the top of College Street, is one of the city's original medieval gateways, housing St Swithun's church.

Practicalities

Winchester **train station** is about a mile northwest of the cathedral on Stockbridge Road; if you arrive by **bus**, you'll find yourself on the Broadway, opposite the **tourist office** in the imposing Guildhall (late May to Sept Mon–Sat 10am–6pm, Sun 11am–2pm; Oct–May Mon–Sat 10am–5pm; ☎01962/840500). The classiest **accommodation** is at the *Wykeham Arms*, 75 Kingsgate St (☎01962/853834; ⑤), where the art of inn-keeping has not yet vanished. Nearly as central but not as expensive is the *Portland House Hotel*, 63 Tower St (☎01962/865195; no credit cards; ②), a Georgian house in a quiet mews between the cathedral and the train station. *Dellbrook*, on Hubert Road (☎01962/865093; ②), is a pleasant Edwardian-era, family-run B&B by the water meadows near St Cross, one mile south of the city centre. Winchester has an exceptionally lovely **youth hostel** in the eighteenth-century mill on Water Lane (☎01962/853723; closed mid-Dec to Feb).

The city's best **pub** is the *Wykeham Arms*, 75 Kingsgate St, unprepossessing from outside but inside a maze of characterful, intimate spaces with imaginative, moderately priced food. The *Eclipse Inn*, on The Square, is an archetypally picturesque old inn specializing in inexpensive pies and casseroles. A good-value **lunch** spot is the *Cathedral Refectory*, on The Close, run by the Friends of Winchester Cathedral. *Nine The Square*, 9 Great Minster St, offers inexpensive light meals at the downstairs wine bar, while *Noah's*, Jewry Street, is a cheap café/restaurant, serving home-cooked dishes with Thai, Caribbean and Mediterranean influences.

The Watercress Line and Chawton

Alresford, six miles east of Winchester, is the beginning of the **Mid-Hants Watercress Line** (☎01962/733810; £8), a jolly, steam-powered train, so named because it passes through the former watercress beds which once flourished here. The train chuffs ten miles east to Alton, with gourmet dinners served on board on Saturday evenings and traditional Sunday lunches too.

A mile southwest of Alton lies **Chawton**, where Jane Austen lived from 1809 to 1817 during the last and most prolific years of her life and where she wrote or revised most of her books, including *Sense and Sensibility* and *Pride and Prejudice*. **Jane Austen's house** (Jan & Feb Sat & Sun 11am–4.30pm; rest of year daily 11am–4.30pm; £2.50), in the centre of the village, is a plain red-brick building, containing first editions of some of her greatest works.

The New Forest

The name of the **NEW FOREST** is misleading, for much of this region's woodland was cleared long before the Normans arrived, and its poor sandy soils support only a meagre covering of heather and gorse in many areas. The forest was requisitioned by William the Conqueror in 1079 as a game reserve, and the rights of its inhabitants soon became subservient to those of his precious deer. Fences to impede their progress were forbidden, and terrible punishments were meted out to those who disturbed the animals – hands were lopped off, eyes put out. Later monarchs gradually restored the forest-dwellers' rights, and today the New Forest enjoys a unique patchwork of ancient laws and privileges, enveloped in an arcane vocabulary dating from feudal times. The forest boundary is the "perambulation", and owner-occupiers of forest land have common rights of obscure practices such as "turbary" (peat-cutting), "estover" (firewood-collecting), and "mast" (letting pigs forage for acorns and beech mast), as well as the right of pasture, permitting domestic animals to graze freely.

The **trees** of the New Forest are now much more varied than they were in pre-Norman times, with birch, holly, yew, Scots pine and other conifers interspersed with the ancient oaks and beeches. The main wooded areas are around **Lyndhurst**, the "capital" of the New Forest, and one of the most venerable trees is the much visited **Knightwood Oak**, just off the A35 three miles southwest of Lyndhurst, which measures about 22 feet in circumference at shoulder height. The most obvious species of

New Forest **fauna** are the New Forest **ponies** (reputedly descendants from the Armada's small Spanish horses which survived the battle), now thoroughly domesticated – you'll see them grazing nonchalantly by the roadsides and ambling through some villages. The local deer are less likely to be seen now that some of the faster roads are fenced, although several species still roam the woods, including the tiny **sika deer**, descendants of a pair which escaped from Beaulieu in 1904.

Covering about 144 square miles – a third now in private ownership, the rest administered by the Forestry Commission – the New Forest is one of southern England's main rural playgrounds, and about eight million visitors annually flock here to enjoy a breath of fresh air, often after spending hours in traffic jams. To get the best from the region, you need to walk or ride through it, avoiding the places cars can reach. There are 150 miles of car-free gravel roads in the forest, making cycling an appealing prospect. The *Ordnance Survey Leisure Map* of the New Forest is worth getting if you want to explore in any detail, and in Lyndhurst you can pick up numerous specialist walking books and natural history guides. The forest also has ten Forestry Commission **campsites** – to get the full list, call or write to 231 Corstorphine Rd, Edinburgh EH12 7AT (☎0131/334 0066); and there's a **youth hostel** in Cottesmore House, Cott Lane, Burley (☎01425/403233; closed Nov–Feb).

RUFUS STONE

The Forest's most visited site, the **Rufus Stone**, stands a few hundred yards from the M27 motorway, three miles northwest of Lyndhurst. Erected in 1745, the monument marks the putative spot where the Conqueror's ghastly son and heir, **William II** – aka William Rufus after his ruddy complexion – was killed in 1100. The official version is that a crossbow bolt fired by a member of the royal hunting party glanced off a stag and struck the king in the heart. Sir William Tyrrell took the rap for the "accident" and fled incriminatingly to France, though he later swore on his deathbed that he had not fired the fatal arrow. As William II was a tyrant with many enemies, his death probably was a political assassination – a strong suspect was William's brother Henry, also in the shooting party, who promptly raced to Winchester to claim the crown, leaving Rufus to be carted ignominiously to the cathedral by a passing charcoal burner. The stone is remarkably unimpressive for such a landmark: the Victorians encased it in a protective layer of metal to deter vandals, and now it can't be seen at all clearly.

Lyndhurst and Brockenhurst

LYNDHURST, its town centre skewered by an agonizing one-way system, isn't a particularly interesting place, though the brick **parish church** is worth a glance for its William Morris glass, Lord Leighton fresco, and the grave of one Mrs Reginald Hargreaves, better known as Alice Liddell, Lewis Carroll's model for Alice. It's mainly valuable for the resources of the **New Forest Museum & Visitor Centre** off the High Street (daily: summer 10am–6pm; winter 10am–5pm; ☎01703/282269) where you can buy bus passes and maps for cycling and riding; AA Bike Hire in Gosport Lane **rents bikes** (☎023/8028 3349). For **accommodation** try *Forest Cottage* (☎023/8028 3461; no credit cards; ①), a B&B at the west end of the High Street, or *Ormonde House* (☎023/8028 2806; ④) on Southampton Road. *Le Café Parisien* sells snacks and the *Crown Hotel* does larger meals – both are on the High Street.

BROCKENHURST, four miles to the south of Lyndhurst, is a useful centre for visitors without their own transport. There's a train station right in town and by the level crossing New Forest Cycle Experience (☎01590/624204) offers **bikes for rent** for

£6–10 a day. The town also has some decent places to **stay**: try the *Cottage Hotel* on Sway Road (☎01590/622296; ⑤) or *Cater's Cottage*, Latchmoor (☎01590/623225; no credit cards; ②), an above-average B&B on the southern outskirts; while a short distance further south in Sway, there's a quiet B&B at *Little Purley Farm* in Chapel Lane Lane (☎01590/682707; no credit cards; ①), with views over to the Isle of Wight. The *Snakecatcher* on Lyndhurst Road is a pleasant **pub** with terrific bar food.

Beaulieu and Buckler's Hard

The village of **BEAULIEU** (originating from the French, but pronounced "Bewley"), in the southeast corner of the New Forest, was once the site of one of England's most influential monasteries, a Cistercian house founded in 1204 by King John – in remorse, it is said, for ordering a group of supplicating Cistercian monks to be trampled to death. Built using stone ferried from Caen and Quarr on the Isle of Wight, the **abbey** managed a self-sufficient estate of ten thousand acres and became a famous sanctuary, offering shelter to Queen Margaret of Anjou among many others. The abbey was dismantled soon after the Dissolution, and its refectory now forms the parish church, which, like everything else in Beaulieu, has been subsumed by the Montagu family who have owned a large chunk of the New Forest since one of Charles II's illegitimate progeny was created duke of the estate.

The estate has been transformed with a prodigious commercial vigour into **Beaulieu** (daily: Easter–Sept 10am–6pm; Oct–Easter 10am–5pm; £8), a tourist complex comprising **Palace House**, the attractive if unexceptional family home, the abbey and the main attraction, Lord Montagu's **National Motor Museum**. An undersized monorail and a more fitting old London bus ease the ten-minute walk between the entry point and Palace House. The house, formerly the abbey's gatehouse, contains masses of Montagu-related memorabilia while the undercroft of the adjacent abbey houses an exhibition depicting medieval monastic life. Inside the celebrated Motor Museum, a collection of 250 cars and motorcycles includes a Formula One McLaren, spindly antiques and recent classics, as well as a couple of svelte land-speed racers such as the record-breaking *Bluebird*. The entertaining *Wheels*, a dizzying ride-through display, takes you on a trip through the history of motoring.

If Beaulieu amply deserves its name, **BUCKLER'S HARD**, a couple of miles downstream on the River Beaulieu, has an even more wonderful setting. It doesn't look much like a shipyard now, but from Elizabethan times onwards dozens of men-of-war were assembled here from giant New Forest oaks. Several of Nelson's ships, including *HMS Agamemnon*, were launched here, to be towed carefully by rowing boats past the sandbanks and across the Solent to Portsmouth. The largest house in this hamlet of shipwrights' cottages – now a part of the Montagu estate – belonged to Henry Adams, the master builder responsible for most of the Trafalgar fleet. The **Maritime Museum** stands at the top of the village, tracing the history of the great naval ships (daily: summer 10am–6pm; winter 10am–4.30pm; £3.20).

Lymington

The most pleasant point of access for the Isle of Wight (see p.215) is **LYMINGTON**, a sheltered haven linked by ferry to Yarmouth and now one of the busiest leisure harbours on the south coast. Rising from the quay area, the old town is full of cobbled streets and Georgian houses and has one unusual building – the partly thirteenth-century church of **St Thomas the Apostle**, with a cupola-topped tower built in 1670.

Places to **stay** in town include *Albany House*, Highfield (☎01590/671900; no credit cards; ③), a Regency house near the public gardens, and *Wheatsheaf House*, a quaint listed building on Gosport Lane, (☎01590/679208; no credit cards; ③). *Jack in the Basket* at 7 St Thomas St, off the High Street (☎01590/673447; ①), offers light **meals** and also has some rooms for B&B. The town's best **pubs** are the *Chequers* on Ridgeway Lane, on the Pennington (west) side of town; the *Bosun's Chair* on Station Road; and the harbour-front *Ship Inn*, on the quayside, with seats outside overlooking the water.

Signposted two miles east of Lymington, is the **Sammy Miller Museum** on Gore Road, New Milton (daily: 10am–4.30pm; £3.50), gives classic motorcycles the "Beaulieu" treatment. Many of the once eminent British marques from Ariel to Vincent are displayed, as well as exotica from MV, NSU and several acclaimed trials bikes ridden by Sammy Miller himself, one of Britain's most successful trials riders.

Bournemouth and around

Renowned for its clean sandy beaches, the resort of **Bournemouth** is the nucleus of Europe's largest non-industrial conurbation stretching between Lymington and Poole harbour. The resort has a single-minded holidaymaking atmosphere, though neighbouring **Poole** and **Christchurch** are more interesting historically. North of this coastal sprawl, the pleasant old market town of **Wimborne Minster** has one of the area's most striking churches, while the stately home of **Kingston Lacy** contains an outstanding collection of old masters and other paintings.

The City

BOURNEMOUTH dates only from 1811, when a local squire, Louis Tregonwell, built a summer house on the wild, unpopulated heathland that once occupied this stretch of coast, and planted the first of the pine trees that now characterize the area. Sadly, the blandly modern town that you see today has little to remind you of Bournemouth's Victorian heyday. Bournemouth does, however, abound in public gardens – over two thousand acres of them, most notably **Compton Acres** (March–Oct daily 10am–6pm or dusk; £4.95), at the west end of town, off the Poole road. Here you'll find seven gardens each with a different international theme, the best of which are the elegantly understated Japanese Garden, and the more familiar, formal Italian Garden.

The excellent **Russell-Cotes Museum** on East Cliff Promenade (Tues–Sun 10am–5pm; free) is central Bournemouth's sole non-horticultural attraction. It houses a collection of oriental souvenirs gathered from around the world by the Russell-Cotes family, hoteliers who grew wealthy during the late Victorian tourist boom. The benefactors' lavishly decorated former home, featuring unusual stained glass and ornate painted ceilings, is jam-packed with their eclectic collections of which the Japanese artefacts are especially interesting. About a mile and a half east of the museum in the suburb of Boscombe, the **Shelley Rooms** in Shelley Park off Beechwood Avenue (Tues–Sun 2–5pm; free) house memorabilia relating to the Romantic poet Percy Bysshe Shelley, the husband of Mary Shelley, who wrote the Gothic horror tale *Frankenstein* in 1818 when aged only 21. She is buried with the poet's heart in the graveyard of St Peter's Church, just east of The Square.

Practicalities

The **train station** is just under a mile east of the centre; frequent **buses** run into town from the bus station opposite. The **tourist office** is on Westover Road, in the centre of town (mid-July to mid-Sept Mon–Sat 9.30am–7pm, Sun 10.30am–5pm; rest of year Mon–Sat 9.30am–5.30pm; ☎01202/451700). Bournemouth has **accommodation** to suit all budgets: try *Sea Dene Hotel*, 10 Burnaby Rd (☎01202/761372; ②), near the beach at Alum Chine, or the *Kensington Hotel*, 18 Durley Chine Rd (☎01202/557434;

④); *Tudor Grange*, 31 Gervis Rd, East Cliff (☎01202/291472; ③), has an attractive interior and gardens; the Edwardian *Langtry Manor*, 26 Derby Rd, East Cliff (☎01202/553887, *lillie@langtrymanor.com*; ⑦), is the former hideaway of Edward VII and his mistress, Lillie Langtry.

The *Brass House*, opposite the tourist office on Westover Rd, is one of Bournemouth's most popular **pubs**, also serving meals, though it can get rowdy in the evening; *CH2*, 37 Exeter Rd, is a moderately priced, elegant **restaurant** specializing in steaks and mussels with a variety of sauces (closed Sun & Mon). Countering its staid image, Bournemouth has produced some sizzling **clubs** in recent years: try the *Zoo* and *The Cage*, both housed in the same building in Firvale Road, right in the centre of town (☎01202/311178), or the *Opera House* at 570 Christchurch Road, Boscombe (☎01202/399922). More traditional resort entertainment can be found at the Pavilion Theatre, with its own ballroom, and the Winter Gardens, home of Bournemouth's symphony orchestra. Things get lively during two weeks in late June and early July, when the Bournemouth International Festival of art, dance and music takes place.

Christchurch

CHRISTCHURCH, five miles east of Bournemouth, is best known for its colossal parish church, **Christchurch Priory** (Mon–Sat 9.30am–5pm, Sun 2.15–6pm; £1 donation requested), bigger than most cathedrals. Built on the site of a Saxon minster dating from 650 AD but exhibiting chiefly Norman and Perpendicular features, the church is the longest in England at 311ft; its fan-vaulted North Porch is also the country's biggest. Fine views can be gained from the top of the 120-foot tower (irregular opening – ask at desk; 50p). The area round the old town quay has a carefully preserved charm. The **Red House Museum and Gardens** on Quay Road (Tues–Sat 10am–5pm, Sun 2–5pm; £1) contains an affectionate collection of local memorabilia.

Accommodation options around town are fairly pricey. The best option is the central *Kings Arms Toby Hotel*, 18 Castle St (☎01202/484117; ③); otherwise try *Grosvenor Lodge*, 53 Stour Rd (☎01202/499008; ④), one of a row of unexciting but reliable guest houses a ten-minute walk from the centre. For **something to eat**, try *La Mamma Pizzeria* at 51 Bridge St which serves Italian classics at moderate prices, or the pricier French restaurant, *Le Petit St Tropez*, at 3 Bridge St (☎01202/482522). Recommended **pubs** include the *King's Arms Hotel* right by the priory with a nice garden area, or check out Christchurch's oldest pub, *Ye Olde George Inn*, 2a Castle St, which has a beer garden and serves meals at lunchtime. **Boat trips** (several daily Easter to mid-Oct; ☎01202/429119) can be taken from the grassy banks of the riverside quay east to the beach at Mudeford or upriver to the *Tuckton Tea Rooms* to the east of Bournemouth.

Poole

POOLE, west of Bournemouth, is an ancient seaport on a huge, almost landlocked harbour. The town developed in the thirteenth century and was successively colonized by pirates, fishermen and timber traders, more recently replaced by companies speculating for oil in the shallow waters – the harbour's environmental significance ensures that the extraction process is carefully disguised. The old quarter by the quayside is worth exploring: the old Custom House, Scaplen's Court and Guildhall are the most striking of over a hundred historic buildings within a fifteen-acre site.

At the bottom of Old High Street, near the Poole Pottery showroom and crafts centre, the late medieval **Scaplen's Court** once billeted Cromwell's troops (you can see their graffiti around the fireplace), and has now been restored as an educational centre, with reconstructions of a Victorian kitchen, pharmacy and school room, and displays of old-time toys and games (Aug Mon–Sat 10am–5pm, Sun noon–5pm; £2; combined ticket with

Waterfront Museum £4). Over the road, local history is further explored at the **Waterfront Museum** (Mon–Sat April–Oct 10am–5pm, Sun noon–5pm; Nov–March Mon–Sat 10am–3pm, Sun noon–3pm; £2; combined ticket with Scaplen's Court £4), tracing Poole's development over the centuries and featuring well-displayed local ceramics and tiles, a rare Iron Age log boat, as well as changing exhibitions. You can visit **Brownsea Island** (daily: April–Sept 10am–6pm or dusk) on one of the regular boats from the nearby quayside. Now a National Trust property, this five-hundred-acre expanse of heath and woodland is famed for its red squirrels and other wildlife.

For **accommodation**, try the handsome *Antelope Hotel* at the quay end of the High Street (☎01202/672029; ③). Smaller hotels include the *Crown Hotel* (☎01202/672137; no credit cards; ①), an inn on the parallel Market Street, or the *Norfolk Lodge*, 1 Flaghead Rd (☎01202/708614; ③), convenient for the Sandbanks beaches. Less central but great value is the *Harbour Lights Hotel*, 121 North Rd, Parkstone (☎01202/748417; ①). There's a collection of good **restaurants** at the southern end of the High Street; look out for *Mez Creis* seafood restaurant at no. 16 (evenings only), or *Toppers*, next door. At the top end of the High Street, *Alcatraz* is a trendy Italian brasserie with outdoor tables.

Wimborne Minster and Kingston Lacy

An ancient town on the banks of the Stour, just a few minutes' drive north from the suburbs of Bournemouth, **WIMBORNE MINSTER**, as the name suggests, is mainly of interest for its great church, the **Minster of St Cuthberga**. Built on the site of an eighth-century monastery, its massive twin towers of mottled grey and tawny stone dwarf the rest of the town – the church was even more imposing before its spire fell down during a service in 1600. What remains today is basically Norman with later features added – such as the Perpendicular west tower, which bears a figure dressed as a grenadier of the Napoleonic era, who strikes every quarter-hour with a hammer. Inside, the church is crowded with memorials and eye-catching details – look out for the orrery clock inside the west tower, with the sun marking the hours and the moon marking the days of the month, and for the organ with trumpets pointing out towards the congregation instead of pipes. The **Chained Library** above the choir vestry (Mon–Fri 10am–noon & 2–4pm; 50p), dating from 1686, is Wimborne's most prized possession and one of the oldest public libraries in the country.

Wimborne's older buildings stand around the main square near the minster, and are mostly from the late eighteenth or early nineteenth century. The **Priest's House** on the High Street started life as lodgings for the clergy, then became a stationer's shop. Now it is an award-winning **museum** (June–Sept Mon–Sat 10.30am–5pm, Sun 2–4pm; April–Oct closed Sun; £2.20), each room furnished in the style of a different period. A working Victorian kitchen, a Georgian parlour and an ironmonger's shop are among its exhibits, and a walled garden at the rear provides an excellent place for summer teas.

Kingston Lacy (April–Oct Mon–Wed, Sat & Sun noon–5.30pm; £6; NT), one of England's finest seventeenth-century country houses, lies two miles northwest of Wimborne Minster, in 250 acres of parkland grazed by a herd of Red Devon cattle. Designed for the Bankes family, who were exiled from Corfe Castle after the Roundheads reduced it to rubble, the Queen Anne brick building was clad in grey stone during the nineteenth century by Charles Barry, co-architect of the Houses of Parliament. William Bankes, then owner of the house, was a great traveller and collector, and the **Spanish Room** is a superb scrap book of his Grand Tour souvenirs. Kingston Lacy's **picture collection** is also outstanding, featuring Titian, Rubens, Velazquez, and many other old masters. Be warned, though, that this place gets so swamped with visitors that the National Trust has to issue timed tickets at busy weekends.

The Isle of Purbeck

Though not actually an island, the **ISLE OF PURBECK** – a promontory of low hills and heathland jutting below Poole Harbour – does have an insular and distinctive feel. Reached from the east by the ferry from Sandbanks, at the narrow mouth of Poole harbour, or by a long and congested landward journey via the bottleneck of **Wareham**, Purbeck can be an effortful destination, but its villages are immensely pretty, none more so than **Corfe Castle**, with its majestic ruins. **Swanage**, a low-key seaside resort, is flanked by more exciting coastlines, all accessible on the Dorset Coast Path. Like Portland, further west, the area is pockmarked with stone quarries – Purbeck marble is the finest grade of the local oolitic limestone.

Wareham

The grid pattern of its streets indicates the Saxon origins of **WAREHAM**, and the town is surrounded by even older earth ramparts known as The Walls. A riverside setting adds to its charms, though the major road junction at its heart causes gridlock in summer, and the scenic stretch along The Quay also gets fairly overrun. Nearby lies an oasis of quaint houses around **Lady St Mary's Church**, which contains the marble coffin of Edward the Martyr, murdered at Corfe Castle in 978 by his stepmother, to make way for her unready son Ethelred.

   St Martin's Church, at the north end of town, dates from Saxon times. The chancel contains a faded twelfth-century mural of St Martin offering his cloak to a beggar, but the church's most striking feature is a romantic effigy of **T.E. Lawrence** in Arab dress, which was originally destined for Salisbury Cathedral, but rejected by the Dean there who disapproved of Lawrence's sexual proclivities. Lawrence was killed in 1935 in a motorbike accident on the road from Bovington, after returning to Dorset from his Middle Eastern adventures. His simply furnished cottage is at **Clouds Hill**, seven miles northwest of Wareham (April–Oct Wed–Fri & Sun noon–5pm; £2.30; NT). In Wareham the small **museum** next to the town hall in East Street (Easter–Oct Mon–Sat 11am–1pm & 2–4pm) displays some of Lawrence's memorabilia as does the absorbing but overpriced **Tank Museum** in Bovington Camp, five miles west of Wareham (daily 10am–5pm; £6.50).

   Holy Trinity Church, on South Street, contains the **tourist office** (June–Sept Mon–Sat 9.30am–5pm, Sun 10am–1pm; Oct–May Mon–Sat 9.30am–1pm & 1.45pm–5pm; ☎01929/552740). Wareham's best **accommodation** options are *The Anglebury Hotel*, 15 North St, (☎01929/552988; ③), and *The Old Granary Restaurant* on The Quay (☎01929/552010; ②), with views over the river.

Corfe Castle

The romantic ruins crowning the hill behind the village of **CORFE CASTLE** (daily: March & late Oct 10am–4.30pm; April to late Oct 10am–5.30pm or dusk; Nov–Feb 11am–3.30pm; £4; NT) are perhaps the most evocative in England. The family seat of Sir John Bankes, Attorney General to Charles I, this Royalist stronghold withstood a Cromwellian siege for six weeks, gallantly defended by Lady Bankes. One of her own men eventually betrayed the castle to the Roundheads, after which it was reduced to its present gap-toothed state by gunpowder. Apparently the victorious Roundheads were so impressed by Lady Bankes's courage that they allowed her to take the keys to the castle with her – they can still be seen in the library at the Bankes' subsequent home, Kingston Lacy (see opposite).

   The village is well stocked with tearooms and gift shops and has a couple of good pubs too: the *Fox* on West Street and, below the castle ramparts, the *Greyhound* which serves excellent seafood. For **B&B**, try *Brook Cottage*, 5 East St (☎01929/480347; no credit cards; ①), the *Bankes Arms Hotel* (☎01929/480206; ②), an old inn outside the castle entrance, or the Tudor-beamed *Cartshed Cottage*, Whiteway Farm, three miles west at Church Knowle (☎01929/480801; ②).

Swanage

Purbeck's largest seaside resort is **SWANAGE**, which boasts a pleasant sandy beach and an ornate town hall, the facade of which once adorned the Mercer's Hall in the City of London and was brought back here as ballast by a ship after delivering a cargo of stone. The town's station is the southern terminus of the **Swanage Steam Railway** (☎01929/425800), which runs as far as Corfe Castle (about £6 return). Swanage is also a good base for exploring **Shell Bay**, to the north, a magnificent long beach of icing-sugar sand, backed by a remarkable heathland ecosystem that's home to all six British species of reptile – adders are quite common, so be careful.

At the top end of the beach a **ferry** (every 20min; 7am–11pm) crosses the mouth of Poole harbour connecting the Isle of Purbeck with Sandbanks in Poole. The **tourist office** is by the beach on Shore Road (Easter–Oct daily 10am–5pm; Nov–Easter Mon–Thurs 10am–5pm, Fri 10am–4pm; ☎0929/422885), and there's a **youth hostel**, with good views across the bay, on Cluny Crescent (☎01929/422113, *swanage@yha.org.uk*; closed Nov to mid-Feb). There are scores of **B&B**s in Swanage; you'll find a handy trio on Kings Road near the train station, or try the *Purbeck Hotel,* 19 High St (☎01929/425160; ①), which also has a decent pub. Swanage has a wide variety of **places to eat**, the best of which is the excellent *Galley*, 9 High St (☎01929/427299), specializing in well-prepared local fish dishes.

Lulworth Cove and Durdle Door

Highlights of the coast beyond Swanage are the grey-white chalk and limestone cliffs between Durlstone Head and St Alban's Head. Further west still, the geology of the coast changes to blackish beds of shale, which turn into a semi-fluid morass in wet weather, leaving limestone layers above unsupported. At **Lulworth Cove**, a perfect shell-shaped bite in the coastline formed when the sea broke through a weakness in the cliffs and then gnawed away at them from behind, forming a circular cave which eventually collapsed to leave a bay enclosed by sandstone cliffs. Lulworth's scenic charms are well known, and as you descend the hill through the quaint thatch-and-stone village of West Lulworth in summer the sun glints off the metal of a thousand car roofs in the car park behind the cove. The fee to park here (£3) includes entry to the **Lulworth Heritage Centre** where the mysteries of the local geology are explained.

Immediately west of the cove you come to **Stair Hole**, a roofless sea cave riddled with arches that will eventually collapse to form another Lulworth, and a couple of miles west is **Durdle Door**, a famous limestone arch that appeals to serious geologist and casual sightseer alike. Most people take the uphill route to the arch which starts from the car park but, if you want to avoid the steep climb, you can drive a mile from the village towards East Chaldon and park at the *Durdle Door Holiday Park* for a small fee.

West Lulworth is the obvious **place to stay or eat** on this section of coast: best of the bunch are the *Castle Inn* (☎01929/400311; ②), *Cromwell House Hotel* (☎0929/400253; ③) and *Ivy Cottage* (☎01929/400509; no credit cards; ①), a seventeenth-century cottage. The **youth hostel** at the end of School Lane West (☎01929/400564; closed Nov–Feb) is a plain chalet with small rooms, just a stone's throw away from the Dorset Coast Path. In **East Lulworth**, the *Weld Arms* also has rooms (☎01929/400211; ①) and the easily missed *Sailor's Return* in East Chaldon, four miles northwest of Lulworth Cove, is locally unsurpassed for its mouthwatering pub food.

Dorchester and around

The county town of Dorset, **DORCHESTER** still functions as the main agricultural centre for the region, and if you catch it on a Wednesday when the market is in full swing
you'll find it livelier than usual. For the local tourist authorities, however, this is essentially
Thomas Hardy's town – he was born at Higher Bockhampton, three miles east of here,
his heart is buried in Stinsford, a couple of miles northeast (the rest of him is in
Westminster Abbey), and he spent much of his life in Dorchester itself, where his statue
now stands on High West Street. The town appears in his novels as "Casterbridge", and
the countryside all around Dorchester provided the landscapes of his books, particularly
the wild heathland to the east ("Egdon Heath"), and the eerie yew forest of Cranborne
Chase. The real Dorchester has a pleasant central core of mostly seventeenth-century
and Georgian buildings, while to the southwest of town looms the massive hill fort of
Maiden Castle, the most impressive of Dorset's many pre-Roman antiquities.

Dorchester was Durnovaria to the Romans, who founded the town in about 70 AD.
The original Roman walls were replaced in the eighteenth century by tree-lined
avenues called "Walks" (Bowling Alley Walk, West Walk and Colliton Walk), but some
traces of the Roman period have survived. At the back of County Hall excavations have
uncovered a fine Roman villa with a well-preserved mosaic floor, and on the southeast
edge of town you'll find **Maumbury Rings**, where the Romans held vast gladiatorial
combats in an amphitheatre adapted from a Stone Age site. The gruesome traditions
continued into the Middle Ages, when gladiators were replaced by bear-baiting and
public executions or "hanging fairs".

Continuing the sanguinary theme, after the ill-fated rebellion of the Duke of
Monmouth (another of Charles II's illegitimate offspring) against James II, **Judge
Jeffreys** was appointed to punish the rebels. His "Bloody Assizes" of 1685, held in the
Oak Room of the **Antelope Hotel** on Cornhill, sentenced 292 men to death. In the
event, 74 were hung, drawn and quartered, and their heads stuck on pikes throughout
Dorset and Somerset; the luckier suspects were merely flogged and transported to the
West Indies. Judge Jeffreys lodged just round the corner from the *Antelope* in High
West Street, where a half-timbered restaurant now capitalizes on the lurid association.

In 1834 the **Shire Hall**, further down High West Street, witnessed another cause
célèbre, when six men from the nearby village of **Tolpuddle** were sentenced to transportation for banding together to form the Friendly Society of Agricultural Labourers,
in order to present a request for a small wage increase on the grounds that their families were starving. After a public outcry the men were pardoned, and the Tolpuddle
Martyrs passed into history as founders of the trade union movement. The room in
which they were tried is preserved as a memorial to the martyrs, and you can find out
more about them in Tolpuddle itself, eight miles east on the A35, where there's a fine
little **museum** (April–Oct Tues–Sat 10am–5.30pm, Sun 11am–5.30pm; Nov–March
closes at 4pm; free).

The best place to find out about Dorchester's history is in the engrossing **Dorset
County Museum** on High West Street (July & Aug daily 10am–5pm; rest of year
closed Sun; £3), where archeological and geological displays trace Celtic and Roman
history, including a section on Maiden Castle. Pride of place goes to the re-creation of
Thomas Hardy's study, where his pens are inscribed with the names of the books he
wrote with them. Other museums in town include the small **Dinosaur Museum** (daily:
April–Sept 9.30am–5.30pm; Oct–March 10am–4.30pm; £3.50) in Icen Way, appealing
chiefly to children. Best of all is **Tutankhamun: The Exhibition** in the High Street
(daily 9.30am–5.30pm; £3.50), a fascinating and thorough exploration of the young
pharaoh's life and afterlife through to the eventual discovery of his tomb in 1922.

Everything from the mummified remains, complete burial chamber and the celebrated golden mask has been carefully and atmospherically re-created with painstaking detail.

Practicalities

Dorchester has two **train stations**, both of them to the south of the centre: trains from Weymouth and London Waterloo arrive at Dorchester South, while Bristol trains use the Dorchester West station. Most **buses** stop around the car park on Acland Road, to the east of South Street. The **tourist office** is in Antelope Walk (April–Sept Mon–Sat 9am–5pm, Sun 10am–5pm; Oct Mon–Sat 9am–5pm; Nov–March Mon–Sat 9am–4pm; ☎01305/267992).

Dorchester has a good selection of **accommodation**, with the best value being the *Casterbridge Hotel*, 49 High East St (☎01305/26404; ⑤), a superior Georgian guest house, and *Maumbury Cottage,* 9 Maumbury Rd (☎01305/266726; no credit cards; ①), a small, friendly and central B&B. The *King's Arms*, High East Street (☎01305/265353; ②), a historic local landmark, has pricey rooms but serves good food, including vegetarian dishes. The nearest **youth hostel** is at Litton Cheney (☎01308/482340; closed Sept–March), halfway between Dorchester and Bridport, and the closest **campsite** is the *Giant's Head Caravan and Camping Park*, Old Sherborne Road (☎01300/341242), about five miles north of town, above the Cerne Abbas giant (see p.236). When it comes to **food**, your best bet is a pub meal; try the *Royal Oak* or the *Old Ship Inn*, both on High West Street and both highly recommended.

Maiden Castle

One of southern England's finest prehistoric sites, **Maiden Castle** stands on a hill two miles or so south of Dorchester. Covering about 115 acres, it was first developed around 2000 BC by a Stone Age farming community and then used during the Bronze Age as a funeral mound. Iron Age dwellers expanded it into a populous settlement and fortified it with a daunting series of ramparts and ditches, just in time for the arrival of Vespasian's Second Legion. The ancient Britons' sling stones were no match for the more sophisticated weapons of the Roman invaders, and Maiden Castle was stormed in a bloody massacre in 43 AD. What you see today is a massive series of grassy concentric ridges about sixty feet high, creasing the surface of the hill. The main finds from the site are displayed in the Dorset County Museum (see p.231).

Weymouth to Bridport

Whether George III's passion for sea bathing was a symptom of his eventual madness is uncertain, but it was at the bay of **Weymouth** that in 1789 he became the first reigning monarch to follow the craze. Sycophantic gentry rushed into the waves behind him, and soon the town, formerly a workaday harbour, took on the elegant Georgian stamp which it bears today. A likeness of the monarch on horseback is even carved into the chalk downs northwest of the town, like some guardian spirit. Weymouth nowadays plays second fiddle to the vast resort of Bournemouth to the east, but it's still a lively family holiday destination, with several costly new attractions to augment its more sedate charms.

Just south of the town stretch the giant arms of Portland Harbour, and a long causeway links Weymouth to the strange five-mile-long excrescence of the **Isle of Portland**. West of the causeway, the eighteen-mile bank of pebbles known as **Chesil Beach** runs northwest in the direction of **Bridport**.

Weymouth

Weymouth had long been a port before the Georgians popularized it as a resort – it's possible that a ship unloading a cargo here in 1348 brought the Black Death to English shores, and on a happier note it was from Weymouth that John Endicott sailed in 1628 to found Salem in Massachusetts. A few buildings survive from these pre-Georgian times: the restored **Tudor House** in Trinity Street (June–Sept Tues–Fri 11am–3.45pm; Oct–May first Sun of month 2–4pm; £1.50) and the ruins of **Sandsfoot Castle**, built by Henry VIII, overlooking Portland Harbour. But Weymouth's most imposing architectural heritage stands along the Esplanade, a dignified range of bow-fronted and porticoed buildings gazing out across the graceful bay, an ensemble rather disrupted by the garish **Clock Tower** commemorating Victoria's jubilee. The more intimate quayside of the Old Harbour, linked to the Esplanade by the main pedestrianized throroughfare St Mary's Street, is lined with waterfront pubs from where you can view the passing yachts, trawlers and ferries.

Weymouth's slightly faded gentility is now counterbalanced by a number of "all weather" attractions, like the **Sea Life Park** in Lodmoor Country Park east of the Esplanade (daily 10am–4pm, last admission 1hr before closing; £5.50; £4.95 from tourist office), where you can get close to sharks and rays and wander among multichrome birds in the 33°C tropical house. Other attractions include the **Deep Sea Adventure** at the Old Harbour (daily: summer 9.30am–8pm; winter 9.30am–7pm; £3.50), which describes the origins of modern diving and the sobering story of the *Titanic* disaster. Over the river on Hope Square, **The Timewalk** (daily 10am–5.30pm; public & school holidays open until 9.30pm; £3.95), housed in Brewer's Quay, contains an entertaining walk-through exhibition of Weymouth's maritime and brewing past. A fifteen-minute walk southwards, the Palmerston-era **Nothe Fort** (mid-May to mid-Sept daily 10.30am–5.30pm; hours are variable in winter, call to check; ☎01305/787243; £3) has a number of displays on military themes plus a museum on the centuries-old practice of coastal defence, made obsolete in 1956 by advancing technology.

Practicalities

Weymouth **train** station is a couple of blocks west of the Bay, where you'll find the **tourist office**, at the northern end of the Esplanade (daily: April–Sept 9am–5pm; Oct–March 10am–3pm; ☎01305/785747). For **accommodation** in the centre, try the *Chatsworth*, 14 Esplanade (☎01305/785012; ④); *Bay Lodge*, 27 Greenhill (☎01305/782419; ④), a better than average B&B with sea views; or *Cavendish House*, 5 Esplanade (☎01305/782039; ②). *Perry's*, 4 Trinity Rd (☎01305/785799), is an attractive **restaurant** overlooking the quayside, serving good-value seafood. Trinity Road also has the *Old Rooms Inn*, a popular pub serving inexpensive meals, and the family-run *Seagull Café*, where you can eat cheap battered fish and lashings of chips. The *Nothe Tavern*, on Barrack Road, is one of Weymouth's better **pubs**, doing a good range of food and Eldridge Pope beer, with harbour views from the garden.

Portland

Stark, wind-battered and treeless, the **ISLE OF PORTLAND** is famed above all for its hard white limestone, which has been quarried here for centuries – Wren used it for St Paul's Cathedral, and it clads the UN headquarters in New York. It was also used for the six-thousand-foot breakwater that protects Portland Harbour – the largest artificial harbour in Britain, which was built by convicts in the mid-nineteenth century. Poorer grades of Portland stone are pulverized for cement – the industrial stone-crushing plant is a prominent and unlovely feature of the island.

The causeway road by which Portland is approached stands on the easternmost section of the Chesil shingle. To the east you get a good view of the harbour, a naval base since 1872, but now jeopardized by the post-Cold-War rundown of Britain's defences. The first place you come to, **Fortuneswell**, overlooks the huge harbour and is itself surveyed by a 450-year-old Tudor fortress, **Portland Castle** (April–Sept 10am–6pm; Oct 10am–5pm; £2.50; EH), commissioned by Henry VIII. South of **Easton**, the main village on the island, Wakeham Road holds Pennsylvania Castle (now a private house), built in 1800 for John Penn, governor of the island and a grandson of the founder of Pennsylvania. A couple of hundred yards beyond the house, the seventeenth-century Avice's Cottage is home to a small **museum** (April–July, Sept & Oct Mon, Tues & Fri–Sun 10.30am–1pm & 1.30–5pm; Aug daily 10.30am–1pm & 1.30–5pm; £1.70), with exhibitions on local shipwrecks, smuggling and quarrying. The cottage owes its name to Thomas Hardy, who described it in his novel *The Well-Beloved*. Nearby, in Church Ope Cove, you can see the ruins of St Andrew's church and eleventh-century Rufus Castle.

The craggy limestone of the island rises to 496 feet at **Portland Bill**, where a lighthouse has guarded the promontory since the eighteenth century. The present one, dating from 1906, now houses Portland's **tourist office** (Easter–Sept Mon, Tues & Thurs–Sun 10am–4pm, Wed 11am–4pm; ☎01305/861233), which can update you on **accommodation** options in the area, for instance *Sturt Corner* (☎01305/822846; no credit cards; ③) or the *Pulpit Inn* (☎01305/821237; ①), both nearby on Portland Bill.

Chesil Beach and Bridport

Chesil Beach is the strangest feature of the Dorset coast, a two-hundred-yard-wide, fifty-foot-high bank of pebbles that extends for eighteen miles, its component stones gradually decreasing in size from fist-like pebbles at Portland to "pea gravel" at Burton Bradstock in the west. This sorting is an effect of the powerful coastal currents, which make this one of the most dangerous beaches in Europe. Though not a swimming beach, Chesil is popular with sea anglers, and its wild, uncommercialized atmosphere makes an appealing antidote to the south coast resorts. Chesil Beach encloses a brackish lagoon called The Fleet for much of its length – setting for J. Meade Faulkner's classic smuggling tale, *Moonfleet*.

At the point where the shingle beach attaches itself to the shore is the pretty village of **ABBOTSBURY**, all tawny ironstone and thatch. The village **Swannery** (April–Oct daily 10am–6pm; last admissions 1hr before closing; £4.80), a wetland reserve for mute swans, dates back to medieval times, when presumably it formed part of the abbot's larder. Other attractions include the **Sub-Tropical Gardens** (daily: April–Oct 10am–6pm, last admission 1hr before closing; Nov–March 10am–dusk; £4.40), where delicate species thrive in the micro-climate created by Chesil's stones, which act as a giant radiator to keep out all but the worst frosts. Up on the downs two miles inland is a monument to **Thomas Hardy**, this time not the writer, but the flag captain in whose arms Admiral Nelson expired. There are good **accommodation** options in Abbotsbury, notably the *Swan Lodge* B&B, 1 Rodden Row (☎01305/871249; no credit cards; ②), and the handsome *Ilchester Arms* in the village centre, which also serves fine **food** (☎01305/871243; ②).

BRIDPORT, just beyond the far end of Chesil Beach, is a nice old town of brick rather than stone, with unusually wide streets, a hangover from its rope-making days when cords made of locally grown hemp and flax were stretched between the houses. If you want to know about the rope and net industry head for the little fishing resort of **West Bay**, Bridport's access to the sea, where the **Harbour Museum** (April–Sept daily 10am–6pm; £1.50) will fill you in about "Bridport daggers" (hangmen's nooses) and more besides.

The local **tourist office** is at 32 South St (April–Oct Mon–Sat 9am–5pm; Nov–March Mon–Sat 10am–3pm; ☎01308/424901). Across the harbour, the *Bridport Arms Hotel* (☎01308/422994; ②) offers good **accommodation** near the beach; alternatively try *Cranston Cottage*, 27 Church St in the centre of Bridport (☎01308/456240; no credit cards; ①). West Bay has the area's best place to **eat**, the *Riverside Restaurant* (☎01308/422011), a renowned but informal fish place with good views out to sea.

Lyme Regis

LYME REGIS, Dorset's most westerly town, shelters snugly between steep hills, just before the grey, fossil-filled cliffs lurch into Devon. Its intimate size and undeniable photogeneity make Lyme so popular that in high summer car-borne crowds jostle with pedestrians for the limited space along its narrow streets. For all that, the town lives up to the classy impression created by its regal name, which it owes to a royal charter granted by Edward I in 1284. It has some upmarket literary associations to further bolster its self-esteem – Jane Austen resorted to a seafront cottage here and penned *Persuasion*, while novelist John Fowles is the town's most famous current resident; the filming of his novel *The French Lieutenant's Woman*, shot on location here, did more than any tourist board production ever could to place the resort firmly on the map.

Colourwashed cottages and elegant Regency and Victorian villas line its seafront and flanking streets, but Lyme's best-known feature is a briskly practical reminder of its commercial origins. As you walk along the seafront and out towards **The Cobb**, the curving harbour wall first constructed in the thirteenth century, look for the outlines of ammonites in the walls and paving stones. The cliffs around Lyme are a complex layer-cake of limestone, greensand and unstable clay, a perfect medium for preserving fossils, which are exposed by landslips of the waterlogged clays. In 1811, after a fierce storm caused parts of the cliffs to collapse, twelve-year-old Mary Anning, a keen fossil-hunter, discovered an almost-complete dinosaur skeleton, a thirty-foot ichthyosaurus now displayed in London's Natural History Museum (see p.127).

Hammering fossils out of the cliffs is frowned on by today's conservationists, and is in any case rather hazardous. Hands-off inspection of the area's complex geology can be enjoyed on both sides of town: to the west lies the **Undercliff**, a fascinating jumble of overgrown landslips, now a nature reserve. East of Lyme, you can either walk along the Dorset Coastal Path as far as jaded **Charmouth** (Jane Austen's favourite resort) or, at low tide, walk for two miles along the beach then, just past Charmouth, rejoin the path to the headland of **Golden Cap**, an outcrop of sandstone crowned with gorse.

Lyme's excellent **Philpot Museum** on Bridge Street (April–Oct Mon–Sat 10am–5pm, Sun 10am–noon & 2.30–5pm; Nov–March Sat 10am–5pm, Sun 10am–noon & 2.30–5pm; also school holidays Mon–Fri 10am–5pm; £1.20) provides a crash course in local history and geology, while **Dinosaurland** on Coombe Street (daily: 10am–5pm; Aug 10am–6pm; £3.20) fills out the story on ammonites and other local fossils. Also worth seeing is the small **marine aquarium** on The Cobb (Easter–Oct 9am–5pm, later closing in July & Aug; £1.50), where local fishermen bring unusual catches, and the fifteenth-century **parish church** of St Michael the Archangel, up Church Street, which contains a seventeenth-century pulpit and a massive chained Bible.

Practicalities

Lyme's nearest **train station** is in Axminster, five miles north; the hourly #31 **bus** (Mon–Sat) runs from here to Lyme Regis (on Sun take #378, running three times). The **tourist office** is on Church Street by the museum (May–Sept Mon–Fri 10am–6am, Sat & Sun 10am–5pm; April & Oct Mon–Sat 10am–5pm; Nov–March Mon–Fri 10am–4pm, Sat 10am–2pm; ☎01297/442138). Lyme's sole seafront **hotel** is the pricey *Bay Hotel* on Marine Parade (☎01297/442059; ⑤). However, the *Old Monmouth Hotel* is centrally located at 12 Church St (☎01297/442456; ②) and *Cliff Cottage* on Cobb Rd (☎01297/443334; no credit cards; ①) also has a tea garden and fish restaurant. Reasonably priced **meals** can be had at the *Kersbrook Hotel* on Pound Road, which is also a pleasant place to **stay** (☎01297/442596; ④), or the moderately priced *Millside Restaurant and Wine Bar*, 1 Mill Lane (☎01297/442049). The best **pubs** are the *Royal Standard* on Ozone Parade, or the *Pilot Boat* on Bridge Street, which also does smashing seafood meals.

Inland Dorset and Southern Wiltshire

The main pleasures of inland Dorset come from unscheduled meandering through its ancient landscapes and tiny rural settlements, many of which boast preposterously winsome names such as Ryme Intrinseca, Piddletrenthide, Up Sydling and Plush. The county's most photographed site is the rumbustious chalk-carved giant outside the village of **Cerne Abbas**. The major tourist honey pots, though, are the towns of **Blandford Forum**, **Shaftesbury** and **Sherborne**, the landscaped garden at **Stourhead** across the county boundary in Wiltshire, and the brasher stately home at **Longleat**, an unlikely hybrid of safari park and historic monument.

Blandford Forum

BLANDFORD FORUM, the gateway into mid-Dorset from Bournemouth, owes its latinate name not to the Romans but to medieval pedantry – the original Saxon name Cheping, meaning "market", was translated as *forum* by Latin-speaking tax officials in the thirteenth century. The Romans weren't far away, however – their main route from Old Sarum to Dorchester ran through the Iron Age fortification of Badbury Rings, just east of the town, where it made an uncharacteristic bend. In 1731 Blandford was all but destroyed by fire, the fourth such conflagration since the end of the sixteenth century. The phoenix that rose from these ashes was designed by the unfortunately named Bastard brothers, John and William, whose "Blandford School" produced buildings characterized by mellow dapplings of brick and stone.

Sleepy Blandford still boasts one of the most harmonious and complete Georgian townscapes in England, with its centrepieces being the **Town Hall** and the **Church of St Peter and St Paul**, built in 1739. Outside, the church's distinguishing feature is the cupola perched on its handsome square tower; inside it has fine box pews and huge Ionic columns. It doesn't quite look as John Bastard intended, though: the church was altered at the end of the nineteenth century, when the chancel was sawn off the nave, stuck on wheels, rolled out the way so that a new section could be built in the gap, and then stuck back on to the extension. The town **museum** in Bere's Yard, opposite the church (closed until mid-2000; call ☎01297/450710, or ask at the tourist office for information), offers a pithy account of local history.

Blandford's **tourist office** is in the car park on West Street (April–Oct Mon–Sat 10am–5pm; Nov–March Mon–Sat 10am–12.30pm; ☎01258/454770). There are many **B&Bs** along Whitecliff Mill Street; try *Gone Walkabout*, at 3 Alexandra St (☎01258/455699, *101454.1674@compuserve.com*; no credit cards; ①), a Georgian house close to the town centre and welcoming walkers and cyclists. The local Hall & Woodhouse brewery supplies many local **hostelries** – *The Greyhound*, in quiet Greyhound Place, is a good-looking pub with outdoor seating and great food.

Cerne Abbas

The most visited site in Dorset lies sixteen miles west of Blandford, just off the A352, on the regular bus route between Dorchester and Sherborne (#216). **CERNE ABBAS** has bags of charm in its own right, with gorgeous Tudor cottages and abbey ruins, not to mention a clutch of decent pubs. Its main attraction, however, is the enormously priapic **giant** carved in the chalk hillside, standing 180 feet high and flourishing a club over his disproportionately small head. The age of the monument is disputed, some authorities believing it to be pre-Roman, others thinking he might be a Romano-British figure of Hercules, but in view of his prominent feature it's probable that the giant originated as some primeval fertility or protective symbol. Today it is in the care of the National Trust, who do their best to stop people wandering over it and eroding the two-foot trenches that form the outlines – a school of thought maintains that lying on the outsize member will induce conception.

Shaftesbury

Ten miles north of Blandford, **SHAFTESBURY** perches on a spur of lumpy green-gold hills, with severe gradients on three sides of the town. On a clear day views from the town are terrific – one of the best vantage points is **Gold Hill**, quaint and cobbled and very steep. The local history **museum** (Easter–Oct daily 10.30am–4.30pm; also some winter weekends 11am–4pm; £1) at the top is worth a glance – its contents include a collection of locally made buttons. Pilgrims once flocked to Shaftesbury to pay homage to the bones of Edward the Martyr, brought to the **Abbey** in 978, though now only the footings of the abbey church survive, just off the main street (Easter–Oct daily 10am–4.30pm; £1). **St Peter's** church on the market place is one of the few reminders of Shaftesbury's medieval grandeur, when it boasted a castle, twelve churches and four market crosses.

The **tourist office** is on Bell Street (mid-March to Oct daily 10am–5pm; Nov to mid-March Mon–Wed 10am–1pm, Thurs–Sat 10am–5pm; ☎01747/853514). The *Mitre Inn* on the High Street serves good pies and has **rooms** (☎01747/852488; ②) as has *The Knoll* in Bleke Street (☎01747/855243; no credit cards; ②). Three miles south of town in the village of **Compton Abbas**, the *Old Forge* (☎01747/811881; no credit cards; ②) on Chapel Hill offers B&B in an eighteenth-century cottage with log fires.

Stourhead

Landscape gardening was a favoured mode of display among the grandest eighteenth-century landowners, and **Stourhead**, ten miles northwest of Shaftesbury, is one of the most accomplished survivors of the genre. The Stourton estate was bought in 1717 by Henry Hoare, who commissioned Colen Campbell to build a new villa in the Palladian style. Hoare's heir, another Henry, returned from his Grand Tour in 1741 with his head full of the paintings of Claude and Poussin, and determined to translate their images of well-ordered, wistful classicism into real life. He dammed the Stour to create a lake, then planted the terrain with blocks of trees, domed temples, stone bridges, grottoes and statues, all mirrored vividly in the water. In 1772 the folly of King Alfred's Tower was added and today affords fine views across the estate and into neighbouring counties. The house itself is fairly run-of-the-mill, though it has some good Chippendale furniture (house April–Oct Mon–Wed, Sat & Sun noon–5.30pm or dusk; garden daily 9am–7pm or dusk; tower April–Oct Tues–Fri 2–5.30pm or dusk, Sat & Sun 11.30am–5.30pm or dusk; house £4.50; garden £4.50; tower £1.50; combined ticket £8; NT). A mile to the southeast in the showpiece village of **Stourton**, also now owned by the National Trust, the *Spread Eagle Inn* is a good place to have lunch and also has **rooms** (☎01747/840587; ⑤).

Longleat

If Stourhead is an unexpected outcrop of Italy in Wiltshire, the African savannah intrudes even more bizarrely at **Longleat** (house Easter–Oct 10am–6pm; Nov–Easter 10am–4pm; safari park Easter–Oct 10am–5pm; house £5; safari park £6; combined ticket £13), south of the road from Warminster to Frome. In 1946 the sixth Marquess of Bath became the first stately-homeowner to open his house to the paying public on a regular basis to help make ends meet, and in 1966 he turned Longleat's Capability Brown landscapes into a drive-through **safari park** – the first in the country. Once committed to such commercial enterprise, the bosses of Longleat knew no limits: other attractions now include the world's largest hedge maze, a Doctor Who exhibition, a hi-tech simulation of the world's most dangerous modes of travel, and the seventh Marquess' steamy murals encapsulating his interpretation of life and the universe (children may not be admitted). Beyond the brazen razzmatazz, though, there's an exquisitely furnished Elizabethan house, with the largest private library in Britain and a fine collection of pictures, including Titian's *Holy Family*.

Longleat is about four miles from the train stations of Frome and Warminster and is currently served by a Lion-Link bus that leaves Warminster train station at 11.10am and returns from the Information Centre at Longleat at 5.15pm – the service is provided free to coach- and rail-ticket holders, and otherwise costs £1.50. Otherwise it's a matter of catching the #53 bus (Mon–Sat) which shuttles roughly every hour between Warminster and Frome train stations – though be prepared to walk the two and a half miles from the entrance of the house to its grounds.

Sherborne

Tucked away in the northwest corner of Dorset, the attractive town of **SHERBORNE** was once the capital of Wessex, holding cathedral status until Old Sarum usurped the bishopric in 1075. This former glory is embodied by the magnificent **Abbey Church** (daily: summer 10am–6pm; winter 10am–4pm), which was founded in 705, later becoming a Benedictine abbey. Most of its extant parts date from the fifteenth-century rebuilding, and it is one of the best examples of Perpendicular architecture in Britain, particularly noted for its outstanding **fan vaulting**. The church also has a famously weighty peal of bells, led by "Great Tom", a tenor bell presented to the abbey by Cardinal Wolsey. Among the abbey church's many tombs are those of Alfred the Great's two brothers, Ethelred and Ethelbert, and the Elizabethan poet Thomas Wyatt, all located in the northeast corner. The **almshouse** on the opposite side of the Abbey Close was built in 1437 and is a rare example of a medieval hospital; another wing provides accommodation for Sherborne's well-known public school.

Sherborne also has two "castles", both associated with Sir Walter Raleigh. Queen Elizabeth I first leased, then gave Raleigh the twelfth-century **Old Castle** (April–Sept daily 10am–6pm; Oct daily 10am–5pm; Nov–March Wed–Sun 10am–1pm & 2–4pm; £1.50; EH), but it seems that he despaired of feudal accommodation and built himself a more comfortably domesticated house, **Sherborne Castle** (April–Oct Tues, Thurs, Sat & Sun 12.30–5pm; £4.80), in adjacent parkland. When Sir Walter fell from the queen's favour by seducing her maid of honour, the Digby family acquired the house and have lived there ever since; portraits, furniture and books are displayed in a whimsically Gothic interior, remodelled in the nineteenth century. The Old Castle fared less happily, and was pulverized by Cromwellian cannonfire for the obstinately Royalist leanings of its occupants. The **museum** on Half Moon Street (Tues–Sat 10.30am–4.30pm, Sun 2.30–4.30pm; £1) includes a model of the Old Castle and photographs of parts of the fifteenth-century Sherbourne Missal, a richly illuminated tome weighing nearly fifty pounds, now housed in the British Library.

The **tourist office** is at 3 Tilton Court, Digby Rd (Easter–Nov Mon–Sat 9.30am–5.30pm; Nov–Easter Mon–Sat 10am–3pm; ☎01935/815341). For an **overnight stay** try *The Half Moon Hotel* on Half Moon Street (☎01935/812017; ②), the *Britannia Inn* on Westbury, just down from the abbey (☎01935/813300; ①) or the *Cross Keys Hotel*, 88 Cheap St (☎01935/812492; ④), which has a few tables out front for drinks and meals. *Oliver's* on Cheap Street and the *Church House Gallery* close to the abbey on Half Moon Street are both good for teas and light lunches.

Salisbury

SALISBURY, huddled below Wiltshire's chalky plain in the converging valleys of the Avon and Nadder, looks from a distance very much as it did when Constable painted his celebrated view of it from across the water meadows, even though traffic may clog its centre and military jets scream overhead from local air bases. Prosperous and well kept, Wiltshire's only city is designed on a pleasantly human scale, with no sprawling suburbs or high-rise buildings to challenge the supremacy of the cathedral's immense

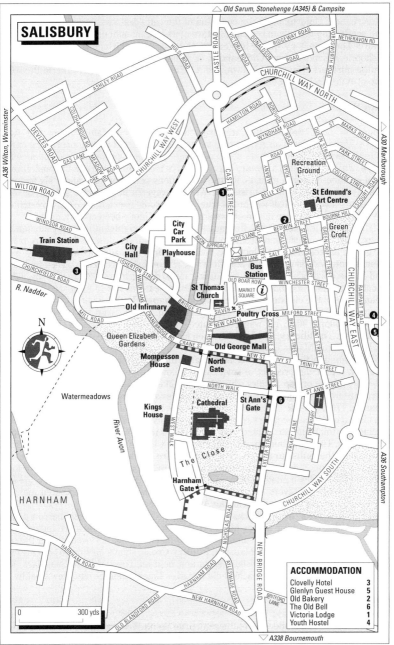

SALISBURY

Old Sarum, Stonehenge (A345) & Campsite

A36 Wilton, Warminster

A30 Marlborough

A36 Southampton

A338 Bournemouth

Train Station

City Hall

City Car Park

Playhouse

St Thomas Church

Old Infirmary

Queen Elizabeth Gardens

Mompesson House

North Gate

Kings House

Cathedral

St Ann's Gate

Harnham Gate

Watermeadows

HARNHAM

R. Nadder

River Avon

The Close

West Walk

North Walk

Recreation Ground

St Edmund's Art Centre

Green Croft

Bus Station

Market Square

Poultry Cross

Old George Mall

CHURCHILL WAY NORTH

CHURCHILL WAY WEST

CHURCHILL WAY EAST

CHURCHILL WAY SOUTH

CASTLE ROAD

CASTLE STREET

WILTON ROAD

WINDSOR ROAD

CHURCHFIELDS ROAD

MILL ROAD

DEVIZES ROAD

ASHLEY ROAD

COLDHARBOUR RD

GAS LANE

MEADOW RD

YORK ROAD

HULSE ROAD

VICTORIA ROAD

DONALDSON ROAD

RIDGEWAY ROAD

NETHERAVON RD

WORDSWORTH ROAD

HAMILTON ROAD

WYNDHAM ROAD

BOURNE HILL

ROLLESTONE STREET

ENDLESS STREET

BEDWIN STREET

SALT LANE

GREENCROFT STREET

CHIPPER LANE

OLD BOAR ROW

WINCHESTER STREET

MILFORD STREET

BROWN STREET

GIGANT STREET

CATHERINE STREET

IVY ST

TRINITY STREET

ST ANN STREET

THE FRIARY

FRIARY LANE

EXETER STREET

ST JOHN'S

NEW ST

NEW CANAL

SILVER ST

HIGH STREET

BRIDGE ST

CRANE ST

CRANEBRIDGE RD

WATER LANE

FISHERTON STREET

AVON APPROACH

ST MARKS ROAD

PARK STREET

COLLEGE STREET

ESTCOURT ROAD

RAMPART ROAD

ALBANY ROAD

BELLE VUE

SCOTS LANE

AVON

NEW BRIDGE ROAD

ST NICHOLAS ROAD

HARNHAM ROAD

AYLESWADE ROAD

OLD BLANDFORD ROAD

NEW HARNHAM ROAD

BRITFORD LANE

QUEEN STREET

N

0   300 yds

ACCOMMODATION	
Clovelly Hotel	3
Glenlyn Guest House	5
Old Bakery	2
The Old Bell	6
Victoria Lodge	1
Youth Hostel	4

© Crown copyright

spire – with unusual sensitivity, the local planners have imposed a height limit on new construction. Unfortunately, the condition of the cathedral itself remains problematic, and scaffolding is likely to remain a feature of its elegant silhouette for the foreseeable future. The town itself sprang into existence in the early thirteenth century, when the bishopric was moved from **Old Sarum**, an ancient Iron Age hill fort which now stands on the northern fringe of the town, just a bit closer than **Wilton House** to the west, one of Wiltshire's great houses.

The City

Begun in 1220, **Salisbury Cathedral** (daily: May–Sept 7am–8.15pm; Oct–April 7am–6.15pm; £3 donation requested) was mostly completed within forty years and is thus uniquely consistent in its style, with one extremely prominent exception – the **spire**, which was added a century later and at 404 feet is the highest in England. Its survival is something of a miracle, for the foundations penetrate only about six feet into marshy ground, and when Christopher Wren surveyed it he found the spire to be leaning almost two and a half feet out of true. The tie-rods inserted by Wren arrested the problem, but didn't cure it, and engineers have once more been at work on it.

The interior is over-austere after James Wyatt's brisk eighteenth-century tidying, but there's an amazing sense of space and light in its high nave, despite the sombre pillars of grey Purbeck marble, which are visibly bowing beneath the weight they bear. Monuments and carved tombs line the walls, where they were neatly placed by Wyatt, and in the north aisle there's a fascinating clock dating from 1386, one of the oldest functioning clock mechanisms in Europe. Other features not to miss are the vaulted colonnades of the **cloisters** and the octagonal **chapter house** (late April to early Sept Mon–Sat 9.30am–7.45pm, Sun 9.30am–5.30pm; early Sept to late April daily 9.30am–5.30pm; 30p), its walls decorated with a frieze of scenes from the Old Testament. The **library**, which is only open for research purposes, contains a rare original copy of the Magna Carta.

Surrounding the cathedral is **The Close**, the largest and most impressive in the country, a peaceful precinct of lawns and mellow old buildings. Most of the houses have seemly Georgian facades, though some, like the Bishop's Palace and the deanery, date from the thirteenth century. **Mompesson House**, built by a wealthy merchant in 1701, is a fine example of a Queen Anne house and contains some beautifully furnished eighteenth-century rooms and a superbly carved staircase – the entry price includes a thirty-minute guided tour (April–Oct Mon–Wed, Sat & Sun noon–5.30pm; £3.40; NT). The other building to head for in The Close is the **King's House**, in which you'll find the **Salisbury and South Wiltshire Museum** (July & Aug Mon–Sat 10am–5pm, Sun 2–5pm; rest of year closed Sun; £3) – an absorbing account of local history. It includes a good section on Stonehenge as well as focusing on the life and times of Keith Pitt-Rivers, the father of modern archeology who excavated many of Wiltshire's prehistoric sites, including Avebury (see p.244).

The Close's **North Gate** opens onto the centre's older streets, where narrow pedestrianized alleyways bear names like Fish Row and Salt Lane, which are indicative of their trading origin. Many half-timbered houses and inns have survived all over the centre, and the last of four market crosses, **Poultry Cross**, stands on stilts in Silver Street, near the Market Square. Salisbury's market, held on Tuesdays and Saturdays, still serves a large agricultural area, as it did in earlier times when the city grew wealthy on the wool trade.

Practicalities

Trains arrive half a mile west of the centre, on South Western Road; the **bus station** lies north of the Market Place, on Endless Street. The **tourist office** is on Fish Row, just off the Market Place (May, June & Sept Mon–Sat 9.30am–6pm, Sun 10.30am–4.30pm; July & Aug Mon–Sat 9.30am–7pm, Sun 10.30am–5pm; Oct–April Mon–Sat 9.30am–5pm; ☎01722/334956).

For **accommodation**, try the *Victoria Lodge*, 61 Castle St (☎01722/320586, *viclodge@interalpha.co.uk*; ③), one of several inexpensive B&Bs along this road; the *Clovelly Guest House*, on Mill Road (☎01722/322055, *clovelly.hotel@virgin.net*; ③) near the train station; or the oak-beamed *Old Bakery*, 35 Bedwin St (☎01722/320100; ②), closer to the city centre. *The Old Bell*, 2 St Ann St (☎01722/327958; ②), is an attractive inn near the cathedral, or else there's *Glen Lyn Guest House*, 6 Bellamy Lane, Milford Hill (☎01722/327880, *glen.lyn@btinternet.com*; ②), ten minutes' walk east of the centre. Salisbury's **youth hostel** is in a 220-year-old building ten minutes' walk east of the cathedral, on Milford Hill (☎01722/327572, *salisbury@yha.org.uk*). *Salisbury Camping and Caravanning Club Site*, Hudson's Field (☎01722/320713), is a well-appointed **campsite** a mile and a half north of Salisbury close to Old Sarum (see below).

For **food and drink**, sample the popular *Michael Snell Tea Rooms*, on St Thomas's Square, or the *Bishop's Mill Tavern*, a popular pub with outdoor seating, right in the city centre on Bridge Street. Another pub worth mentioning is the atmospheric *Haunch of Venison* on Minster Street, which also serves good food. The atmospheric fifteenth-century *Pheasant Inn*, Salt Lane, serves inexpensive, traditional pub food and good vegetarian dishes. *Café Prague*, 2 Salt Lane, is a comfortable café-pub behind the bus station, with good atmosphere and mellow sounds.

Old Sarum

The ruins of **OLD SARUM** (daily: April–Sept 10am–6pm; Oct 10am–5pm; Nov–March 10am–4pm; £2; EH) occupy a bleak hilltop site two miles north of the city centre; it's an easy thirty-minute walk from Salisbury, but there are also plenty of buses that make the journey if you'd prefer not to walk: take #3, #5, #7, #8, #9 or #X19 (Sat only). Possibly occupied up to 5000 years ago, then developed as an Iron Age fort whose double protective ditches remain, it was settled by Romans and Saxons before the Norman bishopric of Sherborne was moved here in the 1070s. Within a couple of decades a new cathedral had been consecrated, and a large religious community was living alongside the soldiers in the central castle. Old Sarum was an uncomfortable place, parched and windswept, and in 1220 the dissatisfied clergy – additionally at loggerheads with the castle's occupants – appealed to the pope for permission to decamp to Salisbury (still known officially as New Sarum). When permission was granted, the stone from the cathedral was commandeered for Salisbury's gateways, and once the church had gone the population waned. By the nineteenth century Old Sarum was deserted, but it continued to exist as a political constituency (William Pitt was one of its representatives), the most notorious of the "rotten boroughs", returning two MPs right up until the 1832 Reform Act.

Wilton

WILTON, five miles west of Salisbury, is renowned for its carpet industry and the splendid **Wilton House** (Easter–Oct daily 10.30am–5.30pm, last entry 1hr before closing; £6.75), of which Daniel Defoe wrote, "One cannot be said to have seen anything that a man of curiosity would think worth seeing in this county, and not have been at Wilton House." The Tudor house, built for the first Earl of Pembroke on the site of a dissolved Benedictine abbey, was ruined by fire in 1647 and rebuilt by Inigo Jones, whose classic hallmarks can be seen in the sumptuous Single Cube and Double Cube rooms, so called because of their precise dimensions. Sir Philip Sidney, illustrious Elizabethan courtier and poet, wrote part of his magnum opus *Arcadia* here – the dado round the Single Cube Room illustrates scenes from the book. The easel **paintings** are what makes Wilton really special, however – the collection includes Van Dyck, Rembrandt, two of the Breugel family, Poussin, Andrea del Sarto and Tintoretto. In the grounds, the famous **Palladian Bridge** has been joined by ancillary attractions including an adventure playground, garden centre and an audio-visual show on the colourful earls of Pembroke, all designed to subsidize the cost of upkeep.

Salisbury Plain

The Ministry of Defence is the landlord of much of **SALISBURY PLAIN**, the 100,000 acres of chalky upland to the north of Salisbury. Flags warn casual trespassers away from MoD firing ranges and tank-training grounds, while rather stricter security cordons off such secretive establishments as the research centre at Porton Down, Britain's centre for chemical and biological warfare. As elsewhere, the army's residency has ironically saved much of the Plain from modern agricultural chemicals, thereby inadvertently nurturing species all but extinct in more trampled landscapes.

Though now largely deserted except by forces' families living in ugly, temporary-looking barracks quarters, Salisbury Plain was once positively thronged with communities. Stone Age, Bronze Age and Iron Age settlements left hundreds of burial mounds scattered over the chalklands, as well as major complexes at Danebury, Badbury, Figsbury, Old Sarum and, of course, the great circle of **Stonehenge**. North of Salisbury Plain, beyond the A342 Andover–Devizes road, lies the softer Vale of Pewsey, traversed by the Kennet and Avon canal. **Marlborough**, to the north of the Vale, is the centre for another cluster of ancient sites, including the huge stone circle of **Avebury**, the mysterious grassy mound of **Silbury Hill** and the chamber graves of **West Kennet**. Malmesbury, though in Wiltshire, is covered in the following chapter, as it feels more closely allied to the Cotswolds area than to the rest of its county, from which it's cut off by the M4 and rail line.

Stonehenge

No ancient structure in England arouses more controversy than **Stonehenge** (daily Mid-March to May & Sept to mid-Oct 9.30am–6pm; June–Aug 9am–7pm; mid-Oct to end Oct 9.30am–5pm; end Oct to mid-March 9.30am–4pm; £4; NT & EH), that mysterious ring of monoliths nine miles north of Salisbury. While archeologists argue over whether it was a place of ritual sacrifice and sun-worship, an astronomical calculator or a royal palace, the guardians of the site struggle to accommodate its year-round crowds, resentful at no longer being able to walk among the stones. Annual battles between the police and gatherings of Druids and New Age travellers trying to celebrate the summer solstice are a thing of the past since the passage of the draconian Criminal Justice Act – but the site is nonetheless securely patrolled on midsummer's dawn. Conservation of Stonehenge, one of UNESCO's 380 designated World Heritage Sites, is obviously an urgent priority, and the current custodians are trying to address the dissatisfaction that many feel on visiting this landmark. A new visitor centre is on the drawing board, but in the meantime, visitors are issued with handsets programmed to dispense a range of information on the site – some of the soundtrack is interesting, but much is misleading and patronizing.

What exists today is only a small part of the original prehistoric complex, as many of the outlying stones were plundered by medieval and later farmers for building materials. The construction of Stonehenge is thought to have taken place in several stages. In about 3000 BC the outer circular bank and ditch were constructed, and the massive Heel Stone placed outside the entrance to the central enclosure; just inside the ditch was dug a ring of 56 pits, which at a later date was filled with a mixture of earth and human ash. Around 2100 BC the first stone circle was raised within the earthworks, comprising approximately eighty great blocks of dolerite (bluestone), whose ultimate source was Preseli in Wales. Some archeologists have suggested that these monoliths were found lying on Salisbury Plain, having been borne down from the Welsh mountains by a glacier in the last Ice Age, but the lack of any other glacial debris on the plain would seem to disprove this theory. It really does seem to be the case that the stones were cut from quarries in Preseli and dragged or floated here on rafts, a prodigious task in view of the fact that some are 25 feet high and weigh as much as forty tons. Scientists recently claimed to have dated a bluestone's removal from its source, which may finally solve some part of the enigma.

The crucial phase in the creation of the site came in 1500 BC, when the incomplete bluestone circle was transformed by the construction of a circle of 25 **trilithons** (two uprights crossed by a lintel) and an inner horseshoe formation of five trilithons. Hewn from Marlborough Downs sandstone, these colossal stones (called sarsens) were carefully dressed and worked – for example, to compensate for perspectival distortion the uprights have a slight swelling in the middle, the same trick as the builders of the Parthenon were to employ several hundred years later. More bluestones were used to form a small circle and horseshoe within the trilithons, but the purpose of all this work remains baffling. The symmetry and location of the site (a slight rise in a flat valley with even views of the horizon in all directions), as well as its alignment towards the points of sunrise and sunset on the summer and winter solstices, tend to support the supposition that it was some sort of observatory or time-measuring device.

Marlborough

An obvious base from which to explore Salisbury Plain is **MARLBOROUGH**, a peaceful spot now that the M4 deflects traffic from the old stagecoach route passing through the town. It's a handsome town too: the wide High Street, a dignified assembly of Georgian buildings, has a fine Perpendicular church standing at each end, and half-timbered cottages rambling up the alleyways behind. The famous public school is not especially old – it was established in 1843 – but incorporates an ancient coaching inn among its red-brick buildings.

Marlborough **tourist office** is in the car park on George Lane, accessible from the High Street via Hilliers Yard (Easter–Oct Mon–Sat 10am–5pm, Sun 10.30am–4.30pm; Nov–Easter Mon–Sat 10am–4.30pm; ☎01672/513989) and there are several inns and guest houses offering **accommodation** along the High Street. Top of the range are *Ivy House* (☎01672/515333; ⑤) and the *Castle & Ball* (☎01672/515201; ④); less expensive B&B options include the *Merlin* pub (☎01672/512151; ④) and the guest house at 5 Reeds Ground, London Road (☎01672/513926; no credit cards; ①). **Eating** is no problem in central Marlborough: the bistro food at *Ivy House* is reasonable, while the *Polly Tea Rooms* serves good snacks and ice cream.

Silbury Hill, West Kennet and Avebury

The neat green mound of **Silbury Hill**, five miles west of Marlborough, is probably overlooked by a majority of drivers whizzing by on the A4. At 130 feet it's no great height, but when you realize it's the largest prehistoric artificial mound in Europe, and was made by a people using nothing more than primitive spades, it commands more respect. It was probably constructed around 2600 BC, but like so many of the sites of Salisbury Plain, no one knows quite what it was for, though the likelihood is that it was a burial mound. You can't actually walk on the hill – so having admired it briefly from the car park, cross the road to the footpath that leads half a mile to the **West Kennet**

Long Barrow. Dating from about 3250 BC, this was definitely a chamber tomb – nearly fifty burials have been discovered at West Kennet.

Immediately to the west, the village of **AVEBURY** stands in the midst of a **stone circle** (free access; NT & EH) that rivals Stonehenge – the individual stones are generally smaller, but the circle itself is much wider and more complex. A massive earthwork 20-feet high and 1400-feet across encloses the main circle, which is approached by four causeways across the inner ditch, two of them leading into wide avenues stretching over a mile beyond the circle. The best guess is that it was built soon after 2500 BC, and presumably had a similar ritual or religious function to Stonehenge's. The structure of Avebury's diffuse circle is quite difficult to grasp but there are plans on the site, and you can get an excellent overview at the **Alexander Keiller Museum**, at the western entrance to the site, which displays excavated material and explanatory information (April–Oct daily 10am–6pm; Nov–March Mon–Sat 10am–4pm; £1.70; NT & EH). Thus clued up, you can wander round the peaceful circle, accompanied by sheep and cattle grazing unconcernedly among the stones.

Avebury is on good **bus** routes from Marlborough and Devizes (see below), with *Stone's Restaurant* providing teas and snacks, and the *Red Lion* pub also offering **accommodation** (☎01672/539266; ②).

Devizes

DEVIZES, seven miles down the A361 from Avebury at the mouth of the Vale of Pewsey, is a pleasant place, with some attractive eighteenth-century houses, a stately semicircular market place and a couple of fine churches, St Mary's and St John's. It's chiefly worth a stop, however, for the excellent **museum** at 41 Long St (Mon–Sat 10am–5pm; £2, free Mon), housing an exceptional collection of prehistoric finds from barrows and henges throughout the county. Star exhibit is the so-called *Marlborough Bucket*, decorated with bronze reliefs from the first century BC.

Devizes has a very helpful **tourist office** at Cromwell House, Market Place (Mon–Sat 9.30am–5pm; ☎01380/729408). The best place **to stay** is the *Castle Hotel* on New Park Street, a former coaching inn with a bar and restaurant (☎01380/729300; ④); less expensive are the *Craven B&B* on Station Road (☎01380/723514; no credit cards; ③) and the *White Bear Inn* on Monday Market Street (☎01380/722583; no credit cards; ③). If you just want to **eat**, try the *Wiltshire Kitchen* across from the tourist office off the market square, which serves good lunches and snacks, as does *The Cheesecake* on Market Place. Also on Market Place, you'll find the *Seafoods Restaurant*, a fish-and-chip takeaway which also provides more substantial sit-down meals at cheap prices.

Lacock and Corsham Court

LACOCK, ten miles northwest of Devizes, is the perfect English feudal village, albeit one gentrified by the National Trust to within a hair's-breadth of natural life, and besieged by tourists all summer. Appropriately for so photogenic a spot, it has a fascinating museum dedicated to the founding father of photography, Henry Fox Talbot, a member of the dynasty which has lived in the local abbey since it passed to Sir William Sharington on the Dissolution of the Monasteries in 1539. Sir William's descendant, Fox Talbot, was the first person to produce a photographic negative, and the **Fox Talbot Museum** (March–Oct daily 11am–5.30pm; £3.60; NT), in a sixteenth-century barn by the abbey gates, captures something of the excitement he must have experienced as the dim outline of an oriel window in the abbey steadily imprinted itself on a piece of silver nitrate paper. The postage-stamp-sized result is on display in the museum. The **abbey** itself (April–Oct Mon & Wed–Sun 1–5.30pm; £3.60; combined ticket with museum £5.70; NT) preserves a few monastic fragments amid the eighteenth-century Gothic, while the church of **St Cyriac** contains the opulent tomb of the nefarious Sir William Sharington, buried beneath a splendid barrel-vaulted roof.

Another sight within a short drive of Lacock is **Corsham Court** (April–Oct Tues–Sun 11am–5.30pm; Nov & Jan–March Sat & Sun 2–4.30pm; £4.50), three miles to the west. It dates from Elizabethan times, though what you see now bears the Georgian stamp of Nash and Capability Brown, and the house contains a fine collection of art, including pieces by Caravaggio, Rubens, Reynolds and Michelangelo. The village of **Corsham** is another dignified little cloth-making town of Bath stone, riddled with underground limestone quarries and a long railway tunnel engineered by Brunel. The delightfully Chaucerian-sounding hostelry *At the Sign of the Angel*, back in Lacock, is a good if expensive **hotel** and **restaurant** (☎01249/730230; ⑥).

Ten miles east of Corsham, off the A342 Chippenham–Devizes road and just outside the village of Calne, **Bowood House** (April–Oct daily 11am–5.30pm; £5.50) was first built in the seventeenth century, though its present appearance is the fruit of a thorough overhaul in the eighteenth century by such eminent architects as Henry Keene, Charles Barry and Robert Adam. The last was chiefly responsible for what's left of the main building, including the great south front and the Orangery. The library owes more to Charles Robert Cockerell, architect of Oxford's Ashmolean Museum, who also built the Neoclassical chapel. But it is the magnificent grounds of Bowood that are the real draw, with rhododendron gardens, a Doric temple on the banks of its placid lake and a waterfall in the woods; there's also an adventure playground for kids, and a restaurant.

Bradford on Avon and around

With its buildings of mellow auburn stone, reminiscent of the townscapes over the county border in Bath and the Cotswolds, **BRADFORD ON AVON** is the most appealing town in the northwest corner of Wiltshire. Sheltering against a steep wooded slope, it takes its name from its "broad ford" across the Avon, replaced in the thirteenth century by a **bridge** that was in turn largely rebuilt in the seventeenth. The domed structure at one end is a quaint old jail converted from a chapel. The local industry, based on textiles like that of its Yorkshire namesake, was revolutionized with the arrival of Flemish weavers in 1659, and many of the town's handsome buildings reflect the prosperity of this period. Yet Bradford's most significant building is the tiny **St Laurence Church** on Church Street, an outstanding example of Saxon architecture dating from about 700. Wrecked by Viking invaders, and later used as a school and a simple dwelling, it was rehabilitated by a local vicar in 1856. Its distinctive features are the carved angels over the chancel arch.

Bradford's **train station** is on St Margaret's Street close to the town centre. A well-equipped **tourist office** lies near the bridge at 34 Silver St (daily: April–Oct 10am–5pm; Nov–March 10am–4pm; ☎01225/865797). Bradford has a good range of **accommodation**, none more characterful than *Bradford Old Windmill*, a non-smoking B&B at 4 Mason's Lane (☎01225/866842; ⑨) that offers an imaginative vegetarian menu. *Priory Steps* (☎01225/862230; ⑨), closer to the centre on Newtown, has excellent views over a roofscape of weavers' cottages. The *Riverside Inn*, 49 St Margaret's St (☎01225/863526; ②), lives up to its name, with private facilities in all rooms. For light **lunches**, try the *Bridge Tea Rooms* on Bridge Street; for more substantial food, head for the *Bunch of Grapes* **pub** on Silver Street.

travel details

Trains

Bournemouth to: Brockenhurst (3 hourly; 30min); Dorchester (hourly; 40min); London (2 hourly; 1hr 45min–2hr); Poole (2–4 hourly; 15min); Southampton (2–3 hourly; 30min); Weymouth (hourly; 1hr); Winchester (3 hourly; 1hr).

Dorchester to: Bournemouth (hourly; 40min); Brockenhurst (hourly; 1hr); London (hourly; 1hr); Weymouth (hourly; 10min).

Portsmouth to: London (3–6 hourly; 1hr 30min–2hr); Southampton (2 hourly; 50min); Winchester (hourly; 1hr).

Ryde to: Shanklin (2 hourly; 30min).

Salisbury to: London (hourly; 1hr 30min); Portsmouth (hourly; 1hr 15min); Southampton (1–3 hourly; 30min).

Southampton to: Bournemouth (3–4 hourly; 30min); Brockenhurst (2–3 hourly; 15min); London (2 hourly; 1hr 15min); Portsmouth (2 hourly; 45min); Salisbury (1–3 hourly; 30min); Weymouth (hourly; 1hr 30min); Winchester (4 hourly; 20min).

Winchester to: Bournemouth (3 hourly; 1hr); London (2–3 hourly; 1hr); Portsmouth (hourly; 1hr); Southampton (2 hourly; 20min).

Buses

Bournemouth to: London (hourly; 2hr 30min); Lyndhurst (8 daily; 1hr 30min); Poole (every 10min; 20min).

Dorchester to: Bournemouth (3 daily; 1hr 15min); London (3 daily; 3hr–4hr 40min); Poole (4 daily; 1hr 15min); Salisbury (2 daily; 1hr 45min); Weymouth (4 hourly; 30min).

Lymington to: Beaulieu (6 daily; 40min).

Lyndhurst to: Bournemouth (7 daily; 1hr 20min); Southampton (hourly; 30min–1hr).

Poole to: Bournemouth (every 10min; 20min); Corfe (hourly; 1hr).

Portsmouth to: London (10 daily; 2hr 30min); Southampton (hourly; 30min); Winchester (hourly; 1hr 40min).

Salisbury to: London (2–3 daily; 2hr 30min–3hr); Poole (5 daily; 1hr 40min); Stonehenge (hourly; 40min).

Southampton to: London (hourly; 2hr 30min); Winchester (3 hourly; 50min).

Weymouth to: Dorchester (4 hourly; 30min).

Winchester to: London (7 daily; 2hr); Portsmouth (hourly; 1hr 40min); Southampton (3 hourly; 50min).

CHAPTER FOUR

FROM LONDON
TO THE SEVERN

Southern central England, the slab of land running west **from London to the River Severn**, is a disparate region of Roman towns and new towns, tree-clad hills and rolling downs, encompassing no fewer than six counties. The chief physical link within this swathe of England is the **River Thames**, whose 215-mile course from its source in the western Cotswolds makes it the second longest river in the country. Transport routes create a further continuity, the oldest of them being the **Ridgeway**, a prehistoric track – and now a national trail – running northeast from Wiltshire and continuing along the length of the Chiltern Hills. Of more practical use to the majority of visitors, the M40/A40 slices right through the heart of the region, linking London to Gloucester via Oxford and the Cotswolds, while the M4 motorway and the rail line between London and Bristol mark the region's approximate southern edge. Densely populated, this is one (especially well-heeled) part of England where remote and "undiscovered" spots are thin on the ground.

Of the places covered in this chapter, a prime target is Hertfordshire's **St Albans**, an ancient and dignified town with Roman remains and a superb cathedral – but marooned amidst a knot of motorways and new towns on the fringes of London. These new towns – places like Welwyn Garden City and Hemel Hempstead – have little obvious appeal, but there are a few surprises hereabouts, not least **Hatfield House**, one of the country's finest ancestral homes.

The best of adjacent **Buckinghamshire**, just to the west, lies in the **Chiltern Hills**. These picturesque chalk uplands, with their heavy covering of beech trees, rise near Luton, beside the M1, and stretch southwest across Buckinghamshire before petering out at the Thames in Oxfordshire. The range provides some of the best walking in the region, chiefly around **Marlow** and **Henley-on-Thames**, either of which makes a convenient base, with the tiny villages that dot the Chilterns possessing a scattering of accommodation too. **Berkshire**, which extends west from the M25 to just beyond

---

ACCOMMODATION PRICE CODES

Throughout this guide, hotel and B&B accommodation is priced on a scale of ① to ⑨, the number indicating the **lowest price** you could expect to pay per night in that establishment for a **double room** in high season. The prices indicated by the codes are as follows:

① under £40	④ £60–70	⑦ £110–150
② £40–50	⑤ £70–90	⑧ £150–200
③ £50–60	⑥ £90–110	⑨ over £200

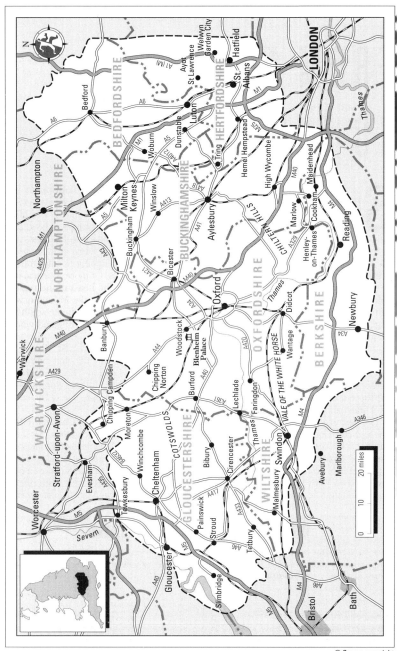

© Crown copyright

Newbury, is blighted in its eastern part by workaday towns such as **Reading** and Slough, though the former does host two of the most prestigious rock festivals in Europe. By contrast, the Berkshire Downs, divided from the Chilterns by the Thames but linked to them by the Ridgeway, stretch west beyond the county boundary to include the **Vale of White Horse**, one of the highlights of this whole region.

Bordering Berkshire to the north, **Oxfordshire** is firmly centred on its county town. With its ancient university, superb museums and lively student population, **Oxford** can keep you busy for days, and it's an excellent base for the **Cotswolds**, which lie mostly in **Gloucestershire**. Throughout the Cotswolds, beautifully preserved mansions and churches attest to the fortunes made through the medieval wool trade, and the remarkable continuity of Cotswold architecture has created villages as attractive as any in England, though the tourist deluge makes some spots nightmarish in summer. Tourism is less of a nuisance in the southern areas of the Cotswolds, around the busy working towns of **Cirencester** and **Stroud**, and of course there's plenty of good walking country in which to escape the crowds.

In the west, the land drops sharply from the Cotswold escarpment down to **Cheltenham**, an elegant Regency spa town most famous these days for its horse racing. It's a rather staid place, however, with much less to offer than **Gloucester**, with its superb cathedral and rejuvenated docklands. From here, the Vale of Gloucester follows the route of the **River Severn** northeast towards Worcestershire, the stone cottages of the Cotswolds giving way to the thatched, half-timbered and red-brick houses which are characteristic of **Tewkesbury**, a solidly provincial town with a superb abbey.

The line between London's Paddington station and Bristol provides the backbone of the **rail network** through this region, with branch lines running north to Reading, Maidenhead, Didcot and Swindon. Trains from King's Cross, St Pancras, Euston and Marylebone stations serve the northeasterly area, including St Albans, Bedford and the northern Chilterns. The area covered in this chapter is threaded by four motorways, the M1, M40, M4 and M25, giving swift access from all sides, whether by private car or **bus**.

St Albans and around

ST ALBANS is one of the most appealing towns on the peripheries of London, its well-blended medley of medieval and modern features grafted onto the site of Verulamium, the town founded by the Romans soon after the invasion of 43 AD. Boudicca and her followers burned this settlement to the ground eighteen years later, but reconstruction was swift and the town grew into a major administrative base. It was here, in 209 AD, that a Roman soldier became the country's first Christian martyr when he was beheaded for giving shelter to a priest. Pilgrims later flocked to the town that had come to bear his name, where the place of execution was marked by a hilltop cathedral, once one of the largest churches in the Christian world.

St Albans' best-known attraction is its **cathedral**, but the town also possesses the outstanding **Verulamium Museum**, home to several breathtaking Roman mosaics, as well as a likeable riverside park and a number of charming old streets. All the town's main sights are within easy walking distance of each other, making St Albans an ideal day out, but if you do decide to stay the night be sure to try out some of the excellent pubs.

The City

You can begin a tour of the city by climbing the 93 steps to the top of the fifteenth-century **Clock Tower** on the High Street (Easter to Sept Sat & Sun 10.30am–4.30pm;

30p), a tight squeeze but worth it for the view. The colossal brick and flint **Cathedral** (daily 9am–5.30pm; £2.50 donation requested), looming to the south, is accessible down a narrow passageway across from the foot of the tower. An abbey was constructed here in 1077, on the site of a Saxon abbey founded by King Offa of Mercia, and despite subsequent alterations – including the ugly nineteenth-century west front – the legacy of the Normans remains the most impressive aspect. The sheer scale of their design is breathtaking: the nave, almost 300 feet long, is the longest medieval nave in Britain, even if it isn't the most harmonious – the massive Norman pillars on the north side stand out from those in the later Early English style opposite. Two- and three-tone geometric designs decorate the Norman arches in the nave and at the central crossing, where the impact of the original design reaches its peak with the mighty Norman tower.

A few yards to the west of the cathedral's main entrance, the **abbey gateway** is the only other part of the original complex to have survived the Dissolution. From here, Abbey Mill Lane leads down past the *Fighting Cocks* (one of the oldest pubs in the country) and across the trickle of the River Ver to **Verulamium Park**, whose sloping lawns and duck-happy ponds occupy the site of the Roman city. The park holds a scattering of Roman remains – primarily fragments of the old Roman wall and the remains of a town house with its underfloor heating system (hypocaust) – but these are hardly riveting. Instead, follow the signs to the **Verulamium Museum** (Mon–Sat 10am–5pm, Sun 2–5pm; £3), which occupies an attractive circular building on the northern edge of the park. Inside, a series of well-conceived displays illustrate and explain life in Roman Britain, but these are eclipsed by the **mosaic** room, containing five wonderful floor mosaics unearthed here on the site of Verulamium in the 1930s and 1950s. Dated to about 200 AD, the *Sea God Mosaic* has created its share of academic debate, with some arguing it depicts a god of nature with stag antler horns rather than a sea god with lobster claws, but there's no disputing the subject of the *Lion Mosaic*, in which a lion carries the bloodied head of a stag in its jaws. The most beautiful of the five is the *Shell Mosaic*, a simply gorgeous work of art whose semi-circular design depicts a beautifully crafted scallop shell within a border made up of rolling waves.

Close by, the **Verulamium Theatre** (daily: April–Sept 10am–5pm; Oct–March 10am–4pm; £1.50), across the busy road from the museum, was built around 140 AD but reduced to the status of municipal rubbish dump by the fifth century. It's nothing but a small hollow in comparison with the Colosseum, but the site is impressive if only for the fact that nothing else quite like it exists in Britain. From here, you can walk back to the centre along St Michael's Street, over one of the prettier stretches of the Ver, past a sixteenth-century **watermill** (now a museum and café; Easter–Oct Tues–Sat 11am–6pm, Sun noon–6pm; Nov–Easter closes 4.45pm; free), and up the gently curving **Fishpool Street**, a quiet road lined with medieval inns and handsome Georgian houses.

Practicalities

Trains bound for Bedford from London King's Cross arrive at St Albans' City Station, from where it's a ten-minute walk up the hill to the main drag, St Peter's Street. Trains from Euston serve the small Abbey Station a similar distance from the centre at the bottom of Holywell Hill, a southerly continuation of St Peter's Street. Most **buses** terminate at City Station, but virtually all services stop along St Peter's Street too. The **tourist office** is in the Town Hall, on the Market Place at the bottom of St Peter's Street (Easter–Oct Mon–Sat 9.30am–5.30pm; Nov–Easter Mon–Sat 10am–4pm; ☎01727/864511).

As for accommodation, there are several inexpensive **B&Bs** near City Station, including the *Care Inns*, 29 Alma Rd (☎01727/867310; no credit cards; ②), a Victorian house with three comfortable and attractively furnished en-suite bedrooms. Fishpool Street is, however, a much prettier spot to head for and it's here you'll find the pleasant *Black Lion Inn*, at no. 198 (℡01727/851786; ②), an ancient pub with sixteen agreeable rooms. Indeed, you can't move for **pubs** in St Albans – the Campaign for Real Ale has its headquarters here, and seems to have a benign influence. Benskins is, by most accounts, the brew to look for. *The Goat*, on Sopwell Lane off Holywell Hill, serves some of the best food (not Fri–Sun eve) and beer in town, and has jazz on Sunday lunchtimes, while the *Blue Anchor*, on Fishpool Street, is a more solidly local pub with an open fire in winter and garden seating in summer. The antique *Fighting Cocks*, on Abbey Mill Lane, has been chopped around a bit and does get mightily crowded on sunny summer days, but still has lots of enjoyable nooks and crannies to nurse a pint. As for **restaurants**, the low prices at *La Cosa Nostra*, a no-nonsense Italian place at 62 Lattimore Rd (℡01727/832658; closed Sun), off Victoria Street out near City Station, is a popular spot, and the best Indian restaurant in town is the moderately priced *New Gulshan Tandoori*, 141 Victoria St (℡01727/830201).

Hatfield House

Hatfield House, six miles east of St Albans (late March to late Sept Tues–Thurs & Sat noon–4pm, Sun 1–4.30pm; £6), is one of the most impressive houses in England. Henry VIII and his heirs used the original building as a country retreat, though for Elizabeth, kept here by her half-sister Mary, it was more a prison than a home. James I, on inheriting the throne, decided he disliked Hatfield and did a house-swap with his chief minister, Sir Robert Cecil. The new owner, fancying himself as an architect, proceeded to destroy most of the Tudor house, but he died in 1612 shortly before the completion of his work. Cecil's descendants still live here.

From the awesome brick exterior to the dark wood panelling inside, Hatfield House has a grand and heavy atmosphere, but some magnificent Tudor and Jacobean portraits bring the **interior** alive, supplying a roll-call of the important people of the day. Elizabeth I provides a central theme, her memorabilia including a pair of silk stockings and an extraordinary pedigree tracing her descent from Adam and Eve via Noah and King Lear. The banqueting hall survives from the Tudor building but is rarely open, being used mainly for "Elizabethan banquets". The extensive grounds include part of the **formal gardens** laid out by John Tradescant, the greatest gardener ever engaged by the Stuarts.

Hatfield House can be reached easily on public transport. Its entrance is opposite Hatfield town's **train station**, on the King's Cross–Cambridge line; there are also frequent local **buses** from St Albans.

Ayot St Lawrence and Shaw's Corner

The tiny village of **AYOT ST LAWRENCE**, nine miles northeast of St Albans, hides among gentle hills in one of the prettiest corners of Hertfordshire. The village boasts the romantic ruins of a Gothic church and a fine pub, but its fame stems from its association with **George Bernard Shaw**, who lived in the house known as **Shaw's Corner** from 1906 until his death in 1950. The house (April–Oct Wed–Sun 1–5pm; £3.30; NT) has been left much as it was – Shaw's fans may be particularly delighted at the chance to have a pee in the playwright's loo. The shed at the bottom of the garden, where Shaw used to write, is little more than a cell, the only luxuries being a telephone and the hut's ability to revolve in order to maximize the available sunlight.

There is no direct **bus service** to the village: the closest public transport gets is Wheathampstead (B653), two miles to the west and served by weekday buses from Hatfield, St Albans and other nearby towns.

The Chilterns

The chalk downs of the **Chiltern Hills** extend southwest from the humdrum town of Luton, beside the M1, rolling across Buckinghamshire and Oxfordshire as far as the River Thames. Dotted with pretty villages and homely pubs, the Chilterns are particularly delightful just to the south of High Wycombe (and the M40) in the vicinity of **Henley**, a smart Thameside town that makes a good base for exploring the range, though there are hotels and B&Bs in the hills too. This is magnificent walking country and some of the best hikes incorporate stretches of the **Ridgeway National Trail**. Beside the Thames at the southern tip of the Chilterns is **Reading**, skirted by the M4 and of interest for its two big festivals, Reading Rock Festival and the World Music extravaganza, Womad. Almost as popular is **Whipsnade Zoo**, perched high up on the downs at the northern end of the Chilterns.

Woburn Abbey and Safari Park

Not strictly speaking in the Chilterns, but worth a detour neverthless, the grandiloquent Georgian facade of **Woburn Abbey** (guided tours: late March to Sept Mon–Sat 11am–4pm & Sun 11am–5pm; Jan to late March & Oct Sat & Sun 11am–4pm; house & grounds £7; £3.50 with ticket to the safari park) overlooks a huge area of parkland just fifteen miles northwest of Luton via the M1. Called an "abbey" since it was built on the site of a Cistercian foundation, the house is the ancestral pile of the dukes of Bedford, whom Queen Victoria once dismissed as a dull lot. Judging from the family's penchant for canine portraits, she may have had a point, but the lavish state rooms also contain some wonderful paintings, including an exquisite set of **Tudor portraits** hanging in the Long Gallery, most notably the famous *Armada Portrait* of Elizabeth I by George Gower. Elsewhere are works by Van Dyck, Velazquez, Gainsborough and Rembrandt, whilst Reynolds and Canaletto each have a room to themselves.

You can explore the grounds immediately around the house on foot, but only motorists can enter the part given over to **Woburn Safari Park** (March–Oct daily 10am–dusk; Nov–Feb Sat & Sun 11am–3pm; £11.50 in summer; £6.50 rest of year; half price if you've already paid to get into the abbey), the largest drive-through wildlife reserve in Britain. The animals include endangered species such as the African white rhino and bongo antelope, and appear to be in excellent health. A posse of guards tours around on the lookout for drivers in distress, but the main danger is an over-heated engine rather than an attack by an enraged animal. The Safari Park is extraordinarily popular and in high season the traffic can achieve rush-hour congestion, so turn up as early as possible for a quieter experience.

Whipsnade Zoo

Whipsnade Zoo (Mon–Sat 10am–6pm or dusk, Sun 10am–7pm or dusk; £9.50), the free-range menagerie of the Zoological Society of London, perches high up on the downs about six miles southwest of Luton, at the northern end of the Chilterns. Whipsnade takes its educational role seriously and runs a number of major breeding programmes – there's a flourishing cheetah population, and the rare Burmese elephant has also been bred successfully. Most animals, from tigers to wallabies, are kept in large enclosures, separated from the public by a fence or a ditch. You can drive around the zoo (March–Nov £7.50 per car; rest of year free), but it's possible to see everything perfectly well on foot. Alternatively, you could hop on the free Safari bus that stops at the main enclosures, or take a ride in the little steam train which offers an "Asian Railway Safari" as it puffs past herds of elephants and one-horned rhinos.

THE RIDGEWAY

The **Ridgeway** has existed for several thousand years and was probably once part of a route extending from the Dorset coast to the Wash in Norfolk. Today, it comprises one of England's fourteen national trails, running from **Overton Hill**, near Avebury in Wiltshire (see p.244), to **Ivinghoe Beacon**, 85 miles to the northeast near Tring, which is itself just a few miles southwest of Luton. Crossing five counties, the trail avoids densely populated areas, following the top of the chalk downland ridge for most of its course, except where the Thames slices through the ridge at **Goring Gap**, which marks the transition from the wooded valleys of the Chilterns to the more open Berkshire Downs. By and large, the Ridgeway is fairly easy hiking and over half of it is accessible to cyclists and RVs. The prevailing winds mean that it is best walked in a northeasterly direction. The Ridgeway is strewn with prehistoric monuments of one description or another, though the finest archeological remains are in the **Vale of White Horse** and around **Avebury** (see p.267 and p.244). There are several youth hostels within reach of the Ridgeway – most notably the *Ridgeway Centre Youth Hostel* (see Wantage, p.267) – and numerous B&Bs. A *Ridgeway Information and Accommodation Guide* is available from the National Trails Office, Cultural Services, Holton, Oxford OX33 1QQ (☎01865/810224). There's also a useful Web site: *www.nationaltrails.gov.uk*

To reach Whipsnade by **car**, leave the M1 at Junction #9 (approaching from the south) or #12 (from the north) and follow the elephant signs. The nearest **train station** is at Luton, from where there are regular **buses** to the zoo (for details, call ☎0345/788788).

Henley-on-Thames

Three counties – Oxfordshire, Berkshire and Buckinghamshire – meet at **HENLEY-ON-THAMES**, a long-established stopping place for travellers between Oxford and London. Henley is a good-looking, affluent commuter town that is at its prettiest among the brick and half-timbered buildings which flank the main drag, Hart Street, with the Market Place at one end and the easy Georgian curves of Henley Bridge at the other. The bridge is also overlooked by the parish church of St Mary, whose sturdy square tower sports a set of little turrets worked in chequerboard flint and stone. A pleasant spot for most of the year, Henley becomes positively arrogant during the **Royal Regatta**, the world's most important amateur rowing tournament. Established in 1839, it's the boating equivalent of the Ascot races (see p.63), a quintessentially English parade ground for the rich, aristocratic and aspiring, whose champagne-swilling antics are inexplicably found thrilling by large numbers of the hoi polloi. The competitions, featuring past and potential Olympic rowers, run from the last Wednesday in June through to the first week in July. Information is available from the Regatta Headquarters on the Berkshire side of the Thames (☎01491/572153).

The Paddington–Reading rail line runs through Twyford, where you change trains for the five-mile journey north along the branch line to Henley; there are no services on Sundays between September and May. From the **train station**, it's a five-minute walk north to Hart Street, Henley's short main street and most useful reference point. Henley is easy to reach by bus with regular services from Oxford, London and Marlow. **Buses** stop in New Street, just to the north of Hart Street. The **tourist office** is in the basement of the town hall (daily: April–Sept 10am–7pm; Oct–March 10am–4pm; ☎01491/578034), on the Market Place, at the top of Hart Street. Henley has several first-rate **B&Bs**, including the smart and tastefully furnished *Alftrudis*, 8 Norman Ave (☎01491/573099; no credit cards; ②), which occupies a Victorian townhouse a couple of minutes' walk south of Hart Street – take Duke Street and watch for the turning on the right. Another good option is *Lenwade*, 3 Western Rd (☎01491/573468, *lenwadeuk@compuserve.com*; no credit cards; ②), which has three comfortable guest rooms in an attractive, semi-detached, Victorian house about five minutes' walk from Hart Street. The best **hotel** is the *Red Lion*, an old wisteria-clad coaching inn near the bridge on Hart Street (☎01491/572161; ⑤). For **food**, stick to the pubs on Hart Street. The *Angel* by the bridge, the *Three Tuns* and the *Argyll* further up all offer good quality, reasonably-priced bar food and the tasty brews of Brakspears, the local brewery.

Reading

READING is a modern, prosperous town on the south bank of the River Thames, ten miles south of Henley. Guarding the western approaches to the capital, it has always been important, a stopping-off point for kings and queens from earliest times and once home to one of the country's richest abbeys. Henry VIII took care of the abbey, seizing its lands and hanging the abbot from the main gate, and today almost nothing remains of the old town except the shattered remains of the aforementioned abbey, a short walk to the east of the pedestrianized shopping centre.

There is a flourishing **arts scene** in the town, with both the Reading Film Theatre (☎0118/9868497) and the Hexagon Theatre (☎0118/9606060) offering a good programme of shows, but you wouldn't make a beeline for the place were it not for its two big summertime **music festivals**. The first, the three-day **Womad** festival, held each July, is a celebration of World Music Arts and Dance originally inspired by Peter Gabriel. Since the first Womad in 1982, there have been about a hundred spin-off events in twenty countries, but the Reading festival remains the focus, held at the Rivermead Leisure Complex, Richfield Ave, just to the north of the town centre. For details on Womad, write to Millside, Mill Lane, Wiltshire SN13 8PN (☎01225/744494, ticket line ☎0118/9390930, *www.realworld.on.net/womad*). Also held at the Rivermead Leisure Complex, but a little later in the summer, is the **Reading Festival**, also held over three days and featuring many of the big names of contemporary music. Details of who is performing are published in the music press at least a couple of months in advance and tickets are available from record shops across the country. The vast majority of festival-goers **camp on site** and special buses run there in their hundreds, or you can walk from Reading train station – it only takes fifteen minutes.

Reading can be reached by train from London Paddington and Waterloo. The **tourist office**, in the town hall, in the town centre on Blagrave Street (Mon–Fri 10am–5pm; ☎0118/9566226), runs an accommodation-booking service – be sure to reserve a room months in advance if you're planning on being here for either festival.

Oxford and around

The image of **OXFORD** that crystallizes in the minds of most British people is one of upper-class students talking in nasal accents, living in oak-panelled rooms and drinking port into the early hours. While such a vision cannot be dismissed as entirely obsolete, it would be a mistake to reduce the city simply to a bastion of privileged scholarship. The average Oxford student looks much the same as a student from any other university, and what fills the local press is not the latest college gossip but reports of joy-riding on local housing estates. The university might dominate central Oxford both physically and mentally, yet the wider city has developed out of the prosperity generated not by the colleges but by the nearby Cowley factory, which launched Britain's first mass-produced car in the 1920s. Thousands of workers have been laid off over the last decade, but the motor industry remains vital to the city's economy.

Oxford started life late, in Saxon times, and blossomed even later, under the Normans, when the cathedral was built and Oxford was chosen as the royal residence. It seems that the presence of **Henry I**, the so-called "Scholar King", helped attract students in the early twelfth century, their numbers increasing with the expulsion of English students from the Sorbonne in 1167. The first colleges, founded mostly by rich bishops, were essentially ecclesiastical institutions – reflected in both their design (most had cloisters and a chapel) and discipline (until 1877 lecturers were not allowed to marry, and women have been granted degrees only since 1920). That said, each of the 39 colleges has its own character and often a particular label, whether it's the richest (St John's), most left-wing (Wadham and Balliol) or most public-school-dominated (Christ Church). Collegiate rivalries are long established, usually based upon success in sports, and so is tension between the university and the city (or "Town" and "Gown"), with the privileges accrued by the colleges particularly resented – until 1950, for example, the university had two MPs of its own. This flares into the occasional confrontation, but a non-communicative coexistence is more typical.

For all its idiosyncrasies, Oxford should not be missed, and can keep you occupied for several days. The university buildings include some of England's greatest architecture, and the city can also boast some excellent museums and numerous bars and restaurants. Getting there is easy too: from London the journey takes just an hour by train and ninety minutes by bus.

Arrival, information and accommodation

Oxford **train station** is fifteen minutes' walk west of the centre, linked by a shuttle bus. Long-distance National Express **buses** terminate at the Gloucester Green bus station at the bottom of George Street, less than five minutes from the centre; many services, including private buses from London, make other city stops prior to arriving at Gloucester Green, while some buses from the surrounding area, including the Cotswolds, terminate on St Giles instead. Intense competition between companies means that **city buses** run reasonably frequently, most leaving from Cornmarket and the High Street. The Oxford Bus Company produces a useful map of routes within the city, which you can pick up at the Gloucester Green station or at the **tourist office** in the Old School, also in Gloucester Green (summer Mon–Sat 9.30am–5pm, Sun 10am–3.30pm; rest of year Mon–Sat 9.30am–5pm; ☎01865/726871), where you can find copies of the free annual *Oxford Guide*, containing a wealth of information about the city sights, as well as services, pubs and restaurants in the area (copies are less easy to find in winter). Oxford's frustrating one-way system and lack of convenient parking space means **driving** around town can be a hassle, so use the **Park and Ride** scheme which operates from the main access routes into the city.

Expensive **hotels** predominate in the heart of Oxford, although there are a few cheaper options close to the train station. While you won't find a great number of **B&Bs** right in the centre, there are plenty scattered along all the main roads heading out of the city, mostly within a half-hour walk or a short bus ride. Wherever you stay, book ahead in high season; you can do this yourself by telephone, or through the tourist office, which levies a £2.50 charge (plus a returnable ten percent deposit).

Hotels & B&Bs

Becket House, 5 Becket St (☎01865/724675). Close to the train station, but less convivial than most. ①.

Cotswold House, 363 Banbury Rd (☎01865/310558). A topnotch B&B, three miles north of the centre (bus #2 or 7). ④.

Isis Guest House, 45–53 Iffley Rd (☎01865/741024). Large college house, just across Magdalen Bridge, open from late June through September; good value. ①.

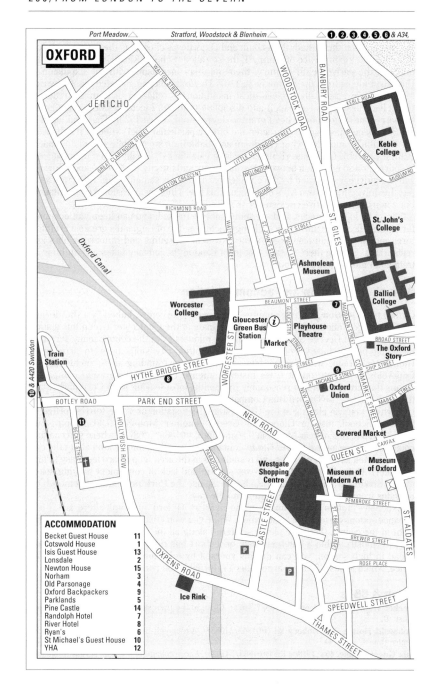

Port Meadow △   Stratford, Woodstock & Blenheim △   △ ❶,❷,❸,❹,❺,❻ & A34,

OXFORD

JERICHO

WALTON STREET

WOODSTOCK ROAD

BANBURY ROAD

KEBLE ROAD

GREAT CLARENDON STREET

CLARENDON STREET

LITTLE CLARENDON STREET

Keble College

BLACKHALL ROAD

MUSEUM RD

WALTON CRESCENT

WELLINGTON SQUARE

RICHMOND ROAD

Oxford Canal

WALTON STREET

ST. JOHN'S STREET

PUSEY STREET

PUSEY LANE

ST. GILES

St. John's College

Ashmolean Museum

Worcester College

BEAUMONT STREET

Balliol College

❼

MAGDALEN STREET

Gloucester Green Bus Station

Market

ℹ

GLOUCESTER STREET

Playhouse Theatre

BROAD STREET

The Oxford Story

Train Station

WORCESTER ST.

HYTHE BRIDGE STREET

❽

GEORGE STREET

SHIP STREET

ST. MICHAEL'S STREET

CORNMARKET STREET

❾

Oxford Union

MARKET STREET

& A420 Swindon

❿

BOTLEY ROAD

PARK END STREET

NEW INN HALL STREET

⓫

HOLLYBUSH ROW

NEW ROAD

Covered Market

BECKET STREET

🅣

PARADISE STREET

Westgate Shopping Centre

QUEEN ST.

CARFAX

Museum of Oxford

Museum of Modern Art

Museum of Oxford

CASTLE STREET

PEMBROKE STREET

ST. ALDATES

🅿

ST. EBBE'S STREET

BREWER STREET

OXPENS ROAD

🅿

ROSE PLACE

Ice Rink

SPEEDWELL STREET

THAMES STREET

ACCOMMODATION

Becket Guest House	11
Cotswold House	1
Isis Guest House	13
Lonsdale	2
Newton House	15
Norham	3
Old Parsonage	4
Oxford Backpackers	9
Parklands	5
Pine Castle	14
Randolph Hotel	7
River Hotel	8
Ryan's	6
St Michael's Guest House	10
YHA	12

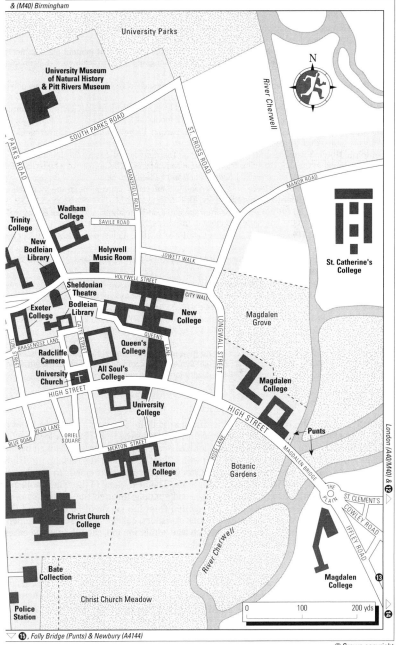

& (M40) Birmingham

University Parks

University Museum
of Natural History
& Pitt Rivers Museum

River Cherwell

N

SOUTH PARKS ROAD

PARKS ROAD

ST CROSS ROAD

MANSFIELD ROAD

MANOR ROAD

Wadham
College

SAVILE ROAD

Trinity
College

New
Bodleian
Library

Holywell
Music Room

JOWETT WALK

HOLYWELL STREET

St. Catherine's
College

Sheldonian
Theatre

CITY WALL

Exeter
College

Bodleian
Library

New
College

CATTE STREET

QUEENS LANE

Magdalen
Grove

BRASENOSE LANE

Queen's
College

LONGWALL STREET

Radcliffe
Camera

University
Church

All Soul's
College

Magdalen
College

HIGH STREET

University
College

HIGH STREET

BEAR LANE

BLUE BOAR
ST

ORIELL
SQUARE

MERTON STREET

ROSE LANE

Punts

MAGDALEN BRIDGE

London (A40/M40) &

Merton
College

Botanic
Gardens

THE
PLAIN

ST CLEMENT'S

COWLEY ROAD

Christ Church
College

River Cherwell

Magdalen
College

IFFLEY ROAD

Bate
Collection

Police
Station

Christ Church Meadow

River Cherwell

0   100   200 yds

, Folly Bridge (Punts) & Newbury (A4144)

Lonsdale, 312 Banbury Rd (☎01865/554872). Away from the centre, but good transport links into town. No credit cards. ②.

Newton House, 82–84 Abingdon Rd (☎01865/240561). The most central of the south Oxford B&Bs, and well placed for evening strolls along the Thames. ②.

Norham Guest House, 16 Norham Rd (☎01865/515352). A quiet and genteel place in north Oxford, an area dominated by large Victorian houses belonging mostly to academics. Fifteen minutes' walk from town, just off the Banbury Rd. ③.

Old Parsonage Hotel, 1 Banbury Rd (☎01865/310210). A small classy hotel in a handsome house at the top of St Giles'. ⑦.

Parklands, 100 Banbury Rd (☎01865/554374). Homely place with a garden, licensed restaurant and bar; a good deal at this price. Standard or en-suite rooms. ⑤.

Pine Castle, 290–292 Iffley Rd (☎01865/241497). A spacious Victorian house in a similar mould to *Parklands*, although marginally closer to the centre. ③.

Randolph Hotel, 1 Beaumont St (☎01865/247481). The most famous, most overrated and most overpriced hotel in the city, suffering from all the disadvantages of being part of a chain. Scenes from the *Inspector Morse* TV series and *Shadowlands* were shot here. ⑧.

River Hotel, 17 Botley Rd (☎01865/243475). Friendly, comfortable, convenient for the train station and the only hotel in Oxford with river frontage. ④.

Ryan's, 164 Banbury Rd (☎01865/558876). Well appointed, with mostly en-suite rooms. A long walk from the centre, but on the bus route and close to the shops. No credit cards. ②.

St Michael's Guest House, 26 St Michael's St (☎01865/242101). Almost permanently full, but the most central of the B&Bs. ②.

Hostels and camping

Oxford Backpackers, 9A Hythe Bridge Rd (☎01865/721761, *oxford@hostels.demon.co.uk*). An eighty-bed independent hostel that's far more central and less institutional than the YHA. There's a late-night bar. Advance booking recommended.

Oxford Camping International, 426 Abingdon Rd (☎01865/244088). The closest campsite to the city, just over a mile south of Carfax. Take bus #35 or #36 from St Aldate's.

Youth Hostel, 32 Jack Straw's Lane (☎01865/762997, *oxford@yha.org.uk*). Off the Marston Road a couple of miles east of the centre, accessible on minibuses #13, #14 or #14A from the High Street, or bus #10 from the bus station. Beds are in great demand, but camping is available in the attractive wooded garden. Inexpensive meals available in addition to good self-catering facilities.

The City

Oxford straddles the confluence of the **Thames** and the **Cherwell** rivers. In theory, and on most maps, the former is known within the city as the "Isis", but few locals actually use the term. Central Oxford's main point of reference is **Carfax**, overlooked by the Saxon remnant of St Martin's tower, from which the city's main axes radiate: the **High** runs east to Magdalen Bridge and the Cherwell, **Cornmarket** north to the broad avenue of St Giles', and **St Aldate's** south to the Thames. Many of the oldest colleges face onto the High, a lovely, though busy, road running through the centre, or onto streets on either side of it: most can be spotted from the tangle of bikes around the entrance. Owing to the ever-growing number of visitors, colleges have restricted opening hours to the afternoon only and a few charge admission too, though in some cases only at weekends and during holiday periods.

South of Carfax

The **Town Hall**, an ostentatious Victorian creation, spreads down the hill from Carfax, with a staircase on the south side giving access to the **Museum of Oxford** (Tues–Fri 10am–4pm, Sat 10am–5pm; £1.50), which makes good use of photographs to tell the history of the city. In the face of tough competition this museum often gets ignored, but you'll learn far more here than at the "Oxford Story" in Broad Street (see p.87).

ON THE RIVER

Punting is a favourite summer pastime both among students and visitors, but handling a punt – a traditional flat-bottomed boat ideal for the shallow waters of the Thames and Cherwell – requires some practice. The Cherwell, though much narrower than the Thames and therefore trickier to navigate, provides more opportunities for pulling to the side for a picnic – an essential part of the punting experience. For **boat rental**, Magdalen Bridge, at the east end of the High, is the most central place (☎01865/202643), but in summer it's so busy that you're better off going a mile or so north to the Cherwell Boat House by Wolfson College off Banbury Road (☎01865/515978). Expect to pay about £10 per hour for a boat plus a £25 deposit, and sometimes ID is required. Five people make an ideal group – four sitting and one punting – though there is room for six. If you're determined not to do any actual punting, chauffeured punts are available for around £20 per half-hour, with free booze.

Just down from the museum, the huge Tom Tower, designed by Christopher Wren, marks the entrance to **Christ Church** (Mon–Sat 9am–5pm, Sun 9am–1pm; £3), Oxford's largest, most prestigious and some would say most pretentious college. The former college of Albert Einstein, William Gladstone and no fewer than twelve other British prime ministers, it claims the distinction of having been founded twice, first by Cardinal Wolsey in 1525, and then again in 1546 following the cardinal's fall from grace and decease. Visitors must enter via the **Memorial Garden**, which takes you directly to the **Cathedral**, which is also the college chapel. This largely Norman building once formed part of a priory said to have been founded by the Saxon princess later canonized as St Frideswide, whose shrine was the impetus to Oxford's growth. The cathedral has been hacked about – Wolsey destroyed part of the west end to make space for a quad and Sir Gilbert Scott made alterations last century – but it still possesses a lovely freshness and sense of space. The Norman legacy remains in the glorious choir, where massive Norman columns rise to delicate fifteenth-century stone vaulting.

From the cathedral you enter the striking but unfinished **Tom Quad**, the raised terrace that was originally designed to be a cloister. Through the smaller Peckwater quad you reach Canterbury quad, where the **Christ Church Picture Gallery** (Easter–Sept Mon–Sat 10.30am–1pm & 2–4.30pm, Sun 2–5.30pm; Oct–Easter Mon–Sat 10.30am–1pm & 2–4.30pm, Sun 2–4.30pm; £1) provides a pokey home for works by many of Italy's finest artists from the fifteenth to eighteenth centuries, including some by Leonardo da Vinci and Michelangelo.

Christ Church Meadow stretches south from the college, where you can follow a shady path first south along the Thames and then north by the Cherwell. Back on St Aldate's and just south of Christ Church, the **Bate Collection** (Mon–Fri 2–5pm, Sat during term 10am–noon; free) contains England's most comprehensive collection of European woodwind instruments. In addition to rows of flutes and clarinets, there are all sorts of other instruments on show, from medieval crumhorns, looking like rejected walking sticks, to the country's finest gamelan, which is played regularly.

Back towards Carfax and off to the left along Pembroke Street, the **Museum of Modern Art** or Moma (Tues–Sun 11am–6pm, Thurs 11am–9pm; £2.50, free Wed till 1pm & Thurs from 6pm) is always worth checking out. The gallery usually has two exhibitions on the go, featuring international contemporary art in a wide variety of media; the basement café serves good coffee and vegetarian food. The gallery may be closed in between exhibitions.

East of Carfax – the High Street and around

As you walk east along the High from Carfax, the first building to demand attention is **St Mary's** or the University Church. Its handsome Baroque porch, flanked by chunky corkscrewed pillars, and the elaborately pinnacled tower take precedence over an unexceptional interior. (You can climb the tower from Radcliffe Square; see opposite.) Across the High from St Mary's, an alley called Magpie Lane leads to Merton Street, cobbled and uncharacteristically tranquil, and to **Merton College** (Mon–Fri 2–4pm, Sat & Sun 10am–4pm; free), historically the city's most important college. Balliol and University colleges may have been founded earlier, but it was Merton – opened in 1264 – which set the model for colleges in both Oxford and Cambridge, being the first to gather its students and tutors together in one place. Furthermore, unlike the other two, Merton retains some of its original medieval buildings, which are therefore the oldest part of the university. Famous Merton alumni include T.S. Eliot, J.R.R. Tolkien and Kris Kristofferson.

The best of the thirteenth-century architecture can be seen in **Mob Quad**, a delightful courtyard complete with mullioned windows and Gothic doorways, and in the Chapel. Here, a curious monument in the antechapel shows Thomas Bodley (founder of Oxford's most important library) surrounded by masculine-looking women in classical garb. Merton's other gem is its fourteenth-century **Library**, one of the finest medieval libraries in Britain. Much of the woodwork, including the panelling, screens and bookcases, dates from the Tudor period, but some fittings are original.

Back on the High, **University College** (known as "Univ"), founded in 1249, has a rightful claim to be the city's first college, but nothing of that period survives – what you see dates mostly from the seventeenth century. A year Univ may prefer to forget is 1811, when it expelled **Percy Bysshe Shelley** for distributing a paper called *The Necessity of Atheism*. Guilt later induced Univ to accept a mawkish memorial to the poet after he drowned in Italy in 1822 – it occupies a shrine-like room by Staircase 3. The college's most famous recent alumnus was Bill Clinton, the non-inhaling Rhodes Scholar; former Australian premier Bob Hawke also studied here.

Queen's College, across the High from Univ (and closed to the public), cuts an altogether more impressive figure. The only Oxford college to have been built in one period (1672–1760), Queen's benefited from the skills of some of the country's finest architects: Nicholas Hawksmoor did much of the work and his teacher, Christopher Wren, designed the chapel, a grand room with a ceiling of cherubs and foliage and a massive oak screen. Unfortunately, the chapel can be visited only on a tour arranged at the tourist office.

Oscar Wilde's college, **Magdalen** (daily 2–6pm; £2.50), pronounced "Maudlin", dominates the eastern end of the High, its majestic medieval tower worthy of a cathedral. A handsome reredos saves the **Chapel** from complete gloom, but you must admire it from a distance since a stone screen confines you to the rather spiritless ante-chapel. The adjacent **cloisters**, with bizarre and grotesque stone figures perched atop delicate buttresses, are the best in Oxford, and Magdalen boasts better **grounds** than most too: a bridge across the Cherwell joins **Addison's Walk**, which you can follow around a water meadow where rare wild fritillaries flower in spring.

Retracing your steps back to Queen's, you can cut north up Queen's Lane, past some of the best gargoyles in Oxford, to **New College** (April–Oct 11am–5pm; Nov–March 2–4pm; £2, free in winter). Founded in 1379, the college has splendid Perpendicular architecture in the Front Quad, though the addition of an extra storey in 1675 spoiled the overall effect. The **Chapel** has been mucked about too, yet it remains perhaps the finest in Oxford after the cathedral, not so much for its design as its contents. The ante-chapel contains some original fourteenth-century glass, but the Nativity in its west window was designed by Sir Joshua Reynolds in 1777. Beneath it, shoved up against the wall, stands the wonderful *Lazarus* by Jacob Epstein – Khrushchev, after a visit to the college, claimed that the memory of this haunting sculpture kept him awake at night. A magnificent nineteenth-century stone reredos takes up the entire east wall of the main chapel, consisting of about fifty canopied figures, mostly saints and apostles, with Christ for a centrepiece. The misericords, the other highlight, sadly are cordoned off.

An archway on the east side of Front Quad leads through to the grounds, a pleasant lawn skirted by the best-preserved part of the thirteenth-century **city walls**. You can leave the college either through the north entrance into Holywell Street or back the way you came and into New College Lane: heading west along either street brings you to the top of Broad Street.

The Broad Street area

Oxford's most monumental architecture prevails over the eastern end of Broad Street. The semicircular **Sheldonian Theatre** (Mon–Sat 10am–12.30pm & 2–4.30pm; £1.50), placed with its facade directed away from the street, was Christopher Wren's first major work: a reworking of the Theatre of Marcellus in Rome, it was conceived in 1663, when the 31-year-old Wren's main job was as professor of astronomy. Designed as a stage for university ceremonies, nowadays it functions mainly as a concert hall. The interior, painted in gold and a dull brown, lacks any sense of drama, and even the views from the cupola (50p) are disappointing.

Wren's colleague Hawksmoor designed the **Clarendon Building**, set at right angles to the Sheldonian and now part of the university library. Across the courtyard, a doorway leads to the **Old Schools Quad**, a beautifully proportioned, symmetrical space created in the seventeenth century by an unknown architect. On the east side, the so-called Tower of the Five Orders of Architecture gives a lesson in design, with tiers of columns built according to the five classical styles: from top to bottom, Tuscan, Doric, Ionic, Corinthian and Composite. The heart of one of the country's great centres of learning occupies the building opposite. Set up by Thomas Bodley in the seventeenth century, the **Bodleian Library** has expanded greatly since then, becoming the second largest library in the UK. An estimated eighty miles of shelves are distributed among various buildings, including the ugly modern annexe on the other side of Broad Street. Though only members can enter the main part, you can go on a guided tour of Duke Humfrey's library (summer Mon–Fri 10.30am, 11.30am, 2pm & 3pm, Sat 10.30am & 11.30am; winter Mon–Fri 2pm & 3pm, Sat 10.30am & 11.30am; £3.50), founded in 1439 and restored by Bodley – sign up for a tour in the Exhibition Room, on the south side of the quad. Entered through the shop on the west side of the quad, the **Divinity School** (Mon–Fri 9am–4.30pm, Sat 9am–12.30pm; free) has a fifteenth-century vaulted ceiling, a riot of pendants and decorative bosses that should be seen on a bright sunny day, when light streams onto the still fresh stone.

The **Radcliffe Camera** (closed to the public) seems rather isolated behind the Old Schools Quad, but this only adds to the majesty of this mighty Italianate rotunda, built from 1737 to 1749 by James Gibbs, architect of London's St Martin-in-the-Fields. For a less intimidating perspective, climb the 125-step tower of the **University Church** (July & Aug daily 9am–7pm; rest of year Mon–Sat 9am–5pm, Sun 11.30pm–5pm; £1.60), which backs onto Radcliffe Square. The views can't be bettered, particularly over **All Souls College** (Mon–Fri 2–4pm; closed Aug; free), with its twin mock-Gothic towers (the work of Hawksmoor) and a coloured sundial designed by Wren.

Back on Broad Street, a series of classical heads, their eyes blackened by pollution, stare menacingly across the street at Blackwells, Oxford's largest and most famous bookshop. The heads continue along the front of the **Museum of the History of Science** (Tues–Sat noon–4pm; free), where microscopes and early calculators are immaculately displayed alongside Islamic and European astrolabes that seem more like works of art than tools of science. The museum is due to re-open in April 2000, a Lottery grant having funded the addition of new galleries and visitor facilities.

Exeter College (daily 2–5pm; closed Christmas week; free), next to the museum but entered from Turl Street, has Oxford's most elaborate **chapel**: modelled by Sir Gilbert Scott on Sainte Chapelle in Paris, it's a cramped conglomeration of fussy neo-Gothic features. A tapestry of the *Adoration of the Magi*, a fine collaboration between William Morris and Edward Burne-Jones, who met at Exeter, is ill-served by its setting. The chapel in **Trinity College** (daily 10.30am–noon & 2–5pm; £2), on the north side of Broad Street, couldn't be more different. Grinling Gibbons did some of his finest carving here, a distinctly secular performance with cherubs' heads peering out from delicate foliage. **Balliol** (daily 2–5pm; £1), next door, is as left-wing as Trinity is conservative, and the two are bitter rivals. Architecturally, Balliol is an unexceptional assembly of buildings, haphazardly gathered around two quads.

The **Oxford Story** (daily: April–June, Sept & Oct 9.30am–5pm; July & Aug 9am–6pm; Nov–March Mon–Fri 10am–4.30pm, Sat & Sun 10am–5pm; £5.50), towards the Cornmarket end of Broad Street, involves sitting at a desk and being pulled sluggishly past scenes illustrating the history of the university, while listening to a commentary through headphones. You can spend a more pleasurable half-hour around the corner at the **Oxford Union** in St Michael's Street, home of the university debating society. The Union has hosted a mixed bag of internationally famous celebrity speakers in recent years, among them Archbishop Desmond Tutu, Ronald Reagan and Diego Maradona. The original debating hall, shaped rather like an upturned boat and now the union library (closed to the public), is decorated with Pre-Raphaelite murals illustrating the Arthurian legend, created (but never completed) in the 1850s by William Morris, Rossetti, Burne-Jones and a few like-minded friends.

The Ashmolean, University and Pitt-Rivers museums

The university's best museums grew up around the collections of **John Tradescant**, gardener to the kings James I and Charles I. During extensive travels around the world he built up a huge collection of artefacts and natural specimens which became known as Tradescant's Ark. The collection eventually passed to the university, was split up – mainly between the Ashmolean and the Pitt-Rivers museums – and has been added to ever since.

The **Ashmolean** (Tues–Sat 10am–5pm, Sun 2–5pm; free), the oldest public museum in the country, was established as a home for Tradescant's Ark in 1683. Originally, the university's vast collection of art and archeology, which includes some of Britain's greatest treasures, was housed in the History of Science Museum in Broad Street but was later moved to a mammoth Neoclassical building on Beaumont Street. If you don't have time to make more than one visit, you'll have to just pick out the highlights. Until late 1998, however, the museum will be in a state of flux pending the completion of work on three new ground-floor galleries (to accommodate Islamic, ancient Greek and Oriental artefacts hitherto locked in the vaults), and many of its prize pieces are difficult to locate. Nor is the glossy Museum Guide (50p) much help; the best way to find something is to ask one of the attendants.

Downstairs, the **Egyptian** displays should not be missed: in addition to the well-preserved mummies and coffins, there are unusual frescoes, rare textiles from the Roman and Byzantine periods and several fine examples of relief carving, such as on the shrine of Taharqa. The **Eastern Art** section includes superb Islamic ceramics and early Chinese pottery, whilst the Beazley Room contains an excellent display of ceramics from the Geometric Period (ninth and eighth centuries BC), and the Arthur Evans or "Minoan" room (no. 28) houses the largest collection of ancient Cretan objects outside Greece. A small part of the Ashmolean's original exhibits can be seen in the **Tradescant Room**, an offbeat group of exhibits including Guy Fawkes's lantern and Oliver Cromwell's death mask.

The Department of Western Art straddles the first and second floors. The Fortnum Gallery has the best of the **Italian art** and it's followed by a strong showing of **French paintings**, including a dash of Picasso and Van Gogh. Look out for what's on in the Eldon Gallery, which stages exhibitions from the Ashmolean's vast hoard of **prints**, and for the Michelangelo and Raphael drawings by the staircase. Up on the second floor, the Combe Gallery is devoted to mostly nineteenth-century **British paintings** with Samuel Palmer's visionary paintings running rings around the rest.

By the *Lamb & Flag* pub on the far side of St Giles' from the Ashmolean, an alley cuts through to Parks Road and the **University Museum of Natural History** (daily noon–5pm; free), opposite the mottled brick facade of Keble College. The building, constructed under the guidance of John Ruskin, looks more like a cross between a railway station and a church than a museum – particularly inside, a high Victorian-Gothic fusion of cast iron and glass, featuring soaring columns and capitals decorated with animal and plant motifs. Exhibits include a working beehive and some impressive fossil dinosaurs, though the museum's natural history displays are outdone by the **Pitt-Rivers Museum** (Mon–Sat 1–4.30pm; free), reached through a door at the far end. Founded in 1884 from the bequest of grenadier guard turned archeologist Augustus Henry Lane Fox Pitt-Rivers, this is one of the world's finest ethnographic museums and an extraordinary relic of the Victorian age, arranged like an exotic junk shop with each bulging cabinet labelled meticulously by hand. The exhibits, brought to England by several explorers, Captain Cook among them, range from totem poles and mummified crocodiles to African fetishes and gruesome shrunken heads from Ecuador. For a breather afterwards, go and sit in the nearby University Parks on the banks of the Cherwell.

Eating, drinking and nightlife

With so many students to cater for, Oxford has developed a huge choice of places to eat and drink. For a midday bite, the numerous **sandwich bars** are ideal – the best are listed below, and you'll find several others in the Covered Market between the High and Cornmarket, an Oxford institution as essential to local shoppers as the Bodleian is to academics. If you prefer to make your own picnic, *Parmenters*, 58 High St, and *Taylors* at the top of St Giles', are recommended delicatessens. Reasonable food is served at most **pubs** – those listed below have been singled out for their ambience or selection of beers rather than for their menus, which are pretty uniform. For **restaurant** meals, Oxford is not exactly a gourmet haven, but it does have a few high-class choices amid the welter of unpretentious and good-value places.

This is not a town for wild nights: lovers of **classical music** are well catered for, but the city has a fairly paltry offering of other forms of entertainment. In addition to the city's main concert halls, certain college chapels – primarily Christ Church, Merton and New College – are good venues for classical recitals. The proximity to London and Stratford-on-Avon means that most Oxonians head out of town to go to the **theatre**. Student productions dominate the city repertoire, but the quality of acting varies, particularly when they tackle Shakespeare, the favourite for the open-air college productions put on for tourists during the summer.

The live-music and club scenes are pretty lame. Part of the reason for this is that the students tend to fall back on college discos, an option closed to the rest. **Listings** are given in the *Oxford Times*, out on Friday; in *Daily Information* (weekly out of term time), a broadsheet posted up in pubs and cafés, and in *This Month in Oxford*, a monthly booklet which you can pick up free at the tourist office. In addition, there is the free monthly *Oxford Magazine* which lists forthcoming gigs and club nights in and around Oxford; you can usually get copies at the train station, the tourist office and other places around town. **Tickets** to most musical events are on sale at Blackwells Music Shop, 38 Holywell St (☎01865/792792).

Snacks and cafés

Café Coco, Cowley Rd. Chic American-style brasserie just off the Plain, offering a great selection of aperitifs, classy shorts and delicious coffee. The food is mainly Mediterranean (*mezes*, pizzas and *merguez*), and a touch pricey, but the service is slick and the atmosphere lively.

Carfax Fish and Chips, Carfax Passage, off the High. Oxford's best-loved chippy. Open Mon–Fri until midnight.

Convocation Coffee House, Radcliffe Square, attached to the University Church. Ideal for coffee and cake or quiche-and-salad lunches, served in an atmospheric stone-vaulted room. No smoking.

Felson's, 32 Little Clarendon St. Another hot contender for Oxford's best sandwich bar, this tiny, friendly place has a huge range of fillings in massive baguettes and rolls.

George and Davies, Little Clarendon St. An old-established ice-cream parlour that stays open well after the pubs and cinemas.

Heroes, 8 Ship St. Sandwich bar with some of the best (and most adventurous) fillings in town.

Kebab Kid, Gloucester Green. The city's best kebab stand is close to the bus station, has tables (a rarity), and serves its grilled lamb and chicken in freshly baked *naan* breads rather than the usual limp pittas. Plenty of vegetarian options, too.

Nosebag, 6 St Michael's St. A civilized but unassuming place, with Laura Ashley decor and classical background music. The hot and cold food attracts queues at lunchtime; not so in the evening, when it is a good place for a quick but wholesome meal. Good selection of veggie food.

Restaurants

Aziz, 228–230 Cowley Rd (☎01865/798033). Lively, spacious and bright Bangladeshi restaurant, with bamboo furniture and rugs. The food's delicious, too, and they do an exceptional range of vegetarian dishes. Reservations recommended at weekends. Inexpensive.

Bangkok House, 42a Hythe Bridge St (☎01865/200705). Best oriental restaurant in town, with superb Thai food and excellent service. The mixed starter and the coconut-milk curries are particularly good. Closed Sun & Mon lunch. Moderate.

Browns, 5–9 Woodstock Rd (☎01865/511995). Buzzing and stylish restaurant with abundant foliage. Main courses from hamburgers to fresh salmon, in addition to legendary Guinness pies. No booking allowed, although queueing is part of the experience. Also open for breakfast. Moderate.

Cherwell Boathouse, Bardwell Rd, off Banbury Rd (☎01865/552746). A deservedly popular spot for an unhurried meal at a riverside setting, about a mile north of town. Closed all Mon & Tues, plus Sun eve. Reservations essential. Moderate.

Hi-Lo Jamaican Eating House, 70 Cowley Rd (☎01865/725984). Legendary West Indian restaurant with oodles of atmosphere and imported Jamaican beer; the menu's meat-oriented (curried goat often features), the lighting low and the background music heavy reggae. Moderate.

Le Petit Blanc, 71–72 Walton St (☎01865/510999). Renowned French chef Raymond Blanc's affordable, and much hyped, alternative to his famous *Manoir aux Quat' Saisons* in Great Milton east of Oxford. It's been criticized for lack of space but the food is a refreshing mix of French gourmet (corn-fed quail with lime leaf and ginger) and traditional English (pan-fried Gloucester old spot pork). If you want to splash out, this is the place to do it. Expensive.

Pizza Express, Golden Cross, Cornmarket (☎01865/790442). Lovely Tudor building and the best-value pizzas in central Oxford, with superb garlic bread starter, but a pricey wine list. Expect a long wait at weekends. Inexpensive.

Shimla Pinks, 16 Turl St (☎01865/245564). One of the best Indian restaurants in the centre and part of a fashionable chain. This one has excellent-value set lunches, friendly service and good tandoori dishes, with vegetarian versions of most curries. Inexpensive.

Pubs and bars

Eagle & Child, 49 St Giles'. Known variously as the "Bird & Baby", "Bird & Brat" or "Bird & Bastard", this pub was cnce the haunt of J. R. R. Tolkien, C.S. Lewis and other literary types, and attracts a fairly genteel mix of professionals and academics.

Isis, by Iffley Lock. Lovely spot amid the flood meadows, just under two miles' walk southeast along the Thames from Folly Bridge: definitely a summer pub. Iffley village nearby has one of the finest

Romanesque churches in the country. Bus #4 from Queen Street or any service running along the Abingdon Road to Donnington Bridge, from which it's a ten-minute walk along the river.

Jolly Farmers, 20 Paradise St, behind the Westgate Centre. Oxford's most popular gay pub; mainly male and packed at weekends.

King's Arms, 40 Holywell St. Prone to student overkill over term-time weekends, but otherwise very pleasant, with snug rooms at the back. Good choice of beers. Walk northwest of the centre across Port Meadow, a large area of common land between the Thames and the rail line.

The Perch, Binsey. Big garden, good (though not particularly cheap) food, busy at Sunday lunchtime. It's a pleasant thirty-minute walk northwest of the centre across Port Meadow, a large area of common land between the Thames and the rail line.

The Turf, Bath Place, off Holywell St. Small seventeenth-century pub with a fine range of beers, and mulled wine in winter, but slowish service because of the tiny bar. Abundant seating outside.

Victoria Arms, 90 Walton St. Northwest of the centre in Jericho, formerly where college servants resided and now Oxford's most atmospheric suburb. At one stage very run down, the area is now popular among students, academics, yuppies and hippies.

White Horse, 52 Broad St. A tiny pub that was used as a set for the *Inspector Morse* series.

Clubs, music venues and discos

The Coven (☎01865/242770), Oxpens Rd. Formerly a gay disco, but now gone more or less straight. Tacky grottoes for tête-a-têtes, but generally a good atmosphere and decent music. Thursday is best night for techno/acid/hard-house. Open 9pm–2am.

Northgate Hall, 16 St Michael's St. A lesbian and gay centre with discos on certain nights (eg women only on Friday, mixed on Saturday). Vastly improved since it got a late licence, but still unpredictable.

Old Fire Station (aka OFS), 40 George St (☎01865/794490). Has found a niche for itself as a testing-ground for West End musicals; tickets for these workshop productions are cheap by London standards. DJs play dance sounds on Friday and Saturday, and there's a popular 1970s cheese night on Thursday. Admission £4–£6.

Philanderer and Firkin, 56 Walton St (☎01865/727265). Good indie bands play here, both local and moderately well-known ones on nationwide tours. The small room above the pub cannot cope with the crowds attracted by the latter. Go prepared to sweat.

Zodiac, 190 Cowley Rd (☎01865/420042). Far and away Oxford's most respected indie and dance venue, with live bands throughout the week, and the excellent *Transformation* club (guitar-driven indie pop) on Saturday.

Theatre, classical music, opera and dance

Apollo, George St (☎01865/244544). Known locally as the "Appalling", but the UK's top opera and ballet companies occasionally break up the monotonous programme of ageing pop acts and pantomimes.

Holywell Music Room, 32 Holywell St (☎01865/798600). This small, plain, Georgian building opened in 1748 as the first public music hall in England. Haydn once conducted here. It has a varied programme, from straight classical to experimental music, with occasional jazz.

Pegasus Theatre, Magdalen Rd (☎01865/722851). Low-budget, avant-garde productions dominate the programme of this east Oxford theatre.

Playhouse, Beaumont St (☎01865/798600). The city's best theatre. Professional touring companies (including the excellent Oxford Stage Company) perform a mixture of plays, opera and concerts, with the odd production by Oxford University Dramatic Society (OUDS), the top student group.

Sheldonian Theatre, Broad St. Hard seats and less-than-perfect acoustics, but still Oxford's top concert hall. Tickets and programme available from Blackwells Music Shop, 36 Holywell Street.

Listings

Banks and exchanges All the major banks are on or near Cornmarket; American Express is at 4 Queen St (☎01865/792066).

Bike rental Bikezone, 6 Lincoln House, Market St, off Cornmarket (☎01865/728877); and Cycle King, 55 Walton St (☎01865/516122).

Books and maps Blackwells Travel Shop and Dillons, both on Broad Street, are the best source of literature on Oxford and the surrounding area.

Bus information Buses to London are operated by Oxford Tube (☎01865/772250) and Citylink (☎01865/785 400), both running every 20 minutes or so during the day and hourly in the evening; the Oxford Tube continues through the night. These companies also serve Birmingham, Gatwick, Heathrow, Henley and Stratford-on-Avon, but most other long-distance services are in the hands of National Express (☎0990/808080). Buses within Oxfordshire are run by the Oxford Bus Company (☎01865/785400) and a number of private companies including Swanbrook (☎01452/712386).

Car rental Avis, 1 Abbey Rd (☎01865/249000); Budget, Park End St, next to the train station (☎01865/724884); Hertz, City Motors, Wolvercote Roundabout, Woodstock Rd (☎01865/319972); National Car Rental, 2 Dawson St, bottom of Cowley Rd (☎01865/240471).

Hospital John Radcliffe Hospital, Headington (☎01865/741166).

Internet Daily Information, 31 Warnborough Rd (Mon–Wed 9am–9pm, Thurs–Sat 9am–6pm, Sun 2–6pm; ☎01865/310011); Internet Exchange Café, Costa Coffee, 8–12 George St (daily 9am–5.30pm; ☎01865/241601); Pickwick Papers, 90 Gloucester Green (daily 9am–6pm; ☎01865/793149).

Laundry Coin Wash Launderette, 127 Cowley Rd; Safari Launderette, 113 Walton St, Jericho.

Pharmacies Boots, 6 Cornmarket St (Mon–Wed, Fri & Sat 8.45am–6pm, Thurs 8.45am–7pm, Sun 11am–5pm; ☎01865/247461).

Police St Aldate's (☎01865/266000).

Post Office 102 St Aldate's (Mon–Fri 9am–5.30pm, Sat 9am–6pm; ☎01865/202863). All services, including fast cash currency transactions.

Taxis ABC (☎01865/775577); City Taxis (☎01865/201201); Euro Taxis (☎01865/430430).

Train enquiries For all enquiries, call ☎0345/484950.

Woodstock and Blenheim

WOODSTOCK, seven miles north of Oxford, has royal associations going back to the Saxon kings, who were first attracted by the area's potential for hunting. Henry I built the first royal lodge here, which was enlarged by Henry II into the palace in which the Black Prince was born in 1330. During the Civil War the Woodstock estate became a Royalist garrison, and in the following century Blenheim Palace was built on the site. The town has clearly benefited from the traffic of successive monarchs and grandees, though its handsome stone buildings and spruce streets are maintained nowadays mainly as a provider of food, drink and beds for visitors to Blenheim. Nonetheless, it's worth having a stroll around and spending half an hour at the **Oxfordshire Museum** on Park Street (Tues–Sat 10am–5pm, Sun 2–5pm; £1), a neat review of the archeology, social history and industry of the county. A refurbishment programme lasting until summer 2000 means that the permanent exhibition will be closed until then.

There are plenty of good **pubs** in the town, the best being the *Black Prince*, a five-minute walk north along Oxford Street away from the crowds; it has a varied menu and serves real ale. **Buses** from Oxford run every thirty minutes (reduced service on Sun), with some continuing to Stratford.

Blenheim Palace

Military achievement nowadays is rewarded with a medal or promotion, but in 1704, as a thank-you for his victory over the French in the Battle of Blenheim, John Churchill, first Duke of Marlborough, got money to build himself the only non-royal residence in the country grand enough to bear the name "palace". The chosen site was the royal estate at Woodstock, where the old residence was demolished to make way for the gargantuan **Blenheim Palace** (mid-March to Oct daily 10.30am–5.30pm; £8.50), designed by Sir John Vanbrugh, architect of Castle Howard in Yorkshire.

Acrimony on all sides characterized the building of Blenheim. Vanbrugh found himself at loggerheads with the duke's formidable wife, Sarah Jennings, who had wanted

Christopher Wren as architect, while Queen Anne's parliament, which had reluctantly approved the sum of £300,000 to finance the project, never paid the full amount. The house was finished only after the death of the man for whom it was built, owing its completion to the widowed duchess, who made up the financial shortfall and was responsible for much of the interior design. The Italianate palace, the country's greatest example of Baroque civic architecture, as well as its largest private residence, is too awesome to be beautiful and is more a monument than a house – as was always Vanbrugh's intention. Other than the first Duke of Marlborough, the only member of the family to have made any real mark was **Sir Winston Churchill**, born here in 1874. Several rooms are dedicated to the wartime prime minister, who is buried with his parents and wife in the graveyard of **Bladon Church**, visible from the palace.

Highlights of the **interior** of the palace include the dining salon with murals by Louis Laguerre, furniture from Versailles, stone and marble carvings by Grinling Gibbons and several fine goldleaf ceilings by Nicholas Hawksmoor. Unfortunately, you don't get much of a chance to relish it all: guides whisk visitors through Blenheim in around 45 minutes, reeling off stultifying statistics that make the Chippendale chairs, family portraits and tapestries all merge into a spiritless inventory.

Formal **gardens** stretch southwards from the palace, but the open parkland remains the chief attraction, especially just north of the house, where the ground falls away dramatically to an exquisite artificial lake. It's said that Capability Brown, who landscaped the grounds, laid out the trees and avenues to represent the Battle of Blenheim. Whatever the truth of the tale, fine vistas fan out in every direction, including one from Vanbrugh's own bridge up to the Column of Victory, erected by Sarah Jennings and topped by a statue of her husband posing heroically in a toga.

There are two **entrances** to Blenheim Palace, one just south of Woodstock on the Oxford road and another through the Triumphal Arch at the west end of Park Street. If you wish to visit the **grounds** only (daily 9am–5pm; £6 with car, £2 for pedestrians) and are driving, use the free car park in Woodstock.

The Vale of White Horse

Extending southwest from Oxford, the **Vale of White Horse** takes its name from the prehistoric figure carved into the chalk of the Berkshire Downs above Uffington, eighteen miles from the city. Burial mounds and Iron Age forts pepper the downs, linked by the **Ridgeway National Trail** which runs along the top – paralleled below by the London–Swindon rail line and the A420 Oxford–Swindon road. In addition to the attraction of the White Horse and adjacent prehistoric sites, the downs provide fine and breezy walking country. Most paths follow the old drove roads, along which sheep were once taken to and from market, but nowadays horses are a more common site. The well-drained downland turf provides an ideal training ground for racehorses, and special areas known as "gallops" are used by numerous local stables, particularly around **Lambourn** on the southern slopes. You can see the horses in action at Newbury racecourse, just off the M4 to the south.

Wantage

Twelve miles southwest of Oxford, **WANTAGE** is a sleepy, slightly run-down market town, useful above all as a base from which to begin exploring the downs and Ridgeway. Its main claim to fame is as the birthplace of King Alfred the Great, whose statue dominates the Market Place. **Buses** from Oxford and Didcot pull in here every hour or so; for timetable information, call Thames Transit on ☎01865/772250. The *Alfred Lodge* at 23 Ormond St (☎01235/762409; ③) is an unassuming, friendly B&B, about five minutes' walk east of the centre, or a mile south of Wantage in the hamlet of Letcombe

Regis (ask directions for the footpath or catch bus #38), try *The Old Vicarage* (☎01235/765827; no credit cards; ②), a spacious Victorian house with a pretty garden opposite the village pub. A mile further south there's the Ridgeway Centre **youth hostel** (☎01235/760253) converted from five former barns, with spectacular views over the vale and just a stone's throw from the Ridgeway; take bus #38 from Wantage to Letcombe Regis, and walk a mile and a half uphill to the hostel from there.

Wantage has a fair selection of **places to eat**, the pick being *Fox's* restaurant (☎01235/760568), just off the square on Newbury Street, which serves a constantly changing menu of gourmet food in cosy, congenial surroundings. For a less expensive pub meal, try *The Lamb* (☎01235/766768), a recently revamped thatched seventeenth-century building at the bottom of Mill Street (head northwest from the square).

The quickest way to reach the **Ridgeway** direct from Wantage is to take bus #38 beyond Letcombe Regis to **Letcombe Bassett**, less than a mile from the path – and the model for Cresscombe village in Hardy's *Jude the Obscure*. The best walks along the Ridgeway take you westwards from Letcombe, the stretch between Wantage and Wayland's Smithy via White Horse Hill being one of the finest along the whole route. Before setting off, it's worth visiting the **Vale and Downland Museum** on Church Street (Tues–Sun 10.30am–4.30pm; £1.50), which gives an excellent history of the local landscape and has a shop with useful books and maps.

White Horse Hill and Uffington

White Horse Hill, six miles along the Ridgeway west of Wantage, follows close behind Stonehenge and Avebury in the hierarchy of Britain's ancient sites, though it attracts nothing like the same number of visitors. Carved into the north-facing slope of the downs, the 374ft-long **horse** looks like something created with a few swift strokes of an immense brush, and there's been no lack of weird and wonderful theories as to the origins of this stylized creature. Some people have suggested it was a glorified signpost, created to show travellers where to join the Ridgeway. The idea that it was supposed to represent the horse (or even the dragon) of St George is scarcely less fanciful, though the saint's story is associated with other parts of this region. In Victorian and Edwardian times the best-loved legend, popularized in a ballad by G.K. Chesterton, claimed that it was cut by King Alfred as an emblem of his victory over the Danes at the Battle of Ashdown, fought nearby in 871 AD. The first record of the horse's existence dates from the time of Henry II, but recent research has suggested that its origin goes back some two thousand years earlier, as far back as the second millennium BC, making it by far the oldest chalk figure in Britain.

Legend has it that the small flat-topped and possibly artificial hillock below the horse, known as **Dragon Hill**, was where St George killed and buried the dragon, a theory supposedly proved by the bare patch at the top and the channel down the side, where blood trickled from the creature's wounds. The **Uffington Castle**, the prehistoric fort above the Horse, now shown to date back to the same era as the White Horse, provides a grazing ground for sheep and the best vantage point in the area for visitors. The Ridgeway runs along its south side and continues west two miles to **Wayland's Smithy**, a five-thousand-year-old burial mound encircled by trees. It is one of the best Neolithic remains along the Ridgeway, though heavy restoration has rather detracted from the mystery of the place. Among a number of conflicting myths, the most romantic suggests that Wayland's Smithy was named after an invisible smith who made invincible armour and reshod travellers' horses.

White Horse Hill can be reached up two narrow roads leading off the B4507, a Roman route otherwise known as the Portway, which follows a lovely undulating route along the foot of the downs. Getting to White Horse Hill on public transport is difficult, the only **bus service** to speak of being the #68 bus between Wantage and Faringdon on Wednesday and Friday. **UFFINGTON**, six miles west of Wantage, is the closest village to the horse, thirty minutes' walk due south. A metropolis compared with the other villages along the Portway, Uffington has a couple of **B&Bs**, the better being the *Craven* on Fernham Road (☎01367/820449, *carol.wadsworth@cwcom.net*; ②); a less pricey option is the pleasant *Norton House*, next to the post office on the main street (☎01367/820230, *106436.145@compuserve.com*; no credit cards; ①). The *White Horse* **pub** (☎01367/820726; ④) in Woolstone, a hamlet hidden among the trees about a mile southwest, has overpriced rooms but serves tastier food than its counterparts in Uffington. There is limited **camping** space at Britchcombe Farm, in a fabulous spot by the Portway just east of the Uffington turn-off.

The Cotswolds

The limestone hills of the **Cotswolds** are preposterously photogenic, strewn with countless picture-book villages built by merchants enriched by the wool trade. Wool was important here as far back as the Roman era, but the greatest fortunes were made between the fourteenth and sixteenth centuries, during which period many of the region's fine manors and churches were built. Largely bypassed by the Industrial Revolution, which heralded the area's commercial decline, much of the Cotswolds is a relic, its architecture preserved in often immaculate condition. Numerous churches are decorated with beautiful Norman carving, for which the local limestone was ideal: soft and easy to carve when first quarried, but hardening after long exposure to the sunlight. The use of this local stone is a strong unifying characteristic, though its colour modulates as subtly as the shape of the hills, ranging from a deep golden tone in **Chipping Campden** to a silvery grey in **Painswick**.

The consequence of all this is that the Cotswolds have become one of the country's main tourist attractions, with many towns afflicted by plagues of tea and souvenir shops – this is Morris Dancing country. To see the Cotswolds at their best, you should visit in winter or avoid the most popular towns and instead escape into the hills themselves. This might be a tamed landscape, but there is good scope for walks, either in the gentler valleys that are most typical of the Cotswolds or along the dramatic escarpment which marks the boundary with the Severn Valley. A long-distance path called the **Cotswold Way** runs along the top of the ridge, stretching about one hundred miles from Chipping Campden past Cheltenham, Gloucester and Stroud as far as Bath. A number of prehistoric sites provide added interest along the route, with some – such as **Belas Knap** near Winchcombe – being well worth a diversion.

There are few large settlements in this region, the biggest true Cotswold town being **Cirencester**, a buzzing community dating back to the Romans. Nearby **Cheltenham** actually sits on the wrong side of the western escarpment and has little in common with Cotswold wool towns, but it likes to present itself as a gateway to the hills and is included here for that practical reason.

Lechlade and around

LECHLADE marks the westernmost navigable point of the Thames and thus in summer is teeming with pleasure boats, but for most people it's handy as a springboard for exploring the southern fringe of the Cotswolds. For **overnight stops** try the *Cambrai Lodge* (☎01367/253173; no credit cards; ②), the *New Inn* (☎01367/252296, *newinnlech@aol.com*; ②) or the *Flour Bag* B&B (☎01367/252322; no credit cards; ①), which doubles as a bakery. You can pitch a tent either at the St John's Priory **campsite** (☎01367/252360), a mile southeast along the A417 (follow the signs for Faringdon), or in the field by the *Trout* pub (☎01367/252313) next door. The boating fraternity congregates at the *Trout*, a real anglers' pub with stuffed fish on the wall

WILLIAM MORRIS AND THE PRE-RAPHAELITES

William Morris, the nineteenth-century socialist, writer and craftsman, had a profound influence on his contemporaries and on subsequent generations. In some respects he was an ally of Karl Marx, railing against the iniquities of private property and the squalor of industrialized society. Where he differed from Marx, however, was in his belief that machines necessarily enslave the individual, and in his vision of a world in which each person would be liberated through a sort of communistic, crafts-based economy. His prose/poem story *News from Nowhere* vaguely described his Utopian society, but his main legacy was the **Arts and Crafts Movement**, a direct offshoot of his work and a lasting influence on British crafts.

His career as an artist began at Oxford, where he met Edward Burne-Jones, who shared his admiration for the arts of the Middle Ages. After graduating they both ended up in London, painting under the direction of Dante Gabriel Rossetti, the leading light of the **Pre-Raphaelites** – a loose grouping of artists intent on regaining the spiritual purity characteristic of art before Raphael and the Renaissance tainted the world with humanism. In 1861 Morris founded **Morris & Co** ("The Firm"), whose designs came to embody the ideas of the Arts and Crafts Movement, one of whose basic tenets was formulated by its founder: "Have nothing in your houses that you do not know to be useful or believe to be beautiful." Rossetti and Burne-Jones were among the designers, though the former remains better known for his paintings of Jane Morris, his friend's wife and his own mistress, whom he turned into the archetypal Pre-Raphaelite woman. Morris's own designs for fabrics, wallpapers and numerous other products were to prove a massive – some would say negative – influence in Britain, as evidenced by the success of the Laura Ashley aesthetic, a lineal descendant of Morris's rustic nostalgia.

Morris's energy was not exhausted by his work for The Firm. In 1890 he set up the **Kelmscott Press**, named after but not located at his summer home, whose masterpiece was the so-called *Kelmscott Chaucer*, the collected poems of one of the Pre-Raphaelites' great heroes, with woodcuts by Burne-Jones. Morris also pioneered interest in the architecture of the Cotswolds – it was in response to hideous restoration work in this region that Morris instigated the **Society for the Protection of Ancient Buildings**, still an active force in preserving the country's architectural heritage.

(and live jazz on Tuesday and Sunday) a footpath leads there across the meadow from by the church.

There's lots to see around Lechlade, with the tiny church at **Inglesham**, by a farm about a mile south, one of the best sights in the entire region. Its oldest parts are Saxon and the whole building breathes history, its wooden screens twisted with age, its stone floor worn and uneven. You can walk to the church along the east bank of the Thames, though you must rejoin the A361 for a short distance at the end. Isolated among fields just three miles east of Lechlade, **Kelmscott** has become a place of pilgrimage for devotees of **William Morris**, who used the Tudor manor as a summer home from 1871 to his death in 1896. The simple beauty of the house (April–Sept Wed 11am–1pm & 2–5pm; £6) is enhanced by the furniture, fabrics, wallpapers and tapestries – some rescued from dog baskets – that were created by Morris or his Pre-Raphaelite friends, including Burne-Jones and Rossetti. Morris and his wife Jane are buried in the southeast corner of the churchyard, in the shadow of the minuscule church. Kelmscott is a pleasant stroll along the north bank of the Thames from Lechlade.

Burford and the Windrush Valley

The A40 runs west from Oxford, whisking traffic through the heart of the Cotswolds. The **River Windrush**, flanked by gentle hills, meanders between willows alongside it, a contrastingly peaceful valley – at least until you reach **BURFORD**, twenty miles from

Westminster Abbey, London

Derek Jarman's garden, Kent

Canary Wharf, London

Notting Hill Carnival, London

Hertford College, Oxford

COLLECTIONS/MICHAEL ST MAUR SHIEL

Glyndebourne

COLLECTIONS/BRIAN SHUEL

Cheese Rolling, Gloucestershire

TATE GALLERY, ST IVES

Tate Gallery, St Ives, Cornwall

JAMES MANN

Cornish cottages

Crantock Beach, Cornwall

Punts, Cambridge

Chamberlain Square, Birmingham

Ely Cathedral

Albert dock, Liverpool

Oxford. The time to appreciate the town's magnificent sloping High Street is not in summer, when cars battle for space while tourists fight it out on the pavements and in the antique shops. But the huge **parish church**, originally Norman but remodelled in the fifteenth century, is a delight at any time. An unusual monument to Henry VIII's barber, Edmund Harman, shows four Amazonian Indians, said to be the first representation of native Americans in Britain.

Spare a morning to follow the footpath along the Windrush through **WIDBROOK**, a hamlet with an idyllic medieval chapel built in the middle of a field on the site of a Roman villa, and on to **SWINBROOK**, just under three miles east of Burford. The church in this immaculate village contains a monument showing six members of the Fettiplace family reclining comically on their elbows: the Tudor effigies rigid and stony-faced, their Stuart counterparts stylish and rather camp. The best place for lunch or a drink in Swinbrook is the *Swan Inn*.

Burford straddles several main Cotswold routes. **Buses** along the A40 between Oxford and Cheltenham stop several times a day, and there are buses daily except Sunday from Lechlade; buses along other routes are mostly once-a-week market-day services. Many of Burford's old inns have metamorphosed into expensive **hotels**, but the *Highway Hotel* at 117 High St (☎01993/822136, *rbx20@dial.pipex.com*; ②) is good value. There are several **B&Bs**, including the *Chevrons* on Swan Lane (☎01993/823416; no credit cards; ①), parts of which date back to the sixteenth century; it's on a side street off the High Street. A good fallback is *Langley Farm* (☎01367/878686; closed Oct–April; ①), a former hunting lodge three and a half miles northeast near the village of Leafield.

Stow-on-the-Wold

Straddling eight roads, including the Roman Fosse Way (now the A429), windswept **STOW-ON-THE-WOLD** sucks in a disproportionate number of visitors for its size and attractions, which essentially comprise an old market place surrounded by brassy pubs, antiques shops and souvenir boutiques. The narrow walled alleyways, or "tunes", running into the square were designed for funnelling sheep into the market, dominated by an imposing Victorian hall and, just to the south, a medieval cross allegedly raised to instil honesty among the traders.

Stow is the logical springboard for trips deeper into the region with its good bus connections from Moreton-in-Marsh and Cheltenham, and its abundant selection of accommodation options. The **tourist office** on the market square (April–Oct Mon–Sat 9.30am–5.30pm, Sun 10.30am–4pm; Nov–March Mon–Sat 9.30am–4.30pm; ☎01451/831082) sells National Express bus tickets and keeps a list of local **B&Bs**, among them the conveniently central and good value *Pear Tree Cottage*, on High Street (☎01451/831210; no credit cards; ①). Tucked away on Union Street (take the short cut passage through the *King's Arms* pub from the square) is secluded *Clover Cottage* (☎01451/832210; no credit cards; ①), a good option for non-smoking vegetarians, or you could try *Tall Trees* (☎01451/831296; no credit cards; ③), on the edge of town off the Oddington road (A436), which has sweeping views, central heating and a cosy wood burner in its modern sitting room annexe. Close to the tourist office stands the popular **youth hostel** (☎01451/830497), but if you're **camping** you'll have to press on a mile or so east along the Oddington road (A436) to the Stow Rugby Club (☎01451/830887), the nearest campsite. For **food**, you've a choice of several old coaching inns on the square, including the *White Hart*, which specializes in down-to-earth meat-and-two-veg meals for under £6. Nearby, the *Royalist*, on the corner of Park and Digbeth streets, is yet another pub billing itself the oldest in Britain, a claim in part substantiated by wooden beams carbon-dated at around one thousand years old.

Moreton-in-Marsh and around

MORETON-IN-MARSH, five miles north of Stow and fifteen miles northwest of Burford, has more of a buzz than most Cotswold towns, particularly on Tuesdays, when the High Street disappears beneath a huge market. But the thing not to miss in Moreton is the **Batsford Arboretum** (March to mid-Nov daily 10am–5pm; £3.50), a fifteen-minute walk from the High Street. The largest private collection of rare trees in the country, it was planted in the 1880s by Lord Redesdale following his return from a posting in Tokyo. The hilly gardens have a distinctly Japanese flavour, and you can sit here amid magnolias and Chinese pocket-handkerchief trees enjoying wonderful views. Beside the entrance to the arboretum is the **Cotswold Falconry Centre** (March–Nov daily 10am–5pm; £3) which, in addition to a collection of beautiful birds of prey, gives flying displays (at 11.30am, 1.30pm, 3pm & 4.30pm; no 4.30pm flight in Nov) against a backdrop of the sweeping Evenlode Valley.

Moreton has better **public transport** services than most other towns in the region, with daily **buses** (except Sun) to Stow-on-the-Wold, Chipping Campden, Evesham, Malvern, Stratford and Cheltenham. In addition, Moreton is on the London–Oxford–Worcester **train** line. There's little in the way of **hotels**, however, *Moreton House* (☎01608/650747, *moretonhouse@msm.com*; ②) being the best value of those on the High Street. For **B&B**, try *Acacia*, an attractive period cottage on New Road, on the way to the station (☎01608/650130; no credit cards; ①). **Places to eat** line the main street, where blackboards advertise any number of inexpensive pub lunches. For a splash-out gourmet meal, head for the *Marsh Goose* **restaurant** (☎01608/652111), on the east side of the thoroughfare, which serves superb fresh seafood and game dishes, with an *à la carte* menu or set dinners for around £25 per head. **Bike rental** is available from Brian Jeffrey's toyshop on the High Street (☎01608/650756).

Two miles southwest along the A44, just before you reach Bourton-on-the-Hill, are the blue onion domes and miniature minarets of **Sezincote** (May–July & Sept Thurs & Fri 2.30–5.30pm; garden Jan–Nov Thurs & Fri 2–6pm; house & garden £4.50; garden only £3), tucked gracefully if incongruously among the Cotswold hills. This extraordinary house, built in the early nineteenth century, was the result of a collaboration between architect Samuel Pepys Cockerell (a distant relative of the diarist), and artist Thomas Daniell, both of whom had spent some time in India and been inspired by Mogul architecture. The end result so impressed the Prince Regent on a visit in 1806 that he ordered the designs for Brighton Pavilion to be changed along these exotic lines. Inside, a curious classical-cum-Chinese style takes precedence; outside, temples, statues and unusual trees and shrubs are scattered about the small but exquisite garden – and in the early months of the year the snowdrops and aconites make a glorious display.

Chipping Campden

CHIPPING CAMPDEN, six miles northwest of Moreton-in-Marsh, gives a better idea than anywhere else in the Cotswolds as to what a prosperous wool town might have looked like in the Middle Ages. The houses have undulating, weather-beaten roofs and many retain their original mullioned windows, while the fine Perpendicular **church** dates from the fifteenth century, the zenith of the town's wool-trading days. Inside, an ostentatious monument commemorates the family of Sir Baptist Hicks, a local benefactor who built the nearby almshouses and the market hall in the High Street. His own home was burnt down during the Civil War, but you can glimpse the ruins over the wall beside the church.

A fine panoramic view rewards those who make the short but severe hike up the Cotswold Way northwest to **Dover's Hill** (follow Hoo Lane north off the High Street).

Since 1610 this natural amphitheatre has been the stage for an Olympics of rural sports, though the event was suspended last century when games such as shin-kicking became little more than licensed thuggery. A more civilized version, the **Cotswold Games**, has been staged each June since 1951: no shin-kicking, but still the odd bit of hammer-throwing.

Such a museum-piece as Chipping Campden must inevitably cope with herds of visitors in summer. Try to stay overnight and explore in the evening or at dawn, when the streets are empty and the golden hues of the stone at their richest. **Public transport** to the area is good, with frequent bus services to Moreton, Evesham and Stratford. You can't move for **guest houses** along the High Street, most of which can be booked through the **tourist office** (daily 10am–5.30pm; ☎01368/841206). Distinguished by its blue door, *Mrs Benfield's* on Lower High Street (☎01386/840163; no credit cards; ②) has fewer lacy trimmings than most (with correspondingly low prices), as does the *Volunteer Inn* on Park Road (☎01386/840688; no credit cards; ③). Most other **pubs** have rooms but are in a different price bracket, such as the *Noel Arms* (☎01386/840317; ⑥). The standard of **pubs** is good, but the *Eight Bells Inn*, around the corner from the church, is particularly cosy, and it serves top food. There's a window in the floor showing the passage once used by Catholic priests escaping from the church.

Winchcombe and around

The journey to **WINCHCOMBE**, twelve miles southwest of Chipping Campden, is stunning, whether you take the dramatic descent over the escarpment or the exhilarating ride down the B4632, which weaves along the lower folds of the cliff. Under the Saxons, Winchcombe became the provincial capital of the kingdom of **Mercia**, and it was the most important town in the Cotswolds until the early Middle Ages. The Saxon abbey didn't survive the Dissolution, and the town's main place of worship is the rather plain fifteenth-century church, most notable for its gargoyles. Apart from that, Winchcombe has an attractive blend of stone and half-timbered buildings and a couple of museums, but the real attractions are Sudeley Castle, Belas Knap and Hailes Abbey, all located just outside the town (see below). These, together with some of the finest scenery in the region and Tewkesbury only a short hop away, make Winchcombe a much more appealing place to base yourself than Cheltenham, or indeed, any number of more touristy towns and villages in the Cotswolds.

Bus #606 runs about once an hour through the day from Cheltenham to Winchcombe bound for Broadway; services from Chipping Campden run three times a day. Winchcombe's efficient **tourist office** (April–Oct Mon–Sat 10am–1pm & 2–5pm, Sun 10am–1pm & 1.30–4pm; ☎01242/602925) has a list of virtually all the **B&Bs** in Winchcombe. Among the best is the Jacobean *Great House* on Castle Street (☎01242/602490; no credit cards; ②), whose rooms all have four-poster beds; the *Gower House* at 16 North St (☎01242/602616; no credit cards; ①) offers a good, though noisier, alternative (it's on the main road), while *Clevely*, three miles out of the village on Corndean Lane (☎01242/602059; no credit cards; ②), is the least expensive option in the area. The nearest campsite is *Winchcombe Caravan Club Site* at Alderton (☎01242/620259), three miles north along the Stow road (B4077).

There's little to choose between the town's two main **pubs**, the *White Hart* and the *Plaisterers Arms*, which are both on the main street and serve food, but *Harvest Home* in the hamlet of Greet, one-and-a-half miles along the Evesham road, sometimes includes delicious German specialities on its eclectic menu.

Sudeley Castle

A short walk west of Winchcombe, **Sudeley Castle** (March–Oct daily 10.30am–5.30pm; castle & garden £6; castle only £4.95) was once a favourite country retreat of Tudor and Stuart monarchs, though it never belonged to the royal family. It has a particularly strong connection with Catherine Parr, the sixth wife of Henry VIII, who came to live here after her marriage to Thomas Seymour, Lord of Sudeley, following the king's death. During the Civil War the house became a base for the Royalists (Charles I sought refuge here several times), then was later all but destroyed by the Parliamentarians. What remained stood empty until 1830, when the ruins were bought by the Dent family, whose work re-created an extremely handsome exterior but not the atmosphere of a fifteenth-century home. The motley collection inside includes paintings by Turner and Constable, a bed Charles I once slept in and one of Catherine Parr's teeth – her tomb is in the chapel. The real joy of Sudeley lies outside: in the **Queen's Garden** (closed March), with its huge yew hedges cut like masonry; in the creeper-covered ruins of the banqueting hall; and, above all, in the setting, with the green slopes of the escarpment behind.

Belas Knap

Up on the ridge overlooking Winchcombe, the Neolithic long barrow of **Belas Knap** occupies one of the most breathtaking spots in the Cotswolds. Dating from around 3000 BC, this is the best-preserved burial chamber in England, stretching out like a strange sleeping beast cloaked in green velvet. The two-mile climb up the Cotswold Way from Winchcombe contributes to the fun, giving good views back over Sudeley Castle. The path strikes off to the right near the entrance to Sudeley; when you reach the road at the top, turn right and then left up into the woods, from where it's a ten-minute hike to Belas Knap.

Hailes Abbey

Hailes Abbey (April–Sept daily 10am–6pm; Oct daily 10am–5pm; Nov–March Sat & Sun 10am–4pm; £2.60), a two-mile stroll northeast of Winchcombe, was once one of England's great Cistercian monasteries. Pilgrims came here from all over the country to pray before the abbey's phial of Christ's blood, a relic shown to be a fake at the time of the Dissolution, when the thirteenth-century monastery was demolished. Not much of the original complex remains beyond the foundations, but some cloister arches survive, worn by wind and rain. The ruin is undramatic, but Hailes is still worth visiting for the attached museum, for the tranquillity of the spot and for the nearby **church**, which is older than the abbey and contains beautiful wall paintings dating from around 1300. The cartoon-like hunting scene was probably a warning to Sabbath-breakers.

Cheltenham

Until the eighteenth century **CHELTENHAM** was like any other Cotswold town, but then the discovery of a spring in 1716 transformed it into Britain's most popular **spa**. During Cheltenham's prime, a century or so later, the royal, the rich and the famous descended in hordes to take the waters, which were said to cure anything from constipation to worms. Nowadays, it's not a place you're likely to want to linger in, though it is a natural stopping-off place; the haughty elegance of the Regency architecture, characterized by fancy ironwork and Greek columns, can be a pleasant change after the homely Cotswolds. The town is also a thriving arts centre, famous for its festivals of **jazz** (April), **classical music** (July) and **literature** (October) – and then, of course, there's the **racecourse**, Britain's main steeplechasing venue, whose three-day National Hunt Festival in March attracts 40,000 people each day. In terms of specific sights, the wide sweep of the **Promenade**, long the focus of Cheltenham, is lined with the town's grandest houses, smartest shops and most genteel public gardens. Once you've had your fill of old spa architecture, the **Art Gallery and Museum** on Clarence Street (Mon–Sat

CHELTENHAM RACES

Cheltenham racecourse, a ten-minute walk north of Pittville Park at the foot of Cleeve Hill, is Britain's main steeplechasing venue. The principal event of the season, the three-day **National Hunt Festival** in March, attracts forty thousand people each day. A fair proportion of them come from Ireland, the birthplace of some of the greatest horses to have raced here, including the supreme steeplechaser, **Arkle**. Other meetings take place in December, January, March, April and November: a list of fixtures is posted up at the tourist office. For the cheapest but arguably the best view, pay £5 (rising to £15 during the Festival) for entry to the Courage Enclosure, as the pen in the middle is known. For schedules and other information, call ☎01242/226226.

A popular pre-meet watering hole is the *King's Arms*, a short walk east of the racecourse in **Prestbury**; an old Cotswold village with a reputation for being the most haunted village in England, it has now been subsumed into the town. **Fred Archer**, considered by many to have been the finest Flat jockey of all time, was brought up here, and he features prominently among the pub's racing memorabilia. The pub has sadly lost much of its character since becoming part of a chain, and you might find the nearby *Royal Oak* more congenial.

10am–5.20pm; free) marks the high point of Cheltenham. It is good on social history and has a fine room dedicated to the Arts and Crafts Movement, containing several pieces by Charles Voysey and Ernest Gimson, two of the period's most graceful designers. Also on display is an array of rare Chinese ceramics and a section devoted to the story of Edward Wilson, a local man who died on Scott's ill-fated expedition to the Antarctic.

Practicalities

All long-distance **buses** arrive at the station in Royal Well Road, just west off the Promenade. The **train station** is on Queen's Road, southwest of the centre; buses G and F run into town every fifteen minutes, otherwise it's a twenty-minute walk. Among the many leaflets and brochures handed out at the **tourist office**, at 77 Promenade (July & Aug Mon–Sat 9.30am–5.15pm, Sun 9.30am–1.30pm; rest of year Mon–Sat 9.30am–5.15pm; ☎01242/522878), is one giving a rundown of bus services to and from most destinations in the area. They also sell tickets for walking **tours** of the town (Mon–Fri at 2.15pm, £2.50), and for guided bus tours stopping at several destinations in the Cotswolds that are otherwise difficult to reach on public transport (mid-June to mid-Oct Tues, Wed, Thurs & Fri; £12); they're popular so book in advance.

Accommodation is plentiful, with many hotels, B&Bs and guest houses located in fine Regency houses; rooms are easy to come by, except during the races, when you should book weeks in advance. Three good choices are the *Lawn Hotel*, 5 Pittville Lawn (☎01242/526638; no credit cards; ③), a short walk from the centre; the *Lypiatt House*, Lypiatt Rd (☎01242/224994; ⑤); and the *Regency House*, 50 Clarence Square (☎01242/582718; *penny@regency1.demon.co.uk*; ④), an upmarket choice with period furnishings and leafy views from its well-equipped rooms.

Restaurants in central Cheltenham cater mainly for the upper end of the market. The best value is *Below Stairs* at 103 Promenade (☎01242/234599; closed Sun), which serves scrumptious fish and seafood at moderate prices. Two other places worth trying are *Le Champignon Sauvage* at 24 Suffolk Rd (☎01242/573449; closed Sun & Mon), which is very expensive, but has a quite reasonable fixed-price menu at lunchtimes; and *Le Petit Blanc* by the side of the Queen's Hotel on the Promenade (☎01242/266800; closed Sun), an outpost of Raymond Blanc's famed *Manoir Aux Quat' Saisons* where you can eat contemporary French cooking at prices which become distinctly affordable at lunchtime. Vegetarians and vegans are well catered for at the *Axiom Art Centre's* bright little café on Winchcombe Street, where you can enjoy wholesome salads, snacks and main meals at bargain prices.

On the whole, Cheltenham's **pubs** are dreary; the *Restoration Inn* on the High Street is worth a visit if only as one of the few survivals from the town's pre-spa days; less formal is the *Old Swan*, a few doors along, which serves fairly standard bar food as well as tea and coffee.

Cirencester and around

Fifteen miles south of Cheltenham, on the very fringes of the Cotswolds, **CIRENCESTER** makes a refreshing change from its neighbours – you'll see groups of young people around here, and for once green wellies and Barbours are not the predominant fashion. Nor does the town peddle the "olde-worlde" image that many Cotswold towns indulge in, though it has an endearingly old-fashioned atmosphere, generated partly by shops that haven't changed for decades.

Under the Romans, the town was called Corinium and ranked second only to Londinium in size and importance. A provincial capital and a centre of trade, it flourished for three centuries and had one of the largest forums north of the Alps. Few Roman remains are visible in Cirencester itself thanks to the destruction meted out by the Saxons in the sixth century. The new occupiers built an abbey (the longest in England at the time), but the town's prosperity was restored only with the wool boom of the Middle Ages, when the wealth of local merchants financed the construction of one of the finest Perpendicular churches in England. Cirencester has survived as one of the most affluent towns in the area, hence the much-vaunted title "Capital of the Cotswolds".

Cirencester's heart is the delightful swirling **Market Place** (where all the buses stop). An irregular line of eighteenth-century facades along the north side contrasts with the heavier Victorian structures opposite, but the parish church of **St John Baptist**, built in stages during the fifteenth century, dominates. The extraordinary flying buttresses which support the tower had to be added when it transpired that the church had been constructed upon a filled-in ditch. Its three-tiered south porch – large enough to function as the town hall at one stage – leads to the nave, where slender piers and soaring arches create a superb sense of space, enhanced by clerestory windows that bathe the nave in a warm light. The church contains much of interest, including a wineglass **pulpit**, carved in stone in around 1450 and one of the few pre-Reformation pulpits to have survived in Britain. North of the chancel, superb fan vaulting hangs overhead in the **chapel of St Catherine**, who appears in a still vivid fragment of a fifteenth-century wall painting. In the adjacent **Lady Chapel** are two good seventeenth-century monuments, to Humphrey Bridges and his family and to the dandified Sir William Master. Outside, one of the best views of the church is from the **Abbey Grounds**; site of the Saxon abbey, it's now a small park skirted by the modest river Churn and a fragment of the Roman city wall.

Few medieval buildings other than the church have survived in Cirencester. The houses along the town's most handsome streets – Park, Thomas and Coxwell – date mostly from the seventeenth and eighteenth centuries. One of those on Park Street houses the **Corinium Museum** (April–Oct Mon–Sat 10am–5pm, Sun 2–5pm; Nov–March Tues–Sat 10am–5pm, Sun 2–5pm; £2.50), which devotes itself mainly to the Roman era. Given that the museum has one of the largest Roman collections in Britain, the number of exhibits on display is disappointing, but a lot of space is taken up by **mosaic pavements**, which are among the finest in the country.

Practicalities

The **tourist office** (Jan–March Mon–Sat 9.30am–5pm; April–Dec Mon–Sat 9.30am–5.30pm; ☎01285/654180) is in the Corn Hall on the Market Place. There are a string of **B&Bs** along Victoria Road, a short walk east of here: facilities and prices barely differ, though the non-smoking *Abbeymead*, at no. 39a (☎01285/653740; no credit cards; ①), *Warwick Cottage* at no. 75 (☎01285/656279; no credit cards; ①) and *The Leauses*, at no. 101 (☎01285/653643; no credit cards; ①), are cheaper than most. For a little more luxury, stay at the *Crown of Crucis Hotel* in Ampney Crucis (☎01285/851806; ④), a sixteenth-century former coaching inn with riverside gardens, a good restaurant and a no-smoking rule; it's two-and-a-half miles east of town on the A417. There's a **youth hostel** in Duntisbourne Abbots (☎01285/821682), a lovely rural spot five miles west; there's an infrequent bus service.

For **snacks** you can't do much better than *Keith's Coffee Shop* on Blackjack Street, which also serves the best coffee in town. The *Café Bar* **restaurant**, next to the Brewery Centre, is inexpensive and goes out of its way to make its vegetarian dishes interesting (no credit cards; closed Sun). The best choice for a relaxing evening meal, however, is *Harry Hare's* at 3 Gosditch St (☎01285/652375), just behind the church, which specializes in classy renditions of down-to-earth English dishes; most three-course meals cost under £20, and they offer a good selection of wines. If you're splashing out and have transport, the *Crown of Crucis* in Ampney Crucis (see accommodation, above) is another option also worth considering.

Cirencester has plenty of **pubs**, their clientele swollen by tweedy students from the nearby Royal Agricultural College. Try the *Kings Head* on the Market Place or, for bar meals, the *Waggon & Horses* on Blackjack Street, and the *Butcher's Arms* in Ampney Crucis.

Malmesbury

The striking half-ruin of a Norman abbey presides over the small hilltown of **MALMESBURY**, one of the oldest boroughs in England. Lying eleven miles south of Cirencester (and only five miles north off the M4 motorway), it's not part of the Cotswolds geologically, though the town's early wealth was based on wool. Malmesbury certainly lacks the tweeness of the Cotswold towns to the north, with new housing estates encircling the centre, and modern developments marring views over the Avon. But none of this can detract from the splendour of the abbey, a majestic structure with some of the finest Romanesque sculpture in the country. **Buses** connect Cirencester and Malmesbury every one or two hours Monday to Saturday. Coming from Bath, it's best to catch a train to Chippenham and pick up a bus from there.

The High Street, which begins at the bottom of the hill by the old silk mills (converted into flats) and heads north across the river and up past a jagged row of ancient cottages, ends up at the octagonal **Market Cross**. Built in around 1490 to provide shelter from the rain, nowadays it is a favourite haunt of the local youth, whatever the weather. Nearby, the eighteenth-century **Tolsey Gate** leads through to the **Abbey** (daily: April–Oct 10am–6pm; Nov–March 10am–4pm). Founded in the seventh century and once a powerful Benedictine foundation, the abbey burnt down in about 1050; the twelfth-century building which replaced it was damaged during the Dissolution, and other parts collapsed at a later date. The **nave** is the only substantial Norman part to have survived, which it has done beautifully. A multitude of figures, in three tiers depicting scenes from the Creation, the Old Testament and the life of Christ, surround the doorway of the south porch, the pride of the abbey, while inside the porch, the apostles and Christ are carved in deep relief. Within the main body of the church, the pale stone brings a dramatic freshness, particularly to the carving of the nave arches and of the clerestory. To the left of the high altar, the pulpit virtually hides the **tomb of King Athelstan**, grandson of Alfred the Great and the first Saxon to be recognized as king of England; the tomb is empty, the location of the king's remains is unknown. The abbey's greatest surviving treasures are housed in the parvise, reached via a narrow spiral staircase right of the main doorway, where pride of place is given to four **medieval Bibles**, written on parchment and sumptuously illuminated with gilt ink and exquisite miniature paintings.

There are several **B&Bs** in town. The **tourist office** in the town hall off Cross Hayes car park (Easter–Sept Mon–Thurs 8.30am–4.50pm, Fri 8.30am–4.20pm & Sat 10am–4pm; ☎01666/823748) has an accommodation list outside. The *Whole Hog*, a stone-walled tearoom-cum-pub overlooking the Market Place, serves good, inexpensive **food**, including Wiltshire ham and Malmesbury sausages, and a selecton of real ale. *Summer Café* on the High Street is better for teas and coffees and also does food. The *Guild Hall Bar* on Oxford Street, opposite the tourist office, is a free house with good ale and pool.

Stroud and around

Five heavily populated valleys converge at **STROUD**, twelve miles west of Cirencester, creating an exhausting jumble of hills and a sense of high activity untypical of the Cotswolds. The bustle is not a new phenomenon. During the heyday of the wool trade the Frome River powered 150 mills, turning Stroud into the centre of the local cloth industry. Even now, Stroud is very much a working town, and one which doesn't need to peddle its heritage to the tourists in order to survive. While some of the old mills have been converted into flats, others contain factories – a few even continue to make cloth, including the so-called Stroudwater Scarlet used for military uniforms. That said, a string of boarded-up shopfronts in the High Street bears witness to a sharp econom-ic decline over past decades, as employment possibilities have dwindled and shoppers travel to malls and out-of-town commercial complexes around Gloucester.

For visitors, interest centres around Stroud's industrial past: as a primer, you could spend half an hour at the **Lansdown Hall Museum**, which is due to move to new premises at the Mansion House, in Stratford Park Leisure Centre – check the current situation with the tourist office. Industrial archeology is strewn the length of the Frome Valley – the so-called Golden Valley. Council offices occupy one of the valley's finest mills, **Ebley Mill**, a twenty-minute walk west of the centre along the old Stroudwater Canal – for the best view you should then walk south across the field to the village of **Selsley**.

Trains on the London–Gloucester rail line stop at Stroud, which is also well served by **buses** from Cirencester. These and other bus services arrive at the station on Merrywalks. The **tourist office** is in the Subscription Rooms on Kendrick Street (April–Sept Mon–Sat 10am–5.30pm; Oct–March Mon–Sat 10am–4.30pm; ☎01453/765768). Most **guest houses** are at the top of steep hills, but the B&B at *Wilmington* (☎01453/752366, *greg@gholder.free-online.co.uk*; no credit cards; ①) is on a level street five minutes' east of the centre on the Cirencester road. The (non-smoking) *Lay-Bye* at 7 Castlemead Rd (☎01453/751514; no credit cards; ①), fifteen minutes' walk south of the centre, offers the best value among the places further out of town, while the *Downfield Hotel* at 134 Cainscross Rd (☎01453/764496; ②), in a Georgian building five minutes from the High Street, is a dependable choice further up the scale. You'll find the nearest **youth hostel** and **campsite** at Slimbridge (see opposite).

Many artists and New Agers live in the local valleys, and they make their mark on Stroud's restaurants. For **food** in the daytime go straight to *Mills Café* in Withey's Yard off High Street, which sells scrumptious cakes, home-made soups and other whole-some concoctions. Vegetarian and organic meals are also served in the town on Union

Street at the *Pelican*, which calls itself an "ethnic pub" and has live jazz and folk. For more conventional surroundings, eat at the *Retreat* wine bar in Church Street, which is smartish but not overpriced.

Uley

The B4066 cuts a glorious route along the valley ridge southwest of Stroud, passing through **ULEY**, six miles from town. Boasting one of the best settings in the region, the village **church** lords it over the small green and the *Old Crown* pub, where the local brews include one called Pigor Mortis. **Uley Bury**, among the largest hill forts in Britain, extends along the ridge above the village. The path from the church takes you up the shortest and steepest route, though motorists can opt to drive up to the car park right by the fort. Fences prevent you from clambering on top of the bury, but you can walk around the edge – a distance of about two miles altogether – and take in some staggering views. The atmosphere peaks on a winter's day, when bracing winds blow across the ridge while mist gathers in the valley below.

Slimbridge

Eight miles southwest of Stroud, out of the Cotswolds, **SLIMBRIDGE** sits in a narrow corridor between the M5 and the Severn – a surprising location for the **Slimbridge Wildfowl and Wetlands Centre** (daily: summer 9.30am–5pm; winter 9.30am–4pm; £5.25), covering 880 acres between Sharpness Canal and the river. Since ornithologist Sir Peter Scott created it in 1946, the centre has become Britain's largest **wildfowl sanctuary**, and a breeding ground with an important conservation role. Geese, swans, ducks and a huge gathering of flamingos make up the bulk of the birdlife. While some birds are resident all year round, many are migratory: the greatest numbers congregate in the winter months, when Bewick swans, for example, migrate from Russia. There is an extensive network of trails around the sanctuary, with hides for observation.

There is a comfortable, purpose-built **youth hostel** (☎01453/890275) and a **campsite**, the *Tudor Caravan Park* (☎01453/890483), midway between the village and the wildfowl centre, about half a mile from each. The only **buses** to go anywhere near Slimbridge are those between Gloucester and Bristol or Dursley, which stop by the turn-off on the A38, just over a mile east of the village.

Painswick

The A46 and the B4070 are equally attractive routes linking Stroud and Cheltenham, but the former has the edge because after four miles you reach the old wool town of **PAINSWICK**, where ancient buildings jostle for space on narrow streets running downhill off the busy main street. The fame of Painswick's **church** stems not so much from the building itself as from the surrounding **graveyard**, where 99 yew trees, cut into bizarre bulbous shapes resembling lollipops, surround a collection of eighteenth-century table-tombs unrivalled in the Cotswolds. However, it's the **Rococo Garden** (mid-Jan to June & Sept–Nov Wed–Sun 11am–5pm; July & Aug daily 11am–5pm; £3), about half a mile north up the Gloucester road and attached to Painswick House (not open to the public), that ranks as the town's main attraction. Created in the early eighteenth century and later abandoned, the garden is being restored to its original form with the aid of a painting dated 1748. Although unfinished, it is already beautiful and the country's only example of Rococo garden design – a short-lived fashion typified by a mix of formal geometrical shapes and more naturalistic, curving lines. With a vegetable patch as an unusual centrepiece, the Painswick garden spreads across a sheltered gully – for the best vistas, walk around anticlockwise. In February and March people flock to see the snowdrops which smother the slopes beneath the pond.

The best **bus** service to Painswick is the #46 between Stroud and Cheltenham, which runs hourly during the week and four times on Sundays. The number of **guest houses** and **hotels** attests to the amount of people who find Painswick a more congenial place than Stroud, and the **tourist office**, housed in an old school at the bottom of the main street (Tues–Fri 10am–4pm, Sat & Sun 10am–1pm; ☎01452/813552), can help you find somewhere at the right price if the following places are booked: for quiet and reasonable rooms try the *Thorne Guest House* on Friday Street (☎01452/812476; no credit cards; ②) or *Cardynham House* on St Mary's Street (☎01452/814006; ③), where all rooms have four-posters – one has a private pool, open fires and lounge, and is available for £100 a night. Nearby, the *Royal Oak* **pub** is reckoned to be the best in town. Alternatively, you might consider heading out of Painswick, to the village of Edge, half a mile west, where *Upper Dorey's Mill* (☎01452/812459, *sylvia@painswick.co.uk/doreys*; ②) offers plenty of rural atmosphere in a converted eighteenth-century cloth mill by the riverside (non-smokers only).

Gloucester

For centuries life was good for **GLOUCESTER**. The Romans chose the spot for a garrison to guard the Severn and spy on Wales, and later for a *colonia* or home for retired soldiers – the highest status a provincial Roman town could dream of. Commercial prestige came with trade up the River Severn, which developed into one of the busiest trade routes in Europe. The city's political importance hit its peak under the Normans, when William the Conqueror met here frequently with his council of nobles. The Middle Ages saw Gloucester's rise as a religious centre, and the construction of what is now the cathedral, but also saw its political and economic decline: navigating the Severn as far up as Gloucester was so difficult that most trade gradually shifted south to Bristol. In a brave attempt to reverse the city's decline, a canal was opened in 1827 to link Gloucester to Sharpness, on a broader stretch of the Severn further south. Trade picked up for a time, but it was only a temporary stay of execution.

Today, the canal is busy once again, though this time with pleasure boats. The Victorian dockyards too have undergone a facelift and are touted as the city's great new tourist attraction – and indeed they house some of the region's best museums. Gloucester's most magnificent possession, however, is the **cathedral**, its tower visible for miles around. Few other buildings in the city have survived the ravages of history and the twentieth century, with the centre a mish-mash of medieval ruins swallowed up by ugly new buildings. Gloucester is solidly downmarket, discount stores taking the place of the boutiques that characterize nearby Cheltenham.

A web of roads engulfs Gloucester, surrounding the city like the tentacles of an octopus. If you're **driving**, head for the docks (well signposted) and park there. National Express runs **buses** from all neighbouring cities and beyond, and there are additional local services from Cheltenham (bus #94). **Trains** arrive every one or two hours from London, Cheltenham, Cardiff, Worcester and Bristol.

The City

Gloucester lies on the east bank of the Severn, its centre spread around a curve in the river. **The Cross**, once the entrance to the Roman forum, marks the heart of the city and the meeting-point of Northgate, Southgate, Eastgate and Westgate streets, all Roman roads. **St Michael's Tower**, the remains of an old church, overlooks it. The main shopping area lies east of the Northgate–Southgate axis, with the **cathedral** and the **docks**, the focus of interest, to the west of it. The bus and train stations are opposite one another across Bruton Way, five minutes' walk east of the Cross.

Southgate and Westgate streets

The most interesting parish church in Gloucester is **St Mary de Crypt** on Southgate Street, mostly late medieval but with some of its original Norman features. A soft, soothing light filters through the stained glass windows, and a sixteenth-century wall painting of the Adoration of the Magi in the chancel shows unusual detail for work of that period. Greyfriars runs alongside St Mary's, past the ruins of a Franciscan church and the Eastgate Market to the **City Museum** on Brunswick Road (July–Sept Mon–Sat 10am–5pm, Sun 10am–4pm; rest of year Mon–Sat 10am–5pm; £2; combined ticket with Folk Museum £3), with a good archeological collection including a fragment of the Roman city wall, preserved *in situ* below ground level. Westgate Street, quieter and many times more pleasant than its three Roman counterparts, retains several medieval buildings. One of them, a creaking timber-framed house at the bottom of the street, contains the **Folk Museum** (July–Sept Mon–Sat 10am–5pm, Sun 10am–4pm; rest of year Mon–Sat 10am–5pm; £2; combined ticket with City Museum £3), which illustrates the social history of the Gloucester area using an impressive collection of objects, from huge wrought-iron cheese presses to salt-filled rolling pins used to scare off witches. College Court alley leads from Westgate Street to the haven of the cathedral, passing the Beatrix Potter shop and museum – the house sketched by the children's artist and author while she was on holiday here in 1897 and subsequently appearing in every copy of *The Tailor of Gloucester* – but it's really only for the seriously obsessed.

The Cathedral

The superb condition of Gloucester **Cathedral** (daily 8am–6pm) is striking in a city that has lost so much of its past. An abbey was founded on this spot by the Saxons, but four centuries later Benedictine monks came and built their own church, begun in 1069. As a place of worship it shot to importance after the murder at Berkeley Castle of Edward II in 1327: Bristol and Malmesbury wouldn't take his body, but Gloucester did, and the king's shrine became a major place of pilgrimage. The money generated helped to finance the conversion of the church into the country's first and greatest example of the **Perpendicular style**: the magnificent 225ft tower crowns the achievement. Henry VIII recognized the church's prestige by conferring on it the status of cathedral.

Beneath the reconstructions of the fourteenth and fifteenth centuries, some Norman aspects remain, best seen in the **nave**, flanked by sturdy pillars and arches adorned with immaculate zigzag mouldings. Only when you reach the choir and transepts can you see how skilfully the new church was built inside the old, the Norman masonry hidden beneath the finer lines of the Perpendicular panelling and tracery. The **choir** has extraordinary fourteenth-century misericords, and also provides the best vantage point for admiring the east window, completed in around 1350 and – at almost eighty feet tall – the **largest medieval window** in Britain. In the nearby **Lady Chapel**, delicate carved tracery holds a staggering patchwork of windows, virtually creating walls of stained glass. There are well-preserved monuments here too, but the tomb of Robert II, back in the **presbytery**, is far more unusual. Robert, eldest son of William the Conqueror, died in 1134, but the painted wooden effigy dates from around 1290. Dressed as a crusader, he lies in a curious pose, with his arms and legs crossed, his right hand gripping his sword ready to do battle with the infidel.

The innovative nature of the cathedral's design can perhaps be best appreciated in the beautiful **cloisters**, completed in 1367 and featuring the first fan vaulting in the country. The fine quality of the work is outdone perhaps only by Henry VII's Chapel in Westminster Abbey, which it inspired. Back inside, an **exhibition** in the upstairs galleries, reached from the north transept (April–Oct Mon–Fri 10.30am–4pm, Sat 10.30am–3pm; £1), traces the history of the cathedral, putting it into context with that of the city as a whole. Try out the **Whispering Gallery** here, where you can pick up the tiniest sounds from across the vaulting.

The Docks

The **Docks** complex was developed during the fifty years following the opening of the Sharpness canal in 1827. The import of corn represented the bulk of the port's business at that time, and huge **warehouses** were built for storing the grain. Fourteen of them have survived, mostly now converted into municipal offices, shops and museums, a redevelopment at its most crudely commercial in the **Merchants' Quay** shopping centre, an oversized greenhouse full of forlorn shoppers.

The museums, however, are excellent. The **Robert Opie Museum of Packaging and Advertising** (March–Sept daily 10am–6pm; Oct–Feb Tues–Sun 10am–5pm; £3.50) gathers together a collection of packets and tins spanning almost a century, from late Victorian times to the 1990s. The first part takes you through the last hundred years decade by decade – something of a nostalgia trip, going back to the good old days of British manufacturing industry.

The much bigger **National Waterways Museum** (daily 10am–5pm; £4.75), in the southernmost Llanthony Warehouse, completely immerses you in the canal mania which swept Britain in the eighteenth and nineteenth centuries, touching on everything from the engineering of the locks to the lives of the horses that trod the towpaths. You walk round to a lively background of recordings, including imaginary dialogues spoken in good West Country accents and readings of contemporary accounts; there's also a series of excellent hands-on displays.

Practicalities

The **tourist office** is at 28 Southgate St (Mon–Sat 10am–5pm; ☎01452/421188). Of the few **hotels** within easy walking distance of the train station and centre, the *Albert* at 56–58 Worcester St (☎01452/502081; ②) and the *Edward* at 88 London Rd (☎01452/525865; ②) offer the best value. A central, inexpensive B&B is *Spalite* (☎01452/380828; ②), at the bottom of Southgate Street near the docks, although it's right on the main road and a bit prone to traffic noise. For organic breakfasts and evening meals, try *Bienvenue* at 54 Central Rd (☎01452/523284; no credit cards; ②; closed Nov & Jan), half a mile south of the centre off the Stroud road. There are more B&Bs on or near London Road, north of the centre, but this area has little to recommend it beyond slightly cheaper room rates and proximity to the train station; elsewhere, a good-value choice is *Lulworth* at 12 Midland Rd (☎01452/521881; ①), in a quiet location behind the park.

The selection of **restaurants** is only slightly more remarkable than its hotels, and many places are open only during the day. You'll find some of the best food in the city at the *Undercroft Restaurant* in the cathedral, open until 4pm and at the bar-café in the Guildhall on Eastgate Street – open until 11pm and always lively. *Ye Olde Fish Shoppe* on Hare Lane, even more of a Gloucester institution, occupies a sixteenth-century building and is the fanciest takeaway for miles; it serves excellent crispy fish until 6.30pm, though the attached restaurant stays open later (☎01452/255502; no credit cards; closed all Sun & Mon eve). You'll hunt in vain for a more conventional restaurant serving classier food, though the *College Green Eating House* at 9 College St is reasonably good (☎01452/520739; closed Sun in winter). For pizzas go to *Pizza Piazza* at Merchants' Quay – the only reason to venture to the docks in the evening.

There isn't a huge choice of **pubs**, the best are all within spitting distance of the Cross. The rambling fifteenth-century *New Inn* in Northgate Street has a good atmosphere, a splendid galleried courtyard and cheap meals, but for really tasty hot food at rock-bottom prices go to the *Fountain Inn*, down a narrow alley off Westgate Street; this pub pulls a sublime pint of Abbot ale and has tables in an olde-worlde adjacent courtyard – ideal for a sunny day.

Tewkesbury and around

The small market town of **TEWKESBURY**, ten miles north of Gloucester, stands hemmed in by the Avon and Severn rivers, which converge nearby. It was bypassed by the Industrial Revolution and the threat of floods has limited town-centre development, a result being that elegant Georgian houses and medieval timber-framed buildings still line several of the town's main streets – especially Church Street. The Norman abbey has also survived as one of the greatest in England.

The site of **Tewkesbury Abbey** was first selected for a Benedictine monastery in the eighth century, but virtually nothing of the Saxon complex survived a sacking by the Danes, and a new abbey was founded by a Norman nobleman in 1092. The work took about sixty years to complete, with some additions made in the fourteenth century. Two hundred years later the Dissolution brought about the destruction of most of the monastic buildings, but the abbey itself survived. The sheer scale of the abbey's exterior makes a lasting impact: its colossal **tower** is the largest Norman tower in the world, while the west front's soaring recessed arch – 65 feet high – is the only exterior arch in the country to boast such impressive proportions. In the nave, fourteen stout Norman pillars steal the show, and the roof of the fourteenth-century **choir** is equally staggering. The brightly painted bosses include a ring of Yorkist suns, said to have been put there by Edward IV after the defeat of the Lancastrians at Tewkesbury in 1471, the last important battle of the Wars of the Roses. (The battlefield, known as Bloody Meadow, is off Lincoln Green Lane, southwest of the abbey.) The abbey's medieval **tombs** celebrate Tewkesbury's greatest patrons, the Fitzhamons, De Clares, Beauchamps and Despensers, who turned the building into something of a mausoleum for themselves. In particular, look out for the handsome monument of Sir Edward Despenser, standard-bearer to the Black Prince, who died in 1375 and is shown as a kneeling figure on the roof of the **Trinity Chapel** to the right of the high altar: you can see it best from beside the Warwick Chantry Chapel in the north aisle. Nearby, in the ambulatory, the macabre so-called **Wakeman Cenotaph**, carved in the fifteenth century but of otherwise uncertain origin, represents a decaying corpse being consumed by snakes and other creatures.

Practicalities

The **tourist office** at 64 Barton St (April–Oct Mon–Sat 9am–5pm, Sun 10am–4pm; rest of year closed Sun; ☎01684/295027) has inexpensive town and walking maps, plus a small museum upstairs. You won't have to look far to find a **room**, though noise can be a problem. There are several guest houses and B&Bs on Barton Road, the busy Evesham Road, including the cheap and cheerful *Bali-Hai* at no. 5 (☎01684/292049; no credit cards; ①). More genteel are the *Two Back of Avon*, a beautiful period building on Riverside Walk (☎01684/298935; no credit cards; ②), or the quiet *Carrant Brook House* on Rope Walk (☎01684/290355; no credit cards; ③). Most of Tewkesbury's smart old **hotels** are run by chains, but for style you can't beat Tewkesbury's two top hotels, the *Tudor House*, High St (☎01684/297755; ④), and the *Bell* at 52 Church St (☎01684/293293; ⑤); both are housed in splendid old buildings, but the latter, overlooking the abbey, has the edge.

The town has a curious line in **tea shops**, several of which make you feel as if you're in someone's sitting room; try the one in the *Bible Bookshop* on Nelson Street (closed Sun

& Mon), or the *Hen & Chicken* on Barton St (closed Sun am & all Mon). If quality takes priority over local colour, you'll do better at *Ye Olde Black Bear* at the top of the High Street, which also pulls some of the best pints in town. *Le Bistro André* at 78 Church St (☎01684/290357; closed Sun & Mon) is a lively, moderately priced French restaurant serving anything from snails to venison; credit cards entail a five percent surcharge.

Bredon Hill

The most important Iron Age fort in the area once crowned **Bredon Hill**, which lies six miles northeast of Tewkesbury and is visible for miles around in the flat Severn Vale. Excavation of the site revealed more than fifty bodies, all hacked to pieces, seemingly the victims of a final assault by unknown attackers in the first century AD. Inside the rampart, a huge expanse covering eleven acres, an eighteenth-century tower called Parson's Folly is an incongruous centrepiece, but the views are supreme, with deer often grazing on the slopes.

Bredon Hill can be approached from various places around the southern foot of the hill. From **Overbury**, one of the prettier villages, the climb takes less than an hour. If you're relying on public transport, buses bound for Evesham from Tewkesbury pass through the village of **Bredon** (except Sun), from where you should allow about three hours to walk to the hill and back.

travel details

Trains

Cheltenham to: Birmingham (1–2 hourly; 40min–1hr); Bristol (hourly; 1hr); Gloucester (1–2 hourly; 10min); London (1–2 hourly; 2hr); Worcester (every 2hr; 30min).

Gloucester to: Birmingham (1–2 hourly; 1hr); Bristol (hourly; 40min); Cheltenham (1–2 hourly; 15min); London (1–2 hourly; 2hr); Stroud (7 daily; 20min).

Oxford to: Birmingham (hourly; 1hr 30min); London (1–2 hourly; 1hr); Moreton-in-Marsh (hourly; 40min); Worcester (hourly; 1hr 10min).

St Albans to: Bedford (1–2 hourly; 40min); London (14 daily; 20–40min).

Buses

Cheltenham to: Bath (daily; 2hr); Birmingham (4 daily; 1hr 10min); Bristol (5 daily; 1hr 15min); Broadway (4 daily; 1hr); Burford (3 daily; 45min); Chipping Campden (Thurs & Sat, also Wed July–Sept; 1hr); Cirencester (Mon–Sat 5 daily; 40min); Gloucester (2–4 hourly; 30–45min); London (11 daily; 2hr 40min); Malvern (Sat 3 daily; 1hr 30min); Moreton-in-Marsh (5 daily, 1 on Sun;

1hr); Oxford (Mon–Sat 5 daily, Sun 3 daily; 1hr 30min); Painswick (Mon–Sat 10 daily, Sun 3 daily; 40min); Stow-on-the-Wold (Mon–Sat 7–9 daily, Sun 1 daily; 50min); Stratford-upon-Avon (2 daily; 1hr 30min); Stroud (10 daily; 45min); Tewkesbury (9 daily; 30min); Warwick (1 daily; 2hr); Winchcombe (hourly; 30min).

Cirencester to: Cheltenham (Mon–Sat 5 daily; 40min); Gloucester (7 daily; 50min); Lechlade (8 daily; 20min); London (8 daily; 2hr 30min); Malmesbury (4 daily; 45min); Stroud (Mon–Sat 7 daily, Sun 1 daily; 45min); Swindon (5–12 daily; 50min); Tetbury (6–9 daily, Sun 2 daily; 45min).

Gloucester to: Bath (Wed & Sat 1 daily; 1hr 30min); Birmingham (4 daily; 1hr 15min); Bristol (5 daily; 50min); Cheltenham (2–4 hourly; 30–45min); Cirencester (7 daily; 50min); Exeter (4 daily; 3hr 10min); Hereford (2 daily; 50min); Oxford (Mon–Sat 5 daily, Sun 3 daily; 2hr); Stroud (hourly; 30min); Tewkesbury (Mon–Sat 10 daily, Sun 5 daily; 40min–1hr); Worcester (5 daily; 1hr 30min).

Henley to: London (8 daily; 1hr 40min); Oxford (9 daily; 1hr 15min).

Oxford to: Bath (3 daily; 2hr); Birmingham (9–12 daily; 1hr 30min); Bristol (5 daily; 2hr 30min); Burford (11 daily; 30–50min); Cambridge (9 daily; 3hr); Cheltenham (Mon–Sat 5 daily, Sun 3 daily; 1hr 10min–1hr 30min); Gloucester (Mon–Sat 5 daily, Sun 3 daily; 1hr 30min–2hr); Henley (15 daily; 1hr); London (hourly; 1hr 45min); Stratford (3 daily; 1hr 30min); Tewkesbury (1 daily; 2hr 30min); Woodstock (2 hourly; 30min); Worcester (1 daily; 2hr).

Stroud to: Cheltenham (Mon–Sat 7 daily; 45min); Cirencester (Mon–Sat 7 daily, Sun 1 daily; 45min); Gloucester (hourly; 30min); Painswick (Mon–Sat 8 daily, Sun 4 daily; 10min); Tetbury (6–8 daily; 40min).

Tewkesbury to: Cheltenham (9 daily; 30min); Gloucester (Mon–Sat 10 daily, Sun 5 daily; 40min–1hr); Oxford (1 daily; 2hr 30min–3hr); Worcester (Mon–Sat 10 daily; 40min–1hr 10min).

CHAPTER FIVE

THE WEST COUNTRY

England's **West Country** – comprising the counties of Somerset, Devon and Cornwall, and the city of Bristol – is a region encompassing everything from genteel, cosy villages to vast, Atlantic-facing strands of golden sand and wild expanses of granite moorland. It would be impossible to do justice to this great peninsula by basing yourself in any one place – the country beckons ever westwards into rural backwaters where increasingly exotic place names and idiosyncratic pronunciations recall that this was once England's last bastion of Celtic culture.

The biggest city in the West Country is also its easternmost – **Bristol**, a cosmopolitan and sophisticated place which, although overrun by traffic and defaced by office blocks, preserves traces of every phase in its long maritime history. Bristol is within reach of some superb countryside, and only a few miles from Georgian **Bath**, whose symmetrical, honey-toned terraces perfectly complement its scenic location. The exquisite cathedral city of **Wells** lies close at hand, over the Somerset border and just up the road from **Glastonbury**, one of many sites steeped in Arthurian legend in this part of the country. Straddling Somerset's border with Devon, **Exmoor** offers a foretaste of the wilderness to be found on **Dartmoor**, which takes up much of the southern half of inland Devon. The greatest of the region's massifs, Dartmoor lies between **Exeter** and **Plymouth**, the West Country's only major cities except for Bristol. Exeter is by far the more interesting, dominated by the twin towers of its medieval cathedral; Plymouth, though holding some reminders of its role as an Elizabethan naval port, is for the most part spoiled by postwar development.

Warmed by the Gulf Stream, and enjoying more hours of sunshine than virtually anywhere else in England, this part of the country can sometimes come fairly close to the atmosphere of the Mediterranean, and indeed Devon's principal resort, **Torquay**, styles itself the capital of the "English Riviera". Cornwall too has its concentrations of tourist development – chiefly at **Newquay**, **Falmouth** and **St Ives** – but this county is essentially less domesticated than its agricultural neighbour. In part this is due to the overbearing presence of the turbulent Atlantic, which is never more than half an hour's drive away, and gives Cornwall's old fishing ports an almost embattled character, especially on the north coast. The fortified headland of **Tintagel** and the clenched little harbour of **Boscastle** are typical of the craggy appeal, but the full elemental power of the ocean can best be appreciated on Cornwall's twin pincers of **Lizard Point** and **Land's**

ACCOMMODATION PRICE CODES

Throughout this guide, hotel and B&B accommodation is priced on a scale of ① to ⑨, the number indicating the **lowest price** you could expect to pay per night in that establishment for a **double room** in high season. The prices indicated by the codes are as follows:

① under £40	④ £60–70	⑦ £110–150
② £40–50	⑤ £70–90	⑧ £150–200
③ £50–60	⑥ £90–110	⑨ over £200

End, where the splintered cliffs resound to the constant thunder of the waves. And there's another factor contributing to Cornwall's starker feel: unlike Devon, this county was once considerably industrialized, and is dotted with remnants of its now defunct mining industries, their ruins presenting a salutary counterpoint to the tourist-centred seaside towns.

The best way to explore the coast of Devon and Cornwall is along the **South West Coast Path**, which allows the dauntless hiker to cover almost six hundred miles from the north coast, at Somerset's border with Devon, heading west around the peninsula via Land's End, and east again to the edge of Bournemouth in Dorset. Getting around by **public transport** in the West Country can be a convoluted and lengthy process, especially if you're relying on the often skimpy bus network. By train, you can reach Bristol, Exeter, Plymouth and Penzance, with a handful of branch lines wandering off to the major coastal resorts – though there's nothing like the extensive network enjoyed by the Victorians.

BRISTOL AND SOMERSET

At the forefront of new developments in arts and technology, the busy commercial city of **Bristol** has a vibrant youth culture which has generated some of the best nightlife in the country. The city also boasts magnificent examples of Victorian engineering, though the most attractive neighbourhoods are those dating from the Georgian era, showing a style perfected over the Somerset border in **Bath**. The graceful lines of this urban masterpiece have echoes in **Wells** and **Glastonbury**, but these two towns belong to two very different timeframes, the former's cathedral offering one of England's most powerful medieval images, the latter's ruined abbey possessing a mystique fuelled by a mixture of Celtic myth, Christian folklore and New Age fantasy. The nearby **Mendip Hills** are characterized by chasms and caverns – notably Cheddar Gorge and Wookey Hole – while in the neighbouring **Quantock Hills** you enter the heartlands of Somerset, a region of verdant glens, thatched pubs and village greens. The mood changes very quickly at **Exmoor**, a protected wilderness that extends as far as the coast, where the cliffs and sea create a perfect setting for such villages as **Porlock** and **Lynton**.

Bristol and around

BRISTOL has long been the most dynamic town in the West Country. Weaving through the centre of town, the River Avon forms part of the system of waterways that made Bristol a great inland port, and in later years it boomed on the transatlantic trafficking of rum, tobacco and slaves. In the nineteenth century the illustrious **Isambard Kingdom Brunel** laid the foundations of a tradition of engineering, creating two of Bristol's greatest monuments – the *SS Great Britain* and the lofty Clifton Suspension Bridge. More recently, spin-offs from the aerospace industry have given the city a high profile in the fields of communications, computing and finance, and a massive renewal of the old docks area is nearly complete, with sparkling new leisure and entertainment complexes. Beneath the prosperous surface, Bristol has its negative aspects – homelessness, some notorious housing estates and an overabundance of cars. Nonetheless, it remains an attractive, predominantly hilly city, surrounded by rolling countryside. The obvious half-day jaunt from Bristol is to **Berkeley Castle**. To the south of town, the Bristol Channel gives the first taste of the West Country's coastal resorts: the nearest, **Clevedon**, also offers the opportunity of seeing a fine Tudor manor house.

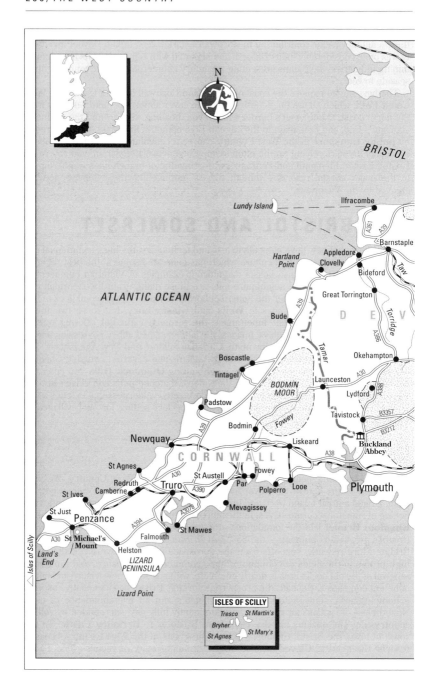

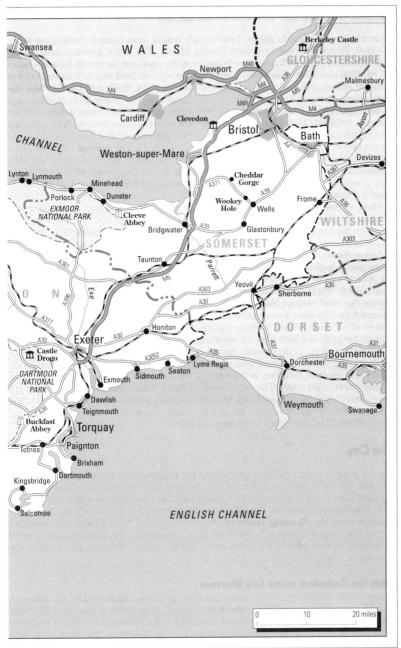

© Crown copyright

Arrival, information and accommodation

Bristol is an easy place to get to. Twice-hourly **trains** from London Paddington arrive at either Bristol Parkway or Bristol Temple Meads. The latter, a twenty-minute walk from the centre, is used by services to and from the west, and served by frequent buses #8, #9, #508 and #509, which pass through the centre on their way to Clifton. Parkway is too far out of town to walk in: take bus #73 (on Sundays, #573 or #583). The **bus station**, where National Express coaches from London arrive hourly, is in Marlborough Street, right next to Broadmead, the modern shopping centre. Cheaper Bakers Dolphin Coaches (☎01934/413000) also connect Bristol with London's Marble Arch, stopping around the corner from the bus station on the Haymarket. For bus timetables and routes in the Bristol and Bath area, call ☎0117/955 5111. The **tourist office** is in the Georgian-Gothic St Nicholas church on St Nicholas Street (June–Sept daily 9.30am–5.30pm; Oct–May Mon–Sat 9.30am–5.30pm, Sun 11am–4pm; ☎0117/926 0767); they offer a free booking service for rooms in hotels and B&Bs – though you'll have to leave a ten percent deposit.

Most of Bristol's **accommodation** is in the leafy Georgian areas of Cotham and Clifton, which are also the districts where the majority of the city's students live. For price, it's hard to beat *St Michael's Guest House*, 145 St Michael's Hill (☎0117/907 7820; ①), situated over one of Cotham's most popular cafés, near the university. In Clifton, try *K Linton Homes*, 3 Lansdown Rd (☎0117/973 7326; no credit cards; ①), located in one of the area's leafiest nooks, or *Downs View*, 38 Upper Belgrave Rd (☎0117/973 7046; ②), which enjoys great views in both directions. Also in Clifton, *Oakfield Hotel*, 52 Oakfield Rd (☎0117/973 5556; ①), provides adequate if uninspiring accommodation, or choose the more elegant *Naseby House Hotel*, 105 Pembroke Rd (☎0117/973 7859; ⑤), a beautifully furnished Victorian building ten minutes' walk from the centre. Best location of all is *Glenroy Hotel*, Victoria Square, near Clifton Village (☎0117/973 9058; ⑤), though the price is a little high for what's offered.

Bristol's modern, central **youth hostel** is in a refurbished warehouse at 14 Narrow Quay (☎0117/922 1659, *bristol@yha.org.uk*). The university also offers B&B during the Easter and summer vacations in the heart of the university district on Woodland Road, Clifton (☎0117/954 5900). The city's cramped *Baltic Wharf* **campsite**, on Cumberland Road (☎0117/926 8030; closed Oct–March), occupies a prime riverside location in the centre. There's more space at *Brook Lodge Farm*, Cowslip Green, Redhill (☎01934/862311), nine miles southwest of Bristol.

The City

A good place to start exploring Bristol is at the **Centre**, once an extension of the port but now the traffic-ridden nucleus of the city, with cars swirling round the statues of Edmund Burke and local benefactor Edward Colston. The Centre is only a few minutes' walk from the cathedral and the oldest quarter of town, and linked by water taxi to the sights around the **Floating Harbour**, the waterway that runs through the southern part of town and connects with the River Avon. You could cover Bristol's other central attractions on foot without too much sweat, but it's worth catching a bus to more distant sights, especially in the hilly Clifton district.

From the Cathedral to the City Museum

A short walk southwest of the Centre lies College Green, dominated by the crescent-shaped Council House and the **Cathedral**. Founded as an abbey in around 1140, on the supposed spot of St Augustine's convocation with Celtic Christians in 603, it became a cathedral church only after the Dissolution. The two towers on the west front were erected in the last century in an act of homage to Edmund Knowle, architect and abbot at the start of the fourteenth century. Inside the cathedral, Abbot Knowle's **choir** offers one of the country's most exquisite examples of the early Decorated style of Gothic, while the adjoining early thirteenth-century **Elder Lady Chapel** contains some fine tombs and eccentric carvings of animals, including a monkey playing the bagpipes accompanied by a ram on the violin. The ornate **Eastern Lady Chapel** has some of England's finest examples of heraldic glass. From the south transept, a door leads through to the **Chapter House**, a richly carved piece of late Norman architecture.

Climbing steeply up from College Green, the shop-lined **Park Street** has some elegant Georgian terraces leading off it – including Great George Street and Berkeley Square, from either of which you can enter **Brandon Hill Park**, site of the landmark **Cabot Tower**, built at the end of the last century to commemorate the 400th anniversary of John Cabot's voyage to America. You can clamber up the 105-foot tower for the city's best panorama. At the top of Park Street stands central Bristol's other chief landmark, the **Wills Memorial Tower**, erected in the 1920s to lend some stature to the newly opened university. One of the last great neo-Gothic buildings in England, the tower was the gift of the local Wills tobacco dynasty, the university's main benefactors. Behind it, and extending uphill into the Cotham area, lie most of the university faculties.

Next to the tower, on Queen's Road, the **City Museum and Art Gallery** (daily 10am–5pm; free) occupies another building donated by the Wills clan. The sections on local archeology, geology and natural history are predictable, but the scope of the museum is occasionally surprising – it has the largest collection of Chinese glass on show outside China, and some magnificent Assyrian reliefs. The second-floor gallery of paintings and sculptures includes work by Pre-Raphaelites and Impressionists, as well as a few choice older pieces, among them a portrait of Martin Luther by Cranach and Giovanni Bellini's *Descent into Limbo*.

From the Centre to Broadmead

One of Bristol's oldest churches, **St Stephen's**, stands just at the east side of the Centre. It was established in the thirteenth century, rebuilt in the fifteenth, and thoroughly restored with plenty of neo-Gothic trimmings in 1875. On nearby **Corn Street**, the city's financial centre, you'll find the Georgian Corn Exchange, designed by John Wood of Bath, which hosts the covered St Nicholas markets. Outside the entrance stand four engraved bronze pillars, dating from the sixteenth and seventeenth centuries and transferred from a nearby arcade where they served as trading tables – thought to be the "nails" from which the expression "pay on the nail" is derived.

West of Corn Street and edging Castle Park, where Bristol Castle once stood, extends Bristol's **Broadmead** shopping centre, an uninspiring development laid out on the ruins left by wartime bombing. A couple of relics survive: accessible from both the central strip of Broadmead, and the Horsefair, **John Wesley's Chapel** was the country's first Methodist chapel, established in 1739 by Wesley himself (Jan & Feb Mon–Sat 11am–2.30pm; March–Dec Mon–Sat 10am–4pm; free; tours £2). Lying very much as Wesley left it, the chapel has a double-deck pulpit beneath a hidden upstairs window, from which the evangelist could observe the progress of his trainee preachers. Nearby, another testimony to Bristol's close links with nonconformist sects is **Quakers' Friars**, a thirteenth-century construction whose name derives from the Dominican friars who first used the building, and the Quakers who took it over in the sixteenth century. William Penn, founder of Pennsylvania, was married here, as was the Quaker founder George Fox.

King Street to St Mary Redcliffe

King Street, a short walk east from the Centre, was laid out in 1633 and still holds some fine seventeenth-century buildings, among them the **Theatre Royal**, the oldest

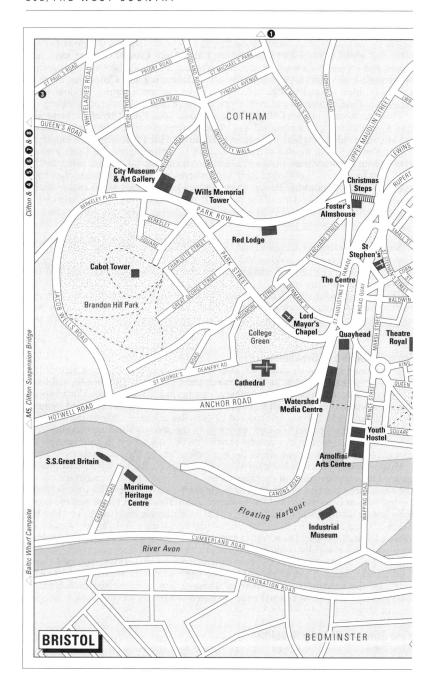

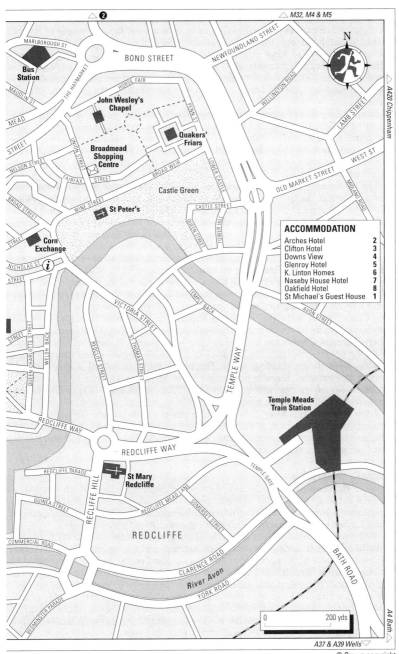

△ ❷

△ M32, M4 & M5

MARLBOROUGH ST

BOND STREET

NEWFOUNDLAND STREET

N

Bus
Station

THE HAYMARKET

HORSE FAIR

WELLINGTON ROAD

△ A420 Chippenham

MAUDLIN ST

LAMB STREET

John Wesley's
Chapel

MEAD

PENN ST

STREET

UNION STREET

WEST ST

Quakers'
Friars

Broadmead
Shopping
Centre

LOWER CASTLE ST

NELSON STREET

BROAD WEIR

OLD MARKET STREET

FAIRFAX   STREET

MIDLAND ROAD

BROAD STREET

WINE STREET

Castle Green

CASTLE STREET

St Peter's

QUEEN STREET

TOWER HILL

STREET

Corn
Exchange

ACCOMMODATION

NICHOLAS ST

ⓘ

Arches Hotel   2
Clifton Hotel   3
Downs View   4
Glenroy Hotel   5
K. Linton Homes   6
Naseby House Hotel   7
Oakfield Hotel   8
St Michael's Guest House   1

STREET

VICTORIA STREET

TEMPLE BACK

QUEEN CHARLOTTE STREET

WELSH BACK

REDCLIFF STREET

ST THOMAS STREET

AVON STREET

STREET

TEMPLE WAY

▽

Temple Meads
Train Station

REDCLIFFE WAY

REDCLIFFE WAY

REDCLIFFE PARADE

St Mary
Redcliffe

RECLIFFE HILL

TEMPLE GATE

REDCLIFFE MEAD LANE

GUINEA STREET

SOMERSET STREET

REDCLIFFE

COMMERCIAL ROAD

CLARENCE ROAD

BATH ROAD

BEDMINSTER PARADE

River Avon

YORK ROAD

A4 Bath

0   200 yds

A37 & A39 Wells ▽

© Crown copyright

working theatre in the country, opened in 1766 and preserving many of its original Georgian features. The theatre hosted most of the most famous names of its time, including Sarah Siddons, whose ghost is said to stalk the building.In a different architectural style, one of King Street's most prominent buildings is the timber-framed **Llandoger Trow pub**, its name taken from the flat-bottomed boats that traded between Bristol and the Welsh coast. Traditionally the haunt of seafarers, it is reputed to have been the meeting place of Daniel Defoe and Alexander Selkirk, the model for Robinson Crusoe.

Behind King Street spreads **Queen Square**, an elegant grassy area focused on a statue of William III by Michael Rysbrack, reckoned to be the best equestrian statue in the country. The square was the site of some of the worst civil disturbances ever seen in England when the Bristolians rioted in support of the Reform Bill of 1832, burning houses on two sides of the square, though among the survivors is no. 37, where the first American consulate in Europe was established in 1792.

The southeast corner of the square leads to Redcliffe Bridge and on to the area of Redcliffe, where the spire of **St Mary Redcliffe** provides one of the distinctive features of the city's skyline. Described by Elizabeth I as "the goodliest, fairest and most famous parish church in England," the church was largely paid for and used by merchants and mariners who prayed here for safe voyage. The present building was begun at the end of the thirteenth century, though it was added to in subsequent centuries and the spire was constructed in 1872. Inside, memorials and tombs recall some of the figures associated with the building, including the arms and armour of Sir William Penn, admiral and father of the founder of Pennsylvania, on the north wall of the nave. The Handel Window, in the North Choir aisle, was installed in 1859 on the centenary of the composer's death – he composed on the organ here. The whale bone above the entrance to the Chapel of St John the Baptist is thought to have been brought back from Newfoundland by John Cabot. Above the church's north porch is the muniment room, where **Thomas Chatterton** claimed to have found a trove of medieval manuscripts in 1768; the poems, distributed as the work of a fifteenth-century monk named Thomas Rowley, were in fact dazzling fakes. The young poet committed suicide when his forgery was exposed, thereby supplying English literature with one of its most glamorous stories of self-destructive genius. The "Marvellous Boy" is remembered by a memorial stone in the south transept.

A few minutes' walk away, Bristol's **Old Station** stands outside Temple Meads station, the original terminus of the Great Western Railway linking London and Bristol. The terminus, like the line itself, was designed by Brunel in 1840, and was the first great piece of railway architecture.

Bristol's waterways

Bristol's **Harbourside** is the focus of a grand development project which is scheduled to open in the spring of 2000. The twin pivots of the scheme are Explore@Bristol, an interactive science centre, and Wildscreen@Bristol, a multi-media wildlife complex, though plans encompass a range of other consumer-friendly installations.

At the southern end of the Centre, the River Frome disappears underground at the **Quayhead**, a spot marked by a statue of Neptune and a memorial plaque to Samuel Plimsoll, inventor of the eponymous line that's painted on the hulls of merchant ships. **St Augustine's Reach**, the central part of the Floating Harbour, is flanked by the Arnolfini and Watershed arts centres, bastions of Bristol's cultural scene and both housed in refurbished Victorian warehouses. Outside the Arnolfini is a statue of **John Cabot**, the Genoan-born explorer licensed by Henry VII to sail from Bristol in 1497; his landing at Newfoundland formed the basis of England's later claims on the New World. He disappeared on his second expedition the following year.

A **ferry** service leaves from near Neptune's statue at the Quayhead (every 40min: April–Sept daily 11am–4pm; Oct–March Sat & Sun 11am–4pm; £1 flat fare; £3.30 one hour return trip). The first stop is the **Industrial Museum**, featuring a diverse collection of vehicles, mostly with Bristol connections, and a display of maritime models and reconstructions (April–Oct Mon–Wed, Sat & Sun 10am–5pm; Nov–March Sat & Sun 10am–5pm; free). From the museum, you can either catch the ferry or use the steam train of the **Bristol Harbour Railway** (March–Oct occasional weekends every 15min noon–6pm; £1 return; ☎0117/9251470) to the **SS Great Britain**. Built in 1843 by Brunel, the *Great Britain* was the first propeller-driven ocean-going iron ship, used initially between Liverpool and New York, then between Liverpool and Melbourne, circumnavigating the globe 32 times over 26 years. Her ocean-going days ended in 1886 when she was caught in a storm off Cape Horn, and subsequently abandoned in the Falkland Islands; she was recovered in 1968. Now berthed in the same dry dock where she was constructed, the *Great Britain* is still undergoing restoration, but is open to visitors (April–Sept 10am–5.30pm; Oct–March closes 4.30pm; £6). Alongside is the much smaller **Matthew** (same times and ticket), the vessel in which John Cabot sailed to America in 1497. She was rebuilt in time for Cabot's voyage to be re-enacted on its 500th anniversary, and may be moved to a new anchorage in future. The adjoining **Maritime Heritage Centre** (same times and ticket) gives a full history of both ships and the few facts which are known about Cabot and his exploits. The museum also illustrates the port's long shipbuilding history from the eighteenth century, when it was second only to London, to its decline in the last century.

Clifton

North and west of the **Wills Tower** extends **Clifton**, once an aloof spa resort and now Bristol's most elegant quarter. Clifton Village, its select enclave, is centred on The Mall, close to **Royal York Crescent**, the longest Georgian crescent in the country, offering splendid views over the steep drop into the Avon Gorge. A few minutes' walk behind the Crescent is Bristol's most famous symbol, **Clifton Suspension Bridge**, 702ft long, poised 245ft above the river. Money was first put forward for a bridge by a Bristol wine merchant in 1753, though it was not until 1829 that a competition was held for a design, won by Isambard Brunel, and not until 1864 that the bridge was completed, five years after Brunel's death. Hampered by financial difficulties, the bridge never quite matched the engineer's original ambitious design, which included Egyptian-style towers topped by sphinxes on each end. You can see copies of his plans in the **Visitor Centre** on Sion Place (daily: Easter–Sept 10am–5.30pm; Oct–Easter 11am–4pm; £1.20). The three rooms here give the full background on the competitions and the various problems which accompanied construction.

Just above the bridge in Clifton, a small **observatory** sits on an arm of Clifton Downs overlooking the gorge, and contains a working camera obscura (daily: summer 11am–5.30pm; winter 11–4pm; closed on cloudy days, call ☎0117/9741242 to check; £1). Adjoining the Downs is **Bristol Zoo** (daily: summer 9am–6pm; winter 9am–5pm; £6), renowned for its animal conservation work, and featuring a collection of rare trees and shrubs.

Eating, drinking and nightlife

Bristol's good selection of **pubs** and **restaurants** are always crowded, with a predominantly young clientele, and the vibrant club scene usually means you can find something happening till late – pick up a copy of *Venue*, the fortnightly Bristol and Bath listings magazine (£1.90).

Restaurants

Bell's Diner, 1 York Rd (☎0117/924 0357). In the heart of the fashionable Montpelier district, a ten-minute-walk north from the Centre, this corner bistro offers an inventive menu with good-value, award-winning food. Closed Sat & Mon lunch, plus Sun eve. Moderate.

Browns, 38 Queen's Rd. Spacious and relaxed place for a cocktail or a burger; in the former university refectory, a Venetian-style structure next to the City Museum. Closed Sun. Moderate.

Harvey's, 12 Denmark St (☎0117/927 5034). Showcase restaurant in a medieval cellar complex adjoining a museum of wine that's an attraction in itself. Formal atmosphere, French food and an encyclopedic wine list. Closed Sat lunch & all Sun. Very expensive.

Las Iguanas, 10 St Nicholas St (☎0117/927 6233). Boisterous Mexican joint with a swinging basement bar. Closed Sun lunch. Moderate.

Michael's Fusion Restaurant, 129 Hotwell Rd (☎0117/927 6190). A range of innovative international dishes served in beautifully furnished Victorian surroundings. Open Tues–Sat eve, plus Sun lunch. Moderate.

River Station, The Grove (☎0117/914 4434). A former river police station artfully transformed into two great restaurants: an informal deli-bar downstairs and a restaurant above with a bigger range of international dishes. Inexpensive to Moderate.

Pubs, bars and cafés

The Albion, Boyces Avenue. Tucked away in an alley in Clifton Village (accessible from Victoria Square or Clifton Down Rd), this is a cosy old tavern with real ales and courtyard seating.

Arnolfini, Narrow Quay. This arts centre serves excellent vegetarian and meat dishes, plus drinks at the bar.

Café Tasca, 12 York Rd. A Montpelier institution for breakfasts, lunches and evening meals (Thurs–Sat only). Newspapers always available.

Cadbury House, 68 Richmond Rd, Montpelier. Loud and crowded with a good jukebox.

Fleece and Firkin, 12 St Thomas St. Loud and sweaty pub in a stone-flagged ex-wool warehouse, with regular live music and comedy.

Mud Dock Café, 40 The Grove. A winning if unlikely combination of bike shop and café/bar/restaurant by the river. Moderately priced, barbecue on the balcony in summer, and DJs most nights.

Highbury Vaults, St Michael's Hill. Amenable student-friendly pub with heated beer-garden and Smiles beers.

Nova Scotia, Cumberland Basin. Traditional waterside pub with seats by the original nineteenth-century lock.

Clubs and venues

Bierkeller, All Saints St, off Broadmead. Steamy venue for live music from thrash metal to world sounds.

Colston Hall, Colston Ave (☎0117/922 3686). Major names appear in this mainstream venue. Most of the events in the classical Proms Festival, at the end of May, take place here.

Lakota, 6 Upper York St. Bristol's most celebrated club, attracting the biggest DJs and often queues to get in. Dress up on Saturdays (no jeans or trainers).

The Maze, Hepburn Rd. Keeps Bristol's club culture kicking, attracting big crowds at weekends for techno, garage and drum'n'bass.

Thekla, Phoenix Wharf, off Queen Square. Steamy, youthful riverboat venue staging regular club nights. Open Thurs–Sat.

Berkeley Castle

Though quite secluded within a swathe of meadows and neat gardens, **Berkeley Castle** (April & May Tues–Sun 1–5pm; June & Sept Tues–Sat 11am–5pm, Sun 1–5pm; July & Aug Mon–Sat 11am–5pm, Sun 2–5pm; Oct Sun 1–5pm; castle & grounds £5.20;

grounds only £1.85) dominates the little village of Berkeley, twenty miles north of the city on the A38. The fortress has an agreeably turreted medieval look, the robust twelfth-century walls softened by later accretions acquired in its gradual transformation into a family home. The interior is packed with mementoes of its long history, including its grisliest moment in 1327 when Edward II was murdered here – apparently by a red-hot iron thrust into his bowels. Outside, the grounds include an Elizabethan terraced garden and a Butterfly Farm (£1.75). Within easy walking distance, in Berkeley village, is the **Jenner Museum** (April–Sept Tues–Sat 12.30–5.30pm, Sun 1–5.30pm; Oct Sun 1–5.30pm; £2.50), dedicated to Edward Jenner, discoverer of the principle of vaccination. From Bristol, **bus** #31 runs once daily to Berkeley Castle and bus #308 (Mon–Sat) stops here en route to Gloucester.

Clevedon

Fifteen miles south of Bristol, **CLEVEDON** is centred on hills inland from the sea, but its handsome beach promenade invites a stroll, with wind-bent trees and views across to Wales. The focal point is the **pier** (April–Oct daily 9am–5pm; Nov–March closed Wed; 75p), from where you can take **cruises** to Bristol, Gloucester, along the coast to Devon, and to Wales; tickets can be obtained from the pier's tollhouse, which doubles as the **tourist office** (same hours as pier; ☎01275/878846). Clevedon is best known for **Clevedon Court** (April–Sept Wed, Thurs & Sun 2–5pm; £4; NT), a fourteenth- and fifteenth-century manor house two miles inland. Since 1709 it has been the property of the Elton family, among whose offspring were Sir Arthur Hallam Elton – inspiration for Tennyson's elegy *In Memoriam* – and his son Edmund, whose internationally known pottery is displayed here. There is also a fascinating collection of glassware, some fine specimens of period furniture, and portraits of and drawings by William Makepeace Thackeray, who wrote much of *Vanity Fair* here, as well as making it the setting of *Henry Esmond*. The chapel is worth a look for its fine tracery, and the terraced gardens give good views seaward. **Buses** from Bristol depart at least hourly.

Bath and around

Though only twelve miles from Bristol, **BATH** has a quite different feel to its neighbour – more harmonious, compact, leisurely and complacent: it was here that Jane Austen wrote *Persuasion* and *Northanger Abbey* and Gainsborough established himself as a portraitist and landscape painter. Nowadays Bath ranks as one of Britain's top ten tourist cities, yet the place has never lost its exclusive air. Bath owes its name and fame to its **hot springs** – the only ones in the country – which made it a place of reverence for the local Celtic population, though it had to wait for Roman technology to create a fully fledged bathing establishment. The baths fell into decline with the departure of the Romans, but the town later regained its pre-eminence under the Saxons, its abbey seeing the coronation of the first king of England, Edgar, in 973. A new Tudor bathing complex was popularized by the visit of Elizabeth I in 1574, and the city reached its fashionable zenith in the eighteenth century, when Beau Nash ruled the town's social scene. It was at this time that Bath acquired its ranks of Palladian mansions and town houses, all of them built in the local **Bath stone** which is now enshrined in building regulations as an obligatory element in any new constructions in the city. Three miles southeast of the centre, near Bath University's campus, **Claverton** holds a museum of Americana amid gorgeous rolling countryside.

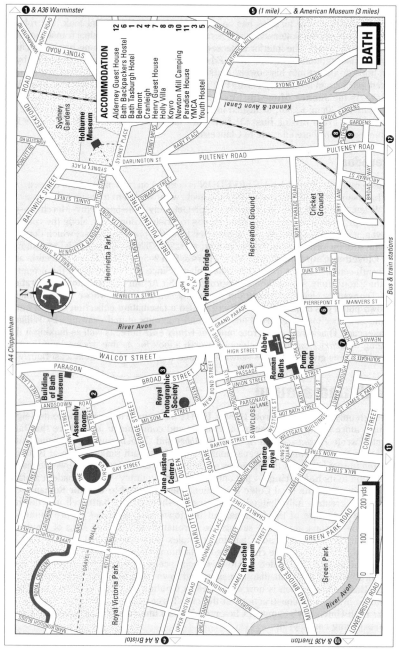

BATH

① & A36 Warminster   ⑤ (1 mile) & American Museum (3 miles)

ACCOMMODATION

Alderney Guest House	12
Bath Backpackers Hostel	6
Bath Tasburgh Hotel	1
Belmont	2
Cranleigh	4
Henry Guest House	7
Holly Villa	8
Koyro	9
Newton Mill Camping	10
Paradise House	11
YMCA	3
Youth Hostel	5

© Crown copyright

Arrival, information and accommodation

Bath Spa **train station** and the city's **bus station** are both on Manvers Street, a short walk from the centre. The **tourist office** is right next to the Abbey, on Abbey Churchyard (June–Sept Mon–Sat 9.30am–6pm, Sun 10am–4pm; Oct–May Mon–Sat 9.30am–5pm, Sun 10am–4pm; ☎01225/477101).

    Accommodation in the centre tends to get full fast, so call ahead for the likes of *Henry Guest House*, 6 Henry St (☎01225/424052; no credit cards; ②), just round the corner from the abbey, or *Alderney Guest House*, 3 Pulteney Rd (☎01225/312365; no credit cards; ①), one of the cheapest of a row of guest houses close to the train station. *Belmont*, 7 Belmont, Lansdown Rd (☎01225/423082; no credit cards; ①), has huge rooms in a house designed by John Wood, very near the Royal Crescent. Strewn with *objets d'art* and period fittings, *Cranleigh*, 159 Newbridge Hill (☎01225/310197, *cranleigh@btinternet.com*; ⑤), is situated above the city, with fine views from some of the back rooms. The YHA **hostel** is an Italianate mansion on Bathwick Hill (☎01225/465674, *bath@yha.org.uk*), a mile from the centre (buses #18 or #418), with gardens and panoramic views. More central are the independent *Bath Backpackers Hostel*, at 13 Pierrepoint St (☎01225/446787), and the YMCA, International House, Broad St (☎01225/460471, *info@ymcabath.u-net.com*). *Newton Mill Touring Centre* (☎01225/333909) is the nearest **campsite**, three miles west of the centre at Newton St Loe – take bus #5 to Newton Mill.

The City

Although Bath could easily be seen on a day-trip from Bristol, it really deserves a couple of days on the spot, particularly to explore some of the out-of-town attractions. The city itself is chock-full of museums, but some of the greatest enjoyment comes simply from the streets, with their pale gold architecture and sweeping vistas.

The Baths and the Abbey

Bath's centrepiece is, naturally enough, the **Roman Baths** (daily: April–July & Sept 9am–6pm; Aug 9am–6pm & 8–10pm; Oct–March 9.30am–5pm; £6.70; combined ticket with Museum of Costume £8.70), located in front of the abbey in the pedestrianized Abbey Church Yard. You could happily spend two or three hours here, with an audio handset allowing you to wander at your own pace around the temple and bathing complex, where a spring still issues water at a constant 46.5°C. Highlights of the remains are the open-air – but originally covered – Great Bath, its vaporous waters surrounded by nineteenth-century pillars, a terrace and statues of famous Romans; the Circular Bath, where bathers cooled off; the Norman King's Bath; and part of the temple of Minerva. Among a quantity of coins, jewellery and sculpture exhibited are the gilt bronze head of Sulis Minerva, the local deity, and a grand, Celtic-inspired gorgon's head from the temple's pediment. Models of the complex at its greatest extent give some idea of the awe which it must have inspired, while the graffiti salvaged from the Roman era – mainly curses and boasts – give a nice personal slant on this antique leisure centre. You can get a free glimpse into the baths – and taste the waters – at the next-door **Pump Room**, the social hub of the Georgian spa community and still redolent of that era, housing a tearoom and restaurant.

    Although there has been a church on the site since the seventh century, **Bath Abbey** did not take its present form until the end of the fifteenth century, when Bishop Oliver King began work on the ruins of the previous Norman building, some of which was incorporated into the new church. The bishop was said to have been inspired by a vision of angels ascending and descending a ladder to heaven, which the present facade recalls on the turrets flanking the central window. The west front also features the founder's signature in the form of carvings of olive trees surmounted by crowns, a play on his name. The interior is in a restrained Perpendicular style, and boasts splendid fan vaulting on the ceiling, which was not properly completed until the nineteenth century. The floor and walls are crammed with elaborate monuments and memorials, and traces of the grander Norman building are visible in the Norman Chapel.

To The Circus and the Royal Crescent

From Abbey Churchyard, the elegantly colonnaded Bath Street leads onto Hot Bath Street, from which turn right into Westgate Street and Sawclose, where you can take a glance at the **Theatre Royal**, opened in 1805 and one of the country's finest surviving Georgian theatres. Up from the Theatre Royal, off Barton Street, the gracious Georgian **Queen Square** was the first Bath venture of the architect **John Wood**, who with his son – also John – was chiefly responsible for the Roman-inspired developments outside the confines of the medieval city.

Just north of the square, at 40 Gay St, the **Jane Austen Centre** (daily 9.30am–5pm; £3.50) collects various objects associated with the writer in a Georgian town house just down from no. 25, one of the many places Austen inhabited in Bath. The Centre gives a good overview of Jane Austen's various connections with the town and includes a formal Georgian garden, a Georgian shopfront and sundry film costumes, though the gift shop takes up a good proportion of the place. West of the square, at 19 New King St, another typical Bath townhouse was where the musician and astronomer Sir William Herschel, in collaboration with his sister Caroline, discovered the planet Uranus in 1781. You can take a brisk whirl around the small **Herschel Museum** here (March–Oct daily 2–5pm; Nov–Feb Sat & Sun 2–5pm; £2.50), showing contemporary furnishings, musical instruments, a replica of the telescope with which Uranus was identified, and various nick-nacks from the Herschels' life.

Up from Queen Square, at the end of Gay Street, is the elder John Wood's masterpiece, **The Circus**, consisting of three crescents arranged in a tight circle of three-storey houses, with a carved frieze running round the entire circle. Wood died soon after laying the foundation stone for this enterprise, and the job was finished by his son. The painter Thomas Gainsborough lived at no. 17 from 1760 to 1774. Brock Street links The Circus to **Royal Crescent**, grandest of Bath's crescents, begun by the younger John Wood in 1767. The stately arc of thirty houses is set off by a spacious sloping lawn from which a magnificent vista extends to green hills and distant ribbons of honey-coloured stone. The interior of **1 Royal Crescent**, on the corner with Brock Street (mid-Feb to Oct Tues–Sun 10.30am–5pm; Nov to mid-Dec Tues–Sun 10.30am–4pm; £4), has been restored to reflect as nearly as possible its original Georgian appearance. At the bottom of the Crescent, Royal Avenue leads onto **Royal Victoria Park**, the city's largest open space, containing an aviary and botanical gardens.

The Assembly Rooms, the Paragon and Milsom Street

The younger John Wood's **Assembly Rooms**, east of The Circus on Bennett Street, were, with the Pump Room, the centre of Bath's social scene. A fire virtually destroyed the building in 1942, but it has now been perfectly restored and houses a **Museum of Costume** (daily 10am–5pm; £3.90), an entertaining collection of clothing from the Stuart era to the latest Japanese designs. From the Assembly Rooms, Alfred Street leads to the Paragon, at the top of Milsom Street. Here, an old Methodist chapel houses the **Building of Bath Museum** (mid-Feb to Nov Tues–Sun 10.30am–5pm; £3), which provides models and displays illustrating the construction and architecture of Bath.

At the bottom of the Paragon, off George Street, lies **Milsom Street**, a wide shopping strand designed by the elder Wood as the main thoroughfare of Georgian Bath. A former private chapel from the period now contains the **Royal Photographic Society** (daily 9.30am–5.30pm; last entry 4.45pm; £2.50), with regular exhibitions and a permanent display of equipment and prints illustrating the history of photography.

The river and Great Pulteney Street

The flow of the River Avon – a crucial ingredient in the city's charm – is interrupted by a graceful V-shaped weir just below the shop-lined **Pulteney Bridge**, an Italianate structure designed by the eighteenth-century architect Robert Adam. The bridge was intended to link the city centre with **Great Pulteney Street**, a handsome avenue originally planned as the nucleus of a large residential quarter on the eastern bank. The work ran into financial difficulties, however, so the roads running off it now stop short after a few yards, though there is a lengthy vista to the imposing classical facade of the **Holburne Museum** (late Feb to Easter Tues–Sat 11am–5pm, Sun 2.30–5.30pm; Easter to mid-Dec Mon–Sat 11am–5pm, Sun 2.30–5.30pm; £3.50), at the end of the street. The three-storey building contains an impressive range of decorative and fine art, mostly furniture, silverware, porcelain and paintings – one by Gainsborough – from the eighteenth century, plus a good collection of twentieth-century craftwork.

Behind Holburne House **Sydney Gardens** was formerly a venue for concerts and fireworks, as witnessed by Jane Austen, whose family had lodgings at 4 Sydney Place in 1801. The park makes a delightful place to take a breather, the bosky slopes cut through today by the railway and the **Kennet and Avon Canal**, which you can explore at leisure from here: it's a one-and-a-half-mile saunter to *The George* pub along a designated nature trail, and if you want to go further the canal eventually ends up at Reading. There are also summer cruises on the canal from Sydney Wharf, near Bathwick Bridge. As for the river, which runs eastwards parallel to the canal, you can rent a skiff, punt or canoe in summer from the Boating Station at the end of Forester Road, north of Holburne House, while there are organized **river trips** from Pulteney Bridge and weir.

Eating, drinking and nightlife

Bath has a reputation for gourmet cuisine, even if too many of the town's **restaurants** do over-exploit the period trappings, but there are also several decent, inexpensive places to eat. Try to be in Bath for the **Bath International Festival** (two weeks in late May & early June), which features big names in classical music, jazz, folk and blues, with a plethora of fringe events accompanying the official programme, plus fireworks, literary and art events, and lots of busking. During the rest of the year, refer to *Venue*, the fortnightly listings magazine (£1.90). **Theatre** and **ballet** fans should check out what's showing at the Theatre Royal, on Sawclose (☎01225/448844), which stages more experimental productions in the Ustinov Studio. The best of the town centre's **clubs** is *Moles* on George Street, which has live music for half the week and DJs playing dance sounds the other half, while *Hush*, The Paragon, is a pre- and post-club hang-out with three bars, lots of tables and chairs and a small dance area. The best gay/lesbian venue is Club Eros, situated under the *Bath Tap* pub at 19 St James's Parade, open on Fridays and Saturdays until 2am. There are three floors in all, including a chill-out zone.

Restaurants

Circus Restaurant, 34 Brock St (☎01225/318918). Homely but elegant, just around the corner from The Circus, serving mainly French cuisine. Non-smoking. Moderate.

Demuth's, 2 North Parade Passage (☎01225/446059). Bath's Mecca for veggies and vegans, with organic beers and wines. Reservations advisable on Fri, Sat & Sun. Non-smoking. Moderate.

The Hole in the Wall, 16 George St (☎01225/425242). Smart, pricey but classy modern British cuisine in a basement retreat. Closed Sun evening. Moderate to Expensive.

Maxson's Diner, 7 Argyle St (☎01225/444 440). A lively, sometimes crowded American-style burger bar off Pulteney Bridge. Inexpensive to Moderate.

Pump Room, Abbey Church Yard (☎01225/444477). If you don't want to splash out on a champagne breakfast or a full meal here, make sure you have at least a sandwich or tea to absorb the atmosphere, though be prepared to queue. Open daytime only, plus evenings during the Bath Festival. Moderate.

Rascals, 8 Pierrepont Place (☎01225/330280). Music and high-quality bistro food in this network of snug cellars off Manvers Street, near Parade Gardens. Moderate.

Walrus and Carpenter, 25 Barton St. Popular spot near the Theatre Royal, serving steaks, burgers, poultry dishes and a full vegetarian menu. Closed Sun. Inexpensive to Moderate.

Pubs

Coeur de Lion, Northumberland Place, off High St. Centrally located on a flagstoned shopping alley, this is Bath's smallest boozer and invariably packed, but makes for a good lunchtime stop, with some bench seating outside.

The George, Mill Lane, Bathampton. Popular canalside pub a twenty-minute walk from the centre, with decent bar food.

Hat & Feather, London St. Further up from Walcot Street, this continues the quarter's alternative theme, with plenty of atmosphere and occasional live music.

Pig & Fiddle, corner of Saracen and Walcot streets. Real ales and outside terraces, north of Pulteney Bridge. Table football and food help to pull in the crowds.

St James' Wine Vaults, St James' St. A varied clientele is attracted to this dive north of The Circus, which has music in the basement.

Claverton

For a quick sample of the lovely countryside around Bath you could make an easy excursion to the **American Museum** (museum: late March to early Nov Tues–Sun 2–5pm; Aug also open Mon 2–5pm; grounds only: Tues–Fri 1–6pm, Sat & Sun noon–6pm; museum £5; grounds £2.50) in **CLAVERTON**, on the eastern edge of Bath. Occupying the early nineteenth-century Claverton Manor, where Winston Churchill made his maiden political speech in 1897, this was the first museum of Americana to be established outside the US, and consists of a series of reconstructed rooms illustrating life in the New World from the seventeenth to the nineteenth centuries, as well as special sections devoted to textiles, whaling, the opening of the West, Native Americans and Hispano-American culture. The glorious **grounds** contain a replica of George Washington's garden, an arboretum, and assorted relics resembling items from a movie set. **Bus #418** runs throughout the year to The Avenue, from where it's a ten-minute walk.

Wells, the Mendips and Glastonbury

Wells, twenty miles south of Bristol across the Somerset border, and the same distance from Bath, is a miniature cathedral city that has not significantly altered in eight hundred years. You might also decide to make it a base for visiting the **Wookey Hole** caves or **Cheddar Gorge** in the nearby **Mendip Hills**. On the southern edge of the range, the town of **Glastonbury** has for centuries been one of the main Arthurian sites of the West Country, and is now the country's biggest New Age centre.

Wells

Technically the smallest city in England, **WELLS** owes its status entirely to its **cathedral**, begun in 1180. Hidden from sight until you pass into its central enclosure from the Market Place, the building presents a majestic spectacle, the broad lawn of the former graveyard providing a perfect foreground. The **west front** teems with some three hundred thirteenth-century figures of saints and kings, once brightly painted and gilded, though their present honey tint has a subtle splendour of its own. The **interior** is a supreme example of early English Gothic, the long nave punctuated by a dramatic "scissor arch", one of three that were constructed in 1338 to take the extra weight of the newly built tower. Though some wax enthusiatic about the ingenuity of these strainer arches, others view them as grotesque intrusions from an artistic point of view.

Other features worth scrutinizing are the narrative carvings on the **capitals and corbels** in the transepts – including men with toothache and an old man caught pilfering an orchard. In the north transept, don't miss the 24-hour astronomical clock, dating from 1390, whose jousting knights charge each other every quarter-hour, as announced by a figure known as Jack Blandiver, who kicks a couple of bells from his seat high up on the right – on the hour he strikes the bell in front of him. Opposite the clock, a doorway leads to a graceful, much-worn flight of steps rising to the **Chapter House**, an octagonal room elaborately ribbed in the Decorated style. There are some gnarled old tombs to be seen in the aisles of the **choir**, at the end of which is the richly coloured stained glass of the fourteenth-century **Lady Chapel**.

The row of clerical houses on the north side of the cathedral green are mainly seventeenth- and eighteenth-century, though one, the **Old Deanery**, shows traces of its fifteenth-century origins. The chancellor's house is now a **museum** (Easter–June, Sept & Oct daily 10am–5.30pm; July & Aug daily 10am–8pm; Nov–Easter Wed–Sun 11am–4pm; £2), displaying, among other items, some of the cathedral's original statuary, placed here for conservation reasons (and replaced by replicas), as well as a good geological section with fossils from the surrounding area, including Wookey Hole. A little further along the street, the cobbled, medieval **Vicars' Close** holds more clerical dwellings, linked to the cathedral by the Chain Gate and fronted by small gardens. Built in the mid-fourteenth century, they have been continuously occupied by members of the cathedral clergy ever since.

On the other side of the cathedral – and accessible through the cathedral shop – are the cloisters, from which you can enter the tranquil grounds of the **Bishop's Palace** (April–July, Sept & Oct Tues–Fri 11am–6pm, Sun 2–6pm; Aug daily 10.30am–6pm; £3). The residence of the Bishop of Bath and Wells, the palace was walled and moated as a result of a rift with the borough in the fourteenth century, and the imposing gatehouse still displays the grooves of the portcullis and a chute for pouring oil and molten lead on would-be assailants. Its tranquil gardens contain the springs from which the city takes its name.

Practicalities

Wells **bus station** is off Market Street, while the **tourist office** is on Market Place (daily: April–Oct 9.30am–5.30pm; Nov–March 10am–4pm; ☎01749/672552). Among the best **B&Bs** are the seventeenth-century *Tor Guest House*, overlooking the cathedral (☎01749/672322; ②), and *Bekynton House*, 7 St Thomas St (☎01749/672222, *desmond@bekynton.freeserve.co.uk*; ②). On the High Street there's the *Market Place Hotel* (☎01749/672616; ⑤) and *The Star Hotel* (☎01749/670500; ④), both old coaching inns. For **food**, try *Chapel's*, on Union Street, off High Street, a modern café-bar with a varied menu, or Sadler Street, where you'll find the Italian-run *Ancient Gate House* (☎01749/672 029) and *Ritcher's* (☎01749/679085), which has a downstairs bistro and serves topnotch dishes in the plant-filled restaurant in the loft. *Good Earth*, on Priory Road (closed Sun), offers great wholefood, while you can find decent **pub** fare at the *City Arms* on Cuthbert Street – formerly the city jail.

The Mendips

The **Mendip Hills**, rising to the north of Wells, are chiefly famous for Wookey Hole – the most impressive of many caves in this narrow limestone chain – and for the **Cheddar Gorge**, where a walk through the narrow cleft might make a starting point for more adventurous trips across the Mendips. From Monday to Saturday there's an hourly bus service to Wookey Hole from Wells (#172), from where there's also an hourly bus to the gorge (#126 or #826).

Wookey Hole

Hollowed out by the River Axe a couple of miles outside Wells, **Wookey Hole** is an impressive cave complex of deep pools and intricate rock formations, but it's folklore rather than geology that takes precedence on the guided **tours** – the only way to visit (daily: April–Oct 10am–5pm; Nov–Feb 10.30am–4.30pm; £7). The highlight of the tour is the alleged petrified remains of the Witch of Wookey, a "blear-eyed hag" who was said to turn her evil eye on crops, young lovers and local farmers until the Abbot of Glastonbury intervened – he dispatched a monk who drove the witch into the inner cave, sprinkled her with holy water and turned her into stone. Beside her were found two skeletons, the remains of goats tied to a stake. At the end of the hour-long tour, you can visit a functioning Victorian paper mill by the river, and rooms containing speleological exhibits. On a less earnest note is the gaudy range of Edwardian amusements laid on by Madame Tussaud's, owners of the complex.

Cheddar Gorge

Six miles west of Wookey on the A371, Cheddar has given its name to Britain's best-known cheese – most of it now mass-produced far from here. However, the biggest selling point of this rather plain village is the **Cheddar Gorge**, lying beyond the neighbourhood of Tweentown about a mile to the north. Cutting a jagged gash across the Mendip Hills, the limestone gorge is an impressive geological phenomenon, though its natural beauty is undermined by the minor road running through it and by the Lower Gorge's mile of shops, its coach park and **tourist office** (Easter–Oct daily 10am–5pm; Nov–Easter Sat & Sun 10am–5pm; ☎01934/744071).

Few trippers venture further than the first few curves of the gorge beyond the shops, which admittedly hold its most dramatic scenery, though each turn of the two-mile length presents new, sometimes startling vistas. At the narrowest part of the gorge, the road squeezes between cliffs towering almost 500ft above. Alternatively, avoid the road altogether by taking cliff-top paths that wind along the rim of the gorge. Sticking on the gorge road, you can continue as far as **Priddy**, the highest village in the Mendips, though you can reach more dramatic destinations by branching off on foot along marked paths to such secluded spots as **Black Rock**, just two miles from Cheddar, or **Black Down** (1067ft), the Mendips' highest peak.

Beneath the gorge, the **Cheddar Caves** (daily: Easter to mid-Sept 10am–5pm; mid-Sept to Easter 10am–4.30pm; £7.50) were scooped out by underground rivers in the wake of the Ice Age, and later occupied by primitive communities. Today the chambers, adorned with tortuous rock formations that resemble organ pipes, waterfalls and giant birds, have floodlighting and laser effects to pick out the pinks, greys, greens and whites in the rock. Outside, close to Cox's Caves, the 274 steps of **Jacob's Ladder** (same ticket as caves) lead to a cliff-top viewpoint towards Glastonbury Tor, Exmoor and the sea. It's a muscle-wrenching climb – anyone not in a state of honed fitness can reach the same spot via a narrow lane winding up behind the cliffs. You can also survey the panorama from **Pavey's Lookout Tower** nearby.

Among Cheddar's handful of **B&Bs**, *Chedwell Cottage*, on Redcliffe St (☎01934/743268; no credit cards; ①), has two en-suite rooms, or try the similarly priced *Innishbeg*, West Lynne, off Tweentown (Easter–Aug; ☎01934/743 494; no credit cards; ①). Alternatively, there's a **youth hostel** opposite the fire station, off the Hayes (☎01934/742494; closed Jan), and two central **campsites**, *Froglands* (☎01934/742058; closed Nov–Easter) and *Church Farm* (☎01934/743048; closed Nov–Easter), across the road.

Glastonbury

Six miles south of Wells, **GLASTONBURY** lies at the centre of the so-called **Isle of Avalon**, a region rich with mystical associations. At the heart of it all is the early Christian legend that the young Jesus once visited this site. The Romans had a heavy presence in the area, mining lead in the Mendips, and one of these mines was supposedly owned by **Joseph of Arimathea**, a well-to-do merchant said to have been related to Mary. A legend has grown up around the theory that the merchant took his kinsman on one of his many visits to his property, in a period of Jesus's life of which nothing is recorded. It was this possibility to which William Blake referred in his *Glastonbury Hymn*, better known as *Jerusalem*: – "And did those feet in ancient time/ Walk upon England's mountains green?" Another legend relates how Joseph was imprisoned for twelve years after the crucifixion, miraculously kept alive by the **Holy Grail**, the chalice of the Last Supper, in which the blood was gathered from the wound in Christ's side. The Grail, along with the spear which had caused the wound, were later taken by Joseph to Glastonbury, where he founded the abbey and commenced the conversion of Britain.

According to the official version, however, **Glastonbury Abbey** (daily: June–Aug 9am–6pm; Sept–May 10am–dusk; £3) was a Celtic monastery founded in the fourth or fifth century – making this the oldest Christian foundation in England – and enlarged by St Dunstan, under whom it became the richest Benedictine abbey in the country. Three Anglo-Saxon kings – Edmund, Edgar and Edmund Ironside – were buried here, the library had a far-reaching fame, and the church had the longest known nave of any monastic church, at 580ft, 165ft longer than Wells Cathedral's. The original building was destroyed by fire in 1184 and the ruins are the rather scanty remains of what took its place, reduced to their present state at the Dissolution. Hidden behind walls at the centre of town, surrounded by grassy parkland and shaded by trees, the ruins only hint at the extent of the building, which was financed largely by a constant procession of medieval pilgrims. The most prominent and photogenic remains are the transept piers and the shell of the Lady Chapel, with its carved figures of the Annunciation, the Magi and Herod.

The abbey's **choir** introduces another strand to the Glastonbury story, for it holds what is alleged to be the tomb of **Arthur and Guinevere**. As told by William of Malmesbury and Thomas Malory, the story relates how, after being mortally wounded in battle, King Arthur sailed to Avalon, where he was buried alongside his queen. The discovery of two bodies in an ancient cemetery outside the abbey in 1191 – from which they were transferred here in 1278 – was taken to confirm the popular identification of Glastonbury with Avalon. In the grounds, the fourteenth-century **abbot's kitchen** is the only monastic building to survive intact, with four huge corner fireplaces and a great central lantern above. Behind the main entrance to the grounds, look out for the thorn-tree that is supposedly from the original **Glastonbury Thorn** – said to have sprouted from the staff of Joseph of Arimathea when he arrived here, seeking converts.

On the edge of the abbey grounds, the medieval abbey barn forms the centrepiece of the engaging **Somerset Rural Life Museum** (April–Oct Tues–Fri 10am–5pm, Sat &

Sun 2–6pm; Nov–March Tues–Sat 10am–3pm; £2.50), illustrating a range of local rural occupations, from cheese- and cider-making to peat-digging, thatching and farming.

From the ruins it's a mile-long hike to **Glastonbury Tor**, at 521ft a landmark for miles around. The conical hill is topped by the dilapidated **St Michael's Tower**, sole remnant of a fourteenth-century church; it commands stupendous views encompassing Wells, the Quantocks, the Mendips, the Somerset Levels – once marshy peat moors rolling out to the sea – and sometimes the Welsh mountains. Pilgrims once embarked on the stiff climb here with hard peas in their shoes as penance – nowadays people come to feel the vibrations of crossing ley lines. If you don't fancy the steep ascent, there's an easier path further up Wellhouse Lane, the road that leads to the Tor Park from the centre of town. At the bottom of Wellhouse Lane, in the middle of a lush garden intended for quiet contemplation, the **Chalice Well** (daily: April–Oct 10am–6pm; Nov–March noon–4pm; £1.50) is meant to be the hiding place of the Holy Grail. The iron-red waters were considered to have curative properties, making the town a spa for a brief period in the eighteenth century, and they are still prized – bring a flask if you want to take some, or there's a tap in Wellhouse Lane when the garden is closed.

Back in town, you might take a glance at the fifteenth-century church of **St John the Baptist**, halfway along the High Street. The tower is reckoned to be one of Somerset's finest, and the **interior** has a fine oak roof and stained glass illustrating the legend of St Joseph of Arimathea, both from the period of the church's construction. The Glastonbury thorn in the churchyard is the biggest in town. Further down the street, the fourteenth-century **Tribunal** (daily: April–Sept 10am–5pm; Oct–March 10am–4pm; £1.50) was where the abbots presided over legal cases; it later became a hotel for pilgrims, and now holds a small **museum** of finds from the Iron Age lake villages that once fringed the marshland below the Tor.

Practicalities

Glastonbury's **tourist office** is in the Tribunal on High Street (same hours as above; ☎01458/832954). **Bicycles** can be rented at Pedalers, 8 Magdalene St. Among the town's less expensive **accommodation** choices, the seventeenth-century *Waterfall Cottage*, 20 Old Wells Rd, boasts a garden and views (☎01458/831707; no credit cards; ①). *The Bolthole*, 32 Chilkwell St (☎01458/832800; no credit cards; ①), is a comfortable **B&B**, though not as grand as the *Ramala Centre*, on nearby Dod Lane (☎01458/832459; ②), a meditation hostel which also offers accommodation without strings. If you prefer a more medieval mood, opt for the oak-panelled *George and Pilgrims*, High St (☎01458/831146; ⑤). The nearest **youth hostel** (☎01458/442961; closed Sept–March) lies a couple of miles outside the village of Street, an easy bus ride away, while *Glastonbury Backpackers*, 4 Market Place (☎01458/833353, *glastonbury@backpackers-online.com*), offers a livelier atmosphere. There's a decent **campsite** at the *Isle of Avalon* (☎01458/833618), a ten-minute walk up Northload Street to Godney Road, off the B3151.

There are some decent **cafés** wedged between the esoteric shops of Glastonbury's High Street, including the *Excalibur* and the *Global Café*, whose felafel and bean salads are sometimes accompanied by live music. The *Blue Note Café* is another good place to hang out over coffees and cakes, often with live music. Halfway up the High Street, the *Assembly Rooms* has a wholefood café, but is better known as the venue for talks, and musical and theatrical **performances**. Concerts and miracle plays are staged within the abbey grounds during the summer (☎01458/832267), though Glastonbury is best known for its **music festival** outside the nearby village of Pilton, usually over three days in the third week of of June. Prices are steep (over £80) and tickets are snapped up early in the year: contact the promoters (☎01749/890470) or the tourist office, which also sells tickets.

Taunton and the Quantocks

Travelling west from the Glastonbury region, your route could take you through **Taunton**, which makes a handy starting point for excursions into the gently undulating **Quantock Hills**, a mellow landscape of snug villages set in scenic wooded valleys or "combes". Public transport is fairly minimal round here, but there are horseriding facilities at many local farms, and you can see quite a lot on the **West Somerset Railway** between Bishops Lydeard and the coastal resort of Minehead, with stops at some of the thatched, typically English villages along the west flank of the Quantocks.

Taunton

TAUNTON, Somerset's county town, lies in the fertile Vale of Taunton Deane, wedged between the Quantock, Brendon and Blackdown hills. The region is famed for its production of cider and scrumpy (cider's less refined cousin), while Taunton itself is host to one of the country's biggest cattle markets. Taunton's **Castle**, started in the twelfth century, staged the trial of royal claimant Perkin Warbeck, who in 1490 declared himself to be the Duke of York, the younger of the "Princes in the Tower", sons of Edward IV, who were murdered seven years earlier. Most of the castle was pulled down in 1662, but a part of it now houses the **County Museum** (Tues–Sat 10am–5pm; £2.50), which includes a portrait of the infamous Judge Jeffreys – whose Bloody Assizes in the wake of the Monmouth Rebellion created a folk-memory in Somerset of gibbets and gutted carcases – among other memorabilia of local interest. Overlooking the county cricket ground are the pinnacled and battlemented towers of the town's two most important churches: **St James** and **St Mary Magdalene**, both fifteenth century, though remodelled by the Victorians. St Mary's is worth a look inside for its roof bosses carved with medieval masks.

Otherwise Taunton should only detain you as a base to visit the Quantock villages or Exmoor. Information is on hand at the **tourist office** in Paul Street (Mon–Fri 9.30am–5.30pm, Sat 9.30am–5pm; April–Oct open till 7pm on Fri; ☎01823/336344), in the library under the multistorey car park. If you want to stay here, head for Wellington Road, in the centre, where there are three **B&Bs**: *Brookfield*, at no. 16 (☎01823/272786; no credit cards; ②), *Beaufort Lodge*, at no. 18 (☎01823/326420; no credit cards; ②), and *Acorn Lodge*, at no. 22 (☎01823/337613; no credit cards; ①). For a snack or **meal**, walk for about ten minutes from Fore Street down East Street to *Porter's*, a congenial and inexpensive wine bar at 49 East Reach.

The Quantocks

Geologically closer to Devon than Somerset, the **Quantock Hills** are a cultivated outpost of Exmoor, similarly crossed by clear streams and grazed by red deer. Just twelve miles in length, the range is enclosed by a triangle of roads leading up from Bridgwater and Taunton, within which snake a tangle of narrow lanes connecting secluded hamlets, reached by local buses from these two towns.

North of Taunton, the first villages you pass through on the A358 give you an immediate introduction to the flavour of the Quantocks. **BISHOPS LYDEARD**, four miles up, has a splendid church tower in the Perpendicular style, and the church's interior is also worth a look for its carved bench ends. The village is the terminus of the **West Somerset Railway**, linked by buses #28 and #28A from Taunton train station. From mid-March to early November (plus some dates in December) steam and diesel trains depart up to eight times daily, stopping at renovated stations on the way to Minehead, some twenty miles away (see p.309).

Across the Quantocks, and eight miles north of Taunton on the A39, the pretty village of **NETHER STOWEY** is best known for its association with **Samuel Taylor Coleridge**, who walked here from Bristol at the end of 1796, to join his wife and child at their new home. This "miserable cottage", as Sara Coleridge called it, was visited six months later by William Wordsworth and his sister Dorothy, who soon afterwards moved into Alfoxton House, near Holford, a couple of miles down the road. Coleridge composed some of his best poetry at this time, including *The Rime of the Ancient Mariner* and *Kubla Khan*, and the two poets in collaboration produced the *Lyrical Ballads*, the poetic manifesto of early English Romanticism.

In **Coleridge's cottage** (April–Sept Tues–Thurs & Sun 2–5pm; £2.50; NT), not such an "old hovel" now, you can see his parlour and reading room, and upstairs, the bedroom and an exhibition room containing various letters and first editions, and a portrait of the poet. The village library in nearby Castle Street houses the **Quantock Information Centre** (☎01278/732845) offering walking itineraries and local information. For **accommodation**, a good choice in the village is *Castle Cottage*, at 12 Castle St (☎01278/733453; no credit cards; ①), a seventeenth-century house which also serves light meals and teas to non-guests. **Holford** has *Quantock House*, a beautiful Elizabethan thatched cottage (☎01278/741439; no credit cards; ②), and a **youth hostel** (☎01278/741224; closed Sept–March), in whose grounds you can **camp**, a signposted two-mile walk from Holford's centre. Holford's *Plough Inn*, where Virginia and Leonard Woolf spent their honeymoon, serves simple **snacks**, and is also a stop on the #15 Bridgwater–Minehead bus route. If you want to do some **pony trekking**, contact *Mill Farm* at Fiddington, near Nether Stowey (☎01278/732286) – also a useful **campsite**.

Exmoor

A high bare plateau sliced by wooded combes and splashing rivers, **EXMOOR** can be one of the most forbidding landscapes in England, especially when the sea mist descends. When it's clear, though, the moorland of this national park reveals rich swathes of colour and an amazing diversity of wildlife, from buzzards to the short and stocky **Exmoor ponies**, a species closely related to prehistoric horses. In the treeless heartland of the moor around Simonsbath, it's not difficult to spot these unique animals, though fewer than 1200 are registered, and of these only about 180 are free-living on the moor. Much more elusive are the **red deer**, England's largest native wild animal, of which Exmoor supports England's only wild population; around 2500 are thought to inhabit the moor today.

Endless permutations of **walking routes** are possible along a network of some six hundred miles of footpaths and bridleways. There are four obvious bases: **Dulverton** in the southeast, site of the main information facilities; **Simonsbath** in the centre; **Exford**, near Exmoor's highest point of Dunkery Beacon; and the attractive village of **Winsford**, close to the A396 on the east of the moor. Exmoor's coastline offers an alluring alternative to the open moorland, all of it accessible via the **South West Coast Path**, which embarks on its long coastal journey at **Minehead**, though there is more charm to be found further west at the sister villages of **Lynmouth** and **Lynton**, just over the Devon border. **Horseback** is another way of getting the most out of Exmoor's desolate beauty, and stables are dotted throughout the area – the most convenient are mentioned below.

Dulverton

The village of **DULVERTON**, on the southern edge of the national park near Brompton Regis, is the Park Authority's headquarters and so makes a good introduction to Exmoor. Information is available at the **Visitor Centre**, at 7 Fore St (daily:

Easter–Oct 10am–1.15pm & 1.45–5pm; Nov–Easter 10.30am–2.30pm; ☎01398/323841).
Accommodation in Dulverton includes *Town Mills* (☎01398/323124; no credit cards;
①), an old millhouse in the centre of the village. If you hanker after beams and four-
posters, try the *Lion Hotel*, in Bank Square (☎01398/323444; ③). *Crispin's*, in a nook off
26 High St, does moderately priced **food**, including vegetarian. **Pony trekking** is
offered at *West Anstey Farm* (☎01398/341354), two miles west of Dulverton, which also
provides accommodation for riders.

Winsford, Exford and Dunkery Beacon

Five miles north of Dulverton, **WINSFORD** lays good claim to being the moor's prettiest village. A scattering of thatched cottages ranged around a sleepy green, it is
watered by a confluence of streams and rivers – one of them the Exe – giving it no fewer
than seven bridges. *Larcombe Foot*, a mile to the north (☎01643/851306; no credit
cards; ①; closed Jan & Feb), offers excellent **B&B** overlooking the Exe, and there's a
campsite nearby at *Halse Farm* (☎01643/851259; closed Nov–Feb). The *Royal Oak*, a
thoroughly thatched and rambling old inn on the village green (☎01643/851455; ⑤),
can offer you drinks, snacks and full restaurant **meals**.

The hamlet of **EXFORD**, an ancient bridging point on the River Exe, is popular with
walkers for the four-mile hike from here to **Dunkery Beacon**, Exmoor's highest point
at 1700ft. The village also holds Exmoor's main **youth hostel**, a large Victorian house
in the centre (☎01643/831288; closed Nov to mid-Feb). Three miles east at Luckwell
Bridge, and convenient for Dunkery Beacon, *Cutthorne* (☎01643/831255; ③) is a
secluded eighteenth-century farmhouse offering **B&B**, while *Westermill Farm*
(☎01643/831238; closed Nov–March) provides a tranquil **campsite** on the banks of the
Exe. **Riding** at all levels can be arranged at *Stockleigh Stables*, half a mile north of
Exford (☎01643/831166).

Simonsbath and around

At the centre of the National Park stands **Exmoor Forest**, the barest part of the moor,
scarcely populated except by roaming sheep and a few red deer; the word "forest"
denotes simply that it was a hunting reserve. In the middle of it stands the village of
SIMONSBATH (pronounced "Simmonsbath"), home to the Knight family, who
bought the forest in 1818 and, by introducing tenant farmers, building roads and
importing sheep, brought systematic agriculture to an area that had never before produced any income. The Knights also built a wall around their land – parts of which can
still be seen – as well as the intriguing Pinkworthy (pronounced "Pinkery") Pond, four
miles to the northwest, whose exact function has never been explained. The *Exmoor
Forest Hotel* (☎01643/831341, *helen@exforest.freeserve.co.uk*; ①) offers comfortable
accommodation, and also space for free **camping**. There's a decent restaurant here
too, *Boevey's*, in a converted barn near the *Simonsbath House Hotel* (☎01643/831259;
⑤), a cosy bolt-hole with agreeably gnarled rooms. A couple of miles outside the village
on the Brayford road, the *Poltimore Arms* at **Yarde Down** is a classic country **pub**,
serving excellent food including vegetarian dishes.

Minehead and around

Once a major port on the Somerset coast, **MINEHEAD** quickly became a favourite
Victorian watering hole with the arrival of the railway, and has ever since retained a
cheerful holiday-town atmosphere. Steep lanes containing some of the oldest houses
link the two quarters of **Higher Town** on North Hill, and the livelier **Quay Town**, the
harbour area. It is in Quay Town that the "Hobby Horse" performs its dance in the
town's three-day May Day celebrations, snaring maidens under its prancing skirt and
tail in a fertility ritual resembling the more famous festivities at Padstow (see p.351).

THE SOUTH WEST COAST PATH

The **South West Coast Path**, the longest footpath in Britain, starts at Minehead and tracks the coastline along Devon's northern seaboard, round Cornwall, back into Devon, and on to Dorset. The path was conceived in the 1940s, but it is only in the last fifteen or so years that – barring some insignificant gaps – the full **six-hundred-mile route** has been open, much of it on land owned by the National Trust, and all of it well signposted.

The relevant Ordnance Survey maps can be found at most village shops on the route, while many newsagents, bookshops and tourist offices will stock books or pamphlets containing route plans and details of local flora and fauna. The Countryside Agency, in conjunction with Ordnance Survey, produces a series of books (published by Aurum Press) describing different parts of the path, while the South West Coast Path Association, Windlestraw, Penquit, Ermington, Devon PL21 0LU (☎01752/896237) publishes an annual guide (£5.99 incl. postage & packing) to the whole path, including accommodation lists, ferry timetables and so forth.

The **tourist office** is midway between Higher Town and Quay Town, at 17 Friday St, off the Parade (April–June, Sep & Oct Mon–Sat 9.30am–5pm; July & Aug Mon–Sat 9.30am–5pm, Sun 10am–1pm; Nov–March Mon–Sat 10am–4pm; ☎01643/702624). If you want to **stay** in Minehead, try *Avill House*, on Townsend Rd, a short walk from the seafront past the tourist office (☎01643/704370; no credit cards; ①), or the central *Mayfair Hotel*, 25 The Avenue (☎01643/702719; ③; closed Dec–March). There's a **youth hostel** a couple of miles southeast, outside the village of Alcombe (☎01643/702595; closed Nov–March), in a secluded combe on the edge of Exmoor.

The old village of **DUNSTER** is about a mile from the first stop on the **West Somerset Railway**, three miles inland of Minehead. The main street is dominated by the towers and turrets of **Dunster Castle** (castle: April–Sept Mon–Wed, Sat & Sun 11am–5pm; Oct Mon–Wed, Sat & Sun 11am–4pm; grounds: April–Sept daily 11am–5pm, Oct–March daily 11am–4pm; castle & grounds £5.40; grounds £2.90; NT), most of whose fortifications were demolished after the Civil War. After that the castle became something of an architectural showpiece, and Victorian restoration has made it into something more like a Rhineland *schloss* than a Norman stronghold. On a tour of the castle you can see a bedroom once occupied by Charles I, a fine seventeenth-century carved staircase and a richly decorated banqueting hall. The grounds include terraced gardens and riverside walks – and drama productions are periodically staged here in summer. The nearby hilltop tower is a Georgian-Gothic folly, **Conygar Tower**, dating from 1776.

Despite the influx of seasonal visitors, Dunster village preserves relics of its wool-making heyday: the octagonal **Yarn Market**, in the High Street below the castle, dates from 1609, while the three-hundred-year-old **water mill**, at the end of Mill Lane (April–June, Sept & Oct Mon–Fri & Sun; July & Aug daily 10.30am–5pm; £2.10; NT), is still used commercially and its riverside garden provides a decent place to eat lunch. For somwhere to **stay**, try the elegant old *Dollons House*, 10 Church St (☎01643/821880, *hannah.bradshaw@virgin.net*; ③).

Porlock

The real enticement of **PORLOCK**, six miles west of Minehead, is its extraordinary position in a deep hollow, cupped on three sides by the hogbacked hills of Exmoor. Unfortunately, the thatch-and-cob houses and dripping charm of the village's long main street have led to invasions of tourists, some of whom are also drawn by the place's literary links. According to Coleridge's own less than reliable testimony, it was a "man from Porlock" who broke the opium trance in which he was composing *Kubla Khan*, while the High Street's beamed *Ship Inn* prides itself on featuring prominently in the Exmoor romance *Lorna Doone* (see below), and in real life having sheltered the poet Robert Southey, who staggered in, rain-soaked after an Exmoor ramble.

The best **accommodation** in town is on the High Street: try the atmospheric *The Ship* (☎01643/862507, *theship@btconnect.com*; ③) or the Victorian *Lorna Doone Hotel* (☎01643/862404, *lorna@doone99.freeserve.co.uk*; ②). Further down, *The Cottage* is smaller and quainter (☎01643/862687; ③). Porlock has a convenient central **campsite**, *Sparkhayes Farm* (☎01643/862470; closed Nov–March). Both *The Cottage* and *Lorna Doone* serve snacks and **meals**.

Lynton and Lynmouth

West from Porlock, the road climbs 1350ft in less than three miles, though there is a gentler and more scenic alternative via a toll road (cars £2, bikes 50p). Nine miles along the coast, on the Devon side of the county line, the Victorian resort of **LYNTON** perches above a lofty gorge, with splendid views over the sea. Almost completely cut off from the rest of the country for most of its history, the village struck lucky during the Napoleonic Wars, when frustrated grand tourists – unable to visit their usual continental haunts – discovered in Lynton a domestic piece of Swiss landscape. Coleridge and Hazlitt trudged over to Lynton from the Quantocks, but the greatest spur to the village's popularity came with the publication in 1869 of R.D. Blackmore's Exmoor melodrama *Lorna Doone*, a book based on the outlaw clans who inhabited these parts in the seventeenth century. The imposing **town hall** on Lee Road epitomizes the Victorian-Edwardian accent of Lynton. It was the gift of publisher George Newnes, who also donated the nearby hydraulic cliff railway connecting Lynton with Lynmouth (daily: March–June, Oct & Nov 9am–7pm; July–Sept 9am–10pm; 50p, £1 after 7pm).

Lynton's **tourist office** is in the town hall (Easter–Oct daily 9.30am–6pm; Nov–Easter Mon–Sat 10am–4pm; ☎01598/752225). There's a good choice of inexpensive **B&Bs**, among them the Victorian *The Turret*, 33 Lee Rd (☎01598/753284; no credit cards; ①), and the more central *St Vincent*, on Castle Hill (☎01598/752244, *keenstvincent@lineone.net*; ①), with spacious bedrooms and a garden. The *Lynhurst Hotel*, Lyn Way (☎01598/752241; ②), is further out from the centre, but has striking

---

WALKS FROM LYNTON AND LYNMOUTH

The major year-round attraction in these parts is walking, not only along the coast path but inland. The one-and-a-half-mile tramp to **Watersmeet**, for example, follows the East Lyn river to where it is joined by Hoar Oak Water, a tranquil spot transformed into a roaring torrent after a bout of rain. From the fishing lodge here – now owned by the National Trust and open as a café and shop in summer – you can branch off on a range of less trodden paths, such as the three-quarters-of-a-mile route south to **Hillsford Bridge**, at the confluence of Hoar Oak and Farley Water.

North of Watersmeet, a path climbs up **Countisbury Hill** and the higher **Butter Hill** (nearly 1000ft), giving riveting views of Lynton, Lynmouth and the north Devon coast, and there is also a track leading to the lighthouse at **Foreland Point**, close to the coastal path. East from Lynmouth you can reach the point via a fine sheltered shingle beach at the foot of Countisbury Hill – one of a number of tiny coves that are accessible on either side of the estuary.

From Lynton, an undemanding expedition takes you west along the North Walk, a mile-long path leading to the **Valley of the Rocks**, a steeply curved heathland dominated by rugged rock formations. At the far end of the valley, herds of wild goats range free, as they have done for centuries.

views over the valley. There is a **youth hostel** (☎01598/753237; closed Jan to mid-Feb) about a mile inland from Lynton's centre, signposted off Lynbridge Road. **Snacks** and coffees are served at *Lily May's*, opposite St Mary's Church.

Five hundred feet below Lynton, **LYNMOUTH** lies at the confluence and estuary of the East and West Lyn rivers, in a spot described by Gainsborough as "the most delightful place for a landscape painter this country can boast". The picturesque scene was shattered in August 1952 when Lynmouth was almost washed away by floodwaters coming off Exmoor, a disaster of which there are many reminders around the village. Having recovered its calm, Lynmouth is only ruffled now by the summer crowds, though nothing could compromise the village's unique location. Shelley spent his honeymoon here with his sixteen-year-old bride Harriet Westbrook, making time in his nine-week sojourn to write his polemical *Queen Mab*; two different houses claim to have been the Shelleys' love nest. Nearby, you can explore the walks and waterfalls of the wooded **Glen Lyn Gorge** (daily: 9am–dusk; exhibition Easter–Oct 9am–dusk; £2), which has displays on the uses and dangers of water-power – this was the course taken by the destructive floods of 1952.

Lynmouth has a **National Park Visitor Centre** at the harbour (April–Oct daily 10am–5pm; ☎01598/752509). The most inspiring **place to stay** is *Harbour Point*, a B&B right on the harbour, at 1 The Esplanade (☎01598/752321; no credit cards; ②). Next door is the *Rising Sun Hotel* (☎01598/753223; ⑥), a fourteenth-century thatched inn. Other good choices are the posh *Bath Hotel*, Harbourside (☎01598/752238; ③), and the *Orchard House Hotel*, 12 Watersmeet Rd (☎01598/753247; ①; closed Jan & Dec). The *Village Inn*, on Lynmouth St, does inexpensive **lunches**, though you'll find better fare at the *Rising Sun* and the *Bath Hotel*.

DEVON

With its rolling meadows, narrow lanes and thatched cottages, **Devon** has long been the urbanite's ideal vision of a pre-industrial, "authentic" England, and a quick tour of the county might suggest that this is a region of cosy, gentrified villages inhabited largely by retired folk and urban refugees. Certainly Devon suffers from an excess of cloying nostalgia, but its popularity has a positive side to it as well – chiefly that zealous care is taken to preserve the undeveloped stretches of countryside and coast in the condition that has made them so popular. Pockets of genuine tranquillity are still to be found all over the county, from Dartmoor villages with an appeal that goes deeper than the merely picturesque, to quiet coves on the spectacular coastline.

Devon has played a leading part in England's **maritime history**, and you can't go far without being reminded of the great Tudor and Stuart seafarers, particularly in the two cities of **Exeter** and **Plymouth**. These days the nautical tradition is perpetuated by yachtspeople taking advantage of Devon's numerous creeks and bays, especially on its southern coast. Land-bound tourists flock to the sandy beaches and seaside resorts, of which **Torquay** on the south coast and **Ilfracombe** on the north are the busiest, though the most attractive are those which have retained something of their nineteenth-century elegance, such as **Sidmouth** and **Dartmouth**. Other seaside villages retain a low level of fishing activity but otherwise live on a stilted Old World image, of which **Clovelly** is the supreme example. Inland, Devon is characterized by swathes of lush pasture and a scattering of sheltered villages, the county's low population density dropping to almost zero on **Dartmoor**, the wildest and bleakest of the West's moors.

Exeter and around

EXETER's sights are richer than those of any other town in Devon or Cornwall, the legacy of an eventful history since its Celtic foundation and the establishment here of the most westerly Roman outpost. After the Roman withdrawal, Exeter was refounded by Alfred the Great, and by the time of the Norman Conquest had become one of the largest towns in England, profiting from its position on the banks of the River Exe. The expansion of the wool trade in the Tudor period sustained the city until the eighteenth century, and Exeter has maintained its status as a commercial centre and county town, despite having much of its ancient centre gutted by World War II bombing.

The coast south and east of Exeter holds an architectural oddity, **A La Ronde**, and a string of old-fashioned seaside resorts, none of them over-commercialized, though still best seen outside the summer peak season. **Sidmouth** is a good choice for an overnight stop, as are the neighbouring villages of **Beer** and **Seaton**. A La Ronde is served by **bus** #57 from Exeter (hourly), while #52, #52A and #52B are best for Sidmouth. A minibus service, #899, also hourly, connects Sidmouth with Beer and Seaton.

Arrival, information and accommodation

Exeter has two mainline **train stations**, Exeter Central and St David's, the latter a little further out of town, though closer to some of the cheaper B&Bs. South West trains on the London Waterloo–Salisbury line stop at both, as do those on to Barnstaple and Exmouth, but Great Western trains from London Paddington only serve St Davids. **Buses** stop at the station on Paris Street, right across from the **tourist office** (July & Aug Mon–Fri 9am–5pm, Sat 9am–1pm & 2–5pm, Sun 10am–4pm; rest of year closed Sun; ☎01392/265700).

For really luxury **accommodation** look no further than the *Royal Clarence Hotel*, Cathedral Yard (☎01392/319955; ⑦), built in 1769. More affordable lodgings a short walk from Central Station include *Maurice*, 5 Bystock Terrace (☎01392/213079; ①), the *Bendene Hotel*, 15 Richmond Rd (☎01392/213526; ②), which has a swimming pool, and *Raffles* at 11 Blackall Rd (☎01392/270200; ②), which is furnished in Victorian style. The *Park View Hotel*, 8 Howell Rd (☎01392/271772; ①), is equidistant from Central and St David's stations. For the bus station, *The Edwardian*, 30 Heavitree Rd (☎01392/276102; ②), is a handy choice. The official **youth hostel**, 47 Countess Wear Rd (☎01392/873329, *exeter@yha.org*), lies two miles outside the city; take minibus #K or #T from High Street or South Street, or #57 from the bus station, to the Countess Wear post office on Topsham Road (15min), then walk for another ten minutes.

The City

The most distinctive feature of Exeter's skyline, **St Peter's Cathedral**, is a stately monument made conspicuous by the two great Norman towers flanking the nave. Close up, it is the facade's ornate Gothic screen that commands attention: its three tiers of sculpted figures – including Alfred, Athelstan, Canute, William the Conqueror and Richard II – were begun around 1360, part of a rebuilding programme which left only the Norman towers from the original construction. The cathedral boasts the longest unbroken **Gothic ceiling** in the world, its **bosses** vividly sculpted – one shows the murder of Thomas à Becket. The **Lady Chapel** and **Chapter House** – respectively at the far end of the building and off the right transept – are thirteenth

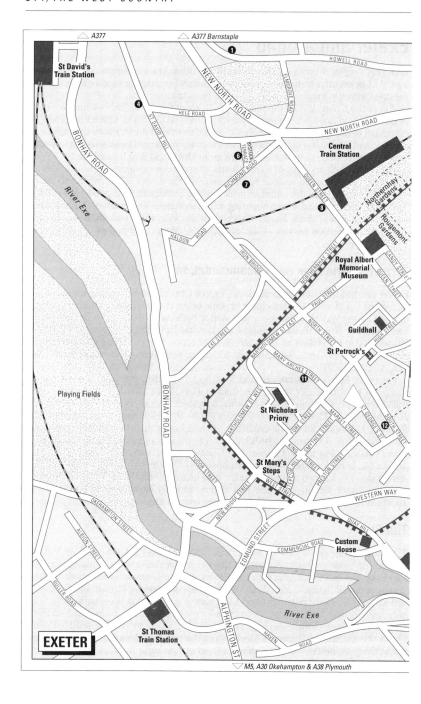

A377

A377 Barnstaple

HOWELL ROAD

St David's
Train Station

ELMGROVE ROAD

NEW NORTH ROAD

HELE ROAD

NEW NORTH ROAD

ST DAVID'S HILL

BONHAY ROAD

BYSTOCK TERRACE

Central
Train Station

RICHMOND ROAD

QUEEN STREET

River Exe

Northernhay Gardens

Rougemont Gardens

HALDON ROAD

IRON BRIDGE

NORTHERNHAY STREET

Royal Albert
Memorial
Museum

CANDY STREET

QUEEN STREET

PAUL STREET

EXE STREET

NORTH STREET

HIGH STREET

Guildhall

BARTHOLOMEW ST EAST

St Petrock's

MARY ARCHES STREET

Playing Fields

BONHAY ROAD

BARTHOLOMEW ST WEST

St Nicholas
Priory

FORE STREET

MARKET STREET

ST GEORGE'S ST

SMYTHEN STREET

SOUTH STREET

TUDOR STREET

KING STREET

PRESTON STREET

St Mary's
Steps

STEPCOTE HILL

WEST STREET

WESTERN WAY

NEW BRIDGE STREET

OKEHAMPTON STREET

QUAY HILL

ALBION STREET

EDMUND STREET

Custom
House

COMMERCIAL ROAD

BUTLER ROAD

ALPHINGTON ST

River Exe

St Thomas
Train Station

HAVEN ROAD

EXETER

M5, A30 Okehampton & A38 Plymouth

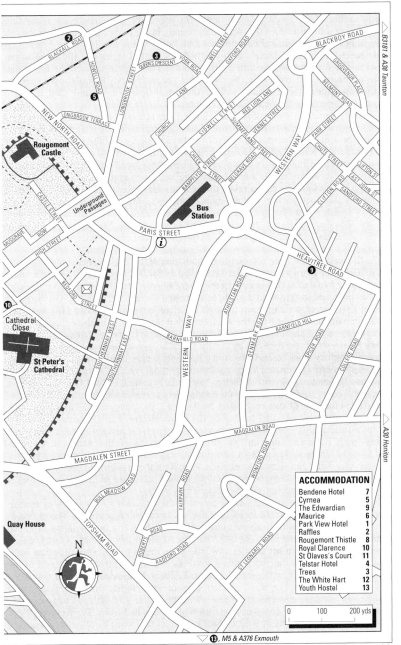

ACCOMMODATION

Bendene Hotel	7
Cyrnea	5
The Edwardian	9
Maurice	6
Park View Hotel	1
Raffles	2
Rougemont Thistle	8
Royal Clarence	10
St Olaves's Court	11
Telstar Hotel	4
Trees	3
The White Hart	12
Youth Hostel	13

century, but the main parts of the nave, including the lavish rib vaulting, are from the full flowering of the English Decorated style, a century later. There are many fine examples of sculpture from this period, including, in the minstrels' gallery on the left side, angels playing musical instruments and, below them, the figures of Edward III and Queen Philippa. Dominating the cathedral's central space are the huge organ pipes installed in the seventeenth century, harmonizing perfectly with the linear patterns of the roof and arches. In the **choir** don't miss the sixty-foot **bishop's throne**, or the **misericords** – decorated with mythological figures in around 1260, they are thought to be among the oldest in the country.

Outside, a graceful statue of Richard Hooker, one of Exeter's early bishops, surveys the **Cathedral Close**, a motley mixture of architectural styles from Tudor to Regency, though most display Exeter's trademark red brickwork. One of the finest buildings is the Elizabethan **Mol's Coffee House**, impressively timbered and gabled, now a bookshop. Some older buildings can also be found amid the banal concrete of the modern town centre, including Exeter's finest civic building, the fourteenth-century **Guildhall**. Standing not far from the cathedral on the pedestrianized High Street, it's fronted by an elegant Renaissance portico, and the main chamber merits a glance for its arched roof timbers, which rest on carved bears holding staves, symbols of the Yorkist cause during the Wars of the Roses. Just down from here, opposite **St Petrock's** – one of medieval Exeter's six surviving medieval churches – you'll find the impossibly narrow Parliament Street, just 25 inches wide at this end.

On the west side of Fore Street, the continuation of the High Street, a turning leads to **St Nicholas Priory** (Easter–Oct Mon, Wed & Sat 3–4.30pm; free), part of a small Benedictine foundation that became a merchant's home after the Dissolution; the interior has been restored to what it might have looked like in the Tudor era. On the other side of Fore Street, trailing down towards the river, cobbled **Stepcote Hill** was once the main road into Exeter from the west, though it is difficult to imagine this steep and narrow lane as a main thoroughfare. Another of central Exeter's ancient churches, **St Mary Steps**, stands surrounded by mainly Tudor houses at the bottom, with a fine seventeenth-century clock on its tower and a late Gothic nave inside.

Exeter's centre is bounded to the southwest by the River Exe, where the port area is now mostly devoted to leisure activities, particularly around the old **Quayside**. Pubs, shops and cafés share the space with handsomely restored nineteenth-century warehouses and the smart **Custom House**, built in 1681, its opulence reflecting the former importance of the cloth trade. Next door, the **Quay House**, from the same period, has an information desk and, upstairs, a video on Exeter's history (Easter–Oct daily 10am–5pm). The area comes into its own at night, but it's worth a wander at any time, and you can cross the river by a pedestrian suspension bridge or frequent **ferries** (Easter–Oct daily; Nov–Easter weekends only; 20p); there is little to see or do on the other side most of the time, but various exhibitions take place in the summer months in the ex-Maritime Museum, 60 Haven Banks.

Back at the north end of the High Street is the entrance to a network of **underground passages** excavated to bring water to the cathedral precincts. The passages can be visited as part of a 35-minute guided tour (July–Sept & school holidays Mon–Sat 10am–5.30pm; Oct–June Mon–Sat 2–5.30pm; £2.50, £3.50 July & Aug). Nearby, Castle Street leads to **Rougemont Castle**, now little more than a perimeter of red-stone walls best appreciated from the surrounding gardens. On Queen Street, at the end of the parks, you could drop in at the excellent **Royal Albert Memorial Museum** (Mon–Sat 10am–5pm; free). Exuding the Victorian spirit of wide-ranging curiosity, this motley assortment includes everything from a menagerie of stuffed animals to fascinating examples of the building styles used at different periods in the city. The picture gallery has some good specimens of West Country art alongside work by other artists associated with Devon.

Eating, drinking and nightlife

The café inside the Royal Albert Memorial Museum sells wholesome **snacks** in a convivial atmosphere. A few steps down on Queen Street, *Café Rouge* is good for breakfasts, baguettes and coffees, while *Coolings Wine Bar* (closed daytime Sun), on
medieval Gandy Street, is a popular spot for more substantial **meals**. Exeter's only
wholefood restaurant, *Herbie's*, is at 15 North St, with organic ice cream on the menu
(☎01392/258 473; closed Mon eve & all Sun). Alluring garlic smells waft out of *Maryam*
(closed Sun), an unpretentious trattoria at 28 South St; reasonably priced Mexican and
Italian staples are on the menu at *Harry's*, in a converted church at 86 Longbrook St
(☎01392/202 234). The *Well House*, in front of the cathedral, is an old **pub** offering
good-value lunches, as does the *Ship Inn* in St Martin's Lane, which claims to have
been Sir Francis Drake's local. Down at the Quayside, you can eat outside at the seventeenth-century *Prospect Inn*.

 Exeter Arts Centre (☎01392/667080), behind the Royal Albert Memorial Museum,
is the focus of the city's cultural pursuits, presenting regular non-mainstream films,
exhibitions and gigs, and there's a good café here. Of the town's **theatres**, the
Northcott, near the university on Stocker Rd (☎01392/493493), and the *Barnfield*, on
Barnfield Rd (☎01392/27180), have the best productions, with the former also staging
ballet and opera performances. The **Exeter Festival**, held in the first three weeks of
July, features jazz and blues concerts as well as classical and cabaret, at various venues
around town. **Clubbers** can soak up the latest sounds at the *Cavern Club*, between
Queen Street and Gandy Street, *Timepiece*, on Little Castle Street, or at the trio of
venues by the Quayside – the studenty *Warehouse* and *Boxes*, and the more mainstream
Volts.

A La Ronde

The Gothic folly of **A La Ronde** (April–Oct Mon–Thurs & Sun 11am–5.30pm; £3.20),
two miles outside Exmouth off the A376, was the creation of two cousins, Jane and
Mary Parminter, who were inspired by their 1790s European grand tour to construct a
sixteen-sided house, possibly based on the Byzantine basilica of San Vitale in Ravenna.
The end product is filled with mementos of the Parminters' tour as well as a number of
their more offbeat creations, such as a frieze made of feathers culled from game birds
and chickens. In the upper rooms is a gallery and staircase completely covered in
shells, too fragile to be visited, though part of it can be glimpsed from the completely
enclosed octagonal room on the first floor – a closed-circuit TV system enables visitors
to home in on details. The women intended that the house should be inherited only by
female descendants, though the conditions of Mary Parminter's will were broken at the
end of the nineteenth century, when the building was inherited by the Reverend
Oswald Reichel. Reichel added the dormer windows on the second floor, which give out
superb views over the Exe Estuary to Haldon Hill, and Dawlish Warren.

Sidmouth

Set amid shelf of crumbling red sandstone, cream-and-white **SIDMOUTH** is the chief
resort on this stretch of coast and boasts nearly five hundred buildings listed as having
special historic or architectural interest, among them the stately Georgian homes of
York Terrace behind the Esplanade. Moreover, the **beaches** are better tended than
many along this coast, not only the mile-long pebbled main town beach but also Jacob's
Ladder, a cliff-backed shingle and sand strip beyond Connaught Gardens to the west of
town. To the east, the South Devon Coast Path (part of the South West Coast Path)
climbs steep Salcombe Hill to follow cliffs that give sanctuary to a range of birdlife.

Further on, the path descends to meet one of the most isolated and attractive beaches in the area, **Weston Mouth**.

The **tourist office** is on Ham Lane, off the eastern end of the Esplanade (March & April Mon–Thurs 10am–4pm, Fri & Sat 10am–5pm, Sun 10am–1pm; May–July & Sept Mon–Sat 10am–5pm, Sun 10am–1pm; Aug & Oct Mon–Sat 10am–6pm, Sun 10am–4pm; Nov–Feb Mon–Sat 10am–1.30pm; ☎01395/516441). The string of **guest houses** along Salcombe Road offers a choice of similarly priced lodgings, including *Berwick House* (☎01395/513621; no credit cards; ②). Elsewhere, seek out *The Old Farmhouse*, on Hillside Rd (☎01395/512284; no credit cards; ②; closed Dec & Jan), or *Ferndale*, 92 Winslade Rd (☎01395/515495; no credit cards; ②), a Victorian house about a mile from the sea. For **snacks**, *Osborne's* on Fore Street offers light meals, while 200yd from the seafront, on Old Fore Street, the *Old Ship* and *Anchor* **pubs** provide excellent bar meals and suppers as well as a good range of ales. Sidmouth hosts what many consider to be the country's best **folk festival**, held over about eight days at the beginning of August. For details, call the tourist office, or call ☎01296/433669. Book early for the main acts.

Beer and Seaton

Eight miles east along the coast, the fishing village of **BEER** lies huddled within a small sheltered cove between gleaming white headlands. A stream rushes along a deep channel dug into Beer's main street, and if you can ignore the crowds in high summer much of the village looks unchanged since the days when it was a smugglers' eyrie, its inlets used by such characters as Jack Rattenbury, who published his *Memoirs of a Smuggler* in 1837. The village is best known for its quarries, which were worked from Roman times until the last century: Beer Stone was used in many of Devon's churches and houses. You can tour the complex of **underground quarries** (Easter–Sept 10am–5pm; Oct 11am–4pm; £3.50) a mile or so west of the village, where there's a small exhibition including pieces carved by medieval masons. *Bay View*, overlooking the sea on Fore Street (☎01297/20489; no credit cards; ①; closed Nov–Easter), is easily the best of the **B&Bs**; Beer's **youth hostel** is on a hillside half a mile northwest at Bovey Combe, Townsend (☎01297/20296; closed Nov–March).

SEATON, a smooth stroll less than a mile eastwards, has a steep, pebbly beach like Beer's, but this is a much more developed resort, mutating from a placid, slow-moving haven at its western end to a much gaudier affair to the east. One of the main attractions is the open-top **tramway** which follows the path of the old railway line to the inland village of Colyton. Seaton's **tourist office** is on the Underfleet, in the main car park on Harbour Road (April–June, Sept & Oct Mon–Sat 10am–5pm; July & Aug Mon–Sat 10am–5pm, Sun 1.30–5.30pm; Nov–March Mon–Fri 10am–2pm; ☎01297/21660). On Trevelyan Road, at the eastern end of the Esplanade you'll find *Beach End* (☎01297/23388; ②; closed Nov–March), a bright and roomy Edwardian **B&B**, while on the west side, just across from the tourist office, is *Beaumont*, on Castle Hill (☎01297/20832, *tony@lymebay.demon.co.uk*; no credit cards; ②) – both have sea views.

The "English Riviera" region

The wedge of land between Dartmoor and the sea contains some of Devon's most fertile pastures, backing onto some of the country's most popular coastal resorts. Chief of these is **Torbay**, an amalgam of **Torquay**, **Paignton** and **Brixham**, together forming the nucleus of an area optimistically known as "**The English Riviera**". To the south, the port of **Dartmouth** offers another calmer alternative, linked by riverboat to historic and almost unspoilt **Totnes**.

Torquay and Paignton

The coast is heavily urbanized around **Torbay**, a tourist conglomeration entirely dedicated to the exploitation of the bay's sheltered climate and exuberant vegetation. **TORQUAY**, the largest component of this super-resort, comes closest to living up to the self-penned "English Riviera" sobriquet, sporting a mini-corniche and promenades landscaped with flowerbeds. The much-vaunted palm trees (actually New Zealand cabbage trees) and the coloured lights that festoon the harbour by night contribute to the town's unique flavour, a slightly frayed combination of the exotic and the classically English. Torquay's transformation from a fishing village began with its establishment as a fashionable haven for invalids, among them the consumptive Elizabeth Barrett Browning, who spent three years here. In recent years the most famous figures previously associated with Torquay – crime writer Agatha Christie and traveller Freya Stark – have given way to the fictional TV hotelier Basil Fawlty, whose jingoism and injured pride perfectly encapsulate the town's adaptation to the demands of mass tourism.

The town is focused on the small **harbour** and marina, on one side of which stands the copper-domed **Pavilion**, an Edwardian building that originally housed a ballroom and assembly hall, now refurbished with shops. Behind the Pavilion, limestone cliffs sprouting white high-rise hotels and apartment blocks separate the harbour area from Torquay's main beach, **Abbey Sands**. If this gets too crowded, follow the pretty half-mile coastal walk north through Daddyhole Plain, a large chasm in the cliff caused by a landslide locally attributed to the devil ("Daddy"). The path descends to meet the seawall at **Meadfoot Beach**, where boats and pedalos can be hired. If you're searching for something a little more low-key, continue round the point to where a string of beaches extends as far as the cliff-backed coves of **Watcombe** and **Maidencombe**.

Torquay's **train station** is off Rathmore Road, next to the Torre Abbey gardens; most **buses** leave from outside the Pavilion. The **tourist office** is on Vaughan Parade, near the Pavilion (June–Sept Mon–Sat 9am–6pm, Sun 10am–6pm; Oct–May Mon–Sat 9am–5.15pm; ☎01803/297428). There's plenty of **accommodation** in Torquay, with most of the budget choices away from the sea. The *Chesterfield Hotel*, 62 Belgrave Rd (☎01803/292318; ②), and *Kingston House*, 75 Avenue Rd (☎01803/212760; ②), are both a short walk from the train station and the marina. Behind the station, on Old Mill Road, the Victorian *Torbay Rise* (☎01803/605541; ③; closed Nov–March) stands on a hill overlooking the harbour and has an outdoor pool. You can find friendly **hostel** accommodation at the central *Torquay Backpackers*, 119 Abbey Rd (☎01803/299924), a ten-minute walk from the station – they'll pick you up free if you ring ahead. Torquay's **restaurants** are of a surprisingly high standard, one of the best being the *Mulberry Room*, 1 Scarborough Rd (☎01803/213639; ③), which also has also three en-suite rooms. The earthier *Jingles*, 34 Torwood St, offers low-priced Tex-Mex meals, or you can relish French provincial cuisine at the moderate *Flynn's Bistro*, 14 Parkhill Rd (evenings only; closed Sun).

Not so much a rival to Torquay as its complement, **PAIGNTON** lacks the gloss of its neighbour, but also its pretensions. Activity is concentrated at the southern end of the wide town beach, around the small harbour that nestles in the lee of the appropriately named Redcliffe headland. Otherwise, diversion-seekers could wander over to **Paignton Zoo** (summer daily 10am–6pm; winter closes at dusk; £7), a mile out on Totnes Road, or board the **Paignton & Dartmouth Steam Railway** (June–Sept daily; April, May, Oct & Dec less frequent), which connects with Paignton's other main beach, **Goodrington Sands**, before trundling alongside the Dart estuary to Kingswear, seven miles away. You could make a day of it by taking the ferry from Kingswear to Dartmouth, then a river-boat up the Dart to Totnes, and finally a bus back to Paignton.

Paignton's **bus and train stations** are next to each other off Sands Road. Five minutes away, the seafront has a **tourist office** (June–Sept Mon–Sat 9am–6pm, Sun 10am–6pm; Oct–May Mon–Sat 9am–5.15pm; ☎01803/558383).

Brixham

From Torquay, it's a thirty-minute bus ride (15min from Paignton) down to **BRIXHAM**, the prettiest of the Torbay towns. Fishing was for centuries Brixham's lifeblood and it still supplies fish to restaurants as far away as Bristol. Among the trawlers on Brixham's quayside is moored a full-size reconstruction of the **Golden Hind** (March–Oct daily 10am–dusk; £1.50), the surprisingly small vessel in which Sir Francis Drake circumnavigated the world. The harbour is overlooked by an unflattering statue of William III, a reminder of his landing in Brixham to claim the crown of England in 1688. From here, steep lanes and stairways thread up to the older centre around Fore Street, where the bus from Torquay pulls in. From the harbour, you can reach the promontory of **Berry Head** along a path winding up from the *Berry Head House Hotel*. Fortifications built during the Napoleonic War are still standing on this southern limit of Torbay, which is now a conservation area.

The town's **tourist office** (June to mid-Oct Mon–Sat 9.30am–6pm, Sun 10am–6pm; mid-Oct to May Tues–Sat 9.30am–5.15pm; ☎01803/852861) is on the quayside, next to William's statue. **Accommodation** includes two B&Bs on King Street, overlooking the harbour: *Sampford House* at no. 59 (☎01803/857761; no credit cards; ②), and the *Harbour View Hotel*, at no. 65 (☎01803/853052; ②), the latter a former harbour master's house. Behind the quayside, the *Brioc Hotel*, 11 Prospect Rd (☎01803/853540; no credit cards; ①), is also good value. The nearest **youth hostel** (☎01803/842444; closed Nov–March) is four miles away, one and a half miles from Churston Bridge (bus #12 or #12A), or one stop on the Paignton & Dartmouth Steam Railway (see p.319). For **eating**, Brixham offers fish and more fish, from the takeaway shops on the harbourside to the moderate-to-expensive *Poopdeck*, at 14 The Quay (☎01803/852 254), above the Harbourside Bookshop. For a relaxed pint, try the *Blue Anchor*, on Fore Street, which has coal fires and low beams.

Totnes

Most of the Plymouth buses from Paignton and Torquay make a stop at **TOTNES**, on the west bank of the River Dart. The town has an ancient pedigree, its period of greatest prosperity occurring in the sixteenth century, when this inland port exported cloth to France and brought back wine. Some handsome structures from that era remain, and there is still a working port down on the river, but these days Totnes has mellowed into a residential market town, enjoying an esoteric fame as a centre for the New Age arts-and-crafts crowd.

The town centres on the long main street that starts off as Fore Street, site of the **Museum** (April–Oct Mon–Fri 10.30am–5pm; £1.50), which occupies a four-storey Elizabethan house at no. 70. Showing how wealthy clothiers lived at the peak of the town's success, it is packed with domestic objects and furniture, and also has a room devoted to local mathematician Charles Babbage, whose "analytical engine" was the forerunner of the computer in the nineteenth century. Fore Street becomes the **High Street** at the East Gate, a much retouched medieval arch. Beneath it, Rampart Walk trails off along the old city walls, curling around the fifteenth-century church of **St Mary's**. Inside, an exquisitely carved rood screen stretches across the full width of the red sandstone building. Behind the church, the eleventh-century **Guildhall** (April–Sept Mon–Fri 10.30am–1pm & 2–4.30pm; 90p) was originally the refectory and kitchen of a Benedictine priory. Granted to the city corporation in 1553, the building still houses the town's council chamber, which you can see together with the former jail cells and courtroom.

Totnes Castle (April–Sept daily 10am–6pm; Oct daily 10am–5pm; Nov–March Wed–Sun 10am–1pm & 2–4pm; £1.60; EH), on Castle Street, leading off the High Street – is a classic Norman structure of the motte and bailey design, its simple crenellated keep atop a grassy mound offering wide views of the town and the Dart valley. Totnes assumes a much livelier air at the bottom of Fore Street, at river level. This is the highest navigable point on the **River Dart** for sea-going vessels, and there is constant activity around the craft arriving from and leaving to European destinations. You can take a **cruise** to Dartmouth from here (Easter–Oct 1–5 daily; 1hr 15min–1hr 45min), leaving from the far side of the river, and, near the railway bridge, board a steam train of the **South Devon Railway** on its run along the course of the Dart to Buckfastleigh, adjacent to Buckfast Abbey (see p.328).

Totnes' **tourist office** is in the Town Mill, off the Plains, near the Safeway car park (Easter–Oct Mon–Sat 9.30am–5pm, Sun 10am–1pm; Nov–Easter Mon–Fri 10am–12.30pm & 1.30–4pm; ☎01803/863168). There is a good **B&B** below the castle at 2 Antrim Terrace (☎01803/862638; no credit cards; ①). For a bit extra, pamper yourself at the *Royal Seven Stars Hotel* on The Plains (☎01803/862125; ③), or, just over the river in Seymour Place, at *The Old Forge* (☎01803/862174; ③). The **youth hostel** (☎01803/862303; closed Nov–March), in a sixteenth-century cottage, lies next to the River Bidwell two miles from Totnes and half a mile from Shinner's Bridge, one stop on the #X80 Torquay–Plymouth bus route.

Willow, at 87 High St (☎01803/862 605), and *Tolivers*, 67 Fore St (☎01803/862 604), are inexpensive vegetarian **restaurants**, while *Rickshaws* serves Indonesian fare at 87 High St (open daytime only). There are also several decent **pubs**: try the *Bull Inn*, at the top of the High Street, or the riverside *Steampacket*, on St Peter's Quay.

Dartmouth

South of Torbay, and eight miles downstream from Totnes, **DARTMOUTH** has thrived since the Normans recognized the potential of this deepwater port for trading with their home country, and today its activities embrace fishing, freight and a booming leisure industry – as well as the education of the senior service's officer class at the Royal Naval College.

Behind the enclosed boat basin at the heart of town stands Dartmouth's most photographed building, the four-storey **Butterwalk**, built in the seventeenth century for a local merchant. Richly decorated with woodcarvings, it overhangs the street on eleven granite columns, forming an arcade now holding shops and Dartmouth's small **Museum** (Mon–Sat: April–Sept 11am–5pm; Oct–March noon–3pm; £1), mainly devoted to maritime curios, including old maps, prints and models of ships. Nearby **St Saviour's**, rebuilt in the 1630s from a fourteenth-century church, has long been a landmark for boats sailing upriver. The building stands at the head of Higher Street, the old town's central thoroughfare and the site of another tottering medieval structure, *The Cherub* inn. More impressive is **Agincourt House**, on the parallel Lower Street, built by a merchant after the battle for which it is named.

Lower Street leads down to **Bayard's Cove**, a short, cobbled quay lined with well-restored eighteenth-century houses, where the Pilgrim Fathers touched en route to the New World. A twenty-minute walk from here along the river takes you to **Dartmouth Castle** (April–Sept daily 10am–6pm; Oct daily 10am–5pm; Nov–March Wed–Sun 10am–1pm & 2–4pm; £2.60; EH), one of two fortifications on opposite sides of the estuary. The site includes coastal defence works from the last century and from World War II, though the main interest is the fifteenth-century castle, the first in England to be constructed specifically to withstand artillery. The castle was never actually tested in action, and consequently is excellently preserved. If you don't relish the return walk, you can take advantage of a ferry back to town (Easter–Oct every 15min).

Continuing south along the coastal path brings you through the pretty hilltop village of **Stoke Fleming** to **Blackpool Sands** (45min from the castle), the best beach in the area. The unspoilt cove, flanked by steep, wooded cliffs, was the site of a battle in 1404 in which Devon archers repulsed a Breton invasion force sent to punish the privateers of Dartmouth for their raiding across the Channel. **Summer cruises** depart from Dartmouth's quay up the River Dart to Totnes; this is the best way to see the river's deep creeks and the various houses overlooking the river, among them the **Royal Naval College** and **Greenway House**, birthplace of Sir Walter Raleigh's three seafaring half-brothers, the Gilberts, and later rebuilt for Agatha Christie.

Dartmouth's **tourist office** is on Mayor's Avenue (Easter–Oct Mon–Sat 9.30am–5.30pm, Sun 10am–4pm; Nov–Easter Mon–Sat 10am–4pm; ☎01803/834224). The hilltop **accommodation** choices have the best views: try the spacious and elegantly furnished *Avondale*, at 5 Vicarage Hill (☎01803/835831; no credit cards; ②), or the comfortable, welcoming *Campbells*, slightly further out at 5 Mount Boone (☎01803/833438; no credit cards; ③). If the uphill hike is too much for you, try *Capritia* the convenient and friendly B&B at 69 Victoria Rd (☎01803/833 419; no credit cards; ①). Dartmouth has a good range of restaurants, including the expensive *Carved Angel*, at 2 South Embankment (☎01803/832465; closed Sun eve, all Mon & Jan to mid-Feb), a high-class restaurant with views over the riverfront that specializes in fish and also game in winter. There's a more reasonably priced offshoot at 7 Foss St, the *Carved Angel Café* (closed Sun & all Jan), while the casual *Café Alf Resco* on Lower Street is good for breakfasts, coffees and snacks (closed Mon & Tues).

Plymouth

PLYMOUTH's predominantly bland and modern face belies its great historic role as a naval base, when it enjoyed the patronage of such national heroes as John Hawkins and Sir Francis Drake. It was from here that the latter sailed to defeat the Spanish Armada in 1588, and 32 years later the port was the last embarkation point for the Pilgrim Fathers, whose New Plymouth colony became the nucleus for the English settlement of North America. The sustained prominence of the city's Devonport dockyards as a shipbuilding and military base made it a target in World War II, when the Luftwaffe reduced much of the old centre to rubble. Subsequent reconstruction has done nothing to enhance the place. That said, it would be difficult to spoil the glorious vista over **Plymouth Sound**, the basin of calm water at the mouth of the combined Plym, Tavy and Tamar estuaries, which has remained largely unchanged since Drake played his apocryphal game of bowls on the Hoe before joining battle with the Armada.

One of the best of the local day excursions is to **Mount Edgcumbe**, where woods and meadows provide a welcome antidote to the urban bustle, and are within easy reach of some fabulous sand. East of Plymouth, the aristocratic opulence of **Saltram House** includes some fine art and furniture, while to the north of town you can visit Drake's old residence at **Buckland Abbey**.

The City

A good place to start a tour of the centre is **Plymouth Hoe**, an immense esplanade studded with reminders of the great events in the city's history. Resplendent in fair weather, with glorious views over to sea, the Hoe can also attract some pretty ferocious winds, making it well-nigh impossible to explore in wintry conditions. The most distinctive landmark is a tall, white naval war memorial, standing alongside smaller monuments to the defeat of the Spanish Armada and to the airmen who defended the city

SIR FRANCIS DRAKE

Born around 1540 near Tavistock, **Francis Drake** worked in the domestic coastal trade from the age of thirteen, but was soon taking part in the first English slaving expeditions between Africa and the West Indies, led by his Plymouth kinsman John Hawkins. Later Drake was active in the secret war against Spain, raiding and looting merchant ships in actions unofficially sanctioned by Elizabeth I. In 1572 he became the first Englishman to sight the Pacific, and soon afterwards, on board the **Golden Hind**, became the first one to circumnavigate the world, for which he received a knighthood on his return in 1580. The following year Drake was made mayor of Plymouth, settling in Buckland Abbey (see p.325), but was back in action before long – in 1587 he "singed the king of Spain's beard" by entering Cadiz harbour and destroying 33 vessels that were to have formed part of Philip II's **armada**. When the replacement invasion fleet appeared in the English Channel in 1588, Drake – along with Raleigh, Hawkins and Frobisher – played a leading role in wrecking it. The following year he set off on an unsuccessful expedition to help the Portuguese against Spain, but otherwise most of the next decade was spent in relative inactivity in Plymouth, Exeter and London. Finally, in 1596, Drake left with Hawkins on a raid on Panama, a venture that cost the lives of both captains.

Drake has come to personify the Elizabethan age's swashbuckling expansionism and patriotism, but England's naval triumphs were as much the consequence of John Hawkins' humbler work in building and maintaining a new generation of warships as they were of the skill and bravery of their captains. Drake was simply the most flamboyant of a generation of reckless and brilliant mariners who broke the Spanish hegemony on the high seas, laying the foundations for England's later imperialist pursuits.

during the wartime blitz, and a rather portly statue of Sir Francis Drake, gazing grandly out to the sea. Appropriately, there's a bowling green back from the brow.

In front of the memorials, the red-and-white-striped **Smeaton's Tower** (Easter–Sept 10.30am–4.30pm; 75p) was erected in 1759 by John Smeaton on the treacherous Eddystone Rocks, fourteen miles out to sea. When replaced by a larger lighthouse in 1882, it was reassembled here, where it gives the loftiest view over Plymouth Sound. Below Smeaton's Tower is the **Plymouth Dome** leisure complex (daily: April–Sept 9am–5pm; Oct–March 11am–5pm; £3.95), which includes tricksy audio-visual exhibitions on Plymouth's history and the lives of its local heroes. On the seafront, Plymouth's **Royal Citadel** was constructed in 1666 to intimidate the populace of the only town in the southwest to be held by the Parliamentarians in the Civil War. Though it's still used by the military, there are guided tours through some of its older parts, including the seventeenth-century Governor's House and the Royal Chapel of St Katherine (tours May–Sept 2.30pm; £2.50); tickets are available from the Plymouth Dome or the tourist office.

Round the corner is **Sutton Harbour**, the old town's quay, still used by the trawler fleet and scene of a boisterous early-morning fish market. The **Mayflower Steps** here commemorate the sailing of the Pilgrim Fathers and a nearby plaque lists the names and professions of the 102 Puritans on board. All three of Captain Cook's voyages to the South Seas, Australia and the Antarctic also started from here, as did the nineteenth-century transport ships to Australia, carrying thousands of convicts and colonists. The **Barbican** district, which edges the harbour, is the heart of old Plymouth. Most of the buildings are now shops and restaurants, but off the quayside, New Street holds most of the oldest buildings, among them the **Elizabethan House** (April–Sept Wed–Sun 10am–5.30pm; £1; NT), a captain's dwelling with a lovely pole staircase. Cross the bridge over Sutton Harbour to reach Plymouth's newest attraction, the grand **National Marine Aquarium** (daily: April–Oct 10am–5pm; Nov–March 11am–5pm; £6.50) which includes Europe's largest collection of seahorse species.

In the centre of town, the mainly seventeenth-century **Merchant's House Museum**, at 33 St Andrew Street (April–Sept Tues–Fri 10am–1pm & 2–5.30pm, Sat 10am–1pm & 2–5pm; 90p), goes into various aspects of Plymouth's history. Behind it, off Royal Parade, stands the city's chief place of worship, **St Andrew's**, a reconstruction of a fifteenth-century building that was almost completely gutted by a bomb in 1941. The entrails of the navigator Martin Frobisher are buried here, as are those of Admiral Blake, the Parliamentarian who died as his ship entered Plymouth after destroying a Spanish treasure fleet off Tenerife.

Practicalities

Plymouth's **train station** is off Saltash Road, from where bus #25 leaves every fifteen minutes for the central Royal Parade. The **bus station** is just over St Andrew's Cross from the Royal Parade, at Bretonside. The **tourist office**, off Sutton Harbour, at 9 The Barbican (Easter to mid-Oct Mon–Sat 9am–5pm, Sun 10am–4pm; mid-Oct to Easter Mon–Fri 9am–5pm, Sat 10am–4pm; ☎01752/304849), gives information on guided tours.

Most of the city's central **accommodation** is a short walk from here, on or around the long Citadel Road: try *The Acorns and Lawns* at no. 171 (☎01752/229474; no credit cards; ①), or *Avalon* at no. 167 (☎01752/668127; no credit cards; ①). On the other side of the Hoe, the *Osmond Guest House*, 42 Pier St (☎01752/229705; ①), is close to the seafront, and offers a pick-up service from the bus or train station. The *Bowling Green Hotel* overlooks Sir Francis Drake's fabled haunt on Plymouth Hoe, at 9–10 Osborne Place, Lockyer St (☎01752/209090; ②). The most convenient stop for the train station is the good-value *Grosvenor Park Hotel*, 114 North Rd East, off the North Cross roundabout (☎01752/229312; ②). Plymouth's **youth hostel** lies on the west side of town, on Devonport Rd (☎01752/562189, *plymouth@yha.org*), a short walk from Devonport train station or a bus ride from the centre (#33, #34, #14A, #15A or #81). There's a more central independent hostel, the *Backpackers Hotel*, at 172 Citadel Rd (☎01752/225158).

Most of Plymouth's eclectic range of **restaurants** are located in and around the Barbican area. *Pavarotti's*, 54 Notte St (☎01752/250 240), has a good-value selection of *meze*; in the same road the trendy and inexpensive *Revival* features a mixed Mexican/Italian/American menu with lots of jazzy ambience. Nearby, Southside Street has the *Barbican Pasta Bar* and one of the best fish restaurants, *Piermaster's* (☎01752/229345; closed Sun), whose kitchen is supplied straight from the nearby harbour. The *Plymouth Arts Centre*, 38 Looe St, has a self-service vegetarian restaurant until around 8pm, though the major reason for coming here is to see its films and live performances. The *Dolphin* **pub** on Southside Street, a landmark in the Barbican, is crowded with fishermen in the morning and a mix of locals and boisterous boozers at night.

Mount Edgcumbe

Lying on the Cornish side of Plymouth Sound and visible from the Hoe, **Mount Edgcumbe** features a Tudor house, landscaped gardens and acres of rolling parkland and coastal paths. The **house** (April to mid-Oct Wed–Sun 11am–5pm; £4) is a reconstruction of the bomb-damaged Tudor original, though inside the predominant note is eighteenth century, the rooms elegantly restored with authentic Regency furniture. The highlight, though, is the grounds, including impeccable **gardens** divided into French, Italian and English sections – the first two a blaze of flowerbeds adorned with classical statuary, the last an acre of lawn shaded by exotic trees. You can reach the house by the passenger **ferry** to Cremyll, leaving at least hourly from Admiral's Hard (bus #33 or #34 from the Guildhall). In summer there's also a direct motor launch between the Mayflower Steps and the village of **Cawsand**, an old smugglers' haunt two hours' walk from the house. Cawsand itself is just a mile from the southern tip of the huge **Whitsand Bay**, the best bathing beach for miles around.

Saltram House

The remodelled Tudor mansion **Saltram House** (house: April–Oct Mon–Thurs & Sun noon–5pm; garden: also open March Sat & Sun 11am–4pm; house and garden £5.70; garden £2.70; NT), two miles east of Plymouth off the A38, is Devon's largest country house, featuring work by the great architect Robert Adam and fourteen portraits by **Joshua Reynolds**, who was born in nearby Plympton. The showpiece is the Saloon, a fussy but exquisitely furnished room dripping with gilt and plaster, and set off by a huge Axminster carpet especially woven for it in 1770. Saltram's landscaped park provides a breather from this riot of interior design, though it is marred by the proximity of the road. You can get here on the hourly #22 bus (not Sun) from Royal Parade to Cott Hill, from where it's a ten-minute signposted walk.

Buckland Abbey

Six miles north of Plymouth, close to the River Tavy and on the edge of Dartmoor, stands **Buckland Abbey** (April–Oct Mon–Wed & Fri–Sun 10.30am–5.30pm; Nov–March Sat & Sun 2–5pm; house & grounds £4.40, £2.30 in winter; grounds only £2.30, free in winter; NT), once the most westerly of England's Cistercian abbeys. After its dissolution, Buckland was converted to a private home by the privateer Richard Grenville, a cousin of Sir Walter Raleigh, from whom the estate was acquired by Sir Francis Drake in 1582, the year he became mayor of Plymouth. It remained his home until his death, though the house reveals few traces of Drake's residence. There are, however, numerous maps, portraits and mementoes of his buccaneering exploits on show, most famous of which is Drake's Drum, which was said to beat a supernatural warning of impending danger to the country. The house stands in majestic grounds which contain the fine fourteenth-century **Great Barn**, buttressed and gabled and larger than the abbey itself. To get to the abbey, take bus #83, #84 or #86 to Tavistock, changing at Yelverton to the #55 minibus (not Sun).

Dartmoor

Occupying the main part of the county between Exeter and Plymouth, **DARTMOOR** is southern England's greatest expanse of wilderness, some 365 square miles of raw granite, barren bogland, sparse grass and heather-grown moor. It was not always so desolate, as testified by the remnants of scattered Stone Age settlements and the ruined relics of the area's nineteenth-century tin-mining industry. Today, desultory flocks of sheep and groups of ponies are virtually the only living creatures to be seen wandering over the central vastnesses of the National Park, with solitary birds – buzzards, kestrels, pipits, stonechats and wagtails – wheeling and hovering high above.

The core of Dartmoor, characterized by tumbling streams and high tors chiselled by the elements, is **Dartmoor Forest**, which has belonged to the Duchy of Cornwall since 1307, though there is almost unlimited public access. Camping is permitted out of sight of houses and roads, but fires are strictly forbidden. Though networks of signposts or painted stones do exist to guide **walkers**, map-reading abilities are a prerequisite for any but the shortest walks, and a good deal of experience is essential for longer distances. Information on walks and on pony-trekking centres can be found at the National Park Visitor Centres in Dartmoor's major towns and villages, and from information points in smaller villages.

Much to the irritation of locals and visitors alike, the **Ministry of Defence** has appropriated a significant portion of northern Dartmoor, an area that contains

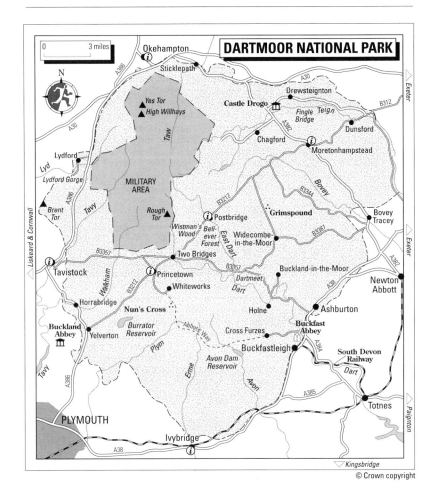

Dartmoor's highest tors and some of its most famous beauty spots. The MoD firing ranges are marked by red and white posts; when firing is in progress, red flags or red lights signify that entry is prohibited. As a general rule, you can assume that if no warning flags are flying by 9am between April and September, or by 10am from October to March, there is to be no firing on that day.

Princetown and the central moor

PRINCETOWN owes its growth to the proximity of Dartmoor Prison, a high-security jail originally constructed for PoWs captured in the Napoleonic wars. The grim presence seeps into the village, which has a somewhat oppressed air and functional grey stone houses, some of them – like the parish church of St Michael – built by French and American prisoners. What Princetown lacks in beauty is amply compensated by the surrounding country, the best of which lies immediately to the north.

Information on all of Dartmoor is given by the main **National Park information centre**, on the village's central green (daily: April–Oct 10am–5pm; Nov–March 10am–4pm; ☎01822/890414). The best places to stay are *Lamorna*, a friendly **B&B** on Two Bridges Road (☎01822/890360; no credit cards; ①), and *Duchy House* (☎01822/890552; no credit cards; ①), which also operates a **café**. Two pubs in Princetown's central square offer accommodation: the *Railway Inn* (☎0822/890232; no credit cards; ①) and the *Plume of Feathers* (☎0822/890240; ①), which has dormitory accommodation in two bunkhouses as well as a convenient **campsite**; staple bar food is always available.

Four miles northeast of Princetown, the largest and best preserved of Dartmoor's **clapper bridges** crosses the East Dart river at **POSTBRIDGE**, to which it gives its name. Used by tin-miners and farmers since medieval times, these simple structures consist of huge slabs of granite supported by piers of the same material. Walkers from Postbridge can explore up and down the river, or press further south through **Bellever Forest**, on the edge of which lies one of Dartmoor's two **youth hostels** (☎01822/880227; closed Nov–March). There's also a bunkhouse and **campsite** close to Bellever Forest, at *Runnage Farm* (☎01822/880222), where you'll get a farmhouse breakfast. You'll find more luxury, and inexpensive meals, in the *Lydgate House Hotel*, half a mile southwest of Postbridge (☎01822/880209; ④; closed Dec–Feb), offering easy access to Bellever Forest.

Two miles northeast of Postbridge, the solitary *Warren House Inn* offers warm, fire-lit comfort in an unutterably bleak tract of moorland. About a mile south of the B3212 lies the Bronze Age village of **Grimspound**, the most complete example of Dartmoor's prehistoric settlements, consisting of 24 circular huts scattered within a four-acre enclosure. Grimspound itself is thought to have been the model for the Stone Age settlement in which Sherlock Holmes camped in *The Hound of the Baskervilles*, while **Hound Tor**, an outcrop three miles to the southwest, was the inspiration for Conan Doyle's tale. According to local legend, phantom hounds were sighted racing across the moor to hurl themselves on the tomb of a hated squire at his death in 1677.

Buckland, Widecombe and the southeastern moor

Four miles east of the crossroads at Two Bridges, **Dartmeet** marks the place where the East and West Dart rivers merge after tortuous journeys from their remote sources. Crowds home in on this beauty spot, but the valley is memorably lush and you don't need to walk far to leave the car park and ice-cream vans behind. From here the Dart pursues a more leisurely course, joined by the River Webburn near the pretty moorland village of **Buckland-in-the-Moor**, one of a cluster of moorstone-and-thatched hamlets on this southeastern side of the moor.

Four miles north, another popular Dartmoor village, **WIDECOMBE-IN-THE-MOOR**, is set in a hollow amid high, granite-strewn ridges. Its church of **St Pancras** provides a famous local landmark, the pinnacled tower dwarfing the fourteenth-century main building, whose interior boasts a beautiful painted rood screen. Look out for the carved one-eared rabbits – an alchemist's symbol – above the communion rail. The nearby **Church House** was built in the fifteenth century for weary churchgoers from outlying districts, and was later converted into almshouses. Widecombe's other claim to fame is the traditional song *Widdicombe Fair*; the **fair** is still held annually on the second Tuesday of September, but is now primarily a tourist attraction. You can **stay** in Widecombe in the plain *Sheena Tower* (☎01364/621308; no credit cards; ①; closed Dec & Jan); half a mile out, *Higher Venton Farm* (☎01364/621235; no credit cards; ①) is a peaceful thatched longhouse close to a couple of good pubs. You can **camp** at *Cockingford Farm*, one and a half miles south of Widecombe (☎01364/621258; closed mid-Nov to mid-March).

A couple of miles east, the Dart weaves through a wooded green valley to enter the grounds of **Buckfast Abbey** (daily: May–Oct 9am–5.30pm; Nov–April 10am–4pm; free), a modern monastic complex occupying the site of an abbey founded in the eleventh century by Canute. The present buildings were built by exiled French Benedictine monks who consecrated their new abbey in 1932, though work on the other monastic buildings has continued until recently. The church itself is in a traditional Anglo-Norman style, following the design of the Cistercian building razed in 1535.

The northeastern moor

The essentially unspoilt market town of **MORETONHAMPSTEAD**, lying on the northeastern edge of the moor, makes an attractive entry point from Exeter. Local **information** is handled by a Community Information Point on The Square (Easter–Oct daily 10am–1pm & 2–5pm; Nov–Easter Fri, Sat & Sun 10am–1pm & 2–4pm; ☎01647/440043). There is classy **accommodation** in the central *White Hart* (☎01647/440406; ③), a Georgian posting house that also provides coffees and meals, and at *Cookshayes*, on the edge of the village at 33 Court St (☎01647/440374; ②; closed Nov–Feb), which offers good home cooking. The Steps Bridge **youth hostel** (☎01647/252435; closed Oct–March) sits on the outskirts of **Dunsford**, three miles northeast of Moretonhampstead and right on the boundary of the National Park. Its woodland setting overlooking the Teign Gorge makes it a popular overnight stop for hikers – buses #359 and #82 stop nearby.

Moretonhampstead has a historic rivalry with neighbouring **CHAGFORD**, a Stannary town (a chartered centre of the tin trade) that also enjoyed prosperity as a centre of the wool trade. It stands on a hillside overlooking the River Teign, with a fine fifteenth-century church on its edge and enough attractions within and around to keep its pubs and hotels in business. The ancient *Three Crowns*, next to the former guildhall on the main square, is one of a number of decent **pubs** in the village, and offers **accommodation** in raftered rooms (☎01647/433444; ⑤). An alternative is the seventeenth-century *Lawn House*, close to the centre on Mill Street (☎01647/433329; no credit cards; ①; closed Nov–Easter).

There are numerous **walks** to be made in the immediate vicinity, for instance downstream along the Teign to the twentieth-century extravaganza of **Castle Drogo** (castle: April–Oct Mon–Thurs, Sat & Sun 11am–5.30pm; grounds: daily 10.30am–dusk; castle £5.30; grounds £2.50; NT), which occupies a stupendous site overlooking the Teign gorge. Having retired at the age of 33, grocery magnate Julius Drewe unearthed a link that suggested his descent from a Norman baron, and set about creating a castle befitting his pedigree. Begun in 1910, to a design by **Sir Edwin Lutyens**, it was not completed until 1930, but the result was an unsurpassed synthesis of medieval and modern elements. Paths lead from Drogo east to the beauty spot of **Fingle Bridge**, where shaded green pools hold trout and salmon. The *Angler's Rest* pub has an adjoining restaurant.

Okehampton

The main centre on the northern fringes of Dartmoor, **OKEHAMPTON** grew prosperous as a market town for the medieval wool trade, and some fine old buildings survive between the two branches of the River Okement that meet here, among them the prominent fifteenth-century tower of the **Chapel of St James**. Across the road from the seventeenth-century town hall, a granite archway leads into the **Museum of Dartmoor Life** (Easter–June & Oct Mon–Sat 10am–5pm; June–Sept daily 10am–5pm; Nov–Easter Mon–Fri 10am–4pm; £2), an excellent overview of habitation on the moor since earliest times. Loftily perched above the West Okement, **Okehampton Castle** (daily: April–Sept 10am–6pm; Oct 10am–5pm; £2.30; EH) is the shattered hulk of a stronghold laid waste by Henry VIII; its ruins include a gatehouse, Norman keep and the remains of the Great Hall, buttery and kitchens.

An old goods line provides Okehampton with a useful Sunday rail connection (May–Sept), linking the town with Exeter (40min) via Crediton: ask about the Sunday Rover ticket (£5) which also covers the Plymouth–Gunnislake rail link and bus travel on Dartmoor (☎01837/55330). The station is a fifteen-minute walk up Station Road from the **tourist office** on Fore Street (Easter–June & Oct Mon–Sat 10am–5pm; July–Sept daily 10am–5.30pm; Nov–Easter Mon, Fri & Sat 10am–5pm; ☎01837/53020), next to the museum and the *White Hart* (☎01837/52730; ③). There's plenty of other decent **accommodation** in the centre of town, with basic rooms at the *Fountain Hotel*, further up Fore Street (☎01837/53900; no credit cards; ①); *Meadowlea*, further out at 65 Station Rd (☎01837/53200; ①); and, half a mile north of the centre, *Upcott House*, Upcott Hill (☎01837/53743; no credit cards; ①). Okehampton's new **youth hostel** (☎01837/53916; closed Dec & Jan) provides six-bed bunkrooms in a converted goods shed at the old station, and there's a small **campsite**, *Yertiz*, three quarters of a mile east of Okehampton on the B3260 (☎01837/52281). Back in the centre of town, *The Coffee Pot*, on Fairplace Terrace, behind the museum, is a cheap retreat for breakfasts, coffees and **meals**.

Lydford

Eight miles southwest of Okehampton, the village of **LYDFORD** boasts the sturdy but small-scale **Lydford Castle**, a Saxon outpost with a Norman keep which was later used as a prison. The picturesque *Castle Inn* sits right next to the castle (☎01822/820242; ④), and has a fire-lit sixteenth-century bar and a pricey but first-rate restaurant. The chief attraction here, though, is **Lydford Gorge** (daily: April–Sept 10am–5.30pm; Oct 10am–4pm; Nov–March as far as the White Lady Waterfall only 10.30am–3pm; £3.40; NT), whose main entrance is a five-minute walk downhill. There is a second entrance at the southern end of the gorge nearer the White Lady Waterfall, which is the only access in winter, when the river can flood (and when the waterfall is the only part of the gorge open). Two routes – one above, one along the banks – follow the ravine burrowed through by the River Lyd as far as the hundred-foot White Lady Waterfall from which a riverside walk continues to a series of whirlpools including the fierce Devil's Cauldron, from which you can return via the opposite bank. Overgrown with thick woods, the one-and-a-half-mile gorge is alive with butterflies, spotted woodpeckers, dippers, herons and clouds of insects. The full course would take you roughly two hours at a leisurely pace.

Tavistock

The main town of the western moor, **TAVISTOCK** owes its distinctive Victorian appearance to the building boom that followed the discovery of copper deposits here in 1844. Originally, however, this market and stannary town on the River Tavy grew around what was once the West Country's most important Benedictine abbey, established in the eleventh century. Scanty remnants still survive in the churchyard of **St Eustace**, a mainly fifteenth-century building with some fine monuments inside and a William Morris window in the south aisle. If you can, try to catch the town's bustling Friday **Pannier Market**, a fixture since 1105. Half a mile south of Tavistock, on the Plymouth Road, stands a statue of Sir Francis Drake, who was born and raised on Crowndale Farm, a mile south of town; the statue on Plymouth Hoe is a replica of this one.

There is a **tourist office** in the town hall on Bedford Square (April–June, Sept & Oct Mon–Sat 10am–5pm; July & Aug 10am–5.30pm; Nov–Easter Mon, Tues, Fri & Sat

10am–4pm; ☎01822/612938) and **bikes** can be rented from Tavistock Cycles, Paddons Row, Brook Street (☎01822/617630). For **accommodation**, *Mallards Guesthouse* is a reliable B&B, at 48 Plymouth Rd (☎01822/615171; no credit cards; ①); another good choice is the Georgian *Eko Brae* at 4 Bedford Villas, in the Springhill quarter of town (☎01822/614028; no credit cards; ①).

North of Tavistock, a four-mile lane wanders up to **Brent Tor**, 1130ft high and dominating Dartmoor's western fringes. Access to its conical summit is easiest along a path gently ascending through gorse on its southwestern side, leading to the small church of St Michael at the top. Bleak, treeless moorland extends in every direction, wrapped in silence that's occasionally pierced by the shrill cries of stonechats and wheatears. A couple of miles eastwards, **Gibbet Hill** looms over Black Down and the ruined stack of the abandoned Wheal Betsy silver and lead mine.

North Devon

From Exeter the A377 runs alongside the scenic Tarka Line railway to **North Devon**'s major town, **Barnstaple**. A few miles north of here, the resort of **Ilfracombe** draws the crowds, though there are acres of broad beaches in the area which give ample opportunity to find your own space, not least at **Woolacombe Sand**. The river port of **Bideford** gives its name to a long bay that holds the precipitous village of **Clovelly**, perhaps Devon's most famous beauty spot. Inspiring coastal walks follow the bay, particularly to the stormy **Hartland Point** and beyond. Away from the coast, there is plenty of scope for walking and cycling along the Tarka Trail long-distance path, passing through some of the region's loveliest countryside, while for a complete break, the tiny island of **Lundy** offers almost complete isolation and a cleansing air.

Barnstaple

BARNSTAPLE, at the head of the Taw estuary, makes an excellent springboard for exploring the area, being well connected to the resorts of Bideford Bay, Ilfracombe (bus #3) and Woolacombe (bus #303), as well as to the western fringes of Exmoor. The town's centuries-old role as a market place is perpetuated in the daily bustle around the huge timber-framed **Pannier Market** off the High Street, alongside which runs **Butchers Row**, its 33 archways now converted to a variety of uses. In the High Street itself, fourteenth-century **St Anne's Chapel** was converted into a grammar school in 1549, and later numbered amongst its pupils John Gay, author of the *Beggar's Opera*; the inside is currently closed to visitors. At the end of Boutport Street, the **Museum of North Devon** (Tues–Sat 10am–4.30pm; £1, free Sat 10am–noon) holds a lively miscellany including wildlife displays and a collection of the eighteenth-century pottery for which the region was famous. The museum lies alongside the Taw, where footpaths make for a pleasant riverside stroll, with the colonnaded **Queen Anne's Walk** – built as a merchants' exchange at the end of the eighteenth century – providing some architectural interest.

A well-equipped **tourist office** lies opposite Butchers Row on Boutport Street (Mon–Sat 9.30am–5pm; ☎01271/375000). Cyclists on the Tarka Trail can **rent bikes** from Tarka Trail Cycle Hire at the train station or Rolle Quay Cycle Hire on Rolle Street, at the top end of the High Street, conveniently placed for the northern section of the Trail towards Braunton. The *Rolle Quay Inn* can provide lunches to eat there or take as a picnic. There are plenty of **places to stay** in town, two of them at the bottom of the High Street: the Georgian *Nelson House*, at 99 Newport Rd (☎01271/345929; no credit cards; ①); and, around the corner on Victoria Road, the equally spacious *Ivy House* (☎01271/371198; no credit cards; ①). A little further out on Landkey Road is the

THE TARKA LINE AND THE TARKA TRAIL

Henry Williamson's **Tarka the Otter** (1927), rated by some as one of the finest pieces of nature writing in the English language, has been appropriated as a promotional device by the Devon tourist industry. As parts of the book are set in the Taw valley, it was inevitable that the Exeter to Barnstaple rail route – which follows the Taw for half of its length – should be dubbed the **Tarka Line**. Leaving hourly from Exeter St David's station, this branch line cuts through the sparsely populated heart of Devon, the biggest town en route being Crediton, ancient birthplace of St Boniface (patron saint of Germany and the Netherlands) and site of the bishopric before its transfer to Exeter in the eleventh century.

Barnstaple forms the centre of the figure of eight traced by the **Tarka Trail**, which tracks the otter's wanderings for a distance of over 180 miles. To the north, the trail penetrates Exmoor then follows the coast back, passing through Williamson's home village of Georgeham on its return to Barnstaple. South, the path takes in Bideford, following a disused railway line to Meeth, and continuing as far as Okehampton before swooping up via Eggesford, the point at which the Tarka Line joins the Taw valley.

Twenty-three miles of the trail follow a former railway line that's ideally suited to **bicycles**, and there are rental shops at Barnstaple, Instow and Bideford. A good ride from Barnstaple is to Torrington (15 miles south), where you can eat at the *Puffing Billy* pub, formerly the train station. Tourist offices give out leaflets on individual sections of the trail, but the best overall book is *The Tarka Trail Guide* (Devon Books, £4.95), available from tourist offices or bookshops.

first-rate *Mount Sandford* (☎01271/342354; no credit cards; ①), which has a beautiful garden. For gourmet dining, as well as accommodation, head south of the centre, to *Lynwood House*, on Bishops Tawton Rd (☎01271/343695, *thelynwood@email.com*; ④), which serves a moderate set lunch and expensive but choice seafood dishes in the evening. Two good, inexpensive **restaurants** in town, both on Boutport Street, are the Italian *La Viennetta* and *Chamber's Brasserie*, good for baguettes and salads until about 9pm.

Ilfracombe and around

The most popular resort on Devon's northern coast, **ILFRACOMBE** is essentially little changed since its evolution into a Victorian and Edwardian tourist centre, large-scale development having been restricted by the surrounding cliffs. Nonetheless, the relentless pressure to have fun and the ubiquitous smell of chips can become oppressive, though in summer you can always pop down to the small harbour and escape on a coastal tour, a cruise to Lundy Island (see p.334) or a fishing trip. If you're moving on east into Somerset, take bus #300 (3 daily), which follows the coast road to Lynton and beyond.

The best **beaches** in the area are around **Morte Point**, five miles west of Ilfracombe. Below the promontory stretches a rocky shore whose menacing sunken reef inspired the Normans to give it the name Morte Stone. A break in the rocks makes space for the pocket-sized **Barricane Beach**, famous for the tropical shells washed here from the Caribbean by the Atlantic currents. Luckily there's room for everyone on the two miles of **Woolacombe Sand**, served by buses #31 and #31a from Ilfracombe five miles southwest, a broad, west-facing expanse much favoured by surfers and families alike. The quieter southern end is bracketed by **Baggy Point**, where from September to November the air is a swirl of gannets, shags, cormorants and shearwaters. Round the point, **Croyde Bay** is another surfers' delight, more compact than Woolacombe, with stalls on the sand renting surfboards and wet suits.

The Ilfracombe **tourist office** is at the Landmark Theatre on the seafront (May, June, Sept & Oct daily 10am–6pm; July & Aug daily 10am–8pm; Nov–April Mon–Fri 10am–5pm, Sat 10am–4pm, Sun 10am–2pm; ☎01271/863001). One of Ilfracombe's less expensive **hotels** is *Kinvara*, very centrally located at 6 Avenue Rd (☎01271/863013; no credit cards; ①; closed Nov–Easter), but if you want views, try the *Cavendish*, at 9 Larkstone Terrace (☎01271/863994; ②; closed Nov–Feb), or, on the same road, the *Harbourside Hotel* (☎01271/862231; ④). Ilfracombe's **youth hostel** sits above the harbour on Hillsborough Terrace (☎01271/865337; closed Oct–March). The area's best **campsites** are around Morte Point: try *North Morte Farm* (☎01271/870381; closed Oct–Easter), 500yd from the beach. Near Ilfracombe's bus station, on Broad Street, the *Landpiper Inn* has a good selection of **food**.

Bideford Bay

Bideford Bay (also called Barnstaple Bay) encapsulates the variety of Devon, encompassing the downmarket beach resort of **Westward Ho!**, the savage wind-lashed rocks of **Hartland Point** and the photogenic village of **Clovelly**. **Bideford** itself is mainly a transit centre, with some decent accommodation and bus connections to all the towns on the bay, and regular boats for Lundy.

Bideford

Like Barnstaple, nine miles to the east, the estuary town of **BIDEFORD** formed an important link in the north Devon trade network, mainly due to its **bridge**, which still straddles the River Torridge. First built in 1300, the bridge was reconstructed in stone in the following century, and subsequently reinforced and widened, hence the irregularity of its 24 arches, no two of which have the same span. Bideford's greatest prosperity arose in the seventeenth and eighteenth centuries, when it enjoyed a flourishing trade with the New World, and today the tree-lined quay along the west riverbank is still the focal point for the knot of narrow shop-lined streets.

From the Norman era until the eighteenth century, the port was the property of the Grenville family, whose most celebrated scion was **Richard Grenville**, commander of the ships that carried the first settlers to Virginia in the sixteenth century, and later a major player in the defeat of the Spanish Armada. Grenville also featured in *Westward Ho!*, the historical romance by **Charles Kingsley**, who wrote part of the book in Bideford and is thus commemorated by a statue at the quay's northern end. Behind, **Victoria Park** extends up the riverbank, containing guns captured from the Spanish in 1588.

Alongside the park is the **tourist office** (Easter–June & Sept Mon–Sat 10am–5pm, Sun 10am–1pm; July & Aug Mon–Sat 10am–5pm, Sun 10am–4pm; Oct–Easter Mon–Fri 10am–4.30pm, Sat 10am–4pm; ☎01237/477676). A useful **B&B** nearby is the *Cornerhouse*, at 14 The Strand, two minutes from Victoria Park (☎01237/473722; no credit cards; ①). Further out, on Northam Road, is the attractive *Mount* (☎01237/473748, *alex@laugharne1.freeserve.com*; ②), set in its own walled gardens. Cooper Street, running up from the quay, has a good-value **restaurant**, the *Vagabond Cavalier*, and *Cooper's* for coffees and daytime snacks. Alternatively, try the bar meals round the corner at the *Heavitree Arms*, on Mill Street. For exploring the Tarka Trail by **bike**, Bideford Bicycle Hire is on Torrington Street (☎01237/424123), a couple of hundred yards south of the bridge on the far riverbank.

Clovelly

The steep cobbled lanes and whitewashed cottages of **CLOVELLY** must have featured on more calendars, biscuit boxes and tourist posters than anywhere else in the West

Country. It was put on the tourist map in the second half of the nineteenth century by two books: Charles Dickens' *A Message From the Sea* and, inevitably, *Westward Ho!* – Charles Kingsley's father was rector here for six years. To an extent, the tone of the village has been preserved since then by limiting hotel accommodation and precluding holiday homes, but on crowded summer days it's impossible to see past the artifice. The first hurdle to surmount is the horrific **visitor centre** (daily 9am–5pm; £2.50), where you are charged for access to the centre's shops, snack bars, audio-visual show and car park. Walkers, cyclists and users of public transport have right of way to the village, though it involves a tiresome detour round the oversized complex. Below the centre, the cobbled, traffic-free main street plunges past neat, flower-smothered cottages where sledges are tethered for transporting goods – the only way to carry supplies since the use of donkeys ceased.

Clovelly's stony beach and tiny harbour lie snuggled at the bottom of a cleft in the cliff wall. A lifeboat operates from here, and a handful of fishing boats are the only remnants of a fleet which provided the village's main business before the herring stocks became depleted. The jetty was built in the fourteenth century to shelter the coast's only safe harbour between Appledore and Boscastle in Cornwall. If you can't face the return climb, take the Land Rover which leaves from behind the *Red Lion* (Easter–Oct 9am–5.30pm; every 15min) back to the top of the village. It is here, immediately below the visitor centre, that **Hobby Drive** begins, a three-mile panoramic cliff-side walk.

You can reach Clovelly by bus #319 from Barnstaple. There are just two **hotels** in the village: the *New Inn*, halfway down the High Street (☎01237/431303; ⑤), and, enjoying the best position of all, the *Red Lion*, at the harbour (☎01237/431237; ⑥), which is also the best place to **eat**. Below the *New Inn* is a small **B&B**, *Donkey Hill Cottage* (☎01237/431601; no credit cards; ①), where you are advised to reserve rooms a long time in advance. There's a greater selection of guest houses a twenty-minute walk up from the visitor centre in Higher Clovelly: try *The Old Smithy*, on the main road (☎01237/431202; no credit cards; ①).

Hartland Point and around

You could drive along minor roads to **Hartland Point**, ten miles west of Clovelly, but the best approach is on foot along the coastal path. Shortly before arriving, the path touches at the only sandy beach between Westward Ho! and the Cornish border, **Shipload Bay**. The headland presents one of Devon's most dramatic sights, its jagged black rocks battered by the sea and overlooked by a solitary lighthouse 350ft up. This sheer stretch of coast has seen dozens of shipwrecks over the centuries, though many must have been prevented by the sight of the tower of fourteenth-century **St Nectan's** – a couple of miles south of the point in the village of Stoke – which acted as a landmark to sailors before the construction of the lighthouse. At 128ft, it is the tallest church tower in North Devon, and overlooks a weathered old graveyard containing memorials to various members of the Lane family – of the Bodley Head and Penguin publishing empire – who were associated with the area; inside, the church boasts a finely carved rood screen and a Norman font, all overlooked by a repainted wagon-type roof. Tea and homemade scones are served in summer at *Stoke Barton Farm*, just opposite, which also provides **B&B** year-round (☎01237/441238; no credit cards; ①) and basic **camping** facilities.

Half a mile east of the church, gardens and lush woodland surround **Hartland Abbey** (May, June & Sept Wed, Thurs & Sun 2–5.30pm; July & Aug Tues–Thurs & Sun 2–5.30pm; £4.25), an eighteenth-century country house incorporating the ruins of an abbey dissolved in 1539. There are just three pubs and a café in **Hartland** itself, further inland, while **HARTLAND QUAY** is a scatter of houses round the remains of a once busy port, financed in part by the beneficence of the mariners Raleigh, Drake and Hawkins, but mostly destroyed by storms in the last century. The *Hartland Quay* **hotel** provides an excellent opportunity to stay in the area (☎01237/441218; ②), and there is a **youth hostel** in a converted Victorian schoolhouse at Elmscott, two miles south and about half a mile inland (☎01237/441367; closed Sept–March). The only public transport is **bus** #319 from Barnstaple and Clovelly; alight at Hartland.

Lundy Island

There are fewer than twenty full-time residents on **Lundy**, a tiny windswept island twelve miles north of Hartland Point. Now a refuge for thousands of marine birds, Lundy has no cars, just one pub and one shop – indeed little has changed since the Marisco family established itself here in the twelfth century, using the shingle beaches and coves to terrorize shipping along the Bristol Channel. The family's fortunes only fell in 1242 when one of their number, William de Marisco, was found to be plotting against the king, whereupon he was hanged, drawn and quartered in London.

After the Mariscos, Lundy's most famous inhabitants were Thomas Benson, MP for Barnstaple in the eighteenth century – who was discovered using slave labour to work the granite quarries, and later found guilty of a massive insurance fraud – and William Hudson Heaven, who bought the island in 1834 and established what became known as the "Kingdom of Heaven". His home, **Millcombe House**, an incongruous piece of Georgian architecture in the desolate surroundings, is one of many relics of former habitation scattered around the island, like the **castle** standing on Lundy's southern end, erected by Henry III following the downfall of the Mariscos.

Tracks and footpaths interweave all over the island, and walking is really the only thing to do here. Inland, the grass, heather and bog is crossed by dry-stone walls and grazed by ponies, goats, deer and the rare Soay sheep. The shores – mainly cliffy on the west, softer and undulating on the east – shelter a rich variety of **birdlife**, including the **puffins** after which Lundy is named – from the Norse *Lunde* (puffin) and *ey* (island). They can only be sighted in April and May, when they come ashore to mate. Offshore, grey seals can be seen all year round.

The *Oldenburg* crosses to Lundy **from Bideford** throughout the year (2–4 weekly; 2hr 15min; ☎01237/470422) apart from a few weeks in January and February, with additional sailings **from Ilfracombe** from April to September (1–4 weekly). **Accommodation** on the island can be booked up months in advance, and B&B is only available in houses which have not already been taken for weekly rentals. Since B&B bookings can only be made within two weeks of the proposed visit, this limits the options, though outside the holiday season it is still eminently possible to find a double room for under £45 per night. **Bookings** must be made through the Landmark Trust's Shore Office in Bideford (☎01237/470422). Options range from the remote *Admiralty Lookout* (lacking electricity and with only battery-pumped water) to the two-storey granite *Barn*, a hostel sleeping fourteen. More comfort can be found at the *Old House*, where Charles Kingsley stayed in 1849, or the *Old Light*, a lighthouse built in 1820 by the architect of Dartmoor Prison. There's also a **campsite** on the island, open all year, though it can get pretty harsh in winter.

CORNWALL

When D.H. Lawrence wrote that being in **Cornwall** was "like being at a window and looking out of England," he wasn't just thinking of its geographical extremity. Virtually unaffected by the Roman conquest, Cornwall was for centuries the last English haven for a **Celtic culture** elsewhere eradicated by the Saxons – a land where princes communed with Breton troubadours, where chroniclers and scribes composed the epic tales of Arthurian heroism, and where itinerant men from Welsh and Irish monasteries disseminated an elemental and visionary Christianity. Primitive granite crosses and a crop of Celtic saints remain as traces of this formative period, and though the Cornish language had ebbed away by the eighteenth century, it is recalled in Celtic place names that have grown more exotic as they have become corrupted over time.

Another strand of Cornwall's folkloric character comes from the **smugglers** who thrived here right up until the last century, exploiting the sheltered creeks and hidden anchorages of the southern coasts. For many fishing villages, such as Polperro and Mousehole, contraband provided an important secondary income, as did the looting of the ships that regularly came to grief on the reefs and rocks. Further distinguishing it from neighbouring Devon, Cornwall has also had a strong **industrial economy**, based mainly on the mining of **copper** and **tin** in the north, centred on the towns of Redruth and St Agnes, and in the south on the deposits of **china clay**, which are still being mined in the area around St Austell.

Nowadays, of course, Cornwall's most flourishing industry is tourism. The repercussions of the holiday business on Cornwall have been uneven, for instance shamefully defacing **Land's End** but leaving Cornwall's other great promontory, **Lizard Point**, untainted. Examples of what happens when all the stops are pulled out can be seen in the thronged resort of **Falmouth** and its north-coast equivalent **Newquay**, the west's chief surfing centre, though the quainter villages such as **Mevagissey**, **Polperro** and **Padstow** have also succumbed to the sell-out. Others, such as **Boscastle** or **Charlestown**, are hardly touched, however, and you couldn't wish for anything more remote than **Bodmin Moor**, a tract of wilderness in the heart of Cornwall – and even **Tintagel**, site of what is fondly known as King Arthur's castle, has preserved its sense of desolation. Other places have reached a happy compromise with the seasonal influx, like **St Ives**, **Fowey** and **Bude**, or else are saved from overexploitation by sheer distance, as is the case with the **Isles of Scilly**.

From Looe to Veryan Bay

The southern strip of the Cornish coast from Looe to Veryan Bay holds a string of medieval harbour towns tarnished by various degrees of commercialization, but there are also a few spots where you can experience the best of Cornwall, including some wonderful coastline. The main rail stop is **St Austell**, the capital of Cornwall's china clay industry, though there is a branch line connecting nearby **Par** with the north coast at Newquay, and another one east of St Austell Bay to **Looe** from Liskeard. The touristy **Polperro** is easily accessible by bus from Plymouth, Looe and the estuary town of **Fowey**, though this port, in a niche of Cornwall closely associated with the author Daphne Du Maurier, is most easily reached by bus from St Austell, as is **Mevagissey** to the west.

Looe and Polperro

LOOE was drawing crowds as early as 1800, when the first "bathing machines" were wheeled out, but the arrival of the railway in 1879 was what really packed its beaches. Though Looe now touts itself as something of a shark-fishing centre, most people come here for the sand, the handiest stretch being the beach in front of East Looe – the busier half of the river-divided town. If you walk a mile eastwards you'll find a cleaner spot to swim at **Millendreath**. If you're not enticed by Looe's boating and bathing attractions, there's always the **Old Guildhall Museum** (May–Sept Mon–Fri & Sun 11.30am–4.30pm; £1), a diverse collection of maritime models and exhibits, though none so interesting as the building itself, a fifteenth-century construction preserving its prisoners' cells and raised magistrates' benches.

East Looe's **tourist office** is at the Guildhall on the main Fore Street (Easter week & May–Oct daily 10am–5pm; Easter–May daily 10am–2pm; ☎01503/262072). There's plenty of **accommodation** here: try *Osborne House*, a converted cottage in Lower Chapel Street, close to the harbour (☎01503/262970; ②; closed Nov & Jan), or *Sea Breeze*, a B&B further up the same street (☎01503/263131; ①) – both have moderately priced **restaurants**.

From the bus stop and car park at the top of neighbouring **POLPERRO**, it's a ten-minute walk following the River Pol down to the minuscule harbour. The tightly packed houses rising on each side of the stream present an undeniably pretty sight, little changed since the village's heyday of smuggling and pilchard fishing, but the "discovery" of Polperro has almost ruined it, its straggling main street – The Coombes – now an unbroken row of tourist shops and fast-food outlets. The best places to **stay** are *New House*, on Talland Hill, right on the harbour (☎01503/272206; no credit cards; ②), or *Fernhill*, on The Coombes – centrally positioned by the river with precious parking space (☎01503/272491; no credit cards; ①). For **eating**, the *Plantation Café*, on The Coombes, is good for cream teas and snacks (closed Sat); also on the main road, *The Kitchen* is well known for vegetarian and seafood dishes.

Fowey

The ten miles west from Polperro to **Polruan** are among the best stretches of the coastal path in south Cornwall, giving access to some beautiful secluded sand beaches. There are frequent **ferries** across the River Fowey from Polruan, giving a fine view of the quintessential Cornish port of **FOWEY** (pronounced "Foy"), a cascade of neat, pale terraces at the mouth of one of the peninsula's greatest rivers. The major port on the county's south coast in the fourteenth century, Fowey finally became so ambitious that it provoked Edward IV to strip the town of its military capability, though it continued to thrive commercially, coming into its own as the leading port for china clay shipments in the last century. In addition to the bulkier freighters sailing from wharves north of the town, the harbour today is crowded with trawlers and yachts, giving the town a brisk, purposeful character lacking in many of Cornwall's south coast ports.

Fowey's steep layout centres on the church of **St Fimbarrus**, a distinctive fifteenth-century construction replacing a church that was sacked by the French. Next door, the **Literary Centre**, on South Street, has a small exhibition on Daphne Du Maurier's life and work (daily mid-May to mid-Sept 10am–5pm; free), while behind the church stands **Place House**, an extravagance belonging to the local Treffry family, with a Victorian Gothic tower grafted on to the fifteenth- and sixteenth-century fortified building. Below the church, the **Ship Inn**, sporting some fine Elizabethan panelling and plaster ceilings, was originally home to the Rashleighs – a recurring name in the annals of this region – and held the local Roundhead HQ during the Civil War. From here, Fore Street, Lostwithiel Street and the Esplanade fan out, the **Esplanade** leading to a footpath that gives access to some splendid walks around the coast. Past the remains of a blockhouse that once supported a defensive chain hung across the river's mouth lies the small beach of **Readymoney Cove**. Close by stand the ruins of **St Catherine's Castle**, built by Thomas Treffry on the orders of Henry VIII, and offering fine views across the estuary.

Practicalities

Separated from eastern routes by its river, Fowey is most accessible by bus #24 from St Austell (every 30min). There is a small **tourist office** in the town's post office on Custom House Hill (May–Sept Mon–Fri 9am–5.30pm, Sat 9am–5pm; Oct–April Mon–Fri 9am–1pm & 2–5pm, Sat 9am–1pm; ☎01726/833616). All of the central pubs offer **B&B**: try the *Safe Harbour*, on Lostwithiel Street (☎01726/833379; no credit cards; ②). On Fore Street, the *Dwelling House*, at no. 6 (☎01726/833662; ②), is a good B&B, while the *Old Quay House Hotel* at no. 28 (☎01726/833302; ②) has lovely views from its airy rooms and patio. The plush *Marina Hotel*, on the Esplanade (☎01726/833315; ⑤), has stylish rooms, a garden and river views. The **youth hostel** is in the nearby riverside hamlet of Golant (☎01726/833507, *golant@yha.org.uk*; closed Nov–Jan). The nearest **campsite** is at *Yeate Farm* (☎01726/870256; closed Nov–March), on the eastern bank of the river, three quarters of a mile up from the Bodinnick ferry crossing. Fowey has some good seafood **restaurants**, among them *Ellis's*, at 3 The Esplanade· (☎01726/832359), specializing in lobster, and *Food For Thought* on the quay, which serves mainly French dishes – both are quite formal, expensive places. The area is also well provided with worthy **pubs**, such as Golant's four miles north of Fowey on the riverside *Fisherman's Arms*, the *Old Ferry Inn* at Bodinnick directly across the river from Fowey, and Polruan's excellent *Lugger Inn*.

St Austell and its bay

It was the discovery of china clay, or kaolin, in the downs to the north of **ST AUSTELL** that spurred the town's growth in the eighteenth century. An essential ingredient in the production of porcelain, kaolin had until then only been produced in northern China, where the high ridge, or *kao-lin*, was the sole known source of the raw material. Still a vital part of Cornwall's economy, the clay is now mostly exported for use in the manufacture of paper, as well as paint and medicines. The conical spoil heaps left by the mines are a feature of the local landscape, especially on Hensbarrow Downs to the north, the great green-and-white mounds making an eerie sight.

St Austell's nearest link to the sea is at **CHARLESTOWN**, an easy downhill walk from the centre. This unassuming and unspoilt port is named after the entrepreneur Charles Rashleigh, who in 1791 began work on the harbour, widening the streets to accommodate the clay wagons passing through daily. The wharves are still used, loading clay onto vessels that appear oversized beside the tiny jetties. Behind the harbour, the **Shipwreck Museum** (March–Oct daily 10am–6pm; £4.45) is entered through tunnels once used to convey clay to the docks, and shows a good collection of photos and relics as well as tableaux of historical scenes.

On each side of the dock, the coarse sand and stone **beaches** have small rock pools, above which cliff walks lead around St Austell Bay. Eastwards, you soon arrive at overdeveloped **Carlyon Bay**, whose main resort is **Par**. The beaches here get clogged with clay – the best swimming is to be found further on at the sheltered crescent of **Polkerris**. The easternmost limit of St Austell Bay is marked by **Gribbin Head**, near which stands Menabilly House, where Daphne Du Maurier lived for over twenty years – it was the model for the "Manderley" of *Rebecca*. The house is not open to the public, but you can walk down to **Polridmouth Cove**, where Rebecca met her watery end.

Trains on the main London–Penzance line serve St Austell, with most services also stopping at Par. An hourly **bus** #31 links St Austell, Charlestown, Par and Polkerris. Charlestown has two really attractive **places to stay**: *T'Gallants* (☎01726/70203; ②), a smart Georgian B&B at the back of the harbour, and the *Pier House Hotel* (☎01726/67955; ④), with a premium harbourside location and a good **restaurant**. Behind *T'Gallants*, the *Rashleigh Arms* offers real ale and a range of food.

Mevagissey to Veryan Bay

MEVAGISSEY was once known for the construction of fast vessels, used for carrying contraband as well as pilchards. Today the tiny port might display a few stacks of lobster pots, but the real business is tourism, and in summer the maze of backstreets is saturated with day-trippers, converging on the inner harbour and overflowing onto the large sand beach at **Pentewan** a mile to the north.

Past the headland to the south of Mevagissey, the small sandy cove of **Portmellon** retains little of its boatbuilding activity but is freer of tourists. Further still, **GORRAN HAVEN**, a former crab-fishing town, has a neat rock-and-sand beach and a footpath that winds round to the even more attractive **Vault Beach**, half a mile south. South of here juts **Dodman Point**, the most striking headland on Cornwall's southern coast and the cause of many a wreck. The stark granite cross on the summit was built by a local parson as a seamark in 1896. The promontory holds the substantial remains of an Iron Age fort, with an earthwork bulwark cutting right across the point.

Curving away to the west, the elegant parabola of **Veryan Bay** is barely touched by commercialism. Just west of Dodman Point lies one of Cornwall's most beautiful coves, **Hemmick Beach**, an excellent swimming spot with rocky outcrops affording a measure of privacy. Visually even more impressive is **Porthluney Cove**, a crescent of sand whose centrepiece is the battlemented **Caerhays Castle**, built in 1808 by John Nash and surrounded by beautiful gardens (house: mid-March to mid-April Mon–Fri 2–4pm; grounds: mid-March to mid-May Mon–Fri 10am–4pm; house £3.50; grounds £3.50; house & grounds £6). A little further on, the minuscule and whitewashed **Portloe** is fronted by jagged black rocks that throw up fountains of sea spray, giving it a good, end-of-the-road atmosphere.

Sequestered inland, **VERYAN**, two miles west of Portloe, is best known for its curious, circular, white houses, built in the nineteenth century. A lane from Veryan leads down to one of the cleanest swimming spots on Cornwall's southern coast, **Pendower Beach**. Two thirds of a mile long and backed by dunes, Pendower joins with the neighbouring **Carne Beach** at low tide to create a long sandy continuum. If you want to stay in Veryan, try the *New Inn*, a friendly **B&B** which serves wholesome meals (☎01872/501362; ②).

Practicalities

From St Austell's train station, **buses** #26 and #26A leave hourly for Mevagissey, some continuing to Gorran Haven. Veryan and Portloe are reachable on bus #51 from Truro. The old *Ship Inn*, in Mevagissey (☎01726/843324; ③), offers reasonable **accommodation**; otherwise try *Mevagissey House*, on Vicarage Hill (☎01726/842427; no credit cards; ③; closed Nov–Feb). You might be better off staying in Portmellon, where the weathered old *Rising Sun Inn* (☎01726/843235; ③; closed Nov to mid-March) confronts the sea. In Gorran Haven, the well-situated *Llawnroc Inn* (☎01726/843461; ③) is the only budget option. The nearest **youth hostel** (☎01726/843234; closed Nov–March) is in a former farmhouse at **Boswinger**, a remote spot half a mile from Hemmick Beach, and a mile from the bus stop at Gorran Church Town (bus #26). Boswinger also has a **campsite**, *Sea View* (☎01726/843425; closed Oct–Easter), overlooking Veryan Bay. There's no shortage of **restaurants** in Mevagissey, most specializing in fish – try the large, harbourfront *Shark's Fin Hotel*. The *Cellar Bar*, on Church Street, and the *Fountain Inn*, on Fore Street, are **pubs** that serve food.

St Mawes to Falmouth

Lush tranquillity collides with frantic tourist activity around **Carrick Roads**, the complex estuary basin to the south of **Truro**, the region's main centre for accommodation and transport. On the eastern shore, the luxuriant **Roseland** peninsula is a backwater of woods and sheltered creeks between the River Fal and the sea. **St Mawes** is the main draw here, chiefly on account of its castle, a twin of Pendennis across the neck of the estuary in **Falmouth**, a major resort at the end of a branch line from Truro.

St Mawes and the Roseland peninsula

Stuck on the end of a prong of land at the bottom of Carrick Roads, secluded, unhurried **ST MAWES** has an attractive walled seafront below a hillside of villas and abundant gardens. Out of sight at the end of the seafront stands small and pristine **St Mawes Castle** (April–Sept daily 10am–6pm; Oct daily 10am–5pm; Nov–March Mon–Wed & Fri–Sun 10am–1pm & 2–4pm; £2.50; EH). Built during the reign of Henry VIII to a clover-leaf design, with a central round keep surrounded by robust gun emplacements, the castle owes its excellent condition to its early surrender when under siege by Parliamentary forces in 1646. The dungeons and gun installations contain various artillery exhibits as well as some background on local social history.

Out of St Mawes, you could spend a pleasant afternoon poking around the Roseland peninsula between the Percuil River and the eastern shore of Carrick Roads. It's only two and a half miles to the scattered hamlet of **ST JUST-IN-ROSELAND**, where the strikingly picturesque church of St Just stands right next to the creek, surrounded by palms and subtropical shrubbery, its gravestones tumbling down to the water's edge.

In summer, there's a **ferry** (May–Sept 2 hourly 10am–4.30pm) from St Mawes to the southern arm of the Roseland peninsula, where you'll find the twelfth- to thirteenth-century church of **St Anthony's** and the **lighthouse** on St Anthony's Head, marking the entry into Carrick Roads. There's also a ferry crossing from St Mawes to Falmouth (every 30min in summer, less frequent in winter). St Mawes makes an attractive – though pricey – place **to stay**. Right on the seafront, *St Mawes Hotel* (☎01326/270266; ⑨; closed Nov to mid-Feb) enjoys a glorious view over the estuary; the price includes dinner. You'll find a more relaxed reception down the road at the *Rising Sun* (☎01326/270233; ③), also with a good restaurant. Less expensive rooms can be found away from the sea, for example at the *Malt House* (☎01326/270129; ②), which has just one spacious en-suite room with sea views. There's a decent **campsite** at Trethem Mill, three miles inland of St Mawes (☎01872/580504; closed Nov–March). The *Victory Inn* is a good old oak-beamed **pub** just off the seafront in St Mawes.

Truro

TRURO, seat of Cornwall's law courts and other county bureaucracies, has a distinctly small-scale provincial feel, even if its Georgian houses do reflect the prosperity that came with the tin-mining boom of the 1800s. Blurring the town's overall identity, its modern shopping centre stands alongside the powerful but chronologically confused **Cathedral**. Completed in 1910, this was the first Anglican cathedral to be built in England since St Paul's, but it incorporates part of the fabric of the old parish church that previously occupied the site. The airy interior's best feature is the neo-Gothic baptistry, with its emphatically pointed arches and elaborate roof vaulting. To the right of the choir, St Mary's aisle is a relic of the original Perpendicular building, other fragments of which adorn the walls, including – in the north transept – a colourful Jacobean memorial to local Parliamentarian John Robartes and his wife. The only other item to keep you in Truro is the **Royal Cornwall Museum** (Mon–Sat 10am–5pm; £2.50), housed in an elegant Georgian building on River Street. The exhibits include minerals, toys and paintings by Cornish artists.

Truro's **tourist office** is on Boscawen Street (Easter–May, Sept & Oct Mon–Fri 9am–5.15pm, Sat 10am–1pm; June–Aug Mon–Fri 9am–6pm, Sat 10am–5pm; Nov–Easter Mon–Thurs 9am–5.15pm, Fri 9am–5.45pm; ☎01872/274555). **Buses** stop nearby at Lemon Quay, or near the **train station** on Richmond Hill, five minutes' walk west of the centre. The best **accommodation** near the train station is at *The Gables*, 49 Treyew Rd (☎01872/242318; ①); *The Bay Tree*, which lies halfway between the station and the centre at 28 Ferris Town (☎01872/240274; ①); and *Patmos*, at 8 Burley Close, where Lemon Street meets Falmouth Road (☎01872/278018; ①). The nearest **camp-site** is *Carnon Downs*, three miles outside Truro on the Falmouth road (☎01872/862283; closed Nov–March). A good selection of Truro's **restaurants** lie on or around Kenwyn St, including the inexpensive *Number Ten*, at no. 10, which serves wholesome dishes from around the world, and the *Feast*, at no. 15, which cooks up excellent wholefoods to eat in or take away. On the corner of Francis and Castle streets, the *Wig and Pen* is a decent **pub** with bar food and a separate restaurant, while the *Globe Inn* next door also serves hot snacks.

Falmouth

The construction of Pendennis Castle on the southern point of Carrick Roads in the six-teenth century prepared the ground for the growth of **FALMOUTH**, then no more than a fishing village. The building of its deepwater harbour was proposed a century later by Sir John Killigrew, and Falmouth's prosperity was assured when in 1689 it became the chief base of the fast Falmouth Packets, which sped mail to the Americas. This centu-ry, though, Falmouth has shed most of its Cornishness and, barring its castle, has lit-tle to offer anyone who wants to get away from the hard sell.

The long main drag, comprising High Street, Market Street and Church Street, is crammed with humdrum bars and cafés, though at its southern end, Arwenack Street, it does have the Tudor remains of the Killigrews' **Arwenack House**. The peculiar granite pyramid standing opposite the house, built in 1737, is probably intended to com-memorate the local family, though its exact significance has never been clear. Apart from this, the centre of town only offers a clamber up the precipitous 111 steps of **Jacob's Ladder** from The Moor, the old town's main square, for a bird's-eye view of the harbour. From the Prince of Wales Pier, below The Moor, frequent ferries leave for St Mawes, accompanied in summer by boats touring the local estuaries.

Standing sentinel at the tip of the promontory that separates Carrick Roads from Falmouth Bay, **Pendennis Castle** (daily: April–June & Sept 10am–6pm; July & Aug 9am–6pm; Oct 10am–5pm; Nov–March 10am–4pm; £2.70; EH) shows little evidence of its five-month siege by the Parliamentarians during the Civil War, which ended only when half its defenders had died and the rest been starved into submission. Facing right out to sea on its own pointed peninsula, the stout ramparts offer the best all-round views of Carrick Roads and Falmouth Bay. Beyond Pendennis Point stretches a long sandy bay with various **beaches** backed by expensive hotels. If you want to swim, the best spot is **Swanpool Beach**, accessible by cliff path from the more popular **Gyllyngvase Beach** – or walk a couple of miles further on to **Maenporth**, from where there are some fine cliff-top walks.

Falmouth's **tourist office** is off The Moor, on Killigrew Street (Easter–June & Sept Mon–Sat 9am–5pm; July & Aug Mon–Sat 9am–5pm, Sun 10am–4pm; Oct–Easter Mon–Fri 9am–1pm & 2–5pm; ☎01326/312300). Most of the town's **accommodation** is in the southern part of town, including the good-value *Ivanhoe*, at 7 Melvill Rd (☎01326/319083; ②). For the beach area, expect to pay more: *Chellowdene*, on Gyllyngvase Hill (☎01326/314950; ②; closed Oct–April), has more reasonable rates than most. There's a perfectly sited **youth hostel** inside Pendennis Castle (☎01326/311435, *pendennis@yha.org.uk*; closed Jan). Among the overdeveloped cara-van parks on the coast south of Falmouth, a decent-sized **campsite**, *Tremorvah Tent Park* (☎01326/318311), lies off the coast path behind Swanpool Beach. The best fish in town is to be found at *The Seafood Bar*, Lower Quay Hill (☎01326/315129; evenings only; closed Sun & Mon). The *Quayside Inn*, further up on Arwenack Street, is the pick of the **pubs**.

The Lizard peninsula

The **Lizard peninsula** – from the Celtic *lys ardh*, or "high point" – preserves a thankfully undeveloped appearance in contrast to many other areas of Cornwall. If this flat and treeless expanse can be said to have a centre, it is **Helston**, a junction for buses running from Falmouth and Truro to the spartan villages of the peninsula's interior and the tiny fishing ports on its coast.

The east coast to Lizard Point

To the north of the peninsula, the snug hamlets sprinkled in the valley of the **River Helford** are a complete contrast to the rugged character of most of the Lizard. At the river's mouth stands **MAWNAN**, whose granite church of St Mawnan-in-Meneage is dedicated to the sixth-century Welsh missionary St Maunanus – Meneage means "land of monks". Upstream on the south side, **Frenchman's Creek** is one of a splay of creeks and arcane inlets running off the river, and was the inspiration for Daphne Du Maurier's novel of the same name. Her evocation of it holds true: "still and soundless, surrounded by the trees, hidden from the eyes of men". Mawnan and Helford Passage are linked to Helston by frequent #T1 and #T4 buses.

You can get over to the south bank by the seasonal ferry from Helford Passage to **Helford**, an agreeable old smugglers' haunt where you can have teas and snacks at *Rose Cottage* or pub lunches in the garden of the *Shipwright's Arms*, overlooking the river. South of here, on the B3293, the road meets the coast at the fishing port of **COVERACK**, whose name – "Hideaway" – gives some indication of its one-time role as a centre of contraband. Three miles offshore lurk the dreaded **Manacles** rocks, the cause of numerous shipwrecks over the centuries, many of which were gleefully claimed by the local wreckers. Coverack has a few decent **places to stay**, including the pleasant *Bakery Cottage* (☎01326/280474; no credit cards; ①), with home cooking; at the seafront, ask in the *Harbour Lights* restaurant about vacancies in a neighbouring cottage (☎01326/280507; ①). There's a **youth hostel** just west of Coverack's centre, in a country house overlooking the bay (☎01326/280687; closed Nov–March). Two #T3 buses daily run to Coverack from Helston in about one hour.

Beyond the safe and clean swimming spot of **Kennack Sands** – where *Sea Acres* (☎01326/290064; closed Nov–Feb) is one of a cluster of **campsites** – the south tip of the promontory, **Lizard Point**, is marked by a plain lighthouse and a couple of low-key cafés and gift shops. Sheltered from the ceaselessly churning sea, a tiny cove holds a disused lifeboat station. Behind the point, a road and footpath lead a mile inland to the nondescript village called simply **The Lizard**, where you can sleep and eat at the *Caerthillian* (☎01326/290019, *caerthillian@connexions.co.uk*; ②). A mile to the west lies the peninsula's best-known beach, **Kynance Cove**. With its sheer hundred-foot cliffs, its stacks and arches of serpentine rock and its offshore islands, the beach has an irresistible wild grandeur, and the water quality is excellent – but take care not to be stranded on the islands by the tide, which submerges the entire beach at its flood. Bus #T3 also runs to Kynance Cove from Helston, though #T1 is the most useful connection for the Lizard, running hourly (five times on Sun) in about fifty minutes.

The west coast

Four miles north of Kynance Cove, **MULLION**, the Lizard's biggest village, has a fifteenth- to sixteenth-century church dedicated to the Breton **St Mellane** (or St Malo), with a dog door for canine churchgoers. In the centre of the village, *Alma House* (☎01326/240509; ②) provides good **accommodation**. A mile away on the coast, **Mullion Cove** has rock sculptures and a small beach outside its sheltered harbour, while the neighbouring beaches of **Polurrian** and **Poldhu** are more popular with surfers. At the cliff edge, the Marconi Monument marks the spot from which the first transatlantic radio transmission was made in 1901. The freshwater **Loe Pool**, three miles north, is separated from the sea by a shingle bar, and is one of the two places claiming to be where the sword Excalibur was restored to its watery source (the other is on Bodmin Moor). Mullion and Poldhu are stops on the frequent #T1 bus route.

Nearby **Porthleven** is a sizeable port that once served to export tin ore from the Stannary town of **HELSTON**, three miles inland. This transport junction is best known for its **Furry Dance** (or Floral Dance), which dates from the seventeenth century. Held on May 8 (unless this falls on a Sunday or Monday, when the procession takes place on the nearest Saturday), it's a stately procession of top-hatted men and summer-frocked women performing a strange, rather solemn dance through the town's streets and gardens. Other than this, the town's most famous attraction is the garish **Flambards Theme Park** (daily: April to mid-July & Sept–Oct 10.30am–5pm; mid-July & Aug 10am–6pm; sometimes closes Mon & Fri in April, May, Sept & Oct, call ☎01326/564093; £7.50), a riot of pseudo-Victoriana.

Helston's **tourist office** is at 79 Meneage St (Easter–Sept Mon–Sat 10am–1pm & 2–5pm; Oct–Easter Mon & Sat 10am–1pm, Tues, Thurs & Fri 10am–1pm & 2–5pm; ☎01326/565431). Just along the street, at no. 95, is *Hutchinson's* award-winning fish and chip shop. For a drink or a **pub** snack, check out the *Blue Anchor*, at 50 Coinagehall St, once a fifteenth-century monastery rest house, now a cramped pub with flagstone floors and mellow beer brewed on the premises. You can **rent bikes** at Bike Services, on Meneage Rd (☎01326/564564).

The Penwith peninsula

Though more densely populated than the Lizard, the **Penwith peninsula** has a more rugged landscape, with a raw appeal that is still encapsulated by the headland at **Land's End**, despite the commercial paraphernalia. The seascapes, the quality of the light and the slow tempo of the local fishing communities made this area a hotbed of artistic activity in the late nineteenth century, when the painters of Newlyn, near **Penzance**, established a distinctive school of painting. More innovative figures – among them Ben Nicholson, Barbara Hepworth and constructivist Naum Gabo – were soon afterwards to make **St Ives** one of England's liveliest cultural communities, and their enduring influence has been marked with the opening of a St Ives branch of the **Tate Gallery**.

From Penzance, the terminus for **rail** services from London and Birmingham, **buses** #1 and (Sun only) #10A go straight to Land's End in about an hour; buses #5A, #5B, #6B and #6C also take in Newlyn and Mousehole. North of Land's End, the comparatively neglected headland of Cape Cornwall is served by bus #10 from Penzance to St Just, while Zennor, St Just, Sennen Cove and Land's End are served by bus #15 from St Ives (Mon–Sat).

Penzance and around

Occupying a sheltered position at the northwest corner of Mount's Bay, **PENZANCE** has always been a major port, but most traces of the medieval town were obliterated at the end of the sixteenth century by a Spanish raiding party. Today the dominant style of Penzance is Georgian, particularly at the top of **Market Jew Street** (from *Marghas Jew*, meaning "Thursday Market"), which climbs from the harbour and the train and bus stations. At the top of the street lies the green-domed, Victorian **Market House**, before which stands a statue of **Humphry Davy**, the local woodcarver's son who pioneered the science of electrochemistry in the early nineteenth century, and invented the life-saving miners' safety lamp, which his statue holds.

Turn left here into **Chapel Street**, which has some of the town's finest buildings, including the flamboyant **Egyptian House**, built in 1835 to contain a geological museum but subsequently abandoned until its restoration twenty-odd years ago. Across the street, the **Union Hotel** dates from the seventeenth century, and originally housed the town's assembly rooms. At no. 19, the **Maritime Museum** (Easter–Oct Mon–Sat 10.30am–4.30pm; £2) holds a good collection of seafaring articles, including an array of items salvaged from local wrecks and a full-size section of an eighteenth-century man-of-war.

If your interest is roused by the art scene that flourished hereabouts at the turn of the century, head for Morrab Road, between the Promenade and Alverton Street (a continuation of Market Jew Street), where the **Penlee House Gallery and Museum** (July & Aug Mon–Sat 10.30am–4.30pm, Sun 12.30–4.30pm; rest of year closed Sun; £2, free on Sat) holds the biggest collection of the works of the Newlyn School – the colony of artists who gathered here around the Irish painter Stanhope Forbes – comprising impressionistic maritime scenes, frequently sentimentalized but often bathed in an evocatively luminous light. Newlyn itself, Cornwall's biggest fishing port, lies immediately south of Penzance.

Penzance's **tourist office** (May & Sept Mon–Fri 9am–5pm, Sat 10am–4pm; June–Aug Mon–Fri 9am–5pm, Sat 10am–4pm, Sun 10am–1pm; Oct–April Mon–Fri 9am–5pm, Sat 10am–1pm; ☎01736/362207) is right next to the **train** and **bus stations**, near the harbour. Most of the cheaper **B&Bs** are ranged along Morrab Road and its surroundings: try *Kimberley House* at no. 10 (☎01736/362727; no credit cards; ①). If you're looking for an atmospheric hotel on Chapel Street, the seventeenth-century *Trevelyan* (☎01736/362494; no credit cards; ①) and *Union* (01736/362319; ④) nicely fit the bill, or splash out on the *Abbey Hotel*, just round the corner on Abbey Street (☎01736/366906; ⑥), which has lashings of old-fashioned comfort and an excellent restaurant. The parallel Alexandra Road is the location of the *Blue Dolphin* (☎01736/363836), a backpackers' **hostel** with dorm beds. The official YHA hostel is a two-mile hike out of town, at Castle Horneck, in Alverton (☎01736/362666, *penzance@yha.org.uk*; closed Jan) – buses #5B, #6B or #10B run from the station as far as the *Pirate Inn*, from where it's a five-minute walk.

Penzance's most congenial **restaurant** is *Co-Co's Tapas Bar*, on Chapel St, good for coffees and cakes as well as beers and tapas, while vegetarians can try either *Dandelions*, a tiny café on the pedestrianized Causeway, or *Brown's*, in the basement of a gallery on Bread Street (both daytime only). Penzance has a couple of characterful **pubs** on Chapel Street: the *Admiral Benbow*, crammed with gaudy ships' figureheads and other nautical items, and the *Turk's Head*, which dates back to the thirteenth century. For **bike rental**, head for Blewett & Pender, on Albert Street, at the bottom of Market Jew Street.

St Michael's Mount

Buses from Penzance bus station leave every thirty minutes for Marazion, five miles east, from where the medieval chimneys and towers of **St Michael's Mount** (April–Oct Mon–Fri 10.30am–5.30pm, plus most weekends; Nov–March call for opening times; ☎01736/710507; £4.40; NT) can be seen a couple of hundred yards offshore. A vision of the archangel Michael led to the building of a church on this granite pile around the fifth century, and within three centuries a Celtic monastery had been founded here. The present building derives from a chapel raised in the eleventh century by Edward the Confessor, who handed over the chapel to the Benedictine monks of Brittany's Mont St Michel, whose island abbey was the model for this one. After the Civil War, when it was used to store arms for the Royalist forces, it became the residence of the St Aubyn family, who still inhabit the castle. A good number of the buildings date from the twelfth century, but the later additions are more interesting, such as the battlemented **chapel** and the seventeenth-century decorations of the Chevy Chase Room the former refectory. At low tide, the promontory can be approached via a cobbled causeway; at high tide there are boats from Marazion (£1).

Mousehole to Land's End

Accounts vary as to the derivation of the name of **MOUSEHOLE** (pronounced "Mouzle"), though it may be from a smugglers' cave just south of town. In any case, the name evokes perfectly this minuscule harbour, cradled in the arms of a granite breakwater three miles south of Penzance. The village attracts more visitors than it can handle, so hang around until the crowds have departed for a walk through its tight tangle of lanes and a drink in the *Ship Inn*. Half a mile inland, the churchyard at **Paul** holds a monument to Dolly Pentreath, a resident of Mousehole who died in 1777 and was reputed to have been the last person to speak only the Cornish language.

PORTHCURNO's name means "Port Cornwall", but its beach of tiny white shells suggests privacy and isolation rather than the movement of ships. Steep steps lead up from here to the cliff-hewn **Minack Theatre**, created in the 1930s and since enlarged to hold 750 seats, though the basic Greek-inspired design has remained intact. The spectacular backdrop of Porthcurno Bay makes this one of the country's most inspiring theatres. The summer season lasts seventeen weeks from May to September, presenting a gamut of plays, opera and musicals, with inexpensive tickets (☎01736/810181). Bring a cushion and a rug.

The best way to approach **Land's End** is unarguably on foot along the coastal path Although nothing can completely destroy the potency of this extreme western tip of England, the colossal theme park built behind this majestic headland in 1987 comes close to violating irreparably the spirit of the place. The trivializing **Land's End Experience** (daily: summer 10am–6pm; winter 10am–5pm; £8.95) substitutes a tawdry panoply of lasers and unconvincing sound effects for the real open-air experience, but the location is still a public right of way (drivers pay a parking fee), and once past the paraphernalia, nature takes over. Turf-covered sixty-foot-high cliffs provide a platform to view the Irish Lady, the Armed Knight, Dr Syntax Head and the rest of the Land's End outcrops, beyond which you can spot the Longships lighthouse, a mile and a half out to sea, and sometimes the Wolf Rock lighthouse, nine miles southwest, or even the Isles of Scilly, 25 miles away.

Whitesand Bay to Zennor

To the north of Land's End, the rounded granite cliffs fall away at **Whitesand Bay** to reveal a glistening mile-long shelf of beach that offers the best swimming on the Penwith peninsula. The rollers make for good surfing and boards can be rented at **Sennen Cove**, the more popular southern end of the beach. There are a few places to **stay** around here, including *Myrtle Cottage* on Old Coastguard Row (☎01736/871698 no credit cards; ①), which also has a cosy café open to non-residents, and the nearby *Polwyn Cottage*, tucked away on Old Coastguard Row (☎01736/871349; no credit cards ①). The pleasant *Whitesands Lodge* **hostel** (☎01736/871776) lies a few minutes' walk inland, with dorms and private rooms.

Cape Cornwall, three miles to the north, shelters another superb beach, overlooked by the chimney of the Cape Cornwall Mine, which closed in 1870. Half a mile inland, the grimly grey village of **ST JUST-IN-PENWITH** was a centre of the tin and copper industry, and the rows of trim cottages radiating out from Bank Square are redo lent of the close-knit community that once existed here. The tone is somewhat light-ened by the grassy open-air theatre where the old Cornish miracle plays were staged; it was later used by Methodist preachers as well as Cornish wrestlers. Off Bank Square, the *St Just Tea Rooms* serves inexpensive **meals**, as does the traditional *Star Inn*, which also has **rooms** (☎01736/788767; ③). There's a signposted **youth hostel** on the out-skirts of the village (☎01736/788437; closed Nov–Feb).

East of St Just, the landscape is all rolling moorland and an abundance of granite, the chief building material of **ZENNOR**. D.H. and Frieda Lawrence came to live here in 1916: "It is a most beautiful place," Lawrence wrote, "lovelier even than the Mediterranean". The Lawrences were soon joined by John Middleton Murry and Katherine Mansfield, with the hope of forming a writers' community, but the new arrivals soon left for a more sheltered haven near Falmouth. Lawrence stayed on to write *Women in Love*, before being given notice to quit by the local constabulary, who suspected Lawrence and his German wife of unpatriotic sympathies. His Cornish expe-riences were later described in *Kangaroo*. At the bottom of the village, the **Wayside Museum** (mid-April to Sept daily 10am–6pm; Oct Mon–Fri & Sun 11am–5pm; £2.20) is dedicated to Cornish life from prehistoric times. Right next door, the *Old Chapel Backpackers Hostel* makes a fun place **to stay** (☎01736/798307), while the nearby *Tinners Arms*, where Lawrence stayed before moving into Higher Tregerthen, is a homely place to **eat** and drink.

St Ives

East of Zennor, the road runs for four hilly miles on to the steeply built town of **ST IVES**, a place that has smoothly undergone the transition to holiday haunt from its pre-vious role as a centre of the fishing industry. So productive were the offshore waters that a record sixteen and a half million fish were caught in one net on a single day in 1868, and the diarist Francis Kilvert was told by the local vicar that the smell was some-times so great as to stop the church clock. By the time the reserves dried up around the early years of this century, St Ives was beginning to attract a vibrant **artists' colony**, precursors of the wave later headed by Ben Nicholson, Barbara Hepworth, Naum Gabo and the potter Bernard Leach, who in the 1960s were followed by a third wave including Terry Frost, Peter Lanyon, Patrick Heron, Bryan Winter and Roger Hilton.

Sunday painters dominate the dozens of galleries sandwiched between the town's restaurants and bars. The better work created in the region can be seen at the **St Ives Tate Gallery**, opened in 1993, overlooking Porthmeor Beach on the north side of town (Tues–Sun 10.30am–5.30pm; £3.90; combined ticket with Hepworth Museum £6). The beachfront, viewed through a grand concave window, is a constant presence inside the airy and gleaming white building, creating a dialogue with the gallery's paintings, sculptures and ceramics, most of which date from 1925 to 1975. Apart from these, the Tate has some specially commissioned contemporary works on view. The museum's rooftop **café** is one of the best places in town for tea and cake.

A short distance away on Barnoon Hill, the **Barbara Hepworth Museum** (July, Aug & public holidays daily 10.30am–5.30pm; rest of year closed Mon; £3.50) gives another insight into the local arts scene. One of the foremost non-figurative sculptors of her time, Hepworth lived in the building from 1949 until her death in a studio fire in 1975. Apart from the sculptures, which are arranged in positions chosen by Hepworth in the house and garden, the museum has masses of background on her art, from pho-tos and letters to catalogues and reviews.

The wide expanse of **Porthmeor Beach** dominates the northern side of St Ives, the stone houses tumbling almost onto the yellow sands. Unusually for a town beach, the water quality is excellent, and the rollers make it popular with surfers. South of the station, **Porthminster Beach** is another favourite spot for sunbathing and swimming, but if you hanker for a less peopled stretch you need to head east of town to the magnificent golden beaches of **St Ives Bay** – the strand is especially fine on the far side of the port of Hayle, at the mouth of the eponymous river.

Practicalities

The **train station** is off Porthminster Beach, just north of the **bus station** on Station Hill. The **tourist office** is in the Guildhall, on Street An Pol, two minutes' walk away (mid-May to Aug Mon–Sat 9.30am–5.30pm, Sun 10am–1pm; Sept Mon–Sat 9.30am–5.30pm; Oct to mid-May Mon–Thurs 9.30am–5.30pm, Fri 9.30am–5pm; ☎01736/796297). You can rent **surfing equipment** on Porthmeor Beach and from the surf specialist WindanSea on Fore Street, with an outlet on the harbour.

St Ives has several good **B&Bs** bordering the seafront near the bus and train stations, including *Kynance*, 24 The Warren (☎01736/796636; ②; closed Nov–Feb), and *Kandahar*, 11 The Warren (☎01736/796183; ②; closed Nov–Jan); both are near Porthminster Beach, so book early. The *Grey Mullet*, 2 Bunkers Hill, just twenty yards from the harbour (☎01736/796635; no credit cards; ②), is said to be the oldest house in town, while *Penclawdd*, 1 Sea View Place (☎01736/796869; ②), has harbour views in the picturesque Downalong area of town. The *St Ives Backpackers* **hostel**, The Stennack (☎01736/799444, *st-ivesbackpackers@dial.pipex.com*) has a good central location in a restored Wesleyan chapel school. St Ives has no **campsite** on the seafront, though *Ayr*, half a mile west of the town centre, above Porthmeor Beach (☎01736/795855; closed Nov–March), has a good sea prospect.

The Café, on Island Square, serves inexpensive vegetarian **snacks**, while *Peppers*, 22 Fore St, is a relaxed pizza and pasta parlour, also serving fish and steaks. For fresh local fish, try *The Grapevine*, a bistro and coffee house on the High Street, or *Pig 'n' Fish*, Norway Lane (closed Sun & Mon).

The Isles of Scilly

The **Isles of Scilly** are a compact archipelago of about a hundred islands 28 miles southwest of Land's End, none of them bigger than three miles across, and only five of them inhabited – **St Mary's, Tresco, Bryher, St Martin's** and **St Agnes**. In the annals of folklore, the Scillies are the peaks of the submerged land of Lyonesse; in fact they form part of the same granite mass as Land's End, Bodmin Moor and Dartmoor. All are swept by an energizing briny air filled with the cries of sea birds, and though the water is cold the beaches are well-nigh irresistible, ranging from small coves to vast, unvisited strands. Other points of interest include Cornwall's greatest concentration of prehistoric remains, some fabulous rock formations, and masses of **flowers**. Along with tourism, the main source of income here is flower-growing, for which the equable climate and the long hours of sunshine – their name means "Sun Isles" – makes the islands ideal.

Free of traffic, theme parks and amusement arcades, the Scillies are a welcome respite from the tourist trail, the main drawbacks being the shortage of **accommodation** – making advance booking essential at any time – and the high cost of reaching the islands. If you're coming between May and September, try to time your visit to be here on a Wednesday or Friday evening to witness the **gig races**, the most popular sport on the Scillies, performed by six-oared vessels some 30ft in length.

St Mary's

The island of **St Mary's** holds the overwhelming majority of the archipelago's population and most of its tourist accommodation. From the airport there are buses to shuttle

The islands are accessible by sea or air. **Boats from Penzance to St Mary's** are operated by the Isles of Scilly Steamship Company, on the South Pier (☎0345/105555). Sailings take place daily at different times according to day and season and take nearly three hours; return tickets are £62–72 with discounts for students, families and children. There are ferries between each of the inhabited islands, though these are sporadic in winter.

The main departure points for **flights** (also operated by the Isles of Scilly Steamship Company) are **Land's End**, near St Just (Mon–Sat 3–15 daily; 15min; £54–92 return), **Newquay** (Mon–Sat 2 daily; 30min; £65–99 return), **Plymouth** (Mon, Wed & Fri 1 daily; 45min; £102–139 return), **Exeter** (Mon–Sat 1–3 daily; 50min; £133–166 return) and **Bristol** (Mon, Tues, Thurs & Fri 1 daily; 1hr 10min; £148–199 return). In winter, there is no service from Newquay and Plymouth, and a much reduced service from Bristol and Exeter, with only Land's End operating a full timetable. For up-to-date times and fares call ☎08457/105555, *www.islesofscilly-travel.co.uk*. In addition to these, **helicopter** flights from the heliport a mile east of Penzance are run by British International to St Mary's (Mon–Sat 4–20 daily; less frequently in winter) and Tresco (Mon–Sat 1–4 daily; less frequently in winter). These take about twenty minutes, with return fares costing about £95, though you can get discounted "Late Saver Returns" if you buy them the day before departure for a one- to three-night stay (call ☎01736/363871).

passengers the mile to **HUGH TOWN**, straddling a neck of land at the southwestern end of the island. Ferries from Penzance dock on the north side of town, under a knob of land still known as The Garrison, where the eight-pointed **Star Castle**, built in Elizabeth I's reign after the scare of the Spanish Armada, has been converted into a hotel. Hugh Town has the engaging **Isles of Scilly Museum** on Church Street, well worth an hour or two's wander (July–Sept Mon–Sat 10am–noon, 1.30–4.30pm & 7.30–9pm; rest of year 10am–noon & 1.30–4.30pm; £1). Most of the exhibits are relics salvaged from the many ships foundered on or around the islands.

The sheltered bay of Porthcressa, a short way south, has the town's best bathing **beach** and offers bike rental at Buccabu Bike Hire, a good way to get around the island if you don't want to take advantage of the circular **bus** service (4–7 daily), though neither is ideal for exploring the remoter coastal sections. From Porthcressa a path wanders south to skirt **Peninnis Head**, passing some impressive sea-sculpted granite rocks. The path follows the coast to **Old Town Bay**, around which the modern houses of **OLD TOWN** give little hint of its former role as the island's chief port. The town has cafés and a sheltered south-facing beach, where there's a **diving** school (☎01720/422732).

Three quarters of a mile east, **Porth Hellick** is the next major inlet on the island's southern coast, marked by a rugged quartz monument to the fantastically named Sir Cloudesley Shovell, who in 1707 was washed up here from a shipwreck which claimed four ships and nearly 1700 lives. On one side of the bay is another rock shape, the **Loaded Camel**, near which a gate leads to a 4000-year-old **barrow**, probably used by the Bronze Age people from the Iberian peninsula, who were the Scillies' first colonists. **Pelistry Bay**, on the northeastern side of St Mary's, less than two miles from Hugh Town, is one of the most secluded spots on the island, its crystal-clear waters sheltered by the outlying **Toll's Island**, joined to St Mary's at low tide by a slender strand. The best remnants of early human settlement on the Scillies are to be found further round the coast at **Innisidgen** and at **Halangy Down**, a mile or so north of Hugh Town. Innisidgen is a Bronze Age burial chamber, as is **Bant's Carn**, the oldest and most complete survival of the complex of stone huts on Halangy Down, most of which dates from around 200 BC.

Hugh Town's **tourist office**, on Porthcressa Beach (Easter–June, Sept & Oct Mon–Sat 8.30am–5.30pm; July & Aug Mon–Sat 8.30am–6pm, Sun 10am–noon; Nov–Easter Mon–Thurs 8.30am–5pm, Fri 8.30am–4.30pm; ☎01720/422536), has information on available accommodation for all the Scillies. The town is relatively well supplied with **B&Bs**: Porthcressa Road has the small *Pieces of Eight* (☎01720/422163; no credit cards; ②), and *The Boathouse*, on the Thoroughfare (☎01720/422688; ③; closed Nov–Feb). In a superb position right on the quay where the ferries dock, the *Harbourside Hotel* (☎01720/422352; ⑦) is one of St Mary's best options; higher up, in The Garrison, there's *Veronica Lodge* (☎01720/422585; no credit cards; ②; closed Jan & Dec). The island's only **campsite** is at *Garrison Farm*, near the playing field at the top of the promontory (☎01720/422670; closed Nov–Feb). The *Pilot's Gig* is a basement **restaurant** below the Garrison Gate at the end of the main Hugh Street, offering lunchtime snacks and fish dinners. In the middle of Hugh Street, the *Kavorna Bakery* has simple snacks as well as coffees and buns. The *Star Castle Hotel*, in The Garrison, has a good-value fixed-price menu, and inexpensive snacks in the bar.

Tresco

After St Mary's, **TRESCO** is the most visited island of the Scillies, yet the boatloads of visitors somehow manage to lose themselves on the two-miles-by-one island, the second largest in the group. Once the private estate of Devon's Tavistock Abbey, Tresco still retains a cloistered, slightly privileged air, and it has no budget accommodation. Depending on the tide, boats pull in at **New Grimsby**, halfway up the west coast, the smaller quay at Old Grimsby, on the east coast, or the southernmost point of Carn Near. Wherever you dock, it's only a few minutes' walk to the entrance of **Abbey Gardens** (daily 10am–5pm; £5.50), featuring a few ruins from the priory amid subtropical gardens first laid out in 1834. Many of the plants were grown from seeds taken from London's Kew Gardens, others were brought here from Africa, South America and the Antipodes. The entry ticket also admits you to a collection of figureheads and other curiosities taken from shipwrecked vessels.

You don't need to walk far to find alluring sandy beaches: one of the best – **Appletree Bay** – is only a few steps from the southern ferry landing at Carn Near. **Old Grimsby**, on the island's eastern side, has another lovely sand beach, looking out to a submarine-shaped rock offshore. North of here, Tresco's tidy fields give way to untended heathland, while a narrow path traces the coast to **Charles' Castle**, built in the 1550s. Strategically positioned on a height to cover the lagoon-like channel separating Tresco from Bryher, the castle was in fact badly designed, its guns unable to depress far enough to be effective, and it was superseded in 1651 by the much better-preserved **Cromwell's Castle**, actually no more than a gun-tower, built at sea level next to a pretty sandy cove. Northwest from here, a path winds across the moor to the northern coast's **Piper's Hole**, a deep underground cave accessible from the cliff edge.

Apart from the exclusive *Island Hotel* at the centre of the island (☎01720/422883; ⑨; closed Nov–Feb), the only **accommodation** on the island is the *New Inn*, at New Grimsby (☎01720/422844; ⑦; closed Nov–Feb). The latter has a **restaurant** with a three-course set menu, and you can eat pub snacks in its garden. For gourmet cuisine splash out at the *Island Hotel*, specializing in fresh fish.

Bryher

Covered with a thick carpet of bracken, heather and bramble, **BRYHER** is the wildest of the inhabited islands, but the seventy-odd residents have introduced some pockets of order in the form of flower plantations, mostly confined to the small settlement around the quay and climbing up the slopes of **Watch Hill**, on the island's eastern side. The exposed western seaboard takes the full brunt of the Atlantic, nowhere more spectacularly than at the aptly named **Hell Bay**, cupped by a limb of land on the north-western shore. In contrast to this sound and fury, peace reigns in the southern cove of **Rushy Bay**, one of the island's best beaches. From the quay there is a daily **boat service** to the other islands, and frequent tours to seal and bird colonies as well as fishing expeditions. You could also make a quick hop to the small isle of **Samson**, deserted since 1855 when the last impoverished inhabitants were ordered off by the island's proprietor.

Soleil D'Or (☎01720/422003; ②; closed Nov–Feb) and *Chafford* (☎01720/422241; ②; closed Oct–March) are among the least expensive of Bryher's **B&Bs**, both on the eastern side of the island near Watch Hill, and both with meals available. There is a **campsite** at Jenford Farm on Watch Hill (☎01720/422886; closed Nov–March). The island's one hotel, the *Hell Bay*, located near the pool below Gweal Hill (☎01720/422947; ⑧; closed Nov–March), has a bar and **restaurant**, and you can also eat inexpensively at the *Vine Café*, on Watch Hill, and *Fraggle Rock Café*, near the post office.

St Martin's

The main landing stage at **ST MARTIN'S** is on the southern promontory, at the head of the majestic sweep of **Par Beach** – a fitting entry to the island that boasts the best of the Scillies' beaches. From the quay, a road leads up to **HIGHER TOWN**, the main concentration of houses and location of the only shop. The waters hereabouts are among the clearest in Britain, and are much favoured by **scuba** enthusiasts: contact the St Martin's Diving Centre (☎01720/422848) for tuition. Beyond the church, follow the road westwards to **LOWER TOWN**, a cluster of cottages on the western extremity, where there's a second quay. The town overlooks the uninhabited isles of **Teän** and **St Helen's**, the latter holding the remains of a tenth-century oratory, monks' dwellings and a chapel, as well as a pest house, erected in 1756 to house plague carriers entering British waters.

Along the southern shore, the gentler side of the island, you'll find the long strand of **Lawrence's Bay** and large areas of flowerbeds. On the northern side, the coast is rougher, with the exception of **Great Bay**, a beautiful secluded half-mile of sand ideal for swimming. From its western end, you can climb across boulders at low tide to the hilly and wild **White Island**, on the northeastern side of which is a large cave, **Underland Girt**, accessible at low tide. At **St Martin's Head** on the northeastern tip of the main island lies the red and white Daymark erected in 1683 (not 1637 as inscribed) as a warning against shipping. Below St Martin's Head, on the southeastern shore, lies another fine beach, **Perpitch**, looking out to the scattered Eastern Isles, slivers of rock to which boats take trippers to view puffins and grey seals.

St Martin's has two good **B&Bs**, *Glenmoor Cottage* (☎01720/422816; no credit cards; ②) and *Polreath* (☎01720/422046; ③), both in Higher Town. In Middletown, there is a **campsite**, just off the road near Lawrence's Bay (☎01720/422888). The only **pub** on the island is the *Sevenstones Inn*, in Lower Town, where snacks are available.

St Agnes

Visitors to the southernmost island of **ST AGNES** disembark at **Porth Conger**, from where a road leads to the western side of the island, passing the disused **Old Lighthouse**, which dates from 1680 – one of the oldest lighthouses in the country and the most significant landmark on the island. From here the right-hand fork leads to **Periglis Cove**, a mooring for boats on the western side of the island, while the left-hand fork goes to **St Warna's Cove**, where the patron saint of shipwrecks is reputed to have landed from Ireland, the exact spot being marked by a holy well. **Beady Pool**, an inlet on the eastern side of the headland, gained its name from the trove of beads washed ashore from the wreck of a seventeenth-century Dutch trader; some of the reddish-brown stones still occasionally turn up. The eastern side of St Agnes faces the smaller isle of **Gugh**, linked by a sand bar at low tide, when a lovely sheltered beach is formed.

The best of the **B&Bs** on St Agnes is the *Coastguards*, one of a smart row of cottages past the Old Lighthouse and post office on the island's western side (☎01720/422373; ③). Others are *Covean Cottage*, above Porth Conger (☎01720/422620; ③; closed Dec–Feb), and the *Parsonage*, nestled below the lighthouse, behind a copse of Cornish elms (☎01720/422370; no credit cards; ②). There's a good **campsite** at *Troy Town Farm*, above Periglis Cove (☎01720/422360; closed Nov–Feb), enjoying superb views over to the Western Rocks. Just above the jetty at Porth Conger, the *Turk's Head* serves pasties to go with its beer.

Newquay to Bude

Though generally harsher than the county's southern seaboard, the north Cornish coast is punctuated by some of the finest beaches in England, the most popular of which are around **Newquay**, the surfers' capital. Other major holiday centres are around the Camel estuary, where the port of **Padstow** makes a good base for some remarkable beaches. North of the Camel, the coast is an almost unbroken line of cliffs as far as the Devon border, the gaunt, exposed terrain making a melodramatic setting for **Tintagel**, though the strand at **Bude** attracts legions of surfers and holidaymakers. Parts of the more westerly stretches are littered with the derelict stacks and castle-like ruins of the engine-houses that once powered the region's **copper** and **tin mines**, industries that at one time led the world.

Newquay

It is difficult to imagine a lineage for **NEWQUAY** that extends more than a few years back, but the "new quay" was built in the fifteenth century in what was already a long-established fishing port. Up to then it had been more colourfully known as Towan Blistra, and was concentrated in the sheltered west end of the bay. The town was given a boost in the nineteenth century, when its harbour was expanded for coal import and a railway was constructed across the peninsula for china clay shipments. With the trains came a swelling stream of seasonal visitors, drawn to the town's superb position on a knuckle of cliffs overlooking fine golden sands and Atlantic rollers, natural advantages which have made Newquay the premier resort of north Cornwall.

The centre of town is a somewhat tacky parade of shops and restaurants, partly pedestrianized, from which lanes lead to ornamental gardens and sloping lawns on the cliff-tops. Below, adjacent to the small harbour in the crook of the massive Towan Head, **Towan Beach** is the most central of the seven miles of firm sandy beaches that follow in an almost unbroken succession. You can reach all of them on foot, though for some of the further ones, such as the extensive **Watergate Bay**, you can take local buses #53 and #56. The beaches get unbearably crowded in season, and all are popular with surfers, particularly Watergate and – west of Towan Head – **Fistral Bay**, the largest of the town beaches. On the other side of East Pentire Head from Fistral, **Crantock Beach** – reachable over the River Gannel by ferry or upstream footbridge – is usually less crowded, and has a lovely backdrop of dunes and undulating grassland.

Practicalities

Newquay is accessible by train via a branch line off the main Penzance line, for which you must change at Par. The town's **train station** is off Cliff Road, a couple of hundred yards from the **bus station** on East Street. The **tourist office** lies opposite the bus station, at Marcus Hill (May–Sept Mon–Sat 9am–6pm, Sun 10am–4pm; Oct–April Mon–Sat 9am–5pm; ☎01637/871345). There's no problem finding **surfing equipment**: one of the trendiest places to rent or buy is Tunnel Vision, 6 Alma Place, off Fore Street, offering a huge range of gear; lessons are run by the Offshore Surfing School on Tolcarne Beach (☎01637/851487; closed Nov–April).

There's plenty of **accommodation** in Newquay, though rooms can still be at a premium in July and August. In the centre of town, the *Bay View House Hotel* offers good value and superb views (☎01637/871214; ③), while fans of Fistral Beach will appreciate the proximity of the *Links Hotel*, on Headland Rd (☎01637/873211; no credit cards; ②). Dorm beds can be found in the two independent **hostels**: *Towan Backpackers Hostel*, 16 Beachfield Av (☎01637/874668), and *Newquay International Backpackers*, 69 Tower Rd (☎01637/879366, *backpackers@dial.pipex.com*). The area's **campsites** are all megacomplexes, many of them – such as the most convenient site, *Porth Beach* (☎01637/876531; closed Nov to mid-March), right next to one of Newquay's best beaches – unwilling to take same-sex groups, or even couples. A little further inland, on Trevelgue Road, *Trevelgue* (☎01637/851851) is also family-oriented.

There's no lack of places to **eat**, but most are mediocre. There are a few casual cafés just up from the beach on Tower Rd, including the *Lifebuoy Café*, which serves very inexpensive all-day breakfasts and baguettes at outdoor tables. Just above Towan Beach, *Chy-an-Mor* is a large café-bar on Beach Road, serving various snacks on its terrace, while you can find fuller and good-value meals at the *Bay View House Hotel*. **Nightclubbers** are also well catered for: the town's hot spots include the *Sailors Arms* and *The Beach* on Fore Street, and Berties on East Street – though if you want to explore the livelier surfhead culture, ask around and watch for posters.

Padstow and around

The small fishing port of **PADSTOW** is nearly as popular as Newquay, but has a very different feel. Enclosed within the estuary of the Camel – the only river of any size that empties on Cornwall's north coast – the town long retained its position as the principal fishing port on this coast, and still has something of the atmosphere of a medieval town. Its chief annual festival is also a hangover from times past: the **Obby Oss**, a May Day romp where one of the locals garbs himself as a horse and prances through the town preceded by a masked and club-wielding "teaser" – a spirited if rather institutionalized re-enactment of old fertility rites.

THE SAINT'S WAY

Padstow's St Petroc church is the traditional starting point for one of Cornwall's oldest walking routes, the **Saints' Way**. Extending for some thirty miles between Cornwall's north and south coasts, and connecting the principal ports of Padstow and Fowey, the path originates from the Bronze Age when traders preferred the cross-country hike to making the perilous sea journey round Land's End. The route was later travelled by Irish and Welsh missionaries crossing the peninsula between the fifth and eighth centuries, on pilgrimage to some of the principal shrines of Cornwall's Celtic culture.

Skirting Bodmin Moor, the reconstructed Saints' Way is rarely dramatic, though it passes through a variety of scenery and there are several points of interest along the way, from Neolithic burial chambers to medieval churches and the more austere lines of Wesleyan chapels. The route is well marked and can be walked in stages, the country paths that constitute it stretching for two to six miles each; although it crosses several trunk roads, these do not impinge too much. Pick up guides and leaflets giving detailed directions in the local tourist offices.

On the hill overlooking Padstow, the church of **St Petroc** is dedicated to Cornwall's most important saint, a Welsh or Irish monk who landed here in the sixth century, later died here, and gave his name to the town – "Petrock's Stow". The building has a fine fifteenth-century font, an Elizabethan pulpit and some amusing carved bench ends. The walls are lined with monuments to the local Prideaux family, who still occupy nearby **Prideaux Place**, an Elizabethan manor house with grand staircases, richly furnished rooms full of portraits, fantastically ornate ceilings and formal gardens (Easter–Sept Mon–Thurs & Sun 1.30–5pm; house & grounds £4.50; grounds only £2.50). The harbour is jammed with launches and boats offering cruises in Padstow Bay, while a regular **ferry** (summer daily; winter closed Sun) carries people across the river to **ROCK** – close to the sand-engulfed church of **St Enodoc** (John Betjeman's burial place) and to the good beaches around Polzeath (see below).

The coast on the **south side** of the estuary also offers some good **beach** country, which you can get to in summer on bus #56 (not Sat). Round **Stepper Point** you can reach the sandy and secluded Harlyn Bay and, turning the corner southwards, **Constantine Bay**, the area's best surfing beach. The dunes backing the beach and the rock pools skirting it make this one of the most appealing bays on this coast, though the tides can be treacherous and bathing hazardous near the rocks. Three or four miles further south lies one of Cornwall's most dramatic beaches, **Bedruthan Steps**. Traditionally held to be the stepping stones of a giant called Bedruthan, a legendary figure conjured into existence in the nineteenth century, these slate outcrops can be readily viewed from the cliff-top path, at a point which drivers can reach on the B3276.

Practicalities

Padstow's **tourist office** is on the harbour (April–Sept Mon–Fri 10am–5pm, Sat 10am–4pm, Sun 11am–4pm; Oct–March Mon–Fri 10am–4pm; ☎01841/533449). Central **accommodation** includes the *London Inn*, on Lanadwell Street (☎01841/532554; no credit cards; ①), converted from a row of fishermen's cottages in 1802, and the posher *Old Ship Hotel*, Mill Square (☎01841/532357; ④). The nearest **youth hostel** has stunning views and is excellently sited almost on the beach at Treyarnon Bay (☎01841/520322; closed Nov–March) – take bus #55 or #56. Behind the hostel there is a **campsite** at *Trethias Farm* (☎01841/520323; closed Oct–March). Padstow's quayside is lined with snack bars and pasty shops as well as **pubs** where you can sit outside, such as the *Shipwright's* on the harbour's north side. Foodies know the town best for its high-class **restaurants**, particularly those associated with star chef Rick Stein, all of which also offer accommodation. The *Seafood Restaurant*, at Riverside (☎01841/532485; ⑨; closed Sun), is now one of England's top fish eateries, but it's very expensive and the waiting list can be months long. Alternatively, try Stein's slightly less expensive and more French-inspired *St Petroc's Bistro*, at 4 New St (☎01841/532700; ⑨; closed Mon), or the casual *Middle Street Café*, nearby (☎01841/532700; ④). For those with more modest means, you could do a lot worse than *Rojano's* pizza and pasta place, on Mill Square (closed Mon), with an attached gelateria.

Polzeath to Port Isaac

Facing west into Padstow Bay, the beaches in and around **POLZEATH** are the finest in the vicinity, pelted by rollers which make this one of the best surfing sites in the West Country. Polzeath has a small **tourist office** behind the beach (Easter to mid-Oct Mon–Sat 10am–5pm; ☎01208/862488). *Pheasants Rise*, Trebetherick (☎01208/863190; no credit cards; ①; closed Nov–Easter), is a useful **B&B** a few minutes' walk from both Polzeath and Daymer bays, and the *Tristram* **campsite** (☎01208/862215; closed Nov–Easter) sits on a cliff overlooking the beach. On the beach, *Finn's* does full meals as well as cream teas; the *Oyster-Catcher* pub is a lively evening hangout just up the hill. Surf's Up on the beach offers **surfing** tuition; the gear can be rented from shops.

The next settlement of any size is **PORT ISAAC**, northeast of Polzeath, wedged in a gap in the precipitous cliff wall and dedicated to the crab and lobster trade. Narrow lanes focus on a couple of pubs at the seafront, where a pebble beach and rock pools are exposed by the low tide. The village offers good **accommodation**, best of all the sixteenth-century *Slipway Hotel*, opposite the harbour (☎01208/880264; ②), with a bar and excellent restaurant. Cheaper choices are outside the centre and away from the sea, among them *Fairholme*, at 30 Trewetha Lane (☎01208/880397; no credit cards; ①), and *St. Andrew's Hotel*, 18 The Terrace (☎01208/880240; ①), with plain but adequate rooms, some with views overlooking the neighbouring Port Gaverne. The *Golden Lion* is Port Isaac's most cheerful **pub** and has an adjoining bistro. Port Isaac is famous for crab – you can buy it to take away at the harbourfront, or try it at the moderately priced *Old School*, at the top of the village (☎01208/880721; ④), also offering rooms with views.

Tintagel and Boscastle

East of Port Isaac, the coast is wild and unspoiled, making for some steep and strenuous walking and providing an appropriate backdrop for the black, forsaken ruins of **Tintagel Castle** (daily: April to mid-July & mid-Aug to Sept 10am–6pm; mid-July to mid-Aug 10am–8pm; Oct 10am–5pm; Nov–March 10am–4pm; £2.80; EH). It was the twelfth-century chronicler Geoffrey of Monmouth who first popularized the notion that this was the **birthplace of King Arthur**, son of Uther Pendragon and Ygrayne, but by that time local folklore was already saturated with tales of King Mark of Cornwall, Tristan and Iseult, Arthur and the knights of Camelot. Twin influences were at work in Geoffrey's story, which merges the historic figure of Arthur – now thought to have been a Celtic warlord who resisted the Saxon advance in the fifth century – with a separate body of legend centring on the missionary activity of the Celtic monastery that occupied this site in the sixth century. Tintagel is certainly a plausibly resonant candidate for the abode of the "Once and Future King", but the **castle** ruins in fact belong to a Norman stronghold that was once occupied by the earls of Cornwall, who after sporadic spurts of rebuilding allowed it to decay, most of it having washed into the sea by the sixteenth century. The remains of the **Celtic monastery** are still visible on the headland and are an important source of knowledge of how the country's earliest monastic houses were organized.

From the village of **Tintagel**, the shortest access is from the signposted path, a well-trodden route. The only building of note in this dreary collection of cafés and B&Bs is the **Old Post Office** (April–Oct daily 11am–5.30pm; £2.20; NT), a rickety-roofed, slate-built fourteenth-century construction. The village has plenty of **accommodation**: try *Bosayne*, Atlantic Rd (☎01840/770514; no credit cards; ①), one of a tier of B&Bs looking out over the cliff, offering basic rooms. The *Old Malt House* (☎01840/770461; ②; closed Jan) and the *Tintagel Arms Hotel* (☎01840/770780; ②), both on Fore Street, are conveniently located for the castle. Three quarters of a mile outside the village at Dunderhole Point, past St Materiana, the offices of a former slate quarry now house a **youth hostel** (☎01840/770334; closed Oct–March). At the end of Atlantic Road, the *Headland* site offers scenic **camping** (☎01840/770239; closed Nov–March).

Three miles east of Tintagel, the port of **BOSCASTLE** lies compressed within a narrow ravine drilled by the rivers Jordan and Valency, its tidy riverfront bordered by thatched and lime-washed houses giving on to the twisty harbour. Above and behind, a collection of seventeenth- and eighteenth-century cottages can be seen on a circular walk, starting either from Fore Street or the main car park. The walk traces the valley of the Valency for about a mile to reach Boscastle's graceful **parish church**, tucked away in a peaceful glen. Another mile and a half up the valley lies another church, **St Juliot's**, restored by Thomas Hardy when he was plying his trade as a young architect.

Boscastle's best **accommodation** is *St Christopher's Hotel*, a restored Georgian manor house at the top of the High Street (☎01840/250412; ②; closed Jan). The *Old Coach House*, on Tintagel Rd (☎01840/250398; ①), is another well-equipped old building. The harbour has a lovely old **youth hostel** (☎01840/250287; closed Nov–Feb) right by the harbour and sea; nearby, you can eat at the *Harbour Café*, which serves hot meals all day. The village has three good **pubs**, though the *Napoleon* has the advantage of a good vegetarian menu and a spacious garden with distant views of the sea. The *Cobweb* is busier but rates highly on atmosphere.

Bude and around

There is little distinctively Cornish in Cornwall's northernmost town of **BUDE**, four miles west of the Devon border. Built around an estuary surrounded by a fine expanse of sands, the town has sprouted a crop of holiday homes and hotels, though these have not unduly spoiled the place nor the magnificent cliffy coast surrounding it.

Of the excellent beaches hereabouts, the central **Summerleaze** is clean and wide, though the mile-long **Widemouth Bay**, two and a half miles **south** of Bude, is the main focus of the holiday hordes – it has the cleanest water monitored between Bude and Polzeath, though bathing can be dangerous near the rocks at low tide. Surfers also congregate five miles down the coast at **Crackington Haven**, wonderfully situated between 430-foot cliffs at the mouth of a lush valley. The cliffs on this stretch are characterized by remarkable zigzagging strata of shale, limestone and sandstone, a mixture which erodes into vividly contorted detached formations.

To the **north** of Bude, acres-wide **Crooklets beach** is the scene of **surfing** and lifesaving demonstrations and competitions. A couple of miles further, **Sandy Mouth** holds a pristine expanse of sand with rock pools beneath the encircling cliffs. It is a short walk from here to another surfers' delight, **Duckpool**, a tiny sandy cove flanked by jagged reefs at low tide and dominated by the three-hundred-foot **Steeple Point**.

Bude's **tourist office** is in the centre of town at The Crescent (April–Sept Mon–Sat 10am–5pm, Sun 10am–4pm; Oct–March Mon–Fri 10am–4pm, Sat 10am–2pm; ☎01288/354240). For **accommodation**, *Clovelly House*, 4 Burn View (☎01288/352761; no credit cards; ②), and *Links View*, 13 Morwenna Terrace (☎01288/352561; no credit cards; ①), are both near the golf course, while *16 The Rowans*, off Hawthorne Ave, is a homely B&B (☎01288/355151; no credit cards; ①). At the top end of the scale is the *Falcon Hotel*, an old coaching inn on Breakwater Road (☎01288/352005; ⑧). Bude's nearest **campsite** is *Wooda Park* (☎01288/352069; closed Nov–March), away from the sea at Poughill (pronounced "Poffil"), two miles north of Bude. The *Falcon Hotel* offers good **food** at its bar and has a more formal and expensive restaurant. There's a choice of **surfing equipment** rental outlets, including Zuma Jay on Belle Vue Lane and, visible at the end of the street, XTC, on Princes St.

Bodmin and Bodmin Moor

Long the county town of Cornwall (though most public offices are now down the road in Truro), **Bodmin** is today an undistinguished straggle of houses and shops, though it retains a relaxed, friendly feel. The town stands at the threshold of **Bodmin Moor** which, though just ten miles in diameter, conveys a sense of loneliness quite out of proportion to its size. The smallest, mildest and most accessible of the West Country's great moors, it has some beautiful tors, torrents, and rock formations, but much of its fascination lies in the strong human imprint, particularly the wealth of relics left behind by its **Bronze Age** population, including such important sites as Trethevy Quoit and the stone circles of The Hurlers. Separated from these by some three millennia, the churches in the villages of **St Neots**, **Blisland** and **Altarnun** are among the region's finest examples of fifteenth-century art and architecture. Despite its Arthurian associations, the small town of **Camelford**, in the northern reaches of the moor, has little of historical interest, though it has good accommodation and a couple of museums worth visiting.

Bodmin

The town of **BODMIN** lies on the western edge of Bodmin Moor, equidistant from the north and south Cornish coasts and the Fowey and Camel rivers, a position that encouraged its growth as a trading town. It was also an important ecclesiastical centre after the establishment of a priory by St Petroc, who moved here from Padstow in the sixth century. The priory disappeared but Bodmin retained its prestige through its church of St Petroc, built in the fifteenth century and still the largest in Cornwall. Though officially the county town, Bodmin sacrificed much of its administrative role by refusing access to the Great Western Railway in the 1870s, as a result of which much local business transferred down the road to Truro. Bodmin does have a train stop now, though **Bodmin Parkway** station lies three miles outside town, with a regular bus connection to the centre.

Bodmin's most prominent landmark is the **Gilbert Memorial**, a 144-foot obelisk honouring a descendant of Sir Walter Raleigh and occupying a commanding location on Bodmin Beacon, a high area of moorland near the centre of town. Below, at the end of Fore Steet, stands **St Petroc's** church; inside it has an extravagantly carved twelfth-century font and an ivory casket that once held the bones of Petroc, while the south-west corner of the churchyard holds a sacred well. Close by, the notorious **Bodmin Jail** (daily: Easter–Oct 10am–6pm; Nov–Easter 11am–4pm; £3) glowers darkly on Berrycombe Road, redolent of the public executions that were guaranteed crowd-pullers until 1862, when the hangings retreated behind closed doors. You can visit part of the original eighteenth-century structure, including the condemned cell and some grisly exhibits chronicling the lives of the inmates.

From Parkway it's less than two miles' walk to one of Cornwall's most celebrated country houses, **Lanhydrock** (April–Oct Tues–Sun 11am–5.30pm; house & grounds £6.40; grounds only £3.20; NT), originally seventeenth century but totally rebuilt after a fire in 1881. The granite exterior remains true to its original form, but the forty-odd rooms show a very different style, including a long picture gallery with a plaster ceiling depicting scenes from the Old Testament, and – most illuminating of all – servants' quarters that reveal the daily workings of a Victorian manor house. The grounds have magnificent beds of magnolias, azaleas and rhododendrons, and a huge area of wooded parkland bordering the River Fowey.

Practicalities

Bodmin's **tourist office** (May–Sept Mon–Sat 10am–5pm; Oct–April Mon–Fri 10am–1pm; ☎01208/76616) is at the bottom of St Nicholas Street. All buses stop directly outside on Mount Folly. If you want to **rent a bike**, Glyn Valley Cycle Hire (☎01208/74244), in Cardinham Woods, three miles east of Bodmin, has mountain bikes available.

Basic **B&B** is available at *Higher Windsor Cottage*, 18 Castle St (☎01208/76474; no credit cards; ①), or try the *George and Dragon* pub, at 3 St Nicholas St (☎01208/72514; no credit cards; ①). Outside town, close to the Lanhydrock estate, the handsome *Bokiddick Farm*, at Lanivet (☎01208/831481; no credit cards; ②), has rooms and fantastic views. There's a good **campsite** on Old Callywith Road, a fifteen-minute walk from the centre (☎01208/73834; closed Dec–Feb). Off Fore Street, the *Hole in the Wall* **pub** on Crockwell Street has an agreeable backroom bar in what used to be the debtors' prison, with exposed fourteenth-century walls enclosing a collection of antiquities and bric-a-brac. You can drink in the courtyard in summer, bar lunches are available, and there's an upstairs **restaurant** specializing in fish.

Blisland and the western moor

BLISLAND stands in the Camel valley on the western slopes of Bodmin Moor, three miles northeast of Bodmin. Georgian and Victorian houses cluster around a village green and a church whose well-restored interior has an Italianate altar and a startlingly painted screen. On **Pendrift Common**, above the village, the gigantic **Jubilee Rock** is inscribed with various patriotic insignia commemorating the jubilee of George III's coronation in 1809. From this seven-hundred-foot vantage point you look eastward over the De Lank gorge and the boulder-crowned knoll of **Hawk's Tor**, three miles away. On the shoulder of the tor stand the Neolithic **Stripple Stones**, a circular platform once holding 28 standing stones, of which just four are still upright. Blisland lies just a couple of miles east of the **Merry Meeting** crossroads, a point near the end of the Camel Trail cycle route. The most convenient **B&B** is the plain but comfortable *Lavethan*, a ten-minute walk outside the village towards St Mabyn (☎01208/850487; no credit cards; ③). Alternatively, try *Riverdale* at Key Bridge, which offers one comfortable double (☎01208/851390; no credit cards; ①). If you want to **camp**, the nearest site is *Glenmorris Park*, on Longstone Road, St Mabyn (☎01208/841677; closed Nov–Easter).

Bolventor and Dozmary Pool

The village of **Bolventor**, lying at the centre of the moor, midway between Bodmin and Launceston, is an uninspiring place close to one of the moor's chief focuses for walkers and sightseers alike – **Jamaica Inn** (☎01566/86250; ③). A staging post even before the precursor of the A30 road was laid here in 1769, the inn was described by Daphne Du Maurier as being "alone in glory, four square to the winds", and the combination of its convenient position and its association with her has led to its growth into a hotel and restaurant complex. One corner exhibits the room where the author stayed in 1930, soaking up inspiration for her smuggler's yarn. At the other end of the building is an entertaining **Museum of Curiosities** (daily: Easter–Oct 10am–5pm, open until 8pm during school holidays; winter 11am–4pm; closed Jan; £2.50).

The inn's car park is a useful place to leave your vehicle and venture forth on foot. Just a mile away, **Dozmary Pool** is another link in the West Country's Arthurian mythologies – after Arthur's death Sir Bedevere hurled Excalibur, the king's sword, into the pool, where it was claimed by an arm raised from the depths. Loe Pool, near Porthleven on the Lizard, also claims the same honour (see p.342). Despite its proximity to the A30, the diamond-shaped lake usually preserves an ethereal air, though it's been known to run dry in summer, dealing a bit of a blow to the legend that the pool is bottomless. The lake is also the source of another, more obviously Cornish, legend, that of John Tregeagle, a steward at Lanhydrock whose unjust dealings with the local tenant farmers in the seventeenth century brought upon his spirit the curse of endlessly baling out the pool with a perforated limpet shell. As if this were not enough, his ghost is further tormented by a swarm of devils pursuing him as he flies across the moor in search of sanctuary; their infernal howling is sometimes audible on windy nights.

Liskeard and St Neot

LISKEARD, a bus and rail junction just off the southern limits of the moor, makes a decent overnight stop, with accommodation at *Elnor*, 1 Russell St (☎01579/342472; no credit cards; ①), and *The Nebula*, 27 Higher Lux St (☎01579/343989; ③). From here, buses go on to **ST NEOT**, one of Bodmin Moor's prettiest villages, approached through a lush wooded valley. Its fifteenth-century **church** contains some of the most impressive stained glass windows of any parish church in the country, the oldest glass being the fifteenth-century **Creation Window**, at the east end of the south aisle. Next along, **Noah's Window** continues the sequence, but the narration soon dissolves into windows portraying patrons and local bigwigs, while others present cameos of the ordinary men and women of the village. If you want to stay here, head straight for the 350-year-old *Dye Cottage* (☎01579/321394; no credit cards; ③), which has excellent rates and offers dinners by prior arrangement, including vegetarian meals.

This southern edge of the moor is far greener and more thickly wooded than the northern reaches, due to the confluence of a web of rivers into the Fowey. One of the moor's best-known beauty spots is a couple of miles east, below Draynes Bridge, where the Fowey tumbles through the **Golitha Falls**, less a waterfall than a series of rapids. Dippers and wagtails flit through the trees, and there's a pleasant woodland walk you can take to the dam at the **Siblyback Lake** reservoir, just over a mile away.

Camelford and the northern tors

The northern half of Bodmin Moor is dominated by its two highest tors, both of them easily accessible from **CAMELFORD**, a town once associated with King Arthur's Camelot, while Slaughterbridge, which crosses the River Camel north of town, is one of the contenders for his last battleground. The town has resisted trading on the Arthurian myths, but does have a couple of museums providing some diversion: the **British Cycling Museum** (Mon–Thurs & Sun 10am–5pm; £2.40), housed in the old station one mile north of town on the Boscastle road, is a cyclophile's dream, containing some four hundred examples of bikes through the ages and a library of books and manuals, while the more conventional **North Cornwall Museum** (April–Sept Mon–Sat 10am–5pm; £1.50), in Camelford's centre, contains domestic items and exhibits showing the development of the local slate industry, and also has a **tourist office** (same hours; ☎01840/212954).

Although it lacks excitement, Camelford makes a useful touring base. Among its **accommodation** is the central *Countryman Hotel*, at 7 Victoria Rd (☎01840/212250; ②). The *Mason's Arms*, on Market Place (☎01840/213309; no credit cards; ①), also has rooms and a beer garden. *The Orangery*, opposite Camelford House, makes a convenient coffee stop. There are two **campsites** in the area, at *King's Acre* (☎01840/213561; closed Nov–Easter), just over half a mile away on the Boscastle road, and, another half-mile or so further out, *Lakefield Caravan Park*, Lower Pendavey Farm (☎01840/213279; closed Nov–March), the latter also offering **pony trekking**.

Rough Tor, the second highest peak on Bodmin Moor, at 1311ft, is four miles' walk southeast from Camelford. The hill presents a different aspect from every angle: from the south an ungainly mass, from the west a nobly proportioned mountain. A short distance to the east stand the Little Rough Tor, where there are the remains of an Iron Age camp, and Showery Tor, capped by a prominent formation of piled rocks. Easily visible to the southeast, **Brown Willy** is, at 1375ft, the highest Bodmin peak in Cornwall, as its original name signified – Bronewhella, or "highest hill". Like Rough Tor, Brown Willy shows various faces, its sugar-loaf appearance from the north sharpening into a long multi-peaked crest as you approach. The tor is accessible by continuing from the summit of Rough Tor across the valley of the De Lank, or, from the south, by footpath from Bolventor. The easiest ascent (2hr) is by the worn path which climbs steeply up from the northern end of the hill.

Altarnun and the eastern moor

ALTARNUN is a pleasant, granite-grey village snugly sheltered beneath the eastern heights of the moor. Its prominent **church**, dedicated to St Nonna, mother of David, patron saint of Wales, contains a fine Norman font and 79 bench ends carved at the beginning of the sixteenth century depicting saints, musicians and clowns. The village also has a Methodist chapel, over the door of which there is a nineteenth-century effigy of John Wesley – a regular visitor to the neighbourhood – by Nevill Northey Burnard. Outside the village, *Trecollas Farm* (☎01566/86386; no credit cards; ①; closed Nov–Feb) offers good **accommodation** and a four-course breakfast.

South of Altarnun, **Withey Brook** tumbles 400ft in less than a mile of gushing cascades before meeting up with the River Lynher, which bounds Bodmin Moor to the east. Beyond the brook, on **Twelve Men's Moor**, lie some of Bodmin Moor's grandest landscapes. The quite modest elevations of Hawk's Tor (1079ft) and the lower Trewartha Tor appear enormous from the north, though they are overtopped by **Kilmar**, highest of the hills on the moor's eastern flank at 1280ft. Withey Brook starts life about six miles from Altarnun on **Stowe's Hill**, site of the moor's most famous stone pile, **The Cheesewring**, a precarious pillar of balancing granite slabs, marvellously eroded by the wind. Gouged out of the hillside nearby, the disused Cheesewring Quarry is a centre for rock climbing. A mile or so south down Stowe's Hill stands an artificial rock phenomenon, **The Hurlers**, a wide complex of three circles dating from about 1500 BC. The purpose of these stark upright stones is not known, though they owe their name to the legend that they were men turned to stone for playing the Celtic game of hurling on the Sabbath.

The Hurlers are easily accessible just outside **MINIONS**, Cornwall's highest village, three miles south of which stands another Stone Age survival, **Trethevy Quoit**, a chamber tomb nearly 9ft high surmounted by a massive capstone. Originally enclosed in earth, the stones have been stripped by centuries of weathering to create Cornwall's most impressive megalithic monument. **Bus** #73 from Liskeard (hourly, 3 on Sun) calls at St Cleer and Darite, both of which are close to Trethevy Quoit; alternatively, it's a three-mile walk from Liskeard.

travel details

Trains

Bath to: Bristol (every 20min; 20min); Exeter (5 daily; 1hr 15min); London (hourly; 1hr 30min).

Bodmin to: Exeter (1–2 hourly; 1hr 40min); London (hourly; 4hr); Penzance (hourly; 1hr 20min); Plymouth (hourly; 40min).

Bristol to: Bath (every 20min; 20min); Birmingham (hourly; 1hr 30min); Exeter (1–2 hourly; 1hr 20min); London (2 hourly; 1hr 40min); Penzance (9 daily; 4hr); Plymouth (8–9 daily; 2hr); Truro (9 daily; 3hr 20min).

Exeter to: Bodmin (1–2 hourly; 1hr 40min); Bristol (1–2 hourly; 1hr 20min); Exmouth (every 30min; 25min); Liskeard (hourly; 1hr 30min); London (hourly; 2hr 30min); Par (hourly; 1hr 50min); Penzance (hourly; 3hr); Plymouth (2 hourly; 1hr); Salisbury 1hr 45min–2hr 20min); Torquay (hourly; 45min); Truro (7 daily; 2hr 15min).

Falmouth to: Truro (10–12 daily; 25min).

Liskeard to: Exeter (hourly; 1hr 30min); London (8 daily; 4hr); Looe (8 daily; 30min); Penzance (hourly; 1hr 30min); Plymouth (hourly; 25min); Truro (hourly; 50min).

Newquay to: Par (4–6 daily; 45min).

Par to: Exeter (hourly; 1hr 50min); Newquay (4–6 daily; 50min); Penzance (hourly; 1hr 10min); Plymouth (hourly; 55min).

Penzance to: Bodmin (hourly; 1hr 20min); Bristol (9 daily; 4hr); Exeter (hourly; 3hr); Liskeard (hourly; 1hr 30min); London (9 daily; 5hr 15min–6hr 30min); Par (hourly; 1hr 10min); Plymouth (hourly; 2hr); St Ives (3–5 daily; 20min); Truro (1–2 hourly; 40min).

Plymouth to: Birmingham (6 daily; 3hr 25min); Bodmin (hourly; 40min); Bristol (8–9 daily; 2hr); Exeter (2 hourly; 1hr); Liskeard (hourly; 25min); London (9 daily; 3hr–3hr 45min); Par (hourly; 55min); Penzance (hourly; 2hr); St Ives (hourly; 1hr 50min); Truro (hourly; 1hr 15min).

St Ives to: Penzance (3–5 daily; 20min).

Torquay to: Exeter (hourly; 45min).

Truro to: Bristol (9 daily; 3hr 20min); Exeter (7 daily; 2hr 15min); Falmouth (10–12 daily; 25min); Liskeard (hourly; 50min); London (9 daily; 4hr 40min); Penzance (1–2 hourly; 40min); Plymouth (hourly; 1hr 15min).

Buses

Bath to: Bristol (every 15–30min; 50min); Frome (hourly; 50min); London (8 daily; 3hr 20min); Salisbury (hourly; 1hr 20min–2hr 20min); Wells (hourly; 1hr 20min).

Bodmin to: Bristol (1 daily; 4hr); Newquay (2–3 daily; 45min–1hr); Plymouth (2–4 daily; 1hr 10min); St Austell (hourly; 45min).

Bristol to: Bath (every 15–30min; 50min); Bodmin (1 daily; 3hr 50min); Exeter (5 daily; 1hr 40min–2hr); Glastonbury (hourly; 1hr 20min); London (hourly; 2hr 25min); Newquay (2–3 daily; 4hr–4hr 35min); Plymouth (5 daily; 2hr 30min–3hr); St Austell (1 daily; 4hr 25min); Torquay (2–3 daily; 2hr 45min–3hr); Truro (1 daily; 5hr); Wells (hourly; 1hr).

Exeter to: Bristol (5 daily; 1hr 45min–2hr); Falmouth (1 daily; 3hr 35min); London (8 daily; 4hr–4hr 40min); Plymouth (every 30min; 1hr–1hr 10min); St Austell (3 daily; 2hr 25min–3hr 40min); Torquay (1–2 hourly; 55min); Truro (3 daily; 3hr 10min).

Falmouth to: Exeter (1 daily; 4hr); Helston (8 daily; 1hr); Penzance (7 daily; 1hr 45min);

Plymouth (2 daily; 2hr 30min); St Austell (2 daily; 1hr 30min); Truro (2–3 hourly; 25–40min).

Glastonbury to: Bristol (hourly; 1hr 20min); Taunton (5 daily; 1hr 35min); Wells (every 30min; 20min).

Newquay to: Bodmin (2–3 daily; 45min–1hr); Bristol (2–3 daily; 4hr–4hr 35min); Plymouth (5 daily; 1hr 30min–2hr); St Austell (hourly; 1hr).

Penzance to: Falmouth (7 daily; 1hr 45min); Plymouth (7 daily; 2hr 50min–3hr 30min); St Austell (6–7 daily; 1hr 30min–2hr 10min); St Ives (2–3 hourly; 35min); Truro (hourly; 1hr 45min).

Plymouth to: Bodmin (2–4 daily; 1hr 10min); Bristol (5 daily; 2hr 30min–3hr); Exeter (every 30min; 1hr–1hr 10min); Falmouth (2 daily; 2hr 30min); London (8 daily; 4hr 40min–5hr 30min); Newquay (5 daily; 1hr 30min–2hr); Penzance (7 daily; 2hr 50min–3hr 30min); St Austell (7–9 daily; 1hr 15min–2hr); St Ives (4 daily; 2hr 25min–3hr); Torquay (hourly; 2hr); Truro (7 daily; 1hr 30min–1hr 50min).

St Austell to: Bodmin (hourly; 45min); Bristol (1 daily; 4hr 25min); Exeter (3 daily; 2hr 25min–3hr 40min); Falmouth (2 daily; 1hr 30min); Newquay (hourly; 1hr); Penzance (6–7 daily; 1hr 30min–2hr 10min); Plymouth (7–9 daily; 1hr 15min–2hr); St Ives (3 daily; 1hr 40min); Truro (1–2 hourly; 35–50min).

St Ives to: Penzance (2–3 hourly; 25min); Plymouth (4 daily; 2hr 25min–3hr); St Austell (3 daily; 1hr 40min); Truro (12 daily; 1hr 15min–1hr 45min).

Taunton to: Bridgwater (4 daily; 30min); Glastonbury (5 daily; 1hr 35min); Wells (5 daily; 1hr 45min).

Torquay to: Bristol (2–3 daily; 2hr 45min–3hr); Exeter (1–2 hourly; 55min); London (8 daily; 5hr 15min); Plymouth (hourly; 2hr).

Truro to: Bristol (1 daily; 5hr); Exeter (2 daily; 3hr 10min); Falmouth (2–3 hourly; 25–40min); Penzance (hourly; 1hr 45min); Plymouth (7 daily; 1hr 30min–1hr 50min); St Austell (1–2 hourly; 35–50min); St Ives (12 daily; 1hr 15min–1hr 45min).

Wells to: Bath (hourly; 1hr 20min); Bridgwater (5–9 daily; 1hr 20min); Bristol (4–12 daily; 1hr); Frome (5–8 daily; 1hr); Glastonbury (every 30min; 15min); Taunton (5 daily; 1hr 50min).

CHAPTER SIX

EAST ANGLIA

Strictly speaking, **East Anglia** is made up of just three counties – Suffolk, Norfolk and the old county of Cambridgeshire – which were settled by Angles from Holstein in the fifth century, though in more recent times, it's come to be loosely applied to parts of Essex and Huntingdonshire too. As a region it's renowned for its wide skies and flat landscapes, and of course such generalizations always contain more than a grain of truth – if you're looking for mountains, you've come to the wrong place. That said, East Anglia often fails to conform to its stereotype: parts of Suffolk are positively hilly, and its coastline can induce vertigo; the north Norfolk coast holds steep cliffs as well as wide sandy beaches; and even the pancake-flat fenlands are broken by wide, muddy rivers and hilly mounds, on one of which perches Ely's magnificent cathedral. Indeed, the whole region is sprinkled with fine medieval churches, the legacy of the days when this was England's most progressive and prosperous region.

Of all the East Anglian counties, **Suffolk** is the most varied. Its undulating southern reaches, straddling the River Stour, are home to a string of picturesque, well-preserved little towns – **Lavenham** and **Kersey** are two excellent examples – which enjoyed immense prosperity during the thirteenth to sixteenth centuries, the heyday of the wool trade. Elsewhere, **Bury St Edmunds** can boast not just the ruins of its once-prestigious abbey, but also some fine Georgian architecture on its grid-plan streets. Even the much-maligned county town of **Ipswich** has more to offer than it's generally given credit for. Nevertheless, for many visitors it's the north Suffolk coast that steals the local show. In **Southwold**, with its comely Georgian high street, Suffolk possesses a delightful seaside resort, elegant and relaxing in equal measure, while neighbouring **Aldeburgh** hosts one of the best music festivals in the country.

Norfolk, as everyone knows thanks to Noël Coward, is very flat. It's also one of the most sparsely populated and tranquil counties in England, a remarkable turnaround from the days when it was an economic and political powerhouse – until, that is, the Industrial Revolution simply passed it by. Its capital, **Norwich**, is still East Anglia's largest city, renowned for its Norman cathedral and castle, and for its high-tech Sainsbury Centre, a provocative collection of twentieth-century art. The one part of Norfolk which has been well and truly discovered is the **Broads**, a unique landscape of reed-ridden waterways that has been over-exploited by farmers and boat-rental companies for the last twenty years. Too far from London to attract day-trippers, the Norfolk

ACCOMMODATION PRICE CODES

Throughout this guide, hotel and B&B accommodation is priced on a scale of ① to ⑨, the number indicating the **lowest price** you could expect to pay per night in that establishment for a **double room** in high season. The prices indicated by the codes are as follows:

① under £40	④ £60–70	⑦ £110–150
② £40–50	⑤ £70–90	⑧ £150–200
③ £50–60	⑥ £90–110	⑨ over £200

coast – with the exception of touristy **Great Yarmouth** and, to a lesser extent, the Victorian resort of **Cromer** – remains one of the most unspoilt in England, with **Blakeney Point** and the surrounding marshes among the country's top nature reserves. Meanwhile, sheltering inland, are two outstanding stately homes – **Blickling Hall** and **Holkham** – with several more within easy striking distance of **King's Lynn**, a strange, almost disconcerting mixture of fenland town and ancient seaport.

Cambridge is, however, the one place in East Anglia everyone visits, largely on account of its world-renowned university, whose ancient colleges boast some of the finest medieval and early modern architecture in the country. The rest of Cambridgeshire is dominated by the landscape of the **Fens**, for centuries an inhospitable marshland, which was eventually drained to provide rich alluvial farming land.

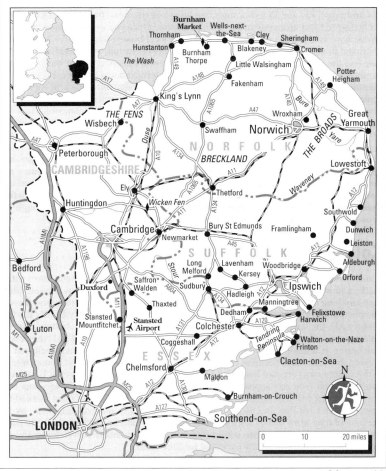

The one great highlight here is the cathedral town of **Ely**, settled on one of the few areas of raised ground in this region and an easy and popular day-trip from Cambridge. The old county of Huntingdonshire, now the western part of Cambridgeshire, has its moments too, most notably in **Peterborough**'s splendid cathedral.

Heading into the region from the south almost inevitably takes you through Essex, though there's little here to divert you. Not properly part of East Anglia but generally lumped together with the region, Essex's proximity to London has turned many places into soulless commuter towns, while its inhabitants – "Essex man and woman" – are dubbed archetypally brash, Conservative and uncultured by the rest of the English. The county capital, Chelmsford, is no great shakes and instead it's in historic towns like **Colchester** and the coastal resort of **Southend-on-Sea** where Essex is at its most diverting.

Getting around

The **train** network is at its best to and from London, with quick and frequent services from the capital to all the major towns. As places like Colchester, Ipswich and Norwich, or Cambridge, Ely and Peterborough, are linked on the same train lines, it's also relatively easy to move from one major town to another. Once you get away from the major towns, however, you're going to have to rely on local **buses**, whose services are often restricted in winter and on Sundays. In parts of north Norfolk and inland Suffolk, you may find the only way to get about is to take your own transport. Major bus routes are dominated by a handful of major operators like Eastern National in Essex, First Eastern Counties in Norfolk and Stagecoach Cambus in Cambridgeshire. Each of these companies sells rover tickets of some description, providing unlimited travel for one day or more on their buses and sometimes on services operated by other companies too. For instance, First Eastern Counties' BusRanger ticket is valid on Eastern National and some Thamesway routes. For more information, contact the operators' offices, as listed in the text.

Hiking, naturally enough, is less strenuous here than in most English regions, and there are several **long-distance footpaths** worth considering. The main routes run through Norfolk, starting with the **Peddars Way**, from Knettishall near Thetford and heading north to the coast at Hunstanton. The route then continues east as the **Norfolk Coast Path** as far as Cromer, from where the **Weaver's Way** then wends through the Broads to Great Yarmouth. Any local tourist office can provide trail guides.

Colchester and around

If you visit anywhere in Essex, it should be **COLCHESTER**, an agreeable town with a castle, a university and a large army base, fifty miles or so northeast of London. More than anything else, Colchester prides itself on being England's oldest town and there is documentary evidence of a settlement here as early as the fifth century BC. By the first century AD, the town was the region's capital under King Cunobelin – better known as Shakespeare's Cymbeline – and when the Romans invaded Britain in 43 AD they chose Colchester (Camulodunum) as their new capital, though it was soon eclipsed by London, becoming a retirement colony for legionaries instead. The first Roman temple in the country was erected here, and in 60 AD the colony was the target of Boudicca's abortive revolt (see box opposite). A millennium later, the conquering Normans built one of their mightiest strongholds in Colchester, but the conflict that most marked the town was the Civil War. In 1648, Colchester was subjected to a gruelling siege by the Parliamentarian army led by Lord Fairfax; after three months, during which the population ate every living creature within the walls, the town finally surrendered and the Royalist leaders were promptly executed for their pains.

BOUDICCA

Boudicca – aka Boadicea – was the wife of Prasutagus, chief of the Iceni tribe of Norfolk, who allied himself to the Romans during the conquest of Britain in 43 AD. Five years later, when the Iceni were no longer useful, the Romans attempted to disarm them and, although the Iceni rebelled, they were soon brought to heel. On Prasutagus's death, the Romans ignored his will and confiscated his property – and when Boudicca protested, the Romans flogged her and raped her daughters. Boudicca quickly rallied the Iceni and their allies and set off on a rampage through southern Britain in 60 AD.

As the ultimate symbol of Roman oppression, the Temple of the Deified Claudius in Colchester was the initial focus of hatred, but once Colchester had been demolished Boudicca turned her sights elsewhere. She laid waste to London and St Albans, massacring over seventy thousand citizens and inflicting crushing defeats on the Roman units stationed there. She was far from squeamish, ripping traitors' arms out of their sockets and torturing every Roman and collaborator in sight. She was eventually defeated by the Roman governor Suetonius Paulinus in a pitched battle which cost the Romans just four hundred lives, and the Britons countless thousands. Boudicca committed suicide, while the Romans took their revenge on the surviving rebel tribes.

Today, Colchester makes a good base for further explorations of the surrounding countryside – particularly the Stour valley towns of Constable country (see p.365).

Arrival, information and accommodation

Colchester has two **train stations**. Services from London and Harwich arrive at the mainline Colchester North Station, from where it's a fifteen-minute walk south into town – follow North Station Road and its continuation North Hill until you reach the west end of the High Street. Trains from Frinton, Walton and Clacton-on-Sea arrive at Colchester Town Station, to the south of the centre at the bottom of St Botolph's Street. The **bus station** is off Queen Street, the northerly continuation of St Botolph's Street, and is a couple of minutes' walk from the High Street. You can get bus timetables here from the First Eastern National office (Mon–Fri 9am–5pm, Sat 9am–1pm; ☎01206/572478), which also sells Bus Ranger tickets (£5.50) valid for a day's travel throughout much of East Anglia.

The **tourist office** is at 1 Queen St (April–Sept Mon–Sat 9.30am–6pm, Sun 10am–5pm; Oct–March Mon–Sat 10am–5pm; ☎01206/282920), just behind the castle. As well as helping with accommodation, they sell leaflets detailing local walks and coordinate daily **guided walks** around town (June–Sept; £2). You can rent a **bike** from Bicycle Breaks (☎01206/868 254; £6 per day) – who deliver the bikes to you if you're staying in or close to the town centre – a good way of getting out to see the nearby "Constable Country" (see p.366).

For **accommodation**, Colchester has more than its fair share of old hotels as well as a cluster of pleasant, well-located B&Bs. *Colchester Mill Hotel*, East St (☎01206/865022; ③), is located in a refurbished flourmill down by the River Colne, a few minutes' walk east from the High Street; the *George Hotel*, 116 High St (☎01206/578494; ⑤), is an attractive old coaching inn, whose recently refurbished rooms come with all mod cons; *The Old Manse*, 15 Roman Rd (☎01206/545154; no credit cards; ①), is the best of the many B&B options along Roman Road, with three pleasant guestrooms; and the *Red Lion*, 43 High St (☎01206/577986; ③), is another old timer, a fifteenth-century timber building containing 24 modernized en-suite rooms.

The Town

Most visitors start off at the town's rugged, honey-coloured **Castle**, the perfect introduction to Colchester's long history, set in attractive parkland, which stretches down
to the River Colne. Begun less than ten years after the Battle of Hastings, it boasts a
phenomenally large keep – the largest in Europe at the time – built on the site of the
defunct Roman temple. The castle's **museum** (March–Nov Mon–Sat 10am–5pm, Sun
2–5pm; Dec–Feb Mon–Sat 10am–5pm; £3.60) contains the best of the region's
Romano-British archeological finds, although, apart from a fine bronze of Mercury,
the messenger of the gods, this amounts to little more than a smattering of coins,
tombstones, statues and mosaics. Perhaps the most impressive mosaic – depicting
sea beasts pursuing dolphins – is on display at the castle entrance, next to the castle
well. The museum also covers the Boudicca revolt and the 1648 siege, and you can
sign up for a **guided tour** of the underground tunnels (45min; £1), which give access
to the foundations of the Roman temple and the Norman chapel and walls – parts not
otherwise accessible to regular visitors.

The castle stands at the eastern end of the wide, and largely pedestrianized, **High
Street**, which lies pretty much along the same route as it did in Roman times. The most
arresting building here is the flamboyant **Town Hall**, built in 1902 and topped by a statue of St Helena, mother of Constantine the Great and daughter of "Old King Cole" of
nursery-rhyme fame – after whom, some say, the town was named. Immediately north
of the High Street is the so-called **Dutch Quarter**, where Flemish refugees settled in
the sixteenth century giving a boost to the town's ailing cloth trade. The area's lofty
buildings still make this a pleasant place to stroll, particularly along West and East
Stockwell streets. South of the High Street, much of the medieval street plan has been
subsumed within a vast open-air shopping precinct, complete with three separate
indoor shopping centres and an open-air **market** held every Friday and Saturday in
Vineyard Street. Nearby, narrow Trinity Street is home to the **Tymperleys Clock
Museum** (April–Oct Tues–Sat 10am–1pm & 2–5pm; free), featuring locally made
clocks and housed in a wonderful fifteenth-century timber-framed building with its own
little garden.

Looming above the western end of the High Street is the town landmark, "**Jumbo**",
a disused nineteenth-century water tower, considerably more imposing than the nearby **Balkerne Gate**, which once marked the western entrance of Roman Colchester.
Built in AD 50, this is the largest surviving Roman gateway in the country, though with
the remains at only a touch over six feet in height, it's far short of spectacular. The
town's **Roman Walls**, to which the gate is joined, are somewhat more impressive –
erected only after Boudicca had sacked the city in AD 60 and, as such, a case of too little too late. The overall effect of this particular section is spoiled by the adjacent ring
road, but there are other more tranquil fragments in the park below the castle.

Eating, drinking and nightlife

Colchester's oysters have been highly prized since Roman times and the local vine-
yards have an equally long heritage, so it's no surprise to find the town has a good
choice of first-rate **restaurants**. Pickings are slim on Sundays, however, when most
places are closed. The best food in town is to be had at the *Warehouse Brasserie*, on
Chapel Street North (☎01206/765656; closed Sun eve), which offers tasty dishes at
moderate prices from a wide-ranging, contemporary menu. Alternatively, try *Ruan
Thai*, 82a East Hill (☎01206/870770), an excellent and moderately priced Thai restaurant near the top of East Hill; or *Tilly's*, 22 Trinity St (closed Sun), a Victorian tearoom
that serves snacks and full English meals. *The Lemon Tree*, 48 St John's St

(☎01206/767337; closed Sun), is a moderately priced option, popular for its lunch specials and sunny courtyard seating. For pizza, try *Pizza Express*, 1 St Runwald's St, off West Stockwell (☎01206/760680), or *Toto's*, 5–7 Museum St (☎01206/573235).

Colchester's town centre is crowded with **pubs**, with three of the best being the *Red Lion*, 43 High St, the *Foresters Arms*, a nice backstreet local on Castle Road, and the *Goat and Boot*, just one of several lively spots down East Hill. And, as you'd expect in a university town, the town rates reasonably well when it comes to the **arts and nightlife**. The Colchester Arts Centre, on Church Street next to the Balkerne Gate (☎01206/500900), puts on a good programme of rock, folk, jazz, theatre and dance, plus some club nights – all in a converted Victorian church. Nearby is the Mercury Theatre (☎01206/573948), the town's main drama venue. In term time it's also worth checking what's on at the university's Lakeside Theatre (☎01206/873261), a mile or so east of the centre, where they provide a varied programme of theatre and music.

The Stour Valley and the old wool towns of south Suffolk

A few miles north of Colchester, the **Stour Valley** forms the border between Essex and Suffolk for much of its length, and signals the beginning of East Anglia proper. Compared with much of the region it is positively hilly, a handsome landscape of farms and woodland latticed by dense, well-kept hedges and thick grassy banks that once kept the Stour in check. The valley is dotted with lovely little villages, where rickety, half-timbered Tudor houses and elegant Georgian dwellings cluster around medieval churches, proud buildings with square, self-confident towers. The Stour's prettiest villages are concentrated along its lower reaches – to the east of the A134 – in **Dedham Vale**, with **Stoke-by-Nayland** and **Dedham** arguably the most appealing of them all. This is also known as **"Constable Country"**, as it was the home of John Constable, one of England's greatest artists, and the subject of his most famous works. Inevitably, there's a Constable shrine – the much-visited complex of old buildings down by the river at **Flatford Mill**.

The villages along the River Stour and its tributaries were once busy little places at the heart of East Anglia's weaving trade, which boomed from the thirteenth to the fifteenth centuries. By the 1490s, the region produced more cloth than any other part of the country, but in Tudor times production shifted to Colchester, Ipswich and Norwich and, although most of the smaller settlements continued spinning cloth for the next three hundred years, their importance slowly dwindled. Bypassed by the Industrial Revolution, south Suffolk had, by the late nineteenth century, become a remote rural backwater, an impoverished area whose decline had one unforeseen consequence. With few exceptions, the towns and villages were never well enough off to modernize, and the architectural legacy of medieval and Tudor times survived. The best-preserved village is **Lavenham**, though the place heaves with sightseers on summer weekends; there are other attractive spots too, notably **Sudbury**, which boasts an excellent museum devoted to the work of Thomas Gainsborough, another great English artist and a native of the town who spent much of his time painting the local landscape.

Seeing the region by **public transport** is problematic – distances are small (Dedham Vale is only about ten miles long), but buses between the villages are infrequent and you'll find it difficult to get away from the towns. Several rail lines cross south Suffolk, the most useful being the London–Colchester–Sudbury route. The area is crisscrossed by **footpaths**, some of the most enjoyable of which are in the vicinity of Dedham village.

East Bergholt, Flatford Mill and John Constable

"I associate my careless boyhood to all that lies on the banks of the Stour," wrote **John Constable**, who was born to a miller in **EAST BERGHOLT**, nine miles northeast of Colchester in 1776. The house in which he was born has long since disappeared, so it has been left to **Flatford Mill**, a mile or so to the south, to take up the painter's cause. The mill was owned by his father and was where Constable painted his most famous canvas, *The Hay Wain* (now in the National Gallery, London), which created a sensation when it was exhibited in 1824. To the chagrin of many of his contemporaries, Constable turned away from the landscape-painting conventions of the day, rendering his scenery with a realistic directness that harked back to the Dutch landscape painters of the seventeenth century. Typically, he justified this approach in unpretentious terms, observing that, after all, "no two days are alike, nor even two hours; neither were there ever two leaves of a tree alike since the creation of the world." The mill itself – not the one he painted, but a Victorian replacement – is not open to the public, but the sixteenth-century thatched **Bridge Cottage** (March, April & Oct Wed–Sun 11am–5.30pm; May–Sept daily 10am–5.30pm; Nov to early Dec Wed–Sun 11am–3pm; Jan & Feb Sat & Sun 11am–3pm; free, but parking £1.80), which overlooks the scene, has been painstakingly restored and stuffed full of Constabilia. Unfortunately, none of Constable's paintings are displayed here, though the adjacent granary contains mezzotints of the artist's works and there's a pleasant riverside tearoom to take in the view. Beyond stands **Willy Lott's Cottage** (also closed to the public), which does actually feature in *The Hay Wain*.

Dedham

Constable went to school in **DEDHAM**, just upriver from Flatford Mill. It's one of the region's most attractive villages, with a scattering of ancient timber-framed houses strung along the wide main street. The only sights as such are **St Mary's Church**, an early sixteenth-century structure which Constable painted on several occasions, and the **Sir Alfred Munnings Art Museum**, in Castle House (May–July & Sept Wed & Sun 2–5pm; Aug Wed, Thurs, Sat & Sun 2–5pm; £3), just south of the village on the road to Ardleigh, which displays works of the locally born academician, best known for his portraits of horses. It is, however, the general flavour of Dedham which appeals most

The only way to reach Dedham by **bus** is on the twice-weekly service from Colchester, but Stratford St Mary, just over a mile to the west, is easily reached on the regular Colchester–Ipswich bus route. Dedham has one of the smartest **hotels** in the area, *Maison Talbooth* (☎01206/322367; ⑦), which occupies a good-looking Victorian country house about fifteen minutes' walk southwest of the village on the road to Stratford St Mary. Each of the hotel's ten large bedrooms are individually decorated in sumptuous style and dinner can be had close by at *Le Talbooth* (☎01206/323150), an expensive but notch **restaurant** in an ancient timber-framed house down by the River Stour. Alternatively, there's *Dedham Hall* (☎01206/323027; ⑨), an old manor house set in its own grounds on the east side of the village off Brook Street – be sure to ask for a room in the house itself. The restaurant here is very good too (closed Mon). You can also stay in the heart of Dedham itself at the *Marlborough Head* pub (☎01206/323250; ③), where a handful of very pleasant rooms are available above the bar, and excellent, moderately priced **food** can be had from its inventive and wide-ranging menu.

Stoke-by-Nayland and Nayland

Heading northwest from Dedham, the B1029 dips beneath the A12 to reach the byroad to Higham, an unremarkable hamlet where you pick up the road to **STOKE-BY-NAYLAND**, four miles to the west. This is the most picturesque of villages, where a knot of half-timbered, pastel-painted cottages snuggle up to **St Mary's Church**. With its pretty brick and stone-trimmed tower, the church was one of Constable's favourite subjects. The doors of the south porch are sumptuously covered by the carved figures of a medieval Jesse Tree. The village also boasts a great old pub, the *Angel Inn* (☎01206/263245; ④), known for its adventurous food (eat in the bar or book for the restaurant) and cosy rooms. There are several other good places to stay in and near the village, including *Thorington Hall* (☎01206/337329; ②), which offers four bedrooms in a seventeenth-century house.

Southwest from here, it's two miles back to the River Stour at **NAYLAND**, a workaday little place that is chiefly remarkable for its church's altar painting, *Christ Blessing the Bread and Wine*. It's one of only two attempts by Constable at a religious theme – and, dated to 1809, it was completed long before he found his artistic rhythm. You can wet your whistle and sample quality bar food at Nayland's venerable *White Hart*, 11 High St. Local **accommodation** is available at *Hill House*, Gravel Hill (☎01206/262782; ②), on the edge of the village and at *Gladwins Farm*, Harper's Hill (☎01206/262261; ③), a secluded timber-framed farmhouse with its own indoor pool.

Sudbury

SUDBURY – the fictional "Eatanswill" of Dickens's *Pickwick Papers* – has doubled in size in the last thirty years, to become easily the most important town in this part of the Stour Valley. A handful of timber-framed houses hark back to its days of wool-trade prosperity, but its three Perpendicular churches were underwritten by another local industry, silk weaving, which survives on a small scale to this day. Sudbury's most famous export, however, is **Thomas Gainsborough**, the leading English portraitist of the eighteenth century, whose statue, with brush and palette, stands on Market Hill, the town's predominantly Victorian market place. A superb collection of the artist's work is on display in the house where he was born – **Gainsborough's House** at 46 Gainsborough St (April–Oct Tues–Sat 10am–5pm, Sun 2–5pm; Nov–March Tues–Sat 10am–4pm, Sun 2–4pm; £3). Gainsborough left Sudbury when he was just thirteen, moving to London where he was apprenticed to an engraver. But it seems he was soon moonlighting and the earliest of his surviving portrait paintings – his *Boy and Girl*, a remarkably self-assured work dated to 1744 – is displayed here. In 1752, Gainsborough moved on to Ipswich, where he soon established himself as a portrait painter to the Suffolk gentry – though, sadly, none of the portraits of high-society ladies with which he made his name are to be found in the museum's collection.

Sudbury is just seven miles northwest of Nayland – and twice that from Colchester – along the A134. It's accessible by **train** from Colchester (change at Marks Tey) and is the hub of **bus** services to and from neighbouring towns and villages including Colchester and Ipswich. Once you've seen Gainsborough's house, though, there's little reason to hang around. If you do decide to stay, the **tourist office** in the town hall on Market Hill (Easter–Sept Mon–Sat 10am–4.45pm; Oct–Easter Mon–Sat 10am–2.45pm; ☎01787/881320) can provide **accommodation** details.

Lavenham

Seven miles from Sudbury, off the A134, lies **LAVENHAM**, formerly a centre of the region's wool trade and today one of the most visited villages in Suffolk, thanks to its unrivalled ensemble of perfectly preserved half-timbered houses. The whole place has changed little since the demise of the wool industry in the seventeenth century, owing in part to the zealous local preservation society, which has carefully maintained the village's museum-like quality by banning from view such excrescences of twentieth-century life as TV aerials.

The village is at its most beguiling in the triangular **Market Place**, an airy spot flanked by pastel-painted, medieval dwellings whose beams have been bent into all sorts of wonky angles by the passing of the years. It's here you'll find Lavenham's most celebrated building, the pale-white, timber-framed **Corpus Christi Guildhall** (April–Oct daily 11am–5pm; £2.80; NT), erected in the sixteenth century as the head-quarters of one of Lavenham's four guilds. In the much-altered interior (used successively as a prison and workhouse), there's an exhibition on the woollen industry, but most visitors quickly reach the walled garden and the teashop. The other building worthy of special notice is the Perpendicular church of **St Peter and St Paul** (daily: summer 8.30am–5.30pm; winter 8.30am–3.30pm), though it's sited a short walk southwest of the centre, at the top of Church Street. Local merchants endowed the church with a nave of majestic proportions and a mighty flint tower, at 141ft the highest for miles around, partly to celebrate the Tudor victory at the Battle of Bosworth in 1485, but mainly to show off their wealth.

There are fairly frequent **buses** to Lavenham from Colchester via Sudbury and Long Melford, with the service continuing on to Bury St Edmunds. The **tourist office** is located on Lady Street (Easter to Oct daily 10am–4.45pm; ☎01787/248207), just south of Market Place. They can help with accommodation and sell a detailed, street-by-street walking guide. Rooms at the *Swan* **hotel** (☎01787/247477; ⑦), a splendid old inn on the High Street, are some of the most comfortable in town; the building incorporates part of the Elizabethan Wool Hall and has a whole host of cosy lounges and courtyard gardens. Less expensive options on the Market Place include the ancient *Angel Hotel* (☎01787/247 388; ④), which has eight pleasant rooms above its bar, and the dinky *Angel Gallery* (☎01787/248417; ②), where the three guest rooms are situated above a pocket-sized art shop. For cheaper B&B options, you'll probably end up staying outside Lavenham itself; the tourist office will provide you with details. For **food**, the *Angel Hotel* serves up excellent, moderately priced bar meals, as does the *Swan*. The other choice in Market Place is the *Great House* (☎01787/247431; closed Sun eve), whose outstanding restaurant serves moderately priced food on both its à la carte and set menus.

Bury St Edmunds

BURY ST EDMUNDS started out as a Benedictine monastery, founded to house the remains of Edmund, the last Saxon king of East Anglia, who was tortured and beheaded by the marauding Danes in 869. Almost two centuries later, England was briefly ruled by the kings of Denmark and the shrewdest of them, King Cnut, made a gesture of reconciliation to his Saxon subjects by conferring on the monastery the status of abbey. It was a popular move and the abbey prospered, so much so that before its dissolution in 1539, it had become the richest religious house in the country. Most of the abbey disappeared long ago, and nowadays Bury is better known for its graceful Georgian streets, its flower gardens and its sugar beet plant than for its ancient monuments. Nonetheless, it's an amiable, eminently likeable place, one of the prettiest towns in Suffolk, and with good transport connections on to Cambridge, Colchester, Ipswich or Norwich it demands at least half a day of anyone's time.

The Town

The town centre has preserved its Norman street plan, a grid plan in which Churchgate was aligned with – and sloped up from – the abbey's high altar. It was the first planned town of Norman Britain and, for that matter, the first example of urban planning in England since the departure of the Romans. Beside the abbey grounds is

Angel Hill, a broad, spacious square partly framed by Georgian buildings, the most distinguished being the ivy-covered **Angel Hotel**, which features in Dickens's *Pickwick Papers*. Dickens also gave readings of his work in the **Athenaeum**, the Georgian assembly rooms at the far end of the square (occasionally open for exhibitions and sales). A twelfth-century wall runs along the east side of Angel Hill, with the bulky fourteenth-century **Abbey Gate** forming the entrance to the abbey gardens and ruins.

The **abbey ruins** themselves are like nothing so much as petrified porridge, with little to remind you of the grandiose Norman complex that dominated the town. Thousands of medieval pilgrims once sought solace at St Edmund's altar and the cult was of such significance that the barons of England gathered here to swear that they would make King John sign their petition – the Magna Carta of 1215. The only significant remnants of the abbey are behind the more modern cathedral (see below) on the far side of the public **gardens** – the suntrap rose garden, hemmed in by giant yew hedges, is a particular delight. Here, the rubbled remains of a small part of the old **abbey church** have been integrated into a set of unusual Georgian houses, one of which holds the **Abbey Visitor Centre** (Easter–Oct daily 10am–5pm; free). The centre traces the history of the abbey and rents headsets (£1.50) for an audiotape tour of the grounds and ruins. In front, across the green, is the imposing **Norman Tower**, once the main gateway into the abbey and now a solitary monument with dragon gargoyles and fancily decorated capitals.

Incongruously, the tower is next to the front part of Bury's **Cathedral of St James** (daily: June–Aug 8.30am–8pm; rest of year 8.30am–5.30pm; £2 donation requested), with chancel and transepts added as recently as the 1960s. That its thousand-odd kneelers are often cited as one of its major highlights gives an idea of the paucity of the interior, notwithstanding the hammer-beam roof and a couple of quality stained glass windows. In fact, it was a toss-up between this place and **St Mary's Church**, further down Crown Street, as to which would be given cathedral status in 1914. The presence of the tomb of Mary Tudor in the latter was probably the clinching factor.

The town's main commercial area is on the west side of the centre, a five-minute walk up from Angel Hill at the top of Abbeygate Street. There's been some intrusive modern planning here, but dignified Victorian buildings flank both Cornhill and Buttermarket, the two short main streets, as well as the narrower streets in between. Older still is the Cornhill's flint-walled **Moyse's Hall**, one of the few surviving Norman houses in England, while the streets to the south are lined by an attractive medley of architectural styles, from elegant Georgian town houses to Victorian brick terraces. You'll see the best by strolling along Guildhall and turning left down Churchgate, which brings you back to Angel Hill.

Practicalities

Bury St Edmunds' **train station** is ten minutes' walk from Angel Hill, south along Northgate Street, and the **bus station** is on St Andrew Street North, near Cornhill. The town's **tourist office**, at 6 Angel Hill (Easter–May Mon–Fri 9.30am–5.30pm, Sat 10am–3pm; June–Sept 9.30am–5.30pm, Sat & Sun 10am–3pm; Oct–Easter Mon–Fri 10am–4pm, Sat 10am–1pm; ☎01284/764667), provides free town maps.

The pick of the town's **hotels** is the *Angel*, on Angel Hill (☎01284/753926; ⑤), an immaculately maintained, county-set hotel with thick carpets, oodles of wood panelling and suitably luxurious rooms. A good alternative is the *Chantry Hotel*, 8 Sparhawk St (☎01284/767427; ④), which has fifteen comfortable rooms in a converted Georgian building near the Manor House Museum. The town has a good supply of **B&Bs**, including the excellent *South Hill House*, 43 Southgate St (☎01284/755650; no credit cards; ②), a handsome old town house with many Georgian features and three large en-suite bedrooms.

For **restaurants**, *Maison Bleue at Mortimer's*, 31 Churchgate St (☎01284/760623; closed Sat lunch & Sun), serves wonderfully fresh seafood at moderate prices. *The Vaults*, inside the medieval undercroft at the *Angel Hotel*, is also first rate, with tasty main dishes from £6.50. Otherwise, aim for coffee, cakes and snacks in the Cathedral Refectory (closed Sun), or at the café in the Manor House Museum, which has courtyard garden seating.

Of the **pubs**, one you shouldn't miss is the *Nutshell* (closed Sun), on The Traverse at the top of Abbeygate, which, at sixteen feet by seven and a half, claims to be Britain's smallest. Greene King's brewery tap is the ancient-looking *Dog & Partridge*, 29 Crown St. For entertainment, there's a year-round programme of cultural events held at the **Theatre Royal**, on Westgate St (☎01284/769505).

Ipswich and around

Situated at the head of the Orwell estuary, **IPSWICH** was a rich trading port in the Middle Ages, but its appearance today is mainly the result of a revival of fortunes in the Victorian era. The town centre itself has been mauled by the developers in the last few decades, but two surviving reminders of old Ipswich – **Christchurch Mansion** and the splendid **Ancient House** – plus the recently renovated quayside are all reason enough to spend at least an afternoon here. Ipswich also boasts a wealth of medieval flint churches, some now locked and slowly rusting away, but others sympathetically restored. One now houses the tourist office, from where **guided walks** depart a couple of times a week during the season (May–Sept, Tues & Thurs 2.15pm; £1.50) – perhaps the best way to see the town on a quick visit.

The Town

The ancient Saxon market place, **Cornhill**, is still the town's focal point, a likeable urban space flanked by a bevy of imposing Victorian edifices – the Italianate town hall, the old Neoclassical post office and the pseudo-Jacobean Lloyds building. To get to Ipswich's most famous building, walk halfway along Tavern Street and duck down the mock-Tudor arcade on the right, known as the Walk, to pedestrianized Buttermarket, a little way along which stands the **Ancient House**. The exterior of this Tudor building was decorated around 1670 in extravagant style, a riot of pargeting and stucco work that is one of the finest examples of Restoration artistry in the country. There are plasterwork reliefs of pelicans and nymphs as well as representations of the four continents known at the time. Europe is symbolized by a Gothic church, America a tobacco pipe, Asia an Oriental dome and Africa, eccentrically enough, by an African astride a crocodile. Since the house is now a shop, you're free to take a peek inside to view yet more of the decor, including the hammer-beam roof on the first floor.

From the Ancient House, head up Dial Lane past the fifteenth-century church of **St Lawrence** and back onto Tavern Street, where two wonderful mock-Tudor shops, built in the 1930s, face the **Great White Horse Hotel**, the "overgrown tavern" which appears in Dickens's *Pickwick Papers*. Heading north from here up Northgate Street takes you past the much-restored sixteenth-century, half-timbered **Oak House**, once an inn and now housing office space, to busy St Margaret's Plain and the gates of **Christchurch Mansion** (Tues–Sat 10am–5pm, Sun 2.30–4.30pm; free). This handsome, if much restored, Tudor building, sporting seventeenth-century Dutch gables, is set in 65 acres of parkland, an area larger than the town centre itself. The mansion's labyrinthine interior is well worth exploring, with period furnishings and a good collection of paintings by Constable and Gainsborough, as well as more contemporary art exhibitions.

Back in the town centre, the western half of old Ipswich has been transformed by some fairly hideous postwar development along **Civic Drive**, but there is one modern building which puts the rest to shame. It's the **Willis Corroon Building**, designed by Norman Foster in the 1970s, whose smoked glass exterior snakes its way along Princes Street at Franciscan Way, reflecting the older buildings around it by day but allowing a startling X-ray vision of the illuminated interior after dusk. From here, it's a short stroll to College Street, named after the college that Cardinal Wolsey, a native of Ipswich, established here in 1528, but failed to complete before his fall from grace. All that remains of Cardinal College now is the solitary **Wolsey's Gateway**, next to the fourteenth-century St Peter's Church.

Pressing on, head east along College Street and, after rounding St-Mary-at-Quay, another medieval church, follow Key Street one block north to reach the **Wet Dock**, the largest in Europe when it opened in 1845 and looking much as it did then, apart from the rash of yachts in the marina. The smell of malt and barley still wafts across the dockside, and several of the granaries continue to function, though other warehouses have been turned into pubs, restaurants and offices. Halfway along the quayside stands the proud Neoclassical **Customs House**, built for the opening of the dock.

Practicalities

Ipswich **train station** is on the south bank of the Orwell, ten minutes' walk from Cornhill along Princes Street. The **bus station** is more central, occupying part of the Old Cattle Market, one block south of the Ancient House. The **tourist office** (Mon–Sat 9am–5pm; ☎01473/258070) is in the converted St Stephen's Church in St Stephen's Lane, between the bus station and the Ancient House. The town is compact enough to walk around, though a special summer **bus** (June to late July Sun only; late July to Aug daily) runs a circular route, connecting the train station to all the main sights, including the Wet Dock and the brewery on Cliff Road.

There's no real need **to stay**, especially with the Suffolk coast so close, but a full list of B&Bs is available from the tourist office. One of the best is *Burlington Lodge*, 30 Burlington Rd (☎01473/251868, *nortonburlodge@msn.com*; ①), an attractive Victorian detached house with five comfortable bedrooms about ten minutes' walk west of Cornhill. Alternatively, try the ultra-modern, spick and span *Novotel Hotel*, in the centre near Wolsey's Gateway, Grey Friars Rd (☎01473/232400; ⑤).

There are several good **restaurants** down by the Wet Dock. *Il Punto* (☎01473/289748), which offers good-quality French cuisine at moderate prices, has the most distinctive premises – on board a Dutch pleasure boat – while the more expensive *Mortimer's Seafood Restaurant* (☎01473/230225), in one of the old red-brick warehouses down on Wherry Quay, specializes in seafood. Meals here range from £20–30 a head, though it's cheaper at lunch. **Cafés** in town include *Bensons* at 1 St Stephen's Lane and *Pickwick's*, 1 Dial Lane, with courtyard seating next to St Lawrence's Church.

For a **drink**, try either the *Black Horse* on Black Horse Lane, or the busy *Brewery Tap*, next to the Tolly Cobbold brewery, at the far end of Cliff Road. For **entertainment**, try the Ipswich Film Theatre, in the Corn Exchange complex (☎01473/215544), behind the town hall, which shows mainstream and art movies.

Woodbridge and around

Stringing along the banks of the River Deben eight miles northeast of Ipswich, **WOODBRIDGE** is a pleasant if somewhat unremarkable town whose easy access to the sea – along the river's long and sheltered estuary – once nourished a thriving seaport and shipbuilding industry. These heady nautical days are recalled by the yachts in the marina and the adjacent **Tide Mill** (April & Oct Sat & Sun 11am–5pm; May–Sept daily 11am–5pm; £1), which comes complete with its antique milling machinery. From the waterfront, it's an easy five-minute walk up Quay and Church streets to **Market Hill**, the heart of the town since the Middle Ages. Here you'll find two moderately diverting museums, the **Woodbridge Museum** (Easter–Oct Thurs–Sat 10am–4pm, Sun 2.30–4.30pm; £1), tracing the town's history and the discovery of the Sutton Hoo treasure (see below); and the **Suffolk Horse Museum** (Easter–Sept daily 2–5pm; £1.50) housed in the eye-catching sixteenth-century Shire Hall and featuring paintings, photographs and exhibits celebrating the Suffolk Punch breed, heavy working horses bred in the town since the fifteenth century.

Woodbridge **train station** is handily located at the foot of Quay Street, beside the waterfront. **Buses** pull in here too. The **tourist office** is at the train station (Easter–Sept Mon–Fri 9am–5.30pm, Sat & Sun 9.30am–5pm; Oct–Easter Mon–Fri 9am–5.30pm, Sat 10am–4pm, Sun 10am–1pm; ☎01394/382240) and can help with accommodation as well as providing sketch maps of the town. Among several **hotels** and **B&Bs**, two of the more appealing are the *Old Station House Hotel*, at the station (☎01394/384831; ③), which has pleasant en-suite rooms and river views, and the *Bull Hotel* on Market Hill (☎01394/382089; ④), a well-run seventeenth-century coaching inn opposite Shire Hall. There are several first-rate **restaurants**, but the best is *Spice*, 17 The Thoroughfare (☎01394/382557; closed Sun), which serves delicious Malaysian and eastern-influenced dishes at moderate prices; it also has a **bar** with a buzz. Alternatively, there's the *Bull Hotel*, on Market Hill, which offers tasty bar meals and prides itself on its puddings, while the *King's Head*, 17 Market Hill, has good beer and bar meals which make full use of the products of nearby Orford's fine smokehouses (see opposite).

Sutton Hoo

In the summer of 1939, at **Sutton Hoo**, a couple of miles east of Woodbridge on the opposite side of the River Deben, a local landowner stumbled across the richest single archeological find in Britain, an Anglo-Saxon royal burial site belonging to Raedwald, king of East Anglia, who died around 625 AD. A forty-oar open ship was discovered, containing a wooden tomb stuffed with gold and jewelled ornaments. Further archeological research was conducted on the site in the 1980s, and in November 1991 a second undisturbed grave was uncovered. The artefacts are now on display in the British Museum in London. The National Trust, who now own Sutton Hoo, are currently revamping visitor facilities and constructing an exhibition area explaining the history and significance of the finds, but the work won't be completed until 2001. In the meantime, the only access is provided on hour-long **guided tours** organized by the Sutton Hoo Society (Easter–Oct Sat & Sun 2pm & 3pm; £2). To join the tour, take the A1152 out of Woodbridge, cross the railway line and then turn down the B1083, the Bawdsey road, at the roundabout. After nearly one mile, opposite the junction to Hollesley, you'll find the footpath to Sutton Hoo signposted on the right; the walk takes twenty minutes.

The Suffolk coast

The **Suffolk coast** feels detached from the rest of the county: the road and rail lines from Ipswich to Lowestoft funnel traffic five miles inland for most of the way, and patches of marsh and woodland make the separation still more complete. Dotting the empty coastline are remnants of the circular brick **Martello towers** built to repel Napoleonic invasion at the turn of the nineteenth century, part of a chain of defences deemed necessary along the sparsely inhabited Suffolk and Essex littoral. Coastal erosion continues to plague the region, and has contributed to the virtual extinction of the local fishing industry, and, in the case of Dunwich, has destroyed virtually the entire town. What is left, however, is undoubtedly one of the most unspoilt shorelines in the country, if you leave aside the Sizewell nuclear power station. The sleepy isolation of **Orford** is rarely broken even in the height of summer, and even more well-established resorts like **Southwold** have managed to escape the lurid fate of other English seaside towns. There are scores of delightful **walks** hereabouts, easy routes along the coast that are best followed with either OS map 156 or 169, or the simplified *Footpath Maps* (£1) available at most tourist offices. The Suffolk coast is also host to East Anglia's most compelling cultural gathering, the three-week-long **Aldeburgh Festival**, which takes place every June.

Orford

Twelve miles east of Woodbridge, on the far side of the storm-racked Forest of Rendlesham, the tiny village of **ORFORD** is dominated by two buildings, both of them medieval. The more impressive is the twelfth-century **Castle** (April–Oct daily 10am–6pm; Nov–March Wed–Sun 10am–4pm; £2.30; EH), built on high ground to the southwest of the village by Henry II, and under siege within months of its completion from Henry's rebellious sons. Most of the castle disappeared centuries ago, but the lofty keep remains, its impressive stature hinting at the scale of the original fortifications. Orford's other medieval edifice, on the far side of the main square, is **St Bartholomew's Church**, where Benjamin Britten premiered his most successful children's work, *Noye's Fludde*, as part of the 1958 Aldeburgh Festival (see box overleaf).

From the top of the castle keep, there's a great view across **Orford Ness**, a six-mile-long spit of shingle deposits that has all but blocked off Orford from the sea since Tudor times. Its mud flats and marshes harbour sea lavender beds, which act as feeding and roosting areas for wildfowl and waders. The National Trust offers **boat trips** (April–Oct Thurs–Sat 10am–2pm; last ferry back 5pm; £5.20; NT members £3.20; call ☎01394/450057) across to the Ness from Orford Quay, four hundred yards down the road from the church, and a five-mile hiking trail threads its way along the spit, passing the occasional military building. Some of the pioneer research on radar was carried out here, but the station was closed at the beginning of World War II because of the threat of German bombing. There are also plenty of walks to be had around Orford itself. One of the best is the five-mile hike north along the river wall that guards the west bank of the River Alde, returning via Ferry Road, a narrow country lane.

Orford's gentle, unhurried air is best experienced on a night's stay. **Rooms** are available at the *Crown & Castle* (☎01394/450205; ④), an attractive inn across from the castle with comfortable bedrooms kitted out with all mod cons, and at the marginally less enticing *King's Head* (☎01394/450271; ②), on Market Hill, the main square. For **meals**, don't miss the Butley Orford Oysterage, also on Market Hill. This has a very reasonably priced café/restaurant, whose menu focuses on fresh oysters and oak-wood smoked fish. Finally, down near the quay, the *Jolly Sailor Inn* serves bar meals, teas and coffee.

Aldeburgh and around

ALDEBURGH is best known for its annual arts festival, the brainchild of composer Benjamin Britten, who is buried in the village churchyard alongside the tenor Peter Pears, his lover and musical collaborator. They lived by the seafront in Crag House on Crabbe Street – the street named for the poet who provided Britten with his greatest inspiration (see box overleaf). Outside of June, when the festival takes place, and November, when the international poetry festival fills the town, Aldeburgh is the quietest of places, with just a small fishing fleet selling its daily catch from wooden shacks along the pebbled shore. The wide main street, parallel to the sea, and its backstreets are, in fact, all that's left of a once extensive medieval town, scoured away by centuries of erosion. Consequently, the seafront is something of a hotchpotch as it was not designed to face the sea.

Aldeburgh's oldest building, the sixteenth-century **Moot Hall** (Easter–May & Sept Sat & Sun 2.30–5pm; June daily 2.30–5pm; July & Aug daily 10.30am–12.30pm & 2.30–5pm; 50p), which began its days in the centre of town, now finds itself on the seashore. It's a handsome building made out of a mixture of red brick, flint and timber and the interior accommodates a modest museum of local finds and history. Aldeburgh's newest building, the **RNLI Lifeboat Station**, is situated bang in the middle of the seafront opposite the Jubilee Hall. From the public viewing deck you can look at the town's lifeboat and the tractor used to drag it out to sea.

Practicalities

Aldeburgh's **tourist office** is located in the half-timbered cinema at 51 High St (April–Oct Mon–Fri 9am–5.15pm, Sat & Sun 10am–5.15pm; ☎01728/453637). The Festival Box Office (see box below) is further down the street at no. 150 (Mon–Fri 10am–4pm, Sat 10am–2pm) and can answer general enquiries when the tourist office is closed. Getting hold of **accommodation** should be no problem, except of course during the festivals when you should book months in advance. The town boasts several

---

BENJAMIN BRITTEN AND THE ALDEBURGH FESTIVAL

Benjamin Britten was born in Lowestoft in 1913, and was closely associated with this part of Suffolk for most of his life. However, it was during his self-imposed exile in the USA during World War II – he was a conscientious objector – that Britten first read the work of the nineteenth-century Suffolk poet George Crabbe. Crabbe's *The Borough*, a grisly portrait of the life of the fishermen of Aldeburgh, was the basis of the libretto of Britten's best-known opera, *Peter Grimes*, which was premiered in London in 1945 to great acclaim.

In 1947 Britten founded the English Opera Group and the following year launched the **Aldeburgh Festival** as a showpiece for his own works and those of his contemporaries. He lived in the town for the next ten years, achieving much of his best work as a conductor and pianist there. For the rest of his life he composed many works specifically for the festival, including his masterpiece for children, *Noye's Fludde*, and the last of his fifteen operas, *Death in Venice*.

By the mid-1960s, the festival had outgrown the parish churches in which it began, and moved into a collection of disused malthouses, five miles west of Aldeburgh on the River Alde, just south of the small village of **Snape** along the B1069. **Snape Maltings** were subsequently converted into one of the finest concert venues in the country. In addition to the concert hall, there is now a recording studio, a music school, various craft shops and galleries, a tearoom, and a nice pub, the *Plough & Sail*. Even if there's nothing specific on, it's worth calling into the complex to browse in the shops or perhaps take one of the daily summer **river trips** (Easter–Oct; 1hr; £3.50) along the Alde estuary to see the birdlife.

For more information on the Aldeburgh Festival, contact the **Festival Box Office** on Aldeburgh High Street (Mon–Fri 10am–4pm, Sat 10am–2pm; ☎01728/453543; *www.aldeburgh.co.uk*). Tickets for the concerts, talks, exhibitions and other special events go on sale to the public around the middle of April, and often sell out fast for the big-name recitals; prices range from £8 to £25. There are concerts at other times of the year too – again details are available from the booking office – with showcase events including the Easter Music Festival, the Proms season in August, the week-long Britten Festival at the end of October and December's Winter Concerts.

splendidly sited **hotels**, including the *Wentworth* (☎01728/452312; ⑥), a family-owned hotel along the seafront from the Moot Hall. Of the **B&Bs**, the *Ocean House*, 25 Crag Path (☎01728/452094; no credit cards; ③), is probably the best. An immaculately maintained Victorian dwelling right on the seafront in the centre of town, it's decorated in period style, with two of its three guest rooms overlooking the beach; dinner is available by prior arrangement. Also in the town centre is *East Cottage*, 55 King St (☎01728/453010; ①), a brightly painted Victorian cottage a block back from the sea. Another option is the *Wateringfield*, on Golf Lane (☎01728/453163; ①), a spacious 1930s house overlooking the golf course on the edge of town. There's also a **youth hostel** on Heath Walk in the hamlet of Blaxhall (☎01728/688206; closed Nov–March), a couple of miles west of the concert facilities at Snape Maltings (see opposite). The hostel has forty beds and is housed in a former village school.

There are tearooms and takeaway fish-and-chip shops on the High Street, but Aldeburgh is the place for miles around to splash out on a decent meal – the town's highbrow leanings sustaining a glut of terrific **restaurants**. *Café 152*, 152 High St (☎01728/454152), is the most moderately priced, a simple painted wooden café where stylishly cooked fresh fish is served at lunch and dinner. There are more Mediterranean flavours and adventurous use of local ingredients at both the *Lighthouse*, 77 High St (☎01728/453377), and the *Regatta*, 171–173 High St (☎01728/452011; closed Mon & Tues through winter), each moderately priced and the latter open to the pavement in summer. For **drinks**, head for the *White Lion Hotel*, just along the seafront from the Moot Hall.

Southwold

Perched on more robust cliffs further north along the coast, **SOUTHWOLD** had, by the sixteenth century, overtaken all its local rivals. Its days as a busy fishing port are now long gone, though a small fleet still brings in herring, sprats and cod, and nowadays it's a genteel seaside resort, an eminently appealing little town with none of the crassness of many of its competitors. There are fine old buildings, a long sandy beach, open heathland, a dinky harbour and even a little industry – in the shape of the Adnams brewery – but no burger bars and certainly no amusement arcades. This gentility was not to the liking of George Orwell, who lived for a time at his parents' house at 36 High St (a plaque marks the house). Orwell heartily disliked the town's airs and graces, and has left no trace of his time here – apart from disguised slights in a couple of early novels.

Southwold's breezy High Street is framed by attractive, mainly Georgian buildings, which culminate in the pocket-sized Market Place. From here, it's a brief stroll along East Street to the curious **Sailors' Reading Room** (daily 9am–5pm; free), decked out with model ships and nautical texts, and the bluff above the **beach**, where row upon row of candy-coloured huts march across the sands. Queen Street begins at the Market Place too, quickly leading to **South Green**, the prettiest of several greens dotted across town. In 1659, a calamitous fire razed much of Southwold and when the town was rebuilt the greens were left to act as fire-brakes. Beyond, both Ferry Road and the Ferry Footpath lead down to the **harbour**, at the mouth of the River Blyth, an idyllic spot, where fishing smacks rest against old wooden jetties and nets are spread out along the banks to dry.

Back on the Market Place, it's a couple of hundred yards north along Church Street to East Green, with Adnams' Brewery on one side, the stumpy lighthouse on another. Close by is Southwold's architectural pride and joy, the **Church of St Edmund** (daily June–Aug 9am–6pm; Sept–May 9am–4pm; free), a handsome fifteenth-century structure whose solid symmetries are balanced by its long and elegantly carved windows. Inside, the slender, beautifully proportioned nave is distinguished by its panelled roof, embellished with praying angels, and its intricate rood screen. The latter carries paintings of the apostles and the prophets, though the Protestants defaced them during the Reformation. Beyond the screen, the choir stalls carry finely carved human and animal heads as well as grotesques – look out for the man in the throes of toothache.

Practicalities

With frequent services from other towns along the coast, Southwold is easy to reach by **bus**. These stop on the Market Place, opposite the **tourist office** (Easter–Sept Mon–Sat 10am–1pm & 1.45–5pm, Sun 11am–1.15pm & 1.45–4pm; ☎01502/724729), which has details of local attractions and sells walking maps. The town has two well-known **hotels** beside the Market Place, both owned and operated by Adnams. The smarter of the two is the *Swan* (☎01502/722186; ⑥), which occupies a splendid Georgian building with lovely period rooms, though the bedrooms – in the main house and in a garden annexe behind – are a little on the small side. The *Crown,* just along the High Street (☎01502/722275; ⑤), has just twelve simple bedrooms, nine of which are en suite. The best **B&B** in town is the delightful *Acton Lodge*, 18 South Green (☎01502/723217; no credit cards; ②), which occupies a grand Victorian house complete with its own neo-Gothic tower. The interior is decorated in period style and the three comfortable bedrooms are all en suite. Breakfasts are delicious, too. Alternatively, there's a string of **guesthouses** down along the seafront on North Parade: try the *North Parade*, at no. 21 (☎01502/722573; ②), a well-tended Victorian house with sprucely decorated bedrooms; or the attractive *Dunburgh*, at no. 28 (☎01502/723253; ③), housed in a rambling building with its own mini-tower.

Southwold has two outstanding **places to eat**. The *Crown*'s front bar provides superb informal meals, encompassing daily fish and meat specials combined with an enlightened wine list where all the choices are available by the glass. Turn up, wait for a table and expect to pay just £12 or so for two courses; you'll have to make a booking if you want to eat in the adjacent restaurant, which is pricier, slightly more adventurous and just as terrific. The *Swan*'s more formal dining room is the place for a gourmet blow-out, offering a choice of set dinners at £20–30 a head. For a **drink**, sample Adnams' brews in the *Crown*'s wood-panelled back bar or stroll along to the *Red Lion* on South Green.

Norwich

One of the five largest cities in Norman England, **NORWICH** once served a vast hinterland of cloth producers in the eastern counties, whose work was brought here by river and exported to the continent. Its isolated position beyond the Fens meant that it enjoyed closer links with the Low Countries than with the rest of England – it was, after all, quicker to cross the North Sea than to go cross-country to London. The local textile industry, based on worsted cloth (named after the nearby village of Worstead), was further enhanced by an influx of Flemish and Huguenot weavers, who made up more than a third of the population in Tudor times. By 1700, Norwich was the second richest city in the country after London.

With the onset of the Industrial Revolution, Norwich lost ground to the northern manufacturing towns – the city's famous mustard company, Colman's, is one of its few industrial success stories. This, and its continuing geographical isolation, has helped preserve many of the city's older buildings and much of its ancient street plan. It has also meant that the population has never swelled to any great extent and today, with just 130,000 inhabitants, Norwich remains an easy and enjoyable city to negotiate. Yet the city is no provincial backwater. In the 1960s, the foundation of the University of East Anglia (UEA) made Norwich more cosmopolitan and bolstered its arts scene, while in the 1980s it's attracted new high-tech companies, who created something of a mini-boom, making the city one of England's wealthiest. As East Anglia's unofficial capital, Norwich also lies at

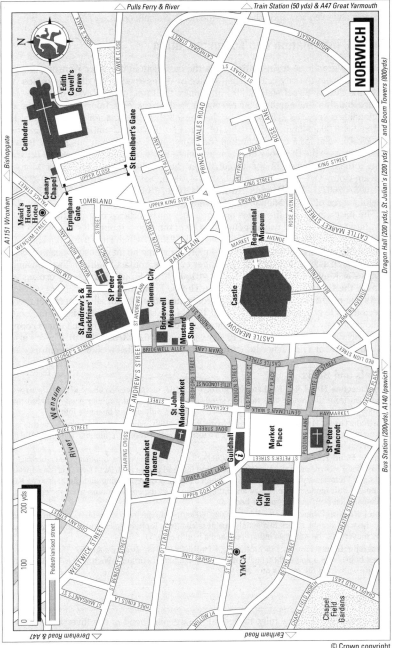

Pulls Ferry & River

Train Station (50 yds) & A47 Great Yarmouth

NORWICH

Dragon Hall (200 yds), St Julian's (200 yds) and Boom Towers (800 yds)

CATTLE MARKET STREET

Bus Station (200yds), A140 Ipswich

MOUNTERGATE

ST VEDAST ST

CATHEDRAL STREET

ROSE LANE

GREYFRIARS RD

ROSE AVENUE

KING STREET

KING STREET

CROWN ROAD

PRINCE OF WALES ROAD

ST FAITH'S LANE

UPPER KING STREET

BANK PLAIN

Edith Cavell's Grave

Cathedral

Bishopgate

St Ethelbert's Gate

LOWER CLOSE

DUKE'S WALK

UPPER CLOSE

Canary Chapel

Maid's Head Hotel

PALACE STREET

Erpingham Gate

TOMBLAND

WENSUM STREET

A1151 Wroxham

ELM HILL

WENSUM STREET

HOLL STREET

PRINCES STREET

QUEEN STREET

ST ANDREWS PLAIN

St Andrew's & Blackfriars' Hall

St Peter Hungate

Cinema City

Bridewell Museum

Mustard Shop

BRIDEWELL ALLEY

SWAN LANE

Castle

CASTLE MEADOW

Regimental Museum

Market

AVENUE

ROSE AVENUE

BELL AVENUE

FARMER'S AVENUE

ST GEORGE'S STREET

ST ANDREW'S STREET

EXCHANGE STREET

BEDFORD STREET

LITTLE LONDON ST

LONDON STREET

OLD POST OFFICE CT

DAVEY PLACE

ROYAL ARCADE

CASTLE STREET

WHITE LION STREET

RED LION STREET

ORFORD PLACE

GENTLEMAN'S WALK

St John Maddermarket

Maddermarket Theatre

DUKE STREET

CHARING CROSS

DOVE STREET

Guildhall

Market Place

HAYMARKET

St Peter Mancroft

PUDDING LANE

Wensum River

Pedestrianised street

200 yds

100

0

COSLANY STREET

WESTWICK STREET

ST BENEDICT'S STREET

ST MARGARET'S ST

THREE KINGS LA

WILLOW LA

CHAPEL FIELD NORTH

ST GILES STREET

FISHERS LANE

POTTERGATE

LOWER GOAT LANE

UPPER GOAT LANE

ST PETER'S STREET

City Hall

BETHEL STREET

THEATRE STREET

CHAPEL FIELD EAST

Chapel Field Gardens

YMCA

Dereham Road & A47

Earlham Road

© Crown copyright

the hub of the region's transport network and serves as a useful base for visiting the Broads, and even as a springboard for the north Norfolk coast.

Arrival, information and accommodation

Norwich's grandiose **train station** is on the east bank of the River Wensum, ten minutes' walk from the city centre along Prince of Wales Road. Long distance **buses** pull in at the Surrey Street station, also little more than ten minutes' walk from the town centre, but this time north via Surrey and St Stephen's streets. Information on local and regional bus services is provided by the Norfolk Bus Information Centre, 4 Goal Hill (Mon–Sat 8.30am–5pm; ☎0500/626116). The First Eastern Counties' Bus Ranger ticket (£5.50), valid for a day's unlimited travel on most East Anglian bus routes, is available here, as is the three-day ticket for unlimited travel on three days in seven (£13.50). The **tourist office** is in the Guildhall on the Market Place (June–Sept Mon–Sat 9.30am–5pm; Oct–May Mon–Fri 9.30am–4.30pm, Sat 9.30am–1pm & 1.30–4.30pm; ☎01603/666071). The **Broads Authority Office**, 18 Colegate (☎01603/610734), is a useful source of information for those heading for the Broads.

The best way to see the city is on foot – the tourist office's **city walking tour** (1hr 30min; £2.25) is a good way of getting the lie of the land – though it's also worth bearing in mind the **riverbus** (May–Sept, 3–4 daily; £1.50), which runs from Elm Hill to the Thorpe Road Quay, opposite the train station, providing an inexpensive means of cruising Norwich's central waterway. For longer **cruises**, contact Southern River Steamers (Easter & May–Sept daily; from £2.50; ☎01603/624051), which runs city cruises and trips to the Broads from Elm Hill and the Thorpe Road quay.

As you might expect, Norwich has **accommodation** to suit all budgets, but there's precious little in the town centre. Most **B&Bs** are strung along the Earlham Road, a tedious, mostly Victorian street running west towards UEA, which itself offers **rooms**, primarily during the summer and Easter vacations (☎01603/592092; ②). There's also a **youth hostel** at 112 Turner Rd (☎01603/627647), two miles west of the centre.

Hotels and B&Bs

The Beeches Hotel, 4–6 Earlham Rd (☎01603/621 167, *reception@beeches.co.uk*). Just across the ring road from the centre, this medium-sized hotel occupies a fully modernized Victorian townhouse. All 25 rooms are en suite and the place is popular with visiting business folk. ⑤.

Earlham Guest House, 147 Earlham Rd (☎01603/454169). Spick and span lodgings at this family-run guest house, located in a two-storey Victorian house a good ten minutes' walk from the centre. Seven bedrooms, each with a TV. ②.

Maid's Head Hotel, Tombland (☎01603/209955). Bang in the centre, opposite the cathedral, this smart hotel incorporates all sorts of architectural bits and pieces from Art Deco flourishes through to heavy Victorian-style wood panelling. The end result is quite pleasing and the bedrooms come complete with modern furnishings and fittings. The most expensive rooms have ancient beamed ceilings, open fires and four-poster beds. ⑥.

Hotel Nelson, Prince of Wales Rd (☎01603/760260). This modern, riverside hotel, directly opposite the train station, caters to a mainly business clientele. It offers spick and span rooms, some of which overlook the water, an indoor pool and a health club. ⑥.

Rosedale Guest House, 145 Earlham Rd (☎01603/453743, *drcbac@aol.com*). Typical Victorian guest house containing eight frugal but perfectly adequate bedrooms, each with a TV. A good ten-minute walk from the town centre. ①.

The City

Norwich is surprisingly hilly, tucked into a sweeping bend of the River Wensum, and with its irregular street plan, a Saxon legacy, orientation in the city can be confusing.

There are, however, some obvious landmarks to help you find your way: the cathedral with its giant spire, the Norman castle on its commanding mound and the distinctive clocktower of City Hall. The **Cathedral** and the **Castle** are the town's premier attractions and the latter also holds one of the region's most satisfying collections of fine art. Finally, note that **Sunday** can be a distastrous day to visit if you want to see anything other than the cathedral: most museums and attractions are closed, not to mention most restaurants.

The Cathedral

Norwich **Cathedral** (daily 7.30am–6pm; free tours June–Oct Mon–Sat; £2 donation requested) is distinguished by its prickly octagonal spire which rises to a height of 315ft, second only to Salisbury. It's best viewed from Bishopgate to the east, where the thick curves of the flying buttresses, the rounded excrescences of the ambulatory chapels – unusual in an English cathedral – and the straight symmetries of the main body can all be seen to perfection.

The **interior** is pleasantly light thanks to the pale pink stone and clear glass of much of the nave, where the thick pillars are a powerful legacy of the Norman builders who began the cathedral in 1096 for Bishop Herbert de Losinga. Look up to spy the nave's fan vaulting, delicate and geometrically precise carving adorned by several hundred roof **bosses** recounting – from east to west – the story of the Old and New Testaments. In **St Luke's Chapel**, on the ambulatory's east side, is the cathedral's finest work of art, the *Despenser Reredos*, a superb painted panel commissioned to celebrate the crushing of the Peasants' Revolt of 1381. Accessible from the south aisle of the nave are the cathedral's unique **cloisters**. Built between 1297 and 1310, and the only two-storey cloisters left standing in England, they contain a remarkable set of sculpted **bosses** depicting scenes from the Bible, similar to the ones in the main nave, but close enough to be scrutinized without binoculars.

Outside, beside the main entrance, stands the medieval **Canary Chapel**. This is the original building of Norwich School, whose blue-blazered pupils are often visible during term time – the rambling school buildings are next door. A statue of the school's most famous boy, Horatio Nelson, faces the chapel, standing on the green of the Upper Close, which is guarded by two ornate and imposing medieval gates, **Erpingham** and, a few yards to the south, **St Ethelbert**. These lead onto the old Saxon market place, **Tombland**, a wide and busy thoroughfare whose name derives from the Saxon word for an open space. The Upper Close itself is but a small part of the much larger **Cathedral Close**, which extends east to the river, covering around one-fifth of the old walled city. Crisscrossed by footpaths, the Close is a pleasant place for a stroll, beginning with the Upper Close and then the adjoining Lower Close, where a scattering of silver birches and cherry trees is flanked by an attractive terrace of Georgian buildings. Keeping straight, the footpath continues east to **Pull's Ferry**, a landing stage at the city's medieval watergate, named after the last ferryman to work this stretch of the river. It's the most picturesque spot in town and from here you can wander along the riverbank either south to the railway station or north to Bishopgate.

From Elm Hill to the Market Place

At the north end of Tombland, fork left at the Maid's Head Hotel and **Elm Hill**, more a gentle slope than a hill, will eventually appear on the left. As you pass along Elm Hill's cobbles, admiring the half-timbered houses which make it Norwich's most photographed spot – be sure to take a look at **Wright's Court**, down a passageway at no. 43, one of the few remaining enclosed courtyards which were once a feature of the street. At the far end Elm Hill opens out into a triangular space centred on a plane tree, planted on the spot where the eponymous elm tree from Henry VIII's time once stood.

Beyond, veering left up Elm Hill, you soon reach **St Peter Hungate** (April–Sept Mon–Sat 10am–5pm; free), a good-looking flint church dating from the fifteenth century and now a brass-rubbing centre and museum of church art. Turn right at the church and it's just a few yards to **St Andrew's Hall** and **Blackfriars Hall**, two adjoining buildings that were originally the nave and chancel, respectively, of a Dominican monastery church. Imaginatively recycled, the two halls are now used for a variety of public events, including concerts, weddings and antique fairs; the crypt of the former now serves as a café (closed Sun).

South of here, off St Andrew's Street and along Bridewell Alley, stands the **Bridewell Museum** (April–Sept Tues–Sat 10am–5pm; £1.30), one of the city's more enjoyable museums. Formerly the city jail, the Bridewell holds a pot-pourri of old machines, adverts, signs, and reconstructed shops celebrating Norwich's old trades and industry. Inevitably, there's much on the all-important mustard industry and there's even more just up the alley at no. 3, where the Colman's-run **Mustard Shop** (closed Sun) sells all sorts of unlikely permutations on the basic mustard theme.

From the top of Bridewell Alley, Bedford Street and then Pottergate lead west to **St John Maddermarket** (June–Sept Wed–Fri 10am–4pm), one of thirty medieval churches standing within the boundaries of the old city walls. Most are redundant and are rarely open to the public, but this is one of the more accessible, courtesy of a dedicated volunteer. St John is a good example of the Perpendicular style. Apart from the stone trimmings, the church is almost entirely composed of flint rubble, the traditional building material of east Norfolk, an area chronically short of decent stone. By comparison, the interior is something of a disappointment, its furnishings and fittings thoroughly remodelled at the start of the twentieth century.

From Pottergate, several narrow alleys lead to the city's **Market Place**, site of one of the country's largest open-air markets (closed Sun), with stalls selling everything from bargain-basement clothes to local mussels and whelks. Three very different but equally distinctive buildings oversee the market's stripy awnings, the oldest of them being the fifteenth-century **Guildhall**, an attractive flint and stone structure that now houses the tourist office. Opposite, commanding the heights of the market place, is the austere **City Hall**, a lumbering brick pile with a landmark clocktower built in the 1930s in a Scandinavian style – it bears a striking resemblance to the city hall in Oslo. On the south side is the finest of the three buildings, **St Peter Mancroft** (Mon–Fri 9.30am–4.30pm, Sat 10am–12.30pm), whose long and graceful nave leads to a mighty stone tower, an intricately carved affair surmounted by a spiky little spire. Just below the church is the bubble-gum-pink **Sir Garnet Wolseley** pub, sole survivor of the 44 ale houses that once crowded the Market Place – and stirred the local bourgeoisie into endless discussions about the drunken fecklessness of the working class. Opposite the pub, across **Gentlemen's Walk**, the town's main promenade, which runs along the bottom of the market place, is the brightly painted **Royal Arcade**, an Art Nouveau extravagance from 1899. The arcade has been beautifully restored to reveal the swirl and blob of the tiling, ironwork and stained glass, though it's actually the eastern entrance, further from the Walk, which is the most appealing section.

The Castle

High on a mound in the centre of town above an incongruous modern shopping mall, stands the twelfth-century **Castle Keep** (Mon–Sat 10am–5pm, Sun 2–5pm; July–Sept £3.40, Oct–June £2.50, includes entry to Regimental Museum) replete with blind arcading, an unusually decorative touch on a military structure. You can join a guided tour (an extra £2) of the battlements and dungeons (the castle served as the county jail for over six hundred years), or simply wander at will around the museum and art gallery inside. The latter contains a selection of work by the early nineteenth-century **Norwich School** of landscape painters, whose leading lights were John Sell Cotman and John Crome.

A long and dark (and one-way) tunnel leads down from the Castle Museum to the **Royal Norfolk Regimental Museum** (same times as castle), which tracks through the history of the regiment with remarkable candour – there's even an even-handed account of the Norfolks' peace-keeping role in Northern Ireland. The exit leaves you below the castle on Market Avenue.

King Street and the river

Behind the castle, **King Street** possesses one or two surprises, beginning with the **Dragon Hall**, at no. 115–123 (April–Oct Mon–Sat 10am–4pm; Nov–March Mon–Fri 10am–4pm; £1.50), an extraordinarily long, half-timbered showroom built for the cloth merchant Robert Toppes in the fifteenth century. Bowed and bent by age, you get a good impression of the building from the outside, but enthusiasts can pop in to have a closer look at the roof – there's nothing else to see. A right turn opposite the hall up St Julian's Alley leads to **St Julian's Church** (daily 7am–6pm; free) and an adjoining monastic cell, thatched and standing in open countryside as late as the mid-nineteenth century. One of the smallest of the city's religious foundations, this was the retreat of St Julian, a Norwich woman who took to living here after experiencing visions of Christ in 1373. Her mystical *Revelations of Divine Love* – written after twenty years' meditation on her visions – was the first widely distributed book written by a woman in the English language, and has been in print ever since.

Still further down King Street, at Carrow Bridge near the football ground, are the ruins of two medieval **boom towers**, which formed part of the city's defences. From here, a **riverside walk** – initially on the east bank – follows the Wensum around the city centre to Bishopgate, switching to the inner (west) bank at Foundry Bridge, beside the train station. The walk is at its most appealing between Pull's Ferry (see p.379) and **Cow Tower**, a 50-foot-high watchtower where the bishop's retainers collected river tolls. This is one of the few survivors of Norwich's **fortified walls** which once stretched for over two miles, surrounding the city and incorporating thirty such circular towers and ten defensive gates. Up until the 1790s, the gates were closed at dusk and all day on Sundays.

The University

The **University of East Anglia** (UEA) occupies a sprawling campus on the western outskirts of the city. Its buildings are resolutely modern concrete-and-glass blocks of varying designs – some quite ordinary, others, like the prize-winning "ziggurat" halls of residence designed by Denys Lasdun, eminently memorable. The high-tech **Sainsbury Centre for Visual Arts** (Tues–Sun 11am–5pm; £2) is an amazing piece of architectural art built by Norman Foster in 1978. The hangar-like interior houses one of the most unusual collections of sculpture and painting in the country, donated by the family which owns the Sainsbury supermarket chain, in which the likes of Giacometti, Bacon and Henry Moore rub shoulders with Mayan and Egyptian antiquities. The centre also runs a first-rate programme of temporary exhibitions (call ☎01603/593199 for further details). **Buses** #26, #27 and #35 run to the UEA from the railway station and Castle Meadow.

Cafés and restaurants

Adlard's, 79 Upper Giles St (☎01603/633522). Engaging Modern-British restaurant with accomplished seasonal cooking. Closed all Sun & Mon lunch. Expensive.

The Last Wine Bar, 72 St George's St (☎01603/626626). Converted factory building holding a smart wine bar, which serves up tasty bistro-style dishes. A couple of minutes' walk north of the river. Closed Sun. Moderate.

Pinocchio's, 11 St Benedict St (☎01603/613318). Relaxed Italian restaurant with inventive food combinations and featuring live music a couple of times a week. Occupies a pleasantly converted old general store. Closed Sun. Moderate.

Pizza Express, 15 St Benedict's St. No surprises, of course, on the menu, but you get the city centre's best pizzas. Inexpensive.

St Andrew's Hall Crypt Coffee Bar, St Andrew's Plain at St George's St. Very cheap spot for budget meals or just a coffee and cake. Closes 4.30pm & all Sun. Inexpensive.

Take 5, at Cinema City, St Andrew's Plain. Imaginative, budget bistro food served in amenable surroundings. There's courtyard seating and a friendly bar, too. Closed Sun. Inexpensive.

Tree House, 14 Dove St, above the Rainbow wholefood shop. Vegetarian wholefood café-restaurant offering a daily changing menu of soups, salads and main courses, plus organic wines and beers. Closed Sun. Inexpensive.

Pubs, bars and clubs

Adam & Eve, Bishopgate. There's been a pub on this site for seven hundred years and it's still the top spot in town for the discerning drinker – with a changing range of real ales and an eclectic wine list supplied by Adnams.

Coach & Horses, Bethel St. Pleasant city-centre pub – across the street from City Hall – with lived-in furnishings and fittings. Good for a quiet drink.

Fat Cat, 49 West End St. Award-winning real-ale pub, twenty minutes' walk west of the centre, down the Dereham Road. Lots of great beer in traditional surroundings.

Waterfront, 139–41 King's St (☎01603/632717). Norwich's principal club and alternative music venue, with gigs and DJs most nights. Sponsored by UEA.

Entertainment

Predictably, Norwich has its fair share of multi-screen **cinemas** showing Hollywood blockbusters, but it also has the art-house Cinema City, in Suckling House on St Andrew's Plain (☎01603/622047). For **theatre**, there's the mainstream Theatre Royal, on Theatre Street (☎01603/630000), while the Maddermarket, St John's Alley, off Pottergate (☎01603/620917), offers an interesting programme of modern plays. There's also the Norwich Arts Centre, Reeves Yard, off St Benedict's Street (☎01603/660352), which hosts a **jazz festival** in the last two weeks of November and features an eclectic year-round programme of cultural events, with everything from acid-jazz to small-scale theatre. Predictably enough, **UEA** is a major source of entertainment for students and locals alike, with gigs at the Union and classical concerts at the Music Centre. The annual **Norfolk and Norwich Festival** each October (call the Ticket Shop ☎01603/764764 for details) features music, film, theatre, comedy, dance, walks and talks at venues all over the city.

The Norfolk Broads

Three rivers – the Yare, Waveney and Bure – meander across the flatlands to the east of Norwich, converging on Breydon Water before flowing into the sea at Great Yarmouth. In places these rivers swell into wide expanses of water known as "broads", which for years were thought to be natural lakes. In fact they're the result of extensive peat cutting, several centuries of accumulated diggings made in a region where wood was scarce and peat a valuable source of energy. The pits flooded when sea levels rose in the thirteenth and fourteenth centuries to create the **Norfolk Broads**, now one of the most important wetlands in Europe – a haven for such species as swallowtail butterflies, kingfishers, great crested grebes and Cetti's warblers – and the county's major tourist attraction.

The Broads' delicate ecological balance suffered badly during the 1970s and 1980s. The careless use of fertilizers poisoned the water with phosphates and nitrates, encouraging the spread of algae; the decline in reed cutting – previously in great demand for thatching – made the Broads partly unnavigable; while the enormous increase in pleasure-boat traffic began to erode the banks. National Park status was, however, accorded to the area in 1988, and efforts are now under way to clear the waters and protect the ecosystem. Co-ordinating the clean-up is the **Broads Authority**, which maintains a series of information centres throughout the region. At any of these locations, you can pick up a free copy of the *Broadcaster*, a useful newspaper guide to the Broads as a whole.

The region is crossed by several **train** lines, with connections from Norwich to Wroxham, Acle and Reedham, as well as Berney Arms, near Breydon Water, one of the few places in England that can be reached by rail but not road. The best – really the only – way to see the Broads themselves is **by boat**, and you could happily spend a week or so exploring the 125 miles of lock-free navigable waterways, visiting the various churches, pubs and windmills en route. Among many **boat rental** companies, two of the more established are Blakes Holidays (☎01603/784458) and Broads Tours Ltd (☎01603/782207), both of whom operate out of Wroxham (see below). Prices start at £600 a week for four people in peak season, but less expensive, short-term rentals are widely available, too.

Trying to explore the Broads by car is – as you might imagine – pretty much a waste of time, but cyclists and walkers have a much better time, taking advantage of the region's network of footpaths and cycling trails. There are eight Broads Authority **bike rental** points dotted round the Broads (£8 per day; ☎01603/782281). **Walkers** should head for the 56-mile Weavers' Way, a long-distance footpath that winds through the best parts of the Broads on its way from Cromer to Great Yarmouth. The easiest boating centre to reach from Norwich is **WROXHAM**, accessible by train, bus and car. Seven miles northeast of the city, the village itself is short on charm, but it has a useful **information centre**, on Station Road (Easter–Oct daily 9am–1pm & 2–5pm; ☎01603/782281), and plenty of places where you can stock up with food before heading out on a cruise.

Five miles east of Wroxham, the village of **LUDHAM** straggles along the roadside at the tip of Womack Water, an offshoot of the River Thurne. Just north of the village is How Hill, where the Broads Authority maintain **Toad Hole Cottage** (daily: Easter–May & Oct 11am–5pm, June–Sept 10am–5pm; free), an old eel catcher's cottage housing a small exhibit on the history of the trade, which was common hereabouts until the 1940s. Behind the cottage is the narrow River Ant where there are hour-long boat trips in the *Electric Eel* (Easter–May & Oct Sat & Sun 11am–3pm, June–Sept daily 10am–5pm; £2.50; reservations advised, call ☎01692/678763) to view the wildlife. **Bus** #54 runs to Ludham from Norwich.

A couple of miles east of Ludham, **POTTER HEIGHAM** is the nominal capital of the Broads, taking its name from the pottery which once stood here on the River Thurne and from the Saxon lord of Heacham who founded the first settlement. Again, there's not much to keep your attention, though you can watch boaters struggling with the village's fourteenth-century bridge, regarded as one of the most difficult passages in the Broads. All the major boat rental companies have outlets here and there's also an **information centre** (Easter–Oct daily 9am–1pm & 2–5pm; ☎01692/670779). The only public transport to Potter Heigham is by bus from Great Yarmouth.

Great Yarmouth

First and foremost, **GREAT YARMOUTH** is a seaside resort, its promenade a parade of amusement arcades and rainy-day attractions, deserted in winter, heaving in summer.

But it's also a port with a long history and, despite extensive wartime bomb damage, it retains a handful of sights that give some idea of the place Daniel Defoe thought "far superior to Norwich".

Yarmouth was a major trading port by the fourteenth century, its economy underpinned by its control of the waterways leading inland to Norwich. It also benefited from fishing, especially during the nineteenth century when there was a spectacular boom in the herring industry. The fishing finally fizzled out in the 1960s, but the town was saved by the timely discovery of gas and oil deposits off the Norfolk coast, and these have since made it a major base for the offshore gas industry, second only to Aberdeen for North Sea oil.

Arriving by train or car from Norwich, initial impressions are favourable thanks to the appealing silhouette of the church of **St Nicholas**, which boasts one of the widest naves in the country and, consequently, an impressive west front. The church stands at the northern end of the broad market place, centre of what was medieval Yarmouth, but now mostly undistinguished. The one exception is the **Hospital for Decayed Fishermen**, founded in 1702, which opens out into a lovely little courtyard flanked by Dutch gables, its central cupola topped by a chilly-looking statue of the fishermen's friend himself, St Peter. Next to the hospital is Sewell House, the childhood home of Anna Sewell, author of *Black Beauty*.

Despite considerable wartime damage, sections of the **medieval walls** remain, with one of the best-preserved portions located along Ferrier Road, just north of St Nicholas. Other interesting features of the old town are the narrow parallel alleys, known locally as "rows", which used to link the River Yare with the seashore. Sixty-nine have survived, and at the **Old Merchant's House** in Row 117 (Easter–Oct daily 10am–5pm; £1.75; EH), three blocks west of the town hall along South Quay, you can join up with one of English Heritage's guided tours of several of them.

The vast majority of tourists simply head for the Victorian-built seafront, **Marine Parade**, whose wide sandy beach was the unlikely setting for many of the most dramatic events in Dickens's *David Copperfield*. There are the usual promenade gardens and seafront attractions here, bolstered by the presence of the town's **Maritime Museum** (June–Sept Mon–Fri & Sun 10am–5pm), which traces the history of the herring industry and the inland waterways. Great Yarmouth also shares the last steam herring-drifter, the 1930s *Lydia Eva*, and when it's here you'll find it berthed on South Quay.

Practicalities

It's a good ten-minute walk east from Great Yarmouth's **train station** to the central market place – cross the river by the footbridge and you'll find yourself on North Quay from where The Conge leads straight there. **Buses** terminate one block from the sea on Wellesley Road. There are two **tourist offices**: one in the town hall, on South Quay (Mon–Fri 9am–5pm; ☎01493/846345), and a seasonal office on Marine Parade (June–Sept Mon–Sat 9.30am–5.30pm, Sun 10am–5pm; April & May daily 10am–1pm & 2–5pm; ☎01493/842195). There's also a useful **Broads Information Centre** in the North West Tower, North Quay (July–Sept daily 10am–4pm; ☎01493/332095).

B&Bs line every street, with price a fair indication of quality, but if you don't have much luck, call in at the tourist office for assistance. Among many, the Willow Guest House, 26 Trafalgar Rd (☎01493/332355; ①), offers sea views from several of its ten bedrooms, while Senglea Lodge, 7 Euston Rd (☎01493/859632; ①), is a cosy, well-maintained terrace house with seven pleasant bedrooms a short walk from Marine Parade. For a **hotel**, try the Royal, 4 Marine Parade (☎01493/844215; ③), arguably Yarmouth's grandest – and where Dickens stayed. Yarmouth's **youth hostel** is in a large Victorian house near the bus station at 2 Sandown Rd (☎01493/843991; closed Sept–March).

Far and away the best **restaurant** in town is the reasonably priced *Seafood Restaurant*, 85 North Quay (☎01493/856 009; closed Sun), which does a superb fish soup and Mediterranean-influenced seafood dishes.

The north Norfolk coast

For thirty miles beyond Yarmouth, there are no estuaries, harbours and very little in the way of habitation along the **north Norfolk coast**. The first place of any note is **Cromer**, a down-at-heel seaside town whose bleak and blustery cliffs have drawn tourists for over a century. A few miles to the west is another well-established resort, **Sheringham**, but thereafter the shoreline becomes a ragged patchwork of salt marshes, dunes and shingle spits which form an almost unbroken series of nature reserves, supporting a fascinating range of flora and fauna. It's a lovely stretch of coast and the villages bordering it, principally **Cley-next-the-Sea**, **Blakeney** and **Wells** are prime targets for an overnight stay. The other major attraction along this northern stretch of the coast is the large number of stately homes a short distance inland – some, like **Felbrigg** and **Holkham Hall**, among the finest in the region.

Cromer and Sheringham are the only places connected by **train**, with an hourly service from Norwich on the Bittern Line. Local **bus** services fill in the gaps, connecting most of the towns and villages. There's also the **Coastliner bus** (June–Sept Tues–Fri & Sun; ☎0500/626116), which provides regular services along the whole length of the coast from Cromer to Hunstanton, with some buses continuing to Great Yarmouth, King's Lynn and Sandringham. The Norfolk Coast Rover ticket (£3.50) gives a day's unlimited travel on the route. For **walkers**, there's also the **Norfolk Coast Path**, which runs from Hunstanton to Cromer (where it joins the Weavers' Way), an exhilarating route through the dunes and salt marshes; a National Trail Guide covers the route in detail, otherwise you'll need OS Landranger maps 132 and 133.

Cromer and around

Dramatically poised on a high bluff, **CROMER** should be the most memorable of the Norfolk coastal resorts, but its fine aspect is undermined by a dispiriting shabbiness in the streets and shopfronts – an "atrophied charm" as Paul Theroux called it. The tower of **St Peter and St Paul**, at 160ft the tallest in Norfolk, attests to the port's medieval wealth, but it was the advent of the railway in the 1880s that heralded the most frenetic flurry of building activity. A bevy of grand Edwardian hotels was constructed along the seafront and for a moment Cromer became the most fashionable of resorts, but the gloss soon wore off and only the seen-better-days **Hotel de Paris** has survived. A small fleet of crab boats resting on the beach with their attendant tractors is all that remains of the town's traditional industry. Cromer's **pier** was badly damaged in a storm in November 1993, but has since been repaired and struggles gamely on.

Somewhat miraculously Cromer has managed to retain its rail link with Norwich; the **train station** is a five-minute walk west of the centre. **Buses** terminate on Cadogan Road, next to the **tourist office** (daily: Easter–Oct 10am–5pm; Nov–March 10am–1pm & 1.30–4pm; ☎01263/512497), which is just 200 yards from the cliff-top promenade. An hour or two in Cromer is probably enough, though the beach is first-rate and the cliff-top walk exhilarating. There's no shortage of inexpensive **accommodation** – the tourist office has all the details.

Felbrigg Hall

Just a couple of miles southwest of Cromer off the A148, **Felbrigg Hall** (April–Oct Mon–Wed, Sat & Sun 1–5pm; £5.50; NT) is a charming Jacobean mansion. The main

facade is particularly appealing, the soft hues of the ageing limestone and brick inter-
cepted by three bay windows which together sport a large, cleverly carved inscription
– *Gloria Deo in Excelsis* – in celebration of the reviving fortunes of the family who then
owned the place, the Windhams. The interior is splendid too, with the studied informality of both the dining room and the drawing room enlivened by some magnificent
seventeenth-century plasterwork ceilings and sundry *objets d'art*. Many of the paintings in the hall were purchased by William Windham II, who did his Grand Tour in the
1740s.

The surrounding **parkland** (daily dawn to dusk) divides into two, with woods to the
north and open pasture to the south. Footpaths crisscross the park – a popular spot to
head for is the medieval church of **St Margaret's** in the southeastern corner, which
contains a fine set of brasses and a fancy memorial to William Windham I and his wife
by Grinling Gibbons. Nearer the house, there's the extensive **walled garden**, which
features flowering borders and an octagonal dove house, and the stables, which have
been converted into very pleasant **tearooms**.

Blickling Hall

Blickling Hall (April–Oct Tues & Wed–Sun 1–4.30pm; house & gardens £6.20; gardens only £3.50; NT), set in a sheltered, wooded valley ten miles south of Cromer, is
another grand Jacobean pile. Built for Sir Henry Hobart, a Lord Chief Justice, the hall
dates from the 1620s and although it was extensively remodelled over a century later,
the modifications respected the integrity of the earlier design. Consequently, the long
facade, with its slender chimneys, high gables and towers, is the apotheosis of Jacobean
design. Inside, highlights include a superb plasterwork ceiling in the Long Gallery and
an extraordinarily grand main staircase. There's also a gargantuan tapestry depicting
Peter the Great defeating the Swedes, given to one of the family by Catherine the Great.

The surrounding **parkland** (daily dawn to dusk) incorporates a mile-long lake and a
weird pyramidal mausoleum holding the earthly remains of the last of the male
Hobarts.

Sheringham

SHERINGHAM, a popular seaside town four miles west of Cromer, has an amiable,
easy-going air and makes a reasonable overnight stop, though frankly you're still only
marking time until you hit the more appealing places further west. One of the distinctive features of the town is the smooth local beach pebbles that face and decorate the
houses, a flinting technique used frequently in this part of Norfolk – the best examples
here are off the High Street. The downside is that the power of the waves which makes
the pebbles smooth has also forced the local council to spend thousands rebuilding the
sea defences. The resultant mass of reinforced concrete makes for a less than pleasing
seafront – all the more reason to head, instead, for **Sheringham Park**, the 770-acre
woodland park a couple of miles southwest of the town, laid out by Humphrey Repton
in the early 1800s. The park boasts a wonderful array of rhododendrons and azaleas, at
their best in late May to early June, and a series of look-out posts from which you can
admire the view down to the coast. The other out-of-town jaunt is on the **North
Norfolk Railway**, whose steam trains operate along the five miles of track from
Sheringham to the modest market town of Holt (June–Sept daily; all-day ticket £6.50;
☎01263/822045).

Sheringham's two **train stations** are opposite each other on either side of Station
Road. The main station, the terminus of the Bittern Line from Norwich, is just to the
east, the North Norfolk Railway station to the west. The **tourist office** (Easter–Oct
Mon–Sat 10am–5pm, Sun 10am–4pm; ☎01263/824329) is in between them on Railway
Approach. From the tourist office, it's a five-minute walk north to the seafront, straight

down Station Road and its continuation, the High Street. You can rent **bikes** from Bike Riders, 7 St Peter's Rd (☎01263/821906), adjacent to the North Norfolk Railway station.

There are plenty of **B&B** options, with one of the best being *Oak Lodge* at 2 Morris St (☎01263/823158; ②), a smart Edwardian house with four attractive bedrooms right in the centre of town. A good alternative is the *Two Lifeboats*, 2 High St (☎01263/822401; ②), a small hotel on the promenade offering sea views from most of its bedrooms. The **youth hostel** is a short walk south of the main train station at 1 Cremer's Drift (☎01263/823215), set in its own grounds just off the Cromer road. The *Two Lifeboats* serves inexpensive **bar meals** and more formal dinners in its **restaurant**, and prides itself on its fresh fish.

Cley-next-the-Sea and Blakeney Point

Travelling west from Sheringham, the A149 meanders through a pretty rural landscape offering occasional glimpses of the sea and a shoreline protected by a giant shingle barrier erected after the catastrophic flood of 1953, a disaster which claimed over a thousand lives. After seven miles you reach **CLEY-NEXT-THE-SEA**, once a busy wool port but now little more than a row of flint cottages and Georgian mansions set beside a narrow, marshy inlet that (just) gives access to the sea. The original village was destroyed in a fire in 1612, which explains why Cley's fine medieval **Church of St Margaret** is located half a mile inland at the very southern edge of the current village, overlooking the green. The Black Death brought church construction to a sudden halt, hence the contrast between the stunted, unfinished chancel and the splendid nave, which boasts several fine medieval brasses and some folksy fifteenth-century bench ends depicting animals and grotesques. Cley's other great draw – housed in an old forge on the main street – is the excellent Cley Smoke House, selling local smoked fish and other delicacies, while nearby Picnic Fayre has long been one of the finest delis in East Anglia.

It's about 400 yards east from the village to the mile-long byroad that leads to the shingle mounds of **Cley beach**. This is the starting point for the four-mile hike west out along the spit to **Blakeney Point**, a nature reserve famed for its colonies of terns and seals. The seal colony is made up of around four hundred common and grey seals and the old lifeboat house, at the end of the spit, is now a National Trust information centre. The shifting shingle can, however, make the going difficult, so keep to the low-water mark – which also means that you won't accidentally trample any nests. The easier alternative is to take one of the boat trips to the point from Blakeney or Morston (see below). The Norfolk Coast Path passes close to the beach too, continuing south along the edge of the **Cley Marshes**, which attract a bewildering variety of waders – and, of course, "twitchers".

Cley has several great places **to stay**, beginning with the *Cley Mill B&B* (☎01263/740209; ③) housed in a converted windmill complete with sails and a balcony offering wonderful views over the surrounding salt marshes and seashore. Other options in the village include the attractive *Whalebone House*, on the main street (☎01263/740336; ②), and the *Three Swallows* pub (☎01263/740526; ②) on the green by the church, which has several pleasant en-suite rooms and serves good **food**.

Blakeney

BLAKENEY is delightful. Once a bustling port exporting fish, corn and salt, it's now a dreamy little place of pebble-covered cottages sloping up from a narrow harbour just a mile west of Cley. Crab sandwiches are sold from stalls at the quayside, the meandering high street is flanked by family-run shops, and footpaths stretch out along the sea wall to east and west, allowing long, lingering looks over the salt marshes. The only sight as such is the **Church of St Nicholas**, beside the A149 at the south end of the village, whose sturdy tower and nave are made of flint rubble with stone trimmings, the traditional building materials of north Norfolk. Curiously, the church has a second, much smaller tower at the back. In the nineteenth century this was used as a lighthouse to guide ships into harbour, but its original function is unknown. Inside, the oak and chestnut hammer-beam roof and the delicate rood screen are the most enjoyable features of the nave, which is attached to a late thirteenth-century chancel, the only survivor from the original Carmelite friary church.

Blakeney **harbour** is linked to the sea by a narrow channel, which pierces its way through the salt marshes. The channel is, however, only navigable for a few hours at high tide – at low tide the harbour is no more than a muddy creek. Depending on the tides, there are **boat trips** from Blakeney or Morston quay, a mile or two to the west, to Blakeney Point; as well as the two-hour round trips which land passengers at the National Trust information centre on Blakeney Point (see p.387) there are also hourlong seal-watching trips. The main operators advertise departure times on blackboards by the quayside.

For **accommodation**, the quayside *Blakeney Hotel* (☎01263/740797; ②) is one of the most charming hotels in Norfolk, a rambling building with high-pitched gables and pebble-covered walls. The hotel has a heated indoor swimming pool, a secluded garden, cosy lounges decorated in soft pastel colours, sea views and serves excellent food. The cheaper rooms can be poky and somewhat airless, but you can pay a little more to get a room with splendid views across the harbour and the marshes. There are discounts for longer stays with full board. A very good alternative is the *Manor Hotel* (☎01263/740376; ④), which occupies a low-lying courtyard complex a few yards to the east of the harbour; or the *King's Arms*, just back from the quay on Westgate (☎01263/740341; ③), a traditional pub, with low, beamed ceilings and seven pleasant en-suite bedrooms, that also serves up excellent, reasonably priced **bar food**. For longer stays, contact *Blakeney Cottage Holidays* (☎01692/405188), who rent some super local cottages – there's an office halfway up the High Street.

Wells-next-the-Sea and around

Despite its name, **WELLS-NEXT-THE-SEA** is situated a good mile or so from open water. In Tudor times, when it enjoyed much easier access to the sea, it was one of the great ports of eastern England, a major player in the trade with the Netherlands. It's still one of the more attractive towns on the north Norfolk coast, and the only one to remain a commercially viable port. There's nothing specific to see among its narrow lanes, but it makes a very good base for exploring the surrounding coastline.

The town divides into three distinct areas, starting with the broad rectangular green to the south, lined with oak and beech trees and some very fine Georgian houses, and known as **The Buttlands** since the days when it was used for archery practice. North from here, across Station Road, are the narrow lanes of the town centre with **Staithe Street**, the tiny main drag, flanked by quaint old-fashioned shops. At the bottom end of Staithe Street stands the **quay**, a slightly forlorn affair inhabited by a couple of amusement arcades and fish-and-chip shops. A few yards away is the mile-long road to the **beach**, a handsome sandy tract backed by pine-clad dunes. The road is shadowed by a high flood defence and a tiny narrow-gauge railway, which scoots down to the beach every forty minutes or so during the season.

Buses to Wells stop on the Buttlands, a short stroll from the **tourist office** at the foot of Staithe Street (March to mid-July, Sept & Oct Mon–Sat 10am–5pm, Sun 10am–4pm; mid-July to Aug Mon–Sat 9.30am–7pm, Sun 9.30am–6pm; ☎01328/710885). Several of the best **guest houses** are along Standard Road, which runs up from the eastern end of the quayside. First choice should be the elegant *Normans* (☎01328/710657; ②), whose seven spacious and tastefully decorated rooms are all en suite; the TV lounge has a log fire and racks of games and the first-floor look-out window provides a wide view over the marshes – binoculars are provided. Other options include *Mill House*, a dignified old millowner's home on Northfield Lane (☎01328/710739; ①), and *Ilex House* on Bases Lane (☎01328/710556; ②); the latter is a good-looking Georgian villa sitting in its own grounds, just to the west of the centre. There's also a **campsite**, the sprawling Pinewoods Caravan and Camping Park, by the beach (☎01328/710439; closed Nov to mid-March).

Wells' best **restaurant** is the *Moorings*, by the quay on Freeman Street (☎01328/710949), which offers unusual and beautifully prepared dishes (local fish a speciality) at moderate prices. *Nelson's*, 21 Staithe St, is a tea and coffee shop which serves inexpensive meals. For **pub** food, head straight for the *Crown* on the Buttlands, the best pub in town.

Holkham Hall

One of the most popular outings from Wells is to **Holkham Hall** (June–Sept Mon–Thurs & Sun 1–5pm; £4), three miles to the west and a stop on the Coastliner bus (see p.385). This grand and self-assured stately home was designed by the eighteenth-century architect William Kent for the first Earl of Leicester and is still owned by the family. The severe sandy-coloured Palladian exterior belies the warmth and richness of the interior, which retains much of its original decoration, notably the much-admired marble hall, with its fluted columns and intricate reliefs. The rich colours of the state rooms are an appropriate backdrop for a fabulous selection of **paintings**, including canvases by Van Dyck, Rubens, Gainsborough and Gaspar Poussin. One real treat is the Landscape Room where around twenty landscape paintings are displayed in the cabinet style of the eighteenth century. Most depict classical stories or landscapes, a poetic view of the past that enthralled the English aristocracy for decades.

The **grounds** are laid out on sandy, saline land, much of it originally salt marsh. The focal point is an eighty-foot-high obelisk, atop a grassy knoll, from where you can view both the hall to the north and the triumphal arch to the south. In common with the rest of the north Norfolk coast, there's plenty of **birdlife** to observe in and around the park – Holkham's lake attracts Canada geese, heron and grebes and several hundred deer graze the open pastures.

A footpath leads north from the estate across the marshes to **Holkham Bay**, where one of the finest sandy beaches on this stretch of coast is fringed by pine-studded sand dunes. Waders inhabit the mud and salt flats, while farther inland you can see warblers, flycatchers and redstarts.

Burnham Market and Burnham Thorpe

A quick diversion off the A149 five miles west of Wells puts you in the picturesque village of **BURNHAM MARKET**, whose Georgian houses are ranged around an appealing green. The target here is the *Hoste Arms* (☎01328/738777; ⑤), an old coaching inn which offers some of the best restaurant and bar food on the coast – and attracts a well-heeled crew to match.

A mile or so to the east, **BURNHAM THORPE** was the birthplace of **Horatio Nelson**, who was born in the parsonage on September 29, 1758. Nelson joined the navy at the tender age of twelve, and was sent to the West Indies, where he met and married Frances Nisbet, retiring to Burnham Thorpe in 1787. Back in action by 1793, his bravery cost him first the sight of his right eye, and shortly afterwards his right arm. His personal life was equally eventful – famously, his infatuation with Emma Hamilton, wife of the ambassador to Naples, caused the eventual break-up of his marriage. His finest hour was during the Battle of Trafalgar in 1805, when he led the British navy to victory against the combined French and Spanish fleet, a crucial engagement that set the scene for Britain's century-long domination of the high seas. The victory, as everyone knows, didn't do Nelson much good – he was shot in the chest during the battle and even the kisses of Hardy failed to revive him.

The parsonage was demolished years ago, but Nelson is celebrated in the **All Saints Parish Church**, where the lectern is made out of timbers taken from the *Victory*, the chancel sports a Nelson bust, and the south aisle has a small exhibition on his life. It was actually Nelson's express wish that he should be buried here, but instead he was laid in state at Greenwich and then buried at St Paul's. The other place to head for here is the **village pub** (no prizes for guessing the name) where Nelson held a farewell party for the locals in 1793.

Hunstanton

The Norfolk coast pretty much ends at **HUNSTANTON**, a Victorian seaside resort that grew up to the southwest of the original fishing village. Like Yarmouth, it has its fair share of amusement arcades, crazy golf, and entertainment complexes, but it has also hung on to its genteel origins – and its sandy beaches, backed by stripy gateau-like cliffs, are among the cleanest in Norfolk. Incidentally, in "The World of Fun" on Greevegate, Hunstanton possesses the self-proclaimed largest joke shop in Britain with more whoopee cushions and Dracula fangs than even the most unpleasant ten-year-old could want.

The **tourist office** is in the town hall (daily: April–Sept 9.30am–5pm; Oct–March 10.30am–4pm; ☎01485/532610) on the wide sloping green, the focal point of the town, and can help out with **accommodation**, though it's easy enough to find. The nicest and priciest places, like *Le Strange Arms* (☎01485/534411; ⑤), whose gardens run down to the beach, are to be found among the cottages of Old Hunstanton, a mile northeast of the town centre. At the other end of the market, the **youth hostel** occupies a Victorian townhouse at 15 Avenue Rd (☎01485/532061; closed Nov–March) south of the green.

King's Lynn and around

An ancient port built on an improbably marshy location, **KING'S LYNN** straddles the mouth of the Great Ouse, a mile or so before it flows into the Wash. Strategically placed for easy access to seven English counties, the merchants of Lynn grew rich importing fish from Scandinavia, timber from the Baltic and wine from France, while exporting wool, salt and corn to the Hanseatic ports. The town stagnated when the focus of maritime trade moved to the Atlantic seaboard, but its port facilities have been reinvigorated since the UK joined the EU. Much of the old centre was demolished during the 1950s and 1960s to make way for commercial development. As a result, Lynn lacks the concentrated historic charm of towns such as Bury St Edmunds, though it does have a number of well-preserved buildings, the oldest guildhall in the country and a handful of excellent stately homes and medieval castle ruins within easy reach.

There are several notable attractions within easy reach of the town, most notable of which are **Houghton Hall**, an extravagant Palladian mansion with baroque flourishes, and **Sandringham**, one of the Queen's country residences.

The Town

Lynn's historic core lies in the two blocks between the High Street and the quayside. A good place to begin is the **Saturday Market Place**, the older and smaller of the town's two market places, presided over by the hybrid **Church of St Margaret**, which contains two of the most fanciful medieval brasses in East Anglia. These are the

Walsoken brass, adorned with country scenes, and the Braunche brass, named after a certain Robert Braunche and depicting the lavish feast he laid on for Edward III. Across the square is Lynn's prettiest building, the **Trinity Guildhall**, its wonderful chequered flint and stone facade dating to 1421 and repeated in the Elizabethan addition to the left and in the adjoining Victorian Town Hall. Next door to the Guildhall is the entrance to the **Old Gaol House** (April–Oct daily 10am–5pm; Nov–March Mon, Tues & Fri–Sun 10am–4pm; £2.20), which incorporates a series of eighteenth-century cells within a small museum on local baddies. There's also access to the guildhall undercroft, which displays an exhibition of the town's rich collection of civic regalia. This is actually more stimulating than you might think, since the treasures include King John's Cup and Sword, the latter a gift to the town prior to the king's ill-fated and ill-timed dash across the Wash, during which he caught the incoming waters and saved himself, but lost the crown jewels.

Of the medieval warehouses which survive along the quayside, the most evocative is the **Hanseatic Warehouse**, built around 1475, whose half-timbered upper floor juts unevenly over the cobbles of St Margaret's Lane. The other architectural highlight is a short stroll north, at the end of the gentle Georgian curve of Queen Street. It's here you'll find the splendid **Custom House**, erected in 1683 in a style clearly influenced by the Dutch. There are classical pilasters, petite dormer windows and a rooftop balustrade, but it's the dinky little cupola that catches the eye. The Custom House holds the tourist office (see below) and overlooks **Purfleet Quay**, a short and stumpy harbour once packed with merchant ships.

Beyond the Custom House, King Street, with its much wider berth, continues where Queen Street left off. On the left, just after Ferry Lane, stands Lynn's most precious building, **St George's Guildhall** (Mon–Sat 10am–5pm; free), dating from 1410 and the oldest surviving guildhall in England. It was a theatre in Elizabethan times and is now part of the King's Lynn Arts Centre. Beyond the guildhall is the later and much larger **Tuesday Market Place**, with the pastel-pink Duke's Head Hotel, dating from 1689, and the Neoclassical **Corn Exchange** – imaginatively converted into a second arts centre for the town – standing out against an otherwise unspectacular assemblage.

Practicalities

From the **train station**, it's a short walk west along Waterloo Street to Railway Road, the principal thoroughfare, which borders the eastern edge of the town centre. The **bus station** is nearer the centre, a few yards to the west of Railway Road from where signs point you to the **tourist office** in the Custom House (April–Oct Mon–Sat 9.15am–5pm, Sun 10am–5pm; Nov–March daily 10.30am–4pm; ☎01553/763044). **Accommodation** presents few problems except during the arts festival at the end of July. Most of the budget **B&Bs** lie southeast of the train station, easily reached by walking through the park behind the station. Aim for Tennyson Avenue and Goodwins Road, its continuation to the south. Here you'll find the *Old Rectory*, 33 Goodwins Rd (☎01553/768544; ②), and *Fairlight Lodge*, 79 Goodwins Rd (☎01533/762234; ②), and the more upmarket *Russet House Hotel*, 53 Goodwins Rd (☎01553/773098; ④). Lynn's finest **hotel** is the *Duke's Head* on the Tuesday Market Place (☎01533/774996; ⑧) – make sure you get a room overlooking the square – which offers good-value year-round deals where evening meals are included. The town's **youth hostel** enjoys a central location in the converted Thorseby College on College Lane (☎01533/772 461; closed Sept–March).

Tasty **pub meals** are available at the Tudor Rose on St Nicholas St, off Tuesday Market Place, and this is also the best place for a **drink**. There's a good café, *Crofter's*, in the undercroft of the Guildhall arts centre, and the town has two highly recommendable, if expensive, **restaurants**. The first is the *Riverside Rooms*, 27 King St (☎01553/773134; closed Sun), in an old fifteenth-century warehouse round the back of the arts centre, where the food – light lunches and dinner – is excellent; you get river views and tables outside in decent weather too. The second is *Rococo*, a modish little outfit on the Saturday Market Place (☎01533/771483; closed all Sun, & Mon lunch), which offers everything from game to veggie dishes.

Entertainment in Lynn revolves around the King's Lynn Arts Centre, housed in St George's Guildhall on King Street (☎01553/764864). Their galleries, cinema and theatre stage much of the annual festival held in July. The Corn Exchange, on the Tuesday Market Place (same number as Guildhall), offers a wide-ranging programme from theatre and music to comedy and dance.

Sandringham House

About seven miles south of Hunstanton looms the seven-thousand-acre estate of **Sandringham House** (Easter–Sept daily 11am–4.45pm; closed for two weeks late-July or early Aug; £5), bought in 1861 by Queen Victoria for her son, the future Edward VII. The house is billed as a private home, but few families have a drawing room crammed with Russian silver and Chinese jade. The **museum**, housed in the old coach and stable block, contains an exhibition of royal memorabilia from dolls to cars, but much more arresting are the beautifully maintained **grounds**, a mass of rhododendrons and azaleas in spring and early summer. The estate's sandy soil is also ideal for game birds, which was the attraction of the place for the terminally bored Edward, whose tradition of New Year shooting parties is still followed by the royals. Local **buses** #410 and #411 make the journey from King's Lynn, as does the summer Coastliner service (see p.385).

Houghton Hall

Five miles due east of Sandringham is the early Palladian masterpiece of **Houghton Hall** (Easter–Sept Thurs & Sun 2–5.30pm; £6), rejected by the future Edward VII in favour of Sandringham. It was built in the 1720s for Sir Robert Walpole, a leading Whig politician whose roller-coaster career included a couple of terms as prime minister and a period of imprisonment for corruption. As at Holkham, the exterior, with its classical portico, is formal and severe, though the four corner domes do add a touch of frivolity. Inside, the lavishness of the state rooms is at its most overpowering in the stone hall and saloon, the ceilings dripping with fancy plasterwork. Look out also for the overmantels in the parlour, the work of Grinling Gibbons. The original Walpole art collection was flogged to Catherine the Great of Russia in 1779 to pay off family debts, but there are still plenty of *objets d'art* on display, notably Sèvres porcelain and Mortlake tapestries.

There's no bus service to the hall.

Ely and around

ELY began its life as a seventh-century Benedictine abbey built on the Isle of Ely, a rare patch of upland in the soggy fens. Until the draining of the fens in the seventeenth century, this was to all intents and purposes a true island – the name Ely means "eel island" – surrounded by treacherous marshland, accessible only with the aid of "fen-slodgers" who knew the terrain. Under Hereward the Wake, the island became a centre of Anglo-Saxon rebellion, holding out against the Norman invaders until 1071. To mark their victory, the Normans constructed a new "cathedral of the fens", a towering structure visible for miles across the flat landscape. With a population of less than ten thousand, Ely has changed very little since medieval times, and the cathedral remains its main attraction. You could easily see the town on a day-trip from Cambridge, but it makes a pleasant night's stop in its own right, and is close to Cambridgeshire's other leading historic sight – the cathedral at **Peterborough**.

The Town

Ely **Cathedral** (June–Sept daily 7am–7pm; Oct–May Mon–Sat 7.30am–6pm, Sun 7.30am–5pm; £3.50) is seen to best advantage from the south, the crenellated towers of the west side perfectly balanced by the prickly finials to the east with the distinctive timber lantern rising above them both. To approach from this direction, follow the footpath leading up the hill into the cathedral precincts from **Broad Street**, the second turning on the right as you walk up Station Road from the train station. At the top of the footpath, pass through the medieval **Porta**, once the principal entrance to the monastery complex, and turn right to reach the main entrance on the lopsided **west front** – one of the transepts collapsed in a storm in 1701.

The first things to strike you as you enter the **nave** are the sheer length of the building and the lively nineteenth-century painted ceiling, largely the work of amateurs. The procession of plain late-Norman arches, built around the same time as Peterborough, leads to the architectural feature that makes Ely so special, the **octagon** – the only one of its kind in England – built in 1322 to replace the collapsed central tower. Its construction, employing the largest oaks available in England to support some four hundred tons, is one of the wonders of the medieval world, and the effect, as you look up into this Gothic dome, is simply breathtaking. **Octagon tours** (£2.50) depart several times a day from the desk at the entrance up into the octagon itself.

When the central tower collapsed, it fell eastwards, and the choir was rebuilt in a fussier decorative style. The thirteenth-century presbytery, beyond, houses the relics

---

THE FENS

One of the strangest of all English landscapes, the **Fens** cover a vast area from just north of Cambridge right up to Boston in Lincolnshire. For centuries, they were an inhospitable wilderness of quaking bogs and marshland, punctuated by clay islands on which small communities eked out a livelihood cutting peat for fuel, using reeds for thatching and living on a diet of fish and wildfowl. Piecemeal land reclamation took place throughout the Middle Ages, but it wasn't until the seventeenth century that the systematic draining of the fens was undertaken – amid fierce local opposition – by the Dutch engineer **Cornelius Vermuyden**. The transformation of the fens had unforeseen consequences: as it dried out, the peaty soil shrank to below the level of the rivers, causing further flooding, a situation only exacerbated by the numerous windmills, erected to help drain the fens, but which actually resulted in further shrinkage. The problem of shrinkage was only resolved in the 1820s with the introduction of steam-driven pumps, as these leviathans could control water levels with much greater precision, enabling the fens to be turned into the valuable agricultural land that you see today.

At **Wicken Fen** (visitor centre daily 9am–5pm; ☎01353/720274; £3.50; NT), nine miles south of Ely, you can visit one of the few remaining areas of undrained fenland. Its survival is thanks to a group of Victorian entomologists who donated the land to the National Trust in 1899, making it the oldest nature reserve in the UK. The seven hundred acres are undrained but not uncultivated – sedge and reed cutting are still carried out to preserve the landscape as it is – and the reserve also features one of the last surviving fenland wind pumps. Traditional "droves" (wide footpaths) enable visitors to explore the fen and a boardwalk nature trail gives access to several hides. The NT also organizes a variety of events and guided walks – call ahead for details.

of **St Ethelreda**, founder of the abbey in 673, who, despite being twice married, is honoured liturgically as a virgin. At the east end are three chantry chapels, the most charming of which (on the left) is an elaborate Renaissance affair dated to 1533. The other marvel at Ely is the **Lady Chapel**, in actual fact a separate building accessible via the north transept. It lost its wealth of sculpture and all its stained glass during the Reformation, but its fan vaulting remains an exquisite example of the English Gothic style. Retracing your steps, the south triforium near the main entrance holds the **Stained Glass Museum** (April–Sept Mon–Sat 10.30am–5pm, Sun noon–6pm; Oct–March Mon–Sat 10.30am–4.30pm, Sun noon–4.15pm; £2.50), another Anglican money-spinner exhibiting examples of this applied art from 1240 to the present day.

The **precincts** of the cathedral boast a fine ensemble of medieval domestic architecture, a higgledy-piggledy assortment of old stone, brick and half-timbered buildings that runs south from the Infirmary complex, abutting the presbytery, to the Prior's buildings near the Porta gate. Many of the buildings are used by the King's boarding school – where the cathedral's choristers are trained – others by the clergy, but although you can't go in any of them, it's still a pleasant area to stroll; a free map and brochure is available from the cathedral.

The rest of Ely is pretty enough, but hardly compelling after the wonders of the cathedral. To the north, the **High Street**, with its Georgian buildings and old-fashioned shops, makes for an enjoyable browse and, if you push on past the Market Place down Forehill, you'll soon reach the riverside **Maltings arts centre**, where you can grab a bite to eat. Alternatively, head west from the cathedral entrance across the triangular Palace Green, to **Oliver Cromwell's House** at 29 St Mary's St (April–Sept daily 10am–5.30pm, Oct–March Mon–Sat 10am–5pm; £2.70), a timber-framed former vicarage, which holds a small exhibition on the Protector's ten-year sojourn in Ely, when he was employed as a tithe collector.

Practicalities

Ely lies on a major rail intersection, with direct **trains** from as far afield as Liverpool, Norwich and London, as well as from Cambridge, just twenty minutes to the south. The **train station** is a ten-minute walk from the cathedral straight up Station Road and its continuation Back Hill. **Buses** (from King's Lynn and Cambridge) stop on Market Street immediately to the north of the cathedral. The **tourist office** is in Oliver Cromwell's House (April–Sept daily 10am–5.30pm, Oct–March Mon–Sat 10am–5pm; ☎01353/662062).

Ely has several appealing **B&Bs**, the best being the handy *Cathedral House*, 17 St Mary's St (☎01353/662124; ②), an attractive Georgian townhouse with three comfortable en-suite bedrooms. Other good options are concentrated along Egremont Street, about five minutes' walk north from the cathedral via the Lynn Road. Possibilities here include the spacious *Old Egremont House*, at no. 31 (☎01353/663118; ②), with cathedral views and a walled garden, and the more modern *Post House*, at no. 12a (☎01353/667184; ①).

Of the numerous **tearooms** in town, the *Almonry*, in the grounds to the north of the cathedral, is by far the best sited, with garden seats granting great views of the cathedral. Another good choice is the *Steeplegate Tea Rooms* on Steeple Row (closed Sun), backing on to the cathedral grounds from the High Street. For **restaurants**, there's a choice of *Dominique's*, 8 St Mary's St (☎01353/665011; closed Sun eve, Mon & Tues), a café by day and a reasonably priced bistro by night; and the *Old Fire Engine House*, 25 St Mary's St (☎01353/662582; closed Sun eve), a long-standing and more expensive gourmet English restaurant. Ely's friendliest **pub** is the Prince Albert, on Silver Street.

Peterborough

There are direct train services from Ely to **PETERBOROUGH**, thirteen miles from Wisbech in the far northwestern corner of Cambridgeshire, whose distinct and unmissable attraction is its superb Norman **Cathedral** (daily 8.30am–5.15pm; £3 suggested donation). A site of Christian worship since the seventh century, the first two churches were destroyed – the original Saxon monastery by the Danes in 870, its replacement by fire in 1116. Work on the present structure began a year after the fire and was pretty much completed within the century. The one significant later addition is the thirteenth-century **west facade**, one of the most magnificent in England, made up of three grandiloquent, deeply recessed arches, though the purity of the design is marred slightly by an incongruous central porch added in 1370.

The **interior** is a wonderful example of Norman architecture – round-arched rib vaults and shallow blind arcades line the nave, while up above the painted wooden ceiling, dating from 1220, is an exquisite example of medieval art, one of the most important in Europe. There are several notable tombs here too, beginning with that of **Catharine of Aragon**, who is buried in the north aisle of the presbytery under a slab of black Irish marble. Catharine was Henry VIII's first wife and the king's determination to divorce her in favour of Anne Boleyn precipitated the English Reformation. The marriage was finally declared void in 1533, but much to the king's chagrin, Katharine insisted till her death (in 1536) that she remained Henry's lawful wife.

The cathedral lies immediately to the east of Peterborough's pedestrianized town centre. To reach it from the **train station**, follow the signs, which bring you to the top of Cowgate in a couple of minutes from where the cathedral is visible straight ahead. The **tourist office** is at 45 Bridge St, to the left as you emerge from the cathedral gate (Mon–Fri 9am–5pm, Sat 10am–4pm; ☎01733/452336).

Cambridge

An agricultural market town at heart, **CAMBRIDGE** is, on the whole, a much quieter and more secluded place than Oxford, though for the visitor, what really sets it apart from its scholarly rival are "the Backs" – the green swathe of land straddling the languid River Cam – which overlook the backs of the old colleges, and provide the town's most enduring image. Cambridge is an extremely compact place, and you can walk round the historic centre in an afternoon – though once you begin to explore the individual colleges, pay a visit to the Fitzwilliam Museum and spend a leisurely afternoon on a punt, you could easily find yourself staying here for several days.

If possible you should avoid coming in high summer when the students are replaced by hordes of sightseers and posses of foreign language students. Faced with such crowds the more popular colleges have had to restrict their opening times, and are now introducing summer admission charges. Bear in mind, too, that during the exam period (May to early June), most colleges close their doors to the public.

Tradition has it that Cambridge was founded in the late 1220s by scholastic refugees from Oxford who fled the town after one of their number was lynched by hostile townsfolk – the first proper college wasn't founded until 1271, however. Rivalry has existed between the two institutions ever since – epitomized by the annual Boat Race on the River Thames – while internal tensions between "town and gown" have inevitably plagued a place where, from the late fourteenth century onwards, the university has tended to dominate local life. The first (but by no means the last) rebellion against the scholars occurred during the Peasants' Revolt of 1381, and had to be put down with armed troops by the Bishop of Norwich; five townsfolk were hanged as a result.

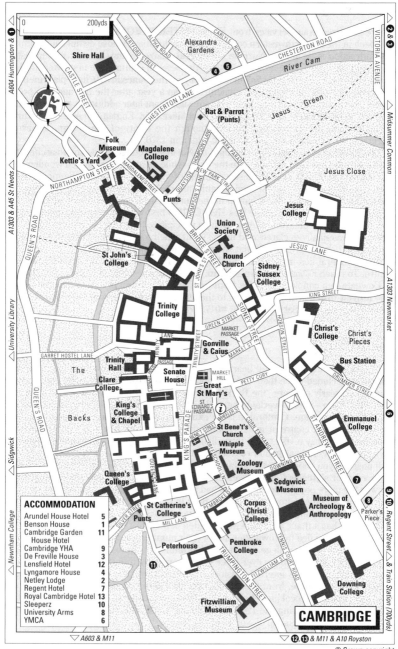

CAMBRIDGE

ACCOMMODATION

Arundel House Hotel	5
Benson House	1
Cambridge Garden House Hotel	11
Cambridge YHA	9
De Freville House	3
Lensfield Hotel	12
Lyngamore House	4
Netley Lodge	2
Regent Hotel	7
Royal Cambridge Hotel	13
Sleeperz	10
University Arms	8
YMCA	6

© Crown copyright

In the sixteenth century, Cambridge became a centre of church reformism, educating some of the most famous Protestant preachers in the country, including Cranmer, Latimer and Ridley, all of whom were martyred in Oxford by Mary Tudor. Later, during the Civil War, Cambridge once again found itself at the centre of events: Cromwell himself was both a graduate of Sidney Sussex College and the local MP, while the university was largely Royalist. After the Restoration, the university regained most of its privileges, though by the eighteenth century it was in the doldrums, better known, as Byron put it, for its "din and drunkenness" than for its academic record.

The nineteenth century witnessed the biggest changes in the balance between town and gown, as the number of students increased dramatically with the broadening of the curriculum to include new subjects such as natural science and history. The university finally lost its ancient privileges over the town, which was expanding rapidly thanks to the arrival of the railway; the population quadrupled in the years between 1800 and 1900. This century, change has been much slower in coming to Cambridge, particularly when it comes to equality of the sexes. The first two women's colleges were founded in the 1870s, yet it was only after 1947 that women were actually awarded degrees. Another women's college, New Hall, was established in 1954, but these three remained the only colleges to accept women until the mid-1970s, with some colleges holding out until the late 1980s. In the meantime, the city and university have been rapidly acquiring a reputation as a **high-tech centre** of excellence, what locals refer to half-seriously as "Silicon Fen". Cambridge has always been in the vanguard of scientific research – its almuni have garnered no fewer than 90 Nobel prizes over the years – and it's currently poised to corner the lucrative electronic communications industry, with the recent announcement that Bill Gates is to establish a Microsoft development centre in the city.

Arrival and transport

The **train station** is a mile or so southeast of the city centre, off Hills Road. It's an easy but tedious twenty-minute walk into the centre, or take shuttle bus #1, which runs into town every eight minutes or so (not Sun). The **bus station** is centrally located on Drummer Street, right by Christ's Pieces. **Stansted**, London's third airport, with its striking terminal building designed by Norman Foster, is just thirty miles south of Cambridge on the M11; there are hourly trains from here to the city, and regular bus services too. Arriving by **car**, you'll find much of the city centre closed to traffic and on-street parking well-nigh impossible – for a day-trip, at least, the best option is a **Park-and-Ride** car park; they are signposted on all major approaches.

The city centre is small enough to walk round comfortably, so apart from getting to and from the train station, you shouldn't have to use the city buses. Instead, you'll immediately be confronted by the fact that Cambridge is a cycling city, with almost every student and local owning one. **Bike rental** outlets are dotted all over town (see p.408), including a handy summer desk right outside the train station. Whenever you leave your bike, padlock it to something immovable – bike theft is rampant.

Information and tours

Cambridge **tourist office** is conveniently situated in the ornate, domed former public library on Wheeler Street, off King's Parade (April–Oct Mon–Fri 10am–6pm, Sat 10am–5pm, Sun 11am–4pm; Nov–March Mon–Fri 10am–5.30pm, Sat 10am–5pm; ☎01223/322640). They issue city maps, have lots of leaflets on local attractions and sell an in-depth guide to the city (£4). They can also help with accommodation (see below), which is a useful service especially in the summer when vacant rooms can be hard to find. The best source of information on eating out and entertainment is Adhoc's Pocket *What's On?*, a free, monthly brochure available at the tourist office and larger bookshops.

The tourist office runs very popular **walking tours** of the centre (2hr; April–Sept daily; Oct Mon–Sat; Nov–March Sat; £6.25), which are expensive but include entrance to at least one college that normally charges for the privilege. Book well in advance in summer. The other high-profile tour is Guide Friday's open-top **bus tour** (daily; £8; ☎01223/362444), which runs in a continuous loop around the city centre – tickets allow you to get on and off at will and are on sale from the driver, at the tourist office and from the Guide Friday Tourism Centre in the train station.

Accommodation

Cambridge is short of central accommodation and those few **hotels** that do occupy prime locations are expensive. That said, Chesterton Road, the busy street running east from the top of Magdalene Street, has several reasonably priced hotels and guest houses. There are lots of **B&Bs** on the outskirts of town, especially along Huntingdon Road, a ten-minute walk north of the centre, and near the train station on Tenison Road, a right turn a couple of hundred yards down Station Road, where you'll also find the **youth hostel**. In high season, when rooms are often difficult to find, the tourist office's **accommodation booking service** can be very useful (Mon–Fri 9.30am–4pm; ☎01223/457581).

Hotels, guest houses and B&Bs

Arundel House Hotel, 53 Chesterton Rd (☎01223/367701). A converted row of late-Victorian houses overlooking Jesus Green makes for one of the better mid-range B&B choices. Neat and tidy rooms with mundanely modern furnishings. Breakfasts are good. ④.

Benson House, 24 Huntingdon Rd (☎01223/311594). The best of the B&Bs in the neighbourhood, opposite New Hall and just five minutes from Magdalene Bridge. Some rooms are en suite. ②.

Cambridge Garden House Hotel, Granta Place, Mill Lane (☎01223/259988). Cambridge's best central hotel, set in its own gardens with a fine riverside location, rooms with balconies, indoor pool and health club. ⑧.

De Freville House, 166 Chesterton Rd (☎01223/354993). Six large and tastefully furnished en-suite rooms in an attractive, high-gabled Victorian house. A little bit too far out from the centre for comfort, but otherwise a very good choice. No credit cards. ③.

Lensfield Hotel, 53 Lensfield Rd (☎01223/355017). Small, family-owned hotel on the ring road just round the corner from the Fitzwilliam Museum. ⑤.

Lyngamore House, 35–37 Chesterton Rd (☎01223/312369, *karen.dowling@lineone.net*). Inexpensive, comfortable B&B whose front rooms overlook Jesus Green. No credit cards. ①.

Netley Lodge, 112 Chesterton Rd (☎01223/363845). Cosy B&B, in an Edwardian townhouse not far from the river and Midsummer Common. Three attractively furnished bedrooms, one en suite. No credit cards. ②.

Regent Hotel, 41 Regent St (☎01223/351470, *reservations@regenthotel.co.uk*). Small-scale, family-owned hotel in a historic townhouse and with a nice café-bar on the south side of the centre overlooking Parker's Piece. ⑤.

Royal Cambridge Hotel, Trumpington St (☎01223/351631, *royalcambridge@msihotels.co.uk*). One of the city's more gracious old hotels, with a slight heavy hand in the traditionally decorated rooms, but no quibbles about the location, just down from the Fitzwilliam. ⑦.

Sleeperz Hotel, Station Rd (☎01223/304050, *info@sleeperz.com*). A popular hotel occupying an imaginatively converted granary warehouse, right outside the train station. Most of the rooms are bunk-style affairs done out in the manner of a ship's cabin, though there are a few doubles too. All are en suite, with shower and TV. ①, doubles ②.

University Arms Hotel, Regent St (☎01223/351241, *devere.uniarms@airtime.co.uk*). The traditionalist's choice, this comfortable Victorian pile lords it over Parker's Piece, on the south side of the city centre. Most rooms enjoy the view, as does the *Parker's Bar*. ⑤.

Hostels and campsite

Cambridge YHA, 97 Tenison Rd (☎01223/354601). Close to the train station, with a small courtyard garden and games room.

Cherry Hinton Caravan Club Site, Lime Kiln Road, Cherry Hinton (☎01223/244088). Three miles east of the city centre in the village of Cherry Hinton, this pleasantly landscaped camping and caravan site spreads over five acres. Closed Nov–March.

YMCA, Gonville Place, at Parker's Piece (☎01223/356998). Central singles and doubles, with breakfast included in the price, but very busy during summer – book well in advance.

The City

Cambridge's main shopping street is Bridge Street, which becomes Sidney Street, St Andrew's Street and finally Regent Street; the other main thoroughfare is the procession of St John's Street, Trinity Street, King's Parade and Trumpington Street. The university developed on the land west of this latter route along the banks of the Cam, and now forms a continuous half-mile parade of **colleges** from Magdalene to Peterhouse, with sundry others scattered about the periphery. The **Fitzwilliam Museum**, easily the city's best, is just along Trumpington Street south of Peterhouse. The account below starts with **King's College**, whose chapel is the university's most celebrated attraction, and covers the rest of the town in a clockwise direction.

King's College

The first buildings of **King's College** (☎01223/331212), founded in 1441 by Henry VI, are no longer part of the college, but lie tucked away behind the glum-looking facade of the Old Schools building, now administrative offices immediately to the north on Trinity Lane. Not content with his initial effort, Henry cleared away half of medieval Cambridge to make room for a much grander foundation, one of the few successes of a spectacularly unsuccessful reign. Henry spared no expense, but although the overall layout of his Great Court survives, the existing college – facing King's Parade – is largely neo-Gothic, built in the 1820s to a design by William Wilkins. The main exception is the much-celebrated **King's College Chapel** (term time Mon–Fri 9.30am–3.30pm, Sat 9.30am–3.15pm, Sun 1.15–2.15pm; rest of year Mon–Sat 9.30am–4.30pm, Sun 10am–5pm; £3), on the north side of Great Court, though visitors usually enter via Trinity Lane. Committed to canvas by Turner and Canaletto, and eulogized in three sonnets by Wordsworth, it's now best known for its **boys' choir**, whose members process across the college grounds during term time in their antiquated garb to sing evensong (Tues–Sat 5.30pm) and carols on every Christmas Eve. Begun in 1446 and over sixty years in the making, the chapel is an extraordinary building. From the outside, it seems impossibly slender, its streamlined buttresses channelling up to a dainty balustrade and four spiky turrets, but the exterior was, in a sense at least, a happy accident – its design predicated by the carefully composed interior. Here, in the final

---

COLLEGE ADMISSION CHARGES AND OPENING TIMES

All of the more visited colleges now impose an **admission charge**, partly to control the number of tourists and partly to raise cash. It is, however, a creeping trend, so don't be surprised if other, lesser-known colleges follow suit. **Opening times** are fairly consistent throughout the year, though term-time hours tend to be a little more restrictive than out of term especially on the weekend. It's also worth noting that during the exam season, which stretches from late April to early June, all the colleges have periods when they are closed to the public. Where no opening hours are given, you're usually free to tour the grounds at any time during the day. For more specific information, call the relevant college; **phone numbers** are given in the text.

flowering of the Gothic style, the mystery of the Christian faith was expressed by a long, uninterrupted **nave** flooded with kaleidoscopic patterns of light filtering in through copious stained glass windows. Paid for by Henry VIII, the **stained glass** was largely the work of Flemish glaziers, with the lower windows portraying scenes from the New Testament and the Apocrypha, and the upper windows displaying the Old Testament. Henry VIII also paid for the intricately carved wooden choir screen, one of the earliest examples of Italian Renaissance wood carving in England, but the choir stalls beyond date from the 1670s. Above the altar hangs Rubens' *Adoration of the Magi*. Finally, an exhibition in the chantries puts more historical flesh on Henry's grand plans.

Like Oxford's New College, King's enjoyed an exclusive supply of students from one of the country's public schools – in this case, Eton – and until 1851 claimed the right to award its students degrees without taking any examinations. The first non-Etonians were only accepted in 1873. Times have changed since those days, and if anything, King's is now one of the more progressive colleges, having been one of the first to admit women in 1972. Among its most famous alumni are E.M. Forster, who described his experiences in *Maurice*; film director Derek Jarman; poet Rupert Brooke; and John Maynard Keynes, whose economic theories did much to improve the college's finances when he became the college bursar.

From King's Parade to Clare College

King's Parade, originally the medieval High Street, is inevitably dominated by King's college and chapel, but the higgledy-piggledy shops opposite are an attractive foil to William Wilkins's architectural screen. At the northern end of King's Parade is **Great St Mary's**, the university's pet church, a sturdy Gothic structure dating from the fifteenth-century. Its tower (Easter–Sept Mon–Sat 9am–6pm, Sun 10am–4pm; Oct–Easter Mon–Sat 9am–4.15pm, Sun 10am–2pm; £1.50) offers a good overall view of the colleges and a bird's-eye view of **Market Hill**, east of the church, where food and bric-a-brac stalls are set out from Monday to Saturday. Opposite the church stands **Senate House**, an exercise in Palladian classicism by James Gibbs, and the scene of graduation ceremonies on the last Saturday in June, when champagne corks fly around the rabbit-fur collars and black gowns. It's not usually open to the public, though you can wander around the quad if the gate's open.

The northern continuation of King's Parade is Trinity Street, a short way along which is the main entrance to **Gonville and Caius College** (☎01223/332400), known simply as Caius (pronounced "keys"), after the co-founder John Keys, who latinized his name, as was the custom with men of learning. The design of the college owes much to Keys, who placed a gate on three sides of two adjoining courts, each representing a different stage on the path to academic enlightenment: the Gate of Humility, through which the student entered the college, now stands in the Fellows' Garden; the Gate of Virtue, sporting the female figures of Fame and Wealth, marks the entrance to Caius Court; while the Gate of Honour, capped with sundials and decorated with classical motifs, leads to Senate House Passage and on to Senate House.

Senate House Passage continues west beyond the Gate of Honour to Trinity Lane, which gives access to the North Gate of King's (for the chapel) and to other two well-concealed colleges. The first, **Trinity Hall** (☎01223/332500) – not to be confused with Trinity College – offers little to detain you, though its Elizabethan library retains several of its original chains designed to prevent students from purloining the texts. **Clare College** (daily 10am–5pm; £1.75; ☎01223/333200), just to the south, is much more interesting. One of seven colleges founded, rather surprisingly, by women, its plain period-piece courtyards, completed in the early eighteenth century, lead to one of the most picturesque of all the bridges over the Cam, **Clare Bridge**. Beyond lies the Fellows' Garden, one of the loveliest college gardens open to the public (times as college).

Trinity and St John's

Trinity College, on Trinity Street (daily 10am–6pm; £1.75; ☎01223/338400), is the largest of the Cambridge colleges and to ram home the point it also has the largest courtyard. It comes as little surprise then that its list of famous alumni is longer than any other college: literary greats, including Dryden, Byron, Tennyson and Vladimir Nabokov; the Cambridge spies Blunt, Burgess and Philby; two prime ministers, Balfour and Baldwin; William Thackeray, Isaac Newton, Lord Rutherford, Vaughan Williams, Pandit Nehru, Bertrand Russell, Ludwig Wittgenstein, Edward VII, George VI and Prince Charles.

A statue of Henry VIII, who founded the college in 1546, sits in majesty over Trinity's Great Gate, his sceptre replaced with a chair leg by a student wit. Beyond lies the vast asymmetrical expanse of **Great Court**, which displays a fine range of Tudor buildings, the oldest of which is the fifteenth-century clock tower – the annual race against its midnight chimes is now common currency thanks to the film *Chariots of Fire*. The centrepiece of the court is the delicate fountain, in which, legend has it, Lord Byron used to bathe naked with his pet bear – the college forbade students from keeping dogs.

To get through to **Nevile's Court** – where Newton first calculated the speed of sound – you must pass through "the screens", a passage separating the hall from the kitchens, a common feature of Oxbridge colleges. The west end of the court is enclosed by the university's most famous building after King's College Chapel, the **Wren Library** (term time Mon–Fri noon–2pm, Sat 10.30am–12.30pm; rest of year Mon–Fri noon–2pm; free). Viewed from the outside, it's impossible to appreciate the scale of the interior thanks to Wren's clever device of concealing the internal floor level. In contrast to many modern libraries, natural light pours into the white stuccoed interior, which contrasts wonderfully with the dark lime-wood bookcases, also Wren-designed and housing numerous valuable manuscripts including Milton's *Lycidas*, Wittgenstein's journals and A.A. Milne's *Winnie the Pooh*.

Next door, **St John's College**, on St John's Street (daily 10am–5.30pm; £1.75; ☎01223/338600), sports a grandiloquent Tudor gatehouse, distinguished by the coat of arms of the founder, Lady Margaret Beaufort, the mother of Henry VII, held aloft by two spotted, mythical beasts. Beyond, three successive courts lead to the river, but there's an excess of dull reddish brickwork here – enough for Wordsworth, who lived above the kitchens on F staircase, to describe the place as "gloomy". The arcade on the far side of Third Court leads through to the celebrated **Bridge of Sighs**, a covered bridge built in 1831 but in most other respects very unlike its Venetian namesake. The wooden bridge is closed to the public, and in any case is best viewed either from a punt or from the much older, more stylish Wren-designed bridge a few metres to the south. The Bridge of Sighs links the old college with the fanciful nineteenth-century **New Court**, a crenellated neo-Gothic extravaganza topped by a feast of pinnacles and a central cupola – and known as "the wedding cake".

From the Round Church to Magdalene

Back on St John's Street, it's a few seconds' walk to Bridge Street and the **Round Church** (daily: summer 10am–5pm; winter 1–4pm), built in the twelfth century on the model of the Holy Sepulchre in Jerusalem. It's a curious-looking structure, squat with an ill-considered nineteenth-century spire, but the Norman pillars remain inside. The church now accommodates the town's brass-rubbing centre, whose staff will instruct you in the art, and it's also the starting point for Christian heritage walks around the city (Feb–Nov Wed 11am, Sun 2.30pm; free).

Set back from the road, down a footpath beside the church, is the **Union Society**, a bastion of male-dominated debating culture, founded in 1815, which only admitted women in the 1960s. The society likes to think of itself as a miniature House of Commons – its debating chamber is designed as such – and its debates continue to

---

ON THE RIVER

Punting is the quintessential Cambridge activity, though it's a good deal harder than it looks. First-timers find themselves zigzagging across the water and "punt jams" are very common on the stretch of the Cam beside the Backs in summer. Punt rental is available at several points, including the boatyard at Mill Lane (beside the Silver Street bridge), at Magdalene Bridge, and at the *Rat & Parrot* pub on Jesus Green. It costs around £8 an hour (and most places charge a deposit of £40), with up to six people in each punt. If you find it all too daunting you can always hire a **chauffeur punt** from most of the rental places, which usually works out at around a fiver a head.

Cambridge is also famous for its **rowing clubs**, which are clustered along the north bank of the river on Midsummer Common, the only stretch of water that is punt-free. The most important inter-college races are the **May Bumps**, which, confusingly, take place in June; fight your way to the bar of the *Fort St George* on Midsummer Common and watch the spectacle.

---

attract many of the leading politicians and speakers of the day. These are presided over by the Union's officers, who tend to be made up of the university's more ambitious, conservative elements. In the normal scheme of things, election to the Union presidency leads about twenty years later to a place in Cabinet – the last Tory administration barely contained a minister who hadn't been Union president.

Saving nearby Jesus College till later (see below), it only takes a minute or two to stroll up from the Round Church to Magdalene Bridge, site of the old Roman ford, and then **Magdalene College** (☎01223/332100) – pronounced "maudlin" – founded as a hostel by the Benedictines and a university college since 1542. Magdalene was the last of the colleges to admit women, finally succumbing in 1988. Here, the main focus of attention is the **Pepys Building** (Oct to early Dec & mid-Jan to mid-March Mon–Sat 2.30–3.30pm; late April to Aug Mon–Sat 11.30am–12.30pm & 2.30–3.30pm; free), in the second of the college's ancient courtyards. Samuel Pepys, a Magdalene student, bequeathed his entire library to the college, where it has been displayed ever since in its original red-oak bookshelves – though his famous diary, which also now resides here, was only discovered in the nineteenth century.

A short walk away at the top of Magdalene Street are two less touristed sites: the **Folk Museum**, 2–3 Castle St (April–Sept Mon–Sat 10.30am–5pm, Sun 2–5pm; Oct–March closed Mon; £1) and, further up Castle Street, the grassy mound which is all that remains of **Cambridge Castle**. Between the two, adjacent to the Folk Museum is **Kettle's Yard**, a deceptively spacious open-plan conversion of some old slum dwellings, originally owned by the art critic and curator Jim Ede. The house is packed full of works of art, including many by the St Ives primitivist Alfred Wallis, but it is much more than a simple gallery – it's the sense of art within a living space, amid house plants, lounge chairs and an extensive library of art books, which makes the place so special. In 1970 a formal exhibition gallery (Tues–Sat 12.30–5.30pm, Sun 2–5.30pm; free) was added as a forum for contemporary artists.

Jesus and Sidney Sussex

Back down Magdalene Street then Bridge Street, take the first left after the Round Church to reach **Jesus College** (☎01223/339339), whose wide open spaces and intimate cloisters are reminiscent of a monastic institution. This is not too surprising as the bishop of Ely founded the college on the grounds of a suppressed Benedictine nunnery in 1496. The main red-brick gateway is approached via a distinctive walled walkway strewn with bicycles and known as "the Chimney". Beyond, much of the ground plan of the nunnery has been preserved, especially around **Cloister Court**, the prettiest of the college's courtyards, dripping with ivy and overflowing hanging baskets. The college chapel, entered from the court, occupies the former priory chancel and looks more like a medieval parish church; it was imaginatively restored in the nineteenth century, using ceiling designs by William Morris and Pre-Raphaelite stained glass. The poet Samuel Taylor Coleridge was the college's most famously bad student, absconding in his first year to join the Light Dragoons, and returning only to be kicked out for a combination of bad debts and unconventional opinions.

From Jesus Lane, Bridge Street becomes Sidney Street and soon after **Sidney Sussex College** (☎01223/338800) appears on the left, its sombre facade engulfed by mock-Gothic cement rendering that was plastered over the college walls in the 1830s. The college's main claim to fame is that Oliver Cromwell studied here, and in 1960 it was the lucky recipient of the Protector's head, now buried in a secret location in the college chapel.

St Andrew's Street

Just beyond Sidney Sussex, on St Andrew's Street, you hit the hustle and bustle of the town's central shopping area, dominated by the **Lion Yard** shopping centre – one of the few town-planning mistakes in the centre of Cambridge. The greatest outrage was foisted upon **Petty Cury**, formerly a cobbled curve of leaning half-timbered houses and now a dreary string of modern shops. To escape from all this, head through the turreted gateway of **Christ's College** (☎01223/334900), which features the coat of arms of the founder, Lady Margaret Beaufort, who also founded St John's. Passing through First Court you come to the Fellows' Building, attributed to Inigo Jones, whose central arch gives access to the **Fellows' Garden** (Mon–Fri 10.30am–12.30pm & 2–4pm; free). The poet John Milton is said to have either painted or composed beneath the garden's elderly mulberry tree, though there's no definite proof that he did either; Christ's other famous undergraduate was Charles Darwin, who showed little academic promise and spent most of his time hunting and shooting. If you continue walking through the college, you come to its modern adjunct, Denys Lasdun's concrete pyramidal accommodation block, dubbed "the typewriter".

A little further along St Andrew's Street is **Emmanuel College** (☎01223/334200), whose stolid Neoclassical facade hides a pair of Wren buildings – the Cloister Gallery and Chapel on the Front Court. The college was founded in 1584 to train a new generation of Protestant clergy following the Reformation. Emmanuel men were numbered among the Pilgrims who settled New England, which not only explains the derivation of the place name Cambridge in Massachusetts but also accounts for Harvard University – John Harvard, another alumnus, is remembered by a memorial window in Wren's chapel.

Still further along the street, but on the opposite side, is the uncompromisingly Neoclassical ensemble of **Downing College** (☎01223/334800), established in 1800 after more than eighty years of costly litigation between the university and the heirs of the original benefactor, Sir George Downing. It is unique among Cambridge colleges in being laid out like a campus around a central lawn, rather than enclosed in separate courtyards.

Downing Street and the museums

A group of scientific and specialist museums occupy the land either side of **Downing Street** and its continuation Pembroke Street, which run between St Andrew's and Trumpington. Each is connected to one of the university faculties and forms an important resource for students, but is also open to the public. There's the **Sedgwick**

Geology Museum (Mon–Fri 9am–1pm & 2–5pm, Sat 10am–1pm; free), which displays fossils and skeletons of dinosaurs, reptiles and mammals, plus the oldest geological collection in the world; the **Museum of Zoology** (Mon–Fri 2.15–4.45pm; free); the **Whipple Museum of Science** (Mon–Fri 1.30–4.30pm; free), crammed with hundreds of scientific instruments; and the **Museum of Archeology and Anthropology** (Mon–Fri 2–4pm, Sat 10am–12.30pm; free). The last is probably the pick of the bunch for the non-specialist, covering the development of the city from prehistoric times to the nineteenth century and, better still, holding a superb ethnographical gallery. This is centred on a soaring 50-foot native totem pole and many of the exhibits derive from the "cabinets of curiosities" collected by eighteenth-century explorers. Several pieces on show were gathered on Captain Cook's first voyage to the South Pacific between 1768 and 1771.

From St Catherine's to Peterhouse

There are four more town-centre colleges clustered around the foot of King's Parade and the top of Trumpington Street. One of them is **St Catherine's College** (☎01223/338300) – popularly known as "Catz" – founded in 1473 by the provost of King's on land just to the south of that college. In contrast to its glamorous neighbour, the Principal Court here is a cheerless affair, whose dour, heavy-duty buildings mirror the college's relative impecuniousness – in 1880 St Catherine's was so broke that it was nearly forced to merge with King's. Much more enticing is **Corpus Christi College** (☎01223/338000), just across King's Parade, founded by two of the town's guilds in 1352. Ignore the first court and head north into Old Court, which dates from the foundation of the college and is where Christopher Marlowe wrote *Tamburlane* before graduating in 1587. The college library, on the south side, contains a priceless collection of Anglo-Saxon manuscripts, while the north side is linked by a gallery to **St Bene't's Church**, which served as the college chapel, but is of much earlier Saxon origin. Inside, Thomas Hobson's Bible is exhibited in the case in the right-hand corner; Hobson was the owner of a Cambridge livery stable, where he would only allow customers to take the horse nearest the door – thus giving rise to the phrase "Hobson's choice".

Queens' College (daily 10am–4.30pm; £1; ☎01223/335511), accessed through the gate on Queen's Lane, just off Silver Street, is the most popular college with university applicants, and it's not difficult to see why. In the Old Court and the Cloister Court, Queens' possesses two fairy-tale Tudor courtyards, with the first of the two the perfect illustration of the original collegiate ideal with kitchens, library, chapel, hall and rooms all set around a tiny green. Cloister Court is flanked by the Long Gallery of the President's Lodge, the last remaining half-timbered building in the university, and, in its southeast corner, by the tower where Erasmus is thought to have beavered away during his four years here, probably from 1510 to 1514. Be sure to pay a visit to the college hall, off the screens passage, which holds mantel tiles by William Morris, and portraits of Erasmus and one of the co-founders, Elizabeth Woodville, wife of Edward IV. Equally eye-catching is the wooden **Mathematical Bridge** over the Cam (visible for free from the Silver Street bridge), a copy of the mid-eighteenth-century original which, it was claimed, would stay in place even if the nuts and bolts were removed.

Back on Trumpington Street, **Pembroke College** (☎01223/338100) contains Wren's first ever commission, the college **chapel**, paid for by his Royalist uncle, erstwhile bishop of Ely and a college fellow, in thanks for his deliverance from the Tower of London after seventeen years' imprisonment. It boasts a particularly fine, though modern, stained glass East Window and a delicate fifteenth-century marble relief of St Michael and the Virgin, the product of an unusually skilled early English workshop. Outside the library there's a statue of William Pitt the Younger, clad here in a toga, who entered the college at fifteen and was prime minister at twenty-five, and is just one of a long list of college alumni, which includes poets Edmund Spenser, Thomas Gray and Ted Hughes.

Across the road from Pembroke is the oldest and smallest of the colleges, **Peterhouse** (☎01223/338200), founded in 1284. Few of the original buildings have survived, the principal exception being the thirteenth-century hall, entered from the main court, whose interior was remodelled by William Morris. As at Corpus Christi, Peterhouse used the church next door – in this case Little St Mary's – as the college chapel, until the present one, with its light-hearted Baroque gables, was erected in the main court in 1632.

The Fitzwilliam Museum

Of all the museums in Cambridge, the **Fitzwilliam Museum**, on Trumpington Street (Tues–Sat 10am–5pm, Sun 2.15–5pm; £3 donation suggested), stands head and shoulders above the rest. The building itself is a splendidly grandiloquent interpretation of Neoclassicism, built in the mid-nineteenth century to house the vast collection bequeathed by Viscount Fitzwilliam in 1816. Since then, the museum has been gifted a string of private collections, most of which are focused on a particular specialism. Consequently, the Fitzwilliam says much about the changing tastes of the British upper class.

The **Lower Galleries** contain a wealth of antiquities including Egyptian sarcophagi and mummies, fifth-century BC black- and red-figure Greek vases, plus a bewildering display of European porcelain. Further on, there are rooms dedicated to armour, glass and pewterware, fans, portrait miniatures and illuminated manuscripts, and – right at the far end – galleries devoted to Far Eastern applied arts and Korean ceramics.

The **Upper Galleries** concentrate on painting and sculpture with three of the first five rooms holding an eclectic assortment of mostly nineteenth- and early twentieth-century European paintings. Among many, there are works by Picasso, Matisse, Monet, Renoir, Delacroix, Cézanne and Degas. The other two rooms concentrate on British painting, with works by William Blake, Constable and Turner, Hogarth, Reynolds, Gainsborough and Stubbs. Moving on, the Italian section boasts works by Fra Filippo Lippi and Simone Martini, Titian and Veronese, while Frans Hals and Ruisdael feature in the Flemish section. The twentieth-century gallery is packed with a fascinating selection including pieces by the likes of Lucian Freud, David Hockney, Henry Moore, Ivon Hitchens, Ben Nicholson and Barbara Hepworth.

To the Botanic Garden

Past the Fitzwilliam Museum, turn left along busy Lensfield Road for the **Scott Polar Research Institute** (Mon–Sat 2.30–4pm; free), founded in 1920 in memory of the explorer, Captain Scott, with displays from the expeditions of various polar adventurers, plus exhibitions on native cultures of the Arctic. There's more general interest near at hand in the shape of the **University Botanic Garden** on Bateman Street, to the south (daily 10am–4pm; £1.50), founded as early as 1846 and providing a quiet end to a day's sightseeing.

Newnham and the Sidgwick Site

Over the last hundred years, the university has spread its tentacles across the west bank of the Cam, beyond the Backs. The first institution established here was **Newnham College** on Sidgwick Ave (☎01223/335700), built in red-brick Dutch style in the 1870s for women undergraduates. Opposite Newnham is the **Sidgwick Site**, where the arts faculties have been based since 1954, and where Cambridge's most notorious modern building, James Stirling's glass-skinned **History Faculty**, was erected in 1968. The critics loved it at the time, though the students and university authorities were somewhat less amused with a building which was like a hothouse in summer and leaked throughout the winter. The equally brutal brick tower, visible to the north, belongs to the **University Library**. Built in the 1930s and looking like something out of *1984*, it's one of the country's five copyright libraries, which receives a free copy of every book published; it now holds over five million books.

Eating and drinking

Students are not the world's greatest customers for restaurateurs, so although the **takeaway** and **café** scene is good in the centre, decent **restaurants** are a little thin on the ground. On any kind of budget, the myriad Italian places – courtesy of Cambridge's large Italian population – will stand you in good stead; otherwise, choose carefully, particularly in the more touristy areas, where quality isn't always all it should be. Happily, Cambridge abounds in excellent **pubs**, and our list rounds up the best of the traditional student and local drinking haunts.

Cafés

Café 31, 2 Quay Side. Bustling, modern coffee house beside the punt rental point at Magdalene Bridge.

Caffé Uno, 32 Bridge St. Popular, gleamingly new café-bar beside the punt rental point at Magdalene Bridge. Outside seating available.

Clowns, 54 King St. Italian-style cappuccino and cakes, sandwiches and snacks, and plenty of newspapers are available in this popular student café.

Copper Kettle, 4 King's Parade. Generations of students have whiled away time in this resolutely old-fashioned café opposite King's College, sipping coffee, eating pastries and putting the world to rights.

Roof Garden, Cambridge Arts Theatre, 6 St Edward's Passage. Conservatory-style rooftop café serving home-made snacks and sandwiches, as well as main meals and pre-theatre dinners. Closed Sun.

Nadia's, 11 St John's St. Good sandwich and cake takeaway in the centre, opposite St John's. One of several outlets.

Pret-a-Manger, 19 Petty Cury. Designer coffee and sandwiches from the trendy London chain.

Restaurants

Brown's, 23 Trumpington St. Breezy brasserie with a wide-ranging menu housed in a former hospital outpatients department. The grand setting – all plants and fans – sets the meal off a treat. Inordinately popular, but no reservations – wait in line or at the bar. Moderate.

Clowns Two, 8 Market Passage (☎01223/322312). The coffee bar's sister outlet, next to the Arts Cinema, makes its mark with pizza and pasta as well as the coffee and cakes it's best known for. Moderate.

Don Pasquale, 12 Market Hill (☎01223/367063). Great location, with seats on the square for lunchtime diners. Tasty food and an especially good place for a quick pick-me-up espresso and slice of pizza. Moderate.

Eraina Taverna, 2 Free School Lane (☎01223/368786). Packed Greek taverna which satisfies the hungry hordes with huge platefuls of stews and grills, as well as pizzas, curries and a whole host of other menu madness. Try to avoid getting stuck in the basement, though at weekends (when you'll probably have to queue) you'll be lucky to get a seat anywhere. Inexpensive.

La Margherita, 15 Magdalene St (☎01223/315232). Cheapish and cheerful Italian outfit offering pizzas and pastas as well as standard meat and fish dishes. Inexpensive to Moderate.

Panos, 154 Hills Rd (☎01223/212958). Best Greek restaurant in town – try the scotch steak or any of the other charcoal grills. Closed Sun. Moderate.

Pizza Express, 28 St Andrew's St and 7A Jesus Lane. Superior pizza chain with an intimate branch at the first address and a grander, marbled hall at the second (in the former Pitt Club). Inexpensive.

Rainbow Vegetarian Bistro, 9a King's Parade (☎01223/321551). The only vegetarian restaurant in Cambridge, with main courses – ranging from couscous to lasagne and Indonesian *gado-gado* – all under £6. Good-value breakfasts, and organic wines served with meals. Inexpensive.

Twenty-Two, 22 Chesterton Rd (☎01223/351880). Consistently the best restaurant in Cambridge, a candlelit townhouse in which the good-value fixed-price menu touches all the modern bases. Closed Sun & Mon. Expensive.

Pubs and bars

Anchor, Silver St. Very popular riverside tourist haunt with views of the Backs, adjacent punt rental and an outdoor deck.

Champion of the Thames, 68 King St. Gratifyingly old-fashioned central pub with decent beer and a student/academic clientele.

Dadie's, Cambridge Arts Theatre, 6 St Edward's Passage. The ground-floor wine bar at the theatre makes a civilized meeting spot, though it's only open until 9pm – and closed Mon eve.

Eagle, Bene't St. An ancient inn with a cobbled courtyard where Crick and Watson sought inspiration in the 1950s, at the time of their discovery of DNA. It's been tarted up since and gets horribly crowded, but is still worth a pint of anyone's time.

Elm Tree, 42 Orchard St. Cosy local with frequent live music, mainly jazz. Just to the north of Parker's Piece and full of furiously smoking refugees from the nearby *Free Press*.

Free Press, 7 Prospect Row. Classic backstreet local with an admirable no-smoking policy, good beer, fine food and a clientele often made up of the university's rowing fraternity.

Fort St George, Midsummer Common. Pleasant riverside location, overlooking the boathouses, and with a series of cosy rooms – shame about the beer, though.

Maypole, 20A Park St. Small pub near the ADC serving world-class cocktails to student thespians.

Portland Arms, 129 Chesterton Rd. A real locals' pub near river and green, with Greene King beer, jazz every other Sunday night and few pretensions.

Arts, entertainment and festivals

The arts scene is at its best during term time, with numerous student **drama** productions, **classical concerts** and **gigs** culminating in the traditional orgy of excess following the exam season, though the more firmly town-based venues, like the Corn Exchange, put on events throughout the year. Apart from the places highlighted below, each college and several churches contribute too – the **King's College choir** is of course the main attraction, but the choral scholars who perform at the chapels of St John's and Trinity are also exceptionally good. For all the week's events, check the listings section of the student weekly, *Varsity*, or Adhoc's Pocket *What's On?*, both of which are widely available from bookshops and newsagents. For advance information, call into the Corn Exchange (see below), which sells tickets for various venues, or at the tourist office.

June and July are the busiest times in Cambridge's calendar of **events**. The fortnight of post-exam celebrations, which take place in the first two weeks of June and are confusingly known as **May Week**, herald the ball and garden-party season, and include boat races, known as the "May Bumps", on the Cam by Midsummer Common. The vaguely hippified **Midsummer Fair**, descendant of the town's famous medieval Stourbridge Fair, discontinued in 1934, takes place in mid-June on Midsummer Common, with bands, theatre and much more besides – all for free. By contrast, you'll have to pay out around £50 for a tent pitch and entry into the three-day **Cambridge Folk Festival**, held annually at the end of July at Cherry Hinton, and attracting a wide variety of loosely folk-based acts.

Boat Race, 170 East Rd (☎01223/508533). Lively pub venue for all kinds of music, with gigs every night.

Cambridge Arts Cinema, 8 Market Passage, off Market St (☎01223/504444), has an excellent, wide-ranging programme.

Cambridge Arts Theatre, 6 St Edward's Passage, off King's Parade (☎01223/503333). The city's main repertory theatre, founded by John Maynard Keynes, and launching pad of a thousand-and-one famous careers, from Derek Jacobi to Stephen Fry, offers a topnotch range of cutting-edge and classic productions.

Corn Exchange, Wheeler St (☎01223/357 851). Revamped nineteenth-century trading hall, now the main city-centre venue for opera, ballet, musicals and comedy as well as regular rock and folk gigs.

Junction, Clifton Rd (☎01223/511511). Rock, indie, jazz, reggae or soul gigs, plus occasional comedy acts and dance groups at this popular arts and entertainments venue.

Listings

Airport Stansted Airport flight enquiries (☎01279/680500); late availability (☎0345/118118).

Banks and exchanges There are banks all over the city centre, and you can exchange traveller's cheques at the main post office (see below); at American Express, 25 Sidney St (☎01223/461410); and Thomas Cook, in the Grafton Centre (☎01223/322611) and at 18 Market Hill (☎01223/366141).

Bike rental Cambridge Recycles, 61 Newnham Rd at Fen Causeway (☎01223/506035) plus a summer stall at the train station; Geoff's Bike Hire, 65 Devonshire Rd (☎01223/365629); Mike's Bikes, 28 Mill Rd (☎01223/312591). Rates start at around £7 a day.

Bookshops Heffers is the biggest outfit in town with the main branch at 20 Trinity St. Cambridge University Press has a shop at 1 Trinity St. For secondhand books try the shops down St Edward's Passage off King's Parade: G. David, at no. 3, is an antiquarian's and hardback hunter's paradise; the Haunted Bookshop, at no. 9, is better for first editions, travel and illustrated books.

Buses Most departures are from Drummer Street bus station. Stagecoach Cambus (☎01223/423554) is the main city and regional operator and has a call-in information office at the Premier Travel Agency, Drummer Street. Cambridge Coach Services (☎01223/423900) operates direct services to Oxford, Norwich, Great Yarmouth and the London airports; National Express (☎0990/808080) runs services to London and other major cities.

Car rental Avis, 245 Mill Rd (☎01223/212551); Budget, 303–305 Newmarket Rd (☎01223/323838); Thrifty, 2a Elizabeth Way (☎01223/321321); Wilhire, Barnwell Rd (☎01223/414600).

Dentist ☎01223/415126.

Hospitals Addenbrooke's Hospital, Hills Road (☎01223/217118).

Left luggage 24-hour lockers at the train station only.

Pharmacies Boots, 28 Petty Cury and 65 Sidney St (☎01223/350213); Lloyds, 54 Burleigh St (☎01223/352917) and 30 Trumpington St (☎01223/359449).

Police The main station is on Parkside (☎01223/358966).

Post office The main office is at 9–11 St Andrew's St (Mon–Fri 9am–5.30pm, Sat 9am–7pm).

Taxis There are ranks at the train station, Drummer Street bus station, King's Parade/Market Hill, and St Andrew's St near the post office. To book, call Intercity (☎01223/312233) or Panther (☎01223/715715).

Trains ☎0345/484950.

Travel agent STA, 38 Sidney St (☎01223/366966).

Around Cambridge

Within easy reach of Cambridge, across the flat fen landscapes, are several absorbing day-trip destinations. South of the city is **Grantchester**, a smart little place that's typical of the villages hereabouts – though the real draw is that you can cycle or punt there through open countryside. A little further afield, south along the M11, comes **Duxford Imperial War Museum** and then, among the rolling hills of northwest Essex, the straggling market town of **Saffron Walden**. Horseracing aficionados will, however, have little truck with all of this, heading straight for **Newmarket**. Each is accessible by bus or train from Cambridge.

Grantchester

The pretty little village of **GRANTCHESTER**, replete with thatched cottages and chestnut trees, is just a couple of miles up the Cam from Cambridge, and a popular destination on sunny days since it's an easy bike or punt ride away through **Grantchester Meadows** – the signposted route starts at the southern end of Newnham Road. The poet Rupert Brooke, who died in World War I, lodged in the old vicarage here as an undergraduate, penning the much-quoted lines "Stands the church clock at ten to three? And is there honey still for tea?" The clock in the pub named after Brooke stands permanently at ten to three, though of the three village **pubs**, you're better off heading for the *Red Lion* or the *Green Man*, both sited where the path from Cambridge emerges on the village's main street.

Duxford: Imperial War Museum

Eight miles south of Cambridge, and visible from the M11 (it's next to junction 10), are the giant hangars of the **Imperial War Museum** (daily mid-March to mid-Oct 10am–6pm; mid-Oct to mid-March 10am–4pm; £7.20), based at Duxford airfield. Throughout World War II, East Anglia was the centre of operations for the RAF and this flat, unobstructed landscape was dotted with dozens of airfields. Duxford itself was a Battle of Britain station, equipped with Spitfires, and there's a reconstructed Operations Room in one of the control towers. In total, Duxford holds over 150 historic aircraft, a wide-ranging collection of civil and military planes from the Sunderland flying boat to Concorde and the Vulcan B2 bombers, which were used for the first and last time in the Falklands; the Spitfires remain the most enduringly popular. Most of the planes are kept in full working order and are taken out for a spin several times a year at **Duxford Air Shows**, which attract thousands of visitors. There are usually four Air Shows a year and tickets cost around £12–15. For further details on these and on the free courtesy bus service linking Duxford with Cambridge, call ☎01223/835000.

Saffron Walden and Audley End

Some ten miles south of Cambridge, the fenlands are left behind for the hillier landscapes of Uttlesford, the district council's euphemism for the northwest corner of Essex. The main event here is **SAFFRON WALDEN**, a good-looking town that possesses dozens of antique timber-framed houses. There are several particularly fine examples on the main road, but the nicest areas of town to explore are away from the thundering traffic in the network of alleyways around the Market Place and the book and antique shops of Church Street. Many of these old houses sport fancy decorative plasterwork, known as pargeting – the last word on which is provided by the stepped gables of the **Old Sun Inn**, on Church Street, which Cromwell once used as his headquarters. The town's prefix was coined in medieval times when saffron crocuses were cultivated here for their dye and medicinal qualities. You can learn more about this and other aspects of the town's history at the **museum** on Museum Street, off Church Street (March–Oct Mon–Sat 10am–5pm, Sun 2.30–5pm; Nov–Feb Mon–Sat 10am–4pm, Sun 2.30–4.30pm; £1). Behind the museum are the scant ruins of the twelfth-century **castle**.

A mile or so to the west of town – beyond the village that bears its name – the palatial Jacobean mansion of **Audley End** (April–Sept Wed–Sun 11am–6pm, Oct Wed–Sun 10am–3pm; house & ground £5.75; grounds only £3.50; EH) was built for the Earl of Suffolk at the start of the seventeenth century. A spectacularly lavish building, it was soon the talk of the aristocracy, so much so that Charles II purchased it in 1668, staying here whenever he went to the races at Newmarket. Returned to the Suffolks after the king's death, Audley End was modified on several later occasions, most notably when one of the Suffolks demolished the east wing in 1735 to reduce his overheads. Highlights of the guided tours include the striking wood panelling and plasterwork of the Great Hall and, less ostentatiously, the subtle elegance of Robert Adam's two drawing rooms. English Heritage has worked hard on renovating the **grounds**, which were first laid out by Capability Brown and contain a river, a lake and a splendid flower garden.

Buses to Saffron Walden stop near the Market Place, where the **tourist office** (April–Oct Mon–Sat 9.30am–5.30pm; Nov–March Mon–Sat 10am–5pm; ☎01799/510 444) has plenty of leaflets on local attractions. The nearest **train station** is in Audley End village, a mile to the west of town off the B1383 and a long walk from Audley End house. In Saffron Walden, Castle and Church streets are just to the north of the Market Place, to the west is the High Street and its continuation Bridge Street, also the B184. The only access to Audley End is off the B1383 – take Audley End Road out of Saffron Walden and follow the signs. The best **pub** in town is the ancient *Eight Bells*, on Bridge Street.

Newmarket

NEWMARKET, twelve miles east of Cambridge, on springy heathland just over the county border in Suffolk, is famous for just one thing – **horseracing**. According to legend, Boudicca's tribe were keen on Ben-Hur style chariot-racing, but history gives James I the honour of founding modern horseracing here. James may have started it off, but Charles II brought the sport to prominence, visiting twice a year and bringing the entire royal court – and Nell Gwynne – with him. Two of the country's five flat-racing classics are held at Newmarket, the One Thousand Guineas and the Two Thousand Guineas, both held early in the season, which runs from the middle of April to October.

Coming from Cambridge, you'll pass the Rowley Mile Racecourse – named after one of Charles's own steeds – on your way into town. The approach roads are flanked by bridleways, and in the morning there are hundreds of racehorses being exercised along them. Newmarket itself is a one-horse town, with the Georgian Jockey Club, founded in 1752, occupying pride of place on the High Street. Next door is the **National Horse Racing Museum** (April–June, Sept & Oct Tues–Sun 10am–5pm; July & Aug daily 10am–5pm; £3.50), telling you more than you'll ever want to know about the sport. It also offers a variety of guided tours, including trips to the equine pool, the National Stud and the adjacent Jockey Club (for further details, call ☎01638/560622). Several **buses** make the half-hour journey to town from Cambridge and there's also a regular **train** service.

travel details

Trains

Cambridge to: Audley End (2 hourly; 15min); Birmingham (hourly; 2hr 50min); Bury St Edmunds (8 daily; 40min); Ely (hourly; 15min); Ipswich (6 daily; 1hr 20min); King's Lynn (hourly; 45min); Leicester (hourly; 1hr 50min); London (2 hourly; 1hr); Newmarket (8 daily; 20min); Norwich (hourly; 1hr); Peterborough (hourly; 50min); Stansted (10 daily; 40min); Thetford (hourly; 20–30min).

Colchester to: Ipswich (2 hourly; 25min); London (2 hourly; 30min); Norwich (hourly; 1hr).

Ely to: King's Lynn (hourly; 30min); Liverpool (hourly 4hr 30min); Manchester (hourly; 3hr 30min); Nottingham (hourly 1hr 45min); Peterborough (hourly; 30min).

Ipswich to: Bury St Edmunds (10 daily; 30min); Ely (7 daily; 1hr); London (2 hourly; 1hr 10min); Lowestoft (every 1–2hr; 1hr 30min); Norwich (hourly; 45min); Peterborough (7 daily; 1hr 50min); Woodbridge (every 1–2hr; 15min).

Norwich to: Cromer (every 1–2hr; 50min); Ely (hourly; 50min); Great Yarmouth (hourly; 30min); Liverpool (hourly; 5hr 30min); London (hourly; 2hr); Lowestoft (hourly; 30–45min); Manchester (hourly; 4hr 30min); Nottingham (hourly 2hr 30min); Peterborough (hourly; 1hr 30min); Sheringham (every 1–2hr; 1hr).

Peterborough to: Bury St Edmunds (6 daily; 1hr); Cambridge (hourly; 50min); Liverpool (hourly; 4hr); London (2 hourly; 1hr); Manchester (hourly; 3hr); Norwich (hourly; 1hr 30min); Nottingham (hourly; 1hr 10min).

Buses

Bury St Edmunds to: Colchester (8 daily; 2hr); Lavenham (10 daily; 30min); Sudbury (10 daily; 1hr).

Cambridge to: Bury St Edmunds (5 daily; 50min); London (hourly; 2hr); Newmarket (6 daily; 30min); Oxford (9 daily; 3hr); Peterborough (6 daily; 1hr 50min); Stansted Airport (9 daily; 45min); Saffron Walden (5 daily; 1hr).

Colchester to: Dedham (4 daily; 30min); Lavenham (8 daily; 1hr 30min); Long Melford (every 1–2hr; 1hr); Sudbury (every 1–2hr; 50min).

Ely to: Cambridge (6 daily; 40min); Newmarket (5 daily; 1hr).

Ipswich to: Aldeburgh (2–6 daily; 1hr 45min); Colchester (6 daily; 30min); Orford (1–2 daily; 1hr 15min).

King's Lynn to: Castle Rising (hourly; 15min); Hunstanton (every 30min; 50min); Norwich (every 2hr; 1hr 30min); Peterborough (every 2hr; 1hr); Sandringham (8 daily; 30min); Wisbech (every 2hr; 30min).

Norwich to: Bury St Edmunds (3 daily; 1hr 30min); Cromer (hourly; 50min); Great Yarmouth (hourly; 1hr 30min); King's Lynn (every 2hr; 1hr 30min); Sheringham (hourly; 1hr 20min); Wells-next-the-Sea (Mon–Sat 4–5 daily; 1hr 45min); Wroxham (2–4 hourly; 30min).

Saffron Walden to: Duxford (every 2hr; 20min); Thaxted (Mon–Sat 3–5 daily; 45min).

Sheringham to: Blakeney (Tues–Fri & Sun 3–5 daily; 20min); Hunstanton (Tues–Fri & Sun 1–4 daily; 1hr 40min); Wells-next-the-Sea (Tues–Fri & Sun 1–5 daily; 50min).

Sudbury to: Bury St Edmunds (hourly; 50min); Lavenham (Mon–Sat hourly; 30min).

Wells-next-the-Sea to: Hunstanton (1–5 daily; 1hr); King's Lynn (Mon–Sat 1–3 daily; 1hr 30min).

CENTRAL ENGLAND

entral England is the most diffuse region of the country, bracketed to the west by the Welsh border and to the east by the North Sea, but otherwise difficult to define geographically. At least there can be no doubt about the location of its economic and demographic focus – **Birmingham**, Britain's second city and once the world's greatest industrial metropolis. Long saddled with a reputation as a culture-hating, car-loving backwater, Birmingham has redefined its image in recent years with some bold artistic and redevelopment projects, most notably the construction of the complex that houses the country's best concert hall. Although it may still be few people's idea of a good-looking town, it's certainly one of the liveliest spots in the region, with nightlife encompassing everything from Royal Ballet productions to all-night raves, and a great spread of restaurants and pubs.

The urban sprawl clinging to the western side of Birmingham, known as the **Black Country**, more amply fulfils the negative stereotypes, although even here you'll find a few pleasant surprises, in the shape of several excellent museums and galleries. In the region to the south of this giant West Midlands conurbation lie the wide and fertile vales of the rivers **Severn** and **Avon**. These hold central England's biggest tourist draws – **Stratford-upon-Avon**, a place now perhaps over-burdened with Shakespeare-related paraphernalia, and the castle of nearby **Warwick**. However, the crowds and commercialism of these two towns fade away in neighbouring **Worcestershire**, a predominantly pastoral county typified by the handsome hills around the spa town of **Great Malvern** and by the low-key old cathedral city of **Worcester** itself.

Further west still is **Herefordshire**, a large and sparsely populated county that's home to several charming market towns, most notably the cathedral city of **Hereford**, pocket-sized **Ross-on-Wye** and **Hay-on-Wye**, where there's the largest concentration of secondhand bookshops in the world. Next door, rural **Shropshire** weighs in with **Ludlow**, one of the region's prettiest towns, awash with antique half-timbered buildings, and the amiable county town of **Shrewsbury**. Shropshire has a fascinating industrial history too, for it was here in the **Ironbridge Gorge** that British industrialists built the first iron bridge and pioneered the use of coal as a smelting fuel – two key events of the Industrial Revolution. To the north lies **Staffordshire**, where the halcyon days when the potteries of **Stoke-on-Trent** dominated the world market are recalled by an

---

ACCOMMODATION PRICE CODES

Throughout this guide, hotel and B&B accommodation is priced on a scale of ① to ⑨, the number indicating the **lowest price** you could expect to pay per night in that establishment for a **double room** in high season. The prices indicated by the codes are as follows:

① under £40	④ £60–70	⑦ £110–150
② £40–50	⑤ £70–90	⑧ £150–200
③ £50–60	⑥ £90–110	⑨ over £200

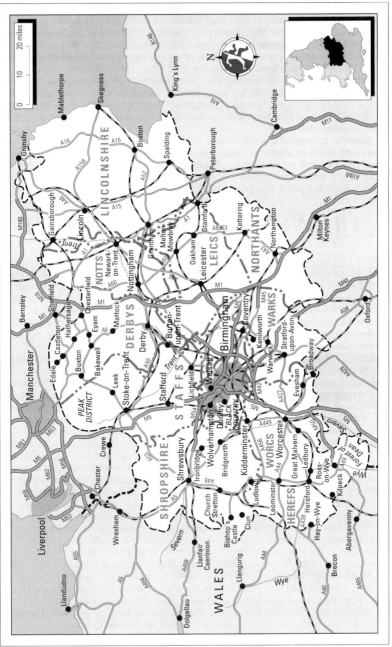

outstanding museum or two, and **Derbyshire**, whose northern reaches incorporate the region's finest scenery in the rough landscapes of the **Peak District**.

Most tourists bypass the counties of the East Midlands – **Nottinghamshire**, **Leicestershire**, **Northamptonshire** and **Lincolnshire** – on their way to more obvious destinations. It's true they miss little of overriding interest, though **Nottingham** and **Leicester** are boisterous cities and the rural charms of much of **Northamptonshire** hold some appeal. **Lincolnshire** is an agricultural backwater in comparison to its neighbours, but its sights – as distinct from the mostly dreary landscape – are far more diverting, most remarkably the cathedral at **Lincoln**, the alluring stone-built town of **Stamford** and the superb parish **churches** that are spread out across the county.

Travel in this region is simple. Birmingham sits at the heart of central England's rail and coach networks, with most of the region's main towns and cities enjoying easy links from there, as well as from London, Bristol, Manchester and points farther north. It is only really when you get into the outbacks of Shropshire, Herefordshire or Lincolnshire that public transport can be problematic.

THE WEST MIDLANDS AND THE PEAK DISTRICT

The factories of central England were the powerhouses of the Industrial Revolution, and the knot of towns at the very heart of the West Midlands – the **Black Country** – still carries a name redolent of a period that has long gone. Post-recession dereliction is the principal problem now facing an area that has taken the brunt of Britain's decline as a manufacturing power – **Birmingham**, for example, lost over a third of its manufacturing jobs between 1974 and 1983. In recent years many of the area's moribund towns have undergone something of a transformation, as the economy has been realigned with a new emphasis on service industries, a process exemplified by Birmingham itself, a city that's now making money from the business convention and exhibition trades. England's second city has also initiated some ambitious architectural and environmental schemes, jazzed up its museums and industrial heritage sites and given itself a higher profile on the British cultural scene than it's ever had before. Though there are signs that the investment in prestige projects is waning, in favour of schemes aimed at the creation of long-term employment, tourists will continue to benefit from the legacies of Birmingham's high-cost revamp.

The counties to the south and west of Birmingham and the Black Country –**Warwickshire**, **Worcestershire**, **Herefordshire** and **Shropshire** – comprise a rural stronghold that maintains an emotional and political distance from the conurbation: the left-wing politics of the big city seem remote indeed when you're in Shrewsbury, but in fact it's only seventy miles from Birmingham. For the most part, the four counties constitute a quiet, unassuming stretch of pastoral England whose beauty is rarely dramatic, but whose charms become more evident the longer you stay. Of the four counties, **Warwickshire** is the least obviously scenic, but draws by far the biggest number of visitors, for – as the huge road-signs declare at every entry point – this is "Shakespeare's County". Too many visitors spend a couple of hours wedged into the crowded streets of **Stratford**, and then take in **Warwick Castle** before heading on, but there is plenty more to this area than this, most notably the great medieval castle at **Kenilworth**, and the gritty city of **Coventry**, worth a call for its magnificent modern cathedral.

Neighbouring **Worcestershire** and **Herefordshire** cover a vast area stretching from the urban fringes of the West Midlands and the mellow Cotswolds to the stark mountains along the Welsh border. Both contain ancient towns bursting with picture-postcard images, although, as in much of rural England, nightlife and entertainment can be less than thrilling. The main centres are the twin cathedral cities of **Worcester** and its smaller sibling, **Hereford**, both within easy reach of the picturesque villages and lush hills that characterize the two counties. Between the two cities lies **Great Malvern**, a mannered inland resort spread along the rolling contours of the **Malvern Hills**, while the rivers Wye and Severn meander southwards past the **Forest of Dean**, one of England's most extensive ancient woodlands.

Shropshire and **Staffordshire** are also mainly rural, albeit with zones of still-productive industry and several reminders of the manufacturing heyday. At **Ironbridge Gorge** a phalanx of museums commemorates the pioneering work of the Darby dynasty of engineers and of Thomas Telford, while the potteries of **Stoke-on-Trent** remain large-scale employers in a part of the country that has been badly dented by the decline in British manufacturing. Both counties boast some appealing historic towns as well: in Shropshire there's a glut of old settlements to enjoy – from the county town of **Shrewsbury**, to the tiny cluster of streets that is **Much Wenlock** and the extraordinarily pretty **Ludlow**, dripping with rickety half-timbered buildings. In Staffordshire, the main attraction is **Lichfield**, which takes its tone from its spectacular cathedral and the legacies of its Regency high times. As for the countryside, little in central England can match the borderlands of Shropshire, where the ancient ridges of the **Long Mynd** and **Wenlock Edge** offer some of the region's wildest walks. But further east lies the extravagantly scenic **Peak District National Park**, whose soft contours offer great opportunities for moderately strenuous walks, as well as the diversions of the former spa town of **Buxton**, the limestone caverns of **Castleton** and a couple of fine country houses, grandiose **Chatsworth** and fascinating **Haddon Hall**.

Birmingham, the nucleus of the region, is easily accessible by **rail** from London Euston, Liverpool, Manchester, Leeds, York and a score of other towns. It is also well served by the National Express **bus** network, with dozens of buses leaving every hour for destinations all over Britain. Local **bus** services are excellent around the West Midlands conurbation – mostly run by West Midlands Travel (WMT) – but tend to dwindle the farther you move from Birmingham.

Stratford-upon-Avon and around

Despite its worldwide fame, **STRATFORD-UPON-AVON** is, at heart, an unassuming market town with an unexceptional pedigree. Its first settlers forded, and later bridged, the River Avon, developing commercial links with the inhabitants of the rich local farmland and the Forest of Arden. A charter for Stratford's weekly market was granted in the twelfth century, a tradition continued to this day, and the town later became an important stopping-off point for stagecoaches between London, Oxford and the north. Like all such places, Stratford had its clearly defined class system and within this typical milieu John and Mary **Shakespeare** occupied the middle rank, and would have been forgotten long ago had their first son, **William**, not turned out to be the greatest writer ever to use the English language. A consequence of their good fortune is that this ordinary little place is nowadays all but smothered by package-tourist hype and its central streets groan under the weight of thousands of tourists. Try not to let that deter you: dodging the multitudes is possible by avoiding the busiest attractions – principally the Birthplace Museum – and the Royal Shakespeare Company offers superb theatre. Moreover, Stratford still has the ability to surprise and delight, whether in the excellence of some of its restaurants or by the river views at the Holy Trinity Church.

Arrival and information

Stratford's **train station** is on the northwestern edge of town, ten minutes' walk from the centre. Now the end of the line, it receives hourly shuttles from Birmingham (Moor Street or Snow Hill stations) and frequent trains from Warwick (for connections to London Paddington or London Marylebone) except on Sundays, when there are only a couple of services all day. Local **bus services**, arrive and depart from the central Bridge Street; National Express services pull into the Riverside station on the east side of the town centre, off Bridgeway.

The **tourist office** (April–Oct Mon–Sat 9am–6pm, Sun 11am–5pm; Nov–March Mon–Sat 9am–5pm; ☎01789/293127) is located a couple of minutes' walk from the bus station by the bridge at the junction of Bridgeway and Bridgefoot. They have oodles of information on local attractions and operate an accommodation booking service (see below), which is very useful during the height of the summer when rooms can be in very short supply. It also issues bus timetables and sells bus tickets. General tourist information is also available from the Guide Friday office in the centre at 14 Rother St (☎01789/294466), but they basically exist to flog tickets for their bus tours of the town and environs (£8 excluding admission to properties). The tourist office will sell you an all-in ticket for all five **Shakespeare Birthplace Trust** properties (£11), or a **Three In-Town Shakespeare Property Ticket** (£7.50) for the three Trust properties in Stratford – both tickets are also available from any of the sites themselves.

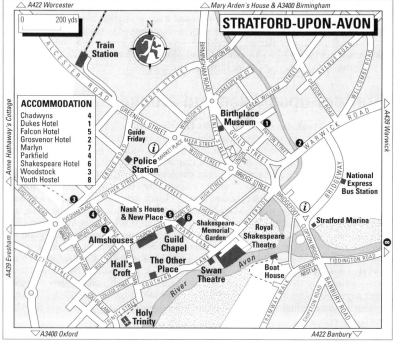

© Crown copyright

Accommodation

As one of the most popular tourist destinations in England, Stratford's **accommodation** is distinctly pricey and gets booked up well in advance. In peak months, and during the Shakespeare birthday celebrations around April 23, it's essential to book ahead. The town has a couple of dozen **hotels**, the pick of which occupy old half-timbered buildings right in the centre of town, but most visitors choose to stay in a **B&B**. These have sprung up in every part of Stratford, but there's a particular concentration to the southwest of the centre around Grove Road, Evesham Place and Broad Walk. The tourist office operates an efficient and extremely useful **Accommodation Booking Hotline** (☎01789/415061; Mon–Fri 9.30am–4.30pm; £3).

Hotels

Dukes, Payton St (☎01789/269300). On the north side of the town centre, a couple of minutes' walk from the Birthplace Museum, this comfortable, privately owned hotel has a pleasant interior dotted with antiques. ⑤.

Falcon, Chapel St (☎01789/279953). Handily situated in the middle of the town centre, the half-timbered facade dates from the sixteenth century, though the rest is an unremarkable modern rebuild. ④.

Grosvenor, Warwick Rd (☎01789/269213). Close to the canal, just a couple of minutes' walk from the town centre, the *Grosvenor* occupies a row of pleasant, two-storey Georgian houses. The interior is done out in a crisp modern style and there's ample parking at the back. Discounted short break deals available. ⑤.

The Shakespeare, Chapel St (☎01789/294771). Right in the centre of town. Now part of a chain, this old hotel, with its mullion windows and half-timbered facade, is one of Stratford's best known. The interior has low beams and open fires and represents a fairly successful amalgamation of old and new features. ⑦.

B&Bs

Chadwyns, 6 Broad Walk (☎01789/269077). Just off Evesham Place, this B&B occupies pleasant Victorian premises and offers three en-suite rooms. ①.

Marlyn, 3 Chestnut Walk (☎01789/293752). More central and secluded than most B&Bs, and good value, with comfortable rooms. ②.

Parkfield, 3 Broad Walk (☎01789/293313). Very pleasant, accommodating B&B in a rambling Victorian house down a residential street off Evesham Place. They have a private car park – a useful facility in crowded Stratford – and most of the rooms are en suite. Less than ten minutes' walk from the centre. ②.

Woodstock, 30 Grove Rd (☎01789/299881). A smart and neatly kept B&B ten minutes' walk from the centre, by the start of the path to Anne Hathaway's Cottage. It has five extremely comfortable bedrooms, most en suite. No credit cards. ②.

Hostels and camping

Stratford Youth Hostel, Hemmingford House, Alveston (☎01789/297093). Two and a half miles east of town on the B4086 and served by Stagecoach Midland Red bus #18 and #X18, which runs every one or two hours from Wood Street. The hostel occupies a rambling Georgian mansion on the edge of the pretty village of Alveston and has dormitories and family rooms with en-suite facilities. Bike rental available too.

The Town

Spreading back from the River Avon, Stratford's **town centre** is fairly flat and compact, its mostly modern buildings filling out a simple gridiron just two blocks deep and four blocks long. Running along the northern edge of the centre is **Bridge Street**, the main thoroughfare lined with shops and choc-a-bloc with local buses. At its west end, Bridge

SHAKESPEARE: WHAT'S IN A NAME?

Over the past hundred years or so, the deification of **William Shakespeare** (1564–1616) has been dogged by a loony backlash among a fringe of revisionist scholars and literary figures known as **"Anti-Stratfordians"**. According to these heretics, the famous plays and sonnets were not written by a wool merchant's son from Stratford at all, but by someone else, and William Shakespeare was merely a *nom de plume*. The American novelist Henry James, among the most notorious arch-sceptics, once claimed that he was "haunted by the conviction that the divine William is the biggest and most successful fraud ever practised on a patient world".

A variety of candidates have been proposed for the authorship of Shakespeare's works, and they range from the faintly plausible (Christopher Marlowe, Ben Jonson, and the earls of Rutland, Southampton and Oxford) to the manifestly whacko (Queen Elizabeth I, King James I and Daniel Defoe, author of *Robinson Crusoe*, who was born six years after publication of the First Folio). The wildest theories, however, have been reserved for Francis Bacon. In his book *The Great Cryptogram*, American congressman Ignatius Donnelly postulates that the word "honorificabilitudinitatibus", which crops up in *Love's Labour Lost*, was actually an anagram for the Latin "Hi ludi F Baconis nati tuiti orbi" ("These plays, F. Bacon's offspring, are preserved for the world"). Others have rallied around the Earl of Oxford's banner; Sigmund Freud maintained that Oxford wrote the plays, and Orson Welles agreed, saying that otherwise there were ". . . some awfully funny coincidences to explain away".

Lying at the root of the authorship debate are several unresolved questions that have puzzled scholars for years. How could a man of modest background from the provinces have such an intimate knowledge of royal protocol? How could he know so much about Italy without ever having travelled there? Why was he allowed to write potentially embarrassing love poems to one of England's most powerful aristocrats? Why did he not leave a library in his will, when the author of the plays clearly possessed an intimate knowledge of classical literature? Why, given that Shakespeare was supposedly a well-known dramatist, did no death notice or obituary appear in publications of the day?

The speculation surrounding Shakespeare's life stems from the fact that far less is known about the man himself than about his work. The few details that have been preserved come mostly from official archives – birth, marriage and death certificates and

Street divides into Henley Street, home of the **Birthplace Museum**, and Wood Street, which leads up to the market place. It also intersects with High Street. This, and its continuation Chapel and Church streets, cuts south to pass most of the old buildings that the town still possesses, most notably **Nash's House** and, on neighbouring Old Town Street, **Hall's Croft**. From here, it's a short hop to the charming **Holy Trinity Church**, where Shakespeare lies buried, and then only a few minutes back along the river past the **theatres** to the foot of Bridge Street. In itself, this circular walk only takes about fifteen minutes, but it takes all day if you potter around the attractions. In addition, there are two outlying Shakespearean properties, **Anne Hathaway's Cottage** in Shottery and **Mary Arden's House** in Wilmcote – though you have to be a really serious sightseer to want to see them all.

The Birthplace Museum

Top of everyone's Bardic itinerary is the **Birthplace Museum**, an ugly modern visitor centre attached to the heavily restored half-timbered building on Henley Street (late March to mid-Oct Mon–Sat 9am–5pm, Sun 9.30am–5pm; mid-Oct to late March Mon–Sat 9.30am–4pm, Sun 10am–4pm; £4.90). The visitor centre pokes into every corner of Shakespeare's life and times, making the most of what little hard evidence there court records. From these we know that on April 22 or 23, 1564, a certain John Shakespeare, variously described as a glove maker, butcher, wool merchant and corn trader, and his wife, Mary, had their first son, William; that the boy attended a local grammar school until financial problems forced him into his father's business; and that at the age of eighteen he married a local woman, Anne Hathaway, seven years his senior, who five months later bore a daughter, Susanna, the first of three children. Several years later, probably around 1587, the young Shakespeare was forced to flee Stratford after being caught poaching on the estate of Sir Thomas Lucy at nearby Charlecote. Five companies of players passed through the town on tour that year, and it is believed he absconded with one of them to London, where a theatre boom was in full swing. *Henry VI*, Shakespeare's first play, appeared soon after, followed by the hugely successful *Richard III*. Over the next decade, Shakesepare's output was prodigious. Thirty-eight plays appeared, most of them performed by his own theatre troupes based in the **Globe**, a large timber-framed theatre overlooking the south bank of the River Thames, in which he had a one-tenth share.

Success secured Shakespeare the patronage of London's fashionable set, among them the dashing young courtier, Henry Wriothesley, Earl of Southampton, with whom the playwright is believed to have had a passionate affair (Southampton is thought to have been the "golden youth" of the Sonnets). The ageing Queen Elizabeth I, bewigged and decked in opulent jewellery, regularly attended the Globe, as did her successor, James I, whose Scottish ancestry and fascination with the occult accounts for the subject matter of *Macbeth*. Shakespeare realized the commercial importance of appealing to the rich and powerful. This, as much as his extraordinary talent, ensured his plays were the most acclaimed of the day, earning him enough money to retire comfortably to Stratford, where he largely abandoned literature in the last years of his life to concentrate on business and family affairs.

Ultimately, the sketchy details of Shakespeare's life are of far less importance than the plays, sonnets and songs he left behind. Whoever wrote them – and despite all the conjecture, William Shakespeare almost certainly did – the body of work attributed to this shadowy historical figure comprises some of the most inspired and exquisite English ever written. The greatest irony is not that *King Lear* and *The Tempest* were penned by a provincial middle-class merchant's son, but that of all the millions of visitors who pass through Stratford each year, the majority appear to be more interested in the writer himself than in what he wrote.

is. His will is interesting in so far as he passed all sorts of goodies to his daughter, but precious little to his wife – the museum commentary tries to gainsay this apparent meanness, but fails to convince. Next door, the half-timbered dwelling is actually two buildings knocked into one. The west half, now fitted out in the style of a sixteenth-century domestic interior, was the business premises of the poet's father, who is thought to have worked as a glover, though some argue that he was a wool merchant or a butcher. Neither is it certain that Shakespeare was born in this building nor that he was born on April 23, 1564 – it's just known that he was baptized on April 26, and it's an irresistible temptation to place the birth of the national poet three days earlier, on St George's Day. However, both suppositions are now treated as fact at this shrine, where the east half of the building – bought by John Shakespeare in 1556 – displays a modest range of period artefacts designed to illuminate a life which remains distinctly enigmatic.

Nash's House and New Place

Follow the High Street south from the junction of Bridge and Henley streets, and you'll soon come to another Birthplace Trust property, **Nash's House** on Chapel Street (late March to mid-Oct Mon–Sat 9.30am–5pm, Sun 10am–5pm; mid-Oct to late March Mon–Sat 10am–4pm, Sun 10.30am–4pm; £3.30, includes New Place). The house was the property of Thomas Nash, first husband of Shakespeare's granddaughter, Elizabeth Hall, and is mostly taken up by a very dry history of Stratford. The adjacent gardens contain the foundations of **New Place** (same hours), Shakespeare's last residence, which was demolished in 1759 by its owner, the Reverend Francis Gastrell. It was quite deliberate: Gastrell was so plagued by Shakespeare pilgrims that he began by chopping down a mulberry tree that Shakespeare himself was reputed to have planted and, when this didn't work, he knocked down the house as well. An alleged descendant of the notorious mulberry is to be seen in the adjacent **Great Garden of New Place**, a formal affair of topiary and flowerbeds whose entrance is on Chapel Lane (March–Oct Mon–Sat 9am–dusk, Sun 10am–dusk; Nov–Feb Mon–Fri 9am–4pm, Sun noon–4pm; free).

On the other side of Chapel Lane stands the **Guild Chapel**, with its chunky tower and plain interior, containing some rather kitsch stained glass windows. The adjoining King Edward VI **Grammar School**, where it's assumed Shakespeare was educated, incorporates a creaky line of fifteenth-century almshouses, just round the corner on Church Street.

Hall's Croft

Chapel Street continues south as Church Street. At the end, turn left along Old Town Street for Stratford's most impressive medieval house, the Birthplace Trust's **Hall's Croft** (late March to mid-Oct Mon–Sat 9.30am–5pm, Sun 10am–5pm; mid-Oct to late March Mon–Sat 10am–4pm, Sun 10.30am–4pm; £3.30). The former home of Shakespeare's elder daughter, Susanna, and her doctor husband, John Hall, the immaculately maintained Croft, with its creaking wooden floors, beamed ceilings and fine kitchen range, holds a scattering of period furniture and a fascinating display on Elizabethan medicine. Hall established something of a reputation for his medical know-how and published some of his case notes in a volume entitled *Select Observations on English Bodies*. You can peruse Hall's casebook – noting that Joan Chidkin of Southam "gave two vomits and two stools" after being "troubled with trembling of the arms and thighs" – and then suffer vicariously at the displays of eye-watering forceps and other implements. The best view of the building itself is at the back, in the neat walled garden.

Holy Trinity Church

Beyond Hall's Croft, Old Town Street veers right to reach the handsome **Holy Trinity Church** (March–Oct Mon–Sat 8.30am–6pm, Sun 2–5pm; Nov–Feb Mon–Sat 9am–4pm, Sun 2–5pm; free), whose mellow, honey-coloured stonework dates from the thirteenth century. Enhanced by its riverside setting and flanked by the yews and weeping willows of its graveyard, the dignified proportions of this quintessentially English church are the result of several centuries of chopping and changing, culminating in the replacement of the original wooden spire with today's stone version in 1763. At the entrance, the **Sanctuary Knocker** is a reminder of medieval times when local criminals could seek refuge from the law here, but only for 37 days. This, so local custom dictated, was long enough for them to negotiate a deal with their persecutors. Inside, the nave is bathed in light from the **stained glass windows**, some of which (predominantly along the south aisle) date from the fourteenth century. Quite unusually, you'll see that the nave is built on a slight skew from the line of the chancel – supposedly to represent Christ's inclined head on the cross. Beside the north transept is the **Clopton Chapel**, where the tomb of George Carew is a superbly carved Renaissance extravagance decorated with military insignia appropriate to George's job as Master in Ordnance to James I. But poor old George is long forgotten, unlike William Shakespeare, who lies buried in the **chancel** (60p), his remains overseen by a sedate memorial plaque and effigy added just seven years after his death.

The theatres

Strolling north along the riverbank from the church, you'll soon reach Southern Lane and its continuation, Waterside, home to the town's three Royal Shakespeare Company **theatres** – The Other Place, the Swan Theatre and the Royal Shakespeare Theatre. There was no theatre in Stratford in Shakespeare's day and indeed the first home-town festival in his honour was only held in 1769 at the behest of London-based David Garrick. Thereafter, the idea of building a permanent home in which to perform Shakespeare's works slowly gained momentum, and finally, in 1879, the first Memorial Theatre was opened on land donated by local beer baron Charles Flower. A fire in 1926 necessitated the construction of a new theatre, and the ensuing architectural competition was won by Elisabeth Scott. Her theatre is today's **Royal Shakespeare Theatre**. In the 1980s, the burnt-out original theatre round the back was turned into a replica "in-the-round" Elizabethan stage – the **Swan**; it's used for works by Shakespeare's contemporaries, classics from all eras and one annual piece by the man himself. The third auditorium, **The Other Place**, showcases modern and experimental pieces. The RSC also organizes a number of behind-the-scenes tours – ask at the box office for details.

Anne Hathaway's Cottage and Mary Arden's House

Anne Hathaway's Cottage (late March to mid-Oct Mon–Sat 9am–5pm, Sun 9.30am–5pm; late Oct to mid-March Mon–Sat 9.30am–4pm, Sun 10am–4pm; £3.90), also operated by the Birthplace Trust, is located just over a mile west of the town centre in **Shottery**. The most agreeable way to get there is on the signposted footpath from Evesham Place, at the south end of Rother Street. The cottage, complete with its dinky wooden beams and thatching, was the home of Anne Hathaway before she married Shakespeare in 1582. A few yards away, the **Shakespeare Tree Garden** has a patch that is planted with species mentioned in the plays.

The Birthplace Trust also keeps **Mary Arden's House**, three miles northwest of the town centre in Wilmcote (late March to mid-Oct Mon–Sat 9.30am–5pm, Sun 10am–5pm; late Oct to mid-March Mon–Sat 10am–4pm, Sun 10.30am–4pm; £4.40). Mary Arden was Shakespeare's mother, the only unmarried daughter when her father, Robert, died in 1556. Unusually for the time, she inherited the house and land, thus becoming one of the neighbourhood's most eligible women – John Shakespeare, eager for self-improvement, married her within a year. The house is a well-furnished example

---

TICKETS FOR THE RSC

As the Royal Shakespeare Company works on a repertory system, you could stay in Stratford for a few days and see four or five different plays. Tickets for the **Royal Shakespeare Theatre** start at around £5 for standing room and a restricted view, rising to £39 for the best seats in the house. However, very popular shows get booked up months in advance. **Swan** tickets are generally between £5 and £36, with tickets for **The Other Place** hovering between £10 and £20.

The RSC's **box office** (Mon–Sat from 9am; ☎01789/403403) serves as the central booking agent for all three houses, although you collect your tickets from the theatre in question. At the Royal Shakespeare Theatre, one hundred tickets are kept back for that evening's performance and sold at just £10 each; for a real blockbuster, arriving to queue at 5am will not be too early. Stand-by tickets (for unsold seats) are also available on the day of performance, but only concessionary groups (OAPs, students, etc) are eligible. If all else fails, turn up about an hour before the performance and try your luck – though last-minute **returns** are quite rare. The RSC runs a **ticket availability information line** (☎01789/403404) and has a **Web site**, *www.rsc.org.uk*.

of an Elizabethan farmhouse and, though the labelling is rather scant, a platoon of guides fills in the details of family life and traditions.

Eating and drinking

Stratford is used to feeding and watering thousands of visitors, so finding refreshment is never difficult. The problem is that many places are geared to serving the day-tripper as rapidly as possible – not a recipe for much gastronomic delight. That said, there is a scattering of very good **restaurants**, several of which have been catering to theatregoers for many years, and a handful of **pubs** and **cafés** offer good food too. The best restaurants are concentrated along Sheep Street, running up from Waterside near the theatres.

Restaurants and cafés

Kingfisher Fish Bar, 13 Ely St. The best fish-and-chip shop in town. A five-minute walk from the theatres. Takeaway only. Closed Sun.

Lamb's Café Bistro, 12 Sheep St (☎01789/292554). Smart restaurant serving a mouthwatering range of stylish English and continental dishes. A good option for pasta lovers. Moderate.

Number 6, 6 Union St (☎01789/269106). Stratford's one and only specialist seafood restaurant. Moderate.

The Opposition, 13 Sheep St (☎01789/269980). Top-quality, imaginative international cuisine in a busy but amiable atmosphere. The dishes of the day, chalked up on a board inside, are excellent value. Moderate.

Pubs

Dirty Duck, 53 Waterside. The archetypal actors' pub, stuffed to the gunwales every night with a vocal entourage of RSC employees and hangers-on. Essential viewing.

The Garrick Inn, 25 High St. Arguably the town's most photogenic and best-preserved old ale house: exposed beams, real ales and good food.

Queen's Head, 54 Ely St. Attracts a mixed straight and gay crowd, and has a good range of ales.

Windmill Inn, Chapel St. Popular, youthful pub with a quirky, olde-worlde interior.

Listings

Banks and exchanges There are lots of banks in the town centre and all of them will change foreign currency and travellers' cheques. American Express has a bureau in the tourist office.

Bike rental Clarke's Cycles, 3 Guild St (☎01789/205057); Dawes & Lee Cooper, Greenhill St (☎01789/298333). Mountain bikes cost around £10 per day plus deposit.

Boat rental In the summertime, row boats (£4.50 an hour) and motor boats (£6 for 30min) can be rented at Stratford Marina, close to the tourist office in between the north end of Clopton Bridge (Bridge Foot) and the Moat House Hotel.

Books Waterstones, 18 High Street (☎01789/414418).

Buses Stagecoach Midland Red (☎01788/535555).

Car rental Ford, Arden Garages, Arden St (☎01789/267446); Hertz, at the train station (☎01789/298827).

Hospital Stratford General Hospital, Alcester Road – on the west side of the town centre (☎01789/205831).

Laundry Sparklean, 74 Bull St, off Old Town (daily 8am–9pm).

Pharmacy Boots, 11 Bridge St (Mon–Sat 9am–5.30pm; late opening roster posted on the door).

Police Rother Street near the junction with Ely Street (☎01789/414111).

Post office Henley Street, on the town side of the Birthplace Museum (Mon–Fri 8.30am–5.30pm, Sat 8.30am–6pm).

Taxis Stratford Taxis ☎01789/415888.

Trains ☎0345/484950.

Warwick

WARWICK, just eight miles northeast of Stratford and easily reached by bus and train, is famous for its massive castle, but it also possesses several charming streetscapes erected in the aftermath of a great fire in 1694, and a couple of particularly interesting buildings. An hour or two is quite enough time to nose around the compact town centre, but you'll need the whole day if, braving the crowds, you're set on exploring the castle too. Either way, Warwick is the perfect day-trip from Stratford.

Towering above the River Avon at the foot of the town centre, **Warwick Castle** (daily: April–Oct 10am–6pm; Nov–March 10am–5pm; £10.50) is locally proclaimed the "greatest medieval castle in Britain" and, if bulk equals greatness, then the claim is certainly valid, although much of the existing structure is the result of extensive nineteenth-century restoration. It's likely that the first fortress here was raised by Ethelfleda, daughter of Alfred the Great, in about 915 AD, but it was the eleventh Earl of Warwick who turned the stronghold into a formidable stone castle – complete with elaborate gatehouses, multiple turrets and a keep – in the fourteenth century. The earl and his descendants played a prominent part in the Hundred Years' War. One of their number was the executioner of Joan of Arc and they all brought prisoners back to Warwick and incarcerated them in the dingy dungeons of Caesar's Tower pending ransom negotiations.

The entrance to the castle is through the old stable block, beyond which a footpath leads round to the imposing east gate. Over the footbridge and beyond the protective towers is the main courtyard. You can stroll along the ramparts and climb the towers, but most visitors head straight for one or other of the special displays installed inside by the present owners, Madame Tussauds. Among several displays, one of the most popular is the "Royal Weekend Party, 1898", an extravaganza of waxwork nobility hobnobbing in the private apartments which were rebuilt in the 1870s after fire damage. Another display, "Kingmaker – a preparation for Battle", adds smells and atmospheric sounds to a lifelike waxwork scene of the preparations for Richard Earl of Warwick's – as in "Warwick the Kingmaker" – final battle in 1471.

Re-emerging from the castle at the stables, Castle Street leads up the hill for a few yards to its junction with the High Street. Turn left and it's a brief stroll to another outstanding monument, the **Lord Leycester Hospital** (June–Sept Tues–Sun 10am–5pm; Oct–May Tues–Sun 10am–4pm; £2.75), a tangle of half-timbered buildings that lean at fairytale angles against the old West Gate. The complex represents one of Britain's best-preserved examples of domestic Elizabethan architecture. It was established as a hostel for old soldiers by the Earl of Leicester, a favourite of Queen Elizabeth I, and incorporates several beamed buildings, principally the Great Hall and the Guildhall, as well as a wonderful galleried courtyard and an intimate chantry chapel. There's a modest regimental museum here too – appropriately enough as retired servicemen (and their wives) still live here.

Doubling back along the High Street, turn left up Church Street – opposite Castle Street – for the **Church of St Mary** (daily 10am–4pm), which was rebuilt in a weird Gothic-Renaissance amalgam after the fire of 1694. One part remained untouched, however – the **chancel**, a glorious specimen of the Perpendicular style with splendid flying ribs in the roof. On the right hand side of the chancel, the **Beauchamp chapel** contains several beautiful tombs, exquisite works of art beginning with that of Richard Beauchamp, Earl of Warwick, who is depicted in an elaborate suit of armour of Italian design from the tip of his swan helmet down. The adjacent tomb of Ambrose Dudley is of finely carved alabaster, as is that of Robert Dudley, Earl of Leicester, one of Elizabeth I's most influential advisers.

Warwick's **train station** is on the northern edge of the centre, about ten minutes' walk from the castle. **Buses** stop beside the Market Place, from where it's a couple of minutes' walk east to St Mary's and a couple more along Church Street to the **tourist office**, in the Courthouse at the corner of Church and Jury streets (daily 9.30am–4.30pm; ☎01926/492212). The tourist office has a list of local hotels and B&Bs, but with Stratford so near and easy to reach, there's no special reason to stay here. For a bite to **eat**, head for the inexpensive *Charlotte's Restaurant and Tearoom*, 6 Jury St (☎01926/498930; closed Mon). For a drink, try the traditional *Zetland Arms*, 11 Church St.

Kenilworth

Five miles to the north of Warwick is workaday **KENILWORTH**, a town that received something of a boost when Sir Walter Scott wrote his novel of the same name, but has become little more than an upmarket dormitory to Coventry (see p.454). It does, however, have one remarkable sight – the **Castle** from which Scott took his inspiration (April–Oct daily 10am–6pm; Nov–March daily 10am–4pm; £3.10; EH). Begun in the twelfth century – the keep dates from then – the castle was one of the key strategic strongholds in the Midlands, alternately held by the king or a leading noble. The Dudleys acquired the castle in the sixteenth century and one of the family, Robert, Earl of Leicester, pleased Elizabeth I no end by turning the draughty fortress into an elegant palace in preparation for her visit. Kenilworth then became one of England's most fashionable country houses, hosting spectacular pageants and entertainments, but following Dudley's death the castle slid into gradual decay, hastened by the attention of Cromwell's troops in the Civil War. Today, the substantial red sandstone ruins still maintain a tremendous presence, with large remnants from each era still easily discernible.

Worcestershire

In geographical terms, **Worcestershire** can be compared to a huge saucer, with the low-lying plains of the Vale of Evesham and Severn Valley rising to a lip of hills: the Malverns in the west, the Cotswolds in the south, the Abberley and Clee hills to the northwest and the Clents and Lickeys in the northeast. In character, the county divides into two broad belts. To the north lie the industrial and overspill towns – Droitwich and Redditch for instance – that have much in common with the Birmingham conurbation, while the south is predominantly rural. Marking the transition between the two is **Worcester** itself, where the main event is the splendid cathedral. The south holds the county's finest scenery in the **Malvern Hills**, excellent walking territory and home to the amiable little spa town of **Great Malvern**. South Worcestershire's rural lifestyle is famously portrayed in *The Archers*, the BBC's never-ending radio soap, which attracts a massive and extraordinarily dedicated audience.

The proximity of Birmingham ensures Worcestershire has a good network of **trains** and **buses**, though services do become less frequent to the villages in the south of the county. Worcestershire's **bus timetable information line** is ☎0345/125436.

Worcester

Right at the heart of the county, both geographically and politically, **WORCESTER** is a robust, slightly schizophrenic city, where timbered Tudor and refined Georgian buildings are overshadowed by charmless modern developments. The chief offender is the award-winning, £85-million Crowngate shopping mall, which obliterates a large swathe of the city centre. Postwar clumsiness apart, the biggest single influence on the city has always been the River Severn, which flows along Worcester's west flank. Because the

Severn is prone to flood, building is prohibited in the meadows flanking the river, leaving clear space by the cathedral, which rises high above the muddy brown river on the eastern bank.

The City

Worcester's skyline is dominated by the squat sandstone bulk of its **Cathedral** (daily 7.30am–6pm; £2 suggested donation), a rich stew of architectural styles, and best approached from the path that runs along the river's edge and through a gate bearing marks of the city's flood levels. The oldest section of the cathedral is its multi-columned **crypt**: built underneath the Saxon monastery founded here by St Oswald in 983, it's the largest Norman crypt in the country. The large circular **Chapter House**, off the cloisters, is the other main Norman portion, and has the distinction of being the first such building constructed without the use of a central supporting pillar. Inside the main part of the cathedral, the western end of the twelfth-century **nave** displays the transition between the rounded Norman and pointed Gothic arches. The pillars of the nave are decorated with bunches of fruit, carved by stonemasons from Lincoln, most of whom succumbed to the Black Death, leaving inferior successors to finish the job. Built in the mid-twelfth century, the Early English **east end** is one of the most elaborate sections, with the choir's forest of slender pillars soaring over the intricately worked choir stalls. In front of the **high altar** is the tomb of England's most reviled monarch, King John. Before he died in 1216, the ailing John explicitly instructed that he was to be buried between the tombs of St Wulstan and St Oswald. Close by is the cathedral's richest monument: **Prince Arthur's Chantry**, a delicate lacy confection of carved stonework built as a memorial in 1504 by King Henry VII for his young son, Arthur, who died on his honeymoon with Catherine of Aragon – later to become the first wife of his younger brother, Henry VIII. The chantry is liberally plastered with heraldic and symbolic depictions of the houses of York and Lancaster, united by the Lancastrian Henry VII after his victory at Bosworth Field and subsequent marriage to Elizabeth, daughter of the Yorkist king Edward IV. Tucked behind the cathedral in Severn Street, alongside the canal, the **Royal Worcester Porcelain** complex (Mon–Sat 9am–5.30pm, Sun 11am–4pm; £7, including factory tour Mon–Fri) contains a factory shop, a museum where a large sample of old Worcester porcelain is displayed in period settings, and the factory itself. Beginning in the mid-eighteenth century, porcelain manufacture was long the city's main industry.

Lower Broadheath

One of Worcestershire's most famous sons was the composer **Sir Edward Elgar**, whose statue faces the cathedral back at the bottom of the High Street. Inevitably, there's an Elgar Trail meandering round the county and its focus is his **birthplace** – a tiny, rustic brick cottage in **LOWER BROADHEATH**, a couple of miles west of Worcester on the B4204 (May–Sept Mon, Tues & Thurs–Sun 10.30am–6pm; Oct to mid-Jan & mid-Feb to April 1.30–4.30pm; £3). Inside, the crowded rooms contain Elgar's musical manuscripts, personal correspondence in his spidery handwriting, press cuttings, photographs and miscellaneous mementoes centred on the desk at which he worked. Regular buses #311 and #317 go directly to Broadheath Common and the cottage is a short walk from there.

Practicalities

Of Worcester's two **train stations**, Foregate Street, at the northern end of the High Street, is the more central, although some express services stop only at Shrub Hill, a fifteen-minute walk to the east of the city centre. The **bus station** is on the city side of the main river bridge, off The Butts behind the Crowngate shopping mall. From here, it's a brief stroll south to the **tourist office** (mid-March to Oct Mon–Sat 10.30am–5.30pm; Nov to mid-March Mon–Sat 10.30am–4pm; ☎01905/726311), in the Georgian Guildhall, towards the cathedral end of the High Street. **Bike rental** is available from Peddlers, 46 Barbourne Rd (☎01905/24238).

The best **hotel** options are the *Fownes' Hotel*, in an old glove factory at the cathedral end of City Walls Road ☎01905/613151; ⑤); the nearby *Loch Ryan*, 119 Sidbury (☎01905/351143; ④), which is noted for its food and terraced garden; and the *Star*, almost next to Foregate Street station (☎01905/24308; ⑤). Recommended central **B&Bs** include *Osborne House*, in a traditional Victorian villa at 17 Chestnut Walk (☎01905/22296; no credit cards; ②), and the excellent *Burgage House*, 4 College Precincts (☎01905/25396; no credit cards; ②), which occupies a Georgian town house with views over to the cathedral.

A few popular café-bars and restaurants serve **meals** all day along Friar Street – try *Osteria* at no. 21, a moderately priced Mediterranean restaurant offering tasty *tapas* (☎01905/745902). Friar Street continues north to become New Street, along which you'll find the pricier *King Charles II* (☎01905/22449), with a rather contrived seventeenth-century ambience but an outstanding traditional English menu. Alternatively, there's *Saffron's*, 15 New St (☎01905/610505), an unpretentious bistro serving mainly chargrilled steaks and chicken at around £10 per main course. A short walk further north, the friendly Worcester Arts Workshop in Sansome Street contains gallery space, an innovative theatre and enjoyable café, making it a useful place to find out about local events.

You'll find a bunch of pleasant old **pubs** in the city centre, among them the *Cardinal's Hat*, 31 Friar St, a sixteenth-century building complete with half-timbered interior; it serves good-value lunches. The *Plough*, tucked away on the corner of Fish Street and Deansway, is among the liveliest places to drink, with a barrel-strewn patio that gets packed out on warm summer evenings. Less touristy are the *Horn & Trumpet* in Angel Street, which has live music, and the minuscule *Lamb & Flag* at 30 The Tything, one of the city's most popular pubs, and a must for Guinness drinkers.

The Malverns

One of the most exclusive and well-heeled areas of the Midlands, **The Malverns** is the generic name for a string of towns stretched along the lower slopes of the **Malvern Hills**, which rise spectacularly out of the flat plains and offer expansive views. The main centre of the region is **GREAT MALVERN**, a pretty little place served by rail from Worcester, Birmingham, Oxford and London. The town's medicinal waters became popular towards the end of the eighteenth century, but it was the Victorians who came here in droves, making the steep hike up to **St Anne's Well** on the hill behind town, where you can still try the stuff yourself. The peculiarities of Great Malvern's spa waters are explained in the town **museum**, housed in the delicately proportioned Abbey Gateway, plum in the centre on Abbey Road (Easter–Oct Mon, Tues & Thurs–Sun, also Wed in school holidays 10.30am–5pm; £1.50). Nineteenth-century cartoons show patients packed into cold wet sheets before hopping gaily away from their crutches and wheelchairs – exaggerated claims perhaps, but poor hygiene did bring on a multitude of skin complaints and the relief the spa waters brought was real enough.

The main sight in town is the **Priory Church**, adjacent to the museum, its patchwork exterior contrasting with the ordered interior, which is notable for its stained glass and hundreds of detailed wall tiles, all added to the building in the mid-fifteenth century. The window of the north transept is especially fine and contains a portrait of Prince Arthur, Henry VII's son – the same Arthur who is commemorated in Worcester cathedral (see p.424). Among the priory's graves is that of Darwin's granddaughter, who died here as a child despite being bathed with Malvern water. From the church, it's a short walk to the **Winter Gardens pavilion**, one of the key venues for the wide range of special events the town puts on each year, including the excellent **Almeida Drama Festival** held in August.

Great Malvern has two other claims to fame: one is the Morgan motor car, which is still handmade in a small factory here; the other is the composer **Edward Elgar**, who lived in the adjacent village of **MALVERN LINK** at the turn of the century. The views from his house on Alexandra Road formed a backdrop for Elgar while he composed his most enduring work, including the famous *Enigma Variations*, whose more lyrical passages have become anthems of the English countryside. Stare out across the Severn Valley from the flank of the Malverns on a fine summer's evening and it's not hard to see why England's most celebrated composer found such inspiration here.

For **walkers**, the Malvern Hills offer splendid day hikes and a number of historical landmarks, including the remains of an Iron Age fort high on the ridge to the south of town. The panorama from here takes in the contrasts of the Malvern valley: plains to the east, and gentle hills rolling towards the gloomy Black Mountains in the west. The hike along the ridge and back takes about four-and-a-half hours. Start from the southern end at **Chase End Hill**, which is reachable by bus (depart Church Street, Great Malvern Wed & Sat at around 9am), and work your way north; alternatively, take the same bus to **British Camp**, midway along the route, and begin there.

Practicalities

Great Malvern **train station** is on the east edge of town, a mile or so from the centre along Avenue Road and Church Street. A range of inexpensive hiking leaflets are sold at the town's **tourist office**, right in the centre across from the priory church at 21 Church St (April–Nov daily 10am–5pm; Dec–March Mon–Sat 10am–5pm, Sun 10am–4pm; ☎01684/892289). They also sell the three excellent large-scale **maps** (£3.75) which are indispensable if you're planning on walking the length of the Malverns. This is also a rewarding, though physically demanding, area to explore by **bike** – you can rent cycles from Spokes & Saddles, 164 Worcester Rd, Malvern Link (☎01684/576141), less than a mile from the centre of town or one stop up the rail line.

Accommodation is plentiful. Right in the heart of town is the rambling old *Great Malvern Hotel*, 7 Graham Rd (☎01684/563411; ⑤), and, just along the street, at no. 23, are the Georgian symmetries of the charming *Montrose Hotel* (☎01684/572335; ⑥). Great Malvern **B&Bs** include the inexpensive *Kylemore*, 30 Avenue Rd (☎01684/563753; no credit cards; ①); the *Chalet House*, an impressive Edwardian house with garden access to the hills at 24 Wyche Rd (☎01684/572995; no credit cards; ②); and *Elm Bank*, an elegant Regency townhouse with en-suite rooms at 52 Worcester Rd (☎01684/566051; ②). The homely **youth hostel**, serving simple meals, is a couple of miles south of Great Malvern, off the main A449 at 18 Peachfield Rd, Malvern Wells (☎01684/569131; closed Nov–March).

For **food**, Great Malvern has oodles of cafés and tearooms – one of the more distinctive is *St Anne's Well*, a cosy vegetarian café serving inexpensive wholefood snacks, salads and cakes from its Victorian premises at the Well; just follow the signs up through the park from the centre. They'll also give you a glass to sample the spring water that babbles into a basin outside the door. The town's other café with character lies downhill from the tourist office at the train station. Known as the *Lady Foley Tea Room* during the day, and *Passionata* in the evening (☎01684/893033; Fri & Sat only), it's actually on one of the station platforms and makes the most of its Victorian surroundings. Finally, *Cridlans' Brasserie* (☎01684/562676), a French-style brasserie just outside the abbey gates, is a slightly pricier, but good-value place to eat, serving light lunches and tasty continental dishes on red-and-white-check tablecloths; try their delicious home-made sausage sandwich.

Herefordshire and the Forest of Dean

The rolling agricultural landscapes of **Herefordshire** have an easy-going charm, but the finest scenery hereabouts is along the banks of the **River Wye**, which wriggles and worms its way across the county linking most of the places of interest. Plonked in the middle of the county on the Wye is **Hereford**, a sleepy, rather old-fashioned sort of place whose proudest possession, the remarkable Mappa Mundi map, was almost flogged off in a round of ecclesiastical budget cuts back in the 1980s. To the west of Hereford, hard by the Welsh border, the key attraction is **Hay-on-Wye**, which – thanks to the purposeful industry of Richard Booth – has become the world's largest repository of secondhand books, on sale in a score of secondhand bookshops. Elsewhere, **Leominster** to the north of Hereford, and **Ledbury** to the east are amiable market towns distinguished by their Tudor and Stuart half-timbered buildings – sometimes called "Black and Whites." In the southeast corner of the county is **Ross-on-Wye**, a genial little town with a picturesque river setting which is the ideal base for explorations into the **Forest of Dean**, nestling in between the rivers Wye and Severn, across the county boundary in Gloucestershire.

Herefordshire possesses one **rail line**, linking Ledbury, Hereford and Leominster, but otherwise you'll be restricted to the county's **buses**, which provide a reasonable service between the villages and towns (not Sun). For information on services, telephone the **County Bus Line** (☎0345/125436).

Hereford

Once a border garrison town against the Welsh, **HEREFORD** owed its military importance to its strategic position beside the River Wye. To the Saxons it was also a religious centre. One of their kings, Ethelbert, was murdered by the Welsh and legend has his ghost insisting his remains be interred here in Hereford Cathedral. The fortifications that once girdled the city have all but vanished, but the cathedral has survived to form the main focus of architectural interest. Otherwise, Hereford is a drowsy market town set amid some of the least spoilt rural landscapes in England. Indeed, the town remains dependent on its agricultural base – the local **cider** industry is one of the city's biggest trades. The Wye meanders around the southern side of the city centre, with the medieval **Wye Bridge** and its twentieth-century neighbour, **Greyfriars Bridge**, connecting the two banks. The **cathedral** and its well-proportioned close sit on the northern bank, at the heart of the city centre, with the main shopping streets spreading out around them.

The City

The **Cathedral** is a curious building, an uncomfortable amalgamation of architectural styles, beginning with the dumpy red sandstone **tower**, constructed in the early fourteenth century to eclipse the western tower built by the Normans, which collapsed under its own weight in 1786. As a result of the accident, a great section of the **nave** was destroyed, leaving architects with a problem that was never satisfactorily resolved. The replacement nave lacks the grandeur of most other English cathedrals, though at least the Norman arches at its eastern end are impressive. The **north transept**, however, is a flawless exercise in thirteenth-century taste; designed by Bishop Aquablanca, probably to house his own tomb, it has soaring windows that are among the finest extant examples of Early English architecture. On the opposite side of the church, in the Norman **south transept**, unusual features include a German *Adoration of the Magi* that dates from the sixteenth century and an early fireplace, one of the few still surviving within an English church.

In the late 1980s, dire financial difficulties prompted the cathedral authorities to plan the sale of their most treasured possession, the **Mappa Mundi**. This parchment map was drawn in 1289, and at 65 by 53 inches it is the largest known example of such a work from that period. Its detail is astonishing, showing the complete world from its centre at Jerusalem, with Britain and Ireland sitting on the edge of the void. Eventually, a scheme was hatched to keep the map in Hereford by raising funds from sharehold-ers, visitors and wealthy patrons, including oil-tycoon John Paul Getty Jnr, who donat-ed nearly half of the £2.6 million needed to construct a splendid new building at the southeast corner of Cathedral Close. Entered via the cloisters, the ground floor of this **Mappa Mundi Centre** (Easter–Oct Mon–Sat 10am–4.15pm, Sun 11am–3.15pm; Nov–Easter Mon–Sat 11am–3.15pm; £4) features a state-of-the-art interpretative exhi-bition that's an ideal primer for the Mappa, displayed in a dimly lit air-conditioned chamber along with the cathedral's other main treasures. Among the latter is an exquis-itely enamelled casket alleged to contain relics of Thomas à Becket and a remarkable twelve-hundred-year-old Saxon gospel written on calf vellum. Also housed in the new building is the world's largest **Chained Library**, a collection of some 1400 books and manuscripts dating from the eighth to the fifteenth century.

Cider enthusiasts should make their way to the **Cider Museum and King Offa Distillery**, over the ring road to the west of the city centre, a thirty-minute walk from the train station off the A438 at 21 Ryelands St (April–Oct daily 10am–5.30pm; Nov–March Tues–Sun 11am–3pm; £2.20). The museum tracks through the history of cider-making and you can view the distillation process and sample King Offa ciders, including a particularly tasty Cider Brandy. If this whets your appetite, there are guid-ed tours of the more commercial **Bulmers' Cider Factory** on Plough Lane (Mon–Fri; £2.95; ☎01432/352000); tours must be booked at least one week in advance.

Practicalities

Hereford's **train station** is about half a mile northeast of the town centre and its **bus station** is nearby, just off Commercial Road. The **tourist office** is almost directly oppo-site the cathedral, at 1 King St (May–Sept Mon–Sat 9am–5pm & Sun 10am–4pm; Oct–April Mon–Sat 9am–5pm; ☎01432/268430). **Bike rental** is available from Coombes Cycles, 94 Widemarsh St (☎01432/354373).

Recommended central **B&Bs** include the *Collins House*, in a Georgian villa at 19 St Owen St (☎01432/272416; ②) and *Charades*, 34 Southbank Rd (☎01432/269444; no credit cards; ①); further out in the countryside, about two miles south of town off the A49, *Grafton Villa Farm* (☎01432/268689; no credit cards; ②; closed Nov–Jan), offers three tastefully decorated bedrooms in the Georgian farmhouse of a working farm. As for **hotels**, the *Green Dragon*, Broad Street (☎01432/272506; ⑤), occupies a grand Neoclassical building right in the centre; it's now one of the Forte Heritage chain.

For **food**, two good options are the inexpensive *Firenze*, 21 Commercial Rd, a pasta and pizza place, and the *Aroon Rai*, 50 Widemarsh St (☎01432/279971), a moderately priced Thai restaurant. In a town where the **cider** industry is so important, you should at least sample some of the finished product. There are shops at both Bulmers' and the Cider Museum (see above), or you could head straight for one of Hereford's many **pubs**. Appealing choices include the *Black Lion*, down near the cathedral in Bridge Street, and *The Barrels* in St Owen Street, which serves Hereford's widest selection of real ales.

Hay-on-Wye

Straddling the Welsh/English border some twenty miles west of Hereford, the sleepy little town of **HAY-ON-WYE** is known to most people for one thing – secondhand book-shops. Richard Booth, whose family originates from the area, opened the first in 1961 and since then the town has become a bibliophile's paradise, with just about every spare inch of Hay being given over to the trade, including the old cinema and the ramshackle stone castle. Most of Hay's inhabitants are outsiders, which means that it has little indigenous feel, but its setting, against the spectacular backdrop of Hay Bluff and the Black Mountains, together with its creaky little streets, is delightful. In summer, the town bursts with life as it plays host to a succession of riverside parties and travelling fairs, the pick of which is the **Hay Literary Festival** in the last week of May, when London's literary world decamps here.

Before you start browsing, pick up one of the free leaflets from the tourist office giving a rundown of the various shops and their specialities, along with a handy street plan. A good place to start is **Richard Booth's Bookshop**, 44 Lion St (☎01497/820322), the largest secondhand bookshop in Europe: a huge, draughty warehouse of almost unlimited browsing potential. It's owned – like just about everything in Hay – by Richard Booth, who lives in part of the castle, a fire-damaged Jacobean mansion built into the walls of a thirteenth-century fortress right in the centre of Hay. In another part of the mansion, Booth's wife runs the **Hay Castle Booth Books** (☎01497/820503), a sedate collection of fine art, antiquarian and photography books.

On Castle Street, **H.R. Grant & Son** at no. 6 (☎01497/820309) and **Castle Street Books** at no. 23 (☎01497/820160) are two of the prime bookshops in town for historical guides and maps. Nearby Broad Street holds **Y Gelli Auctions** (☎01497/821179), with regular sales of books, maps and prints. Also on Broad Street is **West House Books** (☎01497/821225), best for Celtic and women's works.

Practicalities

Buses from Hereford stop in the car park in the town centre off Oxford Road. The adjacent **tourist office** (daily: Easter–Oct 10am–5pm; Nov–Easter 11am–1pm & 2–4pm; ☎01497/820144) stocks an exhaustive range of hiking books and maps, and can help arrange accommodation in the area. **Bike rental** is available from Paddles & Peddles, 15 Castle St (☎01497/820604).

Accommodation in town is plentiful, although things get booked up long in advance for the Hay Literary Festival. Arguably the best option is the *Old Black Lion*, Lion St (☎01497/820841; ③), a captivating inn dating back to medieval times with beamed ceilings and a penchant for candlelight in the evenings; try also *Belmont House*, Belmont Rd (☎01497/820718; no credit cards; ①), a classy guest house crammed with antiques inside an appealing Georgian villa; or the *Old Post Office*, Llanigon (☎01497/820008; no credit cards; ①), a wonderful seventeenth-century B&B two miles south of Hay. The last is well placed for local walks and serves up delicious vegetarian breakfasts. The nearest **campsite** is *Radnors End* (☎01497/820780 or 820233) in a beautiful setting, five minutes' walk from town across the Wye bridge on the Clyro road; washing and toilet facilities here are rudimentary, but pitches are cheap (£3) and the views over Hay and the Black Mountains are great.

Several of Hay's **pubs** offer top-quality bar food and meals, but you'll be hard pushed to find anywhere better than the *Old Black Lion* on Lion Street. Another favourite is *Pinocchio's*, an intimate, mid-priced Italian **restaurant** on Broad Street where you can pick up freshly cut *panini* at lunchtime for £3, while the *Granary*, also on Broad Street is the vegetarian's choice, specializing in wholefood snacks, soups and filling main meals made mostly with organic produce; it also has a roadside terrace that is a great place to kick off your boots and relax over a pint if you've been hiking.

Leominster and Croft Castle

LEOMINSTER (pronounced "Lemster"), thirteen miles north of the county town on the Hereford–Shrewsbury rail line, is Herefordshire's second town, and an increasingly important centre for the **antiques** trade. Worth an hour or two of exploration, the town's attractive centre is a largely half-timbered patchwork of medieval streets with overhanging gables, fanning out from the cramped confines of Corn Square. On the northeast edge of the centre, the chunky **Priory Church** has preserved several original Norman features, from the rounded windows in the clerestory and the sturdy pillars in the nave to the carved "green man" fertility symbol by the west door. The church also possesses a rare example of a **ducking stool**, used to dunk dishonest tradesmen, scolds and the odd "wayward" wife up until 1809.

The **tourist office**, on Corn Square (April–Sept Mon–Sat 9.30am–5pm; Oct–March Mon–Sat 10am–4pm; ☎01568/616460), hands out brochures listing local **accommodation** and, although there's no special reason to hang around, the *Copper Hall*, a large old building with its own walled garden at 134 South St (☎01568/611622; ②), is a pleasant enough spot to hang your hat.

From Leominster, it's just five miles northwest to **Croft Castle** (May–Sept Wed–Sun 1.30–5.30pm; April & Oct Sat & Sun 1.30–4.30pm; £3.40; NT) via the B4361. Here, the sturdy pink stone towers and walls of the original medieval fortress have been embellished by a string of subsequent owners. Mock-Gothic castellated bays lie each side of the gabled front and inside there's an exuberant Georgian-Gothic staircase as well as a kitschy Blue and Gold Room, complete with a vast gaudy chimney piece.

Ledbury

If you're heading east from Hereford to the Malverns (see p.426), then drop by **LEDBURY**, a busy little town whose Market Place is home to the dinky **Market House**, a Tudor beamed building raised on oak columns and with herringbone pattern beams. Running off the Market Place is Church Lane, which possesses a particularly fine ensemble of Tudor and Stuart buildings. Among them is a Heritage Centre, the Butchers' Row Folk Museum and, pick of the bunch, the so-called **Painted Room** (June–Sept Mon–Fri 11am–3pm, Sat & Sun 2–5pm; rest of year closed Sat & Sun; £2 donation requested), featuring a set of bold symmetrical floral frescoes painted on wattle-and-daub walls some time in the sixteenth century. At the far end of Church Lane is **St Michael's parish church**, whose strong and slender spire pokes high into the sky. The nucleus of the church is Norman – note the round pillars and zigzag stonework – but the most interesting features are the funerary monuments inside, including the spectacular seventeenth-century **Skynner Tomb**, where five sons and five daughters kneel beneath the canopied slab on which their parents also kneel.

Ledbury **train station** is inconveniently situated on the northern edge of town, but **buses** stop on the High Street, metres from both the Market House and the **tourist office** (daily 10am–5pm; ☎01531/636147).

Ross-on-Wye

ROSS-ON-WYE, perched high above a loop of the river sixteen miles southeast of Hereford, is the obvious base for exploring the Forest of Dean (see p.432) and makes an agreeable stop if you're heading for Gloucester and the Cotswolds (see pp.269–283). It's a relaxed town with a pleasing sense of proportion, thanks mainly to the efforts of pioneering seventeenth-century town planner John Kyrle, also responsible for laying out **The Prospect**, the cliff-top public garden whose mock-Gothic walls overlook the slender, tapering spire of the parish **Church of St Mary's**. Dating from the early thirteenth century, the church was clumsily renovated by the Victorians, but the interior contains – in the tomb of a certain William Rudhall – one of the last great alabaster sculptures from the specialist masons of Nottingham, whose work was prized right across medieval Europe. Look out also for a rare **Plague Cross** in the churchyard, commemorating the three hundred or so townsfolk who were buried here by night without coffins during a savage outbreak of the plague in 1637. The other item of architectural interest is the seventeenth-century **Market Hall**, a sturdy two-storey sandstone structure bang in the middle of town on the Market Place.

If you've strolled long enough around town but still have time to spare, strike out along one of the many well-defined **footpaths** that thread their way through the riverine fields and woodland bordering the Wye. A collection of leaflets giving detailed descriptions of several circular routes is available at the tourist office.

Practicalities

There are no trains to Ross, but the **bus station** is handily located on Cantilupe Road, a couple of minutes' walk from the Market Place and the **tourist office**, on the corner of High and Edde Cross streets (Easter–Sept Mon–Sat 9am–5pm, Sun 10am–4pm; rest of year closed Sun ☎01989/562768). Ross is strong on **B&Bs** with one of the best being the *Linden House*, next to a gnarled row of old Tudor almshouses opposite St Mary's on Church Street (☎01989/565373; no credit cards; ①), and offering tasty vegetarian breakfasts. Another first-rate choice is *Vaga House*, an immaculately maintained Georgian building just below the tourist office on Wye Street (☎01989/563024; no credit cards; ①). If you're **camping**, your only option is the *Broadmeadow Caravan Park*, occupying a field beside an artificial lake on the northeast edge of Ross (☎01989/768076; closed Nov–March). **Bikes** can be rented from Revolutions on Broad Street (☎01989/562639).

Restaurants range from the *Oat Cuisine*, a straightforward daytime wholefood café in Broad Street, to *Cloisters Wine Bar*, 24 High St (☎01989/567717; evenings only), the best mid-range place to eat, serving copious meat and fish dishes in an attractive wood, stone and candle-lit interior. In a similar mould is the moderately priced *Meader's* (☎01989/562803), at the bottom of Copse Cross Street near the Market Place, where you can try Hungarian specialities. Of the **pubs**, the ancient, oak-beamed *King Charles II* on Broad Street is the most appealing.

The Forest of Dean and around

Wedged between the Rivers Wye and Severn to the south of Ross-on-Wye, the **Forest of Dean** is among the oldest and most extensive tracts of broadleaf woodland in Britain. It was designated a Royal Forest by the Normans in the early eleventh century, but as timber and metal extraction gathered pace during the Tudor era, it was thinned to the brink of extinction, forcing Henry VIII to embark on a massive replanting programme. This was intensified by Charles II, who also ordered the wholesale destruction of the region's iron mines in order to reduce the massive consumption of charcoal essential for the smelting process. Yet it was not until the early nineteenth century, when some thirty million acorns were planted by the government, that the forest's decline was finally reversed. Today, an estimated twenty million trees, predominantly silver birch, huge oaks and ash, cloak the area's winding river valleys, while greenery and wild flowers have largely reclaimed the ruined coal and iron mines, slag heaps and foundries that formerly flourished here.

With so many large towns and cities less than an hour away by road, it's not surprising that tens of thousands of visitors congregate here every year, most of them to picnic at sites set aside by the Forestry Commission. However, the central core – the part of the forest between Coleford and Cinderford – is still large enough to absorb even the heavy bank holiday crowds. A network of marked trails enables you to penetrate this area, both on foot and by bicycle, while bus services connect the major towns and cities. For timetable information, check with the Gloucestershire public transport line (☎01452/527516).

A good primer if you've just arrived in the region is the **Dean Heritage Centre**, at Soudley near Cinderford, in the northeast corner of the forest (daily: April–Sept 10am–6pm; March–Oct 10am–4pm; £3.30), which covers local history with exhibitions on mining, forestry and local crafts. From here, bypass soulless Cinderford, an incongruously grey town surrounded by industrial estates, and head straight through the heart of the forest on the B4226 towards Coleford. No buses cover this route, but the road passes within a stone's throw of **Beechenhurst Inclosure**, a picnic site and park information centre that's a good starting point for nature walks and the famous **Forest of Dean Sculpture Trail**. An easy walk (3.5 miles), the trail is dotted with contemporary artwork and sculptures, including a giant chair on the crest of a hill.

This part of the forest is also a great area for **cycling**: Pedalabikeaway, 500 yards west of Beechenhurst (☎01594/860065), rents hybrid trail bikes, Victorian trikes, wheelchair tandems and mountain bikes at very reasonable rates; they also hand out maps showing the best routes.

Coleford and St Briavels

Four miles further west, the B4226 emerges from the woods at **COLEFORD**, bereft of trees but the most attractive of the larger forest towns and home of the area's main **tourist office**, on the High Street (July & Aug Mon–Sat 10am–4pm, Sun 10am–1.30pm; rest of year closed Sun; ☎01594/812388). Coleford, along with the surrounding villages, is the principal **accommodation** base for the forest. Two good **B&Bs** hereabouts are *Rookery Farmhouse*, a tastefully converted stable just over a mile west of town in Newland (☎01594/832432; no credit cards; ②); and the inexpensive *Allary House*, occupying a Victorian town house in Coleford at 14 Boxbush Rd (☎01594/835306; no credit cards; ①).

Pushing on from Coleford along the B4228, it's a short hop to the pretty rose-stone village of **ST BRIAVELS**, perched on a ridge overlooking the Wye. A forbidding Norman **castle** (April–Sept daily 1–4pm) crowns a bluff in the centre of the village, its weathered stonework encircled by a dry moat. Formerly used by King John as a hunting lodge, and the region's administrative centre since medieval times, it now accommodates one of England's most impressive **youth hostels** (☎01594/530272; closed Nov–Jan). Beneath the keep extends a network of tunnels originally excavated in the thirteenth century by local miners. As a reward for their work, men over the age of 21 and born within one hundred miles of St Briavels were granted the right to mine for coal and iron ore anywhere in the Forest. This law is still in place, and within living memory a significant number of foresters made their living as "**Free Miners**", paying a royalty each year from their earnings to the Crown. Today only a couple of commercial Free Miners survive, but some locals continue to exercise their ancient right to extract coal for household consumption from disused surface mines, known as "scowle holes".

If you're tempted to **stay**, the hostel is the obvious choice, though there are also a handful of en-suite rooms upstairs in *The George*, a friendly old pub beside the castle (☎01594/530228; ②). The pub also serves good food – mostly tasty local fish, meat and game – inside and on the rear terrace overlooking the castle moat.

Shropshire

One of England's largest and least populated counties, **Shropshire** stretches from its long and winding border with Wales to the very edge of the urban West Midlands. Its most unique attraction is industrial: it was here that the Industrial Revolution made a huge stride forward with the spanning of the River Severn by the very first **iron bridge**. The assorted industries that subsequently squeezed into the gorge are long gone, but a series of **museums** celebrate their craftsmanship – from tiles and iron through to porcelain and even clay pipes. The River Severn also flows through the county town of **Shrewsbury**, whose antique centre holds dozens of old half-timbered buildings, though **Ludlow**, further to the south, has the edge when it comes to handsome Tudor and Jacobean houses. Some of the most beautiful parts of Shropshire are to the south and east of Shrewsbury in the twin ridges of **Wenlock Edge** and the **Long Mynd**, both of which are prime hiking areas, best explored from the attractive little towns of **Much Wenlock** and **Church Stretton** respectively. Out west, the hills become increasingly barren and dramatic as they approach the Welsh border. This is one of the remotest parts of England, a solitary landscape dusted with tiny hamlets and the occasional town, amongst which **Bishop's Castle** and **Clun** are perhaps the most appealing.

Yet, for all its attractions, Shropshire remains well off the main tourist routes, one factor protecting the county's remoteness being the paucity of its **public transport**. Shrewsbury and Telford are connected to Birmingham, and Ludlow, Craven Arms and Church Stretton are connected to Shrewsbury on the Hereford line, but that's about the limit of the **train** services, whilst rural **buses** tend to connect outlying villages on just a few days of the week. Precise bus timetable details are available on either the **Shropshire Traveline** (☎0345/056785) or for Telford, Ironbridge and Much Wenlock, the **Telford Traveline** (☎01952/200005).

Ironbridge Gorge

Both geographically and culturally, **Ironbridge Gorge**, the collective title for a cluster of small villages huddled in the wooded Severn valley to the south of new-town Telford, looks to the cities of the West Midlands conurbation rather than rural Shropshire. Ironbridge Gorge was the crucible of the Industrial Revolution, a process encapsulated by its famous span across the Severn gorge – the world's first iron bridge, engineered by Abraham Darby and opened on New Year's Day, 1781. He was the third innovative industrialist of that name – the first Abraham Darby started iron-smelting here back in 1709 and the second invented the forging process that made it possible to produce massive single beams in iron. Under the guidance of such creative figures as the Darbys and Thomas Telford, the area's factories once churned out engines, rails, wheels and other heavy-duty iron pieces in quantities unmatched in England. Manufacturing has now all but vanished, but the surviving monuments make the gorge the most extensive industrial heritage site in the country – and one that has been granted World Heritage Site status by UNESCO.

Arrival, information and accommodation

There are regular **buses** to Ironbridge Gorge from Telford and less frequent services from Shrewsbury and Birmingham, but travelling round the gorge by bus is well-nigh impossible – the shuttle that used to transport visitors between sights no longer operates and regular buses are few and far between. The best bet, therefore, is to hire a **bike** from Ironbridge by Bicycle (☎01952/884391), beside the toll house on the iron bridge itself: advance reservations are advised.

Ironbridge Gorge contains five museums and an assortment of other industrial attractions spread along a four-mile stretch of the River Severn Valley. A thorough exploration takes at least a day – two for comfort. Each museum charges its own admission fee, but if you're intending to visit several, then buy a **passport ticket** (£9.50), which allows access to each of them once in any calendar year. Passport tickets are available at all the main sites. **Parking** is free at all the museums, but not in the village of Ironbridge itself. Pick up local maps and information from the **Ironbridge Visitor Information Centre** (Mon–Fri 9am–5pm, Sat & Sun 10am–5pm; ☎01952/432166), beside the iron bridge in Ironbridge village.

Most visitors to the gorge come for the day, but there are several pleasant **B&Bs** in Ironbridge village, which is where you'll want to be. Two of the best are *The Library House*, which occupies a charming Georgian villa just yards from the iron bridge at 11 Severn Bank (☎01952/432299; no credit cards; ②), and *Eley's Bridge View*, whose spick and span rooms are also a stone's throw from the bridge at 10 Tontine Hill (☎01952/432541; ②). Alternatively, *Coalbrookdale Villa* is an attractive Victorian Gothic ironmaster's house up the hill from the bridge in tiny Paradise (☎01952/433450; no credit cards; ②). The gorge also boasts two **youth hostels**: one in the old Workers' Institute opposite the Coalbrookdale Museum of Iron, the other in the old Coalport China factory. They share the same telephone number (☎01952/588755) and are open all year.

Ironbridge village

There must have been an awful lot of nervous sweat during the construction of the world's first ever **iron bridge** over the River Severn in the late 1770s. No one was quite sure how the new material would wear and although the single-span design looked sound, the fear was the bridge would tumble into the river. To compensate, Abraham Darby used more iron than was strictly necessary, but the end result still manages to appear graceful, arching between the steep banks with the river way down below. The settlement at the north end of the span was promptly renamed **IRONBRIDGE**, and today its brown-brick houses climb prettily up the river bank. The village is also home to the Ironbridge Visitor Information Centre (see above), which introduces you to the site and its history with a short audio-visual show and small exhibition.

Coalbrookdale's Museum of Iron

Just to the west of Ironbridge village, the gorge's big industrial deal was once **COALBROOKDALE**'s iron foundry, which boomed throughout the nineteenth century and employed up to 4000 men and boys. The foundry has been imaginatively converted into the **Museum of Iron** (daily 10am–5pm; £4.50), with a wide range of displays on ironmaking in general and the history of the company in particular. There are superb examples of Victorian and Edwardian ironwork including art castings – stags, dogs and water fountains for instance – that became the house speciality. In the complex too is the restored **furnace** where Abraham Darby pioneered the use of coke as a smelting fuel in place of charcoal. From the furnace, it's about 100 yards up to a pair of old ironmaster's homes, **Dale House** and **Rosehill** (admission included with Coalbrookdale museum), which contains items that once belonged to the Darby family.

The Tar Tunnel and Coalport China Museum

From Ironbridge, it's a couple of miles east along the river's edge to the **Tar Tunnel** (April–Oct daily 10am–5pm; £1), where bitumen oozes naturally from the walls. Close by, the **Coalport China Museum** (daily 10am–5pm; £3.80) occupies the restored factory where Coalport porcelain and china was manufactured from 1792 until the works transferred to Stoke-on-Trent in 1926. The complex has several well-preserved examples of the conical bottle-kilns that were long the hallmark of the pottery industry, and inside the museum there's an engrossing assortment of the gaudy crockery for which the company was famous.

Jackfield Tile Museum

On the opposite bank of the river, accessible either by footbridge from near the Tar Tunnel or the roadbridge a mile upstream, is the **Jackfield Tile Museum** (daily 10am–5pm; £3.80). Housed in an old tile factory, the museum features a superb collection of brightly coloured tiles, from the fancy, flowery patterns of washstand splashbacks through to intricate Victorian fireplace tiles and a folksy *Punch and Judy* panel from the 1920s.

Broseley Clay Tobacco Pipe Museum

Heading west from Jackfield, along the south bank of the River Severn, follow the signs to the enjoyable **Broseley Clay Tobacco Pipe Museum** (April–Oct daily 10am–5pm; £2.50). During the late seventeenth and early eighteenth centuries, the satellite settlement of Broseley, formerly a source of raw materials for the foundries across the river, became a boom town in its own right, producing clay pipes for the swelling ranks of tobacco smokers in Britain. Occupying one of three factories that once existed here, the museum charts the history of smoking with a lively exhibition that culminates with some priceless film footage showing how the arm-length "Church Warden" pipes were made. After the rise of the cigarette eventually brought about the factory's closure, the building and its contents were left exactly as they were the day the workers downed tools. To their credit, the museum's creators have done their best to preserve this time-capsule effect, shunning actors in period costume in favour of informative panels.

Blists Hill Victorian Town

Doubling back to the north bank of the River Severn, **Blists Hill Victorian Town** (daily 10am–5pm; £6.80) lies a mile or so up the hill from the riverbank. Staffed by period-dressed employees, the rambling site encloses various reconstructed Victorian buildings – among them a school, a candlemaker's, a doctor's surgery complete with horrific instruments, a gas-lit pub, a wrought iron works and a slaughterhouse. Jam-packed on most summer days, it's especially popular with school parties.

Eating and drinking

For **food** in the Ironbridge Gorge, try the excellent *Meadow Inn* pub (☎01952/433193), down by the river on Buildwas Road about a mile west of the bridge, or the equally renowned *Horse and Jockey*, 15 Jockey Bank (☎01952/433798), just north of Coalport, whose legendary steak and kidney pie draws punters from miles away. If you're looking for something other than a pub meal, a good bet is the moderately priced *Oliver's Vegetarian Bistro* (☎01952/433086; closed Mon), on the High Street by the bridge. Anyone on a tight budget should head for the youth hostel in Coalport, where you can sit down to a filling three-course meal for under a fiver; they also offer healthy vegetarian options. **Real-ale** buffs will enjoy the *Coalbrookdale Inn*, past the Museum of Iron, which has the CAMRA stamp of approval for its excellent selection of beers.

Much Wenlock and the Wenlock Edge

Heading west from Ironbridge village along the northern bank of the River Severn, it's only a couple of miles along the A4169 to **Buildwas Abbey** (April–Oct daily 10am–6pm; £1.75; EH), a roofless but otherwise well-preserved twelfth-century structure in meadowland by the River Severn. In many ways its setting and isolation lend it more atmosphere than the skeletal ruin of the eleventh-century **priory** (April–Oct daily 10am–6pm; Nov–March Wed–Sun 10am–4pm; £2.30; EH) at **MUCH WENLOCK**, five miles to the south. With some solid Norman carving in its chapter house and lavatorium, the priory stands amid fine topiary in a dipped basin of green fields on the edge of the tiny town. Unfailingly quaint, Much Wenlock itself is a patchwork of Tudor, Jacobean and Georgian buildings, their style captured perfectly by the **Guildhall**, sitting pretty on sturdy oak columns in the middle of the Butter Market. The town is well stocked with accommodation, most of it listed by the **tourist office** on The Square (June–Aug daily 10.30am–1pm & 2–5pm; April–May & Sept–Oct Mon–Sat 10.30am–1pm & 2–5pm, Sun 2–5pm; ☎01952/727679). Pick of the **hotels** hereabouts has to be the charming *Talbot Inn* (☎01952/727077; ⑥), an old coaching inn that was formerly part of the abbey, with exposed beams, fresh flowers in summer and open fires during the winter. Of the **B&Bs**, one place in Sheinton Street at the top of town stands out – the *Old Police Station*, which offers two comfortable en-suite rooms and delicious breakfasts (☎01952/727056; no credit cards; ②).

A good reason to base yourself in this area for a night or two is to walk the beautiful **Wenlock Edge**, a limestone escarpment running twenty-odd miles southwest from the Ironbridge Gorge to Craven Arms (see p.441). Much of the Edge is owned by the National Trust, and a network of waymarked trails, graded by colour according to length and difficulty, winds through the woodland from a string of car parks along the B4371, which hugs the ridge from Much Wenlock to **Longville-in-the-Dale**. Two excellent **hostels** provide inexpensive accommodation for walkers and cyclists in the area, although neither is easily accessible by public transport. At Newton House Farm, one mile west of Much Wenlock on the main Shrewsbury road, the *Stokes Barn Bunkhouse* offers beds in a converted barn (☎01952/727293), while the YHA have one of their flagship properties at **Wilderhope Manor** (mid-Feb to Oct; ☎01694/771363). This magnificent Elizabethan mansion is set deep in idyllic countryside one-and-a-half miles south of the B4371. Wilderhope tends to be block-booked by school groups during the summer term, but usually has vacancies at other times, although reservations are recommended throughout the year. Midland Red West **bus** #712 runs to within striking distance of the youth hostel from Ludlow on Mondays and Fridays, or you can catch one of the more frequent services from Ludlow and Bridgnorth to nearby Shipton, a couple of miles across the fields, and walk from there.

Bridgnorth

BRIDGNORTH, nine miles southeast of Much Wenlock along the A458, may be in Shropshire, but – with Wolverhampton just thirty minutes' drive away – it has all the bustle of the West Midlands. Spilling down a sheer-sided bluff beside the River Severn, the town prospered throughout the medieval era as a bridging point for the river, but was badly mauled and its economy dislocated by the Parliamentary army during the Civil War. Today, Bridgnorth is at its prettiest on top of the bluff in the **High Town**, where the High Street is interrupted by the seventeenth-century **Town Hall**, a half-timbered building perched on an arcaded base. At its southern end, High Street runs into West Coast Street. This soon leads to the domed **St Mary's church**, a solemn-looking edifice designed by Thomas Telford, and the shattered thirty-foot **tower** which is all that remains of the medieval castle: the ruin leans at a precarious angle of seventeen degrees. From here, a short but pleasant walkway tracks along the bluff above the river, ending up at the century-old **cliff railway** (Mon–Sat 8am–8pm, Sun noon–8pm; 50p), which clanks up the steepest rail gradient in Britain to connect Bank Street (off West Coast Street) to the Low Town below.

Bridgnorth is also the northern terminus of the **Severn Valley Railway**, whose trains steam down the valley to Kidderminster, some thirteen miles away. Trains operate all year on a minimum of three days a week (Jan & Feb), increasing to a daily service for most of the summer (2–9 times daily). It takes a little over an hour for the train to travel from Bridgnorth to Kidderminster with the return fare costing between £9 and £20 (further details on ☎01299/403816). In Bridgnorth, the SVR station is in High Town across the footbridge from West Coast Street.

It only takes an hour or two to look round Bridgnorth and afterwards there are regular **bus** services on to Shrewsbury and Ludlow amongst many possible destinations. Most countywide services arrive and depart from the bus stops on the High Street. If you do decide to stay, the **tourist office**, in the library on Listley Street off the south end of High Street (April–Oct Mon–Wed & Fri–Sat 9.30am–5pm, Thurs 10am–1pm & 2–5pm, Sun 11am–1pm & 2–4pm; Nov–March Mon–Wed & Fri–Sat 9.30am–5pm; ☎01746/763257), has a list of local **B&Bs**. For **food**, try *Quaints*, a neat and inexpensive vegetarian bistro on St Mary's Street, just off the High Street near the Town Hall.

Shrewsbury and around

SHREWSBURY, the county town of Shropshire, sits in a narrow loop of the River Severn, a three-hundred-yard spit of land being all that keeps the town centre from becoming an island. It would be difficult to design a better defensive site, and fortifications were first built on this narrow neck in the fifth century, after the departure of the Roman legions from the nearby garrison town of Wroxeter. The Normans were swift to realize the strategic potential of the site too, building the first stone castle, which was expanded and strengthened by Edward I in the late thirteenth century. As the town grew prosperous on the back of the Welsh wool trade its importance grew, reaching its apogee when Shrewsbury briefly became capital-in-exile for King Charles I during the early years of the Civil War. The eighteenth century saw the town evolve as a staging post on the busy London to Holyhead route and, although this traffic withered with the arrival of the railways, the town had by then become the host of a lively social season, patronized by the sort of people who could afford to send their offspring to the famous Shrewsbury School. The top notch gatherings are, however, long gone and nowadays Shrewsbury is an easy-going, middling market town, albeit with several especially fine Tudor and Jacobean streetscapes.

Arrival, information and accommodation

Shrewsbury is well connected by **train** to the rest of the country, and its station, at the northeast edge of the centre, is a popular departure point for scenic rail journeys into mid-Wales. **Buses** from London, Birmingham and beyond pull into the National Express stand at the Raven Meadows bus station, off the Smithfield Road, five minutes' walk west of the train station. The **tourist office** is up the hill from the two stations, on The Square (May–Sept Mon–Sat 10am–6pm, Sun 10am–4pm; Oct–April Mon–Sat 10am–5pm; ☎01743/350761). The labyrinthine lanes and alleys of Shrewsbury's centre can be baffling, but fortunately it's too small an area to be lost in for long. As a general guide, Castle Gates/Castle Street runs from the train station up to Pride Hill, a short pedestrianized street that meets St Mary's Street/Dogpole at one end and High Street/Wyle Cop at the other. The Square off the High Street is at the heart of the city centre.

Shrewsbury has one particularly good **hotel**, the *Prince Rupert*, which occupies a tastefully converted old building, right in the centre of town off Pride Hill on Butcher Row (☎01743/499955; ⑤). Less expensive options in the centre include *The Lion*, a classic Georgian coaching inn on the Wyle Cop (☎01743/353107; ④), and the *College Hill Guest House*, a pleasant **B&B** in an old listed building at 11 College Hill, near The Square (☎01743/365744; no credit cards; ②). Most of the town's B&Bs are beyond the centre, with several dotted along Abbey Foregate, which runs east from the English Bridge at the foot of Wyle Cop: try the unassuming, neat and tidy *Abbey Court Guest*

House, at no. 134 (☎01743/364416; no credit cards; ①). The **youth hostel**, housed in a former Victorian ironmaster's house, is about one mile east of the centre, at the far end of Abbey Foregate (☎01743/360179); it's near Lord Hill's Column, the monument erected in memory of Wellington's sidekick at the Battle of Waterloo. Take bus #8 or #26 from the bus station.

The Town

The sandstone **Castle**, sitting high above the castellated train station, rests on the site of fortifications that go back a millennium and a half. Today's buildings date mainly from the thirteenth century, although the great architect and engineer Thomas Telford was brought in during the 1780s to shore up the remains and turn the castle into an extravagant private home for local bigwig Sir William Pulteney. It is now home to the dull **Shropshire Regimental Museum** (Tues–Sat plus Easter–Sept Sun 10am–4.30pm; £2), a far less interesting attraction than the annual World Music Day (☎01743/231142), which takes place here in July and makes the most of the castle's dramatic setting.

Castle Gates winds up the hill from the station into the heart of the river loop where the medieval town took root. Off Pride Hill, there are several especially appealing half-timbered buildings dotted along **Butcher Row**, which leads into the quiet precincts of St Alkmund's Church, where there's a charming view of the fine old buildings of **Fish Street**. From the church, Bear Steps clambers down to the High Street on the far side of which, in the narrow Georgian confines of The Square, is the **Old Market Hall**, a heavy-duty stone structure built in 1596. To the south of The Square is College Hill, home of the lacklustre **Clive House Museum** (Tues–Sat plus mid-May to Sept Sun 10am–4pm; £2). Occupying the Georgian town house of Robert Clive of India (1725–1774), the museum focuses on period Georgian and Victorian interiors rather than plumping for an examination of Clive's extraordinary career. The conqueror of a vast chunk of India, locally born Clive was elevated to the peerage following his defeat of the ruler of Bengal, but was later the subject of a full-scale parliamentary enquiry into his conduct; though acquitted, he ended up committing suicide shortly afterwards.

A short stroll to the west, on Barker Street near the Welsh Bridge, is Shrewsbury's best museum and the main showpiece for both the town and its county, **Rowley's House** (Tues–Sat plus mid-May to Sept Sun 10am–5pm; £2). An ostentatious 1590s townhouse with a seventeenth-century brick residence tacked on, it houses a wide range of displays relating to local life, with the most interesting exhibits coming from the nearby Roman city of **Wroxeter**, including a unique silver mirror from the third century AD.

From The Square, High Street snakes down the hill to become **Wyle Cop**, lined with elegant Georgian buildings and leading to the **English Bridge**, which provides a handsome view of the town as it crosses the Severn. Beyond the bridge is Shrewsbury's most important ecclesiastical building, the **Abbey** (daily: Easter–Oct 9.30am–5.30pm; Nov–Easter 10.30am–3pm; free), founded in the middle of a traffic intersection on Abbey Foregate. Founded in the 1080s by Roger de Montgomery, who was also responsible for the first stone castle here, the abbey was a Benedictine monastery that became a major political and religious force in Shropshire until the Dissolution. Unusually, the church and monastery buildings were not destroyed by the king's henchmen – indeed, the abbey church continued life as a parish church. Inside, the best feature is the huge west window of heraldic glass, dating from the fourteenth century. The monastery stood largely intact until the 1830s when a new road swept away most of the buildings. More recently, the remaining monastic outhouses have been converted into a new heritage centre, **The Shrewsbury Quest** (daily: April–Oct 10am–6.30pm; Nov–March 10am–5.30pm; £4.25), which recreates the living conditions of medieval monks, basing the whole thing around Ellis Peters' *Brother Cadfael* stories.

Eating and drinking

For daytime **food**, try the *Goodlife Wholefood Restaurant* in the antique surroundings of Barrack's Passage, off Wyle Cop, or snack at *Philpotts Quality Sandwiches*, which deserves its name and is located at 15 Butcher Row. In the evening, there's the *Sol*, 82 Wyle Cop (☎01743/340560; closed Sun), an outstanding if pricey restaurant featuring local ingredients like Shropshire lamb cooked in a broadly Mediterranean style, and tasty tandoori at *Shalimar*, by the abbey at 23 Abbey Foregate (☎01743/366658). Some of the best **pub food** in the centre is served at *Loggerheads*, in St Alkmund's Place, with wood-panelled walls and exposed beams; try their filling "Big Head Pie" – steak pieces topped with puff pastry and served with chips, salad and a pint for around £5. Other good **pubs** are the *Severn Stars* on Coleham Head, just over the English Bridge from the town centre; the smoke-free *Three Fishes*, in an ancient building on Fish Street; and the lively *Coach & Horses*, on Swan Hill just south of The Square. The *Music Hall* **cinema**, next door to the tourist office on The Square, screens art-house as well as mainstream releases (☎01743/244255).

Hawkstone Park

A common activity for eighteenth- and nineteenth-century gentry was to convert their estates into pleasure parks for strolling, hunting and contemplating nature. **Hawkstone Park** (Easter–Oct 10am–4/5pm, Nov–Easter Sat & Sun only 10am–dusk; £4.75), which lies about ten miles north of Shrewsbury between Hodnet and Weston, is an outstanding example of this. The park, which consists of a maze of tree-lined avenues, high ridges and sandstone cliffs, has lain undisturbed by all but a few locals for almost a hundred years. It was designed by the Hill family, who owned the estate from 1748 until 1895, and made good use of the lay of the land – rocky outcrops and two roughly parallel ridges in an otherwise flat land. On one ridge is a tall monument, a tower with 150 spiral steps leading to its windswept balcony. More unusual features along the one- or two- hour circular walk around the park include Swiss Bridge – two tree trunks spanning a deep gully – a hermit's cave and a curious set of dim and eerie grottos on Grotto Hill, from the top of which the views stretch for miles across the plains to the Welsh hills. Parts of the path are a little tricky underfoot, especially towards Foxes Knob, a sandstone outcrop reached via dark passageways snaking through the rock. Bus #572 runs from Shrewsbury to Hodnet (30min) on Tuesdays and Sundays, from where it's a two-mile walk to the park.

The Long Mynd and Church Stretton

Beginning about ten miles south of Shrewsbury, the upland heaths of the **Long Mynd**, ten miles long and between two to four miles wide, run parallel to and just to the west of the A49. This is prime walking territory and the heathlands are latticed with footpaths, the best of which offer sweeping views over the border to the Black Mountains of Wales. Nestled at the foot of the Mynd beside the A49 is **CHURCH STRETTON**, a tidy little place and one-time fashionable Victorian resort that makes the best base for hiking the area. The village also possesses the dinky parish church of St Lawrence, parts of which – especially the nave – are Norman. Look out also for the carving over the north doorway – it's a Sheila-na-gig (fertility symbol). In the centre of the village near the church is the **tourist office** (Easter–Sept Mon–Sat 10am–1pm & 2–5pm; ☎01694/723133), which stocks a wide range of leaflets detailing local walks, hikes and mountain bike routes. Perhaps the most obvious hike is the short, half-mile stroll west up along the National Trust's **Carding Mill Valley** to the **Chalet Pavilion** tearoom and information centre (April–Oct daily 11am–5pm; Nov–March Sat & Sun 11am–4pm). Alternatively, strike up **Caer Caradoc**, the steep hill that looms directly east of the village; crowned by an extensive iron-age hill fort, its summit affords superb views of the

Mynd and the rolling pasture land that extends east towards Birmingham. Waymarked trails lead to the top and down the other side to the picturesque hamlet of **CARDING-TON**, whose cosy village pub serves filling bar meals and fine pints of *Shropshire Lad* bitter. You can do the round walk in three to four hours.

Church Stretton is accessible from Shrewsbury and Ludlow by **train** and **bus**. Most buses stop in the centre of the village; the train station is a short walk from the tourist office just off the A49. There's no shortage of good-value accommodation in and around Church Stretton, much of it on lovely farms overlooking the Mynd. Recommended **B&Bs** include *Acton Scott Farm*, a seventeenth-century building one mile out of Stretton on the A49 with log fires and a choice of standard or en-suite rooms (☎01694/781260; no credit cards; ①), and *Dalesford*, on the western edge of town at the mouth of the Carding Mill Valley (☎01694/723228; no credit cards; ①). For a little more luxury, try *Jinlye*, on Castle Hill in All Stretton, one mile north, which backs on to the Long Mynd and has great views (☎01694/723243; ③). **Campers** have a choice of several sites. These include *Small Batch* (☎01694/723358; closed Oct–Easter), one mile south at Little Stretton, which enjoys a gorgeous situation but is pretty simple, and the pricier and better equipped *Ley Hill Farm* (☎01694/771366; closed Nov–Feb), deep in the countryside near Cardington, with panoramic views of the surrounding hills. **Bike rental** is available from Terry's, 6 Castle Hill, All Stretton (☎01694/724334).

The **youth hostel** at **Bridges Long Mynd** (☎01588/650656), five miles' hike west from Church Stretton near Ratlinghope, is a splendid base for walks, sitting between the Long Mynd and the **Stiperstones**, a remote range of boggy heather dotted with ancient cairns and earthworks. Marooned amid gentler country east of the town on the B4371, near Longville-in-the-Dale, **Wilderhope Manor** is this area's other hotel; it's featured on p.437, along with an account of the Wenlock Edge.

Craven Arms and Stokesay Castle

CRAVEN ARMS, the next stop down the rail line from Church Stretton, lies half a mile or so north of the hamlet of **STOKESAY**, site of one of England's most appealing manor houses. **Stokesay Castle** (April–Oct daily 10am–6pm; Nov–March Wed–Sun 10am–4pm; £2.95; EH), as it's known, comprises a collection of leaning, half-timbered buildings that span a range of over three hundred years, gathered around a neat grassy courtyard. The main block is a thirteenth-century fortified manor, originally built by a prosperous wool merchant for the princely price of a sparrowhawk. Beautifully restored by English Heritage, it contains a vast banqueting hall that retains its central fireplace, vaulted timbers and large windows. The size of the windows is actually very significant: Edward I's suppression of the Welsh had made border life a good deal more secure for the English, so they could afford to weaken the walls to let more light in. Across the central courtyard is the black and yellow gatehouse, built over three hundred years after the manor house yet forming a harmonious group with the main building and the tiny parish church next door. The church was largely rebuilt in the mid-seventeenth century, but some of the original Norman features remain.

From Stokesay, it's just seven miles south to Ludlow (see p.442) or you can double back up the A49 for a mile or two and take the A489 west to Bishop's Castle and Clun.

Bishop's Castle and Clun

BISHOP'S CASTLE, midway between Offa's Dyke and the southern edge of the Long Mynd, is a real treat – uncluttered, very pretty and full of fine secondhand bookshops and junk stores. **Buses** from Shrewsbury and from Montgomery, Knighton, Clun and Ludlow, drop you at the bottom of the High Street, which winds past half-timbered frontages to the miniature Georgian **Town Hall** – this was England's smallest borough until 1967 – and the lurching **House on Crutches**. Stroll up past the town hall and veer to the right to reach the most renowned building in Bishop's Castle, the seventeenth-century **Three Tuns brewery** and its time-warped pub in Salop Street, which serves up traditional home-brew – a pale cider-coloured concoction that's deceptively potent; they also do excellent and imaginative bar meals here. What must be England's most eccentric **tourist office** is housed in a secondhand shop called *Old Time*, at 29 High St (daily 10am–10pm; ☎01588/638467; no credit cards; ①) – staff here can sort out accommodation, and offer rooms of their own.

Five miles south of Bishop's Castle, the modest village of **CLUN** is an excellent base for forest walks and jaunts out across the surrounding hills that roll west over the Welsh border. The village also embraces the battered ruins of a medieval **castle** (dawn–dusk; free), built by the Normans but abandoned in the sixteenth century. The castle's only noteworthy feature today is the chunky masonry of the ruined keep, but the setting more than compensates – the keep is raised on an earthen mound cradled by the river below. In and around Clun are several excellent **B&Bs**. Amongst them is the *Old Farmhouse* (☎01588/640695; no credit cards; ①), an eighteenth-century farmhouse with a pretty garden one mile from – and 300 feet above – Clun. The small **youth hostel** (☎01588/640582) is in a converted watermill, on the northern edge of Clun, about ten minutes' walk from the nearest bus stop. As regards to **pubs**, Clun has two good ones – the *Buffalo Inn*, which offers excellent bar food, and the *Sun Inn* (☎01588/640559), whose à la carte restaurant is first rate. There are **buses** to Clun from Shrewsbury, Ludlow and Bishop's Castle.

Ludlow

LUDLOW, perched on a hill nearly thirty miles south of Shrewsbury, is one of the most picturesque towns in the Midlands, if not in England – a cluster of beautifully preserved black-and-white half-timbered buildings packed around a craggy stone castle, with rural Shropshire forming a dreamy backdrop. Close to the Welsh border, the defensive qualities of the site were recognised by the Saxons, but it was the Normans who got down to business when Roger Montgomery turned up here with his men in 1085. Over the next decades, Montgomery's fortifications were elaborated into an immense **Castle** (May–July & Sept daily 10am–5pm; Aug daily 10am–7pm; rest of year daily 10am–4pm, but closed Jan weekdays; £3), strong enough to keep the Welsh at bay and the natural headquarters for the Council of Wales and the Marches, as the borders were then known. Slighted by Parliamentary troops in the Civil War, the rambling ruins of today include towers and turrets, gatehouses and concentric walls as well as the remains of the 110-foot Norman keep and an unusual Round Chapel built in 1120. With its spectacular setting above the River Teme, the castle also makes a fine open-air theatre during the **Ludlow Festival** every June and July.

The castle entrance opens out on to the main market place, home to the intriguing **Castle Lodge** (daily 10am–5pm; £2), predominantly Elizabethan in style. In the ground-floor oak-panelled rooms, stained-glass windows depict the coats of arms of Germans summoned by Henry VIII to help sack England's monasteries. In low-beamed chambers upstairs, there's a display of Ludlow's chequered history, which omits the popular rumour that Mary, Queen of Scots hid from Elizabeth's henchmen in the lodge's basement.

To the south and east of the market place, the gridiron of streets laid out by the Normans has survived intact, though most of the buildings date from the eighteenth century. It's the general appearance that appeals rather than any special sight, but steeply sloping **Broad Street**, running south from the market place, is particularly attractive, flanked by many of Ludlow's five hundred half-timbered Tudor and red-brick Georgian listed buildings. At its east end, the market place pushes into the Buttercross, off which the magnificently proportioned, fifteenth-century interior of the **church of St Laurence** (daily 10am–5pm; free) boasts vast stained glass windows and some of the country's finest misericords. In its turn the Buttercross nudges King Street which intersects with the **Bull Ring**, home of the *Feathers Hotel*, an extraordinary Jacobean building with the fanciest wooden facade imaginable.

Practicalities

On the Shrewsbury–Hereford line, Ludlow **train station** is on the north side of town, a five-minute walk from the centre – just follow the signs. Most **buses** stop on Mill Street, across the market place from the castle entrance. Ludlow's **tourist office**, on the market place (Mon–Sat 10am–5pm, plus summer Sun 10.30am–5pm; ☎01584/875053), has a wide range of maps and books for walkers, and a selection of inexpensive leaflets detailing day hikes in the area. **Accommodation** is plentiful, though rooms can get scarce during the festival. First choice if you can afford it has to be the beautiful *Feathers Hotel* on the Bull Ring (☎01584/875261; ⑨), an intricately decorated Jacobean town house with luxury rooms and period furnishings to match. Two other, less expensive **B&B** options are the *Wheatsheaf Inn*, a quaint little pub next to the town gate at the foot of Broad Street (☎01584/872980; ②), and the excellent *Number Twenty Eight*, in a couple of old properties beyond the town gate at 28 Lower Broad St (☎01584/876996; ④). Ludlow's **youth hostel** (advance bookings essential; ☎01584/872472) is at the bottom of Lower Broad Street by the River Teme in Ludford Lodge.

For **food and drink**, the *Feathers* serves up excellent snacks and meals at its café-bar; the popular *Olive Branch*, on the Bull Ring (daily 10am–3pm), specializes in inexpensive light meals and salads; and the *Rose and Crown*, off the market place, serves up a good range of beers and delicious bar food and has a sheltered courtyard.

Birmingham

If anywhere can be described as the first purely industrial conurbation, it is **BIRM-INGHAM**. Unlike the more specialist industrial towns that grew up across the north and Midlands, "Brum" turned its hand to every kind of manufacturing, gaining the epithet "the city of 1001 trades". It was here that the pioneers of the Industrial Revolution – James Watt, Matthew Boulton, William Murdock, Josiah Wedgwood, Joseph Priestley and Erasmus Darwin (grandfather of Charles) – formed the Lunar Society, a melting-pot of scientific and industrial ideas that spawned the world's first purpose-built factory, the distillation of oxygen, the invention of gas lighting and the mass-production of the steam engine. A Midlands market town swiftly mushroomed into the nation's economic dynamo – in the fifty years up to 1830 the population more than trebled to 130,000.

Now the second largest city in Britain, with a population of over one million, Birmingham has long outgrown the squalor and misery of its boom years. Nowadays, its industrial legacy is chiefly to be seen in a crop of excellent heritage museums, an extensive network of canals and a multi-racial population that makes this one of Britain's more cosmopolitan cities. The shift to a post-manufacturing economy is symbolized by the new conference centre and by the enormous National Exhibition Centre on the outskirts, while Birmingham's cultural initiatives – enticing a division of the Royal Ballet to take up residence here, and building a fabulous new concert hall for the City of Birmingham Symphony Orchestra – have no equal outside the capital.

Arrival, information and city transport

Birmingham's **airport** is eight miles east of the city centre at Elmdon; the main terminal is connected to Birmingham International train station, from where there are regular services into the centre. **New Street train station**, to which all InterCity and the vast majority of local services go, is right in the heart of the city. However, trains on the Stratford-upon-Avon, Warwick, Worcester and Malvern lines usually use **Snow Hill** and **Moor Street** stations, both about ten minutes' signposted walk from New Street. National Express **coach** travellers are dumped in the grim surroundings of **Digbeth coach station**, from where it is a ten-minute uphill walk to the centre.

Free accommodation booking, maps and transport information are provided by all the city's **tourist offices**. The main office is located opposite the Council House on Victoria Square at 130 Colmore Row (Mon–Sat 9.30am–6pm, Sun 10am–4pm; ☎0121/693 6300). Five minutes' walk from New Street station in the other direction, there's a smaller branch and useful city ticket shop at 2 City Arcade, off New Street (Mon–Sat 9.30am–5.30pm; ☎0121/643 2514). There are also offices open Monday to Friday 9am to 5pm and during major conferences in the International Convention Centre (ICC) in Centenary Square and in the National Exhibition Centre (NEC), next to the airport. The city council runs its own office in the Central Library, Chamberlain Square (Mon–Fri 9am–8pm, Sat 9am–5pm; ☎0121/236 5622).

With much of the cheaper accommodation located out of the city centre, you are likely to be using local **buses** at some point. West Midlands Travel (WMT) is the largest operator (the blue and silver buses), although vehicles of every hue can be seen jostling for custom on the city's streets. The off-peak day pass for WMT buses (also valid on most other operators and the metro) is good value for money (£2.50) and can be bought on the first bus used. If you're using **local trains** as well, it makes sense to buy a Centro Daytripper (£4). For information on all local public transport, call the Centro Hotline (☎0121/200 2700).

Accommodation

B&Bs and cheaper **hotels** are concentrated two miles west of the centre along the A456 **Hagley Road** (buses #9, #19, #120, #123, #124, #126, #136–8, #192, #193, #292 from Centenary Square) and in **Acocks Green**, four miles southeast of the centre (trains from Moor Street or Snow Hill, or buses #1, #11, #37–8). In general, central hotels are geared up for the expense-account trade, although a few new cheaper places have made staying centrally more viable. The NEC tourist office co-ordinates cut-price weekend short stays (☎0121/780 4321) in most of the city-centre hotels, with prices starting at around £19 per person per night. These are available for Friday, Saturday and Sunday nights all year round and every night in July and August. In the centre of town there are also a couple of places offering B&B for gay and lesbian visitors – see the "Lesbian and Gay Birmingham" section on p.451.

Hotels and B&Bs

Atholl Lodge Guest House, 16 Elmdon Rd, Acocks Green (☎0121/707 4417). Comfortable guest house in a south-eastern suburb, handy for the airport and NEC. ①.

Ashdale House, 39 Broad Rd, Acocks Green (☎0121/706 3598). Well-situated B&B, serving good vegetarian and organic food. ②.

Brentwood Hotel, 127 Portland Road, Edgbaston (☎0121/454 4079). Good-value small hotel near the Hagley Road, also offering self-catering apartments (☎0121/420 2301) on a weekly basis for £245. ②.

Birmingham Hotel, 55 Irving St (☎0121/622 4925). Medium-size, slightly downbeat hotel, handily placed just off Bristol Street, in the city centre. ③.

Chamberlain Hotel, Alcester St, Highgate (☎0121/606 9000). Splendid conversion of a magnificent Victorian workhouse within easy walking distance of the city centre, offering excellent-value doubles. ③.

Holiday Inn Crowne Plaza, Central Square, Broad St (☎0121/631 2000). Large, anonymous central hotel with good health and fitness facilities. ⑦.

Hotel Ibis, Ladywell Walk, Arcadian Centre (☎0121/622 6010). Rather characterless, but well-situated hotel, bang in the Chinese Quarter, near the major theatres and nightclubs. ②.

Old Farm Hotel, 108 Linden Rd, Bournville (☎0121/458 3146). Friendly hotel, just 250 yards from Cadbury World museum. ③.

Oxford Hotel, 21 Oxford Rd, Moseley (☎0121/449 3298). Decent, comfortable place in this trendy southerly suburb. ⑤.

Travelodge, 230 Broad St (☎0121/644 5266). Ultra-anonymous central chain hotel (in the thick of bars and clubs), but worth trying for good-value doubles, all en suite. ②.

The City

The focus of Birmingham's city centre is where the main shopping thoroughfares of New Street and Corporation Street meet at right angles, just outside the shopping complex that houses New Street station. **New Street** runs west to the Council House and Town Hall in Victoria Square, with access from there to the central **Museum and Art Gallery** and through Paradise Forum to Centenary Square and the International Convention Centre. In the other direction, New Street heads towards the circular **Rotunda** office block, at the intersection with the **High Street**, where subways lead down to the **Bull Ring**. **Corporation Street** – planned in the 1870s as a mile-long boulevard cutting a swathe through congested slums – leads to the exuberant nineteenth-century terracotta Victoria Law Courts and Methodist Central Hall; a short walk west of Corporation Street brings you to **St Philip's Cathedral** and its surrounding square.

With the scaling down of the inner ring road, pleasant old districts on the fringe of the city centre are being reintegrated into its framework – these include the **Chinese Quarter**, home of many of the best bars and clubs, the **Jewellery Quarter**, complete with an excellent museum and hundreds of workshops and retail outlets, and **Digbeth**, where the city first began. Farther out, to the southwest of the centre, is the well-heeled area of **Edgbaston**, home of the county cricket ground, the principal university and many of the city's best parks. To the south is the planned workers' village of **Bournville**, established in 1879 by the Cadbury family and, true to their Quaker beliefs, still without a pub.

The city centre

The principal Corporation, New and High streets are flanked by chainstores and shopping precincts – more interesting are the multifarious **markets** in and around the **Bull Ring**, yawning under the Rotunda at the intersection of New and High streets. Bulls used to be tethered and baited here, in the belief that if the animal died angry, the meat was better. The Bull Ring indoor shopping centre is scarcely a more edifying spectacle, fulfilling every miserable cliché about 1960s town planning – it's cheap, tatty, hugely disorientating and, thankfully, due to be demolished in the next few years. On the far side of the complex, on the edge of the market stalls, stands **St Martin's**, the city's grime-blackened parish church. It dates back to the fourteenth century, but was completely rebuilt in the last quarter of the nineteenth.

From St Martin's, **Digbeth** – the old main thoroughfare through medieval Birmingham – falls away to the southeast. It's now a busy main road, though the streets to the north house some great examples of imposing industrial architecture. Just beyond the coach station on Gibb Street is the blue-and-white-painted **Custard**

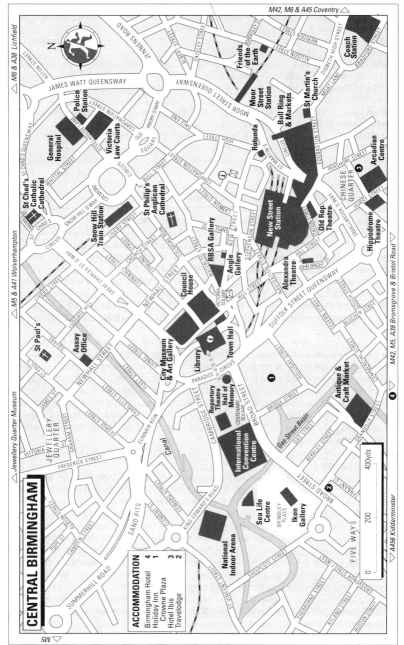

CENTRAL BIRMINGHAM

ACCOMMODATION
Birmingham Hotel 4
Holiday Inn 1
Crowne Plaza 3
Hotel Ibis 2
Travelodge 2

Factory, an arts complex fashioned out of the old Alfred Bird custard works. As well as a couple of chic poolside café-bars, there are small arts workshops and galleries within the complex.

Back in the centre, the finest church in the city is **St Philip's**, a bijou example of English Baroque, occupying a grassy knoll on Colmore Row, to the west of Corporation Street. Consecrated in 1715 as an overspill for the packed St Martin's, it became the city's cathedral in 1905 at the expense of the parish church, largely due to its superior position in a less congested, more upmarket corner of the city centre. The church was extended in the 1880s, when four new stained glass windows were commissioned from local boy **Edward Burne-Jones**, a leading light of the Pre-Raphaelite movement. The windows are typical of his style – intensely coloured, fastidiously detailed and rather sentimental.

One of the world's most comprehensive collections of **Pre-Raphaelite art**, including an entire room of Burne-Jones's work, is housed in the **City Museum and Art Gallery** in Chamberlain Square (Mon–Thurs & Sat 10am–5pm, Fri 10.30am–5pm, Sun 12.30–5pm; free), 200 yards along Colmore Row. Founded in 1848, the Pre-Raphaelite Brotherhood consisted of seven young artists, of whom Rossetti, Holman Hunt, Millais and Madox-Brown are best known. The name of the group was selected to express their commitment to honest observation, which they thought lost with the Renaissance. Many of the Brotherhood's most important paintings are displayed here, including Brown's powerful image of emigration, *The Last of England*, and Rossetti's seminal *First Anniversary of the Death of Beatrice* (1849), inspired by Dante. Such was the group's dedication to realism (as they conceived it) that Hunt visited the Holy Land to prepare a series of religious paintings including his extravagant *The Finding of the Saviour in the Temple*. It's a splendid collection, and one that richly deserves at least a couple of hours, but the museum has much more to offer. To begin with, there's a first-rate sample of eighteenth- to twentieth-century British art including an extensive collection of watercolour landscapes from 1750 to 1850 and numerous works by David Cox, Constable's Birmingham contemporary. Moving on, the **international collection** has its main strengths in seventeenth-century Italian paintings and sculpture, and a small showing of Impressionists.

Birmingham's industrial prowess is amply demonstrated throughout the museum. The ground-floor **Industrial Gallery**, housed in the original Victorian building complete with ornate skylights and huge gas lights, contains beautiful stained glass and local ceramics – and leads to the genteel **Edwardian tea room**, one of the most pleasant places in Birmingham for a midday break. Elsewhere in the building you'll find galleries devoted to **silver**, base metalwork and **jewellery**. Upstairs is a large and rather old-fashioned **natural history** collection, linked to a couple of rooms looking at ancient worlds. Tucked down by the back entrance off Great Charles Street are two interesting **local history** galleries, which focus mainly on the industrial beginnings and development of the city. The adjoining **Gas Hall** (same times; £4.95) is one of the country's most impressive venues for touring art exhibitions.

Chamberlain Square is also bounded by the huge municipal monolith of the domed **Council House**, and the classical **Town Hall** (1832–46), which is based on the Roman temple in Nîmes, whereas the glum **Central Library** looks like it's been modelled on a multistorey car park. The central focus is a fountain commemorating **Joseph Chamberlain** (1836–1914), whose political career took him from the Birmingham mayor's office to national prominence as leader of the Liberal Unionists and figurehead of the resistance to Irish home rule. On the steps is a statue of the city's first MP, Thomas Attwood, his coat-tails tumbling down the concrete.

On its south side Chamberlain Square opens onto the beautifully refurbished **Victoria Square**, whose centrepiece is a stunning fountain designed by Dhruva Mistry. Just across the raised flowerbeds you'll see a far less popular piece of contemporary sculpture – Anthony

Gormley's rusting, thrusting *Iron Man*. On the corner of Victoria Square and New Street is the gallery of the **Royal Birmingham Society of Artists** (Mon–Sat 10.30am–5pm; £1), which hosts some enjoyable temporary exhibitions. Nearby, just along New Street, on the fourth floor of the Piccadilly arcade, is the **Angle Gallery** (Mon–Sat 11am–6pm, Sun 11am–5pm; prices vary), a good bet for radical art and installations. Retracing your steps to the far side of Chamberlain Square, walk through the hideously kitsch **Paradise Forum** – entered through the library complex – to get to **Centenary Square**, laid out as a complement to the showpiece **International Convention Centre** (ICC) and the **Birmingham Repertory Theatre**. Centre-stage on the wide paving is a butter-coloured sculpture called *Forward*, a rousing image of the city's history by Birmingham-born Raymond Mason.

On the **canals** at the back of the ICC, turn left for the bright, boat-filled **Gas Street Basin** (regular public boat trips operate from here and the ICC quayside), or turn right for a canalside wander up to the huge dome of the National Indoor Arena, where the canal forks. This whole area has been the focus of Birmingham's recent redevelopment, principally in the waterside bars, shops and clubs of **Brindley Place**, named after the eighteenth-century Birmingham town engineer who was responsible for many of Britain's early canals. Beside the main canal junction, the shell-like **National Sea Life Centre** (daily 10am–5pm; £7.50) can't help but raise a few eyebrows, given the city's inland location. Nevertheless, it's an enterprising educational venture, giving Birmingham's landlubbers an opportunity to view and even touch many unusual varieties of fish and sea life, even, at one point, from within a 360° glass tunnel. A couple of blocks back, in the heart of the Brindley Place complex, an imposing old Victorian school has now become the home of the city's celebrated **Ikon Gallery** (Tues–Fri 11am–7pm, Sat & Sun 11am–5pm; free), one of the most imaginative British galleries for touring exhibitions of contemporary art.

Where the canals fork at the Sea Life Centre, if you take the right turn along the Birmingham and Fazeley Canal, you'll pass by (and even under) everything from Victorian warehouses to the 500ft Telecom Tower. After about half a mile, you'll reach St Chad's Circus and the twin steeples of the Pugin-designed **St Chad's Catholic Cathedral** (1839–41), the first Catholic cathedral to be built in England since the Reformation. Perhaps more rewarding is Birmingham's long-established **Jewellery Quarter**, immediately northwest of the city centre, and well signposted from it. Bucklemakers and toymakers first colonized the area in the 1750s, opening the way for hundreds of silversmiths, jewellers and goldsmiths. There are still around five hundred jewellery-related companies in the area and most of the jewellery shops are now concentrated along Vittoria Street, Warstone Lane and Frederick Street. A short walk north of the Frederick Street/Warstone Lane intersection, the engrossing **Museum of the Jewellery Quarter**, 75–79 Vyse St (Mon–Fri 10am–4pm; Sat 11am–5pm; £2.50), is built around a factory that was abandoned in 1980 but had remained virtually unchanged since the 1950s. A visitor centre starts proceedings, detailing the growth and decline of the trade in Birmingham, but it's the old factory that steals the show. Here, the atmosphere and conditions of the old works are superbly recreated – the jewellers were wedged into tiny, hot and noisy spaces to churn out hundreds of earrings, brooches and rings. Their modern counterparts use the old machines to show how some of the most common designs were produced. Incidentally, the museum is only a couple of minutes' walk from the new Jewellery Quarter station, on the train line from Moor Street and Snow Hill stations to points west.

Bournville

The most noteworthy of Birmingham's suburbs is the planned village of **BOURNVILLE**, four miles southwest of the city centre (train from New Street or buses #61, #62 & #63 from Corporation Street), founded by the **Cadbury** family in 1879. The first of this Quaker dynasty, John Cadbury, opened a grocery store in Birmingham in

1824 and from it he sold his home-produced "Cocoa Nibs," part soothing night-cap, part a way of weaning the working class from alcohol by providing a cheap and tempting alternative to beer. The popularity of this sweet concoction exceeded John's wildest dreams and just over fifty years later his sons, George and Richard, were able to move the family business out of the city centre to Bournville, a purpose-built "factory in a garden". Much influenced by the utopian ideas of William Morris and the Arts and Crafts movement, the Cadburys' Bournville scheme included gardens for every worker's house, a village green and a half-timbered parade of shops. The brothers also uprooted a pair of Tudor houses, **Selly Manor** and **Minworth Greaves**, and plonked them on Maple Road – they are now open as a museum of Tudor and Jacobean furniture (Tues–Fri 10am–5pm, plus April–Sept Sat & Sun 2–5pm; £1.50). The Bournville Village Trust still operates today, laying down basic rules (no unkempt gardens, for example) to which all inhabitants, even those who own their property, must subscribe.

Cadbury World, tacked onto the huge factory off Linden Road (daily 10am–4pm; booking advised on ☎0121/451 4159; £6.50), takes visitors through the histories of the cocoa bean and the Cadbury dynasty – with excellent displays on advertising. But for chocoholics the point of the tour is the opportunity to gorge on free samples from the production line and stock up on the cut-price finished product.

Edgbaston

Leafy and prosperous, the suburb of **EDGBASTON**, just to the southwest of the city centre, was developed in the 1790s by the Calthorpe family as a genteel residential estate from which industry and commerce were explicitly banned. It's here, on Westbourne Road, you'll find the **Birmingham Botanical Gardens** (Mon–Sat 9am–7pm or dusk, Sun 10am–7pm or dusk; £4.20, Sun £4.50), whose ornamental gardens and glasshouses extend over fifteen acres. The gardens are parcelled up into a number of distinct areas, everything from a rhododendron garden, brilliant herbaceous borders, a rock garden to an Alpine yard. Buses #10, #21, #22, #23, #29 and #103 from the city centre pass close by.

Arguably the most agreeable of Birmingham's many public parks is **Cannon Hill Park**, off the Pershore and Edgbaston roads two miles south of central Birmingham – buses #45 and #47 from the city centre stop nearby. There are boating lakes and bowling greens, tennis courts and woodland, and the greenhouses hold a national collection of tropical plants. Cannon Hill is also home to the excellent **Midland Arts Centre** (see p.452), which has a good bar, café, cinema and bookshop and hosts an imaginative programme of art, craft and photography exhibitions.

Birmingham University, on the southern fringe of Edgbaston (trains from New Street or buses #61, #62, #63), is visible for miles around, thanks to the 328ft clock tower that dominates the campus. For the casual visitor, the university campus has one big draw, the **Barber Institute of Fine Arts**, at the east gate off Edgbaston Park Road (Mon–Sat 10am–5pm, Sun 2–5pm; free). Opened in 1939, this superb gallery contains a world-class collection of European paintings from the thirteenth century onwards. Notable pieces include a fine collection of Rembrandt studies, an unusual Rubens – *Landscape near Malines* – and Degas's *Jockeys Before the Race*, a characteristically audacious piece of off-centre composition. The Barber also houses a good collection of Impressionists, including Monet, Pissarro and Boudin, as well as works by Magritte, Bellini, Whistler, Van Gogh, Gainsborough, Gauguin and Turner.

Eating and drinking

Birmingham's central **restaurants** have long had a reputation as soulless places which empty quickly, but this is changing rapidly, with new venues opening up in the slipstream of the growth in the conference and trade-fair business, particularly along

Broad Street, near the ICC. There's also a concentration of decent, reasonably priced restaurants around the Chinese Quarter, at the top of Hurst Street – also the focus of the gay scene. Birmingham's gastronomic speciality is the **balti**, a delicious and astoundingly cheap Kashmiri stew cooked and served in a small wok-like dish called a *karahi*, with *naan* bread instead of cutlery. Although balti houses have opened up within the city centre, the original and arguably the best balti houses are in the inner-city southern suburbs of **Balsall Heath** and **Sparkhill**. Some of these are listed here – all are unlicensed, so take your own booze.

The city centre **pubs** vary as much as you'd expect: those on Broad Street, in the immediate vicinity of the Convention Centre, are garish places aimed at the delegates and weekend lager-lovers, but more traditional pubs abound throughout the centre and out into the livelier suburbs, such as Bearwood, Handsworth, Moseley and Balsall Heath.

Restaurants

Chez Jules, 5A Ethel St, off New Street (☎0121/633 4664). Best medium-priced French restaurant in the city centre, with especially good lunchtime offers. Moderate.

Chung Ying, 16–18 Wrottesley St (☎0121/622 1793). The best Cantonese dishes in the Chinese Quarter, and always busy. Moderate.

Grand Tandoori, 345 Stratford Rd, Sparkhill (☎0121/773 9244). Extensive balti menu in a concentration of other balti houses. Buses #4, #31, or #41. Inexpensive.

Green Room Café-Bar, Hurst St. Popular and relaxed café-bar opposite the Hippodrome Theatre for anything from a cup of tea or glass of wine through to a full meal. Inexpensive.

I Am The King Balti, 230–232 Ladypool Rd, Balsall Heath (☎0121/449 1170). The name may be ridiculous, but this really is one of the best in the city's main "balti belt". Inexpensive.

Kushi, 558 Moseley Rd, Balsall Heath (☎0121/449 7678). Excellent, award-winning balti house that's unlicensed, dirt cheap and deservedly popular. Inexpensive.

Left Bank, 79 Broad St (☎0121/643 4464). Swish and classy French and continental restaurant that mops up its fair share of ICC delegates. Moderate.

Punjab Paradise, 377 Ladypool Rd, Balsall Heath (☎0121/449 4110). One of the city's classic balti houses, specializing in milder dishes. Bus to the Moseley Dance Centre, then a ten-minute walk. Inexpensive.

Ronnie Scott's Café Bar, 258 Broad St (☎0121/643 4525). Serves an imaginative selection of snacks and meals, with jazz sounds and memorabilia as background. Late licence. Inexpensive.

San Carlo, 4 Temple St (☎0121/633 0251). Best all-round Italian restaurant in the centre, although somewhat lacking in atmosphere. It's near St Philip's Cathedral, just up from the pizza and pasta chain restaurants on New Street. Moderate.

Warehouse Café, 54 Allison St, Digbeth (☎0121/633 0261). Imaginative vegan and vegetarian café open daytimes and evenings, above Friends of the Earth. Bring your own wine. Inexpensive.

Pubs and bars

Circo, 6–8 Holloway Circus. Serious pre-club posing palace, offering pricey designer beers, pastas and salads.

The Cube, Brindley Place. In the centre of fashionable Brindley Place, the terrace of this lively bar teems with drinkers on summer evenings.

The Dubliner, 57 Digbeth. Rather overdone Irish theme park just up from the coach station, but serves excellent Guinness and has nightly live bands.

Fiddle and Bone, 4 Sheepcote St (☎0121/200 2223). Canalside pub-cum-restaurant owned by members of the City of Birmingham Symphony Orchestra, hence its musical name and theme. Has become very popular very quickly. Live music nightly.

James Brindley, next to the *Hyatt* off Bridge St. Frequented by businesspeople in the week, but on weekends the jazz brunches give this place a relaxed air. Great canalside location.

Medicine Bar and **Cafe des Artistes**, Custard Factory, Gibb Street, Digbeth. Popular pre-club haunts in a cheerful arts complex.

Ministry Bar, 55 Broad St. Second home to the Ministry of Sound, this bar boasts the best underground house and garage on the best sound system outside of their London base.

Old Contemptibles, 176 Edmund St. Real old spit-and-sawdust saloon, packed with business folk at lunch and in the early evening. Excellent lunchtime food.

Nightlife and entertainment

Nightlife in Birmingham is thriving, and the club scene is recognized as one of Britain's best, spanning everything from word-of-mouth underground parties to meatmarket clubs. Live music, theatre and comedy surface in pubs and larger venues, including a strong Irish scene around Digbeth.

Birmingham's showpiece **Symphony Hall** and the Birmingham Royal Ballet are the spearheads of the city's resurgent high-cultural scene, and the social calendar gets an added boost from the range of new **festivals**, all of which offer many events for free. These include the **Readers' and Writers' Festival** in May and November, the **Jazz Festival** in the first two weeks in July, and the **Film and TV Festival** in November.

For current information on all events, performances and exhibitions, pick up a free copy of *What's On Birmingham and Midlands* (not to be confused with the inferior *What's On West Midlands*) from tourist offices, galleries or public venues.

Clubs

Baker's, 163 Broad St (☎0121/633 3839). Small, artily designed disco-club with a wide range of speciality evenings.

Bobby Brown's, 52 Gas St (☎0121/643 2573). Chart and retro sounds for the over-25s.

House of God, various venues. Birmingham's ever-popular techno night is still going strong and loud. This is the sound of the city.

Pulse, Hurst Street. Charts and drink promotions most of the week, but on Sunday the all-day "Sundissential" (☎0121/643 4715) is a wild dance party to finish the weekend off.

Que Club (and **The Chapel**), Central Hall, Corporation Street (☎0121/212 0550). Brum's premier "superclub", a conversion of the old Methodist Central Hall into a full-on, 2000-capacity groove. Allnighters every weekend.

Ronnie Scott's, 258 Broad St (☎0121/643 4525). Second of the late maestro's jazz clubs, good also for big names in blues and world music.

Sanctuary, Digbeth High Street (☎0160/447 4591). Opposite the coach station, the old Civic Hall now thumps to some big house tunes during a variety of one-nighters.

Lesbian and gay Birmingham

Angels Café-Bar, 127–131 Hurst St. Enormously popular gay and lesbian bar, with all-day snacks and meals.

Fountain Inn, 102 Wrentham St (☎0121/622 1452). A mainly male real-ale pub with B&B accommodation (②) and occasional cabaret.

The Fox, 17 Lower Essex St. Mostly women at this pub with an excellent atmosphere and a courtyard garden.

Brooks, 92–95 Smallbrook Queensway. Glammy pre-club bar.

The Nightingale, Essex House, Kent St (☎0121/622 1718). Birmingham's foremost gay club: fun, unpretentious and open every night except Mon & Thurs.

Subway City, Livery St, Snow Hill (☎0121/233 0310). Out of the Hurst Street "gay village", but worth the trek. Great weekend club, with dance music and groovy times.

The Village, 152 Hurst St (☎0121/622 4742). Mainly male and enjoyably stylish bar, with a camp garden and B&B accommodation (②).

Classical music, theatre, comedy and dance

Alexandra Theatre, Suffolk Street, Queensway (☎0870/607 7544). Mainstream pop concerts, musicals and plays.

City Tavern, Bishopsgate St, Five Ways (☎0121/643 4394). Pub theatre and live music in a cheerful backstreet local.

The Crescent Theatre, Sheepcote Street, Brindley Place (☎0121/643 5858). Adventurous theatre group and venue for visiting companies.

Glee Club, Arcadian Centre, Hurst Street (☎0121/693 2248). Dedicated comedy club, with top national names and up-and-coming stars.

Hippodrome Theatre, Hurst Street (☎0121/622 7486). Home of the Birmingham Royal Ballet and regular hosts of the Welsh National Opera. Also touring plays and big pre- and post-West End productions, plus "Britain's biggest pantomime" every Christmas.

Midland Arts Centre, Cannon Hill Park, Edgbaston (☎0121/440 3838). Venue for touring theatre companies and some local groups.

Old Rep Theatre, Station Street (☎0121/616 1519). Britain's oldest repertory theatre, now home to the imaginative Birmingham Stage Company.

Repertory Theatre, Centenary Square (☎0121/236 4455). Mixed diet of classics and new work, including some local and experimental writing in the Studio.

Symphony Hall, International Convention Centre, Centenary Square (☎0121/212 3333). Acoustically one of the most advanced concert halls in Europe, home of the acclaimed City of Birmingham Symphony Orchestra (CBSO), as well as a venue for touring music and opera.

Listings

Airport enquiries ☎0121/767 5511.

Banks Lloyds, 125 Colmore Row; HSBC, 130 New St; NatWest, 103 Colmore Row.

Bookshops Dillons, 128 New St; Bookscene, 35 Pallasades Shopping Centre; Waterstone's, 24 High St.

Bike rental In the city centre at On Yer Bike, 10 Priory Queensway (☎0121/627 1590).

Bus enquiries Local services ☎0121/200 2700; National Express ☎0990/808080.

Car rental Avis, 71a Park St and at the airport (both ☎0870/606 0100); Budget, 95 Station St (☎0121/643 0493).

Cricket Warwickshire County Cricket Ground, Edgbaston Rd, Edgbaston (☎0121/446 4422).

Exchange American Express, Bank House, Cherry St (☎0121/644 5533); Thomas Cook, 130 New St (☎0121/643 5057).

Football Aston Villa, based at Villa Park (☎0121/327 5353) is the city's big club. One-time equal Birmingham City, based at St Andrews (☎0121/772 0101), is always threatening a revival – so they say.

Hospital Heartlands Hospital, Bordesley Green East (☎0121/766 6611), or Selly Oak Hospital, Raddlebarn Road, Selly Oak (☎0121/627 1627).

Laundry Nearest to the city centre is Clean & Care, 758 Alum Rock Road. Convenient for the hotels and B&Bs listed above is the Laundry & Dry Cleaning Centre, 236 Warwick Road.

Left luggage New Street station (Mon–Sat 6.45am–9.45pm, Sun 11.15am–6.45pm).

Lesbian and gay switchboard Daily 7–10pm ☎0121/622 6589.

Lost property At the police station.

Pharmacies Boots, 67 High Street (☎0121/236 6027).

Police Main city centre stations in Steelhouse Lane and on the corner of Digbeth and Allison St (both ☎0121/626 6000).

Post office Main post office at 1 Pinfold St, on the corner with Victoria Square (Mon–Fri 9am–5.30pm, Sat 9am–6pm).

Taxis Toa Taxis ☎0121/427 8888.

Train enquiries Long-distance services ☎0345/484950; local services ☎0121/200 2700.

Women's advice and information centre 191 Corporation Street (☎0121/212 1881).

The Black Country

To outsiders the area known as the **Black Country** appears to be an undifferentiated mass sprawling away from the western side of Birmingham, but in fact it's composed of several tightly knit industrial communities, which have gradually expanded until each is touching its neighbours. The region earned its name in the mid-nineteenth century when smoke from hundreds of ironworkings choked the air and sooted the buildings – the environment is much cleaner today. Some of these towns grew on the basis of one or two staple products – leather in Walsall, locks in Willenhall, glass in Stourbridge – whilst the rest exploited the abundant local resources (chiefly coal and limestone) to develop a range of industries, with heavy engineering predominant. Although many of the older trades have long gone, this is still an area where manufacturing is regarded as the only real work, so it's unsurprising that the Black Country's industrial heritage is the main reason for visiting the area.

Dudley

Nine miles west of Birmingham, **DUDLEY** (from Birmingham, take bus #87 from New Street or #126 from Corporation Street) lays fair claim to being the capital of the Black Country as it was here in the seventeenth century that coal was first used for smelting iron. The town is actually much older – as evidenced by its ruined Norman **castle**, perched on the hill above town with grounds that now contain a zoo (Easter to mid-Sept daily 10am–4.30pm; mid Sept–Easter closes 3pm; £6.50) – but the main attraction is the **Black Country Museum** on the Tipton Road, over the far side of Castle Hill from the town centre (March–Oct daily 10am–5pm; Nov–Feb Wed–Sun 10am–4pm; £7.50). Buildings from the surrounding district – shops, a chapel, a pub, workshops, forges and homes – have been re-erected here and populated with local people in period costume, mimicking forms of labour that once employed thousands in these parts. For added authenticity you can take a trip down an underground coal seam, watch a silent movie in the cinema, or enjoy a canal trip into a tunnel under Castle Hill, through some floodlit limestone caverns – but note this adds £2.70 to the admission fee.

The area is also noted for its **beer** – if you only try one Black Country pub, make it the *Vine* (known locally as *"The Bull and Bladder"*), the Batham's brewery outlet on Delph Road, Brierley Hill. It stands at the top of a run of excellent pubs that wind down the hill to the bottom of the Delph Nine Locks on the Dudley no. 1 canal.

Walsall

Some ten miles north of Birmingham, and readily reached by train or bus, **WALSALL** is a pleasantly stoic town, now attempting to diversify into tourism after years as a centre of the leather industry. Its prime attraction is the **Walsall Museum and Art Gallery**, currently on Lichfield Street (Tues–Sat 10am–5pm, Sun 2–5pm; free), but due to move to new premises on Wolverhampton Street in the near future. The gallery contains a wide-ranging collection of paintings, drawings, prints and sculpture assembled by Kathleen Epstein, the widow of Jacob Epstein, and her friend Sally Ryan. Among the paintings, there are works by Blake, Degas, Modigliani, Van Gogh, Picasso, Ruskin, Turner and – of course – Jacob Epstein.

Of more local significance, the **Walsall Leather Museum** (April–Oct Tues–Sat 10am–5pm, Sun noon–5pm; Nov–March Tues–Sat 10am–4pm, Sun noon–4pm; free), on the ring road (A4148 – Littleton Street West), provides a surprisingly interesting look at the industry's development and its effect on the town.

Wolverhampton and around

WOLVERHAMPTON, around fourteen miles northwest of Birmingham, doesn't win any beauty contests, but it does possess the excellent **Wolverhampton Art Gallery and Museum**, on Lichfield Street (Mon–Sat 10am–5pm; free). There's a healthy sample of English paintings here, featuring the likes of Gainsborough, Paul Nash, Stanley Spencer and Landseer, but the gallery is best known for its extensive collection of American and British Pop Art. Amongst many, Hamilton, Hockney, Warhol, Allen Jones and Lichtenstein are all featured, and there are also purposeful temporary exhibitions plus an eclectic selection of contemporary art.

Three miles west is the mock-half-timbered **Wightwick Manor** – pronounced "Witick" – at Wightwick Bank, off the A454 (March–Dec Thurs & Sat 2.30–5.30pm; £5.40 for house and garden; NT). Built in 1887, it was designed by Edward Ould, a devotee of William Morris, and the extravagant furnishings, fittings and paintings all reflect the Pre-Raphaelite influence. The garden (Wed & Thurs 11am–6pm, Sat 1–6pm; £2.40) is maintained in its Victorian form, complete with lush orchards and ostentatious topiary. Buses #516 (Midland Red) and #890 (Green Bus) from Wolverhampton stop at the bottom of the road.

Located four miles to the north of town is **Moseley Old Hall** (mid-March to May Sat & Sun 1.30–5.30pm; June, Sept & Oct Wed, Sat & Sun 1.30–5.30pm; July–Aug Tues, Wed, Sat & Sun 1.30–5.30pm; £3.90; NT), a much-modified Elizabethan country mansion famous for its association with Charles II. The king took refuge here after the Battle of Worcester in 1651 and you can see the bed he slept in and the hole in which he sheltered for the best part of two days as Parliamentarian troops scoured the area. An exhibition in the barn fills out the history. Buses #870–2 and #613 from Wolverhampton pass nearby, leaving a fifteen-minute walk.

Coventry

In medieval times, **COVENTRY**, twenty miles east of Birmingham, was one of England's most prosperous cities, its wealth founded on the cloth, thread and dyeing industries, precursors of the engineering plants that were to become the staple of the city's economy during the nineteenth century. It was here in 1898 that the Daimler Company manufactured the first British motor car, and thereafter the city rapidly became a major centre of car production. As a sign of the good times, the population quadrupled between 1900 and 1930 – from 70,000 to 250,000 – and the future looked rosy. However, Coventry's industrial success attracted the attentions of the Luftwaffe and, on November 14, 1940, in one of the biggest bombing raids of World War II, the Germans destroyed most of the city. The postwar period has not been easy for Coventry. Heavy industry has been on the skids and the motor production lines have waned to near-extinction. Neither has the new Coventry built to replace the old been an architectural success and – with the exception of the splendid **cathedral** – the city is lumbered with more than its fair share of unsightly buildings.

Arrival, information and accommodation

Coventry is an important rail junction and its **train station**, just south of the central ring road near Warwick Road, has direct services to and from London, Birmingham, and many major British cities. The recently re-vamped Pool Meadow **bus station** lies a short way north of the cathedral, and is served by National Express coaches to London, Birmingham, Bath and Bristol, and many other destinations. The bus station is also the hub of the local bus network, with regular connections to Warwick, Warwick University, Leamington and Stratford on Stagecoach Midland Red.

TELEPHONE NUMBERS

On April 22, 2000, all **telephone numbers** in Coventry will change. There will be a **new area code, 024**, and all local numbers will be prefixed with **76**, making the new local numbers eight digits long. For further information on the changes to the telephone numbering system in the UK, see the box on p.42.

For free town maps and glossy local brochures, head for the **tourist office** on Bayley Lane, right in the centre of town opposite the old cathedral (June–Aug Mon–Fri 9.30am–5pm, Sat & Sun 10am–4.30pm; rest of year Mon–Fri 9.30am–4.30pm, Sat & Sun 10am–4.30pm; ☎01203/832303). Their main city guidebook has a list of all the town's **accommodation** and they will also book a room on your behalf at no cost – though comparatively few casual visitors choose to stay here. One particularly pleasant **B&B** is the *Abigail Guest House*, 39 St Patrick's Rd (☎01203/221378; ①), whose five spick and span guest rooms occupy a Victorian terraced house a short walk south of the cathedral, close to the central ring road.

The City

The city centre is dominated by Sir Basil Spence's **St Michael's Cathedral** (daily Easter–Oct 9.30am–6pm, Nov–Easter 9.30am–5.30pm; £2 donation requested), raised alongside the shell of the blitzed old cathedral and dedicated with a performance of Benjamin Britten's specially written *War Requiem* in 1962. Easily the most successful of Coventry's postwar buildings, the cathedral's pink sandstone is light and graceful, the main entrance adorned by a stunningly forceful *St Michael Defeating the Devil* by Jacob Epstein. Inside, Spence's high and slender nave is bathed in light from the soaring stained glass windows, a perfect setting for the magnificent and immense **tapestry** of *Christ in Glory* by Graham Sutherland. The choice of artist could not have been more appropriate. A painter, graphic artist and designer, Sutherland (1903–1980) had been one of Britain's official war artists, his particular job being to record the effects of German bombing. A canopied walkway links the new cathedral with the ruins of the old, used every three years as an atmospheric venue for the **Coventry Mystery Plays** – the next cycle is due to be held in 2000. Finally, the cathedral's visitor centre (Easter–Oct Mon–Sat 10am–4pm, Nov–Easter Mon–Sat 11am–3pm; £1.25) features an historical exhibition on the city and cathedral with showings of a short video, *The Spirit of Coventry*.

A stone's throw southeast of the Cathedral on Jordan Well stands the **Herbert Art Gallery and Museum** (Mon–Sat 10am–5.30pm, Sun noon–5pm; free). The most outstanding exhibits here are Luca della Robbia's gigantic *Bacchus and Ariadne*, which fills an entire wall on the first floor, a famous portrait of King George III by Sir Thomas Lawrence, and a row of Lady Godivas that includes John Collier's much-photographed Pre-Raphaelite version. Also of interest here are Sutherland's sketch studies for the cathedral tapestry, followed up with a trial piece made by French weavers. Downstairs on the ground floor, the go-ahead *Godiva City* exhibition covers one thousand years of local history with a succession of lively interactive displays. Among the original artefacts on show are a large bronze Saxon bowl, known as the Bagington Bowl, sundry items of pristine medieval leatherwork, and drawers of ornate ribbons, including one, woven for the Great Exhibition of 1851, that is allegedly the most complicated ever made.

Coventry has been home to dozens of carmakers, including such almost-forgotten names as Singer, Riley, Humber and Hillman. These connections are celebrated at the **Museum of British Road Transport** (daily 10am–5pm; free), on Hales Street, opposite

LADY GODIVA

The story of **Lady Godiva** riding naked on horseback through the streets of Coventry is one of England's favourite folk tales – and the city milks the connection with postcards, key rings and statues. According to the most popular version of the story, Lady Godiva, the beautiful wife of the local lord, Leofric, the Earl of Mercia, was appalled by the poverty she saw around her, and begged her husband to abolish the crippling taxes he levied on his people. Wearying of his wife's philanthropy, Leofric said he would do as she asked on condition that she ride naked through the town, never suspecting that a woman of her rank would agree to such a proposal. Lady Godiva, however, got around the dilemma by ordering the townsfolk to lock themselves in their houses and bolt their windows on the appointed day. Only one local lad, the original **"Peeping Tom"**, dared disobey the countess's command, and he was struck blind before he had a chance to see Godiva, her long hair covering her body like a cape as she rode through the city, eyes lowered. The ordeal over, Godiva returned to her husband, who kept his word and repealed the taxes.

The story first appeared in 1188, but the historical figures it depicted lived nearly a century and a half before. Leofric was the Anglo-Saxon earl who, in 1043, built the Benedictine priory that helped transform Coventry from a small settlement into medieval England's fourth-largest town. His wife, Godgifu, outlived him by ten years, and may have been a powerful ruler in her own right after her husband's death; she was also pious and donated land and money to the Church. Beyond this, little is known about the couple. The Godiva story probably evolved from some kind of pagan fertility ritual, and was popularized in the writings of the Norman chronicler Roger of Wendover, during the thirteenth century. "Peeping Tom" was a later embellishment, seemingly inspired by a particularly odd chain of events. In 1586, Coventry council asked a certain Adam van Noort (1562–1641) to paint the Godiva legend. He did so, but he placed Leofric in a window looking down at Godiva on her horse. For reasons that remain obscure, the city fathers exhibited the painting outside on Coventry's main square and, mistakenly, the populace took Leofric to be a peeper – and the sub-plot stuck. Researchers in the Herbert Art Gallery (where this painting now hangs) have sorted all this out and also believe that the notion of Godiva's nudity may have been a fanciful elaboration too. It seems more likely that Leofric, if he challenged his wife at all, dared her to ride through the city stripped of her jewellery and finery.

Whatever the truth of the matter, locals kept the story going and "Godiva Processions" kicked off Coventry's annual summer fair from its introduction in the seventeenth century until the 1800s, when all this public flaunting proved too much for the Victorians. More recently, the tradition has been revived in the form of a canny PR exercise to mark the start of the Spirit of Coventry Festival in June, when a local woman rides through the streets dressed in a body stocking.

Pool Meadow bus station, which contains the world's largest collection of British vehicles. Inevitably, the older vehicles attract most of the attention – there's a 1908 Riley, a bull-nosed Morris of 1922 and lots more – but there are more modern cars too, including the XJ6 Jaguar and the phallus-like "Thrust 2", in which Richard Noble set the world land speed record of 633.468mph. The museum also has a display devoted to the Coventry Blitz and a gift shop selling motor memorabilia.

Eating and drinking

Coventry hardly heaves with great places to **eat**, but *Pizza Express*, near the cathedral at 10A Hay Lane, is a safe bet for moderately priced, quality pizza and pasta, and they have a congenial rear terrace opening on to Castle Yard. Alternatively, for a snack or light meal, head for the *Bar Coast*, over in the shopping mall on Broadgate, where you can tuck into tasty Tex-Mex dishes, ciabattas, and healthy salads, or the *Tete à Tete* (Mon–Fri 8am–3pm, Sat 8am–4pm), a flowery tearoom at 188 Spon Street. The *Old*

Windmill, also on Spon Street, at no. 22, has an attractive interior with flagstones and exposed wooden beams, serves a good range of brews and provides inexpensive bar food. Otherwise, Coventry's pub scene is rather too rough and ready for most tastes and many retreat to the campus of Warwick University, four miles to the south of the city. Here the **Warwick Arts Centre** is the largest arts complex outside London, with two theatres, a cinema, an art gallery, a bar and restaurant. For details of what's on, telephone the box office (☎01203/524524).

Staffordshire

Spreading north from the Birmingham conurbation, the miscellaneous and low-key landscapes of **Staffordshire** don't enthral too many people. The county's main historic attraction and prettiest town is the cathedral city of **Lichfield**, at the southern end of Staffordshire. Lichfield also makes a handy base for visiting **Stoke-on-Trent**, famous for its pottery and factory shops. Stoke is also within easy striking distance of **Alton Towers** theme park, Britain's answer to Disney glitter, and the nation's most popular tourist attraction, with several million visitors annually.

Mainline **rail** services pass through Lichfield and Stoke en route between London, Birmingham and the northwest. Wedged in between the major urban centres of the West Midlands and northwest England, the area is also well served by **coaches** and has a decent network of local **buses** and trains.

Lichfield

Just eighteen miles from the centre of Birmingham, the pocket-sized town of **LICH-FIELD** is a slow-moving but amiable place that demands a visit for one reason – its magnificent sandstone **Cathedral** (daily 7.40am–6.30pm; £3 donation requested). Begun in 1085, but substantially rebuilt in the thirteenth and fourteenth centuries, the cathedral is unique in possessing three spires – an appropriate distinction for a bishopric that once extended over virtually all of the Midlands. The church stands on the site of a shrine built for the relics of Saint Chad, an English bishop noted for his humility, who died here in Lichfield in 672.

The cathedral's **west front** is adorned by over one hundred statues of biblical figures, English kings and the supposed ancestors of Christ, some of them dating back to the thirteenth century but mostly Victorian replacements of originals destroyed by Cromwell's troops. Even the central spire was demolished during the skirmishes – Lichfield justly claims to be the cathedral that was most damaged during the Civil War. Extensive and painstaking rebuilding and restoration work, which was begun immediately on the restoration of the monarchy in 1660, has gone on ever since, although the bulk of it was only completed at the end of the nineteenth century.

The **interior** is no less impressive, even if the dimensions are surprisingly modest. The finest part of the main body of the church is the east end, where the choir is set at an angle of ten degrees to the line of the nave. The first three bays of the choir are the oldest part of the church, completed in the Early English style of the twelfth century, but the rest of the choir is middle Gothic – or Decorated. On the south side of the choir nave stands a two-storey thirteenth-century extension whose upper level, with its fine minstrels' gallery, was where the head of Saint Chad used to be displayed to the faithful. Most impressive of all, however, is the **Lady Chapel**, at the far end of the choir, which boasts a set of magnificent sixteenth-century windows, purchased from the Cistercian abbey at Herkenrode in southern Belgium in 1802.

The cathedral's greatest treasure, the **Lichfield Gospels**, is displayed in the beautiful chapter house. One of most exquisite and valuable surviving Anglo-Saxon artefacts

SAMUEL JOHNSON

Eighteenth-century England's most celebrated wit and critic, **Samuel Johnson** was born above his father's bookshop in Lichfield's market square in 1709. From Lichfield he went to Pembroke College, Oxford, which he left in 1731 without having completed his degree. Disgruntled with academia, Johnson returned to Staffordshire as a teacher, before settling in Birmingham for three years, a period that saw his first pieces published in the *Birmingham Journal*.

In 1735 Johnson married Elizabeth Porter, a Birmingham friend's widow twenty years his senior, returning to his home district to open a private school in the village of Edial, three miles southwest of Lichfield. The school was no great success, so after two years the Johnsons abandoned the project and went to London with the young David Garrick, their star pupil. Journalism and essays were the mainstay of the Johnsons' penurious existence until publisher Robert Dodsley asked Samuel to consider compiling a **Dictionary of the English Language**, a project that nobody had undertaken before, and which was to occupy him for eight years prior to its publication in 1755. Massively learned and full of mordant wit ("lexicographer: a writer of dictionaries; a harmless drudge"), the *Dictionary* is one of Johnson's greatest legacies, although he was financially and emotionally stretched to breaking point by the workload it imposed upon him. Money problems continued to dog the writer – in 1759 he wrote the novel *Rasselas* in one week, in order to raise money for his mother's funeral – but a degree of financial stability came at last in the early 1760s, when the new king, George III, granted him a bursary of £300 per year.

In 1763 Johnson met James Boswell, a pushy young Scot who clung tenaciously to the cantankerous older man until he learned to like him. Their journey to Scotland resulted in one of the finest travel books ever written, **A Journey to the Western Isles of Scotland** (1775), in which Johnson's fascinated incredulity at the native way of life makes for utterly absorbing reading. Other publications from his final decade included a preface to Shakespeare's plays, a series of political tracts and the magnificent **Lives of the English Poets**. However, the work by which he is now best known is not one that he himself wrote – it is Boswell's **The Life of Samuel Johnson**, commenced on its subject's death in 1784, published in 1791 and still the English language's most full-blooded biography.

in the country, this 1250-year-old illuminated manuscript contains the complete gospels of Matthew and Mark, and a fragment of the gospel of Luke, written in Latin and embellished with elaborate decoration. No one knows who wrote it, but experts believe it was produced locally and records certainly show it was stolen in a raid and carried off to Wales, from where it was eventually returned in medieval times. The page on display is the gorgeous Carpet Page, showing a decorative cross whose blend of Coptic, Celtic and Oriental influences make it the equal of the more famous Irish Book of Kells and Lindisfarne Gospels (see p.652). The fact that the book ends mid-way through St Luke means it's almost certainly one of a pair – and rare book specialists have long been on the look-out for the matching volume.

The south transept contains a bust of the city's most famous son, **Samuel Johnson**, and if you walk a couple of hundred yards south from the cathedral to Breadmarket Street, on the corner of the market place, you'll come to the **Samuel Johnson Birthplace Museum** (daily 10.30am–4.30pm; £2 or £3.20 joint ticket with Heritage Exhibition). Crammed with books, manuscripts and pictures, the museum pays handsome tribute to the great man, and produces a useful leaflet on the "Johnson Trail", for those who want to retrace his footsteps round his home patch. Opposite Johnson's house, in the middle of the market square, the twelfth-century parish church of **St Mary** is now home to the **Lichfield Heritage Centre** (daily 10am–5pm; £2), an over-designed but comprehensive presentation of the city's history, with illuminating sections on the Civil War and Regency periods. Outside the church, on either side of the market square, stand ponderous statues of Samuel Johnson and his biographer, James Boswell. Near the latter is a memorial to Edward Wightman, who was burnt at the stake for heresy on this very spot in 1612. It was dashed hard luck – he was the last Englishman to be so punished for this particular crime.

As for the rest of the centre, Lichfield is graced by dozens of elegant Georgian houses, with an especially handsome ensemble flanking **The Close**, by the cathedral. Another Georgian property to look for is **Donegal House**, a warm red-brick building tucked in the southwestern corner of the market square on Bore Street. It's now home to both the tourist office, on the ground floor, and the uninspiring **Lichfield Sketchbook** of local history up above (Mon–Sat 9am–5pm; free).

Practicalities

Frequent **trains** from Birmingham call at the Lichfield City central station before continuing to Lichfield Trent Valley station, on the northern fringe of the city and served by mainline trains from London Euston and the northwest. The **tourist office** is in Donegal House on Bore Street, just off the market place (Mon–Sat 9am–5pm; ☎01543/252109).

Lichfield has a reasonable range of **accommodation**. Best value among the hotels is *Oakleigh House*, 25 St Chad's Rd (☎01543/262688; ③), a large Victorian building overlooking the cathedral pool – or pond – with a popular conservatory restaurant (open to non-residents). **B&Bs** within easy reach of the cathedral include the excellent *Gaialands*, 9 Gaiafields Rd (☎01543/263764; no credit cards; ①), whose bright and cheerful rooms occupy part of a large and attractive Victorian home, and Mrs Jones's appealing B&B, in a listed nineteenth-century town house by the cathedral at 8 The Close (☎01543/418483; ①).

Most of the better-value **restaurants** are around Bore Street and St John Street, including a few Indian and Chinese places – the inexpensive *Prince of India*, 9 Bore St, is as good as anywhere. Alternatively, the *Olive Tree*, 34 Tamworth St, is a fashionable bistro serving up tasty Mediterranean-style dishes at reasonable prices.

Stoke-on-Trent

The inhabitants of **STOKE-ON-TRENT**, some thirty miles northwest of Lichfield, have been making pottery since Roman times, but mass production only began in the eighteenth century. Then, in the space of forty years, the development of local coalfields, the securing of a regular supply of fine-quality clay from Devon and Cornwall and the digging of the Trent–Mersey canal transformed the town and its environs into the biggest centre of pottery production in the world – known, logically enough, as **The Potteries**. It was all a terrible eyesore and the district, with its belching smoke stacks and fuming bottle kilns, became synonymous with industrial squalor, but the profits were enormous – quite enough to attract a string of talented entrepreneur-designers. The first of them, and still the most renowned, was Josiah Wedgwood, who opened a factory here in 1769. More recently, the industry has been in decline, hit hard by cheap foreign imports, but Britain's department stores are still stacked with The Potteries' products and local companies – such as Royal Doulton, Spode, Royal Worcester and Wedgwood – are making a fight of it. All this industrial activity doesn't spell much in the way of tourist delight, but Stoke-on-Trent's heritage museums and factory shops are enough to keep most visitors happy for a few hours at least.

The city of Stoke-on-Trent is, in fact, an amalgam of **six towns** – confusing for fans of locally born Arnold Bennett, who wrote about the five towns in novels such as *Clayhanger* and *Anna of the Five Towns*, ignoring the smallest of the six, **Fenton**. Of the other five, the major two are **Stoke** itself, which feels as if it has been left to wither to the benefit of **Hanley**, a mile to the north, which has all the main shops and the main civic museum. **Tunstall** and **Burslem** to the north and **Longton** to the southeast are the remaining Stoke towns, all largely autonomous communities. Trains arrive at **Stoke** station, whereas buses use the **Lichfield Street bus station** in central Hanley.

The **Potteries Museum and Art Gallery** in Bethesda Street, Hanley (Mon–Sat 10am–5pm, Sun 2–5pm; free), holds a magnificent and colossal collection of English pottery and ceramics. The museum tracks through the industry's eighteenth-century artistic heyday and the boom of the nineteenth with examples from all the leading manufacturers. There is also a section of Art Deco pieces – look out for the work of Clarice Cliff – and examples of present-day production. An excellent social history department includes a poignant memorial to three local people who died in the 1984–85 miners' strike – two men on picket duty and one boy scavenging for coal in the winter. For an introduction to the industry itself, head for the excellent **Gladstone Pottery Museum** in Uttoxeter Road, Longton (daily 10am–5pm; £3.95). Distinguished by the large bottle kilns that used to dominate the entire city, the museum employs craftspeople to demonstrate the skills of pottery production, and details the evolution of the six towns and the social conditions of their people.

Dozens of pottery workshops and factories are open to visitors – the **tourist office** in the Potteries Shopping Centre on Quadrant Road in Hanley (Mon–Sat 9.15am–5.15pm; ☎01782/236000) can supply details. One of the better-known companies is Royal Doulton, who have a factory shop at the Regent Works, Lawley Street, Longton (Mon–Sat 9am–5.30pm, Sun 11am–5pm; ☎01782/291172). Without a car, the most convenient way to get around all the main sites is with a China Day Rider bus ticket (£4), timetables for which are also available at the tourist office.

Alton Towers

About thirteen miles east of Stoke **Alton Towers** (mid-March to early Nov 9.30am–7pm or dusk; £19.50; ☎0990/204060; *www.alton towers.co.uk*) is Britain's largest amusement park, which preserves its number-one ranking by introducing more terrifying rides each season, with names like Nemesis and Oblivion. If the white-knuckle stuff is too strong for you, there are endless food outlets to escape into, along with landscaped and themed gardens and an array of less stomach-churning fairground attractions. There's a "family friendly" **hotel** onsite (☎0990/001100; ⑦ for four-person family rooms). The Alton experience doesn't come cheap; as well as the hefty entry fee (which covers all rides), be prepared to pay over the odds for food and drink.

Derby and the Peak District

In 1951, the hills and dales of the **PEAK DISTRICT**, at the southern tip of the Pennine range, became Britain's first national park. Wedged between **Derby**, Manchester and Sheffield, it is effectively the backyard for the fifteen million people who live within an hour's drive of its boundaries, though somehow it accommodates the huge influx with the minimum of fuss.

Landscapes in the Peak District come in two forms. The brooding high moorland tops of **Dark Peak**, fifteen miles east of central Manchester, take their name from the underlying gritstone, known as millstone grit for its former use – a function commemorated in the millstones demarcating the park boundary. Windswept, mist-shrouded and inhospitable, the flat tops of these peaks are nevertheless a firm favourite with walkers on the **Pennine Way**, which meanders north from the tiny village of **Edale** to the Scottish border (see box on p.646). Altogether more forgiving, the southern limestone hills of the **White Peak** have been eroded into deep forested dales populated by small stone villages and often threaded by walking trails along former rail routes. The limestone is riddled with complex cave systems around **Castleton** and under the region's largest centre, **Buxton**, a former spa town just outside the park's boundaries, at the end of an industrialized corridor reaching out from Manchester. Two of the country's most distinctive manorial piles, **Chatsworth House** and **Haddon Hall**, stand near **Bakewell**, a town famed locally not just for its cakes but also for its **well-dressing**, a possibly pagan ritual of thanksgiving for water that is observed in about twenty Peak villages throughout the summer.

Access and accommodation

Trains penetrate only as far as Buxton from the north and cut through Edale on the Manchester to Sheffield route. The main **bus access** is via the Trent bus company's TransPeak service from Nottingham to Manchester via Derby, Matlock, Bakewell and Buxton; otherwise bus #272 runs regularly from Sheffield to Castleton, via Hathersage and Hope, and the Peak Express connects Sheffield to Buxton. If you're not planning on walking between towns and villages, you'll need the essential, encyclopaedic *Peak District Timetable* (published twice-yearly; 60p), from local tourist and national park information offices, which lists all the local **public transport** services. Buses are more widespread than you might imagine, though there are limited winter and Sunday services throughout the region, and often only sporadic links between the major centres. Various one-day **transport passes** allow unlimited travel to and within specified zones. It's a complicated system, but broadly speaking the Peak Explorer (£8) covers the chunk of the park in Yorkshire, the Peak Wayfarer Manchester (£6.60), and the Derbyshire Wayfarer (£7.25) covers the rest. For all Peak District bus information call **Busline** on ☎01298/23098 (daily 7am–8pm).

A joint Derbyshire County Council/National Park venture provides for a series of **Peak Cycle Hire Centres**, which rent out **bikes** for £8 per day (plus a £20 deposit; discounts for YHA members). There's a full network of dedicated cycle lanes, tracks and old railway lines and the centres are located at: Ashbourne (Mapleton Lane, ☎01335/343156), Derwent (Fairholmes, ☎01433/651261), Hayfield (Information Centre, Station Rd, ☎01663/746222), Middleton Top (Visitor Centre, Middleton-by-Wirksworth, ☎01629/823204), Parsley Hay (☎01298/84493), and Waterhouses (Old Station Car Park, ☎01538/308609).

There's plenty of **accommodation** in and around the park, mostly in B&Bs, with a dozen youth hostels and numerous campsites scattered among them. A network of YHA-operated **camping barns** is also available. These are located in converted farm buildings and provide simple and inexpensive self-catering accommodation for between 6 and 24 people. For further details contact the YHA Camping Barns Reservation Office, 16 Shawbridge St, Clitheroe, Lancashire BB7 1LY (☎01200/428366). The Peak District National Park Authority office is at Aldern House, Baslow Road, Bakewell, DE45 1AE (☎01629/816200). They have an excellent **Web site** (*www.peakdistrict.org*) and also operate a string of **information centres**. These are supplemented by village tourist offices and in some smaller places by local stores doubling up as information points. Maps and trail guides are widely available (OS *Outdoor Leisure* maps 1 and 24 cover the Peak District) and guided countryside walks are commonplace – sign up locally. Finally, make sure to pick up a copy of the free *Peakland Post*, crammed with useful information.

Derby

The proximity of the Peak District might lead you to think that **DERBY**, eleven miles northeast of Burton, could prove to be an interesting stopping-off point. Sadly, the city – a status conferred as recently as 1977 – is an unexciting place, though its workaday centre is partly redeemed by several long and handsome nineteenth-century terraces and its **cathedral**, whose pinnacled tower soars high above its modest surroundings on Queen Street. Of the city's several museums, easily the best is the **Derby Museum and Art Gallery** on the Strand (Mon 11am–5pm, Tues–Sat 10am–5pm, Sun 2–5pm; free), a five-minute walk from the central market place. The museum exhibits a splendid collection of Derby porcelain, three thousand pieces tracking through the different phases and styles from the late eighteenth century until today: the painted scenes created by John Brewer during the Crown Derby period of 1784–1811 are especially charming. The museum also holds far and away the most comprehensive collection of the work of **Joseph Wright** (1734–1797), a local artist generally regarded as one of the most talented English painters of his century. Wright's bread and butter came from portraiture, though his attempt to fill the boots of Gainsborough, when the latter moved from Bath to London, came unstuck – his more forceful style did not satisfy his genteel customers and Wright soon high-tailed it back to Derby. Wright was one of the few artists of his period to find inspiration in technology and his depictions of the scientific world were hugely influential.

The train station, on the lines between London and Sheffield and between Birmingham and the northeast, is a mile to the southeast of the city centre. Right in the heart of town, on the market place, is the city's **tourist office** (Mon–Fri 9.30am–5.30pm, Sat 9.30am–5pm, Sun 10.30am–2.30pm; ☎01332/255802) – worth a call if you're on your way into the Peaks.

Buxton

BUXTON was founded in 79 AD by the Romans, who happened upon a spring from which 1500 gallons of pure water gushed every hour at a constant 28°C. So famous did the spring become that Mary, Queen of Scots was allowed by her captors to come here for treatment of her rheumatism. Its heyday came in the last two decades of the eighteenth century, with the fifth Duke of Devonshire's grand design to create a northern answer to Bath or Cheltenham, a plan thwarted by the climate, but not before some distinguished eighteenth-century buildings had formed the gracious Lower Buxton.

Like many former British spas, the town's heritage has been marred by a lack of money to refurbish ageing properties, though a belated attempt has been made to rescue some of the finer buildings. The thermal baths were closed in 1972, though the sweep of the **Crescent**, incorporating the former *St Ann's Hotel* – its grandest architectural feature, modelled on the Royal Crescent in Bath – has been preserved thanks to a hefty government grant. It's hoped that some of the public rooms will re-open in the future, but no firm plans have yet been made. The little street fountain in front of the Crescent, supplied by **St Ann's Well**, is still used to fill local water bottles and the nearby **Pump Room**, first erected in 1894, provides space for temporary art exhibitions in the summer. At the eastern end of the Crescent, a glass and cast-iron canopy hides the entrance to the Cavendish Arcade shopping centre, which makes a hash of preserving the original eighteenth-century bath houses.

The spa remnants apart, the town is at its best in the nearby landscaped **Pavilion Gardens**, just to the southwest of the Crescent, where the thousand-seat **Opera House** (tours most Sats at 11am; £1; call ☎01298/72190 to check), facing Water Street, is the main venue for the **Buxton Opera Festival** held during the last two weeks of July. The glasshouse gardens next to the Opera House shelter an array of exotic foliage and you can walk through to the double-decker glass-and-iron pavilion itself, overlooking the formal gardens, where there's a bar, coffee shop and restaurant with nice views.

Fronting the Crescent, an attractive park known as **The Slopes** – laid out in 1818 in the last flush of municipal enthusiasm – leads up to the traffic-choked Market Place. The top of The Slopes offers the best prospect over the Crescent to the *Palace Hotel* (see below) and the **Devonshire Hospital**; the latter, built in 1790 as a riding school, is covered by what for a long time was the world's widest domed roof. Just down Terrace Road from Market Place, the **Buxton Museum and Art Gallery** (Tues–Fri 9.30am–5.30pm, Sat 9.30am–5pm, Sun in summer only 10.30am–5pm; £1) houses a collection of ancient fossils, rocks and pots found in the Peak District, among them jaw bones from Neolithic lions and bears. The displays on the first floor document the history of the region from the Bronze Age through to more recent times.

As rewarding as any of Buxton's architectural attractions is **Poole's Cavern** (Easter–Oct daily 10am–5pm; £4.50; ☎01298/26978), a mile to the south of town: follow the Broadwalk through the Pavilion Gardens and then take Temple Road. The guided-tour patter is irksome, but the orange and blue-grey stalactite formations are amazingly complex and the chambers impressively large; one marks the underground source of the River Wye. A twenty-minute walk up through the Grinlow Woods from the mouth of the cave leads to **Solomon's Temple**, a Victorian folly with great views across Buxton and the hills to the west.

Practicalities

There's an hourly train service from Manchester Piccadilly to Buxton, terminating two minutes' walk from the centre at the **train station** on Station Road. The TransPeak **bus** runs every two hours between Manchester (Chorlton Street Coach Station) and Nottingham, and stops in Buxton's Market Place, as do the regular buses from Sheffield Interchange. Although the town isn't actually in the National Park, its **tourist office** in the old Natural Mineral Baths on the Crescent (March–Oct daily 9.30am–5pm; Nov–Feb daily 10am–4pm; ☎01298/25106) covers the whole of the Peak District.

Accommodation is plentiful, but at the cheaper end of the market it is none too inspiring, many of the cheaper guest houses being located in dreary backstreets away from the centre. *Lakenham Guest House*, 11 Burlington Rd (☎01298/79209; no credit cards; ③), is a good first choice, overlooking Pavilion Gardens. *Hartington Hotel*, 18 Broad Walk (☎01298/22638; ③), also has a nice parkside location and reasonable facilities. For cheaper beds, try the streets off Market Place, where Grange Road and South Avenue provide several budget choices. At the upper end of the market, start with the friendly *Grosvenor House Hotel*, 1 Broad Walk (☎01298/72439; ③), near The Slopes, which has a variety of rooms and its own coffee shop. The historic associations of the *Old Hall Hotel*, in The Square, near the Opera House (☎01298/22841; ⑤), resonate with some – Mary, Queen of Scots stayed here in 1573 – while pride of the old spa was the *Palace Hotel* on Palace Road (☎01298/22001; ⑦, includes dinner), still sitting pretty above the town and with fantastic views. It is a twenty-minute walk to the *Sherbrook Lodge* **youth hostel**, set in wooded grounds on Harpur Hill Road, at the end of London Road (☎01298/22287); and a further five from there up Dukes Drive to the nearest **campsite**, *Lime Tree Park* (☎01298/22988; closed Dec–Feb).

The town's **eating** options are all fairly down to earth, typified by the bakeries and cafés along Spring Gardens, the main pedestrianized street. *Hargreave's Coffee Shop*, 18 Spring Gardens, has a bit more about it than most, an Edwardian tearoom above a china and nick-nack emporium. The *Wild Carrot*, 5 Bridge St (closed Mon & Tues), at the end of Spring Gardens, is an adventurous (mostly vegetarian) café offering Friday-night dinners. Otherwise, you're left with a motley collection of restaurants and a couple of pubs around Market Place, with *Firenze Pizzeria Ristorante*, 3 Eagle Parade (closed Mon; dinner only), about the best of the bunch. The annual **Buxton Festival** takes place every July, featuring a full programme of classical music, opera and drama, with supporting fringe events, including a film festival. Details from the Festival Office (☎01298/70395), the Opera House, where many events are staged, or from the tourist office.

Castleton

The limestone hills of the White Peaks are riddled with water-worn cave systems, best explored in the four show caves within walking distance of **CASTLETON**, ten miles northeast of Buxton. It's an agreeable small town, overlooked by Mam Tor (see box below), ringed by hills and cut through by a babbling river lined with stone cottages: as a base for local walks it's hard to beat, and the hikers resting up in the quiet Market Place near the church have the choice of a fine spread of local accommodation and services. Overseeing the whole ensemble is **Peveril Castle** (April–Oct daily 10am–6pm; Nov–March Wed–Sun 10am–4pm; £2; ☎01433/620613), from which the village gets its name. Its construction was started by William I's illegitimate son William Peveril to protect the king's rights to the forest that then covered vast areas of the Peak District. After a stiff climb up to the keep, you can trace much of the surviving curtain wall, which commands great views of the Hope Valley.

The closest cavern to town, the **Peak Cavern** (Easter–Oct daily 10am–5pm; Nov–Easter weekends 10am–4pm; £4.75) is tucked in a gully at the back of the town, its gaping mouth once providing shelter for a rope factory and a small village, of which a vague floorplan remains. Daniel Defoe, visiting in the eighteenth century, noted the cavern's colourful local name, the "Devil's Arse", after the fiendish fashion in which the interior contours twisted and turned. Twenty minutes' walk out of town along the road to Whinnat's Pass (there's a parallel route, across the fields) lies **Speedwell Cavern** (daily 9.30am–4.30pm; summer till 5.30pm; last entry 30min before closing; £5.25); at 600ft below ground, it's the deepest cave accessible to the public in Britain. That said, there's precious little to see, with the main drama coming with the means of access itself – down a hundred dripping steps and then by boat through a quarter-mile-long claustrophobic tunnel that was blasted out in search of lead. At the end lies the Bottomless Pit, a pool where 40,000 tons of mining rubble were dumped without raising the water level.

The other two caves are the world's only source of the sparkling fluorspar known as **Blue John**. Highly prized for ornaments and jewellery for the past 250 years, this semi-

---

WALKS AROUND CASTLETON

Several routes take you up from the Hope Valley onto the tops which ring Castleton, some taking in the show caves along the way and most being easy to follow in good weather: you'll need OS map *Outdoor Leisure 1*, or one of the trail leaflets from the information office.

A path runs west from town, climbing past Peak, Speedwell and Treak Cliff caverns before bending around a bluff to reach the Blue John Cavern: if you're sightseeing, you can complete the short circular walk here by following the minor road back down the precipitous **Whinnat's Pass**, emerging again at Speedwell Cavern. For the best views, though, keep following the signposted path from Blue John for the slow climb up the National-Trust-owned **Mam Tor** (1696ft) and its barely discernible Iron Age hill fort (3km from Castleton, 1hr 30min). It's the Peak District's second-highest peak and the NT's most tramped-upon outdoor site, attracting over 250,000 visitors a year – hence the flagstoned path up to the top and along the ridge, whose stone was helicoptered in. This channels the summer crowds along something of a hikers' motorway, but it has allowed the hillside to regenerate itself and the nesting birds to return. The views – to Kinder Scout, Castleton, Edale and down the Hope Valley – remain unsurpassed.

From the peak the ridge rolls along to the northeast and opportunities to drop back down to Castleton can be taken at either Hollins Cross, Back Tor or from Losehill Pike, making the complete walk anything from three to six hours. Hollins Cross is also the lowest crossing-point on the two-hour walk from Castleton to Edale, which could also form part of a circuit involving scaling Mam Tor.

precious stone comes in a multitude of hues from blue through deep red to yellow, depending on its hydrocarbon impurities. Before being cut and polished it must be soaked in pine resin, a process originally carried out in France, where the term *bleu-jaune* (after its primary colours) provided the source of its English name. The **Treak Cliff Cavern** (March–Oct daily 9.30am–5.30pm; Nov–Feb daily 10am–4pm, last entry 40min before closing; £4.50; ☎01433/620571), a few hundred yards along the hillside from Speedwell, contains the best examples of the stone in situ and a good deal more in the shop. This is also the best cave to visit in its own right, dripping – literally – with stalactites (some up to 100,000 years old), flowstone and bizarre rock formations, all visible on an entertaining forty-minute walking tour through the main cave system. Water collected in one of the caves is used to make tea in the café at the entrance since it's much purer than the stuff that pours from the local taps. Tours of the **Blue John Cavern** (daily 9.30am–5.30pm; reduced hours in winter; £5; ☎01433/620638) dive deeper into the rock, with narrow steps and sloping paths following an ancient water-course through whirlpool-hollowed chambers down to the Dining Room Cavern, where a former owner once held a banquet. Blue John Cavern is another fifteen minutes' sign-posted walk beyond Treak Cliff, or there's direct access off the A625, just west of Castleton.

Practicalities

The A625 runs through the centre of Castleton as the high street, with approaches from the west sidetracking down B roads and descending the steep Whinnat's Pass into town. From the east it's a clear run along the A625 from Sheffield. The main approach by public transport is by **bus** from Sheffield on the (roughly) hourly #272, though there are also limited local services from Bakewell and Buxton. The regular Manchester Piccadilly–Hope Valley–Sheffield trains stop at **Hope train station** two miles east of town, which is linked to Castleton by the #272 bus and other local services. The **Peak National Park Information Centre** is on Castle Street, near the church (daily: Easter–Oct 10am–1pm & 2–5.30pm; Nov–Easter 10am–1pm & 2–5pm; ☎01433/620679).

    Accommodation is plentiful, but should be booked in advance at popular holiday times; the information office can help if you're stuck. The lively **youth hostel** (☎01433/620235, *castleton@yha.org.uk*) is housed in eighteenth-century Castleton Hall and the adjacent old vicarage on Market Place, just up past the church from the information office. The most welcoming **B&B** is the slightly eccentric *Bargate Cottage*, also on Market Place (☎01433/620201; no credit cards; ②), whose frilly rooms are overseen by a friendly proprietor who offers conversation, good breakfasts and welcome extras like drying baskets for hiking boots. Two or three other B&Bs are sited just over the road from here. *Cryer House*, a little way back down Castle Street (☎01433/620244; no credit cards; ②), opposite the church, has a lovely conservatory, or try for space at the popular *Kelseys Swiss House*, on How Lane (☎01433/621098; no credit cards; ②), the eastern continuation of the main road through town. All the local pubs have rooms, such as *Ye Olde Cheshire Cheese*, How Lane (☎01433/620330; ③). The best lodgings are at *Ye Olde Nag's Head* at Cross Street on the main road (☎01433/620248; ⑤), a comfortable, if slightly sniffy, seventeenth-century coaching inn with some good weekend – and dinner, room and breakfast – deals. The nearest **campsite** is in Hope, two miles east of Castleton, where the *Laneside Caravan Park* (☎01433/620215; closed Nov–Easter) lies five minutes from Hope's pubs and shops.

    The pubs are the mainstay for **eating out** in Castleton, and aren't bad to boot. *Ye Olde Cheshire Cheese* welcomes muddy boots and fills their owners with generous portions, while the *Castle* on Castle Street has an appealing series of rooms warmed by open fires. Best of all are the bar meals at *Ye Olde Nag's Head*, boasting treats like *bruschetta* and wild mushrooms; you can eat more expensively, and equally well, in their restaurant too.

Edale

There's almost nothing to **EDALE** except for a couple of pubs, a scattering of local B&Bs and a train station, and it's this isolation which is immediately appealing. Walkers arrive in droves throughout the year to set off on the 250-mile **Pennine Way** (see box opposite) across England's backbone to Kirk Yetholm on the Scottish border; its starting-point is signposted from outside the *Old Nag's Head* at the head of the village.

An excellent **circular walk** (9 miles; 1300ft; 5hr) uses the first part of the Pennine Way, leading up onto the bleak gritstone table-top of **Kinder Scout** (2088ft), below which the village cowers. The route cuts west from the *Nag's Head* along a packhorse route once used by Cheshire's salt exporters. From the campsite and camping barn at *Upper Booth Farm* (☎01433/670250), you climb the Jacob's Ladder path continuing half a mile west to the carved medieval **Edale Cross**. Backtracking a couple of hundred yards, the Pennine Way branches north along the broken plateau edge to **Kinder Downfall**, Derbyshire's highest cascade. This was the site of the **Kinder Scout Trespass** of 1932, when dozens of protesters walked onto unused but private land, five subsequently receiving prison sentences. It was the turning-point in the fight for public access to open moorland, leading, three years later, to the formation of the Ramblers' Association. At Kinder Downfall turn east then southeast across the often boggy peat towards the wind-sculpted **Wool Pack** rocks, then across to the eastern rim, where a path to the south along Grindslow Knoll and down into Edale avoids Grindsbrook Clough, the highly eroded route of the original Pennine Way. It can be extremely wet up here among the bare furrows of peat – long-distance walker John Hillaby, on his *Journey Through Britain*, had to resort to removing his footwear to make his way across the sodden top of Kinder Scout, which to his appalled mind looked as if it were "entirely covered in the droppings of dinosaurs".

Edale is around four miles northwest of Castleton by road, slightly more direct by path. Hourly **trains** from Manchester or Sheffield (stopping in Hathersage, too; see p.470) provide surprisingly easy access; the only **bus** is a summer-only Sunday service from Castleton. Walking straight up the road 400 yards from the train station takes you to the **National Park Information Centre** (Easter–Oct daily 9am–1pm & 2–5.30pm; rest of the year closes at 5pm; ☎01433/670207) at Fieldhead. This sells all manner of trail leaflets and hiking guides and can advise about local **accommodation** options. The nearest **youth hostel**, the highly popular *Edale YHA Activity Centre* (☎01433/670302, *edale@yha.org.uk*), is a mile and a half northeast of Edale station, at Rowland Cote, Nether Booth. It's accessible along the road to Nether Booth or through the *Fieldhead* **campsite** (which may, or may not, still be in operation) behind the information centre. However, there is also camping at *Cooper's* at Newfold Farm (☎01433/670372), in the centre of Edale near the *Old Nag's Head*. Other options used by Pennine Way walkers include the **camping barns** at Upper Booth and at *Cotefield Farm*, Ollerbrook (☎01433/670273), which lies on the path to the youth hostel.

Those without hair shirts, or with more money, will do better at the **B&Bs**, starting with the *Old Parsonage*, behind the *Nag's Head* (☎01433/670232; no credit cards; ①; closed Oct–Easter). *Stonecroft*, a detached Victorian house on the village road near the church (☎01433/670262; no credit cards; ③), is good, too, while other private home and farmhouse options lie scattered out along the Nether Booth road: attractive *Edale House* (☎01433/670399; no credit cards; ①) is typical, a twenty-minute walk from the pub. The *Ramblers' Inn* (☎01433/670268; ③), close to the train station at the bottom of the village, has rooms, and is one of only two places to **eat** and drink. Those things, though, are best done at the hiker-friendly *Old Nag's Head* (☎01433/670291), at the top of the village, though you'll be forced down to the *Ramblers'* a couple of times a week in winter when the *Old Nag's Head* is closed.

Bakewell

BAKEWELL, flanking the banks of the River Wye twelve miles east of Buxton, is famous for its **Bakewell Pudding**. Known throughout the rest of the country as a Bakewell tart, this is a wonderful flaky, almond-flavoured confection invented here around 1860 when a cook botched a recipe for strawberry tart. Almost a century before this fortuitous mishap, the Duke of Rutland set out to develop a spa here to surpass the work his rival, the Duke of Devonshire, was doing at Buxton. The frigidity of the water made failure inevitable, leaving only Bath Gardens beside Rutland Square as a reminder of the venture.

Today, there's little reason to linger in town, though it makes a useful base for the surrounding countryside. Stone houses cling to the handful of surviving old lanes near the river, but the heavily trafficked market town (market day is Monday) does itself few other favours. Pop in at least to the **parish church**, All Saints, which sits on a rise at the top of town. Here you'll find a Saxon cross in the churchyard and handsome six-teenth-century tombs inside. One is of local bigwig Sir George Vernon, the other of his daughter Dorothy Manners and her husband John Manners (see Haddon Hall, p.468). Signs behind the churchyard point you up the lane to the **Old House Museum** in Cunningham Place (daily: April–Oct 1.30–4pm; July & Aug 11am–4pm; £2), a Tudor house once owned by Richard Arkwright, now housing rustic tools and costumes from Bakewell's past. The energetic can head off along the **Monsal Trail**, which cuts eight miles north through some of Derbyshire's finest limestone valleys to Wyedale, three miles east of Buxton.

THE PENNINE WAY

The 250-mile-long **Pennine Way** was the country's first long-distance footpath, offi-cially opened in 1965 and stretching north from the boggy plateau of Kinder Scout, through the Yorkshire Dales and Teesdale, crossing Hadrian's Wall and the Northumberland National Park, before entering Scotland to fizzle out at the village of Kirk Yetholm. People had been using a similar route for over thirty years before the offi-cial opening, inspired by Tom Stephenson, Secretary of the Ramblers' Association, who had first identified the need for such a long-distance path in the 1930s. His idea was to stick to the crest of the Pennines where practicable and link up existing tracks, bridle-ways and footpaths, only descending to the valleys for overnight accommodation and ser-vices. The problem was that much of the route lay on private land, so years of negotia-tion and re-routing were necessary before the Pennine Way could be officially declared open.

Now it's one of the most popular walks in the country, either taken in sections or com-pleted in two to three weeks, depending on your level of fitness and experience. It's a challenge in the best of weather, since it passes through some of the most remote coun-tryside in England – you must be properly equipped, able to use a map and compass and be prepared to follow local advice about current diversions and re-routing; changes are often made to avoid erosion of the existing path. The National Trail Guides, *Pennine Way: South* and *Pennine Way: North* (Aurum Press), are essential, though some still prefer to stick to Wainwright's *Pennine Way Companion* (Michael Joseph). National park **infor-mation** centres along the route – particularly the one at Edale – stock a full selection of guides and associated trail leaflets and can offer advice. The YHA also operates a Pennine Way **room-booking service** (☎01629/581061) for its hostels. Finally, on reach-ing the end, you can get your certificate stamped at Edale's *Old Nag's Head* in the south or Kirk Yetholm's *Border Hotel* in the north.

Practicalities

The nearest **train** stations are at Matlock and Buxton, leaving **bus** services such as the TransPeak Manchester to Nottingham service, the Peak Express from Sheffield, the infrequent bus from Castleton, and the #R32/32A from Derby/Matlock as the main routes into town. All services stop in central Rutland Square, with the **tourist office** in the restored, seventeenth-century Old Market Hall (Easter–Oct daily 9.30am–5.30pm; Nov–Easter daily 9.30am–5pm, closed Thurs afternoon; ☎01629/813227), just a couple of hundred yards down the road. This is very well equipped with local biking and hiking leaflets and guides.

For **B&B**, try the *Avenue House*, whose three attractively furnished rooms occupy part of a spacious Victorian house on Haddon Road, near the river (☎01629/812467; no credit cards; ②; closed Nov–Jan). Alternatively, the homely *Castle Inn*, on Castle Street (☎01629/812103; ①), is a sympathetic old inn by the bridge over the Wye with four straightforward, comfortable rooms. The town's **youth hostel**, at Fly Hill (☎01629/812313), north of the church off the Buxton road, is pretty central, while the closest **campsite**, *Greenhills Caravan Park* (☎01629/813052), lies a mile and a half north on the Buxton road. More upmarket is the luxurious *Hassop Hall Hotel* (☎01629/640488; ⑤), a cannily refurbished old manor house with beautiful bedrooms set in charming parkland just 2.5 miles north of Bakewell along the A619 and then the B6001.

There are several good **restaurants** in town, especially *Aitch's Wine Bar & Bistro*, 4 Buxton Rd, near North Church Street, which serves Mediterranean-style dishes, and the French *Renaissance* (closed Sun evening & Mon) on nearby Bath Street, which has a set three-course dinner for around £15. **Bar meals** at the *Castle Inn* are of a good standard too. Excellent **bakeries** all over town claim to bake Bakewell Pudding to the original recipe, with the favourite being the *Old Original Bakewell Pudding Shop* on Rutland Square – open until 9pm in summer and with a full restaurant menu as well as gargantuan, family-sized puddings for a fiver. *Bloomer's* on Water Lane is a fine deli and bakery, known for its home-made sweet and savoury pies.

For a walk or ride to a **country pub**, the wonderfully sited *Lathkil Hotel* (☎01629/812501; ⑤) in Over Haddon, two miles southwest of Bakewell, takes some beating. Its picture windows look out over Lathkil Dale, down into which footpaths meander, while there's reasonable bar food and a more adventurous evening menu in the restaurant.

Haddon Hall

The simple, understated **Haddon Hall** (April–Sept daily 11am–5pm; £5.50; parking 50p), two miles south of Bakewell on the banks of the Wye (by the A6 and on the TransPeak bus route), is one of the finest medieval manor houses in England. In the mid-twelfth century it passed from its Norman founders, the Avenells, to the Vernons, who owned it for four hundred years until 1558 when the sole heir, **Dorothy Vernon**, married John Manners, scion of another powerful family who later became Dukes of Rutland. Their union is commemorated on their joint tomb in Bakewell church, but the romantic story of their elopement is probably apocryphal. At the start of the eighteenth century, when the Devonshires outdid the Rutlands by building nearby Chatsworth, the hall fell into two hundred years of neglect, thereby sparing it from Georgian and Victorian meddling.

Restoration at the beginning of this century revealed the **chapel**'s wall paintings of exotic plants and animals, plastered over at the Reformation. Across the courtyard, the fourteenth-century kitchens – originally detached from the house for fear of fire – are now connected by a passage to the banqueting hall, complete with a beautifully restored roof. A couple of less interesting domestic rooms lead to the house's highlight, the **Long Gallery**, built by John Manners for indoor promenades during inclement weather. The **gardens**, too, are gorgeous, and the whole heady ensemble turned up to great effect as Mr Rochester's Thornfield in Zeffirelli's *Jane Eyre*.

Chatsworth House

Chatsworth House (Easter–Oct daily 11am–5.30pm; last admission 4.30pm; house & grounds £6.25, grounds only £3.60, parking £1), four miles east of Bakewell via the A619, was built in the seventeenth century by the first Duke of Devonshire, and has been in the family ever since. The monumental Palladian frontage beautifully sets off the hundred acres of formal gardens, but they are tiny in comparison to the vast **park**, redesigned in the 1750s by Capability Brown. In the 1820s, the sixth Duke instigated more substantial changes when he added the north wing and set Joseph Paxton (designer of London's Crystal Palace) to work on the gardens, creating the **Emperor Fountain**. At 296ft, the fountain was the world's highest gravity-fed jet, but it now attains a meagre third of that. Inside the house, a maze of balconies and grand staircases lead, eventually, to the **State Apartments**, their ceilings daubed with overblown cherubic figures. None of the rooms is finer than the **Dining Room** in the north wing, its table set as it was for the visit of George V and Queen Mary in 1933, and its wall hung with seven Van Dycks. Vases of the semi-precious Blue John stone flank the door through to the **Sculpture Gallery**, where you can admire a Rembrandt and a Frans Hals before exploring the gardens, restaurant, estate shop or children's playground.

The principal approach to Chatsworth leads through the immaculately maintained estate village of **Edensor**, remodelled by the sixth Duke for his employees, and well worth a few minutes in its own right. There's an infrequent bus service from both Bakewell and Baslow to Edensor, but otherwise the best bet is to catch any Bakewell to Baslow bus and walk from the bus stop through the park to the house – a distance of around a mile. Walking back to Bakewell from Chatsworth is also enjoyable, and Bakewell tourist office has a leaflet outlining a possible route.

If you are looking for **accommodation**, try *Fischer's Baslow Hall* on Calver Road (☎01246/583259; ⑥), on the outskirts of the village of **BASLOW**, a mile or so north of Chatsworth. The hall is one of the Peak's greatest luxuries, an Edwardian "restaurant-with-rooms" – there are just half a dozen – with superb food, in both the expensive restaurant and the less formal café. There are some more economical **B&Bs** in the village too – the Bakewell tourist office has the list and will make reservations.

Eyam

Within a year of September 7, 1665, the attractive hillside lead-mining settlement of **EYAM** (pronounced "Eem"), seven miles north of Bakewell, had lost almost half of its population of 750 to the bubonic plague, a calamity that earned it the enduring epithet "The Plague Village". The first victim was one George Viccars, a journeyman tailor who is said to have released some infected fleas from a package of cloth brought from London into one of the so-called **plague cottages** next to the church. The ensuing epidemic was prevented from spreading to other villages by a self-imposed quarantine led by the rector, William Mompesson, who arranged for food to be left at places on the parish boundary – such as **Mompesson's Well**, half a mile up the hill to the north and still accessible by footpath from the village. Payment was made with coins left in pools of disinfecting vinegar – the stone bowls in which they were immersed can still be seen. The rector closed the church and held services in the open air at a natural rock arch to the south of the village – and every year since 1906 (on the last Sunday in August), a commemorative service has been held here, at Cucklet Delph. Mompesson himself survived the plague, though his wife succumbed; she lies buried in the shadow of a richly carved eighth-century Celtic cross in the churchyard (red roses are placed on her tomb on remembrance day). Informative panels inside the **parish church** (Easter–Sept Mon–Sat 9am–6pm, Sun 1–5.30pm; Oct–Easter Mon–Sat 9am–4pm, Sun 1–5.30pm) tell more of the village's history, highlighting a number of plague sites dotted around the town. The most harrowing of these are the **Riley Graves**, half a mile east of the village in open country, where a Mrs Hancock buried her husband, three sons and three daughters within eight days in August 1666.

Six years after the plague ended, **Eyam Hall** (April–Oct Wed, Thurs, Sun & bank hols, guided tours 11am–5.30pm, last entry 4.30pm; £4) was built for Thomas Wright a hundred yards west of the church, possibly in an attempt to install his son as the squire of the depleted village. Wright's heirs have lived in it ever since, building up a fine collection of furnishings that can be seen on a intriguingly anecdotal hour-long guided tour. Make time, too, for the **Eyam Museum** up Hawkshill Road (March–Oct Tues–Sun 10am–4.30pm; £1.50), beyond the hall, signposted off the main street. This goes into fascinating detail about the history, transmission and effect on society of the bubonic plague – still carried by rats in national parks in certain parts of the western United States.

Practicalities

Eyam makes a great overnight stop, though you should try and book accommodation in advance, since facilities are limited. There are **buses** to the village from Sheffield, Manchester, Buxton and Baslow. All run to the village, stopping outside the *Royal Oak* on the long, main Church Street.

First choice among the handful of **B&Bs** is the luxurious *Delf View House* (☎01433/631533; no credit cards; ③), a beautifully kept Georgian house set in its own grounds just along from the church; breakfast is served in a superb old dining room with its flagstone floor, imposing fireplace and beamed ceiling. Nearby *Aughton House* (☎01433/630381; ②) is of a similar age and appeal but a tad less grand in its outlook. Otherwise, both the *Royal Oak*, at the top of the village, and the *Bull's Head*, opposite the church, are pubs with rooms, though the finest inn is the *Miner's Arms* on Water Lane (☎01433/630853; ③), off the main square. This has nice modern rooms, some of them self-contained in a separate building next to the pub. Eyam **youth hostel**, a large Victorian house on Hawkhill Road (☎01433/630335; closed Dec–March), is a steep twenty-minute walk out of the village, past the museum. The best place **to eat** is the *Miner's Arms* which serves bar meals at lunch (Tues–Sat) and more formal, but very enjoyable, traditional British dinners and Sunday lunch in its restaurant.

Hathersage

The busy little town of **HATHERSAGE** on the A625, nine miles north of Bakewell and just eleven from Sheffield, has a hard time persuading people not to pass straight through into the heart of the national park. It's worth at least an hour though, particularly in its quieter reaches on the heights around the much-restored village **church of St Michael and All Angels**, where a prominent gravesite is said to be that of Sherwood outlaw Little John. The footpath up to the church starts by the side of the *Hathersage Inn* on the main road. Hathersage's other claim to fame is as the "Morton" of Charlotte Brontë's **Jane Eyre** – a village name borrowed by the author from the landlord of the *George* in Hathersage, who met Charlotte off the stagecoach from Haworth when she came to stay here in 1845. She was visiting a friend, whose brother was the local vicar and, in the church, Charlotte doubtless was shown the memorial

"Eyre brasses." She also used several other local names and buildings for her novel, notably North Lees Hall (Rochester's Thornfield Hall) and Moorseats (St John Rivers' Moor House) – all of which can be taken in on a four-mile circular walk around the town.

Hathersage also boasts its share of craft and cottage industries, most notably the impressive **Round Building**, just outside town on the B6001 (Mon–Sat 10am–5pm, Sun 11am–5pm; ☎01433/650220), where Sheffield designer David Mellor produces wonderful cutlery, tableware and kitchenware. There are several first-rate B&Bs – like *Moorgate*, on Castleton Road (☎01433/650293; no credit cards; ①) – and rooms in half a dozen pubs, including the fancy *George* itself (☎01433/650436; ⑤) or the *Scotsman's Pack* (☎01433/650253; ③), a flagstoned, eighteenth-century inn on School Lane, the way to the church. Real Brontë fans will be delighted to know that two apartments in the beautifully restored *North Lees Hall* can be rented – contact the *Vivat Trust* (☎0171/930 8030); prices run between £340 and £435 a week for the two-person and £440–570 for the larger five-person apartment. All the **pubs** serve bar meals, while the restaurant at the *George* is probably the best in town. Otherwise, *Longland's Eating House* on Main Road is a laid-back, licensed, mainly vegetarian, café above a good hiking/outdoors shop. The local **youth hostel** (☎01433/650493) is on the edge of the village, on the Castleton road, a hundred yards past the *George*. The #272 Sheffield–Castleton **bus** stops right outside the *George* and Hathersage is also on the Manchester–Sheffield **train** line.

THE EAST MIDLANDS

The four major counties of the East Midlands – **Nottinghamshire**, **Leicestershire**, **Northamptonshire** and **Lincolnshire** – have much in common. Their county towns, each with a long and eventful history, have been badly bruised by twentieth-century town planning and industrial development, but have soldiered on, becoming busy, bustling places with a positive, sometimes adventurous outlook. Embedded in the modernity are a few historical landmarks – a particularly fine church in Northampton, the castle in Nottingham, traces of Roman baths in Leicester and the magnificent cathedral at Lincoln – but by and large these are the frills rather than the substance. With the exception of Lincoln, few would describe the region's cities as especially good-looking, whereas the countryside around about them can be absolutely delightful.

Leicestershire is probably the most scenic of the counties, with the rocky, forested landscapes around **Ashby** and **Calke Abbey** in the western part of the county. Not far behind comes Northamptonshire, with its beautifully preserved villages and country towns, such as **Fotheringhay** and **Oundle**, plus rolling country estates, the best known of which is **Althorp**, the final resting place of Princess Diana. Elsewhere, tiny Rutland, the region's fifth and final county, weighs in with the little old town of **Oakham**, close to the watersports centre of Rutland Water reservoir. North of Oakham, the eastern reaches of Leicestershire and Nottinghamshire are dotted with antique market towns – the pick of which are **Southwell** and **Newark** – set within fine agricultural landscape that rolls over the county borders to form the western part of Lincolnshire. The majestic cathedral city of **Lincoln** and the splendidly intact stone town of Stamford are the chief urban attractions in this county, but Lincolnshire's most distinctive zone is **The Fens**, whose pancake-flat fields have taken centuries to reclaim from the marshes and the sea. Fenland villages and towns are generally short of charm, but the **churches**, whose spires regularly interrupt the wide-skied landscape, are simply stunning, the most impressive of the lot being St Botolph's in **Boston**. In north Lincolnshire, the low-lying chalky hills of the **Lincolnshire Wolds** contain the county's most diverse scenery, including woodland clustered round **Woodhall Spa**, and a string of sheltered valleys concentrated in the vicinity of **Louth**, the prettiest of the region's towns. To the east of the Wolds, the coast comprises miles of bungalows, campsites and caravan parks beside a sandy beach which extends, with a few marshy interruptions, from Mablethorpe to **Skegness**, the main resort.

Nottinghamshire

With a population of over 270,000, **Nottingham** is one of England's big cities, a long-time manufacturing centre for bikes, cigarettes, pharmaceuticals and lace. It is, however, more famous for Nottingham Forest football team (or rather, for its mercurial ex-manager, Brian Clough), for the Trent Bridge cricket ground and for its association with **Robin Hood**, the legendary thirteenth-century outlaw. Unfortunately the fortress-lair of Hood's bitter enemy, the Sheriff of Nottingham, is long gone, and today the city is at its most diverting in the Lace Market, whose cramped streets are crowded with the mansion-like warehouses of the Victorian lacemakers.

The county town is flanked to the north by the gritty towns and villages of what was, until Thatcher and her cronies decimated it, the Nottinghamshire coalfield, and to the south by the commuter villages of the Nottinghamshire Wolds, neither of which will hold your attention. Moving east, the thin remains of **Sherwood Forest** form **The Dukeries**, named after the five dukes who owned most of this area and preserved at least part of the ancient broad-leaved forest. Three of the four remaining estates – Thoresby, Worksop and Welbeck – are still in private hands, but **Clumber Park** is now owned by the National Trust and offers charming woodland walks. Beyond lie the market towns of eastern Nottinghamshire – **Newark** is the most important town here but nearby **Southwell** has the main attraction, the fine Norman church of Southwell Minster.

Fast and frequent **trains** connect Nottingham with, among many destinations, London, Birmingham, Newark, Lincoln and Leicester. County-wide bus services radiate out from the city too, making Nottingham the obvious base for a visit, though Newark is a palatable alternative except during the Newark International Antiques Fair, Europe's biggest such event, held six times a year, when accommodation here is all but impossible to find.

Nottingham and around

Controlling a strategic crossing over the Trent, the Saxon town of **NOTTINGHAM** was built on one of a pair of sandstone hills whose 130-foot cliffs look out over the river valley. In 1068, William the Conqueror built a castle on the other hill, and the Saxon and Norman communities traded on the low ground in between, the Market Square. The castle was a military stronghold and royal palace, the equal of the great castles of Windsor and Dover, and every medieval king of England paid regular visits. In August 1642, Charles I stayed here too, riding out of the castle to raise his standard and start the Civil War – not that the locals were overly sympathetic. Hardly anyone joined up, even though the king had the ceremony repeated for the next three days.

After the Civil War, the Parliamentarians slighted the castle and, in the 1670s, the ruins were cleared by the Duke of Newcastle to make way for a palace, whose continental – and, in English terms, novel – design he chose from a pattern book, probably by Rubens. Beneath the castle lay a market town which, according to contemporaries, was handsome and well kept – "One of the most beautiful towns in England", commented Daniel Defoe. But in the second half of the eighteenth century, the town was transformed by the expansion of the lace and hosiery industries. Within the space of fifty years, Nottingham's population increased from ten thousand to fifty thousand, the resulting slum becoming a hotbed of radicalism. In the 1810s, a recession provoked the

hard-pressed workers into action. They struck against the employers and, calling themselves **Luddites**, after an apprentice-protester by the name of Ned Ludlam, raided the
factories to smash the knitting machines. This was but the first of several troubled periods. During the Reform Bill riots of 1831, the workers set fire to the duke's home in
response to his opposition to parliamentary reform and, in the following decade, they
flocked to the Chartist movement.

The worst of Nottingham's slums were cleared in the late nineteenth century, when
the city centre assumed its present structure, with the main commercial area ringed by
alternating industrial and residential districts. Crass postwar development, adding
tower blocks, shopping centres and a ring road, has embedded the remnants of the
city's past in a townscape that will be dishearteningly familiar if you've seen a few other
English commercial centres.

Arrival, information and accommodation

Nottingham train station is on the south side of the city centre, a five- to ten-minute
walk from the Market Square – just follow the signs. Long-distance buses arrive at the
Broad Marsh bus station down the street from the train station. Details of bus services

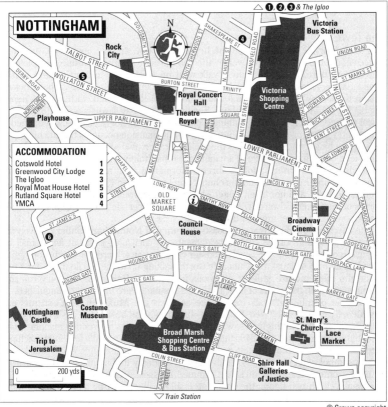

© Crown copyright

across Nottinghamshire are available on the excellent Buses Hotline (daily 7am–8pm; ☎0115/924 0000). The city's tourist office is on the ground floor of the Council House, 1 Smithy Row (Easter to Oct Mon–Fri 9am–5.30pm, Sat 9am–5pm, Sun 10am–3pm; Nov–Easter Mon–Sat 9am–5.30pm; ☎0115/915 5330).

As you might expect of a big city, Nottingham has a good range of accommodation, with the more expensive **hotels** concentrated in the centre, the cheaper places and the **B&Bs** mostly located on the outskirts and the main approach roads. Finding a room is rarely difficult, but the tourist office will assist if required.

Cotswold Hotel, 330 Mansfield Rd (☎0115/955 1070). Comfortable popular mid-range hotel with cheery half-timbered facade. On a main road about one mile north of the city centre. ②.

Greenwood City Lodge, 5 Third Ave, off Sherwood Rise (☎0115/962 1206). Attractive five-bedroomed guest house in a quiet corner of the city, down a narrow lane about a mile north of the city centre. Highly recommended. ②.

The Igloo Tourist Hotel, 110 Mansfield Rd (☎0115/947 5250). Backpackers' haven in the town centre, opposite the *Golden Fleece* pub, with a convivial atmosphere, good showers and free tea and coffee. Bunk-beds in mixed or single-sex dorms for £9 per person.

Royal Moat House Hotel, in the Royal Centre on Wollaton Street (☎0115/936 9988). Impressively plush, modern hotel in the city centre, with all facilities. ⑥.

Rutland Square Hotel, Rutland St, off St James' Street (☎0115/941 1114). Attractive and tastefully furnished modern hotel in a great location, just by the castle. ⑤.

YMCA, 4 Shakespeare St (☎0115/956 7600). In a handy location, with clean and frugal rooms, but fills up fast. Single rooms are a real bargain at £16 a night.

The Town

The **Old Market Square** is still the heart of the city, an airy open area, its shops, offices and fountains watched over by the neo-Baroque **Council House**, completed in 1928. From here, it's a five-minute walk west up Friar Lane to **Nottingham Castle** (daily 10am–5pm, but closed Fri Nov–Feb; free except Sat & Sun £2), whose heavily restored gateway stands above a folkloric bronze of Robin Hood, with plaques depicting his Merry Men on the wall behind. Beyond the gateway, lawns slope up to the squat ducal **palace**, which – after remaining a charred shell for forty years – was opened as the country's first provincial museum in 1878. The mansion occupies the site of the castle's upper bailey and, just outside the main entrance, two sets of steps (guided tours only) lead down into the maze of ancient caves that honeycomb the cliff beneath. One set leads into **Mortimer's Hole**, a three-hundred-foot shaft along which, so the story goes, the young Edward III and his chums crept in October 1330 to capture the Queen Mother, Isabella, and her lover, Roger Mortimer – his would-be usurpers and the murderers of his father, Edward II. Although the incident certainly took place, it's unlikely that this was the secret tunnel Edward used.

The interior of the ducal mansion boasts the **Story of Nottingham Gallery**, a lively and entertaining account of the city's development – in particular, look out for a small but exquisite collection of late medieval **alabaster carvings**, an art form for which Nottingham once had an international reputation. It's worth walking up to the top floor too, for a turn round the main **picture gallery**, a curious assortment of nineteenth-century romantic paintings in which the works of Richard Parkes Bonington are the most distinguished.

A couple of minutes' walk east of the castle is the **Museum of Costume and Textiles**, 51 Castle Gate (Wed–Sun 10am–4pm; free), the best of the city's other museums. In the 1760s, Nottingham saw the earliest experiments to produce machine-made lace, but it was not until the 1840s that the city produced the world's first fully machined lace garments. After that the industry boomed until its collapse after World War I when lace, a symbol of an old and discredited order, suddenly had no place in the wardrobe of most women. The museum's lace-trimmed dresses, accessories and underclothes are displayed on two floors, the changing fashions illustrated by a sequence of dioramas. At the bottom of the stairs there's also an intriguing collection of **samplers**, tryouts made on linen scraps before work on the handmade garments began. A few minutes' walk away, on the east side of the Market Square up along Victoria Street, is the **Lace Market**, whose narrow lanes and alleys surround the church of **St Mary**, a handsome, mostly fifteenth-century structure built on top of the hill that was once the Saxon town. The church abuts High Pavement, the administrative centre of Nottingham in Georgian times, and here you'll find the **Shire Hall**, whose Neoclassical columns and dome date from 1770. Now housing the **Galleries of Justice** (Tues–Sun 10am–4pm; £7.95), the building boasts two superbly preserved Victorian courtrooms as well as some spectacularly unpleasant old cells, a women's prison with bath house and a prisoners' exercise yard. A tour of the whole complex takes around four hours, but note that the interactive nature of a visit (on arrival you are issued with a criminal identity number, and so it continues) is not to everyone's liking. The surrounding sandstone-trimmed Victorian warehouses are at their most striking along **Broadway** and adjacent **Stoney Street**, where – at the corner of Woolpack Lane – a particularly fine warehouse boasts an extravagant stone doorway and slender windows, as well as long attic windows to light the mending and inspection rooms. Nearby, on Byard Lane, is the first shop of local lad **Paul Smith**, the great success story of recent British fashion.

Eating

Nottingham's **restaurant** scene has improved immeasurably in the last five years. French and Mediterranean cuisine are in vogue at present, but the Asian places continue to prosper. In the last couple of years, **cafés** have sprung up all over the city centre. Almost without exception, they've adopted the same formula – angular and ultra-modern furnishings and fittings and a wide range of bottled beers. Many offer tasty, broadly Mediterranean food as well.

Bentons Café Bar, corner of Heathcote Street and Lower Parliament Street. Pleasant café-bar offering tasty dishes from an imaginative menu – salads and pastas through to steaks. Inexpensive.

Café De Paris, 2 Kings Walk, off Upper Parliament Street near the Theatre Royal (☎0115/947 3767). Arguably the best restaurant of its type in town, offering delicious bistro-style French cuisine in neat and informal surroundings. Moderate.

The Indian, 5 Bentinck Rd (☎0115/942 4922). Outstanding Indian restaurant – the best in the city – a mile or so northwest of the centre. Lively and wide-ranging menu and attractive décor too. Moderate.

Pizza Express, 20 King St (☎0115/952 9095). Fashionable pizza and pasta spot serving the chain's usual delicious pizzas. Also at 24 Goose Gate, Hockley (☎0115/912 7888). Moderate.

Saagar Tandoori Restaurant, 473 Mansfield Rd (☎0115/962 2014). Excellent and very popular Indian restaurant, a mile or so north of the city centre. A local favourite. Moderate.

Salamander Vegetarian Restaurant, 23 Heathcote St (☎0115/941 0710). Nottingham's best vegetarian restaurant, with a sound menu. Inexpensive.

Sonny's Restaurant, 3 Carlton St (☎0115/947 3041). Well-prepared, unpretentious food in smart café-style surroundings. Main courses start at around £12.

Wax Café Bar, 27 Broad St. Amongst the city's burgeoning band of café-bars, this is perhaps the trendiest. The food here is especially good – all light Mediterranean dishes at very reasonable prices. Inexpensive.

Pubs and nightlife

Nottingham's **nightclub** scene is boisterous and fast-moving, with clubs regularly opening and closing. The **pubs** around Market Square have a tough edge to them, especially at the weekends, but within a few minutes' walk there's a selection of lively and more enjoyable drinking-holes. For **live music**, both popular and classical, most big names play at the Royal Centre Concert Hall on Wollaton Street, and nearby **Rock City** pulls in some star turns too. The Broadway, 14 Broad St (☎0115/952 6611), is the best **cinema** in town, featuring the pick of mainstream and avant-garde films.

The Bomb, 45 Bridlesmith Gate. The frontrunner in the club scene with regular house, techno and jungle nights.

Broadway Cinema Bar, Broadway Cinema, 14 Broad St. Informal, fashionable bar serving an eclectic assortment of bottled beers to a cinema-keen clientele; can get too smoky for comfort.

Deluxe, 22 St James St. Heaving and huge nightclub featuring dance and indie. Gay nights too.

Essance, Wollaton Street. This cavernous and immensely popular club is the city's best mainstream nightspot. The emphasis is on house, but the programme is lively and varied.

Gatsbys, Huntingdon Street. One of the more established of the city's gay bars, with a busy active scene.

The Limelight, Wellington Circus. The bar of the Nottingham Playhouse is a popular, easy-going spot with courtyard seating on summer nights. Good supply of real ales.

Lincolnshire Poacher, 161 Mansfield Rd. Very popular and relaxed pub, with a wide selection of bottled and real ales. Boorish, beer-swilling rugby players can rattle the equilibrium on the weekend. The *Forest Tavern*, just up the street, is a comparable pub, with a particularly good range of unusual draft beers.

Pitcher & Piano, High Pavement. Lively, fashionable pub in an imaginatively converted Victorian church on the edge of the Lace Market. Good fun.

Rock City, Talbot Street. Giant-sized, crowded nightclub/music venue, with different sounds and crowds each night, from Goth to metal to indie. Regularly hosts name bands on UK tours.

Ye Olde Trip to Jerusalem Inn, below the castle in Brewhouse Yard. Carved into the castle rock, this ancient inn may well have been a meeting point for soldiers gathering for the Third Crusade. Its cave-like bars, with their rough sandstone ceilings, are delightfully secretive.

Eastwood

D.H. Lawrence was born in the coalmining village of **EASTWOOD**, about six miles west of Nottingham. The mine closed years ago, and Eastwood is something of a post-industrial eyesore, but Lawrence's childhood home, a tiny two-up, two-down terraced house, has survived, refurbished as the **D.H. Lawrence Birthplace Museum**, 8A Victoria St (daily: April–Oct 10am–5pm; Nov–March closes 4pm; £1.75), though none of the original furnishings and fittings have lasted. Rainbow bus #1 departs for the thirty-minute trip to Eastwood from Nottingham's Victoria bus station every half-hour.

Newstead Abbey and Hardwick Hall

In 1539, Henry VIII granted **Newstead Abbey** (house April–Sept daily noon–5pm, £2; grounds daily 9am–dusk, £2), eleven miles north of Nottingham, to Sir John Byron, who demolished most of the church and converted the monastic buildings into a family home. In 1798, **Lord Byron** inherited Newstead, then little more than a ruin. He restored part of the complex, but most of the present structure dates from later renovations, which maintained much of the shape and feel of the medieval original while creating the warren-like mansion that exists today. Inside, a string of intriguing period rooms includes everything from a neo-Gothic Great Hall to the Henry VII Bedroom, fitted with carved panels and painted house screens imported from Japan. Some of the rooms are pretty much as they were when Byron lived here – notably his bedroom and dressing room – and in the Library is a small collection of the poet's possessions, from letters and manuscripts through to his pistols and boxing gloves. In the West Gallery, look out also for the painting of Byron's favourite dog, Boatswain, a perky beast who was buried just outside the house – the conspicuous memorial, with its absurdly extravagant inscription, marks the spot. The surrounding **gardens** are simply delightful, a secretive and subtle combination of walled garden, lake, Gothic waterfalls, yew tunnels and Japanese-style rockeries, complete with eccentric pagodas. There's a fast and frequent **bus** service from Nottingham's Victoria bus station to the gates of Newstead Abbey, a mile from the house, every twenty minutes or so; the journey takes about 25 minutes.

Some nine miles northwest of Newstead Abbey, just over the Derbyshire border, lies **Hardwick Hall** (house April–Oct Wed, Thurs, Sat & Sun 12.30–5pm; gardens same months daily noon–5.30pm; house & gardens £6, gardens only £3; NT), a startling sixteenth-century house whose walls comprise more glass than stone. Inside, there's a magnificent show of furniture and tapestries, many of which were listed in an inventory taken in 1601; outside, longhorn cattle roam the grounds, mingling with a flock of Whiteface Woodland sheep.

Sherwood Forest and Clumber Park

Most of **Sherwood Forest**, once a vast royal forest of oak, birch and bracken covering all of west Nottinghamshire, was cleared in the eighteenth century, and nowadays it's difficult to imagine the protection it provided for generations of outlaws, the most famous of whom was **Robin Hood**. There's no "true story" of Robin's life – the earliest reference to him, in Langland's *Piers Plowman* of 1377, treats him as a fiction – but to the balladeers of fifteenth-century England, who invented most of the folklore, this was hardly the point. For them, Robin was a symbol of yeoman decency, a semi-mythological opponent of corrupt clergymen and evil officers of the law; in the early tales, although Robin shows sympathy for the peasant, he has rather more respect for the decent nobleman, and he's never credited with robbing the rich to give to the poor. This and other parts of the legend, such as Maid Marion and Friar Tuck, were added later.

Robin Hood may lack historical authenticity, but it hasn't discouraged the county council from spending thousands of pounds sustaining the **Major Oak**, the creaky tree where Maid Marion and Robin are supposed to have "plighted their troth". The Major Oak is a few minutes' walk from the visitor centre at the main entrance to **Sherwood Forest Country Park** (daily dawn–dusk; free), which comprises 450 acres of oak and silver birch criss-crossed with footpaths. The visitor centre is half a mile north of the village of Edwinstowe, itself twenty-odd miles north of Nottingham.

North of Ollerton, Edwinstowe's immediate neighbour, the A614 trims the edge of Thoresby Park to reach, after six miles, the eastern entrance to **Clumber Park** (daily dawn–dusk; NT), four thousand acres of park and woodland lying to the south of Worksop. The estate was once the country seat of the dukes of Newcastle, and it was here in the 1770s that they constructed a grand mansion overlooking Clumber Lake. The house was dismantled in 1938, when the duke sold the estate, and today all that remains of the lakeside buildings are the Gothic Revival **Chapel** (daily April–Oct 10.30am–6pm, Nov–March 10.30am–4pm), built for the seventh duke in the 1880s, and the adjacent stable block, which now houses a National Trust office (April–Oct daily 10.30am–5pm, Nov–March Sat & Sun only 10.30am–4pm), shop and **café** – located about two and a half miles from the A614. The woods around the lake offer some delightful strolls through planted woodland interspersed with the occasional patch of original forest, or you can go for an easy cycle ride by hiring a bike here.

Stagecoach East Midlands **bus** #33 leaves Nottingham's Victoria bus station hourly for the fifty-minute trip to Edwinstowe, before travelling on up the west side of Clumber Park en route to Worksop – get off at Carburton for the two-mile walk to the NT office in Clumber Park. The excursion is best done as a day-trip from Nottingham.

Southwell and Newark

SOUTHWELL, some fourteen miles northeast of Nottingham, is a sedate backwater distinguished by **Southwell Minster**, whose twin towers are visible for miles around, and the fine Georgian mansions facing it along Church Street. The Normans built the minster at the beginning of the twelfth century and, although some elements were added later, the Norman design predominates, from the imposing west towers through to the forceful, dog-tooth-decorated doorways. Inside, the nave's heavy stonework ends abruptly with the clumsy mass of the fourteenth-century screen, beyond which lies the Early English **choir** and the extraordinary **chapter house**. The latter is embellished with naturalistic foliage dating from the late thirteenth century, among the earliest carving of its type in England.

From Southwell, it's eight miles east to **NEWARK**, an amiable, low-key river port and market town that was once a major staging point on the Great North Road. Fronting the town as you approach from the west are the gaunt riverside ruins of **Newark Castle**, all that's left of the mighty medieval fortress that was pounded to pieces during the Civil War. A brief but pleasant riverside walk takes you from the castle past ancient houses to the old town lock, and a couple of minutes' walk away from the river lies the expansive **Market Place**. This square, surrounded by alleys of old-fashioned shops, is framed by a sequence of attractive Georgian and Victorian facades, as well as the mostly thirteenth-century church of **St Mary Magdalene**, whose massive spire, at 252ft, towers over the town centre.

There's a regular **bus** service from South Parade, on Nottingham's Old Market Square to Newark via Southwell, and Newark is also on the Nottingham–Lincoln **rail** line. The Newark Castle **train station** is on the west side of the River Trent, a five-minute walk from both the castle and the adjacent **tourist office**, on Castlegate (daily 9am–5/6pm; currently ☎01636/678962). The **bus station** is on Lombard Street, a couple of minutes' walk south from the tourist office along Castlegate. Newark has a reasonable range of **hotels** and **B&Bs**, with one good option being the trim *Millgate House Hotel*, a short walk south along the river from the castle at 53 Millgate (☎01636/704445; ⑤). For **food**, make for the excellent *Gannets*, 35 Castlegate (☎01636/702066), which has a downstairs coffee bar serving daytime snacks and a smashing restaurant upstairs in the evenings, or the superb *Café Bleu* (☎01636/610141), a pricey French restaurant serving top-class meals from an inventive menu; it's one of the best restaurants in the county.

Leicestershire and Rutland

The compact county of **Leicestershire** is one of the more anonymous of the English shires, though **Leicester** itself is saved from mediocrity by its role as a focal point for Britain's Asian community. To the west of Leicester, the rolling landscape is blemished by a series of industrial settlements, but things pick up markedly at **Ashby-de-la-Zouch**, a pleasing little town graced by the substantial remains of its medieval castle. Close by is **Calke Abbey**, where a dishevelled country house is surrounded by some of the region's most beguiling scenery. To the east of Leicester, the farmland is studded with long-established market towns. None of them are particularly enthralling, but genial **Melton Mowbray** holds several attractive old buildings and is the pork-pie capital of the world, while nearby **Belvoir Castle** exhibits the art collection of the Duke and Duchess of Rutland.

To the east of Leicestershire lies England's smallest county, **Rutland**, reinstated in 1997 following 23 unpopular years of merger with its larger neighbour. As part of their spirited publicity campaign to revive their ancient county, Rutland's well-heeled burghers issued "passports" to locals and created quite a stir, breaking through the profound apathy which characterizes the English attitude to local government. Rutland has one place of note, **Oakham**, the county town, a handsome rural centre with elegant Georgian architecture.

Getting around Leicestershire and Rutland can be problematic. **Train** lines radiate out from Leicester, most usefully to Market Harborough and Oakham, and there's a good network of **bus** services between the market towns, but these fade away in the villages where, if there is a bus at all, it only runs once or twice a day. For all bus timetable enquiries, ring the **Busline** (☎0116/251 1411).

Leicester

On first impression, **LEICESTER** is a resolutely modern city, but further inspection reveals traces of its medieval and Roman past, situated immediately to the west of the centre, near the River Soar. The Romans, choosing this site in the middle of the territory of the rebellious Coritani, developed Leicester's precursor, Ratae Coritanorum, as a fortified town on the Fosse Way, the military road running from Lincoln to Cirencester, and Emperor Hadrian kitted it out with huge public buildings. Subsequently, in the eighth century, the Danes colonized the town and later still its medieval castle became the base of the earls of Leicester, the most distinguished of whom was Simon de Montfort, who forced Henry III to convene the first English parliament in 1265. Since the late seventeenth century, Leicester has been a centre of the hosiery trade and it was this industry that attracted hundreds of Asian immigrants to settle here in the 1950s and 1960s. Today, about one third of Leicester's population is Asian and the city elected the country's first Asian MP, Keith Vaz, in 1987. Leicester's Hindus put on a massive and internationally famous **Diwali**, Festival of Light, in October or November, while the city's sizeable Afro-Caribbean community celebrates its culture in a whirl of colour and music on the first weekend in August. The latter is the country's second biggest street festival after the Notting Hill Carnival (see p.129).

Arrival, information and accommodation

On the northern line from London's St Pancras station, Leicester **train station** is situated on London Road just to the southeast of the city centre, and ten minutes' walk from **St Margaret's bus station**, which is on the north side of the centre, just off Gravel Street. The **tourist office** is in between the two at 7/9 Every St, on Town Hall Square (Mon–Wed & Fri 9am–5.30pm, Thurs 10am–5.30pm & Sat 9am–5pm; ☎0116/299 8888).

Some of the best **accommodation** options are grouped within walking distance of the train station: try *Belmont House Hotel* on De Montfort Street (☎0116/254 4773; ⑤), a comfortable Georgian house 500 yards south of the train station; or nearby *Spindle Lodge*, 2 West Walk (☎0116/233 8801; ②), an attractively converted Victorian guest house off New Walk. Further out of town there's the *Beaumaris*, 18 Westcotes Drive (☎0116/254 0261; ①), a small and unassuming family-run hotel a mile west of the centre off the Narborough Road (the A46), and the *Scotia* at no. 10 (☎0116/254 9200; ②), a large B&B with eleven bedrooms, four of them en suite. For cheaper accommodation, try the central *YMCA*, 7 East St (☎0116/255 6507), or *YWCA*, 236 London Rd (☎0116/270 5083), both of which are within easy reach of the station and offer basic accommodation for both sexes; or the independent hostel, *Richards Students and Backpackers Lodge*, 157 Wanlip Lane, Birstall (☎0116/267 3107; under-26s only), housed in a tiny suburban semi on the northern edge of town, with patio, summerhouse, and copious inexpensive meals.

The Town

Leicester's landmark Victorian **clock tower** stands right in the heart of the city centre at East Gates, midway between the bus and train stations. From here, the old High Street runs west past the Shires shopping centre with Silver Street (subsequently Guildhall Lane) branching off it to reach **St Martin's Cathedral**, a much-modified eleventh-century structure that incorporates a fine medieval wooden roof in the north porch. Next door is the **Guildhall** (Mon–Sat 10am–5.30pm, Sun 2–5.30pm; free), a half-timbered building which has served, variously, as the town hall and police station, and now contains a small museum. Several items from the old cells are on display – fearsome-looking manacles and the like.

From the Guildhall, it's a short walk west to the ring road and, just beyond, the Saxon church of **St Nicholas**. Footsteps away, the **Jewry Wall** is a chunk of Roman masonry some eighteen feet high and seventy-three feet long that was originally part of Hadrian's public baths. The project was a real irritation to the emperor. Hadrian's grand scheme was spoilt by the engineers, who miscalculated the line of the aqueduct that was to pipe in the water, and so bathers had to rely on a hand-filled cistern replenished from the river – which wasn't what he had in mind at all. The adjacent **Jewry Wall and Archaeology Museum** (Mon–Sat 10am–5.30pm, Sun 2–5.30pm; free) charts Leicester's history from prehistoric to medieval times. Highlights include a fine assortment of Roman relics – from Fosse Way milestones to the splendid Peacock mosaic pavement – and some beautiful medieval glass.

Dodging the traffic, cross St Augustine Road to the south to arrive at the **Castle Gardens**, which, running alongside a canalized portion of the Soar, incorporate the castle motte, the mound where Leicester's Norman fortifications once stood. Walking through the gardens, you re-emerge on the Newarke, the location of the **Newarke Houses Museum** (Mon–Sat 10am–5.30pm, Sun 2–5.30pm; free), two Jacobean houses that make a delightful setting for an extensive exploration of the town's social history. In particular, look out for the display of Victorian toilets in the delicately titled "Hygiene Gallery" and some early twentieth-century furniture designed by a local man, Ernest Gimson, who was much influenced by William Morris.

Nearby, stranded between the carriageways of the ring road stands the distinctive **Magazine Gateway**, once the medieval entrance to the Newarke. From here, it's a short walk south via the pedestrian underpass to the **Jain Centre**, on Oxford Street. The rites and beliefs of the Jains, a long-established Indian religious sect, focus on an extreme reverence for all living things – traditional customs include the wearing of gauze masks to prevent the inhalation of passing insects. The centre's splendid marble-fronted main building contains one of the few Jain temples in western Europe, and visitors may enter the lobby or, better, view the interior (Mon–Fri 2–5pm; call first if visiting outside these hours ☎0116/254 3091; donation requested).

From the Jain Centre, it's about ten minutes' walk southeast to New Walk, a tree-lined promenade that's the home of the **Leicester City Museum and Art Gallery**, at no. 53 (Mon–Sat 10am–5.30pm, Sun 2–5.30pm; free). Upstairs you'll find the country's largest collection of German Expressionists, as well as works by Walter Sickert, Jacob Epstein, Laura Knight and Stanley Spencer. On the ground floor, a collection of mummies, brought from Egypt as souvenirs in the 1880s, fills the Egyptian Gallery, which is next door to a display of crystals and minerals.

About half a mile north of the city centre, **Abbey Park** is a pleasant place to take a stroll, though nothing remains of the Augustinian abbey where Cardinal Wolsey died in 1530, on his way to London to face charges of high treason. The purported plan of the abbey is laid out on the lawns. Further out still, to the northeast, is **Belgrave**, the focus of Leicester's Asian community. Both Belgrave Road and its northerly continuation, Melton Road, are lined with Indian and Pakistani goldsmiths and jewellers, sari shops, Hindi music stores and curry houses; there's even a large cinema, the Bollywood, screening the latest releases from Bombay. It's never dull down here, but Sunday afternoons are particularly enjoyable, when locals have time to stroll the streets in their finest gear. Belgrave celebrates two major Hindu festivals – **Diwali**, the Festival of Light, held in October or November, when six thousand lamps are strung out along the Belgrave Road and 20,000 come to watch the switch-on alone, and **Navrati**, a nine-day celebration in October held in honour of the goddess Ambaji. During these two festivals there are all sorts of events held across the city – further information on ☎0116/266 8266.

Eating, drinking, nightlife and entertainment

With every justification, people come from miles around to browse Leicester's massive open-air **market** (Mon–Sat), right in the centre on the Market Place, and to eat in the **Indian restaurants** on the Belgrave Road – though the opening of lots of balti places in the Highfields area has provided some intense competition. The most famous of the Belgrave Road restaurants is *Bobbys*, no. 154–156 (π0116/266 0106). Run by Gujaratis, this moderately priced place is strictly vegetarian and uses no garlic or onions; if you're here on a weekend, try their delicious house speciality, *undhyu*, or the multi-flavoured *Bobbys Special Chaat*. Excellent alternatives include the *Sayonara Thali*, at no. 49 (π0116/266 5888), which specializes in set *thali* meals, where several different dishes, breads and pickles are served together on large steel plates, and the *Chaat House* (π0116/266 0513), south of *Bobby's* on the same side of the road. The latter does wonderful *masala dosas* and other south Indian snacks – legendary cricket captain Kapil Dev and his Indian team ate here when they were on tour. In the city centre, the *Case*, 4 Hotel St (π0116/251 7675), is a chic place to eat with an imaginative, moderately priced menu, while the *Alhambra*, 70 High St (π0116/253 2448), offers moderately priced and authentic Arabic cuisine – try the Maghreb couscous.

As for **pubs**, the *Rainbow and Dove*, on Charles Street, attracts real-ale enthusiasts, the *Charlotte*, on Oxford Street, features bands most nights and the *Magazine*, Newarke Street, is a favourite student haunt. Amongst a deluge of new city-centre café-bars, two of the trendier, clubbier spots are *Left Bank*, just west of the river on Braunston Gate, and *Tabasco Jaz* on Albion Street. The excellent Phoenix Arts Centre, Newarke Street (π0116/255 4854), is Leicester's top venue for the performing arts and doubles up as an independent cinema. The city's main concert hall is De Montfort Hall, Granville Road (π0116/233 3111).

Ashby-de-la-Zouch, Calke Abbey

ASHBY-DE-LA-ZOUCH, fourteen miles from Leicester, takes its fanciful name from two sources – the town's first Norman overlord was Alain de Parrhoet la Souche and the rest means "place by the ash trees". Nowadays Ashby is far from rustic, not least because its wide main drag, Market Street, serves as the main road between Leicester and Burton-on-Trent. Nevertheless, it's an amiable little place and just off Market Street stands its main attraction, the **Castle** (April–Sept daily 10am–6pm; Nov–March Wed–Sun 10am–4pm; £2.50; EH). Originally a Norman manor house, the stronghold was the work of Edward IV's chancellor, Lord Hastings, who received his "licence to crenellate" in 1474. But Hastings didn't enjoy his new home for long. Just nine years later, he was dragged from a Privy Council meeting to have his head hacked off on a log by the order of Richard III, his crime being his lacklustre support for the Yorkist cause. Today, there's little left of the castle's external walls, but the hundred-foot-high **Hastings Tower**, a self-contained four-storey stronghold, has survived pretty much intact and incorporates a room where Mary, Queen of Scots was once imprisoned. The climb up the tower's well-worn spiral staircase leads to a grand view. For much of the nineteenth century, Ashby was a spa town, popularized by Thomas Cook's tours to its extensive Grecian-style baths. None remain now, but the steaming open-air swimming pool at Hood Park Leisure Centre, behind the tourist office, makes for a refreshing diversion (May–Sept Mon–Fri 9am–8pm, Sat & Sun 9am–1pm & 2–6pm; £2.20).

Another potential outing is to **Staunton Harold Church** (April–Sept Sat–Wed 1–5pm; Oct Sat & Sun 1–5pm only; £1; NT), a rare example of Commonwealth ecclesiastical architecture, complete with delightful painted ceilings, wood panelling and even the original seventeenth-century prayer cushions. The church is located in parkland five miles north of Ashby along the B587 – and just twenty minutes' walk (or a short drive) from **Calke Abbey** (April–Oct Sat-Wed 1–5.30pm; £5; NT), an enchanting early eighteenth-century mansion, whose rambling rooms are kept in a partial state of disrepair – just as they were when the house was recently donated to the National Trust. Footpaths criss-cross the surrounding estate, whose sharp rocky contours pre-figure the harsher topography of the Peak District to the northwest.

There are fast and frequent **buses** from Leicester to Ashby and, if you're tempted to stay, the **tourist office** (Mon–Fri 10am–5pm, Sat 10am–3pm; ☎01530/411767), across Market Street from the castle, can help you find **accommodation**. Alternatively, you could try the comfortable *Cedars Guest House*, five minutes' walk north of the castle at 60 Burton Rd (☎01530/412017; ①), or the central *Queen's Head Hotel*, 79 Market St (☎01530/412780; ②), which also serves excellent traditional pub food.

Melton Mowbray and around

MELTON MOWBRAY, fifteen miles northeast of Leicester, is famous for pork pies, an unaccountably popular English snack made of compressed balls of meat and gristle encased in wobbly jelly and thick pastry. The pie is the traditional repast of the fox-hunting fraternity, for whom the town of Melton, lying on the boundary of the region's most important hunts – Belvoir, Cottesmore and Quorn – has long been a favourite spot. The antics of some of the aristocratic huntsmen are legend – in 1837 the Marquis of Waterford literally painted the town's buildings red, hence the saying – but with the snowballing opposition to blood sports, the days of the tally-ho brigade may well be numbered. If you want to sample the genuine traditional hunters' pie, it is available in Melton only at Dickinson & Morris, on Nottingham Street.

Most of Melton Mowbray is Victorian, but a short walk south from the central market place is the medieval church of **St Mary**, distinguished by its impressive size (150ft long and the tower soaring to over 100ft) and by some of its detail. The clerestory is an especially fine illustration of the Perpendicular style, its 48 windows encircling the church and bathing the interior with great shafts of light. You could also drop by the town's **museum** (Mon–Fri 10am–5pm, Sat 10am–4pm, Sun 2–5pm; free), five minutes' walk from the market place down Sherrard Street, which features the work of John Ferneley, a local artist who made a small fortune selling hunting scenes to the gentry. There are plans for another museum too – this one dedicated to hunting.

Central **trains** runs frequent services from Leicester to Oakham via Melton Mowbray and Barton **buses** link Nottingham, Melton and Oakham.

Belvoir Castle

Heading northeast from Melton Mowbray along the A607, it's about ten miles to the lip of the escarpment overlooking the Vale of Belvoir (pronounced "beaver"). William the Conqueror gave the rich farmland of the valley to his standard-bearer Robert de Todeni, who built a castle down below on the largest hill he could find. In successive centuries the castle was destroyed and rebuilt several times, and the present **Belvoir Castle** (April–Sept Tues–Thurs & Sat–Sun 11am–5pm; £5), an incoherent castellated pile, dates from 1816. The exterior of the castle may not be much to look at, but inside, the Duke and Duchess of Rutland's hoard of art is another story. Particular highlights of the collection include the enormous Gobelin tapestries in the Regent's Gallery and the paintings in the Picture Gallery, notably Jan Steen's *Grace before Meat*, *Proverbs* by David Teniers the Younger and Hans Holbein's portrait of Henry VIII. German-born Holbein was introduced to the king on his second visit to England, in 1532, and Henry was so pleased by his first portraits, which picked a delicate line between flattery and honesty, that he kept him employed until the artist's death in 1543. Belvoir attracts day-trippers in their hundreds for its weekend "medieval" jousts and other special events. **Buses** from Melton, operated by Vale Runner (☎0116/251 1411), leave twice daily, at 10.10am and 11.30am.

Oakham and around

Some twenty miles east from Leicester, well-heeled **OAKHAM**, Rutland's county town, has a long history as a commercial centre, its prosperity bolstered by Oakham School, a late sixteenth-century foundation that's become one of the country's more exclusive private schools. The town's stone terraces and Georgian villas are too often interrupted by the mundanely modern to assume any grace, but the town has its architectural moments – particularly in the L-shaped **Market Place**, where the sturdy awnings of the octagonal Butter Cross shelter the old town stocks. On the north side of the Market Place stands **Oakham Castle** (April–Oct Tues–Sat 10am–1pm & 2–5.30pm, Sun 2–5.30pm; Nov–March Tues–Sat 10am–1pm & 2–4pm, Sun 2–4pm; free), a fortified house dating from 1191 of which the banqueting hall is pretty much all that remains. The hall is a good example of Norman domestic architecture and, inside, the white-washed walls are covered with horseshoes, the result of an ancient custom by which every lord or lady, king or queen, is obliged to present an ornamental horseshoe when they first set foot in the town.

Close by, Oakham School is housed in a series of impressive ironstone buildings along the west edge of the Market Place. On the right-hand side of the school, a narrow lane allows you to see more of the buildings on the way to **All Saints'** church, whose heavy tower and spire rise high above the town. Dating from the thirteenth century, the church is an architectural hybrid, but the light and airy interior is distinguished by the medieval carvings along the piers beside the chancel, with Christian scenes and symbols set opposite dragons, grotesques, devils and demons.

Practicalities

With regular services from Leicester, Melton Mowbray and Peterborough, Oakham **train station** lies on the west side of town, five minutes' walk from the centre. **Buses** connect the town with Leicester, Nottingham and Melton Mowbray and these arrive at St John Street, close to the Market Place. A thorough exploration of Oakham only takes a couple of hours, but, should you decide to stay, the **tourist office**, at Flore's House, 34 High St (Mon–Sat 9.30am–5pm, Sun 10.30–3.30; Nov–March Mon–Sat 10am–4pm; ☎01572/724329), will book accommodation. Alternatively, there are a couple of handy **B&Bs** near the High Street: *Angel House*, 20 Northgate (☎01572/756153; ③), and *Serpentine House*, 8 Lodge Gardens (☎01572/757878; ③), a quiet place with a spacious walled garden. Otherwise, the *Whipper-In Hotel*, on the Market Place (☎01572/756971; ④), has smartly decorated modern rooms behind its old facade. For **food**, the *Whipper-In* also serves excellent bar snacks, as does the *Rutland Angler*, nearby on Mill Street.

Rutland Water

Rutland Water, the horseshoe-shaped reservoir immediately to the east of Oakham, was created by the damming of the River Gwash in 1976. With a shoreline over twenty miles long, it's the second largest artificial lake in England and although few would say it's especially beautiful, it's a pleasant enough area – and a string of leisure developments have developed along its periphery. On the north side of the water, beside the A606 about three miles east of town, lies the **Whitwell** site (buses from Oakham), where the emphasis is on watersports, especially windsurfing, canoeing and sailing. Here also is Rutland Water Cycling (☎07000/292546), which rents out standard range bikes from around £10.50 a day, £7.50 for four hours – a popular cycle path runs right round the lake. A mile or so to the east of Whitwell, the **Butterfly Farm and Aquatic**

Centre (daily April–Aug 10.30am–5pm, Sept & Oct 10.30am–4.30pm; £3), on Sykes Lane in **Empingham**, exhibits Blue Emperors and Paris Peacocks among many species of butterfly, and these share a hothouse with tarantulas and giant stick insects. On the west side of the lake, just south of Oakham, the **Egleton nature reserve** is noted for its wildfowl, has hides, and is attached to the **Anglian Water Birdwatching Centre** (daily 9am–4/5pm; £3), with a viewing gallery and a video remote camera. Finally, on the south side of the lake, just beyond the dinky little village of **Edith Weston**, is Rutland Water's main landmark-cum-trademark, **Normanton Church**, a good-looking mix of Georgian and Victorian features that now houses a small **museum** of local history (March–Oct daily 11am–4/5pm; 80p).

The reservoir's most opulent hotel is *Hambleton Hall* (☎01572/756991; ⑦), a vast Victorian pile of luxury on the peninsula jutting into the western end of Rutland Water. If you fancy the view, but not the cost, try the excellent food at the neighbouring *Finch's Arms* pub.

Hallaton

HALLATON, some ten miles southwest of Oakham along steep and winding country lanes, is one of the region's most attractive villages, its postcard prettiness composed of neat ironstone cottages around a well-kept village green, embellished by a medieval church, a conical Butter Cross and a duck pond. Every Easter Monday, this tranquil scene is disturbed by the **Hare Pie Scramble and Bottle Kicking** contest, when the inhabitants of Hallaton fight for pieces of pie with the people of nearby Medbourne. The participants gather at the *Fox Inn* by the village pond, then proceed to kick small barrels of ale around a hill and across a stream, as has been the custom for several hundred years – though no one has the faintest idea why. The village **museum** (May–Oct Sat & Sun 2.30–5pm; donation requested) does its best to shed some light on the business. For a pint and a ploughman's, head for the green, where the *Bewicke Arms* is one of Leicestershire's oldest-established and most characterful pubs.

Northamptonshire

Northamptonshire is one of the region's less visited counties, generally regarded as somewhere you pass through on the way to somewhere else. Part of the problem is that three of the county's four big towns – Wellingborough, Corby and Kettering – are primarily industrial and whatever charms they offer to their inhabitants, there's not much to attract the casual visitor. The fourth town, **Northampton**, is, however, a good deal more interesting, possessed of several fine old buildings and an excellent museum devoted to shoe-making, the industry that has long made the place tick. Northampton is also just five miles from **Althorp**, family home of the Spencers and the burial place of Princess Diana.

Away from the towns, Northamptonshire comprises a wedge of gentle hills and patchy woodland dotted with good-looking villages, stately homes and country estates. The M1 forms an easy if arbitrary dividing line with west Northamptonshire on one side and the larger **east Northamptonshire** on the other. The prime target in the latter is the good-looking country town of **Oundle**, which makes the best base for visiting the charming hamlet of **Fotheringhay**.

Getting to Northampton by **public transport** is no problem, but to reach the villages and stately homes, you'll mostly need your own vehicle – or some careful planning around infrequent bus services. That said, the County Council now fund the Saunterbus service which links key attractions on specified days from April to September. A day ticket costs £3.70 and is available from the driver; timetable details from any Northamptonshire tourist office or Stagecoach buses (☎01604/620077).

Northampton and around

Spreading north from the banks of the River Nene, **NORTHAMPTON** is a workaday modern town whose appearance largely belies its ancient past. Throughout the Middle Ages, this was one of central England's most important towns, a flourishing commercial centre whose now demolished castle was a popular stopping-off point for travelling royalty. A fire in 1675 burnt most of the medieval city to a cinder and the Georgian town that grew up in its stead was itself swamped by the industrial revolution when Northampton swarmed with boot and shoe manufacturers. The town continues to grow, making room for London's overflow population, and light industries are settling on the outskirts, but the centre does hold several diverting old buildings and is the obvious place to gather information before checking out the rest of the county. Half a day is enough for a quick gambol round the sights, but if you're tempted to stay the night there's a reasonable supply of hotel accommodation and a light scattering of B&Bs. The only times of the year when finding a room here can be difficult are during the annual **Balloon Festival** in August, which attracts 200,000 visitors, and over the weekend of the British Grand Prix, held in mid-July at the nearby **Silverstone** race track. Northampton has one other claim to fame: it was here that Errol Flynn got his start in repertory in 1933, though he high-tailed it out of town the following year leaving a whopping tailor's debt behind him.

Arrival, information and accommodation

A tiny section of the castle remains beside Northampton's **train station**, which has regular services to London Euston and Birmingham, and is ten minutes' walk west of the town centre. Buses pull into the **bus station** on Lady's Lane, right in the centre behind the Grosvenor Shopping Centre. From here, it's just five minutes' walk south to the **tourist office** (Mon–Fri 9.30am–5pm, Sat 9.30am–4pm; late May to Aug also Sun noon–4pm; ☎01604/622677), opposite the Guildhall on St Giles Square. They operate an accommodation service, have oodles of information on the county and issue bus timetables.

The smartest **hotel** in the centre is the *Northampton Moat House*, a dependable chain hotel in a large modern block on Silver Street (☎01604/739988; ⑤). More distinctive is the *Lime Trees Hotel*, 8 Langham Place, Barrack Road (☎01604/632188; ④), in pleasant Georgian premises half a mile north from the centre. The pick of the more central **B&Bs** is the *St Georges Private Hotel*, 128 St Georges Ave (☎01604/792755; ②). This attractive place has spacious, comfortable guest rooms and occupies a large Edwardian house about a mile and a half from the centre, overlooking Racecourse Park.

The Town

Northampton's finest building is **All Saints** church (daily 9am–3pm), just south of the main Market Square on George Row. Crowned by a heavy clock tower and a lavish glass dome, it was rebuilt after being destroyed in the Great Fire of 1675. The pillared portico is reminiscent of St Paul's Cathedral, but this one is topped by a statue of Charles II in a toga, raised to commemorate his donation of a thousand tons of timber after the fire and dressed with oak leaves each year on Oakapple Day (29 May). Inside, the breezy interior looks more like a ballroom than a church, its high ceiling coated in delicately sculpted plasterwork designed around a central rose, the shire's motif.

In front of the west end of the church, a patchwork of flower beds surrounds one of Lutyens's less inspiring monuments, a plain, blunt **war memorial** dating from 1926. In the opposite direction, round the back of the church, is the **Guildhall** (tours Thurs 2.15pm; £2.50), a flamboyant Victorian edifice constructed in the 1860s to a design by

Edward Godwin, one of the period's most inventive architects. The Gothic exterior, with its high-pointed windows and dinky balustrade, sports kings and queens as well as scenes central to the county's history – look out for Mary, Queen of Scots with her head on the block, the Battle of Naseby and the fire of 1675.

The **Central Museum and Art Gallery** (Mon–Sat 10am–5pm, Sun 2–5pm; free), a hundred yards south on Guildhall Road, celebrates the town's industrial heritage with an extensive and surprisingly interesting display of shoes. Along with silk slippers, clogs and high-heeled nineteenth-century court shoes, there's one of the four boots worn by an elephant during the British Expedition of 1959, which retraced Hannibal's putative route over the Alps into Italy. There's celebrity footwear too – almost inevitably, a pair of Elton John shoes: the boots he wore in *Tommy* – but perhaps the most original gear is a *kadaitcha*, made by Australian aborigines from emu feathers and women's hair, and used to fool trackers. The rest of the museum is given over to an excellent display charting the town's history from its Roman days to the present, paying particular attention to the significance of the shoe industry, which employed half the town's population in 1920.

Back at All Saints, a narrow alley leads the few paces north to the vast cobbled **Market Square**, whose stalls brim with produce and bargains every day except Sunday. From the north side of the square, a lane leads through to Sheep Street, where the **Church of the Holy Sepulchre** (May–Sept Mon, Tues & Thurs 2–4pm, Wed & alternate Fri noon–4pm; free) is Northampton's oldest building and one of only five Norman round churches extant in the country. As its name suggests, the church's design was inspired by contact with the Holy Land – in this case, the founder, Simon de Senlis, was a veteran of the First Crusade. The only disturbance to the original circular plan is the eastern portion, which was added in 1860.

Eating and drinking

A good spot for daytime **snacks** is the *Corner House Coffee Bar*, at the corner of George Row and Bridge Street, or *Morelli's Cappuccino*, on Princes Walk. For more substantial **meals**, head for the moderately priced *Sorrentino Don Giovanni*, 64 Gold St (☎01604/602222), the town's most popular pizza and pasta joint, or treat yourself to a slap-up dinner at the smart and pricey *Lime Trees Hotel*, 8 Langham Place, Barrack Road (☎01604/632188). For a **drink**, the *Malt Shovel*, down by the Carlsberg brewery at 121 Bridge St, is a recently refurbished Edwardian pub with a wide range of bottled and draught beers plus inexpensive bar food.

Althorp

Some five miles northwest of Northampton off the A428, the ritzy mansion of **Althorp** is the focus of the Spencer estate. The Spencers have lived here for centuries, but this was no big deal until one of the tribe, **Diana**, married Prince Charles in 1981. The disintegration of the marriage and Diana's elevation to sainthood/stardom is a story known to millions – and most perceptively analysed by B. (for Beatrix) Campbell in her *Diana Princess of Wales: How Sexual Politics Shook the Monarchy*. The public grief following Diana's death in 1997 was quite astounding and Althorp became the focus of massive media attention as the coffin was brought up the M1 motorway from London to be buried on an island in the grounds of the family estate. The estate is open to visitors on timed-entry tickets in July and August only (9am–5pm; £9.50). Tickets must be purchased in advance (bookings on ☎01604/592020; *www.althorp.com*) – and they give access to the **Diana exhibition**, in the old stable block, as well as the adjacent Althorp house, where there's a large collection of priceless paintings, including works by Gainsborough, Van Dyke and Rubens. From the house, a footpath leads round a lake in the middle of which is the islet (no access) on which Diana is buried.

Brixworth

Crowning a low rise above **BRIXWORTH** village, just off the A508 about six miles
north of Northampton, **All Saints Church** (usually open daily 10am–5pm, call
☎01604/880286 to check; bus #62 or #61) is one of England's finest surviving Anglo-
Saxon churches, dating from around 680 AD. From a distance, its most striking feature
is its unusual cylindrical stair-turret, added to the western tower in the ninth century as
part of a plan to fortify the church against Viking raids. Closer inspection reveals something even rarer – Roman tiles, probably salvaged from a nearby villa, are stuck into the
church, often at irregular angles, and form part of the fabric of the building. Inside, the
uncluttered nave's whitewashed walls set off the stonework, notably in the triple archway set high up on the west wall. In 1400, a second, larger triple archway – which once
led into the presbytery – was replaced by a single arch, thereby opening the church up
to the congregation. At the east end, the rounded apse, modelled on a Roman basilica,
has been modified, but still incorporates three eighth-century pillars. To its right (as
you face the altar), a curtained archway leads from the presbytery into the Lady
Chapel, built in the thirteenth century by a local baron, Sir John de Verdun. His carved
stone effigy lies in a recess in the south wall, with legs crossed and his finely carved
suit of chain mail still visible. Further along the wall, look out for a small niche fronted
with glass; this was where Brixworth's famous **reliquary**, two boxes containing fragments of bone thought to be Saint Boniface's larynx, was re-discovered in the nineteenth century. The relic was probably hidden here for safe keeping when Viking raids
were at their peak.

East Northamptonshire

The River Nene wriggles its way across **east Northamptonshire** passing through a
string of little villages and towns, amongst which **Oundle** is by far the most diverting.
Within easy striking distance of Oundle is the historic hamlet of **Fotheringhay** and several country houses, amongst which hilltop **Rockingham Castle** is the most dramatic.

Oundle

Oundle's most conspicuous building is the parish church of St Peter's, right in the centre, with a magnificent two-hundred-foot Decorated spire, but the town's real appeal is
the overall effect of pale limestone houses clinging to streets, whose layout has
changed little over several centuries. Indeed, Oundle boasts some of the finest seven-
teenth- and eighteenth-century streetscapes in the Midlands, and provides a suitably
exclusive setting for one of England's better-known private schools, **Oundle School**,
which has been running since 1556 and owns many of the town's most prized buildings.

If you have your own transport, Oundle makes a good base for exploring the rural
nooks and crannies of this part of the county. **Buses** from Peterborough, Stamford and
Northampton stop in Oundle Market Place, a short walk from the **tourist office**, at 14
West St (Mon–Sat 9am–5pm, plus April to mid-Oct Sun noon–3pm; ☎01832/274333).
They issue maps and bus timetables, have comprehensive details of local attractions
and operate an **accommodation** service. The best place to stay is the *Talbot Hotel*, on
New Street (☎01832/273621; ⑨). This charming hotel looks much the same today as it
did when it was rebuilt in 1626, complete with what is thought to be the very oak staircase Mary, Queen of Scots used on her way to her execution at Fotheringhay Castle
(see below). Apparently the queen's executioner stayed at the *Talbot* and both his and
Mary's ghost are said to wander the upper floor. For somewhere less expensive, head
for the comfortable *Ship Inn*, 18 West St (☎01832/273918; ①).

Fotheringhay

Nestling the River Nene just four miles northeast of Oundle, the tiny hamlet of **FOTHERINGHAY** once boasted an imposing medieval castle which witnessed two key events – the birth of Richard III in 1452 and the beheading of Mary, Queen of Scots in 1587. On the orders of Elizabeth I, Mary was executed in the castle's Great Hall with no one to stand in her defence – apart, that is, from her dog, who is said to have rushed from beneath her skirts as her head fell. Not long afterwards, the castle fell into disrepair and nowadays only a thistle-covered mound remains to mark its position; it's down a narrow lane on the bend of the road near the east end of the village.

Fotheringhay is itself distinguished by its old thatched cottages and the **church of St Mary and All Saints**, whose octagonal lantern tower soars high above the meadows flanking the river. Dating from 1415, the church is supported by a long series of flying buttresses and the interior holds two fancily carved medieval pieces – a pulpit and a fine stone font. On either side of the altar are the tombs of Elizabeth I's ancestors the dukes of York, Edward and Richard. Elizabeth found the tombs in disarray in 1573, and promptly had them rebuilt in a smooth white limestone that still looks like new.

Bus #6 links Oundle and Fotheringhay once daily (except Sun) in each direction.

Rockingham Castle

Some eleven miles west of Oundle, on the outskirts of Corby, **Rockingham Castle** (Easter to mid-Oct Thurs, Sun and bank hol Mon, plus Tues in Aug, 1–5pm; £4.20), stands high above the Welland river valley in the heart of Rockingham Forest, which once stretched all the way to Northampton. A favoured hunting retreat of England's monarchs, from William Rufus and King John through to Edward I, the castle incorporates the original fortifications built by the Normans, but is mostly Tudor, a handsome, honey-coloured brick-and-stone complex designed by Edward Watson, ancestor of the present owners. The highlight is the timber-beamed **Great Hall**, the kernel of the original Norman castle, with grand fireplaces and trellised windows added by Edward I.

Lincolnshire

The obvious place to start a visit to **Lincolnshire** is **Lincoln** itself, where the cathedral, the third largest church in England, remains the region's outstanding attraction – give or take the long sandy beaches of the coast, so different from the rest of the county, their brashness encapsulated by the booming resort of **Skegness.** Lincoln also stands not too far away from **The Fens**, whose most appealing villages lie along the A17, a road that runs close to the old fenland port of **Boston**, now Lincolnshire's second town. The other chief towns of southern Lincolnshire are **Grantham**, birthplace of Margaret Thatcher, and **Stamford**, in the southwest corner of the county, a delightfully attractive old stone-built town boasting one of the great monuments of Elizabethan England, **Burghley House**.

Getting around Lincolnshire by public transport can be difficult, but there are reasonable **bus** services between Lincoln and the larger market towns, like Louth, and **trains** connect Lincoln with Gainsborough and Skegness via Boston. Covering the whole of the county, the **bus timetable hotline** number is ☎01522/553135.

Lincoln

Reaching high into the sky from the top of a steep hill, the triple towers of the mighty cathedral of **LINCOLN** are visible for miles across the flatlands. This conspicuous spot was first fortified by the Celts, who called their settlement Lindon, "hill fort by the lake", a reference to the pools formed by the River Witham in the marshy ground below. In 47 AD the Romans occupied Lindon and built a fortified town which subsequently became, as Lindum Colonia, one of the four regional capitals of Roman Britain.

Today, only fragments of the Roman city survive, mostly pieces of the third-century town wall, and these are outdone by reminders of Lincoln's medieval heyday, which began during the reign of William the Conqueror with the building of the castle and cathedral. Lincoln flourished, first as a Norman power base and then as a centre of the wool trade with Flanders, until 1369, when the wool market was transferred to neighbouring Boston. It was almost five hundred years before the town revived, the recovery based upon its manufacture of agricultural machinery and drainage equipment for the fenlands. As the nineteenth-century town spread south down the hill and out along the old Roman road – the Fosse Way – so Lincoln became a place of precise class distinctions: the "Up hill" area, sloping north from the cathedral, became synonymous with middle-class respectability, "Down hill" with the proletariat. It's a distinction that remains – locals selling anything from secondhand cars to settees still put "Up hill" in brackets to signify a better quality of merchandise.

For the visitor, almost everything of interest is confined to the "Up hill" part of town, and it's here also you'll find the best pubs and restaurants.

Arrival and information

Both Lincoln's **train station**, on St Mary's Street, and its **bus station**, close by off Norman Street, are located "Down hill" in the city centre. From either, it's a steep, twenty-minute walk to the cathedral, which can also be reached by city buses #1A, #7A and #8. There are two **tourist offices**. One is in the shopping centre on The Cornhill, close to the train and bus stations (Easter–Sept Mon–Thurs 9am–5.30pm, Fri 9am–5pm, Sat 10am–5pm; Oct–Easter same hours, but only till 4pm; ☎01522/873703), the other is at 9 Castle Hill, between the cathedral and the castle (Easter–Sept Mon–Thurs 9am–5.30pm, Fri 9am–5pm, Sat & Sun 10am–5pm; Oct–Easter same hours, but only till 4pm; ☎01522/873700). Both have a useful range of literature on Lincoln and its surroundings, take bookings for guided tours of the city, and operate an accommodation service.

Accommodation

Lincoln has a good supply of competitively priced **hotels** and **B&Bs**, though surprisingly few of them are in the vicinity of the cathedral – "Up hill" – and this is precisely where you want to be. All the places below are "Up hill", unless otherwise indicated. On occasion, demand can exceed supply, in which case head for the tourist office, who operate an efficient accommodation service. The town's **youth hostel** is at 77 South Park (☎01522/522076; closed Jan) in a Victorian villa opposite South Common park, half a mile south of the train station.

Carline Guest House, 1–3 Carline Rd (☎01522/530422). One of the best B&Bs in the city, *Carline* occupies a spick and span Edwardian house just five minutes' walk down from the cathedral – take Drury Lane from the top of Steep Hill and keep straight. Breakfasts are first rate, the rooms smart and tastefully furnished. No credit cards. ②.

D'isney Place Hotel, Eastgate (☎01522/538881). This delightful hotel occupies a lovely eighteenth-century building close to the cathedral. Breakfast is served in the bedrooms, some of which have four-poster beds and spa baths. Highly recommended. ⑤.

Edward King House, The Old Palace, Minster Yard (☎01522/528778). For something a little different, head for this unusual B&B in a former residence of the bishops of Lincoln. The exterior is a good bit grander than the rooms, but these are perfectly adequate and some have fine views over the city. Next to the cathedral. ①.

St Clements Lodge, 21 Langworth Gate (☎01522/521532). In a modest side street a short walk from the cathedral, this comfortable B&B offers a handful of pleasant guestrooms. To get there, follow Eastgate east from beside the cathedral. ②.

The City

Approached through the arch of medieval Exchequergate, the west front of **Lincoln Cathedral** (June–Aug Mon–Sat 7.15am–8pm, Sun 7.15am–6pm; Sept–May Mon–Sat 7.15am–6pm, Sun 7.15am–5pm; £3 donation) is a glorious sight, a cliff-face of blind arcading mobbed by decorative carving. Most striking of all is the extraordinary band of twelfth-century carved panels which depict biblical themes with a passionate intimacy, their inspiration being a similar frieze at Modena Cathedral in Italy. The west front's apparent homogeneity is deceptive, and further inspection reveals two phases of construction – the small stones and thick mortar of much of the facade belong to the original church, completed in 1092, whereas the longer stones and finer courses date from the early thirteenth century. These were enforced modifications, for in 1185 an earthquake shattered much of the Norman church, which was then rebuilt under the auspices of **Bishop Hugh of Avalon**, the man responsible for most of the present cathedral, with the notable exception of the fourteenth-century towers.

The cavernous **interior** is a fine example of Early English architecture, with the nave's pillars conforming to the same general design yet differing slightly, their varied columns and bands of dark Purbeck marble contrasting with the oolitic limestone that is the building's main material. Pre-Christian images are still visible around the cathedral; above the doorway to the left of the decorative stone rood screen at the head of the nave, the "cheeky green man" (an early fertility symbol) peers out from behind some foliage, watched by the beady eye of a stealthy dragon.

Beyond the central tower lies **St Hugh's Choir**, its fourteenth-century misericords carrying an eccentric range of carvings, with scenes from the life of Alexander the Great and King Arthur mixed up with biblical characters and folkloric parables. Farther on is the Gothic **Angel Choir**, completed in 1280, its roof embellished by dozens of finely carved statuettes, including the tiny Lincoln Imp (see below). Finally, a corridor off the choir's north aisle leads to the wooden-roofed **cloisters** and the ten-sided **chapter house**, where Edward I convened some of the first English parliaments.

Hidden behind a high wall immediately below (and to the south of) the cathedral on Minster Yard are the ruins of what would, in its day, have been among the city's most impressive buildings. This, the medieval **Bishop's Palace** (April–Oct daily 10am–6pm; Nov–March Sat & Sun 10am–1pm & 2–4pm; £1.30; EH), once consisted of two grand halls, a lavish chapel, kitchens and ritzy private chambers, but today the only significant survivor is the battered and bruised Alnwick Tower and the undercroft. The damage was done during the Civil War when a troupe of Roundheads occupied the palace until they themselves had to evacuate the place after a fierce fire.

From the west front of the cathedral, it's a quick stroll across to **Lincoln Castle** (summer Mon–Sat 9.30am–5.30pm, Sun 11am–5.30pm; winter closes 4pm; £2.50). The castle walls incorporate bits and pieces from the twelfth to the nineteenth century and the wall walkway offers great views over town. The earliest remains are those of the **Lucy Tower**, built on the mound of the first Norman keep. Behind the walls, in the spacious castle grounds, is the dour red-brick old jail, now housing one of the four surviving copies of the **Magna Carta** and a remarkable **prison chapel**. Here, prisoners were locked in high-sided cubicles where they could see the preacher and his pulpit but not their fellow internees, an arrangement founded on the pseudo-scientific theory that defined crime as a contagious disease. Unfortunately for the theorists, their system of "Separation and Silence" drove many prisoners crazy, and it had to be abandoned, though nobody bothered to dismantle the chapel.

Leaving the castle via the west gate, you reach **The Lawn**, formerly a lunatic asylum and now a leisure complex incorporating a modest exhibition on mental health in the **Charlesworth Suite** (Mon–Fri 9am–4.30pm, Sat & Sun 10am–4/5pm; free), in the grandly porticoed building at the front. Adjoining the Charlesworth Suite is a display devoted to now-disbanded no. 50 and no. 61 squadrons, both active in bombing raids during

World War II and both based in Lincolnshire. Close by, and also part of The Lawn, is the **Sir Joseph Banks Conservatory** (same hours; free), a large tropical glasshouse named after the local botanist who travelled with Cook on his first voyage to Australia.

As for the rest of **"Up hill" Lincoln**, it's scattered with historic remains, notably several slabs of Roman wall, the most prominent of which is the second-century **Newport Arch** straddling Bailgate, once the main north gate into the city. It's in fine condition, despite being crunched by a truck in the 1970s, and remains the only Roman arch in Britain that's still used by traffic. There's also a bevy of medieval stone houses, at their best on and around the aptly named Steep Hill as it cuts down to the city centre. In particular, look out for the tidily restored twelfth-century **Jew's House**, a reminder of the Jewish community that flourished in medieval Lincoln – a rare and superb example of domestic Norman architecture, it now houses the *Jew's House Restaurant* (see below).

The **Usher Gallery**, Lindum Road (Mon–Sat 10am–5.30pm, Sun 2.30–5pm; £2), is on the hillside too, its well-presented displays featuring some fine watercolours of the cathedral and its environs, a pleasing sample of seventeenth-century Dutch and Italian paintings, and memorabilia celebrating Lincolnshire's own Alfred Tennyson (1809–92), one of Victorian England's favourite poets. There's also an eclectic collection of coins, porcelain, and watches and clocks dating from the seventeenth century. The timepieces were given to the gallery by its benefactor, James Ward Usher, a local jeweller and watchmaker who made a fortune by devising the legend of the **Lincoln Imp**, which he turned into the city's emblem in the 1880s. His story has a couple of imps hopping around the cathedral, until one of them is turned to stone for trying to talk to the angels carved into the roof of the choir. His chum made a hasty exit on the back of a witch, but the wind is still supposed to haunt the cathedral awaiting their return.

Eating and drinking

Lincoln's **café** and **restaurant** scene is a little patchy – too many places offer mundane food geared to the day-tripping trade – but there are excellent places too, mostly within shouting distance of the cathedral. First stop must be *Browns Pie Shop*, 33 Steep Hill, which has a lively menu where the emphasis is on British ingredients; a main course here will cost you about £10. Next door, and similarly enticing, is the *Wig and Mitre* pub-restaurant, where a wide-ranging, moderately priced menu lists everything from sandwiches through to fillet steak. Another recommendable spot on Steep Hill is the more expensive – and more formal – *Jew's House Restaurant* (☎01522/524851). As for **pubs**, the obvious target is the *Victoria*, opposite the Lawn at 6 Union Rd, an amiable, traditional and long-established local that serves great-value down-to-earth food along with a vast array of guest beers.

Skegness and the coast

SKEGNESS has been a busy resort ever since the railways reached the Lincolnshire coast in 1875. Its heyday was before the 1960s, when the Brits began to take themselves off to sunnier climes, but it still attracts tens of thousands of city-dwellers each year, who come for the wide, sandy beaches and for a host of attractions ranging from nightclubs to bowling greens. Every inch the traditional English seaside town, Skegness gets the edge over many of its rivals by keeping its beaches clean and its parks spick and span, whilst a massive leisure complex in neighbouring Ingoldmells has Europe's largest indoor "fun pool". Indeed, Skegness has a tradition of keeping ahead of its competitors: in 1908 it came up with the ground-breaking "Skegness is So Bracing" slogan beneath a picture of a "Jolly Fisherman" and it was here in 1936 that ex-showman Billy Butlin opened the first "Butlin's Holiday Camp". All that said, the seafront, with its rows of tacky souvenir shops and amusement arcades, can be dismal, especially on rainy days, and you may well decide to sidestep the whole caboodle by heading south along the coastal road to **Gibraltar Point Nature Reserve** (daily dawn to dusk), where a series of footpaths crisscross a narrow strip of salt marsh, sand dune and beach.

The **tourist office** (April–Sept daily 9am–6pm; Oct–March Mon–Fri 9am–5pm, Sat 10am–4pm, Sun noon–4pm; ☎01754/764821), behind the beach in the Embassy Centre on Grand Parade, can provide a colossal list of accommodation, including scores of **B&Bs** and **guest houses**. A series of convenient choices is strung out along South Parade and Drummond Road, a few minutes' walk from the Embassy Centre: try the *Belle View Hotel*, 12 South Parade (☎01754/765274; ②), the *Singlecote Hotel*, 34 Drummond Rd (☎01754/764698; ②), or *Scarborough House*, 54 South Parade (☎01754/764453; ②). For something a little more original, there's the *Old Mill Guest House*, an old and imaginatively converted windmill five miles inland at Westend, Burgh Le Marsh (☎01754/810081; ②). Skegness **bus** and **train** stations are ten minutes' walk inland from the clock tower beside the tourist office, straight up Lumley Road.

The Lincolnshire Fens

The Lincolnshire section of **The Fens**, the great chunk of eastern England extending from Cambridge to Boston, encompasses some of the most productive farmland in Europe. With the exception of the occasional hillock, this pancake-flat, treeless terrain has been painstakingly reclaimed from the marshes and swamps that once drained into the Wash, a process that has taken almost two thousand years. In earlier times, outsiders were often amazed by the dreadful conditions hereabouts – as one medieval chronicler put it: "There is in the middle part of Britain a hideous fen which [is] oft times clouded with moist and dark vapours having within it divers islands and woods as also crooked and winding rivers." These dire conditions spawned the distinctive culture of the so-called **fen slodgers**, who embanked small portions of marsh to create pastureland and fields, supplementing their diets by catching fish and fowl, and gathering reed and sedge for thatching and fuel. Their economy was threatened by the large-scale land reclamation schemes of the late fifteenth and sixteenth centuries, and time and again the fenlanders sabotaged progress by breaking down the banks and dams. But the odds were stacked against the saboteurs, and a succession of great landowners eventually drained huge tracts of the fenland; by the end of the eighteenth century the fen slodgers' way of life had all but disappeared. Nonetheless, the Lincolnshire fens remain a distinctive area of introverted little villages, with just one major settlement, the old port of **Boston**.

Boston

Bisected by the muddy River Witham as it nears the Wash, **BOSTON** (a corruption of Botolf's stone, or Botolph's town) was named after the Anglo-Saxon monk-saint who first established a monastery here, overlooking the estuary and main river crossing point, in 645 AD. In the thirteenth and fourteenth centuries, the settlement expanded to become England's second largest seaport, its flourishing economy dependent on the wool trade with Flanders. Local merchants, revelling in their success, built the magnificent medieval church of St Botolph, whose 272-foot tower still presides over the town and surrounding fenland. The church was completed in the early sixteenth century, but by then Boston was in decline as trade drifted west towards the Atlantic and the Witham silted up. The town's fortunes only revived in the late eighteenth century when, after the nearby fens had been drained, it became a minor agricultural centre with a modest port that has, in recent times, been modernized for trade with the EU. A handsome town with a distinctive fenland feel, Boston is an appealing place to break a journey along England's east coast between Lincoln and Norfolk. On Saturdays and Wednesdays, a busy market livens up the main square, and the surrounding flatlands are peppered with pubs that make ideal targets for forays into the fens.

Mostly edged by Victorian red-brick buildings, the narrow streets of Boston's cramped centre radiate out from the massive bulk of **St Botolph** (Mon–Sat 8.30am–4.30pm, Sun 8.30am–4pm; winter closes Sun noon). Most of the church's exterior masonry, embellished by the high-pointed windows of the Decorated style, dates from the fourteenth century, but the huge and distinctive tower, whose lack of a spire earned the church the nickname "**Stump**", is of later construction. The octagonal lantern, added in the early sixteenth century, is visible from twenty miles away and once sheltered a beacon that guided travellers in from the fens and the North Sea. A tortuous spiral staircase leads to a balcony near the top, from where the views over Boston and the fens amply repay the price of the ticket (£2) and stiff climb.

Down below, St Botolph's light and airy interior contains some intriguing fourteenth-century **misericords**, bearing a lively mixture of vernacular scenes, such as organ-playing bears, a pair of medieval jesters squeezing cats in imitation of bagpipes and a schoolmaster birching a boy, watched by three more awaiting the same fate. There's also the **Cotton Chapel**, dedicated to John Cotton, vicar here in 1612 and later a leading light among the Puritans of Boston, Massachusetts. In the early seventeenth century, Lincolnshire's Boston became a centre of non-conformism, providing a stream of emigrants for the colonies of New England.

It was here too, in 1607, that several of the **Pilgrim Fathers** were incarcerated after their failed attempt to escape religious persecution by slipping across to Holland. They were imprisoned for thirty days in the **Guildhall** (Mon–Sat 10am–5pm, plus April–Sept Sun 1.30–5pm; £1.20, free on Thurs), on South Street near St Botolph, and this now accommodates a small museum containing several old cells, one of which has been returned to its seventeenth-century appearance.

It's ten minutes' walk east from Boston **train station** to the town centre via West Street, where the back of the Regal cinema overlooks the **bus station**. Close to St Botolph, in the Market Place beneath the Assembly Rooms, is the **tourist office** (Mon–Sat 9am–5pm; ☎01205/356656), where you can pick up details of several **B&Bs**. Among them is the likeable *Ailsa Villa*, 16 Sleaford Rd (☎01205/352253; ①), just west of the train station, and the *Bramley House*, a converted eighteenth-century farmhouse one mile further down Sleaford Road at no. 267 (☎01205/354538; ①).

For **food**, try *Goodbarn's*, beneath the north side of the Stump on Wormgate, which serves copious pub meals inside or out in a relaxing back garden overlooking the river. Tucked away in the corner of Church Close, *Monsuda* (☎01205/355671) is an authentic Thai restaurant, with a bona fide Thai chef, where a three-course meal will set you back around £15. Vegetarians should head for *Maud Foster Windmill*, at the west edge of town on Willoughby Road (☎01205/352188; Wed & Sat 11am–5pm, Sun 1–5pm, plus July & Aug Thurs & Fri 11am–5pm), whose tearoom serves a range of vegetarian and vegan meals, as well as a good selection of delicious cakes.

Heckington

The village of **HECKINGTON**, twelve miles west of Boston on the A17, is a tidy little place draped around the church of **St Andrew**, a splendid example of the Decorated style, with a pinnacled spire and elaborate canopied buttresses framing the flowing tracery of the windows. Inside, the original fourteenth-century chancel fittings have survived, including the tomb of the founder, Richard de Potesgrave, and an **Easter Sepulchre**, whose exquisitely carved figures are set against a dense undergrowth of foliage. The sepulchre, one of the finest in England, was built to accommodate the host between Good Friday and Easter morning. The **sedilia** is intriguing too, boasting a cartoon strip of domestic scenes on the subject of food – a man eating fruit, a woman feeding the birds and suchlike. Heckington has one other attraction, its unique eight-sailed **windmill**, near the train station on Station Street, which is worth visiting when it's in operation (Easter to mid-July Thurs–Sun noon–5pm; mid-July to mid-Sept daily noon–5pm; mid-Sept to Easter Sun 2–5pm; £1.50). Afterwards, pop over to the *Nag's Head*, 34 High St (☎01529/460218; ②), where the **food** is excellent.

Stamford

STAMFORD is delightful, a handsome little limestone town of yellow-grey seventeenth- and eighteenth-century buildings edging narrow streets that slope up from the River Welland. It was here that the Romans forded this important river, establishing a fortified outpost that the Danes subsequently selected for one of their regional capitals. Later the town became a centre of the medieval wool and cloth trade, its wealthy merchants funding a series of almshouses known as "callises", after Calais, the English-occupied port through which most of them traded. Indeed, Stamford cloth became famous throughout Europe for its quality and durability, a reputation confirmed when Cardinal Wolsey used it for the tents of the "Field of the Cloth of Gold", the conference of Henry VIII and Francis I of France outside Calais in 1520. Stamford was also the home of William Cecil, Elizabeth's chief minister, who built his splendid mansion, Burghley House, close by. The town survived the collapse of the wool trade, prospering as an inland port after the Welland was made navigable to the sea in 1570, and, in the eighteenth century, as a staging point on the Great North Road from London. More recently, Stamford escaped the three main threats to old English towns – the Industrial Revolution, wartime bombing and postwar development – and was designated the country's first Conservation Area in 1967. Thanks to this, its unspoilt streets lent themselves perfectly to the filming of the TV adaptation of George Eliot's *Middlemarch* in 1993.

The Town

Above all, it's the harmony of Stamford's architecture that pleases, rather than any specific sight. There are, nevertheless, a handful of buildings of some special interest in the compact centre, beginning with the church of **St Mary**, set beside a mixed Georgian and medieval close on St Mary's Street. The church, with its splendid spire, has a small, airy interior that incorporates the Corpus Christi chapel, whose intricately embossed, painted and panelled roof dates from the 1480s.

From St Mary's, several lanes thread through to the carefully maintained High Street, where Ironmonger Street leads north to Broad Street, the site of **Browne's Hospital** (May–Sept Sat & Sun 11am–4pm), the most extensive of the town's almshouses. This paupers' hospital was inelegantly remodelled by the Victorians, but the chapel preserves much of its fifteenth-century stained glass, as does the nearby church of **St John**, just to the west on Red Lion Square. Back on Broad Street, the **Stamford Museum** (April–Sept Mon–Sat 10am–5pm, Sun 2–5pm; Oct–March Mon–Sat 10am–5pm; free) features a tasteless exhibit comparing the American midget Tom Thumb with **Daniel Lambert**, the Leicester fat man who died at Stamford in 1809, aged 39 and weighing 52st 11lb (336kg). After Lambert's death his clothes were displayed in a local inn which Tom Thumb, otherwise Charles Stratton, visited several times to perform a few party tricks, like standing in Lambert's waistcoat armhole.

Down the hill from St Mary's, on the other side of the Welland, is the **George Hotel**, on High Street St Martin's, a splendid old coaching inn whose Georgian facade supports one end of the gallows that span the street – not a warning to criminals, but an advertising hoarding. Close by, the late fifteenth-century church of **St Martin** shelters the magnificent tombs of the lords Burghley, with a recumbent William Cecil carved beneath twin canopies. Just behind, the early eighteenth-century effigies of John Cecil and his wife show the couple as Roman aristocrats, propped up on their elbows to gaze across at their distinguished ancestor.

From St Martin's Church, it's a fifteen-minute stroll south along High Street St Martin's to **Burghley** (pronounced "Burlee") **House** (April–Sept daily 11am–4.30pm; £6.10; guided tours Mon–Fri), an extravagant Elizabethan mansion standing in parkland landscaped by Capability Brown. Completed in 1587 after 22 years' work, the house sports a mellow-yellow ragstone exterior, embellished by dainty cupolas, a pyramidal clock tower and skeletal balustrading, all to a plan by **William Cecil**, the long-serving adviser to Elizabeth I. A shrewd and cautious man, Cecil steered his queen through all sorts of difficulties, from the wars against Spain to the execution of Mary, Queen of Scots, vindicating Elizabeth's assessment of his character when she appointed him secretary of state in 1558: "You will not be corrupted with any manner of gifts, and will be faithful to the state."

With the notable exception of the Tudor kitchen, little remains of Burghley's Elizabethan interior. Instead, the house bears the heavy hand of John, fifth Lord Burghley, who toured France and Italy in the late seventeenth century, commissioning furniture, statuary and tapestries, as well as buying up old Florentine and Venetian paintings, such as Paolo Veronese's *Zebedee's Wife Petitioning our Lord*. To provide a suitable setting for his old masters, John brought in Antonio Verrio and his assistant Louis Laguerre, who between them covered many of Burghley's walls and ceilings with frolicking gods and goddesses. These gaudy and gargantuan murals are at their best in the Heaven Room, an artfully painted classical temple that adjoins the Hell Staircase, where the entrance to the inferno is through the gaping mouth of a cat. Have a close look also at the fine portraits in the Pagoda Room, in particular the querulous Elizabeth I and a sublimely self-confident Henry VIII by Joos van Cleve.

Finally, if you're in Stamford in June, July or August, head out to **Tolethorpe Hall**, a graceful Elizabethan mansion that's home to Stamford Shakespeare Company. The troupe gives outdoor performances, but the audience is safely covered by a vast open-fronted marquee; call ☎01780/754381 for details.

Practicalities

With frequent services from Peterborough and Oakham, Stamford **train station** is five minutes' walk from the town centre, which is just to the north across the river. The **bus station** is in the centre off All Saints' Street, a short stroll from the **tourist office**, inside Stamford Arts Centre at 27 St Mary's St (Mon–Sat 9.30am–5pm, plus April–Oct Sun 10am–3pm; ☎01780/755611).

Stamford has several charming **hotels**, the most celebrated of which is the delightful *George Hotel*, High Street St Martin's (☎01780/755171, *www.stamford.co.uk/george*; ⑦), an old and cleverly remodelled coaching inn with flagstone floors and antique furnishings, where the most appealing rooms overlook the cobbled courtyard. Just along the street is the attractive *Garden House Hotel* (☎01780/763359, *www.stamford.co.uk/gardenh*; ⑤), which occupies a tastefully modernized eighteenth-century building with twenty smart bedrooms. Stamford also possesses lots of first-rate **B&Bs**. As ever, the tourist office has the full list, but one especially good place is *Martins*, 20 High St St Martin's (☎01780/752106, *www.stamford.co.uk/bb/martins.htm*; ③), a Georgian house whose three spacious guestrooms are immaculately maintained and tastefully decorated. Breakfasts are delicious, guests have access to the walled garden and dinner is served by prior request. Another less expensive but highly recommendable option is *Mrs Swithinbank's B&B*, 16 St George's Square (☎01780/482099, *www.stamford.co.uk/bb/16stgeor.htm*; ①), in a pleasant Victorian house overlooking St George's church and with a walled garden and a tiled and beamed main hall.

For **food**, it has to be the *George Hotel* – either in the formal and expensive restaurant, where the emphasis is on British ingredients served in imaginative ways, or in the moderately priced and informal Garden Lounge. There's delicious and inexpensive bar food too, served in the York Bar at lunchtimes.

Grantham and around

GRANTHAM, midway between Stamford and Lincoln, was once a major staging point on the Great North Road from London, but today its lengthy high street is no more than a provincial thoroughfare flanked by an unappetizing combination of modern offices and Victorian red brick. The town's more successful days are recalled by two ancient inns, the stone-fronted *Angel and Royal*, founded by the Knights Templar in the twelfth century, and the *George*, where Charles Dickens's Nicholas Nickleby stopped on his way to Dotheboys Hall – and now guzzled up into a shopping centre. Grantham's present pride and joy is the church of **St Wulfram** (Mon–Sat 10.30am–3.30pm, Sun 7.30am–noon & 6–8pm; free), set within its own close on Swinegate, near – and to the left of – the Guildhall, standing halfway along the main drag.

St Wulfram's most obvious feature is its 282-foot central spire, a fourteenth-century construction whose angular lines are emphasized by pointed blind arcading, slim window openings and the narrowest of columns. Inside, highlights are the sinuous window tracery in and around the south chancel aisle, and the late sixteenth-century, 150-volume **chained library** (Mon 10am–noon & 2–4pm, Thurs & Fri 2–4pm) above the south porch. The high altar is of interest too, not for itself, but because its position prompted a bitter wrangle in 1627. Believing the altar should be more conspicuous, the High Church party turned it round to look down the nave, but the Puritans objected and came to move it back again. The resulting brawl, something of a cause célèbre, hardened attitudes in the run-up to the Civil War.

Beside the church is King's private school, whose original sixteenth-century classroom, with its mullioned windows and high-pitched stone roof, fronts Church Street. This was where **Isaac Newton** received his initial education in the 1650s. There's a statue of the great physicist and mathematician outside the Guildhall and a room of mementoes, including a plaster-cast death mask, in the adjacent **museum** (Mon–Sat 10am–5pm; free), which also has a display on **Margaret Thatcher**, who was born in Grantham in 1925. In a moment of gay abandon, Mrs Thatcher gave several of her dresses to the museum, though her absurdist handbags and threatening hairstyle were always more memorable. Her childhood home is up along the main street at 2 North St: originally a grocer's store, it's been turned into a chiropractic clinic.

Grantham **train station** is ten minutes' walk from the Guildhall: follow Station Road to the four-way junction and turn right along Wharf Road, where you'll also find the **bus station**. Next door to the Guildhall is the **tourist office** (Mon–Sat 9.30am–5pm; ☎01476/406166). Grantham's smartest **hotel** is the *Angel and Royal*, down the road on the High Street (☎01476/565816; ④), and another establishment claiming to be England's oldest inn; more certain is that King John held court here, and that Richard III signed the Duke of Buckingham's death warrant in one of its rooms. The handiest **B&B** is the *Archway House*, by St Wulfram's at 15 Swinegate (☎01476/561807; ③), in an attractive old house with an oak-panelled dining room. The *Beehive Inn*, close by on Castlegate, serves tasty **bar snacks**; it also boasts its own hive of South African bees, fixed to the tree outside the pub.

Belton House

The honey-coloured limestone facade of **Belton House** (April–Oct Wed–Sun 1–5pm; gardens & park 11am–5.30pm; combined ticket £5.20; NT), three miles northeast of Grantham beside the A607, is Restoration design at its finest, its delicate symmetry enhanced by formal gardens and by a later landscaped park. Belton was built in the 1680s for a local family of lawyer-landowners, the Brownlows, whose subsequent climb up the aristocratic ladder prompted them to remodel the interior of their home in the sumptuous Neoclassical style of the late eighteenth century. Entry is through the Marble Hall, where a sequence of family portraits, including three by Reynolds, are framed by the intricate limewood carvings that remain Belton's most distinctive feature. Several of them, both here and in the **saloon**, are thought to be the work of **Grinling Gibbons**, the great Rotterdam-born wood carver and sculptor. Belton is also noted for its pastel-shaded, Adam-style plasterwork ceilings and, on display in the Chapel Drawing Room, a pair of splendid tapestries, which, despite their Indian and Japanese themes, were made in John Vanderbank's workshop in Soho, London. In the park is one of the region's best adventure playgrounds, complete with a railway ride through the woods.

It's easy to reach Belton by **bus** from Grantham: service #601 makes the ten-minute trip roughly every hour from Monday to Saturday.

Woolsthorpe Manor

The birthplace and family home of Sir Isaac Newton, **Woolsthorpe Manor** (April–Oct Wed–Sun 1–5.30pm; £2.70; NT) lies seven miles south of Grantham, just off the A1 in the hamlet of **WOOLSTHORPE-BY-COLSTERWORTH**. The house is a pleasantly modest affair of mullioned windows and heavy-beamed ceilings and was where Newton (1642–1727) sat out the plague years of 1665–7 working on all manner of scientific theories. The apple orchard in front of the house contains a descendant of the illustrious tree whose apple dropped on Newton's head to such great, gravitational effect.

travel details

Trains

Birmingham New Street to: Birmingham International (2–4 hourly; 15min); Coventry (2–4 hourly; 30min); Derby (hourly; 45min); Great Malvern (2 hourly; 1hr); Hereford (10 daily; 1hr 50min); Leicester (hourly; 50min); Lichfield (4 hourly; 45min); London (2 hourly; 1hr 40min); Shrewsbury (hourly; 1hr 20min); Stoke-on-Trent (hourly; 1hr); Worcester (hourly; 1hr).

Birmingham Snow Hill to: Stratford-upon-Avon (Mon–Sat hourly; 50min); Warwick (Mon–Sat hourly; 40min).

Derby to: Birmingham (3 hourly; 45min); Leicester (hourly; 30min); London (hourly; 1hr 50min); Nottingham (3 hourly; 40min).

Grantham to: Derby (hourly; 1hr); Lincoln (every 30min; 45min); London (hourly; 1hr 15min); Nottingham (every 30min; 35min); Skegness (hourly; 1hr 20min).

Hereford to: Birmingham (hourly; 1hr 40min); Great Malvern (hourly; 30min); London (5 daily; 2hr 45min); Ludlow (hourly; 30min); Shrewsbury (hourly; 1hr); Worcester (1–2 hourly; 40min).

Leicester to: Birmingham (2 hourly; 1hr); Coventry (hourly; 45min); Derby (hourly; 40min); Lincoln (hourly; 1hr 40min); London (2 hourly; 1hr 30min); Melton Mowbray (hourly; 15min); Nottingham (2 hourly; 20min); Oakham (hourly; 30min); Stamford (hourly; 50min).

Lincoln to: Birmingham (hourly; 3hr); Boston (hourly; 1hr); Cambridge (hourly; 1hr); Grantham (every 30min; 45min); Leicester (hourly; 1hr 30min); London (hourly; 2hr 15min); Newark (hourly; 30min); Nottingham (hourly; 45min); Peterborough (hourly; 1hr 20min); Skegness (hourly; 1hr 40min).

Northampton to: Birmingham (2 hourly; 1hr); Coventry (hourly; 40min); London Euston (2 hourly; 1hr 10min–1hr 40min).

Nottingham to: Leicester (2 hourly; 30min); Lincoln (hourly; 1hr 15min); London (hourly; 1hr 50min); Newark (hourly; 30min).

Shrewsbury to: Birmingham (2–4 hourly; 1hr 10min); Church Stretton (2 hourly; 15min); Craven Arms (hourly; 25min); Hereford (2–3 hourly; 1hr); Ludlow (hourly; 30min).

Stamford to: Cambridge (hourly; 1hr 20min); Leicester (hourly; 40min); Oakham (hourly; 10min); Peterborough (hourly; 15min).

Stoke-on-Trent to: Birmingham (hourly; 1hr).

Stratford-upon-Avon to: Birmingham (Mon–Sat hourly; 1hr); Oxford (4 daily; 1hr 10min); Warwick (Mon–Sat 8 daily; 30min).

Worcester to: Birmingham (2 hourly; 40min–1hr); Hereford (13 daily; 40min).

Buses

Birmingham to: Derby (5 daily; 1hr); Dudley (2 hourly; 50min); Hereford (Mon–Sat 6 daily; 3hr); Ironbridge (5 daily; 1hr); Leicester (5 daily; 1hr); Lichfield (hourly Mon–Sat; 1hr); London (hourly; 2hr 30min); Ludlow (Mon–Sat hourly; 2hr); Nottingham (5 daily; 1hr 20min); Shrewsbury (5 daily; 1hr 45min); Stoke-on-Trent (10 daily; 1hr); Stratford-upon-Avon (hourly; 1hr); Worcester (2 hourly; 1hr 30min).

Boston to: Skegness (hourly; 45min–1hr).

Bridgnorth to: Ironbridge (Mon–Sat 6 daily; 35min); Kidderminster (Mon–Sat 8 daily; 45min); Ludlow (Mon–Fri 2 daily; 1hr 15min); Much Wenlock (Mon–Sat 8 daily; 20min); Shrewsbury (Mon–Sat 6–8 daily; 1hr); Wolverhampton (hourly; 50min).

Coventry to: Kenilworth (Mon–Sat hourly; 30min); Stratford-upon-Avon (Mon–Sat hourly; 1hr 15min); Oxford (3 daily; 1hr 30min); Warwick (Mon–Sat hourly; 40min).

Derby to: Ashbourne (5 daily; 30min); Birmingham (5 daily; 1hr); Leek (5 daily; 1hr); Leicester (7 daily; 1hr); Lichfield (2 daily; 40min).

Grantham to: Lincoln (hourly; 1hr); Nottingham (2 daily; 45min–1hr 10min); Stamford (3 daily Mon–Sat; 30min).

Hereford to: Birmingham (2 daily; 2hr); Great Malvern (1 daily; 40min); Worcester (Mon–Sat 8 daily; 1hr–1hr 30min).

Leicester to: Ashby-de-la-Zouch (hourly; 1hr); Birmingham (6 daily; 1hr); Bristol (5 daily; 4hr); Melton Mowbray (hourly; 50min); Northampton (6 daily; 1hr 20min); Nottingham (9 daily; 45min); Oxford (2 daily; 2hr 20min).

Lincoln to: Boston (3 weekly; 1hr 30min); Grantham (hourly; 1hr); Peterborough (1 daily; 2hr); Skegness (Mon–Sat 5 daily, Sun 1 daily; 1hr 45min); Stamford (1 daily; 1hr 30min).

Ludlow to: Birmingham (Mon–Sat hourly; 2hr); Bishop's Castle (Mon–Sat 3 daily; 1hr); Bridgnorth (Mon–Fri 1 daily; 1hr 15min); Church Stretton (Mon–Sat 6 daily; 30min); Hereford (Mon–Sat 7 daily; 1hr); Shrewsbury (Mon–Sat 5 daily; 1hr 20min).

Northampton to: Birmingham (2 daily; 1hr 30min); Coventry (2 daily; 1hr); Leicester (10 daily; 45min–1hr); Lincoln, via Birmingham (1 daily; 5hr); Nottingham (1 daily; 2hr 30min).

Nottingham to: Leicester (hourly; 45min); Newark (hourly; 1hr 20min); Northampton (1 daily; 2hr 30min).

Shrewsbury to: Birmingham (3–4 daily; 1hr 50min); Bishop's Castle (Mon–Sat 3 daily; 1hr 45min); Bridgnorth (Mon–Sat 6–8 daily; 1hr); Church Stretton (Mon–Sat 5–8 daily; 45min); Ironbridge (6 daily; 45min); Ludlow (Mon–Sat 5 daily; 1hr 20min); Much Wenlock (Mon–Sat 6 daily; 40min); Stoke-on-Trent (Mon–Sat 6 daily; 1hr 50min).

Stamford to: Nottingham (1 daily; 1hr 15min).

Stoke-on-Trent (Hanley) to: Alton Towers (1 daily; 1hr); Birmingham (9 daily; 1hr); Buxton (3 daily; 1hr); Coventry (7 daily; 2hr 20min); Shrewsbury (6 daily; 1hr 50min); Stratford-upon-Avon (2 daily; 2hr 30min).

Stratford-upon-Avon to: Birmingham (hourly; 1hr); Blenheim Palace (3 daily; 1hr 10min); Coventry (Mon–Sat hourly, 5 on Sun; 1hr 15min); Kenilworth (hourly; 1hr); Oxford (3 daily; 1hr 30min); Warwick (hourly; 20min); Worcester (3 daily; 45min).

Worcester to: Birmingham (2 hourly; 1hr–1hr 30min); Great Malvern (every 30min; 30min); Hereford (Mon–Sat 8 daily; 1hr 30min); Tewkesbury (Mon–Sat 6 daily, Sun 2 daily; 1hr 10min).

CHAPTER EIGHT

THE NORTHWEST

Within the **northwest** of England lie some of the ugliest and some of the most beautiful parts of the country. The least attractive zones of this region are to be found in the inchoate sprawl connecting the country's third and sixth largest conurbations, Manchester and Liverpool, but even here the picture isn't unrelievedly bleak, as the cities themselves have an ingratiating appeal. **Manchester** surprises many who don't expect to see beyond its dour, industrial heritage. Where once only a handful of Victorian Gothic buildings lent any grace to the cityscape Manchester today is rapidly building on its past, with an eye firmly on the 2002 Commonwealth Games, which it is hosting, and a thriving café and club scene, which places it at the leading edge of the country's youth culture. **Liverpool**, set on the Mersey estuary, is less appealing at first glance, though Georgian town houses, its twin cathedrals and a burgeoning café scene soon change perceptions. At the redundant docks that once made the city's fortune, many of the old warehouses have been redeveloped as part of the Albert Dock scheme, housing a fine swathe of museums.

To the south, **Cheshire** boasts the county town of **Chester**, with its complete circuit of town walls and partly Tudor centre. This is as alluring as any of the country's northern towns, capturing the essence of what has always been one of England's wealthiest rural counties. **Lancashire**, which historically lay directly to the north of Cheshire, reached industrial prominence in the last century primarily due to the cotton-mill towns around Manchester and to the thriving port of Liverpool. However, today, neither of those cities is part of the county, having been excised when England's first substantial county boundary changes since the Domesday Book were enacted in 1974. The urban counties of Merseyside and Greater Manchester chopped off the southern section of Lancashire while Cumbria grabbed a substantial northern chunk leaving Lancashire little more than half its former size. Still, it retains the charming towns and villages of the **Ribble Valley** while along the coast to the north of the major cities stretches a line of **resorts** – from Southport to Morecambe – which once formed the mainstay of the northern British holiday trade. Only **Blackpool** is worth visiting for its own sake, a rip-roaring resort which has stayed at the top of its game by supplying undemanding entertainment with more panache than its neighbours. For anything more culturally invigorating you'll have to continue north to the historically important city of **Lancaster**, with its Tudor castle. Finally,

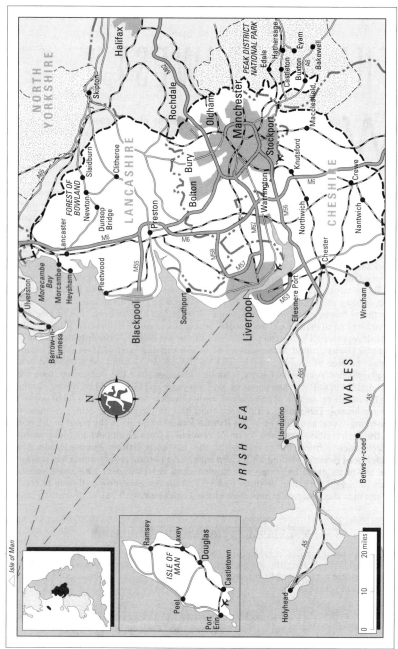

© Crown copyright

the semi-autonomous **Isle of Man**, 25 miles off the coast and served by ferries from Liverpool and Heysham (or short flights from Liverpool), provides a terrain almost as rewarding as that of the Lake District but without the seasonal overcrowding.

Manchester

Whether you approach from the north or south, your first glimpse of **MANCHES-TER** takes in the monuments to a history of prosperity, decline and revival that is still unfolding. Stoic tower blocks and empty shells of mills and factories reach for the skyline beside rows of back-to-back houses whose slate roofs and cobbled back alleys glisten in the seemingly ever-present rain. All this reinforces traditional images of the struggling post-industrial city, but Manchester is being treated to an urban facelift unequalled in Britain. In part this was prompted by the city's selection as the venue for the **Commonwealth Games** in the year 2002, following a succession of failed bids to host the Olympics. But the main engine of change was the devastating IRA bomb, which exploded in June 1996 and wiped out much of the city's commercial infrastructure. The redesign and rebuilding of the city centre was quick and impressive, and millennium projects have given further impetus to Manchester's contemporary renaissance. The city today boasts a thriving **social and cultural scene** that few, if any, English cities can rivals: its cutting-edge sports facilities, concert halls, theatres, clubs and café society are boosted by England's largest student population and a pioneering Gay Village.

Manchester's rapid growth was the equal of any flowering of the Industrial Revolution – from little more than a village in 1750 to the world's major cotton-milling centre in only a hundred years. The spectacular rise of **Cottonopolis**, as it became known, came from the production of competitively priced imitations of expensive Indian calicoes, using machines evolved from Arkwright's first steam-powered cotton mill, which opened in 1783. The rapid industrialization of the area brought prosperity for a few but a life of misery for the majority. Exploitation had worsened still further by the time the 23-year-old Friedrich Engels came here in 1842 to work in his father's cotton plant, and the suffering he witnessed – recorded in his *Condition of the Working Class in England* – was a seminal influence on his later collaboration with Karl Marx, the *Communist Manifesto*.

Waterways and railway viaducts form the matrix into which the city's principal buildings have been bedded – as early as 1772 the Duke of Bridgewater had a canal cut to connect the city to the coal mines at Worsley, and the railway to Liverpool, opened in 1830, was the world's first passenger rail line. The **Manchester Ship Canal**, constructed to entice ocean-going vessels into Manchester, was completed in 1894, and played a crucial part in reviving Manchester's competitiveness. A century later, with the docks, mills and canals no longer in industrial use, it's the splendid behemoths of Victorian Gothic that echo the city's past. Meanwhile, entire new city-centre districts are taking shape as once-blighted areas are reclaimed for retail and residential use.

Arrival, information and city transport

Manchester Airport, ten miles south of the city, is an increasingly popular point of entry into Britain. Trains to Piccadilly (every 15min 5.15am–10.15pm, reduced service through the night; 25min) cost £2.25, £2.65 before 9.30am. It's slightly cheaper (£2.15) – though a journey of around 45 minutes – to take one of the buses from the airport to Piccadilly Gardens or Chorlton Street (every 15–30min, 6am–10.45pm). A taxi from the airport to the centre costs around £12.

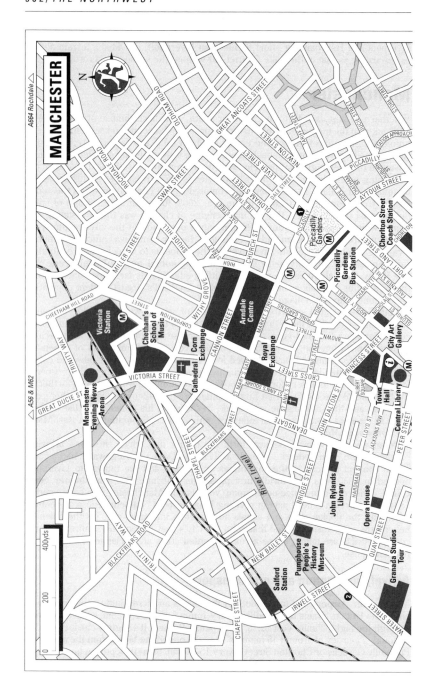

© Crown copyright

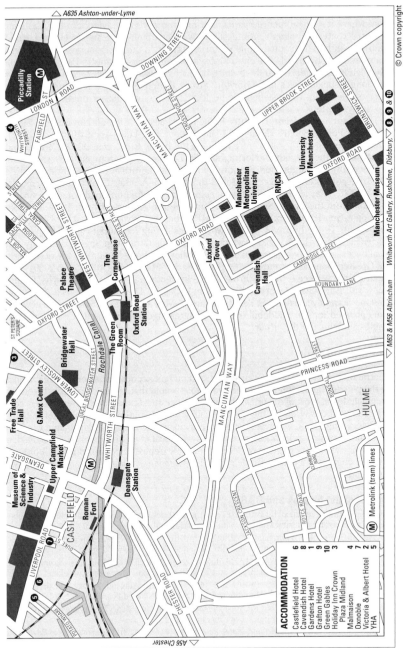

△ A635 Ashton-under-Lyme

DOWNING STREET

Piccadilly Station Ⓜ

LONDON ROAD

LONDON ST

FAIRFIELD STREET

WHITWORTH STREET

❹

MANCUNIAN WAY

UPPER BROOK STREET

BRUNSWICK STREET

▷ 8 9 & 10

University of Manchester

OXFORD ROAD

Manchester Museum

▷ Whitworth Art Gallery, Rusholme, Didsbury,

CANAL STREET

SACKVILLE STREET

BLOOM ST

MAJOR ST

WEST WHITWORTH STREET

CHARLES STREET

OXFORD ROAD

Manchester Metropolitan University

RNCM

The Cornerhouse

Palace Theatre

Loxford Tower

Cavendish Hall

CAMBRIDGE STREET

BOUNDARY LANE

▷ M63 & M56 Altrincham

OXFORD STREET

ST PETERS SQUARE

❸

LOWER MOSLEY STREET

Bridgewater Hall

The Green Room

Oxford Road Station

Rochdale Canal

GREAT BRIDGEWATER STREET

MANCUNIAN WAY

PRINCESS ROAD

BONSALL STREET

Free Trade Hall

G.Mex Centre

WHITWORTH STREET

HULME

DEANSGATE

Upper Campfield Market

Ⓜ

Deansgate Station

JACKSON CRESCENT

Museum of Science & Industry

CASTLEFIELD

Roman Fort

❼

❻

LIVERPOOL ROAD

DUKE ST

ROYCE ROAD

CHORLTON ROAD

❺

POTATO WHARF

CHESTER ROAD

△ A56 Chester

Ⓜ Metrolink (tram) lines

ACCOMMODATION

Castlefield Hotel	6
Cavendish Hotel	8
Gardens Hotel	1
Grafton Hotel	9
Green Gables	10
Holiday Inn Crown Plaza Midland	3
Malmaison	4
Oxnoble	7
Victoria & Albert Hotel	2
YHA	5

© Crown copyright

Mainline trains pull into **Piccadilly Station**, facing London Road, on the east side, from where it's a few hundred yards west into the city's core, via Piccadilly Gardens. Regional routes to points south, east and west call both here and at **Oxford Road Station**, south of the centre, while **Victoria Station**, in the north, serves the northern hinterland and Bradford. The city's Metrolink tram service connects Piccadilly station (the platform is underneath the train station) to Victoria and G-Mex. National Express and long-distance buses use **Chorlton Street Coach Station**, a few hundred yards west of Piccadilly train station. Some local and regional buses might instead use Piccadilly Gardens.

The **Manchester Visitor Centre** in the town hall extension on Lloyd Street, facing central St Peter's Square (Mon–Sat 10am–5.30pm, Sun 11am–4pm; ☎0161/234 3157), offers a free map of the city centre and sells the handy *City Guide* (£1.50). To find out **what's on** in the city, buy the fortnightly *City Life* magazine, from any newsstand.

Piccadilly Gardens Bus Station is the hub of the urban bus network, though a new transport interchange at **Shudehill** (north of the Arndale Centre; due for completion by 2001) may affect the location of some routes. **Information** about all services is available from the Travel Shop, on the southern side of Piccadilly Gardens (Mon–Sat 7am–6pm, Sun 10am–6pm); or call the GMPTE bus enquiry line (☎0161/228 7811 daily 8am–8pm). The only **travel passes** worth considering for tourists are the seven-day Stagecoach Mega-Rider (£6.50), which gives unlimited travel on Stagecoach's city and local buses, and the Wayfarer (£6.60), which allows 24 hours' unlimited travel throughout Greater Manchester and into the Peak District. **Metrolink** (☎0161/205 2000) – the electric tram service – whisks through the city centre and out to the suburbs, linking Bury with Altrincham (every 6–15min 6am–11.30pm). There are stations at Piccadilly Station, Piccadilly Gardens, St Peter's Square, G-Mex and Victoria Station; and new stations planned for the Shudehill transport interchange, the Eastlands Commonwealth Games stadium and the airport.

Accommodation

Central Manchester is not overburdened with budget **accommodation**, though almost all the plusher hotels offer weekend reductions – note that, during the week, breakfast isn't included at most of the pricier hotels. Cheaper guest-house accommodation is concentrated some way out of the centre, mainly on the southern routes out of the city. B&B accommodation in private houses is easy to arrange, too, though again it won't be particularly central, which makes the city's well-located youth hostel, in Castlefield, a first choice for most budget travellers. The Visitor Centre's **accommodation booking service** charges a fee, though their free *Accommodation Guide* lists most of the city's possibilities.

Hotels, guest houses and B&Bs

Castlefield Hotel, Liverpool Rd (☎0161/832 7073). Red-brick, warehouse-style development, opposite the Science and Industry Museum, with leisure club and pool. Midweek ⑤, ③ at weekends.

Cavendish Hotel, 402 Wilbraham Rd, Chorlton (☎0161/881 1911). Edwardian guest house three miles south of the centre. Decent rooms with TV and tea- and coffee-making facilities. ②.

Gardens Hotel, 55 Piccadilly (☎0161/236 5155). Right on Piccadilly Gardens, this accommodating three-star place has an en-suite bathroom and TV with each room. Midweek ⑤, weekend ③.

Grafton Hotel, 56–58 Grafton St (☎0161/273 3092). Six knocked-through terrace houses, south of the university. En-suite rooms fall into the next category up. No credit cards. ①.

Green Gables, 152 Barlow Moor Rd, West Didsbury (☎0161/445 5365). Traditional guest house in a residential area, with regular bus service into town. ①.

Holiday Inn Crowne Plaza Midland Hotel, Peter St (☎0161/236 3333). The apotheosis of Edwardian style, with impressive public rooms and hefty weekend reductions. Midweek ⑧, ⑦ at weekends.

Malmaison, Piccadilly (☎0161/278 1000, *manchester@malmaison.com*). An ornate Edwardian facade given sleek interior lines and contemporary design from the Malmaison group. Midweek ⑥, ⑤ at weekends.

The Oxnoble, 71 Liverpool Rd (☎0161/839 7740). Rooms above a popular pub opposite the Science and Industry Museum. ②.

Victoria & Albert Hotel, Water St, Castlefield (☎0161/832 1188). Superb restoration job for a canalside warehouse, with exposed beams, pipes and brickwork part of the interior fabric. Midweek ⑦, ⑥ at weekends.

Hostels and university accommodation

International Backpackers Hostel, 41–43 Greatstone Rd, Stretford; 64 Cromwell Rd, Stretford (☎0161/872 3499 or 865 9296, mobile ☎0411/556157, *manchester.backpacker@good.co.uk*). Three miles out of the centre, on the Metrolink line (to Old Trafford stop). No credit cards.

Manchester YHA, Potato Wharf, Castlefield (☎0161/839 9960, *manchester@yha.org.uk*). Excellent hostel, whose en-suite rooms sleep one to four people.

University accommodation, University of Manchester/UMIST Central Accommodation Office (Mon–Fri 9.30am–5pm; ☎0161/275 2888). Call for vacancies at the various university hostels (summer vacations only).

The City

If Manchester can be said to have a centre, it's **St Peter's Square** and the cluster of buildings focused on it. South of here, the huge vault of the former Central Station now functions as the **G-Mex** exhibition centre, with the Hallé orchestra's home, the Bridgewater Hall, opposite. There's been a general spruce-up spreading west to the **Castlefield** district, site of the city's two most popular tourist attractions – the **Museum of Science and Industry** and **Granada Studio Tours.** Many of the city's remaining attractions, museums and galleries, and the majority of eating and drinking spots, are scattered over a broad expanse to the north along the central spine of **Deansgate** and east towards **Piccadilly.** Other diversions string out along the main southern artery **Oxford Road,** strictly Oxford Street until a quarter of a mile out but always referred to by the former name.

The Town Hall and around

One of Manchester's boldest Victorian neo-Gothic buildings, Alfred Waterhouse's **Town Hall** (Mon–Fri 9am–5pm; free), finished in 1877, divides the plain expanse of St Peter's Square from the more harmonious Albert Square to the north. Enter into the echoing stone-vaulted interior and climb one of the grand staircases to the **Great Hall,** with its stained glass windows, double hammer-beam roof and paintings by Ford Madox-Brown depicting decisive moments from Manchester's past. **Guided tours** of the building set off from Albert Square (Easter–Sept Sat & every other Wed 2pm; Oct–Dec Sat 2pm; times vary, call ☎0161/274 3157 to check; £3).

On the south side of the Town Hall, the circular **Central Library** (Mon–Thurs 10am–8pm, Fri & Sat 10am–5pm) faces St Peter's Square – built in 1934 as the largest municipal library in the world. Over on Peter Street, the Edwardian interior of the **Midland Hotel** – now the *Holiday Inn Crowne Plaza Midland* – has worn well. Its earlier visitors ventured out for an evening's entertainment at the **Free Trade Hall** further up Peter Street, original home of the city's own Hallé Orchestra. The Italianate facade will be retained as part of any future development on the site.

South of St Peter's Square, Lower Mosley Street runs past the **G-Mex Centre** (Greater Manchester Exhibition and Events Centre), opposite which rises the **Bridgewater Hall** at the junction of Bridgewater Street. This, one of Britain's finest purpose-built concert halls – venue for concerts by the Hallé – is, uniquely, balanced on shock-absorbing springs to guarantee clarity of sound. The other way up Mosley Street, north of St Peter's Square, rises Charles Barry's porticoed **City Art Gallery**, where the array of high Victorian art includes the country's finest public collection of works by the Pre-Raphaelite Brotherhood. Unfortunately, the gallery is closed for major renovations until 2001.

Castlefield

Castlefield, Britain's first "urban heritage park", lies fifteen minutes' walk southwest of the town hall. Since the early 1980s, an influx of money allied to a fair amount of speculative vision has resulted in a cobbled canalside, cleaned-up water, outdoor events arena and new bars. Find out about its various festivals, the September carnival, bank-holiday street markets, and canal cruises at the **Castlefield Visitor Centre** at 101 Liverpool Rd (Mon–Fri 10am–4pm, Sat & Sun noon–4pm; free; ☎0161/834 4026).

The castle-in-the-field itself is a **Roman fort** whose reconstructed scant remains can be seen a few hundred yards from the considerably more diverting **Museum of Science and Industry** (daily 10am–5pm; last admission 4pm; £5), mixing technological displays and special blockbuster exhibitions with trenchant analysis of the social impact of industrialization. Pride of place goes to a working replica of Robert Stephenson's *Planet* – for which his father George's *Rocket* was the prototype. Built in 1830, the *Planet* reliably attained a scorching 30mph but had no brakes; the museum's version does, and uses them at weekends (Easter–Nov Sat & Sun noon–4pm; Dec–Easter Sun only), dropping passengers a quarter-mile away at the **world's oldest passenger railway station**. A reconstructed Victorian sewer below the station illustrates the problems of sanitation in the 1870s, while the improvements brought about by domestic electrification are brought home in a suite of period rooms. There's also a hands-on science centre, where the kids hog all the best experiments, while the museum's comprehensive selection of carding machines, bobbin threaders and cotton looms crash into action at weekends in the Textile Gallery.

Good though the Museum of Science and Industry is, as a tourist attraction it can't compete with the nearby **Granada Studios Tour** around the corner on Water Street (Easter–Sept daily 9.45am–6pm; Oct–Easter Mon–Fri 9.45am–4.30pm, Sat & Sun 9.45am–5.30pm; last admission 2hr before closing; £14.99). Each year 700,000 people file through the studio doors to undergo various different "experiences", ranging from motion simulator rides to special effects shows and a smoothly orchestrated backstage tour. The indoor TV show sets – Sherlock Holmes' Baker Street, the House of Commons, *Blind Date* – provide more entertainment, but it's the allure of Britain's longest-running soap opera that keeps the turnstiles moving, even though most of the footage for *Coronation Street* is now shot elsewhere.

Along and off Deansgate

Central **Deansgate** cuts through the city from the canal to the cathedral, its architectural reference points ranging from Victorian industrialism to Sixties functionalism. Just south of Bridge Street is the beautifully detailed **John Rylands Library** (Mon–Fri 10am–5.30pm, Sat 10am–1pm; free; guided tours Wed noon; £1), the city's supreme example of Victorian Gothic. Now part of Manchester University, it was founded in 1890 by Enriqueta Ryland to house the theological works collected by her late husband. Temporary exhibitions highlight the library's assets, though you should venture inside whatever's showing to see the superb interior. From the library, continue up Deansgate and left onto Bridge Street to reach the **Pumphouse People's History Museum** (Tues–Sun 11am–4.30pm; £1, free on Fri), an exhibition recording the lives and protests of England's working class over the last two hundred years. Posters, press reports, charters and anti-government cartoons show the struggles of suffragettes, reformers and radicals, fighting for equal representation, votes and fair pay.

St Ann's Square, tucked away off the eastern side of Deansgate, was severely damaged by the IRA bomb but has emerged to provide an anchor for the remarkable transformation taking place between here and the cathedral to the north. The square's crowning glory is the restored **Royal Exchange**, which houses the famous **Royal Exchange Theatre**, the country's largest theatre-in-the-round, whose steel-and-glass cat's cradle sits plonked under the building's immense glass-domed roof. The pedestrianized area around St Ann's Square and **King Street** to the south provides Manchester's best shopping, boasting most of the popular designer and high street outlets. To the north, the **Arndale Centre** – a concrete horror of which the Sixties could be truly proud – is also slowly emerging a better place.

Deansgate ends with the Perpendicular **Cathedral** (daily 7.30am–6pm), the third church on this site since its foundation in the ninth century. A fragment of stone by the choir and a fourteenth-century arch by the tower are all that remain of the earlier structures, and in truth it's been hacked about too much to have any real coherence – the famed widest nave in England (114ft, as opposed to York Minster's 106ft) is entirely a result of rich families adding side chapels to the fifteenth-century church, which were later opened out to provide space for Manchester's burgeoning nineteenth-century population of worshippers.

Chinatown, the Northern Quarter and the Gay Village

The grid of streets east of the Town Hall, between Princess and Charlotte streets, marks the boundaries of Britain's largest **Chinatown**. North of here, across **Piccadilly Gardens**, the still shabby but improving Oldham Street has been adopted by "alternative" entrepreneurs who have dubbed it the **"Northern Quarter"** and helped populate the area with trendy clothes and shoe boutiques, record shops and cafés – notably in the five floors of Affleck's Palace at the junction with Church Street and in the Coliseum on Church Street itself. There are rather more lasting skills and crafts on display in the excellent **Manchester Craft Centre**, 17 Oak St (Mon–Sat 10am–5.30pm; free) – a great place to pick up ceramics, fabrics, earthenware, jewellery and decorative art. To the southeast, the roads off Portland Street lead down to

---

THE REDEVELOPMENT OF MANCHESTER

On 15 June 1996 the IRA exploded a 3300lb bomb in the centre of Manchester causing the largest explosion on the mainland since the war: no one was killed, though over two hundred people were injured and seven hundred businesses were put out of action, most in the devastated area around the Arndale Centre and the Royal Exchange. Rather than simply patch up the buildings, the planning authorities embarked on an ambitious £500,000,000 **rebuilding scheme**.

At its heart is a plan to create a pedestrian boulevard ("New Cathedral Street") from the cathedral to St Ann's Church, which will incorporate a new **Exchange Square**, a restored Arndale Centre, and relocated historic buildings (including the *Old Wellington Inn* and *Sinclair's Oyster Bar*) within its parameters. The Sixties eyesore that was the **Arndale Centre** is being modernized and clad in glass; while the largest Marks & Spencer's store in the world sports a gigantic glazed wall down one side of Exchange Square. The **Corn Exchange** across from the cathedral has been refurbished completely, retaining its facade and glass dome, with its interior transformed into a high-tech leisure and retail centre. A second wave of building through to 2001 intends to refashion the area around the cathedral as a **Millennium Quarter**. A new traffic-free **City Park** will feature **Urbis** at its core – a visitor centre with cafés, shops, a "Wonderwall" of city information, and various new virtual and technological attractions. The former Mirror Building nearby is being turned into the futuristic **Printworks Entertainment Centre**, with an IMAX screen, cinema megaplex and various retail units and themed restaurants.

the Rochdale Canal, heart of Manchester's thriving **Gay Village**. The pink pound has transformed this part of the city, and canalside cafés, clubs, bars and businesses have turned a formerly abandoned warehouse district into something with the verve of San Francisco.

Along Oxford Road

From St Peter's Square, **Oxford Road** – initially Oxford Street – stretches through a mile of faculty buildings to Rusholme (by which time it's become **Wilmslow Road**) and the leafy suburbs beyond. Oxford Road Station lurks behind the **Cornerhouse,** the dynamo of the Manchester arts scene, with its cinema and three floors of gallery space (Tues–Sat 11am–6pm, Sun 2–6pm; free) devoted to contemporary and local artists' work. A Gothic Revival building, half a mile south along Oxford Road, houses the **Manchester Museum** (Mon–Sat 10am–5pm; free), one of the city's great unsung treats, which makes a fine display of its superb Egyptian exhibits. The museum is undergoing long-term refurbishment until 2001, which means certain galleries may be closed from time to time. But when it's complete, there will be new geology and ethnology galleries, an interactive "Science for Life" exhibit and Discovery Centre.

Another half-mile away is the city's modern-art collection, housed in the red-brick **Whitworth Gallery** (Mon–Sat 10am–5pm, Sun 2–5pm; free). The gallery forms two distinct halves, with its pre-1880 historic collection incorporating watercolours by Turner, Constable, Cox and Blake. The modern collection concentrates on post-1880 British staples, with Moore, Frink and Hepworth setting off contributions from lesser-known artists. With Manchester's cotton connections it is perhaps not surprising that the gallery also displays the country's widest range of textiles outside London's Victoria and Albert Museum.

Out of the centre

The Metrolink extension to **Salford Quays** provides easy access to one of the city's first urban development projects, which transformed the run-down quays on the western edge of the city centre into a waterfront residential and leisure complex. The Quays will host the country's New Imperial War Museum, though that isn't expected to open until 2002. For now, the major attraction is the spectacular **Lowry Centre** (☎0161/995 2000) which opens for business in 2000. No artist is more closely linked with an English city than Lowry is with Manchester, and the centre will house the most extensive Lowry exhibition in the country, illustrating his early views on the desolation and sadness of Manchester's mill workers and his changing outlook in later life when he repeated earlier paintings changing the greys and sullen browns for lively reds and pinks.

Manchester United, arguably the most famous football team in the world, plays at **Old Trafford** – around three miles from the city centre. Only season ticket holders can ever attend games, but tours of Old Trafford and its museum are available (daily: April–Oct 9.30am–9pm; Nov–March 9.30am–5pm; museum & tour £7.50, museum only £4.50; advance booking essential, call ☎0161/877 4002). In recent years Manchester City has struggled in the lower leagues, and though their support remains high you're more likely to get in to see a game. The ground, **Maine Road** in Moss Side, hosts a rather humbler tour (call for times; £3; ☎0161/226 1782).

Eating, drinking and nightlife

The greatest central concentration of **restaurants** is around Portland Street, especially in and around **Chinatown**, while out at **Rusholme** (along the "curry mile" along Wilmslow Rd; buses #11, #40, #41, #42, #43, #44, #45, #47, #48 or #49) you'll find the best range of **curries** this side of the Pennines. For a more modish snack or drink, European-style **café-bars** are burgeoning around the centre of town, in the Northern Quarter, and especially in the Gay Village – as a general rule, they're open daily from 11am until around 11pm or midnight. Manchester has a full complement of great **pubs**, including two historic establishments damaged by the 1996 bomb – *Sinclair's Oyster Bar* and the *Old Wellington Inn* – both now relocated at a new site on New Cathedral Street.

For the best part of two decades, Manchester has been vying with London as Britain's capital of **youth culture**. Banks of fly posters advertise what's going on in the numerous **clubs** which, as elsewhere, frequently change names and styles on different nights of the week; the most enduring are listed below and you can expect to pay £3–15 cover depending on what's on. Manchester has an excellent **live music** scene in pubs and clubs, with tickets for local bands (and Oasis were a local band once) ranging from £2 to £5. Mega-star gigs take place either at the **G-Mex Centre**, Windmill St (☎0161/832 9000), the **Manchester Apollo**, Ardwick Green (☎0161/242 2560), or the **Manchester Evening News Arena** (formerly the NYNEX), Victoria Station, Hunts Bank (☎0161/930 8000). For the broadest coverage of Manchester's musical happenings, check the fortnightly *City Life* magazine, Friday's *Manchester Evening News* and the monthly freesheet *Alive*.

Café-bars

Barça, Arch 8 & 9, Catalan Square. Trendy Castlefield bar/restaurant tucked into the restored railway arches, boasting Mick Hucknall as part-owner and excellent, if pricey, Spanish food.

Cornerhouse, 70 Oxford St. The place to sip a cappuccino after viewing the galleries or catching a movie. Soups, dips, sandwiches and baked spuds until 8.30pm, an arty bar downstairs.

Cyberia, 12 Oxford St, opposite the Odeon cinema. The city's first dedicated Internet café, with PC access from £5 an hour. Also DJ nights, and a bar, which stays open until 2am Fri, Sat & Sun.

Dry 201, 28–30 Oldham St. The earliest of the designer café-bars on the scene, *Dry* is still as cool as they come, with tapas-like snacks and an Internet café.

Java Bar Espresso, Station Approach, Oxford Rd; Smithfield Building, 55 Oldham St. Coffee vendors, serving up terrific brews. Oxford Road branch closes 9pm, Oldham Street 7pm.

J.W. Johnson's, 78 Deansgate. The place to be seen with the city's rich kids, wannabes and the Man United youth team. Streetside tables and all-day food.

Manto, 46 Canal St. Gay Village stalwart whose chic crowd laps up the contemporary art exhibitions and fashion shows.

Metz, 3 Brazil St. Classy converted warehouse bar and restaurant, with deck seating, opposite *Manto* and with a similar gay/straight mix.

Night & Day, 26 Oldham St. Unpretentious café-bar with a late licence until 2am Fri & Sat, excellent food and live music – jazz, blues, Latin and funk – from local musicians. Closed Sun.

TeN, 10 Tariff St. More informal and cosy than the other café-bars, with sounds ranging from techno to Latin. Closes 2am, 10.30pm on Sun.

Velvet, 2 Canal St. The red-brick facade hides a stylish, laid-back basement cavern, with good food, outrageous staff, campy clientele, late-night sounds (Thurs–Sat until 1am) and Sunday jazz.

Restaurants

Abbaye, 44 Canal St (☎0161/236 5566). Belgian mussels-and-beer joint, with mussels served five ways and a stack of speciality beers. Moderate.

Brasserie St Pierre, 57–63 Princess St (☎0161/228 0231). Wonderful French restaurant with a traditional feel and welcoming service. Closed all Sun, & Mon eve. Expensive.

Café Istanbul, 79 Bridge St (☎0161/833 9942). Delicious Turkish dishes, including a great *meze* selection, and an extensive wine list. Closed Sun. Inexpensive to Moderate.

Darbar, 65–67 Wilmslow Rd, Rusholme (☎0161/224 4392). Award-winning Asian food; try the chef's special *nihari*, a slow-cooked lamb dish. Take your own booze. Inexpensive.

Dimitri's, 1 Campfield Arcade (☎0161/839 3319). Pick and mix from the Greek/Spanish/Italian menu (there's lots of choice for vegetarians) and grab an arcade table. Moderate.

Felix, 156 Burton Rd, West Didsbury (☎0161/445 1921). Mediterranean flavour in a hip south Manchester haunt. Good for Sunday brunch. Closed Mon lunch. Moderate.

Lime Tree, 8 Lapwing Lane, West Didsbury (☎0161/445 1217). Fashionable, Modern-British menu that chargrills as if its life depended on it. Closed all Sat & Mon lunch. Moderate to Expensive.

Little Yang Sing, 17 George St (☎0161/228 7722). Basement forerunner of its bigger Cantonese brother (see below), with lots of choice under £8. Good, especially for *dim sum*. Moderate.

The Market Restaurant, 104 High St (☎0161/834 3743). This is a very relaxing spot for dinner with a regularly changing, eclectic menu. Wed–Sat eve. Expensive.

Mash & Air, 40 Chorlton St (*Mash* ☎0161/661 6161; ☎*Air* 0161/661 1111). Converted cotton mill, named after a stage in the brewing process – it brews its own beer on the premises. Expect to queue for the cheaper *Mash* (chargrill/pizza dishes); reserve for the more intimate *Air*. Moderate to Expensive.

Nico Central, Mount St (☎0161/236 6488). Nico Ladenis' Manchester brasserie (inside the *Midland Hotel*) serves excellent Modern-French cuisine. Expensive, with attitude.

Pizza Express, 6–8 South King St (☎0161/834 0145). The centre's most reliable pizzas, served in familiar surroundings. Inexpensive to Moderate.

Sangam, 13–15 Wilmslow Rd, Rusholme (☎0161/257 3922). The ever-expanding *Sangam* can do no wrong – great curry-house classics, every time. Moderate.

Simply Heathcote's, Jackson Row (☎0161/835 3536). Massive, minimalist dining rooms operated by Michelin-starred Lancastrian chef Paul Heathcote. Moderate to Expensive.

Yang Sing, 34 Princess St (☎0161/236 2200). One of the best Cantonese restaurants in the country – nothing more, nothing less. Moderate to Expensive.

Pubs

The Beer House, 6 Angel St. The best place for ale-tasting, with a constant stock of more than thirty brands of beer.

Britons Protection, 50 Great Bridgewater St. Elegantly decorated traditional pub opposite Bridgewater Hall, with a couple of cosy rooms, a brickyard beer garden, and a mixed crowd.

Circus Tavern, 86 Portland St. Manchester's smallest pub – a Victorian drinking-hole that's many peoples' favourite city-centre pit-stop. You may have to knock on the door to get in.

Dukes '92, Castle St. Old warehouse on the Duke of Bridgewater's canal in Castlefield, classily revamped with art on the walls. Serves a wide range of pâtés and cheeses.

The Lass o' Gowrie, 1 Charles St. Outside, glazed tiles and Victorian styling; inside, stripped floors and a micro-brewery. All in all, one of the city's better studenty pubs.

Marble Arch, 73 Rochdale Rd. Curious real-ale house with a sloping floor, some fine internal decor and – more importantly – scores of bottled beers and a great atmosphere.

The Mark Addy, 2 Stanley St. A popular pub serving a choice of fifty cheeses and eight pâtés (including vegetarian). Eat inside, or outside by the River Irwell.

Mr Thomas' Chop House, 52 Cross St. Victorian classic with a Dickensian feel to its nooks and crannies. There's good-value food served in the ornate dining room, too.

Peveril of the Peak, 127 Great Bridgewater St. The pub that time forgot – one of Manchester's best real-ale houses, with a youthful crowd and some superb Victorian glazed tilework outside.

Via Fossa, Canal St. The elaborate mock-Gothic rooms pack in a high-energy (largely gay) crowd – just the place to ratchet up the atmosphere after the laid-back café-bar antics down the road.

Clubs and live music

Academy, Oxford Rd, on university campus (☎0161/275 2930). Small venue for new and established bands.

Band on the Wall, 25 Swan St (☎0161/832 6625). Cosy joint with a great reputation for its live bands – from world and folk to jazz and reggae – and club nights, too.

THE GAY SCENE

Manchester has one of Britain's most vibrant gay scenes, centred along the Rochdale Canal between Princess and Sackville streets, in the so-called **Gay Village**. The area hosts the annual gay **carnival** (August bank holiday) and the bi-annual lesbian and gay arts **festival**, "It's Queer Up North", to be held next in 2000 and 2002. During the rest of the year, early evenings kick off by the lock at *Manto, Metz, Bar 38* or *Velvet* – at the extravagant *Via Fossa* pub or at the more macho *New Union*, 111 Princess St, just off Canal Street (☎0161/228 1492). An older crowd drinks in the *Rembrandt Hotel*. A camp neon Liberty beckons you into *New York, New York*, 98 Bloom St (☎0161/236 6556), for live DJs. And there are regular **club nights** for gays and lesbians at *Cruz 101*, 101 Princess St (☎0161/237 1554), the main party place in town; *Follies*, 6 Whitworth St (☎0161/236 8149), a lesbian favourite; and *Glide*, on Charles St (☎0161/273 3722).

For further **information**, call the Manchester Lesbian and Gay Switchboard (☎0161/274 3999 daily 4–10pm).

The Boardwalk, 15 Little Peter St (☎0161/228 3555). One of the hot venues for new bands – a nervy Oasis played their first gig here. There are good club nights here, too.

The Brickhouse, 6 Whitworth St West (☎0161/236 4418). Indie, techno, Seventies or glam, depending on the night.

Paradise Factory, 112–116 Princess St (☎0161/228 2966). One of the hottest clubs on the scene, in the old Factory Records building. There's a gay night on Fridays. Closed Sun & Mon.

South, 4a South King St (☎0161/831 7756). Funk to house to Northern Soul played on different nights.

Star & Garter, Fairfield St (☎0161/273 6726). Thrash/punk pub venue; late bar until 2am.

5th Avenue, 121 Princess St (☎0161/236 2754). Student indie/retro scene Mon & Thurs–Sat.

Arts and culture

Manchester is blessed with the North's most highly regarded **orchestra**, the Hallé, which is based at the Bridgewater Hall. Here, and at several other venues, including the city's churches and its cathedral, the orchestra stages classical **concerts** throughout the year. The Cornerhouse is the local **arts** mainstay, while a full range of mainstream and fringe **theatres** produce a year-round programme of events. The biggest annual fest is autumn's **Manchester Festival**, an arts and TV extravaganza, with events in the city's clubs, theatres and open spaces.

Bridgewater Hall, Lower Mosley St (☎0161/907 9000). Home of the Hallé (founded 1857) and the Manchester Camerata (the acclaimed chamber orchestra).

Contact Theatre, 15 Oxford Rd (☎0161/274 4400). One of the most innovative theatre companies in provocative new premises. Puts on predominantly modern works and has a good café-bar.

Cornerhouse, 70 Oxford St (☎0161/200 1500). Engaging arts centre with three cinema screens, changing art exhibitions, recitals, talks, bookshop, café and bar.

Dancehouse Theatre, 10 Oxford Rd (☎0161/237 9753). Home of the Northern Ballet School, and venue for dance, drama and comedy. Also has a café-bar.

Green Room, 54–56 Whitworth St West (☎0161/950 5900). Rapidly changing fringe programme which includes dance, mime and cabaret.

Library Theatre, St Peter's Square (☎0161/236 7110). Classic drama and new writing, in a theatre beneath the Central Library.

Royal Exchange Theatre, St Ann's Square (☎0161/833 9833). The theatre-in-the-round has been thoroughly refurbished, and a Studio Theatre (for works by new writers) added.

Royal Northern College of Music (RNCM), 124 Oxford Rd (☎0161/273 4504). Stages top-quality classical and modern-jazz concerts, including performances by Manchester Camerata.

Listings

Airport General enquiries ☎0161/489 3000; flight enquiries ☎0839/888747.

Banks and exchanges There are branches of all the major banks in the city centre: Barclays, 51 Mosley St, 12 Piccadilly, 133 Deansgate; NatWest, 55 King St, 33 Piccadilly, 115 Deansgate; HSBC, 100 King St, 22 Cross St, 8 High St; Lloyds, 67 Piccadilly, Market St, King St. The only late-night exchanges, other than the big hotels, are at the airport (6am–midnight) and at the Castlefield YHA (daily 7am–11pm); at other times head for American Express, 10–12 St Mary's Gate (☎0161/833 0121); or Thomas Cook 23 Cross St, 2 Oxford St (☎0161/236 8575).

Bookshops The main chains have outlets on Deansgate and around St Ann's Square. Frontline Books, Wilmslow Rd, Rusholme, is Manchester's foremost outlet for radical literature. Gibb's Bookshop, 10 Charlotte St, is great for secondhand books and classical music.

Bus information For all city services, call GMPTE (☎0161/228 7811); for intercity services, call National Express (☎0990/808 080).

Car rental Avis, 1 Ducie St (☎0161/236 6716) and at the airport (☎0161/436 2020); Budget, 660 Chester Rd, Old Trafford (☎0161/877 5555) and at the airport (☎0161/499 3042); Europcar/InterRent, York St, Piccadilly Plaza (☎0161/832 4114) and at the airport (☎0161/436 2200); Hertz, 31 Aytoun St, near Piccadilly Station (☎0161/236 2747) and at the airport (☎0161/437 8208).

Dentist Dental Hospital of Manchester, Higher Cambridge St (☎0161/275 6666).

Hospital Manchester Royal Infirmary, 13 Oxford Rd (☎0161/276 1234).

Lost property Contact the Police Station (see below) or call GMPTE if you think you lost the item on a bus.

Internet *Cyberia* (see Cafés and café-bars, p.509); Net-Works Centre at the Central Library (Tues & Thurs 10am–7.30pm, Wed 1–7.30pm, Fri & Sat 10am–4.30pm).

Laundry There are several launderettes along Wilmslow Road in Rusholme, or you could use the facilities at the YHA hostel.

Left luggage Chorlton Street coach station (daily 9.30am–5.30pm; £1 per bag); Piccadilly train station (Mon–Sat 7am–7pm, Sun 11am–7pm; from £2).

Pharmacy Cameolord Ltd, 7 Oxford St (daily 8am–midnight; ☎0161/236 1445).

Police Greater Manchester Police, Bootle St (☎0161/872 5050).

Post Office 26 Spring Gardens; 63 Newton St. The Spring Gardens office has a *bureau de change* and *poste-restante* section.

Taxis Mantax (☎0161/236 5133); Taxifone (☎0161/236 9974); and, for cabs to the airport, Airtax (☎0161/499 9000).

Train information Local rail information from GMPTE (☎0161/228 7811). National Rail Enquiries (☎0345/484950) for all other services. Piccadilly Station has a walk-in Travel Centre (Mon–Sat 8am–8.30pm, Sun 11am–7pm) for national and international train enquiries.

Travel Agents USIT Campus in the YHA shop, 166 Deansgate (☎0161/273 1721); and branches at UMIST, Manchester Metropolitan University, Manchester Academy and the University of Manchester. STA Travel, 75 Deansgate (☎0161/834 0668).

Chester

In 1779 Boswell wrote to Samuel Johnson: "Chester pleases me more than any town I ever saw." **CHESTER**, forty miles southwest of Manchester, has changed since then, but not so much. A glorious two-mile ring of medieval and Roman walls encircle a neat kernel of Tudor and Victorian buildings, including the unique raised arcades called the "Rows". Very much the commercial hub of Cheshire, its county, Chester has enough in the way of sights, restaurants and atmosphere to make it an enjoyable base for a couple of days.

In 79 AD the Romans built Deva Castra here, their largest known fortress in Britain. Later, Ethelfleda, the daughter of King Alfred the Great, extended and refortified the place, only to have it brutally sacked by William the Conqueror's armies. Trade routes to Ireland made Chester the most prosperous port in the northwest, a status it recovered after the English Civil War, which saw a two-year-long siege of the town at the hands of the Parliamentarians. By the middle of the eighteenth century, however, silting of the port had forced the Irish trade to be re-routed first through Parkgate on the Dee estuary, and then to Liverpool. Things improved a little with the Industrial Revolution, as the canal and railway networks made Chester an important regional trading centre, a function it still retains.

Arrival and information

National Express and regional bus services (including the hourly #X8 from Liverpool) arrive at **Chester bus station**, between Delamere and George streets, close to the northern city walls and Northgate Street, down which you'll find the main **tourist office** in the town hall (May–Oct Mon–Sat 9am–5.30pm, Sun 10am–4pm; Nov–April Mon–Sat 9am–5.30pm; ☎01244/402111). Merseyrail **trains** from Liverpool and all other regional and national services call at the **train station**, northeast of the centre, from where it's a ten-minute walk down City Road and along Foregate Street to the central Eastgate Clock. A second tourist office, the **Chester Visitor Centre**, is on Vicars Lane opposite the amphitheatre (May–Oct Mon–Sat 9am–6.30pm, Sun 10am–5pm; Nov–April Mon–Sat 10am–5pm, Sun 10am–4pm; ☎01244/402111).

Accommodation

Simple **B&B accommodation** can be in short supply, as can space in the more characterful old inns. The places reviewed below are the best of the central choices: if you arrive late, or strike out in the centre, there are lots of budget-rated B&Bs to try along Brook Street, just a couple of minutes from the train station, and several moderate hotels down City Road, also near the station.

Castle House, 23 Castle St (☎01244/350354). B&B in a sixteenth-century house with good facilities; bang in the centre and excellent value for money. No credit cards. ②.

The Chester Grosvenor, Eastgate St (☎01244/324024). Superbly appointed luxury hotel with comfortable bedrooms and a whole host of facilities, not least two fine restaurants. ⑨, ⑧ at weekends.

Chester Town House, 23 King St (☎01244/350021). High-standard B&B in a comfortably furnished seventeenth-century town house, off Northgate Street. No credit cards. ③.

Commercial Hotel, St Peters Church Yard (☎01244/320749). Friendly inn with half-a-dozen pleasant rooms. ②.

Grosvenor Place Guest House, 2–4 Grosvenor Place (☎01244/324455). Pleasant townhouse B&B in a good, if noisy, location near the museum. ②.

Mill Hotel, Milton St (☎01244/350035). Sensitive warehouse conversion on the canal, with its own car park and a nice waterside bar; rooms with balcony attract a £10 supplement. ④.

Pied Bull, Northgate St (☎01244/325829). Characterful old coaching inn, close to the walls and cathedral. ②.

Youth Hostel, Hough Green House, 40 Hough Green (☎01244/680056, *yhachester@compuserve.com*). Victorian house a twenty-minute walk from the centre; family rooms available.

The City

The main thoroughfares of Chester's Roman grid plan meet at **the Cross**, where the town crier welcomes visitors to the city (May–Aug Tues–Sat at noon). Both sides of all four streets leading from here are lined by **the Rows**, unique galleried arcades running on top of the ground-floor shops. The engaging tableau is a blend of genuine Tudor houses and Victorian half-timbered imitations, with the finest Tudor buildings on

Watergate Street – though Eastgate Street is the most picturesque, leading to the filigree **Eastgate Clock**. There's no clear explanation of the origin of the Rows – they were first recorded soon after the fire that wrecked Chester in 1278, and may originally have been built on top of the heaped rubble left after the blaze.

You can get the best insight into Chester's Roman heritage at **Dewa Roman Experience** tucked away up Pierpoint Lane, off Bridge Street (daily 9am–5pm; £3.80). There's a more general introduction to the town in the **Chester Heritage Centre** at the bottom of Bridge Street (March–Oct Mon–Sat 11am–5pm, Sun noon–5pm; £1.25), housed in what used to be St Michael's Church. North of the Cross, the neo-Gothic town hall dominates its square at the end of Northgate Street across from the heavily restored **Cathedral** (daily 9.30am–6pm; free tours Mon–Sat 2.30pm). This Benedictine church is dedicated to St Werburgh, a seventh-century Anglo-Saxon princess who became Chester's patron saint. Parts of the eleventh-century structure can still be seen in the north transept but the highlights in an otherwise simple interior are the fourteenth-century choir stalls, with their intricately carved misericords. Doors in the north wall of the nave lead into the shady sixteenth-century cloisters.

East of the cathedral, steps provide access to the top of the two-mile girdle of the medieval and Roman **city walls** – the most complete set in Britain, though in places the wall is barely above street level. You can walk past all its towers, turrets and gateways in an hour or two, including the fifteenth-century **King Charles Tower** (April–Oct Sat 10am–5pm, Sun 2–5pm; 50p), in the northeast corner, and the **Water Tower** (same hours; 50p), at the northwest. South from the tower you'll see the **Roodee**, England's oldest racecourse, laid out on a silted tidal pool where Roman ships once unloaded wine, figs and olive oil from the Mediterranean.

Until nineteenth-century excavation work, much of the wall near the Water Tower was propped up by scores of sculpted tomb panels and engraved headstones, items probably used to rebuild the walls in a hurry in the turbulent fourth century. Many are now on display at the **Grosvenor Museum**, 27 Grosvenor St (Mon–Sat 10.30am–5pm, Sun 2–5pm; free), near the southern end of the Roodee. This is the best investigation of Roman Chester, with good displays about the legionary system, city buildings, grave sites, defences, daily life and culture. Across the traffic roundabout on Castle Street, the dull **Cheshire Military Museum** (daily 10am–5pm; 50p) inhabits part of the same complex as the Norman **Chester Castle** (Easter–Sept daily 10am–6pm; Oct–Easter daily 10am–4pm; free; EH). Most of what you see today is little older than the eighteenth-century Greek Revival Assize Courts and council offices on the same site, the building of which led to the demolition of much of the medieval structure.

South of the castle, the wall is buried under the street, but it rises again alongside the **Roman Gardens** (unrestricted access) on Souters Lane at Little John Street, where Roman foundations dug up during redevelopment are on display. Across the road stands the half-excavated remains of the **Roman Amphitheatre** (Easter–Sept daily 10am–6pm; Oct–Easter daily 10am–1pm & 2–4pm; free; EH); it is estimated to have held seven thousand spectators, making it the largest amphitheatre in Britain, but the stonework is barely head-high now.

The partly ruined pink-stone **Church of St John the Baptist** (daily 9.15am–6pm), a little to the east in Grosvenor Park, was founded by the Saxon king Ethelred in 689 and briefly served as the cathedral of Mercia. Rebuilt in its entirety by the Normans, the solid Norman pillars of the nave rise to a Transitional triforium and Early-English clerestory. Outside are the romantic eastern ruins, left to deteriorate having been cut off from the rest of the church after the Reformation. Steps from the church gardens and from the southern edge of the city walls lead to the tree-shaded **Groves**, on the banks of the Dee, with its bandstand, slender iron footbridge and villas overlooking the willows draped along the opposite bank. Bithells Boats runs half-hour **cruises** on the river (April–Nov 10am–6.30pm; Dec–March Sat & Sun 11–4pm; every 15min; £3) and two-hour trips in the summer (Wed & Sat 11am & 8.15pm, rest of week 11am only).

Eating and drinking

You can't walk more than a few paces in Chester without coming across somewhere good to **eat and drink**, as often as not housed in a medieval crypt or Tudor building. Some of the **pubs** are highly atmospheric and most serve bar meals, though the quality isn't always up to much. For something different, reserve for the *Mill Hotel*'s one-hour bar-meal **cruise** (£2.50 plus lunch; ☎01244/350035); they also run evening and champagne cruises.

Alexander's Jazz Theatre and Café Bar, 2 Rufus Court (☎01244/340005). Continental style café-bar with *tapas* from the counter and live music or comedy nightly.

Boulevard de la Bastille, Bridge St Row. One of the nicest of the arcade cafés, with tables looking over the street.

The Brasserie, *Chester Grosvenor Hotel*, Eastgate St (☎01244/324024). The *Grosvenor*'s informal brasserie is a great place for a coffee and pastry, or inventive French and fusion cooking. Moderate.

Boot Inn, Eastgate Row. A characterful pub in the upper gallery with a backroom where fourteen Roundheads were killed and a highbacked seat once used by soliciting prostitutes.

Cathedral Refectory, Chester Cathedral, St Werburgh St. Bistro-style dishes served in the thirteenth-century monks' dining room. Closed Sun. Inexpensive.

Chez Jules, 69 Northgate St (☎01244/400014). Classic brasserie menu, including a terrific-value £6 set lunch. Inexpensive.

The Falcon, Lower Bridge St. This half-timbered Samuel Smith's pub was once a town house built by the Grosvenor family by enclosing part of a Row.

Francs, 14 Cuppin St (☎01244/317952). An excellent and very French bistro with good-value set meals. You can also just drop in for a coffee and cake. Moderate.

The Garden House, 1 Rufus Court, off Northgate St (☎01244/320004). A highly praised bistro in a Georgian house by the walls, with a sunny courtyard garden. Moderate to Expensive.

Mamma Mia, 87 St Werburgh St (☎01244/314663). Popular with a party crowd, this pizzeria-restaurant serves speciality fish and vegetarian dishes along with the pizzas. Moderate.

Old Harkers Arms, 1 Russell St, below the City Road bridge. Canalside real-ale boozer imaginatively sited in a former warehouse.

Telford's Warehouse, Tower Wharf, Raymond St (☎01244/390090). Warehouse-style wine-bar pub with regular live music. It's just off the city walls by the Water Tower.

Around Chester

Chester's most popular attraction, **Chester Zoo** (daily: April–Sept 10am–6pm; Oct–March 10am–4pm; last admission 2hr before closing; £9), is the second largest in Britain and one of the best in Europe, spreading over 110 landscaped acres, with new attractions opening all the time. Animals are grouped by region in large paddocks viewed from a maze of pathways or from the creeping monorail, with main attractions being the baby animals (elephants, giraffes and orang-utans), the new rainforest habitat, complete with jaguars, and the Twilight Zone bat cave. The zoo is reached by bus #4, #14 or #40 (Mon–Sat; every 30min) from Chester's bus exchange, or the #11c and #12c (Sun & public holidays; every 30min) to Liverpool's Albert Dock. Merseyrail stations sell a combined train, bus and zoo-admission ticket, using the #40 bus link from Bache Merseyrail station, one stop north of Chester.

It's claimed that the **Ellesmere Port Boat Museum**, seven miles north of Chester (April–Oct daily 10am–5pm; Nov–March Mon–Wed, Sat & Sun 11am–4pm; £5.50), has Britain's largest collection of floating canal vessels, a contention that seems completely plausible when you see the flotilla. Indoor exhibits trace the history of canals and their construction, and you can even take a short ride on a narrow boat (£2.30). The museum is five minutes' walk from Ellesmere Port train station (change at Hooton from Chester) or take bus #3 (every 30min) or the hourly #X8 (Liverpool bus) from Chester bus station on Delamere Street.

Liverpool

Once the country's main transatlantic port and the empire's second city, **LIVERPOOL** spent too many of the twentieth-century postwar years struggling against adversity. Things are looking up at last, as economic and social regeneration brightens the centre and old docks. Yet – as even any short-term visitor to the city could tell you – nothing ever broke Liverpool's extraordinary spirit of community, a spirit that emerged strongly in the aftermath of the Hillsborough football stadium disaster of 1989, when the deaths of 95 Liverpool supporters seemed to unite the whole city. Indeed, acerbic wit and loyalty to one of the city's two football teams are the linchpins of Scouse culture – though Liverpool makes great play of its musical heritage, which is reasonable enough from the city that produced The Beatles.

Although it gained its charter from King John in 1207, Liverpool remained a humble fishing village for half a millennium until the silting-up of Chester and the booming slave trade prompted the building of the first dock in 1715. From then until the abolition of slavery in Britain in 1807, Liverpool was the apex of the **slaving triangle** in which firearms, alcohol and textiles were traded for African slaves, who were then shipped to the Caribbean and America. The holds were filled with tobacco, raw cotton and sugar for the return journey. After the abolition of the trade, the port continued to grow into a seven-mile chain of docks, not only for freight but also to cope with wholesale European **emigration**, which saw nine million people from half of Europe leave for the Americas and Australasia between 1830 and 1930. Some never made it further than Liverpool and contributed to a five-fold increase in population in fifty years. An even larger boost came with immigration from the Caribbean and China, and especially Ireland in the wake of the potato famine in 1845. The resulting mix became one of Britain's earliest multi-ethnic communities, described by Carl Jung as "the pool of life".

The docks were busy until the middle of the twentieth century when cheap air fares saw off the lucrative liner business; trade with the dwindling empire declined, while European traffic boosted southeastern ports at Tilbury, Harwich and Southampton; and containerization meant reduced demand for handling and warehousing. The arrival of car manufacturing plants in the 1960s, like Ford at Halewood, stemmed the decline for a while, but Liverpool never really recovered from the bodyblow of losing its fundamental business. EU development funds have been forthcoming since Liverpool was classified as one of Europe's poorest areas, and millennium money has kick-started other projects, though – compared to the wholesale redevelopment of neighbouring Manchester – the city still has a fair hill to climb.

Arrival, information and city transport

Mainline trains pull in to **Lime Street** station, while the suburban **Merseyrail** system (for trains from Chester) calls at several underground stations in the city, including Lime Street, Central (under the main post office on Ranelagh Street) and James Street (for Pier Head and the Albert Dock). National Express **buses** use the station on Norton Street, just northeast of Lime Street. Local buses depart from a variety of terminals: Queen Square (for eastbound, cross-river and Chester services); Paradise Street Bus

Station (southbound and a few northbound services); and St Thomas Street (north-bound). Liverpool **airport**, eight miles southeast of the city centre, handles flights for Belfast, Dublin, the Isle of Man, Nice, Malaga and Amsterdam. A **taxi** to Lime Street costs around £10, or take bus #80/180 from outside the main entrance (every 30min 6am–11pm) into the city centre. **Ferry** arrivals – from the Isle of Man, Dublin and Belfast – dock at the terminals just north of Pier Head, close to Albert Dock and not far from James Street Merseyrail station.

The **Merseyside Welcome Centre** is centrally located in Queen Square (Mon–Sat 9.30am–5.30pm, Sun 10am–5pm) and there's also the **Atlantic Pavilion tourist information centre** at the Albert Dock (daily 10am–5.30pm), which both share the same telephone enquiries number (☎0151/708 8838). Both also sell the **National Museums and Galleries on Merseyside** (NMGM) Eight Pass (£3) which gives unlimited access into eight local museums for twelve months.

The local transport authority is **Merseytravel**, which co-ordinates all buses, trains and ferries. Their main office is at 24 Hatton Gardens (Merseytravel Line ☎0151/236 7676 daily 8am–8pm), and there are information centres at Queen Square, at the Merseyside Welcome Centre, Paradise Street Bus Station and Pier Head. Daily off-peak, zonal Saveaway tickets (£2.10–4.30) for unlimited use on most city buses, trains and ferries are available from post offices, newsagents and the Merseytravel offices.

Accommodation

Liverpool has very limited central **accommodation**, with just a few business-oriented four-stars at the top end of the range and a clutch of budget hotels along Mount Pleasant. What the city does have, however, is a wide range of hostels and halls of residence, including a terrific youth hostel a short walk from Albert Dock. You might snag a cheap B&B in the surrounding suburbs – the tourist offices can help. There is no useful campsite. Both tourist offices (see above) will book rooms for you for free; call ☎0345/585291 for their details of special-offer weekend breaks and packages.

Hotels and B&Bs

Aachen, 89–91 Mount Pleasant (☎0151/709 3477). The most popular of the Mount Pleasant budget choices, with a range of value-for-money rooms, big breakfasts and a bar. ②.

Britannia Adelphi Hotel, Ranelagh Place (☎0151/709 7200). The *Adelphi* ("star" of TV's fly-on-the-wall series *Hotel*) once catered to passenger-liner customers, but it's lost its lustre since. ⑤.

Feathers Hotel, 117–125 Mount Pleasant (☎0151/709 9655). Converted terrace of Georgian houses, with en-suite rooms and a help-yourself buffet breakfast included in the price. ⑤.

The Gladstone, Lord Nelson St (☎0151/709 7050). Standard accommodation, just behind Lime Street station, with summer and weekend deals knocking a tenner off the room rate. ③.

Holiday Inn Express, Britannia Pavilion, Albert Dock (☎0151/709 1133, *liverpool@ premierhotel.co.uk*). Gives the rest of the city-centre accommodation a run for its money, as all the 170 en-suite rooms go for the same bargain price. ③.

Liverpool Moat House, Paradise St (☎0151/471 9988). Well-equipped, modern hotel a short walk from the Albert Dock, with a fine indoor pool and spa. Midweek ⑦, ⑥ at weekends.

Swallow Hotel, 1 Queen Square (☎0151/476 8000). Stylish new city-centre hotel, handy for Lime Street and the museums, and featuring a pool and hot tub, restaurant and bar. ⑦.

Hostels and halls of residence

Embassie Youth Hostel, 1 Falkner Square (☎0151/707 1089). Relaxed hostel twenty minutes' walk from Lime Street station (bus #80), in a Georgian terrace west of the Anglican cathedral. Free showers, tea, toast and coffee.

John Moores University, Cathedral Park, St James Rd (☎0151/709 3197). Self-catering accommodation in the shadow of the metropolitan cathedral. July to early Sept only.

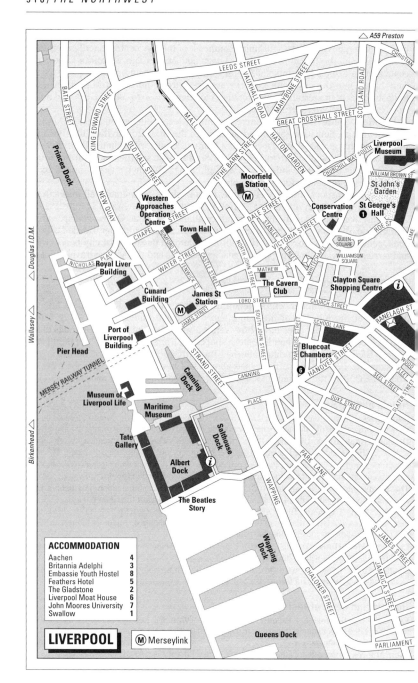

△ A59 Preston

LEEDS STREET

VAUXHALL ROAD

MARYBONE STREET

SCOTLAND ROAD

CHRISTIAN

BATH STREET

KING EDWARD STREET

MALL

GREAT CROSSHALL STREET

HATTON GARDEN

Princes Dock

OLD HALL STREET

NEW QUAY

TITHE BARN STREET

Liverpool Museum

CHURCHILL WAY SOUTH

WILLIAM BROWN ST

St John's Garden

Moorfield Station (M)

Western Approaches Operation Centre

CHAPEL STREET

Town Hall

DALE STREET

STANLEY STREET

VICTORIA STREET

Conservation Centre

St George's Hall ❶

QUEEN SQUARE

ROE ST

LIME

WILLIAMSON SQUARE

NICHOLAS PLACE

Royal Liver Building

WATER STREET

RUMFORD ST

FENWICK ST

CASTLE STREET

NORTH JOHN STREET

MATHEW

WHITECHAPEL

Clayton Square Shopping Centre ℹ

RANELAGH ST

Cunard Building

James St Station (M)

JAMES STREET

LORD STREET

The Cavern Club

CHURCH STREET

SCHOOL LANE

Port of Liverpool Building

SOUTH JOHN STREET

PARADISE STREET

Bluecoat Chambers ❻

HANOVER STREET

WOOD ST

FLEET

Pier Head

STRAND STREET

CANNING

SEEL STREET

SLATER'S ST

MERSEY RAILWAY TUNNEL

Museum of Liverpool Life

Canning Dock

PLACE

DUKE STREET

Maritime Museum

Tate Gallery

Salthouse Dock

Albert Dock ℹ

PARK LANE

WAPPING

The Beatles Story

ST JAMES STREET

JAMAICA STREET

Wapping Dock

CHALONER STREET

PARLIAMENT

Wallasey △   Douglas I.O.M. △   Birkenhead △

ACCOMMODATION

Aachen	4
Britannia Adelphi	3
Embassie Youth Hostel	8
Feathers Hotel	5
The Gladstone	2
Liverpool Moat House	6
John Moores University	7
Swallow	1

LIVERPOOL   (M) Merseylink

Queens Dock

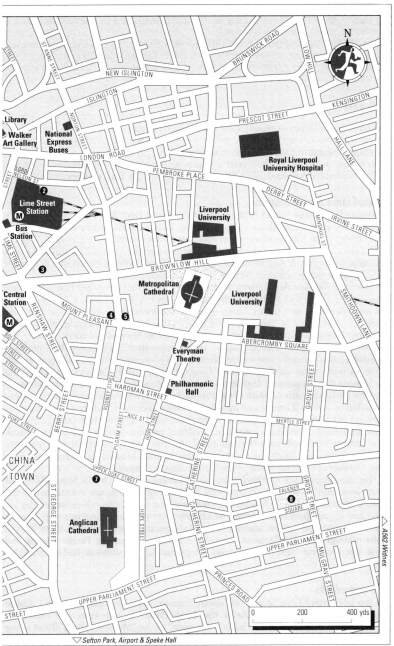

Library
Walker
Art Gallery

National
Express
Buses

NEW ISLINGTON

ISLINGTON

ST ANNE STREET

NORTON STREET

BRUNSWICK ROAD

LOW HILL

N

KENSINGTON

PRESCOT STREET

HALL LANE

LONDON ROAD

PEMBROKE PLACE

LORD NELSON ST

Royal Liverpool
University Hospital

② Lime Street
Station
M

Bus
Station

LIME STREET

DERBY STREET

MINSHULL ST

IRVINE STREET

Liverpool
University

③

BROWNLOW HILL

Central
Station

M

RENSHAW STREET

MOUNT PLEASANT

④ ⑤

Metropolitan
Cathedral

Liverpool
University

ABERCROMBY SQUARE

SMITHDOWN LANE

POLE STREET

Everyman
Theatre

HARDMAN STREET

RODNEY STREET

Philharmonic
Hall

GROVE STREET

BERRY STREET

PILGRIM STREET

RICE ST

HOPE STREET

CATHERINE STREET

MYRTLE STREET

DUKE STREET

CHINA
TOWN

UPPER DUKE STREET

ST GEORGE STREET

⑦

HOPE STREET

Anglican
Cathedral

CATHERINE STREET

FALKNER
⑧
SQUARE

GROVE STREET

UPPER PARLIAMENT STREET

MULGRAVE STREET

PRINCES ROAD

A562 Widnes

UPPER PARLIAMENT STREET

STREET

0   200   400 yds

▽ *Sefton Park, Airport & Speke Hall*

© Crown copyright

Liverpool Youth Hostel, Wapping (☎0151/709 8888, *liverpool@yha.org.uk*). One of the YHA's best, just south of Albert Dock, a new building decorated with Beatles memorabilia. Accommodation is in smart two-, three-, four- or six-bed rooms.
YMCA, 56 Mount Pleasant (☎0151/709 9516). Separate floors of basic accommodation for men and women; singles and twins available. Breakfast included. The restaurant has bargain meals.
YWCA, 1 Rodney St (☎0151/709 7791). Cheap rooms for women only. Centrally heated and with communal kitchens and laundry facilities.

The City

Liverpool has a legacy of magnificent municipal buildings – best seen en masse from across the river or on the Mersey ferry – and these are the chief attractions of the cityscape, along with its two famous **cathedrals**. The city's mercantile past and aspects of its recent history are well covered in a number of museums and galleries, especially in the rejuvenated warehouses of **Albert Dock**, site of the **Tate Gallery**.

Around Lime Street Station

Emerging from **Lime Street Station** you can't miss **St George's Hall**, one of Britain's finest Greek Revival buildings and a testament to the wealth generated from transatlantic trade. Once Liverpool's concert hall and crown courts, its tunnel-vaulted Great Hall is open to the public for monthly craft and antique fairs and for daily **guided tours** in summer (late July & Aug Mon–Sat 11am–4pm; £1.50), when the exquisite floor, tiled with thirty thousand precious Minton tiles, is on show.

Liverpool's **Walker Art Gallery** on William Brown Street (Mon–Sat 10am–5pm, Sun noon–5pm; £3; free with NMGM Eight Pass) houses one of the country's finest provincial art collections, with pieces dating from the fourteenth century to the present day. There's a good range of Italian work on show, while an assertive Rembrandt self-portrait from 1630 is displayed alongside works by Poussin, Rubens and other seventeenth-century masters, but British painting occupies centre stage. George Stubbs, England's greatest animal painter – and native Liverpudlian – shows off his preoccupation with horse anatomy in his painting of *Molly Longlegs* (1762), while Turner's maturing style is captured in the romantic *Linlithgow Palace*. Nothing could contrast more strongly than the contemporaneous work of the Pre-Raphaelites, whose nostalgic fastidiousness is typified by Millais' *Lorenzo and Isabella*. A twentieth-century gallery sees a changing selection of paintings and sculptures, while the museum also displays exhibits from its large applied-art collection – glassware, ceramics, precious metals, and sculpted furniture, largely retrieved from the homes of the city's early industrial businessmen. Contemporary work floods the building during the John Moores Exhibition, held here from October of odd-numbered years to the following January.

The collections at the nearby **Liverpool Museum**, William Brown Street (Mon–Sat 10am–5pm, Sun noon–5pm; £3; free with NMGM Eight Pass), are eclectic to say the least, from tarantulas in its basement "Vivarium" to a space research rocket on the top floor, and it's an appealing diversity which grows on you the longer you stay. There's also a full dinosaur section, starring a set of dinosaur footprints found on the Wirral, while ethnographical collections from the Americas, Egypt, the Pacific Islands and West Africa contain much of interest too. A top-floor café has views of the Liverpool skyline.

The cathedrals

On the hill behind Lime Street, off Mount Pleasant, rises the funnel-shaped Catholic **Metropolitan Cathedral of Christ the King** (Mon–Sat 8am–6pm, Sun 8am–5pm; free), denigratingly known as "Paddy's Wigwam" or the "Mersey Funnel". Built in the 1960s, it was raised on top of the tentative beginnings of Sir Edwin Lutyens's grandiose project to outdo St Peter's in Rome. Bits of Lutyens's cathedral can be seen in the crypt. At the other end of the aptly named Hope Street, the Anglican **Liverpool Cathedral** (daily 8am–6pm; £1 donation requested) looks much more ancient but was actually completed eleven years later, in 1978, after 74 years in construction. The last of the great neo-Gothic structures, Sir Giles Gilbert Scott's masterwork claims a smattering of superlatives: Britain's largest and the world's fifth largest cathedral, the world's tallest Gothic arches and the highest and heaviest bells. On a clear day, a trip up the 330-foot **tower** (11am–4pm; £2) through the cavernous belfry is rewarded by views to the Welsh hills.

The city centre

Having seen the Walker Art Gallery, Liverpool Museum and the cathedrals, you've seen the central showpiece attractions, but you may as well trace a route back through the city centre. **Bold Street** and its backstreet offshoots – Slater Street, Wood Street, Fleet Street – are busy reinventing themselves as café-land, with an increasing number of places opening in which you can sip a latte, neck a late-night beer or shop for vintage clothing. Concert Square, just off Bold Street, its space once occupied by a factory, was levelled to provide room for a warehouse-style bar development, whose outdoor seats are at a real premium in the summer. On neighbouring Wood Street, the **Open Eye Gallery**, at no. 28–32 (Tues–Fri 10.30am–5.30pm, Sat 10.30am–5pm; free), features renowned temporary exhibitions of photography and the media arts. Bold Street ends at Hanover Street, with the pedestrianized shopping street Church Street continuing beyond. To the left, School Lane throws up the beautifully proportioned **Bluecoat Chambers**, built in 1717 as an Anglican boarding school for orphans and now a contemporary art gallery (Tues–Sat 10.30am–5pm; free) with a decent café and arts centre. The **Quiggins Centre**, a bit further along at 12–16 School Lane (Mon–Sat 10am–6pm), is a converted warehouse packed with ever-changing shoplets hawking posters, jewellery, clubwear and skateboards.

The Pier Head

Though the tumult of shipping which once fought the current here has gone, the **Pier Head** landing stage remains the embarkation point for the **Mersey Ferries** to Woodside (for Birkenhead) and Seacombe (Wallasey). Ride one if only for the magnificent views of the Liverpool skyline and the prominent, 322-foot-high **Royal Liver Building** (tours April–Sept by appointment only; call ☎0151/236 2748) – it's topped by the "Liver Birds", a couple of cormorants which have become the symbol of the city.

Straightforward ferry shuttles operate every thirty minutes during morning and evening rush hours (95p each way); at other times the boats run circular **heritage cruises** (hourly: Mon–Fri 10am–3pm, Sat & Sun 10am–6pm; £3.30; ☎0151/630 1030), complete with sappy commentary and repeated renditions of Gerry Marsden's *Ferry 'cross the Mersey*. If you're going to stop off at the **Seacombe Aquarium** (daily: summer 10am–6pm; winter 10am–4pm; £1.55), buy the joint ticket (£4.30).

The Albert Dock

Albert Dock, five minutes' walk south of the Pier Head, was built in 1846 when Liverpool's port was a world leader. It started to decline at the beginning of this century, as the new deep-draught ships were unable to berth here, and last saw service in 1972. A decade later the site was given a complete scrubdown and refit, and billed as "Liverpool's Historic Waterfront" it's a type of rescued urban heritage that's been copied throughout the country. There are **buses** every twenty minutes during the day from Queen Square bus station. All the museums have admission charges: the Maritime Museum, HM Customs Museum and Museum of Liverpool Life are part of the NMGM Eight Pass scheme, while the **Waterfront Pass** (£9.50) saves you money if you want to see the lot.

A trip through the **Merseyside Maritime Museum** (daily 10am–5pm; £3; free with NMGM Eight Pass), filling one wing of the Albert Dock, can easily take two hours. Spread over four floors, it has sections on the history of Liverpool's evolution as a port and ship-building centre, and models of seacraft – from Samoan rafts to opulent passenger liners. An illuminating display details Liverpool's pivotal role as a springboard for over nine million emigrants – the Irish potato famine and a multiplicity of European wars, combined with the lure of gold and free land, brought people scurrying here to buy their passage to North America or Australia. On board the ships – there's a walk-through example – people were packed into dark, noisy ranks of bunks where they "puffed, groaned, swore, vomited, prayed, moaned and cried". The museum is at its best in its "Transatlantic Slavery" exhibit, which manages to be enlightening, shocking and refreshingly honest, and banishes years of Eurocentric excuses to expose the true horror of the exploitation of African slaves who were kidnapped, abused and sold as property. The conditions they endured on the transatlantic voyage are illustrated by a reconstruction of a slave ship, echoing with haunting voices reading from diaries of slaves and slavers, telling of rape, torture and death. Meanwhile, the *HM Customs and Excise Museum*, inside the Maritime Museum, gives the lowdown on smuggling and revenue collection.

The **Museum of Liverpool Life** (daily 10am–5pm; £3, free with NMGM Eight Pass) lies across the dock. Particularly revealing about the hardships that have moulded the

---

THE BEATLES IN LIVERPOOL

Liverpool has sustained its musical impetus ever since the Sixties and is still turning out some excellent bands, but none is ever likely to eclipse **The Beatles**. Mathew Street, ten minutes' walk west of Lime Street station, is where *The Cavern* used to be – once the womb of Merseybeat, it's become a little enclave of Beatles nostalgia, typified by the Cavern Walks Shopping Arcade, with an awful bronze statue of the boys in the atrium. *The Cavern* itself was where the band was first spotted by Brian Epstein; the club closed in 1966 and was partly demolished in 1973, though a latterday successor, the *Cavern Club* at 10 Mathew St, complete with souvenir shop, was rebuilt on half of the original site. The *Cavern Pub*, immediately across the way, is also a musical arriviste, boasting a coiffed Lennon lounging against the wall and an exterior "Cavern Wall of Fame", highlighting the names of all the bands who appeared at the club between 1957 and 1973.

For the history, head to the Albert Dock for **The Beatles Story** in the Britannia Vaults (daily: April–Sept 10am–6pm; Oct–March 10am–5pm; £6.45), tracing The Beatles' rise from the early days at *The Cavern* to their disparate solo careers. Dedicated pilgrims will get more from the two-hour Beatles **Magical Mystery Tour** (July & Aug Mon–Fri & Sun 2.20pm, Sat 11.50am & 2.20pm; rest of year 2.20pm; book through Mersey Tourism, ☎0151/709 3285; £9.50), on board a customized double-decker bus staffed by guides with – in some cases – first-hand acquaintance with The Beatles. It leaves Albert Dock, visiting Strawberry Fields (a Salvation Army home), Penny Lane (an ordinary suburban street) and the terraced houses where the lads grew up. One of these, **20 Forthlin Road**, home of the McCartney family from 1955–1964, has been preserved by the National Trust and is now open to visitors who duly tramp round the 1950s terraced house where John and Paul wrote songs and where Paul's mother Mary died. The house is only accessible on a pre-booked minibus tour (June–Oct Wed–Sat; £4.50; £1.50; NT), which leaves half-a-dozen times daily from Speke Hall (see opposite) – the price includes the tour, the minibus to Forthlin Road and free access to Speke Hall grounds. Beatlemania is wholeheartedly celebrated on August Bank Holiday Monday (the last Monday of the month) at the culmination of the annual Beatles Week and **Mathew Street Festival**, filling the town centre with wannabe moptops.

resilient Scouse character, it has excellent sections on the city's traditional work, with investigations of the lives of ordinary shipwrights, stevedores, carters and seamen. The role of trade unions is traced, from protests in the eighteenth century to the 1981 and 1983 Peoples' March for Jobs, and there's space too for coverage of topics as diverse as the women's suffrage movement and the social unrest that led to the Toxteth riots in the 1980s. In the popular-culture sections, Merseyside football gets good coverage, as does Aintree's Grand National, music from the Sixties to the Nineties, the homegrown soap *Brookside* and local writers like Alan Bleasdale, Willy Russell, Beryl Bainbridge and Carla Lane.

The neighbouring **Tate Gallery Liverpool** (Tues–Sun 10am–6pm; free; special exhibitions usually £2.50–5) is the country's foremost twentieth-century art showcase outside the capital, drawing from the same pool of paintings and sculpture as its London cousin, and often displaying them more successfully in its spacious and well-lit rooms.

Out of the centre

North of the city centre, Liverpool's suburbs form the backdrop for the city's most popular recreational activity, **football**. Liverpool football club has never quite recovered its glory days of the Seventies and Eighties, but its supporters are counted among the nation's best and most loyal. Everton, the city's less glamorous and recently far less successful side, commands equally intense devotion. Liverpool plays at **Anfield** (ticket office ☎0151/260 8680) and offers a tour around the museum, trophy room and dressing rooms (daily 10am–5pm; museum & tour £8; museum only £5; booking essential ☎0151/260 6677). Everton plays at **Goodison Park** (ticket office ☎0151/330 2300; tours Mon, Wed, Fri & Sun 11am & 2pm; £4; booking advised).

Further north still, at Aintree, the first Saturday in April is **Grand National Day** – the "World's Greatest Steeplechase". The race is the culmination of a meeting that starts on the previous Thursday, with prices of entry into the grounds ranging from £7 to £65. Catch the Merseyrail to Aintree and buy a ticket on the gate or book on ☎0151/523 2600. A new Visitor Centre (☎0151/522 2922) lets you ride the National on a race simulator.

Six miles southeast of the centre, **Speke Hall** (Easter–Oct Tues–Sun 1–5.30pm; Nov to mid-Dec Sat & Sun 1–4.30pm; gardens Easter–Oct Tues–Sun 1–5.30pm; Nov–Easter Tues–Sun 1–4.30pm; house & gardens £4.10; gardens only £1.50; NT) is one of the country's finest examples of Elizabethan timbered architecture. Sitting in an oasis of rhododendrons, the house encloses a beautifully proportioned courtyard overlooked by myriad diamond panes. Highlights of the interior are the Jacobean plasterwork in the Great Parlour and the Great Hall's carved oak panel. Bus #80/180 from Paradise Street in the city centre to the airport runs within half a mile of the entrance.

For a glimpse of one of the more benign aspects of Merseyside's industrial past, take the Merseyrail under the river to **Port Sunlight**, a garden village created in 1888 by industrialist William Hesketh Lever for the workers at his soap factory. The project, similar in scope to those of Titus Salt at Saltaire near Bradford and John Cadbury at Bournville in Birmingham, is explained at the **Port Sunlight Heritage Centre**, 95 Greendale Rd (April–Oct daily 10am–4pm; Nov–March Sat & Sun 10am–4pm; 40p), set amid the open-planned housing estates. Off Greendale Road, a little further from Port Sunlight station, the **Lady Lever Art Gallery** (Mon–Sat 10am–5pm, Sun noon–5pm; £3; free with NMGM Eight Pass) houses a small collection of English eighteenth-century furniture and Pre-Raphaelite paintings by artists such as Rossetti and Ford Madox-Brown.

Eating, drinking and nightlife

Liverpool's dining scene is slowly shifting up a gear and there's now a fair choice of classy **restaurants** alongside a great selection of cafés and budget places. Most are around Hardman and Bold streets, at Albert Dock, and along spruced-up Nelson Street, heart of Liverpool's **Chinatown**, which stretches around the corner onto Berry Street. **Café-bars** have made a belated appearance, both down at the Albert Dock and in the central streets off Bold Street: Concert Square, especially, has three of them, where you can hog the pavement tables until 2am at the weekends.

Liverpool's **pubs** stay open later than most, with many now serving until 1am or 2am. Several act as **live music** venues for up-and-coming bands, who tend to disappear from the local circuit as soon as they achieve fame. The rise of late-opening bars has stolen a good deal of trade from the **clubs**, which are mainly notable for their lack of pretence, fashion playing second string to dancing and drinking. The evening paper, the *Liverpool Echo*, has listings of what's going on, and there are usually plenty of flyers in the shops, bars and cafés.

Cafés and café-bars

Beluga Bar, 40 Wood St. Cool basement space that's great for just a drink, or come to eat – there's a changing, seasonal menu. Mon–Sat 11am–2am.

Bluecoat Café Bar, Bluecoat Chambers, School Lane. Mainly vegetarian food – salad bar, baked potatoes and dips – served throughout the day. Closed Sun.

Brook Café, Quiggins Centre, 12–16 School Lane. Hipster hangout on the top floor for breakfast (10am–noon) and all-day café meals. Closed Sun.

Café Blue, Albert Dock. Brick-vaulted café-bar for budget lunches, cappuccino, a tapas dinner or a late-night drink. Mon–Thurs & Sun noon–11pm, Fri & Sat noon–1am.

Café Tabac, 126 Bold St. Popular licensed café with veggie bohemian leanings. Mon–Sat till 11pm, Sun till 5pm.

Everyman Bistro, 9–11 Hope St. Cool theatre-basement hangout with great quiche, pizza and salad type meals for around a fiver. Mon–Sat noon–midnight.

Taste, Tate Gallery, Albert Dock. The Tate's café-bar serves nachos, salads and sandwiches during the day, and varied tapas and paella in the evening. Sun, Tues & Wed 10am–6pm, Thurs–Sat 10am–11pm.

Restaurants

Armadillo Restaurant, 31 Mathew St (☎0151/236 4123). Mediterranean-style dishes with a vegetarian bias. Closed Sun & Mon. Moderate to Expensive.

Becher's Brook, 29A Hope St (☎0151/707 0005). The city's best restaurant. Seasonal Modern-British dishes served with panache. Closed Sat lunch & all Sun. Expensive.

Est Est Est, Unit 6, Edward Pavilion, Albert Dock (☎0151/708 6969). Authentic pizza and pasta – you may have to wait in line at weekends. Inexpensive.

Far East, 27–35 Berry St (☎0151/709 6072). One of the longest-serving and most reliable of Liverpool's Cantonese eating houses. Moderate.

The Lower Place, Philharmonic Hall, Hope St (☎0151/210 1955). Fast winning friends with its chargrilling, oven-roasting, sun-drying ways. Closed Sun. Expensive.

Not Sushi, Imperial Court, Exchange St East (☎0151/709 8894); and at Bar XS, 80 Bold St (☎0151/707 8777). Japanese noodle bar serving grilled chicken, gyoza dumplings *and* sushi. Inexpensive to Moderate.

Number Seven Café, 7 Falkner St (☎0151/709 9633). Laid-back restaurant (with adjacent deli) with a daily changing blackboard menu of contemporary flavours. Kitchen closes at 9pm. Moderate.

Ziba, 15–19 Berry St (☎0151/708 8870). Stylish space serving cutting-edge Modern-British food along with risottos, oriental flourishes and vegetarian specialities. Closed Sun eve. Expensive.

Pubs, bars and clubs

The Baltic Fleet, 33A Wapping. Restored pub with age-old shipping connections, across from the youth hostel. It's got a great period feel and is known for its fine food and local beer.

Cream, Wolstenholme Square, off Hanover St (☎0151/709 1693). One of Liverpool's most popular clubs, often featuring big DJ names (when the cover charge will be steep).

The Dispensary, 87 Renshaw St. Entirely synthetic but highly sympathetic recreation of a Victorian pub using rescued and antique wood, glass and tiles. A real-ale choice.

The Flying Picket, 24 Hardman St. A friendly local tucked in behind the Trade Union centre. *The Picket*, upstairs, is one of the best venues for local bands.

The Grapes, 25 Mathew St. Busy city-centre pub in the Cavern Quarter, where John, Paul, George and Ringo once downed pints between sets at *The Cavern*.

The Lomax, 34 Cumberland St (☎0151/707 9977). Indie band venue with nightly gigs. Cover £3–10.

Metz, Baker House, Rainford Gardens, off Mathew St. Great sounds, food and drink in the Cavern Quarter.

The Philharmonic, 36 Hope St. A superb, traditional watering-hole where the main attractions – the beer aside – are the mosaic floors, tiling, and the marble decor in the gents.

Ye Cracke, 13 Rice St. Crusty backstreet pub off Hope Street, much loved by the young Lennon, and with a great jukebox.

Arts and culture

The Royal Liverpool Philharmonic Orchestra, up with Manchester's Hallé as the north-west's best, dominates the city's **classical music scene** and often plays at the Philharmonic Hall and the Everyman Theatre. Annual **festivals** include the Hope Street Art Festival (June); a celebration of African arts and music in Africa Oye (June); the Summer Pops (July), when the Royal Philharmonic sets itself up beneath a huge marquee on King's Dock to perform a series of classical concerts; the **Brouhaha Street Theatre Festival** (August), which involves performances by a host of European theatre groups; and the **Mathew Street Festival** (August), a free shindig, with local and national street performers playing the best of The Beatles.

Bluecoat Arts Centre, School Lane (☎0151/709 5297). Eclectic mix of events – drama, dance, poetry, comedy, music and art exhibitions; always worth a look.

Everyman Theatre, Hope St (☎0151/709 4776). Presents everything from Shakespeare to Jarman, as well as concerts, exhibitions, dance and musical performances.

Liverpool Empire Theatre, Lime St (☎0151/709 1555). The city's largest theatre, a venue for touring West End shows, opera, ballet and music. The Beatles' first major gig was here in 1962.

Philharmonic Hall, Hope St (☎0151/709 3789). Home of the Royal Liverpool Philharmonic Orchestra, and with a full programme of other concerts. Shows classic films once a month.

Royal Court Theatre, Roe St (☎0151/709 4321). Refurbished Art Deco theatre and concert hall, which sees regular pop and rock concerts among other events.

Listings

Airport ☎0151/486 8877 or 448 1234.

Banks and exchanges American Express, 54 Lord St (☎0151/708 9202); Thomas Cook, 55 Lord St (☎0151/236 1951). You can also change money at the two tourist offices, the two main post offices (see below) and at the airport.

Bookshops Most of the bookshops are along Bold Street: Dillons at no. 14, Waterstones at no. 52 and the more radical News from Nowhere at no. 112.

Buses National Express (☎0990/808080); Merseytravel (☎0151/236 7676).

Car rental Avis, 113 Mulberry St (☎0151/709 4737); Budget, 418 Scotland Rd (☎0151/298 1888); Europcar, St Vincent St (☎0151/708 9150); Hertz, 8 Brownlow Hill (☎0151/709 3337).

Ferries Isle of Man Steam Packet Company (☎08705/523523); Norse Irish Ferries (☎0151/944 1010); Sea Cat (☎08705/523523).

Hospital Royal Liverpool University Hospital, Prescot Street (☎0151/706 2000).

Laundry Liver Launderette, 2B Princess Rd (Mon–Fri 9am–6pm, Sun 9am–4pm).

Left luggage Lime Street Station, daily 7am–10pm; £2.

Pharmacy Moss Chemists, 68–70 London Rd. Open daily until 11pm.

Police The Cop Shop, Church St (☎0151/709 6010).

Post offices City-centre offices at 23–33 Whitechapel, and The Lyceum, 1 Bold St.

Taxis Mersey Cabs (☎0151/298 2222); Davy Liver (☎0151/709 4646); Computer Cabs (☎0151/709 5553).

Travel agent Discounted and student tickets from USIT Campus, at YHA shop, 25 Bold St (☎0151/709 9200), plus branches at both universities.

Trains for all enquiries, call ☎0345/484950.

Blackpool

Shamelessly brash **BLACKPOOL** is the archetypal British seaside resort, its "Golden Mile" of piers, fortune-tellers, amusement arcades, tram and donkey rides, fish-and-chip shops, candyfloss stalls, fun pubs and bingo halls making no concessions to anything but low-brow fun-seeking of the finest kind. There are seven miles of wide sandy beach backed by an unbroken chain of hotels and guest houses, and though the sea-water quality is still highly debatable, even after heavy investment in a new sewage system, there's nothing wrong with the beach itself – except for the crowds packing the central stretches on hot summer days. Sixteen million people come here each year, and love every minute.

Wealthy visitors were already summer holidaying in Blackpool at the end of the eighteenth century, and while it took a day to get there from Manchester by carriage and two days from Yorkshire, the town remained a select destination. The coming of the railway in 1846 made Blackpool what it is today: within thirty years, there were piers, promenades and theatres for the thousands who descended. The **Winter Gardens**, with its barrel-vaulted ballroom, the Baroque **Grand Theatre** on Church Street, and other refined diversions were built to cater to the tastes of the first influx, but it was the Central Pier's "open air dancing for the working classes" that heralded the crucial change of accent. Suddenly Blackpool was favoured destination for the "Wakes Weeks", when whole Lancashire mill towns descended for their annual seven days' holiday.

Where other British holiday resorts have suffered from the rivalry of cheap foreign packages, Blackpool has simply gone from strength to strength by shrewdly providing exactly what its visitors want. Underneath the populist veneer there's a sophisticated marketing approach which balances ever more elaborate rides and attractions with well-grounded traditional entertainment. When other resorts begin to close up for the winter, Blackpool's main season is just beginning, as over half a million light bulbs are used to create **the Illuminations** which decorate the promenade from the beginning of September to early November.

The town and attractions

With seven miles of beach – the tide ebb is a full half a mile, leaving plenty of sand at low tide – and accompanying promenade, you'll want to jump on and off the electric **trams** if you plan to get up and down much between the piers. South Pier to North Pier – between which lies most of what there is to see and do – costs 80p.

The major event in town is Blackpool's **Pleasure Beach** on the South Promenade (March–Easter, Nov & Dec weekends only, Easter–Oct daily; hours vary, call ☎01253/341033), just south of South Pier – billed as "Britain's biggest tourist attraction". Entrance to the amusement park is free, but you'll have to fork out for the superb array of "white knuckle" rides including "The Big One", the world's fastest roller-coaster, or the "PlayStation", which whooshes you up a 200-foot steel tower at 80mph and then drops you back down in free-fall. If you're not leaving until you've been on everything – a sensible course of action – buy one of the ticket books (£20), which saves you paying a pound or two a time to ride (£4.20 for "The Big One"). Across the road, the

Sandcastle (June–Oct daily 10am–5.30pm; Nov–May Sat & Sun only; £5) is the only place you are likely to want to swim. With every aquatic diversion kept at a constant 29°C it can be a welcome respite from the biting sea air. Jump a tram for the ride up to **Central Pier** with its 108-foot-high revolving Big Wheel. The **Sea Life Centre** (summer Mon–Thurs & Sun 10am–6pm, Fri & Sat 10am–10pm; rest of year daily 10am–6pm; £5.50) here is one of the country's best, with eight-foot sharks looming at you as you march through a glass tunnel.

Between Central and North piers stands the 518-foot **Blackpool Tower** – the skyline's only real touch of grace – erected in 1894 when it was thought that the northwest really ought not to be outdone by Paris. It's now marketed as "Tower World" (Easter to early Nov daily 10am–11pm; rest of year Sat 10am–11pm, Sun 10am–6pm; £6.50; times and prices can vary, call ☎01253/622242) which offers a ride up to the top (where there's a postbox), an unnerving walk on the see-through glass floor, plus a visit to the Edwardian ballroom and various other attractions. From the very early days, there's been a Moorish-inspired **circus** (June–Oct 2 shows daily except Fri; £6.50; combined ticket with Tower £9) between the tower's legs, which in the spirit of the times is now animal-free.

Practicalities

Blackpool's main **train station** is Blackpool North half a dozen blocks up Talbot Road from North Pier. A few steps down Talbot Road, towards the sea, stands the combined National Express and local **bus station**. The main **tourist office** at 1 Clifton St (Easter to early Nov Mon–Sat 9am–5pm, Sun 10am–3.45pm; rest of year Mon–Thurs & Sat 8.45am–4.45pm, Fri 8.45am–4.15pm; ☎01253/478222) is on the corner of Talbot Road, five minutes' walk from the stations; a seasonal office sits on the prom opposite Blackpool Tower.

Blackpool claims to have more **hotel beds** than Portugal, and prices are generally low (from £15 per person, even less out of season), but rise on weekends during the Illuminations. *The Garfield*, 22 Springfield Rd (☎01253/628060; ①), two blocks west of Talbot Road, is convenient for station and town; *Boltonia*, 124–126 Albert Rd (☎01253/620248; ②), marks a qualitative step up. The non-smoking *Wildlife Hotel*, 39 Woodfield Rd (☎01253/346143; no credit cards; ①), halfway between Central and South piers, is a vegan guest house. Along North Shore, a mile or so from the action, the grid west of Warbreck Hill Road has hundreds more options, including detached properties like *Grosvenor View*, 7–9 King Edward Ave (☎01253/352851; ③). The *Imperial*, on North Promenade (☎01253/623971; ⑧), is the politician's conference favourite.

GAY BLACKPOOL

Blackpool has become one of the most popular gay resorts in the country, with around forty hotels and guest houses that welcome, or cater specifically for, a gay clientele. Blackpool tourist office can supply a full gay **accommodation** list, but good places to try first include *Raffles Hotel*, set back from Central Pier at 73–75 Hornby Rd (☎01253/294713; ②); *Mardi Gras*, 41–43 Lord St (☎01253/751087; ②); the all-male *Trades Hotel*, 51–55 Lord St (☎01253/294812; ②); and the *Amalfi Guest House*, for women, at 19–21 Eaves St (☎01253/622971; ①).

There's **nightlife** to match, with *Funny Girls* (see p.528) the most high-profile venue. *Flamingos*, opposite the train station at the top of Talbot Road (☎01253/624901), is the largest and liveliest gay club outside London, with four storeys of dancefloors. Gay **bars** include the *Flying Handbag*, 170 Talbot Rd (☎01253/625522); *Basil's on the Strand*, 9 The Strand (☎01253/294 109); *Lucy's Bar*, beneath *Rumours* in Talbot Square (☎01253/293204); and the *Cow Bar*, inland at Cookson and Church streets (☎01253/623537).

Eating revolves around fish and chips, available all over town, but at its supreme best in *Harry Ramsden's*, 60–63 The Promenade, on the corner of Church Street near the Tower. Even more traditional seaside food is available from the wood-panelled, 120-year-old *Robert's Oyster Bar*, 92 The Promenade, near the base of the Tower, where you wash your oysters, cockles and mussels down with a Guinness from the *Mitre* pub around the corner. *Lagoonda*, 37 Queen St (☎01253/293837), off Talbot Square, is a party-time Afro-Caribbean restaurant, though if you really want a blowout, head for the expensive *September Brasserie*, 15–17 Queen St (☎01253/623282; closed Sun & Mon).

If you like your **nightlife** late, loud and libidinous, summertime Blackpool has few English peers. *Yates' Wine Lodge* has two popular branches, in Talbot Square and between Central and South piers. There's a rowdy bar in the *Clifton Hotel*, at North Pier; and a plethora of Irish theme bars, notably *O'Neill's* on the corner of Talbot Road and Abingdon Street, and *Finn's* on Talbot Square. The *Pump & Truncheon*, 13 Bonny St, behind the Sea Life Centre, is a real-ale pub. For **dancing**, local opinion favours *Main Entrance*, at the Central Promenade. *Funny Girls*, a transvestite-run bar on Queen St at Queen Square, has nightly shows which attract long (gay and straight) queues. Specific **music** spots to look out for include the *Tache* in Cookson Street, behind the Talbot Road bus station, which has live rock, pop and indie bands, while the *Blackpool Opry*, 181–189 Church St, is the place for country music and line dancing.

Clitheroe and the Ribble Valley

When the nineteenth-century cotton weavers of Preston enjoyed a rare break from their industry they took to the bucolic retreats of the **Ribble Valley** which cuts through the heart of northern Lancashire to the River Ribble's source in the Yorkshire Dales. In stark contrast to the conurbations to the south, the valley – then, as now – parades a stream of small market towns and isolated villages set among verdant fields and rolling hills.

A tidy little market town on the banks of the River Ribble, **CLITHEROE** (regular trains from Manchester) is best seen from the terrace of its empty **Norman keep**. From here, the small centre is laid out before you and, if there's little else specific to see – save a **Castle Museum** (May–Sept daily 11am–5pm; rest of the year closed Thurs & Fri; £1.50) in the extensive grounds – you can at least spend an hour or two browsing around the shops and old pubs. An obvious target is Pendle Hill, a couple of miles to the east, where the ten **Pendle Witches** allegedly held the diabolic rites that led to their hanging in 1612. The evidence against them came mainly from one small child, but nonetheless a considerable mythology has grown up around the witches, who are remembered in a hilltop gathering each Halloween.

Much of the northwestern part of the region is occupied by thinly populated grouse moorland known as the **Forest of Bowland** – the name "forest" is used in its traditional sense of "a royal hunting ground", and much of the land still belongs to the Crown. From Clitheroe, buses run out to Dunsop Bridge, Newton and Slaidburn, the three tiny villages in the heart of the region. Pedal Power on Waddington Road in Clitheroe (☎01200/422066) can sort you out with a **mountain bike** for in-depth exploration. **SLAIDBURN** is the most substantial and attractive of the Forest's settlements. Hoary stone cottages fronted by a strip of aged cobbles set the tone – a truly ancient **inn**, the *Hark to Bounty* (☎01200/446246; ③), and a popular **youth hostel** (☎01200/446656; closed Oct–March), itself a former inn, complete the picture.

Lancaster

LANCASTER, Lancashire's county town, dates back at least as far as the Roman occupation, though only the scant remains of a bath-house and traces of the fort wall survive from that period. It became an important port on the slave triangle, and it's the legacy of predominantly Georgian buildings from that time that gives the town its character. It's no surprise that many people choose to spend a night here on the way to the Lakes or Dales to the north, and it's an easy side-trip the few miles west to the resort of Morecambe if the lure of the beach becomes too strong.

Lancaster Castle (tours: Easter–Oct daily 10.30am–5pm; last tour at 4pm; £3.50) has been the city's focal point since Roman times, when there was a fort on this site. About a quarter of the building can be visited on an hour's tour beginning around the back in the Shire Hall, though as the prison is due to close in the next few years it's hoped that more of the building should eventually be open to the public. The castle's neighbour, the former Benedictine **Priory Church of St Mary** (Easter–Oct daily 9.30am–5pm; free), has a Saxon doorway at the west end and some finely carved fourteenth-century choir stalls.

A two-minute walk down the steps between the castle and church brings you to the seventeenth-century **Judges' Lodging** (Easter–June & Oct Mon–Sat 2–5pm; July–Sept Mon–Fri 10am–1pm & 2–5pm, Sat & Sun 2–5pm; £2), once used by visiting magistrates and now home to two museums. The ground and first floors house furniture by Gillows of Lancaster, one-time boat builders who, in the eighteenth century, took to cabinet-making with the tropical timber which came back as ballast in their boats. Their high-quality work eventually earned them contracts to fit the great Cunard transatlantic liners, the *Queen Mary* and *Queen Elizabeth*. The finely worked pieces on display mainly come from the earlier period, with an especially beautiful Regency writing desk and a magnificent billiards table – Gillows are credited with first putting the slate under the baize.

Continuing down the hill and left onto Dameside you arrive on the riverbank, where the top floor of one of the eighteenth-century warehouses is taken up by part of the **Maritime Museum**, St George's Quay (daily: Easter–Oct 11am–5pm; Nov–Easter 12.30–4pm; £2), entered through the Old Custom House. The museum's ample coverage of life on the sea and inland waterways of Lancashire is complemented by the **City Museum** on Market Street (Mon–Sat 10am–5pm; free), based in the former town hall, built in 1781, five minutes' walk east of the Judges' Lodging. This explores the city's history through Neolithic, Roman, medieval and Georgian Lancaster.

Practicalities

From the combined local bus and National Express **station** on Cable Street it's a five-minute walk to the **tourist office** at 29 Castle Hill (April–June & Oct Mon–Sat 10am–5pm; July–Sept Mon–Sat 10am–6pm, Sun noon–4pm; Nov–March Mon–Sat 10am–4pm; ☎01524/32878), in front of the castle, which is well signposted from the **train station**, a couple of hundred yards away in Meeting House Lane.

Victoria House, 35 West Rd (☎01524/381489; ②), is an amiable **B&B** in a restored Victorian house. The *Waggon & Horses*, St George's Quay (☎01524/846094; ②), has pleasant rooms above a riverside pub, just past the Maritime Museum, or for a central hotel, try the *Royal King's Arms*, Market St (☎01524/32451; ⑤), opposite the castle. Cheaper lodgings are available at the *Shakespeare Hotel*, 96 St Leonardsgate (☎01524/841041; ②), a popular non-smoking townhouse hotel. For **meals**, the *Fortune Star*, Thurnham St, is a cheap and cheerful Cantonese restaurant; you can fill up for around £8 at *Pizza Margherita*, 2 Moor Lane; and vegetarians should head for the *The*

Whale Tail, an amiable café at 78A Penny St. If you want to splash out, *Il Bistro Morini*, 26 Sun St (☎01524/846252), is the best Italian in town and is moderately priced. The city's main **arts centre**, *Dukes*, on Moor Lane (☎01524/66645), has a cinema, theatre and other concerts events. Best **pub** is *Ye Olde John O'Gaunt*, Market Street, near the City Museum, serving home-cooked food, and with live trad jazz and R&B and a beer garden.

The Isle of Man

The **Isle of Man**, almost equidistant from Ireland, England, Wales and Scotland, is one of the most beautiful spots in Britain, a mountainous, cliff-fringed island just thirty-one miles by thirteen, into which are shoehorned austere moorlands and wooded glens, sandy beaches, fine castles, beguiling narrow-gauge railways and scores of standing stones and Celtic crosses. It takes some effort to reach, and the weather is hardly reliable, factors which have seen tourist numbers fall since its Victorian heyday, when the island developed as rapidly as the other northwestern coastal resorts. This means, though, that the Isle of Man has been spared the worst excesses of the British tourist trade: there's peace and quiet in abundance, picket fences and picnic spots, rural villages straight out of a 1950s picture-book, steam trains and cream teas – a yesteryear ensemble only slightly marred by the island's reputation of being a tax haven for greedy Brits and a refuge for the sort of people who think that even Victorian values were a bit on the lax side.

St Patrick is said to have come here in the fifth century bringing Christianity, which struggled for a while when the **Vikings** established garrisons here in the eleventh century, though they converted while they reigned as **Kings of Mann**. The Scots under Alexander wrested power from the Norsemen in 1275, the beginning of an ultimately unsuccessful 130-year struggle with the English for control of the island. The distinct identity of the island remained intact, however, and many true Manx inhabitants, who comprise a shade under fifty percent of the island's 72,000 population, insist that the Isle of Man is not part of England, nor even of the UK. Indeed, the island has its own government, **Tynwald**, arguably the world's oldest democratic parliament, which has run continuously since 979 AD. The island has its own sterling currency; its own laws, though they generally follow Westminster's; an independent postal service; and a Gaelic-based language which nearly died out but is once again being taught in schools. It also, of course, produces its own tailless version of the domestic cat, as well as famously good kippers and queenies (scallops). At its turn-of-the-century height, tourism was bringing in half a million visitors a year, but in recent times the real moneyspinner has been the **offshore finance industry**, exploiting the island's low income tax and absence of capital gains tax and death duties. More than fifty banks have been established on the island since 1991, whole streets in **Douglas**, the capital, are taken up by consultancies and the island is dotted with the houses and swanky cars of British tax exiles. This hasn't helped the island's image problem, which largely stems from its archaic human rights legislation. Homosexuality was illegal here until 1992, while the death penalty and corporal punishment were only abolished in 1993, in response to pressure from Westminster and the European Union.

Though the landscapes are wonderful, the island's main tourist draw is the **TT (Tourist Trophy) motorcycle races** in the first two weeks in June, a frenzy of speed and burning rubber that's shattered the island's peace annually since 1907. Thousands of bikers swamp the place to watch a non-stop parade of maniacs hurtling round the roads on a 37-mile circuit at speeds approaching 120mph. This is only the most famous of a summer-long list of **rallies and races** on the island's roads, from the Manx Rally (May), International Rally and Manx Classic (both September) to the Kart Racing

Festival (July). If you want to stay on the island at these times, book your accommodation well in advance.

Getting to the island

Most visitors arrive at Douglas, the main port, on **ferries** or **SeaCats**, both run by The Isle of Man Steam Packet Company (☎08705/523523 Mon–Sat 7am–8pm, Sun 9am–8pm), from either Heysham (near Lancaster; ferries only) or Liverpool (ferries and SeaCat). **Heysham** (3hr 30min) has the most frequent service, with two or three sailings a day in July and August dropping to one or two daily during the rest of the year. **Liverpool** manages two to three SeaCat services a day (2hr 30min) between April and September, with a much-reduced ferry service (4hr) at other times. One-way **fares** start at £16 for foot passengers and £95 for cars (the car, driver and one passenger), with five-day deals costing from £55/£152; but advance-purchase tickets, special offers and night-time sailings offer substantial savings. The best **flight** deals are from Liverpool, with Manx Airlines (☎0345/256256) charging from £60–90 return for the forty-minute flight (up to 6 flights daily). Manx Airlines also has flights from Manchester (from £99; 2–3 flights daily; 50min) and several of the UK's other regional airports. Jersey European (☎0870/567 6676) flies from Blackpool (from £70–125; 2 daily; 35min).

Douglas

DOUGLAS has the vast majority of the island's hotels and good restaurants, and it makes as good a base as any, since all roads lead here. A mere market town as late as 1850, with one pier and an undeveloped seafront, Douglas was a product of Victorian mass tourism and displays many similarities to Blackpool, just across the water. However, whereas Blackpool thrives, Douglas – despite its financial acumen – has that permanent end-of-season feel. You can still have a thoroughly enjoyable time in town, but put aside thoughts of state-of-the-art entertainment and sophisticated nightlife. Instead, pull up a candy-striped deckchair and enjoy the extensive sands. When it rains, stroll the covered arcades, ride the trams or attend the afternoon tea dances.

The seafront vista has changed little since Victorian times, and is still trodden by heavy-footed carthorses pulling **trams**. On Harris Promenade the opulent **Gaiety Theatre**, fronted by a stained glass canopy, is unique among the nine theatres designed by Frank Matcham, which include the Grand in Blackpool. Up Victoria Street, past the Manx Legislative Building, the **Manx Museum**, on the corner of Kingswood Grove and Crellins Hill (Mon–Sat 10am–5pm; free), makes a good start for anyone wanting to get to grips with Manx culture and heritage. Various rooms provide an absorbing synopsis of the island's history, packed with Neolithic standing stones, Celtic grave markers and other artefacts, notably some excellent displays relating to Viking burials and runic crosses. Much of the current understanding of Manx culture was pieced together from digs at Peel Castle in the 1980s, which turned up a cache of silver coins minted in Dublin in 1030, and evidence of a pagan sacrifice, in the form of a woman's severed scalp, on display next to the trove.

Practicalities

The island's **airport, Ronaldsway** (☎01624/821600 or 826000), is ten miles southwest of Douglas at Ballasalla, close to Castletown. Buses (every 30min–1hr 7am–11pm) connect the airport with Castletown, Port St Mary and Douglas. **Ferries** and SeaCats dock by the **Sea Terminal** at the southern end of the Douglas waterfront. Fifty yards beyond the forecourt taxi rank, the Lord Street **bus station** is the hub of the island's dozen or so bus routes; the **Travel Shop** here (Mon–Sat 8am–5.40pm;

☎01624/662525), at the bottom of Lord Street, has timetable information and sells islandwide **discount travel tickets** for buses and trains. North Quay runs 300 yards west from the bus station alongside the river and fishing port to Douglas Station, the northern terminus of the **steam railway** to Port Erin. The waterfront (progressively Loch, Central and Queen's promenades) runs a mile and a half north to Derby Castle Station for the **electric railway** to Laxey and Ramsey – take the horse-drawn tram along the promenade or bus #23, #24, #25 or #26 from Douglas bus station. The **tourist office** is in the Sea Terminal building (Easter & mid-May to Sept daily 9am–7.30pm; April & Oct daily 9am–5pm; Nov–Easter Mon–Thurs 9am–5.30pm, Fri 9am–5pm, Sat 9.30am–12.30pm; ☎01624/686766).

B&Bs are packed in along Douglas's front and up the roads immediately off Harris Promenade, particularly along Broadway, Castle Mona Avenue, Empress Drive and Empire Terrace. *Blossoms*, 4 The Esplanade (☎01624/673360; ①), and *Seafield*, 14 Empire Terrace (☎01624/674372; ①), are typical of what's on offer. If you're prepared to spend a bit more for proper **hotel** facilities, comparative bargains abound. Top choices include the *Empress Hotel*, Central Promenade (☎01624/661155; no credit cards; ⑤), the fine castellated mansion that is the *Castle Mona Hotel*, Central Promenade (☎01624/624540; ④), and the luxury *Admiral House Hotel*, on Loch Promenade (☎01624/629551; ⑤). The nearest **campsite** backs onto Nobles Park Grandstand on Glencrutchery Road, a mile north of the tourist office (☎01624/621132; closed Oct–May and during TT and Manx Grand Prix races).

The *Bay Room Restaurant*, in the Manx Museum (closed Sun), and *Greens Vegetarian Restaurant*, in the ticket office at the steam railway station, serve inexpensive **food** – though both close at 5pm. *Scotts Bistro*, 7 John St, has queenies in garlic sauce alongside its other Anglo-French choices. The formal *Waterfront Restaurant*, at the top of North Quay (☎01624/673222; closed Sat lunch & all Sun), offers the island's finest dining though the moderate *Blazers Wine Bar* next door (same phone number; closed Sat lunch & all Sun) is run by the same people. *La Tasca*, in the basement of the *Admiral House Hotel* on Loch Promenade (☎01624/629551), has great tapas and Spanish dishes. For **drinking**, the funky *Bushy's Brew Pub* on Victoria Street at the harbour serves own-brewed "Old Bushy Tail", which will soon revive flagging spirits.

The rest of the island

With a car you could see almost everything in a couple of days; even on foot, it only takes around five days to circumnavigate the entire island. But don't miss a trip on one of the two century-old **rail services** which still provide the best public transport to all the major towns and sights except for Peel. The carriages of the **Steam Railway** (Easter–Oct daily 10am–5pm; £7.60 return to Port Erin) rock their fifteen-mile course from Douglas to Castletown, Port St Mary and Port Erin at a spirited pace. The rolling terrain due north of Douglas was too steep for conventional trains, but by 1893 fledgling technology was available to construct the **Manx Electric Railway** (Easter–May, Sept & Oct daily 10am–5pm; June–Aug daily 10am–7.30pm; £6.20 return) which runs for seventeen miles from Douglas's Derby Castle Station to Ramsey via Laxey. It may be worth buying a **day-rover ticket** (£10.70), which covers the electric and steam train routes as well as the trip to Snaefell summit; seven days' unlimited travel on these routes plus free bus and horse-tram rides costs £29.40; there are also separate one-day (£5.20) and three-day (£11.90) **bus rover** tickets.

Laxey

The straggling town of **LAXEY**, seven miles north of Douglas, spills down from its train station to a small harbour and long, pebbly beach, squeezed between two bulky headlands. The Manx Electric Railway from Douglas drops you at the station used by the

Snaefell Mountain Railway. Shops and a couple of cafés here attempt to divert the crowds who disembark and then head inland and uphill to Laxey's pride, the **"Lady Isabella" Great Laxey Wheel** (Easter–Oct daily 10am–5pm; £2.75), the world's largest working waterwheel. Otherwise Laxey is at its best down in **Old Laxey**, around the harbour, half a mile below the station, where large car parks attest to the popularity of the beach and river.

Hourly **buses** #15, #15A and #15C run to Laxey from Douglas; the #15C runs directly to Old Laxey four times a day (not Sun). Old Laxey has several **guest houses** to choose from, but most have only one or two rooms, so book in advance – you can check on space at Douglas tourist office. The *Mines Tavern*, by the station, has some shaded outdoor seats and serves **lunch**, or you can try the *Riverside Studio* close to the waterwheel (☎01624/862121; closed Mon); there's live jazz and blues here on Wednesdays and at weekends. Down at the harbour, the *Shore Hotel* is a nice **pub** by the bridge which brews its own bitter.

Snaefell

Every few minutes, the tram cars of the **Snaefell Mountain Railway** (Easter–Oct daily 10.30am–3.30pm; £6.40 return) begin their thirty-minute wind from Laxey through increasingly denuded moorland to the island's highest point, the top of **Snaefell** (2036ft) – the Vikings' "Snow Mountain" – from where you can see England, Wales, Scotland and Ireland on a clear day. The four-and-a-half miles of track were built in seven months over the winter of 1895 by two hundred men; one gang worked down from the summit, the other up from Laxey, an unimaginable effort in bitter conditions. At the summit, most people are content to pop into the inelegant café and bar and then soak up the views for the few minutes until the return journey.

Maughold and Ramsey

The Manx Electric Railway trains stop within a mile and a half of **MAUGHOLD**, seven miles northeast of Laxey, a tiny hamlet just inland of the cliffside lighthouse at **Maughold Head**. It's an isolated spot which only adds to the attraction of Maughold's parish church, in whose grounds is maintained an outstanding collection of early Christian and Norse **carved crosses** – 44 pieces, dating from the sixth to the thirteenth centuries, and ranging from fragments of runic carving to a six-foot-high rectangular slab. Look inside the church at the old parish cross, fourteenth century in date and sporting the earliest known picture of the Three Legs of Mann apart from that on the twelfth-century Sword of State.

RAMSEY marks the northern terminus of the Electric Railway, 45 minutes beyond Laxey. The Victorian tourist boom left behind the island's only iron pier and a solitary grand terrace along the front, but the bulk of the town, by the harbour – once more important than that in Douglas – is a dispiriting swatch of build-by-numbers modernity. The beach really isn't worth hanging around for and the only sight, the **Grove Rural Life Museum** (Easter–Sept daily 10am–5pm; £2.75), is a mile north on the A9.

St Johns

The trans-island A1 (and hourly bus #5 or #6 from Douglas) follows a deep twelve-mile-long furrow between the northern and southern ranges from Douglas to Peel. A hill at the crossroads settlement of **ST JOHNS**, nine miles along it, is the original site of **Tynwald**, the ancient Manx government, which derives its name from the Norse *Thing Völlr*, meaning "Assembly Field". Nowadays the word refers to the Douglas-based House of Keys and Legislative Council, but acts passed in the capital only become law once they have been proclaimed here on July 5 (ancient Midsummer's Day) in an annual open-air parliament that also hears the grievances of the islanders.

Tynwald's four-tiered grass mound – made from soil collected from each of the island's parishes – stands at the other end of a processional path from the stone **St John Chapel**, which traditionally doubled as the courthouse.

Peel

The main settlement on the west coast, **PEEL** immediately captivates, with its fine castle rising across the harbour and a popular sandy beach running the length of its eastern promenade. It's a town of some antiquity and its enduring appeal is as one of the most "Manx" of all the island's towns, a character that is manifested in various ways – from an age-old Tuesday market in the market place above the harbour to the line of smoke-belching kipper factories along the harbourside. Archeological evidence indicates that **St Patrick's Isle**, which guards the harbour, has had a significant population since Mesolithic times. What probably started out as a flint-working village on a naturally protected spot gained significance with the foundation of a monastery in the seventh or eighth century, parts of which remain inside the ramparts of the red sandstone **Peel Castle** (Easter–Sept daily 10am–5pm; £3; NT & EH). The Vikings built the first fortifications and the site became the residence of the Kings of Mann until 1220, when they moved to Castle Rushen in Castletown.

On the way to the castle from the town, walking around the river harbour, you'll have passed the excellent harbourside House of Mannannan **heritage centre** (daily 10am–5pm; £5; combined ticket with castle £7; NT & EH) named after the island's ancient sea-god. You'll should allow at least two hours to get around the museum, which concentrates strongly on participatory exhibits – whether it's listening to Celtic legends in a replica longhouse, examining the contents and occupants of a life-sized Viking ship, walking through a kipper factory or steering a steamer.

The hourly #5 and #6 **bus** from Douglas run into town along the promenade to Crown Street. The much less frequent #8 (not Sun) connects Peel to Port Erin, via St Johns and Castletown. Central **accommodation** includes the Georgian *Merchant's House*, 18 Castle St (☎01624/842541; no credit card; ②), and a couple of B&Bs on Bridge Street, just off the seafront Marine Parade. For sea views, try one of the guest houses which huddle together at the end of Marine Parade; *Fernleigh* (☎01624/842435; no credit card; ②) and *Waldick Hotel* (☎01624/842410; no credit cards; ③). The *Peel Camping Park*, on Derby Road (☎01624/842341; closed mid-Sept to mid-May), is signposted about half a mile out on the Douglas road. When it comes to **eating**, *Chez Cousteau* at Castle Court on the promenade (☎01624/844761) is as good as anything on the island, a wonderful seafood café and oyster bar. The **pub** opposite the House of Mannannan, the *Creek Inn*, also serves reasonable food at its outdoor tables.

Port Erin to Port St Mary

Plans for the southern branch of the steam railway beyond Castletown included the speculative construction of the new resort of **PORT ERIN**, at the southwestern tip of the island, just over an hour's ride from Douglas. The aspect certainly demanded a resort: a wide, fine sand beach backing a deeply indented bay sits beneath green hills, which climb to the tower-topped headland of Bradda Head to the northwest. Families relish the beach here, and the timewarped atmosphere, which appears to have altered little in forty years. When you tire of the sand, it's time to take one of the **cruises** (April–Oct daily; £6–8) to the **Calf of Man** bird sanctuary, half a mile off the southwest coast.

The **train station** is on Station Road, a couple of hundred yards above and back from the beach. **Buses** #1 and #2 (Douglas–Castletown), and #8 (Peel–St Johns), stop on Bridson Street, across Station Road and opposite the *Cherry Orchard* hotel. Most **accommodation** is in holiday apartments or long-stay hotels, booked by the week.

Still, you could try one of the large hotels on the cliff-top promenade, like the *Royal*, *Imperial* or *Countess* (all part of the same group; ☎01624/833116; ④), which offer out-of-season discounts. The *Balmoral Hotel*, further down the Promenade (☎01624/833126; ③), and the nearby *Falcon's Nest*, at the seafront end of Station Road (☎01624/834077; ③), are cheaper options. The beachfront **cafés** serve the usual daytime snacks and meals – you're better off heading instead for *La Patisserie* on Church Road, a deli-bakery which will make up sandwiches to take away.

The harbour at Port Erin marks the start of a six-mile loop around Meayll Hill on the coastal path past **Spanish Head**, the island's southern tip, to **Port St Mary**. It's one of the best short walks on the island, giving the opportunity of a detour to **Cregneash Village Folk Museum** (Easter–Sept daily 10am–5pm; £2.75), a picturesque cluster of nineteenth-century thatched crofts on the slopes above Spanish Head. It's peopled at weekends with spinners, weavers, turners and smiths dressed in period costumes.

The fishing harbour still dominates little **PORT ST MARY**, with its houses strung out in a chain above the busy dockside. The best beach is away to the northeast, reached from the harbour along a well-worked Victorian path which clings to the bay's rocky edge.

Castletown

From the twelfth century until 1869, **CASTLETOWN** was the island's capital, but then the influx of tourists and the increase in trade required a bigger harbour, so Douglas took over. So much the better for Castletown, which is a much more pleasant place than it might otherwise have been. Its sleepy harbour and low-roofed cottages are all dominated by **Castle Rushen** (Easter–Sept daily 10am–5pm; £4), one of the most complete and compact medieval castles in Britain. Formerly home to the island's legislature and still the site of the investiture of new lieutenant-governors, the present structure was probably started in the thirteenth century, its limestone walls well under way by the time the last Viking monarch, Magnus, died here in 1256. The heavy defences, comprising three concentric rings of stone-clad ramparts, fosses and a complex series of doors and portcullises, must have made entry a forbidding objective. Today, a mannequin archer guards access to displays on the castle's history, a prelude to five floors of rooms furnished in medieval and seventeenth-century styles, the most evocative being the tapestry-draped banqueting hall.

The **Old Grammar School** was the former capital's first church, built around 1200, and used as a school from 1570. There's not a lot to see, but it does house a handy **tourist office** (Easter–Sept daily 10am–5pm). Below the castle boats and yachts bob about in the harbour, while something of the island's nautical heritage can be gleaned from the little **Nautical Museum** on Douglas Street (daily 10am–5pm; £2.75), just across the harbour footbridge.

The **steam train station** is five minutes' walk from the centre of Castletown, out along Victoria Road from the harbour; **buses** #8 (Peel–Port Erin) and #1 (Douglas–Castletown) stop in the main square. You may find signs advertising local B&Bs, but otherwise the only **accommodation** is the swanky *Castletown Golf Links Hotel* at Derbyhaven (☎01624/822201; ⑤, room only), on the Langness peninsula, east of town. For an outdoor view of the harbour head for the *Chablis Cellar*, 21 Bank St (☎01624/823527; closed Sun eve), which does inexpensive **bistro** lunches and evening meals. The *Castle Arms*, across on the quayside, also serves food.

travel details

Trains

Blackpool to: Manchester (hourly; 1hr 10min).

Chester to: Liverpool (2 hourly; 45min); Manchester (2 hourly; 1hr–1hr 20min).

Lancaster to: Barrow-in-Furness (17 daily; 1hr); Carlisle (hourly; 1hr); Heysham (1 daily; 30min); Morecambe (every 40min; 10min).

Liverpool to: Chester (2 hourly; 45min); Manchester (hourly; 50min).

Manchester to: Barrow-in-Furness (Mon–Sat 7 daily, 3 on Sun; 2hr 15min); Blackpool (hourly; 1hr 10min); Buxton (hourly; 50min); Carlisle (2 daily; 2hr 30min); Chester (2 hourly; 1hr–1hr 20min); Liverpool (every 30min; 50min); Oxenholme (4–6 daily; 40min–1hr 10min); Penrith (2–4 daily; 2hr).

Buses

Blackpool to: Manchester (every 2hr; 1hr 50min); Preston (every 2hr; 40min); Windermere (2 daily; 1hr 40min).

Chester to: Liverpool (hourly; 1hr); Manchester (4 daily; 1hr 15min).

Lancaster to: Barrow-in-Furness (1 daily; 2hr); Carlisle (4–5 daily; 1hr 10min–4hr 30min); Kendal (hourly; 1hr); Keswick (Mon–Sat 10 daily, 5 on Sun; 2hr 50min); Manchester (2 daily; 2hr); Windermere (hourly; 1hr 45min).

Liverpool to: Blackpool (Mon & Fri–Sun 1 daily; 2hr); Chester (hourly; 1hr); Leeds (2 hourly; 2hr 40min); Manchester (hourly; 1hr); Preston (2 daily; 1hr).

Manchester to: Blackpool (every 2hr; 1hr 50min); Buxton (6–7 daily; 1hr 15min); Carlisle (2–3 daily; 2hr 30min); Chester (4 daily; 1hr 15min); Kendal (1–3 daily; 2hr 45min); Keswick (1–3 daily; 3hr 50min); Lancaster (2 daily; 2hr); Liverpool (hourly; 1hr); Preston (9 daily; 1hr 10min); Windermere (1–3 daily; 3hr).

CHAPTER NINE

CUMBRIA AND THE LAKES

The **Lake District** is England's most hyped scenic area, and for good reason. Within an area a mere thirty miles across, sixteen major lakes are squeezed between the steeply pitched faces of England's highest mountains, an almost alpine landscape that's augmented by waterfalls and picturesque stone-built villages packed into the valleys. Most of what people refer to as the Lake District – or simply the Lakes – lies within the **Lake District National Park**, England's largest national park, established in 1951. This, in turn, falls entirely within the northwestern county of **Cumbria**, formed in 1974 from the historic counties of Cumberland and Westmorland, and the northern part of Lancashire. Consequently Cumbria contains more than just its lakes, stretching south and west to the **coast**, and north to its county town of **Carlisle**, a place that bears few traces of a pedigree that stretches back beyond the construction of Hadrian's Wall. To the east, **Penrith** and the **Eden Valley** separate the lakes from the near wilderness of the northern Pennines.

Everywhere in the Lakes is connected by local **bus**, with Stagecoach Cumberland the biggest operator; their **Explorer Tickets** (one-day £5.50, four-day £13.60) are valid on the entire network. The dozens of routes are all spelled out in detail in the free Lakeland Explorer timetable, available from tourist offices; or call Stagecoach Cumberland's **timetable information line** (☎01946/63222 Mon–Sat 7am–7pm, Sun 9am–5.30pm). **Cumbria County Council**'s Journey Planner department (☎01228/606000 Mon–Fri 9am–5pm, Sat 9am–noon) can advise about all the region's bus, coach, rail and ferry services.

The Lake District

Eighteen million visitors a year now pour into the Lake District, making some of the villages even busier than the cities the tourists have come from. Given a week you could

---

ACCOMMODATION PRICE CODES

Throughout this guide, hotel and B&B accommodation is priced on a scale of ① to ⑨, the number indicating the **lowest price** you could expect to pay per night in that establishment for a **double room** in high season. The prices indicated by the codes are as follows:

① under £40	④ £60–70	⑦ £110–150
② £40–50	⑤ £70–90	⑧ £150–200
③ £50–60	⑥ £90–110	⑨ over £200

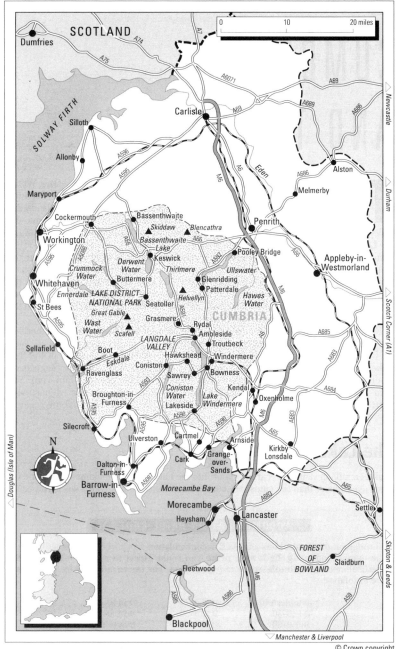

WALKING IN THE LAKE DISTRICT

An almost unchartable network of Lake District paths connects the lakes themselves, tracks the broken knife-edge ridges of the fells and mountains or weaves easier courses around the flanks and onto the tops. The various walks detailed in this section are large-ly aimed at the moderate walker with half a day or so on their hands and require no real experience. Even so, you should always be **properly equipped**: wear strong-soled, sup-portive shoes or boots, carry water, and take a map (and know how to use it). Bad weath-er can move in quickly, even in the height of summer, so before starting out you should check the weather forecast – many hotels and outdoor shops post a daily forecast – call ☎017687/75757 (24-hour line).

The best general **map** of the area is the Ordnance Survey inch-to-the-mile (1:63,360) Touring Map and Guide 3. Essential for **walking** are the 1:50,000 OS *Landranger* maps 89, 90, 96 and 97, or even the yellow 1:25,000 OS *Outdoor Leisure* series, which cover the whole Lake District except the northern flanks of Skiddaw, and are detailed enough to show fences. Many shops and tourist offices also sell local walk leaflets, and regional trail and hiking guides, of which Wainwright's are the best known.

see most of the famous settlements and lakes – a circuit taking in the towns of Ambleside, Windermere and Bowness, all on **Windermere**, the Wordsworth houses and sites in pretty villages like **Hawkshead** and **Grasmere**, and the more dramatic northern scenery near **Keswick** and **Ullswater** would give you a fair sample of the whole. But it's away from the crowds that the Lakes really begins to pay dividends, so aim if you can to steer by central valleys like **Langdale** and **Eskdale**, and the lesser vis-ited lakes of **Wast Water** and **Buttermere**. Of course, it's only when you start to walk and climb around the Lakes that you can really say you've explored the region. Four peaks top out at over 3000 feet – including **Scafell Pike**, the highest in England – but there are literally hundreds of other mountains, crags and fells to roam.

Human interaction has played a significant part in the shaping of the region. Before Neolithic peoples began to colonize the region around five thousand years ago, most of the now bare uplands were forested with pine and birch, while the valleys were blan-keted with thickets of oak and alder. As these first settlers learned to shape flints into axes, they began to clear the upland forests, a process accelerated by the road-building Romans. An even greater impact was made by the Norse Vikings in the ninth and tenth centuries, who farmed the land extensively and left their mark on the local dialect: a mountain here is referred to as a "fell", a waterfall is a "force", streams are "becks", a mountain lake is a "tarn", while the suffix "-thwaite" indicates a clearing. Two factors spurred the first waves of **tourism**: the re-appraisal of landscape brought about by such painters as Constable and the writings of Wordsworth and his contemporaries, and the outbreak of the French Revolution, which put paid to the idea of the continental Grand Tour. At the same time, as the war pushed food prices higher, farmers began to reclaim the hillsides, a tendency sanctioned by the General Enclosure Act of 1801. Most of the characteristic dry-stone walls were built at this time, a development that alarmed Wordsworth, who wrote in his *Guide to the Lakes* that he desired "a sort of national property, in which every man has a right and interest who has an eye to perceive and a heart to enjoy". His wish finally came to fruition in 1951 when the government des-ignated 880 square miles of the Lake District as England's largest national park.

Kendal and around

The limestone-grey town of **KENDAL** might be billed as the "Gateway to the Lakes", but it's nearly ten miles from Windermere – the true start of the lakes – and has more in common with the market towns to the east. As the largest of the southern Cumbrian towns Kendal can be a congested place, but it offers rewarding rambles around the "yards" and "ginnels" which make an engaging maze on both sides of Highgate and Stricklandgate, the main streets. The old **Market Place** has long since succumbed to development, with the market hall now converted to the Westmorland Shopping Centre, but traditional stalls still do business outside every Wednesday and Saturday. The town's most visible product is **Kendal Mintcake**, a solid block of sugar and peppermint oil, an energy-giving confection that has been hoisted to the top of the world's highest mountains.

Of the town's three museums (all daily: April–Oct 10.30am–5pm; Nov–March 10.30am–4pm; £2.50; £1 with a ticket for one of the other museums), the least captivating is the **Kendal Museum**, on Station Road, which houses a fairly run-of-the-mill study of Cumbria's natural history and archeological finds, redeemed by reverential displays on the life of **Alfred Wainwright**. In 1952 this one-time borough treasurer, dissatisfied with the accuracy of existing maps of the paths and ancient tracks across the fells, embarked on what became a series of 47 walking guides, all but two of them painstakingly handwritten with mapped routes and delicately drawn views. The other two museums are in the Georgian **Abbot Hall** and its stable block, by the river to the south. The main hall, painstakingly restored to its 1760s town-house origins, houses the **Art Gallery**, where cherubic portraits by society painter George Romney line the walls, along with works by Constable, Ruskin, Turner, Edward Lear and lesser local artists. The small modern-art collection upstairs is rounded out with Barbara Hepworth's *Oval Form*, gracing the grass between the hall and the stables which house the **Museum of Lakeland Life and Industry**. Here, reconstructed seventeenth-, eighteenth- and nineteenth-century house interiors stand alongside workshops which make a fairly vivid presentation of rural trades and crafts, from spinning and weaving to tanning – medieval Kendal was on the main north–south cattle-trade routes and leather production was once an important local industry. There's also a mock-up study of **Arthur Ransome**, author of the children's classic *Swallows and Amazons*, while John Cunliffe, creator of *Postman Pat*, whose adventures are set just north of Kendal, gets more laid-back treatment next door.

Just behind Abbot Hall, the wide aisles of the Early English **parish church** (daily: Easter–Oct 9.20am–4.30pm; Nov–Easter 9.20am–noon) house a number of family chapels, including that of the Parr family, who once owned **Kendal Castle**, which stands on a hillock to the east across the river. It's claimed as the birthplace of Catherine Parr, Henry VIII's sixth wife, but the story is probably apocryphal – she was born in 1512, at which time the building – now a ruin – was in an advanced state of decay.

Practicalities

Kendal's **train station** is the first stop on the Windermere branch line, five minutes from the **Oxenholme** mainline station. National Express buses stop opposite the **bus station** on Blackhall Rd (off Stramongate) on their way south, but opposite the post office on Stricklandgate going north. The **tourist office** (Easter–Oct Mon–Sat 9am–5pm, Sun 10am–4pm; Nov–Easter Mon–Sat 9am–5pm; ☎01539/725758) is in the town hall on Highgate.

Most of the local **B&Bs** lie along the road to Windermere, north of the centre, though *Bridge House*, 65 Castle St (☎01539/722041; ②), is close to the train station. In the centre itself are the *Hillside Guest House*, 4 Beast Banks (☎01539/722836; ②; closed Dec–Feb), just off All Hallows Lane opposite the town hall, and *Da Franco's Hotel and Restaurant*, 101 Highgate (☎01539/722430; ②). *Lakeland Natural Vegetarian Guesthouse* at Low Slack, Queen's Rd (☎01539/733011; ③), backs onto woods five minutes walk west of the centre. There's a **youth hostel** at 118 Highgate (☎01539/724066), which is attached to The Brewery arts centre. while the most convenient **campsite** is

Ashes Lane at Staveley, four miles northwest of town, off the Windermere Road
(☎01539/821 119; closed mid-Jan to mid-March) – take bus #555.

Kendal certainly doesn't lack decent **cafés**, starting with the *1657 Chocolate House*,
on Branthwaite Brow. For inexpensive veggie wholefood lunches and riverside seating,
visit the *Waterside Café* on Gulfs Road, at the bottom of Lowther Street, or at the highly regarded *Moon*, 129 Highgate (☎01539/729254; dinner only, closed Mon in winter),
an easy-going bistro. The **Brewery Arts Centre**, Highgate (☎01539/725133), with its
café, bar, cinema, theatre and concert hall, is always a good bet.

Sizergh Castle and Levens Hall

Three miles south of Kendal stands **Sizergh Castle** (April–Oct Mon–Thurs & Sun
1.30–5.30pm; gardens open 12.30pm; £4.50; gardens only £2.20; EH), tucked away off
the A591 amid acres of parkland – take bus #555. Home of the Strickland family for
eight centuries, Sizergh is more of a grand manor house than a castle, but owes its epithet to the fourteenth-century peel tower (which you'll often see spelled "pele") at its
core, one of the best examples of the towers built throughout the region as safe havens
during the protracted border raids of the Middle Ages. Like much of the rest of the
house, the Great Hall underwent significant changes in Elizabethan times, when extensions were added to the house and most of its rooms were panelled in oak with their
ceilings layered in elaborate plasterwork.

Two miles south of Sizergh, just of the A590 (also bus #555), **Levens Hall** (April to
mid-Oct Mon–Thurs & Sun noon–5pm; gardens open 10am; house & gardens £5.30;
gardens only £3.90; ☎015395/60321) is also built around an early peel tower, but is
more uniform in style than Sizergh, since the bulk of it was built or refurbished in classic Elizabethan style between 1570 and 1640 by James Bellingham. The main entrance
opens into the spacious Great Hall, its panelled walls lined with coats of arms; to the
left of the hall are the large and small drawing rooms. The other end of the Great Hall
leads to the most splendid apartment, the dining room, panelled not with oak but with
goat's leather, printed with a deep green floral design – one goat was needed for every
forty or so squares. Upstairs, the bedrooms offer glimpses of the beautifully trimmed
topiary gardens.

Windermere, Bowness and around

WINDERMERE town was all but non-existent until 1847 when a railway terminal
was built here, making England's longest lake (after which the town is named) an
easily accessible resort. Most of the guest houses and amenities built for the
Victorians still stand, and Windermere remains the transport hub for the southern
lakes, but there's precious little else to keep you in the slate-grey streets. Instead, all
the traffic pours a mile down hill to its older twin town, **BOWNESS** – bus #599
leaves Windermere train station for the ten-minute run down to Bowness's lakeside
piers. Undoubtedly the more attractive of the two settlements, Bowness spills back
from the lake, though as Cumbria's most popular resort – packed with trinket shops,
cafés and souvenir-hunting tourists – it's a victim of its own popularity. Most tourists,
it seems, bypass everything in Bowness bar the lake for the chance to visit **The
World of Beatrix Potter** in the Old Laundry on Crag Brow (daily: Easter–Sept
10am–6.30pm; Oct–Easter 10am–4pm; £3.25), whose conveyor-belt approach will
soon rid you of any enthusiasm you might have had for the children's story writer.
Five hundred yards north of Bowness, on Rayrigg Road, the **Windermere
Steamboat Museum** (Easter–Oct daily 10am–5pm; £3.25) is a better target – its
star exhibit the 1850 *Dolly*, claimed to be the world's oldest mechanically driven

boat, and extremely well preserved after spending 65 years in the mud at the bottom of Ullswater.

Both, however, come second-best to a trip on **Windermere** itself. Windermere Lake Cruises (☎015394/43360) operates stylish steamers and vintage cruisers to Lakeside at the southern tip (£4 one-way; £5.90 return) or to Waterhead (for Ambleside) at the northern end (£3.80 one-way; £5.70 return). There's also a shuttle service between Bowness piers and Sawrey (£1.20 one-way, £2 return), saving pedestrians the walk down to the car-ferry (see below). A 24-hour **Freedom-of-the-Lake ticket** costs £9.50. Services on both routes are frequent between Easter and October (every 30–60min at peak times and weekends), but much reduced during the winter. The **car-ferry service** across the water to Sawrey (Mon–Sat 7am–10pm, Sun 9am–10pm; departures every 20min; 40p; cars £2), from a pier just south of Bowness, provides access to Beatrix Potter's former home at Hill Top.

Three miles northwest of Windermere, the Lake District National Park has its headquarters at **Brockhole Visitor Centre** (Easter–Oct daily 10am–5pm; grounds & gardens open all year; free; parking £2), a lakeside mansion set in landscaped grounds, with permanent natural history and geological displays. The bookshop is one of the best in the region for local guides and maps, and there's a café with an outdoor terrace overlooking the lake. Buses between Windermere and Ambleside run past the visitor centre, or you can get there by Windermere Lake Cruises launch from Waterhead, Ambleside (hourly 10.45am–4.45pm; £4.30 return).

Cruises also head south down the lake the five or so miles to **Lakeside**, the terminus of the **Lakeside and Haverthwaite Railway** (Easter–Oct 6 daily; £3.40 return; ☎015395/31594), whose steam-powered engines chuff along four miles of track through the forests of Backbarrow Gorge. The boat arrivals at Lakeside connect with train departures throughout the day and you can buy a joint boat-and-train ticket (£8.80 return) at Bowness. Also on the quay at Lakeside is the **Aquarium of the Lakes** (daily 9am–5.30pm; £4.95), an entertaining natural history exhibit centred on the fish and animals found in and along a lakeland river, including a pair of captive otters and a walk-through-tunnel aquarium. Again, there's a combined ticket available with the boat ride from Bowness (£9.10 return).

Practicalities

National Express and most local **buses** stop outside Windermere **train station**, itself only a few yards from the **tourist office** on Victoria Street (daily: July & Aug 9am–7.30pm; rest of the year 9am–5pm; ☎015394/46499). There's a second information office down in Bowness, by the piers on Glebe Road (Easter–Oct Mon–Thurs & Sun 9.30am–6pm, Fri & Sat 9.30am–6.30pm; Nov–Easter Fri–Sun 9.30am–5pm; ☎015394/42895). For **bike rental**, contact Country Lanes, The Railway Station, Windermere (☎015394/44544).

The cheapest **rooms** in Windermere are at the *Backpackers Hostel* in the Old Bakery at the top of the High St (☎015394/46374; no credit cards; ①), across from the tourist office. Otherwise, top **B&B** choices include *Ashleigh Guesthouse* at 11 College Rd (☎015394/42292; no credit cards; ②), and the *Archway* at no. 13 (☎015394/45613; ②); *Brendan Chase*, 1–3 College Rd (☎015394/45638; ②); *Haven*, 10 Birch St (☎015394/44017; no credit cards; ①); *Broadlands Guest House*, 19 Broad St (☎015394/46532; *broadlands@clara.co.uk*; no credit cards; ①); and *Village House*, 5 Victoria St (☎015394/46041; no credit cards; ①). Best hotel choice in Windermere – and a candidate for best in the Lakes – is *Miller Howe*, on Rayrigg Road, the A592 (☎015394/42536, *lakeview@millerhowe.com*; ⑨; closed Jan), whose rooms come with supremely theatrical dinners and breakfasts.

In **Bowness** *Montclare House* on Crag Brow (☎015394/42723; no credit cards; ①), the main street, is as cheap as the **B&Bs** get. *Above The Bay*, 5 Brackenfield (☎015394/88658; no credit cards; ③), has lake views, as does the pricey *The Old England*, Church St (☎015394/42444; ⑦), a relaxed grande-dame hotel opposite the church, with heated outdoor pool and terraced lakeside gardens. For **food**, budget pizza and pasta is on offer at *Rastelli's*, on Lake Road. The most rewarding restaurant is the excellent, upmarket Anglo-Italian *Porthole Eating House*, 3 Ash St (☎015394/42793; closed Tues), with operatic warbling and open fires in winter. For a drink, look no further than *The Hole in't Wall* **pub**, the town's oldest hostelry, in Falbarrow Road behind Bowness church.

Troutbeck

Troutbeck Bridge, a mile northwest of Windermere along the A591, heralds the start of a gentle valley below Wansfell, where you'll find Windermere's local **youth hostel**, *High Cross* at Bridge Lane (☎015394/43543), almost a mile uphill from the bridge. A YHA shuttle-bus service operates to the hostel from Windermere train station (meeting arriving trains) and from Ambleside youth hostel, or there's a fine cross-country walking route (3 miles, 1hr 30min) via **Orrest Head** (784ft), whose summit gives panoramic views over the Yorkshire fells, the Langdales and Troutbeck Valley – the path branches off the main road a hundred yards south of Windermere train station.

A little further up the minor valley road from the hostel, **Townend** (Easter–Oct Tues–Fri & Sun 1–5pm; £3; NT) has been preserved as a seventeenth-century yeoman farmer's house, complete with original furniture and decorative woodwork. Troutbeck's expensive **inn**, the *Mortal Man* (☎015394/33193; ⑦; closed mid-Nov to mid-Feb), has terrific valley views from its rooms and beer-garden, while the *Queen's Head*, down on the main A592 (☎015394/32174; ④; minimum two-night stay at weekends), serves good food.

Ambleside

AMBLESIDE, five miles northwest of Windermere, is at the heart of the southern lakes region, making it a first-class base for walkers, but also ensuring it high-season crowds second only to Windermere's. The town centre consists of a cluster of grey-green stone houses, shops and B&Bs hugging a circular one-way system, which loops round just south of the narrow gully of stony Stock Ghyll. The rest of town lies a mile south at **Waterhead**, a harbour on the shores of Windermere that's filled with ducks, swans and rowboats and overlooked by the landscaped gardens of several plush hotels. There's precious little to look at in Ambleside itself, but you could spare a few minutes for the mural of the rush-bearing ceremony in **St Mary's Church**, whose spire is visible from all over town. A couple of hundred yards north, **Bridge House** (Easter–Oct daily 10am–5pm; free), now a National Trust information centre, straddles Stock Ghyll – scurrilous legend has it that a Scotsman built the two-storey, two-roomed house to evade land taxes. Behind this is **Adrian Sankey's Glass Works** (daily 9am–5.30pm; 30p), where you can watch glass being blown, then splash out on one of the unique finished products. For more on Ambleside's history, stroll a couple of minutes' along Rydal Road to **The Armitt** (daily 10am–5pm; £2.50), whose collection catalogues the very distinct contribution to Lakeland society made by John Ruskin, Beatrix Potter and longtime Ambleside resident, writer Harriet Martineau.

Practicalities

Buses (including National Express) all stop on Kelsick Road, opposite the library. The **tourist office** is just up the road, in Central Buildings on Market Cross (daily 9am–5pm; ☎015394/32582). Lake Road, running between Waterhead and Ambleside, is lined with dozens of **B&Bs**. About the cheapest rates are at *Linda's B&B and Bunkhouse* on Compston Rd (☎015394/32999; no credit cards; ①). The *Waterwheel Guesthouse*, Bridge St (☎015394/33286; no credit cards; ①), fills quickly; it's up the cobbled alley off Rydal Road right by the bridge across Stock Ghyll. Another popular choice is *3 Cambridge Villas*, Church St (☎015394/32307; no credit cards; ②). One of the Lake District's most agreeably sited **youth hostels** is at Waterhead on the A591 (☎015394/32304), a huge lakeside affair, while the nearest **campsite** is the lakeside *Low Wray National Trust Campsite* (☎015394/32810; closed Nov–Easter) three miles south of town – hourly bus #505/506 (to Hawkshead/Coniston) passes within a mile.

Pippins, at 10 Lake Rd, is great for all-day breakfasts, burgers and night-time pizzas, while *Zeffirelli's*, Compston Road (☎015394/33845), specializes in inexpensive vegetarian pizzas and pasta and offers a three-course dinner with cinema-ticket special. Easily the best **restaurant** in town is the *Glass House* (☎015394/32137; closed Mon in winter), a renovated, split-level fulling mill with waterwheel on Rydal Road – expect accomplished Mediterranean/Modern-British cooking, for around £25–30 a head.

Skelwith Bridge, Elterwater and the Great Langdale Valley

Three miles west of Ambleside along the A593, **Skelwith Bridge** marks the start of **Great Langdale**, a U-shaped glacial valley overlooked by the prominent rocky summits of the **Langdale Pikes**, the most popular of the central Lakeland fells. The #516 Langdale Rambler **bus** (April–Oct) from Ambleside's Kelsick Road runs to Skelwith Bridge, Elterwater and the Old Dungeon Ghyll Hotel (see below) at the head of the valley.

A cluster of houses and businesses huddle along either side of the river at Skelwith Bridge, and once you've splashed in the water by the bridgeside picnic area, you can set off on the rustic stroll along a signposted footpath to **ELTERWATER**, just a mile away. This is an attractive settlement fringed by sheep-filled commonland and centered on a tiny village green. It sees its fair share of hikers, not least because of its two local **youth hostels**: *Elterwater Langdale,* just across the bridge from the village (☎015394/37245), and *Langdale High Close*, a mile from Elterwater (☎015394/37313), with a more spectacular setting, high on the road over Red Bank from Skelwith Bridge to Grasmere. Best place to **stay** is the *Britannia Inn* (☎015394/37210, *britinn@edi.co.uk*; ④), an old Lakeland pub on the green.

The Cumbria Way footpath runs to the New Dungeon Ghyll Hotel, three miles from Elterwater. A path indicated by the "Stickle Ghyll" sign follows the beck straight up to **Stickle Tarn**, around to the right then left up to the top of **Pavey Ark** (2297ft). It is fairly easy from then on to **Harrison Stickle** (2414ft), down to the stream forming the headwaters of Dungeon Ghyll and slowly up to **Pike of Stickle** (2326ft). Backtracking a short distance, you reach a path leading to the right almost parallel with Dungeon Ghyll, back to the start (4 miles; 2400ft ascent; 4hr).

The traditional **accommodation** for anyone visiting the upper end of the valley is the peerless *Old Dungeon Ghyll Hotel* (☎015394/37272; ⑤, ⑥ with dinner), superbly isolated at the end of the B5343, seven miles northeast of Ambleside; it offers great three-course dinners in its restaurant (book in advance) and also has a stone-flagged hikers' bar, filled in the evenings with refugees from the nearby *Great Langdale* **campsite** (☎015394/37668).

Grasmere and around

Four miles northwest of Ambleside, the village of **GRASMERE** consists of an intimate cluster of grey-stone houses on the old packhorse road which runs beside the babbling River Rothay. It's an eminently pleasing ensemble, set back from one of the most alluring of the region's small lakes, but it loses much of its charm in summer thanks to the hordes who descend on the trail of the village's most famous former resident, **William Wordsworth** (1770–1850). The poet, his wife Mary, sister Dorothy and other members of his family are buried beneath the yews in **St Oswald's churchyard** (Mon–Sat 10am–4pm, plus Sun services), in whose interior you can admire the unique twin naves, split by a solid arched partition.

On the southeastern outskirts of the village, on the main A591, stands **Dove Cottage** (daily 9.30am–5.30pm; closed mid-Jan to mid-Feb; £4.80), home to William and Dorothy Wordsworth from 1799 to 1808 and where Wordsworth wrote some of his best poetry. Guides bursting with anecdotes lead you around rooms which reflect Wordsworth's guiding principle of "plain living but high thinking" and are little changed now but for the addition of electricity and internal plumbing. If you visit the cottage, you've already paid for the **museum** full of paintings, manuscripts and bric-a-brac once belonging to the Wordsworths, Southey, Coleridge and Thomas De Quincey. In good weather, the garden is open for visits as well (during house hours).

WRITERS IN THE LAKE DISTRICT

William Wordsworth was not the first to praise the Lake District – Thomas Gray wrote appreciatively of his visit in 1769 – but he dominates its literary landscape, not solely through his poetry but also through his still useful *Guide to the Lakes* (1810). Born in Cockermouth in 1770, he was sent to school in Hawkshead before a stint at Cambridge, a year in France and two in Somerset. In 1799 he returned to the Lake District, settling in the Grasmere district, where he spent the last two-thirds of his life with his sister Dorothy, who not only transcribed his poems but was an accomplished diarist as well.

Wordsworth and fellow poets **Samuel Taylor Coleridge** and **Robert Southey** formed a clique that became known as the "Lake Poets", a label based more on their fluctuating friendships and their shared passion for the region than on any common subject matter in their writings. A fourth member of the Cumbrian literary elite was the critic and essayist **Thomas De Quincey**, chiefly known today for his *Confessions of an English Opium-Eater*. One of the first to fully appreciate the revolutionary nature of Wordsworth's and Coleridge's collaborative *Lyrical Ballads*, De Quincey became a long-term guest of the Wordsworths in 1807, taking over Dove Cottage from them in 1809. He stayed there until 1820, but it was only in the 1830s that he started writing his *Lake Reminiscences*, offending Wordsworth and Coleridge in the process.

Meanwhile, after short spells at Allan Bank and The Vicarage, both in Grasmere, the Wordsworths made Rydal Mount their home, supported largely by William's position as Distributor of Stamps for Westmorland and his later stipend as Poet Laureate. After his death in 1850, William's body was interred in St Oswald's churchyard in Grasmere, to be joined five years later by Dorothy and by his wife Mary four years after that.

Inspired by Wordsworth's writings and by the terrain itself, the social philosopher and art critic **John Ruskin** also made the Lake District his home, settling at Brantwood outside Coniston in 1872. His letters and watercolours reflect a deep love of the area, also demonstrated by his unsuccessful fight to prevent the damming of Thirlmere. Much of Ruskin's feeling for the countryside permeated through to two other literary immigrants, **Arthur Ransome**, also a Coniston resident and writer of the children's classic *Swallows and Amazons*, and **Beatrix Potter**, whose favourite Lakeland spots feature in her children's stories.

Another mile and a half southeast along the A591 from Grasmere, the hamlet of **RYDAL** consists of an inn, a few houses and **Rydal Mount** (March–Oct daily 9.30am–5pm; Nov–Feb Wed–Mon 10am–4pm; £3.50), home of William Wordsworth from 1813 until his death in 1850. Parts of the house have been redecorated, but furniture and portraits give a good sense of its former occupants, as does Wordsworth's airy attic study. For many, the highlight is the garden, which has been preserved as Wordsworth designed it. Bus #555 passes the house on the way to Grasmere from Windermere/Ambleside.

Practicalities

Buses stop on the village green. The **tourist office** (April–Oct daily 9.30am–5pm; some winter weekends; ☎015394/35245), five minutes away down Langdale Road, is tucked in by the main **car park** on Red Bank Road at the southern end of the village.

Accommodation can be hard to come by in summer – book well in advance, especially for popular central places like the *Harwood*, Red Lion Square (☎015394/35248, *hardwoodlan@aol.com*; no credit cards; ③). Some of the nicest places are a little way out of the centre: *Banerigg Guest House* (☎015394/35204; no smoking; no credit cards; ②) is a lakeside property ten minutes' walk out on the Ambleside road (A591); or there's *Titteringdales Guesthouse*, on Pye Lane (☎015394/35439, *Titteringdales@grasmere.net*; no credit cards; ②; closed Jan), to the north, just off the A591. Top of the pile is *White Moss House* (☎015394/35295, *dixon@whitemoss.demon.co.uk*; ⑧, incl dinner; closed Dec–Feb), a house once owned by Wordsworth, a mile south on the A591, at the northern end of Rydal Water. Lesser budgets are required for *How Foot Lodge*, at Town End (☎015394/35366; ③; closed Jan), a Victorian house owned by the National Trust, just yards from Dove Cottage. Grasmere has two very popular **youth hostels**: *Butterlip How*, a Victorian house 150 yards north of the green on Easedale Road (☎015394/35316), and *Thorney How*, a characterful former farmhouse, just under a mile further along the unlit road (☎015394/35591).

Bar **meals** are available in the village pubs, or try the *Rowan Tree Licensed Restaurant*, on Church Bridge, Stock Lane, opposite the churchyard, for vegetarian dishes on a terrace overlooking the river. The fanciest local **restaurant** is at *White Moss House* (see above). The only enjoyable **pub** in the village is the *Red Lion*.

Coniston Water

At five miles long and half a mile across at its widest point, **Coniston Water** is not one of the most immediately imposing of the lakes, yet it has a quiet beauty which sets it apart from the more popular destinations. The nineteenth-century art critic and social reformer **John Ruskin** made the lake his home and his isolated house today provides the most obvious target for a day-trip, but the plain village grows on visitors after a while, especially those who base themselves at Coniston for some of the central Lakes' most rewarding walking. In the mid-1960s, the long uninterruptedly glass-like surface of Coniston Water attracted the attention of national hero **Donald Campbell**, who in 1955 had set a world water speed record of 202mph on Ullswater, bumping it up to 276mph nine years later in Australia. On January 4, 1967 he set out to better his own mark on Coniston Water, but just as his jet-powered *Bluebird* hit an estimated 320mph, a patch of turbulence sent it into a somersault. Campbell's shoes, helmet, oxygen mask and teddy bear mascot were recovered from the water, but his body and boat were destroyed completely.

Coniston village and Brantwood

A memorial plaque to Campbell decorates the green in the slate-grey village of **CONISTON**, hunkered below the craggy and copper-mine-riddled bulk of **The Old Man of**

Coniston. The excellent **Ruskin Museum** on Yewdale Road (Easter to mid-Nov daily 10am–5.30pm; £3) combines local history exhibits with a fascinating look at Ruskin's life and work through his watercolours, manuscripts and personal memorabilia. **Coniston Water** itself is hidden out of sight, half a mile southeast of the village. Boat speeds here are now limited to 10mph, a graceful pace for the sumptuously upholstered **Steam Yacht Gondola** (Easter–Oct 4 daily; £4.75 round trip; ☎015394/36003), built in 1859, which leaves Coniston Pier for hour-long circuits, calling at Park-a-moor landing stage then Ruskin's Brantwood. The wooden Coniston **motor launches** (Easter–Oct hourly; Nov–Easter 4 daily depending on the weather; ☎015394/36216) also operate a year-round service to Brantwood on two routes, north (£3.40 return) or south (£5.40) around the lake.

Both steam yacht and motor launches dock beneath the magnificently sited **Brantwood** (mid-March to mid-Nov daily 11am–5.30pm; mid-Nov to mid-March Wed–Sun 11am–4pm; house, gardens & launch £7; house only £4; gardens only £2), two and a half miles by road from Coniston, where art critic and moralist **John Ruskin** lived from 1872 until his death in 1900. Champion of J.M.W. Turner and the Pre-Raphaelites and proponent of the supremacy of Gothic architecture, Ruskin insisted upon the indivisibility of ethics and aesthetics, and was appalled by the conditions in which the captains of industry made their labourers work and live, while expecting him to applaud their patronage of the arts. A twenty-minute video expands on his philosophy and whets the appetite for rooms full of his watercolours. His study – hung with handmade paper to his own design – and dining room boast superlative lake views, bettered only by those from the Turret Room where he used to sit in later life in his bathchair. Various other exhibition rooms and galleries display Ruskin-related arts and crafts, while the *Jumping Jenny Tearooms* – named after Ruskin's boat – has outdoor terrace seating for meals and drinks.

Practicalities

Buses stop on the main road through the village, outside the **tourist office** (April–Oct daily 9.30am–5.30pm; limited weekend hours in winter; ☎015394/41533). You can **rent bikes** from Meadowdore (☎015394/41638) on the main road near the *Crown*, as well as from Summitreks, 14 Yewdale Rd (☎015394/41212).

The most comfortable **B&Bs** are *Shepherds Villa*, Tilberthwaite Ave (☎015394/41337; no credit cards; ③) – the B5285 into the village – and the vegetarian *Beech Tree Guesthouse*, Yewdale (the Ambleside) Road (☎015394/41717; no credit cards; ③). All the **pubs** have rooms, but the best are those at the *Sun Hotel* (☎015394/41248; ④), minimum two-night stay at weekends), an inn 200 yards uphill from the bridge in the centre of Coniston. Of the two **youth hostels**, *Coniston Holly How* (☎015394/41323) is closer, a few minutes' walk north of Coniston on the Ambleside road, but *Coniston Coppermines* (☎015394/41261) is more peaceful, in a dramatic mountain setting a steep mile or so from the village – follow the "Old Man" signs past the Sun Hotel. The nearest **campsite** is the *Coniston Hall Campsite*, Haws Bank (☎015394/41223; booking essential; closed Nov–March), a mile south of town by the lake.

Eating opportunities outside the pubs are limited, but in any case you shouldn't look much further than the *Sun Hotel*, whose cosy bar has filling meals.

Hawkshead and around

Grey-stone **HAWKSHEAD**, between Coniston and Ambleside, wears its beauty well, its patchwork of cottages and cobbles backed by woods and fells and barely affected by twentieth-century intrusions. This is partly due to the enlightened policy of banning traffic in the centre – huge car parks at the village edge take the strain and when the crowds of day-trippers leave, Hawkshead regains its natural tranquillity.

The town was an important wool market at the time Wordsworth was studying at **Hawkshead Grammar School** (Easter–Oct Mon–Sat 10am–12.30pm & 1.30–4.30pm, Sun 1–5pm; £2), founded in 1585, whose entrance lies opposite the tourist office – pride of place is given to the desk on which William carved his signature. While there he attended the fifteenth-century **Church** (daily 9am–6pm) above the school, which harks back to Norman and Romanesque designs in its rounded pillars and patterned arches. From its knoll the churchyard gives a good view over the village's twin central squares, and of Main Street, housing the **Beatrix Potter Gallery** (Easter–Oct Mon–Thurs & Sun 10.30am–4.30pm; £2.90; NT), occupying rooms once used by her solicitor husband. With their timed-entry ticket, fans get bustled into rooms full of Potter's original illustrations, though the less devoted might find displays on her life as keen naturalist, conservationist and early supporter of the National Trust more diverting – Potter bequeathed her farms and land in the Lake District to the Trust on her death.

The main **bus service** to Hawkshead is the #505/506 between Bowness, Ambleside and Coniston; on reaching Hawkshead it loops down to Hill Top and back for the Beatrix Potter house at Near Sawrey (see below). The **tourist office** is at the main car park (Easter–Oct daily 9.30am–5.30pm; limited weekend hours in winter; ☎015394/36525). Some contend that Wordsworth briefly boarded at what is now *Ann Tyson's Cottage*, Wordsworth Street (☎015394/36405; no credit cards; ②), behind the fifteenth-century Minstrel's Gallery. Georgian *Ivy House*, Main Street (☎015394/36204; ④), also makes a characterful base; and there are reasonable rooms at *Greenbank House Hotel*, fifty yards further along Main Street (☎015394/36497; ③), at the edge of the village. All four of the village's **pubs** also have accommodation, with the sixteenth-century *Queen's Head* on Main Street (☎015394/36271; ④) the pick of the bunch. The **youth hostel**, *Esthwaite Lodge* (☎015394/36293), is a mile to the south down the Newby Bridge road. **Camping** is available at Hawkshead's busy *Croft Caravan and Campsite* (☎015394/36374; closed Nov to mid-March), on North Lonsdale Road, right by the village. Of the **tearooms**, *Whig's* on The Square (closed Thurs) serves its eponymous speciality baked rolls; while *Room With a View* in Laburnum House, immediately below the church, is a rated vegetarian restaurant.

Grizedale Forest

If the weather looks promising, time is well spent among the remarkable sculptures in **Grizedale Forest**, three miles southwest of Hawkshead. There's a summer bus service (#515, from Ambleside and Hawkshead or Ulverston and Newby Bridge) to **Grizedale Forest Centre** (Feb–Dec daily 10am–5pm; free; parking £2; ☎01229/860010); otherwise you'll have to **rent a bike** from the *Croft* campsite in Hawkshead. Grizedale Mountain Bikes at the centre (daily 9am–5pm; call ☎01229/860369 to reserve in advance) also has bikes available, or just head out on foot along ten miles of the Silurian Way, which links the majority of the eighty-odd stone and wood sculptures scattered among the trees. Since 1977 artists have been invited to come here, often for six months at a time, to create a sculptural response to their surroundings using natural materials. Some of the resulting works are startling, as you round a bend to find a hundred-foot-long wave of bent logs or a dry-stone wall slaloming the conifers. If you're planning to use the **campsite** (☎01229/860257; closed Oct–Feb), just past the visitor centre, call ahead as it's very popular.

Tarn Hows

A minor road off the Hawkshead–Coniston B5285 winds the couple of miles northwest to **Tarn Hows**, a body of water surrounded by spruce and pine and circled by paths and picnic spots. It takes an hour to walk around the tarn, during which you can ponder on the fact that this miniature idyll is in fact almost entirely artificial – the original owners enlarged two small tarns to make the one you see today, planted and landscaped the surroundings and dug the footpaths. It's now a Site of Special Scientific Interest – keep an eye out for some of the Lakes' (and England's) few surviving native red squirrels. A free National Trust **bus service** runs between Hawkshead and Coniston on Sundays from Easter to the end of October, linking with the regular #505/#506.

Near and Far Sawrey and Hill Top

It's two miles from Hawkshead, down the eastern side of Esthwaite Water (B5285) to the pretty twin hamlets of **NEAR** and **FAR SAWREY**, the first the site of Beatrix Potter's beloved **Hill Top** (Easter–Oct Mon–Wed, Sat & Sun 11am–5pm; £4; NT). A Londoner by birth, Potter bought the farmhouse here with the proceeds from her first book, *The Tale of Peter Rabbit*, and retained it as her study long after she moved out following her marriage in 1913. Its furnishings and contents have been kept as they were during her occupancy – a condition of Potter's will – and the small house is always busy with visitors; so much so that numbers are often limited. In summer, expect to have to wait in line.

Keswick and Derwent Water

Standing on the shores of **Derwent Water** at the junction of the main north–south and east–west routes through the Lake District, **KESWICK** makes a good base for exploring delightful Borrowdale – the start of many walking routes to the central peaks around Scafell Pike – or Skiddaw and Blencathra, which loom over the town. For those not up to a day on the fells, the town remains a popular place throughout the year, with a big enough population (around five thousand) to warrant a bevy of local museums and sights.

Granted its market charter by Edward I in 1276 – **market day** is Saturday – Keswick was an important wool and leather centre until around 1500, when these trades were supplanted by the discovery of local graphite. **The Cumberland Pencil Museum**, west of the centre at Greta Bridge, on Main Street (daily 9.30am–4pm; £2.50), tells the story, beginning with its early application as moulds for cannon balls. With the Italian idea of putting graphite into wooden holders, Keswick became an important pencil-

---

WALKS FROM KESWICK

Rising sharply through coniferous forests above Keswick, the walk up **Latrigg Fell** (4–6 miles; 900ft ascent; 2–3hr) gives splendid views across Derwent Water to Borrowdale and the high fells. Follow Station Road past the youth hostel and museum and, as it bends around to the right to become Brundholme Road/Briar Rigg, look for the right turn up Spooney Green Lane across the A66. From here skirt the west flank of Latrigg before zigzagging to the summit from the north. Return either directly down the southern gully or follow the longer eastern ridge to Brundholme, returning through Brundholme wood or along the railway path.

More demanding, but the easiest of the region's true mountain walks, is the hike up **Skiddaw** (5 miles; 3000ft ascent; 5hr), a smooth mound of splintery slate. Follow the walk above, skirting the west flank of Latrigg, but continue straight ahead when the path branches right to the Latrigg summit. It is pretty much a steady walk (with a possible diversion up Little Man along the way) before reaching a false summit and finally the 3054ft High Man.

The climb up **Cat Bells** (launch to Hawes End) takes you to a renowned vantage-point (1481ft) above the lake's western shore – allow two and a half hours for the scramble to the top and a return along the wooded lake shore.

making town, and remained one until the late eighteenth century, when the French discovered how to make pencil graphite cheaply by binding the common amorphous graphite with clay.

In Fitz Park, on Station Road, you'll find the **Keswick Park Museum and Art Gallery** (Easter–Oct daily 10am–4pm; £1), a quirky Victorian collection of ancient dental tools, fossils and some prized manuscripts and letters written by the Lakeland Poets. Less relevant, but perhaps more entertaining, is the **Cars of the Stars Motor Museum**, Standish Street (Easter to early Jan daily 10am–5pm; £3), showcasing The Saint's Volvo, James Bond's Lotus, Lady Penelope's Rolls Royce, and Chitty Chitty Bang Bang among others.

Keswick's most celebrated landmark is the **Castlerigg Stone Circle** – from the end of Station Road, take the Threlkeld rail line path (signposted by the *Keswick Country House Hotel*) and follow the signs. Thirty-eight hunks of Borrowdale volcanic stone, the largest almost eight feet tall, form a circle a hundred feet in diameter; another ten blocks delineating a rectangular enclosure within. The array probably had an astronomical or timekeeping function when it was erected four or five thousand years ago. Back on the rail path, you can can easily continue all the way to **Threlkeld** itself, three miles from town, on a delightful riverside walk with the promise of a drink in one of Threlkeld's old pubs at the end. Keener hikers use Threlkeld as the starting point for the gut-busting climb up **Blencathra**, whose five great ridges loom above the A66.

On any reasonably decent day, the best move in Keswick is down to the shores of **Derwent Water**, five minutes' walk south of the centre along Lake Road and through the pedestrian underpass. It's among the most attractive of the lakes, ringed by crags and studded with islets, and is most easily seen by hopping on the **Keswick Launch** (Easter–Nov daily 10am–6pm, until 7.30pm in summer; £4.85 round-trip, or 75p per stage; ☎017687/72263), which runs right around the lake calling at several points en route.

Arrival, information and accommodation

Most **buses**, including National Express services, use the terminal behind Lakes Foodstore, off Main Street. The joint **tourist office** and **National Park Information Centre** is in the Moot Hall on Market Square (daily: April–June, Sept & Oct 9.30am–5.30pm; July & Aug 9.30am–7pm; Nov–March 10am–4pm; ☎017687/72645). George Fisher, at 2 Borrowdale Rd (☎017687/72178), is one of the most celebrated **outdoors stores** on the Lakes, with a full range of equipment and maps, a daily weather information service and café. For **bike rental**, try Keswick Mountain Bikes on Southey Hill (☎017687/75202).

You should have no trouble finding **accommodation**, and competition at the lower end of the market keeps the prices keen. B&Bs cluster along Bank Street and Stanger Street, near the post office, and around Southey, Blencathra and Eskin streets, in the grid near the start of the A591 Penrith road. Smarter places line *The Heads*, overlooking Hope Park, a couple of minutes south of the centre on the way to the lake. The nearest **campsite** is *Derwentwater Caravan Club and Camping Site* (☎017687/72392; closed Dec & Jan), less than ten minutes' walk from the centre, down by the lake. There are two **youth hostels**, the *Derwentwater Youth Hostel*, in Borrowdale, a couple of miles south of Keswick along the B5289 (☎017687/77246), and *Skiddaw House Youth Hostel* (phone *Carrock Fell* hostel: ☎016974/78325), one of the most remote buildings in England, on the Cumbria Way, six miles from Keswick by path.

Bluestones, 7 Southey St (☎017687/74237). Well-kept guest house used to walkers; big breakfasts and on-street parking. No credit cards. ①.

Bridgedale Guesthouse, 101 Main St (☎017687/73914). The cheapest central rooms, just around the corner from the bus station; No credit cards. ①.

The Great Little Teashop, 26 Lake Rd (☎017687/73545). Relaxed teashop B&B, with discounts for multi-night stays. No credit cards. ②.

Greystones, Ambleside Rd (☎017687/73108). Non-smoking Victorian terrace house close to the centre at the end of St John's St. En-suite rooms with fell views and TVs. No credit cards. ②.

Highfield Hotel, The Heads (☎017687/72508). Beautifully restored hotel whose stylish feature rooms include two turret rooms and a converted chapel. ③, ④ for feature rooms.

Howe Keld, 5–7 The Heads (☎017687/72417). Welcoming, non-smoking, mid-sized hotel with a reputation for great breakfasts (vegetarian specialities included) and cosy rooms. Car park. ③.

Keswick Country House Hotel, Station Rd (☎017687/72020). Grand Victorian hotel, built for the nineteenth-century railway trade and sitting in landscaped grounds. ⑦, with dinner.

Keswick Youth Hostel, Station Rd (☎017687/72484). A converted woollen mill by the river in town; good location, and free tea and coffee on arrival.

Lane's End, 4 High St (☎017687/74436). Delightful flower-clad cottage with just three rooms, tucked away off St John's St. No credit cards. ①.

Eating, drinking and entertainment

Many of the **places to eat** cater to a walking crowd, which means large portions and few airs. Several of the **pubs** also have meals worth investigating, while there's a fair amount of entertainment in Keswick throughout the year: a **cinema** on St John's Street (closed Dec–Feb), the annual **jazz festival** each May, **beer festival** in June, and traditional country shows in the locality during the summer.

Abraham's Tea Rooms, in George Fisher's outdoor store, 2 Borrowdale Rd. The top-floor tearoom comes to your aid with warming mugs of *glühwein* and big breakfasts. No credit cards. Inexpensive.

Brysons, 42 Main St. Topnotch bakery and tearooms with breakfasts, traditional main dishes and cream teas. No credit cards. Inexpensive.

The Four in Hand, Lake Rd, opposite George Fisher's. Popular pub for its food – grilled Cumberland ham and eggs, local trout and other Lakeland specialities. Inexpensive to Moderate.

Loose Box Pizzeria, King's Arms Courtyard, Main St (☎017687/72083). Popular pizza-and-pasta joint – the house special is *spaghetti rustica* (tomato, garlic, chilli and prawns). Moderate.

Mayson's, 33 Lake Rd. Licensed, self-service café serving bakes, pies and stir-fries (until 8.45pm in summer). No credit cards. Inexpensive.

La Primavera, Greta Bridge (☎017687/74621).The town's top restaurant, with classic pastas, meats and fish; closed Mon. Moderate to Expensive.

Borrowdale and Scafell

It is difficult to overstate the beauty of **Borrowdale**, with its river flats and yew trees, lying at the head of Derwent Water and overshadowed by the peaks of **Scafell** and **Scafell Pike**, the highest in England. Climbs up these, as well as up Great Gable, one of the finest-looking mountains in England, start from the head of the valley, accessible on the #77, #77a and #79 **buses** from Keswick, which run south along the B5289.

Just before the Derwentwater youth hostel, a narrow road branches left for a steep climb to the photogenic **Ashness Bridge**. The minor road ends two miles further south at **Watendlath**, an idyllic little tarn and tearooms which can be hopelessly overrun at times in summer – the National Trust's free Watendlath Wanderer bus runs here every couple of hours from Keswick on summer Sundays, via Ashness.

Back on the B5289, a path at the agreeable *Stakis Lodore Hotel* (☎017687/77285; ⑧, incl dinner) heads to the **Lodore Falls**, only really worth the diversion after sustained wet weather. Further south, past the wonderfully sited *Borrowdale Hotel* (☎017687/77224; ⑦, incl dinner), which has an excellent restaurant, there's a slight detour across an old packhorse bridge to **GRANGE**, a peaceful riverside hamlet, peered down upon by Borrowdale's forested crags. At Grange, it's under a mile south to the 1900-tonne **Bowder Stone**, a house-sized lump of rock scaled by way of a wooden ladder and worn to a shine on top by thousands of pairs of feet.

Shaded paths through the wood, and the B5289, lead in around a mile to the straggling hamlet of **ROSTHWAITE**, which sustains the most concentrated batch of accommodation in the valley. As well as two or three B&Bs, there are comfortable rooms at the hiker-friendly *Royal Oak Hotel* (☎017687/77214; ⑤, with dinner) and the smarter, neighbouring *Scafell Hotel* (☎017687/77208; ⑤), whose attached *Riverside Inn* – the only local pub – serves popular bar meals. A nice **youth hostel**, *Borrowdale Longthwaite* (☎017687/77257), is a mile south of Rosthwaite, on the riverside footpath to Seatoller, opposite *Chapel House Farm* **campsite** (☎017687/77602).

Another mile on, **SEATOLLER** and the **Seatoller Barn National Park Information Centre** (Easter–Nov daily 10am–5pm; ☎017687/77294) marks the end of the #79 bus route from Keswick. *Seatoller House* (☎017687/77218; no credit cards; ③; closed Dec–Feb) has **rooms** (and dinner available), and there's an informal **campsite** in a small field by the beck along the minor road south to **SEATHWAITE**, twenty minutes' walk away. This is a popular base for walks up the likes of Great Gable and Scafell Pike (see below): the trout farm at the foot of the valley has a fine **café** (Easter–Sept daily 10am–6.30pm), and there's another basic **campsite** used by Great Gable climbers.

Scafell, Scafell Pike and Great Gable

In good weather, the minor road to Seathwaite is lined with parked cars by 9am as hikers take to the paths for the rugged climbs up the three major peaks of Scafell, Scafell Pike and Great Gable. Technically, the hikes are not too difficult, though, as always, you should be well prepared and reasonably fit.

The summit of **Scafell Pike** (3205ft), the highest point in England, is close to the second highest point in the Lakes, **Scafell** (3163ft), and an eight-mile, six-hour, loop walk taking in both leaves Seathwaite via Stockley Bridge to the south, branching up Styhead Ghyll to **Styhead Tarn**. This is as far as many get, and on those all-too-rare glorious summer days the tarn is a fine place for a picnic. A direct but very steep approach to **Great Gable** (2949ft) is also possible from Styhead Tarn, though most people cut west at Seathwaite campsite up Sourmilk Ghyll and approach via **Green Gable** (2628ft), also an eight-mile, six-hour return walk.

Buttermere and Crummock Water

Overlooked by the steep Borrowdale Fells, the B5289 cuts west at Seatoller, up and over the dramatic **Honister Pass**. Buses #77 and #77a come this way, making the initial, steep mile-and-a-quarter grind to the car park at the top of Honister Pass, by the *Honister House* **youth hostel** (☎017687/77267). Great Gable climbers start from here and follow a path (6 miles; 4hr) past Grey Knotts and Brandreth to Green Gable, before rounding Great Gable and returning along an almost parallel path to the west.

Back at the pass, the B5289 follows Gatesgarthdale Beck for three miles and makes a dramatic descent into the **Buttermere valley** by *Gatesgarth Farm* **campsite** (☎017687/70256), then runs another mile beside the lake – past more camping at *Dalegarth* (☎017687/70233; closed Nov–March) – to the **youth hostel** (☎017687/70245) just before **BUTTERMERE** village. The village has two hotels: the *Bridge Hotel* (☎017687/70252; ⑥, ⑦ with dinner) and the smaller *Fish Hotel* (☎017687/70253; ③) – both serve reasonable meals, while the *Bridge* has a popular, traditional flagstoned, bar. There's **camping** at *Syke Farm* right by the lake.

The village itself – set between the two expanses of Buttermere and neighbouring **Crummock Water** – makes a good walking base, with a particularly easy two-mile hike out along Crummock Water's southwestern edge to the 125ft **Scale Force** falls. The four-mile, **round-lake** stroll circling Buttermere itself shouldn't take more than a couple of hours; you can always detour up Scarth Gap to Haystacks if you want more of a climb and some views.

The scenery flattens out as the road heads north from Crummock Water and into the pastoral **Lorton vale**, with Cockermouth just a few miles beyond. A minor road south just beyond Brackenthwaite leads directly to minuscule **Loweswater**, one of the less frequented lakes, around which there's a gentle, four-mile (2hr) walk. En route, you'll pass the *Kirkstile Inn* (☎01900/85219; no credit cards; ③), a welcoming sixteenth-century inn with decent bar meals.

Wast Water and Eskdale

Great Gable and Scafell stand as a formidable last-gasp boundary between the mountains of the central lakes and the gentler land to the southwest, which smoothes out its wrinkles as it descends to the Cumbrian coast. **Wast Water**, which points its slender finger towards the pass between both ranges, remains one of the most isolated of the region's lakes. **Public transport** is very limited; in fact, there's none to Wast Water, which makes it one to savour if you fancy getting right off the beaten track. The highest slopes in England frame the northern shores, while on the wild southeastern banks rise the impassable screes which separate the lake from Eskdale to the south. The only road winds from the main coastal A595, through remote settlements, before meeting the lake at its southwestern tip, at the *Wasdale Hall* **youth hostel** (☎019467/26222). The minor road then hugs the shore of the lake, ending four miles away at **Wasdale Head**, a clearing between the mountain ranges, where you'll find the *Wasdale Head Inn* (☎019467/26229; ⑤), with good food and rooms and nearby, the National Trust's *Wasdale Head* **campsite** (☎019467/26220; closed Nov–March).

Eskdale is accessed either by the Ravenglass and Eskdale Railway (see p.559), which drops you right in the heart of superb walking country around the hamlet of Boot; or by the east–west minor road route between the coast, via Eskdale Green, and Little Langdale, just west of Skelwith Bridge. The attractive rural ride by road or train through the valley from the west begins to peter out as you approach Dalegarth station (terminus of the Ravenglass and Eskdale Railway), just beyond which nestles the dead-end hamlet of **BOOT**. Three miles beyond Boot and 800ft up, the remains of granaries, bath houses and the commandant's quarters for **Hardknott Roman Fort** command a strategic and panoramic position. After negotiating the appalling, narrow switchbacks of **Hardknott Pass**, the road drops to Cockley Beck, before making the equally alarming ascent of **Wrynose Pass**; at the col, the **Three Shire Stone** marks the old boundary of Cumberland, Westmorland and Lancashire.

Boot has a fair smattering of **accommodation and services**. The nearest place to Dalegarth station is *Brook House Hotel* (☎019467/23288; ③), which serves meals in its *Poachers Bar*. Further up, in Boot itself, the *Burnmoor Inn* (☎019467/23224, *burnmoor@montrose.demon.co.uk*; ③) is the traditional hikers' choice. Continue up the road past the hamlet and it's 500 yards to *Hollins Farm* **campsite** (☎019467/23253) and

---

A RIVERSIDE WALK FROM ESKDALE

An easy riverside walk (2 miles; 1hr) starts 200 yards east of Dalegarth station down a track to St Catherine's church opposite the road to Boot. In low water you can cross the river below the church by stepping stones; you turn right, then left, up a path beside a stream to **Stanley Ghyll Waterfall**. Returning along the path beside the stream, a branch on the left leads back to Dalegarth station via a bridge over a swimming hole. If you don't cross the stepping stones, you can take a path following the right bank to Doctor Bridge where you can cross and double back for Stanley Ghyll or continue to the road and the *Woolpack Inn*.

another three quarters of a mile to the *Woolpack Inn* (☎019467/23230; ③), serving filling food – another 400 yards beyond the pub you'll find *Eskdale* **youth hostel** (☎019467/23219).

Cockermouth

The farming community of **COCKERMOUTH**, midway between the coast and Keswick at the confluence of the Cocker and Derwent rivers, is yet another station on the Wordsworth trail: the **Wordsworth House** on Main Street (Easter–June Mon–Fri 11am–5pm; July & Aug Mon–Sat 11am–5pm; £2.80; NT) is where William and Dorothy were born and spent their first few years. The terracotta-hued eighteenth-century building was nearly replaced by a bus station in the 1930s, but was saved and given to the National Trust who have furnished it with imports from their vaults. The rest of Cockermouth tries hard to please, but after the dramatic fellside approaches from the south and east the town itself falls a little flat. Next door to the Wordsworth House, you can get your hands dirty at **The Printing House**, 102 Main St (Easter–Oct Mon–Sat 10am–4pm; £2.50), where visitors are invited to tackle some of the seventy-odd printing machines ranging from wood-block to Linotype. Otherwise it's a toss-up on a rainy day between **The Cumberland Toy and Model Museum**, Banks Court (Feb–Nov daily 10am–5pm; £2), and the ninety-minute-long **Jenning's Brewery Tour**, on Brewery Lane nearer the river (Easter–June & Oct Mon–Fri 11am & 2pm; July–Sept Mon–Fri 11am & 2pm, Sat 11am; £3; booking advisable; ☎01900/823214), which culminates with a tasting.

All **buses** stop on Main Street, from where you can follow the signs east to the **tourist office** in the Town Hall, off Market Place (April–June & Oct Mon–Sat 10.30am–4.30pm; July–Sept Mon–Sat 10am–6pm, Sun 2–5pm; Nov–March Mon–Sat 10.30am–4pm; ☎01900/822634). Two of the best **B&Bs** are fairly central: *Castlegate Guest House*, 6 Castlegate (☎01900/826 749; no credit cards; ②), and *Manor House*, 23 St Helen's St (☎01900/822416; no credit cards; ③), beyond the end of Market Place. Ten minutes' walk south along Station Road then Fern Bank brings you to the *Double Mills* **youth hostel** (☎01900/822561) in a seventeenth-century watermill. *Wyndham Holiday Park* (☎01900/822571; closed Dec–Feb) lies a similar distance east along St Helen's Street and St Helen's Road.

Eating options include the *Norham Coffee House*, 73 Main St (closed Sun), which trades on its history – formerly the home of John Christian, grandfather of *Mutiny on the Bounty's* Fletcher Christian. *Beatfords* (closed Sun), further along Main Street in the Lowther Went Shopping Centre, is also worth a look. In the evening, choose between the *Riverside Restaurant*, at 2 Main St, on the bridge at the eastern end (☎01900/823871; closed Tues), and the *Quince and Medlar*, 12 Castlegate (☎01900/823579; closed Sun & Mon), serving excellent vegetarian dishes.

Ullswater

Wordsworth declared **Ullswater** "the happiest combination of beauty and grandeur, which any of the Lakes affords", a judgement that still holds good. At over seven miles long, it's the second longest lake in Cumbria and much of its appeal derives from its serpentine shape, a result of the complex geology of this area: the glacier that formed the trench in which the lake now lies had to cut across a couple of geological boundaries, from granite in the south, through a band of Skiddaw slate, to softer sandstone and limestone in the north. The only **public transport** is the #108 bus service (May–Oct) from Penrith, which runs via Pooley Bridge, Gowbarrow and Glenridding to Patterdale. On summer weekends, three daily buses continue south over the Kirkstone Pass to Bowness.

The chief lakeside settlements, **PATTERDALE** and **GLENRIDDING**, are less than a mile apart at the southern tip of Ullswater, each with a smattering of cafés and B&Bs. In Glenridding the best place to stay is the lakeside *Glenridding Hotel* (☎017684/82228; ⑥), though there are plenty of cheaper spots, like the *Fairlight Guest House* (☎017684/82397; no credit cards; ①), by Glenridding's main car park; *Cherry Holme* (☎017684/82512; no credit cards; ②), a little way north of the village on the A592; or *Moss Crag Guest House* (☎017684/82500; no card; ②; closed Dec), near the shops. *Gillside Caravan & Camping* (☎017684/82346; closed Nov–Feb) lurks a little way up the valley behind the **tourist office** (Easter–June, Sept & Oct daily 9am–5.30pm; July & Aug 9am–6pm; Nov–Easter Fri–Sun 10am–4pm; ☎017684/82414) in the main car park. In Patterdale, the cheapest and most popular bed is at the **youth hostel** (☎017684/82394), just south of the hamlet on the A592. For central **B&Bs** try *Barco House* (☎017684/82474; no credit cards; ②; closed Nov to mid-March), *Home Farm* (☎017684/82370; no credit cards; ①; closed Nov–Feb) or the *White Lion* (☎017684/82214; ③), a pub which also serves bar meals. *Side Farm* (☎017684/82337), in the centre, is open all year for **camping**.

Around the lake

On busy summer days the A592 up the western side of the lake is packed with traffic, all looking for space in one of the few designated car parks. Busiest is usually that below **Gowbarrow Park**, three miles north of Glenridding, where the A5091 meets the A592; the hillside still blazes green and gold in spring, as it was doing when the Wordsworths visited; it's thought that Dorothy's recollections of the visit in her diary inspired William to write his famous "Daffodils" poem. The car park at Gowbarrow is also the start of an easy, brief walk up to **Aira Force**, a bush-cloaked seventy-foot fall that's spectacular in spate and can be viewed from bridges spanning the top and bottom of the drop.

The lake itself is traversed by the **Ullswater Steamer** (☎01539/721626), which has services from Glenridding to Howtown, halfway up the lake's eastern side (Easter–Oct daily; £2.75 one way; 35min) and from Howtown to Pooley Bridge, at the northern end of the lake (Easter–Oct daily; £3.30; 20min). **HOWTOWN** is tucked into a little clearing at the foot of beautiful Fusedale, where the *Howtown Hotel* makes a great spot for lunch. A minor road from here hugs the eastern shore of the lake the four miles to **POOLEY BRIDGE**, passing the incomparable *Sharrow Bay* (☎017684/86301; ⑨, incl dinner) on the way, one of England's finest hotel-restaurants. Pooley Bridge itself is a cute retreat – packed to distraction in summer – with a church and three pubs, most notably the *Pooley Bridge Inn* (☎017684/86215; ④), and a smattering of local B&Bs.

ULLSWATER WALKS

Using the Ullswater Steamer to travel from Glenridding to **Howtown**, the easiest walk back (5 miles; 3hr) follows the shore of Ullswater around Hallin Fell (or over, climbing 263ft) to **Sandwick**, then crosses fields before rejoining the shore at **Long Crag** for the final two miles to the south end of the lake at Patterdale.

A considerably more strenuous route (8 miles; 4–5hr) from Howtown cuts past the *Howtown Hotel* and then heads up lovely **Fusedale**, at the head of which there's a sharp and unrelenting climb up to the **High Street**, a broad-backed ridge that was once a Roman road. Once on top the path is clearly visible for miles, and following the ridge south you meet the highest point, **High Raise** (2632ft) – 2hr from Howtown – where there's a cairn and glorious views. The route then runs south and west, via the stone outcrops of **Satura Crag**, past **Angle Tarn** and finally down to the A592, just shy of Patterdale's pub and post office.

Climbing Helvellyn

Helvellyn (3114ft) is the most popular of the four 3000ft mountains in Cumbria, with most visitors tending to make a day-long circuit from either Glenridding or Patterdale. You are unlikely to be alone or get lost on the yard-wide approaches – on summer weekends and bank holidays the car parks below and paths above are full by 10am – but the variety of routes up and down at least offers a chance of escaping the crowds.

Indeed, if you are hoping to escape the crowds, avoid the most frequently chosen approach via the infamous **Striding Edge**, an alarming, undulating rocky ridge offering the most direct access to the summit. With **Red Tarn** – the highest Lake District tarn – a dizzying drop below, purists negotiate the very ridge top of Striding Edge; slightly safer, but no less precipitous tracks follow the line of the ridge, just off the crest. However you get across there's a final, sheer, hands-and-feet scramble to the flat **summit** (2hr 30min from Ullswater). If you're at all nervous of heights you'll find it a challenge to say the least; in poor weather, it's madness even to contemplate it.

The good news is that once you're up the various descents all seem like child's play. The classic return is to the northeast via the less demanding **Swirral Edge**, where a route leads down to Red Tarn, then follows the beck to the disused slate quarry workings and the dramatically sited **Helvellyn youth hostel** (☎017684/82269), two miles from Glenridding.

Penrith

Once a thriving market town on the main north–south trading route, **PENRITH** today suffers from undue comparisons with the improbably pretty settlements of the nearby Lakes. The brisk streets, filled with no-nonsense shops and shoppers, have more in common with the towns of the North Pennines than the stone villages of south Cumbria, and even the local building materials emphasize the geographic shift. Its deep-red buildings were erected from the same rust-red sandstone used to construct **Penrith Castle** (daily: June–Sept 8am–9pm; Oct–May 8am–4.30pm; free) in the fourteenth century, as a bastion against raids from the north; it's now a crumbling ruin, opposite the train station. The town is at its best in the narrow streets, arcades and alleys off **Market Square**, and around St Andrew's churchyard, while if you call into the tourist office on Middlegate, you'll find it shares its seventeenth-century schoolhouse premises with a small local **museum** (April–Sept Mon–Sat 10am–6pm, Sun 1–6pm; Oct–March Mon–Sat 10am–5pm; free).

Penrith **train station** is five minutes' walk south of Market Square and Middlegate. The **bus station** is on Albert Street, behind Middlegate, and has regular services to Patterdale, Keswick, Cockermouth, Carlisle and Alston. The **tourist office** on Middlegate (April–Oct daily 10am–6pm; Nov–March Mon–Sat 10am–5pm; ☎01768/867466) can help you find **accommodation**. The bulk of the B&Bs line Victoria Road, the continuation of King Street running south from Market Square: *Victoria Guest House*, at no. 3 (☎01768/863 823; no credit cards; ①), and *Blue Swallow*, at no. 11 (☎01768/866 335; no credit cards; ②), are both comfortable and convenient. The *George Hotel*, on Devonshire Street by Market Square (☎01768/862696; ④), is a central old coaching inn with cosy wood-panelled lounges. For **picnic** food, the fantastically-stocked J. & J. Graham's deli-grocery in Market Square can't be beaten, though for a sit-down **meal** head for *Chataways Bistro* (closed all Mon & Sun eve), set on the edge of St Andrew's churchyard.

The Cumbrian coast

South and west of the national park, the **Cumbrian coast** attracts much less attention than the spectacular scenery inland, but it would be a mistake to write it off. It splits into two distinct sections, the most accessible being the **Furness peninsulas** area, just a few miles from Windermere's lakeside, where varied attractions include the resort of **Grange-over-Sands**, the monastic priory at **Cartmel**, and market towns like **Ulverston**. Parts of this region share nearby Lancashire's industrial heritage and in the shipbuilding port of **Barrow-in-Furness** it's possible to see a slow revival that's only just starting to pay dividends in terms of tourism – though the dramatic ruins of nearby **Furness Abbey** have been attracting visitors for almost two hundred years. The **Cumbrian coast** itself is generally judged to begin at **Silecroft** near Millom and stretches for more than sixty miles to the small resort of **Silloth**, on the shores of the Solway Firth. In between lie isolated beaches and the headland of **St Bees** as well as the delights of the **Ravenglass and Eskdale Railway** and the Georgian port of **Whitehaven**.

Grange-over-Sands

Before the coming of the railways, the main route to the Lake District was the "road across the sands" from near Lancaster to **GRANGE-OVER-SANDS**, travellers being led by monks from Cartmel Priory, then from the sixteenth century by a royally appointed guide. The tradition continues today with one guide left, who can be hired by groups to lead the way around the slip sands and hidden channels. The eight-mile walk takes the best part of a day; ask at the Grange tourist office for further details. Otherwise, genteel Grange is a bit of a let-down, despite its solid Victorian buildings and formal gardens. Having been attracted here by the mild climate (supposedly the warmest in the north of England), and after tramping along the mile-long esplanade with its fine views of the marshy bay, you've just about covered all it's got to offer, other than the walk to the top of **Hampsfell** (750ft; 3hr; 4 miles).

Grange **tourist office** is in Victoria Hall, on Main Street (mid-March to Oct daily 10am–5pm; ☎015395/34026), four hundred yards left from the **train station** and National Express stop. Keep walking up Main Street to the top of town to reach Kents Bank Road, which has plenty of **accommodation** lining both sides on the way out of town. *Thornfield House* (☎015395/32512; ②; closed Nov–Feb) and *Methven Hotel* (☎015395/32031; ③) are typical of places in their price ranges. The nearest **youth hostel** is a ten-minute train ride away at the smaller resort of Arnside, on Redhills Road (☎01524/761781). **Eating** options aren't great in Grange, though you can fill up in the cafés along Main Street.

Cartmel

Sheltered several miles inland of Morecambe Bay, **CARTMEL** grew up around its twelfth-century Augustinian priory and is still dominated by the proud **Church of St Mary and St Michael** (daily: summer 9am–5.30pm; winter 9am–3.30pm; tours Easter–Oct Wed 11am & 2pm; free), the only substantial remnant to survive the Dissolution. A diagonally crowned tower is the most distinctive feature outside, while the light and spacious Norman-transitional interior climaxes at a splendid chancel, illuminated by the 45-foot-high **East Window**. You can spend a good half-hour scanning the immaculate misericords and numerous tombs, chief among them the **Harrington Tomb** in the Town Choir, to the south of the chancel – the weathered figure is that of John Harrington, who rebuilt this section in 1340. Everything else in the village is modest in scale, centred on the attractive **market square**, beyond the church, with its Elizabethan cobbles, water pump and fish slabs.

Trains stop at Cark-in-Cartmel, two miles southwest of the village; **buses** #530 and #531 from there or from Grange train station (originating in Kendal) run to the village. On Market Square, *Market Cross Cottage* (☎015395/36143; no credit cards;

③) is a seventeenth-century **B&B**. *Blue Bell House* in Devonshire Square (☎015395/36658; no credit cards; ③), down towards the church, is of a similar age and hue, while the cheapest rooms are at *Bank Court Cottage* (☎015395/36593; no credit cards; ①), through the arch in Market Square. Rooms at the celebrated *Cavendish* on Cavendish St (☎015395/36240, *thecavendish@compuserve.com*; ⑤), just off the square, have been refurbished while retaining their original sixteenth-century features. There's **camping** at *Wells House Farm* (☎015395/36270), just a couple of minutes' walk from the square. The *Cavendish* is the oldest and most characterful of the **pubs**, sitting on the site of a monastic guest house and offering good food and its own award-winning beer.

Ulverston

The railway line winds westwards from Cartmel to **ULVERSTON**, a close-knit market town, which formerly prospered on the cotton, tanning and iron-ore industries. It's an attractive place, enhanced by its dappled grey limestone cottages and a jumble of cobbled alleys and traditional shops zigzagging off the central **Market Place**. Stalls still set up here and in the surrounding streets every Thursday and Saturday; on other days (not Wed) the **market hall** on New Market Street is the centre of commercial life.

Ulverston's most famous son is Stan Laurel (born Arthur Stanley Jefferson), the whimpering, head-scratching half of Laurel and Hardy who are celebrated in a mind-boggling collection of memorabilia at the **Laurel and Hardy Museum** up an alley at 4C Upper Brook St (daily 10am–4.30pm; £2; closed Jan), near Market Place. The copy of Stan's birth certificate (16 June 1890, in Foundry Cottages, Ulverston) lists his father's occupation as "comedian" – young Arthur Stanley could hardly have become anything else. Down from the museum, in Lower Brook Street, Ulverston's **Heritage Centre** (Mon, Tues & Thurs–Sat 9.30am–4.30pm; £2) gives a good overview of the town's history and its various industrial achievements.

Ulverston **train station** is only a few minutes' walk from the town centre – head up Princess Street and turn right at the main road for County Square. **Buses** arrive on nearby Victoria Road. The **tourist office** is in Coronation Hall on County Square (Mon–Sat 10am–5pm; ☎01229/587120). Pick of the **B&Bs** is the *White House*, a three-hundred-year-old beamed cottage at the bottom of Market Street (☎01229/583340; no credit cards; ①; closed Nov–Easter). There's also a great *Walker's Hostel* on Oubas Hill (☎01229/585588; no credit cards; ①), on the A590 as you come into town. **Cafés** include the *Ship's Wheel Café*, King Street, renowned for its frothy coffees and traditional cooking. Out of town, follow the A590 briefly and then turn off at the signpost for **Canal Foot**, running through an industrial estate to reach the beautifully sited *Bay Horse Inn* (☎01229/583972, *reservations@bayhorse.furness.co.uk*; ⑦, ⑧ incl dinner), whose cooking is celebrated far and wide.

Furness Abbey

Furness Abbey (April–Sept daily 10am–6pm; Oct daily 10am–4pm; Nov–March Wed–Sun 10am–4pm; £2.50; EH), a set of roofless red sandstone arcades and pillars hidden in a wooded vale – the so-called "Valley of Deadly Nightshade" – lies a mile and a half out of Barrow-in-Furness on the Ulverston road (local buses to Dalton-in-Furness and Ulverston pass close by). Now one of Cumbria's finest ruins, it was once the most powerful abbey in the northwest, possessing much of southern Cumbria as well as land in Ireland and the Isle of Man. By the fourteenth century it had become such a prize that the Scots raided it twice, though it survived until April 1536, when Henry VIII chose it to be the first of the large abbeys to be dissolved. The transepts stand virtually at their original height, while the massive slabs of stone-ribbed vaulting, richly embellished arcades and intricately carved *sedilia* in the presbytery are the equal of any of Yorkshire's far busier abbey ruins. A small **museum** houses some of the best carvings, including rare examples of effigies of armed knights with closed helmets and – as medieval custom dictated – crossed legs. Only seven others have ever been found intact. The *Abbey Tavern* at the entrance serves drinks at tables scattered about some of the ruined outbuildings

Ravenglass

On its way between Barrow and Whitehaven, the Cumbrian coast railway stops at **RAVENGLASS**, which preserves a row of characterful nineteenth-century cottages, facing out across the mud flats and dunes. The village dates back to the arrival of the Romans who established a supply post here in the first century AD for the northern legions manning Hadrian's Wall. Look for the sign to the "Roman Bath House", just past the station: 500 yards up a single-track lane lie the fairly extensive remains of a fort which survived in Ravenglass until the fourth century. Local **accommodation** includes *Rose Garth* (☎01229/717275; no credit cards; ②), a guest house on the main street, and the *Holly House Hotel* (☎01229/717230; ②), further up, which also has a public bar.

Ravenglass station is the starting point for the toy-like **Ravenglass and Eskdale Railway** (summer daily; winter Sat & Sun, departures roughly 10am–5pm; £6.50 return; ☎01229/717171), known affectionately as La'al Ratty. Opened in 1875 to carry ore from the Eskdale mines to the coastal railway. the tiny train, running on a 15-inch gauge track, takes forty minutes to wind its way through seven miles of forests and fields between the fell sides of the Eskdale Valley to Dalegarth station (and the nearby hamlet of Boot, see "Wast Water and Eskdale", above).

St Bees

The close-knit central streets in the coastal village of **ST BEES** give it the feel of a retirement colony. It's a suitably elderly settlement, with a nunnery established here as early as the seventh century, succeeded by **St Bees Priory**, just north of today's train station, in the twelfth century. This was slightly damaged in the Dissolution, but retains huge Norman arches above its entrance porch; it also houses a small exhibition of Celtic crosses and headstones in the nave. The long sands lie a few hundred yards west of the village, while the steep, red sandstone cliffs of **St Bees Head** to the north are good for windy walks and bird watching. The headland's lighthouse marks the start of Wainwright's 190-mile **Coast-to-Coast Walk** to Robin Hood's Bay in Yorkshire.

St Bees is on the Cumbrian coast train line and lies just five miles south of Whitehaven, from where there's a regular bus service. *Tomlin Guest House*, out of the centre on Beach Road (☎01946/822284; no credit cards; ①), is a good first **accommodation** choice; the *Queen's Hotel*, Main Street (☎01946/822287; ③), is a nice old pub with a beer-garden.

Whitehaven

Some fine Georgian houses mark out the centre of **WHITEHAVEN**, one of the few grid-planned towns in England. The economic expansion that forced this planning was as much due to the booming slave trade as to the more widely recognized coal traffic. Whitehaven spent a brief period during the eighteenth century as Britain's third busiest port (after London and Bristol), making it a prime target for an abortive raid led by Scottish-born American lieutenant **John Paul Jones**. Disgusted with the slave trade he witnessed while ship's mate in America, Jones returned to the port of his apprenticeship to rebel but, let down by a drunk and potentially mutinous crew, he damaged only one of the two hundred boats in dock and his mini-crusade fell flat. All this and more is explained in the **Beacon** (Easter–Oct Tues–Sun 10am–5.30pm; Nov–Easter 10am–4.30pm; £3.80), an enterprising heritage centre on the harbour. There's a **market** held in town every Thursday and Saturday, which adds a bit of colour. Otherwise, stroll up to the seventeenth-century church of **St Nicholas** on Lowther Street, where all that stands is its tower; the rest succumbed to a fire in 1971, but there's a lovely garden now surrounding the former nave. Also on Lowther Street, don't miss Michael Moon's secondhand **bookshop** at no. 19 (closed Sun), a bookworm's treasure trove.

The #X5 **bus** links Whitehaven with Cockermouth, Keswick and Penrith, while **trains** follow the coastal route south to Barrow and north to Carlisle. The **tourist office** is in the Market Hall on Market Place (Easter–Oct Mon–Sat 9.30am–5pm, Sun 10am–4.30pm; Nov–Easter Mon–Sat 10am–4.30pm; ☎01946/852939). There's little choice of **places to eat**: best spots are the *Westminster Café*, opposite St Nicholas' on Lowther Street, for light lunches, sandwiches and espresso, and *Bruno's*, 9–11 Church St, where a full Italian meal can be had for under £20.

Carlisle and around

CARLISLE, the county town of Cumbria and its only city, is also the repository of much of the region's history. Its strategic location has been fought over for more than 2000 years. The original Celtic settlement was superseded by a Roman town, whose first fort was raised here in AD72. Carlisle thrived during the construction of Hadrian's Wall and then, long after the Romans had gone, the Saxon settlement was repeatedly fought over by the Danes and the Scots. The struggle with the Scots defined the very nature of Carlisle as a border city: William Wallace was repelled in 1297 and Robert the Bruce eighteen years later, but Bonnie Prince Charlie's troops took Carlisle in 1745 after a six-day siege, holding it for only six weeks before surrendering to the Duke of Cumberland, who bombarded the city with cannon dragged from Whitehaven. It's not surprising then that Carlisle still trumpets itself as the "great border city" and it's well worth a day of anyone's time to explore its compact centre and visit the trio of top-class sights: cathedral, castle and Tullie House Museum.

The main thoroughfare of English Street is pedestrianized as far as the expansive **Green Market** square, formerly heart of the medieval city, though a huge fire in 1392 destroyed its buildings and layout. The only historic survivors are the market cross (1682), the Elizabethan former town hall behind it, which now houses the tourist office, and the timber-framed Guildhall beyond that (at the southern end of Fisher Street). The much-restored Guildhall now contains a small **museum** (Easter–Sept Thurs–Sun 1–4pm; 50p) of guild and civic artefacts.

It's only a few steps along to **Carlisle Cathedral** (Mon–Sat 7.30am–6.15pm, Sun 7.30am–5pm; £2 donation requested), founded in 1122 but embracing a considerably older heritage. Christianity was established in sixth-century Carlisle by St Kentigern (often known as St Mungo), who became the first bishop and patron saint of Glasgow. The cathedral's sandstone bulk has endured the ravages of time and siege: Parliamentarian troops during the Civil War destroyed all but two powerful arches of the original eight bays of the Norman nave, but there's still much to admire in the ornate fifteenth-century choir stalls and the glorious **East Window**, which features some of the finest pieces of fourteenth-century stained glass in the country.

For more on Carlisle's history, head for the **Tullie House Museum and Art Gallery** (Mon–Sat 10am–5pm, Sun noon–5pm; £3.75), reached up Castle Street or through the cathedral grounds, via Abbey Street. This takes a highly imaginative approach to Carlisle's turbulent past, with special emphasis put on life on the edge of the Roman Empire – climbing a reconstruction of part of Hadrian's Wall you learn about catapults and stone-throwers, while other sections elaborate on domestic life, work and burial practices. There's also plenty on the Jacobite siege of 1745, as well as a dramatic attempt to convey the intensity of the feuds between the "reivers" border families who lived beyond the jurisdiction of the Scottish and English authorities from the fourteenth to the seventeenth century in the so-called "Debatable Lands".

Across the fast Castle Way road stands **Carlisle Castle** (daily Easter–Oct 9.30am–6pm; Nov–Easter 10am–4pm; £3; EH), originally built by William Rufus on the site of a Celtic hill fort. Having clocked up over nine hundred years of continuous military use, the castle has undergone considerable changes, most evident in its outer bailey, which is filled with fairly modern buildings named after battles from the Napoleonic Wars and World War I. Apart from the gatehouse, with its reconstructed warden's quarters, it's the **inner bailey** surrounding the keep that's the real draw. It was here, in 1568, that Elizabeth I kept Mary Queen of Scots as her "guest". There's a **Military Museum** located in the former armoury, but much more interesting are the excellent displays in the **keep** and the elegant heraldic carvings made by prisoners in a second-floor alcove. Don't leave without climbing to the battlements for a view of the Carlisle rooftops.

Practicalities

From the **train station**, just off Botchergate, outside the Citadel, it's a five-minute walk to the **tourist office** in the Old Town Hall on Green Market (June–Aug Mon–Sat 9.30am–6pm, Sun 10.30am–4pm; Sept, Oct & March–May Mon–Sat 9.30–5pm, Sun 10.30am–4pm; Nov–Feb Mon–Sat 10am–4pm; ☎01228/625600).

The **bus station** is off Lowther Street, parallel to English Street, and most of the budget **accommodation** is east of here, concentrated between Victoria Place and Warwick Road. Good choices include *Ashleigh House*, 46 Victoria Place (☎01228/521631; no credit cards; ②); *Cornerways Guest House*, 107 Warwick Rd (☎01228/521733; no credit cards; ①); *Courtfield House*, 169 Warwick Rd (☎01228/522767; no credit cards; ②); and *Howard House*, 27 Howard Place (☎01228/529159; no credit cards; ②). The nearest **campsite** is *Orton Grange* caravan park (☎01228/710252) on the A595 four miles southwest of the city – take bus #300.

For daytime **meals** head for *Café Courtyard*, Treasury Court (enter through the gates on Scotch Street or Fisher Street) or *Delifrance*, behind the tourist office at the southern end of Fisher Street. In the evening, choose between *Franco's*, the pizzeria-restaurant occupying the ground floor of the Guildhall on Fisher Street, or *Fat Fingers* on Abbey Street (☎01228/511774), near Tullie House and the cathedral, a café-bar whose menu trawls the world for inspiration.

travel details

Trains

Carlisle to: Barrow-in-Furness (5 daily; 2hr 20min); Lancaster (hourly; 1hr); Manchester (2 daily; 2hr 30min); Whitehaven (hourly; 1hr 10min).

Oxenholme (Lake District) to: Carlisle (14 daily; 40–50min); Manchester (3–9 daily; 1hr 40min); Penrith (14 daily; 30min).

Buses

Carlisle to: Keswick (Mon–Sat 4 daily, 1 on Sun; 1hr 30min–2hr); Lancaster (4 daily; express services 1hr 10min, some services up to 4hr 30min); Manchester (2 daily; 2hr 30min); Whitehaven (1 hourly; 1hr 30min); Windermere/Bowness (3 daily; 2hr 20min).

Kendal to: Ambleside (1 hourly; 40min); Cartmel (7 daily; 1hr); Grasmere (1 hourly; 1hr); Keswick (1 hourly 1–2hr; 1hr 30min); Lancaster (1 hourly; 1hr); Manchester (Mon–Sat 3 daily, 1 on Sun; 2hr 45min); Windermere/Bowness (1 hourly; 30min).

Keswick to: Ambleside (1 hourly; 1hr); Buttermere (2 daily; 30min); Carlisle (Mon–Sat 4 daily, 1 on Sun; 1hr 30min–2hr); Cockermouth (7 daily; 35min); Grasmere (1 hourly; 40min); Kendal (1 hourly; 1hr 30min); Lancaster (5–10 daily; 2hr 50min); Manchester (1–3 daily; 3hr 50min); Seatoller (Mon–Sat 9 daily, 5 on Sun; 30min); Whitehaven (5 daily; 1hr 40min); Windermere (1 hourly; 1hr).

Windermere to: Ambleside (up to 3 hourly; 15min); Barrow-in-Furness (Mon–Sat 3 daily, 1 on Sun; 1hr 40min); Carlisle (3 daily; 2hr 20min); Grasmere (1 hourly; 30min); Kendal (1 hourly; 30min); Keswick (1 hourly; 1hr); Lancaster (1 hourly; 1hr 45min); Manchester (Mon–Sat 3 daily, 1 on Sun; 3hr).

CHAPTER TEN

YORKSHIRE

F ew visitors pass through **Yorkshire**, England's largest county, without spending time in history-soaked **York**, for centuries England's second city. Famed primarily for its minster, the city is an ensemble of tiny medieval alleys, castle ruins, tucked-away churches, Roman remains, riverside gardens and topnotch museums. York's mixture of medieval, Georgian and Victorian architecture is mirrored in miniature in the prosperous north and east of the county by towns such as **Beverley**, centred on another soaring minster; **Richmond**, banked under a crag-bound castle; and **Ripon**, gathered around its honey-stoned cathedral. **Knaresborough** shares similar attributes, but is overshadowed by the faded gentility of neighbouring **Harrogate**, a spa town geared these days towards the conference trade rather than health-seeking visitors. The Yorkshire coast, too, retains something of the grandeur of the days when its towns were the first to promote themselves as resorts: places like **Bridlington** and **Scarborough** boomed in the nineteenth century and again in the postwar period, though these days they're living on past glories. Instead, it's in characterful, historic places like **Whitby** and **Robin Hood's Bay** that the best of the coast is to be found.

The engine of growth during the Industrial Revolution was not in the north of the county, but in the south and west. By the nineteenth century, Leeds, Bradford, Sheffield and their satellites were the world's mightiest producers of **textiles** and **steel**. Ruthless economic logic left some of the cities battered by depression in the later years of the twentieth century, though a new vigour has infused South and West Yorkshire during the last decade. The city-centre transformations of **Leeds** and **Sheffield** in particular have been remarkable, both now featuring a series of high-profile attractions, from the Royal Armouries to the National Centre for Popular Music, while **Bradford** and its **National Museum of Photography, Film and Television** waylays people on their way to **Haworth** – the wretchedly over-visited birthplace of the Brontë sisters.

During even the worst of times, broad swathes of moorland survived above the slum- and factory-choked valleys. The **Yorkshire Dales**, to the northwest, form a lovely patchwork of limestone hills and serene valleys, ranging from the gentle, grassy spans of **Wharfedale** and **Wensleydale** to the majestic heights of Ingleborough, Whernside and Pen-y-ghent, and the wilder valleys of **Swaledale**, **Dentdale**, **Ribblesdale** and **Malhamdale**. Numerous stone-built villages provide often idyllic centres from which to walk, the whole area being covered by tracks, long-distance paths and old drove

---

ACCOMMODATION PRICE CODES

Throughout this guide, hotel and B&B accommodation is priced on a scale of ① to ⑨, the number indicating the **lowest price** you could expect to pay per night in that establishment for a **double room** in high season. The prices indicated by the codes are as follows:

① under £40	④ £60–70	⑦ £110–150
② £40–50	⑤ £70–90	⑧ £150–200
③ £50–60	⑥ £90–110	⑨ over £200

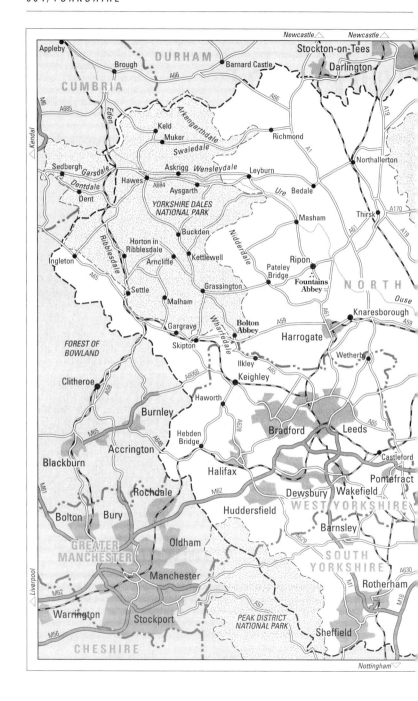

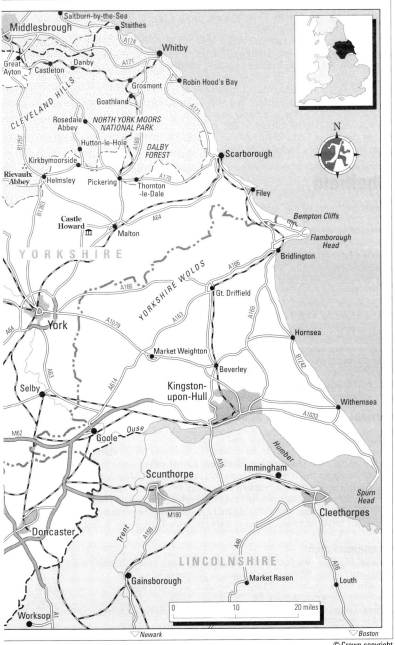

© Crown copyright

roads. Less visited, but still worth as much time as you can spare, is the county's other national park, the **North York Moors**, divided into bleak upland moors and with a tremendous rugged coastline.

The region is also scattered with a host of historic sites and buildings. The stately home of **Castle Howard** stands out, but there are also imperious relics of the Industrial Revolution, notably the Italianate pastiche of **Saltaire**, a millworkers' village on the outskirts of Bradford. In an earlier age, before the Reformation, Yorkshire had more monastic houses than any other English county, centres not only of religious retreat but also of a commercial acumen that was to lay the foundations of the region's great woollen industry. Many beautifully situated **ruins** survive today at Fountains, Rievaulx, Bolton Abbey, Whitby and elsewhere, graceful counterpoints to the more solid remains of the **castles** at York, Richmond, Scarborough and Pickering – the foremost of more than twenty castles raised in Yorkshire by the Normans.

Sheffield

Yorkshire's second city, and England's fourth largest, **SHEFFIELD** remains inextricably linked with its steel industry, in particular the production of high-quality cutlery. As early as the fourteenth century, the carefully fashioned, hard-wearing knives of hard-working Sheffield enjoyed national repute. Technological advances in steel production later turned Sheffield into one of the country's foremost centres of heavy and specialist engineering, which meant the city suffered heavy bombing in World War II, yet several of its grand civic buildings emerged remarkably unscathed. However, more damaging than bombs to the the city's pre-eminence was the steel industry's subsequent downturn, which by the 1980s had tipped parts of Sheffield into dispiriting decline. As with Leeds, the economic and cultural revival has been marked and rapid, spurred on by dogged local business incentives, an enthusiastic council and bundles of lottery money. Urban regeneration is in full swing: the "Heart of the City" project is fast transforming the centre; a glut of **sports facilities** (including the Ski Village, Europe's largest artificial ski resort) backs Sheffield's claim to be considered "National City of Sport"; while the city that gave the world the iconoclastic Jarvis Cocker of Pulp houses the **National Centre for Popular Music**.

Arrival, transport and accommodation

Sheffield's **train station** is just east of the city centre off Sheaf Square. The **bus station**, known as the Sheffield Interchange, is on Pond Street about two hundred yards to the north. The **Destination Sheffield** tourist office is on Surrey Street (Mon–Fri 9.30am–5.15pm, Sat 9.30am–4.15pm; ☎0114/273 4671). Most local **buses** depart from the High Street, while the **Supertram** system (☎0114/272 8282) connects the city centre with the massive shopping mall at Meadowhall. For fare and timetable **information**, call the Travel Line (☎01709/515151). A one-day TravelMaster Pass (£4.95) gives unlimited travel on buses, trains and trams throughout South Yorkshire.

Accommodation

Bristol, Blonk St (☎0114/220 4000, *sheffield@bhg.co.uk*). Breezy business hotel near the river, quays and markets. All rooms are en suite. ⑤, ④ at weekends.

Cutlers, George St (☎0114/273 9939). City-centre inn with budget en-suite rooms, all with TV and tea-and-coffee-making facilities. ④.

Priory Lodge, 40 Wolstenholme Rd (☎0114/258 4670). Suburban accommodation, a mile southwest of the centre. ②.

Rutland Arms, 86 Brown St (☎0114/272 9003). Victorian pub with pleasant beer-garden and a few standard rooms, just seconds from the music centre. No credit cards. ②.

Stakis, Victoria Quays (☎0114/252 5500). Makes superb use of its revitalized canalside site, with a range of leisure facilities. ⑦.

University of Sheffield, Halifax Hall, Endcliffe Vale Rd (☎0114/222 8811). Two miles west of the centre (bus #M60, from Flat St). Hall of residence rooms – some with en-suite facilities (mid-June to mid-Sept only). ①.

The City

Millions of pounds have been earmarked to turn Sheffield city centre away from the twin legacies of Victorian solidity and late twentieth-century sterility. There's been most progress in the re-vamped post-industrial area near the train station – known as the **Cultural Industries Quarter** – where clubs and galleries exist alongside high-tech arts and media businesses. The major player here is the **National Centre for Popular Music** on Paternoster Row (daily 10am–6pm, last admission 3.30pm; £5.95, £7.25 at weekends, on bank holidays and throughout July & Aug), whose main exhibition areas are set within four giant stainless-steel drums – a nod to the city's most prominent industry. It's an interactive arts and education centre and not a traditional museum, so you're encouraged to make, record and mix music, have a go at designing an album sleeve, and sit in the world's first 3-D surround-sound auditorium. The ground-floor café-bar shows signs of rivalling the **Showroom** cinema-and-bar complex across the road, and you can probably find someone to debate the relative merits of famous Sheffield popsters and rocksters, from Def Leppard and the Human League through to Jarvis Cocker and Babybird.

North of the centre, near the River Don, **Castlegate** and its traditional **markets** are still undergoing ambitious redevelopment. In the centre itself, the main development is around the impressive **Town Hall**, at the junction of Pinstone and Surrey streets, topped by the figure of Vulcan, the Roman god of fire and metalworking. The city's new centrepiece, the **Millennium Gallery and Winter Garden**, is destined to hold the Hawley collection of Sheffield hand tools and, of more general interest, the city's Ruskin collection, founded by John Ruskin in 1875 to "improve" the working people of Sheffield. North of the town hall, Fargate meets Church Street, where the city's **Cathedral of St Peter and St Paul** retains elements of its fifteenth-century origins. Across Cathedral Square sits the **Cutler's Hall** of 1832, an imposing reminder of Sheffield's traditions. The Company of Cutlers was first established in 1624 to regulate the affairs of the cutlery industry, and this is the third hall on the site. South of the town hall, the pedestrianized **Moor Quarter** draws in shoppers, though the nearby **Devonshire Quarter**, centred on Division Street, is the trendiest shopping area.

The **Graves Art Gallery** (Tues–Sat 10am–5pm; free), on the top floor of the City Library (entrance on Surrey Street), leans most heavily towards nineteenth- and twentieth-century British artists like Turner, Nash and the Pre-Raphaelites. Sheffield's most instructive museums, however, are those devoted to its industrial past. The **City Museum** (Wed–Sat 10am–5pm, Sun 11am–5pm; free), in Weston Park (a mile west of the city centre; bus #52 from High Street), contains the definitive collection of cutlery and Sheffield ware, but it's eclipsed by the **Kelham Island Museum**, Alma Street (Mon–Thurs 10am–4pm, Sun 11am–4.45pm; £3), one mile north of the city centre (bus #47 or #48 from Flat Street). Exhibits here reveal the breadth of the city's industrial output, ranging from a colossal twelve-thousand horsepower steam engine to a silver-plated penny-farthing made for the Tsar of Russia. Many of the old machines are still working, arranged in period workshops.

Eating, drinking and nightlife

Sheffield has plenty of great **café-bars** and the good-value **restaurants** are all pretty adept at making a play for the student pound. The **pubs** listed below are those with a bit of character and staying power, but for the best insight into what makes Sheffield tick as a party destination take a night-time walk on the wild side along **West Street** where competing theme and retro bars go in and out of fashion (and business). The Crucible, Lyceum and Studio **theatres** in Tudor Square (☎0114/276 9922) host a full programme of theatre, dance, comedy and concerts. The Showroom, 7 Paternoster Row (☎0114/275 7727), is the biggest independent **cinema** outside London. Friday's *Sheffield Telegraph* lists the week's performances, events, concerts and films; look out also for the *Dirty Stop Out's Guide*, a comprehensive listings booklet, available at the tourist office.

Café-bars

All Bar One, 15 Leopold St. Roomy café-bar with a blackboard menu, decent wine (racked above the long bar), pine tables, stripped floors and fans.

The Forum, 127–129 Division St. Long the mainstay of the Devonshire Quarter, the Forum has a great menu and laid-back clientele. Closed Sun.

Halcyon, 113–117 Division St. Designer bar with cosy sofas and a touch of class.

Nonna's 2, Brown St. Italian deli-café, serving *frittata* or scrambled eggs and smoked salmon for breakfast, and ciabatta sandwiches, salads and coffee until 8pm. Closed Sun.

Showroom, 7 Paternoster Row. The relaxed *Showroom* has a café on one side serving Mediterranean-style food, and a great bar on the other.

Restaurants

Antonio's Flying Pizza, 255 Glossop Rd (☎0114/273 9056). Long-established and rumbustious Italian pasta and pizza place. Inexpensive.

Blue Room Café, 22a Norfolk Row. Cheap and cheerful daytime vegetarian/wholefood café, with a few outdoor seats in the summer. Inexpensive.

Encore, Crucible Theatre, Tudor Square (☎0114/275 0724). Accomplished Modern-British cooking in the theatre restaurant; pre-show dinner and meal-and-ticket deals offer the best value. Moderate.

Nirmals, 189–193 Glossop Rd (☎0114/272 4054). The most highly rated Indian restaurant in town, open until 1am at the weekend. Inexpensive.

Trippet's Wine Bar, 89 Trippets Lane (☎0114/278 0198). Unstuffy wine bar behind West Street. The bistro food is popular and there's live jazz and blues on occasion. Moderate.

Pubs, clubs and live music

Arena, Broughton Lane (☎0114/256 5656). Stadium venue on the edge of town.

Bath Hotel, 66 Victoria St. Timeless Victorian classic off Glossop Road – no frills, but well-kept real ale and handsome original features.

The Boardwalk, Snig Hill (☎0114/279 9090). Popular venue for indie bands, rock, folk and comedy.

Capitol, 14–16 Matilda St (☎0114/276 3523). A converted warehouse where the night's clubbing continues until well into the following day.

Don Valley Stadium, on Worksop Rd (☎0114/278 9199). Stadium venues on the edge of town.

Fat Cat, 23 Alma St. Cosy, old-fashioned and famed for its umpteen real ales. It's in old steel-land, about a quarter of an hour's walk north from the city centre.

Frog & Parrot, Division St. A boisterous pub with some dark little nooks and crannies, lots of beers and a good jukebox. Decent mix of locals and students.

Leadmill, 6–7 Leadmill Rd (☎0114/275 4500), in the Cultural Industries Quarter, hosting live bands and DJs most nights of the week.

Niche, 87–91 Sydney St (☎0114/275 1414). Sheffield's finest all-nighter, staying open until 8am – a free minibus service takes people on to the *Capitol* (see above).

Republic, 112 Arundel St (☎0114/249 2210). Club housed in an old steel and engineering works.
The Washington, 79 Fitzwilliam St. A good pub with good beer that's a favoured muso's hangout.
Just two minutes from Division Street.

Leeds

Yorkshire's commercial capital, and one of the fastest-growing cities in the country,
LEEDS has undergone a radical transformation in recent years. There's still a true
northern grit to its character, and in many of its dilapidated suburbs, but the grime has
been removed from the Victorian centre and the city is revelling in its renaissance as a
financial, administrative and cultural boomtown. The most obvious manifestation of
change has been the advent of late-opening cafés, bars, clubs and eclectic restaurants,
and the arrival of the swanky department store Harvey Nichols. The formerly run-
down city quarters have been revitalized and have made Leeds a noted nightlife destination. It's long been the region's cultural centre, home to Opera North, the noted West
Yorkshire Playhouse and a triennial international piano competition that ranks among
the world's top musical events. The **Royal Armouries** aside, the **City Art Gallery** has
the best collection of British twentieth-century art outside London; **Leeds City
Museum** and **Armley Mills Museum** take care of the city's historical legacy; while
further from the city are the ruins of **Kirkstall Abbey** and one of the country's great
Georgian piles, **Harewood House**.

Arrival and transport

National and local Metro trains use **Leeds City Station** off City Square on the southern flank of the city centre, which also houses the Gateway Yorkshire **tourist office** in
the Arcade (Mon–Sat 9.30am–6pm, Sun 10am–4pm; ☎0113/242 5242). The **bus and
coach station** occupies a sprawling site to the east, behind Kirkgate Market, on St
Peter's Street, close to the West Yorkshire Playhouse. The **Metro Travel Centre** at the
bus station has up-to-date service details (Mon–Fri 8.30am–5.30pm, Sat 9am–4.30pm),
or call **Metroline** (Mon–Sat 8am–7pm, Sun 9am–5.30pm; ☎0113/245 7676). If you're
planning to see a slice of West Yorkshire over a day or two, consider buying a bus/train
day rover (£4.50), or separate bus or train day rovers (£3.80 each).

Accommodation

There's a good mix of **accommodation** in Leeds, including some fairly central budget
places near the university campus. Plenty of other cheaper B&Bs lie out to the northwest
in Headingley, though these are all a bus ride away. The tourist office can **book you a
room**; call their booking line on ☎0800/808050. The nearest **youth hostel** is in Haworth
(see p.574), and the nearest **campsite** near Roundhay Park on Elmete Lane (☎0113/265
2354), three miles northeast of the city – buses #10 and #12 (#19 or #19a Sun).

42 The Calls, 42 The Calls (☎0113/244 0099, *hotel@42thecalls.co.uk*). Leeds' top choice – fashionably converted from an old grain mill on the canal. ⑦.
Avalon Guest House, 132 Woodsley Rd (☎0113/243 2545). Decent budget B&B near the university in a large Victorian house. ①.
Glengarth, 162 Woodsley Rd (☎0113/245 7940). Homely B&B, with good rates and a variety of
rooms; the cheapest do not have en-suite facilities. No credit cards. ②.
The Griffin, 31 Boar Lane (☎0113/242 2555). Central Victorian hotel, handily placed for shopping
and café life. Weekend rates are an especially good deal, when prices drop by £20 or so. ⑤.
Malmaison, Sovereign Quay (☎0113/398 1000). Designer waterside premises (behind Swinegate),
with the signature *Malmasion* style. Breakfast is not included. ⑥, ⑤ at weekends.

Moorlea, 146 Woodsley Rd (☎0113/243 2653). Amiable place near the university, with comfortable singles and doubles. No credit cards. ①.

Queen's Hotel, City Square (☎0113/243 1323). Refurbished Art Deco landmark, with period *Palm Court Lounge*, bar, restaurant and free car parking. ⑦, ⑨ at weekends.

University of Leeds (☎0113/233 6100). Rents rooms and self-catering apartments in various halls of residence during university holidays – call well in advance; two-night minimum stay. ①.

The City

There's much to be said for starting **Leeds Town Hall**, one of the finest expressions of nineteenth-century civic pride in the country. It's a classical colossus of great skill, colonnaded on all sides, guarded by white lions and topped by a perky clocktower. Nearby, on the Headrow, in **Leeds City Museum** (Tues–Sat 10am–5pm; free) dark galleries dutifully run through local history from prehistoric times, highlighting fossils, Roman finds, and somewhat incongruously, an unusually large array of stuffed animals. The adjacent **Leeds City Art Gallery** (Mon–Sat 10am–5pm, Wed 10am–8pm, Sun 1–5pm; free) comprises one of the best arrays outside London of twentieth-century British art, with an understandable bias towards pieces by Henry Moore and Barbara Hepworth, both former students at the Leeds School of Art. Moore's *Reclining Woman* lounges at the top of the steps outside the gallery. From the Gallery, a slender bridge connects to the adjacent **Henry Moore Institute** (daily 10am–5.30pm, until 9pm on Wed; free), devoted to showcasing temporary exhibitions of sculpture from all periods and nationalities, and not, as you might imagine, pieces by the masterful Moore.

Most people make a beeline for the brimming, shop-filled **arcades**, further along on either side of **Briggate**. These nineteenth-century palaces of marble, mahogany, stained glass and mosaics have been magnificently restored to house the shops and businesses which are at the heart of Leeds' revival. Perhaps the most splendidly decorated of all is the light-flooded **Victoria Quarter**, with Harvey Nichols as its designer lodestone. Across Vicar Lane, the restored **Kirkgate Market** (closed Wed afternoon & Sun) is the largest market in the north of England. Housed in a superb Edwardian building, it's a descendant of the medieval woollen markets that were instrumental in making Leeds the early focus of the region's textile industry. On the corner of Vicar Lane and Duncan Street, the elliptical, domed **Corn Exchange** (open daily) was built in 1863, and is now a hip market for jewellery, clothes, furnishings, music and other bits and bobs. Behind here, under the railway arches on Assembley Street and along Call Lane, Leeds' **Exchange Quarter** flexes its fashionable muscles in a series of hip cafés and restaurants.

The biggest transformation in Leeds has been along the **Leeds–Liverpool Canal**, formerly a stagnant relic of industrial decline. At **Granary Wharf**, a couple of minutes' walk from the train station, craftshops fill the extensive cobbled, vaulted arches (the "Dark Arches"), while every weekend (and bank holiday) a market with stalls, bands and entertainers spills out onto the canal basin. Further up on the south side, **Tetley's Brewery Wharf** (daily 10.30am–5pm; brewery tours at noon, 1pm & 3pm; £3.95; over-14s only) stands in front of one of the region's oldest, and most favoured, breweries. The **Royal Armouries** (daily: April–Oct 10.30am–5.30pm; Nov–March 10.30am to 4.30pm; £7.95) is five minutes further along the canal footpath, and was purpose-built to house the arms and armour collection from the Tower of London. Themed galleries cover concepts like "War" and "Hunting", while there are enough demonstrations (jousting to falconry), interactive displays, hands-on exhibits and computer simulations to keep everyone interested. Bus #63b runs every fifteen minutes direct to the Armouries from Leeds City Square, a five-minute ride.

Out of the city

The **Thackray Medical Museum**, on Beckett Street (Tues–Sun 10am–5.30pm; daily during school holidays; £4.40), a mile east of the city centre, is next to St James' Hospital ("Jimmy's" from the TV series) – catch bus #5a, #13, #17, #41, #42, #43, #50 or #88. Essentially a medical history museum, it's a hugely entertaining place – and positively ghoulish when it delves into topics like surgery before anaesthetics, and the workings of the human intestine. For Leeds' industrial past, visit the vast **Armley Mills Museum**, two miles west of the centre off Canal Road (Tues–Sat 10am–5pm, Sun 1–5pm; £2; bus #5a, #14, #66 or #67). There's been a mill on the site since at least the seventeenth century, and the present building was one of the world's largest woollen mills until its closure in 1969. You can also visit the ruins of **Kirkstall Abbey** (dawn to dusk; free), the city's most important medieval relic, built between 1152 and 1182 by Cistercian monks from Fountains Abbey. It lies three miles northwest of the city centre on Abbey Road (bus #732, #733, #734, #735 or #736). Four miles east of the city, the Jacobean house of **Temple Newsam** (April–Oct Tues–Sat 10am–5pm, Sun 1–5pm; £2; bus #27) contains many of the paintings and much of the decorative art owned by Leeds City Art Gallery.

If you were to see just one stately home within the area, however, it should be **Harewood House**, seven miles north of Leeds (house: Easter–Oct daily 11am–4.30pm; Nov–Easter Sat & Sun 11am–4.30pm; grounds & bird garden: Easter–Oct daily 10am–6pm; Nov–Easter Sat & Sun 10am–6pm; house, grounds & bird garden £6.95; grounds & bird garden £5.75). The house was conceived in 1759 by York architect John Carr, the building was finished by Robert Adam, the furniture made by Thomas Chippendale and the landscaped gardens laid out by Capability Brown. To cap it all a sweeping terrace designed by Sir Charles Barry (architect of the Houses of Parliament) overlooks the garden, while the ensemble is further enhanced by paintings by artists of such mettle as Turner, Gainsborough, Reynolds, El Greco and a whole host of Italian masters. There are guided tours of the house and galleries throughout the summer every Tuesday and Thursday at 2pm. There are frequent buses to Harewood from Leeds (including the #36, #781 and #X35).

Eating, drinking and nightlife

Eating out in Leeds has been transformed in recent years, with a plethora of **restaurants** and **brasseries** opening up in converted warehouses and grain mills offering up-to-the-minute Modern-British food. Michelin stars are not unknown, but there's a down-to-earth approach to prices, with even the fanciest places offering special lunch or early-bird deals. It's all a long way from when the big name in local cooking was *Harry Ramsden's*, a byword for "proper" fish and chips, but now franchised all over England and even as far away as Hong Kong. Along with its restaurants, Leeds rivals Manchester in the number of late-opening, continental-style **café-bars**, while some sterling spruced-up Victorian **pubs** still pull in the punters, who then move on to one of the city's **clubs**, many of which have a nationwide reputation – not least because Leeds lets you dance until 5 or 6am most weekends. For information about what's on and local **listings**, the *Yorkshire Evening Post* is your best bet.

Café-bars and restaurants

Art's Café, 42 Call Lane (☎0113/243 8243). Bare-bones, stripped-floor café/restaurant in the Exchange Quarter. Moderate.

Brasserie 44, 44 The Calls (☎0113/234 3232). Informal but trendy brasserie, serving everything from Whitby cod to Middle Eastern *meze*. Closed Sat lunch & Sun. Moderate to Expensive.

Café Rouge, Assembley St (☎0113/245 1551). Housed in the old Assembley Rooms, where Leeds' gentry once schmoozed and gambled. Breakfast, lunch or dinner, inside or out. Moderate.

Cornucopia, Corn Exchange, Call Lane. Long-standing favourite in the bowels of the Corn Exchange. Self-service croissants, coffee and lunch specials.Inexpensive.

The Courtyard, 25–37 Cookridge St. Huge café-bar that gets a bit too packed at night, but slip in during the day for snacks and drinks in the brick-paved courtyard (heated in winter). Inexpensive.

Espresso Bar, Harvey Nichols, Victoria Quarter Arcade, Briggate. Domain of the high-fashion shopper. Inexpensive to Moderate.

Fourth Floor Café, Harvey Nichols, Briggate (☎0113/204 8000). Souped-up classics (fish and chips, bangers and mash) and exotic flavours. Closed Mon–Wed eve & Sun. Moderate (lunch) to Expensive (dinner).

Harry Ramsden's, White Cross, Guiseley (☎01943/879531). Expect to wait in line before entering the portals of gastronomic heaven itself. Bus #732,733,734 or 736. Moderate.

Norman, Call Lane. Industrial-chic juice-and-booze bar, with Asian noodle-and-satay menu and Saturday-night club sounds. Inexpensive.

Oporto, 31–33 Call Lane (☎0113/245 4444). Funky Exchange Quarter bistro-bar where the flavours mix and match. Moderate.

Pasta Romagna, 26 Albion Place. Outdoor tables, pizza slices, cappuccino and a mixed crowd of shoppers and slackers. Inexpensive.

Pitcher & Piano, Assembley St. Exchange Quarter magnet for city hipsters, drinking at the outdoor tables or chowing down on Modern-British food and snacks in the gargantuan interior. Moderate.

Pizza Express, White Cloth Hall, Crown St. No menu surprises from this popular chain, but a great building (behind the Corn Exchange) with soaring conservatory. Jazz on Sundays. Inexpensive to Moderate.

Pool Court at 42, 42–44 The Calls (☎0113/244 4242). This is the sharp end of the business – cutting-edge Modern-British cuisine. Closed Sat lunch & Sun. Expensive to Very Expensive.

Rascasse, Canal Wharf, Water Lane (☎0113/244 6611). Pushes all the right buttons – if it's not seared, it's roasted or chargrilled. Closed Sat lunch & Sun. Moderate to Expensive.

Pubs, clubs and live music

Club Uropa, 54 New Briggate (☎0113/242 2224). Immensely popular club nights, with great guest DJs.

Duchess of York, 71 Vicar Lane (☎0113/245 3929). Great pub venue for indie bands and stand-up comedy.

NATO, 66–69 Boar Lane (☎0113/244 5144). Hip happenings at one of Leeds's most enjoyable clubs. Thursday is the locals' night out; watch for flyers.

The Pleasure Rooms, 9 Lower Merrion St (☎0113/245 0923). House, disco, dance and trance on various nights of the week, with top-name DJs on the list.

Queen's Court, Queen's Court (☎0113/245 9449). The city's newest, and most enjoyable, gay club and bar, with midweek cabaret nights and weekend dance parties. Call for schedules.

The Ship, Ship Inn Yard, off Briggate. The yard tables – crammed into a space about three feet wide – take the city's obsession with continental outdoor ways to extremes.

Town & Country Club, 55 Cookridge St (☎0113/280 0100). High-profile live bands and regular weekend retro club nights. Also check out *The Underground*, Portland Crescent (☎0113/244 3403), behind the *T & C* for highly popular Latin, salsa, funk, Motown and soul nights.

The Warehouse, 19–21 Somers St (☎0113/246 8287). One of the biggest clubs in the city, with house, garage and techno sounds bringing in clubbers from all over the country.

The Whip, Duncan St/Briggate. Unchanged Victorian courtyard pub serving great Tetley's beer.

Whitelocks, Turk's Head Yard, off Briggate. Leeds' oldest and most atmospheric pub retains its traditional decor, though you'll be hard pushed to see any of it at peak times.

Arts, festivals and entertainment

Opera North, based at the Grand Theatre, gives a free performance each summer at Temple Newsam, as does the **Northern Ballet Theatre**; both events attract thousands. The **Grand Theatre and Opera House**, 46 New Briggate (☎0113/222 6222), is the regular base of Opera North and also puts on a full range of theatrical productions. The city's most innovative playhouse is the **West Yorkshire Playhouse**, Quarry Hill Mount (☎0113/213 7700). The **City Varieties**, Swan St, off Briggate (☎0113/243 0808), is one of the country's last surviving music halls, though it's less music-hall fare these days and more tribute bands, middle-of-the-road comedians and cabaret – great building and bar though. Hyde Park Picture House, Brudenell Road, Headingley (☎0113/275 2045), is a classic vintage cinema with **independent and art-house shows**; bus #56, 57 or 63 from the city centre.

Bradford

In its Victorian heyday **BRADFORD** – England's fourth largest metropolitan area – was the world's biggest producer of worsted cloth, its skyline etched black with mill chimneys, and its hills clogged with some of the foulest back-to-back houses of any northern city. Today the city has left this nether world behind and is valiantly laying on tourist attractions to rinse away its associations with urban decrepitude. A few spruced-up buildings and the rejuvenation of the late Victorian woollen warehouse quarter, Little Germany, signify an attempt to beautify the city centre, but in truth Bradford itself no longer has the architectural heritage or the cultural interest with which to wage a tourist war.

The only thing of general interest in the city centre is the superb **National Museum of Photography, Film and Television** (Tues–Sun & public holidays 10am–6pm; free). It has recently emerged from a major refit, but still wraps itself around Britain's largest cinema screen (52ft by 64ft), whose daily **IMAX** and 3-D film screenings (£5.80) are billed as "so real you'll think you're there". The ground floor kicks off with the Kodak Gallery, a museum-within-a-museum which houses the contents of Kodak's private collection, crammed with memorabilia and hundreds of cameras. Successive floors are devoted to every nuance of film and television, including some emphasis on state-of-the-art topics like digital imaging and computer animation, and detours into subjects like advertising and news-gathering.

No one should pass up the chance to drop in on **SALTAIRE**, three miles north of the city, a model industrial village built by the industrialist Sir Titus Salt, who garnered his fortune through the innovative use of alpaca and mohair. **Salt's Mill**, designed to emulate an Italian palazzo and larger than St Paul's Cathedral in London, was the biggest factory in the world when it opened in 1853, and was surrounded by schools, hospitals, a train station, parks, baths and wash-houses, 45 almshouses and around 850 houses. Salt's Mill itself is the fulcrum of the village, its several floors now housing art, craft and furniture shops, but its enterprising centrepiece is the **1853 Gallery** (daily 10am–6pm; free), an entire floor of the old spinning shed given over to the world's largest retrospective collection of the works of Bradford-born David Hockney. *Salt's Diner* (☎01274/530533) on the same floor has a Hockney-designed logo, menu and crockery. Trains run to Saltaire from Bradford Forster Square, or take buses #662, #663, #664, or #665 from the Interchange. Saltaire's **tourist office**, 2 Victoria Rd (daily 10am–5pm; ☎01274/774993), is housed in one of the original shops and offers hour-long **guided walks** of the village (Sat at 2pm, Sun & public holidays at 11am & 2pm; £2).

Practicalities

Trains and **buses** arrive at Bradford Interchange on Croft Street, south of the city-centre grid. The **tourist office** (Mon–Fri 9am–5.30pm, Sat 9am–5pm; ☎01274/753678) is located in the Central Library on Prince's Way. The best-value **accommodation** within half a mile of the centre is to be found at the *Ivy*, 3 Melbourne Place (☎01274/727060;

no credit cards; ①), and the *New Beehive Inn*, Westgate (☎01274/721784; no credit cards; ①). More luxurious digs are available at the Victorian-era *Pennington Midland Hotel*, on Forster Square (☎01274/735735; ⑤), or the equally venerable *Quality Victoria Hotel*, on Bridge Street (☎01274/728706; ⑤).

Bradford's large Asian population has made the city famous for its **curry houses**, which are scattered all over the city. General opinion still favours the *Kashmir*, 27 Morley St, close to the National Museum (☎01274/726513), Bradford's first-ever curry house. Nearby, the *International*, at 40–42 Mannville Terrace (☎01274/721449), also has its long-standing adherents. In the centre, the upmarket *Bombay Brasserie* (☎01274/737564), in a converted church on Simes Street, off Westgate, packs diners in for more refined meals. A short drive up Great Horton Road, past the university, more excellent curries are to be found at the Muslim *Mumtaz Paan House*, 386–392 Great Horton Rd (☎01274/571861; no alcohol allowed).

Haworth

Of English literary shrines, probably only Stratford sees more visitors than the quarter of a million who swarm annually into **HAWORTH** to tramp the cobbles once trodden by the Brontë sisters. Quite why the sheltered life of the Brontës should exert such a powerful fascination is a puzzle, though the contrast of their pinched provincial existences with the brooding moors and tumultuous passions of *Wuthering Heights* probably forms part of the answer. Whatever the reasons, during the summer the village's steep, cobbled **Main Street** is lost under huge crowds, herded by multilingual signs around the various stations on the Brontë trail.

Of these, the **Brontë Parsonage Museum**, at the top of the main street (April–July & Sept daily 10am–5.30pm; Aug Wed 10am–7pm, rest of the week 10am–5.30pm; Oct to mid-Jan & early Feb to March daily 11am–5pm; £4.20), is the obvious focus, a modest Georgian house bought by Patrick Brontë in 1820 to bring up his family. After the tragic early loss of his wife and two eldest daughters, the surviving four children – Anne, Emily, Charlotte and their brother, Branwell – spent most of their short lives in the place, which is furnished as it was in their day, and filled with the sisters' pictures, books, manuscripts and personal treasures. The bluff **Parish Church** in front of the parsonage – substantially rebuilt since the Brontës lived here – contains the family vault; Charlotte was married here in 1854. At the **Sunday School**, between parsonage and church, Charlotte, Anne and even Branwell did weekly teaching stints; Branwell, however, was undoubtedly more at home in the **Black Bull**, a pub within staggering distance of the parsonage near the top of Main Street. He got his opium at the pharmacist's over the road (now a gift shop).

The most popular local walk runs to **Brontë Falls** and **Bridge**, reached via West Lane and a track from the village, and to **Top Withens**, a mile beyond, a ruin fancifully thought to be the model for Wuthering Heights (3hr round trip). A plaque here bluntly points out that "the buildings, even when complete, bore no resemblance to the house she [Emily] described." The moorland setting, however, beautifully evokes the flavour of the book, and to enjoy it further you could walk on another two and a half miles to **Ponden Hall**, perhaps the Thrushcross Grange of *Wuthering Heights*.

Practicalities

There are frequent **buses** (#663, #664, #665 and #699) to Haworth from Bradford Interchange, eight miles away, with services every hour during the day; they stop at the bottom of the cobbled Main Street. The Haworth **tourist office** is at 2–4 West Lane, at the top of Main Street (daily 9.30am–5pm; ☎01535/642329).

You'll need to book ahead for **accommodation** at most times of the year. You can join Bramwell's ghost in the *Black Bull Hotel* in Main Street (☎01535/642249; ②); the

THE BRONTËS AT HAWORTH

Patrick Prunty or Bronty (it's unclear which) was born in Ireland and became a school master at the age of sixteen. He later won a place at St John's, Cambridge, where he changed his name to **Brontë**, perhaps influenced by naval hero Lord Nelson, who was made the Duke of Brontë. Later ordained, the Reverend Brontë, and his wife Maria, took up a living at Thornton, just outside Bradford, where the four youngest of their six children – Maria, Elizabeth, Charlotte, Branwell, Emily and Anne – were born between 1816 and 1820. Later that year, the Brontë family moved into the draughty parsonage in nearby Haworth.

It could hardly be called an auspicious start to life in a new home. Mrs Brontë died within the year and her sister was despatched to help look after the children. The four oldest girls were sent away to school, but withdrawn after first Maria, then Elizabeth, died after falling ill. The surviving daughters, and smothered Branwell, were kept at home, where they amused themselves by making up convoluted stories and writing miniature books. As they came of age, the girls took up short-lived jobs as governesses at various local schools; Charlotte and Emily even spent a year in Brussels, learning French. **Branwell**, meanwhile, was already sowing the dissolute seeds of his disappointing future: he had a certain talent for art, but got into debt, and then spent two years as a junior station master near Halifax but was later dismissed in disgrace. He then took a tutor's job but was dismissed again after developing what was darkly referred to as an "unwise passion" for his employer's wife. He retreated to Haworth, made himself overly familiar with the beer in the *Black Bull* and began experimenting with drugs.

Charlotte's, Emily's and Anne's continuing attempts to amuse themselves with their writings led to the private publication, in 1846, of a series of poems, paid for using part of a legacy from their aunt. They used the (male) pseudonyms Currer, Ellis and Acton Bell – keeping their own initials – though few copies of the collection were ever sold. Using the same name, **Charlotte** wrote a novel the same year, which was rejected by various publishers; but her *Jane Eyre*, submitted in 1847, was an instant success. **Emily**'s *Wuthering Heights* and **Anne**'s *Agnes Grey* received similar acclaim the same year; Anne's second novel, the better-known *Tenant of Wildfell Hall*, was published in 1848. As far as the public was concerned, the brilliant Bell brothers were a publishing sensation.

But the next two years destroyed the family, as it was ravaged by consumption. First Branwell, who had sunk ever deeper into addictive misery and ill-health, died in September 1848, followed by Emily in December of that year, and Anne in May of the following year. Charlotte lived on for another six years, writing two more novels – *Shirley* (1849) and *Villette* (1853) – and becoming something of a literary figure once she had revealed her identity, making friends with fellow author Elizabeth Gaskell, who later wrote Charlotte's biography. Charlotte finally married Reverend Brontë's curate, Arthur Bell Nicholls, who moved into the parsonage, but she died after nine months of marriage in the early stages of pregnancy. The Reverend Brontë lived on until 1861 – the entire family, except Anne (who is buried in Scarborough), lies in the Brontë vault in the village church, next to the house.

Old White Lion Hotel, a little further up (☎01535/642313; ③), is a more comfortable old inn. The best guest house is the *Apothecary*, 86 Main St (☎01535/643642, *apot@sisley86.freeserve.co.uk*; ②), opposite the church. For something a bit more luxurious, try *Weaver's*, 15 West Lane (☎01535/643822; ⑤), a converted row of weavers' cottages which also contains one of the best restaurants (dinner only, closed Sun & Mon) in the county. The **youth hostel**, *Longlands Hall* (☎01535/642234), is a mile from the centre at Longlands Drive, Lees Lane, off the Keighley road; the Bradford buses stop on the main road nearby.

The Yorkshire Dales

The **Yorkshire Dales** – "dales" from the Viking word *dalr* (valley) – form a lovely and varied upland area of limestone hills and pastoral valleys at the heart of the Pennines, wedged between the Lake District to the west and the North York Moors to the east. Protected as a **national park**, the region is crammed with opportunities for outdoor activities: the area is crisscrossed by several long-distance footpaths; there's a specially designated circular cycle way; and a host of centres are geared up for caving and other more specialist pursuits.

Most approaches are from the industrial towns to the south, via the superbly engineered **Settle to Carlisle Railway**, or along the main A65 road from towns such as **Skipton**, **Settle** and **Ingleton**. This makes southern dales like **Wharfedale** the most visited, while neighbouring **Malhamdale** is also immensely popular, thanks to the fascinating scenery squeezed into its narrow confines around **Malham**, perhaps the single most visited village in the region. **Ribblesdale**, approached from Settle, is more sombre, its villages in demand from hikers intent on tackling the Dales' famous **Three Peaks** – the mountains of Pen-y-ghent, Ingleborough and Whernside. To the northwest lies the more remote **Dentdale**, one of the least known but most beautiful of the valleys. Moving north, there are two parallel dales, **Wensleydale** and **Swaledale**, the latter pushing Dentdale as the most rewarding overall target. Both flow east, with Swaledale's lower stretches encompassing the appealing historic town of **Richmond**.

Public transport throughout the Dales is surprisingly good; pick up the invaluable, free *Dales Connection* bus timetable (published twice a year), available from tourist offices and from the various **national park information centres**. There are main centres at Grassington, Aysgarth Falls, Malham, Reeth, Hawes and Clapham, as well as numerous national park **information points** in shops, post offices and cafés throughout the region. In addition to the region's youth hostels there's a series of **bunkhouse barns** – basic self-catering accommodation for around £7 a night per person; **camping barns** are usually more rudimentary versions. Hikers will need the OS *Outdoor Leisure* series of **maps** (nos. 2, 10 and 30). The **Pennine Way** cuts right through the heart of the Dales, and the region is crossed by the Coast-to-Coast Walk, but the principal local route is the **Dales Way**, an 84-mile footpath from Ilkley to Bowness in the Lake District; Colin Speakman's *Dales Way* guidebook (Dalesman Press) is useful.

Skipton

Almost any trip to the southern dales is going to pass through **SKIPTON**, particularly if you want to see Wharfedale, five miles to the east. Apart from practical advantages, however, the town's worth a few hours in its own right, particularly on one of its four weekly **market** days (Mon, Wed, Fri & Sat), when the streets and pubs are filled with what seems like half the Dales population.

Sceptone, or "Sheeptown", was a settlement long before the arrival of the battling Normans, whose **Castle**, located at the top of the High Street (March–Sept Mon–Sat 10am–6pm, Sun noon–6pm; Oct–Feb Mon–Sat 10am–4pm, Sun noon–4pm; £4), provided the basis for the present fortress, among England's best preserved, thanks mainly to the efforts of Lady Anne Clifford, who rebuilt much of her family seat between 1650 and 1675 following the pillage of the Civil War. Little survives in the way of furniture or fittings, but starting with the proud battlements – emblazoned with the Clifford cry, *Desormais* ("Henceforth") – the castle very much looks the part. Lady Anne also displayed her restorative skills on the **Church of the Holy Trinity**, which stands in front of the castle at the top of the High Street (daily: summer 8.15am–5.30pm; winter 8.15am–dusk; £1 donation requested), and has a fine bossed fifteenth-century roof, beautiful chancel screen (dating from 1533) and a twelfth-century font crowned with a towering wooden Jacobean cover. Down the High Street, on the first floor of the town hall, drop into the entertaining **Craven Museum** (April–Sept Mon & Wed–Sat 10am–5pm, Sun 2–5pm; Oct–March Mon & Wed–Fri 1.30–5pm, Sat 10am–noon & 1–4pm; free), a brief introduction to the geology, flora, fauna, folk history and archeology of Craven, the region cradled between Wharfedale and the Lancashire border. The alleys on the western side of the High Street emerge on to the banks of the **Leeds–Liverpool Canal**, which runs right through the centre of Skipton. You can rent boats from the Canal Basin, off Coach Street: Pennine Boat Trips at Waterside Court (☎01756/790829), next to the George Fisher outdoor store, runs daily **canal cruises** (April–Oct, call for times; £3).

If you're heading for the Settle to Carlisle Railway, note that most **trains from Skipton** are direct – you shouldn't need to change at Settle unless you want to break your journey. The **bus station** is on Keighley Road, just before Devonshire Place at the bottom of the High Street. The **tourist office** is on narrow Sheep Street, parallel with the bottom of High Street (April–Oct Mon–Sat 10am–5pm; Nov–March Mon–Sat 10am–4pm; ☎01756/792809). Best central **accommodation** is the *Woolly Sheep Inn*, 38 Sheep St (☎01756/700966; ②), a restored seventeenth-century inn. B&Bs tend to lie on the outskirts, ten minutes or so out of the centre, on Gargrave (west) and Keighley (south) roads. *Peace Villas*, 69 Gargrave Rd (☎01756/790672; no credit cards; ①), and the *Skipton Park Guest 'Otel*, virtually opposite at 2 Salisbury St (☎01756/700640; no credit cards; ②), are the best places on Gargrave Road; the *Highfield Hotel*, 58 Keighley Rd (☎01756/793182; no credit cards; ②), is one of a clutch on that road. At night, make for the *Woolly Sheep Inn* which has inventive bar **food**, decent beer and a garden. The *Aagrah*, on Keighley Road near the bus station, has a loyal local following for its fresh, tasty Indian dishes.

Wharfedale

The best of **Wharfedale** starts just east of Skipton at **Bolton Abbey**, and then continues north in a broad, pastoral swathe scattered with villages as picture-perfect as any in northern England. **Grassington** is the main village, a popular walking centre, packed to capacity in summer; lesser hamlets in Upper Wharfedale, like **Kettlewell** and **Buckden**, make less frenetic bases. Upland roads lead from the head of the valley up minor dales to cross the watershed into Wensleydale, though the most attractive itinerary would take you up lonely Littondale to **Arncliffe**, a village almost too good to be true, and then over the tops to either Malham or Ribblesdale. Throughout the year, the #71 **bus** runs roughly hourly (not Sun) to Grassington from Skipton (via Cracoe and Threshfield), and less frequently on up the B6160 to Kettlewell, Starbotton and Buckden. This is augmented by two seasonal services: the **Dalesbus** (Easter–May & Oct Sun; June–Sept Sat & Sun; Aug Tues, Sat & Sun), from Leeds or Bradford; and the Sunday-only **Wharfedale Wanderer** (end-May to end-Aug) which leaves Ilkley, southeast of Skipton, hourly for Grassington via Bolton Abbey, and then travels on to Kettlewell, Starbotton and Buckden.

Bolton Abbey

BOLTON ABBEY, five miles east of Skipton, is the name of a whole village rather than an abbey, a confusion compounded by the fact that the place's main monastic ruin is known as **Bolton Priory** (Mon–Sat 8.30am–7pm, or dusk if earlier; Fri 8.30am–4pm; free), founded here in the 1150s. Turner painted the site, and Ruskin described it as the most beautiful in England, though the priory is now mostly ruined, a consequence of the Dissolution; only the nave, which was incorporated into the village church in 1170, has survived in almost its original state. The priory is the starting point for several highly popular riverside walks, including a section of the Dales Way footpath that follows the river's west bank to take in Bolton Woods and the **Strid** (from "stride"), an extraordinary piece of white water two miles north of the abbey, where softer rock has allowed the river to funnel into a cleft just a few feet wide. Numerous people have drowned trying to make the leap (the river here is 30ft deep), and the quite obvious dangers are underlined by the lifebelts hung nearby. Beyond the Strid, the path emerges at Barden Bridge, four miles from the priory, where the fortified **Barden Tower** was another little restoration job for Lady Anne Clifford; there's a tearoom here.

The Wharfedale Wanderer summer **bus** service calls at Bolton Abbey, or take a taxi from Skipton (around £8 each way). You can also use the **Steam Railway** (☎01756/794727; £5 return) from the station at **Embsay**, two miles east of Skipton on the A59; the Bolton Abbey station is a mile and a half from the priory ruins. At Bolton Abbey the main **accommodation** is the sumptuous *Devonshire Arms* (☎01756/710441; ⑧), just south of the village, owned by the Duke and Duchess of Devonshire. Considerably easier on the pocket is B&B at *Hesketh Farm*, a mile west of the village (☎01756/710541; no credit cards; ①), and at *Holme House Farm*, a quarter of a mile south of Barden, overlooking the river (☎01756/720661; no credit cards; ①). *Barden Tower Barn*, right by the tower (☎01756/720330), is a useful bunkhouse bar (reserved for groups only at weekends).

Grassington and around

GRASSINGTON, the dale's popular main village, is nine miles from Bolton Abbey. The village is at its best by the river and around the cobbled Market Square, home to several inns and to the **Upper Wharfedale Museum** (Easter–Sept daily 2–4.30pm; Oct–Easter Sat & Sun 2–4.30pm; 50p), an occasionally eccentric collection of minerals, farming implements and local miscellanea. The **national park information centre** on Hebden Road (April–Oct daily 10am–4pm; Nov–March most weekends 10am–4pm; ☎01756/752774), across from the **bus stop**, provides wide-ranging information.

Central **B&Bs** include *Kirkfield*, on Hebden Road (☎01756/752385; no credit cards; ①), just past the National Park Centre; and the more central *Town Head Guest House*, 1 Low Lane (☎01756/752811; no credit cards; ②), off Main Street. Costlier, but with a good reputation, is seventeenth-century *Ashfield House* on Summers Fold (☎01756/752584; ④; closed Dec & Jan), fifty yards off the square (behind the *Devonshire Hotel*). Right on the square, there's the Georgian *Grassington House Hotel* (☎01756/752406; ④), or the *Black Horse*, Garrs Lane (☎01756/752770; ④). The local **youth hostel** (☎01756/752400) is at the village of **Linton**, a mile southwest across the river; the rooms are a bit basic, but you can eat well across the green at the *Fountaine Inn*. The nearest **campsite** is the small *Bell Bank*, Skirethorns Lane, in Threshfield (☎01756/752321), a mile west of Grassington. The *Dales Kitchen*, 51 Main St, serves traditional and Mediterranean dishes during the day; all the **pubs** serve bar meals; or head over to **Threshfield** where the stone-flagged *Old Hall Inn* (☎01756/752441; closed Sun eve & Mon) wins plaudits for its food.

Southeast of Grassington, at **Appletreewick**, as well as the odd B&B, there's a campsite, *Mason's*, at Ainhams Farm (☎01756/720236; closed Nov–Easter), while the cosy *Craven Arms* doles out filling meals to walkers. Nearby **Burnsall**'s *Red Lion* (☎01756/720204; ⑤, ⑦ with dinner) has river views and inventive meals, while the Skipton bus runs up the B6265 through **Cracoe**, a couple of miles south of Grassington, whose beamed *Devonshire Arms* (☎01756/730237; ③) makes a comfortable base. The *Angel Inn*, in **Hetton** (☎01756/730263), a mile southwest from Cracoe, serves some of the best food and wine in the region.

Littondale

A mile beyond the dramatic, glacially carved overhang of Kilnsey Crag (three miles from Grassington), a minor road branches off left into **Littondale**, a pristine dale with stunning scenery and views. **ARNCLIFFE**, halfway up the dale, is as idyllic a village as you'll find. The ivy-covered *Falcon* (☎01756/770205; ③, ④ with dinner) on the village green attracts walkers from far and wide. There's a **campsite** back down the road, a mile and a half southeast of Arncliffe, at *Hawkswick Cote Farm* (☎01756/770226; closed Nov–Feb). On foot, the ideal way to see the dale is to follow the valley-floor **footpath** from Arncliffe to **LITTON** (2–3 miles), where the ancient and unspoilt *Queen's Arms* (☎01756/770208; ②) could serve as a base for climbing Pen-y-ghent. There's B&B available at *Litton Hall* (☎01756/770238; no credit cards; ①).

Upper Wharfedale

The landscapes in the last six miles of Wharfedale and its continuation, **Langstrothdale**, hardly suffer by comparison with Littondale. **KETTLEWELL** (Norse for "bubbling spring"), three miles north of Kilnsey, is the main centre for the upper dale, with an informal **national park information point** in the Over and Under outdoor shop, a **campsite** (☎01756/760886) just to the north at Fold Farm, and the *Whernside House* **youth hostel** (☎01765/760232) in the centre of the village. There's plenty of other **accommodation** in the village, notably the very agreeable *Langcliffe Country House* (☎01756/760243; ④), a few hundred yards up a road opposite the *King's Head* pub.

It's lovely country north of Kettlewell, accessed either via the dale's single lonely road (B6160) or the Dales Way path, both of which push to the dale's upper limit. At **STARBOTTON**, two miles away, the *Fox & Hounds* (☎01756/760269; ③; closed Mon in winter & all Jan) has ancient flagged floors, a huge fire and popular food. Topnotch pub accommodation is also available in **BUCKDEN**, another couple of miles to the north, at the *Buck Inn* (☎01756/760228; ⑤). A mile upstream, the river flows through Langstrothdale to **HUBBERHOLME** and the stone-flagged, whitewashed *George* (☎01756/760223; ②), the favourite pub of archetypal Yorkshireman J.B. Priestley, who is buried in the churchyard nearby. There's also a year-round bunkhouse barn in Hubberholme at *Grange Farm* (☎01756/760259).

Malhamdale

A few miles west of Wharfedale lies **Malhamdale**, the uppermost reaches of Airedale and one of the national park's most heavily visited regions, thanks to its three outstanding natural features: **Malham Cove**, **Malham Tarn** and **Gordale Scar**. Unfortunately for those seeking solitude, all three main attractions are within easy hiking distance of Malham village, so any walking you do locally is likely to be in company, with the Pennine Way further adding to the column of walkers processing through the area. The approach by **public transport** is on the #210 bus or postbus from Skipton (not Sat or Sun).

Malham

Unless you're here off-season, some idea of what to expect in **MALHAM** comes at the vast peripheral car park, likely to be packed solid with hikers and day-trippers. The village is home to barely more than a couple of hundred people, who inhabit the huddled stone houses on either side of a bubbling river, but this microscopic gem attracts perhaps half a million visitors a year. Your first stop should be the **national park information centre** on the southern edge of the village (Easter–Oct daily 9.30am–5pm; Nov–Easter Sat & Sun 10am–4pm; ☎01729/830363). In summer, you'll need to book ahead to get a bed at the **youth hostel** (☎01729/830321, *malham@yha.org.uk*). However, there's also a **bunkhouse barn** at *Hill Top Farm* (☎01729/830320), immediately north of the national park information centre, and several good village **B&Bs**, among them *Beck Hall* (☎01729/830332; ②), set in its own streamside gardens a couple of hundred yards from the fork in the village centre; and *Miresfield Farm* (☎01729/830 414; ②), on the edge of the village near the information centre. The comfortable *Riverhouse Hotel* (☎01729/830315; ③), on the road through the village, serves great evening meals. You can **camp** at *Townhead Farm* (☎01729/830287), near the cove, and under Gordale Scar at *Gordale Scar House Campsite* (☎01729/830333; closed Nov–March). Meals are served in the **pubs**, notably at the *Buck*, with a popular walkers' back bar.

Malham Cove, Malham Tarn and Gordale Scar

Malham Cove appears in spectacular fashion a mile north of Malham, a white-walled limestone amphitheatre rising three hundred feet above its surroundings. Like Gordale Scar's ramparts to the east, it was formed by a shear along the Mid-Craven Fault, a geological tear that runs 22 miles from Wharfedale to Kirkby Lonsdale in Cumbria. A broad track leads to the cove, passing some of England's most visible prehistoric field banks en route. Fewer people make the breath-sapping haul to the top, where the rewards are fine views and the famous **limestone pavement**, an expanse of clints (slabs) and grykes (clefts) created by water seeping through weaker lines in the limestone rock. Unusual plants and ferns such as dog's mercury and hart's tongue shelter in the crevices, making this a favoured spot for botanists. A simple walk over the moors abruptly brings **Malham Tarn** into sight, a lake created by an impervious layer of glacial debris. You can then turn south for **Gordale Scar**, which is also easily approached direct from Malham village. Here the cliffs are if anything more spectacular than at Malham Cove, complemented by a deep ravine to the rear caused by the collapse of a cavern roof. A little to the south of the scar, off the road, lies **Janet's Foss**, a gem of a waterfall set amidst green-damp rocks and overarching trees.

A classic circuit which takes in Malham's trio of sights is a clockwise **walk from Malham** (8 miles; 3hr 30min), the only problem being at Gordale Scar, where it may be difficult to scramble down the stream-cut gorge after heavy rain for the last leg back to Malham. If you don't want to see the Tarn and open moorland, the walk is easily cut short by taking a waymarked track from the northern edge of the pavement, above Malham Cove, down to Gordale Bridge and thus onto Gordale Scar (5 miles; 2hr 30min).

Ribblesdale

Ribblesdale, to the west of Malhamdale, is more dour and brooding than the bucolic valleys to the east. It's entered from Settle, starting point of the superbly engineered **Settle to Carlisle Railway**, among the most scenic rail routes in the country (see box opposite). The valley's only village of any size is **Horton in Ribblesdale**, not only a focus for the Ribble Way and Pennine Way, but also where most people start the **Three Peaks Walk**, an arduous hike around the Dales' highest peaks. Settle is the **transport** junction for Ribblesdale, with daily **trains** heading north through Horton to Carlisle and south to Skipton, Keighley and Leeds; a limited service operates on Sundays. The hourly #580 **bus** (not Sun) also connects Skipton with Settle, from where a useful service runs three or four times daily (not Sun) north to Horton but no further, and northwest to Ingleton in the western dales.

Nestled under the wooded knoll of Castleberg, **SETTLE** is well placed for upper Ribblesdale to the north and a pleasant enough base if you haven't the time to find a more intimate overnight stop within the national park. The **tourist office** is in the town hall on Cheapside, just off Market Place (daily 10am–5pm; ☎01729/825192); the **train station** is less than five signposted minutes from here. Two comfortable pubs, the *Royal Oak* on Market Place (☎01729/822561; ④), and the *Golden Lion*, just off Market Place

---

THE SETTLE TO CARLISLE RAILWAY

With the nineteenth-century railway boom at its height, the Midland Railway company – eager to muscle in on the profits made by its rival, the London and North Western Railway on its successful west coast route – applied to Parliament to build a line which would link the industrial heartlands of West Yorkshire with Carlisle and the Scottish borders beyond. In the six years between 1869 and 1875, when the 72-mile **Settle to Carlisle** line opened, herculean efforts were made by thousands of navvies to blast a route through the unforgiving Dales mountainsides. Living in squalid shanty towns by the sides of the track, and even in the newly opened railway tunnels themselves, six thousand men built twenty viaducts and bored fourteen tunnels in a feat of Victorian engineering that has few equals in Britain. Over two hundred of the workers died, some of smallpox and other diseases, others in horrific accidents; many now lie buried in the village churches that line the route.

The attraction in riding the line is the chance to experience what the operators – with no hint of hype – dub "England's most scenic railway". From Settle, the drag up Ribblesdale brings ever more spectacular views – between Horton and Ribblehead the line climbs two hundred feet in five miles, before crossing the famous 24-arched Ribblehead viaduct. Dent is the highest, and bleakest, mainline station in England. Further on, the route heads through Ais Gill, 1100 feet above sea level, before it finally drops into the gentler Eden Valley and on to Carlisle.

The journey from Settle to Carlisle takes just under an hour and forty minutes, so it's easy to make a **return trip** (£18 day-ranger for unlimited travel) along the whole length of the line. There are connections from Skipton and Leeds (2hr 40min); full **timetable** details are available from National Rail Enquiries, ☎0345/484950, or from the **Web site** (*www.settle-carlisle.co.uk*). The **best section** is that between Settle and Garsdale (30min), though note that you'll typically have a very short or very long wait for the return train.

---

along Duke Street (☎01729/822203; ③), are the best **places to stay**, while B&B accommodation is at the *Liverpool Guest House* on Chapel Square (☎01729/822247; no credit cards; ①) or the *Yorkshire Rose* on Duke Street (☎01729/822032; no credit cards; ②). For **food** both pubs have reasonable bar meals, though during the day it's hard to see anyone resisting the lure of *Ye Olde Naked Man Café* (closed Wed) – the name, apparently, is a reference to an eighteenth-century landlord's disgust at clothing fashions.

STAINFORTH, two miles north of Settle, has several B&Bs; a pub, the *Craven Heifer* (☎01729/822599; ③); a **youth hostel** set in extensive grounds about a quarter of mile south of the centre (☎01729/823577, *stainforth@yha.org.uk*); and a **campsite** at *Knight Stainforth Hall*, Little Stainforth (☎01729/822200). The nicest route to the village is by the footpath from Settle, which runs gently alongside the river, reaching Stainforth Force waterfall in around an hour, the village itself ten minutes later.

The noted walking centre of **HORTON IN RIBBLESDALE** dates from Norman times but the village expanded in the nineteenth century when the arrival of the Settle to Carlisle Railway allowed it to expand its age-old quarrying operations. The celebrated **Pen-y-ghent Café** (also known as the *Three Peaks Café*) in the village is a **national park information point** (summer Wed–Fri & Mon 9am–6pm, Sat & Sun 9am–8pm; rest of the year Wed–Mon 9am–6pm; ☎01729/860333) and an unofficial headquarters for the famous **Three Peaks Walk**, a 25-mile, 12-hour circuit of Pen-y-ghent (2273ft), Whernside (2414ft) and Ingleborough (2376ft). The village is most convenient for the ascent of sphinx-shaped **Pen-y-ghent** (3–4hr round trip), arguably the most dramatic of the three summits, just to the east on the Pennine Way; the other peaks are more easily climbed from Ingleton, Chapel-le-Dale or Dentdale.

Horton straggles along an L-shaped mile of the Settle–Ribblehead road (B6479), with the **train station** at the northern end and the church at the southern end. In between are the café, a post office/store and a campsite. **Accommodation** should be booked in advance. B&Bs include the *Willows* (☎01729/860373; no credit cards; ②) and the more elegant *Rowe House* (☎01729/860 212; no credit cards; ②), both left out of the station and a little way up the Ribblehead road. Of the two **pubs**, the *Crown Hotel* (☎01729/860209; ②), by the bridge, is the clear winner, a popular walkers' haunt with good bar food served until 8.30pm. *Dub Cote* (☎01729/860238) is a **bunkhouse barn** at Brackenbottom, just out of the village on the Settle road; and there's also a central tents-only **campsite** at *Holme Farm* (☎01729/860281), near the church.

The Western Dales

The **Western Dales** is a term of convenience for a couple of tiny dales running north from **Ingleton**, a village perfectly poised for walks up **Ingleborough** and **Whernside**, and for exploration of **Dentdale**. Unless you have a car or are hiking from stop to stop, any extensive exploration is difficult, though Ingleton is linked by bus to Clapham and Settle (for Skipton), and the Settle to Carlisle Railway offers access to upper Dentdale, with fine walks possible virtually off the station platforms.

Clapham

CLAPHAM, four miles north of Settle at the southern foot of Ingleborough, makes a fine introduction to the region. Pop into the **national park information centre** (April–Oct daily 10am–5pm; Nov–March occasional weekends; ☎01524/251419), alongside the car park, for a leaflet on the nature trail through Clapdale Woods to **Ingleborough Cave** (March–Oct daily 10am–5pm; Nov–Feb Sat & Sun 10.30am–dusk; £4), the Pennines' oldest show cave. Follow the footpath beyond the caves, and after a little over a mile you reach **Gaping Ghyll**, 365ft deep and 450ft long, probably the most famous of the Dales' many potholes; carry on another two miles northwest from Gaping Gill and the summit of Ingleborough looms – a more interesting approach than the haul up from Ingleton.

The **train station** (on the Leeds/Skipton–Lancaster line) offers another entry to the Dales, but lies over a mile south of the village. There's a post office, general store, a café or two, and the riverside *New Inn* (☎01524/251203; ④). Cheaper **rooms** are available at *Arbutus House*, on Riverside (☎01524/251240; no credit cards; ②), and by the station at the *Flying Horseshoe* pub (☎01524/251229; ②), which also serves meals.

Ingleton and around

INGLETON, four miles beyond Clapham, caters for a fair share of tourists, cavers and climbers, and sits at the confluence of two streams, the Twiss and the Doe, whose beautifully wooded valleys are easily the area's best features. The four-and-a-half-mile **Falls Walk** (entrance fee £1.50) is the main local attraction, a lovely circular walk up the tree-hung Twiss Valley, past viewing points over the Pecca Falls and Thornton Force. More serious hikers tackle **Ingleborough**, one of the Three Peaks, whose flat plateau is reached by a slightly laborious route to the east (3 miles; 2hr 30min).

Ingleton's **tourist office** is in the community centre car park, just off Main Street (May–Oct daily 10am–4.30pm; ☎015242/41049), with the **bus** stop just outside. Inglesport, a **hiking store** on Main Street in the village, is the place for maps, equipment and weather forecasts. There's a **youth hostel**, *Greta Tower* (☎015242/41444), an old stone house in its own gardens, located centrally in a lane between the market square and the swimming pool. Other than that a dozen other overnight options are strewn along Main Street; the best **guest houses** include the no-smoking *Seed Hill* on Main Street, near the church (☎015242/41799; no credit cards; ②); *Ingleborough View*, much further down Main Street past the tourist office (☎015242/41523; ②); and the *Bridge End Guest House* on Mill Lane (☎015242/41413; ①), close to the Falls Walk entrance. You can **camp** at nearby *Moorgarth Farm* (☎015242/41428), while *Stacksteads Farm*, also a mile south but off the minor road to High Bentham (☎015242/41386; ②), has tent space and a **bunkhouse barn**.

Northeast of Ingleton, one and a half miles away, is the entrance to the **White Scar Caves** (daily 10am–5pm; £5.95), the longest show cave in England. Don't be put off by the steep price – it's worth every penny for the eighty-minute tour of dank underground chambers, contorted cave formations and glistening stalactites. Three miles farther up the road the flagstoned **Hill Inn** (☎015242/41256; ①), near Chapel-le-Dale, is a lively, unpredictable place, with occasional live music, lots of climbers and cavers, and a **campsite** nearby – ask at the bar.

Dentdale

Any rail or road route to **Dentdale** has plenty of scenic rewards, but the most breath-taking is the minor-road route from Ingleton up Kingsdale and down Deepdale, with the vast whalebacks of Gragareth and Whernside rising to each side of the windswept lit-tle road. As you might expect, there's next to nothing to do locally except walk or revel in the scenery, but there are few better spots to do either, with **DENT** village an unbeat-able base. Here, the main road gives way to grassy cobbles, while the huddled stone cottages sport blooming window-boxes trailing over ancient lintels. The village's two pubs, the *Sun Inn* (☎01539/625208; ①) and the *George & Dragon* (☎01539/625256; ②), are next to each other in the centre and under the same management; or there's the non-smoking *Stone Close Guest House* (☎01539/625231; ①; closed Jan), which has a café doubling as a **national park information point**.

Confusion – and not a few sore feet – is caused by Dent's **train station** (on the Settle to Carlisle line) not being in Dent at all, but five miles to the east. Between mid-May and mid-October a **bus** runs between station and village twice a day (Sun only). If you get stuck, head for the hamlet of Cowgill, half a mile below the station, which has the *Sportsman's Inn* (☎01539/625282; ②). **Dentdale youth hostel** at *Dee Side House* (☎01539/625251) is a couple of miles south of here down the Dales Way.

Wensleydale

Best known of the Dales to outsiders, if only for its cheese, **Wensleydale** is the largest, least varied and most serene of the national park's dales. Known in medieval times as Yoredale, after its river (the Ure), the dale today takes its name from a now-inconse-quential village, and while there are towns to detain you – including one of the area's biggest in **Hawes** – it's Wenselydale's rural attractions that linger longest in the mind. Many will be familiar to devotees of the **James Herriott** books and TV series, set and filmed in the dale; elsewhere, there are several well-known waterfalls – notably **Aysgarth Falls** – and, as it opens into the Vale of York, a variety of historic buildings, including the stately remains of **Castle Bolton**.

The dale is traversed by the national park's only east–west **main road** (A684), and linked by high moor roads to virtually all the park's other dales of note. Year-round **public transport** is limited to a postbus from Hawes on varied routes (Mon–Fri 2–3 daily, Sat 1 daily) via Bainbridge, Askrigg, Aysgarth and Castle Bolton to Leyburn (for Richmond), and the Arriva services (#156, #157, #159) along the same route between Hawes and Richmond.

Hawes

HAWES – from the Anglo-Saxon *haus*, a mountain pass – is head of Wensleydale in all respects: it is its chief town, main hiking centre, and home to its tourism, cheese and rope-making industries. The cheese trail invariably leads to the **Wensleydale Creamery** on Gayle Lane (Mon–Sat 9.30am–5pm, Sun 10am–4.30pm; £2), a few hundred yards (signposted) south of the centre. The first cheese in Wensleydale was made by medieval Cistercian monks from ewes' milk, and after the Dissolution local farmers made a version from cows' milk which, by the 1840s, was being marketed as "Wensleydale" cheese. The first commercial creamery was founded in Hawes at the turn of the twentieth century, and production continues again today, after the industry was rescued in the 1990s from recession and neglect. The Creamery's "Cheese Experience" tours tell you all this and more, with plenty of opportunity to see the stuff being made, to sample and purchase in the shop. All three of Wensleydale's industries come together in the **Dales Countryside Museum** (Easter–Oct daily 10am–5pm; Nov–Easter Wed, Fri, Sat & Sun 11am–4pm; £2.50), housed in Station Yard's former train station and warehouses. The comprehensive and well-presented collection embraces lead-mining, farming, peat-cutting, knitting (hand-knitted hosiery was a speciality) and all manner of rustic minutiae. Alongside it, in a long shed, the **Hawes Ropemakers Museum** (July–Oct Mon–Fri 9am–5.30pm, Sat 10am–5.30pm; rest of year closed Sat; free) presents popular demonstrations of traditional rope-making. A mile and a half out of town to the north, people cough up the 70p toll at the *Green Dragon* pub (☎01969/667392; ②) to walk to **Hardraw Force**. It's about all the fall is worth for much of the year, for though this is the highest above-ground waterfall in the country there's often barely a trickle dribbling over the edge.

The **national park information centre** shares the same buildings as the Countryside Museum (July–Oct Mon–Fri 9am–5.30pm, Sat 10am–5.30pm; rest of year closed Sat; ☎01969/667450). **Buses** stop in Market Place (except for the postbuses which depart from outside the post office), over the road from the information office car park. There's B&B **accommodation** at the *Steppe Haugh Guest House*, Town Head (☎01969/667645; no credit cards; ①); the *Old Station House*, on Hardraw Road, opposite the museum (☎01969/667785; ②); and at *Laburnum House*, The Holme (☎01969/667717; no credit cards; ①), at the turn-off from the main road to the museum. All the **pubs** on and around the market square have rooms; the best are those at the *Board* (☎01969/667223; ②) and the *White Hart Inn* (☎01969/667259; ②). There's a smart **youth hostel** (☎01969/667368) at Lancaster Terrace, at the junction of the main A684 and B6255. **Camping** is at the *Bainbridge Ings* site (☎01969/667354), half a mile east of the centre, just off the A684 (Aysgarth road). Pub **food** aside, you can pick from coffees, snacks and lunches at *Wensleydale Pantry* on the main road through town; or pricier French-influenced meals at *Herriot's Hotel*, Main Street, opposite the *White Hart Inn*. The weekly **Tuesday market** – crammed with farmers and market traders – is still going strong.

Askrigg

The mantle of "Herriott country" lies heavy on **ASKRIGG**, a mile across the valley from Bainbridge, the TV series *All Creatures Great and Small* having been filmed in and around the village. There's little to see or do, though the pubs and Georgian houses have their charms, and you might stroll to a couple of nearby falls, **Whitfield Force** and **Mill Gill Force**, both a mile west of the village. There's an **information point** in the village shop in the Market Place and plenty of **accommodation**, too, starting with the *King's Arms* in Market Place (☎01969/650258; ⑥), or the *Apothecary's House* (☎01969/650626; no credit cards; ②), a fine-looking period house in Market Place. For a rural retreat, you can't beat *Helm Country House* (☎01969/650443; no credit cards; ④), a seventeenth-century farmhouse a mile west – dinner (£16 a head) is served in the stone-flagged dining room.

Aysgarth and around

The ribbon-village of **AYSGARTH**, straggling along and off the A684, is the vortex that sucks in Wensleydale's largest number of visitors, courtesy of the twin **Aysgarth Falls**, half a mile below the village (there's a path through the fields). Water crashes down a series of limestone steps, while in summer the riverbanks alongside are choked with picnicking families. A marked nature trail runs through the surrounding woodlands and there's a big car park and **information centre** on the north bank (Easter–Oct daily 10am–5pm; Nov–Easter occasional weekends; ☎01969/663424). The **Upper Falls** and picnic grounds lie just back from here, by the bridge and church; the more spectacular **Lower Falls** are a half-mile stroll to the east through shaded woodland.

B&Bs along the main road include *Marlbeck* (☎01969/663610; no credit cards; ①), while the village's only **pub**, the *George & Dragon* (☎01969/663358; ③), has pleasant en-suite rooms and a bar-meal menu with plenty of choice. Other local choices are down by the falls, where the *Wensleydale Farmhouse* (☎01969/663534; ②) is on the main road at the turn-off for the falls, with the well-regarded **youth hostel** (☎01969/663260) just behind. Bar **meals** are served at the *Palmer Flatt* pub on the main road. There's a **campsite**, *Westholme Caravan Park* (☎01969/663268; closed Nov–Easter), half a mile east on the A684.

There's a superb **circular walk** northeast from Aysgarth via Castle Bolton (6 miles; 4hr), a route detailed in a national park pamphlet available from the information centres in Hawes or Aysgarth. The walk starts at the falls themselves and climbs up through Thoresby, with the foursquare battlements of **Castle Bolton** (March–Oct daily 10am–5pm; restricted winter opening; £3) themselves a magnetic lure from miles away across the fields. Built in 1379 by Richard le Scrope, Lord Chancellor to Richard II, it's a massive defensive structure in which Mary Queen of Scots was imprisoned for six months in 1568.

Swaledale

The national park's northernmost dale, **Swaledale** is rivalled only by Dentdale and Garsdale for the lonely grandeur of its landscapes. Narrow and steep-sided in its upper reaches, it emerges rocky and rugged in its central tract, which takes in the remote villages of **Keld**, **Thwaite** and **Muker**, before more typically pastoral scenery cuts in at **Reeth**. From Richmond, **bus** #30 runs up the valley along the B6270 as far as Keld, but it's a limited service (Mon–Sat 3–4 daily); this is one dale where it really pays to have your own transport.

Keld

No more than a straggle of hardy buildings, **KELD** is surrounded by relics of the lead-mining industry that once brought a prosperity of sorts to much of the valley. Here you'll also see the incredible profusion of ancient field barns, or **laithes**, for which the dale is renowned, the legacy of a system of husbandry that dates back to Norse times. Keld's busy **youth hostel** is *Keld Lodge*, an old shooting lodge near the telephone kiosk (☎01748/886259), B&B at *Butt House* (☎01748/886374; no credit cards; ①; closed Sept–Easter) is a more tempting proposition. There's also a **campsite** at *Park Lodge* (☎01748/886274; closed Oct–Easter), but no pub, nor any other facilities.

Any number of local walks are possible, the shortest being to **Kisdon Force**'s triple-stacked waterfall and its wooded gorge half a mile east of Keld, though the best is the hike southeast along the River Swale to Muker, below the circular bulk of Kisdon Hill (2–3 miles; 1hr 30min). The valley road cuts round Kisdon to the south, following part of the so-called **Corpse Way**, a lane used by those paying their last respects when the nearest church was ten miles away at Grinton – footpaths follow its still obvious route down the valley. North and west of Keld, the upper reaches of Swaledale are wild indeed, with an atmosphere bordering on desolate even in summer. The Pennine Way shadows the very minor Stonesdale road for the three or four miles across Stonesdale Moor to the splendid **Tan Hill Inn** (☎01833/628246; ②), reputedly the highest pub in

Britain (1732ft above sea level), and built to serve the coal mines that fed the lead mines and smelting mills of the lower dale.

Thwaite to Reeth

THWAITE, another Norse-founded settlement, is the first hamlet south of Keld, just a two-mile walk away and with **accommodation** and meals available at *Kearton Guest House* (☎01748/886277; no credit cards; ②). Some of the loveliest scenery follows beyond the little village of **MUKER** (the name derives from the Norse for "meadow"), a mile or so to the east, distinguished by tiny side-valleys such as Oxnop Beck, south of Oxnop. Muker has a **national park information point** in the village store and a couple of B&Bs, including *Hylands* (☎01748/886003; no credit cards; ②), an immaculate seventeenth-century cottage off the main road, near the church. There are also a couple of teashops and a nice Dales' pub, the *Farmers Arms*. Further east at **Low Row**, there's a **bunkhouse barn** at the *Punch Bowl Inn* (☎01748/886233; ①), with inexpensive B&B and basic bar meals also available.

A couple of miles east of here lies **REETH**, set in a bowl of bleak moorland. It's the dale's main village and market centre – market day is Friday – and its desirable cottages are gathered around a triangular green. The **national park information centre** on the green (daily 10am–5pm; ☎01748/884059) has local maps and brochures. Some cottages around the green post **B&B** signs in their windows, while other choices for accommodation include two places on the Grinton Road at the edge of the village: the house at 2 Bridge Terrace (☎01748/884572; no credit cards; ①; closed Nov–Easter); and *Hackney House*, also on Bridge Terrace (☎01748/884302; no credit cards; ①). There are also several good **pubs** offering rooms and food, most obviously the *Black Bull* (☎01748/884213; ②) and the *King's Arms* (☎01748/884259; ③), opposite the green.

There are numerous paths across the fields on the south side of the river, letting you complete a circular walk from Reeth via **Grinton**, whose attractive bridge, church and riverside inn, *The Bridge*, are just a mile away by road. The local **youth hostel**, *Grinton Lodge*, is housed in a former shooting lodge spectacularly sited in the hills (☎01748/884206), ten minutes' walk from Grinton.

Richmond

RICHMOND is the Dales' single most tempting historical town, thanks mainly to its magnificent castle, whose extensive walls and colossal keep cling to a precipice above the River Swale. Indeed, the entire town is an absolute gem, centred on a huge cobbled market square backed onto by hidden alleys and gardens housing mainly Georgian buildings of great refinement. The town itself is much older, having been dubbed Riche-Mont ("noble hill") by the Normans who first built a castle here in 1071. That heritage is also celebrated in local street names like Frenchgate and Lombard's Wynd (a "wynd" being a narrow alley).

There's no better place to start than **Richmond Castle** (daily: April–Sept 10am–6pm; Oct 10am–1pm & 2–6pm; Nov–March 10am–1pm & 2–4pm; £3; EH), reached by signposted alleys from the market square. Originally built by Alan Rufus, first Norman earl of Richmond, it retains many features from its earliest incarnation, principally the gatehouse, curtain wall and Scolland's Hall, the oldest Norman great hall in the country. Most of medieval Richmond – all cobbled streets and narrow wynds – sprouted around the castle, but much of the town now radiates from the vast **Market Place**, with the Market Hall alongside (market days are Thursday, Friday and Saturday). The most unusual structure is the defunct **Holy Trinity Church**, built in 1135 and now serving as the **Green Howards Museum** (Feb Mon–Fri 10am–4.30pm;

March & Nov Mon–Sat 10am–4.30pm; April–Oct Mon–Sat 9.30am–4.30pm, Sun 2–4.30pm; £2), honouring North Yorkshire's Green Howards regiment. The **Richmondshire Museum**, reached down Ryder's Wynd, off King Street on the northern side of the square (Easter–Oct daily 11am–5pm; £1.50), is of more general interest. Best of all, though, is the town's **Theatre Royal** (Easter–Oct Mon–Sat 10.30am–4.30pm, Sun 11am–2pm; £1.50) – on the corner of Friar's Wynd (a narrow alley running north of the Market Place) and Victoria Road – dating from 1788, making it one of England's oldest extant theatres. Unassuming from the outside, the theatre's tiny interior is one of England's finest pieces of Georgian architecture – **tours** leave roughly every 45 minutes, while a museum at the rear gives an insight into eighteenth-century theatrical life.

A signposted walk runs along the north bank out to the beautifully situated church of St Agatha and adjacent **Easby Abbey** (daily: April–Sept 10am–6pm; Oct 10am–1pm & 2–6pm; Nov–March 10am–1pm & 2–4pm; free; EH), whose golden stone walls stand a mile southeast of the town centre. Founded in 1152 by Premonstratensian canons – the so-called White Monks – the abbey is now ruined, the greatest damage having been caused in 1346 when the English army was billeted here on its way to the Battle of Neville's Cross. However, the evocative remains are extensive, and in places – notably the thirteenth-century refectory – still remarkably intact.

Practicalities

Buses all stop in the Market Place. The **tourist office**, at Friary Gardens, Victoria Road (summer daily 9.30am–5.30pm; winter Mon–Sat 9.30am–4.30pm; ☎01748/850252), organizes free **guided walking tours** (April–Sept, 1–2 weekly) around the town. Recommended **accommodation** includes the *Old Brewery Guest House*, 29 The Green (☎01748/822460; ②), a tempting spot on a quiet green west of (and below) the castle. The nearby *Restaurant on the Green*, on the corner at 5–7 Bridge St (☎01748/826229; ①), also has a couple of rooms available. Central Frenchgate features *Willance House*, at no. 24 (☎01748/824467; no credit cards; ②); *Carlin House* at no. 6 (☎01748/826771; no credit cards; ①); and *Channel House* at no. 8 (☎01748/823844; no credit cards; ②) – though they only have a couple of rooms each. The tatty but genial *Windsor House*, 9 Castle Hill (☎01748/823285; no credit cards; ①), is about as cheap as you'll find, while top choice is the *King's Head Hotel*, on Market Place (☎01748/850220; ⑤). The nearest **campsite** is three miles west of town on the Reeth Road at *Swaleview Caravan Park* (☎01748/823106; closed Nov–Easter). For **meals**, try *The Bistro*, a pleasant place with an indoor patio on Chantry Wynd (☎01748/850792), off Finkle Street; it stays open for dinner from Wednesday to Saturday (6–9.30pm). There are more Mediterranean flavours at the *Frenchgate Café*, 29 Frenchgate (☎01748/824949), while down on The Green, *Restaurant on the Green*, at 5–7 Bridge St (Thurs–Sat dinner; ☎01748/826229), makes a mark with its inventive bistro food.

Harrogate to Ripon

Somewhat off the beaten track unless you're driving between York and the Dales, **Ripon** – despite its ancient cathedral – would hardly merit a visit on its own were it not for nearby **Fountains Abbey**, Britain's largest and most beautiful monastic ruin. Easily seen from Ripon, it has the added bonus of being the focal point of **Studley Royal**, an eighteenth-century landscaped garden complete with lake, temples, water garden and deer park. With time and transport you could take in a handful of other historic buildings nearby, though better excursions are perhaps made from the refined spa town of **Harrogate**: either to **Knaresborough** for its castle, or to

Nidderdale, an often overlooked adjunct to the Dales proper – for which Harrogate's bus and train connections make the town a perfect gateway.

Harrogate

HARROGATE – the very picture of genteel Yorkshire respectability – owes its airy planned appearance and early prosperity to the discovery of Tewit Well in 1571. This was the first of over eighty ferrous and sulphurous springs that, by the nineteenth century, were to turn the town into one of the country's leading spas. These days local pockets are lined more by a year-round panoply of conferences, exhibitions and festivals but many monuments to its past splendours are left standing. Harrogate's spa heritage begins with the **Royal Baths Assembly Rooms** on Crescent Road, built in 1897, where you can still take a **Turkish bath** in the plush, tiled Victorian surroundings (call ☎01423/556746 for hours; from £8 a session); the public entrance is on Parliament Street. The contemporaneous **Royal Hall**, built as a concert hall, stands across the way (corner of Ripon Road and King's Road), while just around the corner from the Assembly Rooms stands the **Royal Pump Room** (built 1842) in Crown Place, built over the sulphur well that feeds the Royal Baths. The **museum** here (April–Oct Mon–Sat 10am–5pm, Sun 2–5pm; Nov–March closes at 4pm; £1.75) re-creates something of the town's health-fixated past and also lets you sample the water; free **guided walks** leave here several times a week between Easter and October (information from the tourist office). To the southwest, the 120-acre **Valley Gardens** are the venue for the annual Spring Flower Show and Sunday band concerts in summer. Site of the original springs, the gardens are now a continuation of **The Stray**, a jealously guarded green belt that curves around the south of the town centre.

National Express buses drop you on Victoria Avenue, near the library; local and regional services use the **bus station** on Station Parade. The **train station** is on the same road, just a few minutes from all the central sights. Harrogate's **tourist office** (May–Sept Mon–Sat 9am–6pm, Sun noon–3pm; Oct–April Mon–Fri 9am–5.15pm, Sat 9am–12.30pm; ☎01423/537300) is in the Royal Baths Assembly Rooms (Crown Place entrance). Of Harrogate's many **festivals**, the most famous are the **flower shows** (second weeks of April and Sept); but there's also the **Great Yorkshire Show** (second week in July) and the Northern Antiques Fair (second half of Sept).

Accommodation

There are scores of **accommodation** options, starting with the B&Bs on King's Road and Franklin Road, north of the centre. Side streets like Studley Road, off King's Road beyond the conference centre, are quieter.

Alexander Guest House, 88 Franklin Rd (☎01423/503348). Recommended Victorian-era guest house on a residential street, under ten minutes' walk from the centre. No credit cards. ②.

Cavendish Hotel, 3 Valley Drive (☎01423/509637). A comfortable, friendly place. The best rooms here (all en-suite) overlook the Valley Gardens. ③.

The Imperial, Prospect Place (☎01423/565071). The doyen of spa-era hotels, the *Imperial* was once the home of Lord Carnarvon, discoverer of the tomb of Tutankhamen. ⑦.

Lynton House, 42 Studley Rd (☎01423/504715). A relaxed B&B on a quiet side road. No credit cards. ①.

Old Swan Hotel, Swan Rd (☎01423/500055). Large ivy-covered inn set in its own grounds, much rebuilt in Victorian times. Agatha Christie hid out here during her disappearance in 1926. ⑦.

Ruskin Hotel, 1 Swan Rd (☎01423/502045). Appealing Victorian villa with six characterful en-suite rooms, terraced bar and charming gardens. ⑤.

The White House, 10 Park Parade (☎01423/501388). Classy place overlooking The Stray on the Knaresborough road. A delightfully furnished country-house-style villa with a good restaurant. ⑦.

Eating and drinking

Betty's, 1 Parliament St (☎01423/502746). The Harrogate branch, founded in the 1920s, is the original of this famous teashop chain – open daily until 9pm. Inexpensive to Moderate.

The Bistro, 1 Montpellier Mews (☎01423/530708). Fashionable food – polenta, roast scallops, pan-seared salmon and the like – served in a cosy mews cottage. Closed Sun & Mon. Expensive.

Drum and Monkey, 5 Montpellier Gardens (☎01423/502650). Long-standing fish and seafood restaurant, a firm favourite with locals and out-of-towners alike. Closed Sun. Moderate to Expensive.

Est Est Est, 16 Cheltenham Crescent (☎01423/566453). Harrogate's best Italian, a stylish place with classy pizzas, and interesting fish and meat dishes. Moderate to Expensive.

Montey's, 3 Corn Exchange Buildings, The Ginnel (☎01423/526652). Café-cum-music bar with inexpensive lunches and live music most evenings. Inexpensive.

Rick's Just for Starters, 7 Bower Rd (☎01423/502700). Amiable mix-and-match bistro where most things cost under £5. Closed Sun lunch. Inexpensive.

Salsa Posada, 4 Mayfield Grove (☎01423/565151). Funky Mexican restaurant churning out nachos, burritos, fajitas and the rest. Closed Sun lunch. Moderate.

Knaresborough

A four-mile hop east from Harrogate, **KNARESBOROUGH** rises spectacularly above the River Nidd's limestone gorge, its old town houses, pubs, shops and gardens clustered together on the wooded northern bank, with the river itself crossed by two bridges ("High" and "Low"). The rocky crag above the town is crowned by the stump of a **Castle** (Easter–Sept daily 10.30am–5pm; £1.75) dating back to Norman times. Built on the site of Roman and Anglo-Saxon fortifications, it's now little more than a fourteenth-century keep in landscaped grounds, thanks to Cromwell's wrecking tactics during the Civil War. It was here that Henry II's knights fled after the murder of Thomas à Becket in Canterbury Cathedral; here, too, that Richard II was held before being removed to Pontefract, where he was murdered in 1400. In Castle Yard, close to the castle entrance, stands the **Old Court House Museum** (same hours & ticket as castle), with an original Tudor court and displays on local history and the Civil War.

The town's two novelty acts are to be found on the west side of the river. **Mother Shipton's Cave** (daily: Easter–Oct 9.30am–5.45pm; Nov–Easter 10am–4.45pm; £4.55) was home to a sixteenth-century soothsayer who predicted the defeat of the Armada, the Great Fire of London, world wars, cars, planes, iron ships – falling short, however, in the most important oracular chestnut of them all, of the End of the World: "The world to an end will come," she prophesied, "in eighteen hundred and eighty one." Close by is an equally tourist-thronged spot, the **Petrifying Well**, where dripping, lime-soaked waters coat everyday objects – gloves, hats, coats, toys – in a brownish veneer that sets rock-hard in a few weeks. Both cave and well are contained within a riverside estate, reached along a fine eighteenth-century wooded "Long Walk", studded with picnic areas; the main entrance is just over the High Bridge, north of the town, which you can reach by walking along the river from below the castle.

The **bus station** is on the High Street, while **trains** pull up at the station just off the High Street, in the backstreets high above the river. The **tourist office** is at 35 Market Place (Easter–Oct Mon–Sat 10am–5.30pm, Sun 2–5pm; ☎01423/866886). Free **guided walks** around the town leave from the Castle Yard outside the Old Court House Museum (June–Sept 2 weekly; ☎01423/500600); while summer ghost walks depart from the Market Cross (☎01423/860162; £3). Best central **place to stay** is the half-timbered *Villa Hotel*, 47 Kirkgate (☎01423/865370; no credit cards; ②), with fine river and valley views. B&Bs are plentiful: try *Ebor Mount*, 18 York Place (☎01423/863315; no credit cards; ②), or *Grove House*, 14 Boroughbridge Rd (☎01423/868857; no credit cards; ①). There are also rooms (and not bad food) at the *Yorkshire Lass* on High

Bridge (☎01423/862962; ③). Nearest **campsite** is the *Lido Leisure Park*, on the Wetherby road south of the centre (☎01423/865169; closed Dec–Easter). A couple of **pizzerias** offer value for money – the *Bella Rosa*, 25 Castlegate (closed Sun), opposite the tourist office, and *Da Mario's* at 15 Waterside (evenings only, closed Tues). Drink in *Blind Jack's* **pub** in the Market Place or in the *Mother Shipton Inn* at Low Bridge.

Nidderdale

Nidderdale's beautiful upper reaches stand comparison with its more famous neighbours, yet remain relatively unknown and undervisited. Onward itineraries are pretty limited, however: the main approach is along the east–west B6265 between Grassington in Wharfedale and Ripon, with the only available route north the wild road from **Pateley Bridge**, the dale's main village, to Masham and, ultimately, Wensleydale. The **bus** service is restricted to the regular #24 from Harrogate to Pateley Bridge, which on summer Sundays continues on to Grassington; another summer Sunday service runs between Bradford/Leeds and Ripon via Pateley Bridge and Brimham Rocks.

The lower vale is a patchwork of farming land, its first obvious distraction coming at **RIPLEY** (bus #36 from Ripon or Harrogate), four miles north of Harrogate, an impeccably kept village whose bizarre appearance is due to a whim of the Ingilby family, who between 1827 and 1854 rebuilt it in the manner of an Alsace-Lorraine village, for no other reason than they liked the style. Summer crowds pile in for the cobbled square, original stocks and the twee cottages and shops, not to mention the Ingilby house, parkland and **Castle** (castle: June–Sept Thurs & Fri 11.30am–4.30pm, Sat & Sun 10am–3pm; April, May & Oct Sat, Sun & bank hols 10am–3pm; gardens March–Dec daily 10am–5pm, Jan & Feb weekends only; castle & gardens £4.50; gardens only £2.25), with its museum of armour, weapons, furniture and such like. The *Boar's Head* (☎01423/771888; ⑦), part of the estate, has pricey **rooms**, but there's a lovely bar and beer-garden, too.

PATELEY BRIDGE serves as the dale's focus, housing the **tourist office** at 14 High St (Easter–Sept daily 10am–5pm; ☎01423/711147). Its **Nidderdale Museum** (Easter–Sept daily 2–5pm; Oct–Easter Sat & Sun 2–5pm; £1; ☎01423/711225), in the old council offices opposite the church on the edge of the village, provides a run-through of dale life in days gone by. Several local guest houses and hotels provide **accommodation**, one of the nicest the *Sportsmans Arms* (☎01423/711306; ④), an inn a couple of miles out off the Nidderdale road at Wath-in-Nidderdale – there's really good **food** served here.

Five miles west of the village on the Grassington road lie the **Stump Cross Caverns** (Easter–Oct daily 10am–5.30pm; Nov–Easter Sat & Sun 10.30am–4pm; £4), though only one massive stalagmite-filled cavern of the three-mile complex is open to the public. About the same distance east of the village, signposted off the B6265, are the extraordinary **Brimham Rocks**, nearly four hundred acres of strangely eroded millstone grit outcrops scattered over one-thousand-foot high moors. After a clamber on the rocks, you can follow the path up to the **information centre** at Brimham House (April–Oct daily 9am–6pm; free), from where the views are superlative, stretching over the Vale of York, with York Minster visible on clear days. In the upper valley, seven miles from Pateley Bridge, **How Stean Gorge** (daily 10am–6pm; £2) is a terrific ice-gouged ravine of surging waters and overhanging rocks. Take a torch and you can explore Tom Taylor's Cave, a dark, narrow squeeze through an underground cavern. There's summer **camping** (call ☎01423/755666) behind the gorge **café** (closed Mon & Tues in Jan & Feb). A minibus service runs from Pateley Bridge to the gorge (30min), but only on summer Sundays and bank holiday Mondays (end May–Sept).

Blackpool, Lancashire

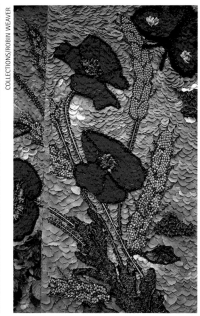

Manto bar, Manchester

Well dressing, Etwall, Derbyshire

Ullswater and Howtown (view from Martindale)

Askrigg, Yorkshire

Tyne and Swing Bridges, Newcastle upon Tyne

Henry Moore Institute, Leeds

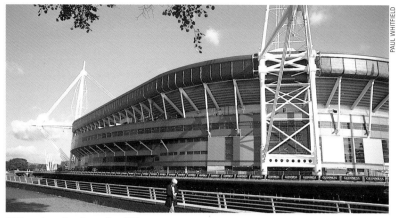

PAUL WHITFIELD

Millennium Stadium, Cardiff

CHARLES AITHIE

Sheepdog near Llanwrtyd

CHARLES AITHIE

St Govan's Chapel, Pembroke

CHARLES BOWMAN

Portmeiron

Ripon

The unassuming market town of **RIPON**, eleven miles north of Harrogate, only really diverts by virtue of its **Cathedral** (daily 8am–6.30pm; £2 donation requested), which can trace its ancestry back to foundation in 672 by St Wilfrid; the original crypt is still extant below the central tower. The rest of the building was destroyed by the Danes in the ninth century, then a second church fell foul of the Normans, part of whose replacement remains, though the bulk of the present building dates from the reign of Archbishop Roger of York (1154–81). Although having a rather plain exterior there's plenty that pleases here, from the subtle, twin-towered, thirteenth-century west front to the choir's misericords, full of painted figures of miserable clergymen, executed by the same team that carved the impressive stalls at Beverley. The town's other focus is its **market place**, "...the finest and most beautiful square...in England", according to Defoe, linked by Kirkgate to the cathedral; market day is Thursday. At the **Prison and Police Museum** on St Marygate (July & Aug daily 11am–5pm; May, June & Sept daily 1–5pm; April & Oct daily 1–4pm; free) behind the cathedral, the old cells serve as the backdrop for an exhibition on the evils of previous punishments. It's questionable whether conditions in the nineteenth century were worse here or in the nearby **Ripon Workhouse**, on Allhallowgate (same hours as museum) where the "undeserving" poor were incarcerated for such heinous crimes as being unable to pay their bills.

The **bus station** is just off the Market Place, while the town's **tourist office** is on Minster Road opposite the cathedral (April–Oct Mon–Sat 10am–5.30pm, Sun 1–4pm; ☎01765/604625). The range of **accommodation** options includes the *Riverside Guest House*, 20 Iddesleigh Terrace (☎01765/602707; no credit cards; ②); the *Coopers*, 36 College Rd (☎01765/603708; no credit cards; ①); *Bishopton Grove House*, Bishopton (☎01765/600888; no credit cards; ①); and the *Unicorn Hotel*, the Market Place (☎01765/602202; ④), central Ripon's finest. There are several small **restaurants** along Kirkgate, though the best place to eat is at the *Old Deanery* (☎01765/603518; closed Sun dinner, & Mon; ⑦, includes dinner), across from the cathedral.

Fountains Abbey and Studley Royal

It's tantalizing to imagine how the English landscape might have appeared had Henry VIII not dissolved the monasteries, with all the artistic ruin and impoverishment precipitated by that act. **Fountains Abbey**, four miles southwest of Ripon, gives a good idea of what might have been, and is the one ruin amongst Yorkshire's many monastic fragments you should make a point of seeing. Linked to it are the elegant water gardens of **Studley Royal**, landscaped in the eighteenth century to form a setting for the abbey, but only reunited as a single 680-acre National Trust estate in 1983.

The site is signposted off the B6265 Ripon to Pateley Bridge road, ten miles north of Harrogate. The closest **rail link** is Harrogate, with a **bus** connection on to Ripon; buses also run to Ripon from York train station. In addition, summer bus services connect the abbey visitor centre with Ripon, Harrogate, York and Leeds – call (Mon–Fri ☎01765/608888, Sat & Sun ☎01765/601005) for details. The **abbey, gardens** and **visitor centre** are open daily – except Friday in November, December and January – for the following hours: April to September 10am to 7pm, October to March 10am to 5pm, or dusk if earlier; Fountains Hall is open daily from April to October from noon to 3pm. **Admission** is £4.30, though you don't have to pay to get into Studley's deer park (all year in daylight hours) or St Mary's Church (Easter & May–Sept daily 1–5pm).

The abbey

Beautifully set in a narrow, wooded valley, through which the River Skell flows to join the Ure at Ripon, **Fountains Abbey** was founded in 1133 by thirteen dissident Benedictine monks from the wealthy abbey of St Mary's in York (perhaps encouraged by the success of Rievaulx, founded a year earlier) and formally adopted by the Cistercians two years later. Within a hundred years, it had become the wealthiest Cistercian foundation in England, a century which saw the three main phases of the abbey's structural development: the church's nave and transepts, the domestic buildings, and the church's east end. At the Dissolution the abbey was sold to Sir Richard Gresham, and ultimately became a source of building stone for the nearby Fountains Hall. Further desecration was avoided when in 1768 it became part of Studley Royal (see below) under William Aislabie, who extended the landscaping exploits of his father to bring the ruined abbey within the estate's orbit.

Most immediately eye-catching is the abbey church, in particular the **Chapel of the Nine Altars** at its eastern end, whose delicacy is in marked contrast to the austerity of the rest of the nave. A great sixty-foot-high window rises over the chapel, complemented by a similar window at the nave's western doorway, over 370ft away. The **Perpendicular Tower**, almost 180ft high, looms over the whole ensemble, added by the eminent early sixteenth-century Abbot Marmaduke Huby, who presided over perhaps the abbey's greatest period of prosperity. Equally grandiose in scale is the undercroft of the **Lay Brothers' Dormitory** off the cloister, a stunningly vaulted space over 300ft long that was used to store the monastery's annual harvest of fleeces. Its sheer size gives some idea of the abbey's entrepreneurial scope, some thirteen tons of wool a year being turned over, most of it sold to Venetian and Florentine merchants who toured the monasteries. The size of the lay buildings – including a substantial **Lay Brothers' Infirmary** – indicates the importance of the lay brothers at the abbey: all are considerably larger than the corresponding monks' buildings, of which the most prepossessing are the **Chapter House** and **Refectory**. Outside the abbey perimeter, between the gatehouse and bridge, are the Abbey Mill and **Fountains Hall**, the latter a fine example of early seventeenth-century domestic architecture.

Studley Royal

A bucolic riverside walk, marked from the visitor centre, takes you through the abbey and past Fountains Hall to a series of ponds and ornamental gardens, harbingers of **Studley Royal** (which can also be entered via the village of Studley Roger, where there's a separate car park). This lush medley of lawns, lake, woodland and **deer park** was laid out in 1720 by John Aislabie, MP for Ripon and chancellor of the exchequer until his involvement with the South Sea Company – one of the great financial scandals of the century – led to his resignation. There are some scintillating views of the abbey from the gardens, though it's the cascades and **water gardens**, fed by canals from the Skell, which command most attention, framed by several small temples positioned for their aesthetic effect. Just within the park stands the church of **St Mary** (1871), neatly approached by an avenue of limes that frame the distant towers of Ripon Cathedral. You could easily spend an afternoon whiling away time in the gardens: the full circuit, from visitor centre to abbey and gardens and then back is a good couple of miles' walk.

York

YORK is the north's most compelling city, a place whose history, said George VI, "is the history of England". This is perhaps overstating things a little, but it reflects the significance of a metropolis that until the Industrial Revolution was second only to

London in population and importance, not only at the heart of the country's religious life, but also a key player in some of the major events that have shaped the nation. These days a more provincial air hangs over the city, except in summer when York feels like a heritage site for the benefit of tourists. That said, no trip to this part of the country is complete without a visit to the city. York is well placed for any number of **day-trips**, the most essential being that to **Castle Howard**, the gem amongst English stately homes.

A brief history of York

The **Romans** chose York's swampy position, at the confluence of two minor rivers, as the site of a military camp during their campaigns against the Brigantes in 71 AD, and in time this fortress became a city – **Eboracum**, capital of the empire's northern European territories. The base for Hadrian's northern campaigns, it was also ruled for three years by Septimius Severus, one of two emperors to die in the city. The other, Constantine Chlorus, was the father of Constantine the Great, first Christian emperor and founder of Constantinople; at Chlorus's death, his son was proclaimed Roman emperor here – the only occasion an emperor was enthroned in Britain.

Much fought over after the decline of Rome, the city emerged as a **Saxon** vassal, Eoforwic, and later became the fulcrum of Christianity in northern England. It was here, on Easter Day in 627, that Bishop Paulinus, on a mission to establish the Roman Church, baptized King Edwin of Northumbria in a small timber chapel. Six years later the church became the first Minster and Paulinus the first Archbishop of York. In 867 the city fell to the **Danes**, who renamed it **Jorvik**, and later made it the capital of eastern England (Danelaw), following a treaty in 886 between Alfred the Great and Guthrum the Dane. Later Viking raids culminated in the decisive **Battle of Stamford Bridge** (1066) six miles east of the city, where English King Harold defeated Norse King Harald – a pyrrhic victory in the event, for his weakened army was defeated by the Normans just a few days later at the Battle of Hastings, with well-known consequences for all concerned. In York, aside from the physical remains left by the Vikings on show in several of the museums, the very street names tell of their profound influence – the suffix "-gate" is derived from an old Norse word for street.

The **Normans** devastated much of York's hinterland in their infamous "Harrying of the North", building two castles astride the Ouse in the city itself. Stone walls were thrown up during the thirteenth century, when the city became a favoured Plantagenet retreat and commercial capital of the north, its importance reflected in the new title of Duke of York, bestowed ever since on the monarch's second son. The 48 **York Mystery Plays**, one of only four surviving such cycles, date from this era, created by the powerful guilds which rose with the city's woollen industry. Although Henry VIII's Dissolution of the Monasteries took its toll on a city crammed with religious houses, York remained strongly wedded to the Catholic cause, and the most famous of the Gunpowder Plot conspirators, **Guy Fawkes**, was born here. During the **Civil War** Charles I established his court in the city, which was strongly pro-Royalist, inviting a Parliamentarian siege which was eventually lifted by Prince Rupert of the Rhine, a nephew of the king. Rupert's troops, however, were routed by Cromwell and Sir Thomas Fairfax at the **Battle of Marston Moor** in 1644, another seminal battle in England's history, which took place just six miles west of York.

The city's eighteenth-century history was marked by its emergence as a social centre for Yorkshire's landed elite. Whilst the Industrial Revolution largely passed it by, the arrival of the **railways** brought renewed prosperity, thanks largely to the enterprise of pioneering "Railway King" **George Hudson**, lord mayor during the 1830s and 1840s. Chocolate, in the shape of Terry and Rowntree-Nestlé, is now the financial mainstay, together with the proceeds from several million annual tourists.

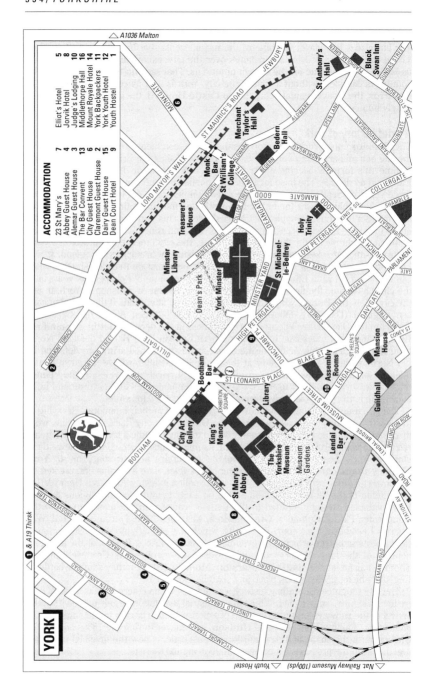

YORK

△ A1036 Malton

ACCOMMODATION

23 St Mary's	7
Abbey Guest House	4
Alemar Guest House	3
The Bar Convent	13
City Guest House	6
Claremont Guest House	2
Dairy Guest House	15
Dean Court Hotel	9
Elliot's Hotel	5
Jorvik Hotel	8
Judge's Lodging	10
Middlethorpe Hall	16
Mount Royale Hotel	14
York Backpackers	11
York Youth Hotel	12
Youth Hostel	1

△ ❶ & A19 Thirsk

St Anthony's Hall
Black Swan Inn
Merchant Taylor's Hall
Bedern Hall
Monk Bar
St William's College
Treasurer's House
Holy Trinity
Minster Library
York Minster
St Michael-le-Belfrey
Dean's Park
Bootham Bar
High Petergate
Mansion House
Assembly Rooms
Guildhall
City Art Gallery
King's Manor
St Mary's Abbey
The Yorkshire Museum
Museum Gardens
Lendal Bar
Library
Exhibition Square

▽ Nat. Railway Museum (100yds)   ▽ Youth Hostel

© Crown copyright

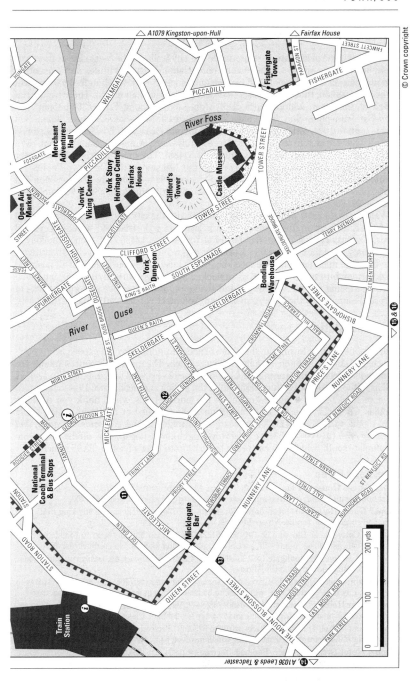

A1079 Kingston-upon-Hull

Fairfax House

Fishergate Tower

FISHERGATE

FAWCETT STREET

PARAGON ST

PICCADILLY

WALMGATE

River Foss

Merchant Adventurers' Hall

TOWER STREET

FOSSGATE

PICCADILLY

York Story Heritage Centre

Jorvik Viking Centre

Fairfax House

Castle Museum

PAVEMENT

Open Air Market

Clifford's Tower

COPPERGATE

TERRY AVENUE

STREET

CASTLEGATE

TOWER STREET

SKELDERGATE BRIDGE

HIGH OUSEGATE

CLIFFORD STREET

CLEMENTHORPE

MARKET STREET

SPURRIERGATE

KING'S STREET

York Dungeon

CLIFFORD STREET

SOUTH ESPLANADE

OUSEGATE

KING'S RAITH

Bonding Warehouse

BISHOPGATE STREET

BATTE HILL TERRACE

15 & 16

River   Ouse

QUEEN'S RAITH

SKELDERGATE

CROMWELL ROAD

BRIDGE ST

OUSE BRIDGE

SKELDERGATE

KYME STREET

NUNNERY LANE

NORTH STREET

FETTER LANE

BUCKINGHAM ST

ST BENEDICT ROAD

BISHOPHILL SENIOR

VICTOR STREET

NEWTON TERRACE

PRICE'S LANE

i

GEORGE HUDSON ST

HAMPDEN STREET

FAIRFAX STREET

MICKLEGATE

TANNER

ROW

12

ROUGIER STREET

STATION

National Coach Terminal & Bus Stops

MICKLEGATE

TRINITY LANE

BISHOPHILL

LOWER PRIORY STREET

VICTOR STREET

SWANN STREET

ST BENEDICT RD

PRIORY STREET

NUNNERY LANE

DALE STREET

SCARCROFT LANE

11

BLOSSOM STREET

LEXBY TERRACE

Micklegate Bar

NORTHORPE ROAD

TOFT GREEN

STATION ROAD

13

QUEEN STREET

THE MOUNT

MOSS STREET

SOUTH PARADE

SCARCROFT ROAD

DALE STREET

EAST MOUNT ROAD

PARK STREET

Train Station

i

14, A1036 Leeds & Tadcaster

0   100   200 yds

A1036 Leeds & Tadcaster

Arrival, information, transport and tours

Trains arrive at **York Station**, just outside the city walls on the west side of the River Ouse, just under a mile from the historic core. National Express **buses** and most other regional bus services drop off and pick up on Rougier Street, two hundred yards north of the train station, though some services call at the train station, too. There's a **tourist office** at the train station (April–Sept Mon–Sat 9am–8pm, Sun 9.30am–5pm; Oct Mon–Sat 9am–6pm, Sun 9.30am–5pm; Nov–March Mon–Sat 9.30am–5.30pm, Sun 10am–4pm; ☎01904/621756), and the **York Tourism Bureau**, at 20 George Hudson St, around the corner from Rougier Street (July–Sept Mon–Sat 9am–5.30pm, Sun 10am–4pm; rest of year closed Sun; ☎01904/554488). The **main tourist office** is over Lendal Bridge, two hundred yards west of the Minster in the De Grey Rooms, on Exhibition Square (April–June, Sept & Oct daily 9am–6pm; July & Aug Mon–Sat 9am–7pm, Sun 9am–6pm; Nov–March Mon–Sat 9am–5pm, Sun 9.30am–3pm; ☎01904/621756).

Walking is the best way to acquaint yourself with the city, and often the only way to get from A to B, given the confused historic layout of pedestrianized streets, alleys and yards. City **bus routes** are operated by First York (☎01904/435600) – you're unlikely to get full use out of their Minstercard, valid for one week's unlimited travel (£9) and available from the main tourist office or on board the buses. The tourist offices all push the Guide Friday **bus tours** (£7.50, £5.50 if booked in advance; ☎01904/640896), but much more interesting are the various **guided walks** on offer, from evening ghost walks to historical tours led by the York Association of Voluntary Guides (☎01904/640780; £3–4).

Accommodation

York is a busy tourist town, with the range of **accommodation** you'd expect, from countless cheap B&Bs to a clutch of topnotch luxury hotels. The main B&B concentrations are in the sidestreets off **Bootham and Clifton** (immediately west of Exhibition Square), as well as in the **Mount** area (turn right out of the station and head down Blossom Street). If you're stuck for a bed, make straight for the tourist offices, who'll **book you a room**. Thomas Cook also has an accommodation booking office at the train station (daily 8am–10pm; ☎01904/673411). The nearest **campsite** is the *Riverside Caravan and Camping Park* (☎01904/705812; closed Nov–March) in Bishopsthorpe, off the A64, a couple of miles south, which you can reach by ferry from King's Staithe (£3.95 return).

Hotels and B&Bs

Abbey Guest House, 14 Earlsborough Terrace, Marygate (☎01904/627782). Riverside terraced guest house with bright, pretty, bargain-priced rooms, two of which are en suite. ②.

Alemar Guest House, 19 Queen Anne's Rd (☎01904/652367). Well-kept, non-smoking B&B, with clean and comfortable rooms. No credit cards. ①.

The Bar Convent, 17 Blossom St (☎01904/643238). Georgian building next to Micklegate Bar, housing a café as well as rooms with access to a self-catering kitchen. No credit cards. ②.

City Guest House, 68 Monkgate (☎01904/622483). Central, non-smoking, family-run guest house with budget rates, not far from the Minster. ②.

Claremount Guest House, 18 Claremount Terrace, Gillygate (☎01904/625158). Fine B&B with just two rooms (one en suite, one with separate bathroom) in a quiet Victorian cul-de-sac. ②.

Dairy Guest House, 3 Scarcroft Rd (☎01904/639367). Victorian house half a mile south of the station, with rooms heavy on stripped pine and flowery furnishings. Closed mid-Dec to Jan. ②.

Dean Court Hotel, Duncombe Place (☎01904/625082). Perfectly sited neo-Victorian hotel with views of the Minster from the front rooms, which means it's pricey. ⑦.

Elliott's Hotel, Sycamore Place, Bootham Terrace (☎01904/623333). A detached Victorian house tucked away in a peaceful and convenient spot. ③.

Jorvik Hotel, 52 Marygate, Bootham (☎01904/653511). In an extremely good position opposite the western entrance to St Mary's Abbey – you'll pay more to overlook the abbey gardens. ③.

Judge's Lodging, 9 Lendal (☎01904/638733). One of the top central, historic choices, located in the eighteenth-century Georgian residence of the former assize court judges. ⑥–⑦.

Middlethorpe Hall, Bishopsthorpe Rd (☎01904/641241). Eighteenth-century mansion two miles south of the city. Set in its own parkland, with a pool, and restaurant. ⑧.

Mount Royale Hotel, The Mount (☎01904/628856). Luxurious, antique-filled, family-run retreat south of the station with superb garden-suites set around a private garden. ⑥.

23 St Mary's, 23 St Mary's, Bootham (☎01904/622738). Very pleasant and amiable family-house hotel just west of St Mary's Abbey and gardens. No credit cards. ③.

Hostels

York Backpackers Hostel, 88–90 Micklegate (☎01904/627720). Dorm space, doubles and family rooms in a Grade 1 listed building. There's a self-catering kitchen, laundry, Internet facilities, TV and games room, and licensed bar. Self-service breakfast costs extra.

York International Youth Hostel, Water End, Clifton (☎01904/653147). Large Victorian mansion about a twenty-minute walk along Bootham from the tourist office and then a left turn at Clifton Green. Beds mostly in four-bedded dorms; also a café with licence for alcohol with meals.

York Youth Hotel, 11–13 Bishophill Senior (☎01904/625904). Centrally located, on the west side of the river, off Micklegate – dorm, single and twin rooms available. Also a late-night bar, kitchen, laundry and bike rental.

The City

Take a look at one of the maps dotted around the city centre and you're confronted with a baffling and intimidating prospect. If the city council and tourist office are to be believed, there are around sixty churches, museums and historic buildings crammed within York's walls. In fact the tally of things you really want to see is surprisingly limited, with most sights within easy walking distance of one another. Even so, it's hard to get round everything in less than two days, and equally difficult to stick to any rigid itinerary. The **Minster** is the obvious place to start, followed by the cluster of buildings that circle it; then you might cut south to the **Shambles**, central to the city's old centre and pedestrianized grid, or walk around **the walls** from the Minster to **Exhibition Square** and Museum Street for the **City Art Gallery**, **Yorkshire Museum** and **St Mary's Abbey**, evocative ruins surrounded by the city's loveliest gardens. Thereafter you could walk through the main shopping streets to take in the **Merchant Adventurers' Hall**, most striking of the city's smaller medieval buildings, then deal with **Clifford's Tower** and the nearby **Jorvik Viking Centre** and **Castle Museum**. Lastly, be sure to leave time to take in the **National Railway Museum**, a superb museum whose appeal goes way beyond railway memorabilia.

York Minster

York Minster (daily: June–Sept 7am–8pm; Oct–May 7am–5pm; £2 donation requested) ranks as one of the country's most important sights. Seat of the Archbishop of York, it is Britain's largest Gothic building and home to countless treasures, not least of which is the world's largest medieval stained glass window and an estimated half of all the medieval stained glass in England. In its earliest incarnation the Minster was probably the wooden chapel used to baptize King Edwin of Northumbria in 627, though the first significant stone foundations were laid around 1080 by the first Norman archbishop, Thomas of Bayeux. The oldest surviving fabric, in the south transept, dates from 1220 and the reign of Archbishop Walter de Grey. A new chapter house, in the Decorated style, appeared in 1300, and a new nave in the same style was completed in 1338. The Perpendicular choir was realized in 1450 and the western towers in 1472. In

1480, the thirteenth-century central tower, which had collapsed in 1407, was rebuilt, thereby bringing the Minster to more or less its present state. In the 1960s, it was found that the 20,000-ton, 234-foot central tower was resting on only a shallow bed of loose stones, a discovery which prompted a £2 million project to pack the foundations with thousands of tons of concrete and over six miles of reinforced steel rods. In 1984 lightning struck the Minster, unleashing a disastrous fire which raged through the south transept, destroying the timber-framed central vault and all but two of its extraordinary roof bosses.

Nothing else in the Minster can match the magnificence of the stained glass in the nave and transepts. The **West Window** (1338) contains distinctive heart-shaped upper tracery (the "Heart of Yorkshire"), whilst in the nave's north aisle, the second bay window (1155) contains slivers of the oldest stained glass in the country. The north transept's **Five Sisters Window** is named after the five fifty-foot lancets, each glazed with thirteenth-century *grisaille*, a distinctive frosted, silvery-grey glass. Opposite, the south transept contains a sixteenth-century, 17,000-piece **Rose Window**, commemorating the 1486 marriage of Henry VII and Elizabeth of York, an alliance which marked the end of the Wars of the Roses. The greatest of the church's 128 windows, however, is the majestic **East Window** (1405), at 78ft by 31ft the world's largest area of medieval stained glass in a single window. Its themes are the beginning and the end of the world, the upper panels showing scenes from the Old Testament, the lower sections mainly episodes from the book of Revelation.

Before leaving the main body of the interior, give some time to the north transept's four-hundred-year-old wooden clock with its oak knights, and the stone **choir screen**, knotted with incredibly intricate carvings and decorated with life-size figures of English monarchs from William I to Henry VI. The painted **stone shields** round much of the nave and choir are those of Edward II and the barons who in 1309–10 held a "parliament" in York. Amongst the many tombs, those of most interest are the monument in the south transept to Walter de Grey, a beautiful grey-green canopy protecting a recumbent stone figure, and the tomb of the ten-year-old William, second son of Edward III, in the choir aisle.

Be sure also to go down to the **crypt** (60p), the spot that transmits the most powerful sense of antiquity, as it contains portions of Archbishop Roger's choir and sections of the 1080 church, including pillars with fine Romanesque capitals. The font stands over the supposed site of Paulinus' timber chapel, while a small illuminated doorway opens onto the base of a pillar belonging to the guardhouse of the original Roman camp. The foundations, or **undercroft** (£1.80), are more intriguing still. Most of the area's seven separate chambers have been turned into a museum, whose concrete consequences contrast with capitals, sculpture and fabric from the present Minster, its Norman predecessor and the ancient Roman fort. Amongst precious church relics in the adjoining treasury are silver plate found in Walter de Grey's tomb and the eleventh-century Horn of Ulf, presented to the Minster by a relative of the tide-turning King Canute. Access to the foundations is from the south transept, also the entrance to the **central tower**, (£2) which you can climb for rooftop views over the city. Finally pop into the **Chapter House** (70p), an architectural novelty whose buttressed octagonal walls remove the need for a central pillar.

Around the Minster

Past the Minster's west front a gateway leads into **Dean's Park**, a quiet green oasis bordered by a seven-arched fragment of arcade from the Norman archbishop's palace and by **York Minster Library** (Mon–Fri 9am–5pm; free), housed in the thirteenth-century chapel of the same palace. Among its more interesting exhibits is the baptismal entry for Guy Fawkes (dated April 16, 1570), removed from **St Michael-le-Belfrey** on High Petergate (open for Sunday services only), immediately south of the Minster.

Walk through Dean's Park with the Minster on your right, then through the gate at the top to reach the **Treasurer's House** in Chapter House Street (Easter–Oct Mon–Thurs, Sat & Sun 10.30am–4.30pm; £3.50; NT), a seventeenth-century town house that stands on the site of houses used by the Minster's treasurers until the Dissolution. Just around the corner in College Street stands **St William's College** (daily 10am–5pm; 60p), a half-timbered building studded with oriel windows, initially dedicated to the great-grandson of William the Conqueror who was Archbishop of York. It serves as a visitor centre for the Minster and a conference hall and banqueting centre, though three of the medieval rooms are open for viewing provided they're not in use.

The walls

Although much restored, the city's superb **walls** date mainly from the fourteenth century, though fragments of Norman work survive, particularly in the gates (or "bars"), whilst the northern sections still follow the line of the Roman ramparts. **Monk Bar** at the northern end of Goodramgate is as good a point of access as any, tallest of the city's four main gates and host to a small **Richard III Museum** (daily March–Oct 9am–5pm; Nov–Feb 9am–4pm; £1), where you're invited to decide on the guilt or innocence of England's most maligned king. For just a taste of the walls' best section, take the ten-minute stroll west from Monk Bar to Exhibition Square (see below) and **Bootham Bar**, the only gate on the site of a Roman gateway and marking the traditional northern entrance to the city. A stroll round the walls' entire two-and-a-half-mile length will take you past the southwestern **Micklegate Bar**, long considered the most important of the gates. It was built to a Norman design reputedly using ancient stone coffins as building stone, and was later used to exhibit the heads of executed criminals and rebels. The engaging **Micklegate Bar Museum** (daily 10am–dusk; £1.50) occupies a surviving fortified tower. **Walmgate Bar** in the east is the best preserved and has traditionally been the city's strongest bar.

The Shambles

The Shambles, off King's Square at the southern end of Goodramgate, could be taken as the epitome of medieval York, though the crowds and self-conscious quaintness take the edge off what would otherwise be a perfect medieval thoroughfare. Flagstoned, almost impossibly narrow and lined with perilously leaning timber-framed houses, it was the home of York's butchers, its erstwhile stench and squalor now difficult to imagine, though old meat hooks still adorn the odd house. At no. 35, there's a **shrine** (closed to the public) to Margaret Clitherow, the Catholic wife of a butcher, martyred in 1586 for allegedly sheltering priests; she was pressed to death with rocks piled on top of a board on the city's Ouse Bridge. Newgate **market** (daily 8am–5pm) lies off the Shambles, together with the core of the city's shopping streets.

Exhibition Square to St Helen's Square

Exhibition Square, outside Bootham Bar, holds the city's main tourist office in the De Grey Rooms, opposite which stands the **City Art Gallery** (Mon–Sat 10am–5pm, Sun 2.30–5pm; free), an extensive collection of British, early Italian and northern European paintings. South of Exhibition Square on Museum Street stands the entrance to the **Yorkshire Museum** (April–Oct daily 10am–5pm; Nov–March Mon–Sat 10am–5pm, Sun 1–5pm; £3.60), which lies within the beautifully laid-out grounds of St Mary's Abbey, itself now in ruins. It's one of York's better museums, strong on archeological remains which it presents in a series of rooms examining the Roman presence in the city – grave effects, cooking utensils in a reconstructed Roman kitchen, glassware, farming equipment and jewellery. There are impressive displays of

Viking and Anglo-Saxon artefacts, too, though chief exhibit is the fifteenth-century Middleham Jewel – a diamond-shaped jewel with an oblong sapphire, claimed as the finest piece of Gothic jewellery in England.

Part of the museum basement incorporates the fireplace and chapter house of **St Mary's Abbey**, whose ruins lie around the Museum Gardens, the abbey's former grounds (abbey & gardens free). Founded around 1080, the abbey later became an important Benedictine foundation, additionally significant as it was from here that disenchanted monks fled to found Fountains Abbey (see p.591).

The street called **Lendal** cuts down from Museum Street to **St Helen's Square** – marking the entrance to the Roman city – whose Georgian **Mansion House** is the private home of the city's mayor. However, you can visit the six-hundred-year-old **Guildhall** (May–Oct Mon–Fri 9am–5pm, Sat 10am–5pm, Sun 2–5pm; Nov–April Mon–Fri 9am–5pm; free) behind, which was almost totally destroyed by bombing in 1942, but has since been restored to an almost mirror image of its original, timber-roofed state. Back up Blake Street from the square, have a look inside the **Grand Assembly Rooms**, built between 1732 and 1736 by the third Earl of Burlington. An epicentre of chic during York's eighteenth-century social heyday, the building attempted to emulate London's grander salons; its 52-columned Central Hall is a tribute to the Egyptian Hall of the capital's Mansion House.

Back at St Helen's Square, **Stonegate** leads northeast towards the Minster, a street as ancient as the city itself. Originally the Via Praetoria of Roman York, it's now paved with thick flags of York stone, which were once carried along here to build the Minster, hence the street name. Guy Fawkes' parents lived on Stonegate (there's a plaque opposite *Mulberry Hall*) and its Tudor houses retain their considerable charm – an alley at no. 52A leads to the scant remains of a twelfth-century Norman stone house, a rarity in England.

South to the Jorvik Viking Centre

At the **Merchant Adventurers' Hall**, off Fossgate (mid-March to mid-Nov daily 8.30am–5pm; mid-Nov to mid-March Mon–Sat 8.30am–3.30pm; £1.90), the whiff of wood polish prepares you for one of the finest medieval timber-framed halls in Europe. The beautiful building was raised by the city's most powerful guild, dealers in wool from the Wolds, woollens from the Dales and lead from the Pennines, commodities that were traded for exotica from far and wide. Castlegate throws up the **York Story**, a heritage centre housed in the former St Mary's Church (Mon–Sat 10am–5pm, Sun 1–5pm; £1.90; combined ticket with Castle Museum £5.95), with a video introduction to the city among other less than gripping exhibits. You may get more out of the adjacent **Fairfax House**, also on Castlegate (Aug & Sept Mon–Sat 11am–5pm, Sun 1.30–5pm; rest of year closed Fri; £3.75), a Georgian town house restored to take an eighteenth-century collection of fine arts left by Noel Terry, scion of one of the city's chocolate dynasties.

These though are all small fry compared to the blockbuster exhibit that is Coppergate's **Jorvik Viking Centre** (daily April–Oct 9am–7pm; Nov–March 9am–5.30pm; last admission 2hr before closing; £4.99), a multi-million pound affair that takes you on a twenty-minute "time-car" ride back through time to experience the sights, smells and sounds of a riverside Viking village – with the voice of Magnus Magnusson for company. You need to get here bang on opening time to have any chance of beating the queues (though a timed-ticket system means you can always come back later at a pre-arranged time). It's worth noting that the museum organizes York's annual **Viking Festival** every February when themed events take place throughout the city – details from the Festival Office at the centre.

York Castle and the Castle Museum

Despite the rich architectural heritage elsewhere in the city, there's precious little left of **York Castle**, one of two established by William the Conqueror. Only the perilously leaning **Clifford's Tower** (daily: Easter–June & Sept 10am–6pm; July & Aug 10am–7.30pm; Oct–Easter 10am–4pm or dusk; £1.80; EH) remains, as evocative a piece of military engineering as you could wish for: a stark and isolated stone keep built on one of William's mottes between 1245 and 1262. The old Norman keep was destroyed in 1109 during one of the city's more shameful historical episodes, when 150 Jews were put inside the tower for their own protection during an outburst of anti-Semitic rioting. The move did little to appease the mob, however, and faced with starvation or slaughter the Jews committed mass suicide by setting the tower on fire.

Immediately east of the tower lies the **Castle Museum** (April–Oct Mon–Sat 9.30am–5.30pm, Sun 10am–5.30pm; Nov–March Mon–Sat 9.30am–4pm, Sun 10am–4pm; £4.75), a remarkable collection founded by a Dr Kirk of Pickering, who realized, even eighty years ago, that many of the everyday items used in rural areas were in danger of disappearing. He took the unusual step of accepting bric-a-brac from his patients in lieu of fees. A whole range of early craft, folk and agricultural ephemera is complemented by costumes, militaria, workshops, two entire reconstructed streets, plus rambling dungeons and period rooms. Pride of place is given to a dazzling Viking helmet, discovered during the Coppergate excavations and the only one of its kind ever found.

The National Railway Museum

The **National Railway Museum** on Leeman Road (daily 10am–6pm; £5; ☎01904/621261), ten minutes' walk from the station, is a must if you have even the slightest interest in railways, history, engineering or Victoriana. The Great Hall alone features some fifty restored locomotives dating from 1829 onwards, among them the *Mallard*, at 126mph the world's fastest steam engine. The South Hall, a former goods station, complete with tracks and platforms, holds the major permanent exhibitions, where you can see the plush splendour of the royal carriages ("Palaces on Wheels") and the bleak segregation of classes in the Victorian coaches. Dotted around the hall is a welter of miscellaneous memorabilia: posters, models, paintings and period photographs, even a lock of George Stephenson's hair. New projects include a walk-round backstage storage area of the museum's reserve collection, and visits to the engineering workshop and a track-and-signal viewing area which has been established over the east coast mainline.

Eating and drinking

It's impossible to walk more than about fifty yards in central York without coming across either a pub, teashop, café or restaurant. In keeping with much else in the city, many establishments are relentlessly and self-consciously old-fashioned, though there are some real highlights – truly historic **pubs**, the remarkable *Betty's*, the ultimate **teashop** experience, and a scattering of well-regarded **restaurants**.

Tearooms and cafés

Betty's, 6–8 St Helen's Square. If there are teashops in heaven they'll be like *Betty's*, a York institution founded in 1919, with an Art Nouveau cladding and a permanent queue. Daily 9am–9pm.

Blake Head Vegetarian Café, 104 Micklegate. Bookstore-café with patio for freshly baked cakes, pâtés, quiche, brunch, salads and soups. Closed Sun.

Mulberry Hall Coffee Shop, Stonegate. Wend through the fifteenth-century house, now York's poshest china and glassware shop, for fine snacks in snazzy surroundings. Closed Sun.

Spurriergate Centre, St Michael's Church, Spurriergate. Quiche, salads and baked potatoes served in the interior of twelfth-century St Michael's. Closed Sun.

Treasurer's House, Minster Yard. Superior tearoom in the cellars of a National Trust property. Closed Fri & Nov–Easter.

Restaurants

19 Grape Lane, 19 Grape Lane (☎01904/636366). Town-house restaurant serving top-quality Modern-British dishes, including some great puddings. Closed Sun. Expensive.

Melton's, 7 Scarcroft Rd (☎01904/634341). Simple, classy cooking, including very good fish dishes, and imaginative vegetarian food. Closed Mon lunch & Sun dinner. Expensive.

La Piazza, 45 Goodramgate (☎01904/642641). Authentic Italian coffee-bar out front, courtyard restaurant out back, tucked into a nice Tudor building. Inexpensive to Moderate.

Pizza Express, River House, 17 Museum St. Grand old riverside club rooms with sought-after balcony, and good-quality pizzas. Inexpensive to Moderate.

The Rubicon, 5–7 Little Stonegate (☎01904/676076). All the veggie classics – nut roast among them – in a laid-back wholefood restaurant. Closed Sun lunch. Inexpensive to Moderate.

St William's College Restaurant, 3 College St (☎01904/634830). Candlelight and jazz in an historic building next door to the Minster; also a superior café during the day. Closes 9.30pm & all Sun. Moderate.

Pubs

Black Swan, Peasholme Green. York's oldest (sixteenth-century) pub and a Grade II listed building with some superb stone-flagging and wood-panelling. Home of the city's folk club.

Hole in the Wall, High Petergate. Very close to the Minster, yet rarely crowded, this pleasant, stripped-down retreat is something of a find in the city centre.

Judge's Lodging Cellar Bar, 9 Lendal. Cosy drinking hole with good beer, in the eighteenth-century cellars of the *Judge's Lodging*, now a smart hotel.

King's Arms, King's Staithe. Close to the Ouse Bridge, this pub has a fine riverside setting with outdoor tables – and accordingly gets very busy in summer.

Tap & Spile, Monkgate. Traditional bare-bones pub with a great range of real ales.

Ye Olde Starre, Stonegate. Vies with the *Black Swan* for historic precedence, with good beer, a cramped beer-garden and plenty of atmosphere.

Nightlife and entertainment

There are healthy helpings of **live music** and **nightlife**, much of it detailed in free weekly handouts like *York What's On* and *YourKmusic*. Most bigger bands bypass the city in favour of Leeds, though the Barbican Centre pulls in its fair share of major mainstream artists, while the pub **music scene** flourishes. **Cultural entertainment** is wide and varied: the annual **Early Music Festival**, held in July, is perhaps the best of its kind in Britain, with dozens of events spread over ten days – details are available on ☎01904/658338. The famous **York Mystery Plays** are held every four years – next performances are in 2004.

Barbican Centre, Barbican Road (☎01904/656688). Country, rock, folk and MOR stalwarts all appear here sooner or later.

Black Swan, Peasholme Green (☎01904/632922). Regular Thursday folk nights with a full range of quality bands and singer-songwriters.

Bonding Warehouse, Skeldergate, by the bridge (☎01904/622527). Live bands several times a week in a fine riverside venue – and good for a drink at other times.

Fibbers, Stonebow (☎01904/651250). A sister venue to the *Duchess* in Leeds, with indie bands playing most nights of the week.

Punch Bowl Inn, Stonegate (☎01904/622305). Pub venue for jazz and blues, a couple of nights a week.

Theatre Royal, St Leonard's Place (☎01904/623568). Musicals, pantos and mainstream theatre.

York Arts Centre, Micklegate (☎01904/627129). Independent theatre productions, as well as gigs, poetry, and dance.

Castle Howard

Immersed in the deep countryside of the Howardian Hills, fifteen miles northeast of York, off the A64, **Castle Howard** (house: March–Oct daily 11am–5pm; gardens:

10am–5pm; housed & grounds £7; grounds only £4.50) is the seat of one of England's leading aristocratic families and among the country's grandest stately homes. Since providing the setting for the television version of *Brideshead Revisited*, the house's car parks have been packed every weekend, but fitting it into a public transport itinerary is something of a problem. In summer there are just two buses a day (1 on Sun) from York, and three (1 on Sun) from Malton and Pickering, but there are also various bus tours from York.

The colossal main house was designed by **Sir John Vanbrugh** in 1699 and was almost forty years in the making – remarkable enough, were it not for the fact that Vanbrugh was, at the start of the commission at least, best known as a playwright. He had no formal architectural training but shrewdly recognized his limitations and called upon the assistance of Nicholas Hawksmoor, who had a major part in the house's structural design – the pair later worked successfully together on Blenheim Palace. If Hawksmoor's guiding hand can be seen throughout, Vanbrugh's influence is clear in the very theatricality of the building, notably in the palatial **Great Hall**. This was gutted by fire in the 1940s, but has subsequently been restored from old etchings and photographs to something approaching its original state.

Vanbrugh soon turned his attention to the estate's thousand-acre **grounds** where he could indulge his playful inclinations to excess, and the formal gardens, clipped parkland, towers, obelisks and blunt sandstone follies stretch in all directions, sloping gently to a large artifical lake. He completed the **Temple of the Four Winds** before his death in 1726, leaving Hawskmoor to design the Howard family **Mausoleum**, which is taller than the house itself. Take a look, too, at the fine **stables** which have been converted into the Costume and Regalia Gallery, Britain's largest private collection of period clothes.

Hull, the Humber and the East Yorkshire coast

Generations of Yorkshire people, born and bred in the historic **East Riding**, were outraged to wake up one morning and find themselves part of "Humberside", just one of the notorious local government conveniences created by the 1974 bastardization of the English counties. Consequently, there was almost universal rejoicing when the Lincolnshire adjuncts from across the **River Humber** were dropped in 1996 and towns like **Hull** could once again revel in their Yorkshire ancestry. Historic **Beverley**, with its marvellous Minster, can be easily reached by **buses** from Hull (or York), while Hull is also linked to Doncaster by the main London–York **train** line. Northeast, up the **East Yorkshire coast**, lonely beaches and wild foreshores draw curious tourists to the bucket-and-spade resorts of **Bridlington** and **Filey**.

Hull

HULL's most famous adopted son, the poet and university librarian Philip Larkin, wrote "I wish I could think of just one nice thing to tell you about Hull, oh yes . . . *it's very nice and flat for cycling*," capturing something of the character of a town which reaches few heights, physical or otherwise. The town – rarely known by its full grandiose title of **Kingston-upon-Hull** – undoubtedly suited the poet's curmudgeonly temperament, but he might have mentioned Hull's self-reliant and no-nonsense atmosphere, or that the restored docks and old town centre are surprisingly appealing. Hull's **maritime** pre-eminence dates back to 1299, when it was laid out as a seaport by Edward I. It quickly became England's leading harbour, and was still a vital garrison when the gates were closed against Charles I in 1642, the first serious act of rebellion of what was to become the English Civil War. The central **Princes Dock** sets the tone for Hull's modern refurbishment, overlooked by Princes Quay, a multi-tier, glass-spangled shopping centre, with the revamped **marina** beyond.

The town's maritime legacy is exhaustively detailed in the **Town Docks Museum** (Mon–Sat 10am–5pm, Sun 1.30–4.30pm; free), on the east side of Queen Victoria Square, immediately north of Princes Quay. The main boost to the town's coffers in the eighteenth and nineteenth centuries was whaling, and the museum tells the story well, displaying gruesome whaling equipment, such as a blubber pot cauldron, alongside model ships, old photographs, Innuit relics and a whale skeleton. Leave Queen Victoria Square on its east side by pedestrianized Whitefriar Gate, turn right on Trinity House Lane after two hundred yards, and you're in front of **Holy Trinity** (Easter–Sept Tues & Fri 10am–4pm, Wed & Thurs noon–4pm, Sat 9.30am–4pm; Oct–Easter Tues & Fri 10am–4pm, Sat 9.30am–4pm), among the largest and most pleasing parish churches in the country. Across Market Place is perhaps Hull's most revered relic – the **Old Grammar School**, a red-brick edifice built in 1583 and which for 120 years doubled as the town's Merchant Adventurers' Hall. As a school, it numbered amongst its pupils William Wilberforce, instigator of the abolition of slavery in the British Empire, and seventeenth-century poet Andrew Marvell, also MP for Hull. (Hull-born Stevie Smith, incidentally, completes the town's poetic triumvirate.)

The **train station** is on the west side of town, on the main drag of Ferensway, with the **bus station** a couple of blocks north. The main **tourist office** is on Paragon Street at Victoria Square (Mon 10am–6pm, Tues–Sat 9.30am–6pm, Sun noon–4pm; ☎01482/223559). The most central **B&B** options include the *Clyde House Hotel*, 13 John St, Kingston Square (☎01482/214981; ②), and the *Pines Hotel*, 138 Spring Bank (☎01482/215480; no credit cards; ①), while the best-sited hotel is the *Forte Marina* on Castle Street overlooking Hull Marina (☎01482/225221; ⑥). For **food**, eat Italian at the expensive *Cerutti's* (☎01482/328501; closed Sat lunch & Sun), on dockside Nelson Street, or the moderately priced *Operetta*, 56–58 Bond St (☎01482/218687; closed Sun lunch). Of Hull's many **pubs**, the *Olde White Harte*, 25 Silver St, has a history going back to the seventeenth century; at the dockside *Minerva* on Nelson Street they brew their own (*Pilot's Pride*).

Beverley

BEVERLEY ranks as one of northern England's premier towns, its Minster the superior of many an English cathedral, its tangle of old streets, cobbled lanes and elegant Georgian and Victorian terraces the very picture of a traditional market town. Over 350 buildings are listed as possessing historical or architectural merit, and though you could see its first-rank offerings in a morning, this is one of a handful of places in this part of the world that you might want to stay in for its own sake.

Approaches to the town are dominated by the twin towers of **Beverley Minster** (Mon–Sat 9am–dusk, Sun 2.30am–5pm; £1 donation requested). Initiated as a modest chapel, the Minster became a monastery under John of Beverley, later ordained Bishop of York, who was buried here in 721 and canonized in 1037 – his body lies under the crossing at the top of the nave. Fires and the collapse of the central tower in 1213 paved the way for two centuries of rebuilding, funded by bequests from pilgrims paying homage to the saint, and the result was one of the finest Gothic creations in the country. The **west front**, which crowned the work in 1420, is widely considered without equal, its survival due in large part to Baroque architect Nicholas Hawksmoor, who restored much of the church in the eighteenth century. Similar outstanding work awaits in the interior, most notably the fourteenth-century **Percy Tomb** on the north side of the altar, its sumptuously carved canopy one of the masterpieces of medieval European ecclesiastical art. Other incidental carving throughout the church is magnificent, particularly the 68 misericords of the oak **choir** (1520–24), one of the largest and most accomplished in England. Much of the decorative work here and elsewhere is on a musical theme. Beverley had a renowned guild of itinerant minstrels, which provided funds in the sixteenth century for the carvings on the transept aisle capitals, where you'll be able to pick out players of lutes, bagpipes, horns and tambourines.

Beverley is most easily reached by regular **train** or **bus** (#121, #122, #X46 or #246) from Hull, though there are also several daily buses from York (#X46). Station Square is just a couple of minutes' walk from the Minster. The **tourist office** is at 34 Butcher Row in the main shopping area (June–Aug Mon–Fri 9.30am–5.30pm, Sat 10am–5pm, Sun 10am–2pm; rest of year closed Sun; ☎01482/867430). There's plenty of local **accommodation**, including the *Eastgate*, 7 Eastgate (☎01482/868464; no credit cards; ②), very close to the Minster. Among the hotels, top central choices include the *King's Head*, 38 Market Place (☎01482/868103; ③), and the *Beverley Arms*, North Bar Within (☎01482/869241; ⑥). The **youth hostel** (☎01482/881751) occupies one of the town's finer buildings, a restored Dominican friary that was mentioned in the *Canterbury Tales*. It's located in Friar's Lane, off Eastgate.

The East Yorkshire coast

The **East Yorkshire coast** curves in a gentle arc between the cliffs of Flamborough Head in the north before bending inland at Spurn Head in the south, a finger-thin isthmus formed by the constant erosion and shifting currents that scour much of England's eastern shores. Between the two lie a handful of old-style resorts, tranquil villages and miles of windswept dunes and mud flats, noted bird sanctuaries, and superbly lonely retreats accessible to anyone prepared to cycle or walk the paths and lanes that fan out amidst the dunes. The two main resorts, Bridlington and Filey, are linked by the regular **train** service between Hull and Scarborough. There's also an hourly bus service between Bridlington, Filey and Scarborough.

Like many coastal stations, **BRIDLINGTON** flourished in Edwardian times as a resort, but spent recent decades in decline. Renovations have smartened up the seafront promenade, which looks down upon the town's best asset – its sweeping sandy **beach** – and as an out-and-out family resort, there's plenty of candy-floss, amusement arcades, rides and diversions. The **tourist office**, 25 Prince St (Easter–Oct Mon–Sat 9.30am–5.30pm, Sun 9am–5pm; Nov–Easter Mon–Sat 9.30am–5.30pm; ☎01262/673474), has full lists of local accommodation – the Flamborough Road has a fair choice, with places like *The Ryburn* at no. 31 (☎01262/674098; no credit cards; ②) a fair bet.

FILEY, half a dozen miles further north up the coast has a deal more class as a resort, retaining many of its Edwardian features, including some splendid panoramic gardens. It, too, claims miles of wide sandy beach, stretching most of the way south to **Flamborough Head** and north the mile or so to the jutting rocks of **Filey Brigg**. If you're going to clamber around on the brigg, check the tide tables first since people get caught unawares by the incoming waters at times. **Bus and train** stations are just west of the centre on Station Road. Walk down Station Avenue and Murray Street to Filey's **tourist office** in the borough council offices on John Street, at the top of the foreshore road (May–Sept daily 9.30am–5.30pm; Oct–April Sat & Sun 10am–12.30pm & 1–4.30pm; ☎01723/512204). You'll find a clutch of standard **B&Bs** on Rutland Street, off West Avenue, which runs from the church in the centre of town.

Around fourteen miles of precipitous four-hundred-foot cliffs gird **Flamborough Head**, just to the northeast of Bridlington. To see the best of Flamborough Head's coastline, try to walk at least part of the grassy cliff-top track, a signposted Heritage Coast path. From **BEMPTON**, two miles north of Bridlington, a quiet lane leads to **Bempton Cliffs**, an RSPB sanctuary and the best single place to see the area's thousands of cliff-nesting birds. This is the only mainland gannetry in England, while Bempton also boasts the second largest **puffin colony** in the country, with around seven thousand returning to the cliffs between March and August. Late March and April is the best time to see the puffins, when they display before nesting in the cliff's deep crevices, but the **Visitor Centre** (March–Oct daily 10am–5pm; Nov & Feb Sat & Sun 9.30am–4pm; ☎01262/851179) can advise on other breeds' activities (best between May and July) and rent you a pair of binoculars (£2). RSPB puffin and seabird **cruises** (most Saturdays, June–Sept; £7.50; reserve on ☎0191/212 0353) last three to four hours and depart from Bridlington.

The North York Moors

Virtually the whole of the **North York Moors**, from the Hambleton and Cleveland hills in the west to the cliff-edged coastline to the east, is protected by one of the country's finest national parks. The moors are lonely, heather-covered, flat-topped hills cut by deep, steep-sided valleys, and views here stretch for miles, interrupted only by giant cultivated forests, pale shadows of the woodland that covered the region before it was cleared by Neolithic and later peoples. Barrows and ancient forts provide memorials of these early settlers, mingling on the high moorland with the **Roman remains** of Wades Causeway, the battered stone crosses of the first Christian inhabitants and the ruins of great monastic houses such as Rievaulx.

Helmsley is the best starting point for any exploration of the western and central moors; **Pickering** (actually just outside the national park) for the eastern moors and northern Esk Valley. The central moors offer the best walking and the most noted landscapes, with **Hutton le Hole** the most picture-perfect village in the region. Any exploration of the district should also include the religious ruins of **Rievaulx Abbey**; the views from **Sutton Bank**; the gentle landscapes of the **Esk Valley**, blessed with its own small train line; and any one of countless deep-rural pubs, isolated hamlets or woodland walks.

The main southern artery linking the western, central and eastern divisions is the A170, which runs from Thirsk, through Helmsley and Pickering to Scarborough. Two trans-moor roads, the Helmsley–Stokesley B1257 (west side) and the Pickering–Whitby A169 (east), offer access into the very heart of the moors. The **steam trains** of the North York Moors Railway operate between Pickering and Grosmont, while at Grosmont you can connect with the regular **trains** on the Esk Valley line, running east to Whitby and the coast, or west to more remote settlements (and ultimately to Middlesbrough). The main **bus** approaches to the moors are from Scarborough and York to Helmsley and Pickering, though beyond these towns local

---

THE MOORSBUS

The National Park Authority is making sterling efforts to reduce traffic congestion in the region by promoting public transport, in particular its bus service, the **Moorsbus** (☎01439/770657), which runs every Sunday and bank holiday Monday from the end of May to the end of October, and daily in the summer school holidays (late July to late Aug). All local tourist and national park information offices have timetables, but the various **services** basically connect Helmsley to Sutton Bank, Rievaulx, Coxwold and Kilburn; Pickering to Hutton le Hole, Castleton and Danby, to Rosedale Abbey and to Dalby Forest; and Helmsley and Pickering to each other. Departures are usually four times daily (hourly on the main routes), and timed so that day-trips are possible to the various sights; all-day **tickets** cost £2.50. Long-distance services (£5) from York (1hr 10min), Hull (1hr 40min), Beverley (1hr), Darlington (2hr) and Middlesbrough (1hr) let you commute into the park for a day's moorland sightseeing.

services are limited. You'll need the free *Moors Connections* booklet, a summary of all rail and bus routes on and around the moors, available from tourist offices and park information centres.

The western moors

The **western moors** are marked on their western edge by the scarp of the **Hambleton Hills** – crowned by the Cleveland Way – and the ruler-straight line of the A19 road between York, **Thirsk** (just outside the park) and Middlesbrough. To the east they are closed by Rye Dale, one of the region's more bucolic valleys, and the B1267 from **Helmsley**. Most outings are likely to centre less on the scenery – except for the walks and staggering views from **Sutton Bank** on the A170 – than on a cluster of historic buildings, of which the most prepossessing is **Rievaulx Abbey**, a couple of miles from Helmsley.

Thirsk and Mount Grace Priory

The small market town of **THIRSK**, 23 miles north of York, made the most of its strategic crossroads position on the ancient drove road between Scotland and York and on the historic east–west route from dales to coast. Its medieval prosperity is clear from the large, cobbled **Market Place** (market days are Monday and Saturday), while later well-to-do citizens endowed the town with a bevy of commendable Georgian houses and halls. However, Thirsk's main draw is its attachment to the legacy of local vet Alf Wight, better known as **James Herriott**. Thirsk was the "Darrowby" of the Herriott books, not least because the town was where the vet had his actual surgery. Following a £1.5m refurbishment, this building at 23 Kirkgate has emerged as the hugely popular **World of James Herriott** (daily: Easter–Oct 10am–5.30pm; Nov–Easter 10am–5pm; last admission 1hr before closing; £4), an entertaining recreation of the vet's 1940s' surgery, dispensary, operating theatre, sitting room and kitchen, each crammed with period pieces and Herriott memorabilia.

Buses stop in the Market Place; the **train station** is a mile west of town on the A61 (Ripon road); minibuses run to the town centre. The **tourist office** is inside the World of James Herriott, 23 Kirkgate (daily: Easter–Oct 10am–5.30pm; Nov–Easter 10am–5pm; ☎01845/522755). For **accommodation**, try *Lavender House*, 27 Kirkgate (☎01845/522224; no credit cards; ③), or *Kirkgate House*, 35 Kirkgate (☎01845/525015; ③). The *Golden Fleece* and *Three Tuns* both serve **meals**, while the nicest daytime choice is the *Yorks Tearooms*, next to the clocktower on Market Place.

Eleven miles north of Thirsk (straight up the busy A19), the fourteenth-century **Mount Grace Priory** (Easter–Oct daily 10am–6pm; Nov–March Wed–Sun 10am–1pm & 2–4pm; £2.70; NT & EH) is the most important of England's nine Carthusian ruins and the only one in Yorkshire. The Carthusians took a vow of silence and lived, ate and prayed alone in their two-storey cells, each separated from its neighbour by a privy, small garden and high walls. The foundations of the cells are still clearly visible, together with one which has been reconstructed to suggest its original layout and the monks' way of life. Take the train from Thirsk to Northallerton, six miles southwest of the priory, and then any of the regular Northallerton–Osmotherley buses (hourly, not Sun).

Sutton Bank, Coxwold and around

The main A170 road enters the national park from Thirsk as it climbs five hundred feet in half a mile to **Sutton Bank** (960ft), a phenomenal viewpoint whose panorama extends across the Vale of York to the Pennines on the far horizon. At the top of the climb stands a huge car park and a lavish **North York Moors National Park Visitor Centre** (Easter–Oct daily 10am–5pm; Nov–March daily 11am–4pm; ☎01845/597426), where you can pick up details about local walks – like the marked **White Horse Nature Trail** (2–3 miles; 1hr 30min) which skirts the crags of Roulston Scar en route to the **Kilburn White Horse**, northern England's only turf-cut figure, at 314ft long and 228ft high.

The first serious diversion off the A170 is **COXWOLD**, as attractive a little village as they come. The majority of its many visitors come to pay homage to the novelist **Laurence Sterne**, who is buried by the south wall (close to the porch) in the churchyard of **St Michael's**, where he was vicar from 1760 until his death in 1768. **Shandy Hall**, 150 yards further up the road past the church (house June–Sept Wed 2–4.30pm, Sun 2.30–4.30pm; gardens June–Sept Mon–Fri & Sun 11am–4.30pm; house & gardens £3; gardens only £1.50), was Sterne's home, and is now a museum crammed with literary memorabilia. It was here that he wrote *A Sentimental Journey through France and Italy* and the wonderfully eccentric *The Life and Opinions of Tristram Shandy, Gentleman*, which prompted Samuel Johnson loftily and misguidedly to declare "nothing odd will last". **Buses** run to Coxwold from Thirsk on Mondays, Fridays and Saturdays (and on to Helmsley), and the Moorsbus runs here from Helmsley in summer. The *Fauconburg Arms* (☎01347/868214; ③), a superb old **pub** on Main Street, has the most to recommend it, with good bar food, a more formal restaurant and pleasant **rooms**.

The pub is named after the viscount who married Mary, daughter of Oliver Cromwell, whom he brought to live in **Newburgh Priory**, half a mile south of the village (April–June Wed & Sun 2–6pm; also Easter weekend & Aug Bank Hol 2–6pm; £4; grounds only £2.50). Raised on the site of an Augustinian monastery founded in 1150, the house is famous for reputedly containing a tomb with the headless body of Oliver Cromwell. Laurence Sterne talked of "A delicious Walk of Romance" from Coxwold to twelfth-century **Byland Abbey** (Easter–Sept daily 10am–6pm; Oct daily 10am–4pm; Nov–Easter Wed–Sun 10am–1pm & 2–4pm; £1.70; EH), a mile and a half northeast of the village. His description captures the appeal of the ruins which, though larger in ground area than the Cistercian houses at Fountains and Rievaulx, are far less well preserved.

Helmsley

One of the moors' most appealing towns, **HELMSLEY** makes a perfect base for visiting the western moors and Rievaulx Abbey. Local life revolves around a large cobbled market square (market day is Friday), dominated by a vaunting monument to the second Earl of Feversham, whose family were responsible for rebuilding most of the village in the last century. The old **market cross** marks the start of the 110-mile Cleveland Way (see below). Close to the square is **Helmsley Castle** (April–Sept daily 10am–6pm; Nov–March Wed–Sun 10am–1pm & 2–4pm; £2.20; EH), its unique twelfth-century D-shaped keep ringed by massive earthworks.

To the southwest of the town, overlooking a wooded meander of the Rye, stands the Fevershams' country seat, **Duncombe Park** (parkland & visitor centre: May–Sept Mon–Fri & Sun 10.30am–6pm; April & Oct Mon–Thurs & Sun 10.30am–6pm; house & gardens same days 11am–5.30pm; house, gardens & parkland £5.50; gardens & parkland £3.50; parkland only £2), built for the Fevershams' ancestor Sir Thomas Duncombe in 1713. The **grounds** are perhaps more appealing than the house (which was extensively rebuilt after a fire in 1879), boasting swathes of landscaped gardens and a brace of artfully sited temples.

Helmsley is a hub for the **Moorsbus**, which takes trippers out to Sutton Bank, Rievaulx, Byland Abbey, Coxwold and Kilburn. Make sense of all the connections in the **tourist office** in the town hall on Market Place (Easter–Oct daily 9.30am–6pm; Nov–Easter Sat & Sun 10am–4pm; ☎01439/770173), which also has full details about the **Cleveland Way**, one of England's premier long-distance National Trails, which embraces both the northern rim of the moors and Cleveland Hills and the cliff scenery of the North Yorkshire coast. The *Cleveland Way Project* (The Old Vicarage, Bondgate, Helmsley, YO6 5BP; ☎01439/770657) produces an annual *Accommodation and Information Guide*, an invaluable route-planning aid. There's plenty of **accommodation** in Helmsley itself, starting with the *Castle View Guest House*, 19 Bridge St, just off the square (☎01439/770618; no credit cards; ①). Slightly more expensive is *Stilworth House*, 1 Church St, behind the tourist office (☎01439/771072; no credit cards; ②), while pricier hotels include the *Feversham Arms*, 1 High St, behind the church (☎01439/770766; ⑤), and the *Black Swan*, also on Market Place (☎01439/770466; ⑦). The **youth hostel** (☎01439/770433) is a few hundred yards east of Market Place – follow Bondgate to Carlton Road and turn left. The old **pubs** in the Market Place – the *Royal Oak* and the *Feathers* – are both atmospheric places for a drink and a bite to eat. Best place for a snack or **meal** is *Monet's* on Bridge Street.

Rievaulx Abbey and Terrace

From Helmsley you can easily hike across country to **Rievaulx Abbey** (daily April–Sept 10am–6pm; Oct–March 10am–1pm & 2–4pm; £2.90; EH), the most heavily visited historic building on the moors. The signposted path follows the opening two miles of the Cleveland Way, plus a mile's diversion off the Way, and takes around an hour and a half – a trail leaflet is available from the tourist office in Helmsley. Founded in 1132, the abbey became the mother church of the Cistercians in England, quickly developing from a series of rough shelters on the deeply wooded banks of the Rye to become a flourishing community with interests in fishing, mining, agriculture and the woollen industry, the latter supported by a chain of associated moorland farms. At its height, 140 monks and up to 500 lay brothers lived and worked at the abbey, though numbers fell dramatically once the Black Death (1348–49) had done its worst. Nemesis came with the Dissolution, when many of the walls were razed and the roof lead stripped – the beautiful ruins, however, still suggest the abbey's former splendour.

Although they form some sort of ensemble with the abbey, there's no access between the ruins and **Rievaulx Terrace and Temples** (Easter–Oct daily 10.30am–6pm, or dusk if earlier; £2.80; NT), a site entered from the B1257, northwest of town. This half-mile stretch of grass-covered terraces and woodland was laid out as part of Duncombe Park in the 1750s, and as with Studley Royal at Fountains Abbey, the Terrace was engineered partly to enhance the views of the abbey. The resulting panorama over the ruins and the valley below is superb, and this makes a great spot for a picnic or simply for strolls along the lawns and woodland trail.

The central moors

The highest and wildest terrain in the North York Moors is in the **central moors**, bounded by Rye Dale in the west and by **Rosedale** in the east. Purple swathes of summer heather carpet the tops, where ancient crosses and standing stones provide hints of the moorland's distant past. It's the one part of the national park where having your own transport is vital if you don't plan to hang around too long, though the Moorsbus connects most of the better-known destinations.

Lying around eight miles northeast of Helmsley, one of Yorkshire's quaintest villages, **HUTTON LE HOLE**, has become so great a tourist attraction that you'll have to come off-season to get much pleasure from its tidy gardens, its stream-crossed village green and the sight of sheep wandering freely through the lanes. The big draw is the **Ryedale Folk Museum** (Easter–Oct daily 10am–5.30pm; £3), an ever-expanding set of displays of local life and work over a two-acre site. The museum also houses a

national park information centre (☎01751/417367). For **accommodation**, try the *Barn Hotel* (☎01751/417311; ②), on the through road just down from the museum, or the Georgian *Hammer and Hand* (☎01751/417300; ②), a comfortable period B&B on the village green.

Farndale is entered from the south by a minor road from Gillamoor, a little to the west of Hutton le Hole. Further up the vale the country lanes are packed in spring with tourists come to see the area's wild daffodils, protected by the two-thousand-acre **Farndale nature reserve**. The flowers grow in several parts of the dale, but the best area is north of **Low Mill**, where roads from Gillamoor and Hutton le Hole meet, about four miles north of the latter. The Moorsbus runs a special "Daffodil" service every Sunday in April and over Easter, shuttling visitors from Hutton le Hole to Farndale.

Rosedale, a couple of miles east of Farndale, has a good network of wild upland roads ranging over its moors, which are densely studded with prehistoric tumuli and ancient stone crosses, like **Ralph Cross** standing sentinel at the isolated crossroads at the top of the dale. The largest of its communities, **ROSEDALE ABBEY**, four miles northeast of Hutton le Hole, preserves only a few fragments of the Cistercian priory (1158) which gave it its name, most of them incorporated into **St Lawrence's** parish church. It's hard to believe now, but in the last century the village had a population of over five thousand, most employed in the ironstone workings whose remnants lie scattered all over the high moors round about. Rosedale village itself gets packed on summer weekends, a fair proportion of visitors here to sit outside the *Milburn Arms* (☎01751/417312; ⑤), overlooking the small green. There's a popular **campsite** at *Rosedale Caravan Park* (☎01751/417272) down by the river, while north of Rosedale Abbey, you can reach the *Lion Inn* (☎01751/417320; ③) on windswept **Blakey Ridge**, a couple of miles south of the junction with the Hutton le Hole–Castleton road (along which the Moorsbus travels).

Pickering and the eastern moors

The biggest centre for miles around, **Pickering** takes for itself the title "Gateway to the Moors", which is pushing it a bit, though it's certainly a handy place to stay if you're touring the villages and dales of the **eastern moors**. Its undoubted big pull, and biggest plus if you're using public transport, is the **North Yorkshire Moors Railway**, which provides a beautiful way of travelling up (and walking from) spectacular **Newtondale**. Otherwise, Moorsbus services radiate from Pickering and there are regular bus services to and from Helmsley, Scarborough, York and Leeds.

Pickering

A thriving market town at the junction of the A170 and the trans-moor A169 (Whitby road), **PICKERING**'s most attractive feature is its **Castle** on the hill north of the market place (Easter–Oct daily 10am–6pm; Nov–March Wed–Sun 10am–4pm; £2.50; EH), reputedly used by every English monarch up to 1400 as a base for hunting in nearby Blandsby Park. Eight monarchs certainly put up here, including Edward II after his trouncing by the Scots at the Battle of Byland Abbey in 1322, and possibly a ninth, Richard II, was kept here as a prisoner shortly before his murder in Pontefract.

The **tourist office**, on Eastgate car park (Easter–Oct Mon–Sat 9.30am–6pm, Sun 9.30am–5.30pm; Nov–Easter Mon–Sat 10am–4.30pm; ☎01751/473791), just above the Malton/Whitby/Scarborough roundabout, can provide full timetables for the **North Yorkshire Moors Railway (NYMR)** (see box opposite). For **accommodation**, tree-lined Eastgate (the Scarborough road) has *Eden House* at no. 120 (☎01751/472289; no credit cards; ②) and *Heathcote House* at no. 100 (☎01751/476991; no credit cards; ②).

THE NORTH YORKSHIRE MOORS RAILWAY

One of the northeast's big tourist draws, the volunteer-run **North Yorkshire Moors Railway** connects **Pickering** with the Esk Valley (Middlesbrough–Whitby) line at **Grosmont**, eighteen miles to the north. The line was completed by George Stephenson in 1835, just nine years after the opening of the Stockton and Darlington Railway, making it one of the earliest lines in the country. Even by the standards of later projects it was a remarkable feat of engineering, navigating 1-in-15 gradients and using thousands of tons of brushwood and heather-stuffed sheepskins to provide bedding for the track through the dale's extensive bogs. For twelve years carriages were pulled by horse, with steam locomotives only arriving in 1847. The line closed in 1965 and was formally re-opened in 1973.

Scheduled **services** operate between late March and early November (plus Christmas specials), with trains running hourly to three times daily depending on the time of year; for timetable information ring ☎01751/472508 or pick up a leaflet from local tourist offices. A day-return **fare** along the whole line costs £9.20. Part of the line's attraction, of course, are the **steam trains**, though be warned that diesels are pulled into service when the fire risk in the forests is high.

Bramwood, 19 Hallgarth (☎01751/474066; no credit cards; ②), lies through an arch off the Whitby road. The nearest **youth hostel** is at the *Old School*, Lockton (☎01751/460376), five miles northeast off the A169 – about two miles' cross-country walk from the NYMR station at Levisham, or ask to be dropped at the turn-off by the Whitby bus. Best place to **eat and drink** in Pickering is the *White Swan*, for good beer, lunchtime bar snacks and a fine restaurant with a French-tinged menu.

Walks from the North Yorkshire Moors Railway

Most people make a full return journey for the superb scenery of the roadless **Newtondale**, but if you want to combine some walking with the train rides, stop en route at one of the minor stations. The first is **Levisham**, perfect for walks to **LEVISHAM** village, a mile and a half to the east, where the *Horseshoe Inn* (☎01751/460240; ②) is a favourite target. A steep winding road continues another mile beyond Levisham to **LOCKTON**, where there's a youth hostel and a path north to the **Hole of Horcum**, a bizarre natural hollow gouged by the glacial meltwaters that carved out Newtondale – the paths run back to Levisham station from here, and the entire seven-mile circuit is one of the Moors' best short walks. In the other direction, a couple of miles west of the station – and reached along a minor road – the fascinating **Cawthorn Camps** (free access) are the only Roman camps of their kind in the world. The site's jumbled collection of earthworks, spreading over 103 acres, puzzled archeologists for years, as all the previously discovered Roman marching camps in Europe were built on precise geometrical plans. It's now known that this was a military training area, troops from York's Ninth Legion garrison being sent here on exercises, many of which obviously involved building camps.

The second stop, **Newtondale Halt**, is handy for the hike to the archetypal high moors community of **STAPE** – three miles southwest through the forest – which lies just two miles south of the best-preserved stretch of Roman road in Europe, **Wheeldale Roman Road**: the remains show a twenty-foot-wide stretch of sand and gravel studded by sandstone slabs and edged with kerbs and ditches. It's signposted off the untarred road from Stape to Goathland, perhaps the wildest and most adventurous north–south route over the moors. Just to the east of the road, down in Wheeldale Beck, **Wheeldale youth hostel** (☎01947/896350), housed in a former shooting lodge, is one of the most isolated and basic in England.

The Esk Valley

The northernmost reaches of the national park are crossed by the east–west **Esk Valley**, whose pretty river flows into the sea at Whitby. It's a part of the North York Moors overlooked by many visitors – partly, one suspects, because its very attractions, at least in the eastern stretches, are its valley characteristics: there's not much moorland tramping to be done until you reach **Danby**, one of the finest of all moorland villages. Train access is easy: the North York Moors Railway connects at **Grosmont**, where you're on the **Esk Valley line** which runs between Middlesbrough and Whitby (4–5 daily, including Sunday).

GROSMONT, little more than a level-crossing, station and a couple of tearooms, sees plenty of summer traffic as does **EGTON BRIDGE** – similarly tiny but with the bonus of a beautifully sited riverside pub, the *Horse Shoe*. Further west, the scenery becomes tinged with the looming moors until, at the isolated stone village of **DANBY**, you're once again within striking distance of some excellent walks, all detailed on trail leaflets available from the **Moors Centre** (Easter–Oct daily 10am–5pm; Nov–Easter Sat & Sun 11am–4pm; ☎01287/660654). The *Stonehouse Bakery & Tea Shop* is great for daytime snacks, while a mile out of the village at **Ainthorpe**, the *Fox & Hounds* (☎01287/660218; ②) looks out over the moors, its refurbished rooms and tasty home-cooked food both good reasons to stop.

South of Grosmont, train, footpath and beck climb out of the Esk Valley towards Goathland. Only on foot will you be able to stop at **BECK HOLE**, after a couple of miles, an idyllic bridgeside hamlet focused on the *Birch Hall Inn*, one of the finest rural pubs in all England. A gentle path from the hamlet runs the mile through the fields up to **GOATHLAND**, another highly attractive village, this time set in open moorland beneath the great expanses of Wheeldale and Goathland moors. If it seems oddly familiar – and if it seems unduly crowded – it's because it's widely known as "Aidensfield", the fictional village at the centre of the *Heartbeat* TV series.

Signposts point you to the local sight, the **Mallyan Spout**, a seventy-foot-high waterfall. This lies half a mile or so from the imposing stone *Mallyan Spout Hotel* on the common (☎01947/896486; ⑤), itself the best place to **stay**, and certainly the best place to **eat and drink**.

The North Yorkshire coast

A bracing change after the flattened seascapes of much of East Yorkshire, the **North Yorkshire coast** is the southernmost stretch of a cliff-edged shore that stretches almost unbroken to the Scottish border. **Scarborough** is the biggest town and resort, and the terminus for bus and rail links from York and beyond. Cute **Robin Hood's Bay** is the most popular of the many Yorkshire villages, with fishing and smuggling traditions, while bluff **Staithes** – a fishing harbour on the far edge of North Yorkshire – has yet to tip over into full-blown tourist mode. **Whitby**, in between the two, is the best stopover, its fine sands and resort facilities tempered by its abbey ruins, cobbled streets, Georgian buildings and maritime heritage. For those who want to sample the most dizzying cliff-tops, the **Cleveland Way** provides a marked path along virtually the entire length of the coast.

Hourly **buses** (fewer on Sundays) run along the A171 between Scarborough and Whitby, and a similarly frequent service operates to Robin Hood's Bay, and north between Whitby and Staithes. The Yorkshire Coastliner service connects Leeds and York with Scarborough (hourly) or Whitby (2–4 daily). You can also reach Scarborough direct by **train** from York (1hr) or Hull (1hr 30min).

Scarborough

The oldest resort in the country, **SCARBOROUGH** first attracted early seventeenth-century visitors to its newly discovered mineral springs. Fashionable among the Victorians – to whom it was "the Queen of the Watering Places" – Scarborough saw its biggest transformation after World War II, when it (and many other resorts) became a holiday haven for workers from the industrial heartlands. All the traditional ingredients of a beach resort are here in force, from superb, clean sands, kitsch amusement arcades and Kiss-Me-Quick hats to the more refined pleasures of its tightknit old-town streets and a genteel round of quiet parks and gardens.

There's no better place to acquaint yourself with the local layout than from the walls of **Scarborough Castle** (April–Oct daily 10am–6pm; Nov–March Wed–Sun 10am–1pm & 2–4pm; £2.30; EH), mounted on a jutting headland between two golden-sanded bays east of the town centre. Bronze and Iron Age relics have been found on the wooded castle crag, together with fragments of a fourth-century Roman signalling station, Saxon and Norman chapels and a Viking camp, reputedly built by a Viking with the nickname of *Scardi* (or "harelip"), from which the town's name derives. The present castle consists mainly of a three-storey keep (1158–64), a thirteenth-century barbican and raking buttressed walls which trace the cliff edge. As you leave the castle, drop into the **Church of St Mary** (1180), immediately below on Castle Road, whose graveyard contains the tomb of Anne Brontë, who died here in 1849.

Most of what passes for family entertainment takes place on the **North Bay** –water slides, kids' amusements, and the miniature North Bay Railway (Easter–Sept daily), which runs up to the **Sea Life Centre**, with its pools of flounders, rock-pool habitats and fishy exhibits. The **South Bay** is more refined, backed by the pleasant Valley Gardens and the Italianate meanderings of the South Cliff Gardens, and topped by an esplanade from which a hydraulic lift putters down to the beach. Here, Scarborough's Regency and Victorian glories are still evident in hotels like the Crown and, most impressively of all, the **Grand Hotel** built in 1867. It's a fair hike from one end of Scarborough to the other; ease the strain by taking one of the **seafront buses** (60p) which run throughout the summer from the *Corner Café* in North Bay to the Spa Complex in South Bay.

Arrival, information and accommodation

The **train station** is at the top of town facing Westborough; buses pull up outside, though the National Express services stop in the car park behind the station. Scarborough's **tourist office** is in Pavilion House, Valley Bridge Road (daily May–Sept 9.30am–6pm; daily Oct–April 10am–4.30pm; ☎01723/373333), just over the road from the station.

Scarborough is crammed with inexpensive **hotels and guest houses**. Happy hunting grounds include North Bay's Queen's Parade, where most of the guest houses have bay views. The cheapest places in town are those without the sea views – try along central Aberdeen Walk (off Westborough), or on North Marine Road and Trafalgar Square, behind Queen's Parade. Above South Bay, hotels tend to be pricier, though there's a clutch of B&Bs along and around West Street. The **youth hostel** occupies a converted watermill at the White House, Burniston Road, Scalby Mills (☎01723/361176); it's a mile or so north of the town centre on the A165 and ten minutes' walk from the Sea Life Centre. Most of the town's huge **campsites** are in this area, too, handy for the North Bay: *Scalby Manor Caravan Park* (☎01723/366212; closed Nov–Easter) and *Scalby Close Park* (☎01723/365908; closed Nov–Easter), both on Burniston Road, have tent spaces.

Hotel Anatolia, 21 West St (☎01723/360864). Nice old Victorian red-brick, one block back from the Esplanade, on a street full of similar choices. No credit cards. ②.

Crown Hotel, Esplanade (☎01723/373491). Built in 1847 in a Regency terrace above South Bay, the *Crown* makes the most of its period features, views and genteel feel. ⑥.

Interludes, 32 Princess St (☎01723/360513). Quiet, theatrically themed, Georgian town house in the old-town streets behind the harbour. Call for details of Stephen Joseph Theatre breaks. ③.

Red Lea Hotel, Prince of Wales Terrace (☎01723/362431). Part of a stylish terrace above South Bay, boasting sea-view rooms and a small indoor pool. ⑤.

Riviera, St Nicholas Cliff (☎01723/372277). Restored Victorian hotel opposite the Grand (down Bar Street, off Westborough) with super bay views and en-suite rooms. ③.

Whiteley Hotel, 99 Queen's Parade (☎01723/373514). Formerly a Victorian merchant's house, this is one of the best Queen's Parade options with good-value en-suite rooms. ②.

Cafés and restaurants

Café Italia, 36 St Nicholas Cliff. Italian coffee-bar next to the *Grand Hotel*, where genuine coffee, foccaccia slices and ice cream keep a battery of regulars happy. Inexpensive.

Il Castello, 34–36 Castle Rd (☎01723/377312). The town's best pizzas, and some inventive home-made pastas and other Italian dishes. Closed Mon & Tues. Moderate.

Gianni's, 13 Victoria Rd (☎01723/507388). The most immediately welcoming of the town's Italian restaurants. Quality pizzas, pastas and quaffable wine by the carafe. Moderate.

The Golden Grid, 4 Sandside (☎01723/360922). The harbourside's choicest fish-and-chip establishment, "catering for the promenader since 1883". Closed Mon–Thurs dinner in winter. Inexpensive to Moderate.

Stephen Joseph Theatre Restaurant, Westborough (☎01723/368463). Fashionable food in the theatre restaurant. Closed Sun, and other evenings when there's no performance. Moderate.

Drinking, nightlife and entertainment

The best **pub** by miles is the *Hole in the Wall* on Vernon Road, a cosy, real-ale haunt with beer-knowledgeable staff and good food (noon–2pm). The *Highlander*, next to the Crown on the Esplanade, has a traditional lounge-bar with beer garden, and its owner has a collection of over a thousand bottles of whisky – drams from around fifty of them are for sale.

The cultural heart of Scarborough is not the Spa Complex or Futurist Theatre and their end-of-pier summer shows but the **Stephen Joseph Theatre** (☎01723/370541), on the corner of Westborough and Valley Bridge Road, opposite the train station. Housed in a former Art Deco cinema, this premieres every new play of local playwright Alan Ayckbourn and promotes strong seasons of theatre and film; a good café-restaurant (see above) and bar is open daily except Sunday.

Robin Hood's Bay

Although known as Robbyn Huddes Bay as early as Tudor times, there's nothing except half-remembered myth to link **ROBIN HOOD'S BAY** with Sherwood's legendary bowman – locals anyway prefer the old name, Bay Town or simply Bay. Perhaps the best-known and most heavily visited spot on the coast, the village fully lives up to its reputation, with narrow streets and pink-tiled cottages toppling down the cliff-edge site, evoking the romance of a time when this was both a hardbitten fishing community and smugglers' den par excellence. From the upper village, lined with Victorian villas, now mostly B&Bs, it's a 1-in-3 walk down the hill to the harbour. Here, Bay is little more than a couple of narrow streets lined with gift shops and cafés, and a steep slipway that leads down to the curving, rocky **shoreline**. When the tide is out, the massive rock beds are exposed, split by a geological fault line and studded with fossil remains. There's an easy walk to **Boggle Hole** and its youth hostel, a mile south, returning inland via South House Farm and the path along the old Scarborough–Whitby railway line.

Buses from Scarborough or Whitby, seven miles north, drop you at the top of the village. Whitby has the nearest train station; **walkers** can make Whitby to Robin Hood's Bay in around three hours along the coastal Cleveland Way. **Accommodation** is often in short supply during high season: the *Victoria Hotel*, Station Road (☎01947/880205; ④), in the upper village has fine views from some of its rooms, or try the *Bay Hotel*, right on the harbour (☎01947/880278; ②), which is the traditional start or end of the Coast-to-Coast Walk. The tiny *Laurel* **pub**, on Main Street (☎01947/880400; ①; minimum stay of two nights), has a bar carved from solid rock. For **food**, the *Bay Horse* is probably the best and the eighteenth-century *Dolphin* in King Street, the oldest pub in the village, has folk nights every Friday. Boggle Hole's **youth hostel**, housed in a former mill, is located in a wooded ravine about a mile south of Robin Hood's Bay at Mill Beck (☎01947/880352). Note that a torch is essential after dark, and that you can't access the hostel along the beach once the tide is up.

Whitby

If there's one essential stop on the North Yorkshire coast it's **WHITBY**, whose historical associations, atmospheric ruins, fishing harbour and intrinsic charm make it many people's favourite northern resort. The seventh-century abbey here made Whitby one of the key foundations of the early Christian period, and a centre of great learning, though little interfered with the fishing community which scraped together a living on the harbour banks of the River Esk below. For a thousand years, the local herring boats landed their catch until the great whaling boom of the eighteenth century transformed the fortunes of the town. Melville's *Moby Dick* makes much of Whitby whalers like William Scoresby, while James Cook took his first seafaring steps from the town in 1746, on his way to becoming a national hero. All four of Captain Cook's ships of discovery – the *Endeavour, Resolution, Adventure* and *Discovery* – were built in Whitby.

Hemmed in by steep cliffs and divided by the River Esk, the town splits into two distinct halves joined by a swing bridge: the **old town** to the east, centered on a curving cobbled street of great character, and the newer (though mostly eighteenth- and nineteenth-century) town across the bridge, generally known as **West Cliff**.

Cobbled **Church Street** is the old town's main thoroughfare, barely changed in aspect since the eighteenth century, though now lined with tearooms and gift shops. At the end of Church Street, you climb the famous **199 steps** of the Church Stairs – now paved, but originally a wide wooden staircase built for pallbearers carrying coffins to the church of St Mary above. Having made the climb, you've followed in the fictional footsteps of Bram Stoker's **Dracula**, who in the eponymous novel (see box overleaf) takes the form of a large dog that bounds up the steps after the wreck of the ship bearing his coffin. The parish church of **St Mary** at the top of the steps, loftily removed from the town it served, is an architectural dog's dinner dating back to 1110, boasting a Norman chancel arch, a profusion of eighteenth-century panelling, box pews unequalled in England and a triple-decker pulpit – note the built-in ear trumpets, added for the benefit of a nineteenth-century rector's deaf wife.

The cliff-top ruins of **Whitby Abbey** (daily: April–Sept 10am–6pm; Oct–March 10am–4pm; £1.70; EH), beyond St Mary's, are some of the most evocative in England, the nave, soaring north transept and lancets of the east end giving a hint of the building's former delicacy and splendour. Its monastery was founded in 657 by Saint Hilda of Hartlepool, daughter of King Oswy of Northumberland, and by 664 had become important enough to host the **Synod of Whitby**, an event of seminal importance in the development of English Christianity. It settled once and for all the question of determining the date of Easter, and adopted the rites and authority of the Roman rather than the Celtic Church. One of the burning issues decided was whether priests should shave their tonsures in the shape of a ring or a crescent. **Caedmon**, one of the brothers at the abbey during its earliest years, has a twenty-foot cross in his memory which stands in front of St Mary's, at the top of the steps. His nine-line *Song of Creation* is the earliest surviving poem in English, making the abbey not only the cradle of English Christianity, but also the birthplace of English literature.

Whitby likes to make a fuss of Captain Cook who served an apprenticeship here from 1746–49 under John Walker, a Quaker ship-owner. The **Captain Cook Memorial Museum** (Easter–Oct daily 9.45am–5pm; £2.60), housed in Walker's rickety old house in Grape Lane (just over the bridge on the east side, on the right), contains an impressive amount of memorabilia, including ships' models, letters and paintings by artists seconded to Cook's voyages.

Final port of call should be the gloriously eccentric **Whitby Museum** in Pannett Park (May–Sept Mon–Sat 9.30am–5.30pm, Sun 2–5pm; Oct–April Mon–Tues 10.30am–1pm, Wed–Sat 10.30am–4pm, Sun 2–4pm; £1), at the back of West Cliff, back from the train station. There's more Cook memorabilia, including various of the ethnic objects and stuffed animals brought back as souvenirs by his crew, as well as casefuls of exhibits devoted to Whitby's seafaring tradition, its whaling industry in particular. Some of the best and largest fossils of Jurassic-period reptiles unearthed on the east coast are also preserved here.

Arrival, information and accommodation

The **train station** lies a couple of hundred yards south of the bridge to the old town. **Buses** from the adjacent bus station run hourly to Robin Hood's Bay, Scarborough, Middlesbrough and points between, and there's a regular summer bus service to Grosmont. Yorkshire Coastliner services from Leeds, York and Pickering drop here,

BRAM STOKER AND DRACULA

Bram Stoker (1847–1912) was born in Dublin and wrote his first stories while working in the Irish civil service. A meeting with Sir Henry Irving in 1877 led him to quit his job and move to London, where he became Irving's manager and close friend. Forgettable adventure novels followed, until in 1890, on holiday in Whitby, Stoker began to become interested in writing a story of vampires and the undead, already popularized in "Gothic" novels earlier that century. Using first-hand observation of a town he knew well – he stayed at a house on the West Cliff, now marked by a plaque – Stoker built a story which mixed real locations, legend, myth and historical fact: the grounding of Count Dracula's ship on Tate Hill Sands was based on an actual event reported in the local papers. The novel was published in 1897 and became synonymous with Stoker's name; it's been filmed, with varing degrees of faithfulness, dozens of times since.

With many of the early chapters recognizably set in Whitby, it's hardly surprising that the town has cashed in on its **Dracula Trail** – ask at the tourist office for details. The various sites – Tate Hill Sands, the abbey, church and steps, the graveyard, Stoker's house – can all be visited, while down on the harbourside the Dracula Experience attempts to pull in punters to its rather lame horror-show antics. Keen interest has also been sparked amongst the **Goth** fraternity, who now come to town en masse a couple of times a year (usually in late spring and around Halloween) for a vampire's ball, concerts and readings; at these times the streets are overrun with pasty-faced characters in Regency dress, wedding gowns, top hats and capes, meeting and greeting at their unofficial headquarters, the otherwise sedate *Elsinore* pub on Flowergate. A kind of truce has been called with the authorities at St Mary's Church, who understandably objected to the more lurid goings-on in the churchyard at midnight; these have largely been curtailed and now there's even a special Goths service held at the church.

too, as do National Express buses from London and York. Whitby's **tourist office** (daily: May–Sept 9.30am–6pm; Oct–April 10am–4.30pm; ☎01947/602674) is a right turn outside the train station to the corner of Langborne Road and New Quay Road.

Most **B&Bs** are on West Cliff, in the streets stretching back from the elegant Royal Crescent, while across the river in the old town, several pubs have rooms. The popular **youth hostel**, East Cliff (☎01947/602878), is a stone's throw from the abbey – book well in advance. There's a backpackers' hostel, *Harbour Grange*, at Spital Bridge, also on the eastern side of the river (☎01947/600817). The nearest **campsite** is a mile west of town on the Sandsend road, at *Sandfield House Caravan Park* (☎01947/602660; closed Nov to mid-March), though it only has a few tent sites.

The Dolphin, Bridge St (☎01947/602197). The pub by the swing bridge has riverside views from some of its B&B rooms. ②.

Duke of York, Church St (☎01947/600324) At the bottom of the 199 steps, this popular pub has en-suite rooms overlooking the harbour, and is only a few steps from the harbour beach. ②.

Lavinia House, 3 East Crescent, Khyber Pass (☎01947/602945). Comfortable family-run guest house with five rooms, the largest at the front boasting sea views. No credit cards. ②.

Number Five, 5 Havelock Place (☎01947/606361). Amiable West Cliff B&B which provides a good breakfast and has a good atmosphere. No credit cards. ①.

Shepherd's Purse, 95 Church St (☎01947/820228). Popular wholefood shop and restaurant with its best rooms set around a galleried courtyard; vegetarian breakfast available. ②.

White Horse & Griffin, Church St (☎01947/604857). Easily the most atmospheric place to stay in the old town – a welcoming eighteenth-century coaching inn with comfortable en-suite rooms, open fires and a good fish restaurant. ②.

Cafés and restaurants

Ditto, 26 Skinner St (☎01947/601404). Smashing Italian restaurant – the blackboard menu changes daily and you need to book in advance. Dinner only, closed Sun & Mon. Moderate to Expensive.

The Dolphin, Bridge St (☎01947/602197). Great fresh fish meals in the pub – from calamari with salsa to grilled tuna or paella – as well as a popular carvery.

Grapevine, 2 Grape Lane (☎01947/820275). Best café in town, whose tiny kitchen dishes up tasty tapas-style lunches and dinners (dinners, weekends only in winter). Inexpensive to Moderate.

Magpie Cafe, 14 Pier Rd (☎01947/602058). The traditional fish-and-chip choice in town for over forty years, with a wide-ranging menu. Closes 9pm. Moderate.

Shepherd's Purse, 95 Church St (☎01947/820228). Daytime wholefood café meals give way to pizza, pasta and fish dinners in hippy-rustic surroundings. Moderate.

Trenchers, New Quay Rd (☎01947/603212). Highly rated fish-and-chip restaurant, with booth seating, snappy service and mountainous portions. Closed Nov–March. Moderate.

Drinking, music and festivals

There are scores of **pubs** in Whitby, including the *Duke of York* on Church Street, at the bottom of the 199 steps, which has harbour views and, on the other side of the river, the mock-rustic *Tap & Spile*, on New Quay Road – a real-ale haunt, with live folk music nearly every night. Whitby is at the centre of the local **music scene** – English folk's first family, the Waterson/Carthys, are from nearby Robin Hood's Bay. Matters all come to a head during the annual **Whitby Folk Week** in August (the week immediately preceding the bank holiday), where the town's streets, pubs and concert halls are filled day and night with singers, bands, traditional dancers, storytellers and music workshops. A special festival campsite is usually set up, but if you want regular accommodation for this week, book well in advance. Other festivals throughout the year also make a splash, some with a seafaring theme; the **Regatta** every August is a weekend of fairground rides, spectacular harbourside fireworks and boat races; and the Goths descend a couple of times a year (see box opposite) for a good-natured vampiric vacation.

Staithes

A fine coastal walk from Whitby through pretty Runswick Bay leads in around four hours to the fishing village of **STAITHES**. At first sight, it's an improbably beautiful grouping of huddled stone houses around a small harbour, backed by the severe outcrop of Cowbar Nab, a sheer cliff-face which protects the northern flank of the village. There's much less tourism here than in Robin Hood's Bay, which means few if any gift shops and only a smattering of cafés and B&Bs. Storms and floods have battered Staithes for centuries: the *Cod & Lobster*, the pub at the harbour, has been rebuilt three times and is shuttered against the wind, while the draper's shop in which James Cook first worked before moving to Whitby collapsed completely in 1745 – its rebuilt successor is now marked by a plaque. Cook is remembered in the **Captain Cook and Staithes Heritage Centre**, on the High Street (daily 10am–5.30pm; £1.75), which recreates an eighteenth-century street among other interesting exhibits.

You could stay at one of the B&Bs in the houses at the top of the village, but better **accommodation** is available down below, either at the *Endeavour Restaurant* (☎01947/840825; no credit cards; ③; closed Sun in winter) – itself the best place to eat for miles around – or at *York House*, High Barrass (☎01947/841187; no credit cards; ②), up a flight of steps off the High Street, at the bottom of the village. There's **camping** back up the road out of the village at *Staithes Caravan Park*, Warp Mill (☎01947/840291; closed Nov–Feb).

travel details

Trains

Harrogate to: Knaresborough (2 hourly; 15min); Leeds (2 hourly; 45min); York (hourly; 30min).

Hull to: Beverley (Mon–Sat hourly, 4 daily on Sun; 15min); Leeds (hourly; 1hr); Scarborough (every 2hr; 1hr 30min); York (10 daily; 1hr 15min).

Leeds to: Bradford (4 hourly; 20min); Harrogate (2 hourly; 45min); Hull (hourly; 1hr); Knaresborough (2 hourly; 45min); Settle (3–8 daily; 1hr); Sheffield (2 hourly; 45min–1hr 15min); Skipton (hourly; 40min); York (2 hourly; 40min).

Pickering to: Grosmont (April–Oct 5–8 daily, plus limited winter service; 1hr).

Scarborough to: Hull (every 2hr; 1hr 30min); York (8–15 daily; 45min).

Sheffield to: Leeds (2 hourly; 45min–1hr 15min); York (hourly; 1hr 20min).

Whitby to: Danby (June–Sept 4 daily; Oct–March Mon–Sat 4 daily; 40min); Grosmont (June–Sept 4 daily; Oct–March Mon–Sat 4 daily; 15min).

York to: Bradford (every 1–2hr; 1hr); Harrogate (hourly; 40min); Hull (hourly; 1hr 15min); Leeds (2 hourly; 40min); Scarborough (8–15 daily; 45min); Sheffield (hourly; 1hr 20min).

Buses

Harrogate to: Knaresborough (4 hourly; 20min); Leeds (1–2 hourly; 40min); Pateley Bridge (Mon–Sat hourly, 2 daily on Sun; 50min); Ripon (2 hourly; 30min); York (Mon–Sat hourly; 1hr 15min).

Helmsley to: Pickering (hourly; 40min); Scarborough (hourly; 1hr 40min); York (Mon–Sat 3 daily ; 1hr 30min).

Pickering to: Castle Howard (May–Sept 1–3 daily; 30min); Helmsley (3–7 daily; 40min); Scarborough (Mon–Sat hourly, 6 daily on Sun; 1hr); Whitby (5 daily; 1hr); York (Mon–Sat hourly, 3 daily on Sun; 1hr 20min).

Scarborough to: Helmsley (3–6 daily; 1hr 40min); Hull (1 daily; 2hr); Leeds (hourly; 3hr); Malton (hourly; 1hr); Middlesbrough (4–8 daily; 2hr); Pickering (hourly; 1hr); Robin Hood's Bay (hourly; 45min); Whitby (hourly; 1hr); York (hourly; 1hr 45min).

Settle to: Horton-in-Ribblesdale (Mon–Sat 3–5 daily; 15min); Ingleton (Mon–Sat 3–4 daily; 30min); Skipton (Mon–Sat hourly; 40min).

Skipton to: Buckden (Mon–Sat 1–2 daily; 1hr); Grassington (Mon–Sat hourly; 30min); Harrogate (5–6 daily; 1hr); Ilkley (hourly; 20min); Keighley (Mon–Sat hourly; 30min); Kettlewell (Mon–Sat 1–2 daily; 1hr); Knaresborough (4 daily; 1hr 30min); Malham (Mon–Fri 2–3 daily; 40min–1hr 15min); Settle (Mon–Sat hourly; 40min); York (Mon–Sat 4 daily; 1hr 50min).

Whitby to: Castle Howard (May–Oct 1 daily; 1hr 15min); Goathland (Mon–Fri 2 daily; 30min); Grosmont (July–Sept 7 daily; 30min); Hull (1 daily; 2hr 45min); Malton (5 daily; 1hr 30min); Pickering (5 daily; 1hr); Robin Hood's Bay (hourly; 30min); Staithes (hourly; 30min); York (Mon–Sat 4 daily, 1 on Sun; 2hr).

York to: Beverley (4 daily; 1hr 15min); Bradford (5 daily; 1hr 45min); Castle Howard (1–2 daily; 1hr); Harrogate (Mon–Sat hourly; 1hr 15min); Hull (5 daily; 1hr 30min); Leeds (10 daily; 45min); Pickering (Mon–Sat hourly, 4 daily on Sun; 1hr 20min); Sheffield (4 daily; 2hr 15min); Skipton (5 daily; 1hr 50min); Whitby (Mon–Sat 4 daily, 1 on Sun; 2hr).

CHAPTER ELEVEN

THE NORTHEAST

For England's northeastern region – in particular the counties of **Northumberland** and **Durham** – the centuries between the Roman invasion and the 1603 union of England and Scotland were a period of almost incessant turbulence. To mark the empire's limit and to contain the troublesome tribes of the far north, **Hadrian's Wall** was built along the seventy-odd miles between the North Sea and the west coast, an extraordinary military structure that is now one of the country's most evocative ruins. When the Romans departed the northeast was plunged into chaos and divided into unstable Saxon principalities until order was restored by the kings of Northumbria, who dominated the region from 600 until the 870s. It was they who nourished the region's early Christian tradition, which achieved its finest flowering with the creation of the **Lindisfarne Gospels** on what is now known as Holy Island. The monks abandoned their island at the end of the ninth century, in advance of the Vikings' destruction of the Northumbrian kingdom, and only after the Norman Conquest did the northeast again become part of a greater England.

The Norman kings and their immediate successors repeatedly attempted to subdue Scotland, passing effective regional control to powerful local lords. Their authority is recalled by a sequence of formidable coastal fortresses, most impressively those at **Bamburgh**, **Alnwick** and **Warkworth**, and also by **Durham Cathedral**, the magnificent twelfth-century church of the Prince Bishops of Durham, who ruled the whole of County Durham. Long after the northeast had ceased to be a critical military zone, its character and appearance were transformed by the **Industrial Revolution**. Coal had been mined here for hundreds of years, but exploitation only began in earnest towards the end of the eighteenth century, when two main coalfields were established – one dominating County Durham from the Pennines to the sea, the other stretching north along the Northumberland coast from the Tyne. The world's first **railway**, the **Darlington and Stockton** line, was opened in 1825 to move coal to the nearest port for export, while local coal and ore also fuelled the foundries of **Middlesbrough**, which in turn supplied the shipbuilding and heavy-engineering companies of Tyneside. The region boomed, creating a score of sizeable towns, amongst which Newcastle was preeminent – as it remains today.

Most visitors dodge the industrial areas, bypassing the towns along the **Tees Valley** – Darlington, Stockton, Middlesbrough and Hartlepool – on the way to **Durham**. From

---

ACCOMMODATION PRICE CODES

Throughout this guide, hotel and B&B accommodation is priced on a scale of ① to ⑨, the number indicating the **lowest price** you could expect to pay per night in that establishment for a **double room** in high season. The prices indicated by the codes are as follows:

① under £40	④ £60–70	⑦ £110–150
② £40–50	⑤ £70–90	⑧ £150–200
③ £50–60	⑥ £90–110	⑨ over £200

Durham it's a short hop to **Newcastle**, an earthy city distinguished by some fine Victorian buildings and a vibrant cultural scene and nightlife. North, past the old colliery villages, the brighter parts of the Northumberland coast boast some fine castles, as well as **Holy Island**, the extravagant ramparts of **Berwick-upon-Tweed**, a string of superb, if chilly, beaches, and the desolate archipelago of the **Farne Islands**. Inland there are the scenic Durham **dales** and the harsh landscapes of **Northumberland National Park**, a huge chunk of moorland and tree plantations that edges the most dramatic portion of Hadrian's Wall. The wall itself is easily visited from the appealing abbey-town of **Hexham**, just half an hour from Newcastle.

The **Northeast Explorer Pass** (1-day, £4.95) pays for itself on long journeys, giving unlimited travel on local buses; and pick up a copy of the **Northumberland Public Transport Guide** (£1), available from local tourist offices. The main long-distance footpath through the northeast is the **Pennine Way**, which crosses Hadrian's Wall and climaxes in a climb through the Northumberland National Park and Cheviot Hills. Less demanding is the 63-mile **St Cuthbert's Way**, which links Holy Island with Melrose, in Scotland.

Durham

The view from **DURHAM** train station is one of the finest in northern England – a panoramic prospect of Durham Cathedral, its towers dominating the skyline from the top of a steep sandstone bluff within a narrow bend of the River Wear. This dramatic site has been the resting place of St Cuthbert since 995, when his body was moved here from nearby Chester-le-Street, over one hundred years after his fellow monks had fled from Lindisfarne in fear of the Vikings, carrying his coffin before them. Cuthbert's hallowed remains made Durham a place of pilgrimage for both the Saxons and the Normans, who began work on the present cathedral at the end of the eleventh century. In the meantime, William the Conqueror, aware of the defensive possibilities of the site, had built a castle that was to be the precursor of ever more elaborate fortifications. Subsequently, the bishops of Durham were granted extensive powers to control the troublesome northern marches of the kingdom, ruling as semi-independent **Prince Bishops**, with their own army, mint and courts of law. The bishops were at the peak of their power in the fourteenth century, but thereafter their office went into decline, especially in the wake of the Reformation, yet they clung to the vestiges of their powers until 1836, when they ceded them to the Crown. They abandoned Durham Castle for their palace in Bishop Auckland and transferred their old home to the fledgling **Durham University**, England's third oldest seat of learning after Oxford and Cambridge.

The City

Surrounded on three sides by the River Wear, Durham's surprisingly compact centre is readily approached by two small bridges which lead from the western, modern part of town across the river to the spur containing castle and cathedral. The commercial heart of this "old town" area is the triangular **Market Place**, inappropriately dominated by an equestrian statue of the third Marquis of Londonderry, a much-hated nineteenth-century colliery owner.

From Market Place, it's a five-minute walk up Saddler Street to the majestic **Durham Cathedral** (daily May–Sept 9.30am–8pm; Oct–April Mon–Sat 9.30am–6pm, Sun 2.30–5pm; £2 suggested donation), facing the castle across the manicured Palace Green. Built to house the remains of St Cuthbert, the present cathedral was completed in 1133, and has survived the centuries pretty much intact, a supreme example of the Norman-Romanesque style. Entry is through the northwest porch, where a replica of

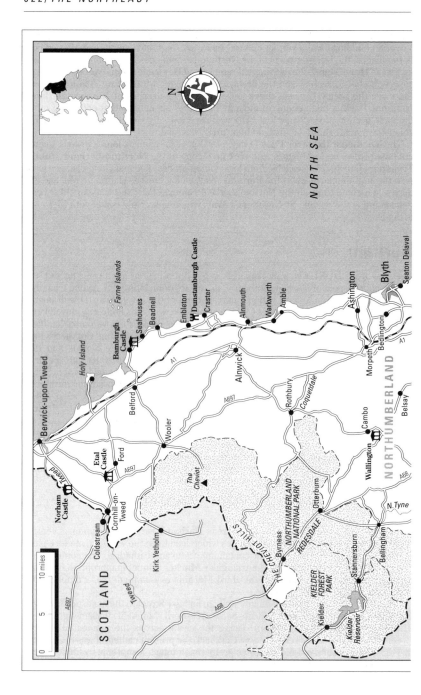

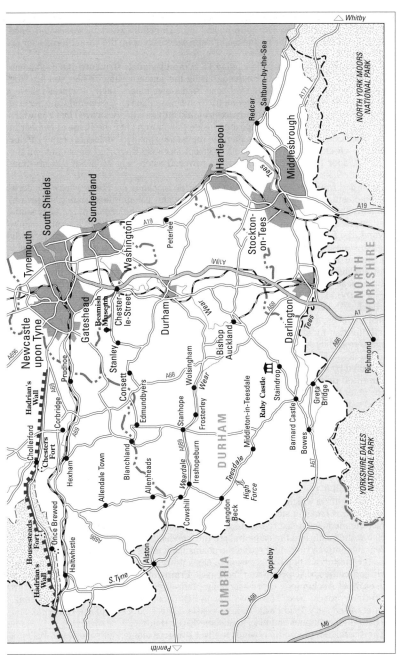

△ Whitby

NORTH YORK MOORS NATIONAL PARK

Saltburn-by-the-Sea

A171

Redcar

Hartlepool

Middlesbrough

Tees

A19

Stockton-on-Tees

A19

South Shields

Sunderland

Washington

A19

Peterlee

NORTH YORKSHIRE

Tynemouth

A1(M)

A596

Newcastle upon Tyne

Gateshead

Beamish Museum

Chester-le-Street

Durham

Wear

Bishop Auckland

A68

Darlington

Tees

A1

A66

Richmond

Hadrian's Wall

Prudhoe

Stanley

Consett

Wolsingham

Raby Castle

Staindrop

Corbridge

A69

Edmundbyers

A68

Stanhope

Frosterley

Wear

Middleton-in-Teesdale

Barnard Castle

Greta Bridge

Chollerford

Chesters Fort

Hexham

Blanchland

A689

Weardale

Treshopeburn

Teesdale

Bowes

A67

YORKSHIRE DALES NATIONAL PARK

Allendale Town

Allenheads

DURHAM

High Force

Housesteads Fort

Once Brewed

Haltwhistle

A596

Cowshill

Langdon Beck

Hadrian's Wall

Alston

Appleby

CUMBRIA

A69

S. Tyne

M6

▽ Penrith

© Crown copyright

the lion-head **sanctuary knocker** is a reminder of the medieval distinction between secular and religious law. The church used to be ringed by wooden crosses and, once a fugitive reached them, he or she could claim sanctuary from the lay authorities for up to 35 days.

The awe-inspiring **nave**, completed in 1128, is an inventive structure that used pointed arches for the first time in England, raising the vaulted ceiling to new and dizzying heights. The weight of the stone is borne by massive pillars, their heaviness relieved by striking Moorish-influenced geometric patterns – chevrons, diamonds and vertical fluting. Most of the cathedral's early fixtures and fittings were destroyed by Cromwell's Scottish prisoners, who were deposited inside the church after the Battle of Dunbar in 1650. The Scots did not, however, damage the gaudily painted, sixteenth-century **Prior Castell's clock**, located in the south transept, because it sported their emblem, the thistle. A door here gives access to the **tower** (Easter–Sept Mon–Sat 9.30am–4pm; Oct–Easter 9.30am–3pm; £2).

Separated from the nave by a Victorian marble screen is the **choir**, where the dark-stained Restoration stalls are overshadowed by the vainglorious **bishop's throne**, reputedly the highest in medieval Christendom, built on the orders of the fourteenth-century Bishop Hatfield, whose militaristic alabaster tombstone lies just below. Beyond, the **Chapel of the Nine Altars** dates from the thirteenth century, its Early English stonework distinguished by its delicacy of detail. Here, and around the adjoining **Shrine of St Cuthbert**, much of the stonework is Frosterley marble, each dark shaft bearing its own fancy pattern of fossils.

Back near the entrance, at the west end of the church, the **Galilee Chapel** was begun in the 1170s, its light and exotic decoration in imitation of the Great Mosque of Cordoba. Subdivided by twelve slender columns, each surrounded by a medley of geometric patterns, the chapel contains the simple tombstone of the **Venerable Bede**, the Northumbrian monk credited with being England's first historian. Bede died at the monastery of Jarrow in 735 and his remains were transferred here in 1020. An ancient wooden doorway opposite the main entrance leads into the spacious **cloisters**, which are flanked by what remains of the monastic buildings. These include the undercroft of the **monks' dormitory** (April–Sept Mon–Sat 10am–3.30pm, Sun 12.30–3pm; 80p) and, more potently, the **Treasury** (Mon–Sat 10am–4.30pm, Sun 2–4.30pm; £2), which is stuffed with bishops' rings and seals, vestments, illuminated manuscripts and relics of St Cuthbert – principally fragments of his much-travelled oak coffin. The original sanctuary knocker is here, too, dating from 1140.

Across Palace Green from the cathedral, **Durham Castle** (Easter & July–Sept Mon–Sat 10am–12.30pm & 2–4pm, Sun 10am–noon & 2–4pm; Oct–June Mon, Wed & Sat 2–4pm; £3) lost its medieval appearance long ago, during refurbishments arranged by a succession of Prince Bishops, but the university went further by renovating the old keep as a hall of residence. It's only possible to visit the castle on a 45-minute guided tour, highlights of which include rapid visits to the fifteenth-century kitchen, a climb up the enormous hanging staircase and the jog down to the so-called "Norman chapel" – in fact the medieval treasure room.

Below the castle and the cathedral are the wooded banks of the **River Wear**, where a pleasant footpath runs right round the peninsula. It takes about thirty minutes to complete the circuit, passing a succession of elegant bridges with fine vantage points over town and cathedral. On the riverbank, past **Framwellgate Bridge**, the university's **Museum of Archeology** (April–Oct daily 11am–4pm; Nov–March Mon, Thurs & Fri 12.30–3pm, Sat & Sun 11.30am–3.30pm; £1) occupies an old stone fulling mill. Eighteenth-century **Prebends Bridge** boasts celebrated views of the cathedral, and the path then continues round to handsome **Elvet Bridge**.

The alternate route from Prebends to Elvet Bridge is along South and North Bailey, a cobbled thoroughfare lined by Georgian houses, many of them occupied by university

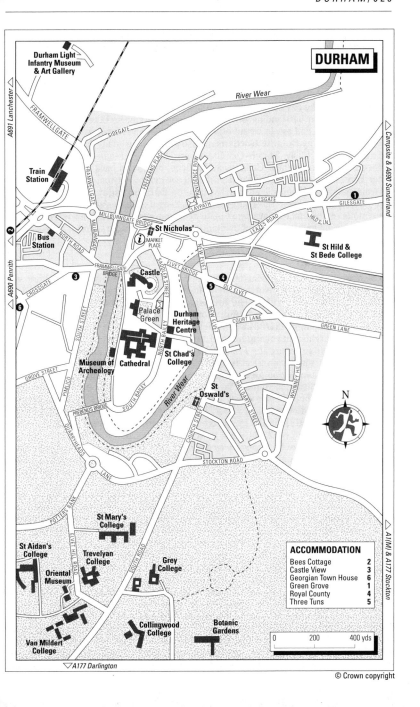

DURHAM

Durham Light Infantry Museum & Art Gallery

River Wear

A691 Lanchester

FRAMWELLGATE

SIDEGATE

FREEMANS PLACE

PROVIDENCE ROW

Campsite & A690 Sunderland

Train Station

MILLBURNGATE

FRAMWELLGATE

CLAYPATH

GILESGATE

GILESGATE

ST HILD'S LN.

❶

A690 Penrith

❷

Bus Station

NORTH ROAD

MILLBURNGATE BRIDGE

St Nicholas'

ⓘ MARKET PLACE

LEAZES ROAD

NEW ELVET

St Hild & St Bede College

FRAMWELLGATE BRIDGE

CROSSGATE

❸

SADDLER STREET

ELVET BRIDGE

Castle

❹

❻

SOUTH STREET

Palace Green

NORTH BAILEY

Durham Heritage Centre

OLD ELVET

NEW ELVET

COURT LANE

GREEN LANE

GROVE STREET

PIMLICO

Museum of Archeology

Cathedral

St Chad's College

SOUTH BAILEY

River Wear

St Oswald's

CHURCH STREET

HALLGARTH STREET

WHINNEY HILL

N

PREBENDS BRIDGE

QUARRYHEADS LANE

STOCKTON ROAD

A1(M) & A177 Stockton

POTTERS BANK

St Aidan's College

ELVET HILL ROAD

St Mary's College

Trevelyan College

Oriental Museum

SOUTH ROAD

Grey College

ACCOMMODATION

Bees Cottage	2
Castle View	3
Georgian Town House	6
Green Grove	1
Royal County	4
Three Tuns	5

Van Mildert College

Collingwood College

Botanic Gardens

| 0 | 200 | 400 yds |

▽*A177 Darlington*

© Crown copyright

college buildings. The church of St Mary-le-Bow, on North Bailey, immediately below the cathedral, does duty as the **Durham Heritage Centre** (Easter to late May Sat & Sun 2–4.30pm; late May to June & Sept daily 2–4.30pm; July & Aug daily 11.30am–4.30pm; £1), a pot-pourri of audio-visual displays, dioramas and exhibitions.

Durham's other noteworthy attraction is the university's **Oriental Museum** (Mon–Fri 9.30am–5pm, Sat & Sun 2–5pm; £1.50), set among college buildings a couple of miles south of the city centre on Elvet Hill (off South Road), whose wide-ranging collection contains an outstanding display of Chinese ceramics. Take bus #5 or #6 (to Bishop Auckland) and ask to be put off on South Road. You may as well then continue on foot to the nearby **Botanic Gardens**, whose glasshouses (daily 9am–4pm; £1), café and visitor centre (daily: March–Oct 10am–5pm; Nov–Feb 11am–4pm; £1) are set in eighteen wooded acres near Collingwood College; buses run back to the centre from either Elvet Hill Road or South Road. North of the centre, a twenty-minute walk from the train station up Framwellgate takes you to the **Durham Light Infantry Museum and Art Gallery** (Tues–Sat 10am–5pm, Sun 2–5pm; £2), at Aykley Heads, whose eponymous regimental displays won't be to everyone's taste, though it's worth enquiring about the art gallery's current exhibitions and concert programme.

Practicalities

Durham **train station** is about ten minutes' walk from the city centre, either via Millburngate Bridge or via North Road – the site of the **bus station** – then the pedestrianized Framwellgate Bridge. The **tourist office** is in Market Place (June & Sept Mon–Sat 9.30am–5.30pm; July & Aug Mon–Sat 9.30am–6pm, Sun 2–5pm; Oct–May Mon–Sat 10am–5pm; ☎0191/384 3720); pick up a copy of *What's on in Durham*, listing local events. You can rent **rowing boats** from Brown's Boathouse, Elvet Bridge, or take the one-hour **cruise** aboard the *Prince Bishop* (☎0191/386 9525; £3), which has regular summer departures from Elvet Bridge.

Durham has a long list of **guest houses** and **B&Bs**, with particular concentrations on Gilesgate, northeast of Market Place, and around Crossgate, south of the bus station. Good budget bets include *Green Grove*, 99 Gilesgate (☎0191/384 4361; no credit cards; ①), and *Bees Cottage Guest House*, Bridge Street, off Sutton Street, not far from the train station (☎0191/384 5775; no credit cards; ③). *Castle View Guest House*, 4 Crossgate (☎0191/386 8852; ③), next to St Margaret's Church, does indeed have a great castle view, while the *Georgian Town House*, 10 Crossgate (☎0191/386 8070; no credit cards; ③), has some rooms with cathedral views. The *Royal County*, Old Elvet, just across Elvet Bridge (☎0191/386 6821; ⑦), is Durham's top hotel; its sister hotel, the *Three Tuns*, New Elvet (☎0191/386 4326; ⑦), is a former sixteenth-century coaching inn. The cheapest beds in town are at the various colleges of **Durham University** (available at Christmas, Easter & July–Sept) – either dormitory-style accommodation or private rooms (②, including breakfast). Call University College (☎0191/374 3863), whose rooms are inside the castle, and St Hild and St Bede on Leazes Road (☎0191/374 3069); the tourist office has a full list. The nearest **campsite**, the *Grange Camping and Caravan Site* (☎0191/384 4778), beside the junction of the A1(M) and the A690, is two miles northeast of the city on Meadow Lane; take bus #220 or #222 for Sunderland.

Vennel's, Saddler's Yard – named after the skinny alley or "vennel" where it stands (next to Waterstone's, off Saddler St) – serves light lunches in a little hidden courtyard. Further up the hill, on Palace Green, the *Almshouse* conjures up mostly vegetarian meals for around £5 (open until 8pm in summer). For Italian food, try *Emilio's*, 96 Elvet Bridge, or *Pizzeria Venezia*, 4 Framwellgate Bridge (closed Sun). The resolutely modern Med-British dishes at *Bistro 21*, a converted farmhouse at Aykley Heads (☎0191/384 4354; closed Sun), north of the centre, make for a good night out. For riverside views, eat a **pub** lunch at the *Coach & Eight* opposite or the *Swan & Three Cygnets* on the west side of Elvet Bridge. Durham's other central **pubs** include the *Court Inn*, on Court Lane, and the lively *Hogshead*, 58 Saddler St, with its selection of real ales.

For more highbrow entertainment, the university sponsors an annual season of **classical concerts** at various venues around the city, while **Durham Art Gallery** (☎0191/384 2214) at Aykley Heads hosts piano recitals and other concerts. Durham Student's Union (☎0191/374 3310) puts on **gigs** during term time, with rock, jazz and comedy most regularly performed at Dunelm House, New Elvet. In June the **Durham Regatta** packs the riverbanks and river, and the same month sees the start of the university's **arts week**. The **Miners' Gala** in July – when the traditional lodge banners are paraded through the streets – recalls the city's proud industrial past; sorrows about its demise are drowned at two respected annual **beer festivals**, one in February, one in September.

The rest of County Durham

In the 1910s, **County Durham** produced 41 million tons of coal each year, raised from three hundred pits by 170,000 miners. This was the heyday of an industry that since the 1830s had transformed the county's landscape, spawning scores of pit villages which matted the rolling hills from the Pennines to the North Sea, between Newcastle and Stockton-on-Tees. The miners' union, waging a long struggle against serf-like pay and conditions, achieved a gradual improvement of the miners' lot, but could not prevent the slow decline of the Durham coalfield from the 1920s: just 127 pits were left when the mines were nationalized in 1947, and only 34 in 1969. Today, only a mere handful of pits remain strung out along the coast to exploit the broader seams that run under the sea.

For a taste of the old days, most people troop off to the reconstructed colliery village (and much more) at the open-air **Beamish Museum**, north of Durham. The county's other obvious tourist attractions are to the west of the coalfield. There's **Raby Castle**, a stately home to the east of the market town of **Barnard Castle**, itself the setting for the opulent art collection of the **Bowes Museum**. Farther west lie the Pennine valleys of **Teesdale** and **Weardale**, whose upper reaches boast some enjoyable moorland scenery, most dramatically at Teesdale's **High Force** waterfall. You may need to make use of Durham County Council's public transport **enquiry line** (☎0191/383 3337 Mon–Thurs 8.30am–5pm, Fri 8.30am–4.30pm).

Beamish Museum

Established in 1970, the open-air **Beamish Museum** (April–June, Sept & Oct daily 10am–5pm; July & Aug 10am–6pm; Nov–March Tues–Thurs, Sat & Sun 10am–4pm; last admission 2hr before closing; £3–10 depending on season) spreads out across the fields beside the A693 about ten miles north of Durham. It's extremely popular with local people, who come to chew the fat with the costumed guides, most of whom are recruited for their real-life experience. The collier who takes you down the re-opened drift mine was once a miner, and the blokes driving the steam engine used to work for British Rail, adding a touch of authenticity and sadness to the proceedings, as those industries continue to deteriorate in tandem with the boom in heritage museums like this one.

The museum divides into four main sections: a pint-sized colliery village as of 1913, complete with cottages, Methodist chapel, old stone winding house and drift mine; a train station and goods yard; an early nineteenth-century manor and farm with traditional breeds of livestock; and a large-scale recreation of a 1920s north country town, its High Street lined by shops, bank, pub, dentist's surgery, printer's workshop, newspaper office, garage and solicitor's office. Reckon on around five hours to get round the lot in summer, much less in winter when only the town and train station are open.

The #720 **bus** from Durham bus station (hourly) or the #709 from Newcastle (hourly from Eldon Square) drop you close to the main entrance. The on-site **Beamish tourist office** (same hours as the museum; ☎0191/370 2533) lists accommodation in the nearby village and around the park. There's also a good **pub**, the *Shepherd & Shepherdess* just outside the main gate.

Bishop Auckland

Eleven miles southwest of Durham city, **BISHOP AUCKLAND** has been the country home of the bishops of Durham since the twelfth century and their official residence for more than a hundred years. Their palace, the gracious **Auckland Castle** (May, June & Sept Fri & Sun 2–5pm; July Thurs, Fri & Sun 2–5pm; Aug Wed–Sun 2–5pm; £3), standing in 800-acre grounds, is approached through an imposing gatehouse just off the town's Market Place. The palace has been extensively remodelled since its medieval incarnation, redesigned to satisfy the whims of such occupants as the seventeenth-century Bishop Cosin who refurbished the original banqueting hall to create today's splendid marble and limestone **chapel**. Here, the stained glass windows relate the stories of early Christian saints familiar throughout the northeast, especially Cuthbert, Bede and Aidan. The town itself plays second fiddle to the castle, though the Market Place is handsome enough. Or you could follow the mile-long lane that leads north to the remains of **Binchester Roman Fort** (Easter & May–Sept daily 11am–5pm; £1.50) – Roman Vinovia – which boasts the country's best example of a **hypocaust**, built to warm the private bath suite of the garrison's commanding officer.

Bishop Auckland is linked by **train** to Darlington while **buses** drop you just a few minutes' west of the town hall, in Market Place, which houses the **tourist office** (April–Sept Mon–Fri 10am–5pm, Sat 9am–4pm Sun 1–4pm; rest of year closed Sun; ☎01388/604922). **Accommodation** options include the *Queen's Head Hotel*, 38 Market Place (☎01388/603477; ③), and the *Albion Cottage Guest House*, on Albion Terrace (☎01388/602 217; no credit cards; ①). For **food**, the *Laurel Room* in the Town Hall, Market Place, is open until 4pm for snacks and drinks (closed Sat & Sun), or try *Rossi's Tea Room*, also in Market Place (closes 3.30pm & all Sun).

Raby Castle

The #8 bus between Bishop Auckland and Barnard Castle runs down the A688 to provide access to the sprawling battlements of **Raby Castle** (Easter week daily 1–5pm; May & June Wed & Sun 1–5pm; July–Sept Mon–Fri & Sun 1–5pm; castle & gardens £4; gardens only £1.50), roughly halfway between the two. The castle mostly dates from the fourteenth century, reflecting the power of the Neville family, who ruled the local roost until 1569. It was then that Charles Neville helped plan the "Rising of the North", the abortive attempt to replace Elizabeth I with Mary Queen of Scots. The revolt was a dismal failure, and Neville's estates were confiscated, with Raby subsequently passing to the Vanes, now the Lords Barnard, who still live in the castle. Raby's focal point is the first-floor Baron's Hall, still of cathedral-like dimensions in spite of the floor being raised ten feet in 1787 to let carriages pass through the neo-Gothic entrance below. Outside the castle, in the two-hundred-acre **deer park**, are the walled **gardens** (same days as castle 11am–5.30pm), where peaches, apricots and pineapples once flourished under the careful gaze of forty Victorian gardeners. Heated cavity walls and curtains protected the trees from frost – above the last remaining apricot tree you can still see the hooks for the curtain rail.

Barnard Castle

Fifteen miles southwest of Bishop Auckland, the remains of **Barnard Castle** (Easter–Oct daily 10am–6pm; Nov–Easter Wed–Sun 10am–4pm; EH; £2.30), poking out from a cliff high above the River Tees, overlook the town which grew up in its shadow. First fortified in the eleventh century, the castle was long a stronghold of the Balliols, an Anglo-Scottish family interminably embroiled in the struggle for the Scottish crown. It was one of this clan, Bernard, who built the circular tower which survives to this day, an impressive thirteenth-century fortification just to the right of the later Round Tower, where a beautiful oriel window carries the emblematic boar of Richard III, one of the subsequent owners.

Castle aside, the prime attaction is the grand French-style chateau that constitutes the **Bowes Museum** (daily 11am–5pm; £3.90), half a mile west of the centre, up Newgate. Begun in 1869, the chateau was commissioned by John and Josephine Bowes, a local businessman and MP and his French actress wife, who spent much of their time in Paris collecting ostentatious treasures and antiques – including furniture, paintings, tapestries, ceramics and incidental curiosities, notably a late eighteenth-century mechanical silver swan in the lobby which still performs twice daily, preening to a brief forty-second melodic burst. Among the paintings, look out for El Greco's *The Tears of St Peter*, elsewhere, there's varied interest in the French decorative and religious art, English period furniture, and an excellent toy collection – whose nineteenth-century lead soldiers were made possible by the new industry in nearby Stanhope. Back in the town centre, it's a pleasant mile-and-a-half walk from the castle, southeast along the banks of the Tees, to the shattered ruins of **Egglestone Abbey** (free access), a minor Premonstratensian foundation dating from 1195. You can also get here on bus #79 from Barnard Castle, getting off at Abbey Bridge End.

Buses stop on either side of central Galgate – once the road out to the town gallows, hence the name. The **tourist office**, in Woodleigh on Flatts Road, is at the end of Galgate by the castle (daily: April–Oct 10am–6pm; Nov–March 11am–4pm; ☎01833/690909). There are several convenient **B&Bs**, such as *The Homelands*, 85 Galgate (☎01833/638757; no credit cards; ②), and *Marwood View*, 98 Galgate (☎01833/637493; no credit cards; ②). The nearest **campsite** is two miles southwest of the centre at *West Roods Farm*, Boldron (☎01833/690116; closed Oct–March), on the way to Bowes. For **food**, the *Hayloft*, in Horsemarket off Galgate (closed Sun in winter), and the *Market Place Teashop*, 29 Market Place, both get the gastronomical thumbs-up. *Oldfield's*, at 7 The Bank (☎01833/630700; closed all Sun & Tues eve), serves light meals during the day, but is also open for dinner.

Teesdale

Extending twenty-odd miles northwest from Barnard Castle, Teesdale begins calmly enough, though the pastoral landscapes of its lower reaches are soon replaced by wilder Pennine scenery. **MIDDLETON-IN-TEESDALE**, the valley's main settlement, was once the archetypal "company town", owned lock, stock and barrel by the Quaker-run London Lead Company, which began mining here in 1753. There are no specific sights in the village, but it's a quiet and remote spot to spend the night, either at *Bluebell House* in the central Market Place (☎01833/640584; no credit cards; ①) or the nearby seventeenth-century *Teesdale Hotel* (☎01833/640264; ④). The nearest **campsite** is the *Daleview Caravan Park* (☎01833/640233; closed Nov–Feb), half a mile south, down Bridge Street and across the river.

Past Newbiggin, the countryside becomes harsher and the Tees more vigorous as the B6277 travels the two miles on to **Bowlees Country Park and Visitor Centre**

(April–Sept daily 10.30am–5.30pm; 50p), the halt for the short walk to the rapids of **Low Force**. Close by is the altogether more impressive **High Force**, a seventy-foot cascade which rumbles over an outcrop of the Whin Sill, a black dolerite ridge that pokes up in various parts of northern England. The waterfall is on private Raby land, and visitors must pay 50p to view the falls and £1 to use the nearby car park, by the B6277. By the car park, the *High Force* **pub** and **hotel** (☎01833/622222; ③) brews its own beer (a Teesdale Bitter and the stronger, award-winning, Cauldron Snout) to accompany the bar meals.

The Pennine Way – which passes the falls – continues the six miles upstream to **Cauldron Snout**, near the source of the Tees, where the river rolls two hundred feet down a dolerite stairway as it leaves **Cow Green Reservoir**. It's also possible to reach the reservoir by car: turn off the main road at **Langdon Beck** – about a mile north of the stone-built **youth hostel** on the B6277 at Forest-in-Teesdale (☎01833/622228, *langdonbeck@yha.org.uk*) – and follow the three-mile-long lane to the car park, a mile's walk from the Snout.

Weardale

Lead and iron-ore mining flourished in and around Weardale from the 1840s to the 1880s, leaving today's landscape scarred with old workings. One of the bigger mines, situated three miles west of Cowshill, a chilly 1500ft above sea level, has been turned into the **Killhope Lead Mining Centre** (April–Oct daily 10.30am–5pm; Nov Sun 10.30am–4pm; £3.40, £5 including mine visit), whose 34-foot high waterwheel still turns, using six thousand gallons of water per minute from a string of diverted streams. Descending Park Level Mine with hard hat and lamp gives you a taste of the miserable mining life. Farther east down the main road, tiny **IRESHOPEBURN** is the home of the **Weardale Museum** (Easter, May–July & Sept Wed–Sun 2–5pm; Aug daily 2–5pm; £1), which footnotes the history of the local lead-mining industry with a gruesome display of miners' ruined lungs.

About nine miles downstream from Ireshopeburn lies **STANHOPE**, the main village of the valley and a useful base for walks across the moors – the **tourist office** (Easter to mid-Nov daily 10am–5pm; mid-Nov to Easter Mon–Fri 10am–4pm, Sat & Sun 11am–4pm; ☎01388/527650), in the Durham Dales Centre, Castle Gardens, opposite Market Place, has all the trail details and a list of **B&Bs**. From Stanhope, it's two miles to **FROSTERLEY**, where quarries once produced the exquisite, fossil-encrusted black limestone "marble" used to such effect in Durham Cathedral. The *Black Bull Inn* here (☎01388/527784; no credit cards; ②) is a nice old pub.

Blanchland

The trans-moorland B6278, which cuts north from Weardale at Stanhope for ten extraordinarily wild miles, runs to tiny **BLANCHLAND**. Little more than a handful of ancient, lichen-stained cottages huddled round an L-shaped square, the hamlet was once the site of a Premonstratensian abbey, founded in the twelfth century. Blanchland has been preserved and protected since 1721, when Lord Crewe, the childless Bishop of Durham, bequeathed his estate to trustees on condition that they rebuilt the old conventual buildings, for Blanchland had slowly fallen into disrepair after the abbey's dissolution. The original trustees obliged and their successors have allowed but the faintest whiff of the twentieth century to intrude. Consequently, the village bears many reminders of its monastic past, from the sturdy gatehouse that now accommodates the post office to the parish church where the medieval chancel and tower were all used to good effect during the rebuilding of 1752. But it's the **Lord Crewe Arms Hotel** (☎01434/675251; ⑦) that steals the show, boasting dark vaulted basements, two big fireplaces left over from the canons' kitchen and a priest's hideaway stuck inside the chimney. The **restaurant** serves expensive table d'hote dinners but there's a fine public bar with cheaper food in the undercroft. By **bus**, you need the #773 from Consett (not Sun), which is itself linked by hourly bus to Newcastle; or the very infrequent, once-weekly (currently Tues) #869 from Hexham.

Darlington and the Tees Valley

In a region whose physical face was blighted first by industrial success and then by urban neglect, the towns along the **Tees Valley** take some beating. Driving north especially, from Yorkshire, it seems that from Middlesbrough onwards a view isn't considered a view unless it's blocked by towers and pipes, clouded by smoking chimneys and framed by rusting machinery. This, of course, is a harsh judgement and only half the story – the **River Tees**, along with the Tyne farther north, was one of the great engines of British economic power in the late nineteenth century. Few tourists stop now, but there were once rich pickings here, in places like **Darlington**, twenty miles south of Durham city, where the first steam train, George Stephenson's *Locomotion*, made its inaugural run. The line ran first to **Stockton-on-Tees** and was then extended to ports at **Middlesbrough** and **Hartlepool**, to enable ever-increasing amounts of Durham coal to be unloaded and exported.

Darlington

DARLINGTON hit the big time in 1825, when George Stephenson's *Locomotion* hurtled from here to nearby Stockton-on-Tees, with the inventor at the controls and flag-carrying horsemen riding ahead to warn of the onrushing train, which reached a terrifying fifteen miles per hour. This novel form of transport soon proved popular with passengers, an unlooked-for bonus for Edward Pease, the line's instigator: he had simply wanted a fast and economical way to transport coal from the Durham pits to the docks at Stockton. Subsequently, Darlington grew into a rail-engineering centre, and didn't look back till the pruning of the network and the closure of the works in 1966.

It's little surprise, then, that all signs in town point to the **Darlington Railway Centre and Museum** (daily 10am–5pm; £2.20), housed in Darlington's North Road station, a twenty-minute walk up Northgate from the central market place. The museum's pride and joy is the original *Locomotion*, actually built in Newcastle, which continued in service until 1841 – other locally made engines superseded it, and some of these are on show, too. Darlington's origins lie deep in Saxon times, following which it enjoyed a long history as an agricultural centre and staging post on the Great North Road. The monks carrying St Cuthbert's body from Ripon to Durham stopped in Darlington, the saint lending his name to the graceful central, riverside church of **St Cuthbert** (Easter–Sept daily 11am–2pm), where the needle-like spire and decorative turrets herald the delicate Early English stonework inside. One of England's largest market squares spreads beyond the church up to the restored Victorian covered **market** (Mon–Sat 8am–5pm), next to the clocktower.

From the **train station**, walk up Victoria Road to the roundabout and turn right down Feethams for the central Market Place. You'll pass the town hall on Feethams, behind which is the **bus station**. The town's **tourist office** is on the south side of Market Place at 13 Horsemarket (Mon–Fri 9am–5pm, Sat 10am–4pm; ☎01325/388666). Central **accommodation** options include the *King's Head*, on Priestgate (☎01325/380222; ⑤), and the *Cricketers Hotel*, at 53 Parkgate (☎01325/384444; ③). Cheap and basic board is available at the town's *Arts Centre* (☎01325/483271; ①), about half a mile west of the centre in Vane Terrace – follow Duke Street from central

Skinnergate. The *Hole in the Wall* pub on the main square serves spicy Thai lunches (closed Sun) for a fiver.

Middlesbrough

MIDDLESBROUGH, the region's largest town, fifteen miles east of Darlington, is entirely a product of the early industrial age, with nineteenth-century iron and steel barons throwing up factories and housing almost as fast as they could ship their products out of the docks on the River Tees. What was a mere hamlet at the turn of the nineteenth century was a thriving industrial town of 100,000 people by the turn of the twentieth. When iron and steel declined in importance and the local shipbuilding industry collapsed (the last shipyard closed in 1986), Middlesbrough took to the chemical industry. Add to this a contemporary renaissance in light engineering and, compared to many of its neighbours, Middlesbrough can boast relative success in keeping its economic head above water.

Only a pair of bridges recall earlier engineering feats – the **Transporter Bridge** (1911) at Ferry Road, just north of the centre, is the sole working example left in the country, its central section carting cars and pedestrians across the Tees (Mon–Sat 5am–11.05pm, Sun 2–11.05pm; cars 80p, pedestrians 30p) towards Hartlepool; further southwest, the **Newport Bridge** (1934) was the first vertical lift bridge built in England. Instead the town prefers to trumpet its position as "Gateway to Captain Cook Country", fair enough given that he was born a mile and a half away in Marton in 1728. Here, at the **Captain Cook Birthplace Museum** in Stewart Park (June–Sept Tues–Sun 10am–5.30pm; Oct–May Tues–Sun 9am–4pm; £2), are artefacts brought back from the South Seas on Cook's voyages, touch-screen terminals providing contemporary testimony by his botanist Sir Joseph Banks, and background information about a sailor's lot at sea. Buses #28, #29, #30, #66 and #90 from the bus station run every fifteen minutes.

From the **train station** it's just a short walk up Albert Road to the main Corporation Road. Turn right for the **bus station** – five minutes further up on its continuation, Newport Road – and left for the **tourist office**, 51 Corporation Rd (Mon–Thurs 9am–5pm, Fri 9am–4.30pm, Sat 9am–1.30pm; ☎01642/243425).

Newcastle upon Tyne

At first glance **NEWCASTLE UPON TYNE** – virtual capital of the area between Yorkshire and Scotland – may appear to be just another grimy industrial conurbation, but the banks of the Tyne have been settled for nearly two thousand years and the city consequently has a greater breadth of attractions than many of its northern rivals. The Romans were the first to bridge the river here, and the "new castle" appeared as long ago as 1080. In Elizabethan times a regional monopoly on **coal** export brought wealth and power to Newcastle and – as well as giving a new expression to the English language – engendered its other great industry, shipbuilding. At one time, a quarter of the world's shipping was built here, and the first steam train and steam turbine also emerged from Newcastle factories. In its Victorian heyday, Newcastle's engineers and builders gave the city an elegance which has survived the ravages of recent development. Industrial decline hit Newcastle early, as highlighted by the **Jarrow March** of 1936, but this remains a vibrant place, with a commercial resilience that's symbolized by the hugely successful **MetroCentre** across the river at Gateshead. Culturally, Newcastle is way ahead of its local rivals, boasting the best art gallery in the Northeast and a slew of good theatres and music venues. The **International Centre for Life**, a biotechnology research centre, is the city's main

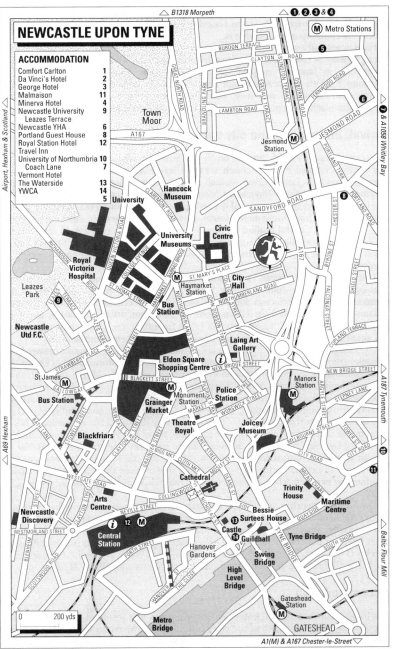

NEWCASTLE UPON TYNE

ACCOMMODATION

Comfort Carlton	1
Da Vinci's Hotel	2
George Hotel	3
Malmaison	11
Minerva Hotel	4
Newcastle University Leazes Terrace	9
Newcastle YHA	6
Portland Guest House	8
Royal Station Hotel	12
Travel Inn	
University of Northumbria	10
Coach Lane	7
Vermont Hotel	
The Waterside	13
YWCA	14
	5

millennium project, while by 2001 work should have been completed on transforming the old **Baltic Flour Mill** on the Gateshead side of the river into a state-of-the-art centre for contemporary visual arts.

Hard times and a sense of remoteness from the capital have given Newcastle's inhabitants, known as **Geordies**, a partisan pride in their city, which finds its most evident expression in fanatical support for the **Newcastle United** football team (the "Magpies"). With the stadium still anchored in the city centre (despite periodic attempts to relocate it), and every other young (and not so young) supporter wearing the familiar black-and-white shirt, it's difficult to overstate the team's importance.

Arrival, information and city transport

The train station, **Central Station**, on Neville Street, is a five-minute walk south of the city centre. National Express **coach** services arrive at Gallowgate station (St James Metro) opposite St James's Park football ground, while regional **bus** services use the **Haymarket** bus station (Haymarket Metro), close to the university. Most other city and local bus services arrive at and depart from the underground bus station at **Eldon Square** (not far from Monument Metro). Newcastle's **airport**, six miles north of the city, is linked to Central Station by Metro (5.50am–11.10pm every 8–15 min; 25min; £1.70). **Ferry arrivals** from Scandinavia dock at Royal Quays, North Shields, seven miles east of the city. Connecting bus services run you into the centre, stopping at Central Station.

There are **tourist offices** in **Central Station** (June–Sept Mon–Fri 10am–8pm, Sat 9am–5pm, Sun 10am–4pm; Oct–May Mon–Sat 10am–5pm; ☎0191/230 0030), in the **Central Library** on Princess Square, behind Northumberland Street (Mon & Thurs 9.30am–8pm, Tues, Wed & Fri 9.30am–5pm, Sat 9am–5pm; ☎0191/261 0610), and at the **airport** (☎0191/214 4422). Reading *The Crack* (monthly; free) is the best way to find out about clubs and bars: it's available from the Central Library tourist office.

City **buses** depart from Eldon Square, although the #33 to Jesmond leaves from Bewick Street, near Central Station. East of Eldon Square, **Monument** is site of the main interchange for the conurbation's efficient rail system, the **Metro** (6am–11.30pm every 4–15min). This runs on two lines: Greenline, connecting South Shields, Jarrow, Gateshead, Central Station, Monument and Jesmond with the airport; and the circular Yellowline connecting Monument with Jesmond, North Shields and Whitley Bay. One-way tickets for short hops start at 55p, while the Day Rover (£3.50) or Weekend Rover (Fri 6pm to Sun midnight; £6.30) offer unlimited travel in Tyne and Wear – or there's the Metro Day Saver (£2.80) for unlimited metro and ferry rides (after 9.30am). For all **public transport enquiries**, call Nexus (☎0191/232 5325 Mon–Sat 8am–8pm, Sun 9am–5pm). To get out on the Tyne, sign up for one of River Tyne Cruises' three-hour **sightseeing cruises**, which depart from the Quayside (June–Aug 2pm; £7; ☎0191/251 5920).

The Metro network connects most of the **day-trip destinations** along the Tyne, and a Day/Weekend Rover or Metro Day Saver ticket enables you to get the best out of the local transport systems. In addition to the Metro, the Day/Weekend Rover is valid for most buses in the county of Tyne and Wear and the ferry between North and South Shields (Mon–Sat 6.30am–10.50pm, Sun 10.30am–6pm; every 15–30min; 7min; 65p one-way). For all timetable and route information, call Nexus on ☎0191/232 5325.

Accommodation

The biggest concentration of **hotels** and **guesthouses** is in Jesmond, along and around Osborne Road, a mile north of the city centre: take the Metro to Jesmond or the #33 bus from Bewick Street, opposite the train station. Many hotels offer discounts for

Friday and Saturday nights, especially at the upper end of the scale where savings can be considerable.

Hotels and guest houses

Comfort Carlton, 82–86 Osborne Rd (☎0191/281 3361). Excellent value, with tasteful en-suite rooms, bar and restaurant. ④.

Da Vinci's Hotel, 73 Osborne Rd (☎0191/281 5284). Light, well-furnished rooms above a classy restaurant complete with piano and Leonardo prints. Midweek ④, weekends ③.

George Hotel, 88 Osborne Rd (☎0191/281 4442). Victorian town-house hotel with some of the city's cheapest rooms. No credit cards. ②.

Malmaison, Quayside (☎0191/245 5000, *newcastle@malmaison.com*). Chic lodgings in the former Co-op building. Rooms come with CD players and modems. ⑥.

Minerva Hotel, 105 Osborne Rd (☎0191/281 0190). Family-run place with pleasant rooms (ones with shower in the next price category), inexpensive dinners, and secure parking. No credit cards. ①.

Portland Guest House, 134 Sandyford Rd (☎0191/232 7868). Simple rooms in a renovated Georgian house, a ten-minute walk from the centre (close to Jesmond Metro). No credit cards. ①.

Royal Station Hotel, Neville St (☎0191/232 0781). The city's original Victorian station hotel, built in 1858 and now fully modernized. Great central location and surprisingly low weekend prices. ⑤.

Travel Inn, City Rd (☎0191/232 6533). When all you want is a bed and a bath you can't beat the reliable Travel Inn chain, now installed near the Quayside. ②.

The Waterside, 48–52 Sandhill (☎0191/230 0111). Small, luxury hotel right in the centre of the Quayside night-time action, and with its own decent bar. ⑤.

Hostels and university accommodation

Newcastle University, Leazes Terrace Student House (☎0191/222 8150). Student accommodation near the football ground, available early July to late Sept. Singles and doubles available.

Newcastle YHA, 107 Jesmond Rd (☎0191/281 2570, *newcastle@yha.org.uk*). Popular townhouse hostel near Jesmond Metro station – reserve in advance in summer. Closed Dec & Jan.

University of Northumbria, Coach Lane Campus Halls of Residence, Coach Lane (☎0191/227 4024). Student hall of residence offering cheap B&B, available April & July–Sept.

YWCA, Jesmond House, Clayton Rd (☎0191/281 1233). Purpose-built B&B accommodation for both sexes (age limit 18–50), near the YHA. Evening meals available.

The City

Anyone arriving by train from the north will get a sneak preview of the **Castle** (April–Sept Tues–Sun 9.30am–5.30pm; Oct–March Tues–Sun 9.30am–4pm; £1.50), as the rail line splits the keep from its gatehouse, the Black Gate, on St Nicholas' Street. A wooden fort was built here on the site of an Anglo-Saxon cemetery by Robert Curthose, eldest son of William the Conqueror, but the present keep dates from the twelfth century. Staircases and rooms, including a bare Norman chapel, lie off a draughty Great Hall, where displays relate to the Civil War siege of 1644 by a Scottish army supporting the Parliamentarian cause; a small museum room shows various archeological finds. Little remains of the outer fortifications except the Black Gate, added in 1242 and topped by a seventeenth-century house.

Further along St Nicholas' Street stands the **Cathedral** (Mon–Fri 7am–6pm, Sat 8am–4pm, Sun 9am–noon & 4–7pm; free), remarkable chiefly for its tower – erected in 1470, it is topped with a crown-like structure of turrets and arches supporting a lantern. Inside, behind the high altar, is one of the largest funerary brasses in England, commissioned by Roger Thornton, who arrived penniless and died its richest merchant in 1430. Much of the interior was given a neo-Gothic remodelling in the late nineteenth century under Sir George Gilbert Scott.

From between castle and the cathedral a road known simply as Side, formerly the main road out of the city, descends to the **Quayside** and the area known as **Sandhill**, where the first bridges across the Tyne stood. There have been fixed river crossings here since Roman times and today the Tyne is spanned by six bridges in close proximity, the most prominent being the looming **Tyne Bridge** of 1929 – symbol of the city – which became the model for the Sydney Harbour bridge. To the west of it, road and rail lines cross the river on the **High Level Bridge**, built by Robert Stephenson in 1849.

Protected by the towering castle, the quayside district became the commercial heart of the city and in the sixteenth and seventeenth centuries its half-timbered houses were the homes of Newcastle's wealthiest merchants. One is **Bessie Surtees' House**, at 41–44 Sandhill (Mon–Fri 10am–4pm; free; EH), the residence of a well-heeled eighteenth-century woman who scandalously eloped to Scotland with a local yokel; all ended well and the groom in question went on to become Lord Eldon, Chancellor of England. Opposite is the **Guildhall**, rebuilt many times since its foundation in 1316, where court sessions were held; John Wesley preached here in 1742 and had to be rescued from a volatile crowd by a hefty fishwife. On Sundays (9am–2.30pm) a busy **market** spreads around the nearby hydraulic **Swing Bridge**, which was erected in 1876. East along the quay, up Broad Chare, lies the unspoiled ensemble of **Trinity House**, with its enclosed courtyard and own graciously carved chapel, built in 1505 for the Mariners' Guild and still run by the Brethren of Master Mariners. Next door, at no. 29, the **Trinity Maritime Centre** (April–Oct Mon–Fri 11am–4pm; £1.50) housed in an old ship chandler's warehouse has a few rooms of maritime mementoes and some lovingly detailed model ships. Beyond Broad Chare, the modern-day regeneration of Quayside is in full swing. A landscaped promenade, public sculpture and pedestrianized squares have paved the way for a series of fashionable new bars and restaurants, while across on the other side of the river, the former **Baltic Flour Mill** is slowly being converted into a visual arts centre (due to be open in 2001).

By the mid-nineteenth century, Newcastle's centre of balance had shifted away from the river, uphill to the rapidly expanding Victorian town. In a few short years, businessmen-builders and architects like Richard Grainger, Thomas Oliver and John Dobson fashioned the best-designed Victorian town in England, with classical facades of stone lining splendid new streets, most notably **Grey Street** – "that descending, subtle curve", as John Betjeman described it. The street takes its name from the Northumberland dynasty of political heavyweights whose most illustrious member was the second Earl Grey, prime minister from 1830 to 1834. In the middle of his term of office he carried the Reform Bill through parliament, an act commemorated by **Grey's Monument** at the top of the street. Grey Street still shows off much of its Victorian elegance, best exemplified by the **Theatre Royal**, halfway down, and by **Grainger Market** (Mon–Sat 8am–5pm), near Grey's Monument, Europe's largest undercover market when built in the 1830s.

West of here, behind Gallowgate, is the most complete stretch of the old **city walls**, leading down to Westgate Road. Once encircling the whole of medieval Newcastle, they remained in place until the sixteenth century, after which time many sections were plundered for building stone. Several towers remained in use by the city guilds as meeting houses and one, the **Morden Tower**, alongside Stowell Street, gained more recent prestige as the haunt of poets such as Allen Ginsberg, Basil Bunting and Tom Pickard. Through the arch, the outer defensive ditch has been restored. Stowell Street, incidentally, is Newcastle's small **Chinatown**. Across Stowell Street from the tower is the tranquil courtyard of **Blackfriars** (usually Mon–Sat 10am–5pm, though times vary; closed Mon in winter; free), a thirteenth-century cloistered monastery, now housing a crafts centre.

Just to the south of here, off Blenheim Street, the **Discovery Museum** in Blandford House, Blandford Square (Mon–Sat 10am–5pm, Sun 2–5pm; free) attempts to put the city's history into context, with various galleries concentrating on Newcastle's maritime history, its pioneering inventors, armed forces, local costumes and fashion, and community groups.

Newcastle's – indeed, the Northeast's – premier art collection is the **Laing Gallery** on New Bridge St (Mon–Sat 10am–5pm, Sun 2–5pm; free), off John Dobson Street, behind the library. It's a splendidly organized museum, in which local pottery, glassware, costume and sculpture play their part, while on permanent display is a sweep through British art from Reynolds to John Hoyland, with a smattering of Pre-Raphaelites, so admired by English industrial barons. The real treat though is the lashings of **John Martin** (1789–1854), a self-taught Northumberland painter with a penchant for massive biblical and mythical scenes inspired by the dramatic northeastern scenery. The other must-see in the gallery is the **Art on Tyneside** exhibition, which romps through the history of art and applied art in the region since the seventeenth century with considerable gusto.

Newcastle University, opposite Haymarket Metro, contains a knot of fine museums and galleries, located off King's Walk: the **Museum of Antiquities** (Mon–Sat 10am–5pm; free) makes a good place to get to grips with the history of Hadrian's Wall; the **Greek Museum** (Mon–Fri 9.30am–12.30pm & 2–4.30pm; free) contains a valuable collection of armour, jewellery and pottery; while the celebrated **Hatton Gallery** (Mon–Sat 10am–5.30pm; free), attached to the Fine Art Department, features a collection of African sculpture, the only surviving example of Kurt Schwitters' *Merzbau* (a sort of architectural collage) and a variety of temporary exhibitions. Also attached to the university is the **Hancock Museum** on adjacent Claremont Road (Mon–Sat 10am–5pm, Sun 2–5pm; £2.25). Based on an eighteenth-century natural history collection, it's grown to immense dimensions – with more than 150,000 insect specimens. Beyond the University of Newcastle stretch the 1200 acres of the **Town Moor**, the city's green lung. It's the site of the annual "Hoppings" in June, a huge week-long **fair** of rides, stalls and other attractions which keeps going until well after dark.

Eating, drinking and nightlife

Newcastle's tastes have moved a long way from traditional dishes, such as black pudding or the gargantuan bread rolls called "stottie cakes". At the budget end of the market Italian, Indian and Chinese food dominates the scene, while at the top end of the scale the city is beginning to attract some top-class chefs. The Quayside and the streets around it are where the most fashionable hang-outs are situated. If you're counting the pennies, aim to eat early – many city-centre restaurants offer **early-bird/happy hours** deals before 7pm, while others serve **set lunches** at often ludicrous low prices.

Newcastle's boisterous **nightlife** centres on the pubs and clubs in the older parts of town: between Grainger Street and the cathedral in the area called the Bigg Market – spiritual home of Sid the Sexist and the Fat Slags, from the locally based *Viz* magazine – and around Sandhill and the Quayside. Top brew is, of course, **Newcastle Brown Ale** – known locally as "Dog" – produced in this city since 1927.

Cafés and coffee shops

Blakes Coffee House, 53 Grey St. Near the Theatre Royal, this is one of the longest-standing coffee houses in town, serving sandwiches, mountainous ciabatta included. Closed Sun.

Café Churchill, corner of Mosley and Dean streets. Proper coffee, sandwiches, pasta, crepes and Brit-Med lunch specials in a gloriously tiled Victorian relic. Closed Sun.

The Side Café Bistro, 1–3 The Side. Pasta, salad, bruschetta and cappuccino in an amiable little place near the Quayside.

Tyneside Coffee Rooms, 2nd floor, Tyneside Cinema, 10–12 Pilgrim St. Coffee, snacks and arthouse movie talk in the cinema café.

Restaurants

21 Queen Street, 21 Queen St (☎0191/222 0755). Newcastle's premier restaurant serves inventive seafood and meat dishes. Set lunches (under £20) are the best deal. Closed Sat lunch & Sun. Very Expensive.

Barn Again, 21 Leazes Park Rd (☎0191/230 3338). Anglo-French cooking, in a bistro hidden away up an alley close to the football ground. Closed Sun & Mon. Moderate (lunch) to Expensive (eve).

Café Sol, Pink Lane (☎0191/221 0122). Off-the-shelf tapas bar (checked tablecloths, bullfight posters, flamenco nights) with food a cut above the average. Closed Sun. Inexpensive.

Courtney's, 5–7 Side (☎0191/232 5537). Modern-British food of distinction, pressing all the right trendy buttons (oven-roasting, wok-frying). Closed Sat lunch & all Sun. Expensive.

Est Est Est, Quayside (☎0191/260 2291). Super-stylish Italian on the Quayside, with terrific pizzas (try the pizza Spago with red onions, sour cream and smoked salmon). Moderate to Expensive.

La Tasca, Quayside (☎0191/230 4006). A veritable tapas barn (next to *Est Est Est*) with Spanish tiling and cast-iron candelabras. Moderate.

Leela's, 20 Dean St (☎0191/230 1261). A rare treat among the flock-wallpaper curry houses, *Leela's* serves high-quality South Indian cuisine. Closed Sun. Moderate to Expensive.

Metropolitan, 35 Grey St (☎0191/230 2306). City-centre brasserie that's great at all times of the day: sandwiches, snacks and an all-day bar, early-bird suppers, or brasserie favourites. Closed Sun. Moderate.

Rupali, 6 Bigg Market (☎0191/232 8629). Budget Indian food in the most boisterous part of town. Inexpensive.

Sabatini, 25 King St (☎0191/261 4415). Quayside Italian with Neo-Impressionist daubs on the wall, good pizzas and a full menu besides. Closed Sun. Moderate.

Pubs, bars and clubs

BieRRex, 2a Hancock St. Café-bar whose *raison d'être* is its long list of punishingly strong continental beers. There's decent food served here too.

The Cooperage, 32 The Close, Quayside. Cosy Quayside pub, originally a sixteenth-century house, just along from the Tyne Bridge, with a good range of guest beers and, often, live bands.

Crown Posada, 31 Side. Local beers and guest ales in a highly attractive wood-and-glass-panelled Victorian pub down by the Quayside.

Old George, Old George Yard, off Bigg Market. Rambling, former coaching inn with courtyard that's worth a drink at quieter times.

Pitcher & Piano, Quayside. The Quayside's most spectacular design – sinuous roof, huge plate-glass walls – is a great place to drink. Live jazz Sun eve.

Planet Earth, Low Friar St. Popular city dance club, hosting 60s, 70s and 80s music nights, plus the usual weekend house and dance shenanigans. Closed Sun.

Powerhouse, Waterloo St. The city's best gay club attracts a friendly crowd. Mon is cabaret night, Thurs is popular. Closed Sun, Tues & Wed.

Quayside Bar, 35 The Close, Quayside. Newcastle's only surviving medieval warehouse, now a quayside pub-restaurant (under the High Level Bridge) with outdoor tables.

Tuxedo Royale, Quayside, Gatsehead. Floating nightclub, on the south side of the river below the Tyne Bridge, with a raucous 18–25-year-old set rolling back the pop years. Closed Sun.

Arts, culture and music

Buddle Arts Centre, 258 Station Rd, Wallsend (☎0191/200 7132). Friendly community arts centre with a fine range of events and concerts, and easy to reach from central Newcastle. Wallsend Metro.

Customs House, Mill Dam, South Shields (☎0191/454 1234). Arts centre on the banks of the Tyne, hosting gigs, films and theatre. There's also a bar and a restaurant. South Shields Metro.

The Jazz Café, 23 Pink Lane (☎0191/232 6505). Intimate jazz club with a late licence, near the station. Closed Sun.

Live Theatre, 27 Broad Chare (☎0191/232 1232). Enterprising theatre company promoting local actors and writers. Folk, blues, roots and jazz at its weekly *Jumpin' Hot Club*. Central Station Metro.

Newcastle Arts Centre, Black Swan Court, Westgate Road (☎0191/261 5618). Art gallery, and concert and drama venue – always worth checking what's on. Central Station Metro.

Newcastle Playhouse, Barras Bridge (☎0191/230 5151). Home of Newcastle's Northern Stage company and the Gulbenkian Studio (for theatre, dance and recitals). Good café-bar (closed Sun). Haymarket Metro.

The Riverside, 57–59 Melbourne St (☎0191/261 4386). Best spot in the city for touring live bands and club nights.

Theatre Royal, Grey St (☎0191/232 2061). Drama, ballet, opera and dance; and the annual RSC season in Sept and Oct. Monument Metro.

Tyneside Cinema, Pilgrim St (☎0191/232 1507). The city's premier art-house cinema. Hosts an acclaimed annual International Film Festival in Nov. Monument Metro.

Tyne Theatre & Opera House, Westgate Rd (☎0191/232 0899). Restored Victorian theatre with productions by the English Shakespeare Company and concerts by the Northern Sinfonia. Central Station Metro.

Listings

Airport and flight enquiries Flight info ☎0191/214 3334; general & airline info ☎0191/286 0966.

Banks and exchanges Banks are concentrated around Grey and Northumberland streets. There's a bureau de change at the airport and in the main post office.

Books Waterstone's, 104 Grey St; Blackwells, Grand Hotel Buildings, Percy St.

Buses For all city and local bus enquiries, call Nexus (☎0191/232 5325). National Express for long-distance routes (☎0990/808080); Arriva Northumbria for most regional services (☎0191/212 3000); Arriva Northeast (☎0345/124125) for Teesside, Middlesbrough and North Yorkshire; Stagecoach for Newcastle area (☎0191/276 1411) or Carlisle and Cumbria (☎01946/592000).

Car rental Avis (☎0191/232 5283), Europcar (☎0191/286 5070), and Hertz (☎0191/286 6748) all have outlets at the airport. The best local rates are offered by Auto Hire, 79–81 Blenheim St (☎0191/232 7774).

Dentist In an emergency, contact the dental school at the Royal Victoria Infirmary, Queen Victoria Rd (☎0191/232 5131).

Ferries North Shields ferry terminal at Royal Quays, seven miles east of the city, has sailings to Scandinavia, Amsterdam and Germany. Contact Fjord Line (for Bergen, Haugesund and Stavanger; ☎0191/296 1313) or Scandinavian Seaways (Gothenberg/Kristiansand, Hamburg and Amsterdam; ☎0990/333000). Buses leave from Central Station to the terminal before each sailing; nearest Metro station is Percy Main, a twenty-minute walk from the ferry terminal.

Hospital Royal Victoria Infirmary, Queen Victoria Rd (☎0191/232 5131), behind the university, just 400 yards from Haymarket bus station. Also, emergency doctor at the Saville Medical Centre, 7 Saville Place (☎0191/232 4274).

Internet Check email and get on line at McNulty's, a café at 26–30 Market St (☎0191/232 0922).

Left luggage Lockers available at the train station.

Lost property Contact Nexus (see Buses, above) for property left on bus and Metro; or the police (below) for general lost property enquiries.

Pharmacies Local, late-opening pharmacies are listed in the local press; or visit the main branch of Boots, Monument Mall, Grey St (☎0191/232 4423), open to 7pm.

Police Corner of Market and Pilgrim streets (☎0191/214 6555).

Post Office St Mary's Place, near the Civic Centre, at Haymarket (☎0345/223 344), for money exchange and *poste restante.*

Taxis There are ranks all over the centre, including those at Haymarket, Bigg Market, and outside Central Station. Weekend nights are the most difficult times to hail a cab; the queues at the Bigg Market ranks can be horrendous. Call Noda (☎0191/222 1888) at Central Station for advance bookings.

Trains For all enquiries, call ☎0345/484950.

Travel agents Usit Campus, Level 5, Student Union Building, King's Walk (☎0191/232 2881).

East of Newcastle: Jarrow

The major attraction is at **JARROW**, five miles east of Newcastle, on the south side of the Tyne, which has been ingrained on the national consciousness since the 1936 **Jarrow Crusade**, a march to London by unemployed protesters which became the most potent image of the hardships of 1930s Britain. However, the town made a mark rather earlier, as the seventh-century St Paul's church and monastery was one of the region's early cradles of Christianity. The first Saxon church was built in 681 AD by monks from St Peter's at Monkwearmouth, and its monastic buildings soon attracted a reputation for scholastic learning. It was here that the **Venerable Bede** (673–735 AD) came to live as a boy, growing to become one of Europe's greatest scholars and England's first historian – his *History of the English Church and People*, describing the struggles of the island's early Christians, was completed at Jarrow in 731. Access to the tranquil stone church of **St Paul's** (Mon–Sat 10am–4pm, Sun 2.30–4pm) is free, although it stands within the wider development that is **Bede's World** (April–Oct Tues–Sat 10am–5.30pm, Sun noon–5.30pm; Nov–March Tues–Sat 10am–4.30pm, Sun noon–4.30pm; £3), which provides a fascinating exploration of early medieval Northumbria. The main **museum** traces the development of Northumbria and England through the use of extracts from Bede's *Ecclesiastical History* set alongside archeological finds and reconstructions. After this you can take a turn through "*Gyrwe*", the eleven-acre demonstration **farm** which features reconstructed timber buildings from the early Christian period, as well as demonstrating contemporary agricultural methods. Bede's World is at Church Bank, a signposted fifteen-minute walk from **Bede Metro station**.

North of Newcastle: the stately homes

One of Vanbrugh's great Baroque houses, **Seaton Delaval Hall**, lies eleven miles northeast of Newcastle, its gloomy north facade looking over the bleak terrain towards the port of Blyth. Fire badly damaged the hall in 1822, a century after it was built, but subsequent restorations have done ample justice to the grandeur of a building that exemplifies the architect's desire to create country houses with "something of the castle air". Take **bus** #363 (hourly) or #364 (hourly; not Sun) from Haymarket.

 Belsay Hall, Castle and Gardens (daily: April–Sept 10am–6pm; Oct 10am–5pm; Nov–March 10am–4pm; £3.80; EH), fourteen miles northwest of Newcastle, were inherited in 1795 by Sir Charles Monck, who eleven years later decided to build a brand new hall here after his return from a honeymoon-cum-Grand-Tour of Europe. Sir Charles planned a majestic Doric house, an austere one-hundred-foot-square sandstone block raised on a podium of three steps. Built between 1807 and 1817, the **Hall** has now been impressively restored, while to the west a footpath threads through to the lush **Quarry Gardens**, planned by Sir Charles as a Romantic antidote to the severity of the house. The track also leads to the substantial remains of the medieval **castle**, its battlements punctuated by four formidable corner turrets. **Belsay village**, on the main road a mile from the Hall, is readily reached by **bus** from Newcastle; the #808 from Eldon Square (not Sun), or #508 from Haymarket (summer Sun only).

 Eight miles northwest of Belsay lies the tiny village of **Cambo**; the summer Sunday #508 service (twice a day) links the two. Just outside the village stands **Wallington House** (April–Oct Mon & Wed–Sun 1–5pm; £5.20; NT) an ostentatious mansion rebuilt by Sir Walter Blackett, the coal- and lead-mine owner, in the 1740s. The interior's highlight is the Rococo plasterwork, though William Bell Scott's Pre-Raphaelite decorations in the central hall are good fun, too. There's a separate charge if you only want to see the **grounds** and walled gardens (daily: April–Oct 10am–7pm; Nov–March 10am–4pm; £3.80).

South of Newcastle: Washington

South of Newcastle, the New Town of **WASHINGTON** is the focus of much of the region's contemporary investment and manufacture. Split into planned, numbered districts, and organized on American lines, it's not an obvious stop, although the original **Old Village** has been zealously preserved as a conservation area. Just off the village green, past the leafy churchyard on The Avenue, stands the ancestral home of the family which spawned the first **US president**. The "de Wessyngtons" – later the Washingtons – originally came over with William the Conqueror, and by 1183 were based at the **Old Hall** (April–Oct Mon–Wed & Sun 11am–5pm; £2.75; NT), where they lived until 1613. Carefully preserved as a Jacobean showpiece, the echoing, stone-flagged house has a fine kitchen and Great Hall, and some exemplary wood panelling, and although none of the furniture is original to the Washington family, it is contemporaneous. Every Fourth of July, the raising of the US flag heralds a day of independence celebrations; entry to the Old Hall is free that day.

The other main attraction in the area is the **Washington Wildfowl and Wetlands Centre** (daily: June–Sept 9.30am–5pm; Oct–May 9.30am–4pm; £4.50), east of town and north of the River Wear in District 15, its hundred acres designed by Sir Peter Scott. The trails, hides, play areas, information centre and children's activities make for an enjoyable day out.

For Washington Village and the Old Hall, the best service is on the #185 bus from Sunderland Central Bus Station (not Sun). The Wildfowl Centre is reached on the #189 from Newcastle's Eldon Square (not Sun) or the #X4 from either Newcastle's Eldon Square or Sunderland's Park Lane (not Sun). All these buses (and many others from Newcastle or Sunderland) call or terminate at **Washington Galleries Bus Station**, from where you'll be able to reach either site. Most buses prefixed with a "W" run to Washington Village from the Galleries.

Along Hadrian's Wall

In 55 and 54 BC, Julius Caesar launched two swift invasions of southeast England from his base in Gaul, his success proving that Britain lay within the Roman grasp. The full-scale assault began under Claudius in 43 AD and, within forty years, Roman troops had reached the Firth of Tay. In 83 AD, the Roman governor Agricola ventured farther north, but Rome subsequently transferred part of its army to the Danube, and the remaining legions withdrew to the frontier which was marked by the **Stanegate**, a military roadway linking Carlisle and Corbridge.

Emperor Hadrian, who toured Roman Britain in 122 AD, found this informal arrangement unsatisfactory. His imperial policy was quite straightforward – he wanted the empire to live at peace within stable frontiers, most of which were defined by geographical features. In northern Britain, however, there was no natural barrier and so Hadrian decided to create his own by constructing a 76-mile **wall** from the Tyne to the Solway Firth. It was not intended to be an impenetrable fortification, but rather a base for patrols that could push out into hostile territory. It was to be punctuated by **milecastles**, which were to serve as gates, depots and mini-barracks, and by observation **turrets**, two of which were to stand between each pair of milecastles. Before the Wall was even completed, major modifications were made: the bulk of the garrison had initially been stationed along the Stanegate, but they were now moved into the Wall, occupying a chain of new **forts**, which straddled the Wall at six- to nine-mile intervals. These new arrangements concentrated the Wall's garrison in a handful of key points and brought them nearer the enemy, making it possible to respond quickly to any threat. Simultaneously, a military zone was defined by the digging of a broad ditch, or **vallum**, on the south side of the Wall, crossed by cause-

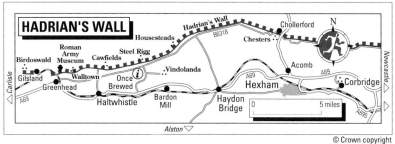

© Crown copyright

ways to each of the forts, turning them into the main points of access and rendering the milecastles, in this respect, largely redundant. The revised structure remained in operation until the last Roman soldiers left in 411 AD.

Approached from Newcastle along the valley of the Tyne, via the Roman museum and site at **Corbridge**, the prosperous-looking market town of **Hexham**, with its fine eleventh-century abbey, makes an ideal base. Most visitors stick to the best-preserved portions of the Wall, which are concentrated between the hamlet of **Chollerford**, three miles north of Hexham, and **Haltwhistle**, sixteen miles to the west. It's here, especially between **Housesteads** and **Steel Rigg**, that the Wall is at its most beautiful, as it clings to the edge of the Whin Sill, a precipitous line of dolerite crags towering above the austere Northumberland National Park moorland. Scattered along this section are a variety of key archeological sites and museums, notably **Chesters Roman Fort and Museum**, near Chollerford, the remains of **Housesteads Fort** and that of **Vindolanda**, and the milecastle remains at **Cawfields**, north of Haltwhistle.

Visiting the Wall

There's a special **Hadrian's Wall Bus Service** which links Hexham with Chesters, Housesteads, Once Brewed Visitor Centre, Vindolanda, the Milecastle Inn, Cawfields car park, Haltwhistle, the Roman Army Museum and Greenhead, Birdoswald and Carlisle. This operates between late May and late September, three to four times a day in either direction; it's an hour from Hexham to Haltwhistle, with one-way tickets costing £2 (Day Rover tickets, from the driver or local tourist offices, £5); holders of Northeast Explorer/Stagecoach Cumberland Explorer passes get half-price travel. A reduced winter service (mid-Oct to late May) runs between Carlisle and Houseteads, via Brampton and Haltwhistle, with two to three departures a day (not Sun). There's also a year-round, hourly service (every 2hr on Sun), the #685, which runs along the A69 between Carlisle, Greenhead, Haltwhistle and Newcastle (Eldon Square). Finally, the #880 or #882 bus from Hexham to Bellingham runs via Chollerford, from where Chesters is just half a mile's walk along the road to the west. Full timetables are available from Hexham, Carlisle or Haltwhistle tourist offices. Call Cumbria County Council Journey Planner (☎01228/606000) or the Northumberland County Council Transport Enquiries Line (☎01670/533128) for further details. The nearest **train** stations are on the Newcastle–Carlisle line at Hexham, Bardon Mill and Haltwhistle, leaving you a fair walk to Chesters, Vindolanda and Cawfields/Greenhead respectively.

Corbridge

Buses from Newcastle and trains on the Newcastle–Hexham–Carlisle line stop at **CORBRIDGE**, a well-heeled town overlooking the River Tyne from the top of a steep ridge.

This spur of land was first settled by the Saxons, and their handiwork survives in parts of the **Church of St Andrew**, on the central Market Place, but it's the adjacent **Vicar's Pele** that catches the eye, a well-preserved fourteenth-century fortified tower-house.

One mile west of the Market Place, accessible by road or along the riverside footpath – take the street opposite the *Watling Coffee House* – lies **Corbridge Roman Site** (Easter–Oct daily 10am–6pm; Nov–Easter Wed–Sun 10am–1pm & 2–4pm; £2.80; EH), the location of the garrison town of Corstopitum. This is the oldest fortified site in the region, first established as a supply base for the Roman advance into Scotland in 80 AD (and thus predating the Wall itself). It remained in regular military use until the end of the second century, after which it became surrounded by a fast-developing town – most of the visible archeological remains date from this period, when Corstopitum served as the nerve centre of Hadrian's Wall. The extensive remains provide an insight into the layout of the civilian town, showing the foundations of temples, public baths, garrison headquarters, workshops and houses as well as the best-preserved Roman granaries in Britain. The site **museum** displays the celebrated *Lion and Stag* fountainhead – the so-called "Corbridge Lion"; to the Romans, the lion and its prey symbolized the triumph of life over death.

Corbridge **train station** is half a mile outside the town, across the river; **buses** stop outside the *Angel Inn* on Main Street or near the post office on Hill Street, around the corner. Corbridge **tourist office** is also on Hill Street, at the library (Easter–Oct Mon–Sat 10am–1pm & 2–6pm, Sun 1–5pm; ☎01434/632815). There are convenient **B&Bs** near the train station on Station Road – try *Holmlea* (☎01434/632486; no credit cards; ①) – and, more centrally, on Main Street – the *Riverside Guest House* (☎01434/632942; no credit cards; ②). You'll need to book in advance for the ivy-covered *Angel Inn* on Main Street (☎01434/632119; ⑤). The *Watling Coffee House*, on Watling Street just off the main square, and *Chadwick's* on Middle Street, both serve light **meals** throughout the day. For **bar meals** and beer, visit the *Wheatsheaf*, on Watling Street (visible at the end of the road, beyond the *Watling Coffee House*), a seventeenth-century former farmhouse with a couple of Roman stones in the stableyard.

Hexham and around

In 671, on a bluff above the Tyne, four miles west of Corbridge, St Wilfrid founded a Benedictine monastery whose church was, according to contemporary accounts, the finest to be seen north of the Alps. Unfortunately, its gold and silver proved irresistible to the Vikings, who savaged the place in 876, but the church was rebuilt in the eleventh century as part of an Augustinian priory, and the town of **HEXHAM**, governed by the Archbishop of York, grew up in its shadow.

The stately exterior of **Hexham Abbey** (daily: May–Sept 9am–7pm; Oct–April 9am–5pm; £2 donation suggested) still dominates the west side of the Market Place. Entry is through the south transept, where there's an impressive first-century tombstone honouring Flavinus, a standard-bearer in the Roman cavalry, who's shown riding down his bearded enemy. The memorial lies at the foot of the broad, well-worn steps of the canons' **night stair**, one of the few such staircases – providing access from the monastery to the church – to have survived the Dissolution. Beyond, most of the high-arched nave dates from an Edwardian restoration and it's here that you gain access to the **crypt**, a Saxon structure made out of old Roman stones, where pilgrims once viewed the abbey's reliquaries. At the end of the nave is the sixteenth-century **rood screen**, whose complex tracery envelops the portraits of local bishops. Behind the screen, the chancel displays the inconsequential-looking **frith stool**, an eighth-century stone chair that was once believed to have been used by Saint Wilfrid. Nearby, close to the high altar, there are four panels from a fifteenth-century **Dance of Death**, a grim, darkly varnished painting.

The rest of Hexham's large and irregularly shaped **Market Place** (main market day is Tuesday) is peppered with remains of its medieval past. The massive walls of the fourteenth-century **Moot Hall** were built to serve as the gatehouse to "The Hall", a well-protected enclosure that was garrisoned against the Scots. Nearby, the archbishops also built their own prison, a formidable fortified tower dating from 1330 and constructed using stones plundered from the Roman ruins at Corbridge. Now, as the **Old Gaol**, this accommodates the tourist office and the **Border History Museum** (Easter–Oct Mon–Sat 10am–4.30pm; Feb–Easter & Nov Mon, Tues & Sat 10am–4.30pm; £1.80).

Hexham's **train station** sits on the eastern edge of the town centre, a ten-minute walk from the abbey and the **tourist office** on Hallgate (Easter to mid-May & Oct Mon–Sat 9am–5pm, Sun 10am–5pm; mid-May to Sept Mon–Sat 9am–6pm, Sun 10am–5pm; Nov to Easter Mon–Sat 9am–5pm; ☎01434/605225). The **bus station** is situated off Priestpopple, a few minutes' south of the tourist office. Good **accommodation** options include the Edwardian *Kitty Frisk House*, a little way from the centre on Corbridge Road (☎01434/601533; no credit cards; ②); the secluded *West Close House*, on Hextol Terrace off the B6305 Allendale Road (☎01434/603307; no credit card; ②); and the bright and breezy *Topsy Turvy*, 9 Leazes Lane (☎01434/603152; no credit cards; ①). Alternatively, try the *Royal Hotel* on Priestpopple (☎01434/602270; ④), which has a dozen en-suite rooms. The **youth hostel** (☎01434/602864) occupies converted stable buildings in the village of **Acomb**, two miles from Hexham (bus #880 or #882). The **campsite** at Acomb, at *Fallowfield Dene Caravan Park* (☎01434/603553; closed Nov–Feb), is a nice place with proper laundry facilities.

Mrs Miggins, on St Mary's Wynd, just off Beaumont Street, is a good-value **coffee shop**, and *O'Kane's*, 3 Old Church, St Mary's Chare, a pleasant little bistro. **Bar meals** are served at most of the pubs, but top honours go to the *Priestpopple Brasserie* on Priestpopple, part of the Royal Hotel. Out of town on Dipton Mill Road, a mile or so south of the centre, the *Black House* (closed Mon all year, plus Tues & Wed in winter) is set in an old stable house – come for morning coffee, afternoon tea and home-cooked lunches. The main focus of **entertainment** in town is the **Queen's Hall Arts Centre** on Beaumont Street (☎01434/607272), which puts on a year-round programme of theatre, dance, music and art exhibitions.

Chollerford and Chesters Roman Fort

At **CHOLLERFORD**, around four miles north of Hexham, a bridge crosses the North Tyne river, overlooked by the *George Hotel* (☎01434/681611; ⑧). Two thousand years ago, the main river crossing was a little way downstream, half a mile west of present-day Chollerford, where **Chesters Roman Fort** (daily: Easter–Oct 10am–6pm; Nov–Easter 10am–4pm; £2.80; EH), otherwise known as *Cilurnum*, was built to guard the erstwhile Roman bridge over the river. Enough remains of the original structure to pick out the design of the fort, and each section has been clearly labelled, but the highlight is down by the river where the vestibule, changing room and steam range of the garrison's **bath-house** are still visible. Back at the entrance, the **museum** has an excellent collection of Roman stonework, including a sculpture of Mars from Housesteads.

Housesteads to Vindolanda

Overlooking the bleak Northumbrian moors from the top of the Whin Sill, **Housesteads Roman Fort** (daily: Easter–Oct 10am–6pm; Nov–Easter 10am–4pm; £2.80; EH & NT), eight miles west of Chesters, has long been the most popular site on the Wall. The fort was built in the second phase of the Hadrianic construction and is of standard design but for one enforced modification – forts were supposed to straddle the line of the Wall, but here the original stonework tracked along the very edge of the cliff, so Housesteads was built on the steeply sloping ridge to the south. Access is via the tiny **museum**, from where you stroll across to the south gate, beside which there are a few remains of the civilian settlement that was dependent on the one thousand infantrymen stationed within. You don't need to pay for entrance to Housesteads if you simply intend to walk west along the Wall from here. The three-mile hike past the lovely wooded **Crag Lough** to **Steel Rigg** offers the most fantastic views, especially when you spy the course of the Wall as it threads over the crags ahead.

Leaving the Wall at Steel Rigg, it's roughly half a mile south to the main road and the **Once Brewed National Park Visitor Centre** (May–Oct daily 10am–6pm; much reduced hours in winter, call for details; ☎01434/344396). The popular *Once Brewed* youth hostel (☎01434/344360, *oncebrewed@yha.org.uk*) is next to the visitor centre, or you can cut the three miles southeast across the back roads to the one-shop-one-pub village of **Bardon Mill** (also a stop on the Hexham–Carlisle train line), where the *Bowes Hotel* (☎01434/344237; ②) has reasonable rooms and food. At **Haydon Bridge**, another four miles to the east, the *General Havelock Inn* (☎01434/684376; closed Sun eve, Mon & Tues) is the best place to **eat** hearty Northumbrian cooking. There's also a very well-equipped backpackers' hostel, *Hadrian's Lodge*, on isolated North Road (☎01434/688688), under two miles north of Haydon Bridge – from the Wall and the B6318, take the turning for Haydon Bridge about a mile east of Housesteads.

Vindolanda

The excavated garrison fort of **Vindolanda** actually predates the Wall itself, though most of what you see today dates from the second to third century AD, when the fort was a thriving metropolis of five hundred soldiers with its own civilian settlement attached. The **site** (daily: May & June 10am–6pm; July & Aug 10am–6.30pm; April & Sept 10am–5:30pm; March & Oct 10am–5pm; Nov & Feb 10am–4pm; closed Dec & Jan; £3.80) is operated by the private Vindolanda Trust, which has done an excellent job of presenting its finds. The **excavations** are spread over a wide area, with civilian houses, inn, administrative building, commander's house and main gates all clearly visible; a full-scale recreated section of the Wall gives an idea of what a miletower would have looked like. The path through the excavations descends to the café, shop and **museum** (same hours as site), the latter housing amongst other finds the largest collection of Roman leather items ever discovered on a single site – dozens of shoes, belts, even a pair of baby boots. More intriguing is the excavated hoard of **writing tablets**, many of which depict graphically the realities of military life in Northumberland: soldiers' requests for more beer, birthday party invitations, and letters from home containing gifts of underwear for freezing frontline grunts.

Haltwhistle to Greenhead

There's not much to the small town of **HALTWHISTLE**, three miles west of Once Brewed/Steel Rigg and a mile south of the wall, but there is a **tourist office** (Easter–Sept Mon–Sat 10am–1pm & 2–6pm, Sun 1–5pm; Oct–Easter Mon–Fri 10am–1pm & 1.30–3.30pm; ☎01434/322002) in the **train station**, at the western edge of town, and a selection of **B&Bs**, including the attractive, stone *Hall Meadows*, right at the top of Main Street (☎01434/321021; no credit cards; ①). Alternatively, *Ashcroft* on Lantys Lonnen, very near the tourist office (☎01434/320213; ②), has nice rooms. The *Haltwhistle Camping Site* is in Burnfoot Park (☎01434/320106; closed Nov–Feb), beside the Tyne on the southeast edge of town. For beer and **bar meals**, the *Spotted Cow Inn*, down on Castle Hill, the eastern extension of Main Street, is an agreeable spot.

A further four-mile trek west along the wall takes you past the remains of **Great Chesters Fort** before reaching a spectacular section of the Wall, known as the

Walltown Crags. The views from here are marvellous. Adjacent to the crags, at Carvoran, the Vindolanda Trust's **Roman Army Museum** (daily: May & June 10am–6pm; July & Aug 10am–6.30pm; April & Sept 10am–5:30pm; March & Oct 10am–5pm; Nov & Feb 10am–4pm; closed Dec & Jan; £3; combined ticket with Vindolanda £5.60) does its best to inject some interest into its dioramas, reconstructions and exhibits.

Push on just a mile southwest, and you're soon in minuscule **GREENHEAD**, where the *Greenhead Hotel* (☎016977/47411; ②) sits opposite the **youth hostel** (☎016977/47401), located in a converted Methodist chapel. Up a track behind the hostel, *Holmhead Guest House* (☎016977/47402; ③) is an old stone farmhouse, serving an excellent set-menu dinner (£17).

Northumberland National Park

Northwest Northumberland, the great triangular chunk of land between Hadrian's Wall and the coastal plain, is dominated by the wide-skied landscapes of the **Northumberland National Park**, whose four hundred windswept square miles rise to the **Cheviot Hills** on the Scottish border. These uplands are interrupted by great slabs of forest, mostly the conifer plantations of the Forestry Commission, and a string of river valleys, of which Coquetdale, Tynedale and Redesdale are the longest. Remote from lowland law and order, these dales were once the homelands of the **Border reivers**, turbulent clans who ruled the local roost from the thirteenth to the sixteenth century. The reivers took advantage of the struggles between England and Scotland to engage in endless cross-border rustling and general brigandage, activities recalled by the ruined **bastles** (fortified farmhouses) and **peels** (defensive tower-houses) that lie dotted across the landscape.

Good walking country can be found right across the National Park. The most popular trail is the **Pennine Way**, which, entering the National Park at Hadrian's Wall, cuts up through Bellingham on its way to The Cheviot, the park's highest peak at 2674ft, finishing at Kirk Yetholm, over the border in Scotland. This part of the Pennine Way is 64 miles long, but it's easy to break the hike up into manageable portions as the footpath passes through a variety of tiny settlements, several of which have youth hostels, B&B accommodation and campsites. As an introduction, it's hard to beat the lovely moorland scenery of the fifteen-mile stretch from Housesteads at Hadrian's Wall to **Bellingham**, a pleasant town on the banks of the North Tyne. Bellingham is also on the road to **Kielder Water**, a pine-surrounded reservoir which has been vigorously promoted as a water-sports centre and nature reserve since its creation in 1982. Farther north, **Rothbury**, in Coquetdale, is close to both the Simonside Hills and **Cragside**, the nineteenth-century country home of Lord Armstrong.

Bellingham

The stone terraces of **BELLINGHAM** (pronounced Bellinjum) slope up from the banks of the Tyne on the eastern edge of the Northumberland National Park. It's a restful spot set in splendid rural surroundings, and it contains the much-modified medieval **Church of St Cuthbert**, which has an unusual stone-vaulted roof – designed (successfully) to prevent raiding Border reivers from burning the church to the ground. The **Heritage Centre** on Front Street (May–Sept Mon & Fri–Sun 1.30am–4.30pm; 50p) has more on this turbulent period.

Buses stop in the centre on Market Place, a few hundred yards down from the **tourist office** on Main Street (Easter–Oct Mon–Sat 10am–1pm & 2–6pm, Sun 1–5pm; Nov–Easter reduced hours, call for details; ☎01434/220616). Central **lodgings** are available at *Lyndale Guest House* (☎01434/220361; ②), just past the *Rose & Crown* pub.

Westfield House, opposite the fire station (☎01434/220340; ③), is rather grander. Bellingham's pubs – the *Rose & Crown*, the *Black Bull* and the *Cheviot* – all have a few rooms, too; those at the *Cheviot* (☎01434/220696; ③) are the nicest. The **youth hostel** (☎01434/220313) is six hundred yards west of the centre, above the village on Woodburn Road (signposted from Main Street). The local **campsite** is at *Demesne Farm* (☎01434/220258; closed Nov–Feb), right in the centre near the police station.

Kielder Water and Forest

West of Bellingham, the road follows the North Tyne River and skirts the forested edge of **Kielder Water**, passing the assorted visitor centres, waterside parks, picnic areas and anchorages that fringe its southern shore. First stop is the Visitor Centre at **Tower Knowe** (daily: May–Sept 10am–5pm; Oct–April 10am–4pm; ☎01434/240398), eight miles from Bellingham, with a café and an exhibition (£1) on the history of the valley and lake. Another four miles west, at **Leaplish**, the waterside park (daily: April & Oct 10am–4pm; May–Sept 10am–5pm; ☎01434/250312), lodge, bar and restaurant are the focus of most of Kielder's outdoor activities: watersports, bike rental, pony trekking and fishing. Leaplish also has **bunk-barn accommodation**, plus a drying room, kitchen and shower. An hour-and-a-half's **cruise** on the Osprey ferry (April–Oct 5 daily; £4) is always a pleasure; departures are from the piers at either Tower Knowe or Leaplish.

Eighteen miles from Bellingham, at the top of the reservoir, just three miles from the Scottish border, stands **Kielder Castle** (Easter–July & Sept daily 10am–5pm; Aug daily 10am–6pm; Oct–Easter Sat & Sun 11am–4pm; ☎01434/250209; free; parking £1), built in 1775 as the hunting lodge of the Duke of Northumberland, and now an information centre and exhibition area praising the work of the Forestry Commission. The castle is surrounded by the **Border Forest Park**, several million spruce trees subdivided into a number of approximately defined forest areas: Wark and Kielder are broadly to the south of the reservoir, Falstone and Redesdale to the north. Several easy and clearly marked **footpaths** lead from the castle into the forest – try the "Duke's Trail" through Ravenshill Wood, a slice of ancient and semi-natural woodland. There's **mountain bike rental** available from Kielder Bikes (☎01434/250392) at the castle. On the road in from Bellingham, a couple of miles before the water, the early seventeenth-century *Pheasant Inn* (☎01434/240382; ③) at **Stannersburn** has comfortable rooms and decent meals. The hamlet of **Falstone**, a mile to the north, boasts the smaller *Blackcock Inn* (☎01434/240200; ③). *Kielder* **campsite** (☎01434/250291; closed Oct–Easter) is by the banks of the Tyne, half a mile north of the castle.

Redesdale

From Bellingham, it's a fifteen-mile trek north along the Pennine Way to **BYRNESS** in **Redesdale**, which can also be reached direct from Kielder Castle via a rough, eleven-mile forestry road. Byrness is a tiny place, but it is fairly well equipped for walkers, with both a **youth hostel** at 7 Otterburn Green (☎01830/520425; closed Oct–Feb), and a **hotel** with public bar, the *Byrness* on the main road (☎01830/520231; ②). At the *Border Forest* **campsite** (☎01830/520259; closed Nov–Easter), a mile south of Byrness off the A68, there's a bunkhouse and small chalets available, too.

Redesdale has only one settlement of any size, **OTTERBURN**, ten miles southeast of Byrness down the A68. It's an undistinguished place today, with little except the name of the local pub, the *Percy Arms*, to recall its most notable hour. It was at Otterburn in August 1388 that an English army led by Sir Henry Percy ("Hotspur") was defeated by the Scots under James, Earl of Douglas. Douglas was killed in battle, as were 1800 English troops, while Hotspur was taken prisoner – a chain of events later made the subject of the medieval ballad of *Chevy Chase*. The battle site is about a mile northwest of the village, off the A68, marked by a stone cross set in a little pinewood. There are several places **to stay**, including the *Butterchurn Guest House*, opposite the church on Main Street (☎01830/520585; ②), and the comfortable *Percy Arms* itself (☎01830/520261; ⑤), further down the road. The *Border Reiver* (☎01830/520682) is part village shop, part coffee-house-restaurant, with just about every other service you could think of – from lottery tickets to dry-cleaning – thrown in to boot.

Rothbury and Cragside

ROTHBURY, straddling the River Coquet some eighteen miles northeast of Otterburn, prospered as a late Victorian resort because it gave ready access to the forests, burns and ridges of the Simonside Hills. Rothbury remains a popular spot for walkers, and the **Northumberland National Park Visitor Centre**, near the Cross on Church Street (daily: Easter–Oct 10am–5pm; July & Aug 10am–6pm; ☎01669/620887), offers advice on local trails, several of which begin in the Simonside Hills car park, a couple of miles southwest of town.

Victorian Rothbury was dominated by Sir William, later the first **Lord Armstrong**, the nineteenth-century engineer and arms manufacturer, who built his country home at **Cragside** (Easter–Oct Tues–Sun 1–5.30pm; £6.20; gardens only £3.95; NT), a mile to the east of the village. At first, Armstrong was satisfied with his modest house, but in 1869 he decided to build something more substantial, and hired Richard Norman Shaw, one of the period's top architects, to do the job. Work continued until the mid-1880s, the final version being a grandiose Tudor-style mansion, whose black and white timber-framed gables are entirely out of place in the Northumbrian countryside. The interior is stuffed with Armstrong's furnishings and fittings, heavy dark pieces enlivened by the William Morris stained glass in the library and the dining-room inglenook. Armstrong was an avid innovator, fascinated by hydraulic engineering and by hydroelectric power. At Cragside he could indulge himself, damming the Debdon Burn to power several domestic appliances, like the dumb waiter in the massive kitchen, as well as heating his personal Turkish-style plunge bath and steam room. In 1880, he also supplied Cragside with electricity, making this the first house in the world to be lit by hydroelectric power. The remains of the original system – including the powerhouse and pumping station – are still visible in the **grounds**, which, together with the **formal gardens**, have longer opening hours (same days 10.30am–7pm or dusk).

Buses from Newcastle's Haymarket station stop on the High Street, outside the *Queen's Head*. You can get local **tourist information** from the nearby National Park Visitor Centre (see p.646). There are several convenient **B&Bs** – like the *Orchard Guest House*, at the top of the High Street (☎01669/620684; ②), which also serves dinner. The *Queen's Head Hotel* (☎01669/620470; ②), at the other end of the High Street, has a few cheaper rooms without shower. Most of the places to **eat** are strung out along the High Street: the *Vale Café* serves all-day breakfasts and basic meals, and the *Sun Kitchen* is an old-fashioned tearoom.

Brinkburn Priory and Longframlington

From Rothbury the B6344 runs four miles southeast through pretty **Coquetdale**, following the course of the river, to reach **Brinkburn Priory** (Easter–Oct daily 10am–6pm; £1.60; EH), nestling in a loop of the Coquet. Founded as an Augustinian priory in 1135, its church – the only surviving building – was built fifty years later and it's this that provides the focus of interest today. Thoroughly but sympathetically restored in the nineteenth century, it's a superb example of northern Transitional architecture, featuring a fine Norman doorway and an echoing nave, empty save for a remarkable series of enormous contemporary wooden religious sculptures by Durham sculptor Fenwick Lawson. A couple of miles north of the priory, up the A697, you could make your base at the village of **LONGFRAMLINGTON**; there are half a dozen buses a day from Rothbury. The eighteenth-century *Granby Inn* (☎01665/570228; ③), on the High Street, is renowned for its large breakfasts, excellent home-made food and a range of malt whiskies in the bar.

The Northumberland coast

The low-lying **Northumberland coast**, stretching 64 miles north from Newcastle to the Scottish border, boasts many of the region's principal attractions, but first you have to clear the disfigured landscape of the old Northumbrian coalfield. Beyond Amble you emerge into a pastoral landscape that spreads over the thirty-odd miles to Berwick-upon-Tweed. On the way there's a succession of mighty fortresses, beginning with **Warkworth Castle** and **Alnwick Castle**, the stronghold-cum-stately-home of the Percys, the county's biggest landowners. Further along, there's the formidable fastness of **Bamburgh** and then, last of all, the magnificent Elizabethan ramparts surrounding **Berwick-upon-Tweed**. In between you'll find splendid sandy beaches – notably at Bamburgh and the small resort of **Alnmouth** – as well as Lindisfarne monastery on **Holy Island** and the sea-bird and nature reserve of the **Farne Islands**.

Warkworth

WARKWORTH, a coastal hamlet set in a loop of the River Coquet a couple of miles from Amble, is best seen from the north, from where the grey-stone terraces of the long main street slope up towards the commanding remains of **Warkworth Castle** (daily: April–Oct 10am–6pm; Nov–March 10am–1pm & 2–4pm; £2.40; EH). Enough remains of the outer wall to give a clear impression of the layout of the medieval bailey, but – apart from the well-preserved gatehouse through which the site is entered – nothing catches your attention as much as the **keep**. Mostly built in the fourteenth century, this three-storeyed structure, with its polygonal turrets and high central tower, has a honeycomb-like interior, a fine example of the designs developed by the castle-builders of Plantagenet England. The castle's cellars were used to good effect in the torture-chamber scenes in the Oscar-nominated film *Elizabeth* (1998). The main Castle Street sweeps down into the attractive village, flattening out at Dial Place, beyond which stands the church of **St Laurence**, whose many Norman features include the impressive ribbed vaulting of the chancel. A delightful path – signposted "Mill Walk" – heads the half-mile inland along the right bank of the Coquet to the boat that shuttles visitors across to **Warkworth Hermitage** (April–Sept Wed & Sun 11am–5pm; £1.60; EH), hewn out of the cliff above the river sometime in the fourteenth century.

Warkworth is on the route of the **bus service** linking Alnwick, Alnmouth and Newcastle, and **buses** stop in Dial Place, near the church. Alnmouth has the nearest **train station**, and is better placed for the beach, so you probably won't want to **stay** in Warkworth, though the village does possess a handful of B&Bs, including *Roxbro House*, 5 Castle Terrace (☎01665/711416; no credit cards; ①). Superior meals and teas are available at the *Greenhouse*, Dial Place (closed Sun eve & Mon), near the church. *Topsey Turvey's*, over the way at 1 Dial Place, is also open for bistro meals (closed Sun & Mon). Next door, the *Mason's Arms* has more traditional **pub food**.

Alnmouth

It's just three miles north from Warkworth to the seaside resort of **ALNMOUTH**, whose narrow, mostly nineteenth-century centre is strikingly situated on a steep spur of land between the sea and the estuary of the Aln. Alnmouth was a busy and prosperous port up until 1806, when the sea, driven by a freakish gale, broke through to the river and changed its course, moving the estuary from the south to the north side of Church Hill and rendering the original harbour useless. Alnmouth never really recovered, though it has been a low-key holiday spot since Victorian times, as attested by the elegant seaside villas.

There are local bus services from Alnwick and Warkworth, while the regular Newcastle to Alnwick **bus** passes through Alnmouth and calls at its **train station** at Hipsburn, a mile and a half west of the centre. Most of the **accommodation** lies along or just off the main Northumberland Street. Best central B&B is *The Grange* opposite the church (☎01665/830401; no credit cards; ②); a few yards further down Northumberland Street, at no. 56, *Copper Beach* (☎01665/830443; no credit cards; ②) has rooms in a period stone cottage. The *Tea Cosy Tea Room*, at no. 23 (☎01665/830393), serves bistro dinners at weekends in summer, or eat at the oak-beamed *Beaches* (underneath *Copper Beach B&B*), which dishes up meals of local cod, filo-stuffed chicken, beef stir-fries and the like.

Alnwick

The unassuming town of **ALNWICK** (pronounced "Annick"), thirty miles north of Newcastle and four miles inland from Alnmouth, is renowned for its castle – seat of the dukes of Northumberland – which overlooks the River Aln immediately to the north of the town centre. Alnwick itself is an appealing market town of cobbled streets and Georgian houses, centred on the old cross in Market Place, site of a weekly **market** (Saturdays) since the thirteenth century. Other than catching the market in full swing, the best time to visit is during the boisterous week-long **Alnwick Fair**, a medieval re-enactment which starts on the last Sunday in June. There's a costumed procession on that day, preceded by street entertainment, with stalls doing a roaring trade in roast ox sandwiches.

The Percys – raised to the dukedom of Northumberland in 1750 – have owned the **Castle** (Easter–Sept daily 11am–5pm; £5.95) since 1309, when Henry de Percy rein-forced the original Norman keep and remodelled its curtain wall. In the eighteenth cen-tury, the castle was badly in need of a refit, so the first duke had the interior refurbished by Robert Adam in an extravagant Gothic style – which in turn was supplanted by the gaudy Italianate decoration preferred by the fourth duke in the 1850s. Entry to the cas-tle is through the carriageway to the right of the fourteenth-century barbican, whose sturdy battlements sport a number of stone soldiers, a piece of eighteenth-century flummery replacing the figurines of medieval times, set up there to ward off the evil eye. Beyond, the broad lawns of the bailey surround the heavy walls of the **keep**, where the **entrance hall** is covered with the armaments of the Percy Tenantry Volunteers, a private force raised by the second duke during the Napoleonic Wars. The hall leads to the **grand staircase**, a marble pomposity that climbs up to the guard chamber, whose Renaissance-style decor, from the mosaic floor to the stucco ceiling, is typical of the work of the Italian craftsmen hired by the fourth duke. The most lavish decoration is in the **red drawing room**, where the rich polygonal panels of the ceiling bear down on damask-covered walls and some magnificent ebony cabinets rescued from Versailles during the French Revolution.

Alnwick **bus station** is on Clayport Street, a couple of minutes' walk west of the Market Place, where you'll find the **tourist office**, in the arcaded Shambles (April–Sept Mon–Sat 9am–5pm, Sun 10am–4pm; Oct–March Mon–Fri 9am–5pm, Sat 10am–4pm; ☎01665/510665). Several **B&Bs** lie just beyond the gatehouse at the end of Bondgate. Here, among others along Bondgate Without, you'll find the *Lindisfarne* at no. 6 (☎01665/603430; no credit cards; ①) and the *Oronsay Guest House*, a Victorian villa at no. 18 (☎01665/603559; no credit cards; ①). Alnwick's main **hotel** is the *White Swan*, on Bondgate Within (☎01665/602109; ⑤) – the hotel's fine panelled dining room was swiped from an old ocean liner, the *Olympic*, which was the twin of the *Titanic*. You can **camp** at *Alnwick Rugby Club* in Greensfield Park (☎01665/602987; closed Nov–March), a little way south of the centre. *Copperfields Coffee House*, 11 Market St, opposite the tourist office, serves daytime **meals**, or visit the *Gate Bistro*, 14 Bondgate Within (closed Mon, plus Tues & Sun eves in winter). The "Dirty Bottles" in *Ye Olde Cross*'s window on Narrowgate have supposedly not been moved for two centuries, since the person who put them there dropped down dead immediately afterwards. Check to see what's on at the **Alnwick Playhouse**, just through the arch on Bondgate Without (☎01665/510785), a venue for theatre, music and film throughout the year.

Craster and Dunstanburgh Castle

Heading northeast out of Alnwick along the B1340, it's a six-mile hop to the region's kipper capital, the tiny fishing village of **CRASTER**, perched above its minuscule harbour. There's not a great deal to make you stop long, but you can buy kippers here at Robson's factory and have a pot of tea in the *Bark Pots*. Even better is the *Jolly Fisherman*, the **pub** above the harbour, with sea views from its back window and famously good crab sandwiches. Most spectacularly, however, the village provides access to **Dunstanburgh Castle** (April–Oct daily 10am–6pm; Nov–March Wed–Sun 10am–4pm; £1.80; NT & EH), whose shattered medieval ruins occupy a magnificent promontory about thirty minutes' windy walk up the coast. Originally built in the fourteenth century, parts of the surrounding walls survive – offering heart-stopping views down to the crashing sea below – though the dominant feature is the massive keep-gatehouse which stands out from miles around on the bare coastal spur.

In summer, half-a-dozen **buses** a day (the #501 and #401) run to Craster from Alnwick, a half-hour journey; the service continues to Seahouses and Bamburgh.

Seahouses and the Farne Islands

From Craster, it's twelve miles north to **SEAHOUSES**, a desultory fishing-port-cum-resort that's the embarkation point for **boat trips** to the windswept and treeless **Farne Islands**, a rocky archipelago lying a few miles offshore. Owned by the National Trust and maintained as a nature reserve, the Farnes are the summer home of many species of migrating seabirds, especially puffins, guillemots, terns and kittiwakes. To protect the birds, only two of the islands are open to visitors: **Inner Farne** (April–Sept daily; landing fee £4) and **Staple Island** (same months & prices). The crossing can be rough, but the islands have a wild beauty that makes it all worthwhile, and on Inner Farne you can also visit a tiny, restored fourteenth-century chapel built in honour of Saint Cuthbert, who spent much of his life here. Weather permitting, several boat owners operate daily **excursions**, usually starting at around 10am: Billy Shiels (Easter–Oct; ☎01665/720308), the best of the bunch, runs a varied programme, from two-and-a-half-hour **cruises** round either island (£8), to all-day trips landing at both (£15); all trips also visit the grey seal colonies off the islands. For more information, call the **National Trust Shop**, 16 Main St, Seahouses (☎01665/721099), across from the *Olde Ship*, 9 Main St (☎01665/720200; ④), easily the most atmospheric place in Seahouses to stay, eat and drink.

Bamburgh

Flanking a triangular green in the lee of its castle, three miles north of Seahouses, the tiny village of **BAMBURGH** is only a five-minute walk from two splendid sandy beaches, backed by rolling, tufted dunes. From the sands **Bamburgh Castle** (April–Oct daily 11am–5pm; £4) is a spectacular sight, its elongated battlements crowning a formidable basalt crag high above the beach. This beautiful spot was first fortified by the Celts, but its heyday was as an Anglo-Saxon stronghold, one-time capital of Northumbria and the protector of the preserved head and hand of Saint Oswald, the seventh-century king who invited Saint Aidan over from Iona to convert his subjects. Rotted by centuries of seaspray and buffeted by winter storms, Bamburgh Castle struggled on until 1894, when a new owner, Lord Armstrong, demolished most of the structure to replace it with a cumbersome castle-mansion, whose focal point is a Great Hall featuring an exquisite collection of Fabergé stone animal carvings. In the basement of the keep, the stone-vaulted ceiling maintains its Norman appearance, making a suitable arena for a display of suits of armour.

Bamburgh is also the home of the **Grace Darling Museum** (Easter to mid-Oct Mon–Sat 11am–7pm, Sun 2–6pm; donation requested), which celebrates the daring sea rescue accomplished by Grace and her lighthouseman father, William, in September, 1838. It began when a gale dashed the steamship *Forfarshire* against the rocks of the Farne Islands. Nine passengers struggled onto a reef, where they were subsequently saved by the Darlings, who left the safety of the lighthouse to row out to them. *The Times* trumpeted Grace's bravery, offers of marriage and requests for locks of her hair streamed into the Darlings' lighthouse home and for the rest of her brief life Grace was plagued by unwanted visitors – she died of tuberculosis aged 26 in 1842. The museum details the rescue and displays the fragile boat the Darlings used; in the churchyard of thirteenth-century **St Aidan's** opposite is the Gothic Revival memorial that covers Grace's body.

A regular **bus** service links Alnwick and Berwick-upon-Tweed with Bamburgh; it stops on Front Street by the green. There are several places **to stay**, including the *Lord Crewe Arms Hotel*, Front Street (☎01668/214243; ⑤; closed Nov–Feb), an old inn with oak beams and open fires. Nearby *Green Gates*, 34 Front St (☎01668/214 535; no credit cards; ②), has a couple of rooms with castle views, and there are also rooms at the *Green House*, 5–6 Front St (☎01668/214513; ②; closed Jan), at the top of the village. There are a couple of tearooms, a bucket-and-spade general store, and meals in the *Green House* restaurant (closed Sun) of local meat and fish.

Holy Island

There's something rather menacing about the approach to **Holy Island**, past the barnacle-encrusted marker poles that line the causeway. The danger of drowning is real enough if you ignore the safe crossing times posted at the start of the three-mile trip across the tidal flats. (The island is cut off for about five hours every day, so to avoid a tedious delay consult the tide timetables at one of the region's tourist offices.) Once here, it's easy to picture the furious Viking hordes sweeping across Holy Island, giving no quarter to the monks at this quiet outpost of early Christianity. Today's sole village is plain in the extreme, which doesn't deter summer day-trippers from clogging the car parks as soon as the causeway is open. But Holy Island has a distinctive and isolated atmosphere, especially out of season.

Once known as **Lindisfarne**, Holy Island has an illustrious history. It was here that Saint Aidan of Iona founded a monastery at the invitation of King Oswald of Northumbria in 634. The monks quickly evangelized the northeast and established a reputation for scholarship and artistry, the latter exemplified by the **Lindisfarne Gospels**, the apotheosis of Celtic religious art, now kept in the British Museum. The monastery had sixteen bishops in all, the most celebrated being **Saint Cuthbert**, who only accepted the job after Ecgfrith, another Northumbrian king, pleaded with him. But Cuthbert never settled here and, within two years, he was back in his hermit's cell on the Farne Islands, where he died in 687. His colleagues rowed the body back to Lindisfarne, which became a place of pilgrimage until 875, when the monks abandoned the island in fear of marauding Vikings, taking Cuthbert's remains with them – the first part of the saint's long posthumous journey to Durham. In 1082 Lindisfarne, renamed Holy Island, was colonized by Benedictines from Durham, but the monastery was a shadow of its former self, a minor religious house with only a handful of attendant monks, the last of whom was evicted at the Dissolution.

Just off the green, the pinkish sandstone ruins of **Lindisfarne Priory** (daily: Easter–Oct 10am–6pm; Nov–Easter 10am–4pm; £2.80; EH) are from the Benedictine foundation. Enough survives to provide a clear impression of the original structure, notably the tight Romanesque arches of the nave and the gravity-defying stonework of the central tower's last remaining arch. Behind lie the scant remains of the monastic buildings while adjacent is the mostly thirteenth-century church of **St Mary the Virgin**, whose delightful churchyard overlooks the ruins. The **museum** (entrance included in priory fee) features a collection of incised stones that constitute all that remains of the first monastery. The finest of them is a round-headed tombstone showing armed Northumbrians on one side, and kneeling figures before the Cross on the other – presumably a propagandist's view of the beneficial effects of Christianity.

Stuck on a small pyramid of rock half a mile away from the village, past the dock and along the seashore, **Lindisfarne Castle** (April–Oct Mon–Thurs, Sat & Sun 1–5.30pm; £4; NT) was built in the middle of the sixteenth century to protect the island's harbour from the Scots. It was, however, merely a decaying shell when Edward Hudson, the founder of *Country Life* magazine, stumbled across it in 1901. Hudson bought the castle and turned it into a holiday home to designs by Edwin Lutyens, who used the irregular levels of the building to create the L-shaped living quarters that survive today. The two historic sites are all that most people bother with, but a **walk** around the island's perimeter is a fine way to spend a couple of hours. Most of the northwestern portion of the island is maintained as a **nature reserve**: from a bird hide you can spot terns and plovers, and then plod through the dunes and grasses to your heart's content.

Practicalities

The #477 **bus** from Berwick-upon-Tweed to Holy Island has a twice-daily service (not Sun) from mid-July to the end of August; services two or three days a week on either side, between May and September; and a severely reduced service between October and March. Departure times vary with the tides, and the journey takes thirty minutes; call the Berwick Bus Shop (☎01289/307283) for details. All walkers and drivers must check the **tide tables** (at any local tourist office) to see when it's safe to cross.

The island is short on places **to stay** and you should make an advance booking, whenever you visit. Two good places are the *North View Guest House*, on Marygate (☎01289/389222; ③; closed Jan), which offers comfortable rooms in a sixteenth-century listed building; or the friendly *Britannia House* (☎01289/389218; no credit cards; ②; closed Nov–Feb), just by the green. Camping isn't allowed anywhere on the island. Guests at *North View* are lucky since they can partake of the good-value set dinner. Otherwise you have to take your chances in the *Ship* – pick of the **pubs**, with good Holy Island Bitter – the *Lindisfarne Hotel* or the *Manor House Hotel*, all of which have similarly uninspiring menus.

Berwick-upon-Tweed

Before the union of England and Scotland in 1603, **BERWICK-UPON-TWEED**, some twelve miles north of Holy Island, was the quintessential frontier town, changing hands no fewer than fourteen times between 1174 and 1482, when the Scots finally ceded the stronghold to the English. Interminable cross-border warfare ruined Berwick's economy, turning the prosperous Scottish port of the thirteenth century into an impoverished garrison town, which the English forcibly cut off from its natural trading hinterland up the River Tweed. By the late sixteenth century, Berwick's fortifications were in a dreadful state of repair and Elizabeth I, apprehensive of the resurgent alliance between France and Scotland, had the place rebuilt in line with the latest principles of military architecture.

The new design recognized the technological development of artillery, which had rendered the traditional high stone wall obsolete. Consequently, Berwick's **ramparts**

– one and a half miles long and still in pristine condition – are no more than twenty feet high but incredibly thick: a facing of ashlared stone protects ten to twelve feet of rubble, which, in turn, backs up against a vast quantity of earth. Further protected by ditches on three sides and the Tweed on the fourth, the walls are strengthened by immense bastions, whose arrowhead-shape ensured that every part of the wall could be covered by fire. Begun in 1558, the defences were completed after eleven years at a cost of £128,000, more than Elizabeth paid for all her other fortifications put together. And, as it turned out, it was all a waste of time and money: the French didn't attack and, once England and Scotland were united, Berwick was stuck with a white elephant.

The Town

Today, the easy **stroll** along the top of the ramparts offers a succession of fine views out to sea, across the Tweed and over the orange-tiled rooftops of a town that's distinguished by its elegant Georgian mansions. These, dating from Berwick's resurgence as a seaport between 1750 and 1820, are the town's most attractive feature, with the tapering **Lions' House**, on Windmill Hill, and the daintily decorated facades of **Quay Walls**, beside the river, of particular note. The three bridges spanning the Tweed are worth a second look too – the huge arches of the **Royal Border Railway Bridge**, built in the manner of a Roman aqueduct by Robert Stephenson in the 1840s, contrasting with the desultory concrete of the **Royal Tweed**, completed in 1928 and the modest seventeenth-century **Berwick Bridge**.

Within the ramparts, the Berwick skyline is punctured by the stumpy spire of the eighteenth-century **Town Hall** at the bottom of Marygate, right at the heart of the compact centre. This retains its original jailhouse, now housing the **Cell Block Museum** (Easter–Oct Mon–Fri tours at 10.30am & 2pm; £1) with its tales of crime and punishment in Berwick. From here, it's a couple of minutes' walk along Church Street to **Holy Trinity Church**, one of the few churches built during the Commonwealth, the absence of a tower supposedly reflecting the wishes of Cromwell, who found them irreligious. Opposite the church, the elongated **Barracks** (Easter–Oct daily 10am–6pm; Nov–Easter Wed–Sun 10am–4pm; £2.60; EH) date from the early eighteenth century and were in use until 1964, when the King's Own Scottish Borderers regiment decamped. Inside, there's a predictable regimental museum, rescued only by the fine proportions of the barracks buildings themselves, and by a superior **Borough Museum and Art Gallery**, sited in the so-called Clock Block. Geared up for school parties, the museum features imaginative dioramas, recordings and displays of local traditional life, even a model of a local clergyman haranguing visitors from his pulpit.

Practicalities

From Berwick **train station** it's ten minutes' walk down Castlegate to the town centre. Most regional **buses** also stop in front of the station, though some also stop closer in on Golden Square (where Castlegate meets Marygate), on the approach to the Royal Tweed Bridge. For all local bus information, call in at the **Berwick Bus Shop**, 125 Marygate (☎01289/307283). Eastern Lane runs off Marygate, where you'll find the **tourist office** in the Maltings arts centre (July & Aug Mon–Wed 10am–6pm, Thurs–Sat 10am–8pm, Sun 10am–4pm; rest of year Mon–Wed 10am–6pm, Thurs–Sat 10am–8pm; ☎01289/330733).

In the centre, the best-value **B&B** is at *3 Scott's Place* (☎01289/305323, *scottsplace@btinternet.com*; ②), a Georgian town house off Castlegate. Also highly recommended is *No.1 Sallyport*, 41 Bridge St (☎01289/308827; ③), a seventeenth-century house next to the city walls (above the Bridge Street Bookshop). Other options include *Clovelly House*, 58 West St (☎01289/302337; ②), and the *Riverview Guest House*, 11 Quay Walls (☎01289/306295; ②; closed Jan & Feb). The finest central **hotel** is the *King's Arms*, Hide Hill (☎01289/307454; ⑤), one of the myriad English coaching inns that Charles Dickens is supposed to have slept and lectured in. Across Berwick Bridge in Tweedmouth, you can't beat the delightful *Old Vicarage Guest House*, a spacious Victorian villa at 24 Church Rd (☎01289/306909; ③).

For daytime **snacks**, **coffee** and **lunches**, you're best off at *Popinjays* café on Hide Hill. Berwick's best **restaurant** is *Foxton's*, 26 Hide Hill (☎01289/303939), a brasserie serving a full menu (with chargrilled specialities) alongside its daytime menu of sandwiches and coffees. The *Barrels Ale House*, 59–61 Bridge St at the foot of the Berwick Bridge, has guest beers, tapas lunches and an extraordinary back room with over-the-top sculpted tables and chairs. The Maltings on Eastern Lane is Berwick's **arts centre** (☎01289/330999), with a year-round programme of music, theatre, film and dance, and river views from its licensed café.

travel details

Trains

Darlington to: Bishop Auckland (every 1–2hr; 30min).

Durham to: Darlington (2 hourly; 20min); London (hourly; 3hr); Newcastle (2 hourly; 20min); York (hourly; 50min).

Hexham to: Carlisle (hourly; 1hr); Haltwhistle (hourly; 20min); Newcastle (hourly; 40min).

Middlesbrough to: Durham (hourly; 50min); Newcastle (hourly; 1hr 10min); Saltburn (hourly; 40min).

Newcastle to: Alnmouth (Mon–Sat 5 daily, 3 on Sun; 30min); Berwick-upon-Tweed (hourly; 45min); Carlisle (7 daily; 1hr 30min); Corbridge (Mon–Sat hourly, 4 on Sun; 40min); Durham (2 hourly; 20min); Haltwhistle (hourly; 1hr); Hexham (hourly; 40min); London (hourly; 3hr 15min).

Buses

Alnwick to: Bamburgh (4–6 daily; 1hr); Berwick-upon-Tweed (3 daily; 2hr).

Bamburgh to: Alnwick (4–6 daily; 1hr); Craster (4–5 daily; 30–40min); Seahouses (Mon–Sat 9 daily, 4 on Sun; 10min).

Barnard Castle to: Bishop Auckland (Mon–Sat 9 daily, 6 on Sun; 50min); Darlington (hourly; 35–45min); Middleton-in-Teesdale (hourly; 25–35min); Raby Castle (9 daily; 15min); Staindrop (Mon–Sat 9 daily, 6 on Sun; 15min).

Berwick-upon-Tweed to: Holy Island (2 daily; 30min); Newcastle (Mon–Sat 6 daily, 3 on Sun; 2hr 20min–3hr 10min).

Bishop Auckland to: Barnard Castle (Mon–Sat 9 daily, 6 on Sun; 50min); Darlington (Mon–Sat hourly; 40min); Hexham (1 weekly; 1hr 50min); Newcastle (hourly; 1hr 15min); Stanhope (Mon–Sat 7 daily, Sun 4; 45min).

Darlington to: Barnard Castle (hourly; 35–45min); Bishop Auckland (every 20min; 45min); Carlisle (1 daily; 3hr 15min); Middleton-in-Teesdale (Mon–Sat 9 daily, Sun 3; 1hr 20min).

Durham to: Barnard Castle (1 daily; 1hr); Beamish (May–Sept 1–3 daily; 30min); Bishop Auckland (2 hourly; 30min); Darlington (2 hourly; 1hr); Newcastle (hourly; 1hr); Stanhope (June–Sept 1–2 weekly; 45min).

Haltwhistle to: Greenhead (mid-July to early Sept Mon–Sat 4 daily, 1 on Sun; 5min); Hexham (hourly; 40min).

Hexham to: Bellingham (Mon–Sat 5 daily; 40min); Bishop Auckland (1 weekly; 1hr 50min); Blanchland (1 weekly; 45min); Chesters (mid-July to early Sept 1–4 daily; 15min); Haltwhistle (hourly; 40min); Housesteads (mid-July to early Sept Mon–Sat 4, 1 on Sun; 30min); Once Brewed (mid-July to early Sept Mon–Sat 4 daily, 1 on Sun; 40min); Otterburn (1 weekly; 1hr); Vindolanda (mid-July to early Sept Mon–Sat 4 daily, 1 on Sun; 40min).

Middlesbrough to: Newcastle (hourly; 1hr); Redcar (hourly; 30min); Saltburn (hourly; 40min).

Middleton-in-Teesdale to: High Force (Tues, Wed, Fri, Sat & Sun 2–3 daily; 12min); Langdon Beck (Tues, Wed, Fri, Sat & Sun 2–3 daily; 18min).

Newcastle to: Alnmouth (hourly; 1hr 30min); Alnwick (Mon–Sat 6 daily, 3 on Sun; 1hr

10min–1hr 45min); Bamburgh (3 daily; 2hr 30min); Barnard Castle (1 daily; 1hr 30min); Berwick-upon-Tweed (Mon–Sat 6 daily, 3 on Sun; 2hr 20min–3hr 10min); Carlisle (hourly; 2hr); Corbridge (Mon–Sat 2 hourly, 1 every 2hr on Sun; 1hr); Craster (3 daily; 1hr 50min); Durham (hourly; 1hr); Hexham (Mon–Sat 2 hourly, 1 every 2hr on Sun; 1hr 15min); Middlesbrough (hourly; 1hr); Otterburn (2 daily; 2hr); Rothbury (Mon–Sat 7 daily, 2 on Sun; 1hr 15min); Seahouses (3 daily; 2hr 10min); Stanhope (1–2 weekly; 1hr 10min); Warkworth (hourly; 1hr 20min); Wooler (Mon–Fri 1–2 daily, 4 on Sat; 2hr–2hr 20min).

PART THREE

WALES

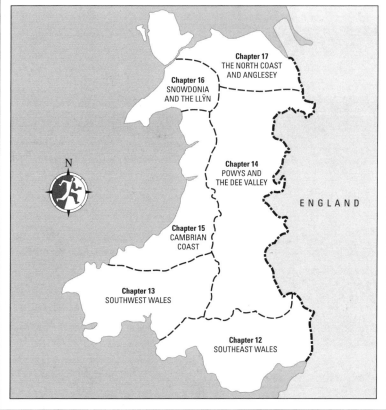

Chapter 17
THE NORTH COAST
AND ANGLESEY

Chapter 16
SNOWDONIA
AND THE LLŶN

Chapter 14
POWYS AND
THE DEE VALLEY

ENGLAND

N

Chapter 15
CAMBRIAN
COAST

Chapter 13
SOUTHWEST WALES

Chapter 12
SOUTHEAST WALES

CHAPTER TWELVE

SOUTHEAST WALES

H ome to almost 1.8 million people, sixty percent of Wales's population, the south-eastern corner is also one of Britain's most industrialized regions. Population and industry are most heavily concentrated in the seaports on the south coast, and in the former coal mining valleys sliced into the mountainous terrain to the north.

Beguilingly rural **Monmouthshire** is the easternmost county in Wales, abutting the English border. The **River Wye** crisscrosses between the two countries to its mouth at the fortress town of **Chepstow**, where you'll find one of the most impressive castles in a land where few towns are without one. In the Wye's beautiful valley lie the spectacularly placed ruins of **Tintern Abbey**, downstream of the old county town of **Monmouth**.

Monmouthshire becomes increasingly industrialized as you travel west towards **Newport**, Wales's third largest conurbation. Although it is hardly likely to feature on a swift tour of Wales, the town has an excellent museum and the remains of an extensive Roman settlement at **Caerleon**, a northern suburb of the town. Western Monmouthshire and northern Glamorgan constitute the world-famous **Valleys**, once the coal- and iron-rich powerhouse of the nation. This is the Wales of popular imagination: hemmed-in valley floors packed with lines of blank, grey houses, slanted almost impossibly towards the pithead. Although nearly all of the mines have since closed, the area is still one of tight-knit towns, with a rich working-class heritage that displays itself in some excellent museums and colliery tours, such as **Big Pit** at Blaenafon and the **Rhondda Heritage Park** in Trehafod. The valleys course down past the foursquare moated castle at **Caerphilly** to the great ports of the coast, which once shipped Wales's products all over the world. The greatest of them all was **Cardiff**, now long past its heyday as the world's busiest coal port, but bouncing back in its comparatively new status as Wales's upbeat capital. Excellent museums, a massive castle, exciting rejuvenation projects around the Victorian docks and Wales's best cultural pursuits make the city an essential stop.

The west of Glamorgan is dominated by Wales's second city, **Swansea**, rougher, tougher and less anglicized than the capital. Like Cardiff, Swansea grew principally on the strength of its docks, and sits on an impressive arc of coast that shelves round from the belching steel works of Port Talbot in the east to **Mumbles** and **Oystermouth**, holiday towns of amusement arcades, copious pubs and chip shops, on the jaw of the

---

ACCOMMODATION PRICE CODES

Throughout this guide, hotel and B&B accommodation is priced on a scale of ① to ⑨, the number indicating the **lowest price** you could expect to pay per night in that establishment for a **double room** in high season. The prices indicated by the codes are as follows:

① under £40	④ £60–70	⑦ £110–150
② £40–50	⑤ £70–90	⑧ £150–200
③ £50–60	⑥ £90–110	⑨ over £200

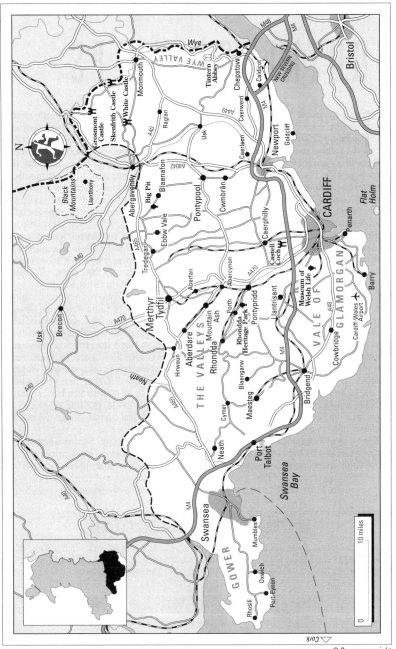

© Crown copyright

delightful **Gower Peninsula** in the west. One of the country's favourite playgrounds, Gower juts out into the sea like a mini-Wales of grand beaches, rocky headlands, bracken heaths and ruined castles.

The Wye Valley

Perhaps the most anglicized corner of Wales, the **Wye Valley** – along with the rest of Monmouthshire – was only finally recognized as part of Wales in the local government reorganization of 1974. Before then, the county was officially included as part of neither England nor Wales, so that maps were frequently headlined "Wales and Monmouthshire". Most of the rest of Monmouthshire is firmly and redoubtably Welsh, but the woodlands and hills by the meandering River Wye have more in common with the landscape over the border. The two main centres are **Chepstow**, with its massive castle radiating an awesome strength high above the muddy flats and waters of the river estuary; and the spruce, old-fashioned town of **Monmouth**, sixteen miles upstream. Six miles north of Chepstow lie the inspirational ruins of the Cistercian **Tintern Abbey**.

Chepstow and around

Of all the places that call themselves "the gateway to Wales", **CHEPSTOW** (Cas-Gwent) has probably the greatest claim, situated on the western bank of the River Wye, the current border, just over a mile from where its tidal waters flow out into the muddy Severn estuary. Chepstow is a sturdy place robbed of the immediate charm of many other Welsh market towns by soulless modern developments. Nonetheless, there's an identifiably medieval street plan hemmed in by the thirteenth-century **Port Wall**, which encases a tight loop of the River Wye and the strategically-sited **Chepstow Castle** (June–Sept daily 9.30am–6pm; April, May & Oct daily 9.30am–5pm; Nov–March Mon–Sat 9.30am–4pm, Sun 11am–4pm; £3). Guarding one of the most important routes into Wales, Chepstow was the first stone castle to be built in Britain, the Great Tower keep being built in 1067 to help subdue the restless Welsh. The Lower Ward is the largest of the three enclosures and dates mainly from the thirteenth century. Here you'll find the **Great Hall**, the home of a wide-ranging exhibition on the history of the castle, with particular emphasis on the English Civil War years, when Royalist Chepstow was twice besieged. Twelfth-century defences separate the Lower Ward from the Middle Ward, which is dominated by the still imposing ruins of the **Great Tower**. Beyond this is the far narrower Upper Ward, which leads up to the Barbican **watchtower** from where there are superb views looking down the cliff to the river estuary.

Opposite is the **Chepstow Museum** (Mon–Sat 11am–1pm & 2–5pm, Sun 2–5pm; £1) containing nostalgic photographs and paintings of the trades supported in the past by the River Wye, and recording Chepstow's brief life in the early part of this century as a shipbuilding centre.

Practicalities

Chepstow's **train station** is five minutes' walk to the south of the High Street; its **bus station** is behind the shops on the other side of the western Town Gate. The **tourist office** is located in the castle car park, off Bridge Street (daily: Easter–Oct 10am–6pm; Nov–Easter 10am–1pm & 2–4pm; ☎01291/623772). Inexpensive B&B **accommodation** can be found at *Mrs Batchlor*, 7 Lancaster Way (☎01291/626344; ①), fifteen minutes' walk from the centre of town towards Tintern; *Afon Gwy*, 28 Bridge St (☎01291/620158, ②); and, a mile east of town, over the Wye, the wonderful *Upper*

Sedbury House, Sedbury Lane (☎01291/627173; ①). The nearest **YHA hostel**, *St Briavels Castle* (☎01594/530272, *stbriavels@yha.org.uk*; ①), is seven miles northeast over the border, in England.

Chepstow has a handful of decent **restaurants** and a host of good **pubs**. *The Grape Escape*, on St Mary's Street, by the river, is best for reasonably inexpensive dining. For gourmet meals, try the moderately priced *Wye Knot*, on The Back (☎01291/622929). For an earthy local pub, pop into the *Five Alls*, at the bottom of High Street.

Tintern Abbey

Six miles north of Chepstow, along one of the River Wye's most spectacular stretches, **Tintern Abbey** (June–Sept daily 9.30am–6pm; April, May & Oct daily 9.30am–5pm; Nov–March Mon–Sat 9.30am–4pm, Sun 11am–4pm; £2.40; CADW) has inspired writers and painters – Wordsworth and Turner among them – for over two hundred years. Such is the place's enormous popularity, however, that it's advisable to go out of season or at either end of the day when the hordes have thinned out. The abbey was founded in 1131 by Cistercian monks from Normandy. Most of the remaining buildings, however, date from the massive rebuilding and expansion plan in the fourteenth century, when Tintern was at its mightiest. Its survival after the depredations of the Dissolution is largely thanks to its remoteness, as there were no nearby villages ready to use the abbey stone for rebuilding.

The centrepiece of the complex is the magnificent Gothic **church**, whose remarkable tracery and intricate stonework remains intact. Around the church are the less substantial ruins of the monks' domestic quarters and cloister, mostly reduced to one-storey rubble. The course of the abbey's waste disposal system can be seen in the Great Drain, an irregular channel that links kitchens, toilets and the Infirmary with the nearby Wye. The **Novices' Hall** lies handily close to the Warming House, which together with the kitchen and Infirmary would have been the only heated parts of the abbey, suggesting that novices might have gained a falsely favourable impression of monastic life before taking their final vows.

Monmouth and around

Enclosed on three sides by the rivers Wye and Monnow, **MONMOUTH** (Trefynwy), fifteen miles north of Chepstow, retains some of its quiet charm as an important border post and county town, and makes a good base for a drive – or a long hike – around the **Three Castles** of the pastoral border country to the north.

The centre of the town is **Agincourt Square**, a handsome open space at the top of the wide, shop-lined Monnow Street, which descends gently to the thirteenth-century bridge over the River Monnow. The cobbled square is dominated by the arched, Georgian **Shire Hall**, in which is embedded an eighteenth-century statue of the Monmouth-born King Henry V, victor of the Battle of Agincourt, in 1415. In front is the pompous statue of another local, the Honourable Charles Stewart Rolls – the co-founder of Rolls-Royce, and, in 1910, the first man to pilot a double-flight over the English Channel. Almost opposite Shire Hall is **Castle Hill**, which you can walk up to glimpse some of the scant ruins of the **castle**, founded in 1068.

Priory Street leads north from Agincourt Square to the market hall, where the **Nelson Museum** (Mon–Sat 10am–1pm & 2–5pm, Sun 2–5pm; £1) attempts to portray the life of one of the most successful sea-going Britons through use of the Admiral's personal artefacts – collected by Charles Rolls' mother, who was an admirer. At the very bottom of Monnow Street, the road narrows to squeeze into the confines of the seven-hundred-year-old **Monnow bridge**, crowned with its hulking stone gate of 1262, that served both as a means of defence for the town and a toll-collection point.

Buses operate from the **bus station** behind Kwik Save, at the bottom of Monnow

Street. The **tourist office** is in the Shire Hall, Agincourt Square (daily: April–Oct 10am–6pm; Nov–March 9.30am–5.30pm; ☎01600/713899). **Accommodation** in town is thin on the ground: try the simple but good *Burton Guesthouse*, on Street James Square (☎01600/714958; ①), the intimate *Riverside Hotel*, on Cinderhill Street, over the Monnow Bridge (☎01600/715577; ③), or the excellent *Church Farm Guesthouse*, two miles south, in the village of Mitchel Troy (☎01600/712176; ②). The nearest tent-friendly **campsites** are both on Drybridge Street (through Monnow Bridge then right): the *Monnow Bridge* (☎01600/714004), behind the *Three Horseshoes* pub, and the slightly pricier *Monmouth Caravan Park* (☎01600/714745), a quarter of a mile beyond.

Inexpensive daytime **eating** can be had at either *Maltsters Coffee Shop*, on St Mary's Street, or at *Cygnet's Kitchen*, White Swan Court, off Church Street, which serves more substantial soups and casseroles, and has outside seating. The *French Horn* (☎01600/772733), handsomely situated at 24 Church St, serves moderately priced French fare for lunch and dinner. You can opt for inexpensive pub grub at the *Punch House*, in Agincourt Square, or the *Green Dragon*, in St Thomas Square, down by the Monnow Bridge.

Raglan

RAGLAN (Rhaglan), seven miles west of Monmouth, is an unassuming village worth visiting for its glorious **Castle** (June–Sept daily 9.30am–6pm; April, May & Oct daily 9am–5pm; Nov–March Mon–Sat 9.30am–4pm, Sun 11am–4pm; £2.40; CADW), whose fussy and comparatively intact style make it stand out from so many other crumbling Welsh fortresses. The last medieval fortification built in Britain, the design of which combines practical strength with ostentatious style, Raglan was begun on the site of a Norman motte in 1435 by Sir William ap Thomas. The **gatehouse**, still used as the main entrance, houses the best examples of the castle's showy decoration in its heraldic shields, intricate stonework edging and gargoyles. In the mid-fifteenth century, ap Thomas's grandson, William Herbert II, was responsible for the two inner courts, built around his grandfather's original gatehouse, hall and keep. The first is the cobbled **Pitched Stone Court**, designed to house the functional rooms like the kitchen, with its two vast, double-flued chimneys, and the servants' quarters. To the left is **Fountain Court**, a well-proportioned grassy space surrounded by opulent residences that once included grand apartments and state rooms. Separating the two are the original hall, from 1435, the buttery, the remains of the chapel and the dank, cold cellars below.

The Three Castles

The fertile, low-lying land between the Monnow and Usk rivers was important as an easy access route into the agricultural lands of South Wales, and in the eleventh century the Norman invaders built a trio of strongholds here to protect their interests. In 1201, Skenfrith, Grosmont and White castles were presented by King John to Hubert de Burgh, who employed sophisticated new ideas on castle design to replace the earlier, square-keeped castles. In 1260, the advancing army of Llywelyn ap Gruffydd began to threaten the king's supremacy in South Wales, and the three castles were refortified in readiness. Gradually, the castles were adapted as living quarters and royal administration centres, and the only return to military usage came in 1404–5, when Owain Glyndŵr's army pressed down to Grosmont, only to be defeated by the future King Henry V. The castles slipped into disrepair, and were finally sold separately in 1902, the first time since 1138 that the three had fallen out of single ownership.

White Castle (April–Sept daily 10am–5pm; £2), eight miles northwest of Monmouth and six miles east of Abergavenny (see p.711), is the most awesome of the three, sited in rolling countryside with some superb views over to the hills surrounding the River Monnow. A few patches of the white rendering that gave the castle its name can be seen

---

THE CHARTISTS

In an era when wealthy landowners bought votes from the enfranchised few, the struggles of the **Chartists** were perhaps a historical inevitability. Thousands gathered around the 1838 People's Charter that called for universal male franchise, a secret, annual ballot for Parliament and the abolition of property qualifications for the vote. Demonstrations in support of these principles were held all over the country, with some of the most vociferous and bloodiest taking place in the radical heartlands of industrial South Wales. On November 4, 1839, Chartists from all over Monmouthshire marched on Newport and descended Stow Hill, whereupon they were gunned down by soldiers hiding in the Westgate Hotel; 22 protesters were killed. The leaders of the rebellion were sentenced to death, although the self-righteous and wealthy leaders of the town subsequently commuted their punishment to transportation. Queen Victoria even knighted the mayor who ordered the shooting.

---

on the exterior walls. The grassy Outer Ward is enclosed by a curtain wall with four towers, divided by a moat from the brooding mass of the Inner Ward. A bridge leads to the dual-towered Inner Gatehouse, where you can climb the western tower for its sublime vantage point. At the back of the Inner Ward are the massive foundations of the Norman keep, demolished in about 1260.

Seven miles northeast of White Castle, in the attractive border village of Skenfrith (Ynysgynwraidd), is the thirteenth-century **Skenfrith Castle** (free access), dominated by the circular keep that replaced an earlier Norman structure. Whilst not as impressive as White Castle, Skenfrith has a pretty riverside setting, its castle walls built of a sturdy red sandstone arranged in an irregular rectangle. In the centre of the ward is a low, round keep, raised slightly on an earth mound, containing the vestiges of the private apartments of the castle's lord on the upper floors.

Five miles upstream of Skenfrith, right on the English border, the most dilapidated of the Three Castles, **Grosmont Castle** (free access), sits on a small hill above the village. Entering over the wooden bridge above the dry moat brings you into the small central courtyard, dominated on the right-hand side by the ruins of a large Great Hall dating from the first decade of the thirteenth century.

Newport and Caerleon

Dominating the once industrious valley towns of southern Monmouthshire, **Newport**, Wales's third largest town, is a downbeat, working-class place that grew up around the docks at the mouth of the River Usk. Its rich history has been largely swept away by the twentieth century, but isolated nuggets remain, most notably at Roman **Caerleon** – the "old port" on the River Usk – now a northern suburb of Newport, but predating the town by about a thousand years.

Newport

NEWPORT, fifteen miles west of Chepstow, is hardly the most prepossessing of towns, with its modern city centre strung along the banks of the foul and muddy River Usk. Overlooking these waters stand both the pathetic remains of **Newport Castle**, and Peter Fink's giant red sculpture, **Steel Wave**, a nod to one of Newport's great industries.

The central High Street leads to Newport and Westgate squares, and the ornate, Victorian **Westgate Hotel** (currently closed) where, in 1839, soldiers sprayed a crowd of Chartist protesters with gunfire (see box above), killing at least twenty – the hotel's original pillars still show bullet marks. A hundred yards along Commercial Street, in John Frost Square, the quirky **Newport clock** shudders, shakes, spits smoke, and comes near to apparent collapse every hour, usually drawing an appreciative crowd. In front of the clock is the town's library, tourist office and imaginative civic **museum** (Mon–Thurs 9.30am–5pm, Fri 9.30am–4.30pm, Sat 9.30am–4pm; free). Starting with the origins of the county of Gwent, the displays examine the county's original occupations and early lifestyles, and include a section on mining, with a roll call of those killed in local pit accidents – 3,508 men between 1837 and 1927. Newport's spectacular growth from 1000 townspeople in 1801 to a grimy port town of 70,000 people by the turn of this century is well charted, but the two most interesting sections deal with the Chartist uprising and a fine Roman mosaic.

Dominating the Newport skyline with its comical, spidery legs is the **Transporter Bridge** (Mon–Sat 8am–6pm, Sun 1–5pm; car toll 50p, free for cyclists and pedestrians), built in 1906 to enable cars and people to cross the river without disturbing the shipping channel, gliding them across the Usk on a dangling platform.

Newport's **tourist office** is in the museum complex in John Frost Square (daily 9.30am–5pm; ☎01633/842962), a hundred yards from Kingsway **bus station** and five minutes' walk south of the **train station**. Staying in Caerleon is a more amenable option, but there are some decent **B&Bs**, including *Craignair*, 44 Corporation Rd (☎01633/259903; ①), and the genteel *St Etienne*, 162 Stow Hill (☎01633/262341; ②). At the western end of Bridge Street, Caerau Road rises up sharply to the south, passing the relaxed, hospitable *Kepe Lodge*, at no. 46A (☎01633/262351; ②). There's a **campsite** at *Tredegar House* (☎01633/815600), a couple of miles west – take bus #315 or #30 from the town centre. For **food**, make for the *Oriel* café, on the top floor of the museum, the vegetarian *Hunky Dory's*, at 17 Charles St, or *Ristorante Vittorio*, at 113 Stow Hill (☎01633/840261), up by the cathedral. With rock music buoyant in Newport (the "British Seattle"), the best place to catch the vibe is at the legendary *TJ's*, 14 Clarence Place, where Kurt Cobain proposed to Courtney Love.

Caerleon

Compact **CAERLEON** (Caerllion), three miles north of central Newport (bus #2; every 15min), but still within city limits, is peppered with the remnants of the major Roman town of Isca, named after the River Usk (Wysg). The settlement was built to provide administrative and military services for the smaller, outlying camps in the rest of South Wales and grew to a size and importance on a par with the better-known York and Chester, in the north of England. Although the town fell gradually into decay after the Romans had left, there were still some massive remains standing when, in 1188, episcopal envoy Giraldus Cambrensis noted with evident relish the "immense palaces, which, with the gilded gables of their roofs, once rivalled the magnificence of ancient Rome".

Although time has had an inevitable corrosive effect on the remains since Giraldus' time, there's a powerful sense of history running through the Roman **fortress baths** (April–Oct daily 9.30am–5.15pm; Nov–March Mon–Sat 9.30am–5pm, Sun noon–4pm; £2; combined ticket with Legionary Museum £3.30; CADW). The bathing houses, cold hall and communal pool area are remarkably intact and beautifully presented, with highly imaginative uses of audio-visual equipment, sound commentary and models. On the High Street, the Victorian Neoclassical portico is the sole survivor of the original **Legionary Museum** (April–Oct Mon–Sat 10am–6pm, Sun 2–6pm; Nov–March Mon–Sat 10am–4.30pm, Sun 2–4.30pm; £2.10; combined ticket with baths £3.30), now housed in a modern building behind and laden with artefacts unearthed here, including everything from amulets to tweezers.

Opposite the Legionary Museum, Fosse Lane leads down to the hugely atmospheric Roman **amphitheatre** (free access), the only one of its kind preserved in Britain.

Hidden under a grassy mound until the 1920s, the amphitheatre was built around 80 AD, at the same time as the Colosseum in Rome. Up to six thousand would take seats to watch animal baiting, military exercises or the gory combat of gladiators.

Caerleon's **tourist office** (daily: April–Oct 10am–6pm; Nov–March 10am–4.30pm; ☎01633/422656) lies next to the legionary museum, or there's more informal information in the Ffwrrwm craft centre, down the main street. There's central, shared-bathroom **B&B** at *Pendragon*, 18 Cross St (☎01633/430871; ②), and *Great House*, Isca Rd (☎01633/420216; ②). The best place to **eat** in Caerleon is *Oriel*, a bistro in the courtyard of the Ffwrrwm centre.

The Valleys

No other part of Wales is as instantly recognizable as the **Valleys**, a generic name for the string of settlements packed into the narrow gashes in the mountainous terrain to the north of Newport and Cardiff. Arriving from England, the change from rolling countryside to sharp contours and a post-industrial landscape is almost instantaneous. Each of the valleys depended almost solely on coal mining which, although nearly defunct as an industry, has left its mark on the staunchly working-class towns: row upon row of brightly painted terraced housing, tipped along the slopes at some incredible angles, are broken only by austere chapels, the occasional remaining pithead and the dignified memorials to those who died underground.

This is not traditional tourist country, and yet is doubtless one of the most interesting and distinctive corners of Wales, dripping with sociological and human interest. Some of the former mines have re-opened as gutsy and hard-hitting museums – **Big Pit** at Blaenafon and the **Rhondda Heritage Park** at Trehafod being the best – while other excellent civic museums include those at **Pontypridd** and **Merthyr Tydfil**. A few

---

WORKING THE BLACK SEAM

The land beneath the inhospitable South Wales Valleys had some of the most abundant and accessible natural seams of **coal** and **iron ore** to be found, readily milked in the boom years of the nineteenth and early twentieth centuries. Wealthy, predominantly English, capitalists came to Wales and ruthlessly stripped the land of its natural assets, while simultaneously exploiting those who risked life and limb underground. The mine owners were in a formidably strong position as thousands flocked to the Valleys in search of work and some sort of sustainable life. By the turn of the twentieth century, the Valleys – virtually unpopulated a century earlier – became packed with pits, chapels and immigrant workers from Ireland, Scotland, Italy and all over Wales.

In 1920, there were 256,000 men working in the 620 mines of the South Wales coalfield, providing one third of the world's coal. Vast Miners' Institutes jostled for position with the Nonconformist chapels, whose fervent brand of Christianity was matched by the zeal of the region's politics – trade-union-led and avowedly left-wing. Great socialist orators rose to national prominence, cementing the Valleys' reputation as a world apart from the rest of Britain, let alone Wales. Even Britain's pioneering National Health Service, founded by a radical Labour government in the years following World War II, was based on a Valleys' community scheme devised by locally born Aneurin Bevan.

Over half of the original pits closed in the harsh economic climate of the 1930s as coal seams became exhausted and the political climate changed. In the 1980s, further closures threatened to bring the number of men employed in the South Wales coalfields down to four figures, and the miners went on strike in 1984 and 1985. No coalfield was as solidly behind the strike as South Wales but, fifteen years on, all of the deep pits – bar one reprieved and taken over in a workers' buy-out in April 1994 – have closed.

older sites, such as vast **Caerphilly Castle** and the sixteenth-century manor house of **Llancaiach Fawr**, have been attracting visitors for hundreds of years.

Blaenafon and Big Pit

Fourteen miles north of Newport, the valley of the Llwyd opens out at the airy iron and coal town of **BLAENAFON**, whose population has shrunk to five thousand, a quarter of its nineteenth-century size. The town's boom kicked off at the Blaenafon **ironworks**, just off the Brynmawr road (April–Oct Mon–Fri 9.30am–4.30pm, Sat 10am–5pm, Sun 10am–4.30pm; £1.50; CADW), founded in 1788. Limestone, coal and iron ore – ingredients for successful iron-smelting – were abundant locally, and the Blaenafon works grew to become one of the largest in Britain in the early nineteenth century, until it closed 1900. The line of Georgian blast furnaces, the water-balance lift and the **museum** in the workers' cottages offer a thorough picture of both the process and the lifestyle that went with it. The ironworks also contains the town's **tourist office** (same hours; ☎01495/792615).

Just as it is now possible to visit the home of Blaenafon's iron industry, the town's defunct coal trade has also been transformed smoothly into the site which most clearly evokes the experience of a miner's work and life. At **Big Pit** (March–Nov daily 9.30am–5pm; last underground tour 3.30pm; full tour £5.75; surface tour £2), a mile west of the town and reached by a half-hourly shuttle bus from Blaenafon, you are kitted out with lamp, helmet and very heavy battery pack and lowered three hundred feet into the labyrinth of shafts and coal faces for a guided tour. The guides – all of whom are ex-miners – lead you through explanations and examples of the different types of coal mining, from the antiquated, risky stack-and-pillar operation to modern, mechanized seam-working. Constant streams of rust-coloured water flow by, adding to the dank and chilly atmosphere that must have terrified the small children who were once paid twopence for a six-day week – of which one penny was taken out for the cost of their candles – pulling the coal wagons along the tracks. Back on the surface, the old pithead baths, smithy, miners' canteen and winding engine house have all been preserved and filled with some fascinating displays about the local mining industry, including a series of characteristically feisty testimonies from the miners made redundant here in 1980.

The Taff and Cynon valleys

The River Taff flows out into the Bristol Channel at Cardiff, after passing through a condensed couple of dozen miles of industry and population. The first town in the Taff vale is **Pontypridd**, one of the most cheerful in the Valleys, and probably the best base. Continuing north, the river splits again at Abercynon, where the River Cynon flows in from Aberdare, site of Wales's only remaining deep mine. Just outside Abercynon is the enjoyable, sixteenth-century **Llancaiach Fawr** manor house. To the north, the Taff is packed into one of the tightest of all the Valleys, passing **Aberfan** five miles short of the imposing valley head town of **Merthyr Tydfil**.

Pontypridd

PONTYPRIDD, twelve miles north of Cardiff, is built up around its quirky arched **bridge**. Once the largest single-span stone bridge in Europe, it was built in 1775 by local amateur stonemason William Edwards, whose previous attempts had crumbled into the river below. Across the river is **Ynysangharad Park**, where Sir W. Goscombe John's gooey statue honours Pontypridd weaver Evan James, who composed the stirringly nationalistic *Mae Hen Wlad fy Nhadau* (*Land of My Fathers*) that has become the

Welsh national anthem. By the bridge at the end of Taff Street, a lovingly restored church houses the **Pontypridd Historical and Cultural Centre** (Mon–Sat 10am–5pm; 25p), one of the best museums in the Valleys. A treasure trove of photographs, videos, models and exhibits succeeds in painting a warm and human picture of the town and its outlying valleys, as well as paying homage to the town's famous sons, crooner Tom Jones and opera star and actor Sir Geraint Evans.

Pontypridd is well connected to bus, train and road networks. The **tourist office** (Mon–Sat 10am–5pm; ☎01443/409512) is in the Historical and Cultural Centre, on Bridge Street. **Accommodation** is rather scarce: in the town centre, try the lively *Millfield Hotel*, Mill Street, near the station (☎01443/480111; ②), or, right in the thick of the action, the bustling *Market Tavern*, Market Street (☎01443/485331; ①). Better bets are a few miles out, notably the well-kept and extremely friendly *Fairmead* guest house (☎01443/411174; ②), almost opposite Llancaiach Fawr (see below), and the floral *Llechwen Hall* (☎01443/742050; ④), signposted off the A470 a couple of miles north of Pontypridd.

Llancaiach Fawr

Five miles north of Pontypridd, the river divides at **Abercynon**, a stark, typical valley town of punishingly steep streets lined with blank, grey houses that fade out into a coniferous hillside. Two miles east, just north of the village of Nelson, is the sixteenth-century **Llancaiach Fawr** (Tues–Fri 10am–5pm, Sat 10am–6pm, Sun noon–6pm; £4.50), a Tudor house, built around 1530, that has been transformed into a living history museum set in 1645, the time of the Civil War, with all of the guides dressed as house servants, speaking the language of seventeenth-century Britain. Although potentially tacky, it is quite deftly done, with well-researched period authenticity and numerous fascinating anecdotes from the staff; visitors are even encouraged to try on the master of the household's armour. Regular **buses** from Pontypridd and Cardiff pass the entrance.

Merthyr Tydfil

Downtown **MERTHYR TYDFIL**, ten miles north of Pontypridd, is a dispiriting, modern place made tolerable by its location at the top of the Taff Valley, on the cusp of the industrial coal country to the south and the grand, windy heights of the Brecon Beacons to the north. In the eighteenth century it became the largest iron-producing town in the world, as well as by far the most populous town in Wales, with four massive ironworks exploiting the local abundance of the key ingredients: iron ore, coal and

---

ABERFAN

North of Abercynon, the Taff Valley contains one sight that is hard to forget. Two neat lines of distant arches mark the graves of 144 people killed in October 1966 by an unsecured slag heap collapsing on Pantglas primary school, in the village of **Aberfan**. Thousands of people still make the pilgrimage to the village graveyard, to stand silent and bemused by the enormity of the disaster. Among the dead were 116 children, who died huddled in panic at the beginning of their school day. A humbling and beautiful valediction can be seen on one of the gravestones, that of a ten-year-old boy, who, it simply records, "loved light, freedom and animals". Official enquiries all told the sorry tale that this disaster was almost inevitable, given the cavalier approach to safety so often displayed by the coal bosses. Gwynfor Evans, then newly elected as the first Plaid Cymru MP in Westminster, spoke with well-founded bitterness when he said, "Let us suppose that such a monstrous mountain had been built above Hampstead or Eton, where the children of the men of power and wealth are at school . . .". But that, of course, would never have happened.

limestone. A century earlier, what was then a village became a rallying point for Dissenter and Radical movements, which gained adherents as the profits from growing industrialization lined the pockets of the works owners, with little cash finding its way to the workers. Merthyr's radicalism bubbled furiously, breaking out into occasional riots and prompting the election of Britain's first socialist MP, Keir Hardie, in 1900.

The sights listed here are all around the River Taff, to the immediate northwest of the town centre. The **Ynysfach Engine House** (enquire in advance at the castle for access, see below; £1) contains a gritty exhibition on social conditions in the urban chaos of the nineteenth century. Half a mile further up the Taff, just off Nant-y-Gwenith Street, the lower end of Neath Road, is **Chapel Row**, a line of skilled ironworkers' cottages built in the 1820s, one of which holds composer **Joseph Parry's Birthplace** (March–Sept Thurs–Sun 2–4pm; Oct–Feb enquire in advance at the castle, see below; 60p). Parry wrote the national favourite, *Myfanwy*, which is now piped into the rooms, some of which are given over to a display on his life and music.

Back across the other side of the river, just beyond the Brecon Road, is a home in absolute contrast to Parry's humble and cramped birthplace. **Cyfartha Castle** (April–Sept daily 10am–5.30pm; Oct–March Mon–Fri 10am–4pm, Sat & Sun noon–4pm; £1.60) was built in 1825 as an ostentatious mock-Gothic castle for William Crawshay II, boss of the town's original ironworks. The castle is set within vast, attractive parkland which slopes down to the river and once afforded Crawshay a view over his iron empire. The old wine cellars contain a varied and enjoyable walk through the history of Merthyr, with the political turmoil and massive exploitation of the past couple of centuries picked over in gory detail. Upstairs, the castle's grand main rooms house an art **gallery** with an impressive collection of Welsh pieces, including works by Augustus John, Cedric Morris, Vanessa Bell, Jack Yeats and Kyffin Williams.

The **train station** is a minute's walk from the High Street. North up the High Street from here is Glebeland Street, on which stands the **bus** station and, at 14A, the **tourist office** (Mon–Sat 9.30am–5.30pm; ☎01685/379884). Municipal **bike rental** is available at Cyfartha Castle. **Accommodation** is varied and includes the unpretentious *Tregenna Hotel*, in Park Terrace, next to Penydarren Park (☎01685/723627; ③), as well as the humbler surroundings of the *Hanover Guest House*, 31 Hanover St (☎01685/379303; ①), and *Penylan*, 12 Courtland Terrace (☎01685/723179; ①). There's a **campsite** four miles north of town in the beautiful surroundings of *Grawen Farm*, Cwmtaf, near Cefn-Coed (☎01685/723740).

The Rhondda

Pointing northwest from Pontypridd, the **Rhondda Fawr** – sixteen miles long and never as much as a mile wide – is undoubtedly the most famous of all the Welsh valleys, as well as being the heart of the massive South Wales coal industry. For many it immediately conjures up Richard Llewellyn's 1939 book – and subsequent Oscar-winning weepie – *How Green Was My Valley*, although this was, strictly speaking, based on the author's early life in nearby Gilfach Goch, outside the valley. Between 1860 and 1910 the Rhondda's population grew from 3000 to nearly 160,000, squeezed into ranks of houses grouped around sixty or so pitheads. The Rhondda, more than any other of the valleys, became a self-reliant, hard-drinking, chapel-going, deeply poor and terrifically spirited breeding ground for radical religion and firebrand politics. The Communist Party ran the town of Maerdy (nicknamed "Little Moscow" by Fleet Street in the 1930s) for decades. The last pit in the Rhondda closed in 1990, but what was left behind was not some dispiriting ragbag of depressing towns, but a range of new attractions, cleaned-up hillsides and some of the friendliest pubs and working men's clubs to be found anywhere in Britain.

Specific attractions are few, however. The only one which really stands out is the colliery museum of the **Rhondda Heritage Park** (April–Sept daily 10am–6pm, last

---

■ MALE VOICE CHOIRS

Fiercely protective of its reputation as a land of song, the voice of Wales is most commonly heard amongst the ranks of **male voice choirs**. Although found all over the country, it is in the southern, industrial heartland that they are loudest and strongest. Their roots lie in the Non-conformist religious traditions of the seventeenth and eighteenth centuries, when Methodism in particular swept the country, and singing was a free and potent way of cherishing the frequently persecuted faith. Classic hymns like *Cwm Rhondda* and the Welsh national anthem, *Mae Hen Wlad Fy Nhadau* (*Land of My Fathers*), are synonymous with the choirs, whose full-blooded interpretation of them continues to render all others insipid. Each valley's town still has its own often depleted choir, most of whom happily accept visitors to sit in on rehearsals. A leaflet, available from tourist offices, gives contact phone numbers for each choir's secretary. Contact them directly, and take the chance to hear one of the world's most distinctive choral traditions in full, roof-raising splendour.

---

admission 4.30pm; Oct–March Tues–Sun 10am–6pm, last admission 4.30pm; £5.50), at **Trehafod**, formed by locals when the Lewis Merthyr pit closed in 1983. You can explore the engine-winding houses, lamp room and fan house, and take a simulated "trip underground", with stunning visuals and sound effects, re-creating 1950s and late nineteenth-century life through the eyes of colliers. The display concludes with a chilling roll call of pit deaths and a moving final narration by Neil Kinnock, the former head of the Labour party, about the human cost of mining – particularly for the valley women.

A **train** line from Cardiff, punctuated with stops every mile or so, runs the entire length of the Rhondda, stopping at Trehafod, a few minutes walk from the Heritage Park. **Buses** also cover the route, continuing up into the mountains and the Brecon Beacons. **Accommodation** within reach of the main bus and train routes is non-existent. Drivers should make for *The Rickards*, Trebanoy Rd, Porth (☎01443/688023; ③), or *Tegfan*, Celyn Isaf, Tonyrefail (☎01443/670831; ②), a couple of miles south of Porth.

Cardiff and around

Official capital of Wales since only 1955, the buoyant city of **CARDIFF** (Caerdydd) has swiftly grown into its new status. A number of progressive developments, not least the new, sixty-member Welsh National Assembly, are giving the city the feel of an international capital, if not always a very Welsh one: compared with Swansea, Cardiff is very anglicized – you'll rarely hear Welsh on the city's streets.

The second Marquis of Bute built Cardiff's first dock in 1839, opening others in swift succession. The Butes, who owned massive swathes of the rapidly industrializing South Wales valleys, insisted that all coal and iron exports use the family docks in Cardiff, and it became one of the busiest ports in the world. In the hundred years up to the turn of the twentieth century, Cardiff's population had soared from almost nothing to 170,000, and the spacious and ambitious new civic centre in Cathays Park was well under way. The twentieth century has seen swinging fortunes: the dock trade slumped in the 1930s and the city suffered heavy bombing in World War II, but with the creation of Cardiff as capital in 1955, optimism and confidence in the city have blossomed. Many large governmental and media institutions have moved here from London, and the development of the dock areas around the new Assembly building to be built in Cardiff Bay has given a positive boost to the cityscape.

Arrival, information and accommodation

The main **bus station** is on the southwestern side of the city centre. Across the fore-court is Cardiff Central **train station**, for all intercity services, as well as many subur-ban and Valley Line services. Queen Street station, at the eastern edge of the centre, is for local services only. The **tourist office**, at 16 Wood St, opposite Cardiff Central (April–Sept Mon–Sat 9am–6.30pm, Sun 10am–4pm; Oct–March Mon–Sat 9am–5.30pm, Sun 10am–4pm; ☎029/2022 7281), will provide good free maps of the city and a copy of *Buzz!*, a free monthly guide to arts in the city.

Cardiff is compact enough to walk around, as even the bay area is within thirty minutes' stroll of Central station. Once you're out of the centre, however, it's best to fall back on the extensive **bus** network, most reliably operated by the garish-orange liveried Cardiff Bus Company. Information and passes are available from the counter next to the tourist office, on Wood Street (Mon–Sat 8.30am–5.30pm). A number of useful **travel passes**, which can also be bought on the bus, include the City Rider ticket (£2.50), which gives unlimited travel around Cardiff and Penarth for a day; the Network Rider (£4.50), which extends the range to Caerphilly and Newport; and the great-value Cardiff Card (£12) which gives unlimited travel on all Cardiff Bus and Valley train services for two days, a bus tour of the city and free access to the major local sights, including Newport's Tredegar House, the Roman Legionary Museum at Caerleon, Caerphilly Castle, and the Rhondda Heritage Park.

Accommodation

The main belt of guest houses and **hotels** lies along the genteel and leafy Cathedral Road, fifteen minutes' walk from the city centre. In addition there are a couple of bud-get **hostels**, but currently no really convenient **campsite**, although the *Pontcanna Fields*, off Cathedral Road (☎029/2039 8362), may soon accept tents again. Otherwise there is only *Lavernock Point Holiday Estate* (☎029/2070 7310), over five miles away at Fort Road, Lavernock Point, near Penarth. Buses #P4, #P5 and #P8 pass within a mile of the site.

Acorn Lodge, 182 Cathedral Rd, Pontcanna (☎029/2022 1373). One of the least expensive B&Bs on this street, yet pleasant and quiet. Some en-suite rooms. ①.

Arosa House, 24 Plasturton Gardens, Pontcanna (☎029/2039 5342). Very friendly and reasonably priced B&B in a quiet street just off Cathedral Road. ①.

Cardiff International Backpacker, 98 Neville St (☎029/2034 5577). Very well-kept hostel with Internet access, pool table, onsite café and bar. The self-catering facilities are fairly cramped, but there's easy access to downtown restaurants. Some private rooms (①), plus single-sex and mixed dorms (up to eight beds).

Cardiff Youth Hostel, 2 Wedal Rd, Roath Park (☎029/2046 2303). Large, purpose-built, red-brick building, situated just underneath the A48 Eastern Avenue flyover at the top of Roath Park, almost two miles from the city centre. Buses #78, #80 or #82 go from the central bus station. No curfew. ①.

Churchills Hotel, Cardiff Rd, Llandaff (☎029/2056 2372). Mock-Edwardian hotel in a quiet part of the city, near the cathedral. ④.

Courtfield Hotel, 101 Cathedral Rd, Pontcanna (☎029/2022 7701). Popular, comfortable and nice-ly furnished hotel with a sizeable gay clientele. ③.

Ferriers, 130 Cathedral Rd, Pontcanna (☎029/2038 3413). Not the cheapest, but one of the best-value B&Bs in Cardiff, with excellent service, a warm welcome and some en-suite rooms. ②.

Lincoln House Hotel, 118 Cathedral Rd (☎029/2039 5558). Elegant, small hotel restored in Victorian style, with heavy brocade and even a couple of four-poster beds. Rates for bed and breakfast. ④.

Scott's of St Fagans, Greenwood Lane, St Fagans (☎029/2056 5400, *scottsofstfagans@btinternet.com*). Four miles from Cardiff, this old post office has been completely remodelled in minimalist style: all white walls, blond ash furniture, chic spotlighting and top quality fittings. Rates include a full break-fast. ③.

△ M4 Junction 29a, Bristol & London   △ Newport

CARDIFF

500 yds

N

ROATH

WATERLOO ROAD

PEN-Y-LAN ROAD

ROATH COURT ROAD

NEWPORT ROAD

BROADWAY

RAILWAY STREET

CARLISLE STREET

CLIFTON STREET

Royal Infirmary

College of Art

MARLBOROUGH ROAD

PEN-Y-LAN RD

ALBANY ROAD

CITY ROAD

Roath Park

TY-DRAW ROAD

NINIAN ROAD

NORTHERN AVENUE

PEN-Y-LAN ROAD

MACKINTOSH PLACE

RICHMOND ROAD

SALISBURY ROAD

STUTTGART STRASSE

COBURN ST

SHIRLEY ROAD

WYEVERNE ROAD

SENGHENNYDD ROAD

WOODVILLE ROAD

ROATH ROAD

CRWYS ROAD

FAIROAK ROAD

WEDAL ROAD

ALLENSBANK ROAD

△ M4 Junction 32

Cathays Station

Nat. Mus. of Wales

PARK PLACE

STUTTGART STRASSE

BLVD DE NANTES

Welsh University Office

Cardiff

MUSEUM AVE

City Hall

CATHAYS TERRACE

KING GEORGE VII AVE

County Hall

MAENDY ROAD

COLUM ROAD

WHITCHURCH ROAD

NORTH ROAD

Welsh Institute of Sport

Bute Park

Glamorgan Cricket Ground

CATHEDRAL ROAD

Sophia Gardens

River Taff

△ M4, Merthyr & Brecon

1

3 4 5 6 7 8

▽ Llandaff & 2

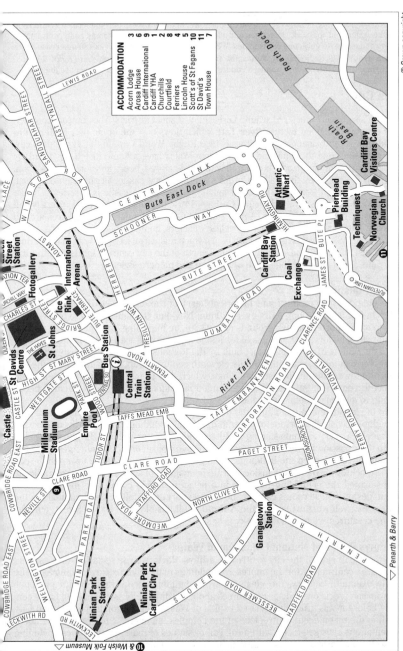

ACCOMMODATION
Acorn Lodge   3
Arosa House   6
Cardiff International 9
Cardiff YHA   1
Churchills   2
Courtfield   8
Ferriers   4
Lincoln House   5
Scott's of St Fagans 10
St David's   11
Town House   7

© Crown copyright

St David's Hotel and Spa, Havannah St, Cardiff Bay (☎029/2045 4045, *reservations@ fivestar-htl-wales.com*). Easily the most luxurious hotel in Cardiff: a tall post-modern structure right on the waterfront that's all clean lines and elegant, understated decor. Rooms come with superb views and access to gorgeous spa facilities. Weekend rates ⑥, including breakfast; otherwise ⑦–⑧.

Town House, 70 Cathedral Rd, Pontcanna (☎029/2023 9399, *thetownhouse@msn.com*). Restored Victorian house with en-suite rooms, a comfortable lounge and better-than-average facilities. ③.

The City

Cardiff's sights are clustered around fairly small, distinct districts. The compact commercial centre is bounded by the **River Taff**, which flows past the brand new **Millennium Stadium**, recently inaugurated with the 1999 Rugby World Cup. In this rugby-mad city, the atmosphere in the pubs and streets when Wales have a home match – particularly against old enemy England – is charged with good-natured, beery fervour. Just upstream, the Taff is flanked by the wall of Cardiff's extraordinary **castle**, an amalgam of Roman remains, Norman keep and Victorian fantasy. North of the castle is a series of white Edwardian buildings grouped around **Cathays Park**: the City Hall, Cardiff University and the superb **National Museum**. A mile south of the commercial centre, the area around **Cardiff Bay** is now one of the city's liveliest quarters, home to the new Welsh Assembly and a welter of new waterfront developments which make it an ideal place for eating, drinking or just ambling about. A couple of miles north of the city centre, **Llandaff Cathedral** warrants a visit for its strange clash of Norman and modern styles.

Cardiff Castle

The political, geographical and historical heart of the city is **Cardiff Castle** (daily: March–Oct 9.30am–5pm, tours every 20min; Nov–Feb 9.30am–3.30pm, 5 tours a day; full tour £5; shorter tour £3; grounds only £2.30), an intriguing hotchpotch of remnants of the city's history. The fortress hides inside a vast walled yard corresponding roughly to the outline of the original fort built by the Romans, Cardiff's first inhabitants. The neat Norman motte, crowned with its eleventh-century **keep**, looks down onto the turrets and towers of the domestic buildings, which date in part from the fourteenth and fifteenth centuries, but were much extended in Tudor times, when residential needs began to overtake military priorities.

In the late nineteenth century, the third Marquis of Bute, one of the richest men on the globe, lavished a fortune on upgrading his pile – although he only lived there for six weeks a year – commissioning architect and decorator William Burges to aid him. With their passion for the religious art and the symbolism of the Middle Ages, they systematically overhauled the buildings, adding a spire to the octagonal tower and erecting a clocktower. But it was inside that their imaginations ran free, and they radically transformed the crumbling interiors into palaces of vivid colour and intricate, high-camp design. These rooms can only be seen as part of the full guided tour, making the extra cost well worthwhile. On the **Animal Wall**, visible from Castle Street, outside, stone creatures are frozen in cheeky poses.

Cathays Park and National Museum of Wales

On the north side of the city centre is **Cathays Park**, a large rectangle of grass that forms the centrepiece for the impressive buildings of the **civic centre**. Dating from the early twentieth century, the gleaming white buildings are arranged with pompous Edwardian precision, and speak volumes about Cardiff's self-assertion, even half a century before it was officially declared capital of Wales. The dragon-topped, domed **City Hall** is the magnificent centrepiece of the complex, an exercise in every cliché about ostentatious civic self-glory, with a roll call of statues of male Welsh heroes, including Lywelyn, St David, Giraldus Cambrensis and Owain Glyndŵr.

To the right stands the **National Museum of Wales** (Tues–Sun 10am–5pm; £4.50), one of Britain's finest, attempting both to tell the story of Wales and to reflect the nation's place in the wider, international sphere. Start off at the back of the entrance lobby with the epic **Evolution of Wales** exhibition, a fabulous mix of natural history, hi-tech gizmos and hugely detailed displays. To the right of the main lobby are various temporary exhibitions and an extensive botany collection, including some stunning silk, paper and wax plant and flower models. In the first-floor archeology gallery, don't miss the Bronze Age remains and the comparatively sophisticated **Caergwrle Bowl**, a delicate, gold-leafed ornament that's 3000 years old. Nearby is the **Tregwynt Treasure Trove**, an impressive cache of gold and silver coins dating back to the Civil War, uncovered near Fishguard in 1996.

The bulk of the East Wing is given over to fine art, with ten galleries on the first floor containing the majority of the museum's extraordinary art collection. The oldest part of the collection starts with the fifteenth- and sixteenth-century **Italian schools**, pushing on to seventeenth-century galleries rich in **Flemish** and **Dutch** work, including Rembrandt's coolly aloof portrait of *Catrina Hooghsaet* and Jacob van Ruisdael's mesmerizing *Waterfall*. The most famous, or perhaps infamous, pieces here are the **Cardiff Cartoons**, four monumental tapestries bought at great expense in 1979 and, at the time, presumed to be the work of Rubens. The first of the great Welsh artists is shown to maximum effect in the **eighteenth-century** galleries, where landscapes by Richard Wilson include *Caernarfon Castle* and *Dolbadarn Castle*. The **nineteenth-century** galleries include a round-up of some of the century's greater painters, including J.M.W. Turner, whose *Thames Backwater, with Windsor Castle* is a characteristic wash of diffuse colour and light.

The most exciting art works are contained in galleries eleven through fifteen, kicking off with a fabulous **sculpture collection**, including many by the one-man Welsh Victorian statue industry, Goscombe John, that contrast with the more delicate Rodin pieces nearby. Gallery Thirteen is home to the National Museum's pride, the Davies collection of **Impressionist paintings**. Cézanne, Monet and Degas figure predominantly, alongside Corot's legendary *Distant view of Corbeil, morning*, Pissaro's classic views of Rouen and Paris, and Renoir's chirpy portrait of *La Parisienne*. Gallery Fourteen houses a hearty collection of Post-Impressionists, Futurists and Surrealists, while Fifteen showcases abstract work with a strong Welsh bent.

Cardiff Bay

A thirty-minute walk from the city centre (bus #8 and the train to Cardiff Bay station from Queen Street station run every 30 min) is the area known as **Cardiff Bay**, the spicier tag of Tiger Bay immortalized by Cardiff-born Shirley Bassey being rarely used these days. The first impression is one of immense and exciting change: the bay has become one of the world's biggest regeneration projects, slowly being transformed from the seedy dereliction of the old docks into an area of landscaped walkways, gardens and public attractions. It is now among the most fascinating parts of Cardiff, where ostentatious Victorian shipping company headquarters rub shoulders with spruced-up dockers' housing, and sleek restaurants lurk in the shadow of glittering, postmodern corporate headquarters. Central to the whole project is the **Cardiff Bay Barrage**, across the Ely and Taff estuaries, which has transformed a vast mud flat into a freshwater lake, controversially depriving the wading bird population of a prime habitat.

First stop is the modern, tubular **Cardiff Bay Visitor Centre** (May–Sept Mon–Fri 9am–7.30pm, Sat & Sun 10am–7.30pm; Oct–April Mon–Fri 9am–5pm, Sat & Sun 10.30am–5pm; free), looking out on to the bay like a giant eye. It's a thinly disguised PR job containing a fabulous scale model of the entire docks area, though, like much else hereabouts, there is great uncertainty about eventual outcomes and timeframes, so the centre may not be long for this world.

The adjacent park is graced by the gleaming white spire of the **Norwegian church** (daily 10am–4pm), an old seamen's chapel in which Roald Dahl was christened, now converted into a excellent café (see opposite) and exhibition space. Alongside is the site of the new **National Assembly of Wales** building, due to open in 2001, which uses so much glass that you'll be able to watch the politicians in action from outside. The Assembly may also make use of the magnificent, but currently empty, **Pierhead Building**, adjacent, a typically rich, neo-Gothic terracotta pile which perfectly embodies the wealth and optimism of the Bute family in late Victorian times.

On the other side of a newly landscaped basin and the mammoth **Exchange Building**, built in the 1880s as Britain's central Coal Exchange, is **Techniquest** (Mon–Fri 9.30am–4.30pm, Sat & Sun 10.30am–5pm; £4.50), a fun, "hands-on" science gallery – perfect for kids. Backing the whole area you'll see the sweeping wavy roofline and vast glass-brick wall of the **Atlantic Wharf**, which makes a striking impression for what is essentially just a big box filled with a twelve-screen multiplex, a bowling alley and a few restaurants.

Llandaff Cathedral

Two miles northwest of the city centre along Cathedral Road, the small, quiet suburb of **Llandaff** is home to a church that has now grown up into the city's **Cathedral**. It is believed to have been founded in the sixth century by Saint Teilo, but was rebuilt in Norman style in around 1120, and worked on well into the thirteenth century. From the late fourteenth century onwards, the cathedral declined into an advanced state of disrepair, and one of the twin towers and the nave roof eventually collapsed. Restoration only began in earnest in the early 1840s, when Pre-Raphaelite artists such as Edward Burne-Jones, Dante Gabriel Rossetti and the firm of William Morris were commissioned to make colourful new windows and decorative panels. Their work is best seen in the south aisle.

The fusion of different styles and ages is evident from outside, especially in the mismatched western towers. Inside, the nave is dominated by Jacob Epstein's overwhelming *Christ in Majesty*, a concrete parabola topped with a soaring Christ figure. At the west end of the north aisle, the **St Illtyd Chapel** features Rossetti's cloying triptych *The Seed of David*. In the south presbytery is a tenth-century Celtic cross, the only survival of the pre-Norman cathedral.

Eating, drinking. and nightlife

The city's long-standing internationalism has paid handsome dividends in the range of **restaurants**, with the influence of Italian immigrants particularly evident in the number of cafés, bistros and trattorias. There are numerous places right in the city, most notably in the "café quarter" along Mill Lane. Most other places are within easy walking distance of the city centre, although there are also good hunting grounds in the cheaper quarters of Cathays and Roath, particularly the curry houses along Crwys, Albany and City roads, a stone's throw from the centre, beyond the University. Cardiff's **pub** life has expanded exponentially over recent years, and there are some wonderful Edwardian palaces of etched, smoky glass and deep red wood, where you'll find Cardiff's very own Brains bitter.

Top-flight **concert venues** such as St David's Hall and the Cardiff International Arena have brought internationally acclaimed orchestras and performers to the city, although these sterile environments are no match for the sweatier gigs and traditional rock found in some of Cardiff's earthier pubs and clubs. The burgeoning Welsh rock scene, both English- and Welsh-language, breaks out regularly in the capital. Cardiff also has a modest **gay scene**: the best sources for current information are Friend (Tues–Sat 8–10pm; ☎029/2034 0101) and Lesbian Line (Tues 8–10pm; ☎029/2037 4051).

Theatre in Cardiff encompasses everything from the radical and alternative at the Sherman and the Chapter to big, blowzy productions at the New Theatre, home of the Welsh National Opera. **Classical music** is best heard at St David's Hall.

Cafés and restaurants

Blas ar Gymru, 48 Crwys Rd, Cathays (☎029/2038 2132). Meaning "taste of Wales", this is a comfortable restaurant with a highly imaginative, moderately priced menu made up of delicious traditional recipes from every corner of Wales. Leave room for the selection of Welsh cheeses. Closed Sun. Moderate to Expensive.

Celtic Cauldron, Castle Arcade. A friendly daytime café, dedicated to bringing a range of simple Welsh food – soups, stews, laver bread, cakes – to an appreciative public. Inexpensive.

Cibo, 83 Pontcanna St, off Cathedral Rd (☎029/2223 2226). A slice of Italy in Cardiff: a small, inexpensive and welcoming trattoria serving ciabatta sandwiches and simple, well-cooked food. No credit cards. Moderate.

Giovanni's, The Hayes (☎029/2022 0077). One of Cardiff's best Italian restaurants, lively and enormously friendly, with a wide menu of old favourites and some unusual house specialities. Closed Sun. Moderate.

Greenhouse, 38 Woodville Rd (☎029/2023 5731). Licensed vegetarian restaurant with a modern take on traditional dishes, often with an inventive twist. Closed Sun & Mon. Moderate.

Jags, 4 Church St. Eat-in and take-out sandwich bar serving stuffed baguettes and good coffee. Inexpensive.

Louis Restaurant, 32 St Mary St. Charming 1950s tea rooms with a clientele of genteel old ladies and bargain-hungry students. Food is basic, lavish in quantity and superb in quality. Last orders 7.45pm; closed Sun. Inexpensive.

Noble House, 9–10 St David's House, Wood St (☎029/2038 8317). Excellent Chinese restaurant, with a good range of Peking and Szechuan dishes. Moderate.

Norwegian Church Café, Harbour Drive. Cosy spot for Norwegian open sandwiches, salads, some scrumptious cakes and filter coffee. Inexpensive.

Porto's, St Mary's St (☎029/2022 0060). Authentic restaurant in a dark, wood-beamed room serving massive portions of Portuguese and Madeiran favourites, including endless variations on dried cod. Moderate.

Woods Brasserie, Stuart St (☎029/2049 2400). One of Cardiff's most stylish establishments, where you'll definitely need to book in advance to sample the excellent Modern-British cuisine. Moderate (lunch) to Expensive (eve).

Bars, pubs and clubs

Chapter, Market Rd, Canton (☎029/2030 4400). A couple of smart bars in the arts complex with a good choice of real ales and whiskies.

Club Metropolitan, Bakers Row (☎029/2022 2615). Slightly scruffy venue for some of the best indie dance nights in town, with plenty of students drawn by the drink specials.

Clwb Ifor Bach, Womanby St (☎029/2023 2199). A sweaty and enjoyable live-music and DJ club with nightly gigs and sessions, many featuring Welsh-language bands.

Exit Bar, 48 Charles St. Frantic, noisy disco-bar, popular among the gay community for pre-club drinks before heading to *Club X*, opposite. Open till midnight.

Golden Cross, 283 Hayes Bridge Rd. Laid-back restored Victorian pub, rich in atmosphere and with some beautiful tiled pictures of yesteryear Cardiff. A great bet for an unhurried pint.

Sam's Bar, 63 St Mary St (☎029/2034 5189). Lively club-bar, with everything from live heavy metal through comedy and drag shows to house DJs. A good place to check the pulse of the Mill Lane "cafe quarter".

Theatre, cinema and classical music

Cardiff International Arena, Bute Terrace (☎029/2022 4488). For mega concerts, both rock and classical.

Chapter Arts Centre, Market Rd, Canton (☎029/2039 9666). Multi-use arts complex that hosts British and touring theatre and dance companies, as well as Cardiff's main art-house cinema.

New Theatre, Park Place (☎029/2039 4844). Splendid Edwardian city-centre theatre that plays host to big London shows. Currently the home of the Welsh National Opera.

The Point, West Bute St, Cardiff Bay (☎029/2049 9979). Experimental performance space in an old church.

Sherman Theatre, Senghenydd Rd, Cathays (☎029/2023 0451). An excellent, two-auditorium repertory theatre hosting a mixed bag of classic Welsh-language pieces (both new and translated), stand-up comedy, children's entertainment, drama classics, music and dance.

St David's Hall, The Hayes (☎029/2087 8444). Part of the massive St David's shopping centre, this large and glamorous venue is possibly the most architecturally exciting building in town. Home to visiting orchestras and musicians from jazz to opera, it's frequently used by the excellent BBC Welsh Symphony Orchestra and Chorus.

Listings

Banks and exchange All major banks have branches along High Street or Queen Street. For exchange, American Express is at 3 Queen St (Mon–Fri 9am–5.30pm, Sat 10am–1pm; ☎029/2066 5843), and Thomas Cook at 16 Queen St (Mon–Fri 9.30am–5pm, Sat 10am–1pm; ☎029/2022 4886).

Bike rental Waterfront Bike Hire (☎029/2048 4110) rent decent machines from their stand in Britannia Park, right by the Cardiff Bay Visitor Centre.

Bus information Cardiff Bus (☎029/2039 6521); National Express (☎029/2034 4751).

Car rental Avis, 14–22 Tudor St (☎029/2034 2111); Enterprise, 45 Penarth Rd (☎029/2038 9222); Hertz, 9 Central Square (☎029/2022 4548).

Emergencies University of Wales Hospital, Heath (☎029/2074 7747). For emergency dental work: Riverside Health Centre, Wellington St, Canton (☎029/2037 1221).

Laundries Drift Inn, 104 Salisbury Rd, Cathays Park; GP, 244 Cowbridge Rd, Canton; Launderama, 60 Lower Cathedral Rd.

Left luggage At Central Station.

Pharmacy Boots, 5 Wood St (Mon–Sat 8am–8pm, Sun 6–7pm; ☎029/2023 4043).

Police Cardiff Central Police Station, King Edward VII Ave, Cathays Park (☎029/2022 2111).

Post office The Hayes (Mon–Fri 9am–5.30pm; Sat 9am–12.30pm; ☎029/2022 7363).

Travel agencies Usit, in the YHA shop, 13 Castle St (☎029/2022 0744); John Cory Travel, Park Place (☎029/2037 1878); Welsh Travel Centre, 240 Whitchurch Rd, Cathays (☎029/2062 1479).

Around Cardiff

On the edge of the northern Cardiff suburbs, the thirteenth-century fairy-tale castle of **Castell Coch** stands on a hillside in the woods, while just further north is the massive **Caerphilly Castle**. West of the city, the massively popular **Museum of Welsh Life**, in the grounds of the rambling Elizabethan country house of **St Fagans Castle**, tells the country's history through a collection of buildings salvaged from all over Wales.

Castell Coch

Four miles north of Llandaff, the turreted **Castell Coch** (April, May & Oct daily 9.30am–5pm; June–Sept daily 9.30am–6pm; Nov–March Mon–Sat 9.30am–4pm, Sun 11am–4pm; £2.50; CADW) was once a ruined thirteenth-century fortress. Like Cardiff Castle, it was rebuilt and transformed into a fantasy structure in the late 1870s by

William Burges for the third Marquess of Bute. With its working portcullis and draw-bridge, Castell Coch is the ultimate wealthy man's medieval fantasy, isolated on its almost Alpine hillside, yet only a few hundred yards from the motorway and Cardiff suburbs. There are many similarities with Cardiff Castle, notably the outrageously lav-ish decor, culled from religious and moral fables, that dazzle in each room. **Bus** #136 from Central station turns round at the castle gates, while bus #26 drops in Tongwynlais village, ten minutes' walk away.

Caerphilly

Caerphilly (Caerffili), seven miles north of Cardiff, is a flattened and colourless town, notable only for its **castle** (April, May & Oct daily 9.30am–5pm; June–Sept daily 9.30am–6pm; Nov–March Mon–Sat 9.30am–4pm, Sun 11am–4pm; £2.50; CADW), the first in Britain built concentrically, with an inner system of defences overlooking the outer ring. Looming out of its vast surrounding moat, the medieval fortress with its cock-eyed tower occupies over thirty acres, presenting an awesome promise not entire-ly fulfilled inside.

The castle was begun in 1268 by Gilbert de Clare as a defence against Llywelyn the Last. Two years later, Llywelyn largely destroyed the castle. It was swiftly rebuilt, but for the next few hundred years Caerphilly was little more than a decaying toy, given at whim by kings to their favourites. By the turn of the twentieth century, Caerphilly Castle was in a sorry state, sitting amidst a growing industrial town that saw fit to build in the then-dry moat and castle precincts. Houses and shops were demolished in order to allow the moat to be reflooded in 1958.

You enter the castle through the much restored **gatehouse**, where there's an exhi-bition on the castle's history. A platform behind the barbican wall exhibits medieval war and siege engines, overlooked on the left by the southeastern tower, out-leaning its rival in Pisa. Of the rest of the castle, the most interesting section is the massive east-ern gatehouse, which includes an impressive upper hall and oratory and, to its left, the wholly restored and reroofed **Great Hall**.

Caerphilly is also known for its crumbly white **cheese**, made in dairies around the town, and available in a ploughman's lunch at the *Courthouse* pub, on Cardiff Rd, right by the castle and a five minute stroll from the **bus** and **train** stations.

The Museum of Welsh Life and St Fagans Castle

St Fagans (Sain Ffagan), four miles west of the city centre, has a rural feel that is only partially disturbed by the bus loads of tourists that roll in regularly to visit the excellent **Museum of Welsh Life** (daily: May–Aug 10am–6pm; Sept–April 10am–5pm; £5.50), built around **St Fagans Castle**, a country house erected in 1580 and furnished in early nineteenth-century style. The most impressive part of the museum is the fifty-acre outdoor collection of buildings from all corners of Wales which have been carefully dismantled and rebuilt on this site since the museum's inception in 1946. There are particular highlights, including the diminutive, white-washed Pen-Rhiw Chapel, built in Dyfed in 1777; the pristine and evocative St Mary's Board School, built in Lampeter in Victorian times; and the stern mini-fortress of a tollhouse that once guarded the southern approach to Aberystwyth, from 1772. The superb Rhyd-y-car **ironworkers' cottages**, from Merthyr Tydfil, were originally built in around 1800. Each of the six houses, with its accompanying strip of garden, has been furnished in the style of a different period, stretching between 1805 to 1985. Even the frontages and roofs are true to their age, offering a wade through working-class Welsh life over the past century. **Buses** #32 (hourly) and #C1 (variable times), leave from Central station.

Swansea

Dylan Thomas called his birthplace an "ugly, lovely town" and poet Paul Durcan updated the epithet to "pretty, shitty city" – both ring true. Large, sprawling and boisterous, **SWANSEA** (Abertawe), with around 200,000 people, is the second city of Wales. It has great aspirations to be the first, and is certainly far more of a Welsh town than Cardiff. The city centre was massively rebuilt after devastating bomb attacks in World War II, and a jumble of tower blocks now dots the horizon. But closer inspection reveals Swansea's multifarious charms: some intact old corners of the city centre, the spacious and graceful suburb of Uplands, a wide seafront overlooking Swansea Bay and a bold marina development around the old docks. Spread throughout are some of the best-funded museums in Wales. **Ferries to Cork**, in Ireland (☎01792/456116) leave roughly once a day from the docks, around a mile east of the town centre.

The city's Welsh name, Abertawe, refers to the settlement at the mouth of the River Tawe, a grimy ditch that is slowly being teased back to life after centuries of use as a sewer for Swansea's metal trades. The first reliable mention of Swansea dates from 1099, when a Norman castle was built here as an outpost of William the Conqueror's empire. A small settlement grew near the coalfields and the sea, developing into a mining and shipbuilding centre that, by 1700, was the largest coal port in Wales. Copper smelting became the area's dominant industry in the eighteenth century, soon attracting other metal trades to pack out the lower Tawe Valley, making it one of the world's most prolific metal-bashing centres. Over the years, the valley became a five-mile stretch of rusting, stagnant land and water that has only recently begun to be re-landscaped.

Arrival, information and accommodation

The **train station** is at the top end of the High Street, a ten-minute hike from the **bus station**, where you'll find the **tourist office** (Mon–Sat 9.30am–5.30pm; ☎01792/468321). **Getting around** Swansea is easy: most of the sights are within walking distance of each other. Popular suburbs, such as Uplands and Sketty, near the University, are a bracing thirty-minute walk from the centre, although buses cover the suburbs extremely thoroughly.

As a lively city on the edge of some of Wales's most popular and inspirational coastal and rural scenery, Swansea makes a logical base. Transport out into the surrounding areas is good, and beds tend to be less expensive in the city than in the more picturesque parts of Gower. There are dozens of dirt-cheap **hotels** and **B&Bs** stretched out along the seafront Oystermouth Road, whose trade is largely pitched at those catching the Swansea–Cork ferry. Better places congregate in leafy Uplands, a ten- to fifteen-minute walk from town. There are no **campsites** or **hostels** in the city itself, although nearby places in Gower are easily reached.

Crescent, 132 Eaton Crescent, Uplands (☎01792/466814). Large, pleasant, well-converted Edwardian guest house. All rooms have en-suite showers, and half have superb views over the city and the bay. ②.

Harlton, 89 King Edward Rd, Brynmill (☎01792/466938). Budget guest house that is a little yellow around the edges but perfectly adequate – and very inexpensive. ①.

Oyster, 262 Oystermouth Rd (☎01792/654345). Small and friendly hotel with some en-suite rooms. Serves great local cuisine. ①.

St James, 76B Walter Rd, Uplands (☎01792/649984). Small, welcoming hotel in an airy Victorian house. ②.

Uplands Court, 134 Eaton Crescent, Uplands (☎01792/473046). Appealing guest house in a gracious Victorian villa situated in a pleasant area. ①.

White House Hotel, 4 Nyanza Terrace, Uplands (☎01792/473856). Excellent-value and extremely well-kept guest house: all the well-appointed rooms have satellite TV and some have en-suite facilities. ①.

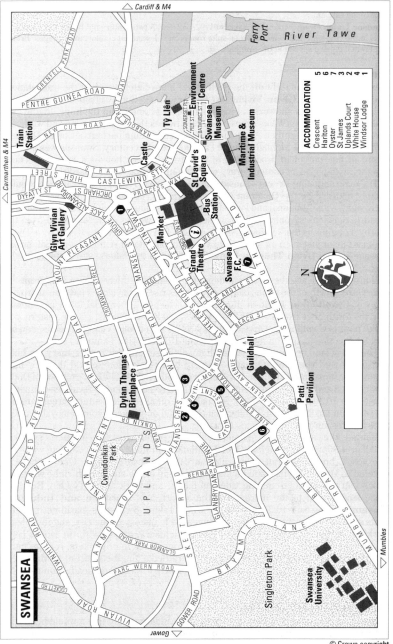

SWANSEA

Cardiff & M4

River Tawe

Ferry Port

ACCOMMODATION
Crescent 5
Harlton 6
Oyster 7
St James 3
Uplands Court 2
White House 4
Windsor Lodge 1

GRENFELL PARK ROAD

PENTRE GUINEA ROAD

NEW CUT ROAD

HARBOUR

SOMERSET PL
PIER ST
BATHURST ST

Tŷ Llên

Environment Centre

Swansea Museum

Maritime & Industrial Museum

Train Station

Castle

STRAND

HIGH STREET

CASTLEWIND STREET

ORCHARD ST

PRINCESS WAY

St David's Square

DYFATTY ST

GROVE PLACE

ALEXANDRA ROAD

Glyn Vivian Art Gallery

MOUNT PLEASANT

MANSEL STREET

CROMWELL STREET

THE KINGSWAY

PAGE ST

Market

Bus Station

i

Grand Theatre

Swansea F.C.

7

WELLINGTON ST

ORCHARD ST

OXFORD ST

WEST WAY

ST HELENS ROAD

WESTERN ST

ARGYLE ST

BEACH ST

OYSTERMOUTH ROAD

N

Dylan Thomas' Birthplace

WALTER ROAD

TERRACE ROAD

3

BRYN-Y-MOR ROAD

5

KING EDWARDS ROAD

ST HELENS AVENUE

Guildhall

Patti Pavilion

2

4

UPLANDS CRES

EATON CRES

6

GLANBRYDAN AVENUE

BERNARD STREET

BRYN ROAD

DYFED AVENUE

PANT-Y-CELYN ROAD

BRYAN CRESCENT

GLANMOR ROAD

PARC WERN ROAD

GLANMOR PARK ROAD

SKETTY ROAD

UPLANDS

Cwmdonkin Park

NIXON RD

NIXON ST

BRYN MILL LANE

MUMBLES ROAD

Singleton Park

Swansea University

Mumbles

Gower

VIVIAN ROAD

GOWER ROAD

TOWNHILL ROAD

COCKETT RD

Carmarthen & M4

© Crown copyright

Great breakfasts, and good three-course evening meals for £10. You can even check your email for the price of the call. ①.

Windsor Lodge Hotel, Mount Pleasant (☎01792/642158). A two-century-old house like a country hotel in the city, with nicely decorated en-suite rooms and elegant but comfortable lounges. British and French cuisine served in the evenings. ④.

The City

Alexandra Road forks right off the High Street immediately south of the train station, leading down to the **Glynn Vivian Art Gallery** (Tues–Sun 10.30am–5.30pm; free), a delightful Edwardian showcase of inspiring Welsh art including the huge, frantic canvases of Ceri Richards, Wales's most respected twentieth-century painter, and works by Gwen John and her brother, Augustus, whose mesmerizing portrait of Caitlin Thomas, Dylan's wife, is a real highlight. In the early nineteenth century, Swansea was a noted centre of fine porcelain production, of which the gallery houses a large collection, together with pieces of contemporary works from Nantgarw, near Cardiff.

The main shopping streets – considerably tarted-up in recent years – lie to the south, notably underneath the Quadrant Centre where the curving-roofed **market** makes a lively sight, with traditional and long-standing stalls selling local delicacies such as laver bread (a delicious savoury made from seaweed), as well as cockles trawled from the nearby Loughor estuary, typical Welsh cakes, fish and cheeses. If you're a Dylan Thomas fan, or just keen on books, it is worth popping down Wind Street to Salubrious Passage for the **Dylan Thomas Bookshop**, filled to the rafters with material on the poet.

Hourly buses leave the Quadrant depot for Uplands, a thirty-minute walk from the city centre. North of the main road, leafy avenues rise up the slopes past the sharp terraces of **Cwmdonkin Park**, at the centre of which is a memorial to Dylan Thomas inscribed with lines from *Fern Hill*, one of his best-known poems. On the eastern side of the park is Cwmdonkin Drive, a sharply rising set of solid Victorian semis, notable only for the blue plaque on no. 5, birthplace in 1914 of Dylan Thomas.

The spit of land between Oystermouth Road, the sea and the Tawe estuary has been christened the **Maritime Quarter** – tourist-board-speak for the old docks – built around a vast marina surrounded by legions of modern flats. The city's old South Dock, now cleaned and spruced up, features the enticingly old-fashioned **Swansea Museum** (Tues–Sun 10.30am–5.30pm; free). A small grid of nineteenth-century streets around the museum has been thoughtfully cleaned up and now houses some enjoyable cafés, pubs and restaurants.

Behind the museum, in Somerset Place, is the airy **Tŷ Llên** (Tues–Sun 10.30am–4.30pm; free), the new Welsh national literature centre, complete with theatre space, book and craft shops, a great café, and two galleries. One of these is devoted to Dylan Thomas, and includes a mock-up of the shed in which he wrote, in which you can see a fascinating video on his life and work. From Tŷ Llên, Burrows Place leads down to the marina and the superb new **Maritime and Industrial Museum** (Tues–Sun 10.30am–5.30pm; free). Taking Swansea's maritime tradition as its starting point, the museum presents a lively history of the city, and includes a working woollen mill, where rows of black machinery, greasy with the wool's lanolin, are operated by staff who gradually turn raw fleece into blankets. A large number of vehicles include an old tram that once rattled along the seafront to Mumbles, and a rare example of Gilbern cars, Wales's principal – and long-dead – contribution to the motor industry.

Eating, drinking and nightlife

Swansea's metamorphosis from a working-class, industrial city into a would-be tourist centre is well demonstrated in the **pubs**, **restaurants** and **entertainment** venues of the city. For nightlife, the city is well placed as a major centre in Wales, with most passing theatre, opera and music of all sorts being obliged to make a stop here. The BBC Welsh Symphony Orchestra appears at the Brangwyn Hall in the Art Deco Civic Centre. Thomas' classics get a regular airing at the Dylan Thomas Theatre, by the marina, while the Taliesin Arts Centre, in the University, is the city's more offbeat venue.

219 High St (☎01792/459050). Swansea's finest modern restaurant serving imaginative cuisine with influences from around the globe. Closed Sun & Mon. Expensive.

Adam and Eve, 205 High St. Traditional pub, with a great atmosphere and varied clientele. Well known for the excellence of its beer.

Bengal Brasserie, 47 Walter Rd (☎01792/643747). Best of the many Indian restaurants in Swansea, well worth the ten-minute hike from the city centre. Moderate.

Bizzie Lizzie's, 55 Walter Rd (☎01792/473379). Relaxed and informal cellar-bar bistro, with a good range of Welsh, international and vegetarian dishes. Reservations recommended. Inexpensive to Moderate.

Duke of York, Princess Way. Home of *Ellington's* club (small cover charge), Swansea's best venue for jazz and blues music, which hosts nightly gigs.

Escape Club, Northampton Lane, off Kingsway. Enormous and glitzy mainstream dance club.

Hanson's, Pilot House Wharf (☎01792/466200). Low-key restaurant on the far side of the marina, at the end of Bathurst Street, serving tasty and well-presented British and Mediterranean dishes. Closed Sun eve. Moderate.

Hwyrnos, Green Dragon Lane, off Wind St (☎01792/641437). Fixed evening menu of Welsh food, plus harp-twanging entertainment in an extremely convivial, bordering on boozy, atmosphere. Caters specifically to groups, but if you call ahead they'll try to match you up with another party. Moderate.

Monkey Café, 13 Castle St. Groovy, mosaic-floored café with a relaxed atmosphere, great sandwiches and cakes, and a selection of Mexican and Italian dishes, including many vegetarian options. Inexpensive.

New Capriccio, 89 St Helen's Rd (☎01792/648804). Popular Italian restaurant, with a bargain lunch menu. Closed Mon & Sun eve. Inexpensive.

Palace, 156 High St. Small, cheerful gay club five minutes' walk north of the station.

Po Na Na, 22 Wind St. New but thriving club with Moroccan "souk" décor, playing mostly garage and hip hop. Small cover charge on Sat & DJ nights.

Queen's Hotel, Gloucester Place, near the marina. Large old seafaring hotel and pub, with good ales, snack lunches and Sunday roasts. Inexpensive.

Gower

A fifteen-mile-long peninsula of undulating limestone, **GOWER** (Gŵyr) points down into the Bristol Channel to the west of Swansea. The area is fringed by sweeping yellow bays and precipitous cliffs, with caves and blowholes to the south, and wide, flat marshes and cockle beds to the north. Bracken heaths dotted with prehistoric remains and tiny villages lie between, and there are numerous castle ruins and curious churches to be found. Out of season, the winding lanes afford wonderful opportunities for exploration, but in the height of the summer – July and August especially – they are congested with caravans shuffling between one overpriced car park and the next.

Gower can be said to start in Swansea's western suburbs, along the coast of Swansea Bay that curves round to a point at the pleasantly old-fashioned resort of **Mumbles**. It finishes with **Rhossili Bay**, a spectacular four-mile yawn of sand backed by the village of Rhossili and occupying the entire western end of the peninsula. The southern coast is punctuated by the village of **Port Eynon**, home to an excellent **YHA hostel** (☎01792/390706; closed Nov–March) and a beautiful beach. West of Port Eynon, the coast becomes a wild, frilly series of inlets and cliffs, topped by a five-mile path that stretches all the way to the peninsula's glorious westernmost point, **Worms Head**. The northern coast merges into the tidal flats of the estuary.

The Mumbles and Oystermouth

At the far westernmost end of Swansea Bay, **The Mumbles** (Mwmbwls) derives its name from the French *mamelles*, or breasts, a reference to the twin islets off the end of Mumbles Head, and is now used as the name for all of the loose sprawl around **OYS-TERMOUTH** (Ystumllwynarth). Here, the seafront is an unbroken curve of budget hotels, breezy pubs and cafés, leading down to the old-fashioned pier and funfair, and the rocky plug of Mumbles Head. Around the headland, reached either by the longer, barren coast road or by a short walk over the hill, is the district of **Langland Bay**, whose sandy beach is fairly popular with surfers. The small **tourist office** (daily: April, May, Sept & Oct 10am–4pm; June–Aug 9.30am–5.30pm; ☎017792/361302) is on the seafront, close to the foot of Newton Road, which leads up to the hilltop ruins of **Oystermouth Castle** (hours vary; generally April–Oct daily 11am–5.30pm; £1). Founded as a Norman watchtower, the castle was strengthened to withstand attacks by the Welsh, before being converted for more amenable residential purposes during the fourteenth century. Today you can see the remains of a late thirteenth-century keep next to a more ornate three-storey ruin incorporating an impressive banqueting hall and state rooms.

The Mumbles is a lively and enjoyable base for the southern Gower coast, with a good clutch of typically tacky seaside entertainment on offer. **Accommodation** is plentiful: try *Henfaes Guesthouse*, 4 Rotherslade Rd (☎01792/366003; ①); the shorefront Victorian *Tides Reach*, 388 Mumbles Rd (☎01792/404877; ②); the superb *Alexandra House*, 366 Mumbles Rd (☎01792/406406; ②); or the sumptuous *Osborne Hotel* (☎01792/366274; ⑥), high on a cliff-top on Rotherslade Road, Langland Bay. There are several good **places to eat** including the inexpensive *Coffee Denn*, 34 Newton Rd, which is good for light lunches and imaginative ice cream sundaes. *Seafront 604*, 604 Mumbles Rd, does moderately priced light meals, while the expensive, fairly formal *Patricks*, 636 Mumbles Rd (☎01792/360199; closed Sun eve), serves an eclectic range of wonderful modern dishes. The scores of pubs along the seafront constitute the **Mumbles Mile**, one of Wales's most notorious pub crawls. The ones to linger in are *The Antelope*, the *Oystercatcher* and the *White Rose*.

Rhossili and Worms Head

The village of **RHOSSILI** (Rhosili), at the western end of Gower, is a centre for walkers and beach loungers alike. Dylan Thomas described the terrain to the west of the village as "rubbery, gull-limed grass, the sheep-pilled stones, the pieces of bones and feathers", and you can tread in his footsteps to **Worms Head**, an isolated string of rocks, accessible for only five hours, at low tide. At the head of the road, near the village, is a well-stocked **National Trust information centre** (April–Oct daily 10.30am–5.30pm; Nov & Dec Sat & Sun 11am–4pm; ☎01792/390707). They post the tide times outside for those heading for Worms Head, and hold details of local companies renting surfing and hang-gliding equipment.

Below the village, a great curve of white sand stretches away into the distance, a dazzling coastline vast enough to absorb the crowds, especially if you are prepared to head north towards **Burry Holms**, an islet that is cut off at high tide. The northern end of the beach can also be reached along the small lane which runs from Reynoldston, in the middle of the peninsula, to **LLANGENNITH**, on the other side of the towering, 633-foot **Rhossili Down**. In the village, PJ's Surfshop (☎01792/386669) rents a wide range of **surfboards** (£7/day) and boogie boards (£5/day), and there's a Surf School (☎01792/386426), a mile away at the Hillend campsite (see below), which runs half-day (£18) and full-day (£28) **surfing courses**.

In Rhossili village, there are great **B&Bs** at: *Hampstead* (☎01792/390545; ②), almost half a mile back from the beach but with superb views from the large rooms; and the very friendly *Meadow View*, a mile from the beach (☎01792/390518; ①), with small but nicely furnished rooms. **Campsites** can be found at *Pitton Cross Park* (☎01792/390593), close to Meadow View, at the foot of the northern slopes of Rhossili Down; and at *Hillend* (☎01792/386204), at the end of the southern lane from Llangennith, behind the dunes that bump down to the glorious beach. There's a rather dingy **restaurant** and bar in Rhossili, but you're better off at the *King Arthur*, in nearby Reynoldston, which serves hearty meals and hosts live folk and rock music nights.

travel details

Trains

Cardiff to: Abergavenny (hourly; 40min); Bristol (every 30min; 50min); Caerphilly (every 20min; 20min); Carmarthen (5 daily; 1hr 30min); Chepstow (hourly; 30min); Fishguard Harbour (1-2 daily; 2hr 20min); Haverfordwest (5 daily; 2hr 40min); London (hourly; 2hr); Merthyr Tydfil (hourly; 1hr); Newport (every 15–30min; 10min); Pontypool (hourly; 30min); Swansea (hourly; 50min); Tenby (4 daily; 2hr 30min); Ystrad Rhondda (every 30min; 50min).

Newport to: Abergavenny (hourly; 30min); Cardiff (every 15–30min; 10min); Chepstow (hourly; 20min).

Swansea to: Cardiff (hourly; 50min); Carmarthen (hourly; 50min); Fishguard (1–2 daily; 1hr 30min); Haverfordwest (7 daily; 1hr 30min); Llandrindod Wells (4 daily; 2hr 20min); London (2 daily; 3hr); Newport (hourly; 1hr 20min); Pembroke (6 daily; 2hr); Tenby (7 daily; 1hr 40min).

Buses

Cardiff to: Abergavenny (hourly; 1hr 20min); Blaenafon (hourly; 1hr 40min); Brecon (1 daily; 1hr 20min); Caerphilly (every 30min; 40min); Cardiff–Wales Airport (hourly; 30min); Chepstow (hourly; 1hr 20min); London (6 daily; 3hr 10min); Merthyr Tydfil (every 30min; 45min); Newport (every 30min; 30min); Swansea (every 30min; 1hr).

Chepstow to: Monmouth (16 daily; 50min); Newport (hourly; 50min); Tintern (8 daily; 20min); Usk (6 daily; 45min).

Merthyr Tydfil to: Abergavenny (hourly; 1hr 30min); Brecon (10 daily; 40min); Cardiff (every 30min; 45min).

Monmouth to: Abergavenny (6 daily; 40min); Chepstow (16 daily; 50min); Raglan (8 daily; 20min); Tintern (8 daily; 30min).

Newport to: Abergavenny (hourly; 1hr 10min); Blaenafon (every 30min; 1hr 10min); Cardiff (every 20min; 40min); Chepstow (hourly; 50min).

Swansea to: Brecon (2–3 daily; 1hr 30min); Cardiff (every 30min; 1hr); Dan-yr-ogof (4 daily; 1hr); Merthyr Tydfil (hourly; 1hr); Mumbles (every 10min; 15min); Oxwich (6 daily; 40min); Port Eynon (7 daily; 50min); Rhossili (Mon–Sat 10 daily, none on Sun; 1hr).

Ferries

Swansea to: Cork (4–7 weekly; 8hr).

CHAPTER THIRTEEN

SOUTHWEST WALES

Pembrokeshire, the most westerly outpost of Wales, attracts thousands of visitors each year to a glorious coastline that is so rocky and indented that large sections have been brought together as the **Pembrokeshire Coast National Park**, through which runs the very popular **Pembrokeshire Coast Path**. It is typically approached through **Carmarthenshire**, a county divided into sweeping flatlands along **Carmarthen Bay** and bucolic hill country inland. Of all the routes that spoke out of the county town of **Carmarthen**, the most glorious is the winding road to **Llandeilo** along the Tywi Valley, past ruined hilltop forts and two of the country's finest gardens. Immediately west sits Wales's most impressively sited castle at **Carreg Cennen**, high up on the dizzy plug of rock of the Black Mountain. Further inland, the sparsely populated landscape of remote hills and tiny valleys is broken only by endearing small market towns, including **Llandovery**, a good base for a visit to the Roman gold mines at **Dolaucothi**.

The wide sands of southern Carmarthenshire, which lie just beyond Dylan Thomas's adopted home town of **Laugharne**, stretch towards the popular south Pembrokeshire bucket-and-spade seaside resort of **Tenby**. Tenby sits at the entrance to the south Pembrokeshire peninsula, divided from the rest of the country by Milford Haven and the Daugleddau estuary, which bring their tidal waters into the heart of the area. The peninsula's turbulent, rocky coast is dotted by some remote historical sites, including the Norman baronial castle at **Manorbier** and **St Govan's Chapel**, a minute place of worship wedged into the rocks of a sea cliff near Bosherston. At the top of the peninsula is the old county town of **Pembroke**, dominated by its fearsome castle, and the market town and transport interchange of **Haverfordwest**, a dull place but seemingly difficult to avoid. The rutted coastline of **St Bride's Bay** is the most glorious part of the coastal walk, which leads north to brush past the impeccable mini-city of **St David's**, whose exquisite cathedral shelters in its own protective hollow. St David's is a magnet for visitors; aside from its own charms, there are opportunities locally for spectacular coast and hill walks, dinghy crossings to local islands and numerous other outdoor activities.

The coast turns towards the north at St David's, becoming the southern stretch of Cardigan Bay where the coast path nips and tucks over windswept headlands and into tight bays. The pretty port of **Fishguard** is primarily of interest as the terminus for ferries to Rosslare in Ireland; **Newport** makes a better base for exploring the area.

ACCOMMODATION PRICE CODES

Throughout this guide, hotel and B&B accommodation is priced on a scale of ① to ⑨, the number indicating the **lowest price** you could expect to pay per night in that establishment for a **double room** in high season. The prices indicated by the codes are as follows:

① under £40	④ £60–70	⑦ £110–150
② £40–50	⑤ £70–90	⑧ £150–200
③ £50–60	⑥ £90–110	⑨ over £200

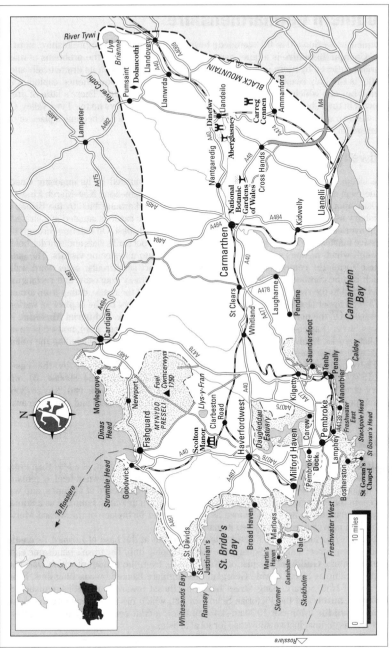

© Crown copyright

Southern Carmarthenshire

Frequently overlooked in the stampede towards the resorts of Pembrokeshire, **southern Carmarthenshire** is a quiet part of the world, with few of the problems of mass tourism suffered by more popular parts of Wales. **Kidwelly**, with its dramatically sited castle, is the only reason to stop before **Carmarthen**, the unquestioned capital of its region but one which fails to live up to the promise of its status. There's little of great interest in town, but it does make a good enough base for forays up the Tywi Valley. On the western side of the Taf estuary, the village of **Laugharne** has become a place of pilgrimage for Dylan Thomas devotees.

Kidwelly

The sleepy little town of **KIDWELLY** (Cydweli) is dominated by its imposing **Castle** (June–Sept daily 9.30am–6pm; April, May & Oct daily 9.30am–5pm; Nov–March Mon–Sat 9.30am–4pm, Sun 11am–4pm; £2.20; CADW). Established around 1106 by the Bishop of Salisbury as a satellite of Sherborne Abbey in Dorset, the castle is situated at a strategic point overlooking the River Gwendraeth and vast tracts of coast. On entering through the massive fourteenth-century gatehouse, you can still see portcullis slats and murder holes, through which noxious substances could be tipped onto unwelcome visitors. The **gatehouse** forms the centrepiece of the impressively intact semicircular outer ward walls, which can be climbed for some great views over the grassy courtyard and rectangular inner ward to the river. This is the oldest surviving part of the castle, dating from around 1275. The upper stories were added in the fourteenth century by the nephew of warlord Edward I. On the northwest edge of the town is the small-scale **Industrial Museum**, on Priory Street (Easter–Sept Mon–Fri 10am–5pm, Sat & Sun 2–5pm; free), housed in an old tin-plate works. Many of the original features have been preserved, including the rolling mills where long lines of tin were rolled and spun into wafer-thin slices.

There's decent pub **accommodation** at the *Old Malthouse*, by the castle (☎01554/891091; ③), and superb B&B at *Penlan Isaf Farm* (☎01554/890084; ①), on a dairy farm overlooking the town. You can **camp** at *Tanylan Farm* (☎01267/267306), which perches alongside the estuary west of Kidwelly. Good **food** and drink are available at the cosy *Boot & Shoe*, 2 Castle St.

Carmarthen and around

CARMARTHEN (Caerfyrddin), the ancient capital of the region, is a less than enticing place to stay for long. While its atmosphere is undeniably down-at-heel, it remains the major town in west Wales where the native language is heard at all times, and was once – in the early eighteenth century – the largest town in Wales. Founded as a Roman fort, Carmarthen is now best known as the supposed birthplace of the wizard Merlin (Myrddin in Welsh gives the town its name).

The most picturesque part of town lies spread out at the base of Edward I's **castle**, around King Street and Nott Square, the main shopping hub. The town's handsome eighteenth-century **Guildhall** sits just off Nott Square, from the bottom of which Darkgate leads to Lammas Street, a wide Georgian thoroughfare flanked by coaching inns. From the top of Nott Square, King Street heads northeast towards the undistinguished **St Peter's Church** and the Victorian School of Art, which has now metamorphosed into **Oriel Myrddin** (Mon–Sat 10.30am–4.45pm; free), a craft centre and excellent gallery that acts as an imaginative showcase for local artists.

The severe grey Bishop's Palace at **Abergwili**, two miles east of Carmarthen, was the seat of the Bishop of St David's between 1542 and 1974, and now houses the **Carmarthenshire County Museum** (Mon–Sat 10am–4.30pm; free), a spirited amble through the history of the area. This surprisingly interesting exhibition covers the history of Welsh translations of the New Testament and *Book of Common Prayer* – both first translated here, in 1567. Local pottery, archeological finds, wooden dressers and a lively history of local castles are presented in well-annotated displays. The upstairs section examines a number of topics including geology, the local coracle industry and the origins of Wales's first eisteddfod (Welsh cultural festival), held in Carmarthen in 1450.

The **train station** lies over Carmarthen Bridge, on the south side of the river. All **buses** terminate at the bus station on Blue Street, just on the north side of the bridge, and many connect with trains. The town's **tourist office** is on Lammas Street, close to the Crimea Monument (daily: Easter–Oct 9.30am–5.30pm; Nov–Easter 10am–4.30pm; ☎01267/231557). For **bike rental**, go to Ar Dy Feic, over the river on Llangunnor Road (☎01267/221182).

There's lots of **accommodation** in town, especially on Lammas Street, where you'll find the *Boar's Head* (☎01267/222789, *kaw@boars-head-hotel.demon.co.uk*; ②), one of the town's grandest old coaching inns, and the *Drovers Arms* (☎01267/237646; ②). The best B&Bs are *Y Dderwen Fach*, 98 Priory St (☎01267/234193; ①), and the *Old Priory* guest house, 20 Priory St (☎01267/237471; ①), both out along the main road to Lampeter and Llandeilo. If you're looking for something a little more remote, don't pass up *Tŷ Mawr* (☎01267/202332; ⑤), an oak-beamed country house hotel in the entirely unspoilt village of **Brechfa**, some twelve miles northeast of Carmarthen. You can find good snack **food** at the old-fashioned *Morris Tea Rooms*, almost opposite the Lyric Theatre in King Street, and at the vegetarian café in the Waverley Stores health-food shop, on 23 Lammas St. The best meals in town can be found at the wonderful *Quayside Brasserie*, on the Tywi quay (☎01267/223000).

Laugharne

The village of **LAUGHARNE** (Talacharn), on the western side of the Taf estuary, is a delightful spot, with its ragged castle looming over the reeds and tidal flats and narrow lanes snuggling in behind. Catch it in high season though and you're immediately aware that Laugharne is increasingly being taken over by the legend of the poet Dylan Thomas.

At the end of a narrow lane bumping along the estuary is the **Dylan Thomas Boathouse** (daily: Easter & May–Oct 10am–5.30pm; Nov–Easter 10.30am–3.30pm; £2.75), the simple home of the Thomas family from 1949 until Dylan's death in 1953. It's an enchanting museum, with views of the peaceful, ever-changing water and light of the estuary and its "heron-priested shore". Inside, a period wireless set in the intact living room regales you with the rich tones of the poet reading his own work, while contemporary newspaper reports of his demise show how he was, while alive, a fairly minor literary figure. Back along the narrow lane, you can peer into the blue garage where he wrote: curling photographs of literary heroes, a pen collection and numerous scrunched-up balls of paper on the cheap desk suggest quite effectively that he is about to return at any minute. Thomas is buried in the graveyard of the parish church in the village centre, his grave marked by a simple white cross.

Laugharne has numerous Thomas connections, and plays them with curiously disgruntled aplomb – none more so than the great alcoholic's old boozing hole, **Brown's Hotel** on the main street where, in the nicotine-crusted front bar, Thomas's cast-iron table still sits in a window alcove. At the bottom of the main street, the gloomy hulk of **Laugharne Castle** (May–Sept 10am–5pm; £2; CADW) broods over the estuary. Two

DYLAN THOMAS

Dylan Thomas was the stereotypical Celt – fiery, verbose, richly talented and habitually drunk. Born in 1914 into a snugly middle-class family in Swansea's Uplands district, Dylan's first glimmers of literary greatness came when he was posted, as a young reporter, to the *South Wales Evening Post* in Swansea. Some of his most popular tales in the *Portrait of the Artist as a Young Dog* were inspired during this period.

Rejecting the coarse provincialism of Swansea and Welsh life, Thomas arrived in London as a broke twenty-year-old in 1934, weeks before the appearance of his first volume of poetry, which was published as the first prize in a *Sunday Referee* competition. Another volume followed shortly afterwards, cementing the engaging young Welshman's reputation in the British literary establishment. He married in 1937, and the newlyweds returned to Wales, settling in the hushed, provincial backwater of Laugharne. Short stories – crackling with rich and melancholy humour – tumbled out as swiftly as poems, further widening his base of admirers, though, like so many other writers, Thomas has only gained star status posthumously. Perhaps better than anyone, he writes in an identifiably Welsh, rhythmic wallow in the language.

Thomas, especially in public, liked to adopt the persona of what he perceived to be an archetypal stage Welshman: sonorous tones, loquacious, romantic and inclined towards a stiff tipple. This role was particularly popular in the United States, where he journeyed on lucrative lecture tours. It was on one of these that he died, in 1953, poisoned by a massive whisky overdose. Just one month earlier, he had put the finishing touches to what many regard as his masterpiece: *Under Milk Wood*, a "play for voices". Describing the dreams, thoughts and lives of a straggling Welsh seaside community called Llareggub – mis-spelt Llaregyb by the po-faced BBC, who couldn't sanction the usage of the expression "bugger all" backwards – it is loosely based on Laugharne, New Quay in Cardiganshire and a vast dose of Thomas's own imagination.

of the early medieval towers survive, although most of the ruins are those of the Tudor mansion built over the original for Sir John Perrot. The views from the domed roof over the tight, huddled little town are sublime.

Surprisingly, Laugharne has very little B&B **accommodation**. *Castle House*, in the village centre (☎01994/427616, *charles@laugharne.co.uk*; ③), has large en-suite rooms and gorgeous estuary views from some rooms; while *Swan Cottage*, at 20 Gosport St (☎01994/427409; ②), is very welcoming. The nearest **campsite** is *Ants Hill Camping Park*, just north of Laugharne (☎01994/427293). For **eating**, the choice is a little wider: try the moderately priced *Stable Door* (closed Mon & Tues), near the central town hall, or the *Under Milk Wood Inn*, on the square.

The Tywi Valley

The **River Tywi** curves and darts its way east from Carmarthen through some of the most magical scenery in south Wales. The thirty-mile trip to Llandovery is punctuated by gentle, impossibly green hills topped with ruined castles, notably the wonderful **Carreg Cennen**. It's not hard to see why the Merlin legend has taken such a hold in these parts – the landscape does seem infused with a kind of eerie splendour. Along the way, a couple of budding gardens have sprung up in the last couple of years: one completely new in the form of the **National Botanic Garden of Wales**; the other a faithful reconstruction of linked walled gardens around the long-abandoned house of **Aberglasney**. Further upstream, the market town of **Llandovery** makes a good base for visiting the Roman gold mine at **Dolaucothi**.

The National Botanic Garden and Aberglasney

The brand new **National Botanic Garden of Wales**, nine miles west of Carmarthen (call for opening hours: ☎01558/668768; £6.50), centres on a vast glasshouse designed by Norman Foster. Inside are plants from regions with a Mediterranean climate: the Cape region of South Africa, southwestern Australia, Chile, California, and the Mediterranean itself. As yet, many of the specimens are only half-grown, but you can already wander through a small olive grove and see an abundance of species. Outside, one-acre plots are dedicated to regions with wet and mild climates similar to the Tywi Valley, and an adjacent hillside gets the same treatment for moorland environments. The garden has been designed around the principle of sustainability: rainwater is caught and used for irrigation; the glasshouses are heated by burning wood coppiced on the grounds; and human waste is transformed into essentially pure water by means of a series of reed beds. The theme runs through to a large section of the surrounding land which is being turned over to organic farming using Welsh breeds of cattle and sheep – which eventually end up on a plate in the visitors' **restaurant**.

A complementary and much older garden has recently opened a few miles to the east, around the dilapidated stately home of **Aberglasney** (April–Oct daily 9.30am–6pm; £4), half a mile south of the A40 near Broad Oak. There's little to see in the stabilized shell of the house itself, but archeological work has pretty much peeled back half a century of neglect to reveal a set of interlinking walled gardens mostly constructed between the sixteenth and eighteenth centuries. The basic framework — the walls, ponds and outline of the beds — is largely intact, but detailed digging continues to uncover more about the site, and extensive restoration is underway in the kitchen garden and secular cloister garden – thought to be the only one in Britain. A walkway leads around the top of the cloister, giving access to a set of six Victorian aviaries from where there are great views over the Jacobean pool garden. The highlight of the garden must be the yew tunnel, planted around three hundred years ago and trained over to root on the far side.

Llandeilo, Dinefwr and Carreg Cennen

Fifteen miles east of Carmarthen, the main street – Rhosmaen Street – of the handsome small market town of **LLANDEILO** climbs up from the Tywi bridge. Although there is little in the way of actual sights in the town, Llandeilo is brilliantly situated in a bowl of hills, a quiet, rustic place whose few streets cluster around the main thoroughfare. Behind the Tywi bridge are the **tourist office** (Easter week & May–Sept Mon–Sat 10am–5pm; ☎01558/824226) and the **train station**. You can **stay** at inexpensive B&Bs like *Tŷ Teilo*, 41 Alan Rd (☎01558/822437; ①), or the relatively plush *Cawdor Arms*, on Rhosmaen St (☎01558/823500; ④), which serves expensive but beautifully cooked evening meals. The *Y Capel Bach* bistro, a couple of doors down, serves tasty, moderately priced **meals**, and there is good drinking to be had across the road at the *Castle Hotel*, which brews its own beer.

A mile west of Llandeilo is the gorgeous parkland of **Plas Dinefwr**, site also of two splendid castles. On a wooded bluff above the Tywi sits the tumbledown shell of **Dinefwr Old Castle** which became ill-suited to the needs of the landowning Rhys family, who aspired to something a little more luxurious. The "new" castle, now named **Newton House** (April–Oct Mon & Thurs–Sun 11am–5pm; house £2.80, grounds £2; NT), was built in 1523, and given a new limestone facade in the 1860s.

Isolated in rural hinterland, four miles southeast of Llandeilo, is one of the most magnificently sited castles in the whole of Wales, **Carreg Cennen Castle** (daily: April–Oct 9.30am–7.30pm; Nov–March 9.30am–4.30pm; £2.50; CADW), just beyond the tiny hamlet of Trapp. Sir Urien, one of King Arthur's knights, is said to have built his fortress on the fearsome rocky outcrop, although the first known construction dates from 1248. Carreg Cennen fell to the English in 1277, during Edward I's initial invasion of Wales, and was finally abandoned after being partially destroyed in 1462 by the Earl of Pembroke, who believed it to be the base of a group of lawless rebels. The most astounding aspect of the castle is its commanding position, 300ft above a sheer drop down into the green valley of the small River Cennen. The highlights of a visit are the views down into the river valley and the long descent down into a watery, pitch-black **cave** that is said to have served as a well. Torches are essential(rented from the excellent tearoom near the car park) – it's worth continuing as far as possible and then turning them off to experience absolute darkness.

Llandovery

Twelve miles beyond Llandeilo, the town of **LLANDOVERY** (Llanymddyfri) has architecture and a layout that have changed little for centuries. As with so many mid-Wales settlements to the north, an influx of New Agers in the 1960s had a discernible effect on the town: there's a thriving independent theatre, and bookshops and wholefood stores abound. Alongside this more alternative flavour, Llandovery is still a major centre for its cattle market, held every other Tuesday.

On the south side of the main Broad Street, a grassy mound holds the scant remains of the town's **castle**. Broad Street has been the main thoroughfare for years, as can be seen from the solid early nineteenth-century town houses and earlier inns that line the road as it widens towards the cobbled, rectangular Market Square. Above the tourist office on Kings Road, the excellent **Llandovery Heritage Centre** (Easter–Sept daily 10am–5.30pm; Oct–Easter Mon–Sat 10am–4pm, Sun 2–4pm) depicts some powerful local legends and tales. Stone Street heads north from the Market Square to the **Llandovery Theatre**, a shadow of its former self but worth keeping an eye on for an update on events in the area.

Llandovery **train station** sits on the main A40 just before Broad Street; **buses** leave from Broad Street and Market Square. The joint **tourist office** and **Brecon Beacons National Park office** (Easter–Sept daily 10am–5.30pm; Oct–Easter Mon–Sat 10am–4pm, Sun 2–4pm; ☎01550/720693) is on Kings Road, the continuation of Broad Street.

The best central **accommodation** is at *The Drovers*, 9 Market Square (☎01686/721115; ①), an eighteenth-century town house full of antique furniture. Less central B&Bs include: *Mrs Billingham's*, Pencerrig New Road, on the way out of town towards Llandeilo (☎01550/721259; ①); the superb Gothic-styled en-suites at *Cwm Rhuddan Mansion* (☎01550/721414; ②), a mile west on the A4069; and, a mile further out on the same road, *Cwm Gwyn Farm*, Llangadog Road (☎01550/720410; ①). The nearest **campsite**, a mile east of Llandovery off the A40, is the *Erwlon* (☎01550/720332). Llandovery has precious few good **places to eat**, though there are a number of daytime cafés and tearooms, mainly around the Market Square, and the *Castle Hotel*, on Broad Street, offers delicious, moderately priced lunchtime and evening food. For **drinking**, the eccentric and bizarrely old-fashioned *Red Lion*, a red, colonnaded house nestled in an easy-to-miss corner at 2 Market Square, can't be beaten.

The Dolaucothi Gold Mine

The countryside to the west of Llandovery is blissfully quiet, with just a handful of main roads and lanes that rarely contain traffic of any volume. The principal route off the A40 between Llandeilo and Llandovery, the A482, heads towards the straggling village of **PUMSAINT** (Five Saints). The origin of the name is explained by a stone found near the entrance of the **Dolaucothi Gold Mine** (late May to mid-Sept daily 10am–5pm; £2.60; NT), half a mile off the main road. Indentations in the rock are said to be the marks left by five sleeping saints, who rested here one night. Pumsaint is the only place in Britain where it is certain that the Romans mined gold, laying complicated and astoundingly advanced systems to extract the precious metal from the rock. The remains of Roman workings – a few water channels and an open cast mine – can still be seen around the site. An underground **tour** (£3.60) goes deep into the mine workings and usually allows visitors to prospect for gold themselves.

Tenby and Caldey Island

On a natural promontory of great strategic importance, the beguilingly old-fashioned resort of **TENBY** (Dynbych-y-Pysgod), wedged between two sweeping beaches fronting an island studded seascape, is everything a seaside resort should be. Narrow streets wind down from the medieval centre to the harbour past miniature gardens fashioned to catch the afternoon sun. Steps lead down the steeper slopes to dockside arches which still house fishmongers selling the morning's catch.

Tenby has a long pedigree. First mentioned in a ninth-century bardic poem, the town grew under the twelfth-century Normans, who erected a castle on the headland in their attempt to colonize south Pembrokeshire and create a "Little England beyond Wales" – an appellation by which the area is still known today. Three times in the twelfth and thirteenth centuries the town was ransacked by the Welsh. In response, the castle was fortified once more and the stout town walls – which largely still exist – were built. Tenby prospered as a major port for a wide variety of foodstuffs and fine goods between the fourteenth and sixteenth centuries, and although decline followed, the arrival of the railway brought renewed wealth as the town became a fashionable resort. Lines of neat, prosperous hotels and expensive shops still stand haughtily along the seafront.

Although the town is extremely conservative, with a large population of retired people, there is plenty of entertainment and a huge number of pubs and restaurants. In the middle of summer, it can seem full to bursting point, with heavy traffic restrictions and a considerable rush on decent accommodation. Tenby is also one of the major stopping-off points along the **Pembrokeshire Coast Path**, a welcome burst of glitter and excitement amidst mile upon mile of undulating cliff scenery. The **National Park** boundary skirts around the edge of the town. A couple of miles offshore from Tenby, the old monastic ruins of **Caldey Island** make for a pleasant day-trip.

Tenby

Tenby is shaped like a triangle, with two sides formed by the coast meeting at Castle Hill. The third side is formed by the remains of the twenty-foot-high town **walls**, first built in the late thirteenth century and massively strengthened by Jasper Tudor, Earl of Pembroke and uncle of Henry VII, in 1457. Further refortification came in the 1580s, when Tenby was considered to be in the frontline against a possible attack by the Spanish Armada. In the middle of the remaining stretch is the only town gate still standing, at **Five Arches**, a semicircular barbican that combined practical day-to-day usage with hidden look-outs and angles acute enough to surprise invaders.

The centrepiece and most notable landmark of the town centre is the 152-foot spire of the largely fifteenth-century **St Mary's Church**, between St George's Street and Tudor Square. A pleasantly light interior shows the elaborate ceiling bosses in the chancel to good effect, and fifteenth-century tombs of local barons demonstrate Tenby's important mercantile tradition.

Wedged between the town walls and the two bays, the **old town** is a great place to wander, with many of the original medieval lanes still intact in the immediate area around the parish church. **Sun Alley** is a tiny crack between overhanging whitewashed stone houses that connects Crackwell and High streets. Due east, on the other side of the church, **Quay Hill** runs parallel, a narrow set of steps and cobbles tumbling down past some of the town's oldest houses to the top of the harbour. Wedged in a corner of Quay Hill is the **Tudor Merchant's House** (April–Sept Mon, Tues & Thurs–Sat 10am–5pm, Sun 1–5pm; Oct Mon, Tues, Thurs & Fri 10am–3pm, Sun noon–3pm; £1.80; NT), built in the late fifteenth century for a wealthy local merchant at the time when Tenby was second only to Bristol as an important west coast port. The rambling house is on three floors, packed with period furniture from the sixteenth century, although more notable are the tapering Flemish-style chimney pieces, a prominent local fashion.

During the day, the **harbour** is the scene of considerable activity as the departure point for numerous excursion boats, the most popular being the short trip over to Caldey Island (see below). Above the harbour is the headland and **Castle Hill**, where paths and flower beds have been planted around the remaining **gatehouse** of the Norman castle. Here, the town **Museum** (Easter–Oct daily 10am–6pm; Nov–Easter Mon–Fri 10am–5pm; £1.80) doubles as a small art gallery and is typical of Tenby: slightly ponderous and municipally minded, but still interesting.

Practicalities

The **train station** is at the western end of the town centre, at the bottom of Warren Street. Some **buses** stop at South Parade, at the top of Trafalgar Rd, although most call at the bus shelter on Upper Park Road. The **tourist office** faces the North Beach, on The Croft (daily: Easter to mid-July & Sept 10am–6pm; mid-July to Aug 10am–9pm; Oct 10am–5.30pm; Nov–Easter Mon–Sat 10am–4pm; ☎01834/842402).

As a major resort, Tenby has dozens of **hotels** and **guest houses**, all pressed from pretty much the same mould, though paying more gets you a wider range of facilities and a sea view. The best budget place is the spotless *Boulston Cottage*, 29 Trafalgar Rd (☎01834/843289; ①). *Lyndale Guest House*, Warren Street (☎01834/842836; ①), is a welcoming B&B near the station, happy to cater for vegetarians; and *Ashby House*, 24 Victoria St (☎01834/842867; ②), is good too. The *Atlantic*, The Esplanade (☎01834/842881; ⑤), is at the top of the range, with a couple of good restaurants and even a small indoor pool. There are a couple of **YHA hostels** nearby: bus #350 runs to *Pentlepoir*, four miles north, near Saundersfoot railway station (☎01834/812333; ①; closed Oct–March); while four miles west of Tenby, overlooking the cliffs, is the bright and modern *Manorbier*, at Skrinkle Haven (☎01834/871803; ①; closed Nov–Feb). You can **camp** there, and at the small and semi-official *Meadow Farm*, Northcliff, on the northern fringes of town (☎01834/844829; closed Oct–March).

There are dozens of **cafés** and **restaurants** around town. For ice cream and Italian snacks, try *Fecci and Sons*, Upper Frog Street. *Quay Room*, on Quay Hill, is good for coffee and snacks, while the moderately priced *La Cave*, Upper Frog Street (☎01834/843038), and the more expensive *Plantagenet*, Quay Hill (☎01834/842350), offer well-cooked local specialities. For **pubs**, head for the *Lifeboat Tavern*, Tudor Square, or the *Coach and Horses*, Upper Frog Street. The *Three Mariners*, on St George's Street, has good beer and live music.

Caldey Island

Looming large over Tenby's seascape is **Caldey Island** (Ynys Pyr), a couple of miles offshore. Celtic monks first settled here in the sixth century, perhaps establishing an offshoot of St Illtud's monastery at Llantwit Major. Little is then known of the island until 1136, when it was given to the Benedictine monks of St Dogmael's at Cardigan, who founded their priory here. Upon the Dissolution of the monasteries in 1536, the Benedictine monks left the island and a fanciful succession of owners bought and sold it on a whim, until it was, once again, sold to a Benedictine monastic order in 1906 and subsequently to an order of Reformed Cistercians. The island has been a monastic home almost constantly ever since.

Boats leave Tenby Harbour (mid-May to mid-Sept Mon–Fri 9.45am–4pm every 15min; Easter to mid-May & mid-Sept to Oct occasional sailings; school summer holidays also Sat 1–4pm; ☎01834/842402; £6). Tickets for the twenty-minute journey (not tied to any specific sailing) are sold at the kiosk in Castle Square, directly above the harbour. On landing at Caldey's jetty, a short walk leads through the woods to the island's main settlement.

The village itself is the main hub of Caldey life. As well as a tiny post office and popular tearoom, there's a **perfume shop** selling the herbal fragrances distilled by the monks from Caldey's abundant flora. The narrow road going to the left leads down to the heavily restored **chapel of St David**, whose most impressive feature is the round-arched Norman door. Opposite is the gathering point for **tours** (July & Aug every 2 hours; rest of year daily; men only) of the garish twentieth-century **monastery**, a white, turreted heap that resembles a Disney castle. A lane leads south from the village to the old **priory**, abandoned at the Dissolution and restored at the turn of this century. The centrepiece of the complex is the remarkable, twelfth-century **St Illtud's Church**, which houses one of the most significant pre-Norman finds in Wales, the sandstone **Ogham Cross**, found under the stained glass window on the south side of the nave. It is carved with an inscription from the sixth century which was added to, in Latin, during the ninth. The lane continues south from the site, climbing up to the gleaming white island **lighthouse**, built in 1828, from which there are memorable views.

Southern Pembrokeshire

The southern zigzag of coast that darts west from Tenby is a strange mix of caravan parks, Ministry of Defence shooting ranges, spectacularly beautiful bays and gull-covered cliffs. From Tenby, the A4139 passes through **Penally**, with its wonderful beach, and continues past idyllic coves, the lily ponds at **Bosherston** and the remarkable and ancient **St Govan's Chapel**, squeezed into a rock cleft above the crashing waves. The ancient town of **Pembroke** really only warrants a visit to its impressive castle before pressing on to neighbouring **Lamphey**, with its fine Bishop's Palace. Bus **transport** to most corners of the peninsula radiates out from Haverfordwest (see p.698).

Penally to Bosherton

Just over a mile down the A4139 from Tenby, the dormitory village of **PENALLY** is unremarkable save for its vast beach. The coastal path hugs the cliff-top from the viewpoint at Giltar Point, just below Penally, reaching the glorious privately owned beach at the headland of **Lydstep Haven** after two miles (fee charged for the sands). A mile further west is the cove of **Skrinkle Haven**, and above it the excellent Manorbier **YHA hostel** (☎01834/871803), where you can also **camp**.

The next part of the coast path heads inland to avoid the artillery range that occupies the beautiful outcrop of **Old Castle Head**, then leads straight into the quaint village of **MANORBIER**, pronounced "Manner-beer" (Maenorbŷr), birthplace in 1146 of Giraldus Cambrensis. Manorbier's **castle** (April–Sept daily 10.30am–5pm; £2), founded in the early twelfth century as an impressive baronial residence, sits above the village and its beach on a hill of wild gorse. The Norman walls are in a good state of repair, surrounding an inner grass courtyard in which the extensive remains of the castle's chapel and state rooms jostle for position with the nineteenth-century domestic residence. In the walls and buildings are a warren of dark passageways to explore, occasionally opening out into little cells with lacklustre wax figures purporting to illustrate the castle's history.

The rocky little harbour at **Stackpole Quay**, reached via the small lane from Freshwater East through East Trewent, is a good starting point for walks along the

THE PEMBROKESHIRE NATIONAL PARK AND COASTAL PATH

The **Pembrokeshire Coast** is Britain's only predominantly sea-based national park, hugging the rippled coast around the entire western section of Wales. Established in 1952, the park is not one easily identifiable mass, rather a series of occasionally unconnected coastal and inland scenic patches.

Crawling around almost every wriggle of the coastline, the **Pembrokeshire Coast Path** winds 186 miles from St Dogmael's near Cardigan in the north to its southern point at Amroth. For the vast majority of the time, the path clings precariously to cliff-top routes, overlooking seal-basking rocks, craggy offshore islands, unexpected gashes of sand and shrieking clouds of sea birds. The most popular and ruggedly inspiring segments of the coast path are: either side of St Bride's Bay, around St David's Head and the Marloes Peninsula; the stretch along the southern coast from the castle at Manorbier to the tiny cliff chapel at Bosherston; and the generally quieter northern coast either side of Fishguard, past undulating contours, massive cliffs, bays and old ports.

Of all the seasons, spring is perhaps the finest for walking as the crowds are yet to arrive and the cliff-top flora is at its most vivid. There are numerous publications available about the coast path, of which the best is Brian John's *National Trail Guide* (£11), which includes sections of 1:25,000 maps of the route. The National Park publishes a handy *Coast Path Accommodation* guide (£2), detailing B&Bs and campsites along its entire length.

breathtaking cliffs to the north. Another walk leads half a mile south to one of the finest beaches in Pembrokeshire, **Barafundle Bay**, with its soft beach fringed by wooded cliffs at either end. The path continues around the coast, through the dunes of **Stackpole Warren**, to **BROAD HAVEN**, where a pleasant small beach overlooks several rocky islets, now managed by the National Trust. Basing yourself here gives good access to the nearby **Bosherston Lakes** inland, three artificial fingers of water beautifully landscaped in the late eighteenth century. The westernmost lake is the most scenic, especially in late spring and early summer when the lilies that form a carpet across its surface are in full bloom.

Another lane dips south from the village of **BOSHERSTON**, across the MoD training grounds, to a spot overlooking the cliffs where tiny **St Govan's Chapel** is wedged: it's a remarkable building, known to be at least eight hundred years old. Steps descend straight into the sandy-floored chapel, now devoid of any furnishings save for the simple stone altar.

Pembroke and around

The old county town of **PEMBROKE** (Penfro) and its fearsome castle sit on the southern side of the River Pembroke, a continuation of the massive Milford Haven waterway, described by Nelson as the greatest natural harbour in the world. Despite its location, Pembroke is surprisingly dull, with one long main street of attractive Georgian and Victorian houses, some intact stretches of medieval town wall but little else to catch the eye. The town grew up solely to serve the castle, the mightiest link in the chain of Norman strongholds built across southern Wales. The walled town, drawn out along a hilltop ridge, flourished as a port for Pembrokeshire goods, which were sold throughout Britain and exported to Ireland, France and Spain. The castle was destroyed by Cromwell during the Civil War, and though the town developed as a centre of leather making, weaving, dyeing and tailoring, it never really regained its former importance.

Pembroke's history is inextricably bound up with that of its impregnable **Castle** (daily: April–Sept 9.30am–6pm; March & Oct 10am–5pm; Nov–Feb 10.30am–4.30pm; £3), founded by the Normans, but rebuilt between 1189 and 1245. During the Civil War, Pembroke was a Parliamentarian stronghold until the town's military governor suddenly switched allegiance to the king, whereupon Cromwell's troops sacked the castle after a 48-day siege. Yet despite Cromwell's battering, and centuries of subsequent neglect, Pembroke still inspires feelings of awe at its sheer, bloody-minded bulk, even if it is largely due to extensive restoration over the last century. The soaring gatehouse leads into the large, grassy courtyard around the vast, round Norman **keep**, 75ft high and with walls 18ft thick, crowned by a dome. In the domestic quarters, there's a dungeon tower, a Norman hall where the period arch has been disappointingly over-restored and reinforced, and the Oriel or Northern hall, a Tudor re-creation of an earlier antechamber. The intact towers and battlements contain many heavily restored communal rooms, now empty of furniture and, to a large extent, atmosphere too, although some of the rooms, mainly in the gatehouse, are used to house some excellent displays on the history of the castle and the Tudor empire.

Opposite the castle walls is the delightfully eccentric **Museum of the Home**, at 7 Westgate Hill, the northward continuation of Main Street (May–Sept Mon–Thurs 11am–5pm; £1.20). Packed into the steep town house is a collection of utterly ordinary items dating from the eighteenth to the twentieth centuries. The objects are loosely gathered into themes, including toiletries, bedroom accessories and children's games – all demonstrated with great enthusiasm.

Pembroke's **train station** is east of the town centre on Station Road. The **tourist office**, on Commons Road, parallel to Main Street (Easter–Oct daily 10am–5.30pm; Nov Tues, Thurs & Sat 10am–4pm; ☎01646/622388), provides a useful, free town guide and has limited information on the Pembrokeshire National Park. If you decide to **stay**, don't miss *Beech House B&B*, 78 Main St (☎01646/683746; ③), which easily outdoes places charging twice as much – one room even boasts a four-poster. If it is full, try the slightly pricier *Merton Place House*, a few doors up at 3 East Back (☎01646/684795; ③), which has a pleasant walled garden at the back. More expensive places in town aren't great shakes, but you could stay in Lamphey (see below), a couple of miles away.

For **food**, try *The Pantry*, 4 Main St, during the daytime and early evening, or the well-cooked bar food at the *King's Arms Hotel*, 13 Main St. Further along, at no. 63, the expensive *Left Bank* (☎01646/622333) serves well-thought-out French cuisine in stylish surroundings. The best of the dozens of **pubs** is the *Old Cross Saws*, at 109 Main St, although it's hard to beat a summer evening on the veranda, overlooking the Mill Pond, at the *Waterman's Arms*, over the bridge on Northgate Street.

Lamphey and Carew

The humdrum village of **LAMPHEY**, two miles southeast of Pembroke, is best known for the ruined **Bishop's Palace** (daily 10am–5pm; £2; CADW), off a quiet lane to the north of the village. A country retreat for the bishops of St David's, the palace dates from around the thirteenth century, but was abandoned following the Reformation. Stout walls surround the ruins, which are scattered over a large area. Many of the palace buildings have long been lost under grassy banks. Most impressive are the remains of the Great Hall, extending across the entire eastern end of the complex. You can still see Bishop Gower's hallmark arcaded parapets running along the top, similar to those he built in the Bishop's Palace of St David's.

A tiny village that can become unbearably packed in high season, **CAREW**, four miles east of Pembroke, by the River Carew, is a pretty place. Just south of the river crossing, by the main road, is the village's **Celtic cross**, the graceful, remarkably intact taper of the shaft covered in fine tracery of ancient Welsh designs. A small hut beyond the cross serves as the ticket office for **Carew Castle and Mill** (Easter–Oct daily 10am–5pm; castle £1.80; castle & mill £2.65). The castle, a hybrid of Elizabethan fancy and earlier defensive necessity, is reached across a field. A few hundred yards to the west is the **Carew French Mill**, used commercially until 1937 and now the only tide-powered mill in Wales. The impressive eighteenth-century exterior belies the rather pedestrian exhibitions and audio-visual displays inside, which describe the milling process.

Haverfordwest to Newport

The most western point of Wales – and the very furthest you can get from England – is one of the country's most enchanting areas. The chief town of the region, **Haverfordwest**, remains rather soulless despite some handsome architecture, but it is useful as a jumping-off point for **St Bride's Bay**. The coast here is broken into rocky outcrops, islands and broad, sweeping beaches curving between two headlands that sit like giant crab pincers facing out into the warm Gulf Stream. The southernmost headland winds around every conceivable angle, offering calm, east-facing sands at **Dale** and sunny expanses of south-facing beach at **Marloes**. Near **Martin's Haven**, boats depart for the offshore islands of **Skomer**, **Skokholm** and **Grassholm**. To the north, the spectacularly lacerated coast veers to the left and the **St David's peninsula**, along stunning cliffs interrupted only by occasional strips of sand. Just north of **St Non's Bay**, the tiny cathedral city of **St David's** is definitely a highlight. Rooks and crows circle above the impressive ruins of the huge Bishop's Palace, sitting beneath the delicate bulk of the cathedral, the most impressive in Wales.

The north-facing coast that forms the very southern tip of Cardigan Bay is noticeably less commercialized and far more Welsh than the touristy shores of south and mid-Pembrokeshire. From the crags and cairns above St David's Head, the coast path perches precariously on the cliffs where only the thousands of sea birds have access. There are only the modest charms of small bays and desolate coves to detain you en route to the charming town of **Newport** – unless you're heading for **Fishguard**, and the ferries to Ireland.

Haverfordwest

In the seventeenth and eighteenth centuries, the town of **HAVERFORDWEST** (Hwlffordd), ten miles north of Pembroke, prospered as a port and trading centre, but despite its natural advantages, it is scarcely a place to linger. A cursory look at the dingy shell of the thirteenth-century **castle** and the less-than-exciting **town museum** (Easter–Oct Mon–Sat 10am–4pm; £1) is enough, though as the main transport hub and shopping centre for western Pembrokeshire you are likely to pass through.

The **tourist office** (May–Sept Mon–Sat 10am–5.30pm; Oct–April Mon–Sat 10am–4pm; ☎01437/763110) is next to the bus terminus, at the end of the Old Bridge, and there is also a highly informative **National Park office** at 40 High St. Next to the tourist office, the Holiday Information Centre includes an excellent booking agency (☎01437/765765) for self-catering cottages in Pembrokeshire. Low-cost **accommodation** is provided at *College Guest House*, 93 Hill St (☎01437/763710; ①), and the *Villa House*, St Thomas Green (☎01437/762977; ①); and there are slightly pricier rooms at the solidly Georgian *Castle Hotel*, in Castle Square (☎01437/769322; ③). For **lunch**, duck into *Morillo's*, on the pedestrian Bridge Street, a successful combination of Italian café and chippy. Evening meals are best at *George's* pub, on Market Street (closed Sun).

Four miles northeast of town, along the B4329, **Scolton Manor** (April–Oct Tues–Sun 10.30am–5.30pm; £1) is a modest stately home that now forms the nucleus of the diverting **Pembrokeshire County Museum**. Aside from the enchanting period rooms indoors, outhouses showcase all manner of quirky exhibits, and there is a good café and an environmentally aware visitor centre on site.

Marloes and Dale peninsula

DALE, fourteen miles west of Haverfordwest, can be unbearably crowded in peak season, but it is a pleasant enough village, whose east-facing shore makes it excellent for watersports in the lighter seas. All the activity happens around the beachside shack of West Wales Wind, Surf and Sailing, who give instruction in windsurfing, surfing, sailing and kayaking (£30–50 per half day), and offer lively B&B **accommodation** on the waterfront in Dale (☎01646/636642; ①). The *Post House Hotel* (☎01646/636201; ②), in the middle of the village just behind the real-ale *Griffin Inn*, has en-suite rooms and optional evening meals; and for a touch of luxury, there's *Allenbrook* (☎01646/636254; ②; closed Dec), a charming country house close to the beach.

The calm waters of Dale are deceptive, and as soon as you head further south towards **St Ann's Head**, one of the most invigoratingly desolate places in the county, the wind speed whips up, with waves and tides to match. The coast path sticks tight to the undulating coastline, passing tiny bays en route to the St Ann's lighthouse.

The coast turns and heads north from St Ann's Head to the unexciting hamlet of **MARLOES**. Only a mile away from the village, the broad, deserted beach is a safe place to swim, and looks out towards the island of Skokholm. From here, the coast path and a narrow road continue for two miles to the National Trust-owned swathe of **Deer Park** – which has no deer but is the name given to the grassy far tip of the southern peninsula of St Bride's Bay – and **Martin's Haven**, from where you can take a **boat** out to the islands of Skomer, Skokholm and Grassholm.

Marloes is tolerably well off for **accommodation**, with the excellent *Foxdale Guesthouse*, Glebe Lane, opposite the church (☎01646/636243; ①), and the en-suite *Lobster Pot* (☎01646/636233; ③), nearby in the centre of the village, above the village's only real restaurant. You can pitch a **tent** behind *Foxdale*, up the street at the field-and-toilets *Greenacre* site, and at *Runwayskiln* (☎01646/636257), close to the *Marloes Sands* YHA **hostel** (☎01646/636667; closed Nov–March), which consists of a series of converted farm buildings overlooking the northern end of the beach. *West Hook Farm*, near Martin's Haven (☎01646/636424), also has **camping**. The most useful **bus** for accessing the central Pembrokeshire coast is the #400 summer service (2 daily) which runs from Milford Haven to Dale (25min), Martin's Haven (40min), Broad Haven (1hr 15min) and St David's (2hr).

Skomer, Skokholm and Grassholm islands

Boats run from Martin's Haven to **Skomer Island** (April–Oct Tues–Sun 10am, 11am & noon; £12), a 722-acre flat-topped island rich in sea birds and spectacular carpets of wild flowers, perfect for bird watching and walking. You can also cross to **Skokholm Island** (June–Aug Mon 10am; £15.50; booking essential, call ☎01646/636234), a couple of miles south of Skomer and far smaller, more rugged and remote, noted for its warm red cliffs of sandstone. Britain's first bird observatory was founded here as far back as the seventeenth century, and there is still a huge number of petrels, gulls, puffins, oystercatchers and rare Manx shearwaters. The trip includes a guided tour by the island's warden. The final boat trips head out even further, to the tiny outpost of **Grassholm Island**, over five miles west of Skomer (boats June–Sept; landing trip Mon 10am & Fri noon; guided trip Thurs 5pm; £20; ☎01646/601636). Visiting the island is an unforgettable experience, largely due to the 70,000 or so screaming gannets who call it home. No booking is required for Skomer trips or the guided trips to Grassholm on Thursdays, although these can be arranged via National Park centres.

St David's

ST DAVID'S (Tyddewi) is one of the most enchanting spots in Britain. This miniature city sits back from its purple- and gold-flecked cathedral at the very westernmost point of Wales in bleak, treeless countryside. Spiritually, it is the centre of Welsh ecclesiasticism. Traditionally founded by the Welsh patron saint himself in 550 AD, the see of St David's has drawn pilgrims for a millennium and a half – William the Conqueror included – and by 1120, Pope Calixtus II decreed that two journeys to St David's were the spiritual equivalent of one to Rome. The surrounding city – in reality, never much more than a large village – grew up in the shadow cast by the cathedral, and St David's today still relies on the imported wealth of incomers and visitors to the area, attracted by its savage beauty.

The Town

The main road from Haverfordwest enters St David's past the tourist office, before descending to the main square, around a **Celtic cross**, and continuing under the thirteenth-century **Tower Gate**, which forms the entrance to the serene **Cathedral Close**, backed by a windswept landscape of treeless heathland. The cathedral lies down to the right, hidden in a hollow by the River Alun. This apparent modesty is explained by reasons of defence, as a towering cathedral, visible from the sea on all sides, would have been vulnerable to attack. On the other side of the babbling Alun lie the ruins of the Bishop's Palace. New Street heads north past the enjoyable **Oceanarium** (daily: April–Sept 10am–6pm; Oct–March 10am–4pm; £3), complete with a shark tank overlooked by a viewing gallery.

From beyond the powerfully solid Tower Gate, the Thirty-nine Articles – steps named after Thomas Cranmer's key tenets of Anglicanism – approach the purple and golden stone **Cathedral**. The 125-foot tower, topped by pert golden pinnacles, has clocks on only three sides – the people of the northern part of the parish couldn't raise enough money for one to be constructed facing them. You enter through the south side of the low, twelfth-century nave in full view of its most striking feature, the intricate latticed oak **roof**. This was added to hide emergency restoration work carried out in the sixteenth century, when the nave was in danger of collapse. The nave floor still has a discernible slope and the support buttresses inserted in the northern aisle look incongruously new and temporary. At the crossing, an elaborate **rood screen** was constructed under the orders of fourteenth-century Bishop Gower, who envisaged it as his own tomb. Behind the screen and the organ, the choir sits directly under the magnificently bold and bright lantern ceiling of the tower, another addition by Gower. At the back of the south choir stalls is a unique **monarch's stall**, complete with royal crest, for, unlike any other British cathedral, the Queen is an automatic member of the St David's Cathedral Chapter.

Separating the choir and the presbytery is a finely traced, rare **parclose screen**. The back wall of the **presbytery** was once the eastern extremity of the cathedral, as can be seen from the two lines of windows. The upper row has been left intact, while the lower three were blocked up and filled with delicate gold mosaics in the nineteenth century. The colourful fifteenth-century roof, a deceptively simple repeating medieval pattern, was extensively restored by Gilbert Scott in the mid-nineteenth century. At the back of the presbytery, around the altar, the **sanctuary** has a few fragmented fifteenth-century tiles still in place. On the south side is a beautifully carved sedilla, a seat for the priest and deacon celebrating mass. To its right are thirteenth-century tombs of two thirteenth-century bishops, Iorwerth and Anselm de la Grace, and on the other side of the sanctuary is the disappointingly plain thirteenth-century tomb of St David, largely destroyed in the Reformation.

From the cathedral, a path leads to the splendid **Bishops' Palace** (April, May & Oct daily 9am–5pm; June–Sept daily 9.30am–6pm; Nov–March Mon–Sat 9.30am–4pm, Sun 11am–4pm; £2; CADW), built by Bishops Beck and Gower around the turn of the fourteenth century. The huge central quadrangle is fringed by a neat jigsaw of ruined buildings built in extraordinarily richly tinted stone. The **arched parapets** that run along the top of most of the walls were a favourite feature of Gower, who did more than any of his predecessors or successors to transform the palace into an architectural and political powerhouse. Two ruined but still impressive halls – the **Bishops' Hall** and the enormous **Great Hall**, with its glorious rose window – lie off the main quadrangle, above and around a myriad of rooms adorned by some eerily eroded corbels. Underneath the Great Hall are dank vaults containing an interesting exhibition about the palace and the indulgent lifestyles of its occupants. The destruction of the palace is largely due to sixteenth-century Bishop Barlow, who supposedly stripped the buildings of their lead roofs to provide dowries for his five daughters' marriages to bishops.

Practicalities

The main road from Haverfordwest enters St David's past the attractive new **tourist office** (Easter–Oct daily 9.30am–5.30pm; Nov–Easter Mon–Sat 10am–4pm; ☎01437/720392), and continues for two hundred yards down High Street to the **bus station** in New Street. You can **rent bikes** at Ramsey Island Cruises, located behind TYF No Limits, at 1 High St, who rent surf gear and kayaks, as well as running various **outdoor courses**. The best among these is "coasteering" (full day £45; half day £35), which involves scrambling over rocks, jumping off cliffs and swimming across the narrow bays of St David's Peninsula.

There are numerous **places to stay** in St David's. Good, inexpensive options in town are *Pen Albro*, 18 Goat St (☎01437/721865; ①), and *Y Glennydd*, 51 Nun St (☎01437/720576; ①), which has some en-suite rooms. *The Waterings*, on High Street, by the tourist office (☎01437/720876; ③), has luxurious suites in a former marine research establishment, while *Twy-y-Felin*, High Street (☎0800/132588; ②), offers B&B and a lively bar in a converted windmill. *Ramsey House*, Lower Moor (☎01437/720321; ⑤), is an excellent small hotel a quarter of a mile out on the road to Porth Clais, with superb Welsh evening meals included in the price.

St David's nearest campsite is at *Caerfai Farm*, Caerfai Bay (☎01437/720548; closed Oct–April), a fifteen-minute walk from the city. A delightful thirty-minute walk west of town are the cliff-top camping fields of *Pencarnon Farm* (☎01437/720324), just short of St Justinian's, with amazing views and a virtually private beach below; and there's a YHA hostel in a former farmhouse, two miles northwest, near Whitesands Bay (☎01437/720345; closed Nov–March).

For inexpensive eating, there are a number of adequate tearooms and the traveller-oriented *Low Pressure Café*, at 1 High St. For more of a treat, *Morgan's Brasserie*, 20 Nun St (☎01437/720508), serves meals made with wonderfully fresh local produce. Nightlife boils down to the lively *Farmers Arms*, Goat Street, the city's only pub, with a terrace overlooking the cathedral.

St David's peninsula

Surrounded on three sides by inlets, coves and rocky stacks, St David's is an easy base for some excellent walking around the headland of the same name. A mile due south, accessed along the signposted lane from the main Haverfordwest road just near the school, popular **Caerfai Bay** provides a sandy gash in the purple sandstone cliffs, rock which was used in the construction of the cathedral. To the immediate west is the craggy indentation of **St Non's Bay**, reached from Goat Street in St David's down the tiny rhododendron-flooded lane signposted to the *Warpool Court Hotel*. St Non reputedly gave birth to St David at this spot during a tumultuous storm around 500 AD, when a spring opened up between Non's feet, and despite the crashing thunder all around, an eerily calm light filtered down on to the scene. St Non's Bay has received pilgrims for centuries, resulting in the foundation of a tiny, isolated chapel in the pre-Norman age. The ruins of the subsequent thirteenth-century chapel now lie in a field to the right of the car park, beyond the sadly dingy well and coy shrine where the nation's patron saint is said to have been born.

The road from St David's to St Non's branches at the *St Non's Hotel*, where Catherine Street becomes a winding lane that leads a mile down the tiny valley of the River Alun to its mouth at **Porth Clais**. Supposedly the place at which St David was baptized, Porth Clais was the city's main harbour, the spruced-up remains of which can still be seen at the bottom of the turquoise river creek. Today, commercial traffic has long gone, replaced by a boaties' haven.

Running due west out of St David's, Goat Street ducks past the ruins of the Bishop's Palace and over the rocky plateau for two miles to the harbour at **St Justinian's**, little more than a lifeboat station and ticket hut for the boats over to **Ramsey Island**. This dual-humped plateau, less than two miles long, has been under the able stewardship of the RSPB since 1992 and is quite enchanting. Birds of prey circle the skies above the island, but it is better known for the tens of thousands of sea birds that noisily crowd the sheer cliffs on the island's western side. On the beaches, seals laze sloppily below the paths beaten out by a herd of red deer. Two companies run boats – weather permitting – around Ramsey, but the only ones that land are Thousand Islands Expeditions' trips (April–Oct Mon & Wed–Sun; ☎0800/163621; £10); you can stay up to five hours. During the springtime nesting season you actually see more from boats which circle the island but don't land: try Ramsey Island Cruises (April–Oct daily; ☎01437/721911; £10). Thousand Island Expeditions operate a similar Ramsey circumnavigation from **Whitesands Bay** (Porth Mawr), two miles to the north and reached from St David's, via the B4583 off the Fishguard road.

Fishguard

From St David's, the coast road runs northeast, parallel to numerous small and less-commercialized bays, to **Strumble Head**, which protects the harbour at **FISHGUARD** (Abergwaun), an attractive, hilltop town seldom seen as anything more than a brief stopoff place for the ferries, which leave regularly for Rosslare in Ireland from the suburb of **Goodwick** (Wdig).

Near the town hall is the **Royal Oak Inn**, where the bizarre Franco-Irish attempt to conquer Britain in 1797 at nearby Carregwastad Point is remembered. The hapless forces arrived to negotiate a cease-fire, which was turned by the assembled British into an unconditional surrender. Part of the invaders' low morale – apart from the drunken farces in which they'd become embroiled – is said to have been sparked off by the sight of a hundred local women marching towards them. The troops mistook their stovepipe hats and red flannel dresses for the outfit of a British infantry troop and instantly capitulated. Even if this is not true, it is an undisputed fact that 47-year-old cobbler Jemima Nicholas, the "Welsh Heroine", single-handedly captured fourteen French soldiers. Her grave can be seen next to the uninspiring Victorian **parish church**, St Mary's, behind the pub. You'll need to cross the street to the church hall to see the **Fishguard Tapestry** (April–Oct Mon–Sat 10am–5pm, Sun 2–5pm; Nov–March Mon–Sat 11am–4pm, Sun 2–4pm; £1.50), a local spin on the Bayeux Tapestry, similarly embroidered to celebrate the bicentennial of the event it depicts.

Look especially for a grim, Amazonian Jemima surrounded by a dozen dejected-looking Frenchmen.

Buses stop by the town hall in the central Market Square, right outside Fishguard's **tourist office** (April, May, Sept & Oct daily 10am–5pm; June–Aug daily 10am–5.30pm; Nov–March Mon–Sat 10am–4pm; ☎01348/873484). There's a subsidiary tourist office in the foyer of the Ocean Lab in Goodwick (same hours as main office; ☎01348/872037), around half a mile from the terminus for **ferries to Rosslare** (2 daily; ☎0990/707070). The **train station** is next to the ferry terminal on Quay Road. Buses usually meet ferries (2 daily), though seldom the catamarans (3—4 daily); a **taxi** (☎01348/874491) into town costs around £3.

Accommodation is plentiful and cheap, with most places well used to visitors coming and going at odd times. Next to the port is the faded elegance of the *Fishguard Bay Hotel*, on Quay Road (☎01348/873571; ④); and you'll find comfortable rooms at *Glanmoy Lodge*, on Tref-Wrgi Road, ten minutes' walk from the port (☎01348/874333; ②). In Fishguard proper is *Three Main Street* (☎01348/874275; ③), easy to find, and with an expensive and highly praised restaurant; or there are dorms at *Hamilton Backpackers Lodge*, 21–23 Hamilton St (☎01348/874797; ①), just a minute's walk from the tourist office. The nearest **camping** is at *Tregroes Touring Park* (☎01348/872316), a mile southwest of Fishguard just off the A40.

Newport

NEWPORT (Trefdraeth) is an ancient and proud little town set on a gentle slope that courses down to the estuary of the Afon Nyfer. There's little to do except stroll around, but you'd be hard pressed to find a better place to do just that. Just short of the Nevern estuary bridge, on the town side, **Carreg Coetan Arthur**, a well-preserved, capped Neolithic burial chamber, can be seen behind the newish holiday bungalows. The footpath that runs along the river either side of the bridge is marked as the Pilgrims' Way; follow it eastwards for a delightful riverbank stroll to Nevern, a couple of miles away. On Lower St Mary Street, the old school has metamorphosed into the excellent **West Wales Eco Centre** (Mon–Fri 9.30am–4.30pm; variable extended hours in summer; free), a venue for exhibitions, advice and resources on various aspects of sustainable living.

Newport's nearest beach, **the Parrog**, is complete with sandy stretches at low tide. On the other side of the estuary is the vast dune-backed **Traethmawr beach**, reached over the town bridge down Feidr Pen-y-Bont. Newport also makes a good jumping-off point for exploring the wooded vales and gnarled hills of **Mynydd Preseli**, just inland, which are scattered with prehistoric remains, notably the four-thousand-year-old capstone at **Pentre Ifan**, a couple of miles south of Newport.

The **tourist office** (April–Sept Mon–Sat 10am–5.30pm; ☎01239/820912) is on Long Street, just off the main road. **Bike rental** is available in town from the *Llysmeddyg* guest house, on East Street. There's plenty of **accommodation**: the *Golden Lion* pub, on the main street (☎01239/820321; ①), does inexpensive B&B, as does *Trewarren*, half a mile to the north (☎01239/820455; ②), overlooking the estuary and with great views – follow Feidr Pen-y-Bont from town. For more luxury, try the superb *Cnapan Country House*, on East Street (☎01239/820575; ③; closed Jan & Feb). The spanking new **YHA hostel** is tucked in behind the Eco Centre (☎01239/820080; ①; closed Nov–March); and a mile south of town, there's a great independent bunkhouse at *Brithdir Mawr*, on Ffordd Cilgwyn, at the bottom of the slopes of Carn Ingli (☎01239/820164; ①). The nearest **campsite** is the *Morawelon* (☎01239/820565), just west of town, at the Parrog, with nice gardens and its own café. For **food**, the *Cnapan Country House* serves exquisite meals, or there are solid pub classics, including a good veggie menu, at the *Royal Oak*, on Bridge Street. Great snacks can be found at the *Fountain House Foods* deli, and *Fronlas Café*, both on Market Street.

travel details

Trains

Carmarthen to: Cardiff (5 daily; 1hr 30min); Fishguard (1–2 daily; 1hr); Haverfordwest (9 daily; 40min); Pembroke (8 daily; 1hr 10min); Swansea (hourly; 50min); Tenby (8 daily; 40min).

Haverfordwest to: Carmarthen (9 daily; 40min); Swansea (7 daily; 1hr 30min).

Pembroke to: Lamphey (7 daily; 3min); Manorbier (7 daily; 10min); Pembroke Dock (7 daily; 10min); Tenby (7 daily; 20min).

Tenby to: Carmarthen (8 daily; 40min); Pembroke (7 daily; 20min); Swansea (7 daily; 1hr 40min).

Buses

Carmarthen to: Haverfordwest (5 daily; 1hr); Kidwelly (hourly; 25min); Laugharne (hourly; 30min); Llandeilo (15 daily; 40min); Swansea (hourly; 1hr 30min); Tenby (2 daily; 1hr).

Fishguard to: Cardigan (hourly; 50min); Haverfordwest (hourly; 40min); Newport, Pembrokeshire (hourly; 20min); St David's (7 daily; 50min).

Haverfordwest to: Carmarthen (5 daily; 1hr); Fishguard (hourly; 40min); Manorbier (hourly; 1hr 10min); Newport, Pembrokeshire (hourly; 1hr 10min); Pembroke (hourly; 50min); St David's (hourly; 40min); Tenby (hourly; 1hr 20min).

Llandovery to: Brecon (Mon–Sat 5 daily, none on Sun; 40min); Llandeilo (9 daily; 45min).

Newport, Pembrokeshire to: Fishguard (hourly; 20min); Haverfordwest (hourly; 1hr 10min).

Pembroke to: Bosherston (Mon–Fri 2 daily, none on Sat & Sun; 1hr); Haverfordwest (hourly; 50min); Manorbier (hourly; 20min); Pembroke Dock (every 10min; 10min); Stackpole (Mon–Fri 2 daily, none on Sat & Sun; 50min); Tenby (hourly; 40min).

St David's to: Broad Haven (2 daily; 40min); Fishguard (7 daily; 50min); Haverfordwest (hourly; 40min).

Tenby to: Carmarthen (2 daily; 1hr); Haverfordwest (hourly; 1hr 20min); Manorbier (hourly; 20min); Pembroke (hourly ; 40min).

Ferries

Fishguard to: Rosslare, Ireland (4–6 daily; ferry 3hr 30min; catamaran 1hr 40min).

Pembroke Dock to: Rosslare (2 daily; 4hr).

CHAPTER FOURTEEN

POWYS AND THE DEE VALLEY

The great tranche of rural **mid-Wales** is often seen as little more than a corridor by which to reach the coast. Discard that notion, for here you will find some of the country's most enjoyable little towns set amongst sparkling upland scenery. A quarter of the area of Wales is occupied by **Powys**, whose name harks back to a fifth-century Welsh kingdom. The county stretches from the fringes of the Glamorgan valleys, south of the Brecon Beacons, to the sparsely populated lakelands of Radnorshire, just short of the Dee Valley.

By far the most popular attraction is **Brecon Beacons National Park**, at the southern end of Powys, stretching from the dramatic limestone country of **Fforest Fawr** in the west, through the gentler Beacons themselves, and out to the English border beyond the **Black Mountains**. The best base for the National Park is the tiny city of **Brecon**, a curious mix of traditional market town, army garrison and often very pretty tourist centre. To the southeast, the market town of **Abergavenny** and nearby village of **Crickhowell** are set in quiet river valleys. Both make excellent bases for hiking in the Beacons or exploring the northern reaches of the South Wales Valleys. A few roads cut through the glowering countryside, connecting popular attractions such as the immense **Dan-yr-ogof caves** and the caves and waterfalls around the popular walking centre of **Ystradfellte**.

North of the Beacons, beyond the peaks of Mynydd Eppynt, lie the old spa towns of Radnorshire, among them earthy **Llanwrtyd Wells** and twee **Llandrindod Wells**. The quiet, occasionally harsh countryside to the north, crossed by spectacular mountain roads such as the **Abergwesyn Pass** from Llanwrtyd, is barely populated and beautiful, dotted with ancient churches and introspective villages. In the east, the border town of **Knighton** is the home of the flourishing **Offa's Dyke path** industry, while inland **Rhayader** makes a good base for the grandiose reservoirs of the **Elan Valley**.

Montgomeryshire is the northern portion of Powys, similarly underpopulated and remote. Like many country towns in mid-Wales, beautiful **Llanidloes** has a healthy stock

---

ACCOMMODATION PRICE CODES

Throughout this guide, hotel and B&B accommodation is priced on a scale of ① to ⑨, the number indicating the **lowest price** you could expect to pay per night in that establishment for a **double room** in high season. The prices indicated by the codes are as follows:

① under £40	④ £60–70	⑦ £110–150
② £40–50	⑤ £70–90	⑧ £150–200
③ £50–60	⑥ £90–110	⑨ over £200

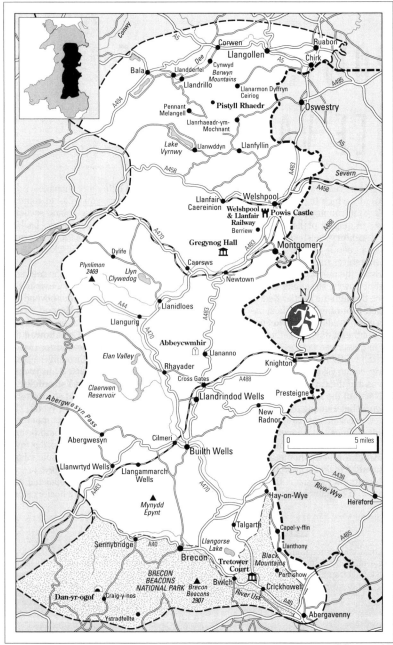

© Crown copyright

of old hippies amongst its population, contributing to a thriving arts and crafts community and a relaxed atmosphere. The west of the county is flecked with boggy heathland and gloomy reservoirs, while the east is home to the anglicized old county town, **Montgomery**, between robust **Welshpool** on the English border, and the charmless centre of Newtown. The northern segment of the county is even quieter. **Llanfyllin** and **Llanrhaeadr-ym-mochnant**, the regional centres, are little more than villages, leaving the few crowds seen around here to cluster along the banks of **Lake Vyrnwy**, a flooded-valley reservoir which has harmoniously moulded itself into the landscape around it.

To the immediate north are the mountains that course down into the **Dee Valley**, a fertile landscape much fought over between the English and the Welsh. With the language still thriving hereabouts, there's more of a tangibly Welsh feel to towns like the fabulous **Llangollen**, a great base for a variety of ruins, rides and rambles, as well as the venue each summer for the colourful International **Eisteddfod** festival. Further west is the resilient, firmly Welsh market town of **Bala**, which, thanks to nearby **Llyn Tegid** (Bala Lake), has become the major Welsh watersports centre.

The Brecon Beacons National Park

With the lowest profile of Wales's three National Parks, the **Brecon Beacons National Park** is the destination of thousands of urban walkers, largely from the industrial areas of South Wales and the West Midlands of England. Rounded, spongy hills of grass and rock tumble and climb around river valleys that lie between sandstone and limestone uplands, peppered with glass-like lakes and villages that seem to have been hewn from one rock. The National Park straddles Powys from west to east, covering 520 square miles. Most remote is the area at the far western side, where the vast, open terrain of **Fforest Fawr** forms miles of tufted moorland tumbling down to a rocky terrain of rivers, deep caves and spluttering waterfalls around the village of **Ystradfellte** and the chasms of the **Dan-yr-ogof caves**. The heart of the national park comprises the **Brecon Beacons** themselves, a pair of 2900-foot hills and their satellites which lend their name to the whole park. East of Brecon, the **Black Mountains** – not to be confused with the Black Mountain some distance to the west – stretch all the way to the English border, and offer the region's most varied scenery, from rolling upland wilderness to the gentler **Vale of Ewyas**, with its ruined abbey and isolated churches.

The Monmouthshire and Brecon Canal defines the northern limit of the Beacons and forges a passage along the Usk Valley between them and the Black Mountains. This is where you're likely to end up staying; in towns such as the sturdy county seat of **Brecon**, the overgrown village of **Crickhowell**, or **Abergavenny**, nestled below the Black Mountains.

Fforest Fawr

Covering a vast expanse of hilly landscape west of the central Beacon Beacons, **Fforest Fawr** (Great Forest) seems something of a misnomer for an area of largely unforested sandstone hills dropping down to a porous limestone belt in the south. The name, however, refers to its former status as a hunting area. The hills rise up to the south of the A40, west of Brecon, with the A4067 piercing the western side of the range and the A470 defining the Fforest's eastern limit. Between the two, a twisting mountain road crosses a bleak plateau and descends into one of Britain's classic limestone landscapes, around the tiny hamlet of **YSTRADFELLTE**. With a dazzling countryside of lush, deep ravines on its doorstep it has become a phenomenally popular centre for its walks over great pavements of bone-white rock next to cradling potholes, disappearing rivers and crashing waterfalls.

A mile to the south, the River Mellte tumbles into the dark mouth of the **Porth-yr-ogof** (White Horse Cave), emerging into daylight a few hundred yards further south. A signposted path heads south from the Porth-yr-ogof car park and into the green gorge of the River Mellte. After little more than a mile, the first of three waterfalls is reached at **Sgwd Clun-Gwyn** (White Meadow Fall), where the river crashes fifty feet over two huge, angular steps of rock before hurtling down course for a few hundred yards to the other two falls – the impressive **Sgwd Isaf Clun-Gwyn** (Lower White Meadow Fall) and, around the wooded corner, the **Sgwd y Pannwr** (Fall of the Fuller). The path continues to the confluence of the rivers Mellte and Hepste, half a mile further on. A quarter of a mile along the Hepste is the most popular of the area's falls – the **Sgwd yr Eira** (Fall of Snow), whose rock below the main tumble has eroded back six feet, allowing people to walk directly behind a dramatic twenty-foot curtain of water. A shorter two-mile walk to Sgwd yr Eira leads from **PENDERYN** village, off the A4059, three miles north of Hirwaun: to get there, catch **bus** #9 (hourly) from Merthyr Tydfil to Hirwaun and change to bus #15 to Penderyn (every 30min). There's a cosy **YHA hostel** (☎01639/720301; closed Nov–March) at **TAI'R HEOL**, half a mile south of Ystradfellte and just a short walk from Porth-yr-ogof. There are numerous informal **camping** spots in the woods.

Dan-yr-ogof Showcaves

Six miles of upland forest and squelchy moor lie between Ystradfellte and the **Dan-yr-ogof Showcaves** (April–Oct daily 10am–4pm; Nov–March times vary, call ☎01639/730801; £7), off the A4067 to the west. Only discovered in 1912, they are claimed to form the largest system of subterranean caverns in northern Europe, and, although relentless marketing has turned them into something of an overdone theme park, the caverns are truly awesome in their size. A concrete path leads into the first of three caverns, the **Dan-yr-ogof** cave, and a bewildering subterranean warren, the crags and walls framed by stalactites and frothy limestone deposits. Emerging back outside, you pass a downbeat recreated Iron Age "village" and a hideous park of fibreglass dinosaurs, and walk through a succession of spookily lit caverns, where water cascades relentlessly down the walls. A swelling classical soundtrack and a dancing light show come together in the final 150-foot-long **Cathedral Cave** – impressive despite its tawdriness. A precarious path leads to the **Bone Cave** where the owners have fenced off an assortment of dressed-up mannequins that make Bronze Age woman look like a reject from Miss Selfridge. **Camping** is available just up the road at the *Tafarn-y-Garreg* pub (☎01639/730236).

Brecon

BRECON (Aberhonddu) is a sturdy county town at the northern edge of the central Beacons. The proliferation of well-proportioned Georgian buildings and its proximity to the hills and lakes of the National Park make it a popular stopping-off place and a good base for day walks in the well-waymarked hills to the south.

The town's highlight is the **Brecknock Museum** (April–Sept Mon–Fri 10am–5pm, Sat 10am–1pm & 2–5pm, Sun noon–5pm; Oct–March Mon–Fri 10am–5pm, Sat 10am–1pm & 2–5pm; £1), at the junction of the Bulwark and Glamorgan Street. Displays include agricultural implements unique to the area, a nineteenth-century assize court last used in 1971, and an antique collection of painstakingly carved Welsh "love spoons" – betrothal gifts for courting Welsh lovers. Running east from the Bulwark is the Watton, where you'll find the diverting **Oriel Jazz** gallery (daily 1–4pm; free). Capitalizing on the town's astonishingly successful annual **jazz festival**, held over a long weekend in mid-August, the gallery presents an entertaining romp through the archives of twentieth-century music, with rare video footage of some of the jazz greats.

From the town-centre crossroads, northwest of the Bulwark, High Street Superior goes north, becoming The Struet, running alongside the rushing waters of the Honddu. Off to the left, a footpath climbs up to the **Cathedral**. The building's dumpy external appearance belies its lofty interior, graced with a few Norman features from the eleventh century, including a hulking font. The mid-sixteenth-century **Games Monument**, in the southern aisle, is made of three oak beds and depicts an unknown woman whose hands, clasped in prayer, remain intact, but whose arms and nose have been unceremoniously hacked off.

Practicalities

The **tourist office** (daily: Easter–Oct 10am–6pm; Nov–Easter 9am–4.45pm; ☎01874/622485) and **Brecon Beacons National Park office** (Easter–Oct daily 9.30am–5.30pm ☎01874/623156) share the same building in the Lion Yard car park off Lion Street, next to the new Safeway supermarket. **Bike rental** is available at the Brecon Cycle Centre, Ship Street (☎01874/622557).

Brecon, and adjacent Llanfaes, is bulging with **accommodation** to suit all pockets, except during the jazz festival. Best bets are the budget *Tirbach Guest House*, 13 Alexandra Rd (☎01874/624551; ①), up behind Safeway, and a couple of lovely places costing a little more: the warm and welcoming *Pickwick House*, St John's Road (☎01874/624322, *isobel@pickwick.prestel.co.uk*; ③), with excellent, predominantly organic breakfasts and evening meals; and *Cantre Selyf*, 5 Lion St (☎01874/622904; *cantreselyf@imaginet.co.uk*; ③), an imposing seventeenth-century townhouse, all creaking floors and moulded plaster ceilings. There are a couple of **YHA hostels**, the closest of which is *Ty'n-y-Caeau*, Groesffordd (☎01874/665270; ①), two miles east of the town. It can be reached via Slwch Lane, a path from Cerrigcochion Road in Brecon, or it's a one-mile walk from the bus stops at either Cefn Brynich lock (Brecon–Abergavenny buses) or Troedyrharn Farm (Brecon–Hereford buses). *Brynich Caravan and Camping Park*, Brynich (☎01874/623325), is situated a mile east of town, just off the A470, overlooking the town and the river.

Brecon is a lively and cosmopolitan town. The inexpensive *Waterfront Bistro*, Canal Basin, is open in the daytime for tasty café **food**; the *Beacons Guest House*, at 16 Bridge St, Llanfaes, is open to non-residents for excellent meals, many inspired by local produce and traditional Welsh recipes. The *Bull's Head*, The Struet, is the pick of the town's **pubs**, or you could make your way four miles north along the B4520 to the *Seland Newydd*, at Pwllgloyw, a peaceful country pub that offers much the best eating around Brecon.

The Brecon Beacons

Far more popular for walking and pony trekking than the Fforest Fawr, the central **Brecon Beacons**, grouped around the two highest peaks in the National Park, are easily accessible from Brecon, just six miles to the north. This is classic old red sandstone country: sweeping peaks rising up out of glacial scoops of land. Although the peaks never quite reach 3000ft, the terrain is unmistakably, and dramatically, mountainous. The panorama fans out from the **Brecon Beacons Mountain Centre** (daily: March–June, Sept & Oct 9.30am–5pm; July & Aug 9.30am–6pm; Nov–Feb 10.30am–4.30pm; ☎01874/623366; small parking fee), on a windy ridge just off the A470 turn-off at Libanus, six miles southwest of Brecon. As well as a café, there are interesting displays on the flora, fauna, geology and history of the area, together with a well-stocked shop of maps, books and guides.

Pen y Fan (2907ft) is the highest peak in the Beacons, indeed in all South Wales. Together with **Corn Du** (2863ft), half a mile to the west, they form the most popular ascents in the park, particularly along the well-trampled muddy red path that starts from Pont ar Daf, half a mile south of Storey Arms, on the A470, midway between Brecon and Merthyr Tydfil. This is the most direct route from a road, where a comparatively easy five-mile round trip gradually climbs up the southern flank of the two peaks. A longer and generally quieter ascent leads up to the two peaks along the "Gap" route, the ancient road that winds its way north from the Neuadd reservoirs, immediately south of Brecon. This passes through the only natural break in the sandstone ridge of the central Beacons, heading to the bottom of the lane that eventually joins the main street in Llanfaes, Brecon, as Bailihelig Road. Although the old road is no longer accessible for cars, car parks at either end open out onto the track for an eight-mile round-trip ascent up Pen y Fan and Corn Du from the east.

The Black Mountains

The easternmost section of the National Park centres on the **Black Mountains**, far quieter than the central belt of the Brecon Beacons and skirted by the wide valley of the River Usk. The only exception to the Black Mountains' unremitting sandstone is an isolated outcrop of limestone, long divorced from the southern belt, that peaks due north of Crickhowell at Pen Cerrig-calch (2302ft). The Black Mountains have the feel of a landscape only partly tamed by human habitation: tiny villages, isolated churches and delightful lanes are folded into an undulating green landscape which levels out to the south around the pretty villages of **Tretower** and **Crickhowell**.

Tretower

Rising out of the valley floor, dominating the view from both the A40 and A479 mountain road, the solid round tower of the **Castle and Court** (daily: March 10am–4pm; April, May & Oct 10am–5pm; June–Sept 10am–6pm; £2.20; CADW) at **TRETOWER** (Tre-tûr), ten miles southeast of Brecon, was built to guard the pass. The bleak, thirteenth-century round tower replaced an earlier Norman fortification, and in the late fourteenth century was supplemented by a comparatively luxurious manor house, itself being gradually expanded over the ensuing years. An enjoyable audioguide tour takes you around an open-air gallery and wall walk, and explains late medieval building methods using the exposed plaster and beams where work is still under way. In the summer, contemporary and Shakespeare **plays** are performed in the inspirational surroundings of the fully restored court (box office ☎01874/730279), with its ostentatious, beam-ceilinged Great Hall facing in on the central cobbled courtyard and square sandstone gatehouse.

Crickhowell

Compact **CRICKHOWELL** (Crucywel), four miles southeast of Tretower, on the northern bank of the wide and shallow Usk, makes for a lively base from which to explore the surrounding area. There isn't much to see in town, however, apart from a grand seventeenth-century **bridge**, with thirteen arches visible from the eastern end and only twelve from the west, spawning many a local myth. **Table Mountain** (1481ft) provides a spectacular northern backdrop, topped by the remains of the 2500-year-old hill fort (*crug*) of Hywel, accessed on a path past The Wern, off Llanbedr Road. Many walkers follow a route north from Table Mountain, climbing two miles up to the plateau-topped limestone hump of **Pen Cerrig-calch** (2302ft).

The **tourist office** (April–Oct daily 9am–1pm & 2–5pm; ☎01837/812105) is in Beaufort Chambers, on Beaufort Street. Mountain and Water, in the Riverside Centre, on New Road (☎01873/831825), **rents bikes. Accommodation** is abundant, with a grandiose coaching inn, the *Bear Hotel*, on Beaufort Street (☎01873/810408; ④), and the *Dragon*, on High Street (☎01873/810362; ②); for cheaper B&B, try *Greenhill Villas*, Beaufort Street (☎01873/811177; ①). The town-centre *Riverside Park* **campsite** lies on New Road (☎01873/810397). Just beyond the turning for the delightful nearby village of Llanbedr, *Perth-y-pia* (☎01873/810050; ②) is an outdoor centre with excellent **hostel** accommodation, B&B and home-cooked evening meals; it's handily close to Llanbedr's *Red Lion* pub. Across the river from Llanbedr, *Gellirhydd Farm* (☎01873/810466; ①) offers great B&B and woodcraft classes.

For straightforward snacks and **lunches** at low, low prices you can't go past the *Queen Coffee Tavern* on Standard Street, just off High Street, even if you're not immediately drawn to dining to the strains of Cliff Richard overlooked by floor-to-ceiling Cliff photos and memorabilia. If you really can't bear it, visit the *Cheese Press* on the High Street. The *Bear Hotel* wins legions of awards for its delectable, pricier-than-average bar and inexpensive to moderately priced restaurant food. The *Bridge End* pub, by the town bridge, offers inexpensive local delicacies and veggie specialities.

Abergavenny and around

Flanking the Brecon Beacons National Park, the lively market town of **ABERGAVEN-NY** (Y Fenni), seven miles southeast of Crickhowell, makes one of the best bases for an extended stay. There's not a whole lot to do, but there's a fine range of places to eat, drink and sleep, and the town is surrounded by commanding hills, a magnet to walkers bound for the local mountains: **Sugar Loaf** and the legend-infused **Holy Mountain** (Skirrid Fawr). Stretching north from town, the **Vale of Ewyas** runs along the foot of the Black Mountains, where the astounding churches at **Partrishow** and **Cwmyoy** are lost in rural isolation. A couple of miles north, **Llanthony Priory** has many features in common with Tintern Abbey, although only a fraction of the crowds. Abergavenny also makes a good base for visiting Monmouthshire's "three castles" (see p.663), set in the pastoral border country to the east.

Although only a couple of miles and a few hills away from the iron and coal towns of the Valleys (see p.666), Abergavenny grew on the basis of its weaving and tanning trades, giving it an entirely different feel. These industries prospered alongside a flourishing market, which is still the focal point for a wide area, drawing many people up from the Valleys every Tuesday. In World War II, Hitler's deputy, Rudolf Hess, was kept in the town's mental asylum as a prisoner, after his plane crash-landed in Scotland in 1941. He was allowed a weekly walk in the nearby hills, growing, it is said, to love the Welsh countryside.

From the train station, Monmouth Road rises gently, eventually becoming High Street, off which you'll find the fragmented remains of the medieval **castle** with its **town museum** (March–Oct Mon–Sat 11am–1pm & 2–5pm, Sun 2–5pm; Nov–Feb Mon–Sat 11am–1pm & 2–4pm; £1), which displays ephemera from the town's history and a reconstruction of Basil Jones's grocery shop, once on Main Street. After the death of Jones's son in 1989, the contents of the shop were transported to the museum lock, stock and biscuit barrel. Some goods are of recent origin, but much dates from the 1930s and 1940s – some even from the nineteenth century. Abergavenny's parish **church of St Mary**, on Monk Street, contains some superb tombs that span the entire medieval period. There are effigies of members of the notorious de Braose family, along with the tomb and figure of Sir William ap Thomas, founder of Raglan Castle. Look out for the **Jesse Tree**, a recumbent, twice-life-size statue of King David's father which would once have formed part of an altarpiece tracing the family lineage from Jesse to Jesus.

Practicalities

Abergavenny's **train station** lies on the well-used line between Newport and Hereford. Buses depart from Swan Meadow **bus station**, right by the joint **tourist office** (daily: April–Oct 9.30am–6pm; Nov–March 10am–4.30pm; ☎01873/857588) and **Brecon Beacons National Park office** (Easter–Sept daily 9.30am–5.30pm; ☎01873/853254). Bob Hemmings (☎01873/856563) **rents bikes**, as do Pedalabikeaway (☎01873/830219), who are based out of town but deliver. **Narrowboats** for exploring the Monmouthshire and Brecon Canal can be rented from the British Waterways office at the village of Govilon, three miles west (☎01873/830328).

Accommodation comes in the form of B&Bs, many on the Monmouth Road between the town centre and the train station: *Maes Glas*, Raglan Terrace, Monmouth Road (☎01873/854494; ①), is the best. Nearby, the *Georgian Park Guest House*, 36 Hereford Road (☎01873/853715; ①), is also very good, while the central *King's Arms* pub, on Neville Street (☎01873/855074; ②), has inexpensive and well-appointed rooms. The nearest place to pitch a **tent** is *Pyscodlyn Farm Caravan and Camping Site* (☎01873/853271), two miles west of town, off the A40. There are plenty of **places to eat** in Abergavenny, including the moderately priced *Greyhound Vaults*, Market Street, great for a wide range of tasty Welsh and English specialities, including the best vegetarian dishes in town. The very expensive *Walnut Tree Inn* (☎01873/852797), on the B4521 at Llanddewi Sgyrrid, two miles north of town, is a famous foodies' paradise for Mediterranean cuisine. Of Abergavenny's **pubs**, the best is the staunchly traditional *Hen & Chickens*, Flannel Street, just off the High Street, with a separate dining room for inexpensive food.

The Vale of Ewyas

In total contrast to the urban blights in the northern Valleys, just a few miles to the south, the northern finger of Monmouthshire, stretching along the English border, is one of the most enchanting and reclusive parts of Wales. The main A465 Hereford road leads six miles north out of Abergavenny to Llanfihangel Crucorney, where the B4423 diverges off to the north along the beautiful **Vale of Ewyas**, along the banks of the Honddu River.

After a mile, a lane heads west towards the enchanting valley of **Gwyrne Fawr**, and the delightful church and well of St Issui in the hamlet of **Partrishow**. First founded in the eleventh century, the tiny church was refashioned in the thirteenth and fourteenth centuries. In the fifteenth century, it acquired the lacy rood screen, carved out of solid Irish oak and adorned with crude symbols of good and evil – most notably in the corner, where an evil dragon consumes a vine, a symbol of hope and well-being. The rest of the whitewashed church breathes simplicity by comparison. Of special note are the wall texts painted over the doom picture of a skeleton and scythe. Before the Reformation, such pictures were widely used to teach an illiterate population about the scriptures, until King James I ordered that such "Popish devices" should be whitewashed over and repainted with scripture texts.

Back on the main B4423, the road winds its way up the valley's western side, past the fork at the *Queen's Head* inn (☎01873/890241; ④), excellent for B&B and **pony trekking**, and a budget place to **camp**. In the adjacent village of **Cwmyoy**, the parish **church of St Martin** has substantially subsided due to geological twists in the underlying rock. Nothing squares up: the tower leans at a severe angle from the bulging body of the church, and the view inside from the back of the nave towards the sloping altar, askew roof and straining windows is unforgettable.

Four miles further up this most remote of valleys is the hamlet of **LLANTHONY**, little more than a small cluster of houses, an inn and a few outlying farms around the wide open ruins of **Llanthony Priory** – a grander setting, and certainly a quieter one than Tintern, though the buildings are far more modest in scale. It was founded in around

1100 by the Norman knight William de Lacy, who, it is said, was so captivated by the spiritual beauty of the site that he renounced worldly living and founded a hermitage, attracting like-minded recluses and forming Wales's first Augustinian priory. The roofless church, with its pointed transitional arches and squat tower, was constructed in the latter half of the twelfth century and retains a real sense of spirituality and peace. There are two good **places to stay**: the *Abbey Hotel* (☎01873/890487; ②), fashioned out of part of the tumbledown priory, was built in the eighteenth century as a hunting lodge; along the road is the *Half Moon Inn* (☎01873/890611; ①), serving superb beer and good-value meals.

From Llanthony, the road slowly climbs four miles alongside the narrowing Honddu River to the isolated hamlet of **Capel-y-Ffin**, from where it's a further mile to the **YHA hostel** (☎01873/890650; ①; closed Dec & Jan), which also has **camping**. The road then weaves a tortuous route up over **Gospel Pass** and onto the howling, windy moor of **Hay Bluff**, on the glorious roof of the Black Mountains, before descending five miles to Hay-on-Wye (see p.429).

The Wells towns

The spa towns of mid-Wales, strung out along the Heart of Wales rail line between Swansea and Shrewsbury, were once all obscure villages, but with the arrival of the great craze for spas in the early eighteenth century, anywhere with a decent supply of apparently healing water joined in on the act. Royalty and nobility spearheaded the fashion, but the arrival of the railways opened them to all. The westernmost, **Llanwrtyd Wells**, was a popular haunt of the Welsh middle classes, some of whom arrived over the bleak moors by the **Abergwesyn Pass**, a narrow road still connecting the area to the Cambrian Coast. Far prettier – although considerably more twee and anglicized – is **Llandrindod Wells** to the north, whose spa is the only one of the four in any state of decent repair. In between, the larger town of Builth Wells was very much the spa of the Welsh working classes and there's no reason to stop other than to change buses. The fourth spa town, Llangammarch Wells, warrants even less attention.

Llanwrtyd Wells and around

Of the four spa towns, **LLANWRTYD WELLS**, twenty miles northwest of Brecon, is the most appealing. It's more Welsh, less spoilt and in more beautiful surroundings than the other three. This was the spa to which the Welsh – farmers of Dyfed alongside the Non-conformist middle classes from Glamorgan – came to the great *eisteddfodau* (festivals of Welsh music, dance and poetry) in the valley of the Irfon.

South of where the Main Street crosses the turbulent Irfon, a lane winds for half a mile along the river to the *Dolecoed Hotel*, built near the original sulphurous spring. Although the distinctive aroma had been noted in the area for centuries, it was truly "discovered" in 1732 by the local priest, Theophilus Evans, who drank from an evilsmelling spring after seeing a rudely healthy frog pop out of it. The spring, named **Ffynon Droellwyd** (Stinking Well), can still be sniffed out in the fields beyond the hotel, now erupting around a dome-shaped extension behind the dilapidated red-and-white spa buildings. The **Neuadd Arms** pub is the base for a wide range of bizarre and entertaining annual events, including a Man-versus-Horse race and a Drovers' Walk (both in June); a town festival (first weekend in Aug); a snorkelling competition in a local bog (end of Aug); a beer festival (Nov); and a torchlight procession through the town (New Year's Eve).

Llanwrtyd's **tourist office** is in *Tŷ Barcud*, on the main square (June–Aug daily 10am–5.30pm; rest of year Mon–Sat 10am–4pm; ☎01591/610666). **Accommodation** includes the *Neuadd Arms*, on the square (☎01591/610236; ③), which also rents out **bikes**; the solidly Victorian *Belle Vue Hotel*, a few yards away (☎01591/610237; ④); and the cheaper *Oakfield House*, Dol-y-coed Road (☎01591/610605; ④). The *Stonecroft Inn*, on Dol-y-coed Road (☎01591/610332; ④), is a superb pub with great food and regular live music, plus a self-catering **hostel** with bunks. Both the *Neuadd Arms* and the *Belle Vue* provide cheap, hearty **food**. The moderately priced *Drovers' Rest*, by the bridge, serves wholesome and highly acclaimed traditional Welsh dishes.

Abergwesyn and the Pass

A lane from Llanwrtyd meets up with another road from Beulah at the riverside hamlet of **ABERGWESYN**, five miles north of Llanwrtyd. From here, you can drive the quite magnificent winding thread of an ancient cattle drovers' road – the **Abergwesyn Pass** – up the perilous **Devil's Staircase** and through dense conifer forests to miles of wide, desolate valleys where sheep graze unhurriedly. At the little bridge over the tiny Tywi River, a track heads south past an isolated, gas-lit **YHA hostel**, at **Dolgoch** (☎01974/298680; ④; closed Oct–April). This is as remote a walking holiday as can be had in Wales. Paths lead from the hostel through the forests and hillsides to the tiny chapel at **Soar-y-Mynydd** and over the mountains to the next, and equally primitive, **hostel** at Ty'n-y-cornel (☎01550/740225; ④; closed Oct–March), five miles from Dolgoch. Although the entire route is less than twenty miles long, it takes a good hour to negotiate the twisting, narrow road safely. The old drovers, driving their cattle to Shrewsbury or Hereford, would have taken a day or two to cover the same stretch.

Llandrindod Wells

If anything can sum up a town succinctly, it is the plaque at **LLANDRINDOD WELLS** station, commemorating the 1990 "Revictorianisation of Llandrindod railway station". The town, fifteen miles northeast of Llanwrtyd, has not been slow to follow suit, peddling itself as Wales's most upmarket Victorian inland resort despite its one-time reputation for licentiousness. It was the railway that made Llandrindod, bringing carriages full of well-to-do Victorians to the fledgling spa from 1864 onwards. The town blossomed, new hotels were built, neat parks were laid out and it came to rival many of the more fashionable spas and resorts over the border. Even now, Llandrindod can seem like a breath of fresh air, with its finer buildings swabbed and sandblasted, its ornate cast-iron railings restored, and the spa brought back to some kind of life.

Llandrindod's Victorian opulence is still very much in evidence in the town's grandiose public buildings, especially the lavishly restored **spa pump room** in the pleasant **Rock Park**, with its trickling streams and well-manicured glens. EU regulations only sanction the use of one of Llandrindod's spa taps in the café inside: a tiny – but more than ample – glass costs 10p, or you can step outside for a free gulp from the chalybeate fountain outside. The architecture around the park entrance is Llandrindod at its most confidently Victorian, with elaborately carved terracotta frontages and expansive gabling.

The High Street, running from here to the centre, contains antique, junk and book shops. The tourist office, on Temple Street, behind, houses the small **Radnorshire Museum** (Tues–Thurs 10am–1pm & 2–5pm, Fri 10am–1pm & 2–4.30pm, Sat & Sun 10am–5pm; £1), which is largely dedicated to excavated remains from the Roman fort at Castellcollen, a mile northwest of Llandrindod. Kitsch Victoriana makes up the bulk of the rest of the collection, although there's also one of the better **red-kite galleries**, including a video with stunning footage. The **National Cycle Exhibition**, on the corner of Temple Street and Spa Road (daily 10am–4pm; £2.50), is a nostalgic collection of over 250 bikes, from a reproduction 1818 Hobbyhorse to relatively modern folding bikes and choppers, including styles that look far too uncomfortable to have been a success.

Buses pull in at the **train station** in the heart of town, between High Street and Station Crescent. The **tourist office** is on Temple Street (April–Sept Mon–Fri 9.30am–5.30pm, Sat & Sun 9.30am–5pm; Oct–March daily 10am–1pm & 2–5pm; ☎01597/822600). **Bikes** can be rented from the Greenstiles Bike Shed (☎01597/824594), next to the Cycle Exhibition.

As mid-Wales's major tourist centre for the past 130 years, Llandrindod is well served for **accommodation**. For something smart and reasonably close to the station, try *Greylands*, High Street (☎01597/822253; ③), or nearby *Rhydithon*, Dyffryn Road (☎01597/822624; ③). The *Kincoed Hotel*, Temple St (☎01597/822656; ③), is well appointed but not a patch on the faded elegance of the *Metropole Hotel*, on the same street (☎01597/822881; ⑤), an old spa hotel with a pool, the centrepiece of the town. It has a refined dining room, open to non-residents. For reasonably priced **food**, head for *The Herb Garden*, Spa Road, a welcoming veggie and wholefood restaurant, or the *Llanerch Inn*, Llanerch Lane, central Llandrindod's only **pub**, and an excellent one at that – a cosy sixteenth-century inn that predates most of the surrounding town, serving a solid menu of good-value, well-cooked classics.

North and East Radnorshire

Radnorshire has long been one of the most sparsely populated counties in England and Wales, the north and east still being especially remote. In the northwest, Rhayader is the only settlement of any size, a gateway to the four interlocking reservoirs of the **Elan Valley** and the surrounding wild, spartan countryside of waterfalls, bogland and bare peaks. The countryside to the northeast of Rhayader is tamer, and lanes and bridle paths delve in and around the woods and farms, occasionally brushing through minute settlements like the village of **Abbeycwmhir**, whose name is taken from its deserted Cistercian abbey. The hills roll eastwards towards the handsome town of **Knighton**, perched right on the English border, beside some of the most intact parts of **Offa's Dyke**.

Elan Valley and around

The poet Shelley spent his honeymoon in buildings now submerged by the waters of the **Elan Valley** reservoirs, a nine-mile-long string of four lakes built between 1892 and 1903 to supply water to the rapidly growing industrial city of Birmingham, 75 miles away. Although the lakes enhance an already beautiful and idyllic part of the world, the way in which Welsh valleys, villages and farmsteads were seized and flooded to provide water for English cities is something that Welsh nationalists have long protested. The tourist board prefers to advertise the profusion of rare plants and birds that resulted, notably the red kites. **Bus #103** from Llandrindod and Rhayader runs to the Elan Valley visitor centre (Mon–Fri; 2 daily).

From the workaday market town of **Rhayader**, ten miles west of Llandrindod Wells, the B4518 heads southwest four miles to **Elan** village, a curious collection of stone houses built in 1909 to replace the reservoir constructors' village that had grown up on the site. Just below the dam of the first reservoir, **Caban Coch**, the **Elan Valley Visitor Centre** (mid-March to Oct daily 10am–6pm; ☎01597/810898) incorporates a tourist office and a permanent exhibition stressing just how awful conditions were in nineteenth-century Birmingham, how rich the wildlife and flora around the lakes is and even how some of the water is now drunk in Wales. Frequent guided **walks** and even **Land Rover safaris** head off from the centre, and a road tucks in along the bank of Caban Coch to the **Garreg Ddu** viaduct, where it winds along for four spectacular miles to the vast, rather chilling 1952 dam on **Claerwen Reservoir**. More remote and less popular than the Elan lakes, Claerwen is a good base for a **serious walk** from the far end of the dam across eight or so harsh but beautiful miles to the monastery of Strata Florida (see p.732). Alternatively, follow the path that skirts around the northern shore of Claerwen and leads to the lonely **Teifi Pools**, glacial lakes from which the River Teifi springs.

Back at the Garreg Ddu viaduct, a more popular road continues north along the long, glassy finger of Garreg Ddu reservoir, before doubling back on itself just below the awesome **Pen-y-garreg** dam and reservoir; if the dam is overflowing, the vast wall of foaming water is mesmerizing. At the top of Pen-y-garreg lake, it's possible to drive over the final dam on the system, at **Craig Goch**. Thanks to its gracious curve, elegant Edwardian arches and neat little green cupola, this is the most photographed of all the dams.

Abbeycwmhir (Abaty Cwm Hir), seven miles northeast of Rhayader, takes its name from the abbey whose sombre ruins lie behind the village. Cistercian monks founded the site in 1146, planning one of the largest churches in Britain. Destruction by Henry III's troops in 1231 scuppered plans to continue building, but the sparse ruins – a rocky outline of the floor plan – lie in a conifer-carpeted valley alongside a gloomy green lake, lending weight to the site's melancholic associations. Llywelyn ap Gruffydd's body was rumoured to have been buried here, and a new granite slab carved with a Celtic sword lies on the altar to commemorate this last native prince of Wales.

Practicalities

The main accommodation base in the area is the *Elan Valley Hotel* (☎01597/810448; ③), an imposing, neocolonial pile on the Rhayader side of Elan village. It's also very good for eating, drinking and entertainment. Otherwise, you may want to make use of **Rhayader**, where buses stop opposite the **tourist office** (April–Oct daily 9.30am–12.30pm & 1.30–5.30pm; Nov–March Mon, Tues & Thurs–Sat 10am–4pm; ☎01597/810591), housed in the leisure centre. Eighteenth-century coaching inns, including the *Elan Hotel*, West Street (☎01597/810373; ②), still line the main streets, or there's more modern **accommodation** at the *Bryncoed* B&B, on Dark Lane (☎01597/811082; ①), opposite the tourist office; the *Elan Hotel*, West Street (☎01597/810109; ②); and *The Mount*, East Street (☎01597/810585; ①), a friendly B&B and the base for Clive Powell Mountain Bikes, from whom you can either **rent bikes** or join one of his organized trips around the tracks of mid-Wales. There's a **campsite** (☎01597/810183) at Wyeside, off the A44 north of town.

Knighton

A town that straddles King Offa's eighth-century border as well as the modern Wales–England divide, **KNIGHTON** (Tref-y-clawdd, "the town on the dyke"), twenty miles northeast of Llandrindod, has come into its own as the most obvious centre for those walking the **Offa's Dyke Path**. Located almost exactly halfway along the route, Knighton, although without many specific sights, is a lively, attractive place that easily warrants a stopoff. The town is so close to the border that its **train station** is actually in England. From here, Station Road crosses the River Teme into Wales and climbs a couple of hundred yards to Brookside Square. Further up the hill is the town's Alpine-looking Victorian clock tower, at the point where Broad Street becomes West Street and the steep High Street soars off up to the left, past rickety Tudor buildings and up to the mound of the old **castle**.

In West Street, the excellent **Offa's Dyke Centre** also houses the **tourist office** (Easter–Oct daily 9am–5.30pm; Nov–Easter Mon–Fri 9am–5pm; ☎01547/529424). **Accommodation** is plentiful: try *Fleece House*, Market Street (☎01547/520168; ②), the basic but cheerful *Red Lion*, West Street (☎01547/528231; ①), or the bargain *Offa's Dyke House*, 4 High Street (☎01547/528634; ①), which serves evening meals and offers

OFFA'S DYKE

George Borrow, in his classic *Wild Wales*, notes that once "it was customary for the English to cut off the ears of every Welshman who was found to the east of the dyke, and for the Welsh to hang every Englishman whom they found to the west of it". Certainly, **Offa's Dyke** has provided a potent symbol of Welsh–English antipathy ever since it was created in the eighth century as a demarcation line by King Offa of Mercia, ruler of central England.

The earthwork – up to 20ft high and 60ft wide – made use of natural boundaries like rivers in its run north to south, and is best seen in the sections near Knighton. Today's England–Wales border crosses the dyke many times, although the basic boundary has changed little since Offa's day. The glorious, 177-mile **long-distance footpath**, opened in 1971, runs from Prestatyn in the north to Chepstow, and is one of the most rewarding walks in Britain.

camping. For **eating** and drinking, it's hard to beat the comfortable *Horse & Jockey*, at the town end of Station Road, though there's folk and jazz in the *Plough*, Market Street.

Montgomeryshire

The northern part of Powys is made up of the old county of **Montgomeryshire** (Maldwyn), an area of enormously varying landscapes and few inhabitants. The best base for the spartan and mountainous southwest of the county is the solid little town of **Llanidloes**, less than ten miles north of Rhayader, a base for ageing hippies on the River Severn (Afon Hafren). Gentle, green contours characterize the east of the county, where the muted old county town of **Montgomery**, with its fine Georgian architecture, perches above the border and Offa's Dyke. The Severn runs a few miles to the west, near the impeccable village of **Berriew**, home of the bizarre Andrew Logan Museum of Sculpture. In the north of the county, **Welshpool** forms the only major settlement, packed in above the wide floodplain of the Severn. An excellent local museum, the impossibly cute toy rail line that runs to **Llanfair Caereinion**, good pubs and reasonable hotels make the town a fair stop for a day or two. On the southern side of Welshpool is Montgomeryshire's one unmissable sight, the sumptuous **Powis Castle** and its exquisite terraced gardens. The very north of the county is pastoral, deserted and beautiful. The few visitors head to **Lake Vyrnwy** and make their way down the dead-end lane to the **Pistyll Rhaedr** waterfall.

Llanidloes and around

Thriving when so many other small market towns seem in danger of atrophying, the secret of success for **LLANIDLOES**, twelve miles north of Rhayader, seems to be in its adaptability. It has developed from a rural village to a weaving town, and has latterly become a centre for artists, craftspeople and assorted alternative lifestylers. One of mid-Wales's prettiest towns, the four main streets meet at the black and white **market hall**, built on timber stilts in 1600 to allow the market – which has long since moved – to take place on the cobbles beneath. Running parallel with the length of the market hall are China Street and Longbridge Street, the latter good for some interesting little shops, including the very browsable Nature Gallery art store. Off Longbridge Street is Church Street, which opens out into a yard surrounding the dumpy parish **church of St Idloes**, whose impressive fifteenth-century hammer-beam roof is said to have been poached from Abbeycwmhir.

From the market hall, the broad Great Oak Street heads west to the **Town Hall**, originally built as a temperance hotel to challenge the boozy **Trewythen Arms** opposite. A plaque on the hotel commemorates Llanidloes as an unlikely-seeming place of industrial and political unrest, when, in April 1839, Chartists stormed the hotel, dragging out and beating up special constables who had been despatched to the town in a futile attempt to suppress political activism amongst the town's flannel weavers. In the town hall, you'll also find the wonderfully eclectic town **museum** (Easter–Sept daily 9.30am–5pm; Oct–Easter Mon–Sat 9.30am–5pm; free), with its inevitable red-kite centre.

China Street curves down to the car park, from where all **bus** services operate. The **tourist office** (Mon–Sat 10am–5pm; ☎01686/412605) is just north of the market hall, on Longbridge Street. One alternative happening worth investigating is the annual **Fancy Dress Night**, held on the first Friday of July, when the pubs open late, the streets are cordoned off and virtually the whole town gets kitted out. **Accommodation** includes the *Red Lion Hotel*, Longbridge Street (☎01686/412270; ②), the genteel *Unicorn*, on the same street (☎01686/413167; ①), and the *Severn View* B&B, China Street (☎01686/412207; ①). You can **camp** at *Dol-llys Farm* (☎01686/412694), on the northern fringe of town. Among the many options for **food**, the best bet is the wholesome fare in the laid-back *Great Oak Café*, on Great Oak Street. The lively *Red Lion* **pub** also does good food, or you could treat yourself at the *Orchard House*, China Street (☎01686/413700).

Montgomery and around

Tiny **MONTGOMERY** (Trefaldwyn), around twenty miles northeast of Llanidloes, is Montgomeryshire at its most anglicized. From the mound of its **castle**, situated just on the Welsh side of Offa's Dyke, there are wonderful views over the lofty church tower and the handsome Georgian streets, notably the impressively symmetrical main street – well-named Broad Street – which swoops up to the perfect little red-brick **Town Hall**, crowned by a pert clocktower. The rebuilt tower of Montgomery's parish **Church of St Nicholas** dominates the snug proportions of the buildings around it. Largely thirteenth-century, the highlights of its spacious interior include a 1600 monument to local landowner Sir Richard Herbert and his wife. Their eight children – including prominent Elizabethan poet George – have been carved in beatific kneeling positions behind them. Call in too at the engaging **Old Bell Museum**, just by the town hall (April–July & Sept Wed–Fri & Sun 1.30–5pm, Sat 10.30am–5pm; Aug Mon–Fri & Sun 1.30–5pm, Sat 10.30am–5pm; £1), an enjoyable collection of excavated artefacts, scale models of local castles and mementoes from Montgomery civic life.

Montgomery is within striking distance of one of the best-preserved sections of **Offa's Dyke**, traced by the long-distance footpath (see box on p.717), which runs on either side of the B4386. Ditches almost twenty feet high give one of the best indications of the dyke's original appearance. To the south of the main road, the England–Wales border still runs along the line of the dyke, twelve hundred years after it was built. If you want to **stay** here, *Little Brompton Farm*, two miles north on the B4385 (☎01686/668371; ②), is handily close to the Offa's Dyke Path or, in town, the *Bronwylfa*, Broad Street (☎01686/668630; ①), is a good B&B in a Georgian town house. For **food** and **drink** there's *The Checkers* pub, on Broad Street.

Berriew

Three miles north of Montgomery, the neat village of **BERRIEW** is more redolent of the Tudor settlements over the English border than anywhere in Wales. Its black and white houses are grouped picturesquely around a small church, the shallow waters of the River Rhiw and the slightly twee *Lion Hotel* (☎01686/640452; ⑤). Just over the river bridge, the **Andrew Logan Museum of Sculpture** (April, Nov & Dec Sun 2–6pm;

May, June, Sept & Oct Sat & Sun 2–6pm; July & Aug Wed–Sun 2–6pm; £2) makes for an incongruous attraction in such a setting, with a good selection of the notable modern sculptor's work. Andrew Logan inaugurated the great 1970s drag-and-grunge ball known as the "Alternative Miss World Contest", from which astounding costumes and memorabilia form a large chunk of the exhibits at the museum. Logan's oversized horticultural sculpture, including giant lilies encrusted with shattered mirrors and vast metal irises, rises to scrape the roof, while his smaller-scale jewellery and model goddesses only add to the sublime camp of the exhibition.

Welshpool

Eastern Montgomeryshire's chief town of **WELSHPOOL** (Y Trallwng), seven miles north of Montgomery, was formerly known as just Pool, its prefix added in 1835 to distinguish it from the English seaside town of Poole, in Dorset. Welshpool lies in the valley of the River Severn, just three miles from the English border, and was dependent largely upon the patronage of English landlords and kings. As a result, the town never developed a very Welsh character, but it's an attractive place to visit, with a number of attractive Tudor, Georgian and Victorian buildings in the centre, and the sumptuous **Powis Castle** nearby.

Along Severn Street from the **train station**, a hump-backed bridge over the much-restored **Montgomery Canal** hides the wharf, from where gaudily painted **boats** will chug you up the navigable section for a few miles and a couple of hours (☎01938/553271; £3.50). Nearby, a carefully restored warehouse contains the **Powysland Museum** (May–Sept Mon, Tues, Thurs & Fri 11am–1pm & 2–5pm, Sat & Sun 10am–1pm & 2–5pm; Oct–April Mon, Tues, Thurs & Fri 11am–1pm & 2–5pm, Sat & Sun 2–5pm £1). The impressive local history collection has a display about the impact of the Black Death here – half the town's population died – and displays Roman remains from the now obliterated local Cistercian abbey of Strata Marcella.

From the *Royal Oak Hotel*, at the centre of town, follow Broad Street – which changes name five times as it rises up the hill – towards the tiny Raven Square terminus station of the **Welshpool and Llanfair Light Railway** (April & May Sat & Sun 1 daily; June–Sept 1 daily; ☎01938/810441; return ticket £7.50). The eight-mile narrow gauge rail line was open for less than thirty years to passengers prior to its closure in 1931. Now, scaled-down engines once more chuff their way along to the almost eerily quiet village of **Llanfair Caereinion**, a good base for daytime walks, with good pub food at the *Goat Hotel*. The post office, opposite the church, stocks free leaflets of some good local circular walks.

Practicalities

The pompous neo-Gothic turrets of the old Victorian **train station** (its modern replacement is directly behind) sit at the top of Severn Street, which leads down into the town centre – the intersection of Severn, Berriew, Broad and Church streets. The **tourist office** (daily 9.30am–5.30pm; ☎01938/552043) is fifty yards up Church Street in the Vicarage Gardens car park.

There is plenty of **accommodation** in town, including the central *Royal Oak* (☎01938/552217; ⑤), a traditional coaching inn at the main crossroads. Dozens of **B&Bs** line Salop Road; *Montgomery House* (☎01938/552693; ①) is the surest bet. Further from the centre are a couple of options: the beautiful *Lower Trelydan Farm* (☎01938/553105; ②), out towards the village of Guilsfield (Cegidfa); and *Severn Farm*, on Leighton Road (☎01938/553098; ①), just beyond the industrial estate to the east of the station, which allows **camping**. The best **eating** in town is either at the moderately priced *Tyler's Brasserie*, High Street (☎01938/555006; closed Mon & Tues lunch, plus all Wed & Sun), or up the street at the *Talbot* pub, which serves excellent lunchtime and evening meals.

Powis Castle

In a land of ruined castles, the sheer scale and beauty of **Powis Castle** (April–June, Sept & Oct Wed–Sun 1–5pm; July–Aug Tues–Sun 1–5pm; castle £7.50; gardens & museum only £5; NT), a mile from Welshpool up Park Lane, is reason enough for coming to the town. On the site of an earlier Norman fort, the castle was started in the reign of Edward I by the Gwenwynwyn family; to qualify for the site and the barony of De la Pole, they had to renounce all claims to Welsh princedom. In 1587, Sir Edward Herbert bought the castle and began to transform it into the Elizabethan palace we see today. Inside, the **Clive Museum** – named after Edward Clive, son of Clive of India, who married into the family in 1784 – forms a lively account of the British in India, through diaries, letters, paintings, tapestries, weapons and jewels. But it is the sumptuous period rooms that impress most, from the vast, kitsch frescoes by Lanscroon, above the balustraded staircase, to the mahogany bed, brass and enamel toilets and decorative wall hangings of the state bedroom. The elegant **Long Gallery** has a rich sixteenth-century plasterwork ceiling overlooking winsome busts and marble statuettes of the four elements, placed between the glowering family portraits. The **gardens**, designed by Welsh architect William Winde, are spectacular. Dropping down from the castle in four huge stepped terraces, the design has barely changed since the seventeenth century, with a charmingly precise orangery, and topiary that looks as if it is shaved daily. In summer, outdoor **concerts**, frequently with firework finales, take place in the gardens.

Llanfyllin and around

The hills and plains of northern Montgomeryshire conceal a maze of deserted lanes and farm outposts along the contours that swell up towards the north and the foothills of the Berwyn Mountains. The only real settlement of any size is **Llanfyllin**, ten miles northwest of Welshpool, a peaceful but friendly hillside town with a Thursday market. There is really nothing to do though, and you are better continuing on to the hiking and nature communing around **Lake Vyrnwy**, or pressing north to **Pistyll Rhaeadr**, Wales's highest waterfall.

Llanrhaeadr-ym-mochnant and Pistyll Rhaeadr

For a place so near the English border, **Llanrhaeadr-ym-mochnant**, five miles north of Llanfyllin, is surprisingly Welsh in its language and appearance. The small, low-roofed village, six miles north of Llanfyllin, is remembered as the serving parish of Bishop William Morgan, who translated the Bible into Welsh in 1588, but it's mostly visited as a base for **Pistyll Rhaeadr**, Wales's highest waterfall, at 150ft. The village lies at the foot of a lane which runs four miles northwest alongside the River Rhaeadr through an increasingly rocky valley to the falls. The river tumbles down the crags in two stages, flowing furiously under a natural stone arch that has been christened the Fairy Bridge. When it's quiet, tame chaffinches swoop and settle all around this enchanting spot, although the charms are a little hard to appreciate amid the tourists on a warm summer Sunday.

The summer-only *Tan-y-Pistyll* licensed café, by the waterfall car park, is tolerable and they run a decent **B&B** (☎01691/780392; ②) with a **campsite** in the back field. The village has a bargain B&B, *Powys House*, on the central square (☎01691/780201; ①), and two great **pubs** – the *Three Tuns* and the *Wynnstay Arms*.

Lake Vyrnwy

A monument to the self-aggrandizement of the Victorian age, **Lake Vyrnwy** (Llyn Efyrnwy) combines its functional role as a water supply for Liverpool with a touch of architectural genius in the shape of the huge nineteenth-century dam at its southern end and the Disneyesque turreted straining tower which edges out into the icy waters. It's a magnificent spot, and a popular centre for walking and bird watching, with nature trails. The village of Llanwddyn was flattened and rebuilt at the eastern end, the inhabitants receiving compensation of just £5 for losing their homes. The story is told, somewhat apologetically, in the **Vyrnwy Visitor Centre** (April–Dec daily 10.30am–5.30pm; Jan–March Sat & Sun 10.30am–5.30pm; free) which combines with the **tourist office** (Easter–Oct daily 10am–5pm; Nov–Easter Mon & Fri–Sun 10am–4pm; ☎01691/870346) and a **bird-watching centre**, in the cluster of buildings on the western side of the dam. **Bikes** can be rented from Mandy's Tea Shop, next door.

Lake Vyrnwy's immediate surroundings have some of the best **accommodation** in the region, notably the grand *Lake Vyrnwy Hotel* (☎01691/870692; ⑦), overlooking the waters above the southeastern shore. If you just want a look, the hotel serves a full afternoon tea in a chintzy lounge overlooking the lake. Close by, *Tŷ Uchaf* (☎01691/870286; ②) has B&B and a good tearoom. Farmhouse B&B is available not far away at *Tynymaes* (☎01691/870216; ①), a couple of miles east of Llanwddyn, on the B4393; and at the sublime, ivy-draped *Cyfie Farm* (☎01691/648451; ③), just over a mile south of Llanfihangel-yng-Ngwynfa.

The Dee Valley

Llangollen, along with the smaller town of Bala, grew up partly as a market centre, but also served the needs of cattle drovers who used the passage carved by the River Dee (Afon Dyfrdwy) through the hills – the easiest route from the fattening grounds of northwest Wales to the markets in England. Long before rail and road transport pushed the dwindling numbers of drovers out of business at the end of the nineteenth century, they had already been joined by early tourists. Most made straight for Llangollen, where the ruins of both a Welsh castle and a Cistercian abbey lent a gaunt Romantic charm to a dramatic gorge naturally blessed with surging rapids. The arrival of the railway, in the middle of the nineteenth century, made Llangollen a firm favourite with tourists from the mill towns of northwest England. The line closed in the 1960s, but **Bala** has fought neglect to become one of Wales's top **watersports** venues, a mecca for windsurfing and white-water kayaking. Between Llangollen and the English border, the Dee is joined by one of its major tributaries, the Ceiriog, which flows down its peaceful valley to the Marcher fortress of **Chirk Castle**.

Llangollen and around

LLANGOLLEN, thirty miles north of Welshpool, is the embodiment of a Welsh town in both setting and character, clasped tightly in the narrow Dee Valley between the shoulders of the Berwyn and Eglwyseg mountains. Along the valley's floor, the waters of the River Dee run down to the town, licking the angled buttresses of the weighty Gothic bridge, which has spanned the river since the fourteenth century. On its south bank, half a dozen streets, their houses harmoniously straggling up the rugged hillsides, are labelled in both Welsh and English, and form the core of the scattered settlement flung out across the low hills. Every July, the town comes alive for the **International Music Eisteddfod**.

As the only river crossing point for miles, Llangollen was an important town long before the early Romantics arrived at the end of the eighteenth century, when they were cut off from their European Grand Tours by the Napoleonic Wars. Turner came to paint the swollen river and the Cistercian ruin of **Valle Crucis**, a couple of miles up the valley; John Ruskin found the town "entirely lovely in its gentle wildness"; and writer George Borrow made Llangollen his base for the early part of his 1854 tour

---

THE LLANGOLLEN INTERNATIONAL MUSIC EISTEDDFOD

Llangollen is heaving in summer, but never more so than during the first week of July, when for six days the town explodes into a frenzy of music, dance, poetry and colour. The **International Music Eisteddfod** comes billed as "the world's greatest folk festival" but unlike the National Eisteddfod, which is a purely Welsh affair, the Llangollen event draws amateur performers from thirty countries, all competing for prizes in their chosen disciplines. Throughout the week, performers present their works at numerous sites around the town, but mainly in the much-derided 6000-seat white plastic structure designed to evoke the shape of the traditional marquee which was formerly erected on the site each year.

The Eisteddfod has been held in its present form since 1947, when it was started more or less on a whim by one Harold Tudor. Forty choirs from fourteen countries performed at the first event. Today, more than 12,000 musicians, singers, dancers and choristers from countries around the world descend on this town of 3000 people, further swamped by up to 150,000 visitors. While the whole set-up can seem oppressive, there is an irresistible *joie-de-vivre* as brightly costumed dancers walk the streets and fill the fish-and-chip shops.

Unless you are going specifically for the Eisteddfod, the week from the first Tuesday of July is probably a good time to stay away. If you come, book early for both accommodation and tickets (☎01978/860236).

---

detailed in *Wild Wales*. The rich and famous came not just for the scenery, but to visit the **Ladies of Llangollen**, an eccentric pair of lesbians who became the toast of society from their house, **Plas Newydd**. But by this stage some of the town's rural charm had been eaten up by the works of one of the century's finest engineers, Thomas Telford, squeezing both his London–Holyhead trunk road and the **Llangollen Canal** alongside the river.

The Town

Standing in twelve acres of formal gardens, half a mile up Hill Street from the southern end of Castle Street, the two-storied mock-Tudor **Plas Newydd** (Easter–Oct daily 10am–5pm; £2.50) was, for almost fifty years, home to the celebrated **Ladies of Llangollen**. Lady Eleanor Butler and Sarah Ponsonby were a lesbian couple from Anglo-Irish aristocratic backgrounds, who tried to elope together at the end of the eighteenth century. After two botched attempts dressed in men's clothes, they were grudgingly allowed to leave in 1778 with an annual allowance of £280, enough to settle in Llangollen, where they became the country's most celebrated lesbians. Despite their desire for a "life of sweet and delicious retirement", they didn't seem to mind the constant stream of gentry who called on them. Walter Scott was well received, though he found them "a couple of hazy or crazy old sailors" in manner, and like "two respectable superannuated clergymen" in their mode of dress. Visitors' gifts of sculpted **wood panelling** formed the basis of the riotous friezes of gloomy woodwork that weigh on your every step around the modest black and white timbered house. Most of the rooms have been left almost empty, so as not to hide the panelling; only one upper room has been devoted to a few of the ladies' possessions and panels detailing their life story.

Llangollen takes its name from the **Church of St Collen**, on Bridge Street (May–Sept daily 1.30–6.20pm; free), outside which is a triangular railed-off monument to the Ladies' maid. On nearby Castle Street is the site of the **European Centre for Traditional and Regional Cultures** (May–Sept Mon–Fri 10am–5pm, Sat & Sun 10am–6pm; Oct–April Mon–Sat 9am–5pm, Sun 10am–4pm; free), primarily a centre for folk studies, but also presenting an exhibition on each of the EU countries every six months, focusing on such diverse topics as lesser-used languages, ceramics and, pointedly, the effect of tourism on fragile communities.

The hills around Llangollen echo to the shrill cry of steam engines easing along the **Llangollen Steam Railway** (June–Oct daily; plus weekends and holidays throughout the year; ☎0800/834820), shoe-horned into the north side of the valley. From Llangollen's time-warped station it runs along a restored section of the disused Ruabon–Barmouth line, the belching steam engines creeping west along the riverbank, hauling ancient carriages which proudly sport the liveries of their erstwhile owners. The restored line currently runs the eight miles to Carrog, although plans to push through to Corwen are well in hand.

A short riverside walk from the station leads to Lower Dee Exhibition Centre, Mill Street, home to the **Doctor Who Exhibition** (daily 10am–5.30pm; £5.50; joint ticket with Model Railway World £9), an endearing homage to this much-loved British sci-fi drama, and **Model Railway World** (same hours; £4.50), with plenty of layouts and engines to play with. Entry to either gives you the opportunity to watch model-making in progress in the parent Dapol toy factory.

Across the street is the Llangollen Canal, one of the finest feats of British canal building. Its architect, Thomas Telford, succeeded in building a canal without locks through fourteen miles of hilly terrain, most spectacularly by means of the thousand-foot-long **Pontcysyllte Aqueduct**, passing 127ft over the River Dee at Froncysyllte, four miles east. **Canal trips** (Easter–Oct daily; £6; ☎01978/860702) over the aqueduct leave from Llangollen Wharf, just above the steam train station, on Wharf Hill.

Walking west from the town bridge, you'll soon come to the site of the International Eisteddfod, crowned by the extraordinary **Royal International Pavilion**, which – especially from the walk up the hill to Dinas Brân – resembles some giant armoured reptile dropped from a great height into the valley. Outside the Eisteddfod season, the auditorium acts as a concert venue and sports hall, with temporary exhibitions in the foyer (Mon–Fri 10am–4pm; free).

Practicalities

Buses stop on Market Street, while the nearest **train station** is five miles away at Ruabon, which is passed by frequent buses on the Llangollen–Wrexham run. The **tourist office**, on Castle Street (daily: Easter–Oct 10am–6pm; Nov–Easter 9.30am–5pm; ☎01978/860828), is fifty yards from the bridge and less than a hundred yards from the bus stop on Market Street. There's **Internet** access at The Gallery Computer World, 22 Chapel St (☎01978/869384; £3 per half hour), and **bike rental** from the town's youth hostel – you don't have to be staying there.

Finding **rooms** in Llangollen can be a chore in summer, especially during the Eisteddfod. Low-cost B&Bs worth checking out include: the bright, simply furnished rooms at *Greenbank Guesthouse*, Victoria Square (☎01978/861835; ①); *Bryant Rose*, 31 Regent St (☎01978/860389; ①), a central B&B with large, airy rooms; and *Jonkers*, 9 Chapel St (☎01978/861158; ①), which has a couple of compact, low-beamed rooms in an ancient house with uneven floors and narrow stairways. Moving upmarket, go for *Gales*, 18 Bridge St (☎01978/860089; ③), a comfortable guest house above a wine bar; *Fron Deg* (☎01978/860126; ②), a top-class B&B a mile west along Abbey Road; or *Bodidris Hall* (☎01978/790434; ⑥), seven miles north of Llangollen on the A5104, which offers secluded luxury in a largely Tudor building with log fires, oak beams and an award-winning restaurant. The excellent **YHA hostel**, on Tyndwr Road (☎01978/860330; ①), is a mile and a half from town – go along the A5 towards Shrewsbury, turn right up Birch Hill, then right again. *Eirianfa* (☎01978/860919), a mile west of the town on the A5, is the closest **campsite** – they also rent out bikes.

Though not extensive by city standards, Llangollen boasts a fairly good selection of **restaurants** and no shortage of cafés around town. *The Gallery*, 15 Chapel St (☎01978/860076), is a good start for moderately priced pizza and pasta dishes. *Jonkers*, steps away at 9 Chapel St (☎01978/861158; closed Sun & Mon), is well worth the extra pound or two for its classy meals, and there's outside seating in summer. *Gales Wine Bar*, 18 Bridge St (☎01978/860089; closed Sun), has great old church pews and an extensive cellar, and serves decent bistro-style food. The *Hand Hotel*, 26 Bridge St, is a straightforward local **pub** where you can listen to a male voice choir in full song (Mon & Fri 7.30pm). Another good watering hole is *Jenny Jones*, Abbey Road, with live country and western music (Wed) and jazz (Thurs).

Around Llangollen

The panoramic view, especially at sunset, justifies a 45-minute slog up to **Castell Dinas Brân** (Crow's Fortress Castle), perched on a hill eight hundred feet above the town, and reached by a path beginning near Llangollen Wharf. The lure certainly isn't the few sad – if powerfully evocative – stumps which stand as a poor testament to what was once the district's largest and most important Welsh fortress. Built in the 1230s by the ruler of northern Powys, Prince Madog ap Gruffydd Maelor, the castle rose on the site of an earlier Iron Age fort. Edward I soon captured it as part of his first campaign against Llywelyn ap Gruffydd, but the castle was left to decay. In 1540, John Leland, Henry VIII's antiquarian, found it "all in ruin".

The gaunt ruin of **Valle Crucis Abbey** (May–Sept daily 10am–5pm, £2; rest of year free access; CADW), a mile or so west of Llangollen, greets you with its best side, the largely intact west wall of the church pierced by the frame of a rose window. Though one of the last Cistercian foundations in Wales, and the first Gothic abbey in Britain, it is no match for Tintern Abbey (see p.662), but nevertheless stands majestically in a pastoral – and much less visited – setting. Despite a devastating fire in its first century, and a complement of far from pious monks, it survived until the Dissolution, in 1535. The church fell into disrepair, after which the monastic buildings, in particular the monks' dormitory, were employed as farm buildings. Now they hold displays on monastic life, reached by a detour through the mostly ruined cloister and past the weighty vaulting of the chapter house.

Chirk Castle

Seven miles southeast of Llangollen, the busy Dee Valley contrasts with the parallel valley of the River Ceiriog, its entrance guarded by the massive, drum-towered **Chirk Castle** (April–Sept Wed–Sun noon–5pm; Oct Sat & Sun noon–5pm; £4.80; NT), squatting ominously on a rise half a mile to the west of **Chirk** (Y Waun). Construction was begun in the thirteenth century, at the behest of Edward I, who wanted to control the borderlands between England and Wales. The structure is designed to mimic Beaumaris Castle, although it lacks its purity and symmetry. At the end of a long avenue of oaks, the approach is guarded by a magnificent Baroque gate screen, the finest work done by the Davies brothers of Bersham, who wrought it between 1712 and 1719. The ebullient floral designs are capped by the coat of arms of the Myddletons who have lived here for the past four hundred years. The exterior has been extensively remodelled, as have the interiors, leaving a legacy of sumptuous rooms reflecting sixteenth- to nineteenth-century tastes, many now returned to their former states after some Victorian meddling by Pugin in the 1840s.

Bala

The little town of **BALA** (Y Bala), twenty miles west of Llangollen, is set at the northern end of Wales's largest natural lake, **Llyn Tegid** (Bala Lake). The town was renowned for its piety in the nineteenth century, but these days it has become a major

watersports centre, and there's little else to do here now. The lake is perfect for wind-surfing in particular, due to the winds buffeting up the Talyllyn valley, which slices thirty miles northeast from the coast, along the Bala geological fault.

Slalom kayak fans can make for the **Canolfan Tryweryn** white-water course, four miles west up the A4212. When water is released from the dam, around two hundred days a year, it crashes down a mile and a half through the slalom site, the venue for frequent summer-weekend competitions and commercial **white-water rafting** trips (☎01678/521083). It is a fairly steep £10 for a single heart-stopping run down the roughest part, but for a minimum of £150 a group of up to seven can rent a raft and instructor for two hours, or about four runs. Down on the shores of Llyn Tegid, by the tourist office, the Bala Adventure and Watersports Centre (☎01678/521059) runs courses and rents equipment for **windsurfing, kayaking** and **sailing**.

The only **bus** is the #94, which runs from Llangollen to Dolgellau, stopping on the High Street. The **tourist office** (April–Oct daily 10am–6pm; Nov–March Sat & Sun 10am–1pm & 2–5pm; ☎01678/521021) is on the lakeside, five minutes' walk away, on Pensarn Road. Bala has plenty of **places to stay**, or you can make the most of the surrounding countryside by staying in the Vale of Edeyrnion, northeast of the town. Centrally, try the welcoming and good-value *Traian*, 95 Tegid St (☎01678/520059; ①). A little further out there's *Abercelyn*, a fine country house half a mile south of Bala on the A494 (☎01678/521109, *aercelyn@celtrail.com*; ②; closed Jan & Dec), and *Fron Feuno Hall* (☎01678/521115; ⑤), a gracious place with lots of thoughtful touches. One and a half miles north on the A494, there's a great independent **hostel**, *The Coach House*, at Tomen Y Castell (☎01678/520738; ①). *Pen-y-Bont*, on the B4402 Llandrillo road (☎01678/520549; April–Oct), is the nearest **campsite**.

travel details

Trains

Abergavenny to: Cardiff (hourly; 40min); Hereford (hourly; 20min); Newport (hourly; 30min).

Knighton to: Llandrindod Wells (4 daily; 40min); Llanwrtyd Wells (4 daily; 1hr 10min); Swansea (4 daily; 3hr 10min).

Llandrindod Wells to: Knighton (4 daily; 40min); Llanwrtyd Wells (4 daily; 30min); Shrewsbury (4 daily; 1hr 40min); Swansea (4 daily; 2hr 10min).

Welshpool to: Aberystwyth (6 daily; 1hr 30min); Birmingham (6 daily; 1hr 30min); Machynlleth (6 daily; 1hr).

Buses

Abergavenny to: Brecon (Mon–Sat 7 daily, none on Sun; 1hr); Cardiff (hourly; 1hr 20min); Crickhowell (Mon–Sat 7 daily, none on Sun; 20min); Llanfihangel Crucorney (6 daily; 15min); Merthyr Tydfil (hourly; 1hr 30min); Monmouth (6 daily; 40min); Raglan (6 daily; 20min).

Bala to: Dolgellau (9 daily; 40min); Llangollen (8 daily; 1hr).

Brecon to: Abergavenny (Mon–Sat 7 daily, none on Sun; 1hr); Cardiff (1 daily; 1hr 20min); Craig-y-nos/Dan-yr-ogof (2–3 daily; 30min); Crickhowell (Mon–Sat 7 daily, none on Sun; 25min); Hay-on-Wye (6 daily; 50min); Libanus (9 daily; 10min); Llandrindod Wells (Mon–Sat 1–3 daily, none on Sun; 1hr); Merthyr Tydfil (10 daily; 40min); Swansea (2–3 daily; 1hr 30min).

Knighton to: Ludlow (3 daily; 1hr 10min); Presteigne (5 daily; 30min).

Llandrindod Wells to: Abbeycwmhir (Mon–Fri 1 postbus daily; 2hr); Aberystwyth (1 daily; 1hr 40min); Brecon (Mon-Sat 1–3 daily, none on Sun; 1hr); Elan Village (Mon–Fri 1 postbus daily;

40min); Hay-on-Wye (Wed & Sat 1 daily; 1hr); Rhayader (3 daily; 30min).

Llanfyllin to: Llanwddyn for Lake Vyrnwy (Mon–Sat 3–4 daily, none on Sun; 30min); Welshpool (Mon–Sat 1 daily; 40min).

Llangollen to: Bala (8 daily; 1hr); Chirk (7 daily; 20min); Wrexham (at least hourly; 30min).

Llanidloes to: Aberystwyth (1 daily; 1hr); Welshpool (5 daily; 1hr 10min).

Llanwrtyd Wells to: Abergwesyn (Mon–Fri 1 postbus daily; 20min); Builth Wells (2 daily; 50min).

Welshpool to: Berriew (Mon–Sat 6 daily, none on Sun; 20min); Llanidloes (5 daily; 1hr 10min); Llanfyllin (Mon–Sat 1 daily, none on Sun; 40min); Montgomery (school bus; 25min).

CHAPTER FIFTEEN

THE CAMBRIAN COAST

Cardigan Bay (Bae Ceredigion) takes a huge bite out of the west Wales coast, leaving behind the Pembrokeshire peninsula in the south and the Llŷn peninsula in the north. Between them lies the Cambrian Coast, a loosely defined mountain-backed strip stretching from Cardigan in the south to Harlech and Porthmadog in the north. Before the railway arrived, the Cambrian Coast was isolated from the rest of Wales, the Cambrian Mountains presenting an awkward barrier only breached by narrow passes – droving routes to the markets in England. Today, large sand-fringed sections are peppered with low-key coastal resorts packed with English families from the Midlands in summer, a fact which still creates some local antipathy in this staunchly nationalistic part of the country.

The Cardigan coast starts where the rugged seashore of Pembrokeshire ends, continuing in much the same vein of great cliffs, isolated beaches and swirling sea birds around the spirited former county town of **Cardigan**. The rocky coast is broken at a few popular seaside resorts and the robust and cosmopolitan "capital" of mid-Wales, **Aberystwyth**.

Inland, the best sights are grouped around two river valleys: the lush and quiet Teifi and the dramatic ravines around the Rheidol. Along the **Teifi**, which flows out into the sea at Cardigan, the best base is **Lampeter**, home of a branch of the University of Wales. The **Rheidol** is great walking country, accessed on the narrow-gauge railway that climbs out of Aberystwyth to the popular tourist honey pot of **Devil's Bridge**, where three bridges, one on top of the other, span a turbulent chasm of waterfalls. **Machynlleth** lies to the north, a magical place, the seat of Owain Glyndŵr's putative fifteenth-century Welsh parliament and still a thriving market centre. It's also the base of the **Centre for Alternative Technology**, an impressive showpiece for community living and renewable energy resources.

Due north from Machynlleth, the southern reaches of **Snowdonia National Park** are dominated by the mountain massif of **Cadair Idris**, its southern, crag-fringed faces best explored from the narrow-gauge Talyllyn railway. Cadair Idris's northern flank slopes down to the scenic Mawddach Estuary, flanked by the market town of **Dolgellau** and the likeable resort of **Barmouth**. Further north again, the castle at **Harlech** stands high on its rocky promontory, the southernmost link in Edward I's chain of thirteenth-century castles, overlooking the coast as it sweeps north towards the Llŷn peninsula and the timeless backdrop of Snowdonia.

ACCOMMODATION PRICE CODES

Throughout this guide, hotel and B&B accommodation is priced on a scale of ① to ⑨, the number indicating the **lowest price** you could expect to pay per night in that establishment for a **double room** in high season. The prices indicated by the codes are as follows:

① under £40	④ £60–70	⑦ £110–150
② £40–50	⑤ £70–90	⑧ £150–200
③ £50–60	⑥ £90–110	⑨ over £200

Cardigan and around

An ancient borough and fomer port at the lowest bridging point of the Teifi Estuary, **CARDIGAN** (Aberteifi) was founded by the Norman lord Roger de Montgomery around its castle in 1093. From the castle mound by the bridge, Bridge Street sweeps through

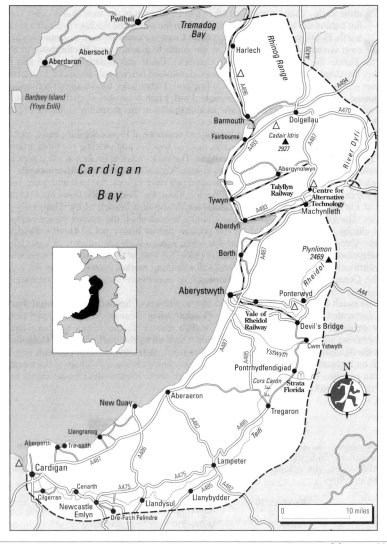

High Street to the turreted oddity of the **Guildhall**, with the Welsh flag skewered adamantly to its grey frontage. Through the Guildhall courtyard is the town's **covered market**, a typically eclectic mix of fresh food, local craft and secondhand stalls. Across the bridge from the town centre, the **Cardigan Heritage Centre** (March–Oct daily 10am–5pm; £2), housed in an old granary, tells the story of the port's rise and fall.

The helpful **tourist office** (Easter–Sept daily 10am–6pm; Oct–Easter Mon–Sat 10am–5pm; ☎01239/613230) is in the foyer of Theatr Mwldan, Bath House Road. There's plenty of **accommodation**, with numerous B&Bs along the Gwbert Road, off North Road: the *Brynhyfryd*, at the town end (☎01239/612861; ②), and the *Maes-a-Mor*, in Park Place, further up Gwbert Road (☎01239/614929; ②), are the best. On the High Street, the old-fashioned *Black Lion* pub (☎01239/612532; ③) does good B&B and evening meals. There's a YHA **youth hostel** four miles away at Poppit Sands, at the end of the Pembrokeshire Coast Path (☎01239/612936; closed Nov–Feb). Buses connect in July and August, but for the rest of the year they terminate at St Dogmael's, two miles short. For **food**, try the inexpensive Theatr Mwldan café or *Jackets*, 58 North Rd, which serves pizzas, potatoes, kebabs and pies. The best pub food is at the *Eagle*, at the southern end of the town bridge.

Tre-Saith and Llangranog

The most popular stopping-off point on the stretch of coast north of Cardigan has to be Aberporth, an elderly resort built around two less than appealing bays, easily shown up by the neighbouring hamlet of **TRE-SAITH**, a mile to the east, which staggers down the tiny valley to a delightful beach. There are **dinghy races** from the beach every Sunday in summer. Around the rocks to the right of the beach, the River Saith plummets over the mossy black rocks in a waterfall. Among the **places to stay** in Tre-Saith, the *Bryn Berwyn* B&B, a ten-minute walk up the hill from Tre-Saith beach (☎01239/811126; ②), is a good bet. You could also **camp** right above the beach in one of the quieter outlying fields of the *Llety Caravan Park*, reached by road en route to Aberporth (☎01239/810354).

Three miles north of the A487, **LLANGRANOG** is the most attractive village on the Ceredigion coast, wedged in between bracken and gorse-beaten hills, the main streets winding to the tiny seafront. The beach can become horribly congested in mid-summer, when it's better to follow the cliff path to **Cilborth Beach**, and on to the glorious NT-owned headland, **Ynys Lochtyn**. In Llangranog, you can **stay** on the seafront either at the excellent *Ship Inn* (☎01239/654423; ③) or the earthier *Pentre Arms* (☎01239/654345; ②); both do good **food**. Between Penbryn and Llangranog is the *Maesglas* caravan park (☎01239/654268), which takes **tents**.

New Quay

Along with Laugharne in Carmarthenshire, **NEW QUAY** (Cei Newydd) lays claim to being the original Llareggub in Dylan Thomas's *Under Milk Wood*. Certainly, it has the little tumbling streets, prim Victorian terraces, cobbled stone harbour and air of dreamy isolation that Thomas evoked in his play but, in the height of summer, the quiet isolation can be hard to find. Although there is a singular lack of excitement in New Quay, it is a truly pleasant base for good beaches, walking, eating and drinking.

The pretty **harbour** and small, curving beach are backed by a higgledy-piggledy line of multi-coloured shops and houses. The beachfront streets comprise the **lower town** – the more traditionally "seaside" part of New Quay, full of cafés, pubs and beach shops. Tucked away down the slipway above the beach is the interesting **Marine Wildlife Centre** (April–Sept daily 10am–5pm; donation requested), with some good displays on the dolphins, seals and sea birds of Cardigan Bay. Acutely inclined streets lead to the residential **upper town**, with some delightful views over the sweeping shoreline below.

The northern beach soon gives way to a rocky headland, **New Quay Head**, where an invigorating path steers along the top of the the the aptly named **Bird Rock**.

Buses stop on Park Street, from where it's a walk down any of the steep streets to the seafront, where you'll find the **tourist office**, centrally located at the junction of Church Street and Wellington Place (daily: April–June & Sept 10am–5pm; July & Aug 10am–6pm; ☎01545/560865). **Accommodation** includes cheap B&Bs at *Elvor*, on George Street, the main road to Llanarth, in the upper town (☎01545/560554; ②); *The Moorings*, on Glanmor Terrace, near the beach (☎01545/560375; ②); and the chintzy luxury of *Ffynnon Feddyg*, out towards Cei Bach on the eastern edge of town (☎01545/560222; ②). The nearest **campsite** is the *Neuadd* (☎01545/560709), fifteen minutes' walk away, behind the *Penrhiwllan Inn*, at the top of the hill on the way to Synod Inn. New Quay contains innumerable cheap, stodgy **cafés**, amongst which the *Mariner's Café*, by the harbour wall, is a sure bet. Most of the **pubs** serve food, the best being the *Seahorse*, Margaret Street, and the *Wellington*, by the tourist office on the seafront.

Aberaeron

ABERAERON, seven miles up the coast, seems marginally more exciting than New Quay but is almost unique amongst the Ceredigion resorts for being on an unappealing stretch of coastline. Nonetheless, the town, with its pastel-shaded houses encasing a large harbour inlet, has a rare unity of design, the result of a complete nineteenth-century rebuilding by the Reverend Alban Gwynne. He spent his way through his wife's inheritance by dredging the Aeron Estuary and constructing a formally planned town around it as a new port for mid-Wales.

The A487 runs straight through the heart of town, down Bridge Street and past the large **Alban Square**, named after the rich rector. On the north side of the town bridge, a grid of streets stretches down to a neat line of ordered, colourful houses on the seafront. Right on the harbour, the **Hive on the Quay** (late May to mid-Sept daily 10am–1pm & 2–5pm; £1.20) combines an exhibition of bees with chances to sample honey products, including delicious ice cream. Quay Parade runs down the side of the seafront past some of the old fisherman's houses and pubs to the fairly humdrum **Sea Aquarium** (Easter–Oct daily 10am–5pm; £3.50).

A trip to the exquisite kitchen gardens at **Llanerchaeron**, three miles east of Aberaeron (April–Oct Thurs–Sun 11am–5pm; £2; NT), makes an excellent excursion. Once an integrated smallholding typical of this region, the estate is currently undergoing restoration; occasional open days allow access to the Nash-designed main house.

The **tourist office** is on Quay Parade, the seafront road (Easter–June & Sept daily 10am–5pm; July & Aug daily 10am–6pm; Oct–Easter Mon–Sat 10am–5pm; ☎01545/570602). There are two town-centre **B&Bs**, both on Cadwgan Place: *Fairview* (☎01545/571472; ②) and *Arosfa* (☎01545/570120; ②). The nearest local **campsite** is the *Aeron Coast*, on the A487 just north of town (☎01545/ 570349). For **food**, there's the moderate *Arosfa*, at 8 Cadwgan Place, for traditional and new Welsh specialities, and an excellent fish restaurant at the *Hive on the Quay*. Good seafood, together with some imaginative French cuisine, can be found at the *Harbourmaster* pub, by the tourist office.

The Teifi Valley

The Teifi is one of Wales's most eulogized rivers, for its rich spawn of fresh fish, its meandering rural charm and the coracles that were a regular feature from pre-Roman times. On the way to its estuary at Cardigan, it flows through some gloriously green and undulating countryside, winding its way over the falls at **Cenarth** and passing the massive ramparts of **Cilgerran Castle**. Further upstream, the river also takes in the proudly Welsh university town of **Lampeter**, and the river's infancy can be seen near the ruins of **Strata Florida Abbey**, beyond which the river emerges from the dark and remote **Teifi Pools**.

Cilgerran Castle

Just a couple of miles up the Teifi River from Cardigan, the attractive village of **CIL-GERRAN** clusters around its wide main street. Behind is the bulk of the **Castle** (April–Oct daily 9.30am–6.30pm; Nov–March daily 9.30am–4pm, Sun 2–4pm; £2; CADW), founded in 1100 at a commanding vantage point on a high wooded bluff above the river, then still navigable for sea-going ships. This is the legendary site of the 1109 abduction of Nest (the "Welsh Helen of Troy") by a love-struck Prince Owain of Powys. Her husband, Gerald of Pembroke, escaped by slithering down a toilet waste chute through the castle walls. The two massive drum towers still dominate the castle, and the outer walls, some four feet thicker than those facing the inner courtyard, are traced by vertiginously high walkways. The outer ward, over which a modern path now runs from the entrance, is a good example of the keepless castle evolving throughout the thirteenth century. The views over the forested valley towards the pink and grey Georgian fantasy castle of **Coedmore**, on the opposite bank, are inspiring.

A footpath runs down from the castle to the river's edge and an exhibition at the quay about local industries – coracles included – which also covers the story of America-bound emigrants leaving from Cardigan. Guided two-hour Canadian **canoe trips** leave from the quay in summer.

Cenarth and Dre-Fach Felindre

A tourist magnet since it was swooped on by nineteenth-century Romantics and artists, **CENARTH**, five miles east of Cilgerran, is a pleasant spot, but hardly merits the mass interest that it receives. The village's main asset, its **waterfalls**, are close to the main road, connected by a path from opposite the *White Hart* pub. This runs past the **National Coracle Centre** (Easter–Oct Mon–Fri & Sun 10.30am–5.30pm; £2.50), a small museum with displays of original coracles from all over the world, before continuing to a restored seventeenth-century flour mill by the falls' edge.

The area's prolific past as a weaving centre is best seen at the **Museum of the Welsh Woollen Industry** (April–Sept Mon–Sat 10am–5pm; Oct–March closed Sat; £3), in the village of **Dre-Fach Felindre**, eight miles southeast of Cenarth, which once had over forty working mills.

Lampeter

Twenty miles east of Cenarth, **LAMPETER** (Llanbedr Pont Steffan) is the home of possibly the most remote university in Britain. St David's University College, now a constituent of the University of Wales, was Wales's first university college, founded in 1822 by the Bishop of St David's to aid Welsh students who couldn't afford the trip to England to receive a full education. With a healthy student population and large numbers of resident hippies, the small town is well geared up for young people and visitors.

There's not a great deal to see in Lampeter, and what you are able to visit is fairly low-key. **Harford Square** forms the hub of the town. Around the corner, at 2 Bridge St, is **Celtic Edge**, a showcase for local artists' work at the back of the Mulberry Bush health-food shop, which has a good bulletin board. The main buildings of the **University College** lie off College Street, and include a quadrangle modelled on an Oxbridge college and the motte of Lampeter's long-vanished castle – looking incongruous amidst such order. The High Street is the most architecturally distinguished part of town, its eighteenth-century coaching inn, the *Black Lion*, dominating the streetscape; you can see its old stables and coach house through an archway.

There is a basic **tourist office** in the new civic buildings at the back of Market Street (Mon–Fri 9am–5pm; ☎01570/422718). *Haulfan*, 6 Station Terrace, behind University College (☎01570/422718; ②), is the best **B&B**, or you could try the recently refurbished *Black Lion*, High Street (☎01570/422172; ④). Just off the B4343 is one of the area's best farmhouse B&Bs, at *Pentre Farm*, near Llanfair Clydogau, five miles from Lampeter (☎01570/493313; ③). The nearest **campsite** is five miles northeast, at Moorlands, near Llangybi (☎01570/493543). There are plenty of fine **places to eat** in town. *Lloyds* is an upmarket fish-and-chip restaurant in Bridge Street; the *Cottage Garden* restaurant, opposite the University, on College Street, is cheap and popular with students, as is the *King's Arms*, on Bridge Street, a small stone pub with well-kept beer. Don't miss *Conti's Café*, on Harford Square, a wonderfully timewarped place renowned for its home-made ice-cream. Just south of town, where the A485 joins the A482, the *Cwmann Tavern* is the best bet for catching the extremely lively local **music** scene.

Strata Florida Abbey

Twenty miles northeast of Lampeter, the mighty **Strata Florida Abbey** (May–Sept 10am–5pm; Oct–April open access; £2; CADW) dominates the bucolic Ystrad Fflur, the Valley of the Flowers. This Cistercian abbey was founded in 1164, swiftly growing into a centre for milling, farming and weaving, and becoming an important political centre for Wales. In 1238, Llywelyn the Great, whose conquering exploits throughout the rest of Wales had brought him to the peak of the Welsh feudal pyramid, summoned the lesser Welsh princes here. He was near death, and worried that his work of unifying Wales under one ruler would disintegrate, so he commanded the assembled princes to pay homage not just to him but also to his son, Dafydd, so sealing the succession. The church here was vast – larger than the cathedral at St David's – and, although very little survived Henry VIII's Dissolution of the monasteries, the huge Norman west doorway gives some idea of its dimensions. Fragments of one-time side chapels include beautifully tiled medieval floors, and there's also a serene cemetery, but it's really the abbey's position that impresses most, in glorious rural solitude amongst wide open skies and fringed with a scoop of sheep-spattered hills. A sinewy yew tree reputedly shades the spot where Dafydd ap Gwilym, fourteenth-century bard and contemporary of Chaucer, is buried.

Aberystwyth and around

The liveliest seaside resort in Wales, **ABERYSTWYTH** is an essential stop along the Ceredigion coast. Being rooted in all aspects of Welsh culture, it is possibly the most enjoyable and relaxed place to gain an insight into the national psyche. As the capital of sparsely populated mid-Wales, and with one of the most prestigious colleges of the University of Wales in the town, there are plenty of cultural and entertainment diversions here, as well as an array of Victorian and Edwardian seaside trappings. In 1907, the National Library was inaugurated, and the Cymdeithas yr Iaith (Welsh Language Society) was founded here in 1963. Aberystwyth's politics are firmly radical Welsh, and in a country that still struggles with its inherent conservatism, the town is a fresh blast of air.

The Town

With two long, gentle bays curving around between rocky heads, Aberystwyth's position is hard to beat. **Constitution Hill** (430ft), at the north end of the long Promenade, rises sharply away from the rocky beach. It is a favourite jaunt, crowned with a tatty jumble of amenities – café, picnic area, telescopes and an octagonal **camera obscura** (Easter–Oct daily 10am–5.30pm; free) – reached on foot or by the clanking 1896 **cliff**

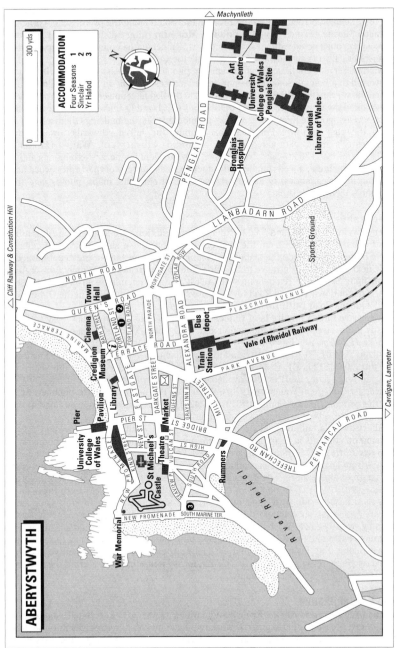

ABERYSTWYTH

△ Machynlleth

300 yds
0

ACCOMMODATION
Four Seasons   1
Sinclair   2
Yr Hafod   3

N

◁ Cliff Railway & Constitution Hill

Art
Centre

University
College of Wales
Penglais Site

National
Library of Wales

PENGLAIS ROAD

Bronglais
Hospital

LLANBADARN ROAD

Sports Ground

NORTH ROAD

Town
Hall

QUEEN'S ROAD

NORTHGATE ST

POPLAR ROW

PLASCRUG AVENUE

Cinema

MARINE TERRACE

BATH STREET

PORTLAND ST

PORTLAND ROAD

NORTH PARADE

ALEXANDRA ROAD

Bus
depot

Credigion
Museum

TERRACE ROAD

Vale of Rheidol Railway

Library

EASTGATE

DARKGATE STREET

QUEENS ST

Train
Station

PARK AVENUE

Pier

Pavilion

PIER ST

NEW ST

Market

GRAYS INN RD

MILL STREET

University
College
of Wales

KING STREET

NEW PROMENADE

VULCAN ST

BRIDGE ST

HIGH ST

TREFECHAN RD

PENPARCAU ROAD

St Michael's
Castle

Theatre

SOUTH ROAD

BAVIEW PL

Rummers

River Rheidol

War Memorial

NEW PROMENADE

SOUTH MARINE TER.

▽ Cardigan, Lampeter

railway (Easter–Oct daily 10am–6pm; £2 return) from the grand terminus building at the top of Queen Street, behind the Promenade. South along the promenade – officially called Marine Terrace – the **Ceredigion Museum** (Mon–Sat 10am–5pm; £1) houses cosy reconstructed cottages, a dairy and a nineteenth-century pharmacy in the atmospherically ornate Edwardian music hall, the Coliseum.

Marine Terrace continues past the spindly **pier** to a John Nash-designed **villa**, later converted to a hotel to soak up the anticipated masses arriving on the new railway line. When the venture failed, the building was sold to the fledgling university. The Promenade cuts around the front of the building to the ruins of Edward I's thirteenth-century **Castle** (free access), notable more for its breezy position than for the buildings themselves.

To the east of town, Penglais Road climbs the hill northwards towards the **University**'s main campus and the **National Library of Wales** (Mon–Fri 9.30am–6pm, Sat 9.30am–5pm; free), which has excellent temporary exhibitions and **A Nation's Heritage**, a well-rounded introduction to the history of the written word and printing in Wales, shown in an absorbing range of old texts, maps, photos, and the Morgan's 1588 Welsh Bible.

Practicalities

Aberystwyth's mainline and Vale of Rheidol **train stations** are adjacent on Alexandra Road, a ten-minute walk from the seafront on the southern side of the town centre. Local **buses** stop outside the station, with long-distance ones using the depot immediately next door, by the entrance to the park. The busy **tourist office** (daily: July & Aug 10am–6pm; Sept–June 10am–5pm; ☎01970/612125) is a ten-minute stroll from the station, straight down Terrace Road towards the seafront. On Your Bike, in the Old Police Yard, Queens Road (☎01970/626996), does bike rental.

Aberystwyth has hundreds of **places to stay**, so beds are generally easy to find, mostly in the streets around the station and along South Marine Terrace, where you'll find *Yr Hafod*, at no. 1 (☎01970/617579; ②). The intimate *Sinclair* guest house, 43 Portland St (☎01970/615158; ②), is another good choice. *Four Seasons*, 50–54 Portland St (☎01970/612120; ④), is an upmarket Victorian town house behind the seafront. Outside term time, B&B is also available on the Penglais and seafront sites of the University College of Wales (☎01970/621960; ②). The nearest place to pitch a **tent** is the *Aberystwyth Holiday Village* (☎01970/624211), off the main Penparcau Road to the south of town, a twenty-minute walk from the station.

Aberystwyth's cultural and gastronomic life is an ebullient, all-year-round affair, thriving on students in term-time and visitors in the summer. Just behind the market, *Gannets Bistro*, at 7 St James Square (closed Tues), creates imaginative, inexpensive dishes from local farm and sea produce. *Y Graig*, 34 Pier St, is a trendy wholefood **café** with a great atmosphere. The delicious, fresh food at the moderate *Yoskins*, 49 North Parade (☎01970/615374), makes for a superb treat. The *Castle Hotel*, South Road, doubles as a harbourside **pub**, built in the style of an ornate Victorian gin palace, and serves vegetarian specialities; *Y Cŵps* (Coopers Arms), Llanbadarn Road, is fun and friendly, with regular Welsh folk and jazz nights. Many pubs open until 1am in the summer. For a slice of Edwardian gentility, take afternoon tea in any of the seafront hotels along the Promenade, and visit the **Aberystwyth Arts Centre**, at the University's Penglais site (☎01970/623232), for art-house cinema, touring theatre and wide-ranging temporary exhibitions.

The Vale of Rheidol

Inland from Aberystwyth, the River Rheidol winds its way up to a secluded, wooded valley, where occasional old industrial workings have moulded themselves into the contours, rising up past waterfalls and minute villages to Devil's Bridge. It's a glorious route, and by far the best way to see it is on board one of the trains of the **Vale of Rheidol railway** (April–Oct; £10.50 return), a narrow-gauge steam train that wheezes its way along sheer rock faces from the terminus in Aberystwyth to Devil's Bridge. It was built in 1902, ostensibly for the valley's lead mines but with a canny eye on its tourist potential as well, and has run ever since. Part way along, a punishing path on the north side of the river from the Rhiwfron stop scrambles up over the mines for a mile to the sombre little village of Ystumtuen, a former lead-mining community whose school has been converted into a basic **youth hostel** (☎01970/890693). From here it's a couple of miles' walk to Devil's Bridge.

Folk legend, idyllic beauty and travellers' lore combine at **DEVIL'S BRIDGE** (Pontarfynach), twelve miles east of Aberystwyth, a tiny settlement built solely for the growing visitor trade of the last few hundred years. Be warned, however, that Devil's Bridge is a seriously popular day excursion – in order to escape some of the inevitable congestion, it is wisest to come here at the beginning or end of the day, or out of season.

The main attraction here is the bridge itself, which is actually three stacked bridges spanning the chasm of the churning River Mynach, yards upstream from its confluence with the Rheidol. The road bridge in front of the striking, but distinctly antiquated, *Hafod Arms* **hotel** (☎01970/890693; ④) is the most modern of the three, dating from 1901. Immediately below it, wedged between the rock faces, are the stone bridge from 1753 and, at the bottom, the original bridge, dating from the eleventh century and reputedly built by the monks of Strata Florida Abbey (see p.732). For a remarkable view of the bridges, you have to enter the turnstile (£1) downstream of the bridge and head down slippery steps to the deep cleft of the **Punch Bowl**, where the water pounds and hurtles through the gap crowned by the bridges. More dramatic still, the gate on the other side (Easter–Oct daily 9.30am–5.30pm; £2.20; rest of year and evenings access through turnstiles; £2) leads west to a path that tumbles down into the valley below the bridges, descending ultimately to the crashing **Mynach Falls**. The scenery here is magnificent: sharp, wooded slopes rise away from the frothing river and distant mountain peaks surface on the horizon. Platforms overlook the series of falls, from where a set of steep steps takes you further down to a footbridge dramatically spanning the river at the bottom of the falls.

There's a **campsite** – *Woodlands Caravan Park* (☎01970/890233) – by the petrol station, just beyond the bridges.

Machynlleth and around

The flat river plain and rolling hills of **Dyfi Valley** lay justifiable claims to being "one of the greenest corners of Europe", an area replete with B&Bs and other businesses started up by idealistic New Agers who have flocked to this corner of Wales since the late 1960s. The focal point is the genial town of **MACHYNLLETH** (pronounced Ma-hun-thleth), often referred to as "Mach", a candidate for the Welsh capital in the 1950s and site of Owain Glyndŵr's embryonic fifteenth-century Welsh parliament. In the hills to the north, the renowned, self-contained **Centre for Alternative Technology** runs on co-operative lines and makes for one of the most interesting days out in Wales.

It is difficult to imagine that the nation's capital could have consisted essentially of just two streets. The wide main street, **Heol Maengwyn**, is busiest on Wednesdays, when a lively market springs up out of nowhere; **Heol Penrallt** intersects at a fussy clocktower. Glyndŵr's partly fifteenth-century **Parliament House** (Easter–Sept daily 10am–5pm; Oct–Easter by appointment, call ☎01654/702827; free) sits halfway along Heol Maengwyn, a modest looking black and white fronted building, concealing a large interior. Displays chart the course of Glyndŵr's life, his military campaign, his downfall and

OWAIN GLYNDŴYR

No name is so frequently invoked in Wales as that of **Owain Glyndŵyr**, a potent figure-head of Welsh nationalism since he rose up against the occupying English in the early fif-teenth century. Little is known about the real Glyndŵyr, although he is described in Shakespeare's *Henry IV, Part I* as "not in the roll of common men". There's little doubt that the charismatic Owain fulfilled many of the mystical medieval prophecies about the rising up of the red dragon. Born in the late fourteenth century to an aristocratic family, he had a conventional upbringing, part of it in England studying English in London, where he became a loyal and distinguished soldier of the English king. He returned to Wales to take up his claim as Prince of Wales, being directly descended from the princes of Powys and Cyfeiliog, but became the focus of a rebellion born of discontent simmer-ing since Edward I's stringent policies of subordinating Wales.

Goaded by a parochial land dispute in North Wales in which the courts failed to back him, Glyndŵyr garnered four thousand supporters and declared anew that he was Prince of Wales. He attacked Ruthin, and then Denbigh, Rhuddlan, Flint, Hawarden and Oswestry, before encountering English resistance at Welshpool, but whole swathes of North Wales were his for the taking. The English king, Henry IV, despatched troops and rapidly drew up a range of severely punitive laws against the Welsh, even outlawing Welsh-language bards and singers. Battles continued to rage until, by the end of 1403, Glyndŵyr controlled most of Wales.

In 1404, Glyndŵyr assembled a parliament at Machynlleth, drawing up mutual recog-nition treaties with France and Spain, and being crowned king of a free Wales. A second parliament in Harlech took place a year later, with Glyndŵyr making plans to carve up England and Wales into three as part of an alliance against the English king. The English army, however, attacked the Welsh uprising with increased vigour, and the Tripartite Indenture was never realized. From then on, Glyndŵyr lost battles, ground and castles, and was forced into hiding, dying, it is thought, in Herefordshire. The draconian anti-Welsh laws stayed in place until the accession to the English throne of Henry VII, who had Welsh origins, in 1485. Wales became subsumed into English custom and law, and Glyndŵyr's uprising became an increasingly powerful symbol of frustrated Welsh inde-pendence. Even in the 1980s, the shadowy organization that razed several English holi-day homes took the name Meibion Glyndŵyr – the Sons of Glyndŵyr.

the 1404 parliament, when he controlled almost all of what we now know as Wales. The sorriest tales are from 1405 onwards when tactical errors and the sheer brute might of the English forced a swift retreat and an ignominious end to the greatest Welsh uprising.

On the Aberystwyth road, at Y Plas, the new **Celtica** exhibition (daily 10am–6pm; last admission 4.40pm; £4.95) combines audio-visual trickery with tales of the Celtic peoples in a thunderous romp through history. The overall effect is certainly impres-sive, even if the Welsh tendency for sentimentality is evident on occasion. Upstairs are more detailed exhibitions relating to Celtic history and language. On the other side of the central clocktower, on Heol Penrallt, is **Y Tabernacl** (Mon–Sat 10am–4pm; free), a serene old chapel whose spectacular new sculpted entrance by David Thomas is an audacious addition to the Machynlleth streetscape. The chapel has now been convert-ed into a cultural centre, with a programme of temporary exhibitions augmenting the small collection of the **Wales Museum of Modern Art**. It also hosts films, theatre and the annual **Gŵyl Machynlleth** festival in mid- to late August, with a combination of classical music, debate, theatre and some folk music.

The old Victorian **train station** and **bus stop** are both a five-minute walk from the clocktower up Heol Penrallt and its continuation, Heol Doll. The **tourist office** (daily: Easter–Sept 9.30am–6pm; Oct–Easter 10am–5pm; ☎01654/702401) is next to the Glyndŵyr Parliament House on Heol Maengwyn. **Bike rental** is available across the road from Greenstyles Cycles, 4 Heol Maengwyn (☎01654/703543).

B&B **accommodation** includes the *Maenllwyd*, on Newtown Road, the eastern extension of Heol Maengwyn (☎01654/702928; ②), and *Gwelfryn*, in the town centre at 6 Greenfields, Bank Street (☎01654/702532; ①). Among the hotels are the grand *Wynnstay Arms,* on Heol Maengwyn (☎01654/702941; ③), and the earthier *Glyndŵyr Hotel*, on Heol Doll, towards the station (☎01654/703989; ②). There's a lovely **camp-site** three miles north, opposite the Centre for Alternative Technology, at *Llwyngwern Farm* (☎01654/702492), or a very simple tent site at *Plas Forge* (☎01654/703228), a mile or so out on the road to Dylife. There are plenty of **cafés**, **restaurants** and **pubs** in town, including a great wholefood shop and café at *Siop y Chwarel*, opposite the post office on Heol Maengwyn. The *Wynnstay Arms* does reasonable evening meals, and the *Glyndŵyr*, on Heol Doll, has live music at the weekend. The bar at *Y Tabernacl* is the most arty hangout in town.

Centre for Alternative Technology

Since its foundation in the middle of the oil crisis of 1974, the **Centre for Alternative Technology** – or Canolfan y Dechnoleg Amgen (daily: April–Oct 10am–7pm; £6.90; Oct–March 10am–5pm; £4.90; discounts for visitors arriving by bike or public transport) – just over two miles north of Machynlleth off the A487, has become one of the biggest attractions in Wales. A former derelict slate quarry, covering seven acres, over the last 25 years the centre has become an entirely self-sufficient community, generating its own power and water from onsite equipment. It's not a museum, but it is open to the public. It's a fascinating place to visit, combining earnest education about renewable resources and practices with flashes of pzazz, such as the water-powered cliff rail line (April–Oct) that whisks the visitor 197ft up from the car park. Whole houses have been constructed to showcase energy-saving ideas and the fifty-strong staff – who all live communally and receive identical (very low) wages – are ebullient and helpful in explaining the ideas. There are also organic gardens, beehives, a water wheel, an adventure playground and numerous hands-on exhibits. The wholefood **restaurant** and adjoining bookshop are excellent.

The Cadair Idris area

The southern coastal reaches of Snowdonia National Park are almost entirely dominat-ed by **Cadair Idris** (2930ft), a five-peaked massif standing in isolation, which has some demanding but very rewarding walks. Tennyson claimed never to have seen "anything more awful than the great veil of rain drawn straight over Cader Idris"; catch it on a good day, and the views are stunning. During the last Ice Age, the heads of glaciers scalloped out two huge cwms (steep-sided horseshoe valleys) from Cadair Idris's dis-tinctive dome, leaving thousand-foot cliffs dropping away on all sides to cool, clear lakes. The largest, the **Chair of Idris**, may take its name from the seat-like rock for-mation on the summit ridge, where, it is said, anyone spending the night will become a poet, go mad or die.

To the north lies the Mawddach, which Wordsworth found to be "a sublime estu-ary" – romantic hyperbole perhaps, but these broad tidal flats gouging deep into the heart of the mid-Wales mountains create dramatic backdrops from every angle. The sands here contain gold, though not enough for mining company Rio Tinto Zinc, who thankfully abandoned their plans to dredge for the stuff in the early 1970s. Spasmodic outbursts of gold fever still occasionally hit the region's main town, **Dolgellau**, but most people are content to come here for some excellent walking up Cadair Idris and along the estuary around **Barmouth**, or to ride the **Talyllyn Railway**, one of Wales's most popular narrow-gauge lines, to the languid pleasures of the Talyllyn and Dysynni valleys.

Tywyn and around

TYWYN is primarily of interest as a base for the **Talyllyn** and **Dysynni valleys**, although the town does have miles of sandy beach and the five-foot-high **Ynysmaengwyn**, or St Cadfan's Stone, within the Norman nave of the **Church of St Cadfan** (daily 9am–5pm; later in summer; church tour Wed 5pm), which bears the earliest example of written Welsh, dating back to around 650 AD.

Tywyn's three main roads meet at the joint **train station** and main **bus stop**, a short walk from the **tourist office**, opposite the entrance to the leisure centre on High Street (Easter–Oct daily 10am–1pm & 2–6pm; ☎01654/710070), and, two hundred yards to the south, the Talyllyn narrow-gauge train station (Tywyn Wharf). The Talyllyn Valley is served by the #30 **bus**, running from Tywyn to Abergynolwyn, continuing to Minffordd (where you can catch #2 to Dolgellau) and Machynlleth. Decent **accommodation** can be found at the *Ivy Guest House*, High Street (☎01654/711058; ②), opposite the tourist office, or the cheaper, non-smoking *Glenydd Guest House*, 2 Maes Newydd (☎01654/711373; ②), two hundred yards from the beach off Pier Road. The handiest **campsite** is *Ynysmaengwyn Caravan Park*, a mile out on the Dolgellau road (☎01654/710684; closed Oct–March). The best **eating** in town is upstairs at moderately priced, non-smoking *The Proper Gander*, High St.

The Talyllyn and Dysynni valleys

The **Talyllyn narrow-gauge railway** (April–Oct 2–8 daily; return £8.50; ☎01654/710472) belches seven miles inland through the delightful wooded Talyllyn Valley to Nant Gwernol. From 1866 to 1946, the rail line was used to haul slate to Tywyn Wharf station. Just four years after its closure, enthusiasts restarted services, making this the world's first volunteer-run railway. At a leisurely 15mph, the round trip takes two hours, longer if you get off to take in some fine broadleaf forest walks. The best of these starts at Dolgoch Falls station, where three well-marked trails (maximum 1hr) lead off to the lower, mid and upper falls. At the end of the line, more woodland walks take you around the site of the old slate quarries.

From Tywyn, the road runs parallel to the Talyllyn Railway, meeting it at Dolgoch Falls, a couple of miles short of the largest settlement, **Abergynolwyn**, comprising a few dozen quarry workers' houses and two pubs. The Dysynni Valley branches northwest here, but Talyllyn Valley continues northeast to **Tal-y-llyn Lake** (Llyn Mwyngil) and the fifteenth-century **St Mary's**, a fine example of a small Welsh parish church, unusual because of its chancel arch painted with an alternating grid of red and white roses, separated by grotesque bosses.

The **Dysynni Valley** has more to offer in the way of sights, though the lack of public transport makes it difficult to get to. A mile and a half northwest of Abergynolwyn, a side road cuts northeast to the hamlet of **Llanfihangel-y-Pennant** and the scant, but impressive, ruins of **Castell-y-Bere** (free access; CADW), a fortress built by Llywelyn the Great in 1221 to protect the mountain passes. One of the most massive of the Welsh castles, it was besieged twice before being consigned to seven centuries of obscurity and decay. There's still plenty to poke around, with large slabs of the main towers still standing, but it's primarily a great place just to sit gazing at Cadair Idris, or three miles seaward to **Craig yr Aderyn** (Birds' Rock), a 760-foot-high cliff where thirty breeding pairs of cormorants have remained loyal to the spot as, over the centuries, the sea has receded. Also worth seeing is the fabulous three-dimensional patchwork map of the Dysynni Valley that can be found just up the road in the vestry of Llanfihangel-y-Pennant church.

Good **places to stay** include *Tan-y-Coed-Uchaf* (☎01654/782228; ②; closed Dec–Feb), a superb farmhouse B&B close to Dolgoch Falls; the excellent *Riverside*

Guesthouse, Cwrt, in Abergynolwyn (☎01654/782235; ②); or the *Minffordd Hotel* (☎01654/761665; ⑥; closed Jan & Feb), an eighteenth-century farmhouse and coaching inn by Tal-y-llyn Lake, open to non-residents for moderately priced traditional British **dinners** (Thurs–Sat). There is a basic **campsite** at *Cedris Farm*, a mile northeast of Abergynolwyn (☎01654/782280), and plenty of others dotted about the two valleys.

Dolgellau

Its distance from England and its historical position in the heartland of Welsh nationalism should make **DOLGELLAU** (pronounced Dol-geth-laye) the most Welsh of towns, but the town's granite architecture draws more from nineteenth-century England, with a dour series of small neo-Georgian squares all bearing English names. Victorian tourists came to marvel at Cadair Idris and the Mawddach Estuary, still the best policy, as the town has little to offer beyond the **Quaker Interpretive Centre**, above the tourist office. This details the lives of Quakers forced by persecution to seek a better life in Pennsylvania, where some towns still bear Welsh names: Bangor, Bryn Mawr and others.

Dolgellau has no train station but is well served by **buses**, all of which pull into the central Eldon Square, close by the **tourist office** (Easter–Oct daily 10am–1pm & 2–6pm; Nov–Easter Mon & Thurs–Sun 10am–5pm; ☎01341/422888). Central **accommodation** is best found at the *Aber Café*, Smithfield Street (☎01341/422460; ②), and the good-value *Clifton House Hotel*, Smithfield Square (☎01341/422554; ③). Outside

---

▌ WALKS AROUND DOLGELLAU ▐

Dolgellau is a good base for walks, whether fairly easy rambles, like the first two described here, or more strenuous mountain hiking. For the Cadair Idris ascent, youll need a map and walking equipment. You're best off with the 1:25,000 OS *Outdoor Leisure* map #23, "Cadair Idris & Bala Lake", though the 1:50,000 map #124, "Dolgellau", will do.

Torrent Walk
Victorians seldom missed the lowland, beechwood Torrent Walk (2 miles; 100ft ascent; 1hr) which follows the course of the River Clywedog as it carves its way through bedrock to the *Clywedog Tea Garden*, where home-baked scones are served beside the river. Bus #2 takes you the two miles east along the A470 to the start, by the junction of the B4416.

Precipice Walk
Nowadays, more people head for the not remotely precipitous Precipice Walk (3–4 miles; negligible ascent; 2hr), a circuit around the bracken and heather-covered Foel Cynach, with great views along the Mawddach Estuary and towards the thousand-foot ramparts of Cadair Idris. Best done in the late afternoon, when the sun is low on the estuary, the walk is fairly well signposted from the start, three miles north of Dolgellau along the Llanfachreth road, which turns off the A494 by Big Bridge. Bus #33 runs to the start three times on Tuesdays and Fridays only.

Pony Path
More ambitious Victorians climbed **Cadair Idris** on the since-eroded Fox's Path, now widely ignored in favour of the straightforward, classic Pony Path (6–7 miles; 2500ft ascent; 4–5hr), starting three miles up Cadair Road in the car park at Ty Nant. As you begin by the sign near the telephone box, the view to the craggy flanks of the massif are tremendous, but they disappear as you climb steeply to the col, where a left turn leads to the summit shelter on **Penygadair** (2930ft).

town, the eighteenth-century *Tyddyn Mawr Farmhouse*, Islawrdref (☎01341/422331; ③), stands on the slopes of Cadair Idris at the foot of the Pony Path, while the superb seventeenth-century *George III Hotel*, Penmaenpool (☎01341/422525; ⑤), overlooks the Mawddach Estuary, two miles west of Dolgellau. The tent-only *Bryn-y-Gwyn* **campsite**, Cader Road (☎01341/422733), is less than a mile southeast of town. There's a fair choice for **eating** in Dolgellau: the best bets are the creative and moderately priced *Bwyty Dylanwad Da*, 2 Smithfield St (☎01341/422870), and the *Tyn-y-Groes Hotel*, Glanllwyd (☎01341/440275), four miles north of town in the Coed y Brenin forest, with good beer, fine bar meals and à la carte dinners. Back in town, the *Tafarn Caetanws*, Smithfield Street, is a great **pub** for food and occasional music and comedy. Dolgellau's Sesiwn Fawr folk and rock **festival** (mid-July) has rapidly grown into one of Wales's finest.

Barmouth and around

The best approach to **BARMOUTH** (Abermaw) is from the south, where the Cambrian coast rail line sweeps across the Mawddach River from tiny Fairbourne, over 113 rickety-looking wooden spans. It's still the haunt of English holidaymakers from the midlands, who fashioned Barmouth as a sea-bathing resort in the nineteenth century, but also warrants some attention for breezy rambles on the cliffs of **Dinas Oleu**, above the town, and a great walk around the mouth of the estuary (see box below). Central attractions don't extend beyond the **Tŷ Gwyn Museum** (July–Sept Tues–Sun 10.30am–5pm; free), a medieval tower house – now a Tudor museum – where Henry VII's uncle, Jasper Tudor, is thought to have plotted Richard III's downfall; and the **Tŷ Crwn Roundhouse**, on the hill behind (same times) which once acted as a lockup for drunken sailors.

Buses from Harlech and Dolgellau stop in the leisure centre car park by the train station, just a few yards from the **tourist office** on Station Road (Easter–Oct daily 10am–6pm; ☎01341/280787). **Accommodation** is plentiful, and best at *The Gables*, Mynach Road (☎01341/280553; ①), ten minutes' walk north of town and particularly welcoming to walkers, or the *Wave Crest Hotel*, 8 North Parade (☎01341/280330; ②). The closest of a long string of **campsites** is *Hendre Mynach*, Llanaber Road (☎01341/280262; closed Nov–Feb), a mile north of town and just off the beach. Basic **cafés** are plentiful, though for just a little more money you can get mammoth French sticks and pancakes at the *Anchor Restaurant*, The Quay, and good pizzas next door at the *Isis*. Close to The Quay, in Church Street, *The Last Inn*, in a former cobbler's shop, serves good **pub** meals.

WALKING THE BARMOUTH–FAIRBOURNE LOOP

The best lowland walk in the Cambrian Coast region, the **Barmouth–Fairbourne Loop** (5 miles; 300ft ascent; 2–3hr) is a fine way to spend an afternoon with impressive mountain scenery, and estuarine and coastal views all the way. The walking component can be virtually eradicated by using both the mainline and Fairbourne railways. The route first crosses the estuary rail bridge (30p) to Morfa Mawddach mainline station, then follows the lane to the main road, crossing it onto a footpath that loops behind a small wooded hill to Pant Einion Hall, then follows another lane back to the main road near Fairbourne. In Fairbourne, turn north, either walking along the beach to the quay at the end of the spit or catching the **Fairbourne Railway** (Easter–Oct 3–6 daily) to the **passenger ferry** (Easter–Oct; hourly) across the estuary mouth back to Barmouth.

Harlech

It's hard to dislike **HARLECH**, ten miles north of Barmouth, with its time-worn castle dramatically clinging to its rocky outcrop, and the town cloaking the ridge behind commanding one of Wales's finest views over Cardigan Bay to the Llŷn. There are good beaches nearby, and the town's twisting, narrow streets harbour places where you can eat and sleep surprisingly well for such a small place.

Harlech's substantially complete **Castle** (April–Oct daily 9.30am–6.30pm; Nov–March Mon–Sat 9.30am–4pm, Sun 11am–4pm; £3; CADW) sits on its 200-foot-high bluff, a site chosen by Edward I for one more link in his magnificent chain of fortresses. Begun in 1285, it was built of a hard Cambrian rock, known as Harlech grit, hewn from the moat. The sea, which originally protected one side of the fortress, has now receded, leaving the castle dominating a stretch of duned coastline. Harlech withstood a siege in 1295, but was taken by Owain Glyndŵr in 1404. The young Henry VII withstood a seven-year siege at the hands of the Yorkists until 1468, when the castle was again taken. It fell into ruin, but was put back into service for the king during the Civil War; in March 1647, it was the last Royalist castle to fall. The first defensive line comprised the three successive pairs of gates and portcullises built between the two massive half-round towers of the **gatehouse**, where an exhibition now outlines the castle's history. Much of the castle's outermost ring has been destroyed, leaving only the twelve-foot-thick curtain walls rising up forty feet to the exposed battlements. Only the towering gatehouse prevents you from walking the full circuit.

Harlech's **train station** is on the main A496, overlooked by the castle. Most **buses** call both here and on High Street, a few yards from the **tourist office** (Easter–Oct daily 10am–6pm; ☎01766/780658). The pick of the local **places to stay** are the friendly *Aris Guesthouse*, 4 Pen y Bryn (☎01766/780409; ③), just above the village, past the *Lion Hotel*, and the cosy, informal *Castle Cottage* hotel, on Pen Llech, near the castle (☎01766/780479; ③), which has the trappings of a place charging twice as much. Other possibilities include the *Plas Newydd* youth hostel (☎01341/241287), three miles south in Llanbedr (buses #38 & #94), where the lane also heads west to the sprawling **camping** resort at Shell Island (☎01341/241453), great for camp fires in the dunes and walks on the beach. If you want to camp in Harlech itself, head for the *Min y Don* campsite, Beach Road (☎01766/780286; closed Oct–Easter), three minutes' walk from the beach; take the first right out of the station. There are some wonderful **places to eat** on High Street, including the inexpensive but licensed *Plâs Café*, with a good range of food and fabulous views from the garden and conservatory; the bistro-style *Yr Ogof*, where you'll find a good-value range of inventive vegetarian and meat dishes; and the classy, modern *Castle Cottage*.

travel details

Trains

Aberystwyth to: Birmingham (6 daily; 3hr); Machynlleth (7 daily; 30min); Shrewsbury (6 daily; 2hr); Welshpool (6 daily; 1hr 30min).

Barmouth to: Harlech (6 daily; 30min); Machynlleth (6 daily; 1hr); Porthmadog (6 daily; 45min).

Harlech to: Barmouth (6 daily; 30min); Birmingham (5 daily; 4hr 15min); Machynlleth (6 daily; 1hr 20min); Porthmadog (8 daily; 20min).

Machynlleth to: Aberystwyth (7 daily; 30min); Barmouth (6 daily; 1hr); Birmingham (7 daily; 2hr 30min); Harlech (5 daily; 1hr 20min); Porthmadog (6 daily; 1hr 45min); Shrewsbury (7 daily; 2hr).

Buses

Aberaeron to: Aberystwyth (hourly; 40min); Cardigan (6 daily; 1hr 10min); Carmarthen (5 daily; 1hr 45min); Lampeter (7 daily; 40min); New Quay (hourly; 20min).

Aberystwyth to: Aberaeron (hourly; 40min); Caernarfon (1 daily; 2hr 40min); Cardigan (5 daily; 2hr); Carmarthen (1 daily; 2hr 40min); Devil's Bridge (2 daily; 40min); Dolgellau (5 daily; 1hr 30min); Lampeter (5 daily; 1hr 30min); Machynlleth (5 daily; 45min); New Quay (hourly; 1hr).

Barmouth to: Bala (8 daily; 1hr); Blaenau Ffestiniog (4 daily; 1hr); Dolgellau (8 daily; 20min); Harlech (9 daily; 30min); Llangollen (7 daily; 1hr 50min); Wrexham (7 daily; 2hr 20min).

Cardigan to: Aberaeron (6 daily; 1hr 10min); Aberporth (hourly; 30min); Aberystwyth (5 daily; 2hr); Carmarthen (hourly; 1hr 30min); Fishguard (hourly; 50min); Newcastle Emlyn (hourly; 30min); Newport, Pembrokeshire (hourly; 30min); New Quay (hourly; 1hr).

Dolgellau to: Aberystwyth (5 daily; 1hr 30min); Bala (9 daily; 40min); Barmouth (8 daily; 20min); Blaenau Ffestiniog (3 daily; 50min); Caernarfon (4 daily; 1hr 40min); Llangollen (8 daily; 1hr 30min); Machynlleth (6 daily; 40min); Porthmadog (6 daily; 50min); Tywyn (6 daily; 50min); Wrexham (8 daily; 2hr).

Harlech to: Barmouth (9 daily; 30min); Blaenau Ffestiniog (4 daily; 40min).

Lampeter to: Aberaeron (7 daily; 40min); Aberystwyth (5 daily; 1hr 30min); Carmarthen (8 daily; 1hr 10min); Machynlleth (1 daily; 2hr 30min).

Machynlleth to: Aberystwyth (5 daily; 45min); Bala (4 daily; 1hr 20min); Cardiff (1 daily; 5hr 15min); Dolgellau (6 daily; 40min); Lampeter (1 daily; 2hr 30min); Llangollen (6 daily; 3hr); Porthmadog (4 daily; 1hr 45min); Tywyn (4–6 daily; 40min).

New Quay to: Aberaeron (hourly; 20min); Aberporth (hourly; 40min); Aberystwyth (hourly; 1hr); Cardigan (hourly; 1hr).

SNOWDONIA AND THE LLŶN

W ithout doubt, Snowdonia is the crowning glory of North Wales. This tightly packed bundle of soaring cliff faces, jagged peaks and plunging waterfalls measures little more than ten miles by ten, but packs enough mountain paths to keep even the most jaded walking enthusiast happy for weeks. The last Ice Age left a legacy of peaks ringed by cwms – huge hemispherical bites out of the mountainsides. The ranges were left separated by steep-sided valleys, a challenge for even the most light-footed climber. Even if lakeside ambles and rides on antiquated steam trains are more your style, you can't fail to appreciate the natural grandeur of the scenery, occasionally revealing an atmospheric Welsh castle ruin or decaying piece of quarrying equipment. The area's small settlements – well geared up for walking and other outdoor activities – make for lively bases, whether long-standing tourist towns like Betws-y-Coed and Llanberis, or old mining and quarry towns such as Beddgelert and Blaenau Ffestiniog.

Snowdonia is the heart – and undisputed highlight – of the massive **Snowdonia National Park** (Parc Cenedlaethol Eryri), an 840-square-mile area which extends north and south, beyond the bounds of Snowdonia and this chapter, to encompass the Rhinogs, Cadair Idris (see p.737) and 23 miles of superb coastal scenery. To the west, this coast is the highlight, in the gentle rockiness of the **Llŷn peninsula**, which juts out into the Irish Sea at almost a right angle to the Cambrian Coast. Here, Wales ends in a flourish of small coves and seafaring villages, offering almost unlimited rambling potential around the high-hedged lanes. Finally, roads loop back along the Llŷn to the tip of the north coast, where **Caernarfon** sits overshadowed by its stupendous castle.

ACCOMMODATION PRICE CODES

Throughout this guide, hotel and B&B accommodation is priced on a scale of ① to ⑨, the number indicating the **lowest price** you could expect to pay per night in that establishment for a **double room** in high season. The prices indicated by the codes are as follows:

① under £40	④ £60–70	⑦ £110–150
② £40–50	⑤ £70–90	⑧ £150–200
③ £50–60	⑥ £90–110	⑨ over £200

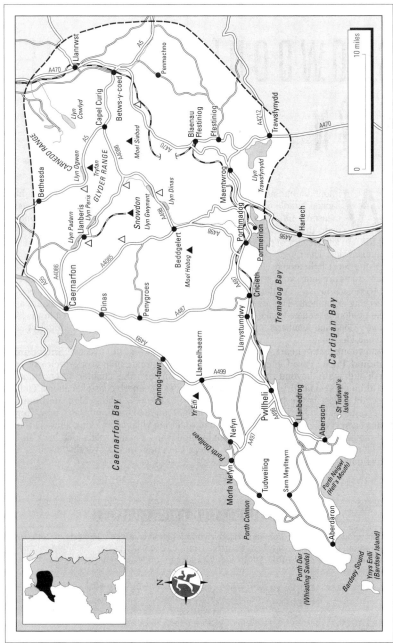

© Crown copyright

Snowdonia

What the coal valleys are to the south of the country, the mountains of **Snowdonia** (Yr Eryri) are to the north: the defining feature, not just in their physical form, but in the way they have shaped the communities within them. To Henry VIII's antiquarian, John Leland, the region seemed "horrible with the sight of bare stones"; now it is widely acclaimed as the most dramatic and alluring of all Welsh scenery, a compact, barren land of tortured ridges dividing glacial valleys, whose sheer faces belie the fact that the tallest peaks only just top three thousand feet. It was to this mountain fastness that Llywelyn ap Gruffydd, the last true Prince of Wales, retreated in 1277 after his first war with Edward I; it was also here that Owain Glyndŵr held on most tenaciously to his dream of regaining for the Welsh the title of Prince of Wales. Centuries later, the English came to remove the mountains: slate barons built huge fortunes from Welsh toil and reshaped the patterns of Snowdonian life forever, as men looking for steady work in the quarries left the hills and became town dwellers. By the mid-nineteenth century, those with the means began flocking here to marvel at the plunging waterfalls and walk the ever-widening paths to the mountaintops. Numbers have increased rapidly since then and thousands of hikers arrive every weekend for some of the country's best walks over steep, exacting and constantly varying terrain.

Not surprisingly, the **Snowdon** massif (Eryri) is the focus of the Snowdonia National Park, the first such area in Wales. Several of the ascent routes are superb, and you can always take the cog railway up to the summit café from **Llanberis**. But the other mountains are as good or better, often far less busy and giving unsurpassed views of Snowdon. The **Glyders** and **Tryfan** – best tackled from the **Ogwen Valley** – are particular favourites.

If you are serious about doing some **walking** – and some of the walks described here are serious, especially in bad weather (Snowdon gets 200 inches of rain a year) – you need a good map such as the 1:50,000 OS *Landranger* #115 or the 1:25,000 OS *Outdoor Leisure* #17; bear in mind that conditions, especially on higher ground, are notoriously changeable. Weather reports and walking conditions are often posted on the doors or noticeboards of outdoor shops and tourist offices.

But Snowdonia isn't all about walking. Small settlements are dotted in the valleys, usually coinciding with some enormous mine or quarry. Foremost among these are **Blaenau Ffestiniog**, the "Slate Capital of North Wales", where a mine opens its caverns for underground tours, and **Beddgelert** whose former copper mines are also open to the public. The only place of any size not associated with slate mining is **Betws-y-Coed**, a largely Victorian resort away from the higher peaks, and a springboard for the walkers' hamlets of **Capel Curig** and **Pen-y-Pass**.

Betws-y-Coed and around

Sprawled out across a flat plain at the confluence of the Conwy, Llugwy and Lledr valleys, **BETWS-Y-COED** (pronounced Betoos-er-Coyd), the much-vaunted "Gateway to Snowdonia", is hard to avoid. Its riverside setting, overlooked by the conifer-clad slopes of the Gwydyr forest, is undeniably appealing, and the town boasts the best selection of hotels and guest houses in the region, but after an hour mooching around the outdoor equipment shops and drinking tea you may well be left wondering what to do. For serious mountain walkers, the best advice is to continue on, but for everyone else there are some delightful – and fairly easy – strolls from town into the surrounding hills and river valleys. Particularly good are the two local beauty spots of the **Conwy** and **Swallow** falls, though these can get pretty congested in high summer.

This one-time lead-mining town remained a backwater until 1815 when, as part of his A5 toll road, Telford completed the graceful **Waterloo Bridge** (Y Bont Haearn),

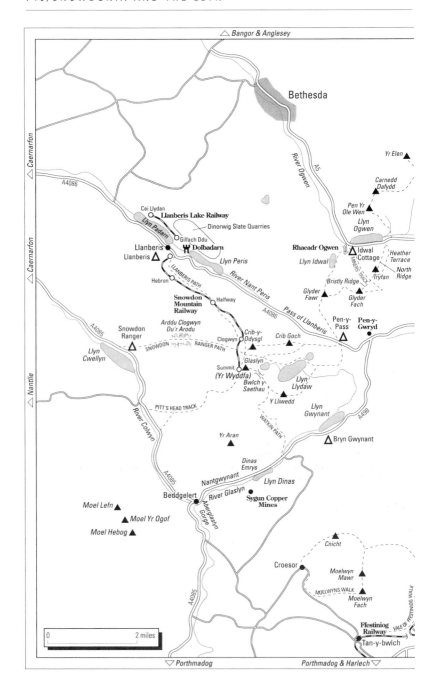

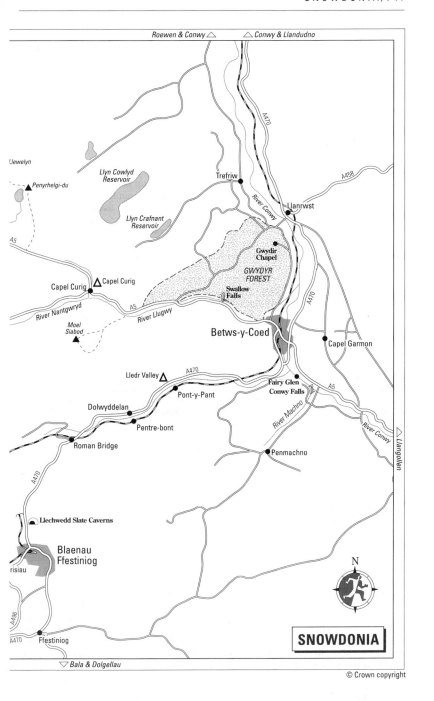

speeding access for the leisured classes already alerted to the town's beauty by J.M.W. Turner's landscapes. The arrival of the railway line in 1868 lifted its status from coaching station to genteel resort, an air the town tries to maintain, albeit without much success. By the station, the **Conwy Valley Railway Museum** (Easter–Oct daily 10.15am–5.30pm; Nov–Easter Sat & Sun 10.30am–4.30pm; £1) presents a fairly standard collection of memorabilia and shiny engines, enlivened by the chance of a short ride on a miniature train or tram. The **Motor Museum** (Easter–Oct daily 10am–6pm; £1.50), a couple of hundred yards away behind the tourist office, is little better, with a half-dozen classic bikes and fifteen cars, including a 1934 Bugatti Straight 8 and a Model T Ford.

Practicalities

The **train station**, for services from Llandudno Junction up the Conwy Valley and on to Blaenau Ffestiniog, is just a few paces across the grass from the **tourist office**, at Royal Oak Stables (daily: Easter–Oct 10am–6pm; Nov–Easter 9am–1pm & 2–4pm; ☎01690/710426), and the **bus stop**, outside St Mary's church, on the main street. Whether you're a beginner or intermediate climber, **scrambling**, **climbing** and **abseiling** courses can be arranged with Snowdonia Mountain Guides (☎01690/710720; £30–45 a day) – ask at the Climber and Rambler shop opposite Pont-y-Pair bridge for more information. **Mountain bikes** can be rented from Beics Betws, on Church Hill, at the top of the road beside the post office; permits and information on routes through the Gwydyr Forest are obtainable from the tourist office.

The town has plenty of **accommodation**, but has to cope with an ever-larger number of visitors pushing prices up in the summer, when you need to book ahead. The cheapest rooms are above the award-winning *Riverside Restaurant*, Holyhead Road, near the central Pont-y-Pair bridge (☎01690/710650; ①). *Glan Llugwy*, on the A5, a short way beyond Pont-y-Pair (☎01690/710592; ①), is another inexpensive option, while *Tŷ Gwyn*, also on the A5 (☎01690/710383; ③), is a prettified old coaching inn half a mile east of the centre, just over Waterloo Bridge. The luxury option is *Tan-y-Foel*, Capel Garmon (☎01690/710507; ④), with a heated indoor pool and superb cuisine; take the A470 towards Llanrwst then turn right after about a mile. The nearest **youth hostel** is at Capel Curig (see opposite); the closest **campsite** is *Riverside* (☎01690/710310; closed Nov–Easter), right behind the station.

For a town so geared to tourism that you can hardly turn around without knocking someone's cream tea to the floor, there are surprisingly few places to **eat** other than the pubs. The aforementioned *Tŷ Gwyn*, on the A5, is the best place to eat in town, whether you want a tasty pub meal or one of their praiseworthy table d'hôte meals. The low-cost bar meals at the lively *Royal Oak Hotel*, High Street, are decent value.

The Conwy and Swallow Falls

Nothing in Betws-y-Coed can compete with getting out to the gorges and waterfalls in the vicinity, and walking is the ideal way to see them. In the final gorge section of the River Conwy, a couple of miles above Betws-y-Coed, the river plunges fifty feet over the **Conwy Falls** into a deep pool. The *Conwy Falls Café*, reached by the #49 bus (4 daily), collects a small fee entitling you to view the falls and a series of rock steps which once formed part of a primitive fish ladder.

After carving out a mile or so of what kayakers regard as some of North Wales's toughest white water, the Conwy negotiates a staircase of drops and enters the **Fairy Glen**, a cleft in a small wood which takes its name from the Welsh fairies, the *Tylwyth Teg*, who are said to be seen hereabouts. The two sights are linked by a mile-long path following a cool green lane giving glimpses of the river through the woods. The path continues a short distance to Beaver Bridge from where you can walk back along the road to Betws-y-Coed – an excellent round trip.

The **Swallow Falls**, two miles west along the A5 towards Capel Curig, are the region's most visited sight, a straightforward, pretty waterfall with the occasional mad kayaker scraping down the precipitous rock. Pay your 50p and you can walk down to a series of viewing platforms. Better still, leave the car park on the north side of Pont-y-Pair, in town, and follow the **Llugwy Valley Walk** (3 miles; 400ft ascent; 1hr 30min), a forested path following the twisting and plunging river upstream towards Capel Curig. Less than a mile from Pont-y-Pair you first reach the steeply sloping **Miners' Bridge**, which linked miners' homes at Pentre Du, on the south side of the river, to the lead mines in Llanrwst. Just beneath the bridge are a series of idyllic plunge pools, perfect for swimming. The path follows the river on your left for another mile to a slightly obscured view of **Swallow Falls**. Detailed maps are available from the tourist office showing numerous routes back through the Gwydyr Forest, or you can continue half a mile to the road bridge from where you can wait for the bus back to Betws-y-Coed.

Capel Curig

Tantalizing flashes of Wales's highest mountains are glimpsed through the forested banks of the Llugwy as you climb west from Betws-y-Coed on the A5, but Snowdon eludes you until the final bend before **CAPEL CURIG**. The tiny, scattered village, six miles west of Betws-y-Coed, is the site of a major centre for outdoor enthusiasts. A quarter of a mile along the A4086 to Llanberis from the main road junction, Plas-y-Brenin, the **National Mountaineering Centre** (☎01690/702214), was built around a former coaching inn and hotel, and now runs renowned residential courses. Two-hour abseiling, canoeing and dry-slope skiing sessions are held during July and August, there's a state-of-the-art climbing wall open throughout the year (daily 10am–11pm; £2–3), and the opportunity to hear talks or watch slide shows of expeditions (usually Mon–Thurs & Sat 8pm; free).

There are plenty of **places to stay**, though none is especially luxurious. The best is either the *Bron Eryri* (☎01690/720240; ①), a comfortable and welcoming B&B half a mile outside the village towards Betws-y-Coed, or the *Bryn Tyrch Hotel* (☎01690/720223; ②), also on the A5, but closer to the main road junction. The *Llugwy Guesthouse* (☎01690/720218; ①) is on the A4086 towards the adventure centre of Plas-y-Brenin (☎01690/720214; ①), which has a limited amount of accommodation. The cheapest option in the village is the **youth hostel** (☎01690/720225; closed Jan), five hundred yards along the A5 towards Betws-y-Coed. Two and a half miles west down the Ogwen Valley you can stay for a good deal less in the *Williams Barn* bunkhouse and **campsite** (see p.751). During the day, walkers patronize the *Pinnacle Café*, grafted onto the post office and general store at the main road junction. In the evening they retire to the warm and lively **bar** of the *Bryn Tyrch Hotel*, which serves great **food**, much of which is vegan and vegetarian, or head for the sociable bar at the Plas-y-Brenin centre.

The Ogwen Valley

Prising apart the Carneddau and Glyder ranges northwest from Capel Curig, the A5 forges through the **Ogwen Valley** to Bethesda, where one of Wales's last surviving slate quarries continues to tear away the end of the Glyders range, only just keeping the tatty town viable. To the north, the frequently mist-shrouded Carneddau range glowers across at the **Glyders** range and its triple-peaked **Tryfan**, arguably Snowdonia's most demanding mountain, which forms a fractured spur out from the main ridge, blocking the view down the valley. West of Tryfan, the road follows a perfect example of a U-shaped valley, carved and smoothed by rocks frozen into the undersides of the glaciers that creaked down **Nant Ffrancon** ten thousand years ago.

WALKS FROM OGWEN: TRYFAN AND THE GLYDERS

Tourists hike up Snowdon, but mountain connoisseurs invariably prefer the sharply angled peaks of Tryfan and the Glyders, with their challenging terrain, cantilevered rocks and views back to Snowdon. The sheer number of good walking paths on the Glyders make it almost impossible to choose one definitive circular route. The individual sections of the walk have therefore been defined separately in order to allow the greatest flexibility. All times given are for the ascents: expect to take approximately half the time to get back down. **Maps** are essential for all these walks: the OS *Outdoor Leisure* 1:25,000 "Snowdonia" #17 is highly recommended.

If you've got the head for it, the **North Ridge of Tryfan**, at 3002ft (1 mile; 2000ft ascent; 1hr–1hr 30min), is one of the most rewarding scrambles in the country. It's never as precarious as Snowdon's Crib Goch, but you get a genuine mountaineering feel as the valley floor drops rapidly. The route starts in the lay-by at the head of Idwal Lake and goes left across rising ground, until you strike a path heading straight up, following the crest of the ridge to the twin monoliths of **Adam and Eve** on the summit. The courageous, or foolhardy, make the jump between them as a point of honour at the end of every ascent. In fact, the leap is trivial, but the consequences of overshooting would be disastrous.

There are two other main routes up Tryfan. The first follows the so-called **Miners' Track** (2 miles; 1350ft ascent; 2hr) from Idwal Cottage, taking the path to Cwm Idwal then, as it bears sharply to the right, keeping straight ahead and making for the gap on the horizon. This is **Bwlch Tryfan**, the col between Tryfan and Glyder Fach, from where the **South Ridge** of Tryfan (800yd; 650ft ascent; 30min) climbs past the Far South Peak to the summit. This last section is an easy scramble. The second route, which is more often used in descent, follows **Heather Terrace** (1.5 miles; 2000ft ascent; 2hr), which keeps to a fault in the rock running diagonally across the east face.

The assault on **Glyder Fach** (3260ft) begins at Bwlch Tryfan, reached either by the Miners' Track from Idwal Cottage or by the south ridge from Tryfan's summit. The trickier route follows **Bristly Ridge** (1000yd; 900ft ascent; 40min) which isn't marked on OS maps but runs steeply south from the col up past some daunting-looking towers of rock. It isn't that difficult in dry conditions, and saves a long hike southeast along a second section of the **Miners' Track** (1.5 miles; 900ft ascent; 1hr 30min). The summit lies to the west of the ridge, a chaotic jumble of huge grey slabs that many people don't bother climbing up, preferring to be photographed on a massive cantilevered rock a few yards away.

From Glyder Fach, it's an easy enough stroll to **Glyder Fawr** (3280ft), reached by skirting round the tortured rock formations of **Castell y Gwynt** (The Castle of the Winds) then following a cairn-marked path to the dramatic summit of frost-shattered slabs angled like ancient headstones (1 mile; 40min; 200ft ascent). Glyder Fawr is normally approached from Idwal Cottage, following the **Devil's Kitchen Route** (2.5 miles; 2300ft ascent; 3hr) past Idwal Lake, then to the left of the Devil's Kitchen, zigzagging up to a lake-filled plateau. Follow the path to the right of the lake and turn left for the summit where two paths cross.

The time-compacted moraine left by the retreating ice formed Llŷn Ogwen. On its shores, **Idwal Cottage**, a settlement so small it isn't named on maps, provides the valleys with a mountain rescue centre, a snack bar and a YHA **youth hostel**, all clustered around the car park. This is the start of some of Wales's most demanding and rewarding hikes (see box above), and the easier half-hour walk to the magnificent cirque, **Cwm Idwal**. The cwm's scalloped floor traps the beautifully still **Llŷn Idwal**, which reflects the precipitous grey cliffs behind, split by the jointed cleft of Twll Du, **The Devil's Kitchen**. Down this, a fine watery haze runs off the flanks of **Glyder Fawr**, soaking the crevices where early botanists found rare Arctic-Alpine plants, the main reason for designating

Cwm Idwal as Wales's first **nature reserve** (NT) in 1954. An easy, well-groomed path leads up to the reserve from the car park, where the café (daily 8.30am–5pm; later on summer weekends) will sell you a nature trail booklet for 60p. A five-minute walk down from the car park, the road crosses a bridge over the top of **Rhaeadr Ogwen** (Ogwen Falls), which cascade down a step in the valley floor.

A couple of inconveniently timed **buses** run along the valley daily between Betws-y-Coed and Bangor. **Accommodation** in the valley is limited to a self-catering bunkhouse and **campsite** at *Williams Barn*, Gwern-y-Gof Isaf Farm, two and a half miles west of Capel Curig (☎01690/720276; ①), the smaller *Gwern Gof Uchaf* campsite, a mile further west, and the Idwal Cottage YHA **youth hostel** (☎01248/600225), at the western end of Llŷn Ogwen, five miles from Capel Curig. Residents can get meals at the youth hostel; the valley is otherwise self-catering.

Llanberis and Snowdon

Mention **LLANBERIS**, ten miles west of Capel Curig, to any mountain enthusiast and they will think of **Snowdon**. The two seem inseparable, and it's not just the five-mile-long umbilical of the **Snowdon Mountain Railway**, Britain's only rack and pinion railway, which bonds the town to the summit, nor the popular path running parallel to it (see box opposite). This is the nearest you'll get to an Alpine climbing village in Wales, its single main street thronged with weather-beaten walkers and climbers decked out in Gore-Tex and fleeces, high fashion for what is otherwise a dowdy town. At the same time, Llanberis is very much a Welsh rural community, albeit a depleted one now that slate is no longer being torn from the flanks of Elidir Fawr, the mountain across the town's twin lakes. The quarries, which for the best part of two centuries employed up to three thousand men, closed in 1969, making way for the construction of the Dinorwig Pumped Storage Power Station.

Three of the routes up Snowdon start five miles east of Llanberis at the top of the Llanberis Pass, one of the deepest, narrowest and craggiest in Snowdonia. At the summit, a **youth hostel**, café and car park comprise the settlement of **PEN-Y-PASS**. Frequent, year-round Sherpa **buses** travel up daily to Pen-y-Pass, and from mid-July to August there is also the #96 Pen-y-Pass shuttle from Llanberis, the recommended approach even if you have a car, since the Pen-y-Pass car park is expensive and almost always full. Use the "Park and Ride" car park at the bottom of the pass, near the *Vaynol Arms*.

The Town

Scattered remains are all that is left of thirteenth-century **Dolbadarn Castle** (free access; CADW), on the road to **Parc Padarn**, where lakeside oak woods are gradually recolonizing the discarded workings of the defunct Dinorwig Slate Quarries. Here, the **Welsh Slate Museum** (Easter–Oct daily 9.30am–5.30pm; £3.50) occupies the former maintenance workshops of what was once one of the largest slate quarries in the world. The line shafts and flapping belts driven by a fifty-foot-diameter waterwheel provide a backdrop to workbenches where former quarry workers demonstrate their skills at turning an inch-thick slab of slate into six, even eight, perfectly smooth slivers. The craftsmen here operate an ageing foundry, producing pieces for the scattered branches of the National Museum of Wales, as well as repairing the rolling stock belonging to the nearby **Llanberis Lake Railway** (March–June & Sept to early Oct Mon–Fri & Sun 3–6pm; July & Aug 4–11pm daily; £4.25 return), which formerly transported slate and workers between the Dinorwig quarries and Port Dinorwig on the Menai Straits. It's a tame forty-minute round trip with little to do at the end except come back and explore the old slate workings.

In 1974, five years after the quarry closed, work began on hollowing out the vast underground chambers of the **Dinorwig Pumped Storage Hydro Station**, designed to provide power on demand. If you can bear the thinly disguised electricity industry advertisement which comes before it, you can take an hour-long minibus tour around the enormous pipework in the depths. For this, you need to call at **Electric Mountain** (Feb–Easter Thurs–Sun 10.30am–4.30pm; Easter–Sept daily 9.30am–5.30pm; Oct–Dec daily 10.30am–4.30pm; £5), by the lake beside the A4086, the town-centre bypass. The museum complex has some tolerably interesting displays on local glaciation, flora and fauna, and an exhibition about mammoths.

Practicalities

All **buses** to Llanberis stop near the **tourist office**, 41A High St (April–Sept daily 10am–6pm; Oct daily 10am–4pm; Nov–March Wed–Sun 10am–4pm; ☎01286/870765). Adventurous types should contact Gwynedd Mountaineering Services, 13 Stryd y Ffynnon (☎01286/871128), or High Trek Snowdonia, Tal y Waen, Deiniolen (☎01286/871232), for guided walking and courses. Padarn Watersports at Bryn Du, Tydu Road (☎01286/870556), offer organised climbing, abseiling, canoeing and other mountain activities. The Llanberis Path (see box opposite), Snowdon Ranger Path and Pitt's Head Track to Rhyd-Ddu are open to **cyclists**, although a voluntary agreement exists restricting cycle access to and from the summit between 10am and 5pm from June to September.

There is plenty of low-cost **accommodation** in or close to town: *The Heights*, 74 High St (☎01286/871179; ①–②), caters to the walking and climbing set, offering B&B and dorms, not to mention a climbing wall, good restaurant and lively bar. Two other options on the High Street are the *Dolafon Hotel* (☎01286/870933; ②), a comfortable B&B in its own grounds, and the family-run *Padarn Lake Hotel* (☎01286/870260; ③). The only luxurious place is the *Royal Victoria Hotel*, opposite the Mountain Railway (☎01286/870253; ⑤). Llanberis **youth hostel**, Llwyn Celyn (☎01286/870280), is half a mile uphill along Capel Goch Road, signposted off High Street. Outside town, the *Pen-y-Pass* YHA youth hostel (☎01286/870428) is four miles east and the *Pen-y-Gwryd Hotel* (☎01286/870211; ②; closed Nov–Feb & Mon–Fri in winter), a mile further west; they're used to muddy boots in the bar. A cheaper option is *Gwastadnant B&B and Bunkhouse*, three miles east of Llanberis in Nant Peris (☎01286/870356; ①), which also has **camping** facilities.

For **food** of gut-splitting proportions, climbers and walkers flock to *Pete's Eats*, 40 High St, while *Y Bistro*, 43–45 High St (☎01286/871278; closed Sun), is the best restaurant for miles around. The *Vaynol Arms*, two miles east of Llanberis and the only pub before Pen-y-Gwryd, serves good beer and very tasty food in a convivial atmosphere; it's usually full of campers from across the road.

Snowdon and the Snowdon Mountain Railway

The highest British mountain outside Scotland, the **Snowdon massif** (3560ft) forms a star of shattered ridges with four major peaks: Crib Goch, Crib-y-ddysgl, Y Lliwedd and the main summit, **Yr Wyddfa**. Snowdon sports some of the finest walking and scrambling in the park and, in winter, the longest season for ice climbers and cramponed walkers. Hardened outdoor enthusiasts dismiss it as overused, and it can certainly be crowded, especially in summer, when a thousand visitors a day can be pressed into the postbox-red carriages of the Snowdon Mountain Railway, while another 1500 pound the well-maintained paths.

Opprobrium is chiefly levelled at the **Snowdon Mountain Railway** (mid-March to Oct 6–25 trains daily, call ☎01286/870223; £15 return) for its sheer existence. Completed in 1896, seventy-year-old carriages pushed by equally old steam locos still climb, in just under an hour, from the eastern end of Llanberis opposite the *Royal Victoria Hotel* to the summit café and bar (open when the trains are running to the top). A "Railway Stamp" (10p) affixed to your letter – along with the usual Royal Mail one – entitles you to use the highest postbox in the UK and enchant your friends with a "Summit of Snowdon – Copa'r Wyddfa" postmark. Times, type of locomotive and final destination vary with demand and ice conditions at the top. To avoid disappointment, buy your tickets early on clear summer days. If you walk up by one of the routes detailed in the "Walks on Snowdon" box, you can take the train down, if there is space (£7.50).

WALKS ON SNOWDON

The following are justifiably the most popular of the seven accepted routes up Snowdon. Maps are essential for all these walks: the OS *Outdoor Leisure* 1:25,000 map of "Snowdonia" #17 is highly recommended.

Llanberis Path

The easiest, longest and most derided route up Snowdon, the **Llanberis Path** (5 miles to summit; 3200ft ascent; 3hr) follows the rail line past the Halfway Station café (March to late Sept daily; winter Sat & Sun only); posted on the wall inside are the barely believable times of the annual Snowdon Race, which passes on the fourth Saturday in July. Continuing up, the path gets steeper to the "Finger Stone" at **Bwlch Glas** (Green Pass), marking the arrival of the Snowdon Ranger Path, and three routes coming up from Pen-y-Pass to join the Llanberis Path for the final ascent to **Yr Wyddfa**, the summit.

The Miners' and Pig tracks

The **Miners' Track** (4 miles to summit; 2400ft ascent; 2hr 30min) is the easiest of the three routes up from Pen-y-Pass, a broad track leading south then west to the dilapidated remains of the former copper mines in Cwm Dyli. Skirting around the right of a lake, the path climbs more steeply to the lake-filled Cwm Glaslyn, then again to Upper Glaslyn, from where the measured steps of those ahead warn of the impending switchback ascent to the junction with the Llanberis Path.

The stonier **Pig Track** (3.5 miles to summit; 2400ft ascent; 2hr 30min) is really just a variation on the Miners' Track, leaving from the western end of the Pen-y-Pass car park and climbing up to **Bwlch y Moch** (the Pass of the Pigs) before meeting the Miners' Track prior to the zigzag up to the Llanberis Path.

Snowdon Horseshoe

Some claim that the **Snowdon Horseshoe** (8 miles round; 3200ft ascent; 5–7hr) is one of the finest ridge walks in Europe. The route makes a full anticlockwise circuit around the three glacier-carved cwms of Upper Glaslyn, Glaslyn and Llydaw. Not to be taken lightly, it includes the knife-edge traverse of **Crib Goch**, which requires a minimum of an ice axe and crampons in winter. The path follows the Pig Track to Bwlch y Moch, then pitches right for the moderate scramble up to Crib Goch. If you balk at any of this, turn back: if not, pick your way along the sensational ridge to **Crib-y-ddysgl** (3494ft) and, on easier ground, to the summit. The return to Llyn Llydaw and the Miners' Track is via **Bwlch-y-Saethau** (Pass of the Arrows) and **Y Lliwedd** (2930ft).

Watkin Path

The most spectacular of the southern routes up Snowdon, the **Watkin Path** (4 miles to summit; 3350ft ascent; 3hr) begins at Bethania Bridge, three miles northeast of Beddgelert in Nantgwynant. The path starts on a broad track, lined with oaks, which narrows before heading past a disused tramway to a series of cataracts. A natural amphitheatre contains the ruins of a slate works and **Gladstone Rock**, at which, in 1892, the 83-year-old prime minister officially opened the route.

Beddgelert

Almost all of the prodigious quantity of rain which falls on Snowdon spills down either the Glaslyn or Colwyn rivers, which meet at the huddle of grey houses, prodigiously brightened with floral displays in summer, that make up **BEDDGELERT**. A sentimental tale fabricated by a wily local publican to lure punters tells how the town got its name. **Gelert's Grave** (bedd means burial place), an enclosure just south of town, is supposedly the final resting place of Prince Llywelyn ap Iorwerth's faithful dog, Gelert, who was left in charge of the prince's infant son while he went hunting. On his return, the child was gone and the hound's muzzle was soaked in blood. Jumping to conclusions, the impetuous Llywelyn slew the dog, only to find the child safely asleep beneath its cot and a dead wolf beside him. Llywelyn hurried to his dog, which licked his hand as it died.

Beyond the "grave", the river crashes down the bony and picturesque **Aberglaslyn Gorge** towards Porthmadog. You can walk along the right bank of the river, past Gelert's Grave, crossing over the bridge onto the disused track bed of the narrow-gauge Welsh Highland rail line. This then hugs the left bank for a mile, heading gently down to Pont Aberglaslyn, at the bottom of the gorge. The more adventurous Fisherman's Path runs just below, giving a closer look at the river's course through chutes and channels in sculpted rocks. You have to return the same way.

A mile in the opposite direction up Nantgwynant, the **Sygun Copper Mine** (daily 10am–5pm; £4.75) is the dilapidated remnant of what, until a century ago, had been the valley's prime source of income from Roman times. Restored and made safe, the multiple levels of tunnels and galleries can now be visited on a 45-minute guided tour, accompanied by the disembodied voice of a miner describing his life in the mine.

Buses all stop by the National Trust shop and **information centre** (daily: April, May, Sept & Oct 11am–5pm; June–Aug 11am–6pm; ☎01766/890293) which houses some interesting exhibits on Snowdonia and the Victorian Romantics, and is the nearest thing in the village to a tourist office. The best **places to stay** are the *Beddgelert Antiques and Tea Rooms*, Waterloo House, directly opposite the bridge (☎01766/890543; ②), with limited accommodation above the restaurant; *Ael-y-Bryn*, Caernarfon Road (☎01766/890310; ①), with good views and inexpensive home-cooked evening meals; and *Sygun Fawr Country House*, three quarters of a mile away off the A498 (☎01766/890258; ③), a partially sixteenth-century house in its own grounds with a sauna and good, moderately priced evening meals. The excellent *Beddgelert Forest Campsite* (☎01766/890288) is a mile out on the Caernarfon road, four miles before the highly rated *Snowdon Ranger* **YHA hostel** (☎01286/650391; closed Jan to mid-Feb); another YHA hostel, the *Bryn Gwynant* (☎01766/890251; closed Nov & Dec), is beautifully sited in Nantgwynant, four miles northeast of Beddgelert on the A498, and has a **campsite** where you can use the hostel's facilities for half the adult rate.

Blaenau Ffestiniog and around

Every approach to **BLAENAU FFESTINIOG** is dramatic, but none more so than the train journey through the Lledr Valley from Betws-y-Coed. Following the twists of the river, the railway passes through broadleaf woods which give way to the smooth, grassy slopes of the Moel Siabod, where the the longest rail tunnel in Wales bores through over two miles of slate to suddenly emerge in the town. Blaenau means "head of the valley", in this case the lush Vale of Ffestiniog, a dramatic contrast to the forbidding town, hemmed in by stark slopes strewn with heaps of discarded, splintered slate. When clouds hunker low in this great cwm and rain sheets the grey roofs, grey walls and grey paving slabs, it can be a terrifically gloomy place. Thousands of tons of slate per year were once hewn from the labyrinth of underground caverns here, but these days the

THE WELSH SLATE INDUSTRY

Slate derives its name from the Old French word *esclater*, meaning to split, an apt reflection of its most highly valued quality. The Romans recognized the potential of the substance, roofing the houses of Segontium with it, and Edward I used it extensively in his Iron Ring of castles around Snowdonia. It wasn't until around 1780 that Britain's Industrial Revolution kicked in, leading to greater urbanization and boosting the demand for Welsh roofing slates. Cities grew; Hamburg was re-roofed with Welsh slate after its fire of 1842, and it is the same material which still gives that rainy-day sheen to interminable rows of English mill-town houses.

By 1898, Welsh quarries – run, like the coal and steel industries of the south, by the English – were producing half a million tons of dressed slate a year, almost all of it from Snowdonia. At Penrhyn and Dinorwig, mountains were hacked away in terraces, sometimes rising 2000ft above sea level, with the teams of workers negotiating with the foreman for the choicest piece of rock and the selling price for what they produced. They often slept through the week in damp dormitories on the mountain, and tuberculosis was common, exacerbated by the slate dust. At Blaenau Ffestiniog, the seams required mining underground rather than quarrying, but conditions were no better with miners even having to buy their own candles, the only light they had. In spite of this, thousands left their hillside smallholdings for the burgeoning quarry towns. Few workers were allowed to join Undeb Chwarelwyr Gogledd Cymru (The North Wales Quarrymen's Union), and in 1900 the workers in Lord Penrhyn's quarry at Bethesda went out on strike. They stayed out for three years, but failed to win any concessions. Those who got their jobs back were forced to work for even less money as a recession took hold, and although the two World Wars heralded mini-booms as bombed houses were replaced, the industry never recovered its nineteenth-century prosperity, and most quarries and mines closed in the 1950s.

For the 1862 London Exhibition, one skilled craftsman produced a sheet ten feet long, a foot wide and a sixteenth of an inch thick – so thin it could be flexed – firmly establishing Welsh slate as the finest in the world. Sadly, much of what little is produced today is used for things besides roofing: floor tiles, road aggregate and an astonishing array of nasty ashtrays and coasters etched with mountainscapes.

town is only kept alive by its extant slate cavern tour, and by tourists who change from the Lledr Valley train line onto the wonderful, narrow-gauge Ffestiniog Railway (see p.757), which winds up from Porthmadog.

The Llechwedd Slate Caverns

It is difficult to get a real feeling of what slate means to Blaenau Ffestiniog without a visit to the **Llechwedd Slate Caverns** (daily: March–Sept 10am–5.15pm; Oct–Feb 10am–4.15pm; single tour £6.95, both tours £10.50), on the edge of town on the road to Betws-y-coed. There are two tours available: on the **Miners' Tramway Tour**, you are plied with facts about slate mining as a small train takes you a third of a mile along one of the oldest levels to the enormous Cathedral Cave and the open-air Chough's Cavern. The awe-inspiring scale of the place justifies going on the tour even without the tableaux of Victorian miners at work. On the more dramatic **Deep Mine Tour**, a steeply inclined railway takes you down to a labyrinth of tunnels through which you are guided by an irksome taped spiel of a Victorian miner. The long caverns angling back into the gloom are increasingly impressive, culminating in one filled by a beautiful opalescent pool.

Practicalities

The **train station** on the High Street serves both the Ffestiniog line to Porthmadog and mainline train services from Betws-y-Coed, and is a short walk up the main drag

---

A WALK FROM BLAENAU FFESTINIOG

One of the most scenic, and easiest, walks around Blaenau Ffestiniog leads down into the **Vale of Ffestiniog** (4–5 miles; descent only; 2–3hr) following the Ffestiniog Railway (see opposite) past its 360° loop, through sessile oak woods and past several cascades all the way to Tan-y-bwlch. From here, you can return to Blaenau Ffestiniog, or continue on to Porthmadog by train; check the times at the station and buy your ticket to ensure a place on the return train.

The walk can be done from Blaenau Ffestiniog, but it involves a fairly dull first mile easily avoided by catching the railway or driving to the reservoir at Tanygrisiau. From the station, turn right past the Tanygrisiau information centre then take the second left, not the road beside the reservoir but the next one, following the footpath signs. Cross the train line, then pass a car park on your left before turning left down a track and skirting behind the powerhouse. The path then sticks closely to the train line, occasionally crossing it. Even when there are several paths you can't go far wrong if you keep the train lines in sight. *The Grapes* pub at Maentwrog, half a mile beyond Tan-y-bwlch, is a great place to while away the time until the next train – or the one after that.

---

from the **tourist office** (April–Oct daily 10am–6pm; ☎01766/830360), opposite the *Queen's Hotel*. **Buses** stop either in the car park around the back or outside *Y Commercial* pub, on High Street. A vast number of Blaenau Ffestiniog's visitors ride the train up from Porthmadog, visit a slate mine and leave, and this is reflected in the limited range of **accommodation**. But try the excellent, welcoming cheapie *Afallon*, Manod Road (☎01766/830468; ①), almost a mile south of the tourist office, or, in town itself, *The Don*, 147 High St (☎01766/830403; ②). For a few extra pounds, you might want to travel the mile or so south on the A470 to *Cae Du*, Manod Road (☎01766/830847; ②), in a seventeenth-century farmhouse.

Good **food** isn't especially abundant in Blaenau Ffestiniog. *Caffi Glen*, south of the tourist office, at 36 High St, does decent all-day breakfasts and snacks, but for something more substantial you're limited to the moderate, broad-ranging menu at *Myfanwys*, 4 Market Place (☎01766/830059), or a bar meal at the *Queen's Hotel*. Most locals head for *The Grapes* (☎01766/590208) at Maentwrog, four miles south down the A496, where there's the moderately priced and gamey *Flambard's* restaurant, although the place is lauded for their gargantuan and inexpensive bar meals.

The Llŷn

The Llŷn takes its name from an Irish word for peninsula, an apt description for this most westerly part of North Wales, which, until the fifth century, had a significant Irish population. The cliff- and cove-lined finger of land juts out south and west, separating Cardigan and Caernarfon bays, its hills tapering away along the ancient route to Aberdaron, where pilgrims sailed for Ynys Enlli (Bardsey Island). Today, it's the beaches that lure people to the south coast family resorts of **Cricieth**, **Pwllheli** and **Abersoch**, and unless you want to rent windsurfers or canoes, it's preferable to press on along the narrow roads that dawdle down towards Aberdaron. Not even Snowdonia can match the remoteness of the tip of the Llŷn, and nowhere in Wales is more staunchly Welsh: road signs are still bilingual but the English is frequently obliterated; Stryd Fawr is used instead of High Street, and in most local shops you'll only hear Welsh spoken.

The Llŷn is reached through one of the two gateway towns, Porthmadog and Caernarfon, linked by the A487, an effective boundary between Snowdonia proper and the peninsula's gentler contours. **Porthmadog**, nestling into the crook of the elbow where the Cambrian coast takes a sharp left turn, is of interest for its proximity to the private "dream village" of **Portmeirion**, reached on Wales's finest narrow-gauge train line, the **Ffestiniog Railway**. The Llŷn's northern coast comes to an abrupt end at the mouth of the Menai Strait, guarded by the magnificent fortress which forms the centrepiece of **Caernarfon**, a good base for both the Llŷn and central Snowdonia.

Porthmadog and around

Located right at the point where the Llŷn peninsula turns sharply south down the Cambrian coast, **PORTHMADOG** was once the busiest slate port in North Wales. Nowadays, it's a pleasant enough town to spend a night or two, although it sadly makes little of its situation on the north bank of the vast, mountain-backed estuary. Two things it does make a fuss about are the Italianate folly of Portmeirion, two miles east of town, and the Ffestiniog Railway that originally carried slates up Blaenau Ffestiniog through thirteen miles of verdant mountain scenery. Porthmadog would never have existed at all without the entrepreneurial ventures of a Lincolnshire MP named William Alexander Madocks, who named the town after both himself and the Welsh Prince Madog, who some say sailed from the nearby Ynys Fadog (Madog's Island) to North America in 1170. Between 1808 and 1812, Madocks fought tides and currents to build the mile-long embankment of The Cob, southeast of present-day Porthmadog, enclosing 7000 acres of the estuary. A wharf was built and, with the completion of the Blaenau Ffestiniog Railway in 1836, the town spread along a waterfront thick with orderly heaps of slate and the masts of merchant ships.

Without a doubt, the **Ffestiniog Railway** (Easter–Oct 4–10 daily; Nov–Easter mainly weekends; return to Blaenau Ffestiniog £13.80, to Tan-y-Bwlch £8.40; ☎01766/512340) ranks as Wales's finest narrow-gauge rail line, twisting and looping up 650ft from the wharf at Porthmadog to the slate mines at Blaenau Ffestiniog, thirteen miles away. When the line opened in 1836, it carried slates from the mines down to the port with the help of gravity, horses riding with the goods then hauling the empty carriages back up again. Steam had to be introduced to cope with the 100,000 tons of slate a year that Blaenau Ffestiniog was churning out by the late nineteenth century, but the slate roofing market collapsed between the wars and the line was abandoned in 1946. Most of the tracks and sleepers had disappeared by 1954, when a bunch of dedicated volunteers began reconstruction, only completing the entire route in 1982. Leaving Porthmadog, trains cross The Cob and then stop at Minffordd, a mile from Portmeirion and a convenient place to change onto the mainline railway. Two stops later is Tan-y-Bwlch, from where it's a short stroll to *The Grapes* pub at Maentwrog (see box opposite) and the start of the Vale of Ffestiniog walk (see box opposite).

Practicalities

Cambrian coast trains pull into the mainline **train station** at the north end of the High Street; the **Ffestiniog station** is located down by the harbour, about half a mile to the south. In between the two, National Express **buses** stop on Avenue Road outside the *Royal Sportsman*; local bus services stop outside the *Australia Inn*, on High Street. The helpful **tourist office**, adjoining the community centre on the High Street (Easter–Oct daily 10am–6pm; Nov–Easter Mon & Wed–Sun 10am–5pm; ☎01766/512981), is over the bridge from the Ffestiniog Railway station.

While limited budgets are well catered for, there's not much really decent **accommodation**, unless you're prepared to splash out for a night at the swanky *Portmeirion Hotel*, in Portmeirion (☎01766/770000; ⑦). *Skellerns*, 35 Madog St, near the Ffestiniog train station (☎01766/512843; ①), is a good budget place. *Eric's Bunkhouse*, at Prenteg (☎01766/512199), two miles north of Porthmadog on the A498 to Beddgelert, opposite *Eric Jones' Café,* has acceptable dorms for around £3 a night. At the top of High Street,

Bank Place forks left, becoming Borth Road, on the way out to numerous family-oriented **campsites** at Black Rock and Morfa Bychan. Along this way, about fifteen minutes' walk from town, you'll come to the pleasant enough *Tyddyn Llwyn* site (☎01766/512205).

For **food**, there's *Yr Hen Fecus*, Lombard Street (☎01766/514625), an unpretentious place with some good veggie options, or the seafood specialities of the excellent *Harbour Restaurant*, High Street (☎01766/512471; closed Sun–Wed in winter), almost opposite the tourist office. For bar meals, try *The Ship*, a popular pub on Lombard Street, noted for its oriental beer and its food – predominantly Thai and Malaysian, with some vegetarian options.

Portmeirion

The area's main lure is the unique, Italianate private village of **PORTMEIRION** (daily 9.30am–5.30pm; £4), set on a small rocky peninsula in Tremadog Bay, three miles east, near Minffordd. Both the mainline and Ffestiniog trains, as well as buses #1 and #2, stop in Minffordd, from where it's a 25-minute walk to Portmeirion. Perhaps best known as "The Village" in the Sixties British cult TV series *The Prisoner*, Portmeirion is the brainchild of eccentric architect Clough Williams-Ellis, and his dream to build an ideal village which enhances rather than blends in with the surroundings, using a "gay, light-opera sort of approach". The result is certainly theatrical: a stage set with a lucky dip of buildings arranged to distort perspectives and reveal tantalizing glimpses of the seascape behind.

In the 1920s, Ellis bought the site and turned an existing house into a hotel, the income from this providing funds for Ellis's "Home for Fallen Buildings". Endangered buildings from all over Britain and abroad were broken down, transported and rebuilt, every conceivable style being plundered: a Neoclassical colonnade from Bristol, siamese figures, a Jacobean town hall, and the Italianate touches, a campanile and a pantheon. Ellis designed his village around a Mediterranean piazza, piecing together a scaled-down nest of loggias, grand porticoes and tiny terracotta-roofed houses and painting them in pastels: turquoise, ochre and buff yellows. Continually surprising, with hidden entrances and cherubs popping out of crevices, the ensemble is eclectic, yet never quite inappropriate.

It is in need of a lick of paint here and there, but even so, more than three thousand visitors a day come to ogle in summer, when it can be a delight; there are fewer in winter, when it seems just bizarre. In the evening, when the village is closed to the public, patrons at the opulent, waterside *Portmeirion Hotel* (see Porthmadog "Practicalities") get to see the place at its best: peaceful, even ghostly. Other than walking in the delightful grounds, there's little to actually do, except for viewing a film on Portmeirion, popping into the shops selling china and *Prisoner* memorabilia, and eating.

Cricieth and Llanystumdwy

When sea bathing became the Victorian fashion, English families descended on the sweeping sand and shingle beach at **CRICIETH** (sometimes Criccieth), five miles west of Porthmadog, a quiet, amiable resort which curiously abounds with good places to stay and great restaurants, making it a good touring base for the peninsula and Porthmadog. There isn't much here, however, other than the battle-worn remains of **Cricieth Castle** (April–Oct daily 10am–6pm; free access in winter; £2.20; CADW), dominating the coastline with its twin-towered gatehouse. Started by Llywelyn ap Iorwerth in 1230, it was strengthened by Edward I around 1283, and razed by Owain Glyndŵyr in 1404, leaving little besides a plan of broken walls. It's a great spot to sit and look over Cardigan Bay to Harlech, but leave time for the ticket office, where there's a fairly workaday exhibition on Welsh castles and a wonderful animated cartoon based on the twelfth-century Cambrian travels of Giraldus Cambrensis as he gathered support for the Third Crusade.

A mile west, the village of **LLANYSTUMDWY** celebrates its most famous son, the Welsh patriot, social reformer and British prime minister David Lloyd George. He grew up in Highgate House, now part of the **Lloyd George Museum** (Easter–May Mon–Fri 10.30am–5pm; June Mon–Sat 10.30am–5pm; July–Sept daily 10.30am–5pm; Oct Mon–Fri 11am–4.30pm; £3), comprising a fairly dull collection of gifts, awards and caskets honouring the statesman, displays full of anecdotes and little-known facts, and a couple of short films giving a broad sweep of his life. Lloyd George is buried by the River Dwyfor under a memorial – a boulder and two simple plaques designed by Portmeirion designer Clough Williams-Ellis. **Bus** #3 runs from Porthmadog and Cricieth, passing through the village on its way to Pwllheli.

Buses and **trains** along the Cambrian coastline stop a couple of hundred yards west of Y Maes, the open square at the centre of Cricieth. **Accommodation** is plentiful, with *Trefaes Guesthouse*, Y Maes (☎01766/523204; ①), a superb option at the cheaper end and the *Moelwyn*, 27–29 Mona Terrace (☎01766/522500; ②), a good seafront choice. More luxurious places are further afield: *Mynydd Ednyfed*, Caernarfon Road (☎01766/523269; ③), is a classy country hotel a mile north on the B4411, while *Bron Eifion Country House Hotel* (☎01766/522385; ⑤) is a beautiful Victorian country house set in its own grounds a mile west of town. You'll find the **campsite**, *Mynydd Du*, a mile towards Porthmadog on the A497 (☎01766/522533; closed Nov–March).

For such a small town, good **restaurants** are surprisingly abundant and offer the best range of eating on the peninsula. The two plusher hotels listed above both serve innovative and moderately priced meals. *Tir-a-Môr*, 1–3 Mona Terrace (☎01766/523084; closed Sun), isn't strictly Italian, but offers a large range of expensive Italian-influenced dishes in airy surroundings; *Moelwyn* (see above) has a superb seafacing restaurant; and the *Prince of Wales*, Stryd Fawr, offers a great **pub** atmosphere and decent bar meals.

Pwllheli

PWLLHELI (pronounced "Poolth-heli") is the market town for the peninsula, a role it has maintained since 1355, when it gained its charter, though there's little sign of its history nowadays. The overall tenor is one of low-brow fun-seeking, as holidaymakers flood in from the nearby holiday camp. Pwllheli's one defining feature is its Welshness. Even in the height of summer, you'll hear far more Welsh spoken here than English.

As the terminus for National Express **buses**, which stop on Y Maes, the main square, and the final stop for Cambrian coast **trains**, Pwllheli is hard to avoid, but you should push on if possible, only stopping at the **tourist office**, Station Square (daily: April–Oct 10am–6pm; Nov–March 10am–5pm; ☎01758/613000). During the summer you can rent **mountain bikes** at Llŷn Cycle Hire, Ala Road (£10 per day; ☎01758/612414). If you decide to **stay**, try *26 Stryd Fawr* (☎01758/613172; ①) or, 400yd away, *Llys Gwyrfai*, 14 West End Parade (☎01758/614877; ①), a comfortable guest house with sea views and home-cooked meals.

Abersoch

After the distinctly Welsh feel of Pwllheli, **ABERSOCH**, seven miles southwest along the coast, comes as a surprise. This former fishing village pitched in the middle of two golden bays has, over the last century, become a thoroughly anglicized resort, with a haughty opinion of itself. Such high self-esteem isn't really justified, but at high tide the harbour is attractive, and the long swathe of the beach-hut-backed Town Beach is a fine spot, even if it is barely visible under towels at busy times. A short walk along the beach shakes off most of the crowds, but a better bet is to make for three-mile-long **Porth Neigwl** (Hell's Mouth), two miles to the southwest, which ranks as one of the country's best surf beaches; you'll need your own gear, and beware of the undertow if you are swimming. You can **rent windsurfers**, surfboards and wetsuits from Abersoch Watersports, Lôn Pont Morgan (☎01758/712483), by the harbour.

Buses from Pwllheli make a loop through the middle of Abersoch, stopping by the **tourist office**, Lôn Pen Cei (Easter to mid-Sept daily 10.30am–5pm; ☎01758/712929). For **accommodation**, try the *Trewen*, Lôn Hawen, just off Lôn Sarn Bach (☎01758/712755; ①). Two good places on Lôn Sarn Bach itself are *Angorfa Guest House* (☎01758/712967; ②; closed Dec), and the superb *Neigwl Hotel* (☎01758/712363; ③). There are some decent **places to eat**: *Mañana*, on Lôn Pen Cai, serves Mexican and Italian food, or you can get bar meals at the *Vaynol Arms*, on Lôn Sarn Bach, and the excellent *Ship*, out of town in Llanbedrog, near Pwllheli.

Aberdaron and Bardsey Island

The small, lime-washed fishing village of **ABERDARON** backs a pebble beach two miles short of the tip of the Llŷn. For a thousand years, from the sixth century onwards, it was the last stop for pilgrims to **Bardsey Island**, or Ynys Enlli (The Island of the Currents), just offshore; three visits were proclaimed equivalent to one pilgrimage to Rome. Many pilgrims came to die there, earning Bardsey its epithet "The Isle of Twenty Thousand Saints". The final gathering place before the treacherous crossing is the fourteenth-century *Y Gegin Fawr* (Great Kitchen), a stone building which still operates as a **café**. Today, pilgrims are more likely to be attracted by poetry, as until 1978, **R.S. Thomas** was the minister at Aberdaron's seafront church of **St Hywyn**.

Without your own transport, the only way to get to Aberdaron is to catch the #17 **bus** from Pwllheli (Mon–Sat). **Accommodation** is fairly limited; the least expensive option is *Brynmor* (☎01758/760344; ①), overlooking the bay, just up the road to Porth Oer, the "whistling sands". The best and quietest **campsite** around is *Mur Melyn* (no phone) just over a mile out from Aberdaron, mid-way to Porth Oer. Take the B4413 west, fork right, then turn left at Pen-y-Bont house.

Caernarfon

It was in **CAERNARFON**, in 1969, that Charles, the current heir to the throne, was invested as Prince of Wales, a ceremony which re-affirmed English sovereignty over Wales in this, one of the most nationalist of Welsh-speaking regions. Since 1282, when the English defeated Llywelyn ap Gruffydd, the last Welsh Prince of Wales, the title has been bestowed on heirs to the English throne, but it wasn't until 1911 that the machinations of Lloyd George – MP for Caernarfon and future prime minister – brought the ceremony to the centre of his constituency: an odd move for a proto-nationalist considering the symbolic implications. Caernarfon's vastly imposing castle and near-complete rectangle of town walls make it an appealing place, but apart from the castle, there isn't too much to see: you can only walk a small section of the wall and the rest of the town has been ripped through by a dual carriageway and boxed in by modern buildings. That said, it is well situated on the Menai Strait, between the mainland and Anglesey (see p.776), and has good bus connections to Llanberis and Snowdonia.

The Town
In 1283, Edward I started work on **Caernarfon Castle** (April–May & Oct daily 9.30am–5pm; June–Sept daily 9.30am–6pm; Nov–March Mon–Sat 9.30am–4pm, Sun 11am–4pm; £4.20; CADW), the strongest link in his Iron Ring (see box on p.771), a decisive

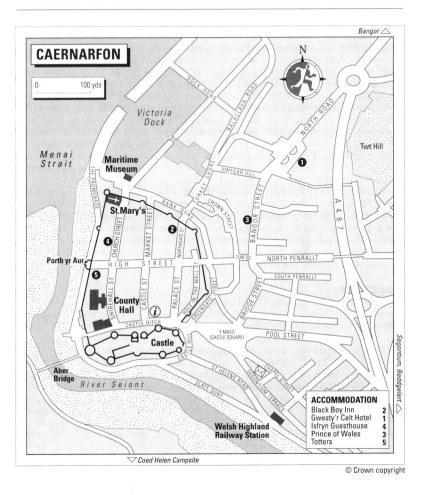

CAERNARFON

0   100 yds

Bangor △

Victoria Dock

Menai Strait

Maritime Museum

St.Mary's

Porth yr Aur

County Hall *(i)*

Castle

Aber Bridge *River Seiont*

Twt Hill

NORTH PENRALLT

SOUTH PENRALLT

Y MAES (CASTLE SQUARE)

POOL STREET

ST HELENS ROAD

Welsh Highland Railway Station

Segontium, Beddgelert △

ACCOMMODATION
Black Boy Inn	2
Gwesty'r Celt Hotel	1
Isfryn Guesthouse	4
Prince of Wales	3
Totters	5

▽ *Coed Helen Campsite*

hammer blow to any Welsh aspirations to autonomy and the ultimate symbol of Anglo-Norman military might. With the Welsh already smarting from the loss of their prince, Edward is said to have promised "a prince born in Wales who could speak never a word of English", a vow he fulfilled to the letter by moving his pregnant wife to Caernarfon. The story is almost certainly apocryphal. Instead, Edward attempted to appease the Welsh by paying tribute to aspects of local legend. The Welsh had long associated their town with the eastern capital of the Roman Empire: Caernarfon's old name, Caer Cystennin, was also the name used for Constantinople, and Constantine himself was believed to have been born at Segontium (see p.762). Edward's architect, James of St George, exploited this connection in the distinctive limestone and sandstone banding and the polygonal towers, both reminiscent of the Theodosian walls in present-day Istanbul.

In military terms, the castle is supreme. It was taken once, before building was complete, but then withstood two sieges by Owain Glyndŵr with a garrison of only

28 men-at-arms. Entering through the **King's Gate**, the castle's strength is immediately apparent. Embrasures and murder holes between the octagonal towers face in on no fewer than five gates and six portcullises, and that's once you have crossed the moat, now bridged by an incongruous modern structure. Inside, the huge lawn gives a misleading impression since both the wall dividing the two original wards and all the buildings which filled them crumbled away long ago. The towers are in a much better state, and linked by an exhausting honeycomb of wall-walks and tunnels. The tallest and most striking is the **King's Tower**, at the western end, whose three slender turrets are adorned with eagle sculptures, and give the best views of the town. To the south, the Queen's Tower is entirely taken up by the numbingly thorough **Museum of the Royal Welch Fusiliers**, while the Northeast Tower houses the **Prince of Wales Exhibition**, just outside which is the Dinorwig slate dais used for Charles' investiture.

A ten-minute walk along the A4085 Beddgelert road brings you to the western end of the Roman road from Chester, at **Segontium Roman Fort** (April–Oct Mon–Sat 10am–5pm, Sun 2–5pm; Nov–March Mon–Sat 10am–4pm, Sun 2–4pm; £1.25; CADW). The Romans occupied this five-acre site for three centuries from around 78 AD, though most of the remains are from the final rebuilding after 364 AD. The ground plan is seldom more than shin-high and somewhat baffling, making the museum and displays in the ticket office pretty much essential.

Practicalities

With no mainline train station, the hub of Caernarfon's public transport system is Y Maes (Castle Square), right under the walls of the castle, where **buses stop**. The **tourist office** is on Castle Street (Easter–Oct daily 10am–6pm; Nov–Easter closed Wed; ☎01286/672232), just a few steps away.

There are a number of **accommodation** options close to the centre: try *Isfryn Guesthouse*, 11 Church St (☎01286/675628; ①), or the *Prince of Wales* pub on Bangor Street (☎01286/673367; ②). The characterful *Black Boy Inn*, Northgate Street (☎01286/673023; ②), is one of the town's oldest buildings, but for more upmarket accommodation, your best bet is the *Gwesty'r Celt Hotel*, Bangor Street (☎01286/674477; ⑤), which comes complete with an indoor pool and smart restaurant. Away from town are some excellent country houses, including *Pengwern Farm*, Saron, three miles southwest of Caernarfon (☎01286/830717; ②; closed Dec & Jan), which has a lovely rural setting, and serves inexpensive, farm-fresh evening meals. Take the A487 south across the river then turn right towards Saron – Pengwern is just over two miles down on the right. For independent **hostel** accommodation, *Totters*, at Plas Porth Yr Aur, 2 High St (☎01286/672963; ①), is superb and very friendly. The *Coed Helen* **campsite** (☎01286/676770; closed Nov–Feb) sits right on the Seiont River, just across the footbridge from the base of the castle.

Caernarfon boasts a number of low-key and likeable **restaurants**: you can sample the eclectic menu at *Courteney's*, 9 Segontium Terrace (closed Mon, Tues lunch & Sun), or the bistro-style fare at *Stone's*, 4 Hole in the Wall St (closed Sun). The cheapest option is the excellent **bar meals** at the aforementioned *Black Boy Inn*. For **nightlife**, everyone heads ten miles north to Bangor, though you might catch a Welsh-language band at *Tafarn Yr Albert*, 11 Segontium Terrace, on Saturday nights, or live music at the *Prince of Wales*, Bangor Street. Thursday's *Caernarfon Chronicle* has gig information for both Bangor and Caernarfon.

travel details

Trains

Betws-y-Coed to: Blaenau Ffestiniog (6 daily; 30min); Llandudno Junction (6 daily; 30min).

Blaenau Ffestiniog to: Betws-y-Coed (6 daily 30min); Llandudno Junction (6 daily; 1hr); Porthmadog by Ffestiniog Railway (April–Oct 4–10 daily; 1hr).

Cricieth to: Barmouth (7 daily; 55min); Machynlleth (7 daily; 1hr 45min); Porthmadog (7 daily; 10min); Pwllheli (6 daily; 15min).

Porthmadog to: Barmouth (7 daily; 45min); Blaenau Ffestiniog by Ffestiniog Railway (Easter–Oct 4–10 daily; 1hr); Harlech (7 daily; 20min); Machynlleth (7 daily; 1hr 40min); Pwllheli (6 daily; 25min).

Pwllheli to: Cricieth (7 daily; 15min); Machynlleth (7 daily; 2hr); Porthmadog (7 daily; 25min).

Buses

Aberdaron to: Pwllheli (9 daily; 40min).

Abersoch to: Pwllheli (9 daily; 20min).

Beddgelert to: Caernarfon (8 daily; 30min); Llanberis (5 daily; 40min); Porthmadog (8 daily; 30min).

Betws-y-Coed to: Bangor (2 daily; 50min); Blaenau Ffestiniog (1 daily; 30min); Capel Curig (9 daily; 15min); Conwy (6 daily; 55min); Llanberis (3 daily; 40min).

Blaenau Ffestiniog to: Caernarfon (roughly hourly; 1hr 30min); Harlech (4 daily; 35min); Porthmadog (hourly; 30min).

Caernarfon to: Bangor (every 20min; 30min); Beddgelert (6 daily; 30min); Blaenau Ffestiniog (roughly hourly; 1hr 25min); Cricieth (3 daily; 40min); Llanberis (every 30min; 25min); Llandudno (hourly; 1hr 40min); Porthmadog (hourly; 45min); Pwllheli (at least hourly; 45min).

Capel Curig to: Bangor (2 daily; 40min); Betws-y-Coed (7 daily; 15min); Llanberis (3 daily; 30min).

Cricieth to: Caernarfon (3 daily; 40min); Llanystumdwy (hourly; 5min); Porthmadog (hourly; 15min); Pwllheli (hourly; 20min).

Llanberis to: Bangor (7 daily; 40min); Beddgelert (4 daily; 40min); Betws-y-Coed (3 daily; 40min); Caernarfon (every 30min; 25min).

Porthmadog to: Beddgelert (6 daily; 30min); Blaenau Ffestiniog (hourly; 30min); Caernarfon (at least hourly; 45min); Cardiff (1 daily; 6hr 40min); Cricieth (hourly; 15min); Dolgellau (6 daily; 50min); Machynlleth (3 daily; 1hr 45min); Pwllheli (hourly; 40min).

Pwllheli to: Aberdaron (7 daily; 40min); Abersoch (9 daily; 15min); Caernarfon (at least hourly; 45min); Cricieth (hourly; 20min); Porthmadog (hourly; 40min).

CHAPTER SEVENTEEN

THE NORTH COAST AND ANGLESEY

Wales's north coast and its natural offshoot, the Isle of Anglesey, not only encompass the geographical extremities of the country, but take in an area exhibiting the extremes of Welsh life. As you walk around most of the brash seaside towns along the eastern section of the coast, only the street signs give any indication that you are in Wales at all; further west, there are places where English is seldom spoken other than to visitors. Scattered along the coast, dramatically sited castles act as a superb antidote to low-brow fun-seeking. Head inland and there's further contrast in the urban sprawl of Wrexham, tempered by the picture-perfect tranquillity of the Vale of Clwyd.

In the thirteenth century, the might of the English king Edward I had all but crushed the aspirations of the Welsh princes as their armies were forced west towards Anglesey and Edward set about building the Norman castles which hammered them into subjugation. Walled towns grew up around Edward's castles at **Conwy** and **Caernarfon** that were entirely the preserve of the English, thereby economically and politically marginalizing the Welsh who retreated west, where the English wielded less influence. As a response, Edward sited his final castle at **Beaumaris** to protect the entrance to the **Menai Strait**, the treacherous channel that separates the Isle of **Anglesey** from the mainland. The castle's concentric design was militarily more advanced than either Conwy or Caernarfon, but so complete was the English dominance by this stage that Edward never bothered to complete its construction.

The second sweeping change came in the late nineteenth and early twentieth centuries, when the benefits of the Industrial Revolution finally loosened the shackles on English mill-town factory workers enough for them to take holidays. Tatty beachfront towns sprang up, epitomized by the stretch of coast from Rhyl to **Colwyn Bay**. In contrast, Victorian **Llandudno**, always the posher place to stay, remains a cut above the rest, lying at the foot of the **Great Orme** limestone peninsula.

ACCOMMODATION PRICE CODES

Throughout this guide, hotel and B&B accommodation is priced on a scale of ① to ⑨, the number indicating the **lowest price** you could expect to pay per night in that establishment for a **double room** in high season. The prices indicated by the codes are as follows:

① under £40	④ £60–70	⑦ £110–150
② £40–50	⑤ £70–90	⑧ £150–200
③ £50–60	⑥ £90–110	⑨ over £200

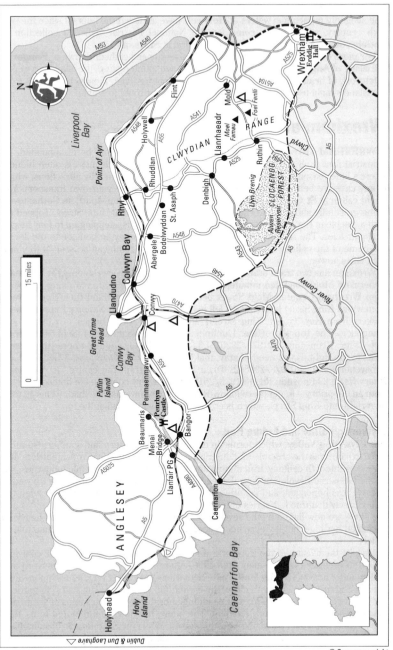

© Crown copyright

A few surprises come embedded into this matrix of bingo halls and caravan sites. The allegedly miraculous waters at **Holywell** have attracted the hopeful since the seventh century, while others come for the National Portrait Gallery's collection at **Bodelwyddan**, and Britain's smallest cathedral at **St Asaph**.

For more beaches, head up through the university and cathedral town of **Bangor** to the island of **Anglesey**. Often dismissed as flat and uninteresting, the island is a gentle patchwork of beautiful beaches and sites of ancient heritage. Finally, the ferries from the island's main town, **Holyhead**, provide the fastest route to Dublin.

Wrexham and around

If **WREXHAM** (Wrecsam) is your introduction to Wales, don't be disappointed. Its industrial past is all too evident and, as a border town, its Welshness is often hidden. There's little reason to stop except to use it as a base for the nearby attractions, which in any case are better visited from Llangollen – if you have your own transport. You might call in at **St Giles' Church** (Easter–Oct Mon–Fri 10am–4pm), its Gothic tower rising gracefully above the kernel of small lanes at the end of Hope Street. Topped off with a steeple in the 1520s, the tower has five distinct levels, stepping up to four hexagonal pinnacles. The same design was used at Yale University, in homage to the ancestral home of the college's benefactor, Elihu Yale, whose tomb can be seen at the base of St Giles' tower.

Wrexham has two **train stations**, half a mile apart, all services stopping at Wrexham General on Mold Road, ten minutes' walk northwest of the centre. Walking into town from Wrexham General, Mold Street becomes Regent Street and then Hope Street, from which King Street branches off left to the **bus station**, for National Express buses (tickets from Key Travel, King Street) and frequent **local buses** to Chester and Llangollen. The **tourist office**, Lambpit Street (Mon–Sat: Easter–Sept 10am–5pm; Oct–Easter 10am–4pm; ☎01978/292015), is reached by turning left where Hope Street turns to the right. If you need to **stay**, make for *Lyndhurst Guesthouse*, 3 Gerald St, off Grosvenor Road (☎01978/290802; ①), a short walk from the centre, or *Abbotsfield Priory Hotel*, 29 Rhosddu Rd (☎01978/261211; ③), a very comfortable hotel converted from an old priory – to get there follow Regent Street towards Wrexham General, then turn right into King Street, which is crossed by Rhosddu Road at the top.

Clywedog Valley and Erddig Hall

The **Clywedog Valley**, which forms an arc around the western and southern suburbs of Wrexham, was the crucible of industrial success in the northern Welsh borders during the eighteenth century. Iron mining and smelting were the principle industries, but as the Industrial Revolution forged ahead, water power harnessed from the Clywedog became less important, and factories moved closer to their raw materials, leaving the valley barely disturbed. A series of former industrial sites – ironworks, lead mines and the like – are now linked by the seven-mile-long **Clywedog Trail**. It's all a bit heavy on packaged heritage, but if you're interested, pick up a leaflet from the Wrexham tourist office.

Despite the closure of the ironworks and the consequent drop in demand, coal continued to be mined in the valley until 1986. After World War II, coal mines were tunnelled under nearby **Erddig Hall** (April–Sept Mon–Wed, Sat & Sun; house: noon–5pm; gardens: 11am–6pm; Oct both close 1hr earlier; full tour £6, "below stairs" & gardens £4; NT), two miles south of Wrexham, adding subsidence to the troubles of an already decaying seventeenth-century building. The house has now been restored to its 1922 appearance, but it isn't particularly distinguished. While the State Rooms upstairs have their share of fine furniture and portraits – including one by Gainsborough – the real interest lies in the quarters of the servants, whose lives were fully documented by their unusually benevolent masters. Eighteenth- and early nineteenth-century portraits of staff are still on display in the Servants' Hall, and each has a verse written by one of the Yorkes. You can also see the blacksmith's shop, lime yard, stables, laundry, kitchen and still-used bakehouse.

Holywell to Colwyn Bay

Making for the coastal resorts or mountains of Snowdonia, you might be tempted to charge headlong through northern Clwyd – not a bad idea considering the paucity of significant sights. No sooner have you cleared the industrial hinterland that spreads over the border from Chester than you hit the North Wales coast, a twenty-mile stretch from the end of the Dee estuary to Colwyn Bay which constitutes the ugliest piece of Welsh coastline: almost the entire length is taken up by caravan parks. "Amusements" aimed at the ubiquitous families from northwest England are liberally scattered along the promenades and beachfronts, and seem designed to keep you off the beaches: a good idea even in the hottest weather since the sea hereabouts is none too clean.

The country flanking the salt marshes of the Dee estuary was once contested by Marcher lords, but skirmishes were quashed by the construction of Flint Castle, the earliest of Edward I's Iron Ring of fortresses and now an insubstantial ruin overlooking the estuary at Flint. Understated **Holywell** has been an important pilgrimage site for the last thirteen hundred years, but now quietly ticks by almost unvisited. Much the same can be said of **St Asaph**, home to Britain's smallest cathedral. Two miles to the north is the second of Edward I's castles at **Rhuddlan**, and a few miles west, the National Portrait Gallery's Welsh outpost at **Bodelwyddan**; both are easily accessed from the brash resort town of Rhyl.

Holywell and around

A place of pilgrimage for thirteen hundred years, **HOLYWELL** (Treffynnon), just off the A55, fifteen miles northwest of Chester, comes billed as "The Lourdes of Wales", but without the tacky souvenir stalls, it doesn't really warrant such a comparison. **St Winefride's Well** (daily: mid-May to Sept 9.30am–5.15pm; Oct to mid-May 10am–4pm) – half a mile from the bus station at the far end of the High Street, then turn right and follow the signs – is the source of all the fuss, a calm pool capacious enough to accommodate the dozens of the faithful who dutifully wade through the waters three times in the hope of curing their ailments, a relic of the Celtic baptism by triple immersion.

The existence of the spring was first noted by the Romans, who used the waters to relieve rheumatism and gout. The traditional legend, however, states that in around 660 AD, the virtuous Winefride (Gwenfrewi in Welsh) was decapitated here after resisting the amorous advances of Prince Caradoc; the well is said to have sprung up at the spot where her head fell. Richard I and Henry V provided regal patronage, ensuring a steady flow of believers to what became one of the great shrines of Christendom, and James II came here to pray for a son and heir. Pilgrims formerly spent the night praying in the Perpendicular **St Winefride's Chapel** (key from the ticket office; CADW), built in around 1500 to enclose three sides of the well. The site's importance is waning, but pilgrimages do still take place, mainly on St Winefride's Day, the nearest Sunday to June 22, when a couple of thousand pilgrims are led through the streets behind a relic, part of Winefride's thumb bone.

From St Winefride's Well, a mile-long path runs past the remains of the copper and brass factories which now constitute the **Greenfield Valley Heritage Park** (April–Oct daily 10am–5pm), whose farm and museum perserves mainly agricultural buildings from around the area. Over the way are the ruined domestic buildings used by the abbot and twelve monks of the Savignac order at **Basingwerk Abbey** (free access; CADW).

Holywell has no train station, but frequent **buses** run to Rhyl and Chester from the station at the southern end of High Street. From the bus station, head a hundred yards down High Street and turn left to get to the **tourist office**, in the library on North Street (Mon 10am–5.30pm, Wed 10am–1pm, Tues, Thurs & Fri 10am–7pm, Sat 9.30am–12.30pm; ☎01352/713157).

St Asaph and around

ST ASAPH (Llanelwy), ten miles further west off the A55, ranks as Britain's second smallest city after St David's in Pembrokeshire, and its **cathedral** (open daily 8am–dusk) is the country's most diminutive, no bigger than many village churches. It was founded around 570 AD by St Kentigern, the patron saint of Glasgow, and takes its name from the succeeding bishop, St Asaph. Both are commemorated in the eastern-most window in the north aisle of the cathedral. From 1601 until his death in 1604, the bishopric was held by **William Morgan**, whose grave under the presbytery has gone unmarked since Giles Gilbert Scott's substantial restoration in the 1870s. Morgan was responsible for the translation of the first Welsh-language Bible in 1588, replacing the English ones used up until that time. Over 25 years, he and three other clergymen produced a translation so successful that the Privy Council decreed that a copy of *Y Beibl* should be allocated to every Welsh church, thereby setting a standard for prose and codifying the language. Without his efforts, many claim, Welsh would have died out. One thousand Morgan bibles were printed, of which only nineteen remain, one of them displayed in the north transept along with notable prayer books and psalters.

Buses stop right outside the cathedral. The best central **rooms** are at the *Kentigern Arms*, towards the bottom of the High Street (☎01745/584157; ③). The nicely furnished, non-smoking *Chalet*, The Roe (☎01745/584025; ②), is a quarter of a mile away – across the river bridge then right – while the plush *Plas Elwy*, The Roe (☎01745/582263; ④), is further down the same road. St Asaph's best **food** is served at the moderately priced *Barrow Alms*, High Street (☎01745/582260), followed by the bar meals at the *Kentigern Arms*, which is the most alluring **pub**.

Rhuddlan

RHUDDLAN, two miles north of St Asaph, lies on the banks of a tidal reach of the Clwyd River (Afon Clywedog), which finally meets the sea at Rhyl. The town would be an insignificant suburb of Rhyl but for the diamond-shaped ruin of **Rhuddlan Castle** (May–Sept daily 10am–5pm; £2; CADW), built between 1277 and 1282 as a garrison and royal residence for Edward I. The impressive castle commands a canalized section of the river protected by **Gillot's Tower**. Behind, the castle's massive towers were the work of James of St George, who was responsible for the concentric plan that allowed archers on both outer and inner walls to fire simultaneously. Important though the castle was, Rhuddlan earns its position in history as the place where Edward I signed the **Statute of Rhuddlan** on March 19, 1284, consigning Wales to centuries of subjugation by the English. A large – and somewhat ironic – plaque in Rhuddlan's main street details the terms of the statute.

Bodelwyddan

Barrelling west along the A55 expressway towards the coast brings you to the small village of **BODELWYDDAN**. The slender 202-foot limestone spire of **Marble Church** heralds the finest art showcase in North Wales, **Bodelwyddan Castle** (April–June,

Sept & Oct Mon–Thurs, Sat & Sun 10am–5pm; July & Aug daily 10am–5pm; Nov–March Tues–Thurs, Sat & Sun 11am–4pm; castle £4.50, gardens £1), set amidst landscaped gardens on its hill, half a mile south of the village. The opulent Victorian interiors of what is essentially a nineteenth-century mansion were restored in the 1980s to house one of four provincial outposts of the **National Portrait Gallery**, specializing in works contemporary with the castle.

Most of the two hundred-odd paintings are on the ground floor, approached through the "Watts Hall of Fame", a long corridor specially decorated in William Morris style to accommodate a chair by Morris and 26 portraits of eminent Victorians by G.F. Watts, among them Millais, Rossetti, Browning and Walter Crane. In the Ladies' Drawing Room opposite, a beautiful Biedermeier sofa outshines paintings of little-celebrated nineteenth-century women around the walls. Of the three main rooms, it is the Dining Room that stands out. Two sensitive portraits here highlight the Pre-Raphaelite support for social reform: William Holman Hunt's portrayal of the vociferous opponent of slavery and capital punishment, Stephen Lushington; and Ford Madox-Brown's double portrait of Henry Farell, prime mover in the passing of the 1867 Reform Bill, and suffragette Millicent Garrett. Works by John Singer Sargent and Hubert von Herkamer also adorn the room, which, like the others, is furnished with pieces from the Victoria and Albert Museum in London. Upstairs, nineteenth-century portraiture, portrait photography and works by female artists get generous coverage along with animal painters, Landseer in particular.

Llandudno

Set on a low isthmus, four miles northwest of Colwyn Bay, **LLANDUDNO** has an undeniably dignified air, its older set of promenading devotees often huddled in the glassed frontages of once-grand hotels, content to sit and watch the more rumbustious younger visitors. Almost invariably, the wind funnels between the limestone hummocks of the 680-foot **Great Orme** and its southern cousin the **Little Orme**, which flank the gently curving Victorian frontage; but don't let that put you off visiting this archetype of the genteel British seaside town.

Llandudno's early history revolves around the Great Orme, where St Tudno, who brought Christianity to the region in the sixth century, built the monastic cell that gives the town its name. When the early Victorian copper mines looked about to be worked out, in the mid-nineteenth century, local landowner Edward Mostyn exploited the growing craze for sea bathing and set about a speculative venture to create a seaside resort for the upper middle classes. Work got under way around 1854 and the town rapidly gained popularity over the next fifty years, becoming synonymous with the Victorian ideal of a respectable resort.

Despite the pavilion being destroyed by fire in early 1994, Llandudno's nineteenth-century **pier** (open all year; free) is one of the few remaining in Wales. It juts out into Llandudno Bay, a leisurely ten-minute stroll along The Promenade from Vaughan Street and the region's premier contemporary art gallery, the **Oriel Mostyn**, 12 Vaughan St (Mon–Sat 10am–1pm & 1.30–5pm; free), which hosts temporary shows featuring works by artists of international renown, with a particular leaning towards the current Welsh arts scene.

Kids are better entertained at the **Alice in Wonderland Visitor Centre**, 3–4 Trinity Square (April–Oct daily 10am–5pm; Nov–March closed Sun; £2.95), where they are guided through the "Rabbit Hole", full of fibre-glass Mad Hatters and March Hares, while a headset treats them to readings of *Jabberwocky* and the like. The Alice books were inspired by Lewis Carroll's meeting with one Alice Liddell, the daughter of friends, here in Llandudno.

The Great Orme

The view from the top of the **Great Orme** (Pen y Gogarth) ranks with those from the far loftier summits in Snowdonia, combining the seascapes east towards Rhyl and west over the sands of the Conwy Estuary with the brooding, quarry-chewed northern limit of the Carneddau range where Snowdonia crashes into the sea.

This huge lump of carboniferous limestone was subject to some of the same stresses that folded Snowdonia, producing fissures filled by molten mineral-bearing rock. A Bronze Age settlement developed when people began to smelt the contents of the malachite-rich veins, supplying copper – if current speculation turns out to be true – throughout Europe. The result of their labour is evident at the **Great Orme Copper Mines** (March–Oct daily 10am–5pm; £4.20), accessed via the tramway (see below). What were, until recently, considered to be Roman workings have recently revealed 4000-year-old animal bones which had been used as scrapers. Hard hats and miner's lamps are provided for the **guided tour** through just a small portion of the tunnels, enough to get a feel for the cramped working conditions and the dangers of rock fall.

The base of the Great Orme is traditionally circumnavigated on **Marine Drive**, a five-mile anticlockwise circuit from just near Llandudno's pier. To ascend to the dry ski slope and toboggan run at the **Summit Complex** (Easter–Oct daily; Nov–Easter Sat & Sun only), you can take the road, which runs past the mines, or the San Francisco-style **Great Orme Tramway** (April–Sept 10am–6pm; Oct–March 10am–4pm; £3.80 return), which creaks up from the bottom of Old Road, much as it has done since 1902. Alternatively, a **Cabin Lift** (Easter–June, Sept & Oct daily 10am–1pm & 2–4.30pm; July & Aug 10am–5.30pm; £4.80) carries you up over the Orme from the **Happy Valley** formal gardens, at the base of the pier.

Practicalities

The **train station**, at the corner of Augusta and Vaughan streets, is five minutes' walk southeast from the **tourist office**, 1–2 Chapel St (Easter–Sept daily 9.30am–6pm; Oct–Easter Mon–Sat 9.30am–5pm; ☎01492/876413). Chapel Street runs parallel to Mostyn Street, where local **buses** stop. Less than ten minutes' walk south, National Express buses pull in to the coach park on Mostyn Broadway. **Bike rental** is available from West End Cycles, 22 Augusta St, across the road from the train station.

With over seven hundred **hotels**, finding a place to stay is not usually a problem, though in high summer and especially on bank holidays, booking ahead is wise. The greatest concentration of budget places is along St David's Road, just west of the station, where you'll find the *Cliffbury Hotel*, 34 St David's Rd (☎01492/877224; ①). *Fernbank*, 9 Chapel St (☎01492/877251; ①), is one of the least expensive and best equipped of a string of low-cost hotels just along from the tourist office, while the *Gwesty Leamore Hotel*, 40 Lloyd St (☎01492/875552; ①), is one of the few guest houses in Llandudno actually run by Welsh people. If you've a head for heights, try *The Lighthouse*, Marine Drive (☎01492/876819; ⑥), three miles from Llandudno, and 370ft above the Irish Sea. Topnotch accommodation is available at *St Tudno Hotel*, a superb, small, seafront hotel on North Parade, just behind the pier (☎01492/874411; ④). The closest **camping** is at *Dinarth Hall Farm*, Dinarth Hall Road, Rhos-on-Sea (☎01492/548203), three miles east of Llandudno, accessible on buses #13, #14 and #15.

Llandudno is blessed with the widest range of **restaurants** in North Wales. The basement bistro at *Richards*, 7 Church Walks, dishes up imaginative, seafood-based meals, while the *Garden Room* at the *St Tudno Hotel* is one of Wales's best restaurants, serving French cuisine based on fresh Welsh produce. For substantial, tasty bar food, try the *Cottage Loaf*, Market Street, a flag-floored **pub** built from old ships' timbers on top of an old bakehouse, or the *King's Head*, on Old Road, the oldest pub in town, where Edward Mostyn and his surveyor mapped out the town.

Around the turn of the century, all the best performers clamoured to play Llandudno but today you're lucky to get anything more than faded stars plying the resorts throughout the summer. However, with the new 1500-seat **North Wales Theatre** (Theatr Gogledd Cymru), The Promenade (☎01492/872000) and the Llandudno **October Festival**, with concerts, theatre and exhibitions, things are looking a little rosier.

Conwy and around

CONWY has been much prettified since completion of a bypass tunnel under the Conwy River (Afon Conwy), making it one of the highlights of the north coast. Backed by a forested fold of Snowdonia, the town boasts a fine castle, a nearly complete belt of town walls and a wonderful setting on the Conwy estuary. Nowhere in the core of medieval and Victorian buildings is more than two hundred yards from the irregular triangle of protective masonry formed by the town walls. This makes it wonderfully easy to potter around and though you'll get to see everything you want to in a day, you may well want to stay longer.

Conwy Castle

Conwy Castle (April–May & Oct daily 9.30am–5pm; June–Sept daily 9.30am–6pm; Nov–March Mon–Sat 9.30am–4pm, Sun 11am–4pm; £3.50; CADW), now entered through a separate ticket office and over a modern bridge, is the toughest-looking link in Edward I's "Iron Ring" fortresses. After advancing west of the Conwy River in 1283, Edward decided to maintain a bridgehead by establishing another of his bastide towns (see box below). He chose a strategic knoll at the mouth of the river and set James of

---

THE IRON RING

Dotting the North Wales coast, each within a day's march of the next, Edward I's fearsome **Iron Ring** of colossal fortresses represents Europe's most ambitious and concentrated medieval building project, designed to prevent the recurrence of two massively expensive military campaigns. After Edward's first successful campaign in 1277, he was able to pin down his adversary, Llywelyn ap Gruffydd ("the Last") in Snowdonia and on Anglesey. In his first attempt at subjugation, this gave Edward room and time enough to build the now largely ruined castles at **Flint**, **Rhuddlan**, **Builth Wells** and **Aberystwyth**, as well as to commandeer and upgrade Welsh castles.

Llywelyn's second uprising, in 1282, was also ultimately unsuccessful, and Edward, determined not to have to fight a third time for the same land, set about extending his ring of fortifications in an immensely costly display of English might. Together with the Treaty of Rhuddlan in 1284, this saw the Welsh resistance effectively crushed. The castles at **Harlech**, **Caernarfon** and **Conwy**, though nearly contemporary, display a unique progression towards the later, highly evolved concentric design of **Beaumaris**. All this second batch, including the town walls of Caernarfon and Conwy, were the work of the master military architect of his age, James of St George d'Espéranche, whose work in Conwy is now recognized with **UN World Heritage Site** status.

Each of the castles was integrated with a **bastide town** – an idea borrowed from Gascony in southwest France, where Edward I was duke – the town and castle mutually reliant on each other for protection and trade. The bastides were always populated with English settlers, the Welsh permitted to enter the town during the day but not to trade and certainly not to carry arms. It wasn't until the eighteenth century that the Welsh would have towns they could truly call their own.

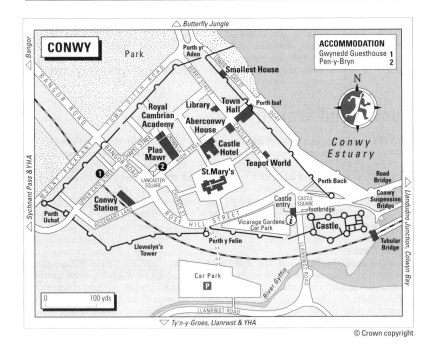

CONWY

Park

Butterfly Jungle

Porth yr Aden

Smallest House

ACCOMMODATION
Gwynedd Guesthouse 1
Pen-y-Bryn 2

N

Royal Cambrian Academy

Library

Town Hall

Aberconwy House

Plas Mawr

Castle Hotel

Porth Isaf

Conwy Estuary

Teapot World

St.Mary's

Conwy Station

Porth Uchaf

LANCASTER SQUARE

Porth Bach

Castle entry

CASTLE SQUARE

footbridge

Road Bridge

Conwy Suspension Bridge

Vicarage Gardens
Car Park

Castle

Llewelyn's Tower

Porth y Felin

Tubular Bridge

Car Park
P

0   100 yds

LLANRWST ROAD

River Gyffin

Ty'n-y-Groes, Llanrwst & YHA

© Crown copyright

St George to fashion a castle to fit its contours. With the help of 1500 men it took only five years.

Richard II stayed at the castle on his return from an ill-timed trip to Ireland in 1399, until lured from safety by Bolingbroke's vassal the Earl of Northumberland. Northumberland swore in the castle's chapel to grant the king safe passage, but Richard was taken and Bolingbroke became Henry IV. Just two years later, on Good Friday, when the fifteen-strong castle guard were at church, two cousins of Owain Glyndŵr took the castle and razed the town for Glyndŵr's cause. The castle then fell into disuse, and was bought in 1627 for £100 by Charles I's Secretary of State, Lord Conway of Ragley, who then had the task of refortifying it for the Civil War. At the restoration of the monarchy in 1665, the castle was stripped of all its iron, wood and lead, and was left substantially as it is today.

Being overlooked by a low hill, the castle appears less easily defended than others along the coast, but James constructed eight massive towers in a rectangle around the two wards, the inner one separated from the outer by a drawbridge and portcullis, and further protected by turrets atop the four eastern towers, now the preserve of crows. Strolling along the wall-top gallery, you can look down onto something unique in the Iron Ring fortresses, a roofless but largely intact interior. The outer ward's 130-foot-long Great Hall and the King's Apartments are both well preserved, but the only part of the castle to have kept its roof is the **Chapel Tower**, named for the small room built into the wall whose semicircular apse still shows some heavily worn carving. On the floor below, there's a small exhibition on religious life in medieval castles which won't detain you long from exploring the passages.

The rest of the town

Anchored to the castle walls as though a drawbridge, Telford's narrow **suspension bridge** (April–June & Sept–Oct Wed–Mon 10am–5pm; July & Aug daily 10am–5pm; £1; combined ticket with Aberconwy House £2.50; NT) was part of the 1826 road improvement scheme, prompted by the need for better communications to Ireland after the Act of Union, and contemporary with his far greater effort spanning the Menai Strait. Restored to its original state, without tarmac, signs or street lighting, it now operates as a footbridge.

The approach to the modern replacement bridge has created the only breach in the thirty-foot high **town walls**, which branch out from the castle into a three-quarter-mile-long circuit, enclosing Conwy's ancient quarter. Inaccessible from the castle they were designed to protect, the walls are punctuated by 21 evenly spaced horseshoe towers, a third of which can be visited on the **wall walk**, starting from Porth Uchaf on Upper Gate Street and running down to a spur into the estuary. Here, you come down off the walls beside brightly rigged trawlers, mussel boats and the self-proclaimed **smallest house in Britain** (daily: Easter–June & Sept to mid-Oct 10am–6pm; July & Aug 10am–9pm; 50p), only 9ft by 5ft in total. Porth Isaf, the nearby gate in the town walls, leads up Lower High Street to the fourteenth-century timber and stone **Aberconwy House**, Castle Street (April–Oct Mon & Wed–Sun 10am–5pm; £2; combined ticket with suspension bridge £2.50; NT), a former merchant's house, its rooms decked out in styles that recall its past. Continue along the High Street to the Dutch-style **Plas Mawr** at no. 20 (Tues–Sun: April–May & Sept 9.30am–5pm; June–Aug 9.30am–6pm; Oct 9.30am–4pm; £4; CADW), a beautifully restored Elizabethan town house, built in 1576 for Robert Wynn, one of the first Welsh people to live in the town. Much of the dressed stonework was replaced during renovations in the 1940s and 1950s, but the interior sports more original features, in particular the friezes and superb moulded plaster ceilings depicting fleurs de lis, griffons, owls and rams. The tour concludes with a wonderfully scatological exhibition on sixteenth- and seventeenth-century ideas about disease and cleanliness.

Light relief from all the worthy history is on hand across the road from Aberconwy House, at the **Teapot World**, Castle Street (Easter–Oct Mon–Sat 10am–5.30pm, Sun 11am–5.30pm; £1.50), which has a thousand pots, mostly dating from before the 1950s: Wedgwood and majolica to Bauhaus and Clarice Cliff.

Practicalities

Llandudno Junction, less than a mile across the river to the east, serves as the main **train station**; only slow, regional services stop in Conwy itself. National Express **buses** pull up outside the town walls on Town Ditch Road, while local buses use the stops in the centre, mostly on Lancaster Square or Castle Street. The **tourist office** (April–Oct daily 9.30am–6.30pm; Nov–March Mon–Sat 9.30am–4pm, Sun 11am–4pm; ☎01492/592248) shares the same building as the castle ticket office.

Accommodation right in the centre of town is a bit thin, so booking ahead is advisable in summer: *Gwynedd Guesthouse*, 10 Upper Gate St (☎01492/596537; ①), is the least expensive central B&B and consequently often full. *Glan Heulog*, Llanrwst Road, on the outskirts of town half a mile towards Llanrwst on the B5106 (☎01492/593845; ②), is about the best B&B within easy walking distance of Conwy. *Pen-y-Bryn*, 28 High St (☎01492/596445; ②), is another central B&B worth trying; it's housed in a sixteenth-century building above some excellent tearooms. Further afield, there's *Castle Bank Hotel*, Mount Pleasant (☎01492/593888; ⑤), a licensed, non-smoking hotel with country house atmosphere, ten minutes' walk from the town centre: turn first left outside the town walls on the Bangor road. Take bus #19 to the nearest **campsite**, the family-oriented *Conwy Touring Park*, a mile or so south along the B5106 (☎01492/592856; closed

Nov–March). The **YHA hostel** (☎01492/593571) is on Lark Hill, a ten-minute hike from town up the road to Sychnant Pass, and there's another one nearby in the simple but superbly set *Rowen*, a mile up a steep hill above Rowen village, four miles south of Conwy (☎01492/650089; closed Oct–Easter); bus #19 connects hourly in summer.

Conwy has relatively few **restaurants**. In town, you're best off going veggie at *The Wall Place*, Bishop's Yard, Chapel Street, which is fast becoming Conwy's trendiest spot; it even has the occasional night of live folk and Welsh music. Otherwise, you can eat Italian at *Alfredo's*, Lancaster Square (closed Sun), or Austrian at the *Austrian Restaurant*, west of town on Old Conwy Road, Capelulo (closed Sun eve & Mon). Good **pubs** are easier to find: try *Ye Olde Mail Coach*, at 16 High St, for decent beer, food and occasional music, or the unpretentious *Malt Loaf*, opposite the station on Rosehill Street, where you'll find regular live folk and other music. The best pub in the vicinity is the fifteenth-century *Groes Inn*, in Tyn-y-Groes, two miles south on the B5106 to Llanrwst, which serves excellent bar meals and good cask ales.

Around Conwy

The best short walk from Conwy is on to **Conwy Mountain** and the 800-foot peaks behind, all giving great views right along the coast. Follow a sign up Cadnant Park off the Bangor road just outside the town walls, then take the road around until Mountain Road heads off on the right towards a hill fort on the summit. This group is separated from the foothills of the Carneddau range by the narrow cleft of **Sychnant Pass**.

Thousands come to Conwy specifically to see **Bodnant Garden** (mid-March to Oct daily 10am–5pm; £4.60; NT), beside the lower reaches of the Conwy, eight miles to the south. During May and June, the Laburnum Arch flourishes and banks of rhododendrons are in full and glorious bloom all over what ranks as one of the finest formal gardens in Britain. Laid out in 1875 around Bodnant Hall (closed to the public) by its then owner, English industrialist Henry Pochin, the garden spreads out over eighty acres of the eastern Conwy Valley. Facing southwest, the bulk of the gardens – divided into an upper terraced garden and lower pinetum and wild garden – catch the late afternoon sun as it sets over the Carneddau range. Though it's arranged so that shrubs and plants provide a blaze of colour throughout the opening season, autumn is a perfect time to be here, with hydrangeas still in bloom and fruit trees shedding their leaves. The #25 bus runs here from Llandudno every two hours, calling at Llandudno Junction, or it's a two-mile walk from the Tal-y-Cafn train station on the Conwy Valley line.

Bangor and Penrhyn

After spending a few days travelling through mid-Wales or in the mountains of Snowdonia, **BANGOR** makes a welcome change. It is not big, but as the largest town in Gwynedd and home to **Bangor University**, it passes in these parts for cosmopolitan. The students decamp for the summer, leaving only a trickle of visitors to replace them. The presence of a large non-Welsh student population inflames the passions of the more militant nationalists in what is a staunchly Welsh-speaking area, a dramatic change from the largely English-speaking north-coast resorts.

The university takes up much of upper Bangor, straddling the hill that separates the town centre from the Menai Strait. The shape of the college's main building is almost an exact replica of the thirteenth- to fifteenth-century **cathedral** (daily 11am–5pm), which boasts the longest continuous use of any cathedral in Britain, easily predating the town. Pop in if only to see the sixteenth-century wooden **Mostyn Christ**, depicted bound and seated on a rock.

Just over the road, the **Bangor Museum and Art Gallery**, Ffordd Gwynedd (Tues–Fri 12.30–4.30pm, Sat 10.30am–4.30pm; free), offers snippets of local history enlivened by a traditional costume section and an archeology room, containing the most complete Roman sword found in Wales. The art gallery concentrates on predominantly Welsh contemporary works. For a good look down the Menai Strait to Telford's bridge, walk along Garth Road to Bangor's rejuvenated and pristine **Victorian Pier** (50p), which reaches halfway across to Anglesey.

Penrhyn Castle

There can hardly be a more vulgar testament to the Anglo-Welsh landowning gentry's oppression of the rural Welsh than the oddly compelling **Penrhyn Castle** (Mon & Tues–Sun: April–June, Sept & Oct noon–5pm; July & Aug 11am–5pm; castle & grounds £5; grounds only £3; NT), two miles east of Bangor, which overlooks Port Penrhyn from its acres of isolating parkland. Built on the backs of slate miners for the benefit of their hated bosses, this monstrous nineteenth-century neo-Norman fancy, with over three hundred rooms dripping with luxurious fittings, was funded by the quarry's huge profits. The sugar and slate fortune built by anti-abolitionist Richard Pennant, first Baron Penrhyn, provided the means for his self-aggrandizing great-great-nephew George Dawkins to hire architect Thomas Hopper, who spent thirteen years from 1827 encasing the neo-Gothic hall in a Norman fortress complete with monumental five-storey keep.

Sour grapes aside, the decoration is glorious, and fairly true to the Romanesque style, with its deeply cut chevrons, billets and double-cone ornamentation. Hopper even looked to Norman architecture for the design of the furniture, but abandoned historical authenticity when it came to installing the central heating system, which piped hot air through ornamental brass ducts at the cost of twenty tons of coal a month. Everything is on a massive scale. Three-foot-thick oak doors separate the rooms, ebony is used to dramatic effect and a slate bed was built for, but declined by, Queen Victoria when she visited. The family amassed Wales's largest private painting collection, including numerous family likenesses, a Gainsborough landscape, Canaletto's *The Thames at Westminster* and a Rembrandt portrait.

Gleaming examples of rolling stock from Richard Pennant's slate railway and the country's other private industrial lines are on display in the **Industrial Railway Museum** (same times as castle; entry with castle ticket), including Lord Penrhyn's luxurious coach, linked to a quarrymen's car. Buses #5, #6 and #7 run frequently from Bangor to the gates, from where it is a mile-long walk to the house.

Practicalities

All trains on the North Coast line stop at Bangor **train station**, on Station Road, at the bottom of Holyhead Road. The **tourist office** is in the Town Hall on Deiniol Road (Easter–Sept daily 10am–6pm; Oct–March Tues–Sat 10am–5pm; ☎01248/352786). Bangor doesn't have a huge choice of places to stay, with most of the cheaper **accommodation** bundled at the northern end of Garth Road, about twenty minutes' walk from the train station: try *Dilfan* (☎01248/353030; ②). *Eryl Môr Hotel*, 2 Upper Garth Rd (☎01248/353789; ③), is a quiet and comfortable hotel with views over Bangor's pier and the Menai Strait. The University lets out clean, functional rooms on Ffriddoedd Road (☎01248/372104; ①) from late June to late September and over the Easter vacation. Bangor's **YHA hostel**, Tan-y-Bryn (☎01248/353516), is signposted off the A56, ten minutes' walk east of the centre (bus #6 or #7 along Garth Road). The nearest **campsite** is the very laid-back *Treborth Hall Farm* (☎01248/364104), fifteen minutes' walk (or bus #5) from Upper Bangor, on the road out towards the Menai Bridge.

With the possible exception of Llandudno, Bangor offers the widest selection of **eating** possibilities in North Wales. Packed out with students and locals, the *Fat Cat Café Bar*, 161 High St, has a menu ranging from huge burgers to salmon and broccoli pasta quills; another good bet is the classy *Greek Taverna Politis*, 12 Holyhead Rd. The expensive restaurant of the *Menai Court Hotel*, Craig-y-Don Road, earns plaudits from foodies for its traditional British and European dishes. If you've tried to learn any of the language you can put it to good use at *Tafarn Y Glôb*, a traditional **pub** on Albert Street, where ordering in Welsh is pretty much *de rigueur*. For a pint of beer try "un peint o cwrw, os gwelwch yn dda", pronounced "een paint o cooroo, os gweloch un tha". *Y Castell*, on Glanrafon, a street opposite the cathedral, is a very popular and studenty pub, while *O'Shea's*, on High Street, is your best bet for local **live music**.

Anglesey

Anglesey (Ynys Môn) welcomes visitors to "Mam Cymru", the Mother of Wales, attesting to the island's former importance as the national breadbasket. In the twelfth century Giraldus Cambrensis noted that "When crops have failed in other regions, this island, from its soil and its abundant produce, has been able to supply all Wales", and while feeding their less productive kin in Snowdonia is no longer a priority, the land remains predominantly pastoral, with small fields, stone walls and white houses reminiscent of England. Linguistically and politically, though, Anglesey is intensely Welsh. One of the four Plaid Cymru MPs represents the islanders, seventy percent of whom are Welsh-speakers. The island was the crucible of pre-Roman druidic activity in Britain, and there are still numerous neolithic remains in which to soak up the atmosphere of a pagan past. Many people charge straight through to **Holyhead** and the Irish ferries, missing out on the ancient town of **Beaumaris**, with its fine castle, the Whistler mural at **Plas Newydd** and some superb coastal scenery: a necklace of fine sandy coves and rocky headlands that's a match for anywhere in the country.

Beaumaris

The original inhabitants of **BEAUMARIS** (Biwmares) were evicted by Edward I to make way for the construction of his new castle and bastide town (see p.771), dubbed "beautiful marsh" in an attempt to attract English settlers. Today the place can still seem like the small English outpost Edward intended, with its elegant Georgian terrace along the front (designed by Joseph Hansom, of cab fame) and more plummy English accents than you'll have heard for a while. Many of their owners belong with the flotilla of yachts, an echo of the port's fleet of merchant ships, which disappeared with the completion of bridges to the mainland and subsequent growth of Holyhead. While Beaumaris repays an afternoon mooching around and enjoying the views across the Strait, it also boasts more sights than the rest of the island put together, inevitably drawing the crowds in summer.

Beaumaris Castle (April–May & Oct daily 9.30am–5pm; June–Sept daily 9.30am–6pm; Nov–March Mon–Sat 9.30am–4pm, Sun 11am–4pm; £2.20; CADW) might never have been built had Madog ap Llywelyn not captured Caernarfon in 1294. When asked to build the new castle, James of St George abandoned the Caernarfon design in favour of a concentric plan, developing it into a highly evolved symmetrical octagon. Sited on flat land at the edge of town, the castle is denied the domineering majesty of Caernarfon or Harlech, its low outer walls appearing almost welcoming until you begin to appreciate the concentric layout of the defences protected by massive towers, a moat linked to the sea and the Arab-influenced staggered entries through the two gatehouses. Despite over thirty years' work, the project was never quite finished, leaving most of the inner ward empty and the corbels and fireplaces built into the walls unused. You can explore the internal passages in the walls but the low-parapet wall-walk, from where you get the best idea of the castle's defensive capability, remains off limits. Impressive as they are, none of these defences was able to prevent siege by Owain Glyndŵyr, who held the castle for two years from 1403, although they did withhold a Parliamentarian siege during the Civil War.

Almost opposite the castle stands the Jacobean **Beaumaris Courthouse** (Easter & June–Sept Mon–Fri 11am–5.30pm, Sat & Sun 2–5.30pm; May Sat & Sun 2–5.30pm; £1.50; combined ticket with jail £2.95), built in 1614 and the oldest active court in Britain. It is now used only for the twice-monthly Magistrates Court, but until 1971, when they were moved to Caernarfon, the quarterly Assize Courts were held here. These were traditionally held in English, giving the jury little chance to follow the proceedings and Welsh-speaking defendants no defence against prosecutors renowned for slapping heavy penalties on minor offences. On session days you can watch the trials, but won't be able to take the recorded tour or inspect *The Lawsuit*, a plaque in the magistrates' room depicting two farmers pulling the horns and tail of a cow while a lawyer milks it.

Many citizens were transported from the courthouse to the colonies for their misdemeanours; others only made it a couple of blocks to **Beaumaris Gaol**, Steeple Lane (Easter & June–Sept daily 11am–5.30pm; £2.30; combined ticket with courthouse £2.95) which, when it opened in 1829, was considered a model prison, with running water and toilets in each cell, an infirmary and eventually heating. Women prisoners did the cooking and were allowed to rock their babies' cradles in the nursery above by means of a pulley system. Advanced perhaps, but nonetheless a gloomy place: witness the windowless punishment cell, the yard for stone-breaking and the treadmill water pump operated by the prisoners. The least fortunate inmates were publicly hanged, the fate of a certain Richard Rowlands, whose disembodied voice leads the recorded tour of the building and various displays on prison life.

Practicalities

With no trains, long-distance coaches or tourist office, Beaumaris seems poorly served, but it does have a regular **bus** service to Bangor (#53 & #57; infrequent on Sun). The best of the **hotels** is the ancient and luxurious *Ye Olde Bull's Head Inn*, 18 Castle St (☎01248/810329; ⑤), used as General Mytton's headquarters during the Civil War. The *Bishopsgate House Hotel*, 54 Castle St (☎01248/810302; ④; closed Jan to mid-Feb), is only a stone's throw away and almost of the same standard. The first of the **B&Bs** to head for is the antique-furnished *Swn-y-Don*, 7 Bulkeley Terrace (☎01248/810794; ②). *Kingsbridge* is the nearest **campsite**, two miles north in Llanfaes (☎01248/490636). There are plenty of daytime cafés serving snacks, and more substantial **restaurants** are also in good supply, the best being *Ye Olde Bull's Head Inn* and the moderately priced *Bishopsgate House Hotel*, both of which also do filling bar meals. *The Cockleshell*, at 13 Castle St, offers good seafood specialities.

Llanfair PG and Plas Newydd

In the 1880s a local tailor invented the longest place name in Britain in a successful attempt to draw tourists. However, it is an utter disappointment to arrive at Llanfairpwllgwyngyllgogerychwyrndrobwllllantysiliogogogoch, which translates as "St Mary's Church in the hollow of white hazel near a rapid whirlpool and the Church of St Tysilio near the red cave" – commonly known as **LLANFAIR PG** – to find only a vast car park, a tacky wool shop and a **tourist office** (April–Sept Mon–Sat 9.30am–5.30pm, Sun 10am–5pm; Oct–March Mon–Sat 9.30am–5pm, Sun 10am–5pm; ☎01248/713177), the only one worth its salt on the island.

The marquises of Anglesey still live at **Plas Newydd** (April–Oct Mon–Wed, Sat & Sun noon–5pm; house & garden £4.20, garden only £2.20; NT), a mile and a half south of Llanfair PG, a modest three-storey mansion with incongruous Tudor caps on slender octagonal turrets. Inside, architect James Wyatt was given free stylistic rein, producing a Gothic music room followed by a Neoclassical staircase hall with a cantilevered staircase and deceptively solid-looking Doric columns – actually just painted wood. Endure the slog through corridors of oils and period rooms to the highlight, a 58-foot-long wall consumed by a trompe l'oeil painting by Rex Whistler, who spent a couple of years here in the 1930s. Walking along his imaginary seascape, your position appears to shift by over a mile as the mountains of Snowdonia and a whimsical composite of elements, culled from Italy as well as Britain, change perspective. Portmeirion (see p.758) is there, as are the Round Tower from Windsor Castle and the steeple from St Martin-in-the-Fields in London. Whistler himself appears as a gondolier, and again as a gardener in one of the two right-angled panels at either end, which appear to extend the room further. The prize exhibit in the **Cavalry Museum**, a few rooms further on, is the world's first articulated leg, all wood, leather and springs, designed for the first marquis, who lost his leg at Waterloo.

Holy Island and Holyhead

Holy Island (Ynys Gybi) is blessed with Anglesey's best scenery and cursed with its most unattractive town. The spectacular sea cliffs around South Stack, and the Stone Age and Roman remains on Holyhead Mountain are just a couple of miles from workaday Holyhead, whose ferry routes to Ireland and good transport links mean you'll probably find your way there at some stage.

The local council's valiant attempts to brighten up **HOLYHEAD** (Caergybi) somehow make this town of dilapidated shopfronts and high unemployment even more depressing. In 1727, Swift found it "scurvy, ill provided and comfortless", and little has changed. Fortunately, train and ferry timings are reasonably well integrated, so you shouldn't need to spend much time here. From the combined **train station**, **bus station** and **ferry terminal**, a pedestrian bridge over London Road, past the A5, leads into the town centre. The **tourist office** (daily 10am–6pm; ☎01407/762622) is temporarily housed in a Portakabin on the A5 approach to town, opposite the aluminium smelting works.

Shun the bunch of poor **B&Bs** along the A5 into the town in favour of those around Walthew Avenue, most easily reached by turning left just before the tourist office onto the beachfront Prince of Wales Road, then left again into Walthew Avenue. *Glan Ifor*, at no. 8 (☎01407/764238; ①), and *Orotavia*, at no. 66 (☎01407/760259; ①), are both good, as is *Yr Hendre*, Porth-y-Felin, at the top of Walthew Avenue (☎01407/762929;

②), a former manse where you can get inexpensive evening meals. Fast **food** is the staple diet in Holyhead, but you can still eat well: the budget *Omar Khayyam Tandoori*, 8 Newry St, serves the tastiest curries around.

Holyhead Mountain and South Stack

The northern half of Holy Island is ranged around the skirts of the 700-foot **Holyhead Mountain** (Mynydd Twr), its summit ringed by the seventeen-acre **Caer y Twr** (unrestricted access; CADW), one of the largest Iron Age sites in North Wales. The best approach is by car or bus #44 to the car park at **South Stack** (Ynys Lawd), two miles west of Holyhead, from where a path (30min) leads to the top of Holyhead Mountain. Most visitors only walk the few yards to the cliff-top **Ellin's Tower Seabird Centre** (Easter–Sept daily 11am–5pm; free) where, from April until the end of July, binoculars and closed-circuit TV give an unparalleled opportunity to watch up to three thousand birds – razorbills, guillemots and the odd puffin – nesting on the nearby sea cliffs while ravens and peregrines wheel outside the tower's windows. When the birds have gone, rock climbers picking their way up the same cliff face replace them as the main interest. A twisting path leads down from the tower to a suspension bridge over the surging waves. Nearby, nineteen low stone circles make up the **Cytiau'r Gwyddelod** or the "huts of the Irish" – a common name for any ancient settlement – in this case late Neolithic or early Bronze Age.

travel details

Trains

Bangor to: Chester (25 daily; 1hr); Colwyn Bay (20 daily; 30min); Conwy (7 daily; 20min); Holyhead (21 daily; 30–40min); Llandudno Junction (20 daily; 20min); Llanfair PG (7 daily; 10min).

Conwy to: Bangor (7 daily; 20min); Holyhead (8 daily; 1hr); Llandudno Junction (8 daily; 5min).

Holyhead to: Bangor (20 daily; 30–40min); Chester (15 daily; 1hr 40min); Llandudno Junction (20 daily; 1hr); Llanfair PG (7 daily; 30min).

Llandudno to: Betws-y-Coed (5 daily; 40min); Blaenau Ffestiniog (5 daily; 1hr 10min); Llandudno Junction (at least hourly; 10min).

Llandudno Junction to: Bangor (20 daily; 20min); Betws-y-Coed (6 daily; 30min); Holyhead (20 daily; 1hr).

Llanfair PG to: Bangor (7 daily; 10min); Holyhead (7 daily; 30min).

Wrexham to: Chester (every 2hr; 20min); Chirk (every 2hr; 10min); Liverpool (change at Bidston; hourly; 1hr 15min).

Cardiff (1 daily; 7hr 45min); Chester (2 daily; 2hr 40min); Conwy (every 30min; 45min); Holyhead (every 30min; 1hr 15min); Llanberis (every 30min; 30min); Llandudno (every 30min; 1hr); Llanfair PG (every 30min; 15min).

Beaumaris to: Bangor (at least hourly; 30min).

Conwy to: Bangor (every 30min; 45min); Betws-y-Coed (5 daily; 1hr); Llanberis (4 daily; 1hr 30min); Llandudno (every 30min; 20min).

Holyhead to: Bangor (every 30min; 1hr 15min); Chester (1 daily; 3hr 30min); Llanfair PG (every 30min; 1hr).

Llandudno to: Bangor (every 30min; 1hr); Betws-y-Coed (5 daily; 1hr 15min); Caernarfon (every 30min; 1hr 40min); Llanberis (4–6 daily in summer, none in winter; 2hr).

Llanfair PG to: Bangor (every 30min; 15min); Holyhead (every 30min; 1hr).

Wrexham to: Barmouth (7 daily; 2hr 20min); Chester (every 15min; 40min); Chirk (hourly; 40min); Dolgellau (8 daily; 2hr); Llangollen (at least hourly; 40min).

Buses

Bangor to: Beaumaris (at least hourly; 30min); Betws-y-Coed (2 daily; 50min); Caernarfon (every 20min; 30min); Capel Curig (2 daily; 40min);

Ferries

Holyhead to: Dublin (4 ferries daily; 3hr 45min; 3 catamarans daily; 3hr 45min); Dun Laoghaire (4 catamarans daily; 1hr 45min).

PART FOUR

SCOTLAND

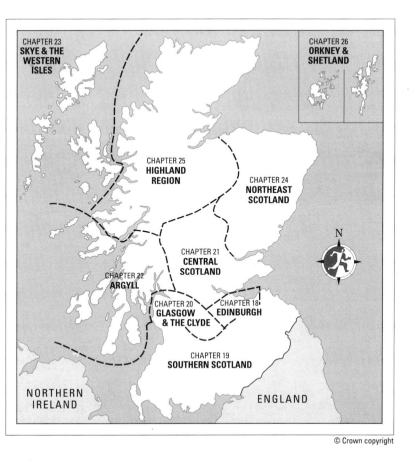

CHAPTER 23
SKYE & THE WESTERN ISLES

CHAPTER 26
ORKNEY & SHETLAND

CHAPTER 25
HIGHLAND REGION

CHAPTER 24
NORTHEAST SCOTLAND

CHAPTER 21
CENTRAL SCOTLAND

CHAPTER 22
ARGYLL

CHAPTER 20
GLASGOW & THE CLYDE

CHAPTER 18
EDINBURGH

N

CHAPTER 19
SOUTHERN SCOTLAND

NORTHERN IRELAND

ENGLAND

© Crown copyright

CHAPTER EIGHTEEN

EDINBURGH AND AROUND

Well-heeled **EDINBURGH**, the showcase capital of Scotland, is a cosmopolitan and cultured city. The setting is wonderfully striking: the city is perched on a series of extinct volcanoes and rocky crags which rise from the generally flat landscape of the Lothians, with the sheltered shoreline of the Firth of Forth to the north. "My own Romantic town", Sir Walter Scott called it, although it was another native author, Robert Louis Stevenson, who perhaps best captured the feel of his "precipitous city", declaring that "No situation could be more commanding for the head of a kingdom; none better chosen for noble prospects."

Despite its relatively small population of just under half a million, Edinburgh is spread out over a wide area, although most of the main attractions are within walking distance of each other in the historic heart of the city. The centre has two distinct parts, the Old and New Towns, divided by **Princes Street Gardens**, which run roughly east–west under the shadow of **Castle Rock**. Set on the crag which sweeps down from the towering fairytale **Castle** to the royal **Palace of Holyroodhouse**, the **Old Town** preserves all the key reminders of its role as a capital. Its tortuous alleys and tightly packed closes are unrelentingly medieval, associated in popular imagination with the underworld lore of Deacon Brodie, inspiration for Stevenson's *Dr Jekyll and Mr Hyde*, and the body snatchers Burke and Hare. Edinburgh earned its nickname of "Auld Reekie" for the smog and smell generated by the Old Town, which for centuries swam in sewage tipped out of the windows of cramped tenements.

In contrast, a tantalizing glimpse of the wild beauty of Scotland's countryside can be found immediately beyond the palace in **Holyrood Park** – an extensive area of open countryside dominated by **Arthur's Seat**, the largest and most impressive of the volcanoes. To the north of Princes Street Gardens, the dignified, Neoclassical **New Town** was immaculately laid out during the Age of Reason, after the announcement of a plan to improve conditions in the city.

Among Edinburgh's suburbs, the most lively is **Leith**, the city's medieval port, whose seedy edge is now softened by a series of great bars and upmarket seafood restaurants. Outside the city boundaries, the village of **Roslin**, to the south, draws visitors to its mysterious fifteenth-century chapel, while to the northwest of the city, the dramatic lines of the **Forth Rail Bridge** are best seen from the parallel Road Bridge.

In August and early September, around a million visitors flock to the city for the **Edinburgh Festival**, in fact a series of separate festivals that make up the largest arts extravaganza in the world. Among the host of permanent attractions is the exciting new **National Museum of Scotland**, housing ten thousand of Scotland's most precious artefacts, while the **National Gallery of Scotland** and its offshoot, the **Scottish National Gallery of Modern Art**, have two of Britain's finest collections of paintings.

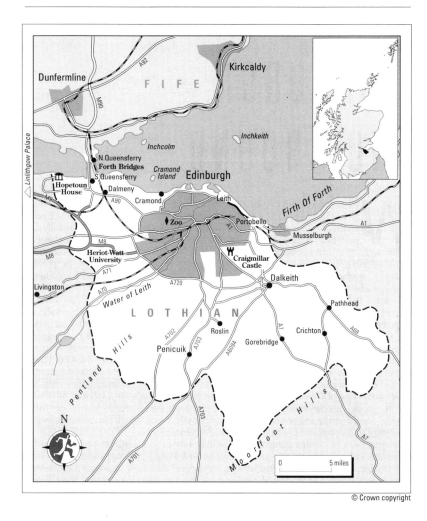

© Crown copyright

On a less elevated theme, the city's distinctive howffs (pubs), allied to its brewing and distilling traditions, make it a great **drinking** city, though the relatively recent arrival of café culture and some topnotch **restaurants** have added a cosmopolitan hue to the traditional image. The presence of three **universities**, plus several colleges, means that there is a youthful presence for most of the year – a welcome corrective to the stuffiness which is often regarded as Edinburgh's Achilles heel.

Some history

It was during the **Dark Ages** that the name of Edinburgh – at least in its early forms of Dunedin or Din Eidyn ("fort of Eidyn") – first appeared. Castle Rock, a strategic fort atop one of the volcanoes, served as the nation's **southernmost border post** until 1018, when King Malcolm I established the River Tweed as the frontier. In the reign of

Malcolm III, the castle became one of the main seats of the court, and the town, which was given privileged status as a **royal burgh**, began to grow. In 1128 King David established Holyrood Abbey at the foot of the slope, later allowing its monks to found a separate burgh, known as **Canongate**.

Robert the Bruce granted Edinburgh a **new charter** in 1329, giving it jurisdiction over the nearby port of Leith, and during the following century the prosperity brought by foreign trade enabled the newly fortified city to establish itself as the **permanent capital** of Scotland. Under King James IV, the city enjoyed a short but brilliant **Renaissance** era, which saw not only the construction of a new palace alongside Holyrood Abbey, but also the granting of a royal charter to the College of Surgeons, the earliest in the city's long line of academic and professional bodies.

This period came to an abrupt end in 1513 with the calamitous defeat by the English at the **Battle of Flodden**, which led to several decades of political instability. In the 1540s, King Henry VIII's attempt to force a royal union with Scotland led to the sack of Edinburgh, prompting the Scots to turn to France for help; French troops arrived to defend the city and the young queen Mary was dispatched to Paris as the promised bride of the Dauphin. While the French occupiers succeeded in removing the English threat, they themselves antagonized the locals, who had become increasingly sympathetic to the ideals of the **Reformation**. When the radical preacher John Knox returned from exile in 1555, he quickly won over the city to his **Calvinist** message.

James VI's rule saw the foundation of the University of Edinburgh in 1582, but following the **Union of the Crowns** in 1603, the royal court headed south and Edinburgh was totally upstaged by London. Although James promised to visit every three years, it was not until 1617 that he made his only return trip. In 1633 Charles I visited Edinburgh for his coronation, but soon afterwards precipitated a crisis by introducing episcopacy to the Church of Scotland, in the process making Edinburgh a bishopric for the first time. Fifty years of religious turmoil followed, culminating in the triumph of **Presbyterianism**. Despite these vicissitudes, Edinburgh expanded throughout the seventeenth century and, constrained by its walls, was forced to build upwards.

The **Union of the Parliaments** in 1707 dealt a further blow to Edinburgh's political prestige, though the guaranteed preservation of the national church and the legal and educational systems ensured that it was never relegated to a purely provincial role. On the contrary, it was in the second half of the eighteenth century that Edinburgh achieved the height of its intellectual influence, led by an outstanding group of visionary thinkers, including David Hume and Adam Smith. Around the same time, the city began to expand beyond its medieval boundaries, laying out a **New Town**, a masterpiece of the Neoclassical style.

Industrialization affected Edinburgh less than any other major city in the nation, and it never lost its white-collar character. Nevertheless, the city underwent an enormous **urban expansion** in the course of the century, annexing, among many other small burghs, the large port of Leith.

In 1947, Edinburgh was chosen to host the great **International Festival** which served as a symbol of the new peaceful European order; despite some hiccups, it has flourished ever since, in the process helping to make tourism a mainstay of the local economy. In 1979, the inconclusive referendum on **Scottish devolution** robbed Edinburgh of the chance of reviving its role as a governmental capital, and Glasgow, previously the poor relation but always a tenacious rival, began to challenge the city's status as a cultural centre.

While the 1990s have seen Glasgow establish a clear lead in driving Scotland's contemporary arts scene, they have also seen the return of power and influence to Edinburgh. Following the general election of May 1997, Britain's new Labour government held another referendum on devolution. This time, Scotland voted resoundingly in favour of its own **parliament** with tax-levying powers. Formally opened by the queen on July 1, 1999, it now sits in a temporary home in the twin-towered Church of Scotland

Assembly Halls, just off the Royal Mile. With real political power over domestic issues being wielded from Edinburgh for the first time in nearly three hundred years, the city has every right to feel and act like a proper capital again. Meanwhile, construction teams are at work on the modern parliament building, which will take its place opposite the ancient Palace of Holyroodhouse at the foot of the Royal Mile.

Arrival, information and city transport

Edinburgh International Airport (☎0131/333 1000) is at Turnhouse, seven miles west of the city centre, close to the start of the M8 motorway to Glasgow. Regular shuttle buses (£3.60) and taxis (£14) connect to **Waverley Station**, the terminus for all mainline **trains**, conveniently situated in the heart of the city, at the eastern end of Princes Street. There's a second mainline train stop, **Haymarket Station**, just under two miles west on the lines from Waverley to Glasgow, Fife and the Highlands, although this is only really of use if you're staying nearby. The **bus terminal** for local and intercity services is on **St Andrew Square**, two minutes' walk from Waverley, on the opposite side of Princes Street. One of the major bus companies, First Edinburgh, has a shop (☎0131/557 5061) at the southeastern corner of the bus station, where **timetables** are kept and **tickets** sold for a number of the local bus operators.

Information

Edinburgh's main **tourist office** is found on top of Princes Mall, near the northern entrance to the station (July Mon–Fri 9am–6pm, Sat 9am–5.30pm, Sun 9.30am–5pm; Aug Mon–Fri 9am–7pm, Sat 9am–6pm, Sun 9am–5pm; Sept–June Mon–Fri 9am–5.30pm, Sat 9am–4.30pm, Sun 9.30am–2.30pm; ☎0131/473 3800). Although its staff are inevitably flustered at the height of the season, it's efficiently run, with scores of free leaflets; when the office is closed, there's a 24-hour computerized information service at the door. The much smaller **airport branch** is in the main concourse, directly opposite Gate 5 (daily April–Oct 6.30am–10.30pm; Nov–March 7.30am–9.30pm). For free backpacker-related information head to the **Haggis Office**, at 60 High St (daily 9am–6pm; ☎0131/557 9393). Although their main function is to run minibus tours of Scotland, they're a good source of general information about the backpacker scene around Scotland and you can book both SYHA and independent hostels in Edinburgh from here. Up-to-date **maps** of the city can be bought at the tourist office or from one of the major book stores – Waterstones, at 13–14 Princes St, is the nearest to Waverley Station.

City transport

Most **public transport** services terminate on or near Princes Street, the city's main thoroughfare, which lies at the extreme southern end of the symmetrical New Town, with the maze-like Old Town on the heights immediately to the rear. Most places worth visiting lie within the compact city centre, which is easily explored on **foot**.

Edinburgh is well served by **buses**, although, confusingly, several companies offer competing services along similar routes. Each bus stop usually lists the different companies together with the route numbers that stop there. Most useful for the central area are the maroon buses operated by Lothian Regional Transport (LRT); all buses referred to in the text are run by them unless otherwise stated. Tickets can be bought from the driver, for which you'll need exact change – the most common fare is 65p. The green and green-and-yellow buses link the capital with **outlying towns** and villages. Most services depart from and terminate at the St Andrew Square bus station.

A good investment, especially if you're staying far out or want to explore the suburbs, is the £10.50 **pass** allowing a week's unlimited travel on LRT buses; you'll need a passport photo. You can also buy an LRT day pass for £2.40 (£4.20 including the airport service). Timetables and passes are available from their ticket centres on Waverley Bridge or 27 Hanover St (☎0131/554 4494), or from the City Council-run Traveline, at 2 Cockburn St (☎0800/232323).

The city has numerous **taxi** ranks, especially around Waverley Bridge. Black cabs are the only taxis you can hail on the street, but as these are the safest and most reliable it's best to stick to these. For journeys to and from the airport, use designated Airport Taxis. For telephone numbers for black cabs and Airport Taxis see p.831.

Edinburgh is a reasonably **cycle**-friendly city – although hilly – with several cycle paths. The local cycling action group, Spokes (☎0131/313 2114), publishes an excellent cycle map of the city. For **rental**, see p.830.

Accommodation

As befits its status as a top tourist city, Edinburgh has a greater choice of **accommodation** than any other place in Britain outside London. In addition to Edinburgh's large central **hotels**, there's a wide choice of smaller hotels and **guest houses** with a dozen rooms or less, as well as hundreds of private houses offering bed-and-breakfast, but in order to protect the guest-house trade from excessive competition, they are only open between Easter and October. There is also a decent choice of both official and private **hostels**, and three **campsites** attached to caravan parks within striking distance of the centre.

Advance reservations are very strongly recommended during the Festival: just turning up entails accepting whatever is left, which is unlikely to be good value, or else commuting from the suburbs. The **tourist office** (see opposite) sends out accommodation lists for free, and can reserve any type of accommodation in advance for a non-refundable £5 fee. In Waverley Station, Capital Holidays runs an accommodation reservation service (daily 9am–5pm; ☎0131/556 0030), which makes no charge for bookings but requires the first night to be paid in advance by credit card. The centrally located accommodation options we've listed are shown on the map overleaf.

Hotels and guest houses

In the centre of the city, Edinburgh's **hotels** tend to fall into two categories: grand and traditional at the upper end of the market, and modern, continental-style hotels in the middle price range. While a number of stylish upmarket hotels have recently arrived around the edges of the city centre, in the suburbs and beyond the country-house-style hotel dominates. Edinburgh's many **guest houses** and **small hotels** generally offer much better value for money, and are far more homely places to stay.

ACCOMMODATION PRICE CODES

Throughout this guide, hotel and B&B accommodation is priced on a scale of ① to ⑨, the number indicating the **lowest price** you could expect to pay per night in that establishment for a **double room** in high season. The prices indicated by the codes are as follows:

① under £40	④ £60–70	⑦ £110–150
② £40–50	⑤ £70–90	⑧ £150–200
③ £50–60	⑥ £90–110	⑨ over £200

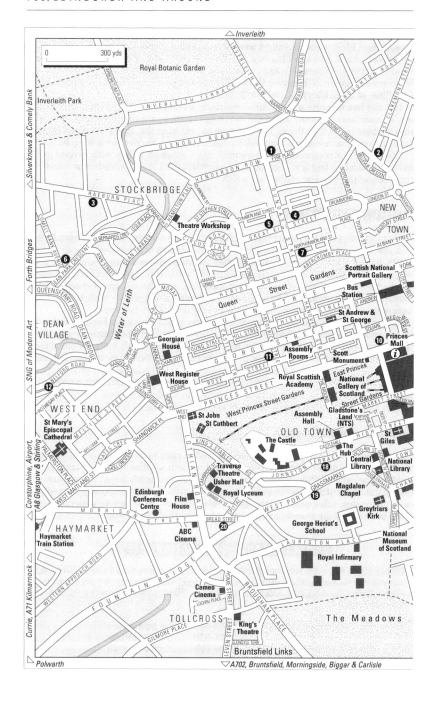

△ Inverleith

0 ————— 300 yds

Royal Botanic Garden

Inverleith Park

INVERLEITH TERRACE

GLENOGLE ROAD

HENDERSON ROW

STOCKBRIDGE

RAEBURN PLACE

Theatre Workshop

St Bernard's Cres

CIRCUS PLACE

ROYAL CIRCUS

NEW TOWN

Scottish National Portrait Gallery

Gardens

Queen Street

Bus Station

St Andrew & St George

DEAN VILLAGE

Georgian House

West Register House

Princes Mall

Assembly Rooms

Scott Monument

Royal Scottish Academy

National Gallery of Scotland

WEST END

St Mary's Episcopal Cathedral

PRINCES STREET

West Princes Street Gardens

East Princes Street Gardens

Gladstone's Land (NTS)

St John St Cuthbert

Assembly Hall

OLD TOWN

The Castle

St Giles

Traverse Theatre

Usher Hall

Royal Lyceum

The Hub

Central Library

National Library

Edinburgh Conference Centre

Film House

Magdalen Chapel

HAYMARKET

Haymarket Train Station

ABC Cinema

George Heriot's School

Greyfriars Kirk

National Museum of Scotland

Royal Infirmary

Cameo Cinema

TOLLCROSS

King's Theatre

The Meadows

Bruntsfield Links

△ Polwarth

▽ A702, Bruntsfield, Morningside, Biggar & Carlisle

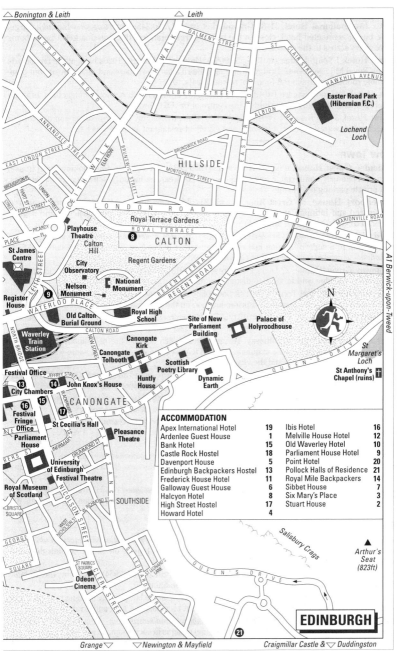

△ Bonington & Leith   △ Leith

Easter Road Park
(Hibernian F.C.)

Lochend
Loch

HILLSIDE

▷ A1 Berwick-upon-Tweed

Royal Terrace Gardens

CALTON

Playhouse
Theatre

St James
Centre

Calton
Hill

City
Observatory

Regent Gardens

Nelson
Monument

National
Monument

Register
House

Old Calton
Burial Ground

Royal High
School

Site of New
Parliament
Building

Palace of
Holyroodhouse

St
Margaret's
Loch

Waverley
Train
Station

Canongate
Kirk

Canongate
Tolbooth

St Anthony's
Chapel (ruins)

Festival Office

Huntly
House

Scottish
Poetry Library

Dynamic
Earth

13 City Chambers

14 John Knox's House

16 Festival
Fringe
Office

St Cecilia's Hall

Parliament
House

15

17

CANONGATE

Pleasance
Theatre

University
of Edinburgh

Festival Theatre

Royal Museum
of Scotland

SOUTHSIDE

ACCOMMODATION

Apex International Hotel	19		Ibis Hotel	16
Ardenlee Guest House	1		Melville House Hotel	12
Bank Hotel	15		Old Waverley Hotel	10
Castle Rock Hostel	18		Parliament House Hotel	9
Davenport House	5		Point Hotel	20
Edinburgh Backpackers Hostel	13		Pollock Halls of Residence	21
Frederick House Hotel	11		Royal Mile Backpackers	14
Galloway Guest House	6		Sibbet House	7
Halcyon Hotel	8		Six Mary's Place	3
High Street Hostel	17		Stuart House	2
Howard Hotel	4			

Odeon
Cinema

Salisbury Crags

▲
Arthur's
Seat
(823ft)

EDINBURGH

Grange ▽   ▽ Newington & Mayfield   Craigmillar Castle & ▽ Duddingston

Old Town

Apex International Hotel, 31–35 Grassmarket (☎0131/300 3456, *mail@apexhotels.co.uk*). Large, new, business-oriented hotel, close to the bars and restaurants of the Grassmarket. Upper rooms have views across to the castle. ⑥.

Bank Hotel, 1 South Bridge (☎0131/556 9043). Unique location in a 1920s bank at the crossroads of the Royal Mile and South Bridge, with Logie Baird's bar downstairs and nine unusual but comfortable rooms upstairs in the theme of famous Scots. ⑤.

Ibis Hotel, 6 Hunter Square (☎0131/240 7000). Part of the French economy-hotel chain, offering smart if uncharacterful rooms right at the centre of the Old Town. ③.

Point Hotel, 34–59 Bread St (☎0131/221 5555). Chic, thoroughly modern conversion of a former supermarket, with a popular "style bar" and excellent restaurant at street level. ⑥.

New Town

Ardenlee Guest House, 9 Eyre Place (☎0131/556 2838). Welcoming, non-smoking guest house, with exceptionally comfortable and spacious rooms. Breakfast includes some vegetarian options, and private parking is available. ③.

Davenport House, 58 Great King St (☎0131/558 8495, *davenporthouse@btinternet.com*). A well-priced and intimate alternative to some of the nearby hotels, in an attractive and regally decorated New Town town house. ④.

Frederick House Hotel, 42 Frederick St (☎0131/226 1999, *frederickhouse@ednet.co.uk*). Smart and well priced, in a superb location just off George Street in the New Town. Continental breakfasts included – served across the road at *Café Rouge*. ④.

Galloway Guest House, 22 Dean Park Crescent (☎0131/332 3672). Friendly, family-run place in elegant Stockbridge, within walking distance of the centre. ②.

Halcyon Hotel, 8 Royal Terrace (☎0131/556 1032). A very reasonably priced, unpretentious hotel, one of a number along a terrace in a prime location on the north side of Calton Hill. ④.

Howard Hotel, 34 Great King St (☎0131/557 3500, *reserve@thehoward.com*). Top-of-the-range, elegant town-house hotel. Lavishly decorated; serves classy Modern-Scottish food. ⑨.

Melville House Hotel, 3 Rothesay Terrace (☎0131/225 5084). One of Edinburgh's grandest Victorian dwellings, with some exquisite internal features and decent rooms, some with outstanding views over Dean Village and the city skyline. ⑥.

Old Waverley Hotel, 43 Princes St (☎0131/556 4648). Large, grand and recently refurbished, in an ideal location right across from Waverley Station, with sweeping city views. ⑧.

Parliament House Hotel, 15 Calton Hill (☎0131/478 4000). Smart new hotel in a great central location halfway up Calton Hill; includes three rooms suitable for disabled visitors. ⑧.

Sibbet House, 26 Northumberland St (☎0131/556 1078, *sibbet.house@zetnet.co.uk*). Small, sumptuous family guest house, with beautifully decorated rooms and high standards. Breakfast times are often lively. Non-smoking throughout. ⑥.

Six Mary's Place, Raeburn Place (☎0131/332 8965, *sixmarysplace@btinternet.com*). Collectively run "alternative" guest house; has a no-smoking policy and offers excellent home-cooked vegetarian meals. ③.

Stuart House, 12 E Claremont St (☎0131/557 9030, *stuartho@globalnet.co.uk*). Homely, bright, refurbished Georgian house in the New Town, a few minutes' walk from the bus station. No smoking. ④.

Leith and Inverleith

A-Haven Town House, 180 Ferry Rd, Leith (☎0131/554 6559, *reservations@a-haven.co.uk*). A terrifically friendly place – among the best of a number of guest houses on one of Edinburgh's main east–west arteries. ⑤.

Ashlyn Guest House, 42 Inverleith Row, Inverleith (☎0131/552 2954). Right by the Botanic Garden, and within walking distance of the centre. No smoking. ③.

Bar Java, 48–50 Constitution St, Leith (☎0131/467 7527). Simple but brightly designed rooms above one of Leith's funkiest bars, where you can get a great breakfast and food and drink till late. ②.

Malmaison, 1 Tower Place (☎0131/468 5000, *edinburgh@malmaison.com*). Smart, modern hotel in a converted harbourside building with bold, original designs in each room, as well as CD players and cable TV. Also has gym, room service, Parisian-style brasserie and café-bar serving lighter meals. ⑦.

Ravensdown Guest House, 248 Ferry Rd, Inverleith (☎0131/552 5438). Good-quality B&B with fine panoramic views across Inverleith playing fields to the city centre. ②.

South of the centre

Allison House Hotel, 15–17 Mayfield Gardens, Mayfield (☎0131/667 8049, *dh007ljh@msn.com*). Well run and recently expanded, with an "honesty" bar, where guests serve themselves and pay on departure. ④.

Ashdene House, 23 Fountainhall Rd, Grange (☎0131/667 6026, *Ashdene_House_Edinburgh @compuserve.com*). Well-run, non-smoking and environmentally friendly guest house in the quiet southern suburbs. ③.

Braid Hills Hotel, 134 Braid Rd, Braid Hills (☎0131/447 8888, *bookings@braidhillshotel.co.uk*). Old-fashioned, baronial-style hotel in a residential area up in the hilly southern outskirts, with fine views across the city. A ten-minute drive from the centre. ⑦.

Bruntsfield Hotel, 69–74 Bruntsfield Place, Bruntsfield (☎0131/229 1393, *bruntsfield @queensferry-hotels.co.uk*). Large, comfortable and peaceful, overlooking Bruntsfield Links, a mile south of Princes Street. ⑦.

Hopetoun Guest House, 15 Mayfield Rd, Mayfield (☎0131/667 7691, *hopetoun@aol.com*). There are just three rooms, but all are bright and friendly, and have great views of Arthur's Seat and Blackford Hill. ②.

International Guest House, 37 Mayfield Gardens, Mayfield (☎0131/667 2511). One of the best of the Mayfield guest houses, with comfortable, well-equipped rooms. ②.

Prestonfield House Hotel, Priestfield Rd, Bruntsfield (☎0131/668 3346). Luxury hotel in a seventeenth-century mansion set in its own grounds below Arthur's Seat. A new wing, sympathetic to the old building, has been added. Peacocks strut around on the lawns and Highland cattle low in the adjacent fields. ⑦.

The Stuarts, 17 Glengyle Terrace, Bruntsfield (☎0131/229 9559, *reservations@the-stuarts.com*). A five-star B&B in central Edinburgh, with three attractively furnished rooms with excellent facilities in a basement beside Bruntsfield Links. ⑥.

Teviotdale House Hotel, 53 Grange Loan, Grange (☎0131/667 4376, *teviotdale.house @btinternet.com*). Peaceful non-smoking hotel, offering luxurious standards at reasonable prices. Particularly good (and huge) home-cooked Scottish breakfasts. ③.

East of the centre

Devon Guest House, 2 Pittville St, Portobello (☎0131/669 6067). Pleasant rooms and good breakfasts at this family-run guest house, only two minutes from the shore. ②.

Joppa Turrets Guest House, 1 Lower Joppa (☎0131/669 5806, *stanley@joppaturrets.demon.co.uk*). The place to come if you want an Edinburgh holiday by the sea: a quiet establishment right by the beach in Joppa, five miles east of the city centre. ②.

Stra'ven Guest House, 3 Brunstane Rd North, Joppa (☎0131/669 5580). Splendid lounge and friendly service in an elegant, well-kept guest house. No smoking. ②.

Hostels and student halls

Edinburgh now has a wealth of **hostels**, including two grand SYHA-run establishments and a cluster of independent outfits on or near the Royal Mile. **Campus accommodation** is also available, varying from tiny single rooms in long lonely corridors to relatively comfortable places in small shared apartments; much of it, however, is quite a trek from the centre of town.

Argyle Backpackers Hotel, 14 Argyle Place, Marchmont (☎0131/667 9991, *iolaire@sol.uk*). Quieter, less intense version of the typical backpackers hostel. The small dorms have single beds and there are a dozen double/twin rooms. Located near the Meadows, in studenty Marchmont.

Belford Hostel, 6–8 Douglas Gardens, West End (☎0131/225 6209, reservations ☎0800/096 6868, *info@hoppo.com*). Housed in a converted Arts and Crafts church, just west of the centre, close to St Mary's Cathedral and the Gallery of Modern Art. The dorms are in box rooms with the vaulted church ceiling above. No curfew.

Bruntsfield Hostel, 7 Bruntsfield Crescent, Bruntsfield (☎0131/447 2994, reservations ☎0541/553255). Large SYHA youth hostel overlooking Bruntsfield Links a mile south of Princes Street; take bus #11, #15 or #16. Curfew at 2am; breakfast included in price. Note that SYHA also take over two wonderfully central student residences during July and August – one on The Pleasance and one on Cowgate; both have over a hundred single bedrooms (☎0131/337 1120 or book on the central reservations line).

Castle Rock Hostel, 15 Johnston Terrace, Old Town (☎0131/225 9666). Busy 200-bed hostel tucked below the castle ramparts. Dorms are large but bright, and the communal areas include a games room with pool and table tennis tables. No curfew.

Edinburgh Backpackers Hostel, 65 Cockburn St, Old Town (☎0131/539 8695, reservations ☎0800/0966868, *info@hoppo.com*). Big hostel with a great central location on a side street off the Royal Mile. Accommodation is mostly in large but bright dorms, although a few doubles are available. No curfew.

Eglinton Hostel, 18 Eglinton Crescent, Haymarket (☎0131/337 1120, reservations ☎0541/55 32 55). Slightly more expensive, but the more central of the two main SYHA hostels, in a characterful town house west of the centre, near Haymarket Station. Curfew at 2am; breakfast included in price.

High Street Hostel, 8 Blackfriars St, Old Town (☎0131/557 3984). Large, but lively and well-known hostel in a sixteenth-century building just off the Royal Mile. Open 24hr.

Napier University, 219 Colinton Rd, Merchiston (☎0131/455 4291). Halls of residence for those staying two nights or more, in a reasonable location in the southern inner suburbs, reached by buses #23 and #37 from Princes Street. Three- to five-person self-catering flats are also available by the week in more central locations near Haymarket (☎0131/455 4427). Closed mid-Sept to May.

Royal Mile Backpackers, 105 High St, Old Town (☎0131/557 6120). Small, friendly hostel with numerous longer-term residents. Onsite communal areas are limited, but facilities are shared with the nearby High Street Hostel. No curfew.

University of Edinburgh Pollock Halls of Residence, 18 Holyrood Park Rd, Newington (☎0131/651 2011). Unquestionably the best setting of any of the campuses, right beside the Royal Commonwealth Pool and Holyrood Park. Although expensive for its type, it's a lot less than other self-catering accommodation in the city centre. Open Easter and late June to mid-Sept only.

Campsites

Drummohr Caravan Park, Levenhall, Musselburgh (☎0131/665 6867). A large, pleasant site in this coastal satellite town to the east of Edinburgh, with excellent transport connections to the city, including buses #15, #15A, #26, #44, #66 (SMT) and #85. Closed Nov–Feb.

Mortonhall Caravan Park, 38 Mortonhall Gate, Frogston Rd E (☎0131/664 1533). A good site, five miles out, near the Braid Hills; take bus #11 from Princes Street. Closed Nov–Feb.

Silverknowes Caravan Site, Marine Drive, Silverknowes (☎0131/312 6874). Pleasant all-year campsite close to the shore in the northwestern suburbs, thirty minutes' ride from the centre; take bus #14.

The Old Town

The **Old Town**, although only about a mile long and three hundred yards wide, represents the total extent of the twin burghs of Edinburgh and Canongate for the first 650 years of their existence, and its general appearance and character remain indubitably medieval. Containing as it does the majority of the city's most famous tourist sights, it makes by far the best starting point for your explorations.

The obvious goals of the **Castle**, the **Palace of Holyroodhouse** and **Holyrood Abbey** are linked by scores of historic buildings along the length of the **Royal Mile**. Inevitably, much of the Old Town is sacrificed to hard-sell tourism, and it can be uncomfortably crowded throughout the summer, especially during the Festival. Yet the area remains at the heart of Edinburgh, with daily business of the greatest importance being conducted in **Parliament House**, home of the Scottish Parliament until

1707 and now the location of Scotland's highest Law Courts, and in the **Assembly Hall**, temporary home of the new Scottish Parliament. It's well worth extending your explorations to the area immediately to the south of the Royal Mile, and in particular to the stunning new **National Museum of Scotland**; and, no matter how pressed you are, make sure you spare time for the wonderfully varied scenery and breathtaking vantage points of **Holyrood Park**, an extensive tract of open countryside on the eastern edge of the Old Town.

The Castle

The history of Edinburgh, and indeed of Scotland, is indissolubly bound up with its **Castle** (daily: April–Oct 9.30am–6pm; Nov–March 9.30am–5pm; £6.50), which dominates the city from its lofty seat atop an almost-sheer volcanic rock. Would-be attackers, like modern tourists, were forced to approach the castle from the crag to the east, on which the Royal Mile runs down to Holyrood.

The castle's disparate styles reflect its many changes in use, as well as advances in military architecture: the oldest surviving part, **St Margaret's Chapel**, is from the twelfth century, while the most recent additions are less than a hundred years old. Having been lost to (and subsequently recaptured from) the English on several occasions, the defences were dismantled by the Scots themselves in 1313, and only rebuilt in 1356. It last saw action in 1745, when the Young Pretender's forces, fresh from their victory at Prestonpans, made a half-hearted attempt to storm it. Subsequently, advances in weapon technology diminished the Castle's importance, but under the influence of the Romantic movement it came to be seen as a great national monument. The castle still has a working military garrison, provided by the British Army.

Though you can easily take in the views and wander round the Castle yourself, you might want to take advantage of **audioguides**, available in various languages from a booth just inside the gatehouse. Both these and guided tours by staff members are included in the entrance price.

The Esplanade and the lower defences

The Castle is entered via the **Esplanade**, a parade ground laid out in the eighteenth century and enclosed a hundred years later by ornamental walls, the southern one commanding fine views towards the Pentland Hills. Each evening during the Festival (see p.828), the Esplanade is the setting for the city's most shameless and spectacular demonstration of tourist kitsch, the Edinburgh Military Tattoo, although plans have been mooted to move the Tattoo to a permanent auditorium in Princes Street Gardens.

The **Gatehouse** to the Castle is a Romantic addition of the 1880s, complete with the last drawbridge ever built in Scotland. It was later adorned with appropriately heroic-looking statues of William Wallace and Robert the Bruce. Rearing up behind is the most distinctive and impressive feature of the Castle's silhouette, the sixteenth-century **Half Moon Battery**, which marks the outer limit of the actual defences.

Continuing uphill, you pass through the **Portcullis Gate**, a handsome Renaissance gateway of the same period, marred by the addition of a nineteenth-century upper storey equipped with anachronistic arrow slits rather than gunholes. Beyond is the six-gun **Argyle Battery**, built in the eighteenth century by Major-General Wade, whose network of military roads and bridges still forms an essential part of the transport infrastructure of the Highlands. Further west, on **Mill's Mount Battery**, a well-known Edinburgh ritual takes place – the daily firing of the one o'clock gun. Originally designed for the benefit of ships in the Firth of Forth, it's now used as a time signal by city-centre office workers. Both batteries offer wonderful panoramic views over the New Town to the coastal towns and hills of Fife across the Forth.

Up the tortuously sloping road is the **Governor's House**, a 1740s mansion whose harled masonry and crow-stepped gables are archetypal features of vernacular Scottish architecture. It now serves as the officers' mess for members of the garrison, while the governor himself lives in the northern side wing. Behind stands the largest single construction in the Castle complex, the **New Barracks**, built in the 1790s in an austere Neoclassical style. The road then snakes round towards the enclosed citadel at the uppermost point of Castle Rock, entered via **Foog's Gate**.

St Margaret's Chapel

At the eastern end of the citadel, **St Margaret's Chapel** is the oldest surviving building in the Castle, and probably the oldest in Edinburgh itself. Used as a powder magazine for three hundred years, this tiny Norman church was rediscovered in 1845 and rededicated in 1934, after sympathetic restoration. Externally, it is austere, but the interior preserves an elaborate zigzag archway dividing the nave from the sanctuary. Although once believed to have been built by the saint herself, and mooted as the site of her death in 1093, its architectural style suggests that it actually dates from about thirty years later, and was thus probably built by King David I as a memorial to his mother.

The battlements in front of the chapel offer the best of all the Castle's panoramic views. They are interrupted by the **Lang Stairs**, which provide an alternative means of access from the Argyle Battery via the side of the Portcullis Gate. Just below the battlements there's a small, immaculately kept **cemetery**, the last resting place of the **soldiers' pets**. Continuing eastwards, you skirt the top of the Forewall and Half Moon Batteries, passing the 110-foot **Castle Well** en route to Crown Square, the highest, most secure and most important section of the entire complex.

Crown Square

The south side of **Crown Square** is occupied by the **Great Hall**, built in the reign of James IV as a venue for banquets and other ceremonial occasions. The meeting place of the Scottish Parliament until 1639, it later underwent the indignity of conversion and subdivision, firstly into a barracks, then a hospital. During this time, its hammer-beam roof – the earliest of three in the Old Town – was hidden from view. It was restored towards the end of the last century, when the hall was decked out in the full-blown Romantic manner.

The eastern side of the square is occupied by the **Palace**, a surprisingly unassuming edifice built round an octagonal stair turret heightened last century to bear the Castle's main flagpole. Begun in the 1430s, the Palace's present Renaissance appearance is due to King James IV, though it was remodelled for Mary Queen of Scots and her consort Henry, Lord Darnley. Their entwined initials (MAH), together with the date 1566, can be seen above one of the doorways. This door gives access to a few historic rooms, the most interesting of which is the tiny panelled bedchamber at the extreme southeastern corner, where Mary gave birth to James VI. Along with the rest of the Palace, the room was revamped for James's triumphant homecoming in 1617, though this was to be the last time it served as a royal residence.

Another section of the palace houses the magnificent Honours of Scotland – the only pre-Restoration set of crown jewels in the United Kingdom – along with a detailed audio-visual presentation. Slow-moving queues shuffle past the **Crown Room**, where the magnificent regalia, one of the most potent images of Scotland's nationhood, are on display. They were last used for the Scottish-only coronation of

THE STONE OF DESTINY

Legend has it that the **Stone of Destiny** (also called the Stone of Scone) was "Jacob's Pillow", on which he dreamed of the ladder of angels from earth to heaven. Its real history is obscure, but it is known that it was moved from Ireland to Dunadd by missionaries, and thence to Dunstaffnage, from where Kenneth MacAlpine, king of the Dalriada Scots, brought it to the abbey at Scone in 838. There it remained for almost five hundred years, used as the coronation throne on which all kings of Scotland were crowned.

In 1296, an over-eager Edward I stole what he believed to be the Stone and installed it at Westminster Abbey, where, apart from a brief interlude in 1950 when it was removed by Scottish nationalists and hidden in Arbroath for several months, it remained for seven hundred years. All this changed in December 1996 when, after an elaborate ceremony-laden journey from London, the Stone returned to Scotland, in one of the doomed attempts by the Conservative government to convince the Scottish people that the Union was a good thing. Much to the annoyance of the people of Perth and the curators of Scone Palace (see p.914), and to the general indifference of the people of Scotland, the Stone was placed in Edinburgh Castle.

However, speculation surrounds the authenticity of the Stone, for the original is said to have been intricately carved, while the one seen today is a plain block of sandstone. Many believe that the canny monks at Scone palmed this off onto the English king, and that the real Stone of Destiny lies hidden in an underground chamber, its whereabouts a mystery to all but the chosen few.

Charles II, in 1651, an event which provoked the wrath of Oliver Cromwell, who made exhaustive attempts to have the jewels melted down. Having narrowly escaped his clutches by being smuggled out of the Castle and hidden in a rural church, the jewels later served as symbols of the absent monarch at sittings of the Scottish Parliament before being locked away in a chest following the Union of 1707. For over a century they were out of sight, and were eventually presumed lost, before being rediscovered in the Castle in 1818, as a result of a search initiated by Sir Walter Scott. Of the three pieces comprising the Honours, the oldest is the **sceptre**, given to James IV in 1494 by Pope Alexander VI; even finer is the **sword**, a swaggering Italian High Renaissance masterpiece presented to James IV by the great artistic patron Pope Julius II; the jewel-encrusted **crown**, made for James V by the Scottish goldsmith James Mosman, incorporates the gold circlet worn by Robert the Bruce and is surmounted by an enamelled orb and cross. The glass case containing the Honours has recently been rearranged to create space for its newest addition, the **Stone of Destiny** (see box above). This remarkably plain object now lies incongruously next to the opulent crown jewels.

The Vaults

From Crown Square, you can descend to the **Vaults**, a series of cavernous chambers erected by order of James IV to provide an even surface for the showpiece buildings above. They were later used as a prison for captured foreign nationals, who have bequeathed a rich legacy of graffiti. One of the rooms houses the famous fifteenth-century siege gun, **Mons Meg**, which could fire a five-hundred-pound stone nearly two miles. A seventeenth-century visitor, the London poet John Taylor, commented: "It is so great within, that it was told me that a child was once gotten there." In 1754, Mons Meg was taken to the Tower of London, where it stayed till Sir Walter Scott persuaded George IV, on the occasion of his 1822 state visit to Scotland, to return it.

The Royal Mile

The **Royal Mile**, the name given to the ridge linking the Castle with Holyrood, was described by Daniel Defoe in 1724 as "the largest, longest and finest street for Buildings and Number of Inhabitants, not in Bretain only, but in the World". Almost exactly a mile in length, it is divided into four separate streets – **Castlehill**, **Lawnmarket**, **High Street** and **Canongate**. From these, branching out in a herringbone pattern, a series of tightly packed closes and steep lanes are entered via archways known as pends. After the construction of the New Town, the Royal Mile degenerated into a notorious slum, but has since shaken off that reputation, becoming once again a highly desirable place to live. Although marred somewhat by rather too many tacky tourist shops and the odd misjudged new development, it is still among the most evocative parts of the city, and one that particularly rewards detailed exploration.

Castlehill

The narrow uppermost stretch of the Royal Mile is known as **Castlehill**. The first building on the northern side of the street as you leave the Castle Esplanade is the former reservoir for the Old Town, which has been converted into the **Edinburgh Old Town Weaving Centre** (Mon–Sat 9am–5.30pm, Sun 10am–5pm; £4). Very much a commercial enterprise, the centre sells kilts, rugs and other tartan adornments while noisy looms rhymically churn the stuff out on the floors below. You can see these up close and even try your hand at weaving.

On the corner of the wall of the Weaving Centre, facing the castle, the pretty Art Nouveau **Witches' Fountain** commemorates the three hundred or more women burnt at this spot on charges of sorcery, the last of whom died in 1722. Rising up behind are the picturesque apartment buildings of **Ramsay Gardens**, the oldest part of which is the octagonal **Goose Pie House** – home of the eighteenth-century poet Allan Ramsay, author of *The Gentle Shepherd* and father of the better-known portrait painter of the same name – while the rest dates from the 1890s and was the brainchild of Patrick Geddes, a pioneer of the modern town-planning movement.

Opposite the Weaving Centre, at the top of the southern side of Castlehill, the so-called **Cannonball House** takes its name from the cannonball embedded in its masonry, which, according to legend, was the result of a poorly targeted shot fired by the Castle garrison at Bonnie Prince Charlie's encampment at Holyrood. The truth is far more prosaic: the ball marks the gravitation height of the city's first piped water supply. Alongside, the **Scotch Whisky Heritage Centre** (daily: June–Sept 9.30am–6pm; Oct–May 10am–5.30pm; tours £3.25 & £4.95) features a gimmicky ride in a "barrel" through a series of uninspiring historical tableaux with a free dram (a measure of whisky) at the end. The longer tour also offers a detailed explanation of aspects of production and blending, although there's little on offer here which you won't find done rather better on a tour of a real distillery.

Across the street, the **Outlook Tower** (April–Oct Mon–Fri 9.30am–6pm, Sat & Sun 10am–6pm; Nov–March 10am–5pm; £3.95) has been one of Edinburgh's top tourist attractions since 1853, when the original seventeenth-century tenement was equipped with a **camera obscura**. It makes a good introduction to the city: live images are beamed through a periscope mounted at the highest point of the tower onto a white table in the auditorium, accompanied by a running commentary. For the best views, visit at noon when there are fewer shadows. The viewing balcony is one of Edinburgh's best vantage points, and there are exhibitions on pinhole photography, holography, Victorian photographs of the city, and topographic paintings made between 1780 and 1860.

A few doors further on is the **Assembly Hall**, normally used as the meeting place of the annual General Assembly of the Church of Scotland but since May 1999, the home of the Scottish Parliament while it awaits more permanent accommodation (see p.802). From the Royal Mile side, the Hall is unimpressive; at its northern entrance, however, on Mound Place, are the twin towers which feature so prominently on vistas of the Old Town skyline. It is possible to visit the debating chamber of the Parliament by going to the public entrance in Milne's Court, one of the closes off the Royal Mile, just past the Assembly Hall (open Mon–Fri 10am–noon & 2–4pm; free). When Parliament is in session, you can sit and watch the debates from the large public gallery – tickets are available on an ad hoc basis from the desk at the public entrance.

The imposing black church building opposite the Assembly Hall, at the foot of Castlehill, is **the Hub** (daily 8am to around midnight), which in 1999 became the first permanent home of the Edinburgh International Festival; it is open year-round, providing performance, rehearsal and exhibition space, a ticket centre and a café. The building itself was constructed in 1845 to designs by James Gillespie Graham and Augustus Pugin, the latter being one of the co-architects of the Houses of Parliament in London – a connection obvious from the superb neo-Gothic detailing and the sheer presence of the building, whose spire is the highest in Edinburgh. Worth checking out is the main hall upstairs, where the original neo-Gothic woodwork and high-vaulted ceiling is enlivened with a fabulous fabric design in Rastafarian colours. Permanent works of art have been incorporated into the centre, including over two hundred delightful foot-high statues by Scottish sculptor Jill Watson, representing Festival performers and audiences.

Lawnmarket

Below the the Hub, the Royal Mile opens out into the broader expanse of **Lawnmarket**, which, as its name suggests, was once a market place. At its northern end is the entry to **Milne's Court**, whose excellently restored tenements now serve as student residences. Immediately beyond is **James Court**, one of Edinburgh's most fashionable addresses prior to the advent of the New Town: David Hume and James Boswell were among those who lived there.

Back on Lawnmarket itself, **Gladstone's Land** (April–Oct Mon–Sat 10am–5pm, Sun 2–5pm; £3.20) takes its name from the merchant Thomas Gledstane (sic), who acquired a modest dwelling on the site in 1617, transforming it into a magnificent six-storey mansion. The Gledstane family are thought to have occupied the third floor, renting out the rest to merchants, in the style of tenement occupation still widespread in the city today. The arcaded ground floor, the only authentic example left of what was once a common feature of Royal Mile houses, has been restored to illustrate its early function as a shopping booth. Several other rooms have been kitted out in authentic period style to give an impression of the lifestyle of a well-to-do household of the late seventeenth century; the Painted Chamber, with its decorated wooden ceiling and wall friezes, is particularly impressive.

A few paces further on, steps lead down to **Lady Stair's Close** and Lady Stair's House (Mon–Sat 10am–5pm; also Sun 2–5pm during the Festival; free), another fine seventeenth-century residence, albeit one subject to a considerable amount of Victorian refurbishment. It now serves as Edinburgh's literary museum, featuring a collection of personal mementoes (among them locks of hair and walking sticks) of the three lions of Scottish literature – Robert Burns, Sir Walter Scott and Robert Louis Stevenson. In the courtyard outside – called the Makars' Court, after the Scots word for the "maker" of poetry or prose – look out for quotations from twelve of Scotland's most famous writers, inscribed on the paving stones.

The High Kirk of St Giles

Across George IV Bridge is the third section of the Royal Mile, known as the **High Street**, which occupies two blocks either side of the intersection between North Bridge and South Bridge. The dominant building on the southern side of the street is the **High Kirk of St Giles** (April–Sept Mon–Fri 9am–7pm, Sat & Sun 9am–5pm; Oct–March Mon–Sat 9am–5pm, Sun 1–5pm; free), which closes off Parliament Square from High Street. The sole parish church of medieval Edinburgh, from which John Knox (see box opposite) launched and directed the Scottish Reformation, the Kirk is almost invariably referred to as a cathedral, although it has only been the seat of a bishop on two brief and unhappy occasions in the seventeenth century. According to one of the city's best-known legends, the attempt in 1637 to introduce the English prayer book, and thus episcopal government, so incensed a humble stallholder named Jenny Geddes that she hurled her stool at the preacher, prompting the rest of the congregation to chase the offending clergy out of the building. A tablet in the north aisle marks the spot from where she let rip.

In the early nineteenth century, St Giles received a much-needed but over-drastic restoration, covering most of the Gothic exterior with a smooth stone coating that gives it a certain Georgian dignity while sacrificing its medieval character almost completely. The only part to have been spared this treatment is the late fifteenth-century tower, whose resplendent crown spire is formed by eight flying spurs. The **interior** has survived in much better shape. Especially notable are the four massive piers supporting the tower, which date back, at least in part, to the church's Norman predecessor. In the nineteenth century, St Giles was adorned with several Pre-Raphaelite **stained glass** windows, the best of which can be seen on the facade wall of the north aisle.

At the southeastern corner of St Giles, the **Thistle Chapel** was built by Sir Robert Lorimer in 1911 as the private chapel of the sixteen knights of the Most Noble Order of the Thistle, the highest chivalric order in Scotland. Self-consciously derivative of St George's Chapel in Windsor (see p.142), it's an exquisite piece of craftsmanship, with an elaborate ribbed vault, huge drooping bosses, and extravagantly ornate stalls.

Parliament Square

The open cobbled area in front of the main door to St Giles is **Parliament Square**, dominated on its southern side by the Neoclassical facades of the **Law Courts**, originally planned by Robert Adam but, due to shortage of funds, eventually built by Robert Reid, who faithfully quoted from Adam's architectural vocabulary without matching his flair. William Stark, the mentor of William Playfair, was more flamboyant in his design, and his **Signet Library**, which occupies the west side of the square, is one of the most beautiful interiors in Edinburgh, its sumptuous colonnaded hall a perfect embodiment of the ideals of the Age of Reason. Unfortunately it can only be seen by prior written application, except on very occasional open days.

Around the corner, facing the southern side of St Giles, is **Parliament House** (Mon–Fri 9am–5pm), built in the 1630s for the Scottish Parliament, a role it maintained until the Union, when it passed into the hands of the legal fraternity. The most notable features of the impressive main hall are the extravagant hammer-beam roof and the delicately carved stone corbels from which it springs – in addition to some vicious grotesques, they include accurate depictions of Edinburgh Castle. In the far corner is a small exhibition explaining the history of the building and courts, but it's more fun simply to watch the everyday business, with solicitors and bewigged advocates in hushed conferral.

Outside on the square, an imposing equestrian **monument to King Charles II** depicts him in fetching Roman garb. Back on the High Street, beside a bloated memorial to the fifth Duke of Buccleuch, the brickwork pattern set in the pavement is known as the **Heart of Midlothian**. Immortalized in Scott's novel of the same name, it marks the site of a demolished tollbooth; you may see passers-by spitting on it for luck. Public proclamations have traditionally been read from the **Mercat Cross** at the back of St Giles. The present structure, adorned with coats of arms and topped by a sculpture of a unicorn, looks venerable enough, but most of it is little more than a hundred years old.

JOHN KNOX

Little is known about Protestant reformer **John Knox**'s early years: he was born between 1505 and 1514 in East Lothian, and trained for the priesthood at St Andrews University. Ordained in 1540, Knox then served as a private tutor, together with Scotland's first significant Protestant leader, **George Wishart**. After Wishart was burnt at the stake for heresy in 1546, Knox became involved with a group which had carried out the revenge murder of the Scottish primate, Cardinal David Beaton, and subsequently took up residence in his castle in St Andrews. The following year, the castle was captured by the French, and Knox was carted off to work as a galley slave.

He was freed in 1548, as a result of the intervention of the English, who invited him to play an evangelizing role in the spread of their own Reformation. Following successful ministries in Berwick-upon-Tweed and Newcastle-upon-Tyne, Knox turned down the bishopric of Rochester, less from an intrinsic opposition to episcopacy than from a wish to avoid becoming embroiled in the turmoil he guessed would ensue if the Catholic Mary Tudor acceded to the English throne. When this duly happened in 1553, Knox fled to the continent, ending up as minister to the English-speaking community in Geneva, which was then in the grip of the theocratic government of the Frenchman **Jean Calvin**. Knox was quickly won over to Calvin's radical version of Protestantism, declaring Geneva to be "the most perfect school of Christ since the days of the Apostles". In exile, Knox wrote his most infamous treatise, *The First Blast of the Trumpet Against the Monstrous Regiment of Women*, a specific attack on the three Catholic women then ruling Scotland, England and France, which has made his name synonymous with misogyny ever since.

When Knox was allowed to return to Scotland in 1555, he took over as spiritual leader of the Reformation, becoming minister of St Giles in Edinburgh, where he established a reputation as a charismatic preacher. However, the establishment of Protestantism as the official religion of Scotland in 1560 was dependent on the forging of an alliance with Elizabeth I, which Knox himself rigorously championed: the swift deployment of English troops against the French garrison in Edinburgh dealt a fatal blow to Franco-Spanish hopes of re-establishing Catholicism in both Scotland and England. Although the return of Mary Queen of Scots the following year placed a Catholic monarch on the Scottish throne, reputedly Knox was always able to retain the upper hand in his famous disputes with her. Before his death in 1572, Knox began mapping out the organization of the Scots Kirk, sweeping away all vestiges of episcopal control and giving lay people a role of unprecedented importance.

For all his considerable influence, Knox was not responsible for many of the features which have created the popular image of Scottish Presbyterianism – and of Knox himself – as austere and joyless. A man of refined cultural tastes, he did not encourage the iconoclasm that destroyed so many of Scotland's churches and works of art; indeed, much of this was carried out by English hands. Nor did he promote the unbending Sabbatarianism, the obsessive work ethic or even the inflexible view of the doctrine of predestination favoured by his far more fanatical successors. Ironically, though, by fostering an irrevocable rift in the "Auld Alliance" with France, he did do more than anyone else to ensure that Scotland's future was to be linked irrevocably with that of England.

Upper High Street

The first main building on the northern side of the **High Street**, after the George IV Bridge and Bank Street intersection, is the High Court of Justiciary, Scotland's highest criminal court, outside which is a statue of the philosopher David Hume. A little further on, opposite the Mercat Cross, are the U-shaped **City Chambers**, designed by John Adam, brother of Robert, as the Royal Exchange. Local traders never warmed to the exchange, however, so the town council established its headquarters there instead. Beneath the City Chambers lies **Mary King's Close**, one of Edinburgh's most unusual attractions. Built in the early sixteenth century, it was closed off for many years, following the devastation of the 1645 plague, and was entirely bricked in following the building of the City Chambers in 1753. The only way to see this rather spooky "lost city" is on the brief tours run regularly through the day by Mercat Tours (☎0131/225 6591).

Across the road is the **Tron Kirk**, best known as the focal point for Hogmanay revellers. The church was built in the 1630s to accommodate the Presbyterian congregation ejected from St Giles when the latter became the seat of a bishop; the spire is an 1820s replacement for one destroyed by fire. Today the building houses the **Old Town Information Centre** (Easter–May Thurs–Mon 10am–1pm & 2–5pm; June–Sept daily 10am–7pm), where you can peruse information boards on the buildings of the Old Town and look down from raised walkways on excavations of an old close being carried out in the floor of the building.

Lower High Street

Beyond the intersection of North Bridge and South Bridge, **Trinity Apse**, in Chalmers Close, is a poignant reminder of the fifteenth-century Holy Trinity Collegiate Church. Formerly one of Edinburgh's most outstanding buildings, it was demolished in 1848 to make way for an extension to Waverley Station. The stones were carefully numbered and stored on Calton Hill so that it could be reassembled at a later date, but many were pilfered before sufficient funds became available, and only the apse could be reconstructed on this new site. A few years ago, it was transformed into a **Brass Rubbing Centre** (Mon–Sat 10am–5pm; also Sun 2–5pm during the Festival; free), where you can rub your own impressions from Pictish crosses and medieval church brasses (£1.20 upwards).

On the other side of High Street, the noisy **Museum of Childhood** (Mon–Sat 10am–5pm; also Sun 2–5pm during the Festival; free) was, oddly enough, founded by an eccentric local councillor who heartily disliked children. Although he claimed that the museum was a serious social archive for adults, and dedicated it to King Herod, it has always attracted swarms of kids, who delight in the dolls' houses, teddy bears, train sets, marionettes and other paraphernalia.

Almost directly opposite is what's thought to be the city's oldest surviving dwelling, the early sixteenth-century **Moubray House** (closed to the public). The uses of the four-storey house have included tavern, bookshop and even, towards the end of the nineteenth century, temperance hotel. It also served as Daniel Defoe's office during his stay as an English government representative in 1707. Next door lies the picturesque **John Knox's House** (Mon–Sat 10am–4.30pm; £1.95), built some thirty years later. With its outside stairway, biblical motto, and sundial adorned with a statue of Moses, it gives a good impression of how the Royal Mile must have once looked. Whether or not it was ever really the home of Knox is debatable: he may have moved here for safety at the height of the religious troubles. The rather bare interiors, which give a good idea of the labyrinthine layout of Old Town houses, display explanatory material on Knox's life and career.

Canongate

For over seven hundred years, the district through which **Canongate** runs was a burgh in its own right, officially separate from the capital. In recent decades, it has been the subject of some of the most ambitious restoration programmes in the Old Town, two notable examples of which can be seen at the top of the street. On the south side is the residential **Chessel's Court**, a mid-eighteenth-century development with fanciful Rococo chimneys. It was formerly the site of the Excise Office, scene of the robbery that led to the arrest and execution of Deacon Brodie. Over the road, the **Morocco Land** is a reasonably faithful reproduction of an old tenement, incorporating the original bust of a Moor from which its name derives.

Dominated by a turreted steeple, the late sixteenth-century **Canongate Tolbooth** stands a little further down the north side of the street. Once a prison, it now houses **The People's Story** (Mon–Sat 10am–5pm; also Sun 2–5pm during the Festival; free), a lively museum devoted to the everyday life and work of Edinburgh people down the centuries, with sounds and tableaux on various aspects of city living, including a typical Edinburgh pub. Next door, **Canongate Kirk** was built in the 1680s to a curiously archaic design, still Renaissance in outline, and on a cruciform plan wholly at odds with the ideals and requirements of Protestant worship. Its churchyard, one of the city's most exclusive cemeteries, commands a superb view across to Calton Hill. Among those buried here are Adam Smith, Mrs Agnes McLehose (better known as Robert Burns' "Clarinda") and Robert Fergusson. The latter is regarded by some as Edinburgh's greatest poet, despite his death at the age of 24; his headstone was donated by Burns, a fervent admirer, who also wrote the inscription.

Opposite the church, the local history museum in **Huntly House** (Mon–Sat 10am–5pm; also Sun 2–5pm during the Festival; free) includes a quirky array of old shop signs, some dating back to the eighteenth century, as well as displays on indigenous industries such as glass, silver, pottery and clockmaking, and on the dubious military career of Earl Haig. Also on view is the original version of the National Covenant of 1638; modern investigations have failed to resolve whether or not some of the signatories signed with their own blood, as tradition has it.

Holyrood

At the foot of Canongate lies **Holyrood**, Edinburgh's royal quarter. The **legend** of its foundation, in 1128, is described in a fifteenth-century manuscript still kept in the palace: King David I, son of Malcolm Canmore and St Margaret, went out hunting one day and was suddenly confronted by a stag who threw him from his horse and seemed ready to gore him. In desperation, the king tried to protect himself by grasping its antlers, but instead found himself holding a crucifix, whereupon the animal ran off. In a dream that night, he heard a voice commanding him to "make a house for Canons devoted to the Cross"; he duly obeyed, naming the abbey Holyrood (rood being an alternative name for a cross). A more prosaic explanation is that David, the most pious of all Scotland's monarchs, simply acquired a relic of the True Cross and decided to build a suitable home for it.

Holyrood soon became a favoured **royal residence**, its situation in a secluded valley making it far more agreeable than the draughty castle. At first, monarchs lodged in the monastic guest house, to which a wing for the exclusive use of the court was added during the reign of James II. This was transformed into a full-blown palace for James IV, which in turn was replaced by a much larger building for Charles II, although he never actually lived there. Indeed, it was something of a white elephant until Queen Victoria started making regular trips to her northern kingdom, a custom that has been maintained by her successors.

The precincts

On the north side of **Abbey Strand**, which forms a sort of processional way linking Canongate with Holyrood, Abbey Lairds is a four-storey sixteenth-century mansion which once served as a home for aristocratic debtors and is now occupied by royal flunkies during the summer seat of the court.

Legend has it that Mary Queen of Scots used to bathe in sweet white wine in the curious little turreted structure nearby known as **Queen Mary's Bath House**; it is more likely, however, that it was either a summer pavilion or a dovecote. Its architecture is mirrored in the **Croft an Righ**, a picturesque L-shaped house in a quiet, generally overlooked corner beside the eastern wall of the complex.

The Scottish Parliament Site and around

Tthe massive construction site immediately opposite the Palace, at the foot of the Royal Mile, is where the new **Scottish Parliament** is being built. For decades, campaigners for home rule for Scotland lifted their eyes to the Old Royal High School building on Calton Hill (see p.813) as the ideal place for a Scottish parliament to sit. In the run-up to devolution becoming a reality, however, the Scottish Office unexpectedly announced that the Old Royal High School was too small to accommodate the proposed Parliament and its offices, and eventually the site of a disused brewery at the foot of the Royal Mile was identified as the ideal location. Designed by Catalan architect Enric Miralles in the form of a series of petal-shaped buildings which have been compared – both favourably and unfavourably – to upturned boats, the structure will cost something in the region of £100 million, and is due to be ready by 2002. Until then, Parliament sits in the Church of Scotland Assembly Hall on the Mound (see p.809).

On the Holyrood Road side of the construction site, beneath a pin-cushion of white metal struts, is **Our Dynamic Earth** (April–Oct daily 10am–6pm; Nov–March Wed–Sat 10am–5pm; £5.95), a new, hi-tech attraction aimed mainly at families. A "time machine" elevator takes you on a tour of the creation of the universe and the formation of the landscape, using video graphics, film footage, eerie music and a deep-throated commentary.

The Palace of Holyroodhouse

In its present form, the **Palace of Holyroodhouse** (daily: April–Oct 9.30am–5.15pm; Nov–March 9.30am–3.15pm; £5.50) is largely a seventeenth-century creation, planned for Charles II. However, the tower house of the old palace was skilfully incorporated to form the northwestern block, with a virtual mirror image of it erected as a counterbalance at the other end. The three-storey **courtyard** is an early exercise in Palladian style, exhibiting a punctiliously accurate knowledge of the main Classical orders to create a sense of absolute harmony and unity.

Inside, the **State Apartments**, as Charles II's palace is known, are decorated with oak panelling, tapestries, portraits and paintings, all overshadowed by the magnificent white stucco **ceilings**, especially in the Morning Drawing Room. The most eye-catching chamber, however, is the **Great Gallery**, which takes up the entire first floor of the northern wing. During the 1745 sojourn of the Young Pretender, this was the setting for a banquet – reconstructed in detail in Scott's novel *Waverley* – and it is still used for big ceremonial occasions. Along the walls are ninety or so portraits commissioned from

---

ADMISSIONS TO HOLYROODHOUSE

Guided tours of Holyroodhouse only take place from November to March; at other times of the year, visitors are free to move at their own pace. It is worth remembering that Holyrood is still a working palace, so the buildings are closed to the public for long periods during state functions; you won't be able to visit during a fortnight in the middle of May, or at the time of the annual royal visit, which usually takes place in the last two weeks of June and the first week of July.

the seventeenth-century Dutch artist Jacob de Wit to illustrate the royal lineage of Scotland from its mythical origins in the fourth century BC; the result is unintentionally hilarious, as it is clear that the artist's imagination was taxed to bursting point by the need to paint so many different facial types without having an inkling as to what the subjects actually looked like. In the adjacent **King's Closet**, de Wit's *The Finding of Moses* provides a biblical link to the portraits, the Scottish royal family claiming descent from Scota, the Egyptian pharaoh's daughter, who discovered Moses in the bulrushes.

The oldest parts of the palace, the **Historical Apartments**, are mainly of note for their associations with Mary Queen of Scots and in particular for the brutal murder, organized by her husband, Lord Darnley, of her private secretary, David Rizzio, who was stabbed 56 times and dragged from the small closet, through the Queen's Bedchamber, and into the Outer Chamber. Until a few years ago, visitors were shown apparently indelible bloodstains on the floor of the latter, but these are now admitted to be fakes, and have been covered up. A display cabinet in the same room shows some pieces of **needlework** woven by the deposed queen while in English captivity; another case has an outstanding **miniature portrait** of her by the French court painter, François Clouet.

Holyrood Abbey

In the grounds of the Palace are the wonderfully evocative ruins of **Holyrood Abbey**. Of King David's original Norman church, the only surviving fragment is a doorway in the far southeastern corner. Most of the remainder dates from a late twelfth- and early thirteenth-century rebuilding in the Early Gothic style. The surviving parts of the **west front**, including one of the twin towers and the elaborately carved entrance portal, show how resplendent the abbey must once have been. Unfortunately, its sacking by the English in 1547, followed by the demolition of the transept and chancel during the Reformation, all but destroyed the building. Charles I attempted to restore some semblance of unity by ordering the erection of the great east window and a new stone roof, but the latter collapsed in 1768, causing grievous damage to the rest of the structure. By this time, the Canongate congregation had another place of worship, and schemes to rebuild the abbey were abandoned.

Holyrood Park

Holyrood Park – or Queen's Park – a natural wilderness in the very heart of the modern city, is unquestionably one of Edinburgh's main assets, as locals (though relatively few tourists) readily appreciate. Packed into an area no more than five miles in diameter is an amazing variety of landscapes – mountains, crags, moorland, marshes, glens, lochs and fields. It represents something of a microcosm of Scotland's scenery, although **Duddingston Loch**, a bird sanctuary, is the only natural stretch of water in the park. Perched above the loch, just outside the park boundary, **Duddingston Kirk** dates back in part to the twelfth century, and is the focus of one of the most unspoilt old villages within modern Edinburgh.The park is a great place for outdoor activities, with toddlers, cyclists and rock-climbers all being catered for. A single tarred road, the **Queen's Drive**, circles the park, enabling many of its features to be seen by car, though you really need to stroll around to appreciate it fully.

Two of the most rewarding **walks** begin opposite the southern gates of the Palace: one, a pathway nicknamed the Radical Road, traverses the ridge immediately below the **Salisbury Crags**, one of the main features of the Edinburgh skyline, while you can also walk along the top of the basalt crags, from where there are excellent views of the Palace of Holyroodhouse and Holyrood Abbey.

Dunsapie Loch, towards the eastern side of the park, is the usual starting point for the ascent of **Arthur's Seat**, a majestic extinct volcano rising 823ft above sea level. The Seat is Edinburgh's single most prominent landmark, resembling a huge crouched lion when seen from the west. The climb from Dunsapie, up a grassy slope, followed by a rocky path near the summit, is considerably less arduous than it looks: it's no more than a fairly straightforward twenty-minute walk. The views from the top are all you'd expect, covering the entire city and much of the Firth of Forth; on a clear day, you can even see the southernmost mountains of the Highlands. The composer, Felix Mendelssohn, climbed Arthur's Seat in July 1829, and noted: "It is beautiful here! In the evening a cool breeze is wafted from the sea, and then all objects appear clearly and sharply defined against the gray sky; the lights from the windows glitter brilliantly."

The rest of the Old Town

Although most visitors to the Old Town understandably concentrate on the Royal Mile, the area has many other intriguing, and less commercial, corners, notably the **Grassmarket**, famous as the site of public executions in previous centuries, and the rather gloomy **Cowgate**, which runs between the Grassmarket and the Holyrood area. The area around the University contains the Adam-designed **Old College**, the excellent **National Museum of Scotland** and the historic kirkyard at **Greyfriars**.

Cowgate

Immediately south of the Royal Mile, following a roughly parallel course from the Lawnmarket to St Mary's Street, is **Cowgate**. One of Edinburgh's oldest surviving streets, it was also formerly one of the city's most prestigious addresses. However, the construction of the great **viaducts** of George IV Bridge and South Bridge entombed it below street level, condemning it to decay and neglect and leading the nineteenth-century writer, Alexander Smith, to declare that "the condition of the inhabitants is as little known to respectable Edinburgh as are the habits of moles, earthworms, and the mining population". In the last decade or so Cowgate has experienced something of a revival, with various nightclubs and Festival venues establishing themselves, though few tourists venture here and the contrast with the neighbouring Royal Mile remains stark.

At the corner with Niddry Street, which runs down from the High Street near its junction with North Bridge and South Bridge, the unprepossessing **St Cecilia's Hall** (Wed & Sat 2–5pm; £3) was built in the 1760s for the Musical Society of Edinburgh. Inside, Scotland's oldest and most beautiful concert room, oval in shape and set under a shallow dome, makes a perfect venue for concerts of Baroque and early music held during the Festival, and occasionally at other times of the year. Otherwise, the building is primarily worth visiting for the **Russell Collection** of antique keyboard instruments.

Towards the western end of Cowgate stands the **Magdalen Chapel** (Mon–Fri 9.30am–4.30pm), a sixteenth-century almshouse under the jurisdiction of the Incorporation of Hammermen, a guild to which most Edinburgh workers, other than goldsmiths, belonged. The Hammermen added a handsome tower and steeple in the 1620s, and later transformed the chapel into their guildhall, which was suitably adorned with fine ironwork. However, the main feature of the interior is the only significant pre-Reformation stained glass in Scotland still in its original location. That it escaped the iconoclasts is probably due to the fact that it is purely heraldic.

Grassmarket and George IV Bridge

At its western end, Cowgate opens out into the **Grassmarket**, which has played an important role in the murkier aspects of Edinburgh's turbulent history. The public gallows were located here, and it was the scene of numerous riots and other disturbances down the centuries. It was here, in 1736, that Captain Porteous was lynched, after he ordered shots to be fired at a crowd watching a public execution. The notorious duo William Burke and William Hare had their lair in a now-vanished close just off the western end of Grassmarket, luring to it victims whom they murdered with the intention of selling their bodies to the eminent physician Robert Knox. Eventually, Hare betrayed his partner, who was duly executed in 1829, and Knox's career was finished off as a result. Today, the Grassmarket can still have a seedy edge, though the cluster of busy bars and restaurants along its northern side are evidence of a serious attempt to clean up its image.

At the northeastern corner of the Grassmarket are five old tenements of the old **West Bow**, which formerly zigzagged up to the Royal Mile. The rest of this was replaced in the 1840s by the curving **Victoria Street**, an unusual two-tier thoroughfare, with arcaded shops below and a pedestrian terrace above. This sweeps up to **George IV Bridge** and the **National Library of Scotland**, which holds a rich collection of illuminated manuscripts, early printed books, historical documents, and the letters and papers of prominent Scottish literary figures, displayed in regularly changing thematic exhibitions (usually Mon–Sat 10am–5pm, Sun 2–5pm; free).

Greyfriars and around

The **statue of Greyfriars Bobby** at the southwestern corner of **George IV Bridge** must rank as Edinburgh's most sentimental tourist attraction. Bobby was a Skye terrier acquired as a working dog by a police constable named John Gray. When John Gray died in 1858, Bobby began a vigil on his grave which he maintained until he died fourteen years later. In the process, he became an Edinburgh celebrity, fed and cared for by locals who gave him a special collar (now in the Huntly House Museum; see p.801) to prevent him being impounded as a stray. His statue, originally a fountain, was modelled from life, and erected soon after his death; his story has gained international renown, thanks to a spate of cloying books and tear-jerking movies.

The grave Bobby mourned over is in the **Greyfriars Kirkyard**, which among its clutter of grandiose seventeenth- and eighteenth-century funerary monuments boasts the striking mausoleum of the Adam family of architects. Greyfriars is particularly associated with the long struggle to establish Presbyterianism in Scotland: in 1638, it was the setting for the signing of the National Covenant, while in 1679, some 1200 Covenanters were imprisoned in the enclosure at the southwestern end of the yard. Set against the northern wall is the Martyrs' Monument, a defiantly worded memorial commemorating all those who died in pursuit of the eventual victory.

The graveyard rather overshadows **Greyfriars Kirk** itself, completed in 1620 as the first new church in Edinburgh since the Reformation. It's a real oddball in both layout and design, having a nave and aisles but no chancel, and adopting the anachronistic architectural language of the friary that preceded it, complete with medieval-looking windows, arches and buttresses.

At the western end of Greyfriars Kirkyard is one of the most significant surviving portions of the **Flodden Wall**, the city fortifications erected in the wake of Scotland's disastrous military defeat of 1513. When open, the gateway beyond offers a short cut to **George Heriot's Hospital**, otherwise approached from Lauriston Place to the south. Founded as a home for poor boys by "Jinglin Geordie" Heriot, James VI's goldsmith, it is now one of Edinburgh's most prestigious fee-paying schools; although you can't go inside, you can wander round the quadrangle, whose array of towers, turrets, chimneys, carved doorways and traceried windows is one of the finest achievements of the Scottish Renaissance.

The National Museum of Scotland

Immediately opposite Greyfriars Bobby, on the south side of Chambers Street, stands the striking honey-coloured sandstone **National Museum of Scotland** (Mon & Wed–Sat 10am–5pm, Tues 10am–8pm, Sun noon–5pm; £3, free after 4.30pm Tues). Opened in 1998 to deserved acclaim, both for its elegant design and for its respectful but imaginative treatment of the nation's treasures, this is undoubtedly Scotland's premier museum. The fresh, open atmosphere of the building is combined with excellent features: specially commissioned art works; the **Discovery Centre**, specifically aimed at 5–14-year-olds; the **exhibIT** computer bank with databases of the museum's collections; and the **Tower Restaurant**, a sleek, stylish place with fabulous views which is also open in the evenings (see opposite).

The main entrance to the museum is at the base of the tower, although you can also enter from the neighbouring Royal Museum of Scotland (see opposite). Hawthornden Court, the central atrium of the museum, contains the museum shop and access to the Royal Museum **café**. Free **guided tours** on different themes take place through the day, and free audio headsets give detailed information on artefacts and displays.

BEGINNINGS AND EARLY PEOPLE

The first section, **"Beginnings"**, is down on Level 0. Here, Scotland's story before the arrival of man is presented with audio-visual displays, artistic recreations and a selection of rocks and fossils, including some Lewisian gneiss, the oldest rock in Europe, and "Lizzie" (*Westlothiana lizziae*), the oldest known fossil reptile in the world.

The second section, **"Early People"**, also on Level 0, which covers the period up to the end of the first millennium AD, is arguably the most engaging in the whole museum, both for the quality of its artefacts and the innovative use of contemporary art: eight giant bronze figures in the distinctive post-industrial style of Edinburgh-born sculptor Sir **Eduardo Paolozzi** "wear" different artefacts such as prehistoric bracelets and necklaces in small display compartments. Also look out for **Andy Goldsworthy**'s *Enclosure* – four curved walls of slate roof tiles. Among the **artefacts** on display, highlights are the Trappain treasure hoard, 44lb of silver plates, cutlery and goblets found buried in East Lothian; the Cramond Lioness, a sculpture from a Roman tombstone found recently in the Firth of Forth (see p.818); and the beautifully detailed gold, silver and amber Hunterston brooch, dating from around 700 AD.

THE KINGDOM OF THE SCOTS

"The Kingdom of the Scots", on Level 1, covers the period between Scotland's development as a single independent nation and the union with England in 1707. At the entrance to the section, in Hawthornden Court, is the **Dupplin Cross**, a symbol of the different peoples who united under Kenneth MacAlpin to form a single kingdom in 843. Star exhibits include the **Monymusk reliquary**, an intricately decorated box said to have carried the remains of St Columba; the **Lewis chessmen**, exquisitely idiosyncratic twelfth-century pieces carved from walrus ivory; and the **"Maiden"**, an early form of the guillotine. The section on the church is of interest not only for the craftsmanship of some of the objects, most notably the silver gilt **St Fillan's crozier**, but also because just outside the window you can glimpse Greyfriars Kirkyard, where the National Covenant was signed in 1638.

SCOTLAND TRANSFORMED

Level 3 shows exhibits under the theme **"Scotland Transformed"**, covering the century or so following the Union of Parliaments in 1707. This was the period which saw the last of the Highland uprisings under the Young Pretender (whose silver travelling canteen is on display), yet also witnessed the expansion of trade links with the Americas and developments in industries such as weaving and iron and steel production. Dominating the floor is a reconstructed steam-driven **Newcomen engine**, which was still being used to pump water from a coal mine in Ayrshire in 1901. Alongside it, in contrast, is part of a thatched, cruck-frame house of the 1720s of a type in which many Scots still lived during this time.

INDUSTRY, EMPIRE AND THE TWENTIETH CENTURY
Following the early innovations of steam and mechanical engineering, Scotland went on to pioneer many aspects of heavy engineering, with ship and locomotive production to the fore. Largest of the exhibits in **"Industry and Empire"** is the steam locomotive *Ellesmere*. Other fields are covered too, including domestic life, leisure activities and the influence of Scots around the world, both as a result of emigration, and through such luminaries as James Watt, Charles Rennie Mackintosh and Robert Louis Stevenson.

For the **Twentieth Century Gallery**, on Level 6, a range of Scots, from schoolchildren to celebrities, were asked to pick a single representative object. Choices are intriguing, controversial and unexpected, from computers to football strips, cans of Irn Bru to a black Saab convertible. The obvious challenge is implicitly made: what would you choose, and why? A lift gives access to the **roof garden**, from which there are fine views across the city and beyond.

The Royal Museum of Scotland

Interlinked with the National Museum, though also with its own entrance, is the Royal Museum of Scotland (Mon & Wed–Sat 10am–5pm, Tues 10am–8pm, Sun noon–5pm; £3, free after 4.30pm Tues), a dignified Venetian-style palace with a cast-iron interior modelled on that of the Crystal Palace in London. The **sculptures** in the lofty entrance hall begin with a superb Assyrian relief from the royal palace at Nimrud, and range via Classical Greece, Rome and Nubia to Buddhas from Japan and Burma and a totem pole from British Columbia. Also on the ground floor are collections of stuffed animals and birds, and the **Power Collections**, with a double-action beam engine designed by James Watt in 1786 alongside a section of the Inchkeith lighthouse and the control desk from Hunterston A nuclear reactor. Upstairs there's a fine array of Egyptian mummies, ceramics from ancient Greece to the present day, costumes, jewellery, natural-history displays and a splendid selection of European decorative art, ranging from early medieval liturgical objects via Limoges enamels and sixteenth-century German woodcarving to stunning **French silverware** made during the reign of Louis XIV. Finally, on the top floor, you'll come to a distinguished collection of historic scientific instruments, a small selection of arms and armour, plus sections on geology, fossils, ethnology, and the arts of Islam, Japan and China.

Old College

Immediately alongside the Royal Museum is the earliest surviving part of the **University of Edinburgh**, variously referred to as the **Old College** or Old Quad, although nowadays it houses only a few University departments; the main campus colonizes the streets and squares to the south.

The Old College was designed by Robert Adam, but it was completed in a considerably modified form by William Playfair, one of Edinburgh's greatest architects, in 1834. Playfair built just one of Adam's two quadrangles – the dome was not added until 1879 – and his magnificent **Upper Library** is now mostly used for ceremonial occasions. The **Talbot Rice Art Gallery** (Tues–Sat 10am–5pm; free), housed in the Old College, includes many splendid seventeenth-century works from the Low Countries, with Teniers, Steen and van de Velde well represented. There are also some outstanding bronzes, notably the *Anatomical Horse* by an unknown Italian sculptor of the High Renaissance, and *Cain Killing Abel* by the Dutch Mannerist Adrian de Vries. The first and largest exhibition hall displays contemporary art.

The New Town

The **New Town**, itself well over two hundred years old, stands in total contrast to the Old Town: the layout is symmetrical, the streets broad and straight, and most of the buildings are Neoclassical. The entire area, right down to the names of its streets, is something of a celebration of the Union, which was then generally regarded as a proud development in Scotland's history. Originally intended to be residential, today the New Town is the bustling hub of the city's professional, commercial and business life, dominated by shops, banks, offices and increasing numbers of bars and restaurants.

The existence of the New Town is chiefly due to the vision of **George Drummond**, who made schemes for the expansion of the city soon after becoming Lord Provost in 1725. Work began on the draining of the Nor' Loch below the Castle in 1759, a job that was to last some sixty years. The North Bridge, linking the Old Town with the port of Leith, was built between 1763 and 1772 and, in 1766, following a public competition, a plan for the New Town by 22-year-old architect **James Craig** was chosen. Its gridiron pattern was perfectly matched to the site: central George Street, flanked by showpiece squares, was laid out along the main ridge, with the parallel Princes Street and Queen Street on either side below, and two smaller streets, Thistle Street and Rose Street in between the three major thoroughfares to provide coach houses, artisans' dwellings and shops. Princes and Queen streets were built up on one side only, so as not to block the spectacular views of the Old Town and Fife. Architects were accordingly afforded a wonderful opportunity to play with vistas and spatial relationships, particularly well exploited by **Robert Adam**, who contributed extensively to the later phases of the work. The First New Town, as the area covered by Craig's plan came to be known, received a whole series of extensions in the first few decades of the nineteenth century, all carefully in harmony with the Neoclassical idiom.

In many ways, the layout of the New Town is its own most remarkable sight, an extraordinary grouping of squares, circuses, terraces, crescents and parks, with a few set-pieces such as Register House, the north frontage of **Charlotte Square** and the assemblage of curiosities on and around Calton Hill. However, it also contains an assortment of Victorian additions, notably the **Scott Monument**, as well as two of the city's most important public collections – the **National Gallery of Scotland**, and the **Scottish National Gallery of Modern Art**.

Princes Street

Although only allocated a subsidiary role in the original plan of the New Town, **Princes Street** had developed into Edinburgh's principal thoroughfare by the middle of the nineteenth century, a role it has retained ever since. Its unobstructed views across to the Castle and the Old Town are undeniably magnificent. Indeed, without the views, Princes Street would lose much of its appeal; its northern side, dominated by ugly high-street chains, is almost always crowded with shoppers, and few of the original eighteenth-century buildings remain. It was the coming of the railway, which follows a parallel course to the south, that ensured Princes Street's rise to prominence. The tracks are well concealed at the far end of the sunken gardens that replaced the Nor' Loch, which provide ample space to relax or picnic during the summer. Thomas de Quincey, author of *Confessions of an English Opium Eater*, spent the last thirty years of his life in Edinburgh and is buried in the graveyard of St Cuthbert's Church, at the western end of the gardens.

The East End

Register House (Mon–Fri 10am–4pm; free), Princes Street's most distinguished building, is at its extreme northeastern corner, framing the perspective down North

Bridge. Unfortunately, the majesty of the setting is marred by the **St James Centre** to the rear, an ugly grey behemoth incorporating a covered shopping arcade now regarded as the city's worst ever planning blunder. Register House was designed in the 1770s by Robert Adam to hold Scotland's historic records, a function it has maintained ever since. Its exterior is a model of restrained Neoclassicism; the interior, centred on a glorious Roman rotunda, has a dome lavishly decorated with plasterwork and antique-style medallions.

Opposite is one of the few buildings on the south side of Princes Street, the Balmoral Hotel, formerly known as the **North British**. Among the most luxurious hotels in the city, it has always been associated with the railway, and the timepiece on its bulky clocktower is always kept two minutes fast in order to encourage passengers to hurry to catch their trains. Alongside the hotel, the **Waverley Market** is a fairly sensitive modern commercial development. The open-air piazza on its street-level roof is home to Edinburgh's tourist office (see p.706), and a favourite haunt of street theatre groups and other performing artists during the Festival.

The Scott Monument and the Royal Scottish Academy

Facing the Victorian shopping emporium Jenners, and set within East Princes Street Gardens, the 200-foot-high **Scott Monument** (March–May daily 10am–6pm; June–Sept Mon–Sat 9am–8pm, Sun 10am–6pm; Oct daily 10am–6pm; Nov–Feb daily 10am–4pm; £2.50) was erected in memory of the writer by public subscription within a few years of his death. The world's largest monument to a man of letters, its magisterial, spire-like design was created by George Meikle Kemp, a carpenter and joiner whose only building this is; while it was still under construction, he stumbled into a canal one foggy evening and drowned. The architecture is closely modelled on Scott's beloved Melrose Abbey (see p.838), while the rich sculptural decoration shows sixteen Scottish writers and 64 characters from the *Waverley* novels. Underneath the archway is a **statue** of Scott with his deerhound Maida, carved from a thirty-ton block of Carrara marble.

The Princes Street Gardens are bisected by the **Mound**, which provides a road link between the Old and New Towns. Its name is an accurate description: it was formed in the 1780s by dumping piles of earth brought from the New Town's building plots. At the foot of the Mound, on the Princes Street side, Playfair's **Royal Scottish Academy** (Mon–Sat 10am–5pm, Sun 2–5pm; price varies) is a Grecian-style Doric temple used somewhat infrequently for temporary exhibitions during the year, notably for the RSA annual exhibition held from April to July.

The National Gallery of Scotland

To the rear of the Royal Scottish Academy, the less elaborate **National Gallery of Scotland** (Mon–Sat 10am–5pm, Sun 2–5pm; free) is another Playfair construction, built in the 1850s and now housing a choice display of Old Masters, many of which belong to the Duke of Sutherland. A few years ago, the original Playfair rooms on the ground floor were controversially restored to their 1850s appearance, with the pictures hung closely together, often on two levels, and intermingled with sculptures and *objets d'art* to produce a deliberately cluttered effect (some lesser works, which would otherwise languish in the vaults, are a good 15ft up). Two small, late nineteenth-century works in Room 12 – one anonymous, the other by A.E. Moffat – show the gallery as it was in the nineteenth century, with paintings stacked up even higher than at present.

Though individual works are frequently moved, the layout is broadly chronological, starting in the upper rooms above the entrance, and continuing clockwise around the ground floor. The upper part of the rear extension is devoted to smaller panels of the eighteenth and nineteenth centuries, while the basement contains the majority of the Scottish collection. There are no guided tours; instead, **audioguides** (£2) provide commentaries on the gallery's more important works.

EARLY NETHERLANDISH AND GERMAN WORKS

Among the gallery's most valuable treasures are the *Trinity Panels*, the remaining parts of the only surviving pre-Reformation altarpiece made for a Scottish church. Painted by **Hugo van der Goes** in the mid-fifteenth century, they were commissioned for the Holy Trinity Collegiate Church by its provost, Edward Bonkil, who appears in the company of organ-playing angels in the finest and best preserved of the four panels. On the reverse sides are portraits of James III, his son (the future James IV) and Queen Margaret of Denmark. Their feebly characterized heads, which stand in jarring contrast to the superlative figures of the patron saints accompanying them, were modelled from life by an unknown local painter after the altar had been shipped to Edinburgh.

Of the later Netherlandish works, **Gerard David** is represented by the touchingly anecdotal *Three Legends of St Nicholas*, while the *Portrait of a Notary* by **Quentin Massys** is an excellent early example of northern European assimilation of the forms and techniques of the Italian Renaissance. Many of his German contemporaries developed their own variations on this style, among them **Cranach**, by whom there is a splendidly erotic *Venus and Cupid*, and **Holbein**, whose *Allegory of the Old and New Testaments* is a Protestant tract painted for an English patron.

ITALIAN RENAISSANCE WORKS

The Italian section includes a wonderful array of **Renaissance** masterpieces. Of these, *The Virgin Adoring the Child* is a beautiful composition set against a ruined architectural background shown in strict perspective: although known to have been painted in the workshop of the great Florentine sculptor **Andrea del Verrocchio**, its authorship remains a mystery. Equally graceful are the three works by **Raphael**, particularly *The Bridgewater Madonna* and the tondo of *The Holy Family with a Palm Tree*, whose striking luminosity has been revealed after recent restoration.

Of the four mythological scenes by **Titian**, the sensuous *Three Ages of Man*, an allegory of childhood, adulthood and old age, is one of the most accomplished compositions of his early period, while the later *Venus Anadyomene* ranks among the great nudes of Western art, notwithstanding its rough state of preservation. The companion pair of *Diana and Acteon* and *Diana and Callisto*, painted for Philip II of Spain, show the almost impressionistic freedom of his late style. **Bassano**'s truly regal *Adoration of the Kings*, a dramatic altarpiece of *The Descent from the Cross* by **Tintoretto**, and several other works by **Veronese**, complete a fine Venetian collection.

SEVENTEENTH-CENTURY SOUTHERN EUROPEAN WORKS

Among the seventeenth-century works is the gallery's most important sculpture, **Bernini**'s *Bust of Monsignor Carlo Antonio dal Pozzo*. **El Greco**'s *A Fable*, painted during his early years in Italy, takes a mysterious subject whose exact meaning is unclear, while *The Saviour of the World* is a typically intense, visionary image from his mature years in Spain. Indigenous Spanish art is represented by **Velázquez**'s *An Old Woman Cooking Eggs*, an astonishingly assured work for a lad of nineteen, and by **Zurbaran**'s *The Immaculate Conception*, part of his ambitious decorative scheme for the Carthusian monastery in Jerez. There are two small copper panels by the short-lived but enormously influential Rome-based German painter **Adam Elsheimer**; of these, *Il Contento*, showing Jupiter's descent to earth to punish the ungodly, is a *tour de force* of technical precision.

The series of *The Seven Sacraments* by **Poussin** are displayed in their own room, whose floor and central octagonal seat repeat some of the motifs in the paintings. Based on the artist's extensive research into biblical times, the series marks the first attempt to portray scenes from the life of Jesus and the early Christians in an authentic manner, rather than one overlaid by artistic conventions. Poussin's younger contemporary **Claude**, who likewise left France to live in Rome, is represented by his largest canvas,

Landscape with Apollo, the Muses and a River God, which radiates his characteristically idealized vision of Classical antiquity.

SEVENTEENTH-CENTURY FLEMISH AND DUTCH WORKS
Rubens' *The Feast of Herod*, an archetypal example of his grand manner, was executed, like all his large works, with extensive studio assistance, whereas the three small *modellos* are all from his own hand. The trio of large upright canvases by **Van Dyck** date from his early Genoese period; of these, *The Lomellini Family* shows his mastery at creating a definitive dynastic image. Among the four canvases by **Rembrandt** is a poignant *Self-Portrait Aged 51*, and the ripely suggestive *Woman in Bed*. The largest and probably the earliest of the thirty or so surviving paintings by **Vermeer**, *Christ in the House of Martha and Mary*, is here, too, while **Hals** is represented by a typical pair of portraits plus a brilliant caricature, *Verdonck*. There's also an excellent cross-section of the specialist Dutch painters of the age, highlights being the mischievous *School for Boys and Girls* by **Jan Steen**, and the strangely haunting *Interior of the Church of St Bavo in Haarlem* by **Pieter Saenredam**.

EUROPEAN WORKS OF THE EIGHTEENTH AND NINETEENTH CENTURIES
Of the large-scale eighteenth-century works, **Tiepolo**'s *The Finding of Moses*, a gloriously bravura fantasy, stands out. Other decorative compositions of the same period are **Goya**'s *The Doctor*, a cartoon for a tapestry design, and the three large upright pastoral scenes by **Boucher**. However, the gems of the French section are the smaller panels, in particular **Watteau**'s *Fêtes Vénitiennes*, an effervescent Rococo idyll, and **Chardin**'s *Vase of Flowers*, a copybook example of still-life painting. There's also a superb group of Impressionist and Post-Impressionist masterpieces, including a particularly good showing of the works of **Degas**, three outstanding examples of **Gauguin**'s work, set respectively in Brittany, Martinique and Tahiti, **Cézanne**'s *The Tall Trees*, and one of the most famous paintings from **Monet**'s haystacks series.

ENGLISH AND AMERICAN WORKS
The gallery has relatively few English paintings, but those here are impressive. **Hogarth**'s *Sarah Malcolm*, painted in Newgate Prison the day the murderess was executed, once belonged to Horace Walpole, who also commissioned **Reynolds'** *The Ladies Waldegrave*, a group portrait of his three great-nieces. **Gainsborough**'s *The Honourable Mrs Graham* is one of his most memorable society portraits, while **Constable** himself described *Dedham Vale* as being "perhaps my best". There are two wonderful Roman views by **Turner**, by whom the gallery owns a wonderful array of watercolours, faithfully displayed each January, when the light is at its weakest. More unexpected than the scarcity of English works is the presence of some exceptional American canvases: **Benjamin West**'s Romantic fantasy, *King Alexander III Rescued from a Stag*; **John Singer Sargent**'s virtuoso *Lady Agnew of Lochnaw*; and **Frederic Edwin Church**'s *View of Niagara Falls from the American Side*.

SCOTTISH WORKS
On the face of it, the gallery's Scottish collection, which shows the entire gamut of Scottish painting from seventeenth-century portraiture to the Arts and Crafts movement, is something of an anticlimax. There are, however, some important works: **Gavin Hamilton**'s *Achilles Mourning the Death of Patroclus*, for example, painted in Rome, is an unquestionably arresting image. **Allan Ramsay**, who became court painter to George III, is represented by his intimate *The Artist's Second Wife* and *Jean-Jacques Rousseau*, in which the philosopher is shown in Armenian costume. Of **Sir Henry Raeburn**'s large portraits, note the swaggering masculinity of *Sir John Sinclair* or *Colonel Alistair MacDonell of Glengarry*, both of whom are shown in full Highland

dress. Raeburn's technical mastery was equally sure when working on a small scale, as shown in one of the gallery's most popular pictures, *The Rev Robert Walker Skating on Duddingston Loch*.

Other Scottish painters represented include the versatile **Sir David Wilkie** and **Alexander Nasmyth**, whose tendency to gild the lily can be seen in his *View of Tantallon Castle and the Bass Rock*. More recent Scottish work is best represented in works such as Sir William McTaggart's *The Storm*, and James Guthrie's *A Hind's Daughter*, along with Phoebe Anna Traquair's exquisite Arts and Crafts panels.

George Street

The street parallel to Princes Street to the north is **George Street**, rapidly changing its role from a thoroughfare of august financial institutions to a high-brow version of Princes Street, lined with bars and designer shops. George Street was designed to be the centrepiece of the First New Town, joining two grand squares. At its eastern end lies **St Andrew Square**, in the middle of which is the Melville Monument, a statue of Lord Melville, Pitt the Younger's Navy Treasurer. On the eastern side of the square stands a handsome eighteenth-century town mansion, designed by Sir William Chambers. Headquarters of the Royal Bank of Scotland since 1825, the palatial mid-nineteenth-century banking hall is a symbol of the success of the New Town. On the south side of the street, the oval-shaped **church of St Andrew** (now known as St Andrew and St George) is chiefly famous as the scene of the 1843 Disruption led by Thomas Chalmers, which split the Church of Scotland in two. Famous visitors to George Street have included Percy Bysshe Shelley, who stayed at no. 60 with the sixteen-year-old Harriet Westbrook during the summer of 1811, and Charles Dickens, who gave a number of readings in the Assembly Rooms in the 1840s and 1850s.

At the western end of the street, **Charlotte Square** was designed by Robert Adam in 1791, a year before his death. For the most part, his plans were faithfully implemented, an exception being the domed and porticoed church of St George, which was simplified on grounds of expense. Its interior was gutted in the 1960s and refurbished as **West Register House**; like its counterpart at the opposite end of Princes Street, it features exhibitions of documents and manuscripts (Mon–Fri 10am–4pm; free).

The **north side** of the square has deservedly become the most exclusive address in the city. Number 6 is the official residence of the First Minister of the Scottish Parliament, and also where Scottish cabinet meetings take place, while the upper storeys of no. 7 are the home of the Moderator of the General Assembly, the annually elected leader of the Church of Scotland. Restored by the NTS, the lower floors are open to the public under the name of the **Georgian House** (April–Oct Mon–Sat 10am–5pm, Sun 2–5pm; £4.40), whose contents give a good idea of what the house must have looked like during the period of the first owner, the head of the clan Lamont. The rooms are decked out in period furniture, including a working barrel organ which plays a selection of Scottish airs, and hung with fine paintings, among which are portraits by Ramsay and Raeburn, and a beautiful *Marriage of the Virgin* by El Greco's teacher, the Italian miniaturist Giulio Clovio.

The Scottish National Portrait Gallery

Queen Street, the last of the three main streets of the First New Town, is bordered to the north by gardens, and commands sweeping views across to Fife. Much the best preserved of the area's three main streets, its principal attraction is the excellent **Scottish National Portrait Gallery** (Mon–Sat 10am–5pm, Sun 2–5pm; free), at the far eastern end. The building is itself a fascinating period piece, its red sandstone exterior modelled on the Doge's Palace in Venice, and encrusted with statues of famous Scots.

This theme is taken up in the stunning entrance hall, which has a mosaic-like frieze procession by William Hole of great figures from Scotland's past, with heroic murals by the same artist of stirring episodes from the nation's history adorning the balcony above.

The permanent exhibitions are located on the two floors above, and are devoted to portraits, accompanied by potted biographies, of famous Scots, forming an engaging procession through Scottish history. The gallery in fact owns two portraits of Prince Charlie (not always shown at the same time): one, by **Antonio David**, shows him as an aristocratic, rosy-cheeked twelve-year-old; the other, by **Maurice-Quentin de la Tour**, depicts him as an older, dashing warrior in armour, and was purchased by the prince himself. From the seventeenth century, there's an excellent **Van Dyck** portrait of Charles Seton, second Earl of Dunfermline, and the tartan-clad Lord Mungo Murray, who died in the disastrous attempt to establish a Scottish colony in Panama. Eighteenth-century highlights include portraits of the philosopher David Hume, by **Allan Ramsay**, and the bard Robert Burns by his friend, **Alexander Nasmyth**, plus a varied group by **Raeburn**: subjects include Sir Walter Scott, the fiddler Niel Gow and the artist himself. The star portrait from the nineteenth century is that of physician Sir Alexander Morison by his patient, the mad painter **Richard Dadd** – Edinburgh's fishing port of Newhaven is in the background. Twentieth-century portraits on the first floor include a very angular Alec Douglas-Home, briefly prime minister in the 1960s, Sean Connery depicted by the Scottish artist **John Bellany**, and photomontages of sporting stars Stephen Hendry and Sir Alex Ferguson.

Temporary **exhibitions** are displayed in the galleries on the ground floor, where you'll also find the gallery shop and **café** (closes 4.30pm), a favourite spot with locals.

Calton

Of the various extensions to the New Town, the most intriguing is **Calton**, which branches out from the eastern end of Princes Street and encircles a volcanic hill. For years the centre of a thriving **gay** scene (see p.826), it is an area of extraordinary showpiece architecture, dating from the time of the Napoleonic Wars or just after, and intended as an ostentatious celebration of the British victory. While the predominantly Grecian architecture led to Calton being regarded as a Georgian Acropolis, it is, in fact, more of a shrine to local heroes.

Waterloo Place forms a ceremonial way from Princes Street to Calton Hill. On its southern side is the sombre and overgrown **Old Calton Burial Ground**, in which you can see Robert Adam's plain, cylindrical memorial to David Hume and a monument, complete with a statue of Abraham Lincoln, to the Scots who died in the American Civil War. Hard up against the cemetery's eastern wall, perched above a sheer rockface, is a picturesque castellated building, the only surviving part of the **Calton Gaol**, once Edinburgh's main prison. Next door is the massive **St Andrew's House**, built in the 1930s to house civil servants. Further east, set majestically in a confined site below Calton Hill, is one of Edinburgh's greatest buildings, the Grecian **Old Royal High School**, which for many years was assumed to be where Scotland's new parliament would sit.

Robert Louis Stevenson reckoned that **Calton Hill** was the best place to view Edinburgh, "since you can see the Castle, which you lose from the Castle, and Arthur's Seat, which you cannot see from Arthur's Seat". Though the panoramas from ground level are spectacular enough, those from the top of the **Nelson Monument** (April–Sept Mon 1–6pm, Tues–Sat 10am–6pm; Oct–March Mon–Sat 10am–3pm; £2, or £4 joint ticket with Scott Monument) are even better. Begun just two years after Nelson's death at Trafalgar, this is one of Edinburgh's oddest buildings, resembling a gigantic spyglass. Alongside, the **National Monument**, had it been completed, would have been a reasonably accurate replica of the Parthenon, but funds ran out with only twelve columns

ROBERT LOUIS STEVENSON

Though **Robert Louis Stevenson** (1850–94) is sometimes dismissed for his deceptively simple manner, he was undoubtedly one of the best-loved writers of his generation, and one whose travelogues, novels, short stories and essays remain enormously popular a century after his death.

Born in Edinburgh into a distinguished family of engineers, Stevenson was a sickly child, with a solitary childhood dominated by his governess, Alison "Cummie" Cunningham, who regaled him with tales drawn from Calvinist folklore. Sent to the University to study engineering, Stevenson rebelled against his upbringing by spending much of his time in the lowlife howffs and brothels of the city, and eventually switched to law. Although called to the bar in 1875, by then he had decided to channel his energies into literature. While still a student, he had already made his mark as an **essayist** – he eventually had over a hundred essays published, ranging from light-hearted whimsy to trenchant political analysis. A set of topographical pieces about his native city was later collected together as *Edinburgh: Picturesque Notes*, which conjures up nicely its atmosphere, character and appearance – warts and all.

Stevenson's other early successes were two **travelogues**, *An Inland Voyage* and *Travels with a Donkey in the Cevennes*, kaleidoscopic jottings based on his journeys in France, where he went to escape Scotland's weather, which was damaging his health. It was there that he met Fanny Osbourne, an American ten years his senior, who was estranged from her husband and had two children in tow. His voyage to join her in San Francisco formed the basis for his most important factual work, *The Amateur Emigrant*, a vivid first-hand account of the great nineteenth-century European migration to the United States.

Having married the now-divorced Fanny, Stevenson began an elusive search for an agreeable climate that led to Switzerland, the French Riviera and the Scottish Highlands. He belatedly turned to the novel, achieving immediate acclaim in 1881 for **Treasure Island**, a highly moralistic adventure yarn that began as an entertainment for his stepson and future collaborator, Lloyd Osbourne. In 1886, his most famous short story, **Dr Jekyll and Mr Hyde**, despite its nominal London setting, offered a vivid evocation of the atmosphere of Edinburgh's Old Town: an allegory of its dual personality of prosperity and squalor, and an analysis of its Calvinistic preoccupations with guilt and damnation. The same year saw the publication of **Kidnapped**, a historical romance and lively adventure tale which exemplified Stevenson's view that literature should seek above all to entertain.

In 1887 Stevenson left Britain for good, travelling first to the United States, where he began one of his most ambitious novels, *The Master of Ballantrae*. A year later, he set sail for the **South Seas**, and eventually settled in Samoa; his last works include a number of stories with a local setting, such as the grimly realistic *The Ebb Tide* and *The Beach of Falesà*. However, Scotland continued to be his main inspiration: he wrote *Catriona* as a sequel to *Kidnapped*, and was at work on two more novels with Scottish settings, *St Ives* and *Weir of Hermiston*, a dark story of father–son confrontation, at the time of his sudden death from a brain haemorrhage in 1894. He was buried on the top of Mount Vaea, overlooking the Pacific Ocean.

built. At the opposite side of the hill, the grandeur of Playfair's Classical **Monument to Dugald Stewart** seems totally disproportionate to the stature of the man it commemorates – a now-forgotten professor of philosophy at the University. Playfair also built the **City Observatory** for his uncle, the mathematician and astronomer John Playfair, whom he honoured in the cenotaph outside.

The rest of the New Town

The **Northern New Town** was the earliest extension to the First New Town, begun in 1801, and today roughly covers the area north of Queen Street between India Street to the west and Broughton Street to the east, and as far as Fettes Row to the north. This has survived in far better shape than its predecessor: with the exception of one street, almost all of it is intact, and it has managed to preserve a predominantly residential character. One of the area's most intriguing buildings is the neo-Norman **Mansfield Place Church**, on the corner of Broughton and East London streets, designed in the late nineteenth century for the strange, now defunct Catholic Apostolic sect. Having lain redundant and neglected for three decades, it has suddenly acquired cult status, its preservation the current obsession of local conservation groups. The chief reason for this is its cycle of **murals** by the Dublin-born **Phoebe Anna Traquair**, a leading light in the Scottish Arts and Crafts movement. She laboured for eight years on this decorative scheme, which has all the freshness and luminosity of a medieval manuscript, yet it was almost lost due to leaks and rot in the fabric of the building in recent decades. It was only when the building was acquired by a trust in 1998 that its future was secured and the precious murals saved.

Dean Village, Stockbridge and the West End

Work began on the western end of the New Town in 1822, in a small area of land northwest of Charlotte Square. Instead of the straight lines of the earlier sections, there were now the gracious curves of Randolph Crescent, Ainslie Place and the magnificent, twelve-sided Moray Place. Round the corner from Randolph Crescent, the four-arched **Dean Bridge**, a bravura feat of 1830s engineering by Thomas Telford, carries the main road high above Edinburgh's placid little river, the **Water of Leith**. Down to the left lies **Dean Village**, an old milling community that is one of central Edinburgh's most picturesque yet oddest corners, its atmosphere of terminal decay now arrested by the conversion of some of the mills into designer flats. The riverside path into Stockbridge passes **St Bernard's Well**, a pump room covered by a mock Roman temple, commissioned in 1788 by Lord Gardenstone to draw mineral waters from the Water of Leith.

Stockbridge, which straddles both sides of the Water of Leith on the other side of Dean Bridge, is another old village which has retained its distinctive identity, and is particularly renowned for its antique shops and "alternative" outlets. The residential upper streets on the far side of the river were developed by Sir Henry Raeburn, who named the finest of them **Ann Street** which, after Charlotte Square, is the most prestigious address in Edinburgh (writers Thomas de Quincey and J.M. Ballantyne were residents); alone among New Town streets, its houses each have a front garden.

A little further west, the streets between Dean Bridge and Haymarket were the last of the extensions to the New Town to be built, deviating from the area's overriding Neoclassicism with a number of Victorian additions. Because of this, the huge **St Mary's Episcopal Cathedral**, an addition of the 1870s, is less intrusive than it would otherwise be, its three spires forming an eminently satisfying landmark for the far end of the city centre. The last major work of Sir George Gilbert Scott, the cathedral is built in imitation of the Early English Gothic style and was, at the time of its construction, the most ambitious church built in Britain since the Reformation.

The Scottish National Gallery of Modern Art

Set in spacious wooded grounds at the far northwestern fringe of the New Town, about ten minutes' walk from either the cathedral or Dean Village, the **Scottish National Gallery of Modern Art**, on Belford Road (Mon–Sat 10am–5pm, Sun 2–5pm; free), was established as the first collection in Britain devoted solely to twentieth-century painting and sculpture. The grounds serve as a sculpture park, featuring works by Jacob Epstein, Henry Moore and Barbara Hepworth, while inside, the display space is divided between temporary loan exhibitions and selections from the gallery's own holdings; the latter are arranged thematically, but are almost constantly moved around. What you get to see at any particular time is therefore a matter of chance, though the most important works are nearly always on view.

APPROACHES TO THE MODERN ART AND DEAN GALLERIES

One of the most pleasant ways of arriving at the neighbouring Modern Art and Dean galleries is along the **Water of Leith walkway**, which can be picked up at Stockbridge or Dean Village. Alternatively, a **free bus** runs on the hour (Mon–Sat 10am–5pm, Sun 2–5pm) from outside the National Gallery on the Mound, stopping at the National Portrait Gallery on the way. The only regular **public transport** running along Belford Road is bus #13, which leaves from the western end of George Street.

French painters are particularly well represented, beginning with Bonnard's *Lane at Vernonnet* and Vuillard's jewel-like *Two Seamstresses*, and by a few examples of the Fauves, notably Matisse's *The Painting Lesson* and Derain's dazzlingly brilliant *Collioure*; there's also a fine group of late canvases by Leger, notably *The Constructors*. Among some striking examples of **German Expressionism** are Kirchner's *Japanese Theatre*, Feininger's *Gelmeroda III*, and a wonderfully soulful wooden sculpture of a woman by Barlach entitled *The Terrible Year, 1937*. Highlights of the **Surrealist** section are Magritte's haunting *Black Flag*, Miró's seminal *Composition* and Giacometti's contorted *Woman with her Throat Cut*, while **Cubism** is represented by Picasso's *Soles* and Braque's *Candlestick*.

Of works by Americans, Roy Lichtenstein's *In the Car* is a fine example of his Pop Art style, while Duane Hanson's fibreglass *Tourists* is typically unflinching. English artists on show include Sickert, Nicholson, Spencer, Freud and Hockney, but, as you'd expect, considerably more space is allocated to Scottish artists. Of particular note are the **Colourists** – S.J. Peploe, J.D. Fergusson, Francis Cadell and George Leslie Hunter – whose works are attracting fancy prices on the art market, as well as ever-growing posthumous critical acclaim. Although they did not form a recognizable school, they all worked in France and displayed considerable French influence in their warm, bright palettes. Also worth exploring is the vivid realism of the more recent **Edinburgh School**, whose members include Anne Redpath, Sir Robin Philipson and William Gillies. The gallery also shows works by many contemporary Scots, among them **John Bellany**, a portraitist of striking originality, and the poet-artist-gardener **Ian Hamilton Finlay**.

The Dean Gallery

Opposite the Modern Art Gallery, on the other side of Belford Road, is the latest addition to the National Galleries of Scotland, the **Dean Gallery** (same hours; free), housed in an equally impressive Neoclassical building completed in 1833. The interior of the gallery has been dramatically refurbished specifically to make room for the huge collection of the work of Edinburgh-born sculptor **Sir Eduardo Paolozzi**.

Visitors are given an awesome introduction to Paolozzi's work by the huge *Vulcan*, a half-man, half-machine which squeezes into the Great Hall immediately opposite the main entrance. In the rooms to the right of the main entrance, the artist's London studios have been expertly re-created, right down to the clutter of half-finished casts and empty pots of glue. Hidden among this chaos is a large part of his bequest, with half-finished casts piled four or five deep on the floor and designs stacked randomly on shelves.

Also on the ground floor is the **Roland Penrose Gallery**, which houses an impressive collection of **Dada** and **Surrealist** art: Marcel Duchamp, Max Ernst and Man Ray are all represented in the gallery, along with Dalí, Picasso and Miró. In the adjoining **Gabrielle Keiller Library**, which is open to all and contains a unique collection of surrealist literature, manuscripts and correspondence, there is a wonderful pen and ink caricature of Picasso by De Chirico, as well as a series of Picasso's own cartoons satirizing General Franco.

The outskirts

Edinburgh's principal sights are by no means confined to the city centre, with a number of its popular tourist draws – the **Royal Botanic Garden**, the **Zoo** and **Craigmillar Castle** – out in the suburbs. To the north of the city is the fashionable port area of **Leith**, home to the retired royal yacht *Britannia*, while to the northwest of the capital, at South Queensferry, is one of Scotland's most celebrated sights, the **Forth Rail Bridge**, best seen from the parallel Road Bridge. East of the bridges is the area's finest country pile, **Hopetoun House**, while ruined **Linlithgow Palace** has seen many significant moments in Scottish history. South of the city, the main draw is the ornate chapel at **Roslin**, with its vivid gargoyles and unusual imagery.

The Royal Botanic Garden

Just beyond the northern boundaries of the New Town, with entrances on Inverleith Row and Arboretum Place, is the seventy-acre site of the **Royal Botanic Garden** (daily: March & Sept 9.30am–6pm; April–Aug 9.30am–7pm; Oct & Feb 9.30am–5pm; Nov–Jan 9.30am–4pm; free), particularly renowned for its rhododendrons, which blaze out in April and May. In the heart of the grounds, a group of hothouses designated the **Glasshouse Experience** (daily: March–Oct 10am–5pm; Nov–Feb 10am–3.30pm; free, but donation requested) displays orchids, giant Amazonian water lilies, and a 200-year-old West Indian palm tree. Many of the most exotic plants were brought to Edinburgh by the aptly named George Forrest, who made seven expeditions to southwestern China between 1904 and 1932. **Buses** # 23, 27 and 37 go down Inverleith Row from the centre of town.

The Zoo

Edinburgh Zoo (daily: April–Sept 9am–6pm; Oct & March 9am–5pm; Nov–Feb 9am–4.30pm; £6) lies three miles west of Princes Street on an eighty-acre site on the slopes of Corstorphine Hill (**bus** #2, #26, #31, #36, #69, #85 or #86). Here you can see over a thousand animals, including a number of endangered species such as white rhinos, red pandas, pygmy hippos and Madagascar tree boas. Making the most of the space offered by Corstorphine Hill, the **African Plains Experience** and a new **Lion Enclosure** have walkways leading you out over the animals to viewing platforms, while other popular new additions include the Magic Forest, showcasing smaller primates, and a water-filled Evolution Maze. However, the zoo's chief claim to fame is its crowd of penguins, the largest number in captivity anywhere in the world, a legacy of Leith's whaling trade in the South Atlantic. The **penguin parade** (April–Sept daily at 2pm, plus sunny days in March and Oct) has gained something of a cult status.

Craigmillar Castle

Craigmillar Castle (April–Sept daily 9.30am–6pm; Oct–March Mon–Wed & Sat 9.30am–4pm, Thurs 9.30am–noon, Sun 2–4pm; £1.80) lies in a green belt three miles southeast of the centre. It's one of the best-preserved medieval fortresses in Scotland, and before Queen Victoria set her heart on Balmoral, it was being considered as her royal castle north of the border, a possibility which seems odd now given its proximity to the ugly council housing scheme of Craigmillar, one of Edinburgh's most deprived districts. The oldest part of the complex is the L-shaped **tower house**, which dates back to the early 1400s: it remains substantially intact, and the great hall, with its resplendent late Gothic chimneypiece, is in good enough shape to be rented out for functions. Take **bus** #30, #33 or #82, or any bus heading for Hawick or Jedburgh, from the city centre to the district called Little France, from where the castle is a ten-minute walk along Craigmillar Castle Road.

Leith

For several hundred years, **Leith** was separate from Edinburgh. As Scotland's major east coast port, it played a key role in the nation's history, even serving as the seat of government for a time. In 1920, it was incorporated into the capital and, in the decades that followed, went into seemingly terminal decline. The 1980s, however, saw an astonishing turnaround, and the port now boasts arguably the best concentration of **restaurants** and **pubs** in Edinburgh. The surviving historic monuments were spruced up too, and a host of housing developments built or restored, a renaissance crowned by the completion of a vast new building housing civil servants from the Scottish Office. To reach Leith from the city centre, take one of the many **buses** going down Leith Walk, northeast of the centre. Otherwise, it's a brisk stroll of around twenty minutes.

Although the shipbuilding yards have gone, Leith remains an active port with a rough-edged character. Most of the showpiece Neoclassical buildings lie on or near **The Shore**, the tenement-lined road along the final stretch of the Water of Leith, just before it disgorges into the Firth of Forth. To the west, set back from The Shore, is **Lamb's House**, a seventeenth-century mansion built as the home of the prosperous merchant Andro Lamb.

The most recent developments have focused on the old harbour itself, half a mile to the west of The Shore, where the former royal yacht **Britannia** (daily 10.30am–4.30pm; bookings advised, call ☎0131/555 5566; £7.50) is settling into retirement. For over forty years, the ship was used by the royal family for state visits, diplomatic functions and royal holidays. A visitor centre displays royal holiday snaps and video clips of Britannia's most famous moments, after which you are given an audio handset and allowed to roam around the yacht, which largely preserves her 1950s dowdiness – the guide loyally attributes this to the Queen's good taste and astute frugality in the lean postwar years. Regular shuttle **buses** operated by both Guide Friday and LRT run direct between Waverley Bridge and Britannia.

The Forth Bridges and Inchcolm

Everything in South Queensferry, ten miles northwest of Edinburgh's centre, is overshadowed, quite literally, by the two great bridges, each about a mile and a half in length, which traverse the Firth of Forth at its narrowest point. The cantilevered **Forth Rail Bridge**, built from 1883 to 1890 by Sir John Fowler and Benjamin Baker, ranks among the supreme achievements of Victorian engineering. Some 50,000 tons of steel were used in the construction of a design that manages to express grace as well as might. The suspension format chosen for the **Forth Road Bridge** makes a perfect complement to the older structure, although it finally killed off the 900-year-old ferry service. It's well worth walking (or cycling) across its footpath to Fife for tremendous views of the Rail Bridge and the Forth estuary. To get to South Queensferry, take the **train** to Dalmeny station or **buses** #43, #53, #55, #56 or #57.

From South Queensferry's Hawes Pier, just west of the Rail Bridge, pleasure boats leave for a variety of **cruises** on the Forth (Easter, May & June Sat & Sun; July to mid-Sept daily; ☎0131/331 4857; £7.50–10). Be sure to check in advance as sailings are always subject to cancellation in bad weather.

The most enticing destination is the island of **Inchcolm**, whose beautiful ruined **Abbey** was founded in 1123 by King Alexander I in gratitude for the hospitality he received from a hermit (whose cell survives at the northwestern corner of the island) when his ship was forced ashore in a storm. The best-preserved medieval monastic complex in Scotland, the abbey's surviving buildings date from the thirteenth to the fifteenth centuries, and include a splendid octagonal chapter house. Although the church is almost totally dilapidated, its tower can be ascended for a great aerial view of the island, which is populated by a variety of nesting birds and a colony of grey seals.

Hopetoun House

Immediately beyond the western edge of South Queensferry, **Hopetoun House** (April–Sept daily 10am–5.30pm, Oct Sat & Sun 10am–5.30pm; house & grounds £5; grounds only £2.80) is one of Scotland's grandest stately homes. The original house was built at the turn of the eighteenth century by Sir William Bruce, the architect of Holyroodhouse. A couple of decades later, William Adam carried out an enormous extension, engulfing the house in a curvaceous main facade and two projecting wings – superb examples of Roman Baroque swagger. The scale and lavishness of the Adam interiors, most of which were carried out by his sons after the architect's death, make for a stark contrast with the intimacy of those designed by Bruce. Particularly impressive are the Red and Yellow Drawing Rooms, with their splendid ceilings by the young Robert Adam. Among the house's furnishings are seventeenth-century tapestries, Meissen porcelain, and a distinguished collection of paintings, including portraits by Gainsborough, Ramsay and Raeburn. The grounds of Hopetoun House are also open, with magnificent walks along the banks of the Forth and great opportunities for picnics. To get here it's a two-mile walk from South Queensferry, or you can catch **buses** #47, #455 or #456 from St Andrew Square to the nearby village of Newton.

Linlithgow Palace

Fifteen miles west of Edinburgh, in the ancient royal burgh of Linlithgow, lies **Linlithgow Palace** (April–Sept daily 9.30am–6pm; Oct–March Mon–Sat 9.30am–4pm, Sun 2–4pm; £2.50), a splendid fifteenth-century ruin romantically set on the edge of Linlithgow Loch and associated with some of Scotland's best-known historical figures – including the ubiquitous Mary Queen of Scots, who was born here in 1542. Fire razed an earlier manor house in 1424, after which James I began construction of the present palace, a process that continued through two centuries and the reign of no fewer than eight monarchs. From the top of the northwest tower, Queen Margaret looked out in vain for the return of James IV from the field of Flodden in 1513. The ornate octagonal **fountain** in the inner courtyard, with its wonderfully intricate figures and medallion heads, flowed with wine for the wedding of James V and Mary of Guise. Bonnie Prince Charlie visited during the Forty-five, and one year later the palace was burnt, probably accidentally, whilst occupied by General Hawley's troops.

This is a great place to take children; the rooflessness of the castle creates unexpected vistas and the elegant rooms with their intriguing spiral staircases seem labyrinthine. The galleried **Great Hall** is magnificent, as is the adjoining kitchen, which has a truly cavernous fireplace. Don't miss the dank downstairs **brewery**, which produced vast quantities of ale; 24 gallons were apparently a good nightly consumption in the sixteenth century. **St Michael's Church,** adjacent to the palace, is one of Scotland's largest pre-Reformation churches, consecrated in the thirteenth century. The present building was completed three hundred years later, with the exception of the hugely incongruous aluminium spire, tacked on in 1946. Inside, decorative woodcarving around the pulpit depicts queens Margaret, Mary and Victoria. Linlithgow can be reached by **train** from Waverley or Haymarket, or by **buses** #38, #455 or #456 from St Andrew Square.

Roslin

In the tranquil village of **Roslin**, seven miles south of the centre of Edinburgh, is the mysterious, richly decorated late-Gothic **Rosslyn Chapel** (Mon–Sat 10am–5pm, Sun noon–4.45pm; £3). Only the choir, Lady Chapel and part of the transepts were built of what was intended to be a huge collegiate church dedicated to St Matthew: construction halted soon after the founder's death in 1484, and the vestry built onto the facade nearly four hundred years later is the sole subsequent addition. After a long period of neglect, a massive restoration project has recently been undertaken: a canopy has been placed over the chapel which will remain in place for several years in order to dry out the saturated ceiling and walls, and other essential repairs are due to be carried out within the chapel. Roslin can be reached by **buses** #87a or #66C from St Andrew Square.

The foliage carving inside the chapel is particularly outstanding, with botanically accurate depictions of over a dozen different leaves and plants. Among them are cacti and Indian corn, providing fairly convincing evidence that the founder's grandfather, the daring sea adventurer Prince Henry of Orkney, did indeed, as legend has it, set foot in the New World a century before Columbus. The rich and subtle figurative sculptures have given Rosslyn the nickname of "a Bible in stone", with allegorical portrayals of the Dance of Death, the Seven Acts of Mercy and the Seven Deadly Sins.

The greatest and most original carving of all is the extraordinary knotted **Prentice Pillar**, at the southeastern corner of the Lady Chapel. According to local legend, the pillar was made by an apprentice during the absence of the master mason, who killed him in a fit of jealousy on seeing the finished work. A tiny head of a man with a slashed forehead, set at the apex of the ceiling at the far northwestern corner of the building, is popularly supposed to represent the apprentice, his murderer the corresponding head at the opposite side. The entwined dragons at the foot are symbols of Satan, and were probably inspired by Norse mythology.

Cafés and restaurants

Style, sophistication and good taste are breaking out all over Edinburgh. **Café culture** has hit the centre of the city, with tables spilling onto the pavements in the summer. Small **diners** and **bistros** predominate, many adopting a casual French style and offering good-value set menus. Traditional **Scottish cooking** can still be found at some of the more formal restaurants, but it's worth keeping an eye out for more unusual contemporary Scottish places. There are plenty of **fish** specialists – seafood fans should head to **Leith**, whose waterside restaurants serve consistently good food. The city's ethnic communities, despite their small size, ensure that the perennial favourites are well represented, in particular with some great **Italian** trattorias and a host of excellent **Indian** restaurants. **Vegetarians** and vegans are well catered for, while influences from around the world, from Spain to Southeast Asia, can all be found. It's worth bearing in mind that most **pubs** (which are covered in the following section) serve food, and that many have restaurants attached.

Brasseries, cafés and diners

Bell's Diner, 7 St Stephen St, Stockbridge (☎0131/225 8116). Unpretentious little diner with good, inexpensive burgers. Open daily until 11pm. Moderate.

Café Q, 87 Clerk St, Newington (☎0131/668 3456). Well-prepared salads, vegetarian dishes, soups and puddings in the Queen's Hall, a respected music and arts venue. Closed Sun & evenings. Inexpensive.

Clarinda's, 69 Canongate, Old Town (☎0131/557 1888). Spruce olde-worlde café serving home-cooked breakfasts and light lunches. Closed evenings. Inexpensive.

Common Grounds, 2–3 North Bank St, Old Town (☎0131/226 1146). American-style coffee shop on two levels, non-smoking upstairs. Open till 10pm, and live music most evenings. Inexpensive.

Cyberia, 88 Hanover St, New Town (☎0131/220 4403, *manager@cybersurf.co.uk*). Bright Internet café with fifteen computers (£2.50 per 30min) and a wide range of snacks. Inexpensive.

Daniel's, 88 Commercial St, Leith (☎0131/553 5933). Top-grade bistro in an attractive setting on the ground floor of a converted warehouse, with food from the Alsace region of France. Moderate.

Elephant House, 21 George IV Bridge, Old Town (☎0131/220 5355). Attractive and popular café with a large selection of coffees, teas, sandwiches and cakes and wonderful views of the castle from the cavernous back room. Mon–Sat 8am–11pm, Sun 10am–8pm. Inexpensive.

The Gallery Café, Scottish National Gallery of Modern Art, Dean Village (☎0131/332 8600). The cultured setting and strong menu attract reassuring numbers of locals for salads, light meals and the like. Open Mon–Sat 10am–4.30pm, Sun 2–4.30pm. Moderate.

Glass & Thompson, 2 Dundas St, New Town (☎0131/557 0909). An unusually airy deli with an extensive cheese counter and made-to-order sandwiches. Closed evenings. Inexpensive.

Kaffe Politik, 146–148 Marchmont Rd, Marchmont (☎0131/446 9837). Café culture hits the student fiefdom of deepest Marchmont. Open till 10pm. Inexpensive.

Lost Sock Diner, 11 East London St, Broughton (☎0131/557 6097). Fill up on burgers, wraps and blackboard specials while your dirty clothes take a spin in the adjacent launderette. Open till 10pm Tues–Sat. Inexpensive.

Lower Aisle, in the High Kirk of St Giles, High Street, Old Town (☎0131/225 5147). Popular with bewigged advocates for good-value light lunches. Closed evenings. Inexpensive.

Mango & Stone, 165A Bruntsfield Place, Bruntsfield (☎0131/229 2987). Juice bar serving sandwiches and coffee. Closed evenings. Inexpensive.

Ndebele, 57 Home St, Tollcross (☎0131/221 1141). Colourful African café offering delicious sandwiches and fruit juices, plus a great selection of teas and coffees. Open daily till 10pm. Inexpensive.

Netherbow Café, Netherbow Arts Centre, 43 High St, Old Town (☎0131/556 9579). Excellent wholefood and vegetarian soups and light meals, with a courtyard for sunny days. Lunchtimes only. Inexpensive.

Patisserie Florentin, 8–10 St Giles St, Old Town (☎0131/225 6267). French-style café off High Street – a popular late-night rendezvous. Open daily 7am–11pm, till 3am during the Festival. Inexpensive.

Terrace Café, Royal Botanic Garden, Inverleith (☎0131/552 0616). Stunning views of the city skyline from the outside tables, though the food (hot dishes, sandwiches, cakes) is not that exciting. Inexpensive.

Valvona and Crolla, 19 Elm Row, Leith Walk, Broughton (☎0131/556 0616). Authentic and delicious breakfasts, lunches and snacks served in the café at the back of an exquisite Italian deli. Closed Sun & evenings. Moderate.

Chinese and Southeast Asian

Bamboo Garden, 57A Frederick St, New Town (☎0131/225 2382). Popular with Edinburgh's Chinese inhabitants for great *dim sum* at Sunday lunchtime – the waiters will explain the choices. Moderate.

Chinese Home Cooking, 34 West Preston St, Southside (☎0131/668 4946). Plain, straightforward and perenially popular BYOB café: three-course lunch for £4.50, with daily chef's specials in the evening. Inexpensive.

Oriental Dining Centre, 8–14A Morrison St, Tollcross (☎0131/221 1288). Three distinct restaurants, the most popular being the *Ho-Ho-Mei Noodle Shak*. Inexpensive to moderate.

Siam Erewan, 48 Howe St, New Town (☎0131/226 3675). Excellent Thai restaurant. Closed Sun. Moderate.

Szechuan House, 12 Leamington Terrace, Bruntsfield (☎0131/229 4655). Unassuming setting in a Bruntsfield hotel, but a real find for lovers of genuine spicy Chinese food. BYOB. Closed Mon. Moderate.

French

La Bonne Vie, 49 Causewayside, Newington (☎0131/667 1110). Very popular French restaurant serving a £15 set dinner. Moderate.

Chez Jules, 1 Craigs Close, off Cockburn St, Old Town (☎0131/225 7007). French food in a fine, no-frills establishment. Open daily 5.30–10.30pm. Moderate.

La Cuisine d'Odile, French Institute, 13 Randolph Crescent, West End (☎0131/225 5685). Genuine French home cooking in a West End basement. Lunch only (noon–2pm). Closed Mon, Sun & all July. Inexpensive.

Malmaison Café Bar, 1 Tower Place, Leith (☎0131/468 5001). Successful attempt to create the feel of a French café, serving excellent steak and chips and great fish dishes, plus incredibly rich mashed potato. Expensive.

Pierre Victoire, 10 Victoria St, Old Town (☎0131/225 1721). The PV phenomenon started here, and lives on – great French food in an easy-going atmosphere, at decent prices. Moderate.

Le Sept, Old Fishmarket Close, Old Town (☎0131/225 5428). Long-established French brasserie tucked down a cobbled close off the Royal Mile. Three-course set lunch for £6. Moderate.

Restaurant Martin Wishart, 52 The Shore, Leith (☎0131/553 3557). Scotland's latest "it-chef" wows the gourmets with French-influenced Scottish food right by the Water of Leith. Closed Sun & Mon. Expensive.

Indian

Ann Purna, 45 St Patrick Square, Southside (☎0131/662 1807). Excellent-value restaurant serving authentic Gujarati and southern Indian cuisine (so mainly vegetarian) – try the three-course lunch for £4.95. Moderate.

Kalpna, 2 St Patrick Square, Southside (☎0131/667 9890). Outstanding vegetarian restaurant serving authentic Gujarati dishes. Eat-as-much-as-you-like lunchtime buffet for £5. Closed Sun. Moderate.

Khushi's, 16 Drummond St, Old Town (☎0131/556 8996). More a café than a restaurant, with only the basic comforts, but the food is reliable and cheap. Bring your own drink. Closed Sun. Inexpensive.

Shamiana, 14 Brougham Place, Tollcross (☎0131/228 2265). Established, first-class North Indian and Kashmiri restaurant. The interior is oddly stark, but it's well worth it. Mon–Sat 6–9.30pm, Sun 6–8pm. Moderate.

Suruchi, 14A Nicolson St, Southside (☎0131/556 6583). Popular establishment serving genuine south Indian dishes – the menu is written in bizarre but entertaining broad Scots. Emphasis on rice and vegetables, with a few splendid poultry dishes. The set lunches go for £3.50–6.50. Moderate.

Italian

Cosmo, 58A N Castle St, New Town (☎0131/226 6743). Straightforward, delicious Italian cuisine in a long-established trattoria. Closed Sun. Expensive.

Est Est Est, 135 George St, New Town (☎0131/225 2555). Popular, modern Italian with an irresistibly stylish feel. Serves the old favourites, with designer touches. Open daily till 1am. Moderate.

Lazio's, 95 Lothian Rd, Tollcross (☎0131/229 7788). Pick of the family-run trattorias on this block, handy for a late-night meal after a show. Closes 1.30am daily. Moderate.

Mamma's, 30 Grassmarket, Old Town (☎0131/225 6464). The best pizzas in this part of town, popular with students and larger groups, with outside tables in the summer and reasonably priced wine. Open till 11pm Sun–Thurs, midnight Fri & Sat. Inexpensive to moderate.

Tinelli, 139 Easter Rd, Hillside (☎0131/652 1932). Reputed to be Edinburgh's best Italian. Specializes in northern Italian food – try the spinach and pumpkin-stuffed pasta. Closed Sun. Moderate.

Umberto's, 2 Bonnington Road Lane, Bonnington (☎0131/554 1314). The best place in Edinburgh for anyone with children. Play areas, sympathetic staff and good food. Moderate.

Scottish

The Atrium, 10 Cambridge St (☎0131/228 8882). This award-winning restaurant is considered by many to be the city's best, serving innovative nouvelle food and focusing on high-quality Scottish produce. Tables made from railway sleepers; lit by flaming torches. Closed Sunday. Very expensive.

Blue, Traverse Theatre, 10 Cambridge St, off Lothian Rd (☎0131/221 1222). Stunning décor and equally impressive food – original and tasty dishes for under £10 per main course. Open Sun & Mon till midnight & Tues–Sat till 1am. Inexpensive to Moderate.

Martin's, 70 Rose St North Lane, New Town (☎0131/225 3106). Long-standing restaurant hidden in an unlikely-looking backstreet, with an emphasis on organic, unfarmed ingredients – salmon, venison and unpasteurized cheeses. Closed Sun & Mon. Expensive.

Point Hotel, 34 Bread St, Tollcross (☎0131/221 5555). Classy, modernist decor, and great food based on fresh local fish and meat, yet one of the best-value deals in town. Moderate.

Stac Polly, 8A Grindlay St, off Lothian Rd (☎0131/229 5405). Unusual mix of traditional and contemporary Scottish fare, with an emphasis on game, fish and meat. Evenings only. Expensive.

The Tower, Museum of Scotland, Chambers Street, Old Town (☎0131/225 3003). Modern, Scottish food in the self-consciously chic setting of the new Museum of Scotland, with spectacular views to the floodlit castle. Expensive.

The Witchery by the Castle, 352 Castlehill, Royal Mile, Old Town (☎0131/225 5613). The restaurant that only Edinburgh could create, with Gothic panelling, tapestries and heavy stonework – only a broomstick-hop from the castle. The superb fish and game dishes are pricey, but you can steal a sense of it all with a pre- or post-theatre set menu (£10). Expensive.

Seafood

Café Royal Oyster Bar, 17A W Register St, New Town (☎0131/556 4124). Splendidly ornate Victorian interior featured in *Chariots of Fire*. Classic seafood dishes, including freshly caught oysters, served in a civilized, chatty atmosphere. Very expensive.

Creelers, 3 Hunter Square, Old Town (☎0131/220 4447). Excellent seafood restaurant priding itself on fresh produce. Bistro section at the front, with a more expensive restaurant at the back. Moderate to expensive.

Marinette, 52 Coburg St, Leith (☎0131/555 0922). Slightly insalubrious location gives this well-regarded restaurant even more of a Leith feel. French flair, an informal ambience and great food. Closed Sun & Mon. Expensive.

Ship on the Shore, 24–26 The Shore, Leith (☎0131/555 0409). The homeliest and least expensive of the waterfront brasseries, serving good fresh fish and with a changing range of cask ales. Moderate.

Sweet Melinda's, 11 Rosneath St, Marchmont (☎0131/229 7953). Friendly restaurant serving seafood and Scottish fare. On Tuesday nights you pay only what you think the food is worth. Closed Sun & Mon. Moderate.

Vegetarian

Bann's Vegetarian Café, 5 Hunter Square, Old Town (☎0131/226 1112). Reliable, informal café, halfway up the Royal Mile, with an original and appealing menu. Daily 10am–11pm. Moderate.

Black Bo's, 57 Blackfriars St, Old Town (☎0131/557 6136). Inventive non-meat diner with an earthy atmosphere and friendly service. Open after 11pm for drinks only. Closed Sun lunch. Moderate.

Henderson's Salad Table, 94 Hanover St, New Town (☎0131/225 2131). Self-service vegetarian basement restaurant, with freshly prepared hot dishes, plus a great choice of salads, soups, sweets and cheeses. A busy Edinburgh institution. Light jazz every evening. Open Mon–Sat 8am–10.30pm. Inexpensive.

Susie's Diner, 51 W Nicolson St, Southside (☎0131/667 8729). Popular café serving tasty and unusual soups, savouries and puddings, as well as a range of vegan food, to crowds of students. Inexpensive.

Other

Blue Parrot Cantina, 49 St Stephen's St, Stockbridge (☎0131/225 2941). Cosy Stockbridge basement, with a small, frequently changing menu which dares to deviate from the Mexican clichés. Moderate.

Daruma-Ya, 82 Commercial St, Leith (☎0131/554 7660). Smart, stylish interior, with the best sushi and sashimi in Edinburgh. Closed Sun. Moderate to expensive.

Igg's, 15 Jeffrey St, Old Town (☎0131/557 8184). A Spanish-owned hybrid, offering tapas snacks and Mediterranean dishes, plus traditional Scottish food. Good lunchtime tapas for around £5. Closed Sun. Expensive.

Marrakech, 30 London St, Broughton (☎0131/556 4444). Scotland's only Moroccan restaurant, dishing up superb, authentic couscous, and *tajine*, plus a range of soups, fresh bread and pastries. BYOB. Moderate.

Phenecia, 55–57 W Nicolson St, Southside (☎0131/662 4493). A basic joint beside the main University campus, serving mostly Tunisian food but drawing on a variety of Mediterranean cuisines; three-course lunch £4.40. Moderate.

Tampopo, 25A Thistle St, New Town (☎0131/220 5254). Japanese noodle bar offering filling meals from around £5. Open Mon–Sat noon–2.30pm & 6–9pm. Inexpensive.

The Tapas Tree, 1 Forth St, Broughton (☎0131/556 7118). Authentic, lively and extremely friendly tapas bar, featuring Spanish guitar music on Wednesday evenings and flamenco on Thursdays. Moderate.

Viva Mexico, 10 Anchor Close, off Cockburn Street, Old Town (☎0131/226 5145). Long-standing restaurant, with plenty of choice for vegetarians, and bargain options at lunchtimes. Moderate.

Pubs and bars

Many of Edinburgh's **pubs**, especially in the Old Town, have histories that stretch back centuries, while others, particularly in the New Town, are unaltered Victorian or Edwardian period pieces that rank among Edinburgh's outstanding examples of interior design. Add in the plentiful supply of trendy modern bars, and there's a variety of styles and atmospheres to cater for all tastes. The standard licensing hours are 11am–11pm (12.30–11pm on Sundays), but many honest howffs stay open later and it's no problem to find bars open till at least 1am. Currently, Edinburgh has three **breweries**, including the giant Scottish and Newcastle (who produce McEwan's and Younger's). The small, independent Caledonian Brewery (tours ☎0131/337 1286) uses old techniques and equipment to produce some of the best beers in Britain, and there's also the tiny Rose Street Brewery, which has its own pub.

Edinburgh's main drinking strip was once the near-legendary **Rose Street**, a pedestrianized lane tucked between Princes and George streets, and the ultimate Edinburgh pub crawl was to drink a half-pint in each of its dozen or so establishments. Things are a bit more sophisticated these days, with **George Street** taking a lead. Most of the **student pubs** are in and around the Grassmarket, with a further batch on the Southside, an area overlooked by most tourists. **Leith** has a nicely varied crop of bars, ranging from the rough spit-and-sawdust places to polished pseudo-Victoriana.

The Old Town

Bannermans, 212 Cowgate. The best pub in the street, formerly a vintner's cellar, with a labyrinthine interior and good beer on tap. Tasty, bargain veggie lunches on weekdays; breakfasts served at weekends 11am–4pm. Open daily till 1am.

Bar Kohl, 54 George IV Bridge. Trendy vodka bar with a huge choice. Open Mon–Sat till 1am. Closed Sun.

Bennets Bar, 8 Leven St, Tollcross. Edwardian pub with mahogany-set mirrors and Art Nouveau stained glass; packed in the evenings. Lunch served Mon–Sat. Open till midnight.

Blue Blazer, 2 Spittal St. Traditional Edinburgh howff with oak-clad bar, church pews and a good selection of ales. Open Wed & Thurs till midnight, Fri & Sat till 1am.

Bow Bar, 80 West Bow. Old wood-panelled bar that won an award as the best drinkers' pub in Britain a few years back. Nearly 150 whiskies and a changing selection of cask beers. Closed Sun afternoons.

City Café, 19 Blair St. Longstanding but determinedly trendy American-style bar on the street linking the Royal Mile to the clubbers' hub along the Cowgate.

Doric Tavern, 15 Market St. Long-established upstairs wine bar, a favoured watering hole of journalists and artists. The downstairs *McGuffie's Tavern* is a traditional Edinburgh howff, while the brasserie serves reliable, good-quality Scottish food. Open till 1am.

Fiddlers Arms, 9–11 Grassmarket. Traditional bar serving excellent McEwan's 80 Shilling. Fiddlers play on Monday nights. Open Mon–Thurs till 11.30pm, Fri & Sat 1am.

Greyfriars Bobby, 34 Candlemaker Row. Long-established favourite with both students and tourists. Open daily till 1am.

Jolly Judge, 7A James Court. Atmospheric, low-ceilinged bar in a close just down from the Castle. Cosy in winter and pleasant outside in summer.

Last Drop, 74–78 Grassmarket. The "Drop" refers to the Edinburgh gallows, which were located in front. Cheapish pub food, and, like its competitors in the same block, mainly student clientele. Open daily till 1am.

Malt Shovel, 11–15 Cockburn St. Dimly lit, comfortable bar with an excellent range of cask beers and single malt whiskies; serves big portions at lunchtime. Open Mon–Thurs & Sun 11am–12.30am, Fri & Sat 11am–1am.

Sandy Bell's, 25 Forrest Rd. Small but busy folk-music institution, hosting regular impromptu sessions. The city's favourite chess-playing pub. Open Mon–Sat till 12.30am.

Traverse Bar Café, Traverse Theatre, 10 Cambridge St. Spacious, modern bar with a lively, sophisticated crowd. Good food available in the bar.

New Town and Stockbridge

Abbotsford, 3 Rose St. Large-scale pub whose original Victorian decor, complete with wood panelling and "island bar", is among the finest in the city. Good range of ales, and the restaurant upstairs serves hearty Scottish food. Closed Sun.

Baillie Bar, 2 St Stephen St, Stockbridge. Traditional basement bar at the corner of Edinburgh's most self-consciously Bohemian street. Open Mon–Thurs till midnight, Fri & Sat till 1am, Sun till 11pm.

The Basement, 10A Broughton St, Broughton. Packed out, especially at the weekends, with a pre-club crowd; serves cheap Mexican food till 10pm every day. Open till 1am.

Café Royal Circle Bar, 17 W Register St. The pub part of this stylish Victorian restaurant, and worth a visit just for its decor. Open Thurs till midnight, Fri & Sat till 1am.

The Dome Bar, 14 George St. Opulent conversion of a massive New Town bank and probably the most impressive bar interior in Edinburgh, though the ultra-chic atmosphere can be a bit intense. Open Sun–Thurs till 11.30pm, Fri & Sat till 1am.

Indigo Yard, 7 Charlotte Lane, West End. Designer chic hits Edinburgh's West End: great for those who want Thai fish cakes with their draught beer. Daily till 1am.

Kenilworth, 152–154 Rose St. Attractive high-ceilinged pub dating from 1899, with good beer and food. There's a family room at the back, with a special children's menu. Open Fri & Sat till 1am.

Mathers, 25 Broughton St, Broughton. Relaxed, old-fashioned pub which attracts a mixed crowd and gets noisy during big TV sporting occasions. Open Mon–Thurs till midnight, Fri & Sat till 12.30am.

Milne's Bar, 35 Hanover St. Cellar bar once beloved of Edinburgh's literati, earning the nickname "The Poets' Pub". Serves a good range of cask beers.

Po-Na-Na, 43B Frederick St. Trendy and very popular Moroccan-style "souk" bar, offering simple snacks. On Thurs (£2) and Fri & Sat (£3), admission is charged after 11pm. Open daily 8pm–3am.

Rose Street Brewery, 55 Rose St. Edinburgh's only micro-brewery; the two beers made in the upstairs restaurant are also on tap in the ground-floor bar.

The Standing Order, 62–66 George St. A former bank with a vast central hall which has had the chain makeover, but the vast central hall is impressive and there are comfy chairs in the library. Real ales and good-value meals available. Open till 1am.

Leith

Carriers Quarters, 42 Bernard St, Leith. Intimate pub that dates back to 1775, and is still preserved in its original state, with a blazing log fire. Specializes in high-quality cask beers.

Kings Wark, 36 The Shore, Leith. Real ale and good food in a restored eighteenth-century pub.

Ye Olde Peacock Inn, Lindsay Road, Newhaven (☎0131/552 8707). Serves cheap, homely food, including the best fish and chips in the city. Advance reservations are advisable for the main bar and restaurant; otherwise try for a table in the small lounge. Don't miss the gallery displaying prints of the pioneering Hill and Adamson calotypes of Newhaven fishwives.

Elsewhere in the city

Athletic Arms (The Diggers), 1 Angle Park Terrace, Polwarth. Out in the western suburbs, near Murrayfield rugby stadium. Long-standing reputation as Edinburgh's best pub for serious ale drinkers. Open Mon–Sat till midnight; Sun till 6pm.

Canny Man's (Volunteer Arms), 237 Morningside Rd, Morningside. Atmospheric and idiosyncratic pub/museum adorned with anything that can be hung on the walls or from the ceiling. Mon–Sat open till midnight.

Peartree House, 36 W Nicolson St, Southside. Fine bar in an eighteenth-century house with a courtyard, one of Edinburgh's very few beer-gardens; serves decent bar lunches. Open Mon–Wed & Sun until midnight, Thurs–Sat until 1am.

Sheep Heid Inn, 43 The Causeway, Duddingston. Eighteenth-century inn with a family atmosphere: an ideal refreshment stop at the end of a tramp through Holyrood Park. Decent home-cooked meals, plus an old-fashioned skittle alley – always popular with students.

Stewart's, 14 Drummond St. A Southside institution since the beginning of the century, and seemingly little changed since then; popular with lecturers and students. Open Mon–Sat till midnight.

Nightlife and entertainment

Not surprisingly, Edinburgh's **nightlife** is at its best during the Festival (see box on p.828), which can make the other 49 weeks of the year seem like one long anticlimax. However, when not compared to this misleading yardstick, the city has a lot to offer, especially in the realm of performing arts and live music.

The **nightclub** scene is lively, with some excellent venues hosting a changing selection of one-nighters. In the bigger venues, you may find different clubs taking place on each floor. Most city-centre clubs stay open till around 3am. While you can normally hear live **jazz**, **folk** and **rock** every evening in one or other of the city's pubs, for the really big rock events, ad hoc venues – such as the Castle Esplanade, Murrayfield Stadium or the exhibition halls of the Royal Highland Show at Ingliston, which hosts occasional raves – are often pressed into service.

With an estimated homosexual population of around 15,000–20,000, Edinburgh has a dynamic **gay culture**, for years centred round the top of Leith Walk and Broughton Street. Since the start of the 1990s, more and more gay enterprises, especially cafés and nightclubs, have moved into this area, now dubbed the "Pink Triangle".

The best way to find out **what's on** is to pick up a copy of *The List*, a fortnightly listings magazine covering both Edinburgh and Glasgow (£1.95). Alternatively, get hold of the listings column of the *Edinburgh Evening News*, which appears daily except Sunday. Information on nightclubs can be found on posters and piles of leaflets distributed to most of the pre-club bars around town. Box offices of individual halls and theatres are likewise liberally supplied with promotional leaflets about forthcoming music and theatre, and some are able to sell tickets for more than one venue.

Nightclubs

La Belle Angèle, 11 Hasties Close (☎0131/225 2774). A rotating selection of Latin, soul, hip-hop and jazz. Edinburgh's best drum'n'bass club on Fri, with house on Sat. Occasionally hosts important touring bands.

The Bongo Club, 14 New St (☎0131/556 5204). Great venue above a car park near Waverley Station, attracting some of the most interesting DJs around. Look out for the mighty Messenger Sound System on Saturday nights.

Café Graffiti, Mansfield Place Church, at the foot of Broughton Street (☎0131/557 8003). Great venue in a church basement, with Latin and jazz playing at the weekend. Usually sells out very quickly, so arrive before 11.30pm.

The Cavendish, West Tollcross (☎0131/228 3252). Slightly dingy, but still packed on Friday for roots, ragga and reggae; *The Mambo Club* on Saturday plays African and Latin rhythms.

Club Mercado, 36–39 Market St (☎0131/226 4224). Cheesy music night on Friday starts at 5pm for the after-work crowd, while sharp clothes are required to get into Saturday's house nights.

Honeycomb, 36–38A Blair St (☎0131/220 4381). A great sound system plays thumping house, hip-hop and garage Thurs–Sun and live jazz Mon–Wed.

Rocking Horse, Cowgate (☎0131/225 3326). Rock nights including heavy metal, Goth-rock and grunge.

The Venue, 15 Calton Rd (☎0131/557 3073). Each of the three levels hosts a variety of different one-nighters specializing in house, funk and garage. Friday nights see the long-running, popular *Pure* with techno and live acts; Saturdays alternate between 1970s disco and house/garage.

Wilkie House, Cowgate (☎0131/225 2935). *Sublime*, held on alternate Fridays, is a busy techno and trance event, while *Joy*, a popular gay night, takes place monthly on a Saturday.

Gay clubs and bars

Blue Moon Café, 1 Barony St (☎0131/556 2788). Coffee, drinks and light meals available at this stylish café/bar. Attracts a mixed crowd. Mon–Fri 11am–12.30am, Sat & Sun 9am–12.30am.

CC Bloom's, 23 Greenside Place (☎0131/556 9331). Big dance floor, stonking rhythms and a young, friendly crowd.

Newtown Club Bar, 26B Dublin St (☎0131/538 7775). Men-only, with a high number of professionals. The raunchy *Intense Cellar Bar* downstairs is particularly good fun.

Planet Out, 6 Baxter's Place (☎0131/556 5991). Loud and outrageous bar beside the Playhouse Theatre.

Nexus Café, 60 Broughton St (☎0131/478 7069). Light meals, snacks and drinks in a relaxed atmosphere at the Edinburgh Gay, Lesbian and Bisexual Centre. Open 11am–11pm.

Live music pubs and venues

La Belle Angèle, 11 Hasties Close (☎0131/225 2774). Home to both indie bands and Latin divas.

Canon's Gait, 232 Canongate (☎0131/556 4481). Local folk and jazz, in a Royal Mile basement bar serving good beer.

Cas Rock, 104 W Port (☎0131/229 4341). A mixture of sedate folk and raucous punky sounds.

Cellar No. 1, 1 Chambers St. Traditional cellar bar which sways to jazz, salsa or flamenco every night of the week. Open till 1am.

Kulu's Jazz Joint, 8 Morrison St, off Lothian Road (☎0131/221 1288). Edinburgh's premier jazz and hip-hop venue, with live music every night and regular top performers.

The Liquid Room, 9C Victoria St (☎0131/225 2528). Good-sized venue frequented by visiting indie and local R&B bands.

Negociants, 45–47 Lothian St (☎0131/225 6313). An upstairs brasserie serves food from 8am till 2.30am, and specializes in Belgian fruit beers. The downstairs bar hosts varied live bands and DJs and is popular with students. Open until 3am.

The Queen's Hall, 37 Clerk St (☎0131/667 2019). Housed in a former Southside church, with some pews still in place, hosting African, funk and rock bands, as well as smaller jazz, folk concerts and comedy nights with well-established comedians.

Sandy Bell's, 25 Forrest Rd (☎0131/225 2751). A friendly bar, and a reliable place to find folk music every night of the week.

Tron Ceilidh House, 9 Hunter Square (☎0131/226 0931). Busy, huge complex of bars on different levels, with regular jazz and folk nights. Comedy on Friday nights.

The Venue, 15 Calton Rd (☎0131/557 3073). Small, intimate, sweaty club hosting up-and-coming indie bands.

THE FESTIVAL

The **Edinburgh Festival**, now the largest arts festival in the world, first took place in August 1947. Driven by a desire for reconciliation and escape from postwar austerity, the Austrian Rudolf Bing, administrator of the Glyndebourne Opera, brought together a host of distinguished musicians from the war-ravaged countries of central Europe. The symbolic centrepiece of his vision was the emotional reunion of Bruno Walter, a Jewish refugee from Nazi tyranny, and the Vienna Philharmonic Orchestra. At the same time, eight theatrical groups, both Scottish and English, turned up in Edinburgh, uninvited, performing in an unlikely variety of local venues, thus establishing the Fringe. Today more than a million people come to the city during August and early September to see several separate festivals, each offering a bewildering variety of artists and events – everything is on show, from the word's finest orchestras to controversial body-mutilating circus acts.

The legacy of Rudolf Bing's Glyndebourne connections ensured that, for many years, the official **Edinburgh International Festival** was dominated by opera. Although efforts were made in the 1980s to involve locals and provide a broader cultural mix of international theatre, dance and classical music, the official Festival is still very much a high-brow event. The International Festival now has a prominent year-round base at The Hub on the Royal Mile (see p.796), which has a café, performance space and a ticket centre. The **programme** is published in April by the Edinburgh International Festival Society, 21 Market St, EH1 1BW (☎0131/473 2000, *www.edinburghfestivals.co.uk*); bookings begin shortly afterwards.

For many years largely the domain of student revues – notable exceptions include Joan Littlewood's distinguished Theatre Workshop, with their early 1950s production of *The Other Animal*, about life in a concentration camp, and work by the great Spanish playwright, Lorca – the **Festival Fringe** really began to take off in the 1970s and it is now what most people think of as the Edinburgh Festival. Despite the arrival of nearly a thousand acts – from national theatre groups to stand-up comedians – using around two hundred venues, the Fringe remains loyal to its original open policy and there is still no vetting of performers. This means that the shows range from the inspired to the truly diabolical and ensures a highly competitive atmosphere, in which one bad review in a prominent publication means box-office disaster. Performances go on round the clock: if so inclined, you could sit through twenty shows in a day. The full **programme**

Theatre and comedy

Assembly Rooms, 54 George St (☎0131/220 4349). Varied complex of small and large halls. Used all year, but really comes into its own during the Fringe, featuring large-scale drama productions and mainstream comedy.

Bedlam Theatre, 2A Forrest Rd (☎0131/225 9893). Housed in a converted Victorian church and used predominantly by student groups.

Festival Theatre, Nicolson Street (☎0131/529 6000). The largest stage in Britain, principally used for Scottish Opera and major orchestral performances.

King's Theatre, 2 Leven St (☎0131/228 5955). Stately Edwardian civic theatre offering the most eclectic programme in the city – includes major touring theatre companies, Shakespeare, pantomime and comedy.

Netherbow Arts Centre, 43 High St (☎0131/556 9579). Small auditorium used heavily through the Festival but with an adventurous year-round programme concentrating on children's and Scottish theatre.

Playhouse Theatre, 18–22 Greenside Place (☎0131/557 2590). Recently refurbished, and used largely for extended runs of popular musicals and occasional rock concerts.

Royal Lyceum Theatre, 30 Grindlay St (☎0131/229 9697). Fine Victorian civic theatre with compact auditorium. The city's leading year-round venue for mainstream drama.

is usually available in June from the Festival Fringe Office, 180 High St, EH1 1QS (☎0131/226 5257, *www.edfringe.com*). Postal and telephone (☎0131/226 5138) bookings can be made immediately afterwards, while during the Festival tickets can be bought from the office or at various locations around the city. Each day during the Fringe, a free daily guide is published listing everything showing in the Fringe that day.

The **Film Festival** also began at the same time as the main Festival, making it the longest-running in the world. After a period in the doldrums, it has become a respected fixture on the international circuit, incorporating both mainstream and independent new releases and presenting a series of valuable retrospectives. It also hosts interviews and discussions with film directors – visitors have included Kenneth Anger, the Coen brothers, Clint Eastwood and Steve Martin. A particular feature has been the high-profile support given to Scottish film: from Bill Douglas's austere and brilliant *Childhood* trilogy, through the lighter style of Bill Forsyth, to the recent hits *Shallow Grave* and *Mrs Brown*. Tickets and information are available from the main venue: the Filmhouse, 88 Lothian Rd, EH3 9BZ (☎0131/228 2688, *www.edfilmfest.org.uk*). The programme is usually ready by late June, when bookings start.

Meanwhile, other Festivals have emerged: the **Jazz Festival**, which has attracted the likes of Teddy Wilson and Benny Waters, takes place in the first week of August. The programme is available at the end of May from the office at 29 St Stephen's St, EH3 5AN (☎0131/225 2202, *www.jazzmusic.co.uk*). The **Book Festival** evolved from existing meet-the-author sessions to become an important annual jamboree held in the douce setting of a marquee-covered Charlotte Square. Hundreds of established authors from throughout the English-speaking world come to take part in readings, lectures, panel discussions and audience question-and-answer sessions, along with a particularly strong programme of children's events. For further information, contact the Scottish Book Centre, 137 Dundee St, EH11 1BG (☎0131/228 5444, *www.edbookfest.co.uk*).

Although officially a separate event, the **Edinburgh Military Tattoo**, held in a splendid setting on the Castle Esplanade, is very much part of the Festival scene and an unashamed display of the kilt-and-bagpipes view of Scottish culture. Pipes and drums form the kernel of the programme, with a lone piper towards the end; performing animals, gymnastic and daredevil displays, plus at least one guest regiment from abroad, provide variety. Tickets for the Tattoo are like gold dust during August and it's best to get hold of them in advance: contact the Tattoo Office, 32 Market St, EH1 1QB (☎0131/225 1188, *www.edintattoo.co.uk*).

The Stand Comedy Club, 5 York Place (☎0131/558 7272). The city's top comedy spot, with an excellent bar, even when the stage is quiet.

Theatre Workshop, 34 Hamilton Place (☎0131/226 5425). Enticing programmes of innovative international theatre and performance art all year round.

Traverse Theatre, 10 Cambridge St (☎0131/228 1404). A byword in experimental theatrical circles, and unquestionably one of Britain's premier venues for new plays.

Concert halls

Queen's Hall, 89 Clerk St (☎0131/667 2019). Converted Georgian church with a capacity of around eight hundred, though many seats have little or no view of the platform. Home of both the Scottish Chamber Orchestra and Scottish Ensemble, and much favoured by jazz, blues and folk groups. Also hosts established comedians.

Reid Concert Hall, Bristo Square (☎0131/650 2423). Narrow, steeply pitched Victorian hall owned by the University; hosts classical concerts.

St Cecilia's Hall, corner of Cowgate and Niddry Street (☎0131/650 2805). A Georgian treasure that is again University-owned and not used as frequently as it deserves to be.

Usher Hall, corner of Lothian Road and Grindlay Street (☎0131/228 1155). Edinburgh's main civic concert hall, seating over 2500. Excellent for choral and symphony concerts, but less suitable for solo vocalists. The upper circle seats are cheapest and have the best acoustics.

EDINBURGH'S OTHER FESTIVALS

Quite apart from the Edinburgh Festival, the city is now promoting itself as a year-round festival city, beginning with Edinburgh's **Hogmanay** (contact the tourist office ☎0131/473 3800 or the Hub ☎0131/473 2010 for more information about ticketed events), which claims to be one of the world's largest New Year street parties, involving torchlight processions, folk and rock concerts and fireworks galore. The Shoots and Roots **folk festival** has sessions in April and November (☎0131/557 1050), drawing local and international performers, while the **Science Festival**, also in April (☎0131/530 2001), incorporates hands-on children's events as well as numerous lectures on a vast array of subjects. There is a **Puppet and Animation Festival** in March (☎0131/556 9579), and a **Children's Festival** in May (☎0131/225 8050), with readings, magicians and so on. In the summer, a series of concerts (usually free), ranging from tea dances to world music, is held in the Ross Bandstand in Princes Street Gardens. The Caledonian Brewery, 42 Slateford Rd, runs its own German-style **beer festival** in early June.

The **Doors Open Day**, around late September, is an opportunity to visit a number of noteworthy buildings otherwise closed to the public. In recent years, these have included private homes in the New Town, the High Court and the Central Mosque. Contact the Cockburn Association (☎0131/557 8686) for details. The **Filmhouse** (☎0131/228 2688) also has a number of annual seasons of international cinema, notably French (in November) and Italian (April), and a gay season (June).

The useful **Web site** *www.edinburghfestivals.co.uk* has links to the home pages of most of Edinburgh's main festivals.

Cinemas

The heart of Edinburgh's cinema-land is, appropriately, in the area of town where Sean Connery was born, around Lothian Road in the west of the city. There are also three excellent independents:

Cameo, 38 Home St, Tollcross (information ☎0131/228 2800; bookings ☎0131/228 4141). New art-house and more challenging mainstream releases, as well as cult late-nighters.

Filmhouse, 88 Lothian Rd (☎0131/228 2688). Eclectic programme of independent, art-house and classic films.

The Lumière, Royal Museum of Scotland (enter from Lothian Street; ☎0131/247 4219). Art-house movies grouped into special themes and seasons. Open Fri–Sun only.

Listings

Airlines British Airways, 32 Frederick St (☎0345/222111); British Midland, Edinburgh Airport (☎0131/344 5600); Easyjet (☎0870/600 0000); Ryanair (☎0541/569569).

Banks & exchange American Express, 139 Princes St (☎0131/225 9179); Bank of Scotland, The Mound (head office), 38 St Andrew Square, 103 George St; Barclays, 1 St Andrew Square; Clydesdale, 20 Hanover St; Lloyds, 113–115 George St; Midland, 76 Hanover St; NatWest, 80 George St; Royal Bank of Scotland, 36 St Andrew Square; TSB, 109 George St; Thomas Cook, 28 Frederick St (Mon–Sat 9am–5.30pm; ☎0131/465 7600). There are currency exchange bureaux in the main tourist office and beside platform 1 at Waverley Station (Sept–June Mon–Sat 7.30am–9pm, Sun 8.30am–9pm; July & Aug Mon–Sat 7am–10pm, Sun 8am–10pm). To change money after hours, try one of the upmarket hotels – but expect to pay a hefty commission charge.

Bike rental Central Cycles, 13 Lochrin Place (☎0131/228 6333); Scottish Cycle Safaris, 29 Blackfriars St (☎0131/556 5560).

Books Bauermeisters, 19 George IV Bridge (☎0131/226 5561); James Thin, 53–59 South Bridge (☎0131/556 6743) and 57 George St (☎0131/225 4495). For second hand books: Broughton Books, 2A Broughton Place (☎0131/557 8010); Second Edition, 9 Howard St (☎0131/556 9403).

Car rental Arnold Clark, Lochrin Place (☎0131/228 4747); Avis, 100 Dalry Rd (☎0131/337 6363); Budget, 111 Glasgow Rd (☎0845/606 6669); Carnies, 46 Westfield Rd (☎0131/346 4155); Europcar,

24 E London St (☎0131/557 3456); Hertz, Waverley Station (☎0131/557 5272); Mitchells, 32 Torphichen St (☎0131/229 5384); Thrifty Car Rental, 24 Haymarket Terrace (☎0131/313 1613).

Consulates Australia, 37 George St (☎0131/624 3333); Canada, 30 Lothian Rd (☎0131/220 4333); USA, 3 Regent Terrace (☎0131/556 8315).

Dentist The National Health Service Line (☎0800/224488) will tell you where your nearest surgery is. For emergencies go to Edinburgh Dental Institute, Lauriston Place (☎0131/556 4913), or the Western General Hospital, Crewe Rd South (☎0131/537 1338).

Hospital Royal Infirmary, 1 Lauriston Place (☎0131/536 1000), has a 24-hour casualty department.

Internet *Cyberia*, 88 Hanover St (Mon–Sat 10am–10pm, Sun noon–7pm; ☎0131/220 4403, *www.cybersurf.co.uk*); *Web 13*, 13 Bread St (Mon–Wed & Fri 9am–5.30pm, Thurs 9am–7pm, Sat 9am–6pm, Sun 11am–5pm; ☎0131/229 8883, *www.web13.co.uk*).

Laundry Capital Launderette, 208 Dalkeith Rd, Newington; Sundial Launderette, 7–9 East London St, Broughton; Tarvit Launderette, 7–9 Tarvit St, Tollcross.

Left luggage Lockers are available at Waverley Station (Mon–Sat 7am–11pm, Sun 8am–11pm) and St Andrew Square bus station (Mon–Sat 6.35am–10pm, Sun 8am–10pm).

Lost property Edinburgh Airport (☎0131/333 1000); Edinburgh Police HQ (☎0131/311 3141); Lothian Regional Transport (☎0131/554 4492); Scotrail (☎0141/332 9811).

Pharmacy Boots, 48 Shandwick Place (Mon–Fri 8am–9pm, Sat 8am–7pm, Sun 10am–5pm; ☎0131/225 6757), has the longest opening hours.

Police Lothian and Borders Police HQ, Fettes Ave (☎0131/311 3131). Local police stations include: Queen Charlotte St, Leith (☎0131/554 9350); and Torphichen Place, West End (☎0131/229 2323).

Post office 8–10 St James Centre (Mon 9am–5.30pm, Tues–Fri 8.30am–5.30pm, Sat 8.30am–6pm; ☎0345/223344).

Taxis Airport Taxis (☎0131/344 3344); Central Radio Taxis (☎0131/229 2468); City Cabs (☎0131/228 1211).

Travel agents Usit/Campus Travel (student and youth specialist), 53 Forrest Rd (☎0131/225 6111) and 5 Nicolson Square (☎0131/668 3303); Edinburgh Travel Centre (student and youth specialist), 196 Rose St (☎0131/226 2019) and 3 Bristo Square (☎0131/668 2221). For three- and six-day coach trips to the Highlands, try Haggis Backpackers, 11 Blackfriars St (☎0131/558 1177) or MacBackpackers, 105 High St (☎0131/558 9900).

travel details

Trains

Edinburgh to: Aberdeen (hourly; 2hr 40min); Aviemore (5 daily; 3hr); Birmingham (6 daily; 5hr 30min); Bristol (3 daily; 6hr 30min); Dundee (hourly; 1hr 45min); Fort William (change at Glasgow; 3 daily; 5hr); Glasgow (every 30min; 50min); Inverness (6 daily; 3hr 30min); Leuchars for St Andrews (hourly; 1hr); London (every 30min; 4hr–4hr 30min); Manchester (4 daily; 4hr); Newcastle upon Tyne (every 30min; 1hr 30min); Oban (change at Glasgow; 3 daily; 4hr 10min); Oxford (2 daily; 9hr); Perth (6 daily; 1hr 15min); Southampton (1 daily; 9hr); Stirling (every 30min; 45min); York (hourly; 2hr 30min).

Buses

Edinburgh to: Aberdeen (hourly; 3–4hr); Campbeltown (3 daily via Glasgow; 6hr); Dundee (hourly; 1hr 30min–2hr); Fort William (2 direct daily; 5hr); Glasgow (every 20min; 1hr 10min); Inverness (hourly; 3–4hr); London (6 daily; 7hr 50min); Newcastle upon Tyne (3 daily; 3hr 15min); Oban (3 daily via Glasgow; 5hr); Perth (hourly; 1hr 20min); Pitlochry (hourly; 2hr); York (1 daily; 5hr).

Flights

Edinburgh to: Birmingham (Mon–Fri 9 daily, Sat & Sun 4 daily; 1hr); London (Gatwick Mon–Fri 5 daily, Sat & Sun 3 daily; Heathrow Mon–Fri 20 daily, Sat & Sun 15 daily; Stansted Mon–Fri 13 daily, Sat & Sun 7 daily; 1hr 15min); Manchester (Mon–Fri 9 daily, Sat & Sun 2 daily; 50min).

CHAPTER NINETEEN

SOUTHERN SCOTLAND

Although southern Scotland doesn't have the high tourist profile of other areas of the country, in many ways the region is at its very heart. Its inhabitants bore the brunt of long wars with the English, its farms have fed Scotland's cities since industrialization, and two of the country's literary icons, Sir Walter Scott and Robbie Burns, lived and died here. The main roads – the fast routes from northern England to Glasgow and Edinburgh – bypass the best of the region, but if you make an effort to get off the highways, there's plenty to see, from the ruins of medieval castles and abbeys to well-preserved market towns and seaports set within a wild, hilly countryside.

Geographically, southern Scotland is dominated by the **Southern Uplands** – a chain of bulging flat-peaked hills and weather-beaten moorland punctuated by narrow glens, fast-flowing rivers and blue-black lochs. These extend south and west from an imaginary line drawn between Peebles and Jedburgh, in central southern Scotland, over to the Ayrshire coast. They are at their most dramatic in the west, in the **Galloway Forest Park**, with peaks soaring over 2000ft, crisscrossed by **walking trails**.

South of Edinburgh, the **Pentland**, **Moorfoot** and **Lammermuir** ranges form the southern edge of the Central Lowlands. These Lowlands spread east beyond Edinburgh, where they become the slender coastal plain of **East Lothian**, which rolls down towards a string of fine sandy beaches. Further south, the coastline becomes more rugged, its cliffs and rocky outcrops harbouring a series of ruined castles, including the ruined **Tantallon Castle**, overlooking the sea east of **North Berwick**.

North of the inhospitable Cheviot Hills, which straddle the border with England, is the region known as the Borders, inspiration for countless folkloric ballads telling of bloody battles with the English and clashes between the notorious warring families, the Border reivers. Its nucleus is the valley of the **River Tweed**, where a clutch of tiny towns – including **Peebles**, **Melrose** and **Kelso** – make good bases for exploring the valley's castles, Adam-designed houses and ruined abbeys. South of Kelso is the useful transport hub of **Jedburgh**, a former garrison town with another imposing abbey and the bleak **Hermitage Castle** nearby.

The gritty town of **Dumfries** is gateway to southwest Scotland, where on the marshy Solway coast you can visit the magnificent remains of **Caerlaverock Castle** and the charming town of **Kirkcudbright**, on the Dee estuary. Further west, the **Rhinns of**

ACCOMMODATION PRICE CODES

Throughout this guide, hotel and B&B accommodation is priced on a scale of ① to ⑨, the number indicating the **lowest price** you could expect to pay per night in that establishment for a **double room** in high season. The prices indicated by the codes are as follows:

① under £40	④ £60–70	⑦ £110–150
② £40–50	⑤ £70–90	⑧ £150–200
③ £50–60	⑥ £90–110	⑨ over £200

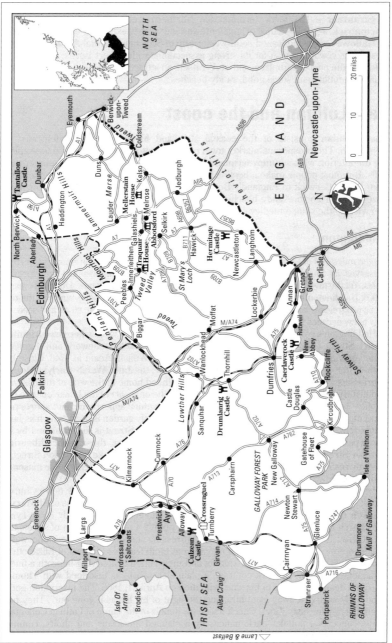

© Crown copyright

Galloway, a hilly peninsula at the end of the Solway coast, encompasses the grimy town of **Stranraer** – the ferry terminal for Northern Ireland – and pretty, seaside **Portpatrick**, as well as a host of smaller towns and villages extending down to the **Mull of Galloway**, the wind-lashed southwestern tip of Scotland. Pastoral **Ayrshire**, on the west coast, rewards a visit for its strong associations with Robert Burns, especially at **Alloway**, the poet's birthplace, and at **Ayr** itself, an attractive seaside resort with an air of faded gentility and some good, sandy beaches.

East Lothian and the coast

East Lothian consists of the coastal strip and hinterland immediately east of Edinburgh. The prosperous market town of **Haddington** serves as a base for exploring the interior, whose bumpy farmland is bordered to the south by the Lammermuir Hills. But most people make a beeline for the fifty miles or so of **coastline** extending from North Berwick to England's Berwick-upon-Tweed. There's something for most tastes here, from the sandy beaches and volcanic islets around the resort of **North Berwick** to the ruined medieval stronghold of **Tantallon**.

Haddington

Fifteen miles east of Edinburgh, **HADDINGTON**, the birthplace of John Knox (see p.799), preserves an intriguing ensemble of seventeenth- to nineteenth-century architectural styles. Yet the town's otherwise staid appearance belies an innovative past. During the early 1700s, Haddington became a byword for modernization as its merchants supplied the district's progressive landowners with all sorts of new-fangled equipment, stock and seed. In only a few decades Lothian agriculture was utterly transformed.

Haddington's compact centre is best approached from the west, where tree-trimmed **Court Street** ends suddenly with the soaring spire, stately stonework and dignified Venetian windows of the **Town House**, designed by William Adam in 1748. Close by, to the right, and next door to a fine Italianate facade, the **Jane Welsh Carlyle House** (April–Sept Wed–Sat 2–5pm; £1.50) was the childhood home of the wife of the essayist and historian Thomas Carlyle. The dining room – the only part of the house open to the public – has been restored to its early nineteenth-century appearance, and sports pictures of the influential personalities of the day. The lovely garden is pretty much as Jane would have known it too. Continuing straight on, **High Street** is distinguished by its pastel-painted gables and quaint pends, a tad prettier than those in neighbouring **Market Street**. Keep an eye open, however, for **Mitchell's Close** on Market Street, a recently restored seventeenth-century alley with crow-stepped gables, rubble masonry and the narrowest of staircase towers.

Leaving the town centre to the east along High Street, it's a brief walk down Church Street – past the hooped arches of **Nungate Bridge** – to the hulking mass of **St Mary's Church** (Mon–Sat 10am–4pm, Sun 1–4pm; free). Built close to the reedy River Tyne, the church dates from the fourteenth century, but it's a real hotchpotch of styles, the squat grey tower uneasy above clumsy buttressing and pinkish-ochre stone walls. Inside, on the **Lauderdale Aisle**, a magnificent tomb features the best of Elizabethan alabaster carving, moustachioed knights and their ruffed ladies lying beneath a finely ornamented canopy. In stark contrast, a plain slab nearby is inscribed with Thomas Carlyle's beautiful tribute to his wife, who died on April 21, 1866. The inscription ends: "Suddenly snatched away from him, and the light of his life as if gone out". They had been married for forty years. Check inside for details of the Lamp of Lothian Collegiate Trust concerts – popular perfomances by acclaimed musicians and choirs, running through the summer months.

Practicalities

Fast and frequent **buses** connect Haddington with Edinburgh, and North Berwick. All services stop on High Street. There's no tourist office, but orientation is easy and *A Walk around Haddington* (£1), detailing every building of any conceivable consequence, is available from local newsagents. There are several central **B&Bs** including *Mrs Richards*, whose well-kept Georgian town house is at 19 Church St (π01620/825663; ②), and the *Plough Tavern*, 11 Court St (π01620/823326; ②). Alternatively, try the more pricey and luxurious *Brown's Hotel*, 1 West Rd (π01620/822254; ⑥). *Monks' Muir Caravan Park* (π01620/860340), on the edge of town by the A1, also takes **tents**. For daytime eating, try *Simply Scrumptious*, next to the Town House. The best places for an evening meal are the *Waterside Bistro*, on the far side of Nungate Bridge; *Poldrate's Restaurant*, on the Gifford road, and *Brown's Hotel* restaurant, where you'll need to reserve a table (π01620/822254).

North Berwick and around

NORTH BERWICK, on the coast ten miles northeast of Haddington, has an old-fashioned air, its guest houses and hotels extending along the shore in all their Victorian and Edwardian sobriety. Set within sight of two volcanic heaps – the Bass Rock and North Berwick Law – the resort's pair of wide and sandy **beaches** are the main attraction.

Little now remains of the original medieval town, but the fragmentary ruins of the **Auld Kirk**, next to the harbour, bear witness to one of the most extraordinary events in Scottish history. In 1590, **King James VI** spent the summer in Denmark wooing his prospective wife. In his absence, Francis Stuart, **Earl of Bothwell**, summoned the witches of Lothian to meet the Devil in the Auld Kirk. Bothwell turned up disguised as the Devil and instructed his two hundred acolytes to raise a storm that would shipwreck the king. To cast the spell, they opened a few graves and engaged in flagellation before kissing the bare buttocks of the "Devil" – reportedly "as cold as ice and as hard as iron" as it hung over the pulpit. Despite these shenanigans, the king returned safely, and since he refused to believe the rumours of Bothwell's treachery, the earl went unpunished.

Resembling a giant molar, the **Bass Rock** rises 350ft above the sea some three miles east of North Berwick. This massive chunk of basalt, formerly a prison, fortress and monastic retreat, is home to millions of nesting sea birds. Weather permitting, there are regular ninety-minute **boat trips** round the island from North Berwick harbour (Easter to early Oct daily; £3.50), but only Fred Marr (π01620/892838; £11.50) has landing rights. The other volcanic monolith, 613-foot-high **North Berwick Law**, is about an hour's walk from the beach – take the Law road off High Street and follow the signs. On the summit, you can see the remains of a Napoleonic watchtower and an arch made from the jaw bone of a whale; on a clear day, the views out across the Firth of Forth make the effort of the climb well worthwhile.

Practicalities

It's ten minutes' walk east from North Berwick **train station** to the town centre along Abbey Road, Westgate and High Street. **Buses** from Edinburgh stop on High Street and those from Haddington outside the **tourist office** on Quality Street (April & May Mon–Sat 9am–6pm; June & Sept also Sun 11am–4pm; July & Aug Mon–Sat 9am–7pm, Sun 11am–6pm; Oct–March Mon–Fri 9am–5pm; π01620/892197).

Several excellent **B&Bs** are open from April to September, including *Mrs Duns*, 20 Marmion Rd (π01620/892066; ①), and *Mrs McQueen*, 5 West Bay Rd (π01620/894576; ①). Out of season, try *Mrs Ralph*, 13 Westgate (π01620/892782; ①), *Mrs Gray*, 115 High St (π01620/892884; ②), or *Craigview*, 5 Beach Rd (π01620/892257; ②), a well-maintained

guest house. *Point Garry*, 20 West Bay Rd (☎01620/892380; ⑤; closed Nov–March), is an upmarket **hotel**. The nearest **campsite**, *Tantallon Rhodes Caravan Park* (☎01620/893348, *TantallonP@aol.com*; closed Nov–Feb), occupies a prime cliff-top location a couple of miles east of the centre – take the Dunbar bus.

Several little **cafés**, such as the *Buttercup*, on High Street, sell inexpensive snacks, and for an evening meal most of the hotels will serve bar meals, including *The Grange*, *The County Hotel* and *The Tantallon Inn*.

Tantallon Castle

The melodramatic ruins of **Tantallon Castle** (April–Sept Mon–Sat 9.30am–6.30pm; Oct–March Mon–Wed & Sat 9.30am–4.30pm, Thurs 9.30am–noon, Sun 2–4.30pm; £2.50) lie three miles east of North Berwick, on the precipitous cliffs facing the Bass Rock. This pinkish sandstone edifice, with its imposing cylindrical towers, protected the powerful "Red" Douglases, earls of Angus, from their enemies for over three hundred years. With a sheer drop down to the sea on three sides and a sequence of moats and ditches on the fourth, the castle's desolate invincibility is daunting, with the wind howling over the remaining battlements and the surf crashing on the rocks far below. In fact, the setting is more striking than the ruins: Cromwell's army savaged the castle in 1651 and only the impressive 50-foot-high and 14-foot-thick curtain wall has survived relatively intact. To reach Tantallon Castle from North Berwick, a fifteen-minute trip, take the Dunbar bus.

The Borders

Rising in the hills far to the west, the **River Tweed** snakes its way across the Borders until it reaches the North Sea at Berwick-upon-Tweed. In the higher reaches, it passes throught the pleasant country town of **Peebles**, often visited as an excursion from Melrose, twenty miles or so to the west. On the way, savour the wooded scenery and drop into historic **Traquair House**, just off the main road at Innerleithen.

Melrose, with its Gothic **abbey**, makes a great base for exploring, as well as being a beautiful town in its own right. The rich, forested scenery of this part of the Tweed Valley inspired Sir Walter Scott, and the area's most outstanding attractions – the elegaic ruins of **Dryburgh Abbey** and lonely **Smailholm Tower**, not to mention Scott's purpose-built creation, **Abbotsford House** – bear his mark. Fortunately, perhaps, Scott died before the textile boom industrialized parts of the Tweed Valley, turning his beloved Selkirk and Galashiels into mill towns.

The eastern reaches of the river, for the most part, form the boundary between Scotland and England. For the English, the gentle, rural landscape of the east Borders was the quickest land route to the centre of Scotland and time and again they launched themselves north, destroying everything in their way. Indeed, the English turned Berwick-upon-Tweed into one of the most heavily guarded frontier towns in northern Europe, and the massive fortifications survive today (see p.653). The region also witnessed one of the most devastating of medieval battles when the Scots, under James IV, were decimated by the English at **Flodden Field**, over the border from Coldstream, in 1513. Nowadays, the Lower Tweed Valley really has only one place of note, **Kelso**, a busy agricultural centre distinguished by the Georgian elegance of its main square and its proximity to **Floors Castle**.

Some ten miles south of Melrose and the same distance north of the border with England is the former royal burgh of **Jedburgh**. Although the castle is long since destroyed, the town makes a good starting point for a tour of the four Border abbeys due to its transport connections and the presence of grim **Hermitage Castle**, to the south.

THE BORDER REIVERS

From the thirteenth to the early seventeenth century, the wild, inhospitable border country stretching from the Solway Firth in the west to the Tweed Valley in the east, well away from the power bases of both the Scottish and English monarchs, was overrun by outlaws known as the **Border reivers**. This was no cross-border dispute, but an open struggle for power among the great families of the region. Cattle-rustling, blackmail and kidnapping led to an almost anarchical mind set, where feuding families would wreak havoc and devastation on each other almost as a way of life.

The causes of this behaviour can be found in the constant destruction and devastation brought about by continual warfare between England and Scotland, and the scorched earth tactics of the era. With so many unable to find sustenance from the land, crime became the only way to survive. Those who "shook loose the Border" included people from all walks of life: agricultural labourers, gentleman farmers, smallholders, even peers of the realm.

The legacy of the Border reivers can still be felt today in the region's fortified farms and churches; in its traditions – notably the "Common Riding", in which riders beat the bounds in an annual pageant; and in the great family names – Armstrong, Graham, Kerr, Nixon – that once filled the heart of every borderer with dread.

Peebles and around

Straddling the Tweed twenty miles south of Edinburgh, **PEEBLES** has a genteel, relaxing air, its wide High Street bordered by a complementary medley of architectural styles, mostly dating from Victorian times. A stroll around town should include a visit to the **Tweeddale Museum**, on High Street (April–Oct Mon–Fri 10am–1pm & 2–5pm, Sat 10am–noon, Sun 2–4pm; Nov–March closed Sat & Sun; free). William Chambers, a local worthy, presented the building to the town in 1859, complete with an art gallery dedicated to the enlightenment of his neighbours. He stuffed the place with casts of the world's most famous sculptures, and, although most were lost long ago, today's "Secret Room" boasts two handsome friezes: one a copy of the Elgin marbles, the other of the Triumph of Alexander cast in 1812 to honour Napoleon. Make time to walk out to **Neidpath Castle** (Easter–Sept Mon–Sat 11am–5pm, Sun 1–5pm; £2), a dramatic medieval tower house whose location above the river failed to protect it from English invasions from the fifteenth to the seventeenth centuries.

Traquair House

Six miles east of Peebles, a mile or so south of the main road, near the village of Innerleithen, **Traquair House** (April, May & Sept daily 12.30–5.30pm; Jun–Aug daily 10.30am–5.30pm; Oct Fri–Sun 2–5pm; house & grounds £5; grounds only £2) is the oldest continuously inhabited house in Scotland, with the present owners – the Maxwell Stuarts – living here since 1491. Persistently Catholic, the family paid for their principles: Protestant mill workers repeatedly attacked their property, and by 1800 little remained of the family's once enormous estates.

Nevertheless, the house has kept many of its oldest features, including the original vaulted cellars, where locals once hid their cattle from raiders; the twisting main staircase as well as the earlier medieval version, later a secret escape route for persecuted Catholics; and even a **Priest's Room**, where a string of resident chaplains lived in hiding until the Catholic Emancipation Act freed things up in 1829. In the **Museum Room** there are several fine examples of Jacobite or **Amen glass**, inscribed with pictures of the Bonnie Prince or verses in his honour; and the cloak worn by the fourth earl during his dramatic escape from the Tower of London. Under sentence of death for his part in the Jacobite Rising of 1715, the earl was saved by his wife, Lady Winifred Herbert, who got his jailers drunk and smuggled him out disguised as a maid. It's worth sparing time for the surrounding gardens where you'll find a maze, several craft workshops and a working brewery, whose products are on sale at the tearoom – or better, at the vibrant Traquair Fair which is held here in August.

Practicalities

Buses to Peebles stop outside the post office, a few doors down the High Street from the well-stocked **tourist office** (April & May Mon–Sat 10am–5pm, Sun 10am–2pm; June & Sept Mon–Sat 10am–5.30pm, Sun 1–4pm; July & Aug Mon–Sat 9am–7pm, Sun 10am–6pm; Oct Mon–Sat 10am–4.30pm, Sun 10am–2pm; Nov & Dec Mon–Sat 10am–12.30pm & 1.30–4.30pm; ☎01721/720138). Of the many **B&Bs**, try *Rowanbrae*, on Northgate, off the High Street (☎01721/721630; ①); the *Minniebank Guest House*, Greenside (☎01721/722093; ②), by the main bridge; or *Viewfield*, 1 Rosetta Rd (☎01721/721232; ①), west of the bridge. The best of the more upmarket **hotels** is *The Park Hotel*, Innerleithen Road (☎01721/720451; ⑤), followed by the relaxing *Kingsmuir Hotel*, south of the river on Springhill Road (☎01721/720151, *chrisburn@kingsmuir.scotborders.co.uk*; ⑥). For **camping**, the *Rosetta Caravan and Camping Park* (☎01721/720770; closed Nov–March) is fifteen minutes' walk north of the High Street. For **food**, *The Olive Tree* serves great snacks; the *Crown Hotel*, High Street, features good daily specials; and the *Kingsmuir Hotel*, Springhill Road, has more expensive but excellent bar meals.

Melrose and around

Tucked in between the Tweed and the Eildon Hills, just over twenty miles downstream from Peebles, minuscule **MELROSE** is the most beguiling of towns. Its narrow streets are trimmed by a harmonious ensemble of styles, from pretty little cottages and tweedy shops to high-standing Georgian and Victorian facades. The town is renowned as the birthplace of the famous **Rugby Sevens**, which takes place in the second week of April, although the weekend of the **Melrose Music Festival** (September) is gaining prominence as another popular event in the town's calendar.

The ochre-tinted stone ruins of **Melrose Abbey** (April–Sept daily 9.30am–6.30pm; Oct–March Mon–Sat 9.30am–4.30pm, Sun 2–4.30pm; £3.50; HS) soar above their riverside surroundings. The abbey, founded in 1136 by David I, grew rich selling wool and hides to Flanders, but its prosperity was fragile: the English repeatedly razed Melrose, most viciously under Richard II in 1385 and the Earl of Hertford in 1545. Most of what remains dates from the intervening period, when extensive rebuilding abandoned the original austerity for an elaborate, Gothic style inspired by the abbeys of northern England.

The site is dominated by the **Abbey Church**, where the elegant window arches of the nave lead down to the **monk's choir**, whose grand piers are disfigured by the masonry of a later parish church. The adjacent **presbytery** is better preserved, its dignified lines illuminated by a magnificent Perpendicular window. The legend that the heart of Robert the Bruce was buried here beneath the window was proven in 1996, when it was publicly exhumed. The location didn't, however, accord with the dying king's wishes: he actually told his friend, James Douglas, to carry his heart on a Crusade to the Holy Land. Douglas tried his best, but was killed fighting the Moors in Spain – and Bruce's heart ended up in Melrose. In the **south transept**, another fine fifteenth-century window sprouts yet more delicate, foliate tracery and the adjacent cornice is enlivened by angels playing musical instruments. Outside, all sorts of **gargoyles** adorn the majestic lines of the church, from peculiar crouching beasts to a pig playing the bagpipes on the south side of the nave.

The fragmentary ruins of the old monastic buildings edge the church and lead across to the **Commendator's House** (same times as the abbey), the headquarters of the abbey's lay administrators in the sixteenth century, where a modest collection of ecclesiastical bric-a-brac can be seen. Next door to the abbey, in the opposite direction, is the delightful **Priorwood Garden** (April–Sept Mon–Sat 10am–5.30pm, Sun 1.30–5.30pm; Oct–Dec Mon–Sat 10am–4pm, Sun 1.30pm–4pm; free; NTS), whose walled precincts are given over to flowers that are suitable for drying – there's a dried flower shop too. Melrose's other museum, the **Trimontium Exhibition**, just off Market Square (April–Oct daily 10.30am–4.30pm; £1.25), is a quirky affair, where the sound of a Roman blacksmith you can see Celtic bronze axe heads and learn about the three Roman occupations of the region.

Practicalities

Buses to Melrose stop in Market Square, a brief walk from the **tourist office** (March–May Mon–Sat 10am–5pm, Sun 10am–1pm; June & Sept Mon–Sat 10am–6pm, Sun 10am–2pm; July & Aug Mon–Sat 9.30am–6.30pm, Sun 10am–6pm; Oct Mon–Sat 10am–1pm; ☎01896/822555). Melrose has a clutch of **hotels**, including the smart and tidy *Burts Hotel* on Market Square (☎01896/822285, *burtshotel@aol.com*; ⑤), the neat, ten-bedroom *Bon Accord*, just across the street (☎01896/822645; ④), and the far less expensive *Station Hotel*, up the hill from Market Square (☎01896/822038; ②). It's among Melrose's **B&Bs**, however, that you'll get the real flavour of the place, most notably at *Braidwood*, Buccleuch Street (☎01896/822488; ②), and *Dunfermline House*, opposite (☎01896/822148; ②). The town also has a **youth hostel** (☎01896/822521), occupying a Victorian villa overlooking the abbey from beside the access road into the bypass. The *Gibson Caravan Park* (☎01896/822969) is at the foot of the High Street opposite the Greenyards rugby grounds.

Some of the B&Bs serve reasonably priced **evening meals** on request. In town, *Marmion's Brasserie*, on Buccleuch Street, offers well-prepared meals from an imaginative menu, as does *Melrose Station*, in the old train station above the square. To work up an appetite, walk across the suspension bridge to the *Hoebridge Inn* at Gattonside, a relaxed restaurant that was once a bobbin mill and now serves wonderful Italian dishes. Back on Market Square, *Russel's* has good coffee and snacks; while the busy *Burts Hotel* serves excellent bar meals, although their attitude to backpackers can be a bit snooty. No such restrictions exist at *Haldane's Fish & Chip Shop* (closed Wed), just off the square, or at the nearby *Ship Inn* on East Port, the liveliest **pub** in town. For alternative entertainment, visit The Wynd, a little theatre hidden in the alley between the High Street and Buccleuch Street.

Dryburgh Abbey

Hidden away on a bend in the Tweed a few miles east of Melrose, the remains of **Dryburgh Abbey** (April–Sept daily 9.30am–6.30pm; Oct–March Mon–Sat 9.30am–4.30pm, Sun 2–4.30pm; £2.50; HS) occupy a superb position against a hilly backdrop. The Premonstratensians founded the abbey in the twelfth century, but they were never as successful as their Cistercian neighbours in Melrose. The abbey, demolished and rebuilt on several occasions, incorporates a number of architectural styles, beginning in the shattered church where the clumsy decoration of the main entrance contrasts with the spirited dog-tooth motif around the east processional doorway. The latter leads through to the **monastic buildings**, a two-storey ensemble that provides an insight into the lives of the monks. Bits and pieces of several rooms have survived, but the real highlight is the barrel-vaulted **Chapter House**, complete with low stone benches, grouped windows and carved arcade. The room was used by the monks for the daily reading of a chapter from either the Bible or their rule book, and was, as they prospered, draped with expensive hangings. Finally, back in the church, the battered **north transept** contains the grave of Sir **Walter Scott**; close by lies Field Marshal Haig, the World War I commander whose ineptitude cost thousands of soldiers' lives.

To get to the abbey from Melrose, take the Jedburgh **bus** as far as Newtown St Boswells, ten minutes away, and walk the signposted last mile down St Cuthbert's Way. Sir Walter Scott's favourite haunt, "**Scott's View**" stands a mile further up the road from the Abbey and is well worth the trip for the fantastic views across the River Tweed to the three Eildon Hills, the famous Border landmark.

Smailholm Tower

The fifteenth-century **Smailholm Tower** (April–Sept daily 9.30am–6.30pm; £1.80; HS) perches on a rocky outcrop a few miles northeast of Dryburgh. A remote and evocative fastness recalling violent reivers' raids and border skirmishes (see p.837), not least for Walter Scott, who was but a "wee, sick laddie" when he was brought here to live in 1773 (see box opposite), the tower was designed to withstand sudden attack. The rough rubble walls average six feet thick and both the entrance – once guarded by a heavy door plus an iron yett (gate) – and the windows are disproportionately small. Inside, ignore the inept costumed models and press on up to the roof, where two narrow wall-walks, jammed against the barrel-vaulted roof and the crow-stepped gables, provide panoramic views. There are **buses** to Smailholm from Earlston and Kelso.

Mellerstain House

Mellerstain House (May–Sept Mon–Fri & Sun 12.30–5pm; £4.50), a couple of miles north of Smailholm, represents the very best of the Adams' work. William designed the wings in 1725, and his son, Robert, the castellated centre, fifty years later. Robert's love of columns, roundels and friezes culminates in a stunning sequence of plaster-moulded, pastel-shaded ceilings, from the looping symmetry of the library ceiling, adorned by medallion oil paintings of *Learning* and *Reading* on either side of *Minerva*, to the whimsical griffin and vase pattern in the drawing room. It takes about an hour to tour the house; afterwards you can wander the formal **Edwardian gardens**, which slope down towards the lake.

Abbotsford House

Abbotsford House (March–May & Oct Mon–Sat 10am–5pm, Sun 2–5pm; June–Sept daily 10am–5pm; £3.50), three miles west of Melrose, was designed to satisfy the Romantic inclinations of Sir Walter Scott, who lived here from 1812 until his death twenty years later. Abbotsford took twelve years to evolve, with the fanciful turrets and castellations of the Scots Baronial exterior incorporating copies of medieval originals; the entrance porch imitates that of Linlithgow Palace, fifteen miles west of Edinburgh, and the screen wall in the garden echoes Melrose Abbey's cloister. Inside, visitors start in the wood-panelled study, with its small writing desk made of salvage from the Spanish Armada. The library boasts an extraordinary assortment of Scottish memorabilia, including a lock of Bonnie Prince Charlie's hair, Flora Macdonald's pocket book, the inlaid pearl crucifix that accompanied Mary Queen of Scots to the scaffold, and even a piece of oatcake found in the pocket of a dead Highlander at Culloden. You can also see Henry Raeburn's famous portrait of Scott, hanging in the drawing room, and all sorts of weapons, notably Rob Roy's sword, dagger and gun, in the armoury. To get to the house, take the fast and frequent Melrose–Galashiels **bus**.

SIR WALTER SCOTT

Walter Scott (1771–1832) was born in Edinburgh to a solidly bourgeois family whose roots were in Selkirkshire. As a child he was left lame by polio and his anxious parents sent him to recuperate at his grandfather's farm in Smailholm, where the boy's imagination was fired by his relatives' tales of derring-do, the violent history of the Borders retold amidst a rugged landscape that he spent long summer days exploring. Scott returned to Edinburgh to resume his education and take up a career in law, but his real interests remained elsewhere. Throughout the 1790s, he transcribed hundreds of old Border ballads, publishing a three-volume collection entitled *The Minstrelsy of the Scottish Borders* in 1802. An instant success, *Minstrelsy* was followed by Scott's own *Lay of the Last Minstrel*, a narrative poem whose strong story and rose-tinted regionalism proved very popular.

More poetry was to come, most successfully *Marmion* (1808) and *The Lady of the Lake* (1810), not to mention an eighteen-volume edition of the works of John Dryden and nineteen volumes of Jonathan Swift. However, despite having two paid jobs, one as the Sheriff-Depute of Selkirkshire, the other as clerk to the Court of Session in Edinburgh, his finances remained shaky. He had become a partner in a printing firm, which put him deeply into debt, not helped by the enormous sums he spent on his mansion, Abbotsford. From 1813, Scott was writing to pay the bills and thumped out a veritable flood of historical novels using his extensive knowledge of Scottish history and folklore. He produced his best work within the space of ten years: *Waverley* (1814), *The Antiquary* (1816), *Rob Roy* and the *The Heart of Midlothian* (both 1818) and, after he had exhausted his own country, two notable novels set in England, *Ivanhoe* (1819) and *Kenilworth* (1821). In 1824 he returned to Scottish tales with *Redgauntlet*, the last of his quality work.

A year later Scott's money problems reached crisis point after an economic crash bankrupted his printing business. Attempting to pay his creditors in full, he found the quality of his writing deteriorating with its increased speed and the effort broke his health. His last years were plagued by illnes, and in 1832 he died at Abbotsford and was buried within the ruins of Dryburgh Abbey.

Although Scott's interests were diverse, his historical novels mostly focused on the Jacobites, whose loyalty to the Stuarts had riven Scotland since the "Glorious Revolution" of 1688. That the nation was prepared to be entertained by such tales was essentially a matter of timing: by the 1760s it was clear the Jacobite cause was lost for good and Scotland, emerging from its isolated medievalism, had been firmly welded into the United Kingdom. Thus its turbulent history and independent spirit was safely in the past, and ripe for romancing – as shown by the arrival of King George IV in Edinburgh during 1822 decked out in Highland dress. Yet, for Sir Walter the romance was tinged with a genuine sense of loss. Loyal to the Hanoverians, he still grieved for Bonnie Prince Charlie; he welcomed a commercial Scotland but lamented the passing of feudal ties; and so his heroes are transitional, fighting men of action superseded by bourgeois figures searching for a clear identity.

Kelso and around

Compact **KELSO**, at the confluence of the Tweed and Teviot, grew up in the shadow of its abbey, once the richest and most powerful in Southern Scotland. The abbey was founded in 1128 during the reign of King David, whose policy of encouraging the monastic orders had little to do with spirituality. The bishops and monks David established here, as well as at Melrose, Jedburgh and Dryburgh, were the frontiersmen of his kingdom, helping to advance his authority in areas of doubtful allegiance. This began a long period of relative stability across the region which enabled its abbeys to flourish, until frequent raids by the English, who savaged Kelso three times in the early sixteenth century, brought ruin.

Such was the extent of the devastation – compounded by the Reformation – that the surviving ruins of **Kelso Abbey** (April–Sept Mon–Sat 9.30am–6pm, Sun 2–6pm; Oct–March Mon–Fri 9.30am–4pm, Sun 2–4pm) are disappointing: a heavy central tower and supporting buttresses represent a scant memorial to the massive Romanesque original that took over eighty years to build. From the abbey, it's a couple of minutes' walk along Bridge Street to **The Square**, a cobbled expanse where the columns and pediments of the **Town Hall** are flanked by a splendid ensemble of three-storey eighteenth- and nineteenth-century pastel buildings. Beyond the general air of elegance, though, there's little to actually see.

Kelso has one other diversion. Leaving The Square along Roxburgh Street, take the alley down to the **Cobby Riverside Walk**, where a brief stroll leads to Floors Castle (see below). En route is the spot where the Teviot meets the Tweed. This junction has long been famous for its salmon fishing, with permits booked years in advance irrespective of the cost: currently around £5000 per rod per week. Permits for **fishing** other, less expensive, reaches of the Tweed and Teviot are available from Tweedside Fishing Tackle, 36 Bridge St (☎01573/225306).

Practicalities

Kelso **bus station** is on Roxburgh Street, a brief walk from The Square, where you'll find the **tourist office** (April–June & Sept Mon–Sat 10am–5pm, Sun 10am–1pm; July & Aug Mon–Sat 9.30am–6.30pm, Sun 10am–6pm; Oct Mon–Sat 10am–4.30pm, Sun 10am–1pm; ☎01573/223464).

The tourist office can provide you with a long list of **B&Bs**, three good choices being the convenient *Wester House*, 155 Roxburgh St (☎01573/224428; ①); *Duncan House*, at Chalkheugh Terrace (☎01573/225682; ①), more basic but with river views; and the mansion house *Abbey Bank*, The Knowes (☎01573/226550; ②). Best of all, however, is *Wooden* (☎01573/224204; ②; closed Oct–April), an ivy-clad country house dating from 1824 half a mile east of Kelso on the B6350. There's also one rather special **hotel**, *Ednam House*, on Bridge Street, near The Square (☎01573/224168; ⑥), a splendid Georgian mansion, whose gardens abut the Tweed. The outstanding *Roxburghe Hotel*, two and a half miles south of Kelso, at Heiton (☎01573/450331; ⑧), serves top-quality **food** at top-quality prices. Otherwise, *The Cottage Garden*, opposite the abbey, is the nicest of the several cafés. For something more substantial try the *Queen's Head*, Bridge Street.

Floors Castle

There's nothing medieval about **Floors Castle** (April–Oct daily 10am–4.30pm; £5), a vast castellated mansion overlooking the Tweed about a mile northwest of Kelso. The bulk of the building was designed by William Adam in the 1720s, and much of the interior demonstrates his uncluttered style, despite the many Victorian modifications. Floors remains privately owned – just ten rooms and a basement are open to the public – the property of the tenth Duke of Roxburghe, whose arrogant-looking features can be seen in a variety of portraits. The duke is a close friend of royalty: it was here, apparently, that Prince Andrew proposed to Sarah Ferguson in 1986. Highlights of the interior include Hendrick Danckerts' splendid panorama of Horse Guards Parade in the entrance hall, paintings by Augustus John and Henri Matisse in the Needle Room, and all sorts of snuff boxes and cigarette cases in the gallery.

Jedburgh and around

Ten miles south of Melrose, **JEDBURGH** nestles in the valley of the Jed Water near its confluence with the Teviot, out on the edge of the wild Cheviot Hills. During the interminable Anglo-Scottish Wars, it was the quintessential frontier town, a heavily gar-

---

JEDBURGH FESTIVALS

Jedburgh is at its busiest during the town's two main festivals. The **Common Riding**, or Callants' Festival, takes place in the first two weeks of July, when the young people of the town – especially the lads – mount up and ride out to check the burgh boundaries, a reminder of more troubled days when Jedburgh was subject to English raids. In similar spirit, early February sees the day-long **Jedburgh Hand Ba'** game, an all-male affair between the "uppies" (those born above Market Place) and "downies" (those born below). In theory the aim of the game is to get hay-stuffed leather balls – originally the heads of English men – from one end of town to the other, but there's more at stake than that: macho reputations are made and lost during the two two-hour games.

---

risoned royal burgh incorporating a mighty castle and abbey. Though the Castle was destroyed by the Scots in 1409, to keep it out of the hands of the English, its memory has been kept alive by local folklore. In 1285, for example, King Alexander III was celebrating his wedding feast in the Great Hall when a ghostly apparition predicted his untimely death and a bloody civil war; sure enough, he died in a hunting accident shortly afterwards and chaos ensued. Today, a stroll round Jedburgh's old town centre is a pleasant way to wile away an hour or two.

The remains of **Jedburgh Abbey** (April–Sept Mon–Sat 9.30am–6.30pm, Sun 2–6.30pm; Oct–March Mon–Sat 9.30am–4.30pm, Sun 2–4.30pm; £3; HS), right in the centre of town, date from the twelfth century. Benefiting from King David's patronage, the monks developed an extravagant complex on a sloping site next to the Jed Water, the monastic buildings standing beneath a huge red sandstone church. All went well until the late thirteenth century, when the power of the Scots kings waned following the death of Alexander III, and a prolonged war ensued. The abbey was subsequently burnt and badly damaged on a number of occasions, the worst being inflicted by the English in 1544. The monastery finally closed in 1560, following the Reformation.

Entry to the site is through the informative **visitor centre**, beside which are the scant remains of the cloister buildings. The **Abbey Church**, however, which remained a parish kirk for another three centuries after the Dissolution, is particularly well preserved. It is entered through the East Processional doorway, an intact example of Romanesque architecture. The splendidly proportioned three-storeyed nave is on your left as you enter, a fine example of the transition from Romanesque to Gothic design, with pointed window arches surmounted by the round-headed arches of the triforium, which, in turn, support the lancet windows of the clerestory. This delicacy of form is not matched at the east end, where the squat central tower is underpinned by the monumental circular pillars and truncated arches of the earlier, twelfth-century choir.

It's a couple of minutes' walk from the abbey round to the tiny triangular market place. Up the hill from here, at the top of Castlegate, **Jedburgh Castle Jail and Museum** (April–Oct Mon–Sat 10am–4.45pm, Sun 1–4pm; £1.25) has displays on prison life throughout the ages. Finally, **Mary, Queen of Scots' House** (April–Oct Mon–Sat 10am–4.30pm; March & Nov Mon–Sat 10.30am–3.45pm, Sun 1–4pm; £2), situated at the opposite end of the town centre, is something of a misnomer as the owner was actually her protector, Sir Thomas Kerr. It's true that Mary stayed here during the assizes of 1566, but she didn't stay long and there's little on show connected with her visit. The attempt to unravel her complex life is cursory, the redeeming features being a copy of Mary's death mask and one of the few surviving portraits of the Earl of Bothwell.

Practicalities

Transport connections around the region are good; Jedburgh's **bus station** is a few yards from the abbey, and the **tourist office** (June & Sept Mon–Sat 9.30am–6pm, Sun noon–4pm; July & Aug Mon–Fri 9am–8.30pm, Sat 9am–7pm, Sun 10am–7pm;

Nov–March Mon–Fri 10am–4.30pm; ☎01835/863435) lies on Murray's Green, just yards from the abbey. For **accommodation**, try *Kenmore Bank Guest House* on Oxnam Road (☎01835/862369; ②), overlooking the Jed Water south of the abbey; the *Glenbank Country House Hotel*, Castlegate (☎01835/862258; ④); or the *Glenfriars Hotel*, The Friars (☎01835/862000; ④), a big old house in its own grounds near the north end of High Street. Alternatively, there are several **B&Bs** among the pleasant and antique row houses of Castlegate, notably *Mrs Poloczek* at no. 48 (☎01835/862504; ③). The *Elliot Park* caravan and **campsite** (☎01835/863393; closed Nov–Feb) is beside the Edinburgh road about a mile north of the centre. Jedburgh has several places to **eat**, including *Simply Scottish*, on the High Street, and the *Castlegate Tea Room and Restaurant*, 26 Castlegate.

Hermitage Castle

Heading south out of Jedburgh on the A68, it's about a mile to the B6357, a narrow byroad that leads over the moors to the hamlet of Bonchester Bridge. From here, the road cuts south through Wauchope Forest and carries on into **Liddesdale**, whose wild beauty is at its most striking between Saughtree and Newcastleton. In between the two, take the turning to **Hermitage Castle** (April–Sept daily 9.30am–6.30pm; Oct–March Sat 9.30am–4.30pm, Sun 2–4.30pm; £1.80; HS), a bleak and forbidding fastness bedevilled by all sorts of horrifying legends. One owner, William Douglas, starved his prisoners to death, whilst another occupant, Lord de Soulis, engaged the help of demons to fortify the castle in defiance of the king, Robert the Bruce. Not entirely trusting his demonic assistants, Soulis also drilled holes into the shoulders of his vassals, the better to yoke them to sledges of building materials. Bruce became so tired of the complaints that he exclaimed, "Boil him if you please, but let me hear no more of him." Bruce's henchmen took him at his word and ambushed the rebellious baron. Convinced, however, that Soulis would be difficult to kill, they bound him with ropes of sifted sand, wrapped him in lead and boiled him slowly.

From the outside, the castle remains an imposing structure, its heavy walls topped by stepped gables and a tidy corbelled parapet. However, the apparent homogeneity is deceptive: certain features were invented during a Victorian restoration, a confusing supplement to the ad hoc alterations that had already transformed the fourteenth-century original. The ruinous interior is a bit of a let-down, but look out for the tight Gothic doorways and gruesome dungeon.

Dumfries and around

With a population of 30,000, bustling **DUMFRIES** crowds the banks of the River Nith a few miles from the Solway Firth, which forms the western border between England and Scotland. Long known as the "Queen of the South", the town flourished as a medieval seaport and trading centre, its success attracting the attention of many English armies. The invaders destroyed much of the settlement in 1448, 1536 and again in 1570, but Dumfries survived to prosper, with its light industries supplying the agricultural hinterland. The town planners of the 1960s badly damaged the town, reducing it to an architectural hotchpotch, the prime example of which is the graceful fifteenth-century lines of Devorgilla Bridge set against cereal-box apartment blocks. Nevertheless, the town makes a convenient base for exploring the Solway coast, and is at least worth a visit for its associations with Robert Burns, who spent the last five years of his life here.

Hemmed in by the river to the north and west, the snout-shaped centre of Dumfries radiates out from the pedestrianized **High Street**, which runs roughly parallel to the Nith. At its northern edge is the **Burns Statue**, a fanciful piece of Victorian frippery featuring the great man holding a posy in one hand, whilst the other clutches at his heart. They haven't forgotten his faithful hound either, who lies curled around his feet.

Heading south down High Street, it's a couple of minutes' walk to **Midsteeple**, the old prison-cum-courthouse, and the narrow alley that leads to the smoky, oak-panelled *Globe Inn*, one of Burns' favourite drinking spots, and still a tavern. Continuing down the street, follow the signs to **Burns' House** (April–Sept Mon–Sat 10am–5pm, Sun 2–5pm; Oct–March Tues–Sat 10am–1pm & 2–5pm; free), a simple sandstone building where the poet died of rheumatic heart disease in 1796. Inside, there's an incidental collection of Burns' memorabilia – manuscripts, letters and the like – and one of the bedroom windows bears his signature, scratched with his diamond ring.

Burns was buried in a simple grave beside **St Michael's Church**, a monstrous eighteenth-century heap just south of his house. Just twenty years later, though, he was dug up and moved across the graveyard to a purpose-built Neoclassical **mausoleum**, whose bright white columns hide a statue of Burns being accosted by the Poetic Muse. The subject matter may be mawkish, but the execution is excellent – notice the hang of the bonnet and the twist of the trousers. All around, in contrasting brownstone, stand the tombstones of the town's bourgeoisie, including many of the poet's friends; a plan indicates exactly where each is interred.

From the mausoleum, saunter back along the Nith and cross Devorgilla Bridge to the tiny **Old Bridge House Museum** (April–Sept Mon–Sat 10am–1pm & 2–5pm, Sun 2–5pm; free) – which contains various rooms restored in Victorian style, including a surgery equipped with a teeth-chattering range of dental gear – and the **Robert Burns Centre** (April–Sept Mon–Sat 10am–8pm, Sun 2–5pm; free), sited in an old water mill, which concentrates on the poet's years in Dumfries. A leaflet on local **walks** is available from the tourist office, one of which covers every Burns connection in the town. On the hill above the Robert Burns Centre, occupying an eighteenth-century windmill, the **Dumfries Museum** (April–Sept Mon–Sat 10am–5pm, Sun 2–5pm; Oct–March Tues–Sat 10am–1pm & 2–5pm; free) traces the region's natural and human history and features a **camera obscura** on its top floor (April–Sept; £1.20). Also worth visiting is the excellent **Gracefield Arts Centre** (May–Oct Tues–Sun; ☎01387/262084), on the Edinburgh road, next to the river. The centre hosts an ever-changing series of exhibitions, runs workshops and painting schools, and has a lively programme of arts activities for kids.

Practicalities

Dumfries **train station**, on the east side of town, is a five-minute walk from the centre. The **bus station** stands at the top of Whitesands, beside the River Nith, on the west edge of the centre. The **tourist office** is also on Whitesands, on the corner of Bank Street (June–Sept daily 9.30am–6pm; April, May & Oct daily 10am–5pm; Nov–March Mon–Sat 10am–4.30pm & 2–5pm; ☎01387/253862). They have information about museums, Burns attractions and town trails, and will book accommodation in the Dumfries area free of charge. If you want to head further afield, Grierson and Graham, 10 Academy St (☎01387/259483), offer **bike rental**, useful for reaching the nearby Solway coast.

There are lots of guest houses and **B&Bs** in the handsome villas clustered round the train station, including *Morton Villa*, 28 Lovers Walk (☎01387/255825; ①) and *Lindean*, 50 Rae St (☎01387/251888; ①), both of which offer clean, comfortable accommodation. For a more distinctive setting try along Kenmure Terrace, a short block of attractive old houses overlooking the Nith from beside the footbridge below the Burns Centre; *The Haven* at no. 1 (☎01387/251281; ①) should be your first port of call. If you're looking for a **hotel**, head for Laurieknowe, a five- to ten-minute walk west from the bus station, where you'll find the *Edenbank Hotel* (☎01387/252759; ④), or, if you fancy splashing out on something with a little more history, try *Comlongon Castle* at Clarencefield, seven miles south of Dumfries on the A75 (☎01387/870283; ⑦). The hotel is in an atmospheric manor house adjacent to the castle proper, and guests get a tour of the castle before dinner.

The cheapest **meals** in town are provided by the popular YMCA café, *Grapevine*, on Castle Street (Mon–Fri 10am–3pm, Sat 10am–2.30pm), behind and beyond the Burns Statue. *Ben Venuto*, at 42 Eastfield Rd, is an Italian and seafood restaurant that welcomes children, while the *Hole in the Wa'* pub, down an alley opposite Woolworth's, on High Street, sells reasonable bar **food**. If you want a **pub** with more atmosphere, however, you should make your way instead to the earthy *Globe Inn*. There's Scottish fare for fans of fish and game at the *Station Hotel*, 49 Lovers Walk, while the *Cairndale Hotel*, on English Street, caters for tourists with their "taste of Burns Country" menu and Sunday night ceilidhs. *Bruno's* fish-and-chip shop, on Balmoral Road, reputedly sells the best chips in the southwest.

Caerlaverock

The remote and lichen-stained **Caerlaverock Castle**, eight miles southeast of Dumfries (April–Sept daily 9.30am–6.30pm; Oct–March Mon–Sat 9.30am–4.30pm, Sun 2–4.30pm; £2.50; HS), is shaped like a dramatic triangle, with its mighty gatehouse at the apex. Close inspection reveals several phases of construction, which reflect Caerlaverock's turbulent past. Time and again, the castle was attacked and slighted, each subsequent rebuilding further modifying the late thirteenth-century original. For instance, the fifteenth-century machicolations of the gatehouse top earlier towers that are themselves studded with wide-mouthed gunports from around 1590. This confusion of styles continues inside, where the gracious Renaissance facade of the Nithsdale Apartments was added by the first earl in 1634. Nithsdale didn't get much value for money: just six years later he was forced to surrender his castle to the Covenanters, who proceeded to wreck the place. It was never inhabited again.

From the castle it's about three miles further east to the **Caerlaverock Wildfowl and Wetlands Centre** (daily 10am–5pm; £3.25; concessions for those arriving by public transport, bicycle or on foot; ☎01387/770200), 1350 acres of protected salt marsh and mud flat edging the Solway Firth. A National Nature Reserve and a Wildfowl and Wetlands Trust Refuge, the centre is equipped with screened approaches that link the main observatory to a score of well-situated bird-watchers' hides. There are bird-watching events, swan feeding and wildlife safaris on most days. The centre is famous for the twelve thousand or so Barnacle Geese which return here each winter. Between May and August, when the geese are away, walkers along a wetlands trail may glimpse the rare natterjack toad.

Both the castle and the centre are reached along the B725; this is the route the Dumfries **bus** takes, usually terminating at the castle but sometimes continuing to the start of the two-mile lane leading off the B725 to the Centre.

Ruthwell

Seven miles east of the Caerlaverock Centre lies the village of **RUTHWELL.** Where the B725 meets the B724, turn down the short, signposted lane to the main attraction, a modest country church. The keys are kept at one of the houses at the foot of the lane; just look for the notice. Inside the church is the **Ruthwell Cross**, an extraordinary early Christian monument possibly dating from as early as the late seventh century, when Galloway was ruled by the Northumbrians. The eighteen-foot-high Cross reveals a striking diversity of influences in its decoration. Written in runic characters running round the edge is the famous Anglo-Saxon poem *The Dream of the Rood*. But it's the biblical carvings on the main face that really catch the eye, notably Mary Magdalene washing the feet of Jesus.

Drumlanrig Castle

Seventeen miles north of Dumfries, the A76 strips along the southern reaches of **Nithsdale**, whose gentle slopes and old forests hide one major attraction, the massive, many-turreted seventeenth-century mansion of **Drumlanrig Castle** (May–Aug daily 10am–4pm; house & grounds £6; grounds only £2.50). It's not in fact a castle at all, but the grandiose stately home of the Duke of Buccleuch and Queensberry. Drumlanrig, which has an imperial, pink-sandstone facade, with cupolas, turrets and towers sur-rounding an interior courtyard, is graced by a charming horseshoe-shaped stairway – a welcome touch of informality to the stateliness of the structure behind.

Inside, a string of luxurious rooms attests to the immense wealth of the family. Among the priceless hoard of antique furnishings and fittings are a trio of famous paintings exhibited in the staircase hall. These are Rembrandt's *Old Woman Reading*, a sensual composition dap-pling the shadow of the subject's hood against her white surplice; Holbein's formal portrait of *Sir Nicholas Carew*; and the *Madonna with the Yarnwinder* by Leonardo da Vinci. Other works are by Breugel, Gossaert and Van Dyck, and there is a host of family portraits by Allan Ramsay and Godfrey Kneller. Also look out for John Ainslie's *Joseph Florence the Chef*, a sharply observed and dynamic portrait much liked by Walter Scott. Apart from the house there are also craft workshops, nature trails, a cycle museum – which rents out mountain bikes – birds of prey flying demonstrations and a teashop. If you're heading here by bus from Dumfries or Ayr, bear in mind it's a one-and-a-half-mile walk from the road to the house.

Sweetheart Abbey

NEW ABBEY, a tidy hamlet eight miles south of Dumfries, is home to the red-sand-stone ruins of **Sweetheart Abbey** (April–Sept daily 9.30am–6.30pm; Oct–March Mon–Wed & Sat 9.30am–4.30pm, Thurs 9.30am–1pm, Sun 2–4.30pm; £1.20; HS). Founded by Cistercians in 1273, Sweetheart takes its name from the obsessive behav-iour of its patron, Devorgilla de Balliol, who carried her husband's embalmed heart around with her for the last sixteen years of her life. The site is dominated by the remains of the **Abbey Church**, a massive structure that abandons the austere simplic-ity of earlier Cistercian foundations. The grand, high-pointed window arches of the nave, set beneath the elaborate clerestory, draw the eye to a mighty central tower with a battlemented parapet and flamboyant corbels. The opulent style reflects the monks' wealth, born of their skill in turning the wastes and swamps of Solway into productive farmland. After seeing the abbey, you can pop into the *Abbey Cottage* tearooms next door for a great cup of coffee and a piece of home-made cake.

There are a couple of **hotels** in the village, the *Criffel Inn* (☎01387/850305; ②), a fine pub with good beer, or the *Abbey Arms* (☎01387/850489; ②), on the main square.

Along the Solway coast

Facing the Irish sea, and edged by tidal marsh and mud bank, much of the **Solway coast** is flat and eerily remote, but there are also some fine rocky bays sheltering beneath wooded hills, most notably at **Rockcliffe** and **Kippford**, about twenty miles west of Dumfries. **Kirkcudbright** and **Gatehouse of Fleet**, once bustling ports, were bypassed by the Victorian train network and so slipped into economic decline, thus preserving their handsome eighteenth- and early nineteenth-century architecture. Both towns are popular with – but not crowded by – tourists, as is **Threave Castle**, a gaunt tower house perched on an river islet just outside **Castle Douglas**.

Within striking distance of the coast are the **Galloway Hills**, whose forested knolls and grassy peaks flank lochs and tumbling burns – classic Southern Upland scenery. Two peninsulas extend south from the western end of the Solway coast: the **Machars**, to the south of the market town of **Newton Stewart**; and the **Rhinns of Galloway**, a hilly, hammer-shaped protusion encompassing the grimy port of **Stranraer**, from where there are regular ferries over to Northern Ireland, and the beguiling resort of **Portpatrick**, the western terminus of the Southern Upland Way. A string of tiny farming villages leads down to the **Mull of Galloway**, the windswept headland at the southwest tip of Scotland.

Castle Douglas and around

The eighteenth-century streets of **CASTLE DOUGLAS**, some eighteen miles southwest of Dumfries, were designed by the town's owner, William Douglas, a local lad who made a fortune trading in the West Indies. Douglas had ambitious plans to turn his town into a prosperous industrial and commercial centre, but, like his scheme to create an extensive Galloway canal system, it didn't quite work. You'll only need to hang around town long enough to get your bearings as the district's two attractions, Threave Garden and Castle, are well outside the centre.

It's about a mile's walk west to **Threave Garden** (daily 9.30am–5.30pm; £4.40; NTS), which can also be reached direct from the A75 – the signposted turning is at the roundabout on the west side of town. The garden features a magnificent spread of flowers and woodland, sixty acres subdivided into over a dozen areas, from the bright, old-fashioned blooms of the Rose Garden to the brilliant banks of rhododendrons in the Woodland Garden and the ranks of primula, astilbe and gentian in the Peat Garden. The **visitor centre** (April to late Oct daily 9.30am–5.30pm) has maps of the garden and the surrounding estate, and a useful restaurant.

To reach **Threave Castle** (April–Sept daily 9am–6.30pm; £1.80; HS), return to the A75 roundabout and cut straight across, down the mile-long country lane which brings you to the start of the footpath to the River Dee. It's a ten-minute walk down to the river where you ring a brass bell for the boat over to the stern-looking stronghold, stuck on a flat and grassy islet. Built for a Black Douglas, Archibald the Grim, in around 1370, the fortress was among the first of its kind, a sturdy, rectangular structure completed shortly after the War of Independence when clan feuding spurred a frenzy of castle-building. The bleak lines of the original structure are, however, partly obscured by a rickety, fifteenth-century curtain wall, thrown up as a desperate – and unsuccessful – attempt to defend the castle against James II. Determined to crush the Black Douglases, the king personally murdered the eighth earl after dinner in Stirling and subsequently appropriated his estate. The Covenanters wrecked the place in the 1640s, but enough remains of the interior to make out its general plan.

Practicalities

The **bus station** is at the west end of the long main drag, King Street; the **tourist office** (April–June, Sept & Oct daily 10am–4.30pm; July & Aug daily 10am–6pm; ☎01556/502611) is at the other end. **Bike rental** is available at Ace Cycles, 11 Church St (☎01556/504542). There is a variety of **accommodation** available, including several **B&Bs** in Castle Douglas itself: try the friendly and welcoming *Craigvar House*, 60 St Andrew St (☎01556/503515; ②), or *Balmaghie House* (☎01556/670234; ②), a huge mansion in its own grounds at Glenlochar, five miles to the northwest, with great home cooking. For considerably more luxury, head thirteen miles south of Castle Douglas to Auchencairn, where the award-winning *Balcary Bay Hotel* (☎01556/640217; ⑦) boasts a stunning location at the water's edge. The pleasant *Lochside* **campsite** is out on the Threave road (☎01556/502949).

Rockcliffe and Kippford

The **Colvend coast** is a six-mile-long, low-key holiday strip, eleven miles southeast of Castle Douglas. In the middle, nestling round a beautiful cove, is **ROCKCLIFFE**, a beguiling little place from where there are some great walks. At low tide you can waddle out across the mud flats to **Rough Island**, a hillocky, twenty-acre bird sanctuary owned by the NTS, though it's out of bounds in May and June when the terns and oystercatchers are nesting. Alternatively, you can stroll up the coast along the "Jubilee Path" a mile or so to the **Mote of Mark**, a Celtic hill fort, and continue a few miles to the village of **KIPPFORD**, once a ship-repair centre, and now a cosy holiday spot strung out along an estuary. There are other walking and cycle tracks around the coast and into nearby Dalbeattie Forest.

Rockcliffe and Kippford have a reasonable range of **accommodation**, but note that reservations are recommended during the summer; try the grand, Victorian *Barons Craig* (☎01556/660225; ⑥; closed Nov–March), on the hill above the bay in Rockcliffe, or the *Anchor Hotel* (☎01556/620205; ③) in Kippford; the *Anchor* serves good bar food. **Camping** is best at *Kippford Caravan Park* (☎01556/620636) or *Sandyhills Leisure Park* (☎01557/870267).

Kirkcudbright

KIRKCUDBRIGHT (pronounced "Kirkcoobrie"), hugging the muddy banks of the Dee ten miles southwest of Castle Douglas, has a quaint harbour and the most beguiling of town centres, a charming medley of simple brick cottages with medieval pends, Georgian villas and Victorian town houses. This is the setting for **MacLellan's Castle** (April–Sept daily 9.30am–6pm; Oct–March Sat 9.30am–4.30pm, Sun 2–4.30pm; £1.50; HS), a sullen pink-flecked hulk towering above the harbourside. Part fortified tower house and part spacious mansion, the castle dates from the late sixteenth century when a degree of law and order permitted the aristocracy to relax its old defensive preoccupations. As a consequence, chimneys have replaced battlements at the wall-heads and windows begin at the ground floor. Keep an eye out for a real curiosity, the "lairds' lug", or peephole, behind the fireplace of the Great Hall, from which Sir Thomas could spy on his guests. The castle was built for Sir Thomas MacLellan, who now lies buried in the neighbouring **Greyfriars Church**, where his tomb is an eccentrically crude attempt at Neoclassicism – it even incorporates parts of someone else's gravestone.

Close by, on the L-shaped High Street, **Broughton House** (April to mid-Oct daily 1–5.30pm; £2.40; NTS) was once the home of Edward Hornel, an important member of the late nineteenth-century Scottish art establishment. Hornel and his buddies – The Glasgow Boys – established a self-regarding artists' colony in Kirkcudbright, and some of their work, Impressionistic in style, is on display here. It's all pretty modest stuff, but Hornel's paintings of Japan, a country he often visited, are bright and cheery, and the house itself a delight. Hornel had the Georgian mansion he bought in 1901 modified to include a studio and a mahogany-panelled gallery decked out with a frieze of the Elgin marbles. He also designed the lovely Japanese garden.

A couple of minutes' walk away is the church-like **Tolbooth**, which once served as court house, prison and town hall. Its clock faces are offset so that they can be viewed down both parts of the High Street. Recently the building has been turned into the **Tolbooth Art Centre** (May & June Mon–Sat 11am–5pm, Sun 2–5pm; July & Aug

Mon–Sat 10am–6pm, Sun 2–5pm; Sept–April Mon–Sat 11am–4pm, Sun 2–5pm; £1.50), featuring more examples of the work of Hornel and his associates, plus a video on the group. Don't miss the nearby **Stewartry Museum** on St Mary Street (same hours; £1.50), which houses an extraordinary collection of local exhibits illuminating the life and times of the Solway Coast.

Practicalities

Buses to Kirkcudbright stop by the harbour, next to the **tourist office** (daily: April–June & Sept–Oct 10am–5pm; July & Aug 9.30am–6pm; ☎01557/330494). The town has several quality **hotels** – the best among them the Georgian *Gladstone House*, 48 High St (☎01557/331734; ③), and the eighteenth-century *Selkirk Arms*, just up the road (☎01557/330402; ⑤). For a convenient **B&B**, try the High Street for *Mrs Durok's* bright, modern house at no. 109A (☎01557/331279; ①); the excellent *Baytree House*, at no. 110, a recently-restored Georgian house (☎01557/330824; ③); or *Mrs Black's*, at 1 Gordon Place, just off the High Street, which is set in an attractive row of whitewashed houses (☎01557/330472; ②). For **camping**, *Silvercraigs Caravan and Camping Site* (☎01557/330123; closed Nov–Easter) is on a bluff overlooking town, at the end of St Mary's Place, five to ten minutes' walk from the centre. Kirkcudbright is light on **restaurants**, though the *Selkirk Arms* serves excellent bar meals. The *Auld Alliance*, 5 Castle St (☎01557/330569), is a superior, if pricey, restaurant offering an imaginative mixture of French and Scottish cuisine.

Gatehouse of Fleet

The quiet streets of **GATEHOUSE OF FLEET**, ten miles east of Kirkcudbright, give no clue that for James Murray, the eighteenth-century laird, this spot was to become the "Glasgow" of the Solway Coast – a centre of the cotton industry whose profits had already made him immeasurably rich. Yorkshire millowners provided the industrial expertise, imported engineers designed aqueducts to improve the water supply, and dispossessed crofters – and their children – yielded the labour. Between 1760 and 1790, Murray achieved much success, but his custom-built town failed to match its better-placed rivals. By 1850 the boom was over and the mills slipped into disrepair. Nowadays, tiny Gatehouse is sustained by tourism and forestry.

It's the country setting that appeals rather than any particular sight, but there are some graceful Georgian houses along High Street, which also has an incongruous, granite clocktower and the **Mill on the Fleet Museum** (March–Oct daily 10am–5.30pm; £2.75), gallantly tracing the history of Gatehouse and Galloway from inside an old bobbin mill. The **tourist office** nearby (daily: March, April & Oct 10am–4.30pm; May, June & Sept 10am–5pm; July & Aug 10am–6pm; ☎01557/814212) sells an excellent leaflet on local **walks**. One of them tracks along Old Military Road, passing through deciduous woodland before circling back near the stark remains of **Cardoness Castle** (April–Sept daily 9.30am–6.30pm; Oct–March Sat 9.30am–4.30pm, Sun 2–4.30pm; £1.80; HS). Perched on a hill, this late fifteenth-century stronghold is a classic example of the fortified tower house, with dense walls and tiny windows.

Accommodation in Gatehouse includes the *Murray Arms Hotel* (☎01557/814207; ⑥), close to the clocktower; and some more affordable and convenient **B&Bs**, such as the *Bay Horse*, 9 Ann St (☎01557/814073; ②). Also worth trying are *High Auchenlarie Farm* (☎01557/814073; ②), six miles off the A75 heading west, and *Holecroft Farm* (☎01557/840250; ①), half a mile further on. In town, the *Murray Arms* offers delicious **meals**, along with advice on local fishing, including permits for guests.

Newton Stewart

To the west of Gatehouse, the A75 skirts the mud flats of Wigtown Bay before cutting up to **NEWTON STEWART**, an unassuming market town beside the River Cree, famous for its salmon and trout fishing. The excellent *Creebridge House Hotel* (☎01671/402121, *creebridge.hotel@daelnet.co.uk*; ⑦), in an old hunting lodge near the main bridge, arranges fishing permits for around £15 per day, can provide personal gillies (guides) for a further £25 daily, and at a pinch they'll even rent you all the tackle. The season runs from March to mid-October. The hotel serves great bar food too – try the fish or the home-made pies.

The Newton Stewart **tourist office** (daily: April & Oct 10am–4.30pm; May, June & Sept 10am–5pm; July & Aug 10am–6pm; ☎01671/402431), just off the main street opposite the **bus station**, has bags of helpful literature. In town, there's good **accommodation** at *Kilwarlin*, 4 Corvisel Rd (☎01671/403047; ①; closed Nov–March) and *Stables Guest House*, on Corsbie Rd (☎01671/402157; ②). Further afield, *Auchenleck Farm* is an excellent place to stay in Glen Trool Forest (☎01671/402035; ③). The convenient *Minnigaff* **youth hostel** can be found in an old schoolhouse, 650yd from the main street, near the bridge (☎01671/402211; closed Oct–March). For **camping**, *Caldons Campsite* (☎01671/402420; closed Nov–March) is near the car park at the western tip of Loch Trool.

The Machars

The **Machars**, the name given to the peninsula of rolling farmland and open landscapes south of Newton Stewart, is a neglected part of the coastline, with a somewhat disconsolate air. From Newton Stewart it's eighteen miles south to **WHITHORN**, with its sloping, airy high street of pastel-painted cottages. This one-horse town occupies an important place in

---

GALLOWAY FOREST PARK AND GLEN TROOL

With its plentiful supply of accommodation and good bus connections along the A75, Newton Stewart has also become a popular base for hikers and cyclists heading for the nearby **Galloway Hills**, most of which are enclosed within **Galloway Forest Park**. Many hikers aim for the park's **Glen Trool** by following the A714 north for about ten miles to Bargrennan, where a narrow lane twists the five miles over to the glen's Loch Trool. From here, there's a choice of magnificent **hiking** and **cycling** trails, as well as lesser tracks laid out by the forestry commission. Several longer routes curve round the grassy peaks and icy lochs of the Awful Hand and Dungeon ranges, whilst another includes part of the Southern Upland Way, which threads through the Minnigaff Hills to Clatteringshaws Loch (see below).

The twenty-mile stretch from Newton Stewart to New Galloway, known as the **Queen's Way**, cuts through the southern periphery of Galloway Forest Park, a landscape of glassy lochs, wooded hills and bare, rounded peaks. You'll pass all sorts of **hiking trails**, some the gentlest of strolls, others long-distance treks. For a short walk, stop at the *Talnotry Campsite*, about seven miles from Newton Stewart, where the forestry commission has laid out three trails, each of which delves into the pine forests beside the road, crossing gorges and burns. The campsite itself (☎01671/402420; closed Nov–March) occupies an attractive spot among the wooded hills of the park. A few miles further on is **Clatteringshaws Loch**, a reservoir surrounded by pine forest, with a fourteen-mile footpath running right round. If you're serious about doing some hiking, be sure to buy the Ordnance Survey maps and *The Galloway Hills: A Walker's Paradise* by George Brittain.

Scottish history, for it was here in 397 AD that **St Ninian** founded the first Christian church north of Hadrian's Wall. Ninian daubed his tiny building in white plaster and called it **Candida Casa**, translated as "Hwiterne" (White House), hence Whithorn, by his Pictish neighbours. Ninian's life is shrouded in mystery, but he does seem to have been raised in Galloway and was a key figure in the Christianization of his country. Indeed, his tomb became a popular place of pilgrimage and, in the twelfth century, a priory was built to service the shrine. For generations the rich and the royal made the trek here, but this ended with the Reformation.

Halfway down the main street, the **Whithorn Dig** (April–Oct daily 10.30am–5pm; £2.70) exploits these ecclesiastical connections. A video gives background details and a handful of archeological finds serve as an introduction for a stroll round the dig. Be sure to take up the complimentary guide service – you won't make much sense of the complex sequence of ruins without one. Beyond the dig the meagre remains of the priory fail to inspire, unlike the adjacent museum, whose impressive assortment of early Christian memorials includes a series of standing crosses and headstones, the earliest being the Latinus Stone of 450 AD. For **lunch**, the *Diner*, near the Dig, offers basic meals.

The pilgrims who crossed the Solway to visit St Ninian's shrine landed at the **ISLE OF WHITHORN**, four miles south of Whithorn. Not an island at all, it's an antique and tiny seaport hiding the minuscule remains of the thirteenth-century **St Ninian's Chapel**. If you're looking for somewhere to **stay**, try the unassuming *Steam Packet Inn* (☎01988/500334; ②), right on the quay; this is also a good place to eat.

The **pilgrims way** is a marked, one-hundred-mile walk – or cycle ride – from Isle of Whithorn to Glenluce, covering all the principal religious sites in the area. A leaflet is available from tourist information offices.

Stranraer

No one could say **STRANRAER** was beautiful. However, if you're heading to (or coming from) **Northern Ireland** you may well have to pass through, and at least nearly everything's convenient. The **train station** is close to the Stena Sealink **ferry terminal** on the Ross Pier, where boats depart for Larne; a couple of minutes' walk away, on Port Rodie, is the town's **bus station**; and nearby, further round the bay, SeaCat **catamaran** services leave from the West Pier to Belfast. Less handy, however, is the P&O ferry to Larne, which leaves from the port of Cairnryan, some five miles north.

While you're waiting for a Stranraer ferry, a walk along the dishevelled main street, variously Charlotte, George and High streets, takes in the town's one specific attraction, a medieval tower which is all that remains of the **Castle of St John** (April–Sept Mon–Sat 10am–1pm & 2–5pm; £1). Inside, an exhibition traces the history of the castle down to its use as a police station and prison in the nineteenth century. The old exercise yard is on the roof.

The **tourist office**, 28 Harbour St (April–June, Oct & Nov Mon–Sat 9.30am–5.30pm, Sun 10am–4pm; July–Sept daily 9.30am–6pm; Dec–March Mon–Sat 10am–4pm; ☎01776/702595), can arrange **accommodation**; alternatively, you could try the excellent family-run *Old Manse,* on Lewis Street (☎01776/702135; ①), or *Fernlea*, on the same street (☎01776/703037; ①). For **camping**, *Aird Donald Camp and Caravan Park* (☎01776/702025) is ten minutes' walk east of the town centre along London Road. Stranraer has plenty of basic snack bars, but it's well worth paying a little extra to enjoy a **meal** at the *Apéritif,* just up the hill from the bus station along Bellevilla Road or at the *Ark House*, on Church Street.

Portpatrick to the Mull

Perched on the west shore of the Rhinns, the pastel houses of **PORTPATRICK** spread over the craggy coast above the slender harbour. Until the mid-nineteenth century, when sailing ships were replaced by steamboats, this was the main embarkation point for Northern Ireland, with coal, cotton and British troops heading in one direction, Ulster cattle and linen in the other. Nowadays, Portpatrick is a quiet, comely resort enjoyed for its rugged scenery and coastal hikes.

Portpatrick has several good **hotels** and **guest houses**, the best of which are the *Portpatrick Hotel* (☎01776/810333; ⑧), a grand turreted Edwardian mansion on the hill above the harbour, the *Mount Stewart Hotel* (☎01776/810291; ②) for great views, the comfortable *Carlton Guest House*, beside the harbour on South Crescent (☎01776/810253; ①) or, close by, the bright, white *Knowe Guest House* (☎01776/810441; ②). For a **meal** and a **drink**, head on down to the *Crown* pub, on the seafront, or the *Auld Acquaintance* coffee shop nearby.

The **Rhinns of Galloway**, which extend about twenty miles farther south from Portpatrick, consist of gorse-covered hills and pastureland crossed by narrow country lanes and dotted with farming hamlets. On the sharper, rockier western coastline, near the village of Port Logan, you'll find the **Logan Botanic Garden** (March–Oct daily 10am–6pm; £3), an outpost of Edinburgh's Royal Botanic Garden. There are three main areas, a peat garden, a woodland and a walled garden noted for its tree ferns and cabbage palms. It's a further twelve miles south to the **Mull of Galloway**, a bleak and precipitous headland where wheeling birds and whistling winds circle a bright whitewashed lighthouse. On clear days you can see over to Cumbria and Ireland.

The Ayrshire coast

Fifty miles from top to bottom, the coast of south Ayrshire north from Stranraer to Ayr is easily seen from the A77 coastal road, which leaves Stranraer to trim thirty miles of low, rocky shore before reaching **Girvan**, a low-key seaside resort where boats depart for **Ailsa Craig**, out in the Firth of Clyde. Back on shore, the A77 presses on through the village of Turnberry, home to one of the world's most famous golf courses, where the A719 branches off for eighteenth-century **Culzean Castle** (pronounced "Cullane"). From the castle, it's twelve miles further to **Ayr**, the largest town on the coast, with a population of around fifty thousand. Ayr is both a commercial centre and holiday resort, its beach and prestigious racecourse attracting hundreds of Scotland's city dwellers. A couple of miles south, the suburb of **Alloway** is notable for a clutch of Burns-related attractions. An alternative route from Culzean is to keep to the main road, passing the medieval remains of **Crossraguel Abbey**.

Girvan and Ailsa Craig

Set beneath a ridge of grassy hills, **GIRVAN** is at its prettiest round the harbour, a narrow slit beside the mouth of the Girvan Water. Here, overlooked by old stone houses, the fishing fleet sets about its business, and, for a moment, it's possible to ignore the amusement arcades and seaside tat elsewhere in town. From late May to September boats leave the harbour for the ten-mile excursion west to the **Ailsa Craig**, "Fairy Rock" in Gaelic – though the island looks more like an enormous muffin than a place of enchantment. With its jagged cliffs and summit, Ailsa Craig (1114ft) is a privately owned bird sanctuary that's home to thousands of gannets. The best time to make the trip is at the end of May and in June, when the fledglings are trying to fly. **Cruises** are operated by Mark McCrindle (1–2 daily; £10 for 6hr, £9 for 4hr; ☎01465/713219), the only operator with permission to land on the island – which you can do, weather permitting.

There are regular **bus** services from Stranraer and Ayr to Girvan, which is also on the Glasgow–Stranraer **train** line. The **tourist office**, on Bridge Street, just up from the harbour (Easter–May Mon–Fri 11am–1pm & 2–5pm, Sat & Sun 11am–5pm; June daily 11am–5pm; July & Aug daily 10am–7pm; Sept daily 11am–5pm; ☎01465/714950), has a full list of accommodation, or try among the attractive Victorian villas along the seafront, such as the neat and tidy *Thistleneuk Guest House*, 19 Louisa Drive (☎01465/712137; ②).

Culzean Castle

Twelve miles southwest of Ayr on the A719, the impressive **Culzean Castle** and its surrounding **country park** (castle: April–Oct daily 10.30am–5pm; grounds: Nov–March 9am–sunset; castle & grounds £7; grounds only £5; NTS), whose 565 acres spread out along the seashore, are Ayrshire's premier tourist attractions. At the **visitor centre** in the modernized Home Farm buildings, you can pick up free maps to help you get your bearings; from here, it's a few minutes' walk over to the castle, whose towers and turrets rise high above the sea cliffs. Nothing remains of the original fifteenth-century structure, since, in 1777, David Kennedy, the tenth Earl of Cassillis, commissioned Robert Adam to remodel the family home. The work took fifteen years to complete, and, although the exterior, with its arrow slits and battlements, preserves a medieval aspect, the interior exemplifies the harmonious Classical designs Adam loved.

On the ground floor, the subtle greens of the old eating room are enlivened by vineleaf-and-grape plasterwork along the cornice, a motif continued in the adjacent dining room. Nearby, there's the brilliantly conceived oval staircase, where tiers of Corinthian and Ionic columns lead up to a huge cupola allowing light to stream down. All this is a fitting prologue to the impressive circular saloon, whose symmetrical flourishes deliberately contrast with the natural land- and seascapes on view through the windows. Further on, a small exhibition celebrates President **Eisenhower**'s military and civilian career as well as his association with Culzean; Ike stayed here on several occasions and the castle's top floor was given to him by the old owners, the Kennedys, for his lifetime.

Crossraguel Abbey

The substantial remains of **Crossraguel Abbey** (April–Sept Mon–Sat 9.30am–6.30pm; Sun 2–6.30pm; £1.80; HS), a further three miles along the main road, are mostly overlooked – something of a surprise considering their singularity. Founded as a Cluniac monastery in the thirteenth century, Crossraguel benefited from royal patronage with its abbots holding land "for ever in free regality". The abbots took the temporal side of their work seriously and became powerful local lords. By the early sixteenth century, they had constructed an extensive private compound complete with a massive gatehouse and sturdy tower house. Both still stand – behind what remains of the abbey church – recalling the corruption of the monastic ideal that sparked off the Reformation. Behind the gatehouse, you'll also spot the well-preserved dovecot, a funnel-shaped affair that was a crucial part of the abbey's economy; the monks not only ate the doves but also relied on them for eggs.

Ayr and around

AYR was an important seaport and trading centre for many centuries, and rivalled Glasgow in size and significance right up until the late seventeenth century. With the relative decline of its seaborne trade, Ayr developed as a market town, praised by

Robert Burns, who was born in the neighbouring village of **Alloway** (see p.855), for its "honest men and bonny lasses". In the nineteenth century, Ayr became a popular resort for middle-class Victorians, with a new town of wide streets and boulevards built behind the long, sandy beach immediately southwest of the old town.

The cramped, sometimes seedy streets and alleys of Ayr's **Old Town** occupy a wedge of land between Sandgate and Alloway Place in the west, and the south bank of the treacly River Ayr to the east. Almost all the medieval buildings were knocked down by the Victorians, but the **Auld Brig**, with its cobbles and sturdy breakwaters, has survived from the thirteenth century. The bridge was saved by Robert Burns, or rather his poem *Twa Brigs*, which made it too famous to demolish; an international appeal raised the capital necessary for its refurbishment in 1907.

The Auld Brig connects with High Street where you should turn left and subsequently left again down Kirk Port, a narrow lane leading to the **Auld Kirk** (July & Aug Tues & Thurs only; erratic hours, call ☎01292/262580). At the lych gate, a plan of the graveyard shows where some of Burns' friends are buried. Notice also the mort-safe (heavy grating) on the wall of the lych gate. Placed over newly dug graves, these mort-safes were a sort of early nineteenth-century corpse security system meant to deter body snatchers at a time when dead bodies were in great demand by medical schools.

Extending southwest of Sandgate to the Esplanade and the **beach**, the wide, gridiron streets of the Victorian **New Town** contrast with the crowded lanes of old Ayr. It was the opening of the Glasgow to Ayr railway line in 1840 that brought the first major influx of holidaymakers and Ayr remains a busy resort today, with many visitors heading for the plethora of trim guest houses concentrated around **Wellington Square**, whose terraces flank the impressive County Buildings dating from 1820. The new town extends north towards the river, spreading over what remains of the walls of a fort, built by Cromwell. It's here, off Bruce Crescent, that you'll find St John's Tower, all that's left of the parish church used by Cromwell as his armoury.

Practicalities

Ayr's **bus station** is at the foot of Sandgate, a ten-minute walk west of both the **train station** and the **tourist office**, on Burns Statue Square (June & Sept to early Oct Mon–Sat 9.15am–6pm, Sun 10am–6pm; July & Aug Mon–Sat 9.15am–7pm, Sun 10am–7pm; Oct–May Mon–Sat 9.15am–5pm; ☎01292/288688).

For a place to stay, head straight for the cluster of **hotels** and **guest houses** around Wellington Square, a couple of minutes' walk south of Sandgate along Alloway Place. In particular, try Queen's Terrace where, among others, there's the *Dargil Guest House* at no. 7 (☎01292/261955; ①), *Queens* at no. 10 (☎01292/265618; ②) and the *Daviot* at no. 12 (☎01292/269678; ②). Ayr's **youth hostel**, 5 Craigweil Rd (☎01292/262322; closed Nov–Feb), occupies a grand neo-Gothic mansion behind the beach, a twenty-minute signposted walk south of the town centre. There is also the *Heads of Ayr Campsite* (☎01292/442269), five miles south of the town along the A719.

The best **restaurant** in Ayr is *Fouters*, 2A Academy St, in a cellar off Sandgate (☎01292/261391); steaks and seafood are its specialities. Another good choice, using local produce, is the *Boathouse*, 4 South Harbour St, beside the river at the foot of Fort Street. For filling and more reasonably priced meals, try *Littlejohn's*, 231 High St, or *Petit Pierre*, 4 River Terrace (☎01292/282087). The most enjoyable **pub** in town is the *Tam o' Shanter*, on the High Street, whose ancient walls sport quotes from Robert Burns. There are also several lively bars on and around Burns Statue Square, including *O'Briens*, which frequently showcases Irish folk bands.

Alloway

There's little beyond Burnsiana in the small village of **ALLOWAY**, a couple of miles south of Ayr. The first port of call in Alloway is the whitewashed **Burns Cottage and**

ROBERT BURNS

The first of seven children, **Robert Burns**, the national poet of Scotland, was born in Alloway on January 25, 1759. His father, William, was employed as a gardener until 1766, when he became a tenant farmer at Mount Oliphant, near Alloway, moving to Lochlie farm, Tarbolton, eleven years later. A series of bad harvests and the demands of the landlord's estate manager bankrupted the family, and William died almost penniless in 1784. These events had a profound effect on Robert, leaving him with an antipathy towards political authority and a hatred of the landowning classes.

With the death of his father, Robert became head of the family and they moved again, this time to a farm at Mossgiel, near Mauchline. Burns had already begun writing poetry and prose at Lochlie, recording incidental thoughts in his *First Commonplace Book*, but it was here at Mossgiel that he began to write in earnest, and his first volume, *Poems Chiefly in the Scottish Dialect*, was published in Kilmarnock in 1786. The book proved immensely popular, celebrated by ordinary Scots and Edinburgh literati alike, with the satirical trilogy *Holy Willie's Prayer*, *The Holy Fair* and *Address to the Deil* attracting particular attention. The object of Burns' poetic scorn was the Kirk, whose ministers had obliged him to appear in church to be publicly condemned for fornication – a commonplace punishment in those days.

Burns spent the winter of 1786–87 in the capital, lionized by the literary establishment. Despite his success, however, he felt trapped, unable to make enough money from writing to leave farming. He was also in a political snare, fraternizing with the elite, but with radical views and pseudo-Jacobite nationalism which constantly landed him in trouble. His frequent recourse was to play the part of the unlettered ploughman-poet, the noble savage who might be excused his impetuous outbursts and hectic womanizing.

Burns had, however, made useful contacts in Edinburgh and as a consequence was recruited to collect, write and rearrange two volumes of songs set to traditional Scottish tunes. These volumes, James Johnson's *Scots Musical Museum* and George Thomson's *Select Scottish Airs*, contain the bulk of his songwriting, and it's on them that Burns' international reputation rests with works like *Auld Lang Syne*, *Scots Wha Hae*, *Coming through the Rye* and *Green Grow the Rushes, O*. At this time too, he produced two excellent poems: *Tam o' Shanter* and a republican tract, *A Man's a Man for a' that*, which was used as an unofficial national anthem for the 1999 opening of the Scottish Parliament.

In 1788, Burns married Jean Armour and moved to Ellisland Farm, near Dumfries. The following year, he was appointed excise officer, moving to Dumfries in 1791. Burns' years of comfort were short-lived, however. His years of labour on the farm, allied to a rheumatic fever, damaged his heart, and he died in Dumfries on July 21, 1796, aged 37.

Burns' work, inspired by a romantic nationalism and tinged with a wry wit, has made him a potent symbol of "Scottishness". Ignoring the Anglophile preferences of the Edinburgh elite, he wrote in Scots vernacular about the country he loved, an exuberant celebration that filled a need in a nation culturally colonized by England. Today Burns Clubs and Scottish people all over the world mark every anniversary of the poet's birthday with the Burns' Supper, complete with Scottish totems – haggis, piper and whisky bottle.

Museum (April–Oct daily 9am–6pm; Nov–March Mon–Sat 10am–4pm, Sun noon–4pm; £1.70), the poet's birthplace, a dark and dank, long thatched cottage where animals and people lived under the same roof. The two-room museum boasts all sorts of memorabilia – the family Bible, letters and manuscripts – plus a potted history of his life.

The modern, faceless **Tam o' Shanter Experience** (daily: April–Oct 9am–6pm; Nov–March 9am–5pm; £2.80 for each video) belies a slightly more interesting interior. Two audio-visual presentations show the life of Burns and a dramatic presentation of *Tam o' Shanter*. It also has a souvenir shop selling a good selection of books about, and by, Burns. Across the road from here are the plain, roofless ruins of **Alloway Church**, where Robert's father William is buried. Burns set much of *Tam o' Shanter* here. Tam, having got drunk in Ayr, passes "By Alloway's auld haunted kirk" and stumbles across a witches' dance, from which he's forced to fly for his life over the **Brig o' Doon**, a hump-backed bridge which still curves gracefully over the river below the **Burns Monument** (April–Oct, same hours & ticket as Cottage), a striking Neoclassical temple in a small carefully manicured garden.

travel details

Trains

Ayr to: Glasgow (approx. every 30min; 50min); Stranraer (5–7 daily; 1hr 20min).

Dumfries to: Carlisle (5–15 daily; 40min); Glasgow (2–7 daily; 1hr 40min).

Edinburgh to: North Berwick (hourly; 30min).

Glasgow to: Ardrossan Harbour (5 daily; 50min); Ayr (every 30min; 50min); Carlisle (2–7 daily; 2hr 15min); Dumfries (2–7 daily; 1hr 40min); Stranraer (3 daily; 2hr 20min).

Stranraer to: Ayr (5 daily; 1hr 20min); Glasgow (3–5 daily; 2hr).

Buses

Ayr to: Castle Douglas (Mon–Sat 2 daily; 2hr); Culzean Castle (hourly; 30min); Girvan (every 30min; 1hr); Glasgow (hourly until 5.30pm; 1hr); Largs (hourly; 1hr 10min); Stranraer (10 daily; 2hr).

Dumfries to: Caerlaverock (Mon–Sat 5 daily; 40min); Carlisle (hourly; 50min); Castle Douglas (2–4 daily; 45min); Edinburgh (2 daily; 2hr 20min); Gatehouse of Fleet (2 daily; 1hr); Glasgow (4 daily; 2hr); Kirkcudbright (2 daily; 1hr 10min); Newton Stewart (2 daily; 1hr 20min); Rockcliffe (2 daily; 1hr 10min); Stranraer (2 daily; 2hr).

Edinburgh to: Carlisle (3–5 daily; 3hr 30min); Galashiels (hourly; 1hr 30min); Haddington (hourly; 1hr); Jedburgh (4–6 daily; 2hr); Melrose (3–9 daily; 2hr 15min); North Berwick (every 30min; 1hr 20min); Peebles (hourly; 1hr).

Galashiels to: Berwick-upon-Tweed (8–11 daily; 1hr 40min); Carlisle (6–7 daily; 2hr); Hawick (9–10 daily; 40min); Selkirk (every 30min; 20min).

Haddington to: North Berwick (Mon–Sat 10 daily, Sun 4 daily; 45min).

Jedburgh to: Hawick (hourly; 40min); Kelso (3–6 daily; 30min).

Melrose to: Galashiels (hourly; 15min); Hawick (Wed & Fri 3 daily, Sat 2 daily; 40min); Jedburgh (hourly; 30min); Kelso (8 daily; 40min); Peebles (7 daily; 1hr 10min); Selkirk (Mon–Sat hourly, Sun 4 daily; 40min).

Newton Stewart to: Ayr (2–5 daily; 2hr 15min); Girvan (2–5 daily;1hr 20min); Glen Trool (2–5 daily; 30min); Isle of Whithorn (3–6 daily; 1hr); Stranraer (2–9 daily; 40min); Whithorn (3–8 daily; 50min).

Stranraer to: Newton Stewart (2–9 daily; 40min); Port Logan (1–2 daily; 40min); Portpatrick (5 daily; 30min).

Ferries

To **Arran**: Ardrossan–Brodick (Caledonian MacBrayne ferry: up to 5 daily, 1hr).

To **Belfast**: Stranraer–Belfast (Stena Sealink hydrofoil: 5 daily, 1hr 45min; SeaCat: 5 daily, 1hr 30min).

To **Larne**: Cairnryan–Larne (P&O jetliner: 6 daily, 1hr; P&O ferry: 3 daily, 2hr 15min).

CHAPTER TWENTY

GLASGOW
AND THE CLYDE

R ejuvenated, upbeat **GLASGOW**, Scotland's largest city, has not enjoyed the best of reputations. Once an industrial giant set on the banks of the mighty River Clyde, today it can initially seem a grey and depressing place, with the M8 motorway screeching through the centre and crumbling slums on its outskirts. However, Glasgow's remarkable overhaul as a dynamic cultural centre has firmly established the city as an important tourist destination, with a buzz and sophistication which sets it apart from Edinburgh's stuffier image.

Glasgow has some of the best-financed and most imaginative museums and galleries in Britain – among them the showcase **Burrell Collection** of art and antiquities – and nearly all of them are free. There's also a robust social scene and nightlife that is remarkably diverse, though somewhat restricted by the Scottish licensing laws. Glasgow's **architecture** is some of the most striking in the nation, from the restored eighteenth-century warehouses of the **Merchant City** to the hulking Victorian prosperity of George Square. Most distinctive of all is the work of local luminary Charles Rennie Mackintosh, whose elegantly streamlined Art Nouveau designs appear all over the city, reaching their apotheosis in the **School of Art**, and newly showcased in the Lighthouse building.

Despite all the hype, however, Glasgow's gentrification has passed by deprived inner-city areas such as the **East End**, home of the **Barras market** and some staunchly change-resistant pubs. This area, along with isolated housing schemes such as Castlemilk and Easterhouse, needs more than a facelift to resolve its complex social and economic problems. These parts of Glasgow have historically been the breeding ground for the city's much-lauded **socialism**, and working people's culture is celebrated in such attractions as the **People's Palace**, one of Britain's most celebrated social history museums, founded in 1898 to extol ordinary lives and achievements, and the **Citizens' Theatre**, formed in 1942 by playwright James Bridie, where the innovative productions still cost next to nothing to see. In addition, Glasgow seems to sustain a remarkable number of cultural events – particularly music festivals – by tapping into the enthusiasm and commitment of its residents.

Quite apart from its own attractions, Glasgow also makes an excellent base from which to explore the **Clyde Valley and coast**, made easy by the region's reliable rail service. **Paisley**, where the distinctive cloth pattern gained its name, is the most interesting of Glasgow's satellite towns to the west, while of the small communities in the Clyde Valley to the southeast, the importance of the remarkable eighteenth-century **New Lanark** mills and workers' village has recently been recognized by its nomination as a World Heritage Site. Nearby, the birthplace of the explorer David Livingstone at **Blantyre** and the impressive red-sandstone citadel of **Bothwell Castle** offer unexpected glimpses of the valley's varied history.

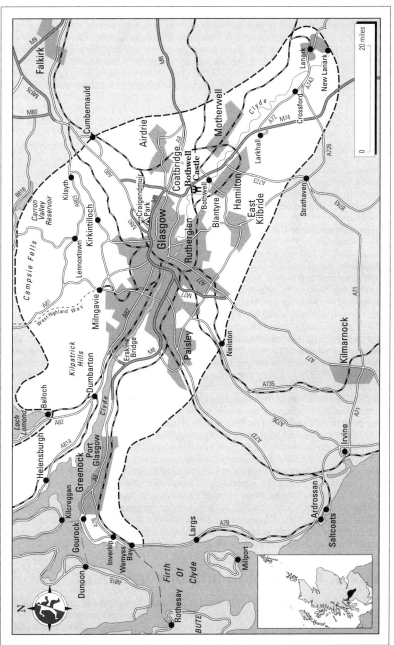

Some history

Glasgow's earliest history, like so much else in this surprisingly romantic city, is obscured in a swirl of myth. The city's name is said to derive from the Celtic *Glas-cu*, which loosely translates as "the dear, green place" – a tag that the tourist board are keen to exploit as an antidote to the sooty images of popular imagination. It is generally agreed that the first settlers arrived in the sixth century to join Christian missionary **Kentigern** – later to become St Mungo – in his newly founded monastery on the banks of the tiny Molendinar Burn.

William the Lionheart gave the town an official charter in 1175, after which it continued to grow in importance, peaking in the mid-fifteenth century when the **University** was founded on Kentigern's site – the second in Scotland after St Andrew's. This led to the establishment of an archbishopric in 1492 and, due to its situation on a large, navigable river, Glasgow soon expanded into a major **industrial port**. The first cargo of tobacco from Virginia off-loaded in Glasgow in 1674, and the 1707 Act of Union between Scotland and England – despite demonstrations against it in Glasgow – led to a boom in trade with the colonies which continued until American independence. Following the **Industrial Revolution**, coal from the abundant seams of Lanarkshire fuelled the ironworks all around the Clyde, worked by the cheap hands of the Highlanders and, later, those fleeing the Irish potato famine of the 1840s.

The Victorian age transformed Glasgow beyond recognition. The population boomed from 77,000 in 1801 to nearly 800,000 at the end of the century, and new tenement blocks swept into the suburbs in an attempt to cope with the choking influxes of people. Two vast and stately **International Exhibitions** were held in 1888 and 1901 to showcase the city and its industries, necessitating the construction of huge civic monoliths such as the Kelvingrove Art Gallery and the Council Chambers in George Square. At this time Glasgow became known as the **"Second City of the Empire"** – a curious epithet for a place that today rarely acknowledges second place in anything.

By the turn of the **twentieth century**, Glasgow's industries had been honed into one massive shipbuilding culture. Everything from tugboats to transatlantic liners was fashioned out of sheet metal in the yards that straddled the Clyde. In the harsh economic climate of the 1930s, however, unemployment spiralled, and Glasgow could do little to counter its popular image as a city dominated by inebriate violence and, having absorbed vast numbers of Irish emigrants, sectarian tensions. The **Gorbals** area in particular became notorious as one of the worst slums in Europe. The city's image has never been helped by the depth of animosity between its two great rival football teams: the Catholic **Celtic** and Protestant **Rangers**, whose warring armies of fans used to clash with monotonous regularity. Nowadays, the "Old Firm" battles continue with the same passion on the field, but without the subsequent post-match violence.

The depressed postwar decades saw the steady decline of almost all of Glasgow's heavy industry, including the iconic shipbuilding, with little arriving to replace it. The city's revival instead came from an unlikely source. A tourist promotion campaign began in the Eighties, snowballing towards the year-long party as **European City of Culture** in 1990. In 1999, Glasgow beat off competition from Edinburgh and Liverpool to become **City of Architecture and Design**, showing off the city's rich architectural heritage and highlighting the role of design in everyday modern living.

Arrival, information and city transport

Glasgow's **airport** (☎0141/887 1111) is out at Abbotsinch, eight miles southwest of the city. To get into town, take one of the frequent Citylink or Airport Express **buses** (both £2.70) from stop 2, both of which run to Buchanan Street **bus station** (☎0141/332

7133), three blocks north of George Square. The main entrance to **Glasgow Central** railway station, the arrival point for **trains** from anywhere south of the city, is on Gordon Street. It's a ten-minute walk from here to **Queen Street** station, at the corner of George Square, for trains to Edinburgh and the north – or take the **shuttle bus** (50p), which runs every ten minutes between the two stations. All buses arrive at Buchanan Street station, except those run by Greater Glasgow and Kelvin Buses to local destinations, which terminate in depots around the city.

The city's excellent **tourist office**, at 11 George Square (May Mon–Sat 9am–6pm, Sun 10am–6pm; June & Sept Mon–Sat 9am–7pm, Sun 10am–6pm; July & Aug Mon–Sat 9am–8pm, Sun 10am–6pm; Oct–April Mon–Sat 9am–6pm; ☎0141/204 4400), can book accommodation (£2 fee), car **rental** and theatre tickets, and sells travel passes. Ask for the free *Guide to Getting Around Glasgow*, which contains an excellent fold-out map of the city centre and West End.

The best way to get around this sprawling city is to use the **Underground** (Mon–Sat 6.30am–10.30pm, Sun 11am–5.30pm), affectionately known as the "Clockwork Orange" – there's just one circular route and the trains are a garish bright orange. Stations are marked with a large "U". There's a flat fare of 80p, or you can buy a **day ticket** for £2.50; a **multi-journey ticket** gives ten journeys for £5.40.

If you're travelling beyond the city centre or the West End, you may need to use the train and buses. There's no easy guide to using the privatized local **bus** network other than picking up individual timetables at the **Strathclyde Travel Centre** (Mon–Sat 8.30am–5.30pm; ☎0141/332 7133), above St Enoch Underground station, though you could try calling First Bus (☎0141/636 3195), the operating company for most local buses. Information on relevant services is given at some bus stops.

The suburban **train** network is swift and convenient. Suburbs south of the Clyde are connected to Glasgow Central mainline station, while trains from Queen Street head into the northeast. The grim but functional **cross-city line**, which runs beneath Argyle Street (and includes a low-level stop below Central station), connects northwestern destinations with southeastern districts as far out as Lanark.

A number of **travel passes** are available from the tourist office of Strathclyde Travel Centre (see above). The Roundabout Glasgow Ticket (£3.50) gives unlimited travel for a day on the Underground and rail network from Milngavie in the north to Motherwell in the south. You can also get a Day Tripper Ticket (one adult and two children £7.50; two adults and four children £13), although you'd need to spend a very busy day sightseeing to make it worthwhile. If you're in the city for at least a week, it's worth investing in a weekly Zonecard, which covers all public transport networks. A two-zone card (£11) gets you from Partick in the west to Rutherglen in the east, and as far as the Burrell Collection in the south; a Zonecard giving you access to all zones within Greater Glasgow is only £14.40. **Taxis** run all day and night, and are very reasonable.

Accommodation

There's a good range of **accommodation** in Glasgow, from an excellent youth hostel in the leafy West End through to some top international hotels in the city centre. Most of the rooms are in the city centre, the West End or down in the southern suburb of Queen's Park. Glasgow's speciality is its profusion of converted Victorian **town houses** in the middle of town, many of which are now privately run B&Bs, offering excellent value for money. In general, prices are significantly lower than in Edinburgh, and given that many hotels are business-oriented, you can often negotiate good deals at weekends.

ACCOMMODATION PRICE CODES

Throughout this guide, hotel and B&B accommodation is priced on a scale of ① to ⑨, the number indicating the **lowest price** you could expect to pay per night in that establishment for a **double room** in high season. The prices indicated by the codes are as follows:

① under £40	④ £60–70	⑦ £110–150
② £40–50	⑤ £70–90	⑧ £150–200
③ £50–60	⑥ £90–110	⑨ over £200

Hotels and guest houses

Adelaide's, 209 Bath St, City Centre (☎0141/248 4970). Eight well-appointed rooms in a beautifully restored, central church building. ②.

Ambassador Hotel, 7 Kelvin Drive, West End (☎0141/946 1018). Smallish, comfortable, family-run hotel in lovely surroundings next to the Botanic Gardens. ③.

Argyll Hotel, 973 Sauchiehall St, West End (☎0141/337 3313, *argyll_angus.hotel@virgin.net*). Well-placed, near Kelvingrove Museum, this newly refurbished hotel has neat rooms and friendly staff. ③.

Babbity Bowster, 16–18 Blackfriars St, Merchant City (☎0141/552 5055). A traditional and very lively hotel, bar and restaurant that makes much of its Scottishness. ⑤.

Boswell Hotel, 27 Mansionhouse Rd, Southside (☎0141/632 9812). Informal, relaxing Queen's Park hotel with a superb real-ale bar. ④.

Brunswick Hotel, 106 Brunswick St, Merchant City (☎0141/552 0001, *brunhotel@aol.com*). Fashionable but good-value designer hotel with minimalist furniture and a smart bar and restaurant. ③.

Cathedral House, 28 Cathedral Square, City Centre (☎0141/552 3519). This intriguing red-sandstone Victorian building has comfortable modern rooms and a good restaurant. ④.

Copthorne Hotel, George Square, City Centre (☎0141/332 6711). Large and impressive eighteenth-century hotel occupying the entire northwestern corner of George Square; prices rocket at the weekend. ⑥.

Drambuie Scottish Chefs Centre, 62 St Andrews Drive, Southside (☎0141/427 1106). Scotland's top school for chefs with a number of great-value guest-house rooms available. ②.

Ewington Hotel, 132 Queen's Drive, Southside (☎0141/423 1152, *ewington@aol.com*). Comfortable and peaceful upmarket hotel facing Queen's Park, with an excellent, moderately priced restaurant. ⑦.

Hillhead Hotel, 32 Cecil St, West End (☎0141/339 7733, *hillhotel@aol.com*). Quiet, welcoming guest house in a student area close to Hillhead Underground and excellent local pubs and restaurants. ②.

Hillview Guest House, 18 Hillhead St, West End (☎0141/334 5585). Small, unassuming and peaceful guest house near the University and Byres Road. ②.

Lomond Hotel, 6 Buckingham Terrace, West End (☎0141/339 2339). Discreet guest house in a beautifully restored Victorian terrace near the Botanic Gardens and Byres Road. ②.

Malmaison, 278 West George St, City Centre (☎0141/572 1000, *glasgow@malmaison.com*). Easily the most stylish hotel in the city centre, with large, elegant rooms and contemporary designer touches everywhere. ⑨.

One Devonshire Gardens, 1 Devonshire Gardens, Great Western Road, West End (☎0141/339 2001). Glasgow's most exclusive and exquisite small hotel, a ten-minute walk up the Great Western Road from the Botanic Gardens. ⑨.

Reidholme Guest House, 36 Regent Park Square, Southside (☎0141/423 1855). Small and friendly guest house in a quiet sidestreet; designed by Alexander "Greek" Thomson. ②.

Rennie Mackintosh Hotel, 218–220 Renfrew St, City Centre (☎0141/333 9992). Small, smart and intimate; the "Mockintosh" theme is elegant rather than tacky. ③.

Sandyford Hotel, 904 Sauchiehall St, West End (☎0141/334 0000). A clean, comfortable, mid-sized hotel, well located for Kelvingrove Park and the SECC (conference centre). ③.

Scott Guest House, 417 Woodside Rd, West End (☎0141/339 3750). Friendly B&B, well situated close to Kelvinbridge underground station. ①.

Victorian House, 212 Renfrew St, City Centre (☎0141/332 0129). Smart but friendly terraced guest house with sixty rooms. ②.

Hostels, student halls and camping

Baird Hall, 460 Sauchiehall St, City Centre (☎0141/553 4148). Student halls of residence in a lavish Art Deco building near the School of Art. Closed mid-Sept to May.

Glasgow Youth Hostel, 7–8 Park Terrace, West End (☎0141/332 3004, reservations ☎0541/553255, *glasgow@syha.org.uk*). A luxurious place nuzzled deep in the splendour of the West End. It's a ten-minute walk south from Kelvinbridge Underground station, or take buses #11, #44 or #59 from the city centre, after which it's a short stroll west up Woodlands Road. Very popular, so book in advance.

Berkeley Globetrotters Independent Hostel, 63 Berkeley St, West End (☎0141/221 7880). A slightly cheaper alternative to the youth hostel. Bus #57 from the city centre runs straight past the door.

University of Glasgow (☎0141/330 5385). Low-priced, self-catering rooms and flats. Closed mid-Sept to June.

University of Strathclyde (☎0141/553 4148). Various sites, mostly around the cathedral; cheaper rates without bed linen or breakfast. Closed mid-Sept to June.

Craigendmuir Park, Campsie View, Stepps (☎0141/779 4159). The only campsite within a decent distance of Glasgow, four miles northeast of the city centre, a 15min walk from Stepps train station; adequate facilities with showers, a laundry and a shop, but only ten pitches.

The City

Glasgow's enormous city centre is ranged across the north bank of the River Clyde, roughly bounded on its western and northern sides by the M8 motorway, and to the east by the High Street running from the Cathedral down to the river. At its geographical heart is **George Square**, a nineteenth-century municipal showpiece crowned by the enormous City Chambers at the eastern end. Behind this lies one of the 1980s greatest marketing successes, the **Merchant City**, an area of massive gentrification partially restored to its nineteenth-century glory. The grand buildings and trendy cafés cling to the borders of the run-down **East End**, a strongly working-class district that chooses to ignore its rather showy neighbour. The oldest part of Glasgow, around the **Cathedral**, lies immediately north of the East End.

Still in the city centre, Glasgow's commercial core spreads west of George Square, and is mostly built on a large grid system – possibly inspired by Edinburgh's New Town; ruler-straight roads rise up severe hills between grand, sand-blasted buildings. The main shopping areas here are **Argyle Street**, running parallel to the river underneath Central train station, and **Buchanan Street**, which crosses it and leads up to the pedestrianized shopping thoroughfare, **Sauchiehall Street**. Just to the north is Rennie Mackintosh's famous **Glasgow School of Art**. To the immediate west of Buchanan Street, crowned by the neat Blythswood Square, the steep Georgian streets of **Blythswood Hill** are remarkably quiet and reserved.

Outside the city centre, the **West End** begins just over a mile west of Central station, and covers most of the area west of the M8. In the nineteenth century, as the East End tumbled into poverty, the West End ascended the social scales with great speed, a process crowned by the arrival of the **University**. Today, this is still very much the student quarter of Glasgow, exuding a decorously well-heeled air, with graceful tree-lined avenues and trendy shops and cafés. Straddling the banks of the cleaned-up River

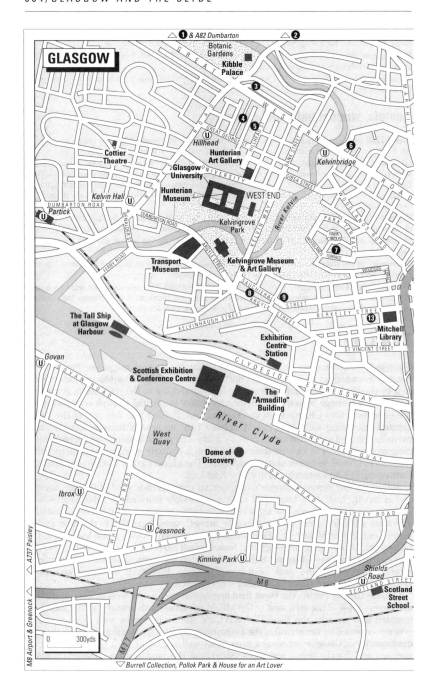

GLASGOW

△ **1** & A82 Dumbarton   △ **2**

Botanic
Gardens

Kibble
Palace

3

GREAT

4

5

Hillhead Ⓤ

GREAT GEORGE ST

HILLHEAD ST

BANK STREET

WESTERN

6

Kelvinbridge Ⓤ

Cottier
Theatre

Hunterian
Art Gallery

Glasgow
University

UNIVERSITY

GIBSA STREET

ROAD

Hunterian
Museum

Kelvin Hall Ⓤ

DUMBARTON ROAD

Partick Ⓤ

DUMBARTON ROAD

BENALDER ST

WEST END

River Kelvin

KELVIN WAY

Kelvingrove
Park

PARK TER

PARK
CIRCUS

WOODLANDS ROAD

7

WOODLANDS
TERRACE

Transport
Museum

ARGYLE STREET

FERRY ROAD

Kelvingrove Museum
& Art Gallery

SAUCHIEHAL

8

ARGYLE

9

STREET

BERKELEY STREET

WOODSIDE

13

Mitchell
Library

The Tall Ship
at Glasgow
Harbour

KELVINHAUGH STREET

STREET

ST VINCENT STREET

Exhibition
Centre
Station

CLYDESIDE

Govan Ⓤ

GOVAN ROAD

Scottish Exhibition
& Conference Centre

EXPRESSWAY

The
"Armadillo"
Building

LANCEFIELD QUAY

River Clyde

West
Quay

Dome of
Discovery

GOVAN ROAD

PAISLEY ROAD

WHITEFIELD ROAD

Ibrox Ⓤ

Cessnock Ⓤ

PAISLEY   ROAD   WEST

Kinning Park Ⓤ

M8

Shields
Road Ⓤ

SCOTLAND STREET

Scotland
Street
School

M8

0   300yds

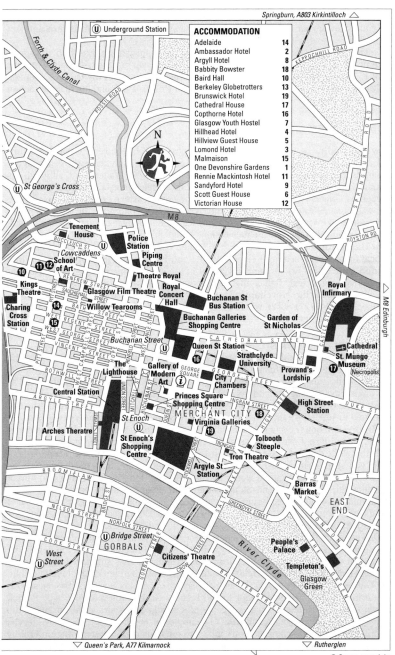

Springburn, A803 Kirkintilloch △

U Underground Station

ACCOMMODATION

Adelaide	14
Ambassador Hotel	2
Argyll Hotel	8
Babbity Bowster	18
Baird Hall	10
Berkeley Globetrotters	13
Brunswick Hotel	19
Cathedral House	17
Copthorne Hotel	16
Glasgow Youth Hostel	7
Hillhead Hotel	4
Hillview Guest House	5
Lomond Hotel	3
Malmaison	15
One Devonshire Gardens	1
Rennie Mackintosh Hotel	11
Sandyford Hotel	9
Scott Guest House	6
Victorian House	12

N

Forth & Clyde Canal

St George's Cross

KEPPOCHHILL ROAD

ROYSTON RD

M8

△ M8 Edinburgh

Tenement House
Police Station
Cowcaddens
School of Art
Piping Centre
Theatre Royal
Kings Theatre
Glasgow Film Theatre
Royal Concert Hall
Royal Infirmary
Charing Cross Station
Willow Tearooms
Buchanan St Bus Station
Garden of St Nicholas
Buchanan Galleries Shopping Centre
Buchanan Street
Queen St Station
Cathedral
St Mungo Museum
Necropolis
The Lighthouse
Gallery of Modern Art
Strathclyde University
Provand's Lordship
Central Station
City Chambers
High Street Station
Princes Square Shopping Centre
MERCHANT CITY
St Enoch
Virginia Galleries
Arches Theatre
St Enoch's Shopping Centre
Tolbooth Steeple
Tron Theatre
Argyle St Station
Barras Market
EAST END
Bridge Street
GORBALS
People's Palace
West Street
Citizens' Theatre
Templeton's
Glasgow Green
River Clyde

BROOMIELAW
NELSON STREET
COOK STREET
NORFOLK STREET

▽ Queen's Park, A77 Kilmarnock   ▽ Rutherglen

Kelvin, the slopes, trees and statues of **Kelvingrove Park** are framed by a backdrop of the Gothic towers and turrets of the university and the **Kelvingrove Museum and Art Gallery**.

Not as genteel as the West End, nor as raffishly downbeat as the East End, the **south side** of the city, across the river, is nevertheless also worth a visit – though you may want to bypass the scruffy and infamous suburbs of Govan and the Gorbals, immediately south of the Clyde, for the leafy enclaves of **Pollok Park** and the main attraction south of the river, the **Burrell Collection**.

George Square and around

Now hemmed in by incessant traffic, the imposing architecture of **George Square** reflects the confidence of Glasgow's Victorian age. Rising high above the centre of the square is an eighty-foot column topped with a statue of Sir Walter Scott, although his links with Glasgow were, at best, sketchy. The florid splendour of the **City Chambers**, opened by Queen Victoria in 1888, occupies the entire eastern end of the square. Built on wealth gained by colonial trade and heavy industry, it epitomizes the aspirations and optimism of late Victorian city elders. Its intricately detailed facade includes high-minded friezes typical of the era: the four nations (England, Ireland, Scotland, Wales) of the then United Kingdom at the feet of the throned queen; the British colonies; and allegorical figures representing Religion, Virtue and Knowledge. It's worth taking a free **guided tour** (Mon–Fri 10.30am & 2.30pm) of the labyrinthine interior to get a look at the intricate gold leaf, Italian marble, Wedgwood ceilings and Rococo trimmings. Equally opulent is the **Merchant's House**, opposite Queen Street station (by appointment only; ☎0141/221 8272), where the grand Banqueting Hall and silk-lined Directors' Room are highlights.

The Gallery of Modern Art

Queen Street leads south from George Square to Royal Exchange Square, where the focal point is the graceful mansion built in 1780 for tobacco lord William Cunninghame. It was the most ostentatious of the Glasgow merchants' homes and, having served as the city's Royal Exchange and central library, now houses the excellent **Gallery of Modern Art** (Mon–Sat 10am–5pm, Sun 11am–5pm; free). Controversial from the day it opened in 1996, the gallery has pleased the punters more than the critics.

The presentation is certainly unusual: the main part of the gallery is divided into four levels, named Fire, Earth, Water and Air, though these themes bear only a tenuous link with the work displayed. Once through the main portals, a mirrored reception area leads you straight into the **Earth Gallery**, a spacious zone that effortlessly absorbs large-scale socially committed works by the "Glasgow Pups" – Peter Howson, Adrian Wiszniewski, Ken Currie and Stephen Campbell. Felipe Linares' beautifully painted papier-mâché skeletons exploring the seven deadly sins shine defiantly from the end of the gallery, along with the evocative photos of Sebastião Salgado, whose most famous pictures record the plight of the world's economic underclasses.

Downstairs is the **Fire Gallery**, a dark place packed with interactive creations, while upstairs you'll find the **Water Gallery**, a brightly lit room dealing with the flow of life and death through art that ranges from Andy Goldsworthy's sun-baked and cracked red clay floor to intricate Aboriginal paintings on canvas and bark. The blinding white **Air Gallery** is a perfect setting for such displays of optical fireworks as *Punjabi*, an eye-shattering study in red, white, violet and green by Bridget Riley, or *Jubilee* by Patrick Hughes, a witty exercise in visual deception. A small set of stairs at the far end of the gallery leads down to an area filled with examples of well-designed everyday objects, from nappies to book shelves. Don't miss the top-floor **café**, where a huge mural by Adrian Wiszniewski competes with the view of rooftops below.

The Merchant City

The grid of streets that lies immediately southeast of the City Chambers is known as the **Merchant City**, an area of eighteenth-century warehouses and homes once bustling with cotton, tobacco and sugar traders. In the last decade or so, it has been sandblasted and swabbed clean with greater enthusiasm and municipal money than any other part of Glasgow in an attempt to bring residents back into the city centre. Expensive designer shops, style bars and bijou cafés continue to flock here, giving the area a pervasive air of sophistication and chic.

Look out for the delicate white spire of the National Trust for Scotland's regional headquarters, **Hutcheson's Hall**, at 158 Ingram St (Mon–Sat 10am–5pm). The NTS have a shop on the ground floor and visitors can see the ornately decorated hall upstairs. In the shop you can pick up a Merchant City Trail leaflet, which guides you around a dozen of the most interesting buildings in the area, including the nearby Robert Adam-designed **Trades House**, on Glassford Street (by appointment only; ☎0141/552 2418; free), easily distinguished by its neat, green copper dome. Built for the purpose in 1794, it still functions as the headquarters of the Glasgow trade guilds. Its history can be traced back to 1605 when fourteen societies of well-to-do city merchants, the forerunners of the trade unions, first incorporated, although they have since become little more than quasi-masonic lodges for men from all sections of Glasgow's business community. The former civic pride and status of the guilds is still evident, however, from the rich assortment of carvings and stained glass windows, with a lively pictorial representation of the different trades in the silk frieze around the walls of the first-floor banqueting hall.

The East End

Before 1846, when the construction of the new train station near George Square shifted the city's emphasis west, **Glasgow Cross**, the junction of **Trongate**, Gallowgate and the High Street, was the city's principal intersection. The turreted seventeenth-century **Tolbooth Steeple** still stands here, although the rest of the building has long since disappeared, and today the stern tower is little more than a traffic hazard at a busy junction. Further east, down Gallowgate, beyond the train lines, lies the **East End**, the district that perhaps most closely corresponds to the old perception of Glasgow. Hemmed in by Glasgow Green to the south, and the old university to the west, this densely packed industrial area essentially created the city's wealth. The Depression caused the closure of many factories, leaving communities stranded in an industrial wasteland. Today, isolated pubs, tatty shops and cafés sit amidst this dereliction, in sharp contrast to the gloss of the Merchant City only a few blocks to the west.

Three hundred yards down either London Road or Gallowgate, **The Barras** is Glasgow's largest and most popular weekend market (Sat & Sun 9am–5pm). Red iron gates announce its official entrance, but boundaries are breached as the stalls – selling inexpensive household goods, bric-a-brac, secondhand clothes and records – spill out into the surrounding cobbled streets.

Between London Road and the River Clyde are the wide and tree-lined spaces of **Glasgow Green**. Reputedly the oldest public park in Britain, the Green has been common land since at least 1178, when it was first mentioned in records. Glaswegians hold it very dear, considering it to be an immortal link between themselves and their ancestors, for whom a stroll on the Green was a favourite Sunday afternoon jaunt. It has also been the site of many of the city's major political demonstrations – the Chartists in the 1830s and Scottish republican campaigners in the 1920s – and was the traditional culmination of the May Day workers' marches until the 1950s, when the celebrations were moved to Queens Park. Various memorials (some in bad states of disrepair) are dotted around the lawns: the 146-foot **Nelson Monument**; the ornate – but derelict – terra-cotta **Doulton Fountain**, rising like a wedding cake to the pinnacle where the forlorn Queen Victoria oversees her crumbling empire; and the stern monument extolling the evils of drink and the glory of God that was erected by the nineteenth-century Temperance movement – today, a meeting place for local drunks.

The People's Palace

On the northern end of Glasgow Green stands the **People's Palace** (Mon–Sat 10am–5pm, Sun 11am–5pm; free), a wonderfully haphazard evocation of the city's history. This squat, red-brick Victorian building, with a vast semicircular glasshouse tacked on the back, was purpose-built as a museum back in 1898 – almost a century before the rest of the country caught on to the fashion for social history collections.

On the top floor, glowing murals by Glasgow artist **Ken Currie** powerfully evoke the spirit of Glasgow, from the Carlton Weavers strike in 1787 to the Red Clydesiders of the 1920s (a radical independent Labour Party formed in the economic slump which followed World War I), and provide a potted history of the city's social and economic development. Exhibits include Suffragette flags, trade union banners and the desk of John MacLean, who became consul to the Bolshevik government in 1918. The west wing contains everything from cast-iron railings to biscuit wrappers together with a giant portrait of Billy Connolly. In the East Gallery, an entertaining sound-and-light show reconstructs a "single-end" or one-roomed house, the focus of the daily life of hundreds of thousands of Glasgow people through the years. On the first floor, various themes with a particular resonance in Glasgow are explored, including alcohol, the traditional holiday excursion "Doon the Water" by steamer to various Clyde coastal resorts, and "the Patter", or Glaswegian dialect. The glasshouse at the back of the palace houses the **Winter Gardens**, whose café, water garden, twittering birds and assorted tropical plants and shrubs make a pleasant place in which to pass an hour or so.

A hundred yards across the road from the People's Palace you can see the riotously intricate orange and blue Venetian-style facade of **Templeton's Carpet Factory**, built in 1889. William Leiper, Templeton's architect, is said to have modelled his industrial cathedral on the Doge's Palace in Venice; today it houses a centre for small businesses.

The cathedral district

Rising north up the hill from the Tolbooth Steeple at Glasgow Cross is Glasgow's **High Street**. In British cities, the name is commonly associated with the busiest central thoroughfare, and it's a surprise to see how forlorn and dilapidated Glasgow's version is, long superseded by the grander thoroughfares further west. The High Street leads up to the **Cathedral**, on the site of Glasgow's original settlement.

Glasgow Cathedral

Built in 1136, destroyed in 1192 and rebuilt soon after, the stumpy-spired **Glasgow Cathedral** (April–Sept Mon–Sat 9.30am–6pm, Sun 2–5pm; Oct–March Mon–Sat 9.30am–4pm, Sun 2–4pm) was not completed until the late fifteenth century, with the final reconstruction of the chapter house and the aisle designed by Robert Blacader, the city's first archbishop. The only Scottish mainland cathedral to have escaped the hands of religious reformers, thanks to the intervention of the city guilds, it is dedicated to the city's patron saint and reputed founder, St Mungo, about whom four popular stories are frequently told – they even make an appearance on the city's coat of arms. These involve a bird that he brought back to life, a bell with which he summoned the faithful to prayer, a tree that he managed to make spontaneously combust and a fish that he caught with a repentant adulterous queen's ring on its tongue.

Because of the sloping ground on which it is built, at its east end the cathedral is effectively on two levels, the crypt actually part of the "lower church". On entering, you arrive in the impressively lofty nave of the **upper church**, completed under the direction of Bishop William de Bondington (1233–58). Either side of the nave, the narrow **aisles** are illuminated by vivid, mostly twentieth-century stained glass windows. Beyond the nave, the **choir** is hidden from view by the curtained stone pulpit, making the interior feel a great deal smaller than might be expected from the outside. In the choir's northeastern corner, a small door leads into the cathedral's gloomy **sacristy**, in which Glasgow University was first founded over 500 years ago. Wooden boards mounted on the walls detail the alternating Roman Catholic and Protestant clergy of the cathedral, testimony to the turbulence and fluctuations of the Church in Scotland.

Steps from the nave lead down into the **lower church**, where you'll see the dark and musty **chapel** surrounding the tomb of St Mungo. The saint's relics were removed in the late Middle Ages, although the tomb still forms the centrepiece. The chapel itself is one of the most glorious examples of medieval architecture in Scotland, best seen in the delicate fan vaulting rising up from the thicket of cool stone columns. Also in the lower church is the spaciously light **Blacader Aisle**, whose bright, frequently gory, medieval ceiling bosses stand out superbly against the simple whitewashed vaulting.

Outside, the atmospheric **Necropolis** rises above the cathedral. Inspired by the Pierre Lachaise cemetery in Paris, developer John Strong created a garden of death in 1833, filled with Doric columns, gloomy catacombs and Neoclassical temples reflecting the vanity of the nineteenth-century industrialists buried here. From the summit, next to the column topped with an indignant John Knox, there are superb views over the cathedral and its surrounding area.

Cathedral Square

Back in Cathedral Square, the **St Mungo Museum of Religious Life and Art** (Mon–Sat 10am–5pm, Sun 11am–5pm; free) focuses on objects, beliefs and art from Christianity, Buddhism, Judaism, Islam, Hinduism and Sikhism. Portrayals of Hindu gods are juxtaposed with the stunning Salvador Dalí painting *Christ upon the Cross*. In addition to the main exhibition, a small collection of photographs, papers and archive material examines a number of themes, including religion in Glasgow, the nineteenth-century Temperance movement and Christian missionaries – local boy David Livingstone, in particular.

Across the square, the oldest house in the city, the **Provand's Lordship** (Mon–Sat 10am–5pm, Sun 11am–5pm; free) dates from 1471, and has been used, among other things, as an ecclesiastical residence and an inn. Many of the rooms have been kitted out with period furniture, including a re-creation of the fifteenth-century chamber of cathedral clerk Cuthbert Simon. As a reminder of the manse's earthier history, the upper floor contains cuttings and pictures telling interesting tales of assorted lowlife characters, including match-sellers, musicians of eighteenth- and nineteenth-century Glasgow and notorious drunkards.

Behind this building lies the small **Garden of St Nicholas**, a herb garden which contrasts medieval and Renaissance aesthetics and approaches to medicine; moving from the muddled clusters of herbs amid stone carvings of the heart and other organs to the controlled arrangement of plants around a small ornate fountain. The garden, bordered by sandstone walkways where you can sit, is an aromatic and peaceful haven away from the High Street.

From Buchanan Street to Sauchiehall Street

The huge grid of streets that extends from Buchanan Street to the M8, a mile to the west, is home to Glasgow's main shopping district as well as its financial and business corporations. On Buchanan Street, **Princes Square**, hollowed out of the innards of a soft sandstone building, is one of the most stylish and imaginative shopping centres in the country. The interior, all recherché Art Deco and ornate ironwork, has lots of pricey, highly fashionable shops. Nearby, on Mitchell Lane, between Buchanan Street and Union Street, is **The Lighthouse** (Mon, Wed, Fri & Sat 10.30am–6pm, Tues 11am–6pm, Thurs 10.30am–8pm, Sun noon–5pm; free), Charles Rennie Mackintosh's first public commission, which once housed the offices of the *Glasgow Herald* newspaper. As Scotland's Centre for Architecture, Design and the City, it now mounts temporary exhibitions alongside the permanent **Mackintosh Interpretation Centre** (£2.50), a great place to come if you want to learn more about the man and his work.

CHARLES RENNIE MACKINTOSH

The work of **Charles Rennie Mackintosh** (1868–1928) has come to be synonymous with the architectural image of Glasgow. Whether his work was a forerunner of the Modernist movement or merely the sunset of Victorian design, he undoubtedly created buildings of great beauty, idiosyncratically fusing Scots Baronial with Gothic, Art Nouveau and modern design. Though the bulk of his work was conceived at the turn of the century, Mackintosh's ideas became particularly fashionable in the postwar years, giving rise to a certain amount of ersatz "Mockintosh" in his home city, with his distinctive lettering and small design features used time and again by shops, pubs and businesses. Fortunately, there are also plenty of examples of the genuine article, making the city something of a pilgrimage centre for art and design students from all over the world.

Although his family did little to encourage his artistic ambitions, as a young child he began to cultivate his interest in drawing from nature during walks in the countryside, taken to improve his health. This talent was to flourish when he joined the **Glasgow School of Art**, in 1884, where the vibrant new director, Francis Newberry, encouraged his pupils to create original and individual work. Here he met Herbert MacNair and the sisters Margaret and Frances MacDonald whose work seemed to be sympathetic with his, fusing the organic forms of nature with a linear, symbolic Art Nouveau style. Nicknamed "**The Spook School**", the four created a new artistic language, using extended vertical design, stylized abstract organic forms and muted colours, reflecting their interest in Japanese design and the work of Whistler and Beardsley.

It was architecture, however, that truly challenged Mackintosh. His big break came in 1896, when he won a competition to design the new **Art School** (see opposite). This is his most famous work, but a number of smaller buildings created during his tenure with the architects Honeyman and Keppie, which began in 1889, document the development of his style. One of his earliest commissions was for a new building to house the **Glasgow Herald headquarters** on Mitchell Street, off Argyle Street. A massive tower rises up from the corner, giving the building its popular name of The Lighthouse; it now houses the Mackintosh Interpretation Centre (see above).

In the 1890s Glasgow went wild for tearooms, where the middle classes could play billiards and chess, read in the library or merely chat over a fine meal. The imposing Miss Cranston, who dominated the Glasgow teashop scene, running the most elegant establishments, gave Mackintosh great freedom of design and in 1896 he started to plan the interiors for her growing business. Over the next twenty years he designed articles from teaspoons to furniture and finally, as in the case of the **Willow Tearooms**, the structure itself.

The spectre of limited budgets was to haunt Mackintosh throughout his career, and he never had the chance to design and construct with complete freedom. These constraints never managed to dull his creativity, as demonstrated by the **Scotland Street School** of 1904, situated near the Burrell Collection (see p.875), while he never saw the **House for an Art Lover** (see p.876), a building which arguably displays Mackintosh at his most flamboyant – it was eventually constructed in Bellahouston Park in 1996, 95 years after plans for it were submitted to a German architectural competition.

Sauchiehall Street runs in a straight line west past some unexciting shopping malls, leading to a few of the city's most interesting sights. Mackintosh fans should head for the **Willow Tearooms**, at 217 Sauchiehall St – not all that easy to spot at first, above a jewellery shop – a faithful reconstruction on the site of the 1904 original. Everything from the fixtures and fittings right down to the teaspoons and menu cards were designed by Mackintosh. Taking inspiration from the word *Sauchiehall*, which means "avenue of willow", he chose the willow leaf as a theme to unify the whole structure. The motif is most apparent in the stylized linear panels of the bow window, which continue into the intimate dining room as if to surround the sitter in a willow grove, and are echoed in the distinctively high-backed silver-and-purple chairs.

At the north edge of the grid, behind the hulking Royal Scottish Academy for Music and Drama lies McPhater Street, home of the immaculate **Piping Centre** – a national centre for the promotion of the infamous bagpipe. For the casual visitor, the **museum** (daily 10.30am–4.30pm; £2) is of most interest, with its collection of instruments and artefacts from the fourteenth century to the present day. Audio headsets provide a commentary – available in a number of languages, Gaelic included – with musical examples.

Glasgow School of Art

Rising above Sauchiehall Street to the north is one of the city centre's steepest hills, where Dalhousie Street and Scott Street veer up to Renfrew Street and, at no. 167, Charles Rennie Mackintosh's **Glasgow School of Art** (guided tours Mon–Fri 11am & 2pm, Sat 10.30 & 11.30am; July & August only Sun 10.30 & 11.30am; booking advised; ☎0141/353 4526; £5). Widely considered to be the pinnacle of Mackintosh's work, the school is a characteristically angular building of warm sandstone which, due to financial constraints, had to be constructed in two sections (1897–99 and 1907–9). There's a clear change in style from the earlier severity of the east wing to the softer lines of the western half. The only way to see the school is by taking one of the student-led guided tours, the extent of which are dependent on curricular activities.

All over the school, from the roof to the stairwells, Mackintosh's unique touches – light Oriental reliefs, tall-backed chairs and stylized Celtic illuminations – recur like leitmotifs. Hanging in the main entrance hall stairwell is the artist's highly personal wrought-iron version of the "bird, bell, tree, ring and fish" legend of St Mungo. You'll see excellent examples of his early furniture in the tranquil **Mackintosh Room**, flooded with soft, natural light. The **Furniture Gallery**, tucked up in the eaves, shelters an Aladdin's cave of designs that weren't able to be housed elsewhere in the school. Building designs are mounted around the room, including the House for an Art Lover, which has recently been built in the South Side's Bellahouston Park.

You can peer down from the Furniture Gallery into the school's most spectacular room, the glorious two-storey **Library**, where sombre oak panelling contrasts with angular lights in primary colours, dangling down in seemingly random clusters. The dark bookcases sit precisely in their fitted alcoves, while of the furniture, the most unusual feature is the central periodical desk, whose oval central strut displays perfect and quite beautiful symmetry.

The Tenement House

Just a few hundred yards northwest of the School of Art – albeit on the other side of the sheer hill that rises and falls to the north – is the **Tenement House**, at 145 Buccleuch St (March–Oct daily 2–5pm; Nov–Feb by appointment only; £3.20; NTS). This is the perfectly preserved home of the habitually hoarding Agnes Toward, who moved here with her mother in 1911, changing nothing and throwing out very little until she was hospitalized in 1965. On the ground floor, there's a fascinating display on the development of urban Scottish housing, plus relics – ration books, letters, bills, holiday snaps and so forth – from Miss Toward's life. Upstairs you have to ring the doorbell to enter the living quarters, which give every impression of still being inhabited, with a roaring hearth and range, kitchen utensils, framed religious tracts and sewing machine all untouched. The only major change since Miss Toward left has been the reinstallation of the flickering gas lamps she would have used in the early days.

The West End

The urbane veneer of the **West End**, an area which contains many of the city's premier museums, seems far removed from the industrial image of Glasgow. In the 1800s, the city's focus moved west as wealthy merchants established huge estates away from the soot and grime of city life, and in 1870 the ancient university was moved from its cramped home near the cathedral to a spacious new site overlooking the River Kelvin. Elegant housing swiftly followed, the Kelvingrove Art Gallery was built to house the 1888 International Exhibition, and in 1896 the Glasgow District Subway – today's Underground – started its circuitous shuffle from here to the city centre.

The hub of life in this part of Glasgow is **Byres Road**, running down from the straight Great Western Road past Hillhead Underground station. Shops, restaurants, cafés, some enticing pubs and hordes of roving young people, including thousands of students, give the area a real sense of style. Glowing red-sandstone tenements and graceful terraces provide a suitably upmarket backdrop to this cosmopolitan district.

Kelvingrove Museum and Art Gallery

Founded on donations from the city's chief industrialists, the huge, red-brick fantasy castle of **Kelvingrove Museum and Art Gallery** (Mon–Sat 10am–5pm, Sun 11am–5pm; free) is a brash statement of Glasgow's nineteenth-century self-confidence. On the ground floor, a fairly dusty hall contains the **Scottish Natural History** display, where local and global events are marked in the rings of a slice of ancient Douglas fir. On the opposite side of the main hall sits an unremarkable exhibition of European and Scottish weapons.

However, it's the **art collections**, the majority of which are upstairs, that are of most interest. **Room 22** contains some superb Italian paintings, notably Botticelli's delicate *Annunciation*, Giorgione's rich and vibrant *The Adulteress Brought before Christ*, and some fervent landscapes by Salvator Rosa. Further down the gallery, Rembrandt's symbolic portrayal of a crucified ox stands out darkly, along with his quiet portrait *The Man in Armour*. Continuing from the seventeenth century and leading up to the early nineteenth century, **Room 23** contains predominantly British work. The space is dominated by two paintings by Jacob More, a Scottish artist who worked in the elegiacally classical style of Claude; the spread of classicism in eighteenth-century Europe is also attested by pieces such as *Vestals Attending the Sacred Fire*, by David Allan, whose figures languish amongst ancient temples.

Room 24 is filled with quality work from Scottish and European artists of the eighteenth to the early twentieth centuries. Among the biggest names here are Courbet, Corot, Degas and Monet. As for the Scots, the angelic face of *Mrs William Urquhart* is testimony to Sir Henry Raeburn's skill as an informal portraitist, while the meticulous detail of *South and North Western View from Ben Lomond* – a dramatic pair of paintings

KELVINGROVE MUSEUM AND ART GALLERY

At the time of going to press, the Kelvingrove Musuem and Art Gallery was on the point of securing a grant for a complete **refurbishment** of the building in time for its centenery in 2001. This would mean that the museum would be closed to the public from spring 2000 for around a year. For an update, contact the tourist office on ☎0141/332 7133.

by John Knox – makes a striking contrast with Turner's radiant *Modern Italy – The Pifferari*, a picture that glows amongst the dark glens and sombre portraits. Catching up on the twentieth century, **Room 26** contains such continental luminaries as Bonnard, Pissarro, Vuillard, Braque and Derain, and more excellent work by undervalued Scottish artists. *The Pink Parasol* by J.D. Fergusson, for example, reveals what he learned from Matisse and Cézanne, and the grittier *Two Children* by Joan Eardley makes use of collage and thick paint to convey the energy of Gorbals children in the 1960s.

In the east wing, **The Scottish Gallery** is entirely devoted to native artists. Here Raeburn's magnificent *Mr and Mrs Robert N. Campbell of Kailzie* almost overwhelms the room, the golden, life-size figures emerging from the loosely brushed background. A statue of Sir Walter Scott gazes upon a row of paintings depicting the romantic, Victorian view of Scotland, as exemplified by Horatio McCulloch's depiction of *Loch Maree*. On the far wall hangs the famous portrait of *Robert Burns* by Alexander Naysmyth, now found on biscuit tins the world over.

The **Glasgow Style** room is dedicated to the era when Charles Rennie Mackintosh was in his prime: this marvellous collection of furniture is crowned by a pair of domino tables and chairs designed by Mackintosh for the Willow Tearooms. The **Glasgow Boys** are well represented, with the decorative *In a Japanese Garden*, by George Henry, balanced by the bovine tranquillity of Crawhall's *Landscape with Cattle*. Works by Guthrie, Hornel and Lavery are also on display.

The Transport Museum

The twin-towered **Kelvin Hall** is home to the excellent and enormous city **Transport Museum** (Mon–Sat 10am–5pm, Sun 11am–5pm; free), a collection of trains, cars, trams, circus caravans and prams, along with an array of old Glaswegian ephemera, whose entrance is in Bunhouse Road. Near the entrance, "Kelvin Street" is a re-created 1950s cobbled street featuring an old Italian coffee shop, a butcher's, a bakery and an old-time Underground station. A cinema shows fascinating films – mostly on themes based loosely around transport – of old Glasgow life, with crackly footage of Sauchiehall Street packed solid with trams and shoppers and hordes of pasty-faced Glaswegians setting off for their annual jaunts down the coast. The Clyde Room displays intricate models of ships forged in Glasgow's yards – everything from tiny schooners to ostentatious ocean liners such as the *QE2*.

Glasgow University

Dominating the West End skyline, the gloomy turreted tower of Glasgow's **University**, designed by Sir Gilbert Scott in the mid-nineteenth century, overlooks the glades of the River Kelvin. Access to the main buildings and museums is from University Avenue, running east from Byres Road. In the dark, neo-Gothic pile under the tower you'll find the **University Visitor Centre** (May–Sept Mon–Sat 9.30am–5pm, Sun 2–5pm; rest of year closed Sun), which distributes leaflets about the various university buildings and the statues around the campus.

Next door to the visitor centre, the collection of the **Hunterian Museum** (Mon–Sat 9.30am–5pm), Scotland's oldest public museum, dating back to 1807, was donated to the university by ex-student William Hunter, a pathologist and anatomist whose eclectic tastes form the basis of a fairly dry, but frequently diverting zoological and archeological museum. Exhibitions include Scotland's only dinosaur, a look at the Romans in Scotland – the chilly farthest outpost of a massive empire – and a vast coin collection.

On the other side of University Avenue is Hunter's more frequently visited bequest: the **Hunterian Art Gallery** (Mon–Sat 9.30am–5pm; free), best known for its works by James Abbott McNeil Whistler – only Washington DC has a larger collection. Whistler's breathy landscapes are less compelling than his portraits of women: look out especially for the trio of full-length portraits.

The gallery's other major collection is of nineteenth- and twentieth-century Scottish art, including the quasi-Impressionist Scottish landscapes of William McTaggart, a forerunner of the Glasgow Boys movement, represented here by Walton, McGregor, Murray, Guthrie and Hornel. From the east coast, the thickly textured, colourful landscapes and portraits by Scottish Colourists Peploe, Fergusson, Hunter and Cadell brighten up the gallery. A small selection of French Impressionists includes Corot's soothing *Distant View of Corbeil* and works by Boudin and Pissarro.

A side gallery leads to the **Mackintosh House**, a re-creation of the exquisitely cool interior of the now-demolished Glasgow home of Margaret and Charles Rennie Mackintosh, with over sixty pieces of Mackintosh furniture on three floors. Among the highlights are the Studio Drawing Room, whose cream and white furnishings are bathed in expansive pools of natural light, and the Japanese-influenced guest bedroom in dazzling, monochrome geometrics.

The Botanic Gardens

At the top of Byres Road, where it meets the Great Western Road, is the main entrance to the **Botanic Gardens** (daily 7am–dusk). Of the glasshouses here, the best-known is the hulking, domed **Kibble Palace** (daily: summer 10am–4.45pm; winter closes 4.15pm). Originally known as the Crystal Palace, it was built in 1863 for wealthy landowner John Kibble's estate on the shores of Loch Long, where it stood for ten years before he decided to transport it into Glasgow, drawing it up the Clyde on a vast raft pulled by a steamer. Today, the palace houses a damp, musty collection of swaying palms from around the world, along with an unremarkable but well-placed **café**. The smell is much sweeter on entering the Main Range glasshouse, home to lurid and blooming flowers and plants – including stunning orchids, cacti, ferns and tropical fruit – luxuriating in the humidity.

South of the Clyde

The southern bank of the Clyde, facing the city centre, is home to the notoriously deprived districts of **Govan**, a community yet to find its niche after the shipbuilding slump, and the **Gorbals**, synonymous with the razor gangs of old. On the southern side of Govan the vast bowl of **Ibrox**, home to the rigidly Protestant Rangers football team, proudly displays the Union flag.

Inner-city decay fades into altogether gentler and more salubrious suburbs, commonly referred to as **South side**. These include Queen's Park, a residential area home to Celtic's Hampden Park football stadium, and the rural landscape of **Pollok Park**, three miles southwest of the city centre, which contains two of Glasgow's major museums: the **Burrell Collection** and **Pollok House**. A further reason to venture south is to see the latest attractions on the Glasgow architects' trail: Charles Rennie

---

CYCLING IN GLASGOW

Around the Glasgow area, a series of converted railway lines, minor roads and the towpath of the Forth and Clyde Canal have been converted into **cycle paths**, with routes extending as far as Loch Lomond, Greenock and Irvine. As some of these routes can be a little confusing, it's worth picking up information from the local tourist office.

Bikes are carried free on Strathclyde Transport and Scotrail trains; you may wish to make use of them one way, as some of the routes are over twenty miles long. Only a few bike shops in Glasgow **rent** out bikes: Dales, 150 Dobbies Loan (☎0141/332 2705), has reasonable weekend rates, and can be found one block north of Buchanan Street bus station; conveniently placed close to the start of the Glasgow to Loch Lomond route, West End Cycles, 16 Chancellor St (☎0141/357 1344), offers cheaper daily and weekly rental.

Mackintosh's **House for an Art Lover** in Bellahouston Park and Alexander "Greek" Thomson's **Holmwood House** in the Cathcart district.

The Burrell Collection

The lifetime collection of shipping magnate Sir William Burrell (1861–1958), the outstanding **Burrell Collection** (Mon–Sat 10am–5pm, Sun 11am–5pm; free) is, for some, the principal reason for visiting Glasgow. Unlike many other art collectors, Sir William's only real criterion for buying a piece was whether or not he liked it, enabling him to buy many "unfashionable" works, which cost comparatively little but subsequently proved their worth. The simplicity and clean lines of the Burrell building are its greatest assets, with large picture windows giving sweeping views over woodland and serving as a tranquil backdrop to the objects inside. The sculpture and antiques are on the ground floor, arranged in six sections that overlap and occasionally backtrack, while a mezzanine above displays most of the paintings.

On entering the building, the most striking piece, by virtue of sheer size, is the Warwick Vase, a huge bowl containing fragments of a second-century-AD vase from Hadrian's Villa in Tivoli. Next to it are the first of a series of sinewy and naturalistic bronze casts of Rodin sculptures, among them *The Age of Bronze, A Call to Arms* and the famous *Thinker*. Beyond the entrance hall, on three sides of a courtyard, are a trio of dark and sombre panelled rooms re-erected in faithful detail from the Burrells' Hutton Castle home, their heavy tapestries, antique furniture and fireplaces displaying the same eclectic taste as the rest of the museum.

From the courtyard, leading up to the picture windows, the **Ancient Civilizations** collection – a catch-all title for Greek, Roman and earlier artefacts – includes an exquisite mosaic Roman cockerel from the first century BC and a four-thousand-year-old Mesopotamian lion's head. The bulk of it is Egyptian, however, with rows of inscrutable gods and kings. Nearby, also illuminated by the enormous windows, the **Oriental Art** section forms nearly one quarter of the complete collection, ranging from Neolithic jades through bronze vessels and Tang funerary horses to cloisonné. Near-Eastern art is also represented, in a dazzling array of turquoise- and cobalt-decorated jugs, and a swathe of intricate carpets.

The collection of **Medieval and Post-Medieval European Art**, which encompasses silverware, glass, textiles and sculpture, ranges across a maze of small galleries, whose most impressive sections are the sympathetically lit stained glass – note the homely image of a man warming his toes by the fire – and the numerous tapestries. Among the church art are simple thirteenth-century Spanish wooden images and cool fifteenth-century English alabaster, while a trio of period interiors cover both the Gothic and Elizabethan eras, and seventeenth and eighteenth centuries. This is interrupted by a selection from Burrell's vast art collection, the highlight of which is one of Rembrandt's characterful early self-portraits.

Upstairs, the cramped and comparatively gloomy **mezzanine** is probably the least satisfactory section of the gallery, not the best setting for its sparkling array of paintings. The selection incongruously leaps from a small gathering of fifteenth-century religious works to Gericault's darkly dynamic *Prancing Grey Horse* and Degas' thoughtful and perceptive *Portrait of Emile Duranty*. Pissarro, Manet and Boudin are also represented, along with some exquisite watercolours by Glasgow Boy Joseph Crawhall, revealing his accurate and tender observations of the animal world.

From both the Pollok Park gates, a free half-hourly minibus runs between 10am and 4.30pm to the Burrell Collection, while the pleasant walk through the grounds of the country park will take about twenty minutes. **Buses** #34 and #34a from Govan Underground station set down outside the gate nearest to the Burrell, on Hagg's Road. Pollokshaws West station, beside the Pollockshaws Road gate, is served by regular trains from Glasgow Central. In addition buses #45, #48 and #57 connect Union Street in the city centre with Pollokshaws West station. However, as Pollok Park is only three miles from the city centre, taking a **taxi** to the Burrell is an inexpensive option (£7–8).

Pollok House

A quarter of a mile away down rutted tracks lies the lovely, eighteenth-century **Pollok House** (daily: April–Oct 10am–5pm; Nov–March 11am–4pm; April–Oct £4; Nov–March free; NTS), the manor of the Pollok Park estate and once home of the Maxwell family, local lords, and owners of most of southern Glasgow until well into this century. Designed by William Adam in the mid-1700s, the house is typical of its age: graciously but sturdily built, looking out onto pristine raked and parterre **gardens** (free access all year), whose stylized daintiness contrasts with the heavy Spanish paintings indoors, among them works by El Greco, Murillo and Goya. The NTS has made a deliberate effort to return the house to the layout and style it would have enjoyed when the Stirling Maxwells were living here in the 1920s and 1930s. The rooms have the flavour of a well-to-do but unstuffy country house, with the odd piece of attractive furniture and some pleasant rooms, but little that can be described as outstanding. The servants' quarters downstairs do manage to capture the imagination – a virtually untouched labyrinth of tiled Victorian parlours and corridors that includes a good tearoom in the old kitchen. Free tours of the house are available from the front desk, or you can wander around at your own pace.

House for an Art Lover

A mile to the northwest of Pollok Park lies the smaller Bellahouston Park, home to Charles Rennie Mackintosh's **House for an Art Lover** (April–Sept Mon–Thurs, Sat & Sun 10am–4pm; Oct–March daily 10am–4pm but closed occasionally for functions; ☎0141/353 4449; £3.50). Designed in 1901 but never constructed, for decades this building existed solely in the minds of wishful architecture lovers. But after years of intensely detailed research and painstaking work, the building opened in 1996 as a centre for Glasgow School of Art's postgraduate students, with some rooms open for public viewing. In an interpretation room on the first floor, a video explains the building's construction; opposite this the delicate **Oval Room** was designed for women to retire to after dinner. The massive windows in the hallway cast a cool light upon the sombre woodwork, in direct contrast to the dazzling white **music room**. The dark, intimate **dining room** is decorated by some beautiful gesso tiles. To reach the house, take the Underground to Cessnock station; coming out of the station, turn right onto Paisley Road West, which runs up to the park. By train from central station, get off at Dumbreck, cross the road and continue straight on until you reach the park. From either, it's about a fifteen-minute walk to the house.

Holmwood House

Four miles south of the city centre, in the suburb of Cathcart, **Holmwood House** (April–Oct daily 1.30–5.30pm; £3.20; NTS), the finest domestic design by rediscovered Glasgow architect Alexander "Greek" Thomson, has recently been restored and opened to the public. A commission by James Couper, co-owner of a paper mill on the nearby River Carth, the house shows off Thomson's bold Classical concepts. The interior shows a highly imaginative attention to detail: look out for the white marble fireplace and nighttime star decorations on the ceiling of the **drawing room**, which contrast with the black marble fireplace and sunburst decorations in the **parlour**, the room immediately beneath. Across the corridor, the **dining room** has a frieze of scenes from the *Iliad*, along with a skylight at the back of the room designed to allow the Greek gods to peer down on the feasting inside. Restoration is ongoing, as you'll see from the patches of exquisite stencilling revealed beneath the wallpaper, and the fact that the rooms are unfurnished.

Cafés and restaurants

Glasgow's renaissance has seen an explosion of fine **restaurants** and European-style **bars** and **cafés**, which, in addition to the input of its diverse and ethnically mixed population, make eating possibilities pretty wide. Traditional **Scottish cuisine** has become very trendy in recent years, too. **Vegetarians** won't have a hard time finding something to eat in Glasgow. Most restaurants and cafés have at least one vegetarian dish on the menu, while others listed below are either exclusively vegetarian, or offer a very good selection of meat-free dishes. For **budget food**, cafés range from the cheapest, greasiest cholesterol-hole through to bars offering reasonable snacks all day, and frequently into the evening. Unlike in staid Edinburgh, where a lot of places close on Sunday, most of Glasgow's restaurants are open seven days a week.

City centre

The **Merchant City** is where you'll find the largest concentration of designer brasseries and some very pricey restaurants, although cafés, bars and restaurants are spread across the wide swathe of the city centre. The shopping precincts of **Buchanan** and **Sauchiehall streets** feature the familiar line-up of fast-food chains, while the area around **Charing Cross**, where a number of clubs are situated, is a good place to head if you're searching for food after 10pm.

Cafés, bars and diners

Babbity Bowster, 16–18 Blackfriars St (☎0141/552 5055). Atmospheric and popular Merchant City bar serving excellent Scottish food – anything from hearty broths to haggis, salmon and kippers. The restaurant upstairs is pricier and more sedate. Closed Sun. Moderate.

Brunswick Café Bar, 106–8 Brunswick St. Self-consciously trendy bistro offering an eclectic menu ranging from Scottish meats to Japanese sushi. Daily 8am–midnight. Moderate.

Café Gandolfi, 64 Albion St. An enduring Merchant City favourite with beautifully distinctive wooden furniture and stained glass, serving up good-quality soup, salads and fish dishes. Closed Sun. Moderate.

Fratelli Sarti, 133 Wellington St & 121 Bath St (☎0141/204 0440). Authentic and popular Italian. The frantic Wellington Street café also has a deli (9am–6pm) serving delicious takeaway pizza and pastas; the Bath Street restaurant, next door, is larger with the same quality menu. Moderate.

Gallery of Modern Art Café, Queen St. Worth visiting for the mural alone and the view over the rooftops. Serves light lunches – the salads are good – and cakes and coffee at other times. Daily 10am–4.30pm. Inexpensive.

GLC Café-Bar, 11 Dixon St. In the Glasgow Gay and Lesbian Centre, this colourful and relaxed establishment has a varied menu. Bar open till midnight. Inexpensive.

Ichiban Noodle Café, 50 Queen St (☎0141/204 4200). Authentic Japanese noodle bar where the staple is a huge bowl of noodle soup with meat or veg topping, to which you can add substantial side orders of fish, salad or dumplings if you're hungry. Inexpensive.

13th Note, corner of King St & Osborne St. This Merchant City bar stands out for its all-vegan menu. Inexpensive.

Toast, 84–86 Albion St. Stylish coffee shop in the heart of the Merchant City with an array of breads, as well as a classic all-day breakfast. Mon–Sat 8am–8pm, Sun 10am–6pm. Inexpensive.

Tron Theatre, 63 Trongate. A trendy wrought-iron café-bar caters for the quick-lunch and coffee crowd, while the old-fashioned Victorian bar is perfect for a laid-back lunch or dinner. Closed Sun evening. Moderate.

Vegville Diner, 93 St Georges Rd. Good-quality, tasty vegetarian dishes. Mon–Sat open till 1am. Inexpensive.

Wee Curry Shop, 7 Buccleuch St. Tiny Indian cafe, serving tasty, filling, well-priced food. Closed Sun lunch. Inexpensive.

Willow Tea Rooms, 217 Sauchiehall St & 97 Buchanan St. Refined elevenses, lunches and afternoon tea in Mackintosh-designed splendour. Of the two, the Sauchiehall Street branch is more authentic. Open till 4.30pm. Inexpensive.

Restaurants

Amber Regent, 50 West Regent St (☎0141/331 1655). Decisively Western decoration matched with authentic Chinese food. Half-price meals every Mon & Tues eve; closed Sun. Moderate.

Cantina Del Rey, 6 Kings Court (☎0141/552 4044). Housed in a converted railway vault, this spacious restaurant serves authentic Mexican cuisine. Evenings only. Moderate.

Canton Express, 407 Sauchiehall St. Formica palace popular with shoppers and late-night clubbers alike, tempted by the Chinese and Sichuan fast food and good prices. Open daily noon–4am. Inexpensive.

City Merchant, 97 Candleriggs (☎0141/553 1577). Popular restaurant in the Merchant City that serves good food using Scottish produce, from Dingwall haggis to fresh lobster. Expensive.

Fire Station, 33 Ingram St (☎0141/552 2929). Merchant City Italian restaurant housed in a huge old fire station dating from 1900. The excellent food is good value, and the half-price pasta from 5pm to 7pm is a real bargain. Moderate.

Gamba, 225A West George St (☎0141/572 0899). A stylish, upmarket basement restaurant with nods to Spain in both the decor and seafood-dominated menu. Closed Sun. Expensive.

Ho Wong, 82 York St, just off Argyle Street (☎0141/221 3550). Secluded restaurant offering a top-class range of Cantonese and Sichuan food – well worth the high prices. Closed Sun lunch. Expensive.

Kama Sutra, 331 Sauchiehall St (☎0141/332 0055). Thick velvet curtains, wrought ironwork and a designer interior with an unusual and wide-ranging Indian menu. Open Mon–Thurs noon–midnight, Fri & Sat noon–1am, Sun 5pm–midnight. Moderate.

Loon Fung, 417 Sauchiehall St (☎0141/332 1240). Long-established Cantonese with great *dim sum*, but lacks vegetarian options. Moderate.

O'Sole Mio, 34 Bath St (☎0141/331 1397). A superb and affordable city-centre restaurant for unusual pasta dishes, as well as pizzas from their log-fired oven. Budget specials 5–6.30pm; closed Sun lunch. Moderate.

Rogano, 11 Exchange Place, near Buchanan Street (☎0141/248 4055). Although the food here is not solely Scottish, the *Rogano* is a Glasgow institution, an absolutely superb but shockingly expensive fish restaurant decked out as a replica of the 1930s Cunard liner, the *Queen Mary*. *Café Rogano*, in the basement, is cheaper but not so deliciously ostentatious.

Taj Mahal, 573–581 Sauchiehall St (☎0141/226 5030). Pleasant restaurant serving huge portions of delicious Indian food. Open till midnight. Moderate.

Tun Ton, 157 Hope St. Hip designer restaurant, with 1970s throwbacks in the design, dazzling light and a creative buzz. The food is "fusion" – leaning to the East, with lots of fresh veggies and fruit. Moderate.

West End

Predominantly due to the large local student population, the **West End** is the best area for cheap, stylish restaurants and cafés, and bars serving food, especially around Hillhead Underground station on Byres Road. Nearby, the restaurants along **Ashton Lane** dish out unreservedly good meals. On the other side of Byres Road from the station, **Ruthven Lane** is home to some lively restaurants well known for their happy hours.

Cafés, bars and diners

Back Alley, 8 Ruthven Lane. Deservedly popular spot serving great burgers smothered in assorted toppings. Early-evening happy hour Mon–Thurs. Open Mon–Sat till midnight. Inexpensive.

Café Alba, 61 Otago St. Situated just off Gibson Street, this popular café sells a good selection of vegetarian food and the best home baking in the west. Mon–Sat 10am–5pm. Inexpensive.

View from the top of Snowdonia

Welsh mountain sheep, Brecon Beacons

JERRY DENNIS

'The Armadillo', Clydeside, Glasgow

MICHAEL JENNER

Victoria Street, Edinburgh

COLLECTIONS/IAN YATES

Playing the bagpipes, Edinburgh Festival

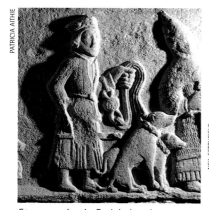

Salmon fishing on the River Tay

Old Man of Hoy, Orkney

Stone carving in Rodel church

Glasgow School of Art

Whisky

Calanais Standing Stones, Lewis

Glen Spean

Café Antipasti, 337 Byres Rd. Two-tier Italian bistro near the Botanic Gardens, serving tasty and well-priced pastas and salads. Mon–Thurs & Sun 9am–11pm, Fri & Sat 9am–midnight. Inexpensive.

Insomnia, 38–42 Woodlands Rd. This crowded 24-hour café lies conveniently on the path from the city centre to the West End. Inexpensive.

Tinderbox, 189 Byres Rd. Very fashionable place for coffee and a snack. Inexpensive.

University Café, 87 Byres Rd. One of the last of a dying race of "caffs", dearly loved by generations of students, serving up fish and chips or mince and tatties. Open daily till 10pm. Inexpensive.

Restaurants

Air Organic, 36 Kelvingrove St. Funky, new designer eatery and downstairs club, serving delicious organic offerings cooked with flair and flavour. Mon–Thurs & Sun 11am–11pm, Fri & Sat 11am–midnight. Expensive.

Ashoka, 19 Ashton Lane (☎0141/337 1115). Traditional but lively West End *dhosa* house and Indian restaurant, popular with local students. Closed Sun lunch. Moderate.

The Big Blue, 445 Great Western Rd (☎0141/357 1038). Subterranean bar and Italian restaurant serving simple but tasty pasta dishes. Moderate.

Fusion, 41 Byres Rd (☎0141/339 3666). The sushi bar that New York, London and Glasgow have – but not Edinburgh. The staff help you sort out your *nigiri* from your *temaki*. Open till midnight Tues–Sun, closed Mon. Moderate.

Mother India, 28 Westminster Terrace, off Sauchiehall St (☎0141/221 1663). Good-quality food at affordable prices in a friendly Indian restaurant. Small corkage fee for bring-your-own. Closed Sun lunch. Moderate.

Murphy's Pakora Bar, 1287 Argyle St (☎0141/334 1550). Over seventy varieties of *pakora* available as a light snack or mountainous meal. Open daily till midnight. Inexpensive.

Stravaigin, 28 Gibson St (☎0141/334 2665). Local meats and fish are given a cosmopolitan make-over with roast vegetables or a shitake mushroom sauce. Moderate (upstairs) to expensive (downstairs).

Ubiquitous Chip, 12 Ashton Lane (☎0141/334 5007). Splendid West End restaurant serving Glasgow's most delicious Scottish food – game, seafood and local cheeses. Very expensive.

Pubs and bars

Not so many years ago, Glasgow's rough image was inextricably associated with its **pubs**, widely thought of as no-go areas for any visitor. Although much of this reputation was exaggerated, there was an element of truth in it. Nowadays, however, you're just as likely to spend an evening in a succession of open and airy café-bars. The centre has an admirable range of reliable places to drink; if you tire of the glossy **Merchant City**, head for the **East End**, where a fair number of local spit-and-sawdust establishments make a welcome change. All in all, though, the liveliest area, once again, has to be the **West End**.

City centre

Bargo, 80 Albion Street. Spacious wood and stainless-steel interior, where the trendy set pose elegantly behind the massive glass frontage.

Bar 91, 91 Candleriggs. Well-designed Merchant City bar, using wrought iron to evoke a stylish atmosphere.

Corinthian, 191 Ingram St. An exquisite renovation of an old bank, complete with huge glass dome, is worth experiencing for cocktails or a light meal in the grill room. Dress smartly.

Corn Exchange, 88 Gordon St. Bang opposite Central station, this bar has successfully re-created the feel of a traditional Victorian Glaswegian pub.

Horseshoe Bar, 17 Drury St. Traditional old pub, reputedly Glasgow's busiest – loud, frantic and great fun, with a very mixed clientele. Karaoke upstairs, with a downstairs bar for quiet conversation.

McChuill's, 40 High St. Glasgow's skateboarders wheel into this brick-lined bar for the Wednesday hip-hop evenings. With live music most other nights, it attracts a faithful crowd.

Nico's, 375–379 Sauchiehall St. Trendy without being painfully so, with a French ambience.

RG's, 73 Queen St. Nostalgia-soaked bar that serves as a focus for Glasgow's rock music heritage. Incongruously, the downstairs section, *Bar Sauza*, is all funky Latin and margaritas.

Saracen Head, 209 Gallowgate (opposite the Barras market). Unchanged East End pub that offers an enjoyably beery, sawdust-floored wallow. Look out for the tax demand from Robbie Burns displayed on the wall, from the days when he was the local tax officer.

Scotia Bar, 112 Stockwell St. Laid-back bar popular with writers and artists. Occasional live folk music – Billy Connolly began his career here, telling jokes in between singing folk songs.

Ten, 10 Mitchell St. Designed by the same crew as Manchester's legendary *Hacienda* club, so it's suitably chic, though with a healthy dose of Glaswegian humour to take off the posey edge.

Variety Bar, 401 Sauchiehall St. Crowded bar with faded Art Nouveau appeal frequented by local art school students.

West End

The Aragon, 131 Byres Rd. Old-fashioned bar with a vast beer selection, which includes European fruit beers and weekly guest ales.

Attic, 44–46 Ashton Lane. Creative attic-conversion bar above the *Cul-de-Sac* restaurant – the smart place to drink on busy Ashton Lane.

Brel, 39–43 Ashton Lane. Narrow, Belgian-themed bar with a wide range of Belgian beers, serving up big pans of mussels and chips.

Brewery Tap, 1055 Sauchiehall St. Well known for its excellent selection of real ales and imported lager, with seating outside for those long summer evenings.

Firebird, 1321 Argyle St. A hip drinking spot with a wood-stoked pizza oven. Downstairs, guest DJs keep the clubbing crowd entertained.

The Halt, 106 Woodlands Rd. Great beer and a vast selection of whiskies in this relaxed music pub, spiritual home of Glasgow cartoon character Lobey Dosser, whose statue is opposite.

Living Room, 5–9 Byres Rd. Hotbed for the young and fashionable, at the southern end of Byres Road. Wrought iron and candles enhance the pre-club atmosphere.

Uisge Beatha, 232 Woodlands Rd. Re-created Scottish atmosphere – all kilts, piped music and stripped wood.

Whistler's Mother, 116–122 Byres Rd. Combines a relaxed restaurant with the more basic bar, which is deservedly popular with students and legions of young people.

Nightlife and entertainment

Glasgow's streets can seem incredibly busy between midnight and 1am, especially on Friday and Saturday nights, but the impression is a little distorted by the city's unique **licensing laws**, which mean that the pubs close up at midnight, and that no one is allowed into a club after 1am. Nevertheless, the clubbing scene is highly rated, with one or two large, mainstream venues: Glasgow consistently attracts some of the top DJs from around the world.

Most **nightclubs** are in the heart of the main shopping areas off Argyle and Buchanan streets, with a further concentration on Sauchiehall Street near Charing Cross. Establishments are pretty mixed, and although there's still a stack of outdated mega-discos with rigorous dress codes, the last couple of years have seen the arrival of far more stylish haunts. Hours hover from around 11pm to 3am, though some are open until 5am, and cover charges are variable – expect to pay around £3 during the week, and up to £10 at the weekend.

While the city's cultural programme doesn't match the heady 1980s and early 1990s, it has maintained an impressive breadth of art, theatre, film and music. Glasgow is firmly established as the home of both Scottish Opera and the Royal Scottish National

Orchestra. The majority of the larger **theatres**, **cinemas** and showpiece **concert halls** are around the shopping streets of the city centre, while the West End is home to student-oriented venues. The city's two trendiest theatres, the Citizens' and the Tramway, are both South side.

You can find **details** of events in the *Herald* or *Evening Times* newspapers, or in the comprehensive fortnightly listings magazine, *The List*, which also covers Edinburgh. To book **tickets** for theatre productions or big concerts, call at the Ticket Centre, City Hall, Candleriggs, on the Trongate end of Argyle Street (Mon–Sat 9am–6pm, Sun noon–5pm; phone bookings Mon–Sat 9am–9pm, Sun noon–6pm; ☎0141/287 5511).

Nightclubs

Archaos, 25 Queen St. Massive nightclub with designer decor, and a mixed, young crowd. Weekends are balanced between house, hip-hop and garage.

The Arches, 30 Midland St, off Jamaica Street. Deservedly popular weekend club in converted railway arches, under Central station. Pounds out predominantly house and techno.

Fury Murray's, 96 Maxwell St, behind the St Enoch Centre. Student-oriented and lively, with music spanning the 1960s to techno.

Lime, 5 Scott St. Busy, studenty club with mainstream music and Seventies and Eighties classics midweek.

Riverside Club, Fox Road, off Clyde Street. Regular weekend ceilidh that gets packed out with good-natured, drunken Scottish dancers, from seasoned experts to visiting novices. Get there early (8–9pm) to ensure a place.

Sub Club, 22 Jamaica St. Well-established nightclub aimed squarely at the cutting edge end of the market. Weekend nights are very trendy.

Trash, 197 Pitt St. Three-room venue playing house and garage, though the popular Sly on Thursday nights draws in a party crowd with cheesy favourites from the Seventies and Eighties.

The Tunnel, 84 Mitchell St. Stylish club with arty decor, though now a bit faded; the gents' toilet has cascading waterfall walls.

The Velvet Rooms, Sauchiehall Street. Consists of a small bar with postage-stamp dance area for the posing set, and a larger bar above playing mainstream dance, garage and soul.

Gay clubs and bars

Bennett's, 90 Glassford St, Merchant City. Glasgow's main gay club: predominantly male, fairly old-fashioned but enjoyable nonetheless. Straight nights on Tues.

Caffe Latte, 58 Virginia St. By day, a café serving food, and a trendy bar by night. Very popular with a gay crowd, although the clientele is usually very mixed.

Del Monica's, 68 Virginia St. Glasgow's liveliest and most stylish gay bar, very near George Square, with a mixed and hedonistic crowd.

Polo Lounge, 84 Wilson St, off Glassford Street. The original decor in this converted insurance office – all marble tiles and open fires – and the dark pounding nightclub underneath attract a mixed crowd.

The Waterloo Bar, 306 Argyle St. Very central, garish but enjoyable gay bar, which gets packed at weekends, mostly with men.

Live music pubs and venues

Barrowlands, 244 Gallowgate (☎0141/552 4601). Legendary East End dance hall hosting some of the sweatiest, liveliest gigs you will ever encounter.

The Garage, 490 Sauchiehall St (☎0141/332 1120). Good-size venue for bands that are just about to make it big.

King Tut's Wah Wah Hut, 272A St Vincent St (☎0141/221 5279). One of the city's best programmes of bands at this splendid city-centre live music pub. Famous as the place where Oasis were discovered.

Nice'n'Sleazy, 421 Sauchiehall St (☎0141/333 9637). Alternative bands most nights in the somewhat cramped downstairs bar.

Scotia Bar, 112 Stockwell St, near the St Enoch Centre (☎0141/552 8681). The folkies' favourite, a mellow musical pub, with regular live gigs and frequent jam sessions.

The 13th Note Café, 50–60 King St (☎0141/553 1638). This relaxed bar and vegetarian restaurant with Art Deco styling is the place to sample local music talent, including jazz and R&B; the club of the same name at 260 Clyde St is a bit louder and livelier.

Theatre and comedy

The Arches, 30 Midland St (☎0141/221 4001). Trendy base for performances by touring theatre and contemporary dance groups; also with club nights.

Blackfriars, 36 Bell St (☎0141/552 5924). The city's premier comedy and cabaret venue, well sited in the Merchant City and renowned for its good-value Sunday-night line-ups. Also live music at the weekend, particularly jazz.

Citizens' Theatre, 119 Gorbals St (☎0141/429 0022). "The Citz" has grown from profound work-ing-class roots to become one of the most respected and adventurous theatres in Britain. Three stages, with truly bargain prices for students and the unemployed.

Cottier Theatre, 935 Hyndland St (☎0141/357 3868). Small, trendy theatre in an old West End church hosting touring shows and regular music gigs.

King's Theatre, 294 Bath St (☎0141/287 5511). Large, grand theatre featuring mainstream shows and comedy, just south of Sauchiehall Street.

Tramway Theatre, 25 Albert Drive, off Pollokshaws Road (☎0141/227 5511). Good venue for experimental theatre, dance, music and regular art exhibitions.

Tron Theatre, 63 Trongate (☎0141/552 4267). Varied repertoire of mainstream and experimental productions from visiting companies, together with one of the city's most laid-back bars.

Concert halls

Royal Concert Hall, 2 Sauchiehall St (☎0141/287 5511). Some big-name rock and soul stars, as well as middle-of-the-road music hall acts, enjoy the acoustics and intimate feel of this relatively new venue. Also features big-name touring orchestras and is home to the Royal Scottish National Orchestra.

Scottish Exhibition and Conference Centre, Finnieston Quay (☎0141/248 3000). Huge, soulless and overpriced shed with the acoustics and atmosphere of an aircraft hangar; visited by megastars on world tours.

Theatre Royal, 282 Hope Street (☎0141/332 9000). The opulent home of Scottish Opera and regular host to visiting classical orchestras, opera companies, theatre blockbusters and occasional comedy.

Cinemas

The most accessible mainstream cinemas are along Sauchiehall and Renfield streets; both are conveniently placed near bus and underground stops. In addition, there are a couple of good independents:

Glasgow Film Theatre, 12 Rose St (☎0141/332 8128). The city's main art-house and independent cinema.

Grosvenor, Ashton Lane (☎0141/339 4298). Eclectic mix of repertory, mainstream and art-house movies on two screens in this tiny West End alley. Occasional theme nights and frequent lates for local students.

Listings

Airlines Aer Lingus, 19 Dixon St (☎0645/737747); British Airways, 66 Gordon St (☎0345/222111); Icelandair, Glasgow Airport (☎0345/581111); Lufthansa, 78 St Vincent St (☎0345/737747); Northwest, 177 W George St (☎0141/226 4991); Qantas, 395 King St (☎0345/747767). Airport enquiries ☎0141/887 1111.

Banks and exchange American Express, 115 Hope St (Mon–Fri 8.30am–5.30pm, Sat 9am–noon; ☎0141/221 4366); Bank of Scotland, 110 Queen St, 63 Waterloo St, 235 Sauchiehall St and 55 Bath St; Barclays, 90 St Vincent St; Clydesdale Bank, 14 Bothwell St, 7 St Enoch Square, 30 St Vincent

Place, 344 Argyle St and 120 Bath St; Lloyds, 12 Bothwell St; National Westminster, 14 Blythswood Square; Royal Bank of Scotland, 98 Buchanan St, 22 St Enoch Square, 140 St Vincent St and 393 Sauchiehall St. Outside banking hours you can change money at Thomas Cook, Central station (Mon–Wed & Sat 8am–7pm, Thurs & Fri 8am–8pm, Sun 10am–6pm; ☎0141/204 4496).

Bike rental see box on p.874.

Books John Smith's, 57 St Vincent St; Waterstone's, 132 Union St; Dillons, 104–108 Argyle St, and the vast Borders, 98 Buchanan St, all have extensive sections on Glasgow.

Bus enquiries Local buses: ☎0141/332 7133. National buses: ☎0990/505050.

Car rental Arnold Clark, 10–24 Vinnicomb St (☎0141/334 9501); Avis, 161 North St (☎0141/221 2827); Budget, 101 Waterloo St (☎0141/226 4141); Eurodollar, airport (☎0141/887 7915); Europcar, 38 Anderston Quay (☎0141/248 8788).

Dentist Glasgow Dental Hospital, 378 Sauchiehall St (☎0141/211 9600); J McDonald, 2 Lansdowne Cres (☎0141/339 0873); Smile Dental Care, 128 Great Western Road (☎0141/331 1366).

Hospital 24-hour casualty department at the Royal Infirmary, 84 Castle St (☎0141/211 4000).

Internet *Café Internet*, 2nd floor, Waterstone's, 153–7 Sauchiehall St (Mon–Fri 8am–10pm, Sat 8am–8pm, Sun 10.30am–7pm); *Link Café*, 569 Sauchiehall St (Mon–Fri 9am–11pm, Sat 10am–7pm, Sun noon–7pm).

Laundry 1110 Argyle St; 39 Bank St; 161 Great Western Rd.

Left luggage Buchanan Street bus station (daily 6.30am–10.30pm); Central and Queen Street train stations (24hr lockers).

Pharmacies Munroe's, 693 Great Western Rd (daily 9am–9pm); Superdrug, Central station (Mon–Wed 8am–8pm, Thurs–Sat 8am–9pm, Sun 10am–8pm).

Police Cranstonhill Police Station, 945 Argyle St (☎0141/532 3200); Stewart Street station, Cowcaddens (☎0141/532 3000).

Post office 47 St Vincent St (Mon–Fri 8.30am–5.45pm, Sat 9am–5.50pm), with branch offices at 85–89 Bothwell St, 228 Hope St and 533 Sauchiehall St.

Taxis TOA Taxis (☎0141/332 7070).

Travel agents Campus Travel, The Hub, Hillhead St (☎0141/357 0608), and 122 George St (☎0141/553 1818); Glasgow Flight Centre, 143 W Regent St (☎0141/221 8989).

The Clyde

The temptation to speed through the **Clyde Valley** is considerable, especially since the raw beauty of the Highlands, Argyll and, of course, Edinburgh are all within easy reach of the city. Although many of the towns and villages surrounding Glasgow are decidedly missable, some receive far fewer visitors than they deserve, tarnished with the frequently redundant image of dejected industrial towns. From the city regular trains dip down the southern bank of the Clyde to **Paisley**, where the distinctive cloth pattern gained its name, before heading up to the Firth of Clyde. Heading southeast out of Glasgow, the river's industrial landscape gives way to a far more attractive scenery of gorges and towering castles, including the bulky **Bothwell Castle**, which endured a long siege by Edward I in the late thirteenth century. Here you can also see the centre dedicated to the missionary and explorer David Livingstone at **Blantyre**, and the stoic town of **Lanark**, where eighteenth-century philanthropists built their model workers' community around the mills of **New Lanark**.

Paisley

Founded in the twelfth century as a monastic settlement around an abbey, **PAISLEY** expanded rapidly after the eighteenth century as a linen-manufacturing town, specializing in the production of highly fashionable imitation Kashmiri shawls. Paisley quickly eclipsed other British centres producing the cloth, eventually lending its name to the swirling teardrop design.

Opposite the town hall, the **Abbey** (Mon–Sat 10am–3.30pm; free) was built on the site of the town's original settlement in the twelfth century, although it was massively overhauled in the Victorian age. The unattractive, fat grey facade of the church does little justice to the renovated interior, which is tall, spacious and elaborately decorated. The elongated choir, rebuilt extensively throughout the last two centuries, is illuminated by jewel-coloured stained glass from a variety of ages and styles. The abbey's oldest monument is the tenth-century Celtic cross of St Barochan, which lurks like a gnarled old bone at the eastern end of the north aisle.

Paisley's tatty High Street leads from the town hall to the west and towards the civic **Museum and Art Gallery** (Tues–Sat 10am–5pm, Sun 2–5pm; free), which shelters behind pompous Ionic columns facing the grim buildings of Paisley University. The local history section, nearest the entrance, contains a collection of local artefacts from song sheets to spinning threads. The most popular part of the museum, which deals with the growth and development of the Paisley pattern, shows the teardrop design from its simplistic beginnings to elaborate later incarnations. Beyond the museum stands the **Thomas Coates Memorial Church** (May–Sept Mon, Wed & Fri 2–6pm), a Victorian masterpiece of hugely overstated grandeur, with massive tower-top buttresses and an interior of seemingly endless marble and alabaster. The harsh reality of eighteenth-century life is re-created in the **Sma' Shot Cottages** (April–Sept only Wed & Sat 1–5pm; free), on George Place, off New Street. Each with individual themes, they contain re-creations of eighteenth- and nineteenth-century daily life complete with bone cutlery and ancient looms.

Regular **trains** from Glasgow Central connect with Paisley's Gilmour Street station in the centre of town. Greater Glasgow **buses** #39, #53 and #54 stop at Paisley Abbey, but the train is faster and more convenient. South of the train station, down Gilmour or Smithills streets, lies the bridge over the White Cart Water and the borough's ponderous town hall. The **tourist office** (April & May Mon–Fri 9am–1pm & 2–5pm; June–Sept Mon–Sat 9am–6pm; ☎0141/889 0711) is a five-minute walk east from here, tucked inside the unremarkable Lagoon Leisure Centre, on Mill Street. Lunchtime and evening bar **meals**, together with a reasonably convivial atmosphere, can be found at *Gabriel's Bar*, 33 Gauze St, near the abbey, and the *Last Post* **pub**, in the old Post Office building in County Square. The *Paisley Arts Centre*, on New Street, has a small bar with seating outside.

Blantyre and Bothwell Castle

BLANTYRE, now a colourless suburb of Hamilton, twelve miles southeast of Glasgow, was a remote Clydeside hamlet when explorer and missionary David Livingstone was born there in 1813. From Blantyre station, a right turn brings you to a quiet country lane, at the bottom of which, painted a brilliant white, is the **David Livingstone Centre** (Mon–Sat 10am–5.30pm, Sun 12.30–5.30pm; hours may be reduced in winter; ☎01698 823140; £2.95; NTS), telling the story of his life from early years as a mill worker up until his death in 1873, while searching for the source of the River Nile. In 1813, the building consisted of 24 one-room tenements, each occupied by an entire family. Today, the Livingstone family room shows the claustrophobic conditions under which he was brought up. Other rooms feature slightly defensive exhibitions on the missionary movement with tableaux of scenes from his life in Africa. Smaller exhibitions on Blantyre and the Clyde Valley area are held inside the main "Africa Pavilion" building.

A mile or so from Blantyre, **Bothwell Castle** (April–Sept daily 9.30am–6.30pm; Oct–March Mon–Wed, Fri & Sat 9.30am–4pm, Thurs 9.30am–12.30pm, Sun 2–4.30pm; £1.80; HS) is one of Scotland's most dramatic citadels, a great red-sandstone bulk looming high above a loop in the river. The oldest section is the solid, circular keep, at the western end, built by the Moray family in the late 1200s to protect themselves against the English king Edward I during the Scottish wars of independence. Such was the might of the castle, that Edward only finally succeeded in capturing it in September 1301, after wheeling a catapult all the way from Glasgow. Over the next two centuries, the castle changed hands numerous times and was added to by each successive owner. The most recent section, dating from the sixteenth century, is the Great Hall, which sits in the grassy inner courtyard. **Bus** #255 from Glasgow to Hamilton will drop you off on the Bothwell Road, near the castle entrance.

Lanark and New Lanark

The neat little market town of **LANARK** is an old and distinguished burgh, sitting in the purple hills high above the River Clyde, its rooftops and spires visible for miles around. Other than the world's oldest bell, cast in 1130 and visible in the Georgian **Church of St Nicholas**, there's little to see in town and most people make their way to the restored heritage village of **NEW LANARK** (daily 11am–5pm; £3.75), a mile below the main town on Braxfield Road.

Although New Lanark is served by an hourly **bus** from the train station, it's well worth the steep downhill walk to get there. The first sight of the village, hidden away down in the gorge, is unforgettable: large, broken, curving walls of honeyed warehouses and tenements, built in Palladian style, lined up along the turbulent river's edge. The community was founded by David Dale and Richard Arkwright in 1785 to harness the power of the Clyde waterfalls in their cotton-spinning industry, but it was Dale's son-in-law, Robert Owen, who revolutionized the social side of the experiment in 1798, creating a "village of unity". Believing the welfare of the workers to be crucial to industrial success, Owen built adult educational facilities, the world's first day nursery and playground, and schools in which dancing and music were obligatory and there was no punishment or reward. The Neoclassical **Institute for the Formation of Character** at the very heart of the village was opened by Owen in 1816, and quickly became the main focus of the community, with a library, chapel and dance hall; today, you can see an introductory video about New Lanark and its founders in the spacious congegational hall. Of the three vast old mill buildings open to visitors, one houses the **Annie McLeod Experience**, where a chair-ride whisks visitors through a representation of life here from the imaginary perspective of a young mill girl.

The village itself is just as fascinating: everything, from the co-operative store to the workers' tenements and workshops, was built in an attempt to prove that industrialism need not be unaesthetic. You can wander through the re-created 1920s shop and explore the **New Buildings** to discover how the workers lived. More recently, **Robert Owen's House** has been brought to life, allowing visitors to glimpse the man behind the visionary mask and poke around the domestic kitchen, study, and living areas. Situated in the Old Dyeworks, **The Scottish Wildlife Trust Visitor Centre** (Feb, March & Oct–Dec Sat & Sun 1–5pm; April–Sept Mon–Fri 11am–5pm, Sat & Sun 1–5pm; £1) provides information about the history and wildlife of the area. Further on, past the visitor centre, a path along the Clyde leads you past the small falls of green water on which the Lanark project was first founded, and past the Bonnington hydroelectric station to the major **Falls of The Clyde**, where at the stunning tree-fringed **Cora Linn**, the river plunges 90ft in three tumultuous stages. It's an excellent marker point for the **Clyde Walkway**, which follows the river from Glasgow Green to this valley forest.

Practicalities

By **train**, Lanark is the terminus on the line from Glasgow Central station. The town's **tourist office** (May–Sept Mon–Sat 10am–6pm, Sun noon–5pm; Oct–April Mon–Sat 10am–5pm; ☎01555/661661) is housed in a circular building in the Horsemarket, just west of the station. By far the most original **accommodation** options in the area make use of reconstructed mill buildings in New Lanark: the **youth hostel** (☎01555/666710) has sixteen four-bed rooms in the cutely named Wee Row, on Rosedale Street, and is an excellent spot for enjoying the surrounding countryside in peace; the *New Lanark Mill Hotel* (☎01555/6672000, *hotel@newlanark.org*; ④) has good views and lots of character, as well as a brasserie serving some tasty dishes. On the edge of town, just off the A73 Glasgow Road, the *Cartland Bridge Hotel* (☎01555/664426; ⑤) is set in spectacular wooded surroundings. The best of the B&Bs are a little out of town: try *Covanhill Farm* (☎01555/811219; ①) or *Jerviswood Mains Farm* (☎01555/663987; ①). For **food**, there are plenty of inexpensive cafés and takeaways on High Street, while the *Courtyard Restaurant*, at 3 Castlegate, has a quiet patio away from the road. The unpretentious *Crown Tavern*, a quiet drinking haunt in Hope Street, serves reasonable food.

travel details

Trains

Glasgow Central to: Ardrossan (every 30min; 45min); Ayr (every 30min; 50min); Birmingham (5 daily; 3hr 50min); Blantyre (every 30min; 20min); Carlisle (hourly; 2hr 30min); Lanark (Mon–Sat hourly; 50min); London (10 daily; 5hr 45min); Manchester (1 daily; 3hr 50min); Newcastle-upon-Tyne (8 daily; 2hr 30min); Paisley (every 15min; 10min); Stranraer (4 daily; 2hr 10min); Wemyss Bay (hourly;1hr); York (7 daily; 3hr 30min).

Glasgow Queen Street to: Aberdeen (hourly; 2hr 40min); Aviemore (3 daily; 2hr 40min); Dundee (hourly; 1hr 20min); Edinburgh (every 30min; 50min); Fort William (3 daily; 3hr 40min); Inverness (3 daily; 3hr 30min); Mallaig (3 daily; 5hr 15min); Oban (3 daily; 3hr); Perth (hourly; 1hr); Stirling (hourly; 30min).

Buses

Glasgow to: Aberdeen (15 daily; 4hr); Aviemore (hourly; 3hr 30min); Campbeltown (3 daily; 4hr 20min); Dundee (hourly; 2hr 15min); Edinburgh (every 15min; 1hr 15min); Fort William (4 daily; 3hr); Glencoe (4 daily; 2hr 30min); Inverness (hourly; 4–5hr); Kyle of Lochalsh (3 daily; 5hr); Loch Lomond (hourly; 45min); London (5 daily; 7hr 30min); Newcastle-upon-Tyne (2 daily; 4hr); Oban (4 daily; 3hr); Perth (hourly; 1hr 40min); Pitlochry (hourly; 2hr 20min); Portree (3 daily; 6hr); Stirling (hourly; 45min); York (1 daily; 6hr 30min).

Flights

Glasgow to: Birmingham (Mon–Fri 11 daily, Sat & Sun 6 daily; 1hr); London Gatwick (Mon–Fri 4 daily, Sat & Sun 3 daily; 1hr 30min); London Heathrow (Mon–Fri 20 daily, Sat & Sun 12 daily; 1hr 30min); London Stansted (Mon–Fri 4 daily, Sat 1 daily, Sun 4 daily; 1hr 30min); Manchester (Mon–Fri 8 daily, Sat 1 daily, Sun 2 daily; 1hr).

CHAPTER TWENTY-ONE

CENTRAL SCOTLAND

Within easy reach of Edinburgh and Glasgow, central Scotland is split by the Highland Boundary Fault, running southwest to northeast across the region, which divides the picture-postcard beauty of the more prosperous Central Lowlands and the wilder, poorer terrain of the Highlands, which officially begin here. The region is much visited, not just for its spectacular and varied countryside, but also for its associations with some of the most important events in Scottish history. Today the landscape is not only littered with remants of the past – well-preserved medieval towns and castles, royal residences and battle sites – but is also coloured by the many romantic myths and legends that have grown up around it.

At the heart of the **Central Lowlands**, above the industrial belt around Falkirk and Grangemouth, is venerable **Stirling**, its imposing castle perched high above the town. Historically one of the most important bridging points across the River Forth, it was the site of two of the most famous battles fought under Robert the Bruce during the **Wars of Independence**. To the west and north of Stirling, the magnificent scenery centres on the fabled mountains, glens, lochs and forests of the **Trossachs**, a unique and beautiful area of high peaks and steep-sided glens that stretches west from **Callander** to the eastern banks of Loch Lomond. The geography and history of the area caught the imagination of **Sir Walter Scott**, who took so much delight in the tales of local clansman **Rob Roy** MacGregor, the notorious seventeenth-century outlaw, that he set them down in his novel of the same name. Visitors flocked to the Trossachs and according to one contemporaneous account, after Scott's *Lady of the Lake* was published in 1810, the number of carriages passing Loch Katrine rose from fifty the previous year to nearly three hundred. Thanks to Scott, and to William and Dorothy Wordsworth's effusive praise, Queen Victoria decided to visit, placing the area firmly on the tourist map. Today however, the trappings of tourism – evident in twee shops and tearooms in every small town – don't impinge too much on the experience.

Lying to the east of the Central Lowlands is **Fife**, the only one of Scotland's seven original Pict kingdoms to survive relatively intact. Neither Norse nor Norman influence found its way to this independent corner, and nine and a half centuries later, when the government at Westminster redrew local boundaries in 1975 and again in 1995, the Fifers stuck to their guns and successfully opposed any changes. Here you'll find coastal fishing villages, sandy beaches and the self-assured town of **St Andrews**, inextricably

---

ACCOMMODATION PRICE CODES

Throughout this guide, hotel and B&B accommodation is priced on a scale of ① to ⑨, the number indicating the **lowest price** you could expect to pay per night in that establishment for a **double room** in high season. The prices indicated by the codes are as follows:

① under £40	④ £60–70	⑦ £110–150
② £40–50	⑤ £70–90	⑧ £150–200
③ £50–60	⑥ £90–110	⑨ over £200

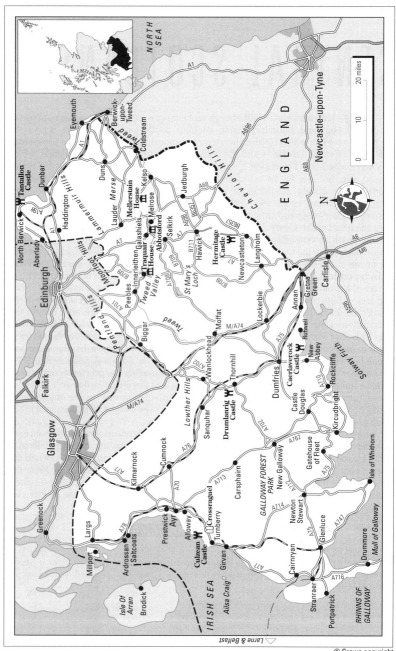

© Crown copyright

linked in the public consciousness with golf, but also notable for a large number of well-preserved medieval buildings and the oldest university in Scotland.

North of St Andrews on the west bank of the River Tay is the ancient town of **Perth**, surrounded by beautiful rugged country. At nearby **Scone**, Kenneth Macalpine established the capital of the kingdom of the Scots and the Picts in 846. When this settlement was washed away by floods in 1210, William the Lion founded Perth as a royal burgh and it stood as Scotland's capital until 1452. The four great monasteries of Perth were all destroyed during the Reformation after a sermon by John Knox at St John's Church. North of Perth, the Highlands begin in earnest. From **Loch Tay** onwards, beyond the agreeable town of **Aberfeldy**, the countryside becomes more sparsely populated and spectacular, with the **Grampian Mountains** to the east offering wonderful walks, especially around **Pitlochry**, and the wild expanses of **Rannoch Moor** to the west. This northerly part of the region also boasts Scotland's most popular tourist attraction, **Blair Castle**.

Stirling and around

Straddling the River Forth a few miles upstream from the estuary at Kincardine, at first glance **STIRLING** appears like a smaller version of Edinburgh – a lively, appealing place with a crag-top castle, steep, cobbled streets and a mixed community of locals and students. As a much-coveted river crossing and the seat of Scotland's first university, Stirling has historic importance, but being geographically trapped equidistant between Scotland's two main cities, it remains at heart decidedly provincial.

The town was the scene of some of the most significant developments in the evolution of the Scottish nation. It was here that the Scots under William Wallace defeated the English at the **Battle of Stirling Bridge** in 1297, only to fight – and win again – under Robert the Bruce, just a couple of miles away at the **Battle of Bannockburn**, in 1314. Stirling enjoyed its golden age between the fifteenth and seventeenth centuries, most notably when its castle was the favoured residence of the Stuart monarchy and the setting for the coronation in 1543 of the young Mary Queen of Scots. By the early eighteenth century, the town was again besieged, its location being of strategic importance during the Jacobite rebellions of 1715 and 1745.

Today Stirling is known for its **Castle** – just as beautiful as its Edinburgh counterpart – and the lofty **Wallace Monument**, a mammoth Victorian monolith high on Abbey Craig to the northeast. The **University**, also, has helped to maintain the town's profile. Stirling is at its liveliest during the summer, with buskers and street artists jostling for performing space in the pedestrianized centre. If you get decent weather – which isn't all that uncommon despite the proliferation of surrounding hills – there's very much a holiday air about the place, with kids rushing around the castle ramparts, backpackers struggling up the steep hill to the youth hostel, and students, many of whom choose to stay here over the summer, spilling out of the cafés.

Arrival, information and accommodation

The **train station** is near the centre of town, on Station Road; the **bus station** is nearby on Goosecroft Road. Stirling's **tourist office** is in the heart of the Lower Town, at 41 Dumbarton Rd (June & Sept Mon–Sat 9am–6pm, Sun 10am–4pm; July & Aug Mon–Sat 9am–7.30pm, Sun 9.30am–6.30pm; Oct–May Mon–Sat 10am–5pm; ☎01786/475019). This is the main office for Loch Lomond, Stirling and the Trossachs, with a wide range of books, maps and leaflets.

If you're in Stirling between May and October, you'll need to book a room by lunchtime at the latest, or you're likely to be stranded; the tourist office carries details of **accommodation**. Most of the B&Bs are concentrated in the residential area nearby, on Causewayhead Road leading to the university, and in the opulent Victorian suburb of King's Park, immediately south of the tourist office; two of the friendliest are *No. 10*, 10 Gladstone Place (☎01786/472681; ②), and *Whitegables*, 112 Causewayhead Rd (☎01786/479838; ②). The *Park Lodge Hotel*, 32 Park Terrace (☎01786/474862; ⑤), is Stirling's finest, overlooking the park and castle, with an *haute-cuisine* restaurant. *The Heritage*, 16 Allan Park (☎01786/473660; ③), on the northern edge of King's Park, also has rooms looking up at the castle, and a good Scottish/French restaurant.

At the top of the town (a strenuous trek with a backpack), the cheapest option is the **youth hostel** in a converted church on St John Street (☎01786/473442). If you prefer to stay out of town, try the **campus accommodation** at Stirling University

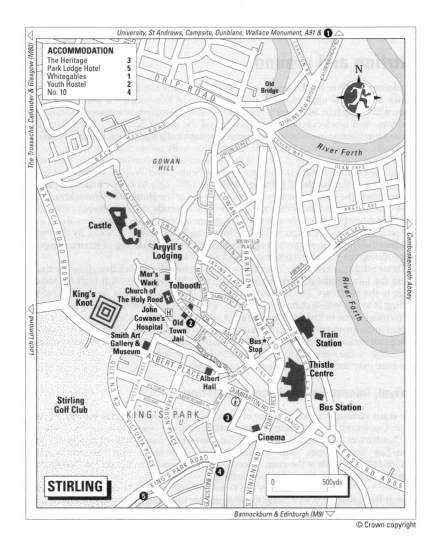

© Crown copyright

(☎01786/467141; ③; closed Sept–May) a couple of miles north of the town centre (bus #53 or #58 from Murray Place). Also on campus is the new Stirling Management Centre (☎01786/451666; ⑦), as popular with tourists as with the conference guests at whom it was originally aimed, with rooms looking out at the Wallace Monument. There's a **campsite**, the *Witches' Craig* at Blairlogie, three miles northeast of the town, off the A91 road to St Andrews (☎01786/474947; closed Nov–May).

The Town

Stirling evolved from the top down, starting with its castle and gradually spreading south and east onto the low-lying flood plain. At the centre of the original **Old Town**, Broad Street was the main thoroughfare, with St John Street running more or less parallel, and St Mary's Wynd forming part of the original route to Stirling Bridge below. In the eighteenth and nineteenth centuries, as the threat of attack decreased, the centre of commercial life crept down towards the River Forth, with the modern town – commonly called the **Lower Town** – growing on the edge of the plain over which the castle traditionally stands guard.

Stirling Castle

Stirling Castle (daily: April–Sept 9.30am–6.30pm; Oct–March 9.30am–5pm; £5, including entry to Argyll's Lodging; HS) presented would-be invaders with a formidable challenge. Its impregnability is most daunting when you approach the town from the west, from where the sheer, 250-foot drop down the side of the crag is most obvious. The rock was first fortified during the Iron Age, though what you see now dates largely from the fifteenth and sixteenth centuries. Presently undergoing a massive restoration scheme (due to be completed in 2001), some parts of the castle may be inaccessible.

The **visitor centre** (same times as castle), on the esplanade, shows an introductory film giving a potted history of the castle, but the best place to get an impression of its gradual expansion is in the courtyard known as the **Upper Square**. Here you can see the magnificent **Great Hall** (1501–03), with its lofty dimensions, superb hammer-beam roof and huge fireplaces making it perhaps the finest medieval secular building in Scotland. The exterior of the **Palace** (1540–42) is richly decorated with grotesque carved figures and Renaissance sculpture, including, in the left-hand corner, the glaring bearded figure of James V in the dress of a commoner. Inside, in the royal apartments, are the **Stirling Heads**, 56 elegantly carved oak medallions, which once adorned the ceiling of the Presence Chamber, where visitors were presented to royalty. Otherwise the royal apartments are bare, their emptiness emphasizing the fine dimensions and wonderful views. The **Chapel Royal** (1594) was built by James VI for the baptism of his son, and replaced an earlier chapel, not deemed sufficiently impressive. The interior is lovely, with a seventeenth-century fresco of elaborate scrolls and patterns.

The castle also houses the Argyll and Sutherland Highlanders **museum**, with its collection of well-polished silver and memorabilia, including a seemingly endless display of Victoria Crosses won by the regiment. The set-up in the restored castle **kitchens** recreates the preparations for the spectacular Renaissance banquet given by Mary Queen of Scots for the baptism of the future James VI. As well as an audio-visual display describing how delicacies for the feast were procured, and an abundance of stuffed animals in various stages of preparation (who, we are assured, died natural deaths), the kitchens feature replica recipe books with such delights as sugar wine glasses, golden steamed custard and dressed peacock.

From the **Douglas Gardens** you can see the surprisingly small window from which the eighth Earl of Douglas, suspected of treachery, was thrown by James II in 1452.

There's a bird's-eye view down to the **King's Knot**, a series of grassed octagonal mounds which in the seventeenth century were planted with box trees and ornamental hedges.

The Old Town

Leaving the castle, head downhill into the old centre of Stirling, fortified behind the massive, whinstone boulders of the **town walls**, built in the mid-sixteenth century and intended to ward off the advances of Henry VIII, who had set his sights on the young Mary as a wife for his son, Edward. The walls now constitute some of the best-preserved town defences in Scotland, and can be traced by following the path known as **Back Walk**. This circular walkway was built in the eighteenth century and in the upper reaches encircles the castle, taut along the edge of the crag, offering panoramic views of the surrounding countryside.

Argyll's Lodging (daily: April–Sept 9.30am–6.30pm; Oct–March 9.30am–5pm; £2.80; HS), five minutes' walk down the hill from the castle's visitor centre, is a romantic Renaissance mansion built by Sir William Alexander of Menstrie. Inside, an extremely informative exhibition examines the history of the building itself and the wealthy families that lived here, from Sir William Alexander, the first Earl of Stirling, to the ninth Earl of Argyll. Laigh Hall, the original reception room that opens out onto the courtyard, is a sparse affair retaining the original 1630s fireplace and mantelpiece, while the Great Kitchen, marked by low ceilings and tiny windows, has an enormous fireplace complete with a special recess for salt. Creaking stairs lead up to the painstakingly restored Furnished Apartments. The refined High Dining Room is surrounded by authentic painted Corinthian pilasters, dating from 1675, while the lavishly decorated Drawing Room contains the earls' imposing chair of state. The Bedchamber used by the earl and countesses is reached via the Drawing Room and is quite homely, with a comfortable four-poster bed and feather mattress – often the most expensive single item in any aristocratic establishment.

The richly decorated facade at the top of Broad Street on Castle Wynd hides the dilapidated **Mar's Wark**, a would-be palace which the first Earl of Mar, Regent of Scotland and hereditary Keeper of Stirling Castle, started in 1570. His dream house was never to be realized, however, for he died two years later and what had been built was left to ruin, its degeneration speeded up by extensive damage during the 1745 Jacobite Rebellion. Below it is the **Church of the Holy Rude** (May–Sept Mon–Fri 10am–5pm, Sat & Sun times vary), a fine medieval structure, the oldest parts of which, including the impressive oak hammer-beam roof, date from the early fifteenth century. Go in during the day and imagine the ceremony that was held here in 1567 for the coronation of the infant James VI – later the first monarch of the United Kingdom – and come back in the evening to the atmospheric graveyard, from where you can watch the sun set. Just south of the church on the edge of the crag, the grand, E-shaped **John Cowane's Hospital** was built in 1649 as an almshouse for "decayed [unsuccessful] members of the Guild of Merchants". Above the entrance, John Cowane, the wealthy merchant who founded the hospital, is commemorated in a statue which, it is said, comes alive at Hogmanay.

Continuing down St John Street brings you to the impressive **Old Town Jail** (daily: April–Sept 9.30am–6pm; Oct–March 9.30am–4pm; guided tours every 30min; £2.75). The sweeping driveway leads up to a formidable crestellated building, rescued from dereliction in 1992 and superbly refurbished to house a replica nineteenth-century jail. Tours are brought to life by costumed guides who assume a variety of costumes and personas. Life-size models inhabit the cells and there is a working example of the dreaded crank, which prisoners had to turn a punishing 14,400 times per day as part of their punishment. Take the glass lift up to the prison roof on the third floor to admire spectacular vews across Stirling and the Forth Valley.

Broad Street was the site of the marketplace and centre of the medieval town. Many of its buildings have been restored in recent years, and preservation work continues. Down here, past the **Mercat Cross** (the unicorn on top is known, inexplicably, as "the puggy"), the **Tolbooth**, sandwiched between Broad and St John streets – and with its entrance on Broad Street – was built in 1705 by Sir William Bruce, who designed the Palace of Holyrood House in Edinburgh. It was used as both a courthouse and, after 1809, a prison, from where the unfortunate were led to execution in the street outside. **Darnley's House**, at the bottom of Broad Street, was where Mary Queen of Scots' husband is believed to have lodged while she lorded it up in the castle; it is now a touristy coffee shop.

The Lower Town

The further downhill you go into Stirling's Lower Town, the more modern the buildings become. Follow St John Street into Spittal Street, and then on down into King Street, where austere Victorian facades block the sun from the cobbled road. Stirling's main **shopping** area is down here, along Port Street and Murray Place, while the **Smith Art Gallery and Museum** is a short walk west up Dumbarton Road (Tues–Sat 10.30am–5pm, Sun 2–5pm; free). Founded in 1874 with a legacy from local painter and collector Thomas Stuart Smith, it houses a permanent exhibition relating the history of Stirling, and a range of changing displays of arts and crafts, contemporary art and photography.

The fifteenth-century **Old Bridge** over the Forth lies on the edge of the town centre, a twenty-minute walk from Murray Place. Although once the most important river crossing in Scotland – the lowest bridging point on the Forth until the new bridge was built in 1831 – it now stands virtually forgotten, an almost incidental reminder of Stirling's former importance. An earlier, wooden **bridge**, now vanished, was the focus of the Battle of Stirling Bridge in 1297.

Eating, drinking and nightlife

The elegant, three-storey *Darnley Coffee House*, on Bow Street, serves reasonably priced **lunches** and teas, amid an impressive plain barrel-vaulted interior. On Albert Place, the *Café Albert* in the Victorian grandeur of Albert Hall is another good choice for lunch. In the evening, the upmarket *Hermann's*, at 32 St John St (☎01786/450632), serves Austrian/Scottish meals in a handsomely austere interior; the downstairs brasserie is open at lunchtime. *Italia Nostra*, 25 Baker St (☎01786/473208), serves good, moderately priced Italian food and is especially lively at weekends, while the *East India Club*, at 7 Viewfield Place, a five-minute walk from the centre (☎01786/471330), offers fabulous Indian food. Slightly more expensive is the delicious and elegantly served Cantonese food at *The Regent*, 30 Upper Craigs (☎01786/472513).

Nightlife in Stirling revolves around **pubs** and **bars** and is dominated by the student population. The lively *Barnton Bar & Bistro* on Barnton Street serves a good selection of beers and food, including huge breakfasts. Also popular with students is the beer at Stirling's oldest ale house, the *Settle Inn*, 91 St Mary's Wynd. Near the university, try *The Meadowpark* pub, on Kenilworth Road. From June to September there are **ceilidhs** in the wonderful venue of John Cowane's Hospital, near the castle (usually Mon 8pm, but check with the tourist office; £3.50). The larger Albert Hall is a good venue for classical and pop/rock **concerts**. The main venue for **theatre** and **film** is the excellent MacRobert Arts Centre (☎01786/461081), on the university campus, which shows a good selection of drama and art-house films.

The Wallace monument and Cambuskenneth Abbey

Overlooking the university, two miles north of Stirling, is the prominent **Wallace Monument** (daily: March–May & Oct 10am–5pm; June & Sept 10am–6pm; July & Aug 9.30am–6.30pm; Nov & Dec 10am–4pm; £3.25), built 1861–69, a rocket-like tribute to Sir William Wallace ("the hammer and scourge of the English"), who was portrayed by Mel Gibson in the 1995 film *Braveheart*. It was from nearby Wallace's Pass that the Scottish hero led his troops down to defeat the English at the Battle of Stirling Bridge in 1297. Exhibits inside the monument include Wallace's long steel sword, the Hall of (Scottish) Heroes – a row of stern white marble busts featuring John Knox and Adam Smith – and, most kitsch of all, a life-size "talking model" of Wallace. If you can manage the climb – 246 spiral steps up – it's well worth it on a clear day, with superb views across to Fife and Ben Lomond from the top of the 220-foot tower. A shuttle bus (70p) runs from the base of the hill to the tower every ten minutes for those who want to avoid the initial steep climb.

A thirty-minute walk weaves its way along a woodland path from the monument to the ruins of **Cambuskenneth Abbey**, about a mile east of Stirling (grounds: free access year-round; ruins: April–Sept only; free; HS). Founded in 1147 by David I on the site of an Augustinian settlement, the abbey is distinguished by its early fourteenth-century bell tower, though there's little else to see there now. Its history, however, makes it worth a brief look: the Scots parliament met here in 1326 to pledge allegiance to Robert the Bruce's son David, and James III and his wife, Queen Margaret of Denmark, are both buried in the grounds, their graves marked by a nineteenth-century monument erected at the insistence of Queen Victoria.

Bannockburn

A couple of miles south of Stirling, just north of the village of **BANNOCKBURN**, the **Bannockburn Heritage Centre** (daily: April–Oct 10am–5.30pm; March, Nov & Dec 11am–3pm; £2.30; NTS) stands close to where Robert the Bruce won his mighty victory over the English at the **Battle of Bannockburn** on June 24, 1314. It was this battle, the climax of the Wars of Independence, which united the Scots under Bruce and led to independence under the Declaration of Arbroath (1320) and the Treaty of Northampton (1328). Outside, a concrete rotunda encloses a cairn near the spot where Bruce planted his standard after beating Edward II. Of the original bore stone, only a fragment remains, safely on display in the visitor centre. Over-eager visitors used to chip pieces off, and the final straw came when a particularly zealous enthusiast attempted to blast enough of it away to make two curling stones. Pondering the scene is an equestrian statue of Bruce, on the spot from where he is said to have commanded the battle.

Dunblane

Frequent trains, and bus #58, make the journey four miles north of Stirling to **DUNBLANE**, a small city now indissolubly linked with the massacre that occurred in one of its primary schools in March 1996. Prior to that atrocity, Dunblane's reputation rested on its **Cathedral** (April–Sept Mon–Sat 9.30am–6.30pm, Sun 2–6pm; Oct–March Mon–Sat 9.30am–4.30pm, Sun 2–4pm; free; HS), a building dating mainly from the thirteenth century, and restored to its Gothic splendour a hundred years ago. Inside, note the delicate, blue-purple stained glass, and the exquisitely carved pews, screen and choir stalls, all crafted in the early twentieth century. Also of interest is the little alcove with its thin stained-glass window, thought to have been a hermit's cell; a tenth-century Celtic cross; and a sadly worn thirteenth-century double effigy of the fifth Earl of

Strathearn and his countess. The cathedral stands serenely amid a clutch of old-world buildings, among them the seventeenth-century Dean's House, which houses the tiny cathedral **museum** (May–Oct Mon–Sat 10am–12.30pm & 2–4.30pm; free), with exhibits on local history. Close by lies the oldest private library in Scotland, **Leighton Library** (same times as museum; donation requested), which allows visitors to browse through some of Scotland's rarest books, including a first edition of Sir Walter Scott's *Lady of the Lake.*

Doune

DOUNE, eight miles northwest of Stirling (bus #59), is worth a call for its ruined, fourteenth-century **Castle** (April–Sept Mon–Sat 9.30am–6pm, Sun 2–6pm; Oct–March Mon–Wed & Sat 9am–4pm, Sun 2–4pm; £2.30; HS), standing magnificently on a small hill in a bend of the River Teith. Built by Robert, Duke of Albany, it eventually ended up in the hands of the earls of Moray (whose descendants still own it), following the execution of the Albany family by James I. In the sixteenth century it belonged to the second earl, James Stewart – son of James V and half-brother of Mary Queen of Scots – murdered in 1592 and immortalized in the ballad the *Bonnie Earl of Moray.* Today the most prominent features of the castle are its mighty 95-foot gatehouse, with its spacious vaulted rooms, and the kitchens, complete with medieval rubbish chute. The present earl has a fabulous collection of flash vintage cars, which are on show one mile northwest of town in the **Doune Motor Museum** (April–Nov daily 10am–5pm; £3) off the A84. Among the examples of gleaming paintwork and tanned upholstery you can see legendary models of Bentley, Lagonda, Jaguar and Aston Martin, as well as the second oldest Rolls Royce in the world (built in 1905).

Dollar and Castle Campbell

Above the town of **Dollar**, twelve miles east of Stirling, the dramatic chasm of Dollar Glen is commanded by **Castle Campbell** (April–Sept daily 9.30am–6.30pm; Oct–March Mon–Wed & Sat 9.30am–4.30pm, Thurs 9.30am–noon, Sun 2–4.30pm; £2.50; NTS & HS). Previously known as Castle Gloom, an evocative corruption of an old Gaelic name, the castle came into the hands of the Campbells in 1481, who changed its name eight years later. John Knox preached here in 1556, although probably from within the castle, rather than from the curious archway in the garden, as is traditionally claimed. In 1654, the castle was burned by Cromwell's troops; the remains of a graceful seventeenth-century loggia and a roofless hall bear witness to the destruction. However, the oldest surviving part of the castle, the fine fifteenth-century tower built by Sir Colin Campbell, survived the fire; look out for the claustrophobic pit prison just off the Great Hall and the latrines with their vertiginous views to the ground. You can also walk round the roof of the tower, where there's a wonderful view of the hills behind the castle, and down the glen to Dollar. The castle is only a mile and half from the main street in Dollar, but the road stops short of the castle, and there's limited parking at the top. There's also a signposted footpath which follows the stream from the bridge at the top of town.

The Trossachs

The **Trossachs** boast a magnificent diversity of scenery, with dramatic peaks and densely wooded slopes that live up to all the images ever produced of Scotland's wild land. This is Rob Roy country, where every waterfall, hidden cave and barely discernible path was supposedly once frequented by the seventeenth-century Scottish outlaw who led

---

ROB ROY

"**Rob Roy**, hero or villain?" ponders the tourist literature, in the great spirit of inquiry. Given that Rob Roy's clan, the MacGregors, have the distinction of having invented the term blackmail, and that Rob Roy himself achieved fame through cattle-rustling and thieving, the evidence seems to point to the "villain" thesis. Born in 1671, in Glengyle, just north of Loch Katrine, Rob Roy (from Rab Ruadh, meaning "Red Robert" in Gaelic) started life as a cattle farmer, supported by the powerful Duke of Montrose. When the duke withdrew his support, possibly having been robbed of £1000 by Rob Roy, the latter became a bankrupt and a brigand, plundering the rich carse land and revenging himself on the duke. He was at the Battle of Sherrifmuir in 1715, ostensibly as a Jacobite but probably as an opportunist – the chaos would have made cattle-raiding easier. Eventually captured and sentenced to transportation, Rob Roy was pardoned and returned to Balquhidder, where he remained until his death in 1734. His life has been much romanticized ever since Sir Walter Scott's 1818 version of the story in his novel *Rob Roy*; a process continued in the film starring Liam Neeson.

---

the Clan MacGregor. Strictly speaking, the name "The Trossachs", normally translated as either "bristly country" or "crossing place", originally referred only to the wooded glen between Loch Katrine and Loch Achray, but today it is usually taken as being the whole area from Callander in the east to Queen Elizabeth Forest Park in the west, right up to the eastern banks of Loch Lomond.

The Trossachs' high tourist profile was largely attributable in the early days to Sir Walter Scott, whose *The Lady of the Lake* and *Rob Roy* were set in and around the area. Since then, neither the popularity – nor beauty – of the region have waned, and in high season the place is jam-packed. Autumn is a better time to come, when the hills are blanketed in rich, rusty colours and the crowds are thinner. In terms of where to stay, **Aberfoyle** has a slightly dowdy air, even at the height of summer, so it is better to opt for the romantic seclusion of the **Lake of Menteith**, or the handsome country town of **Callander**, reached from Aberfoyle by the dramatic **Duke's Pass**.

Aberfoyle and Lake of Menteith

Like Brigadoon waking once a year from a mist-shrouded slumber, each summer the sleepy little town of **ABERFOYLE**, twenty miles west of Stirling, dusts itself down for the annual influx of tourists. Its position in the heart of the Trossachs is ideal, with Loch Ard Forest and Queen Elizabeth Forest Park stretching across to Ben Lomond and Loch Lomond to the west, the long curve of Loch Katrine and Ben Venue to the northwest, and Ben Ledi to the northeast. Don't come here for lively nightlife or entertainment, but for a good, healthy blast of the outdoors. The town itself is well equipped to lodge and feed visitors (though booking is recommended), and is an excellent base for walking and pony-trekking, or simply wandering the hills.

About four miles east of Aberfoyle towards Doune, the **Lake of Menteith** is a superb fly-fishing centre and Scotland's only lake (as opposed to loch), so named due to a historic mix-up with the word *laigh*, the Gaelic for "low-lying ground", which applied to the whole area. To rent a **fishing boat** contact the Lake of Menteith Fisheries (☎01877/385664). From the northern shore of the lake you can take the little ferry boat (April–Sept Mon–Sat 9.30am–6.30pm, Sun 2–6.30pm; £3) to the **Island of Inchmahome** (HS), and explore the lovely ruin of the Augustinian abbey, perhaps Scotland's most beautiful island monastery. Founded in 1238, the priory's remains rise tall and graceful above the trees. Although the church nave is roofless, the choir still shelters the graves of important families from the surrounding area. Most touching is a late thirteenth-century double effigy depicting Walter, the first Stewart Earl of Menteith, and his Countess Mary who, feet resting on lion-like animals, turn towards each other and embrace.

Also buried at Inchmahome is **Robert Bontine Cunninghame Graham**, the adventurer, scholar, socialist and Scottish nationalist, who was Liberal MP for northwest Lanarkshire for 25 years, and the first president of the National Party of Scotland. A pal of Buffalo Bill in Mexico as well as an intimate friend of the novelist Joseph Conrad, Cunninghame Graham had a ranch in Argentina, where he was affectionately known as "Don Roberto". Five-year-old **Mary Queen of Scots** was hidden at Inchmahome in 1547 before being taken to France; there's a knot garden in the west of the island known as Queen Mary's bower, where legend has it the child queen played. Traces remain of an orchard planted by the monks, but the island is thick now with oak, ash and Spanish chestnut.

If you have children, you might like to take them to the **Farm Life Centre** (April–Oct daily 10am–6pm; £3.50), where they can pet a host of farm animals, make oatcakes, milk goats and ride tractors. This converted farm can be found off the main road from Aberfoyle to Callander and has a play and picnic area, smiddy, tearoom and small farm museum – a good distraction on a rainy day.

Practicalities

Regular **buses** from Stirling to Aberfoyle pull into the car park on Main Street. The **tourist office**, directly next door, has full details of local accommodation, sights and outdoor activities (daily: March–June, Sept & Oct 10am–5pm; July & Aug 9.30pm–7pm; ☎01877/382352). For **accommodation**, try the tartan-carpeted *Covenanter's Inn*, at the northern end of town (☎01877/382347; ③), or the *Inverard Hotel*, Loch Ard Road (☎018772/382229; ④), with good views over the River Forth. There are scores of **B&Bs** in the town itself including the Tudor-style *Craigend*, 1 Craiguchty Terrace (☎01877/382716; ②). *The Lake Hotel and Restaurant*, at Port of Menteith (☎01877/385258; ⑥), has a lovely lakeside setting, and a classy restaurant. A couple of miles south of Aberfoyle on the edge of Queen Elizabeth Forest Park, *Cobleland Campsite* (☎01877/382392; closed Nov–Feb) is run by the Forestry Commission; further south is the *Trossachs Holiday Park* (☎01877/382614; closed Nov–March), which rents **bikes**.

Duke's Pass

Whether driving or on foot, don't miss the trip from Aberfoyle to Callander which for part of the way takes you along the **Duke's Pass** – so called because it once belonged to the Duke of Montrose – as it weaves its way through the Queen Elizabeth Forest Park to just south of Loch Katrine.

The A821 twists up out of Aberfoyle, following the contours of the hills and snaking back on itself in tortuous bends. About halfway up is the excellent Queen Elizabeth Forest Park **visitor centre** (April–Oct daily 10am–6pm; Nov–March Sat & Sun only 10am–4pm; car park fee £1; ☎01877/382258), which details the local fauna and flora. From here various marked paths wind through the forests giving splendid views over the lowlands and surrounding hills. A few miles further on, a road branches off to the left, leading to the southern end of Loch Katrine, at the foot of Ben Venue (2370ft), from where the historic steamer, the *SS Sir Walter Scott* (April–Oct Sun–Fri 4 daily, Sat 2 daily; £3.70), has been plying the waters since 1900, chugging up the loch to Stronachlachar and the wild country of Glengyle, where Rob Roy was born. To climb

Ben A'an (1520ft), start from the Trossachs Hotel on the north bank of Loch Achray. No longer a hotel, it retains the splendid exterior designed by the outlandishly named Lord Willoughby d'Eresby in 1852.

The final leg of the pass is along the tranquil shores of **Loch Venachar** at the southern foot of Ben Ledi. Look out for the small **kirk** in a lovely setting at the edge of the loch, where services are still held on the first Sunday of each month at 3pm.

Callander and around

CALLANDER, on the eastern edge of the Trossachs, sits quietly on the banks of the River Teith roughly ten miles north of Doune, at the southern end of the Pass of Leny, one of the key routes into the Highlands. Its wide main street recalls the influence of the military architects who designed the town after Bonnie Prince Charlie's Jacobite Rebellion of 1745.

Callander first came to fame during the Romantic era of the eighteenth and nineteenth centuries, when the glowing reports given by Sir Walter Scott and William Wordsworth prompted the first tourists to venture into the wilds by horse-drawn carriage. Development was given a boost when Queen Victoria chose to visit, and then by the arrival of the train line – long since closed – in the 1860s.

The present community has not been slow to capitalize on its appeal, establishing a plethora of restaurants, tearooms, antique shops, secondhand book shops and shops selling local woollens and crafts. The chief formal attraction is the **Rob Roy and Trossachs Visitor Centre**, at Ancaster Square on the main street (Jan & Feb Sat & Sun only 11am–4.30pm; March–May & Oct–Dec daily 10am–5pm; June & Sept daily 9.30am–6pm; July & Aug daily 9am–10pm; £2.50), an entertaining and partisan account of the life of the diminutive redhead featuring a talking statue huddled next to a fire in some barren glen, musing over the injustice of the lairds and their treatment of the people.

Callander's **tourist office** is in the Rob Roy and Trossachs Visitor Centre (same hours; ☎01877/330342). Good **accommodation** choices include *The Priory*, Bracklinn Road (☎01877/330001; ③), a Victorian house with good views and disabled access; the *Ben A'an Guest House*, on the main street (☎01877/330317; ③); the handsome Victorian *Brook Linn Country House*, on Leny Feus (☎01877/330103; ③), set above the town. Across the river, the *Trossachs Backpackers* is a sparkling new, thirty-bed independent hostel and activity centre with self-catering dorms, family rooms and **bike rental** (☎01877/331100, *trosstel@aol.com*). The *Invertrossachs Country House* (☎01877/331126; ⑥), on the southern shores of Loch Venachar, is a plush Edwardian mansion offering superior **B&B** accommodation. There are few **restaurants** worth recommending in Callander, though the *Myrtle Inn*, on the eastern edge of town, does good pub food.

On each side of Callander, pleasant and less-than-arduous walks wind through a wooded gorge to the **Falls of Leny** to the north and **Bracklinn Falls** to the south – both distances of only a mile or so. North of town, you can walk or ride the scenic six-mile **Callander to Strathyre Cycleway**, which forms part of the network of cycle ways between the Highlands and Glasgow. The route is based on the old Caledonian train line to Oban, which closed in 1965, and runs along the western side of **Loch Lubnaig**.

To the north, Rob Roy is buried in the small yard behind the ruined church at tiny **BALQUHIDDER**, where he died in 1734. Oddly enough, considering the Rob Roy fever that plagues the region, his grave – marked by a rough stone marked with a sword, a cross and a man with a dog – is remarkably underplayed. If you want to **stay** in Balquhidder, go to the award-winning eighteenth-century farmhouse *Monachyle Mhor* hotel (☎01877/384622; ⑦), which has a terrific restaurant looking out to Loch Voil and very comfortable rooms, some with great views of the loch.

Watersports are the life force of the village of **LOCHEARNHEAD**, at the western end of **Loch Earn**, a substantial body of water running east into Perthshire and fed by water off the slopes of **Ben Vorlich** (3201ft), to the south. A more impressive stretch of water is **Loch Tay**, about fifteen miles north of Callander, which points northeastwards, like a fourteen-mile finger, towards Aberfeldy (see p.917).

Loch Lomond

Loch Lomond is the largest stretch of fresh water in Britain (about 24 miles long and up to five miles wide), and is almost as famous as Loch Ness, thanks to the ballad about its "bonnie, bonnie banks". The song is said to have been written by a Jacobite prisoner captured by the English, who, sure of his fate, wrote that his spirit would return to Scotland on the low road much faster than his living compatriots on the high road. However, all is not bonnie at the loch nowadays, especially on its overdeveloped west side, fringed by the A82; on the water itself, speedboats tear up and down on summer weekends, destroying the tranquillity which so impressed the likes of Queen Victoria, the Wordsworths and Sir Walter Scott. Nevertheless, the west bank of the loch is an undeniably beautiful stretch of water, and despite the crowds, gives better views than the heavily wooded east side.

LUSS, the setting for the enormously popular Scottish TV soap *Take the High Road*, is the prettiest village, though its picturesque streets can become unbearably crowded in summer. The **visitor centre**, adjacent to the main village car park (Easter–Oct daily

---

THE WEST HIGHLAND WAY

Opened in 1980, the **West Highland Way** was Scotland's first long-distance footpath, stretching some 95 miles from Milngavie (pronounced "Mull-gye"), about six miles from the centre of Glasgow, to Fort William, where it reaches the foot of Britain's highest mountain.

Though not the most strenuous of Britain's long-distance walks, a moderate degree of fitness is required to undertake it, as there are some fairly steep ascents. Most walkers take between ten to fourteen miles at a time and there's accommodation in various forms dotted along the way. You should be prepared for changeable weather.

Passing through the lowlands north of Glasgow, the West Highland Way traverses the eastern shores of Loch Lomond and the Highlands boundary fault, skirts Crianlarich, then crosses the open heather of the wild Rannoch Moor. The path runs close to Glencoe, famous for the massacre of the MacDonald clan, and the stunning Mamores, the last mountain range before Fort William.

The route follows, for the most part, ancient drove roads, along which highlanders herded their cattle and sheep to market in the lowlands; military roads, built by troops to control the Jacobite insurgence in the eighteenth century; old coaching roads; and even disused railway lines. As well as the stunning scenery, walkers may see some of Scotland's more rare wildlife, including the feral goats left behind after the Highland clearances, red deer, and soaring over the highest peaks, golden eagles.

Several guides are available to accompany walkers. The official guide, published by the Stationary Office, includes Ordnance Survey route maps as well as descriptions of the route and detailed information on the cultural, historical, archaeological and wildlife interest along the way. It's available from bookshops or from the HMSO, 72 Lothian Road, Edinburgh EH3 9AZ. Further information, including an accommodation list, can be obtained from the West Highland Way ranger, Balloch Castle, Balloch, Dunbartonshire G53 8LX (☎01389/758216) or from the very useful West Highland Way Web site, at *www.west-highland-way.co.uk*.

10am–6pm; ☎01436/860601), gives a fascinating glimpse into the loch's landscape, wildlife and history as well as the environmental pressures it faces. **BALLOCH**, a brash holiday resort at the loch's southern tip, is the place to head for if you want to take a **boat trip**. Various operators offer one-hour cruises around the thirty-odd islands scattered near the shore, including *Mullens Cruises*, Riverside (daily; £5; ☎01389/751481), and *Sweeney's Cruises*, Riverside (hourly; £4.50; ☎01389/752376). The tranquil east bank is far better for walking than the west, and can only be traversed in its entirety by the West Highland Way footpath, from where you can head on through Queen Elizabeth Forest Park, or take the hugely rewarding three-hour hike from Rowardennan to the summit of **Ben Lomond**, subject of the Scottish proverb "Leave Ben Lomond where it stands" – just let things be.

Practicalities

The West Highland **train** – the line from Glasgow to Mallaig, with a branch line to Oban – joins Loch Lomond seventeen miles north of Balloch, at Tarbet, and has one other station further on at Ardlui, at the mountain-framed head of the loch. Loch Lomond's **tourist office** (daily: April–June, Sept & Oct 10am–5pm; July & Aug 9.30am–7.30pm; ☎01389/753533) is above the marina in Balloch. They'll reserve a room for you without charge at one of the many local **hotels** and **B&Bs**, such as the comfortable *Balloch Hotel*, Balloch Road (☎01389/752579; ⑤), which also has a decent restaurant, or the *Gowanlea Guest House*, Drymen Road (☎01389/752456; ④). A couple of miles up the west side of the loch at minuscule Arden is Scotland's most beautiful **youth hostel**: a turreted building complete with ghost (☎01389/850226; closed Nov–Feb). Tents are best pitched at the secluded Forestry Commission **campsite** (☎01360/870234; closed Nov–March), two miles south of Rowardennan, at Cashel, on the east bank.

Passenger ferries cross between Inverbeg and Rowardennan, where there is an eponymous **hotel** (☎01360/870251; ⑦) and a wonderfully situated **youth hostel** (☎01360/870259; closed Nov–Feb, except New Year). On the northeast shore of the loch is the *Inversnaid Lodge* (☎01877/386254; ⑥), once the hunting lodge of the Duke of Montrose. There is no road from Rowardennnan up the east of the loch to Inversnaid; you have to take the B829 west from Aberfoyle. From Inversnaid you can take the mile-long loch-side walk to **Rob Roy's cave**, a hideout which is said to have given shelter to both Rob Roy and Robert the Bruce.

Southern Fife

The ancient Kingdom of **Fife**, designated as such by the Picts in the fourth century, is a small area (barely fifty miles at its widest points), but one which has a definite identity, inextricably bound with the waters which surround it on three sides – the Tay to the north, the cold North Sea to the east, and the Firth of Forth along the **south coast**. The recent closure of the coal mines has left local communities floundering to regain a foothold, and the squeeze on the fishing industry up the coast may well lead to further decline. In the meantime, many of the villages have capitalized on their unpretentious appeal and welcomed tourism in a way that has enhanced rather than degraded their natural assets; the perfectly preserved town of Culross is unmissable. East of Culross is Dunfermline, an overdeveloped town with the remains of the first Benedictine abbey in Scotland.

Although the south coast of Fife is predominantly industrial, with everything from cottage industries to the refitting of nuclear submarines, thankfully only a small part has been blighted by insensitive development. Even in the old coal mining areas, disused pits and left-over slag heaps have either been well camouflaged through landscaping or put to alternative use as recreation areas. If you're driving, it's tempting once you've crossed the river to beat a path directly north up the M90 motorway, but if you do decide to stop off, you'll find the area has much to offer.

Fife is linked to Edinburgh by the two **Forth bridges**. You used to be able to take guided walks across the historic rail bridge; today, however, you'll have to be satisfied with seeing it from a train or a boat. West of the bridges, **Culross** was once a lively port enjoying a thriving trade with Holland, but fell into decline for around two hundred years, although it has now been lovingly restored. It was from inland **Dunfermline**, immediately north of the Forth crossing, that Queen Margaret ousted the Celtic Church from Scotland in the eleventh century; her son, David I, founded an abbey here in the twelfth century, which acquired vast stretches of land for miles around. Today, even though the lands no longer belong to the town, Dunfermline remains the chief town and the focus of the coast. East of the bridges, along the north side of the Firth of Forth, are **Aberdour**, a pretty, medieval town and **Kirkcaldy**, a sprawling industrial seaport with a surprisingly good art gallery and museum.

Culross

Crossing the Forth Road Bridge from the south, with unattractive views of the shipyard at Inverkeithing and the naval dock at Rosyth, the A985 then heads west along the Forth before approaching **CULROSS** (pronounced "Cooros"). One of Scotland's most picturesque settlements, the town's development began in the fifth century with the arrival of St Serf on the northern side of the Forth at "Holly Point", and it is said to be the birthplace of St Mungo, who travelled west and founded Glasgow cathedral. The town today is in excellent condition, thanks to the work of the NTS, who have been restoring its whitewashed, red-tiled buildings since 1932.

Make your first stop the **visitor centre** (Easter–Sept daily 11am–5pm; combined ticket for Town House, Palace & Study £4.40; NTS), in the **Town House** on the main road, for an excellent introduction to the burgh's history. Some of the four thousand witches executed in Scotland between 1560 and 1707 were tried here, and imprisoned on the upper floor while awaiting execution in Edinburgh. Behind the ticket office is a tiny prison with built-in manacles, where people were locked up as punishment for minor offences. The focal point of the community is the ochre-coloured **Culross Palace** (Easter–Sept daily 11am–5pm), built by wealthy coal merchant George Bruce in the late sixteenth century. Actually it's not a palace at all, but a grand and impressive house, with lots of small rooms and connecting passageways. The garden is planted with grasses, herbs and vegetables of the period, carefully grown from seed. There's also a café (10.30am–4.30pm), serving home-made food.

A cobbled alleyway known as **Back Causeway**, with a raised central aisle used by noblemen to separate them from the commoners, leads up behind the Town House to the **study** (Easter–Sept daily 1.30–5pm), built in 1610, with oak panelling in Dutch Renaissance style. Further up the hill lie the remains of **Culross Abbey**, founded by Cistercian monks in 1217 on the site of a Celtic church dating from around 450 AD. Although it is difficult to get a sense of what the abbey would have looked like, the overall effect is of grace and grandeur. The most intact part of the abbey, the choir and tower, became a parish church in the seventeenth century, at which time the fine, adjoining **manse** was built. Inside the church, a tenth-century Celtic cross in the north transept is a reminder of the abbey's origins. Recumbent alabaster figures of Sir George Bruce and his lady, with three sons and five daughters kneeling in devotion, decorate the splendid family tomb. The graveyard of the church is fascinating: many of the tombs are eighteenth century, with symbols depicting the occupation of the person who is buried; note, too, the Scottish custom, still continued, of marking women's graves with maiden names, even when they are buried with their husband.

Dunfermline

Scotland's capital until the Union of the Crowns in 1603, **DUNFERMLINE** lies seven miles inland, east of Culross and north of the Forth bridges. This "auld, grey toun" is built on a hill, dominated by the abbey and ruined palace at the top. Up until the late nineteenth century, Dunfermline was one of Scotland's foremost linen producers, as well as a major coal mining centre, and today the town is a busy place, its ever-increasing sprawl attesting to its booming economy. At the heart of the town is the imposing abbey, and the dramatic skeleton of the palace.

In the eleventh century, **Malcolm III** (Canmore) offered refuge here to Edgar Atheling, rightful heir to the English throne, and his family, who while fleeing the Norman Conquest were fortuitously shipwrecked in the Forth. Malcolm married Edgar's sister, the Catholic Margaret, in 1067, and in so doing started a process of reformation that ultimately supplanted the Celtic Church. Margaret, an intensely pious woman who was canonized in 1250, began building a Benedictine priory in 1072; her son, **David I**, raised the priory to the rank of abbey in the following century. In 1303, during the first of the **Wars of Independence**, the English king Edward I occupied the castle. He had the church roof stripped of lead to provide ammunition for his army's catapults, and also appears to have ordered the destruction of most of the monastery buildings, with the exception of the church and some of the monks' dwellings. **Robert the Bruce** helped rebuild the abbey and was finally buried here 25 years after he died of leprosy, although his body went undiscovered until building began on a new parish church in 1821. His heart, however, lies in Melrose Abbey (see p.838).

The Town

Dunfermline's **centre**, at the top of the hill around the abbey and palace, holds an appeal of its own, with its narrow, cobbled streets, pedestrianized shopping areas and gargoyle-adorned buildings. One of the best of these, the **City Chambers**, on the corner of Bridge and Bruce streets, is a fine example of late nineteenth-century Gothic Revival style. Among the ornate porticoes and grotesques of dragons and winged serpents which adorn the exterior are the sculpted heads of Robert the Bruce, Malcolm Canmore, Queen Margaret and Queen Elizabeth I.

Dunfermline Abbey (April–Sept Mon–Sat 9.30am–6.30pm, Sun 2–6.30pm; Oct–March Mon–Wed & Sat 9.30am–4.30pm, Thurs 9.30am–12.30pm, Sun 2–4.30pm; £1.80; HS) comprises the twelfth-century nave of the medieval monastic church, with an early nineteenth-century parish church spliced on. A plaque beneath the pulpit marks the spot where Robert the Bruce's remains were laid to rest, while Malcolm and his queen, Margaret, who died of grief three days after her husband in 1093, have a shrine outside. Nearby, the pink-harled **Abbot House** (daily 10am–5pm; £3) dates from around the fourteenth century, and has been variously used as an abbot's house, an iron foundry, an art school and a doctor's surgery. It's best seen from the outside, since nothing remains of the original interior. The guest house of Margaret's Benedictine monastery, south of the abbey, became the **Palace** (same times as abbey; £1.80) in the sixteenth century, under James VI, who gave both it and the abbey to his consort, Queen Anne of Denmark. Charles I, the last monarch to be born in Scotland, came into the world here in 1600. All that is left of it today is a long, sandstone facade, especially impressive when silhouetted against the evening sky.

Pittencrieff Park, known to locals as "the Glen", covers a huge area in the centre of town. Bordering the ruined palace, the 76-acre park used to be owned by the Lairds of Pittencrieff, whose 1610 estate house, built of stone pillaged from the palace, still stands within the grounds. In 1902, however, the entire plot was purchased by local rags-to-riches industrialist and philanthropist Andrew Carnegie, who donated it to his home town. Today, **Pittencrieff House** (daily: May–Oct 11am–5pm; Oct–April

11am–4pm; free) has exhibits on local history, the glasshouses are filled with exotic blooms, and the Pavilion coffee shop offers refreshment. In the centre of the park are the remains – little more than the foundations – of **Malcolm Canmore's Tower**, which may be the location of Malcolm's residence, known to have been somewhere to the west of the abbey. Dunfermline takes its name from the tower's location: "Dun", meaning hill or fort, "Fearum", bent or crooked, and "Lin", a pool or running water.

Just beyond the southeast corner of the park, the modest little cottage at the bottom of St Margaret Street is **Andrew Carnegie's Birthplace** (April, May, Sept & Oct Mon–Sat 11am–5pm, Sun 2–5pm; June–Aug Mon–Sat 10am–6pm, Sun 2–6pm; Nov–March daily 2–4pm; £1.50). The son of a weaver, the young Carnegie lived upstairs with his family, while the room below housed his father's loom shop. Following the family's emigration to America in 1848, he worked on the railways before becoming involved with the iron and then the steel industries. From 1873 he began his acquisition of steel-production firms, later to be consolidated into the Carnegie Steel Company. When he retired in 1901 to devote himself to philanthropy, Carnegie was a multi-millionaire. His house, an ordinary two-up two-down, has been preserved as it was at the end of the last century, and the adjacent Memorial Hall details his life and work.

Buried incongruously beneath the Glen Bridge car park, just north of the park, lies one of Scotland's holy shrines, **St Margaret's Cave** (Easter–Sept daily 11am–4pm; free). A dimly lit passageway, reminiscent of a wartime underground tunnel, descends deep underneath the ground, past displays and information panels that document the pious life of Margaret, who prayed here daily. At the bottom, the sparse stone praying area is surprisingly small and damp, although in Margaret's day it was decorated with crosses and candles. The climb back to the surface requires some effort.

Practicalities

Dunfermline's **train station** is southeast of the centre, halfway down the long hill of St Margaret's Drive, fifteen minutes' walk down from the **tourist office**, next to Abbot House, Maygate, near the High Street (April–Sept Mon–Sat 9.30am–5.30pm, Sun 11am–4pm; Oct–March Mon–Sat 9.30am–5.30pm; ☎01383/720999). From the **bus station**, cut through the shopping centre to High Street. If you do want to **stay**, options include the *Davaar House Hotel*, 126 Grieve St (☎01383/721886; ④), or a friendly **B&B** at 59 Buffies Brae (☎01383/733677; ①). There are some good, well-priced ethnic **restaurants** in Dunfermline: *Blossom's*, 6–8 Chalmers St, for Chinese food; *Khan's*, 33 Carnegie Drive, for Indian cuisine; and *Café Rene*, also on Carnegie Drive, for cheap and cheerful French cooking. If you want a drink in town, try the *Watering Hole*, New Row.

Aberdour

ABERDOUR, five miles east of the Forth bridges, clings tight to the walls of its **Castle** (April–Sept daily 9.30am–6.30pm; Oct & Nov Mon–Sat 9.30am–4.30pm, Sun 2–4pm; Dec–March Mon–Wed & Sat 9.30am–4pm, Sun 2–4pm; £1.80; HS), at the southern end of the main street. Once a Douglas stronghold, the castle is on a comparatively modest scale, with gently sloping lawns and a large, enclosed seventeenth-century garden and terraces. The fourteenth-century tower is the oldest part of the castle, the other buildings having been added in the sixteenth and seventeenth centuries, including the well-preserved dovecote. Worth more perusal is **St Fillan's Church**, also in the castle grounds, which dates from the twelfth century, with a few sixteenth-century additions, such as the porch restored from total dereliction earlier this century. There's little else to see here apart from the town's popular **silver sands** beach, which, along with its watersports, golf and sailing, has earned Aberdour the rather optimistic tourist board soubriquet of the "Fife Riviera". From Aberdour you can take a ferry to **Inchcolm**

Island to see its ruined medieval **abbey**, one of the best-preserved monastic complexes in Scotland. The abbey's surviving buildings date from the thirteenth to the fifteenth centuries and include a splendid octagonal chapter house and a tower from which there is a fine view of the island.

If you want to **stay**, you could try the friendly *Aberdour Hotel*, on High Street (☎01383/860325; ⑤), which also has an inexpensive **restaurant** downstairs. The real gem though is *Hawkcraig House*, Hawkcraig Point (☎01383/860335; closed Nov–Feb ③), a guest house with a good restaurant, in an old ferryman's house overlooking the harbour.

Kirkcaldy and around

The ancient royal burgh of **KIRKCALDY** (pronounced "Ker-coddy") is familiarly known as "The Lang Toun" for its four-mile-long esplanade, built in 1922–23 – not just to hold back the sea, but also to alleviate unemployment. If you're here in mid-April, you'll see the historic **Links Market**, a week-long funfair that dates back to 1305, and is possibly the largest street fair in Britain. Incidentally, though there's little to show for it today, architect brothers Robert and James Adam were born in Kirkcaldy, as was the eighteenth-century thinker Adam Smith, whose great work *The Wealth of Nations* (1776) established political economy as a separate science.

Kirkcaldy doesn't hold a great deal of interest for the visitor, beyond a stroll along the promenade. The town's history is chronicled in its **Museum and Art Gallery** (Mon–Sat 10.30am–5pm, Sun 2–5pm; free), set in the colourful War Memorial Gardens, between the train and bus stations. The gallery, established in 1925, has built up its collection to around three hundred works by some of Scotland's finest painters from the late eighteenth century onwards, including works by the fine portraitist Sir Henry Raeburn, the historical painter Sir David Wilkie, the Scottish "Colourists", the "Glasgow Boys" and a particularly large collection from the work of William McTaggart. For a town known primarily for linoleum production and whose reputation is firmly rooted in the prosaic, the art gallery is an unexpected boon.

Just beyond the northern end of the waterfront, Ravenscraig Park is the site of the substantial ruin of **Ravenscraig Castle**, a thick-walled, fifteenth-century defence post, which occupies a lovely spot above a beach. The castle looks out over the Forth, and is flanked on either side by a flight of steps – the inspiration, apparently, for the title of John Buchan's novel *The 39 Steps*. Sir Walter Scott also used it, as a setting for the story of "lovely Rosabella" in *The Lay of the Last Minstrel*.

Beyond Kirkcaldy lies the old suburb of **Dysart**, where tall ships once arrived bringing cargo from the Netherlands, setting off again with coal, beer, salt and fish. Well restored, and retaining historic street names such as Hot Pot Wynd (after the hot pans used for salt evaporation), it's an atmospheric place of narrow alleyways and picturesque old buildings. In Rectory Lane, the birthplace of John McDouall Stuart (who in 1862 became the first man to cross Australia from the south to the north) now holds the **McDouall Stuart Museum** (June–Aug daily 2–5pm; free; NTS), and gives an account of his emigration to Australia in 1838 and subsequent adventures.

Practicalities

Kirkcaldy's **train** and **bus stations** are in the upper part of town – keep heading downhill to get to the centre. The **tourist office**, 19 Whytecauseway (Mon–Fri 10am–5pm, Sat 10am–1pm & 2pm–5pm; ☎01592/267775), offers an **accommodation**-booking service, useful for getting you into the *Parkway Hotel*, Abbotshall Road (☎01592/262143; ④), or the smaller, more refined *Dunnikier House Hotel*, Dunnikier Park, Dunnikier Way (☎01592/268393; ④). You can get cheaper rooms along the road in neighbouring **Dysart**, at the *Royal Hotel*, Townhead (☎01592/654112, *Royalhotel@aol.com*; ②), which occupies one of the village's historic buildings. The *Royal Hotel* is a good place for **eating**, as is the

Old Rectory Inn, West Quality Street, also in Dysart. In Kirkcaldy, itself, try *Giovanni's*, 66 Dunnikier Rd, for traditional Italian food, or *Maxin*, 5 High St, for Chinese. There's a good **arts cinema**, with a restaurant and bar, housed in the Adam Smith Theatre, on Bennochy Road in the town centre.

The Howe of Fife

Inland from St Andrews, the rich rolling pastureland at the foot of the heather-swathed Lomond Hills is known as the **Howe of Fife**, "howe" meaning a low-lying stretch of ground. The area's two major towns, **Falkland** – with its fine renaissance palace – and **Cupar**, both preserve a number of handsome seventeenth- and eighteenth-century houses and make ideal stopping points on the way to St Andrews.

Falkland

Nestling in the lower slopes of East Lomond, the narrow streets of **FALKLAND**, eleven miles north of Kirkcaldy, are lined with fine and well-preserved seventeenth- and eighteenth-century buildings. The village grew up around **Falkland Palace** (April–Oct Mon–Sat 11am–5.30pm, Sun 1.30–5.30pm; palace & gardens £5; gardens only £2.30; NTS), home to the Macduffs, the earls of Fife. James IV began the construction of the present palace in 1500, but it was completed and embellished by James V, after which it became a favoured royal residence. Charles II stayed here in 1650, when he was in Scotland for his coronation, but after the Jacobite rising of 1715, and temporary occupation by Rob Roy, the palace was left to ruin. In the late nineteenth century, the third Marquess of Bute acquired the palace and restored it entirely. Today, it is a stunning example of Early Renaissance architecture, complete with corbelled parapet, mullioned windows, round towers and massive walls. The gardens are also worth a look, with their well-stocked herbaceous borders lining a pristine lawn, and the oldest "real" (royal) tennis court in Britain – built in 1539 for James V and still in use.

When not playing tennis, the royal guests at Falkland would hunt deer and wild boar in the forests which then covered the Howe of Fife, stretching towards Cupar, ten miles northeast. There are still deer here today, at the **Scottish Deer Centre** (daily: Easter–Oct 10am–6pm; Nov–Easter 10am–5pm; £3.50), three miles west of Cupar on the A91, which specializes in the rearing of red deer, and is also home to species of sika, fallow and reindeer; there are falconry displays three times daily. It's a good place for children, who can pet the tamer animals, and there are play and picnic areas, and guided nature trails.

For B&B **accommodation**, try the attractive *Oakbank Guest House*, The Pleasance, two minutes' walk from the palace (☎01337/857287; ②). Directly opposite the palace is the *Hunting Lodge Hotel*, High Street (☎01337/857226; ③), and just up the road, the *Covenanter Hotel* (☎01337/857224; ③). There's also a youth hostel, on Back Wynd (☎01337/857710; closed Oct–Feb).

Cupar

Straddling the small River Eden and surrounded by gentle hills, **CUPAR**, twelve miles northwest of Falkland, has retained much of its medieval character – and its self-confident air – from the days when it was a bustling market centre. A livestock auction still takes place here every week and it remains the capital of Fife. In 1276, Alexander III held an assembly in the town, bringing together the Church, aristocracy and local burgesses in an early form of Scottish parliament. For his troubles he subsequently became the butt of Sir David Lindsay's biting play, *Ane Pleasant Satyre of the Thrie Estaitis* (1535), one of the first great Scottish dramas.

Cupar's main street, part of the main road from Edinburgh to St Andrews, is plagued with thundering traffic. The **Mercat Cross**, stranded in the midst of the lorries and cars which speed through the centre, now consists of salvaged sections of the seventeenth-century original, following its destruction by an errant lorry some years ago.

One of the best reasons for stopping off at Cupar is to visit the **Hill of Tarvit** (house: Easter–Sept daily 1.30–5.30pm; gardens: April–Oct daily 9.30am–9pm, Nov–March daily 9.30am–4.30pm; house £3.90; gardens free; NTS), an Edwardian mansion two miles south of town remodelled by Sir Robert Lorimer from a late seventeenth-century building. The estate includes the five-storey, late sixteenth-century **Scotstarvit Tower**, set on a little mound three quarters of a mile west of the present house (keys available from house during season only), and a fine example of the Scots tower house, providing both fortification and comfort. The estate was bequeathed to the NTS in 1949, and the house contains an impressive collection of eighteenth-century Chippendale and French furniture, Dutch paintings, Chinese porcelain and a restored Edwardian laundry.

A couple of miles southeast of Cupar, in **Ceres**, a village set around a green, is the **Fife Folk Museum** (mid-May to Oct Mon–Thurs, Sat & Sun 2–5pm; £2). Occupying several well-preserved buildings dating from the seventeenth to the nineteenth centuries, it exhibits a vast array of historical and agricultural paraphernalia, including a pillory used to restrain miscreants on market days.

The **train station** is immediately south of the centre; **bus** #23 from Stirling to St Andrews stops outside. If you want to **stay**, try the *Eden House Hotel*, 2 Pitscottie Rd (☎01334/652510, *lv@eden.u-net.com*; ④), which serves good inexpensive Scottish food; or *Rathcluan*, on Carslogie Road (☎01334/657857, *reservations@rathcluan.co.uk*; ③). There is no shortage of good **restaurants** in the area – particularly recommended is *Ostler's Close*, 25 Bonnygate (☎01334/655574); for drinks and bar food try *Watts*, on Coal Road.

St Andrews and around

Confident, poised and well groomed, **ST ANDREWS**, Scotland's oldest university town and a pilgrimage centre for golfers from all over the world, overlooks a wide bay on the northeastern coast of Fife. It's often referred to in tourist literature as "the Cambridge of the North", and, like Cambridge, by and large St Andrews *is* its university. According to legend, the town was founded, pretty much by accident, in the fourth century. St Rule – or Regulus – a custodian of the bones of St Andrew on the Greek island of Patras, had a vision in which an angel ordered him to carry five of the saint's bones to the western edge of the world, where he was to build a city in his honour. The conscientious courier set off, but was shipwrecked on the rocks close to the present harbour. Struggling ashore with his precious burden, he built a shrine to the saint on what subsequently became the site of the cathedral: St Andrew became Scotland's patron saint and the town its ecclesiastical capital.

Local residents are proud of their town, with its refined old-fashioned ambience. Thanks to a strong and well-informed local conservation lobby, many of the original buildings have survived. Almost the entire centre consists of listed buildings, while the ruined castle and cathedral have all but been rebuilt in the efforts to preserve their remains. If you're here in early August, make sure to get to the two-day **Lammas Fair**, Scotland's oldest surviving medieval market, complete with town crier. The other main event in the St Andrews calendar is the **Kate Kennedy Pageant**, usually held on the third Saturday in April, which involves a procession of students taking to the streets dressed as characters associated with the university, including Kate Kennedy herself, niece of one of the university founders, Mary Queen of Scots, and more modern figures.

South of St Andrews, the **East Neuk** (*Neuk* is Scots for "corner") is a region of quaint fishing villages, all crow-stepped gables and tiled roofs. The best beaches are at the resorts of **Elie** and **Earlsferry**, which lie next to each other about twelve miles south of St Andrews. The villages between St Andrews and Elie fall into two distinct types: either scattered higgledy-piggledy up the hillside like **Crail** – perhaps the prettiest of the fishing villages, with its pottery and heritage centre – or neatly lined along the harbour like **Anstruther**, where you can visit the excellent Fisheries Museum and take a boat trip to the **Isle of May**.

Arrival, information and accommodation

St Andrews is not on the train line. The nearest **train station** is on the Edinburgh–Dundee–Aberdeen line at **Leuchars**, five miles northwest across the River Eden, from where regular, but not always connecting, buses make the trip into town every fifteen minutes. Frequent **buses** from Edinburgh and Dundee terminate at the bus station on City Road, at the west end of Market Street. The **tourist office** is at 70 Market St (April & May Mon–Sat 9.30am–6pm, Sun 11am–4pm; June to mid-Oct Mon–Sat 9.30am–7pm, Sun 11am–6pm; mid-Oct to March Mon–Sat 9.30am–5pm; ☎01334/472021). If you're driving, the town's fiendish **parking** system requires vouchers (35p per hour) which you can get from the tourist office and from some local shops.

Although rooms in St Andrews cost more than in the surrounding area, they book up fast in the summer, making a reservation in advance is strongly recommended. Most of the **guest houses** are around Murray Place and Murray Park, between The Scores and North Street. Good ones include *Aedel House*, 72 Murray Place (☎01334/472315; ①), and *Bell Craig Guest House*, at 8 Murray Park (☎01334/472962; ②). On North Street, try *Aslar House*, at no. 120 (☎01334/473460, *pardoe@aslar.u-net.com*; ③). Between June and

---

GOLF IN ST ANDREWS

St Andrew's **Royal and Ancient Golf Club** (or "R&A") is the governing body for golf the world over, dating back to a meeting of 22 of the local gentry in 1754, who founded the Society of St Andrews Golfers, being "admirers of the ancient and healthful exercise of golf". It acquired its current title after King William IV agreed to be the society's patron in 1834. The game itself has been played here since the fifteenth century. Those early days were instrumental in establishing Scotland as the home of golf, for the rules were distinguished from those in the French game by the fact that participants had to manoeuvre the ball into a hole, rather than hit an above-ground target. (Early French versions were, in fact, more like croquet.) The game developed, acquiring popularity along the way – even Mary Queen of Scots, was known to have the occasional round. It was not without its opponents, however, particularly James II who, in 1457, banned his subjects from playing since it was distracting them from archery practice.

St Andrews' status as a world-renowned golf centre is particularly obvious as you enter the town from the west, where the approach road runs adjacent to the famous **Old Course**. At the eastern end of the course lies the old clubhouse, a stolid, square building dating from 1854; the modern clubhouse across the fairway is a members-only preserve. The first British Open Championship was held here in 1873, having been inaugurated in 1860 at Prestwick in Ayrshire, and since then, the British Open is held here regularly, pulling in enormous crowds. The eighteenth hole of the Old Course is immediately in front of the old clubhouse, and has been officially christened the "Tom Morris", after one of the world's most famous golfers. Pictures of Nick Faldo, Jack Nicklaus and other golfing greats, along with clubs and a variety of memorabilia which they donated, are displayed in the admirable **British Golf Museum** on Bruce Embankment, along the waterfront below the clubhouse (April–Oct daily 9.30am–5.30pm; Nov–March Thurs–Mon 11am–3pm; £3.75). There are also plenty of hands-on exhibits, including computers, video screens and footage of British Open championships, tracing the development of golf through the centuries.

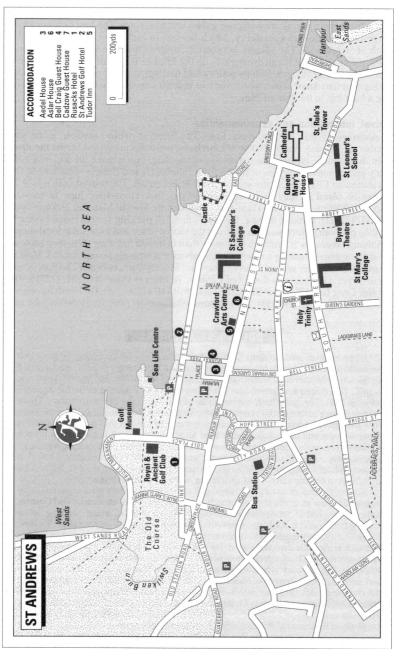

ST ANDREWS

ACCOMMODATION

Aedel House	3
Aslar House	6
Bell Craig Guest House	4
Cadzow Guest House	7
Rusacks Hotel	1
St Andrews Golf Hotel	2
Tudor Inn	5

0   200yds

NORTH SEA

West Sands

The Old Course

Swilken Burn

WEST SANDS ROAD

Royal & Ancient Golf Club

Golf Museum

Sea Life Centre

Castle

St. Rule's Tower

Cathedral

Harbour

East Sands

LONG PIER

SHOREHEAD

St Leonard's School

Queen Mary's House

St Salvator's College

Crawford Arts Centre

St Mary's College

Byre Theatre

Holy Trinity

Bus Station

© Crown copyright

September, the **University** (☎01334/462000; ③) offers about two hundred rooms in various locations, all on a B&B basis with dinner optional. More upmarket are the various **hotels** lining The Scores, beyond the eastern end of the Old Course, overlooking the bay. The *St Andrews Golf Hotel*, at no. 40 (☎01334/472611, *thegolfhotel@standrews.co.uk*; ⑦), occupies a three-storey town house, with great views from the bedrooms at the front. As you come into town from Leuchars, you'll see the entrance to the swanky *Rusacks Hotel*, 16 Pilmour Links (☎01334/474321; ⑦), on the left. A little further up the road is the *Tudor Inn*, 129 North St (☎01334/474906; ③) – its uncharacteristic black and white Tudor facade more English than Scottish.

The Town

The centre of St Andrews still follows the medieval layout. Wandering its three main thoroughfares, North Street, South Street and Market Street, which run west to east towards the ruined Gothic cathedral, are several of the original university buildings from the fifteenth century. Narrow alleys connect the cobbled streets, attic windows and gable ends shape the rooftops, and here and there you'll see old wooden doors with heavy knockers and black iron hinges.

At the east end of town, the ruin of the great **St Andrews Cathedral** (April–Sept Mon–Sat 9.30am–6pm, Sun noon–6pm; Oct–March Mon–Sat 9.30am–4pm, Sun 2–4pm; £1.80, joint ticket with St Andrews castle £3.50; HS) gives only an idea of its former importance. The cathedral was founded in 1160, but not finished and consecrated until 1318, in the presence of Robert the Bruce. But on June 5, 1559, the Reformation took its toll, and supporters of John Knox, fresh from a rousing meeting, plundered the cathedral and left it to ruin. Stone was still being taken from the cathedral for various local building projects as late as the 1820s.

Standing above the harbour where the land drops to the sea, the cathedral site can be a blustery place, with the wind whistling through the great east window and down the stretch of turf that was once the central aisle. In front of the window a slab is all that remains of the high altar, where the relics of St Andrew were once enshrined. It is thought that they were previously kept in **St Rule's Tower**, the austere Romanesque monolith next to the cathedral, which was built as part of an abbey in 1130. A token from the visitor centre (included in entry ticket) allows you to climb the 157 steps of the tower, from which there are great views, particularly of the remains of the monastic buildings which made up the priory. Around the entire complex is a sturdy wall dating from the sixteenth century, over half a mile long and with three gateways. The **visitor centre** houses an archeological exhibition, displaying the sarcophagus of St Andrew, exquisitely carved with pagan and Pictish symbols.

Southwest of the cathedral enclosure lies **the Pends**, a huge fourteenth-century vaulted gatehouse which marked the main entrance to the priory, and from where the road leads down to the harbour, passing prim **St Leonard's**, one of Scotland's leading private schools for girls. The sixteenth-century, rubble-stonework building on the right as you go through the Pends is **Queen Mary's House**, where she is believed to have stayed in 1563. The house was restored in 1927 and is now used as the school library.

Down at the **harbour**, gulls screech above the fishing boats, keeping an eye on the lobster nets strewn along the quay. If you come here on a Sunday morning, you'll see students parading down the long pier, red gowns billowing in the wind, in a time-honoured after-church walk. The beach, **East Sands**, is a popular stretch, although it's cool in summer, and positively biting in winter. A path leads south from the far end of the beach, climbing up the hill past the caravan site and cutting through the gorse; this makes a pleasant walk on a sunny day, taking in hidden coves and caves.

North of the beach, the rocky coastline curves inland to the ruined **St Andrews Castle** (April–Sept Mon–Sat 9.30am–6pm, Sun 9.30am–4pm; Oct–March Mon–Sat

9.30am–4pm, Sun 2–4pm; £2.50, joint ticket with St Andrews Cathedral £3.50; HS), with a drop to the sea on three sides and a moat on the fourth. It was built around 1200 as part of the palace of the Bishops and Archbishops of St Andrews and was consequently the scene of some fairly grim incidents at the time of the Reformation. There's not a great deal left of the castle, since it fell into ruin in the seventeenth century, and most of what can be seen dates from the sixteenth century, the only exception being the fourteenth-century Fore Tower. The Protestant reformer George Wishart was burnt at the stake in front of the castle in 1546, as an incumbent Cardinal Beaton looked on. Wishart had been a friend of John Knox's, and it wasn't long before fellow reformers sought vengeance for his death. Less than three months later, Cardinal Beaton was stabbed to death, his body displayed from the battlements before being dropped into the "bottle dungeon", a 24-foot pit hewn out of solid rock visible in the Sea Tower. The perpetrators then held the castle for over a year, and dug a secret passage which can be entered from the ditch in front.

St Andrews University is the oldest in Scotland, founded in 1410 by Bishop Henry Wardlaw. The nominal founder is James I, to whom the bishop was tutor, and the king was certainly a great benefactor of the university. The first building was on the site of the Old University Library and by the end of the Middle Ages three colleges had been built: St Salvator's (1450), St Leonard's (1512) and St Mary's (1538). At the time of the Reformation, St Mary's became a seminary of Protestant theology, and today it houses the university's Faculty of Divinity. The **quad** here has beautiful gardens and some magnificent old trees, perfect for flopping under on a warm day. A **guided tour** (June–Aug Mon–Sat 11am, 2.30pm & 4.30pm on request, call ☎01334/462000; £3) takes in the main historical areas. Tickets are available from the International Office, Butts Wynd, near St Salvator's Chapel where the tour starts.

If you've got **children** in tow you may want to visit the huge **Sea Life Centre** on The Scores, at the west end of town close to the golf museum (daily 10am–6pm; July & Aug closes 7pm; £4.25), which examines marine life of all shapes and sizes with displays, live exhibits, observation pools and underwater walkways. Also good for children is the fifty-acre **Craigtoun Country Park** (April–Sept daily 10.30am–6.30pm; £2), a couple of miles southwest of town on the B939. As well as several landscaped gardens there's a miniature train, plus boating, trampolining, crazy golf and picnic areas, and a country fair each May with craft stalls, wildlife exhibits, and showjumping displays.

If you want to escape from the bustle of the town, the **Botanic Gardens**, on Canongate (daily: May–Sept 10am–7pm; Oct–April 10am–4pm; glasshouses all year Mon–Fri 10am–4pm; £1.50), offer a peaceful retreat, with hothouses and shady walkways. The gardens are a ten-minute walk south from South Street.

Eating and drinking

St Andrews has no shortage of **restaurants** and **cafés**. In town, *Littlejohns*, at the east end of Market Street, serves hearty burgers and steaks, while *The Vine Leaf Restaurant*, 131 South St (☎01334/477497), is known for its good range of seafood. *Brambles*, 5 College St, offers inexpensive home baking as does *The Merchant's House*, 49 South St, which also has good vegetarian options. The licensed *Victoria Café*, 1 St Mary's Place, a popular student haunt, serves baked potatoes and toasted sandwiches, while *Ma Belle's*, 40 The Scores, in the basement of the *St Andrews Golf Hotel*, is a lively pub serving cheap food and catering for locals as much as students. For the best views of the Old Course, *Rusacks Lounge Bar*, 16 Pilmour Links, has big comfy chairs, where you can watch the golfers through huge windows and sip pricey bar drinks, tea or coffee. For truly great food, head for the *Peat Inn* (☎01334/840206), five miles south of town on the A915 and then one mile west on the B940. This is one of Britain's top restaurants, serving a varied menu of local specialities, and will set you back at least £40 per head.

With its big student population, St Andrews has lots of good **pubs**. Locals and tourists mix with the students at the *Tudor*, 129 North St, which has a late-night licence on Thursdays and Fridays and live bands from time to time. The *Central* on Market Street serves huge pies and a powerful beer brewed by Trappist monks. *Firkins*, St Mary's Place, at the bottom of Market Street, is a popular real-ale bar, attracting a young crowd.

Crail

A maze of streets tumbling down to a picturesque working harbour makes **CRAIL** one of the most attractive villages on this stretch of the coast. Look out for the large blue stone by the gate of the twelfth-century **St Mary's Church** – the legend goes that it was hurled there by the devil, all the way from the Isle of May, offshore. You can trace the history of the town at the intriguing **Crail Museum and Heritage Centre**, 62 Marketgate (Easter–Sept daily 10am–1pm & 2–5pm, Sun 2–5pm; free), which also doubles as the town's **tourist office**. At 75 Nethergate, the **Crail Pottery** (Mon–Fri 8am–5pm, Sat & Sun 10am–5pm) is worth a visit for the wide range of locally made pottery on display, some of which is for sale.

If you want to **stay** in Crail, you could try the small, comfortable *Hazelton Guest House*, 29 Marketplace (☎01333/450250; ①); *Caiplie Guest House*, 53 High St (☎01333/450564; ①), where some of the rooms have sea views and the home cooking is superb; or the small, central *Honeypot Guest House*, 6 High St (☎01333/450935; ①).

Anstruther and the Isle of May

ANSTRUTHER is home to the wonderfully unpretentious **Scottish Fisheries Museum** (April–Oct Mon–Sat 10am–5.30pm, Sun 10am–5pm; Nov–March Mon–Sat 10am–4.30pm, Sun 2–4.30pm; £3.20), quite in keeping with the no-frills integrity of the area in general. Set in a complex of sixteenth- to nineteenth-century buildings, on a total of eighteen different floors, it charts the history of the fishing and whaling industries in ingenious displays, including a Historic Boatyard with a ring netter in dry dock and a reconstruction of a turn-of-the-century fisherman's house.

A lighthouse, erected in 1816 by Robert Louis Stevenson's grandfather, is several miles offshore from Anstruther on the rugged **Isle of May**, where you can also see the remains of Scotland's first lighthouse, built in 1636, which burned coals as a beacon. The island is now a nature reserve and bird sanctuary, and can be reached by boat from Anstruther (May–Sept; 1 daily; £12; ☎01333/310103). Between April and July the dramatic sea cliffs are covered with breeding kittiwakes, razorbills, guillemots and shags, while inland there are thousands of puffins and eider duck. Grey seals also make the occasional appearance. Be sure to check up on departure times, and allow between four and five hours for a return trip: an hour each way, and a couple of hours there. Also take plenty of warm, waterproof clothing.

There's a **tourist office** next to the museum (Easter to mid-Sept (Mon, Fri & Sat 10am–5pm, Tues, Wed & Thurs 10am–1pm & 2–5pm, Sun noon–5pm; ☎01333/311073). Anstruther makes a pretty and peaceful **place to stay**, and there are plenty of good **B&Bs**, including the lovely *Hermitage Guest House*, Ladywalk (☎01333/310909; ②), and *The Sheiling*, 32 Glenogil Gardens (☎01333/310697; ①), plus two places on Pittenweem Road, the *Beaumont Lodge Guest House* (☎01333/310315, *reservations@beau-lodge.demon.co.uk*; ②), and *The Spindrift* (☎01333/310573, *spindrift@east-neuk.co.uk*; ③). You'll also find a **campsite** nearby at Crail, the *Sauchope Links* (☎01337/450460). There's a fine fish **restaurant** in Anstruther, the *Cellar* (☎01333/310378), in one of the village's oldest buildings, once a cooperage and smokehouse.

SCOTLAND'S SECRET BUNKER

Inland, between St Andrews and Anstruther on the B940 (bus #61 takes you to within two miles of the bunker), is the idiosyncratic **Scotland's Secret Bunker** (April–Oct daily 10am–5pm; £5.95), off the secrets list and open to the public since 1994. Entrance is through an innocent-looking farmhouse, then you walk down a vast ramp to the bunker, which is 100ft below ground and encased in 15ft of reinforced concrete. In the event of a nuclear war the bunker would have become Scotland's new administrative centre. From here, government and military commanders would have co-ordinated fire-fighting and medical help for Scotland from a switchboard room with 2800 phone lines. The bunker, which could house 300 people, was due to be equipped with air filters, a vast electricity generator and its own water supply; the best of 1950s technology, today it has a rather kitsch James Bond feel about it. The only concession to entertainment was a couple of cinemas, which now show Fifties newsreels giving painfully inadequate instructions to civilians in the event of nuclear war.

Perth and around

Viewed from the hills to the south, **PERTH** still justifies Sir Walter Scott's glowing description in the opening pages of his novel *The Fair Maid of Perth* as "this exquisite landscape", surrounded as it is by fertile agricultural land and beautiful scenery. For several centuries Scotland's capital, the city's prestige reached its peak when, during the reign of James I, Parliament met here on several occasions. Its glory was short-lived, however: the king was murdered in the town's Dominican priory in 1437 by the traitorous Sir Robert Graham, who was captured in the Highlands and tortured to death in Stirling. During the Reformation, on May 11, 1559, John Knox preached a rousing sermon in St John's Church, which led to the destruction of the town's four monasteries (by those Knox later condemned as "the rascal multitude") and quickened the pace of reform in Scotland. Despite a period of decline in the seventeenth century, the community has prospered ever since – today it's a financial centre, and still an important and bustling market town. Its long history in **livestock trading** is continued throughout the year, notably with the summer Aberdeen Angus sales and the Perthshire Agricultural Show, held in August.

A few miles north of the city, the stately **Scone Palace** stands on the site of an earlier abbey where all Scottish kings were crowned. To the west, **Dunning**, once the capital of the Picts, and **Crieff**, a busy little spa town, are among the highlights of **Strathearn** – the valley of the River Earn – which stretches west towards Loch Earn and the watersports centre at Lochearnhead. Two thousand years ago, the Roman general Agricola was thwarted in this area after subduing most of the lands to the south; later, it was frequented by Bonnie Prince Charlie and Rob Roy, both bound up in the north–south struggle in different ways.

The Town

Perth's **centre** occupies a small area, easily explored on foot, on the west bank of the Tay. Two large areas of green parkland, known as the North and South Inch, flank the centre. The **North Inch** was the site of the Battle of the Clans in 1396, in which thirty men from each of the clans Chattan and Quhele (pronounced "Kay") met in a violent skirmish, while the **South Inch** was the public meeting place for witch-burning in the seventeenth century. Both are now used for more civilized public recreation, with sports matches to the north, and boating and putting to the south.

The usual-high street chains line High Street and South Street, as well as filling St John's shopping centre on King Edward Street. Opposite the entrance to the centre, the imposing **City Hall** is used by Scotland's politicians for party conferences. Behind here lies **St John's Kirk** (daily 10am–noon & 2–4pm; free), founded by David I in 1126, although the present building dates from the fifteenth century and was restored between 1923 and 1928 to house a war memorial chapel designed by Robert Lorimer. It was in St John's that John Knox preached his fiery sermon calling for the "purging of the churches from idolatry" in 1559.

To the north of the centre, the **Fair Maid's House**, on North Port, is arguably the town's best-known attraction, although you can only see it from the outside. Standing on the site of a thirteenth-century monastery, this cottage of weathered stone with small windows and an outside staircase was the setting chosen by Sir Walter Scott as the house of Simon Glover, father of the virginal Catherine Glover, in his novel *The Fair Maid of Perth*. Set in turbulent times at the close of the fourteenth century, the novel tells a traditional story of love, war and revenge, centring on the attempts by various worthies to win the hand of Catherine.

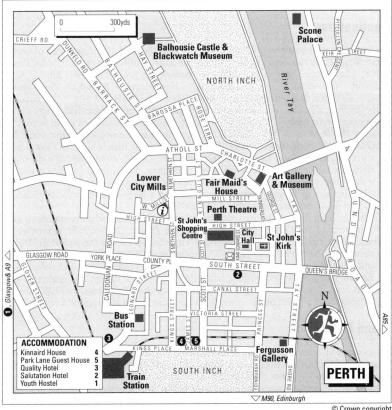

ACCOMMODATION
Kinnaird House 4
Park Lane Guest House 5
Quality Hotel 3
Salutation Hotel 2
Youth Hostel 1

© Crown copyright

The nearby **Art Gallery and Museum**, on George Street (Mon–Sat 10am–5pm; free), gives a good overview of local life through the centuries. In similar vein, at **Lower City Mills**, West Mill Street (April–Nov Mon–Sat 10am–5pm; £1.50), a restored oatmeal mill driven by a massive water wheel is an impressive reminder of Victorian Perth. The Round House, a domed circular structure on Marshall Place, used to house the waterworks, and is the unlikely setting for the excellent **Fergusson Gallery** (Mon–Sat 10am–5pm; free). The gallery holds a collection of the paintings, drawings and sculpture of J.D. Fergusson, the foremost artist of the Scottish "Colourist" movement. His lifelong companion was the dancer and painter Margaret Morris; her summer schools, held annually for forty years, provided Fergusson with models and inspired his monumental paintings of bathers, in pure bright colours.

Beyond the Fair Maid's House, elegantly restored Georgian terraces give way to newer buildings, which have gradually encroached on the former territory of the fifteenth-century **Balhousie Castle**, off Hay Street (May–Sept Mon–Sat 10am–4.30pm; Oct–April Mon–Fri 10am–3.30pm; free). The castle, restored in Scots Baronial style with turrets and crow-stepped gables, sits incongruously in a peaceful residential area and now houses the headquarters and **Museum of the Black Watch**. This historic regiment – whose name refers to the dark colour of their tartan – was formed in 1739, having been built up by General Wade earlier in the century, who employed groups of highlanders to keep the peace.

Practicalities

The **bus** and **train stations** are on opposite sides of the road, at the west end of town, where Kings Place runs into Leonard Street. The **tourist office**, Lower City Mills, West Mill St (April–June, Sept & Oct Mon–Sat 9am–6pm, Sun 11am–4pm; July & Aug Mon–Sat 9am–8pm, Sun 11am–6pm; Nov–March Mon–Sat 9am–5pm; ☎01738/4506000), is a ten-minute walk away. There are **B&Bs** all over town, notably on the approach roads from Crieff and Stirling. In the centre, Marshall Place, overlooking the South Inch, is the place to look. Of the many possibilities along here, try *Kinnaird House*, at no. 5 (☎01738/628021; ②), or the *Park Lane Guest House*, at no. 17 (☎01738/637218, *parklane@aol.co.uk*; ②). Of the numerous **hotels** in Perth's town centre, try the *Quality Hotel*, Leonard Street (☎01738/624141, *admin@gb628-u-net.com*; ⑤), right by the station, or the refurbished *Salutation*, 34 South St (☎01738/630066; ⑤), which claims to be one of Scotland's oldest hotels, dating back to 1699. The **youth hostel** is housed in an impressive old mansion on Glasgow Road (☎01738/623658; closed Nov–Feb), beyond the west end of York Place.

Within striking distance of the youth hostel is a good, basic Indian **restaurant**, the *Café Kamran*, 13 York Place. The *Good Luck Food Palace*, 181 South St, serves well-priced Chinese cuisine, while the best choice for a classier meal is the stylish Art Deco fish restaurant, *Number Thirty Three*, 33 George St (☎01738/633771), with an oyster bar and à la carte restaurant. For delicious wholefood, home baking and coffee, try *The Lemon Tree*, 29–41 Skinnergate, just behind the tourist office; this spacious café closes at 5pm. There are a few **pubs** in the town centre: *Twa Tams*, on Scott Street, and *Brennans*, on St John Street, provide inexpensive meals and regular live music.

Scone Palace

Just a couple of miles north of Perth, along the A93 (bus #7, #26 or #46), **Scone Palace** (pronounced "Scoon") is worth every penny of the admission charge levied by its owners, the Earl and Countess of Mansfield (mid-April to mid-Oct daily 9.30am–5.15pm; £5.40). The two-storey palace, restored in the nineteenth century, consists of a sixteenth-century core that replaced an earlier palace, destroyed by followers of John

Knox, in 1559. The surrounding buildings, complete with battlements and the original gateway, are older, and mostly built of red sandstone. The abbey that stood here in the sixteenth century, and where all Scottish kings until James I were crowned, was one of those destroyed following John Knox's sermon in Perth. In the extensive grounds which surround the palace lies the Moot Hill, which was once the site of the famous Coronation **Stone of Destiny** (see box on p.795).

Inside, a good selection of sumptuous rooms is open to visitors, including the library, which has exchanged its books in favour of an outstanding collection of porcelain, one of the foremost in the world, with items by Meissen, Sèvres, Chelsea, Derby and Worcester. Look out too for the beautiful papier-mâché dishes, Marie-Antoinette's writing desk, and John Zoffany's exquisite eighteenth-century portrait of the second earl's daughter, *Lady Elizabeth Murray with Dido*. You could easily spend at least a morning here, enjoying the gardens, with their strutting peacocks, Highland cattle, picnic spots, donkey park, children's playground. There's also a grand and fragrant pine garden, planted in 1848 with exotic conifers.

Dunning

Heading south of Perth on the busy A9, it's worth taking a detour to the quiet village of **DUNNING**, which has an impressive history. The village was once the capital of the Picts, and the place where Kenneth I, King of the Picts and Scots, died in 860. Dunning was destroyed by the Jacobites and subsequently rebuilt, which accounts for its homogeneous appearance, the houses all being late eighteenth and early nineteenth century. **St Serf's** has survived, a rugged church with a Norman tower and arch. Just west of the village is an extraordinary monument, a pile of stones surmounted by a cross, and scrawled with the words "Maggie Wall, Burnt here, 1657". Maggie Wall was burnt as a witch, and the rumour is that local women replenish the white writing on the monument every year.

Crieff and around

CRIEFF, 15 miles from Perth, lies at the heart of Strathearn, in a lovely position on a south-facing slope of the Grampian foothills. There's a pleasing mixture of Edwardian and Victorian houses, with a busy little centre which still retains something of the atmosphere of the former spa town. Cattle traders used to come here in the eighteenth century, since this was a good location – between Highland and Lowland – for buying and selling livestock, but Crieff really came into its own with the arrival of the railway in 1856. Shortly after that, Morrison's Academy, now one of Scotland's most respected schools, took in its first pupils, and in 1868 the grand old *Crieff Hydro* (☎01764/655555; ⑨), then known as the *Strathearn Hydropathic*, opened its doors. It's still the nicest place to stay in town, despite being dry.

The **Crieff Visitor Centre** (daily 9am–5pm) is a "craftsy" place, crammed with pottery and paperweights. The **tourist office** is in the town hall on High Street (April–June, Sept & Oct Mon–Sat 9.30am–5.30pm, Sun 11am–4pm; July & Aug Mon–Sat 9am–7pm, Sun 11am–6pm; Nov–March Mon–Fri 9.30am–5pm, Sat 9.30am–1.30pm; ☎01764/652578). For those not staying at the hydro, cheaper **B&B** options include *Eastview Guest House*, 98 East High St (☎01764/652132; ③), and *Bank Guest House*, 32 Burrell St (☎01764/653409, *bookings@comelybank.demon.co.uk*; ③).

Glenturret Distillery

From Crieff, it's a short drive or twenty-minute walk to the **Glenturret Distillery** (Jan–Feb Mon–Fri 11.30am–4pm, last tour 2.30pm; March–Dec Mon–Sat 9.30am–6pm,

Sun noon–6pm, last tour 4.30pm; free; guided tour £3.50, with tasting £7.50), just off the A85 to Comrie. To get there on public transport, catch any bus going to Crieff, Comrie or St Fillans and ask the driver to drop you at the bottom of the Glenturret Distillery road, from where it's a five-minute walk. This is Scotland's oldest distillery, established in 1775, and a good one to visit, if only for its splendid isolation.

Drummond Castle Gardens

If you enjoy ornate gardens, on no account miss the **Drummond Castle Gardens** (May–Oct daily 2–6pm; £3) near Muthill, two miles south of Crieff on the A822 (bus #47 from Crieff towards Muthill, then a half-hour walk up the castle drive). The approach to the garden is extraordinary, up an impressive, mile-long dark avenue of trees. Crossing the courtyard of the castle to the grand terrace, you can view the garden in all its symmetrical glory. It was laid out by John Drummond, second Earl of Perth, in 1630, and shows clear French and Italian influence, although the central structural feature of the parterre is a St Andrew's cross. Italian marble statues punctuate the long lines of the cross, and the overall effect is of exceptional harmony and grace. The castle itself (closed to the public) is a wonderful mixture of architectural styles; the blunt fifteenth-century keep on a rocky crag adjoins a much-modified Renaissance mansion house.

Northwest Perthshire

Northwest Perthshire is a place of magnificent beauty, dominated by the mountains of the mighty Grampian range, which fall away down forested slopes to long, deep lochs on the valley floor, influence the weather and tolerate little development. The **Breadalbane Mountains** run between Loch Tay and Loch Earn; as well as providing walking and watersports, the area is dotted with fine towns and villages, like **Aberfeldy** at the western tip of Loch Tay and **Dunkeld** with its eighteenth-century whitewashed cottages and elegant ruined cathedral. Among the wealth of historical sites in the region is the splendid **Blair Castle**, north of the popular holiday centre of **Pitlochry**. Heading west, the spectacular Lochs Tummel and Rannoch lead to the desolate **Rannoch Moor**, a huge, unspoilt tract of bog that has a haunting beauty of its own.

Dunkeld

DUNKELD, fifteen miles up the A9 and the River Tay from Perth, was proclaimed Scotland's ecclesiastical capital by Kenneth MacAlpine in 850. Its position at the southern boundary of the Grampian mountains made it a favoured meeting place for Highland and Lowland cultures, but in 1689 it was burned to the ground by the Cameronians – fighting for William of Orange – in an effort to flush out troops of the Stuart monarch, James VII. Subsequent rebuilding, however, has created one of the area's most delightful communities, and it's well worth at least a brief stop to view its whitewashed houses and historic cathedral. The **tourist office** is at The Cross, in the town centre (April–June, Sept & Oct Mon–Sat 9.30am–5.30pm, Sun 11am–4pm; July & Aug Mon–Sat 9am–7.30pm, Sun 11am–7pm; Nov & Dec Mon–Sat 9.30am–1.30pm; ☎01350/727688).

Dunkeld's partly ruined **Cathedral** is on the northern side of town, in an idyllic setting amid lawns and trees on the east bank of the Tay. Construction began in the early twelfth century, but the building was more or less ruined at the time of the Reformation. The fourteenth-century **choir**, restored in 1600 (and several times since), now serves as the parish church, while the fifteenth-century **nave** remains roofless apart from the clock tower. Inside, note the leper's peep near the pulpit in the north wall, through which they could receive the sacrament without contact with the congregation. Also look out for the great effigy of "The Wolf of Badenoch", Robert II's son, born in 1343. The Wolf acquired his name and notoriety after being excommunicated from the Church for leaving his wife: he took his revenge by burning the towns of Forres and Elgin, and sacking Elgin Cathedral. He eventually repented, did public penance for his crimes and was absolved by his brother Robert III.

Dunkeld is linked to its sister community, **BIRNAM**, by Thomas Telford's seven-arched bridge of 1809. Thanks to Shakespeare, this little village has a place in history, for it was on "Dunsinane Hill" to the southeast of the village that Macbeth declared: "I will not be afraid of death and bane/Till Birnam Forest come to Dunsinane", only to be told by a messenger: "As I did stand my watch upon the Hill/I look'd toward Birnam, and anon me thought/The Wood began to move ...". The **Perthshire Visitor Centre** just south of Birnam, down the A9 at Bankfoot (daily 9am–7pm; £2), offers "The Macbeth Experience", which documents – on film and through talking dummies – the true story of Macbeth, a noble and fair king, and quite the opposite of Shakespeare's scheming villain. Several centuries later another literary personality, Beatrix Potter, drew inspiration from the area, recalling her childhood holidays here when penning the Peter Rabbit stories.

There are plenty of places to stay in Dunkeld, including some large **hotels** in the heart of the village: the *Atholl Arms Hotel* (☎01350/727219; ④), the *Royal Dunkeld* (☎01350/727322; ④) and the Victorian-Gothic *Birnam Hotel* (☎01350/727462; ⑤). Just to the north, the luxurious *Stakis Dunkeld* (☎01350/727771; ⑨) is set in its own extensive grounds, where you can fish, shoot, cycle and stroll. For **B&B**, try the non-smoking *Bheinne Mhor*, Birnam Glen, Dunkeld (☎013502/727779; ②), or the friendly *Heatherbank*, in Birnam (☎01350/727413; ①). There are a few mediocre **places to eat** on Dunkeld's main street; the best food options are lunch at the *Atholl Arms* or a more expensive dinner at the *Stakis Dunkeld*.

Heading north on the A9 to Pitlochry, you can stop off and walk the mile and a half to **The Hermitage** (buses from Perth to Pitlochry also stop near here), set in the wooded gorge of the River Braan. This pretty eighteenth-century folly, also known as Ossian's Hall, was once mirrored to reflect the water, but the mirrors were smashed by Victorian vandals, and the folly more tamely restored. The hall, appealing yet incongruous in its splendid setting, neatly frames a dramatic waterfall.

Aberfeldy

A largely Victorian town twenty miles northwest of Dunkeld, **ABERFELDY** sits at the point where the Urlar Burn – lined by the silver birch trees celebrated by Robert Burns in his poem *The Birks of Aberfeldy* – flows into the River Tay. The river is spanned by **Wade's Bridge**, built in 1733 during efforts to control the unrest in the Highlands. With its humpback and four arches, it is regarded as one of the general's finest remaining crossing points. Overlooking the bridge from the south end is the **Black Watch Monument**, a statue of a pensive, kilted soldier, erected in 1887 to commemorate the peacekeeping troop of Highlanders gathered together by Wade in 1739. The small town centre is a busy mixture of craft and tourist shops, its main attraction the superbly restored, early nineteenth-century **Aberfeldy Water Mill** (Easter–Oct Mon–Sat 10am–5.30pm, Sun noon–5pm; £2), which harnesses the water of the Urlar to stone-grind oatmeal in the traditional Scottish way.

One mile west of Aberfeldy, across Wade's Bridge, **Castle Menzies** (April to mid-Oct Mon–Fri 10.30am–5pm, Sun 2–5pm; £2.30) is an imposing, Z-shaped, sixteenth-century tower house, which until the middle of this century was the chief seat of Clan Menzies. With the demise of the Menzies line the castle was taken over by the Menzies Clan Society, which has been restoring it for the last 25 years. The interior, with its wide stone staircase and fine plasterwork ceilings, is sparsely furnished, apart from some clan memorabilia.

The **tourist office** is at The Square (April–June, Sept & Oct Mon–Sat 9.30am–5.30pm, Sun noon–4pm; July & Aug Mon–Sat 9am–7pm, Sun 11am–6pm; Nov–March Mon–Fri 9.30am–5pm, Sat 9.30am–1pm; ☎01887/820276). For **accommodation**, *Moness House Hotel and Country Club*, Crieff Road (☎01887/820446; ④), occupies a whitewashed country house and offers fishing, golf and watersports, while *Guinach House*, by the Birks – pleasant grounds near the famous silver birches (☎01887/820251; ⑤) – is a tastefully decorated small hotel. *Farleyer House*, a mile out of Aberfeldy on the B846 (☎01887/820332; ⑧), is highly recommended as a hotel and **restaurant**. For B&B, try *Novar*, 2 Home St (☎01887/820779; ①), or *Marvis Bank*, Taybridge Drive (☎01887/820223; ①), both attractive stone cottages.

Loch Tay

Loch Tay, stretching southwest of Aberfeldy, sits below moody **Ben Lawers** (3984ft), Perthshire's highest mountain; from the top there are incredible views towards both the Atlantic and the North Sea. The ascent – which should not be tackled without all the right equipment (see p.51) – takes around three hours. The trail begins at 1300ft, from the NTS **visitor centre** (mid-April to Sept daily 10am–5pm; £1; ☎01567/820397), reached by taking a minor road off the A827, which runs along the northern side of the loch. The centre has an audio-visual show, slides of the mountain's flowers – including the rare Alpine flora found here – and a nature trail with accompanying descriptive booklet.

The mountains of **Breadalbane** (pronounced "Bread-*al*bane") loom over the western end of Loch Tay. Glens Lochay and Dochart curve into the north and south respectively from the small town of **KILLIN**, where the River Dochart comes rushing out of the hills and down the frothy **Falls of Dochart**, before disgorging into Loch Tay. There's little to do in Killin itself, but it does make a convenient base for some of the area's best **walks** and from here you can join the A85 south to Lochearnhead and the Trossachs (see p.895). The **tourist office** is located by the falls (March–May & Oct daily 10am–5pm; June–Sept daily 9.30am–6pm; Nov, Dec & Feb Sat & Sun 10am–4pm) next to the **Breadalbane Folklore Centre** (same times as tourist office; £1). The centre explores the history and mythology of Breadalbane and holds the 1300-year-old 'healing stones' of St Fillan, an early Christian missionary who settled in Glen Dochart. One of the more unusual places to **stay** is the *Dall Lodge Hotel*, Main Street (☎01567/820217; ⑦), which the owner, who lives in the Far East, has filled with all manner of exotic bits and pieces. The dining room serves fine local produce. There is also a **youth hostel** (☎01567/820546; closed Nov–March), in an old country house north of the village, with views out over the loch.

On the other side of the Breadalbane mountains, north of Loch Tay, lies **Glen Lyon** – at 34 miles the longest enclosed glen in Scotland – where, legend has it, the Celtic warrior Fingal built twelve castles. Access to the glen is usually impossible in winter, but the narrow roads are passable in summer. You can either take the road from Killin up to the **Ben Lawers Visitor Centre**, four miles up Loch Tay, and keep going, or take the road from Fortingall, which is a couple of miles north of the loch's northern end. The two roads join up, making a round trip possible, but bear in mind there is no road through the mountains to Loch Rannoch further north. **FORTINGALL** itself is little more than a handful of thatched cottages, although locals make much of their 3000-year-old yew tree – believed (by them at least) to be the oldest living thing in Europe. The village also lays claim to being the birthplace of Pontius Pilate, reputedly the son of a Roman officer stationed here.

Pitlochry

Just beyond the confluence of the Tummel and Tay rivers at Ballinluig, **PITLOCHRY**, 12 miles north of Dunkeld, spreads gracefully along the eastern shore of the Tummel, on the lower slopes of Ben Vrackie. Even after General Wade built one of his first roads through here in the early eighteenth century, Pitlochry remained little more than a village. Queen Victoria's visit in 1842 helped to put the area on the map, but it wasn't until the end of the century that Pitlochry established itself as a popular holiday centre.

Today, the busy main street is a constant flurry of traffic of motor traffic. Beyond the railway bridge at the southern end of the main street (Atholl Road leading to Perth Road) is Bells' **Blair Atholl Distillery** (Easter–Sept Mon–Sat 9am–5pm, Sun noon–5pm; Oct–Easter closed Sat & Sun; tours every 10min; £3, including tasting), where the excellent visitor centre illustrates the process involved in making the Blair Atholl malt. Whisky has been produced on this site since 1798, and production now stands at around two million litres a year – making this only a medium-sized distillery.

A perfect contrast to the Blair Atholl is the **Edradour Distillery** (March–Oct Mon–Sat 9.30am–5pm, Sun noon–5pm; Nov Mon–Sat 10am–4pm), Scotland's smallest, in an idyllic position tucked into the hills a couple of miles east of Pitlochry on the A924. A whistle-stop audio-visual presentation covering more than 250 years of distilling precedes the tour of the distillery itself.

On the western edge of Pitlochry, just across the river, lies Scotland's renowned "Theatre in the Hills", the **Pitlochry Festival Theatre** (Easter to early Oct; ☎01796/472680). Set up in 1951, the theatre started in a tent on the site of what is now the town curling rink, before moving to the banks of the river in 1981. Backstage tours, covering all aspects of theatre production (generally Thurs & Fri 2pm; £3; booking essential), run through the day, while both mainstream and offbeat productions are staged in the evening.

A short stroll upstream from the theatre is the **Pitlochry Power Station and Dam**, a massive concrete wall which harnesses the water of the man-made Loch Faskally, just north of the town, for hydro-electric power. Although the visitor centre (April–Oct daily 10am–5.30pm; £1.90) explains the ins and outs of it all, the main attraction here, apart from the views up the loch, is the **salmon ladder,** up which the salmon leap on their annual migrations in late spring and at the end of summer – a sight not to be missed.

Practicalities

The **bus** stop and the **train** station are on Station Road, at the north end of town, ten minutes' walk from the centre and the **tourist office** at 22 Atholl Rd (April to mid-May & Oct Mon–Sat 9am–6pm, Sun noon–6pm; mid-May to Sept daily 9am–8pm; Nov–March Mon–Fri 9am–5pm, Sat 9am–1.30pm; ☎01796/472215). Two places to **stay**, both with good restaurants, are the *Birchwood Hotel*, East Moulin Road (☎01796/472477, *birchwoodhotel@msn.com*; ⑤), and the *Queens View Hotel*, on the way to Tummel Bridge (☎01796/473291, *queensviewhotel@compuserve.com*; ⑤), which has lovely views of Loch Tummel. Other possibilities include *McKays Hotel*, 138 Atholl Rd (☎01796/473888; ②), *Craigroyston House*, 2 Lower Oakfield (☎01796/472053; ②), *Comar House*, Strathview Terrace (☎01796/473531; ①), and *Ferryman's Cottage*, beautifully situated next to the River Tummel (☎01796/473681; ①). The **youth hostel** is a fine stone mansion on Knockard Road, at the top of town (☎01796/472308). Pitlochry has plenty of tearooms, but is pitifully short of **restaurants** and pubs; the best option in town is the very popular restaurant at the Festival Theatre or the nearby *Port-na-craig Inn & Restaurant*, both of which have beautiful riverside locations.

Killiecrankie and Blair Castle

Four miles north of Pitlochry, the A9 cuts through the **Pass of Killiecrankie**, a breathtaking wooded gorge which falls away to the River Garry below. This dramatic setting was the site of the **Battle of Killicrankie** in 1689, when the Jacobites quashed the forces of General Mackay. Legend has it that one soldier of the Crown, fleeing for his life, made a miraculous jump across the eighteen-foot **Soldier's Leap**, an impossibly wide chasm halfway up the gorge. Exhibits at the slick **visitor centre** (April–Oct daily 10am–5.30pm; £1; ☎01796/473233; NTS) recall the battle and examine the gorge in detail.

Before leading the Jacobites into battle, Graham of Claverhouse, Viscount ("Bonnie") Dundee, had seized the whitewashed **Blair Castle** (April–Oct daily 10am–6pm; £6), three miles up the road at Blair Atholl. Seat of the Atholl dukedom, and dating from 1269, the castle presents an impressive sight as you approach up the drive. A piper may be playing in front of the castle: he is one of the Atholl Highlanders, a select group retained by the duke as his private army – a privilege afforded to him by Queen Victoria, who stayed here in 1844. Today the duke is the only British subject allowed to maintain his own force. More than thirty rooms are open for inspection, and display a selection of paintings, furniture, Brussels tapestries and the like that is sumptous in the extreme, although the vast number of stuffed animals may not be to everyone's liking. The castle has a self-service restaurant, and there's a **riding stable** from where you can take treks and explore the landscaped grounds further.

Loch Tummel and Loch Rannoch

Between Pitlochry and Loch Ericht lies a sparsely populated, ever-changing panorama of mountains, moors, lochs and glens. Venturing into the hills is difficult without a car – unless you're hiking – but infrequent local buses do run from Pitlochry to the outlying communities in the surrounding area, and the train to Inverness runs parallel to the A9.

West of Pitlochry, the B8019/B846 twists and turns along the Grampian mountainsides, overlooking **Loch Tummel** and then **Loch Rannoch**. These two lochs, celebrated by Harry Lauder in his famous song *The Road to the Isles*, are joined by Dunalastair Water, which narrows to become the River Tummel at the western end of the loch of the same name. **Queen's View** at the eastern end of Loch Tummel is a fabulous vantage point, looking down the loch across the hills to the misty peak of Schiehallion (3520ft), the "Fairy Mountain", whose mass was used in early experiments to judge the weight of the Earth. The Forestry Commission's **visitor centre** (April–Oct daily 10am–6pm; ☎01350/727284) interprets the fauna and flora of the area, and also has a café.

Beyond Loch Tummel, **KINLOCH RANNOCH** marks the eastern end of Loch Rannoch. This small community is popular with hikers, who stock up at the local store before taking to the hills again. You can stay at *Cuilimore Cottage* (☎01882/632218; ④), where the atmosphere is rustic and the food delicious. The road follows the loch to its end and then heads six miles further into the desolation of **Rannoch Moor**, the biggest peat moor in Europe, where **Rannoch station**, a lonely outpost on the Glasgow to Fort William West Highland train line, marks the end of the road. The only way back is by the same road as far as Loch Rannoch, where it's possible – but not always advisable, depending on conditions – to return on a very minor road along the south side of the lochs. The round trip is roughly seventy miles.

travel details

Trains

Kirkcaldy to: Aberdeen (hourly; 2hr); Dundee (hourly; 40min–1hr); Edinburgh (hourly; 40min); Perth (7 daily; 40min); Pitlochry (4 direct daily; 1hr 15min; 4 change at Perth; 1hr 25min).

Perth to: Aberdeen (hourly; 1hr 40min); Dundee (hourly; 30min); Edinburgh (9 daily; 1hr 30min); Glasgow Queen Street (hourly; 1hr); Kirkcaldy (7 daily; 40min); Pitlochry (8 daily; 30min).

Pitlochry to: Edinburgh (5 daily; 2hr); Glasgow Queen Street (3 daily; 1hr 45min); Kirkcaldy (4 direct daily; 1hr 15min; 2 change at Perth; 1hr 45min); Perth (8 daily; 30min); Stirling (4 daily; 1hr 15min).

Stirling to: Aberdeen (hourly; 2hr 15min); Dundee (hourly; 1hr); Edinburgh (hourly; 1hr); Glasgow Queen Street (hourly; 30min); Perth (hourly; 30min); Pitlochry (3–5 daily; 1hr 15min).

Buses

Dundee to: Kirkcaldy (10 daily; 1hr 30min); St Andrews (every 30min; 40min); Stirling (hourly; 1hr 30min).

Dunfermline to: Edinburgh (2 daily; 40min); Kirkcaldy (hourly; 1hr); St Andrews (11–13 daily; 2hr).

Perth to: Dunblane (every 30min; 35min); Dunfermline (every 30min; 50min); Edinburgh (hourly; 1hr 20min); Glasgow (20 daily; 1hr 40min); Gleneagles (18 daily; 30min); Inverness (10 daily; 2hr 30min); London (4 daily; 9hr); Stirling (20 daily; 50min).

St Andrews to: Dundee (every 30min; 40min); Dunfermline (11–13 daily; 2hr); Edinburgh (12 daily; 2hr); Glasgow (6 daily; 2hr 50min); Kirkcaldy (16 daily; 1hr); Stirling (6 daily; 2hr).

Stirling to: Callander (11 daily; 45min); Dollar (13 daily; 40min); Doune (14 daily; 30min); Dunblane (20 daily; 1hr 15min); Dundee (12 daily; 1hr 30min); Dunfermline (13 daily; 50min); Edinburgh (hourly; 1hr 40min); Glasgow (every 30min; 1hr 10min); Gleneagles (16 daily; 30min); Inverness (12 daily; 3hr 30min); Killin (2 daily; 2hr); Lochearnhead (2 daily; 1hr 40min); Perth (20 daily; 50min); Pitlochry (2 daily; 1hr 30min); St Andrews (6 daily; 2hr).

CHAPTER TWENTY-TWO

ARGYLL

C ut off for centuries from the rest of Scotland by the mountains and sea lochs that characterize the region, Argyll remains remote, its scatter of offshore islands forming part of the Inner Hebridean archipelago (the remaining Hebrides are dealt with in the next chapter). Geographically, as well as culturally, this is a transitional area between Highland and Lowland, boasting a rich variety of scenery, from lush, subtropical gardens warmed by the Gulf Stream to flat and treeless islands far out in the Atlantic. It's in the folds and twists of the countryside and the views out to the islands that the strengths and beauties of mainland Argyll lie – the one area of man-made sights you shouldn't miss is the cluster of Celtic and prehistoric sites near Kilmartin. The overall population is tiny; even Oban, Argyll's main administrative centre and chief ferry port, has barely even a thousand inhabitants, while the prettiest, Inveraray, boasts a mere four hundred.

The eastern duo of **Bute** and **Arran** are the most popular of Scotland's more southerly islands, the latter – now strictly speaking part of North Ayrshire – justifiably so, with spectacular scenery ranging from the granite peaks of the north to the Lowland pasture of the south. Of the Hebridean islands covered in this chapter, mountainous **Mull** is the most visited, though it is large enough to absorb the crowds, many of whom are only passing through en route to the tiny isle of **Iona**, a centre of Christian culture since the sixth century. **Islay**, best known for its distinctive malt whiskies, is fairly quiet even in the height of summer, as is neighbouring **Jura**, which offers excellent walking opportunities. And for those seeking still more solitude, there are the remote islands of **Tiree** and **Coll**, which, although swept with fierce winds, boast more sunny days than anywhere else in Scotland.

The region's name derives from *Aragàidheal*, which translates as "Boundary of the Gaels", the Irish Celts who settled here in the fifth century AD, and whose **kingdom of Dalriada** embraced much of what is now Argyll. Known to the Romans as Scotti – hence Scotland – it was the Irish Celts who promoted Celtic Christianity, and whose Gaelic language eventually became the national tongue. After a brief period of Norse invasion and settlement, the islands (and the peninsula of Kintyre) fell to the immensely powerful Somerled, who became King of the Hebrides and Lord of Argyll in the twelfth century. Somerled's successors, the MacDonalds, established Islay as their headquarters in the 1200s, but were in turn dislodged by Robert the Bruce. Of Bruce's

---

ACCOMMODATION PRICE CODES

Throughout this guide, hotel and B&B accommodation is priced on a scale of ① to ⑨, the number indicating the **lowest price** you could expect to pay per night in that establishment for a **double room** in high season. The prices indicated by the codes are as follows:

① under £40	④ £60–70	⑦ £110–150
② £40–50	⑤ £70–90	⑧ £150–200
③ £50–60	⑥ £90–110	⑨ over £200

allies, it was the **Campbells** who benefited most from the MacDonalds' demise, and eventually, as the dukes of Argyll, gained control of the entire area – even today they remain one of the largest landowners in the region.

In the aftermath of the Jacobite uprisings, the islands of Argyll, like the rest of the Highlands, were devastated by the **Clearances**, with thousands of crofters evicted from their homes in order to make room for profitable sheep-farming – "the white plague" – and cattle rearing. Today the traditional industries remain under threat, leaving the region ever more dependent on tourism and EU grants to keep things going; while Gaelic, once the language of the majority in Argyll, retains only a tenuous hold on the outlying islands of Islay, Coll and Tiree – all officially part of Scotland's Gaelic-speaking areas.

Gare Loch and Loch Long

Most people approach Argyll from Glasgow, from where there's a choice of two routes: the most popular is along Loch Lomond (see p.899); a quieter route (and the one which

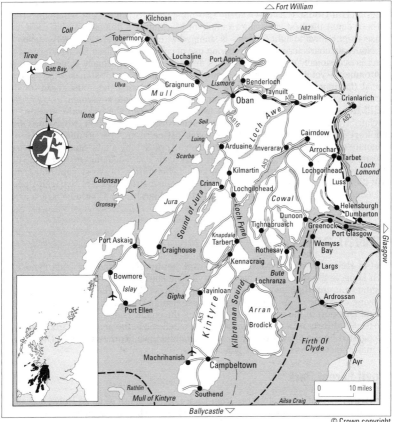

© Crown copyright

the train takes) is along the shores of **Gare Loch** and **Loch Long** to Arrochar, which marks the beginning of Argyll proper. Apart from Helensburgh, however, there's little to see along the shores of either loch. Both are littered with decaying industrial remains, including the nuclear submarine base at Faslane on Gare Loch and the oil tanks at Finnart on Loch Long. Only occasionally is it possible to glimpse the "unspeakably beautiful" landscape described by eighteenth-century travellers.

Helensburgh

HELENSBURGH, twenty miles or more northwest of Glasgow, is a smart, Georgian grid-plan settlement laid out in an imitation of Edinburgh's New Town. In the eighteenth century it was a well-to-do commuter town for Glasgow and a seaside resort, whose bathing-master, **Henry Bell**, invented one of the first steamboats, the *Comet*, to transport Glaswegians "doon the watter". Today Helensburgh is a stop on the route of the *Waverley,* the last sea-going paddle steamer in the world, which does a zigzag tour of the lochs of Argyll throughout the summer (pick up a timetable from the tourist office).

The inventor of TV, John Logie Baird, was born here, as was Charles Rennie Mackintosh, who in 1902 was commissioned by the Glaswegian publisher Walter Blackie to design **Hill House** (Easter–Oct daily 1.30–5pm; £6; NTS), on Upper Colquhoun Street. Without doubt the best surviving example of Mackintosh's domestic architecture, the house – right down to light fittings – is stamped with his very personal interpretation of Art Nouveau, characterized by his sparing use of colour and stylized floral patterns. The effect is occasionally overwhelming – it's difficult to imagine actually living in such an environment – yet it is precisely Mackintosh's attention to detail that makes the place so special (for more on Mackintosh see p.870). After exploring the house, head for the kitchen quarters, which have been sensitively transformed into a tearoom.

Hill House is a twenty-minute walk from Helensburgh Central **train station**, up Sinclair Street, or just five minutes from Helensburgh Upper station (where the Oban and Fort William trains stop). The **tourist office** is on the ground floor of the Italianate old church tower by the loch (daily: April & May 10am–5pm; June & Sept 9.30am–6pm; July & Aug 9.30am–7pm; early Oct 10am–4.30pm; ☎01436/672642). The best **accommodation** options are *Lethamhill*, 20 West Dhuhill Drive (☎01436/676016; ③), set in the attractive leafy villa district near Helensburgh Upper, and *Greenpark* (☎01436/671545; ②; closed Nov–March), on Charlotte Street, near Hill House.

Cowal and Bute

West of Helensburgh, the claw-shaped **Cowal peninsula**, formed by Loch Fyne and Loch Long, is the most visited part of Argyll. The landscape here is extremely varied, ranging from the Highland peaks of the Argyll Forest Park in the north, to the gentle low-lying coastline of the southwest, but most visitors confine themselves to the area around **Dunoon** in the east, leaving the rest of the countryside relatively undisturbed. The island of **Bute** is in many ways simply an extension of the peninsula, from which it is separated by the merest slither of water; its chief town, **Rothesay**, rivals Dunoon as the major seaside resort on the Clyde.

Argyll Forest Park

The **Argyll Forest Park** stretches from Loch Lomond south as far as Holy Loch, providing the most exhilarating scenery on the peninsula. The park includes the **Arrochar**

Alps, north of Glen Croe and Glen Kinglas, whose Munros offer some of the best climbing in Argyll: Ben Ime (3318ft) is the tallest of the range and The Cobbler (2891ft) is easily the most distinctive – all are for experienced walkers only. Less threatening are the peaks south of Glen Croe, between Loch Long and Loch Goil (the latter branches off Loch Long), known as **Argyll's Bowling Green** – no ironic nickname but an English corruption of the Gaelic *Baile na Greine* (Sunny Hamlet).

Approaching from Glasgow by road (A83), you enter the park from **ARROCHAR**, at the head of Loch Long. The village itself is ordinary enough, but the setting is dramatic, and it makes a convenient base for exploring the northern section of the park. There's a **train station**, a mile or so east up the Tarbert road (A83), and numerous **hotels** and **B&Bs** – try the *Lochside Guest House* (☎01301/702467; ①) or the *Mansefield Hotel* (☎01301/702282; ②). Two miles beyond Arrochar at **ARDGARTAN**, there's a lochside Forestry Commission **campsite** (☎01301/702293; closed Nov to mid-March), a **youth hostel** (☎01301/702362; closed Jan) and a **tourist office** (daily: April–June, Sept & Oct 10am–5pm; July & Aug 10am–6pm; ☎01301/702432), which can give you lots of information on the forest park.

Rest-and-be-Thankful to Loch Eck

Approaching Cowal from the east, you're forced to climb **Glen Croe**, a strategic hill pass whose saddle is called Rest-and-be-Thankful, for obvious reasons. From here, continue along the A83 down the grand Highland sweep of **Glen Kinglas** to the head of Loch Fyne. A mile or so around the head of the loch on the main road is the famous *Loch Fyne Oyster Bar* (☎01499/600264), which sells more oysters than anywhere else in the country, plus lots of other fish and seafood treats.

To delve further into Cowal, take the A815 southwest to Strachur before heading inland to **Loch Eck**, an exceptionally narrow freshwater loch, squeezed between steeply banked woods, and a favourite for trout fishing. At the southern tip of Loch Eck are the **Younger Botanic Gardens** (mid-March to Oct daily 10am–6pm; £1.50), an offshoot of Edinburgh's Royal Botanic Gardens, especially striking for its avenue of great redwoods, planted in 1863 and now over 100ft high. There's an excellent inexpensive **café** by the entrance, open in the season with an imaginative menu – you can eat there without visiting the gardens.

Dunoon

In the nineteenth century, Cowal's capital, **DUNOON**, grew from a mere village to a major Clyde seaside resort, a favourite holiday spot for Glaswegians. Nowadays, tourists tend to arrive by ferry from Gourock, and though their numbers are smaller, Dunoon remains by far the largest town in all Argyll, with 13,000 inhabitants. Apart from its practical uses, there's little to tempt you to linger in Dunoon. It's a good idea, however, to take advantage of the **tourist office** – the only one in Cowal – on Alexandra Parade (April & Oct Mon–Fri 9am–5.30pm, Sat 10am–5.30pm, Sun 11am–3pm; May, June & Sept Mon–Fri 9am–5.30pm, Sat & Sun 10am–5pm; July & Aug Mon–Fri 9am–7pm, Sat 10am–7pm, Sun 10am–5pm; Nov–March Mon–Thurs 9am–5.30pm, Fri 9am–5pm; ☎01369/703785). The shorter, more frequent of the two **ferry crossings** across the Clyde from Gourock to Dunoon is the half-hourly Western Ferries service to Hunter's Quay, a mile north of the town centre; CalMac have the prime position, however, on the main pier, and better transport connections for foot passengers.

If you need to **stay**, try the central *Cedars* (☎01369/702425; ②), on the seafront just up Alexandra Parade from the tourist office, the landmark *Argyll,* opposite the pier (☎01369/702059; ②), or the highly reputable *Ardfillayne*, West Bay (☎01369/702267; ③). *Chatters*, 58 John St (closed Mon, Tues & Sun), is Dunoon's finest **restaurant**, offering delicious Loch Fyne seafood and Scottish beef; the *Argyll* serves perfectly decent, filling bar snacks. The town also boasts a two-screen cinema (a rarity in Argyll) on John Street, but by far Dunoon's most famous entertainment is the **Cowal Highland Gathering**, the largest of its kind in the world, held here on the last weekend in August, and culminating in the awesome spectacle of the massed pipes and drums of over 150 bands marching through the streets.

Southwest Cowal

The mellow landscape of **southwest Cowal**, in complete contrast to the bustle of Dunoon or the Highland grandeur of the forest, becomes immediate as soon as you head west to Loch Striven, where, from either side, there are few more beautiful sights than the **Kyles of Bute**, the thin slithers of water that separate the bleak bulk of north Bute from Cowal, and constitute some of the best sailing territory in Scotland.

The most popular spot from which to appreciate the Kyles is the A8003 as it rises dramatically above the sea lochs before descending to the peaceful lochside village of **TIGHNABRUAICH** best known for its sailing school (☎01700/811396), which offers week-long courses from beginners to advanced. The *Royal Hotel* (☎01700/811239; ⑤), by the waterside, does exceptionally fine **bar meals** but it's cheaper to stay in neighbouring **KAMES** at the *Kames Hotel* (☎01700/811489; ②) which has wonderful views over the Kyles.

Isle of Bute

Thanks to its consistently mild climate and Rothesay's ferry link with Wemyss Bay, the island of **Bute** has been a popular holiday and convalescence spot for Clydesiders – particularly the elderly – for over a century. Even considering the island's small size (fifteen miles long and five miles wide) you can find peace and quiet; most of its inhabitants are centred on the two wide bays on the east coast of the island.

Bute's one and only town, **ROTHESAY**, is a long-established resort, set in a wide sweeping bay, backed by green hills, with a classic promenade and pagoda-style Winter Gardens. It creates a better impression than Dunoon, though it, too, has passed its prime. However, even if you're just passing through, you must pay a visit to the ornate Victorian toilets (daily: Easter–Oct 8am–9pm; Nov–March 9am–5pm; 10p) on the pier, which were built in 1899 and have since been declared a national treasure (gentlemen have the best time as the porcelain urinals steal the show). Rothesay also boasts the militarily useless, but architecturally impressive, moated ruins of **Rothesay Castle** (April–Sept Mon–Sat 9.30am–6.30pm, Sun 2–6.30pm; Oct–March closes 4.30pm; £1.50), hidden amid the town's backstreets but signposted from the pier. Built in the twelfth century, it was twice captured by the Vikings in the 1400s; such vulnerability was the reasoning behind the unusual, almost circular, curtain wall, with its four big drum towers, of which only one remains fully intact.

A very good reason for coming to Bute is to visit **Mount Stuart** (Easter & May to mid-Oct Mon, Wed & Fri–Sun 11am–5pm; £5.50), three miles south of Rothesay. Seat of the fantastically wealthy seventh Marquis of Bute, the mansion was built for the third marquis between 1879 and World War II, as an incredible High Gothic fancy, drawing architectural inspiration from all over Europe. The sumptuous interior was decked out by craftsmen who worked with William Burges on the marquis's earlier medieval concoctions at Cardiff Castle. The gardens, established in the eighteenth century by the third Earl of Bute, who had a hand in London's Kew Gardens, are equally lovely.

For the best overall view of the island, take a walk up **Canada Hill** above the freshwater Loch Fad, which all but divides Bute in two. The northern half of the island is hilly, uninhabited and little visited, while the southern half is made up of Lowland-style farmland. The early monastic history of the island is recalled at **St Blane's Chapel**, a twelfth-century ruin beautifully situated in open countryside on the west coast, close to the very southernmost tip. Bute's finest sandy beach is **Scalpsie Bay**, further up the west coast, beyond which lies **St Ninian's Point**, where the ruins of a sixth-century chapel overlook another fine sandy strand and the deserted island of **Inchmarnock**.

Practicalities

Rothesay's **tourist office** is at 15 Victoria St (April & Oct Mon–Fri 9am–5.30pm, Sat 10am–5.30pm, Sun 11am–3pm; May Mon–Fri 9am–5.30pm, Sat & Sun 10am–5pm; June & Sept Mon–Fri 9am–6pm, Sat & Sun 10am–5pm; July & Aug Mon–Sat 9am–7pm, Sun 10am–5pm; Nov–March Mon–Thurs 9am–5.30pm, Fri 9am–5pm; ☎01700/502151). There's no shortage of **places to stay** along the seafront, the grandest being the giant, former spa sanatorium *Glenburn Hotel* on Glenburn Road (☎01700/502500; ⑥). Others, like the *Commodore* at 12 Battery Place (☎01700/502178; ③) or the distinctive *Glendale*, at no. 20 (☎01700/502329; ②), are more modest. **Food** options are limited to the bistro in the Winter Gardens, pasta and steaks at *Oliver's* opposite, or fish and chips from Rothesay's finest, *The West End Café* on Gallowgate. Bute holds its own **Highland Games** on the last weekend in August – Prince Charles, as Duke of Rothesay, occasionally attends – plus a **folk festival** on the third weekend in July, and a mainly **trad-jazz festival** during May Bank Holiday weekend.

Inveraray

A classic example of an eighteenth-century planned town, **INVERARAY** was built on the site of a ruined fishing village in 1745 by the third Duke of Argyll, head of the powerful Campbell clan, in order to distance his newly rebuilt castle from the hoi polloi in the town and to establish a commercial and legal centre for the region. Today Inveraray, an absolute set-piece of Scottish Georgian architecture, has a truly memorable setting, the brilliant white arches of Front Street reflected in the still waters of Loch Fyne, which separate it from the Cowal peninsula.

Squeezed onto a promontory some distance from the duke's new castle, there's not much more to Inveraray's "New Town" than its distinctive **Main Street** (set at a right angle to Front Street), flanked by whitewashed terraces, whose window casements are picked out in black. At the top of the street, the road divides to circumnavigate the town's Neoclassical church, originally built in two parts: the southern half served the Gaelic-speaking community, while the northern half (still in use) served those who spoke English.

East of the church is **Inveraray Jail** (daily: April–Oct 9.30am–6pm; Nov–March 10am–5pm; £4.50), whose attractive Georgian courthouse and grim prison blocks ceased to function in the 1930s. The jail is now an imaginative and thoroughly enjoyable museum, which graphically recounts conditions from medieval times up until the nineteenth century. You can also sit in the beautiful semicircular courthouse and listen to the trial of a farmer accused of fraud.

Slightly removed from the New Town, to the north, the neo-Gothic **Inveraray Castle** (April–June, Sept & Oct Mon–Thurs & Sat 10am–1pm & 2–6pm, Sun 1–6pm; July & Aug Mon–Sat 10am–6pm, Sun 1–6pm; £4) remains the family home of the Duke of Argyll. Built in 1745 by the third duke, it was given a touch of the Loire with the addition of dormer windows and conical roofs in the nineteenth century. Inside, the most startling feature is the armoury hall, whose displays of weaponry – supplied to the Campbells by the British government to put down the Jacobites – rise through several storeys. The **Combined Operations Museum** (Mon–Thurs & Sat 11am–6pm, Sun 1–6pm; £1.25) in the old stables recalls the wartime role of Inveraray as a training centre for the D-Day landings, during which over half a million troops practised secret amphibious manoeuvres around Loch Fyne.

Practicalities

Inverary's **tourist office** is on Front Street (April & mid-Sept to Oct Mon–Sat 9am–5pm, Sun noon–5pm; May & June Mon–Sat 9am–5pm, Sun 11am–5pm; July to mid-Sept daily 9am–6pm; Nov–March Mon–Fri 11am–4pm, Sat & Sun noon–4pm; ☎01499/302063), as is the town's chief **hotel**, the historic *Argyll Hotel* (☎01499/302466; ⑥), where Dr Johnson and Boswell stayed. Also worth considering is the *Fernpoint Hotel* (☎01499/302170; ⑥) round by the pier. For **B&B** accommodation, try *Lorona* on Main Street (☎01499/302258; ②; closed Nov–March). The **youth hostel** (☎01499/302454; closed Nov to mid-March) is just up the Oban road. The **bar** of the *George Hotel* in the middle of town is the liveliest spot. The best place to sample Loch Fyne's delicious fresh fish is the restaurant of the aforementioned *Loch Fyne Oyster Bar* (see p.925), six miles back up the A83 towards Glasgow.

Oban

The solidly Victorian resort of **OBAN** enjoys a superb setting – the island of Kerrera providing its bay with a natural shelter – distinguished by a bizarre granite amphitheatre, dramatically lit at night, on the hilltop above the town. Despite a population of just 8500, it's by far the largest port in northwest Scotland, the second largest town in Argyll, and the main departure point for ferries to the Hebrides. If you arrive late, or are catching an early boat, you may well find yourself staying the night (though there's no real need otherwise); it is a useful base for wet-weather activities and shopping, although it does get uncomfortably crowded in the summer.

The only real sight in Oban is the town's landmark, **McCaig's Folly**, a stiff ten-minute climb from the quayside. An imitation of the Coliseum in Rome, it was the brainchild of a local businessman a century ago, who had the twin aims of alleviating off-season unemployment among the local stonemasons and glorifying his family. Work never progressed further than the exterior walls before McCaig died, but the folly provides a wonderful seaward panorama, particularly at sunset.

You can pass a few hours admiring the fishing boats in the harbour and looking out for scavanging seals in the bay; or you can take a 45-minute guided tour of the **Oban Distillery** (July–Sept Mon–Fri 9.30am–5pm, Sat 9.30am–8.30pm; Easter–Oct Mon–Sat 9.30am–5pm; £3), in the centre of town off George Street, which ends with a dram of whisky (and a refund of the admission fee if you buy a bottle).

Practicalities

The CalMac **ferry terminal** for the islands is on Railway Pier, a stone's throw from the **train station**, itself adjacent to the **bus stops** on Station Square. A host of private **boat operators** can be found around the harbour: their excursions – direct to the castles of Mull, to Staffa and the Treshnish Islands – are well worth considering. The **tourist office** (Mon–Fri 9.30am–5pm, Sat & Sun noon–4pm; longer hours in peak season; ☎01631/563122) is housed in a converted church on Argyll Square, and has a visually attractive, interactive exhibition where the altar used to be.

Oban is positively heaving with **hotels** and **B&Bs**, particularly on Dalriach and Ardconnel Road, Dunollie Terrace and the Esplanade. Top choices are the superior Victorian *Glenburnie Hotel* (☎01631/562089; ③) on the Esplanade, the excellent *Glenburvie Guest House* (☎01631/564770; ①) on Dalriach Road, and *Glengorm* (☎01631/565361; ①), a cheapie on Dunollie Terrace. There are three **youth hostels** in town – the SYHA one is north along the Esplanade (☎01631/562025), the laid-back

Oban Backpackers is on Breadalbane Street (☎01631/562107) and the third, run by the eccentric Jeremy Inglis, is at 21 Airds Crescent (☎01631/565065 or 563064). The nearest **campsite** is south of town on Glenshellach Road (☎01631/562755; closed Dec–Feb); ask the tourist office for directions.

Oban's best **restaurant** is *The Gathering* (☎01631/565421; eves only; closed Jan–Easter), Breadalbane Street, which excels in, among other things, fish and seafood; *F'Eats*, a café at 5 John St, does delicious grilled panini. The town's fish-and-chip shops are also better than average; try *Onorio's*, 86 George St (closed Sun). Oban's one and only half-decent **pub** is the *Oban Inn* opposite the north pier, with a classic flagstone-and-brass bar downstairs and lounge upstairs. You might want to make use of the town's **cinema**, confusingly known as The Highland Theatre (☎01631/562444), at the north end of George Street.

Isle of Mull

The second largest of the Inner Hebrides, **MULL** is by far the most accessible – just forty minutes from Oban by ferry. First impressions largely depend on the weather: without the sun the large tracts of moorland, particularly around the island's highest peak, Ben More (3196ft), can appear bleak and unwelcoming. There are, however, areas of more gentle pastoral scenery around Dervaig in the north and Salen on the east coast, and the indented west coast varies from the sandy beaches around Calgary to the cliffs of Loch na Keal. The most common mistake is to try and "do" the island in a day or two: Mull is a place that will grow on you only if you have the time and patience to explore.

Historically, crofting, whisky distilling and fishing supported the islanders (*Muileachs*), but the population – which peaked at 10,000 – decreased dramatically in the nineteenth century due to the Clearances and the 1846 potato famine. On Mull, it is a trend that has been reversed, mostly due to the large influx of settlers from elsewhere in the country which has brought the current population up to around 2500. One of the main reasons for this resurgence is, of course, tourism – over half a million visitors come here each year – although oddly enough, there are very few large hotels or campsites. Public transport is limited, and the roads are predominantly single-track, which can cause serious congestion in summer.

Craignure and around

CRAIGNURE is the main entry point to Mull, linked daily to Oban by several car ferries; a faster, less frequent car ferry service crosses from Lochaline on the Morvern peninsula to Fishnish, six miles northwest of Craignure. Fishnish is just a slipway and Craignure itself is little more than a scattering of cottages, though it has all the amenities you'd need to make it a base for touring the area – there's a **tourist office** (April to mid-June & Sept to mid-Oct Mon–Thurs 9am–7pm, Fri 9am–5pm, Sat 9am–6.30pm, Sun 10.30am–5pm; mid-June to Aug Mon–Thurs 9am–7pm, Fri 9am–5pm, Sat 9am–8.15pm, Sun 10.30am–7pm; mid-Oct to March Mon–Sat 9am–5pm, Sun 10.30am–5pm; ☎01680/812377), several guest houses – try the snug *Craignure Inn* (☎01680/812305 ③) – a **campsite** (☎01680/812496; closed Nov–March) with hostel accommodation and bike rental, and infrequent bus connections with Tobermory and Fionnphort.

Two castles lie immediately southeast of Craignure. The first, **Torosay Castle** (Easter to mid-Oct daily 10.30am–5pm; £4.50), a full-blown Scottish Baronial creation, is linked to Craignure by the narrow-gauge Mull Rail link (Easter to mid-Oct). The magnificent **gardens** (daily 9am–7pm) with their avenue of eighteenth-century Italianate statues, Japanese section, and views over to neighbouring Duart, are the real highlight.

The house itself, in the mid-nineteenth-century style, is stuffed with junk relating to the present owners, the little-known Guthries.

Lacking the gardens, but on a much more romantic spit of rock, fifteen minutes' walk east of Torosay, **Duart Castle** (May to mid-Oct daily 10.30am–6pm; £3.50) is a restored medieval fortress, the headquarters of the once powerful MacLean clan until the late seventeenth century when it was left to rot by the Campbells. Only in 1911 did the MacLeans manage to buy it back and restore it – the 27th clan chief now lives there. You can learn more about the MacLean clan (and the world scout movement) inside, and peek in the dungeons and ascend the ramparts; but the castle is seen to best advantage from the Oban ferry.

Tobermory

Mull's chief town, **TOBERMORY**, is easily the most attractive fishing port on the west coast of Scotland, its clusters of brightly coloured houses and boats sheltering in a bay backed by a steep bluff. Founded in 1788 by the British Fisheries Society, it never really took off as a fishing port and only survived due to the steady influx of crofters evicted from other parts of the island during the Clearances. If you're staying any length of time on Mull, you're bound to end up here – for one thing, it has the island's sole bank, the Clydesdale.

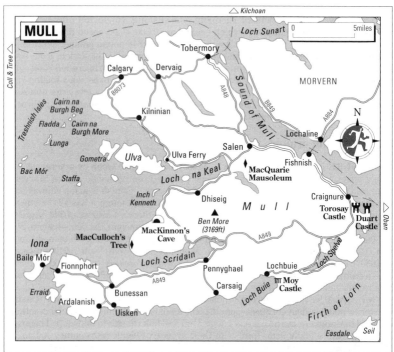

© Crown copyright

Practicalities aside, the harbour's shops are good for browsing, and you could pay a visit to the **Hebridean Whale and Dolphin Trust** (April–Oct Mon–Fri 10am–6pm, Sat & Sun 11am–5pm, Nov–March Mon–Fri 11am–5pm; free), which has lots of information on recent sightings and on how to identify marine mammals. Sea Life Surveys (☎01688/302787), who offer a variety of whale- and dolphin-watching trips, are run from the same office. One endearing feature of the town is its diminutive **clock-tower**, erected by the author Isabella Bird in 1905 in memory of her sister who died of typhoid on the island in 1880.

A stiff climb up Back Brae will bring you to the island's new arts centre, **An Tobar** (Tues–Sat 10am–4pm; free), housed in a converted Victorian schoolhouse. The centre hosts exhibitions, a variety of live events, and contains a café with comfy sofas set before a real fire. Another wet weather retreat is the small **Mull Museum** on Main Street (Easter to mid-Oct Mon–Fri 10.30am–4pm, Sat 10am–1pm; £1). Alternatively, there's the minuscule **Tobermory Distillery** (Easter–Oct Mon–Fri 10.30am–4pm; £2.50) at the south end of the bay, which offers a guided tour finishing off with a tasting.

Practicalities

The **tourist office** (April & mid-Sept to Oct Mon–Sat 10am–5pm, Sun 10am–5pm; May & June daily 9am–5pm; July to mid-Sept daily 9am–6pm; ☎01688/302182) is in the same building as the CalMac ticket office at the northern end of Main Street. There are several **accommodation** options on Main Street – try the excellent *Fàilte* (☎01688/302495; ②), the *Harbour Guest House* (☎01688/302209; ①), or the friendly youth hostel (☎01688/302481; late Feb to Oct). The grand Victorian *Western Isles Hotel* (☎01688/302012; *wihotel@aol.com*; ⑤) sits high above the bay. The nearest **campsite** is *Newdale* (☎01688/302306; closed Dec–March), nicely situated one and a half miles outside Tobermory on the B8073 to Dervaig.

The *Back Brae* (evenings only), on the corner of Main Street, serves good local **food**; for cheaper, filling dishes, head along Main Street to *Gannets* or the lounge bar of the *Mishnish Hotel*. The bar of the *Mishnish* is the local hangout, and the focus of Mull's annual **Traditional Music Festival**, a feast of Gaelic folk music held on the last weekend in April. Mull's other major musical event is the annual **Mendelssohn on Mull Festival**, held over ten days in early July, which commemorates the composer's visit here in 1829.

Along the west coast

The gently undulating countryside west of Tobermory, beyond the Mishnish lochs, provides some of the most beguiling scenery on the island. Added to this, the road out west, the B8073, is exceptionally dramatic, with fiendish switchbacks much appreciated during the annual Mull Rally, which takes place each October. The only village of any size is **DERVAIG**, which nestles beside a narrow sea loch just eight miles southwest of Tobermory, distinguished by its unusual pencil-shaped church spire and the dinky little cottages on its main street. Dervaig is home to **Mull Theatre**, one of the smallest professional theatres in the world, which puts on plays adapted for just two resident actors (April–Sept; ☎01688/400245). The theatre lies within the grounds of the *Druimard Country House* (☎01688/400345; ⑦), which offers pricey but excellent pre-theatre dinners. The best of the **B&Bs** are the vegetarian-friendly *Glen Bellart House* (☎01688/400282; ①; Nov–Easter) on the main street, *Glenview* (☎01688/400239; ②; closed Nov–March), a lovely 1890s house on the edge of the village, or *Balmacara* (☎01688/400363; ③), a modern and extremely luxurious hillside house.

A little beyond Dervaig, the **Old Byre Heritage Centre** (Easter–Oct daily 10.30am–6.30pm; £2) is better than many of its kind, with a video on the island's history and a passable tearoom. The road continues cross-country to **CALGARY**, once a thriving crofting community, now an idyllic holiday spot boasting Mull's finest sandy bay, with wonderful views over to Coll and Tiree. There's just one **hotel**, the delightful *Calgary Farmhouse* (☎01688/400256; ④; closed Nov–March), which has an excellent restaurant, *The Dovecote*, in what was once a dovecote; and an unofficial **campsite** by the beach.

Isle of Staffa

Seven miles off the west coast of Mull, **STAFFA** is the most romantic and dramatic of Scotland's many uninhabited islands. On its south side, the perpendicular rockface features an imposing series of black basalt columns, known as the Colonnade, which have been cut by the sea into cathedralesque caverns, most notably **Fingal's Cave**. The Vikings knew about the island – the name derives from their word for "Island of Pillars" – but it wasn't until 1772 that it was "discovered" by the world. Turner painted it, Wordsworth explored it, but Mendelssohn's *Die Fingalshöhle*, inspired by the sounds of the sea-wracked caves he heard on a visit here in 1829, did most to popularize the place – after which Queen Victoria gave her blessing too. The geological explanation for these polygonal basalt organ pipes is that they were created by a massive subterranean explosion some sixty million years ago. A huge mass of molten basalt ejaculated onto land and, as it cooled, solidified into what are, essentially, crystals. Of course, confronted with such artistry, most visitors have found it difficult to believe that their origin is entirely natural – indeed, the various Celtic folk tales, which link the phenomenon with the Giant's Causeway in Ireland, are certainly more appealing. To **get to Staffa**, join one of the many boat trips from Oban, Dervaig, Ulva Ferry or Fionnphort, weather permitting. Staffa-only trips start at £10 per person on the MB *Iolaire* (☎01681/700358) which sails out of Fionnphort, and with *Turus Mara* (☎01688/400242; *turus.mara@dial.pipex.com*), operating out of Ulva Ferry. However, *Inter-Island Cruises* (☎01688/400264), operating out of Dervaig, is worth the extra money.

Ben More and the Ross of Mull

From the southern shores of Loch na Keal, which almost splits Mull in two, rise the terraced slopes of **Ben More** (3169ft) – literally "big mountain" – a mighty extinct volcano, and the highest mountain on Mull. Stretching for twenty miles west as far as Iona is the island's rocky southernmost peninsula known as the **Ross of Mull**, which, like much of Scotland, appears blissfully tranquil in good weather, and desolate and bleak in bad. Most visitors simply drive through the Ross en route to Iona, but given that **accommodation** is severely limited on Iona, and Fionnphort is not the nicest place to stay, it's worth considering basing yourself near Bunessan, roughly two thirds of the way along the Ross. There's a good selection of places here ranging from the excellent *Assapol House Hotel* (☎01681/700258; ⑥; closed Nov–Easter) to *Ardalanish Farm* (☎01681/700265; ①). The basic *Fidden Farm* **campsite** (☎01681/700427; closed Oct–March), a mile south of Fionnphort along the Knockvologan road by Fidden beach, is the nearest one to Iona. Fionnphort itself now boasts a brand new **Columba Centre** (mid-May to Sept Mon–Sat 10am–6pm, Sun 11am–6pm; £2), with a small museum dedicated to the life of the saint, which is worth investigating.

Isle of Iona

Less than a mile off the southwest tip of Mull, **IONA**, although just three miles long and no more than a mile wide, manages to encapsulate all the enchantment and mystique of the Hebrides. It is frequently tagged "the cradle of Christianity": St Columba arrived here from Ireland in 563 and established a monastery which was responsible for the conversion of more or less all of pagan Scotland as well as much of northern England. This history and the island's splendid isolation have lent it a peculiar religiosity; in the words of Dr Johnson, "that man is little to be envied . . . whose piety would not grow warmer among the ruins of Iona". Today, however, the island can barely cope with its thousands of day-trippers, so to appreciate the special atmosphere and to have time to see the whole island, including the often overlooked west coast, you should plan on staying at least one night.

Baile Mór

The frequent passenger ferry from Fionnphort stops at the island's main village, **BAILE MÓR** (literally "large village"), which is in fact little more than a single terrace of cottages facing the sea. Just inland, you can walk through the ruins of an **Augustinian nunnery** built with pink granite around 1200, but disused since the Reformation – if nothing else, it gives you an idea of the state of the present-day abbey before it was restored. At a bend in the road just beyond the nunnery stands the fifteenth-century **MacLean's Cross**, a fine example of the distinctive, flowing, three-leaved foliage of the Iona school. To the north the **Iona Heritage Centre**

A BRIEF HISTORY OF IONA

Legend has it that **St Columba** (Colum Cille), born in Donegal in 521, was a direct descendant of the Irish king, Niall of the Nine Hostages. A scholar and soldier priest, who founded numerous monasteries in Ireland, he became involved in a bloody dispute with the king when he refused to hand over a copy of the *Book of Psalms* copied illegally from the original owned by St Finian of Moville. At the Battle of Cooldrumman, Columba's forces won, though with great loss of life; repenting this bloodshed, he went into exile with twelve other monks, eventually settling on Iona in 563. Columba became a legend in his own lifetime and is credited with miraculous feats such as defeating the Loch Ness monster and banishing snakes (and, some say, frogs) from the island.

During Columba's lifetime, Iona enjoyed a great deal of autonomy from Rome, establishing a specifically **Celtic Christian** tradition. Missionaries were sent out to the rest of Scotland and parts of England, and Iona quickly became a respected seat of learning and artistry; the monks compiled a vast library of intricately **illuminated manuscripts** – most famously the *Book of Kells* (now on display in Trinity College, Dublin) – while the masons excelled in carving peculiarly intricate crosses. Two factors were instrumental in the demise of the Celtic tradition: a series of Viking raids, the worst of which was the massacre of 68 monks on the sands of Martyrs' Bay in 806, and relentless pressure from the established church, which culminated in the suppression of the Celtic Church by King David I in 1144.

In 1203, Iona became an official part of the mainstream church with the establishment of an Augustinian nunnery, and a **Benedictine monastery**, its masons enjoying a second flowering of stone carving. During the Reformation, the complex was ransacked and all but three of the island's three hundred and sixty crosses were destroyed. Although plans were drawn up at various times to turn the abbey into a Cathedral of the Isles, nothing came of them until 1899, when its then owner, the Duke of Argyll, donated the abbey buildings to the **Church of Scotland**, who restored the abbey church for worship. Iona's modern resurgence began in 1938, when **George MacLeod**, a minister from Glasgow, established a group of ministers, students and artisans to begin rebuilding the remainder of the monastic buildings. What began as a male, Gaelic-speaking, strictly Presbyterian community is today mostly a lay, mixed and ecumenical retreat. The entire abbey complex has been successfully restored and the island, apart from the church land and a few crofts, now belongs to the NTS.

(April–Oct Mon–Sat 10.30am–4.30pm; £1.50), in a manse, built, like the nearby parish church, by the ubiquitous Thomas Telford, has displays on the social history of the island.

The Abbey complex

No buildings remain from Columba's time: the present **Abbey** dates from the arrival of the Benedictines in around 1200, was extensively rebuilt in the fifteenth and sixteenth centuries, and restored virtually wholesale in the 1900s. Adjoining the facade is a small steep-roofed chamber, believed to be St Columba's grave, now a small chapel. The three high crosses in front of the abbey date from the eighth to tenth centuries, and are decorated with the Pictish serpent and boss and Celtic spirals for which Iona's early Christian masons were renowned. For reasons of sanitation, the cloisters were placed, contrary to the norm, on the north side of the church (where running water was available); entirely reconstructed in the late 1950s, they now shelter a useful historical account of the abbey's development.

South of the abbey, Iona's oldest building, **St Oran's Chapel**, has a Norman door dating from the eleventh century. Legend has it that the original chapel could only be completed through human sacrifice. Oran, one of the older monks in Columba's entourage, apparently volunteered to be buried alive, and was found to have survived the ordeal when the grave was opened a few days later. Declaring that he had seen hell and it wasn't all bad, he was promptly re-interred for blasphemy. The chapel stands at the centre of the sacred burial ground, **Reilig Odhráin**, which is said to contain the graves of sixty kings of Norway, France, Ireland and Scotland, including Shakespeare's Duncan and Macbeth. The best of the early Christian gravestones and medieval effigies which once lay in the Reilig Odhráin are now the chief exhibits of the **Infirmary Museum**, behind the abbey. The grave that many visitors now head for is that of the short-lived leader of the Labour Party, **John Smith** (1938–94), who was a frequent visitor to Iona, though he himself was born in the town of Ardrishaig.

Practicalities

There's no **tourist office** on Iona, and, as demand far exceeds supply, you should organize **accommodation** in advance. Of the island's two hotels, the *Argyll* (☎01681/700334; ⑤; closed Nov–March) is by far the nicer. As for **B&Bs**, *Iona Cottage* (☎01681/700569; ④; closed Nov–Easter) is an attractive whitewashed cottage right by the pier; for a more secluded location, try *Kilona* in Sithean (☎01681/700362; ④), a mile from the ferry, on the peaceful west side of the island. **Camping** is not permitted on Iona, and there is no youth hostel. Visitors are not allowed to bring cars onto the island, but **bikes** can be rented from *Finlay Ross* (☎01681/700357). **Food** options are limited: the eclectic bar menu of the *Argyll* is probably your best option, or for something lighter, head for the *Coffee House*, run by the Iona Community, just west of the abbey, which serves home-made soup and delicious cakes.

Coll and Tiree

Coll and **Tiree** are among the most isolated of the Inner Hebrides and, if anything, have more in common with the outlying Western Isles than with their closest neighbour, Mull. Each is roughly twelve miles long and three miles wide, both are low-lying, treeless and exceptionally windy, with white sandy beaches and the highest sunshine records in Scotland. Like most of the Hebrides, they were once ruled by Vikings, and didn't pass into Scottish hands until the thirteenth century. Coll's population peaked at 1440, Tiree's at a staggering 4450, but both were badly affected by the Clearances, which virtually halved their populations in a generation.

The CalMac **ferry** from Oban calls at Coll (2hr 40min) and Tiree (3hr 40min) every day except Thursdays and Sundays throughout the year. Tiree also has an **airport** with daily flights (Mon–Sat) to and from Glasgow. The majority of visitors on both islands stay for at least a week in self-catering accommodation, though there are B&Bs and hotels on the islands. However, choice is limited so it's as well to book as far in advance as possible (and that goes for the ferry crossing, too). The only **public transport** is on Tiree, which has an infrequent bus service and a postbus (both Mon–Sat only), plus a shared taxi system (☎01879/220311 or 220419).

Isle of Coll

The island of **Coll** (population 175) lies less than seven miles off the coast of Mull. The CalMac ferry drops off at Coll's only village, **ARINAGOUR** on the western shore of Loch Eatharna, where half the population now lives. Here, you'll find the island's post office, petrol pump, church, school, two shops, a laundry and a nine-hole golf course to the northwest.

On the southwest coast there are two edifices – Coll's only formal attractions – both known as **Breachacha Castle**, built by the MacLeans. The oldest, at the head of Loch Breachacha, is a fifteenth-century tower house with an additional curtain wall, recently restored, and a training centre for overseas aid volunteers. The "new castle", to the northwest, was built around 1750 and is made up of a central block with two side pavilions added a century later; it has been converted into holiday homes. Other points of interest are the strip of **giant sand dunes** which link the westernmost tip of Coll with the rest of the island, and **Ben Hogh** (at 339ft, Coll's highest point) two miles west of Arinagour.

For **accommodation** on the island head for Arinagour's small, family-run *Coll Hotel* (☎01879/230334; ③), the comfortable, modern *Taigh Solas* (☎01879/230333; ①), overlooking the bay or *Achamore* (☎01879/230430; ③), a traditional nineteenth-century farmhouse B&B, two miles to the west. The island's official **campsite** (☎01879/230374; closed Nov–March), with only basic facilities, is in the old walled gardens of the castle on Breachacha Bay; you can also stay in the *Garden House* B&B (same number as campsite; ①; open all year). The *Coll Hotel* doubles as the island's social centre, does good bar **food** and has a more expensive dining room.

Isle of Tiree

Tiree, as its Gaelic name *Tir-Iodh* (Land of Corn) suggests, was once known as the breadbasket of the Inner Hebrides, thanks to its acres of rich machair. Nowadays crofting and tourism are the main sources of income for the resident population of more than eight hundred and, every October, the windswept sandy beaches attract large numbers of windsurfers for the International Windsurfers' Championships.

The CalMac ferry calls at **SCARINISH**, on a headland to the west of the great sandy beach of **Gott Bay**. It's just one mile across the island from Gott to Vaul Bay, on the north coast, where the well-preserved remains of a drystone broch, **Dun Mor** – dating from the first century BC – lie hidden in the rocks to the west of the bay. From here it's another two miles west along the coast to the *Clach a'Choire* or **Ringing Stone**, a huge glacial boulder decorated with mysterious prehistoric markings, which, when struck with a stone, gives out a metallic sound; the story goes that should the Ringing Stone ever be broken in two, Tiree will sink beneath the waves. A mile further west is the lovely sandy **Balephetrish Bay**.

The most intriguing sights lie in the bulging western half of the island, where Tiree's two landmark hills rise up. The highest of the two, **Ben Hynish** (463ft), is unfortunately occupied by a "golf ball" radar station which tracks incoming transatlantic flights;

the views from the top, though, are great. Below Ben Hynish, to the east, is the abandoned **Hynish harbour**, designed by Alan Stevenson in the 1830s in order to transport building materials for the 140ft **Skerryvore Lighthouse**, which lies on a sea-swept reef some twelve miles southwest of Tiree. The harbour features an ingenious reservoir to prevent silting, and a granite signal tower; the nearby row of lightkeepers' houses has been turned into a **museum** telling the history of the Herculean effort required to erect the lighthouse. Weather permitting, you can glimpse the lighthouse from the top of the signal tower, or from the spectacular headland of Ceann a'Mhara, two miles west of Ben Hynish, across the golden sands of Balephuil Bay. The cliffs are home to literally thousands of sea birds; the islands of Barra and South Uist are also visible on the northern horizon.

Practicalities

The only transport around the island is the **postbus**; otherwise, you'll need to make use of the shared taxi (see above) or **bike rental** from the *Tiree Lodge* on Gott Bay. For **accomodation**, try *Kirkapol House* (☎01879/220729; ②), a converted old kirk, or *The Glassary* (☎01879/220684; ③) over on the west coast in Sandaig. There are no official campsites, but camping is allowed with the crofter's permission. For **food**, try the unpretentious *Glassary*, which serves up local produce.

Isle of Colonsay

Isolated between Mull and Islay, **Colonsay** – eight miles by three at its widest – is nothing like as bleak and windswept as Coll or Tiree. Its craggy hills even support the occasional patch of woodland, plus a bewildering array of plant- and birdlife, wild goats and rabbits, and one of the finest quasi-tropical gardens in Scotland. That said, the population is precariously low at around one hundred, down from a pre-Clearance peak of just under a thousand, and the ferry link with Oban is infrequent and inconvenient.

The CalMac ferry terminal is at **SCALASAIG**, on the east coast, where there's a post office-cum-store, a petrol pump, a restaurant and the island's only hotel. Two miles north, and inland of Scalasaig is **Colonsay House** (not open to the public), built in 1722 by Malcolm MacNeil. In 1904, the island and house were bought by the wealthy Lord Strathcona, who made his fortune building the Canadian Pacific Railway. Giant breakers roll in from the Atlantic across **Kiloran Bay**, Colonsay's most impressive white sandy beach to the north of Colonsay House, though the shell beach at Balnahard, two miles northeast along a rough track, is even more deserted and backed by rabbit-infested dunes. The island's west coast forms a sharp escarpment, at its most spectacular just west of Kiloran around **Beinn Bhreac** (456ft), where hundreds of sea birds nest in spring and summer.

The island's only **hotel** is the *Isle of Colonsay* (☎01951/200316; ⑤) in Scalasaig, while the best **B&B** is the superb *Seaview* (☎01951/200315; ②; closed Nov–March) in Kilchattan. Budget travellers can now stay in the *Backpackers' Lodge* **hostel** in Kiloran (☎01951/200312) All accommodation and ferries need to be booked well in advance. Both places can organize **bike rental**, and there's a limited **bus/postbus** service for those without their own transport.

Isle of Oronsay

Isle of Oronsay, half a mile to the south, is only an island when the tide is in, and, as you can't stay overnight, it can only be visited as a day-trip from Colonsay. The two are separated by "The Strand", a mile of tidal mud flats which act as a causeway for two hours either side of low tide; check locally for current timings. Although legends (and etymology) link saints Columba and Oran with both Colonsay and Oronsay, the ruins of the **Oronsay Priory** only date back to the fourteenth century. Abandoned since the Reformation, it still has the original church and cloisters, but the highlight is the Oronsay Cross, a superb example of late medieval artistry from Iona, and the numerous finely carved grave slabs that lie within the Prior's House.

Mid-Argyll

Mid-Argyll is a vague term which loosely describes the central wedge of land south of Oban and north of Kintyre, extending west from Loch Fyne to the Atlantic. The highlights of this gently undulating scenery lie along the sharply indented west coast, in particular the rich Celtic remains in the **Kilmartin** valley, one of the most important prehistoric sites in Scotland. Public transport is thin on the ground, with buses radiating mainly from Lochgilphead, on the shores of Loch Fyne.

    LOCHGILPHEAD is the administrative capital of Argyll & Bute, though it has little to offer beyond its **tourist office**, at 27 Lochnell St (April & mid-Sept to Oct Mon–Fri 10am–5pm, Sat & Sun noon–5pm; May & June Mon–Sat 10am–5pm, Sun 11am–5pm; July to mid-Sept Mon–Sat 9.30am–6pm, Sun 10am–5pm; ☎01546/602344). For **accommodation** you're best off looking elsewhere, such as Crinan (see below), though there's the pristinely maintained *Lochgilphead Caravan Park* **campsite**, a short distance west of town in Bank Park (☎01546/602003; closed Nov–March). *The Smiddy*, on Smithy Lane (closed Sun), does the best **food** in town.

Kilmartin and Dunadd

The **Kilmartin valley**, fanning out south of the village of the same name, is one of the most important prehistoric sites in Scotland. The most significant relic is the **linear cemetery**, where several cairns are aligned for more than two miles, beginning just south of Kilmartin. Whether these represent the successive burials of a ruling family or chieftains, nobody can be sure. The best view of the cemetery's configuration is from the Bronze Age Mid-Cairn, but the Neolithic **South Cairn**, dating from around 3000 BC, is by far the oldest and the most impressive, with its large chambered tomb roofed by giant slabs.

    Close to the Mid-Cairn, in a small copse, the **Templewood stone circles** appear to have been the architectural focus of burials in the area from Neolithic times to the Bronze Age. Visible to the south are the impressively cup-marked **Nether Largie standing stones**, the largest of which looms over 10ft high. **Cup- and ring-marked rocks** are a recurrent feature of prehistoric sites in the Kilmartin valley and elsewhere in Argyll. There are many theories as to their origin: some see them as Pictish symbols, others as African death symbols, primitive solar calendars and so on. The most extensive markings are at **Achnabreck**, off the A816 towards Lochgilphead.

    KILMARTIN village, situated on high ground to the north of the cairns, has a new interpretive centre, **Kilmartin House** (daily 10am–5.30pm; £3.90), housed in the old manse adjacent to the village church. The museum is excellent, both enlightening about the area's history and environment and entertaining, with numerous hands-on displays. The café/restaurant is equally enticing, with local (often wild) produce on offer, which you can wash down with heather beer. The nearby church is worth a brief reconnoitre as it shelters the badly damaged and weathered **Kilmartin crosses**, while a separate enclosure in the graveyard houses a large collection of medieval grave slabs of the Malcolms of Poltalloch.

    The peaty plain of Mòine Mhór (Great Moss), which opens up to the south of Kilmartin, is home to the Iron Age fort of **Dunadd**, one of Scotland's most important Celtic sites, occupying a distinctive 176-foot-high rocky knoll once surrounded by the sea but currently beside the winding River Add. It was here that Fergus, the first King of Dalriada, established his royal seat, having arrived from Ireland around 500 AD. Its strategic position, the craggy defences and the view from the top are all impressive, but it's the **stone carvings** between the twin summits which make Dunadd so remarkable: several lines of inscription in ogham (an ancient alphabet of Irish origin), the faint outline of a boar, a hollowed-out footprint and a small basin. The boar and the inscriptions are probably Pictish, since the fort was clearly occupied long before Fergus got there, but the footprint and basin have been interpreted as being part of the royal coronation rituals of the kings of Dalriada. It is thought that the Stone of Destiny was used at Dunadd before being moved to Scone Palace (see p.914) and eventually to Westminster Abbey (see p.91) in London before being returned to Edinburgh in 1996 (see p.795).

In terms of **accommodation**, Crinan (see below) is probably the best choice, rather than Lochgilphead. Either that, or you could hole up in the excellent *Cairnbaan Hotel* (☎01546/603668; ⑥), an eighteenth-century coaching inn overlooking the Crinan Canal; it has a great restaurant and bar meals featuring locally caught seafood. The aforementioned café/restaurant at Kilmartin House is a good spot for lunch; alternatively *The Cairn* (☎01546/510254; closed Nov–Feb), opposite the church in Kilmartin, does moderately expensive evening **meals**, featuring superb Scottish and some Mediterranean dishes.

Crinan and the Crinan Canal

In 1801 the nine-mile-long **Crinan Canal** was opened, linking Loch Fyne with the Sound of Jura, thus cutting out the long and treacherous journey around the Mull of Kintyre. John Rennie's original design, although an impressive engineering feat, had numerous faults and by 1816 Thomas Telford had to be called in to take charge of the renovations.

The largest concentration of locks – there are fifteen in total – is around Cairnbaan, but the best place to view the canal in action is at **CRINAN**, the picturesque fishing port at the western end of the canal. Crinan's tiny harbour is, for the moment at least, still home to a small fishing fleet, though the majority of the traffic on the canal itself is now made up of pleasure boats. Every room in the *Crinan Hotel* (☎01546/830261; ⑦) looks across Loch Crinan to the Sound of Jura – one of the most beautiful views in Scotland, especially at sunset when the myriad islets and the distinctive Paps of Jura are reflected in the still, golden waters of the loch. If the *Crinan* is beyond your means, there are some cheaper but less well-appointed **B&Bs**. Lunch at the *Crinan* is recommended, but may be beyond the reach of most. Tea and delicious calorific cakes can be had from the **café** (closed Nov–Easter) right on the quayside.

Kintyre

If it wasn't for the mile-long isthmus between West and the much smaller East Loch Tarbert, **KINTYRE** (from the Gaelic *ceann tire*, "land's end") would be an island. Indeed, in the eleventh century, when the Scottish king, Malcolm Canmore, told Magnus Barefoot, King of Norway, he could lay claim to any island he could navigate his boat round, Magnus succeeded in dragging his boat across the Tarbert isthmus and added the peninsula to his Hebridean kingdom. After the Wars of the Covenant, when the vast majority of the population and property was wiped out by a combination of the 1646 potato blight coupled with the destructive attentions of the Earl of Argyll, Kintyre became a virtual desert until the earl began his policy of transplanting Gaelic-speaking Lowlanders to the region.

Tarbert

A distinctive rocket-like church steeple heralds the fishing village of **TARBERT** (in Gaelic *an tairbeart*, meaning "isthmus"), sheltering an attractive little bay backed by rugged hills. With the local fishing industry under threat from EU quotas, tourism is an increasingly important source of income, as is the money that flows through the town during the last week in May, when the yacht races of the Scottish Series take place. Tarbert's main tourist attraction is the **An Tairbeart Heritage Centre** (Easter–Dec daily 10am–5pm; free), five minutes' walk up the Campbeltown road. The shop and the excellent restaurant both offer local produce, while behind is a nature park, aimed at children, where you can see the local wildlife at close quarters.

The **tourist office** (April Mon–Fri 10am–5pm, Sat & Sun noon–5pm; May & June Mon–Sat 10am–5pm, Sun 11am–5pm; July to mid-Sept Mon–Sat 9.30am–6pm, Sun 10am–5pm; mid-Sept to Oct Mon–Sat 10am–5pm, Sun noon–5pm; ☎01880/820429) is on the harbour. For somewhere to **stay**, try the *Springside* B&B on Pier Road (☎01880/820413; ③) or the *Columba* hotel further along the same road (☎01880/820808; ④). If you're just looking for a fill-up, the **bar snacks** at the *Victoria Hotel* on the harbour should suffice, but for some excellent fish and seafood, head for *The Anchorage* (☎01880/820881; closed Mon & Sun in winter), on the opposite side of the harbour, unforgettable not least for its eccentric proprietor. You can **rent bikes** from Mr Leitch (☎01880/820287).

One reason you might find yourself staying in Tarbert is its proximity to no fewer than four **ferry terminals**: the CalMac service east to Portavadie on the Cowal peninsula leaves from Pier Road in Tarbert itself; the busiest terminal, though, is five miles south at **Kennacraig**, which runs daily sailings to Islay and a once-weekly service to Colonsay; further south is the Gigha ferry from Tayinloan. On the east coast the Claonaig ferry to Lochranza in Arran runs from April to mid-October.

Isle of Gigha

Gigha (pronounced "Geeya", with a hard "g") is a low-lying, fertile island, just three miles off the west coast of Kintyre. The island's Ayrshire cattle produce over a quarter of a million gallons of milk a year, some of it used to manufacture the distinctive fruit-shaped cheese which is one of the island's main exports. Like many of the smaller Hebrides, the island was sold by its original lairds, the MacNeils, and has been put on the market twice in less than ten years, causing great uncertainty amongst the 120 or so inhabitants, who have to endure these periods of instability as best they can.

The ferry from Tayinloan, 23 miles south of Tarbert, deposits you at the island's only village, **ARDMINISH**, where you'll find the post office and shop. The only sight as such is the **Achamore Gardens** (daily 9am–dusk; £2), a mile and a half south of Ardminish. Established by the first postwar owner, Sir James Horlick of hot drink fame, they are best seen in the early summertime, ablaze with rhododendrons and azaleas.

Gigha is so small – six miles by one – that most visitors come here just for the day. However, it is possible to **stay**, either with the McSporrans, at the *Post Office House* (☎01583/505251; ③), or at the *Gigha Hotel* (☎01583/505254; ⑤; closed Nov–Feb), which also runs self-catering flats dotted over the island. Caravans and camping are not allowed on Gigha. The *Gigha Hotel* is the only place to go for tea and cakes – it also does really good **bar meals**. **Bike rental** is available at the McSporrans'.

Campbeltown

CAMPBELTOWN's best feature is its setting, in a deep bay sheltered by Davaar Island and the surrounding hills. What's more, with a population of 6500, it's also one of the largest towns in Argyll, and, if you're staying in the southern half of Kintyre, by far the best place to stock up on supplies. Originally known as Kinlochkilkerran (or *Ceann Loch Cill Chiaran*), the town was renamed in the seventeenth century by the Earl of Argyll – a Campbell – when it became one of the main points for immigration from the Lowlands. As is evident from the architecture, Campbeltown's heyday was the Victorian era, when shipbuilding was going strong, coal was shipped by canal from Drumlemble, the fishing fleet was vast and Campbeltown Loch was said to be made of whisky.

Nineteenth-century visitors to Campbeltown frequently found the place engulfed in a thick fog of pungent peat smoke from the town's 34 **whisky distilleries**. Nowadays, only Glen Scotia and Springbank are left to maintain this regional sub-group of single-malt whiskies, though only the latter is keen on encouraging visitors (☎01586/552085). The town's one major sight is the **Campbeltown Cross**, a fourteenth-century blue-green cross with figural scenes and spirals of Celtic knotting, which presides over the main roundabout on the quayside. Back on the harbour is the "**Wee Picture House**", a dinky little Art Deco cinema on Hall Street, built in 1913 and now doubling as a bingo hall (Tues & Fri) and cinema. Next door is the equally delightful **Campbeltown Museum and Library** (Wed, Fri & Sat 10am–1pm & 2–5pm, Tues & Thurs 10am–1pm & 2–7.30pm; free), built in 1897 in the local sandstone, crowned by a distinctive lantern, and decorated on its harbourside wall with four relief panels depicting each of the town's main industries at the time. Inside, there's a timber-framed ceiling and etched glass partitions to admire, but the museum itself is inferior to the **Campbeltown Heritage Centre** on the Machrihanish Road (April–Oct Mon–Sat noon–5pm, Sun 2–5pm; £2), housed in the church known locally as the "Tartan Kirk", partly due to its Gaelic associations, but mainly for its stripy bell-cote and pinnacles.

Practicalities

Campbeltown's **tourist office** is currently on the Old Quay (April Mon–Sat 10am–5pm; May & June Mon–Sat 9am–5pm, Sun noon–5pm; July to mid-Sept Mon–Sat 9am–6.30pm, Sun noon–5pm; mid-Sept to Oct Mon–Fri 10am–5pm, Sun 10am–4pm; Nov–March Mon–Fri 10am–4pm; ☎01586/552056). **Accommodation** is surprisingly plentiful: the best of the hotels is the delightful family-run *Ardshiel Hotel* (☎01586/552133; ③), one block back from the ferry terminal on Kilkerran Road; another excellent choice is the *Balegreggan Country House Hotel* (☎01586/552062; ④), a fine detached Victorian villa, north of town off the A83; for a cheap, simple, central B&B, head for *Eagle Lodge*, 56 High St (☎01586/551359; ①; closed Dec & Jan). As for **places to eat**, the best bar meals and restaurant are to be found at the aforementioned *Ardshiel Hotel*, while the *Commercial Inn*, on Cross Street, is a good drinking hole. You can **rent bikes** at The Bike Shop, Longrow (☎01586/554443).

Southend and the Mull of Kintyre

The bulbous, hilly end of Kintyre, south of Campbeltown, features some of the most spectacular scenery on the whole peninsula, though slightly surprisingly it also contains large swathes of Lowland-style farmland, too. **SOUTHEND** itself, however, is one of those bleak, blustery spots beloved of fixed caravan sites, and comes as something of a disappointment. It does have a wide sandy beach, but there are nicer sandy beaches at **Carskey Bay** to the west, and **Macharioch Bay**, three miles east, looking out to distant Ailsa Craig in the Firth of Clyde. Below the cliffs to the west of Southend, a ruined thirteenth-century chapel marks the alleged arrival point of St Columba prior to his trip to Iona, and a pair of footprints carved into a rocky knoll nearby are known as **Columba's footprints**, though only one is actually of ancient origin.

Most people venture south of Campbeltown to make a pilgrimage to the **Mull of Kintyre** – the nearest Britain gets to Ireland, whose coastline, just twelve miles away, is visible on clear days. Although the Mull was made famous by the mawkish number one hit by one-time local resident Paul McCartney, with the help of the Campbeltown Pipe Band, there's nothing specifically to see in this godforsaken storm-racked spot but the view. The roads up to the "**Gap**" (1150ft) – where you must leave your car – and down to the lighthouse, itself 300ft above the ocean waves, are terrifyingly precipitous.

There are few places to **stay** in this remote region. Southend's only hotel has been closed for some time and cuts a forlorn figure, set back from the bay; try instead *Ormsary Farm* (☎01586/830665; ①; closed Oct–March), up Glen Breakerie, or the **campsite** at *Machribeg Farm* (☎01586/830249; closed Oct–Easter) right by the beach.

Isle of Arran

Arran is the most southerly (and therefore the most accessible) of all the Scottish islands. The Highland–Lowland dividing line passes right through its centre – hence the tourist board's aphorism about "Scotland in miniature" – leaving the northern half sparsely populated, mountainous and bleak, while the lush southern half enjoys a milder climate. Despite its immense popularity, the tourists, like the population, tend to stick to the southeastern quarter of the island, leaving the west and the north relatively undisturbed.

Although tourism is now by far its most important industry, at twenty miles in length, Arran is large enough to have a life of its own. While the history of the Clearances on Arran, set in motion by the local lairds, the dukes of Hamilton, is as depressing as elsewhere in the Highlands, in recent years it has not suffered from the depopulation which has plagued other, more remote islands. Once a county in its own right (along with Bute), Arran has been left out of the new Argyll and Bute district in the latest county boundary shake-up, and is now coupled instead with mainland North Ayrshire, with which it enjoys closer transport links, but little else.

Transport on the island is pretty good: daily **buses** circle the island (Brodick tourist office has timetables) and there are two **ferry services**, one from Ardrossan (all year) in Ayrshire to Brodick, and a smaller ferry from Claonaig on the remote Kintyre peninsula to Lochranza in the north (April to mid-Oct).

Brodick

Although the resort of **BRODICK** (from the Norse *breidr vik*, "broad bay") is a place of little charm, it does at least have a grand setting in a wide, sandy bay set against a backdrop of granite mountains. Its development as a tourist resort on the Clyde was held back for a long time by its elitist owners, the dukes of Hamilton, though nowadays, as the island's main communication hub, Brodick is by far the busiest town on Arran.

The dukes lived at **Brodick Castle** (daily: April–June, Sept & Oct 11am–4.30pm; July & Aug 11am–5pm; £5; NTS), on a steep bank on the north side of the bay. The interior is undistinguished; but the tearooms are excellent and the flower-filled **gardens** (daily 9.30am–dusk; £2.50) are superb. The **Arran Heritage Museum** (Easter–Oct Mon–Sat 10am–5pm; £1.50) is a somewhat dry collection of old tools and furniture in a converted crofter's farm halfway between the castle and the town centre, and a wet weather retreat only.

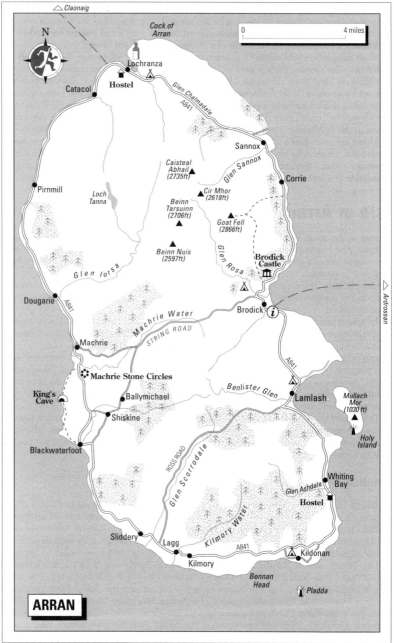

Brodick's **tourist office** (May–Sept Mon–Sat 9am–7.30pm, Sun 10am–5pm; Oct–April Mon–Sat 9am–5pm; ☎01770/302140) is by the CalMac' pier, with reams of information on bus and ferry services, and the numerous outdoor activities possible on the island. Unless you've got to catch an early-morning ferry, there's very little reason **to stay** in Brodick, but should you need to, try the excellent *Dunvegan House Hotel* (☎01770/302811; ④), or the Art Deco *Invercloy Hotel* (☎01770/302225; *invercloyhotel@si.co.uk*; ②; closed Nov–Feb); closer to the castle, the sandstone *Glen Cloy Farm House* (☎01770/302351; *mvpglencloy@compuserve.com*; ②; closed Dec–Feb) has real fires and a warm welcome; the nearest **campsite** is *Glenrosa* (☎01770/302380), two miles from town, off the B880 to Blackwaterfoot. **Food** at the *Kilmichael Country House Hotel* is very expensive, but one of the best choices on the island; also good is the moderately expensive seafood restaurant *Creelers* (☎01770/302810; closed Nov to mid-March), on the road to the castle; and there are above average bar meals at *Brodick Bar & Brasserie* (☎01770/302169) by the post office.

The south

The southern half of Arran is less spectacular, and less forbidding than the north; the land is more fertile, and for that reason the vast majority of the population lives here. The tourist industry has followed them, though with considerably less justification. With its distinctive Edwardian architecture and mild climate **LAMLASH** epitomizes the sedate charm of southeast Arran. Its major drawback is its bay, which is made not of sand but of boulder-strewn mud flats. You can take a boat out to the slug-shaped hump of **Holy Island** which shelters the bay, and is now owned by a group of Tibetan Buddhists who have set up a meditation centre – providing you don't dawdle, it's possible to scramble up to the top of Mullach Mòr (1030ft), the island's highest point, and still catch the last ferry back.

If you want to **stay** in style, head for the *Glenisle Hotel* (☎01770/600559; ⑦; closed Jan), or the much smaller *Lilybank Hotel* (☎01770/600230; ③), which does superb homemade food; cheaper B&Bs are easy enough to find – try *Blairmore House* (☎01770/600004; ②) in the middle of the golf course. You can **camp** at *Middleton's Caravan Park* (☎01770/600255; closed mid-Oct to mid-April), five minutes' walk north of the centre. The best **restaurant** in Lamlash is undoubtedly the *Carraig Mhor* near the pier (☎01770/600453; Mon–Sat eves only), which offers an exclusive and expensive menu featuring fresh local game, fish and seafood; a cheaper alternative is a bar meal at the *Pier Head Tavern*.

Although it has been an established Clydeside resort for over a century now, **WHITING BAY**, four miles south of Lamlash, is actually pretty characterless. However, there are plenty of places to stay, among them *The Royal* (☎01770/700286; ②; closed Nov–Feb), the *Argentine House Hotel*, run (confusingly) by a Swiss couple (☎01770/700662; *argentine.hotel.arran@dial.pipex.com*; ③; closed mid-Jan to mid-Feb), and the *Burlington Hotel* (☎01770/700255; *burlhotel@aol*.com; ③; closed Nov–Easter), all on Shore Road. At the lower end of the price range, *Norwood* (☎01770/700536; ①; closed Nov–Feb), on Smiddy Brae, is the best choice, or the **youth hostel** (☎01770/700339; closed Nov–Feb). On the south coast the easiest point of access to the sea is at **KILDONAN**, a small village off the main road, with a nice sandy beach, and, at its east end, a ruined castle looking out to the tiny island of Pladda. There's a campsite (☎01770/820210) right by the shore.

BLACKWATERFOOT, on the western end of String Road that bisects the island, is even smaller than Kildonan, a good place to escape the worst of Arran's summer crowds. If you want to **stay**, the Victorian *Blackwaterfoot Hotel* (☎01770/860202; ⑤; closed Jan & Feb) is the place to hole up, though there are better B&Bs just up the road in **SHISKINE**, in particular *The Old House* (☎01770/860302; ②; closed Dec–March).

North of Blackwaterfoot, the wide expanse of **Machrie Moor** boasts a wealth of Bronze Age sites. No fewer than six **stone circles** sit east of the main road; although many of them barely break the peat's surface, the tallest surviving monolith is over eighteen feet high.

The north

The desolate north half of Arran – effectively the Highland part – features bare granite peaks, the occasional golden eagle and miles of unspoilt scenery, within reach only to those prepared to do some serious hiking. Arran's most accessible peak is also the island's highest, **Goat Fell** (2866ft), which can be ascended in just three hours from Brodick (return journey 5hr), though it's a strenuous hike (for the usual safety precautions see p.51). From Goat Fell, experienced walkers can follow the horseshoe of craggy summits and descend either from the saddle below Beinn Tarsuinn (2706ft) or from Beinn Nuis (2597ft).

The ruined castle which occupies the mud flats of the bay, and the gloomy north-facing slopes of the mountains which frame it, make for one of the most spectacular settings on the island – yet **LOCHRANZA**, despite being the only place of any size in this sparsely populated area, attracts far fewer visitors than Arran's southern resorts. The finest **accommodation** is at the superb *Apple Lodge* (☎01770/830229; ③), or at the *Lochranza Hotel* (☎01770/830223; *george@lochranza.co.uk*; ②), whose bar is the centre of the local social scene; the most intriguing of the **B&Bs** is the welcoming *Castlekirk* (☎01770/830202; ①; closed Dec & Jan) in a converted nineteenth-century church opposite the castle. Lochranza also has a **youth hostel** (☎01770/830631; closed Jan) overlooking the castle, and a well-equipped **campsite** (☎01770/830273; *camp@lochgolf.demon.co.uk*; closed mid-Oct to Easter) beautifully situated by the golf course.

An alternative is to continue a mile or so southwest along the coast to **CATACOL**, where the friendly *Catacol Bay Hotel* (☎01770/830231; *davecath@aol.com*; ①) takes the prize as the island's best pub by far: good, basic pub food (with several veggie options and real chips), great beer on tap, a small adjoining **campsite**, and seal and shags to view on the nearby shingle. The pub also puts on live music most weeks, and hosts a week-long **folk festival** in early June.

Isle of Islay

Islay (pronounced "eye-la") is famous for one thing – single-malt **whisky**. The smoky, peaty, pungent quality of Islay whisky is unique, recognizable even to the untutored palate, and the six distilleries that still function lay on guided tours, ending with the customary complimentary tipple. Yet despite the fame of its whiskies, Islay remains relatively undiscovered, much as Skye and Mull were some twenty years ago. Part of the reason, no doubt, is that it takes a pricey, two-hour ferry journey from Kennacraig on Kintyre to reach the island.

In medieval times, Islay was the political centre of the Hebrides, with Finlagan Castle, near Port Askaig, the seat of the MacDonalds, lords of the Isles. The picturesque, whitewashed villages you see on Islay today, however, date from the planned settlements founded by the Campbells in the late eighteenth and early nineteenth centuries. Apart from whisky and solitude, the other great draw is the **birdlife**, in particular the scores of white-fronted and barnacle geese who winter here. For two weeks around late May or early June, the Islay Festival *Feis Ile* takes place, with whisky-tasting, pipe bands, folk dancing and other events celebrating Islay's Gaelic culture.

Port Ellen and the south

Laid out as a planned village in 1821 by Walter Frederick Campbell and named after his wife, **PORT ELLEN** is the busiest port on Islay, with the island's largest fishing fleet, and main CalMac ferry terminal. The neat terraces along the harbour are pretty enough, but the bay is dominated by the now disused whisky distillery – the smell of malt which wafts across the harbour comes from the modern maltings just off the Bowmore road. If you need **accommodation** in Port Ellen itself, try *Tighcargaman* (☎01496/302345; ①), set back from the road to Bowmore, half a mile from the ferry. Up the A846 towards the airport, there's the excellent *Glenmachrie Farmhouse* (☎01496/302560; ③), which does superb home cooking. There's also a **campsite** (closed Oct–March), and an **independent hostel** at *Kintra Farm* (☎01496/302051; ③), three miles northwest of Port Ellen, at the southern tip of Laggan Bay.

From Port Ellen, a dead-end road heads off east along the coastline, passing three functioning distilleries in as many miles. First comes **Laphroaig Distillery** (Mon–Fri 10am & 2.15pm; £2; ☎01496/302418) which produces the most uncompromisingly smoky of the Islay whiskies. As every bottle of Laphroaig tells you, translated from the Gaelic the name means "the beautiful hollow by the broad bay", and, true enough, the whitewashed distillery is indeed in a gorgeous setting by the sea. The **Lagavulin Distillery** (Mon–Fri 10.30am & 2.30pm; £2; ☎01496/302400), a mile down the road, produces a superb sixteen-year-old single malt, while **Ardbeg Distillery** (June–Aug Mon–Sat 10am–4pm; rest of year Mon–Fri only; £2; ☎01496/302244), another mile on, sports the traditional pagoda-style roofs of the malting houses.

There are a handful of **B&Bs** further east along the rapidly deteriorating road – try *Tigh-na-Suil* (☎01496/302483; ①). A mile beyond this, the simple thirteenth-century **Kildalton Chapel** boasts a wonderful eighth-century Celtic ringed cross made from the local "bluestone", which is, in fact, a rich bottle-green. The quality of the scenes matches any to be found on the crosses carved by the monks in Iona: Mary and child are on one side with what look like elephants on the other.

Bowmore and Loch Gruinart

BOWMORE, Islay's administrative capital with a population of around nine hundred, was founded as a planned village in 1768 to replace the village of Kilarrow, which was deemed to the local laird to be too close to his own residence. It's a striking place, laid out in a grid plan rather like Inveraray, with Main Street climbing up the hill in a straight line from the pier on Loch Indaal to the town's crowning landmark, the **Round Church**. A little to the west of Main Street is **Bowmore Distillery** (Easter–Sept Mon–Fri 10.30am, 11.30am, 2pm & 3pm, Sat 10.30am; Oct–Easter Mon–Fri 10.30am & 2pm; £2; ☎01496/810441), the first of the legal Islay distilleries, founded in 1779 and still occupying its original whitewashed buildings by the loch.

Islay's only official **tourist office** is in Bowmore (April Mon–Sat 10am–5pm; May & June Mon–Sat 9.30am–5pm, Sun 2–5pm; July to mid-Sept Mon–Sat 9.30am–5.30pm, Sun 2–5pm; mid-Sept to Oct Mon–Sat 10am–4.30pm; Nov–March Mon–Fri noon–4pm; ☎01496/810254), and can help you find **accommodation**. Like Port Ellen, Bowmore itself is, in fact, not the best place in which to stay. If you must, however, try one of the town's better B&Bs, such as *Lambeth House* (☎01496/810597; ①), centrally located on Jamieson Street. If you're looking for more character and comfort, head out to the *Bridgend Hotel* (☎01496/810960; ⑤), a couple of miles up the road. For **food**, the *Harbour Inn* on Main Street is the place; you can sample the local prawns and warm yourself by a peat fire. *The Cottage* (closed Sun) is a cheap and friendly greasy spoon, further up on the same side of the street.

North of Bowmore, an entire working farm was purchased by the RSPB close to the mud flats of **Loch Gruinart** in order to encourage the barnacle and white-fronted geese to winter here rather than on the Islay farmers' land. The **RSPB visitor centre** (daily 10am–5pm; free) is at Aoradh (pronounced "oorig") and houses an observation point with telescopes and a CCTV link with the flats; there's also a hide across the road looking north over the salt flats at the head of the loch itself. The geese begin to arrive in mid-September and by late October there are over 20,000 geese on the reserve. By the third week of April, the geese have all left for Greenland, but in summer you can see numerous lapwing, snipe and redshanks. Bird-watchers should hole themselves up in *Loch Gruinart House* (☎01496/850212; ①) by the reserve, or at the rudimentary *Craigens Farm* **campsite** by the loch (☎01496/850256; closed Nov–March).

Port Charlotte and the Rinns of Islay

PORT CHARLOTTE, named after the founder's mother, is generally agreed to be Islay's prettiest village, the "Queen of the Rinns" (derived from the Gaelic word for promontory), its immaculate cottages hugging the sandy shores of Loch Indaal. East of the village, the imaginative **Museum of Islay Life** (Easter–Oct Mon–Sat 10am–5pm, Sun 2–5pm; £2) has a children's corner and a good library of books about the island. The **Wildlife Information Centre** (Easter–Oct Mon, Tues, Thurs & Fri 10am–3pm, Sun 2–5pm; £1.80), housed in the former distillery warehouse, is also worth a visit for anyone interested in the island's flora and fauna. The welcoming *Port Charlotte Hotel* (☎01496/850360; *carl@portcharlottehot.demon.co.uk*; ⑤) has the best **accommodation**, and a moderately expensive seafood restaurant. For B&B, you're actually better off going for *Octofad Farm* (☎01496/850225; ①; closed Nov–March), a few miles down the road beyond Nerabus. Port Charlotte itself is also home to the SYHA Islay **youth hostel** (☎01496/850385; closed Nov to mid-March), next door to the Wildlife Information Centre. The *Croft Kitchen* (☎01496/850230; closed mid-Oct to mid-March), opposite the museum, serves simple **food**, including delicious, inexpensive seafood.

The coastal road culminates seven miles south of Port Charlotte at **PORTNA-HAVEN**, a fishing and crofting community since the early nineteenth century. The familiar Hebridean cottages wrap themselves around the steep banks of a deep bay; in the distance, you can see Portnahaven's twin settlement, **PORT WEMYSS**, a mile south. A short way out to sea are two islands, the larger of which, Orsay, sports the **Rinns of Islay Lighthouse**, built by Robert Louis Stevenson's father in 1825.

Finlaggan and Port Askaig

Just beyond Ballygrant, on the road to Port Askaig, a narrow road leads off north to **Loch Finlaggan**, site of a number of prehistoric crannogs (artificial islands) and head-quarters of the lords of the Isles from the twelfth to the sixteenth century, rulers of the Hebrides and Kintyre. Unless you need shelter from the rain, you can happily skip the **visitor centre** (Easter & Oct Tues, Thurs & Sun 2–4pm; May–Sept Mon–Fri & Sun 2.30–5pm; £2), to the northeast of the loch, and simply head on down to the site itself (access at any time), which is dotted with interpretive panels. Duckboards allow you to walk out across the reed beds of the loch and explore the main crannog, **Eilean Mor**, where several carved grave slabs can be seen among the ruins, which seem to support the theory that the lords of the Isles buried their wives and children here, while having themselves interred on Iona.

Islay's other ferry connection with the mainland, and its sole link with Colonsay and Jura, is from **PORT ASKAIG**, a scattering of buildings which tumble down a little cove by the narrowest section of the Sound of Islay. The only real reason to come here is to catch one of the ferries; if you've time to kill, you can head half a mile north to the **Caol**

Ila distillery (☎01496/840207; Easter–Sept Mon, Tues, Thurs & Fri 10.30am, 11.15am, 1.30pm & 2.45pm, Wed 10.30am & 11.15am; £2), or the **Bunnahabhainn distillery** (tours by appointment Mon–Fri; ☎01496/840646), a couple of miles further on. Easily the most comfortable **place to stay** is the lovely whitewashed *Kilmeny Farmhouse* (☎01496/840668; ④), southwest of Ballygrant; a more modest alternative is the secluded B&B *The Kennels* (☎01496/840237; ①). The *Ballygrant Inn* is a good **pub** in which to grab a pint, as is the bar of the *Port Askaig Hotel,* which enjoys a wonderful position by the pier at Port Askaig, with views over to the Paps of Jura.

Isle of Jura

Twenty-eight miles long and eight miles wide, the long whale-shaped island of **Jura** is one of the wildest and most mountainous of the Inner Hebrides, its entire west coast uninhabited and inaccessible except to the dedicated walker. The distinctive Paps of Jura – so called because of their smooth breast-like shape, though there are in fact three of them – seem to dominate every view off the west coast of Argyll, their glacial rounded tops covered in a light dusting of quartzite scree. The island's name derives from the Norse *dyr-oe* (deer island), and, appropriately enough, the current deer population of five thousand outnumbers the two hundred humans 25 to 1.

If you're just coming over for the day from Islay, you could happily spend the day in the lovely wooded grounds of **Jura House** (daily 9am–5pm; £2), five miles up the road from Feolin Ferry. Pick up a booklet at the entrance to the grounds, and follow the path which takes you down to the sandy shore, a perfect picnic spot in fine weather. Closer to the house itself, there's an idyllic **walled garden**, divided in two by a natural rushing burn that tumbles down in steps.

Anything that happens on Jura happens in **CRAIGHOUSE**. eight miles up the road from Feolin Ferry. The village enjoys a sheltered setting, overlooking Knapdale on the mainland – so sheltered, in fact, there are even a few palm trees thriving on the seafront. There's a shop/post office, the island hotel and a tearoom, plus the tiny **Craighouse distillery** (tours by appointment; ☎01496/820240), which welcomes visitors.

The family-run *Jura Hotel* in Craighouse is the island's one and only **hotel** (☎01496/820243; ④), and centre of the island's social scene. The hotel does inexpensive bar meals, and has a shower block and laundry facilities round the back for non-residents. For **B&B**, try Mrs Boardman at 7 Woodside (☎01496/820379; ①; closed Oct–March). There's an infrequent **minibus service** on the island (call ☎01496/820314 to find out when it's running). The **ferry** from Port Askaig occasionally fails to run if there's a strong northerly or southerly wind, so bring your toothbrush if you're coming for a day-trip.

In April 1946, Eric Blair (better known by his pen name of **George Orwell**), suffering badly from TB and intending to give himself "six months' quiet" in which to write his novel *1984,* moved to a remote farmhouse called Barnhill, on the northern tip of Jura. He lived out a spartan existence there for two years but was forced to return to London shortly before his death. The house, 23 miles north of Craighouse up an increasingly poor road, is as remote today as it was in Orwell's day, and sadly there is no access to the interior.

travel details

Trains

Glasgow (Queen St) to: Arrochar & Tarbert (4 daily; 1hr 15min); Dalmally (3 daily; 2hr 15min); Helensburgh Central (2 hourly; 45min); Helensburgh Upper (4 daily; 45min); Oban (3 daily; 3hr).

Mainland buses (not including postbuses)

Arrochar to: Carrick Castle (Mon–Sat 3 daily; 1hr); Garelochhead (Mon–Fri 2 daily; 20min); Inveraray (Mon–Sat 5 daily, Sun 2 daily; 40min); Lochgilphead (Mon–Sat 3 daily, Sun 2 daily; 1hr 30min); Lochgoilhead (Mon–Sat 3 daily; 40min).

Campbeltown to: Airport (Mon–Fri 2 daily; 10min); Carradale (Mon–Sat 3–4 daily, Sun 2 daily; 45min); Machrihanish (Mon–Sat 9–11 daily, Sun 3 daily; 15min); Saddell (Mon–Sat 3–4 daily, Sun 2 daily; 30min); Southend (Mon–Sat 5–6 daily, Sun 2 daily; 30min).

Colintraive to: Dunoon (Mon–Fri 1–3 daily, Sat 2 daily; 40min); Tighnabruaich (Mon–Thurs 1–2 daily; 40min).

Dunoon to: Colintraive (Mon–Fri 1–3 daily, Sat 3 daily; 40min); Inveraray (Mon–Fri 5 daily, Sat 3 daily; 1hr 15min).

Glasgow to: Arrochar (Mon–Sat 6 daily, Sun 3 daily; 1hr 10min); Campbeltown (Mon–Sat 3 daily, Sun 2 daily; 4hr 30min); Dalmally (Mon–Sat 4 daily, Sun 2 daily; 2hr 20min); Inveraray (Mon–Sat 6 daily, Sun 3 daily; 1hr 45min); Kennacraig (Mon–Sat 2 daily, Sun 1 daily; 3hr 30min); Lochgilphead (Mon–Sat 3 daily, Sun 2 daily; 2hr 40min); Oban (Mon–Sat 4 daily, Sun 2 daily; 3hr); Tarbert (Mon–Sat 3 daily, Sun 2 daily; 3hr 15min); Taynuilt (Mon–Sat 4 daily, Sun 2 daily; 2hr 45min).

Kennacraig to: Claonaig (Mon–Sat 3 daily; 15min); Skipness (Mon–Sat 3 daily; 20min).

Inveraray to: Dalmally (Mon–Sat 3 daily, Sun 1 daily; 30min); Dunoon (Mon–Fri 5 daily, Sat 3 daily; 1hr 15min); Lochgilphead (Mon–Sat 3 daily, Sun 2 daily; 40min); Oban (Mon–Sat 3 daily, Sun 1 daily; 1hr 5min); Tarbert (Mon–Sat 3 daily, Sun 2 daily; 1hr 30min); Taynuilt (Mon–Sat 3 daily, Sun 1 daily; 45min).

Lochgilphead to: Campbeltown (Mon–Sat 4 daily, Sun 2 daily; 1hr 30min); Crinan (Mon–Fri 1–3 daily, Sat 2 daily; 20min); Inveraray (Mon–Sat 3 daily, Sun 2 daily; 40min); Kilmartin (Mon–Sat 1–5 daily; 15–40min); Oban (Mon–Sat 1 daily; 1hr 30min); Tarbert (2–4 daily; 30min).

Oban to: Appin (Mon–Sat 4 daily, Sun 1 daily; 30min); Benderloch (Mon–Sat 10–14 daily, Sun 6 daily; 20min); Ellenabeich (Mon–Sat 2–4 daily; 45min); Kilmartin (Mon–Sat 1 daily; 1hr 10min); Lochgilphead (Mon–Sat 1 daily; 1hr 30min).

Tarbert to: Campbeltown (Mon–Sat 4 daily, Sun 2 daily; 1hr 10min); Claonaig (Mon–Sat 3 daily; 30min); Skipness (Mon–Sat 3 daily; 40min); Kennacraig (Mon–Sat 5 daily, Sun 1 daily; 15min).

Tighnabruaich to: Portavadie (Mon–Sat 3–4 daily; 30min); Rothesay (Mon–Thurs 1–2 daily; 1hr).

Island buses (not including postbuses)
Arran

Brodick to: Blackwaterfoot (Mon–Sat 15–18 daily, Sun 3 daily; 25min–1hr 10min); Lamlash (Mon–Sat 15–16 daily, Sun 10 daily; 15min); Lochranza (Mon–Sat 5–8 daily, Sun 4 daily; 40min); Whiting Bay (Mon–Sat 15–16 daily, Sun 10 daily; 30min).

Bute

Rothesay to: Kilchattan Bay (Mon–Sat 4 daily, Sun 3 daily; 30min); Mount Stuart (Mon, Wed & Fri–Sun 1 daily every 45min; 15min); Rhubodach (Mon–Sat 1–2 daily; 20min).

Colonsay

Scalasaig to: Kilchattan (Mon–Fri 2–4 daily; 30min); Kiloran Bay (Mon–Fri 2–3 daily; 15min); The Strand (Mon–Fri 1 daily).

Islay

Bowmore to: Port Askaig (Mon–Sat 8–10 daily, Sun 1 daily; 30–40min); Port Charlotte (Mon–Sat 4–6 daily; 30min); Port Ellen (Mon–Sat 5–7 daily, Sun 1 daily; 20–30min); Portnahaven (Mon–Sat 5–7 daily; 50min).

Mull

Craignure to: Fionnphort (Mon–Sat 4 daily, Sun 1 daily; 1hr 10min); Fishnish (Mon–Sat 4 daily, Sun 3 daily; 10min); Salen (Mon–Sat 4 daily, Sun 2 daily; 25min); Tobermory (Mon–Sat 4 daily, Sun 3 daily; 50min).

Tobermory to: Calgary (Mon–Fri 3–6 daily, Sat 2 daily; 45min); Dervaig (Mon–Fri 3–6 daily, Sat 2 daily; 30min); Fishnish (Mon–Sat 4 daily, Sun 3 daily; 40min).

Car ferries (summer timetable)

To Arran: Ardrossan–Brodick (Mon–Sat 5–6 daily, Sun 4 daily; 1hr); Claonaig–Lochranza (10 daily; 30min).

To Bute: Colintraive–Rhubodach (frequently; 5min); Wemyss Bay–Rothesay (every 45min; 30min).

To Campbeltown: Ballycastle (Northern Ireland)–Campbeltown (2 daily; 3hr).

To Coll: Oban–Coll (Mon–Wed, Fri & Sat 1 daily; 2hr 40min).

To Colonsay: Kennacraig–Colonsay (Wed 1 daily; 3hr 40min); Oban–Colonsay (Wed, Fri & Sun 1 daily; 2hr 10min); Port Askaig–Colonsay (Wed 1 daily; 1hr 20min).

To Dunoon: Gourock–Dunoon (hourly; 20min); McInroy's Point–Hunter's Quay (2 hourly; 20min).

To Gigha: Tayinloan–Gigha (hourly; 20min).

To Islay: Colonsay–Port Askaig (Wed 1 daily; 1hr 20min); Kennacraig–Port Askaig (Mon–Sat 1–2 daily; 2hr); Kennacraig–Port Ellen (1–2 daily except Wed; 2hr 10min); Oban–Port Askaig (Wed 1 daily; 4hr).

To Jura: Port Askaig–Feolin Ferry (Mon–Sat 16 daily, Sun 6 daily; 10min).

To Kintyre: Portavadie–Tarbert (hourly; 30min).

To Lismore: Oban–Lismore (Mon–Sat 2–4 daily; 50min).

To Luing: Cuan Ferry (Seil)–Luing (every 30min; 5min).

To Mull: Kilchoan–Tobermory (Mon–Sat 7–8 daily; July & Aug also Sun 5 daily; 40min); Lochaline–Fishnish (hourly; 15min); Oban–Craignure (Mon–Sat 6 daily, Sun 4–5 daily; 40min).

To Tiree: Oban–Tiree (1 daily except Thurs & Sun; 3hr 40min).

Passenger-only ferries (summer only)

To Helensburgh: Gourock–Helensburgh (Mon–Sat 4 daily; 40min); Kilcreggan–Helensburgh (Mon–Sat 3 daily; 30min).

To Iona: Fionnphort–Iona (Mon–Sat frequently, Sun hourly; 5min).

To Lismore: Port Appin–Lismore (daily every 2hr; 5min).

Flights

Glasgow to: Campbeltown (Mon–Fri 2 daily; 40min); Islay (Mon–Fri 2 daily, Sat 1 daily; 40min); Tiree (Mon–Sat 1 daily; 45min).

CHAPTER TWENTY-THREE

SKYE AND THE WESTERN ISLES

A procession of Hebridean islands, islets and reefs off the northwest shore of Scotland, Skye and the Western Isles between them boast some of the country's most alluring scenery. It's here that the turbulent seas of the Atlantic smash up against an extravagant shoreline hundreds of miles long, a geologically complex terrain whose rough rocks and mighty sea cliffs are interrupted by a thousand sheltered bays and, in the far west, a long line of sweeping sandy beaches. The islands' interiors are equally dramatic, a series of formidable mountain ranges soaring high above great chunks of boggy peat moor, a barren wilderness enclosing a host of tiny lakes, or lochans.

Skye and the Western Isles were first settled by Neolithic farming peoples in around 4500 BC. They lived along the coast, where they are remembered by scores of incidental remains, from passage graves through to stone circles – most famously at **Calanais** (Callanish) on Lewis. Viking colonization gathered pace from 700 AD onwards – on Lewis four out of every five place names is of Norse origin – and it was only in 1266 that the islands were returned to the Scottish crown. James VI (and I of England), a Stuart and a Scot, though no Gaelic-speaker, was the first to put forward the idea of clearing the Hebrides, though it wasn't until after the Jacobite uprisings, when many Highland clans disastrously backed the wrong side, that the Clearances began in earnest.

The isolation of the Hebrides exposed them to the whims and fancies of the various merchants and aristocrats who caught "island fever" and bought them up. Time and again, from the mid-eighteenth century onwards, both the land and its people were sold to the highest bidder. Some proprietors were well-meaning – like **Lord Leverhulme**, who tried to turn Lewis into a centre of the fishing industry in the 1920s – while others were simply autocratic – such as **Colonel Gordon of Cluny**, who bought Benbecula, South Uist, Eriskay and Barra, and forced the inhabitants onto ships bound for North

---

ACCOMMODATION PRICE CODES

Throughout this guide, hotel and B&B accommodation is priced on a scale of ① to ⑨, the number indicating the **lowest price** you could expect to pay per night in that establishment for a **double room** in high season. The prices indicated by the codes are as follows:

① under £40	④ £60–70	⑦ £110–150
② £40–50	⑤ £70–90	⑧ £150–200
③ £50–60	⑥ £90–110	⑨ over £200

America at gunpoint – but always the islanders were powerless and almost everywhere they were driven from their ancestral homes. However, their language survived, ensuring a degree of cultural continuity, especially in the Western Isles, where even today the mother tongue of the vast majority is **Gaelic**.

Aficionados of this part of Scotland swear that each island has its own distinct character, which is to some extent true, although you can split the grouping quite neatly into two. **Skye** and the so-called **Small Isles** – the improbably named Canna, Rum, Eigg and Muck – are part of the Inner Hebrides, which also include the islands of Argyll (see the chapter on Argyll). Beyond Skye, across the unpredictable waters of the Minch, lie

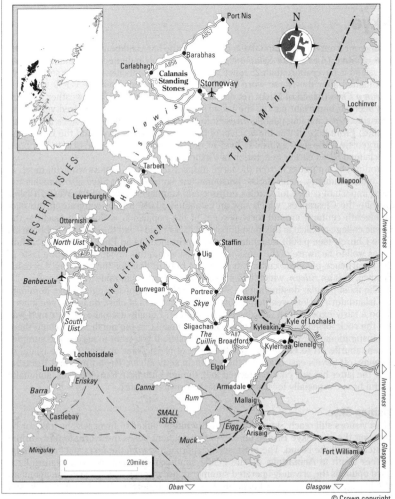

© Crown copyright

the Outer Hebrides or Outer Isles, nowadays known as the **Western Isles**, a 130-mile-long archipelago stretching from **Lewis** in the north to **Barra** in the south.

Although this area is one of the most popular holiday spots in Scotland, the crowds only become oppressive on Skye, and even here, most visitors stick to a well-trodden sequence of roadside sights that leaves the rest of the island unaffected. The main attraction, the spectacular scenery, is best explored on **foot**, following the scores of paths that range from the simplest of cross-country strolls to arduous treks. There are four obvious areas of outstanding natural beauty to aim for: on Skye, the harsh peaks of the **Cuillin** and the bizarre rock formations of the **Trotternish peninsula**, both of which attract hundreds of walkers and mountaineers; on the Western Isles, the mountains of **North Harris**, together with the splendid sandy beaches that string along the Atlantic seaboard of **South Harris** and the **Uists**.

Skye

Jutting out from the mainland like a giant wing, the bare and bony promontories of the **Isle of Skye** (*An t-Eilean Sgiathanach*) fringe a deeply indented coastline that means the island is never more than 25 miles wide – at some points it's as little as seven. Skye was named after the Norse word for cloud (*skuy*), earning itself the Gaelic moniker, *Eilean a Cheo* (Island of Mist). Yet despite the unpredictability of the weather, tourism has been an important part of the island's economy for almost a hundred years now, ever since the train line pushed through to Kyle of Lochalsh in the western Highlands in 1897. From here, it was the briefest of boat trips across to Skye, and the Edwardian bourgeoisie were soon swarming over to walk its mountains, whose beauty had been proclaimed by an earlier generation of Victorian climbers.

You might not guess it from the large number of English settlers who run much of the tourist industry – the B&Bs, museums and so forth – but Skye also remains the most important centre for **Gaelic culture** and language outside of the Western Isles. Despite the Clearances, which saw an estimated 30,000 people emigrate in the mid-nineteenth century, around forty percent of the population is fluent in Gaelic – the Gaelic college on Sleat is the most important in Scotland – and the extreme Sabbatarian Free Church (see p.966) maintains a strong presence. As an English-speaking visitor, it's as well to be aware of the tensions that exist within this idyllic island. For a taste of the resurgence of Gaelic culture, try and get here in time for the Skye and Lochalsh Festival, *Feis an Eilean*, which takes place over two weeks in mid-July.

The most popular destination on Skye is the **Cuillin**, whose jagged peaks dominate the island during clear weather, though, to explore them at close quarters, you'll need to be a fairly experienced and determined walker. Equally dramatic in their own way are the rock formations of the **Trotternish** peninsula, in the north, from which there are inspirational views across to the Western Isles. If you want to escape the summer crush, shuffle off to **Glendale** and the cliffs of Neist Point or head for the island of **Raasay**, off Skye's east coast. Of the two main settlements, **Broadford** and **Portree**, only the latter has any charm attached to it, though both have tourist offices, and make useful bases, especially for those without their own transport.

Visiting Skye

Most visitors still reach Skye via **Kyle of Lochalsh**, linked to Inverness by train, or by crossing the new Skye Bridge on one of the frequent buses over to **Kyleakin**, on the western tip of the island. The more scenic approach is from the **ferry** port of **Mallaig**, further south to **Armadale**, on the gentle southern slopes of the Sleat peninsula. A third option is the privately operated summer-only car **ferry** which leaves the mainland at Glenelg, south of Kyle of Lochalsh, to arrive at **Kylerhea**, between Armadale and

Kyleakin. Most visitors arrive by car, as the **bus** services, while adequate between the villages, peter out in the more remote areas, and virtually close down on Sundays.

The Sleat peninsula

Ferry services (June to mid-Sept 6 daily; rest of year Mon–Sat only; 30min) from Mallaig connect with the **Sleat peninsula** (pronounced "Slate"), Skye's southern tip, an uncharacteristically fertile area that has earned it the sobriquet "the Garden of Skye". The CalMac ferry terminal is at **ARMADALE** (Armadal), an elongated hamlet stretching along the wooded shoreline. If you need a bite **to eat**, pop into the *Pasta Shed* next door, which does a great seafood pizza (eat-in or takeaway). If you want to catch the morning ferry, and need a place **to stay**, try *Skye Batiks* B&B (☎01471/844396; ①) in Armadale itself. Alternatively, Armadale SYHA **youth hostel** (☎01471/844260; closed Oct to mid-March) is a ten-minute walk up the A851 to Broadford, overlooking the bay; *Sleat Independent Hostel* (☎01471/844440) is another two miles up the same road. In neighbouring Ardvasar, a mile to the southwest, the *Ardvasar Hotel* (☎01471/844223; ⑤; closed Nov–Feb) has an excellent restaurant and a lively bar. The SYHA hostel **rents bikes**.

Just past the youth hostel, you'll find the **Clan Donald Visitor Centre** (March–Oct daily 9.30am–5.30pm; gardens open all year 9.30am–5.30pm; centre £3.80, gardens free) whose handsome forty-acre gardens surround the nineteenth-century remains of Armadale Castle. Part of the castle has been turned into a museum that traces the history of the Gaels, concentrating on medieval times when the Donalds were the lords of the Isles. There's a lot of fairly confusing historical text on the walls, and the romantic sound effects – the cries of sea birds and battle songs – don't really compensate for the lack of original artefacts, but the handsome forty-acre **gardens** are the highlight with guided nature walks in the grounds.

Continuing northeast, it's another six miles to **ISLEORNSAY** (Eilean Iarmain), a secluded little village of ancient whitewashed cottages that was once Skye's main fishing port. With the mountains of the mainland on the horizon, the views out across the bay are wonderful, overlooking a necklace of seaweed-encrusted rocks and the tidal **Isle of Ornsay** itself, which sports a trim lighthouse. You can **stay** at the mid-nineteenth-century *Isle Ornsay Hotel* (☎01471/833332; ⑥), a pricey place (also known by its Gaelic name *Hotel Eilean Iarmain*), whose restaurant serves great seafood. The hotel is owned by Sir Iain Noble, an Edinburgh merchant banker who owns a large chunk of the peninsula and is an untiring Gaelic enthusiast.

Kyleakin and Kylerhea

The aforementioned Sir Iain Noble is also one of the leading advocates of (and investors in) the privately financed **Skye Bridge**, which nows links the tidy hamlet of **KYLEAKIN** (Caol Acain) with the Kyle of Lochalsh (see p.1037), just half a mile away on the mainland. The bridge, welcomed by the vast majority of islanders, was built entirely by Anglo-German contractors for a cool £30 million, which they are currently trying to recoup by charging around £5 each way for cars and more than £30 for lorries and coaches, making it the most expensive toll bridge in Europe, and no cheaper than the ferry it replaces. The well-orchestrated campaign by SKAT (Skye & Kyle Against Tolls), 350 of whose members have refused to pay the tolls, are still hoping to succeed in either reducing or abolishing the fee.

With its ferry now defunct, Kyleakin has reinvented itself as something of a backpackers' paradise – to the consternation of many villagers – and in summer, the population more than doubles. The SYHA **hostel** (☎01599/534585) is an ugly, modern building a couple of hundred yards from the old pier; nearby *Skye Backpackers* (☎01599/534510) is a more laid-back option, as is *Dun Caan Hostel* (☎01599/534087). **Bike rental** is available from Skye Bikes (☎01599/534795) on the pier.

You can still avoid crossing the Skye Bridge by taking the ferry service from Glenelg to **KYLERHEA** (mid-March to mid-May, Sept to mid-Oct Mon–Sat 9am–6pm; mid-May to Aug Mon–Sat 9am–8.30pm, Sun 10am–6pm; 15min), a peaceful little place, some four miles down the coast from Kyleakin. **Seal trips**, organized by Castle Moil Seal Cruises, also set off from the ferry pier, taking you to view the seal colony on Eilean Mhal (4 daily; £5.50; ☎01599/534641). Alternatively, you can walk half an hour up the coast to the Forestry Commission **Otter Hide**, where if you're lucky, you may be able to spot one of these elusive creatures.

Broadford

Heading west out of Kyleakin or Kylerhea brings you eventually to the island's second largest village, charmless **BROADFORD** (*An t-Ath Leathann*), whose mile-long main street curves round a wide bay. Despite its rather unlovely appearance, Broadford is a useful base for the southern half of Skye, with a **tourist office** (April, May & Sept Mon–Sat 9.30am–5.30pm; June Mon–Sat 9am–6pm; July & Aug Mon–Sat 9am–7pm, Sun 10am–5pm; Oct Mon–Sat 9.30am–5pm; ☎01471/822361) next door to the Esso garage on the main road, and a bank and bakery at the west end of the village. The SYHA **youth hostel** is on the west shore of the bay (☎01471/822442; closed Jan), or there's the much more beautiful and primitive *Fossil Bothy* (☎01471/822297, *mandeville@sprite.co.uk*), a small, independent hostel on the east side of the bay. You can **rent bikes** from the official youth hostel or from *Fairwinds Guest House* (☎01471/822270; ③; closed Nov–Feb).

Isle of Raasay

Travelling west from Broadford, with the Skye Cuillin to your left and the sea to your right, it's thirteen miles to Sconsor, where a car ferry leaves for the **Isle of Raasay** (Mon–Sat 9–10 daily; 15min), a nature conservancy area, which offers great walks across its bleak and barren hills, and remains well off the tourist trail. The island's ageing population now numbers just 150, most of them members of the Free Presbyterian Church (see p.966). Strict observance of the Sabbath – no work or play on Sundays – is the most obvious manifestation for visitors, who should respect the islanders' feelings.

The ferry docks at the southern tip of the island, an easy fifteen-minute walk from **INVERARISH**, a tiny village set within thick woods on the island's southwest coast. A further half-mile along the coast is the *Raasay Outdoor Centre*, housed in a partially restored Georgian mansion, which offers comfortable **accommodation** in tastefully bohemian rooms (☎01478/660266; ①; closed Nov–Feb), and **camping** in the grounds. Close by, there are comfortable rooms at the likeably old-fashioned *Isle of Raasay Hotel* (☎01478/660222; ③), which sits above the seashore looking out over Skye; they also serve delicious traditional Scottish food.

To the north of the Outdoor Centre, along the coast, lies the hamlet of Oskaig, from where a rough track cuts up the steep hillside to reach, by turning right at the road, Raasay's isolated but beautifully placed **SYHA hostel** (☎01478/660240; closed Oct to mid-May). Most of the rest of Raasay is starkly barren, a rugged and rocky terrain of sandstone in the south and gneiss in the north, with the most obvious feature being the curiously truncated basalt cap on top of **Dun Caan** (1456ft), where Boswell "danced a Highland dance" on his visit to the island with Dr Johnson in 1773.

The Cuillin and the Red Hills

For many people the **Cuillin**, whose sharp snow-capped peaks rise mirage-like from the flatness of the surrounding terrain, are Skye's *raison d'être*. When the clouds finally disperse, they are the dominating feature of the island, visible from every other peninsula on Skye. There are basically three approaches to the Cuillin: from the south, by foot or by boat from Elgol; from the Sligachan Hotel from the north; or from Glen Brittle to the west of the mountains. Glen Sligachan is by far the most popular route, dividing as it does the granite of the round-topped **Red Hills** (sometimes known as the Red Cuillin) to the east from the dark, coarse-grained jagged-edged gabbro of the real Cuillin (also known as the Black Cuillin), to the west. With some twenty Munros between them, these are mountains to be taken seriously, and many routes through the Cuillin are for experienced climbers only (for more on safety see p.51).

Elgol and Loch Coruisk

In summer there's a busy stall at **ELGOL**, fourteen miles southwest of Broadford, serving burgers and seafood because the chief reason for visiting Elgol is, weather permitting, to take a boat across Loch Scavaig (March–Sept 2–4 daily), past a seal colony, to a jetty near the entrance of **Loch Coruisk** (*coire uish*, "cauldron of water"). An isolated, glacial loch, this needle-like shaft of water, nearly two miles long but only a couple of hundred yards wide, lies in the shadow of the highest peaks of the Black Cuillin, a wonderfully overpowering landscape.

The journey by sea takes 45 minutes and passengers are dropped to spend about one and a half hours ashore; for booking (essential) and details of sailing times, ring the *Bella Jane* (☎0800/7313089). From Loch Coruisk, there are numerous possibilities for walking amidst the Red Cuillins; the most popular route, though, is to head north over the pass into **Glen Sligachan**.

The only public transport is the **postbus** from Broadford (Mon–Fri 2 daily, Sat 1 daily), which takes two hours to reach Elgol in the morning (check with the tourist office in Broadford about connections). Rather than stay in Elgol, head for *Rowan Cottage* (☎01471/866287; ①; closed Dec–March), a lovely **B&B** a mile or so east in Glasnakille, or the larger, more luxurious *Strathaird House* (☎01471/866269, *jkubale@compuserve.com*; ③; closed Oct–March) just beyond Kilmarie, three miles up the road to Broadford. By far the most popular place to stay, though, is the **campsite** (closed Nov–March) by the *Sligachan Hotel* (☎01478/650204; ②) on the A87, at the northern end of Glen Sligachan. The hotel's huge *Seamus Bar* serves food for weary walkers until 10pm, and quenches their thirst with the full range of real ales produced by Skye's very own micro-brewery in Uig.

Glen Brittle

Six miles along the Dunvegan road (A863) from the Sligachan Hotel, there's a turning to Carbost, which quickly leads to the entrance to stony **Glen Brittle** (with the settlement, Glenbrittle, at its southern end), edging the western peaks of the Black Cuillin. Climbers and serious walkers tend to congregate at the **youth hostel** (☎01478/640278; closed Oct to mid-March) or the **campsite** (☎01478/640404; closed Oct–March), a mile or so further south behind the wide sandy beach at the foot of the glen. Buses from Portree will drop you at the top of the road, but you'll have to walk the last seven miles; both the youth hostel and the campsite have grocery stores, the only ones for miles.

From the valley a score of difficult and strenuous trails lead east into the **Cuillin**, a rough semicircle of peaks that, rising to about 3000ft, surround Loch Coruisk, to the east. One of the easiest walks is the five-mile round trip from the campsite up **Coire Lagan**, to a crystal-cold lochan squeezed in among the sternest of rockfaces. Above the lochan is Skye's highest peak, Sgurr Alasdair (3257ft), one of the more difficult Munros; Sgurr na Banachdich (3166ft) is considered the most easily accessible Munro in the Cuillin (for the usual walking safety precautions see p.51).

You could while away an afternoon at **Talisker Whisky Distillery** (by appointment; ☎01478/640314), which produces a very smoky, peaty single malt. Talisker is the island's only distillery, situated on the shores of Loch Harport at **CARBOST** (and not, confusingly, at the village of Talisker itself).

Dunvegan and Duirinish

After the Glen Brittle turning, the A863 slips across bare rounded hills to skirt the bony sea cliffs and stacks of the west coast twenty miles or so north to **DUNVEGAN** (Dùn Bheagain). It's an unimpressive place, strung out along the east shore of the sea loch of the same name, though it does make quite a good base for exploring two interesting peninsulas: Duirinish and Waternish. From the jetty outside the castle there are regular seal-spotting **boat trips** out along Loch Dunvegan, as well as longer and less frequent sea cruises.

The main tourist trap in the village is **Dunvegan Castle** (mid-March to Oct daily 10am–5.30pm; £5.20; gardens only £3.70) which sprawls on top of a rocky outcrop, sandwiched between the sea and several acres of beautifully maintained gardens. It's been the seat of the Clan MacLeod since the thirteenth century, but the present greying, rectangular fortress with its uniform battlements and dummy pepper pots dates from the 1840s. Inside, you don't get a lot of castle for your money and the contents are far from stunning, Most intriguing of all are the battered remnants of the **Fairy Flag**, a yellow silken flag from the Middle East thought to have been the battle standard of the Norwegian king, Harald Hardrada, who was commander of the imperial guard in Constantinople.

The hammerhead **Duirinish peninsula** lies to the west of Dunvegan, much of it inaccessible to all except walkers prepared to scale or skirt the area's twin flat-topped peaks known as **MacLeod's Tables**. The main areas of habitation lie to the north, along the western shores of Loch Dunvegan, and in the broad green sweep of **Glen Dale**, attractively dotted with white farmhouses and dubbed "Little England" by the locals, due to its high percentage of "white settlers", English incomers searching for a better life. Glen Dale's current predicament is doubly ironic given its history, for it was here in 1882 that local crofters staged a rent strike against their landlords, the MacLeods. Five locals – who became known as the "Glen Dale Martyrs" – were given two-month prison sentences, and eventually, in 1904, the crofters became (and remain) the only owner-occupiers in the Highlands.

All this, and much more about crofting, is told through contemporary news cuttings at **Colbost Folk Museum** (Easter–Oct daily 10am–6.30pm; £1), the oldest of Peter MacAskill's three Skye museums, situated in a restored black house, four miles up the road from Dunvegan. Further up the road in **BORRERAIG**, where there was once a famous piping college, is the **MacCrimmon Piping Heritage Centre** (Easter to late May Tues–Sun 11am–5.30pm; late May to early Oct daily 11am–5.30pm; £1.50), on the ancestral holdings of the MacCrimmons, hereditary pipers to the MacLeod chiefs for three centuries, until they were sent packing in the 1770s. The plaintive sounds of the *piobaireachd* of the MacCrimmons, founding family of Scottish piping, fill this illuminating museum.

The west coast of Duirinish is mostly uninhabited now, due to the Clearances of the 1830s, when the villagers were given the choice of emigration or prison. For walkers, though, it's a great area to explore, with blustery but easy footpaths leading to the dramatically sited lighthouse on **Neist Point**, Skye's most westerly spot, which features some fearsome sea cliffs, and gives out wonderful views across the sea to the Western Isles.

Practicalities

Dunvegan is by no means the most picturesque place on Skye, but it's a useful base. It has a new **tourist office** (Mon–Sat 9am–5.30pm; ☎01470/521581) and boasts several excellent **hotels** and **B&Bs** dotted along the main road, such as the converted traditional croft *Roskhill House* (☎01470/521317, *stay@roskhill.demon.co.uk*; ③). Other possibilities include the beautifully situated *Silverdale* (☎01470/521251; ①) just before you get to Colbost, or the luxurious *Harlosh House* (☎01470/521367; ⑥; closed Nov–March), four miles south of Dunvegan, plus *Mo Dhachaidh* (☎01470/511210; ①; closed Nov–Easter) in Glendale itself. There's a basic loch-side **campsite** (closed Oct–March) a short distance west along the head of Loch Dunvegan.

The culinary mecca in the area is the expensive *Three Chimneys* **restaurant** (☎01470/511258; closed Sun), located beside Colbost Folk Museum. There are welcoming fires and good food at the sixteenth-century *Stein Inn* (☎01470/592362, *angus.teresa@steininn.demon.co.uk*; ②), in Stein, north of Dunvegan, and outstanding seafood at the *Lochbay Seafood Restaurant* (☎01470/592235; closed Sat & Sun). Eating in Dunvegan is a little problematical; however, there is a snug **café** attached to *Dunvegan Bakery* (closed Sat afternoon & Sun) where you can also pick up sandwich components and home-made carrot cake.

Portree

Although referred to by the locals as "the village", **PORTREE** is the only real town on Skye. It's also one of the most attractive fishing ports in northwest Scotland, its deep cliff-edged harbour filled with fishing boats and circled by multi-coloured restaurants and guest houses. The harbour is overlooked by **The Lump**, a steep and stumpy peninsula with a flagpole on it, that was once the site of public hangings on the island. Up above the harbour is the spick and span town centre, spreading out from **Somerled Square**, built in the late eighteenth century as the island's administrative and commercial centre, and now housing the bus station and car park. The **Royal Hotel**, on Bank Street, occupies the site of the *McNab's Inn* where Bonnie Prince Charlie took leave of Flora MacDonald (see box overleaf), and where, 27 years later, Boswell and Johnson had "a very good dinner, porter, port and punch".

A mile or so out of town on the Sligachan road is one of Skye's most successful tourist attractions, the **Aros Centre** (daily 9am–6pm; open later in summer). Here, you can enjoy the Aros Experience (£2.50), a dramatic and unsentimental presentation of episodes of the island's history, with stunning life-size figures and special effects, ending with an audio-visual show. If it's fine, there are waymarked forest walks and a Gaelic alphabet trail starting just outside. For a view of the contemporary visual art scene, it's well worth seeking out **An Tuireann Arts Centre**, housed in a converted fever hospital on the Struan road (Mon–Sat 10am–6pm; free), which puts on exhibitions, stages concerts, and has an excellent small café where even the counter is a work of art, with an imaginative range of food on offer.

Buses to Portree arrive in Somerled Square, just round the corner from the **tourist office**, off Bridge Street (April–Oct Mon–Sat 9am–5.30pm, Sun 11am–4pm; Nov–March closed Sun; ☎01478/612137); for **bike rental**, go to *Island Cycles* on the Green (☎01478/613121; closed Sun). Portree has a good range of **accommodation**, though prices tend to be higher than elsewhere, especially in the town itself – and it can get very busy. Probably the best **hotel** is the comfortable *Cuillin Hills* (☎01478/612003, *office@cuillinhills.demon.co.uk*; ⑤), ten minutes' walk out of town along the northern

BONNIE PRINCE CHARLIE

Prince Charles Edward Stewart – better known as **Bonnie Prince Charlie** or "The Young Pretender " – was born in Rome in 1720, where his father, "The Old Pretender", claimant to the British throne, was living in exile. At the age of 25, with little military experience, no knowledge of Gaelic, an imperfect grasp of English and a strong attachment to the Catholic faith, the prince set out for Scotland on a French ship, disguised as a seminarist from the Scots College in Paris. He arrived on the island of Eriskay in July 1745, and was immediately implored to return to France by the clan chiefs, who were singularly unimpressed by his lack of army. Charles was unmoved and went on to win the Battle of Prestonpans, marching on London and reaching Derby before finally calling a retreat. Back in Scotland, he won one last victory at Falkirk, before the final disaster at Culloden in April 1746.

The prince spent the following five months in hiding, with a price of £30,000 on his head, and literally thousands of government troops searching for him. He certainly endured his fair share of cold and hunger whilst on the run, but the real price was paid by the Highlanders themselves, who risked their lives (and often paid with them) by aiding and abetting the prince. The most famous of these was, of course, 23-year-old **Flora MacDonald**, whom Charles met on South Uist in June 1746. Flora was persuaded – by either his beauty or her relatives, depending on which account you believe – to convey Charles "over the sea to Skye", disguised as an Irish servant girl by the name of Betty Burke. Flora was arrested just seven days after parting with the prince in Portree, and was held in the Tower of London until her release in July 1747. She went on to marry a local man, had seven children and lived to the age of 68.

Charles eventually boarded a ship back to France in September 1746, but, despite his promises – "for all that has happened, Madam, I hope we shall meet in St James's yet" – never returned to Scotland, nor did he ever see Flora again. After mistreating a string of mistresses, he eventually got married at the age of 52 to the 19-year-old Princess of Stolberg, in an effort to produce a Stewart heir. They had no children, and she eventually fled from his violent drunkenness; in 1788, a none too "bonnie" Prince Charles died in the arms of his illegitimate daughter in Rome. Bonnie Prince Charlie became a legend in his own lifetime, but it was the Victorians who really milked the myth for all its sentimentality, conveniently overlooking the fact that the real consequence of 1745 was the virtual annihilation of the Highland way of life.

shore of the bay, or the atmospheric Victorian pile, *Viewfield House* (☎01478/612217; ⑤), on the southern outskirts of town. The *Bosville Hotel* (☎01478/612846, *bosville@macleodhotels.co.uk;* ④) on Bosville Terrace commands a good view of the harbour. In the lower price range, try *Givendale Guest House* (☎01478/612183; ②; closed Nov–March), ten minutes' walk up the hill from the town centre on Heron Place, or *Conusg* (☎01478/612426; closed Oct–Easter; ②), a B&B in a quiet spot by the *Cuillin Hills Hotel*. Of Portree's year-round **hostels**, the smartest is the *Portree Independent Hostel* (☎01478/613737, *portreeindhostel@hotmail.co.uk*) housed in the Old Post Office on the Green, though the *Portree Backpackers Hostel* (☎01478/613332), ten minutes' walk up the Dunvegan road, enjoys a more secluded location (and will pick you up from town if you ring ahead). Torvaig **campsite** (☎01478/612209; closed Nov–March) lies a mile and a half north of town off the A855 Staffin road.

The best **food** in town is at the *Bosville Hotel*'s *Chandlery* restaurant, a pricey option, with its sister *Bosville* restaurant only slightly cheaper. *Harbour View* has a seafood **restaurant** with candlelit ambience, but better is *Ben Tianavaig,* an excellent veggie and seafood place (☎01478/612152; Tues–Sun eve only). The *Lower Deck Seafood Restaurant* on the harbour has a wood-panelled warmth to it, and is reasonably priced at lunchtime; or you can pop next door to their excellent fish-and-chip shop.

Trotternish

Protruding twenty miles north from Portree, the **Trotternish** peninsula boasts some of the island's most bizarre scenery, particularly on the east coast, where volcanic basalt has pressed down on the softer sandstone and limestone underneath, causing massive landslides. These, in turn, have created sheer cliffs, peppered with outcrops of hard, wizened basalt, which run the full length of the peninsula. These pinnacles and pillars are at their most eccentric in the Quiraing, above Staffin Bay, on the east coast. Trotternish is best explored with your own transport, but an occasional bus service along the road encircling the peninsula gives access to almost all the coast (ask for times at the Portree tourist office).

The east coast

The first geological eccentricity on Trotternish, six miles north of Portree along the A855, is the **Old Man of Storr**, a distinctive column of rock, which along with its neighbours is part of a massive land slip, with huge blocks of stone still occasionally breaking off the cliff face of the Storr (2358ft) above and sliding downhill. At 165ft, the Old Man is a real challenge for climbers – less difficult is the brief and boggy footpath up to the foot of the column from the car park beside the main road, though it's often closed by the forest rangers when it gets too waterlogged. Eight miles further north, there's another car park for the **Kilt Rock**, whose tube-like, basaltic columns rise precipitously from the sea. A mile or two up the minor road which cuts across the peninsula from Staffin Bay, there's a path up to the savage rock formations of the **Quiraing** – a forest of mighty pinnacles including the Needle, the Prison and the Table, where Victorian ramblers used to picnic and play cricket.

The **accommodation** on the east coast is among the best on Skye, with most places enjoying fantastic views out over the sea. Just beyond the Lealt Falls there's the very welcoming and comfortable *Glenview Inn* (☎01470/562248; ③; closed Nov–Feb), with an excellent adjoining restaurant, and a **campsite** (☎01470/562213; closed Oct–March) south of Staffin Bay. In fine weather, you can enjoy good bar snacks on the castellated terrace of the stylish *Flodigarry Country House Hotel* (☎01470/552203; ⑥), three miles up the coast from Staffin. Behind the hotel (and now part of it) is the cottage where local heroine Flora MacDonald lived, and had six of her seven children, from 1751 to 1759. If the hotel's rooms are beyond your means, try the neat and attractive *Dun Flodigarry Backpackers' Hostel* (☎01470/552212), a couple of minutes' walk away – you can ring the hostel to arrange transport or catch the local bus.

The west coast

Beyond **Flodigarry**, the A855 veers off to the west coast, rounding the tip of the Trotternish ridge before reaching the shattered remains of a headland fortress at **DUNTULM**, once a major MacDonald power base, abandoned by the clan in 1732 after a clumsy nurse dropped one of their babies from a window onto the rocks below. The imposing *Duntulm Castle Hotel* (☎01470/552213; ②; closed Dec–Feb) is close by, and provides good bar meals as well as wonderful views across the Minch to the Western Isles. Heading down the west shore of the Trotternish, it's two miles to the **Skye Museum of Island Life** (Easter–Oct Mon–Sat 9.30am–5.30pm; £1.75), an impressive cluster of thatched black houses on an exposed hill overlooking Harris. The museum, run by locals, gives a fascinating insight into a way of life that was commonplace on Skye a hundred years ago. Behind the museum up the hill are the graves of **Flora MacDonald** and her husband. Thousands turned out for her funeral in 1790, creating a funeral procession a mile long – indeed so widespread was her fame that the original family mausoleum fell victim to souvenir hunters, and had to be replaced. The Celtic cross headstone is inscribed with a simple, contemporaneous tribute by Dr Johnson, who visited her in 1773: "Her name will be mentioned in history, if courage and fidelity be virtues, mentioned with honour".

A further four miles south is the ferry port of **UIG** (Uige), which curves its way round a dramatic, horseshoe-shaped bay. If you're arriving from Tarbert (Harris) or Lochmaddy (North Uist), you might like to know there's a **tourist office** (April–Oct Mon–Sat 8.45am–6.30pm; mid-July to mid-Sept also Sun 8.45am–2pm; ☎01470/542404) inside the CalMac office on the pier. If you need an inexpensive **B&B** near the ferry terminal, head for *Braeholm* (☎01470/542396; ①; closed Nov–Feb), the **campsite** (☎01470/542360; closed Nov–Feb), by the shore near the dock, or the **SYHA hostel** (☎01470/542211; closed Nov to mid-March), high up on the south side of the village, with exhilarating views over the bay. The *Pub at the Pier* offers filling meals, and serves the local Skye beers, which are also on sale in the shop of the nearby brewery (tours by appointment Mon–Fri; ☎01470/542477). **Bike rental** is available from North Skye Bicycle Hire.

The Small Isles

The history of the **Small Isles**, which lie to the south of Skye, is typical of the Hebridean islands: early Christianization, followed by a period of Norwegian rule that ended in 1266 when the islands were handed back into Scottish hands. Their support for the Jacobite cause resulted in hard times after the failed rebellion of 1745, but the biggest problems came with the introduction of the **potato**, in the mid-eighteenth century. The consequences were as dramatic as they were unforeseen: the success of the crop and its nutritional value – when grown in conjunction with traditional cereals – eliminated famine at a stroke, prompting a population explosion.

At first, the problem of overcrowding was camouflaged by the **kelp** boom, in which the islanders were employed, and the islands' owners made a fortune, gathering and burning local seaweed to sell for use in the manufacture of gunpowder, soap and glass. But the economic bubble burst with the end of the Napoleonic Wars and, to maintain their profit margins, the owners resorted to drastic action. The first to sell up was Alexander Maclean who sold **Rum** as grazing land for **sheep**, got quotations for shipping its people to Nova Scotia, and gave them a year's notice to quit. He also cleared **Muck** to graze cattle, as did the MacNeills on **Canna**. Only on **Eigg** was some compassion shown; the new owner, a certain Hugh MacPherson, who bought the island from the Clanranalds in 1827, actually gave some of his tenants extended leases.

Since the Clearances each of the islands has been bought and sold several times, though only **Muck** is now privately owned by the benevolent laird, Lawrence MacEwan. **Eigg** hit the headlines in 1997, when the islanders finally managed to buy

---

GETTING TO THE SMALL ISLES

CalMac run passenger-only ferries to the Small Isles every day except Sunday from Mallaig (☎01687/462403). Day-trips to all four islands are possible only on Saturdays, but involve catching the ferry at 5am in the morning. The CalMac ferry can currently only dock at Canna; on the other three islands, you have to be transferred to an island tender.

From May to September, you can also reach Rum, Eigg and Muck seven days a week from Arisaig with **Murdo Grant** (☎01687/450224). Day-trips are possible to Eigg on most days, allowing four to five hours ashore, and to Rum and Muck on a few days. With careful studying of both CalMac and Murdo Grant timetables, you should be able to organize a visit to suit you, especially as Arisaig and Mallaig are linked by railway.

the island themselves and put an end to more than 150 years of property speculation. The other islands were bequeathed to national agencies: **Rum**, the largest and most visited of the group, possesses a cluster of formidable volcanic peaks and the architecturally remarkable Kinloch Castle, passed to the Nature Conservancy Council (now known as Scottish Natural Heritage) in 1957; and **Canna**, by far the prettiest of the Small Isles with its high basalt cliffs, went to the National Trust for Scotland (NTS) in 1981.

Rum

Like Skye, **Rum** is dominated by its Cuillin, which, though only reaching a height of 2663ft at the summit of Askival, rise up with comparable drama straight up from the sea in the south of the island. Rum's chief formal attraction is **Kinloch Castle** (Tues & Thurs guided tours at 2pm; £3), a squat red sandstone edifice fronted by colonnades and topped by crenellations and turrets, that dominates the village of Kinloch. Completed at enormous expense in 1900 – the red sandstone was shipped in from Arran; the soil for the gardens from Ayrshire – its interior is a perfectly preserved example of Edwardian decadence, "a living memorial of the stalking, the fishing and the sailing, the tenantry and plenty of the days before 1914". From the galleried hall, with its tiger rugs, stags' heads and giant Japanese incense burners, to the "Extra Low Fast Cushion" of the Soho snooker table in the Billiard Room, the interior is packed with nick-nacks and technical gizmos accumulated by **Sir George Bullough** (1870–1939), the spendthrift son of self-made millionaire Sir John Bullough, who bought the island as a sporting estate in 1888. As such, it was only really used for a few weeks each autumn, during the "season", yet employed an island workforce of one hundred all year round. Bullough's guests were woken at eight each morning by a piper; later on, an orchestrion, an electrically driven barrel organ (originally destined for Balmoral), crammed in under the stairs, would grind out an eccentric mixture of pre-dinner tunes: *The Ride of the Valkyries* and *Ma Blushin' Rosie*, among others (a demo is included in the tour). The *pièce de résistance*, though, has to be Bullough's **Edwardian bathrooms**, whose baths have hooded walnut shower cabinets, fitted with two taps and four dials, which allow the bather to fire high-pressure water at their body from every angle.

For those with only limited time or energy, there are two gentle waymarked **heritage trails**, both of which start from Kinloch, and take around two hours to complete. For longer walks, you must fill in route cards and pop them into the White House (Mon–Fri 9am–12.30pm). The island's best beach is at **KILMORY**, to the north (5hr return), though this part of the island is only open to the public on the weekend, as it's given over to the study of red deer. When the island's human head count peaked at 450 in 1791, the hamlet of **HARRIS**, on the southwest coast (6hr return), housed a large crofting community – all that remains now are several ruined black houses and the extravagant **Bullough Mausoleum**, built by Sir George to house the remains of his father, in the style of a Greek Doric temple, overlooking the sea.

If you plan to stay the night, you need to book in advance, as **accommodation** is fairly limited. Kinloch lets a few of its four-poster rooms – for which you pay a bit extra – but it's basically run now as an independent **hostel** (☎01687/462037). SNH also run two mountain **bothies** in Dibidil and Guirdil, and basic **camping** on the foreshore near the jetty. You need to book ahead for both, by contacting the reserve manager at the *White House* (☎01687/462026).

Wherever you're staying, you can either self-cater – hostellers can use the hostel kitchen – or eat the unpretentious **food** offered in the hostel's licensed bistro. There is also a small shop, off-licence and post office in Kilmory. Finally, bear in mind that Rum is the wettest of the Small Isles, and is known for having some of the worst **midges** (see p.19) in Scotland – come prepared for both.

Eigg

Eigg is without doubt the most easily distinguishable of the Small Isles from a distance, since the island is mostly made up of a basalt plateau 1000ft above sea level, and a great stump of columnar pitchstone lava, known as An Sgurr, rising out of the plateau another 290ft. It's also by far the most vibrant, populous and welcoming of the Small Isles, with a real strong sense of community.

Visitors arrive in the southeast corner of the island – which measures just five miles by three – at **GALMISDALE**, where **An Laimhrig** (The Anchorage), the island's new community centre, stands, housing a shop, post office, tearoom, and information centre. The island minibus meets incoming ferries, and will take you to wherever you need to go on the island. Many visitors head off to **CLEADALE**, in the north of the island, where the beach, known as the **"Singing Sands"**, is comprised of quartz, which squeaks underfoot when dry (hence the name). With the island's great landmark, **An Sgurr** (1292ft), watching over you wherever you go, many folk feel duty bound to climb it, and enjoy the wonderful views over to Muck and Rum; the return trip takes between three and four hours. A large colony of **Manx shearwater** nests in burrows around the summit; to view the birds, you need to be there around dawn or dusk.

The nicest place **to stay** on Eigg is *Kildonan House* (☎01687/482446; ③, incl dinner), a beautiful eighteenth-century wood-panelled house, where the cooking is superb. Other B&Bs are *Lageorna* (☎01687/482405; ④, incl dinner), a crofthouse that also has a couple of self-catering cottages. As you'll probably notice, as you walk around the island, Eigg has no mains electricity so each house has its own diesel generator.

Muck

Smallest and most southerly of the Small Isles, **Muck** is low-lying, mostly treeless and extremely fertile, and as such shares more characteristics with the likes of Coll and Tiree than its nearest neighbours. Its name derives from *muc*, the Gaelic for "pig" – or, as some would have it, *muc mara*, "sea pig" or porpoise, which abound in the surrounding water – and has long caused much embarrassment to generations of lairds who preferred to call it the "Isle of Monk", because it had briefly belonged to the medieval church. **PORT MÓR**, the village on the southeast corner of the island, is where visitors arrive. A road, just over a mile in length, connects Port Mór with the island's main farm, **GALLANACH**, which overlooks the rocky seal-strewn skerries on the north side of the island. The nicest sandy beach is Camas na Cairidh, to the east of Gallanach. Despite being only 452ft above sea level, it really is worth climbing **Beinn Airein**, in the southwest corner of the island, for the 360-degree panoramic view of the surrounding islands; the return journey from Port Mór takes around two hours. You can **stay** with one of the MacEwen family, who have owned the island since 1896, at *Port Mór House* (☎01687/462365; ③, incl dinner); the rooms are pine-clad and enjoy great views, and the food is delicious. Alternatively, you can stay at the island's **bunkhouse** (☎01687/462042); with permission, you may also **camp rough**, but bring supplies with you as there is no shop.

Canna

Measuring a mere five miles by one, and with a population of just twenty, **Canna** is run as a single farm by the NTS. The island enjoys the best harbour in the Small Isles, a horn-shaped haven at its southeastern corner protected by the tidal island of Sanday, now linked to Canna by a footbridge. For visitors, the chief pastime is walking: from the dock it's about a mile across a grassy basalt plateau to the bony sea cliffs of the north shore, and about the same to the top of Compass Hill (458ft) – so called because its high metal content distorts compasses – from where you get great views across to Rum and Skye. From the buffeted western tip of the island, you can spy the **Heiskeir of Canna**, a curious mass of stone columns sticking up 30ft above the water, some seven miles offshore.

Accommodation is extremely limited. With permission, you may **camp rough** on Canna; otherwise the only option is **B&B** with Wendy MacKinnon (☎01687/462465; ⑤, incl dinner), or the NTS-owned *Tighard*, a **self-catering** cottage half a mile from the jetty, which sleeps a maximum of ten people. Booking forms are available from Holiday Cottages, NTS, 5 Charlotte Square, Edinburgh (☎0131/226 5922). Remember, however, that there are no shops on Canna (bar the post office), so you must bring your own supplies.

The Western Isles

The wild and windy **Western Isles** – also known as the Outer Hebrides – vaunt a strikingly hostile mix of landscapes from windswept golden sands to harsh, heather-backed mountains and peat bogs. An elemental beauty pervades each one of the more than two hundred islands that make up the archipelago, only a handful of which are actually inhabited by a total of just over 30,000 people. The influence of the Atlantic Gulf Stream ensures a mild but moist climate, though you can expect the strong Atlantic winds to blow in rain on two out of every three days even in summer. Weather fronts, however, come and go at such dramatic speed in these parts, there's little chance of mist or fog settling and fewer problems with midges.

The most significant difference between Skye and the Western Isles is that here, tourism is much less important to the islands' fragile economy – still mainly concentrated around crofting, fishing and weaving. The Outer Hebrides also remain the heartland of **Gaelic culture**, with the language spoken by the vast majority of islanders, though its everyday usage remains under constant threat from the national dominance of English. Its survival is, in no small part, due to the all-pervading influence of the Free Church, whose strict Calvinism is the creed of the vast majority of the population, with only South Uist, Barra and parts of Benbecula adhering to the relatively more relaxed demands of Catholicism.

The interior of the northernmost island, **Lewis**, is mostly peat moor, a barren and marshy tract that gives way abruptly to the bare peaks of **North Harris**. Across a narrow isthmus lies **South Harris**, presenting some of the finest scenery in Scotland, with wide sandy beaches trimming the Atlantic in full view of the mountains and a rough boulder-strewn interior lying to the east. Further south still, a string of tiny, flatter islets, mainly **North Uist**, **Benbecula**, **South Uist** and **Barra**, offer breezy beaches, whose fine sands front a narrow band of boggy farmland, which, in turn, is mostly bordered by a lower range of hills to the east.

In direct contrast to their wonderful landscapes, villages in the Western Isles are rarely picturesque in themselves, and are usually made up of scattered, relatively

---

GAELIC IN THE WESTERN ISLES

Except in Stornoway, and Balivanich on North Uist, **road signs** are now exclusively in **Gaelic**, a difficult language to the English-speaker's eye, with complex pronunciation, though as a (very) general rule, the English names can often provide a rough pronunciation guide. Particularly if you're driving, it's essential to buy the bilingual Western Isles map, produced by the local tourist board, *Bord Turasachd nan Eilean*, and available at most tourist offices. In the text, we've put the English first, with the Gaelic in brackets; thereafter we've stuck to the English names.

modern crofthouses strung out along the elementary road system. **Stornoway**, the only real town in the Outer Hebrides, is eminently unappealing. Many visitors, walkers and nature watchers forsake the settlements altogether and retreat to secluded cottages and B&Bs, though for this you really need your own transport.

Visiting the Western Isles
British Regional Airlines and Loganair operate fast and frequent **flights** from Glasgow and Inverness to Stornoway on Lewis, Barra and Benbecula on North Uist. But be warned, the weather conditions on the islands are notoriously changeable, making these flights both prone to delay and sometimes stomach-churningly bumpy. On Barra, the other complication is that you land on the beach, so the timetable is adjusted with the tides. CalMac **car ferries** run from Ullapool in the Highlands to Stornoway; from Uig, on Skye, to Tarbert and Lochmaddy; and from Oban or Mallaig to South Uist and Barra. There's also an inter-island ferry from Leverburgh, on Harris, to Otternish, on North Uist (for more on ferry services, see "Travel details" on p.975).

Lewis (Leodhas)

Lewis is the largest and most populous of the Western Isles and the northernmost island in the Hebridean archipelago. After Viking rule ended in 1266, the island was fought over by the MacLeods and MacKenzies, until eventually being sold by the latter in 1844. The new owner, Sir James Matheson, invested heavily in new industries, as **Lord Leverhulme** did with the fishing industry when he acquired the island (along with Harris) in 1918. Though undoubtedly a benevolent despot, Leverhulme's unpopularity with crofters on Lewis, and his financial difficulties, forced him to give up his grandiose plans in 1923, when he gave the island to its inhabitants. His departure, however, left a big gap in the economy, and between the wars thousands more emigrated.

Most of the island's 20,000 inhabitants – two thirds of the Western Isles' total population – now live in the crofting and fishing villages strung out along the northwest coast, between Callanish and Port of Ness. On this coast you'll find the islands' best-preserved **prehistoric remains** – at Carloway and Callanish – as well as a smattering of ancient crofters' houses in various stages of abandonment. The landscape is mostly flat peat bog – hence the island's name, derived from the Gaelic *leogach* (marshy) – with a gentle shoreline that only fulfils its dramatic potential around the Butt of Lewis, a group of rough rocks on the island's northernmost tip, near Port of Ness. To the south, where it is physically joined with the Isle of Harris, the land rises to just over 1800ft, providing a more exhilarating backdrop for the excellent beaches, peppered along the isolated coastline to the southwest of Callanish.

Most visitors use Stornoway, on the east coast, as a base for exploring the island, though this presents problems if you're travelling by **bus**. There's a regular service to Port of Ness and Tarbert, and although the most obvious excursion – the 45-mile round trip from Stornoway to Callanish, Carloway, Arnol and back – is almost impossible to complete by public transport, the tourist office's minibus tours make the trip on most days from April to October.

Stornoway (Steornabhagh)
In these parts, **STORNOWAY** is a buzzing metropolis, with some eight thousand inhabitants, a one-way system, pedestrian precinct and all the trappings of a large town. It is a centre for employment, the island's social hub, and perhaps most importantly of all, home to the **Comhairle nan Eilean** (Western Isles Council), set up in 1974, which has done so much to promote Gaelic language and culture, trying to stem the tide of anglicization. For the visitor, however, the town is unlikely to win any great praise – aesthetics is not its strong point, and the urban pleasures on offer are limited.

The best thing about Stornoway is the convenience of its services. The island's **airport** is four miles east of the town centre, a £5 taxi ride away; the **ferry** terminal is on South Beach, close to the **bus station**. The **tourist office** is near North Beach at 26 Cromwell St (April–May & Sept to mid-Oct Mon–Fri 9am–6pm, Sat 9am–5pm; June–Aug Mon, Tues, Thurs & Sat 9am–6pm & 8–9pm, Wed & Fri 9am–8pm; mid-Oct to March Mon–Fri 9am–5pm; ☎01851/703088), and will, for a small booking fee, fix you up with accommodation. Of the **hotels**, the *Royal Hotel*, on Cromwell Street (☎01851/702109; ⑤), is your best bet. Another fairly reliable choice is the *Park Guest House* (☎01851/702485; ②) on James Street; the public areas have bags of lugubrious late Victorian character; the bedrooms significantly less. Of the **B&Bs** along leafy Matheson Road, try *Ravenswood*, at no. 12 (☎01851/702673; ②). The *Stornoway Backpackers* **hostel** is a basic affair about five minutes' walk from the ferry at 47 Keith St (☎01851/703628; *hostel@bayble.demon.co.uk*). The nearest **campsite** is the *Laxdale Holiday Park* (☎01851/703234), a mile or so along the road to Barabhas, on Laxdale Lane; the campsite has holiday bungalows (three nights minimum), and a new **bunkhouse**. For **bike rental** go to Alex Dan, 67 Kenneth St (Mon–Sat 9am–6pm; ☎01851/704025).

Decent **food** options are disappointingly limited in Stornoway. One of the best places is the *Thai Café* on Church Street, which serves inexpensive but authentic **Thai** food (☎01851/701811). You can get snacks from the *An Lanntair* tearoom, and from *An Leabharlann*, the coffee shop in the new library on Cromwell Street. Your best bet for local food is the restaurant of the *Park Guest House*, on James Street (closed Mon & Sun), but it's expensive, unless you go for the "early bird" option. The biggest problem is that all the above places are closed on Sunday. The *Stornoway Balti House*, near the bus station on South Beach, opens on Sunday evenings.

As for **pubs**, *MacNeills*, on Cromwell Street, is the liveliest central pub, with a mixed clientele of keen drinkers. *The Criterion*, a tiny, wee pub on Point Street, is another option, as is the very pleasant bar of the *Royal Hotel*. Needless to say, all pubs are closed on Sundays, while hotel bars are open for residents only. Last, but not least, Stornoway is home to the Western Isles' only **Internet café**, *Captions*, 27 Church St (Mon–Sat 10am–10pm; *bayble@captions.co.uk*), where you can check your email, and enjoy tea and home-made cakes..

Barvas (Barabhas) to Port of Ness (Port Nis)

Northwest of Stornoway, the A857 crosses the vast, barren **peat bog** of the interior, an empty wilderness riddled with stretch marks formed by peat cuttings and pockmarked with freshwater lochans. The whole area was once covered by forests, but these disappeared long ago, leaving a smothering deposit of peat that is, on average, 6ft thick, and is still being formed in certain places. For the people of Lewis, peat is a valuable energy resource, with each crofter being assigned a slice of the bog. The islanders spend several very sociable weeks each spring cutting the peat, turning it over and leaving it neatly laid out in the open air to dry, returning in summer to collect the dried sods and stack them outside their houses. Though tempting to take home as souvenirs, these piles are the fruits of hard labour, and remain the island's main source of domestic fuel, its pungent smoke one of the most characteristic smells of the Western Isles.

Twelve miles across the peat bog the road divides, heading southwest towards Callanish (see below), or northeast through **BARVAS** (Barabhas), and a whole string of bleak, fervently Free Church, crofting and weaving villages. Be prepared for the fact that these scattered settlements have none of the photogenic qualities of Skye's whitewashed villages. The churches are plain and unadorned; the crofters' houses are fairly modern and smothered in grey, concrete pebble dash; the stone cottages and enclosures of their forebears often lie half-abandoned in the front garden;

RELIGION IN THE WESTERN ISLES

Sharply divided – although with little enmity – between the Catholic southern isles of Barra and South Uist, and the Protestant north of North Uist, Harris and Lewis, it is difficult to overestimate the importance of **religion** in the Western Isles. Most conflicts arise from the very considerable power the ministers of the Protestant Church, or Kirk, wield in secular life in the north, where the creed of **Sabbatarianism** is very strong. Here, Sunday is the Lord's Day, and virtually the whole community (irrespective of their degree of piety) stops work – all shops close, all pubs close, all garages close and there's no public transport, but perhaps most famously of all, even the swings in the children's playgrounds are padlocked.

The other main area of division is, paradoxically, within the Protestant Church itself. Scotland is unusual in that the national church, the **Church of Scotland**, is presbyterian (ruled by the ministers and elders of the church) rather than episcopal (ruled by bishops). At the time of the main split in the Presbyterian Church – the so-called **1843 Disruption** – a third of its ministers left the Church of Scotland, protesting at the law which allowed landlords to impose ministers against parishioners' wishes, and formed the breakaway **Free Church**. Since those days there has been a partial reconciliation; although, in 1893, there was another break, when a minority of the Free Church became the Free Presbyterian Church, while the rest slowly made their way back to the Church of Scotland. The remaining rump of the Free Church – better known as the **"Wee Frees"** – have their spiritual heartland on Lewis. To confuse matters further, as recently as 1988, the Free Presbyterian Church split over a minister who attended a requiem mass during a Catholic funeral of a friend – he and his supporters have since formed the breakaway Associated Presbyterian Churches.

The various brands and subdivisions of the Presbyterian Church may appear trivial to outsiders, but to the churchgoers of Lewis, Harris and North Uist (as well as much of Skye and Raasay) they are still keenly felt. In part, for social and cultural reasons: Free Church elders helped organize resistance to the Clearances, and the Wee Frees have done the most to help preserve the Gaelic language. A Free Church service is a memorable experience, and in some villages it takes place every evening (and twice on Sundays): there's no set service or prayer book, only Biblical readings, plainchant and a fiery sermon all in Gaelic; the pulpit is the architectural focus of the church, not the altar, and communion is taken only on special occasions.

while a rusting assortment of discarded cars and vans now serves to store peat bags and the like. The main road continues through a string of straggling villages, terminating at the remote village **PORT OF NESS** (Port Nis), nestled round its tiny harbour and golden beach.

From Port Nis, a minor road heads two miles north to the hamlet of **EUROPIE** (Eoropaidh) and the **Teampull Mholuaidh** (St Moluag's Church), an austere stone structure thought to date from the twelfth century. From Europie, a narrow road twists north to the bleak and blustery tip of the island, well known to devotees of the BBC shipping forecast as the **Butt of Lewis** (Rubha Robhanais), where a lighthouse sticks up above a series of sheer cliffs and stacks, alive with a cacophony of sea birds, and a great place for seal spotting.

Several **B&Bs** line the main road between Barvas and Port of Ness. Alternatively, try the *Galson Farm Guest House* (☎01851/850492; ⑤), an eighteenth-century farmhouse in South Galson (Gabhsann Bho Dheas), with a **bunkhouse** close by (phone number as above). Another, more modest option is the modern croft of *Eisdean* (☎01851/810240; ①) in Five Penny Borve (Coig Peighinnean), four miles northeast of Barvas, or *Cross Inn* (☎01851/810378; ①), remarkable primarily for being the only pub in the entire parish.

Arnol to Callanish (Calanais)

Heading southwest from the crossroads near Barvas brings you to the village of **ARNOL**, which meanders down towards the sea. At the far end of the village is the **Black House Museum** (May–Sept Mon–Fri 10am–5pm, Sat 11am–5pm; £1.80; HS), which dates from the 1870s and was inhabited right up until 1964. Built low against the wind, the house's thick walls are made up of an inner and outer layer of loose stone on either side of a central core of earth, a traditional type of construction which attracted the soubriquet "black house" around 1850, when buildings with single-thickness walls were introduced to Lewis from the mainland and were commonly called "white houses" (*tigh geal*) by the locals – even though they weren't all white. Thus traditional dwellings came to be called "black houses" (*tigh dubh*).

Returning to the main road, it's about eight miles to the parish of **CARLOWAY** (Carlabhagh), with its scattering of crofthouses. Just beyond Carlabhagh, about 400yd from the road, **Dùn Charlabhaigh Broch** perches on top of a conspicuous rocky outcrop overlooking the sea. Scotland's Atlantic coast is strewn with the remains of over 500 brochs, or fortified towers, but this is one of the best preserved, its dry-stone circular walls reaching a height of more than 30ft on the seaward side. The broch consists of two concentric walls, the inner one perpendicular, the outer one slanting inwards, the two originally fastened together by roughly hewn flagstones, which also served as lookout galleries reached via a narrow stairwell. The only entrance to the roofless inner yard is through a low doorway set beside a crude and cramped guard cell. As at Callanish (see below), there have been all sorts of theories about the purpose of the brochs, which date from between 100 BC and 100 AD; the most likely explanation is that they were built to provide protection from Roman slave-traders.

Dùn Charlabhaigh now has its very own **Doune Broch Centre** (April–Oct Mon–Sat 10am–6pm; free), situated at a discreet distance, stone-built and sporting a turf roof. It's a good wet weather retreat, and fun for kids, who can walk through the hay-strewn mock-up of the broch as it might have been.

Five miles south of Dùn Charlabhaigh lies the village of **CALLANISH** (Calanais), site of the islands' most dramatic prehistoric ruins, the **Callanish Standing Stones**, whose monoliths – nearly fifty of them – occupy a serene loch-side setting. There's been years of heated debate about the origin and function of the stones – slabs of gnarled and finely grained gneiss up to 15ft high – though almost everyone agrees that they were lugged here by Neolithic peoples between 3000 and 1500 BC. It's also obvious that the planning and construction of the site – as well as several other lesser circles nearby – were spread over many generations. Such an endeavour could, it's been argued, only be prompted by the desire to predict the seasonal cycle upon which these early farmers were entirely dependent, and indeed, many of the stones are aligned with the position of the sun and the stars. This rational explanation, based on clear evidence that this part of Lewis was once a fertile farming area, dismisses as coincidence the ground plan of the site, which resembles a colossal Celtic cross, and explains away the central burial chamber as a later addition of no special significance. These two features have fuelled all sorts of theories ranging from alien intervention to human sacrifice.

You can't actually walk between the stones any more, only by the fence that surrounds them. An adjacent black house has been refurbished as a **teashop**, now upstaged by the much bigger, but less cosy, restaurant at the nearby **Callanish Visitor Centre** (Mon–Sat: April–Sept 10am–7pm; Oct–March closes 4pm; £1.50) now built on the other side of the stones (thankfully out of view). However, with so much information on the panels beside the stones, it's not really necessary to visit the centre's small museum.

There are several inexpensive **B&Bs** in Callanish itself: try Mrs Catherine Morrison, 27 Calanais (℡01851/621392; ①; closed Oct–Feb), or an excellent B&B, which caters

well for veggies and is run by Debbie Nash (☎01851/621321; ②) in neighbouring
Tolastadh a Chaolais (Tolsta Chaolais), three miles north. Callanish also has a modern
Eschol Guest House (☎01851/621357; ③), no beauty from the outside, but very comfort-
able within. If it's just **food** you want, try *Tigh Mealros* (closed Sun), in Gearraidh na h-
Aibhne, which serves good, inexpensive lunches and evening meals, featuring local
seafood. A mile north of Carloway is the beautifully remote coastal settlement of
GARENIN (Gearrannan), where an old thatched crofters' house now serves as a primitive **hostel** (no phone; open all year).

Harris (Na Hearadh)

The "division" between Lewis and **Harris** – they are, in fact, one island – is embedded
in a historical split in the MacLeod clan, lost in the mists of time. The border between
the two was also a county boundary until 1975, with Harris lying in Inverness-shire, and
Lewis belonging to Ross and Cromarty. Nowadays, the dividing line is rarely marked
even on maps, though for the record it comprises Loch Resort in the west, Loch
Seaforth in the east, and the six miles in between. Harris itself is more clearly divided
by a minuscule isthmus, into the wild, inhospitable mountains of North Harris and the
gentler landscape and sandy shores of South Harris.

Along with Lewis, Harris was purchased in 1918 by **Lord Leverhulme**, and after he
pulled out of Lewis in 1923, all his efforts were concentrated here. In contrast to Lewis,
though, Leverhulme and his ambitious projects were broadly welcomed by the people
of Harris. His most grandiose plans were drawn up for Leverburgh, but he also purchased an old Norwegian whaling station in Bunavoneadar in 1922, built a spinning mill

---

HARRIS TWEED

Far from being a picturesque cottage industry, as it's sometimes presented, the production of **Harris tweed** is vital to the local economy with a well-organized and unionized
workforce. Traditionally, the tweed was made by women, from the wool of their own
sheep, to provide clothing for their families, using a 2500-year-old process. Each woman
was responsible for plucking the wool by hand, washing and scouring it, dyeing it with
lichen, heather flowers or ragwort, carding (smoothing and straightening the wool, often
adding butter to grease it), spinning and weaving. Finally the cloth was dipped in sheep's
urine and "waulked" by a group of women, who beat the cloth on a table to soften and
shrink it whilst singing Gaelic waulking songs. Harris tweed was originally made all over
the islands, and was known simply as *clò mór* (big cloth).

In the mid-nineteenth century, the Countess of Dunmore, who owned a large part of
Harris, started to sell surplus cloth to her aristocratic friends, thus forming the genesis
of the modern industry, which serves as a vital source of employment, though demand
(and therefore employment levels) can fluctuate wildly as fashions change. To earn the
official Harris Tweed Association trademark of the Orb and the Maltese Cross – taken
from the Countess of Dunmore's coat of arms – the fabric has to be hand-woven on the
Outer Hebrides from 100 percent pure new Scottish wool, while the other parts of the
manufacturing process must take place only in the local mills.

The main centre of production is now Lewis, where the wool is dyed, carded and spun;
you can see all these processes by visiting the **Lewis Loom Centre** in Stornoway (see
p.964). In recent years, there has been a revival of traditional tweed-making techniques,
with several small producers, like Anne Campbell at **Clò Mór** in Liceasto (Mon–Fri
9am–5pm; ☎01859/530364), religiously following old methods. One of the more interesting aspects of the process is the use of indigenous plants and bushes to dye the cloth: yellow comes from rocket and broom, green from heather, grey and black from iris and oak,
and, most popular of all, reddish brown from crotal, a flat grey lichen scraped off rocks.

at Geocrab and began the construction of four roads. Financial difficulties, a slump in the tweed industry and the lack of market for whale products meant that none was a whole-hearted success, and when he died in 1925, the plug was pulled on all of them by his executors.

Since the Leverhulme era, unemployment has been a constant problem in Harris. Crofting continues on a small scale, supplemented by the Harris Tweed industry, though the main focus of this has shifted to Lewis. Shellfish fishing continues on Scalpay, while the rest of the population gets by on whatever employment is available: roadworks, crafts and, of course, tourism. There's a regular **bus** connection between Stornoway and Tarbert, and an occasional service which circumnavigates South Harris.

Tarbert (Tairbeart)

The largest place on Harris is the ferry port of **TARBERT**, sheltered in a green valley on the narrow isthmus that marks the border between North and South Harris. The town's mountainous backdrop is impressive, and the town is attractively laid out on steep terraces sloping up from the dock. However, it does boast the only **tourist office** (April–Oct Mon–Sat 9am–5pm; also open to greet the ferry; winter opening times to be confirmed; ☎01859/502011) on Harris, close to the ferry terminal. The tourist office can arrange modest, inexpensive B&B **accommodation** and has a full set of bus timetables, but its real value is as a source of information on local walks.

If you wish to base yourself in Tarbert, there's a **hostel**, *Rockview Bunkhouse* on Main Street (☎01859/502211), which also offers **bike rental**. You'll need to book ahead to stay in Tarbert's two most popular **guest houses**: *Allan Cottage* (☎01859/502146; ③; closed Oct–March), and *Leachin House* (☎01859/502157; ⑤), further up the Stornoway road. Another good option is the Victorian B&B *Dunard* (☎01859/502340; ③), or there's the easy-going, old-fashioned *Harris Hotel* (☎01859/502154; ③), five minutes' walk from the ferry. The purpose-built hotel **bar** acts as the local social centre and serves low-grade bar meals; the adjacent *Crofters* **restaurant** serves moderately expensive, fairly ordinary fare. During the day, you're best off heading for the very pleasant *First Fruits* **tearoom** (closed Sun, plus Oct–March), behind the tourist office. The only alternative is the **fish-and-chip shop** (closed Sun, plus Nov–March), next to the hostel.

North Harris (Ceann a Tuath na Hearadh)

The A859 north to Stornoway takes you over a boulder-strewn saddle between mighty **Sgaoth Aird** (1829ft) and the **Clisham** (2619ft), the highest peak in the Western Isles. This bitter terrain offers but the barest of vegetation, with the occasional cluster of crofters' houses sitting in the shadow of a host of pointed peaks, anywhere between 1000ft and 2500ft high. These bulging, pyramidical mountains reach their climax around the dramatic shores of the fjord-like **Loch Seaforth**.

If you're planning on walking in North Harris, and can afford it, consider using the spectacular *Ardvourlie Castle* (☎01859/502307; ⑥; closed Nov–March), ten miles north of Tarbert by the shores of Loch Seaforth, as a launch pad. A cheaper, but equally idyllic spot is the GHHT **youth hostel** (no phone; open all year) in the lonely coastal hamlet of Rhenigdale, until recently only accessible by foot or boat. To reach the hostel without your own transport, walk east five miles from Tarbert along the road to Kyles Scalpay (Caolas Scalpaigh). After another mile or so, watch for the sign marking the start of the path which threads its way through the peaks of the craggy promontory that lies trapped between Loch Seaforth and East Loch Tarbert. It's a magnificent hike, with superb views out along the coast and over the mountains, but you'll need to be properly equipped and should allow three hours for the one-way trip.

South Harris (Ceann a Deas)

The mountains of **South Harris** are less dramatic than in the north, but the scenery is equally breathtaking. There's a choice of routes from Tarbert to the ferry port of Leverburgh, which connects with North Uist; the east coast, known as Bays (Na Baigh), is rugged and seemingly inhospitable, while the west coast is endowed with some of the finest stretches of golden sand in the whole of the archipelago, buffeted by the Atlantic winds. Paradoxically, most people on South Harris live along the harsh eastern coastline rather than the more fertile west side, though not by choice – they were evicted from their original crofts to make way for sheep-grazing.

The main road from Tarbert into South Harris snakes its way west for ten miles across the boulder-strewn interior to reach the **west coast**. Once there, you get a view of the most stunning **beach**, the vast golden strand of **Tràigh Losgaintir**. The road continues to ride above a chain of sweeping sands, backed by rich **machair**, that stretches for nine miles along the Atlantic coast. In good weather, the scenery is stunning, foaming breakers rolling along the golden sands set against the rounded peaks of the mountains to the north and the islet-studded turquoise sea to the west. Nobody bothers much if you **camp** or park beside the dune-edged beach, as long as you're careful not to churn up the machair, and there's the very good B&B, *Moravia* (☎01859/550262; ①; closed Nov–Feb), overlooking the sands at Luskentyre (Losgaintir), but the choicest **accommodation** (and food) is three miles further south at *Scarista House* (☎01859/550238, *ian@caristahouse.demon.co.uk*; ⑦; closed Oct–April) which overlooks a golden beach in the village of Scarista (Sgarasta).

If you're intrigued by the local machair, join one of the guided walks (mid-May to mid-Sept Mon & Fri 2.30pm; £2) across a particularly magnificent stretch by the golden sands close to the village of **NORTHTON** (Taobh Tuath), where you'll find the **MacGillivray Centre** (free access), which houses a small exhibition on the naturalist William MacGillivray (1796–1852), after whom it's named, and a little on crofting and machair. From Northton, the road veers to the southeast to reach the island's south shore, eventually reaching the sprawling settlement of **LEVERBURGH** (An t-Ob), named after Lord Leverhulme, who planned to turn the place into the largest fishing port on the west coast of Scotland. From a jetty about a mile south of the main road, a new CalMac **car ferry** leaves for North Uist. There are several **B&Bs** in and around Leverburgh: try *Caberfeidh House* (☎01859/520276; ①), a lovely stone-built Victorian building by the turn-off to the ferry; or *Sorrel Cottage* (☎01859/520319; ①), which specializes in vegetarian and seafood cooking. A cheaper alternative is the purpose-built timber-clad *An Bothan* **bunkhouse** (☎01859/520251), which has all great facilities, and is only a few minutes' walk from the ferry.

Three miles southeast of Leverburgh and a mile or so from Renish Point, the southern tip of Harris, is the old port of **RODEL** (Roghadal), where a smattering of ancient stone houses lies among the hillocks surrounding the dilapidated harbour. On top of one of these grassy humps is the distinctive castellated tower of **St Clement's Church** (Tur Chliamainn), burial place of the MacLeods of Harris and Dunvegan in Skye. Dating from the 1520s, the church's gloomy interior is distinguished by its wall-tombs, notably that of the founder, Alasdair Crotach (also known as Alexander MacLeod), whose heavily weathered effigy lies beneath an intriguing backdrop and canopy of sculpted reliefs of vernacular and religious scenes – elemental representations of, among others, a stag hunt, the Holy Trinity, St Michael, and an angel and devil weighing the souls of the dead. Look out, too, for the *sheila-na-gig* on the south side of the tower.

North Uist (Uibhist a Tuath)

Compared to the mountainous scenery of Harris, **North Uist** – seventeen miles long and thirteen miles wide – is much flatter and for some comes as something of an anticlimax. Over half the surface area is covered by water, creating a distinctive peaty-brown lochan-studded "drowned landscape". Most visitors come here for the trout and salmon fishing and the deerstalking, both of which (along with poaching) are critical to the survival of the island's economy. Others come for the solitude of North Uist's vast sandy beaches, which extend – almost without interruption – along the north and west coast and the smattering of prehistoric sites.

Despite being situated on the east coast, some distance away from any beach, the ferry port of **LOCHMADDY** (Loch nam Madadh) is easily the best base for exploring the island. The village itself, occupying a narrow, bumpy promontory, is nothing special, though, if you've time to kill, take a look round **Taigh Chearsabhagh** (Mon–Sat 10am–5pm; £1), a converted eighteenth-century merchant's house, which now harbours an excellent local museum, arts centre and café. If the weather's good, take a walk out past the Uist Outdoor Centre, and across the footbridge that leads to the derelict Sponish House. From here a path leads east to Lochmaddy's most intriguing sight, **Both nam Faileas** (Hut of the Shadow), an ingenious dry-stone, turf-roofed camera obscura recently built by sculptor Chris Drury. Right by the **tourist office** (mid-April to mid-Oct Mon–Fri 9am–5pm, Sat 9.30am–5.30pm; also open to greet the evening ferry; ☎01876/500321) is the spick and span *Lochmaddy Hotel* (☎01876/500331; ⑦), whose restaurant and bar serve outstanding seafood. There are also a couple of nice Victorian **B&Bs** – try the *Old Bank House* (☎01876/500275; ①). Not far beyond, the **hostel** in the Uist Outdoor Centre (☎01876/500480) offers four-person bunk rooms. The only **bike rental** on the island is at Morrison Cycle Hire (☎01876/580211), nine miles away in Carinish (Cairinis), but they will deliver to Lochmaddy if you phone them.

Several prehistoric sights lie within easy cycling distance of Lochmaddy (or even walking distance if you use the postbus for the outward journey). The most significant is the **Barpa Langass**, a large, mostly intact, chambered cairn seven barren miles to the southwest along the A867; a mile to the southeast is the small stone circle of **Pobull Fhinn**. Three miles northwest of Lochmaddy along the A865 is **Na Fir Bhreige** (The Three False Men), three standing stones which, depending on your legend, mark the graves of three spies buried alive, or three men who deserted their wives and were turned to stone by a proto-feminist witch.

North Uist's other main draw is the **Baranald RSPB Reserve**, one of the last breeding grounds of the corncrake, among Europe's most endangered birds. Sightings are rare, partly because the birds are very good at hiding in long grass, but the males' loud "craking" is relatively easy to hear from May to July. From the excellent new **visitor centre**, there's a two-hour walk along the headland, marked out by discreet white pegs, giving you ample opportunity for appreciating the wonderful carpet of flowers that covers the machair in summer, and for spotting corn buntings and arctic terns inland and gannets and Manx shearwaters out to sea – guided walks take place throughout the summer (May–Aug Tues & Fri 2pm; ☎01878/602188).

Another hostel worth noting is the *Taigh mo Sheanair* (☎01876/580246), a very welcoming, family-run **hostel**, where you can also **camp**. The hostel is clearly signposted from the main road, south of the crossroads at Clachan; from the main road it's a good fifteen-minute walk.

Berneray (Bearnaraigh)

For those in search of still more seclusion, there's the low-lying island of **Berneray** – two miles by three, with a population of about 140 – now accessible via a brand new causeway from Otternish, eight miles north of Lochmaddy. The island's main claim to fame is as the favoured holiday hideaway of that great eccentric, Prince Charles, lover of Gaelic culture, and royal potato picker to local crofter "Splash" MacKillop. Apart from the sheer peace and isolation of the place, the island's main draw is the three-mile-long sandy beach on the west and north coast. The other great draw is the wonderful GHHT **hostel** (no phone) which occupies a pair of thatched black houses in a lovely spot by a beach, beyond Loch a Bhàigh and the main village. Alternatively you can follow in the prince's footsteps and stay (and help out) at "Splash" MacKillop's *Burnside Croft* **B&B** (☎01876/540235; ②; closed Dec & Jan), and enjoy "storytelling evenings"; bike rental is also available.

Benbecula (Beinn na Faoghla)

Blink and you could miss the pancake-flat island of **Benbecula** (put the stress on the second syllable), sandwiched between Protestant North Uist and Catholic South Uist. Most visitors simply trundle along the main road that cuts across the middle of the island in less than five miles – not such a bad idea, since nearly half the island's 1200 population are Royal Artillery personnel, working at the missile range on South Uist. Nearly all the military personnel live in the depressing barracks-like housing developments of **BALIVANICH** (Baile a Mhanaich), the grim, grey capital of Benbecula in the northwest. The only reason to come here at all is if you happen to be flying into or out of **Benbecula airport** (direct flights to Glasgow, Barra and Stornoway). There's no tourist office and if you've got your own transport, there's no need **to stay** here, but if you're reliant on public transport, try the modern **hostel** *Taigh-na-Cille* (☎01870/602522), within easy walking distance of the airport, on the road to North Uist. The best thing about Balivanich is *Stepping Stone*, the excellent purpose-built **café/restaurant** situated opposite the post office.

South Uist (Uibhist a Deas)

To the south of Benbecula, the island of **South Uist** is arguably the most appealing of the southern chain of islands. The west coast boasts some of the region's finest beaches – a necklace of gold and grey sand strung twenty miles from one end to the other – while the east coast features a ridge of high mountains rising to 2034ft at the summit of Beinn Mhor. The only blot on the landscape is the Royal Artillery missile range, which occupies the island's northwest, shattering the peace and quiet every so often.

The Reformation never took hold in South Uist – or Barra (see below) – and the island remains Roman Catholic, as is evident from the slender modern statue of *Our Lady of the Isles* that stands by the main road below the small hill of **Rueval**, known to the locals as "Space City" for its forest of aerials and golf balls, which help track the missiles heading out into the Atlantic. To the south of Rueval is the freshwater **Loch Druidibeg**, a breeding ground for greylag geese and a favourite spot for mute swans; there's a path through the nature reserve from the phone box on the main road.

One of the best places to gain access to the sandy shoreline is at **HOWMORE** (Tobha Mòr), a pretty little crofting settlement, with a fair number of restored houses, many still thatched, including one distinctively roofed in brown heather. A GHHT **hostel** (no phone; open all year) occupies one such house, near the village church, from which it's an easy walk across the flower-infested machair to the gorgeous beach. Close by the hostel are the shattered, lichen-encrusted remains of no fewer than four medieval churches and chapels, and a burial ground now harbouring just a few scattered graves.

Five miles south of Tobha Mor, the **Kildonan Museum** (Mon–Sat 10am–5pm, Sun 2–5pm; £1.80) contains mock-ups of Hebridean kitchens through the ages; two lovely box beds, and an impressive selection of old photos are accompanied by a firmly unsentimental, yet poetic written text on crofting life in the last two centuries. The museum also runs a café, serving sandwiches and home-made cakes, and has a choice of historical videos for those really wet and windy days.

Without doubt, the best **hotel** on the Uists is the *Orasay Inn* (☎01870/610298; *orasayinn@btinternet.com*; ③), located in a peaceful spot off the road to Loch a Charnain (Lochcarnan), in the northeastern corner of the island. **LOCHBOISDALE** (Loch Baghasdail), the island's chief settlement, has, if anything, even less to offer than Lochmaddy, with just the *Lochboisdale Hotel* for somewhere to have a drink and a proper meal. The **tourist office** (Easter to mid-Oct Mon–Sat 9am–5pm; ☎01878/700286), by the harbour, is also open to meet the night ferry from Oban. There are several small, perfectly ordinary **B&Bs** within comfortable walking distance of the dock, including *Bayview* (☎01878/700329; ②; closed Nov–Feb) and *Lochside Cottage* (☎01878/700472; ②).

If you're heading for Barra, you could take the passenger ferry from **Ludag jetty**, two miles east of the *Polochar Inn*, which lands at Eoligarry on Barra's north coast – and when the causeway to Eriskay is complete in 2001, there are plans to institute a car ferry service to Barra.

Eriskay (Eiriosgaigh)

To the south of South Uist lies the barren, hilly island of **Eriskay**, famous for its patterned jerseys (on sale at the community centre), and a peculiar breed of pony, originally used for carrying peat and seaweed. The island, which measures just over two miles by one, shelters a small fishing community of about 150, and makes a great daytrip from South Uist, as long as the weather's fine. The ferry from Ludag, across the treacherously shallow waters of the Sound of Eriskay, will be made redundant when the new causeway is finished in 2001.

For a small island, Eriskay has had more than its fair share of historical headlines. It was on the island's main beach on the west coast on July 23, 1745, that **Bonnie Prince Charlie** landed on Scottish soil – a pink sea bindweed grows there to this day, said to have sprung from the seeds Charles brought with him from France. Eriskay's other claim to fame came in 1941 when the **SS Politician** sank on its way from Liverpool to Jamaica, along with its cargo of bicycle parts, £3 million in Jamaican currency and 264,000 bottles of whisky, inspiring Compton MacKenzie's book – and the Ealing comedy (filmed here in 1948) – *Whisky Galore!* (released as *Tight Little Island* in the US). The ship's stern can still be seen to the northwest of the Isle of Calvey at low tide, and one of the original bottles (and lots of other related memorabilia) is on show in the island's purpose-built pub, *Am Politician*, on the west coast.

Until the causeway is complete, there are three types of **ferry** to Eriskay from Ludag jetty on South Uist – car ferry, passenger ferry and a rigid inflatable. Which one runs depends on the tides and demand, so get hold of a copy of the monthly timetable from the tourist office or phone the enquiry line (☎01878/720261).

Barra (Barraigh)

Just four miles wide and eight miles long, **Barra** has a well-deserved reputation for being the Western Isles in miniature. It has sandy beaches, backed by machair, glacial mountains, prehistoric ruins, Gaelic culture and a laid-back Catholic population of just over 1300. The only settlement of any size is the old herring port of **CASTLEBAY** (Bagh a Chaisteil), which curves around the barren hills of a wide bay on the south side of the island (ferries from Lochboisdale, on South Uist, and Oban stop here). Barra's religious allegiance is announced by the large Catholic church, Our Lady, Star of the Sea, which overlooks Castlebay; to underline the point, there's a Madonna and Child on the slopes of **Heaval** (1260ft), the largest peak on Barra, and a fairly easy hike from the bay.

As its name suggests, Castlebay has a castle in its bay, the medieval islet-fortress of **Kisimul Castle** (Mon, Wed & Sat 2pm; £3), ancestral home of the MacNeil clan. The

MacNeils owned Barra until 1838, when they sold it to the infamous Colonel Gordon of Cluny, who offered to clear the island and turn it into a state penal colony. The government declined, so the colonel called in the police and proceeded with some of the most cruel forced clearances in the Hebrides. In 1937, the 45th chief of the MacNeil clan bought back the castle (and most of the island). It has since been restored to something of its original appearance, and you can take a tour round it by catching the ferry from the slipway at the bottom of Main Street. To learn more about the history of the island, and about the postal system of the Western Isles, pay a visit to the **Barra Heritage Centre** (Mon–Fri 11am–5pm; £1), housed in an unprepossessing block on the road that leads west out of town.

One of the most fascinating sights on the island is **Barra Airport**, on the north side of the island, where the planes have to land and take off from the crunchy shell sands of Tràigh Mhór, better known as **Cockle Strand**; the exact timing of the flights depends on the tides, since at high tide the beach (and therefore the runway) is covered in water. As its name suggests, the strand is also famous for its cockles and cockleshells, the latter being used to make harling (the rendering used on most Scottish houses).

Barra's **tourist office** (April to mid-Oct Mon–Sat 9am–5pm; also open to greet the ferry; ☎01871/810336) is situated on Main Street in Castlebay, just round from the pier, and can help book **accommodation**. In Castlebay itself, the *Castlebay Hotel* (☎01871/810223; ④) is the most comfortable **place to stay**, followed by *Tigh-na-Mara* (☎01871/810304; ②; closed Nov–March), a guest house a couple of minutes' walk from the pier by the sea; another good choice is *Grianamul* (☎01871/810416, *ronnie.macneil@virgin.net*; ③; closed Nov–March). There's a new GHHT **hostel** (no phone) in Breibhig (Brevig), a couple of miles east of Castlebay, where you can also **camp**; if you're camping rough, there are toilets and a shower in the CalMac office on the pier. Places **to eat** include the *Kisimul Galley*, which serves up breakfast all day every day, and specializes in cheap and cheerful Scottish fry-ups. For more fancy fare, duck inside the *Castlebay Hotel*'s cosy bar which regularly has cockles, crabs and scallops on its menu.

There's a fairly decent **postbus** service which does the rounds of the island (Mon–Sat). **Bike rental** is available at Castlebay Cycle Hire (☎01871/810284), half a mile east of the town centre, and Barra Cycle Hire (☎01871/810284), who will meet you off the passenger ferry from South Uist. **Car rental** is available from Barra Car Hire (☎01871/810243), who will deliver vehicles to the airport or either ferry terminal. Films are occasionally shown to the public on Saturday evenings at the local school – look out for the posters. Those interested in a boat trip to the sea cliffs of the Isle of **Mingulay**, south of Barra, whose last two inhabitants were evacuated in 1934, should phone Mr Campbell (☎01871/810303) or enquire at the *Castlebay Hotel*.

travel details

Trains

Aberdeen to: Kyle of Lochalsh (Mon–Sat 1 daily; 5hr).

Edinburgh to: Kyle of Lochalsh (Mon–Sat 1 daily; 6hr 50min).

Fort William to: Mallaig (Mon–Sat 6 daily, Sun 3 daily; 1hr 30min).

Glasgow (Queen St) to: Mallaig (Mon–Sat 3 daily, Sun 2 daily; 5hr 10min); Oban (Mon–Sat 3 daily, Sun 2 daily; 3hr).

Inverness to: Kyle of Lochalsh (Mon–Sat 3 daily, Sun 1 daily; 2hr 30min).

Buses

Mainland

Edinburgh to: Broadford (1 daily; 6hr 30min); Oban (1 daily; 4hr); Portree (1 daily; 7hr 40min).

Glasgow to: Broadford (3 daily; 5hr 30min); Oban (Mon–Sat 4 daily, Sun 2 daily; 3hr); Portree (3 daily; 6hr 10min); Uig (2 daily; 7hr 40min).

Inverness to: Broadford (Mon–Sat 3 daily, Sun 2 daily; 2hr 50min); Portree (Mon–Sat 3 daily, Sun 2 daily; 3hr 15min).

Kyle of Lochalsh to: Broadford (7 daily; 30min); Portree (7daily; 1hr).

Skye

Armadale to: Broadford (Mon–Sat 5 daily, Sun 2 daily; 45min); Portree (Mon–Sat 6 daily, Sun 1 daily; 1hr 20min); Sligachan (Mon–Sat 4 daily, Sun 1 daily; 1hr 10min).

Broadford to: Portree (10–12 daily; 40min).

Dunvegan to: Glendale (Mon–Sat 1–4 daily; 30min).

Kyleakin to: Broadford (Mon–Sat 12–14 daily, Sun 7 daily; 15min); Portree (Mon–Sat 6–7 daily, Sun 5 daily; 1hr); Sligachan (Mon–Sat 7–8 daily, Sun 5 daily; 45min); Uig (Mon–Sat 2 daily; 1hr 20min).

Portree to: Carbost (Mon–Fri 2–3 daily, Sat 1 daily; 40min); Duntulm (Mon–Sat 2–3 daily; 1hr); Dunvegan (Mon–Sat 4 daily; 50min); Fiskavaig (Mon–Fri 2 daily, Sat 1 daily; 50min); Staffin (Mon–Sat 3 daily; 40min); Uig (Mon–Sat 4–5 daily; 30min).

Lewis/Harris

Stornoway to: Barabhas (Mon–Fri 11–13 daily,

Sat 8 daily; 30min); Calanais (Mon–Sat 5–7 daily; 40min); Carlabhagh (Mon–Sat 4–6 daily; 1hr); Leverburgh (Mon–Sat 4–5 daily; 2hr); Point (Mon–Sat hourly; 40min); Port Nis (Mon–Sat 6–9 daily; 1hr); Siabost (Mon–Sat 6 daily; 45min); Tarbert (Mon–Sat 4–5 daily; 1hr 10min); Timsgearraidh (Mon–Sat 1–2 daily; 1hr–1hr 30min); Tolastadh (Mon–Sat every 1hr 30min; 40min).

Tarbert to: Huisinis (Tues, Fri & schooldays 3–4 daily; 45min); Leverburgh (Mon–Sat 8 daily; 50min); Leverburgh via the Bays (Mon–Sat 3–4 daily; 1hr 10min); Scalpay (Mon–Fri 5 daily, Sat 3 daily; 20min).

Uists/Benbecula

Lochboisdale to: Ludag (Mon–Sat 6–7 daily; 30–45min).

Lochmaddy to: Balivanich (Mon–Sat 4–5 daily; 45min–2hr); Balranald (Mon–Sat 4–5 daily; 50min); Berneray (Mon–Sat 5–6 daily; 30min); Lochboisdale (Mon–Sat 2–3 daily; 2hr).

Otternish to: Balivanich (Mon–Sat 3–4 daily; 1hr–2hr 20min); Lochmaddy (Mon–Sat 6–7 daily; 20–50min).

Barra

Castlebay to: Airport/Eoligarry (Mon–Sat hourly; 35min/45min); Vatersay (Mon–Sat 8 daily; 20min).

Ferries (summer timetable)

To Barra: Lochboisdale–Castlebay (Tues, Thurs, Fri & Sun; 1hr 40min); Mallaig–Castlebay (Sun; 3hr 45min); Oban–Castlebay (Mon, Wed, Thurs & Sat; 5hr).

To Canna: Eigg–Canna (Mon & Sat; 2hr 45min–3hr); Mallaig–Canna (Mon, Wed, Fri & Sat; 2hr 30min–4hr 15min); Muck–Canna (Sat; 2hr 15min); Rum–Canna (Mon, Wed & Sat; 1hr–1hr 15min).

To Eriskay: Ludag–Eriskay (at least 2 daily; 20min).

To Eigg: Canna–Eigg (Fri & Sat; 2hr 15min–3hr); Mallaig–Eigg (Mon, Tues, Thurs & Sat; 1hr 30–1hr 50min); Muck–Eigg (Tues, Thurs & Sat; 45–50min); Rum–Eigg (Fri & Sat; 1hr 15min–2hr).

To Harris: Lochmaddy–Tarbert via Uig (Mon–Sat 1–2 daily; 4hr); Otternish–Leverburgh (Mon–Sat 4 daily; 1hr 10min); Uig–Tarbert (Mon–Sat 1–2 daily; 1hr 45min).

To Lewis: Ullapool–Stornoway (Mon–Sat 2 daily; 2hr 40min).

To Muck: Canna–Muck (Sat; 2hr 15min); Eigg–Muck (Tues, Thurs & Sat; 1hr); Mallaig–Muck (Tues, Thurs & Sat; 2hr 40min–4hr 45min); Rum–Muck (Sat; 1hr 15min).

To North Uist: Leverburgh–Otternish (Mon–Sat 4 daily; 1hr 10min); Tarbert–Lochmaddy via Uig (Mon–Sat 1–2 daily; 4hr); Uig–Lochmaddy (1–2 daily; 1hr 50min).

To Raasay: Sconser–Raasay (Mon–Sat 9–10 daily; 15min).

To Rum: Canna–Rum (Wed, Fri & Sat; 1hr–1hr 15min); Eigg–Rum (Mon & Sat; 1hr 30min–2hr); Mallaig–Rum (Mon, Wed, Fri & Sat; 1hr 45min–3hr 30min); Muck–Rum (Sat; 1hr 15min).

To Skye: Glenelg–Kylerhea (frequently daily; 15min); Mallaig–Armadale (June to mid-Sept 6–7 daily; rest of year not Sun; 30min).

To South Uist: Castlebay–Lochboisdale (Mon, Wed, Thurs & Sat; 1hr 40min); Mallaig–Lochboisdale (Tues; 3hr 30min); Oban–Lochboisdale (Mon, Wed & Thurs–Sat; 5hr–6hr 50min).

Flights

Benbecula to: Barra (Mon–Fri 2 daily; 20min); Stornoway (Mon–Fri 2 daily; 40min).

Glasgow to: Barra (Mon–Fri 2 daily, Sat 1 daily; 1hr); Benbecula (Mon–Sat 1 daily; 1hr); Stornoway (Mon–Sat 2 daily; 1hr);

Inverness to: Stornoway (Mon–Fri 2 daily, Sat 1 daily; 20min).

CHAPTER TWENTY-FOUR

NORTHEAST SCOTLAND

A large triangle of land thrusting into the North Sea, the northeast of Scotland comprises the land to the east of a line drawn roughly from Perth up to Forres, east of Inverness, on the fringe of the Moray Firth. The area takes in the county of Angus and the city of Dundee to the south and, beyond the Grampian Mountains, the counties of Aberdeenshire and Moray and the city of Aberdeen. The northeast has a good deal of fertile farmland, mostly found in the coastal belt and along the lower stretches of the Dee and Don rivers. This is fringed on its seaward side by dramatic cliffs and long sandy beaches, and inland gradually gives way to wooded glens, mountains and increasingly desolate highlands.

The northeast was the southern kingdom of the **Picts**, whose mysterious and beautifully artistic carved stones are found scattered across the region in fields, churchyards and numerous small museums. Remote, self-contained and cut off from the centres of major power in the south, the area never grew particularly prosperous, and a few feuding and intermarrying families, such as the Gordons, the Keiths and the Irvines, grew to wield disproportionate influence, building many of the region's **castles** and religious buildings, and developing and planning its towns.

Farming and fishing were long the mainstays of the northeast's economy, and while fishing is only a fondly held memory in many parts, a number of the ports have been transformed by the discovery of **oil** in the North Sea in the 1960s, particularly **Aberdeen**, Scotland's third largest city. Aberdeen is the region's most stimulating urban centre, a fast, relatively sophisticated city that continues to ride on the crest of the oil boom. In contrast, **Dundee**, the next largest metropolis in the northeast, is low-key and only now emerging from a depressed post-industrial period. Having said that it does boast a splendid site on the banks of the Tay and makes a useful base for visiting the Angus hinterland, including nearby **Glamis Castle**, famous as the setting for Shakespeare's *Macbeth*. A little way up the Angus coast lie the historically important towns of **Arbroath**, home of the Declaration of Arbroath, Scotland's famous fourteenth-century clarion call for independence from England, and **Montrose**, set between the sea and a wildlife-filled basin. Inland, the picturesque **Angus glens** cut into the hills, their villages, such as **Blairgowrie** and **Kirriemuir**, useful centres for hikers and skiers.

North of the glens, **Deeside** is a wild, unspoilt tract of land made famous by the royal family, who have favoured **Balmoral** as one of their prime residences since Queen

---

ACCOMMODATION PRICE CODES

Throughout this guide, hotel and B&B accommodation is priced on a scale of ① to ⑨, the number indicating the **lowest price** you could expect to pay per night in that establishment for a **double room** in high season. The prices indicated by the codes are as follows:

① under £40	④ £60–70	⑦ £110–150
② £40–50	⑤ £70–90	⑧ £150–200
③ £50–60	⑥ £90–110	⑨ over £200

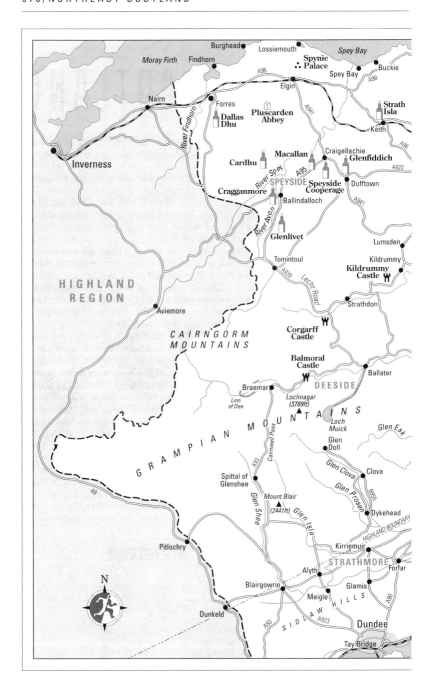

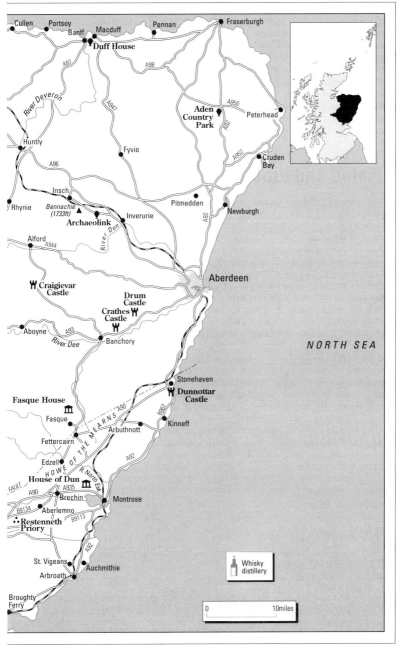

Cullen
Portsoy
Banff
Macduff
Pennan
Fraserburgh
Duff House
A97
A98
River Deveron
A947
A950
Aden Country Park
A92
Peterhead
Huntly
Fyvie
A952
Cruden Bay
A96
Insch
Pitmedden
Newburgh
Rhynie
Bennachie (1733ft)
Archaeolink
Inverurie
River Don
A92
Alford
A944
Craigievar Castle
Drum Castle
Crathes Castle
Aberdeen
Aboyne
A93
River Dee
Banchory

NORTH SEA

Stonehaven
Dunnottar Castle
Fasque House
Fasque
HOWE OF THE MEARNS
A90
Arbuthnott
B967
Kinneff
Fettercairn
A92
Edzell
HOWE OF THE
House of Dun
R North Esk
FAULT
A935
A90
Brechin
Montrose
B9134
Aberlemno
B9113
Restenneth Priory
A92
St. Vigeans
Auchmithie
Arbroath
Broughty Ferry

Whisky distillery

0   10miles

© Crown copyright

Victoria fell in love with it back in the 1840s. Beyond, the **Don Valley** is much quieter, while **Speyside**, a little way northwest, is best known as Scotland's premier **whisky**-producing region. The route around the northeast coast offers the best of Aberdeenshire and Moray, with rugged cliffs, empty beaches and historic fishing villages tucked into the coves and bays.

Northeast Scotland is well served by an extensive **road** network, with fast links between Dundee and Aberdeen, while the area north and east of Aberdeen is dissected by a series of efficient routes. **Trains** from the south connect to Dundee, Aberdeen and other towns on the coast, with an inland line from Aberdeen heading northwest to Elgin and on to Inverness. A reasonably comprehensive scheduled **bus service** is complemented by a network of **postbuses** in the Angus Glens. Only in the most remote and mountainous parts does public transport disappear altogether.

Dundee and around

At first sight, **DUNDEE** can seem a grim place. In the nineteenth century it became famous as the city built on three Js – jam, jute and journalism – but with the passing of industrialization and its maritime connections it became economically depressed and somewhat overshadowed by its northerly neighbour, Aberdeen. Today, however, it's still a refreshingly unpretentious and welcoming city, wonderfully placed on the banks of the Tay, with some good museums, a lively arts scene and useful transport connections throughout Angus.

Even prior to its Victorian heyday, Dundee was a town of considerable importance. It was here in 1309 that Robert the Bruce was proclaimed the lawful King of Scots, and during the Reformation the town earned itself a reputation for tolerance, sheltering leading figures such as George Wishart and John Knox. Destroyed during the Civil War by both Royalists and Cromwellian armies, Dundee was razed again by the early Jacobite John Graham of Claverhouse, Viscount Dundee (popularly known as "Bonnie Dundee"), prior to the Battle of Killiecrankie. The city picked itself up in the 1800s, its train and harbour links making it a major centre for shipbuilding, whaling and the manufacture of jute. Today, however, there's little left of Dundee's former glory, and its self-image hasn't been helped by the imposition of a couple of garish central shopping malls and the seemingly endless spread of 1970s housing estates around the city edges.

The journalism arm of Dundee's triad is maintained by D.C. Thomson, the local publishing giant which produces the timelessly popular *Beano* and *Dandy* comics; also part of the city's literary heritage is the nineteenth-century poet William McGonagall, still peerless as the world's worst poet. Dundee's jam factories resulted from the plentiful soft fruit grown in the Angus hinterland, and it is here that marmalade was invented in the nineteenth century by a local housewife determined not to let a cargo of Seville oranges go to waste.

The City

The best approach to Dundee is across the mile-and-a-half-long **Tay Road Bridge** from Fife. Offering a spectacular panorama of the city spread over the northern bank of the widening River Tay, the bridge, opened in 1966, has a central walkway for pedestrians. An 80p toll is levied on cars leaving the city, but you can enter from the south for free. Running parallel is the **Tay Rail Bridge**, opened in 1887 to replace the spindly structure which collapsed in a storm in 1879 only eighteen months after it was built, killing the crew and 75 passengers on a train passing over the bridge at the time. The present construction, over two miles long, is still claimed as the longest rail bridge in Europe.

Dundee's city centre is focused on **City Square**, a couple of hundred yards north of the Tay. The square and its surrounding streets have been much spruced up in recent years, with fountains, benches and extensive pedestrianization making for a relaxing environment, though the grand old buildings and churches have been rather overwhelmed by large shopping malls filled with the mundane mass of chain stores you see all over Britain.

A hundred yards north of City Square along Reform Street is the attractive **Albert Square**, with the imposing edifices of the D.C. Thomson building, Dundee High School and, on its eastern side, the **McManus Art Galleries and Museum** (Mon–Wed, Fri & Sat 10am–5pm, Thurs 10am–7pm, Sun 12.30–4pm; free), Dundee's most impressive Victorian structure, designed by Gilbert Scott, with curved stone staircases and extravagant Gothic elaborations. The museum gives an excellent overview of Dundee's past, with displays ranging from Pictish stones to the Tay Bridge disaster. On the ground floor, the most impressive exhibit is the skeleton of a whale, washed up on a nearby beach in 1883 and eulogized in one of William McGonagall's wonderfully dreadful poems. Upstairs, the magnificent **Albert Hall** – crowned by a roof of 480 pitchpine panels in a Gothic arch – houses antique musical instruments, decorative glass, gold, silver, sculpture and some exquisite furniture.

Across Ward Road from the museum, the **Howff Burial Ground**, on Meadowside (daily 9am–5pm or dusk), has some great carved tombstones dating from the sixteenth to nineteenth centuries. Five minutes' walk west of here, on West Henderson Wynd, in the Blackness area, an award-winning museum, **Verdant Works**, tells the story of jute from its harvesting in India to its arrival in Dundee on clipper ships (April–Oct Mon–Sat 10am–5pm, Sun 11am–5pm; Nov–March Mon–Sat 10am–4pm, Sun 11am–4pm; £5; combined ticket with Discovery Point £8.75). The museum, set in an old jute mill, recreates the turn-of-the-century factory floor, where you can watch jute being processed on fully operational quarter-size machines originally used for training workers.

Immediately west of the city centre, High Street becomes Nethergate and then Perth Road, which passes the University and as result has the best concentration of pubs, cafés and arts venues in the city. Principal among these is the exciting new **Dundee Contemporary Arts**, at 152 Nethergate (daily 10am–11pm; galleries: Tues–Sun 11.30am–7.30pm), a stunningly designed centre which incorporates galleries, a print studio, two art-cinema screens and an airy café-bar.

Just south of the city centre, at the water's edge alongside the Tay Road Bridge, **Discovery Point** is an impressive development centring on the Royal Research Ship *Discovery* (same hours as Verdant Works; £5). A three-mast, steam-assisted vessel built in Dundee in 1901 to take Captain Scott on his polar expeditions, it has been elegantly restored, with polished wood panels and brass trimmings giving scant indication of the privations suffered by the crew. Temperatures on board would plummet to –28° in the Antarctic, and turns at having a bath came round every 47 days. Enthusiastic guides spin some fascinating yarns about the boat's colourful history. A recent addition, "Polarama", a hands-on gallery, recreates some of the conditions on the polar ice caps.

In total contrast is the endearingly simple wooden frigate **Unicorn** (mid-March to Oct daily 10am–5pm; Nov to mid-March Mon–Fri 10am–4pm; £3.50), moored in Victoria Dock on the other side of the road bridge – there is a pathway between the two. Built in 1824, it's the oldest British warship still afloat and was in active service as recently as 1968. Although the ship is now mastless and the interior is sparse, the cannons, the splendid figureheads and the wonderful model of the ship in its fully rigged glory – 23.5 miles of rope would have been used – are fascinating.

Out from the centre

A mile or so north of town, **Dundee Law** is the plug of an extinct volcano and, at 571ft, the city's highest point. Once the site of a seventh-century defensive hill fort, it is now an impressive lookout, with great views across the whole city and the Tay – although the climb is steep and often windy. It takes thirty minutes to walk to the foot of the law from the city centre, or you can take buses #3 or #4 from Albert Square.

The city's other volcanic plug of rock sits a mile to the west of Dundee Law. **Balgay Hill** is skirted by the wooded **Lochee Park**, while at its summit sits the **Mills Observatory** (April–Sept Tues–Fri 11am–5pm, Sat & Sun 12.30–4pm; Oct–March Mon–Fri 4–10pm, Sat & Sun 12.30–4pm; free), Britain's only full-time public observatory with its own resident astronomer. The best time to go is after dark on winter nights; in summer there's little to be seen through the telescope, but well-explained, quirky exhibits and displays chart the history of space exploration and astronomy, and on sunny days you can play at being a human sundial or a shadow clock and take in the fantastic views over the city through little telescopes. Buses #2, #36 and #37 drop you in Balgay Road, at the entrance to the park.

Four miles east of Dundee's city centre lies the seaside settlement of **BROUGHTY FERRY**, now engulfed by the city as a reluctant suburb. In former days, jute barons built big villas on the hillside and the local fishermen lived in smaller cottages along the shoreline, and something of that eclectic mix is still apparent in the more recent rise of "The Ferry" (as it's called by locals) as a pleasant and relaxing spot with some good restaurants and pubs. It's far more unspoilt than Dundee, and you are much more aware of the sea than in the city, although the pollution levels on the beach itself are pretty dire. Right by the seashore, the striking **Broughty Castle and Museum** (April–Sept Mon–Sat 10am–5pm, Sun 12.30–4pm; Oct–March Tues–Sat 10am–5pm, Sun 12.30–4pm; free) was built in the fifteenth century. It's worth a look for the exhibits on local history, covering the story of Broughty Ferry as a fishing village, the history of whaling, and details of local geology and wildlife.

Practicalities

Dundee's **airport** (☎01382/643242) is five minutes' drive west from the city centre. There are no buses but a taxi will only set you back about £2. By **train**, you'll arrive at Taybridge Station on South Union Street, about 300yd south of the city centre, near the river. Long-distance **buses** arrive at the Seagate bus station, a couple of hundred yards east of the centre. Right in the centre of things, at 21 Castle St, Dundee's very helpful **tourist office** (June–Sept Mon–Sat 9am–6pm, Sun noon–4pm; Oct–May Mon–Sat 9am–5pm; ☎01382/527527) can book accommodation and bus tickets.

In Dundee and its neighbouring suburb, Broughty Ferry, there is a good range of **accommodation**. The *Queens Hotel*, 160 Nethergate (☎01382/322515; ⑤), is the city's grandest old hotel, with fine views of the Tay and good food. The *Shaftesbury Hotel*, 1 Hyndford St (☎01382/669216; ④), is a converted jute-merchant's house very near town, while the *Auld Steeple*, 94 Nethergate (☎01382/200302; ①), is a very central, inexpensive B&B. In Broughty Ferry, there are rooms above the *Fisherman's Tavern*, 12 Fort St (☎01382/775941; ②), and *Stonelee*, 69 Monifieth Rd (☎01382/737812; ①), offers decent B&B accommodation. The *Riverview Hostel*, 127 Broughty Ferry Rd (☎01382/450565), a student residence, has two small dorms and two twins on the upper level.

The West End of Dundee, around the principal university and Perth Road, is the best area for **eating** and drinking. The *Agacan*, 113 Perth Rd (☎01382/644227), is a unique, if tiny, Turkish restaurant with colourful and original paintings crowded onto its rough walls; *Deep Sea*, 81 Nethergate, is the best of Dundee's fish-and-chip restaurants; while *Raffles*, 18 Perth Rd, is a pricey but faultlessly stylish café-bar serving good vegetarian meals. In Broughty Ferry, another good place to head, *Nawab*, 43a Gray St, serves excellent balti and tandoori food, while *Visocchi's*, 40 Gray St, is an inexpensive Italian restaurant in a popular ice-cream café.

Of the city's **pubs**, *Laing's*, 8 Roseangle, off Perth Road, is usually packed on rare warm summer nights thanks to its beer garden and great views over the Tay. *Jute Café-bar*, at Dundee Contemporary Arts, is a hip place to drink with great views and inexpensive light meals, *The Mercantile*, 100 Commercial St, has an excellent range of beers, and the *Ship Inn*, 121 Fisher St, Broughty Ferry, offers great food and views over the Tay from the waterfront.

There are three **nightclubs**, *Fat Sam's*, *De Stihl's* and *Mardi Gras* – all on top of each other in South Ward Road, midway between the centre and the university precincts and popular with a studenty crowd. The prodigious Dundee Repertory Theatre (☎01382/223530), on Tay Square, north of Nethergate, is an excellent place for contemporary **theatre**. The best venue for **classical music**, including visits by the Royal Scottish Orchestra and other bigwigs, is Caird Hall (☎01382/434451), whose bulky frontage dominates City Square.

The Angus coast

Two roads link Dundee to Aberdeen and the northeast coast of Scotland – by far the more pleasant option is the slightly slower A92 coast road which joins the inland A90 at Stonehaven, just south of Aberdeen. Along the coast, which boasts both long, attractive beaches and some impressive cliffs, are the ports of **Arbroath** and **Montrose**, distinctive towns with a rich sense of history and some interesting sights.

Arbroath

Since it was settled in the twelfth century, local fishermen have been landing their catches at **ARBROATH**, situated on the Angus coast where it starts to curve in from the North Sea towards the Firth of Tay. The **Arbroath smokie** – line-caught haddock, smoke-cured over smouldering oak chips and then poached in milk – is one of Scotland's best-known dishes. Although the town has, like Dundee, suffered from messy development around its centre, the harbour area is still lively and interesting and attractive coastal cliffs and sands are within easy walking distance.

Chiefly due to its harbour, Arbroath had, by the late eighteenth century, become a trading and manufacturing centre, famed for boot-making and sail-making – the *Cutty Sark's* sails were made here. Arbroath's real glory days, however, were in the thirteenth century, with the completion of **Arbroath Abbey** (April–Sept daily 9.30am–6pm; Oct–March Mon–Sat 9.30am–4pm, Sun 2–4pm; £1.80; HS), whose rose-pink sandstone ruins, described by Dr Johnson as "fragments of magnificence", stand on Abbey Street, soaring above the rest of the town. Founded with royal patronage in 1178 and completed in 1233, it was the scene of one of the most significant events in Scotland's history when, on April 6, 1320, a group of Scottish barons drew up the **Declaration of Arbroath**, asking the pope to reverse his excommunication of Robert the Bruce and recognize him as king of a Scottish nation independent from England. The wonderfully resonant language of the document still makes for a stirring expression of Scottish nationhood: "For so long as one hundred of us remain alive, we will never in any degree be subject to the dominion of the English, since it is not for glory, riches or honour that we do fight, but for freedom alone, which no honest man loses but with his life." It was duly dispatched to Pope John XXII in Avignon, who in 1324 agreed to Robert's claim.

The abbey was dissolved during the Reformation, and by the eighteenth century it was little more than a source of red sandstone for local houses. However, there is still enough left to get a good idea of how vast the place must have been: the semicircular west doorway is more or less intact, complete with medieval mouldings, and the south transept has a beautiful round window, once lit with a beacon to guide ships. In the early

1950s, the Abbey hit the headlines when the **Stone of Destiny**, daringly stolen from London by a group of Scottish nationalists, mysteriously reappeared, wrapped in a Scottish flag, at the high altar, the place where Scotland's independence had first been so eloquently championed. The stone was taken back to Westminster Abbey but was recently "officially" returned to Scotland and is now kept in Edinburgh Castle.

Down by the harbour, the elegant, Regency **Signal House Museum** (Mon–Sat 10am–5pm; July & Aug also Sun 2–5pm; free) stands sentinel as it has since 1813. The interior is now given over to some excellent local history displays. A school room, fisherman's cottage and lighthouse kitchen have all been carefully re-created, with the addition of realistic smells.

Practicalities

Arbroath's helpful **tourist office**, at Market Place, right in the middle of town (April, May & Sept Mon–Fri 9am–5pm, Sat 10am–5pm; June–Aug Mon–Sat 9.30am–5.30pm, Sun 10am–3pm; Oct–March Mon–Fri 9am–5pm, Sat 10am–3pm; ☎01241/872609), will recommend local walks and can book accommodation. **Buses** stop at the station on Catherine Street, about a five-minute walk south of the tourist office, while **trains** arrive at the station just across the road, on Keptie Street.

The presence of the sea and harbour makes Arbroath a pleasant **place to stay**: the excellent *Five Gables Guest House* (☎01241/871632; ①), above the golf course, one mile south of town on the A92, has a great position overlooking the sea; down by the harbour is the *Harbour House Guest House*, 4 The Shore (☎01241/878047; ①). The harbour is also the place for **eating and drinking**: try the Arbroath smokies at *The Old Brewhouse* (☎01241/879945), a convivial and well-priced restaurant and pub, by the harbour wall at the end of High Street, or check out the *Smugglers Tavern*, on The Shore, where you can try some of the 180 varieties of rum.

Montrose and around

"Here's the Basin, there's Montrose, shut your een and haud your nose." As the old rhyme indicates, **MONTROSE**, a seaport and market town since the thirteenth century, can sometimes smell a little rich, mostly because of its position on the edge of a virtually landlocked two-square-mile lagoon of mud known as the Basin. Flooded and emptied twice daily by the tides, this is a rich nature reserve for the host of geese, swans and waders who frequent the ooze to look for food. On the south side of the basin, a mile out of Montrose along the A92, the **Montrose Basin Wildlife Centre** (daily: April–Oct 10.30am–5pm; Nov–March 10.30am–4pm; £2.50) is an impressive new facility where you can use binoculars, high-powered telescopes, bird hides and even remote-control video cameras to check out the diverse bird- and wildlife. The centre also has a resident ranger who regularly takes parties out for guided walks.

Montrose locals are known as Gable Endies, because of the unusual way in which the town's eighteenth- and nineteenth-century merchants, influenced by architectural styles they had seen on the continent, built their houses gable end to the street. The few original gabled houses which remain line the wide **High Street**, off which are numerous tiny alleyways and quiet courtyards. Two blocks behind the soaring kirk steeple at the lower end of High Street, in Panmure Place on the western side of Mid Links park, the **Montrose Museum and Art Gallery** (Mon–Sat 10am–5pm; free) is one of Scotland's oldest museums, dating from 1842. For a small-town museum, it has some particularly unusual exhibits, among them the so-called Samson Stone, a Pictish relic bearing a carving of Samson slaying the Philistines. On the upper floor, the maritime history exhibits include a cast of Napoleon's death mask and a model of a British man-of-war, sculpted out of bone by Napoleonic prisoners at Portsmouth.

Outside the entrance of the museum, a winsome study of a boy by local sculptor William Lamb is a taster for his work, more of which can be seen in the moving **William Lamb Memorial Studio**, on Market Street (July to mid-Sept Tues–Sun 2–5pm; for entry at other times ask at the museum; free). A superbly talented but largely unheralded modern artist, Lamb's work is made the more impressive by the fact that he re-taught himself to sculpt with his left hand, having suffered a war wound in his right.

Practicalities

The Montrose **tourist office** is squeezed into a former public toilet next to the library, where Bridge Street merges into the lower end of High Street (April–June & Sept Mon–Sat 10am–5pm; July & Aug Mon–Sat 9.30am–5.30pm; ☎01674/672000). Most **buses** stop in High Street, while the **train** station lies a block back on Western Road. For **accommodation**, try *Oaklands*, a B&B over the river bridge at 10 Rossie Island Rd (☎01674/672018, *oaklands12@aol.com*; ①), or the friendly *Murray Lodge Hotel*, 2–8 Murray St, the northern continuation of High Street (☎01674/678880; ③). An unusual alternative is *Kirkside* (☎01674/830780; ②), an isolated converted fishing bothy situated on the edge of the sand dunes by St Cyrus Nature Reserve, just over two miles north of Montrose, at the mouth of the North Esk River.

For **eating**, the liveliest place in Montrose is unquestionably *Roo's Leap*, a sports bar and restaurant by the golf club off the northern end of Traill Drive, near the beach; the food is an unlikely, but excellent, mix of Scottish, American and Australian. Its sister café-bar, the exuberant *Sharky's*, on George Street, serves coffee and light snacks, while the *Salutation Inn*, at 69–71 Bridge St, offers good, cheap food and has a beer garden. The more traditional *Cornerhouse Hotel*, on High Street, hosts folk nights on Tuesdays.

The House of Dun

Across the Basin, four miles west of Montrose, the Palladian **House of Dun** (Easter weekend & May–Sept daily 1.30–5pm; Oct Sat & Sun 1.30–5pm; house and grounds £3.90, grounds only £1; NTS), can be reached on the regular Montrose–Brechin bus (#30) – ask the driver to let you off outside. Built in 1730 for David Erskine, Laird of Dun, to designs by William Adam, the house has an easy-going grandeur not always found in art-laden country houses. It has been extensively restored, and is crammed full of period furniture and *objets d'art*. Inside, the ornate relief plasterwork is the most impressive feature, extravagantly emblazoned with Jacobite symbolism.

The Angus glens

Immediately north of Dundee, the low-lying Sidlaw Hills divide the city from the rich agricultural area of **Strathmore**, along which are found the tidy market towns of **Blairgowrie** and **Kirriemuir**, sprinkled with interesting Pictish stones and small museums. The Strathmore towns lie on a fertile strip along the southernmost edge of the Grampian Mountains, and act as gateways to the **Angus glens** – or "Braes o' Angus", tranquil valleys which penetrate deep into some of the most rugged and majestic landscape of northeast Scotland. The glens are a rain-swept, wind-blown, sparsely populated area, sometimes cut off by snow as early as October, and in the summer plagued by ferocious midges. The rolling hills and dales attract hikers, bird-watchers and botanists in the summer, grouse shooters and deer hunters in autumn and a growing number of skiers in winter.

Blairgowrie and around

The well-heeled town of **BLAIRGOWRIE** (officially Blairgowrie and Rattray), set among raspberry fields on the glen's southernmost tip, is as good a place as any to base yourself. The town is gathered around the Wellmeadow, a pleasant grassy triangle in the town centre, where St Ninian once camped. The **tourist office** (Easter–June, Sept & Oct Mon–Sat 9.30am–5.30pm, Sun 11am–4pm; July & Aug Mon–Sat 9am–7pm, Sun 10am–6pm; Nov–Easter Mon–Fri 9.30am–5.30pm, Sat 10am–2pm; ☎01250/872960) is on the high side of the Wellmeadow, and useful for booking local accommodation. **Bikes** can be rented from the *Blairgowrie Holiday Park* and from Mountains and Glens, on Railway Rd.

The best budget **places to stay** are some way up Glen Shee (see below). In town, try the excellent Ivybank House just across the main road bridge over the river on the Rattray side (☎01250/873056; ①), a B&B offering sweeping views of the river and surrounding hills. For **camping**, try the year-round *Blairgowrie Holiday Park*, on Rattray's Hatton Road (☎01250/872941). There are lots of places to **eat and drink**: for a more formal meal the best is *Cargills* (☎01250/876735; closed Mon), right by the river on Lower Mill Street. For lighter meals and takeaways, try the intriguing *Dome Restaurant*, opened by two local Italian families in the 1920s, and for a good pub meal try the *Brig o'Blair*, on the Wellmeadow, or head out of town up the A93 for six miles to the delightfully situated *Bridge of Cally Hotel* (☎01250/886231; ③), which also has rooms.

Meigle

Six miles east of Blairgowrie along the A926 is the unremarkable Strathmore town of Aylth, three miles south of which along the B954 is one of the foremost collections of Pictish stones in Scotland, located in a small schoolhouse in the unassuming village of **Meigle**. Housed in a modest former school building, the **Meigle Museum** (April–Sept daily 9.30am–6pm; £1.80; HS) holds one of Scotland's most important collections of early Christian and Pictish inscribed stones, with some thirty pieces dating from the seventh to the tenth centuries. Most impressive is the seven-foot-tall, two-tone cross slab, said to be the gravestone of Guinevere, King Arthur's wife; it's carved on one side with Daniel surrounded by lions and mythological creatures, and on the other with the "ring of glory" – a wheel containing a cross carved and decorated in high relief. The exact meaning and purpose of the stones and their enigmatic symbols is obscure, and why so many of the stones were found at Meigle is also a mystery. The most likely theory suggests that the settlement was once an important ecclesiastical centre which attracted secular burials of prominent Picts. Bus #57 runs hourly from Dundee and Perth.

Glen Shee

The most dramatic and best-known of the Angus glens, **Glen Shee** is dominated by its ski-fields, sprawled over four mountains above the Cairnwell mountain pass. In summer it's all a bit sad, with lifeless chair lifts and bare, scree-covered slopes, although hang-gliders take advantage of the crosswinds between the mountains and there are some excellent hiking and mountain biking routes. Nearly twenty miles north of Blairgowrie, at the **SPITTAL OF GLENSHEE**, there is an excellent bunkhouse run by *Cairnwell Mountains Sports* (☎01250/885255; ①), a good place to base yourself for summer or winter sports. They also hire skis, bikes and even offer hang-gliding lessons. This is also the turn-off to one of the nicest places to stay in the area, *Dalmunzie House* (☎01250/885224; ⑥), a gorgeous, turreted, Highland sporting lodge, evoking the peace and tranquillity of the rugged scenery. From the Spittal the road climbs another five miles or so to the ski centre at the crest of the Cairnwell Pass.

SKIING IN THE ANGUS GLENS

During the winter season – December to March – skiers, predominantly from the cities of central Scotland, brave the cold temperatures and bitter winds of Glen Shee. For **information**, call Ski Glenshee (☎013397/41320), which offers ski hire and lessons. Cairnwell Mountain Sports (☎01250/885255), located at the Spittal of Glenshee, rents skis, boards and telemark equipment, and also gives lessons. **Ski rental** starts at around £12 a day, while lessons are around £10 for two hours. **Lift passes** cost £17.50 per day or £70 for a five-day (Mon–Fri) ticket. For the latest snow and weather conditions call the Ski Hotline (☎0891/654656). For **accommodation**, contact Blairgowrie tourist information (☎01250/875800).

Kirriemuir and around

The sandstone town of **KIRRIEMUIR**, known locally as Kirrie, is set on a hill on the cusp of glens Clova and Prosen. Full of narrow closes, twisting wynds and steep braes, the main cluster of streets has all the appeal of an old film set, with the old-fashioned bars, tiled butcher's shop, tartan outlets and haberdasheries somehow managing to avoid being contrived and quaint – although the re-cobbling of the town centre, around a twee statue of Peter Pan, undermines this somewhat.

In the nineteenth century, as a linen manufacturing centre, it was made famous by a local handloom-weaver's son, J.M. Barrie, with his series of novels about "Thrums", in particular *A Window in Thrums* and his third novel, *The Little Minister.* The author was to become more famous still as the creator of Peter Pan, the little boy who never grew up, a story which Barrie penned in 1904 – some say as a response to a strange upbringing dominated by the memory of his older brother, who died as a child. **Barrie's birthplace**, a plain little whitewashed cottage at 9 Brechin Rd (Easter weekend & May–Sept Mon–Sat 11am–5pm, Sun 1.30–5pm; Oct Sat 11am–5pm, Sun 1.30–5pm; £2; NTS), displays his writing desk, photos and newspaper clippings. The washhouse outside – sentimentally billed as Barrie's first "theatre" – was apparently the model for the house built for Wendy in Never-Never Land.

Kirrie's helpful **tourist office** (April–June & Sept Mon–Sat 10am–5pm; July & Aug Mon–Sat 9.30am–5.30pm; ☎01575/574097) is in Cumberland Close, in the new development off the main square, behind *Visocchi's*. **Accommodation** can be found at *Crepto* B&B, Kinnordy Place (☎01575/572746; ①), or the respectable *Airlie Arms*, St Malcolm's Wynd (☎01575/572487; ③). *Visocchi's* is great for daytime **snacks**, while the *Airlie* or the *Thrums Hotel* are a good bet in the evening. The best place to eat in the area is six miles away, at the *Roundhouse Lodge*, at the foot of Glen Isla. Of the Kirrie **pubs**, the *Kilt and Clogs*, behind the tourist office, is the long-standing favourite. **Postbuses** into Glen Clova and Prosen leave from the main post office, Reform Street, at 8.30am (Mon–Sat). A second Glen Clova bus leaves at around 3pm (Mon–Fri) but only goes as far as Clova village before returning to Kirriemuir. Hourly buses connect with Forfar for onward travel.

Glamis Castle

Regular buses (#125; 4 daily; 40min) from Dundee to Forfar or Kirriemuir pass the pink-sandstone **Glamis Castle** (April–Oct daily 10.30am–4.45pm; castle and grounds £5.40, grounds only £2.50), a mile north of the picturesque village of **Glamis** (pronounced "Glahms"). A wondrously over-the-top, L-shaped five-storey pile set in an extensive landscaped park complete with deer and pheasants, this is one of the most famous Scottish castles. Shakespeare chose it as a central location in his *Macbeth*, and its contemporary royal connections – as the childhood home of the Queen Mother and birthplace of Princess Margaret – make it one of the essential stops on every bus tour of Scotland. It is also said to be one of the country's most haunted buildings.

Approaching the castle down the long main drive, the fantastical melee of turrets, towers and conical roofs are framed by the Grampian Mountains. Glamis began as a comparatively humble hunting lodge, used in the eleventh century by the kings of Scotland. In 1372, King Robert II gave the property to his son-in-law, Sir John Lyon, who built the core of the present building. His descendants, the earls of Kinghorne and Strathmore – the fourteenth of which was the Queen Mother's father – have lived here ever since.

Most of the castle can only be seen on the guided tours; these will point out plenty of connections to the Queen Mother, along with the wealth of ornaments, portraits, furniture and plasterwork which adorn the house. The highlight of the tour is the family **Chapel**, completed in 1688. Jacob de Wet was commissioned to reproduce as frescoes illustrations found in the family Bible, although his depictions of Christ wearing a hat and St Peter in a pair of glasses have raised eyebrows ever since. The chapel is said to be haunted by the spectre of a grey lady, the ghost of the sixth Lady Glamis, who was burnt as a witch under orders of James V. A little further on, **Duncan's Hall**, a fifteenth-century guardroom, is the traditional – but inaccurate – setting for Duncan's murder by Macbeth (it actually took place near Elgin).

Glamis' **grounds** are worth a few hours in their own right. Highlights include the lead statues of James VI and Charles I at the top of the main drive, the seventeenth-century Baroque sundial, the formal gardens, and the verdant walks out to Earl John's Bridge and through the woodland.

Glen Clova

Of all the Angus glens, **Glen Clova** – which in the north becomes Glen Doll – with its stunning cliffs, heather slopes and valley meadows, is often declared the finest. Wildlife is abundant, with deer on the mountains, wild hares, grouse and the occasional buzzard. The meadow flowers on the valley floor and arctic plants on the rocks – including great splashes of white and purple saxifrage – also make it something of a botanist's paradise.

The B955 from Dykehead and Kirriemuir divides at the Gella bridge over the swift-coursing River South Esk. Road traffic is unofficially encouraged to use the western branch of the road for travel up the glen and the eastern side heading south. Six miles north of Gella, the two branches of the road join up once more at the hamlet of **CLOVA**, which consists of little more than the hearty *Clova Hotel* (☎01575/550222; ③), which also has a bunkhouse (①). It's seldom a dull place, hosting regular barbecues, ceilidhs and even pleasure flights by helicopter or balloon. Meals and real ale are available in the lively bar. An excellent, if fairly strenuous, four-hour walk from behind the old school at the back of the hotel leads up into the mountains and around the lip of **Loch Brandy**, which legend predicts will one day flood and drown the valley below.

North from Clova village, the road turns into a rabbit-strewn lane coursing along the riverside for four miles to the car park and informal **campsite** in Glen Doll. This is a useful starting point for numerous superb walks. From the car park, it's only a few hundred yards further to the **youth hostel** (☎01575/550236; closed Nov to mid-March), a cheerful restored hunting lodge.

Aberdeen and around

Some 120 miles from Edinburgh, standing between the mouths of the rivers Dee and Don smack in the middle of the northeast coast, **ABERDEEN** is commonly known as the Granite City. The third largest city in Scotland, it's a place that people either love or

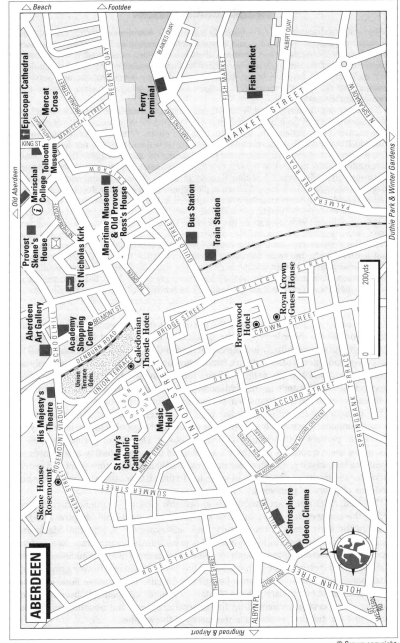

ABERDEEN

△ Beach   △ Footdee
△ Old Aberdeen
▷ Duthie Park & Winter Gardens
▽ Ringroad & Airport

Episcopal Cathedral
Mercat Cross
Marischal College Tolbooth Museum
Provost Skene's House
Maritime Museum & Old Provost Ross's House
St Nicholas Kirk
Ferry Terminal
Fish Market
Bus Station
Train Station
Aberdeen Art Gallery
Academy Shopping Centre
Caledonian Thistle Hotel
His Majesty's Theatre
Skene House Rosemount
St Mary's Catholic Cathedral
Music Hall
Brentwood Hotel
Royal Crown Guest House
Satrosphere
Odeon Cinema

Union Terrace Gdns.

MARKET STREET
BLAIKIE'S QUAY
REGENT QUAY
VIRGINIA STREET
MARISCHAL STREET
KING ST
CASTLE STREET
JUSTICE STREET
SHIPROW
NETHERKIRKGATE
THE GREEN
GUILD STREET
COLLEGE STREET
CROWN STREET
BRIDGE STREET
BELMONT ST
SCHOOLHILL
DENBURN ROAD
ROSEMOUNT VIADUCT
UNION TERRACE
GOLDEN SQUARE
UNION STREET
DEE STREET
HOLBURN STREET
SKENE STREET
ROSE STREET
SUMMER STREET
THISTLE STREET
ALBYN PL.
ALFORD LANE
BON ACCORD STREET
BON ACCORD TERRACE
BON ACCORD CRESCENT
SPRINGBANK TERRACE
PALMERSTONE ROAD
ALBERT QUAY
JAMESON'S QUAY
FISH MARKET
N.ESP(LANADE)
N.ESP W
HOLTON STREET
WEST(ERN) RD

0   200yds

N

© Crown copyright

OIL AND ABERDEEN

When **oil** was discovered in BP's Forties Field in 1970, Aberdonians rightly viewed it as a massive financial opportunity, and, despite fierce competition from other east coast British ports, Scandinavia and Germany, the city succeeded in persuading the oil companies to base their headquarters here. Land was made available for housing and industry, millions were invested in the harbour and offshore developments, new schools opened and the airport expanded to include a heliport, which has since become the busiest in the world.

The city's **population** swelled by 60,000, and earnings escalated from 15 percent below the national average to a figure well above it. Wealthy oil companies built prestigious offices, swish new restaurants, upmarket bars and shops. At the peak of production in the mid-1980s, 2.6 million barrels a day were being turned out, and the price had reached $80 a barrel – from which it plummeted to $10 during the slump of 1986. The effect was devastating – jobs vanished at the rate of a thousand a month, house prices dropped and Aberdeen soon discovered just how dependent it was on oil. The moment oil prices began to rise again, the loss of 167 lives in the **Piper Alpha disaster** deeply scarred the industry and precipitated an array of much-needed but very expensive safety measures.

In recent years production has steadily risen back up to levels not seen since the early Eighties, although with assurances that this time the dangers of boom-and-bust policies have been heeded. Oil remains the cornerstone of the Aberdeen economy, keeping unemployment down to some of the lowest levels in Britain and driving up house prices not just in the city but in an increasingly wide area of the rural northeast hinterland. Predictions of the imminent decline in oil reserves and the end of Aberdeen's economic honeymoon are heard regularly, as they have been ever since 1970, but there are fairly reliable indications that the black gold will still be flowing well into the next millennium.

hate. As Lewis Grassic Gibbon, one of the northeast's most eminent novelists, summed it up: "One detests Aberdeen with the detestation of a thwarted lover. It is the one hauntingly and exasperatingly lovable city of Scotland." Certainly, while some extol the many hues and colours of Aberdeen's famous **granite** architecture, others see only uniform grey and find the city grim, cold and unwelcoming. The weather doesn't help: Aberdeen lies on a latitude north of Moscow and the cutting wind and driving rain can be tiresome, even if it does transform the buildings into sparkling silver.

The presence of the **oil** industry has made Aberdeen an almost obscenely wealthy and self-confident place – only four percent of Scotland's population live in the city, yet it has eight percent of the country's spending power. Despite, or perhaps because of this, it can seem a soulless city; there's a feeling of corporate sterility and sometimes, despite its long history, Aberdeen seems to exist only as a departure point and service station for the transient population of some ten to fifteen thousand who live on the hundred-plus offshore oil platforms.

That said, Aberdeen's **architecture** is undeniably striking – a granite cityscape created in the nineteenth century by three fine architects: Archibald Simpson and John Smith in the early years of the century, and, subsequently, A. Marshall Mackenzie. Classical inspiration and Gothic-revival styles predominate, giving grace to a material once thought of as only good enough for tombs and paving stones. In addition, it sometimes seems like every spare inch of ground has been turned into **flower gardens**, the urban parks being some of the most beautiful in Britain. This positive floral explosion – Aberdeen has been debarred from "Britain in Bloom" competitions because it kept winning – has certainly cheered up the general greyness, but nonetheless the new image, just like the first, is always at the mercy of the weather.

Some history

In the twelfth century, Alexander I noted "Aberdon" as one of his principal towns, and by the thirteenth century, it had become a centre for **trade** and **fishing**, a jumble of timber and wattle houses perched on three small hills, with the castle to the east and St Nicholas' Kirk outside the gates to the west.

It was here that **Robert the Bruce** sought refuge during the Scottish Wars of Independence, leading to the establishment of a garrison in the castle by Edward I and Balliol's supporters. In a night-time raid in 1306, the townspeople attacked the garrison and killed them all, an event commemorated by the city's motto "Bon Accord", the watchword for the night. The victory was not to last, however, and in 1337 Edward III stormed the city – an event which precipitated the rebuilding of the city on a grander scale. A century later, Bishop Elphinstane founded the Catholic **University** in the area north of town known today as **Old Aberdeen**, while the rest of the city developed as a mercantile centre and important port.

Industrial and economic expansion led to the Aberdeen New Streets Act in 1800, setting off a hectic half-century of development that almost led to financial disaster. Luckily, the city was rescued by a boom in trade: in the **shipyards** the construction of **Aberdeen Clippers** revolutionized sea transport, giving Britain supremacy in the China tea trade, and in 1882, a group of local businessmen acquired a **steam** tugboat for trawl fishing: sail gave way to steam and fisher families flooded in. By the mid-twentieth century Aberdeen's traditional industries were in decline, but the discovery of **oil** in the North Sea in the 1970s transformed the place from a depressed port into a boom town.

Arrival, information and city transport

Aberdeen's Dyce **airport**, seven miles northwest of town, is served by flights from most parts of the UK and a few European cities. The #27 airport bus (Mon–Fri roughly every 45min until 5.20pm; £1.30) runs to Union Street and the bus station; after 5.20pm and at weekends, you'll have to depend on the #27A (every 60–90min) or take a taxi (£9). The **train** and **bus stations** are beside each other, on Guild Street, in the centre of the city. Aberdeen is also linked to Lerwick, in Shetland, and Stromness, in Orkney, by P&O **ferries** (☎01224/572615), with regular crossings from Jamieson's Quay in the harbour.

From the stations it's a two-minute walk up the hill to Union Street, Aberdeen's main thoroughfare, and only a little further to the **tourist office**, on Broad Street, just north of Union Street at its eastern, seaward end (June & Sept Mon–Sat 9am–5pm, Sun 10am–2pm; July & Aug Mon–Sat 9am–7pm, Sun 10am–4pm; Oct–May Mon–Fri 9am–5pm, Sat 10am–2pm; ☎01224/632727), which can book accommodation and produces the useful monthly magazine, *Listings Aberdeen*. The best place for more esoteric information – anything from t'ai chi workshops to festivals and ceilidhs – is the Lemon Tree Arts Centre, 5 West North St (☎01224/642230), which produces a glossy bi-monthly programme.

Aberdeen is best explored on foot, but you might need to use **local buses**, almost all of which pass along Union Street, to reach some of the sights, including Old Aberdeen, in the north of the city. **Taxis**, which operate from ranks throughout the city centre, are rarely necessary, except late at night. If you don't manage to hail one, call Mairs Taxis (☎01224/724040).

Accommodation

As befits a high-flying business city, Aberdeen has a large choice of **accommodation**. Unfortunately, though, as most visitors are here on business, much of it is characterless and expensive, although some of the swankier places sometimes offer good-value weekend deals. Predictably, the best budget options are the **B&Bs** and **guest houses**, many of which are strung along Bon Accord and Crown streets (buses #6, #17 and #26 to and from Union Street) and the Great Western Road (buses #18, #19 and #24). Cheaper yet are the **youth hostel** and the **student halls** left vacant for visitors in the summer months. There's also a **campsite** in the suburbs.

Hotels, B&Bs and guest houses

Bracklinn Guest House, 348 Great Western Rd (☎01224/317060). Welcoming Victorian house with elegant furnishings – one of the city's best B&Bs. ②.

Campbell's Guest House, 444 King St (☎01224/625444, *cam444@zetnet.co.uk*). One mile from the city centre and handy for the beach. Highly recommended breakfasts. ②.

Cedars Private Hotel, 339 Great Western Rd (☎01224/583225). Small hotel with a friendly atmosphere. ③.

Ferryhill House Hotel, 169 Bon Accord St (☎01224/590867). One of the most historic pubs in Aberdeen, with colourful rooms and good food. ⑤.

Fourways Guest House, 435 Great Western Rd (☎01224/310218). A converted manse in the west end of town. ②.

The Jay's Guest House, 422 King St (☎01224/638295, *jaysguesthouse@clara.net*). Well-run, non-smoking house located in Old Aberdeen, near the University. ③.

Mannofield Hotel, 447 Great Western Rd (☎01224/315888). Charming old granite building, once a posh private house, a mile west of town. Excellent-value three-course dinners. ④.

Palm Court Hotel, 81 Seafield Rd (☎01224/310351, *info@palmcourt.co.uk*). Plush West End establishment with popular conservatory bistro-bar. ④.

Simpson's Hotel, 59 Queen's Road (☎01224/327777, *address@simpsonshotel.com*). Highly style-conscious, terracotta-coloured modern interior to this large granite terrace house, with an excellent brasserie and good weekend rates. ⑤.

Hostels, campus accommodation and campsites

Crombie Johnstone Halls, College Bounds, Old Aberdeen (☎01224/273301). Private rooms in probably the best of the student halls available, in one of the most interesting parts of the city.

Hazelhead Campsite, five miles west of centre (☎01224/321268). Grassy campsite with a swimming pool nearby. Follow signs from ring road or take buses #14 or #15. Closed Oct–March.

King George VI Memorial Hostel, 8 Queen's Rd (☎01224/646988 or central reservations ☎0541/553255). Rather soulless SYHA youth hostel with rooms for four to six people and a 2am curfew. Bus #14 and #15 from the bus and train stations.

The City

Aberdeen divides neatly into five main areas. The **city centre**, roughly bounded by Broad Street, Union Street, Schoolhill and Union Terrace, features the opulent **Marischal College**, the colonnaded **Art Gallery**, with its fine collection, and homes that predate Aberdeen's nineteenth-century town planning and have been preserved as **museums**. Union Street continues west to the comparatively cosmopolitan **West End**, where much of the city's decent nightlife, plus a couple of sights, can be found amid the tall grey town houses. To the south, the **harbour** still heaves with boats serving the fish and oil industries, while north of the centre lies attractive **Old Aberdeen**, a village neighbourhood presided over by **King's College** and **St Machar's Cathedral** and dominated by the presence of the university. The magnificent **beach** marks the city's entire eastern border.

The city centre

Any exploration of the city centre should begin at the east end of the mile-long **Union Street**, whose impressive architecture, sometimes lost among the shoppers and chain stores, finishes up at **Castlegate**, where Aberdeen's long-gone castle once stood. An open cobbled area, it is now graced by the late seventeenth-century **Mercat Cross**, carved with a unique gallery of Stewart sovereigns alongside some fierce gargoyles. Castlegate was once the focus of city life but nowadays is rather lifeless. However, the view up gently rising Union Street – a jumble of grey spires, turrets and jostling double-decker buses – is quintessential Aberdeen and well worth taking a moment or two to savour.

The granite **Town House** looms over the Union Street end of Castlegate – a discreet door on the side of this leads into the **Tolbooth Museum** (April–Sept Tues–Sat 10am–5pm, Sun 12.30–3.30pm; £2.50; combined ticket with Maritime Museum and Provost Skene's House £5), quarried out of the seventeenth-century prison which lurks behind the steely grey nineteenth-century exterior. The theme of the museum is law and imprisonment; climbing the claustrophobic staircases and squeezing into tiny, airless cells certainly gives plenty of opportunity to appreciate the harsh realities of incarceration. A suitably chilling audio-visual display featuring a talking model of a Jacobite prisoner complete with rattling chains can be seen, along with some fascinating maps and 3D models charting Aberdeen's development from its old-town beginnings.

Heading west down Union Street brings you to Broad Street, where Aberdeen's oldest surviving private house, **Provost Skene's House**, dating from 1545, cowers behind the modern offices at 45 Guestrow (Mon–Sat 10am–5pm, Sun 1–4pm; £2.50, combined ticket with Maritime and Tolbooth museums £5). In the sixteenth century, all the well-to-do houses in the area looked like this, with mellow stone and rounded turrets – yet it was only the intervention of the Queen Mother in 1938 which saved this house from the fate of its neighbours. Little has been altered since the Provost of Aberdeen lived here from 1676 to 1685.

On Broad Street itself stands Aberdeen's most imposing edifice and the world's second largest granite building after El Escorial in Madrid – the exuberant **Marischal College**, whose tall, steely grey pinnacled neo-Gothic facade is in absolute contrast to the eyesore that houses the tourist office opposite. This spectacular architecture, with its soaring, surging lines, has been painted and sketched more than any other in Aberdeen, and though not to everyone's taste – it was once described by a minor art historian as "a wedding cake covered in indigestible grey icing" – there's no escaping the fact that it is a most extraordinary feat of sculpture. The college itself was founded in 1593 by the fourth Earl Marischal, and coexisted for over two centuries as a separate Protestant university from the Catholic college, King's, just up the road. It was long Aberdeen's boast that their city had as many universities as the whole of England, and it wasn't until 1860 that the two were united as the University of Aberdeen. The facade fronts an earlier quadrangle designed by Archibald Simpson in 1837–1841. After the merger, the central tower was more than doubled in height by A. Marshall Mackenzie in 1893 and the profusion of spirelets added, though the facade was not totally completed until 1906.

Behind the tower, through the college entrance, the Mitchell Hall's east window illustrates the history of the university in stained glass. The fan-vaulted lobby, once the college's old hall, now houses the wonderful **Anthropological Museum** (Mon–Fri 10am–5pm, Sun 2–5pm; free), made up of two large rooms that contain a wealth of weird exhibits, among them a series of Eskimo soapstone carvings, an outrigger canoe carved from a breadfruit tree from Papua New Guinea, a macabre Hawaiian head crafted from basketry and a Tibetan prayer wheel. Most bizarre are the high-relief mummy case of an Egyptian five-year-old girl and a stomach-churning foot, unbound and preserved in brine.

Between Upperkirkgate and Union Street stands the long **St Nicholas' Kirk** (May–Sept Mon–Fri noon–4pm, Sat 1–3pm, Oct–April Mon–Fri 10am–1pm; free), actually two churches in one with a solid bell tower rising from the middle, from where the 48-bell carillon, the largest in Britain, regularly chimes across the city. Take time to explore the large peaceful churchyard, which, with its green marble tombs and Baroque monuments, seems a million miles from the bustling main street.

A little further west up Schoolhill, Aberdeen's engrossing **Art Gallery** (Mon–Sat 10am–5pm, Sun 2–5pm; free) was purpose-built in 1884 to a Neoclassical design by Mackenzie. You enter into the airy **Sculpture Court**, whose walls are lined with contemporary British paintings, many by Scottish artists. Highlights of the room are two Barbara Hepworth sculptures, including the central fountain, and the thick pillars running down from the upper balcony, each hewn from a different local marble. Off to one side is the **Contemporary Arts and Crafts Gallery**, which includes work by one of the finest silversmiths in Europe, Malcolm Appleby, who lives in the nearby village of Crathes. Beyond this is the **Memorial Court**, a calming, white-walled circular room under a skylit dome that serves as the city's principal war memorial. The upstairs rooms house the majority of the gallery's painting collection. The displays are changed fairly regularly, but you'll find some impressive works by British Impressionists and Modernists on the balcony overlooking the central Sculpture Court; look out for Stanley Spencer's joyful portrait of the British seaside in *Southwold* and his dramatic *Crucifixion*, Robert Brough's half-dazed *View of Elgin* and Duncan Grant's haunting *Self-portrait*.

West of the gallery, across the rail bridge, the sunken **Union Terrace Gardens**, bordered by the sparkling light-grey granite buildings of Union Terrace, are a welcome relief from the hubbub of heavy traffic on Union Street. In summer you'll catch free brass bands and orchestral performances, making it a great place to have a picnic. From here there are views across to the three domes of the Central Library, St Mark's Church and His Majesty's Theatre, traditionally referred to as "Education, Salvation and Damnation".

The West End

Tatty gentility characterizes much of the **West End**, the area around the westernmost part of Union Street, which roughly begins at the great granite columns of the city's **Music Hall**. A block north is **Golden Square** – a misnomer, as the trim houses, pubs and restaurants surrounding the statue of the Duke of Gordon are uniformly grey. The city has invested much in gentrifying the area north of Union Street, resulting in neat cobbles, old-fashioned lamps and mushrooming designer boutiques. Huntly Street, west of Golden Square, heads off towards the curiously thin spire of **St Mary's Catholic Cathedral** (daily: April–Oct 8.30am–5pm; Nov–March 8.30am–4pm), a typically forbidding example of Victorian-Gothic church architecture.

On the southern side of Union Street, wedged between Bon Accord Street and Bon Accord Terrace, **Bon Accord Square** is a typical, charming Aberdeen square. In the middle, a grassy centre surrounds a great hulk of granite, commemorating **Alexander Sampson**, architect of much of nineteenth-century Aberdeen. West of Bon Accord Terrace is Justice Mill Lane, home to many of the city's favourite bars and nightclubs, and also to the **Satrosphere** (school terms Mon & Wed–Fri 10am–4pm, Sat 10am–5pm, Sun 1.30–5pm; school holidays Mon–Sat 10am–5pm, Sun 1.30–5pm; £4.50, children £2.25), Aberdeen's thoroughly entertaining hands-on science exhibition.

The harbour

The old cobbled road of Shiprow winds down from Castlegate, at the east end of Union Street, to the north side of the harbour. Just off this steep road, peering out to the harbour through a striking modern glass facade, is **Aberdeen Maritime Museum** (Mon–Sat 10am–5pm, Sun noon–3pm; £3.50; combined ticket with Provost Skene's

House and Tolbooth Museum £5), an unlikely combination of a thoroughly modern, airy museum and Aberdeen's oldest surviving building, **Old Provost Ross's House**. The marriage has been very successful, however, and the museum is an engrossing, imaginatively designed tribute to the past and present importance of the sea to Aberdeen. Well-designed displays and audio-visual presentations, many of which draw on personal reminiscences, tell the story of herring fishing, whaling, shipbuilding, lighthouses and the oil and gas industry. Rising up through the centre of the museum is an incredible, 27-foot-high model of an oil rig. Passages lead into Provost Ross's House, where there are displays of intricate ship's models and a variety of nautical paintings and drawings.

At the bottom of Shiprow, the cobbles meet Market Street, which runs the length of the **harbour**. Here, brightly painted oil-supply ships, sleek cruise ships and peeling fishing boats jostle for position to the sounds of an ever-constant clatter and the screech of well-fed seagulls. It's not always the most salubrious area, but follow your nose down the road to the **fish market**, best visited early (7–8am) when the place is in full swing. The current market building dates from 1982, but fish has been traded here for centuries – the earliest record dating back to 1281 when an envoy of Edward I's was charged for one thousand barrels of sturgeon and five thousand salt fish.

Back at the north end of Market Street, Trinity Quay runs to the shipbuilding yards and down York Street to the east corner of the harbour, where you'll come to Aberdeen's **Footdee** or "fitee", a quaint, nineteenth-century fishermen's village – an easy walk (or bus #14) from Union Street. The higgledy-piggledy cottages back onto the sea, their windows and doors facing inwards to protect from storms but also, they say, to prevent the Devil from sneaking in the back door. From Market Street it's a twenty-minute walk (bus #6 from Market Street or buses #16 and #17 from Union Street) to **Duthie Park** (9.30am–dusk; free), situated on the banks of the Dee at the end of Polmuir Road. The rose garden here, known as Rose Mountain due to its profusion of blooms, can be stunning in summer, but the real treat is the **Winter Gardens** – a steamy jungle paradise of enormous cacti, exotic plants and even tropical birds jokingly held to be a favourite haunt with mean Aberdonians saving on their heating bills.

Old Aberdeen

An independent burgh until 1891, the tranquil district of **Old Aberdeen**, a twenty-minute bus ride (#20) north of the city centre, has always maintained a separate, village-like identity. Dominated by King's College and St Machar's Cathedral, its medieval cobbled streets, tiny wynds and little lanes are conserved beautifully, despite the pervasive and sometimes inelegant presence of the university.

The southern half of High Street is overlooked by **King's College Chapel** (Mon–Fri 9am–5pm), the first and finest of the college buildings, completed in 1495 with a chunky Renaissance spire. Named in honour of James IV, the chapel's west door is flanked by his coat of arms and those of his queen. The chapel stands on the quadrangle, whose gracious buildings retain a medieval plan but were built much later. Inside the screen, the stalls – each unique – and the ribbed, arched ceiling are rare and beautiful examples of medieval Scottish wood-carving. The remains of Bishop Elphinstane's tomb and the carved pulpit from nearby St Machar's are also here. A spanking new **visitor centre** (Mon–Sat 10am–5pm, Sun noon–5pm; free) in the main college buildings tells the tempestuous tale of the establishment of the University of Aberdeen.

From the college, the cobbled High Street leads a short way north to **St Machar's Cathedral** (daily 9am–5pm; free), on the leafy Chanonry, overlooking Seaton Park and the River Don. The site was reputedly founded in 580 by Machar, when he was sent by Columba to find a grassy platform near the sea, overlooking a river shaped like the crook on a bishop's crozier. This setting fitted the bill perfectly, and the cathedral was one of the city's first great granite edifices.

The beach

Among large British cities, Aberdeen could surely claim to have the best **beach**. Less than a mile to the east of Union Street is a great two-mile sweep of clean sand, broken by groynes and lined all along with an esplanade. On a sunny day, most of the city seems to be down there. By the southern end of the beach is a burgeoning modern complex of cinemas, fast-food eyesores and concrete-rich expanses. Squeezed between this, a couple of fairly tatty amusement parks and a vast leisure centre, there are a couple of cafés and bars which are established favourites with Aberdonians for ice-cream treats and Sunday morning brunch. As you head further north, most of the beach's hinterland is devoted to successive golf links. Bus #14 runs along the southern esplanade.

Eating, drinking and entertainment

Aberdeen is certainly not short of good places to **eat**, though inevitably you will find it more pricey than elsewhere in northeast Scotland. Union Street and the surrounding area has a glut of attractive **restaurants** and **cafés**. As for **nightlife**, like most ports of call, Aberdeen caters for a transient population with a lot of disposable income and a desire to get drunk as quickly as possible. There is no shortage of loud, flashy bars catering to such needs; however, there are still a number of more traditional old **pubs** which, though usually packed, are well worth a visit.

Restaurants and cafés

Ashvale, 46 Great Western Rd. One of Scotland's finest, and biggest, fish-and-chip shops, with seating for 300. Restaurant open daily until 11pm; takeaway until 1am. Inexpensive.

Café 52, The Green (☎01224/590094). Uncomplicated but original food on the old, cobbled "Green" down below the south side of Union Street. Closed Mon. Inexpensive.

La Lombarda, corner of Castlegate and King Street (☎01224/640916). A smart but lively trattoria which has been serving up pasta since 1922. Inexpensive to moderate.

Lemon Tree, 5 West North St (☎01224/642230). Easy-going arts centre café with good vegetarian and vegan snacks and meals. Inexpensive.

Martha's Vineyard, 1 Alford Lane (☎01224/213795). Highly regarded West End bistro with an excellent menu of European/Scottish cuisine. There's a more formal restaurant upstairs. Moderate. Closed Mon eve & Sun.

Silver Darling Restaurant, Pocra Quay, North Pier (☎01224/576229). Pricey, but the best seafood restaurant in town, located at the mouth of the Dee, in Footdee. Closed Sat lunch & Sun. Expensive.

Soul & Spice Café Bar, 15–17 Belmont St (☎01224/645200). Entertaining and colourful café serving up fantastic African and Caribbean dishes. On Thursday nights you can barter for your food. Moderate. Closed Mon.

Wild Boar, 19 Belmont St (☎01224/625357). Upbeat brasserie with well-priced vegetarian food, soups, salads and oriental-style noodles, as well as great cake and coffee through the day. Food served till 9pm (8pm Fri & Sat), after which DJs move in. Moderate.

Pubs and bars

Bex Bar, Justice Mill Lane. Trendy spot packed at weekends; one of a number of pubs and clubs along this West-End street.

Carriages, *Brentwood Hotel*, 101 Crown St. Unusually lively hotel cellar bar with the city's largest range of real ales and ciders. Also serves excellent bar food.

Ma Cameron's Inn, Little Belmont Street. Aberdeen's oldest pub, though only a section remains of the original. Serves food.

Frankenstein Pub, 504 Union Street. The full horror theme with monsters and test-tubes lining the walls. DJs play at weekends and food is served from 9am until closing time.

Nicky Tam's, 44 Market St. "Olde-worlde" pub but revels in its quirkiness. The only approachable bar in the harbourside area.

The Prince of Wales, 7 St Nicholas Lane. Venerated Aberdeen pub with a long bar and flagstone floor. Very central and renowned for its real ales, it's often crowded.

RSVP, Academy Shopping Centre, Schoolhill. Stylish and busy new venue with designer furniture and live jazz on a Sunday afternoon. Open daily till midnight.

St Machar Bar, 97 High St, Old Aberdeen. The medieval quarter's sole pub, a pokey, old-fashioned bar inevitably full of King's College students.

Clubs and live music venues

Franklyn's, Justice Mill Lane. Part of the same complex as the *Bex Bar*, with three very different rooms: a piano bar; a club bar with live bands (Fri & Sat); and crowd-pleasing chart music pumping out in the main dance area.

Lemon Tree, 5 W North St. The fulcrum of the city's arts scene with a great buzz and regular live music, comedy and folk.

Ministry of Sin, 16 Dee St. The hottest dance club for miles – Sunday nights are legendary. Occasionally has big-name guest DJs.

O'Donnaghue's, 16 Justice Mill Lane. Aberdeen's most popular Irish bar, with a large venue upstairs hosting medium-sized touring gigs.

Oh Henrys, Adelphi Close. Flash studenty club just off Union Street with regular theme nights.

Theatres and concert halls

Tickets to most of the venues listed below can be bought from the **box office** beside the Music Hall on Union Street (Mon–Sat 10am–6pm; ☎01224/641122).

Aberdeen Arts Centre, 33 King St (☎01224/635208). A variety of theatrical productions alongside a programme of lectures and exhibitions.

Cowdray Hall, Schoolhill (☎01224/523700). Classical music, often with visiting orchestras.

His Majesty's, Rosemount Viaduct (☎01224/637788). Aberdeen's main theatre, in a beautifully restored Edwardian building, with a programme that ranges from highbrow drama and opera to pantomime.

Lemon Tree, 5 West North St (☎01224/642230). Avant-garde events with off-the-wall comedians and plays – many are a spin-off from Edinburgh's festival.

Music Hall, Union Street (☎01224/632080). Big-name comedy and music acts.

Stonehaven and Dunottar Castle

South of Aberdeen, the A92 and the main train line follow the coastline to Stonehaven, a pretty harbour town and base for nearby Dunottar Castle. **STONEHAVEN** is a busy, pebble-dashed town, split into two parts, the picturesque working harbour area being most likely to detain you. On the north side of the harbour, Stonehaven's oldest building, the **Tolbooth** (June–Sept Mon & Thurs–Sat 10am–noon & 2–5pm; Wed & Sun 2–5pm; free), built as a storehouse during the construction of Dunnottar Castle, is now a museum of local history and fishing. On calm summer evenings, you can also take **boat trips** from the harbour to the RSPB reserve at Fowlsheugh (June & July Tues and Fri at 6pm). The old High Street connects the harbour and its surrounding old town with the late eighteenth-century planned centre on the other side of the River Carron. On New Year's Eve, High Street is the setting for the ancient ceremony of **Fireballs**, when locals parade its length, swinging metal cages full of burning debris around their heads. This, it is said, wards off evil spirits for the year ahead.

Two miles outside Stonehaven (the tourist office sells a walking guide for the scenic amble), **Dunnottar Castle** (Easter–Oct Mon–Sat 9am–6pm, Sun 2–5pm; Nov–Easter Mon–Fri 9am–dusk; £3) is one of the finest of Scotland's ruined castles, a dramatic ninth-century fortress set on a three-sided sheer cliff jutting into the sea – a setting striking enough to be chosen as the setting for Zeffirelli's movie version of *Hamlet*. Once the principal fortress of the northeast, the ruins are worth a good root around, and there are any number of dramatic views out to the crashing sea. Siege and blood-stained drama splatter the castle's past: in 1297 William Wallace burned the whole English Plantaganet garrison alive here, while one of the more gruesome tales from the castle's history tells of the imprisonment and torture of 122 men and 45 women Covenanters in 1685 – an event, as it says on the Covenanters' Stone in the churchyard, "whose dark shadow is for evermore flung athwart the Castled Rock".

Stonehaven's **tourist office** is at 66 Allardice St, the main street past the square (April–May & Oct Mon–Sat 10am–1pm & 2–5pm; June & Sept Mon–Sat 10am–1pm & 2–6pm, Sun 1–6pm; July & Aug Mon–Sat 10am–7pm, Sun 1–7pm; ☎01569/762806). For **bike rental** and advice about good tracks in local forests and cycling to Dunnottar, seek out Ruftrack Bikes, at 56 Barclay St, one block from the tourist office. Among the **places to stay**, *Arduthie House*, Ann St, is a good B&B (☎01569/762381; ②), as is the *Braemar*, Evan St (☎01569/764841; ①). *Dunottar Mains Farm* (☎01569/ 762621; ①) is a well-situated B&B right by Dunnottar Castle, a few miles south of town. For **food**, the *Tolbooth Seafood Restaurant* (closed Mon; ☎01569/762287), above the museum on the harbour, is well worth its high prices. Try the entertaining *Marine Hotel* and *Ship Inn*, both on the harbour, for **drinking** or pub food.

Deeside

More commonly known as **Royal Deeside**, the land stretching west of the coast along the River Dee revels in its connections with the royal family, who have regularly holi-dayed here, at **Balmoral Castle**, since Queen Victoria bought the estate. Eighty thou-sand Scots turned out to welcome her on her first visit in 1848, but some weren't so charmed – one local journalist remarked that the area was about to be "desolated by cockneys and other horrible reptiles". Today, however, the locals are fiercely protective of their connections, forever retelling stories of their encounters with blue-bloods.

Many of Victoria's guests weren't as enthusiastic about Deeside as she was: Count von Moltke, then aide-de-camp to Prince Frederick William of Prussia, observed, "It is very astonishing that the Royal Power of England should reside amid this lonesome, desolate, cold mountain scenery," while Tsar Nicholas II whined, "The weather is awful, rain and wind every day and on top of it no luck at all – I haven't killed a stag yet." However, the Queen adored the place, and the woods were said to remind Prince Albert of Thuringia, his homeland.

Deeside is undoubtedly handsome in a fierce, craggy, characteristically Scottish way, and the royal presence has helped keep a lid on unattractive mass development. The vil-lages strung along the A93, the main route through the area, are noticeably well-heeled but the facilities for visitors are first class, with a number of bunkhouses and youth hos-tels and some outstanding hotels, as well as plenty of castles and grounds to snoop around. The main centres are **Ballater**, the village closest to Balmoral, with its ranks of shops adorned with royal crests, and **Braemar**, a hardy spot at the junction of three glens where the royals pay an annual visit to watch the Highland Games. It's also an excellent area to use as a base for **outdoor activities**, with hiking routes into both the Grampian and Cairngorm mountains, and good mountain biking, canoeing and skiing.

Ballater and Balmoral

The neat and ordered town of **BALLATER**, attractively hemmed in by the river and fir-covered mountains, was dragged from obscurity in the nineteenth century when it was discovered that the local waters were useful in curing scrofula. Scrofula is no longer a problem, but with a bit of sharp commercialism and some encouraging recent medical tests, Deeside Spring Water is all the rage once more, and you'll find it for sale around town.

It was in Ballater that Queen Victoria first arrived in Deeside by train from Aberdeen back in 1848 – she wouldn't allow a station to be built any closer to Balmoral, eight miles further west, and although the line is long closed, the elegant train station, now housing a tearoom, can be seen. The local **shops**, having provided the royals with household basics, also flaunt their connections, sporting oversized crests above their doorways.

Ballater is an excellent base for local **walks and outdoor activities**. There are numerous hikes from Loch Muik (pronounced 'Mick'), nine miles southwest of town, including a well-worn but strenuous all-day trek up and around Lochnagar (3789ft), the mountain much painted and written about by the current Prince of Wales. The place to set off from, or to find out about a series of free, guided nature walks, is the Balmoral Rangers' **Visitor's Centre**, on the shores of the loch. **Bikes** can be rented from Wheels and Reels, at 2 Braemar Rd, just over the railway bridge from Station Square.

The **tourist office** is opposite the station, on Station Square (Easter–May & Oct Mon–Sat 10am–1pm & 2–5pm, Sun 1–5pm; June & Sept Mon–Sat 10am–1pm & 2–6pm, Sun 1–6pm; July & Aug Mon–Sat 9.30am–7pm, Sun 1–7pm; ☎013397/55306). There are plenty of reasonable **B&Bs** in town, including the excellent *Inverdeen House*, Bridge Square (☎013397/55759; ②), where you're offered a choice of no less than six breakfasts. Other places worth trying include the welcoming *Deeside Hotel*, Braemar Road (☎013397/55420; ②), or *The Green Inn Restaurant*, 9 Victoria Rd (☎013397/55701; ⑥), where the price includes dinner. For **camping**, the *Anderson Road Caravan Park* (☎013397/55727; closed Nov–Easter) is down towards the river. There are numerous **places to eat**, from smart hotel restaurants to bakers and coffee shops; the award-winning *Green Inn* is pricey but excellent, while *Bruno's Restaurant*, 34 Victoria Rd (☎013397/55346; closed Mon & Tues, plus Oct–March), is an unexpectedly authentic if over-the-top Italian in a family house. For non-touristy drinking, try the back bar (the entrance down Golf Street) of the *Prince of Wales*, which faces the main square.

Balmoral Castle and Crathie Church

Originally a sixteenth-century tower house built for the powerful Gordon family, **Balmoral Castle** (mid-April to May Mon–Sat 10am–5pm; June & July daily 10am–5pm; £4) has been a royal residence since 1852, when it was converted to the Scottish Baronial mansion that stands today. The royal family traditionally spend their summer holidays here, but despite its fame, it can be something of a disappointment even for a dedicated royalist: for the three months when the doors are nudged open the general riff-raff are permitted to view only the ballroom and the grounds.

Opposite the castle's gates on the main road is the granite parish church of **CRATHIE**, the royals' local church, which is open to visitors. A small **tourist office** operates in the often-busy car park by the church on the main road in Crathie (daily: April 10am–5pm; May–Aug 9.30am–6pm; Sept & Oct 10am–5.30pm; ☎013397/42414).

Braemar

Continuing for another few miles, the road rises to 1100ft above sea level on the way to the upper part of Deeside and the village of **BRAEMAR**, overlooked by the unimposing **Braemar Castle** (Easter–Oct Mon–Thurs, Sat & Sun 10am–6pm; £2.50). It's a strategically situated spot right at the heart of the Grampians, with passes from the Cairngorms and Glen Shee meeting at the head of the Dee. Signs as you enter Braemar

---

THE MALT WHISKY TRAIL

Speyside's **Malt Whisky Trail** is a clearly signposted seventy-mile meander around a selection of the region's distilleries, although there are others not on the official trail that you can visit by prior arrangement: The Macallan at Craigellachie (☎01340/871471), and Cragganmore at Ballindalloch (☎01807/500202) are both worth trying. Unless you're seriously interested in whisky, it's best to just pick out a couple that appeal, perhaps choosing one for the whisky and another for its setting. All the distilleries offer a guided **tour** (some are free, and some charge an entry fee, then give you a voucher which is redeemable against a bottle of whisky from the distillery shop) with a tasting to round it off – if you're driving you'll be offered a miniature to take away with you. Indeed, most people travel the route by car, though you could cycle it, or even walk using the Speyside Way.

Cardhu, on the B9102 at Knockando (March–Nov Mon–Fri 9.30am–4.30pm; July–Sept also Sat 9.30am–4.30pm & Sun 11am–4pm; Dec–Feb 10am–4pm; £2 with voucher). This distillery was established over a century ago when the founder's wife was nice enough to raise a red flag to warn local crofters when the authorities were on the lookout for their illegal stills. Sells rich, full-bodied whisky which has distinctive peaty flavours, in an attractive bulbous bottle.

Dallas Dhu, Mannachie Road, Forres (April–Sept daily 9.30am–6pm; Oct–March Mon–Wed & Sat 9.30am–4pm, Thurs 9.30am–noon, Sun 2–4pm; £2.50). Located apart from the others, this classic Victorian distillery no longer makes whisky, but all the old equipment is in place and you can look around freely with an audioguide handset.

Glenfiddich, on the A941 just north of Dufftown (April to mid-Oct Mon–Sat 9.30am–4.30pm, Sun noon–4.30pm; mid-Oct to March Mon–Fri 9.30am–4.30pm; free). Probably the best known of the malt whiskies, and the biggest and slickest of all the distilleries. It's a lighter, sweet whisky which comes in familiar triangular shaped bottles. Uniquely, Glenfiddich is bottled on the premises – an interesting process to watch. Informative (and free) tours, though the place is thronged with tourists.

Glenlivet, on the B9008, ten miles north of Tomintoul (April–Oct Mon–Sat 10am–4pm, Sun 12.30–4pm; July & Aug last tour 5pm; £2.50 with voucher). With a famous name and a lonely hillside setting, this was the first licensed distillery in the Highlands, following the 1823 Act of Parliament which aimed to reduce illicit distilling and smuggling. The Glenlivet twelve-year-old malt is a floral, fragrant medium-bodied whisky.

Speyside Cooperage, Craigellachie, four miles north of Dufftown (all year Mon–Fri 9.30am–4.30pm, plus Easter–Sept Sat 9.30am–4pm; £2.95). Gain an insight into the ancient and skilled art of cooperage, and watch the oak casks for whisky being made and repaired.

Strathisla, Keith (Feb & March Mon–Fri 9.30am–4pm, April–Nov Mon–Sat 9.30am–4pm, Sun 12.30–4pm; £4, with a £2 voucher). A small old-fashioned distillery claiming to be Scotland's oldest (1786); it's certainly one of the most attractive, situated in a highly evocative highland location on the Isla River. The malt itself has a rich, almost fruity taste and is pretty rare, but is used as the heart of the better-known Chivas Regal blend.

---

boast that it's an "Award Winning Tourist Village", which just about sums it up, as everything seems to have been prettified to within an inch of its life or have a price tag on it. That said, it's an invigorating, outdoor kind of place, well patronized by committed hikers, although probably best known for its Highland Games, the annual **Braemar Gathering** (first Sat of Sept). Games were first held here in the eleventh century, when Malcolm Canmore set contests for the local clans in order to pick the bravest and strongest for his army. Since Queen Victoria's day it has become customary for successive generations of royals to attend and for all its reputation as the most famous Highland Games in the world it's an overcrowded, rather overblown event. You're unlikely to get in if you just turn up, but if you're keen enough to plan that far in advance, tickets are available after February 1st from the Bookings Secretary, BRHS, Coilacriech, Ballater, AB35 5UH (☎013397/55377).

Braemar's **tourist office** is in the modern building known as the Mews, on Mar Road, in the middle of the village (June daily 10am–6pm; July & Aug daily 9am–7pm, Sept daily 10am–1pm & 2–6pm; Oct–May Mon–Sat 10am–1pm & 2–5pm, Sun noon–5pm; ☎013397/41600). For advice on **outdoor activities**, as well as ski, mountain bike and climbing equipment hire, head to Braemar Mountain Sports, by the river bridge.

Rooms are scarce in Braemar in the lead-up to the gathering, but at other times there's a wide choice. *Clunie Lodge Guest House*, Clunie Bank Road (☎013397/41330; ②), on the edge of town, is a good B&B with lovely views up Clunie Glen, and there's a **youth hostel** at Corrie Feragie, 21 Glenshee Rd (☎013397/41659 or central reservations ☎0541/553255). Alternatively, the cheery *Rucksacks*, an easy-going bunkhouse well equipped for walkers and backpackers, is just behind the Mews complex (☎013397/41517; ①); they also rent bikes, and have a sauna. The *Invercauld Caravan Club Park* (☎013397/41373), just south of the village, off the Glenshee Road, has fifteen **camping** pitches. Standard and fairly pricey hotel **food** can be had from the bars of the various large hotels, or for some cheap stodge try the *Braemar Takeaway*, by the river bridge. For drinking, the *Invercauld Arms* in the middle of town is a youthful hangout with a pool table.

Speyside

Speyside refers to the region around the middle and lower reaches of the Spey River, although to most people the name is synonymous with the production of **whisky**. Indeed there are more whisky distilleries and famous brands concentrated in this small area than in any other region of the country. Running through the heart of the region is the River Spey whose clean, clear waters play such a vital part in the whisky industry and are home to thousands of salmon.

At the centre of Speyside, the cheery community of **DUFFTOWN**, founded in 1817 by James Duff, the fourth Earl of Fife, proudly proclaims itself "Malt Whisky Capital of the World", and indeed it exports more of the stuff than anywhere else in Britain. Following the A941 through the town brings you to the **Glenfiddich Distillery** (see box opposite), past the old Dufftown train station, currently being restored for a steam line through to Keith. Behind the distillery, the ruin of the thirteenth-century **Balvenie Castle** (April–Sept daily 9.30am–6pm; £1.20; HS) sits on a mound overlooking vast piles of whisky barrels. The castle was a Stewart stronghold, which was abandoned after the 1745 uprising, when it was last used as a government garrison.

Four miles north of Dufftown, the small settlement of **CRAIGELLACHIE** sits above the confluence of the sparkling waters of the Fiddich and the Spey. From the village, you can look down on a beautiful old iron bridge over the Spey built by Thomas Telford in 1815.

Practicalities

For maps and information on the **whisky trail**, head straight to the **tourist office** in Dufftown, inside the handsome clocktower at the centre of Main Square (April, May & Oct Mon–Sat 10am–1pm & 2–5pm; June & Sept Mon–Sat 10am–1pm & 2–6pm, Sun 1–6pm; July & Aug Mon–Sat 10am–7pm, Sun 1–7pm; ☎01340/820501). **Bikes** can be rented from Clarke's Cycle Hire (☎01340/881525), beside the *Fiddichside Inn* at Craigellachie.

There's a good range of **places to stay** in Dufftown, as well as in the surrounding countryside. *Morven*, on Main Square (☎01340/820507; ①), offers good, cheap B&B, while there's a tiny **hostel**, *Whisky Capital Backpackers*, a mile out of Dufftown on the

Huntly road (☎01340/821069). In Craigellachie, the most comfortable option is the B&B attached to the Green Hall Gallery, on Victoria St (☎01340/871010, *stewart.johnston@dial.pippex.com*; ③). For unquestionable style and luxury, head to *Mimore House* (☎01807/590378; closed Nov–March; ⑥), the former home of Glenlivet owner George Smith, which sits right beside the distillery on a quiet hillside above the Livet Water. In Archiestown, a few miles west of Craigellachie, the *Archiestown Hotel* (☎01340/810218; ⑥) is a good base for walking or cycling, and serves great seafood.

The *Glenfiddich Café*, just beyond Dufftown's tourist office, on Church Street, does simple **meals** and takeaways, while the popular *Taste of Speyside* on Balverie Street, just off the square, serves a classier, and pricier, Scottish menu. Nine miles out of town along the B9009 towards Glenlivet, the *Croft Inn* is a cosy roadside pub with well-priced local dishes and beautiful views over Ben Rinnes. Unsurprisingly, there's no shortage of **pubs** in the vicinity, with the best selection of malts being at the *Grouse Inn* at Cabrach, ten miles out along the A941 to Rhynie. In Craigellachie, the tiny *Fiddichside Inn*, on the A95 Huntly road, is a wonderfully original and convivial pub with a garden by the river, while the busy *Highlander Inn*, on Victoria Street, serves good pub grub.

The coast to Findhorn

The **coastline** of northeast Scotland from Aberdeen to Inverness is a rugged, and often desolate place, despite the number of small settlements tucked into its bays and inlets. The weather can be wild – as the huddled design of the fishing villages testifies – but if it's good, a couple of days meandering through the various little villages, exploring the cliff-tops and walking along miles of deserted, unspoilt beaches, is as unexpected a piece of escapism as you'll find in Scotland.

Most visitors bypass Peterhead and Fraserburgh, the two largest communities, and head instead for quieter spots such as **Pennan** and nearby **Cullen**, on the Moray Firth Coast. Other attractions are the outstation of the National Gallery of Scotland at Duff House in **Banff**, the ruined cathedral at **Elgin**, with the working abbey at **Pluscarden** close by, and the **Findhorn Foundation**, a controversial spiritual community, near Forres.

Pennan

West of Fraserburgh, along the north-facing Moray coast, the real charm of this area is revealed. You'll need lots of time to meander along the winding coastal roads, and there are countless castle ruins, cliff-top walks and lonely beaches worth stopping to investigate. One of the very best of the coast's tiny fishing hamlets is at **PENNAN**, about twelve miles west of Fraserburgh, a village you don't see until the steep and hazardous road into it brings you down almost on top of the single row of whitewashed stone cottages. If the descent and the village, particularly the red telephone box, seem familiar, it's because Pennan was used for the village scenes in the film *Local Hero*, filmed here in 1982. Such fame brings a steady stream of aficionados, but the nature of the village, tucked in hard against the cliff, means that there's really no room for crass development to have its way. The only **place to stay** here is the *Pennan Inn* (☎01346/561201; ⑤), a convivial, lively place with an excellent seafood **restaurant** and a cosy pub which readily spills out onto the sea wall on still summer evenings.

Macduff and Banff

Just over ten miles west along the coast from Pennan you come to **MACDUFF**, a famous spa town during the nineteenth century which now has a thriving and pleasant harbour. Worth a visit here is the new **Macduff Marine Aquarium** (daily 10am–5pm; £2.75), a showcase for the marine life of the Moray Firth which includes the deepest aquarium tank in Britain. It's a fun place, full of kids splashing water and pressing their noses to the glass tanks, and, by dedicating itself to the local aquaculture, doesn't have the zoo-like associations of more glamorous aquarium centres.

Macduff more or less merges with the town of **BANFF**, just over the River Devoron via a beautiful seven-arched bridge. By the river, on the other side of the golf club, is the area's main attraction, the extravagant **Duff House** (April–Oct daily 11am–5pm; Nov–March Thurs–Sun 11am–4pm; £3; HS), an elegant Georgian Baroque house built to William Adam's design in 1730. Originally intended for one of the northeast's richest men, William Braco, who became Earl of Fife in 1759, the house was clearly built to impress, and could have been even more splendid had Adam been allowed to build curving colonnades either side; Braco's refusal to pay for carved Corinthian columns to be shipped in from Queensferry caused such bitter argument that the laird never actually came to live here and even went so far as to pull down his coach curtains whenever he passed by. The house has been painstakingly restored and reopened as an outpost of the **National Gallery of Scotland**. The artwork kept here is all chosen to fit in with the style and antiquity of the house, although there are a couple of small rooms on the second floor given over to displaying travelling exhibitions sent up from Edinburgh.

Cut off from the rest of the estate by the main road, the **tourist office** (April–June & Sept Mon–Sat 10am–1pm & 2–5pm; July & Aug Mon–Sat 10am–1pm & 2–6pm, Sun 1–6pm; ☎01261/812419) is housed in the Greek Doric lodge of the Duff estate. For a £1 deposit, you can collect a thoroughly enjoyable **audioguide tour** of the town, which introduces both the grand Georgian upper town and, down by the harbour, the older, scruffier **Scotstown**. The tour points out lots of good views, interesting buildings and juicy snippets of ancient gossip.

There are several good **B&Bs** in Banff, including *Castlehill*, 58 Castle St, an extension of the High Street (☎01261/818372; ①), and, over the river in the heart of Macduff, *Mrs Grieg's*, 11 Gellymill St (☎01261/833314; ①). Four miles south of Macduff, off the A497 Turriff road, the elegant and welcoming Regency *Eden House* (☎01261/821282; ⑤) is set in extensive grounds overlooking the Deveron Valley. **Camping** is best near the beach at the *Banff Links Caravan Park* (☎01261/812228; closed Oct–March). There are various cafés and pubs for **food and drink**; you can try the *Aul' Fife*, just along from the tourist office at 12 Low St, or the coarser *Market Arms*, a sixteenth-century town house on High Shore.

Cullen

West of Banff, the coastal trail continues through yet more attractive fishing villages, notably **Portsoy**, renowned for the green marble it once shipped to Versailles. Another, five miles west, is **CULLEN**, served by bus from Aberdeen. The town, strikingly situated beneath a superb series of arched rail viaducts, is made up of two sections – Seatown, by the harbour, and the new town on the hillside. There's a lovely stretch of sheltered sand by Seatown, where the colourful houses – confusingly numbered according to the order in which they were built – huddle end-on to the sea. Also worth the walk is Cullen's lovely old **kirk**, a twenty-minute stroll from the centre, which dates back to the fourteenth century.

A group of locals have established their own **tourist office** (June–Aug daily 11am–5pm) and are enthusiastic purveyors of information and recommendations. Cullen is famous for a tasty fish soup made from cream and smoked haddock called **Cullen Skink**; if you want to try some, the friendly *Three Kings* pub, on North Castle Street, is your best bet – the smarter hotels around town also serve it if you prefer a grander setting. Most of the **B&Bs** are in Seatown. They're all much of a muchness, but Mrs Mair at *Torrach*, 147 Seatown (☎01542/840724; ①; closed Nov–March), is friendly and comfortable.

Elgin and around

Inland, about fifteen miles southwest of Cullen, the lively market town of **ELGIN** grew up in the thirteenth century around the River Lossie. It's an appealing place, still largely sticking to its medieval street plan, with a busy main street opening out onto an old cobbled market place and a tangle of wynds and pends.

On North College Street, just round the corner from the tourist office and clearly signposted, is the still-lovely ruin of **Elgin Cathedral** (April–Sept daily 9.30am–6.30pm; Oct–March Mon–Wed & Sat 9.30am–4pm, Thurs 9.30am–noon, Sun 2–4pm; £2; HS), founded in 1224. Once considered Scotland's most beautiful cathedral, rivalling St Andrew's in importance, today it is little more than a shell, though it does retain its original facade. The so-called Wolf of Badenoch (Alexander Stewart, Earl of Buchan and illegitimate son of Robert II) burnt the place down in 1390, along with the rest of the town, in retaliation for being excommunicated by the Bishop of Moray when he left his wife. The cathedral went on to suffer even more during the post-Reformation, when all its valuables were stripped and the building was reduced to common quarry for the locals. Unusual features include the Pictish cross slab in the middle of the ruins and the cracked gravestones with their memento mori of skulls and cross bones.

At the very top of High Street is the **Elgin Museum** (April–Sept Mon–Fri 10am–5pm, Sat 11am–4pm, Sun 2–5pm; £1.50), one of Britain's oldest, having been housed in the same purpose-built building since 1843. With so many new museums filled with audio-visual displays and interactive computers opening up, it's refreshing to realize just how absorbing a well-looked-after old-style museum can be. Its exhibits include a weird anthropological collection including reptilian skulls, a shrunken head

---

THE FINDHORN FOUNDATION

In 1962, with little money and no employment, Peter and Eileen Caddy, their three children and friend Dorothy Maclean, settled on a caravan site at Findhorn. Dorothy believed she had a special relationship with what she called the "devas", in her own words "the archetypal formative forces of light or energy that underlie all forms in nature – plants, trees, rivers, etc", and from the uncompromising sandy soil they built a garden filled with remarkable plants and vegetables far larger than had ever been seen in the area.

The Original Caravan – as it is marked on the site's map – still stands, surrounded by a whole host of newer timber buildings and other caravans. The Foundation is now home to a couple of hundred people, with around 8000 visitors arriving every year. The buildings, employing solar power, earth roofs and other green initiatives, including a huge greenhouse-type structure called *The Living Machine*, an ecological sewage treatment centre, show the commitment of the Findhorners to a sustainable future.

As can be expected, the Foundation is not without its controversy, a local JP declaring that "behind the benign and apparently religious front lies a hard core of New Agers experimenting with hallucinatory techniques marketed as spirituality", a predictable enough charge from local conservative thought. Findhorn, now a public company, is also accused of being overly well heeled; a glance into the shop or a tally of the large cars parked outside the eco-houses does give some substance to such ideas. However, most people here, although honest about the downsides of community living, are extremely positive about its benefits.

from Ecuador and a grinning mummy from Peru. In addition, there is an excellent collection of fossils and well-explained Pictish relics.

Practicalities

Elgin is well served by public transport, with the Aberdeen–Inverness train stopping here several times a day. The **bus station** (☎01343/544222) is on Alexandra Road, a block from High Street's St Giles Church, while the **train station** is slightly less conveniently situated on the south side of town, on Station Road – turn right out of the station, left at the island and up Moss Street to reach the town centre. The **tourist office**, 17 High St (April–June & Sept Mon–Sat 10am–5pm, Sun 1–5pm; July & Aug Mon–Sat 10am–6pm, Sun 1–6pm; Oct–March Mon–Sat 10am–4pm; ☎01343/542666), will book accommodation.

Among the **places to stay**, *The Lodge*, 20 Duff Av (☎01343/549981; ②), is a good-quality **B&B** in an old tea plantation owner's house; for more luxury, the castle-like *Mansion House Hotel*, by the riverside just to the west of the city centre (☎01343/548811; ⑨), is one of the most exclusive in the region. Elgin has a small backpacker's **hostel**, the *Saltire Bunkhouse* (☎01343/550624), one of the last houses in town heading west along Pluscarden Road, about a 25-minute walk from the centre of town. For **food**, the justifiably popular place to go is *Flanagan's Irish Pub*, on Shepherd Close, 48A High St, which sometimes has live music; the *Ashvale*, on Moss St, is good for fish and chips; otherwise there's *Littlejohn's Brasserie*, 193 High St, a TexMex and Cajun theme chain restaurant. Good places for **drinking** include *Thunderton House* pub, Thunderton Place, off High Street, partly rebuilt from the seventeenth-century Great Lodge of Scottish kings, and *High Spirits*, in an old church on Moss Street.

Pluscarden Abbey

Set in attractive countryside seven miles southwest of Elgin, **Pluscarden Abbey** (daily 4.30am–8.45pm), one of only two abbeys in Scotland with a permanent community of monks, looms impressively large in a peaceful clearing off an unmarked road. Founded in 1230 for a French monastic order, it was another of the properties burnt by the Wolf of Badenoch in 1390; recovering from this, it became a priory of the Benedictine Abbey of Dunfermline in 1454 and continued as such until monastic life was suppressed in Scotland in 1560. The abbey's revival began in 1897 when the Catholic antiquarian, John, third Marquis of Bute, started to repair the building. In 1948 his son donated it to the small group of Benedictine monks from Gloucester who established the present community.

The Findhorn Foundation

The **Findhorn Foundation** on the B9011, about ten miles east of Elgin (Mon–Sat 9am–noon & 2–5pm, Sun 2–5pm; free), is a spiritual community and magnet for soul-searchers from around the world. Set up in 1962 by Eileen and Peter Caddy (see box opposite), the foundation has blossomed from its early core of three adults and three children into a full-blown community, with facilities for hundreds of people. Bizarrely enough, despite its enormous growth, the foundation is still situated on the town's caravan and camping park (☎01309/690203; closed Nov–March), creating an intriguing combination of people on site. Many of the original caravans have metamorphosed into more permanent structures, including some fascinating houses and community spaces employing the latest in ecological methods. It's an amazing place and, however cynical you might be, well worth at least a flying visit. Guided **tours** (Mon, Wed, Fri & Sat 2pm), residential workshops and short-term stays are all available (for details contact the visitor centre on ☎01309/690311), and there's a smart **café** and richly stocked delicatessen/general shop on site.

travel details

Trains

Aberdeen to: Arbroath (every 30min; 1hr); Dundee (every 30min; 1hr 15min); Edinburgh (1–2 hourly; 2hr 40min); Elgin (hourly; 1hr 30min); Forres (hourly; 1hr 45min); Glasgow (1–2 hourly; 2hr 40min); Inverness (hourly; 2hr 10min); Montrose (every 30min; 45min); Nairn (hourly; 2hr); Stonehaven (every 30min; 15min).

Dundee to: Aberdeen (every 30min; 1hr 15min); Arbroath (hourly; 20min); Montrose (hourly; 15min).

Elgin to: Forres (hourly; 15min); Inverness (hourly; 45min); Nairn (hourly; 30min).

Buses

Aberdeen to: Arbroath (hourly; 1hr 20min); Ballater (hourly; 1hr 45min); Banchory (hourly; 1hr); Banff (hourly; 2hr); Braemar (4–6 daily; 2hr 10min); Crathie, for Balmoral (4–6 daily; 2hr); Cruden Bay (hourly; 50min); Cullen (hourly; 1hr 50min–2hr 30min); Dufftown (2 weekly; 2hr 10min); Dundee (hourly; 2hr); Elgin (hourly; 2hr 40min–3hr 40min); Forfar (2 daily; 1hr 20min); Forres (hourly; 2hr 40min); Macduff (hourly; 1hr 50min); Montrose (hourly; 1hr); Stonehaven (every 30min; 25–45min).

Ballater to: Crathie (June–Sept daily; 15min).

Banchory to: Ballater (June–Sept daily; 45min); Braemar (June–Sept daily; 1hr 20min); Crathie (June–Sept daily; 1hr); Spittal of Glenshee (June–Sept daily; 2hr).

Dundee to: Aberdeen (hourly; 2hr); Arbroath (every 15min; 40min–1hr); Blairgowrie (every 30min; 50min–1hr); Forfar (every 30min; 30min); Glamis (2 daily; 40min); Kirriemuir (hourly; 1hr 10min); Meigle (hourly; 40min); Montrose (hourly; 1hr 15min).

Elgin to: Aberdeen (hourly; 3hr 15min); Forres (hourly; 30min); Pluscarden (1 daily; 20min).

Forres to: Elgin (hourly; 30min); Findhorn (Mon–Sat 8 daily; 20min).

Ferries

Aberdeen to: Lerwick, Shetland (6 weekly; 14hr); Stromness, Orkney (1 weekly; 10hr).

Flights

Aberdeen to: Belfast (Mon–Fri 1 daily; 2hr 45min); Birmingham (Mon–Fri 3 daily; 1hr 30min); Glasgow (1 daily; 45min); London (Heathrow 7 daily, Gatwick 5 daily, Luton 2 daily, Stansted 4 daily; 1hr 30min); Manchester (Mon–Fri 9 daily, Sat 3 daily, Sun 4 daily; 1hr 20min); Newcastle (Mon–Fri 5 daily; Sat & Sun 2 daily; 1hr); Shetland (Mon–Fri 4 daily, Sat & Sun 2 daily; 1hr).

Dundee to: London City (Mon–Fri 2 daily; 1hr 15min).

CHAPTER TWENTY-FIVE

THE HIGHLAND REGION

The Highland region of Scotland, covering the northern two-thirds of the country, holds much of the mainland's most spectacular scenery: a classic combination of mountains, glens, lochs and rivers surrounded on three sides by a magnificently pitted and rugged coastline. The inspiring landscape and the tranquillity and space which it offers are without doubt the main attractions of the region. You may be surprised at just how remote much of it still is: the vast peat bogs in the north, for example, are among the most extensive and unspoilt wilderness areas in Europe, while a handful of the west coast's isolated crofting villages can still only be reached by boat.

Exposed to slightly different weather conditions and, to some extent, different historical and cultural influences, each of the three coastlines has its own distinct character. Visitors with limited time tend to just stick to the more scenic **west coast**. The jagged shoreline of sea lochs, rocky headlands and white-sand coves is set against some of Scotland's most dramatic mountains, and looks across to the islands of Skye, Mull and the Outer Hebrides. The **north coast**, stretching from wind-lashed **Cape Wrath** to **John O' Groats**, is wilder and more rugged. Sheer cliffs and sandy bays bear the brunt of fierce Atlantic storms, while in the hinterland is the vast and ecologically unique bog-land of the **Flow Country**. Along the fertile **east coast**, green fields and woodland run down to the sweeping sandy beaches of the Moray, Cromarty and Dornoch firths, while further north, rolling moors give way to peaty wastes and sheep country.

Cutting diagonally through the heart of the Highlands, the **Great Glen** links the key towns of Inverness on the east coast and Fort William in the west with a chain of impressive lochs, most notably **Loch Ness**. **Inverness**, the only major urban centre in the Highlands, has good transport links and facilities, and is an obvious springboard for more remote areas, including the spectacular **Cairngorm Mountains** to the south-east. From mundane **Fort William**, on the west coast, it's possible to branch out to some fine scenery, most conveniently **Ben Nevis** and the beautiful expanses of **Glen Coe**, but also the remote and tranquil **Ardnamurchan peninsula**, the "Road to the Isles" to **Mallaig**, and the lochs and glens that lead up to **Kyle of Lochalsh** – the most direct route to Skye (see p.1037).

Throughout the Highlands, there are many rewarding places to stay in the more remote small towns and villages. The planned eighteenth-century port of **Ullapool**, in

---

ACCOMMODATION PRICE CODES

Throughout this guide, hotel and B&B accommodation is priced on a scale of ① to ⑨, the number indicating the **lowest price** you could expect to pay per night in that establishment for a **double room** in high season. The prices indicated by the codes are as follows:

① under £40	④ £60–70	⑦ £110–150
② £40–50	⑤ £70–90	⑧ £150–200
③ £50–60	⑥ £90–110	⑨ over £200

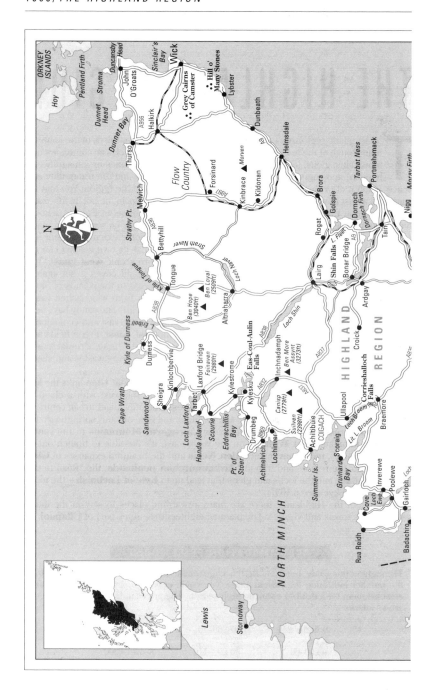

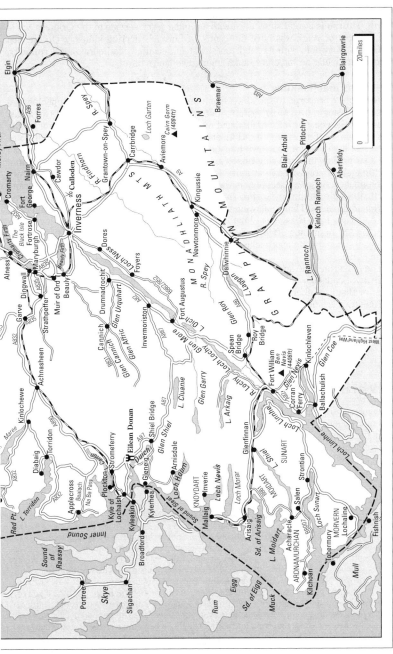

© Crown copyright

the northwest, is well placed for exploration of the spellbinding countryside. In the far north, **Thurso** is a solid stone town with a regular ferry service to the Orkneys, while the old port of **Wick** was once the centre of Europe's herring industry. On the east coast lies **Dornoch**, with its sandstone fourteenth-century cathedral, and **Cromarty**, whose vernacular architecture ranks among Scotland's finest.

Highlands practicalities

Unless you're prepared to spend weeks on the road, the Highlands are simply too vast to see in a single trip. Most visitors, therefore, base themselves in one or two areas, exploring the coast or hills on foot, and making longer hops across the interior by car, bus or train. Getting around the Highlands, particularly the remoter parts, is obviously easiest if you've got your own transport, but with a little forward planning you can see a surprising amount using **buses** and **trains**, especially if you fill in with **postbuses** (timetables are available at most post offices). The A9, a modern fast **road** with some dual-carriageway sections, is the key route into the area, sweeping north from Perth through Strathspey to Inverness and on to John O' Groats, with one of the Highlands' main **rail** lines following broadly the same route. In the west, the main road, the A82, runs from Glasgow to Fort William, then follows the Great Glen to Inverness, with the A87 branching off towards Skye and the A835 linking Inverness with Ullapool. Inverness can also be approached from Aberdeen by train or on the notoriously dangerous A96.

The most romantic approach to the region has to be via the famous **West Highland Railway**, Scotland's most scenic and brilliantly engineered rail route, which crosses country that can otherwise only be seen from long-distance footpaths. From Glasgow, the line travels along the banks of Loch Lomond and traverses desolate Rannoch Moor, circumnavigating Ben Nevis to enter Fort William. The second leg of the journey, from Fort William to Mallaig, traverses the magnificent, curving Glenfinnan Viaduct, and there are superb views of Skye and the Small Isles as the line runs past the famous silver sands of Morar.

Inverness

The largest town in the Highlands, **Inverness**, 105 miles northwest of Aberdeen and 114 miles north of Perth, has an appealing setting on the leafy banks of the River Ness, near the point where it flows into the sea at the Moray Firth. While the town boasts decent shopping, one or two worthwhile museums and a striking sandstone castle, it is not a compelling place to stay for long, as inevitably most visitors are quickly drawn to the attractions of sea and mountains beyond. With plenty of accommodation and places

---

■■■ SAFETY IN THE HILLS ■■■

The mountains of the Scottish Highlands, while not as high or as steep as the Alps, are sufficiently exposed that weather conditions – including blizzards and icy winds of up to 100mph – can be fatal. Every year people die in the Scottish mountains, many of them inexperienced walkers who did not realize the levels of danger involved. It's essential to take proper precautions. Always put **safety** first: never underestimate just how fast the weather can change or how extreme the changes can be; don't venture off track if you're inexperienced; and be sure to set out properly equipped, with warm, waterproof clothing, decent footwear, a compass, all the maps you might need, and some food in case you get stuck. Make sure, too, that someone knows roughly where you have gone and when you expect to be back – and remember to contact them again on your return.

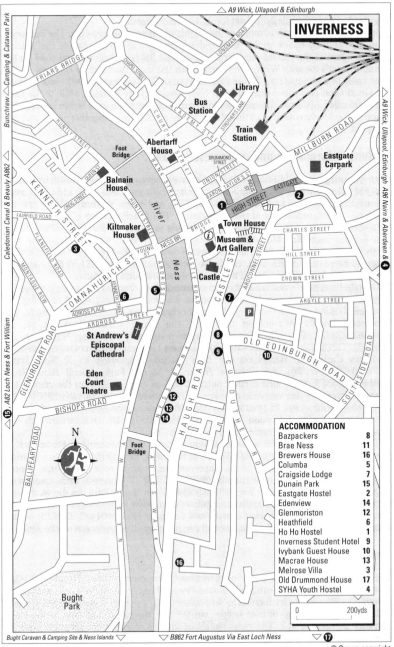

△ A9 Wick, Ullapool & Edinburgh

INVERNESS

Library
Bus Station
Train Station
Eastgate Carpark
Abertarff House
Foot Bridge
Balnain House
Kiltmaker House
Town House
Museum & Art Gallery
Castle
St Andrew's Episcopal Cathedral
Eden Court Theatre
Foot Bridge
Bught Park

N

ACCOMMODATION

Bazpackers	8
Brae Ness	11
Brewers House	16
Columba	5
Craigside Lodge	7
Dunain Park	15
Eastgate Hostel	2
Edenview	14
Glenmoriston	12
Heathfield	6
Ho Ho Hostel	1
Inverness Student Hotel	9
Ivybank Guest House	10
Macrae House	13
Melrose Villa	3
Old Drummond House	17
SYHA Youth Hostel	4

0   200yds

△ Bunchrew △ Camping & Catavan Park
◁ Caledonian Canal & Beauly A862
◁ A82 Loch Ness & Fort William
△ A9 Wick, Ullapool, Edinburgh A96 Nairn & Aberdeen △

Bught Caravan & Camping Site & Ness Islands ▽   ▽ B862 Fort Augustus Via East Loch Ness   ▽ ⑰

to eat and drink, the town is most useful as a base for day-trips deeper into the Highlands or as a jumping-off point for more remote parts.

Inverness is at the hub of much of the Highlands' **transport** network. The approach from the south by rail or on the A9 provides a spectacular introduction to the district, with glimpses of the distant mountains and coastal fringes. Both rail and road routes continue north towards Wick and Thurso, with the main road link to Ullapool on the west coast branching off not far north of Inverness. To the west, the A82 runs through the Great Glen past the depths of Loch Ness towards Fort William, while to the east, the overloaded A96 from Aberdeen and its parallel railway line pass within striking distance of the lovely coastline of the Moray Firth, offering an altogether more pastoral prospect.

Arrival, information and accommodation

Inverness **airport** (☎01463/232471) is at Dalcross, seven miles east of town; from here **bus** #11 (Mon–Sat every 1hr–1hr 30min; 20min; £2.50) goes into town, and a **taxi** costs around £10. The **bus station** (☎01463/233371) and **train station** both lie just off Academy Street, to the east of the town centre. The **tourist office** (June to mid-July Mon–Fri 9am–6pm, Sat & Sun 9am–5pm; mid-July to Aug Mon–Fri 9am–8.30pm, Sat & Sun 9–6pm; Sept–May Mon–Fri 9am–5pm, Sat 10am–4pm; ☎01463/234353) is in a 1960s block on Castle Wynd, just five minutes' walk from the station. It stocks a wide range of literature on the area, can book local accommodation (£1.50 fee), and the friendly staff also hand out useful free maps of the town and environs.

Despite Inverness's vast amount of **accommodation**, demand can outstrip supply in July and especially August. In these months, it's worth phoning ahead or using the advance booking service run through tourist offices. Ness Bank, on the riverside, has two good **hotels** overlooking the river: the smart *Glenmoriston*, at no. 20 (☎01463/223777; ⑥), with a topnotch Italian restaurant; and *Brae Ness* at no. 16 (☎01463/712266; ③; closed Nov–March), a homely Georgian hotel looking across to St Andrews Cathedral. **B&Bs** on the river include *Edenview*, at 26 Ness Bank (☎01463/234397; ②), and *Brewers House,* 2 Moray Park, Island Bank Road (☎01463/235557; ①), a little further out, but still an easy stroll from the centre. On Kenneth Street, on the west side of town, are *Heathfield* at no. 2 (☎01463/230547; ①), and *Melrose Villa* at no. 35 (☎01463/233745; ①), while on the east side, good options are *Craigside Lodge*, 4 Gordon Terrace (☎01463/231576; ②), and, farther out, *Old Drummond House*, Oak Avenue (☎01463/226301; ①).

The good range of **hostel** accommodation includes the non-smoking *Bazpackers*, at the top of Castle Street (☎01463/717663), or the large, new *SYHA Hostel*, on Victoria Drive, off Millburn Road, about three-quarters of a mile from the centre (☎01463/231771; central reservations ☎0541/553255). Inverness's main **campsite**, *Bught Caravan and Camping Site* (☎01463/236920), in Bught Park, on the west bank of the river near the sports centre, can get very crowded at the height of the season. An alternative is the *Bunchrew Caravan and Camping Park* (☎01463/237802), on the shores of the Beauly Firth in Bunchrew, three miles west of Inverness on the A862.

The Town

The logical place to begin a tour of Inverness is the central **Town House**, on High Street. Built in 1878, this Gothic pile hosted Prime Minister Lloyd George's emergency meeting to discuss the Irish crisis in September 1921, and now accommodates council offices. There's nothing of note inside, but the old **Mercat Cross** next to the main entrance is worth a look. The cross stands opposite a small square formerly used by merchants and traders and above the ancient *clach-na-cudainn*, or **"stone of tubs"** – so called because washerwomen used to rest their buckets on it on their way back from the river. A local superstition holds that as long as the stone remains in place, Inverness will continue to prosper.

Looming above the Town House and dominating the horizon is **Inverness Castle** (mid-May to Sept Mon–Sat 10am–5pm; £3), a predominantly nineteenth-century red-sandstone edifice perched picturesquely above the river. The original castle formed the core of the ancient settlement, which had rapidly developed as a port trading with Europe after the town's conversion to Christianity by St Columba in the sixth century. Two famous Scots monarchs were associated with the building: **Robert the Bruce** wrested it back from the English during the Wars of Independence, destroying it in the process, and **Mary, Queen of Scots** had the governor of the second castle hanged from its ramparts after he had refused her entry in 1562. This structure was also destined for destruction, held by the Jacobites in both the 1715 and the 1745 rebellions, and blown up by them to prevent it falling into government hands. Today's edifice houses the Sheriff Court and, in summer, the **Castle Garrison Encounter**, an entertaining and noisy interactive exhibition, in which the visitor plays the role of a new recruit in the eighteenth-century Hanoverian army. Around 7.30pm during the summer, a lone piper clad in full Highland garb performs for tourists on the castle esplanade. The statue of a woman staring south from the terrace is a memorial to **Flora MacDonald**, the clanswoman who helped Bonnie Prince Charlie escape to Skye in the wake of Culloden.

THE TRUTH ABOUT TARTAN

Tartan is big business and an essential part of the tourist industry. Every year, hundreds of visitors return home clutching tartan monsters, foreign-made souvenirs tied with foreign-made tartan ribbon, or lengths of cloth inspiringly named Loch This, Ben That or Glen Something-Else, fondly believing that they are bringing authentic history with them. The reality is that tartan is an ancient Highland craft form that romantic fiction and commercial interest have enclosed within an almost insurmountable wall of myth.

Real tartan, the kind that long ago was called "**Helande**", was a fine, hard and almost showerproof cloth. The wool of the native sheep was spun, dyed with preparations of local plants and woven into patterns by artist-weavers. It was worn as a huge single piece of material, which was belted around the waist and draped over the upper body, rather like a knee-length toga. The colours of old tartans were clear but soft, and the broken pattern gave superb camouflage, unlike modern versions, whose colours are either so strong that the pattern is swamped or so dull that it has no impact.

Tartan did not become popular in the Lowlands until the beginning of the eighteenth century, when it was adopted as the anti-Union badge of **Jacobitism**, and it was not until after 1745 that the Lowlands took it over completely. The 1747 ban on wearing tartan put an end to the making of tartan in Highland glens; instead, whole villages on the Lowland fringes devoted themselves to supplying the needs of the army and emigrant Highlanders in the colonies and, after the ban was lifted in 1782, those of the home market. The wars abated and the colonies became more self-sufficient, and what had become a major industry faced hard times. At first the remedy was sought in a proliferation of new patterns for, despite the existence of a handful with clan names, tartan was, in the main, a small-scale fashion fabric. Then Sir Walter Scott set to work glamorizing the clans, George IV visited Edinburgh in 1822 and wore a kilt, and, finally, Queen Victoria set the royal seal of approval on both the Highlands and tartan.

At about this time, the idea that every **clan** had its own distinguishing tartan became highly fashionable. To have the right to wear tartan, one had to belong, albeit remotely, to a clan, and so the way was paved for the "what's-my-tartan?" lists that appear in the tartan picture books and the souvenir shops. Great feats of genealogical gymnastics were performed in the concoction of these lists, but they could not include every name, so "district", "national" and "political" tartans were developed.

Below the castle, the **Inverness Museum and Art Gallery** (Mon–Sat 9am–5pm; free), on Castle Wynd, gives a good general overview of the development of the Highlands. Informative sections on geology, geography and history cover the ground floor, while upstairs you'll find a muddled selection of silver, taxidermy, weapons and bagpipes, alongside a mediocre art gallery. On the west bank of the river stands one of Scotland's most novel museums, **Balnain House** (July–Aug Mon–Fri 10am–10pm; Sat–Sun 10–6pm; Sept–June Mon–Sat 10am–5pm; £2), which has a modest performance space and an interactive exhibition that will appeal as much to the casual visitor as folk-music aficionados. The exhibition traces the development of Highland **music** from its prehistoric roots – ringing rocks, cast-bronze battle horns and ancient Gaelic songs – to modern electric folk-rock. CD listening posts and a short video allow you to sample snatches of numerous other musical styles from the region, including clan-gathering and spell-casting songs, complex Shetland fiddle reels and the haunting singing of the Hebrides. You can even try to play various instruments, including the bagpipes, clarsach and fiddle. There's also a congenial café downstairs that hosts music events in summer, and a shop selling traditional Highland instruments, CDs and cassettes.

A ten-minute walk upstream (south) from Balnain House brings you to **St Andrews Episcopal Cathedral**, intended by its architects to be one of the grandest buildings in Scotland. However, funds ran out before the giant twin spires of the original design could be completed, and as a result Inverness isn't officially a city, but a town. The interior is pretty ordinary, too, though it does claim an unusual octagonal chapter house. From the cathedral, you can wander a mile or so upriver to the peaceful **Ness Islands**, an attractive, informal public park reached and linked by footbridges. Further upstream still, the river runs close to the **Caledonian Canal**, designed by Thomas Telford in the early nineteenth century as a link between the east and west coasts, joining lochs Ness, Oich, Lochy and Linnhe; today its main use is recreational. Three miles to the west of the town, on the top of **Craig Phadrig** hill, there's a vitrified **Iron Age fort**, reputed to be where the Pictish King Brude received St Columba in the sixth century. The walls of the fort were built of stone laced with timber and, when the timber was set alight, some of the stone fused to glass – hence the term "vitrified".

Eating

There are several good **places to eat** in and around Inverness. Takeaways cluster on Young Street, just across the river, and at the outer ends of Eastgate and Academy Street. Good places for picnic food include *Crumbs*, on Inglis Street, *The Gourmet's Lair*, on Union Street, and *Lettuce Eat*, on Drummond Street. A classic chips-with-everything café is the *Castle Restaurant*, 41 Castle St. The *River Café and Restaurant*, 10 Bank St, near the Grieg Street footbridge (☎01463/714884), serves wholefoods, cakes and good coffee. Decent Italian fare predominates at *Riva*, 4–6 Ness Walk (☎01463/237377), while for Indian food, try *Rajah* (☎01463/237190), nearby on Post Office Avenue. Particularly good restaurants include *Café No. 1*, 75 Castle St (☎01463/226200), offering much the most ambitious cuisine to be found in the centre, and, on the edge of town, on the Fort William road, *Dunain Park Hotel Restaurant* (☎01463/230512), set in lovely gardens. Less expensive is the unpretentious *Le Déja Vu*, 38 Eastgate (☎01463/231075), which serves very good French country food; the set lunch menu is astounding value. The *Glen Mhor Hotel*, 9 Ness Bank (☎01463/234308), has a good bistro at the back specializing in local salmon, beef and game.

Drinking and nightlife

The liveliest **nightlife** in Inverness revolves around the pubs and the town's two main dance venues. The far end of Academy Street has a cluster of good **pubs**: the public bar of the *Phoenix* is the most original town-centre place, while the ersatz-Irish *Lafferty's* next door often has live music, as does the *Blackfriars* across the street. In a basement beside the river, on the corner of Bank and Bridge streets, *Johnny Foxes* also drapes itself in shamrocks but draws eager crowds to its regular live music sessions. Over on Bridge Street, the *Gellions* is a legendary watering hole with several other congenial places in between.

The town's liveliest **nightclub** is *Mr G's*, on Castle Street, while on the north side of the bus station, the larger *Blue* hosts local and nationally known DJs, plus occasional bands. The basement café at Balnain House museum, on the east bank of the Ness, opposite Grieg Street footbridge, has informal **folk sessions** that sometimes turn into ceilidhs (Tues & Thurs nights in summer; Thurs nights in winter). In addition, the museum stages regular recitals and workshops by Highland musicians and touring artists; details of all these are posted in the café, and the lobby upstairs. The 800-seat Eden Court Theatre and the attached Riverside Screen offer a programme of touring **theatre**, an eclectic range of concerts and films.

Around Inverness

The gentle countryside around Inverness makes a good contrast to the scenic splendours you'll encounter once you head further north into the Highlands. Some of the region's most intriguing castles and historic sites make easy afternoon- or day-trips from town and are well-served by public transport. The ill-fated Jacobite uprising of 1745 ended on the outskirts of Inverness at the battlefield of **Culloden**, near the prehistoric burial site of the **Clava Cairns**. A little further east is the whimsical **Cawdor Castle**, which features in Shakespeare's *Macbeth*. On the fertile, sheltered coastal strip of the **Moray Firth**, the low-key seaside resort of **Nairn**, with its championship golf course, is also within easy striking distance of Inverness, as is **Fort George**, one of several impressive Hanoverian bastions erected in the wake of the Jacobite rebellion.

To the north of Inverness, the **Black Isle** is not an island at all, but a fertile peninsula whose rolling hills, prosperous farms, and stands of deciduous woodland make it more reminiscent of Dorset or Sussex than the Highlands. It probably gained its name because of its mild climate: there's rarely frost, which leaves the fields "black" all winter. The area is littered with dozens of prehistoric sites, but the main attraction here is the picturesque eighteenth-century town of **Cromarty**. A string of villages along the south coast, including **Fortrose** and **Rosemarkie**, are also worth stopping off for en route, while **Chanonry Point** is one of the best **dolphin-spotting** sites in Europe (see box on p.1019).

Culloden and around

The windswept **CULLODEN** moor (site free access all year; visitor centre daily: Feb, March, Nov & Dec 10am–4pm; April–Oct 9am–6pm; £3.20; NTS), five miles east of Inverness, witnessed the last ever battle on British soil when, on April 16, 1746, the Jacobite cause was finally subdued – a turning point in the history of the Scottish nation. Ill-fed and exhausted after a pointless night march, the Jacobites were hopelessly outnumbered by the Duke of Cumberland's government troops. The open, flat moorland was also totally unsuitable for the Highlanders' style of courageous but undisciplined fighting, which needed steep hills and lots of cover to provide the element of surprise, and they were routed. After the battle, in which 1500 Highlanders were slaughtered, many of them as they lay wounded on the battlefield, the Young Pretender ("Bonnie Prince Charlie") fled west to the hills and islands, where loyal Highlanders sheltered and protected him. He eventually escaped to France, leaving his erstwhile supporters to their fate – and, in effect, the end of the clan system. The clans were disarmed, the wearing of tartan and playing of bagpipes forbidden, and the chiefs became landlords greedy for higher and higher rents. Culloden also unleashed an orgy of violent reprisals on Scotland, as unruly English troops raped and pillaged their way across the region; within a century, the Highland way of life had changed out of all recognition.

Today you can walk freely around the battle site; flags show the position of the two armies, and **clan graves** are marked by simple headstones. The **Field of the English**, for many years unmarked, is a mass grave for the fifty or so English soldiers who died. Half a mile east of the battlefield, just beyond the crossroads on the main road, is the **Cumberland Stone**, thought for many years to have been the point from where the duke watched the battle. It is more likely, however, that he was much further forward and simply used the stone for shelter. Thirty Jacobites were burnt alive outside the old **Leanach cottage** next to the visitor centre; inside, it has been restored to its eighteenth-century appearance. The **visitor centre** itself provides background information through detailed displays and a film show, as well as a short play set on the day of the battle presented by local actors (June–Sept daily; included in entry price), or you can take the evocative hour-long guided **walking tour** (June–Sept daily; £3). The site is served by Guide Friday **buses** from Bridge Street in Inverness (June–Sept; 10 daily from 10.30am; last bus back to town leaves Culloden at 5.45pm; 25min) and Highland Country bus #12, from Inverness post office (Mon–Sat 8 daily), as well as Highland County's Tourist Trail circular service which leaves from outside the tourist office (daily June–Sept), calling at Fort George, Cawdor Castle and Culloden.

The Clava Cairns

If you're visiting Culloden with your own transport, make a short detour to the **Clava Cairns** (free access), an impressive collection of prehistoric burial chambers clustered around the south bank of the River Nairn, a mile southeast of the battlefield. Erected some time before 2000 BC, the cairns, which are encircled by standing stones in a spinney of mature beech trees, are of two different kinds: one large and one very small **ring-cairn**, and two **passage graves**, which have a narrow passageway from edge to centre. Though cremated remains have been found in both types of structure, and unburnt remains in the passage graves, little is known about the nomadic herdsmen who are thought to have built them.

Cawdor

The pretty if slightly self-satisfied village of **Cawdor**, eight miles east of Culloden, is the site of **Cawdor Castle** (May to mid-Oct daily 10am–5.30pm; £5.40), apocryphally known as the setting for Shakespeare's *Macbeth* – the fulfilment of the witches' prediction that Macbeth is to become Thane of Cawdor sets off his tragic desire to be king. Though visitors descend here in their droves each summer because of the site's literary associations, the castle, which dates from the early fourteenth century, could not possibly have witnessed the grisly historical events on which the Bard's drama was based. However, the immaculately restored monument – a fairy-tale affair of towers, turrets, hidden passageways, dungeons, gargoyles and crenellations whimsically shooting off from the original keep – is still well worth a visit. The Cawdors have lived here for six centuries, and the castle still feels like a family home, albeit one with tapestries, pictures and opulent furniture. As you explore, look out for the **Thorn Tree Room**, a vaulted chamber complete with the remains of an ancient tree, carbon-dated to 1372, an ancient pagan fertility symbol believed to ward off fairies and evil spirits. According to Cawdor family legend, the fourteenth-century thane dreamed he should build on the spot where his donkey lay down to sleep after a day's wandering – the animal chose this tree and building began immediately.

The **grounds** of the castle are possibly the best part of the visit, with an attractive walled garden, a maze of topiary, a small golf course, a putting green and nature trails. It's also worth visiting the village for a drink or meal at the traditional *Cawdor Tavern*, an old **inn** serving beautifully prepared local food. Highland **bus** #12 (Mon–Sat 8 daily; 35min) runs to Cawdor from Inverness post office; the last bus back leaves the castle just after 6pm.

Fort George

Eight miles of undulating coastal farmland separate Cawdor Castle from **Fort George** (April–Sept daily 9.30am–6.30pm; Oct–March Mon–Sat 9.30am–4.30pm, Sun 2–4.30pm; £3.50; HS), an old Hanoverian bastion considered by military architectural historians to be one of the finest fortifications in Europe. Crowning a sandy spit that juts into the middle of the Moray Firth, it was built after Culloden as a base for George II's army, in case the Highlanders should attempt to rekindle the Jacobite flame. By the time of its completion, however, the uprising had been firmly quashed and the fort has been used ever since as a barracks; note the armed sentries at the main entrance and the periodic crack of live gunfire from the nearby firing ranges.

Apart from the sweeping panoramic **views** across the Firth from its ramparts, the main incentive to visit Fort George is the **Regimental Museum** of the Queen's Own Highlanders. Displayed in polished glass cases is a predictable array of regimental silver, coins, moth-eaten uniforms and medals, along with some macabre war trophies, ranging from bloodstained nineteenth-century Sudanese battle robes to Iraqi gas masks gleaned in the Gulf War. The heroic deeds performed by various recipients of Victoria Crosses make compelling reading. The **chapel** is also worth a look: squat and solid outside, and all light and grace within.

Walking on the northern, grass-covered casemates, which look out into the estuary, you may be lucky enough to see the school of bottle-nosed **dolphins** (see box on p.1018) swimming in with the tide. This is also a good spot for bird watching: a colony of kittiwakes occupies the fort's slate rooftops, while the white-sand beach and mud flats below teem with waders and seabirds. The easiest way to get to Fort George by public transport is by Highland **bus** #11B from Inverness post office (Mon–Sat 9 daily; 25min).

Nairn

One of the driest and sunniest places in the whole of Scotland, **NAIRN**, on the southern shore of the Moray Firth sixteen miles east of Inverness, began its days as a peaceful community of fishermen and farmers. The former spoke Gaelic, the latter English, allowing James VI to boast that a town in his kingdom was so large that people at one end of the main street could not understand those at the other end. Nairn became popular in Victorian times, when the train line offered a convenient link to its revitalizing sea air and mild climate, and today it still relies on tourism, with all the ingredients for a traditional seaside holiday – a sandy beach, ice-cream shops and fish-and-chip stalls. Its windy, coastal **golf course**, the Links, is one of the most popular in Scotland (☎01667/462787), and Thomas Telford's **harbour** is filled with leisure rather than fishing boats. Nearby, amid the huddled streets of old Fishertown – the town centre is known as new Fishertown – is the tiny **Fishertown Museum** (June–Aug Mon–Sat 10am–5pm; free), signposted from the town centre and the harbour. The more interesting exhibits focus on the parsimonious and puritanical life of the fishing families.

Nairn's helpful **tourist office** is at 62 King St (Easter–May, Sept & Oct Mon–Sat 10am–5pm; June–Aug daily 9am–6pm; ☎01667/452753). **Bike rental** is available from Nairn Watersports (☎01667/455416), down by the harbour. For **accommodation**, try *Clifton House*, Viewfield Street (☎01667/453119; ⑥), which is stacked with antiques and

---

THE DOLPHINS OF THE MORAY FIRTH

The **Moray Firth**, a great wedge-shaped bay forming the eastern coastline of the Highlands, is one of only three areas of British waters that support a resident population of **dolphins**. Just over a hundred bottle-nosed dolphins (*Tursiops truncatus*) live in the estuary, the most northerly breeding ground for this particular species in Europe, and you stand a good chance of spotting a few, either from the shore or from a boat.

Tursiops truncatus is the largest dolphin in the world, typically growing to a length of around 13ft and weighing between 400 and 660 pounds. The adults sport a tall, sickle-shaped dorsal fin and a distinctive beak-like "nose", and usually live for around 25 years, although a number of fifty-year-old animals have been recorded. During the summer, herds of thirty to forty dolphins have been known to congregate in the Moray Firth; no one is exactly sure why, although experts believe the annual gatherings, which take place between late June and August, may be connected to the breeding cycle. Another peculiar trait of the Moray Firth school is its habit of killing porpoises. Several porpoise corpses with serrated tooth marks have been washed ashore in the area, the dolphins tossing dead or dying porpoises around in the waves as if for fun.

Both adults and calves frequently leap out of the water, "bow riding" in front of boats and performing elegant synchronized swimming routines together. This, of course, makes them spectacular animals to watch, and dolphin-spotting has become something of a craze in the Moray Firth area. One of the best places in Scotland, if not in Europe, to look for them is **Chanonry Point**, on the Black Isle, a spit of sand protruding into a narrow, deep channel, where converging currents bring fish close to the surface, and thus the dolphins close to shore; the hour or so before high tide is the most likely time to see them. **Kessock Bridge**, one mile north of Inverness, is another prime dolphin-spotting location. You can go all the way down to the beach at the small village of North Kessock, underneath the road bridge, near the *North Kessock Hotel*, a decent place to have a drink. Alternatively, stop above the village in the car park just off the A9, where there's a **visitor centre** and listening post (daily 10am–5pm; ☎01463/731866; £1 for the whole season) set up by a team of zoologists from Aberdeen University; hydrophones allow you to eavesdrop on the clicks and whistles of underwater conversations.

In addition, several companies run dolphin-spotting **boat trips** around the Moray Firth. However, researchers claim that the increased traffic is causing the dolphins unnecessary stress, particularly during the all-important breeding period, when passing vessels are thought to force calves underwater for uncomfortably long periods. They have therefore devised a code of conduct for boat operators, based on the experiences of other countries where dolphin-watching has become disruptive. Operators currently accredited under the Dolphin Space Programme include Majestic Cruises, Inverness (☎01463/731661); Karl Nielsen, 21 Great Eastern Rd, Portessie, Buckie (☎01542/832289); Macaulay Charters, Inverness (☎01463/751263); Moray Firth Cruises, Shore Street, Inverness (☎01463/717900); and Dolphin Écosse, Bank House, High Street, Cromarty (☎01381/600323).

paintings and hosts music and arts events, or *Greenlawns*, 13 Seafield St (☎01667/452738; ②), a spacious and friendly B&B with most rooms en suite The most luxurious option is the *Golf View Hotel* (☎01667/452301; ⑥), overlooking the golf course and sea; delicious, moderately priced informal meals are served in the conservatory. The plainer *Longhouse Restaurant*, on the corner of Harbour Street and Watson's Place (☎01667/455532), has moderately priced seafood and inexpensive light meals on its menu.

Fortrose and Rosemarkie

Set on the eastern shores of the Black Isle, the peninsula jutting into the Moray Firth, **FORTROSE** is twelve miles by road from Inverness. The town's main point of interest is its ruined early thirteenth-century **cathedral**, behind the main street. Founded by King David I, it now languishes on a lovely yew-studded green bordered by red-sandstone and colour-washed houses; a hoard of gold coins dating from the time of Robert III was unearthed here in 1880. There's also a memorial to the Seaforth family, whose demise was famously predicted by the Brahan Seer, a well-known local visionary of the seventeenth century. There's another memorial plaque to the seer at nearby **Chanonry Point**, reached by a backroad from the north end of Fortrose; the thirteenth hole of the golf course here marks the spot where he met his death. Jutting into a narrow channel in the Moray Firth, the point, fringed on one side by a beach of golden sand and shingle, is an excellent place to look for **dolphins** (see box opposite).

ROSEMARKIE, a one-street village north of Fortrose at the opposite (northwest) end of the beach, is thought to have been converted to Christianity by St Boniface in the early eighth century. **Groam House Museum** (May–Sept Mon–Sat 10am–5pm, Sun 2–4.30pm; Oct–April Sat & Sun 2–4pm; £1.50), at the bottom of the village, displays a bumper crop of intricately carved standing stones and shows an informative video highlighting Pictish sites in the region. A lovely mile-and-a-half **woodland walk** to Fairy Glen, along the banks of a sparkling burn, begins at the car park just beyond the village, on the road to Cromarty. Inexpensive bar **food** is available at the wonderfully old-fashioned *Plough Inn*, just down the main street from the museum.

Cromarty

An ancient legend recalls that the twin headlands flanking the entrance to the Cromarty Firth, known as The Sutors (from the Gaelic word for shoemaker), were once a pair of giant cobblers who used to protect the Black Isle from pirates. Nowadays, however, the only giants in the area are the colossal oil rigs marooned in the estuary. Built and serviced here for the Forties North Sea oilfield, they form a surreal counterpoint to the web of tiny streets and chocolate-box workers' cottages of **CROMARTY**, the Black Isle's main settlement, at the northeast corner of the peninsula. An ancient ferry crossing point on the pilgrimage trail to St Duthac's shrine in Tain, across the firth, the town has been a royal burgh since the fourth century, but Cromarty didn't became a prominent port until 1772, when the entrepreneurial local landlord, George Ross, founded a hemp mill here. Imported Baltic hemp was spun into cloth and rope in the mill, fuelling a period of prosperity during which Cromarty acquired some of Scotland's finest Georgian houses. These, together with the terraced fishers' cottages of the nineteenth-century herring boom, have earned the town the somewhat corny epithet, "the jewel in the crown of Scottish vernacular architecture".

To get a sense of Cromarty's past, head straight for the award-winning **museum** housed in the old **Courthouse**, on Church Street (daily: April–Oct 10am–5pm; Nov, Dec & March noon–4pm; £3), which tells the history of the town using audio-visuals and animated figures. You are also issued with a personal stereo, a tape and a map for a walking tour around the town. A nineteenth-century stonemason turned author, geologist, folklorist and Free Church campaigner, Hugh Miller, was born in Cromarty, and his **birthplace** (May–Sept Mon–Sat 11am–1pm & 2–5pm, Sun 2–5pm; £2; NTS), a modest thatched cottage on Church Street, has been restored to give an idea of what Cromarty must have been like in his day. Aside from formal sights, there's an excellent **walk** out to the south Sutor stacks, plus **boat trips** to see seals, porpoises, bottle-nosed dolphins and occasionally minke whales just off the coast (see box opposite). The **Dolphin Centre**, in Bank House, on High Street, has all sorts of background information on dolphins and whales, along with some spectacular photographs of the animals. The tiny two-car Cromarty–Nigg **ferry** (May–Sept daily 9am–6pm), Scotland's smallest, also doubles up as a cruiser on summer evenings; you can catch it from the jetty near the lighthouse.

Nine **buses** each day run to Cromarty from Inverness (1hr), returning from the stop near the playing fields on the western outskirts of town. During summer, **accommodation** is in short supply, so book ahead. Most upmarket is the traditional *Royal Hotel* (☎01381/600217; ⑥), down at the harbour, which has rather small but richly furnished rooms overlooking the Firth, and a good bar/restaurant. For B&B, there are a number of attractive old houses on Church Street: try *Mrs Robertson's*, at no. 7 (☎01381/600488; ①). Above the town, *Mrs Ricketts* (☎01381/600308; ①) offers well-equipped rooms and good views. The most down-to-earth **place to eat** is the *Cromarty Arms*, which serves basic, inexpensive bar meals, and a good selection of ales and malts. If you're after something a little more sophisticated, you could try the *Thistle Restaurant*, on Church Street, or the *Royal Hotel*'s restaurant, which features Scottish specialities. Cheaper meals are available in the *Royal's* cosy public bar or, on fine nights, on the terrace outside with great views over the firth.

Dingwall and around

Most traffic nowadays takes the upgraded A9 north from Inverness, bypassing the small provincial town of **DINGWALL**, a royal burgh since 1226 and former port that was left high and dry when the river receded during the last century. Today, it's a tidy but dull service and market town with one long main street that's bustling all day and moribund by dinner time. Dingwall's only real claim to fame is that it was the birthplace of Macbeth, whose family occupied the now ruined castle on Castle Street.

If you need to stay, Castle Street is a good place to look for **B&Bs**: try *The Croft* at no. 25 (☎01349/863319; ①), or *St Clements* at no. 17 (☎01349/862172; ①). The smartest hotel is the stylish *Tulloch Castle*, Castle Drive (☎01349/861325; ⑤), a former Highland clan headquarters, or there's the central *Royal Hotel*, High Street (☎01349/862130; ④).

A few miles east of Dingwall, **STRATHPEFFER**, a Victorian spa town surrounded by wooded hills, is a congenial place to stop over. During its heyday, this was a renowned European **health resort** complete with a Pump Room, where visitors could chat while they sipped the water. Today, sadly, some of its buildings are in a sorry state, including several huge faded hotels, though plans are afoot to restore the Pavilion Ballroom to its former glory. Activity is concentrated around the main square, in the middle of which the **Water Sampling Pavilion** rekindles some of the atmosphere of the Victorian days: bath chairs nestle against the wall and four taps carry sulphur-laden water from various nearby sources – you are free to sample them although for most people the rank smell more than offsets any possible benefit.

Buses run regularly between Dingwall and Strathpeffer (not Sun), dropping passengers in the square, where you'll find a small seasonal **tourist office** (hours variable, but usually open daily June to mid-Sept, Mon–Sat April, May & mid-Sept to mid-Oct; ☎01997/421415) with information on points west as well as local areas. The **hotels** in the village are very popular with bus tours, but often have room: the vast *Ben Wyvis* (☎01997/421323; ④) is adequate, in nice grounds east of the main square on the Dingwall road, while north of the main square a converted Victorian villa, complete with turrets, houses the *Holly Lodge Hotel* (☎01997/421254; ②). The *Inver Lodge*, west of the main square (☎01997/421392; ①), and *Francisville*, just past the church (☎01997/421345; ①), both offer good **B&B**. If you don't mind dorms, head for the rambling fifty-bed **youth hostel** (☎01997/421532 or central reservations ☎0541/553255; closed Oct–March), a mile southwest of the main square, up the hill towards Jameston. Those keen on tackling a broader range of **outdoor pursuits**, including canoeing, mountain biking and assault courses, should head to the excellent Fairburn Activity Centre (☎01997/433397; ②), set in the grounds of a magnificent country estate about three miles outside the village of Marybank, south of Strathpeffer and northwest of Muir of Ord.

The Cromarty Firth

Northeast of Dingwall, the **Cromarty Firth** has always been recognized as a perfect natural harbour. During World War I it was a major **naval base**, and today its sheltered waters are used as a centre for repairing North Sea oil rigs. The A862 road from Dingwall rejoins the A9 just after the main road crosses the firth on a long causeway; shortly after this, **Evanton**, a few miles further west along the A9, is notable for the **Fyrish Monument** rising up from a hill behind the village. It was built by a certain Sir Hector Munro, partly to give employment to the area and partly to commemorate his own capture of the Indian town of Seringapatam in 1781 – hence the design, resembling an Indian gateway. If you want to get a close-up look, it's a tough two-hour walk through pine woods to the top. An easier but no less dramatic walk from the village is to follow the Allt Graad river to the unexpected, mile-long **Black Rock** gorge, a deep furrow cut by glacial meltwaters in a band of softer sandstone. The best approach to the gorge is along a track which leaves from *Evanton Caravan Park*, where there's also a simple but neat **bunkhouse** (☎01349/830917, *mlb@blackrockscot.freeserve.co.uk*), one of only two hostels on this entire stretch between Inverness and Thurso.

Strathspey and the Cairngorms

Rising high in the heather-clad hills above Loch Laggan, forty miles due south of Inverness, the **River Spey**, Scotland's second longest river, drains northeast towards the Moray Firth through one of the Highlands' most spellbinding valleys. Famous for its **ski slopes**, **salmon fishing** and **ospreys**, Strathspey forms a broad cleft between the mighty Monadhliath mountains in the north and the ice-sculpted Cairngorm range to the south. Outdoor enthusiasts flock here year-round to take advantage of the superb hiking, watersports and winter snows, but the valley is also a major transport artery connecting Inverness and the northern highlands with the south.

Of Strathspey's scattered settlements, **Aviemore** absorbs the largest number of visitors, particularly in midwinter when it metamorphoses into the UK's busiest ski resort. The village itself isn't up to much, but the 4000ft summit plateau of the Cairngorm is often snowcapped, providing stunning mountain scenery on a grand scale. Sedate **Kingussie**, further up the valley, is an older established holiday centre, popular more with anglers and grouse hunters than canoeists and climbers, while the Georgian town of **Grantown-on-Spey**, jumping-off point for **Loch Garten**, makes another good base for exploring the area. Most of upper Strathspey is privately owned by the Glen More Forest Park and Rothiemurchus Estate, who provide between them a plethora of year-round outdoor facilities, with masses of accommodation of all types. Both bodies actively encourage the recreational use of their land, which gives you the freedom to go virtually anywhere you want.

Aviemore

AVIEMORE was first developed as a resort in the mid-1960s, as the towering concrete **Aviemore Centre** bears witness: a shabby assortment of cavernous concrete buildings and incongruous high-rise hotels presently undergoing a much-needed redevelopment. The village proper, a sprawling jumble of traditional stone houses and tacky tourist shops set in a sea of car and coach parks, isn't much better. That said, Aviemore is by far the most important service centre in the area, with a wide range of facilities, an advantage which outweighs its lack of aesthetic appeal.

Aviemore's **tourist office** is just south of the train station on the main drag, Grampian Road (April–October Mon–Fri 9am–6pm, Sat 10am–5pm, Sun 10am–4pm, Nov–March Mon–Fri 9am–5pm, Sat 10am–5pm; ☎01479/810363). It offers an accommodation booking service, free maps and endless leaflets on local attractions. **Accommodation** is not a problem around here. One of the nicest places in the area is *Corrour House Hotel* (☎01479/810220; ⑤), a little way out at Inverdruie. *Ver Mont Guest House* (☎01479/810470; ③) on Grampian Road is good value. There are also plenty of **B&Bs**: try Mrs Clark at *Sonas* (☎01479/810409; ①). There's also a large **youth hostel** (☎01479/810345 or central reservations ☎0541/553255), close to the tourist office, while the brand new *Aviemore Independent Bunkhouse* (☎01479/811137) on Dalfaber Road is also very central. The *Old Bridge Inn*, on the east side of the railway, below the bridge, is one of the best **places to eat**. *Café Mambo*, in Aviemore Shopping Centre on Grampian Road, attracts a younger crowd with its bright, funky decor and contemporary menu, and the Loch Insh

---

WINTER AND SUMMER ACTIVITIES IN AVIEMORE

WINTER SPORTS

By continental European and North American standards the **skiing** at Aviemore is on a tiny scale, but occasionally snow, sun and lack of crowds coincide and you can have a great day. February and March are usually the best times, but in some years the snow may still be good until April. Lots of places – not just in Aviemore itself – sell or hire equipment; for a rundown of ski schools and rental facilities in the area, check out the tourist office's *Ski Scotland* brochure. The **Cairngorm Ski Area**, about eight miles southeast of Aviemore, above Loch Morlich in Glen More Forest Park, is well served by buses from Aviemore. You can rent skis and other equipment from the Day Lodge at the foot of the ski area (☎01479/861261), which also has a shop, a bar and restaurant, and sells tickets for the year-round chair lift – soon to be replaced by a highly controversial **funicular railway**.

If there's lots of snow, the area around **Loch Morlich** and into the **Rothiemurchus Estate** provides enjoyable **cross-country skiing** through lovely woods. If you really want to know about survival in a Scottish winter, you could try a week at *Glenmore Lodge* (☎01479/861276) in the heart of the Glen More Forest Park at the east end of Loch Morlich. This superbly equipped and organized centre, run by Sports Scotland, offers winter courses in hill-walking, mountaineering, alpine ski-mountaineering, avalanche awareness and much besides.

SUMMER SPORTS

In summer, the main activities around Aviemore are **watersports**, and there are two centres that offer sailing, windsurfing and canoeing. The Loch Morlich Watersports Centre (☎01479/861221), five miles or so east of Aviemore at the east end of the loch, rents equipment and offers tuition in a lovely setting with a sandy beach, while, up-valley, the Loch Insh Watersports Centre (☎01540/651272) offers the same facilities in more open and less crowded surroundings. It also rents mountain bikes, boats for loch fishing, and gives ski instruction on a 164ft dry slope.

Riding and **pony trekking** are on offer up and down the valley: try Alvie Stables at Alvie near Kincraig (☎01540/651409, mobile 0831/495397), or the Carrbridge Trekking Centre, Station Road, Carrbridge, a few miles north of Aviemore (☎01479/841602). **Fishing** is very much part of the local scene; you can fish for trout and salmon on the River Spey, and the Rothiemurchus Estate has a stocked trout-fishing loch at **Inverdruie**, where success is virtually guaranteed. Instruction and rod hire is available from the centre beside the loch. The area is also a great one for **mountain biking**, with both Rothiemurchus and Glenmore estates more progressive in their attitude to the sport than many. The Rothiemurchus visitor centre at Inverdruie has route maps, and you can also hire bikes here, while Bothy Bikes (☎01479/810787) in the Aviemore Shopping Centre beside the railway station on Grampian Road rents out good-quality mountain bikes with front suspension, as well as offering friendly advice on different grades of local routes.

Watersports Centre has a particularly pleasant **restaurant** overlooking the loch with snacks during the day and delicious meals in the evening. All the hotels do run-of-the-mill bar food.

Walks around Aviemore

Walking is an obvious attraction in the Aviemore area, but always follow the usual safety rules (see p.1010). If you want to walk the high tops, take either the service road and summit path or the chair lift up from the Day Lodge (see below). However, as well as the high mountain trails, there are some lovely **low-level walks** around Aviemore. It takes an hour or so to complete the gentle circular walk around pretty **Loch an Eilean** in the Rothiemurchus Estate, beginning at the end of the backroad that turns east off the B970 two miles south of Aviemore. The estate visitor centres at the loch-side and by the roadside at Inverdruie provide more information on the many woodland trails that crisscross this area. A longer walk starts at the near end of **Loch Morlich**. Cross the river by the bridge and follow the dirt road, turning off after about twenty minutes to follow the signs to Aviemore. The path goes through beautiful pine woods and past tumbling burns, and you can branch off to Coylumbridge and Loch an Eilean. Unless you're properly prepared for a 25-mile hike, don't take the track to the **Lairig Ghru**, which eventually brings you out near Braemar. The routes are all well marked and easy to follow and, depending on what combination you put together, can take anything from two to five hours.

Another good shortish (half-day) walk leads along well-surfaced forestry track from Glenmore Lodge up towards the **Ryvoan Pass**, taking in An Lochan Uaine, known as the "Green Loch" and living up to its name, with amazing colours that range from turquoise to slate grey depending on the weather. The track narrows once past the loch and leads east towards Deeside, so retrace your steps if you don't want a major trek. The Glen More Forest Park Visitor Centre by the roadside at the turn-off to Glenmore Lodge has information on other trails in this section of the forest.

Kingussie

KINGUSSIE (pronounced "King*yoos*ee") lies twelve miles south of Aviemore and is far cosier, stacked around a single main street. Beyond its usefulness as a place to stay, the chief attraction here is the excellent **Highland Folk Museum** (May–Aug Mon–Fri 9.30am–5.30pm, Sat & Sun 1–5pm; April, Sept & Oct guided tours only Mon–Fri 10.30am–4.30pm; £3; combined ticket with Newtonmore £4). The museum is split into two complementary parts: the Kingussie section contains an absorbing collection of artefacts typical to traditional Highland ways of life, as well as a farming museum, an old smokehouse, a mill, a Hebridean "black house", and a traditional herb and flower garden; most days in summer there's a demonstration of various traditional crafts. The larger site at **Newtonmore** (same opening hours; £3; combined ticket with Folk Museum £4), three miles south of Kingussie on the A86, tries to create more of a living history museum, with reconstructions of a working croft, a church where recitals on traditional Highland instruments are given through the summer months, and a small village of black houses being constructed using only authentic tools and materials. An entry ticket for either site (£3) can be upgraded to cover both sites for £1 extra.

Kingussie is also notable for the ruins of **Ruthven Barracks** (free access), standing east across the river on a hillock. The best-preserved garrison built to pacify the Highlands after the 1715 rebellion, it makes for great exploring by day and is stunningly floodlit at night. Taken by the Jacobites in 1744, Ruthven was blown up in the wake of Culloden to prevent it from falling into enemy hands. It was also the place from where clan leader Lord George Murray dispatched his acrimonious letter to Bonnie Prince Charlie, holding him personally responsible for the string of blunders that had precipitated their defeat.

OSPREYS AT LOCH GARTEN

The **Abernethy Forest RSPB Reserve** on the shore of **LOCH GARTEN**, eight miles south of Grantown-on-Spey (or seven miles north of Aviemore), is famous as the nesting site of one of Britain's rarest birds. A little over fifty years ago, the **osprey**, known in North America as the "fish hawk", had completely disappeared from the British Isles. Then, in 1954, a single pair of these exquisite white-and-grey eagles mysteriously reappeared and built a nest in a tree half a mile or so from the loch. Although efforts were made to keep the exact location secret, one year's eggs fell victim to a gang of thieves, and thereafter the area became the centre of an effective high-security operation. Now the birds are well established not only here but elsewhere, and there are believed to be up to 130 pairs nesting across the Highlands. The best time to visit is during the nesting season, between late April and August, when the RSPB opens an **observation centre** (daily 10am–6pm; £2.50) complete with powerful telescopes and television monitoring of the nest. This is the place to come to get a glimpse of osprey chicks in their nest; you'll be luckier to see the birds perform their trademark swoop over water to pluck a fish out with their talons, though nearby Loch Garten, as well as Loch Morlich and Loch Insh, are good places to stake out in the hope of a sighting, while one of the best spots is the Rothiemurchus trout loch at Inverdruie. The reserve is also home to several other species of rare birds and animals, including the Scottish crossbill, capercaillie, whooper swan and red squirrel – **guided walks** leave from the observation centre at 9.30am on Wednesdays.

Kingussie's **tourist office** is in the same building as the entrance to the Highland Folk Museum, on Duke Street (same hours as museum; ☎01540/661297). If you want to base yourself here, try *Greystones* (☎01540/661052, *greystones@lineone.net*; ①) on Acres Road, off Ardbroilach Road, which has good facilities for walkers and cyclists and serves meals, or *Ruthven Farm House* (☎01540/661226; ③), a pleasant **B&B** overlooking the barracks. There are also a couple of decent **hostels** in the area: *The Laird's Bothy* (☎01540/661334) is right on the High Street beside the *Tipsy Laird* pub, while the *Pottery Bunkhouse* (☎01528/544231) is attached to Caoldair Pottery at Laggan Bridge, eleven miles west of Kingussie on the A86. The most ambitious **food** in the area is served at *The Cross* restaurant, in a converted tweed mill on Tweed Mill Brae (☎01540/661166; closed Tues, plus Dec–Feb, except Christmas). Its pricey meals make interesting use of local ingredients and there's a vast wine list; they also have several rooms (⑧ including dinner). Cheaper food is available at *The Tipsy Laird*, which does real ales as well as bistro-style meals.

Carrbridge

Another, smaller centre is **CARRBRIDGE**, a pleasant, quiet village about seven miles northeast of Aviemore. Its **Landmark Heritage Park** (daily: April to mid-July 9.30am–6pm; mid-July to Aug 9.30am–8pm; Sept & Oct 9.30am–5.30pm; Nov–March 10am–5pm; £6.40, families from £20.10) combines multimedia presentations on history and natural history with forest walks, nature trails, a maze and fun rides; it's more tastefully done than some places of this kind and an excellent place for children to let off steam. There are some decent accommodation options, including the friendly *Cairn Hotel* (☎01479/841212; ②), the immaculate *Fairwinds Hotel* (☎01479/841240; ③) and, more basic, the tiny but cosy *Carrbridge Bunkhouse* (☎01479/841250, *christian.j@virgin.net*), half a mile or so north of the village on the Inverness road.

Grantown-on-Spey

Buses run from Aviemore and Inverness to the tiny Georgian town of **GRANTOWN-ON-SPEY**, about fifteen miles northeast of Aviemore, which, if you've got your own transport, makes another good base for exploring Strathspey and the Cairngorm area. Activity is concentrated around the attractive central square, including a small **museum** (Tues–Sat 10am–4pm; £3) on Burnfield Avenue which tells the story of the people and the building of the town. The **tourist office** is on High Street (April–Oct daily 9am–6pm; ☎01479/872773) and there's a wide choice of **accommodation**: *Speyside Backpackers* at 16 The Square (☎01479/873514) has dorms and basic double rooms (①), while, if you're after something more upmarket, head for the large seventeenth-century *Garth Hotel*, at the north end of the square (☎01479/872836; ③), or the slightly less pricey *Tyree House Hotel* (☎01479/872615; ③) on its west side. Both are open all year round and have good **restaurants** that serve Scottish specialities.

The Great Glen

The **Great Glen**, cutting diagonally across the Highlands from Fort William to Inverness, follows a major geological fault-line. This huge rift valley was formed when the northwestern and southeastern sides slid against each other along the fault for more than sixty miles, and were later smoothed by glaciers that only retreated around 8000 BC. The glen is impressive more for its sheer scale than its great beauty, but is an obvious and rewarding route between the east and west coast. Of the Great Glen's four elongated lochs, the most famous is **Loch Ness**, home to the mythical beast and linked to the other three, **lochs Oich**, **Lochy** and **Linnhe** (a sea loch) by the **Caledonian Canal**. Surveyed by James Watt in 1773, this famous waterway was completed in the early 1800s by Thomas Telford to enable ships to pass between the North Sea and the Atlantic without having to navigate Scotland's treacherous northern coast. However, only 22 miles of it are bona fide canal – the other 38 exploit the glen's natural lochs and rivers flowing west to reach the Atlantic.

The traditional and most rewarding way to travel through the glen is by **boat**. A flotilla of kayaks, small yachts and pleasure vessels take advantage of the canal and its old wooden locks during the summer, among them Jacobite Cruises (☎01463/233999 for details). Forest Enterprise has also established an excellent **cycle path** through the glen, divided into twelve manageable stages that make a tranquil alternative to the hazardous A82. A leaflet outlining the route, through winding timber trails, towpaths and stretches of minor roads, is available at most tourist offices, or direct from Forest Enterprise, Strathoich, Fort Augustus PH32 4BT (☎01320/366322). Following a broadly similar route is a long-distance footpath, the seventy-mile **Great Glen Way**, which takes five to seven days to walk in full – details of this can be obtained from tourist offices or Scottish Natural Heritage (☎01463/712221). In addition, the Great Glen is reasonably well served by **buses**, with several daily services between Inverness and Fort William, and a couple of extra buses covering the section between Fort William and Invergarry during school terms.

Loch Ness

Loch Ness is long and undeniably scenic, with rugged heather-clad mountains sweeping up from a steep, wooded shoreline, but if it weren't for its legendary inhabitant, Nessie, the Loch Ness Monster, you'd probably drive past without a second glance – especially as the A82, which runs southwest along the west side of the loch to Fort William, gives little

---

"NESSIE"

The world-famous Loch Ness monster, affectionately known as "Nessie" (and by serious aficionados as *Nessiteras rhombopteryx*), has been around a long time. The first mention of her crops up in St Adamnan's seventh-century biography of St Columba. While on his way to evangelize the pagan inhabitants of Inverness, the saint allegedly calmed the monster after she attacked one of his monks. Present-day interest, however, is probably greater outside Scotland than in, dating from the 1930s when the A82 was built along the loch's western shore. Recent encounters range from glimpses of ripples by anglers, to the famous occasion in 1961 when thirty hotel guests saw a pair of humps break the water's surface and cruise for about half a mile before submerging.

Several seemingly photographic evidence is showcased in the two "Monster Exhibitions" at Drumnadrochit, but the most impressive of these – including the renowned black-and-white movie footage of Nessie's humps moving across the water, and the photo of her neck and head – have been exposed as fakes. Hi-tech sonar surveys carried out over the past two decades have failed to come up with conclusive evidence, but it's hard to dismiss Nessie as pure myth. Too many locals have mysterious tales to tell, which they invariably keep to themselves for fear of ridicule by incredulous outsiders. Loch Ness also has an undeniably enigmatic air; even the most hardened cynics rarely resist the temptation to scan the waters for signs of life, just in case . . .

---

opportunity to pull over. The opposite, eastern side – skirted by the sinuous single-track B862/852 (originally a military road built to link Fort Augustus and Fort George) – affords far more spectacular views. However, buses from Inverness only run as far south as Foyers, so you'll need your own transport to complete the whole loop around the loch.

Drumnadrochit and around

Situated above a verdant, sheltered bay fifteen miles from Inverness, **DRUMNADRO-CHIT**, practically the first chance to draw breath as you head down the A82, is the epicentre of Nessie hype, sporting a rash of tacky souvenir shops and two rival monster exhibitions whose head-to-head scramble for punters occasionally erupts into acrimonious exchanges – detailed with relish by the local press. Of the pair, the **Original Loch Ness Monster Exhibition** (daily: April–June & Sept–Nov 10am–6pm; July & Aug 9am–9pm; Dec–March 10am–4pm; £3.50) is the least worthwhile – basically a gift shop with a shoddy audio-visual show tacked on the side. If you're genuinely interested in "Nessie" lore, the **Official Loch Ness Monster Exhibition** (daily: April–June 9.30am–5.30pm; July & Aug 9am–8pm; Sept & Oct 9am–6.30pm; Nov–March 10am–4pm; £5.95), though more expensive (and no more "official" than the other), is a much better bet, offering an in-depth rundown of eyewitness accounts through the ages and mock-ups of the various research projects carried out in the loch. **Cruises** on the loch aboard the *Nessie Hunter* can be booked at the Original Loch Ness Visitor Centre (Easter–Oct hourly 9.30am–6pm; 50min; £8), though a more relaxing alternative is to head out **fishing** with a local ghillie – the boat can take five to eight people and costs £25 for two hours; contact Bruce on ☎01456/450279 to book.

Most photographs allegedly showing the monster have been taken a couple of miles further south, around the fourteenth-century ruined loch-side **Castle Urquhart** (daily: April–June & Sept 9.30am–6.30pm; July & Aug 9.30am–8.30pm; Oct–March 9.30am–4.30pm; last admission 45min before closing; £3.80). Built as a strategic base to guard the Great Glen, the castle played an important role in the Wars of Independence. It was taken by Edward I of England and later held by Robert the Bruce against Edward III, only to be blown up in 1692 to prevent it from falling to the Jacobites. It's pretty dilapidated today, but looks particularly splendid floodlit at night when all the crowds have gone. The castle receives more visitors each year than any other historic site in the Highlands, and the pressures are inevitably taking their toll: a major project is underway to create a larger car park and visitor centre built into the hillside between the main road and the castle.

There's a good range of accommodation around Drumnadrochit, and in the adjoining village of Lewiston. Two very welcoming **B&Bs** are *Gilliflowers* (☎01456/450641, *gilliflowers@cali.co.uk*; ①), a renovated farmhouse tucked away down a country lane in Lewiston, or the modern *Drumbuie* (☎01456/450634; ①), on the northern approach to Drumnadrochit. **Hotels** include the pleasant and secluded *Benleva* (☎01456/450288; ③) between Lewiston and the loch, and, two miles west from Drumnadrochit along the Cannich road, *Polmailly House* (☎01456/450343, *polmaillyhousehotel@btinternet.com*; ⑤); a family-friendly country-house hotel. For **hostel** beds, head to the immaculate and friendly *Loch Ness Backpackers Lodge* (☎01456/450807, *hostel@lochnessbackpackers.freeserve.co.uk*), at Coiltie Farmhouse in Lewiston; follow the sign to the left when coming from Drumnadrochit. All the hotels in the area serve good bar **food**; in Drumnadrochit the *Glen Café* has a short and simple menu with basic grills, while the slightly more upmarket *Fiddlers' Café Bar*, next door to the *Glen* on the village green, offers local steaks, salmon and appetizing home-baked pizza; it also rents out good-quality **mountain bikes** (☎01456/450223), and provides maps and rain capes on request.

Invermoriston and Fort Augustus

Heading south, **INVERMORISTON** is a tiny, attractive village just above Loch Ness, from where you can follow well-marked woodland trails past a series of grand waterfalls. Dr Johnson and Boswell spent a couple of nights here planning their journey to the Hebrides; you, too, could stay at the *Glenmoriston Arms Hotel* (☎01320/351206; ⑤), an old-fashioned inn with more than a hundred malt whiskies at the bar. Alternatively, the SYHA *Loch Ness Youth Hostel* (☎01320/351274 or central reservations ☎0541/553255; closed Nov–March), three and a half miles north of Invermoriston and overlooking the loch, is a more economical base.

FORT AUGUSTUS, the tiny village at the more scenic southwestern tip of Loch Ness, was named after George II's son, the chubby lad who later became the "Butcher" Duke of Cumberland of Culloden fame; it was built as a barracks after the 1715 Jacobite rebellion. Today, it's dominated by comings and goings along the Caledonian Canal, which leaves Loch Ness here, and by its large **Benedictine Abbey**, a campus of grey Victorian buildings founded on the site of the original fort in 1876. The abbey formerly housed a Catholic boys' school and until recently was home to a small but active community of

---

THE NEVIS RANGE SKI STATION

The **Nevis Range Ski Range** (☎01397/705825), seven miles northeast of Fort William on the A82, boasts Scotland's only cable-car system (daily: July & Aug 9.30am–8pm; Sept to mid-Nov & mid-Dec to June 10am–5pm; £6.50 return), in the **AONACH MHOR** ski area – a popular attraction during both winter and the summer off-season period. Built in 1989 with a hefty grant from the regional council, the one-and-a-half mile gondola ride (15min) gives an easy approach to some high-level walking, but for most tourists it simply provides an effortless means to rise 2000ft and enjoy the spectacular views from the terrace of the self-service restaurant at the top. In July and August, you can also ski on the Nevis Range's 246-foot **dry slope** (July & Aug Mon–Thurs & Sun 11.30am–1pm; £9 including ski rental and group instruction), while a three-kilometre championship-grade **downhill mountain bike course** starting from the top gondola station is presently under construction. Highland County bus #41 from Fort William runs here four times a day (June–Oct).

monks, but this broke up due to financial pressures and the building now lies empty. Traditional Highland culture is the subject of **The Clansmen Centre**'s lively and informative exhibition (Easter to mid-Oct daily 10am–6pm; £3), on the banks of the canal, where the guides sport sporrans and rough woollen plaids to talk you through the daily life of the region's seventeenth-century inhabitants inside a mock-up of a turf-roofed stone croft, followed by demonstrations of weaponry in the back garden. Rather more sedate is the small **Caledonian Canal Heritage Centre** (Easter–Oct daily 10am–6pm; free) in Ardchattan House on the northern bank of the canal, where you can view old photographs and records about the building and history of the canal.

Fort Augustus's small **tourist office** (April–June Mon–Sat 10am–5pm; July & Aug 9am–6pm; Sept & Oct 10am–5pm; ☎01320/366367) hands out useful free maps detailing popular walks in the area. They'll also help sort out fishing permits if you fancy trying your luck in the loch or nearby river. The only **hostel** accommodation in town is at *Morag's Lodge* (☎01320/366289) above the petrol station on the Loch Ness side of town, where the atmosphere livens up with the daily arrival of backpackers' minibus tours. The *Old Pier* (☎01320/366418; ③) is a particularly appealing B&B, right on the loch at the north side of the village. Of the **hotels**, try the small, friendly *Caledonian* (☎01320/366256; ②), overlooking the Abbey, or the *Brae* (☎01320/366289; ④), just off the main road as you approach the village from the north. **Eating** places include the *Gondolier*, on the southern side of the village, which serves ambitious Scottish food at reasonable prices, or you can try the *Bothy Bite* beside the canal for Scottish specialities with a good range of moderately priced fish, steak and pies. The village has a lively **pub**, drawing a mixed clientele of locals, yachties and backpackers, as does *Poachers* on the main road.

Spean Bridge and Glen Roy

The fast A82 runs south from Fort Augustus along the shores of Loch Oich, where, at Invergarry, the A87 strikes westwards towards Kyle of Lochalsh and the Skye Bridge. Continuing south towards **Spean Bridge** and Fort William, there are fine views across Loch Lochy to the Glengarry mountains, including Ben Tee, on its northern side. The road comes into more open country near the **Commando Memorial**, a group of bronze soldiers, sculpted in 1952 by Scott Sutherland in memory of the men who trained in the area and lost their lives during World War II. The statue stands on a raised promontory that overlooks an awesome sweep of moor and mountain, taking in Lochaber and the Ben Nevis massif.

Shortly after the Commando Memorial, the A82 dips into the village of Spean Bridge, where it's met by the A86 trunk road to Dalwhinnie on the A9 and Kingussie in Speyside (see p.1023). The countryside here is attractive but relatively untrammelled, with some good hiking routes leading to a generous sprinkling of pretty glens and Munros. At **Roy Bridge**, three miles along the road from Spean Bridge, a minor road turns off which runs up **Glen Roy**. A couple of miles along the glen, you'll see the so-called "parallel roads": not roads at all, but ancient beaches at various levels along the valley sides which mark the shorelines of a loch confined here by a glacial dam in the last Ice Age. Back on the A86, two miles beyond Roy Bridge, *Aite Cruinnichidh*, 1 Achluachrach (☎01397/712315, *gavin@achluachrach.prestel.co.uk*), is a comfortable **bunkhouse** in a beautiful setting, with good facilities and local advice for climbers, walkers and cyclists. The West Highland Railway line runs right past the hostel, fringing the River Spean and the spectacular Monassie Gorge, which you can view from a footpath leading down from the roadside.

Fort William

With its stunning position on Loch Linnhe and the snow-streaked bulk of Ben Nevis rising behind, **FORT WILLIAM**, known by the many walkers and climbers that come here as "Fort Bill", should be a gem. Sadly, the same lack of taste that nearly saw the town renamed "Abernevis" in the 1950s is evident in the ribbon bungalow development and an ill-advised dual carriageway complete with a grubby pedestrian underpass, which have wrecked the waterfront. The main street and the little squares off it are more appealing, though occupied by some decidedly tacky tourist gift shops.

Fort William's downfall started in the nineteenth century, when the original fort, which gave the town its name, was demolished to make way for the train line. Today, the town is a sprawl of dual carriageways, and there's little to detain you except the splendid and idiosyncratic **West Highland Museum**, on Cameron Square, just off High Street (April–June, Sept & Oct Mon–Sat 10am–5pm; July & Aug Mon–Sat 10am–5pm, Sun 2–5pm; Nov–March Mon–Sat 10am–4pm; £2). Its collections cover virtually every aspect of Highland life and the presentation is traditional, but very well done, making a refreshing change from state-of-the-art heritage centres. There's a good section on Highland clans and tartans and, among interesting Jacobite relics, a secret portrait of Bonnie Prince Charlie, seemingly just a blur of paint that resolves itself into a portrait when viewed against a cylindrical mirror. Look out, too, for the long Spanish rifle used in the assassination of a local factor (the landowner's tax-collector-cum-bailiff) – the murder that subsequently inspired Robert Louis Stevenson's novel *Kidnapped.*

Practicalities

The town's **bus** and **train** stations are next door to each other at the east end of High Street. The **tourist office**, Cameron Square, just off High Street (April, May Mon–Sat 9am–5pm, Sun 10am–4pm; June, Sept & Oct Mon–Sat 9am–6pm, Sun 10am–5pm; July & Aug Mon–Sat 9am–8.30pm, Sun 9am–6pm; Nov–March Mon–Fri 9am–5pm, Sat 10am–4pm; ☎01397/703781), hands out free town maps and can help arrange onward transport to many of the less-visited areas of the west coast. **Mountain bikes** are available for rent at Off Beat Bikes (☎01397/704008) on the High Street; they also have a branch open at the Nevis Range lower gondola station during July and August – good for exploring forest tracks in that area. **Excursions** from town include the popular day-trip to Mallaig (see p.1036) on the **Jacobite Steam Train** (mid-June, July & Sept Mon–Fri; Aug Mon–Fri & Sun; depart Fort William 10.20am, Mallaig 2.10pm; day return £19.75; bookings ☎01463/239026). Several **cruises** also leave from the town pier every day, offering the chance to spot the marine life of Loch Linnhe, including seals, otters and sea birds.

Much the most luxurious **place to stay** is *Inverlochy Castle* (☎01397/702177; ⑨), an exceptional country house hotel two miles north of Fort William. Much less expensive is the *Alexandra Hotel* on The Parade (☎01397/702241, *sales@miltonhotels.com*; ⑤), slap in the town centre. An upper-range **B&B** is *Distillery House* (☎01397/700103; ③), just north of the town centre. More economical but very comfortable and central places are the new *Bank Street Lodge* on Bank Street (☎01397/700070; ①) and *St Andrews West*, on Fassifern Rd (☎01397/703038; ①). **Hostels** include the *SYHA* (☎01397/702336 or central reservations ☎0541 553255) at the foot of Glen Nevis, but often full in summer; the *Ben Nevis Bunkhouse*, at Achintee Farm (☎01397/702240, *achintee.accom@glennevis.com*), a more civilized option; in town there's the *Fort William Backpackers*, on Fort William's Alma Road (☎01397/700711), a friendly independent hostel five minutes' walk from the train station, while in Corpach *Farr Cottage* (☎01397/772315, *farrcottage@sol.co.uk*) is the liveliest of the local backpacker stops.

Most **eating places** in Fort William are pretty basic. However, the *Café Chardon*, up a lane off the High Street next to A.T. Mays, does excellent baguettes, croissants and pastries to eat in or take away. On the High Street, the *Grog and Gruel* does pizzas, pasta and Mexican favourites with real ale. For a treat, the *Crannog Seafood Restaurant*, on the pier, cooks oysters, langoustines, prawns and salmon with flair and the wine list is also excellent.

Glen Nevis

A ten-minute drive out of town, **Glen Nevis** is indisputably among the Highlands' most impressive glens: a classic U-shaped glacial valley hemmed in by steep covered slopes and swathes of blue-grey scree. Herds of shaggy Highland cattle graze the valley floor, where a sparkling river gushes through glades of trees. With the forbidding mass of Ben Nevis rising steeply to the north, it's not surprising this valley has been chosen as the location for scenes in several **movies**, among them *Rob Roy* and *Braveheart*. Apart from its natural beauty, Glen Nevis is also the starting point for the ascent of Scotland's highest peak, and you can rent **mountain equipment** and **mountain bikes** at the trailhead. Highland Country **bus** #42 runs from An Aird, Fort William, approximately hourly through the day as far as the youth hostel; less frequently the service carries on another two and a half miles up the glen to the car park by the Lower Falls (mid-May to Sept only; 10–20 min).

Glen Coe

Breathtakingly beautiful, **Glen Coe** (literally "Valley of Weeping"), sixteen miles south of Fort William on the A82, is one of the best-known Highland glens: a spectacular mountain valley between velvety-green conical peaks, their tops often wreathed in cloud, and cascades of rock and scree. In 1692 it was the site of a notorious **massacre**, in which the MacDonalds were victims of a long-standing government desire to suppress the clans. Fed up with what they regarded as unacceptable lawlessness, and a groundswell of Jacobitism and Catholicism, the government offered a general pardon to all those who signed an oath of allegiance to William III by January 1, 1692. When

---

GLEN NEVIS: WALKS AND HIKES

Harvey's Ben Nevis Walkers Map and Guide

Of all the walks in and around **Glen Nevis**, the ascent of **Ben Nevis**, Britain's highest summit, inevitably attracts the most attention. In high summer, the trail is teeming with hikers, whatever the weather. However, this doesn't mean the mountain should be treated casually. It can snow round the summit any day of the year and more people perish here annually than on Everest, so take the necessary precautions (see p.51); in winter, of course, the mountain should be left to the experts.

The most obvious **route** to the summit, a Victorian pony path up the whaleback south side of of the mountain, built to service the observatory that once stood on the top, starts from the Ionad Nibheis Vistor Centre (Easter–Oct daily 9am–5pm; free), a mile and a half southeast of Fort William along the Glen Nevis road (bus #42 from An Aird in Fort William). From the centre, which has a lot of background information on the mountain, as well as a daily weather forecast written on a board outside, cross the footbridge over the River Nevis, then follow the well-marked path which after about twenty minutes connects with a path leading directly down to the Youth Hostel. Continue upwards, swinging onto a wide saddle followed by a series of seemingly endless zigzags which rises from here over boulderfields on to a plateau, which you cross to reach the summit, marked by cairns, a shelter and a trig point.

If you don't fancy a hike up the mountain, try the great **low-level walk** which runs from the end of the road at the top of the glen. The good but very rocky path leads through a dramatic gorge with impressive falls and rapids, then opens out into a secret hanging valley, carpeted with wild flowers, with a high waterfall at the far end. It's a pretty place for a picnic and if you're really energetic you can walk on over **Rannoch Moor** to **Corrour Station**, where you can pick up one of four daily trains to take you back to Fort William.

clan chief **Alastair MacDonald** missed the deadline, a plot was hatched to make an example of "that damnable sept", and **Campbell of Glenlyon** was ordered to billet his soldiers in the homes of the MacDonalds, who for ten days entertained them with traditional Highland hospitality. In the early morning of February 13, the soldiers turned on their hosts, slaying between 38 and 45 and causing more than 300 to flee in a blizzard, some to die of exposure.

Today, the glen, a property of the NTS since the 1930s, is virtually uninhabited, and provides outstanding climbing and walking. A small **NTS visitor centre** (April–Oct 9.30am–5.30pm; 50p), in the middle of the glen just off the main road, shows a short video about the massacre, and has a gift shop selling the usual books, postcards and Highland kitsch; for information about the area, the **tourist office** at Ballachulish is more useful. There is a shortish walk from the centre through the forest to Signal Rock, which unsurprisingly offers good views up and down the glen. More substantial are the informative ranger-led **guided walks** which leave from the centre (May–Aug): a high-level hike leaves at 10.30am on Thursdays (£10) and a low-level walk at 2.30pm on Tuesdays (£2).

There's a good selection of **accommodation** in the Glen Coe and Ballachulish area, making it a viable alternative to staying in Fort William. Basic options include an SYHA

WALKS AROUND GLEN COE

Ordnance Survey Landranger Map No. 41.
Flanked by sheer-sided Munros, Glen Coe offers some of the Highlands' most challenging **hiking** routes, with long steep ascents over rough trails and notoriously unpredictable weather conditions that claim lives every year. The walks outlined below number among the glen's less ambitious routes, but still require a map. It's essential that you take the proper precautions (see p.51), and stick to the paths, both for your own safety and for the sake of the soil, which has become badly eroded in places.

A good introduction to the splendours of Glen Coe is the half-day hike over the **Devil's Staircase**, which follows part of the old military road that once ran between Fort William and Stirling. The trail, a good option for families and less experienced hikers, starts at the village of **Kinlochleven**, due north across the mountains from Glen Coe at the far eastern tip of Loch Leven (take the B863): head along the single-track road from the British Aluminium Heritage Centre to a wooden bridge, from where a gradual climb on a dirt jeep track winds up to Penstock Farm. The path, a section of the **West Highland Way**, is marked from here onwards by thistle signs, and is therefore easy to follow uphill to the 1804ft pass and down the other side into Glen Coe. The Devil's Staircase was named by 400 soldiers who endured severe hardship to build it in the seventeenth century, but in fine settled weather the trail is safe and affords stunning views of Loch Eilde and Buachaille Etive Mhor. A more detailed account of this hike features in *Great Walks: Kinlochleven* leaflet (No. 4), on sale at most tourist offices in the area.

Another leaflet in the Great Walks series (*No. 5: Glen Coe*) gives a good description of the **Allt Coire Gabhail** hike, another old favourite. The trailhead for this half-day route is in Glen Coe itself, at the car park opposite the distinctive Three Sisters massif on the main A82 (look for the giant boulder). From the road, drop down to the floor of the glen and cross the River Coe via the wooden bridge, where you have a choice of two onward paths; the easier route, the less worn one, peels off to the right. Follow this straight up the Allt Coire Gabhail for a couple of miles until you rejoin the other (lower) path, which has ascended the valley beside the burn via a series of rock pools and lively scrambles. Cross the river here via the stepping stones and press on to the false summit directly ahead – actually the rim of the so-called "Lost Valley" which the Clan MacDonald used to flee to and hide their cattle in when attacked. Once in the valley, there are superb views of Bidean, Gearr Aonach and Beinn Fhada, which improve as you continue on to its head, another twenty- to thirty-minute walk. Unless you're well equipped and experienced, turn around at this point, as the trail climbs to some of the glen's high ridges and peaks.

hostel (☎01855/811219 or central reservations ☎0541/553255) on a back road half-way between Glen Coe village and the *Clachaig Inn*; the year-round *Red Squirrel* **campsite** (☎01855/811256) nearby; and a grassier NTS campsite (☎01855/811397; closed Nov–March) on the main road. Glencoe village has a few comfortable **B&Bs**, such as the secluded *Scorry Breac* (☎01855/811354, *john@tajones.demon.co.uk*; ①), and the *Glencoe Guest House* (☎01855/811244; ①), while the best-known **hotel** in the area is the stark *Clachaig Inn* (☎01855/811252, *inn@glencoe-scotland.co.uk*; ③), a great place to swap stories with fellow climbers, and to reward your exertions with pints of beer and heaped platefuls of food. **Mountain bikes** and **tandems** can be rented from the *Clachaig Inn*.

The West Coast

For many people, the Highlands' starkly beautiful **west coast** – stretching from the **Morvern** peninsula (opposite Mull) in the south, to wind-lashed Cape Wrath in the far north – is the epitome of "Bonnie Scotland". Serrated by long blue sea lochs, deep glens and rugged green mountains that sweep from the shoreline, its myriad islets, occasional white-sand beaches and turquoise bays can, on sunny days, look like a picture postcard of the Mediterranean. This also is the least populated part of Britain, with just two small towns, and yawning tracts of moorland and desolate peat bog between crofting settlements.

The **Vikings**, who ruled the region in the ninth century, called it the "South Land", from which the modern district of Sutherland takes its name. After Culloden, the Clearances emptied most of the inland glens of the far north, however, and left the population clinging to the coastline, where a herring-fishing industry developed. Today, tourism, crofting, fishing and salmon farming are the mainstay of the local economy, supplemented by EU construction grants and subsidies for the sheep you'll encounter everywhere.

For visitors, **cycling** and **walking** are the obvious ways to make the most of the superb scenery, and countless lochans and crystal-clear rivers offer superlative trout and salmon **fishing**. The shattered cliffs of the far northwest are an ornithologist's dream, harbouring some of Europe's largest and most diverse **sea-bird colonies**, and the area's craggy mountaintops are the haunt of the elusive golden eagle.

Tempered by the Gulf Stream, the west coast's weather ranges from stupendous to diabolical. Never count on a sunny morning meaning a fine day; it can rain here at any time, and go on raining for days. Beware, too, as always in this part of the world, of the dreaded **midge**, which drives even the hardiest of locals to distraction on warm summer evenings.

Without your own vehicle, **getting around** the west coast can be a problem. There's a reasonable **train** service from Inverness to Kyle of Lochalsh and from Fort William to Mallaig, and a useful **summer bus** service connects Inverness to Ullapool, Lochinver, Scourie and Durness. However, services peter out as you venture further afield, and you'll have to rely on **postbuses**, which go just about everywhere, albeit slowly and at odd times of day. **Driving** is a lot less problematic: the roads aren't busy, though they are frequently single-track and scattered with sheep. On such routes, refuel whenever you can, as pumps are few and far between, and make sure your vehicle is in good condition because, even if you manage to reach the nearest garage, spares may well have to be sent over from Inverness.

Morvern to Morar: the "Rough Bounds"

The remote and sparsely populated southwest corner of the Highlands, from the **Morvern** peninsula to the busy fishing and ferry port of **Mallaig**, is a dramatic, lonely region of mountain, moorland and almost deserted glens fringed by a coast of stunning white beaches, with wonderful views to Mull and Skye. Its Gaelic name translates as the **"Rough Bounds"**, implying a region geographically and spiritually apart. Even if you haven't got a car, you should spend a few days here exploring by foot – there are so few roads that some determined hiking is almost inevitable.

The southwest Highlands' main road is the A830, which winds in tandem with the rail line through the glens from **Fort William** to Mallaig. Along the way, the road passes **Glenfinnan**, the much-photographed spot at the head of stunning Loch Shiel where Bonnie Prince Charlie gathered the clans to start the doomed Jacobite uprising of 1745. There are regular buses and trains along the main road; elsewhere in the region you'll usually have to rely on daily post- or school buses. If you have your own transport, the five-minute ferry crossing at **Corran Ferry** (every 15min; foot passengers and bicycles go free), a nine-mile drive south of Fort William down Loch Linnhe, provides a more direct point of entry for Morvern and the rugged **Ardnamurchan** peninsula.

Morvern, Sunart and Ardgour

Bounded on three sides by sea lochs and, to the north, by desolate Glen Tarbet, the remote southwest part of the Rough Bounds region, known as **Morvern**, is unremittingly bleak and empty. Most visitors only travel through here to get to **LOCHALINE** (pronounced "Loch*aa*lin"), a scattering of houses and a diving school (☎01967/421627) around a small pier from which a ferry crosses to Fishnish on Mull. There are some good walks, including the one to the nearby fourteenth-century ruins of **Ardtornish Castle**, reached via a track that turns east off the main road one and a half miles north of Lochaline. The *Lochaline Hotel* (☎01967/421657; ①) serves reasonable bar food and has a couple of small but comfortable **rooms**.

The predominantly roadless regions of **Sunart** and **Ardgour** make up the country between Loch Shiel, Loch Sunart and Loch Linnhe, north of Morvern: the heart of Jacobite support in the mid-eighteenth century, and a Catholic stronghold to this day. The area's only real village is sleepy **STRONTIAN**, grouped around a green on an inlet of Loch Sunart. In 1722, lead mines here yielded the first ever traces of the element **strontium**, named after the village. Worked by French POWs, the same mines also furnished shot for the Napoleonic wars. Strontian's other claim to fame is the **"Floating Church"**, which was moored nearby in Loch Sunart in 1843. After being refused permission by the local laird to found their own "kirk", or chapel, on the estate, members of the Free Presbyterian Church (see p.966) bought an old boat on the River Clyde, converted it into a church and then had it towed up the west coast to Loch Sunart.

Travelling by **public transport**, you can get to Strontian (not Sun) on the 8am bus from Kilchoan (see below), or on a bus that leaves Fort William at 12.15pm and Ardgour at 12.50pm. Strontian's **tourist office** (Easter–Oct Mon–Sat 9am–5pm, Sun 10am–3pm; ☎01967/402131) will book accommodation for a small fee. *Loch View* **B&B** (☎01967/402465; ①) is excellent value, while *Sea View* (☎01967/402060; ②), a small and very traditional cottage next door, is friendly but more basic. The modern *Kinloch House* (☎01967/402138; ②) is very comfortable, with stunning views down the loch. Strontian also has a couple of good **hotels**, including the *Strontian Hotel* (☎01967/402029; ②), in a splendid position near the water, and the luxurious *Kilcamb Lodge* (☎01967/402257; ⑤), with dinner; closed Dec–Feb), a restored country house set in its own grounds on the loch-side, whose restaurant serves excellent food.

The Ardnamurchan peninsula

A tortuous single-track road (the B8007) winds west from **Salen** along the northern shore of Loch Sunart to the wild **Ardnamurchan peninsula**, the most westerly point on the British mainland. The unspoilt landscape is relatively gentle and wooded at the eastern end, but as you travel west the trees disappear and are replaced by a wild, salt-sprayed moorland. The peninsula, which lost most of its inhabitants during the infamous Clearances (see p.1055), is today virtually deserted apart from the handful of tiny crofting settlements clinging to its jagged coastline. Ardnamurchan remains a naturalist's paradise, harbouring a huge variety of birds, animals and wildflowers like thrift and wild iris.

An inspiring introduction to the diverse flora, fauna and geology of Ardnamurchan is the superb **Glenmore Natural History Centre** (April–Oct 10.30am–5.30pm; £2.50), nestled near the shore just west of the hamlet of **GLENBORRODALE**. Brainchild of local photographer Michael MacGregor (whose stunning work enlivens postcard stands along the west coast), the centre is housed in a sensitively designed timber building, complete with turf roof and wildlife ponds. TV cameras relay live pictures of the comings and goings of the surrounding wildlife, from a pine marten's nest, a heronry and from underwater pools in the nearby river, while an excellent audio-visual show features MacGregor's photographs of the area accompanied by specially composed music. The small **café** serves sandwiches and good home-baked cakes and there's a useful bookshop. The nearby **RSPB reserve**, a mile to the east, is rich in wildlife too, being home to tree creepers, golden eagles, otters and seals, while for coastal wildlife-spotting – or trips to Tobermory on Mull or Fingal's Cave – contact Ardnamurchan Charters at Glenborrodale (☎01972/500208).

KILCHOAN, nine miles west of the Glenmore Centre, is Ardnamurchan's main village – a straggling but appealing crofting township overlooking the Sound of Mull. Between Easter and mid-October, a **car ferry** runs from here to Tobermory (7 daily; 35min), while in the winter a passenger ferry plies the route for schoolchildren and shoppers. The new community centre in the village houses a **tourist office** (Easter–Oct daily 10am–6pm; ☎01972/510222), who will help with and book accommodation, though year-round the community centre will act as an informal source of local advice and assistance. Accommodation isn't plentiful in Kilchoan, but both the *Meall mo Chridhe Hotel* (☎01972/510328; ⑤, ⑦ with dinner; closed Nov–March), a converted eighteenth-century manse set among trees above the road, and *Doirlinn House* (☎01972/510209; ②; closed Nov–Feb), a B&B with great views, are very pleasant. Further afield, *Feorag House* (☎01972/500248; ⑦, incl dinner) at Glenborrodale is an acclaimed upmarket B&B, while a couple of miles before the Ardnamurchan Point lighthouse (see below), there's the *Sonachan Hotel* (☎01972/510211; ②), a cosy and friendly haven also offering good bar meals, and *Hillview* (☎01972/510322; ①), a traditional cottage about four miles north of Kilchoan at Achnaha (you'll need your own transport). The only direct bus to Kilchoan leaves from Corran Ferry at 12.35pm, arriving two hours later.

Beyond Kilchoan the road continues to wild and windy **Ardnamurchan Point**, with its unmanned **lighthouse** and spectacular views west to Coll, Tiree and across to the north of Mull. The lighthouse buildings house a café and an enthusiastically run **visitor centre** (April–Oct 9.30am–6pm; £2.50; ☎01972/510210), whose main theme is lighthouses, their construction and the people who lived in them. About three miles north of the point, the shell-strewn sandy beach of **Sanna Bay** offers truly unforgettable vistas of the Small Isles to the north, circled by gulls, terns and guillemots.

Moidart

Heading north from Salen on the A861 towards the district of Moidart, the main settlement is **ACHARACLE**, an ancient crofting village lying at the seaward end of Loch Shiel. Surrounded by gentle hills, it's an attractive place whose scattered houses form a real community, with several shops, a post office, and plenty of places to stay. The informal *Loch Shiel House Hotel* (☎01967/431224; ②) has nice rooms and simple but good food including local salmon and haddock. *Belmont* (☎01967/431266; ②) is a comfortable and central B&B, as is *Mrs Crisp's* (☎01967/431318; ①), just across the road. On the south side of the village, *Ardshealach Lodge* (☎01967/431301; ②) is secluded and welcoming. You can get to Acharacle by **boat** with Loch Shiel Cruises on Wednesdays (☎01397/722235), or by **bus** on the infrequent links with Mallaig and Fort William.

A mile north of Acharacle, a side road running north off the A861 winds for three miles or so past a secluded estuary lined with rhododendron thickets and fishing platforms to **Loch Moidart**, a calm and sheltered sea loch. Perched atop a rocky promontory in the middle of the loch is **Castle Tioram** (pronounced "cheerum"), one of Scotland's most atmospheric historic monuments. Reached via a sandy causeway, the thirteenth-century fortress, whose Gaelic name means "dry land", was the seat of the MacDonalds of Clanranald until it was destroyed by their chief in 1715 to prevent it from falling into Hanoverian hands while he was away fighting for the Jacobites. Today, the surviving walls and tower enclose an inner courtyard and a couple of empty chambers.

Glenfinnan to Mallaig

Approaching Moidart from the south by train, or via the fast Fort William–Mallaig road (the A830), you pass **GLENFINNAN**, nineteen miles west of Fort William at the head of Loch Shiel, where Bonnie Prince Charlie raised his standard to signal the start of the Jacobite uprising of 1745. It is a poignant place, a beautiful stage for the opening scene in a brutal drama which was to change the Highlands for ever. The **visitor centre** and café (daily: April, May, Sept & Oct 10am–5pm; June–Aug 9.30am–6pm; £1.50; NTS), opposite the monument, gives an account of the '45 uprising through to the rout at **Culloden** eight months later (see p.1015). For a longer taste of the atmosphere of the spot, a **boat trip** on the loch with Loch Shiel Cruises (April–Oct; ☎01397/722235) is highly recommended.

Glenfinnan is also one of the most spectacular moments on the West Highland Railway line, not only for the glimpse it offers of the monument and graceful Loch Shiel, but also the mighty 21-arched **viaduct** built in 1901 and one of the first ever large constructions made out of concrete. You can learn more of the history of this section of the railway at the **Glenfinnan Station Museum** (June–Sept daily 9.30am–5pm; 50p), set in the old booking office of the station. Right beside the station two old railway carriages have been pressed into use as one of the most original restaurants and bunkhouses along the West Coast. The *Dining Car* (May–Sept daily 9.30am–11pm; ☎01397/722400) is open for light lunches, home baking and excellent evening meals, while the *Sleeping Car*, a converted 1958 "Camping Coach", sleeps ten in bunk beds.

Beyond Glenfinnan, the A830 runs towards a coast marked by acres of white sands, turquoise seas and rocky islets draped with orange seaweed. **ARISAIG**, scattered

---

THE RAISING OF THE STANDARD

On 19 August 1745, surrounded by no more than 200 loyal clansmen, Bonnie Prince Charlie waited at Glenfinnan to see if Cameron of Loch Shiel would join his army. The drone of this powerful chief's pipers drifting up the glen was eagerly awaited, for without him the Stuarts' attempt to claim the English throne would have been sheer folly. Despite strong misgivings, Cameron did decide to support the uprising, and arrived at Glenfinnan late in the day with 800 men, thereby encouraging other less-convinced clan leaders to follow suit. Assured of adequate backing, the prince raised his red-and-white silk colour, proclaimed his father King James III of England, and set off on the long march to London from which only a handful of the soldiers gathered at Glenfinnan would return. The spot is marked by a column, crowned with a clansman in full battle dress, erected as a tribute by Alexander Macdonald of Glenaladale in 1815.

round a sandy bay at the west end of the Morar peninsula, makes a good base for exploring this area. There's nothing in the way of specific attractions, but if the weather's fine you can spend hours wandering along the beaches and quiet backroads. **Accommodation** in the village is plentiful. *Kinloid Farm House* (☎01687/450366; ②, ⑤) with dinner; closed Nov–Feb) is one of several pleasant B&Bs with sea views, while the more upmarket *Old Library Lodge* (☎01687/450651; ⑤; closed Nov–March) has rooms in a 200-year-old converted stable overlooking the waterfront.

The next settlement of any significance is **MORAR**, where the famous beach scenes from *Local Hero* were shot. Since then, however, a bypass has been built around the village, and the white sands, plagued by the rumble of frozen-cod lorries, are no longer the unspoilt idyll Burt Lancaster paddled ecstatically around in the early 1980s. You can still find some pleasant places to stay – of the string of campsites try *Camusdarach* (☎01687/450221), which isn't quite on the beach but is quieter and less officious than others nearby. B&B is also available in the attractive main house (①).

Mallaig

A cluttered, noisy port whose pebble-dashed houses struggle for space with great lumps of granite tumbling down to the sea, **MALLAIG**, 47 miles west of Fort William along the A830 (regular buses and trains run this route), is not a pretty village. Before the railway reached here in 1901, it consisted of only a few cottages, but now it's a busy, bustling place and, as the main ferry stop for Skye and the Small Isles (see p.950), is always full of visitors. The continuing source of the village's wealth is its thriving **fishing industry**: on the quayside, piles of nets, tackle and ice crates lie scattered around a bustling modern market. When the fleet is in, trawlers encircled by flocks of raucous gulls choke the harbour, and the pubs, among the liveliest on the west coast, host bouts of serious drinking.

Apart from the daily bustle of the harbour, the main attraction in town is **Mallaig Marine World**, north of the train station near the harbour (June & Sept Mon–Sat 9am–7pm, Sun 10am–6pm; July & Aug Mon–Sat 9am–9pm, Sun 10am–6pm; Oct–May Mon–Sat 9am–5.30pm, Sun 11am–5pm; £2.75), where tanks of local sea creatures and informative exhibits about the port provide an unpretentious but sensitive introduction to the local waters. Alongside the train station, the **Mallaig Heritage Centre** (May–Sept Mon–Sat 11am–4pm, Sun 1–4pm; £1.80), displaying old photographs of the town and its environs, is worth a browse.

Mallaig is a compact place, concentrated around the harbour, where you'll find both the **tourist office** (April, May, Sept & Oct Mon–Sat 10am–6.30pm; June–Aug Mon–Sat 9am–8pm, Sun 10am–4pm; Nov–March Mon, Wed & Fri 10am–2pm; ☎01687/462170), which will book accommodation for you, and the **bus** and **train stations**. The CalMac ticket office (☎01687/462403), serving passengers for Skye and the Small Isles, is also nearby, and you can arrange transport to Knoydart by telephoning Bruce Watt Cruises (☎01687/462320 or 462233), which sails to Inverie every Monday, Wednesday and Friday morning and afternoon, the later cruise continuing east along Loch Nevis to Tarbet; the loch is sheltered, so crossings are rarely cancelled. Mr Watt also operates cruises (mid-May to mid-Sept) to Loch Scavaig on Skye (see p.955) on Tuesdays and Thursdays (11am).

There are plenty of places **to stay**: the *West Highland Hotel* (☎01687/462210; ③) is pleasantly old-fashioned, if a little shabby in places – some rooms have excellent sea views; while the *Marine* (☎01687/462217; ③) is much smarter inside than first impressions suggest. For **B&B**, head around the harbour to East Bay, where you'll find the immaculate *Western Isles Guest House* (☎01687/462320; ①), with the nearby *Haco Cottage* (☎01687/462434; ①) a good alternative. Budget travellers should head for Sheena's *Backpackers' Lodge* (☎01687/462764), a refreshingly laid-back independent hostel overlooking the harbour, with mixed dorms, self-catering facilities and a sitting room. For **eating**, the *Marine Hotel* serves good-value bar meals featuring fresh seafood which are well above average, while the nearby *Seafood Restaurant* (also known as the *Cabin*) has a more ambitious menu but is very popular, so booking is wise. During the day, the *Tea Garden* at *Sheena's Lodge* is a great place to watch the world go by while you tuck into a bowl of Cullen Skink (soup made from smoked haddock), a pint of prawns, or home-made scones.

Kyle of Lochalsh

KYLE OF LOCHALSH is a busy town, a transit point on the route to Skye and an important train terminal. Straggling down the hill towards the pier and train station, it's not particularly attractive – concrete buildings, rail junk and myriad signs of the fishing industry abound – and is ideally somewhere to pass through rather than linger in. Since the **Skye Road Bridge** was opened in 1995, traffic has little reason to stop in town before rumbling over the channel a mile to the north, leaving its shopkeepers bereft of the passing trade they used to enjoy. The new bridge, built with private sector money, has also sparked controversy over its high tolls (£5.70 for cars), with local protesters doing battle in Dingwall Sheriff Court and Edinburgh's Court of Session.

Buses run to the harbour in Kyle of Lochalsh from Glasgow via Fort William and Invergarry (3 daily; 5hr 30min–6hr 15min), and from Inverness via Invermoriston (4 daily; 2hr); there's also a summer service from Edinburgh (1 daily; 7hr 15min). These routes can become very crowded, so it's wise to book in advance (☎0990/505050). All these services continue at least as far as Portree, on Skye, and a shuttle service runs across the bridge to Kyleakin every thirty minutes or so. Three or four **trains** run daily, with one or two on summer Sundays, from Inverness (2hr 30min); it's a spectacular journey.

The **tourist office** (April, May, Sept & Oct Mon–Sat 9am–5pm; June & Aug Mon–Sat 9am–7pm, Sun 10am–4pm; ☎01599/534276), on top of the small hill near the old ferry jetty, will book accommodation for you, which is useful as there are surprisingly few places to stay, particularly in high summer. If you're feeling flush, splash out at the *Lochalsh Hotel* (☎01599/534202; ⑨), a wonderfully located place looking out at Skye, with fabulous seafood and an air of dated luxury. For **B&B**, try Mrs Henderson at *Glenview* (☎01599/534119; ①), five minutes' walk from the train station, or *Crowlin View* (☎01599/534286; ③), a traditional house with views to Skye, one and a half miles north of Kyle on the Plockton road. There's a simple but neat and clean backpackers in town, *Cúchulainn's* (☎01599/534492), above a pub across the main street from the tourist information. Between Kyle and Plockton, the *Old Schoolhouse* at Erbusaig (☎01599/534369; ②) is a good-quality restaurant with inexpensive and comfortable rooms. The *Seagreen Restaurant and Bookshop* (☎01599/534388), also on the Plockton road on the edge of Kyle of Lochalsh, has excellent fresh seafood and vegetarian meals in a pleasant, unfussy setting, while the *Seafood Restaurant* at the train station is also recommended, if a little pricier.

Loch Duich

Approaching Kyle of Lochalsh by road, you skirt the northern shore of **Loch Duich**, the boot-shaped inlet that forms the northern shoreline of the Glenelg peninsula, and features prominently on the tourist trail, with buses from all over Europe thundering down the road through Glen Shiel on their way to Kyle of Lochalsh and Skye. It's a dramatic approach, with the mountains known as the Five Sisters of Kintail surging up to heights of 3000ft – a familiar sight from countless tourist brochures, but an impressive one nonetheless. With steep-sided hills hemming in both sides of the loch, it's sometimes hard to remember that this is, in fact, the sea. There's a congenial SYHA **youth**

HIKING IN GLEN SHIEL

Ordnance Survey Landranger Map No. 33.
The mountains of **Glen Shiel**, sweeping southeast from Loch Duich, offer some of the best hiking routes in Scotland. Rising dramatically from sea level to over 3000ft in less than a couple of miles, they are also exposed to the worst of the west coast's notoriously fickle weather. Don't underestimate either of these two routes. Tracing the paths on a map, they can appear short and easy to follow; however, unwary walkers die here every year, often because they failed to allow enough time to get off the mountain by nightfall, or because of a sudden change in the weather. Neither of the routes outlined below should be attempted by inexperienced walkers, nor without a map, a compass and a detailed trekking guide – the *SMC's Hill Walks in Northwest Scotland* is recommended. Also make sure to follow the usual safety precautions outlined on p.51.

Taking in a bumper crop of Munros, the **Five Sisters traverse** is deservedly the most popular trek in the area. Allow a full day to complete the whole route, which begins at the first fire break on the left-hand side as you head southeast down the glen on the A87. Strike straight up from here and follow the ridge north along to Scurr na Moraich (2874ft), dropping down the other side to Morvich on the valley floor.

The distinctive chain of mountains across the glen from the Five Sisters is the **Kintail Ridge**, crossed by another famous hiking route that begins at the *Cluanie Inn* on the A87. From here, follow the well-worn path south around the base of the mountain until it meets up with a stalkers' trail, which winds steeply up Creag a' Mhaim (3108ft) and then west along the ridgeway, with breathtaking views south across Knoydart and the Hebridean Sea.

---

hostel just outside Shiel Bridge at **RATAGAN** (☎01599/511243 or central reservations ☎0541/553255; closed Jan), popular with walkers newly arrived off the Glen Affric trek from Cannich.

Eilean Donan Castle

After Edinburgh's hilltop fortress, **Eilean Donan Castle** (April–Oct daily 10am–5.30pm; £3.75), ten miles north of Shiel Bridge on the A87, has to be Scotland's most photographed monument. Presiding over the once strategically important confluence of lochs Alsh, Long and Duich, the forbidding crenellated tower rises from the water's edge, joined to the shore by a narrow stone bridge and with sheer mountains as a backdrop.

The original castle was established in 1230 by Alexander II to protect the area from the Vikings. Later, during a Jacobite uprising in 1719, it was occupied by troops dispatched by the King of Spain to help the "**Old Pretender**", James Stuart. However, when King George heard of their whereabouts, he sent frigates to weed the Spaniards out, and the castle was blown up with their stocks of gunpowder. Thereafter, it lay in ruins until John Macrae-Gilstrap had it rebuilt between 1912 and 1932. Eilean Donan has also been the setting of several major **movies**, including *Highlander*, starring Christopher Lambert, and a recent James Bond adventure, *The World Is Not Enough* (numerous film stills are sold at the ticket office). Three floors, including the banqueting hall, the bedrooms and the troops' quarters, are open to the public, with various Jacobite and clan relics also on display, though the large numbers of people passing through make it hard to appreciate them.

There are several **places to stay** less than a mile away in the hamlet of **DORNIE**, including the *Silver Fir Bunkhouse* (☎01599/555264), little more than a simple hut with two bunk beds and a woodburning stove, but friendly and characterful. Otherwise, the *Dornie Hotel*, Francis Street (☎01599/555205; ④), boasts comfortable rooms, while the *Loch Duich Hotel* (☎01599/555213; ③) has splendid doubles overlooking the loch and a small restaurant serving upmarket bar snacks and evening meals. Another good place for a bar meal is the popular *Clachan*, just along from the *Dornie Hotel*.

Plockton

A fifteen-minute train ride north of Kyle at the seaward end of islet-studded Loch Carron lies unbelievably picturesque **PLOCKTON**: a chocolate-box row of neatly painted cottages ranged around the curve of a tiny harbour and backed by a craggy landscape of heather and pine. Originally known as Am Ploc, the settlement was a crofting hamlet until the end of the eighteenth century, when a local laird transformed it into a prosperous fishery, renaming it "Plocktown". Its fifteen minutes of fame came in the mid-1990s, when the BBC chose the village as the setting for three series of the television drama *Hamish Macbeth*. Though the resulting spin-off has quietened down a little, in high season it's still packed full of tourists, yachtsmen and second-home owners. The unique brilliance of Plockton's light has also made it something of an artists' hangout, and during the summer the waterfront, with its row of shaggy palm trees, even shaggier Highland cattle, flower gardens and pleasure boats, is invariably punctuated by painters dabbing at their easels.

If you want **to stay**, try the friendly, cosy *Haven Hotel*, on Innes Street (☎01599/544223; ⑤), renowned for its excellent food, or the *Plockton Inn*, also on Innes Street (☎01599/544222; ③), which makes an informal and comfortable alternative. The *Plockton Hotel*, Harbour Street (☎01599/544274; ④), overlooking the harbour with some rooms in a nearby cottage, has a friendly bar and serves good seafood. Of the fifteen or so **B&Bs**, *The Shieling* (☎01599/544282; ②) has a great location on a tiny headland at the top of the harbour, the nearby *Heron's Flight* (☎01599/544220; ②) has uninterrupted views across the loch from its upstairs bedrooms, while *The Manse* on Innes Street (☎01599/544442; ②) features beautifully furnished rooms and serves generous breakfasts. There's also the attractive new *Station Bunkhouse* (☎01599/544235), built in the shape of a signal box next to the railway station, which has four- and six-person dorms and a cosy open-plan kitchen and living area. You should have little difficulty finding somewhere good **to eat** in Plockton: both the *Haven* and the *Plockton Inn* have excellent seafood restaurants, while *Off the Rails*, in the train station, serves good-value, imaginative snacks by day and dinner. For **fishing** or **seal-spotting** boat trips from Plockton, try Leisure Marine (☎01599/544306) or Sea Trek Marine (☎01599/544356).

The Applecross peninsula

The most dramatic approach to the **Applecross peninsula** (the English-sounding name is actually a corruption of the Gaelic *Apor Crosan*, meaning "estuary") is from the south, along the infamous **Bealach na Ba** (literally "Pass of the Cattle"). Crossing the forbidding hills behind Kishorn and rising to 2053ft, with a gradient and switchback bends worthy of the Alps, this route, the highest road in Scotland and a popular cycling piste, is hair-raising in places, but the panoramic views across the Minch to Raasay and Skye more than compensate. The other way in is from the north: a beautiful coast road that meanders slowly from Shieldaig on Loch Torridon, with tantalizing glimpses of the Cuillins to the south.

The sheltered, fertile coast around **APPLECROSS** village, where the Irish missionary monk Maelrhuba founded a monastery in 673 AD, comes as a surprise after the bleakness of the moorland approach. It's an idyllic place: you can wander along lanes banked with wild iris and orchids, and explore beaches and rock pools on the shore. It's also quite an adventure to get here by **public transport**. The nearest railhead is seventeen miles northeast at Strathcarron station, near Achnasheen, which you have to reach by 9.50am to catch the postbus to Shieldaig, on Loch Torridon. From here, a second postie leaves for Applecross at 11.30am (90min). No buses of any kind run over the Bealach na Ba. The old *Applecross Inn* (☎01520/744262; ②), right beside the sea, is the focal point of the community, with rooms upstairs and a lively bar serving snacks and tasty platefuls of local seafood. A couple of friendly **B&Bs** lie south of here towards Toscaig, with its pier and inquisitive seals: try Mrs Thompson (☎01520/744260; ①) at *Camusteel*, or Mrs Dickens (☎01520/744206; ①) at *Camusterrach*. **Camping** (☎01520/744268) is provided at the *Flowertunnel*, as you come into the village from the pass. There are a couple of options if you want to explore the area: Applecross Peninsula Visitor Services (☎01520/744262) offer half- or full-day Landrover or walking trips seeking out local history, wildlife and geology, while Applecross Mountain & Sea (☎01520/744393) have more rugged mountain expeditions and kayaking around the coast.

Loch Torridon

Loch Torridon marks the northern boundary of the Applecross peninsula, its awe-inspiring setting backed by the spectacularly rugged mountains of **Liathach** and **Beinn Eighe**, tipped by streaks of white quartzite. The greater part of this area is composed of the reddish 750-million-year-old Torridonian sandstone, and some 15,000 acres of the massif are under the protection of the National Trust for Scotland. They run a **Countryside Centre** (May–Sept Mon–Sat 10am–5pm, Sun 2–5pm) at Torridon village at the east end of the loch, where you can call in and learn a bit more about the local geology, flora and fauna.

The road which runs along the northern shore of the loch from **TORRIDON** village is scenic and dramatic, winding first along the shore then climbing and twisting past lochans, cliffs and gorges to the green wooded slopes of **DIABAIG**. There's a modern **youth hostel** at Torridon (☎01445/791284 or central reservations ☎0541/553255; closed Nov–Jan, except Christmas & New Year), and one of the area's top hotels, the rambling Victorian *Loch Torridon Hotel* (☎01445/791242; ⑧), set amid well-tended lochside grounds. Next door, *Ben Damph Lodge* (☎01445/791242, *ben@ochtorridnhotel.com*; ③) is a modern conversion of an old farmsteading with neat if characterless rooms and a large climber's bar. Also in Diabaig, Miss Ross (☎01445/790240; ①) has comfortable accommodation overlooking the rocky bay, and there's a good B&B, *Tigh Fada* (☎01520/755248; ①), at **DOIREANOR**, on the southwest side of Loch Shieldaig.

Loch Maree

About eight miles north of Loch Torridon, **Loch Maree**, dotted with Caledonian pine-covered islands, is one of the west's scenic highlights, best viewed from the road (A832) that drops down to its southeastern tip through Glen Docherty. It's also surrounded by some of Scotland's finest deerstalking country: the remote, privately owned *Letterewe Lodge* on the north shore, accessible only by helicopter or boat, lies at the heart of a famous deer forest. **Queen Victoria** stayed a few days here in 1877 at the wonderfully sited *Loch Maree Hotel* (☎01445/760288, *lochmaree@easynet.co.uk*; ⑤), which is comfortable and less formal than in her day; another good base if you're heading into the hills is *Cromasaig* B&B (☎01455/760234, *cromasaig@msn.com*; ①) by Kinlochewe, a great place for hill walkers set in the forest right at the foot of the track up Beinn Eighe.

The A832 skirts the southern shore of Loch Maree, passing the **Beinn Eighe Nature Reserve**, the UK's oldest wildlife sanctuary. Parts of the Beinn Eighe reserve are forested with Caledonian pinewood, which once covered the whole of the country, and it is home to pine marten, wildcat, fox, badger, Scottish crossbill, buzzards and

WALKING AROUND TORRIDON

Ordnance Survey Outdoor Leisure map No. 8.

There are difficult and unexpected conditions on virtually all hiking routes around Torridon, and the weather can change very rapidly. If you're relatively inexperienced but want to do the magnificent ridge walk along the Liathach (pronounced "Lee-a-gach", or "Lee-ach") massif, or the strenuous traverse of Beinn Eighe (pronounced "Ben Ay"), join a National Trust Ranger Service guided hike (details from the Torridon Countryside Centre on ☎01445/791221).

For those confident to go it alone (using the above map), one of many possible routes takes you behind Liathach and down the pass, Coire Dubh, to the main road in Glen Torridon. This is a great, straightforward walk if you're properly equipped (see p.51), covering thirteen miles and taking in superb landscapes. Allow yourself the whole day. Start at the stone bridge on the Diabaig road along the north side of Loch Torridon. Follow the Abhainn Coire Mhic Nobuil burn up to the fork at the wooden bridge and take the track east to the pass (a rather indistinct watershed) between Liathach and Beinn Eighe. The path becomes a little lost in the boggy area studded with lochans at the top of the pass, but the route is clear and, once over the watershed, the path is easy to follow. At this point you can, weather permitting, make the rewarding diversion up to the Coire Mhic Fhearchair, widely regarded as the most spectacular corrie in Scotland; otherwise continue down the Coire Dubh stream, ford the burn and follow its west bank down to the Torridon road, from where it's about four miles back to Loch Torridon.

A rewarding walk even in rough weather is the seven-mile hike up the coast from Lower Diabaig, ten miles northwest of Torridon village, to Redpoint. On a clear day, the views across to Raasay and Applecross from this gentle undulating path are superlative, but you'll have to return along the same trail, or else make your way back via Loch Maree on the A832. If you're staying in Shieldaig, the track that winds up the peninsula running north from the village makes a pleasant ninety-minute round walk.

golden eagles. There's also a wide range of flora, with the higher rocky slopes producing spectacular natural alpine rock gardens. A mile north of Kinlochewe, the **Beinn Eighe Visitor Centre** (Easter & May–Sept daily 10am–5pm) on the A832 gives details of the area's rare species and sells pamphlets describing two excellent **walks** in the reserve: a woodland trail through loch-side forest, and a more strenuous half-day hike around the base of Beinn Eighe. Both start from the car park a mile north of the visitor centre.

Gairloch and around

Mostly scattered around the sheltered northeastern shore of the loch of the same name, the crofting township of **GAIRLOCH** thrives during the summer as a low-key holiday resort with several tempting sandy beaches and some excellent coastal walks within easy reach. The **Gairloch Heritage Museum** (April, May & Oct Mon–Sat 11am–4pm; June–Sept Mon–Sat 10am–5pm; for winter times phone ☎01445/712287; £2.50) has eclectic, appealing displays covering geology, archeology, fishing and farming that range from a mock-up of a croft house to an early knitting machine. Probably the most interesting section is the archive – an array of photographs, maps, genealogies, lists of place names and taped recollections, mostly in Gaelic – made by elderly locals.

The area's real attraction, however, is its beautiful **coastline**. To get to one of the most impressive stretches, head around the north side of the bay and follow the single-track B8021 beyond Big Sand (a cleaner and quieter beach than the one in Gairloch) to the tiny crofting hamlet of **Melvaig** (reachable by the 9.05am Gairloch postbus), from where a narrow surfaced track winds out to **Rua Reidh** (pronounced "Roo-a Ree") Point. The converted **lighthouse** here, which looks straight out to Harris in the Outer Hebrides, serves slap-up afternoon teas and home-baked cakes (Easter–Oct Tues, Thurs & Sun noon–5pm). You can also stay in its comfortable and relaxed **bunkhouse**, or **double rooms** (book ahead in high season on ☎01445/771263, *ruareidh@netcomuk.co.uk*; ①), or use it as a base for one of the popular walking or activity holidays organized by the folk who run the bunkhouse. Around the headland from Rua Reidh lies the secluded and beautiful **Camas Mor** beach. For a great half-day walk, follow the marked footpath inland (southeast) from here along the base of a sheer scarp slope, and past a string of lochans, ruined crofts and a remote wood to Midtown on the east side of the peninsula, five miles north of Poolewe on the B8057. However, unless you leave a car at the end of the trail or arrange to be picked up, you'll have to walk or hitch back to Gairloch, as the only transport along this road is an early-morning post van.

A more leisurely way to explore the coast is on a wildlife-spotting cruise: Gairloch Marine Life Centre & Cruises (Easter–Oct ☎01445/712636) at the pier run informative and enjoyable boat trips across the bay in search of dolphins, porpoises, seals and even the odd whale. You can also rent a boat for the day through Gairloch's chandlery shop (☎01445/712458), popular with sea anglers.

Practicalities

There's a late afternoon bus (not Sun) from Inverness to **Gairloch**, though the route and arrival time varies. Without your own transport, you'll have to depend upon postbuses to get around once there. Two postbus services (one for each side of the loch) leave from in front of the post office: one at 8.20am for Melvaig, and the other at 10.35am for Redpoint.

There's a good choice of **accommodation** in Gairloch, most of it mid-range; the central **tourist office** (April, May & mid-Sept to Oct Mon–Fri 10am–5pm, Sat 11–4pm; June Mon–Fri 9.30am–5.30pm, Sat 10am–5pm; July to mid-Sept Mon–Sat 9am–6pm, Sun noon–5pm; ☎01445/712130) will help if you have problems finding a vacancy. If you're looking for a **hotel**, try the family-run *Myrtle Bank Hotel* (☎01445/712004; ⑤), which has a good restaurant and is just above the loch. **B&Bs** are scattered throughout the area. In the village, options include the bright and pleasant *Newton Cottage* (☎01445/712007; ①), a little way up Mihol Road, and the friendly *Bains House* (☎01445/712472; ①), on the main street near the bus stop. A few hundred yards north on the Melvaig road, Gaelic-speaking Miss Mackenzie's *Duisary* (☎01445/712252; ①) is a good choice. Continuing towards Melvaig for about five miles, a little past the North Erradale junction, *Little Lodge* (☎01445/771237; ⑥, incl dinner) is outstanding, with immaculately furnished rooms, a log-burning stove, cashmere goats and dramatic sea views, as well as superb food. At Badachro, the recently built *Lochside* (☎01445/741295; ①) is spacious with a great view over the harbour and the Torridons. For **hostel** accommodation, there's a pleasant SYHA place at **Carn Dearg** two miles up the Melvaig road (☎01445/712219 or central reservations ☎0541 553255; closed Oct to mid-May), and the reasonable if often quiet *Badachro Bunkhouse* (☎01445/741255) overlooking Badachro harbour. **Camping** is possible at Big Sand or at Redpoint.

For **food**, Myrtle Bank's restaurant serves good meals at reasonable prices, while the fact that the chef at the *Scottish Seafood Restaurant* next to the petrol station near the pier is also the harbour master means that the fish and shellfish served up will be the pick of the catch. Another seafood option is *The Steading* beside the Heritage Museum. Inexpensive pasta and pricier seafood and meat are on offer at *Gino's* in the *Millcroft Hotel*, though service can be slow. For **snacks**, *the Serendipity Coffee Shop*, up the lane off the square, is a good bet, while the *Old Inn*, opposite the harbour, is a good real-ale **pub**.

Poolewe

It's a fifteen-minute hop by bus over the headland from Gairloch to the trim little village of **POOLEWE** on the sheltered south side of Loch Ewe, at the mouth of the River Ewe as it rushes down from Loch Maree. One of the area's best **walks** begins near here, signposted from the layby-cum-viewpoint on the main A832, a mile south of the village. It takes a couple of hours to follow the easy trail across open craggy moorland to the shores of Loch Maree, and thence to the car park at **Slatterdale**, seven miles southeast of Gairloch. If you reach Slatterdale just before 7pm on a Tuesday, Thursday or Friday, you should be able to pick up the Westerbus from Inverness back to Poolewe or Aultbea (confirm times on ☎01445/712255). Also worthwhile is the drive along the small side road running along the west shore of Loch Ewe to **COVE**. Here you'll find an atmospheric cave that was used by the "Wee Frees" as a church into this century; it's quite a perilous scramble up, however, and there's little to see once you're there. The route is also covered by a Poolewe **postbus** (1.55pm).

If you want **to stay** in the area, try the *Poolewe Hotel* (☎01445/781241; ③), on the Cove road; it's old-fashioned but very pleasant and serves straightforward food. From September until April they also have a bunkhouse available for hill walkers. Rather more upscale is the *Pool House Hotel* (☎01445/781272, *poolhouse@inverewe.co.uk*; ⑤) which belonged to Osgood MacKenzie (see below); it has lovely views out over the loch and serves up tasty, if pricey, bar and restaurant meals. For **B&B** in Poolewe, *The Creagan* (☎01445/781424; ①), up the track on the village side of the campsite, is a welcoming modern house wreathed with honeysuckle. Up the Cove road, four miles north at **Inverasdale**, *Bruach Ard* (☎01445/781214; ②; closed Nov–March) has mostly en-suite rooms and great views to Assynt. At Cove, Mrs MacDonald (☎01445/781354; ②; closed Nov–March) offers upscale B&B with fine loch views. There's also an excellent **campsite** between the village and Inverewe Gardens (☎01445/781229; closed Nov–March). *The Bridge Cottage Coffee Shop*, just up the Cove road from the village crossroads, serves good coffee and home-baked cakes (closed Sun and Nov–Feb).

Inverewe Gardens

Half a mile across the bay from Poolewe on the A832, **Inverewe Gardens** (daily: mid-March to Oct 9.30am–9pm; Nov to mid-March 9.30am–5pm; £5; NTS), a verdant oasis of foliage and riotously colourful flower collections, form a vivid contrast to the wild, heathery crags of the adjoining coast. Taking advantage of the area's famously temperate climate, **Osgood Mackenzie**, who inherited the surrounding 12,000-acre estate from his stepfather, the laird of Gairloch, in 1862, collected plants from all over the world for his walled garden, still the nucleus of the complex. By the time Mackenzie died in 1922, his garden sprawled over the whole peninsula, surrounded by 100 acres of woodland. Interconnected by a labyrinthine network of twisting paths and walkways, more than a dozen gardens feature exotic plant collections from as far afield as Chile, China, Tasmania and the Himalayas. Mid-May to mid-June is the best time to see the rhododendrons and azaleas, while the herbaceous garden reaches its peak in July and August. Look out, too, for the grand old eucalyptus in the Peace Plot, which is the largest in the northern hemisphere, and the nearby Ghost Tree (*Davidia involucrata*), representing the earliest evolutionary stages of flowering trees.

Gruinard Bay and around

Three buses each week (Mon, Wed & Sat; eastwards in the morning, westwards in the evening) run the twenty-mile stretch along the A832 from Poolewe past **Aultbea**, a small NATO naval base, to the head of **Little Loch Broom**, surrounded by a salt marsh that is covered with flowers in early summer. From **Laide**, the road skirts the shores of **Gruinard Bay**, offering fabulous views and, at the inner end of the bay, some excellent sandy beaches. During World War II, **Gruinard Island**, in the bay, was used as a testing ground for biological warfare, and for years was ringed by huge signs warning the public not to land. The anthrax spores released during the testing can live in the soil for up to a thousand years, but in 1987, after much protest, the Ministry of Defence had the island decontaminated and it was finally declared "safe" in 1990.

The road heads inland before joining the A835 at **Braemore Junction** (three Inverness–Ullapool buses stop here daily) above the head of **Loch Broom**. Just nearby, and easily accessible from the A835, are the spectacular 164ft **Falls of Measach**, which plunge through the mile-long **Corrieshalloch Gorge**. You can overlook the cascades from a special observation platform, or from the impressive suspension bridge that spans the chasm, whose 197-foot vertical sides are draped in a rich array of plant life, with thickets of wych elm, goat willow and bird cherry miraculously thriving on the cliffs. North from the head of Loch Broom to Ullapool is one of the so-called **Destitution Roads**, built to give employment to local people during the nineteenth-century potato famines.

Hotels along here include the excellent *Old Smiddy* (☎01445/731425; ③, ⑥ with dinner; closed Nov–March) on the main road in Laide, on the western shore of Guinard Bay and linked with Braemore and Achnasheen on the Kyle of Lochalsh railway by postbus. Crammed with travel trophies, family memorabilia, books and paintings by local artists (some on sale), the hotel has fine mountain views to the east, and serves outstanding food. Another option is *Cul-na-Mara* (☎01445/731295; ①), up the turning just past the *Sand Hotel*. At the head of Little Loch Broom, the *Dundonnell Hotel* (☎01854/633204, *selbie@dundonnellhotel.co.uk*; ⑤) is smart and comfortable and serves bar meals, while *Sail Mhor Croft* (☎01854/633224, *sailmhor@btinternet.com*) is a small independent hostel in a lovely location on the loch-side a couple of miles before the *Dundonnell Hotel*.

Ullapool

ULLAPOOL, the northwest's principal centre of population, was founded at the height of the herring boom in 1788 by the **British Fisheries Society**, on a sheltered arm of land jutting into Loch Broom. The grid-plan town is still an important fishing centre, though the ferry link to Stornoway on Lewis (see p.964) means that in high season its personality is practically swamped by visitors. Even so, it's still a hugely appealing place and a good base for exploring the northwest Highlands – especially if you are relying on public transport. Regular **buses** run from here to Inverness, Durness and (from May to early Oct) to the railhead at Lairg. Accommodation is plentiful and Ullapool is an obvious hideaway if the weather is bad, with cosy pubs, a new swimming pool and a lively arts centre, the *Ceilidh Place*.

Day or night, most of the action in Ullapool centres on the **harbour**, which has an authentic and salty air, especially when the boats are in. By day, attention focuses on the comings and goings of the ferry, fishing boats and smaller craft, while in the evening, yachts swing on the current, the shops stay open late, and customers from the *Ferry Boat Inn* line the sea wall. During summer, booths advertise trips to the **Summer Isles** – a cluster of uninhabited islets two to three miles offshore – to view seabird colonies, dolphins and porpoises, but if you're lucky you'll spot marine life from the waterfront. Otters occasionally nose around the rocks near the *Ferry Boat Inn*, and seals swim past begging scraps from the boats moored in the middle of the loch.

The only conventional "sight" in town is the **museum**, West Argyle Street (April to mid-July & mid-Aug to Oct Mon–Sat 9.30am–5.30pm; mid-July to mid-Aug Mon–Sat till

8pm; Nov–March, Wed & Sat 11am–3pm; £2), in the old parish church, with displays on crofting, fishing, local religion and emigration. During the Clearances, Ullapool was one of the ports through which evicted crofters left to start new lives in Canada, Australia and New Zealand.

Practicalities

Forming the backbone of its grid plan, Ullapool's two main arteries are the loch-side **Shore Street** and, parallel to it, **Argyle Street**, further inland. **Buses** stop at the pier, in the town centre near the ferry dock, from where it's easy to get your bearings. The well-run **tourist office** is on Argyle Street (April–July & Sept–Nov Mon–Fri 9am–5.30pm, Sat 10am–5pm, Sun noon–5pm; Aug Mon–Sat 9am–6pm, Sun noon–6pm; Oct Mon–Fri 10am–5pm, Sat noon–4pm; Nov & Dec Mon–Fri 11am–4pm; ☎01854/612135).

There's plenty of **accommodation** to choose from, including one of Scotland's most expensive hotels, the world-famous *Altnaharrie Hotel* (☎01854/633230; ⑨), across the loch from town – you're collected by launch. The *Ceilidh Place*, West Argyle Street (☎01854/612103, *reservations@ceilidh.demon.co.uk*; ⑥) is a tasteful and popular hotel, with a laid-back atmosphere. Particularly pleasant guest houses and B&Bs include the *Brae Guest House*, Shore Street (☎01854/612421; ②); *The Shieling* on Garve Road (☎01854/612947; ②) and *Waterside House*, 6 West Shore St (☎01854/612140; ②). There's an excellent youth hostel on Shore Street (☎01854/612254 or central reservations ☎0541 553255; closed Jan), a busy independent hostel, *West House*, on West Argyle Street (☎01854/613126, *r.lindsay@btinternet.com*), while the *Ceilidh Place* also has family-style bunkhouse accommodation (closed Nov–April; ①).

If you're looking for somewhere **to eat** and are a seafood fan, you won't do better than the *Morefield* on Morefield Lane, which serves up some of the best fish dishes on the west coast. The *Ceilidh Place* does filling snacks at the bar, or full meals in the restaurant, with occasional live music. The *Scottish Larder* on Ladysmith Street is worth trying, too. *John MacLean's* on Shore Street is a wholefood shop and deli which offers daytime snacks. The two best pubs are the *Arch Inn*, home of the Ullapool football team, and the *Ferry Boat Inn*, known locally as the "FBI", with good food at moderate prices, washed down with a pint of real ale at the loch-side (midges permitting) and live folk sessions on some nights.

North of Ullapool

North of Ullapool, the landscape changes to consist not of mountain ranges but of extraordinary peaks rising individually from the moorland. As you head further north, the peaks become more widely spaced and settlements smaller and fewer, linked by twisting single-track roads and shore-side footpaths that make excellent hiking trails. You can easily sidestep what little tourist traffic there is by heading down the peaceful backroads, which, after twisting through idyllic crofts, invariably end up at a deserted beach or windswept headland with superb views west to the Outer Hebrides.

Ten miles north of Ullapool, a single-track road winds west off the A835 to squeeze between the northern shore of Loch Lurgainn and the lower slopes **of Cul Beag** (2523ft) and craggy Stac Pollaidh (2012ft) to reach the **Coigach** peninsula. To the southeast, the awesome bulk of **Ben More Coigach** (2439ft) presides over the district, which contains some spectacular coastal scenery including a string of sandy beaches and the Summer Isles, scattered just offshore.

Coigach's main settlement is **ACHILTIBUIE**, an old crofting village stretched above a series of white-sand coves and rocks tapering into the Atlantic, from where a fleet of small fishing boats carries sheep, and tourists, to the island pastures during the summer. The village also attracts gardening enthusiasts, thanks to the space-station-like structure overlooking its main beach. Dubbed "The Garden of the Future", the **Hydroponicum** (Easter–Sept 10am–5pm; £4; tours hourly on the hour) is a kind of glorified greenhouse that concentrates the sun's heat, while protecting the plants inside from winter cold and acidic soil. The results – exotic plants, fruit, fragrant flowers and herbs thriving in four separate "climate rooms" – speak for themselves; you can also taste its strawberries and other produce in the subtropical setting of the *Lily Pond Café*, which serves meals, desserts and snacks. Also worth a visit is the **Achiltibuie Smokehouse** (April–Sept Mon–Sat 9.30am–5pm; free), three miles north of the Hydroponicum at **Altandhu**, where you can see meat, fish and game being cured in the traditional way and can buy some afterwards.

The wonderful *Summer Isles Hotel* (☎01854/622282; ⑤; closed Nov–March), just up the road from the Achiltibuie school, enjoys a near-perfect setting above a sandy beach with views over the islands, and is virtually self-sufficient. The hotel buys in Hydroponicum fruit and vegetables, but has its own dairy, poultry, and even runs a small smokehouse, so the food in its excellent restaurant (open to non-residents) is about as fresh as it comes. A set dinner costs about £35, while superb bar snacks and lunches feature crab, langoustines and smoked mackerel starting from £5. Of Achiltibuie's several **B&Bs**, *Dornie House* (☎01854/622271; ①) in the north of the settlement is welcoming and has particularly fine views. There's also a beautifully situated twenty-bed SYHA **youth hostel** (☎01854/622254 or central reservations ☎0541/553255; closed Oct to mid-May), three miles down the coast at Achininver, which is handy for Coigach's many mountain hikes.

Lochinver

The narrow road north from Coigach through Inverkirkaig is unremittingly spectacular, threading its way through a tumultuous landscape of secret valleys, moorland and bare rock, past the startling shapes of **Cul Beag** (2523ft), **Cul Mor** (2785ft) and the distinctive sugar-loaf **Suilven** (2398ft). A scattering of pebble-dashed bungalows around a sheltered bay heralds your arrival at **LOCHINVER**, the last sizeable village before Thurso, also with the last cash machine. It's a workaday place, with a huge fish market, from where large trucks head off to the rest of Britain. There's a better-than-average **tourist office** (April–June, Sept & Oct Mon–Sat 10am–5pm; July & Aug Mon–Sat 10am–5pm, Sun 11am–4pm; ☎01571/844330), whose **visitor centre** gives an interesting rundown on the area's geology, wildlife and history; a countryside ranger is available to advise on walks. The area is popular with **fishing** enthusiasts, and fly rods and other equipment are available for rent from the newsagent on the main road. **Mountain bikes** are available in the village from Assynt Adventures, on the main road near the police station. Lochinver has a range of good **B&Bs**: on the north side of the harbour, *Ardglas* (☎01571/844257; ①) has superb views, though no en-suite rooms, while nearby *Davar* (☎01571/844501; ②) is better equipped. Lochinver's most imaginative **food** can be found in the *Larder Riverside Bistro* on the main street: it has local seafood, venison and several vegetarian choices at reasonable prices. Decent bar meals are available at the *Caberfeidh* next door, which is also the most convivial place to head for a drink, while the *Seamen's Mission*, down at the harbour, is a good option for filling meals (some vegetarian) if you're on a tight budget.

East of Lochinver

The area to the **east of Lochinver**, traversed by the A837 and bounded by the gnarled peaks of the Ben More Assynt massif, is a wilderness of mountains, moorland, mist and scree. Dotted with lochs and lochans, it's also an angler's paradise, home to the only non-migratory fish in northern Scotland, the brown trout, and numerous other sought-after species, including the Atlantic salmon, sea trout, Arctic char and a massive prize strain of cannibal ferox. **Fishing** permits for the rivers in this area are like gold dust during the summer, snapped up months in advance by exclusive hunting-lodge hotels, but you can sometimes obtain last-minute cancellations (try the *Inver Lodge* on ☎01571/844496); permits for fishing lochs are easier to get hold of.

Although most of the land here is privately owned, nearly 27,000 acres are managed as the **Inverpolly National Nature Reserve**, whose visitor centre (April–Oct daily 10am–5pm; ☎01854/666254) at Knockan Cliff, twelve miles north of Ullapool on the A835, gives a thorough overview of the diverse flora and wildlife in the surrounding habitats. The theory of thrust faults was developed here in 1859 by eminent geologist James Nicol, and an interpretive **Geological Trail** shows you how to detect the movement of rock plates in the nearby cliffs. A few miles further on in the village of Knockan, the *Birchbank Holiday Lodge* (☎01854/666215; ②) is an excellent base if you're planning to hike or fish in the area; it's on a working sheep farm run by one of the area's top outdoor guides, who has a wealth of information on the best routes and places to explore.

Further north, on the rocky promontory that juts into eastern Loch Assynt, stand the jagged remnants of **Ardveck Castle** (free access), a MacLeod stronghold from 1597 that fell to the Seaforth Mackenzies after a siege in 1691. Previously, the Marquis of Montrose had been imprisoned here after his defeat at Carbisdale in 1650. The rebel marquis, whom the local laird had betrayed to the government for £20,000 and 400 bowls of sour meal, was eventually led away to be executed in Edinburgh, lashed back to front on his horse.

The *Inchnadamph Hotel* (☎01571/822202; ④), on Loch Assynt, is a wonderfully traditional Highland retreat; inside, the walls are covered with the stuffed catches of its past guests. The hotel offers fine old-fashioned cooking, usually with good vegetarian options, in its moderately priced restaurant and bar. It's popular with anglers, who get free fishing rights to Loch Assynt, as well as several hill lochs backing onto Ben More, haunts of the infamous ferox trout. Just along the road, the Assynt Field Centre at *Inchnadamph Lodge* (☎01571/822218; ①) has basic but comfortable bunk rooms, as well as more spacious B&B accommodation.

North from Lochinver: the coast road

Heading **north from Lochinver**, there are two possible routes: the fast A837, which runs eastwards along the shore of Loch Assynt to join the northbound A894, or the narrow **coastal road** (the B869) that locals dub "The Breakdown Zone" because its ups and downs claim so many victims during summer. Hugging the indented shoreline, this route is the more scenic, offering superb views of the Summer Isles, as well as a number of rewarding side-trips to beaches and dramatic cliffs. **Postbuses** from Lochinver cover the route as far as Ardvar or Drumbeg (not Sun). Unusually, most of the land and lochs around here are owned by local crofters rather than wealthy landlords. Helped by grants and private donations, the **Assynt Crofters' Trust** made history in 1993 when it pulled off the first ever community buy-out of estate land in Scotland; it's now pursuing a number of projects aimed at strengthening the local economy and conserving the environment. The Trust owns the lucrative fishing rights to the area, too, selling permits for £5 per day (£25 per week) through local post offices and the tourist office in Lochinver. An alternative outdoor activity is **pony trekking**, which is available through Clachtoll Trekking Centre (☎01571/855364), at Clachtoll on the road between Achmelvich and Stoer.

Heading north, the first village worthy of a detour is **ACHMELVICH**, a couple of miles along a side road, whose tiny bay cradles the whitest beach and most stunning turquoise water you'll encounter this side of the Seychelles. There's a noisy **campsite** and a basic forty-bed **youth hostel** (☎01571/844480 or central reservations ☎0541/553255; closed Oct–March) just behind the largest beach. However, for total peace and quiet there are other equally seductive beaches beyond the headlands.

The side road that branches north off the B869 between **Stoer** and **Clashnessie**, both of which have sandy beaches, ends abruptly by the automatic **lighthouse** at **Raffin** – built in 1870 by the Stevenson brothers (one of whom was the author Robert Louis Stevenson's dad) – but you can continue for two miles along a well-worn track to Stoer Point, named after the colossal rock pillar that stands offshore known as "**The Old Man of Stoer**". Surrounded by sheer cliffs and splashed with guano from the seabird colonies that nest on its 200-foot sides, it was climbed for the first time in 1961.

DRUMBEG, nine miles further on, is a major target for trout anglers, lying within reach of countless lochans. Permits to fish them are sold at the post office, but you'll need a detailed map and a compass to find your way in and out of this area without getting hopelessly lost. There's a lot of self-catering accommodation in the area, but few **B&Bs**. A good choice, however, is *Taigh Druimbeag* (☎01571/833209; ③; closed Nov–March), a comfortable old Edwardian house with period furniture and a large garden; to find it, turn off the main road at the primary school and follow the signs.

Kylesku to Kinlochbervie

KYLESKU, 33 miles north of Ullapool and around 6 miles west of Drumbeg, is the site of the award-winning road bridge spanning the mouth of lochs Glencoul and Glendhu. It's a pleasant place for a short stay, with plenty of good walks and a congenial hotel by the water's edge above the old ferry slipway. The family-run *Kylesku Hotel* (☎01971/502231; ④; closed Nov–Feb) has en-suite rooms, a welcoming bar popular with locals, and an excellent restaurant serving outstanding fresh seafood, including lobster, crab, mussels and local salmon (you can watch the fish being landed on the pier). Alternatively, there's *Newton Lodge* (☎01971/502070; ③, ⑤ with dinner), a modern, friendly and comfortable small hotel a few hundred yards up the road towards Ull`apool. Cheaper accommodation is available at *Kylesku Lodges and Backpackers* (☎01971/502003), with twin rooms in a series of reasonable A-frame lodges and, inevitably, a great setting. Statesman Cruises runs entertaining boat trips (March–Oct daily 11am & 2pm; round trip 2hr; £10; ☎01571/844446) from the jetty below the hotel to the 650-foot **Eas-Coul-Aulin**, Britain's highest waterfall, at the head of Loch Glencoul; otters, seals, porpoises and minke whales can occasionally be spotted along the way.

Handa Island

Visible just offshore to the north of Scourie is **Handa Island**, a huge chunk of red Torridon sandstone surrounded by sheer cliffs and carpeted with machair and purple-tinged moorland. Teeming with sea birds, it's an internationally important wildlife reserve and a real treat for ornithologists, with vast colonies of razorbills and guillemots breeding on its guano-splashed cliffs during summer. From late May to mid-July, large numbers of puffins waddle comically over the turf-covered cliff-tops where they dig their burrows.

Apart from a solitary warden, Handa is deserted. Until midway through the last century, however, it supported a thriving, if somewhat eccentric, community of crofters. Surviving on a diet of fish, potatoes and seabirds, the islanders, whose ruined cottages still cling to the slopes by the jetty, devised their own system of government, with a "queen" (Handa's oldest widow) and "parliament" (a council of men who met each morning to discuss the day's business). Uprooted by the 1846 potato famine, most of the villagers eventually emigrated to Canada's Cape Breton; today, Handa is private property, administered as a nature sanctuary by the Scottish Wildlife Trust. If you're landing on the island, you're encouraged to make a donation of around £1.50 towards its upkeep.

You'll need about three hours to follow the footpath around the island – an easy and enjoyable walk taking in the north shore's Great Stack rock pillar and some fine views across the Minch: a detailed route guide is featured in the SWT's free leaflet available from the warden's office when you arrive. Weather permitting, boats (☎01971/502347; £7) leave for Handa throughout the day (until around 4pm) from the tiny cove of **TAR-BET**, three miles northwest of the main road and accessible by postbus from Scourie (Mon–Sat 1 daily; 1.50pm), where there's a small car park and jetty. Alternatively, if you want to see the island and the local coastline, with its attendant sea- and bird-life, from the sea, Laxford Cruises (☎01971/502251) offer two-hour boat trips from **FANAG-MORE** (May–June & Sept Mon–Sat 10am, noon & 2pm; July & Aug Mon–Sat 10am, noon, 2pm & 4pm; £8), a mile further up the coast from Tarbet (reached by the same postbus as above). Camping is not allowed on the island, but the SWT maintains a **bothy** for bird-watchers (reservations must be made on ☎0131/312 7765, or with the warden on the island), while in Tarbet, Rex and Liz Norris (☎01971/502098; ①) run a comfortable little **B&B** overlooking the bay. For food, Tarbet's unexpected *Seafood Restaurant* (closes 7pm & all Sun) serves delicious, moderately priced fish and vegetarian dishes, and a good selection of home-made cakes and desserts, in its airy conservatory just above the jetty.

Kinlochbervie

North of Scourie, the road sweeps inland through the starkest part of the Highlands; rocks piled on rocks, bog and water create an almost alien landscape, and the astonishingly bare, stony coastline looks increasingly inhospitable. After about eight miles, at **Rhiconich**, you can branch off the main road to **KINLOCHBERVIE**, a major fishing port set in a rugged, rocky inlet. Trucks from all over Europe pick up cod and shellfish from the trawlers here, crewed mainly by east coast fishermen. *The Old Schoolhouse Restaurant and Guest House* (☎01971/521383; ③) provides comfortable accommodation and home-cooked meals.

The North Coast

Though a constant stream of sponsored walkers, caravans and tour groups makes it to **John O' Groats**, surprisingly few visitors travel the whole length of the Highlands' wild **north coast**. Those that do, however, rarely return disappointed. Pounded by one of the world's most ferocious seaways, Scotland's rugged northern shore is backed by barren mountains in the west, and in the east by lochs and open rolling grasslands. This is a great area for **bird watching**, too, with huge sea-bird colonies clustered in clefts and on remote stacks at regular intervals along the coast; **seals** also bob around in the surf offshore, and in winter **whales** put in the odd appearance in the more sheltered estuaries of the northwest.

Getting around this stretch of coast without your own transport can be a slow and frustrating business: **Thurso**, the area's main town and springboard for Orkney, is well connected by bus and train with Inverness, but further west, after the main A836 peters into a single-track road, you have to rely on a convoluted series of postbus connections or, in peak season, a single Highland Country bus (#387).

Durness and around

Scattered around a string of sheltered sandy coves and grassy cliff-tops, **DURNESS**, the most northwesterly village on the British mainland, straddles the turning point on the main road as it swings east from the inland peat bogs of the interior to the north coast's fertile strip of limestone machair. First settled by the Picts around 400 BC, the area has been farmed ever since, its crofters being among the few not cleared off estate land during the nineteenth century. Today, Durness is the centre for several crofting communities and a good base for a couple of days, with some good walks. Even if you're only passing through, it's worth pausing here to see the **Smoo Cave**, a gaping hole in a sheer limestone cliff, and to visit beautiful **Balnakiel beach**, to the west. In addition, Durness is the jumping-off point for roadless and rugged **Cape Wrath**, the windswept promontory at Scotland's northwest tip, which has retained an end-of-the-world mystique lost long ago by John O' Groats.

The Smoo Cave

A mile or so east of Durness village lies the 200-foot-long **Smoo Cave**, a natural wonder, formed partly by the action of the sea, and partly by the small burn that flows through it. Tucked away at the end of a narrow sheer-sided sea cove, guides will show you the illuminated interior, although the much-hyped rock formations are less memorable than the short rubber-dinghy trip you have to make in the second of three caverns, where the whole experience is enlivened after wet weather by a **waterfall** that crashes through the middle of the cavern. A boat trip (May–Sept daily, times depending on weather and tide, call ☎01971/511365 or 511284 for details; 1hr 30min; £6.50) leaves from Smoo Cave on a wildlife tour of the coast around Durness, taking in stretches of the shoreline only accessible by sea. The trip takes a close look at **sea-bird colonies**, and sightings of seals, puffins and porpoises are common.

Cape Wrath

An excellent day-trip from Durness begins three miles southwest of the village at **Keoldale**, where a foot-passenger ferry (June–Aug hourly 9.30am–4.30pm; May & Sept usually 4 daily; no motorcycles; ☎01971/511376) crosses the Kyle of Durness estuary to link up with a minibus (☎01971/511287; closed Oct–April) that runs the eleven miles out to **Cape Wrath**. The UK mainland's most northwesterly point, the headland takes its name not from the stormy seas that crash against it for most of the year, but from the Norse word *hvarf*, meaning "turning place" – a throwback to the days when Viking warships used it as a navigation point during raids on the Scottish coast. These days, a lighthouse (another of those built by Robert Louis Stevenson's father) warns ships away from the treacherous rocks. Looking east to Orkney and west to the Outer Hebrides, it stands above the famous **Clo Mor cliffs**, the highest sea cliffs in Britain and a prime breeding site for seabirds. You can walk from here to remote Sandwood Bay, visible to the south, although the route, which cuts inland across lochan-dotted moorland, is hard to follow in places. Hikers generally continue south from Sandwood to the trail end at Blairmore; if you hitch or walk the six miles from here to Kinlochbervie you can, with careful planning, catch a bus back to Durness. Don't attempt this route from south to north, as, if the weather closes in, the Cape Wrath minibus stops running. Note also that much of the land bordering the headland is a military firing range and the area is sometimes closed – check with Durness tourist office before you set off.

Durness practicalities

Public transport in the area is sparse; the key service on the north coast is the Highland Country link (#387) to Thurso (June to mid-Sept Mon–Sat) leaving Thurso at 11.30am and Durness at 3pm. This connects at Durness with the daily Inverness Traction link (June to mid-Sept) from Inverness via Ullapool and Lochinver. Postbuses provide a more complicated year-round alternative; check at the post office, tourist office or youth hostel.

Durness has an enthusiastic **tourist office** (April–June, Sept & Oct Mon–Sat 10am–5pm, July & Aug Mon–Sat 10am–5pm, Sun 11am–4pm; Oct–March Mon–Fri

10am–1.30pm; ☎01971/511259), in the village centre, which can help with accommodation and arranges ranger-guided walks; its small visitor centre also features excellent interpretative panels detailing the area's history, geology, flora and fauna, with some good insights into the day-to-day life of the community. **Accommodation** is fairly limited in Durness itself, but there are further options along nearby Loch Eriboll (see below). Durness's best offering is the *Cape Wrath Hotel* (☎01971/511212; main hotel ④, annex ②), which has a beautiful setting near the ferry jetty at Keoldale. Popular with walkers and fishermen, its rather austere character is offset by friendly service and a stunning view from the dining room. Of the B&Bs, *Puffin Cottage* (☎01971/511208; ③) is a small but pleasant place. The friendly youth hostel (☎01971/511244; closed Oct to mid-May), beside the Smoo Cave car park, a mile and a half east of the village, also rents out mountain bikes. There's camping at *Sango Sands Caravan and Camping Site*, Harbour Road (☎01971/511262), which has the added advantage of a good bar and restaurant. The other good **eating** option is the restaurant at Loch Eriboll's *Port-Na-Con* guest house – you should book in advance.

Loch Eriboll

Ringed by ghost-like limestone mountains, deep and sheltered **Loch Eriboll**, six miles east of Durness, is the north coast's most spectacular sea loch. Servicemen stationed here during World War II to protect passing Russian convoys nicknamed it "Loch 'Orrible", but if you're looking for somewhere wild and unspoilt, you'll find this a perfect spot. Porpoises and otters are a common sight along the rocky shore, and minke whales occasionally swim in from the open sea.

Overlooking its own landing stage at the water's edge, *Port-Na-Con* (☎01971/511367, *shm@capetech.co.uk*; ②; closed Nov to mid-March), seven miles from Durness on the west side of the loch, is a wonderful **B&B**, popular with anglers and divers (it'll refill air tanks for £2.50). Topnotch food is served in its small restaurant (open all year, including Christmas), with a choice of vegetarian haggis, local kippers, fruit compote and home-made croissants for breakfast, and adventurous three-course evening meals for around £12; the menu always includes a gourmet vegetarian dish. Non-residents are welcome, although you'll need to book. Another good option, half a mile further south, is *Rowan House* (☎01971/511347; ①), a child-friendly place overlooking the loch with a tiny eighteen-hole golf course; fresh local oysters often feature on its menu. A further half-mile south, *Choraidh Croft* (☎01971/511235; ①; closed Dec–Easter) offers B&B and has a rare-breeds collection (£2), as well as a good café.

Tongue

It's a long slog around Loch Eriboll and east over the top of A Mhùine moor to the pretty crofting township of **TONGUE**. Dominated by the ruins of **Varick Castle**, the village, an eleventh-century Norse stronghold, is strewn over the east shore of the **Kyle of Tongue**, which you can cross either via a new causeway, or by following the longer and more scenic single-track road around its southern side. When the tide recedes, this shallow estuary becomes a mass of golden sand flats, superb on sunny days, with the sharp profiles of **Ben Hope** (3040ft) and **Ben Loyal** (2509ft) looming large to the south.

In 1746, the Kyle of Tongue was the scene of a naval engagement reputed to have sealed the fate of Bonnie Prince Charlie's **Jacobite rebellion**. In response to a plea for help from the prince, the King of France dispatched a sloop and £13,600 in gold coins to Scotland. However, the Jacobite ship *Hazard* was spotted by the English frigate *Sheerness*, and fled into the Kyle, hoping that the larger enemy vessel would not be able to follow. It did, though, and soon forced the *Hazard* aground. Pounded by

English cannonfire, its Jacobite crew slipped ashore under cover of darkness in an attempt to smuggle the treasure to Inverness, but they were followed by scouts of the local Mackay clan, who were not of the Jacobite persuasion. The next morning, a larger platoon of Mackays waylaid the rebels, who, hopelessly outnumbered and outgunned, began throwing the gold into **Lochan Hakel**, southwest of Tongue (most of it was recovered later). The prince, meanwhile, had sent 1500 of his men north to rescue the treasure, but these too were defeated en route; historians debate whether the missing men might have altered the outcome of the Battle of Culloden three weeks later.

If you want **to stay** in Tongue, try *Rhian Cottage* (☎01847/611257; ②, ④ with dinner), a pretty whitewashed house with an attractive garden, about a mile down the road past the post office, while *Cloisters* (☎01847/601286; ②), two miles out of town at Talmire on the west side of the Kyle, has great views out towards the Orkney Islands and is well worth heading out of town for. The *Ben Loyal Hotel* (☎01847/611216; ④) and *Tongue Hotel* (☎01847/611206; ④; closed Nov–Feb) are more luxurious, and both do excellent food. There's also a beautifully situated and friendly SYHA **youth hostel** (☎01847/611301 or central reservations ☎0541/553255; closed Nov to mid-March), right beside the causeway a mile north of the village centre on the east shore of the Kyle, and two **campsites**: *Kincraig Camping and Caravan Site* (☎01847/611218), just south of Tongue post office, and *Talmine Camping and Caravan Site* (☎01847/601225), just behind a sandy beach at Talmine, five miles north of Tongue on the western side of the Kyle.

Bettyhill to Dounreay

BETTYHILL, a major crofting village, straggles along the side of a narrow tidal estuary, and down the coast to two splendid beaches. Forming an unbroken arc of pure white sand between the rivers Naver and Borgie, **Torrisdale beach** is the more impressive of the pair, ending in a smooth white spit that forms part of the **Invernaver Nature Reserve**. During summer, arctic terns nest here on the river banks, dotted with clumps of rare Scottish primroses, and you stand a good chance of spotting an otter or two. The delightful and loyally maintained **Strathnaver Museum** (April–Oct Mon–Sat 10am–1pm & 2–5pm; £1.90), housed in the old church set apart from the village near the sea, is full of locally donated bits and pieces, and includes panels by local school children telling the story of the Strathnaver Clearances. You can also see some Pictish stones and a 3800-year-old early Bronze Age beaker found in Strathnaver, the river valley south of the village, whose numerous prehistoric sites are mapped on an excellent pamphlet sold at the entrance desk.

Bettyhill's small **tourist office** (April & May Mon–Sat 1–5pm; June Mon–Sat 11am–5pm; July Mon–Sat 10am–5pm; Aug Mon–Sat 10am–6pm, Sun noon–5pm; ☎01641/521342) can book **accommodation** for you. The *Bettyhill Hotel* (☎01641/521230; ③), at the top of the hill, has character, and does good bar food. There are also several good-value B&Bs, including *Shenley* (☎01641/521421; ①; closed Nov–March), a grand but homely detached house in an elevated spot in the middle of the village, and *Bruachmhor* (☎01641/521265; ①; closed Nov–March), a small but comfortable croft house, facing south over the village.

As you move east from Bettyhill, the north coast changes dramatically as the hills on the horizon recede to be replaced by fields fringed with flagstone walls. At the hamlet of **MELVICH**, twelve miles from Bettyhill, the A897 cuts south through Strath Halladale, the Flow Country (see below) and the Strath of Kildonan to Helmsdale on the east coast (see p.1057). Melvich has some good accommodation, including the excellent *Sheiling Guesthouse* by the main road (☎01641/531256; ②; closed Nov–March), whose impressive breakfast menu features locally smoked haddock and fresh herring.

Five miles further east, **Dounreay Nuclear Power Station**, a surreal collection of stark domes and chimney stacks marooned in the middle of nowhere, is still a fairly major local employer, though its three fast breeder reactors were decommissioned in April 1994 and it now reprocesses spent nuclear fuel rather than generating electricity. A permanent **exhibition** (Easter–Sept daily 10am–5pm; free) in the old aircraft control tower details the processes – and, unsurprisingly, the benefits – of nuclear power, and does at least make an attempt to address issues such as the area's "leukemia cluster", and the high levels of radiation reported over the years on the nearby beaches.

South from Melvich: the Flow Country

From Melvich, you can head forty miles or so south towards Helmsdale (see p.1057) on the A897, through the **Flow Country**. This huge expanse of bog-land came into the news a few years ago when ecology experts, responding to plans to transform the area into forest, drew attention to the threat to this fragile landscape, described by one contemporary commentator as of "unique and global importance, equivalent to the African Serengeti or Brazil's rainforest". Some forest was planted, but the environmentalists won the day, and the forestry syndicates have had to pull out. There's an excellent RSPB Flow Country **visitor centre** (Easter–Oct daily 9am–6pm; ☎01641/571225), based in the train station at Forsinard, fifteen miles south of Melvich, which is easily accessible from Thurso, Wick and the south by train. Guided walks through the RSPB **nature reserve** leave from the visitor centre (May–Aug Tues & Thurs) and illuminate the importance of the area and its wildlife.

Thurso

Approached from the isolation of the west, **THURSO** feels like a metropolis. In reality, it's a relatively small service centre visited mostly by people passing through to the nearby port of **Scrabster** to catch the ferry to Stromness in Orkney. The town's name derives from the Norse word *Thorsa*, literally "River of the God Thor", and in Viking times this was a major gateway to the mainland. Later, ships set sail from here for the Baltic and Scandinavian ports loaded with meal, beef, hides and fish. Much of the town, however, dates from the 1790s, when Sir John Sinclair built a large new extension to the old fishing port. The nearby Dounreay Nuclear Power Station ensured continuing prosperity after World War II, when workers from the plant (dubbed "Atomics" by the locals) settled in Thurso in large numbers. Its gradual rundown over recent years has cast a shadow over the local economy, but investment in new industries such as telecommunications has improved matters.

Traill Street is the main drag, turning into the pedestrianized Rotterdam Street and High Street precinct at its northern end. However, the shops are uninspiring, and you're better off heading to the old part of town near the harbour, to see **Old St Peter's Church**, a substantial ruin with origins in the thirteenth century, but which has been much altered over the years. Alternatively, you could visit the **Thurso Heritage Museum**, High Street (Mon–Sat 10am–1pm & 2–5pm; 50p), whose most intriguing exhibit is the Pictish **Skinnet Stone**, intricately carved with enigmatic symbols and a runic cross.

Practicalities

It's a ten-minute walk from the **train station**, with services to Inverness and Wick, down Princes Street and Sir George Street, to the **tourist office** on Riverside Road (April–Oct Mon–Sat 9am–5pm; July & Aug also Sun 11am–4pm; ☎01847/892371). The bus station, close by, runs regular **buses** to John O' Groats, Wick and Inverness and a summer service to Durness. **Ferries** operate daily from adjoining Scrabster to Orkney, which has less frequent links to Shetland and Aberdeen. You can book ahead through P&O Scottish Ferries (☎01224/572615) or through any local tourist office. If you fancy a day-trip to Orkney, see "John O' Groats" (below). The local bus services aren't much help if you're connecting with the ferry at Scrabster – the walk is just over a mile long; a **taxi** (☎01847/892868) will set you back £3.

Thurso is well stocked with **accommodation**, including a decent if tight-fitting hostel, *Sandra's*, 24 Princes St (☎01847/894575, *sandra's-hostel@carson.softnet.co.uk*), with four-bed bunkrooms and drying and self-catering facilities above the lively local café. Inexpensive if tatty dorms and doubles are also available at *Ormlie Lodge* (☎01847/896888), a block of student accommodation on Ormlie Road, close to the station. Of the **B&Bs**, *Murray House*, 1 Campbell St (☎01847/895759; ①), is central, comfortable and friendly, or you could try the welcoming *Mrs Oag*, 9 Couper St (☎01847/894529; ①), east of High Street near the town hall, or *Mrs Budge*, 6 Pentland Crescent (☎01847/893205; ①), next to the beach front. The recently refurbished *Royal Hotel* on Traill Street (☎01847/893191; ④) is the main **hotel** in town and a reasonable choice. The nearest **campsite** (☎01847/805503) is out towards Scrabster alongside the main road. **Food** options include *Le Bistro*, 2 Traill St, with a reasonable-value menu of lunchtime snacks and more ambitious evening meals, and *Upper Deck*, by the harbour at Scrabster, serving large, moderately priced steaks and seafood dishes. You can **rent bikes** at the Bike and Camping shop on the extension of High Street, beyond its junction with Couper Street, while a little further along at 57 High St, Harper's fishing shop (☎01847/893179) is the place to rent wetsuits or boards, or get hold of other **surfing** supplies, before you take on the mighty north-coast breaks.

Dunnet Head to Duncansby Head

Despite the plaudits that John O' Groats customarily receives, Britain's northernmost mainland point is in fact Dunnet Head. The headland is at the far side of Dunnet Bay, a vast sandy beach backed by huge dunes about six miles east of Thurso. The bay is popular with surfers, and even in the winter you can usually spot intrepid figures far out in the Pentland Firth's breakers. There's a **Ranger Centre** (April–Sept Tues–Fri 2–5pm, Sat & Sun 2–6pm) beside the campsite at the east end of the bay, where you can pick up information on good local history and nature walks. Nearby is the small village of **DUNNET**, where it's worth stopping in at **Mary-Ann's Cottage** (June–Sept Tues–Sun 2–4.30pm; £1), a farming croft vacated in 1990 by 93-year-old Mary-Ann Calder, whose grandfather had built the cottage, and maintained just as she left it, full of reminders of the three generations who lived and worked there over the last 150 years.

For **Dunnet Head**, turn off at Dunnet onto the B855, which runs for four miles over windy heather and bog to the tip of the headland, crowned with a Victorian lighthouse. The red cliffs below are startling, with weirdly eroded rock stacks and a huge variety of sea birds; on a clear day you can see the whole northern coastline from Cape Wrath to Duncansby Head, and across the Pentland Firth to Orkney.

John O' Groats

Familiar from endless postcards, **JOHN O' GROATS** comes as something of an anticlimax. The views north to Orkney are fine enough, but the village itself turns out to be little more than a windswept grassy slope leading down to the sea, dominated by an enormous car park that is jammed throughout the summer with tour buses. The village gets its name from the Dutchman, Jan de Groot, who obtained the ferry contract for the crossing to Orkney in 1496. The eight-sided house he built for his eight quarrelling sons (so that each one could enter by his own door) is echoed in the octagonal tower of the much-photographed *John O' Groats Hotel*, which is fast falling into disrepair but remains a good stopoff for a quick drink.

John O' Groats is connected by regular **buses** to Wick (4–5 daily; 50min) and Thurso (Mon–Fri 5 daily, Sat 2 daily; 1hr). John O' Groats Ferries (☎01955/611353) operates a daily passenger ferry across to Burwick in the Orkney Islands (May & Sept 1 daily; June–Aug 4 daily; 45min; £24 return): officially this is a foot-passenger service, but it will take bicycles and motorbikes if it isn't too busy. The company also offers a couple of whistle-stop day-tours of Orkney, as well as a more leisurely afternoon wildlife cruise round the Stacks of Duncansby and the sea-bird colonies of Stroma (1hr 30min; £12). The **tourist office** (April–Oct Mon–Sat 9am–5pm; ☎01955/611373) by the car park can help sort out **accommodation**. Alternatively, try *Swona View* B&B (☎01955/611297; ①; closed Nov–March) on the road to Duncansby Head, or *Creag-Na-Mara* (☎01847/851713; ③), a welcoming B&B serving tasty evening meals at East Mey, west along the Thurso road. *Bencorragh House* (☎01955/611449; ②, ④ with dinner; closed Nov–Feb) offers very pleasant farmhouse accommodation at Upper Gills in Canisbay. If you're on a tight budget, head for the small **youth hostel** at Canisbay (☎01955/611424 or central reservations ☎0541/553255; closed Nov–March), or one of the two local **campsites** – *Stroma View* (☎01955/611313), one mile along the Thurso road, is the more pleasant.

Duncansby Head

If you're disappointed by John O' Groats, press on a couple of miles further east to **Duncansby Head**, which, with its lighthouse, dramatic cliffs and well-worn coastal path, has a lot more to offer. The birdlife here is prolific, and south of the headland lie some spectacular 200-foot cliffs, cut by sheer-sided clefts known locally as *geos*. This is also a good place from which to view Orkney. Dividing the islands from the mainland is the infamous **Pentland Firth**, one of the world's most treacherous waterways. Only seven miles across, it forms a narrow channel between the Atlantic Ocean and North Sea, and for fourteen hours each day the tide rips through here from west to east at a rate of ten knots or more, flooding back in the opposite direction for the remaining ten hours. Combined with the rocky sea bed and a high wind, this can cause deep whirlpools and terrifying 30–40-foot towers of water to form when the ebbing tide crashes across the reefs offshore. The latter, known as the "Bores of Duncansby", are the subject of many old mariners' myths from the time of the Vikings onwards.

The East Coast

The **east coast** of the Highlands, between Inverness and Wick, is nowhere near as spectacular as the west, with gentle undulating moors, grassland and low cliffs where you might expect to find sea lochs and mountains. Washed by the cold waters of the North Sea, it's markedly cooler, too, although less prone to spells of permadrizzle and midges. Although the Inverness–Thurso train line is twice forced by topography to head inland, the region's main transport artery, the A9 – slower here than in the south – follows the coast, which veers sharply northeast exactly parallel with the Great Glen, formed by the same geological fault.

From around the ninth century AD onwards, the **Norse** influence was more keenly felt here than in any other part of mainland Britain, and dozens of Scandinavian-sounding names recall the era when this was a Viking kingdom. Culturally and scenically, much of the east coast is more lowland than highland and Caithness in particular evolved more or less separately from the Highlands, avoiding the bloody tribal feuds that wrought such havoc further south and west. Later, however, the nineteenth-century **Clearances** hit the region hard, as countless ruined cottages and empty glens show. Hundreds of thousands of crofters were evicted, and forced to emigrate to New Zealand, Canada and Australia, or else take up fishing in one of the numerous herring ports established on the coast. The oil boom has brought a transient prosperity to one or two places over the past two decades, but the area remains one of the country's poorest, reliant on sheep farming, fishing and tourism.

Wick, the largest town on this section of coast, has an interesting industrial past, the story of which is told in another good heritage centre, but is otherwise uninspiring. The relatively flat landscapes of this northeast corner – windswept peat-bog and farmland dotted with lochans and grey and white crofts – are a surprising contrast to the more rugged country south and west of here. South of Wick, the area around the port of **Lybster** is littered with the remains of ancient civilizations, while the award-winning Timespan Heritage Centre at **Helmsdale** recounts the human cost of the landlords' greed. Beyond Helmsdale, the ersatz-Loire chateau **Dunrobin Castle** is the main tourist attraction, a monument as much to the iniquities of Clearances as to the eccentricity of Victorian taste. South of Dornoch, a famous golfing resort renowned for its salubrious climate and sweeping beach, lies the Black Isle, an area close to Inverness, covered earlier in this chapter (see p.1015).

Wick and around

Originally a Viking settlement named *Vik* (meaning "bay"), **WICK** has been a royal burgh since 1589. It's actually two towns: Wick proper, and **Pultneytown**, immediately south across the river, a messy, rather run-down community planned by Thomas Telford in 1806 for the British Fisheries Society, to encourage evicted crofters to take up fishing. Wick's heyday was in the mid-nineteenth century, when it was the busiest herring port in Europe, exporting tons of fish to Russia, Scandinavia and the West Indian slave plantations. Pultneytown, lined with rows of fishermen's cottages, is the area most worth a wander, with the acres of largely derelict net-mending sheds, stores and cooperages around the harbour giving some idea of the former scale of the fishing trade. The town's story is told in the excellent **Wick Heritage Centre** in Bank Row, Pultneytown (June–Sept Mon–Sat 10am–5pm; £2), which contains a fascinating array of artefacts from the old fishing days, including fully rigged boats, original boat models, the old Noss Head lighthouse light and a great photographic collection dating from the 1880s.

Rising steeply from a needle-thin promontory three miles north of Wick are the dramatic fifteenth- to seventeenth-century ruins of **Sinclair** and **Girnigoe castles**, which functioned as a single stronghold for the earls of Caithness. In 1570 the fourth earl, suspecting his son of trying to murder him, imprisoned him in the dungeon here until he died of starvation.

The **train** station and **bus** stops are next to each other behind the hospital. Frequent local buses run to Thurso and up the coast to John O' Groats. Wick also has an **airport** (☎01955/602215), a couple of miles north of the town, with direct flights from Edinburgh and Aberdeen, and connections further south. From the train station, head across the river down Bridge Street to the **tourist office**, just off High Street (July–Sept Mon–Sat 10am–5pm, Sun 10am–5pm; rest of year closed Sun; ☎01955/602596), which can organize local **accommodation**. The best value **B&B** in town is the welcoming *Greenvoe* on George Street (☎01955/603942; ①), looking over the river. *Wellington Guest House*, just behind the station at 41–43 High St (☎01955/603287; ②; closed Nov–Feb), is reasonable value, as is *The Clachan* B&B, South Road (☎01955/605384; ②), while The *Harbour Guest House*, on Rose Street, Pultneytown (☎01955/603276; ①) is friendly but more basic. The best of the hotels is *Mackay's*, by the river in the town centre (☎01955/602323, *mackays.hotel@caithness-mm.co.uk*; ③). Good-quality **bikes** can be rented from Wheels Cycle Shop on Glamis Road (☎01955/603636; closed Sun & Oct–Easter).

As for **eating**, the good-value *Lamplighter Restaurant*, High Street, serves enormous helpings of imaginative food; downstairs in the same building, *Houston's Café* cheerfully churns out good burgers. *Cabrelli's*, at the east end of the High Street, opposite the bridge over to Pultneytown, is a real find, trapped in a time warp, and serving piles of fish and chips, along with authentic pizza. A few doors further on, *Carter's* serves unremarkable pub grub, while the adjoining *Camps* is among the liveliest of the **pubs** in the evenings, with occasional live music.

Between Wick and Helmsdale

The stretch of road south of Wick gives great views over the cliffs and out to sea to the oil rigs perched on the horizon. The planned village of **LYBSTER**, established at the height of the nineteenth-century herring boom, once had around two hundred boats working out of its harbour. Today, although still a busy fishing port, it's a grim collection of grey pebble-dashed bungalows centred on a broad main street. Most visitors head straight for the nearby **Grey Cairns of Camster**, seven miles due north and one of the most memorable sights on the northeast coast. Surrounded by bleak moorland, these two enormous prehistoric burial chambers, constructed around four or five thousand years ago, were immaculately designed, with corbelled dry-stone roofs in their hidden chambers, which you can crawl into through narrow passageways. More extraordinary ancient remains lie at **East Clyth**, two miles north of Lybster on the A99, where a path leads to the **"Hill o' Many Stanes"**; here two hundred boulders stand in twenty-two parallel rows that run north to south; no one has yet worked out what they were used for, although archeological studies have shown there were once six hundred stones.

  DUNBEATH, hidden at the mouth of a small strath, twelve miles north of Ord of Caithness, was another village founded to provide work in the wake of the Clearances. The local landlord built a harbour here in 1800, at the start of the herring boom, and the settlement flourished briefly. Today, it's a sleepy place, with lobster pots stacked at the quayside and views of windswept Dunbeath Castle (closed to the public) on the opposite side of the bay. The novelist Neil Gunn was born here, in one of the terraced houses under the flyover that now swoops above the village; you can find out more about him at the **Dunbeath Heritage Centre** (Easter–Oct daily 10am–5pm; £1.50), signposted from the road. The best of the handful of modest **B&Bs** here is *Tormore Farm* (☎01593/731240; ①), a large farmhouse with four comfortable rooms, half a mile north of the harbour on the A9.

Helmsdale

HELMSDALE is an old herring port, founded in the nineteenth century to house the evicted inhabitants of Strath Kildonan, which lies behind it. Today, the sleepy-looking grey village attracts thousands of tourists, most of them to see the **Timespan Heritage Centre**, beside the river (Easter–Oct Mon–Sat 9.30am–5pm, Sun 2–5pm; £3.50). It's a remarkable venture for a place of this size, telling the local story of Viking raids, witch-burning, Clearances, fishing and gold-prospecting through hi-tech displays, sound effects and an audio-visual programme. For a spot of light relief after the exhibition, head across the road to the sugary pink and frilly *Mirage Restaurant*. The proprietor has become something of a Scottish celebrity, modelling herself on the romantic novelist Barbara Cartland, whose shooting lodge is nearby. Photographs proudly displayed on the walls show the peroxide-blonde restaurateuse posing with her heroine, while the fittings and furnishings reflect her predilection for all things pink and kitsch, with fish tanks, fake-straw parasols, and plastic seagulls set off by the country and western soundtrack. She also dishes up great fish and chips, grills and puddings.

  Helmsdale's **tourist office** (April–Sept Mon–Sat 10.30am–4pm; ☎01431/821640) in the Timespan centre will book accommodation for you. Most of the **B&Bs** are on the

---

GOLD AT BAILE AN OR

From Helmsdale the single-track A897 runs up Strath Kildonan and across the Flow Country (see p.1053) to the north coast, at first following the River Helmsdale, a strictly controlled and exclusive salmon river frequented by the royals. Some eight miles up the Strath at **Baile an Or** (Gaelic for "goldfield"), gold was discovered in the bed of the Kildonan Burn in 1869; a gold rush ensued, hardly on the scale of the Yukon, but quite bizarre in the Scottish Highlands. A tiny amount of gold is still found by some hardy prospectors every year: if you fancy gold-panning yourself, you can rent the relevant equipment for £2.50 from Helmsdale's gift and fishing-tackle shop, Strath Ullie, opposite the Timespan Heritage Centre, which also sells a booklet with a few basic tips.

---

outskirts of town: *Broomhill House*, Navidale Road (☎01431/821259; ①), is the best of the bunch, with bedrooms in a turret added to the former croft by a miner who struck it lucky in the Kildonan gold rush (see above). Alternatively, try *Torbuie* (☎01431/821424; ①), in Navidale, on the A9 less than a mile from the village, or *Eastdale*, half a mile up the A897 (☎01431/821334; ①), both of which offer comfortable rooms. There's also a small **youth hostel** (☎01431/821577; closed Oct to mid-May), about half a mile north of the harbour.

Golspie and around

Sixteen miles south of Helmsdale on the A9 lies the straggling red-sandstone town of **GOLSPIE**, whose status as an administrative centre does little to relieve its dullness. It does, however, boast an eighteen-hole **golf course** and a sandy beach, while half a mile further up the coast the **Big Burn** has several rapids and waterfalls that can be seen from an attractive **woodland trail** (beginning at the Sutherland Arms Hotel).

Dunrobin Castle

The main reason to stop in Golspie is to look around **Dunrobin Castle** (May & Oct Mon–Sat 10.30am–4.30pm, Sun noon–4.30pm; June–Sept daily 10.30am–5.30pm; £4.80), overlooking the sea a mile north of town. Approached via a long tree-lined drive, this fairy-tale confection of turrets and pointed roofs – modelled by the architect Sir Charles Barry (designer of the Houses of Parliament) on a Loire chateau – is the seat of the infamous Sutherland family, at one time Europe's biggest landowners, with a staggering 1.3 million acres, and the principal driving force behind the **Clearances** in this area. The castle is on a correspondingly vast scale, boasting 189 furnished rooms, of which the tour only takes in seventeen. Staring up at the pile from the midst of its elaborate **formal gardens**, it's worth remembering that such extravagance was paid for by uprooting literally thousands of crofters from the surrounding glens. Much of the extra income generated by the evictions was lavished on the castle's opulent **interior**, which is crammed full of fine furniture, paintings (including works by Landseer, Allan Ramsay and Sir Joshua Reynolds), tapestries and *objets d'art*.

Set aside at least an hour for Dunrobin's amazing **museum**, housed in an eighteenth-century building at the edge of the garden. Inside, hundreds of disembodied animals' heads and horns peer down from the walls, alongside other more macabre appendages, from elephants' toes to rhinos' tails. Bagged mainly by the fifth Duke and Duchess of Sutherland, the trophies vie for space with other fascinating family memorabilia, including one of John O' Groat's bones, Chinese opium pipes, and such curiosities as a "picnic gong from the South Pacific". There's also an impressive collection of ethnographic artefacts acquired by the Sutherlands on their frequent hunting jaunts, ranging from an Egyptian sarcophagus to some finely carved Pictish stones.

The Sutherland Monument

You can't miss the 100-foot **Monument** to the first Duke of Sutherland, which peers proprietorially down from the summit of the 1293ft **Beinn a'Bhragaidh**, a mile north-west of Golspie. An inscription cut into its base recalls that the statue was erected in 1834 by "... a mourning and grateful tenantry [to] ... a judicious, kind and liberal land-lord ... [who would] open his hands to the distress of the widow, the sick and the trav-eller". Unsurprisingly, there's no reference to the fact that the duke, widely regarded as Scotland's own Josef Stalin, forcibly evicted 15,000 crofters from his million-acre estate – a fact which, in the words of one local historian, makes the monument ". . . a grotesque representation of the many forces that destroyed the Highlands". Campaigners are lobbying, so far unsuccessfully, to have the monument broken into pieces and scattered over the hillside, so that visitors can walk over the remains to a new, more appropriate memorial. However, the Sutherland estate and local council con-tinue to resist such moves.

It's worth the wet, rocky **climb** (1hr 30min return trip) to the top of the hill for the wonderful views south along the coast past Dornoch to the Moray Firth and west towards Lairg and Loch Shin. It's a steep and strenuous walk, however, and there's no view until you're out of the trees, about ten minutes from the top. Take the road oppo-site Munro's TV Rentals in Golspie's main street, which leads up the hill, past a foun-tain, under the railway and through a farmyard – from here, follow the Beinn a'Bhragaidh footpath (BBFP) signs along the path into the woods.

Dornoch

DORNOCH, approximately ten miles south of Golspie, lies on a flattish headland over-looking the **Dornoch Firth**. Surrounded by sand dunes and blessed with an excep-tionally sunny climate by Scottish standards, it's something of a middle-class holiday resort, with solid Edwardian hotels, trees and flowers in profusion, and miles of sandy beaches giving good views across the estuary to the Tain peninsula. The town is also renowned for its championship **golf course**, ranked eleventh in the world and the most northerly first-class course in the world.

Dating from the twelfth century, Dornoch became a royal burgh in 1628. Among its oldest buildings, which are all grouped round the spacious Square, the tiny **Cathedral** was founded in 1224 and built of local sandstone. The original building was horribly damaged by marauding Mackays in 1570, and much of what you see today was restored by the Countess of Sutherland in 1835, though her worst Victorian excesses were removed this century, when the interior stonework was returned to its original state. A later addition were the stained glass windows in the north wall, which were endowed by the expat American-based Andrew Carnegie (see p.903). Opposite, the fortified six-teenth-century Bishop's Palace, a fine example of vernacular architecture, with stepped gables and towers, has been refurbished as an upmarket hotel (see below). Next door, the **Old Town Jail** (Mon–Sat 10am–5pm; free) contains a mock-up of a nineteenth-cen-tury cell accessed through a gift and crafts shop.

Buses from Tain and Inverness stop in the Square, where you'll also find a **tourist office** (May–June, Sept & Oct Mon–Fri 9am–5pm, Sat 9am–4pm; July & Aug Mon–Fri 9am–5pm, Sat 9am–4pm, Sun 11am–5pm; Nov–April Mon–Fri 9am–5pm; ☎01862/810400). There's no shortage of **accommodation**: the *Trentham Hotel* (☎01862/810551; ①), near the golf course on the northeast edge of town, is friendly and comfortable if a bit staid, while the characterful *Dornoch Castle Hotel* (☎01862/810216; ④; closed Nov–March), in the Bishop's Palace on the Square, has a cosy old-style bar and relaxing tea garden. Of the B&Bs, try *Trevose*, on the Square (☎01862/810269; ①; closed Oct–Feb), or, a couple of miles out on the A949, *Evelix Farmhouse* (☎01862/810271; ①; closed Oct–May). Expensive gourmet **meals** are available at the *2 Quail* restaurant on Castle Street (☎01862/811811; closed Sun

& Mon), which also has tasteful rooms available (③), while both the hotels do good bar and restaurant meals and the *Cathedral Café* is open until 9pm in summer and serves delicious soup and snacks.

Bonar Bridge and around

Before the causeway was built across the Dornoch Firth, traffic heading along the coast used to skirt around the estuary, crossing the Kyle of Sutherland at **BONAR BRIDGE**. In the fourteenth and fifteenth centuries, the village harboured a large **iron foundry**. Ore was brought across the peat moors of the central Highlands from the west coast on sledges, and fuel for smelting came from the oak forest draped over the northern shores of the nearby Kyle. These days there's little of note in Bonar Bridge other than the bridge itself, which has had three incarnations up to the present steel construction of 1973, all recalled on a stone plinth on the north side. However, you may want to check out the unusual **airboat** trips (book on ☎01863/766839; 30min–1hr; £8–15), run from the Caledonian Hotel. The unlikely-looking craft, with a huge fan mounted on the back of a flat-bottomed launch, previously saw service in the Everglade swamps of Florida, and is used in similar fashion on the Kyle to skim over shallow water and mud flats to get a closer look at the local wildlife and scenery.

Carbisdale Castle

Towering high above the River Shin, three miles northwest of Bonar Bridge, the daunting neo-Gothic profile of **Carbisdale Castle** (not open to the public) overlooks the **Kyle of Sutherland**, as well as the battlefield where the gallant Marquis of Montrose was defeated in 1650, finally forcing Charles II – if he wanted to be received as king – to accede to the Scots demand for Presbyterianism. It was erected between 1906 and 1917 for the dowager **Duchess of Sutherland**, following a protracted family feud. After the death of her husband, the late Duke of Sutherland, the will leaving her the lion's share of the vast estate was contested by his children from his first marriage. In the course of the ensuing legal battle, the Duchess was found in contempt of court for destroying important documents pertinent to the case, and locked up in Holloway prison for six weeks. However, the Sutherlands eventually recanted (although there was no personal reconciliation) and, by way of compensation, built their stepmother a castle worthy of her rank. Designed in three distinct styles (to give the impression it was added to over a long period of time), Carbisdale was eventually acquired by a Norwegian shipping magnate in 1933, and finally gifted, along with its entire contents and estate, to the SYHA, which has turned it into what must be one of the most opulent **youth hostels** in the world, full of white Italian marble sculptures, huge gilt-framed portraits, sweeping staircases and magnificent drawing rooms alongside standard facilities such as self-catering kitchens, games rooms, TV rooms and thirty dorms, including some recently upgraded four-bed family rooms (☎01549/421232; closed first 2 weeks of May & Nov–Feb). The best way to get here by public transport is to take a train to nearby Culrain station, which lies within easy walking distance of the castle. **Buses** from Inverness (3 daily; 1hr 30min) and Tain (4 daily; 25min) only run as far as **Ardgay**, three miles south.

Lairg

Eleven miles north of Bonar Bridge, the A836 parallels the River Shin for eleven miles, to **LAIRG**, a bleak and scattered place at the eastern end of lonely **Loch Shin**. On fine days, the vast wastes of heather and deergrass surrounding the village can be beautiful, but in the rain it can be a deeply depressing landscape. This workaday village is predominantly a **transport hub** and the railhead for a huge area to the northwest, and there's nothing much to see in town. However, a mile southeast on the A839, there are signs of early settlement at nearby **Ord Hill**, where archeological digs have recently yielded traces of human habitation dating back to Neolithic times. The Ferrycroft Countryside Centre and **tourist office**, on the west side of the river (April–Oct Mon–Sat 9.30am–5.30pm, Sun 10am–5pm; ☎01549/402160), hands out leaflets detailing the locations of hut circles and other sites and is the starting point for forest walks and an archeological trail to Ord Hill. Every August, Lairg hosts an annual lamb sale, the biggest one-day livestock market in Europe, when sheep from all over the north of Scotland are bought and sold.

Lairg, at the centre of the region's **road system**, is distinctly hard to avoid: the A838, traversing some of the loneliest country in the Highlands, is the quickest route for Cape Wrath; the A836 heads up to Tongue on the north coast; and the A839 links up to the A837 to push west through lovely Strath Oykel, to Lochinver on the west coast. For non-drivers, Lairg is on the **train line** connecting Inverness to Wick and Thurso and is the nexus of several **postbus routes** around the northwest Highlands, including one which links Lairg with Ledmore, on the Ullapool–Durness road. Trains arrive north of the main road along the loch; buses stop right on the loch. Should you want **to stay**, *Carnbren* (☎01549/402259; ③), just south of the bridge on the Bonar Bridge road, is comfortable, as is the *Old Coach House* (☎01549/402378; ③; closed Nov–April), three miles south of Lairg on the B864 at Achany.

travel details

Trains

Aviemore to: Edinburgh (Mon–Sat 8 daily, Sun 3 daily; 3hr); Inverness (Mon–Sat 8 daily, Sun 4 daily; 40min); Newtonmore (Mon–Sat 6 daily, Sun 4 daily; 20min).

Dingwall to: Helmsdale (Mon–Sat 3 daily, plus Sun 2 daily in summer; 2hr); Inverness (Mon–Sat 6–7 daily, plus Sun 4 daily in summer; 30min); Kyle of Lochalsh (Mon–Sat 3–4 daily, plus Sun 2 daily in summer; 2hr); Lairg (Mon–Sat 3 daily, plus Sun 2 daily in summer; 1hr 10min); Thurso (Mon–Sat 3 daily, plus Sun 2 daily in summer; 3hr 20min); Wick (Mon–Sat 3 daily, plus Sun 2 daily in summer; 3hr 20min).

Fort William to: Arisaig (Mon–Sat 4 daily, plus Sun 3 daily in summer; 1hr 10min); Crianlarich (Mon–Sat 3–4 daily, Sun 1–3 daily; 1hr 40min); Glasgow (Mon–Sat 3 daily, Sun 1–2 daily; 4hr); Glenfinnan (4 daily; 40min); London (1 nightly; 12hr); Mallaig (Mon–Sat 4 daily, Sun 1–3 daily; 1hr 25min).

Inverness to: Aviemore (Mon–Sat 8 daily, Sun 4 daily; 40min); Dingwall (Mon–Sat 6–7 daily, plus Sun 4 daily in summer; 30min); Edinburgh (Mon–Sat 8 daily, Sun 3 daily; 3hr 30min); Helmsdale (Mon–Sat 3 daily, plus Sun 2 daily in summer; 2hr 20min); Kyle of Lochalsh (Mon–Sat 3–4 daily, plus Sun 2 daily in summer; 2hr 40min); Lairg (Mon–Sat 3 daily, plus Sun 2 daily in summer; 1hr 40min); London (Mon–Fri & Sun 2 daily, Sat 1 daily; 8hr 40min); Plockton (Mon–Sat 3–4 daily, plus Sun 2 daily in summer; 2hr 15min); Thurso (Mon–Sat 3 daily, plus Sun 2 daily in summer; 3hr 45min); Wick (Mon–Sat 3 daily, plus Sun 2 daily in summer; 3hr 45min).

Kyle of Lochalsh to: Dingwall (Mon–Sat 3–4 daily, plus Sun 2 daily in summer; 2hr); Inverness (Mon–Sat 3–4 daily, plus Sun 2 daily in summer; 2hr 40min); Plockton (Mon–Sat 3–4 daily, plus Sun 2 daily in summer; 20min).

Lairg to: Dingwall (Mon–Sat 3 daily, plus Sun 2 daily in summer; 1hr 10min); Inverness (Mon–Sat 3 daily, plus Sun 2 daily in summer; 1hr 40min); Thurso (Mon–Sat 3 daily, plus Sun 2 daily in summer; 2hr); Wick (Mon–Sat 3 daily, plus Sun 2 daily in summer; 2hr).

Mallaig to: Arisaig (Mon–Sat 4 daily, plus Sun 3 daily in summer; 15min); Fort William (Mon–Sat 4 daily, plus Sun 3 daily in summer; 1hr 30min); Glasgow (Mon–Sat 3 daily, Sun 1–2 daily; 5hr 20min); Glenfinnan (Mon–Sat 4 daily, plus Sun 3 daily in summer; 40min).

Newtonmore to: Aviemore (Mon–Sat 6 daily, Sun 4 daily; 20min); Inverness (Mon–Sat 6 daily, Sun 4 daily; 1hr).

Thurso to: Dingwall (Mon–Sat 3 daily, plus Sun 2 daily in summer; 3hr 20min); Inverness (Mon–Sat 3 daily, plus Sun 2 daily in summer; 3hr 45min); Lairg (Mon–Sat 3 daily, plus Sun 2 daily in summer; 2hr).

Wick to: Dingwall (Mon–Sat 3 daily, plus Sun 2 daily in summer; 3hr 20min); Inverness (Mon–Sat 3 daily, plus Sun 2 daily in summer; 3hr 45min); Lairg (Mon–Sat 3 daily, plus Sun 2 daily in summer; 2hr).

Buses

Aviemore to: Grantown-on-Spey (6–9 daily; 40min); Inverness (15 daily; 40min); Newtonmore (8 daily; 20min).

Brora to: Thurso (4–5 daily; 1hr 50min); Wick (5–6 daily; 1hr 15min).

Dornoch to: Brora (5 daily; 40min); Inverness (10 daily; 1hr 10min).

Fort William to: Acharacle (Mon–Sat 2–4 daily; 1hr 30min); Drumnadrochit (6 daily; 1hr 30min); Fort Augustus (6 daily; 1hr); Inverness (6 daily; 2hr); Mallaig (1–2 daily; 2hr).

Gairloch to: Dingwall (3 weekly; 2hr); Inverness (3 weekly; 2hr 20min); Redpoint (1 daily; 1hr 40min).

Inverness to: Aberdeen (hourly; 3hr 40min); Aviemore (Mon–Sat 15 daily, Sun 12 daily; 40min); Cromarty (4 daily; 45min); Drumnadrochit (6 daily; 30min); Durness (May to early Oct 1 daily; 5hr); Fort Augustus (6 daily; 1hr); Fort William (6 daily; 2hr); Gairloch (1 daily; 2hr 20min); Glasgow (7 daily; 3hr 35min–4hr 30min); John O' Groats

(1–2 daily; 3hr 40min); Kirkwall (April–Sept 2 daily; 5hr 20min); Kyle of Lochalsh (3–4 daily; 2hr); Lairg (Mon–Sat 2 daily; 2hr); Lochinver (May to early Oct 1 daily; 3hr 10min); Nairn (Mon–Sat hourly; 40min); Newtonmore (8 daily; 1hr 10min); Oban (Mon–Sat 2 daily; 4hr); Perth (10 daily; 2hr 40min); Portree (3–4 daily; 3hr 20min); Tain (hourly; 1hr 15min); Thurso (Mon–Sat 5 daily, Sun 4 daily; 3hr 30min); Ullapool (2–4 daily; 1hr 30min); Wick (Mon–Sat 3 daily; 2hr).

Kyle of Lochalsh to: Fort William (3 daily; 1hr 50min); Glasgow (3 daily; 5hr); Inverness (3–4 daily; 2hr).

Lochinver to: Inverness (May to early Oct 1 daily; 3hr 10min).

Mallaig to: Acharacle (1–3 daily; 1hr 45min); Fort William (1–2 daily; 2hr).

Thurso to: Bettyhill (2 daily; 1hr 20min); Inverness (Mon–Sat 5 daily, Sun 4 daily; 3hr 30min); Wick (Mon–Sat 2–4 daily, Sun 1 daily; 40min).

Wick to: Inverness (Mon–Sat 3 daily; 2hr); Thurso (Mon–Sat 2–4 daily, Sun 1 daily; 40min).

Ferries

To Lewis: Ullapool–Stornoway, see p.976.

To Mull: Kilchoan–Tobermory, see p.949.

To Orkney: Scrabster–Stromness, see p.1065.

To Skye: Mallaig–Armadale; Glenelg–Kylerhea, see p.976.

To the Small Isles: Mallaig–Eigg, Rum, Muck and Canna, see p.960.

Flights

Inverness to: Amsterdam (1 daily; 1hr 40min); Edinburgh (Mon–Fri 1 daily; 50min); Glasgow (Mon–Fri 2 daily; 50min); Kirkwall (Mon–Fri 2 daily; 40min); London (4 daily; 1hr 30min); Shetland (Mon–Fri 1 daily; 1hr 50min); Stornoway (Mon–Sat 2 daily; 40min).

CHAPTER TWENTY-SIX

ORKNEY AND SHETLAND

R eaching up towards the Arctic Circle, and totally exposed to turbulent Atlantic weather systems, the Orkney and Shetland islands gather neatly into two distinct and very different clusters. Often referring to themselves as Orcadians or Shetlanders, and with unofficial but widely displayed flags, their inhabitants regard Scotland as a separate entity; the mainland to them is the one in their own archipelago, not the Scottish mainland. This feeling of detachment arises partly from geography but also from their distinctive history, culture and landscape, in which they differ not only from Scotland but also from each other.

To the south, just a short step from the Scottish mainland, are the seventy or so **Orkney Islands**. With the major exception of Hoy, which is high and rugged, they are mostly low-lying, gently sloping and fertile, and for centuries have provided a reasonably secure living for their inhabitants from farming and fishing. In spring and summer the days are long, the skies enormous and the meadows thick with wild flowers. There is a peaceful continuity to Orcadian life reflected not only in the well-preserved treasury of Stone Age settlements, such as **Skara Brae**, and standing stones, most notably the **Stones of Stenness**, but also in the rather conservative nature of society here today.

Another sixty miles north, the **Shetland Islands** are in nearly all respects a complete contrast. Dramatic cliffs, teeming with thousands of sea birds, rise straight out of the water to barren, sometimes rugged, heather-coated hills, while ice-sculpted sea inlets cut deep into the land, offering memorable coastal walks in Shetland's endless summer evenings. With little fertile ground, Shetlanders have traditionally been crofters rather than farmers, but most often have looked to the sea for an uncertain living in fishing or the naval and merchant services; today they enthusiastically embrace new opportunities such as fish farming and computing. Nevertheless, the past is seldom forgotten; the Norse heritage is clear in every road sign and there are many well-preserved prehistoric sites such as the remarkable **Broch of Mousa** and **Jarlshof**.

Since people first began to explore the North Atlantic, Orkney and Shetland have been stepping stones on routes between Britain, Ireland and Scandinavia; and both groups have a long history of settlement, certainly from around 3500–4000 BC. The Norse settlers, who began to arrive from about 800 AD, with substantial migration from around 900 AD, left the islands with a unique cultural character. Orkney was a powerful Norse earldom, and Shetland (at first part of the same earldom) was ruled directly from

---

ACCOMMODATION PRICE CODES

Throughout this guide, hotel and B&B accommodation is priced on a scale of ① to ⑨, the number indicating the **lowest price** you could expect to pay per night in that establishment for a **double room** in high season. The prices indicated by the codes are as follows:

① under £40	④ £60–70	⑦ £110–150
② £40–50	⑤ £70–90	⑧ £150–200
③ £50–60	⑥ £90–110	⑨ over £200

Norway for nearly 300 years after 1195. The Norse influence is clearly evident today in place names and in dialect words; neither group was ever part of the Gaelic-speaking culture of Highland Scotland and the Scottish influence is essentially a Lowland one.

It's impossible to overestimate the influence of the **weather** in these parts. The one thing you can say about it is that it's interesting, frequently dramatic. More often than not, it will be windy and rainy, though, as they say in the nearby Faroes, you can have all four seasons in one day. The wind-chill factor is not to be taken lightly, and there is often a dampness or drizzle in the air, even when it's not actually raining. Even in late spring and summer, when there can be long dry spells with lots of sunshine, you still need to come prepared for wind, rain and, most frustrating of all, the occasional sea fog. The one good thing about the almost constant presence of the wind is that midges are generally less of a problem, except on those rare days when the air is still.

DIALECT AND PLACE NAMES

Between the tenth and seventeenth centuries the chief language of Orkney and Shetland was **Norn**, a Scandinavian tongue close to modern Faroese and Icelandic. After the end of Norse rule and with the transformation of the church, the law, commerce and education, Norn gradually lost out to Scots and English. Today, Orkney and Shetland have their own dialects, and individual islands and communities within each group have local variations. The **dialects** have a Scots base, with some Old Norse words; however, they don't sound strongly Scottish, with the Orkney accent – which has been likened to the Welsh one – especially distinctive. Listed below are some of the words you're most likely to hear, including some birds' names and common elements in place names. In most cases, the Shetland form is given; the Orkney terms are very similar, if not identical.

aak	guillemot	*neesick*	porpoise
alan	storm petrel	*noost*	hollow place where a
ayre	beach		boat is drawn up
böd	fisherman's store	*norie*	puffin
bonxie	great skua	(or *tammie-norie*)	
bruck	rubbish	*noup*	steep headland
burra	heath rush	*peerie* (in Orkney,	small
corbie	raven	often *peedie*)	
crö	sheepfold	*plantiecrub*	small dry-stone
du	familiar form of "you"	(or *plantiecrö*)	enclosure for
dunter	eider duck		growing cabbages
eela	rod-fishing from	*quoy*	enclosed, cultivated
	small boats		common land
ferrylouper	incomer (Orkney)	*reestit*	cured (as in *reestit*
fourareen	four-oared boat		mutton)
foy	party or festival	*roost*	tide race
geo	coastal inlet	*scattald*	common grazing land
haa	laird's house	*scootie alan*	arctic skua
hap	hand-knitted shawl	*scord*	gap or pass in a
kame	ridge of hills		ridge of hills
kishie	basket	*shaela*	dark grey
maa	seagull	*shalder*	oystercatcher
mallie (Shetland) or		*simmer dim*	summer twilight
mallimak (Orkney)	fulmar petrel	*sixern*	six-oared boat
mool	headland	*solan*	gannet
moorit	brown	*soothmoother*	incomer (Shetland)
mootie	tiny	*tystie*	black guillemot
muckle	large	*voe*	sea inlet

Orkney

Just a short step from John O' Groats, the **Orkney Islands** are a unique and fiercely independent grouping. In spring and summer the meadows and cliff-tops are a brilliant green, shining with wild flowers, while long days pour light onto the land and sea. For an Orcadian, "Mainland" invariably means the largest island in Orkney, rather than the rest of Scotland, and throughout their history they've been linked to lands much further afield, principally Scandinavia.

Small communities began to settle in the islands around 4000 BC, and the village at **Skara Brae** on the Mainland is one of the best-preserved Stone Age settlements in Europe. This and many of the other older archeological sites, including the **Stones of Stenness** and **Maes Howe**, are concentrated in the central and western parts of the Mainland. Elsewhere the islands are scattered with chambered tombs and stone circles, a tribute to the well-developed religious and ceremonial practices taking place here from around 2000 BC. More sophisticated **Iron Age** inhabitants built fortified villages incorporating stone towers known as brochs, protected by walls and ramparts, many of which are still in place. Later, Pictish culture spread to Orkney and the remains of several of their early Christian settlements can still be seen, the best at the **Brough of Birsay** in the West Mainland, where a group of small houses is gathered around the remains of an early church. Later, around the ninth century, **Norse** settlers from Scandinavia arrived, and the islands became Norse earldoms, forming an outpost of this powerful and expansive culture that was gradually forcing its way south. The last of the Norse earls was killed in 1231, but they had a lasting impact on the islands, leaving behind not only their language but also the great **St Magnus Cathedral** in Kirkwall, one of Scotland's most outstanding pieces of medieval architecture.

After the end of Norse rule, the islands became the preserve of **Scottish earls**, who exploited and abused the islanders, although a steady increase in sea trade did offer some chance of escape. French and Spanish ships sheltered here in the sixteenth century, and the ships of the **Hudson Bay Company** recruited hundreds of Orcadians to work in the Canadian fur trade. The islands were also an important staging post in the **whaling industry** and the herring boom, which brought great numbers of small Dutch, French and Scottish boats. More recently, the naval importance of **Scapa Flow**

GETTING TO ORKNEY

Orkney is connected to the Scottish mainland by three main **ferry** routes. P&O Scottish Ferries (☎01856/850655) runs car ferries to **Stromness** once a week (June–Aug twice weekly) from **Aberdeen** (8hr) and daily services on the much shorter crossing (2hr) from **Scrabster**, about two miles northwest of Thurso on the north coast, which has train and bus connections from Inverness. A new vehicle ferry service is also in the pipeline between St Margaret's Hope on South Ronaldsay, and Gills, east of Thurso, on the north coast (ring the tourist board for the latest). There is also a passenger ferry between **John O' Groats** and **Burwick** on South Ronaldsay (May–Sept 2–4 daily; 45min) with which the Orkney Bus service from Inverness connects directly. A day-trip is also offered from Inverness or John O' Groats, with a tour of some of the major sights on the Mainland; details of both ferry and bus are available from John O' Groats Ferries (☎01955/611353). There's also a weekly or, from June to August, twice-weekly P&O service from Stromness to **Lerwick** in Shetland.

There are **direct flights** to Kirkwall airport from Shetland, Wick, Inverness, Aberdeen, Edinburgh or Glasgow, with good connections from Birmingham, London and Manchester. All of these services can be booked through British Airways (☎0345/222111).

brought plenty of money and activity during both world wars, and left the seabed scattered with **wrecks**, making for wonderful **diving** opportunities, and the cliff-tops dotted with gun emplacements. Since the war, things have quietened down somewhat, although in the last two decades the large **oil terminal** on the island of Flotta and European Community funding have brought surprise windfalls, stemming the exodus

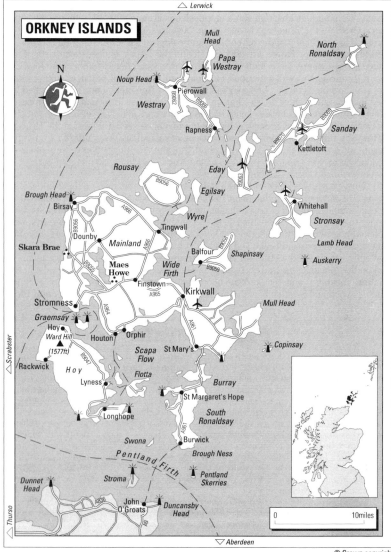

ORKNEY ISLANDS

of young people. Meanwhile, many disenchanted southerners have become "ferry-loupers" (incomers) searching for the peace and apparent simplicity of island life.

Getting around
Bus services on the Orkney Mainland are fairly infrequent, and some of the most interesting areas aren't served at all; on the islands, there will usually be a bus service to and from the ferry terminal and that's all. **Cycling** is cheap and, with few steep hills and modest distances, relatively easy, though the wind can make it hard going. Bikes can be rented in Kirkwall, Stromness and on some of the smaller islands. Bringing a **car** to Orkney is straightforward, if not exactly cheap; alternatively, you can rent one in Kirkwall, Stromness or on several of the islands. Especially if time is limited, it may be worth considering one of the well-organized and informative **tours** available by bus or minibus operated by Wildabout (☎01856/851011) and others; details are available from the tourist offices.

Getting to the other islands from the Mainland isn't difficult; Orkney Ferries (☎01856/872044) operates several sailings daily to Hoy, Shapinsay and Rousay and between one and three, depending on route and season, to all the others except North Ronaldsay, which has a weekly boat on Fridays. There are flights from Kirkwall to Eday, North Ronaldsay, Westray, Papa Westray, Sanday and Stronsay, all of which can be booked through British Airways or Loganair (☎01856/872420). Travel between individual islands by sea or air isn't so straightforward, but careful study of timetables can sometimes reduce the need to come all the way back to Kirkwall. Special sailings on summer Sundays make very useful inter-island connections.

Stromness

Vastly more appealing than most ferry ports, the harbour at **STROMNESS** has been one of the focal points of Orkney life since Viking times or before. It was here, in the sheltered Hamnavoe, on the edge of the great natural harbour of Scapa Flow, that ships from all around the world came and went, sweeping the town into a series of booms, unloading a cargo of sea tales and embarking hundreds of Orcadians on weird and wonderful expeditions.

French and Spanish ships sheltered in Hamnavoe in the sixteenth century, and for a long time European conflicts made it safer for ships heading across the Atlantic to travel around the top of Scotland rather than through the English Channel, many of them calling in to Stromness to take on food, water and crew. Crews from Stromness were also hired for herring and whaling expeditions for which the town was an important centre. By 1842, the town was a tough and busy harbour, with some forty or so pubs and reports of "outrageous and turbulent proceedings of seamen and others who frequent the harbour". The herring boom brought large numbers of small boats to the town, along with thousands of young women who gutted and pickled the fish before they were packed in barrels. Today Stromness is still an important harbour town, serving as the headquarters of the Northern Lighthouse Board as well as being the main ferry terminal.

The Town
The old town of Stromness still hugs the shoreline, its one and only street, a narrow winding affair, built long before the advent of the motor car, and still paved with great flagstones, and fed by a tight network of alleyways or closes. The central section is known as **Victoria Street**, though in fact it takes on several other names – Graham Place, Dundas Street, Alfred Street and South End – as it threads its way southwards. On the east side of the street the houses are gable end on to the waterfront, and originally each one would have had their own pier, from which merchants would trade with passing ships.

You can visit the first of the old jetties, to the south of the modern harbour, as it now houses the **Pier Arts Centre** (July & Aug Tues–Sat 10.30am–12.30pm & 1.30–5pm, Sun 2–5pm; rest of year closed Sun; free). The art gallery is spread over two buildings, divided by a lovely flagstone sun-trap courtyard (access is down an alleyway off the main street): the first building hosts temporary exhibitions, often featuring painting and sculpture by local artists, while the warehouse has a remarkable permanent display of twentieth-century British art. At first it comes as a shock to see abstract works executed by members of the Cornish art scene such Barbara Hepworth, Ben Nicholson, Terry Frost, Patrick Hero and Eduardo Paolozzi, but the marine themes of many of the works, and in particular the primitive scenes by Alfred Wallis, have a special resonance in this seaport.

Ten minutes' walk down the main street, at the junction of Alfred Street and South End, is the newly refurbished **Stromness Museum** (May–Sept daily 10am–5pm; Oct–April Mon–Sat 10.30am–12.30pm & 1.30–5pm; £2), built in 1858, partly to house the collections of the local natural history society. The natural history collection is still there – don't miss the pull-out drawers of birds' eggs, butterflies and moths – and has since been joined by a whole range of salty artefacts gathered from shipwrecks and Arctic expeditions, including barnacle-encrusted crockery from the German High Seas Fleet that sank in Scapa Flow, beaver fur hats, Cree Indian cloth and part of the torpedo that sunk the *HMS Royal Oak*.

Practicalities

Arriving by ferry, you'll disembark at the new ferry terminal, which also houses the **tourist office** (April–Oct Mon–Sat 8am–6pm, Sun 9am–4pm; Nov–March Mon–Fri 9am–5pm; ☎01856/850716). Unfortunately, Stromness has a fairly poor selection of **hotels**, with the venerable Victorian *Stromness Hotel* (☎01856/850610, *stromnesshotel@compuserve.com*; ⑤) probably your best bet. As for **B&Bs**, there's a traditional end-on waterfront house next to the museum at 2 South End (☎01856/850215; ②; closed Nov–March), or, further south still, *Stenigar* (☎01856/850438; ②; closed Nov–March), a converted boatyard which has lots of character, and is situated just before the campsite on the Ness Road. Stromness has an SYHA **youth hostel** in a converted school on Helliehole Road (☎01856/850589; closed Nov to mid-March), signposted off the main street; it has a curfew and single-sex dorms. More laid-back is the independent family-run *Brown's Hostel*, 45–47 Victoria St (☎01856/850661; no curfew), with bunk beds in shared rooms and kitchen facilities. There's also a **campsite** (☎01856/873535; closed mid-Sept to April) in a superb setting a mile south of the ferry terminal at Point of Ness, with views out to Hoy; it's well equipped and even has its own lounge, however it's also extremely exposed, especially if a southwesterly is blowing.

Stromness has a couple of decent **places to eat** on and off the main street. The moderately expensive *Hamnavoe Restaurant,* at 35 Graham Place (☎01856/850606; Thurs–Sun eves only), offers the town's most ambitious cooking in a very pleasant setting. For something less formal, head for the upstairs lounge bar of the *Stromness Hotel*, which does very good bar meals – go for the specials. The nearby *Coffee Shop* offers enormous breakfasts, imaginative lunches, as well as tea and cakes, though it closes at 4 or 5pm. **Takeaway** options include the *Chip Shop* on the main street (closed Thurs eve, Sat lunch & Sun), and *Velzian's*, further south, which does thin or thick-based pizzas and Tex-Mex. The downstairs *Flattie Bar* of the *Stromness Hotel* is a congenial place to warm yourself by the real fire, or sit outside, and have a **drink**; another popular pub is the *Ferry Inn*, opposite the hotel. *Argo's Bakery*, on Victoria Street, has a wide range of **picnic** basics, while *Orkney Wholefoods*, a few doors down, sells seafood, health food, cheese, local ice cream, and delicious made-to-order sandwiches.

West Mainland

The great bulk of the **West Mainland** is fertile, productive farmland, fenced off into a patchwork of fields used either to produce crops or for cattle grazing. The West Mainland is, however, fringed by some spectacular coastline, particularly in the west, and littered with some of the island's most impressive prehistoric sites, such as the village of **Skara Brae**, the standing **Stones of Stenness** and the chambered tomb of **Maes Howe**. Despite the intensive farming, there are still some areas which are too barren to cultivate, and the high ground and wild coastline are protected by several interesting **wildlife reserves**.

Stones of Stenness and Maes Howe

The parish of **STENNESS**, lies along the main road from Stromness to Kirkwall, south of the twin lochs of Stenness and Harray, which are separated by a couple of promontories, that once stood at the heart of Orkney's most important Neolithic ceremonial complex. The most visible part of the complex are the **Stones of Stenness**, originally a circle of twelve rock slabs, now just four, the tallest of which is a real monster, at over sixteen feet, though it's more remarkable for its incredible thinness. The circle is surrounded by a much diminished henge, a circular bank of earth and a ditch, with a couple of entrance causeways. Less than a mile to the northwest is another stone circle, the **Ring of Brodgar**, a much wider circle dramatically sited on raised ground. Here, there were originally sixty stones, twenty-seven of which now stand; of the henge, only the ditch survives.

There are several quite large burial mounds visible to the south of the Ring of Brodgar, but these are entirely eclipsed by the most impressive Neolithic burial chamber in the whole of Europe, **Maes Howe** (April–Sept daily 9.30am–6.30pm; Oct–March Mon–Wed & Sat 9.30am–4.30pm, Thurs 9.30am–noon, Sun 2.30–4.30pm; £2.50; HS), which lies less than a mile northeast of the Stones of Stenness. Dating from around 3000 BC, its incredible state of preservation is partly due to the massive slabs of sandstone from which it was constructed, the largest of which weighs over three tons. The central chamber is reached down a long, low, stone passage and contains three cells built into the walls, each of which was plugged with an enormous stone. When the tomb was opened in 1861, it was found to be virtually empty, thanks to the work of generations of grave-robbers, who had only left behind a handful of human bones. The Vikings broke in here in the twelfth century, probably on their way to the crusades, leaving behind large amounts of runic graffiti on the walls of the main chamber.

Skara Brae and Skaill House

The beautiful white curve of the Bay of Skaill is home to **Skara Brae** (April–Sept daily 9.30am–6.30pm; Oct–March Mon–Sat 9.30am–4.30pm, Sun 2–4.30pm; £4 in summer; £3.20 in winter), where the extensive remains of a small Neolithic fishing and farming village, dating back to 3000 BC, were discovered in 1850 after a fierce storm. The village is very well preserved, its houses huddled together and connected by narrow passages which would originally have been covered over with turf. The houses themselves consist of a single, spacious living room, surrounded by a vast array of domestic detail, including dressers, fireplaces, in-built cupboards, beds and boxes, all carefully put together from slabs of stone.

Unfortunately, the sheer number of people now visiting Skara Brae means that you can no longer explore the site properly, but only look down from the outer walls. Before you reach the site, you must buy a ticket from the new visitor centre, which also contains a small introductory exhibition. You then proceed to a full-scale replica of House 6, complete with fake wood and skin roof. It's all a tad neat and tidy, with fetching up-lighting, rather than dark, smoky and smelly, but you get the general idea.

In the summer months, your ticket to Skara Brae also covers entry to nearby **Skaill House**, a vast range of buildings 300yd inland, that was once the home of the laird of Skaill. The original house was built by Bishop George Graham in the 1620s and has since been much extended. Its contents include Captain Cook's dinner service from the *Resolution* as well as family and military memorabilia.

Birsay and Evie

Occupying the northwest corner of the Mainland, the parish of **BIRSAY** was the centre of Norse power in Orkney for several centuries, until the earls moved to Kirkwall following the construction of the cathedral. Today a tiny cluster of homes is gathered around the sandstone ruins of the **Earl's Palace** at Birsay, which in the second half of the sixteenth century by Robert Stewart, Earl of Orkney, using the forced labour of the islanders. The crumbling walls and turrets retain plenty of their grandeur, although there is little remaining evidence of domestic detail. When it was occupied, the palace was surrounded by flower and herb gardens, a bowling green and archery butts. By comparison, the Earl's Palace in Kirkwall seems almost humble.

Just over half a mile northwest of the palace is the **Brough of Birsay**, a small Pictish settlement on a tidal island that you can get to – and from – only during the two hours each side of high tide. The focus of the village was – and still is – the twelfth-century **St Peter's Church**, which stands significantly higher than the surrounding buildings. To the south, on the other side of Birsay Bay, is **Marwick Head**. On it stands the memorial to Lord Kitchener and the crew of the HMS *Hampshire* who died near here when the ship struck a mine in June 1916. Marwick Head and (just over a mile to the east) the **Loons** are both **RSPB reserves**. Marwick Head is a good place to see guillemots and puffins nesting in summer, while the Loons has a roadside hide, and is an excellent place to watch a variety of waterfowl.

Overshadowed by the great wind turbine on Burgar Hill, the little village of **EVIE**, on the north coast, looks out across the turbulent waters of Eynhallow Sound towards the island of Rousay. Its chief draw is the nearby **Broch of Gurness** (April–Sept daily 9.30am–6.30pm; £2.50), the best preserved broch on an archipelago replete with them, and one which is still surrounded by a remarkable complex of later buildings. As at Birsay, the sea has eaten away half the site, but the broch itself, dating from around 100 BC, still stands, its walls reaching a height of twelve feet in places, its inner cells still intact. The compact group of homes clustered around the broch have also survived amazingly well, with much of their original and ingenious stone shelving and fireplaces still in place.

Practicalities

You can easily base yourself in Kirkwall or Stromness, but many good **places to stay** are scattered throughout the West Mainland. There are welcoming **B&Bs** such as *Duncraigon*, overlooking the Loch of Harray at Sandwick (☎01856/841647; ①). *Netherstove* (☎01856/841625; ①) has comfortable rooms and self-catering cottages with a great view over the Bay of Skaill. Without doubt, the best place to stay, though, is *Woodwick House* (☎01856/751330; ②) near Evie, a secluded, cultured and friendly place, with good food, hosting occasional arts events. Also in Evie, you can stay in the nicely modernized **bothy and campsite**, run by Dale Farm (☎01856/751270; closed Nov–March), right by the junction of the road to Dounby (and not to be confused with the much tattier bothy back down the road to Kirkwall).

Kirkwall

Initial impressions of **KIRKWALL** are not always favourable. It has nothing to match the picturesque harbour of Stromness, and its urban sprawl is far less appealing. However, it does have one great redeeming feature, and that is its sandstone cathedral, without doubt the finest medieval building in the north of Scotland. Part of the reason for Kirkwall's disappointing waterfront is that today's harbour is a largely modern invention; in the mid-nineteenth century, the shoreline ran along Junction Road, and before that it was flush with the west side of main street. Nowadays, the town is divided into two main focal points: the flagstoned **main street**, which twists its way north past the cathedral; and the busy **harbour**, at the north end of the street, where ferries come and go all year round, and where, during the summer, launches off-load smartly dressed holidaymakers from the numerous cruise ships that weigh anchor in the Bay of Kirkwall.

The Town

Towering above the town, the **St Magnus Cathedral** (April–Sept Mon–Sat 9am–6pm, Sun 2–6pm; Oct–March Mon–Sat 9am–1pm & 2–5pm; Sunday service at 11.15am) is the town's most compelling sight. This beautiful red-sandstone building was begun in 1137 by the Orkney Earl Rognvald, who decided to make full use of a growing cult surrounding the figure of his uncle Magnus, who had been killed on the orders of his cousin Haakon in 1115. When Magnus's body was buried in Birsay a heavenly light was said to have shone overhead, and his grave soon became a place of pilgrimage attributed with miraculous powers and attracting pilgrims from as far afield as Shetland. When Rognvald finally took over the earldom he built the cathedral in his uncle's honour, moving the centre of religious and secular power from Birsay to Kirkwall.

The first version of the cathedral, built using yellow sandstone from Eday and red sandstone from the Mainland, was somewhat smaller than today's structure, which has been added to over the centuries, with a new east window in the thirteenth century, the extension of the nave in the fifteenth century and a new west window to mark the building's 850th anniversary in 1987. Today the soft sandstone is badly eroded – the capitals around the main doors are reduced to gnarled stumps – but it's still an immensely impressive building, its shape and style echoing the great cathedrals of Europe. Inside, the atmosphere is surprisingly intimate, the bulky sandstone columns drawing you up to the exposed brickwork arches, while around the walls is a series of mostly seventeenth-century tombstones, many carved with a skull and cross bones and other symbols of death, alongside chilling inscriptions calling on the reader to "remember death waits us all, the hour none knows".

To the south of the church are the ruined remains of the **Bishop's Palace** (April–Sept daily 9.30am–6.30pm; £1.80; HS), residence of the Bishop of Orkney since the twelfth century. Most of what you see now, however, dates from the time of Bishop Robert Reid, the founder of Edinburgh University, in the mid-sixteenth century. The walls still stand, as does the tall round tower in which the bishop had his private chambers; a narrow spiral staircase takes you to the top for a good view of the cathedral and across Kirkwall's rooftops.

VISITING ORKNEY'S HISTORIC SCOTLAND SIGHTS

If you're planning on visiting several of **Orkney's Historic Scotland sights**, it might be worth buying a combined ticket, which costs £9 and covers entry to Skara Brae, the Broch of Gurness, and Maes Howe as well as the Bishop's Palace.

The neighbouring **Earl's Palace**, built by the infamous Earl Patrick Stewart around 1600, using forced labour, is rather better preserved, and a lot more fun to explore. With its grand entrance, fancy oriel windows, dank dungeons, massive fireplaces and magnificent central hall, it has a confident solidity, and is reckoned to be one of the finest examples of Renaissance architecture in Scotland. The roof may be missing, but many domestic details remain, including a set of toilets and the stone shelves used by the clerk to store his filing. Earl Patrick enjoyed his palace for only a very short time before he was imprisoned and eventually executed.

Opposite the cathedral stands the sixteenth-century **Tankerness House**, a former home for the clergy. It has been renovated countless times over the years, most recently in the 1960s in order to provide a home for the **Orkney Museum** (May–Sept Mon–Sat 10.30am–5pm, Sun 2–5pm; rest of year closed Sun; free). Among its more unusual artefacts are a collection of balls used in a traditional Orkney street game, The Ba', played at Christmas and New Year. On a warm summer afternoon, the gardens (which can be entered either from the house itself or from a gate on Tankerness Lane) are thick with the buzz of bees and brilliant blooms.

At the harbour end of Junction Road is the tiny **Orkney Wireless Museum** (April–Sept Mon–Sat 10am–4.30pm, Sun 2–4.30pm; £2) packed to the roof with every sort of radio equipment; only a small part of the huge collection can be displayed at one time.

Further afield, a mile or so south of the town centre on the A961 to South Ronaldsay, is the **Highland Park distillery** (Easter–June, Sept & Oct Mon–Fri 10am–4pm; July & Aug Mon–Sat 10am–4pm, Sun noon–4pm; Nov–March Mon–Fri tours at 2pm; £3), billed as "the most northerly legal distillery in Scotland". It's been in operation for more than 200 years, and still has its own maltings, although it was closed during World War II, when the army used it as a food store and the huge vats served as communal baths. You can decide for yourself whether the taste still lingers by partaking of the regular guided tours of its beautiful old buildings and the customary dram afterwards.

Practicalities

Ferries docking at Stromness are met by buses to Kirkwall (40min), and there are also bus connections (45min) from the Burwick terminal on South Ronaldsay, served by passenger ferry from John O' Groats. The **bus station** is five minutes' walk west of the town centre. Kirkwall **airport** is about three miles southeast of Kirkwall on the A960; it's not served by buses, but a taxi into town should only set you back about £6. The helpful **tourist office**, on Broad Street, beside the cathedral graveyard (April–Sept daily 8.30am–8pm; Oct–March Mon–Sat 9.30am–5pm; ☎01856/872856), books accommodation, changes money and gives out an excellent free leaflet, the *Kirkwall Heritage Guide*, which takes you through all the buildings of interest. Most events are advertised in *The Orcadian*, which comes out on Thursdays, and there's a *What's on Diary* on BBC Radio Orkney (Mon–Fri 7.30–8am, 93.7 FM).

As for **accommodation**, Kirkwall has plenty of small rooms in ordinary B&Bs, and a host of blandly refurbished hotels, but nothing exceptional, so unless you're reliant on public transport, or have business in town, there's really no compelling reason to base yourself here, rather than out in Orkney's wonderful countryside. The SYHA **hostel** (☎01856/872243), on the road to Orphir, is a good ten minutes' walk from the centre of town – it's no beauty from the outside, but it's comfortable enough inside. A more central option is the small *Peedie Hostel* (☎01856/875477), on the waterfront next door to the *Ayre Hotel*. There's also a **campsite** (☎01856/873535; closed mid-Sept to mid-May) behind the new Pickaquoy Leisure Centre, five minutes' walk west of the bus station; the site is well equipped with laundry facilities, but it's hardly what you'd call picturesque.

The *Ayre Hotel* on Ayre Road (☎01856/873001; *reception@ayrehotel.co.uk*; ⑤), smart, friendly and on the waterfront, is the best – and most expensive – in town. Equally central are the *Albert*, on Mounthoolie Lane (☎01856/876000; ③), and the welcoming *West End Hotel*, 14 Main St (☎01856/872368; ③). Of the **B&Bs**, try *Whiteclett*, St Catherine's Place (☎01856/874193; ①), in a listed house right by the waterfront, or *Briar Lea*, 10 Dundas Crescent (☎01856/872747; ①), an attractive stone-built house with its own walled garden.

Given the quality of Orkney beef, and the quantity of shellfish caught in the vicinity, Kirkwall's **food** options are pretty disappointing. *Trenabies* and the *Pomona Café* are both venerable institutions, but the nicest **café** is *The Strynd* tearoom up the alleyway by the tourist office. For something more substantial, there's nothing for it but to head for one of the town's hotels – the *Albert,* and the *West End* are probably the best options, offering both bar meals and à la carte – or opt for Orkney's Indian restaurant, the *Mumutaz*, on Bridge Street.

The **nightlife** scene in Kirkwall is a lot more animated. The liveliest **pub** is the *Torvhaug Inn* on Bridge Street; another good place to try is the *Bothy Bar* in the *Albert Hotel*, which sometimes has live music. The *Ayre Hotel* has a good reputation for **traditional live music**, especially the regular Orkney Accordion & Fiddle Club nights on Wednesdays. Kirkwall's new Pickaquoy Leisure Centre, a short walk from the town centre, up Pickaquoy Road, contains the New Phoenix **cinema** (☎01856/879900).

East Mainland

Southeast from Kirkwall, the narrow spur of the **East Mainland** juts out into the North Sea and is joined, thanks to the remarkable **Churchill Barriers** (see box overleaf), to the smaller islands of Burray and South Ronaldsay. The land here is densely populated and heavily farmed, but there are several interesting fishing villages and a scattering of unusual historical relics. The northern side of the East Mainland consists of a series of exposed peninsulas, the first of which, **Rerwick Head**, is marked by the remains of World War II gun emplacements. **Mull Head** – the furthest east – is an RSPB reserve with a large colony of sea birds, including arctic terns, that swoop on unwanted visitors, screeching threateningly.

On the south coast, just east of the village of **ST MARY'S** and the first of the barriers, is the **Norwood Museum** (May–Sept Tues–Thurs & Sun 2–5pm & 6–8pm; also by arrangement ☎01856/781217; £3), a display of antiques collected from the age of thirteen by local stonemason Norrie Wood. Only about half of the collection is on display, but it's a fascinating and eccentric selection of bits and pieces from around the world, including pottery, painting, medals, furniture, cutlery, clocks and even a narwhal's tusk, all housed in a grand Orkney home.

South Ronaldsay

At the southern end of the series of four barriers is low-lying **South Ronaldsay**, which is the largest of the islands linked to the Mainland, and is, like the latter, heavily cultivated, rich farming country. The main settlement is **ST MARGARET'S HOPE**, which local tradition claims takes its name from Margaret, the Maid of Norway, who is thought to have died here in November 1290 while on her way to marry the English King Edward II (then Prince Edward). Margaret had already been proclaimed the Queen of Scotland, and the marriage was intended to unify the two countries. Today St Margaret's Hope is a lovely little gathering of houses at the back of a sheltered bay, and it makes an excellent base from which to explore the area. The village smithy, on Cromarty Square, has been turned into a **Smiddy Museum** (May & Sept daily 2–4pm;

SCAPA FLOW AND THE CHURCHILL BARRIERS

The presence of the huge naval base in Scapa Flow during both world wars presented an irresistible target to the Germans, and protecting the fleet was always a nagging problem for the Allies. During World War I, blockships were sunk to guard the eastern approaches, but in October 1939, just weeks after the outbreak of World War II, a German U-boat managed to manoeuvre past the blockships and torpedo the battleship *HMS Royal Oak*, which sank with the loss of 833 lives. The U-boat captain claimed to have acquired local knowledge while fishing in the islands before the war. Today the wreck of the *Royal Oak*, marked by a green buoy off the Gaitnip Cliffs, is an official war grave.

The sinking of the *Royal Oak* convinced the First Lord of the Admiralty, Winston Churchill, that Scapa Flow needed better protection, and in 1940 work began on a series of **barriers** – known as the Churchill Barriers – to seal the waters between the Mainland and the string of islands to the south. Special camps were built to accommodate the 1700 men involved in the project; their numbers were boosted by the surrender of Italy in 1942, when Italian prisoners of war were sent to work here.

Besides the barriers, which are an astonishing feat of engineering when you bear in mind the strength of Orkney tides, the Italians also left behind the beautiful **Italian Chapel** on the first of the islands, Lamb Holm. This, the so-called "miracle of Camp 60", must be one of the greatest adaptations ever, made from two Nissen huts, concrete, barbed wire and parts of a rusting blockship. The chapel deteriorated after the departure of the Italians, but its principal architect, Domenico Chiocchetti, returned in 1960 to restore the building. Today it is beautifully preserved and Mass is said regularly.

June–Aug noon–4pm; Oct Sun 2–4pm; free), which is particularly fun for kids, who enjoy getting hands-on with the old tools, drills and giant bellows. There's also a small exhibition on the annual **Boys' Ploughing Match**, in which local boys compete with miniature hand-held ploughs. The competition, which is taken extremely seriously by all those involved, takes place on the third Saturday in August, at the beautiful golden beach at the **Sands O'Right** in Hoxa, a couple of miles west of the Hope.

One of the most enjoyable archeological sights to visit on Orkney is the ancient chambered burial cairn, at the southeastern corner of South Ronaldsay, known as the **Tomb of the Eagles** (daily: April–Oct 10am–8pm; Nov–March 10am–noon; £2.50). Discovered, excavated and still owned by local farmer Ronald Simpson, a visit here makes a refreshing change from the usual interpretative centre. First off, you get to look round the family's private museum of prehistoric artefacts; then, you get a brief guided tour of a nearby Bronze Age **burnt mound**, which is basically a Neolithic rubbish dump; and finally you get to walk out to the **chambered cairn**, by the cliff's edge, where human remains were found alongside talons and carcases of sea eagles. To enter the cairn, you must lie on a trolley and pull yourself in using an overhead rope – something that's guaranteed to put a smile on every visitor's face.

St Margaret's Hope has some very good **accommodation** options. First choice should be the *Creel Restaurant and Rooms* (☎01856/831311; ④) on Front Road, one of the best restaurants in Scotland and winner of all sorts of awards for its superb **food** featuring local produce. It's expensive, but friendly and relaxed, and the rooms are comfortable too. More modest bar meals are available in the popular bar of the nearby *Murray Arms Hotel* (☎01856/831205; ②), and from the *Galley Inn* of *The Anchorage* B&B (☎01856/831456; ③), also on the seafront. Among the Hope's **B&Bs**, *West End House* (☎01856/831495; ②) is outstanding, with appealing rooms and a pleasant garden, as is *Bellevue Guest House* (☎01856/831294; ②), on a hill just east of the village. For more basic accommodation, head for *Wheems* **hostel**, about a mile and a half from the War Memorial in Eastside (☎01856/831537). Mattresses and ingredients for a wholesome breakfast are provided, and organic produce from the croft is on sale.

Hoy

Hoy, Orkney's second largest island, rises sharply out of the sea to the southwest of the Mainland. The least typical of the islands, but certainly the most dramatic, its north and west sides are made up of great glacial valleys and mountainous moorland rising to the 1577-foot mass of Ward Hill and the enormous sea cliffs of St John's Head. This huge expanse is virtually uninhabited, with just the cluster of houses at Rackwick nestling dramatically in a bay between the cliffs. Most of Hoy's four hundred residents live on the fertile land in the southeast in and around the villages of Lyness and Longhope.

Around the island

Much of Hoy's magnificent landscape is embraced by the **North Hoy RSPB Reserve** (which covers most of the northwest end of the island), in which the rough grasses and heather harbour arctic plants and a healthy population of mountain hares, as well as numerous great skuas, plus a few merlins, kestrels and peregrine falcons, while the more sheltered valleys are nesting sites for snipe and arctic skua. Walkers, arriving by passenger ferry from Stromness at Moaness Pier, near the tiny village of **HOY**, and heading for Rackwick, can either catch the minibus or take the well-marked footpath that passes Sandy Loch, and along the large open valley beyond. On the western side of this valley is the narrow gully of **Berriedale**, which supports Britain's most northerly native woodland, a huddle of birch, hazel and honeysuckle. The minibus route to Rackwick is via the single-track road along another valley to the south. En route, duck boards head across the heather to the **Dwarfie Stane**, Orkney's most unusual chambered tomb, cut from a solid block of sandstone and dating back to 3000 BC.

RACKWICK is an old crofting and fishing village squeezed between towering sandstone cliffs on the west coast. Rackwick's crofting community went into a steady decline in the middle of this century and these days many of the houses have been renovated as holiday homes. A small **museum** (free access) beside the hostel tells a little of Rackwick's rough history. Take the time, too, to stroll down to the beach, comprised mostly of giant sandstone pebbles washed smooth by the sea, which make a thunderous noise when the wind gets up.

Despite its isolation, Rackwick has a steady stream of walkers and climbers passing through it en route to the **Old Man of Hoy**, a great sandstone column some 450ft high, perched on an old lava flow which protects it from the erosive power of the sea. The well-trodden footpath from Rackwick is an easy three-mile walk (3hr return) and rewards you with a great view of the stack. The surrounding cliffs provide ideal rocky ledges for the nests of thousands of sea birds, including guillemots, kittiwakes, razorbills, puffins and shags. Continuing north along the cliff-tops, the path peters out before **St John's Head**, which at 1136ft, is one of the highest sea cliffs in the country.

On the opposite side of Hoy, along the sheltered **eastern shore**, the high moorland gives way to a gentler environment, similar to that of the other islands. Hoy marks the western boundary of Scapa Flow, and **LYNESS** played a major role for the British Navy during both world wars. Many of the old wartime buildings have been cleared away over the last few decades, but the harbour and hills around Lyness are still scarred with scattered remains. Among these are the remains of what was – incredibly – the largest cinema in Europe, and the monochrome Art Deco facade of the old Garrison Theatre. Lyness also has a large **naval cemetery**, where many of the victims of various naval disasters, such as the sinking of the *Royal Oak* (see box opposite), now lie.

The old oil pump house, which still stands opposite the new Lyness ferry terminal, has been turned into the **Scapa Flow Visitor Centre** (mid-May to June & first two weeks of Sept Mon–Sat 9am–4.30pm, Sun 10.30am–3.45pm; July & Aug Mon–Sat 9am–4.30pm, Sun 9.45am–6pm; mid-Sept to mid-May Mon–Fri 9am–4.30pm; £2), a fascinating insight into wartime Orkney. The pump house itself retains much of its old equipment, and every hour on the half hour, an audio-visual on the history of Scapa Flow is shown in the sole surviving oil tank, which has the most incredible acoustics.

Practicalities

Two **ferry services** run to Hoy: a passenger ferry from Stromness to the village of Hoy (2–4 daily; 25min), which also serves the small island of Graemsay; and the roll-on/roll-off car ferry from Houton on the Mainland to Lyness (2–5 daily; 30min–1hr), which sometimes calls in at the oil terminal island of Flotta, and begins and ends its daily schedule at Longhope. There's no bus service on Hoy, but those arriving on the passenger ferry from Stromness should find a **minibus** waiting to take them to Rackwick, should they so wish.

If you have time, it's worth staying on Hoy; there are very good, friendly **B&Bs** at *Stonequoy Farm*, south of Lyness (☎01856/791234; ①), and *Burnhouse*, in Longhope (☎01856/701263; ①), plus three **hostels** providing basic rooms. The two SYHA-affiliated hostels, *Hoy Hostel* (closed mid-Sept to April) and *Rackwick Hostel*, can be booked through the council (☎01856/873535 ext 2404); *Burnmouth Cottage* (☎01856/791316) lies in a beautiful setting right at the top of the beach in Rackwick, but has no mattresses. There are shops in Lyness and Longhope, and the *Hoy Inn* in Hoy village offers appetizing bar **food**. A good place for a snack or soup is the *Lyness Visitor Centre Café*.

Shapinsay

Just a few miles northwest of Kirkwall, **Shapinsay** is the most accessible of the northern isles. Its chief attraction for visitors is **Balfour Castle** (May–Sept Wed & Sun guided tours 3pm), the imposing Baronial pile designed by David Bryce and completed in 1848 by the Balfour family of Westray, who had made a small fortune in India the previous century. The Balfours died out in 1960 and the castle was bought by a Polish cavalry officer, Captain Tadeusz Zawadski, whose family now run the place as a hotel. The guided tours are great fun, and go down very well with children too, as they finish off with complimentary tea and home-made cakes in the servants' quarters.

They also reformed the island's agricultural system and built **BALFOUR** village, a neat and disciplined cottage development, to house estate workers. The Balfours' grandiose efforts in estate management have left some appealingly eccentric relics. Melodramatic fortifications around the harbour include the huge and ornate, if not exactly beautiful, **Gatehouse**, now a pub. There's a stone-built **Gasometer** which once supplied castle and harbour with electricity, and, southwest of the pier, the castellated **Dishan Tower**, a seventeenth-century doocot that was converted into a cold salt-water shower in Victorian times. The old village **Smithy** (Mon, Tues & Thurs–Sat noon–4.30pm, Wed & Sun noon–5.30pm; free), on the main street, now serves as a museum of local history, with a tearoom upstairs.

Less than thirty minutes from Kirkwall by **ferry**, Shapinsay is an easy day-trip. If you want to visit the castle, you must buy an all-inclusive ticket (£14.50) – which includes a return ferry ticket and entry to the castle – from Kirkwall tourist office before you set out. It's possible **to stay** in opulent style in *Balfour Castle* (☎01856/711282; *balfourcastle@btinternet.com*; ⑧); room prices include dinner, bed and breakfast. More modest accommodation is available at *Girnigoe* (☎01856/711256; ①, ③ with dinner), a very comfortable B&B close to the north shore of Veantro Bay. The only food option is the **café** in the old smithy (closed Oct–April), which serves teas and sandwiches.

Rousay, Egilsay and Wyre

Just over half a mile away from the Mainland's northern shore, the hilly island of **Rousay** is one of the most interesting of the smaller isles, home to a number of intriguing prehistoric sites, as well as being one of the more accessible. The group of a dozen or so houses above the ferry terminal is the only settlement of any size, but a single road runs around the edge of the island, connecting a string of small farms, which make use of the more cultivable coastal fringes. Many visitors come on a day-trip, as it's easy enough to reach the main points of archeological interest on the south coast by foot from the ferry terminal.

The first trio of archeological sights are spread out over the next couple of miles, on and off the road that leads west from the ferry terminal. **Taversoe Tuick**, the nearest chambered cairn, dates back to 3500 BC, and is unusual in that it exploits its sloping site by having two storeys. A little further west is the **Blackhammar Cairn**, which is divided into "stalls" by large flagstones, rather like the more famous cairn at Midhowe (see below). Finally, there's the **Knowe of Yarso**, another stalled cairn dating from the same period that's a stiff climb up the hill from the road, worth it if only for the magnificent view.

A footpath sets off from beside the Taversoe Tuick tomb off into the **RSPB reserve** that encompasses a large section of the nearby heather-backed hills, the highest of which is **Blotchnie Field** (821ft). This high ground offers good hill walking, with superb panoramic views of the surrounding islands, as well as excellent bird-watching. If you're lucky, you may well catch a glimpse of merlins, hen harriers, peregrine falcons and red-throated divers, although the latter are more widespread just outside the reserve on one of the island's three lochs, which also offer good trout fishing.

The southwestern side of Rousay is home to the most significant of the island's archeological remains. Most lie on the **Westness Walk**, a mile-long heritage trail that begins at Westness Farm, four miles northwest of the ferry terminal. **Midhowe Cairn**, about a mile on from the farm, comes as something of a surprise, both for its immense size – it's known as "the great ship of death", and measures nearly 100ft in length – and for the fact that it's now entirely surrounded by a stone-walled barn with a corrugated roof. Unfortunately, you can't actually explore the roofless communal burial chamber, dating back to 3500 BC, but only look down from the overhead walkway.

A couple of hundred yards beyond Midhowe Cairn is perhaps Rousay's finest archeological site, **Midhowe Broch**, whose compact layout suggests that it was originally built as a sort of fortified family house, surrounded by a complex series of ditches and ramparts. These are now partially obscured by later houses, many of which have shelving and stairs still intact. The broch itself looks as though it's about to collapse – it was obviously shored up with flagstone buttresses back in the Iron Age, and has more recently been given extra sea defences by Historic Scotland. The interior of the broch is divided into two separate rooms, each with their own hearth, water tank and quern stone, all of which date from the final phase of occupation around the second century AD.

Egilsay, the largest of the low-lying islands sheltering close to the eastern shore of Rousay, makes for an easy day-trip. The island is dominated by the ruins of **St Magnus Church**, with its distinctive round tower. It is possible that it was built as a shrine to Earl (later Saint) Magnus, who arranged to meet his cousin Haakon here in 1117, only to be treacherously killed by the latter's cook, Lifolf. A cenotaph marks the spot where the murder took place, about a quarter of a mile southeast of the church. The tiny, neighbouring island of **Wyre**, to the southwest, is another possible day-trip, and is best known for **Cubbie Roo's Castle**, built around 1150 by local farmer Kolbein Hruga. The outer defences have survived well on three sides of the castle, which has a central keep, with walls rising to a height of around six feet, and a central water tank still intact. Close by the castle stands **St Mary's Chapel**, a roofless twelfth-century church, founded by either Kolbein or his son, Bjarni the Poet, who was Bishop of Orkney.

Practicalities

Rousay makes a good day-trip from the Mainland, with regular **car ferry** sailings from Tingwall (20min) which has bus connections to and from Kirkwall. Most ferries call in at Egilsay and Wyre, but some need to be booked the day before at the Tingwall ferry terminal (☎01856/751360). Alternatively, you can join one of the very informative **minibus tours** run by Rousay Traveller (June–Aug Tues–Fri; ☎01856/821234), which connect with ferries and last between two and six hours, the longer ones allowing extended walks. **Bike rental** is available from *Arts, Bikes & Crafts* on Pier Road (☎01856/821398).

Accommodation on Rousay is extremely limited. The only hotel is the *Taversoe Hotel* (☎01856/821325; ②), a modern extension added onto an old croft, a couple of miles west of the terminal at Frotoft. The hotel **restaurant** offers excellent home cooking featuring local produce, especially seafood, and vegetarian options; a bar and beer garden overlook the Eynhallow Sound. Alternatively, *Trumland Farm* (☎01856/821252), half a mile or so west of the terminal, runs a **hostel**, where you can also camp, and two self-catering cottages. As well as the *Taversoe*, the *Pier Restaurant* (☎01856/821359), right beside the terminal, serves bar meals at lunchtime; if you phone in advance, they will pack you a delicious **picnic** of crab, cheese, fruit and bannock bread. In the evenings, the restaurant functions as a pub.

Westray

Although exposed to the full force of the Atlantic weather, **Westray**, in the far northwest of Orkney, shelters one of the most tightly knit and prosperous island communities. It has a fairly stable population of 700 or so, producing superb beef, scallops, shellfish and a large catch of white fish, with its own small fish-processing factory and a highly prized organic salmon-farm. Old Orcadian families still dominate every aspect of life here, giving the island a very strongly individual character.

The main village and harbour is **PIEROWALL** in the north of the island, a good eight miles from the Rapness ferry terminal on the southernmost tip of the island. For the islands, Pierowall is a place of some considerable size, with a school, several shops, a bakery (the only one not on the Mainland), and the excellent **Westray Heritage Centre** (mid-May to mid-Sept Tues–Sat 9.30am–12.30pm & 2–5pm; £2), a very welcoming wet weather retreat if you've got kids, and somewhere to grab a cup of tea.

The island's most impressive ruin is the colossal sandstone husk of **Noltland Castle**, which stands above the village half a mile west up the road to Noup Head. This Z-plan castle, which is pockmarked with over seventy gunloops, was begun around 1560 by Gilbert Balfour, a shady character from Fife, who was Master of the Household to Mary Queen of Scots, and was implicated in the murder of her husband Lord Darnley in 1567. To explore the castle, you must first pick up the key, which hangs outside the back door of the nearby farm.

The northwestern tip of the island rises up sharply, culminating in the dramatic sea cliffs of **Noup Head**, which are particularly spectacular when a good westerly swell is up. The whole area is an RSPB reserve, and during the summer months, the guano-covered rock ledges are packed with over 100,000 nesting sea birds, primarily guillemots, razorbills, kittiwakes and fulmars, plus a fair few puffins, too: a truly awesome sight, sound and smell. The sea cliffs in the southeast of the island, around **Stanger Head**, are not quite as spectacular, but it's here that you'll find **Castle o' Burrian**, a sea stack that was once an early Christian hermitage, and is now the best place on Westray at which to see **puffins** nesting – there's even a signpost to the puffins from the main road.

Practicalities

Westray is served by car **ferry** from Kirkwall (2–3 daily; 1hr 25min; ☎01856/872044), or you can **fly** on Loganair's tiny eight-seater plane from Kirkwall to Westray (Mon–Sat 1–2 daily). **Minibus tours** of the island can also be arranged with Island Explorer (☎01857/677355), which connects with ferries. M & J Harcus of Meadowbank, Pierowall (☎01857/677450), run a **bus service** which will take you from Rapness to Pierowall; they also offer **car rental**. For **bike rental** contact *Sand O' Gill* (☎01857/677374) or *Twiness* (☎01857/677319).

The finest **accommodation** on Westray is at the *Cleaton House Hotel* (☎01857/677508; *cleaton@orkney.com*; ④), a converted Victorian manse about two miles southeast of Pierowall, with great views over to Papa Westray. *Cleaton House* is also the only place on the island where you can sample Westray's organic salmon, either in the expensive hotel **restaurant**, or inexpensively in the hotel's congenial **bar**, washed down with a pint of draught Orkney Dark Island beer. Somewhat bizarrely, the hotel also has a **pétanque** pitch, which residents and non-residents alike are welcome to use. By contrast, the *Pierowall Hotel* (☎01857/677208; ①), in Pierowall itself, is simple but welcoming with a popular bar and a reputation for excellent fish and chips. Alternatively, **B&B** is available at *Sand O' Gill* (☎01857/677374; ①), where you can also **camp** or rent the **self-catering caravan**. If you'd like to play the somewhat eccentric **golf course** on the links northwest of Pierowall, head for Tulloch's shop (☎01857/677373), which rents out clubs.

Papa Westray

Across the short Papa Sound from Westray is the neighbouring island of **Papa Westray**, known locally as "Papay". With a population hovering precariously between sixty and seventy, it's an island that's had to fight hard to keep itself viable over the last couple of decades, helped by a hefty influx of outsiders. To get an idea how life used to be on Papay, when the Traill family ruled over the island, visit the small **museum** (free access) in an old bothy opposite Holland House, at the centre of the island.

A road leads down from Holland House to the western shore, where Papay's prime prehistoric site, the **Knap of Howar**, stands overlooking Westray. Dating from around 3500 BC, this Neolithic farm building makes a fair claim to being the oldest-standing house in Europe. Half a mile north along the coast from the Knap of Howar, is **St Boniface Kirk**, a beautiful pre-Reformation church that has recently been restored.

The northern tip of the island around **North Hill** (157ft), is now an **RSPB reserve**. During the breeding season, you're asked to keep to the coastal fringe, where razorbills, guillemots, fulmar, kittiwakes and puffins nest, particularly around Fowl Craig, on the east coast. To visit the interior of the reserve, which plays host to one of the largest arctic tern colonies in Europe, as well as numerous arctic skuas, contact the warden at Rose Cottage (☎01857/644240), who does regular escorted walks.

With a regular **passenger ferry** service from Pierowall (3–6 daily; 25min), Papa Westray is an easy day-trip from Westray. On Tuesdays and Fridays, the **car ferry** from Kirkwall to Westray continues on to Papa Westray; at other times, you can catch the bus from Rapness to Pierowall to connect with the passenger ferry. Papay is also connected to Westray by the **world's shortest scheduled flight** – two minutes in duration, less with a following wind. Tickets from Loganair cost around £15 one-way; you can also fly direct from Kirkwall to Papa Westray (Mon–Sat 1–2 daily). The island's Community Co-operative (☎01857/644267) runs a **minibus** which will take you from the pier to wherever you want on the island. It also runs a shop, a sixteen-bed SYHA-affiliated **hostel**, a

guest house (②, ⑤ with dinner) and a **self-catering cottage**, all housed within the old estate workers' cottages at Beltane, to the east of Holland House.

Eday

A long, thin island at the centre of Orkney's northern isles, **Eday** shares more characteristics with Rousay and Hoy than with its immediate neighbours, dominated as it is by a great block of heather-covered upland, with farmland confined to a narrow strip of coastal ground. However, Eday's hills have provided huge quantities of peat, which has been exported to the other peatless northern isles for fuel, and Eday's yellow sandstone has also been extensively quarried, and was used to build the St Magnus Cathedral in Kirkwall.

The island is very sparsely inhabited, has no real village as such, and is almost divided in two by the thin waist, where the island's airfield lies. The chief points of interest are all in the northern half of the island, beyond the Eday Community Enterprises shop on the main road. This marks the beginning of the signposted **Eday Heritage Walk**, which covers all the main sights, and takes about three hours to complete. The walk initially follows the road heading northwest, past the RSPB bird hide overlooking **Mill Loch**, where several pairs of red-throated divers regularly breed.

Clearly visible to the north of the road is the 15-foot-high **Stone of Setter**, Orkney's most distinctive standing stone, weathered into thick, lichen-encrusted fingers. From here, you can climb the hill to reach the **Vinquoy Chambered Cairn**, which has a similar structure to that of Maes Howe. You can crawl into the tomb through the narrow entrance; a skylight inside lets light into the main, beehive chamber, but not into the four side-cells. From the cairn, you can continue north to the viewpoint on the summit of **Vinquoy Hill** (248ft), and on to the very northernmost tip of the island, and the dramatic red-sandstone sea cliffs of **Red Head**, where guillemots, razorbills, puffins and other sea birds nest in summer. Alternatively, you can simply head straight down to the east coast and **Carrick House**, the grandest home on Eday (mid-June to mid-Sept Sun 2pm; £2; ☎01857/622260), best known for its associations with the pirate **John Gow,** on whom Sir Walter Scott's novel *The Pirate* is based.

Eday's **ferry** terminal is at Backaland pier in the south, not ideal for visiting the more interesting northern section of the island, although if you haven't got your own transport you should find it fairly easy to get a lift with someone off the ferry (2 daily; 1hr 15min–2hr). Alternatively, you can rent a **taxi** from Mr A. Stewart by the pier (☎01857/622206), or **bicycles** from Martin Burkett at Hamarr, in the valley below the post office (☎01857/622331). It's also possible to catch the Loganair **flight** from Kirkwall to Eday on Wednesdays; for times and fares, contact them on ☎01856/872494.

The best option when it comes to **accommodation** are the new self-catering cottages set in the hacienda-style complex around the local pub, *Pirate Gow's Inn* (Fri–Sun only), in Calfsound (☎01700/505357; ①). All six cottages are well equipped, and can be rented out for anything from one night to a week. Friendly **B&B** is available at *Skaill Farm*, a traditional farmhouse just south of the airport (☎01857/622271; ③ incl dinner; closed April & May). The SYHA-affiliated **hostel**, situated in an exposed spot just north of the airport, is very basic and is run by Eday Community Association (☎01857/622206; closed Oct–March).

Stronsay

A beguiling combination of green pastures, white sands and clear turquoise bays, **Stronsay** has seen two economic booms in the last three hundred years. The first was built on collecting vast quantities of seaweed and exporting the **kelp** for use in the chemical industry, particularly in making iodine, soap and glass. Later, **fishing** on a grand scale came to dominate life here. **WHITEHALL**, the only village, was established as a fishing port in the 1820s; lobster and cod were important, but an astonishing expansion of trade and population in the later nineteenth and early twentieth centuries was based on herring. As well as a small army of coopers, coal-merchants, butchers and bakers, the village boasted several Italian ice-cream parlours and a cinema. Decline set in from the 1930s and, though the form of the village retains its appeal, several of the houses are roofless and others lie empty. The long fish market by the pier has found a new role as a **Heritage Centre** (May–Sept daily 11am–5pm; free), café and hostel. Stronsay's low cliffs and beaches are good for walking and the island attracts many migrant birds in spring and autumn.

Stronsay is served by a regular car **ferry** service from Kirkwall to Whitehall (twice daily; 1hr 35min–2hr), and weekday Loganair **flights** from Kirkwall. There's no bus service, but D.S. Peace (☎01857/616335) operates taxis and **rents cars**. Of the few **accommodation** options available, a good choice is the well-equipped **hostel** in the old fish market, run by the folk at the *Stronsay Hotel* opposite (☎01857/616213; ①), which is currently undergoing a long overdue refurbishment. There's even more basic accommodation at *Torness Camping Barn* in Holland Farm (☎01857/616314), beyond Dishes, in the south of the island. Alternatively, the *Stronsay Bird Reserve* (☎01857/616363; ①) is a nicely positioned **B&B**. The bar in the *Stronsay Hotel* does pub **food**, and there's a takeaway along the street at *Woodlea* that's open sporadically (☎01857/616337); otherwise, you'll need to bring your own supplies and make use of the island's two shops.

Sanday

Sanday, though the largest of the northern isles, is also the most insubstantial, a great low-lying, drifting dune strung out between several rocky points. The island's bays and clean white sands are the finest in Orkney, and in dry, clear weather it's a superb place to spend a day or two. The island has a long history as a shipping hazard, with many wrecks smashed against its shores, although the construction of the **Start Point Lighthouse** (1802–1806), on the island's exposed eastern tip, reduced the risk for seafarers. Today the islanders still survive largely from farming and fishing.

The shoreline supports a healthy seal and otter population, and behind the beaches are stretches of beautiful open grassland, thick with wild flowers during the spring and summer. The entire coastline presents the opportunity for superb walks, with splendid sandy bays protected by jaggy outcrops of rock. Sanday is particularly rich in archeology, with hundreds of sites including cairns, brochs and burnt mounds. The most impressive is **Quoyness Chambered Cairn** on the fertile farmland of Els Ness peninsula, dating from the third millennium BC. The main chamber is thirteen feet long and holds six small side-cells, which contained bones and skulls.

Ferries to Sanday arrive at the new terminal at the southern tip of the island, and are met by the island **minibus** (book on ☎01857/600467), which will take you to most points on the island. The airfield is in the centre of the island and there are Loganair **flights** to Kirkwall twice daily on weekdays, and once on Saturdays. The fishing port of Kettletoft is where the ferry used to dock, and where you'll find the island's two **hotels**, neither of which is spectacularly good. Of the two, the *Belsair Hotel* (☎01857/600206; ②) has the slightly more adventurous restaurant menu, while the *Kettletoft Hotel* (☎01857/600217; ①) has a lively bar that's popular with the locals. Of the island's handful of **B&Bs**, try *Quivals* (☎01857/600418), who can also organize car and bike rental. For a wonderful, reasonably priced **self-catering cottage**, over by Start Point, contact Richard Corser (☎01857/600403).

North Ronaldsay

North Ronaldsay – or "North Ron" as it's fondly known – is Orkney's most northerly island. Separated from Sanday by the treacherous waters of the North Ronaldsay Firth, it has a tangible outpost atmosphere, brought about by its extreme isolation. Measuring just three miles by one, and rising only 66ft above sea level, the island is almost overwhelmed by the enormity of the sky, the strength of wind and, of course, the ferocity of the sea – so much so that its very existence seems an act of tenacious defiance. Despite these adverse conditions, North Ronaldsay has been inhabited for centuries, and continues to be heavily farmed, from old-style crofts, whose roofs are made from huge local flagstones.

The island's **sheep** are a unique, tough, goat-like breed, who feed mostly on seaweed, giving their flesh a dark tone and a rich, gamey taste, and making their thick wool highly prized. A high **dry-stone dyke**, running the thirteen miles around the edge of the island, keeps them off the farmland, except during lambing season. North Ronaldsay sheep are also unusual in that they can't be rounded up by sheepdogs, like ordinary sheep. Instead, the islanders herd the sheep communally into a series of **dry-stone "punds"** near Dennis Head, once a year for clipping and dipping, in what is one of the last acts of communal farming practised in Orkney.

There are very few real sights on the island, and the most frequent visitors are ornithologists, who come here in considerable numbers, to catch a glimpse of the rare migrants who land here briefly on their spring and autumn migrations. The peak times of year for migrants are from late March to early June, and from mid-August to early November, although there are also many breeding species which spend the spring and summer here, including gulls, terns, waders, black guillemots, cormorants, and even the odd corncrake. As on Fair Isle, there's now a permanent **Bird Observatory**, situated in the southwest corner of the island, which can give advice as to which birds have recently been sighted.

The **ferry** from Kirkwall to North Ronaldsay only runs once a week (usually on Fridays; 2hr 40min–3hr), though day-trips are possible on occasional Sundays between late May and early September (phone ☎01856/872044 for details). Probably your best bet is to catch a Loganair **flight** from Kirkwall (Mon–Sat 2 daily), which allows between five and seven hours on the island. You can, of course, **stay** overnight either at the *North Ronaldsay Bird Observatory* (☎01857/633200; *alison@nrbo.prestel.co.uk*), which offers full board either in private guest rooms (③) or in dorms (①). Full-board accommodation is also available at *Garso*, in the northeast (☎01857/633244; *christine.muir@virgin.net*; ③), which also has a self-catering cottage. The *Burrian Inn*, to the southeast of the war memorial, is the island's small **pub**, and does hot food. **Camping** is possible; for further information, phone ☎01857/633222.

Shetland

Many maps place the **Shetland Islands** in a box somewhere off Aberdeen, but in fact Bergen in Norway is a lot closer than Edinburgh and the Arctic Circle nearer than Manchester. The Shetland **landscape** is a product of the struggle between rock and the forces of water and ice that have, over millennia, tried to break it to pieces. Smoothed by the last glaciation, the surviving land has been exposed to the most violent **weather** experienced in the British Isles. In winter, gales are routine and Shetlanders take even the occasional hurricane in their stride, marking a calm fine day as "a day atween weathers". There are some good spells of dry, sunny weather from June to September, but it's the **"simmer dim"**, the twilight which replaces darkness at this latitude, which makes Shetland summers so memorable; in June especially, the northern sky is an unfinished sunset of blue and burnished copper.

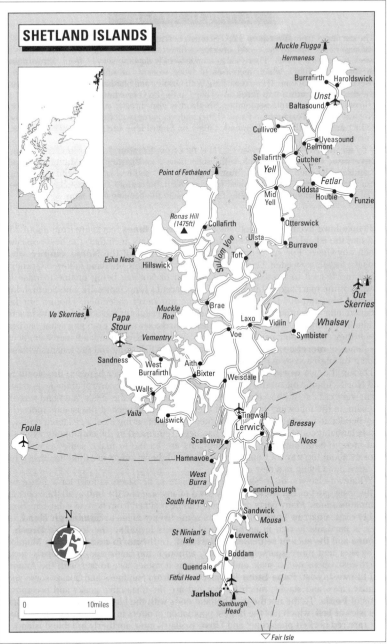

SHETLAND ISLANDS

Muckle Flugga
Hermaness
Burrafirth   Haroldswick
Unst
Baltasound
Cullivoe   Uyeasound
                   Belmont
Sellafirth   Gutcher
Yell   *Fetlar*
Point of Fethaland   Oddsta
                   Houbie   Funzie
Mid
Yell
Ronas Hill   Collafirth
(1475ft)
Otterswick
Ulsta
Burravoe
Esha Ness   Toft
Hillswick
Out
Skerries
Ve Skerries   *Papa*   Muckle   Brae
               Stour   Roe
                              Laxo
Vementry   Voe   Vidlin   *Whalsay*
Sandness   Symbister
          West   Aith
          Burrafirth Bixter
                      Weisdale
          Walls
Vaila
          Culswick   Tingwall
Foula   Lerwick   *Bressay*
          Scalloway   *Noss*
          Hamnavoe
          West
          Burra   Cunningsburgh
          South Havra
                     Sandwick
                       Mousa
N   *St Ninian's*   Levenwick
          Isle
                     Boddam
          Quendale
          Fitful Head
                     Jarlshof
                     Sumburgh
                     Head

0   10miles

▽ Fair Isle

© Crown copyright

GETTING TO SHETLAND

The **car ferry** from **Aberdeen**, P&O Scottish Ferries (☎01224/572615 or 01595/695252, *passenger@poscottishferries.co.uk*), operates a direct overnight service four or five times a week to Lerwick (14hr). There's also a once-weekly daytime service from **Stromness** in Orkney (8–10hr), which increases to twice weekly in summer (June–Aug), one overnight, one daytime. If you're visiting both Orkney and Shetland, be sure to check out the discounted **round-trip fares** advertised in the P&O brochure.

From mid-May to mid-September, Shetland is also directly connected to **Bergen** in Norway (13hr), **Tórshavn** in Faroe (13hr) and, via Faroe, with **Seydisfjördur** in Iceland (33hr) and **Hanstholm** in Denmark (50hr) on Smyril Line (details from P&O Scottish Ferries).

By **air**, British Airways (☎0345/222111) flies from **Edinburgh, Glasgow, Aberdeen, Inverness, Kirkwall** and **Wick**, with connections from **Birmingham, Manchester** and **London.** The main airport is at **Sumburgh**, 25 miles south of Lerwick, with connecting bus services to the latter. Standard fares are high, but various cheaper tickets and special offers are sometimes available if you can meet the booking conditions.

People have lived in Shetland since **prehistoric times**, certainly from about 3500 BC, and the islands display several spectacular remains, including the best-preserved broch anywhere. For six centuries Shetland was part of the **Norse empire** which brought together Sweden, Denmark and Norway. In 1469, Shetland followed Orkney in being mortgaged to Scotland, King Christian of Norway being unable to raise the dowry for the marriage of his daughter Margaret to King James III. The Scottish king annexed Shetland in 1472 and the mortgage was never redeemed. Though Shetland retained links with other North Sea communities, religious and administrative practice gradually became Scottish; and **mainland lairds** set about grabbing what land and power they could. Later, especially in rural Shetland, the economy fell increasingly into the hands of **merchant lairds**; they controlled the fish trade and the tenants who supplied it through a system of truck, or forced barter.

During the two **world wars**, Shetland's role as gatekeeper between the North Sea and North Atlantic meant that the defence of the islands and control of the seas around them were critical. With a rebirth of the local economy in the 1960s, Shetland was able to claim, in the following decade, that the **oil industry** needed the islands more than they needed it. Careful negotiation, backed up by pioneering local legislation, produced a substantial income from oil which has been reinvested in the community. Now that that income is diminishing, local politicians are having to make some very difficult choices about the way they spend what's left and the islanders are thinking afresh how to carve out a living in a new century.

Whatever else you do in Shetland you're sure to be based, at least for a day or two, in the lively port of **Lerwick**, the only town of any size and the hub of all transport and communications. Many parts of Shetland can be reached from here in a day-trip. South of Lerwick, a narrow finger of land runs some twenty miles to **Sumburgh Head**; this area is particularly rich in archeological remains including the Iron Age **Broch of Mousa** and the ancient settlement of **Jarlshof**. To the **north and west**, the Mainland is bleaker and more sparsely inhabited, although the landscape, particularly to the northwest, opens out in scale and grandeur as it comes face to face with the Atlantic. Off the west coast, **Papa Stour** lies just a mile from Sandness and boasts some spectacular caves and stacks; much further out are the distinctive peaks and precipitous cliffs of **Foula**. To the northeast, Shetland ends with the bleak but magnificent northern isles of **Yell**, which has the largest population of otters in Shetland; **Fetlar**, home to the rare red-necked phalarope; and **Unst**, Britain's most northerly inhabited island.

Lerwick and around

For Shetlanders, there's only one place to stop, meet and do business and that's "da toon", **LERWICK**. Very much the focus of Shetland's commercial life, Lerwick is home to about 7500 people, roughly a third of the islands' population. All year, its sheltered **harbour** at the heart of the town is busy with ferries, fishing boats, oil-rig supply vessels and a variety of more specialized craft including seismic survey and naval vessels from all round the North Sea. In summer, the quaysides in the centre of town come alive with visiting yachts, cruise liners, historic vessels, such as the restored *Swan*, and tall sailing ships. Behind the old harbour is the compact town centre, made up of one long main street, Commercial Street; from here, narrow lanes, known as "**closses**", rise westwards to the late Victorian "**new town**".

Lerwick began life as a **temporary settlement**, catering to the Dutch herring fleet in the seventeenth century, who brought as many as 20,000 men. During the nineteenth century, with the presence of ever-larger Scottish, English and Scandinavian boats, it became a major fishing centre, and whalers called to pick up crews on their way to their northern hunting grounds. In 1839, the visiting Danish governor of Faroe declared that "everything made me feel that I had come to the land of opulence". Business was conducted largely from buildings known as **lodberries**, each typically having a store, a house and small yard on a private jetty. **Smuggling** was part of the daily routine and there are reputed to be secret tunnels connecting the lodberries to illicit stores. During the late nineteenth century, the construction of the Esplanade along the shore isolated several lodberries from the sea, but further south beyond the Queen's Hotel are some that still show their original form. Lerwick expanded considerably at this time and the large houses and grand public buildings established then still dominate, notably the impressive **Town Hall**, which remains the town's most prominent landmark.

Arrival, information and accommodation

Arriving by **ferry** you'll come ashore at the P&O terminal in the north harbour, about a mile from the town centre. If you arrive by **plane** at Sumburgh Airport (☎01950/460654) at the southern tip of the Mainland, there are regular buses to Lerwick; taxis (£25) and car rental are also available. **Buses** stop on the Esplanade, very close to the old harbour and Market Cross, or at the bus station on Commercial Road about a quarter of a mile to the north. The **tourist office** at the Market Cross on Commercial Street (May–Sept Mon–Fri 8am–6pm, Sat 8am–4pm, Sun 10am–1pm; Oct–April Mon–Fri 9am–5pm; ☎01595/693434) is a good source of information. For more details of what's on, listen in to "Good Evening Shetland" on BBC Radio Shetland (Mon–Fri 5.30pm, 92.7MHz FM) or buy Friday's *Shetland Times*.

On the whole, Shetland's best **accommodation** is not to be found in Lerwick. Even so, in July, August and over the Folk Festival weekend in April, you should book in advance. The *Kvelsdro House Hotel*, Greenfield Place (☎01595/692195; ⑥), is Lerwick's luxury option, followed by the venerable *Queen's Hotel* on Commercial Street (☎01595/692826; ⑤). *Glen Orchy House*, 20 Knab Rd (☎01595/692031; ④), is an upper-range guest house, while *Carradale Guest House*, 36 King Harald St (☎01595/695411; ①), is more of a B&B. The Lerwick **youth hostel** (☎01595/692114, *islesburgh@atnet.co.uk*; closed Oct–March) at Islesburgh House on King Harald Street offers unusually comfortable surroundings. Lerwick's *Clickimin* **campsite** (☎01595/694555; closed Oct to late April) enjoys the excellent facilities of the neighbouring Clickimin leisure centre, including good hot showers, but its sheltered location, amidst Lerwick's suburbs, is far from idyllic.

The Town

Commercial Street, universally known to locals as "da Street", is still very much the core of Lerwick. Its narrow, winding form provides shelter from the elements even on the worst days, and is where locals meet, shop, exchange news and gossip and bring in the New Year to the sound of a harbourful of ships' sirens. The Street's northern end is marked by the towering walls of **Fort Charlotte** (daily: June–Sept 9am–10pm; Oct–May 9am–4pm; free), originally built for Charles II between 1665 and 1667, during the war with the Dutch, and attacked and burnt down by them in August 1673. In 1782 it was rebuilt and given its name in honour of George III's queen.

Now a desirable place to live, it's not so long ago that the narrow lanes or **"closses"** that connect the Street to Hillhead were regarded as slumlike dens of iniquity, from which the better-off escaped to the Victorian gridiron "new town" laid out to the west. The steep stone-flagged lanes are now fun to explore, each one lined by tall houses with trees, fuchsia, flowering currant and honeysuckle pouring over the garden walls.

Hillhead, up in the Victorian "new town", is dominated by the splendid **Town Hall** (Mon–Fri 10am–noon & 2–3.30pm; free) a Scottish Baronial monument to civic pride, whose castellated central tower occupies the town's highest point. Built by public subscription, the many carved stone panels, coats of arms and stained glass windows celebrate Shetland's history and, in particular, the islands' commercial and cultural links with other parts of Britain and Europe. Opposite the town hall, housed on the first floor of the desperately ugly municipal library, the **Shetland Museum** (Mon, Wed & Fri 10am–7pm, Tues, Thurs & Sat 10am–5pm; free) houses an interesting range of Shetland artefacts relating to the islands' history and prehistory, including replicas of the St Ninian's Isle Treasure. More unusual exhibits include a stone carving by Adam Christie (1869–1950), a Shetlander who is perhaps best known for his application to patent a submarine invisible to enemies because it would be made of glass. There's a small art gallery too.

Clickimin Broch and the Böd of Gremista

A mile or so southwest from the town centre, in the midst of Lerwick's housing estates, lies the fortified **Clickimin Broch**, begun around 700 BC and later enclosed by a defensive wall, whose main tower once rose to around 40ft, though the remains are now around 10ft high. Excavation of the site has unearthed an array of domestic goods that suggest international trade, including a Roman glass bowl thought to have been made in Alexandria around 100 AD.

In earlier times the seasonal nature of the Shetland fishing industry led to the establishment of small stores, known as **böds**, often incorporating sleeping accommodation, beside the beaches where fish were landed and dried. About a mile and a half north of the town centre, right off the A970, stands the beautifully restored **Böd of Gremista** (June to mid-Sept Wed–Sun 10am–1pm & 2–5pm; £1.50), the birthplace of **Arthur Anderson** (1791–1868), co-founder of the Peninsular and Oriental Steam Navigation Company (P&O). The displays inside explore Anderson's life as naval seaman, businessman, philanthropist, Shetland's first native MP and founder of Shetland's first newspaper.

Eating, drinking and entertainment

The most interesting of Lerwick's **eating options** is *Monty's* deli (downstairs) and bistro (upstairs) on Mounthooly Street (both closed Sun); expect good contemporary cooking at moderate prices. Other places to try include a very good Indian restaurant, the *Raba*, 26 Commercial Rd; a Chinese, *Golden Coach*, 17 Hillhead, and *Little Italy*, 33 North Road. *Faerdie-Maet* (closed Sun), near the post office on Commercial Street, serves filled rolls, cakes, teas, good coffees and great ice cream; it's non-smoking.

UP HELLY-AA

On the last Tuesday in January, whatever the weather, the Victorian "new town" of Lerwick is the setting for the most spectacular part of the Lerwick Up Helly-Aa, a huge fire-festival, the largest of several held in Shetland in January to march. Around nine hundred torch-bearing participants, all male and all in extraordinary costumes, march in procession behind a grand Viking longship. The annually appointed Guizer Jarl and his "squad" appear as Vikings and brandish shields and silver axes; each of the forty or so other squads is dressed for their part in the subsequent entertainment, perhaps as giant insects, space invaders or ballet dancers. Their circuitous route leads to the King George V Playing Field at which, after due ceremony, all the torches are thrown into the longship, creating an enormous bonfire. A fireworks display follows, then the participants, known as "guizers", set off in their squads to do the rounds of more than a dozen "halls" (which usually includes at least one hotel, the ferry terminal and the Town Hall) from around 8.30pm in the evening until 8am the next morning, performing some kind of act – often a comedy routine – at each.

Up Helly-Aa itself is not that ancient, dating only from Victorian times; but it replaced an older Christmas tradition of burning tar-barrels and other sorts of mischief. Around 1870, perhaps as a result of frustration at the controls increasingly imposed by the Town Council, the tar-barrellers moved their activities into January, coined the name Up Helly-Aa and introduced both a torchlight procession and an element of disguise; it was some years, though, before the festival took on its Viking associations. Although this is essentially a community event with entry to halls by invitation only, visitors are welcome at the Town Hall, for which tickets are sold in early January; contact the tourist office well in advance. To catch some of the atmosphere of the event check out the annual Up Helly-Aa exhibition in the **Galley Shed** (mid-May to mid-Sept Tues & Sat 2–4pm, Fri 7–9pm; £2.50) on St Sunniva Street, where you can see a full-size longship, costumes, shields and photographs.

Lastly, there's the relaxed, friendly *Havly Centre* (closed Mon & Sun), a Norwegian lunchtime café on Charlotte Street, much frequented by locals and tourists, with excellent snacks. The best fish and chips are to be had from the *Fort Café* (closed Sun), on Commercial Street, below Fort Charlotte.

At weekends or whenever the fishing fleet is confined to harbour, Lerwick's **pubs** are great social centres. The downstairs bar in the *Thule* on the Esplanade is an archetypal seaport pub, usually heaving with serious drinkers. The friendliest pub in town, however, is the upstairs bar in the *Lounge*, up Mounthooly Street, where local musicians usually play Saturday lunchtime and some evenings. If you're desperate to keep going until the early hours, head for the town's main dance venue, *Posers*, a small, lively and smartish nightclub at the back of the *Grand Hotel* on Commerical Street. **Music** features very strongly in Shetland life; in late April, musicians from all over the world converge on Shetland for the excellent **Shetland Folk Festival** (☎01595/694757). In October, there's an **Accordion and Fiddle Festival**: similar format, same contact number, but a different musical focus and separately organized. Throughout the year, there are traditional dances in local halls all over Shetland; the whole community turns up and you can watch, or join in.

Not surprisingly, another Shetland passion – throughout the isles as well as in Lerwick – is **boating and yachting**. There's a regatta somewhere on most summer weekends; lately, the sport of **yoal racing** has caught on in a big way and teams from different districts compete passionately for the honours. Yoals are large six-oared boats which, in their original incarnation, were the backbone of Shetland's fishing industry.

Bressay and Noss

Shielding Lerwick from the full force of the North Sea is the island of **Bressay**, dominated at its southern end by the conical Ward Hill and accessible on an hourly car and
passenger ferry from Lerwick. At the end of the nineteenth century, Bressay had a population of around 800, due mostly to the prosperity brought by the Dutch herring fleet;
now about 350 people live here. The island provides interesting cliff and coastal walks,
notably to the lighthouse, and huge World War I gun batteries at the northern and
southern ends of the island. In the past, Sir Walter Scott and royal visitors have stayed
in the laird's Gardie House, one of the largest and finest of the Shetland laird houses.
If you want to **stay** on Bressay, try the *Maryfield House Hotel* (☎01595/820207; ③) by
the ferry terminal, or enquire at the Lerwick tourist office about the tiny camping böd
at the Bressay Lighthouse.

Just off Bressay's eastern shore the island of **Noss**, which means "a point of rock",
was inhabited until World War II but is now given over to sheep farming and is also a
National Nature Reserve managed by Scottish Natural Heritage. They operate an inflatable as a ferry from the landing stage below the car park at the east side of Bressay
(mid-May to Aug daily except Mon & Thurs 10am–5pm). On the island, the old farmhouse of Gungstie contains a small **visitor centre** where the warden will give you a
quick briefing, and give you a free map and guide. Behind the house is an old stud farm
for **Shetland ponies**, which were sent to work in the mines of county Durham. The
most memorable feature of Noss is its cliffed coastline rising to a peak at the massive
500-foot **Noup**, home to vast colonies of cliff-nesting gannets, puffins, guillemots,
shags, razorbills and fulmars, a truly wonderful sight and one of the highlights of
Shetland. Be warned: if you stray off the marked path, the great skuas will do their best
to intimidate with dive-bombing raids that may hit you hard.

South Mainland

Shetland's South Mainland is a long, thin finger of land, only three or four miles wide,
ending in the cliffs of **Sumburgh Head** and **Fitful Head**. It's a beautiful area with wild
landscapes but also rich farmland, and has yielded some of Shetland's most impressive
archeological treasures.

From Leebitton, halfway to Sumburgh Head, you can take a summer passenger ferry
(☎01950/431367; mid-April to mid-Sept) to the small **Isle of Mousa** on which stands the
best-preserved broch anywhere. **Mousa Broch** features in both *Egil's Saga* and the
Orkneyinga Saga, contemporary chronicles of Norse exploration and settlement. In the former, a couple eloping from Norway to Iceland take refuge after being shipwrecked in 900
AD, while in the latter, the broch is besieged by Earl Harald Maddadarson when his mother is abducted and brought here from Orkney by Erlend the Young, who wants to marry
her. Rising to more than 40ft and with its curving stonework intact, it has a remarkable
presence. The low entrance passage leads through two concentric walls to a central courtyard. Between the walls, there are cells and galleries in which storm petrels breed and a
rough staircase leads to the top (a torch is provided at the entrance). Elsewhere on Mousa,
there are remains of several buildings, some of which housed the eleven families who lived
here in the eighteenth century. **Seals** can often be seen at the bays on the east side.

Of all the archeological sites in Shetland, the largest and most complex is **Jarlshof**
(April–Sept daily 9.30am–6.30pm; £2.50; HS; Oct–March the grounds are always open;
free). There's evidence of more than four thousand years of continuous occupation,
with buildings dating from the Stone Age to the early seventeenth century. The best-
preserved buildings are the Pictish wheelhouses surrounding a Neolithic broch, and

also the Norse longhouses. Sir Walter Scott was responsible for the name: while visiting Shetland in 1814 he decided to use part of the ruins in his novel *The Pirate.* Towering over the whole complex is the laird's house, originally built by Robert Stewart, Earl of Orkney and Lord of Shetland, in the late sixteenth century.

The Mainland comes to a dramatic end at **Sumburgh Head**, about two miles from Jarlshof. The lighthouse, designed by Robert Stevenson, was built in 1821; although not open to the public its grounds offer great views to Noss in the north and Fair Isle to the south. This is also the easiest place in Shetland to get close to **puffins**. During the nesting season, you simply need to look over the western wall by the lighthouse gate to see them arriving at their burrows with beakfuls of fish or giving flying lessons to their offspring; on no account should you try to climb over the wall.

On the west side of the south mainland, there's an **RSPB Bird Reserve** at the **Loch of Spiggie**, important for waterfowl; farther north, the ruined chapel on **St Ninian's Isle** – reached across a spectacular sandy tombolo – was the scene in 1958 of a remarkable discovery of Pictish treasure, perhaps hidden during a Norse raid.

Practicalities

For **accommodation,** you could try the *Sumburgh Hotel* (☎01950/460201; ④), next to Jarlshof, or *Columbine* **B&B** (☎01950/460582; ①) at Boddam. **Hostel** accommodation is available at the *Cunningsburgh Community Club* (☎01950/477241) and there's a **camping böd** at *Betty Mouat's Cottage* (book through Lerwick tourist office; closed Nov–March), immediately southwest of Sumburgh Airport. For **camping**, head for the *Levenwick Campsite* (☎01950/422207; closed Oct–April), which has hot showers and a superb view over the east coast.

Fair Isle

Halfway between Shetland and Orkney and very different from both, **Fair Isle** supports a vibrant community of around seventy. At one time the population was not far short of four hundred, but clearances forced emigration from the middle of the nineteenth century. By the 1950s, the population had shrunk to just 44, a point at which evacuation and abandonment of the island was seriously considered. George Waterston, who'd bought the island and set up a bird observatory in 1948, passed it into the care of the NTS in 1954 and rejuvenation began. The island can now boast an advanced **electricity system** integrating wind and diesel generation; and crafts, including boatbuilding, the making of fiddles, felt and stained glass, have been developed.

The north end of the island rises like a wall; the **Sheep Rock**, a sculpted stack of rock and grass on the east side is one of the island's most dramatic features. The social and natural history of the island is compellingly told in the George Waterston Memorial Centre (☎01595/760244; free). The present **Bird Observatory** dates from 1969, just above the North Haven where the ferry from Shetland arrives; it's one of the major European centres for ornithology and its work in watching, trapping, recording and ringing birds goes on all year. Fair Isle is a landfall for a huge number and range of migrant birds during the spring and autumn passages. Migration routes converge here and more than 345 species have been noted.

Fair Isle is even better known for its **knitting** patterns, still produced with as much skill as ever by the local knitwear co-operative, though not in the quantities which you might imagine from a walk around city department stores; there are demonstrations at the Hall from time to time, and the George Waterson Memorial Centre fills in the history. The idea that the islanders borrowed all their patterns from three hundred shipwrecked Spanish seamen is nowadays regarded as a somewhat patronizing myth.

Practicalities

The passenger **ferry** connects Fair Isle with either Lerwick (alternate Thurs; 4hr 30min) or Grutness, in Sumburgh (Tues, Sat & alternate Thurs; 3hr); for bookings contact J.W. Stout (☎01595/760222) in advance. The crossing can be very rough at times, so if you're at all susceptible to seasickness, it might be worth considering flying from Tingwall (Mon, Wed, Fri & Sat) or Sumburgh (Tues, Thurs & Sat); a one-way ticket costs £36, and day-trips are possible on Mondays and Wednesdays.

If you want **to stay**, try the *Fair Isle Lodge & Bird Observatory* (☎01595/760258; *birdobs@zetnet.co.uk*; ③; ⑤ with dinner), a very friendly and sociable place that offers full board, B&B and hostel-style dorm beds for £25 per person. The bird observatory also offers good home cooking for lunch and dinner. The only other B&B options are *Schoolton* (☎01595/760250; ①, ③ with dinner), or *Upper Lough* (☎01595/760248; ①; ③ with dinner), both in the south of the island.

Scalloway and the Westside

Approaching **SCALLOWAY** from the shoulder of the **Scord**, there's a dramatic view over the town and the islands to the south and west. Once the capital of Shetland, Scalloway's importance waned through the eighteenth century as Lerwick, just six miles to the east, grew in trading success and status. Nowadays, Scalloway is very sleepy indeed, though its prosperity, always closely linked to the fluctuations of the fishing industry, has recently been given a boost with investment in new fish-processing factories, and in the impressive North Atlantic Fisheries College on the west side of the harbour.

In spite of modern developments nearby, Scalloway is dominated by the imposing shell of **Scalloway Castle**, a classic fortified tower house built with forced labour in 1600 by the infamous Earl Patrick Stewart, who held court in the castle and gained a reputation for enhancing his own power and wealth through the calculated use of harsh justice, frequently including confiscation of assets. He was eventually arrested and imprisoned in 1609, though not for his ill-treatment of Shetlanders, but for his aggressive behaviour towards his fellow landowners; his son, Robert, attempted an insurrection and both were executed in Edinburgh in 1615.

On Main Street, a small **museum** (May–Sept Tues–Thurs 2–4.30pm, Sat 10am–12.30pm & 2–4.30pm; free) explains the importance of fishing and tells the story of the **Shetland Bus**, the link between Shetland and Norway which helped to sustain the Norwegian wartime resistance. Four miles or so north of Scalloway, at the head of Tingwall Loch, is the **Law Ting Holm**, a small peninsula which was once an island. This was the site of the **Lawting**, *thing* being old Norse for "parliament".

The best **accommodation** available in Scalloway is at the very comfortable and welcoming *Hildasay Guest House* (☎01595/880822; ②), a Hansel-and-Gretel weatherboarded house on the top of the hill above Scalloway, behind the swimming pool. For **food**, head for *Da Haaf* (closed Sat & Sun), the unpretentious licensed restaurant in the *North Atlantic Fisheries College*, which serves fresh fish, simply prepared, with broad harbour views to enjoy as well.

The Westside

Reached from Lerwick through the attractive coastal landscape of **Whiteness** and the district of **Weisdale**, scene of particularly harsh Clearances, the Westside's rolling brown and purple moorland is scattered with dozens of small picturesque lochs gleaming blue or silver and patches of bright green, where cultivation and reseeding have taken place. The coast, cut by several deep voes, is very varied; aside from dramatic cliffs, there are intimate coves and some fine beaches. The crossroads for the area is effectively Bixter, southwest of which lies the finest Neolithic structure in the Westside, dubbed the **Staneydale Temple** by the archeologist who excavated it because it resembled one on Malta. Whatever its true function, it was twice as large as the surrounding oval-shaped houses (now in ruins) and was certainly of great importance, perhaps as some kind of community centre. The foundations measure more than 40ft by 20ft internally with immensely thick walls, still around 4ft high, whose roof would have been supported by spruce posts (two postholes can still be clearly seen).

On the west coast the rounded form of **Sandness Hill** (750ft) falls steeply away into the Atlantic. It's an attractive spot; its fertile fields and wide beach come as a contrast to the peat moorland around. The modern **spinning mill** (Mon–Fri 8am–5pm; free) produces pure Shetland wool and welcomes visitors; you can watch how they manage to spin the exceptionally fine Shetland wool into yarn.

The only **hotel** in the area is the beautifully situated *Burrastow House* (☎01595/809307; ⑥), about three miles southwest of Walls. Of the few **B&Bs** try wonderfully welcoming *Skeoverick* (☎01595/809349; ①), a lovely modern crofthouse which lies a mile or so north of Walls. The beautifully restored *Voe House* (book through Lerwick tourist office; closed Nov–March) is the largest **camping böd** on Shetland; the modest price includes peat for the fires. *Burrastow House* offers distinguished if expensive **food** – the best in Shetland – in idyllic surroundings by the sea; booking ahead is recommended.

Papa Stour

A mile offshore from Sandness is the quintessentially peaceful island of **Papa Stour** ("big island of the priests"); apart from early Christian connections, it was home, in the eighteenth century, to people who were mistakenly believed to have been lepers. The sea has eroded its volcanic rocks to produce some of the most impressive coastal scenery in Shetland, with **stacks, caves** and **natural arches**. The east side is the most fecund area, partly because much of the soil from the western side was painstakingly transported here. In the nineteenth century, Papa Stour supported around three hundred inhabitants; today the island supports a community of thirty or so. The island's main settlement, **BIGGINGS**, lies in the west near the pier, and it was here that excavation in the early 1980s revealed the remains of a thirteenth-century Norse house, which is thought to have belonged to Duke Haakon, heir to the Norwegian throne. In summer, the passenger **ferry** runs from West Burrafirth on the Westside to Papa Stour (Mon, Wed & Fri–Sun); always book in advance and reconfirm the day before departure (☎01595/810460); day-trips are only possible on Friday, Saturday and Sunday. There's also a **flight** from Tingwall airport every Tuesday, and again a day-trip is feasible. The only accommodation on the island is *North House* **B&B** (☎01595/873238; ①, ③ with dinner).

Foula

Southwest of Walls, at "the edge of the world", the island of **Foula** is separated from the nearest point on Mainland Shetland by about fourteen miles of ocean. Seen from the Mainland, its distinctive form changes subtly, depending upon the vantage point, but the outline is unforgettable. Its western **cliffs**, the second highest in Britain after those of St Kilda, rise at the Kame to some 1220ft above sea level; on a clear day its highest point, the Sneug (1373ft), offers a magnificent panorama stretching from Unst to Fair Isle. On a bad day, the exposure is complete and the cliffs generate turbulent blasts of wind known in Shetland as "flans" which tear down the hills with tremendous force. The cliffs and moorland provide a home for a quarter of a million **birds** – the name of the island is based on the Old Norse for "bird island" – and host the largest colony of great skuas in Britain. The island has been inhabited from prehistoric times; Foula's human population peaked at around two hundred at the end of the nineteenth century, but has fluctuated wildly over the years, dropping to three in 1720 following an epidemic of "muckle fever". Today, the gentler eastern slopes provide crofting land which, with sheep grazing, helps to support a community numbering about forty. The people here take pride in their separateness from Shetland, cherishing local traditions such as the observance of the Julian calendar, officially dropped in Britain in 1752, where Old Yule is celebrated on January 6 and the New Year arrives on January 13.

Practicalities

A day-trip by **ferry** isn't possible, as the summer passenger service to Foula from Walls only runs on Tuesdays, Saturdays and alternate Thursdays (2hr 30min), with a sailing from Scalloway on remaining Thursdays (3hr); it's essential to book and reconfirm (☎01595/753232). The boat arrives at Ham, in the middle of the east coast, and has to be winched up onto the pier to protect it. There are also **flights** from Tingwall, to Foula (Mon–Wed & Fri; ☎01595/840226), with day-trips possible except on Tuesdays; tickets cost around £20 one-way. If you want to stay on the island, the only **B&B** is *Leraback* (☎01595/753226; ②), near Ham, which does full-board only. Even if you go to the island just for the day, bear in mind that there's no shop, so you'll need to take all your supplies with you.

North Mainland

The North Mainland, stretching more than thirty miles north from Lerwick, is wilder than much of Shetland, with some rugged and dramatic coastal scenery; it contains Shetland's highest point. The main road crosses open ground, occasionally dropping in on small coastal settlements, the first of which is **VOE**, where the tight huddle of homes and workshops around the pier has a strongly Scandinavian appearance. The village is dominated by the Sail Loft, a rich, deep-red building, originally used by fishermen and whalers but later for the manufacture of knitwear.

From Voe the main road divides; the northern leg leads to Toft, the ferry terminal for the island of Yell (see opposite), while the other branch cuts northwest to **BRAE**, a sprawling settlement that still has the feel of a frontier town, expanded in some haste in the 1970s to accommodate the workforce for the huge Sullom Voe Oil Terminal to the north. During World War II the deep-water harbour of Sullom Voe was home to the Norwegian Air Force and a base for RAF seaplanes. Although the terminal, built between 1975 and 1982, has passed its production peak, it is still the largest of its kind in Europe.

The peninsula of **Northmavine**, to the north of Brae, is connected by the narrow isthmus of Mavis Grind, at which it's said you can throw a stone from the Atlantic to the North Sea (or at least to Sullom Voe). Northmavine is unquestionably one of the most picturesque areas of Shetland, with its often rugged scenery, magnificent coastline and wide open spaces. **HILLSWICK**, the main settlement in the area, was once served by the steamers of the North of Scotland, Orkney & Shetland Steam Navigation Company and in the early twentieth century the firm also built the **Magnus Bay Hotel**, importing it in the form of a timber kit from Norway; it still stands, albeit somewhat altered. Nearer the shore is the much older Hillswick House and, attached to it, **Da Böd**, formerly the oldest pub in Shetland, said to have been founded by a German merchant in 1684, but now an unpredictable hippy café called *The Booth*.

Just outside Hillswick, a side road leads west to **Esha Ness** (*Ay*shaness), celebrated for its splendid coastline views. Spectacular **cliffs** and **stacks** are spread out before you as the road climbs away from Hillswick, with stacks called **The Drongs** in the foreground and distant views to the Westside and Papa Stour. A mile or so south off the main road is the **Tangwick Haa Museum** (May–Sept Mon–Fri 1–5pm, Sat & Sun 11am–7pm; free), which, through photographs, old documents and fishing gear, tells the often moving story of this remote corner of Shetland. Line fishing far offshore, from bases like **Stenness fishing station**, at the end of the road, was once a major activity; the boats were small and it was a dangerous trade. To the north the road ends at the **Esha Ness Lighthouse**, a great place to view the cliffs, stacks and, in rough weather, blowholes of this stretch of coast, and the starting point for an excellent three-hour walk.

North of Ronas Voe, by the shores of Colla Firth, an unmarked road leads up **Collafirth Hill**, the easiest place from which to approach the rounded contours of **Ronas Hill**, Shetland's highest point (1475ft). The climb, with no obvious path, is exhausting but rewarding (2hr each way): from the top you can look west to one of the most beautifully sculptured parts of the Shetland coast, as the steep slope of the hill drops down to the arching sand and shingle beach called the **Lang Ayre**. Also at the summit is a Neolithic or Bronze Age **chambered cairn**, one of the best preserved in Shetland and useful as a shelter from the wind.

Practicalities

Just across the bay from Brae is one of the best **hotels** in Shetland, *Busta House* (☎01806/522506; ⑤). Even if you're not staying the night here, it's worth coming for afternoon tea in the Long Room, or for a drink and a superb **bar meal** in the hotel's pub-like bar. A cheaper alternative is the modern crofthouse **B&B** of *Westayre* (☎01806/522368; ①), beyond Busta, on the peaceful island of Muckle Roe, which is linked to the mainland by a bridge. Nearer Esha Ness, *Almara* (☎01806/503261; ①) in Urafirth offers good food, a family welcome and excellent views. For more basic accommodation, if you have an airbed or sleeping mat, try the **camping böds** at the *Sail Loft* in Voe or *Johnnie Notions* at Hamnavoe in Esha Ness; book both through Lerwick tourist office. Apart from *Busta House*, the best **food** option is at the *Pierhead Restaurant & Bar* in Voe.

The North Isles

Shetland's three **North Isles** bring Britain to a dramatic, windswept end; north from Unst there's no land until eastern Siberia, beyond the North Pole. These landscapes and seascapes have been shaped by centuries of fierce storms; their beauty is elemental. Nevertheless, the three islands differ markedly from one another. They offer superb **walking** and some interesting **archeological sites**, but it is their **wildlife** which impresses most. **Otters** are abundant around the coast of Yell and all three islands have notable **bird reserves**. They're very easy to reach and, at less windy times of year, they make good cycling country, with few steep hills. Accommodation in the northern isles isn't abundant, so book ahead, especially in summer.

To get to the North Isles, a **bus** service connecting with **ferries** leaves Lerwick for Yell, Unst and Fetlar every morning except Sunday. Get details of all these services from Leasks (☎01595/693162). **Taking a car** is easy; using the inexpensive and frequent ferry services operated by Shetland Islands Council. Booking is wise and you can easily reserve a car space on ☎01957/722259.

Yell

Historically, **Yell**, the largest of the North Isles, hasn't had good write-ups: the Scottish historian Buchanan claimed it was "so uncouth a place that no creature can live therein, except such as are born there". Certainly, if you keep to the fast main road, you'll pass a lot of uninspiring peat moorland, but the landscape is relieved by Whale Firth, Mid Yell Voe and Basta Voe, which cut deeply into it, providing superb natural harbours. Yell's coastline, too, is gentler and greener than the interior and provides an ideal habitat for a large population of **otters**; locals will point out the best places to watch for them.

At **BURRAVOE**, in the southeastern corner of Yell, there's a lovely whitewashed laird's house dating from 1672, with crow-stepped gables, that now houses the **Old Haa Museum** (late April to Sept Tues–Thurs & Sat 10am–4pm, Sun 2–5pm; free), which is stuffed with artefacts, and has lots of material on the history of the local herring and whaling industry; there's a very pleasant wood-panelled café on the ground floor, too. The island's largest village, **MID YELL** has a couple of shops, a pub and a leisure centre with a good swimming pool. In the north of Yell, the area around **CULLIVOE** has relatively gentle, but attractive, coastal scenery with some sandy beaches. To the west is **GLOUP**, with its secretive narrow voe, once the largest haaf-fishing station in Shetland. This area provides some excellent walking, as does the Atlantic coast further west, where there's an Iron Age fort and field system at Burgi Geos.

One of the best **B&Bs** on Yell is *Hillhead* (☎01957/722274; ①) in Burravoe; you can also stay with the Tullochs at Gutcher's post office (☎01957/744201; ①). A cheaper alternative is to stay in the **camping böd** at *Windhouse Lodge* (book through Lerwick tourist office; closed Nov–March), on the main road near Mid Yell. There isn't a great range of **food** options on the island but the non-smoking café in the *Old Haa Museum* (closed Mon & Fri) at Burravoe has soup, snacks and delicious home baking. The *Hilltop Bar* in Mid Yell offers standard bar meals, while the *Seaview Café* at the Gutcher ferry terminal has filled rolls, snacks, soup, teas and coffees.

Fetlar

Known as "the garden of Shetland", **Fetlar** is the most fertile of the North Isles, much of it grassy moorland and lush meadow with masses of summer flowers. Around nine hundred people once lived here; there might well be more than one hundred now were it not for the nineteenth-century Clearances. Today Fetlar's population lives along the southern and eastern shores of the island, where the main settlement, **HOUBIE**, has the excellent **Fetlar Interpretive Centre** (May–Sept Tues–Sun noon–5pm; free) presenting the island's history and offering information on Fetlar's outstanding birdlife through an Internet site as well as by more conventional means.

Of the archeological remains on Fetlar, perhaps the most remarkable is the **Funzie Girt** or Finnigirt, an ancient stone boundary of uncertain date, which divides the island in two. Its southern end has been destroyed, but it is well preserved on the western and northern slopes of Vord Hill, within the **RSPB North Fetlar Reserve**, which is closed for general visiting from mid-May to mid-July; between those dates it's essential to contact the warden at Baelan (☎01957/733246) to find out if a visit is possible. The same applies if you want to seek out the birdlife, which has included regular visits by **snowy owls**. Fetlar is also one of very few places you'll see the rare, graceful **red-necked phalarope** (late May to July); a hide has been provided overlooking the marshes (or mires), to the east of the Loch of Funzie (pronounced "Finnie").

Ferries to Fetlar (5–6 daily; 25min) depart from both Gutcher (on Yell) and Belmont (on Unst). The ferry docks at Oddsta, three miles northwest of Houbie; the only public transport is an infrequent **post car** (Mon, Wed & Fri). If you bring a car, bear in mind that there's no petrol station on Fetlar, so fill up before you come across. If you wish to stay the night, Fetlar's most comfortable **B&B** is the modern *Gord* (☎01957/733227; ①), behind the island shop in Houbie, followed by *The Glebe* (☎01957/733242; ②), which is non-smoking, and is hidden among the trees above Papil Water; both will provide an evening meal. *The Garths* **campsite** (☎01957/733227; closed Oct–April) is in a field just to the west of Houbie, with toilets, showers and drying facilities. There's a post office, shop and **café** (closed Mon) in the middle of Houbie.

Unst

Unst has a population of around 1000, of whom 300 or 400 are connected to the RAF radar base at Saxa Vord, listening out for uninvited intruders. Though much of the landscape is rolling grassland, the coast is more dramatic, a fringe of cliffs relieved by some beautiful sandy beaches. As Britain's most northerly inhabited island, there is a surfeit of "most northerly" sights, which is fair enough, given that many visitors only come here in order to head straight for Hermaness, to look out over Muckle Flugga and the northernmost tip of Britain, to the North Pole beyond.

On the south coast of the island, not far from the ferry terminal, is **UYEASOUND**, with the stone-built Greenwell's Booth, an old Hanseatic merchants' warehouse by the pier. Further east lie the ruins of **Muness Castle**, built in 1598 by Laurence Bruce, half-brother of Robert Stewart and probably designed by Andrew Crawford who shortly afterwards built Scalloway Castle for Robert's son Patrick. The island's main settlement is at **BALTASOUND**, where old jetties around the bay testify to a bygone herring industry; there's an airport, a hotel with a pub, shop, post office and a leisure centre with a pool.

From Baltasound, the main road crosses what appears to be a giant boulder field. What you see is, in fact, serpentine rock, found widely on Unst; most often it's greyish green, but it weathers to rusty orange, and in some stone walls there are pieces which are of an extraordinary deep turquoise hue. The serpentine soil is so poor, it produces unusual vegetation, turning the grass bluish-grey. At the **Keen of Hamar** National Nature Reserve, east of Baltasound, numerous rare plants, including the unique mouse-eared Edmondston's chickweed, grow in an almost lunar landscape.

Britain's most northerly post office is over the hill to the north, at **HAROLDSWICK**. Here, down near the shore, is the **Unst Boat Haven** (May–Sept daily 2–5pm; free), an outstanding and beautifully presented display of historic boats with many tools of the trade and information on fishing; most of the boats are from Shetland, with one from Norway. A little to the northeast, off the main road, is the **Unst Heritage Centre** (May–Sept daily 2–5pm; free) where you can find out about other aspects of Unst life such as crofting and its unique geology. The road ends at Skaw, with a beautiful beach and the very last house in Britain.

Northwest of Haroldswick is **Burra Firth**, a north-facing inlet surrounded by cliffs and guarded by the hills of **Saxa Vord** (936ft), Unst's highest point, and the bleak headland of **Hermaness**. Now a National Nature Reserve, Hermaness is home to more than 100,000 breeding sea birds. A **visitor centre** is located in the former lighthouse keepers' houses; and a marked route into the reserve allows you to look down over the jagged rocks of **Muckle Flugga** and the most northerly bit of Britain, **Out Stack**. There are few more dramatic settings for a lighthouse, and few sites could ever have presented as great a challenge to the builders. The views from here are inevitably marvellous and the walk down the west side of Unst towards Westing is one of the finest in Shetland.

Ferries leave regularly from Gutcher on Yell for Belmont on Unst (every 15–30min; 10min); booking in advance is wise (☎01957/722259). **Flights** to Unst depart from Sumburgh Airport (Mon–Fri only), and arrive at the airport near Baltasound. By far the best **accommodation** on Unst is historic *Buness House* (☎01957/711315, *buness@zetnet.co.uk*; ③), a lovely old haa in Baltasound. Another very good bet is *Prestagaard* (☎01957/755234; ①), a more modest Victorian B&B in Uyeasound, where there's also the very handy, independent *Gardiesfauld Hostel* (☎01957/755259; closed Oct–March), which allows **camping**, and offers **bike rental**. The *Baltasound Hotel* serves **food** to non-residents, and snacks and teas can be had at the tearoom in *NorNova Knitwear* just north of Muness Castle, or, often on a help-yourself basis, at the *Haroldswick Shop*.

ONWARDS TO NORWAY, THE FAROE ISLANDS AND ICELAND

Thanks to the historical ties and the attraction of a short hop to continental Europe, Shetlanders and Orcadians often include Norway in their holiday plans, from where it's easy to move on to the rest of Scandinavia. Norwegians often think of Shetland and Orkney as their western isles and, particularly in west **Norway**, wartime bonds with Shetland are strong. Norwegian yachts and sail training vessels are frequent visitors to Lerwick and Kirkwall.

However, there are two other interesting options from Shetland. By ferry, it's easy to reach the **Faroe Islands**, steep, angular shapes rising out of the North Atlantic, with a strong and independent culture. From Faroe, it's another slightly longer hop to **Iceland**, where the forces which have shaped the planet are laid bare in a quite unforgettable combination of heat, cold, water and dust.

There are weekly **flights** between June and September from Kirkwall, Orkney (1hr 45min), and twice weekly from Sumburgh, Shetland (1hr), to Bergen in Norway. Short inclusive breaks are available by air from Shetland. From June to August the large, comfortable and fast Faroese car ferry *Nörrona* is in almost perpetual motion on a route which, in a week, manages to take in return trips from her home port in Faroe to Shetland, Norway, Iceland and Denmark. From Shetland, Bergen in Norway and Torshavn in Faroe are 13 hours away; to Iceland the journey takes 33 hours northbound including a brief stop in Faroe; on the way back there's a two-day stopover in Faroe while the ship makes a return trip to Denmark.

travel details

ORKNEY

Buses

Kirkwall to: Houton (5–6 daily; 30min); St Margaret's Hope (4 daily; 40 min); Stromness (hourly; 40min); Tingwall (3 daily; 25min).

Ferries

Burwick to: John O' Groats (passengers only; 2–4 daily; 45min).

Houton to: Hoy (Lyness) and Flotta (11 daily; 45min).

Kirkwall to: Eday (1–3 daily; 1hr 15min); North Ronaldsay (1 weekly; 2hr 40min); Papa Westray (2–3 daily; 1hr 15min); Sanday (1–3 daily; 1hr 25min); Shapinsay (4–6 daily; 45min); Stronsay (1–3 daily; 1hr 35min); Westray (2–3 daily; 1hr 25min).

Stromness to: Aberdeen (1 weekly in winter, 2 weekly in summer; 8–10hr); Hoy (passengers only; 2–3 daily in summer; 30min); Lerwick (1 weekly in winter, 2 weekly in summer; 8hr);

Scrabster/Thurso (summer 1–3 daily, winter Mon–Sat only; 1hr 45 min).

Tingwall to: Egilsay (7 daily; 50min); Rousay (7 daily; 30min); Wyre (7 daily; 45min).

Flights

Kirkwall to: Aberdeen (2–4 daily; 45min); Eday (Wed 2 daily; 12min); Edinburgh (1 daily; 2hr); Glasgow (1 daily; 2hr 10min); Inverness (2 daily; 50min); North Ronaldsay (Mon–Sat 2 daily; 15min); Papa Westray (Mon–Sat 1–2 daily; 12min); Sanday (Mon–Sat 1–3 daily; 20min); Stronsay (Mon–Fri 1–2 daily; 25min); Westray (Mon–Sat 1–2 daily; 12min).

SHETLAND

Buses

Cullivoe to: Ulsta (1–3 daily; 50min).

Lerwick to: Brae (3–7 daily; 40min); Culswick (daily; 1hr 20min); Hamnavoe (Mon–Sat 2 daily; 30min); Hillswick (1–2 daily; 1hr 15min); Laxo (2–3 daily; 30min); Sandwick (Mon–Sat 4–6 daily, Sun 3 daily; 35min); Scalloway (Mon–Sat 6 daily; 15min); Sumburgh (3–5 daily; 45min); Unst (Mon–Sat 1–2 daily; 2hr 45min); Vidlin (Mon–Sat 2–3 daily; 40min); Walls and Sandness (3–4 daily, 50min); Yell (Mon–Sat 3 daily, Sun 1 daily; 1hr 20min).

Ferries

Mainland

Grutness to: Fair Isle (May–Sept Tues, Sat & alternate Thurs; 2hr 30min).

Laxo to: Whalsay (16–18 daily; 30min).

Lerwick to: Aberdeen (6 weekly; overnight direct sailings 14hr, via Orkney afternoon/overnight 20hr); Bressay (20–22 daily; 5min); Fair Isle (alternate Thurs, 4hr 30min); Out Skerries (Tues & Thurs, 2hr 30min).

Scalloway to: Foula (May–Sept alternate Thurs; 3hr).

Toft to: Yell (25–28 daily; 20min).

Vidlin to: Out Skerries (Mon 1 daily, Fri, Sat & Sun 3 daily; 1hr 30min).

Walls to: Foula (May–Sept, Tues, alternate Thurs & Sat; 2hr 30min).

West Burrafirth to: Papa Stour (Mon & Wed, 1 daily; Fri–Sun 2 daily; 35min).

Other islands

Unst (Belmont) to: Fetlar (3 daily; 25min).

Yell (Gutcher) to: Fetlar (4–7 daily; 25min); Unst (29 daily; 10min).

Flights

Sumburgh to: Aberdeen (Mon–Fri 5 daily, Sat & Sun 2 daily; 1hr); Fair Isle (1 weekly; 15min); Glasgow (1 daily; 2hr 5min); Kirkwall (1–2 daily; 40min); Unst (Mon–Fri 1 daily; 35min); Wick (Mon–Sat 1 daily; 50min).

Tingwall to: Fair Isle (Mon, Wed, Fri & Sat 1–2 daily; 25min); Foula (Mon–Wed, Fri 1–2 daily; 15min); Out Skerries, calling at Whalsay on request (Mon & Wed–Fri, 1 daily; 30min); Papa Stour (Tues 2 daily; 10min); Unst (Mon–Fri 1 daily; 25min).

GORSAFAWDDACHAIDRAIGDDANHEDDOGLEDDOLLÔNPENRHYNAREURDRAETHCEREDIGION

A BRIEF HISTORY OF BRITAIN

THE BEGINNINGS

Off and on, people have lived in Britain for the best part of half a million years, though the earliest evidence of human life dates from about **250,000 BC**. These meagre remains, found near Swanscombe, east of London across the Thames from Tilbury, belong to one of the migrant communities whose comings and goings depended on the fluctuations of the Ice Ages. Renewed glaciation then made the area uninhabitable once more, and the next traces – mainly roughly worked flint implements – were left around 40,000 BC by cave-dwellers at Creswell Crags in Derbyshire, Kent's Cavern near Torquay and Cheddar Cave in Somerset. The last spell of intense cold began about 17,000 years ago, and it was the final thawing of this **last Ice Age** around 5000 BC that caused the British Isles to separate from the European mainland.

The sea barrier did nothing to stop further migrations of nomadic hunting communities, drawn by the rich forests that covered ancient Britain. In about 3500 BC a new wave of colonists arrived from the continent, probably via Ireland, bringing with them a Neolithic culture based on farming and the rearing of livestock. These tribes were the first to make some impact on their environment, clearing forests, enclosing fields, constructing defensive ditches around their villages and digging mines to obtain flint used for tools and weapons.

Fragments of Neolithic pottery have been found near Peterborough and at Windmill Hill, near Avebury in Wiltshire; others – like the well-preserved village of Skara Brae in Orkney – were near the sea, enabling them to supplement their diet by fishing and to develop their skills as boat builders. The most profuse relics of this culture are their graves, usually stone-chambered, turf-covered mounds (called long barrows, cairns or cromlechs), which are scattered throughout the country – the most impressive ones are at Belas Knap in Gloucestershire, Barclodiad y Gawres in Anglesey, and Maes Howe on Orkney.

The transition from the Neolithic to the **Bronze Age** began around 2000 BC, with the immigration from northern Europe of the so-called **Beaker Folk** – named from the distinctive cups found at their burial sites. Originating in the Iberian peninsula and bringing with them bronze-workers from the Rhineland, these newcomers had a well-organized social structure with an established aristocracy, and quickly intermixed with the native tribes. Many of Britain's stone circles were completed at this time, including **Stonehenge** in Wiltshire, and **Callanish** on the Isle of Lewis, while many others belong entirely to the Bronze Age – for example, the Hurlers and the Nine Maidens on Cornwall's Bodmin Moor. Large numbers of earthwork forts were also built in this period, suggesting a high level of tribal warfare, but none of these were able to withstand the waves of Celtic invaders who, spreading from a homeland in central Europe, began settling in Britain around 600 BC.

THE CELTS

Highly skilled in battle, the **Celts** soon displaced the local inhabitants all over Britain, establishing a sophisticated farming economy and a social hierarchy that was headed by **Druids**, a ritual priesthood with attendant poets, seers and warriors. Through a deep knowledge of ritual, legend and the mechanics of the heavens, the Druids maintained their position between the people and a pantheon of over four thousand gods. Familiar with Mediterranean artefacts through their far-flung trade routes, they introduced superior methods of metalworking that favoured iron rather than bronze, from which they forged not just weapons but also coins. Gold was used for ornamental works – the first recognizable

British art – heavily influenced by the symbolic, patterned **La Tène** style still thought of as quintessentially Celtic.

The principal Celtic contribution to the landscape was a network of hill forts or brochs, and other defensive works stretching over the entire country, the greatest of them at **Maiden Castle** in Dorset, a site first fortified almost 3500 years earlier, and **Mousa** in the Shetland islands. The original Celtic tongue – the basis of modern Welsh and Scottish Gaelic – was spoken over a wide area, gradually dividing into Goidelic (or Q-Celtic) now spoken in Ireland and Scotland, and Brythonic (P-Celtic) spoken in Wales, Cornwall and later exported to Brittany in France. Great though the Celtic technological and artistic achievements were, the people and their pan-European cousins were unable to maintain an organized civic society to match that of their successors, the Romans.

THE ROMANS

Coming at the end of a lengthy but low-level infusion of Roman ideas into the country, the Roman invasion had begun hesitantly, with small cross-Channel incursions by **Julius Caesar** in 55 and 54 BC. Britain's rumoured mineral wealth was a primary motive behind these raids, but the immediate spur to the eventual conquest nearly a century later was the dangerous collaboration between British Celts and the fiercely anti-Roman tribesmen in France, and the need of the emperor **Claudius**, who owed his power to the army, for a great military triumph. The death of the British king Cunobelin, who ruled all southeast England and was the original of Shakespeare's Cymbeline, offered the opportunity Claudius required, and in **August 43 AD**, a substantial force landed in Kent, from where it fanned out, soon establishing a base along the estuary of the Thames. Joined by Claudius and a menagerie of elephants and camels for the major battle of the campaign, the Romans soon reached Camulodunum (Colchester), and within four years were dug in on the frontier of south Wales.

The Catuvellauni chief, Caratacus, continued to conduct a guerrilla campaign from Wales until his eventual betrayal and capture in about 50 AD. About ten years later, a more serious challenge to the Romans arose when the East Anglian Iceni, under their queen **Boudicca** (or Boadicea), sacked Camulodunum and Verulamium (St Albans), and even reached the undefended port of Londinium, precursor of London. The uprising was soon quashed, and turned out to be an isolated act of resistance, with many of the already Romanized southeastern tribes of England probably welcoming absorption into the empire. However, it was not until 79 AD that Wales and the north of England were subdued.

By 80 AD the Roman governor, Agricola, felt secure enough in the south of Britain to begin an invasion of the north, building a string of forts across the Clyde–Forth line and defeating a large force of Scottish tribes at Mons Graupius. The long-term effect of his campaign, however, was slight. In 123 AD the Emperor Hadrian decided to seal the frontier against the northern tribes and built **Hadrian's Wall**, which stretched from the Solway Firth to the Tyne and was the first formal division of the island of Britain. Twenty years later, the Romans again ventured north and built the **Antonine Wall** between the Clyde and the Forth. This was occupied for about forty years, but thereafter the Romans, frustrated by the inhospitable terrain of the Highlands, largely gave up their attempt to subjugate the north, and instead adopted a policy of containment.

The written history of Britain begins with the Romans, whose rule lasted nearly four centuries. For the first time most of England was absorbed into a unified and peaceful political structure, in which commerce flourished and cities prospered, particularly **Londinium**, which immediately assumed a pivotal role in the commercial and administrative life of the province. Although Latin became the language of the Romano-British ruling elite, local traditions were allowed to co-exist with imported customs, so that Celtic gods were often worshipped at the same time as the Roman, and sometimes merged with them. Perhaps the most important legacy of the Roman occupation, however, was the introduction of **Christianity** from the third century on, becoming firmly entrenched after its official recognition by the emperor Constantine in 313.

THE ANGLO-SAXON PERIOD

As early as the reign of Constantine, Roman England was being raided by Germanic Saxon pirates. As economic life declined and rural areas became depopulated, individual military leaders began to usurp local authority, so that by the start of the fifth century England had become irrevocably detached from what remained of the Roman Empire. Within fifty years the **Saxons** were settling on the island, the start of a gradual conquest that – despite bitter resistance led by such semi-mythical figures as King Arthur, who is alleged to have held court at Caerleon in Wales – culminated in the defeat of the native Britons in 577 at the **Battle of Dyrham** (near Bath), at which three British kings were killed. Driving the few recalcitrant Celtic tribes deep into Cumbria, Wales and England's West Country, the invaders eliminated the Romano-British culture and by the end of the sixth century the rest of England was divided into the Anglo-Saxon kingdoms of Northumbria, Mercia, East Anglia, Kent and Wessex.

Only in Scotland and Wales did the ancient Celtic traditions survive, untouched by the Teutonic invaders as they had been by the Romans. In the fifth century, Irish-Celtic invaders formed distinct colonies in parts of Wales, and in the northwest of Scotland. Between the fifth and the eighth centuries the **Celtic Saints**, ascetic evangelical missionaries, spread the gospel around Ireland and western Britain, promoting the middle-Eastern eremitical tradition of living a reclusive life. In south Wales, Saint David was the most popular (and subsequently Wales' patron saint), while in northwest Scotland, Saint Columba founded several Christian outposts, the most famous of which was on the island of Iona.

The revival of Christianity in England was driven mainly by the arrival of **St Augustine**, who was dispatched by Pope Gregory I and landed on the Kent coast in 597, accompanied by forty monks. The missionaries were received by **Ethelbert**, who gave Augustine permission to found a monastery at Canterbury, where the king himself was then baptized, followed by ten thousand of his subjects at a grand Christmas ceremony. Despite some reversals in the years that followed, the Christianization of England proceeded quickly, so that by the middle of the seventh century all of the Anglo-Saxon kings had at least nominally adopted the faith. Tensions and clashes between the Augustinian missionaries and the more freebooting Celtic monks inevitably arose, to be resolved by the

Synod of Whitby in 663, when it was settled that the English church should follow the rule of Rome, thereby ensuring a realignment with the European cultural mainstream.

The central English region of **Mercia** became the dominant Anglo-Saxon kingdom in the eighth century under kings Ethelbald and Offa, the latter being responsible for the greatest public work of the Anglo-Saxon period: **Offa's Dyke**, an earthwork stretching from the River Dee to the Severn, marking the border with Wales. After Offa's death **Wessex** gained the upper hand, and by 825 **Egbert** had conquered or taken allegiance from all the other English kingdoms. The supremacy of Wessex coincided with the first large-scale Norse or **Danish** Viking invasions, which began with coastal pirate raids, such as the one that destroyed the great monastery of Lindisfarne in 793, but gradually grew into a migration, chiefly in the Scottish islands of Orkney, Shetland and the Hebrides.

In 865 a substantial Danish army landed in East Anglia, and within six years they had conquered Northumbria, Mercia and East Anglia, and were attacking Wessex. At about the same time, the leadership of Wessex was assumed by **Alfred the Great**, a warrior whose dogged resistance and acceptance of the need to coexist with the Danes ensured the survival of his kingdom. Having established a border demarcating his domain from the northern **Danelaw**, the part of England in which the rule of the now Christianized Danes was accepted (a border roughly coinciding with the Roman Watling Street), Alfred directed his resources into internal reforms and the strengthening of his defences.

Although Danish attacks had recommenced before the end of Alfred's reign in 899, his successor, **Edward the Elder**, established supremacy over the Danelaw and was thus the *de facto* overlord of all England, acknowledged even by Scottish and Welsh chieftains. In 973, **Edgar**, king of Mercia and Northumberland, became the first ruler to be crowned king of England, but the aggression from the Danes was unrelenting, and in 1016 Ethelred the Unready – having failed to buy off the enemy – fled to Normandy, establishing links there which were to have a far-reaching effect on ensuing events.

The first and best king of the short-lived Danish dynasty was **Canute**, who was followed by his two unexceptional and disreputable sons, after whom the Saxons were restored under Ethelred's son, **Edward the Confessor**. It was said of Edward that he was better suited to have been a priest than a king, and most of his reign was dominated by Godwin, Earl of Wessex, and by Godwin's son Harold. On Edward's death, the Witan – a sort of council of elders – confirmed **Harold** as king, despite the claim of William, Duke of Normandy, that the exiled and childless Edward had sworn himself to be William's vassal, promising him the succession. Harold's brief reign was overshadowed by the events in the last two of its ten months, when he first marched north to fend off an invasion attempt by his brother Tostig (who had been deprived of his earldom of Northumbria) in league with King Harald of Norway. Having defeated their combined forces at Stamford Bridge in Yorkshire, Harold was immediately forced to return south to meet the invading William, who routed his forces at the **Battle of Hastings** in 1066. Harold was killed, and on Christmas Day of that year William the Conqueror was installed as king in Westminster Abbey.

ENGLAND: THE NORMANS AND PLANTAGENETS

Making little attempt to reach any understanding with the indigenous Saxon culture, **William I** imposed a new military aristocracy on his subjects, enforcing his rule with a series of strongholds all over England, the grandest of which was the Tower of London. The sporadic rebellions that broke out during the early years of his reign were ruthlessly suppressed by a scorched earth policy, especially in Yorkshire and its surrounding counties, but perhaps the single most effective controlling measure was the compilation of the **Domesday Book** between 1085 and 1086. Recording land ownership, type of cultivation, the number of inhabitants and their social status, it afforded William an unprecedented body of information about his subjects, providing the framework for the administration of taxation, the judicial structure and feudal obligations.

William was succeeded in 1087 by his son William Rufus, an ineffectual ruler but a notable benefactor of the religious foundations that were springing up throughout the realm. Killed by an arrow while hunting in the New Forest, William was in turn followed by William I's youngest son, Henry I, who spent much of his reign in tussles with the country's barons, but at least was the first Norman king to encourage intermarriage, himself marrying a Saxon princess. On his death in 1135, William I's grandson Stephen of Blois contested the accession of Henry's daughter Mathilda (also called Maud), with the consequence that the nineteen years of his reign were spent in civil war. Mathilda's son was eventually recognized as Stephen's heir, and the reign of **Henry II** (1154–89), the first of the **Plantagenet** branch of the Norman line, provided a welcome respite from baronial brawling. Asserting his authority throughout a domain that reached from the Cheviots to the Pyrenees, Henry presided over immense administrative reforms, including the introduction of trial by jury. His attempts to subordinate ecclesiastical authority to the Crown went terribly awry in 1170, when he sanctioned the murder in Canterbury Cathedral of his erstwhile drinking companion **Thomas à Becket**, whose canonization just three years later created an enduring Europe-wide cult.

The last years of Henry's reign were riven by quarrels with his sons, the eldest of whom, **Richard I** (or Lionheart), spent most of his ten-year reign crusading in the Holy Land. Alienated by the king's rift with the Church in Rome, and by his loss of Henry II's huge legacy of French territory, the barons eventually forced Richard's brother **King John** to consent to a charter guaranteeing their rights and privileges, the **Magna Carta**, which was signed in 1215 at Runnymede, on the Thames. The power struggle with the barons continued into the reign of Henry III, who was defeated by their leader Simon de Montfort at Lewes in 1265, when both Henry and Prince Edward were taken prisoner. Edward escaped, defeated the barons' army at the battle of Evesham in 1265 and killed de Montfort, ascending the throne in 1272 as **Edward I**. A great law-maker in the mould of William I and Henry II, Edward presided over the Model Parliament of 1295, a significant step in the evolution of consensual politics, though he was mostly absorbed in extending his kingdom within the island, annexing Wales and imposing English jurisdiction in Scotland.

THE CONQUEST OF WALES

Though Wales was unable to present a unified opposition to the Norman invaders, William the

Conqueror didn't attempt to annex Wales. Instead, he installed a huge retinue of barons, the **Lords Marcher**, along the border to bring as much Welsh territory under their own jurisdiction as possible. Despite generations of squabbling, the barons managed to hold onto their privileges until Henry VIII's Act of Union over four hundred years later.

The status quo between Wales and England changed irrevocably, however, when Edward I succeeded Henry III and began a crusade to unify Britain. The Welsh chief, Llywelyn the Last, had failed to attend Edward's coronation, and refused to pay him homage. With effective use of sea power Edward had little trouble forcing Llywelyn back into Snowdonia. Peace was restored with the **Treaty of Aberconwy** which deprived Llywelyn of almost all his land and stripped him of his financial tributes from the other Welsh princes, but left him with the hollow title of "Prince of Wales". After a relatively cordial four-year period, Llywelyn's brother Dafydd rose against Edward, inevitably dragging Llywelyn along with him. Edward crushed the revolt, captured Llywelyn, and executed him at Cilmeri, after fleeing from the abortive Battle of Builth in 1282. The **Treaty of Rhuddlan** in 1284 set down the terms by which the English monarch was to rule Wales: much of it was given to the Marcher lords who had helped Edward, the rest was divided into administrative and legal districts similar to those in England. Though the treaty is often seen as a symbol of English subjugation, it respected much of Welsh law and provided a basis for civil rights and privileges. Many Welsh were content to accept and exploit Edward's rule for their own benefit, but in 1294 a rebellion led by **Madog ap Llywelyn** gripped Wales and was only halted by Edward's swift and devastating response. Most of the privileges enshrined in the Treaty of Rhuddlan were now rescinded and the Welsh seemed crushed for a century.

Pent-up resentment towards the English sowed seeds of a rebellion led by the tyrannical but charismatic Welsh hero **Owain Glyndŵr**, who declared himself "Prince of Wales" in 1400, and with a crew of local supporters attacked the lands of nearby barons, slaughtering the English. Henry IV misjudged the political climate and imposed restrictions on Welsh land ownership, swelling the general support Glyndŵr needed to take Conwy Castle the fol-

lowing year. In 1404 Glyndŵr summoned a parliament in Machynlleth, and had himself crowned Prince of Wales, with envoys of France, Scotland and Castile in attendance. He then demanded independence for the Welsh Church from Canterbury and set about securing alliances with English noblemen who had grievances with Henry IV. This last ambitious move heralded Glyndŵr's downfall. A succession of defeats saw his allies desert him and by 1408, when the castles at Harlech and Aberystwyth were retaken for the Crown, this last protest against Edward I's English conquest had lost its momentum.

SCOTLAND IN THE MIDDLE AGES

The victory of the Scottish king, **Malcolm III**, known as Canmore ("bighead"), over Macbeth in 1057 marked the beginning of a period of fundamental change in Scottish society. Having avenged his father Duncan, Malcolm III, who had spent the previous seventeen years at the English court, sought to apply to Scotland a range of ideas he had brought back with him. He and his heirs established a secure dynasty based on succession through the male line and introduced **feudalism** into Scotland, a system that was diametrically opposed to the Gaelic system, which rested on blood ties: the followers of a Gaelic king were his kindred, whereas the followers of a feudal king were vassals bought with land. The Canmores successfully feudalized much of southern and eastern Scotland by making grants to their Norman, Breton and Flemish followers, but beyond that, traditional clan-based forms of social relations persisted.

The Canmores, independent of the local nobility, who remained a military threat, also began to reform the **Church**. This development started with the efforts of Margaret, Malcolm III's English wife, who brought Scottish religious practices into line with those of the rest of Europe and was eventually canonized. **David I** (1124–53) continued the process by importing monks to found a series of monasteries, principally along the border at Kelso, Melrose, Jedburgh and Dryburgh. By 1200 the entire country was covered by a network of eleven bishoprics, although church organization remained weak within the Highlands. Similarly, the dynasty founded a series of **royal burghs**, towns such as Edinburgh, Stirling and Berwick, and bestowed upon them charters recognizing them as centres of trade. The charters usually granted a measure of self-government, vested in the town corporation or guild, and the monarchy hoped this liberality would both encourage loyalty and increase the prosperity of the kingdom. Scotland's Gaelic-speaking clans had little influence within the burghs, and by 1550 Scots – a northern version of Anglo-Saxon – had become the main language throughout the Lowlands.

The policies of the Canmores laid the basis for a cultural rift in Scotland between the Highland and Lowland communities. Before that became an issue, however, the Scots had to face a major threat from the south. In 1286 **Alexander III** died, and a hotly disputed succession gave Edward I, the king of England, an opportunity to subjugate Scotland. In 1291 Edward presided over a conference where the rival claimants to the Scottish throne presented their cases. Edward chose John Balliol, in preference to **Robert the Bruce**, his main rival, and obliged John to pay him homage, thus turning Scotland into a vassal kingdom. Bruce refused to accept the decision, thereby continuing the conflict, and in 1295 Balliol renounced his allegiance to Edward and formed an alliance with France – the beginning of what is known as the "Auld Alliance". In the conflict that followed, the Bruce family sided with the English, Balliol was defeated and imprisoned, and Edward seized control of almost all of Scotland.

Edward had shown little mercy during his conquest of Scotland – he had, for example, had most of the population of Berwick massacred – and his cruelty seems to have provoked a truly national resistance. This focused on **William Wallace**, a man of relatively lowly origins who forged an army of peasants, lesser knights and townsmen that was fundamentally different from the armies raised by the nobility. Figures like Balliol, holding lands in England, France and Scotland, were part of an international aristocracy for whom warfare was merely the means by which they struggled for power. Wallace, by contrast, led proto-nationalist forces determined to expel the English from their country. Probably for that very reason Wallace never received the support of the nobility, and, after a bitter ten-year campaign, he was betrayed and executed in London in 1305.

With Wallace out of the way, feudal intrigue resumed. In 1306 **Robert the Bruce**, the erst-while ally of the English, defied Edward and had himself crowned king of Scotland. Edward died the following year, but the unrest dragged on until 1314, when Bruce decisively defeated a huge English army under Edward II at the battle of **Bannockburn**. At last Bruce was firmly in control of his kingdom, and in 1320 the Scots asserted their right to independence in a successful petition to the pope, now known as the **Arbroath Declaration**.

FROM BANNOCKBURN TO BOSWORTH

The defeat at Bannockburn added to the unpopularity of **Edward II**, and the king was eventually overthrown by his wife Isabella and her lover Roger Mortimer, by whom he was horribly put to death in Berkeley Castle, Gloucestershire. Although **Edward III** was initially preoccupied by Scottish wars, his reign is chiefly remembered for his claim to the French throne, a feeble pretence – he had earlier recognized the king of France and done homage to him – but one that launched the **Hundred Years' War** in 1337. Early English victories such as the Battle of Crécy in 1346, and the capture of Calais the following year, were interrupted by the outbreak of the **Black Death** in 1349, a plague which claimed about a third of the English population. The resulting scarcity of labour produced economic turmoil in the land, and attempts to restrict the rise of wages and to levy a poll tax (a tax on each person irrespective of wealth) provoked widespread riots, which peaked with the **Peasants' Revolt** of 1381. After seizing Rochester Castle and sacking Canterbury, the rebels marched on London, where the boy king **Richard II** met Wat Tyler, the leader of the revolt, at Smithfield. The resulting scuffle led to Tyler's murder and the dispersal of the mob, and soon afterwards the Bishop of Norwich routed the Norfolk rebels, the prelude to a wave of repression and terrible retribution.

Parallel with this social unrest were the clerical reforms demanded by the scholar **John Wycliffe**, whose followers made the first translation of the Bible into English in 1380. Another sign of the elevation of the language was the success enjoyed by **Geoffrey Chaucer** (c.1340–1400), a wine merchant's son, whose *Canterbury Tales* was the first major work written in the vernacular and one of the first English books to be printed.

During the later years of Edward III's reign England had in effect been ruled by his son, **John of Gaunt**, Duke of Lancaster, whose influence remained paramount during the minority of Richard II. In 1399 the vacillating Richard II was overthrown by John of Gaunt's son, who took the title **Henry IV** and founded the **Lancastrian** dynasty. Fourteen years later, he in turn was succeeded by his son, **Henry V**, who promptly renewed the war with France, which had been limping along ingloriously since the victory at Poitiers in 1356. After the much-celebrated triumph at **Agincourt**, Henry forced the French king to sign the Treaty of Troyes in 1420, making the English king the heir to the French throne, but on Henry's death just two years later his son was still an infant, which left regents governing the country on behalf of the monarch. Settling their differences, the French rallied under **Joan of Arc** to beat back the English, and by 1454 only Calais was left in English hands.

Meanwhile **Henry VI**, who was temperamentally more inclined to the creation of such architectural coups as King's College Chapel in Cambridge and Eton College Chapel than to warfare, had suffered lapses into insanity. Strongest of the rival contenders for the throne was Richard, Duke of York, by virtue of his direct descent from Edward III. It was no accident that the **Wars of the Roses** – named from the red rose that symbolized the Lancastrian cause and the white Yorkist rose – broke out just a year after the return of the last English garrisons from France, filling the country with footloose knights and archers accustomed to a life of plunder and war. The instability of the time was signalled by **Jack Cade's Rebellion** of 1450, when a disorganized rabble – though with more participation by dissatisfied gentry than had been the case in the 1381 Peasants' Revolt – challenged the king's authority, winning a battle at Sevenoaks before being scattered. Political disputes within the circle surrounding the mad king were to prove more threatening to the regime. The Duke of York's authority over Henry was challenged by the king's accomplished and ambitious wife, Margaret of Anjou, whose forces defeated and slew Richard at Wakefield in 1460. She and Henry were in turn overwhelmed by Richard's son, who was crowned **Edward IV** in 1461 – the first king of the **Yorkist** line.

The civil strife entered a new stage when Edward attempted to shrug off the overbearing influence of Richard Neville, Earl of Warwick and Salisbury, or "Warwick the Kingmaker", as he became known. Warwick then performed a dramatic volte-face by allying himself with his old enemy Margaret of Anjou, forcing Edward into exile and proclaiming Henry king once more. Henry VI's second term was soon interrupted by Edward's unexpected return in 1471, when Warwick was defeated and killed at the Battle of Barnet and the rest of the Lancastrians were crushed at Tewkesbury three months later. Margaret was captured, Henry's heir was killed and Henry himself was soon afterwards dispatched in the Tower.

Edward IV proved to be a precursor of the great Tudor princes – licentious, cruel and despotic, but also a patron of Renaissance learning. In 1483, his twelve-year-old son succeeded as **Edward V**, but his reign was cut short after only two months, when he and his younger brother were murdered in the Tower of London – probably by their uncle, the Duke of Gloucester, who was crowned **Richard III**. Increasingly unpopular as rumours circulated of his part in the fate of the princes in the Tower, Richard was toppled at Bosworth Field in 1485 by **Henry Tudor**, Earl of Richmond, who took the throne as **Henry VII**.

THE TUDORS

The opening of the **Tudor period** brought radical transformations. A Lancastrian through his mother's descent from John of Gaunt, Henry VII reconciled the Yorkist faction by marrying Edward IV's daughter Elizabeth, putting an end to the internecine squabbling among the discredited gentry. The growth of the wool and cloth trades and the rise of a powerful merchant class brought a general increase of wealth, while England began to assume the status of a major European power partly as a result of Henry's alliances and political marriages – his daughter to James IV of Scotland and his son to Catherine, daughter of Ferdinand and Isabella of Spain.

The relatively easy suppression of the rebellions of Yorkist pretenders Lambert Simnel and Perkin Warbeck ensured a smooth succession for **Henry VIII** in 1509. Although Henry was himself not a Protestant and even received from the pope the title of "Defender of the Faith" for a book he published criticizing Luther's doctrine, this tumultuous king is chiefly noted for the separation of the English Church from Rome. The schism was triggered not by doctrinal issues but by the failure of his wife Catherine of Aragon – widow of his elder brother – to provide Henry with male offspring. Failing to obtain a decree of nullity from Pope Clement VII, he dismissed his long-time chancellor Thomas Wolsey and followed the advice of Thomas Cromwell, forcing the English Church to recognize him as its head. The most far-reaching consequence of this step was the **Dissolution of the Monasteries**, a decision taken mainly to enjoy the profits of the ensuing land sales. The first phase of the Dissolution in 1536, involving the smaller religious houses, was a factor in the only significant rebellion of the reign, the **Pilgrimage of Grace**, a protest largely in the north of the country, which Henry put down with great cruelty, preparing the ground for the closure of the larger foundations in 1539.

In his later years Henry became a corpulent tyrant, six times married but at last furnished with an heir, **Edward VI**, who was only nine years old when he ascended the throne in 1547. His short reign saw Protestantism established on a firm footing, with churches stripped of their images and Catholic services banned, yet on Edward's death most of the country recognized his half-sister **Mary**, daughter of Catherine of Aragon and a fervent Catholic. She restored England to the papacy and married the future Philip II of Spain, forging an alliance whose immediate consequence was war with France and the loss of Calais, last of England's French possessions. Mary's unpopularity increased when she began a savage persecution of Protestants, executing the leading lights of the English Reformation, Hugh Latimer, Nicholas Ridley and Thomas Cranmer, the archbishop of Canterbury who was largely responsible for the first English Prayer Book, published in 1549.

The accession of the Protestant **Elizabeth I** in 1558 took place in a highly volatile atmosphere, with the country riven between opposing religious loyalties and threatened abroad by Philip II. Heresy and treason were the twin preoccupations of the Elizabethan state, a society in which a sense of English nationhood was evolving on an almost mystical level in the vacuum created by the break with Rome. Aided by a team of exceptionally able ministers, the Virgin Queen provided a focal point for national feeling, enthusiastically supported by a mercantile class which was opposed to foreign entanglements or clerical restrictions, and was represented in a parliament made stronger by the constitutional decisions of the preceding fifty years.

The 45 years of Elizabeth's reign saw the efflorescence of a specifically English Renaissance, especially in the field of literature, which reached its pinnacle in the brilliant career of **William Shakespeare** (1564–1616). It was also the age of the **seafarers** Walter Raleigh, Francis Drake, Martin Frobisher and John Hawkins, whose piratical exploits helped to map out the world for English commerce. English navigational skills – as demonstrated by Drake's voyage round the world (1577–80) – and the country's growing naval strength triumphed with the defeat of the **Spanish Armada** in 1588. The commander of the English fleet, Lord Howard of Effingham, was a practising Catholic, a fact that dashed Philip's hope of a Catholic insurrection in England – a hope in part founded on the widespread sympathy for Elizabeth's cousin Mary Queen of Scots, whose twenty-year imprisonment in England had ended with her beheading in 1587.

WALES UNDER THE TUDORS

Welsh allegiance during the Wars of the Roses lay broadly with the Lancastrians, who had the support of the ascendant north Welsh Tewdwr (or Tudor) family. Welsh expectations of the first Tudor monarch, Henry VII, were high. Henry lived up to some of them, removing many of the restrictions on land ownership imposed at the start of Glyndŵyr's uprising, and promoting many Welshmen to high office, but administration remained piecemeal. Control was still shared between the Crown and largely independent Marcher lords until a uniform administrative structure was achieved under Henry VIII.

Wales had been largely controlled by the English monarch since the Treaty of Rhuddlan in 1284, but the **Acts of Union** in 1536 and 1543 fixed English sovereignty over the country. At the same time the Marches were replaced by shires (the equivalent of modern counties), the Welsh laws codified by Hywel Dda were made void and partible inheritance gave way to primogeniture, the eldest son becoming the sole heir. For the first time the Welsh and

English enjoyed legal equality, but the break with native traditions wasn't well received. Most of the people remained poor, the gentry became increasingly anglicized, the use of Welsh was proscribed, and legal proceedings were held in English (a language few peasants understood).

Since Christianity had always been a ritual way of life rather than a philosophical code in Wales, Catholicism was easily replaced by Protestantism during the religious upheavals of Henry VIII's reign. What the Reformation did promote was a more studied approach to religion and learning in general. Under the reign of Elizabeth I, Jesus College was founded in Oxford for Welsh scholars, and the Bible was translated into Welsh for the first time by a team led by Bishop **William Morgan**.

With new land ownership laws enshrined in the Acts of Union, the stimulus provided by the Dissolution hastened the emergence of the Anglo-Welsh gentry, a group eager to claim a Welsh pedigree while promoting the English language and the legal system, helping to perpetuate their grasp. Meanwhile, landless peasants continued in poverty, only gaining slightly from the increase in cattle trade with England and the slow development of mining and ore smelting.

THE STEWARTS IN SCOTLAND

In the years following Bruce's death in 1329, the Scottish monarchy gradually declined in influence. The last of the Bruce dynasty died in 1371, to be succeeded by the "Stewards", hence **Stewarts** (known as Stuarts in England), but thereafter a succession of Scottish rulers, culminating with James VI in 1567, came to the throne when still children. The power vacuum was filled by the nobility, whose key members exercised control as Scotland's regents while carving out territories where they ruled with the power, if not the title, of kings. **James IV** (1488–1513), the most talented of the early Stewarts, might have restored the authority of the Crown, but his invasion of England ended in a terrible defeat for the Scots – and his own death – at the Battle of Flodden Field.

The reign of **Mary Queen of Scots** (1542–87) typified the problems of the Scottish monarchy. Mary came to the throne when just one week old, and immediately caught the attention of the English king, Henry VIII, who sought, first by persuasion and then by military might, to secure her hand in marriage for his five-year-old son, Edward. Beginning in 1544, the English launched a series of devastating attacks on Scotland, an episode Sir Walter Scott later called the "Rough Wooing", until, in the face of another English invasion in 1548, the Scots – or at least those not supporting Henry – turned to the "Auld Alliance". The French king proposed marriage between Mary and the Dauphin Francis, promising in return military assistance against the English. The six-year-old queen sailed for France in 1548, leaving her loyal nobles and their French allies in control, and her husband succeeded to the French throne in 1559. When she returned thirteen years later, following the death of Francis, she had to pick her way through the rival ambitions of her nobility and deal with something entirely new – the religious Reformation.

The **Reformation** in Scotland was a complex social process, whose threads are often hard to unravel. Nevertheless, it is quite clear that, by the end of the sixteenth century, the established Church was held in general contempt. Another spur to the Scottish Reformation was the identification of Protestantism with anti-French feeling. In 1554 Mary of Guise, the French mother of the absent Queen Mary, had become regent, and her habit of appointing Frenchmen to high office caused considerable resentment. In 1557, a group of nobles banded together to form the **Lords of the Congregation**, whose dual purpose was to oppose French influence and promote the reformed religion. With English military backing, the Protestant lords succeeded in deposing the French regent in 1560, and, when the Scottish Parliament assembled shortly afterwards, it asserted the primacy of Protestantism by forbidding Mass and abolishing the authority of the pope. The nobility proceeded to confiscate two thirds of Church lands, a huge prize that did much to bolster their new beliefs.

Even without the economic incentives, Protestantism was a highly charged political doctrine. As the Protestant reformer **John Knox** told Queen Mary at their first meeting in 1561, subjects are not bound to obey an ungodly monarch. Mary ducked and weaved, trying to avoid an open breach with her Protestant subjects. Her difficulties were exacerbated by her disastrous second marriage to **Lord Darnley**, a cruel and politically inept character, whose jealousy led to his involvement in the murder of Mary's favourite, David Rizzio, who was dragged from the queen's supper room at Holyrood and stabbed 56 times. The incident caused the Scottish Protestants more than a little unease, but they were entirely scandalized in 1567, when Darnley himself was murdered and Mary promptly married the **Earl of Bothwell**, widely believed to be the murderer. This was too much to bear, and the Scots rose in rebellion, driving Mary into exile in England at the age of just 25. The queen's illegitimate half-brother, the Earl of Moray, became regent and her son, the infant James, was left behind to be raised a Protestant prince. Mary, meanwhile, became perceived as such a threat to the English throne that, after twenty years' imprisonment in England, Queen Elizabeth I had her executed in 1587.

Knox could now concentrate on the organization of the reformed Church, or **Kirk**, which he envisaged as a body empowered to intervene in the daily lives of the people. **Andrew Melville**, another leading reformer, proposed the abolition of all traces of episcopacy – the rule of the bishops in the Church – and that the Kirk should adopt a **presbyterian** structure, administered by a hierarchy of assemblies, part elected and part appointed. At the bottom of the chain, beneath the General Assembly, Synod and Presbytery, would be the Kirk session, responsible for church affairs, the performance of the minister and the morals of the parish. In 1592, the Melvillian party achieved a measure of success when presbyteries and synods were accepted as legal church courts and the office of bishop was suspended.

James VI (1567–1625) disliked presbyterianism because its quasi-democratic structure – particularly the lack of royally appointed bishops – appeared to threaten his authority. He was, however, unable to resist the reformers until 1610, when, strengthened by his installation as King of England, he restored the Scottish bishops. The argument about the nature of Kirk organization would lead to bloody conflict in the years after James' death.

THE STUARTS AND THE COMMONWEALTH

On Elizabeth's death in 1603, James VI became **James I** of England, thereby uniting the English and Scottish crowns. James quickly moved to end hostilities with Spain – a move resented by the increasingly powerful English Puritans, an extreme Protestant group – but his intention to exercise tolerance towards the country's Catholics was thwarted by the outcry in the wake of the **Gunpowder Plot** of 1605, when Guy Fawkes and a group of Catholic conspirators were discovered preparing to blow up king and Parliament. Puritan fundamentalism and commercial interests converged in the foundation of Virginia in 1608, the first permanent **colony in North America**, followed in 1620 by the landing in New England of the Pilgrim Fathers, the nucleus of a colony that would absorb about 100,000 mainly Puritan immigrants by the middle of the century.

A split was inevitable between James, who clung to the medieval notion of the divine right of kings, and the landed gentry who dominated the increasingly powerful Parliament, a situation exacerbated by the persecution of the Puritans. Recoiling from the demands of the Parliamentarians, the king relied heavily on court favourites, progressing from the skilful Robert Cecil, Earl of Salisbury, and the philosopher Francis Bacon, to the rash and unpopular George Villiers, Duke of Buckingham, who also had a close influence on the second Stuart king, **Charles I** (1625–49).

Raised in Episcopalian England, Charles had little understanding of Scottish reformism, and like his father, he believed in the divine right of kings. In 1637, Charles attempted to impose a new prayer book on the Scottish Kirk, laying down forms of worship in line with those favoured by the High Anglican Church. The reformers denounced these changes as "Popery" and organized the **National Covenant**, a religious pledge that committed the signatories to "Labour by all means lawful to recover the purity and liberty of the Gospel as it was established and professed". Charles declared all the "Covenanters" to be rebels, a proclamation endorsed by his Scottish bishops. Consequently, when the king backed down from military action and called a General Assembly of the Kirk, the assembly promptly abolished the episcopacy. Charles pronounced the proceedings illegal, but lack of finance stopped him from mounting an effective military campaign – whereas the Covenanters, well financed by the Kirk, assembled a proficient army under Alexander Leslie.

In desperation, Charles summoned the English Parliament, the first for eleven years, hoping it would pay for an army. But, like the calling of the General Assembly, the decision was a disaster and Parliament was much keener to criticize his policies than to raise taxes. In 1642, facing the concerted hostility of Parliament, the king withdrew to Nottingham where he raised his standard, the opening military act of the **Civil War**. The Royalist forces were initially successful against the Parliamentarian army, gaining an advantage after the first battle of the war, Edgehill, at which Charles's nephew, the dashing cavalry officer Prince Rupert, displayed the reckless valour which was to distinguish his participation in subsequent engagements. After Edgehill, the Parliamentarian army was completely overhauled by **Oliver Cromwell** as the New Model Army, and won victories at Marston Moor and Naseby. Charles was captured by the Scots at Newark in Nottinghamshire, in 1646 and was finally handed over to the English, by whom, after prolonged negotiations and more fighting, he was executed in January 1649.

The following year, at the invitation of the Earl of Argyll, Charles' son, the future Charles II, came to Scotland. To regain his Scottish kingdom, Charles was obliged to renounce his father and sign the Covenant, two bitter pills taken to impress the population. In the event, the "presbyterian restoration" was short-lived. Cromwell invaded, defeated the Scots at Dunbar and forced Charles into exile. For the next eleven years the whole country was a **Commonwealth** – at first a true republic, then, after 1653, a Protectorate under Cromwell, who was ultimately as impatient of Parliament and as arbitrary as Charles had been. Cromwell's policies were especially savage in Ireland, where his depredations are remembered to this day. At his death in 1658 his son Richard ruled briefly and ineffectually, and in 1660 Parliament voted to restore the monarchy in the person of **Charles II** (1660–85), the exiled son of the previous king.

THE RESTORATION AND THE GLORIOUS REVOLUTION

The turmoil of the previous twenty years had unleashed a furious debate on every strand of legalistic, theological and political thought, an environment that spawned a host of fringe sects – such as the Levellers, who demanded constitutional reform, and the more radical Ranters, who proposed common ownership of all land. Nonconformist religious groups flourished, prominent among them the pacifist **Quakers**, led by the much persecuted George Fox (1624–91), and the Dissenters, to whom the most famous writers of the day, John Milton (1608–74) and John Bunyan (1628–88), both belonged. With the **Restoration**, however, these philosophical eddies gave way to a new exuberance in the fields of art, literature and the theatre, a remarkable transition from the sombreness of the Puritan era, when secular drama and other such fripperies were banned outright. In the scientific arena, just six months after his accession Charles founded the **Royal Society**, which numbered Isaac Newton (1642–1727) among its first fellows.

The low points of Charles II's reign came with the **Great Plague** of 1665 and the **Great Fire of London** the following year, though the latter had the positive consequence of allowing Christopher Wren (1632–1723) and other great architects to redesign the capital along more contemporary classical lines. Moreover, the political scene was not entirely tranquil: tensions still existed between king and Parliament, where the traditional divisions of court and country began to coalesce into **Whig** and **Tory** parties, respectively representing the Low-Church gentry and the High-Church aristocracy. A measure of vengeance was also wreaked on the regicides and other leading Parliamentarians, though its intensity was nothing like that of the anti-Catholic hysteria sparked off by the Popish Plot of 1678, the fabrication of the trickster Titus Oates.

The succession in 1685 of the Catholic **James II** (James VII of Scotland), brother of Charles II, provoked much opposition, though – as one might expect from a country recently racked by civil war – there was an indifferent response when the **Duke of Monmouth**, favourite of Charles II's illegitimate sons, landed at Lyme Regis to mount a challenge to the new king. His undisciplined forces were routed at Sedgemoor, Somerset, in July 1685; nine days later Monmouth was beheaded at Tower Hill, and in the subsequent **Bloody Assizes** of Judge Jeffreys, hundreds of rebels and suspected sympathizers – mainly in Somerset and Devon – were executed or deported.

When seven bishops protested against James's **Declaration of Indulgence** of 1687, removing anti-Catholic restrictions, the king showed something of his father's obstinacy by having them tried for seditious libel, though he was quickly forced to acquit them. When James's son was born, a child destined to be brought up in the Catholic faith, messengers were dispatched to **William of Orange**, the Dutch husband of Mary, the Protestant daughter of James II. William landed in Brixham in Devon, proceeding to London where he was acclaimed king in the so-called **Glorious Revolution** of 1688, the final postscript to the Civil War.

William and Mary were made joint sovereigns, having agreed to a **Bill of Rights** defining the limitations of the monarch's power and the rights of his or her subjects. This, together with the **Act of Settlement of 1701** – among other things, barring Catholics or anyone married to one from succession to the English throne – made Britain the first country to be governed by a **constitutional monarchy**, in which the roles of legislature and executive were separate and interdependent, a model broadly consistent with that outlined by the philosopher and political thinker John Locke (1632–1704), whose essentially Whig doctrines of toleration and social contract were gradually embraced as the new orthodoxy.

Ruling alone after Mary's death in 1694, William regarded England as a prop in his defence of Holland against France, a stance that defined England's political alignment in Europe for the next sixty years. Mary died without leaving an heir and, on William's death in 1702, the Crown passed to her sister **Anne**, who was also childless. In response, the English Parliament secured the Protestant succession through the Act of Settlement, naming the Electress Sophia of Hanover as the next in line to the throne. The Act did not, however, apply in Scotland, and the English feared that the Scots would invite James II's son, James Edward Stuart, back from France to be their king.

Nevertheless, despite the strength of anti-English feeling, the Scottish Parliament passed the **Act of Union** by 110 votes to 69 in 1707. Some historians have explained the vote purely in terms of bribery and corruption, but there were other factors. Scottish politicians were divided between the Cavaliers – Jacobites (supporters of the Stuarts) and Episcopalians – and the Country party, whose presbyterian members dreaded the return of the Stuarts more than they disliked the Hanoverians. There were commercial considerations too. In 1705, the English Parliament had passed the Alien Act, which threatened to impose severe penalties on cross-border trade, whereas the Union gave merchants of both countries free access to each other's markets. The Act of Union also guaranteed the Scottish legal system and the Presbyterian Kirk, though it replaced the two separate parliaments with a new British Parliament based in London.

THE HANOVERIANS

When Anne died in 1714, the succession passed – in accordance with the terms of the Act of Settlement – to a non-English-speaking German, the Elector of Hanover, who became **George I** of England. This prompted the first major **Jacobite uprising** in support of James Edward Stuart, the "Old Pretender" (Pretender in the sense of having pretensions to the throne, Old to distinguish him from his son Charles, the "Young Pretender"). Its timing appeared perfect. Scottish opinion was moving against the Union, which had failed to bring Scotland any tangible economic benefits. Neither were Jacobite sentiments confined to Scotland. There were many in England who toasted the "King across the water" and showed no enthusiasm for the new German ruler. In September 1715, the fiercely Jacobite John Erskine, Earl of Mar, raised the Stuart standard at Braemar Castle. Just eight days later, he captured Perth, where he gathered an army of over 10,000 men, drawn mostly from the Episcopalians of northeast Scotland and from the Highlands. Mar's rebellion took the government by surprise. They had only 4000 soldiers in Scotland, under the command of the Duke of Argyll, but Mar dithered until he lost military advantage. There was an indecisive battle at Sheriffmuir in November, but by the time the Old Pretender arrived the following month, 6000 veteran Dutch troops had reinforced Argyll. The rebellion disintegrated rapidly and James slunk back to exile in France in February 1716.

As power leaked away from the monarchy into the hands of the Whig oligarchy – many Tories having been discredited for suspected

Jacobite sympathies – the king ceased to attend cabinet meetings, his place being taken by his chief minister. Most prominent of these ministers was **Robert Walpole**, regarded as Britain's **first prime minister**, who effectively ruled the country in the period 1721–42. This was a tranquil period politically, with the country standing aloof from foreign affrays, but the financial world was prey to a mania for speculation. Of the numerous fraudulent or ill-conceived financial ventures of this time, the greatest was the fiasco of the **South Sea Company**, which in 1720 sold shares in its monopoly of trade in the Pacific and along the east coast of South America. The "bubble" burst when the shareholders took fright at the extent of their own investments and the value of the shares dropped to nothing, reducing many to penury, and almost wrecking the government, which was saved only by the astute intervention of Walpole.

Peace ended in the reign of **George II**, when in 1739 England declared war on Spain, the prelude to the eight-year War of the Austrian Succession. Then in 1745 the country was invaded by the **Young Pretender**, Charles Edward Stuart (Bonnie Prince Charlie), the Old Pretender's dashing son, in the **Jacobite uprising of 1745**. This second rebellion had little chance of success: the Hanoverians had consolidated their hold on the English throne, Lowland society was uniformly loyalist, and even among the Highlanders Charles only attracted just over half of the 20,000 clansmen who could have marched with him. Nevertheless, after a decisive victory over government forces at Prestonpans, Charles made a spectacular advance into England, getting as far as Derby. London was in a state of panic: its shops were closed and the Bank of England, fearing a run on sterling, slowed withdrawals by paying out in sixpences. But Derby was as far south as Charles got. On December 6, threatened by superior forces, the Jacobites decided to retreat to Scotland.

The Duke of Cumberland was sent in pursuit and the two armies met on **Culloden Moor**, near Inverness, in April 1746. Outnumbered and out-gunned, the Jacobites were swept from the field, losing over 1200 men compared to Cumberland's 300 plus. After the battle, many of the wounded Jacobites were slaughtered, an atrocity that earned Cumberland the nickname

"Butcher". Jacobite hopes died at Culloden and the prince lived out the rest of his life in drunken exile. In the aftermath of the uprising, the wearing of tartan, the bearing of arms and the playing of bagpipes were all banned. Rebel chiefs lost their land and the Highlands were placed under military occupation. Most significantly, the government prohibited the private armies of the chiefs, thereby effectively destroying the clan system.

Meanwhile, the **Seven Years' War** brought yet more overseas territory, as English armies wrested control of India and Canada from France, then in 1768 **Captain James Cook** departed from Plymouth on his voyage to New Zealand and Australia, further widening the scope of the colonial empire.

In 1760, George II had been succeeded by **George III**, the first native English Hanoverian. The early years of his sixty-year reign saw a revived struggle between king and Parliament, enlivened by the intervention of John Wilkes, first of a long and increasingly vociferous line of parliamentary radicals. The contest was exacerbated by the deteriorating relationship with the thirteen colonies of North America, a situation brought to a head by the American **Declaration of Independence** and Britain's defeat in the Revolutionary War. Chastened by this disaster, Britain chose not to interfere in the momentous events taking place across the Channel, where France, its most consistent foe in the eighteenth century, was convulsed by revolution. Out of the turmoil emerged the country's most daunting enemy yet, Napoleon, whose progress was interrupted by Nelson at Trafalgar in 1805, and finally stopped ten years later by the Duke of Wellington at Waterloo.

THE INDUSTRIAL REVOLUTION

Britain's triumph was largely due to its financial strength, itself largely due to the gradual switch from an agricultural to a manufacturing economy, a process generally referred to as the **Industrial Revolution**. The earliest mechanized production lines were constructed in the Lancashire cotton mills, where cotton-spinning was transformed from a cottage industry into a highly productive factory-based system. Water power became a thing of the past after James Watt patented his **steam engine** in 1781, and the utilization of coal as an engine fuel made it convenient to locate mills and factories near coal mines, a tendency that was accelerated as **ironworkers** took up coal as a smelting fuel, vastly increasing the output from their furnaces. Accordingly there was a shift of population towards the Midlands and north of England, where the great coal reserves were located, resulting in the rapid growth of the industrial towns and the expansion of Liverpool as a commercial port, importing raw materials from India and the Americas and exporting manufactured goods. Commerce and industry were served by steadily improving transport facilities, such as the building of a network of **canals** in the wake of the success of the Bridgewater Canal in 1765, which linked coal mines at Worsley with Manchester and the River Mersey. But the great leap forward occurred with the arrival of the **railway** age, heralded by the opening of the Liverpool– Manchester line in 1830, with power provided by George Stephenson's *Rocket*.

Boosted by influxes of Jewish, Irish, French and Dutch immigrants, many of whom intro-

duced new manufacturing techniques, the country's population rose from about seven and a half million at the beginning of George III's reign to more than fourteen million at its end, an increase whose major cause was the slowing-down of the death rate owing to improvements in medical science. But while factories and their attendant towns expanded, the rural settlements of England suffered, inspiring the elegiac pastoral yearnings of Samuel Taylor Coleridge and William Wordsworth, the first great names of the **Romantic** movement in English literature. Later Romantic poets such as Percy Bysshe Shelley and Lord Byron took a more socially engaged stance, inveighing against social injustices that were aggravated by the expenses of the Napoleonic Wars and by its aftermath, when many returning soldiers found their jobs had been taken by machines. Discontent emerged in demands for parliamentary reform, and in 1819 demonstrators in Manchester – centre of the cotton industry and most impor-

THE HIGHLAND CLEARANCES

Once the clan chief was forbidden his own army, he had no need of the large tenantry that had previously been a vital military asset. Conversely, the second half of the eighteenth century saw the Highland population double after the introduction of the easy-to-grow and nutritious **potato**. The clan chiefs adopted different policies to deal with the new situation. Some encouraged emigration, and as many as six thousand Highlanders left for the Americas between 1800 and 1803 alone. Other landowners developed alternative forms of employment for their tenantry, mainly fishing and kelping. **Kelp** (brown seaweed) was gathered and burnt to produce soda ash, which was used in the manufacture of soap, glass and explosives. Other landowners developed **sheep runs** on the Highland pastures, introducing hardy breeds like the black-faced Linton and the Cheviot. But extensive sheep farming proved incompatible with a high peasant population, and many landowners decided to clear their estates of tenants, some of whom were forcibly moved to tiny plots of marginal land, where they were to farm as **crofters**.

The pace of the **Highland Clearances** accelerated after the end of the Napoleonic Wars in 1815, when the market price for kelp, fish and cattle declined, leaving sheep as the only profitable Highland product. As the dispossessed

Highlanders scratched a living from the acid soils of some tiny croft, they learnt through bitter experience the limitations of the clan. Famine followed, forcing large-scale emigration to America and Canada and leaving the huge uninhabited areas found in the region today. The crofters eked out a precarious existence, but they hung on throughout the nineteenth century, often by taking seasonal employment away from home.

In the 1880s, however, a sharp downturn in agricultural prices made it difficult for many crofters to pay their rent. This time, inspired by the example of the Irish Land League, they resisted eviction, forming the **Highland Land Reform Association** and the **Crofters' Party**. In 1886, in response to the social unrest, Gladstone's Liberal government passed the **Crofters' Holdings Act**, which conceded three of the crofters' demands: security of tenure, fair rents to be decided independently, and the right to pass on crofts by inheritance. But Gladstone did not attempt to increase the amount of land available for crofting and shortage of land remained a major problem until the **Land Settlement Act** of 1919 made provision for the creation of new crofts. Nevertheless, the population of the Highlands has continued to decline during the twentieth century, with many of the region's young people finding city life more appealing.

tant of the industrial boom towns still unrepresented in Parliament – were mown down by troops in what became known as the **Peterloo Massacre**.

The following year George III, by now weak, old, blind and insane, died and was succeeded by his son **George IV**. During his reign religious toleration became a reality, as Catholics and Nonconformists were permitted to enter parliament, workers' associations were legalized, and a civilian police force was created, largely the work of **Robert Peel**, a reforming Tory who outlined the basic ideology of modern Conservatism. More far-reaching changes came under **William IV**, with the passing of the **Reform Act** of 1832, whereby the principle of popular representation was acknowledged (though most adult males still had no vote); two years later, the revised **Poor Law** alleviated the condition of the destitute. Significant sections of the middle classes wanted far swifter democratic reform, as was expressed in public indignation over the **Tolpuddle Martyrs** – the Dorset labourers transported to Australia in 1834 for joining an agricultural trade union – and support for **Chartism**, a working-class movement demanding universal male suffrage. Poverty and injustice were the dominant theme of the novels of **Charles Dickens** (1812–70) and the preoccupation of the paternalistic reform movements that were a feature of the nineteenth century. This social concern had been anticipated in the previous century by the Methodism of John Wesley (1703–91) and the anti-slavery campaign promoted by evangelical Christians such as the Quakers and William Wilberforce. As a result of their efforts, slavery was banned in Britain in 1772 and throughout the colonies in 1833 – putting an end to what had been a major factor in the prosperity of ports such as Bristol and Liverpool.

THE VICTORIAN AGE

In 1837 William IV was succeeded by his niece **Victoria**, who, living through a period in which Britain's international standing reached unprecedented heights, came to be as much a national icon as Elizabeth I had been. Though the intellectual achievements of the Victorian age were immense – as typified by the publication of Charles Darwin's *The Origin of Species* in 1859 – the country saw itself primarily as an imperial power founded on industrial and commercial prowess, its spirit perhaps best embodied by the great engineering feats of Isambard Kingdom Brunel and by the **Great Exhibition** of 1851, a display of manufacturing achievements from all over the world.

With trade at the forefront of the agenda, much of the political debate during this period crystallized into a conflict between the **Free Traders** – represented by an alliance of the Peelites and the Whigs, forming the Liberal Party – and the **Protectionists** under Bentinck and **Disraeli**, guiding light of the Tories. During the last third of the century, Parliament was dominated by the duel between Disraeli and the Liberal leader **Gladstone**. Although it was Disraeli who eventually passed the Second Reform Bill in 1867, further extending the electoral franchise, it was Gladstone who had first proposed it, and it was Gladstone's first ministry of 1868–74 that passed some of the century's most far-reaching legislation, including compulsory education, the full legalization of trade unions and an Irish Land Act.

In 1854 troops were sent to protect the Turkish empire against the Russians in the **Crimea**, an inglorious debacle whose horrors were relayed to the public by the first ever press coverage of a military campaign and by the shocking revelations of Florence Nightingale. The fragility of Britain's empire was further exposed by the Indian Mutiny of 1857, though the country's prestige was not sufficiently dented to prevent Victoria from taking the title Empress of India after 1876. Apart from the Chinese Opium War of 1839–42 and some colonial skirmishes in Asia and Africa, the only other serious conflict to occur in Victoria's reign was the **Boer War** against the Dutch settlers in South Africa (1899–1902), another mishandled affair leading to the establishment of self-government there in 1906 and a military shake-up at home that was to be of significance in the coming European war.

FROM WORLD WAR I TO WORLD WAR II

Victoria died in the first month of 1901, to be succeeded by her son, **Edward VII**, whose leisurely and dissolute life could be seen as the epitome of the complacent era to which he gave his name. The Edwardian era came to an end on August 4, 1914, when the Liberal government, honouring the Entente Cordiale signed with

France in 1904, declared war on Germany. World War I was a futile massacre which destroyed millions of lives and eradicated whatever remained of the majority's respect for the ruling classes, whose officers had treated their conscripts as mere cannon fodder.

At the war's end in 1918 the social fabric of the country was changed drastically as the **voting** franchise was extended to all men aged 21 or over and to women of thirty or over, subject to certain residential or business qualifications. This tardy liberalization of women's rights – largely due to the radical **Suffragettes** led by Emmeline Pankhurst and her daughters Sylvia and Christabel – was not completed until 1929, a year after Emmeline's death, when women were at last granted the vote at 21, on equal terms with men.

At around this time the progressive wing of British politics, formerly occupied by the Liberal Party, was taken over by the **Labour Party**, the fruit of an alliance between trade-union interests and middle-class radicals. Labour formed its first government in 1923 under Ramsay MacDonald, but following the publication of the **Zinoviev Letter**, a forged document that seemed to prove Soviet encouragement of British socialist subversion, the Conservatives were returned with a large majority. In 1926, the tensions which had been building up since the end of the war, produced by severe decline in manufacturing and attendant escalating unemployment, erupted with the **General Strike**. Spreading instantly from the coal mines to the railways, the newspapers and the iron and steel industries, the strike lasted nine days and involved half a million workers, provoking the government into draconian action – the army was called in, and the strikers were forced to surrender. The economic situation deteriorated even further after the crash of the New York Stock Exchange in 1929, with unemployment reaching over 2.8 million in 1931, generating a series of mass demonstrations that reached a peak with the **Jarrow March** of 1936. The same year, economist John Maynard Keynes argued in his *General Theory of Employment, Interest and Money* for a greater degree of state intervention in the management of the economy, though the whole question was soon overshadowed by international events.

Abroad, the structure of the British Empire had undergone profound changes since World War I. The status of Ireland had been partly resolved after the electoral gains of the nationalist Sinn Fein in 1918 led to the establishment of the Irish Free State in 1922, from which the six counties of the mainly Protestant North "contracted out". Four years later, the **Imperial Conference** recognized the autonomy of the British dominions, an agreement formalized in the 1931 Statute of Westminster, whereby each dominion was given an equal footing in a Commonwealth of Nations, though each still recognized the British monarch. The royal family itself was shaken in 1936 by the **abdication of Edward VIII**, following his decision to marry a twice-divorced American, Wallis Simpson. Although the succession passed smoothly to his brother **George VI**, the scandal further reduced the standing of the royals, a process which has gathered pace in recent years.

Non-intervention in the Spanish Civil War and the Sino-Japanese War was paralleled by a policy of appeasement towards **Adolf Hitler**, who had massively rearmed Germany in pursuit of his territorial ambitions. In 1938 Prime Minister Neville Chamberlain returned from meeting Hitler and Mussolini at Munich with an assurance of good intentions from the two fascist leaders, and when **World War II** broke out in September 1939, Britain was still seriously unprepared. In May 1940 the discredited Chamberlain stepped down in favour of a national coalition government headed by the charismatic **Winston Churchill**, whose bulldog persistence and heroic speeches provided the inspiration needed in the backs-against-the-wall mood of the time. Partly through Churchill's manoeuvrings, the United States became a supplier of food stuffs and munitions to Britain. Given that the US had broken trade links with Japan in June (in protest at their attacks on China), this factor may have precipitated the Japanese bombing of Pearl Harbor on December 7, 1941 and thus the US's entry into the war as a combatant. This, combined with the heroic resistance of the Russian Red Army, swung the balance.

In terms of the number of casualties it caused, World War II was not as calamitous as the Great War (as World War I is often known), but its impact upon the civilian population was even more terrible. In its first wave of bombing, the Luftwaffe caused massive damage to industrial and supply centres such as London,

Coventry, Manchester, Liverpool, Southampton and Plymouth; in later raids, intended to shatter morale rather than factories and docks, the cathedral cities of Canterbury, Exeter, Bath, Norwich and York were targeted. At the end of the fighting, nearly one in three of all the houses in the nation had been destroyed or damaged, nearly a quarter of a million members of the British armed forces had lost their lives and over 58,000 civilians were dead.

POSTWAR BRITAIN

The end of the war in 1945 was quickly followed by a general election. Hungry for change, the electorate displaced Churchill in favour of the Labour Party under **Clement Attlee**, who, with a large parliamentary majority, set about a radical programme to **nationalize** the coal, gas, electricity, iron and steel industries, as well as the inland transport services. Building on the plans for a social security system presented in Sir William Beveridge's report of 1943, the **National Insurance Act** and the National **Health Service Act** were both passed early in the Labour administration, giving birth to what became known as the **welfare state**. But despite substantial American aid, the huge problems of rebuilding the economy made austerity the keynote, with the rationing of food and fuel remaining in force long after they had ended in most other European countries.

In April 1949 Britain, the United States, Canada, France and the Benelux countries signed the **North Atlantic Treaty** as a counterbalance to Soviet power in eastern Europe, defining the country's postwar international commitments. Yet confusion regarding Britain's post-imperial role was shown up by the Suez Crisis of 1956, when Anglo-French forces invaded Egypt, only to be hastily recalled following international condemnation. Revealing severe limitations on the country's capacity for independent action, the Suez incident resulted in the resignation of Conservative prime minister Anthony Eden and his replacement by the more pragmatic **Harold Macmillan**. Nonetheless, Macmillan maintained a nuclear policy that suggested a continued desire for an international role, and nuclear testing went on against a background of widespread marches under the auspices of the pacifist Campaign for Nuclear Disarmament.

The 1960s, dominated by the Labour premiership of **Harold Wilson**, saw a revival of consumer spending and a corresponding cultural upswing, with London becoming the hippest city on the planet. The good times lasted barely a decade. Though Tory prime minister Edward Heath led Britain into the brave new world of the European Economic Community, the 1970s were a decade of recession and industrial strife. A succession of public-sector strikes and mistimed decisions by James Callaghan's Labour government handed the 1979 general election to **Margaret Thatcher**, who four years earlier had ousted Heath to become the first woman to lead a major political party in Britain.

Thatcher went on to win three general elections, steering the country into a period of ever-greater social polarization. While taxation policies and easy credit fuelled a consumer boom for the professional classes, the erosion of manufacturing industry and the weakening of the welfare state created a calamitous number of people trapped in long-term impoverished unemployment. Despite the intense dislike of her regime among a substantial portion of the population, Thatcher won an increased majority in the 1983 election, partly because of the successful outcome of the 1981 war to regain control of the **Falkland Islands**, partly owing to the fragmentation of the Labour opposition, from which the short-lived Social Democratic Party had split in panic at what it perceived as the radicalization of the party. Social tensions surfaced in sporadic urban rioting and the year-long miners' strike against pit closures (1984–85), an industrial dispute in which the police were given unprecedented powers to restrict the movement of citizens, while the media perpetrated some immensely misleading coverage of events. The violence in Northern Ireland also intensified, and the bombing campaign of the IRA came close to killing the entire Cabinet when it blew up the Brighton hotel in which the Conservatives were staying for their 1984 annual conference.

The divisive politics of Thatcherism reached their apogee with the introduction of the Poll Tax, a lunatic scheme that led ultimately to Thatcher's overthrow by colleagues who feared annihilation should she lead them into another general election. The uninspiring new Tory leader, **John Major**, won the Conservatives a fourth term of office in 1992, albeit with a much-reduced majority in Parliament. While his government presided over a steady growth in economic performance, they gained little credit amid allegations of mismanagement, feckless leadership and what became known as "sleaze" among Conservative MPs, with revelations of extra-marital affairs, cover-ups and financial deceit seized upon with glee by an increasingly cynical British press. Major's unaggressive style was frequently called into question, not least among his own party, among whom vocal right-wing **Euro-sceptics** called for Britain to disassociate itself from the planned integration of the economies of the European Union and the introduction of a Europe-wide currency, the euro.

The government's noncommittal "wait-and-see" policy towards monetary union impressed neither its critics at home nor Britain's European partners, relations with whom plummeted further when it was revealed that a brain-wasting disease in cattle (bovine spongiform encephalopathy – **BSE** – or "mad cow disease") was widespread in British beef. Concerned about the threat of the disease spreading to humans as well as cows, the EU slapped a crippling export ban on British beef, domestic sales of meat plunged (briefly), a programme of slaughter was introduced and amid the hysteria and confusion the government was, yet again, roundly blamed.

Sharing the malaise of the Conservative gov-

SCOTTISH AND WELSH NATIONALISM

In September 1997, the people of Scotland and Wales voted in favour of **devolution** from a centralized British government. The referendum in which they voted was the first Bill to be passed by the new Labour government, led by Tony Blair, which had achieved a landslide victory in the British general election just four months earlier. During its election campaign, Labour had made much of its promise to implement a referendum on devolution and, with nationalist feeling riding high beyond the English borders, this was a smart move: the Conservative Party, which had opposed all talk of devolution during its eighteen years in power, failed to hold a single seat in either Scotland or Wales.

Nationalist aspirations in these two Celtic countries, which have a long history of conflict with England, have taken on a more political expression in the twentieth century. The oldest of the nationalist political parties, **Plaid Genedlaethol Cymru** (The National Party of Wales), was established in 1925. Initially led by the gifted writer Saunders Lewis, Plaid won over an intellectual majority, but failed to gain the support of the masses, who continued to give the Labour Party their vote. Three years later, the putative **Scottish National Party** (SNP) was founded with a similar literary membership of romantics and idealists, including the poet Hugh McDiarmid.

For many years, neither party made much impact on British politics. Indeed, it was not until the 1960s that either won a seat in the British Parliament, with **Gwynfor Evans** becoming the first Plaid MP in 1966, after winning a Carmarthen by-election, and **Winnie Ewing** securing Hamilton for the SNP the following year. Support for the two parties began to grow, with increasing local-government representation and the odd Westminster seat, and the two main political parties – Labour and Conservative – watched nervously as their vote was eroded in Wales and in Scotland. Both the Conservatives and Labour began to fashion policies for limited devolution in an attempt to stave off the new nationalist threat, but the Conservatives shelved their plans after winning the 1970 election – the nationalists had secured too small a share of the vote to pose a serious threat. Meanwhile, the Labour Party continued to encourage devolution, hoping that limited self-government would be enough for the Scots and the Welsh.

Devolution is, of course, something of a compromise between nationalist idealism and the desire to maintain the status quo. The devolution on offer in Labour's 1997 referendum remains firmly rooted within the wider British constitution: total separation has never been on offer. **Scotland**, which has retained a separate legal and educational system since its union with England in 1707, now has the power to levy its own taxes. **Wales**, on the other hand, which has been more closely ruled from Westminster during its seven-hundred-year membership of Britain, was not offered such financial independence and it seems unlikely that the Referendum Bill will lead to any radical changes there. The devolution referendum took place at a time when the mood for greater local government was ripe within the wider European context, and the British government may well find both Scotland and Wales moving towards a far bigger say in their own affairs. Devolution has certainly engendered a feeling of optimism and excitement in both countries.

ernment in the early 1990s was the **Royal Family**, whose credibility cracked with the break-up of the marriages of Charles and Diana and Andrew and Fergie, along with a growing sense that the monarchy had become an anachronistic institution incapable of relating effectively with its subjects. **Diana**, who formally divorced from Charles in 1996, was championed as an example of the humanity and glamour lacking in the other royals, and her death in a car accident in Paris in the summer of 1997 had a profound impact on the entire British population, who joined in spontaneous mourning unprecedented in recent British history. The reaction to her death, as much as her death itself, marked a watershed in the royal family's relationship with both the public and the media.

The Labour Party, itself in disarray through the 1980s, began to regroup under a dynamic young leader, **Tony Blair**, who persuaded the party to distance itself from traditional left-wing socialism and take on a mantle of idealistic, media-friendly populism. The transformation worked to devastating effect, sweeping Blair to power in the general election of May 1997 on a surge of optimism which was immediately reflected in enhanced relations with Europe, progress in the Irish peace talks and even – most unexpected of all – success for British teams in the sporting arena. Blair's electoral touch was repeated in

Labour-sponsored votes in both Scotland and Wales in favour of a devolved regional government (see box opposite).

These changes, along with significant democratizing reform of the **House of Lords**, an institution much derided for its entrenched conservatism and fustiness, have undoubtedly set the tone for a period of re-evaluation and modernism in British affairs. Blair's government still enjoys unprecedented popularity, despite vociferous complaint from certain countryside factions, who formed the amorphous "**Countryside Alliance**" and in 1998 donned their Wellington boots to march through central London. This was a result of discontent about country issues being dictated from Westminster – particularly the proposed ban on fox-hunting – and a feeling that the government wasn't giving sufficiently strong support to beleaguered beef farmers. On the other side of the political spectrum, many find the government's hardline approach to refugees and asylum seekers distasteful, and fear that "New Labour" has abandoned principle and is swayed too strongly by media opinion and American-style focus groups. But, in the words of Labour's election anthem, "things can only get better." For many Britons, after years of dissatisfaction with the increasing disarray that characterized Conservative rule, they already have.

BOOKS

Most of the books listed below are in print and in paperback – those that are out of print (o/p) should be easy to track down in secondhand book shops. Publishers are detailed with the British publisher first, separated by an oblique slash from the US publisher, where both exist. Where books are published in only one of these countries, UK or US precedes the publisher's name; where the book is published by the same company in both countries, the name of the company appears just once.

As regards the wealth of Britain's fiction and poetry, the selection below is intended as a very general guide but is, by its nature, partial and partisan.

TRAVEL AND JOURNALS

Bill Bryson, *Notes from a Small Island* (Doubleday). Bryson's best-selling and highly amusing account of his farewell journey round Britain.

Giraldus Cambrensis, *The Journey through Wales* and *The Description of Wales* (Penguin Classics). Two witty and frank books in one volume, written in Latin by the quarter-Welsh clergyman after his 1188 tour around Wales recruiting for the third Crusade with Archbishop Baldwin of Canterbury.

David Craig, *On the Crofter's Trail* (UK Jonathan Cape). Using anecdotes and interviews with descendants, Craig conveys the hardship and tragedy of the Highland Clearances without being mawkish.

Nick Danzinger *Danzinger's Britain* (UK Flamingo). A well-timed journey through the "other Britain" of council estates and poverty which captures the mood of post-Thatcherite Britain.

Daniel Defoe, *Tour through the Whole Island of Great Britain* (Penguin). Defoe, the son of a

Stoke Newington butcher, was a novelist, pamphleteer, journalist and sometime spy. This classic travelogue opens a fascinating window onto Britain in the 1720s.

Charles Jennings, *Up North* (Little, Brown). A provocative, but very readable account of a journey round the north of England, by a self-confessed southerner.

Jan Morris, *The Matter of Wales* (Penguin). Prolific half-Welsh travel writer Jan Morris immerses herself in the country that she evidently loves. Highly partisan and fiercely nationalistic, the book combs over the origins of the Welsh character and describes the people and places of Wales with precision and affection. A magnificent introduction to a diverse, and occasionally perverse, nation.

Samuel Pepys, *The Diary of Samuel Pepys* (HarperCollins/University of California); *The Illustrated Pepys* (Unwin/University of California). Pepys kept a voluminous diary from 1660 until 1669, recording the fall of the Commonwealth, the Restoration, the Great Plague and the Great Fire, as well as describing the daily life of the nation's capital. The unabridged version is published in eleven weighty tomes; Penguin has published an abridged version; Unwin's is made up of just the choicest extracts.

J.B. Priestley, *English Journey* (Mandarin/University of Chicago Press). Account of Bradford-born author's travels around England in the 1930s.

Dorothy Wordsworth, *Journals* (Oxford University Press). The engaging diaries of William's sister, with whom he shared Dove Cottage in the Lake District, provide a vivid account of walks and visits and reflect Dorothy's fascination with the natural world.

HISTORY, SOCIETY AND POLITICS

Venerable Bede, *Ecclesiastical History of the English People* (Penguin). First ever English history, written in seventh-century Northumbria.

Asa Briggs, *Social History of England* (Weidenfeld & Nicolson/Trafalgar Square). Immensely accessible overview of English life from Roman times to the 1980s.

Vera Brittain, *Testament of Youth* (Virago/Viking Penguin). Vera Brittain was an exemplar of a golden generation – young, gifted and idealistic – whose lives were shattered by the Great War. She lost her fiancé, brother and two close friends to the trenches, and this book stands testament to the dead, to her own pain, and to the burgeoning pacifism which was to shape her brilliant career as an activist and writer.

Alan Clark, *Diaries* (UK Phoenix). Candid and often cutting insight into the heart of Thatcher's government by controversial late minister.

David Daiches (ed), *A Companion to Scottish Culture* (Polygon/Holmes & Meier). More than 300 articles interpreting Scottish culture in its widest sense, from eating to marriage customs, the Scottish Enlightenment to children's street games.

Friedrich Engels, *The Conditions of the Working Class in England* (Penguin/Oxford University Press). Portrait of life in England's hellish industrial towns, written in 1844 when Engels was only 24.

Christopher Hill, *The English Revolution* (Lawrence & Wishart/Beekman Publishers o/p); *The World Turned Upside-Down* (Penguin). Britain's foremost Marxist historian, Hill is without doubt the most interesting writer on the Civil War and Commonwealth period.

Will Hutton, *The State We're In* (UK Vintage). Widely regarded economic and political survey of Major's Britain by the editor of the *Observer*, spoken of as the textbook for Blair's new Labour.

Philip Jenkins, *A History of Modern Wales 1536–1990* (Longman). Magnificently thorough book, placing Welsh history in its British and European contexts. Unbiased and rational appraisal of events and the struggle to preserve Welsh consciousness, with enough detail to make it of valuable academic interest and sufficient good humour to make it easily readable.

J. Graham Jones, *The History of Wales* (University of Wales). A concise, easy-paced overview of Welsh life with a welcome bias towards social history.

Michael Lynch, *Scotland: A New History* (UK Pimlico). Probably the best available overview of Scottish history, going up to 1992 and the bid for a national parliament.

John McLeod, *No Great Mischief If You Fall* (Mainstream/Trafalgar). Gloom and doom on the rape of the Highlands; an enraging, bleak but stimulating book debunking some of the myths upheld by the Highland industry.

George Orwell, *The Road to Wigan Pier*, *Down and Out in Paris and London* (both Penguin). *Wigan Pier* depicts the effects of the Great Depression on the industrial communities of Lancashire and Yorkshire; *Down and Out* is Orwell's tramp's-eye view of the world, written with first-hand experience – the London section is particularly harrowing.

Wynford Vaughan-Thomas, *Wales – a History* (Michael Joseph). One of the country's most missed broadcasters and writers, Vaughan-Thomas's masterpiece is this warm and spirited history of Wales. Working chronologically through from the pre-Celtic dawn to the aftermath of the 1979 devolution vote, the book offers perhaps the clearest explanation of the evolution of Welsh culture, with the author's patriotic slant evident throughout.

Jennifer Westwood, *Albion: A Guide to Legendary Britain* (Grafton/Salem House). Highly readable volume on the development of myth in literature, with a section on Scottish legends.

REGIONAL GUIDES

William Condry, *Snowdonia* (David & Charles). A personal guided tour around the Snowdonia National Park dipping into geology, natural history and industrial heritage. The best detailed approach to the region.

Joe Fisher, *The Glasgow Encyclopedia* (Mainstream/Trafalgar). The essential Glasgow reference book, covering nearly every facet of this complex urban society.

Christopher Hibbert (ed), *Pimlico County History Guides* (UK Pimlico). An informative series giving a detailed history of selected English counties. Currently available are guides to Bedfordshire, Cambridgeshire, Dorset, Lincolnshire, Norfolk, Oxfordshire, Somerset (with Bath and Bristol), Suffolk and Sussex.

Daphne Du Maurier, *Vanishing Cornwall* (Penguin/Doubleday o/p). Good overall account of Cornwall from an author who lived most of her life there.

Pathfinder Guides (UK Jarrold-Ordnance Survey). With more than forty titles covering England, Scotland and Wales, these user-friendly walking guides feature Ordnance Survey maps and clear route details.

Ben Weinreb and Christopher Hibbert, *The London Encyclopaedia* (Papermac/St Martin's Press o/p). More than one thousand pages of concisely presented and well-illustrated information on London past and present – the most fascinating single book on the capital.

ART, ARCHITECTURE AND ARCHEOLOGY

Alan Crawford, *Charles Rennie Mackintosh* (UK Thames & Hudson). Part of the World of Art series, describing the major contribution of Scotland's premier architect.

Samantha Hardingham, *England: A Guide to Recent Architecture* (UK Ellipsis). A handy pocket-sized book detailing the best of England's modern buildings.

Andrew Hayes, *Archaeology of the British Isles* (Batsford/St Martin's Press). Useful introductory history from Stone Age caves to early medieval settlements.

Duncan MacMillan, *Scottish Art 1460–1990* (Mainstream/Trafalgar). Lavish overview of Scottish painting with good sections on landscape, portraiture and the Glasgow Boys.

Nikolaus Pevsner, *The Englishness of English Art* (UK Penguin). Wide-ranging romp through English art concentrating on Hogarth, Reynolds, Blake and Constable, including a section on the Perpendicular style and landscape gardening.

Nikolaus Pevsner and others, *The Buildings of England & Wales* (UK Penguin). Magisterial series, at least one volume per county, covering just about every inhabitable structure in the country. This project was initially a one-man show, but later authors have revised Pevsner's text, inserting newer buildings but generally respecting the founder's personal tone.

FICTION

Peter Ackroyd, *English Music* (UK Penguin). A typical Ackroyd novel, constructing parallels between interwar London and distant epochs to conjure a kaleidoscopic vision of English culture. His other novels, such as *Chatterton*, *Hawksmoor* and *The House of Doctor Dee*, are variations on his preoccupation with the English psyche's darker depths.

Martin Amis, *London Fields* (Penguin/Random House). A gleefully satirical novel which follows its seedy anti-hero, minor crook Keith Talent, through the mean streets of inner-city London. The rusticity suggested by the title is emphatically ironic.

Jane Austen, *Pride and Prejudice*; *Sense and Sensibility*; *Persuasion* (all Penguin). Austen wrote with wit and vigour on manners, society and the pursuit of happiness, never more enjoyably than in *Pride and Prejudice*. Her amusing sense of irony, especially when delineating acquisitive and socially pretentious characters, is never far from the surface.

Iain Banks. An amazingly prolific author, who also writes sci-fi as Iain M. Banks. *The Bridge* (Sphere/HarperCollins) layers fantasy and reality and provides an astonishing psychological insight into a near-death experience; the charming and more accessible *Whit* (UK Abacus) follows a feisty female character who makes an eccentric spiritual and actual journey from her home – a farm housing a Central Scotland cult – to London.

Julian Barnes, *England England* (Picador/Knopf). A satire of the all-pervasive "heritage industry"; a tycoon builds replicas of England's greatest monuments on the Isle of Wight, which gradually come to possess a greater power and importance than the originals.

Arnold Bennett, *Anna of the Five Towns*; *Clayhanger Trilogy* (both Penguin). Bennett's first novel, *Anna*, is the story of a miser's daughter and like the later *Clayhanger* trilogy is set in the Potteries.

R.D. Blackmore, *Lorna Doone* (Penguin/Oxford University Press). Blackmore's swashbuckling, melodramatic romance, set on Exmoor, has done more for West Country tourism than anything else since.

Charlotte Brontë, *Jane Eyre* (Penguin). A wonderful Victorian "progress" story, following Jane from her pinched, unhappy childhood and schooling to her romance with Mr Rochester. The novel features scenes of quintessential Gothic melodrama – the mad woman in the attic wreaking revenge – and also functions as a deep psychological study of emotional repression.

Emily Brontë, *Wuthering Heights* (Penguin). One of the best, and strangest, novels in the English language. Often falsely claimed as a romance, it is more accurately a work about obsession, and still has the power to disturb. The complex intertwining of the narrative voices in the novel is just one aspect of its genius.

George Mackay Brown, *Beside the Ocean of Time* (John Murray). A child's journey through the history of an Orkney island, and an adult's effort to make sense of the place's secrets in the late twentieth century.

John Buchan, *The Complete Richard Hannay* (Penguin/Godine). This one volume includes *The 39 Steps, Greenmantle, Mr Standfast, The Three Hostages* and *The Island of Sheep.* Good gung-ho stories with a great feel for Scottish landscape.

Bruce Chatwin, *On the Black Hill* (Picador). Best known for his travel writing, Bruce Chatwin's talent proved a little too slender for the scope of this subject matter: the sweeping narrative follows the Jones twins' eighty-year tenure of a farm on the Radnorshire border with England. Provides a gentle angle on Welsh–English antipathy.

Joseph Conrad, *The Secret Agent* (Penguin). Spy story based on the 1906 Anarchist bombing of Greenwich Observatory, exposing the hypocrisies of both the police and Anarchists.

Charles Dickens, *Bleak House; David Copperfield; Little Dorrit; Oliver Twist; Hard Times* (all Penguin). Many of Dickens's novels are located in London, including *Bleak House, Oliver Twist* and *Little Dorrit*, and contain some of his most trenchant passages of social analysis; *Hard Times* is set in a Lancashire mill town; while *David Copperfield* draws on Dickens's own unhappy experiences as a boy, with much of the action taking place in Kent and Norfolk.

George Eliot, *Scenes of Clerical Life; Middlemarch* (both Penguin); *Mill on the Floss* (Penguin/Oxford University Press). Eliot (real name Mary Ann Evans) wrote mostly about the county of her birth, Warwickshire, the setting for the three tales from her fictional début, *Scenes of Clerical Life. Middlemarch* is a gargantuan portrayal of English provincial life prior to the Reform Act of 1832, while *The Mill on the Floss* is based on her own childhood experiences.

Henry Fielding, *Tom Jones* (Penguin). Mock-epic comic novel detailing the exploits of its lusty orphan hero, set in Somerset and London.

E.M. Forster, *Howard's End* (Penguin/NAL-Dutton). Bourgeois angst in Hertfordshire and Shropshire; this is the best book by one of the country's most affectionately regarded modern novelists.

John Fowles, *The Collector* (Pan/Dell); *The French Lieutenant's Woman; Daniel Martin* (both Pan/NAL-Dutton). *The Collector*, Fowles's first, is a psychological thriller in which the heroine is kidnapped by a psychotic pools-winner, the story told once by each character. *The*

French Lieutenant's Woman, set in Lyme Regis on the Dorset coast, is a tricksy neo-Victorian novel with a famous DIY ending. *Daniel Martin*, a dense, realistic novel, is set in postwar Britain.

Elizabeth Gaskell, *Sylvia's Lovers; Mary Barton* (both Penguin). *Sylvia's Lovers* is set in a Whitby (Monkshaven in the novel) beset by press gangs, while *Mary Barton* takes place in Manchester and has strong Chartist undertones.

Lewis Grassic Gibbon, *A Scots Quair* (Penguin/Schocken o/p). A landmark trilogy, set in northeast Scotland during and after World War I, the events are seen through the eyes of Chris Guthrie, "torn between her love for the land and her desire to escape a peasant culture". Strong, seminal work.

William Golding, *The Spire* (Faber/Harcourt Brace). An atmospheric novel centred on the building of a cathedral spire, taking place in a thinly disguised medieval Salisbury.

Robert Graves, *Goodbye to All That* (Penguin/Hippocrene Books o/p). Horrific and humorous memoirs of public school and World War I trenches, followed by postwar trauma and life in Wales, Oxford and Egypt.

Alasdair Gray, *Lanark* (Canongate/Braziller o/p). Gray's extraordinary first novel is a postmodern blend of social realism and labyrinthine fantasy featuring his own allegorical illustrations; it takes invention and comprehension to their limits.

Graham Greene, *Brighton Rock* (Penguin); *The Human Factor* (Penguin/Pocket Books). Two of the best from the prolific Greene: *Brighton Rock* is an action-packed thriller with heavy Catholic overtones, set in the criminal underworld of a seaside resort; *The Human Factor*, written some forty years later, probes the underworld of London's spies.

Thomas Hardy, *Far from the Madding Crowd; The Mayor of Casterbridge; Tess of the D'Urbervilles; Jude the Obscure* (all Penguin). Hardy's novels contain some famously evocative descriptions of his native Dorset, but at the time of their publication it was Hardy's defiance of conventional pieties that attracted most attention: *Tess*, in which the heroine has a baby out of wedlock and commits murder, shocked his contemporaries, while his bleakest novel, the Oxford-set *Jude the Obscure*, provoked such a violent response that Hardy gave up novel-writing altogether.

Kazuo Ishiguro, *The Remains of the Day* (Faber & Faber/Random House). An intelligent novel, beautifully economical in style. It tells of an ageing butler who comes to realize that the master to whom he has devoted himself has Nazi sympathies; it is also a restrained and poignant love story.

James Kelman, *The Busconductor Hines* (UK Phoenix); *How Late It Was, How Late* (Secker & Warburg/Norton). *The Busconductor Hines* tells the wildly funny story of a young Glasgow bus conductor with an intensely boring job and a limitless imagination. *How Late It Was* is Kelman's award-winning and controversial look at life from the perspective of a blind Glaswegian drunk. A disturbing study of personal and political violence, with language to match.

Rudyard Kipling, *Stalky & Co* (Oxford University Press). Nine stories about a mischievous trio of schoolboys, drawn from Kipling's experiences of public school in Devon.

D.H. Lawrence, *Sons and Lovers*; *The Rainbow*; *Women in Love*; *Lady Chatterley's Lover* (all Penguin); *Selected Short Stories* (Penguin/Dover). Lawrence wrote magnificently on the social and emotional aspirations of the working class in Nottinghamshire's pit villages. His early short stories contain some of his finest writing, as does *Sons and Lovers*, a rich semi-autobiographical novel. One of the first writers of the century to write seriously about sex, he brought intensity, integrity and finely tuned feeling to the subject.

Laurie Lee, *Cider with Rosie* (Penguin). Reminiscences of adolescent bucolic frolics in the Cotswolds during the 1920s.

Richard Llewellyn, *How Green Was My Valley* (Penguin); *Up into the Singing Mountain* (o/p); *Down Where the Moon is Small* (o/p); *Green, Green My Valley Now* (o/p). Vital tetralogy in eloquent and passionate prose, following the life of Huw Morgan from his youth in a South Wales mining valley through emigration to the Welsh community in Patagonia and back to 1970s Wales. A best seller during World War II and still the best introduction to the vast canon of "valleys novels", *How Green was my Valley* captured a longing for a simple if tough life, steering clear of cloying sentimentality.

Sir Thomas Malory, *La Morte d'Arthur* (Penguin/Northwestern University Press). Fifteenth-century tales of King Arthur and the Knights of the Round Table, written while the author was in London's Newgate Prison.

Daphne Du Maurier, *Frenchman's Creek* (Arrow/Bentley); *Jamaica Inn* (Arrow/Avon); *Rebecca* (Arrow/Avon). *Frenchman's Creek* and *Jamaica Inn* are nail-biting, swashbuckling romantic novels set in the author's adopted home of Cornwall; but *Rebecca* – in which an unnamed and anonymous bride narrates in terrified thrall the story of her predecessor, the shadowy "first Mrs de Winter" – is perhaps Du Maurier's best-known novel.

William McIlvanney, *Docherty* (UK Sceptre). Tale of a hard, poverty-wracked Scottish coal-mining community by one of the country's most respected contemporary authors.

Compton Mackenzie, *Whisky Galore* (UK Penguin). Comic novel based on a true story of the wartime wreck of a cargo of whisky on a Hebridean island. Full of predictable stereotypes but still funny.

Timothy Mo, *Sour Sweet* (Paddleless Press). A dense comic novel set in London's Chinatown in the 1960s, which follows the fortunes of the Chen family as they attempt to set up a restaurant, their malevolent rivals posing an increasingly sinister threat.

Thomas De Quincey, *Confessions of an English Opium Eater* (Penguin/Oxford University Press). Tripping out with the most famous literary drug-taker since Coleridge. In fact, the opium visions only come at the end of the book; the rest is a digressive but entertaining account of the author's childhood and later struggles.

Sir Walter Scott, *The Waverley Novels* (Penguin). The books that did much to create the romanticized version of Scottish life and history. Among them is *Rob Roy*, a rich and ripping yarn which transformed the diminutive brigand into a national hero.

Lawrence Sterne, *Tristram Shandy* (Penguin). Anarchic, picaresque eighteenth-century ramblings based on life in a small English village, and full of bizarre textual devices – like an all-black page in mourning for one of the characters.

R.L. Stevenson, *Dr Jekyll and Mr Hyde* (Penguin/Vintage); *Kidnapped* (Penguin/Signet); *The Master of Ballantrae* (Penguin/Oxford University Press); *Weir of Hermiston* (UK Penguin). Superbly imagined and pacily written nineteenth-century tales of intrigue and adventure.

Graham Swift, *Waterland* (Picador/Random House). Postmodern family saga set in East Anglia's fenlands – excellent on the strange history of this superficially drab landscape. *Last Orders* (Picador/Random House) is a bizarre and deceptively simple tale, which follows four men as they take the ashes of their friend, London butcher Jack Dodds, to the sea.

William Makepeace Thackeray, *Vanity Fair* (Penguin). A sceptical but compassionate overview of English capitalist society by one of the leading realists of the mid-nineteenth century.

Dylan Thomas, *Under Milk Wood; Collected Stories* (Dent Everyman). *Under Milk Wood* is Thomas's most popular play, telling the story of a microcosmic Welsh seaside town over a 24-hour period. *Collected Stories* contains all of Thomas' classic prose pieces: *Quite Early One Morning*, which metamorphosed into *Under Milk Wood*, the magical *A Child's Christmas in Wales* and the compulsive, crackling autobiography, *Portrait of the Artist as a Young Dog*.

Anthony Trollope. *The Warden; The Small House at Allington* (both Penguin). Trollope was an astonishingly prolific novelist who also, in his capacity as a postal surveyor, found time to invent the letter box. His best-known book, *The Warden*, tells of a collision of family and moral duties in an English cathedral city, while *The Small House at Allington* is a tender story of a failed love affair.

Evelyn Waugh, *Sword of Honour Trilogy* (Penguin/Knopf); *Brideshead Revisited* (Penguin/Little, Brown). The trilogy is a brilliant satire of the World War I officer class laced with some of Waugh's funniest set-pieces. The best-selling *Brideshead Revisited* is possibly his worst book, rank with snobbery, nostalgia and money-worship.

Irvine Welsh, *Trainspotting; The Acid House* (both UK Minerva); *Marabou Stork Nightmares* (UK Jonathan Cape). Depending on the strength of your stomach, these trawls through the horrors of drug addiction, sexual fantasy, urban decay and hopeless youth will either make you rejoice at an authentic and unapologetic new voice for the dispossessed, or throw up. Thankfully, Welsh's unflinching attention is not without humour.

Virginia Woolf, *Orlando* (Penguin/Harcourt Brace); *Mrs Dalloway* (Flamingo/Harcourt Brace). Woolf's lover, Vita Sackville-West, was the inspiration for *Orlando*, the life of the eponymous protagonist spanning four centuries and both genders. *Mrs Dalloway*, which relates the thoughts of a London society hostess and a shell-shocked war veteran, is a compelling example of her stream of consciousness style.

POETRY

Simon Armitage, *All Points North* (UK Penguin). An engaging and funny poetic travelogue, moving out from Armitage's home town of Marsden in West Yorkshire and taking in Leeds Airport, Huddersfield Town football ground on a Saturday afternoon, amateur dramatics and nights on the town.

W.H. Auden, *Collected Poems* (UK Faber & Faber). Auden combines the themes of history, politics and love in poems which seem likely to be definitive expressions of his times. The politically committed work of the 1930s gives way to a later religious commitment, but all his work is marked by stylistic virtuosity.

Beowulf, Seamus Heaney trans (Faber & Faber/Farrar, Straus & Giroux). A wonderful verse translation of the tenth-century Anglo-Saxon poem, which relates the epic progress of the warrior Beowulf.

John Betjeman, *Collected Poems* (John Murray). Betjeman (1906–1984) was the English poet laureate; his humorous and often nostalgic work was profoundly concerned with England and the English.

George Mackay Brown, *Selected Poems 1954–1983* (UK John Murray). Brown's work is as haunting, beautiful and gritty as the Orkney islands which inspire it.

William Blake, *Complete Poems* (Penguin). Blake ranges from the limpid wisdom of *Songs of Innocence and Experience* to the mystical complexities of the prophetic books. He is unique among major poets in illustrating his own work, most of which is set in, or has a significant relationship to, London.

Robert Browning, *Selected Poems* (Penguin). Browning's poems are marked by intellectual complexity, technical variety and a wide-ranging engagement with the issues of the Victorian age. He also evokes the Italian Renaissance more richly than any other poet in English.

Robert Burns, *Selected Poems* (Penguin). Comprises the best-known work of Scotland's most famous bard, who employed vigorous vernacular language. Immensely popular all over the world, his famous early poems include *Auld Lang Syne* and *My Love Is Like A Red, Red Rose.*

Byron, *Selected Poems* (Penguin). Byron was a best-seller in his day for exotic poems of adventure such as *The Corsair*, and he is also a master of the Romantic lyric, but the core of his achievement lies in his unfailingly inventive and hilarious satire on all aspects of early nineteenth-century life, *Don Juan.*

Charles Causley, *Collected Poems* (UK Papermac). Contemporary Cornish poet Causley is a champion of the ballad tradition, and writes with precision and beauty about the natural world, and about creativity itself.

Geoffrey Chaucer, *Canterbury Tales* (Penguin/Bantam). Fourteenth-century collection of bawdy verse tales which follows a pilgrimage to Becket's shrine at Canterbury; translated into modern English blank verse.

Samuel Taylor Coleridge, *Selected Poems* (Penguin). Coleridge's output is small, but of the highest quality. *Khubla Khan* and *The Rime Of The Ancient Mariner* are amongst the strangest productions of the Romantic period, but equally noteworthy are the quieter "conversation" poems such as *Frost at Midnight.*

John Donne, *The Complete English Poems* (Everyman). Donne (1572–1631), the greatest of the "metaphysical poets", brought passionate physicality and brilliant intellectual rigour to both his love poetry and religious verse.

T.S. Eliot, *The Wasteland and Other Poems* (Faber & Faber/Harcourt Brace). Published in 1922 and considered one of the cornerstones of Modernist writing, *The Wasteland* offers a revolutionary vision of Western civilization; it is imbued with resonant images of contemporary and ancient London.

Thomas Gray, *Thomas Gray* (Everyman/Charles E. Tuttle). Gray is a minor talent who produced one great poem, *Elegy Written in a Country Churchyard*, a powerful meditation on changes in an apparently changeless English countryside.

George Herbert, *The Complete English Poems* (Penguin). A great seventeenth-century devotional poet, whose passionate dialogues with his Maker ring with energy and deep emotion.

A.E. Housman, *A Shropshire Lad* (UK Penguin). Housman's poem is a richly detailed evocation of English pastoralism shot through with a strong, if suppressed, vein of homoeroticism.

Ted Hughes. Soon before he died, Hughes published *Birthday Letters* (Faber & Faber/Farrar, Straus & Giroux), a moving account of his relationship with the poet Sylvia Plath, and his response to her suicide. *New Selected Poems 1957–1994* (UK Faber & Faber) is the most comprehensive collection of Hughes's work available.

Jackie Kay, *The Adoption Papers; Other Lovers* (UK Bloodaxe). Kay's poetry explores being black, Scottish and gay and deals with personal relationships in an accessibly intimate way.

John Keats, *Selected Poems* (Penguin). Keats was potentially one of the greatest writers who ever lived. Even given his early death – he was only 25 – his achievements in poems such as the *Ode to Autumn* are extraordinary.

Philip Larkin, *Collected Poems* (UK Faber & Faber). Larkin used plain language in his work, the subject of which is often the insignificance of human life. Many of the poems achieve an apparently unstudied beauty, though in fact Larkin published very little, preferring to refine his verse to its basic elements.

London Poems on the Underground (UK Ward Lock). The idea of pasting poems in London tube trains was hugely popular, and enlivened many a dull journey. Perhaps paradoxically, the London-related poems were then translated into this eclectic and entertaining anthology.

MacCaig, Morgan, Lochhead, *Three Scottish Poets* (Canongate/Carcanet). A representative selection from the work of three well-known poets. Differing perspectives – natural, metaphysical, urban, political and feminist – reflect the complexity of the modern Scottish experience.

Sorley Maclean (Somhairle Macgill-Eain), *From Wood to Ridge: Collected Poems* (Birlinn Limited-Carcanet Press/Scholarly Book Services). Written in Gaelic, his poems have been translated into bilingual editions all over the world; they deal with the sorrows of poverty, war and love.

Roger McGough, *Blazing Fruit: Selected Poems* (UK Penguin). A contemporary Liverpool poet, whose witty rhetorical verse is instantly recognizable.

Hugh McDiarmid, *Selected Poems* (UK Penguin). McDiarmid was a poet and nationalist who sought, through his fine lyrical verse, to reinvigorate the use of Scottish literary language.

Edwin Muir, *Collected Poems* (UK Faber & Faber). Muir's childhood on Orkney remained with him as a dream of paradise from which he was banished to Glasgow. His poems are passionately concerned with Scotland.

New Golden Treasury of English Verse (Papermac/Trans-Atlantic Publications). Covers 800 years of English poetry, from medieval verse by the ubiquitous "anon" to contemporary wordsmiths. A real treasure trove.

Wilfred Owen, *The Poems of Wilfred Owen* (Chatto & Windus/Norton). As with Keats, Owen's early death was a tragedy for English literature. His war poetry is at its best in *Strange Meeting*, with its strikingly original use of half rhymes.

Alexander Pope, *Selected Poetry* (UK Oxford Paperback)`; *Complete Poetical Works* (US Oxford University Press). Pope is the great poetic figure of the eighteenth century and invests the apparent rigidities of the heroic couplet with a flexibility unequalled by any other poet. His *Dunciad* is a steely satire of bad writing in an evil society, while *The Rape of the Lock* is a triumph of charm and delicate eroticism.

Christina Rossetti, *A Choice of Christina Rossetti's Verse* (Faber & Faber). Like the American Emily Dickinson, Rossetti is an utterly unpredictable original, capable of producing lyric poems of piercing intensity in addition to the uncanny and gripping long work, *Goblin Market*.

William Shakespeare, *Complete Works* (Oxford University Press/Random House). The entire output at a bargain price. For individual plays, you can't beat the *Arden Shakespeare* series (Routledge), each volume containing illuminating notes and good introductory essays on the great bard.

Percy Bysshe Shelley, *Selected Poetry* (Penguin). Shelley's poetry moves from swooning romantic intensity to vigorously expressed hatred of the establishment of his day. He is a seminal figure in the pantheon of English radical dissent.

Stevie Smith, *New Selected Poems of Stevie Smith* (Norton/New Directions). Smith's best-known poem is *Not Waving But Drowning* (1957), which uses the format of the comic poem but is loaded with economically expressed tragedy.

Alfred Tennyson, *Tennyson's Poetry* (Norton). Tennyson's is perhaps the most purely beautiful and musical poetry in English, filled with sensuous detail and dreamy evocations of natural beauty and the past. *In Memoriam* shows him to be the great poet of Victorian doubt and faith.

Dylan Thomas, *Selected Poems* (UK Everyman). Thomas's beautifully wrought and inventive verse carried a deep, pained concern with mortality and the nature of humanity.

R.S. Thomas, *Counterpoint* (Bloodaxe/Dufour Editions). Welsh poet R.S. Thomas takes as his theme the enduring nature of Christianity, juxtaposed with the fleeting superficialities of contemporary culture. His finest poems have a strong visionary element, distilled in wonderfully still language.

William Wordworth, *Selected Poems* (Penguin). It is impossible to exaggerate Wordsworth's originality and his influence on the future direction of English culture; his presence is clearly felt in the novels of Dickens and George Eliot as well as in later poets. His understanding of what it means to be human can only be described as profound.

Benjamin Zephaniah, *City Psalms* (Bloodaxe/Dufour). Born in Jamaica but brought up in Britain, Zephaniah is an accomplished dub-poet, and a great performer of his own work.

FILM

The British film industry is in a healthier state now than perhaps at any point in its history, with increased state support and strong investments by Film Four, Goldcrest, Palace and Polygram. The current scene is diverse and vital: the Brits have cornered the market in impeccable costume dramas; the social realist tradition of the 1960s still finds expression in critical and popular successes such as Brassed Off; and the much-hyped "Cool Britannia" phenomenon is reflected in zeitgeist movies such as Trainspotting, which depict Britain's edgy urban side. Some film fans opine that, while British TV leads the world in terms of quality, its films can lack a certain scope and confidence – that many are essentially small-screen ventures. But within the last ten years a host of British pictures – The Full Monty and Four Weddings and a Funeral are just two examples – have enjoyed great success internationally, a trend which looks set to continue into the second century of cinema.

The films listed below are all set in England, Scotland or Wales. They are not exclusively greats – though some rank amongst the best movies ever made – but all depict a particular aspect of British life, whether reflecting the experience of immigrant communities, exploring the country's history, or depicting its richly varied landscapes.

Akenfield (Peter Hall, 1974). A powerfully involving evocation of English rural life whose ingredients include glowing cinematography and Michael Tippett's wonderful music. Past and present are skilfully contrasted, but the heart of the film lies in its sometimes ecstatic, but also harsh, rendering of the past.

An American Werewolf in London (John Landis, 1981). Two witty American chums cause heads to swivel in a remote Yorkshire pub in this greatly enjoyable gore-fest. They are subsequently attacked by a wolf, the cue for a great transformation-to-werewolf scene and some genuinely terrifying thrills.

Babylon (Franco Rosso, 1980). A moving account of black working-class London life. We follow the experiences of young Blue through a series of encounters which reveal the insidious forces of racism at work in Britain. Good performances and a great reggae soundtrack: an all too rare example of black Britain taking centre stage in British movies.

Bhaji on the Beach (Gurninder Chadha, 1993). An Asian women's group takes a day-trip to Blackpool in this issue-laden but enjoyable picture. A lot of fun is had contrasting the seamier side of British life with the *mores* of the Asian aunties, though the male characters are cartoon villains all.

Billy Liar! (John Schlesinger, 1963). Tom Courtenay is stuck in a dire job as an undertaker's clerk in a northern town, and spends his time creating extravagant fantasies. His life is lit up by the appearance of Julie Christie, who holds out the glamour and promise of swinging London. Touching and amusing.

Brassed Off (Mark Herman, 1996). A pacy film about British working-class life that eschews pathos, opting instead for uncompromising anger, underscored by robust black humour. With the imminent demise of the town's coal pit, the future for the Grimley Colliery Brass Band looks hopeless. Danny (Pete Postlethwaite) valiantly attempts to keep the band alive as the emotional lives of the musicians collapse.

Braveheart (Mel Gibson, 1995). Cod-Highland high camp, with a shaggy-haired Mel Gibson wielding his claymore as thirteenth-century Independence hero William Wallace. The English are (naturally enough) thieving effete scum, the Scots all warm-blooded noble savages, and history takes a firm back seat. The Battle of Stirling Bridge, mysteriously, has no bridge, and Wallace's putative fathering of England's royal line is about as historically convincing as Mel's accent. Despite much Scot-nat posturing, the picture was largely filmed in Ireland.

Breaking the Waves (Lars von Trier, 1996). A lyrical, deeply moving drama set in a devout community in the north of Scotland. An innocent young woman, Bess (Emily Watson), falls in love with Danish oil-rig worker Jan (Stellan Skarsgaard). Blaming herself for the injury which cripples him, she embarks on a masochistic sexual odyssey, which rapidly takes her into dark and uncharted waters.

Brief Encounter (David Lean, 1945). Extramarital attraction at a railway station is the theme of this mysteriously popular "classic". Noel Coward is responsible for the clipped dialogue, Rachmaninov for the weepy score, Trevor Howard keeps his upper lip stiff and Celia Johnson wears an improbable hat.

Brigadoon (Vincent Minnelli, 1954). Gene Kelly escapes brash New York for the Highland glens, discovering love in the agreeable shape of local lass Cyd Charisse in the eponymous mythical village, which appears from the gloaming only once a century. Despite the slightly awkward studio landscapes, this is a delightful escapist fantasy from the master of serious Hollywood musicals, with some great Lerner and Loewe tunes.

Brighton Rock (John Boulting, 1947). A fine adaptation of Graham Greene's novel, featuring a young, genuinely scary Richard Attenborough as the psychopathic hood Pinkie, who marries a witness to one of his crimes to ensure her silence. Beautiful cinematography and good performances, with a real sense of *film noir* menace.

The Brothers (David MacDonald, 1948). Well worth seeking out as an alternative to cosy Highland mythology. Feisty young Mary moves from Glasgow to the intolerant world of a small Western Isles crofting community, exciting understandable interest from the sons of her savagely patriarchal kinsman. Brilliant interweaving of powerful myth and the hard reality of peasant lives, this has an unusual honesty for its time.

A Canterbury Tale (Michael Powell and Emeric Pressburger, 1944). Set in a wartime Kentish village, where a plucky land girl, a small-town GI and a sardonic English sergeant are billeted. Overseen by a mysterious local magistrate, they make their own pilgrimage to Canterbury, the cathedral glowing high over bomb-damaged streets. A mystical vision of English history is fused with bucolic images of rural life, a restrained exploration of the characters' personal suffering underlying a truly magical masterpiece.

Chariots of Fire (Hugh Hudson, 1981). This hugely successful movie prompted writer Colin Welland to bombastically – and optimistically – proclaim, "The British are coming". Based around the 1924 Olympics, it tells the true story of Scottish missionary Eric Liddell (Ian Charleson) and repressed Cambridge student Harold Abrahams (Ben Cross). Oscar-winning and overblown, it is distinguished only by Charleson's quiet performance, and some great locations, such as the sweeping beach at St Andrews.

The Company of Wolves (Neil Jordan, 1984). A reworking of the Little Red Riding Hood tale from a story by Angela Carter. Riding Hood's studio-bound village home is at the centre of a series of stories-within-stories on the many transformations from childhood to adulthood, and the dangers and pleasures awaiting those who stray from the path. A good fairy-tale, mythic England, and some great werewolf special effects.

Comrades (Bill Douglas, 1986). In 1830s England, a group of farm workers decide to stand up to the exploitative tactics of the local landowner, and find themselves prosecuted and transported to Australia. Based on the true story of the Tolpuddle Martyrs, this combines political education (the founding of the modern union movement) with a moving and visually stunning celebration of working lives.

Culloden (Peter Watkins, 1964). The story of the last battle fought on British soil, made in the style of a BBC documentary, with verité battle footage and interviews with Scottish clansmen and the Duke of Cumberland's opposing modern army. Highly atmospheric, its great strength is the account of the catastrophic aftermath, as Cumberland's men embark on a process of ethnic cleansing.

Distant Voices, Still Lives (Terence Davies, 1988). Beautifully realized autobiographical tale of growing up in Forties and Fifties Liverpool, juxtaposing contemporary popular songs with isolated scenes from the life of a family ruled by a brutal patriarch. The mesmeric pace is punctuated by astonishing moments of drama, and the whole is a very moving account of how the family survives and triumphs, in small ways, against the odds.

East is East (Damien O'Donnell 1999). Seventies Salford is the setting for this lively comedy, with a Pakistani chip-shop owner struggling to keep control of his seven children as they rail against the strictures of Islam and arranged marriages. Inventively made, and with some pleasing performances.

The Edge of the World (Michael Powell, 1937). Michael Powell's first feature, based on the life and evacuation of the tiny isolated island of St Kilda. It is full of embryonic Powell magic, combining an account of the hard life of the islanders and the pull of the modern world with a sense of the power of community and poetry of the island world.

Elizabeth (Shekahar Kapur, 1998). Charismatic Cate Blanchett is – thankfully – the still heart of this madly over-blown production, where all political and emotional nuance is lost in an orgy of decapitations, swirling cloaks and stagy thunderstorms. Features a host of plodding cameos with, most bizarrely, footballing heart-throb Eric Cantona as the French ambassador.

Far From the Madding Crowd (John Schlesinger, 1967). A largely successful and imaginative adaptation of Hardy's doom-laden tale of the desires and ambitions of wilful Bathsheba Everdene. Julie Christie is a radiant and spirited Bathsheba, Terence Stamp flashes his blade to dynamic effect, Alan Bates is quietly charismatic as dependable Gabriel Oak, and the West Country setting is sparsely beautiful.

Fires Were Started (Humphrey Jennings, 1943). One of the best films to come out of the prewar documentary tradition in Britain, this is the story of the experiences of a group of firemen through one night of bombing during the Blitz. The use of real firemen as performers rather than professional actors, and the avoidance of formulaic heroics, gives the film great power as an account of the courage of the ordinary people who fought, often uncelebrated, on the home front.

Frenzy (Alfred Hitchcock, 1972). Hitchcock comes back to Blighty in top form, with the story of a man on the run, under suspicion for the vicious "neck tie" murders carried out in Covent Garden. Trademark sly black humour combines with a disturbing exploration of sexual immaturity.

The Full Monty (Peter Cattaneo, 1997). Six Sheffield ex-steel workers throw caution to the wind and become male strippers, their boast being that all will be revealed: the "full monty". Unpromising physical specimens all, they score an unlikely hit with the local lassies. The film was itself an unlikely hit worldwide: the theme of manhood in crisis is sensitively explored, and the long-awaited striptease is a joy to behold.

Get Carter (Mike Hodges, 1971). Although not the masterpiece some claim, this is still one of the most vivid and interesting British gangster movies, featuring a monumentally evil outing for Michael Caine as the eponymous villain, returning to his native Newcastle to avenge his brother's death. Great use of its Newcastle locations and a fine turn by playwright John Osborne as the local godfather don't quite, however, compensate for its now faintly ridiculous misogyny.

Gregory's Girl (Bill Forsyth, 1981). John Gordon Sinclair is engaging and gangly as Gregory, whose adolescent dreams are filled with football-playing schoolgirl siren Dorothy. Gregory's gauche attempts to woo her keep the gentle plot tripping along nicely, his teachers making sardonic asides and his little sister proffering grave advice.

Hedd Wyn (Paul Turner, 1992). Sentimental and epic Welsh-language feature about World War I poet Ellis Evans, who was mortally wounded on the first day of the Battle of Passchendale.

Henry V (Laurence Olivier, 1944). Featuring glowing Technicolor backdrops, this wonderful piece of wartime propaganda is emphatically "theatrical", the action spiralling out from the Globe Theatre itself. Olivier is a brilliantly charismatic king, the pre-battle scene where he goes disguised amongst his men being delicately muted and atmospheric.

Hope and Glory (John Boorman, 1987). A glorious autobiographical feature about the Blitz seen through the eyes of nine-year-old Bill, who revels in the liberating chaos of bomb-site playgrounds, tumbling barrage balloons and shrapnel collections. His older sister's unfettered romps with a Canadian soldier and the adults' privation and occasional despair are an additional source of amusement for Bill and his tiny sister. Sentimental in the best sense, and deliciously nostalgic.

Howards End (James Ivory, 1991). E.M. Forster's tale of the forward-thinking Schlegel sisters, and their relationship with the conventional, domineering Wilcoxes. One of many immaculate British costume dramas, with precise performances from Vanessa Redgrave, Helena Bonham Carter and, most notably, Emma Thompson as Margaret Schlegel.

I Know Where I'm Going (Michael Powell and Emeric Pressburger, 1945). Utterly charming fantasy following headstrong Wendy Hiller as she travels to the wilds of west-coast Scotland to wed the ageing tenant of an island castle. Waylaid on the mainland by predictably inclement weather, she begins to fall for Roger Livesey's authentic local laird, and under the spell of the wild landscape and its myths.

If... (Lindsay Anderson, 1968). The stifling world of the English public school as a rather inadequate microcosm of society. Malcolm McDowell plays our iconoclastic hero, leading his little cell in revolution against the arbitrary discipline and cruelty of the school hierarchy. Although beautifully shot and well realized in its own caricatural terms, it seems dated now and rather too narrowly of its time.

Jane Eyre (Robert Stevenson, 1943). Joan Fontaine does a fine job of portraying Jane, and Orson Welles is a suavely sardonic Rochester, the scene where he is thrown from his horse in the mist achieving the perfect melodramatic pitch. With the unlikely tagline, "A Love Story Every Woman Would Die a Thousand Deaths to Live!", it briefly features young Elizabeth Taylor as dying Helen Burns.

Kes (Kenneth Loach, 1969). Recently re-released to the highest of praise from reviewers, this is the unforgettable story of a neglected Yorkshire schoolboy who finds solace and liberation in training his kestrel. As a still pertinent commentary on poverty and an impoverished school system it is bleak but idealistic, and pale and pinched David Bradley who plays Billy Caspar is hugely affecting.

Kind Hearts and Coronets (Robert Hamer, 1949). As with the best of the Ealing movies, this is a totally savage comedy on the cruel absurdities of the British class system. With increasing ingenuity, Dennis Price's suave and ruthless anti-hero murders his way through the d'Ascoyne clan (all brilliantly played by Alec Guinness) to claim the family title.

The Ladykillers (Alexander Mackendrick, 1955). Alec Guinness is fabulously toothy and malevolent as "Professor Marcus", a murderous conman who lodges with a sweet little old lady, Mrs Wilberforce. The professor and his ragbag of criminal accomplices – their sinister intent a hilarious counterpoint to Mrs Wilberforce's genteel tea parties – try to pass themselves off as musicians, while, thanks to her innocent interventions, the body count inexorably mounts. Features some evocative London streetscapes.

The Last of England (Derek Jarman, 1987). Derek Jarman was a genuine maverick presence in Eighties Britain; this is his most abstract account of a unique vision of the state of the nation. Composed of apparently unrelated shots of decaying London landscapes, rent boys and references to emblematic national events such as the Falklands War, this may not be to all tastes but it is a fitting testament to a unique talent in British film making.

The Life and Death of Colonel Blimp (Michael Powell and Emeric Pressburger, 1943). An epic celebration of the oft-ridiculed romantic spirit of the English, personified by the wonderful Roger Livesey. We follow him through the actual and emotional duels of his youth, against his equally dashing German foe, to crusty old age in World War II. A daring and visually stunning story of love and friendship, it was hated by Churchill for supposedly being unpatriotic, which is surely recommendation enough.

Little Voice (Mark Herman, 1998). Entertaining screen adaptation of Jim Cartwright's hit play about reclusive "Little Voice" (Jane Horrocks), who comes miraculously to life only on stage, brilliantly impersonating Fifties stars such as Marilyn Monroe. It features a great performance from Michael Caine as the impossibly seedy agent who seeks to exploit her bizarre talent, and offers a great glimpse of seaside England, with all its eccentric charm.

Local Hero (Bill Forsyth, 1983). A genuinely endearing, humane picture which rediscovers some of the subtlety and exuberance of the Ealing comedies. It contrasts the ambitions of a Texan oil baron who wants to buy up a Scottish village with the seductive warmth and vitality of the life of the village. Glorious landscapes, and inspired acting from an imperious Burt Lancaster and a charming Denis Lawson.

Lock, Stock and Two Smoking Barrels (Guy Ritchie, 1998). Four lads attempt to pay off gambling debts by making a drug deal in this overstylized and rather shallow picture, which, though it has a modern setting, pays dubious homage to the London of the Kray twins. However, the suits are sharp, the production is slick and football's hardman turned actor Vinnie Jones turns in a surprisingly solid debut performance.

The Long Good Friday (John MacKenzie, 1979). Despite a maniacal turn from Bob Hoskins as the East End gang boss threatened by powerful, mysterious new arrivals, this is not all it's cracked up to be. Its vision of East End villains seems self-indulgent and dated, and the plodding TV visual style doesn't help to raise the level.

Made in Britain (Alan Clarke, 1982). One of Alan Clarke's series of savage dissections of Eighties Britain, featuring a seventeen-year-old Tim Roth as skinhead Trevor, on a downbeat odyssey of job centre visits, drug-taking and racist explosions. The energy of the central performance, and the energy of the film making itself, transcend the worthy TV aesthetic and deliver a film of real force, and a very powerful indictment of Thatcher's Britain.

The Madness of King George (Nicholas Hytner, 1994). Adapted from an Alan Bennett play, this eighteenth-century royal romp has an irritating staginess, with the king's loopy antics played against a cartoon-like court and an England apparently devoid of real people.

A Man For All Seasons (Fred Zinnemann, 1966). Sir Thomas More versus Henry VIII: one of British history's great moral confrontations made skilfully tedious by this film's stagebound, talky origins in Robert Bolt's play. Despite muted, atmospheric visuals and a heavenly host of theatrical talent (including a cheering appearance by Orson Welles as Cardinal Wolsey), nothing can save this from paralysing dullness.

A Matter of Life and Death (Michael Powell and Emeric Pressburger, 1946). From the wartime golden age of British cinema, this remarkable fantasy opens with David Niven's airman miraculously surviving a fall from his stricken bomber. There follows a tussle between the monochrome bureaucracy of Heaven, who seek to reclaim him, and his fast-evolving Earth-bound love affair. Great performances and beautiful Technicolor images in another of Powell and Pressburger's enchanting romances.

Mona Lisa (Neil Jordan, 1986). This fine London-based thriller has powerful performances from Bob Hoskins, Michael Caine and then-newcomer Cathy Tyson, the latter playing a high-class prostitute who recruits Hoskins to help find her lost friend. This takes him, and us, on a nightmarish exploration of the dark side of Eighties London, lightened only slightly by an utterly convincing, poignant love story, as Bob begins to fall for his beautiful employer.

Mrs Brown (John Madden, 1997). Demonstrates the Brits' tedious preoccupation with royalty, and concerns the did-she-or-didn't-she relationship between widowed Queen Victoria and her kilted Highland "ghillie" John Brown. Well acted but unchallenging, with Judy Dench as the tight-lipped monarch and Billy Connolly as the plain-speaking Highlander.

My Beautiful Laundrette (Stephen Frears, 1985). A slice of Thatcher's Britain, with a young Asian, Omar, on the make, opening a ritzy laundrette. His lover, Johnny, is an ex-National Front glamour boy, angry and inarticulate when forced by the acquisitive Omar into a menial role in the laundrette. The racial, sexual and class dynamics of their relationship are closely observed, and mirror the tensions engendered by the Asian presence in a hostile London. Daring, unexpected and funny, with a wonderful performance from Daniel Day-Lewis as Johnny.

Night and the City (Jules Dassin, 1950). Great *film noir*, with Richard Widmark as an anxious nightclub hustler on the run. Gripping and convincingly sleazy, the London streetscapes have an expressionist edge of horror.

Nil by Mouth (Gary Oldman, 1997). Features strong performances by Ray Winstone (Ray) as a boorish south Londoner and Kathy Burke (Valery) as his battered wife. A brave and bleak realist picture, which depicts Ray as a victim of his own violence, as well as the devastatingly vulnerable Valery. Brace yourself.

Notting Hill (Roger Michell, 1999). More smug, middle-class jollity from the writer (Richard Curtis) who brought you *Four Weddings and a Funeral* (1994). Grant reprises his bumbling floppy-haired Englishman role and falls for a glamorous American (Julia Roberts), again. Spans a year in the life of Notting Hill, perversely failing to feature the event for which this part of London is best known: the biggest and best street carnival in Europe.

On the Black Hill (Andrew Grieve, 1987). A visually absorbing adaptation of Bruce

Chatwin's rather slight novel of Welsh farming folk. Hardyesque characterization and a similar predilection for doom, with a strong performance by Bob Peck as stubborn Amos Jones, trapped in an unhappy marriage to a middle-class woman.

Only Two Can Play (Sidney Gilliat, 1961). Dryly funny if faintly depressing adaptation of Kinsley Amis's farce *That Uncertain Feeling*, with Peter Sellers in convincingly seedy mode as an adulterous Welsh librarian.

Orlando (Sally Potter, 1992). Although modest in budget terms, this is a vivid and visually very beautiful adaptation of Virginia Woolf's novel, following its hero/heroine through 400 years of British history. Tilda Swinton is perfectly cast as the androgynous immortal, and choice moments spanning Elizabethan England to the present day (through the Civil War and Victoria's reign, for example) are perfectly and mysteriously realized.

Performance Nicolas Roeg/Donald Cammell, 1970). Credited with precipitating James Fox's breakdown and subsequent retirement from the movies, this shape-shifting tale of gangsters and pop culture is the best account of the hedonistic end to Britain's psychedelic 1960s. Well known for its strange drug-hazed second half, the film is also brilliantly funny in parts and should be cherished for its hilarious destruction of the myth of Kray-style criminals.

The Ratcatcher (Lynne Ramsay, 1999). Set in 1970s Glasgow during a refuse workers' strike, Ramsay's striking first feature follows twelve-year-old James, who accidentally drowns his friend as the rubbish around the tenement blocks mounts. Weaving rich humour into the gloomy narrative, Ramsay layers poetic images of the city, rejecting realism for a lyrical, symbolic approach.

Rebecca (Alfred Hitchcock, 1940). Hitchcock does Du Maurier: Laurence Olivier is wonderfully enigmatic as Maxim de Winter, and Joan Fontaine glows as her meek second wife, living in the shadow of her mysterious predecessor. Perfectly paced and beautifully shot, Hitch's first Hollywood picture is a true classic.

The Remains of the Day (James Ivory, 1993). Kazuo Ishiguro's masterly study of social and personal repression translates beautifully to the big screen. Anthony Hopkins is the overly decorous butler who gradually becomes aware of his master's fascist connections, Emma Thompson the housekeeper who struggles to bring his real, deeply suppressed feelings to the surface.

Richard III (Richard Loncraine, 1995). A splendid film version of a renowned National Theatre production, which brilliantly transposed the action to a fascist state in the 1930s. The infernal political machinations of a snarling Ian McKellen as Richard are heightened by Nazi associations, and the style of the period imbues the film with the requisite glamour, as does a languorously drugged Kristin Scott-Thomas as Lady Anne. Innovative use of some great London locations, with monumental Battersea Power Station the setting for the Battle of Bosworth.

Rob Roy (Michael Caton-Jones, 1994). Liam Neeson brings a much-needed gravity to the rather sordid goings-on in this moderately successful romanticization of the real-life story of a cattle rustling, blackmailing thug. Some splendid Scottish locations and generally solid performances (including an extravagantly evil Tim Roth) just about redeem the anachronistic script.

Secrets and Lies (Mike Leigh, 1995). Much-loved Mike Leigh slice-of-life drama, with wonderful Timothy Spall at the head of a spectacularly dysfunctional London family. His sister Cynthia (Brenda Blethyn), her heart of gold buried in boozy, cloying unhappiness, is reunited with the black daughter she gave up for adoption at birth. With trademark over-long improvised sequences and a sharp eye for suburban vulgarity which comes uncomfortably close to parody, the film is lifted by stunning ensemble performances and sustained by the simple strength of its central tenet: that secrets and lies in a family will only cause unnecessary pain.

Sense and Sensibility (Ang Lee, 1995). Jane Austen's sprightly essay on the merits of well-modified behaviour is nicely realized by Lee, and neatly scripted by Emma Thompson. Thompson and Kate Winslet are charming as the downtrodden Dashwood sisters: Winslet is a brilliantly over-wrought, romantic Marianne, while Thompson turns in another perfect performance as prudent Elinor.

Shakespeare in Love (John Madden, 1998). This irresistible homage to life, love and Shakespeare has an energetic Joseph Fiennes as the quill-chewing bard and Gwyneth Paltrow as his sparky love interest. Sharply scripted by

Tom Stoppard, it skips a dainty line between parody and over-reverence, and has fun sending up the British over-fondness for cameos, with Rupert Everett as melancholy Kit Marlowe, off on a one-way trip for a drink in Deptford. No mere piece of frivolity though, the film aspires to, and achieves, real feeling.

Small Faces (Gillies MacKinnon, 1995). A moving little saga about the lives of three brothers growing up in 1960s Glasgow amid feuding gangs of local teenagers. We follow the rough education of young Lex, torn between the excitement and real danger of a life of fighting, and the alternative artistic ambitions of his older brother. A convincing and occasionally very funny re-creation of the period.

The Thirty-Nine Steps (Alfred Hitchcock, 1935). Hitchcock's best-loved British movie, full of wit and bold acts of derring-do. Robert Donat stars as innocent Richard Hannay, inadvertently caught up in a mysterious spy ring and forced to flee both the spies and the agents of Scotland Yard. In a typically perverse Hitchcock touch, he spends a generous amount of time handcuffed to Madeleine Carroll, fleeing across the Scottish countryside, before the action returns to London for the film's great music-hall conclusion.

This Sporting Life (Lindsay Anderson, 1963). One of the key British films of the 1960s, *This Sporting Life* tells the story of a northern miner turned star player for his local rugby team. The young Richard Harris gives a great performance as the inarticulate anti-hero, able only to express himself through physical violence, and the film is one of the best examples of the gritty "kitchen sink" genre it helped to usher in.

Trainspotting (Danny Boyle, 1995). Iconic posters of Ewan McGregor looking wet and wasted in a tight T-shirt fuelled intense *Trainspotting* fever in 1995. An innovative, energetic adaptation of Irvine Welsh's novel, the film features a sensational soundtrack and takes a headlong dive into the drug-fuelled dark side of Edinburgh. Exciting and disturbing in equal measure, with almost insolently superb performances from McGregor, Ewen Bremner and Robert Carlyle.

Twin Town (Kevin Allen, 1997). A Welsh take on *Trainspotting*, with amoral twins Julian and Jeremy wreaking elaborate revenge when their father, Fatty, is hospitalized. The attempt at iconic status largely backfires, but Llyr Evans and Rhys Ifans turn in strong performances as the terrifying Port Talbot twins.

Whisky Galore! (Alexander Mackendrick, 1949). When a shipwrecked stock of the amber nectar is washed ashore on a remote Scottish island, the locals contrive all manner of cunning ruses to conceal its presence from the pursuing authorities. A beautiful Ealing comedy, with real sympathy for its eccentric little community as they battle the forces of dull authority in the entirely laudable ambition of having a good time at no expense.

The Wicked Lady (Leslie Arliss, 1945). One of the best of Gainsborough Studio's series of escapist romances, this features a magnificently amoral and headstrong Margaret Lockwood, wooed to a criminal double life by James Mason's quintessentially dashing highwayman. Its opulent recreation of eighteenth-century England is terribly appealing, as are the tempestuous entanglements of its two wayward stars.

The Wicker Man (Robin Hardy, 1973). A classic more by virtue of its unutterable weirdness than any great achievements of film making. Edward Woodward plays a detective investigating the mysterious disappearance of a local girl on an isolated Scottish island, and finds himself drawn into a strange world of maypole-dancing and inadvertently hilarious pagan rites. Christopher Lee manages to keep a straight face throughout, rather surprisingly.

Withnail and I (Bruce Robinson, 1986). Richard E. Grant is superb as the raddled, drunken Withnail, an out-of-work actor with a penchant for drinking lighter fluid. Paul McGann is the "I" of the title – a bemused and beautiful spectator of Withnail's wild excesses, as they abandon an astonishingly grotty London flat for the wilds of a remote cottage, and the attentions of Withnail's randy uncle Monty. A rare look at the Sixties that avoids nostalgia, and opts instead for emotional truth.

Helena Smith and Dan Smith

Stay in touch with us!

ROUGH*NEWS* is Rough Guides' free newsletter. In four issues a year we give you news, travel issues, music reviews, readers' letters and the latest dispatches from authors on the road.

I would like to receive ROUGH*NEWS*: please put me on your free mailing list.

NAME ....

ADDRESS ....

Please clip or photocopy and send to: Rough Guides, 62–70 Shorts Gardens, London WC2H 9AB, England or Rough Guides, 375 Hudson Street, New York, NY 10014, USA.

ROUGH GUIDES: Travel

Amsterdam
Andalucia
Australia
Austria
Bali & Lombok
Barcelona
Belgium &
  Luxembourg
Belize
Berlin
Brazil
Britain
Brittany &
  Normandy
Bulgaria
California
Canada
Central America
Chile
China
Corfu & the
  Ionian Islands
Corsica
Costa Rica
Crete
Cyprus
Czech & Slovak
  Republics
Dodecanese &
  the East Aegean

Dominican
  Republic
Egypt
England
Europe
Florida
France
French Hotels &
  Restaurants
  1999
Germany
Goa
Greece
Greek Islands
Guatemala
Hawaii
Holland
Hong Kong &
  Macau
Hungary
India
Indonesia
Ireland
Israel & the
  Palestinian
  Territories
Italy
Jamaica
Japan
Jordan
Kenya

Laos
London
Los Angeles
Malaysia,
  Singapore &
  Brunei
Mallorca &
  Menorca
Maya World
Mexico
Morocco
Moscow
Nepal
New England
New York
New Zealand
Norway
Pacific
  Northwest
Paris
Peru
Poland
Portugal
Prague
Provence & the
  Côte d'Azur
The Pyrenees
Rhodes & the
  Dodecanese
Romania
St Petersburg

San Francisco
Sardinia
Scandinavia
Scotland
Scottish
  highlands and
  Islands
Sicily
Singapore
South Africa
South India
Southwest USA
Spain
Sweden
Syria

Thailand
Trinidad &
  Tobago
Tunisia
Turkey
Tuscany &
  Umbria
USA
Venice
Vienna
Vietnam
Wales
Washington DC
West Africa
Zimbabwe &
  Botswana

Discover the

AVAILABLE AT ALL GOOD BOOKSHOPS

ROUGH GUIDES: Mini Guides, Travel Specials and Phrasebooks

MINI GUIDES

Antigua
Bangkok
Barbados
Big Island of
  Hawaii
Boston
Brussels
Budapest

Dublin
Edinburgh
Florence
Honolulu
Jerusalem
Lisbon
London
  Restaurants
Madrid
Maui
Melbourne
New Orleans
Seattle
St Lucia

Sydney
Tokyo
Toronto

TRAVEL SPECIALS

First-Time Asia
First-Time
  Europe
Women Travel

PHRASEBOOKS

Czech
Dutch

Egyptian Arabic
European
French
German
Greek
Hindi & Urdu
Hungarian
Indonesian
Italian
Japanese

Mandarin
  Chinese
Mexican
  Spanish
Polish
Portuguese
Russian
Spanish
Swahili
Thai
Turkish
Vietnamese

AVAILABLE AT ALL GOOD BOOKSHOPS

ROUGH GUIDES:
Reference and Music CDs

REFERENCE

Classical Music
Classical:
  100 Essential CDs
Drum'n'bass
House Music
Jazz
Music USA

Opera
Opera:
  100 Essential CDs
Reggae
Reggae:
  100 Essential CDs
Rock
Rock:
  100 Essential CDs
Techno
World Music
World Music:
  100 Essential CDs
English Football
European Football

Internet
Millennium

ROUGH GUIDE MUSIC CDs

Music of the
  Andes
Australian
  Aboriginal
Brazilian Music
Cajun & Zydeco

Classic Jazz
Music of
  Colombia
Cuban Music
Eastern Europe

Music of Egypt
English Roots
  Music
Flamenco
India & Pakistan
Irish Music
Music of Japan
Kenya & Tanzania
Native American
North African
Music of Portugal

Reggae
Salsa
Scottish Music
South African
  Music
Music of Spain
Tango
Tex-Mex
West African
  Music
World Music
World Music Vol 2
Music of
  Zimbabwe

AVAILABLE AT ALL GOOD BOOKSHOPS

NORTH SOUTH TRAVEL

DISCOUNT FARES

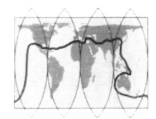

PROFITS TO CHARITIES

- North South Travel is a friendly, competitive travel agency, offering discount fares world-wide.
- North South Travel's profits contribute to community projects in the developing world.
- We have special experience of booking destinations in Africa, Asia and Latin America.
- Clients who book through North South Travel include exchange groups, students and independent travellers, as well as charities, church organisations and small businesses.

To discuss your booking requirements: contact Brenda Skinner between 9am and 5pm, Monday to Friday, on (01245) 492 882: Fax (01245) 356 612, any time. Or write to:
North South Travel Limited, Moulsham Mill Centre, Parkway,
Chelmsford, Essex CM2 7PX, UK

Help us to help others – Your travel can make a difference

the perfect getaway vehicle

low-price holiday car rental.

rent a car from holiday autos and you'll give yourself real freedom to explore your holiday destination. with great-value, fully-inclusive rates in over 4,000 locations worldwide, wherever you're escaping to, we're there to make sure you get excellent prices and superb service.

what's more, you can book now with complete confidence. our £5 undercut* ensures that you are guaranteed the best value for money in holiday destinations right around the globe.

drive away with a great deal, call holiday autos now on **0990 300 400** and quote ref RG.

holiday autos
miles ahead